EDMUND CAMPION

A DEFINITIVE BIOGRAPHY

Richard Simpson

TAN Books
Charlotte, North Carolina

Retypeset and published in 2013 by TAN Books, Charlotte, North Carolina, with Americanization of word spelling.

This edition originally published in England by Gracewing. Copyright © 2010 Peter Mary Joseph, frpjoseph@hotmail.com.

Cover design by Caroline Kiser.

Front cover image: Saint Edmund Campion, from a print made by Jacques Neeffs (engraving), Flemish School, (17th century) / Private Collection / The Bridgeman Art Library.-

Cataloging-in-Publication data on file with the Library of Congress.

ISBN 978-0-89555-444-4

Published in the United States by
TAN Books
P.O. Box 410487
Charlotte, NC 28241
www.TANBooks.com

Printed and bound in the United States of America.

Contents

Foreword

BY CARDINAL GEORGE PELL

IN AN age of religious indifference, waning ecumenical enthusiasms, and turmoil in the Anglican communion, it is too easy to become blasé about the differences between Catholics and Anglicans. In Campion's time, those differences were literally a matter of life and death. One has to be inspired by the life of this man who practised Christian devotion and fidelity at an heroic level, and endured torture and martyrdom.

It was my privilege to live at Campion Hall during four years at Oxford University, where the proceeds from Evelyn Waugh's biography of Campion were used to adorn the Lady Chapel with murals by Charles Mahoney. Campion remains one of my heroes. I concelebrated the celebratory Mass in his old college of St. John's on the day of his canonization in 1970 before a sumptuous feast at Campion itself. Far happier times religiously than the first Elizabethan England.

There is a great passage in Waugh, where he compares the respective careers of Tobie Matthew and Edmund Campion. Tobie Matthew was a young Fellow of Christ Church, Oxford, and, like Campion, highly esteemed by Queen Elizabeth. With Elizabeth's patronage:

> . . . a splendid career lay before him. He became Canon of Christ Church four years later; in 1572, at the unusually early age of twenty-six, he was made President of St. John's . . . four years later he was Dean of Christ Church, later Vice-Chancellor; from there he turned to the greater world, became successively Dean and Bishop of Durham, and, finally, Archbishop of York. He was a talkative little man, always eager to please, always ready with a neat, parsonic witticism; the best of good fellows, everywhere, except in his own family. When, on the Council of the North, he was most busy

hunting down recusants, he was full of little jokes to beguile his colleagues. He was a great preacher ... He married admirably, a widow
of stout Protestant principles and unique place in the new clerical caste, which had sprung naturally from the system of married
clergy: Frances Barlow, widow of Matthew Parker, Junior; she was
notable in her generation as having a bishop for her father, an archbishop for her father-in-law, an archbishop for her husband, and
four bishops for her brothers. Tobie Matthew died full of honors
in 1628. There, but for the Grace of God, went Edmund Campion.

It is my prayer that this biography of St. Edmund may help Catholics to
appreciate the grit and heroism of our saints, and inspire and challenge
other Christians to understand more fully the reasons for the turmoil
that led to their separation from the Catholic Church. It is also an invitation to reconsider the claims of the See of Peter, the divinely sustained
Rock of stability in our marvelous world. After all, unity was, and still is
today, the prayer of St. Edmund Campion.

✝ George Cardinal Pell
Archbishop of Sydney

Preface

The Author

RICHARD SIMPSON (1820–1876) was educated at Oriel College, Oxford, and took his Bachelor of Arts degree in 1843. He was ordained an Anglican clergyman, married, and was appointed vicar of Mitcham in Surrey, but resigned in 1845 to become a Catholic—in the same year as John Henry Newman.

Over the years 1854–62, Simpson contributed articles on philosophy, theology, and the English martyrs to *The Rambler*, of which he became editor in 1858.

Simpson was one of the first to uphold the Catholicity of Shakespeare's religious beliefs. For the purposes of the present biography, it is interesting that *Twelfth Night*, Act IV, sc. ii, clearly refers a number of times—and favorably too—to Campion ("the old hermit of Prague"), as well as Fr. Persons ("master Person").

Among his several works, *Edmund Campion* (1867) is regarded as Simpson's finest, and is a witness to his scholarship, intelligence, and literary talents.

The Revision of "Edmund Campion"

Nearly a century and a half after its publication in 1867, Richard Simpson's biography of Edmund Campion is still the most comprehensive one by far. In 1896, it was reprinted with corrections by the author, who had died already—and it appeared for the third time back in 1907.

Along with his bibliography and endnotes, Simpson's original preface bears witness to the thoroughness of his research. It is printed in the *Editor's Note* near the end of this book, which also gives a full account of the sources and method I have used in the revision of this Life.

Special thanks are due to Maria d'Urso, Anna Krohn, Rose Yazbek, Tanya Rizk, Annabel Sadaka, and Anne Zabodal, who gave valuable help and services for this project. Fr. John Fleming gave much appreciated labor in carefully revising the historical chapter 9, and writing the major portion of chapter 16, an outline of the complex Tower debates. I thank Ranya Helou for doing the maps. I am grateful also to Bishop Geoffrey Jarrett, Fr. Michael Head S.J., Fr. John Parsons, Fr. Luke Joseph, Fr. Nicholas Schofield, Prof. Lubomír Konečný, Eve Dutton, Anusha Jebanasam, John Chifley, Imogen Hitchings, David Kerr, Katharina Barrios Larrañaga, Belle Joseph, Eugenie Joseph, and Jan Graffius at Stonyhurst College, for particular assistance. I thank Sister M. Thelma Cañete P.D.D.M. and Bernadette Samia for their special support. I thank also Brother J. Hodkinson S.J. and Anna Edwards at the Jesuit Archives, London, for supplying me with important material. Kylie Prats was wonderfully generous and skillful in typesetting.

In the narrative and in Simpson's bibliography, the personal pronoun "I" refers always to Simpson. In the endnotes it refers to the current editor. Any references to contemporary time are updated: "today" always means the year A.D. 2010.

The lives of the saints are masterpieces of God, each one showing some aspects of God's infinite perfection. They were weak, sinful human beings, transformed by God's grace.

May God Who is glorified in His saints, may Jesus Christ the King of Martyrs, and may Holy Mary the Queen of Martyrs, grant us all a share in the zeal and sanctity of him whom I like to think of as *Saint Edmund the Great.*

Fr. Peter Mary Joseph
Wagga Wagga
New South Wales
Australia

CHAPTER 1

London and Oxford

Birth in London

E DMUND Campion, the proto-martyr of the English Jesuits, was
born in Paternoster Row,[1] London, on the feast of St. Paul, January
25, 1540, in the thirtieth year of the reign of Henry VIII.[2] It was a year
marked by the suppression of the great religious houses in England, the
inauguration of a persecution of which, forty years later, Campion was
to be a victim—and the solemn Papal approval of the Society of Jesus, of
which he was to be an ornament.

His father, also named Edmund, a man of moderate means, was a citizen of London and a bookseller, of which there were several in Paternoster
Row—a street that still exists, on the north side of old St. Paul's Cathedral.
Mr. Campion was probably from the Sawston (Cambridgeshire) branch
of the family; if not, then the related Campions of Witham (Essex).[3] His
wife was possibly named Anne.[4] Where young Edmund was baptized is
not known.[5]

"His parents were not wealthy in the riches of this world, but very
honest and Catholic," says Father Persons.[6] Campion himself was not
so certain of this; he only "hopes" that they died in the faith.[7] They had
four children—a girl and three boys—of whom Edmund was second. He
and his youngest brother took to books; the other preferred adventure,
and took a wife, who was occasionally left to herself while her husband
served in the wars.[8] The younger brother's name was, possibly, Robert.[9]
His sister is unheard of until the end of Campion's life, when she came to
visit him in prison.

Edmund "signed his name indifferently Campion and Campian.
His signature shows that he was a rapid writer with a firm and beautiful
hand."[10]

First Schooling

When Edmund reached the "years of discretion," or a little later, when he was nine or ten, in 1549 or 1550, his parents planned to apprentice him to some merchant, but the company of Merchant Adventurers, "perceiving his sharp and pregnant wit from his childhood," decided "to maintain him rather at their common charges to study of learning,"[11] and so his parents sent him first to St. Paul's grammar-school, founded in 1509. It was then located in the City of London and close to their home.

In those days there seems to have been a regular competition among the London grammar-schools. Campion is said always to have borne away the prize in all contentions of learning—a fact which he would occasionally in after life "merrily make mention and name the rewards that were given to him, though ever with great modesty, for they touched his own praise and commendation."[12]

On August 23, 1553, young Edmund won a silver pen in a literary contest between three schools: St. Paul's, St. Anthony's, and Christ's Hospital school.[13] One of the contestants was William Fulke, also from St. Paul's. Fulke's biographer comments, "Our aspiring young scholar [Fulke] being unsuccessful bore his disappointment with so ill a grace as to shed tears under it, indignantly looking forward to the reprisals of a future competition."[14] That competition came twenty-eight years later, in 1581, when Edmund was a prisoner in the Tower, and Fulke was placed opposite him in dispute over the true religion—and was beaten there as well.[15]

Edmund changed school, from St. Paul's to Christ's Hospital, possibly some time from August 24 to September 29, 1553.[16] The latter was a new foundation of King Edward VI at Christ-Church, Newgate Street, a school founded in 1552 with confiscated Church property, and known as Christ-Church Hospital, or, later, the Blue Coat School, meant for orphans or other poor children. Perhaps Edmund's father had died, or some change of circumstances induced the change. At this new school, in addition to his education, Edmund could receive lodging free of charge. A 19th-century Protestant account of Christ's Hospital has this to say, with delightful ambivalence, on one of her more famous students: "With Campion's errors Christ's Hospital is not to be charged; and, as a man of learning, she has every right to be proud of her son."[17]

Speech before Queen Mary

Edmund's academic championship was acknowledged a few weeks after winning the silver pen: when Queen Mary, on her coronation procession of September 30, 1553, had to pass by St. Paul's School, Campion was chosen to make the requisite speech—even though he was no longer a student there.[18] It was a long-established custom that a pupil of St. Paul's School would deliver an address to the Sovereign, on occasion of formal royal passages through London past St. Paul's School at the east end of the Cathedral church-yard.[19]

Minds that had faith in functions would have triumphed in the prospects which that day opened to the Church. They could not admit that the enthusiasm could be so soon cooled. London had been dressing itself for the ceremony for three weeks beforehand.[20] About three o'clock the queen set forth from the Tower in a chariot drawn by six white horses all adorned with red velvet. The queen was dressed in a gown of blue velvet, furred with ermine. On her head was a caul of cloth of tinsel beset with pearls and precious stones of inestimable value. There was a grand procession, through the streets of the city of London, as a prologue to the coronation the following day. This was one of Mary's halcyon days; and the procession was distinguished by seventy ladies riding after the queen on horseback, clad in crimson velvet. Five hundred gentlemen, noblemen, and ambassadors preceded her, from the lowest in degree to the highest. Each ambassador was accompanied by a great officer of the Crown. The earl of Sussex bore the queen's hat and cloak, between two squires of honor, who had robes of estate rolled, and worn over the shoulder and round the waist. The Lord Mayor, Sir Thomas White, carried the scepter. Pageantry, in the old-accustomed style, greeted the queen in her progress through the city. At various points on the way there were minstrels playing and singing. The roofs and streets were crowded with citizens too, singing, playing organs, and shouting, "God save Queen Mary!"[21]

It was in the midst of this tumult that little Campion had to spout his address, and to share the honors of a day when good humor ruled, and criticism was mute except to applaud. The queen is said to have been much pleased with him, and the people cheered him heartily, though they probably did not hear a word he said, for at thirteen he had not that "sweet, modulated, full, sonorous bass voice"[22] which afterwards inspired hearts with so high resolves, though there might have been the *Os tibi mellifluum, faciei grata venustas* (your honeyed lips, a pleasing beauty)[23] against whose rhetoric the people could not hold argument, and anticipations of excellence to make citizens proud of their young champion.

Change of Regime

In November 1558, both Queen Mary and Cardinal Pole died. Five years of Catholic rule suddenly came to an end. Elizabeth Tudor succeeded. Within a few weeks the new queen had forbidden the Sacred Host to be elevated in her presence, had chided her preachers for their doctrine, and had excited such suspicion that a bishop could hardly be procured to crown her. After her coronation she threw off the mask, violated the Coronation Oath, and within a short time—against the unanimous decision of the bishops—substituted the Anglican Establishment for the Catholic Church. But it was a long time before the law written on paper became transfused into the life and habits of the English nation.

St. John's College, Oxford

Under the reign of Queen Mary, Sir Thomas White (1492–1567) founded the College of St. John the Baptist, Oxford, in 1555, to teach philosophy, theology, and arts, but it did not really function as a college until 1557.[24] When the College had increased and was ready to operate, Sir Thomas admitted Edmund as a student in 1557,[25] "which he did most willingly after he was informed of his rare towardliness in learning and virtue,"[26] and "it seems probable that he persuaded some of his wealthy business friends, and others, to contribute to the support of some of the poorer students, including Edmund."[27] Initially, Edmund received financial assistance from Sir William Chester. From 1560, he received "forty shillings a year, so long as he is a student in Oxford" from the will of Sir Anthony Hussey, who lived in Paternoster Row. He was a member of the Merchant Adventurers guild, and a Registrar of the chapter of St. Paul's.[28]

Sir Thomas conceived a special affection for Edmund, who had in a very short time grown to be much known for his wit, and especially for his grace of speech and gift of eloquence, in which he came to be thought the best man of his time.

Sir Thomas White and the Character of St. John's

St. John's College was at that time a breeding-ground for Catholics. The founder, Sir Thomas White, was a devout Catholic who as Lord Mayor of London in 1553 had done good service against Thomas Wyatt's rebellion against Queen Mary, and who in Elizabeth's first Parliament had protested, in a reference to the young Cecil and Bedford, that "it was unjust that a religion begun in such a miraculous way, and established by such grave men, should be abolished by a set of beardless boys." White's strong desire to produce a learned clergy is shown in Statute 16, which is original and not borrowed: he is founding the College for "the increase of the orthodox faith and of the Christian profession in so far as it is weakened by the damage of time and the malice of men."[29]

Campion scholar Gerard Kilroy says:

> The dedication of St. John's College to the old religion in those early years can be verified by looking at the donations to the library, most of which are still present in the College Library today. It is still possible to see on the shelves what books Campion could have read in a library with under 500 books. . . . St. John's College Library did not receive any book by a [Protestant] reformer until 1600, by which time . . . Sir Thomas Tresham had donated a further 200 volumes of traditional Catholic theology.[30]

Within a few years it had, in Greek, works of the Fathers, such as St. Basil, plus the classics of Homer, Plato, Thucydides, Aristophanes, Euripides, Lucian, Aristotle and his commentators, Suidas's Greek lexicon, and other dictionaries. In Latin, it possessed a ten-volume collection of the works of St. Augustine, in addition to works of Sts. Ambrose, Gregory the Great, and Anselm. Kilroy gives another indication of the Catholic faith at St. John's: "From 1565 till 1580, some sixteen fellows and two chaplains of the College left Oxford to become Catholic priests at Rheims and Douay."[31]

The College's first years were very difficult. The first president of the College, Alexander Belsyre, appointed in 1555, was deprived of his post by Sir Thomas in 1559, for dishonesty in the use of money.[32]

His successor, William Eley (Elye), was, like Belsyre, a Catholic. He held his post from 1559 till 1560 without acknowledging Queen Elizabeth's supremacy over the Church. In November 1560, however, the oath of supremacy was tendered to him; he chose to resign rather than take it.[33]

William Stock succeeded Eley at the end of 1560. He remained in his post, but not continuously, it seems, until he was replaced in 1564.[34]

In 1564, Sir Thomas White made John Robinson president. He remained so for eight years, till July 1572, when he was appointed precentor of Lincoln Cathedral,[35] which means he conformed to the Protestant Establishment. Certainly as president, up to the Catholic founder's death in 1567, he would not have acted against the Catholic religion at the College.

When Robinson left, the character of the College underwent a complete change. White was dead, and Bishop Horne of Winchester, a Puritan, succeeded in upsetting White's statutes of 1566 that deprived the bishops of that see of the visitation of the College and vested it in trustees—of whom one of the first was William Roper, son-in-law of Sir Thomas More.[36] Another trustee was a strong Catholic, Sir William Cordell, a member of the Privy Council (the queen's cabinet) under Queen Mary.

Tobie Mathew was made president in 1572. The founder dead and his spirit having departed, there was no home now for anything Catholic in the Establishment. Nine out of twenty were expelled from the fellowships as suspected "Papists," and their places were filled by "Puritans." ("Papist" was a derogatory term for Catholics, invented in the 16th century for the followers of Papal teachings and authority. The "Puritans" were those Protestants who, though divided in other important ways among themselves, followed the doctrines of the extremist Calvin—and not only Luther—and aimed to differ from Catholic tradition and worship as far as possible. In contrast, Queen Elizabeth, and other Anglicans, though also divided among themselves, followed a mid-way position, retaining certain Catholic feasts and forms of worship.)

Campion had gone before Tobie Mathew took over, but it is significant that in Campion's first seven years at St. John's, up to 1564, Catholicism was tolerated there, although the presidents had to tread warily.

John Bavand (Bavant), a Master of Arts from Christ's College, was tutor to Edmund Campion and Gregory Martin at St. John's in their first year, 1557.[37] He was a faithful Catholic and left England about 1564 rather than compromise his Catholic principles. Bavand, Campion, and Martin became close friends, and all three were to become priests.

Campion did not frequent the heretical services or churches at all.[38]

In those times, the men at St. John's would never have the (Protestant) Lord's Supper celebrated in their chapel, nor go in search of it. If they had not the same objection to the Anglican *Common Prayer*, they avoided all topics of religious dispute, devoted themselves to philosophy and scholarship, and made Campion promise not to make trouble for himself in his public disputations.

Oxford University

The change of regime in 1558 was sharply felt at Oxford, which from long before had been very resistant to the religious innovations of Protestantism. Within a year of Elizabeth's accession, only one College head was allowed to remain from the previous reign.[39] Over the next decade, more than a hundred fellows and senior members left Oxford for religious reasons, a great proportion of them to enter the priesthood and the work of the English mission.[40] But the undergraduates were reasonably free, at least in Elizabeth's early years; the authorities did not want to make Oxford a desert by forcing too many consciences. Campion was not compelled to take the oath acknowledging the spiritual supremacy of the queen until he took his degree of Bachelor of Arts in 1564. By that time, the seductions of the University, a host of friends, and a large following of disciples had entangled him. "And for the opinion and fame which he had for his eloquence, the orations which he made in the University upon occasions then occurring, were diligently copied and greatly desired by all the scholars of the University."[41] His eloquence was a dangerous gift; as junior in the act of February 19, 1564, he was orator in the schools, "at which time," says Oxford historian Anthony à Wood, "speaking one or more most admirable orations, to the envy of his contemporaries, [he] caused one of them, who was afterwards an archbishop [Tobie Mathew], to say, that rather than he would omit the opportunity to show his parts, and *dominari in una atque altera conciuncula* [to show off in a spouting-match or two], did take the oath against the pope's supremacy, and against his conscience."[42] There is some truth in this envious stab of Tobie's. The success of the orator Edmund tempted him to desert theology and to become a humanist; and why should a humanist and a layman trouble himself with the quarrels of pope and queen? His own path of duty was plain; he was more certain that he ought to obey his superiors, and fulfill his engagements with his pupils, than he could be about the abstract question of the pope's supremacy. The more certain duty eclipses the less; and as a mere layman he had no particular call to certify himself more securely on so very inconvenient a point. Nevertheless, though he took the oath himself, he sometimes saved others from doing so. Over the years 1564–70, "I knew him at Oxford," says Robert Persons, "and it was through him that the oath was not tendered to me when I took my M.A. degree."[43]

Campion's Studies

On November 20, 1561, Campion was admitted as a student for the degree of Bachelor of Arts,[44] and graduated in 1564. He and two others then received license for the degree of Master of Arts on July 3, 1564, but owing to a plague did not incept until February 1565 when the Act was held.[45] In September 1564, Campion was elected a fellow of the College. From 1564–70, he was lecturer in Rhetoric. (At Oxford, a fellow, or "don," is a lecturer, student or researcher, or College appointee, who sits on the College's governing body. The fellows are in effect the trustees of a College.)

Still, however loath, he was obliged by the statutes of the College to enter on the study of theology; but he managed to find a respite, and to stave off the urgent questions. He began in 1564 with natural theology, and read it up from Aristotle—Aristotle says nothing about the pope's supremacy. Then he went on to positive theology, the old settled dogma, which had not much to do with the controversies of the day. Then he determined to study the Fathers, where he could not expect to find much about these abstruse points (or so he imagined). We have his own statement: "First I learned grammar in my native place; then I went to Oxford, where I studied philosophy for seven years [1557–1564], and theology for about six [till 1570]—Aristotle, Positive Theology, and the Fathers."[46] He obtained the M.A. degree in 1566, and that was the last degree he received before leaving St. John's a few years later without the Bachelor of Divinity.[47] "I graduated as Master of Arts at Oxford," he wrote later.[48]

After he had taken his Bachelor's degree in 1564, he had hosts of pupils who followed not only his teaching but his example, and imitated not only his phrases but his gait. He filled Oxford with "Campionists"; he became the mirror wherein the youth did dress themselves, whose speech, gait and diet was the copy and book that fashioned others. Among these Campionists was Robert Turner, afterwards rector of the University of Ingoldstadt, who speaks of his master as the one "who had pinched up, and pulled out, and squared into shape my slovenly style."[49] An other was Richard Stanihurst, poet, historian, and divine; and another, Henry Vaux. None of them approach their master in his brief and brilliant phrases, and forcible and life-like epithets; but they gathered round him and formed a classical public, a brotherhood of scholars, to excite, to appreciate, and to applaud.

Campion Orates

Campion's first public oratorical display at Oxford was at one time thought to have been as early as 1560, at the re-burial of Amy Robsart, Robert Dudley's wife, who had been hastily buried at Cumnor Hall, Berkshire, after her untimely death on September 8, 1560. Whether it was murder, suicide, or accident is not certain, but the people muttered that Dudley directed his servant Anthony Foster, with the help of Sir Richard Varney, to throw her downstairs and break her neck,[50] so that he might enjoy the queen's favors more freely—as afterwards he did for his whole life. To counter this gossip, Dudley decided to display his love and grief by a magnificent funeral in St. Mary's Church, Oxford, where his chaplain, Dr. Babington, made her funeral oration. But either more than one oration was made over her casket, or the event was commemorated in different colleges: for Persons says that "Edmund Campion was chosen, though then but very young [twenty], to make an English oration in the same [funeral], which he performed with exceeding commendation of all that were present."[51] All writers today, however, judge that Persons here repeats an unreliable story.[52]

I have already mentioned his oratorical successes of February 1564. On February 12, 1567, Sir Thomas White died, and, in conformity with his will (in which he bequeathed a black gown to Campion),[53] his body was brought from London to Oxford, "with great celebrity and marvellous concourse of people for the exceeding great opinion that all men had of his virtuous life and extraordinary works"[54] and because he was a known Catholic and had done much to defend and advance his religion.

Therefore, says Persons, Campion was chosen to make the funeral oration in Latin; and in it he so well commended the alms-deeds of Sir Thomas, "that he wonderfully moved his whole auditory [audience] to the esteem and love of alms and pious deeds, and appalled much for many days the new-fangled preachers of that time who had then begun to diminish and abase the merit and value of the same" good works.[55]

There are preserved at least five manuscripts of this oration; one of them is at the Jesuits's Stonyhurst College in Lancashire.[56] It is in very idiomatic and elegant Latin, and my translated extracts below give no idea of its excellence. The author begins with a rhetorical picture of the grief of the thirty towns which White's munificence had enriched, and then turns to the simplicity which governed this liberality.

> What magnificent generosity it was for a wholly unlettered man to found this great home of literature, for a man without learning to patronize the learned, for a wealthy citizen to adopt so many strangers when he had no children of his own, and to give all he had to strangers!

He enlarges on White's childlessness, and declares that it was providential, not natural:

> Wherefore? He was freed from this care that he might be wholly unencumbered for another; and this other care he so entirely embraced, that for the last ten years he devoted all his thoughts, all his means, all his labor upon us; when away from Oxford, his soul was here; waking or sleeping he only thought of us. As soon as his last fatal paralysis attacked him, he immediately sent off for one of us. Our president was away, and I was sent instead. As soon as he saw me, the old man embraced me, and with tears spoke words that I could not hear with dry eyes and cannot repeat without weeping. The sum was, that we should take every care that the College be not harmed, that we should be in charity among ourselves, and educate the youth entrusted to us liberally and piously. We were to tell him if there was anything as yet unfinished, for he was prepared to supply what was needful; and there was yet time to make fresh regulations, or to repeal, remove, or change the old. He had provided for us in his will, and hoped that his wife and [Sir] William Cordell, his executors, would take care of us. He begged that we would not pray

for his recovery, but for faith and patience in his last moments; and nothing annoyed him so much as wishes for a restoration to health.

Then he addresses the absent Sir Thomas, and summarizes his charities—the foundation of Merchant-Tailors's School in London, the restoration of Gloucester Hall, and the foundation of St. John's College, Oxford.

He has beaten all of us students . . . with our holy ways, our sacred teaching, our pious talk, and our hallowed laws. In this man's tongue, manners, and gait, there was nothing polished, dressed up, painted, affected, or false; all was bare, open, plain, pure, sincere, chaste, undefiled.

He and Sir Thomas Pope were the only private persons who had founded colleges; but he did it at a time when there were few incentives to such an act:

when literature was despised, was in prison, in poverty, and in despair, half-dead with sorrow, nearly washed out in tears.

In one of his last letters to the College, January 27, 1567, White had written:

Mr. President, with the Fellows and Scholars, I have me recommended unto you even from the bottom of my heart, desiring the Holy Ghost may be among you until the end of the world, and desiring Almighty God that every one of you may love one another as brethren; and I shall desire you all to apply to your learning, and so doing God shall give you His blessing both in this world and in the world to come. And furthermore if any variance or strife do arise among you, I shall desire you for God's love to pacify it as much as you may; and that doing I put no doubt but God shall bless every one of you.[57]

Campion Speaks and Debates before Queen Elizabeth

The other great occasion of Campion's oratorical triumphs was in the year before, on September 3, 1566, during the queen's visit to the University. He was twenty-six years old, seven years younger than the queen.

The whole university exerted itself in every way to make the best show they could in all kinds of learned and liberal exercises, as orations, disputations, comedies, tragedies, and the like. There were farces and rough horse-pranks, which Elizabeth relished; there were sour theological disputes "moderated" by Bishop John Jewel of Salisbury; and a discussion of physical philosophy, in which Campion bore the chief share. But he had his share in the other revels, "whereof myself," says Persons, "was then an eye-witness also among others, though some six or seven years in standing [age] behind Mr. Campion."[58]

Wood says that Campion welcomed the queen in the name of the University, at her first entry into the city, as thirteen years before he had welcomed Queen Mary to London. His opinions would not be against him at court. Queen Elizabeth notoriously hated the Puritans, and had a taste for many of the externals of the old religion, towards the professors of which she exhibited the moderation of endeavoring to win them by gentle means without exasperating them.[59] Campion's state of mind, however obnoxious to Bishop Jewel or Tobie Mathew, would make him the more interesting to a political coquette who prided herself on her powers of fascination. Nevertheless his friends extorted from him a promise to avoid all controverted points in his orations. Nor was the council less anxious to keep such disputes from the queen's ears. The documents remaining in the State Papers Office[60] are an amusing proof of the industry with which the queen's advisers incubated over this important point. One list of questions in Sir William Cecil's hand carefully eschews all theology, and begins with the inquiry, "Why is ophthalmia catching, but not dropsy or gout?" Another paper proposes to affirm as many heresies as could be stuffed into the budget. The scheme finally adopted by the Council was a clever one for committing the University to the political theology of the court. Its questions in divinity are, "Whether subjects may fight against wicked princes?" "The ministry is not an external power." In moral philosophy, "Princes should be declared by succession, not by election." "The rule of the king alone is better than that of law alone." The political nature of the so-called religious movement in England is well indicated by these questions, and it shows some liberality in the government, that they were allowed to be canvassed at the University in the presence of the queen.

It must have been a relief to his friends to find that Campion was only to be the oracle of two physical mysteries: "Whether the tides are caused by the moon's motion?" and "Whether the lower bodies of the universe are regulated by the higher?" He was respondent; that is, he had first to expose his arguments briefly, then to listen and reply to the objections of his opponents. This display came off on September 3, 1566, before the queen and the handsome Robert Dudley, who was Earl of Leicester, Chancellor of the University, the consoled widower of Amy Robsart, and almost a recognized suitor for the queen's hand, "the chick that sitteth next the hen."[61] His familiarity encouraged her Majesty's faithful Commons, two months afterwards, to petition her to marry, even going so far as to designate him for her husband, "if she intended to marry a subject." But Elizabeth took offense, and commanded him on peril of his life not to aspire to such a thing.[62] Lord Burghley (pronounced "burly") presented, among the reasons why it was inexpedient for Elizabeth to marry Leicester, "that he is infamed by the death of his wife." As yet, however, the drama was not *Love's Labor Lost*, and so the adulatory Oxonians could treat Dudley almost as if he were king, without making the queen jealous. Before this loving pair, Campion was called out to dispute against four challengers, Mr. John Belly being moderator, Campion respondent. The attacking party was composed of John Day (Dee) of Magdalen College; John Meyrick (a peppery Welshman, made bishop of Man in 1573); Richard Bristow of Christ Church (afterwards a Catholic and a dear friend of Campion); and Adam Squire (later to marry the daughter of Bishop Aylmer).[63] In his opening speech, in Latin, Campion, who was an orator, not an astronomer, shows more rhetoric and tact than knowledge:

> Most august Sovereign, even if you are about to watch a young man in an unequal contest, single-handed against pugnacious soldiers: yet it is, by necessity, at the bidding of Philosophy, the princess of letters, before a lettered Princess [Elizabeth].[64]

Then he addressed the eminent Chancellor, Leicester, "whose godly and immortal benefactions to the University I could not deny if I would, and ought not to conceal if I could." It was he who had raised Oxford from her lethargy and encouraged her progress:

> May God preserve these benefits to us; may He preserve your Majesty; [to Dudley] your Honor—you, our mother [the queen]; you, our protector [Dudley]—you, who do these things; you, who advise them.[65]

This Ciceronian see-saw was great clap-trap no doubt, but it effected its purpose. The queen was visibly affected, and turned with smiles to Lord Robert: "You, my lord, must still be one"; words of no great weight, but which thrilled through an ambitious heart, and kindled in it no unkindly feeling to the young orator. Campion did not notice the queen's interruption, but proceeded with his pendulum:

> You [the queen], who watch over these things; you [Dudley], who take care of them; you [the queen], who honor us; you [Dudley], who love us; you, who give us security; you, who give us happiness. For these things, so many and so great . . . we have no gold, dresses, delicacies, paintings, or grand displays, for they are not ours; . . . we can only give what we have within us, something from the veins and womb of philosophy.

Then he philosophizes after this fashion: The moon rules the tides. How do we know? The astronomers tell us that she rules moisture; the physicians, that the humors of the body flow more freely at the changes of the moon; the naturalists, that she expands the sea-water. Directly beneath her, therefore, the sea is always blown out with vapors, like water boiling in a pot. This is the cause of tides. With equal brevity he infers that "the heaven rules all lower bodies," and concludes by asking his hearers' best attention for the sturdy youths who are to oppose him.[66]

Campion Receives Patronage

After the debate, the queen expressed her admiration of Campion's eloquence, and commended him particularly to Lord Robert, who willingly undertook to patronize the scholar. Campion certainly deserved some gratitude for the confession he had drawn from the queen; and his religious tendencies were not then offensive to Robert Dudley, against whom the anonymous author of the time says: "for his gain he was some years their [Catholics] secret friend against you [Protestants], until by his friends he was persuaded, and chiefly by the Lord North, by way of policy, as the said Lord boasteth, in hope of greater gain to step over to the Puritans against us both."[67]

Dudley therefore sent for Campion, bestowed exquisite praises upon him and said,

Truly, my ingenious young man, you are much beholden to the Queen's Majesty. No one would believe how concerned she is for your welfare and progress. I have been commanded by her to ask diligently of you what you would have her do for you or for any of your friends. Make use of this royal generosity and know that you have been taken under her patronage and that you can expect greater things from it each day. Let not any simple or boyish bashfulness deter you from asking whatever you need. In fact, it is not only the queen's command but also my own inclination to bestow most willingly whatever benefits and honors there can be.... This much for the present; hereafter, whatever you desire or ask, the queen and I will make it our care.[68]

But Campion would not make any particular request. The friendship of the Chancellor, he said, was worth more than all gifts. Dudley of course was pleased to gain a brilliant client at no cost. "Valued for his eloquence rather than his theology, he had only to conform to be advanced in either field. Probably Leicester was cognizant of his wavering and made a special effort to lure so gifted a man definitely into the fold of the English Church."[69] For the next five years, the Earl of Leicester (Dudley's title from 1564) showed him no little kindness, as Campion acknowledges in his dedication of his *History of Ireland* to the Earl in May 1571:

There is none that knoweth me familiarly, but he knoweth withal how many ways I am beholden to your Lordship. The regard of your deserts and of my duty hath easily won at my hands this testimony of a thankful mind. I might be thought ambitious if I should recount in particular the times and places of your several courtesies toward me: how oft at Oxford, how oft at the Court, how at Rycott, how at Windsor, how by letters, how by reports, you have not ceased to further with advice, and to countenance with authority, the hope and expectation of me, a single student. Therefore, in sum, it shall suffice me to acknowledge the general heap of your bounties, and for them all to serve your Honor frankly, at the least wise with a true heart. Let every man esteem in your state and fortune the thing that best contenteth and feedeth his admiration; but surely to a judgment seated and rectified, these outward felicities which the world gazeth on are then and therefore to be deemed praiseable, when they lodge those inward qualities of the mind, which (saving for suspicion of flattery) I was about to say, are planted in your breast.

Thirteen years [1558–71] to have lived in the eye and special credit of a prince [Queen Elizabeth],[70] yet never during all that space to have abused this ability to any man's harm, to be kindled neither with grudge nor emulation, to benefit an infinite resort of daily suitors, to let down your calling to the need of mean subjects, to retain so lowly a stomach, such a facility, so mild a nature in so high a vocation, to undertake the tuition of learning and learned men— these are indeed the kernels for the which the shell of your nobility seemeth fair and sightly; this is the sap for whose preservation the bark of your tree is tendered; this is the substance which maketh you worthy of those ornaments wherewith you are attired; and in respect of these good gifts, as I for my part have ever been desirous to discover an officious and dutiful mind towards your Lordship, so will I never cease to betake the uttermost of my power and skill to do you service, nor to beg of Almighty God your plentiful increase in godliness, wisdom and prosperity. Fare you well.

From Dublin May 27, 1571.

Your Lordship's humble to command

Edmund Campion

Campion's admiration of Leicester is certainly a weak point in his early character. His great superiority of intellect and his scholarship were united, say his biographers, with great modesty, and an easy pliability to the wishes of others. Protestant and Catholic writers alike praise his humility, his sweetness, his amiable manners, and his innocent meekness. Charity thinks no evil, and reverence gives honor to great place. If St. Alphonsus Liguori might dedicate a book with fulsome flattery to the anti-clerical Tanucci, Prime Minister of Naples, without suspicion to his sanctity and simplicity, I do not see how we can quarrel with Campion for this preface, though his patron had probably murdered his wife in 1560, and had become notorious to the more knowing ones.

But these crimes were not public; those were days of more than ordinary hypocrisy, and the secret workings of intrigue were harder to discover. Leicester appeared open and free, his manners were engaging, and his treatment of dependents liberal. Several writers of note dedicated works to him.

Campion on Wolsey

Wherever Queen Elizabeth went at Oxford, inscriptions were put up in her honor. One set up over the gate of Christ Church made a painful impression on Campion. That College was one of Cardinal Thomas Wolsey's two magnificent foundations. Later Campion wrote:

> His fall [Wolsey's] was the rising of numbers; for he had extorted for himself enough to set up thirty ordinary magnates. He was Cardinal, Legate, Chancellor, Bishop of York, of Winchester and of Durham, and Abbot of St. Alban's Monastery. He had possessed himself moreover of so many abbeys and priories, of so many rich benefices, that he had gained the name, "guzzler of livings." It was expected that his fall would drive Wolsey to despair, and kill him; but he bore his disgrace with wonderful calmness. If he had but exhibited the same character in his prosperity, all would have been well with him. He went to his house, he lived moderately, he kept up his dignity, but put away his old pomp; he looked after his soul, without being too cast down, or sighing too deeply.
>
> His enemies, who wished rather to rid the world than the court of his presence, envied his happiness, and filed a new bill against him; they embittered the King's counsel, to destroy him entirely. The counts were mostly false, some ridiculous, some wicked: that he had compassed and exercised the power of Legate; that he had written some letters with the phrase, *Ego et rex meus* ("I and my King"); that he had complained of the perversity and the failing discipline of the English Church, and had obtained the office of Papal Legate in order to apply the remedy to this evil; that he had taken the King's seal with him to Flanders; that he had, on private authority, made a pact between Henry [VIII] and the Prince of Ferrara; that he had intruded into the King's presence while laboring under a shameful disease; that he had coined royal money with a cardinal's hat on it; that he had defended the privileges of St. Alban's against the royal commissioners; that he had bought his honors at Rome. Summoned to reply to these counts, he died on the way, and was buried at Leicester.
>
> A man of excellent genius, not unlearned; born at Ipswich, of humble origin, of most lofty ambition; passionate, confident, impure, insincere. He built two colleges: one at Ipswich, which Henry [VIII] destroyed; the other at Oxford, so magnificent that

there is no college in Europe equal to it. This he endowed with an annual income of about £3,000. At the present day Henry is called its founder, simply because he did not upset it and confiscate its revenues after the Cardinal came to the end of his days. Witness the verses carved in great letters over the entrance when Elizabeth made her visit; the last line of the inscription was: *Imperfecta tui subiens monumenta parentis* [Entering the unfinished monument of your father]. I never saw anything more saddening: the memory of the noble patron [Wolsey] obliterated and the honor conferred on one [Henry] who had violated every principle of honor, trampled under-foot all laws, human and divine, and destroyed the Religion and commonwealth of England.[71]

The same thoughts on Wolsey are expressed in Campion's *History of Ireland*,[72] in a passage used and adapted by Shakespeare in his play, *Henry VIII* (Act IV, scene 2), drawing on the version of that *History* in Holinshed's *Chronicles*.

Exhibition from the Grocers' Company

On September 28, 1566, the Grocers' Company gave Campion an annual exhibition of £5.13.4 for his maintenance, which he received for the next two years, "the conditions being that the recipients should have begun the study of divinity, and should be willing to preach at Paul's Cross once a year, if so desired."[73] When this maintenance was discontinued, for reasons explained below,[74] the Company decided, on November 25, 1568, to grant Campion a half-year's exhibition of £3.6.8.[75]

"One of the Diamonds of England"

Anthony à Wood testifies:

> All writers, whether Protestant or Popish, say that he was a man of most admirable parts, an elegant orator, a subtle philosopher and disputant, and an exact preacher whether in English or Latin tongue, of a sweet disposition, and a well-polished man.[76]

Fr. Persons remembers that on account of Campion's

> rare example of his virtuous life, humility, discretion, and modesty, which grew to be scarce and rare in students of those times, the whole University of Oxford did much love and admire him, and did

lay upon him with great good will and applause of all men whatsoever dignities and preferments that University had to give to a man
of his calling and standing.[77]

When the queen asked Guzman, the Spanish ambassador, what he
thought of the Oxford exercises, he replied, "Very well, but I marvel not
thereat considering the variety of good wits and talents there discovered,
and that all the speakers came very well prepared beforehand; but I should
desire to hear something done extempore and without preparation." At
this a number of men were at once sent for to Merton College, where,
in presence of the ambassador, and Dudley, Cecil, and others, they were
made to dispute upon "fire." Persons records that Campion bore away
most praise in this sudden encounter, as he did a little after for a certain
oration that he was forced to extemporise before the queen at Woodstock
Palace, eight miles from Oxford, in which Campion

> confessed afterwards that he was like to have lost himself utterly at
> the beginning, partly by the hastiness of the time [the short notice
> given] and partly by the sudden great pomp wherein the Queen
> came forth to hear him, until after a space (as he was wont to tell) he
> remembered that she was but a woman, and he a man . . . and that all
> that splendor and pomp that glittered in his eyes was but transitory
> vanity, and had no substance in it, by which cogitations and other
> the like he was emboldened to go through with his speech, as he did
> to the great contentation of the Queen and others of the Court and
> to his own high commendation.[78]

Dudley was not alone: Elizabeth's Secretary of State, Sir William
Cecil (Lord Burghley from 1571), also took great interest in Campion's
success, and "gave singular praises to Mr. Campion above all the rest
for his rare learning and talents, and invited him with many hopes and
promises to follow that course."[79] Four years afterwards, when Campion
had left England, Cecil said to Campion's pupil, Stanihurst, "It is a very
great pity to see so notable a man as Campion is, to leave his country, for
indeed he was one of the diamonds of England."[80] Yet in 1581 Cecil was
the chief author of his death, against the wishes of others of the Council,
as Persons was told by one who was present at the deliberations.[81]

Edmund's personal standing and eminence are seen also in the
fact that in March 1565 he was appointed with three Doctors of the

University and four other members to interpret a new statute and so determine whether the Hebrew and Greek lecturers should take part in public disputations.[82]

On the whole, in 1566, Campion was the most popular man in Oxford, where no man envied his triumphs. He did not reside long enough to take his Doctor's degree; but he was made junior proctor at Oxford University on April 18, 1568, the highest post compatible with his standing.[83] As junior proctor, he was second only in importance to the vice-chancellor. It was a position of many and varied responsibilities within the University: he handled all public business, summoned Congregations (university assemblies), licensed bachelors, ministered the oath to inceptors, was a scrutineer in the election of officers, managed University finances, and was responsible for the good order and custody of documents.[84]

Tutor to Henry Vaux

To turn for some time to Edmund's life outside University—Recusant historian and Dominican priest, Godfrey Anstruther, records: "In 1567 or 1568 occurred an event that was to have a far-reaching influence on the whole fortunes of the Vaux [rhymes with "hawks"] family. Lord Vaux's eldest son Henry was then a studious, precocious little boy of nine, and his father looked for a worthy tutor. His choice fell upon the most promising young orator of the day, the idol of Oxford, no less a scholar than Edmund Campion. . . . He was invited to [the family mansion of] Harrowden where he spent several months, and later wrote a long, graceful Latin letter to the little boy":[85]

> Edmund Campion to the Honorable boy Henry Vaux
>
> Hearty greetings.
>
> From the day your father first asked me to see you and to super-intend your education I have become amazingly attached to you. For I marvelled and was almost perplexed when I saw a boy who had not yet completed his ninth year, of a notable family, of such pleasant demeanor and refinement; who wrote and spoke Latin so well; who was equally good at prose and verse, accurate and quick at figures, devoted to the study of letters, diligent in application, able to sketch out and arrange his whole course of study. If circumstances

had permitted it I should have desired nothing better than to give my enthusiastic help to that celebrated man, your father, and to you, a boy of such great promise. But since some unknown fate, yours and mine, has deprived you of me, and me of you, your father (by whom I am dearly loved, and whom I particularly revere) has easily persuaded me that my voice and advice should come to you.

Generally speaking, in any one class of men there are very few who accomplish with praiseworthy passage the full range of the fine arts. But among men of your rank we very seldom come across any who have even a slight acquaintance with literature. Many are over-burdened with leisure; they cling to trifles, waste the possessions of others and squander their own; they ruin their prime of life with unmanly luxury. All the more rightly, then, do I congratulate you on your intellectual outlook, your distinguished father, your grand-mother, your relations and kinsfolk: all of them are and were your teachers, who so formed you that you truly count it a thing admi-rable and noble, excellent and glorious, to consider the ornaments of virtue and not fleeting imaginings to be the real fame; not to waste your talents in idleness, not to gamble away your life, not to be puffed up, not to live licentiously and for pleasure; but to serve God, to curb vicious passions, to seek the best in culture and in art.

Consider well the course you have chosen, how you are going, to where you are voyaging. You have sailed out of the rough waters of elementary studies: away, as it were, from the rocks and shoals of the coast-line. And now with billowing sails and a favorable breeze, you catch sight of the harbor as if from afar. Full steam ahead!

In your own family there are not lacking examples to imitate or to emulate: your grandfather, your mother, your sister. Your grandfather, a man of very wide and expert knowledge of classical and humanist literature has enriched our English language by poeti-cal compositions in various modes. Your mother was noted for her admirable shrewdness, her natural ability and holiness. Your sister is your rival in study and in work; and she is learned in the same academic pursuits. If you underrate her, even a little, and take things easy, she will beat you and outshine you.

Exert yourself, then, all the more and strive for this: both to ful-fil completely the promise that you bear, and to urge on that learned and in every way accomplished maiden, your sister, who is now run-ning her course of her own accord. If you follow this path, you two will be a golden pair; you will reach the delights you seek, you will shine with marvellous lustre, you will be filled with the desire to act dutifully and generously, and you will be surrounded by renown and affection in the sight of all men.

Beware of pride, be modest always, associate with good companions and avoid the company of the wicked like the plague. Love God and serve Him. Honor your parents. Treat your elders with respect and your equals with courtesy.

A more illustrious example of affability and integrity than your father I do not think it is possible for you to see. Take him as your pattern. During the period of several months when I was a guest at your father's house, his daily speech and intimate conversation brought home to me the great work he was doing for all men of learning. I was much impressed by his pleasant and easy manner, his anxious and solicitous care for you all, and the fatherly pride he took in your natural gifts. And although I have been separated from him longer than I anticipated, not by my own wish, but by reason of my way of life, still I shall never cease to favor you and to wish you well, you and your family, by whom I am so sumptuously maintained and so honorably encouraged.

Farewell.

Oxford, July 28, 1570

The letter provides a charming picture of the cultured life of Vaux's house, and the deep friendship between Campion and the whole family, that seems to have been long-standing. It represents Lord Vaux as a patron of letters, and the last sentence seems to mean that he was Campion's patron as well.[86]

Campion's faith in the Anglican Settlement had been waning for some time. What part his stay at Harrowden Hall, Northamptonshire, played in his momentous decision to be no part of it we have no means of knowing, but his friendship was to cost the Vaux family a great deal in the years to come, as we will see a little when Lord Vaux and Henry Vaux re-appear in these pages.[87]

A Struggle of Conscience

All his successes, says Fr. Persons, put Campion into exceeding danger, by enticing him to follow a course of which his conscience disapproved,

> for he was always a sound Catholic in his heart . . . and utterly condemned in his judgment all the whole form and substance of that new religion which the Queen and Council so lately before had chosen to themselves . . . and yet . . . the sugared words of those great persons and especially those of the queen herself, joined with the pregnant hopes of great dignities and preferments . . . [88]

so enticed him that he knew not which way to turn. His youth and ambition, his desire to satisfy the expectations of his friends, and emulation at the advance of his equals and inferiors, pushed him onwards; while remorse of conscience, fear of Hell, and an invincible persuasion of the truth of Catholic doctrine and the falsehood of the Protestant opinion, pulled him back.

He decided to compromise matters by temporizing; his internal combat was long and dangerous, for he lacked the aid of the Sacraments and of spiritual direction; and though he prayed earnestly for light, yet he still hearkened to both sides inwardly, to see whether he could find sufficient reasons to allow his conscience to follow in peace the course to which his worldly interests so strongly inclined him.

This was the case also with Robert Persons for some years, and with many others, especially at the universities; with young men, well accommodated in fellowships or otherwise, and provoked by infinite inducements to seek the preferments which the place and the country yielded, or at least to keep what they had; yet feeling that the religion on which these preferments depended was doubtful and therefore dangerous: hence they lived in great toil and torment of mind, loath to lose the hope of salvation, glad to hold their commodities without molestation of conscience, if possible, ever in suspense, ever ready to listen to any reason that promised to remove their scruples.

The Fathers of the Church

The only safe anchor in this troubled water was, in Persons's opinion, the study of the Fathers—those holy and learned ecclesiastical writers of the first six centuries:

> for whatsoever one of us had heard or conceived in the whole day
> for pulling out this thorn of conscience and for smoothing the way
> to be Protestant, either by good fellowship and conversation with

Protestants themselves, or by hearing their sermons or reading their books and the like, all this was dashed soon after again by one hour's reading of some book or treatise of the old holy Doctors, and the wound of our conscience was made again so green and grievous as ever before, by that which in every leaf and page almost we should find to be spoken by those holy men, either by virtue or austerity of life, or of questions and matters of controversies, and that so directly for the Catholic religion and most perspicuously against all that the Protestants did either teach or practise, as if these ancient Fathers had lived and seen their dealings, and had been their open adversaries in these our days.[89]

It was in 1567 that Campion, having exhausted Aristotle and natural theology for the past three years, had to turn to these authentic reporters of the Christian tradition; and for three whole years he was distracted with the various arguments for and against the open profession of his Catholic belief. He had begun with a conscientious examination of the controverted doctrines one by one; the unhistorical and illogical character of the new tenets was soon discovered; and as truth begets truth, and as a mind once cheated ever suspects fraud, he examined the points which he used to take for granted; here too the ground failed beneath him. But the consequences of his step were too fatal to his worldly interests to allow of any hurry. He consulted his friends. He went to anyone, no matter what his views, who professed to be able to tell him something, but every discussion pushed him on a step further.

An extract from his *Rationes Decem* ("Ten Reasons," Reason No. 5) will illustrate this. Campion is speaking in 1581 of his memory of an event that took place back in 1559, when John Jewel, Bishop of Salisbury, issued a public challenge to Catholics to prove specific doctrines from the Bible, Fathers and early Councils:

> When I was a young man, the following incident occurred. John Jewel, a foremost champion of the Calvinists of England, with incredible arrogance challenged the Catholics, at St. Paul's, London, hypocritically invoking and calling upon the Fathers who had flourished within the first six hundred years of Christianity. His challenge was taken up by the illustrious men who were then in exile at Louvain, although hemmed in with very great difficulties by reason of the iniquity of their times. I dare say that Jewel's craft, ignorance,

roguery and impudence, which those writers happily exposed, did
so much good to our countrymen that scarcely anything in my
recollection has turned out to the better advantage of the suffering
English Church. At once an edict was posted on the doors, forbidding the reading or possession of any of those books—whereas they
had come out, or were wrung out, one could say, by the outcry that
Jewel had raised. The result was that everyone interested in the matter came to see that the Fathers were Catholics, that is to say, were
ours. . . .

   Once also I familiarly questioned Tobie Mathew, now your
leading preacher, whom I loved for his good accomplishments and
his seeds of virtue, and asked him to answer honestly how a man
who read the Fathers assiduously could take the side which he supported. He answered, "If I believed them, as well as read them, I
could not." This is a perfectly true statement, and I do not suppose
that he . . . thinks any differently now.

This challenge, naturally, summoned Tobie, who answered in a
concio apologetica (speech of self-defense), given at the church of Our
Lady at Oxford on October 9, 1581. It was delivered in Latin, printed
or circulated possibly the same year, and, strangely, printed in 1638, ten
years after his death. It is eighty-six small pages, and very tedious, most
of it being strings of quotations from the Fathers, with occasional snide
remarks about Campion. Father Persons describes it as rather vehement
and rhetorical than sincere. Of course, Tobie denied the charge:

> Edmund Campion says that Tobie Mathew in one word repudiated
> all the Fathers. Edmund Campion affirms it, Tobie Mathew denies
> it; will you believe both? . . . I avouch that neither in speech nor in
> writing, in jest or in earnest, waking or sleeping, did I ever say it, or
> anything like it.[90]

However, Campion who had asserted it was soon to be dead for his
faith, and Mathew was enjoying benefices and prospects which might
be risked by the story being believed. He challenged Campion, as if they
were in court together, to say exactly when and where, in whose company,
on what occasion and in what circumstances, he said it.[91] According to
Persons, Campion's friend Richard Stanihurst declared that he had heard
it from Campion at the very time it occured.[92] The admiration of Edmund

for Tobie was, at the time, mutual: there survives a "Latin letter, express-ing many compliments and great friendship" from Tobie to Edmund.[93]

Another of Campion's Christ Church friends was reputed to be as cunning in the Scriptures as Tobie Mathew in the Fathers; this was Philip Sidney's first tutor, Dr. Thomas Thornton[94]—a Latinist, theologian, and staunch Protestant. He professed to prove his religion from the Bible alone, without the Fathers. Campion and he had an argument, in which "each party should allege only bare Scripture, and to strive for the sense, as they could, by those means which the Protestants do assign, which are the help of tongues [languages], and conferring [comparing] one place with another, and prayer."[95] When Campion had produced many strong passages on the Catholic side, and had shown that they could not be evaded in Greek or Hebrew, and perceived that Thornton could not bring any so clear for his side, and could only oppose wrangling inter-pretations out of his own head, Campion, says Persons, fully resolved that he would never follow it for temporal reasons, seeing that both the Scriptures and Fathers were wholly against the Protestant side.

Cheney, Bishop of Gloucester

Campion had access to Leicester's ante-room whenever he pleased. Here, perhaps, he met with Richard Cheney, the Bishop of Gloucester since 1562, a man of congenial nature, tastes, and studies. Cheney was a mild, persuasive, old man, very different from the rest of the Elizabethan bish-ops, from whom he held aloof, as if he had been of a different commu-nion. In the Convocation of 1553, he had tried to commit the Anglican body to the Lutheran doctrine of consubstantiation, but he was so far from being either Lutheran or Calvinist in other respects that in 1568 his flock complained of "very strange, perilous, and corrupt doctrines, contrary to the Gospel,"[96] which he preached in his cathedral of Bristol, where his own fanatical clergy withstood him to the face. He warned his hearers that the new writers differed from each other, and were therefore not safe guides, but that the old Fathers and Doctors alone were to be followed; that any heretic might avouch Scripture, and that controversy would be endless without the appeal to the Fathers; that Luther wrote a very ill book against free will, which Erasmus answered well; and that the consent of the Fathers was the only test by which he would be tried.

There was one more statement with which Cheney's Puritanical accusers were scandalized, though it was addressed, not so much to the Puritans, as to those numerous loose Catholics who would not give up the old faith, but were unwilling to submit to the penalties for not going to church. There was always a large party of this sort in England. In 1562, some of their chief men, via the Portuguese ambassador, had consulted the Fathers of the Council of Trent upon the matter, and had asked whether they might not with a safe conscience attend the Anglican *Common Prayer* and preaching. A committee was appointed to reply, who firmly but kindly gave a decided negative. But one answer was not enough—especially when it was not the answer one hoped for. Many books were printed, and many more circulated in manuscript, on the same question. Many English Catholics persisted in thinking that they might save their freedom and their goods by being present at *Common Prayer* and sermons. Cheney encouraged this idea. He would have recoiled from subverting what remained of Catholic faith. He only undermined it. He did not deny that attendance at the Protestant services was like Naaman the Syrian attending to his king at worship in the pagan temple of Rimmon, which the prophet Elisha allowed Naaman to do (*2 Kgs.* 5:18). He quoted this example to show that political motives might excuse a man's presence at a worship which his conscience abhorred. In a sermon in the cathedral of Bristol in 1562, Cheney said:

> A question may be asked between the young maid and Naaman; whether that a godly man may be at idol-service with his body, his heart being with God, without offense or sin? I say you may, without offense or sin. And because you shall not think that I am of this opinion only, I will bring you Peter Martyr [Vermigli], a learned man, and as famous as ever was in our time, being your own doctor [onetime Professor of Divinity at Oxford]: who saith, a man may be present without offense. Whose very words I will read unto you; which are these: *Non enim simpliciter et omnibus modis interdictum est piis hominibus, ne in fanis praesentes adsint, dum profani et execrandi ritus exercentur.* [It is not utterly and in all manner forbidden for pious men to attend pagan temples in person when profane and execrable rites are being performed].[97]

This was just the doctrine that Campion wanted. The two men agreed in execrating the innovators, and yet maintaining the duty of remaining in the Establishment. Was it not the ancient national Church, founded by apostolic authority, to be the repository of the Faith and Sacraments? If her vineyard was now usurped by the beasts of the forests, if the wild-boar was uprooting her vines, should her children forsake her in her affliction? No; though heretical Calvinists occupied her pulpits, her children need not desert their old homes. If Naaman might attend his king to the house of Rimmon, much more might we accompany our tyrant to our own churches, though heretics for a season occupied our places, and botchers had disfigured our ancient rites. Thus was the instance of Naaman generalized into a universal dispensation for all sects to huddle together, provided it was within the stone walls built for God's service in Catholic times. If he ever lighted on the words of St. Hilary, Cheney chose to ignore the ancient Bishop of Poitiers: "It is ill that a love of walls has seized you; it is ill that your veneration for God's Church lies in houses and buildings; it is ill that under this plea you insinuate the name of peace. Is there any doubt that Antichrist is to sit in these? Mountains and woods and lakes and prisons are to me safer; for in these the prophets, sojourning or sunk, still by God's Spirit prophesy."[98]

The acquaintance soon ripened into affection; Campion was continually visiting Cheney at Gloucester, reading in the bishop's study, and borrowing books from his library, enjoying the closest familiarity, sharing the old man's sorrows, and listening to his complaints of the calumnies that assailed him. The bishop exhorted his young friend never for a moment to swerve from the royal road of Church Councils and Fathers, and ever to put full faith in their consensus. Campion saw the inconsistency of this advice, yet he allowed himself to be persuaded. He saw that the weapons which Cheney wielded against Puritans might be better used by Catholics against Cheney; he saw, and hesitated; yet he could not make up his mind to tell Cheney his doubts, to warn him his position was untenable, or to entreat him, now that he was so near the kingdom of God, to take but one more step and secure it for ever.

Cheney alone of the Elizabethan bishops had the slightest pretensions to orthodoxy; alone confessed the living presence of Christ upon the altar, and the freedom of man's will; alone refused to waste his episcopal property by leases, exchanges, sales of lands, of timber, or even of the lead off the church-roof; he alone refused to persecute the Catholics of his diocese. In his Certificate of Recusants, October 24, 1577, Cheney excused those "supposed to favor popery" as absenting themselves from church on the ground of sickness or fear of process for debt, while he indicted the Puritans as willful recusants.[99] The Council peremptorily ordered him to proceed against the Popish recusants; whereupon, November 20, he sent up a short list, got up, he said, by diligent inquiry.[100] (On "recusants," see chapter 9.)[101] Indeed, so far from Campion influencing his friend, Cheney had, on the contrary, fixed his eyes upon Campion as the man to carry on his hybrid project: a Catholic tradition in a Protestant framework.

Deacon in the Church of England

While in a state of doubt and suspension of mind, Edmund yielded half-reluctantly to the persuasions of his worldly friends, and in 1569 he let himself be ordained deacon, so as to be capable of preferment and to be able to preach. The heretics hoped, says Persons, to bind him fast to their party in this way.

We have no document with the date or even year of his ordination. "He was ordained deacon by Bishop Cheney of Gloucester, but the date is uncertain, for the first volume of the registers of that diocese perished long ago. As the see of Oxford was vacant, many Oxford men were ordained at Gloucester about this time."[102]

However, good reasons lead us to an ordination date between March 19 and July 11, 1569. This is the period reached by Dr. Vossen,[103] who shows that all the early biographers say Campion's ordination was followed by a speedy repentance and then a retreat to Ireland. The evidence for this is given here in an endnote.[104] If we can date the sudden change of heart, we can thereby date the ordination. Vossen says, "On March 19, 1569 Campion supplicated for the degree of bachelor of theology but when the Act was held on July 11 he did not come forward for the degree."[105] Vossen agrees with Stevenson and Salter, who say, "It is evident that in March 1569 Campion thought that he could support the position of the Reformed Church [as a theology candidate had to do], but apparently his opinions changed in the next four months."[106]

Three more pieces of evidence indicate 1569.

First, having repented promptly of his entrance into Anglican ministry, Edmund got permission in October 1569 to travel overseas (although for a year he did not use it).[107]

Secondly, his friend Gregory Martin resigned his fellowship at St.

John's in December 1568 to go to the Duke of Norfolk.[108] Campion recalls, "I remember how from your Prince's house you [Martin] once dealt with me by correspondence to keep me from the ecclesiastical dignity, which . . . you feared might betray me into serving these wretched times."[109] Thus, at the end of 1568 he was not yet a deacon.

Thirdly, in March 1569 he was given the vicarage of Sherborne (Gloucester) by the Bishop of Gloucester and held its benefice for a year or so.[110] It makes sense to say the benefice came with ordination. His regret over the ordination was intense. At the time, he was not thinking, as he afterwards said, "that the matter had been as odious and abominable as upon more light and knowledge he perceived."[111] As soon as he was ordained, troubles began to beset him. Says Persons, he "took presently such a remorse of conscience and detestation of mind."[112] Outwardly, his familiarity with Cheney, and the reports of his opinions, made him suspected by his London friends. Later, Campion would refer to his Holy Orders in the Established Church as "my disorders" and "the mark of the beast."[113] Persons records: "The remembrance of this mark of the English beast, as afterward he was wont to tell us, did make him sad and melancholy."[114] He was tormented by "the memory of which profane degree and schismatic order," "exceedingly molested and stung in conscience with that heretical character and profane mark of ministry."[115] He never advanced to the next step, of Anglican priesthood.

Trouble from the Grocers' Company

He still held his exhibition from the Grocers' Company, when rumors of his heterodoxy (i.e., Catholic opinions) reached them and they began to question him. The Company's records of April 30, 1568, say:

> Agreed that Edmund Campion, the scholar of this Company, to prepare himself to preach before the Company at St. Stephen's Walbrook on the day of the election next, which if he refuse to do the exhibition granted to him to cease and given to another, unless he can show reasonable cause to the contrary.[116]

St. Stephen's church was under the (shared) patronage of the Company.[117]

If the diaconate was a pre-requisite to preach, and a layman could not be compelled or expected to do so—then one wonders why the layman Campion was being summoned to preach publicly. The only possible answer is that Edmund concealed his lay state, and the unaware Grocers' Company presumed he was ordained since the normal due date of diaconate was past.[118] In a letter to them cited below, he says "that to preach . . . he would be very loath to presume unto"—which may mean presumptuous *of a layman*, as he still was, but without saying so.

Their records of July 9, 1568, mention, for the second time, the issue of preaching:

> To avoid and clear the suspicion conceived of Edmund Campion, one of the Company's scholars, and that he may utter his mind in favoring the religion now authorized, it is agreed that between this and Candlemas next [February 2, 1569] he shall come and preach at Paul's Cross, in London, or else the Company's exhibition to cease, and be appointed [assigned] to another; and that he shall have warning thereof within these 13 days from Mr. Warden to provide himself thereunto.

A subsequent entry just a few days later, July 14, 1568, brings it up for the third time:

> Whereas at the last Court it was thought good that Edmund Campion, one of the Company's scholars, "being suspected to be of no sound judgment in religion" and for clearing himself therein, should preach at St. Paul's Cross between that and Candlemas next [February 2, 1569], the said Campion having already had his exhibition for two years at Midsummer and has not to the Company's knowledge ever made one sermon anywhere. After further consideration, it is now agreed that he shall, between this and the second Sunday after Michaelmas [July 14–October 10, 1568] preach a sermon at Paul's Cross, and if he refuse, then his exhibition to cease. The Wardens are with all speed to write to him to answer forthwith.

The required sermon was brought forward by four months—possibly because Campion's failure to preach anywhere was a sign that he was not one in faith with the Established Church. They wanted to ascertain his position soon, and they had no intention to continue funding a dissenter for so long.

If the "exhibition for two years at Midsummer" indicates also the time in which he had "not ever made one sermon anywhere," this would

mean they presumed that he received diaconate in 1566, when he was
twenty-five years old, a usual age for that step; and it fits in with the time
the exhibition was granted, namely, the same year.[119]

Campion disliked the ordeal proposed, and he appeared before them
and petitioned them to postpone the clearing of himself. The record of
August 2, 1568, says:

> The said Campion appeared at this Court [some time earlier] desiring
> to know the Company's pleasure . . . [Campion] discreetly answered
> "that to preach first [give his first sermon] at Paul's Cross is a thing
> he would be very loath to presume unto and therefore desired this
> Court to give him a longer time to prepare himself thereunto." The
> Court, "well liking that he did not utterly refuse to preach," after
> further consideration, agreed that he should come to London and
> preach before the Company at St. Stephen's Walbrook a fortnight
> after Michaelmas next. He was called in and the said agreement read
> to him, but he alleged "that he was this year by office a public per-
> son [because proctor] and cannot at all do what he wills, as also is
> charged with the education of divers worshipful men's children . . ."
> therefore did again beseech to have a longer day, whose request the
> Company thought not good to grant, but fully resolved themselves
> that he shall come and preach at the said church the said day being
> the 17th day of October, unto which in the end the said Campion did
> agree, and desired to have note thereof, which was delivered to him
> in manner and form following. . . . It is agreed by this Company that
> Mr. Edmund Campion shall come to London and make a sermon
> before them at St. Stephen's in Walbrook in London the Sunday
> fortnight after the feast of St. Michael the Archangel next, which
> shall be the 17th of October 1568, on the forenoon of the same day.

The choice of St. Stephen's Church, Walbrook, was a concession,
since it was a less notable place than St. Paul's Cross, an open-air pulpit
in the church-yard of St. Paul's Cathedral, London. The record also says
that the exhibition is to continue as before.

In the end, Campion, resolving not to comply with them, and knowing they would not postpone the sermon again, did not preach. The
Company's record of October 14 says that Campion did not come to
preach but sent a letter

wherein he thanked the Company for the benefit he had received at their hands and frankly yielded up the same, alleging that "he dare not, he cannot, neither was it expedient that he should preach as yet, declaring in his letters divers reasons for the same." Upon the reading of the said letter, it was ordered by the Court that the said exhibition should be bestowed upon some other scholar.

This was not the end of their sponsorship completely, however. The entry of November 25, 1568, says that upon a petition to the Wardens of the Grocers' Company from Mr. Thomas Roe, Lord Mayor of London, a half-year's exhibition of £3.6.8 was granted to Campion.

Gregory Martin and the End of Oxford

Stevenson and Salter explain Campion's next moves, physically and mentally:

> A few months later he shows that he still thought it possible to maintain the doctrine of the Church of England, for on March 19, 1569 he supplicated, in the usual form, that a study of theology for five years *cum multis et crebris exercitiis privatis in eadem, cum reliqua perfecerit et adimpleverit quae per nova statuta requiruntur* [with many and frequent private exercises in the same, when he shall have completed the remainder and fulfilled what is required by the new statutes] should be adequate to admit him to the degree of bachelor in theology; this was granted. The *nova statuta* [new statutes] are apparently the statutes passed in 1564 and 1565, which merely add to the old statutes the regulation that a candidate for the degree of B.D. [Bachelor of Divinity (Theology)] must publicly dispute two questions of theology and that the questions are to be affixed to the door of St. Mary's [Oxford] fourteen days before the day of disputation. It is unnecessary to say that every disputant was expected to maintain the side of the Reformed Church, and that no one would be granted a degree if he was suspected of disloyalty to the Reformation. It is evident that in March 1569 Campion thought that he could support the position of the Reformed Church, but apparently his opinions changed in the next four months. He ceased to be proctor on April 20, 1569, but when the Act was held on July 11, he did not come forward for the degree of B.D.; doubtless he had failed to perform the public disputations demanded by the *nova statuta*.

It is generally said that he resigned his fellowship and withdrew from Oxford on August 1, 1569, but it was at Michaelmas
[September 29] 1570, or a few days earlier, that he went away with
what we should call a travelling fellowship for five years under the
College Statute which permitted a fellow, with the approval of the
College, to travel abroad for that period, continuing to receive the
emoluments of his fellowship at the rate of £8 a year.[120]

He had prepared this move a year earlier, but then delayed it:

On October 6, 1569 he had been given leave by the College to travel
abroad for five years, retaining his fellowship, starting on May 1,
1570; but he did not make use of this permission, and it was renewed
to him on August 7, 1570, to take effect from September 30, and
there can be no doubt that his departure was between August 7 and
September 30.[121]

He may have delayed his departure a year until a new graduate,
Robert Hart, could take over his lectureship in Rhetoric.[122] The understanding was that he would return to St. John's:

The Statute (no. 32), under which Campion was allowed to travel
lays down that after five years the fellow shall return to the College
and give lectures, to the intent that the College may benefit from his
studies; and if he fails to return, that he will repay to the College the
money he has received; and that beyond his oath he shall give a bond
of £40 together with two of his friends ("men of worth and wealth")
that he will fulfill these conditions.[123]

Edmund received the £8 per year, for the next two-and-a-half years,
up to the reception of his theology degree at Douay in January 1573, and
it was only upon entering the Jesuits later that year that he became ineli-
gible to retain the stipend, "as the rule of all Oxford Colleges was that a
fellowship was vacated on marriage or on joining a religious order."[124]

In those days, it was a requirement for a student at a certain point in
his studies to accept the Holy Order of priesthood. Campion was probably due for priestly ordination by Michaelmas 1569, but he managed
to evade ordination (beyond diaconate), by holding the lectureship in
Rhetoric, which exempted one for the time being from entering upon
the priesthood.[125] Then, when the Statutes required that he receive

priesthood during his overseas study, he was given special consideration for his scruples over the matter, and exempted from the requirement. The concession "is worth notice, since eight out of the ten who signed the resolution [granting him the travelling fellowship and not stipulating ordination] remained members of the Church of England, and five of them received, or had already received, holy orders in that church."[126]

Fully occupied as he must have been with his academic duties—he was junior proctor in 1568–69—and with his pupils, and devoted as he was to the course of education, his duties did not occupy his whole attention, or stifle his misgivings of conscience and his distress. When he retired into himself, his thoughts were not the most pleasant. He is reported to have declared more than once that soon after his ordination he began to feel extraordinary mental anguish: his illicit orders could only be cured by Catholicism. The dignities he once dreamed of had lost their allurements. If his ambition had once been to continue Cheney's work, and to succeed to his bishopric, now he plainly saw what a Babylonian captivity those gilded chains disguised. He was one of those favored men whose falls are the direct occasions of their rise, and who may truly exclaim, *O felix culpa!* (O happy fault).

> O benefit of ill! now I find true
> That better is by evil still made better,
> And ruin'd love, when it is built anew,
> Grows fairer than at first, more strong, far greater.
> So I return rebuk'd to my content,
> And gain by ill thrice more than I have spent.
> —Shakespeare, Sonnet [119]

There existed then in his stricken mind a civil war while different opinions about either concealing or professing the Catholic religion fought it out. The Grocers were driving him, his conscience was goading him, and now his dearest friend Gregory Martin was beckoning him away. Edmund Campion and Gregory Martin had been college companions for thirteen years, where they had their meals, their books, their ideas in common; they had studied under the same masters, had loved the same friends, were hated by the same enemies. Martin, like Campion, was a man of mark, "of extraordinary modesty and moderation," "the Hebraist, the Grecian, the poet, the honor and glory"[127] of St. John's

College. Martin had accepted a place in the Duke of Norfolk's family as governor to his boys; and though Philip Howard, afterwards Earl of Arundel, did Martin no present credit, the young nobleman bore witness, by his holy death in 1595, to the good husbandry of his early tutor (he is now St. Philip Howard, one of the Forty Martyrs of England and Wales). In 1569, when the duke's troubles about the Queen of Scots began, all his household were commanded to attend Common Prayer and sermons.[128] Gregory Martin therefore fled overseas to Douay to live as a Catholic and become a priest. But before he left, he wrote to Campion to warn him against the ambition that was leading him astray into the wide path where so many great wits had perished in those evil days. He begged him not to fear for poverty; their friendship was too pure to admit such difficulties. "If we two can but live together," he wrote, "we can live on nothing; if this is too little, I have money; if this fails, one thing is left—'they that sow in tears shall reap in joy,'" (*Ps.* 125:5).[129]

Dr. Gerard Kilroy summarizes Edmund's intentions to keep his options open:

> When Campion walked through the gates of St. John's late in 1570, he had been given a travelling fellowship by the College. His choice of Ireland was, according to Bombino, because he had discovered from friends that "he could more freely—anyway with less certain danger—practice the true religion."[130] More importantly, Campion seems to have been trying to avoid the more radical option of Louvain or Douay; his travelling fellowship allowed him to spend five years abroad without taking [holy] orders, and to continue to receive his stipend as fellow. It seems clear that he intended to return to St. John's, and that for the time he was resisting the appeals of Gregory Martin to join him, along with Richard Bristow, Thomas Stapleton, William Allen and many others in the recently established 'Oxford house" at Douay. Campion was still, in Bombino"swords, "utrinque nutantem": hesitating which way to jump.[131]

Driven one way and drawn another, Campion terminated his office as proctor on April 20, 1569, did not come forward for the degree of Bachelor of Divinity on July 11, 1569; and on the Feast of St. Michael, September 29, 1570, or a few days earlier, he left Oxford,[132] never to see it again.

CHAPTER 2

Ireland

CAMPION HAD no desire to exercise an Anglican ministry; he wished to forget it and to live as a simple layman. But in the cause of education and of letters his enthusiasm never for a moment slackened. He strenuously recommended his pupils to complete the whole circle of sciences, "not to deliquesce into sloth, nor to dance away your time, nor to live for rioting and pleasure; but to serve God, to bridle your passions, to give yourself up to virtue and learning, and to reckon this the one great, glorious, and royal road."[1] To one of his scholars, Richard Stanihurst, who at the age of twenty-three, two years after his matriculation at Oxford, had published an erudite commentary on Porphyry,[2] he was quite dithyrambic in his congratulations

> that our university should possess a youth of rank, learning, and goodness, capable almost in his teens of competing with able men in maturity. Proceed, Stanihurst, with the same pains and toil, bury yourself in your books: complete your course, abjure the snares of vice, keep your mind on the stretch, give yourself to your country, strive for the prizes which you deserve.[3]

He anticipated a splendid future for such precocious attainments, when they had been matured and completed by methodical study; when wit had been confirmed with judgment, judgment with wisdom, and

> wisdom with age. . . . Only persevere, keep doing what you are doing, do not degenerate from what you are, nor suffer the keen edge of your mind to grow dull and rusty. I exhort you ardently, not because I mistrust you, but because it is my duty to be anxious for the fame of men like you.[4]

Lest the reader think Campion was being over-effusive, Stanihurst's work is recognized as extraordinarily learned. It is interesting to note that the printed edition has a prefatory letter by Campion, and commendatory verses by, among others, Laurence Humphrey—who was one day to be a theological foe of Campion.[5]

Campion Goes to Ireland

When he finally left Oxford, it was not because he was weary of university life, but because the opposition to his way of thinking was becoming too strong. The new religion was daily gaining ground at the English university, the whole machinery of which was in the hands of men who were both able and desirous to make it the stronghold of the rising Puritanism.

Campion took himself to Dublin, therefore, at the end of September 1570, with the approbation of the Earl of Leicester, accompanied by Richard Stanihurst.[6]

His first and chief host in Ireland was the Recorder of Dublin and Speaker of the House of Commons, James Stanihurst, the father of Campion's pupil, and at that time a Catholic—but very much compromised by passing the laws legitimizing the Elizabethan settlement of religion in his country. In 1559, Anglicanism was made the religion of Ireland. Catholic bishops not conforming were removed from office. For the next forty years, no solemn Mass was celebrated in Dublin.

James died only three years after hosting Campion, in December 1573, aged fifty-one. His son, Richard Stanihurst (1547–1618), helped Campion collect materials for his *History* of the country. In 1579, Richard's wife, Janet, daughter of Sir Christopher Barnewall, died aged nineteen. In 1581, Richard left for the Low Countries (modern Holland, Belgium, and Flanders) never to return to his native Ireland, or England. He was by then fully committed to Catholicism. His second wife was Helen Copley of Surrey, a Catholic, who had moved with her family to Dunkirk. They had two sons, Peter and William, both of whom became Jesuits. When Helen died in 1602, Richard himself became a priest.

His Activities in Dublin

Campion was cordially received by his pupil's father, and domiciled in his house, where he is said to have lived a kind of monastic life, and to have exhibited such purity and modesty of demeanor, that the Dublin people called him a "Religious in secular garb, an Angel in human flesh." [7]

Here he employed himself in exercises of learning with Richard Stanihurst, in setting forth his ideal of a university education, and, in his spare time, compiling materials on Irish history. He wrote a discourse, *De Homine Academico* ("The University Man"), which has not survived in its original form but in the shape of an oration, *De Juvene Academico* ("The Young Student"), pronounced at Douay a year or two hence, which we look at next chapter.[8]

It used to be said that Campion went to Dublin to take up a post in the university about to be erected there,[9] but this is now known not to have been the case at all. In fact, Simpson was the first to link Campion to this proposed university—and many have repeated it since.[10] However, Dr. Vossen demonstrates clearly this is wrong: no previous biographer mentions it; no source or contemporary record mentions it; such a university, even if achieved, would have been a Protestant one—hardly a place for Campion.[11]—Further, far from entering a public post, he was about to be pursued for his Catholic religion.

Forced into Hiding

For a time—from October 1570 to March 1571—Campion was allowed to pray, study, and research in peace. He lived openly as a Catholic, and the high commissioners had therefore resolved to apprehend him; but, as the persecution was not then very rigorous, they were delayed for a time by the authority and credit of his friends. He was saved from arrest and received special protection from Sir Henry Sidney (1529–1586), Lord Deputy of Ireland, who was regarded by Father Persons as "a very honorable, calm, and civil gentleman, and no thing hot in the new religion, but rather a great friend to Catholics."[12] Henry Sidney was married to Robert Dudley's sister. Sidney secretly promised James Stanihurst that, while he was Governor, "no busy knave of them all (for those were his words) should trouble him for so worthy a guest as Mr. Campion,"[13] and performed it most honorably while he remained in Ireland. Sidney was the residing head of the English government in Ireland, but that was completely subordinate to the Court of England. The Parliament of Ireland had no real power: it was summoned only to approve of measures already decided by the queen, and its opposition to anything was smothered.

Elizabeth's rival—Mary Queen of Scots—entered England in May 1568. The years 1569 and 1570 were disastrous both to the present and future of English Catholics. The 1569 rebellion of the North against Elizabeth had failed, and Elizabeth's ministers had behaved as men usually do when recovering from a crisis of great danger and greater terror. The queen had been further exasperated by St. Pius V's bull of excommunication against her, which a layman, John Felton, had pasted up on the Bishop of London's gates on the feast of Corpus Christi, 1570.

The attention of the Court was especially turned to the designs of Spain upon Ireland. The French ambassador learnt in London, early in January 1571, that Philip II had submitted to the pope, as suzerain of the island, the tender of the Irish crown, made to him by Stukeley in the name of the people, who were anxiously looking for him; that the pope had bidden him God-speed, on condition of his re-establishing the Catholic religion; and that 10,000 men were to be sent over.[14] Before February 12, 1571, Elizabeth had written to Sidney to delay his departure, and to order him to provide for the defense of the country, promising to send him directly all the aid he wanted.[15]

In these circumstances, even Sir Henry Sidney's influence could no longer ensure Campion's safety. But he did what he could; in the middle of March, when Campion was to be seized early the next day, Sidney sent a servant to warn him, by a private message at midnight. James Stanihurst, therefore, procured him a refuge with Sir Christopher and Lady Marion Barnewall, at Turvey, twelve miles north of Dublin. James's sons, Richard and Walter, conducted him through the darkness, and committed him to the hospitable care of his new hosts, who were more earnest in their Catholic faith than Sidney was. Lady Marion (née Sherle) was from Shallon, County Meath. The Barnewalls had five sons and fifteen daughters. The youngest daughter was already married. Sir Christopher was to die in 1575; Lady Marion about 1589. "Owing to its situation on the isthmus between the inlets of Malahide and Donabate it must have been an ideal hiding-place."[16] This was about March 17, 1571, a week before Henry Sidney left Ireland, "with innumerable hearty prayers and with that wish of his return,"[17] to find waiting for him at Chester the queen's letter, which ordered him, too late, to remain at his post.

It appears from his letter that Edmund fell ill at this time. From Turvey House, Campion wrote to Mr. James Stanihurst, March 20, 1571:

Great is the fruit, O splendid man, which I gather both from your
affection and from your esteem: from your affection, that in these
hard days you take as much care of me as if I had sprung from you
(like Minerva from Jupiter); from your esteem, because, when I was
well nigh turned out of home and hearth, you chose not only to give
me hospitality but to embrace me as a friend. . . .

I congratulate myself that on coming into a new country,
I acquired your friendship, indeed your patronage. Unknown
stranger as I was, out of your inborn generosity and goodness, you
kept me in luxury for months in your house. You looked after my
health as carefully as that of your son Richard (who deserves all your
love). You furnished me with all conveniences of place, time, and
company (as the occasion arose). You supplied me with books, and
made such good provision for my time of study that, in all honesty,
away from my rooms at Oxford, I never read more pleasantly.

After this one would think there was nothing more to come; but
there was more. What was it? As soon as I saw that you heard the
first rustlings of the storm which was sure to blow wildly if I stayed
longer in sight of the heretics at Dublin, you opened to me this
secret hiding-place among your country friends. Till now, I had to
thank you for conveniences; now I have to thank you for my safety
and my breath—yes; breath is the word. For they who struggle with
those tyrants are commonly thrust into dismal dungeons, where
they inhale filthy vapors and are not allowed to breathe wholesome
air. But now through your and your children's kindness I shall live,
if Christ is propitious, more free from this peril, and, my mind tells
me, most happily. First of all, your friend Barnewall, an illustrious
man, is profuse in his promises. When he had read your letter [of
introduction], he spoke with grief of the iniquity of the times, but
showed himself as delighted with my coming as if I had done him
a favor.

As he had to go into the city [Dublin], he commended me to his
wife, who treated me most kindly. She is certainly a very religious
and very modest woman.

I was shut up in a convenient place within an inner chamber,
where I have again won the favor of my books. With these companions I lie concealed in my cell.[18]

The letter ends with compliments to Stanihurst's sons and relations,
and with a request to have a book of his by St. Bernard of Clairvaux sent

to him. On the same day, March 20, he wrote a more familiar letter to his pupil Richard:

> Of your countless kindnesses to me, Stanihurst, I make no end or bounds of considering. It is hard that, however grateful I feel, I cannot show it. . . . But I know you neither need nor desire repayment; so I only give you my wishes for the present; the rest when I get back to the land of the living.
>
> Meanwhile if these buried relics have any flavor of the old Campion, their flavor is for you; they are at your service. I am infinitely obliged to you and your brother Walter for the pains you lately took on my behalf. You, up all night; he, torn from his wife's arms besides! Seriously, I owe you much. I have nothing further to write about, unless you have time and inclination to laugh.
>
> Are you silent? Listen, then. The day after I came here, I was settling down to work, when suddenly a poor old woman burst into my chamber, perhaps to tidy up. She saw me on her left hand, and knowing nothing about whence I came, thought I was a ghost. Her hair stood on end, her color fled, she was struck dumb, her jaw fell. "What is the matter?" I asked. Overcome with fright, she almost fainted. She could not speak a word; all she could do was rush out of the room; she could not rest till she had told her mistress that there was some hideous thing, she thought a ghost, writing in the garret.
>
> The story was told me at supper time; the old woman was sent for, and made to tell her fright; everybody died of laughing, and I was found to be alive.[19]

He Writes a *History of Ireland*

Whatever protection came through Sir Henry Sidney was finished with Sidney's departure from Dublin on March 25, 1571. Campion devoted ten weeks[20] at this time to a hasty knocking together of a *History of Ireland*. The original and full title was *Two Bokes of the Histories of Ireland*. The actual writing occupied him from March 19 to May 27 (date of the dedication to Dudley)—but he had researched and collected materials for it from the time he came to Dublin, the previous October. That was done in his spare time, he says in his preface "To the loving reader":

> At my times of leisure from ordinary studies I have since my first arrival hither enquired out antiquities of the land, whereunto being

holpen [helped] by diverse friendly gentlemen, I gave the adventure to frame a story, which I bring from their very first original [origin] until the end of this last year 1570.

He then names some important sources he consulted by Welsh, Scottish, and English chroniclers, plus more recent oral and written sources—but as to Irish ones:

Irish chronicles, all they be reported to be full fraught of lewd examples, idle tales, and genealogies, *et quicquid Graecus mendax audet in historia* [whatever a lying Greek dares put into history], yet concerning the state of that wild people, especially before the Conquest, I am persuaded that with choice and judgment I might have sucked thence some better store of matter, and gladly would have sought them, had I found an interpreter, or understood their tongue: . . . so hard that it asked [required] continuance in the land of more years than I had months to spare upon this business.

He intended his book to be only a contribution to the subject, and hoped the Irish antiquaries would

hereafter at good leisure supply the want of this foundation, and polish the stone rough hewed to their hands. Notwithstanding as naked and simple as it is, it could never have grown to any proportion in such post haste except I had lighted into familiar society and daily table talk with the worshipful esquire, James Stanihurst, Recorder of Dublin, who beside all courtesies of hospitality, and thousand loving turns not here to be recited, both by word and written monuments and by the benefit of his own library, nourished most effectually mine endeavor.

The work is dedicated to Leicester,[21] to whom he freely confesses its shortcomings:

To the Right Honorable Robert Lord Dudley . . .
High Chancellor of the university of Oxford, my singular good lord.
    That my travel into Ireland might seem neither causeless nor fruitless, I have thought it expedient (being one member of your Lordship's honorable charge) to yield you this poor book as an account of my voyage, happly [perhaps] not the last nor the most beautiful present that is extended to your Honor by me, but surely more full of unsavory toil for the time than any plot of work that

ever I attempted; which I write not of vanity to commend my diligence, but of necessity to excuse my imperfection. For whereas it
is well known to the learned in this land how late it was before I
could meet with [find a copy of medieval writer] Gerald of Wales,
the only author that ministereth some indifferent furniture to this
chronicle, and with what search I have been driven to piece out the
rest by help of foreign writers incidentally touching this realm, by a
number of brief extracts, of rolls and records and scattered papers;
these things, I say, considered, I trust this little volume shall seem
great enough in such barren shift [patch], and my defect in penning
the same shall be imputed partly to my haste, who must needs have
ended all before I should leave the land and am even now upon the
point of my departure hence, so as to handle and lay these things
together I had not in all the space of ten weeks. Such as it is, I address
and bequeath it to your good Lordship.

There was much interest in his *History of Ireland;* Richard Stanihurst
says, "His history in mitching [sneaking] wise wandered through sundry
hands."[22] Reginald (Reyner) Wolfe, printer to the queen, had the good
luck to light upon a copy. He gave it to Raphael Holinshed, who gave
it to Richard to edit for publication. But Stanihurst at some point also
had his own copy.[23] Six years after writing, it was published—with major
changes by Stanihurst—in Holinshed's *Chronicles* in 1577. It appeared
in print again, with more revisions by a new editor,[24] in volume 2 of the
1587 edition of Holinshed, but did not get published in its original form
until 1633, edited by Sir James Ware.

The original work re-appeared in 1809, 1940, 1963, 1970, 1971, 2000,
and 2009.[25] The first and only critical and scholarly edition was published
in 1963 by Dutch scholar Alphonsus Vossen.[26] Campion's autograph of
the *History* is lost—but, says Dr. Vossen, "The most valuable transcript
is the Jones MS in the Bodleian [Library, Oxford], which is probably a
direct transcript from the original, and certainly the archetype of all the
other extant copies."[27]

One of Campion's own manuscript copies was seized by an inquisition at Oxford in November 1572. "My *History of Ireland*," he afterwards
wrote, "I suspect has perished; it was a good-sized and neat volume; the
heretical inquisitors seized it."[28] In this letter, he is referring to a raid
upon St. John's College in which many students were arrested and

materials were taken by the Anglican authorities.[29] The occasion of it was the government's interception of letters sent from overseas to Cuthbert Mayne and other fellows of St. John's, urging them to come to Douay. The *History* was handed over to Archbishop Matthew Parker, who in turn sent it to Leicester via Lord Burghley. In his letter to Burghley, November 8, 1572, Parker says:

> The book of Ireland's history we obtained, which here I send to your Lordship, which your Honor may direct to my Lord of Leicester, for it is dedicated to him; and if this Campion could be reclaimed or recovered, I see by his wit that he were worthy to be made [use] of; and thus I wish your good Lordship heartily well to fare.[30]

By that time, the Church of God, and not of Parker, had "reclaimed" Campion, for Edmund had recovered his courage and Catholic faith.

But he was not to recover the manuscript of his Irish history till early 1580.[31]

The Value of the *History*

Campion's *History* is a short work: 151 pages of text (counting the dedication, etc.) in the 1963 edition. Before considering its merits and demerits, let us see the headings of its twenty-five chapters:

FIRST BOOK

1. The site and special parts of Ireland
2. The temporal nobility
3. Nature of the soil and other incidentals
4. The Irish tongue and the name Hibernia, Ireland
5. Dispositions of the people
6. The mere Irish
7. The most ancient inhabitants of Ireland
8. The several inhabitants of Ireland since Bartolenus
9. The arrival of the Spaniards, then called Iberians, into Ireland
10. The coming of the Picts into Ireland
11. How the Irish settled themselves in Scotland
12. The conversion of the Irish to Christendom
13. St. Patrick's Purgatory
14. Irish saints

15. The most notable events in Ireland between the time of St. Patrick and the conquest under Henry II

SECOND BOOK

1. The conquest of Ireland by Henry the second king of England, commonly called Henry FitzEmpress
2. The titles of the crown of England to every part of Ireland and to the whole diverse ways
3. Richard I and King John
4. Henry III and Edward I
5. Edward II
6. Edward III and Richard II
7. The House of Lancaster, Henry IV, Henry V, Henry VI
8. Edward IV and Edward his son, Richard III and Henry VII
9. Henry VIII
10. Edward VI, Mary, Elizabeth

In fifty-six pages, Book 1 covers the geography, characteristics, and peoples of Ireland; then the history of the Irish Celts up to the English conquest.

In eighty-nine pages, Book 2 covers the remainder of the history to the present day—mainly the history of the Anglo-Irish in the Pale. The last nine pages are about the Parliamentary proceedings under James Stanihurst and Henry Sidney.

The work scarcely pretends to greater dignity than that of mere annals. It is not regarded today as a reliable account of Irish geography or history or as a contribution to general science, but is interesting for the light it throws upon the writer's own opinions and powers at the time.

Dr. Vossen says:

> Campion's *Histories* is a Renaissance work. It is a marked improvement on the medieval annals, but on account of the primitive state of Elizabethan chronology and other auxiliary sciences it falls short of modern ideals. . . . It contains little that is of use to modern historians, apart from a few remarks about contemporary conditions or events. Yet it must be assigned a place in Elizabethan historiography.[32]

Fr. Pollen S.J., in evaluating the work, remarks that one finds, on the one hand, many good epigrams and fine passages, and on the other hand, some obvious defects. It is evidently too short and sketchy, he says; the subject is expanded very irregularly. Mythology and ancient legend receive too much space; then generations and centuries pass with hardly a word of record.[33]

Dom Hilary Steuert judges the work

> strong in vigor and dramatic simplicity but loose in structure and often harsh in rhythm. We feel that we are reading the rough draft of a work possessed of both acumen and distinction, but which remains a series of brilliant notes and is not a unified whole. Yet there is cause here for regret rather than for censure: it was want of opportunity rather than want of ability which left the work "unplaned."[34]

Stanihurst himself recognized this, for in his preface he says:

> Master Edmund Campion did so learnedly bequite [prove] himself, in the penning of certain brief notes, concerning that country, as certainly it was greatly to be lamented that either his theme had not been shorter, or else his leisure had not been longer. . . . it was so huddled up in haste . . . it seemed rather to be a work roughly hewed, than smoothly planned. . . . I . . . was fully resolved to enrich Master Campion's chronicle with further additions.[35]

A few years after writing it, and not knowing it was about to be published, Edmund himself referred to it as "a production of ours, and in truth an immature one . . . I would rather it perish altogether than fall into the hands of the public."[36] Still, given the shortness of time, and the pressure that the writer was under, in his hurry-skurry from one residence to another, it is a remarkably eloquent work, and demonstrates, indirectly, the author's calmness, discipline, and powers of concentration amidst much distraction.

Albeit with much of the credulity of his day, Edmund combined a clear insight into the main principles of historical criticism; and he summarily explodes many a fable by a comparison of dates, or by showing that the various testimonies on which it rests reduce themselves to a multiplied echo of a single authority.

On Campion's view of the Irish question of his day, Fr. Pollen remarks:

As to this, we must confess that his position was not altogether cred-
itable to him. In brief, the Irish problem presented itself to him in
this way. The Irish seemed to him to be bent upon going backwards
on the path of civilization, and to wish to return to medieval usages
and the clan system. In his eyes the good of Ireland depended upon
education and assimilation to the ways of Renaissance Europe,
to which it must arrive by adopting the manners and usages of
England. . . . The Anglo-Irish were to him ideals of vigor, enterprise,
and other civic virtues.[37]

One should not conclude, however, that all that Campion says is anti-
Irish. After looking at the original sources of some parts of the *History*,
Pollen observes:

Yet though his information was one-sided, we find that he deliberately diminishes what he found on record against Ireland, and
enlarges what he has to say in its praise. . . .

In fact, when one reads the *History* closely, one finds that
what is favorable is in quantity out of all comparison to what is
unfavorable.[38]

Selections from the *History's* Prose

Evelyn Waugh observes that the short *History*

is remarkable as being Campion's only complete work which has
survived in the English language. The rest of his published work was
in Latin. . . . The History of Ireland is a superb piece of literature,
comparable in vigor and rhythm to anything written in his day.
With all its imperfections of structure and material, it is enough to
show that, had Campion continued in the life he was then planning
for himself, he would, almost certainly, have come down in history
as one of the great masters of English prose. From the lovely cadence
of the opening sentences . . . to the balanced, Ciceronian speeches
at the end it is manifestly the work of a stylist for whom form and
matter were never in conflict; there is no shadow of the effort and
ostentation which clouds all but the brightest genius of the period.[39]

To the ordinary reader, the most interesting parts of the work will
always be those which consist of the writer's own observations upon the
soil and the inhabitants of Ireland, which

lieth aloof in the West Ocean . . . In proportion it resembleth an egg blunt and plain, on the sides not reaching forth to sea nooks and elbows of land, as Britain doth.[40]

Since the book is scarce I will give some extracts from its chapters as specimens of Campion's English style, in his own day greatly admired:

The soil is low and waterish, includeth divers little islands environed with lakes and marshes. Highest hills have standing pools in their top. . . . The air is wholesome, not all so clear and subtle as ours of England. Of bees good store; no vineyards, contrary to the opinion of some writers, who both in this and other errors touching the land may easily be excused, as those that wrote of hearsay.

Cambrensis [13th century historian Gerald of Wales] in his time complaineth that Ireland had excess of wood and very little champagne ground. But now the English Pale is too naked. Turf and sea-coal is their most fuel. It is stored of kine [cows]; of excellent horses and hawks; of fish and fowl. They are not without wolves, and greyhounds to hunt them, bigger of bone and limb than a colt. Their kine, as also the rest of their cattle, and commonly what else soever the country engendereth (except man) is much less in quantity than ours of England. Sheep few, and those bearing coarse fleeces, whereof they spin notable rug mantle. The country is very fruitful both of corn and grass. The grass, for default of husbandry, not for the cause alleged in *Polycronicon* [a 14th century "Universal History"], suffered uncut, groweth to rank in the north parts that oft-times it rotteth their kine. Eagles are well known to breed here, but neither so big nor so many as books tell. . . . Horses they have, of pace easy, in running wonderful swift. Therefore they make great store, as wherein at times of need they repose a great piece of safety. . . . I heard it verified by honorable to honorable that a nobleman offered (and was refused) for one such horse a hundred kine, five pounds lands, and an eyrie [brood] of hawks yearly during seven years. . . .

No venomous creeping beast is brought forth or nourished, or can live here being sent in. And therefore the spider of Ireland is well known not to be venomous. Only because a frog was found living in the meadows of Waterford somewhat before the conquest, they construed it to import their overthrow. . . . Generally it is observed, the further west the less annoyance of pestilent creatures. The want whereof is to Ireland so peculiar that whereas it lay long in question to whether realm, Britain or Ireland, the Isle of Man should pertain, the said controversy was decided, that forasmuch as venomous beasts were known to breed therein, it could not be counted a natural piece of Ireland. Neither is this property to be ascribed to St. Patrick's blessing (as they commonly hold) but to the original blessing of God, who gave such nature to the situation and soil from the beginning. And though I doubt not but it fared the better in many respects for that holy man's prayer, yet had it this condition notified hundreds of years before he was born.[41]

He describes the dispositions of the people, whom he divides into those of English descent, and "the mere Irish"—the "mere" not being pejorative here; it means the pure Irish as opposed to the English residing in Ireland, or the Anglo-Irish there:

The people are thus inclined: religious, frank, amorous, ireful, sufferable of pains infinite, very glorious, many sorcerers, excellent horsemen, delighted with wars, great alms-givers, [sur]passing in hospitality. The lewder sort, both clerks [clerics] and lay, are sensual and loose to lechery above measure. The same being virtuously bred up or reformed are such mirrors of holiness and austerity that other nations retain but a shadow of devotion in comparison of them. As for abstinence and fasting, which these days make so dangerous, this is to them a familiar kind of chastisement. In which virtue and divers others how far the best excel, so far in gluttony and other hateful crimes the vicious they are worse than too bad. They follow the dead corpse to [the] grave with howling and barbarous outcries, pitiful in appearance, whereof grew, as I suppose, the proverb to weep Irish. The uplandish [rustic] are lightly abused to believe and avouch idle miracles and revelations vain and childish. Greedy of praise they be, and fearful of dishonor. And to this end they esteem their poets, who write Irish learnedly, and pen therein sonnets heroical, for the which they are bountifully rewarded; if not, they send out libels in dispraise, whereof the gentlemen, specially the mere [pure] Irish, stand in great awe. They love tenderly their foster-children, and bequeath to them a child's portion, whereby they nourish sure friendship, so beneficial every way that commonly five hundred kine [cows] and better are given in reward to win a nobleman's child to foster. They are sharp-witted, lovers of learning, capable of any study whereunto they bend themselves, constant in travail, adventurous, intractable, kind-hearted, secret in displeasure.

Hitherto the Irish of both sorts, mere and English, are affected much indifferently, save that in these, by good order and breaking, the same virtues are far more pregnant; in those other, by licentious and evil custom, the same faults are more extreme and odious. I say by licentious and evil custom, for there is daily trial of good natures among them; how soon they be reclaimed, and to what rare gifts of grace and wisdom they do and have aspired. Again, the very English of birth, conversant with the brutish sort of that people, become degenerate in short space, and are quite altered into worst rank of Irish rogues. Such a force hath education to make or mar.[42]

The mere Irish are quite another people from the Anglo-Irish; nor must it be supposed that Irish manners are now the same as Cambrensis (Bishop Gerald of Wales) describes; indeed, Campion wishes it to be observed

how much Ireland is beholden to God for suffering [allowing] them to be conquered, whereby many of these enormities were cured, and more might be, would themselves be pliable.[43]

He first notices:

In some corners of the land they used a damnable superstition [of] leaving the right arms of their infant males unchristened (as they termed it) to the intent it might give a more ungracious and deadly blow.[44]

He tells a story of a monk in Ulster asking of a grave gentleman at the end of his confession whether he were guilty of murder:

When he had said his mind, the priest demanded him whether he were faultless in the sin of homicide. He answered that he never wist [knew] the matter so heinous before, but being instructed thereof, he confessed the murder of five—the rest left wounded, so as he knew not whether they lived or no. Then was he taught that both the one and the other were execrable, and very meekly humbled himself to repentance.[45]

He then cites the ancient Greek geographer, Strabo, who asserts that they ate human flesh, counted it honorable for parents deceased to be eaten by their children, and lived together promiscuously without regard to kindred. Though since St. Patrick's days Christianity has never ceased, yet it had but a lax hold before the conquest, especially in matrimonial matters. And this was a fault not corrected even in Campion's time:

> Yea, even at this day, where the clergy is faint, they can be content to marry for a year and a day of probation, and at the year's end to return her home upon light quarrels, if the gentlewoman's friends be unable to avenge the injury. Never heard I of so many dispensations for marriage as these men show. God grant they be all authentic, and builded upon sufficient warrant.[46]

In like manner, Shane O'Neill, Earl of Tyron, Hereditary Lord of North Ireland, wrote to Queen Elizabeth, February 8, 1561, that "his father never refused no child that any woman named to be his."

Campion then continues the list of their old customs, their faithlessness and perjury, their oaths upon St. Patrick's staff, and the pagan ceremonies of crowning the king of Ulster.

> So much of their old customs. Now a few words of their trade at this present.
>
> Clean men they are of skin and hue, but of themselves careless and bestial. Their women are well favored, clear colored, fair-handed, big and large, suffered [allowed] from their infancy to grow at will, nothing curious of their feature and proportion of body.
>
> Their infants of the meaner sort are neither swaddled nor lapped in linen, but folded up stark naked into a blanket till they can go, and then if they get a piece of rug to cover them they are well sped.
>
> Linen shirts the able do wear for wantonness and bravery, with wide hanging sleeves pleated; thirty yards are little enough for one of them. They have now left their saffron, and learn to wash their shirts four or five times in a year. Proud they are of long crisped gleebes [thick hair over forehead and eyes], and the same do nourish with all their cunning. To crop the front thereof they take it for a notable piece of villainy.
>
> Shamrocks, water-cresses, roots, and other herbs they feed upon. Oatmeal and butter they cram together. They drink whey, milk, and beef broth. Flesh they devour without bread; corn, such as they have, they keep for their horses. In haste and hunger they squeeze [out] the blood of raw flesh and ask no more dressing

thereto; the rest boileth in their stomachs with aquavite [whiskey], which they swill in after such a surfeit by quarts and pottles [half-gallons]. Their kine they let blood, which, grown to a jelly, they bake and overspread with butter, and so eat it in lumps.

One office in the house of great men is a tale-teller, who bringeth his lord on sleep with tales vain and frivolous, whereunto the number give sooth and credence. So light [easy] they are in believing whatsoever is with any countenance of gravity affirmed by their superiors, whom they esteem and honor, that a lewd prelate within these few years, needy of money, was able to persuade his parish that St. Patrick in striving with St. Peter to let an Irish galloghlagh [gallowglass, soldier] into Heaven, had his head broken with the keys, for whose relief he obtained a collection.

Without either precepts or observation of congruity they speak Latin like a vulgar language, learned in their common schools of leech craft [medicine] and law, whereat they begin children, and hold on sixteen or twenty years, conning [memorizing] by rote the aphorisms of Hippocrates and the civil institutes, and a few other parings of those two faculties.

I have seen them where they kept school, ten in some one chamber, grovelling upon couches of straw, their books at their noses, them selves lying flat prostrate, and so to chant out their lessons by piece meal, being the most part lusty fellows of 25 years and upwards. Other lawyers they have, liable to [in the service of] certain families, which after the custom of the country determine and judge cases. These consider of wrongs offered and received among their neighbors. Be it murder or felony or trespass, all is redeemed by composition [agreement] (except the grudge of parties seeking revenge). And the time they have to spare from spoiling and preying, they lightly bestow in parling [speaking] about such matters. The Brehon (so they call this kind of lawyer) sitteth him down on a bank, the lords and gentlemen at variance round about him, and then they proceed.

They honor devout friars and pilgrims, suffer [allow] them to pass quietly, spare them and their mansions, whatsoever outrage they show to the country be side them. [That is, the monasteries in Ireland, unlike in England, have not been despoiled]. To rob and prey their enemies they deem it none offense, nor seek any means to recover their loss, but even to watch them the like turn [to retaliate

in kind]. But if neighbors and friends send their caters to purloin
one another, such actions are judged by the Brehons aforesaid.

Toward the living they are noisome and malicious; the same
being dead they labor to avenge eagerly and fiercely. They love and
trust their foster-brethren more than their own.[47]

Campion next descants on what was then a prominent vice—
impurity and promiscuity. He concludes his sketch with the truly Irish
sentence:

"One I hear named which hath (as he calleth them) more than ten
wives in twenty places."[48]

On other customs:

> There is among them a brotherhood of Carrowes, that profess to
> play at cards all the year long, and make it their only occupation.
> They play away mantle and all to the bare skin, and then truss them
> selves in straw or in leaves. They wait for passengers in the highway,
> invite them to game upon the green, and ask no more but compan-
> ions to hold them sport. For default of other stuff they pawn por-
> tions of their gleebe [matted hair], the nails of their fingers and toes
> . . . which they lose or redeem at the courtesy of the winner.
>
> Where they fancy and favor they are wonderful kind. They
> exchange by commutation of wares for the most part, and have
> utterly no coin stirring in any great lord's houses. Some of them be
> richly plated [owning silver]. Their ladies are trimmed rather with
> massy jewels than with garish apparel. It is counted a beauty in them
> to be tall, round, and fat.
>
> The inheritance descendeth not to the son, but to the brother,
> nephew, or cousin german eldest and most valiant. For the child,
> being oftentimes left in nonage [under legal age] or otherwise young
> and unskillful, were never able to defend his patrimony, being his no
> longer than he can hold it by force of arms. But by the time he grow
> to a competent age and have buried an uncle or two, he also taketh
> his turn, and leaveth it in like order to his posterity. This custom
> breedeth among them continual wars and treasons.[49]

Another small extract contains a prognostication of the future fate
both of Campion and of Ireland:[50]

> I remember Cambrensis writeth himself merrily to have objected to
> Morris, then Archbishop of Cashell, that Ireland in so many hundred

years had not brought forth one martyr. The Bishop answered pleasantly (but alluding to the late murder of Thomas of Canterbury):
"Our people" (quoth he), notwithstanding their other enormities,
yet have evermore spared the blood of Saints. Marry, now we are
delivered to such a nation that is properly well acquainted with making martyrs, henceforwards (I trust) this complaint shall cease.[51]

Selections from the *History*'s Speeches

The most striking thing about the book is the vast dramatic power of the
speeches which he introduces, according to the custom of the historians
of his day. The taste which we get here is sufficient to make us regret both
that the tragedies which he afterwards produced at Prague were written
in Latin, and that some are lost. Some of his orations only want meter to
be comparable with those of his great dramatic contemporaries.

Take the following for specimens. The first is a speech of Roderic, a
chief of Scythian redshanks, blown with a few refugees upon the coast of
Ireland, of whose king he demands hospitality:

> Not as degenerate from the courage of our ancestors, but inclining
> ourselves to the sway and bent of fortune, we are become suppliants
> to Ireland that never before have humbled ourselves to any. Look,
> Sir king, and eye us well: It is not light bruise that has caused these
> valiant bodies to stoop. Scythians we are, and the Picts of Scythia.
> Great substance of glory lodgeth in these two names. What shall I
> tell of the civil tumult that hath reft [robbed] us our home, or rip up
> [re-open harshly] old stories to make strangers bemoan us? Let our
> vassals and children discourse it at leisure, if perhaps you vouchsafe
> us any leisure in the land. To which effect and purpose our infinite
> necessities prayeth your favors, a king of a king, men of men. Princes
> can consider how near it concerneth their honor and surety to prop
> up the state of a king defaced by treason, and men will remember
> nothing better beseemeth the nature of man than to feel by compas-
> sion the griefs of men. Admit (we beseech you) these few scattered
> relics of Scythia. If your rooms be narrow, we are not many; if the
> soil be barren, we are born to hardness; if you live in peace, we are
> your subjects; if you war; we are your soldiers. We ask no kingdom,
> no wealth, no triumph in Ireland. We have brought ourselves, and
> left these casualties with the enemy. Howsoever it like you to esteem

of us, we shall easily learn to like it, when we call to mind, not what we have been, but what we are.[52]

The following is a speech of an Irish king, calling upon his countrymen to complete the overthrow of the Danish invaders, begun by the assassination of the Danish chief:

> Lordlings and friends, this case neither admitteth delay nor asketh policy. Heart and haste is all in all. While the feat is young and strong, that of our enemies some sleep, some sorrow, some curse, some consult, all dismayed, let us anticipate their fury, dismember their force, cut their flight, occupy their places of refuge and succor. It is no victory to pluck their feathers, but their necks; nor to chase them in, but to rouse them out; to weed them, not to rake them; nor to tread them down, but to dig them up. This lesson the tyrant himself hath taught me. I once demanded him in parable by what good husbandry the land might be rid of certain crows that annoyed it. He advised to watch where they bred, and to fire the nests about their ears. Go we then upon these cormorants that shroud themselves in our possessions, and let us destroy them so, that neither nest, nor root, nor seed, nor stalk, nor stubble may remain of this ungracious generation.[53]

Another extract gives an exact reproduction in English of Campion's Latin style. It is from the Earl of Kildare's defense of himself against Cardinal Wolsey, who accused him of conniving at the treasons of his kinsman, the Earl of Desmond:

> Cannot the Earl of Desmond shift, but I must be of counsel? Cannot he be hid, except I wink? If he be close, am I his mate? If he befriended, am I a traitor? This is a doughty kind of accusation which they urge against me, wherein they are stabled and mired [stuck in the mud] at my first denial. "You would not see him," say they. Who made them so familiar with mine eyesight, or when was the Earl within my equinus [way], or who stood by when I let him slip, or where are the tokens of my wilful hoodwink? "O, but you sent him word to beware of you." Who was the messenger, where are the letters? Convince [confute] my negative. See how loosely this idle reason hangeth. "Desmond is not taken: well, you are in fault." Why? "Because you are." Who proves it? "Nobody." What conjectures? "So it seemeth." To whom? "To your enemies." Who told it

them? "They will swear it." What other ground? "None." Will they
swear it, my Lords, why? Then of like they know it. If they know it,
either they have my hand to show or can bring forth the messenger,
or were present at a conference or privy to Desmond, or somebody
bewrayed [revealed] it to them, or themselves were my carriers or
vice-regents therein. Which of these parts will they choose?[54]

It is worthwhile to give these specimens of an eloquence that succeeded beyond that of all contemporary rivals in transfusing the vigor
and polish of Cicero into a language that was only struggling into form.
Campion's fame in England was built upon his eloquence; and it is only
by the speeches of this *Irish History*, which his scholar Richard Stanihurst
calls "tickled-tongued (for master Campion did learn it to speak),"[55] and
by the report of his defense at his trial, that we can estimate a power
which appears to have swayed all who listened to him.

In the same dedication just quoted (1577), Stanihurst calls Campion,
"my fast [close] friend, and inward companion," and further down he
praises "so rare a clerk, as Master Campion, who was so upright in conscience, so deep in judgment, so ripe in eloquence."[56] Amazingly, the
1587 edition of Holinshed's *Chronicles* left these compliments untouched,
while printing, in another part of the same work, Anthony Munday's
hostile description of the trial and execution of Campion as a traitor.[57] By
that time Stanihurst himself had become a Catholic and also left England.

Campion finishes his *History* with two speeches, which he professes
to report from his own notes, as near as he could, in the same words
and sentences in which he heard them. They are the speeches of James
Stanihurst, Speaker of the Commons, and of Sir Henry Sidney, the Lord
Deputy, at the prorogation of the Parliament, December 12, 1570.

I quote so much of them as refers to the project of Dublin University,
and the subsidiary schools which were to be founded in every diocese.
At Dublin, the old university had been commenced by Pope John XXI,
at the request of Archbishop Alexander Bigmore, and, as Campion tells
us,[58] had solemnly kept its terms and commencements, and had been
never disfranchised, but only through variety of time discontinued, and
was now, since the subversion of monasteries, utterly extinct. It was to
begin anew. A motion was made in the parliamentary session of 1570 to
erect it again—but the idea was not to be realized until the foundation of
Trinity College, Dublin, in 1592.

Surely [says James Stanihurst], might one generation sip a little of
this liquor, and so be induced to long for more, both our countrymen that live obeisant would ensue with a courage the fruits of
peace, whereby good learning is supported; and our unquiet neighbors would find such sweetness in the taste thereof as it should be a
ready way to reclaim them. In mine own experience, who have not
yet seen much more than forty years, I am able to say that our realm
is at this day in half deal more civil than it was, since noblemen and
worshipful and other of ability have used [been accustomed] to send
their sons into England to the law, to universities, or to schools.
Now when the same schools shall be brought home to their doors
that all that will may repair [go] unto them, I doubt not, considering
the numbers brought up beyond seas, and the good already done in
those few places where learning is professed, but this addition, dis-
creetly made, will foster a young fry likely to prove good members of
this commonwealth and desirous to trade [train] their children the
same way. Neither were it a small help to the assurance of the Crown
of England when babes from their cradles should be inured under
learned schoolmasters with a pure English tongue, habit, fashion,
discipline, and in time utterly forget the affinity of their unbroken
borderers, who possibly might be won by this example, or at the
least wise lose the opportunity which now they have to infect others. And seeing our hap [luck] is not yet to plant a university here at
home . . . me seemeth it is the more expedient to enter so far forth as
our commission reacheth, and to hope for the rest.[59]

The portion of Sidney's reply that related to the schools and university is as follows:

To you belongeth the quickening of this godly statute, which here
again I recommend unto you . . . Show yourselves forward and frank
in advancing the honor, wealth, ease and credit of your counties.
Envy not to your posterity the same path that yourselves have trodden and whereby you flourish at this day in the light and eye of your
commonwealth. Had your opinions matched with mine concerning
the University . . . no doubt the very name and reputation thereof
would have been a spur to these erections [the Schools], as nurses
for babes to suck in till they might repair thither [go there] to be
weaned. But I trust your consents therein are only suspended for
a time, and that so much good labor shall not be utterly lost and

frustrate. What though certain imperfections cannot as yet be salved? What though the sum arise not to make a muster of colleges at the first day? What though the place be not all so commodious? What though other circumstances infer a feeble and raw foundation? These are indeed objections of the multitude, whose backwardness breedeth a necessary stop in this our purpose. But your wisdoms can easily consider that time must ripen a weak beginning, that other universities began with less, that all experience telleth us so. Shall we be so curious or so testy that nothing will please us but all in all, all absolute, all excellent, all furnished, all beautified, all fortified in the very prime and infancy thereof? I remember a tale of Apuleius's ass, who, being indifferently placed between two bottles of hay, because he could not reach them both at once, forbare them both. Let not us so do, but content ourselves by little and little to be fed as the case requireth.[60]

As the work had opened with an overflowing dedication to the Earl of Leicester, so it closed with an extravagant tribute to Sir Henry Sidney as a Lord Deputy Governor of Ireland, who was a true Renaissance man:[61]

The man was surely much loved of them from his first office of Treasurer in the second [year] of Queen Mary; stately without disdain, familiar without contempt, very continent and chaste of body, no more than enough liberal, learned in many languages, and a great lover of learning, perfect in blazing arms, skilful of antiquities, of wit fresh and lively, in consultations very temperate, in utterance happy which his experience and wisdom hath made artificial [skillful], a preferrer of many, a father to his servants, both in war and peace of commendable courage.[62]

On the Run in Ireland

By March 19, 1571, Campion was at Turvey, as we saw—but it was too dangerous to stay in one place for long. In May, he was back in Dublin; and in the beginning of June, at Drogheda.[63] All this time he was dodging the pursuivants (officers empowered to execute a warrant), whom the commissioners, exceedingly offended at being beguiled of their prey, sent to search and to lay wait over all Ireland. His sweet temper carried him well through all, and in the intervals of flight he employed himself in "huddling up in haste"[64] the materials he had collected for his *History*.

If, as some assert, he led a kind of monastic life in Ireland, it was more in this latter period where he had no choice; at Turvey he lived "as though in a cell," and he asked for his copy of St. Bernard.

His Religious Allegiance

Campion's religious allegiance must still, however, have been vacillating; at least, it is uncertain to us now. We have no diary of his private thoughts or reflections at this or any point of his life. On the one hand, in a letter of March 19, given above, Campion speaks of the Protestants pursuing him as "heretics at Dublin"—but, on the other hand, an Anglican could also use such language of a Puritan. His *History* has an opening Dedication to the Earl of Leicester,[65] dated from Dublin, May 27, 1571, which shows that he still considered himself a protégé of the man, for in it he says he hopes that the work not be "the last nor the most beautiful present that is intended to your Honor by me." One study concludes: "This preface, addressed to the Chancellor of Oxford and expressing hopes of future favors from him, should have made it clear that Campion had not broken with Oxford or the Church of England by mid-summer 1571."[66] Yet it is also true he was hunted as an overt Catholic in Ireland. Biographers are not in agreement over his state of mind: other writers conclude that Campion was definitely a Catholic long before, namely, when he arrived in Ireland in 1570; in other words, he had broken with the Church of England but not the University of Oxford. Dr. Vossen is one of these.[67] All the early biographers say that Campion was definitely a Catholic when he arrived in Ireland.

From his *History* we have only small indicators of a Catholic religious position at the time. In all matters where human judgment has course, Campion judged for himself; witness his excellent chapter on the legend of St. Patrick's Purgatory,[68] and the very decided intimations which he gives in many places of his opinions upon the policy or the lawfulness of a rebellion founded upon a papal excommunication, and upon the validity of the pope's claim to the suzerainty of Ireland, and the disposition of the English crown. He writes in such a way as to be taken for a Protestant, though there is nothing decidedly Protestant—and makes few distinctly Catholic statements. The Reformation is passed over almost without notice; he casually mentions that the monasteries were suppressed, that King Henry "cast off" his wife "with much indignation

of all the Spaniards"[69] and made himself head over Ireland to displace the
pope. He makes an ironical remark on King Henry's destructiveness.[70]
Of the changes under queens Mary and Elizabeth, he says nothing.[71] Yet
he does not avoid Catholic subjects, so to speak; he mentions popes, but
without praise or blame; he mentions the foundation of the eleven chief
Irish abbeys; he speaks of saints and their shrines, of revelations and miracles. Here he comes closest to open profession of the Catholic religion:
he refers to the "outrage" against the homes of friars;[72] he dismisses old
hagiographical legends but admits that revelations and miracles may take
place and do take place in the lives of the saints and at their shrines.

Two clear pro-Catholic things to note are a reference to the late
queen as "the blessed Queen Mary,"[73] and a comment on hagiographical legends: "Neither he nor we are bound to believe any story besides
that which is delivered us from the Scriptures and the consent of God's
Church."[74]

Eleanor Rosenberg summarizes his acceptable attitudes, despite his
Catholicism:

> Internal evidence indicates that even while Campion was in flight
> from his Protestant persecutors in Ireland he still believed that his
> work would find acceptance in England and would open a new
> path for advancement to him there. His historical judgment is
> that of a loyal subject of Elizabeth. He asserts the ancient author-
> ity of the British crown in Ireland, rejects the papal claim of [cur-
> rent but not past][75] overlordship there, and writes with respect of
> Elizabeth's father, Henry VIII, who should have been anathema to
> any Catholic.[76] There is nothing in his history which would have
> prejudiced either the policies he supported or his own chances of
> preferment.[77]

But in the end, preferment never came. Campion certainly never
sought out the Earl upon his return to England. He would not see Dudley
again until ten years later, when he was conducted under guard as a prisoner of the Tower to see him for questioning.

Return to England

Gregory Martin, whose letter had much to do in drawing Campion from
Oxford, wrote again to him in Ireland. "I remember," says Campion,

"how earnestly you called upon me to come from Ireland to Douay; how
you admonished me; how effectual were your words."[78] But Campion
was again as much driven as drawn. Seeing, says Persons, that he could
hardly escape the commissioners long, and must endanger his friends,
he resolved to return to England in disguise. On his flight from Dublin
to Turvey in March he had called himself Mr. Patrick, out of devotion to
the apostle of the country. By this assumed name he passed in his various wanderings and concealments, till finally, in the last week of May,
he took ship at Drogheda, a little port twenty miles north of Dublin. He
was in disguise, "apparelled in a lackey's weed"[79] as a servant to Melchior
Hussey,[80] the Earl of Kildare's steward, who was then on his way to
England.

But as he had lamented being forced to leave England, he was now
full sorry, says Persons, to leave Ireland, because of the new and dear
friends to whom he had become attached in that country. And they wept
at his departure, so beloved had he become to them.

As there was some suspicion that he might be on board, some officers were sent to search the ship for him. As they asked for him by name,
he thought he could not escape, and his surprise was too great to allow
him to take any precautions; so he stood quietly on the deck, while the
officers ferreted out every nook and corner, examined the crew, tumbled
the cargo up and down, with plentiful curses upon the seditious villain
Campion. There he stood in his menial livery, and saw everybody but
himself strictly examined; while he called devoutly upon St. Patrick,
whose name he had assumed, and whom, in consideration of the protection he then gave, he ever afterwards invoked for similar voyages.

When the officers had finished their search, the ship was allowed
to sail; and, after an indifferent and prosperous voyage, he landed in
England, to miss the Irish hospitality, but not to miss that which he
chiefly sought to avoid: the prying inquisitions of the queen's officers,
and of the provincial constables. On the east of St. George's Channel, he
found, says Persons, nothing but fears, suspicions, arrests, condemnations, torture, executions, for the risings of the Earls of Northumberland
and Westmoreland, and of Lord Dacres, and for the publication of Pius
V's Bull. The Duke of Norfolk was imprisoned, and other great men confined to their houses, as the Earl of Pembroke and the Earl of Arundel,
suspected of favoring the Queen of Scots, in England since May 1568.

And a new conspiracy was just discovered in Norfolk, for which Mr. John Throgmorton and others were executed in 1570. The queen and Council were so troubled that they could not tell whom to trust, and so fell to rigorous proceedings against all, but especially against Catholics, whom they most feared; so that Campion could not tell where to rest in England, all men being in fear and suspicion of one another.[81] Says Fr. More: "Although they could have nothing against him except his reconciliation to the Mother-Church [Rome], he knew very well a man cannot defend his house by innocence alone once fanaticism has crossed the threshold."[82]

A dramatic trial now showed the way England was going under Elizabeth, Burghley, and Leicester.

The Trial of Dr. Storey

The date of the preface to the *History*, June 9, does not square with Fr. Persons's declaration that Campion witnessed the arraignment and trial of Dr. Storey,[83] which took place in Westminster Hall on May 26 in the same year. Even putting the date back eleven days for the "New Style" (through Pope Gregory's reform of the Calendar in 1582) will not help us. It may be, however, that Campion purposely post-dated his work, perhaps for the purpose of concealing from the officers the real time of his departure from Ireland. Fr. Persons can hardly be mistaken in saying Campion was present at this celebrated trial; so we must overlook the few days' discrepancy in the dates.[84] Or perhaps Campion heard all about the trial, and spoke with such interest to Persons about it (in 1580), as to give the impression he had been there.

Dr. John Storey (1504–71) was a civilian, and the first Regius praelector of civil law in the University of Oxford. He entered Parliament in 1547, and was imprisoned from January 1548 to March 1549 for opposing the Bill of Uniformity. On his release, he retired with his family to Louvain, but after the accession of Queen Mary in 1553, he returned to England the same year and became chancellor to Bishop Bonner. He thus took a prominent part in the ecclesiastical acts of Mary's reign. In Elizabeth's first Parliament, he boldly defended his role under the previous queen:

"I see (said he) nothing to be ashamed of " . . . but rather said that
he was sorry for this, because he had done no more than he did, and
that in executing those laws, they had not been more vehement and
severe.

Their only fault, he said, was

that they labored only about the young and little sprigs and twigs,
while they should have struck at the root and clean have rooted it
out.[85]

In plain terms, not to prosecute barrow-sellers and cobblers for heresy, but to make examples of such tall plants as the Lady Elizabeth and Sir
William Cecil. In 1560, Storey incurred the displeasure of Elizabeth for
his outspoken opposition to the Bill of Supremacy. He was imprisoned
in May 1560, but escaped, was re-arrested and again imprisoned. Again
he broke out, and fled to the Low Countries to escape the vengeance
of Elizabeth and Cecil. There he renounced his English allegiance and
became a Spanish subject. He lived in great poverty at Louvain, with a
wife and four young children dependent upon him, besides nephews and
nieces. In Flanders, upset that many Protestant merchants used to bring
in heretical books to infect the Catholic people, Dr. Storey accepted the
office of inquisitor, to search English ships entering or leaving the port of
Antwerp for contra-band prints. For this, English heretics conspired to
capture him. Cecil and Leicester contrived the plot: in August 1570, their
agents kidnapped Storey while he was searching their English ship. They
fastened the hatches down upon him, and carried him off to England.
He was brought to London and imprisoned in the Tower, where he was
frequently racked, and indicted for having conspired against the queen's
life and for having, at Antwerp, assisted the Northern rebels. The saintly
martyr bore his tortures with fortitude, asserted over and over his innocence of the charges, but refused to make any further plea, on the ground
that he was a Spanish subject, and that consequently his judges had no
jurisdiction.

Campion, says Persons, heard Storey prove that he had committed
nothing treasonable or punishable in going to Flanders, and living under
a prince who would allow him the exercise of his religion, which he could
not have in England; and that, being there, he might accept and exercise

the office of inquisition and search against all such, though they were English, as offended the common laws of the Catholic Church (whereof he was a member, and to which he owed more particular obedience than to his country or prince) or the laws of Flanders. Moreover, any subject whatever, on so just a cause as religion, might renounce his naturalization, and betake himself to the subjection of another prince, as he had to the Catholic king of Spain, and that consequently they could not proceed against him for it. Even if this were not allowed, as the deed for which he was indicted was committed in another country, and he taken there by fraud, and brought into England by force only, he was not punishable for it in England.[86]

John Storey was executed June 1, 1571 (June 12, New Style, i.e., Gregorian calendar), with circumstances of unusual cruelty, in addition to the prescribed drawing, hanging, disembowelling and quartering.[87] In 1886 he was beatified as a martyr under Pope Leo XIII.

Departure from England

The trial was enough to drive Campion from England. He resolved to fly overseas for good, as he saw that there was no longer secure living for Catholics without compromising their conscience. He went, not to escape the danger, but to prepare himself to meet it more usefully. Being neither priest nor theologian, he thought himself of little use at present, and therefore determined to go at once to Douay, and was already half across the Channel on the day of Storey's death.[88] But in mid-channel his ship was stopped by the H.M.S. *Hare*, an English warship cruising there, which despatched a boat to see that the ship's papers were regular, and that each passenger had his passport. Campion had no document of the kind, and his fellow-passengers, though they knew nothing about him, suspected he might be a Catholic. This was enough; he and his baggage were carried off to the *Hare*, and brought to Dover, where the captain took possession of all his money—all donated by Campion's friends in England and Ireland. The captain, having occasion to go to London, would have to carry his prisoner with him. Albeit, says Persons, by the event that ensued, it seems it was rather a show to justify taking Campion's money, which he wanted to keep, than from any desire to get his prisoner to London, where Campion might find some friend to aid him in recovering his funds, seeing in those days there were not so rigorous laws against leaving the realm as afterwards were devised.[89] Campion, suspecting this, began directly to linger behind; each of them, without speaking a word, comprehended what the other wanted, and an understanding was soon established. Campion turned round, and walked off towards the east; his companion pursued him westwards. The fugitive obtained a fresh supply of money from some friends in Kent, and succeeded in getting over to Calais without molestation.

CHAPTER 3

Seminarian at Douay

CALAIS TO Douay was a walk of eighty miles or more. Douay was located in Spanish Flanders; a century later it would be part of France.

Campion at the English Seminary of Douay

At Douay College ("Douay" is the town; "Douay" for the seminary), Campion was delighted at the reunion with his old friends Gregory Martin and Richard Bristow. The three were close in age: Bristow, thirty-three; Campion and Martin, thirty-one.

Gregory Martin of Maxfield, Guestling, Sussex, a brilliant scholar and linguist, a contemporary with Campion among the early students of St. John's College, Oxford, was to become the main translator of the Latin Vulgate Bible into English—which became known as the Douay-Rheims version.[1]

Richard Bristow of Worcestershire, of both Exeter College and Christ Church, Oxford, was Dr. Allen's right-hand man and the first Prefect of Studies of Douay College. A brilliant and eloquent scholar, he authored the celebrated work of apologetics, *Motives Inducing to the Catholic Faith*, first published in 1574.[2]

Douay College, founded only three years earlier and destined to play so crucial a role in English Catholic history, was the brainchild of Dr. William Allen.

Born in 1532 in Lancashire, Allen entered Oriel College, Oxford, in 1547, was elected a Fellow in 1550, and received his Master of Arts in 1553. He became principal of St. Mary's Hall, Oxford, six years later. In 1561 he left the country for Louvain, one of the scholastic towns of

Flanders which, since the first years of Elizabeth's reign, had become a second country to English refugees. Allen returned to Lancashire about 1563. With the intention to become a priest, he went back to the Low Countries (modern Holland, Belgium, and Flanders) in 1565 for further studies and was ordained a priest in Mechlin (Mechelen or Malines, Belgium) in 1567.

Allen went to Rome in 1567 with his lay friend Dr. Jean Vendeville who was professor of canon law at Douay University. On their journey they discussed the possibilities of reviving Catholicism in those countries where Protestantism was established. One outcome of their discussions was the decision to establish a college at Douay (Douay, Doway) where young English Catholics could receive the education they could no longer get at Oxford or Cambridge. So Douay College came to be founded on Michaelmas day, September 29, 1568. The emphasis soon came to be put on training for the priesthood but the general education of youths continued.

Allen had the following clear objectives in mind:

1. The training of English youths in the Low Countries in "common conference and public exercise,"[3] so that if or when they returned to England they would be faithful to their religion. "Our aim," Allen later wrote, "is and has always been, to train Catholics to be plainly and openly Catholics; to be men who will always refuse every kind of spiritual commerce with heretics."[4]

2. To attract young men from England who wished to have a "more exact education than is in these days in either the Universities."

3. To train those who have vocations for the priesthood to replace the diminishing number of priests in England.

Dr. Allen set his great project on foot in full trust that somehow or other the necessary funds would be forthcoming. English Catholics in the Low Countries and friends in England sent donations. William Roper, son-in-law of St. Thomas More, was fined for sending money abroad for this purpose. Another benefactor was Morgan Phillips, Allen's old tutor at Oriel College; and there were other notables. Later on, the popes and King Phillip II gave regular support, but, even so, the College always had difficulty in making ends meet.

The three-year course of training for the priesthood, which followed the general education, was designed with the practical needs of England

in mind. Allen's purpose was not to produce learned scholars and controversialists; the Douay University could supply that need. Allen wanted
to train men who could meet the pastoral situation of the times—but this
did not mean anything makeshift in the education. The training of the
students was very thorough and was in the hands of some of the leading Catholic scholars of the day, many of them graduates of Oxford and
Cambridge.

Primary importance was placed on the study of the Scriptures since
this was the basis of Protestant teaching. With this can be linked the
translation of the *New Testament*, though this was not published until
1582 when, owing to disturbances in the Low Countries, the College
had temporarily moved to Rheims in France (1578–93), after which it
returned to Douay. Over three years, the entire *Old Testament* was gone
through twelve times, and the entire *New Testament* sixteen times. There
were regular disputations on those texts on which Protestants put so
much emphasis, and every week the students had to practice preaching in
English. Great care was taken to train them as catechists and confessors.

Fr. McCoog sums up the method and focus of the seminarians' training, with phrases taken from Dr. Allen:

> The seminarians were trained for disputations. With an eye on cur-
> rent controversial issues, they studied Scriptural passages that either
> confirmed the truths of Catholicism or were favored by Protestants
> in their arguments. Replies to the latter were clearly formulated.
> Once a week there was a public disputation in which selected stu-
> dents would not only defend Catholic doctrine against Protestant
> assault but also sharpen their skills by maintaining Protestant views
> against their colleagues. To augment their knowledge of Scripture,
> the students learned Greek and Hebrew so that they could read both
> Testaments in the original languages and avoid "the sophisms which
> heretics extract from the properties and meanings of words." A sec-
> ond weekly disputation involved chosen articles from the Summa
> [of St. Thomas]. For private study, the decrees of the Council of
> Trent [1545–63]; English church history . . . and selected works of
> Augustine, Cyprian, and Jerome were recommended. Finally the
> students were acquainted "with the chief impieties, blasphemies,
> absurdities, cheats and trickeries of the English heretics, as well as
> their ridiculous writings, sayings and doings."[5]

Dr. Allen wrote one time:

> we teach scholastic theology (without which no one can be solidly
> learned or become an acute disputant) and we teach it chiefly from
> St. Thomas; sometimes also from the Master of the Sentences [Peter
> Lombard]. Once a week we have a disputation on five selected arti-
> cles from the *Summa*.[6]

The first priests were ordained in 1573, and four went to England in
1575. By 1578, seventy-five priests were ordained and fifty-two were in
England "on mission"; by 1579, as many as one hundred were there. By
the end of Elizabeth's reign, Douay College had produced around 450
priests.[7] By 1610, 135 of the students of the seminary had sealed their
mission with their blood.[8] The preparation of young men for the priesthood and for martyrdom gave the place a unique atmosphere of commitment and heroism. Allen bore emphatic witness to their zeal for their
studies and their faithful observance of Catholic morals and discipline.
Students fully knew what they were preparing to face in England. There
was no ecclesiastical ambition or other distraction in this seminary!

On Campion's arrival in May 1571, the foundation was still small but
growing every year. Not counting the president, there were twenty students: seven priests and thirteen candidates for Holy Orders.[9] By 1582,
the number was 120. The reasons for the steady growth will be easily
understood from Cardinal Allen's own account of the "motives and accidents" which had drawn the men together.[10]

The first thought of the founders of the College had been to attract
the young English exiles who were living in Flanders from their solitary
and self-guided study to a more exact method, and to collegiate obedience; and their next, to provide for the rising generation in England a
succession of learned Catholics, especially of clergy, to take the place of
those removed by old age, imprisonment, and persecution.

Their design, then, was to draw together out of England "the best
wits" from the following classes: those inclined to Catholicism; those who
desired a more exact education than could be then obtained at Oxford or
Cambridge, "where no art, holy or profane, was thoroughly studied, and
some not touched at all"; those who were scrupulous about taking the
oath of the queen's supremacy; those who disliked to be forced, as they
were in some colleges of the English universities, to enter the ministry, "a

calling contemptible even to their own conceit, and very damnable in the judgment of others," the dread of being forced into which had (in 1581), yielded to the new College "many, yea some scores, partly before, partly after their entrance into that trade"; "and those who were doubtful which religion was the true one, and were disgusted that they were forced into one without being allowed opportunity of inquiring into the other."

Such a band of zealous young men and converts, all of whom had made some sacrifices, and some of whom had sacrificed all they had for religion, were a real power, because they had fallen into the hands of a man who, with all his political blunders—to use the mildest term—had a true genius for ecclesiastical government. William Allen was not the man to let the force in an educated convert lie fallow, or let him stand all day idle in the market-place for want of employment. The ingenuity of his machinery for utilizing the power of which he disposed may be appreciated from the following example.

One of Allen's rules was, that, while those who were now forgotten in their old circles busied themselves in writing books, or in instructing the scholars, the young men, whose memories were still fresh in the affections of those they had left at home, should write letters to move them to attend to the salvation of their souls, and to beseech them not to damn themselves willfully, on the pretext of preserving their property for themselves and their children.

The letters by which Gregory Martin had drawn Campion to Douay are only specimens of the practical utility of this rule. And before he left Douay, Campion obtained some results from the same practice. He wrote to certain special friends of his in England, some Catholics and some Protestants, with such fervor, that some of them were moved by his words to leave all and follow him to Douay.

To this directive of Dr. Allen we are indebted for Campion's letter of November 1, 1571, to Bishop Cheney of Gloucester, "whom," says Persons, "Mr. Campion for friendship doth so rattle up (but yet with great modesty, and show of reverence, and hearty good will), as it may easily appear how abundantly God had imparted His Holy Spirit unto him, for his letter to him is truly Apostolical."[11]

The Fate of Cheney

His old friend Cheney was now in deep disgrace. While Campion was
being hunted in Ireland, Cheney was being harassed in England. In April
1571 Cheney was summoned to the Clergy Convocation but refused to
attend. In the third session, April 20, he was excommunicated[12] for refusing to accept the official Anglican *Thirty-Nine Articles of Religion*.[13] But,
after a little time, May 12,[14] he sent his chaplain with letters of proxy
to sue for absolution, which was granted. It is sufficient to look at the
visitation articles of Archbishop Grindal, whereby the prelates in this
Convocation tried to sweep away all the lingering remnants of the old
religion, to know why Cheney absented himself.

Holy Communion was no longer to be put into the communicant's
mouth, but into his hands; all ceremonies or gestures not prescribed
in the *Prayer-Book* were to cease; people were to communicate three
times a year—and not at Easter or Christmas, like Catholics, but on Ash
Wednesday, and one of the two Sundays before Easter, Pentecost, and
Christmas. All altars were to be pulled down, and the altar-stones defaced
and put to some common use. All prayers for the dead at funerals or
commemorations were to cease; no person was allowed to wear rosary-
beads, or to pray upon them in Latin or English, or to burn candles on
the feast of the Purification (Candlemas), or to make the sign of the cross
when entering church.[15]

These articles of visitation were only the logical development of the
Act of Uniformity, the enforcing of which throughout the English counties stands in such startling complication with the reports of rebellion
in the Calendar of State Papers for the latter part of the year 1569. Up to
1570, Catholic practices had been allowed to linger in the Establishment;
now, after the defeat of the northern rebels, the Puritans found themselves
strong enough to repress by force what they had hitherto been obliged to
connive at. But Cheney would not sanction by his presence, even though
he was only there to protest, a convocation which was to destroy all that
he loved in Anglicanism; he retired to Gloucester, and, though he took
measures to remove the excommunication, which would have entailed all
kinds of material disasters, he never afterwards had anything to do with
his brother-bishops. After eight years, he died as he had lived, leaving it
doubtful whether he was reconciled to the Catholic Church or not. One of

his successors in the see, Godfrey Goodman, said that "it was certain that he was a Papist, and bred up his servants Papists, as he had been informed by one of them, with whom he had spoken"[16]—but Campion wrote the contrary in 1581, two years after the bishop's death:

> A certain convocation in London even attempted to do this [delete the clause "He descended into hell" from the Creed], as I was told by an eyewitness, Richard Cheney, a most miserable old man, badly mauled by robbers without, and who yet *entered not his father's house.*[17]

Church historian Fuller also contradicts Goodman's story, on the authority of Mrs. Goldsborough, widow to Bishop Goldsborough of Gloucester (second in succession after Cheney), who at a public entertainment avowed that to her knowledge Cheney died a true and sincere Protestant.[18] Protestant historian John Strype gives Cheney a good character for hospitality and good husbandry of his temporal goods: he believed that no truly General Council could err; on this he built his faith in the Real Presence. He also considered the Fathers as the authorized interpreters of Scripture.[19] Camden calls him *Luthero addictis simus* (very much addicted to Luther)[20]—but, in disagreement with Luther, he upheld free-will. The "addiction" to Luther (as opposed to Calvin) meant that, as Luther, he upheld the presence of Christ in the Eucharist, and was not opposed to crucifixes, or pictures of saints in churches, and other old customs.

Still, old Cheney might have been reconciled, but "secretly, for fear of the Jews" (*Jn.* 19:38), and any accident might have prevented the publication of the fact. Certainly, his memory was not in benediction with the Protestants. He died in 1579 and was buried in his Cathedral of Gloucester, but no memorial was erected to him; and, as if to avenge the Puritans (whom he had troubled) on the Papists (whom he had spared), after his death there was no county in England where more malicious cruelty was exercised on Catholics than in Gloucestershire.

(Bishop Godfrey Goodman of Gloucester, born 1582, named above, himself became a Catholic. By 1636, he seems to have been fully a Catholic in heart. In 1640, his Catholic beliefs were so obvious, Archbishop Laud suspended him from episcopal office. Some years after this, he made open profession of the Catholic faith and practiced it till his death in 1656).

Campion's Letter to Cheney

Here is the famous letter written, in Latin, from Douay, on All Saints'
Day, 1571, with all the ardor of a saint and future martyr—to a
compromiser.[21]

Edmund Campion to the most illustrious Richard Cheney:

Greetings.

It is not now, as of old, the dash of youth, or facility of pen, nor
even a dutiful regard of your favors, that makes me write to you. I
used to write from the mere abundance of my heart; now a greater
necessity has forced me to write this letter.

We have already been too long subservient to men's ears, to the
times, to our hopes, to ambition; at length let us say something for
the service of our soul. I beg you by your own natural goodness, by
my tears, even by the pierced side of Christ and by the wounds of
Him nailed to the Cross: listen to me carefully. There is no end nor
measure to my thinking of you; and I never think of you without
being horribly ashamed, praying silently, and repeating the text of
the Psalm, "From the sins of others, spare Thy servant, O Lord" [Ps.
18:13]. What have I done? It is written, "If thou saw a thief, thou
ran with him" [Ps. 49:18]; and again, "The sinner is praised in his
desires, and the man is blessed" [Ps. 9:24]. So often was I with you at
Gloucester, so often in your private chamber, so many hours have I
spent in your inner rooms and personal library, with no one near us,
when I could have done this business, and I did it not; and what is
worse, I have added flames to the fever by assenting and conniving.
And although you were superior to me in your counterfeit dignity,
in wealth, age, and learning; and though I was not bound to look
after your soul or its spiritual nourishment, yet since you were of so
easy and sweet a temper as in spite of your grey hairs to admit me,
young as I was, to frequent and familiar conversation with you, to
say whatever I chose, in all security and secrecy, while you imparted
to me your sorrows, and all the calumnies of the heretics against you;
and since like a father you exhorted me to walk straight and upright
in the royal road, to follow the steps of the Church, the Councils and
the Fathers, and to believe that where there was a consensus of these
there could be no speck of falsehood, I am very angry with myself
that through false modesty or culpable negligence I neglected to use
such a handsome opportunity of recommending the faith, that I did

not address with boldness one who was so near to the kingdom of God, but that while I enjoyed your favor and renown I promoted rather the shadowy notion of my own honor than your everlasting good.

But as I have no longer the occasion that I had of persuading you face to face, it remains that I should send my words to you to witness my regard, my care, my anxiety for you, known to Him to whom I make my daily prayer for your salvation. Listen, I beseech you, listen to a few words. You are sixty years old, more or less, of uncertain health, of weakened body, the hatred of heretics, the pity of Catholics, the talk of the people, the sorrow of your friends, the laughing-stock of your enemies. Against your conscience you falsely usurp the name of a Bishop, by your silence you advance a pestilent sect of which you approve not. You are stricken with anathema, cut off from the body into which alone the graces of Christ flow, you are deprived of the benefit of all devout prayers, sacrifices, and Sacraments. Who do you think yourself to be? What do you expect? What is your life? Wherein lies your hope? In the heretics hating you so implacably, and abusing you so roundly? Because of all the heresiarchs of Britain you are the most tolerably crazy? Because you confess the living presence of Christ on the altar, and the freedom of man's will? Because you have persecuted no Catholics in your diocese? Because you are hospitable to your towns-people, and to good men? Because you plunder not your palace and lands as your brethren do? Surely these things will avail much, if you return to the bosom of the Church, if you suffer even the smallest thing in common with those of the Household of the Faith, or join your prayers with theirs. But now whilst you are outside, and an enemy, whilst like a base deserter you fight under a foreign flag, it is in vain you attempt to cover your countless crimes with the cloak of virtues. You shall gain nothing, except perhaps to be tortured somewhat less horribly in the everlasting fire than Judas or Luther or Zwingli, or than those antagonists of yours, Cooper, Humphrey, and Samson.[22]

What difference does the kind of death make? Death is the same, whether you are thrown from a tall rock into the sea, or pushed from a low bank into the river; whether a man is killed by iron or rope, tortured by the rack or pierced by a bullet, dismembered by sword or by axe, whether pounded by stones or by clubs, whether roasted with fire or boiled in scalding water.

What is the use of fighting for many articles of the faith, and
to perish for doubting of a few? To escape shipwreck and to fall by
the dagger? To flee from the plague and die of famine? To avoid the
flames and be suffocated by the smoke? Whoever refuses to believe
one or other article of the faith, believes in none of them. For as soon
as he knowingly oversteps the bounds of the Church, which is the
pillar and ground of the truth [1 Tim. 3:15], to which Christ Jesus,
the highest, first, and most pure truth, the source, light, leader, measure and pattern of the faithful, reveals all these articles—whatever
else of Catholic doctrine he retains, yet if he obstinately criticizes
one dogma, the remainder that he holds, he holds not by orthodox
faith, without which it is impossible to please God, but by his own
reason, his own conviction.

In vain you defend the religion of Catholics, if you embrace only
that which you like, and cut off all that seems not right in your eyes.
There is one plain known road, not enclosed by your boundaries or
mine, not by private judgment, but by the severe laws of humility
and obedience; when you wander from this you are lost. You must
be altogether within the house of God, within the walls of salvation,
to be safe and sound from all injury. If you wander and walk abroad
ever so little, if you carelessly thrust hand or foot out of the ship, if
you stir up ever so small a mutiny in the crew, you shall be thrust
forth—the ark is shut, the ocean roars, you are lost. He who gathers
not with Me (says the Saviour), scatters. And Jerome explains: He
who is not Christ's is Antichrist's.

You are not so stupid as to follow the heresy of the
Sacramentarians;* you are not so mad as to want to be in all things
a follower of Luther's faction, now condemned in the General
Councils of Constance and Trent (which you yourself think authoritative). And yet you stick in the mire of your imagination, and wish
to appear sharper than the sharpest,[23] and to sit as an honorary arbi-
trator in the disputes of your little brothers.

Do you remember the sober and solemn answer which you
gave me, when three years ago we met in the house of the renowned
Thomas Dutton at Sherborne, where we were to dine? We were talking of St. Cyprian. I objected to you, in order to discover your real
opinions, that Synod of Carthage which erred about the baptism of

---

*   Deniers of Christ's presence in the Eucharist.

heretics.[24] You answered, rightly, that the Holy Spirit was promised
not to one province, but to the Church; that the universal Church is
represented in a full Council; and that no doctrine can be pointed
out, about which such a Council ever erred. Acknowledge your own
weapons, which you used against the adversaries of the mystery of
the Eucharist. You cry up the Christian world, the assemblies of
bishops, the guardians of the deposit, that is, the ancient faith; these
you commend to the people as the interpreters of Scripture. Most
rightly do you ridicule and disparage the impudent figment of certain professors of false Patristic.[25]

Now what do you say? Here you have the most celebrated
Fathers and Patriarchs and Apostolic men, most recently gathered
at Trent, who have all united to contend for the ancient faith of the
Fathers. Legates, prelates, cardinals, bishops, orators, doctors, of
diverse nations, of mature age, rare wisdom, marvellous erudition,
princely dignity, streaming in from all sides: Italians, Frenchmen,
Spaniards, Portuguese, Greeks, Poles, Hungarians, Flemish, Illyrians,
many from Germany, some from Ireland, Croatia, Moravia—even
England was not unrepresented. All these, whilst you live as you are
now living, smite you, hiss you off, turn you out, execrate you. What
reason can you urge? Especially now you have declared war against
your colleagues, why do you not make full submission, without any
exceptions, to the discipline of these prelates? Have you seen anything in the Lord's Supper that they did not see, discuss and resolve?
Dare you equate yourself by even the hundredth part with the lowest
theologians of this Council? I doubt not your discretion, nor your
modesty; you dare not. You are surpassed, then, by your judges in
number, value, weight, and in the serious and clear testimony of the
whole world.

Once more consult your own heart, my poor old friend; give
me back your old splendor, and those excellent gifts which have
been hitherto smothered and stuck in the mire of dishonesty. Give
yourself to your mother, who begot you to Christ, nourished you,
consecrated you. Admit your betrayal. Let confession be the remedy
for your sin.

You have (as they say) one foot in the grave; you must be taken
from this life, perhaps at once, certainly very soon, to stand before
that tribunal, where you will hear, "Give an account of thy steward-
ship"; and unless while you are on the way you make it up quickly

and exactly with the adversary of sin, it shall be required to the last penny, and you shall be driven miserably from the land of the living by Him whom you will never be able to pay. Then those hands which have conferred spurious Orders on so many wretched youths shall for very pain scratch and tear your sulphurous body; that impure mouth, defiled with falsehood and schism, shall be filled with fire and worms and the breath of tempests. That lofty carnal pomp of yours, your episcopal throne, your yearly revenues, spacious palace, honorable greetings, band of servants, elegant furniture—that affluence for which the poor ignorant people esteem you so happy, shall be exchanged for fearful wailings, gnashing of teeth, stench, filth, foulness and chains. There shall the spirits of Calvin and Zwingli, whom you now oppose, afflict you for ever, with Sabellius, Arius, Nestorius, Wycliff, Luther—with the devil and his angels you shall suffer the pains of darkness, and belch out blasphemies.

Spare yourself, spare your soul, spare my grief. Albeit your ship is wrecked, your merchandise lost; nevertheless, seize the plank of penance, swim as you can, and come even naked to the port of the Church. Doubt not that Christ will preserve you with His hand, run to meet you, kiss you, and put the white garment on you; the heavens will rejoice. Take no thought for your life; He will take thought for you "who gives the beasts their food, and feeds the young ravens that call upon Him" [*Ps.* 146:9].

If you but made trial of our banishment, if you but cleared your conscience, and came to behold and consider the living examples of piety which are shown here* by Bishops, Priests, Religious Friars, Provosts, Scholars, Provincial Governors, lay people of every age, rank and sex, I believe that you would exchange six hundred Englands for the opportunity of redeeming the residue of your time by tears and sorrow. But if for diverse reasons you are hindered from going out freely where you would, at least free your soul from its heavy chains; set your body any task rather than let it hold you down with its weight and banish you to the depths of Hell. In whatever place you remain, or wheresoever you roam, "God knows His own, and is near to all that call upon Him in truth" [*2 Tim.* 2:19; *Ps.* 144:18].

Pardon me, my venerated old friend, for these just reproaches

---

*   In the town of Douay

and for my ardor. Permit me to hate that deadly disease, let me ward off the imminent danger to so noble a man, and rescue so dear a friend, with any medicine, however bitter. And now, if Christ gives grace, and if you yourself do not refuse, my hopes of you are equal to my love. I love you as one outstanding in nature, in learning, in gentleness, in goodness, and as doubly dear to me for your many kindnesses and services. If you recover, you make me happy for ever; if you despise me, this letter is my witness. God judge between you and me. Your blood be on yourself. Farewell.

> November 1st [1571]
> From him who most desires your salvation,
> Edmundus Campianus

Balbin says (but one wonders how he could know) that Cheney kept this letter among his archives, and prized it as his chief treasure.[26]

His Activities at Douay

During the time that Campion spent at Douay, he completed his course of scholastic theology, and there he passed the three stages for the degree of Bachelor of Theology on March 21 and November 27, 1572, and January 21, 1573. He did not remain long enough to receive the licentiate.[27]

On August 13, 1571, Edmund bought for himself a newly printed copy, in three volumes folio, of the *Summa Theologica* of St. Thomas Aquinas.[28] This *Summa* was printed by Christopher Plantin at Antwerp in 1569, and it had therefore freshly appeared. In Campion's handwriting, on the title-page of the first volume appears: EDM. CAMPIANUS, Londinensis, Emptus A.D. 1571. Idib. Augusti (Edmund Campion of London. Bought August 13, A.D. 1571). It was in the possession of Fr. Barbier, parish priest of St. Souplet, France, when it was discovered in 1887 by Canon Didiot, Dean of Theology, Catholic University, Lille, France.[29] It is now preserved at the Jesuits' Manresa House, Roehampton, London.[30] It contains many notes in the margins in Campion's own hand, in perfect Latin. On the title-page, he underlined in the long title the words that indicated that the book treats of those passages of the "Holy Scriptures and the ancient Fathers that have been or are now controverted by heretics," showing that he saw how the *Summa* would help him in controversy. His marginal notes show the width of his reading: he refers to Fathers, Councils, philosophers, and theologians of his time.[31] In a passage relating to Baptism of Blood, St. Thomas quotes an authority as saying, "by martyrdom all the sacramental virtue of Baptism is contained."[32] There Edmund wrote in the margin in large bold characters, in a prophetic gesture, the one word: MARTYRIUM (martyrdom).

Edmund received minor orders (porter, lector, exorcist, acolyte) up to and including subdeacon.[33] Perhaps he was employed also as a teacher in the College, just as he would be made Professor of Rhetoric at the Clementine College in Prague, while still a religious novice.[34] If he taught, he had not only to teach the rules, but also to set the example of eloquence; and Persons tells us that, after an oration of his upon the angels, on St. Michael's Day, Dr. Matthew Gallenius, the Chancellor of the University, declared, *Profecto nostra patria non fert tale ingenium* (Truly, our country does not produce such a wit)—which, says Persons, though an exaggeration, considering the great store of rare and eminent men that Belgium yields daily to the world, yet shows his opinion of Master Campion, to whom he was a perfect stranger.[35]

His Ideal Christian Student

Campion wrote in Ireland a discourse, *De Homine Academico* ("The university man"), which has not survived in its original form but in the still more valuable shape of an oration, *De Juvene Academico* ("The young student"),[36] written when his views had been refined by his public submission to the Church. It was pronounced in the presence of Dr. Allen and all the professors and students of the seminary. This oration provides us with Campion's private views on education and his vision of an ideal Catholic student.

His ideal, he says professedly, is of one who excels in every respect, and is not one he has ever met, but can act as a "spur to the acquisition of every virtue and kind of knowledge."

In the first place, his ideas on this subject were not changed by his submission to the Church; he imported into her what he had learned outside her, without any material alterations.

> I will try, out of my observations made during many years, in
> numerous places, and with many minds—taking what I may from

the words of many others—to make a kind of pencil sketch of the university man.

This sketch was not intended merely for the lay ideal, but for the ecclesiastical student, whose education, "up to his twenty-third year, when he begins his theology," is placed before us in a model whose different members are all culled from real examples, and which, though perhaps as a whole unattainable by any individual, is yet the ideal towards which all should strive, according to their various powers.

Campion begins with his ideal youth's social and personal advantages. He is supposed to be

> rich, gently and liberally nurtured, gifted too with such a fine presence that you would say he was fashioned by nature to noble station and dignity. He was healthy and muscular; his mind subtle, fast and clear; his memory most reliable; his voice flexible, sweet and resonant; his walk and all his motions so lively, composed and mature that you would regard him as a dwelling-place fit for wisdom.

He is supposed to have been born of Catholic parents and to have learned his religion with his alphabet, not from any old master but from an accomplished and learned man. He was trained in careful and accurate pronunciation from an early age, and when he grew older he easily acquired the nice turns of eloquence. His first years at school were devoted to Latin, to the rudiments of Greek, and to a mastery over his native tongue, in which he had to write verses and epigrams. His other accomplishments were painting, playing the lute, singing at sight, writing with facility and correctness, quickness in arithmetic, speaking impromptu, and practice in writing-style.

Before entering upon the study of philosophy and other sciences, he had become a good orator and had devoured most of the works of Cicero. He had enlarged his knowledge of Greek, and had become a finished, even an inspired, poet.

> These gifts were rendered more remarkable and attractive by a nature that was simple, sincere and docile, and a character that was truly holy. So it was that by the grace of God and the care of his elders, the good seed begot in this youth the flower of purity and innocence, and produced the good fruits of every virtue.
>
> For what does it avail to cultivate the mind with knowledge

unless a man recognise the Source of knowledge? What purpose
does study serve unless its target be set in sight? What folly to dress
up talent that it may serve the devil! What vanity to furnish the mind
if, enriched and endowed, it be cast down to Hell!

This ideal youth possessed piety and integrity beyond normal measure. Like St. Louis, he had resolved never to commit a mortal sin, no
matter what threats or losses. "He used to say that there was no sun shining that day on which he did not attend Mass." He said daily prayers
to the Blessed Virgin Mary. He prayed with a devout and not a casual
posture. He confessed regularly and often went to Holy Communion.
He opened his soul to a spiritual Father and followed his counsel. He
respected priests and relished penance. "As alms to the poor he often
gave what through abstinence he had withheld from himself." At school,
he befriended and supported those unfairly despised. He looked out for
his companions to render them services, visited them when they were
sick and spoke to them as brothers. He was earnest in his studies, mild
and relaxed at games, and pleasant in his conversation.

The literary studies carried him to his sixteenth year. In the next
seven years he completed his course of philosophy, finished Latin oratory, and studied the eloquence of the Greeks. He read all histories, those
of his own country, then the Roman, then the Greek, and lastly the annals
of other nations. Moral and political philosophy he studied, chiefly in
Aristotle and Plato. He ran through mathematics, and learned all that he
judged useful for his purpose out of every subject of science. This variety
was so methodical that it involved no confusion or hesitation; he was at
once

> in diction and style so pure, elegant and religious, that he seemed to
> have digested and assimilated Cicero; in argument, so intent, concise
> and cogent, that he could refute Chrysippus; in physics, so shrewd
> and acute as to be called an oracle of nature; in history, so deep as
> to be an explorer of the ages; and in the rest, so intelligent and ready
> that he seemed to have investigated every field of knowledge.

How did he reach such heights?

> It was by natural talent, not precocious, but matured and per-
> fected; through learned masters, a well-stored library, and continual

industry; by labor in learning, method in laboring, and constancy in method.

These are the intellectual characteristics of Campion's model. He insists on the collateral necessity of moral virtues in as great perfection as the mental attainments. The only two precepts of intellectual and literary abstinence are the following:

> He did not fill himself with indiscriminate reading, nor stuff himself with the dry bones of books. He did not dull himself by staying up to ungodly times, but slept about seven hours. The day he dedicated to work, the night to rest.

His dress was simple and becoming; there was nothing singular or extravagant to invite comments.

It goes without saying that he avoided blasphemy, drunkenness, unchastity, theft, or hatred. He avoided even small sins. He kept himself free from vanity, curious looks, quarrels, and impatience.

> Holy thus in mind and in body, with equal care and delicacy of conscience he avoided superstitions, scrupulosity, hypocrisy, presumption, sadness and that critical, superior attitude which sometimes lurks around even good works.

He was strict in his judgment upon himself, but lenient with others. He found something to praise in every work, and never gave a simple censure or a contemptuous remark. Yet he always maintained the principle that kindness should be kept clear of flattery, and truth free from bitterness.

In general literature there was one subject which he always avoided: he was "a poet who had never written nor even read amatory compositions"—such as those of the ancient Roman poet Ovid. But he had not avoided the great masters of literature on account of the incidental allusions to this matter. He could express himself in:

> the majesty of Virgil, the festal grace of Ovid, the rhythm of Horace, and the tragic vein of Seneca.

He was an *orator* who knew, as the occasion demanded, how to charm with sweetness, or sway with fervent appeals, or astonish by the weight of his thought, or convince his listeners by the chain of his reasoning. He was "a *historian* who, as a thorough master of geography and chronology, the two eyes of history," could traverse the world over, from creation to the present day. He was a *Greek scholar* who had drunk in ancient Greek wisdom with relish. He was a *logician* capable of appreciating, distinguishing and illuminating all he touched. He was a *philosopher* familiar with the deepest secrets of nature. He was an *astronomer* who could read off the solar system like a book. In his last year, about to begin Theology, he became a good *student of Hebrew.*

But there is one more thing to make him truly well-rounded and perfect. During all this time his religious exercises had included not only attendance at sermons and catechisms, but private discussions with theologians, and the perusal of contemporary Catholic authors, especially those who treated of disputed doctrines in a clear and good style. Thus he had acquired a knack of religious controversy and an insight into the principles of heresy that enabled him to repel with facility, knowledge, and intelligence, whatever attack was made upon his religion.

This model student

> used to say that those old heretics, Arius, Eutyches, Pelagius, Nestorius and the others, could not be properly refuted except by skilled theologians, on account of their shrewd subtlety and knowledge, but that the sophisms of our days were such flagrant and manifest violations of truth that, once put to the test, they immediately crumbled, and required no great force of either skill or knowledge to be brought down.[37]

In short, the student is

> one endowed with every good quality, whose name is on the lips of all, who abounds in virtues and multifarious knowledge, an excellent linguist, and a virtuous ripening theologian.

Evelyn Waugh remarks: "This catalogue no doubt defines the aim which Campion was setting himself and, to a great extent, realizing in that period."[38]

In one of his historical writings,[39] Edmund mentions with complacency the revival of the "salutary knowledge of the three tongues" (Latin, Greek, Hebrew) and the consequent disrepute into which "the subtleties of the old theologians and grammarians" had fallen; and while lamenting the "evils which the young students had with characteristic precipitation imported into this excellent movement," and blaming those who, after turning to the best account the leisure purchased for them by the liberality of prelates and abbots, employed their attainments to ridicule their patrons, who had paid their expenses, he yet saw that the only remedy was to bring the race of "ignorant ecclesiastics, simple preachers, and old-fashioned monks" to a speedy end by a radical change in their education. And how radical was the change he meditated is abundantly shown by the ideal model which he proposed to the president, professors, and students of the great seminary at Douay.

Here is the peroration, in which he exhorts all these seminarians to try to realize his ideal of an academic young man for the sake of the eternal salvation of souls in the current religious crisis:

> Listen to our Heavenly Father asking back His talents with interest; listen to Mother Church who bore us and nursed us, imploring our help; listen to the pitiful cries of our neighbors in danger of spiritual starvation; listen to the howling of the wolves that are plundering the flock. The glory of your Father, the preservation of your mother, your own salvation, the safety of your brethren are at stake, and can you stand idle? If this house were blazing before your eyes, would he not be a juvenile reprobate who went on singing or chortling or playing games or, as Horace puts it,[40] riding a cock-horse, at the height of the common crisis?
>
> Behold, by the wickedness of the wicked the house of God is given over to flames and destruction; numberless souls are being deceived, are being ruined, are being lost—any one of which is worth more than the empire of the whole world. Do not, I pray you, regard such a tragedy as a joke; sleep not while the enemy keeps watch; play not while he devours his prey; relax not in idleness and vanity while he is dabbling in your brothers' blood. It is not wealth nor liberty nor station that suffer but the eternal inheritance of each of us, the very life-blood of our souls, the life of the Holy Spirit. See, then, most dear and learned youths, that you lose none of this precious time but carry away from this seminary a plentiful and rich crop, enough to supply the public wants and to gain for yourselves the reward of dutiful sons.

In Praise of Scripture

The other oration belonging to this period, *De Laudibus Scripturae Sacrae* (On the Praises of Sacred Scripture),[41] is incomplete, and the part that survives is not of great worth; he maintains the most rigid theory of verbal and syllabic dictation.[42] The following simile, however, is aptly and prettily introduced:

> At Down, which is a market-town in the noble island of Ireland, Gerald of Wales, its historian, attests that he saw with his own eyes the relics of the most renowned woman, Saint Brigid, and among these was found a concordance of the four Evangelists, beautified with mystical pictures in the margin, whose colors and workmanship at the first blush were dark and unpleasant, but in the view wonderfully lively and artistic. . . . Is not this most like to the style of Scripture? which seems to him, who only looks in at the door, to speak unlearnedly and pedantically; whereas whoever attends, observes and looks closely, finds the truth of the Prophet's praise: "Thy words are like fire, and as a hammer that breaketh the rock"[43] [*Jeremiah* 23:29].

A Change of Plan

After spending nearly two years at Douay, Campion be came dissatisfied with his position. His biographers attribute this solely to his desire of penance and perfection. His chief study was to acquire the true science of the saints, the knowledge of God and of himself. But the more his self-knowledge increased, the more unhappy he became about that miserable Anglican diaconate. From the first it had given him the most painful scruples, which only grew more painful as his self-knowledge grew deeper, his learning more extensive, and his virtue more mature. He called it "the mark of the English beast," and the thought of being impressed with it grew at last too burdensome to be lightened by counsel of learned friends, or by his own study. So he determined to break entirely with the world, to make a pilgrimage to Sts. Peter and Paul at Rome, and, by their good help, to become a Jesuit.[44] He heard, as his foreign biographers add, an interior voice commanding him to go to Rome,[45] where he should be told what to do. He resolved to obey, and immediately felt such inward comfort, that he decided not to delay.

A diligent study of Campion's writings throws light on a divergence between his views and those of Dr. Allen, which I am disposed to think had almost as much to do with his leaving Douay as his scruples or his vocation. A weak point lay in Dr. Allen's character, a point in which he suffered the usual fate of exiles—ignorance of the movements and feelings of his country, and the crystallization of his brain in those feelings with which he first left England. In Queen Mary's reign, her husband Philip II was king consort of England, and loyalty to him was a proper sentiment. Allen preserved this sentiment all his life, and not without reason, for he lived within the Spanish king's dominions, and was a dependant on his bounty. But he let it lead him into his defense of the treachery of Sir William Stanley at Deventer, Holland, who, fighting for England, freely yielded the city to the Spaniards and offered his services to Spain. It led him also to the composition of the disgraceful pamphlet which he intended to be distributed throughout England as soon as the Spanish Armada should have achieved its first success.[46]

But whatever divergence there might have been politically between Allen and Campion, there was no disturbance to their friendship. Even the resolution of his most promising subject to leave him did not alienate the affections of the great founder of the English seminary. With a vast harvest to gather in, and only few laborers to send; with every interest of heart and mind concentrated on the conversion of England, it would have been very excusable if he had been grievously offended at Campion's desertion, and all the more at his entrance into the Society of Jesus, which as yet had taken no part in the English mission. We might perhaps have expected Allen to offer the most strenuous opposition to the step, to show himself for years afterwards a bitter enemy of the Society, and to guard himself against any future loss of his students by forbidding them to learn from its professors, to listen to its preachers, or to perform its spiritual exercises. But he was too big-hearted and farsighted to be swayed by such petty jealousies; he counted on receiving back his loan with interest, and, though he had to wait a while, his calculations did not fail him in the end.

He Leaves for Rome

We presume Campion waited for winter to be coming to an end before making the long trip from Douay to Rome. Perhaps he waited first for his friends Gregory Martin and Richard Bristow to be ordained priests on March 21, 1573.

As soon as he had decided to depart, and had fixed the day, his preparations did not occupy much time. He went on foot as a poor pilgrim.
He allowed his friends to accompany him one day's journey, but would
receive no other assistance or protection.[47] The rest of his journey he
accomplished alone, and never afterwards spoke of its incidents. But he
was met on the road by an old Oxford acquaintance, a Protestant, who
had known him "in great pomp and prosperity," and who on his return
from a tour to Rome came across a pilgrim in a mendicant's dress. They
passed each other without recognition; but the traveller, struck with
some familiar expression, rode back to see who the poor man was. He
soon recognized him, dismounted, shook hands, exhibited the greatest
sympathy, and asked whether he had fallen among thieves that he was
in such a plight. When he heard that it was all voluntary mortification,
he mocked the idea as unworthy of an Englishman, fit only for a crazy
fanatic, and absurd in a man of moderate means and a frame not over-
robust; so he pulled out his purse, and told Campion to help himself. The
pilgrim refused, and, says Persons, "made such a speech unto him of the
contempt of this world, and eminent dignity of serving Christ in poverty,
as greatly moved the man and us also his acquaintance that remained yet
in Oxford, when the report thereof came unto our ears."[48]

Campion arrived in Rome in spring 1573.

CHAPTER 4

Pilgrim to Rome

C AMPION'S BIOGRAPHERS—THE four Jesuit priests: Persons, Bombino, Bartoli, and More—tell us nothing of what occurred to him at Rome beyond his conformity to the pious customs of pilgrims, his visits to the major churches and saints' tombs, his conviction that he was called to be a Jesuit, and his admission into the Order in April 1573. It appears by his own statements that he had already made up his mind about his vocation when he first arrived.

Meeting with Cardinal Gesualdi

Campion arrived in Rome in spring 1573, most likely mid-April. If we have surmised correctly that March 22 was the day of his departure from Douay,[1] he managed to accomplish the trip in about twenty-five days.[2]

Among those whom he visited there was John Bavand, his first tutor at Oxford, who left England around 1564 and was now a priest. Fr. Bavand gave Edmund introductions, help, and money.[3]

Perhaps one of those introductions was to Cardinal Alfonso Gesualdi.[4] "At my first arrival into Rome," said Edmund at his trial, in November 1581, "which is now about ten years past, it was my hap [fortune] to have access to the said Cardinal, who, having some liking of me, would have been the means to prefer me to any place of service whereunto I should have most fancy; but I, being resolved what course to take, answered that I meant not to serve any man, but to enter into the Society of Jesus, thereof to vow and to be professed."[5]

Then Cardinal Gesualdi began to question him about the Bull of Pius V against Elizabeth. The Cardinal simply wanted to know what had been the effect of this step. If it had failed in effectiveness, there was some wish to make its bearings on the Catholics as easy as possible. "Being demanded farther," Campion continues, "what opinion I had conceived of the Bull, I said, it procured much severity in England, and the heavy hand of her Majesty against the Catholics; where unto the Cardinal replied, that he doubted not it should be mitigated in such sort as the Catholics should acknowledge her highness as their queen without danger of excommunication." For the pope's Bull not only excommunicated the queen but all who continued to obey her.

The Temporal Power of the Popes

Campion urges that his conduct rather implied dissent from, than agreement with, the Bull. That this was his opinion, one might show from his *History of Ireland*, where Campion speaks in strong terms against those Irishmen who had risen against Elizabeth and Henry VIII:

- Shane O'Neill is a "wretched man," who "quenched the sparks of grace that appeared in him with arrogance and contempt against his prince."[6]
- Lord Thomas Fitzgerald, Deputy of Ireland, who, upon the receipt of false intelligence that his father had been put to death in England, had risen in arms, is represented by Campion as saying:

I am none of Henry's deputy, I am his foe. I have more mind to conquer than to govern, to meet him in the field than to serve him in office. If all the hearts of England and Ireland that have cause thereto would join in this quarrel (as I trust they will) then should he [Henry] soon abie [pay the penalty] (as I trust he shall) for his heresy, lechery, tyranny, wherein the age to come may hardly [willingly] score him up among the ancient princes of most abominable and hateful memory.

This is language quite in conformity with that of Paul III's Bull against Henry—yet Campion's comment on it is:

With that he rendered up the sword [of State], and flung away like a bedlam [madman], adding to this shameful oration many other slanderous and foul terms, which for regard of the king's posterity I have no mind to utter.[7]

Campion can hardly have shut his mind against the great Roman question of the day. His *History of Ireland* proves that he was fully instructed in the claims of the popes to the temporal supremacy of all Christian kingdoms. He not only narrates but he believes, that "when Ireland first received Christendom, they gave themselves into the jurisdiction, both spiritual and temporal, of the See of Rome. The temporal lordship Pope Adrian [IV] conferred upon Henry II."[8] Moreover, "Henry II, building upon the pope's favor, his born subject [Adrian was English-born], had sent ambassadors to Rome in the first year of his reign, asking leave to attempt the conquest of Ireland."[9] Adrian had such trust in the king, that he not only gave him leave to conquer the island, but conferred on him a kind of legatine power of correcting its religious abuses. Accordingly, the invasion took place; a religious reformation was enacted in the synod of Cashel; and the Irish clergy, in obedience to the papal Bulls, "denounced curse and excommunication to any that would maliciously gainsay or frustrate"[10] the temporal right over Ireland that the popes had given to Henry.

The popes themselves seem to have founded their right, first on the feudal law, then on the ground of divine right, because they were Vicars of Christ in His temporal as well as in His spiritual power; and then on the ground of the necessity of this right for the government of the Church, after controversialists had shown that they were Vicars of Christ only in those powers which Christ had exercised while upon earth.

If the pope could give Ireland to Henry because "all islands belonged to the Roman See," the same reason was equally applicable to England. But Campion was far from allowing this. He mentions the fact that King John

> made a personal surrender of both his realms in way of submission [to the Pope], and after his assoilment [absolution] received them again. Some add that he gave away his kingdoms to the See of Rome for him and his successors, recognizing to hold the same of the Popes in fee, paying yearly therefore one thousand marks, and in them 300 for Ireland. . . . Sir Thomas More, a man in that calling and office likely to sound the matter to the depth, writeth precisely [*The Supplication of Souls*, 1529] that neither any such writing the Pope can show, nor were it effectual if he could.[11]

Sir Thomas More was clearly a favorite of Campion. In his history of Henry's divorce he talks of the "incredible experience in affairs and penetration of intellect" which the Chancellor displayed, and of his "sublime and almost divine wisdom";[12] and this appeal to his authority on the subject of the pope's rights over England is decisive.

In short, Campion's position was inconsistent, or at least a mixture: he asserts past (but not current) Papal authority over Ireland—yet not over England, while also upholding the English crown's authority over Ireland, given to England by Pope Adrian IV.

The Bull of Pius V

But Pope Pius V had no doubts about his temporal power. Knowing how his predecessor's attempts to send an agent to Elizabeth had failed, he changed his plan, and began to address himself to the people. After having declared the queen a heretic in the Bull *Regnans in excelsis*, dated February 25, 1570,[13] he sent Dr. Nicolas Morton into England:

> to declare by Apostolic authority to certain illustrious and Catholic men, that Elizabeth, who then wore the crown, was a heretic, and therefore had lost all right to the do minion and power which she exercised upon the Catholics, and might be properly treated by them as a heathen and publican; and that they henceforth owed no obedience to her laws or commands. By this declaration many of the higher classes were led not only to consult their own interest, but to consider by what means they could deliver their brethren from the tyranny of the heretics. And they hoped that all the Catholics would join them with all their forces in this pious design. But though the affair turned out contrary to their hopes, either because all the Catholics did not yet properly know that Elizabeth was legally declared a heretic, or because God had determined to punish still more heavily the revolt of England, yet their design was a praise-worthy one, and was by no means without a certain success.[14]

So wrote Fr. Sanders in 1571. The "success" attained was the rebellion of the great earls of the North in 1569. Its failure did not discourage the English advisers of Pius V. They soon picked up a new leader, the Duke of Norfolk, whom they assumed to be a sound Catholic, and to whose standard they fondly expected the whole realm to rally; it only required that the pope's pleasure and censure should be known to the

Catholics, and there would be no place for resistance; and afterwards the whole difficulty might be settled by a marriage between the Duke of Norfolk and Queen Mary of Scotland. Fr. William Watson judged them wrong on all points:

> It is well known that the chief reasons that moved Pius V to yield unto them [Harding, Morton, etc.] were most falsely and surreptitiously suggested to His Holiness, and carried with them very many absurdities; as . . . forsooth, the Duke of Norfolk was a most sound Catholic (which was false); all the realm would follow him (which was absurd); the Pope's pleasure and censure once known to the Catholics, there could be no resistance (which was ridiculous). Besides this, a marriage would follow, that would reform all and work wonders.[15]

Ironically, the same Fr. Watson, who wrote against the Jesuits and any attempts to unseat Elizabeth, was himself, years later, arrested for the "Bye Plot" to kidnap the new king in 1603.

Persuaded by the representations cited above, which had more weight with the pope than the entreaties of King Maximilian of Hungary and Bohemia, and other princes, Pius V publicly launched his Bull, in which he detailed Elizabeth's crimes:

> She has forbidden by the strong hand of power the observance of the true religion . . . She has persecuted those who profess the Catholic faith . . . She has abolished the Sacrifice of the Mass, the Divine Office, fasting, abstinence, celibacy, and Catholic rites. She has ordered the use throughout the realm of books containing manifest heresy, and the observance by her subjects of impious mysteries and ordinances, according to the rule of Calvin . . . She has dared to take away their churches and benefices from the bishops, the pastors and other Catholic priests, and has given them, with other ecclesiastical goods, to heretics. She has made herself a judge in ecclesiastical causes. . . . She has compelled many to take an oath to observe her wicked laws, to renounce the authority of the Roman Pontiff, to refuse to obey him, and to accept her as the sole ruler in temporal and spiritual matters. She has decreed punishments and penalties against those who do not submit to her . . . She has thrown Catholic prelates and pastors into prison, where many, worn out by protracted sufferings and sorrows, have ended their days in misery.[16]

The conduct of "the servant of iniquity, Elizabeth, the pretended queen of England," is contrasted with that of her sister "Mary, the legitimate queen."

The pope asserted in the strongest terms all the Papal claims: that he alone is appointed "prince over all nations and all realms, to pluck up, to destroy, to dissipate, to crush, to plant, and to build." Elizabeth is declared a heretic, and therefore excommunicated, and "deprived of her pretended right to the said kingdom, and all and every dominion, dignity and privilege." All her subjects are forever absolved from all allegiance to her; all are commanded "not to dare obey her, or her monitions, commands and laws." All who do so are anathematized with her.

Fr. Pollen explains:

> According to the medieval idea of Christendom, the Pope should be final arbiter both between prince and prince, and between prince and people, and, by consequence, he should be able to depose an heretical sovereign, who was imposing his creed upon his subjects by force. It is recognized nowadays on all hands that such a right does exist somewhere, and it is held that such tyranny may properly be met with rebellion. The English Reformers had frequently asserted the latter principle, and by it justified their interference in France, Scotland, and Flanders. But the English Catholics still held to their old conservative idea of the Papal referendum, an idea which the makers of the English constitution had cherished, which Henry VIII himself had maintained,[17] but which Protestants now declared to be treasonable.[18]

To many today, it seems absurd to vest such power in one man—but it is no more absurd than to vest it in the people who have to conduct the rebellion, or the United Nations Organization which today makes much the same temporal judgments as the medieval popes but without any higher principles.

Excommunication with deposition had been the recognized punishment for excessive tyranny in the Middle Ages, and was enjoined by the disciplinary decrees of Lateran Council IV, held in Rome in 1215. Even in the 13th century, as in the case of King John of England and Pope Innocent III, such theoretical claims had only had practical effect when political circumstances were favorable to the Papacy. With the appearance of Protestantism, such claims had even less credibility. The Bull was a dead letter in its temporal claims.

Catholics' Reaction to the Bull

Pius V's Bull, says Fr. Sanders, was obeyed by one or two (*unus et alter*) Catholics, who sacrificed their lives in publishing or asserting it. The rest, either because they did not acknowledge the legality of its publication, and observed that the neighboring princes and commonwealths made no difference in their relations with the queen; or because, when Pius V died, they did not know that his successor had renewed and confirmed the Bull; or, at least, through fear (though they alleged the former excuses), remained in their obedience; and their opponents braved the whole thing as a bugbear to frighten children.[19] But Sanders also says the adversaries were really in a great fright, as was proved by their earnest but vain endeavors to get the Bull cancelled.

Some judged that the pope cannot forbid their temporal obedience to their sovereign. The pope is only the interpreter, not the enactor, of the divine law, and therefore his interposition is only required when something obscure has to be cleared up, not in cases which need no explanation. Therefore, when the command is to "render to Caesar what is Caesar's, and to God what is God's" (*Mk.* 12:17), and to "be submissive to rulers and authorities, to be obedient" (*Titus* 3:1), it is the pope's business to define what is Caesar's and what is God's, but not to forbid subjects to give anything whatever to Caesar—for this is not to interpret but to abrogate the law. Our obligation of obedience to the State is comprised within the limits of temporal matters, while all spiritual affairs are reserved to the jurisdiction of the Vicar of Christ and the other bishops. No sovereign is to be obeyed when commanding things contrary to the law of nature or of God, or to good morals. These things are the right of the pope and bishops to determine. But if the Pope commands citizens "not to dare obey" their sovereign, or the sovereign's "monitions, commands and laws," he cannot be obeyed, because this is not interpreting but annulling the divine precept, and is beyond the Papal power.

Sanders (whom Camden[20] follows) and others are sufficient witnesses of the reasons which induced English Catholics to treat the Bull as a dead letter. That Campion shared the common opinions of his brethren I have, I think, made evident. Like them, he at least hesitated about the

Bull; he doubted whether it justified Catholics in throwing off their allegiance; it put him into the same skeptical attitude which precluded any kind of decisive political partisanship.

Evelyn Waugh says:

> After Pius's death an inquiry had been sent to Rome to discover whether the Bull was still in force, and had elicited the following replies: that it had been issued in the hope of the kingdom being immediately restored to Catholicism, and in view of that occasion [the Rising of the North, 1569], and that as long as the Queen remained *de facto* ruler, it was lawful for Catholics to obey her in civil matters and co-operate in all just things; that she might honorably be addressed with her titles as Queen; that it was unlawful for any private person, not wearing uniform and authorised to do so as an act of war, to slay any tyrant whomsoever, unless the tyrant, for example, had invaded his country in arms; that in the event of anyone being authorised to put the Bull into execution, it would not be lawful to Catholics to oppose him.[21]

Waugh names no date or authority—for, indeed, it was a private opinion of a theologian in Rome (possibly Fr. Antonio Possevino S.J.), never promulgated. In effect, the opinion was in accord with how Catholics judged the issue without the benefit of an authoritative statement.

The Bull's effect on Elizabeth and her government was, on the other hand, most decisive. That persecution which drove Campion first from Ireland and then from England was the immediate result; and within two years it had produced a crop of penal laws, the first installment of that sanguinary code which in process of time nearly effaced the Catholic Church from England. The fear that this Bull, and any future Bulls, might lead to mischief, was the occasion of the penal laws—as shown by the very title of the first of them: "An Act against the bringing in and putting in execution of Bulls, Writings, or Instruments, and other superstitious things from the See of Rome." No wonder that Campion, when asked his opinion about the Bull, declared that it procured much severity in England, and the heavy hand of her Majesty against Catholics.

Entrance into the Society of Jesus

When Campion arrived in Rome in spring 1573—most likely mid-April, as we said—the Society of Jesus was without a head at the time.[22] Its third General, (Saint) Francis Borgia, died on October 1, 1572, exactly five months after Pope (Saint) Pius V. Campion had to wait a little, while the third General Congregation was assembled to elect a successor. The choice fell upon Fr. Everard Mercurian, of Liege, Belgium, on April 12, 1573. A few days afterwards, Campion presented himself as the new General's first postulant. Campion gave such a good account of himself that no further trial of his vocation was required than the probation he had imposed upon himself; he was accepted without delay, but as there was then no English Province in the Society of Jesus, the various Provincials disputed who should have him, and he was at last allotted to an Italian priest, Lawrence Maggio, Provincial of the Austrian Province.[23] Persons says he was incredibly comforted with this battle of the provincials for the possession of his body, because he saw that he was no more his own man, but in the hands of others, who, under God, would dispose of him better than he could do for himself; he was perfectly indifferent to all functions and all countries; but as his own inclination was for a country where he might strive against heresy, he was glad that Bohemia had been allotted to him. He thought that England owed some reparation to a country which had been first infected by the disciples of Wycliff.[24] (Wycliff was English; his heresy spread abroad and had great influence in Bohemia from the 1380's.)

Campion was a man of common opinions, which he could urge and adorn with all the resources of rhetoric and the wealth of eloquence, and was consequently more dependent on authority for his ideas than upon any depth of research or originality of thought, and must have hailed the new obedience he had undertaken as a happy deliverance from himself. In England he had held, as we have seen, the popular opinions upon the Papal sovereignty which had been inherited by English Catholics, through Sir Thomas More, from generations of politicians. We find him at Rome with his old opinions, refusing any political place that Cardinal Gesualdi had to offer, and taking refuge from the storms of debate in the Society of Jesus where all his energies might be devoted to his own religious perfection, and to those scholastic employments which he ever cultivated, even in the midst of his greatest religious difficulties.

CHAPTER 5

Jesuit at Prague and Brünn

T HE GENERAL Congregation of the Society of Jesus, having elected a new General in April, proceeded with its other matters and came to an end on June 16, 1573.[1]

Jesuit Novitiate in Prague

Soon afterwards, Father Maggio, the Austrian Provincial, with certain Spanish and German Fathers, and Campion, left Rome for Vienna, where they arrived in August. Campion was immediately sent on to Prague, capital of Bohemia, where the novitiate then was, in the company of Father James Avellanedo, the newly appointed confessor to the Empress. This priest was afterwards known to Fr. Persons at Madrid, and often told him "how exceedingly he was edified in all that journey with the modesty, humility and sweet behavior and angelic conversation of Fr. Campion, for whose sake he remained ever after much affectioned to our whole nation."[2]

Edmund arrived in Prague on August 26, 1573. At his entrance into the Society of Jesus, he was asked, according to custom, whether he had ever defended heretical opinions. He answered, "Never did I defend anything pertinaciously."[3]

The novitiate was a two-year period of probation in which a candidate was tested and observed (to see if this was his vocation) and formed in the Jesuit way of life. It was the time of preparation before the religious vows were taken that bound a man permanently as a member.

One of the first acts required of him was to inscribe in the album or blank book of the novitiate certain particulars about him self, his family, and his education. I have already extracted most of the details, but for convenience I print here the full passage [with years added]:

My name is Edmund Campion, an Englishman of London, in my 34th year [aged thirty-three], born of a legitimate marriage and Christian parents of long-standing, and departed in the Catholic faith, we hope. My father's name was Edmund, a citizen and book-seller, of medium fortune. I have two brothers and one sister. The older brother is married, and serves in the army, as I hear; the younger one is a student. I have the deliberate intention of living and dying .in this Society of Jesus; and this I now decide, if I have not decided before, by no one's coercion, but by my own choice.

First I learned grammar in my native place [London]; then I went to Oxford, where I studied philosophy for seven years [1557–64], and theology for about six [1564–70]—Aristotle, Positive Theology, and the Fathers; then nearly a biennium of scholastic theology at Douay [1571–73]. I graduated as Master of Arts at Oxford [1566], and Bachelor of Theology at Douay [1573]. I have a toler-ably happy memory, an understanding sufficiently penetrating, and a mind inclined to study, and for this purpose, as also for the other duties of the Society, I am quite robust. August 26 [1573].[4]

Transfer to Brünn

Campion's first residence at Prague was of very short duration. Within two months of his arrival there, the novitiate was, in October, transferred 125 miles south-east of Prague to Brünn in Moravia (today Brno, Czech Republic), a city where the prospects of Catholicism were even more gloomy than at Prague. The very names of pope and Catholic were in execration; magistrates and people were alike Protestant, the latter riot-ous and unruly. The clergy of one of the great churches was Catholic, that of the other alternated between the two religions: in 1570 a single ener-getic Jesuit had been sent there, who continued to preach in spite of the tumults that his presence excited. But the diocesan bishop, the Bishop of Olmütz, Moravia (now Olomouc, Czech Republic), saw that one Father was not sufficient for the work, and had therefore procured the transfer of the novitiate from Prague to Brünn, in hopes of being able to utilize the exercises of the novices and the spare time of the Fathers.

Accordingly, October 10, 1573, Fr. John Paul Campana,[5] Master of Novices, conveyed Campion and five other novices from Prague to Brünn, where they were soon joined by six more from Vienna. But in the following January the Bishop of Olomouc died, and for ten years the establishment was in continual peril: its goods were seized, its funds confiscated, its members accused before the tribunals, and its suppression decreed by the Emperor, though the commissioners would not promulgate the edict.[6] But after much inconvenience and continual changes of residence, the foundation was gradually consolidated, and in process of time was able to erect an enormous college with seven quadrangles.

The Jesuit Novitiate

The rules of the Society were such as to make the novitiate an institution of great power and influence in a town like Brünn. Some of the five "experiments" (or experiences) prescribed by the Jesuit *Constitutions*[7] for the novices can be turned to missionary purposes:

1. The novice was to spend one month in complete retirement from work and study, during which time he was to perform the thirty days' *Spiritual Exercises* of St. Ignatius, explained below.
2. Another month was devoted to hospitals, where the novice had to make himself a servant to all the patients.
3. For the length of a month, he had to make a pilgrimage without money, begging alms from door to door, so accustoming himself to discomforts and learning to rely completely upon his Creator and Lord.
4. In the religious house of his residence, he had to take his turn in all the most menial employments of the house, with all care and diligence.
5. At least a month was to be spent in catechizing children and ignorant persons, either publicly or privately.

The fifth was precisely that for which the Bishop of Olmütz wished to have the novitiate at Brünn. This exercise therefore superseded many of the others, and the novices were scarcely settled before their Novicemaster began to send them round into all the neighboring villages to teach Catechism. All had great success, but Campion was always noticed to be the most successful, and the villages around Brünn contained many converts that he had led to the Church.

To show with what hearty fervor Campion entered into these exercises, and how utterly he gave himself body and soul to the new life he had undertaken, I need only quote the two following letters, which he wrote to the novices at Brünn, after he had been transferred to the college at Prague even before finishing his own novitiate:

How much I love you in the viscera of Jesus Christ, my dearest brethren, you may conclude from this, that in spite of my daily occupations, which scarce leave me time to breathe, I have managed to steal time from the' midst of my functions and cares to write to you. How could I do otherwise, directly I heard of a sure messenger to Brünn? How could I help firing up with the remembrance of that house, where there are so many burning souls, fire in their mind, fire in their body, fire in their words—the fire which God came to send upon the earth, that it might always burn there?

O dear walls, that once shut me up in your company! Pleasant recreation room, where we talked so holily! Glorious kitchen, where the best friends—John [Cantensis] and Charles [van Tienen], the two Stephens [Drnoczky and Nagy], Sallitz, Finnit and George [Rous], Tobias [Meinhart] and Gaspar [Puschman][8]—compete for the saucepans in holy humility and unfeigned charity! How often do I picture to myself one returning with his load from the farm, another from the market; one sweating stalwartly and merrily under a sack of rubbish, another under some other toil! Believe me, my dearest brethren, that your dust, your brooms, your chaff, your loads, are beheld by angels with joy, and that through them they obtain more for you from God than if they saw in your hands scepters, jewels, and purses of gold. Would that I knew not what I say; but yet, as I do know it, I will say it: in the wealth, honors, pleasures, pomps of the world, there is nothing but thorns and dirt. The poverty of Christ has less pinching parsimony, less meanness, than the emperor's palace. But if we speak of the spiritual food, who can doubt that one hour of this familiar intercourse with God and with good spirits, is better than all the years of kings and princes?

I have been about a year in religion, in the world thirty-five; what a happy change, if I could say I had been a year in the world, in religion thirty-five! If I had never known any father but the Fathers of the Society; no brothers but you and my other brothers; no business but the business of obedience; no knowledge but Christ crucified! Would that at least I had been as happy as you, who have entered the vineyard of Christ in the morning of your lives! I almost envy [John] Cantensis and Charles [van Tienen], who have been brought in so young that they can spend their childhood with the Child Jesus, and can grow up with Him, and increase to the perfect strength of the fullness of Christ. Rejoice therefore, my brethren, at the good you enjoy, and at the greatness of the honor God has done you. Let the remembrance of this be ever present to you, to resist the devil, the world, the flesh, and the difficulties and storms of all temptations. If we are not very stupid and senseless, let us say from our hearts, "It is no great thing that I should serve God; but it is really a great thing that God should have willed to have me for a servant."

I thank you all most heartily for the extraordinary charity which I experienced when with you, and when away from you, by your letters and remembrances, and at my departure as I was setting off; especially I thank Melchior—and who else is it that I named before?—my dearest brother, my friendly rival, my peer in the society, but how high above me in merits! His letters gave me and will give me the greatest pleasure; so did the things he spoke about in his two letters. I will join with the Father Rector in drawing up a plan, and after the affair is set in order, I will write out the whole for him, before the feast of the Annunciation of the Blessed Virgin, I hope. Stephen the Hungarian said that he would write, but has never written a word. With my whole heart I congratulate George [Rous] and Charles, who have lately made their vows.[9] These are strong chains, my brethren, and most strongly do they bind you to our Lord. Who shall tear you from His hands? Shall this triple cord [of the three vows: poverty, chastity, obedience] be broken by that miserable devil who is so impotent that he could not even drown the swine without leave? Who, then, is he that he should be able to overthrow the image of God? Never can he do so, unless we ourselves blot out the image, and con spire with him to our own mischief. I have spent a long time in writing to you—is that the first bell for schools?

I must leave off; and tomorrow is the feast, when I shall be fully occupied, so I don't think I shall be able to write more; however, I will take the next opportunity. I thank my dearest brother [John] Cantensis, whose letter gave me the greatest pleasure, and I thank my God who has given him so good a mind at his age. I received from him the pictures, the *Agnus Dei* [wax image of the "Lamb of God"], and the relics of our holy father Ignatius—a great treasure, for which I return great thanks.

I salute you all in Christ Jesus from the bottom of my soul. My last request is that you would humbly beg Fr. Rector and Fr. [John Vivarius] Aquensis[10] to pardon my long silence; they must ascribe it to my fault, and not to my forgetfulness of their kindness to me. I commend myself to the prayers of you all.[11]

Farewell.

Prague, February 26, 1575

Edmundus Campianus

The second letter was written when he was a scholastic, i.e., after taking the three religious vows at the end of the novitiate, but not yet ordained to the priesthood:

To my dearest brothers in Christ. Although the words of men, my dearest brothers, ought to have much less weight and influence with you than that Spirit who without sound of words whispers in your ears, yet since this work of love is not altogether useless or unnecessary, your charity will cause you to receive this fraternal letter, the witness of my love and duty, with your usual kindness. I write not to you as though you required the spur, for wherever you go your hearts are ever set upon every virtue; but that I, while I employ my time in writing to you, may spur myself, and may enjoy the perfume of the remembrance of your affection, and may testify my affection towards you. And I would that as I speak, and as you perform, so you might speak and I perform. For I know what freedom there is in obedience, what pleasure in work, what sweetness in prayer, what dignity in humility, what peace in the midst of conflict, what nobility in endurance, what perfection in infirmity. But the task is to reduce these virtues to practice. And this is your work, to run over the portion of your earthly course in the glorious chariots of Paradise. As the poet says, I will follow as I can, *non passibus equis* ["not at the same pace," Virgil: *Aeneid*, II, 724].

My dearest brothers, our life is not long enough to thank Christ for revealing these mysteries to us. Which of us would have believed, unless He had called him and instructed him in this school, that such thorns, such filth, such misery, such tragedies, were concealed in the world under the feigned names of goods and pleasures? Which of us would have thought your kitchen better than a royal palace? your crusts better than any banquet? your troubles than others' contentment? your conflicts than their quiet? your crumbs than their abundance? your mean estate than their triumphs and victories? For I ask you whether, if you could all your lives, as they would like, feed your eyes on spectacles, and changes of scene and of company, your eyes would be the stronger? If you fed your ears with news, would they be the fuller? If you gave your mind its lusts, would it be richer? If you fed your body with dainties, could you make it immortal? This is their blunder who are deceived by vanities, and know not what a happy life means. For while they hope and expect great things, they fancy they are making vast progress, and not one in a hundred obtains what he dreamed; and if perchance one obtains it, yet after making allowance for his pains, and his loads of care, the slipperiness of fortune, his disgraceful servility, his fears, plots, troubles, annoyances, quarrels, crimes, which must always accompany and vex the lovers of the world, he will doubtless find himself to be a very base and needy slave. One sigh of yours for Heaven is better than all their clamors for this dirt; one conversation of yours, where the angels are present, is better than all their parties and debauched drinking bouts, where the devils fill the bowls. One day of yours consecrated to God is worth more than all their life, which they spend in luxury.

My brothers, run as you have begun; acknowledge God's goodness to you, and the dignity of your state. Can any pomp of kings or emperors, any grandeur, any pleasure, I will not say equal, but even shadow your honor and consolation? They (I speak of the good among them) fight under Christ their king, with their baggage on their back; you are eased of your burdens, and are called with the beloved disciple to be familiar followers of your Lord. They are admitted to the palace, you to the presence chamber; they to the common pasture, you to the choicest banquets; they to friend ship, you to love; they to the treasury, you to the special rewards. Think what difficulties they have who even live as they ought in this wicked world; then you will more easily see what you owe to His mercy in calling you out of infinite dangers into His society. How hard it is for them to follow Christ when He marches forth in haste against His enemies, who have wives in their bosoms, children on their shoulders, lands on their backs, cares on their heads, whose feet are bound with cords, whose spirits are well-nigh smothered. Is not your happiness great, whom the King marshals by His side, covers with His cloak, clothes and honors with His own livery? What great thing is it for me to have left friends for Him who left Heaven for me? What great thing for me to be a servant to my brethren, when He washed the feet of the traitor Judas? What marvel if I obey my Fathers, when He complied with Pilate? What mighty thing for me to bear labors for Him who bore His cross for me? What disgrace if I a sinner bear rebukes, when He, an Innocent, was cursed, spat upon, scourged, wounded, and put to death? Whenever we look into this mirror, my brothers, we see clearly that the temptation of no pleasure, the fear of no pain, should tear us away from the arms of such a Master.

You see I have nearly filled my paper, though I have plenty to do. It is time to check myself, and to return you to that Teacher who by His sacred influences can im press these things much more strongly on your minds than I can. Hear Him, for He has the words of eternal life.

I have snatched this time from my duties to address some words to you, both of my own free-will and by authorisation of our Rector, Rev. Fr. Paul [Hoffaeus],[12] who follows the house of Brünn with a special concern. The College of Prague, too, which loves you especially, wanted its goodwill towards you to be mentioned in this same letter, and the warmest greetings addressed to each one of you.

For my part, I kiss not only you, but the prints of your holy footsteps, and I beg you to give me, a poor needy wretch, an alms of the crumbs that fall from your table.

I greet most dutifully Rev. Fr. Rector and the other Fathers and Brothers who live with you. In addition, I thank very much Rev. Fr. [John Vivarius] Aquensis and Master Francis, and I commend myself completely to them who have so often greeted me most warmly in their letters.[13]

Farewell.

> Prague, February 20, 1577
> By authorisation of Rev. Fr. Rector
>   and of The College of Prague.
> Your humble servant in Christ,
> *Edmundus Campianus*

The Jesuit Spirit

The first major exercise of new entrants into the Society of Jesus was to make the thirty days' retreat according to the program of St. Ignatius's *Spiritual Exercises*. The *Exercises* form the basis and whole orientation of a Jesuit's spiritual life. Any account or appreciation of Edmund

Campion's interior life, and of Jesuit life itself, depends upon a proper understanding of the *Spiritual Exercises*. With the other novices, Edmund made these series of meditations and exercises, divided into four parts: (a) a consideration and contemplation on sin; (b) the life of Christ our Lord up to Palm Sunday inclusively; (c) the Passion of Christ; (d) the Resurrection and Ascension.

In the first part, Edmund contemplated the purpose of life and creation in the *Principle and Foundation*:

> Man is created to praise, reverence, and serve God our Lord, and by this means to save his soul. And the other things on the face of the earth are created for man and that they may help him in attaining the end for which he is created.
>
> From this it follows that man is to use them inasmuch as they help him on to his end, and ought to rid himself of them insofar as they hinder him from it.
>
> For this it is necessary to make ourselves indifferent to all created things, in all that is allowed to the choice of our free will and is not prohibited to it; so that, on our part, we want not health rather than sickness, riches rather than poverty, honor rather than dishonor, a long rather than short life, and so in all the rest—desiring and choosing only what is most conducive for us to the end for which we are created.[14]

After having him meditate on the origin and heinousness of sin, Ignatius leads the novice to talk to Christ crucified with familiarity:

> Colloquy: Imagining Christ our Lord present and placed on the Cross, let me make a Colloquy, how as Creator He has come to making Himself man, and from life eternal has come to temporal death, and so to die for my sins.
>
> Likewise, looking at myself: What have I done for Christ? What am I doing for Christ? What ought I to do for Christ?
>
> And so, seeing Him such, and so nailed on the Cross, to go over that which will present itself.
>
> The Colloquy is made, properly speaking, as one friend speaks to another, or as a servant to his master; now asking some grace, now blaming oneself for some misdeed, now communicating one's affairs, and asking advice in them.

At the end of the first part, that is, after making the exercises on sin, and reviewing all the sins of his life up to the present, Edmund no doubt made a general confession (a confession of all the sins of his life) as the *Exercises* encourage the retreatant to do.

In the second part, Ignatius presents the call of an earthly king and contrasts it with the call of Christ the Eternal King. Edmund considered

> Christ our Lord, the eternal King, and before Him the entire world, to which, and each one in particular, He calls, and says: "It is My will to conquer all the world and all enemies and so to enter into the glory of My Father; therefore, whoever would like to come with Me is to labor with Me, that following Me in the pain, he may also follow Me in the glory."
>
> Consider that all those who have judgment and reason will offer their entire selves to the labor. Those who will want to be more devoted and signalize themselves in all service of their Eternal King and Universal Lord, not only will offer their persons to the labor, but, acting against their own sensuality and against their carnal and worldly love, will even make offerings of greater value and greater importance, saying:
>
> "Eternal Lord of all things, I make my oblation with Thy favor and help, in the presence of Thy infinite Goodness and in the presence of Thy glorious Mother and of all the Saints of the heavenly Court. I want and desire, and it is my deliberate determination, if only it be Thy greater service and praise, to imitate Thee in bearing all injuries and all abuse and all poverty of spirit, and actual poverty, too, if Thy most Holy Majesty wants to choose and receive me to such a life and state."

Later in the second part, Edmund made the *Meditation on Two Standards*:

> The one of Christ, our Commander-in-chief and Lord; the other of Lucifer, mortal enemy of our human nature.

The *Spiritual Exercises* contain other specific meditations and directives to free a man from disordered attachments to enable him to serve God freely and wholeheartedly. There are also points of instruction on: degrees of humility; rules to help one make a choice of a state of life; the wiles of the devil; methods of prayer; and a contemplation on divine love leading to a complete offering of oneself to God.

At the end of the *Exercises*, Ignatius proposes eighteen *Rules for thinking with the Church*. The basis for all of them lies in the first Rule:

> All judgment laid aside, we ought to have our mind ready and prompt to obey in all the true Spouse of Christ our Lord, which is our holy Mother the hierarchical Church.

The thirteenth Rule insists upon obedience and adherence to the hierarchical Church,

> believing that between Christ our Lord, the Bridegroom, and the Church, His Bride, there is the same Spirit which governs and directs us for the salvation of our souls. Because by the same Spirit and our Lord Who gave the Ten Commandments, our holy Mother the Church is directed and governed.

For Ignatius, as for all Catholics, there could be no separation of Christ from His Church, or any true union with Christ our Head apart from His Body the Church. In the words of St. Joan of Arc: "About Jesus Christ and the Church, I simply know they are just one, and one should not complicate the matter."[15]

Many of the *Rules* are directed in support of Church teachings, traditions and practices reprobated by Protestants, such as: Mass, confession, religious vows and celibacy; church ornaments and images; veneration, intercession and relics of Saints; Scholastic theology, and so on. Four are written with contemporary controversies in mind as he advises preachers and writers to speak carefully: not to emphasize faith, without distinction or explanation, so as to engender laziness in good works; likewise, not to accentuate grace so much as to deny human liberty its rightful role; and similarly not to speak much of predestination lest one induce fatalism, and negligence in works which lead to salvation.

Apart from obedience—in which St. Ignatius especially desired the Jesuits to excel—in his *Constitutions* we find the particular practices, virtues, and attitudes he wished to inculcate in the members of the religious Order that he founded. The *Constitutions of the Society of Jesus* he wrote in Rome over the years 1544–51, before his death in 1556. A few random extracts will have to suffice:

> *Purpose of the Society:* The end of this Society is to devote itself with God's grace not only to the salvation and perfection of the members'

own souls, but also with that same grace to labor strenuously in
giving aid toward the salvation and perfection of the souls of their
fellowmen.[16]

Spiritual formation and direction: It will be beneficial to have a faithful and competent person whose function is to instruct and teach the
novices in regard to their interior and exterior conduct, to encourage them towards this correct deportment, to remind them of it,
and to give them kindly admonition; a person whom all those who
are in probation may love and to whom they may have recourse in
their temptations and open themselves with confidence, hoping to
receive from him in Our Lord counsel and aid in everything. They
should be advised, too, that they ought not to keep secret any temptation which they do not tell to him or their confessor or the superior, being happy that their entire soul is completely open to them.
Moreover, they will tell him not only their defects but also their penances or mortifications, or their devotions and all their virtues, with
a pure desire to be directed if in anything they have gone astray, and
without desiring to be guided by their own judgment unless it agrees
with the opinion of him whom they have in the place of Christ our
Lord.[17]

Spiritual doctrine: On certain days of each week instruction should
be given about Christian doctrine, the manner of making a good and
fruitful Confession, receiving Communion, assisting at Mass and
serving it, praying, meditating, and reading [good spiritual books],
in accordance with each one's capacity. Likewise, care should be
taken that they learn what is proper and do not let it be forgotten,
and put it into practice; that is, all of them should give time to spiritual things and strive to acquire as much devotion as divine grace
imparts to them.

Mortification, modesty, and mutual respect: All should take special
care to guard with great diligence the gates of their senses (especially
the eyes, ears, and tongue) from all disorder, to preserve themselves
in peace and true humility of their souls, and to give an indication
of it by silence, when it should be kept and, when they must speak,
by the discretion and edification of their words, the modesty of their
countenance, the maturity of their walk, and all their movements,
without giving any sign of impatience or pride. In everything they

should try and desire to give the advantage to the others, esteeming them all in their hearts as better than themselves [Phil 2:3] and showing exteriorly, in an unassuming and simple religious manner, the respect and reverence befitting each one's state, in such a manner that by observing one another they grow in devotion, and praise God our Lord, whom each one should endeavor to recognize in his neighbor as in His image.

Meals: In the refection of the body care should be taken to observe temperance, decorum, and propriety, both interior and exterior, in everything. A blessing should precede the meal and a thanksgiving come after it; and all ought to recite these with proper devotion and reverence. During the meal, food should also be given to the soul, through the reading of some book which is devotional rather than difficult so that all can understand it and draw profit from it, or through having someone preach during that time, according to what the superiors may order, or through doing something similar for the glory of God our Lord.

Discretion in penances: The chastisement of the body ought not to be immoderate or indiscreet in abstinences, vigils and other external penances and labors which damage and impede greater goods. Therefore it is expedient for each one to keep his confessor informed of what he does in this matter. If the confessor thinks that there is excess or has a doubt, he should refer the matter to the superior. All this is done that the procedure may be attended by greater light and God our Lord may be more glorified through our souls and bodies.

Overcoming temptations: Temptations ought to be anticipated by their opposites, for example, if someone is observed to be inclined toward pride, by exercising him in lowly matters thought fit to aid toward humbling him; and similarly of other evil inclinations.

Peace: Passion or any anger of some toward others should not be allowed among the residents of the house. If something of the sort arises, efforts should be made to bring the parties to prompt reconciliation and fitting satisfaction.

Right intention, and love of God above all: All should make diligent efforts to keep their intention right, not only in regard to their state of life but also in all particular details. In these they should always aim at serving and pleasing the Divine Goodness for its own sake

and because of the incomparable love and benefits with which God
has anticipated us, rather than for fear of punishments or hope of
rewards, although they ought to draw help also from them. Further,
they should often be exhorted to seek God our Lord in all things,
stripping off from themselves the love of creatures to the extent that
this is possible, in order to turn their love upon the Creator of them,
by loving Him in all creatures and all of them in Him, in conformity
with His holy and divine will.

A constant refrain of St. Ignatius in his *Constitutions* and his many
letters was *Ad maiorem Dei gloriam* (A.M.D.G., For the greater glory of
God). This was always to be the guide and the purpose of one's actions.
It became a motto emblazoned on many Jesuit buildings and works.
This meant, in effect, emphasis upon spiritual growth, and the avoidance of scandal or disputes as far as possible; it meant seeking the good
of the Church, as opposed to private interests, self-promotion, vanity,
or worldliness. To preserve the Society in a humble state and to curb
the entry of ecclesiastical ambition into it, St. Ignatius's *Constitutions*
directed the professed members to promise God never to seek any office
in the Society—and to expose anyone so doing. In an age when bishoprics were often accompanied by great benefices and extravagant living,
the professed members were likewise directed to promise God never to
seek episcopal office.[18]

Another great gift of St. Ignatius, gained through his own experience
and divine enlightenment, was "discernment of spirits," i.e., discerning
the will or inspirations of God by observing how one is moved this way
and that, especially at times of prayer. The *Exercises* contain rules for discerning spirits, suitable at different times or stages of one's spiritual life.
For example, among the initial and basic rules are the following:

> First Rule: In persons who go from mortal sin to mortal sin, the
> Enemy [the devil] is commonly accustomed to propose to them
> apparent pleasures, making them imagine sensual delights and plea-
> sures in order to hold them more, and make them grow in their vices
> and sins. In these persons the good spirit uses the opposite method,
> pricking them and biting their consciences through the process of
> reason.

Second Rule: In persons who are going on intensely cleansing themselves of their sins, and rising from good to better in the service of
God our Lord, it is the method contrary to that in the first Rule, for
then it is the way of the evil spirit to bite, sadden and put obstacles,
disquieting with false reasons, that one may not go on; and it is
proper to the good to give courage and strength, consolations, tears,
inspirations and quiet, easing, and putting away all obstacles, that
one may go on in well-doing.

The Three Jesuit Vows

At the end of his two years' novitiate, around August 1575, Edmund took
perpetual vows: the three religious vows—poverty, chastity, obedience—
and bound himself to serve God according to the *Constitutions of the
Society of Jesus*. Once he had pledged himself in this way, he could then
place the initials "S.J." (Society of Jesus) after his name to signify his
membership.

By the vow of poverty, Edmund renounced personal property: the
possession or accumulation of any money or goods in his own name.
He thus put aside avarice completely, and, in imitation of the poor and
humble Christ, he could call nothing truly his own and had to ask his
superior for any goods needed for his apostolic work.

Vowing chastity, he renounced the good of marriage for the sake of
the Kingdom of Heaven, and was thus enabled to devote himself to God
with undivided heart in imitation of his celibate Lord, Jesus Christ. St.
Ignatius said in simple and straightforward terms, with no intention to
be original, that chastity "should be preserved through the endeavor to
imitate the angelic purity by the purity of the body and the mind,"[19] and
no one ever impugned the chastity of Edmund, handsome and engaging
though he was. Fr. Persons cites a witness to Campion's chastity even
before he entered the Society of Jesus:

> Mr. Richard Stanihurst, who was his inseparable companion in all
> the years of the most fervor of his youth, hath oftentimes avowed
> to me that he never could note in him as much as one light word or
> wanton look all the time he knew him, so as in matters belonging to
> chastity it is verily thought by all that knew him that he died as true
> a virgin as he was born of his mother.[20]

By the vow of obedience, in imitation of Christ who came not to do His own will but the will of His heavenly Father who sent Him, Edmund renounced his own will and preferences, and bound himself to fulfil the will of God as manifested to him by his superiors within the Jesuit Order. In all his assignments, we see how he faithfully observed both the letter and the spirit of obedience as St. Ignatius explained it in the *Constitutions:*

> All should keep their resolution firm to observe obedience and to distinguish themselves in it, not only in matters of obligation but also in others, even though nothing is perceived but the indication of the superior's will without an express command. They should keep God our Creator and Lord in view, for whom such obedience is practised, and they should endeavor to proceed in a spirit of love and not as men troubled by fear. Hence all of us should exert ourselves not to miss any point of perfection which we can attain in the observance of all the Constitutions . . . by applying all our energies with very special care to the virtue of obedience shown first to the Sovereign Pontiff [the pope] and then to the superiors of the Society.
>
> Consequently, in all things into which obedience can with charity be extended (all those in which some sin is not manifest), we should be ready to receive its command just as if it were coming from Christ our Saviour, since we are practising obedience to one in His place and out of love and reverence for Him. . . . We should perform with great alacrity, spiritual joy, and perseverance whatever has been commanded us, persuading ourselves that everything is just, and renouncing with blind obedience any contrary opinion and judgment of our own in all things which the superior commands and in which (as stated) some species of sin cannot be judged present. We ought to be firmly convinced that everyone of those who live under obedience ought to allow himself to be carried and directed by Divine Providence through the agency of the superior as if he were a corpse which allows itself to be carried to any place and treated in any manner desired, or as if he were an old man's walkingstick which serves in any place and in any manner whatsoever the owner wishes to use it. For in this way the obedient man ought to devote himself joyfully to whatsoever task in which the superior desires to employ him to aid the whole body of the religious Institute; and he ought to hold it as certain that by this practice he is conforming himself with the divine will more than by anything else he could do while following his own will and different judgment.[21]

The similes of a staff and a dead body, and the notion of "blind obedience" (which did not exclude representations to one's superior), so often emphasized by writers, were not original in Loyola; they were used by St. Basil and St. Francis of Assisi, among others.[22] In the same chapter of the *Constitutions*, as in his famous *Epistle on Obedience* of 1553, St. Ignatius explained that there are three degrees of religious obedience. The first degree, obligatory at all times, but of no great merit in itself, is obedience of execution, whereby one does what has been commanded. The second degree is obedience of will: to do willingly what one has been commanded. The third degree, that of perfect obedience, he teaches, is obedience of understanding: to conform one's mind and judgment to what has been commanded. We see, at crucial points in Edmund's life, how he followed this obedience wholeheartedly, and this may be judged a major source of his peace of soul; he knew that by doing what he was commanded he was fulfilling the will of God and not his own, possibly mistaken, will.

Return to Prague

In 1574, Fr. John Paul Campana, the Novice-master of Brünn, was appointed Rector of the house at Prague. Accordingly, he carried off with him, on October 7, Campion and two other novices,[23] in the coach of the Chancellor of Bohemia, Vratislav Pernstein, as it was marked, for these trips of the humble Fathers in the trappings of civil state were remembered with complacency.

The Situation in Bohemia

It would take me too far out of my way to trace the importation of the half-political heresy of Wycliff into Prague; its adoption and propagation there by John Huss; the tumults to which it led; the overthrow of the famous university, which was a natural result of a doctrine that "universities, studies, colleges, degrees and professorships are pagan vanities, and are of as much value to the Church as the devil."[24] (This is a proposition of Wycliff, the 29th of those condemned by Pope Martin V and the Council of Constance in 1415; it was equally an opinion of the Hussites.) At last came the persecution of heretics, in which a remedy was sought for these evils—which Campion thus defends:

Huss would not have been punished, had not that perfidious and pestilent man been captured in an escape which the Emperor Sigismund
had forbidden him under pain of death; and had he not also violated
the conditions which he had agreed to in writing with the Emperor,
and so nullified all the value of that safe-conduct. Huss's malice was
too hasty and he was caught. He was commanded to present himself
at Con stance to answer for the barbarous tragedies he had instigated in his own land of Bohemia; he despised the prerogative of
the Council and sought security from the Emperor. The Emperor
signed, but the Christian world, greater than the Emperor, rescinded
it. The heresiarch refused to come to his senses; he perished. Now,
Jerome of Prague stole to Constance with nobody's protection. He
was caught, he made his appearance, he spoke, was treated with
great kindness, went freely wherever he liked, he was healed, abjured
his heresy; he relapsed, and was burnt.[25]

Cochlaeus, in the first half of the next century, still deplored the fall
of the University of Prague, which had once been the boast of Bohemia,
and also that of the Catholic religion, which was so low that it would be
difficult for it ever to recover its ancient state.[26] Still half a century passed,
and in 1570 religion had made no advance; some doubted whether it ever
could. The Bohemian Catholics were few, and all of the poorest classes;
the only wealthy persons of that religion at Prague were the Italian merchants, who united in a confraternity to assist the priests.[27] The Emperor
also was Catholic, and had sent the Jesuits to the town, bidding them
rely on his assistance in case of any tumults. But the influence of the
new Order was only gradually felt. The toil of all the laborers only produced a harvest of seventy souls in 1573, and of fifty in 1574. In 1575
a few apostate priests were reconciled, one or two Hussite ministers,
and forty-three laymen; and so on till 1580, when the whole influence
of the court was lent to them, and 584 converts responded to their call.
That was the first year of any distinct significance. A few years before,
Campion had exclaimed, "Surely this commonwealth will either return,
through God's favor and the help of the saints, to the unity of the Roman
Church, or else, through the wrath of God, Satan will triumph, and it will
be overwhelmed in the thick and horrible darkness of new sects, and will
perish."[28]

Activities in Prague

October 18, 1574, the studies solemnly commenced at Prague. Campion was made Professor of Rhetoric at the *Clementinum,* the newly built Jesuit College there, and opened the schools with a "glorious panegyric," which Fr. Schmidl, in 1747, was able to read at Prague. The *Clementinum,* founded in 1556, in Prague's Old Town, held great prestige from its establishment. St. Peter Canisius was one of its founding Fathers. Students came to study there from Germany, the Netherlands, Italy and Spain.[29] Its buildings today house the National Library of the Czech Republic.

And now began a series of routine labors, tedious even to describe. He was loaded with offices: besides being Professor of Rhetoric, he was *matutinus excitator* (morning rouser), *nocturnus visitator* (night roundsman) and worked in the kitchen for recreation. He went to bed half an hour before the other Fathers but had to rise and ring for the nightly examination of conscience, and after the lapse of a quarter of an hour to ring again for the lights to be put out. After another quarter of an hour, he looked into each cell to see that all were in bed and all candles extinguished. In the morning, he rose half an hour before the rest; he rang the bell to rouse them and went to each cell to awaken the student and light his candle. After fifteen minutes, he repeated his visits, to see that all were dressing; then he rang for prayers, and again for ending them. It was his place to see that all were decently covered in bed, and to report all habitual defaulters.

Among the other employments of Campion were those of prefect and legislator of the Confraternity of the Immaculate Conception, which he founded on January 16, 1575, composed of ten adolescents.[30] These confraternities or sodalities, which were established in every college of the Jesuits, served many purposes. They were the means of introducing more conformity to Roman customs: thus at Prague, one of Campion's rules was that every member of his sodality should forego the Bohemian liberty of communicating under both kinds (receiving both Host and Chalice at Holy Communion). They also gave the opportunity of more supervision and spiritual formation of the best scholars, to whom it was a special honor and privilege to be admitted into these select associations. Campion's foundation flourished wonderfully, and afterwards branched into three great sodalities. Its name, however, was changed when it was incorporated into the Archconfraternity of the Salutation (Annunciation) at the Roman College.

In 1576 Campion was transferred, for two years, to the Boarders' College, where to his former functions he added the duties of *Proefectus morum* (prefect of discipline) and *Proefectus cubiculi* (dormitory prefect).

Besides these various duties, Campion had to compose a Latin oration or a play for almost every important occasion. Schmidl remarks that he "was then flourishing at Prague by the glory of his teaching and especially his eloquence, and he gave not only those orations but also those dramas, which fill a good-sized volume."[31] Emperor Rudolph II and his court loved to hear his preaching.

At the opening of the autumn scholastic term he made a panegyric of St. Wenceslaus, the patron of Bohemia, on his feast, September 28. The oration, which was much admired, is preserved among his works.[32]

Says Persons:

> In these most godly and Christian exercises thus passed Fr. Campion his time in Prague, doing good to as many as he could, and omitting no occasion or labor to increase his merit for the life everlasting. He preached publicly, made exhortations in private, read in the schools, taught the Christian doctrine unto children, heard confessions, visited prisons and hospitals of sick men, and at the death of sundry great persons made such excellent funeral orations as astonished the hearers, and infinite increase of piety and good works ensured thereof.[33]

Balbin says:

> His companions thought it a miracle that one man could bear so many diverse loads; but whenever a new task was laid upon him, Campion used to go to the Superior, and ask whether he really thought him strong enough to bear it. If the answer was affirmative, Campion made no delay or excuses, but immediately did what he was told, having more confidence in the Rector's judgment about him than in his own about himself.[34]

And his labors did him no harm; he was never better in health. "Why should I not be well, dearest Persons?" he wrote, "I have no time to be ill."[35]

Gregory Martin's verses on Campion's life refer to this extraordinary activity:

> You taught, wrote and spoke much; at the Rector's bidding,
> Everything which he bade, you did so easily.[36]

Persons comments:

> No marvel if Christ his Master prospered him so well and brought
> him to so happy an end, seeing that in all his actions he cast himself
> so confidently upon His holy providence.[37]

His sanctity and innocence, before and after priesthood, were no less remarkable than his diligence. His spiritual director, Portuguese Jesuit Fr. Francis Anthony, used to dismiss him frequently from confession without absolution, for there was no sin to absolve.[38]

Professor of Rhetoric

At the Clementine College, after his morning prayers, meditation, Mass, and private study—Campion went down to the classroom to teach Rhetoric, and to form the minds of the rising aristocracy of Bohemia. His method was rigidly prescribed to him: the object of his lessons was to teach the use of language, and to cultivate the faculty of expression in prose and verse; the art of speaking, the style of writing, and the store of rhetorical materials and commonplaces were to be his care. In speaking and style, Cicero was to be almost the only model; for matter, his store-houses were to be history, the manners and customs of various nations, the Scriptures, and a moderate stock of illustrations from arts and sciences.

In class, he first made his scholars repeat a passage they had learned out of school-hours; then the monitors collected the written exercises, which he looked over and corrected. While he was thus occupied, the boys were trying to imitate a passage of a poet or an orator which he had set them, or to write a brief account of a garden, a church, a storm, or any other visible object; to vary a sentence in all possible ways; to translate it from one language into another; to write Greek or Latin verses; to convert verses from one meter into an other; to write epigrams, inscriptions, epitaphs; to collect phrases from good authors; to apply the figures of rhetoric to a given subject; or to collect all the topics or common places that are applicable to it. After this came a summary of the former day's lesson, and then the lecture of the day, on one of Cicero's speeches, was read, and the boys were examined upon it. The composition of the lecture was to be on a given pattern. First, he was to explain his text, and to discriminate the various interpretations of it. Next, he was to elucidate the writer's art, and to display his tricks of composition, invention, disposition, and style; the reasons of his dignity, his persuasiveness, or his power, and the rules of verisimilitude and illustration which he followed. Thirdly, the professor had to produce parallel or illustrative passages from other authors. Fourthly, he was to confirm the author's facts or sentiments by other testimony, or by the saws of the wise. Fifthly, he was to illustrate the passage in any other way he could think of. Each lecture did not necessarily include all these points; but such was the range and the order prescribed for the points that were adopted.

After two hours thus spent in school, the scholars retired to play, and the professor to the kitchen to wash the dishes. Then came his dinner, followed by his hour of recreation—that innocent hour of guileless wit and harmless fun, which always leaves so pleasing an impression on the remembrance of the visitor to any religious house who has been privileged to witness the inner life of its residents.

After this, the professor spent two more hours with his class. First his scholars repeated the heads of the morning lecture; then he gave them a lesson on one of Cicero's rules of rhetoric. The rule was first explained; then the similar rules of other authors were discussed and compared; then the reason of the rule was investigated; next it was illustrated by passages from the best authors in prose or verse; then any passages or curious facts that served to illustrate it were adduced; and lastly, the professor explained how the rule was to be applied in the various circumstances of modern life and society. All this was to be done in the choicest language and most select phrases, so that the master's example might profit, as well as his precepts.

According to the rule, the second afternoon-hour was occupied with Greek. Campion was not Greek Professor, not because he was unacquainted with the language, but perhaps because he knew less of it than the Ruthenians and other Eastern Europeans who were to be found in the college. The familiar way in which he quotes it in his letters, and the easy fluency of his Greek calligraphy, are sufficient evidence of his scholarship. It was, perhaps, fortunate that in this language no one had obtained a Ciceronian monopoly. Homer, Hesiod, Pindar, Demosthenes, Thucydides, Nazianzen, Basil, and Chrysostom occupied the throne in common.

On holidays, the exercises were more exciting: they were either historical lectures, disputes on questions of scholarship, or brief dramatic scenes. Every Saturday there was a repetition of the week's lectures. The chief aim was to give facility of speech and eloquence of style. All great days were celebrated with epigrams, inscriptions, or copies of verses; every month an oration was pronounced, and a play acted, in the chapel and hall. The boys' minds were always on the alert; and the life and soul of the whole method was the Professor of Rhetoric, who was at once the rule, the model, and the moderator of the exercises, and who had to keep the hall, the refectory, and the chapel alive with daily, weekly, and monthly exhibitions of his pupils. But Campion was not only an instructor; he was a friend and guide to his students.

Campion's Tract on Rhetoric

It was Campion's business to animate and direct this literary enthusiasm. He was well-fitted to stimulate it by his own sanguine and disputatious temperament, and to guide it by his extensive knowledge, his exquisite taste and rare oratorical power.

A portion of his rhetorical course has been preserved—*Tractatus de Imitatione Rhetorica* (tract on rhetorical imitation),[39] written during the years 1577 and 1578.[40] It has six small chapters, each of only two or three pages. Its headings are:

1. There are many models for "invention" and "arrangement" but for style there is only one
2. The imitation of verbal style
3. The history of Latin eloquence
4. How to imitate Cicero
5. The imitation of Cicero's vocabulary
6. Ciceronian phraseology and sentence-structure

Since Campion was renowned as a stylist and orator, it is worthwhile to record a few of his remarks. (Where he speaks of Cicero, an equivalent stylist in English would be John Henry Newman.)

The first two parts of rhetoric, he says, the invention of arguments, and their arrangement, may be learned from any good writer—indeed, the more authorities we have, the better. The great writers have their respective literary merits. "By reading their works we shall enlarge our fund of ideas and improve our power of expression. In each of these authors some one literary quality stands out": vigorous expression, insight into human nature, variety of treatment, grandeur in description, ordered presentation of facts, delicate tact, dignity in conferring praise, sharpness in critique, an abundance of wise observations, subtlety in argument, and so on.

From all outstanding authors we may learn what to say and how to say it—but for *style* we must follow one man only—Marcus Tullius Cicero. By *style*, Campion means "diction and the embellishments of language." Other writers' styles are to be copied sparingly, as one eats rich foods in small portions—but Cicero's eloquence is like healthy food which may be consumed in abundance. It must be learned by imitation, for it does not come by nature; but we cannot imitate all good writers at once. "He who tries to go everywhere will get nowhere. . . . Hence arose the proverb: whoever chases several hares, catches none." Cicero, then, is not to be our chief model, but our only one.

> Nature lavished all her gifts upon him. His mother tongue was Latin and his native ability and taste were enhanced by training in arts and literature. His mastery of style grew and matured with the years, and constant practice in speaking and writing made it a marvellous faculty. His official position in the Roman Republic widened his knowledge and increased his literary diligence. Finally, it was his heart-felt concern to bring Latin eloquence to perfection.[41]

Even in the Golden Age of Latin literature, Cicero towers above the rest. He has none of the defects of his contemporaries, and his language is more fluent and graceful than theirs. His name has become synonymous with eloquence.

Campion warns: some would-be Ciceronians practice ridiculous efforts at imitation and produce only a caricature. They mimic Cicero like monkeys but do not take after him as children take after their father. They quote whole passages, and lug in his words in the wrong context.

Campion offers three short pieces of advice, to grow in Ciceronian style.

First, if we like Cicero's ideas and sentiments, the proper way, when composing, is to clothe them in our own words, not his. If we like his words, use them naturally, and not as if the words were everything and the meaning nothing, and as if all we had to say could only be expressed in a fixed mould of fine phrases. On the contrary, we should first think about the thing, then about the words to express it.

Secondly, beginners may find it helpful, when they have to write a letter or compose an essay or give an address, to find a similar work in Cicero and use it as a model. But this should be done for a time only. To continue the practice betrays one as a slavish imitator or as a person without thoughts of his own.

Further, we should note the various elements of the Ciceronian masterpieces: the openings that win over the reader at once, the narrations that hold one's interest, the convincing arguments, the appeals to emotion, the examples used and topics treated, the matchless diction, his ability to be lofty without being pompous, matter-of-fact without being trite, and pleasant and interesting without recourse to inappropriate humor. "While we admire and imitate these qualities, we shall studiously avoid an affected style."

Campion then speaks at more length on the topics of Ciceronian vocabulary and composition.

It is foolish, he says, to suppose that we may use no words but those authorized by Cicero, as if he had written on every conceivable subject, or as if we possess all that he wrote.

Campion counsels his students: we must not copy Cicero's works but the man himself. We must try to enter into his taste, to hear with his ear, and to speak as he spoke. It is absurd to reject all words that have not his authority. If he uses *perpessio* and not *passio* (passion), and *resipiscentia* instead of *poenitentia* (penance), we need not innovate on our theological terms, nor need we restore the words "sacrament" and "testament" to their classical meanings. (We see that Campion's Ciceronian propensities were under the sway of common sense.)

Cicero's ear for rhythm is unerring. How important rhythm and cadence are in producing literary effect—and how much study and assiduous practice are needed to master the difficult art of fluent and measured prose!

Campion closes his little treatise:

In every art and every line of endeavor, there is only one summit, one
ideal of absolute perfection. The ideal is often something that cannot
be apprehended by the senses but only pictured in the mind. This is
true also of literary style. There is only one absolutely perfect type,
and this is the goal we must strive to attain. To that ideal Cicero has
indisputably come closer than anyone else. Hence we must wholly
emulate his resourcefulness, his effectiveness, his emotional appeal,
his subtlety, his methodical arrangement. We do not banish other
authors from our shelves. No harm, but much good, will come to
us from reading them. Nevertheless, the whole texture of our style,
our diction, phraseology, figures of speech, rhythm—all should be
patterned after Marcus Tullius alone. Words we can borrow from
others, on occasion; but the weaving of words, the style, must be
distinctively Ciceronian. Success in this art must be attributed to a
gift not from men but from God, the source of all wisdom.

And while we should strive to imitate Cicero in our speech, we
must take greater pains to reproduce Christ in our lives.

Jesuit Education Praised

The three great levers of the Jesuit education were excitement of interest, concentration of attention, and application of principles to present
controversies. They saw that they had to do battle for the intellectual and
moral supremacy of the world with the new spirit of inquiry, which had
its roots in the religious innovations of Luther and Calvin, the assertion
of political liberties, the literary enthusiasm of the Humanists, and the
scientific school, which culminated in Francis Bacon. The science and
boldness of the leaders in this fight extorted the admiration of their most
determined opponents. English Protestant Sir Edwin Sandys, in 1599,
after a tour through Europe, wrote:

> Behold also the Jesuits, the great clerks, politicians, and orators of the
> world, who vaunt that the Church is the soul of the world, the clergy
> of the Church, and they of the clergy; do stoop also to this burden
> [of education], and require it to be charged wholly upon their necks
> and shoulders. In all places wherever they can plant their nests, they
> open free schools for all studies of humanity. To these flock the best
> wits and principal men's sons in so great abundance, that wherever
> they settle other colleges become desolate, or frequented only by the
> baser sort, and of heavier metal; and in truth, such is their diligence

and dexterity in instructing, that even the Protestants in some places send their sons unto their schools, upon desire to have them prove excellent in those arts they teach.

But this, he continues, is only a bait; their real object is

> to plant in their scholars with great exactness and skill the roots of their religion, and nourish them with an extreme hatred and detestation of the adverse party. . . . Presuming, perhaps, of the truth beforehand, and laboring for no other thing than the advancing of their party, they endeavor by all means to imbreed such fierceness and obstinacy in their scholars as to make them hot prosecutors of their own opinions, impatient and intractable of any contrary considerations, as having their eyes fixed upon nothing save only victory in arguing. For which cause, to strengthen in them those passions by exercise, I have seen them in their bare grammatical disputations inflame their scholars with such earnestness and fierceness, as to seem to be at the point of flying each in the other's faces, to the amazement of those strangers which had never seen the like before, but to their own great content and glory, as it appeared.[42]

To this graphic account I may add Francis Bacon's testimony to the worth of the education given by the Jesuits:

> The noblest part of the ancient discipline has been restored in the Jesuit colleges. When I consider their industry and skill both in cultivating learning and in forming character, I cannot help saying, *Talis cum sis, utinam noster esses.* [Since you are such, would that you were ours] . . . Partly by their own predilection, partly in consequence of the emulation of their foes, they devote their energies to literature; . . . and as for education, the shortest advice I can give is: Copy their schools; nothing better has yet been brought into use.[43]

Bacon selects for his chief praise the dramatic exercises of the pupils:

> There is a thing which done for a livelihood is infamous, done to discipline the mind is capital; I mean the drama. It strengthens the memory; it tempers the tone of voice and the clearness of pronunciation; it gives grace to the countenance and to the action of the limbs; it gives no small confidence; and it accustoms boys to the eyes of men.

The testimony of John Selden (d. 1654), one of the greatest scholars and statesmen of his day, is equally flattering to the results of their
education:

> The Jesuits, and the lawyers of France, and the Low-Country
> [Netherlands] men, have engrossed all learning. The rest of the
> world make nothing but homilies.[44]

One Eye on England

In 1575 and 1576, he heard of several of his old Oxford friends entering
the Society of Jesus at Rome—Robert Persons of Balliol, William Weston
of All Souls, John Lane of Corpus Christi, Henry Garnet and Giles Gallop
of New College, and Thomas Stephens. Says Persons:

> Of all these, our being in Rome, and entering together into the
> Society of Jesus, when I had given relation by writing to good Fr.
> Campion, he rejoiced exceedingly, and wrote divers letters unto
> me again of his wonderful joy conceived by this matter, and infal-
> lible hope that Almighty God would use mercy one day towards our
> Country, and restore the Catholic faith again, as also vouchsafe to
> serve Himself of some of our labors to that happy end; seeing He
> had so wonder fully drawn so many together in one purpose and
> place for His holy service. And withal he insinuated again his own
> desire to be employed that way when His divine Majesty should like
> [please] thereof, though in the mean space he were well contented
> where he was, and not altogether unprofitable also for England, for
> now and then there passed that way, by reason of the Emperor's
> court, certain English gentlemen, who, finding him there, were con-
> tent to deal with him in matters of religion, and departed commonly
> far better instructed and persuaded than when they came thither.[45]

Visit of Philip Sidney

The year 1577 brought Edmund into contact with the celebrated Sir
Philip Sidney, son of Sir Henry who hosted him in Ireland, and a nephew
of his old patron, Dudley, Earl of Leicester. Sidney was sent by Elizabeth
to Prague to congratulate the new Emperor, Rudolph II (b. 1552), on his
accession to the throne. Sir Philip, who was only twenty-one, had been
in Venice during the year 1574, and his familiarity with Catholics there,
especially with his cousin Shelley, the English prior of Malta, had excited

the misgivings of his friends to such an extent that his Protestant tutor, Hubert Languet, then agent for the Duke of Saxony at the imperial court, wrote to warn him about it:

> I see that your friends have begun to suspect you on the score of religion, because at Venice you were so intimate with those who profess a different creed from your own. I will write to Master Walsing ham on the subject, and if he has entertained such a thought about you, I will do what I can to remove it; and I hope that my letter will have sufficient weight with him not only to make him believe what I shall say of you, but also endeavor to convince others of the same. Meanwhile, I advise you to make acquaintance where you now are [Vienna] with the French ministers, who are learned and sensible men; invite them to visit you, and hear their sermons, and do the same at Heidelberg and Strasburg.[46]

This was written from Prague, March 10, 1575. (Sidney had visited Prague for nine days from February 22, 1575 but there is no evidence of a meeting with Campion then.)[47]

When Sidney reached Prague in April 1577, he wished much to see Campion, whom he had known at Oxford in Campion's last two years there,[48] and whom his father had protected in Ireland. Their meeting, says Persons, was difficult, for Sir Philip was afraid of so many spies sent about him by the English Council. His passport explicitly forbade him to "haunt or keep company with" any unauthorized English exile[49]—but he managed to have several long and secret conferences with his old friend. Even if Sidney professed himself convinced,[50] he was not prepared to make an open profession of faith. He said that it was necessary for him to hold onto the course which he had hitherto followed; yet he promised never to hurt or injure any Catholic, which for the most part he performed; and for Fr. Campion himself he assured him that in whatever matter he could help, he should find him a trusty friend.[51] But he failed to do that—for only four years afterwards, when Campion was condemned to death, Sidney's luck was down: in 1581 he was short of money, compromised by receiving recusant fines for himself, and no longer in such high favor.[52] He held no court office; and though admitted to see the queen in October, he was so "wholly out of comfort"[53] that he could not venture to intercede for any other person. He did, however, occasionally interpose in favor of recusants suffering under the law.[54]

Politically, Sidney always took the side contrary to what were then supposed to be Catholic interests. He loathed the Spaniards and took a very strong national line in opposing Elizabeth's marriage with the French Duke of Anjou in 1581. He was even on the Parliamentary Committee of that year for framing the penal laws against Catholics.

One thing, how ever, is clear, that after his embassy to Prague, in spite of his marriage with Walsingham's daughter, he made no advance in his public career for several years, and held no trust or office except the nominal one of royal cup-bearer. According to a letter of Fr. Thomas Fitzherbert of February 1, 1628, Sidney had the courage to confess in England that "one of the most memorable things he had witnessed abroad was a sermon by Campion, at which he had assisted with the Emperor in Prague." Probably the reports sent home by the spies caused him to be looked upon as wavering in religion. He ever afterwards had a strong party in the Council against him. Campion's own account of his conversations with Sidney will be found farther on, at the end of a letter to John Bavand.[55]

On Sidney's part, one curious memorial of their meeting may be discovered by a critical eye in his official letter as ambassador to Walsingham. After describing his reception by the Emperor, Sidney sets down the following brief character of Rudolph, which is evidently from the hand of the author of the *History of Ireland*:

> The Emperor is wholly by his inclination given to the wars, few of words, sullen of disposition, very secret and resolute, no thing the manners his father had in winning men in his behavior, but yet constant in keeping them; and such a one as, though he promise not much outwardly, but, as the Latins say, *aliquid in recessu* [something in reserve, i.e., more than meets the eye].[56]

According to Persons, Sidney was only one of several Englishmen who met up with Campion in Prague. Campion was:

> not altogether unprofitable also for England, for now and then there passed that way by reason of the Emperor's court certain English gentlemen, who finding him there were content to deal with him in matters of religion, and departed commonly far better instructed and persuaded than when they came thither; and of these I could give divers examples, but it might be prejudicial to the persons yet living and some of them in England.[57]

Playwright

The same year, 1577, Campion wrote a play, *Saulus*, on the subject of King Saul, which was exhibited at the expense of the town, with great magnificence, during Prague fair, in honor of Elizabeth of Austria, widow of Charles IX of France, who had then returned to her family at Prague. Emperor Rudolph II (her brother) and his court attended it. The play lasted six hours, and was repeated the next day, by command of the Emperor.

"Just after this," also in 1577, says Schmidl, "Campion produced a wonderful theatrical piece in which he skillfully depicted the extra-ordinary emotions which the struggling father, Abraham, felt within himself in sacrificing his son Isaac."[58]

In October 1578, he put on another Latin drama, *Ambrosia*, much celebrated among his contemporaries, on St. Ambrose and the Emperor Theodosius. It was attended by Emperor Rudolph, who knew Latin well, as did all well-educated people, and received an enormous applause. It was put on again by command of the empress (Rudolph's mother, Mary of Austria) and the French queen (Elizabeth of Austria).[59] It was also performed in Munich in 1591.[60]

In after times, some German admirer of the author prefixed a title to a German version of it: *Ambrosiana Tragaedia, auctore Beato Edmundo Campiano, Graeco, Latino, Poeta, Oratore, Philosopho, Theologo, Virgine et Martyre* (A Tragedy on Ambrose, by the author Blessed Edmund Campion, a poet in Greek and Latin, an orator, philosopher, theologian, virgin, and martyr).[61] Epigrams were written, complimenting the author on his mellifluous mouth, and on the nectar and ambrosia which distilled from it. One early writer calls the play *Nectar and Ambrosia*.[62] For a long time, no trace of it was found among the manuscripts at Prague. It was finally found at Dillingen (the one on the Danube in Bavaria) around 1896,[63] but how it came there we do not know. It was first printed, along with an English translation, in 1969.[64]

Ambrosia has 1,407 lines, written in a variety of metres. It lacks the organic unity which dramas from Shakespeare onwards are expected to have. In the style of the day, the play is really a series of scenes of separate events, connected only by the identity of the central character, St. Ambrose, Bishop of Milan. Among the events in it are the rediscovery of the relics of Saints Gervase and Protase, the conversion of St. Augustine, and the conflict between Bishop Ambrose and Emperor Theodosius. The play is for the most part true to history, but the characters are stock types, one may say, with straightforward feelings and reactions, without intricate development. The aims of such plays were to teach, to delight or entertain, and to persuade.[65] Our tastes today would find it stylized and artificial—but to judge it on its own terms, it was successfully elegant, dramatic, and didactic.[66]

One might say that the play is prophetic in that it depicts a churchman against a tyrannical sovereign—which would be the very struggle of Campion and the whole Church in England against the tyrant Queen Elizabeth. Campion places in the play an ancient hymn attributed to Ambrose, sung here by the bishop with his clergy. There is one verse in it which corresponds precisely to Edmund's own future fate—to occur in only three years—the fate of those hanged and quartered:

> *Nudata pendent viscera*
> *Sanguis sacratus funditur*
> *Sed permanent immobiles*
> *Vitae perennis gratia.*
> (Their bowels hang up, torn out
> Their holy blood pours forth
> But they remain unshaken
> For the sake of endless life.)

Later in that scene is another hymn, written by Campion exactly in the style of St. Ambrose.

Of Campion's three full-length plays, *Ambrosia* is the only one which survives; the other two are lost.[67]

The only surviving manuscript of this play has at the start an epigram in Latin verse in praise of its author, "the most holy martyr Edmund Campion":

> When Edmund gave to the people and their princes
> The relics of Gervase translated with great triumph
> It augured the time when he himself would be
> A martyr wreathed with a purple crown.
> And it was not a false prophecy, for as a martyr amongst martyrs
> He spends never-ending eternity in gladness and rejoicing.

Sing of the martyrs, therefore, O most holy martyr. For who
Better than a swan can praise others in their swan-song?[68]

The Spectre of the Anglican Diaconate

In an evaluation of March 1577, the Rector Fr. Campana wrote to Jesuit
General Fr. Mercurian that Campion was grappling with and over- coming his difficulties.[69] This could well refer to the specter of the false diaconate. Persons writes:

> The greatest and only difficulty which the Fathers there [at Prague]
> had with him for a time was to appease his conscience about the
> scruple . . . touching his being made deacon in England after the
> heretical fashion; the memory of which profane degree and schis-
> matic order did so much torment his mind every time that he did
> think attentively of it, as it did breed him extreme affliction. Neither
> sufficed it to tell him, which also he knew right well of himself, that it
> was no order, degree, or character at all that he had received, seeing
> that he that gave it to him and laid his hands upon him was no true
> bishop, and consequently had no authority to give any such order
> more than a mere layman, and that it was only an apish imitation of
> the true bishops of the Catholic Church . . . for a show to the peo-
> ple, as though they had holy and ecclesiastical orders among them.
> But indeed themselves did not so esteem thereof that any character
> was given as in Catholic Ordinations by imposition of hands, for
> amongst them a man be a priest or minister for a time, and then a
> soldier or craftsman again, and the Puritans or newer Calvinists did
> deny flatly all spiritual authority of bishops. And therefore, albeit
> the sin was great for a Catholic man, especially such as Mr. Campion
> then was, to take any ordination at the hands of any such heretical,
> schismatic or excommunicated persons; yet was he to believe that
> that sin was now fully forgiven by his hearty repentance and turn-
> ing to Almighty God, and by his satisfaction already done for the
> same; and therefore that he should trouble himself no more with the
> memory thereof, but rather put it wholly out of his mind, and cheer-
> fully proceed in the service of God which he had taken in hand.[70]

These arguments would cheer him for a time, yet every now and then
these "disorders" would sadden him again.

And he would never wholly be delivered of this inward grief until
the absolute order and commandment of his General came from
Rome to trouble himself no more about that scruple, and until he
was made both deacon and priest by the Archbishop of Prague after
the rite of the Catholic Church, for by the receiving of this true
character the other imagination was wholly blotted out and put in
oblivion.[71]

Seven Letters of Campion

Occupied by multiple duties, it may be supposed that he was "very spar-
ing in his correspondence,"[72] but what letters he wrote he composed
with some care, as proved by the copies of several preserved amongst the
Stonyhurst manuscripts.

Several letters written by Campion this year have been preserved;
one, written to the novices at Brünn, I have given above; another, to
Gregory Martin, is published among his *opuscula* (small works) and the
rough copies of six more, in Campion's own hand, are at Stony hurst. I
subjoin translations of all of them; for a man is best known by his familiar
correspondence. The two first relate to the manuscripts of his *History
of Ireland*. His library had been left in England, and Gregory Martin
wrote to him,[73] February 8, 1575, about Campion's books (and some of
Martin's) which their mutual friend from St. John's College, Mr. Henry
Holland,[74] had transferred to the library of Mr. Thomas Cox, married to
Holland's sister, in Cleeve, Gloucester, where those savoring of heresy
were afterwards burnt in 1578.[75]

1. Edmund Campion to Francis Coster, at Cologne

I was troubled about a parcel of manuscripts which is due to me
from France, when Fr. Antonio Possevino,[76] who passed through
this place on his way from Rome into Sweden, told me that it was
possible that you, as having the charge of the next Province, could
lend me your aid in the business. I was glad to hear the name of
Coster, whose friendship I had cultivated at Douay; and I confidently under took to ask you for any favor, both as your former student and as your son.

Gregory Martin, who lives with Allen at Rheims, writes that he
wishes to send me a volume [*History of Ireland*] which I had ordered

[to be sent] to him, but he has no messenger to entrust it to, and does not know how so large a packet can be sent so great a distance. I have ventured to ask you, relying both on our old acquaintance, and on the bond by which the Society has joined us in Christ, to do what you can in this matter, as I am far away, and know nothing about either places or persons.

If Martin manages to convey the book to you, my Father, do manage to have it sent to me at Prague, not by the shortest, but by the surest way. I will say no more in asking this, for I am sure that in this matter you will do whatever you conveniently can. For my part, I confess I shall be much obliged to you for this; for that book is a production of mine, a hasty and immature one;[77] and if I am to lose it, I would rather it perish altogether than fall into the hands of men. For which reason, I am trying hard to make certain it is with you, and then it can get here slowly but surely.

Farewell.[78]

Prague, January 1577

2. Edmund Campion to Francis Coster, Provincial of the Rhine

Although, Reverend Father, I fully expected the assistance which you promised me in your kind letter, for I knew by what spirit you were led yet it was in truth great pleasure to me to renew the taste of your goodness and charity from their impressions in your writing. I am bound to you, not now for the first time, but by old kindnesses, which I will never forget, for they are eternal. This kind office of yours gives me a double pleasure, both because you are going to do something for me, and because you love me so well as to do it willingly. And see what impudence your kindness has inspired me with. I enclose you a letter for Martin; if you can send to him into France I hope that he will do his part. I beg of you also, as Martin tells me that he knows no way of conveying the papers to me, that if you know any trusty person to employ, you will take the whole business upon your own shoulders, and manage to have them sent from Rheims to Cologne, and from Cologne to Prague. But if this cannot be done, let me know, and I will try some other plan, and give you no further trouble. The place where I sojourn compels me not to be too modest in my requests.

Farewell.[79]

July 16, 1577

For various reasons, there were extended delays in the whole business. It was not till August 22, 1578, that Martin wrote to Campion from
Rheims, to say he had in his hands at last the *History of Ireland*, received
from Mr. William Wigges (a former student of St. John's, Oxford),[80] but
that it was too large to send conveniently. On February 13, 1579, having
received no reply, Martin wrote again to say that Dr. Allen was keeping
the manuscript to make a copy before sending it on, in case it gets lost in
its travels. On October 16, 1579, Martin wrote to say that the *History* had
finally started on its way to Prague. If it arrived within six months, which
is quite possible, then Campion saw it again, finally, before he left Prague
for good in March 1580—but without enough time to revise it.[81]

The third letter is to Father Persons, the year before Persons's ordination; in the first part he enters heartily into the "conspiracy" to catch
Gregory Martin and make him a Jesuit: the share that he took in this
nearly successful attempt will be seen from another letter further on; in
the second part he congratulates Persons and the rest who had entered
into the Society, and vaguely refers to some old Oxford events which
Persons had recalled to his mind, and at the same time professes his
agreement with Persons's "philosophical reflections" upon the state of
England. These clearly were, that a good wind, or rather storm of persecution, was the best way to return England to the faith, when the instability of mind, mundane attachment, cowardice, and want of logic that had
allowed Elizabeth's government to deprive England of its religion, would
be the best guarantee for the success of a forcible reaction under such
masters as Philip II or the Duke of Alva.

3. Edmund Campion to Robert Persons, at Rome, Greetings.

> I have received your letter, my brother, teeming not only with
> discretion and weight, but also, what is the chief thing, with love
> and piety. I readily take your advice, and consent to do my duty,
> in which I confess I have been for some time rather lax, somewhat
> more lengthily and liberally than you; but I had written in that time
> to Martin, and my letter, I suppose, is still in Flanders, where it must
> have arrived after his departure. Do let us conspire to de liver that
> good soul; it is good fishing. I love him on many accounts; I can
> say nothing more emphatic, I love him; I congratulate him with
> all my heart upon making the acquaintance of so many of you; my

part shall not be wanting. At the end of his last letter to me there was something that showed that this miserable and slippery world was not altogether to his taste—"I am in peril in the world; let your prayers preserve me." Let us pray God; if he is needed, he will be granted to us. About myself I would only have you know that from the day I arrived here, I have been extremely well—in a perpetual bloom of health, and that I was never at any age less upset by literary work than now, when I work hardest. We know the reason. But, indeed, I have no time to be sick, if any illness wanted to take me. So you may unhesitatingly contradict those reports.

About yourself and [John] Lane [a fellow of Corpus Christi College, now in the Society of Jesus], whom you must greet heartily from me, I feel proud and happy; I can more reasonably rejoice in this than in the memory of my proctorship [since, as proctor, Campion administered the anti-Catholic oath to Persons and others].[82] You are seven [Englishmen who have joined the Society]; I congratulate you; I wish you were seventy times seven. Considering the goodness of the cause, the number is small; but considering the iniquity of the times it is not little, especially since you have all come within two years. If my memory is good, I remember all the names, and your somewhat tall person.

Your reflections on the tears of our orthodox countrymen are quite true; wavering minds, mischievous attachments, cowardly tempers, illogical intellects. But these things will carry them into port when our Lord gives a good wind. I have used up my paper, so I will end. But I will give you a commission, since you have offered yourself to me. When I was at Rome [in 1573], I owed everything to the Rev. Father Ursmar [Goisson].[83] Tell him I have not forgotten him, and greet him most heartily in my name. Farewell.
Prague, St. John the Baptist's day [June 24], 1577

In the fourth letter, to Robert Arden of Warwickshire, another priest of the Society, he speaks of none of those violent measures, to which his gentle spirit was only excited by contact with the fiery temper of Persons, but only of converting England by prayers and tears.

4.   Edmund Campion to Robert Arden, Priest S.J., Greetings.

Father Francis, our common and dear friend, has told me the gratifying intelligence contained in your letter from Lucerne of May 3. He asked me to write to you in reply, and I am doing so; for it seemed to me an excellent opportunity of greeting a fellow-countryman and— nobler bond!—a brother in the Society. If you are the Arden I fancy, this is not our first acquaintance; for we were members of neighboring colleges in Oxford, I of St. John's, you of Trinity. If you are not the man, you need no more be ashamed of being taken for him than of being yourself. But if you had been not only my familiar friend but mine own brother to boot, even then our relationship could not have been dearer, or firmer, or nearer than the union by which we are now united in Christ. For this at least we are indebted to those by whose heresy and persecution we have been driven forth and cast gently on a pleasant and blessed shore.[84] . . . One thing remains; we must rejoice at our deliverance from the hands of the Egyptians, and we must strive to save them, and to catch them by the prayers and tears at which they laugh. We will do them this favor against their wills, and so return them the benefit that they have unwillingly done to us. But to return to you, my father, and to finish my letter. You must know that I have had no greater pleasure for many a day than the perusal of your letter, which gives us good hope of restoring and tilling that vineyard. If you go on so, you shall gather a most abundant harvest.

We here, by God's mercy, can only do penance and pray, dignified by the honor of the college, the numbers of our scholars, the favor of the people, and the gain of souls. That these things may become more abundant, help us by your prayers and sacrifices. Farewell.

Prague, the morrow of Our Lady of the Snows [i.e., August 6], 1577

The fifth letter is to John Bavand (Bavant), M.A., lecturer in Greek at St. John's from 1557 to about 1564.[85] He was Campion's first tutor at Oxford, a faithful Catholic, who had left the country about 1564 rather than submit to the Elizabethan Church order. He made his way to Rome and became one of the chaplains at the English Hospice there. He returned to England for priestly work in June 1581—a month before Campion's capture. He was in prison 1585–6, and thereafter evaded trouble until his death in 1613.[86] The letter, of mid-1577, contains some pleasant recollections of his youth, and his account of his dealings with Sir Philip Sidney. The opening sentence refers to another former pupil of Bavand—Gregory Martin who was in Rome in connection with the founding of the English College.[87]

5. Edmund Campion to John Bavand, His Master, Greetings.

Thanks to our good Martin, who in his last letter to me enlarged
upon your goodness and kindness to him, I am reminded, not by his
precept, but his example, not to shirk my duty, or to loosen any of
those old links by which your undying care of both of us has bound
us to you. I must own that, if I had thought frequent letter-writing
the sum of fidelity and gratitude, I had been too neglectful of what
my respect for you, and your fatherly care and provision for me,
required. But there are other tokens of love and friendship be side
letters, and my sentiments from my earliest childhood have been
so well known to you that they can never be clouded over either by
my epistolary neglect, or by our separation in place. I should be a
mere knave, and unworthy of the liberal education which you gave
me, if, while I have any memory at all, I forgot you, instead of bearing witness, by all sorts of observance, to the care, the prudence,
the sympathy, and the virtue which you displayed in teaching and
educating me. To these I must add the clear proofs of your favor
and affection since bestowed upon me—and they the more pleasant,
because they so plainly manifested an uncommon benevolence. For
though in my youth I was but an indifferent subject, yet, since I was
entrusted to you and clung to your side, hung upon your looks and
lived in your society, I do not much wonder that a good man like
you, so diligent in your duties, took such care of me. But that in after
years, you undertook to feed me and to polish me, as it was all from
your free choice, so does it more redound to the credit of your virtue
and kindness. And what is your last favor? When I was in Rome, did
you not altogether spend yourself upon me? Did you not give me
introductions, help, and money? And that to one who, as you knew,
not only would never repay you, but who was on the point of leaving the world, and, so to speak, of death. One of the greatest works
of mercy is to bury the dead, for they help those to wards whom
neither flesh, blood, nor goods, nor hope, nor favor, nor any thought
of earthly convenience attracts them. You were munificent to me
when I was going to enter the sepulchral rest of religion. Add one
further kindness, my dear father; pray for me, that in this seclusion,
far from the noise of all vanity, I may be buried really and meritori-
ously. For it was the Apostle's declaration, "You are dead, and your
life is hidden with Christ in God." I remember how, on the eve of
your leaving England, you bade me farewell with the words, "I go to

die." For you had decided to let death overtake you anywhere rather than in Egypt [Biblical metaphor, meaning England in its present state]. We must seek to die once for all, and happily, but we must seek it also daily and faith fully. But to where have I wandered? Now listen to my news:

The Emperor Rudolph, a prudent, brave, and good youth, and a sincere son of the Church, has fixed upon himself the eyes and the hearts of the Germans and Bohemians. If he lives, great things are expected of him. The Empress Dowager, Maximilian's widow, and sister of Philip of Spain, is living at Prague. A few months ago [April 1577] Philip Sidney came from England to Prague as ambassador, magnificently provided. He had much conversation with me—I hope not in vain, for to all appearance he was most eager. I commend him to your sacrifices, for he asked the prayers of all good men, and at the same time put into my hands some alms to be distributed to the poor for him, which I have done. Tell this to Dr. Nicholas Sanders, because if any one of the laborers sent into the vineyard from the Douay seminary has an opportunity of watering this plant, he may watch the occasion for helping a poor wavering soul. If this young man, so wonderfully beloved and ad mired by his countrymen, chances to be converted, he will astonish his noble father, the Deputy of Ireland, his uncles the Dudleys, and all the young courtiers, and Cecil himself. Let it be kept secret.

Do you want to know about Bohemia? A mixen and hotch-pot of heresies. But all the chief people are Catholics. The lower orders promiscuous. A pleasant and diversified harvest. For my part, I labor in it with more pleasure since an Englishman, Wycliff, infected the people.

In conclusion, I must ask you to excuse me if I have been re miss in writing. Greet in my name Sanders, Cope, Stoneley, and the priests and fellows of your [English] Hospice. Finally, be merry, and mind your health; love me, and write to me.
Farewell.
When you have opportunity, reverently kiss the hand of the Bishop of St. Asaph for me.[88]

The next letter, to one of his Bohemian pupils, is a specimen of the affectionate terms on which he and his scholars stood.

6. Edmund Campion to Sebastian Pastler, at Passau, greetings.

Your letter was gratifying to me, because I saw by it how grateful you were. For if while you were here we hoped much of you from your rare advance in learning and piety, what must we think of you now you are gone for persevering so constantly in the course which you pursued here! I wish that my services to you had been worth as much as you value them at; anyhow, whatever they were worth, they were given with a real goodwill, which I will take care to pre serve, so as not to let a young man so good and so devoted to us slip from my memory. I read some paragraphs of your letter to the Confraternity at our meeting yesterday, and exhorted them to remember you; I have no doubt they will. This is written in the evening twilight, and the failing light forces me to finish.

Farewell.[89]

Prague, July 18, 1577

The last letter belonging to this year is that written to Gregory Martin, to try and induce him to become a Jesuit. The adroitness which insinuates and implies without indicating, and which stirs up desires without too plainly showing how they may be gratified, is a model of subtle rhetoric.

Martin was at this time in circumstances that facilitated such a move. His position with Allen was uncertain; the English seminary was on the point of being driven from Douay by popular tumults, which Allen attributed to the intrigues of Elizabeth, and by which he partly justified his perpetual intrigues against her. The Cardinal of Guise had not yet offered him a retreat at Rheims, and Martin had been sent to Rome to see what could be obtained there. At this time Allen probably thought with Sanders, who wrote to him a few months later (November 1577):

We shall have no steady comfort but from God, in the Pope, not the King of Spain. Therefore I beseech you to take hold of the Pope, for the King is as fearful of war as a child of fire, and all his endeavor is to avoid all such occasions. The Pope will give two thousand [men], when you shall be content with them. If they do not serve to go to England, at the least they will serve to go into Ireland. The state of Christendom dependeth upon the stout assailing of England.[90]

Martin had gone to Rome in 1576, and had written to Campion in February 1577: "After the first letter which you wrote from Brünn, you received two of mine together, a long while after date. In answer you at once wrote most kindly, in every way corresponding to my hopes, except in your brevity. You called your letter only a precursor; this expression of yours authorized me to look for another and a longer letter, as I have done and still do. I am not at Douay, but at Rome." And then he proceeded (but the letter is lost) to describe the popular risings at Douay against the English. To these "accusations" Campion replied:

7.   Edmund Campion to Gregory Martin

Such accusations as those wherewith you accuse me trouble me not; for they coax you out of a letter full of endearing complaints, and let me see, to my joy, how lovingly you look for my reply. It may perhaps be stale to excuse myself on the plea of business, but I do, and ever will, steal time enough for the religious rites of our friendship, which is always in my heart. I lately sent a parcel to you at Douay; in it there was a long letter to you; and because you did not receive it, you wrangle with me about the postmen. But don't irritate me, though you are tall, and I short. The next sentence in your letter gives me sad news, which nips my jokes in the bud. Are there indeed such troubles in Flanders? Has the peril reached to the English College? How far? Are they to be driven out? Let them be driven anywhere but into their own country. What is it to us, to whom England is imprisonment, the rest of the world transportation! Be of good cheer; this storm will drive you into smooth water.

Make the most of Rome. Do you see the cadavers of that Imperial City? What in this life can be glorious, if such wealth, such beauty, has come to nothing? But what men or what things have outlasted these miserable changes of time? The relics of the Saints and the chair of the Fisherman! A work of Divine Providence! Why is Heaven neglected for worldly glory, when we see with our own eyes that even in this world the kings of this world could not preserve these monuments of their vanity, these trophies of their folly! What will this smoke seem in the ether of Heaven, when it so soon blows away in the atmosphere of earth? How will angels laugh, when even men mock? But no need to tell you this.[91] For your whole letter breathes a noble spirit. Your story, your hopes, and your requests set me in a blaze at all points. Nor is this the first time; all your letters show with what prudence, with what a Christian spirit you love me, when you so heartily congratulate me on the state of life which I have embraced, though it keeps us so far apart. This is the meaning of loving and being loved. I remember too how earnestly you called me from Ireland to Douay, how you admonished me, and how effective were you words. Before that, I remember how from your Prince's house [the Duke of Norfolk] you once dealt with me by correspondence to keep me from the ecclesiastical dignity, which, as a friend, you feared might betray me into serving these wretched times. In these words, as I consider, you were even prompted by the Holy Ghost—"If we two can live together, we can live for no thing; if this is too little, I have money; but if this also fails, one thing remains 'they that sow in tears shall reap in joy.'" What you foretold is fulfilled. I live in affluence, and yet I have nothing; and I would not exchange the sorrows of my Institute [the Society of Jesus] for all England. If our tears are worth all this, what are our consolations worth? And they are quite numberless, and above all measure. So as you rejoice with me, you may always go on rejoicing, for what I have found is indeed most joyful.

As for your praises, I pray you, my dear Father, to commend my soul to God in your sacrifices, that it may become less unworthy of your praise. This is the sum—since for so many years we had in common our college, our meals, our studies, our opinions, our fortune, our degrees, our tutors, our friends, and our enemies, let us for the rest of our lives make a more close and binding union, that we may have the fruit of our friend ship in Heaven. There also I will, if I can, sit at your feet.

Though I have many greetings, Martin, for John Bavand, our old tutor, of whom it would be too long to write all I might and ought to say, yet, as I am writing a letter, I will send him a very brief message. If he receives this letter, he will have three on his conscience (supposing the others arrived), and yet not a word from him. There was some reason, which, though I know it not, I fully admit and approve, in entire confidence of his kindness and friendship. Farewell.[92]

Prague, from the College of the Society of Jesus, July 10, 1577

Deacon and Priest

The next year, 1578, Campion returned from the Boarders' College to that of the Society, and was ordained deacon and priest by the Archbishop of Prague, Antonin Brus of Mohelnice,[93] who knew him well, and said on the occasion that "as from one Englishman, Wycliff, all the evils of

Bohemia had sprung, so God had provided another Englishman to heal the wounds of Bohemia."[94]

In the Jesuit chapel of the *Clementinum*,[95] the new priest said his first Mass on the feast of the Nativity of the Blessed Virgin, September 8, 1578.

As a Catholic priest, he was now empowered to baptize, to offer the sacrifice of the Mass, to give Holy Communion, to absolve penitents in the Sacrament of Penance (confession), to anoint the gravely ill with Extreme Unction, to conduct marriages and funerals, to preach in church, to be a spiritual and moral guide and teacher, to instruct catechumens and receive them into the Church, to lead Lauds and Vespers and other official rites of the Church, and to give any blessings that priests can give to persons, places, and objects.

This year he was appointed Latin preacher, and in that office made an "admirable sermon" before the Archbishop during the Mass of the Lord's Supper on Holy Thursday.[96] In it, he mentioned the Eucharistic devotion of Queen Mary and made a little side-comment: "O how unlike this poor lady is the one who now occupies the throne!"[97]

August 14, he preached at the funeral of the Apostolic Nuncio, Ottavio Santacroce.[98] Among his other productions of this year, Schmidl enumerates a Latin poem in honor of the Archbishop. He also wrote orations for his scholars to deliver, one of them being a spiritual conference, addressed, it seems, to the members of the Sodality of Our Lady, urging his students to take the Blessed Virgin as their patron and commend themselves to her most powerful intercession. Its ardor manifests his own most tender devotion to the Blessed Virgin, mother of mercy. It is printed among his works under the title *De tutela et defensione B. Mariae Virginis* (On the patronage and protection of the Blessed Virgin Mary).[99]

This year, too, he obtained an evil reputation amongst Protestants as a convert-maker. A Protestant youth, Martin Schultes, of Frankfurt, who had been sent to the College because of its superiority, had been converted by Campion. In the vacation the lad's parents became aware of the fact, and were furious; but he ran away from them, and returned to the College.

Professor of Philosophy

In October this year, having finished his course of Rhetoric, Campion was made Professor of Philosophy, teaching both Logic and Physics.[100]

Philosophy was to be the vestibule of theology; Aristotle was to be the professor's great authority, in every point in which the philosopher was not contradicted by the Scholastics or the Creed. The infidel commentators, like Averroes, were not to be used in such a way as to give the pupils a taste for them. St. Thomas was always to be mentioned with honor, and, when not followed, reverently and respectfully treated. Logic, physics, and metaphysics were each to occupy one year; the chief object was to be a right understanding of Aristotle's text. As in rhetoric, there were to be monthly and quarterly disputations in public, in which the scholars were to be made ashamed of all faults in formal arguing, to be taught to adhere rigidly to rules, and never to speak but in their turn.

The Situation in England; Fr. Persons to Campion

Nothing is more notable in most of Campion's letters than the lack of any political allusions; religion and literature were the only spheres which he recognized, except with one passing exception, in a letter to Persons. Persons, however, observed no such reticence, but gave to Campion intelligence about Elizabeth's enemies, to know which, without reporting it, by the laws of those days, rendered a man a traitor.

> PAX CH. [*Pax Christi:* The Peace of Christ]
> Having received this letter, almost a month agone from [Rev.] Mr. [Gregory] Martin I deferred to send it until this time, to th'end I might accompany it with some news touching our English matters. You shall understand, therefore, that Sir Thomas Stukeley, who was made here Marquis before his departure, is now dead in Africa with the King of Portugal; the particulars of his death I have not received. . . . And other provision that went with Sir Thomas, all is dispersed; and so this enterprise is come to nothing.
> Here, in Rome, the English seminary goeth forth well; for there be almost 40 persons under the government of three of our Company [Society of Jesus]. We are here at Rome now 24 Englishmen of the Society, whereof five hath entered within this month. One named Mr. [Fr. William] Holt, which was once of Oriel College, Master of Arts, and the other four came hither from Paris; all excellent towardly youths, and all have ended the courses of philosophy: 2 of them are your countrymen, born in Paternoster Row [London]; one named [Edmund] Harwood and the other [Nicholas] Smith, little

Doctor Smith the physician's nephew. One English[man], of good learning, is presently now here hence sent towards Japan. I hope, e'er it be long, we shall [find] a vent another way. Father [Thomas] Darbyshire [nephew of Bishop Bonner and later to enter the Society] is come hither from Paris, and it may be that I shall go, e'er it be long, in his place thither. Mr. [John] Lane [Fellow of Corpus Christi, Oxford, entered the Society in 1576], as I wrote to you before, is gone to Alcala in Spain, and arrived thither, hath wrote your commendations in a letter to me. And this is as much [as] I have to write to you at this time.

[Rev.] Mr. [Gregory] Martin was called away herehence [from Rome to Rheims] by Mr. Dr. Allen's letters. I think they were half afraid of him, what might become of him; but [Rev.] Mr. [William] Holt, entering of late, hath much amazed them. I pray you, Mr. Campion, pray for me; for I have great need of it. All our countrymen here doth commend themselves heartily to you. From Rome, this 28th of November 1578.

> Your servant in Christ,
> Rob. Persons[101]

The first part of Persons's letter refers to the enterprise of Thomas Stukeley to land in Ireland with a large Spanish force; but the plan got nowhere: the man died in battle in Africa even before setting sail for Ireland. But any communication with such a man, any knowledge of his doings without exposing them, was sufficient to constitute treason. Campion was of much too sweet a temper to rebuke Persons for intruding upon his notice things of which he wished to hold himself quite clear. Probably, too, he had then no idea of ever being sent on the English mission, although he told Persons by letter that "he still had a certain particular inward motion and inclination to be rather employed towards the help of his own country than anywhere else, if God would move his Superior so to dispose of him."[102]

More Letters of Campion

Of the year 1579, we have a letter of Campion to Gregory Martin, still on the subject of his books and the troubles of the seminary, and upon the martyrdom of Cuthbert Mayne, November 30, 1577, which Campion seems to have heard of for the first time a year after the event.

Edmund Campion to Gregory Martin

Father Persons has sent me your letter from Rome; I see the devil is furious with your seminary, and will not allow banished men a place of banishment. Well, he may burst with envy; but these blasts of his will never blow away the Spirit of Christ. Since he is so envious, torture the Enemy daily with your good deeds. I am indeed angry sometimes when I remember what Allen—himself a little angry, I think—wrote in the beginning of Bristow's book, that so good a cause was dashed by men so evil, so ignorant, so few, and so much at variance with each other. But God sees all.

We all thank you so much for your account of the martyrdom of Cuthbert [Mayne]; it gave many of us a real religious joy. Wretch that I am, how that novice has outdistanced me! May he be favorable to his old friend and tutor! Now I shall bask in these titles more than ever.[103]

I have answered your two letters, the latter first. I have left something for the end, that you may know how much I have it at heart. I had written to Fr. Francis Coster, our Provincial of the Rhine Province, asking him if you sent him those small writings[104] of mine about Irish history which you have, to find some way of sending them to me here at Prague in perfect safety. He promised to do it. So now I ask you to get them to Cologne; our people will manage the rest. Tell me or them what you can do (what you would do

I already know); write either to Father Coster, the Provincial of the Rhine, or to your namesake, who is Rector at Cologne; for he is called Fr. Martin. You shall be either Father Martin or Father Gregory, as you choose.

Is there anything else? I had well-nigh forgotten. About the burning of the books I congratulate both of us, and thank [Henry] Holland.[105] I wish he had not spared Erasmus and the Scholiasts, whose prefaces, corrections, antidotes and triflings have deformed the works of the Fathers. I am truly glad that the bill has been honored, and I acknowledge Sheldon's kindness, whose family we have reason to love.[106] I remember them, as I ought, when I say Mass; to your sacrifices also I commend the patrons, companions, entertainers and scholars that we have almost always had in common.

You ask what I am doing: I have finished [lecturing on] the *Organon* of Aristotle; now I go to the *Physics* [of Aristotle]. I shall soon confer the Bachelor degrees, and after finishing this course the

Masters degrees of Prague. Six days we quarrel with the philosophers, the seventh we are friends. I am foolishly supposed to be an
accomplished Sophist. What does it signify?
Prague, July 17, 1579
Salute my honored friend Allen, and Bristow, and the whole
seminary.[107]

Campion eventually caught up to his pupil: Cuthbert and Edmund
are both among the Forty Martyrs of England and Wales canonized in
1970.

Two other letters, concerning Melchior Newhyre, a pupil and convert of his, show with what affectionate care he watched over the fortunes
and progress of his scholars.

Edmund Campion to George Ware, at Olomouc, Greetings.

Melchior Newhyre, my pupil, an honest and well-instructed youth,
and very dear to me, is migrating to you·at Olomouc for the sake
of his studies. There are many and weighty reasons why I wish his
progress and fortune to be well cared for. Wherefore, I beseech you,
let me lighten my anxiety by your friendship, and by the certainty
that you will spend all your love for me in care, favor, help and anything else that the youth may require. Whatever kind office you do
him, you may put to my account; and as I am already your debtor
to an amount which I cannot repay, I have determined to increase
the debt daily.
Farewell.[108]
Prague, January 26, 1579

Edmund Campion to Melchior Newhyre, at Olomouc, Greetings.

I recognize in your letter both the old polish and the old devotion,
and I return praise for the one and affection for the other. In giving me such abundant thanks, you kindly and dutifully preserve the
memory of my love towards you; while in speaking so piously about
the light of faith which God's mercy called you out of darkness to
behold, you faithfully and religiously offer to God the soul which
you owe Him. So I sincerely hope that Christ our Divine Lord may
reward your recollection of His favors by a daily increase of grace.
You have me not only as a friend, whom you reckon far above his
value, but also as a debtor, because you proceed in such a way as not

only to increase but to honor the flock of my Lord. For the rest, I earnestly exhort and beseech you to temper your good disposition with all liberal learning, to endure whatever comes upon you in this short span till you can reap with honor and profit that which you now sow with labor and cost.

Persevere, and farewell.[109]

Prague, May 16, 1579

This year also he preached a celebrated funeral sermon at the burial of Maria Cardona Requesens, the wife of Antonio Cardona, Viceroy of Sardinia. It is published among his works.[110]

Presentiment of Martyrdom

The uncheckered life of Campion at Brünn and Prague has been chronicled with great minuteness by his Bohemian brethren.[111] The historians of the Society in Bohemia reckon it the great glory of the novitiate of Prague and Brünn to have been the preparation of Edmund Campion for his martyrdom. They tell us that before he left Brünn he was warned of the death he was to die. This fact is partly confirmed by his own letters which show that he went to England fully impressed with the certainty of his fate. This presentiment was unreasonable, if Campion only considered what had taken place in England, where, among the bishops and priests and laymen who had died in prison or beneath the gallows, not more than one or two had as yet suffered for religion alone.

The execution of Dr. Storey was to satisfy an old grudge. Felton was hanged for pasting up Pius V's Bull on the Bishop of London's gates. Fr. Thomas Woodhouse, hanged in 1573, was so forward in anathematizing the queen's supremacy[112] that Burghley considered him mad, and only had him hanged to be rid of his importunity. In the market-place at Launceston, (Saint) Cuthbert Mayne, Campion's contemporary at St. John's, was hanged, drawn, and quartered, ostensibly for possessing a copy of a Papal bull of the Jubilee indulgence, but really in order to enable them to enrich one of the queen's cousins with the estates of Mr. Francis Tregian and to convict in a *praemunire* certain gentlemen who had harbored Cuthbert.[113] (*Praemunire* was the offense of asserting Papal jurisdiction in England, thus denying the ecclesiastical supremacy of the sovereign.) Nelson was hanged in 1578 for saying that the queen was a heretic and schismatic—expressions which had a terrible meaning to princes with insecure titles in days when it was widely held that no schismatic or heretic had any right to rule over Catholics. The case of Sherwood was similar; and though these executions evinced a firm determination in the English government to treat as a traitor anyone who questioned the queen's right to the place she claimed, yet they could not have anticipated the extreme persecutions to follow.

Fr. Schmidl tells us that Campion's presentiment of martyrdom was grounded upon a vision he saw in the garden at Brünn where the Blessed Virgin, in a likeness to her picture at the Basilica of St. Mary Major at Rome—copies of which had been distributed by St. Francis Borgia to the various novitiates—appeared to him at an old mulberry tree and exhibited to him a purple cloth, a sign that he was to shed his blood for religion.[114] (Other prophecies of his martyrdom are given in the next section.)

The End of Prague, the Summons to England

This was the last year of Campion's quiet life at Prague. In October, Dr. Allen went to Rome to resolve the major disputes at the English College, and to obtain the assistance of the Jesuits in the English mission. After mature deliberation, the chief points of which I will give in the next chapter, it was decided that two Fathers, Persons and Campion, should be sent.

As soon as Allen had secured his object, he wrote to Campion from Rome in an exulting strain to announce the fact:

> Greetings in Christ Jesus.
>
> My father, brother, son, Edmund Campion, for to you I must use every expression of the tenderest ties of love. Since the General of your Order, who to you is Christ Himself, calls you from Prague to Rome, and thence to our own England; since your brethren after the flesh call upon you for though you hear not their words, God has heard their prayers—I, who am so closely connected with them, with you, and with our common country both in the world and in the Lord, must not be the only one to keep silence, when I should be first to desire you, to call you, to cry to you. Make all haste and come, then, my dearest friend, so that you may meet up with me in the City [Rome] at least by the end of February, or even by mid-month I would prefer; certainly that would suit me. Accordingly, as far as your strength permits (for I make no exception here for

commitments or whatever other obstacles), run and fly with all swiftness. You have done enough at Prague towards remedying the evils that our countrymen inflicted upon Bohemia. It will be dutiful, religious and Christian in you to devote the rest of your life and some part of your extraordinary gifts to our beloved country, which has the greatest need of your labors in Christ. I do not stay to inquire what your own wish and inclination may be, since it is your happiness to live, not by your own will, but by others'; and you would not shrink from the greatest perils or the furthest Indies if your superiors bade you go. Dearest brother, our harvest in England is already great; ordinary laborers are not enough; more practiced men are wanted, and it calls for select men, and especially you yourself and others of your Order [the Jesuits]. Reverend Father General has yielded to all our prayers; the Pope, the true father of our country, has consented; and God, in whose hands are the issues, has at last granted that our own Campion, with his extraordinary gifts of wisdom and grace, should be restored to us.

Prepare yourself then for a journey, for a work, for a trial. You will have an excellent colleague, and though they still live who sought the Child's life [cf. *Matt.* 2:20], yet for some time past a door has been opened for you in the Lord. It is not I that am preparing for you and your Order the place in England that your soul once presaged, but it is you (I hope) who will procure for me and mine the power of returning. We will talk over the rest, my Edmund; and so that may happen the sooner, I beg you to be on your way, for I know not how long I can stay in Rome; and as soon as the winter months pass I mean to go to Rheims or Douay, where our common friends and dearest companions Bristow and Martin now live. You will be astonished to see our Belgian and Roman Colleges, and will easily understand why we have at last such hopes for our country.

In the meantime let us pray the Lord of the harvest to make us worthy of His mercy and visitation, and do you, my father, by your prayers and sacrifices, wash away my sins before Jesus Christ. May He send you to us as soon as may be.[115]

> Entirely thine,
> William Allen
> Rome, the English College,
> December 5, 1579

Campion, though surprised at this intelligence, was on the whole glad. Fr. Persons says that, at the time he first entered the Jesuits, "of his own inclination he most desired" to be "employed in the harvest of his afflicted country," but that, remitting himself wholly to Divine Providence through his superiors, he was sure that if it were God's will, God "would move his Superior to bestow him that way."[116] If there had been any fears, he had conquered them. He wrote to Allen that he was ready to go when the order should arrive; the honor of the cause made him willing, but the command of his superiors made him anxious to go. At their bidding he was willing to fight to the death for his country.

The day before, December 4, 1579, the General had written to Campion, without mentioning England, ordering him to depart for Padua, Italy, as soon as possible, where he would meet people to tell him of his mission. It seems this letter never reached Campion, and Mercurian wrote again, February 6, and March 18, 1580, ordering Campion to come directly to Rome.[117] In March, two letters from the General came to Prague, one to Campana the Rector, the other to Campion. The Rector immediately communicated the command to Campion, who heard it in silence, blushed, and said, "Indeed, what the Fathers seem to suspect about me, I know not. I hope their suspicions may be true. Yet God's will be done, not mine."[118]

The suspicions to which Campion referred had already found vent: the night before, a twenty-seven-year-old Jesuit scholastic, James Gall, of Glogów, Silesia, a simple and pious man known to have ecstasies, rose from his bed to write with a piece of coal in Latin over Campion's door: "P. Edmundus Campianus, Martyr." (P. = Pater, Father.) The writer, when discovered, was given a penance to do for his infringement of discipline, but he declared that he felt moved to do it by a special impulse.[119] Another Jesuit student, John Vitztumb,[120] of Olomouc, Moravia, had previously painted a palm with a garland of roses and lilies, insignia of virginity and martyrdom, on the wall of Campion's room, just above where his head usually rested when seated at his desk.

Persons records:

> For as soon as ever the Rector of Prague had intimated the General's order unto him, he, taking it as coming from God Himself, smiling to the Rector said that he did accept the citation and would make his appearance as he was commanded; and, being scarce able to hold

tears for joy and tenderness of heart, went to his chamber and there upon his knees to God satisfied his appetite of weeping and thanksgiving, and offered himself wholly to His divine disposition without any exception or restraint, whether it were to rack, cross, quartering, or any other torment or death whatsoever.[121]

When he left, Campana the Rector changed habits with him—a common mode in those days of leaving a keepsake with a friend. Campion left Prague promptly and quietly—not taking leave and farewelling everybody, one by one. A Jesuit friend later wrote to him from Prague: "If you had started to say good-bye, and it got around that you were leaving, still today you would not have finished shaking hands and consoling desolate spirits."[122] All of Prague was sorry at his departure.[123] After a few days, Campana wrote in a letter that, "All are affected with the loss who knew his virtue, his powerful eloquence, and his other talents. But obedience is as strong as death so we submit with equanimity, considering that God wills it so."[124]

Arrival in Rome

Campion left Prague about March 4, 1580.[125] He went by carriage as far as Munich (about 240 miles away) with Ferdinand, second son of Albert, recently deceased Duke of Bavaria. There on the feast of St. Thomas Aquinas, March 7, he was induced to give the University students a specimen of his eloquence. He preached in their hall on Aquinas, using the text, *Vos estis sal terrae* (You are the salt of the earth), and explained the office of a Christian doctor. Intending to describe St. Thomas, his hearers said that he described himself. The duke and his brother William were so pleased, that they insisted on conveying the preacher to Innsbruck (about 100 miles further), from which place he set out on foot over the Alps for Padua (nearly 200 miles more). At Padua, he was commanded to take a horse.[126]

On horseback, then, he arrived in Rome on Holy Saturday, April 9, 1580.

CHAPTER 6

Rome and the English Mission

The English College at Rome

FOR THE benefit of the multitude of English pilgrims who in the Middle Ages were ever on the road to and from Rome, there were two houses founded in the Eternal City: the *English Hospice of the Most Holy Trinity and St. Thomas*, in 1362; and *St. Edmund's*, in 1391. But when, after Henry VIII's time, the number of pilgrims had dwindled down, the idea must have occurred to many that these houses could be used to train priests for England. Dr. Allen must have come to some agreement about the matter during his visit to Rome in 1576, for as soon as he returned to Douay, he began to send detachments of students to Rome, with Dr. Gregory Martin to look after them.[1]

So the *Venerable English College* came to be opened on the site of Holy Trinity hospice, via di Monserrato, Rome, where it still functions as a seminary today. The other hospice, St. Edmund's, via dei Genovesi, 22, was eventually let for the College's benefit. The official foundation date of the English College is 1579, when the pope ordered the Society of Jesus to take charge of it, but it had begun to house students from late 1576. In 1579, it had forty-two students, some in the old hospice and some in a neighboring house. By 1585 there were seventy students.

The first president of the new seminary was a distinguished and learned Welsh secular priest who had been appointed warden of the place in 1565 when it was still a hospice. His first two years as seminary head, up to May 1578, were full of tensions. His alleged partiality to his countrymen excited factions and heated disputes. The tumults were not entirely calmed by the appointment of two Italian Jesuits for the moral and literary superintendence of the seminarians, for this only angered the

Welsh faction against the Society of Jesus, which they accused of having stirred up these tumults underhand, so that the Fathers might gain possession of the College—not to send the English students to the mission but to keep them at Rome and make them Jesuits. Dr. Allen feared greatly for broader consequences if these broils continued, and from France he decided to go to Rome, to resolve these conflicts if he could—and for other purposes related to the seminaries and an English mission.

The Jesuits and the English Mission

Allen was in Rome from October 10, 1579, until February 16, 1580. While there, he advocated the participation of the Jesuits in the English mission. He had earlier written a letter of appeal to Mercurian, the General of the Society of Jesus, who had sent many men to distant mission-lands: "The nation and our native land asks, and suppliantly requests, some part of the charity and concern which you bestow upon all nations, Christian and barbarous. Do not repel us, Father, as we ask for justice. And you who through your men gather sheep for Christ in the far-off Indies, do not be disdainful of seeking with us the lost British lamb."[2] The cause was debated between him and Mercurian, and Mercurian's four assistants; also Claudio Acquaviva, the Roman Provincial, afterwards General, and Father Robert Persons.

Back in late 1575 or early 1576, during his earlier stay in Rome, Allen had drawn up a memorandum for a meeting with Mercurian in which he explained the English situation. He even nominated five Jesuits he thought suitable for a mission to England, including Edmund Campion. Not having seen him since Campion left Douay in 1573, Allen was unaware of his whereabouts but recommended him as one commonly acknowledged "a most brilliant orator and of most ready wit."[3]

The arguments for the mission were founded upon several considerations: the piety, necessity, and importance of the work; the desire of English Catholics; the increasing intensity of the persecution, which now required more men; the comfort it would be to the English Catholics to see religious men return there after so long, and especially such religious as could not try to recover any of the alienated property of their Orders (for the Jesuits had never owned any in England); the propriety of the Jesuits' engaging in the mission, since the object of their foundation was to oppose the heresies of the day; the notable encouragement and help it would give to the seminary priests (the diocesan priests now necessarily trained in seminaries abroad, as opposed to those ordained at home in happier times) if they had Jesuits, not only to assist them abroad in their studies, but at home in their conflicts. It was urged also that Englishmen were more neighbors than distant heathens, and had greater claims for spiritual help; for it was more obligatory to preserve than to gain; and a token that the Jesuits were called to accept the mission was to be found in the fact that there were more Englishmen in the Society than in all the other Orders together. (In fact, about seventy Englishmen entered the Society of Jesus over the years 1556–80—and one of them, Fr. Thomas King, was the first to return to his native land. He went back to England in 1564 for his health's sake, with full priestly faculties, and worked zealously among Catholics for nearly a year before he died in May 1565.)[4] Moreover, the Jesuits had been the professors and the directors of the seminary priests, and had exhorted them to undertake their perilous enterprise. It was not seemly for those who were sending men at the risk of their lives to bear the burden of the day and the heat, themselves to stand aloof. How could the Fathers expect to be acceptable to the English nation after the restoration of religion, if they refused to bear their share of the toil and the danger of restoring it? Lastly, as the Order of St. Benedict had first converted England, so the Society of Jesus might fairly hope for the glory of reconverting it.

In reply to these arguments, it was urged that so grave a matter must not be too hastily settled; that it was a hard thing to send men to so dangerous a place as England, where the adversaries, though Christian in name, were more hostile, more eager, more vigilant, and much more cruel than the infidels were then, or than the heathen Saxons formerly were when St. Augustine went over; that the superiors, who would have no difficulty in persuading the English Jesuits to face the risk of martyrdom, had great difficulty in deciding whether the loss of such men did not far outweigh the hope of gain by their labors. Again, the English government would at once publish a proclamation declaring that the Jesuits had not come over for religious, but only for political purposes, and would thus make the missionaries odious and their actions doubtful. It would require more wisdom than could be expected in the mass of men to unravel the web and detect the fallacy. The charge would either be believed, or men would remain in suspense till the outcome was seen.

Again, the method of life which priests were obliged to practice in England was totally incompatible with the *Constitutions of the Society of Jesus*. Whilst the external danger was a recommendation, the spiritual perils must give them pause. They would be obliged to go about in disguise and hide their priesthood and their religious profession; they must live apart from one another, and consort with men of uncertain character; they would be sent back to the world, to leave which they had sacrificed themselves. They would be overwhelmed with business, and there would be no facilities for renewing their relaxing fervor by frequent retreats. They would have no rest or silence; their prayer-life would be irregular and disrupted; they would be in perpetual hurly-burly. They would be accused of treason, and hunted about as traitors. On occasion of disagreements with other priests, there were no bishops in England to exercise ecclesiastical jurisdiction; and it seemed difficult to believe that so many priests and religious could live together in one realm without discord.

It was long before any decision was made. Allen went to the pope, who removed the last difficulty by sending Dr. Thomas Goldwell to be the ordinary (bishop) of all England. He had been Bishop of the Diocese of St. Asaph (1555–59), in Wales, in Queen Mary's reign,[5] and was the only English or Welsh bishop in exile, and was already in his seventies perhaps (born some time 1501–15). The other objections were overruled, chiefly through the arguments of Fr. Claudio Acquaviva, who asked to be sent on the mission, and of Fr. Oliver Manare (Mannaerts), the assistant from Germany, who, as a Belgian, knew the state of England through the English exiles who swarmed in his country. It was decided that the Society of Jesus should take part in the English mission and special instructions be drawn up to guide those first sent.[6]

Instructions for the Spiritual Mission

The *Instructions* drawn up by Jesuit General Fr. Mercurian for the direction of Persons and Campion are important for outlining the nature of the mission and the mode of its conduct. They are in the tradition established by St. Ignatius himself when, for example, he wrote special directives for his priest-theologians attending the Council of Trent. The *Constitutions* required the superior to draw up instructions for special missions and to communicate them in writing.[7] Any deviation from them was against the vow of obedience taken by the Jesuit priests.

The purpose of the mission was defined in the first paragraph:

> The object intended by this mission is, first, if God be propitious, to preserve and to advance in the faith and in our Catholic religion all who are found to be Catholics in England; and secondly, to bring back to it whoever may have strayed from it either through ignorance or at the instigation of others.[8]

We note that the conversion of Protestants was not one of the aims of the mission. Catholics and lapsed Catholics, and Catholics who went to Protestant church ("Church-papists" as they were called) were the primary object of the priests' care.

Two "weapons" were essential to the missionaries:

> It behoves our men to be armed with two weapons especially: first, with virtue and piety beyond the ordinary; and secondly, with prudence.

These arms were crucial for dwelling safely in a nation of "shrewd, experienced, and unscrupulous enemies." To preserve virtue and piety, they were to

> observe exactly the Society's mode of life so far as the conditions allow where they are stationed, yet their chief aid will be a right intention, and a combination of distrust in themselves with a firm confidence in God to whom alone they can look for grace and light.

To observe prudence, they were to study with whom, when, in what way, and about what things they were to speak, and to be especially careful never to commit themselves, either amid the temptations of good fellowship, or by hasty and immoderate zeal.

As a matter of necessity, their dress would be that of laymen, but it was to be

> of modest and sober kind, and to give no appearance of levity and vanity.
>
> They are not to be in possession, however, when they are permanently stationed, of clothes of the sort customary in the Society [of Jesus], unless it is evident that they can have them perfectly safely; and in that case they are only to be used for the purpose of holding services, hearing Confessions and carrying out other duties of this kind.

If it is out of the question for them to live in community, let them at least take care to visit one another as often as possible and have conversation, so that they may console one another and also help one another with advice and assistance as has been our custom.

Fr. Robert [Persons] will be in charge of all who are now being sent . . . and all are to obey him as they would ourselves [the Jesuit General].

On their dealings with laymen:

As regards communication with strangers, this should at first be with the upper classes rather than with the common people, both on account of the greater fruit to be gathered and because the former will be able to protect them against violence of all sorts.

Then, in the case of Catholics, let it be with the reconciled rather than with schismatics.

With heretics they should not have direct dealings at all; but they will urge the Catholics each and all to strive for the conversion of the members of their families, and to enable them to do so let them give them advice and equip them with arguments . . .

If necessity compels them to dispute with heretics, they should refrain from biting and intemperate words and give evidence of their modesty and charity no less than of their learning, and let them make use of solid arguments in preference to bitter wrangling. And as it is a characteristic of heretics, when they are clearly beaten in argument, to be unwilling to give in to anybody, for this reason let them be slow to enter into conversation with them, either at festive gatherings or elsewhere, unless, by reason of those present, there is hope of great gain from it and unless also there is no danger of information being given against them; and that being so, let them be brief and avoid quarrels and altercations . . . and let them produce all their strongest arguments first, so as to get the upper hand from the very beginning.

If there were heretics desiring to convert, the priests were to employ laymen to manage all the preliminaries of conversion, and they themselves were only to apply the finishing stroke. (The priests were not to spend hours of their precious time in disputes, with an uncertain outcome—or even danger if they provoked an opponent.)

To preserve their decorum, gravity, and reputation, "Familiar conversation with women, even the best of them, will be a thing to shun."

They were to take special care never to be garrulous. "As far as possible, convivial gatherings must be avoided, and they should usually have their meals in private." Whether dining alone or with others, temperance in food and drink was necessary lest they offend or disedify their hosts.

Other religious Orders might legitimately want to reclaim stolen property in England—but this could not be a distraction or temptation for the Jesuits, since their Order had never possessed any there. Still, they were not to appear as legacy-hunters in any way:

> They must be very careful not to give rise to any, even the slightest, suspicion of avarice and greed; and to this end, unless the need is pressing, they should not ask or accept alms. And if it should be necessary, it is better to receive from one or two loyal and tried men. Finally, they must so behave that all may see that the only gain they covet is that of souls.

In view of the 1571 Act, under which Cuthbert Mayne had been condemned, they were "to carry about with them none of those articles which have been proscribed under pain of death." They were to observe the same prudence with anything that might compromise them, such as carrying letters.

Except for the strongest reasons, they must never let it be publicly known that they were Jesuits, or even priests.

Most importantly, the spiritual nature of the mission was again emphasized:

> They are not to mix themselves in affairs of State, nor write here [Rome] or there [England] about political matters, nor speak against the Queen, nor allow others to do so in their presence—except perhaps in the company of those whose fidelity has been long and steadfast, and even then not without strong reasons.

The only exception to avoiding matters of state and restricting themselves to religion alone was

> in such cases, as the one were so joined and entangled with the other, as it were not possible to deal in the latter without touching on the former.

It would have been too much to expect the English Jesuits to have no political opinion at all, or to be favorable to Queen Elizabeth. But short of proscribing all political action whatever, the instructions given to the first Jesuits certainly confine such action within the narrowest possible limits; they were to do nothing, and only to give out their opinions in the most select company. The only political action that was to be allowed them was one for which the government of Elizabeth ought to have been thankful to them: they were allowed to acknowledge her authority.

Interestingly, when the *Instructions* were renewed in 1581, adverse criticism of the queen was simply prohibited; the phrase, "except perhaps with those whose fidelity has been long and steadfast," was struck out.[9]

Faculties from the Pope

They asked Pope Gregory for a mitigation of his predecessor's Bull regarding Elizabeth, and received it. It was one of a series of requests made to the Holy Father on April 3, 1580, which were all answered in one general affirmative on April 14.

> An explanation is sought from our sovereign Lord [Pope Gregory XIII] of the declaratory Bull made by Pius V against Elizabeth and her adherents, which Catholics desire to be understood thus: that it should always bind her and the heretics; but that it should in no way bind Catholics while things remain as they are (*rebus sic stantibus*); but only then when public execution of the said Bull is able to occur.[10]

The reader will remember that Pope Pius V excommunicated not only Elizabeth and her abettors, but also all who obeyed her and her laws. So the unfortunate Catholics were placed between two fires: hanged if they did not obey, cursed if they did. Campion, on his first arrival at Rome, had been consulted about the practical effect of this Bull, and had declared that it procured great evils to the Catholics. Cardinal Gesualdi had told him that it might without doubt be so mitigated as to allow the Catholics to acknowledge the queen without censure;[11] and now, before going to England he asked for and obtained only this mitigation, not probably because it was all he thought useful, but because it was all he could hope to get.

It is possible that Fathers Persons and Campion had an audience with Pope Gregory XIII on April 14.[12]

With regard to the lay instructors for the preliminaries of conversion, to begin the building which the Fathers were to finish, and other lay assistants, the pope gave the following encouragement and blessing:

> Since a number of persons, priests and others, in England have determined to imitate the life of the Apostles, and to devote themselves wholly to the salvation of souls and the conversion of heretics; and the better to do this, have determined to be content with food and clothing, and the bare necessities of their state, dedicating the remainder of their goods to the common support of Catholics, and procuring alms for this common fund . . . and to promote the conversion of England in other ways, His Holiness deigns to approve and bless the pious zeal of these men, and to grant a plenary indulgence [on the conditions and feasts named] four times in the year to all those who would exert themselves in this work and volunteer to do it, according to their resources, whether they be in prison or out of prison.[13]

The two Jesuits were given large freedom in matters of law regarding the Sacraments. They were allowed to celebrate Mass up to three hours before dawn, if necessary, or even up to 1:00 p.m. (when, outside of vigils, Mass was normally prohibited after midday). They could carry the Holy Eucharist secretly if necessary, and—where needed, e.g., for the sick—keep the Blessed Sacrament for a time in a decent place, without lights or ceremony. They could bless corporals, palls, and vestments and perform all other blessings not requiring Chrism (which a bishop alone could consecrate).[14] The priests were allowed to use portable altars whether or not they contained relics.[15]

They could administer five Sacraments: Baptism, Holy Eucharist, Penance, Marriage, and Extreme Unction (if they had holy oil blessed by a bishop). For Confirmation and Holy Orders, a bishop was needed.

Given the danger of being arrested conducting Catholic ceremonies, and the difficulty of procuring all the usual vessels or instruments, they were allowed, when administering Sacraments, to omit the customary ceremonies, provided they performed the minimum necessary for validity.[16] This meant, for example, they could perform Baptism by washing with water in the name of the Holy Trinity, and omit all the other prayers and ceremonies preceding and following. Likewise, a marriage could be conducted merely by the pronouncement of vows without the Nuptial Blessing and other prayers.

The Divine Office (psalms and prayers of the Breviary) could be replaced by other prayers or religious work, when it could not be said without apparent danger.[17]

They were allowed to print and issue Catholic books without naming the author, place, or press—a dispensation from the law laid down by the Council of Trent.[18]

These, and other indulgences and faculties, were granted by the pope to Persons and Campion on April 14, 1580; and by a brief dated two days later they were enabled to communicate all their privileges to the secular priests employed on the missions of England, Ireland, and Scotland.[19]

In the following year, they were given power to dispense from certain marriage impediments.[20]

In spite, however, of the extraordinary privileges which the Jesuits enjoyed, they were only part of a band of men which Dr. Allen had persuaded the pope to send into England at this time. They are all listed early in the next chapter.

The Military Mission to Ireland

It would have been well for English Catholicism if there had not been another enterprise in hand, of a very different character, but aiming at the same object, the return of the British islands to the obedience of the pope. Unfortunately the proviso *rebus sic stantibus* (while affairs stand as they do) in the mitigation of the Bull was introduced with an intention only too plain. I have already quoted a letter of 1577 from Dr. Sanders to Dr. Allen, in which he tells of the pope being ready to give 2,000 men for an expedition into Ireland.[21]

Before Allen was at Rome, the Roman government organized this force. The expedition had arrived nine months before the missionaries started from Rome, yet it appears that Persons and Campion knew nothing of it. Dr. Sanders had arrived in Dingle Bay on July 18, 1579.

The expedition, and the part that the Roman government took in it, was no secret to the diplomatic body of Europe. The English government was as well informed as any other, as is evident from the French ambassador's dispatches from London, giving an account of the whole expedition, and of its appalling failure. An Italian named Bastiano San Giuseppe commanded it, and Dr. Sanders, Papal nuncio to Ireland, was attached to it. The enterprise was such a fiasco—no surprise, with a force of merely eighty men—that Jesuit historian Francis Edwards comments, "It belongs to the libretti of comic opera rather than to military history."[22] Historian Godfrey Anstruther notes the effect: "The military value of the gesture was ludicrous, but the propaganda value to the English government was incalculable."[23] Afterwards, whenever a priest was captured in England, he was asked what he thought of the conduct of the pope and Sanders, and generally condemned to die if he refused to qualify it; and at the time of Campion's trial the arrival of the Jesuits was cynically connected with the doings of the rebels in Ireland. Sanders was not slaughtered but lived on for another year or so: he perished some time in April of 1581, in the woods of Cleanglaise, and his resting-place remains unknown.

When it was first planned and decided upon, in 1575–76, no one could have foreseen the great missionary undertaking of 1580. Indeed, had it not been for King Philip's endless delays, the attempt might have been made, and all over, long before this present religious expedition.[24] The policy of combining these two expeditions is hard either to justify or to understand.

Persons himself, in his life of Campion, describes the dismay with which he first heard of the expedition from Dr. Allen at Rheims, just before he and Campion crossed over into England:

We were told also by Mr. Dr. Allen how he had understood, by fresh letters from Spain, that Dr. Sanders, by order of His Holiness's Nuncio [Mgr. Sega] lying there, was newly gone into Ireland, to comfort and assist certain Catholic Irish Lords, as, namely, the Earl of Desmond, the Viscount Baltinglass and others that were said to have taken arms a little before in defense of their religion, and had asked help, counsel and comfort of His Holiness therein. For which journey of Dr. Sanders, though being made by order of his superiors it belonged not to us to mislike, yet were we heartily sorry, partly for we had just cause to suspect and fear that which came to pass, that so rare and worthy a man should be lost in that action; and secondly for we did easily foresee that this would be laid against us and other priests that should be taken in England, as though we had been privy or partakers thereof, as in very truth we were not, nor ever heard or suspected the same until this day. But seeing that it was so and that it lay not in our hands to remedy the matter, our consciences being clear, we resolved ourselves with the Apostle, *per infamiam et bonam famam* [through evil report or good report: *2 Cor* 6:8] to go forward only with the spiritual action we had in hand; and if God had appointed that any of us should suffer in England under a wrong title, as Himself did upon the case of a malefactor, we should lose nothing thereby but rather gain with Him who knew the truth, and to whom only in this enterprise we desired to please; and with this consideration we comforted ourselves.[25]

Pollen explains that, in fact, Sanders had now been ten months in Ireland but had come secretly and had done nothing hitherto to attract publicity.[26] Reinforcements, in a second expedition, of 600 Spaniards and Italians, arrived in September 1580 to help the Irish rebels, but they were defeated by November.

The Lack of a Bishop

The papers that relate to the mission of 1580 reveal another difficulty that was occasioned. Bishop Goldwell was at the head of the mission; but through ill-health he failed to enter England, and no other bishop was sent in his place. After nearly thirty years, ecclesiastical jurisdiction over England was conferred on an Archpriest, and lamentable disorders and disputes followed. Goldwell was taken ill at Rheims, and

before he could recover, the persecution in England grew to be so rigorous after our going in as it seemed not good to the Pope to adventure a man of that age and dignity to so turbulent a time, and so called him back to Rome again, where he lived in the love of all men and in universal opinion of great virtue and sanctity, until he died the year of God [1585].[27]

Goldwell was to be the last surviving member of the ancient English hierarchy and was, with Cardinal Reginald Pole, one of only two English bishops who attended the Council of Trent, where he was treated with great respect. Even before they left Rome, Pope Gregory directed Dr. Goldwell and Dr. Morton to go to Rheims quietly, ahead of the rest, and wait there to see whether it was thought advisable for them to enter England or not.[28] The last survivor of the Catholic bishops still in

England—Bishop Thomas Watson of Lincoln—was kept so isolated in Wisbeach Castle, till his death in 1584, that he could perform no episcopal duties. The Jesuits had no sooner arrived in England than they began to beg for bishops. Bishops were needed to administer Confirmation, consecrate holy oil for Extreme Unction, give dispensations from marriage impediments, release from excommunications, and so forth, where the local priests had no special faculties. In November 1580, Persons wrote, "There is immense want of a bishop to consecrate the holy oils, for want of which we are brought to the greatest straits, and unless His Holiness makes haste to help us in this matter we shall soon be at our wit's end."[29] Again in 1591 he renewed his request, and got Bishop Sarmientos of Jaen to promise him a competent support for two or three bishops.[30] In 1597 he again presented a memorial to the pope and Cardinals, praying for the appointment of two bishops for the English mission;[31] but soon afterwards, finding the objections at Rome insurmountable, he changed his plan, and asked for the appointment of an Archpriest.

The real reason why no substitute was provided for Goldwell was, Persons says, because the pope did not like to endanger the episcopal dignity in such turbulent times. That his supposition was not unfounded is clear from the following letter,[32] written from Rheims to the pope by Goldwell, July 13, 1580, who had been "a month cured of his fever, and yet not well either in mind or body, but waiting for the decision of His Holiness."

> Beatissimo Padre,
>
> If I could have crossed over into England before my coming was known there, as I hoped to do, I think that my going thither would have been a comfort to the Catholics, and a satisfaction to Your Holiness; whereas now I fear the contrary, for there are so many spies in this kingdom, and my long tarrying here [France] has made my going to England so talked about there, that now I doubt it will be difficult for me to enter that kingdom without some danger. Nevertheless, if Your Holiness thinks differently, I will make the trial, though it should cost me my life. Still it would be impossible for me alone to supply the wants of the Catholics, who are more by many thousands than I thought, and scattered over the whole kingdom. The most that I can hope to do is to supply for the city of London and some miles round. And therefore, in my ignorance, I

cannot but marvel how it is that, after God has given Your Holiness grace, as it were, to plant anew and support the Catholic faith in that kingdom, you make so many difficulties about creating three or four titular Bishops to preserve and propagate it—a thing that might be done with as little expense as Your Holiness pleases; for God has so inclined the minds of the priests to spend their lives in promoting the return of that kingdom to the Catholic faith, that, after being made Bishops, they would be content to live as poorly as they do now, like the Bishops of the primitive Church. God inspire Your Holiness to do that which shall be most to His honor, and prosper you many years.

> I humbly kiss your feet.
> Your Holiness's most devoted
> servant,
> The Bishop of St. Asaph

Dr. Allen was of the same mind with Goldwell, and would have been content to live in England on the most beggarly allowance.[33] After this, it will be impossible to doubt from what quarters the difficulties about sending bishops to England originally proceeded. The Jesuits always asked for bishops, and their request was refused or neglected. Dr. Goldwell (in his letter above) proposed titular bishops for England, i.e., bishops with full episcopal authority but not assigned to a particular local diocese. Should the remaining bishops be released and free to return to their sees, there would be no conflict of authority, since the titular ones had not replaced them in their diocese. But the Church in England was left without bishops till the factions among the clergy had grown so furious that the measure which might have been a successful preventive was not strong enough to be an adequate cure.

Fr. Campion and Fr. Persons Compared

We have already mentioned the famed Robert Persons who was to accompany Campion. Persons was born of Catholic parents at Nether Stowey, Somersetshire, on June 24, 1546. He was educated at Stogursey and then Taunton, and from there went to St. Mary's Hall, Oxford, in 1564. In 1566, he transferred to Balliol College, Oxford, where he received the Bachelor of Arts degree in 1568 and became a College fellow. He records the occasion of this Arts degree in his Autobiography, writing in both the first and the third person: In the reception of his [Persons'] first degree, Edmund Campion, who was [Junior] Proctor of the university that year, . . . presided as usual at Congregation [university assembly]. Robert began through his friends

> to deal with Campion (for they were both Catholics at heart) how to contrive some scheme of avoiding that impious oath against the Roman Pontiff, which by the laws of the heretics had to be proposed to everyone taking any degree in Letters. Campion promised to do his best to that effect. However, as he had a companion in office who watched all his proceedings [James Charnock of Brasenose College],[34] and the affair had to take place in a public assembly, he could not manage what had been requested. Accordingly, wicked and ambitious youth that I was, not to lose my degree, I twice pronounced with my lips that abominable oath, though at heart I detested it.[35]

As we saw earlier, on another occasion (his M.A. degree), Persons did manage with Campion's help, to escape the public oath.[36]

Unlike Edmund, Robert was not ordained in the Established Church. He left Oxford with the intention to study medicine in London, but was advised to go rather to the leading medical school of the day at Padua, Italy. Stopping at Louvain on the way, in summer 1574, he made the Spiritual Exercises of St. Ignatius of Loyola under the direction of Fr. William Good S.J. It was a major turning-point of his life. Overcoming his long years of hesitation, he reverted to the Catholic Church. Eventually putting aside a medical career, he followed a priestly vocation and went to Rome where he was received into the Society of Jesus on July 25, 1575. He made his Jesuit novitiate and then studied theology at the Roman College (the forerunner of today's Gregorian University). He was ordained priest in 1578, only three years after his entry—a remarkably short time for a Jesuit's training. From this time up to the English mission, he was occupied in formation of second-year Jesuit novices, was a confessor at St. Peter's Basilica, and was involved in the development of the English College of Rome.[37]

Though Campion's junior in age and in the religious life, Fr. Persons was appointed superior in the mission. Campion had asked not to be made superior. Fr. Pollen S.J., in comparing the characters and gifts of the two men, shows that it was the right decision not to put Campion in charge:

> His brilliant talents, and his seniority, both in years and in the Society, had naturally led to his being given the precedence, but upon consideration Father Mercurian agreed to the change. In truth Campion was one of those delightful, artistic characters who are able to give the greatest scope to their talents when they have at hand a strong, circumspect friend, who will relieve them of the embarrassment which men of genius often feel in deciding on matters of everyday life. It was Campion's special gift to throw his whole soul and all his inspiring enthusiasm into every letter, speech or sermon; it was Persons's special gift to make plans, to provide means, to arrange for all contingencies. . . . there was no hesitation now in putting the younger man into the command.[38]

Fr. Persons had talents better suited for administration and management. Inferior in eloquence, and in enthusiastic simplicity of purpose, he had a deeper knowledge of men and things, greater versatility, a finer and subtler policy, and as strong a will.

Both Persons and Campion were well proved, especially in obedience, and ready to go anywhere without excusing themselves, though Campion had practiced the more complete abnegation of will. They were furnished with the instructions already quoted, which descended to particulars about things and persons in a way that must have given a very diplomatic air to those who followed such orders.

The *Constitutions of the Society of Jesus* prescribed that missionaries should be at least two, and that for a very fervent and courageous man, a more cautious and circumspect companion should be chosen.[39] In this expedition the prudence was Robert's, the zeal was Edmund's. Simple as a child, Robert knew he was marching to his death; still he affected no more courage than he felt, but owned and made a joke of his fears. The flesh was weak, but the will was strong, and though the body trembled and the teeth chattered, in the depths of his soul he loved the danger that he contemplated so clearly, and deliberately courted the self-sacrifice. Everything, he thought, should be risked rather than the salvation of a single soul. Robert was a man of more animal courage, but he did not obtain the grace of martyrdom. *Finis coronat opus* (the end crowns the work), and martyrdom is generally the seal of merit.[40]

CHAPTER 7

The Journey from Rome to England

C AMPION, AS we saw, reached Rome on Holy Saturday, April 9, 1580. He was a sight to behold, for he arrived in the clerical fashion of Bohemia. Persons says:

> And surely I remember he came after so venerable a manner to Rome as he might move devotion, for he came in grave priest's [garb] with long [beard and] hair after the fashion of Germany.[1]

A 16th-century engraving in the British Museum depicts Campion in this style, including a very high collar fully covering the neck. In it, Campion holds a palm, for martyrdom, in one hand, and his heart in the other. In the background are pikes with his flesh exhibited after execution.

In Rome, the youth of the English College wished to have him with them for one or two days, and to hear him preach, and five of them accompanied him to England. The seminarians there were no less heroic than those at Douay College. It was a rule—made at the insistence of the students themselves—that each student, upon entrance into the English College, take an oath binding himself to enter ecclesiastical service, to receive the Sacrament of Holy Orders, and upon completion of his studies, to return to his homeland to work for souls, regardless of danger to life or limb.[2]

Edmund was to stay in Rome only nine days,[3] till April 18. He freed himself from all temporal cares so as to attend to his devotion. Every day he went to pray and say Mass in different churches where Apostles' or Saints' bodies lay.[4] He, with Fathers Sherwin and Kirby (named below):

together used such notable and extraordinary diligence for preparing themselves well in the sight of God and to obtain His holy grace and the assistance of His blessed saints for this mission, as was a matter of edification to all Rome.[5]

The Band of Fourteen Departs from Rome

On the day they left, April 18, a Welsh exile for the faith, Robert Owen, wrote to Dr. Humphrey Ely at Rheims a letter which fell into the hands of Walsingham's agents, and conveyed the first intelligence of the mission to the English government:

> My Lord of St. Asaph [Bishop Goldwell] and Mr. Dr. Morton are gone hence, some say to Venice, some to Flanders, and so further, which if it be true you shall know sooner than we here. God send them well to do whithersoever they go, and specially if they be gone to the harvest. The sale that Mr. Dr. Morton made of all his things maketh many think *quod non habet animum revertendi* [he has no intention of returning]. This day depart hence many of our countrymen thitherward, and withal good Father Campion.[6]

Another agent furnished Walsingham with a list: of the English scholars in Rome; the English gentlemen at Rome, Rheims, Paris, and Douay; and all but one of those that departed from Rome on April 18 with Campion and Persons.[7] "Indeed news of the possibility of such a mission had reached Walsingham more than a year earlier. His informant was Charles Sledd, a servant at the English College, professing to be Catholic, who turned spy. . . . Another spy in Rome about this time was Anthony Munday, the future playwright. Both he and Sledd were to play a part in the trial of Campion and his fellows."[8] Sledd sent a description of Persons, but could not provide a description of Campion as he had arrived in Rome only nine days before the mission left.

The band of fourteen was made up of the following:

Three English Jesuits: (1) Fr. Edmund Campion, (2) Fr. Robert Persons, (3) Br. Ralph Emerson.

Emerson was a Jesuit lay Brother, which means he took the three religious vows of poverty, chastity, and obedience, and was one of the "temporal co-adjutors" as the Jesuit *Constitutions* described the Brothers, who were not ordained priests, and so did not baptize, say Mass, hear confessions, preach and teach, and so on. They contributed physical support and labor to the priests and were their invaluable assistants.

An English priest: (4) Fr. Ralph Sherwin.

Two Welsh priests: (5) Fr. Luke Kirby, (6) Fr. Edward Rishton.

These last three had been transferred from Douay to Rome. Sherwin, a graduate of Exeter College, Oxford, a secular priest of wide philosophical and theological knowledge, outstanding in Latin, Greek, and Hebrew,[9] hanged at Tyburn on December 1, 1581, became the proto-martyr of the English College. Kirby was hanged at Tyburn May 30, 1582. Rishton was imprisoned in 1581 and banished four years later.

Two lay students in their twenties, the first-fruits of the recently erected English College: (7) Thomas Briscoe (Brusco[e], Burscough),[10] (8) John Paschal (Paschall, Pascal, Pasqual).

Four Marian priests: (9) Edward Bromborough (Bromburg, Brombery, Briber) (10) William Giblet (11) Thomas Crayne (Crane) (12) William Kemp.

These four lived at the English Hospice before it became the English College. They were now in their fifties and sixties. ("Marian priests" meant priests surviving from the time of Queen Mary, 1553–58, and included priests ordained even earlier.)

(13) Bishop Thomas Goldwell—the leader of the group, in his late seventies.

(14) Fr. Nicholas Morton, formerly English penitentiary at St. Peter's, Rome.

These last two, being older, took horses and rode on ahead; they were not seen again until Rheims. Both eventually returned to Rome without entering England.[11]

Not counting these last two, Fr. Persons speaks of the happy apostolic number of twelve travellers

Thus all ranks in the Church—a bishop, priests (both secular and religious), a brother, and laymen—had their share in this great spiritual enterprise.

Before leaving Rome, the pilgrims had doubtless originated the custom of the English missionaries, before setting out for the scene of their passion, of going to St. Philip Neri, who was then at San Girolamo (St. Jerome's), opposite the English College—that the full zeal and love pent up in that burning breast might find a vent and flow over from him who was kept at home upon those who were to face the foe. "Therefore," says Fr. John Henry Newman, "one by one, each in his turn, those youthful soldiers came to the old man, and one by one they persevered and gained the crown and the palm—all but one, who had not gone and would not go for the salutary blessing," (*The Second Spring*, 1852). I do not know whether this refers to John Paschal; he was the only one of this company that fell. He was a layman, a great favorite of the pope, an agreeable companion, and a pupil of Sherwin; after his fall it was remembered of him that he had shown great defect of character in his behavior with the pope, whose generosity and kindness he received with too great familiarity. Bombino says this was pride, "for the same arrogance which covets distinctions above one's sphere, makes light of them when gained."[13]

The day after the Octave of Easter, on April 18, 1580, having received the pope's "benediction, which he gave not without tears,"[14] they departed from St. Peter's Basilica and left Rome by the gate known as Porta del Popolo, accompanied as far as the Milvian Bridge by almost all the Englishmen then in Rome, including Sir Richard Shelly, English Prior of the Knights of St. John of Malta, and Father Oliver Manare and other Jesuits sent by the General. At the bridge there was a solemn and affectionate farewell, which, as described by the biographers, was not very consistent with the mystery and secrecy sought to be thrown round the mission.

The pilgrims went by foot. Father Persons managed everything. He records: it was thought convenient that each priest should discard long cassocks, both for better travelling by foot, as also not to be so easily recognized in Germany and other Protestant places, where priests were little favored. When some new clothing was offered to Campion, he would not take it, but only covered himself with old buckram under a bare cloak, and passed with that attire throughout his whole journey, for he said: "To him that goes to be hanged in England any apparel is sufficient." To try the blessed man the more, God sent continual rain for the first eight or ten days after leaving Rome, so that from morning to night he travelled in the wet with that evil apparel, and often got stuck so fast in the mire in those deep and foul paths that he was scarcely able to get out again.[15]

There were a few horses among them for the use of the old and sick. Persons remembers that Campion never rode in the whole journey but once, when he was suffering from ague and diarrhoea. It was ordered also that every man should take a new name, to escape the chance spies by the way, who would reveal each man in particular to the queen's Council. They wanted to call Campion Peter; but he, remembering how well he had escaped from Ireland under St. Patrick's patronage, would take no other name but his old one of Patrick. Albeit, says Persons, when they came to St. Omer's, and were to enter England, they persuaded him to take some other English name, lest the other, being Irish, might bring him in question; for Ireland at that time was reported to be in trouble by the arrival of Dr. Sanders with some soldiers from the pope. So Campion adopted the name Mr. Edmunds "in remembrance of St. Edmund, King and Martyr of England, whom he desired to imitate."[16]

Their Daily Program

The pilgrims had agreed to observe a regular order of the day. Persons so describes it:

> The manner of the whole journey was that one or two only were charged with the care of providing victuals upon the way, so as all the rest might the better attend unto their devotions. In the morning, after the *Itinerarium* [a traditional Latin prayer for a safe journey] . . . each man had his time allotted for their meditations and mental prayer, and after that to say their service of the Breviary and other devotions as each man would, and where commodity of church and of other things necessary was offered, there either all, or as many of the priests as could, or at least some one for all the rest, said Mass.
>
> After dinner also, besides their ordinary service of Evensong, Compline and Matins for the next day, they had their several times appointed for saying their rosary or their beads and divers sorts of Litanies, and towards night the examen of their conscience, which every man did with so great care and diligence as men that supposed that within very few days after they might chance to see themselves before the judgment seat of Almighty God; seeing they knew the entertainment which they were likely to receive in their country if they were apprehended, and for this cause, to prepare themselves the better to this event, the book which they most read and conferred of upon the way was St. Luke's story of the Acts of the Apostles.[17]

It was Campion's practice on this journey, after reciting the *Itinerarium* with the company, to push on a half-mile or more ahead of the rest, to meditate alone for a few hours, pray the Breviary, recite the Litany of the Saints and other prayers, and address Christ in his own zealous fashion without being overheard. Then, some hour before dinner, he would lag to allow the party to catch up to him, and would joke and chatter with them—and talk of suffering for Christ, with such comfort, for such was a common subject of their conversation.

Bologna

With a journey of some eight or nine hundred miles on foot ahead of them, the missionaries knew they could neither loiter nor hurry. To reach Bologna, they would have passed through Viterbo, Siena, Colle di Val d'Elsa, and Florence. In Siena and Florence, they doubtless would have lodged at the Jesuit Colleges.[18]

At Bologna they were obliged to stay some days by an accident to Persons's leg, now badly swollen. They had brought a letter to Cardinal Gabriel Paleotto (or Paleotti) from Fr. Alphonsus Agazzari, Rector of the English College in Rome, a Jesuit from Siena who began his seven-year term as Rector in 1579. The Bishop of Bologna received them hospitably. He was a close friend of St. Charles Borromeo. He was made Bishop of Bologna in 1566; its Archbishop in 1582.

The historian Cardella gives two traits of him worth noting: "Soon after he was Cardinal, he exhibited his Christian liberty by opposing in consistory a tax that was proposed to be laid on the inhabitants of the Papal States to assist the Catholic party in the French civil wars. In this he was against the pope and against the whole body of Cardinals, who advised His Holiness to confiscate his pension. But the pope by the next morning had come round to Paleotto's opinion, and his pension was saved." Again: "He had a chief share in the reconciliation of Henry IV of France; for it was he who induced Clement VIII to come to terms with that sovereign."[19]

This prelate enforced a monastic discipline in his palace. At dinner, after the usual reading, spiritual topics were proposed by the chaplains for discussion, and every man had to give his opinion. Discussion passed into discourse. Campion and Sherwin were both encouraged to speak, and did so excellently, extempore in Latin. To paraphrase Persons: Campion's discourse was very pithy, and fit for the place and time. He began with Cicero's quotation from Pythagoras, who, perceiving by the

light of nature man's difficulty to good, and proneness to vice, said, that
the way of virtue was hard and laborious, but not void of delectation, and
much more to be embraced than the other, which was easy. Which, Fr.
Campion applying to a Christian life, showed very aptly both the labors
and delights thereof, and that the saying of Pythagoras was much more
verifiable in the same than in the life of any heathen philosopher, for
the labors were greater, the helps more potent, the end more high, and
the reward more excellent. Whereby also in fine he came to declare the
nature and quality of the journey and enterprise which his fellows had in
hand, and greatly to encourage them in the same.[20]

We presume the pilgrims visited the tomb of St. Dominic and the
body of St. Catherine of Bologna in her sedentary resting-place.

The rest at Bologna gave Campion time to write to one of his Jesuit
friends at Prague. Here is a translation of his Latin letter:

This is an answer to your two letters, one of which I received as I was
leaving Munich [about March 8],[21] the other when I had reached
Rome [April 9].[22] What you order me for the sake of my health, I
accept as the command of God. Only do not think that your care of
me is ended while I live. You must not wonder that when I wrote
from Munich I did not say a word about your letter, for it was delivered to me after I had folded mine, and had left it with the Rector of
the College [to be posted]. I see you had not read it even when you
wrote your second letter to me; you must therefore speak to Father
Ferdinand, and give him my dutiful salutation. With respect to
Ambrosia [Campion's play] which you ask me about in your other
letter, you must know, my dear Father, that it was not given back to
me after your return from Vienna; but that I saw it in your room,
where I doubt not that it still lies somewhere among your things,
unless it is in somebody's hands who borrowed it from you when
you were engaged, so that you have forgotten about it. If it is acted
again, I pray you let it be made more comprehensible. I submit it
to the experienced judgment of a man such as Father Nicholas; I
remembered him in the Holy House at Loreto, and I read the poem
which he hung up.

I accept with joy Father Urban [Ziffel]'s bargain; I expected
nothing so little as a letter from him, whom in my journey I had
often recommended to God as dead; now at last I learn there was a
mistake in the person, on account of his having the same name as

the one who lately died at Fulda. So I am exceedingly glad that such a pious agreement exists between Father [Urban] Ziffel[23] and me. I have a similar agreement with Fathers [John Vivarius] Aquensis, Gabriel, Stephen of Dalmatia, and [John] Troger,[24] jointly and severally. Now they can be of great service to me in the midst of my infinite perils.

I am now at Bologna, on my return from Rome, and on the way to my warfare in England. Whatever becomes of me, our posterity survives. You would hardly believe me if I told you what comfort I feel when I think of them. If they were not Englishmen I would say more about them. In this expedition there are two Fathers of the Society, Robert Persons and myself, seven other priests, and three laymen, one of whom is also of us. I see them all so prodigal of blood and life, that I am ashamed of my backwardness. I hope to be with Allen, at Rheims, in the beginning of June. We all travel at the Pope's expense. Though we should fall at the first onset, yet our army is full of fresh recruits, by whose victory our ghosts will be pacified.

But let us come to the latter thing first, the completed journey [to Rome]. I was driven in the carriage of Prince Ferdinand as far as Innsbruck, thence I walked to Padua. There, as I was about to bestow what money I had left, according to your directions, I immediately received orders to hasten to Rome. We mounted our horses, another Father and I, for I had stumbled on him by the way. Though I had so much money left at first, yet in a few days I should have had nothing to pay my bills; except my companion had had plenty. I made use of Divine Providence, and your liberality, as you told me. Indeed I was liberal enough to spend more than the whole. At Padua I was shown about by young Matthias Melchior, who scarcely left my side; he has the best dispositions towards the Society, and is of excellent re port. Here I am reminded of my pupils, and of our companions, whom I often think of. There are so many to whom I wished to write severally, and I was so overwhelmed with their number and with my other business, that hitherto I have written to none of them. I am tired when I reach our colleges; in the inns I can scarcely breathe. During my stay in Rome, which was about eight days, I was more pressed for time than during all the rest of my journey. I must ask them therefore, and especially my Fathers and Brothers of Prague, to pardon what I cannot help. The rest I reserve for a fourth letter.

I shall be very glad if I find one from you before I pass over into

England. You may send to Rheims, Paris or Douay, for I suppose that I shall visit these places. But, anyhow, if they are sent to Allen, they will be delivered to me.

In uncertainty whether we shall ever see one another again, I write my will, and I leave to you and all of them the kiss of charity and the bond of peace.

Farewell.

Bologna, April 30, 1580.

Reverend Father, again and again, and for ever, farewell.[25]

Cardinal Borromeo at Milan

The road from Bologna to Milan ran in a nearly straight line for over 130 miles through Modena, Parma, and Piacenza.

They found a saint to welcome them at Milan. St. Charles Borromeo received the pilgrims into his house and kept them there for eight days. He made Sherwin preach before him and he made Campion discourse every day after dinner. Amongst Campion's listeners was Cardinal Nicholas Sfrondato, who ten years later became Pope Gregory XIV.[26]

Says Persons:

> He [Borromeo] received us, I say, all into his house and . . . had sundry learned and most godly speeches with us, tending to the contempt of this world, and perfect zeal of Christ's service, whereof we saw so rare an example in himself and his austere and laborious life; being nothing in effect but skin and bone, through continual pains, fasting, and penance; as without saying any word he preached to us sufficiently so as we departed from him greatly edified and exceedingly animated.[27]

Their stay in Milan seems to have covered parts of the first and second week of May.

St. Charles always showed a partiality for the English exiles. Welshman Owen Lewis had been his vicar-general, and William Giffard, afterwards Archbishop of Rheims, his chaplain. After the pilgrims' visit he wrote to Agazzari, the Rector:[28]

> Most Reverend Father,
> Those Englishmen who departed from here recently, I saw and willingly received, as their goodness deserved, and the cause

for which they had undertaken that journey. If, in future, your Reverence shall send any others to me, be assured that I will take care to receive them with all charity, and that it will be most pleasing to me to have occasion to perform the duties of hospitality, so proper for a Bishop, to wards the Catholics of that nation.

In any case, your Reverence, my sincere best wishes.

Milan, the last day of June, 1580.

> At your service,
> the Cardinal of Santa Prassede

From Milan the party went to Turin, and then on to Susa, at the foot of the Alps. They entered the Alps by the long climb to the pass of Mount Cenis, "all in health, and apt for travel," says Sherwin, and after sundry long marches, winding their way down along the banks of the Arc, they arrived at St. Jean de Maurienne, in Savoy, where they encountered many troops of Spanish soldiers marching from Flanders to Milan. Their numbers blocked the roads, consumed the provisions and occupied every resting-place *en route*.

Theodore Beza at Geneva

The party continued as far as Aiguebelle but then found themselves obliged to turn either to the right or the left. If left, they learned that the road by Lyons was blocked and imperiled by the insurrection of the peasants of Dauphine. So, after deliberation, they resolved to turn right and pass by Geneva in spite of the difficulties that might arise from the difference in religion; for it was a free city, and the laws of the Swiss cantons permitted travellers, whether Catholics or not, to pass that way; and stay for three days, which was a longer delay than they meant to make.

Most of the company also desired to see Calvin's successor, Theodore Beza, of whom they had heard so much in England, where his fame was greater than in any other Calvinist country, much greater than it was then in Geneva itself. Some of them suggested that perhaps the magistrates of the city, who were in confederacy with Elizabeth, might detain them, or send them as prisoners to England, at the instance of Beza or the English residents. But they concluded that, if God would have them taken, He would provide; and it was all the same to them whether they were captured in Geneva or in England.

There remained yet another little consultation, whether they should confess to the magistrates what religion they professed and where they were bound, or only tell them as much as they were obliged; but it was quickly resolved unanimously to declare clearly that they were Catholics, and to begin their confession in the city where the sect of Calvin was first hatched. Nevertheless, before they arrived near that "sink of heresy," as Sherwin called it, every man disguised himself; and Campion, wrote Sherwin, "dissembled his personage in form of a poor Irishman, and waited on Mr. Paschal; which sight, if you had seen how naturally he played his part, the remembrance of it would have made you merry."[29] Thus disguised, they came to the gates of Geneva. It was about mid-May.

Campion and Sherwin were two of the first to enter. The soldiers, who were keeping watch for fear of the Spanish bands passing through the country, asked whence they came, and whither they went. After answer was made, the captain told one of his men to conduct them to be examined by the magistrates, who were in session with certain ministers in the open market-place. They were again asked whence they came, and whither they travelled, and why they passed not the ordinary way. They replied: "To avoid the Spaniards, and the 'Dolphinates' who are up in arms." Then they were asked what countrymen they were, "Some English, some brought up in Ireland," was the reply; and Campion was introduced as Mr. Patrick. "Are you of our religion?" "No," said Paschal. "From the first to the last of us we are all Catholics," said Briscoe boldly. "So are we too," said the magistrates. (At that time, certain Protestants still claimed the ancient name "Catholic" for themselves.)[30] "Yea, but," said Sherwin, who only now came up, "we are all Roman Catholics." "Of that we marvel," said the magistrates, "for your queen and all her realm are of our religion." "As for our queen," answered one (Persons does not remember whether it was Campion), "we cannot tell whether she is of your religion or not, considering the variety of opinions that this age has brought forth; but sure we are she is not of ours. Though for the realm, you must understand that all are not of her religion, nor of yours; but many be good Christian Catholics, and do suffer both losses at home and banishment abroad for the same, of which number are we, who have lived divers years in Italy, and are going now towards the English Seminary in Rheims, but are obliged to pass by Geneva to avoid the Spanish soldiers and Dauphinese insurgents." Then the magistrates promised them free and courteous treatment according to the laws of the country; and seeing them all so resolute, they questioned them no more about religion, but only about the Spaniards, of whom they could give but very little news. So a soldier was ordered to guide them to their inn, a very fair one, bearing the sign of the city, and willed that they should be very well treated for their money—as they were. This was about 11 o'clock in the morning. As they were being examined, they saw the long-bearded ministers of Geneva looking at them from the windows and laughing. "But if we might have had our wills," says Sherwin, "we would have made them to have wept Irish." As they were passing through the streets of the city, some one said, "They are all priests"; others, "They are all monks"; and one, seeing Campion dressed like a servant, thought either to discover him or to chaff him, by asking in Latin, *Cujus es?* (Whose man are you?). Campion had his wits about him, and answered sharply in Italian, *Signor, no!* (No, sir). The fellow was taken aback, and asked, *Potesne loqui latine?* (Can you speak Latin?), no doubt mistaking the Italian for Latin; and Campion answered with "a shrink with his shoulder, and so shaked off the knave."[31]

After dinner, forthwith, Father Persons, Paschal, with his man "Patrick" (Campion) dressed in an old suit of black buckram, Sherwin, Rishton, and Kirby, sallied forth to visit Beza, and, if possible, to have some speech with him, either about the Catholic religion, or about the controversy between the Protestants and Puritans, as he was reckoned one of the chief writers in it. When they knocked at the door, his wife Claudine came and opened it and let them into a little court, where she told them to stay, as Monsieur Beza was busy in his study, and would come forth to them, which it seems he did with annoyance, as he had been informed about them by the magistrates. However, when he came forth in his long black gown and round cap, with ruffs about his neck, and his fair long beard, he saluted them courteously, but did not invite them into his house, or to sit down, but remained on foot, and asked them what they would have. They told him, that being scholars, and passing by Geneva, they could do no less than come to see him, for the fame that they had heard in England of his name: he answered, that he understood it was far greater than he deserved; that he loved all Englishmen heartily, but was sorry to hear his visitors were not of the religion of their country. They answered that their country was large, and held more sorts than one; that they kept to the religion to which it was first converted from paganism, but if he could show more weighty reasons to the contrary than they had yet heard or read, they would be content to hear him. Father Persons then asked how his Church was governed, and he replied, "By equality in the ministry: there are nine of us, and every one rules his week." Then it was said that the English had bishops, and that the queen was the head without any interruption. Beza answered "shamefully" that he did not know it to be so, and after some shuffling declared that he did not approve of it. However, he said, the difference is one of discipline only, not of doctrine; and he could not proceed with the dispute, which would take more time than he could spare, for he was busy, having just received some packets of letters from France. Thus he drew aside the talk from religion to other subjects, and with this would have broken off.

All the while stood Campion in his serving-man's attire, waiting with hat in hand, "facing out the old doting heretical fool," says Sherwin. But, at this point, Campion was unwilling to let Beza escape thus; he broke out of his character of servant, and challenged him: "Sir, though I perceive you are much occupied and would be gone, I pray you let me ask but this question: How do you say that the queen of England and you be of one religion, seeing that you defend the religion of the Puritans, which she so much abhors and persecutes?" Beza replied, with a slight shrug, "I know not what the name 'Puritan' means. The difference you speak of is none at all in effect." On this, Campion offered to prove that the differences were very important, and many, and essential, even on such points as the Sacraments. Beza, fearing a long controversy, made a sign to his wife, who interposed with another packet of letters; on which he said that he could stay no longer, and courteously took leave of them, promising to send to their inn to visit them an English scholar of his, the son and heir of Sir George Hastings.

The youth, however, never came, but instead there came his tutor, Mr. Brown, very fervent in the religion of Geneva, and with him Mr. Powell, a Protestant, a very civil gentleman, a young man of good parts, M.A. of Corpus Christi College, Oxford, where he had been acquainted with Campion, and familiar with Persons and Sherwin. Three or four Irishmen also came.[32]

Campion was absent when they came, and as he was in such strange attire, it was thought advisable not to let them see him. So Persons and the rest walked about the town with them, and had much familiar speech, which ended in an invitation to supper. However, Powell and the rest would not sup with them, but promised to come afterwards. When they came, Persons took Powell in hand, and Sherwin, Kirby, and Rishton attacked Brown, with whom they hotly disputed in the streets of Geneva almost till midnight, sending to Beza through him a challenge to a public controversy on any disputed point, with this condition, that the one justly convicted in the opinion of indifferent judges should be burnt alive in the market-place. Brown promised to convey the message. Sherwin, Kirby and Rishton had lacked Fr. Persons's presence to moderate their ardor and forbid such rashness.

On hearing what had happened, Powell told Persons that he knew the place well, and was sure that if Brown told Beza or the magistrates of the challenge, it might bring Persons's company into trouble; they were within the municipal jurisdiction, and a reason might easily be found for detaining them beyond the three days allowed them by law, in which case it would be hard to get any remedy. Persons profited by this sage and friendly advice, and made peace for that night, resolving to leave the town early the next morning. Powell offered to accompany them, but he was asked not to bring the Puritan schoolmaster Brown.

Early the next morning Powell came again and breakfasted with them, treating them lovingly, and brought them out of the town on their way.

Campion Disputes with a Genevan Minister

All this while Campion had played the serving-man, and not wishing to be recognized by Powell, he and Briscoe were sent forward by themselves. On the top of a hill, about a mile out of Geneva, on the road towards France, they met one of the nine great ministers of Geneva, who seemed to be learning off a sermon.

Campion straightway accosted him, and asked, "How is your Church governed?"

The minister, who supposed Campion, as an Englishman, to be Protestant, explained: "It is governed by nine ministers in their turns."

"Then who is the chief head of it?" asked Campion.

"Christ," said the other.

"But has it no one certain supreme head or governor upon earth under Christ?"

"It needs none."

"Why, then," said Campion, "how can you hold the religion of the queen of England to be true, when she calls herself head and supreme governor of the Church?"

"She does not call herself so," said the minister.

"Yes, but she does," said Campion, "and he that shall deny her supremacy in ecclesiastical causes in England must suffer death for it, for it is treason by statute."

The minister, in a great chafe—"almost mad"—was going to deny it again, when Campion, seeing Powell and the rest approach, suddenly left him.

Persons and Sherwin came up to the man, who seemed in desperation, and told them that there was a fellow beyond who held a strange opinion, and had mocked him about his Church. But instead of receiving any comfort from the new-comers, the whole company "fell upon him, and so shook up the poor shakerell[33] before the soldiers just by the gate." Campion looked back and saw that the dispute was renewed; so, fearing misrepresentation, he went back to tell what had been controverted.

Persons, and Powell who was acquainted with the minister, said that it was undeniable that the queen was taken for head of the Church, and that the first-fruits of all benefices were paid to her, and that Parliament had transferred all the pope's jurisdiction in England to her.

The preacher then suggested: "It may be she calls herself supreme head of the Church *quia Regina est Christiana* [because the queen is Christian]."

"*Ergo* [Therefore]," said Campion, "much more is the King of France head of the Church, because he is called *Rex Christianissimus* [the most Christian king]."

"Nay," said the minister, "I mean *Catholica Christiana* [Catholic Christian]."

"*Ergo* [Therefore]," said Campion, "much more the King of Spain, whose title is *Rex Catholicus* [Catholic king]."

The minister was furious, and declared that Campion was no Englishman but a very Papist.

But Powell, who had now recognized Campion, and saluted him with much affection, quieted the preacher and sent him off, and walked on a mile or more with them. They must have made some impression on him, for he promised them, before taking their leave, to study Catholic books and to visit a Catholic friend in Rome.

The party looked back from the top of a hill upon the miserable city, and said a *Te Deum* for their escape from it; and for penance for their curiosity the whole company made a pilgrimage to the shrine of St. Clodoveus (Clovis), at Saint-Claude, France, about eight or nine miles off, over difficult paths. The miraculously incorrupt body of the saint was there. Alas, no more; it was destroyed by the crazed revolutionaries of 1794 who cut it to pieces and carried it off to be burnt. Only two pieces escaped that destruction.

Afterwards the band went stoutly on their journey till Whit Monday (the day after Pentecost), when eight of them fell sick in one night; so they had to travel to Rheims by short stages, and all but Fr. Kemp reached that city on May 31, having spent nearly six weeks on the journey.

Persons's detailed account mentions only the obvious troubles on the way, and humbly says nothing of his leadership—but we know from private correspondence that it really had been a difficult trip for the companions. At the end of it all, Fr. Sherwin wrote to Fr. Agazzari in Rome to advise him what the next group of missionaries would need: more than twice as much spending money, and a vastly better outfit of clothing. "Believe me, everything has to be new, from the sole of the foot to the top of the head. . . . My heart is broken as I think of the straits we are in . . . and yet Father Robert [Persons] has foreseen all and arranges everything with the greatest zeal and prudence."[34]

Arrival at the English Seminary at Rheims

The seminary of Douay, then in Spanish Flanders, had perforce been transferred to Rheims, in France, just two years before, in 1578, and would stay there until 1593. Unlike at Douay, Dr. Allen had no large college in which to house the students. They lived in separate houses up and down the road, which came to be known as *La Rue des Anglais* (Englishmen's Street).

When the pilgrims came to Rheims on May 31,[35] they were received with the greatest joy by all the confessors and servants of God that lived there. Here they rejoined Bishop Goldwell and Dr. Morton, who had arrived much earlier by horseback. Campion was specially welcomed by William Allen and his dearest of friends, Gregory Martin, and the rest, for old acquaintance's sake: they had not seen him for seven years or more, so there was no end to their embracing and welcoming the good man; and besides, he and his companions were already looked upon as martyrs. Sherwin wrote to a friend: "The College was full of old friends from Rome, and Allen is ever the same as he was. He was simply exultant with delight, embraced and welcomed us like sons, and now looks after us quite tenderly."[36]

Campion spent only a week at Rheims, meeting his old friends for the last time in this life. Gregory Martin was to die of consumption only two-and-a-half years later.

Campion missed his old friend Richard Bristow[37] who was probably at Douay—and would in September return to England for his health's sake. Indeed Bristow was to die before Campion, through consumption, in October 1581, at the home of the Bellamy family, Harrow-on-the-Hill—a family Campion would also visit.

From far way, at Rome, they knew it was no easy thing to get into England without discovery; but fresh difficulties had arisen. At Rheims the missionaries were told of a new proclamation in which Elizabeth declared that she had notice of the pope, the King of Spain, the Duke of Florence and other Catholic princes, having made a league against her to invade her realm, at the persuasion of some of her subjects who lived beyond the sea. This was seen to be a plain introduction to a rigorous persecution awaiting all priests who should convey themselves into the country.

Here also they heard of the unfortunate expedition into Ireland,[38] to which may be attributed much of the severity with which they were to be treated.

Campion, therefore, feeling that the case was somewhat altered, and that there was now less chance of success in the undertaking, went to Allen, and said:[39]

> Well, Sir, here now I am. You have desired my going to England, and I am come a long journey, as you see—from Prague to Rome, and from Rome. And do you think my labors in England may counter-vail with all this travail, as also my absence from Bohemia?—where, though I did not much, yet I was not idle nor unemployed, and yet also against heretics.

The president answered,

> My good father, your labors in Boeme-land [Bohemia], though I
> do not doubt but they were very profit able, yet do I imagine that
> another man of your Society may supply the same, at least two or
> three. But towards England I hope verily that Almighty God will
> give you strength and grace to supply for many men; and seeing that
> your obligation is greater towards that country than towards any
> other, and the necessity of help more urgent, and the talents that
> God has given you more fit and proper for that, than for any other
> land, doubt you not but all is Christ's holy providence for the best;
> and so be you of good comfort.

Dr. Allen gives his own recollection of his words at the same
conversation:

> Father, first, whatsoever you did there may be done by others, one
> or more of your Order. Secondly, you owe more duty to England
> than to Bohemeland, and to London than to Prague—though it lik-
> eth me well that you have made some recompense to that country
> for the old wound it received by us. Thirdly, the recovery of one
> soul from heresy is worth all your pains, as I hope you shall gain a
> great many—because the harvest is both more plentiful and more
> ripe with us, than in those parts. Finally, the reward may be greater,
> for you may be martyred for it at home, which you can not obtain
> lightly there.[40]

To which Campion replied,

> As for me, all is one, and I hope I am and shall be ever indifferent for
> all nations and functions whereinsoever my Superiors under God
> shall employ me. I have made a free oblation of myself to His Divine
> Majesty, both for life and death, and I trust that He will give me
> grace and force to perform, and this is all I desire.

Dr. Allen asked Campion to preach to the students, and Campion
was glad of an opportunity to do so, for he had seldom spoken publicly
in English for many years. On June 5, he preached on the text *Ignem veni
mittere in terram* (I have come to cast fire on the earth: *Lk.* 12:49)—or
possibly *Isaiah* 64:11: "The house of our holiness and of our glory, where
our fathers praised Thee, is burnt with fire; and all our lovely things are

turned into ruins."[41] Persons remembered one principal point which he handled:

> to compare the new religion of England unto a fire which, being once kindled and inflamed in any one house of a city, putteth obligation upon all men, as well friends as enemies of the man whose house is afire, to run to the quenching thereof. And to show the truth of this comparison, the more he repeated briefly the hurts that this fire had already done in our country: how many goodly churches, monasteries and other monuments of piety it had devoured in an instant, which our Catholic ancestors had erected in so many hundred years before; how many holy orders of religion it had dissolved in both sexes; how many [hearts] it had in flamed of weak and [inconstant will, and incited] people to marry or live in incest, that before served God in virginity or chastity; what devilish division and heat of hatred it had enkindled in the hearts of Englishmen, the one against the other, even those that by nature should be most loving. By all which points and other the like he showed the rage and fury of this fire and exhorted his fellow-priests and all the company present to put their helping hands and endeavors to the staying or quenching of the same. And if that water would not serve of Catholic doctrine, nor milk of sweet and holy conversation, they should cast blood also of potent martyrdom, which might be hoped would be accepted for the quenching thereof.[42]

While he was describing the outbreak of the conflagration, Bombino tells us that he cried out "fire, fire, fire," so loud, that passers-by were going to fetch water-buckets to put it out.[43]

Allen, who heard him, wrote: "Whether he was inspired by his subject, or whether it was a miracle of memory, he spoke English as fluently and as correctly as if he had but yesterday come fresh out of England."[44] In a letter to Agazzari, Allen said, "Fr. Edmund gave us an address in our own language to try whether, after eight years disuse, he still remembered his native tongue. But so rapid was the torrent of his words that with impetuous violence it seemed to overflow its boundaries."[45] Allen was probably not aware that sometimes Englishmen visited Campion in Bohemia, such as Philip Sidney.[46] Besides, as a traveller in a group of English-speakers, presumably Campion spoke English with them over the six weeks of the trip to Rheims.

The Party Splits Up

Before the missionaries departed for England, the places of Bishop Goldwell and Dr. Morton, who were obliged to stay behind (and later return to Rome), were filled up by two men of Rheims, Dr. Humphrey Ely (a layman) and Fr. John Hart. They were also joined by Fr. Thomas Cottam, an English Jesuit, who had been long laboring in Poland, and who was only ordered to go to his native country for the recovery of his health. They prudently determined not to risk their whole adventure in one boat, but to divide themselves into small parties and reach England by different routes.

Fr. Bromborough and Mr. Briscoe went by Dieppe.[47]

On June 8, Sherwin left with his pupil Mr. Paschal. They went, via Paris, to Sherwin's priest-uncle, John Woodward, living in exile at Rouen in Normandy.[48] At Rouen, Sherwin found young Edward Throckmorton, by whom he wrote an affectionate letter to his old master at Rome, begging Fr. Alphonsus Agazzari to accept Throckmorton in his place at the English College. It was a fair exchange. Sherwin died a martyr with Campion in England; Throckmorton died after two-and-a-bit years in the odor of sanctity at the English College in Rome.

The three older priests—Giblet, Crayne, and Kemp—went by Abbeville and Boulogne.

Fathers Rishton, Kirby, Hart, and Cottam, with Dr. Ely, went by Douay and Dunkirk.

Campion, Persons, and Emerson to St. Omer

The College diary records the day of the Jesuits' departure:

> June 7. Dr. Edmund Campion and Dr. Robert Persons left us, on their way to England. Both are excellent dialecticians, more than ordinarily skilled in Greek and Latin classics, and good theologians. Campion in speech so polished and eloquent as to have few equals, Persons in act so prudent as to have few betters among men of his years. Our hopes regarding them are high as they well can be, not only because of their gifts and accomplishments, but even more so for the alacrity with which they accepted so great a task, thinking themselves fortunate to be selected first to break through the ice, since there is hardly a man of that Society [of Jesus], now so

numerous and so widely spread, who would not gladly have faced the same dangers. Large indeed is the debt that we afflicted Englishmen owe to this great and truly holy Society.[49]

Campion, Persons, and Br. Ralph Emerson went to a house of their Order at St. Omer, in the Province of Artois, then part of Spanish Flanders and a center for English Catholic exiles. A letter of Sherwin records that Fr. Persons's brother (George) went with them.[50]

Later, in 1592-9, a college would be founded at St. Omer by Fr. Persons. (Its lineal descendant today is Stonyhurst.)

Since all Catholic education was prohibited in England, several colleges had been founded by Englishmen on the Continent—at Douay (1568), later moved to Rheims, and back to Douay again; the English College, Rome (1579); Valladolid (1589) and Seville (1592) in Spain. Their primary object was the education of the clergy, but Fr. Persons recognized the need for a college for the laity, and for this purpose he chose a spot as near as possible to England. St. Omer was twenty-four miles from Calais, the French port of departure for England.

The party of three, says Persons, had to travel through a country filled with soldiers of diverse sorts and conditions, but all perilous to anyone who should fall into their hands—and they went "without guard, defense or escort. But our count [lot] was cast and our hope was in Him that is Master and Commander of all, and He led us through the midst of all without hurt, stay, or trouble, and brought us to St. Omer in health and safety."[51]

When they reached the Jesuit residence at St. Omer, the Flemish Fathers thought their safe coming there to be miraculous, and tried to dissuade them from carrying out their undertaking any further. It would be tempting Providence, they said, to dare such an accumulation of new dangers. The queen and Council had been informed in various ways of their coming, and were much exasperated. Several spies, who knew all their names, who had lived with them in Rome, and could describe their persons and dress, had given particular information to the Council, who in turn had given it to the searchers and officers of all the ports; so that it was impossible to enter without being taken. Their very pictures had been drawn and sent to the officers, to help in identifying them.

These rumors had been spread by the English Catholic exiles who lived at St. Omer. Among these was one wiser than the rest, Mr. George

Chamberlain, a distinguished gentleman, in banishment for his conscience, who had married a Flemish lady. He was brother to Dame Cecily
Stonor, whose family shall appear later in our story.[52] As a discreet and
well-qualified person, he was consulted on the matter, and said that such
reports had certainly come from England, and were likely enough to be
true in general, though he did not believe all the particulars. He did not
think that the Council could have found out so much in so little time; yet
it would be wise to deliberate well before setting out on such a journey.
Persons and Campion replied that the journey itself was deliberated and
decided long ago, and offered to God; so there could be no new deliberation on it, but only about the manner, way, place, and time of effecting
it. On this they asked Chamberlain's advice, and begged him to declare it
in the presence of the Jesuit Fathers of St. Omer, and to hear the reasons
on the other side, so that the journey might be prosecuted with the good
liking and approbation of all, without waiting for a new crop of difficulties and perils.

So Chamberlain went with them to the College, where Persons and
Campion expounded their commission and desires, and the reasons for
their haste: they said that the dangers, granting them to be as great as
was reported would only grow greater daily; that it did not matter if the
Council knew their names, for they had license to change them and their
dress, which they would take care to be very different from the dress in
which the spies had seen them; that many men were like each other, and
the informers could scarcely have so exact a knowledge of their persons
as to identify them under all disguises; that the story about the pictures
was well-nigh impossible—the spies in Rome had no opportunity to have
their pictures drawn from description, and much less have so many copies made and quickly distributed to English ports. So the Flemish Fathers
were asked to commend the matter to God, and let the missionaries go
forward; for this, they were persuaded, was God's will, and the meaning
of their superiors in Rome.[53]

Persons's objective was to secure the acquiescence of Chamberlain
as a representative of the English laity, and of the Flemish Fathers on
the part of the Society, and thus to provide in anticipation an answer to
charges of rashness and want of consideration for the interests of others. His object was attained when Chamberlain and the Fathers professed
themselves content with his reasons, and proceeded to advise with him

on the manner of their going. The result of their consultation was that
Persons alone was to go (with his brother George) through Calais to
Dover, and if he succeeded was to send for Campion.

Persons was to pass for a captain and soldier returning home from
Flanders; Campion for a merchant of jewels. They liked the idea of
deceiving the enemy with a truth—for, in fact, Persons was the superior
in this mission, which was a real warfare, and their business was the merchandise of the "pearl of great price."[54]

Persons Crosses to Dover

Persons departed the next day, furnished by Chamberlain with a captain's uniform of buff trimmed with gold-lace, with hat and feather to
match, and another suit for his brother George, who went as his servant.
He went to Calais on St. Barnabas's Day, June 11, and found a passage
to Dover. Leaving on June 15, he arrived the next morning—his first
time in England for six years.[55] There the searcher examined him, and
so far from doubting him let him pass with all favor, and procured him
a horse to carry him to Gravesend. Persons took heart at this providential courtesy of the searcher and took the opportunity to ease the passage of Campion. He told the man that a friend of his, "Mr. Edmunds"
(Campion's assumed name for the time being), a merchant lying at St.
Omer, would follow him shortly, and entreated that like favor be shown
to him. The searcher even undertook to forward to Edmunds a letter in
which Persons told him that he had thought of certain special and urgent
causes why he should make haste to London for dealings in jewels and
the like—a letter which might be shown to the searcher when he came
over. This was a clever device of Persons by which he could not only
summon Campion over, but facilitate Campion's acceptance and entry
into the country.

Persons reached Gravesend at midnight, and at once got into a tilt
boat proceeding to London. He was horrified to find himself in the midst
of a collection of gentlemen of the Inns of Court and of the queen's
household, who had been merry-making in Kent, and who kept playing
and singing half through the night. In dread of facing inquisitive questions in the daylight, Persons took the opportunity before the gentlemen
were awake of jumping into a wherry, which landed him and George in
Southwark about four o'clock in the morning. But here he was in fresh

difficulties; he had no horse, and so was not acceptable to the hosts of the inns, who were moreover made cautious by the late proclamations and rumors against suspicious people. Besides, they saw that his dress was foreign, and one and all refused to receive him.

The Remarkable Thomas Pounde

After spending all his time from dawn almost to noon in a fruitless search over Southwark for a lodging, he resolved to apply to some Catholic. He knew not where any lived but was sure to find plenty of them at any of the prisons. So he went to the Marshalsea prison, where the wealthier recusants were confined, and inquired after a Thomas Pounde, Esquire, who had lain there and in other prisons for some years for his faith. In fact, he had a letter for Pounde from the Jesuit General, Fr. Mercurian, written on April 15.[56] Why that was, we will soon see.

To us, today, this seems a strange proceeding—to go to prison when in dire need to contact friends for help! E. E. Reynolds explains:

> The prison system—if it can be called such—of Elizabethan times was both more harsh and more humane than ours. The key to understanding much that happened to priests and others is that the prisons were not run by the state but were leased to jailers who were out to get as much return on their investments as possible. So prisoners who had funds were almost like paying guests, and they were even allowed out on occasions; there is no record of this permission being abused. Prisoners without money or friends were almost starved and kept in foul conditions. One of the great demands on Catholics for years to come was to provide funds for the support of their co-religionists, who were in prison and without resources. The power of what was known as "the silver key" explains why Catholics could lead a club-like life and priests could say Mass which outsiders, for a fee, could attend. What we call bribery, often under the guise of fees, was a normal practice from the Court downwards.[57]

Prisons varied greatly in standards and regulations. Conditions in the Fleet prison, for example, for those who could afford the exorbitant fees, were quite tolerable. A prisoner could have a servant, order his own food, see friends, have books and writing materials, and, though locked up at night in a separate cell, meet during the day at specified hours with other prisoners, and sometimes dine with them.

At that time, Marshalsea prison, one of five in Southwark, was immediately south of present-day Guy's Hospital, between Newcomen Street and Mermaid Court.[58]

Thomas Pounde took Persons into his room, was delighted at his safe arrival, and told him that he and the other Catholic prisoners had been praying earnestly for many days for him and Campion, and that they must now return thanks. Persons replied that they must continue their prayers some days longer, for Campion was not yet come over. The prisoners gladly promised to do so. Thomas Pounde of Belmont (or Beaumont), near Bedhampton, born in 1538, was then just over forty years of age. He had already passed some five years in various terms of imprisonment. He was educated in law, and at one time had been a Court favorite, but at Christmas 1569 was converted. He had been in Elizabeth's Court, full of spirits, fun, and vigor, and so admired as a dancer that the queen made him perform before her some intricate measure which needed great agility. At first she applauded his deft footing and graceful springs, when suddenly his foot slipped and down he came with a humiliating crash upon the floor. At this, her Majesty roared with laughter and gave him a kick, crying, with a mock knighthood, "Arise, Sir Ox!"

In that Court, such unqueenly behavior did not mean much, but the lesson was not lost on Pounde. He muttered as he rose, *Sic transit gloria mundi* (thus passes the glory of the world), and left the Court never to return. Applying himself now to the practice of virtue and religion with the same energy which he had before devoted to success at Court, he gradually developed the desire of joining the Jesuits, and was on the point of going abroad to do so, when he was imprisoned, about 1574, and being ever after restrained, now by bail, now by chains, could never leave England.

Unable to accomplish his purpose in the ordinary way, he begged the favor of having his imprisonment for the faith taken in lieu of Jesuit novitiate, and of being admitted to the Society with the obligation of crossing over and living in a Jesuit house abroad, when opportunity should serve and obedience calls. The Jesuit General Mercurian accepted his proposal and admitted him on December 1, 1578, writing to him, "Keep your secret to yourself until better times come."[59] He gave him some spiritual advice in the same letter: "we trust that . . . you will not expose yourself to peril without cause, or hope of result. This would be rashness, not courage. Nor should you put your health in jeopardy though immoderate fasting and abstinence, to which we hear you are prone. . . . Keep up your strength for God!" Pounde was to take vows secretly as a Jesuit in the presence of Fr. Weston S.J., his co-captive in Wisbeach Castle.

The man, therefore, to whom Persons had presented himself had an unusual number of claims on their consideration. He was, in a way, a Jesuit novice, of tried faith, witty, generous, with considerable literary powers, and respectable ability as a controversialist. He had, nevertheless, some of the defects which generally go with the solitary life. "He is very fervent," wrote Fr. Garnet S.J., April 10, 1605, "but somewhat abounding in singularities." For instance, he so loved to suffer for Christ that he would reward his jailer handsomely when he was put into irons or harshly treated, but when freed from bonds and the like, he gave the expectant keeper nothing!

Pounde's austerity in sleep and food were extraordinary. His commitment to several hours of daily prayer was no less remarkable. His charity and liberality were endless. He was most devoted to the sacred mysteries, availing himself of confession frequently, and receiving Holy Communion, when possible, on Sundays and feast-days. He encouraged other Catholics to receive the Sacraments with the same frequency.

Pounde was to spend thirty years in captivity for his religion, becoming an inmate of eleven prisons as he was moved from one cell to another. Of that time, four spells over nearly seven years were spent in the dreaded Tower of London. Bishop Sandys of London offered him liberty one time if he would publicly attend church once and hear a Protestant sermon, to which he replied: "If I cannot recover my liberty otherwise than by offending God, I am firmly resolved that my soul shall be first torn from my body, than that my body shall go forth from prison on such terms."

He was released, about 1603, upon the accession of King James I, sent to his family home by his Jesuit Superiors, and died there in 1613, aged seventy-five.

George Gilbert

Fr. Persons dined with the numerous Catholic prisoners and afterwards entrusted himself to the guidance of one of the current visitors, Mr. Edward Brooksby (married to Eleanor Vaux, sister of Campion's former pupil, Henry). Brooksby led Persons to a Catholic house in Chancery

Lane, in the City, a kind of club, where he found other gentlemen and priests, and notably Mr. George Gilbert, the tenant of the house, who rented it "from a notorious unnamed pursuivant, whose love of money exceeded his devotion to the established Church."[60]

Gilbert was a close friend of Pounde and visited him frequently in jail. He was also a friend of Persons. He was a young gentleman of large property in Suffolk, and other counties, who had succeeded young to his wealth. Born about 1555, he had been brought up in London in the current religion. He was a real favorite at Court, both under Mary and Elizabeth, for his graceful form, pleasing countenance, and gentlemanly address.[61] His earnest nature inclined him rather to Puritanism, in which he had been confirmed by daily frequenting the sermons of Edward Dering, a famous Puritan preacher. However, after he came to the enjoyment of his property, he traveled abroad; and in Paris he providentially fell into the company of Fr. Thomas Darbyshire,[62] the Jesuit, who opened his eyes to the Catholic religion. Fr. Persons, in Rome, in 1579, completed his conversion, and was his godfather at his Confirmation. From that time, though the new convert still pursued his studies, and learned the accomplishments for which Italy was then famous—riding, fencing, vaulting, and the like, for he was of stalwart growth—yet he secretly added all kinds of religious exercises, such as prayer, fasting, mortification, and liberal almsgiving.

Gilbert's friends had induced him to propose to a young heiress. He was about to be married, but when he heard of the mission of Persons and Campion to England, he broke off the engagement and resolved never to marry. He wanted to make a vow—with Persons's approbation as soon as he came to him in England. Persons would not at first permit it, though at last he allowed him to vow chastity till the Catholic religion should be publicly professed in England.

Back in Rome, Gilbert had wished to expend his first fervor in a pilgrimage to Jerusalem. Persons persuaded him rather to return to England, and lay out his money on the care of priests and on other means of advancing the Catholic cause. The result was that he drew together and organized several principal young men for this crucial purpose of organizing the care of newly arrived priests and putting them in touch with Catholics and safe houses.[63]

Among these companions were bearers of the names of leading

Catholic families, such as Vaux, Throgmorton, Titchbourne, and Stonor. These young men took lodging together and sojourned in the chief pursuivant's house in Fetter or Chancery Lane. The pursuivant (Catholic hunter) was a friend of the Bishop of London, John Aylmer, who resided at Fulham Palace. They also had another powerful protector at Fulham, in the person of the bishop's son-in-law, Dr. Adam Squire, who was in their pay. Through the connivance of these men they were able to receive priests and have daily Mass in their house for some years, till the Jesuits entered England, when the times grew much more exasperated. Squire was master of Balliol College, Oxford, during Persons's tenure as bursar there, and sided against Persons in a dispute over college accounts. Back then, Persons was already his enemy for having forced Squire to compensate some men whom Squire had conned out of their modest possessions.[64] Fr. McCoog points out the irony—thanks to Squire's venality, Persons and his confederates had secured the protection of Persons's old adversary through bribes.[65]

The role of these men who loved money more than they hated Catholicism was crucial to the freedom of certain Catholics. Many an official or layman in the pay of Catholic gentry would testify, when their Catholic benefactor was charged for an offense, that the prisoner was "an honest gentleman," thus averting the enforcement of the law for the time being, and assuring for themselves the continuance of money which an imprisoned Catholic could not provide.

After being introduced to this club of men, Persons gave directions about Campion, who was shortly to follow him, and set out, under the guidance of Mr. Henry Orton, to visit certain gentlemen in the counties round London. After three weeks he hoped to return, and to find that his confrère had arrived.

Campion Prepares to Cross

While this was going on in England, Campion was left in doubt and concern at St. Omer, where on June 17 he began a letter to Fr. Everard Mercurian, the General, and finished it on June 20:

> Father Robert, accompanied by his brother George, sailed from Calais after midnight, on the day before I began writing this; the wind was very good, so we hope that he reached Dover some time

yesterday morning, June 16. He was dressed up like a soldier—such a peacock, such a swaggerer, that a man must have very sharp eyes to catch a glimpse of any holiness and modesty shrouded beneath such a garb, such a look, such a strut! We are worried all the same, I will not say by mere rumors but by something positively like a clamor that heralds our approach. Only Divine Providence can counteract this kind of publicity, and we fully acquiesce in its dispositions.

Following orders, I have stayed behind for a time, to try, if possible, to fish some news about Father Robert"s success out of the carriers, or out of certain merchants who are to come to these parts, before I sail across. If I hear anything, I will advise upon it; but in any case I will go over and take part in the fight, though I die for it. It often happens that the first rank of a conquering army takes a thrashing. Indeed, if our Society is to go on with this campaign, the ignorance and sheer wickedness against which this war is declared will have to be overcome.

On June 20 I mean to go to Calais. In the meantime, I live in the College at St. Omer, where I am getting myself fitted out, with my companion Ralph. You may imagine the expense, especially as none of our old things can be used hereafter. As we want to disguise ourselves, and to imitate the vain fashions of this world, we were obliged to buy several trifles which seem to us altogether silly. Our journey, these clothes, and four horses, which we must buy as soon as we reach England, may possibly square with our money; but only with the help of the Providence which multiplied the loaves in the wilderness. But this, in fact, is the least of our difficulties, so let us have done with it.

I will not yet close this letter, that I may add whatever news reaches me during these three days. For though our lot will be cast one way or other before you read this, yet I thought I ought, while I am here, to trace every particular of this great undertaking, and the last doings, on which the rest, as yet unwritten, will hang.

There is a certain English gentleman [George Chamberlain], very well-informed in matters of State, who comes often to me. He tells me that the coming of the Bishop of St. Asaph [Goldwell] is broadcast in letters and in conversation. Great expectations are raised by it; for most people think that such a man, at his age, would never undertake such a task, unless there were something big afoot. I told him in the simplest manner the true cause of his coming.

Still, he did not cease wondering, for the episcopal title and office is indeed held in high honor in England.

Today the wind is falling, so I will move off quickly to the sea.

I have been thoroughly well-treated in St. Omer's College, and helped with all things needful. Indeed, in our whole journey we received incredible comfort in all the residences of our Fathers. On top of this, we enjoyed the hospitality of two most illustrious Cardinals, Paleotto and Borromeo, and of the Archpriest of Colle di Val d'Elsa [Rev. Niccolò Sabolini].[66] We purposely avoided Paris and Douay.

We seem safe enough, unless we are betrayed in these coastal regions. I have stayed a day longer than I meant, and as I hear nothing good or bad of Father Robert, I persuade myself that he got through safely.

I pray God ever to protect Your Reverence, and your Assistants, and the whole Society.

Farewell. June 20, 1580.[67]

Persons's brother, George, named above,[68] and at the start of this letter, was a frequent companion of Fr. Persons, and was later with him at Rome and elsewhere.[69] Since he is not mentioned earlier in any account of the missionaries' travels, we presume he met up with them at Rheims, or a little earlier, since the College diary says he arrived with Campion, Persons, and Emerson on May 31.[70] He went to England with his brother Robert, as we saw—and his return from England is noted in the Rheims College diary on June 1, 1582.[71]

Campion Crosses to Dover

Campion must have received Persons's communication sent from Dover immediately after closing this letter to his General. With full confidence of success, he at once prepared to follow. He was very glad that the feast of his old patron, St. John the Baptist, was so near at hand. Indeed, it happened that he crossed over on the very day; for he was obliged to wait four days at Calais for a good wind, and at last he put to sea on the evening of June 24,[72] the feast of his patron's nativity, and reached Dover, in Kent, before day light, Saturday June 25, 1580.

It was his first time in England for nine years.

CHAPTER 8

The Mission Begins

C AMPION LANDED on the sands of Dover, and retired behind a
great rock, to fall on his knees and commend his cause and his
whole coming to God, whether it might be for life or for death.[1] Then he
and Brother Ralph went to look for the searcher, whom they hoped to
find in as good a humor as Persons had left him; but lately stricter orders
had come down from the Council to look more diligently to his charge,
with a reprimand to him and the Mayor for having, as was supposed,
allowed certain priests to pass that way into the realm.

Danger in Dover

Besides this, some spy had notified the Council from France that Mr.
Gabriel Allen, brother of Dr. Allen, was about to visit his friends in
Lancashire. A description of Gabriel had been provided, agreeing in the
main with the physique and features of Campion. Hereupon Edmund
and Ralph were seized and carried before the Mayor of Dover. He
charged them with being foes of the queen's religion, and friends of the
old faith; with sailing under false names; with having been abroad for
religion; and with returning for the purpose of propagating popery. He
declared Campion was Gabriel Allen; but Campion offered to swear this
was not the case. At last he resolved to send them, under guard, to the
Council, and ordered the horses to be prepared. Campion all the while
stood in a corner, begging the intercession of his patron, St. John the
Baptist, and most earnestly beseeching Almighty God not to call him
from the combat before he had engaged in it, and to grant him but one
year to fight the battle of Christ; and at the end of that year, he would not
ask reprieve from any chains, crosses, or butchery whatsoever.[2] No doubt
Edmund had adopted the Baptist as his patron from the time he went to

199

the College of St. John the Baptist, in Oxford, back in 1557. His heavenly patron did not disappoint him; suddenly an old man came forth from the room where the mayor had retired and said: "Now, it has been decided that you are dismissed. Good-bye."[3]

Arrival in London

He and Ralph thereupon hurried to London, in Middlesex, where he was anxiously expected, and where much prayer was being made for his safety, for the great fear was what he would do when he first arrived. The letter from Persons had summoned him to London without naming any place to go. But it happened that when the boat going up the Thames, in which he was a passenger, came to the Hythe port at London, Thomas Jay (James), one of the Catholic network, was watching out for him. He had never seen him; but partly through Persons's description of his person and dress, partly through seeing him in company with the short Brother Ralph, who had also been described to him, he suspected him to be the man, and so boldly stepped to the boat's side: "Mr. Edmunds, give me your hand. I stay here for you to lead you to your friends."[4] And he led him to the house in Chancery Lane (where Fr. Persons had been led earlier), where George Gilbert and the rest clothed and equipped him like a gentleman, and furnished him with a horse. This was on the morning of Sunday, June 26.

Persons was still out of London, in "a shire nigh adjoining, at the request of certain principal Catholic gentlemen."[5] He had left word that Campion should stay in London for his return, and employ his time in the best manner he could for the comfort of Catholics. Campion set to work at once: the College diary at Rheims records:

> The two Fathers of the Society [of Jesus] gone forth to England sent us letters; the first of whom, namely Fr. Edmund, wrote that at once, on the day after his arrival, in London, he heard confessions of at least forty penitents.[6]

Campion Says Mass

Hereupon the young men entreated him to preach to them on Wednesday, June 29, the feast of Sts. Peter and Paul. There was great difficulty in fixing upon a place, for their house would not hold all that wished to attend, and no public place was safe. So at last they chose the great hall of a house near Smithfield, which Thomas Lord Paget hired for them from Lord Norreys (Norris), where the servants and porters were for the occasion replaced by gentlemen of worship and honor; and while these trusty watchmen guarded the ways, Campion preached on the Gospel, taking for his text both St. Peter's confession, *Thou art the Christ, the Son of the living God,* and Our Lord's answer, *And I say unto thee: Thou art Peter and upon this Rock I shall build My Church.* From the former he animated them to the true confession of Christ in that faith and religion of His which first He sent to England when it was converted from paganism; from the latter, he laid before them the indignity, danger and folly of siding against this invincible rock of Peter and his successors,; and the effect of his whole sermon was to draw forth many tears in consideration of the one, and to plant in all that heard him great courage and fortitude for the execution of the other.

His sermon so strongly affected those who heard him, that each of them supposed that if this loose Catholic or that sincere Protestant could be brought to speak with the preacher, the conversion of the wanderer would be secured. Hence Campion's coming was entrusted as a grand secret to half the world, and after a few days, which he well spent in conferences with all comers, the Council began to suspect what was on hand, and set on foot a diligent search for his apprehension. They at first tried the stratagem of sending false brothers to hear him, and to apprehend him at Mass or preaching. There were spies abroad, yearning for Catholic sermons, especially if any of the Jesuits might be heard. But Campion was advertised of this scheme by some principal persons of the Court, and therefore took greater heed with whom he conversed, employing himself only in private meetings and exhortations in secret friends' houses during eight or ten days.[7]

Persons Returns

Those private conferences went on till about July 8, therefore, when Persons returned to deliberate with him what course to follow to execute their purposes within the realm. He "found Fr. Campion retired for his more safety into a certain poor man's house in Southwark near the Thames where men might repair [go] without great show of suspicion, both by land and water."[8]

Danger in London

But even these quiet proceedings were known to the queen and Council, who only abstained from violent measures in the hopes of being able to capture at one stroke not only the Jesuits but a considerable number of the chief Catholics at some of the conferences. The government was exceedingly stung to hear so many priests had entered the country at once; for besides the band which came from Rome, several had been sent from France and Flanders, "not upon any agreement together," asserts Persons, "but by chance, or rather God's providence, divers of them not knowing the one of the other's journey."[9] These others included the laymen Dr. Ely and Mr. Orton, and the priests Bosgrave, Robert Johnson, Cottam, Hart, and Briant who was to suffer with Campion.

But though the Council kept silence for the present, the searchers of London grew so eager and frequent, and the spies so many and diligent, that scarce an hour passed without some Catholic being reported as taken up on suspicion or detected.

Fr. Henry More describes their activity:

> Spies and public informers were a repulsive breed of men who made it their whole business day and night to keep watch on Catholic houses throughout the city. If they noticed anyone making a visit for the second or third time, or saw a number of people calling, they would lay siege to the doors; even call on neighbors to help them, while they burst in, to lay hold on their man. Having seized him, they would bring him before the magistrate. If he showed the slightest hesitation in answering their questions, they led him away forthwith as a suspected priest to be heavily fined or subjected to prolonged imprisonment, or even killed. At this time, Sledd was the worst of such characters.[10]

As a specimen of the dangers which the two Jesuits were continually incurring, we may take this story. On July 12, Henry Orton, the young gentleman who had been Persons's conductor in his short expedition into the country, set out one morning from his lodging in Smithfield to meet Campion and Persons. On the way, there stood Charles Sledd (Slade or Slaydon), a former servant in the English College at Rome, but turned spy and informer, with a constable, ready to apprehend anyone he might recognize. Sledd had known Orton in Rome; and though he knew the young man was neither priest nor Jesuit, he guessed that he conversed with such as were. So he followed him a while in the street; and if he had followed him a little farther, he would have found the very house where the two Fathers were together, and would have captured them both at once. But Sledd was impatient and had Orton arrested in the street, whereby the Fathers were indirectly warned, and so provided for themselves.

Sledd had already done major harm to Fr. Robert Johnson in London, a revered and holy priest, about forty years of age, who had visited Rome as a pilgrim shortly before the departure of the Fathers for England. Johnson had already labored painfully in his own country for some years. Before he returned to his work he had, on Persons's recommendation, stayed at a Jesuit house where he went through the *Spiritual Exercises* of St. Ignatius. On his way to England he was joined by Sledd, the spy, who was then talking like a most enthusiastic Catholic, but behaving so loosely that Johnson was obliged to reprehend him. Sledd was so angry that he at first considered murdering him on the spot, but after reflection decided to betray him to the English government instead. He therefore went to the English ambassador at Paris, and gave information about Johnson and other priests both to him and to Jerome Vane, a spy attached to the embassy. On the same day that Orton was caught, when Sledd was loitering about London on his treacherous mission, Sledd saw Fr. Johnson going through Smithfield. He followed him till he saw a constable, whom he charged in the queen's name to arrest Johnson as a priest and traitor. The constable, at heart a Catholic, made all sorts of excuses; but on Sledd's threatening to report him to the Recorder (a type of magistrate), he took up his staff, and told Sledd to show him the man who was to be arrested. Sledd did so, and was about to depart, when the constable told him he must follow to uphold the charge, and to bear the possible consequences of a false arrest and imprisonment. The true motive, however, was to expose Sledd as an informer to the people. So Sledd and the constable followed Johnson till he came to the Thames, and saw him hire a wherry to convey him over to Southwark, where Persons and Campion were in council with several other priests. Sledd told the constable to take another boat and row after Johnson; but the constable, guessing something of the errand on which the priest was bound, told his companion that he could not spend all the day tracking a man in a boat, perhaps to miss him at the last; so he cried out to the bystanders to stop the traitor, and arrested him then and there. Johnson was taken, and thrust into a prison, from which he only emerged to pass through Westminster Hall (with Campion) to the scaffold in 1582. But the lesson was not lost; Sledd was at once noted, and expelled from Catholic society before he had time to do much more mischief. Sledd will reappear later in this story as a perjuring witness at the trial of Campion and companions.

Orton and Johnson were on the way to join a small assembly in Southwark. A report of the capture reached the assembled priests, who broke up in haste.

The Synod in Southwark

Amid such perils, and even before these latest arrests, it became clear to the friends of the Fathers that London was no place for them; they were therefore counseled to shorten their stay there, and to despatch with speed such things as were to be considered or decided before their departure.

So it was that on Tuesday, July 12, in a little house near St. Mary Overy's (now St. Saviour's) in Southwark,[11] in the vicinity of the Clink, they therefore collected the most respected priests then to be found in London, among whom were Nicholas Tyrwhitt (Tirwitt), Thomas Metham and George Blackwell (afterwards Archpriest),[12] and also various principal laymen, for their better satisfaction. Assorted points of importance were to be discussed, and it was only natural that in matters of common concern the clergy and laity should take common counsel at a time of danger, when the active cooperation of both classes was necessary in order to secure the interests of either. As the medieval canonical axiom says, *Quod omnes tangit ab omnibus tractari et approbari debet* (what concerns all should be discussed and approved by all). So far as the faith was concerned, there were no questions to discuss among the English Catholics in 1580, but questions of morals, worship, discipline, and political conduct, in which all were equally interested, urgently claimed at that moment the consideration and the agreement of all. This convocation was a small synod, so to speak, but without a bishop. Fr. Persons had no authority over the secular priests gathered, but as he came from Rome, on mission from the pope and the General, and had lately spoken to Dr. William Allen, what he had to say carried much weight.

The Purely Spiritual Mission

The first question to be discussed was the answer to be made, for the satisfaction both of Protestants and Catholics, to the rumor raised on occasion of the entrance of the Jesuits into the realm; it was said to be for treason, conspiracy, and matter of State, and not for religion. Sanders, in his book on the ecclesiastical monarchy, excuses the English Catholics for failing to support the rebellion of the great earls of the north, on the ground that they did not know of the Bull; and the English statesmen retorted that this want of information was diligently and cunningly supplied by sending the Jesuits and seminary priests into the realm.[13] They said also that while a Bull was in existence, declaring that Elizabeth had no right or title to the crown, all who submitted, or were prepared to submit, to the authority which proclaimed it, were in their hearts secret traitors, and only waiting the occasion to declare themselves open traitors; which occasion it was necessary to remove, by preventing the secret promulgation of the Bull by the agency of the missionary priests. Moreover, it would be argued that the famous mitigation obtained by Campion and Persons did not in the least affect the substance of the Bull, whereby the queen still remained excommunicated and deposed, but merely allowed the English Catholics to exhibit to her a temporary and conditional loyalty and obedience (*rebus sic stantibus*, as long as things stood thus) as long as they could not help themselves—but the moment they could, or thought they could, or were told by the pope that the time was come, then their obedience and loyalty were to end; the censures were to resume their full force, and the queen was to be violently assailed. The mitigation would thus be made to appear like a truce obtained upon false pretenses by one belligerent party, only in order to gain time to recruit forces for a new attack. Moreover, it would be called absurd in the Roman missionaries to expect that their master's agents would be allowed all the privileges of a friendly power in England, while he and his agents in Ireland were carrying on an open war against the queen of both realms. It was to be feared that by these considerations all their spiritual and ecclesiastical functions might be brought into obloquy and hatred with the people, and much cruelty inflicted both on the said clergymen themselves when they should be taken, and on all other Catholics for their sake.

But to all this the Fathers said they had but one answer to give: their public and private denial of any such intentions as were imputed to them. So they, then and there, made oaths before Almighty God, and before the priests and laymen assembled, "that their coming only was apostolical, to treat matters of religion in truth and simplicity, and to attend to the gaining of souls, without any knowledge or intention in the world of matters of State."[14] After this oath, they exhibited the *Instructions* they had received; and they declared that they had never heard of Sanders's passage into Ireland till they were at Rheims. This oath, they supposed, would be sufficient to content Catholics and dispassionate Protestants, and to assure them of the falsehood of the reports that were being spread; for they could never think that all these priests would make so light of their souls as to cast them away by willful perjury.

But as for the queen's Council and bishops, whose interest it was to crush the Catholic religion and to defame its ministers, the only way against them was, if any of the Fathers fell into their hands, that he should not only protest on his oath, but also stand to his denial before God and man, and challenge his adversaries to prove any single point against him—which no man living would ever be able to do, because there never was such matter either in fact or thought. And as all this would go by unanimous verdict of a jury of twelve substantial Englishmen, they fondly hoped that a condemnation would be almost impossible, since they knew that no fact, attempt or intention, however slight, could ever be proved.

And here one of the assembly objected, that considering the present hatred against priests, and its probable increase by the conversion of many to the faith, mere conjectures would be enough for a jury to condemn them. The Fathers replied, that if conjectures and probabilities were to have place, it would be easy to bring conjecture against conjecture, and to refute less probabilities by greater. For instance, if foreign princes wished to send political emissaries, they would not choose mere scholars, nor send so many in so public a fashion; nor would ambassadors travel all the way from Rome by foot, dressed as servants. Again, if they were political emissaries, they must be sent to the Catholics alone; but what Catholic would ever listen to them if, after the oath they had just taken, he were to see them meddling with matters of State?

"This," said Campion and Persons, "is the satisfaction that we can give, and if all this will not serve, then our last satisfaction must be to protest the same at our deaths and seal it with our blood"; and then it will not matter, they said, whether we are believed or not, or whether, like Our Lord, we are reckoned among the wicked, and as He and His Apostles, put to death as enemies of Caesar.[15]

Soon after this assembly, a very senior and venerable priest, Fr. Thomas Wilson,[16] put to Fr. Persons, on behalf of a number of priests already on the mission, that the arrival of the Jesuits had as a matter of fact increased the persecution against Catholics, and had caused many gentlemen and noblemen suspected as Catholics to be brought to London and imprisoned, on the grounds that they had dealings with the Jesuits, and that hence it would be better for the Jesuit Fathers to leave now and return at a calmer time and better opportunity. To these concerns, all founded on fear and human prudence, Persons replied that they had not come by their own volition but sent by the highest authority in the Church, who alone could call them forth again, and that they would not endanger other priests needlessly, but go only to where they were summoned. God, whose hand rules over all, would draw forth good fruits from this intensified persecution, which was to be expected whenever there was a new contingent of priests entering. Fr. Wilson took this answer back to his confrères who (most of them) accepted it and thereafter co-operated with the Jesuits most willingly.[17]

The Question of Attending Protestant Church

The second point was practically, and for the time, the most important that this council had to settle: How far could it ever be lawful to go to Protestant churches, especially if the persecution should increase? Several pleas were alleged, and it was said that a man might go if he justly feared or knew that going was the one way to save his goods or person, or to save himself from intolerable vexation; that he would go only for external obedience to the queen and her laws, without respect to religion, just as he would go to any other profane place if commanded by the same authority, not to pray with or among the Protestants, but to go there only for temporal obedience. Or, if this was unlawful or not permissible, might not certain principal men, who were not likely to be hurt or infected, go there at certain times, with protestation at their entering the churches that they went not for the sake of religion, but only by commandment of the sovereign, and no otherwise? Or lastly, if none of these ways were allowed, might not one obtain a dispensation from the pope to permit it, either generally in England, considering the difficulties and dangers that might beset such as refused, or at least to certain principal men who might have more urgent cause to ask such permission?

A negative answer was given to all these questions, and it was determined that nothing could ever justify a Catholic in attending Protestant worship in England. The religions, it was said, were different; the most learned foreign Catholics had been consulted; the Council of Trent had appointed a committee to deliberate the question in 1562, had considered all the circumstances, and had come to this conclusion. The pope was of the same mind, and would never grant a dispensation in so notorious a case, where men were called upon openly to confess or deny God's true religion by an evident and distinctive sign, and by the public act of attending an alien worship where the truth is impugned, and the Catholic Church defaced, calumniated, and ridiculed—an iniquity in which no Catholic could acquiesce without damning his soul. The Catholic, therefore, however pressed to conform externally, ought to resist, at any peril or cost, and even to thank God for so honorable an occasion of confessing Him, remembering that there is no dispensation from the assurance, "Whoever shall deny Me before men, I also will deny before My Father" (Matt 10:33). And it was concluded that this was what all priests in England should uniformly teach to all Catholics on the matter.

Evelyn Waugh remarks:

> If anyone had remained in doubt of the missionaries' innocence of political motive, this verdict [against attending Common Prayer] should have reassured them. If their object in their secret coming and going from house to house had been conspiracy; if, as was said by their enemies, they were using the confessional to prepare a concerted insurrection in support of Spain, they would have instructed their followers to equivocate with "mental reservations," to lie low, to attend the services, take the oaths, and then at the appointed signal fall upon their unsuspecting neighbors; nothing would have been more recklessly imprudent, or fatal to their purposes, than to make their adherents advertise themselves publicly to the authorities.[18]

Both Campion and Persons had tasted the bitter fruits of conformity contrary to conscience. Still, the question was surrounded with difficulties, as may be seen from the following case, which happened afterwards, reported by Persons.

The Example of Fr. Bosgrave

Some time after this small conference, Fr. James Bosgrave was arrested. He was a Jesuit priest, of a good family in England, who had left his country when a boy, and had since worked on the mission in Moravia, Poland, and Lithuania. After a time he lost his health, and was sent back in 1580 to try the effect of his native air; but he was captured at Orford straight after his landing on the Suffolk coast. With all his learning, he was ignorant of the state of religion in England, and so, when brought before the Bishop of London, he astounded people by his answers. "Whence came you?" said the bishop. "From Germany and Poland." "What were you doing there?" "Traveling." "That is well, and befits a gentleman. What is your religion?" "Catholic." "That is ours also [the Anglicans were still then claiming the name, "Catholic," but the question is, will you go to church, or not?" "I see no reason why not." At this answer, the bishop was wonderfully glad, for he hoped he had found a learned man to oppose the other Catholics on this point, which they made of so much importance. Bosgrave was therefore praised to the skies for his discretion and conformity; he was made "extreme much" of, and allowed to go at large. And the bishop took care to publish all over London that one of the most learned Jesuits had yielded in this point, and that those who stuck to the opposite practice were mere simpletons in comparison with him.

This news gave great scandal. Campion and Persons had by this time left London, so that none of his Order remained to deal with Bosgrave; and as the heretics confidently affirmed that he would soon be entirely theirs, the Catholics were afraid of him, and shunned him whenever he sought their company, or desired to enter their houses. He could not guess the reason of this strange conduct, which afflicted him greatly; for he had been so long abroad that he had half forgotten his native tongue, and had no friends in London, and so knew not what to do or where to go.

But at last he met with a near kinsman, a Catholic, who told him roundly what men thought of him, and what scandal he had given by his answers to the bishop. Bosgrave, in amazement, said that he offered to go to their churches just as in Rome or Germany he might go to the Jews' synagogue, and in Constantinople to the Turks' mosques, to hear their folly and confute it. In Germany and Poland, he said, they never made any scruple about it; but any learned man might go freely to the meetings of the Calvinists, Lutherans, Unitarians, or Anabaptists, and hear their folly and blasphemy in order to refute it. And this was all he meant when he promised the bishop to go to church.

Then he was shown how different England was from Germany; for here the question was not whether learned men may for curiosity or controversy go once or twice to heretical churches, but whether a learned man may bind himself to go there ordinarily, and thereby acknowledge that religion to be true, and so give an evil example to simple people, who might be unable to refute what they heard. Here, too, the act was commanded by the legislature as a religious profession, and so very different from the isolated act of a private person. If the same law was enacted in the heretical States of Germany, no doubt it would be as great a sin to obey it there as in England. He was told, too, how this point of discipline was now on its trial in the country, and that numbers of Catholics were at that moment suffering imprisonment and persecution for it; that all the priests, all the Jesuits, and all the learned and zealous among the laity were of one opinion. Bosgrave, therefore, could not swerve from the rest without great scandal; and, indeed, the heretics had already taken occasion from his slight complacence to sow suspicion that he was going to join them.

This moved him exceedingly. He was angry at their malice, and declared that, with God's grace, he would soon cure their false fancies, and satisfy the Catholics about his honest meaning. He therefore wrote an epistle to the Catholics to pardon what he had done, and another to the bishop and the other commissioners to retract his promise of going to church, and to deliver himself up to their hands. To jump ahead in our story, he was therefore sent to the Marshalsea prison,[19] and afterwards to the Tower; there condemned with Campion as a traitor, but reprieved at the request of the king of Poland, and banished with some other priests in 1585, after which he returned to his Order in Poland.

Rules of Fasting

The third point settled in the council at Southwark was whether the old English or the Roman rules of fasting and abstinence were henceforth to prevail. In England, all Fridays were fasts, as well as several vigils that were not observed in Italy. Differences had already begun to grow in different shires, and the priests and good men could not agree about the course most proper for those days of danger. The old priests were proud of the store of national devotions and works of piety which had distinguished England above every other kingdom of the world, since St. Augustine of Canterbury, by command of St. Gregory, transplanted into it the flower of all the devotions that he had noted to be observed in any nation by which he passed. It was decided, therefore, that for the present nothing should be altered, in manner of fasting, from the old customs; but in the shires, wherever the different uses of York, Salisbury, Hereford, or Canterbury and London used to prevail, wherever the Catholics remembered that Fridays or vigils were days of fast, they were to be kept, and the priests were to be the first to observe them. But where the memory had died out, no one was bound to fast, though the voluntary act was always commendable. This was not commanded, but only counseled, for direction of priests and preservation of unity, till God should open the door for an authoritative decision.

The Division of the Work

The fourth point was to determine the various districts that each priest was to frequent. It was agreed that there were three districts that ought specially to be attended to: Wales, because it was not attended to by the Protestants, or, indeed, by the Catholics; and because the ignorant inhabitants, though they had not yet apostatized from the faith, were so little attached to it that they might be led from it by the first preachers of heresy, if they were not previously strengthened by the missionaries. Secondly, Lancashire and the North, which had shown itself so forward in the Catholic cause in 1569. And thirdly, Cambridgeshire, already sapped with Puritanism, which had deeply tainted the University. To these districts the secular priests were sent. The two Jesuits seem to have been appointed to visit the whole country, for we shall trace them from London to Lancashire, and throughout the intervening places.

Fr. Cottam

The last thing to be determined in the small synod was the case of Fr. Thomas Cottam.[20] He had landed at Dover with Dr. Humphrey Ely and Fathers Rishton and Hart. Sledd had sent to the port a very particular description of these last two, and so they were held.

But the mayor and searcher were not sure of Cottam. So he was arrested at Dover, and sent to London in the custody of a fellow-traveler, whom the port authorities took for a Protestant. But he was really a lay Catholic jurist, Dr. Ely, who had passed more than once under the name of Howard, and was not suspected. Ely was commissioned to present Cottam to the Warden of the Cinque Ports, Lord Cobham. Ely promised to do so, and the inn-keeper of Dover, who knew him as Howard, vouched for him.

On the way to London, Dr. Ely of course let Fr. Cottam go, and was afterwards himself arrested for having done so. He thought it would be a greater offense to offer up a priest to the persecutors than to break his promise to the mayor and searcher.

Fr. Cottam conceived some scruple about this, and wanted to give himself up chivalrously to save his friend. So, as he still accounted himself a Jesuit, having been dismissed from the Society only for bad health, with express promise to be re-accepted when he was well, he sought out Campion and Persons, and told them his case.

After consultation, they advised that, as Dr. Ely was the one who promised to take him in, and as Cottam had made no promise to Ely (or to the mayor for that matter), he was not bound to offer himself to so manifest a danger. This decision contented him for a time; but when he heard that Dr. Ely was likely to come into worse trouble on his account, he consulted the Fathers again, who submitted it to the council. This time, they permitted him to do as his conscience persuaded him.

So with a merry countenance, he went to New Fish Street, and gave himself up to a deputy of Lord Cobham, who took him to the court at Oatlands. After three or four days he was committed to the Marshalsea, where he remained till he was arraigned and condemned with Campion for treason.

Dr. Ely, not being a priest, was released as a result (despite being named in the indictment against Campion and others),[21] and he returned to Rheims, to be ordained a priest in 1582. Fr. Cottam, who heroically gave himself up, won the martyr's crown.

The Roman Rite and the Sarum Use

The small synod discussed rules of fasting, as mentioned, but made no mention of the Rite of Mass to be used. By the time the Jesuits came to England in 1580, the Missal promulgated by Pope Pius V in 1570 (seven years after the Council of Trent concluded) was the norm for Jesuits and missionary priests. Undoubtedly there were still many valiant Marian priests who had not conformed to Protestantism who were saying "the old Mass" from Missals of the Sarum Rite (the Rite of Salisbury), according to the surviving books that had escaped being collected and burnt. By at least the early 17th century, post-Tridentine traveling Missals were specifically printed for priests on the English mission. They were abbreviated Missals; being smaller they were easier to hide and carry. Some contained also the Rite of Baptism and other more common Sacraments and rites. A Missal of 1623 is the first to contain a non-Sarum Ritual— extracts from the new Roman Ritual promulgated in 1614.[22]

Since going to the Continent in 1571, and his ordination in 1578, Campion would have been versed in the 1570 Missal of Pius V. Persons and the Jesuits would have regarded the use of the post-Tridentine reform as bringing modernity and conformity to the mission to England; the seculars and older priests from previous reigns would have been happy enough to continue with the Sarum Rite, as most of them did. One can imagine perhaps the new Roman-trained Jesuits and seminary priests smiling at "the old boys" still continuing with the Sarum usages, and the old men deliberately doing so to emphasize their Englishness and their disdain for the new-fangled ways. Although in 1457, more than a century before, it was said that the Sarum Use of the Roman Rite was followed in nearly the whole of England, Wales and Ireland,[23] by the 17th century one hears no more of the Sarum usages in England, unlike the Gallican rites, for example, perduring in France.

If Campion used the old Sarum Missal it would have been in country houses where a surviving copy was the only one available. Substantially, the Sarum Rite has the Prefaces and Canon of the Roman Missal, but there are several differences between the Roman Rite of Mass and the Sarum Use. In the Sarum Rite there are sacristy prayers of preparation, including the first part of the *Hail Mary*. On arrival at the altar there is simply the *Confiteor* and a few versicles. At the *Offertory* the bread and wine are offered together with a single prayer. There is a different form of the *Orate fratres* ("Pray, brethren") and its response. In the Roman Canon, "et rege nostro N." (and our King . . .) is inserted after the pope's name. The priest's prayers before and on receiving Communion are different, and prayers after Communion vary by addition on the Roman ones. The

Last Gospel is not said at the altar but as a devotion as the priest returns to the sacristy. Other differences in the Sarum Rite regard its variations on the Roman chant, and its numerous late medieval sequences used before the 1570 reform reduced them to five only in the Roman Missal.

One can imagine Campion sometimes utilizing an old Sarum Missal but using from memory the Psalm *Judica me* and the new Roman form of the *Prayers at the Foot of the Altar,* the Roman *Offertory Prayers* and *Prayers before Communion* silently, rather than the Sarum ones which he would not have known by heart unless re-learned or remembered from his youth. It is possible the seminary priests, Jesuits, and others would have known some Masses off by heart in case a Missal were not available, as in modern times, in World War II camps, some priests celebrated from memory a daily "dry Mass" (Mass prayers alone, without bread and wine, etc.). However, there may have been occasions when only Sarum Missals were available (they were printed in the reign of Mary), and the priest-martyrs—especially those who were not converts—would have grown up with the Sarum Usage and been familiar with it.

One may wonder what rite of Mass the English celebrated at Douay when it was first founded in 1568, just before the promulgation of St. Pius V's Missal; one guesses the local usage rather than the Sarum one.

Today at Winchester Cathedral, there is an edition of the Sarum Missal printed at Paris in 1510, which made its way into the library of Bishop George Morley, Bishop of Winchester 1662–84. On a blank space within the book is a handwritten inscription signed by a Bartholomew Hussey. Perhaps he was a priest and the owner of the Missal who lived through the troubled times of the reigns of Edward VI and Elizabeth I. The words poignantly express the loss and sorrow of a people who had something beloved and beautiful torn from them:[24]

> I pray God I may live to see the Mass to be said in England again,
> for that to see it would glad my heart so much more than anything
> in this world.

CHAPTER 9

The Religious Situation in 1580

N OW, BEFORE we follow the Jesuits on their mission, it would be well to describe the religious condition of the people to whom they were sent.[1] In 1580, Elizabeth was in the twenty-second year of her reign. A generation had been born and grown to adulthood since she had altered the religion of the land.

Elizabeth's Coming to the Throne

Elizabeth acceded to the throne in 1558 at the age of twenty-five. By the time of her death in 1603, after a long reign of nearly forty-five years, she had become as much a legend as her father, Henry VIII, had become after his reign of thirty-eight years.

Of all the grave problems that had to be faced at the beginning of Elizabeth's reign, the most pressing was that of religion. Ordinary folk must have been in a confused religious state, uncertain as to what they were supposed to adhere to or believe. The Church in England had gone into schism in 1534, had been transformed by Protestantism from 1547, taken back to Catholicism in 1553, and was now, only five years later, on the verge of another reformation.

When Elizabeth was one year old, the breach with Rome took place under Henry VIII when he had himself declared "supreme head of the Church of England" (1534). Then followed the dissolution of the lesser and greater monasteries (1536 and 1539). Henry VIII's vacillations had been baffling, but he was reputed at one time to have been alarmed at the Lutheran views of his last queen, Katherine Parr, who outlived him. Henry himself heard two or three Masses daily, perhaps the abbreviated "hunting Masses" (which suggests superstition or pure habit, rather than true devotion). He did not embrace Protestantism, but his state of belief was fairly confused and very much compromised by his series of "wives" when he died in 1547, leaving money for thousands of Masses to be said for the repose of his soul.

His successor to the throne was his son by his third queen, Jane Seymour. Edward VI reigned from 1547–53. They were six years of pronounced Protestantism. A new English prayer-book of Protestant worship was introduced and promulgated in 1549: *The Book of Common Prayer, and administration of the Sacraments, and other Rites and Ceremonies in the Church of England.* An Act was passed permitting the clergy to marry.

Edward was followed by Mary Tudor, Henry's daughter by Queen Catherine of Aragon. A devout Catholic like her mother, Queen Mary married Philip II of Spain in 1554, who was, therefore, for four years, the king consort of England. In her brief reign (1553–58), Mary did everything possible to restore the Catholic Church and religion in England, and repress Protestantism. Protestant bishops, Latimer, Ridley, and Cranmer, were among those burnt at the stake.

Mary was succeeded by her half-sister, Elizabeth, Henry's daughter by his second queen, Anne Boleyn.

"What is to come now?" the people wondered, as Elizabeth acceded to the throne of England in November 1558.

Elizabeth's Religious Views

Much would depend on the religious outlook of the queen herself, but no one then or since has been able to give a clear account of its nature. Experience had taught her to move cautiously and not to reveal her full mind. This was to prove one of her notable characteristics which, at times, drove her councilors to distraction. She might have taken as her motto her father's saying: "If I thought that my cap knew my counsel, I would cast it into the fire and burn it." Probably she had no fixed religious position herself—so, unable to choose properly between Catholic and Protestant, she avoided the two "extremes" of Catholics who would not conform to her spiritual supremacy, and Puritans who were *too* Protestant for her liking. In 1560, she said, "in the Sacrament of the Altar, some think one thing, some another; whose judgment is best God knows."[2]

Katherine Parr, Henry's last queen, made a home for his three children, Mary, Elizabeth, and Edward, and her leaning towards Protestantism influenced Elizabeth and Edward.

Mary at twenty-seven years of age proved immune to her father's latest consort, but Elizabeth at ten and Edward at six were more susceptible. Not that this meant withdrawal from Mass; King Henry would never have tolerated that. The tutors appointed for Edward and Elizabeth were Cambridge humanists, not outright rejecters of Catholic faith and outlook.

The Princess Elizabeth conformed with reluctance during the last years of Mary's reign, and when she herself was made queen she continued, initially, to have Mass in her own chapel. To quiet apprehensions upon her accession, Elizabeth immediately issued a decree forbidding any alteration to the Latin liturgy until Parliament met after her coronation. The coronation took place on January 16, 1559. In the meantime Elizabeth attended Mass, merely requiring the discontinuance of the Elevation of the Sacred Host. Cardinal Reginald Pole, Archbishop of Canterbury, having died on the same day as Queen Mary, the next senior prelate was Nicholas Heath, Archbishop of York. He declined to accept this condition regarding the Elevation, and would not crown Elizabeth for this and for a second reason that the *Litany of the Saints* was to be sung in English. He also refused to consecrate Matthew Parker as the new Archbishop of Canterbury to succeed Cardinal Pole. In the end, the queen got her way: Parker, ordained a priest in 1527, was consecrated to Canterbury in December 1559 in the Edwardian rite. (But Pope Paul IV in 1555 had already ruled the Edwardian ceremony invalid on account of a major defect in its consecration formula—a judgment definitively confirmed by Pope Leo XIII in *Apostolicae Curae*, 1896. In consequence, Parker remained a priest and was never validly consecrated a bishop. Parker was subsequently chosen to consecrate all the other Anglican bishops. Since he could not transmit Episcopal Orders to anyone else, Holy Orders was lost to the Church of England which, nevertheless, still held to an Episcopal form of government. Informed Catholics understood this at the time.)

The Mass of Christmas 1558 was celebrated for the queen in the Chapel Royal by Bishop Owen Oglethorpe of Carlisle. He ignored the queen's note sent to the sacristy asking him not to elevate the Host. At the Elevation, the queen withdrew.

Nonetheless, a few weeks later, Oglethorpe was the only bishop who could be prevailed upon to crown Elizabeth—which he did, and thereafter regretted up till his death under house arrest on December 31, 1559.

By mid-1559, Elizabeth and Parliament had restored the Protestant *Book of Common Prayer;* yet Elizabeth certainly liked Catholic ceremonial and usages. Thus she had lighted candles on the altar, and her life-long aversion to a married clergy was a vestige of Catholic thinking.

The Act of Supremacy, 1559

The first Parliament of the new reign met on January 25, 1559, and the main business put before it was a bill on the Supremacy (headship of the Church in England). The complicated proceedings resulted in the 1559 Act of Supremacy and the subsequent Act of Uniformity. The nine bishops present in the House of Lords voted against the Supremacy. The Clergy Convocation had already declared in favor of Catholic doctrine on the Eucharist, and Papal primacy, and against interference by Parliament in matters of faith and Church discipline. When the time came, the bishops refused to take the Oath of supremacy. Among the resisters was the venerable Bishop Cuthbert Tunstall of Durham,[3] who had been a friend of St. Thomas More. One by one, from May to November 1559, fifteen of the sixteen bishops were deprived of their sees. One was an invalid; one was sick and died before the year closed; Bishop Goldwell went to the European Continent; the rest were constrained or imprisoned, six of them in the Tower of London.[4] The only one not deprived was Bishop Anthony Kitchin of Llandaff, a bishop since Henry VIII's time. He was the sole Catholic bishop to conform under Elizabeth, and remained in office until his death in 1566.

At Elizabeth's accession, six sees were vacant, including the archbishopric of Canterbury. Four bishops died during the first year of her reign. These ten sees were all filled by conformists.

The title "supreme head of the Church of England" was not to Elizabeth's liking; it was changed to "only supreme governor," but practically there was no difference: it applied "as well in all spiritual or ecclesiastical things or causes as temporal." The queen's purpose may have been to make the supremacy more acceptable to Catholics, as "Governor" implied governance from outside the ecclesiastical body and carried no suggestion of sacerdotal power. Radical Protestants objected to the new title as being the old one in another guise. Both titles implied too much State control of religion, and some thought it incongruous for a woman to exercise such authority.

The Act repealed the heresy laws enacted under Mary, revived those enacted under Henry VIII, and repudiated the claim of any "foreign prince, person, prelate, state or potentate, spiritual or temporal" to exercise any power in England. Without specifically mentioning the pope, this meant rejection of Papal primacy. The next clause vested all power over the national Church in the crown. Catholics thought it worse than comical that Protestants, who objected to the pope's authority over the Church, had simply substituted it with that of a laywoman and were even glad to swear on the Gospels to the profession of this novel doctrine. Most Protestants were happy to do so, but some Puritans openly said they did not acknowledge the queen's religious authority. Some Catholics called it Elizabeth's "female papacy."[5]

The Act penalized all who defended any authority other than that of the queen. For the first offense, the penalty was loss of goods; if these were worth less than £20, a year's imprisonment was imposed. A second offense meant the penalties of *praemunire*—loss of all property and imprisonment for life. (*Praemunire* was the name given to 14th-century statutes that forbade referring to Papal courts matters belonging to the king's courts.) A third offense would be high treason, punishable by death.

Two clauses attempted to circumscribe the nature of heresy: Parliament was now arrogating to itself powers that had formerly been ecclesiastical. Clause 20 states that heresies would be:

> only such as heretofore have been determined, ordered or adjudged to be heresy by the authority of the canonical Scriptures, or by the first four General Councils, or any of them, or by any other General Council wherein the same was declared heresy by the express and plain words of the said canonical Scriptures, or *such as hereafter by the high court of Parliament* of this realm, with the assent of the clergy in their Convocation . . .

The "first four General Councils" recognized by this Act were:

- Nicaea, held in A.D. 325, defining the divinity of Jesus Christ, and promulgating the Nicene Creed.

- Constantinople, 381, defining the divinity of the Holy Spirit, and promulgating the Nicene Creed anew with additions (the version used by Catholics and Anglicans today).
- Ephesus, 431, defining that the Virgin Mary is truly and rightly called "Mother of God."
- Chalcedon, 451, defining that Jesus Christ is one divine Person, with two natures, divine and human.

Significantly, this truncated list did not include the Second Council of Nicaea, A.D. 787, which condemned the heresy of Iconoclasm ("image-smashing"), and declared that images of Our Savior, the Blessed Virgin, the angels and saints—along with relics of saints—could be set up and given honor or veneration, without the worship due to God alone. That omission distinctly favored Protestant iconoclasts, while Anglican believers in sacred art and veneration of Saints had to fight for such things.

The Oath of Supremacy

The Oath of Supremacy was used to apply and enforce the Act of Supremacy. All holders of ecclesiastical and civil office—bishops, priests, judges, mayors, etc.,—and those taking a university degree, were required to take an oath recognizing the queen's spiritual and temporal supremacy.

The oath read:

> I, _____ , do utterly testify and declare in my conscience that the Queen's highness is the only supreme governor of this realm and of all other her highness' dominions and countries, as well in all spiritual or ecclesiastical things or causes as temporal, and that no foreign prince, person, prelate, state or potentate has or ought to have any jurisdiction, power, superiority, pre-eminence or authority, ecclesiastical or spiritual, within this realm; and therefore I do utterly renounce and forsake all foreign jurisdictions, powers, superiorities and authorities . . . so help me God, and by the contents of this book [the Gospels].

Refusal to take the oath brought deprivation of office and benefice. This oath, therefore, marks the beginning of the exclusion of Catholics (and non-conforming Protestants) from public life. But in Tudor times, there was a considerable time-lag between the making of an Act and its enforcement. The administrative machinery did not exist. Thus a number of Catholic magistrates retained office, though this was also, in part, due to the difficulty of finding replacements. Moreover, the oath does not seem to have been systematically applied. We saw already how, one time at Oxford, Robert Persons managed to escape pronouncing the oath before receiving a degree.[6]

Peers were exempted from oath-taking, and some Catholic nobles, though excluded from the Council, were employed by the queen. A good example is Viscount Montague of Cowdray (Anthony Browne). Although he voted against the Acts of Supremacy and Uniformity and made speeches against these and other Protestant measures in the House of Lords, the queen made use of his services until his death in 1591, a year after he had entertained her for a week at Cowdray. Another instance is Richard Shelly, Esquire, of Lewes, Sussex, who had lost a position on the Commission of the Peace through his Catholic religion. He was reinstated in 1578 without conforming—by order of the queen's Council, on account of his faithful service to Her Majesty![7] These examples point to the danger of making generalizations about the position of Catholics under Elizabeth. Often Catholics managed to hold on to office because the numerous "Church Papists"[8] around them (Catholics in heart who went grudgingly to Protestant church) were in complete sympathy with them and did not proceed against them or denounce them. This was true especially in the Inns of Court, and Oxford University, where Catholic lawyers and students continued to operate, much to the frustration of the Council. Other factors, too, impeded the enforcement of national religious uniformity. Local and familial ties could over-ride any notion of loyalty to the queen that included prosecuting friends and neighbors for religion. In strongly Catholic areas, there were simply not enough Protestants to fill the local offices, and some Catholics were needed in office if the government was to have the good-will and cooperation of subjects.[9]

The enforcement of the oath of supremacy seems to have been largely confined to the parish clergy and, even so, was demanded rather haphazardly. "This desire to impose conformity on office holders was not completely successful. Justices of the Peace could, and did, avoid taking the oath."[10] Ten years after the first census of the religious convictions of the Justices of the Peace, the queen's Council still felt it was necessary to deal with justices who absented themselves from church service.[11] Even then, when justices were summoned in a few counties to take the oath, many simply absented themselves.

The Act and Oath of Supremacy Extended, 1563

In 1563, Parliament extended the application of the Act of Supremacy and made its penalties more severe.

Refusal to take the oath no longer brought simple deprivation of office, but loss of goods and life imprisonment. A second refusal was reckoned high treason and entailed the death penalty. This brought more pressure to bear on men of position, and some conformed to save their family and property. Still, any person of the degree of baron or higher was not bound to take the oath.

Not only were ecclesiastics and civil office holders to take the oath but school-masters, private teachers, and members of the House of Commons. As a result, a few years later the Parliament of 1566 would be the first with no Catholics in the Commons. The queen was evidently reluctant to accept this new law, but Protestant opinion in the House of Commons was too strong for her. She got round it by giving instructions through Archbishop Matthew Parker of Canterbury that the oath was not to be proffered a second time without his written approbation.

The Act of Uniformity

The Act of Uniformity (1559) that followed on the Act of Supremacy bore more hardly on Catholics. Its full title was: "An Act for the Uniformity of common prayer and divine service in the church, and the administration of the sacraments." The second Edwardian *Book of Common Prayer* (1552) was adopted, with small but significant changes.

The penal clauses of the Act as these directly affected Catholics:

1. "Any parson, vicar or other whatsoever minister" who "refused to use the said common prayers or to minister the sacraments," for the first offense lost his emoluments·[income] for a year and was imprisoned for six months. For the second offense the term of imprisonment was one year with loss of the benefice. A third offense meant life imprisonment. If not beneficed, he was imprisoned for one year for his first offense, and for life for a second. (The word "priest" was not used in the two Acts.)

2. Anyone who spoke "in derogation, depraving or despising the said book," or who compelled any minister to act contrary to the *Book of Common Prayer*, or who interrupted the prescribed services had to pay a fine of 100 marks for a first offense, 400 for a second, and for a third, loss of goods and life imprisonment. (A mark was two-thirds of a pound, or 13 shillings and 4 pence.)

3. The part of the Act enjoining attendance at Common Prayer said:

> All and every person and persons inhabiting within this realm . . . shall diligently and faithfully, having no lawful or reasonable excuse to be absent, endeavor themselves to resort to their parish church or chapel . . . or . . . to some usual place where Common Prayer and such service of God shall be used . . . upon every Sunday and other days ordained . . . upon pain of punishment by the censures of the church, and also upon pain that every person so offending shall forfeit for every such offense twelve pence, to be levied by the churchwardens of the parish where such offense shall be done.

Our different economy makes it hard to give modern equivalents for these fines, but it is informative to know that in Elizabethan times a skilled carpenter could earn 10 pence a day; so a 12 pence fine (a shilling) was a day's wage for some people, and more than that for many others; and the fine had to be paid for each adult in a family.[12]

In addition, the Act revived the heavy penalties for attending Mass: six months imprisonment for a first offense, twelve months for a second, life imprisonment for a third.[13]

The Book of Common Prayer

King Edward's *Book of Common Prayer* of 1549 provided a rite of Mass in English which was a conservative revision of the Sarum rite in its essential structure, and in its teaching on the Real Presence and the Sacrifice of the Mass. The Eucharistic Rite was entitled, "The Supper of the Lord and the Holy Communion, commonly called the Mass." The priest wore the traditional vestments, and held, in turn, the bread, and chalice of wine, in his hands as he consecrated each with the Lord's words from the Last Supper. There were the commemoration of the Saints, prayers for the dead, and clear references throughout to "altar" and "priest." Two Protestant stipulations, however, were that the Elevation of the

consecrated Host was forbidden, and Communion was to be given in
both kinds, bread and wine, instead of following the then Catholic usage
of the species of bread alone.

The Prayer-Book also introduced people to a complete set of rituals in English for Baptism, Confirmation, visitation of the sick, matins
(morning prayer), evensong (vespers), funerals, and so on.

Three years later, that book was drastically revised in a Protestant
direction to become the second Edwardian *Book of Common Prayer* in
1552, which eradicated and supplanted the Mass with a Communion
service, abolished Eucharistic vestments and the sign of the cross, and
confused the unlearned with deliberately ambiguous wording. One
definitive change unacceptable to Catholics was the final rubric added to
the Communion service (later known as the "Black Rubric")—a doctrinal
statement rather than a rubric—stating that kneeling for Communion
did not in any way imply belief in the Real Presence, let alone worship of
the sacramental elements.[14]

There was, however, barely time for this book to be distributed and
used before Queen Mary promptly banned it upon her accession to the
throne in 1553.

It made a come-back, however, when Elizabeth's Parliament in
1559 restored this second version, with small modifications—some in a
Catholic direction, and others ambiguous or ambivalent. But the over-
whelmingly Protestant character of the book was retained. The queen
would have preferred the first Edwardian *Book of Common Prayer* (1549)
as this was much less objectionable to Catholics, but she gave way to the
strongly expressed Protestant feelings of the House of Commons.

As an example of ambivalence: Communion was in both kinds, as
before, but its words became:

> The body (blood) of our Lord Jesus Christ, which was given (shed)
> for thee, preserve thy body and soul unto everlasting life; and take
> and eat this in remembrance that Christ died for thee; and feed on
> him in thine heart by faith, with thanksgiving (drink this in remem-
> brance that Christ's blood was shed for thee, and be thankful).

This prayer combines, in turn, the two versions of the words used
for administration of Communion from the previous two prayer-books
of 1549 and 1552. We note the ambivalence: the first half is a Catholic

wording (1549), based on the Real Presence; the second half is Protestant (1552), based on remembrance only.

On the other hand, in a Catholic direction, a rubric was added to Morning Prayer prescribing the use of traditional vestments. The wording of the *Litany* was revised, the chief change being the omission of the words added in 1552: "from the tyranny of the Bishop of Rome and all his detestable enormities . . . Good Lord, deliver us." The "Black Rubric" was abolished—and this omission was a cherished grievance of the Puritans. These were probably instances of how the queen as supreme governor exercised her prerogative; she may have been hoping that in this way the most recent *Book of Common Prayer* would be less offensive to Catholics.

The touchstone defect for the fervent Catholic was the abolition of Holy Mass, replaced with a Communion service: "The order for the Administration of the Lord's Supper or holy Communion."

For a Catholic, the essence of the Mass is in the priest's consecration of the bread and wine—by which they become the Body and Blood of Christ, whose Sacrifice is thus made present upon the altar, from which the priest receives Communion; which Sacrifice the laity participate in by co-offering the Sacred Victim and receiving Holy Communion in their turn when they so desire and are rightly disposed. Recognition of the Real Presence and the sacrificing priesthood is shown in different ways by the vestments, the gestures and the words of the prayers.

However, even with the "Black Rubric" gone, the Eucharistic rite was still unacceptable to Catholics, for the Act of Uniformity adopted the Prayer-Book of 1552, which went much further in a Protestant direction than the 1549 Book: altars became tables standing "in the body of the church or in the chancel"; ordinary bread was allowed (but not obligatory) and was to be given in the hands (not onto the tongue, as Catholics did); at the directive for the administration of Communion the term "Sacrament of the Body of Christ" was changed to "bread"; in the Eucharistic prayers, the commemoration of Our Lady and the saints and martyrs was omitted, and also the prayers for the dead; the whole prayer of offering was omitted at the Consecration and placed as an option after all receive Holy Communion (hence no sense of offering the Sacrifice of the Mass); the Lord's Prayer came after Communion (to cancel any link between "our daily bread" and the Sacrament of the Eucharist).

These and other changes to the prayers, actions, and whole shape of
the service made it much less "Catholic" in presentation, and deprived
it of any sense of the Real Presence. Since the Communion service soon
became a rite celebrated only four times a year, Sunday Mass was really
being replaced by the new Morning Prayer, read by a clergyman vested
in a surplice and standing at a desk. Thus "Church Papists" (Catholics
attending the Established church) were deprived of even a semblance of
Sunday Mass, and their children could not have known what the Mass
meant or even looked like in the Catholic Church.

It took some time for knowledge of the Act to reach the remoter
villages. For a longish period there must have been confusion and even
bewilderment among priests and people before the new order could get
stabilized. There was, too, the practical problem of supplying copies of
the *Book of Common Prayer*, and the two volumes of *Homilies* (1547
and 1563) provided for the clergy to read out on Sundays and feast-days.
Except for a few licensed to preach their own sermons, the clergy were
regarded as too uneducated to prepare their own. The role of the *Homilies*
is often overlooked; these prescribed texts, heard year in and year out,
taught that the pope's Church is the filthy harlot foretold in *Revelations*
12, that any reverence to images breeds idolatry, and that the whole world
has been drowned in idolatry these last 800 years or more. The *Homilies*
regularly presented the popes as tyrants, caricatured Catholic beliefs, and
openly attacked specific Catholic doctrines and Sacraments as incompatible with Christianity.[15]

Moreover, the "Royal Injunctions" of 1559 required all clergy to
declare in their sermons, four times a year, that "all usurped and foreign
power" (in other words, the Papacy) has no warrant in the Word of God,
and that the queen alone is the authority between Englishmen and their
God. The clergy were likewise required to teach that the cult of the Saints,
reverence for their relics, and belief in miracles wrought by their intercession is "superstition and hypocrisy." Once a month, when exhorting
to works of faith, clergy were to instruct the people that pilgrimages and
the use of Rosary beads are detested and abhorred by Almighty God. The
Royal Injunctions mandated the destruction of all shrines and images—
even those in private possession—and that all Catholic vestments and
ritual books were to be sought out and destroyed.[16] Still, it was a common lament of the new Protestant bishops in the years to come that the

Injunctions were being evaded. Their ecclesiastical visitations to parishes sought to ensure enforcement.[17]

The Protestant government mandated all of this, but Protestants themselves were far from being all of one mind on Church affairs. There were those who accepted the Edwardian settlement, though they would have liked some changes, especially as to vestments. There were others, more extreme or radical, who were highly critical of that settlement and would have liked a drastic revision of the *Book of Common Prayer*. These included ministers and others who had returned from exile spent in Reformist centers such as Frankfurt, Zurich, and Geneva. (These "Radical Protestants" became known as "Puritans." For convenience, we will use both terms interchangeably.) The Radical Protestants wanted a new prayer-book altogether, on the lines of the Geneva Service-book in which there was no trace of Catholic liturgy. In 1572 they went so far as to describe the *Book of Common Prayer* as "an unperfect book; culled and picked out of that Popish dunghill, the Mass book, full of abominations."[18] Their worship was so bare they objected to such things as wedding-rings in the celebration of marriage, and the sign of the cross at Baptism.

The Queen's Strategy

The queen was unshakably resolved to have no more changes made in the prescribed services. She was aware that in its existing form the Prayer-Book was not wholly unacceptable to lukewarm Catholics, and she wanted things to remain that way. In her plan, the old forms that met the eye were to be altered as little as possible: the vestments were to remain, and the hierarchical constitution, and, if possible, the same pastors. No doctrinal changes were to be made; only those portions of the old liturgy were to be dropped—adoration of the Blessed Sacrament, and the veneration of images and saints—which were most offensive to the new opinions.

The foreign Protestants were furious; they declared emphatically to their English followers that they could not possibly take any ministerial part in a Church thus constituted. The question of wearing vestments was declared a fundamental one.[19] But when it was seen that the queen and government were firm in mandating them, the same counselors advised their friends to dissimulate: "Use those habits either in preaching, or in the administration of the Lord's supper, provided however you persist in speaking and teaching against the use of them."[20] The great fear of the Puritans was that they would be excluded from all share in the new Establishment. They gladly accepted the commission to govern a Church, the constitution of which they thought wrong, in hopes of being able to conform it, in time, to their notions of right. "The Radicals deceived themselves in thinking that the [English] populace was anxious to imitate "the best reformed Churches of Europe." The fact was that most of them became apathetic as a result of being pushed this way and that during the past twenty years in the observance of religion. It was to take many years for Radical Protestantism and, later, Puritanism, to become dominant."[21]

Catholics objected not so much to anything contained in the *Common Prayer* as to its omissions: the Sacrifice of the Mass, certain other Sacraments, the intercession of the Blessed Virgin and the saints, prayers for the dead, naming of the pope.[22] The one thing for which they rejected communion with the Establishment was its "lack of unity," its schism from the rest of Christendom, and its want of homogeneity in itself, "some being therein Protestants, some Puritans, and some of the Family of Love."[23] Yet this lack of unity—of external unity with the rest of Christendom, and of internal unity with itself was the one sacrifice which Elizabeth was determined to make, in order to secure the political unity of the country, and the unity of the State with the Church.

Parliament had gone further than the queen desired. Francis Bacon famously said of her, in a remark often mistakenly attributed to the queen herself, that, "her Majesty (not liking to make windows into men's hearts and secret thoughts, except the abundance of them did overflow into overt and express acts or affirmations), tempered her law so, as it restraineth only manifest disobedience."[24] Even after the Papal Bull of excommunication in 1570, she declared through the Lord Keeper publicly in the Star-Chamber on June 15, 1570:

> That the queen would not have any of their consciences unneces-
> sarily sifted, to know what affection they had to the old religion. . . .
> Her Majesty would have all her loving subjects to understand that
> as long as they shall openly continue in the observation of her laws
> and shall not willfully and manifestly break them by their open acts,
> Her Majesty's meaning is not to have any of them molested by any
> inquisition or examination of their consciences in causes of religion

... [she] being very loath to be provoked by the overmuch boldness and willfulness of her subjects to alter her natural clemency into a princely severity.[25]

This sounds all very reasonable and liberal, except that within the same message, we learn that the laws to be observed regard going to Protestant church!

For although certain persons have been lately convented [summoned] before her Majesty's Council upon just causes, and that some of them have been treated withal upon some matter of religion; yet the cause thereof hath grown merely of themselves [it is all their own fault]; in that they have first manifestly broken the laws established for religion, in not coming at all to the church, to common prayer, and divine service . . .[26]

In other words, Catholics shall be left free in conscience—provided they behave as Protestants!

The protestation of not making "examination of their consciences" was a farce: Campion and others were questioned as to their *thoughts* on passages in certain Catholic writers, their *private views* on the Bull of Pius V, and their future *intentions* in hypothetical scenarios (e.g., invasion by a foreign Catholic power).

Despite this, the queen avoided even more extreme measures for the general public. For instance, she successfully resisted by her veto several attempts by Parliament to enforce the reception of Communion on top of mere attendance at church.

She was swimming against the tide of religious opinion; each Church, Catholic or Protestant, believed itself to be the only rightful Christian Church and wished its particular tenets and forms of worship to be imposed on the whole nation. The idea of toleration was alien to the times and, indeed, for long afterwards. Men felt so deeply and even fiercely about religion that they could not conceive how those professing different creeds could live at peace together. The obvious remedy nowadays for this discord would be toleration for all; but in 1558 such a thought was almost impossible. The unity of religion in a country was reckoned to be a State necessity; there was no concept of a pluralist society.

In Elizabeth's judgment, where opinions were much divided, it was not deemed possible to favor any extreme and exclusive sect, but only to enforce moderation upon all; and this, not by allowing all to differ, but by obliging them all to meet on a common and, as it were, neutral ground. A new formula might satisfy both Catholics and Puritans, by suppressing all that either considered to be blasphemy, and by including only the "fundamentals" on which both were agreed.

At the same time, the queen's attitude was not a precocious exercise in toleration; the most likely explanation is that she herself had no deep religious convictions. She had been an Anglican under her father Henry, a Protestant under her half-brother Edward, and, externally at least, a Catholic under her half-sister Mary. But she was neither a prig like her brother nor a militant like her sister. "A plague on both your houses!" may have expressed her sentiment.

Moreover, not much psychological equilibrium could be expected from Henry VIII's daughter, who was born a princess, but was later declared illegitimate, and three years after her birth, lost her mother, Anne Boleyn, put to death by order of her father.

The Enforcement upon the Clergy

All but one of the Catholic bishops, as said, refused to take the oath of supremacy, and were deprived of their sees before the end of 1559. The full rigors of the law were not applied to them; none of them was executed. Protestant bishops were substituted for them.

In May 1559, a royal commission was issued to a company, partly lay, partly clerical, and all Puritan, to tender the oath of supremacy to the rest of the clergy.[27] They were ordered to proceed with such moderation, as not to exasperate the Catholics, but to bring them gradually, by fair means, to a sense of their duty.[28] The first commission was too zealous; and in October the queen had to modify it, substituting laymen for several of the clergymen.[29] Yet even their moderation had such serious effects that, in December, the queen had to write to the commissioners in both provinces to suspend their proceedings, and only to decide matters already begun.[30] The effect of these arrangements was that, of the multitudes of clergymen who refused to subscribe, not many were immediately deprived; some had three years given them for consideration, and others seem to have been connived at.

The commissioners were not only to see that the clergy were conforming, but to complete the work begun under Edward VI of removing all visible signs of the Catholic religion such as Missals, altars, crucifixes, statues, tabernacles, shrines, reliquaries, and so on.

Before he was removed from his see on September 28, Bishop Tunstall of Durham wrote to Sir William Cecil (Lord Burghley), the Secretary of State:

> If the same visitation shall proceed to such end in my diocese of Durham, as I do plainly see to be set forth here in London, as pulling down of altars, defacing of churches by taking away of the cruci- fixes, I cannot in my conscience consent to it, being pastor there, because I cannot myself agree to be a Sacramentary [denier of the Real Presence] nor to have any new doctrine taught in my diocese.[31]

This company visited the four sees of the province of York in August and September 1559. At the end of their papers, there is an abstract of the numbers of rectors, vicars, and curates who refused to attend the visitation when summoned: 158 for York diocese, 85 for Chester, 36 for Durham, 35 for Carlisle; total: 314 (from 968 parishes). Probably the visi- tation was never completed, but broken off by the queen's letters. This shows, however, that in York province a third of the clergy at least either refused to swear, or would have refused if they had been pressed. In the northern province, the number of priests deprived of their parish upon appearing before the visitors and openly refusing to conform, was 90.[32] Many others, therefore, were tolerated, and perhaps retained their livings for some years yet.

In the province of Canterbury, we hear of the dean and canons of Winchester Cathedral, the warden and fellows of the College, and the master of St. Cross, all refusing the oath.[33] For the whole province, the visitors returned the totals of 49 non-subscribers and 786 conformists,[34] significantly omitting the absentees. Archbishop Parker of Canterbury had orders "not to push anyone to extremities on account of his oath."[35]

However, with the expirations of the three years of grace, and fresh commissions sitting from time to time, the clergy, at first tolerated, were gradually removed, and their places filled up with men who were required to acknowledge the queen as supreme governor of the Church of England upon earth. No great difficulty was raised about other points of doctrine, provided they were willing to obey the laws of the realm.[36] Thus it came to pass that most of the clergy were, as one Puritan called them, "popish priests, consecrated to perform Mass; and the far greater part of the remainder are most ignorant persons,"[37] appointed to recite the prayers, but not allowed to preach.

The priests who refused or avoided the oath had fewer scruples about the *Common Prayer*. When it was first introduced under King Edward, some priests said the Latin Mass, some the English Lord's Supper and Communion; some both; some joined half of one to half of the other.

Fr. Persons summarized the situation:

> And this mingle-mangle did every man make at his pleasure, as he thought it would be most grateful [gratifying] to the people. But that which was of more importance and impiety, some did consecrate bread and wine, others did not, but would tell the people beforehand plainly that they would not consecrate, but restore them the bread and wine back again as they received it from them, only adding to it the Church-benediction. And after consecration, some did hold up the Host to be adored after the old fashion, and some did not. And of those that were present, some did kneel down and adore, others did shut their eyes, others turned their faces aside, others ran out of Church blaspheming, and crying: Idolatry![38]

Under Elizabeth this state of things lasted with some modification. Before the service on Sunday, the priests would celebrate Mass in their own houses, and the Catholics would receive Holy Communion there, while at church the Protestants received the Protestant communion (bread and wine, not the Body and Blood of Christ). Or the priest would take to church the Hosts he had consecrated at home, to give to his Catholic parishioners at the altar-rails, while he gave to Protestants the wafers of bread used in the *Common Prayer* service. Thus the Sacrament of two hostile religious bodies was distributed by the same hands, at the same time, at the same altar-rails, to the discordant and divided flock.[39] State Papers mention instances of incumbent priests (conforming to the law and following the *Book of Common Prayer*) saying Mass in their houses long after 1559. Even in 1592 we find several clergymen in one county giving large sums to a pursuivant (an agent to catch Catholics) not to accuse them of popery. In May 1581, while Persons and Campion were active in England, one parson, William Shepherd, of Haydon, county Essex, was denounced to the Privy Council for several sermons favoring Catholic doctrine and commending the Jesuits.[40]

It is difficult to say nation-wide how many resisted and how many conformed. Fr. Philip Hughes judges that, even taking an optimistic view, namely, that the clergy conformed without necessarily taking an explicit oath, "no less than three-fourths of these priests now abandoned both the Mass and the pope."[41] E.E. Reynolds estimates, "Probably up to eighty percent of the clergy conformed."[42] Fr. Pollen says:

> It is . . . very difficult to speak about them with satisfactory precision, so very defective are the registers and other records on which we have to rely. We cannot, for instance, tell how many priests there then were in England, nor how many actually subscribed to the Oath of Supremacy. Without security on these two fundamental points, all our calculations must needs be left somewhat indefinite. Speaking, therefore, with intentional vagueness, we may estimate the total of the clergy in 1559 at about 8,000, and of these the great majority, roughly about three-quarters—that is, some 6,000—accepted the changes, with the outward man at least.[43]

Publicly they performed Protestant services in church, but privately they could still celebrate Mass and other Catholic rituals. Yet, over the years, a number of these time-servers, seeing that things were not improving, left and reverted to being unswerving Catholic priests.[44]

William Wizeman S.J. says, "nearly half of the Marian clergy of London resigned or were deprived at the beginning of Elizabeth's reign, and numerous canons, deans, archdeacons and diocesan chancellors throughout England as well."[45]

Nation-wide, the usual estimate is that in the first six years of Elizabeth's reign, 200–300 priests were deprived of their parishes.[46]

Over a greater period, roughly 2,000 priests refused to conform. What happened to them? Some were removed from their post, some just retired early or took on a lay job. Others, maybe two or thee hundred, fled abroad. Some took up residence in the houses of Catholic gentry as chaplains or tutors or stewards; some became fugitives, always on the move, saying Mass in secret and bringing the Sacraments to the faithful. Much depended on the presence locally of a lord of the manor, or one of the landed gentry who remained a convinced Catholic. He could shelter the priest and allow neighbors to come to his house for Mass. The country gentry were in fact the key to Catholic survival.

One cannot over-estimate the work of those priests who refused to conform. They were comparatively few in numbers but dauntless in their determination to preserve at least a remnant of the Church. Without their labors, Catholicism would have simply died out in England. Their achievement has been over-shadowed by the missionary work of the seminary priests, but these latter did not begin to enter the country until 1575—sixteen years after the Act of Uniformity was passed.

Many Catholics of means chose to emigrate, but not everyone easily obtained permission to leave. The laws of the day allowed only noblemen and merchants to travel abroad freely as a matter of course. Clergy and religious (friars, monks, and nuns) were free to leave England, and many did.

English Protestants who had fled abroad under Mary returned, and some Protestants oppressed in Holland now migrated to England.

The Administration of the Sacraments

Within the Catholic Church, the seven Sacraments instituted by Jesus Christ are by His ordinance a necessary means of salvation and an abundant source of divine grace. "The whole liturgical life of the Church revolves around the Eucharistic sacrifice and the Sacraments." "The seven Sacraments touch all the stages and all the important moments of Christian life: they give birth and increase, healing and mission to the Christian's life of faith." "Celebrated worthily in faith, the Sacraments confer the grace that they signify. They are *efficacious* because in them Christ Himself is at work: it is He who baptizes, He who acts in His Sacraments in order to communicate the grace that each Sacrament signifies."[47] Given this importance and role of the Sacraments, it was crucial for Catholics to have priests and bishops to guarantee their administration.

Under the Elizabethan persecution, the situation for the seven Sacraments stood thus:

- Baptism and Marriage were celebrated secretly by a priest, or by the laity if no priest was available.
- The Holy Eucharist (Mass and Holy Communion) and Penance (Confession) were celebrated and administered secretly by a priest.

- Since all Catholic bishops were imprisoned or restrained, no candidates received Holy Orders; any new priests had to come from abroad.
- As no bishop was free to bless and consecrate the Holy Oils, or to perform any rite, Confirmation ceased to be administered.
- For the same reason, Extreme Unction (anointing of the gravely ill and dying) continued for a time but ceased when priests ran out of Holy Oil. Priests then had no faculty to bless Holy Oil for the sick or to confirm.

The Thirty-Nine Articles

Assisted by some colleagues, Thomas Cranmer (d. 1556), the heretical Archbishop of Canterbury, drew up 42 Articles of (Anglican) faith, which were issued by Royal Mandate in 1553. The Articles were never enforced, however, on account of the accession of the Catholic Queen Mary in the same year. After Mary's death, the 42 Articles were used as the basis of a set of 39 Articles of Faith approved by the 1563 Convocation meeting under Archbishop Parker. Queen Elizabeth deleted one at the time but allowed it to be restored in 1571—and so the *Thirty-Nine Articles* reached their final form.

Apart from perfectly orthodox declarations concerning the Holy Trinity, the Incarnation, the Passion, Death, and Resurrection of Christ, and so on, *The Thirty-Nine Articles* repudiated certain Catholic teachings and practices, e.g., Purgatory, veneration of images and relics, and invocation of Saints (Article 22), the use of ancient languages in the Liturgy when not understood by the assembly (24), Transubstantiation (28), the Sacrifice of the Mass (31), and the universal authority of the pope (37). They also affirmed that Scripture contains all things necessary for salvation (6); that only two Sacraments—Baptism and the Lord's Supper— were instituted by Christ (25); that both bread and wine should be served to all in the Lord's Supper (30); and that ministers may always marry (32).

In line with the Elizabethan *via media* (middle way), the Articles at other points repudiated some extreme Calvinist and Anabaptist doctrines.

By an Act of Parliament in 1571, bishops and all other clergy were ordered to subscribe to the *Thirty-Nine Articles*. Naturally, this increased the Established Church's separation from the Catholic Church and faith.

"Church Papists"

The effect of Elizabeth's laws was gradually to divide English Catholics into two groups: the temporizers or "schismatics" or "Church Papists" who kept the Faith but frequented the churches; and the open Catholics who braved fines and imprisonment, and refused to go to church: the "recusants." We could add a third group: refugees who went into exile to have religious freedom. Groups of exiles went to the principal university towns of Europe and to the towns of Spanish Netherlands and northern France which were easily accessible from England: Brussels, Antwerp, Mechlin, Douay, Dunkirk, Rouen, Rheims, and Louvain.

There were many variations in the degrees of conformity. Among those who conformed, some just did the minimum to satisfy the law, and strove to save as much of their Catholic practices as possible behind closed doors. Some men conformed and went to the local church, without their wives, to escape the penalties of the law, but ran a Catholic household with chaplains, Catholic tutors for their children's education, family prayers, and Catholic customs, and ensured their daughters married into other recognizably Catholic families.[48]

Some went to church but openly manifested their non-adherence in one way or another: sitting where they could not see the minister; using a Catholic prayer-book; interrupting the service; talking during the sermon; adopting different postures from the congregation's (e.g., sitting while others stood or knelt); ostensibly praying with rosary beads; not joining in the prayers; or paying no attention to the service at all.

Alexandra Walsham remarks:

> Clearly conformity was often a gesture of political loyalty, a congenial solution to the problem of reconciling allegiance to the monarchy with adherence to a religion which had legally been defined as treasonous. But . . . it could also be a form of camouflage for subversive undercover activity, a deceptive cloak behind which dissidents could shelter. Nor should church papistry be seen in terms of surrender, as symbolic of resignation to Protestant hegemony as a

permanent and irreversible state of affairs. Perhaps many conformists thought of themselves as "waiting for the day," quietly biding
their time until the forces of international Catholicism came to their
aid.[49]

The Northern rebellion of 1569 showed that the "Church Papists"
were ready to join the others, and to re-establish the old religion if they
could.

The Rise of the Recusants

In 1562, English Catholics asked the Spanish ambassador to obtain for
them from Rome an authoritative decision on the question of whether
they could attend the services of the government-established Church.
In October 1562, the Roman Inquisition gave a decisive no, quoting the
Lord's words about whoever is ashamed of confessing Him (*Mk.* 8:38)–
but, it seems, this reply never became known to English Catholics.

Also in 1562, Catholic gentlemen asked the Portuguese ambassador[50] to consult the Council of Trent (which closed in 1563) whether
their attendance at Anglican Sunday services could be permitted. A committee was appointed to reply, who firmly but kindly pronounced it quite
inadmissible: "without heinous offense and God's indignation, you may
not be present at such prayers of heretics, or at their sermons."[51] The
decision was confirmed by Pope Pius V in 1566. In 1567 the pope sent
four priests into England, including Fr. Lawrence Vaux, Dr. Sanders, and
Dr. Harding, with episcopal powers to grant faculties for the absolution
of schismatics, but chiefly to declare that "no exception or dispensation can be had for any of the laity" to have their children baptized in
a Protestant church, or themselves to "be present at the communion or
service now used in churches in England."[52]

From this time, large numbers of Catholic laymen began to refuse
to attend Protestant church. As we saw last chapter,[53] this position was
officially recognized in the meeting convened by Persons and Campion
in July 1580. It was: upheld by Cardinal Toletus, June 14, 1581; enforced
in a circular of Dr. Allen, written by the direction of Pope Clement VIII,
in 1592; and finally confirmed by Pope Paul V in a Brief addressed to the
English Catholics in 1606.[54]

Different recusants may or may not have had access to a priest or

Mass, or perhaps only occasionally. While many church-going Catholics were already on the way to losing the Faith in practical terms, the recusants too had to struggle to keep theirs when there was no profession of faith beyond the walls of the home, and possibly no access to Mass or confession or the other Sacraments beyond Baptism and Marriage celebrated by themselves. There were of course many Catholic lay people deeply devoted to their religion. They used the primers and catechisms and other devotional aids that had become so common since the invention of printing. How numerous were these convinced Catholics? Unfortunately statistics do not exist, and any figures would be guesswork. All one can say is that the number of Catholics who were both convinced and fearless was not large enough to influence general opinion. Since the Catholic bishops were all confined, Catholics got no guidance or encouragement save from the handful of priests who chose to go out into the wilderness. There was no concerted leadership. Still, the "problem" of adherence to Catholicism must have been widespread if to overcome it were required laws, fines, informers, spies, raids, arrests, trials, imprisonment, tortures, and gallows.

At the start of Elizabeth's reign, a shilling fine, levied by the church-wardens, was imposed on all persons sixteen or over who failed to attend the Church of England services in their parish. The term "recusant" arose as a consequence of these laws—from the Latin *recusare:* to object or refuse. A "recusant" was someone who refused to attend the obligatory services. (Sometimes the term is applied to those who refused the oath of supremacy, but in documents of the period it meant only non-attendees at church.)

By the Act of Persuasions of 1581, the fine for recusancy rose monstrously, from one shilling per absence, to £20 a month.[55] In addition, to attend Mass now incurred a higher penalty of 100 marks and one year in prison. In the years 1580–81, the queen and Council directed the money raised from wealthy recusants to pay for the horses and lances needed to resist the pope's army in Ireland.

Only recusants formally convicted as such were liable to the financial penalties imposed by law. If the non-attendees were unable to pay, their goods and chattels could be claimed as substitute payment. There are cases of the sale of every bit of furniture, and even of the house itself, over the heads of a family noted for its recusancy. The Arundell family of Lanherne supplies the most notable example of continued payment of the penalty for recusancy. They were still paying in 1680—they were uncommonly rich!

Sometimes wealthy Catholics helped out their poorer brethren. A whole mutual aid system developed for the benefit of impoverished Catholics still at large and the others destitute in prison, where they were expected to pay for their upkeep, or could die of malnutrition. Fr. Persons made it part of his ministry in England to organize such help between Catholics.

In the half-year ending Easter 1575, fines were paid by 150 recusants.[56] What the total number of recusants was at that time is not known, but in 1592 there were at least 3,500, and it is unlikely that the figure was substantially less seventeen years earlier. The only conclusion to be drawn is that whilst convictions for recusancy were to be counted in thousands, the number of recusants who actually paid their fines only ran into hundreds. But those who did pay, paid fairly heavily.

Up to 1581, we do not know how far the weekly shilling fine was exacted, since it was collected by the church-wardens and used (but not always) for local poor relief, and therefore did not come under Exchequer control for record. (Under the laws of 1581, the national government was involved in their collection, and the records are more complete.) The administrative machinery in those times was sparse and the sheer physical problem of supervision defeated the full application of the Act.

There was also the human factor. One Member of Parliament in 1571 complained that the shilling fine was not being exacted. The church-wardens, he said, were "simple, mean men" who "would rather commit perjury than give their neighbors cause for offense." This would particularly apply to small communities where everyone knew everyone else, where there was much inter-marrying, and where all had been brought up together from childhood. The church-warden was one of themselves and, after his year of office, unless re-appointed, would find himself again an ordinary parishioner, so "live and let live" would be the prudent policy. No doubt personal spite was at times active, and perhaps some mild blackmail was extorted, but the general picture was one of neighborly tolerance. Kindly feeling would be found also among the magistrates and landowners, some of whom were Catholics until replacements could be appointed. A magistrate would not be anxious to persecute someone with whom he had gone to school, hunted, and enjoyed social relations. But the intrusion of a Protestant fanatic could upset a whole village, and much bitterness and strife would follow.

As time went on, there were other recusants who were not Catholics, but for one reason or another refrained from attending the services of the Established Church. This fact must be remembered in dealing with the recusancy lists, though, of course, the great majority of recusants were Catholics. Lists of recusants for various counties exist in the *Pipe Rolls* preserved in the Public Record Office, London. Others are to be found in the British Museum, Bodleian Library, and in various local archives.

In March 1587, the £20-a-month fine for non-attendance at the State church, if unable to be exacted, was amended to a possible confiscation of goods and chattels and two-thirds of a recusant's landed property instead.

The recusancy laws were in force from the reign of Elizabeth to that of George III (d. 1820)—though not always enforced with equal vigor. For example, the records of the bishop's Visitation and the High Commission in York indicate that in 1575 the total number of non-communicants was less frequent than ten years earlier, i.e., conformity to the Established Church was increasing. This is attributed to the zeal of Archbishop Edmund Grindal, but when he left York in 1575 there was a resurgence of Catholicism. The York Commission records show a growth from 21 cases in 1578 to 329 in 1582—and this without changing the methods of discovery. Nor was this rise in recusants in the North only. John Aylmer, Bishop of London, after conferring with other Anglican bishops, wrote to Sir Francis Walsingham with a plan to reduce Catholic social standing by fines. The reason given for the proposal was the growth in the number of recusants.[57]

It was in 1592 that the official *Recusant Rolls* were instituted. Lists of Catholics, the numbers in the various parishes, their incomes, etc., had been kept in a more or less systematic way since 1562, but the *Rolls*, which began thirty years later and were kept without a break for over sixty years, gave an account of estates wholly or partly in the hands of the queen by reason of recusancy, and recorded the names of people fined for not attending the service in the parish church. They also included lists of people who heard Mass voluntarily and paid the fine of 100 marks (avoiding imprisonment, it seems)—people of every class:

landed gentry, yeomen, farmers, tradesmen, fishermen, wives, widows, spinsters.[58]

In 1593, "Popish Recusants," as the law now called them, were restricted to particular districts and permanently prohibited to travel more than five miles from home. In that year, a year of severe persecution, the *Recusant Rolls* mention only about 1,400 recusants, roughly one percent of Catholics.[59] More anti-Catholic legislation and penal laws were devised in the century to come: in 1673, Parliament passed the Test Act requiring all civil and military officers to take the Oaths of Allegiance and Supremacy and to make the Declaration against Transubstantiation. From 1692, recusants incurred a double land tax, and from 1699, recusants were barred from purchasing or inheriting land. Penal laws against Catholics (restrictions upon their careers; bars from certain offices and employments, etc.) remained in force in Britain until the Relief Act of 1778, which enabled Catholics to inherit and purchase land, and repealed the Act of William III that rewarded the conviction of priests. The Relief Act of 1791 permitted Catholic clergy to exercise their ministry. The end of all restrictions came in 1829 with the Emancipation Act allowing Catholics to hold office and to sit in Parliament.

Returning to Elizabeth's time, how many Catholics remained defiantly faithful is not known, but it was certainly a dwindling or at least precarious number, and this was a matter of grave concern to those who, in spite of all, clung to the Old Faith.

The situation varied from county to county. In writing to Jesuit General Mercurian one time, Dr. Allen gave an account of the number, location and estimated strength of English recusants. He divided England into Catholic districts: York, Winchester, Newcastle, Durham, Chester, Derby, Lancaster, Richmond, Lincoln, and almost all of northern England. He noted too that Oxford was more responsive to the Ancient Faith than Cambridge, but from the latter University also students came to Douay.[60] Allen's unique position in regularly receiving exiles fresh from all parts of England enabled him to get a full picture of Catholic life in the country. It was in London and Norwich and a few other towns that Protestantism had taken a firm hold. The rest of the country, especially the north and west, was relatively free from such influences. Out of a population of some four million, only half a million lived in the larger towns, including London. The other three-and-a-half million lived in small market towns, villages, and hamlets, and were less accessible to Protestant propaganda, though garbled versions of the Lutheran and other heretical tenets might come from chance travellers.

One recent study shows it took two decades for Elizabeth's Acts to be effectively enforced in Sussex. Another study demonstrates that in Lancashire, Catholics endured persecutions but remained loosely united because the laws bearing on religion were subverted by the gentry.[61]

As mentioned, some Catholics could get to the manor houses of the Catholic gentry where priests risked imprisonment to keep in touch with Catholics of whom they had knowledge. In Devon, Somerset, and Dorset, the practice was adopted of spreading household linen over a hedge, as though for drying or bleaching—as a code that Mass was to be celebrated there that morning. Children used to call it "snow on the hedges."[62] Houses where Mass was said became known as "Massing houses" and there is still the odd road today in England known as "Massing house lane."

Through badgering and fear, isolated Catholics fell away. As the years passed, the outlook became bleaker. The 1563 extension of the Act of Supremacy brought more pressure to bear on men of position, and some conformed for the sake of family and property. The wealthy Catholic laity were being fined into outward submission, or taken off to jails; many secular priests, along with their congregations, were conforming; the old priests were dying and there were none to take their places. There was no Catholic bishop in England free to ordain young men. Every incumbent bishop was now a Protestant. By an inevitable process, many Catholics, little by little, became so accustomed to the new services that they accepted them as normal and forgot their old ways. In all probability, Elizabeth's strategy of a bloodless rise to religious monopoly by the national Church would have succeeded—just as Protestantism gained hegemony in Scandinavia with barely any resistance, as the Catholic Church there faded away quietly and completely. But one man appeared to challenge that strategy.

William Allen Confronts Catholic Compromise

That the Catholic decline was checked was due largely to the work of one remarkable and determined man—William Allen. He was born in 1532 at Rossall, Lancashire. In 1547, he entered Oriel College, Oxford, and was elected a Fellow in 1550. He received his Master of Arts in 1554 and two years later became principal of St. Mary's Hall, Oxford. Even during the reign of Edward VI (1547–53) it was possible for Catholics to continue their studies, provided they kept quiet. The position was less favorable under Elizabeth, but it was not until 1561 that Allen's religious convictions led him to leave the country for Louvain, which had become a center for Catholics who chose exile rather than conform. Allen returned to Lancashire about 1563 for his health's sake, and lived with his family in security. Of the religious state of that county in 1567, the Protestant historian John Strype wrote, "Religion, in Lancashire and the parts thereabouts, went backwards, papists about this time showing themselves to be numerous, Mass commonly said, priests harbored, the *Book of Common Prayer* and the church established by law laid aside, many churches shut up and curés unsupplied, unless with such popish priests as had been ejected."[63]

William Allen did not remain in Lancashire for the whole of his stay in England; he was in the Midlands and in East Anglia, and he found the position there far different from that in his home county; conformity was common among Catholics who were steadily losing their faith. Not that things were perfect in Lancashire: Allen relates that by his teaching and example he had been able to convince many among the nobility and landowners that truth was to be found only in the Catholic Church, but that it had been a far harder task to persuade them to give up going to church, hearing the Ministers' sermons, using the Protestant books, receiving Anglican Communion, and so on. His attempts, he remarks, to separate these Catholics from their lax habits in this regard were bitterly resisted:

> This is a very difficult thing to do over there because of the harsh laws, and the fact that they are punished with prison and various penalties; and also because in the past the Catholics themselves in general gave way to this practice through fear. So much was this the case that not only did well-meaning lay people, otherwise firm in their faith and ready to assist at Mass at home when possible, go to their churches and attend schismatic services, sometimes even receiving Communion—but even many priests, after saying Mass in secret, publicly conducted the heretical services and Supper, thus (a monstrous crime) on the very same day sharing the chalice of

the Lord with the chalice of demons [cf. 1 Cor 10:21]. They did this because they falsely thought it was sufficient if they held to their faith by inward assent while obeying the sovereign in outward actions, especially in singing Psalms and other parts of Scripture in the vulgar tongue, which seemed to be a matter of indifference.[64]

An Italian account published in 1590 confirms this picture. The author notes the practice, in the early years of Elizabeth, of attendance at the *Prayer-Book* service, and indicates that there were Catholics who thought that they could save themselves from taking part in the actual service with the heretics if they came to church before them and refused to leave in their company. They took Communion, or at least got themselves inscribed as having done so, and then went home to hear Mass privately. In this way, they said to themselves, they were merely attending but not participating. They even allowed the heretical Ministers to baptize their children and to bless their marriages. All this, the author continues, was done without scruple because (apart from a few) those priests still in England and at liberty either gave their approval to such conduct by ignorance, or through fear pretended that it was permissible.[65]

There were others who, while quite willing to assist at the *Prayer Book* services, could not bring themselves to receive the Anglican Communion, and found various means to avoid doing so. If they were lucky, they might arrange to be inscribed by a compliant vicar as having fulfilled this legal Easter duty; or, if they were sufficiently prosperous, as for example were Sir John Bourne or Viscount Montague, they would undertake a change of residence on Holy Saturday so as to avoid appearing on the register of either the parish they had just quitted or the one in which, on Easter Sunday, they had just arrived! Others took refuge behind the rubric in the *Prayer-Book* which forbade the Minister to admit to the Lord's Table not only those who were openly evil-doers, but also those betwixt whom he perceived malice or hatred to reign. By claiming or arranging to be "out of charity" with one of their neighbors, some Catholics were able to excuse themselves from receiving Anglican Communion at Easter or at other obligatory times.[66]

Allen returned to the Low Countries (modern Holland, Belgium, and Flanders) in 1565 with the intention of being ordained; he became a priest at Mechlin (Belgium) in 1567. In 1568 his name appears on an edict of Elizabeth, first among the priests whose arrest is demanded of the Sheriff of Lancashire.[67]

Dr. Allen and Douay Seminary

Allen's great project of a place to educate English students abroad came to fruition in the foundation of Douay College in 1568, mentioned in chapter 3.[68] "He chose Douay in Flanders, the seat of a newly founded university, where he had himself just then finished his theological studies."[69] He had recognized the fact that if young men were not trained to replace the dwindling number of loyal Catholic priests in England, the country would surely be lost to the Faith. "At first Allen had thought less of the work of the mission than was the case later on. Like many of his fellow-countrymen, he clung rather to the hope that with a change of the crown the whole of England might once more be recovered for the Church! In that case it would be necessary that as large a number of priests as possible should be ready to take possession of the parishes."[70] Pope Pius V gave his approval to the College in 1568 and in the same year appointed Dr. Allen as superior of the English mission. Later, Pope Gregory XIII confirmed both these acts, and further increased Allen's powers.

There was a quick response after the College opened with six students; within a few years, the numbers reached a few dozen, and climbing,[71] most of them training to return to England as priests. The first priests were ordained in 1573 and four were sent to England in 1575. By 1578, fifty-two priests were "on mission"—"mission," because England was no longer a Catholic country. By the end of Elizabeth's reign, Douay College had produced around 450 priests.[72]

The English government was, naturally, exceedingly hostile to the seminaries and colleges, which were all erected in countries belonging to the "Spanish faction." The College at Rome (first students 1576) was directly under the pope and the Jesuits; that at Douay under the protection of King Philip; that at Rheims, France (whither Douay was transferred), was under the protection of the Duke of Guise. To deal with these seminarians and their teachers, a special Act of 1571 deprived of property and home in England anyone who was overseas without permission or did not return by a specified date and conform to the State religion. More seminaries for Englishmen were also to be founded in Spain: Valladolid

in 1589 and Seville in 1592; plus a school for boys to get a Catholic education at St. Omer's (modern France) in 1593.

Lord Burghley (William Cecil, the administrative head of Elizabeth's
government) declared that the missionaries "under secret masks, some of
priesthood, some of other inferior orders, with titles of seminaries [semi-
nary priests] for some of the meaner sort, and of Jesuits for the stagers
and ranker sort . . . labored secretly to persuade the people to allow of the
pope's foresaid bulls," who, once persuaded in their consciences, were
forthwith secret traitors, and only wanted opportunity to be so openly.[73]
But in the seminaries at Rheims and at Rome, the students wished to
be martyrs, not for a political plot, but for religion; they wished to be
Christ's ministers, not Philip's soldiers. They repudiated honestly and
heartily all designs of political meddling.

For his work, Dr. Allen was called to Rome by Pope Gregory XIII in
1585 and made a Cardinal in 1587. He remained there until his death in
1594.

Fr. Pollen evaluates his role:

> Of William Cardinal Allen, it would be hard indeed to speak too
> highly. If we except Blessed Edmund Campion, there was perhaps
> no one among the English Catholics of his day who can be placed
> higher. Amid all the miseries and sufferings of persecution and exile
> his co-religionists greeted him as "our Moses," "Pater Patriæ" [Father
> of the fatherland], "the man upon whom all depends," though it
> was he who most of all insisted on their enduring those miseries
> without flinching. The explanation is given us by Campion's words
> below, "Neither shall this Church here ever fail, so long as Priests
> and Pastors be found for the sheep; rage man or devil never so
> much."[74] It was, indeed, due to Campion that this assurance could
> be given, for it was his glorious zeal which enkindled the spirit of
> martyrs throughout the whole Catholic community; but it was not
> only due to Allen that "Priests and Pastors" were actually "found for
> the sheep," but he had also been the first to foresee the way out of
> the difficulty. He had done so at the very moment when the fortunes
> of Catholicism seemed desperate, and he had devoted life, fortune,
> influence, everything to the building up of that seminary at Douay
> in which "Priests and Pastors" were taught and ordained.[75]

Priests on the Mission

Ludwig von Pastor writes,

> Many were pronouncing their own death sentence when they entered one of the seminaries, and bound themselves expressly by oath to the English mission. But for all their labors and sufferings, martyrdom was the reward they sought, and that, despite a long life of sacrifice and pain, could never be bought at too great a price, while the harvest they reaped made up for all their privations.[76]

Writing in 1577, Allen provides a vivid account of the dangers to the priests once they returned:

> I could reckon unto you the miseries they suffer in night journeys, in the worst weather that can be picked; peril of thieves, of waters, of watches, of false brethren; their close abode in chambers as in prison or dungeon without fire and candle lest they give token to the enemy where they be; their often and sudden rising from their beds at midnight to avoid the diligent searches of heretics; all which and diverse other discontentments, disgraces and reproaches they willingly suffer . . . and all to win the souls of their dearest countrymen.[77]

The harvest was at times extraordinary. "Day by day," wrote Allen, "many return to the faith and give up their attendance at Protestant worship."[78] Even arrest did not put an end to the labors of the missionary priests. In London, in 1583, Allen says, there were, besides the other Catholics, twenty-four priests in the Marshalsea prison alone, "who live there most sweetly in the Lord":

> They receive visits from Catholics who wish to speak to them or to go to Confession or receive Communion. And what is more, priests are allowed out of jail each day to go to various parts of the city, to minister to the spiritual needs of Catholics, so long as they return to custody for the night. Hence, unbelievably, the salvation of many is promoted there, sometimes as much as if the priests had been at liberty. So God blesses their efforts in every way, and experience itself rebukes those human judgments of many either crying out or murmuring that we ought to keep our men for better times, give in to the persecution, and cease from work. If we made use of these advisers, countless souls would be lost every day, and all hope for the future

salvation and conversion of our country would be extinguished. For
we must not merely look forward to better times, we must bring
them about.[79]

How priests in jail could so easily hear confessions and say Mass is
explained earlier.[80]

In one jail, the prisoners obtained their own keys and gathered
together for early morning Mass each day before their guards were
astir. On another occasion, Catholics came into a prison specifically to
hear Mass—this was the complaint one time of Bishop Aylmer to Lord
Burghley. We hear of jailers so much impressed through their daily contact with priests that they were received into the Church by their own
captives.[81]

In the same letter of 1583, Allen reports that so far 230 priests have
been sent out from the two Colleges: twelve died as martyrs last year
(1582) and three in the last few months; forty are in prison, laboring as
they can manage; and of this vast number—despite all the threats and
promises of their enemies—not one has proved a weakling. Two only
have behaved in a blameworthy fashion, but repented after liberation.
Thus far no scandal has occurred, and this without any local supervision.

In another letter, Allen reports that Bishop Thomas Strong, con-
secrated in Rome on April 5, 1582, for Ossory in Ireland, stopped in
England on his way to his diocese—and Catholics came from all over
London and beyond to ask for their children to receive

> the Sacrament of Confirmation, which among us has always been
> held in greater veneration than anywhere else in the world; many
> came to receive his blessing, many came just to see him, since for
> so long now they have not seen a bishop ordained in a Catholic and
> canonical way, as they understood him to be. In whatever home he
> entered, everyone genuflected right down to the ground with con-
> spicuous joy and devotion. My aforesaid brother [Gabriel] saw him
> confirm many with sacred Chrism.[82]

A Statistical Summary

While we do not have exact figures for priests and laity, Catholics and
Protestants, recusants and conformists, it is worth mentioning what estimates and figures have been given by historians over the last century.

In 1580, the population of England was between 3.5 and 4 million. By 1583, 230 secular priests had been sent to England. There was also an unknown number of surviving Marian priests.

In 1585, i.e., after ten years of missionary priests coming to England, including Jesuits in the last five of those years, Catholics could be numbered at 120,000, of whom 40,000 perhaps were secretly Catholic.[83]

To turn to the end of Elizabeth's reign, Penry Williams estimates, "By 1603 there were perhaps about 30,000–40,000 Catholics including 'church papists,' in a population of about [4] million."[84]

Father Anstruther's catalogue names 780 "seminary priests" who returned to work in England at some time in Elizabeth's reign, 1558–1603.[85]

In martyrdoms, priests far exceeded the laity. Under Elizabeth, 123 priests were put to death: that is, every sixth or seventh priest. Of the laity, sixty were executed: about one in every two thousand.[86] A priest could be executed for performing any priestly function. As a rule, when a layman was executed, it was not merely for attending Mass and so forth, but for having supported or harbored a priest, or helped one to escape prison.[87]

In addition, for every four or five executed for religion, we must add one (priest or layman) who died while in prison, through ill-treatment, or malnutrition, or disease brought on by the conditions. Some were confined in foul and stinking dungeons, and given the worst food and water. Some were tied like animals to a manger, or yoked liked beasts of burden to work a tread-mill and whipped if they did not work willingly or were unable to work from illness.[88]

English Catholic Writers Abroad

A number of school-exiles as well as members of the Thomas More circle had settled at Louvain, Flanders (in modern Belgium). Their leader was Nicholas Sanders (Winchester and New College, Oxford), who had been among the theologians at the Council of Trent (1545–63). With him were Thomas Harding and Thomas Stapleton, both of Winchester and New College, as well as other scholars. Their work was apologetic and controversial, and the books and pamphlets they produced were an important weapon in the war against Protestantism. For several years they were engaged in refuting Bishop John Jewel's *Apologia Ecclesiae Anglicanae* (A Defense of the Anglican Church, 1562), the most effective statement of the Anglican position. Devotional and instructional books were also printed, such as Fr. Laurence Vaux's *Catechism* for children and the unlearned (1567). Vaux had been a Fellow of Corpus Christi, Oxford. He returned to England in 1580 and was almost immediately arrested and spent the remainder of his life in prison.

While William Allen was studying theology at Louvain, he wrote two books: *A Defense and Declaration of the Catholic Church's Doctrine touching Purgatory and Prayer for the Dead* (1565)[89] and *A Treatise made in defense of the lawful power and authority of Priesthood to remit sins* (1567).

Between 1559 and 1570, fifty-eight books were published by these exiles. From 1559–1603, they wrote and published more than two hundred English works.[90] Over one-third of the English Catholic books published during Elizabeth's reign featured an anonymous author or translator. The distribution of these books in England was full of risks and could land the bearer of them in prison for life. Many proclamations were issued against importing Catholic books or possessing them. Special precautions were taken at the ports to search for and examine all books brought in by traders and travellers. The considerable trade between England and the Low Countries presented countless opportunities for smuggling books especially by way of the lesser ports and harbors. Sometimes the carriers were put ashore on lonely parts of the coast. In spite of these difficulties the books were widely distributed by paid agents (a costly business), by private hawkers and, later, by the incoming missionary priests.

Elizabeth's Dangers at Home

Religion was a cause of internal discord, and could also be a source of external threats to power. Wherever Elizabeth turned there were dangers—dangers at home from Mary Queen of Scots (1568) and the Northern Rising (1569)—and dangers to herself and her government from abroad: from Pius V's Bull (1570), the Ridolfi plot (1571), the Stukeley plot (1578), and the Sanders invasion (1580). These all confronted her up to Campion's time (to 1580), but others were still to come—for example, the plots of Throckmorton (1583) and Babington (1586) to assassinate her (although these two never got close to success), and the invasion of the Spanish Armada (1588).

Mary Queen of Scots: Mary Stuart, Queen of Scots, took refuge in England in May 1568. In January 1567, her husband had been murdered; three months later she married James Hepburn, Earl of Bothwell. As he was a divorced Protestant, the marriage was according to a Protestant rite. All this shocked Catholics, but in May 1568, shortly after her incarceration in England under Elizabeth, Mary was reconciled with the Catholic Church, and on November 30 she wrote to Pope Pius V to ask his pardon for her participation in Protestant services and to give satisfaction for any scandal she may have caused.[91] As time went on, Mary became a most devout Catholic. The arrival of the Queen of Scots in England presented Elizabeth with a dilemma that was to bedevil English politics for nineteen years. Mary inevitably became the center of plots; she was, after all, on strict hereditary principle, the heiress to the throne. As a great-grand-daughter of Henry VII, many Catholics thought she had a better claim on the English throne than her "illegitimate" cousin, Elizabeth. Some Catholics, but not all, were prepared to forget her murky past and to see her as the Catholic supplanter of Elizabeth. As the years went by, a romantic mist enshrouded this unfortunate woman. Many went to the gallows or the block on her behalf, while under Elizabeth she was to be held captive from 1568 to her execution in 1587.[92]

The rebellion of the Northern Earls: In November 1569 took place the unsuccessful Catholic Rising of the northern Earls of Northumberland and Westmoreland who sought to free Mary, Queen of Scots, and place her on the English throne. Durham was occupied successfully on November 14, and the priests took the occasion to restore the old service and sing High Mass in Durham Cathedral. The Rising was put down ruthlessly: Thomas Percy, Earl of Northumberland, was beheaded, and 800 of his followers were hanged; they were, for the most part, artisans and rustics.

Dangers from Abroad

In 1580, at the arrival of Persons and Campion, the English government and nation were thoroughly convinced, first, that there was a very dangerous combination of foreign Catholic powers intent on the invasion of England; and secondly, that the invaders counted upon finding an ally in every English Catholic. The system of espionage, which Walsingham had organized with marvelous skill—a skill which far surpassed the attempts of the Spaniards in the same line—had kept the Council well informed of many details of the schemes.

The Ridolfi plot: 1571 saw the grotesque scheme of Roberto Ridolfi, a Florentine banker resident in London since 1560. He plotted with Spanish and Papal support to place Mary Stuart and Thomas Howard, Duke of Norfolk, on the English throne. The execution of Norfolk in June 1572 closed the episode.

The Stukeley plot: Apart from national rebellions within Ireland, Elizabeth feared foreign invasions launched from Ireland. In 1578, such a projected expedition was initiated under the command of Irishman Thomas Stukeley, once a Protestant pirate but now a Catholic adventurer. The attempt was a fiasco—Stukeley did not even get to Ireland. On the way, at Lisbon, he was persuaded to join a Portuguese crusade going to Africa, where he would die in battle in August 1578.

The Sanders invasion: In 1579, a crusade under the leadership of the celebrated soldier, James Fitzmaurice Fitzgerald, cousin of the Earl of Desmond, landed in Ireland, at Smerwick (St. Mary Wick) in Kerry—assisted by General Bastiano San Giuseppe and Rev. Dr. Nicholas Sanders, who were sent by the pope in 1579 as reinforcements. A second expedition, of 600 Spaniards and Italians, arrived in September 1580. Dr. Sanders, says Pollen, "was the last English Catholic to take up arms openly for the Faith."[93] This invasion into Ireland came to a miserable end in November 1580. This offensive was mentioned earlier, where Fr. Persons expressed his dismay at the enterprise, when Dr. Allen told him of it at Rheims.[94] Information came to the Council which proved this expedition to have been contrived by the Papal Roman Curia. Queen Elizabeth vented her anger especially on persons who were innocent, namely, her own Catholic subjects.

Pope Pius V's Bull

A Dominican friar, Cardinal Michael Ghislieri, became pope in 1566 and took the name "Pius V." He continued to wear his Dominican habit, and this was to become the standard form of the Papal vesture thereafter. He was a man of strict, holy living—"food was to be taken as medicine," he said—and in his six years as pope he did much to clean up the Roman Curia and to make bishops and clergy attend to their pastoral duties. He was in no sense a politician; his religion came first and last. So it was that on February 25, 1570, he issued the Bull *Regnans in Excelsis,* in which he excommunicated Queen Elizabeth and declared her dethroned, and her subjects released from all obedience to her. (This Bull has already been related above.)[95]

The pope did this without consulting any of the kings or princes whose duty it was, in his view, to enforce the Bull. Philip of Spain was affronted. His political plans did not include a break with England, and so, as far as he was concerned, the Bull was a dead letter, as it was for other princes. Rome had yet to realize that in a Europe divided into Catholic and Protestant States, the pope now had little influence on a world of power politics.

There has been much discussion on the wisdom or folly of the pope's action. The Bull was issued through high principles and pure intentions— but under a misapprehension as to the local situation, and without the necessary consultation with, and deference to, those who knew the full situation from within.[96] Few Catholics were likely to renounce their allegiance to the queen—eleven years into her reign—though it must have taken a long time for the news of the excommunication to reach most of them, as the Bull was not published in England. A daring layman, John Felton, fixed a copy of the Bull to the Bishop of London's palace gates on May 25. For this he was sent to the Tower of London to be examined under torture, and was hanged in St. Paul's Churchyard on August 8, 1570.

The most serious objection to the Bull was that it put into the hands of the government an additional weapon. Catholics could now be charged with being traitors, and they could be faced with "the bloody question," as it was called (meaning mortal or fatal question): "If a Catholic army invaded the country, would you support the Queen or the Pope?" It is, however, unrealistic to argue that the Bull was responsible for the subsequent persecution; that would have come in any case—for the queen and her councilors, especially William Cecil and Francis Walsingham, were determined to suppress residual Catholicism. The Bull happened to be a welcome and extra cause for doing so. It did not *create* the conflict of loyalties for Catholics; that dilemma was the result of the Act of Uniformity (1559). The "bloody question" itself was an obvious one to put to suspects, whether priests or laymen; Cecil and Walsingham did not need the pope to suggest it to them.

As a historian considering both sides, Fr. Pollen admits first that the Bull caused harm:

> Loss of prestige to the Pope, grievous troubles of conscience to the faithful, and the final loss of many who were previously holding on, though weakly, to the old cause. Against this must be set the inestimable advantage of making it evident to all the world that Elizabeth and her followers were cut off from the Catholic Church, that to accept and submit to her was to reject that Church. The Bull made clear the iniquity of attending Protestant churches at her command, which nothing had hitherto been able to bring home to the Tudor Catholics, with their miserable proclivity to give up religious liberty at the sovereign's whim. Now at last those who refused to attend grew into a body, and won a special name, that of the Recusants.[97]

The Anti-Catholic Laws of 1571

One result of the crisis set by the arrival of the Queen of Scots in the country, and to a lesser extent by the Papal Bull, was that a new penal law was passed in retaliation by Elizabeth's third Parliament (April–May 1571): anyone claiming that Elizabeth was either a heretic or schismatic, and not the legitimate monarch, was guilty of high treason. Reconciliation with the Catholic Church and recognition of Papal authority was forbidden; to bring or receive Papal Bulls, crucifixes and rosaries, etc., was forbidden; and anyone seeking absolution from a Papal representative, or anyone granting absolution, was guilty of high treason. Abettors and harborers were liable to loss of goods and life imprisonment.

Enforcement of these laws varied as local authorities lacked either the will or the means. Before these laws, and for some years after, few transgressors were executed. Between January 4, 1570, and February 3, 1578, seven were executed: laymen and priests.[98]

The effect of the laws was not regular, but it was horrible. Families were broken up, property confiscated, the master of the house imprisoned, the priest murdered. This was what the Catholics were now called upon to face.[99] From 1593, children were abducted from their parents to be educated as Protestants, at their parents' expense.[100]

Dread, suspicion, and distrust became the order of the day:

Any day they might fall into a trap set for them by avowed enemies
or false friends. . . . Marriages were celebrated in secret to avoid the
protestant marriage service, and women about to become mothers
hid themselves in places where no one could take their child away
from them to receive the dreaded baptism of heretics. Even in the
bosom of the family men did not feel safe, for they suspected that
the government spies had their eyes everywhere. . . . Children and
parents were set at variance, husband and wife lost confidence in
one another, one part of a family was betrayed by the other, and the
owner by his heir. The servants of Catholic families were arrested
and examined about their masters. No place, no man was safe any
longer from espionage, not even the prisoners in prison. Men who
enjoyed the full confidence of Catholics entered into an understanding with the government and undertook to sound the prisoners
under the guise of friendly visits.[101]

The period from April 1579 till April or May 1580 was a period
of relaxed severity, although no law was repealed or modified, and no
prison closed in that time. Then came a period of recrudescence of persecution, June to December 1580, beginning with the Jesuits' arrival.
However, it was not simply on account of their arrival or successes. The
Privy Council had issued orders against Jesuits in 1578, two years before
any had landed. After they had landed their name does not appear in the
Privy Council Registers for another three months, i.e., not till September
11, 1580, when Campion was probably the one intended.[102]

In 1581, Parliament passed even sterner laws against Catholics,
which will be mentioned in their place.[103]

Anti-Catholic Legends

The attempted invasions of the realm, and the Bull of Pius V, helped to
raise anti-Catholic feeling among the populace, but there was a literary
force at work also. March 1563 saw the publication of John Foxe's *Acts
and Monuments of these latter and perilous days, touching matters of the
Church, wherein are comprehended and described the great persecutions
and horrible troubles, that have been wrought and practiced by the Romish
Prelates, specially in this Realm of England and Scotland, from the year of
our Lord a thousand, unto the time now present.* This book became commonly known as Foxe's *Book of Martyrs.* It is impossible to exaggerate its
influence on English feeling and opinion. The Catholics angrily named it

Foxe's Golden Legend, but the nickname defines very accurately the place taken by the book in the minds of the common people of England. Clergy Convocation in 1571 ordered that a copy should be made available for public use in every cathedral. Copies were also widely bought for parish churches. A reader would gather people around him to listen to these accounts of the Protestant "martyrs," and those who could not read could turn the pages and study the lurid illustrations.

Five editions of the book were printed during the reign of Elizabeth, and it continued to be in steady demand for more than two centuries. It became a second book to the Bible in many households. Many, many thousands of children and adults received their impressions of Catholicism from this book, and became imbued with dread and horror of the Catholic Church.

Hopes for a Royal Catholic Marriage

One hopeful sign in 1580 that made Catholics anticipate greater liberty—even tolerance—was the long-awaited marriage, then under discussion, of Queen Elizabeth to François Valois, a Catholic, the brother of Henry III of France. News reached Rome too that, to overcome opposition to her marriage, Elizabeth was considering admitting three Catholics to the Privy Council. This optimism may have played a part in Father General Mercurian's decision to send Jesuits to England.[104] But the marriage never happened.

The Catholics, apparently under the inspiration of the French ambassador, made a "combination"[105] in which we find such names as the Earl of Northumberland, the Earl of Oxford, Lord Henry Howard, and Charles Arundel. Their object, apparently, was to promote this royal marriage with François Valois, Duke of Anjou—which the Puritans as resolutely opposed.

Except for the sad end of the drama, the varieties of its progress are a complete comedy. It would certainly have been an odd match if it happened—in 1572, François was seventeen and Elizabeth was thirty-nine! Negotiations for their marriage went on from 1572 until François's natural death in 1584. The Duke visited England three times during this period.

The Puritans were furious against the match. Puritan preachers denounced it when the Duke was invited to Court. The Spanish ambassador, Mendoza, likewise strove to persuade the Catholics to oppose it—for other (Spanish) reasons. The French ambassador, Castelnau, was all in favor of it, exhorting Catholics to be patient, for the end would crown the labor, and the queen's new husband would secure their freedom of worship. There were the counselors: the mysterious Lord Burghley (in favor of the marriage); the profound and devilish Francis Walsingham (against it); the versatile and unprincipled Earl of Leicester; and the rest. Lastly, there was the audacious queen, giving hopes to all, but satisfying none; faithful to her policy of doing little, but letting events work themselves out, and making it her main business to preserve her personal popularity.

So far was she from preferring the Puritans, that some of her personal favorites were as near being Catholics as the irregularities of their lives would permit. She made no objection to the religion of Anjou, a Catholic; indeed, she said that his fidelity to it was a claim on her respect; and in 1578 she agreed with the French ambassador that her husband was to be allowed to do as he liked in his own house, as she hoped to be allowed to do as she liked in hers.[106] And she told Leicester that "this was the year to marry off all the poor old maids in England; they should all be wedded with her." But nothing could make her act; she delayed, the affair dragged on; and nothing had happened before it all came to a close in 1584 with the Duke's death.

The Irresolute Majority

The two striking changes under Elizabeth were the liberty granted to Protestants and the reformation of church services. For thirty years now, the people had been used to liturgical variations, some made on illegitimate authority, some, as Mary's restoration, rightfully; but all had come to the people on the authority of the State, whether it was the State acting schismatically or acting in obedience to Rome. So far as appeared externally, Elizabeth's change might be as authorized as Mary's. Perhaps only the educated and the attentive were aware of its internal character.

For a variety of reasons, the people had in the first years of Elizabeth attended the church, where, for the most part, their old pastors still ministered. But soon scandals arose; tinkers and cobblers succeeded to the pulpits of the grave theologians who were dispossessed. Some of the priests forgot their vows of celibacy; and as early as 1562, during a tour in Essex and Suffolk, Elizabeth was offended at the slovenly way in which the service was being conducted, and at the consequences of clerical marriage. On her return, she issued an order prohibiting women from lodging in cathedrals and colleges.[107]

The Catholic part of the population had been taken unawares at the change of religion. No choice was given them; Protestantism was simply imposed upon them. They saw, for the most part, their pastors retaining their benefices, sometimes displaced to make room for an ignorant ranter; but then, in turn, they saw this ranter's mouth stopped, and himself reduced to a mere reader of prayers and homilies. Many bore it patiently, hoping this would in its turn soon come to an end.

The people, then, to whom the missionaries were sent had no firm conviction against the truth of Catholicism. Their inclinations led them towards it; only their fear or their indolence prevented their profession of it. Their external show of Protestantism was due to cowardice and sloth rather than heresy, helplessness rather than a strong passion. It was their will that had to be strengthened, rather than their mind to be enlightened.

To the missionaries, they were heretics because they despaired of being able to live as Catholics. Strengthen them to do their duty, and they will naturally come back to the faith they learnt at their mothers' knees.

On the other side, English Protestants might be warned that the Established Church was not as secure as they fancied. The queen would die some day, and her successor would restore all; perhaps the pope and the French and Spanish kings would come and dethrone her, and extirpate the heretics. Then and to this day is the saying: "The Catholic religion was the first, and shall be the last."

The committed Catholics were always looking out for a sign of its return.

Portents of the Times

A flood, or a comet, or a monstrous birth, sent a thrill through England, and awakened the expectation of the "golden day" that was to restore the Old Religion (the Catholic religion). No picture of those times is complete that does not catalogue these prodigies, which had so extraordinary an effect on the belief of the people.

On the day of the election of St. Pius V, it is said, two comets with large bloody tails stood over London at midday, and near them, a large hand issued from a cloud, brandishing a sword.[108]

1580—the year the Jesuits entered the country—was distinguished by a profusion of such portents. In his life of Campion, Fr. Persons records from chronicler John Stowe[109] an earthquake in London on April 6 which made the great bell of Westminster toll of itself, and many other clocks and bells. The quake caused a large stone to fall from the roof of Christ Church, Newgate Street, at sermon-time, killing two persons. There were other earthquakes in April and May. In June, there were great storms of lightning, thunder, and monstrous hailstones. After one of these tempests, one Alice Perin, eighty years of age, brought forth a monster with a head like a helmet, a face like a man, a mouth like a mouse, a human body, eight legs, all different, and a tail half a yard long. Not long after this, Agnes, the wife of William, gave birth to a monster that was male and female, with mouth and eyes like a lion, and other parts no less monstrous.[110] On May 18, a vision of a hostile fleet was seen at sea off Bodmin; a pack of hounds was heard and seen in the air in Wiltshire; and in Somersetshire three several companies of sixty men in black appeared in the air, one after another.

At a time when a student of magic, the Holy Roman Emperor Rudolph II, occupied the imperial throne,[111] and Lord Burghley was entreating Edmond Kelly, assistant to Elizabeth's astrologer Dr. John Dee,[112] not to deprive his native country of his good gifts, it is no wonder that such predictions as are found in Moore's *Almanack* had a great effect on men's minds.

The old priests still occasionally warned their flocks of their evil state. A Lincolnshire boor informed the Council how Parson Britton, minister of Bonnington, preached that there was no salvation for those who went without confession and penance. "You must confess," he said, "not to bad fellows like me; but if you seek for them, there be honest men in the country." The boor accordingly sought, and found an honest man, who persuaded him that "there would be amendment this year [1580] of religion," and showed him in a book the cabalistic words, "*E* [Elizabeth] shall fall, and *I* [=?] shall stand instead; and *I* is not *J* [James, b. 1566, son of Mary Queen of Scots], and shall not continue; and there shall be a musing Midsummer, a murdering Michaelmas, a bloody March. All after, merry shall be."[113] One instance is as good as twenty of the sort of

sayings that were current among the people in reference to the immediate restoration of the old Faith.

Such were the people to whom the Jesuits were sent, to bid them
separate themselves from the communion of the heretics and to forbear
going to their churches, whatever the penal consequences might be. They
came to separate what the queen wanted to unite, and accordingly she
issued her proclamations, warning the people against them as enemies of
herself, of Church and State, who were to be diligently hunted as persons
perilous to the public good. Yet when they came, they were found to be
men of peace, churchmen without weapons, teaching the old doctrine,
fasting and praying, preaching confession and restitution, and offering
to dispute about these points with the new ministers, whose lives were
known to be far distant from any of these things.[114]

CHAPTER 10

Campion's *Brag*: The Challenge and the Pursuit

Organization and Precautions

CAMPION AND Persons found London emptied of friends and swarming with spies. Further stay there had become both useless and perilous, and they decided, with the other priests, to go forth on their appointed missions into the shires.

Each Jesuit Father was furnished with two horses and a servant, sixty pounds in money, two suits of traveling clothes, books, vestments, and everything needful for rituals or for the road. George Gilbert provided everything and also promised to supply whatever more might be necessary for them.

Fr. Pollen explains, "Sixty pounds was, of course, a very large sum indeed for those days . . . One must remember, however, that Persons, at least, kept lodgings in London, and had to send letters abroad by special messengers. Gratuities, too, had often to be given suddenly and on a large scale."[1]

Gilbert was the leader of the group of young men mentioned in chapter 7.[2] It was not a formally constituted sodality or confraternity with rules or promises,[3] but their peculiar position forced these young laymen into association. The various difficulties of the missionary priests made the cooperation of some such men absolutely necessary. The penal laws were already very severe, and held out strong inducements to the layman to betray the missionaries. Prudence, therefore, forbade them to compromise themselves, or the person whom they visited, before they knew that their visits at his house would be safe to themselves and acceptable to him. It was for this reason that the Jesuits were ordered to be very

261

careful whom they conversed with; to prefer the gentleman, someone
of the upper classes, because of his greater influence when converted,
his greater power to protect them, as well as the lesser likelihood of his
betraying their secret through the enticement of a quick gain. As their
Instructions dictated, the Jesuits were on no account to have personal
dealings with Protestants till their Catholic friends had sounded their
disposition, secured their impartiality and ascertained that the priests
might speak to them without risk of betrayal.[4] All this required extensive
organization among the Catholic gentry.

Further, as the safety of the priests required that they should know
to whom they were going to entrust themselves, and should be protected
and conducted on their way from house to house, so did the safety of their
host require that he should know whom he was receiving. Missionaries
could not carry about with them certificates of their priesthood or proofs
of their honesty. Unknown strangers might be spies or false brethren or
fallen priests, as easily as honest men. It was necessary, then, that missionaries should be conducted by some well-known and trustworthy person, who could answer for their identity and their honesty at the houses
where they were introduced. Hence this conductor had to be a gentleman
well-known and respected throughout the country.

These active Catholic men performed the functions of preparing
Protestants and conducting priests, besides procuring alms for the common fund out of which the priests were supplied. They made great sacrifices for the cause; they dedicated themselves wholly to the salvation of
souls and conversion of heretics. They contented themselves with basic
food and clothing and the necessities of their state, and bestowed all the
remainder for the good of the Catholic cause.[5]

The enemy called these men "subseminaries" (sub-seminarians),
"conductors, companions, and comforters of priests," "lay brothers,"
out of whom the Jesuits were accused of getting "either all or most part
of their riches," before handing them over to their superiors; "inferior
agents," "lay assistants," to "straggle abroad and bring in game," whose
business it was, "not to argue, but to pry in corners, to get men to entertain conference of the priest, or inveigle youths to fly over sea to the
seminaries."[6]

These "young gentlemen of great zeal and forwardness in religion,"
says Persons,[7] men of birth and property, most without wives or office,

and thus free to devote themselves to the cause, entered on their dangerous and difficult path with "such extraordinary joy and alacrity ... every
man offering himself, his person, his ability, his friends, and whatsoever
God had lent him besides to the service of this cause, which was no small
comfort unto us at that time ... the times being so hard, as they were, and
so many priests in London to be furnished and disposed of and maintained ... But for all, the gentlemen offered to provide, as indeed they did
very sufficiently."[8]

The Network of Catholic Gentry

George Gilbert was one such man, and their leader. Others were:

- Henry Vaux, Campion's former pupil, now aged about twenty-
  one, the eldest son of Lord William Vaux.[9] Persons says his "life
  was a rare mirror of religion and holiness unto all that knew
  him."[10] Although heir, he was never to marry; before the end
  of 1581, he had decided to leave all things and become a Jesuit.
  That did not happen. By 1585, after Gilbert's departure overseas,
  Vaux was leading this network of priest-helpers. Caught for this,
  he spent six months in the Marshalsea prison up to May 1587
  and died peacefully that November.
- Edward Brook(s) (Brooksby, Brookesby) of Sholdby,
  Leicestershire, married to Eleanor, daughter of Lord Vaux. He
  died before mid-1581, three years into marriage, leaving a son
  and daughter.
- William Brooks, brother of Edward. Their father's house was to
  become the site of Fr. Persons's first printing-press.[11] In 1583 he
  entered the Society of Jesus.
- Stephen Brinkley, later to manage this printing-press.
- Thomas Fitzherbert of Swynnerton, Staffordshire, educated at
  Oxford; then newly married, but later a widower, priest, and
  Jesuit in Rome, and Rector of the English College there. As early
  as 1572, he had been imprisoned for recusancy. He was to check
  the references for Campion's book, Ten Reasons.[12]
- John Stonor, who lived at his mother's property of Stonor Park,
  famous as the site where Ten Reasons was printed,[13] for helping
  which he would be arrested.[14]

- Charles Arundel(l), a member of Court, thought by some to be the author or co-author of Leicester's Commonwealth.[15] His mother was sister to Henry VIII's fifth "wife," Catherine Howard. By October he would be under house arrest. He ended life on the Continent as a subject of Spain.

- Charles Basset, great-grandson of Sir Thomas More: his mother was Mary Roper, grand-daughter of St. Thomas. Less than a year hence, May 1581, Basset would leave England with Gilbert, and die at Rouen in 1584.

- Philip Bassett, his younger brother.[16]

- Edward and Francis Throgmorton (Throckmorton), brothers. Francis was to be executed in 1584 for a plot against the queen. Edward was to go to Rome and lead a holy life there and die young in 1582 as a member of the Society of Jesus.[17]

- Richard and William Griffen (Griffin, Griffith), brothers. Richard would later enter the Jesuits.

- Arthur (Joseph) Creswel (Cresswell), who would leave London the following year to become a priest and Jesuit, and eventually an assistant to Fr. Persons in Rome.[18]

- Sir Edward Fitton (Filten) of Gawsworth Hall, Cheshire, married in 1572 to Lady Hesketh's niece, Alice Holcroft, and knighted this year, 1580. His brother, Francis Fitton, was a seminary priest.

- Gervase and Henry Pierrepoint, brothers from a leading Catholic family of Nottinghamshire, who would prove valuable conductors in travels.

- Nicholas Roscarock, a poet and fellow-student with Ralph Sherwin at Oxford. In his London home Sherwin was to be captured. He himself was to be arrested and imprisoned also.[19]

- William Tresham, a member of Court, brother of famous recusant Sir Thomas Tresham. He would flee to Paris in 1582.[20]

- James Hall (Hill), who would later take refuge in France.

- Richard Stanihurst, born in Dublin, an outstanding pupil of Campion at Oxford, mentioned earlier.[21] In 1581, he would leave for the Low Countries, never to return to Ireland or England. Much later he would become a priest.

- Godfrey Foljambe (Fuljambe), who left England for France in 1583, as did many that year.[22]

- Thomas James, who met Campion at the wharf upon his arrival in London.[23] Years later, he would become English consul of Andalucia and play an important role in English Catholic affairs in Spain.[24]
- Anthony Babington, who was to give his name to the plot of 1586 to assassinate Queen Elizabeth—for which he and the next five men listed here were executed.
- Chideock Titchbourne[25]
- Charles Tilney (Tylney)
- Edward Abingdon
- Thomas Salisbury
- Jerome Bellamy, who lived at Harrow-on-the-Hill.[26] He was executed as a traitor merely for feeding two of the plot's fugitives who came to his home.

There were many others whom Persons did not name (in 1594) for fear of compromising them. The ones he did name were dead (twelve), or had entered religious orders overseas (six), were in exile, or had suffered punishment already. Among the unnamed gentlemen must have been, at one time, Lord Oxford, Lord Henry Howard, Mr. Francis Southwell (all reconciled to the Catholic Church in 1576–77),[27] Lord Paget, and prisoner Thomas Pounde.

At Christmas 1580, Lord Oxford (Edward de Vere, son-in-law of Lord Burghley) denounced as traitors his cousin Lord Henry Howard and his onetime friends Francis Southwell and Charles Arundel. He confessed to the queen that he and they had been reconciled to the Church of Rome a few years earlier, but he now craved pardon. As a result of his accusations, Howard, Southwell, and Arundel were arrested for some time. Upon Francis Throgmorton's arrest in November 1583, Arundel and Lord Paget fled to Paris.

The above list shows that the young men belonged to the chief Catholic families of the land.

Meeting at Hoxton

Equipped by this young Catholic society, Persons and Campion rode forth from London in the dark of the evening[28] on Monday, July 18—Persons accompanied by George Gilbert, and Campion by Gervase Pierrepoint or Charles Basset, or both.[29]

Since, for safety, they had at the time been living in separate lodgings in London,[30] the two Fathers agreed to meet again and take leave of each other at Hoxton, Middlesex—at that time a small country village called Hoggsden, a mile or so north of the City of London. They went to the house of a gentleman—possibly Sir William Catesby, not yet a Catholic but married to one, Anne Throgmorton.[31] If not, it was to Mr. Gardiner, Persons's first convert[32]—*Hogsdonii celebris inquilinus* (the renowned lodger of Hoxton) as Fr. More calls him.[33]

Just before the Jesuits left Hoxton, on July 19, there came to them in hot haste Thomas Pounde, a prisoner in the Marshalsea (where Persons had visited him), who had found means to blind the jailer to his temporary absence. He told them that a meeting of the associates, prisoners and others, had been held at the jail to discuss the means of counteracting the rumors which the Privy Council was encouraging.

Pounde's message in effect was this: "It is believed that the Jesuits have come into England for political purposes. The story will grow during your absence from London, and will gain fresh strength with every report of your activities which you are about to start in the shires. You are going into the proximate danger of capture, and if captured you must not expect justice, but every refinement of misrepresentation. You will be asked crooked questions, and your answers to them will be published in some debased form. Be sure that whatever then comes through to the outer world will come out poisoned and perverted. Even well-meaning people will be deceived, and the Catholic cause not a little slandered. I urge you to write now a brief declaration of the true causes of your coming, and leave it in safe custody. Write now what you would wish to have published then, in case infamous rumors should be put about during your incarceration, rumors which you will then not be able to answer or to repudiate."[34]

The proposition seemed to proceed from zeal and mature discretion, and it was accepted by both the Fathers. Campion, however, had been hesitant until prompted by Persons. The similarity in some of their points and ideas suggests that the two of them discussed exactly what to write.

Campion Writes His *Brag*

And Campion, says Persons, being a man of singular good-nature, and easy to be persuaded to whatever religion or piety inclined towards, rose from the company, took a pen, and seated himself at the end of the table. There, in less than half an hour, says Persons,[35] he wrote the declaration which was soon to be so famous. It was written without preparation, and in the hurry of a journey; yet it was so "pithy both for substance and propriety of style in the English language"[36] that it was a triumph to one party and poison to the other. It was addressed to the Lords of the Council, before whom he expected to be examined when he should be apprehended.

Here is the text of this declaration of purpose, Tuesday, July 19, 1580, soon to become known as Campion's *Brag*—which surely ranks as one of the greatest pieces of declamatory prose in the English language:[37]

A Letter to the Lords of the Privy Council

> Right Honorable: Whereas I have come out of Germany and Boëmeland,* being sent by my Superiors, and adventured myself into this noble Realm, my dear Country, for the glory of God and benefit of souls, I thought it like enough that, in this busy, watchful and suspicious world, I should either sooner or later be intercepted and stopped of my course. Wherefore, providing for all events, and uncertain what may become of me, when God shall haply† deliver my body into durance,‡ I supposed it needful to put this writing in a readiness, desiring your good Lordships to give it the[38] reading, for to know my cause. This doing I trust I shall ease you of some labor. For that which otherwise you must have sought for by practice of wit, I do now lay into your hands by plain confession. And to the intent that the whole matter may be conceived in order, and so the better both understood and remembered, I make thereof these 9 points or articles, directly, truly and resolutely opening my full enterprise and purpose.
>
> 1. I confess that I am (albeit unworthy) a priest of the Catholic Church, and through the great mercy of God vowed now these 8

---

*   Bohemia
†   perchance, perhaps
‡   imprisonment

years into the Religion* of the Society of Jesus. Hereby I have taken upon me a special kind of warfare under the banner of obedience, and eke† resigned all my interest or possibility of wealth, honor, pleasure, and other worldly felicity.

2. At the voice of our General Provost, which is to me a warrant from heaven, and Oracle of Christ, I took my voyage from Prague to Rome (where our said General Father is always resident) and from Rome to England, as I might and would have done joyously into any part of Christendom or Heatheness,‡ had I been thereto assigned.

3. My charge is, of free cost to preach the Gospel, to minister the Sacraments, to instruct the simple, to reform sinners, to confute errors—in brief, to cry alarm spiritual against foul vice and proud ignorance, wherewith many my dear Countrymen are abused.

4. I never had mind, and am strictly forbidden by our Father that sent me, to deal in any respect with matter of State or Policy of this realm, as things which appertain not to my vocation, and from which I do gladly restrain and sequester§ my thoughts.

5. I do ask, to the glory of God, with all humility, and under your correction, 3 sorts of indifferent¶ and quiet audiences: *the first,* before your Honors, wherein I will discourse of religion, so far as it toucheth the common weal** and your nobilities: *the second,* whereof I make more account, before the Doctors and Masters and chosen men of both Universities,†† wherein I undertake to avow the faith of our Catholic Church by proofs innumerable, Scriptures, Councils, Fathers, History, natural and moral reasons: *the third,* before the lawyers, spiritual and temporal,‡‡ wherein I will justify the said faith by the common wisdom of the laws standing yet in force and practice.

6. I would be loath to speak anything that might sound of any insolent brag or challenge,§§ especially being now as a dead man

---

* religious life

† also

‡ lands of the heathens

§ seclude

¶ impartial

** commonwealth, common welfare

†† Oxford and Cambridge

‡‡ canon and civil lawyers

§§ Thus did this document become known as Campion's "Brag and Challenge."

to this world and willing to put my head under every man's foot, and to kiss the ground they tread upon. Yet have I such a courage in avouching the Majesty of Jesus my King, and such affiance* in His gracious favor, and such assurance in my quarrel, and my evidence so impregnable, and because I know perfectly that no one Protestant, nor all the Protestants living, nor any sect of our adversaries (howsoever they face men down in pulpits, and overrule us in their kingdom of grammarians and unlearned ears)† can maintain their doctrine in disputation. I am to sue most humbly and instantly for the combat with all and every of them, and the most principal that may be found: protesting that in this trial the better furnished they come, the better welcome they shall be.

7. And because it hath pleased God to enrich the Queen my Sovereign Lady with notable gifts of nature, learning, and princely education, I do verily trust that—if her Highness would vouchsafe her royal person and good attention to such a conference as, in the 2nd part of my fifth article I have motioned, or to a few sermons, which in her or your hearing I am to utter—such manifest and fair light by good method and plain dealing may be cast upon these controversies, that possibly her zeal of truth and love of her people shall incline her noble Grace to disfavor some proceedings hurtful to the Realm, and procure towards us oppressed more equity.

8. Moreover I doubt not but you her Highness's Council being of such wisdom and discreet in cases most important, when you shall have heard these questions of religion opened faithfully, which many times by our adversaries are huddled up and confounded, will see upon what substantial grounds our Catholic Faith is builded, how feeble that side is which by sway of the time prevaileth against us, and so at last for your own souls, and for many thousand souls that depend upon your government, will discountenance error when it is bewrayed,‡ and hearken to those who would spend the best blood in their bodies for your salvation. Many innocent hands are lifted up to heaven for you daily by those English students, whose posterity shall never die, which beyond seas, gathering virtue and sufficient

---

*   confidence

†   The meaning is: "The ministers tyrannize us, as if we were schoolboys and
     unlearned folk, who could listen only, not speak" (J. H. Pollen S.J.).

‡   revealed, unmasked

knowledge for the purpose, are determined never to give you over,* but either to win you heaven, or to die upon your pikes. And touching our Society,† be it known to you that we have made a league—all the Jesuits in the world, whose succession and multitude must overreach all the practices of England—cheerfully to carry the cross you shall lay upon us, and never to despair your recovery, while we have a man left to enjoy your Tyburn,‡ or to be racked with your torments, or consumed with your prisons. The expense is reckoned, the enterprise is begun, it is of God, it cannot be withstood. So the faith was planted, so it must be restored.

9. If these my offers be refused, and my endeavors can take no place, and I, having run thousands of miles to do you good, shall be rewarded with rigor, I have no more to say but to recommend your case and mine to Almighty God, the Searcher of Hearts, who send us His grace, and set us at accord before the day of payment, to the end we may at last be friends in heaven, when all injuries shall be forgotten.

In the judgment of A.C. Southern, "It deserves to rank with the greatest of the short Apologies [i.e., manifestos] of the [English] language. Indeed, in its kind, it is doubtful whether as a piece of prose writing it has ever been surpassed."[39]

The text of this document has never been satisfactorily settled by a collation of the principal texts, of which there are several, with their variations.[40]

Campion wrote his triple challenge with more confidence in his cause, and more trust in the good-will of his opponents, than knowledge of their views. To reconcile the Catholicism which he came to preach with the designs of the politicians of the Council was a task beyond all the powers of reason.

A Confession of Faith for the London magistrates was Persons's lengthy, carefully thought-out statement of position and purpose, twice as long as Campion's piece.[41] In it, he condemned the attempt to make Catholicism synonymous with treason. He acknowledged himself, as

---

*   give up on you
†   The Society of Jesus
‡   Tyburn Tree, London, opposite modern Hyde Park, the execution site of criminals and Catholics

priest and Jesuit, a hater of tyranny, and one rejecting "all the congregations and sects of the Puritans." He was "firmly convinced that there can
no more be a new faith or religion than there can be some kind of new
God." He explained the world-wide evangelizing mission of the Society of
Jesus, vehemently repudiating any intention of stirring up "rebellion and
I know not what unholy plots in our peaceful kingdom." He ended with
a challenge to public disputation with the ministers of the new religion.[42]

It is sometimes said that Persons's manifesto remained sealed, as
planned (for he was never caught) and remained unknown at the time.[43]
This seems not right, as Dr. Allen, in Rheims, in a letter of November 10,
1580, to Fr. Agazzari writes:

> At last there have come into our hands the two declarations written
> some time ago by our Fathers in England . . . if perchance, which
> may God avert, they should be arrested. These written fly-leaves
> pass from hand to hand everywhere among people in England and
> are a source of strength to many.[44]

The College diary also records:

> This very month we heard of copies of letters of Fathers Edmund
> and Robert sent to the Queen's Council, stating the reasons for their
> mission and challenging all the heretics to a debating contest.[45]

In any case, Persons's statement never attained the fame of Campion's
composition, nor received a public rebuttal.

Campion gave a copy to Pounde, keeping the original himself. He
desired that it not be published till there was necessity for so doing; but
he forgot to seal it, as proposed, and as the more wary Persons took care
to do.

The Jesuits Set Out: Campion's First Journey

Off they rode—Persons, with Gilbert, to start his roundabout tour of
shires from west to east; Campion, with Emerson, to counties west of
London.

The *Brag* Is Publicized

Pounde returned to prison, read Campion's challenge and was
thrown into such exultation by it that, though he had no intention of

imparting it to his friends, still less of giving them, or allowing them to take copies of it, he was resolved not to hide its light altogether under a bushel. It gave him an idea to make a challenge of his own, not unlike Campion's.

The Marshalsea in Southwark, one of the chief prisons for recusant Catholics, was at that time infested by two Puritan ministers—Mr. Henry Tripp and Mr. Robert Crowley—who under the protection of the authorities visited the poorer prisoners in their cells, and urged them to conduct some discussion with them, offering that debate which they obstinately refused to hold in public.

Pounde then, bursting with the secret of Campion's challenge, was inspired by it to make a public challenge himself to Tripp and Crowley on September 8, and to back it up with petitions to the Privy Council and to the Bishop of London,.in which he revealed the universal wish of the Catholics for public conferences. He challenged them to allow a disputation, four or six on each side, adding that he knew of two or three who would challenge all the Protestant divines together.[46]

> But let this petition, [he concluded], made in the name of all the Catholic fathers of our nation, remain for a perpetual record and testimony, even to our enemies, of our indifference and of their insufficiency. Muse not, my lords, at this challenge, with a counter-buff, as the soldier saith. For it is made in the further behalf (as it may be presumed) of a perpetual corporation and succession of most learned Fathers, as any with out comparison in the world; with the aid of another good race besides, which cannot die, who have all vowed, as charity hath inflamed them, either to win this realm again to the Catholic faith, and that without any bloodshed except their own, at God's permission, or else to die all upon the pikes of your sharpest laws, and win heaven, as they hope, for themselves.

Much of this, it can be seen, is copied closely from the eighth article of Campion's declaration.

Pounde was right in the importance he attached to public disputation. It soon became one of the chief weapons of the Jesuits, whose unexampled dexterity in wielding it came to be admitted by the Protestants themselves.[47]

Fr. Persons had once before[48] found that Campion could not be safely entrusted to the custody of Gilbert's young associates—a set of youths, as Fr. Bartoli writes, "holy indeed and deserving of every spiritual assistance, but because of their youth and the fervor conceived, more generous than careful."[49]

About September 1st the Bishop of London decided to remove Pounde from his companions in the Marshalsea. Pounde knew of this soon after, and on the 18th, he was sent, heavily ironed, to solitary confinement in the then half-ruined episcopal castle at Bishop's Stortford.[50] After a half-year confinement there, he was transferred to Wisbeach Castle, and afterwards to the Tower, to be questioned there at the same time as Father Campion—where they exchanged letters, as we shall see in due course.[51]

On the eve of his departure, Pounde delivered Campion's paper to the keeping of someone less retentive of a secret than himself, or else communicated it through a conviction that Campion's challenge was much more calculated to embarrass the Council than his own had proved to be. Actuated by one of these motives, Pounde communicated the paper to his neighbor Tichbourne (a fellow Hampshire man), Tichbourne to William Horde, and Horde to several others, including Elizabeth Sanders, a nun, sister to Dr. Sanders who was at this time with the Italian expedition in Ireland. John Watson, the Bishop of Winchester, laid hands upon all these people, on November 18 or thereabouts, committed them to the house of correction at Winchester, confiscated their "lewd and forbidden books," and sent to the Lords of the Council a copy of the "seditious supplication, protestation, or challenge" which, he added, seemed "very plausible" to the people in his part of England.[52] About the same time, another copy was discovered and sent to the Council by the Sheriff of Wilts. From this time it became well-known all over England, and many persons got into trouble for circulating copies of it.[53]

It was written as a masterly protest of innocence—to be broadcast in event of capture and silence—but it became, by premature release, a chivalrous offer of public debate.[54] An unknown hand changed Campion's title *A Letter to the Lords of the Privy Council* to *The Challenge*.[55]

Fr. McCoog summarizes the effect:

> The release of Campion's "Brag" . . . removed the religious debate
> from ambassadorial chambers to the market place. Circulation of

his "Brag" as a broadside challenged authorities. Throwing down the gauntlet made him a champion to Catholics and the most wanted priest in England.[56]

The Protestants' refusal to engage in public debate was proof of their cowardice, fear, and prejudice. The *Brag* angered them and humiliated them, and lifted up Catholics.

Fr. Pollen sums it up:

> From being subdued, cowed and half despondent, the Catholics became courageous, hopeful, and felt the presage of future victory. An audience was won in quarters where previously no hearing could be expected. The Catholic reaction was confirmed and, despite the hurricane of persecution, established on a footing that defied Lord Burghley's fiercest efforts. Such was the remarkable fortune of Campion's *Letter to the Privy Council*, the only piece of his English during his golden period which has survived. Written, we may say, as a swan song, it became a *Challenge* to theological discussion. It fluttered his foes, aroused and rejoiced his friends, and inspired them with secure hopes amid their pressing dangers and daily disasters.[57]

The *Brag* sparked a controversy and public debate about the Jesuits and their purposes in England, which in one sense has never ceased.[58] (See Simpson's bibliography, section 3: "Publications connected with the Brag".)

Two replies were very soon published—the first in December the same year, 1580, by William Charke, a Puritan minister, sometime Fellow of Peterhouse, Cambridge: *An Answer to a seditious pamphlet lately cast abroad by a Jesuit, with a discovery* [exposure] *of that blasphemous sect.* He issued an enlarged edition the next year, which most conveniently did a service for Campion by printing the Challenge in the text of his book—as did the second rebuttal, from Meredith Hanmer, formerly of Corpus Christi College, Oxford, printed January 1581: *The great Brag and Challenge of Mr. Champion a Jesuit, commonly called Edmund Campion, lately arrived in England, containing nine articles here severally laid down, directed by him to the Lords of the Council, confuted and answered.* "In this, as the title suggests, Hanmer follows the familiar device of the time by printing the words of his opponent *in extenso*, and then controverting them passage by passage, thus giving the appearance at least of treating an opponent fairly. As far as the Catholics were concerned, this gave a wider circulation to their books than they could have achieved by their own means, since they could do nothing openly to print or circulate their views."[59] On Hanmer's rather flat reply, Persons remarked, "his book seemeth to very little purpose but only to spread abroad the copies of the other's reasonable offer, which was some labor before to write out to so many hands as desired it."[60]

Hanmer and Charke were very different characters. Hanmer was a cheerful, bombastic Welshman, given to drinking and jesting. Charke was a Puritan, sour and ill-mannered—once in trouble at Cambridge for calling the episcopacy an invention of Satan.[61] Natural and moral reasons, to which Campion appealed, Charke called the "enemies of true religion, and two great nurses of Atheism and Heresy."[62] How could one reason with Puritans who rejected reason itself?

Fr. Persons confuted both of these at once in 1581: *A Brief Censure upon two books written in answer to Mr. Edmund Campion's offer of disputation.* Chapter 12 will speak more of his secret press and its public output.

The Pursuit Intensified

The Council soon knew of Campion's departure from London, and sent pursuivants (hunters for Catholics) into most of the shires of England with authority to apprehend him and Persons wherever they could find them. However, the Jesuits were diligently warned by the Catholics, and easily avoided their pursuers.

Says Persons:

> They lost their labor and we had three or four months free to follow our business, in which period, by the help and direction of the young gentlemen that went with us, we passed through the most part of the shires of England, preaching and administering the sacraments in almost every gentleman's and noble man's house that we passed by, whether he was Catholic or not, provided he had any Catholics in his house to hear us.
>
> We entered, for the most part, as acquaintance or kinsfolk of some person that lived within the house, and when that failed us, as passengers or friends of some gentleman that accompanied us; and

after ordinary salutations, we had our lodgings, by procurement of
the Catholics, within the house, in some part retired from the rest,
where, putting ourselves in priests' apparel and furniture—which we
always carried with us—we had secret conference with the Catholics
that were there, or such of them as might conveniently come, whom
we ever caused to be ready for that night late to prepare themselves
for the sacrament of confession; and the next morning, very early,
we had Mass, and the Blessed Sacrament ready for such as would
communicate, and after that an exhortation; and then we made ourselves ready to depart again. And this was the manner of proceeding
when we stayed least; but when there was longer and more liberal
stay, then these exercises were more frequent.[63]

Persecution Increased

A new proclamation was published on July 15 against "Jesuits and Massing
priests," calling for the recall of all seminarians abroad, the banishment
of all Jesuits and seminary priests from England, and the punishment of
any who assisted them.

Hitherto the government had contented itself with searching for the
missionaries and issuing proclamations. Now new measures were taken,
both energetic and comprehensive. They amounted to a plan for putting
all the Catholic gentry of England under surveillance, and for confining
all the most energetic of them either to prison or to very narrow limits.

Certain castles in various parts of England were selected for the custody of the recusants, and a keeper and two superintendents appointed
for each. Wisbeach Castle, which had been already selected in 1572, on
account of its solitary site, as a place where the chief recusants should be
imprisoned and made "to live at their own charges,"[64] was now made
the prison for such of "the capital doctors and priests" as were found
"busier in matters of State than was meet for the quiet of the realm."[65] Sir
Nicholas Bacon was appointed keeper; and Michell and Carleton were to
be the resident superintendents.[66]

The instructions to the keeper of Wisbeach Castle for the treatment
of Catholic priests[67] will serve as a specimen of the rest. Besides the usual
rules of "close" (solitary) confinement, a minister was to be appointed,
to have "his charge of diet and other necessaries by the contributions of
the recusants"; and the keeper was to see "that due exercise of common

prayer be observed every day, and preaching twice in the week at least."
At this the prisoners were to be present, or, if they refused, they were to
be fined at the pleasure of the Bishop of Ely. Each prisoner, moreover,
was to be, "twice in the week at least, conferred with, as well by the minister as by other learned men sent by the bishop, or that voluntarily of
themselves should come for so charitable a work." The prisoners were
not to have any conference with each other except at meal-time, and then
there was to be "no speech of any matters in controversy." Those who
conferred with the minister were to have more liberty than those who
did not. The only books allowed were a Bible, works of the Fathers, and
others licensed by the minister.

Fr. Persons writes from London in August 1581 to Fr. Alphonsus
Agazzari S.J., Rector of the English College at Rome:

> Into a similar place of captivity, within the last few days, after endur-
> ing the London prisons for so many years, were thrown those very
> respected and reverend gentlemen, [Thomas Watson] the Bishop
> of Lincoln, [John Feckenham] the Abbot of Westminster, and
> many others. In their venerable old age they are sent to Wisbeach
> Castle, a most unhealthy place, in the custody of a sour Puritan
> [Mr. Carleton], where it is certain they cannot survive long. [Bishop
> Watson died there September 25, 1584]. Over and above the dis-
> comfort of the prison, they are treated inhumanely and barbarously
> by their keeper. All books but a single Bible are taken from them,
> nor are they allowed any papers of their own writings or notes.
> Conceited ministers are often let in upon them without warning, to
> argue against them when unprepared, and to taunt and insult them.
> Often, then, false and ridiculous stories about them are circulated,
> and even printed, in order to lessen the high esteem in which they are
> held. Last month a shameless woman was let into their cells without
> their knowledge, so they might acquire a reputation for unchastity.
>   No access to them is allowed, and we are compelled to use this
> ploy which I will now relate. When one of our people wants to give
> them some donation, he walks in the neighboring fields the day
> before, and cries out like a hunter looking for game. At this signal,
> one of them looks out the window, and learns by a sign that the
> hunter has something for them. So, the next night, when everyone
> else is asleep, the hunter cautiously creeps up to the wall, and one of
> the inmates lets down a basket from the same window where the sign

was given, and draws up the gift. Much the same plan is employed for the other prisons also; but the variety of places requires a variety of methods, and the zeal, charity, and bravery of Catholics in working out and executing these designs at very great risk is truly wonderful.[68]

After the coast had been somewhat cleared by confining the "capital doctors and priests" in Wisbeach, and the other recusants, already committed, in other castles, the council undertook a general raid against all the Catholics of England. The chief of them were sent for to London, to answer before the council. Letters were directed to the bishops to summon and commit those who were not summoned to London; but they were told to be careful not to permit them "to come many together at a time," for fear they should know their strength.[69] Those who were summoned to London had first to give bonds for their appearance, and were then committed, some as prisoners to their own houses, some to those of their Protestant friends, and others to the castles prepared for them.

Fr. Persons quotes a long string of names of persons committed. He names several who were actually committed at a later date and were not even converted in July 1580. From his list, and from an official list of prisoners, we can name the following as the chief of them: the Earl of Southampton, Lord Herbert, Lord Compton, Thomas Lord Paget, Sir Thomas Fitzherbert, Sir John Arundel, Sir Alexander Culpeper,[70] Sir John Southworth, Sir Nicholas Poyntz, Sir Thomas Gerard, Sir George Peckham, John Talbot of Grafton, William and Richard Shelly, Ralph Sheldon, Thomas and Francis Throgmorton, John and Edward Gage, Nicholas Thimbleby, William and Robert Tirwhit, Richard Culpeper, John Walker, Mr. Towneley, Mr. Guilford, Robert Price, Peter Titchbourne, Erasmus Wolseley, John Gifford, Brian Fowler, Thomas Cross.[71]

But, gradually the gentry were sent back to their estates and were restricted in their movements. Their arms and horses were taken away.[72]

Both of these events, the proclamation and the persecution, were described by Dr. Allen, who wrote as follows to the Cardinal of Como from Rheims, September 12, 1580:

Most Illustrious and Reverend Lord Cardinal,
     Not long ago I sent your Eminence the late edict [July 15, 1580] which the Queen of England had promulgated against the Catholics

of her dominions; not, indeed, professedly against their religion, but against their suspected treason and conspiracy with the refugees. In it she tells her subjects, that the Pope and the King of Spain had been long and earnestly entreated by her enemies and the refugees to make war against her; she boasts that she is quite prepared for it, and that she fears no foreign forces; she commands her subjects to stand fast in their duty and fidelity; and she says she fears neither rebel citizens, nor the land or sea forces made ready from abroad. Moreover, she declares that in future she means to deal more sharply than her habit or her nature inclines her with those of her subjects who are guilty of any conspiracy with the refugee rebels. Soon after the publication of this edict, by crier, through the whole realm, she orders that in each county all the more powerful and notable Catholics should be apprehended, and committed either to prison or to the custody of heretics. This was immediately, almost suddenly, put in execution; at the same time the strictest search was made for priests, particularly for two lawyers whom we sent over this summer [Dr. Humphrey Ely and Mr. Henry Orton], and for the Jesuits. But the Catholics take such pains, and use such care in concealing them, that up to this time very few have fallen into the enemies' hands. They have only taken two priests of Rheims and one of Rome.

The number of gentlemen now in prison is so great that they are obliged to remove the old prisoners in London for religion—the most reverend Bishop of Lincoln [Dr. Thomas Watson] and several other ecclesiastics—to other strong places far distant from the city, to make room for the new prisoners. The same thing had already been done not long ago at York (which is also a prominent city in that isle). But many think that the reason for this was that the priests detained in those cities were converting all the chief citizens and many of the nobility, and persuading them by their life and example to persevere. They treat citizens or gentlemen more severely who are known to have sons in the seminary of Rome or of Rheims. This persecution is heavier, and extends to more persons, than any of those years prior. For before this, they never committed any of the nobility; who, however, are not in prison for reason of religion, but only given into the custody of heretics.

It is supposed that they do all this exceptional activity to prevent any Catholics joining the enemy, if there is to be any (for they are horribly afraid of what is to be). And perhaps they have made quite sure of those whom they have shut up, whatever eventuates. But as for the rest, who escape the present danger by dissimulation or other shifts, they are rather provoked and irritated to make some attempt, when God gives opportunity, not only to deliver their own souls, but their friends' also, who are so dishonorably imprisoned.

And certainly the whole Catholic population, afflicted in soul and body by this disgraceful tyranny of one woman, awaits some redemption from God with unspeakable yearnings. For this we exiles cry out to our most Holy Father, the highest minister of justice upon earth; for this the prisoners groan to him; for this innumerable afflicted souls, his own sheep, suppliantly stretch forth their hands to him. Not that we doubt that the well-known compassion of the most holy [Pope] Gregory can do more than it does; or that he, our only father upon earth, can wish us greater or better things than he does; but that we may at least somewhat relieve our most just sorrow for our people by communicating our calamities to our most holy Lord and loving Father, and to your kindness. Certainly, all thinking men prognosticate that this new cruelty will do hurt to our enemies themselves. Whether they intend to do more than imprison is as yet uncertain; further measures are expected after the meeting of Parliament, which is supposed to take place soon. Our religion is in fact exalted by this persecution, and by the admirable constancy of many which it calls forth. And it is made clear to all that the question and struggle now are not about religion—of which our enemies have none—but about the stability of the empire, and about worldly prosperity. May the Lord Jesus long preserve your Lordship to be our great defense!

Your Eminence's most humble servant in the Lord,

William Allen

Rheims, Sept. 12, 1580

P.S. I thought to send you this extract of the [English] Calendar, so that from the solemn festival of Elizabeth's birthday kept on September 7th, totally eclipsing the Nativity of the holy Mother of God the following day, you may see to what level of pride the queen has come, who in addition to the splendid festival of her coronation, has chosen to have this celebration of her birthday.[73]

Neither Persons nor Campion, who were on the spot, describe this persecution with so much bitterness as Dr. Allen at Rheims. This we may attribute partly to a generosity which feels more pain at seeing others suffer than at suffering; partly to a consciousness, which Allen must have felt, that the persecution was in some measure attributable to himself and the foreign meddlers who were perpetually interfering in the political affairs of England, with the object of restoring religion there. It is abundantly clear that Allen was deeply implicated in the plots of the day. The last part of the foregoing letter would have been treasonable, especially when we connect his passionate appeal to the pope with the papal expedition against Elizabeth which at the very time had descended upon the coast of Ireland, and about which the nuncio at Paris had just sent off this news to Rome: "The Earl of Desmond, and Dr. Nicholas Sanders [in Ireland from July 1579], and all the Catholic army, are still encamped in their old place—a strong position. They were, at the date of my advice, waiting for foreign aid, without which they can do little or nothing. But we heard yesterday by letter and authentic report that five great ships full of soldiers and munitions of war—sent, it said, by the Holy See—reached in safety some port in Ireland a few days ago."[74] The document goes on to describe the terror of the English Jezebel and her court of heretics, and the measures of precaution she was adopting. The second expedition, of 600 Spaniards and Italians, arrived to help the Irish rebels but they were defeated by November.

The Jesuits' Success

The Jesuits were satisfied with the fruits of this first expedition. They found the country people more inclined to be Catholics than the inhabitants of the towns: "the infection of ministers beareth most rule with artisans and merchants"[75]—but the best part of the nobility and gentry, who dwelt on their estates, together with their tenants and dependants, remembered the virtuous life and just proceeding of those of the ancient religion, especially when they saw and felt the present contrast. It "was a comfortable thing," says Persons, "to see the universal inclination of so infinite a people to the Catholic religion," and "so was an incredible sorrow . . . to see the rents and breaches, the wrenches and disjointures, which the preaching of new doctrines for twenty years had made in the consciences and belief of this good people, which lived before so many ages in one only faith."[76]

The breach between the Protestants and Puritans was already of many years' date. But this year, 1580, Puritanism had given birth to a new sect, that of the "Family of Love," which had already gained several of the queen's household and her guard, and against which she published a proclamation, dated October 3. The peasant mind had already begun to ferment. In May, Matthew Hammond, a ploughman of Hethersett, near Norwich, had suffered the loss of his ears for blaspheming the queen and council, and was afterwards burnt in the castle-ditch at Norwich for saying that the New Testament was a fable; that Christ's blood is not necessary for salvation; that He neither rose again nor ascended into heaven; that there is no Holy Spirit; and that there are no Sacraments. Persons maintains that this denial of all Christianity was a logical development of the principle which renounced the authority of Tradition to determine the canon of Scripture and explain its meaning; rejected all merit in order to amplify God's mercy; denied Christ's descent to the dead, and the assistance of General Councils by the Holy Spirit; and prepared the way for rejecting all the Sacraments by rejecting five of them.[77]

Where the fermentation did not drive men into these sloughs, it led them to seek out the Jesuits to be resolved of their doubts and scruples. For beside the open and obstinate heretics there were many who were only verging to that state, unable by themselves to answer the arguments of the minister, but easily kept right by the priest. Persons gives several examples. Anne Dimocke, a maid of honor to the queen, a great follower of the court preachers, had learnt from them that there was no Hell, "but only a certain remorse of conscience for him that did evil, which was to be understood for Hell, and that all the rest were but bug bears to fright children." To solve this doubt, she applied to Father Persons, under whose instructions she at once became Catholic, and afterwards left the court and the world, and, with one of Lord Vaux's daughters, followed Persons to Rouen, where she entered a convent.

Sir Robert Dimocke (Dymock) was another great hearer of sermons, and had been led into such a maze by them, that he had come to doubt whether there was any God. His friends therefore procured a secret interview between him and Father Persons; and the first point which had to be discussed between them was the existence of God. Persons, during a ride of a few hours, convinced him on this point; but as Sir Robert was still a Protestant, the Father durst not trust himself with him in any town or house. However, Dimocke afterwards sent for a priest, who finished his conversion, and brought him into the Church.

These examples Persons gives to show how those farthest gone out of order were brought back; how those who were going were stayed; how doubters were resolved; how the cold and negligent were warmed; how those whose good desires were paralyzed by fear were put in heart; and how those who were good were confirmed.

The same examples probably led Persons, when revising his *Christian Directory* (1582),[78] to add a large chapter 2 in the 1585 edition, on proofs of the existence of God—because in this confused post-Reformation world, nothing was certain in men's minds anymore, and one truly had to begin at the beginning.

The venture prospered—to use the mercantile phraseology they affected in order to conceal their meaning from the uninitiated—though many slighted their wares, and many defamed them, there were not a few buyers and more admirers. Among the Protestants there was vast talk about the Jesuits, who were as much befabled as mythological monsters. There were wild tales current about their origin, their life, their rule, morals, doctrine, designs, and actions. Almost all agreed, however, that they were spies of the pope, or agents of treason and sedition.[79]

The Catholics' Fervor and Tension

The general tenor of the conduct of the Catholics who received the Jesuits gladly, and the stresses they were under, may be learned from a letter of Persons to fellow-Jesuit Father Agazzari:

> I should never come to an end if I began to talk about the zeal and fervor of the Catholics. When a priest comes to their house, they first salute him as a stranger unknown to them, and then they take him to an inner chamber where an oratory is set up, where all fall on their knees, and humbly beg the priest's blessing. Then they ask how long he will stay with them, which they wish for as long as is possible. If he says he is to go on the following day (as he usually does, to avoid risk from a longer stay) they all prepare to confess their sins that very evening; the next morning they hear Mass and fortify themselves with the most Holy Eucharist; then, after preaching and giving his requested blessing a second time, the priest departs, and is almost invariably conducted on his journey by some of the young noblemen.
>
> The Catholics in various parts of their houses have a number of

secret places (as we read was the practice in the primitive Church) in which to hide the priests from the violence of the officials, who make sudden raids. But now (as happens) owing to their long use and also by reason of the treachery of some false brethren, for the most part they have come to the knowledge of the persecutors. It is the custom of the Catholics themselves to take to the woods and thickets, to ditches and holes even, for concealment, when a raid is made at night. Sometimes when we are sitting merrily at table, conversing familiarly on matters of faith and devotion (for this is the most frequent subject of conversation of all), there comes a hurried knock at the door, sounding like that of a pursuivant; at once—like deer upon hearing the hunts men's voice—we all stand with pricked ears and our souls alert; we leave our food, and commend ourselves to God in a brief aspiration; no word or sound of any sort is heard till the servants report what the matter is. And if it turns out to be nothing dangerous, after the fright they have had, they are more cheerful than ever. It can be truly said they carry their lives ever in their hands.

No one is to be found in these parts who complains of the length of services; nay, if a Mass does not last nearly an hour, many are displeased. If six, eight, or more Masses are said in the same place, and on the same day, as often happens when there is a meeting of priests, the same congregation will attend them all. When they can get priests, they expiate their sins by a salutary confession every week. Quarrels on any matters are scarcely heard of amongst Catholics. If any dispute arises, it is almost always left to the arbitration of the priest. They do not willingly intermarry with heretics, nor will they pray with them, nor do they like to have any dealings with them. A noble-lady was lately given an offer to be let out of prison, if she would only walk once through a church. She refused, adding that she had come into prison with a sound conscience, and she would without harm to her conscience, either leave prison, or die.

See, I beg you, what the Spirit of God has effected by means of this persecution. In the time of King Henry, the father of this Elizabeth, practically the whole kingdom (with all its Bishops and learned men) at one word of the tyrant renounced its faith and the Roman Pontiff's authority. But now, by the supreme mercy of God, when Henry's daughter is persecuting them, there are not lacking boys and women who not only profess their faith openly and boldly even before the tribunals, but refuse to do what might seem to some people a thing of minor importance, even when the alternative is death. This is truly a change brought about by the right hand of God on high [*Ps.* 76:11] and to be accounted among the most signal benefits conferred on this nation.[80]

Persons's Letter to Rome

Campion and Persons returned towards London to meet in October and confer once more, and to compare the results of their labors. The two letters in which they give an account of their doings will fitly conclude this chapter.

On November 17, Persons writes to Fr. Agazzari in Rome:

> The heat of the persecution now raging against Catholics throughout the whole realm is most intense, such as has never been heard of since the conversion of England. Everywhere, noblemen and commoners, men and women, and even children, are being dragged off to prison. They are being bound in iron chains; they are despoiled of their goods, shut out from the light of day, and publicly held up to the contempt of the people in proclamations, sermons and speeches, as traitors and rebels.[81]

He then presents the reasons supposed for this great persecution: the ill-success of the English in Ireland; the demonstration made last summer against England by the Spanish fleet; fear of Scotland whose young king may be more inclined to the Catholic religion; the increase in Spanish power in consequence of her acquisition of Portugal; and lastly, the coming of the Jesuits into the island, and the great number of conversions made by them, which has so astonished the heretics that they know not what to say or do. They are most troubled, he says, about a certain protestation of our faith and religion, and of the reasons of our coming into England, which the Jesuits wrote and signed and placed in the hands of a friend.

> In the meantime it happened that the man [Pounde] to whom the thing [Campion's *Brag*] had been committed, communicated, I know not why, a copy of this writing to another man, and he to someone else, so that in a few days the thing came into the hands

of a countless number of people and even the queen's councilors themselves . . .

We hear that in one month alone more than 50,000 names of persons who refused to go to the heretics' churches were reported. [This figure is vastly exaggerated].[82] Many more, I fancy, have been discovered since. From these it can be guessed what an immense number of secret Catholics there are, when so many are found openly to incur the risk of losing their lives and all their fortunes rather than consent even to go beneath even the roofs of the heretics' conventicles.

When they throw the Catholics into prison, the heretics only ask them one thing—to condescend to come to their churches or conventicles, and to be present at a sermon and divine service. . . .

And so it is a wonderful thing to see now in this realm the strictness and constancy of the Catholics in avoiding and repudiating the heretics' churches, and how almost every day they are giving themselves up to prison of their own accord rather than even pay a visit to the porches of the heretics.

Recently, it was even proposed to certain noblemen to come to the heretics' churches, even only once a year, making a protest in advance that they came not to approve of their religion or doctrine, but only to show an outward obedience to the queen; and if that alone were done, they would be released from prison at once. They replied that this they could not do with a clear conscience.

They gave a certain noble lady this choice, either to stay in prison, or simply to walk through the middle of a church, without stopping there or showing any sign of respect, while the heretics were conducting a service; but she answered that she had entered the prison with a clear conscience, and with the same clear conscience she would leave it; otherwise she was willing to stay there forever.

Some boy, of ten years I believe, was led by some trick of his friends into walking to church before a bride on her wedding day (as the custom is), and afterwards had been blamed by his companions . . . and began to weep inconsolably and was perfectly inconsolable till he found me a few days later, when he ran to me and in a flood of tears threw him self down at my feet to ask pardon for his fault, promising that he would rather be racked with every kind of torment than again consent to so great a sin. I pass over countless other like stories.

Our situation is like this: although by public edict all conversation with us is forbidden, we are most earnestly sought out everywhere; and wherever we go, we are received with the utmost pleasure. Many make long journeys just to speak to us, and put themselves and their possessions entirely at our disposal; clothes, horses and all other equipment they press on us in abundance everywhere.

The secular priests in everything go along with us, or rather, obey us, with the greatest good-will. In short, such is the reputation of our Society with everybody that we fear as to how we can sustain it, especially since we know how far we are from that perfection which they suppose us to have. Hence we need your prayers all the more....

I am left here with the burden of much business, which I cannot easily support without fresh help.... Press by every means for a fresh mission of men of our Society; and if possible, let not fewer than five be sent: one Spaniard, one Italian, and three Englishmen, two of whom also I would wish to be very learned men, which is very necessary to maintain the good opinion that has been conceived of our Society in these parts. Especially the Spaniard who is sent ought to be outstanding, so that he may be able to resolve all the cases of conscience, and very grave ones, that occur here.

Persons's idea, apparently, was to have Spanish and Italian Jesuit Fathers as consultors and confessors, acting as chaplains, protected by the Spanish ambassador. However, it is unlikely they would have been left immune by the English government.[83]

They will do well also to ask for ample faculties from His Holiness so that we can use them for the honor of God and the spread of the Catholic faith, which is greatly hindered by doubtful and complicated cases, which arise from no one here having Apostolic faculties; nor is it possible for us except with extreme peril to consult the Apostolic See about everything, since it is an offense of high treason to consult with the Apostolic See from here on any matter, or to receive any sort of public instrument on any matter from that See.

Priests needed "ample faculties" especially to release any Catholics from excommunication, and to grant dispensations from canonical impediments to marriage.

There is immense need of a Bishop to consecrate for us the holy oils
for Baptism and Extreme Unction, for want of which we are brought
to the greatest straits; and unless His Holiness makes haste to help us
in this, matter, we shall soon be at our wits' end. [Priests then had no
faculty to bless oil for Extreme Unction.] Would that the Reverend
Bishop of St. Asaph [Dr. Goldwell] had succeeded in reaching us
here as he wished. For I had procured everything necessary for him,
and found places that were safe and sound. But his efforts did not
meet with success. We are hoping that His Holiness will very soon
supply us with someone else of more vigorous body. It is certainly in
the interests of the common cause that we get someone soon.

From prison greet you Fr. [Ralph] Sherwin, Fr. Luke [Kirby],
Fr. [Robert] Johnson, Fr. [John] Hart, [Mr. John] Paschal, [Mr.
Henry] Orton. . . .

The adversaries are very mad that by no cruelty can they move a
single Catholic from his resolution—no, not even little girls. A noble
maiden of sixteen [Miss Thomson] was questioned by the pseudo-
bishop of London about the Supreme Pontiff, and answered him
with courage, and even made fun of him in public, and so the bar-
barian ordered her to be consigned to the public residence for pros-
titutes [Bridewell]. On the way she cried out before all that she was
being sent to that shameful place by reason of her conscience and
her Catholic faith, and not for misconduct.

Persons later reported that the notoriously cruel Bishop Aylmer of
London had her beaten with whips as a prostitute.[84]

The safest way of communicating with me from Belgium is through
a certain person by whom at fixed times everything is transmitted to
me quite safely. He has also an appointed place in London where the
letters he sends reach me. For though I have many places in London
where I can stay, yet in none of them do I ever remain more than
two days, because of the strict searches made to catch me. I think,
however, that by the grace of God, I am sufficiently safe from them
owing to the precaution I take, and am going to take, of being in different places from early morning till late at night.

After having performed the divine services [Mass and Divine
Office], and preached, which sometimes I am compelled to do twice
in the same day, I struggle with almost endless business, of which the
chief matters are solving cases of conscience which arise; directing

other priests to suitable places and tasks; reconciling schismatics to the Church; writing letters to those wavering at times under this persecution; and procuring temporal aid to support those in need in prison. For, every day, they send to me, laying bare their needs. In short, there are so many burdens of this kind that I could now easily say that I am weary, except that I perceive clearly that the important work we are doing tends to God's honor....

Hence all Catholics here lift up their hands to heaven and thank God and His Holiness for founding such a College at Rome, beyond all their hopes; and they beseech His Holiness with earnest prayer, by the viscera of the mercy of our Saviour, to defend the College, and to enlarge it for the needs of the present time, so that from it we may be able to look for the ample help of erudite priests to carry on the spiritual battle with the sworn enemies of God and the Church. But I earnestly pray Your Reverence to send us only men who are well-prepared, and especially those well-instructed in controversy, for one learned man is worth more than a hundred illiterate ones.

Two days ago a priest called [Thomas] Clifton [Douay-trained; arrived back in England in January 1580] was led in chains through the streets to his interrogation, and he walked with so cheerful a countenance that the people marveled. When he saw this, he began to laugh so heartily, at which the folks were still more amazed, and asked him why he was the only one to laugh at his own sad case, for which everybody else pitied him. He answered that it was because he, rather than other people, was the one about to make a profit from the business. And are you surprised, he said, that a man rejoices at his gain? [For maintaining the Pope's supremacy he was condemned in 1581 to perpetual imprisonment, where he died probably in 1593.]

At the beginning of this persecution, there were some people in a certain county of England who were overwhelmed by fear, and, yielding to the insistence of the queen's commissars, promised to go thereafter to the Protestant church—but on hearing this, their wives stood out against them, threatening to leave them if out of human respect they left off their obedience to God and the Church. Many like things have taken place among sons who for this cause have said "Farewell" to their parents.[85]

Years later, Persons recorded what he had learnt of the Catholics' zeal and courage shown back in 1577: How boldly those who are Catholics in secret, and not yet captured, serve the Catholic religion, appears by a fact that we have learnt in a recent letter of one who, without being of any great rank or power, nevertheless was not content with one private Mass, but caused two High Masses to be sung in his house, with all ornaments and inferior ministers [deacon, sub-deacon], as though he had been in the middle of Rome and not in England. Another has even gone beyond that: he has actually caused Mass to be celebrated in the house of the Dean of London, a cruel persecutor, for the benefit of the Catholics there kept in custody, while the Dean was away from home.[86]

"The Hottest Blood"

Fr. Persons mentions above the fortitude of certain young girls and women. Men feature more than women in this biography, but the courage of many girls and women—often more than manly—should not be forgotten.[87] One young girl, well-known for her bravery, was Frances Burroughs, adopted by her cousin Eleanor Brooksby (née Vaux)[88] when orphaned at the age of five. It is recorded that, at the age of eleven, Frances boldly confronted pursuivants and constables who came into her house with many swords drawn, to search for priests or "Massing stuff." On another occasion, a pursuivant held a naked dagger at her breast, and threatened to stab her if she refused to say where the priests were concealed. She answered with perfect composure, and in words worthy of Shakespeare:

> If thou dost, it shall be the hottest blood that ever thou sheddest in thy life.[89]

Campion's Account to the Jesuit General

Campion's letter of November 1580 to the Father General in Rome describes the passages of his career since he last wrote from St. Omer. The events to which the first paragraphs refer have already been related; but it will do no harm to repeat them in his own words. The rest refers to his experience during his first journey through England.

> Reverend Father,
>
> Having now passed five months, relying on divine mercy, in these places, I thought it good to inform you by letter of the present state of things here, and what is likely to come. For I am sure, both

for the common care of us all, and special love to me, you long to know what I do, what hope I have, and how I proceed. Of the earlier things, I wrote from St. Omer; what has since happened, I will now briefly recount to you.

It so happened, by the counsel of God, as I construe it, that waiting four days for favorable winds, I finally took to sea on the fifth day in the evening, which was the feast of John the Baptist, my heavenly patron, to whom I had often before commended my cause and journey. The next day, very early, we came to land, at Dover, my little man [Br. Ralph] and I.[90] There we were at the very point of being captured. We appeared, as ordered, before the Mayor of the town, who conjectured many things and took us to be who we were: opponents of the heretical party; lovers of the faith of our fathers; that we dissembled our names; had been abroad for religion; and returned again to spread the same. One thing he specially urged: that I was Mr. [Gabriel] Allen; which I offered to deny under oath, if need be. At length he resolved, and repeated it often, that I should be sent up under guard to the Privy Council. And I cannot tell who inspired him to change his mind, if not God, whom I was then silently beseeching, employing the intercession also of St. John [the Baptist], by whose favor I had come thus far. Suddenly an old man came out—God reward him!—"It has been decided," he said, "you can go. Farewell." The two of us took off. By these and similar events which I experience here, I am confirmed in my opinion that I shall be apprehended one day, when it shall be for the greater glory of God,[91] and not before.

I made it to London, and my good angel guided me unawares into the same house that had previously hosted Father Robert [Persons]. Young gentlemen [George Gilbert and others] came to me on every hand; they greet me, dress me, furnish me, arm me, and convey me out of the City.

I ride about some piece of the country nearly every day. The harvest is wonderfully great. On horseback I meditate my sermon; when I come to the house, I polish it. Then I talk with any who approach me, or hear their confessions. In the morning, after Mass, I preach; with such eagerness their ears strain to listen, and they very often receive the Sacraments, for the ministration of which we are assisted here and there by priests, whom we find in every place, whereby both the people are well served, and the work is made less onerous for us.

Our native priests, themselves being outstanding in learning and holiness of life, have raised such a high opinion of our Order, that I hesitate to describe the exceeding reverence Catholics show unto us. All the more must it be plain that the helpers, of which we have now enormous need, be such as may meet everyone's expectation of them! Above all, let them be well trained in preaching.

We cannot long escape the hands of the heretics; the enemies have so many eyes, so many tongues, so many traps.

I am in clothing very ridiculous to myself; I change it often, and my name too. I read letters myself that in the first page tell the news that "Campion is captured." This so re-echoes in my ears repeatedly now, wherever I go, that fear itself has driven out all my fear. "My life is ever in my own hands" [Ps. 118:109]. Let those coming to help us meditate upon this and keep it in mind.

Truly, the consolations intermingled with these affairs are so great, that they not only countervail the dread of punishment, but by infinite sweetness compensate for any sort of pain. A conscience pure, a courage invincible, zeal incredible, a work so worthy, the number innumerable, of high and middle and lower class, of every age and sex.

Here, even amongst the Protestants themselves who are of a milder nature, it has become a proverb, that Catholics are people who repay the money they owe; to the point that if any Catholic treats someone unfairly, they expostulate with him for behavior least becoming such a person.

In short, heresy hears ill of all men; neither is there any condition of people counted more vile and corrupt than their own ministers, and we are rightly indignant that fellows so unlearned, so evil, so scorned, so base, should in so desperate a cause overrule such a number of noble wits as our realm has.

Threatening edicts besiege us. Yet, by caution, and by the prayers of good people, and, most importantly, by God's gift, we have passed safely through a good part of the island. I find so many being forgetful of themselves, and solicitous for us.

By the will of God, a certain thing fell out these days, which I had not looked for. I had set down in writing in several articles the causes of my coming in, and made certain most reasonable demands. I professed myself to be a priest of the Society; that I returned to spread the Catholic faith, to teach the Gospel, to minister the Sacraments, humbly asking audience of the queen and the nobility of the realm, and challenging my adversaries to a debate. One copy of this writing I determined to keep with me, that it might go with me if I should fall into the officers' hands; another copy I entrusted to a friend [Pounde], that if I myself should be seized with the other copy, another might there upon straightaway be dispersed.

My friend concealed it not, but divulged it, and it was gobbled up; whereat the enemy was furious. They answered from their pulpits, that they themselves were certainly willing to debate, but the queen was not willing to have further disputes on matters already settled. They lash at us with insults, calling us seditious, hypocrites—even heretics too, which is much laughed at. The people hereupon is ours. In a remarkable way, that mistake [of spreading the *Brag*] has much advanced the cause. If we be commanded, and may have safe conduct, we will go into the Court. But they mean nothing like it.

All our prisons are being filled with Catholics, and they are now making new ones. At last they openly admit that it were better to hand over a few traitors to execution than to betray so many souls.

Of their martyrs they now speak no more. We surpass them as regards our cause, our number, our prestige, and the good opinion of all. Instead of a few apostates or retired cobblers of theirs, we have bishops, lords, knights, the old nobility, patterns of learning, integrity and prudence, the choicest youth, noble matrons, and the remainder of a more modest position too numerous to count, either martyred at once, or by consuming imprisonment dying daily. While I write this, a most cruel persecution is raging. The household is sad. They talk of nothing but the death of their own members, or hiding-holes, or chains, or the confiscation of their property; all the same they carry on courageously.

Very many, even at this present, are being restored to the Church. New soldiers enroll their names, while the veterans offer up their blood. By this sacred blood and these oblations God will be pleased, and we shall, no question, soon overcome. You see, then, Reverend Father, how much need we have of your prayers and sacrifices and other heavenly help. There will always be in England men that will have care of their own salvation, and such as shall advance other men's, rage man or devil never so much. This

Church shall stand so long as priests and pastors shall be found for the sheep.

I am hindered by a rumor of a present peril—so no more at this time. "Arise God, His enemies scatter" [*Ps.* 67].

Farewell.

Ed. Camp.[92]

Jesuit General, Fr. Mercurian, did not see this letter; he had died on August 1. It was received and read by the Society's Vicar-General, Fr. Oliver Mannaerts, a strong supporter of the English mission.[93]

CHAPTER 11

Campion's Progress

FATHERS PERSONS and Campion had last seen each other on July 19. On that day, when they parted at Hoxton, they set no date for a reunion, but clearly they intended to meet up again in London. Persons wrote, "Fr. Edmund and I have both left London for the country, with the intention of returning there in two or three months."[1] In the event, Campion was away for eleven weeks, and Persons was away for a little less than that.

At some point, Fr. Robert must have sent word to Fr. Edmund to return to London; and told him of a contact person there who would tell him where Robert was when Edmund should arrive.

Reunion, Review, and Plans at Uxbridge

Persons reached London at the start of October 1580,[2] some days before Campion, for whom he tried to find a convenient lodging. But he found the persecution had become so hot, and Campion especially was so ardently sought, that it was thought unsafe for him to come into the city—for everyone was talking about the *Brag*, with "infinite copies taken thereof."[3] It was therefore indicated to Edmund on the way that he should tarry somewhere in the neighborhood. He accordingly stayed at William Griffith's house at Southland, in Buckinghamshire, near Uxbridge,[4] fifteen miles from London, where Persons and other missionary priests joined him.

Full and exact itineraries of Persons and Campion are not known to us; they wrote letters and reports to Rome, but generally did not name specific Catholics or residences, and of course it was too dangerous to keep a diary or address book. At their first meeting, they related to each other their adventures. They enumerated the shires, towns, and houses they had visited, the dispositions of the people, the successes gained, the souls harvested, the dangers faced, and the perils escaped. Some of it they already knew through the network of Catholic contacts, for, says Persons, while not seeing one another for the previous eleven weeks or so, "albeit often they had heard of each other's journey and partly also of their affairs."[5]

Persons told how, with George Gilbert as companion, he had toured from west to east, passing through the counties of Northampton, Derby, Worcester, Gloucester, and Hereford;[6] how he had reconciled Lord Compton, Thomas Tresham, William Catesby, and his uncle Sir Robert Dimocke (Dymock), the hereditary "Champion of England"[7] who had died for the Faith in Lincoln jail, only a few weeks earlier, September 11, 1580.[8] Among his converts or reverts, Persons may have enumerated certain aldermen of Stratford, John Wheeler, and John Shakespeare, father of William, the dramatist and poet.[9]

Campion, in his turn, told of his travels in counties west of London, namely, Berkshire, Oxfordshire, and Northampton shire, and the conversions he had made there.[10] We can identify one particular visit, to the mansion house of Great Coxwell, about two miles south-west of Faringdon (formerly in Berkshire; now Oxfordshire).[11] An indictment was later issued against: "Edmund Foster," *alias* of Edmund Campion; Mr. and Mrs. Francis and Anne Morris; Edmund, Martha, and Alice Morris; Alice Wicks, widow, of Ashbury; and others to the number of thirty. The charge—written in thoroughly Puritanical language—was that on July 30, 1580, Campion, "in a certain room within the mansion house of Great Coxwell, being vested in alb and other vestments according to papistical rites and ceremonies, did say and celebrate one private and detestable Mass in the Latin tongue, derogatory to the blood of Christ, and contrary to his due allegiance."[12]

Some of the chief converts or reverts that he and Persons had gathered in had their estates in the county of Northamptonshire. Among these were Lord Vaux of Harrrowden, Sir William Catesby of Ashby St. Leger, and Sir Thomas Tresham of Rushton Hall, Northamptonshire.

Tresham (c. 1543–1605) had been reared a Catholic, and if he was reconciled through Fr. Persons' ministry, it was scarcely more than a formality.[13] He spent much of his life from 1581 in prison or under house arrest. Between 1581–88 he was imprisoned for harboring Edmund Campion. He was also imprisoned for recusancy in 1597 and 1599.

Catesby was also persecuted as a recusant.

Their sons, Francis Tresham and Robert Catesby, were among the thirteen conspirators of the Gunpowder Plot of 1605.[14]

Persons found that Campion had reaped a wonderful harvest and that the other priests had gathered plentifully but had been chiefly employed in watering what Campion had sown. They then laid their plans for their next expedition and resolved that Persons should for the present remain in or near London, for it seemed that he was not as yet so diligently sought after as Campion, who, both for this reason and because his presence was most earnestly desired in various places, was sent into the country till the tempest should die down somewhat.

The Catholics of several shires had made suit to have Campion among them, especially those of Lancashire and Norfolk, which he had been unable to visit on his former circuit. (In July of the following year, Campion would set out on another trip, aiming for the county of Norfolk—but was prevented from visiting it, as we shall see.) Lancashire was chosen because it was further from London, generally better disposed to the Catholic religion and because there was more hope to find there a commodity of books to help him answer the heretics, if they should provoke him. It was supposed they would shortly do so, seeing that his *Challenge* or *Brag* was now in their hands, and known over all England— and France too, as the ambassador there, Sir Henry Cobham, wrote to Walsingham.[15] It furnished almost the only common topic at ordinary tables and public meetings. Campion was now a household name. Although an answer had not hitherto been published, it seemed impossible for there not to be one shortly. So it was resolved that Campion should depart again and, with all the secrecy he could, put himself within the compass of Lancashire.

Campion to Write a Book

Moreover, it was moved to him, that as nothing needing a reply had yet appeared, he should do well, whenever he had leisure from preaching and instructing, to write something in Latin to the Universities, considering the love they bore him, and the good opinion they had of his style in times past. After some insistence, he agreed to this, provided the subject

was given him. On this some proposed: "Consolation to Catholics in
this time of persecution"; others, "Encouraging the weak to stand, and
reprehending such as for worldly fear did shrink from God"; others, "To
reprove this manner of the Protestants' proceedings contrary to their
own doctrine and protestations in time past"; and others, finally, that he
should write of some points in controversy.

Campion, after fit pause, said that all these proposals were good;
yet, if it was left to him, he should choose an argument that no one had
named: *De hoeresi desperata* (Heresy in despair)—"to show that heresy
did now despair in England." All present laughed at the paradox and
objected that heresy was then most rampant, triumphant, and persecuting. "Even for this cause," he replied, "seemeth that argument most fit
at this time, for this manner of their cruel proceeding by terror is the
greatest argument that may be of their desperation, for if they had any
confidence at all in the truth of their cause, they would never proceed in
this manner."[16] Whether the company was ready to accept so broad a
principle, Fr. Persons does not inform us.

This notion of "heresy in despair," which was to have been the title of
his work, is the key-note of his famous *Ten Reasons*.

As Fr. Pollen explains,

> Campion did not affirm that heresy was on the point of failing, and
> that Catholicism was on the point of conquering. He knew well
> enough that the elimination of heresy in England would take a long,
> long time, and that the Catholics must pass through fire and water
> before they reached repose. That he himself would probably soon
> be slain is a dominant thought, which shows itself constantly. What
> Campion meant was that heresy was in despair of succeeding in
> the way it had hoped to succeed; that is as a Church, by preaching,
> teaching, or persuasion. It was now discovered to be a sham, a mere
> human tyranny; a thing that could not stand by reason; and by con-
> sequence doomed in time to pass away and end. Its mask was torn
> from its face, and it was desperate at the exposure of its hideousness,
> irrationality, and instability.[17]

His first theme is the "diffidence" which leads men to pervert
Scripture, and the "despair" which made Manicheans, Ebionites, Luther,
and Lutherans alter or maim the Bible. This beginning of Campion's

book shows, as Persons says, "his intention was specially to handle that point of the despairing of heresy, if he had not been drawn to another argument afterward by the answer of Charke" to his *Challenge*. For, says Persons,

> it was Fr. Campion's perpetual opinion that heresy in England was desperate, and that few or no men of judgment did think in their consciences that doctrine to be true and defensible that was commonly taught and practiced, the absurdities thereof being so many and manifest as they were; but that some, of policy, some for present government, others for ease, others for gain, honour, and preferment, and all commonly for some temporal interest or other, did stretch out a hand to hold it up for a time by force and violence.[18]

This idea may be found in several parts of the *Ten Reasons*, especially in the conclusion.

After disposing of the point of Campion's writing, the company proceeded to consult about sending some priests to the Universities to help and direct such youths as God might move to embrace His religion, and to pass over sea to the Seminaries. For this purpose they appointed Frs.. William Hartley and Arthur Pitts (obviously in attendance at this Uxbridge meeting). The fate of Fr. Hartley is narrated at the end of the next chapter. Fr. Pitts was captured eventually, February 1582, treated harshly in the Tower, and banished in 1585.

Campion Goes North for His Second Journey

Finally, Persons tells us, he and Campion agreed to write an account to the General at Rome how matters had passed with them, in what state they were for the present, and what helps they had need of for the time to come. These were chiefly two: the prayers of all good men, and a new supply of other Jesuits for the English mission to come and share their labors—a request that was answered by the mission of Fathers Holt and Heywood. The persecution and the search beginning now to be so vehement, it was thought dangerous for them to stay any longer together. It was decided that Campion should presently depart and write his letter to the General upon the way. His letter was given at the end of the last chapter.

So after prayer and some exhortations, mutual confession and renewal of their vows according to the custom of their Society, they parted, each one committing "his fellow to the grace of Almighty God, with the tenderness of heart which in such a case and so dangerous a time may be imagined, when they might hardly hope to see ever the one the other again, they took their journey"[19] on November 16, 1580: Campion towards Lancashire, with Br. Ralph Emerson—and their superior to London.[20]

In October, just before the priests' conference was being held in Uxbridge, the queen's Council published a new Proclamation for their discovery and capture—the third since the entrance of the Jesuits into England. This caused such great danger and molestation from constables, pursuivants, searchers, and other catchpoles, that Campion found it difficult to pass through the counties and shires where he was to go. Often he lighted upon the searchers, though not they upon him—for his time was not yet come.[21]

Gaps, and Sources of the Narrative

This chapter's narrative began early in October, and has jumped to November 16. If these two dates (both from Persons) are right—the first for the return to London, or rather, Uxbridge; the second for the departure on the next apostolic journey—it is difficult to explain what Campion did in or from Uxbridge for six weeks. At least, we have no knowledge of any works or visits in this time beyond meeting with his superior probably at the start and end of the period.[22]

The biographer now loses the invaluable aid of the manuscript life of Campion by Persons, since he left it unfinished at this point, November 1580. For a few months now of Campion's life (December 1580–July 1581), he has to rely on Bombino and Bartoli, two honest writers who had authentic materials to work from. There is also a skeleton of Persons's intended continuation of his biography, which served as a guide to Bombino; and there are papers in the Public Record Office and the British Museum. Then, from July 1581 on, we have contemporary notes and personal memoirs, in addition to State papers and official records, of a good deal of the proceedings right up to Campion's death.

Campion Travels to the North, End of 1580

After departing from Uxbridge on November 16, 1580, in order to go to Lancashire, Campion, finding himself more than ever beset, was obliged to tarry a long while on the way.

The period up to Christmas is a blank to us, but, "because he mentioned them . . . without precise dates, Campion may have stayed at the homes of Lord William Vaux, Sir Thomas Tresham, and Sir William Catesby in Northamptonshire and [at Lapworth Park] Warwickshire during this period."[23] Burghley's papers, however, say he stayed at these three men's houses in Summer 1580—some months earlier.[24]

On November 15, 1581, Vaux, Tresham, and Catesby were all tried in the Star-Chamber, between 9 and 10 o'clock in the morning, the day after Campion's arraignment.[25] The three were related: Vaux was married to Tresham's aunt; Catesby was brother-in-law of Tresham. Vaux was fined £1,000; Tresham and Catesby 1,000 marks apiece.[26]

One place Campion may have visited before Christmas, on the way north, was the home of Mr. Edward Arden, High Sheriff in Warwickshire in 1575, and second cousin to William Shakespeare's mother, Mary Arden. We know he went there some time, for two years later, around November 1583, Mr. Arden was arrested and executed—hanged, drawn, and quartered—on the pretext of not reporting the treasonous words of his mad brother-in-law, but, in reality, says Persons, for having hosted the Jesuits: "They put to death with a great many odious insults a much respected gentleman, and a most zealous Catholic, named Edward Arden, in whose house Fathers Campion and Persons had been most hospitably received in England."[27]

Another possible host on the way was Mr. Thomas Fitzherbert,[28] whose ancestral home was at Swynnerton, Staffordshire.[29]

Campion in the North, Start of 1581

At Christmas 1580, Gervase Pierrepoint took Campion to the house of his brother, Henry Pierrepoint of Holme Pierrepoint (on the Trent below Nottingham), and Thoresby (near Ollerton), Nottinghamshire, the ancestor of the earls of Kingston.[30]

There he remained till Sunday, January 8, when he and his guide Gervase left for Mr. and Mrs. Walter and Cassandra Powdrell (Powtrell), sergeant-at-law of West Hallam, six miles north-east of Derby.[31] Later that year, on November 15, 1581, Mr. Powdrell was tried before the Star-Chamber, and admitted: "that I have received Mr. Campion, I have confessed it; and I hope I have not offended therein, for bestowing a night's lodging on him who sometime did read to me in the university, and by whom I did never know evil."[32] He was fined 500 marks. His wife Cassandra was the daughter of Francis Shirley of Staunton, Leicester—a Sheriff of the counties of Warwick and Leicester (d. 1571), famous for his charity.[33] The Powdrells had three sons and four daughters.[34] Owing to their fines, they gradually lost their extensive estates. They died on the same day in 1588.[35]

Campion and his guide spent Wednesday, January 11, at the house of Henry Sacheverell, who had been at St. John's, Oxford, with Campion.[36] The house was either at Hopwell Hall, five miles east of Derby—or in Morley, four miles north-east of Derby. Campion said Mass.

Thence he and his guide went to the Langford's (Longford's) at Longford, nine miles west of Derby, towards Uttoxeter, where they spent the Thursday and Friday, January 12 and 13, with Mass on both days. Mr. and Mrs. Nicholas Longford had been recusants in 1577 and are recorded to have harbored three priests there in the 1580s.

Thence Campion went on Saturday, January 14, to Lady Constance Foljambe's (Fuljames) at Throwley Hall, North Wingfield, Staffordshire (or to her other house at Walton, Derbyshire). There they were joined by George Gilbert. Campion said Mass on each of the two days spent there.

Lady Foljambe's husband, Sir James, had died in 1558. In January 1569, she had hosted Mary Queen of Scots (with her servants), who was being transported in the custody of Sir Francis Knowles, who would harass Campion at his execution:[37]

> Mary [Stuart] was herself attacked with violent pain in the side next day, and became so alarmingly ill in the course of a few hours, that Sir Francis Knollys [Knowles], finding it impossible to bring her on to Chesterfield, halted seven miles north of that town, and lodged her at the mansion of Mr. Foljambe, where she and her ladies were honorably received and kindly entertained by their noble hostess, Lady Constance Foljambe, till she was sufficiently recovered to proceed to her destination.[38]

In 1588, Lady Foljambe would be apprehended as a recusant and held for two years. When released, she found herself deprived of her goods, and so made destitute for some time in her old age, until her struggle for their return was successful. She died in 1600. She was one who gave courage to other recusants. When she was held in prison, the Anglican Rector of North Wingfield, John Coke, wrote with pleasure, that "divers of my flock, being made recusants by her means, have very orderly conformed themselves."[39]

From her place they went on Monday, January 16, to a well-known recusant, Mr. Robert Eyre (Ayers) of Spital,[40] Chesterfield, Derbyshire.

There Gervase Pierrepoint handed over his office of conductor to Mr. Tempest who led Campion into Yorkshire on January 17. This could be Henry Tempest, of Broughton Hall, near Skipton-in-Craven, born 1527, a recusant who assigned his estates to his son to avoid confiscation. Alternatively, it could be his son, Stephen, born 1553, and knighted in 1603 by King James, though a convicted recusant and fined as such.[41]

Campion in Yorkshire

After Mr. Tempest took Pierrepoint's place, however, Burghley is obliged to note that "Campion confesseth he went Northwards with Tempest, and that they kept company together about nine days, and will confess no place of their being but at inns."[42] Those nine days will bring us to January 26, roughly, 1581.

The Lord Treasurer managed to light upon a gentleman, John Rooksby (Rokeby, Rookby) of Mortham Tower, Little Danby, by Yafforth, who confessed that Campion was at his house on Saturday, January 28. For this, the man was brought to London in December 1581, and in 1584 is found in the Fleet prison, for religion.[43]

Lord Burghley records as Campion's chief favorers in Yorkshire— at whose houses Campion was to be found between January 28 and February 26, 1581:

- Dr. Thomas Vavasour, a physician, who practiced in York. The Privy Council had named him in July 1580 to be indicted for having Mass at his home. We find him in prison at Hull on August 6, 1580 and in the Gatehouse in 1583.[44] Burghley's notes say that the doctor was in prison when Campion visited, and Mrs.

Dorothy Vavasour summoned her neighbors. Both Dr. and Mrs. Vavasour were to die for the Faith, in separate prisons, in 1585 and 1587, respectively. Their son James became a priest overseas and died in Rheims. Mrs. Vavasour knew well St. Margaret Clitherow, executed in 1586 by crushing to death, and it is reasonable to surmise that Mistress Clitherow was invited to Mass said by Fr. Campion.

- Mrs. Katherine Bulmer (Boulmer),.of Marrick, near Richmond, North Yorkshire.[45] Born Katherine Norton, she had married Francis Bulmer who had died in 1578.
- Sir William Bapthorpe (Babthorpe) of Osgodby, in the East Riding, who in the previous August had given bond of £200 to Archbishop Sandys and the other commissioners, that he and his family would dutifully go to church, and "apprehend all roving popish priests, and other like evil popish subjects, and bring their bodies before the commissioners." Once when pursuivants came to his house to arrest two priests within, Sir William, a tall, strong man, drew out his sword and held them in fear of it until the priests had safely gone. For this action, he was fined such a great sum as brought him to poverty, besides almost a year's imprisonment.[46]
- Mr. Grimston—possibly Blessed Ralph Grimston (Grymeston) of Nidd, hanged at York on June 15, 1598, for aiding, assisting and conducting Blessed Peter Snow, a priest, executed with him. Their skulls are in the altar of the Cathedral of Leeds.
- Or this Grimston could be Thomas, whose main house was Grimston Garth, Holderness, in the East Riding, but who also owned property in Mitton parish, over the West Riding border into Lancashire, and at Little Smeaton in Birkby parish, Allertonshire. At Smeaton, in 1575, Thomas Grimston, with his son Marmaduke and a schoolmaster, had been presented by the church-wardens for recusancy. In 1579 the whole family was at Little Smeaton and put on bond to conform.[47]
- Mr. William Hawkesworth and his wife Rosamund, daughter of Thomas Lister of Westby.[48] He had property in Birkby parish, Mitton, and elsewhere in the West Riding. Both the (second)

Grimstons and the Hawkesworths had sons in the continental
seminaries and were closely related to Dr. Allen.[49]

• Mr. Askulph Cleesby (Cleasby), whose principal estate was
at Cleasby in Gilling East, but he also had two other places in
Cleveland. He had been part of the Catholic uprising of 1569, but
escaped punishment. He died peacefully at his Morton home in
1584.[50]

At mid-Lent, about February 26, Tempest seems to have resigned his
charge of conductor to the hands of Campion's third guide, Mr. Smyth,
who took him to Tempest's sister, married to Mr. William Harrington of
Mount St. John,[51] an isolated house in the parish of Felixkirk, Yorkshire,
about the Tuesday in the third week of Lent (February 28), where they
stayed for fourteen days, to March 13.[52]

It is said that this retreat of Mount St. John, and other stopping-
places in the region, were found for Edmund by a Yorkshire priest, Fr.
Richard Holtby, of Hovingham, later a Jesuit, who had received Campion
into his home.[53]

For sheltering Campion, Harrington was jailed in the Fleet prison,
London, in 1581. Under interrogation, he said that his wife's brother
brought Campion to his house but he "knew him not for Campion until
he was upon departure." He was remitted to the York Assizes. It is possible he conformed occasionally to escape further harassment, as so many
did, but his family kept close to priests for the next twenty years.[54]

Campion Writes *Ten Reasons*, 1581

In those fourteen days at Harrington's, Campion was occupied in writing much of his book *De Hoeresi Desperata*, which afterwards appeared
as *Rationes Decem* (Ten Reasons),[55] a form which better enabled him to
meet the charge of overweening pride which Charke and Hanmer had
made against him, because be had challenged to dispute single-handed
with all the learning of a whole realm; a charge which had become so
general, that every pulpit was ringing with his impudence, and with the
frauds and sedition of the Jesuits. Hence he was forced to show that his
trust was not in his own power, but solely in the strength of his cause,
which he exhibited in ten reasons, *quibus fretus* (relying on which),[56]
he offered to dispute with any or all of the ministers of the Established

Church. He united the two ideas of defending his *Challenge* and address-ing the Universities.

Here, at Mount St. John, his conduct made such an impression on William, one of his host's six sons, that three years afterwards he fled overseas to Rheims, and eventually came back to England a priest, to be hanged, drawn, and quartered: Blessed William Harrington, martyred at Tyburn in 1594, beatified 1929.

From Tuesday, March 14, to Easter Sunday, March 26, we have a gap, best explained by the adept guidance of Fr. Holtby, on account of which Lord Burghley failed to find out anything about Campion's movements in that period.[57] We can surmise, with Fr. Morris S.J., that this time was spent in refining and polishing the *Ten Reasons*.[58]

Campion in Lancashire

At Easter, Campion obtained a fresh conductor, a Yorkshireman, Mr. More, who had once been his pupil,[59] and who now, with his wife, trav-eled with him to protect him, and to introduce him to the houses of the Catholic gentlemen in Lancashire (Lancaster). This was possibly Edward More of the family of More Hall, Bolsterstone, but at that time partly resident on his small property at Cowley, near Sheffield. Alternatively, it was Mr. Edward More of Barnborough Hall, Doncaster,[60] whose father John was the only son of Sir Thomas More. He was born c. 1537 and died in 1620. (Edward More's second son was Henry, later to become a Jesuit priest and biographer of Campion.)[61] Probably Campion traveled as a servant, as he had done in the journey from Rome: a simple enough disguise which also provided a good reason to be travlling with a married couple. By them he was led to visit the homes of:

- The Worthingtons of Blainscough Hall, Standish, near Wigan. Isabel was the surviving widow of Peter. Their fourth son, Thomas, educated at Oxford, trained at Douay, ordained priest in 1577, was at this time also engaged in priestly work in England.[62] Also residing there, it seems, were Thomas and Mary Worthington. Mary was niece to Dr. Allen and cousin to Allen's nephew, the priest, Blessed George Haydock (martyred 1584).[63]
- Thomas Talbot of Bashall.[64]
- Thomas Southworth of Samlesbury Hall: son of Sir John

Southworth. Sir John Southworth, married to Mary Assheton of Middleton, had six sons and four daughters. He was Sheriff of Lancashire in 1562, 1568, and 1569, and was conspicuous as a recusant.[65] He was arrested by the Earl of Derby in 1568 and imprisoned in Chester Castle for speaking against the *Book of Common Prayer*, for never going to church, and for refusing to "take wine with the parson"[66] (as the Lancashire gentry contemptuously called the Protestant Communion). Sir John was also in prison for the Faith at least in the years 1581–84, and was often reported for his unflinching defense of the Faith. He died 1595. His son Thomas was equally staunch in his religion. Another son, Christopher, ordained priest at Rome in 1583, suffered imprisonment at Wisbeach Castle in 1595.[67]

- Bartholomew Hesketh of The Maynes (Mains, or Monks' Hall), Aughton: married to Sir John Southworth's daughter, Alice,[68] who was later imprisoned as a "busy recusant."[69]

- Mrs. Elizabeth Allen (née Westby) of Rossall Grange: widow of Dr. Allen's older brother, George, who died in 1579. In 1586, the Rossall Estate was confiscated from her, on the grounds that she was aiding and abetting Dr. Allen, and she was banished from England. Like other relatives of Dr. Allen, she was marked out for special persecution.[70]

- Richard Hoghton (Houghton, pronounced "Horton") of Park Hall in Charnock Richard: son of the staunch recusant Thomas Hoghton who built Hoghton Tower but had already died in exile. Richard entertained Campion at Hoghton Tower,[71] which had a fine library.[72] Campion left some books and papers there, which Br. Ralph went to fetch in the July coming. Richard and his wife Mary (sister of Fr. Edward Rishton who was then in the Tower of London) would be apprehended shortly after Campion and examined on Campion's visit there with Br. Ralph, and his books. A number of papers were seized there. Richard survived his imprisonment but was persecuted relentlessly to the end of his life.[73]

- John Westby of Mowbrick (Mowbreck Hall), a staunch and determined recusant, later imprisoned for this hospitality.[74] Dr. Allen recorded that one time, "John Westby of Molbreck,

Esquire, was glad to stand for a whole winter's day almost in a pit in water up to the ears, and often forced to duck under the waters, lest he should be espied of the persecutors."[75] He was a brother-in-law of Sir John Southworth and an uncle of Blessed George Haydock.[76]

- Mr. and Mrs. John and Jane Rigmayden of Wedacre (Woodacre) Hall, in the parish of Garstang. Born 1527, John was a staunch Catholic, and in consequence was greatly persecuted, suffering imprisonment in 1567. He died in 1587.[77]

At these houses he spent the time between Easter (March 26) and Whitsuntide (Pentecost, May 14), staying chiefly, according to Burghley, at Mr. Talbot's and Mr. Thomas Southworth's,[78] where he was fully occupied in preaching to the crowds that pressed to have conference with him.

This schedule of visits in the North was drawn up by Burghley after Campion's capture, and it was given out that Campion had confessed it all.[79]

Other people with whom Campion stayed at this and other times are named in other chapters.[80]

The people named here, and elsewhere, by no means make a complete list. If Edmund moved house every one or two days, there were many others who remained undetected. On occasion, however, where an entire household was Catholic, and Mass did not have to be held secretly and early while Protestants in the house were still asleep, he would stay for two, three or four days, in answer to their importunate requests.[81]

Shakespeare

We said above that Fr. Persons in his first circuit may have reconciled or strengthened William Shakespeare's father, John, in Stratford. John's wife was Mary Arden, from a strongly Catholic noble family. Her second cousin, Edward Arden, was executed for hosting Persons and Campion.[82] In 1757, behind the rafters of John Shakespeare's house in Henley Street, was discovered a spiritual *Testament*, or profession of Catholic faith, signed and concealed by him, which he most likely received from Persons or Campion, since the text is an English translation of one composed in Italian by Cardinal Borromeo, whom the two priests had visited in Milan on their way from Rome to England.[83]

The spiritual *Testament* was a long and beautiful document of sixteen paragraphs. It is so called because it is like a *Last Will and Testament*—but a spiritual one, committing one's soul to God and putting one's spiritual affairs in order. In it, the Catholic reaffirmed his faith in the Father, Son and Holy Spirit, and the one, Catholic, and Apostolic Church. He professed his desire to receive the Sacraments of Penance, Extreme Unction, and Holy Communion at the end of life. He thanked the Divine Majesty for his creation, redemption, sanctification, preservation, and vocation. He entrusted his soul to the divine goodness and infinite mercy, and pardoned all offenses and injuries he had received in life. He invoked the protection and intercession of the Blessed Virgin Mary, his Guardian Angel, and patron saints. He accepted death in whatsoever manner it may befall him, and conformed his will unto the will of God, "giving thanks unto His Divine Majesty for the life He has bestowed upon me."[84]

It was at this time that the seventeen-year-old future poet and playwright, William Shakespeare, probably staying at the home of (strong Catholic) Alexander Hoghton, most likely met the Jesuit orator and dramatist. We can only speculate on what passed between them. It is certain Shakespeare's father was a Catholic and that William knew recusant families in Lancashire. One of the school-masters at William Shakespeare's school, Stratford school, was Simon Hunt, from 1571 until 1575, when he went abroad, first to Douay, and then to Rome to become a Jesuit priest. Another master there, who began in 1579, was John Cottam, younger brother to Fr. Thomas Cottam who would be tried and condemned with Campion.[85]

It is noteworthy that Shakespeare's play, *Twelfth Night*, Act IV, scene ii, clearly refers a number of times—and favorably, too—to Campion ("the old hermit of Prague"), as well as Fr. Persons ("master Person").[86] The clown in that scene refers to "the old hermit of Prague, that never saw pen and ink." Campion had spent some years at Prague, in a religious life involving isolation from England; and the phrase, "never saw pen and ink" refers to an episode which occurred in the third Tower debate, on September 23, 1581, in which Campion was opposed by Fulke:[87]

> *Campion.* If you dare, let me show [you] Augustine and Chrysostom, if you dare.

Fulke. Whatsoever you can bring, I have answered already in writing against others of your side. And yet if you think you can add anything, put it in writing, and I will answer it.

Campion. Provide me ink and paper, and I will write.

Fulke. I am not to provide you ink and paper.[88]

Some writers have surmised or invented other connections between Campion and Shakespeare—but what is written above is as far as the evidence goes; there is nothing more documented or recorded.[89]

About 1564, a Mr. Burgess and his family moved to a farm called Denham Hall, one of the properties of the Hoghtons of Hoghton Tower. Denham Hall was in the parish of Brindle and about three miles from Hoghton Tower. Mr. Burgess placed an altar in a large room in the old farm-house, for the convenience of the numerous Catholics living there under the protection of the Hoghtons. In Easter-tide 1581, says one writer, Campion said Mass at this altar, and remained at Denham Hall until the Worthingtons carried him off, in the disguise of a groom, to their home at Blainscough Hall.[90] At their house, he was saved from arrest by an astute maid-servant, who in affected anger pushed him into a pond, and thus effectually disguised him.

Memories of Campion

Father Henry More S.J., writing in 1660, says:

> Even up to my time, Campion's memory has remained fresh in the North, where they have still remembered his sermons on the Hail Mary, on the Ten Lepers, on the King who went off on a journey, on the Last Judgment, and many other subjects, which people were so greedy of hearing that very many persons of notable families spent whole nights in neighboring barns, so that they might be early at the place next day. They were drawn not so much by his eloquence or elocution, although he was admirable in both respects, as by his fire, and by a certain hidden force in his way of speaking which they considered could only flow from the Holy Spirit. He preached daily, except when he sometimes withdrew himself to write his book, and perhaps to avoid the pursuivants, who were always on his track.[91]

CHAPTER 12

Fr. Persons and the Progress of the Mission

W E WILL now trace some of the activities of Fr. Persons and others of the band of twelve who entered England in June, and also consider the state of the English Catholics in the vital year that followed the missionaries' entry.

Persons Stays in London

Having sent Campion towards the north on November 16, 1580, Persons retired to London, where he found the persecution redoubled in vigor. A fourth proclamation came out against the Jesuits in November; for the Council imagined that all the priests had returned to London, and therefore directed the most minute search to be made in all Catholic houses for them. For this cause Persons, and probably other priests likewise, were forced to seek lodging elsewhere. Persons found his sometimes in Bridewell, London (close to Bridewell Church, near the Thames river), sometimes in the suburbs, and sometimes even in one of the queen's palaces. From this time the Catholics found their most secure asylums in the houses of pursuivants, or other civil and ecclesiastical officers whom they had in their pay.

Persons wrote:

> For though I have many places in London where I can stay, yet in none of them do I ever remain beyond two days, because of the extremely careful searches made to capture me. I think, however, that by the grace of God, I am sufficiently safe from them owing to the precaution I take, and will take, of being in different places from early morning till late at night.[1]

It was at this time also that Persons procured the assistance of Bernardino de Mendoza, the Spanish ambassador, who took him under his special protection, and would walk with him as one of his own men, while the queen's officers were watching his house. By him, Persons allowed himself to be altogether detached from the French interest, which was suspected, on account of Castelnau's friendly dealing with the Protestants. Persons discussed with the Spanish ambassador the means of saving England and Scotland from heresy or the dominion of heretics. Persons's biographer notes:

> An important factor was the attitude of the Catholic embassies in London. Bernardino de Mendoza, the Spanish ambassador, was most friendly. Persons spent a long evening with him on October 19 [1580]. He was to be an important link in the communications chain. Letters for Persons from Europe were to be directed in the first instance to the Flemish Jesuit rector at St. Omer, who would send them on as opportunity offered.[2]

His biographer summarizes his activities at this time:

> There were by now many places in London where Persons could stay, but he stayed nowhere more than two days to avoid the hyperactive pursuivants. During the daytime he kept on the move from early morning till late at night. His time was spent in preaching, saying Mass, sometimes twice a day, dealing with the moral problems of individuals, directing other priests to suitable places and ministries, reconciling schismatics, writing letters, and arranging help for those in prison and in want. But not even the myriad problems of the English mission engaged his whole attention. He was now looking towards Scotland.[3]

Persons wrote to the Rector of the English college on August 5, 1580:

> We are encountering many dangers—greater than those which are likely to be met by those who come after us, seeing that they will find many places arranged by us, and also because the enemy have a special hatred for us who are the first to come, as precursors, and they are planning every sort of evil for us. But the dangers are not such as to be inescapable for many years, or at any rate months; and I hope we shall avoid them, although indeed we are not certain of a single day.[4]

Fr. Ralph Sherwin Captured

In London, Persons escaped the dangers, but some of his chief friends were captured, including Ralph Sherwin.

Sherwin had been born at Rodesley, near Longford, in Derbyshire, about 1550. He studied at Oxford University, and was nominated a fellow of Exeter College in 1568. In 1575 he embraced the Catholic faith, left Oxford and entered Douay seminary. After two years' study of theology he was ordained priest by the Bishop of Cambrai on March 23, 1577. On August 2 following, he set out for the newly founded English College where he remained until he left for the English mission.

Sherwin and Persons had not met since they had parted at Rheims; yet he would do nothing without consulting Father Robert. His great anxiety to practice obedience would have driven him into a religious order, if it had not been for a still greater desire to sacrifice himself in the work of the English mission.

Persons writes:

> He met me the night that Bosgrave followed me home from Hoxton; we passed the night together in spiritual conference, wherein he told me of his desire to die. The next day he came to tell me what danger we were in, and then went away to preach; for we had agreed that he should stay in London for the arrival of a certain gentleman who had asked for him, and in the meantime should occupy him self with preaching; and it was while preaching in Mr. [Nicholas] Roscarock's house that he was captured. I think he was the first of our confraternity to be taken, though he was not the first priest caught since our arrival, for Bosgrave and Hart were already in prison.[5]

Sherwin was arrested early November 1580 and committed to the Marshalsea, where he dealt most fruitfully with two members of the "Family of Love" (a spiritualist sect of Dutch origin). He answered a challenge put to the Catholic prisoners to dispute for their religion, but before it happened Sherwin was sent to the Tower, where the registers say that he entered on December 4, 1580, together with Frs.. Thomas Cottam, Robert Johnson, and Luke Kirby, Mr. Henry Orton and his good host Mr. Nicholas Roscarock. All these names are found in the lieutenant's lists as "third-class" prisoners paying a certain amount for their weekly diet, fuel and candles. (The first and second classes paid more per week, for a better diet. From these payments, the lieutenant of the Tower made his profits.)

In the Tower, Sherwin was questioned and racked on December 15 and again on the 16th. He was offered a Protestant bishopric if he would renounce his faith.

Persons's report to the English College shows the extraordinary soul of Sherwin:

> Sherwin, one of your men, who in Rome used to burn with such zeal, has spent, with no less ardor of spirit, almost [four][6] whole months in preaching throughout various counties of the kingdom; and in this undertaking he was given graces and influence which were truly outstanding. And God in his Providence willed that in reward of such great labors he should be taken eventually in the act of preaching at the house of a certain noble youth named [Nicholas] Roscarock, who was committed to prison along with Sherwin, and afterwards, it is said, tortured on the rack.
>
> When Sherwin had been brought to the inner court of the prison, they fastened very heavy fetters on him which he could hardly move; this done, the warders went away for the time being to see into what cave or cell he was next to be confined. He, however, when he had looked around everywhere and saw that he was alone, looked up to heaven with a countenance full of joy and gave thanks to God; again, however, he looked at his feet loaded with chains and tried whether he could move them, and when, on moving them, he heard the sound of the chain, he could not contain himself, but with a loud laugh and shedding tears of joy as well, and raising his hands and eyes to heaven, he gave vent to his feeling of intense joy. The whole of this was witnessed by two heretics, members of the "Family of Love" who were being held prisoners in a place close by, and they were never able to cease from astonishment, and afterwards were in the habit of relating very often the whole sequence of what he had done. . . .
>
> When he had been six days, I think, in prison, he wrote to me thus:
>
> "I have received the alms you sent me yesterday; may God repay you. I had had a small sum, too, before, that; when it is finished, I shall go down to my brother robbers in the pit so as to live from the common basket of alms, and I shall go down assuredly much more

willingly than I have ever gone to any feast before. For the bread out of that basket will represent the cause of my God, sweeter than all honey and banquets of every kind. I have now some little bells [chains] on my feet and legs to remind me who I am and whose I am; I have never experienced such sweet harmony elsewhere. . . . Pray for me that I may complete my course bravely and faithfully."[7]

These captures show that the persecution was increasing in severity.

To add to Persons's perplexity, Adam Squire, the son-in-law of Aylmer, bishop of London, whose protection Gilbert had purchased for Persons, declared himself unable to carry out his agreement because of the quarrels in which it involved him with the bishop, and the danger to which it exposed him from the Council.

John Paschal Falls

It was at this time, late 1580, that young John Paschal fell away (one of the band which came from Rome). He was from Essex,[8] had been Sherwin's pupil at Oxford, and was the gentleman whose servant Campion pretended to be at Geneva. He was apprehended and committed to the Marshalsea while Sherwin was still there. His old master kept him firm, but when he lost the company of Sherwin, he was tripped up by his overconfidence. On his transfer to the Tower about Christmas 1580,[9] his resolution was almost gone. On January 15, 1581, he yielded to fear of torture, and agreed to attend Protestant church, took the oath of supremacy publicly and got his freedom. Persons says that Paschal, "repenting of his weakness and inconstancy, retired with great sorrow and shame from London."[10] He buried himself in some corner of Kent. Sherwin, who mourned over him, used to say to him, when he would burst into zealous speeches offering to bear all for Christ: "John, John, little knowest thou what thou shalt do before thou comest to it."[11] Thus he slips out of our narrative.

The Fate of the Fourteen

In summary, by early 1581, of the original band of fourteen who left Rome:

- The two who went ahead did not enter England (the bishop and Fr. Morton)

- One died naturally "not long after his entrance":[12] Fr. Bromborough
- Four were now imprisoned (Frs. Rishton, Sherwin, Kirby, and Mr. Briscoe)
- One had given in and retired (Mr. Paschal)
- Six were still at large (Frs. Persons, Campion, Crayne, Giblet, Br. Emerson, and possibly still Fr. Kemp)

Persons's Printing Press in Greenstreet

One of the great needs of the times was Catholic literature, both for the sustenance of Catholics and the rebuttal of their enemies' false charges against them. The enterprise of obtaining them or printing them was exceedingly difficult. "Books were seized at the ports or confiscated in the homes of Catholics. Proclamations condemning the importation and the possession of books of religious controversy were frequently issued during the reign [of Elizabeth], beginning with the Proclamation of March 1, 1569, and followed by similar edicts on July 1, 1570, November 14, 1570, and September 28, 1573, all directed against books published on the Continent."[13]

In October of 1580, Persons busied himself in carrying out a recommendation discussed at Uxbridge—the establishment of a press for printing answers to the works which would be sure to swarm against them. He found some allies amongst both the old Marian priests and younger Douay-Rheims men, of whom he names Fathers Edward Chambers, George Blackwell, William Maurice (Morris), Nicholas Tirwhit, Robert Gwynn, George Birkett (Birkhead), and Richard Norris.[14] Fr. Persons must have had this idea before coming to England; we saw that among the special faculties he received from Pope Gregory was permission to print Catholic books anonymously.[15]

Edward and William Brookesby (also Brooks or Brookes) persuaded their father to give permission for certain gentlemen to lodge at his large unoccupied house called Greenstreet (Greensted), now known as Boleyn Castle.[16] This secluded mansion at East Ham in Essex, south of Wanstead Flats and near Barking, was about seven miles east of London, Persons tells us.[17] There he conveyed the necessary materials, chiefly by the assistance of his young friend Mr. Stephen Brinkley who provided the equipment and its management. A "learned and resourceful"[18] Marian priest, William Maurice,[19] offered to procure the paper and other requisites.[20]

Little is known of Brinkley. A Bachelor of Civil Law, in 1579 he had translated and adapted a book by a Spanish Jesuit entitled *The Exercise of a Christian Life*. Persons called him "a gentlemen of excellent parts in literature and virtue,"[21] "a man of exceptional faith and energy, endowed as well with a great variety of talents and with a zeal for religion."[22] George Gilbert financed the press.[23] The secrecy of such a vital enterprise was crucial; not even the owner of the house, Thomas Brookesby, was informed of the doings there.

At Greenstreet, Persons encountered the parson and churchwardens, who urged on the new-comers their duty of going to church. Soon he was frightened by the idea that he had furnished a clue to the discovery of his press by an incautious purchase of paper. Regularly he was told that he would certainly be caught, that Campion was already taken, and that some of his confraternity were being apprehended daily in London. In reality the priests John Hart, Christopher Thompson,[24] James Bosgrave, and layman Thomas Briscoe, were apprehended and committed to the Tower on Christmas Eve 1580.[25]

Persons in Print

The Council of Trent's decree on Catholic literature (1546) had laid down that "it shall not be lawful for anyone to print or get printed any books whatsoever dealing with sacred matters without the name of the author—or in the future to sell them, or even to have them in possession, unless they have first been examined and approved by the ordinary [bishop]."[26] But on April 14, 1580, before leaving Rome, the two Jesuits had received a dispensation making it "licit to print and issue Catholic books without giving the name of the author, place or press, notwithstanding the Council of Trent."[27]

After one by Thomas Hide, and one by Richard Bristow, the third book[28] that issued from Persons's press at Greenstreet House was the first to be composed and printed by himself: *A brief discourse containing certain reasons why Catholics refuse to go to church*. He put the author as I. H., standing for his pseudonym, John Howlet, and the printer as John

Lyon of Douay.[29] It was printed before November 6, 1580.[30]

"At last, by God's favor," says Persons, "we completed the printing amid great difficulties and dangers, and Brinkley dismantled the press."[31] It was a thorough, systematic, and well-written treatment of the subject, the argument being presented in the form of nine reasons why no believing Catholic can go to the churches or services of the contrary religion.[32] In it, among other things, Persons pleaded with the queen for public disputations so that "men's doubts might be resolved." The quickness of its repartee made the government doubly angry. One may think that the proclamation of January 10, 1581, just two months after its printing, ordering all young men to return from the seminaries, and denouncing all receivers and favorers of priests and Jesuits, was a kind of reply to this *Brief Discourse.*[33]

In the following year, three prominent Puritans—William Fulke, John Field, and Perceval Wilburn—each wrote a refutation of it. Fulke's title referred to Persons's nom-de-plume: *a Popish discourse . . . by John Howlet, or some other Bird of the night, under that name.* Field was more sure: his title began, *A Caveat for Parsons Howlet.*

Distributing the Books

Difficulties and risks did not cease with the printing. The books then had to be distributed.

Persons wrote in a letter to Rome:

> With no less zeal and with like disregard of danger on the part of the priests, they are circulated so that what is written may reach the hands of all. Their method is to bring all the books to London before a single copy is given out. Then they are consigned to the priests in parcels of fifty or a hundred, and sent at exactly the same time to different parts of the kingdom. After the day when the pursuivants begin their usual searches of Catholic houses for these books, a number of young gentlemen will be ready to distribute other copies at night in the heretics' residences, in the workshops, as well as in the noblemen's palaces, in the Court also, and about the streets, so that Catholics alone may not be charged with [possessing] them.[34]

By the books' simultaneous appearance in multiple places, the site of the press was concealed, the enemy caught unawares, and the impact magnified.

Campion Libeled by Two Ministers

After printing Persons's first book, Brinkley came with a bright face to Persons, thinking to pass a merry evening with him—but Persons had a new cause for anxiety. On his return to London, he found a book by William Charke, a Puritan minister, preacher at Lincoln's Inn: *An Answer to a seditious pamphlet lately cast abroad by a Jesuit, with a discovery* [exposure] *of that blasphemous sect* (December 1580). It was followed by another pamphlet, *The great Brag and Challenge of Mr. Champion a Jesuit,* by another minister, Meredith Hammer (January 1581), also confuting Campion's *Challenge.*[35] These two books gave Persons a two-fold difficulty; they contained some pestilent accusations against himself and Campion, and he saw no way of refuting them. Brinkley offered to bring the press back if he would write an answer; but Persons lacked access to reference books and a safe place for the press.

The Press Is Moved to Southwark

Brokesby's mansion was not available to house the press again. Mr. Thomas Brokesby began to be anxious about his property. He had been led to suppose that his tenants were a family of gentlemen. Brinkley had dressed up his seven workmen in fine clothes and given them horses to make the story appear more likely, but the signs of labor did not altogether escape the notice of the landlord who was unwilling to let his house be used for illegal purposes.

A new place was urgently needed. At last Sir Francis Browne offered his Southwark house and his books, together with board and service. Sir Francis also had a country house, Henley Park, which according to government spies "was never without three or four priests." (He was the brother of Anthony Browne, Lord Montague, the staunchest Catholic in Elizabeth's first parliament. "In 1581 Montague can be found protecting Catholics who were suspected of fraternizing with Campion, in particular Sir Alexander Culpeper, Montague's wife's brother-in-law . . . already being harassed by the high commission."[36] Culpeper was imprisoned with other recusants for a few months up to Pentecost 1581, but was released through an appeal by Montague, on a bond of £1,000.)

Persons Defends Campion in Print

So Persons set himself to write the *Censure* of Charke and Hanmer. This was to be Persons's second book. Its full title was *A Brief Censure upon two books written in answer to Mr. Edmund Campion's offer of disputation.* Persons put down the publisher again as John Lyon, Douay 1581. It was printed in January, before the 12th,[37] at Browne's house in Southwark.

Here again he incurred great trouble and risk in publishing the book, for his host, Francis Browne, got arrested, in consequence of the trap laid for George Gilbert, whose bailiff had been ordered by the Council to come to London to pay Gilbert his money. Knowing it was most likely a trap, Persons would not allow Gilbert to go in person to receive it, but sent Francis Browne and Charles Basset to Mr. Higgins, an attorney. While they were there, Sir George Carey, Knight Marshal, came in with sword drawn, and seized both the money and the men.[38]

William Fleetwood, the pursuivant, we are told, on finding a copy of *A Brief Censure* outside his door ten days after the publication of Hanmer's *Great Brag*, was amazed at the size of the book and the speed of its production.[39]

The book is in four parts. Persons treats respectively of: "the Society" (of Jesus), "the man" (Campion), "the matter" (petition for a debate) and "the apostate" (Christian Francken, quoted by Charke).[40]

It is worthwhile to give a few sketches from this book. Persons considered Charke to be more venomous than Hanmer, who replied "more quietly, plainly, and good fellow-like, excepting a foul lie or two,"[41] making liberal offer of disputation, though he was never likely to be one of the disputers. He had taken occasion to vent a commonplace book of anti-Popish citations, about anything but the matters in controversy, and had made a book of little purpose but to increase the availability of Campion's *Challenge* (reproduced within it), which had been a tedious labor to write out for all who wanted a copy.

Charke misrepresented the *Challenge*, drew everything to disloyalty and rebellion, flattered the higher powers, and wearied the reader with endless repetitions of "pope" and "popery" and all excesses of abusive speech. He averred all manner of lies without blushing and asserted anything whatever, provided only it was fit to discredit the Jesuits.[42]

Persons thus addresses him on his treatment of Campion:

Concerning the man whom you answer: To let pass all your evil speech towards him, as pardonable in you, who know little civility, you seem to deal otherwise very hardly [harshly] with him—for whatsoever he says or does you will have it to be taken in evil part: if he speak humbly, he dissembles; if he yield commendation, he flatters; if he show confidence in his cause, he vaunts; if he offer trial, he means not performance; if he protest his meaning, he must not be credited; if he desire audience, he must not be admitted; finally, whatsoever he can imagine to utter for justifying of himself or his cause, it must avail nothing. William Charke will have him condemned for unlearned, proud, wicked and traitorous to the State.[43]

Persons found it more convenient to turn off Charke's insinuations with a jest than to answer them. Thus, when Campion is said to have come over "in hopes of a golden day"—a phrase which in those days was interpreted to mean the death or dethronement of Elizabeth, and the restoration of religion—Persons replies that the word "golden" will not serve to express any of Campion's hopes, whom all the gold in England cannot gild, and who despises gold as much as Charke desires it.[44]

As to Charke's claim to settle all matters and believe only according to the written Word of God—the Bible alone (without Tradition, the Church, Councils of bishops, or popes), Persons replied:

For seeing there are at this day the Hussites in Bohemia, the Trinitarians in Transylvania, the Anabaptists in Poland, the Adamites in diverse parts of Germany, the Lutherans in Saxony, the Calvinists in France, the Puritans and Family of Love in England, and other like sects in the world abroad, which all with one voice agree against the Catholic Church in this point, that Scripture only is to be received, and all other testimonies to be rejected: how comes it to pass that these sects, grounding their several religions upon the mere word of God, as they say, can not yet end their controversies? If the Scriptures be so plain, clear, easy, evident, and sufficient to end all controversies, as they say: why do they so long disagree?[45]

After this, some time from April to July,[46] Persons printed another book—most likely at the third press site, Stonor Park[47]—containing his account of John Nichols, who professed to be a pope's scholar (i.e., receiving a burse from the pope) and had given the English government information of what was done in Rome, Rheims, and the other seminaries, wherein truth was so much mixed with fiction that Persons had no very difficult task to discredit him.

The same year, Charke and Hanmer made separate replies to Persons's *Censure.* Persons countered in 1582, from Rouen, France, with a defense of his *Censure.*[48]

Catholic Publications in 1581

A letter from Fr. Persons to Fr. Agazzari, Rector of the English College, in August this year, 1581, gives the following account (while concealing his own role) of the Catholic publications of the period:[49]

> As I have obtained the services of a sure and faithful man who says he is going to set out for you at once, I am going to run briefly through the principal points which I have already written to you about in other letters; for fear that in these very difficult times they may not have been able to reach you. . . .
>
> There has been this year quite a battle of books, and the heretics have not been able to publish anything without its being immediately controverted. Charke and Hanmer; Calvinist ministers, first wrote against Campion, making a strange hash of the whole order of Jesuits in general, and of the life of Ignatius Loyola in particular; but within ten days there appeared in print a short review by an un known author [Persons's second book: *A Brief Censure* [50]] which convicted them of so many lies that both they and their followers were heartily ashamed of them selves. In this book the ministers were for the second and third time challenged to a disputation; and when they showed great offense at this, Campion wrote his luminous little book in Latin to the Universities [*Ten Reasons*—see next chapter], wherein he gave the reasons of that demand.
>
> The Queen published some outrageous proclamations against all Jesuits, priests, scholars of seminaries, and against the foundation of the colleges themselves. But that most learned man, William Allen (who may most justly be called the father of this vineyard), wrote an *Apology*[51] for them with such prudence, moderation and weighty argument that the heretics themselves, ready enough to be offended, praised his book highly, while the Catholics gained no little increase by it. About the same time, one Fulke, a minister, had attacked a book written many years before by Allen on Purgatory [1565][52] . . . but this man, who was bragging ridiculously like a boy, was speedily

put down and all but broken by a man of great authority, who enjoys the highest reputation for erudition, Richard Bristow,[53] Prefect of Studies in the seminary at Rheims.

In these days the Parliament met, and it was said that Catholics were to be condemned for contumacy if they refused to attend the Protestant service at the queen's bidding. There was there fore dispersed in the Parliament itself an English pamphlet printed in England, which gave very many and solid reasons for this refusal, which the adversaries cannot controvert (unless, like atheists, they think that all considerations of conscience in Catholics are to be totally despised).

This last pamphlet was Persons's first: against a position adopted by people such as Clytheroe and Langdale, mentioned below.[54]

The Sad Figure of John Nichols

The same letter continues with the story of the unstable John Nichols:

> I have already written about the apostasy and relapse of John Nichols, who at first was a Calvinist minister, and then a pretended scholar of your [English] College. This man has preached several times in the Tower of London to the imprisoned priests, who were dragged to the church to hear him in the presence of a great concourse of courtiers, who came to grace the comedy.

According to Fr. Hart's diary of the Tower, this kind of thing happened every Sunday from February 5 to Whitsunday. The prisoners used to interrupt the preachers, and hoot them when they had finished.

> It is almost unbelievable what praises are everywhere lavished on this creature. He is held to be the most learned Jesuit of them all, the Pope's scholar, the Cardinals' preacher, a theologian, a philosopher, a scholar of Greek, Hebrew and Syriac—an expert in all languages and sciences. He has printed his renunciation of the faith,[55] in which he tells innumerable lies about Rome, the Pope, the Cardinals, your College, the Jesuits, the scholars, and all orders of monks and priests.
>
> The book was received and distributed by the heretics with mighty triumph; but almost within a month there came out another book, *A Discovery* [exposure] *of J. Nichols* [Persons's third book[56]], proving clearly that he was neither Jesuit nor priest, neither theologian nor philosopher; that he had never preached before Pope

or Cardinals (except once or twice before the Inquisitors when he abjured the heresy of Calvin); that he knew nothing of any learned language or science, but was merely a relapsed minister, an unskilled grammarian, a stray vagabond, and an egregious liar; withal, it was a perfect occasion to explain so many things about Roman matters, the works of charity done in the city, the celebrated munificence of His Holiness and the eminent Cardinals, and the signal piety of all the religious Orders, so that the heretics are not a little regretful at having provided the necessity for us to publish an explanation, whereby their fraud is discovered, and which makes many begin to mistrust their side, and to attach themselves to ours.

So much for the books. With no less zeal on the part of the priests, and danger too, they are circulated, so that what is written can reach the hands of all. The method is: all the books are taken to London before any is distributed, and then they are distributed to the priests in hundreds or fifties, so that they may be issued in all parts of the realm at exactly the same time. And the next day, when the pursuivants begin as usual to search the Catholics' houses, because these books have been distributed, there are plenty of young noblemen who have brought these books at night into the houses, shops, and mansions of the heretics, and disseminated them even about the [Royal] Court, and through the streets, so that Catholics alone cannot be accused of [having] them.[57]

Nichols here mentioned was a Welshman, and student first of White-hall, then Jesus College, Oxford, and later Brazenose College. Afterwards he returned to Wales, and became tutor to a gentleman's sons. He was ordained to a curacy in Somersetshire, 1579, whence he moved to London, thence to Antwerp, so to Rheims, and thence to the English College in Rome, whence he was sent back towards Rheims in 1581, but returned to England, and was apprehended in Islington, and sent to the Tower, where he made a public recantation, was received into Sir Owen Hopton's family, and in 1581 published at least three books: his *Recantation*, his *Oration and Sermon made at Rome* and his *Pilgrimage*. He was at first in such credit that the Privy Council, by a letter to Archbishop Grindal of Canterbury of May 19, 1581, ordered that the English bishops should contribute among them £50 a year for his maintenance.[58] However, the bishops soon grew tired of their liberality. Nichols came to be in want, grew into great contempt and was turned out of doors by Hopton. Even the Privy Council later found one of his books wanting, and rebuked the Bishop of London when he "permitted a book under the name of John Nichols to be printed, containing light matter and tending nothing or little to edification, but giving offense unto some and occasion of slander unto the cause of Religion."[59]

In 1581, after Fr. William Kirby and others had been condemned to death, Nichols even went to visit Kirby in prison, admitting, says Persons, "that he had acted most evilly and ungratefully and had told many lies; he begged forgiveness of his fault and offered to make satisfaction by going to the Secretary Walsingham and clearing them (as far as was in his power) of all suspicion of treachery."[60]

After this, in 1582, he went abroad once more and was apprehended at Rouen, when he made another recantation, and wrote most humble letters to Dr. Allen, confessing his frauds and lies, and beseeching his protection.[61]

He was a weak man, terrified by the mention of the rack, and consenting to any remedy suggested to his fear. He declared that what he wrote, he wrote partly from memory, partly from Hopton's dictation, who made him say whatever he chose. He published many things dangerously compromising the loyalty of the priests; as that in their common talk at Rome and Rheims they were perpetually wishing harm to the queen. He declares, however, that he designedly absented himself from London when Campion and his companions were tried, lest he be compelled to perjure himself by swearing to the truth of what he had written.

Persons's pamphlet against Nichols showed that he had been dismissed from the English College after little more than a year on the grounds of total unsuitability. It was to be Persons's last work printed at Stonor Park.[62]

Robert and Thomas Alfield: Brother against Brother

One or two months after his arrival in England, when Persons needed a servant for a journey, he was met by a young man, Thomas Alfield, about to leave for Rheims to study for the priesthood. He earnestly begged Persons to take his younger brother Robert into service, and promised him solemnly that Robert would be entirely faithful to him. Persons heard Robert's confession, reconciled him to the Church, took him on, and paid him very well. "I took him for my servant on liberal terms, that he might serve with greater cheerfulness and fidelity," says Persons.[63]

After only a few months of service, Alfield wanted to leave Persons and return to his father, who—Persons now learnt to his surprise and dismay—was a Protestant minister and preacher in Gloucester. So Persons paid him his salary, and six gold pieces beside, to keep him happy; and let him go. But some time later, after getting into fights and brawls, and driven by want, Alfield came back. Persons was in a dilemma. If rejected, Alfield could become embittered and go and give the authorities the names and addresses of Catholic houses where they had stayed. But if Persons kept him, he could watch Alfield closely and restrict his contacts. Yet, that also meant Alfield could learn more and cause greater harm in the future—and Catholics might become wary of having Persons visit them with an unreliable companion who might betray them one day.

Following the advice of certain Catholics, Fr. Persons avoided Alfield for a time. From overseas, Thomas Alfield wrote many times to Persons, begging him to reinstate Robert and keep him close to him, lest Robert lose his soul. So Persons took him on again but never thoroughly trusted him afterwards.

After another few months, Robert Alfield again wanted to return to his father. Persons was once more in perplexity. If he sent him back, he could do untold harm if arrested and questioned. But Alfield was now self-conceited through the goodness and generosity of Catholics towards him, and unreliable; too difficult to keep or control. Persons eventually came up with a plan. He asked Robert if he would like to go to Italy, which he did. Robert was paid handsomely, given letters of recommendation for Rome, and set off. He left Persons's service in or after July 1581. In Rome he was very well treated.

This plan worked for a time, but his base ingratitude and other vices led him back again. After Persons left England, Alfield became an apostate in Italy, returned to England to do harm, which he did, and he was possibly the one who betrayed his brother, Thomas, now a priest on the mission.[64]

The elder brother, Thomas, had been a Protestant, educated at Eton and King's College, Cambridge. After his conversion to the Catholic faith, he studied for the priesthood at Douay and Rheims and was ordained in 1581. He returned to the English Mission, and was present at Campion's martyrdom, of which he wrote a most valuable eye-witness account. He was arrested while distributing copies of Dr. Allen's *True, Sincere and Modest Defense of English Catholics*.[65] Blessed Thomas Alfield, as he now is, was martyred at Tyburn, July 6, 1585, and beatified in 1929.

Fr. Alexander Briant Tortured in the Tower

Fr. Briant was arrested about April 28, 1581.[66] In May he was transferred to the Tower from the Counter Prison,[67] Wood St. London, where he had been thrust upon his apprehension. Briant was afterwards connected with Campion; but at this point their histories have no relation. Says Persons, "He was my disciple and my pupil at [Balliol College] Oxford, and ever inclined to virtue; afterwards a priest at Rheims, of the greatest zeal. Just before he came into England, he wrote to Father Richard Gibbon to ask whether he might visit his mother. He reconciled my father, and while he was in England he never willingly left my side."[68] Briant was arrested in a house neighboring Persons's house in Bridewell, London.

When it was found how close a companion of Persons had been taken, and how narrowly Persons himself had escaped, it is scarcely to be wondered at that the eagerness of the catchpoles to get at their great prize carried them still deeper into cruelty. They tried what hunger and thirst could extract out of Briant. This means failing, they sent him where he could be tortured more scientifically. The torments he suffered in the Tower were duly entered in the diary of Fr. John Hart, his fellow-prisoner:

> Alexander Briant, a priest, was brought from another prison, where he had almost perished with thirst, and loaded with the heaviest shackles. Then needles were thrust under his nails, with the hope of forcing him to disclose the place in which he had seen Father Persons; but he resolutely refused to reveal it.
>
> [Ten days later, in May], the same Briant was cast into the Pit [a dark underground cave]; and, eight days later, was led forth to the rack, on which he was immediately stretched with the greatest cruelty. The next day again, he was twice subjected to the same torture; yet from his own lips, only a little before his martyrdom, I afterwards heard the declaration, that, when his body was extended to the utmost, and his tormentors were ferociously endeavoring to increase the intensity of his sufferings, he was actually insensible of pain.[69]

We have a letter Briant wrote describing fully how, miraculously or otherwise, he "was without sense and feeling" during the racking.

Dr. Allen's account records:

> Within two days after his coming to the Tower, he was brought before the Lieutenant, Mr. Dr. Hammond, and Norton, who examined him after their common manner, first in tendering an oath to answer to all, etc. And because he would not confess where he had seen Fr. Persons, how he was maintained, where he had said Mass, and whose confessions he had heard, they caused needles to be thrust under his nails, whereat Mr. Briant was not moved at all, but with a constant mind and pleasant countenance said the psalm *Miserere* [*Ps.* 50], desiring God to forgive his tormentors; whereat Dr. Hammond stamped and stared as a man half beside himself, saying, "What a thing is this? If a man were not settled in his religion, this were enough to convert him." He was, even to the dismembering of his body, rent and torn upon the rack, because he would not confess where Fr. Persons was, where the print [press] was, and what books he had sold.[70]

According to the established practice of Elizabeth's government, when this cruelty was afterwards complained of, Norton, one of the commissioners was called to account for it.[71] The following is an extract of a letter Norton wrote to Walsingham, who had sent him Persons's *Epistle of the Persecution*, published in Rouen in 1582:

> I find in the whole book only one place touching myself, fol. ult. pa. 2. [2nd paragraph of last page]: "Briant, whom Mr. Norton, the rack-master (if he be not misreported), vaunted in the court to have pulled one good foot longer than ever God made him,[72] and yet in the midst of all he seemed to care nothing, and therefore, out of doubt (saith he), he had a devil within him." Surely I never said in that form, but thus. When speech was of the courage of Campion and some other, I said truly that there appeared more courage of a man's heart in Briant than in Campion, and therefore I lamented that the devil had possessed poor unlearned Briant in so naughty a cause; for being threatened by those that had commission (to the intent he might be moved to tell truth without torment), that if he would not for his duty to God and the Queen tell truth, he should be made a foot longer than God made him, he was therewith nothing

moved. And being for his apparent obstinacy in matters that he well knew racked more than any of the rest, yet he stood still with express refusal that he would not tell truth. When he setteth out a miracle that Briant was preserved from feeling of pain, it is most untrue; for no man of them all, after his torture, made so grievous complaining and showed so open sign of pain as he.[73]

Norton carefully avoids denying what Briant asserted—namely, that he felt no pain *whilst* he was being racked. Norton simply asserts that *after* the torture Briant exhibited great signs of pain, which Briant himself also confessed in his own letter to Persons, where he tells not only of his freedom from pain while on the rack, but of the agonies he suffered afterwards.

In a letter to the Rector of the English College, Rome, Persons also recorded the extraordinary steadfastness of the man:

Fr. Briant was quite a young man, and he excelled in patience above the ordinary, combined with an exceeding meekness; and so in the course of his tortures, which were extreme, he never uttered so much as a groan or cry. This the enemy admits and wonders at extremely, since he seemed to be very slender in build and of a very delicate constitution. They kept pressing him, when under torture, just to state where he had seen Fr. Robert. He replied, "You will never learn that from me, do whatever you can. I have seen him and lived with him, and yet I will never tell you where." And although (as the torturers themselves declare), they had stretched his body by force of the rack more than half a foot beyond its natural measure, he remained silent without a groan, as though he felt nothing, absorbed in prayer and meditation.[74]

At his trial in November, it is recorded:

As he stood before the judges, he always looked at the palm of his hand, in which he held a little crucifix of wood, which he himself had made in the prison. When they saw how he kept his eyes down on his hand, those present took it away, and he said, "You cannot take it out of my heart, though you may take it from my hands."[75]

Persons's House Raided

Persons relates the following story; he refers it by mistake to a later period, but it must have been around April 28, 1581, namely, a few days after the time of Briant's arrest. While he was at Stonor Park one night, Fr. Hartley told him that four days ago he heard at Oxford that a servant of Roland Jenks had turned and given evidence against his master.[76]

Jenks was the Catholic stationer at Oxford, lately employed by Persons at his house in Bridewell, London, to bind some books, with the help of that same servant. That house was owned by a Protestant man, and in it Persons had the use of a large room in which priests met, and in which he kept things needed for their mission: vestments, books, and so forth.

Persons at once saw the danger, and next morning sent a man to London, who came back and reported that

> first he passed through the street and found it in fearful and sorrowful silence, except that a woman's lamentations could be heard in a building, who by her extraordinary sorrow [he realized] was Persons's landlady. From her he learnt that, the night before, Thomas Wilkes, secretary of the Council, with a hundred armed guards, first entered the room of that certain unknown gentleman (Persons, he understood, for the woman knew him only by sight), then soon after broke into the next house. From Persons's chamber was carried off all that was found . . . and from her side they took her husband who had taken that man as a lodger. In the next house they apprehended a fine young man for being a priest, it is rumored.[77]

The good woman was clearly a Catholic. So Persons lost all his letters, books, papers, medals, rosaries, and other pious objects, and Fr. Briant was captured in the neighboring house.[78]

Jinx!

Roland Jenks (Jinks), Catholic stationer and bookbinder, was doubtless known to all Oxford men. In July 1577, his name had been noised all over Europe. He had been sentenced to have his ears cut off for a religious offense (Catholic printing activity), when suddenly the judge was taken ill and the infection traveled with marvelous rapidity and struck down by a fever the greater part both of the bench and of the jury. Two judges, twelve justices, other high officials, almost the whole jury, and many others, died within the space of two days. Thus did Jenks, on that earlier occasion at least, escape the enforcement of the law! His good luck and their bad luck is no doubt the origin of the phrase, "to jinx."

The Press Moved to Stonor Park

The great secret which Hammond and Norton wished to rack out of Briant was where Persons printed his books. Now, whatever confidence Persons might have in Briant's resolution, it was clearly the part of prudence to count on the possibility of a moment of weakness or unguardedness, when the secret might be wormed out by some artful question. So Persons took the precaution to transfer the press from Browne's at Southwark to a lodge in Dame Cecily Stonor's park, in Oxfordshire, five miles north of the riverside town, Henley-on-Thames, about forty miles west of London.

In one account, Persons says the move to Stonor Park was provoked by a different event: one of Brinkley's men went to London to buy paper, was somehow recognized when bargaining with the merchant, was arrested, clapt in prison, and tortured.[79]

The printing press was housed, in turn, at Brokesby's of Greenstreet (from October 1580), Browne's of Southwark (around January 1581) and, lastly, Stonor Park (from March to August 1581).[80]

Dame Stonor, the widow of Sir Francis Stonor who had died in 1564, was a niece of the Carthusian martyr, (Blessed) Sebastian Newdigate (Tyburn, 1535), and a cousin of Cardinal Pole's executed mother. Her second son John was one of the Gilbert group. She herself lived at the Lodge in the village. Stonor Park was both secret, being surrounded with beech woods, and easily accessible, for the Thames River at that period was a better highway than any road. The isolation was a great advantage, for the noise of a printing-press at work was always a source of apprehension.[81] Stephen Brinkley organized the transfer of the press with the type and paper to Stonor Park about March 1581. Here *Decem Rationes* was printed without accident, and from here it was in due time dispersed among the academics of Oxford.

The English Clergy

There were at this time three classes of priests in England:

- The Jesuits, newly arrived, with a few more to come over the years (never a large number at any one time)
- The "seminary priests," meaning the secular clergy (i.e., not members of religious orders), educated in "seminaries," special colleges for training priests—an institution of the Council of Trent (concluded in 1563)
- The "Marian priests," surviving from the time of Queen Mary (1553– 58), whose reign had ended 22 years before. This included priests ordained even earlier.

E. E. Reynolds notes here that in contrast to Campion's positive remarks on the local clergy in his letter,[82] Persons seems to under-rate the work of the seminary priests, and the apostolate of the Marian priests, some of whom were still active, but, as McCoog remarks, "we remain relatively ignorant of their number, their organization, and their ministry."[83]

As for the seminary priests from Douay and then Rheims: by 1580 there were probably about 100 priests on the mission, and a few others coming from Rome.[84] The number of entrants to England then rose sharply. In June 1581, Dr. Allen referred to "the fifty priests (at least) who have this year been sent from the two colleges" (Rome and Rheims), of whom "at least thirty priests have entered England since Easter" (March 26).[85]

The English Laity

As for the zeal of the Catholics, Persons wrote in a letter of August 1580:

> As long, then, as Our Lord shall leave us to enjoy this freedom, the hope of a harvest is excellent, for we are so spoilt by the Catholics and kept so busy that we have neither time nor strength sufficient. I am forced two or three times every day on this my tour to give discourses to men of rank, and they are touched by the Spirit of God and are most ready for any distinguished service. More often than not they put at my disposal their persons and all their possessions, and their zeal and fervor are worthy of astonishment principally in these three matters: first in hearing Mass, at which they assist with

such sighs and such a flood of tears that they move even me, dry as I am, to weep against my will. The second thing is the devotion and reverence they have for the Supreme Pontiff. For, greatly as they should and do appreciate his authority, this is not greater than their love. Hence as soon as they hear these words in the Litany [of the Saints]: *Oremus pro Pontifice nostro Gregorio* [Let us pray for our Pope, Gregory], they raise their hands and voices to heaven with a feeling and unanimity that is wonderful. The third thing is that wonderful fortitude of soul that makes them ready to undergo any labor in the cause of religion.[86]

The Treatment of Catholic Prisoners

It is not to be supposed that the excitement caused by the Jesuits' preaching escaped the notice of the government. It induced them to use greater severity to the Catholics in prison, and to search with greater strictness for those not yet apprehended. The first case of torture that we know of being applied to them was on December 10, 1580,[87] when Frs. Luke Kirby and Thomas Cottam were put into the "scavenger's daughter" at the Tower—Kirby for more than an hour (see a description in ch. 15: "Tortures in the Tower").[88] The Council had previously drawn up a paper of questions to be administered to them:

> Why did the Pope send them? To whom were they specially directed to repair [go]? What hopes had they of an invasion of Ireland? Why had the Bishop of St. Asaph, Dr. Morton, and others, come from Rome to Paris? Who had relieved them? Had the Queen of Scots given them anything? Whom had they reconciled? Whom had they heard of as being reconciled? What communications had they held with Campion? Where was he? Whose names are in the catalogues of the Pope's principal favorers? What communication have they had with the [Catholic] Bishop of Ross? [in Scotland; a supporter of Mary Queen of Scots] or with Dr. Sanders in Ireland? and who are the Irishmen most noted as favorers of the rebellion there?

According to Cottam's own account,[89] Hammond and the other commissioners did not confine themselves to these questions, but wanted to know what sins he had confessed, and what penance had been given him.

After this, Ralph Sherwin and Robert Johnson were racked, December 15; Sherwin again the next day; and John Hart, who was brought to the

Tower about Christmas, was with Mr. Henry Orton racked on December 31, 1580; Christopher Thompson, an old priest, January 3, 1581, and Mr. Nicholas Roscarock, at whose house Sherwin had been taken saying Mass, was racked on January 14.

More Anti-Catholic Penal Laws

The government, both ecclesiastical and civil, were by this time convinced that the penal laws against Catholics, bloody as they already were, were not yet sufficient to exterminate the Catholic religion. It was felt that severity must be increased. The first impulse towards a more systematic persecution came from the ecclesiastical side.

In January 1581, the Bishop of Chester, the state of whose diocese prognosticated to him the success that Campion was to achieve there a few months later, wrote to the Council, urging them to bring in a Bill making traitors and felons of "all such vagrant priests as walk about in disguised apparel seducing her Majesty's subjects, etc., by assembling of unlawful conventicles," and of their receivers, felons. He wanted the Council also to enforce preachers to reside on their benefices, to make all work unlawful before eleven o'clock on Sunday, to forbid fairs and markets on Sundays, and to enact some general law to bring all subjects back to conformity. He adds: "In this cathedral church of Chester, neither the dean nor any prebendary has been resident . . . of many years. Neither is any parson or vicar of any parish church within the city a preacher."[90]

Other bishops begged to have the High Commission in their dioceses, to enforce the religious laws. Thus the Bishop of Coventry writes to Burghley in April 1581, about the bad state of Shropshire (Salop): "being one of the best and conformablest parts of my diocese," where, however, "of one hundred almost presented for recusancy, they could get but one only to be bound, the rest refusing most obstinately to come before them."[91] What must it be then, he asks Burghley, in the other shires of the diocese, when it is thus in the best of them?

The Catholics presaged that something severe awaited them. A Royal Proclamation of July 1580 had called for the loyalty of all Englishmen and denounced traitors living abroad. On January 10, 1581, another one was made: "A Proclamation, for revocation [recall] of students from beyond the seas and against the retaining of Jesuits." Students abroad were given three months to return and their parents were forbidden to send them money. This prompted Dr. Allen's *An Apology* [Defense] *and true declaration of the institution and endeavors of the two English colleges, the one in Rome, the other now resident in Rheims: against certain sinister informations given up against the same*—issued by June 1581.[92]

In it, Allen wrote:

> we are not fugitives, as sometimes uncourteously we are called, nor are fled for following any factions or differences of noble families, nor for any crimes or disloyalties done against the Prince or Commonwealth, nor for any disorder in our lives, or worldly discontentment or disagreement with the present civil state and polity, or for mislike of any her Majesty's ministers, whose persons, wisdoms, moderation and prudence in government, and manifold graces, we do honor with all our heart in all things, excepting matters incident to Religion, wherein their Honors cannot be offended if we prefer the judgment of God's Church before their human counsel.

The persecution grew still stronger, and Persons felt that something must be done. He therefore sent Father Edward Gratley to John Bodin then acting as agent for the Duke of Anjou to treat of Anjou's marriage with the queen—to persuade him to advise her Majesty to treat the Catholics with more mildness; but the author of the *Six Books of the Commonwealth* was too good a politician to mix himself up with such irrelevant matters. He said he was in England for the marriage, not for matters of religion.[93]

A meeting of gentlemen was therefore held one Sunday after Communion in the house of Francis Throgmorton—the same who was executed in 1584 for a conspiracy to deliver Mary Stuart—to consider whether a truce could be purchased. Affairs had proceeded to such a pitch, the pursuivants had become so intolerable, that the people began to talk of paying the queen so much per head to be let alone. However, there was no one to propose it to her. The Spanish ambassador would have created a prejudice against them instead of helping them. The French ambassador was mistrusted. Bodin refused to meddle.

Catholic Attempts to Compromise

Another section of Catholics thought it was time to reconsider the question about attending the churches, and to make out a probable case to allow them to save their goods and their liberties, if not their faith too, by an occasional and merely formal attendance at the Anglican service.

In 1580, Fr. Alban Langdale (Viscount Montague's chaplain) wrote an anonymous tract,[94] to prove that attendance at the Protestant church was in itself no sin and might be lawfully submitted to for the purpose of avoiding a persecution so intolerable at present and threatening to grow worse. It was circulated by a legal clerk, Mr. William Clytheroe (Clitherow), later a priest, brother-in-law to St. Margaret Clitherow of Yorkshire,[95] who was to be martyred in 1586.

English Catholics were not unwilling to follow an opinion that so happily saved them from a sea of troubles. Some prominent gentlemen began to compromise as a result and attend the State church. Fr. Persons was informed of the affair—the tract and its effect—in a letter to him of November 6, 1580, from Fr. Edward Chambers.[96]

Langdale's tract was circulated only in manuscript. (Catholic) Ralph Sheldon's copy is in the State Papers Office.[97] It was a scholastic argument on the case whether *for civil reasons* a Catholic may be present at the Protestant church. By the 19th century, the case was partially solved in the affirmative when no Catholic feared to be present at an Anglican marriage or funeral, to listen to an Anglican cathedral chant, or see the functions of the Ritualists. But the import of such behavior was altogether different in Elizabethan England—where, moreover, attendance was required every week.

Persons, however ready he might be to engage in plots against the queen, was, as a Catholic, uncompromising and rigid. He could go a long way with the advocates of equivocation in civil cases, but he could not allow an equivocation in act or word, when the faith, or the honor of religion, seemed at stake. Elizabeth and her ministers declared that the attendance at church was a mere political act, and by no means forced the conscience; but he could not accept the distinction between a religious act and a political or social ceremony. Besides, had not a committee of the Council of Trent decided the matter in 1562? Had not Pius V given the same ruling in 1566? Cost what it might, Catholics must be induced to act on the principles of Tertullian and St. Cyprian, and the Catholic Fathers.

Persons therefore thought it his duty to write a refutation of Langdale's tract, the authorship of which he did not know at the time. He went with Fr. George Blackwell first to the library of the late Dr. Young, in the house of a certain merchant, but finding the books to be too old and the print not easy to read, Persons reminisces, "they departed thence again quickly and would not stay to dinner, as the merchant earnestly entreated them. And it seemed the Providence of God, for soon after they were gone, came in the pursuivants to search the house, and had taken them both together if they had stayed."[98] So they went to the library of Dr. Langdale where, by the marks left in the books, they realized that he was the writer. In collaboration with Blackwell, Persons wrote an answer to this latest tract and disseminated it in manuscript.[99]

The Passing of the Penal Laws

In the midst of these discussions among Catholics, the Legislature intervened with its heavy hand. The Bishop of Chester's recommendations were carried out to the full. The existing Parliament was convoked for the third time, for the express purpose of finding a remedy for the poison of the Jesuits.[100]

On January 25, 1581, Sir Walter Mildmay rose to move the new bill. His speech was an essay which he learned by rote and repeated several times in the Star-Chamber at the trials of recusants, till his hearers must have known it almost as well as himself. It began with an elaborate eulogy of Elizabeth as the refuge of persecuted Protestants, for which cause the pope raged against her, and procured through his confederates all means of annoyance to her; such as the northern rebellion of 1569, the maintenance of the fugitive rebels, the Bull, the recent rebellions and attempts at invasion. The queen had baffled these attempts in a way that redounded to her honor. She had no fear; but she had all cause for caution; for, in spite of the freedom of the pulpit, such had been the secret practices of the pope and his secret ministers, that the

> obstinate and stiff-necked Papist is so far from being reformed, as he hath gotten stomach to go backward, and to show his disobedience, not only in arrogant words [such as Campion's *Challenge*] but also in contemptuous deeds.

The pope he said, comforted papists'

hollow hearts with absolutions, dispensations, reconciliations, and such other things of Rome. You see how lately he hath sent hither a sort of hypocrites, naming themselves Jesuits, a rabble of vagrant friars newly sprung up and coming through the world to trouble the Church of God; whose principal errand was to creep into the houses and familiarities of men of behavior and reputation, not only to corrupt the realm with false doctrine, but also, and under that pretense to stir up sedition.

Mr. Thomas Norton seconded the motion, and proposed referring the matter to a committee, which he named. The House was ready to go further than even the Court desired, and the Bill, which, as the Speaker said, was for the glory of God, the safety of the queen, and the prosperity of the people, received the royal assent on March 18, 1581.

The "Act to retain the Queen's majesty's subjects in their due obedience" fell broadly into two sections: the first, to deal with the work of priest-missionaries; and the second, to stiffen the penalties for ordinary recusancy or refusal to attend Protestant church.

The Act made it treason to absolve any Englishman, to convert him to the Catholic religion, to move him thereto or to do any overt act tending that way. It was also treason to be so absolved or converted. Another clause made it misprision of treason to aid or maintain any persons so offending, or to conceal any such offense, without divulging it to the magistrate within twenty days.

By another clause, the *saying* of Mass was forbidden under penalty upon the priest of 200 marks and one year's imprisonment (a *mark* was thirteen shillings and four pence, i.e., two-thirds of a pound). *Hearing* of Mass was under a similar and now severer penalty of 100 marks and one year in prison.

Lastly, a system of fines was devised, which for half a century became one of the great items in the budget of the Chancellor of the Exchequer; although in fact the receipts of the Exchequer were but a trifle compared with the waste and losses inflicted on the Catholics, and with the vast sums which found their way into the hands of courtiers and parasites—favorites to whom recusants were given to exploit, and pursuivants and informers, who made Catholics pay for their forbearance.

Furthermore, any person above sixteen years of age who did not come to church for one month was fined £20 each month for the first twelve months, when apprehended, as well as a £200 good behavior bond. This was in addition to the shilling fine for each weekly absence. Consequently, not to attend church was to cost each adult, in total, £460 a year. This enactment made any arrangement such as that proposed at Francis Throgmorton's house henceforth impossible. There could be no talk of paying the queen for a license to practice their religion, when she got all the money that could be extorted from them on the ground of their not practicing hers.

One clause imposed a monthly fine of £10 upon every person keeping a school-master who did not regularly attend church. This, coupled with the proclamation of January, which recalled all students from foreign seminaries, was intended to make Catholic education henceforth an impossibility for Englishmen.

E. E. Reynolds sums up the effect:

> Those who did not pay the fines were imprisoned until they either did so or conformed; as a consequence many recusants were to spend years in prison and some died there; their numbers are not known, but recent research has revealed that they must have numbered many thousands over the years. The monthly fine of £20 was a crippling exaction and could only be levied on the well-to-do and rich. . . . A sinister provision was that informers who brought successful actions were rewarded with one-third of the forfeiture; another third went to the Exchequer, and the last third could be used for the local poor. Here was a method that led to all kinds of blackmail, bribery and chicanery.[101]

If this legislation had been tempered with every kind of constitutional consideration, and administered only by responsible agents of the government who kept within the letter of the law, still the legislative persecution would have been almost intolerable. In reality, it was capriciously administered, and gradually fell into the hands of a class of people who traded on the lives and lands of the Catholics: "bloodsuckers," as Fr. William Harrington (martyred at Tyburn 1594) called them.

To jump ahead a little—in 1585, a new Act of Parliament inflicted the penalty of high treason on priests for the mere fact of being within the realm, with proportionate penalties for all who assisted, protected or failed to betray any priest they met. Before the Act was passed, nearly all the priests held in prison were shipped overseas, to face the penalty if they tried to return. These hateful Acts were maintained in force for over a hundred years and kept on the statute-book for a century more.[102]

Under Elizabeth's successor, James I, the evil increased, till in 1605 it had reached such a pitch that one of the Anglican bishops seems to have considered even the Gunpowder Plot to have been a natural, if not a justifiable, attempt to cut short the intolerable evil.

The Catholics had borne with it in Elizabeth's latter days, in hopes, after the old woman's death, to find some mitigation. In those last days the administration of the law had been moderated, the persecutors being uncertain what might succeed after the queen's passing. But after the settlement of James, with no hope of better days, and expecting daily the utmost rigor in the execution of the law, the Catholics became desperate. A lady was hanged for harboring a priest, and a citizen for being reconciled to the Church. Under the penal code, wrote the (Anglican) Bishop Goodman of Gloucester:

> they could not subsist;—what was usually sold in shops and openly bought, this the pursuivant would take away from them as being popish and superstitious. One knight did affirm that in one term he gave twenty nobles [a noble was 100 pence] in reward to the door keeper of the attorney-general; another did affirm, that his third part which remained unto him of his estate did hardly serve for his expense in law to defend him from other oppressions; besides, their children to be taken from home to be brought up in another religion. So they did every way conclude that their estate was desperate; ... they were debarred in any course of life to help themselves; they could not practise law, they could not be citizens, they could have no office; they could not breed up their sons—none did desire to match with them; they had neither fit marriages for their daughters, nor nunneries to put them into ... The Spiritual Court did not cease to molest them, to excommunicate them, then to imprison them; and thereby they were entirely disenabled to sue for their own.[103]

The Political Setting of the New Anti-Catholic Laws

The background to these new laws is summed up by E. E. Reynolds:

> This intensified persecution of Catholics must be seen in its political setting. England was still at peace in 1580 as it had been since

the beginning of the reign twenty-two years earlier. This considerable achievement was largely due to Queen Elizabeth's tortuous policy that baffled her councilors as much as it did foreign rulers and statesmen.

But by 1580 the clouds were gathering for a storm. An undeclared war with Spain had been carried on for more than a decade across the Atlantic by such seamen as Hawkins and Drake, who had made many profitable raids (out of which the queen had her pickings) of a piratical nature. This has antagonized Spain. Tales of how the Inquisition dealt with captured English sailors stirred up national animosity. The long drawn-out struggle of the Protestant Dutch and the Spanish Netherlands excited sympathy in Protestant England. The designs of the papacy for an invasion of England under Spanish leadership further aggravated anti-Catholic feeling. The enemy was Spain, and Douay, where the priests were being trained, was in Spanish territory and was patronized by King Philip. The Fitzgerald-Sander Irish venture seemed a foretaste of what might follow. There was indeed a very real threat of invasion hanging over a country with no standing army. It was a period of rising suspicion and apprehension; and it was at this critical period that the two Jesuit priests arrived in England; they could not have come at a less propitious time. They were inevitably regarded as emissaries of the enemy intent on stirring up trouble from within to coincide with threats from without. We know that such was not their purpose, and in the letters and writings of Campion and Parsons during the mission there is not the slightest hint of any political intention. . . . One obvious measure [on the opposing government side] was to intensify the harassment of Catholics in the hope that they would be forced into conformity. Hence the new legislation and the incessant search for the two Jesuits.

We find it easy to keep religion and politics in separate departments as Queen Elizabeth vainly tried to do. Religion no longer plays a determinative part in the lives of the vast majority of people, but from, say, 1550 to 1650, it was part of men's thinking and was inevitably interlocked with national affairs.[104]

Persons and Campion Discussed in Parliament

During the debates on this bill I find the first attempt on the part of the Protestants to define the different characters of the two Jesuits. Persons was described as "a lurking wolf," Campion "a ubiquitous and vagrant Jesuit."[105] There was more truth in this coloring than in the subsequent notion which Camden promulgated, that Persons was a violent and a fierce-natured man, while Campion was of a sweet disposition and good breeding; the one seditious, turbulent, and confident; the other modest in all things except his *Challenge*. Campion, it seems to me, was the quick-tempered man, open, free, generous, hot, enthusiastic, yet withal modest, gentle, and fair; Persons more slow, subtle, cool, calculating, and capable of exhibiting either violence or modesty as the occasion seemed to demand. If Campion had the wisdom; Persons had the prudence. One knew how to move, the other to guide. If I may use offensive terms without offense, one had the gifts which make an agitator, the other those that make a conspirator. The practice of the Jesuits, as shown above,[106] linked together characters thus dissimilar, in order that united they might act with more force and more completeness. This would have been the case if their functions had been all in common; but though the men were linked together, they generally worked separately. Campion thought that all was done when he had reconciled his convert to the Catholic Church, had taught him the faith, and made him partaker of the Sacraments. Persons looked farther; he desired and labored for the conversion of England, and he thought that nothing could effect this but the overthrow of Elizabeth.

Fathers Heywood and Holt

The second pair of Jesuit missionaries were no less contrasted with each other than the first. Fathers Heywood and Holt had been asked for by name in the letters written from Uxbridge to the General of the Order. Persons could not have known Heywood; but Campion, who suggested him,[107] had met him at Munich at the court of the Duke of Bavaria[108] on his way to Rome, in March 1580.[109]

The two new Jesuits entered England in June 1581. When the two arrived, they went at once to report to their religious superior, Father Persons, at the Bellamys' house at Harrow.

A descendant of Sir Thomas More,[110] Jasper Heywood was a poet and the son of an epigrammist, John Heywood. He had entered the Society in 1562 and had been employed in Germany, far from the center of ecclesiastical politics, and in a country where the coexistence of hostile confessions was, in the midst of violence, laying the foundation of mutual toleration and forbearance. Like Campion in this, he was unlike him in other respects. Heywood, now forty-six years old, had lost his strength, was gouty and was unable to fast or even to abstain—a grave offense in the eyes of some of the more rigid English Catholics. But he was, like Campion, a learned man, a doctor in theology, one deeply versed in theological controversy, and an excellent Hebraist. There was some difficulty in obtaining his services, for he was a great favorite with the Duke of Bavaria, but a letter of Gregory XIII, dated May 27, 1581, overcame the Duke's unwillingness and he was sent on the mission.[111] He was a wonderfully diligent and daring man, and in the judgment of Gabriel Allen, the Cardinal's brother, he was, next to Campion, the most successful of all the missionaries. He himself wrote to Allen: *Stupeo hic in captura piscium . . . quia homo peccator sum* (I am amazed at the catch of fish here, for I am a sinful man).[112] He received into the Church Philip, Earl of Arundel and Henry, Earl of Northumberland. His relaxation of the fasts, and introduction of the Roman custom into England, greatly offended the old-fashioned party. This, together with his gout, determined the General to recall him. He got out of England safely and was in sight of Dieppe when his ship was driven back and he was sent prisoner to the Tower, where he was treated much as Campion before him, and tortured on the rack.[113] Then his treatment became gentler, by comparison, but he never succumbed to bribery or threats. On one occasion, he was visited in the Tower by Fr. William Weston S.J.,[114] who went under the guise of being part of a family visit, which included Heywood's twelve-year-old Catholic nephew, John Donne, later the famous poet, but no longer Catholic. After more than a year in custody, Heywood was deported in January 1585, under pain of death if he returned.[115]

William Holt, his companion, was a Lancashire man, educated at Oxford till 1575, when he passed over to Douay, studied theology and was ordained, after which he went to Rome and became a Jesuit in November 1578. When the Queen of Scots caused it to be notified to Persons that she would be glad to have a Jesuit sent to instruct her son James, the young king, in the faith, Holt was the one chosen by Persons, and he

travelled to Scotland in late December 1581. There he worked most fruitfully until 1586, when he was recalled by Jesuit General Acquaviva and
appointed Rector of the English College in Rome.[116]

I can best conclude this section of narrative by printing two letters, one of Persons to Pope Gregory XIII, and another of Dr. Allen to
Agazzari, the Rector of the English College in Rome.

A Letter of Fr. Persons to the Pope

Robert Persons to the Pope, June 14, 1581

Most Holy Father,

Although I hope Your Holiness knows enough of our affairs
by the other letters I have sent to you, yet as I have found a convenient courier [George Gilbert], to whom I must give some kind of
letter, I wished to add some brief notice of our situation. Today the
French legates have left London without having done their business,
as is generally supposed, for there is dead silence on the marriage
[between Elizabeth and Anjou].

We are daily now expecting a fresh storm of persecution; for
two days ago the Council sent an order to all parts of the realm, to
make search for the Catholic Recusants, as they call them, according
to the form of a new statute made in the last session of Parliament,
which condemns every one above the age of sixteen years to pay 80
crowns [£20] for every month they refuse to come to the Protestant
church. And although there are very few Catholics who are rich
enough to pay, and the rest must therefore expect to be perpetually
imprisoned, yet they are full of joy, and not at all anxious about this
matter, as they hope that their case will be the same as that of the
Israelites, and that the aggravation of their oppression will be the
hopes of a more speedy redemption.

Against us they publish the most threatening proclamations,
books, sermons, ballads, libels, lies, and plays. But the people receive
us with the greatest eagerness, comfort us, and protect us. The number of the faithful is wonderfully increased, and of our shrewdest
foes we have softened many, some we have converted. The contest is
sharp. God give us humility, patience, and fortitude!

Whatever priest or layman they lay hold of, whom they suspect to know anything about us, they torture on the rack or scaffold to make him betray us; and quite lately they tortured one most

atrociously [Fr. Alexander Briant, or a servant of Brinkley], but could get nothing out of him. Meanwhile we live safely enough in their very sight; we talk, preach, write, and do everything else to resist them, expecting every kind of torment when we are taken— yet meanwhile, through God's goodness, we sleep soundly. We earnestly desire supplies of new men, and that soon, for fear we should be taken before they can relieve us. So much concerning religious affairs.

It now remains for me to tell Your Holiness somewhat about the bearer of this letter, who, to tell the truth, is the chief cause of my writing. He is a young gentleman, named George Gilbert, who has afforded the rarest spectacle to all England. He was a man of great wealth, in great favor at Court, and devoted all his property to the defense of the Catholic religion. When we first entered the island, while others were in fear and doubt, he alone took us in, comforted us, clothed us, fed us, helped us with money, horses, servants; then took us about the island at his own expense; he journeyed with us, gave us books and other essentials, bought a press for us, sold some of his property, and gave us a large sum of the money for all purposes whereby the Catholic religion might be promoted; nor was this all; he bestowed continual alms on all prisoners for the Catholic faith, whereby he soon became so hateful to the heretics (especially as he had once been one of them) that they searched for him everywhere, and threatened to put him to a cruel death if caught. Now, although he cared little for this, yet since I saw that he could work no longer, nor stay in England without plain peril to his life, and that we had more trouble and anxiety in protecting him than ourselves, I at last persuaded him to leave all things, and cross over the sea, to keep himself for happier times.

Now, therefore, I most humbly entreat Your Holiness, or rather all we priests entreat you, because this one man was a most munificent patron to us all, that Your Holiness will regard him and console him for that consolation which he has given our souls, or rather sustained the common cause. For if we have done any good, a great part of it is to be attributed to this young man. So, if he finds an equal charity on that side, it will be great edification for all, and no little encouragement to those like him to imitate his example in the time to come.

May Jesus most merciful long preserve Your Holiness to us, as

all Catholics here pray day and night with deepest devotion, who
consider themselves so obliged by the countless and immense benefits you have shown, that they never cease talking of Your Holiness
and to pray for your long life in this world, and your salvation and
eternal happiness in the next. From London, June 14, 1581.

Your Holiness's most unworthy son,
Robert Persons[117]

A Letter of Dr. Allen to Rome

Letter of Dr. William Allen, Rector of the English College in France, to Father Alphonsus Agazzari, Rector of the English College at Rome

We have heard from England, by a letter of Fr. Robert Persons of
your Society that the persecution still rages with the same fury, the
Catholics being hauled away to prison and otherwise vexed, and the
Fathers of the Society being most diligently looked for everywhere;
but by God's singular providence they are still at liberty. However,
one of them in the same room as Fr. Robert was seized and searched
not long ago; but the Father himself was absent at the time. But one
[Fr. Alexander] Briant, who was a student of our college at Rheims,
living in a room next door, was not only taken, but most cruelly
tortured on the rack twice to make him tell where "that Jesuit" was.
But so far from confessing anything of the sort, he laughed at the
torturers; and though nearly killed with the pain, he said, "Is this
all you can do? If the rack is no more than this, bring on a hundred
more for this matter."

The day after, John Nichols, the apostate, who spent last year
in Rome, met Fr. [Anthony] Tyrrell, a student of your College, in
the street, and, as soon as he saw him, cried out "Traitor!" and so
caught him. But he is not committed to the Tower, but to another
prison called the Gatehouse, where he and Fr. Rishton, another of
your pupils, live happily. The Catholics were never more cheerful,
or more ready to suffer.

Two days afterwards, a certain Dr. Ireson[118] was caught, in possession of ten copies of our *Apology* [defense of the English seminaries abroad]; thus it happened that the Lords of the Council came to
know of the books. He is once again confined to his old home, the
Fleet Prison, whence he had been delivered by a friend's favor.

The said heretic, John Nichols, boasts that he made a long oration at Rome before the Cardinals (nothing can be more false), which he has just published in his second book, and has at the same time promised to publish the former turned into Latin, having also published a leaflet of his *Pilgrimage*, in which he copiously sets out the pillage, murders and adulteries of the Catholics, and the evil life of the Jesuits and students. He now preaches publicly in London, but everyone has already had their fill of him; and (I imagine) he will soon be tripped up, especially when that abjuration of heresies that he made in Rome at the Inquisition comes to England; for I have received the authentic copy of it which you sent, containing his whole recantation, and have sent it to Fr. Robert in England. [Fr. Persons used it for his pamphlet against Nichols].

Fr. Robert wants three or four thousand or even more of the English *Testaments*, for many persons desire to have them ["Spiritual Testaments" which Catholics signed to make a profession of Catholic faith—or the forthcoming English *New Testament*].[119] He says that he earnestly hopes and expects more fellow-laborers of your [Jesuit] Order; he says also that everything is going on well there, and that our *Apology* is highly approved.

I enclose a letter for the Holy Father, and another for our Cardinal Protector [John Moroni], which you must see delivered to them. Therein I thank His Holiness for his many favors of this year, namely for the foundation of the English College at Rome, for our college here established for fifteen years, for his late extraordinary subsidy of 500 golden crowns, for assigning so good a Protector to each college, and particularly for not listening to the detractors of the colleges and missions, who, to excuse their own idleness and cowardice, assert that all these attempts on our country are in vain; and I show that it is sufficiently evident that these missions, and the endeavors of the Fathers and seminaries are of incredible utility; and finally I assert and boldly pronounce (from the opinion, sense, and experience of all good men) that the Fathers and priests have gained more souls this one year in their own country than they could possibly have gained in the whole world else in the very longest lifetime. I write also that the dangers are not so great as to make it expedient to relinquish this duty, seeing that of the at least 50 priests who have this year been sent from the two colleges [in Rheims and Rome], not more than ten have fallen into the enemies' hands, and up to this time the Fathers are altogether free, and laboring fruitfully. Lastly, we show that our books are thus moderately worded, and nothing brought forward in anger, but rather directed by pity, because of the vast utility that accrues to every class of persons by reading them. So much for the letter to the Pope.

But to our Cardinal Protector, I merely write to beg him to turn his ears from certain idle and envious men, who say that the work of the Fathers and seminaries for our country is useless; moreover I beseech him for Christ's sake not to forbid my sending five or six young men to that college next autumn, because ours has become so numerous, that we cannot in any way feed them, although His Holiness has given us an extraordinary gift of 500 golden crowns. So much for my letter to him. I am rather afraid to send any students against his express injunction, lest we appear either to have no moderation, or to abuse the Pope's liberality too much. At this very time we are obliged to send for 20 youths—gentlemen for the most part— from Douay to our college here at Rheims, who otherwise would have to return to England, to the manifest damage of soul and body, since, on account of this edict, they can get no money from England. Moreover, within the last fortnight more than 20 young men have come to me from England (poor me!), and where shall we get bread that these may eat, that each one of them may have only a little, lest they faint in this exile? May the Lord God bless and multiply our food!

This week I have heard that the Fathers in England are not only well, but so occupied in the vineyard that they could not write to me, and Fr. Campion is said to have published a Latin book of encouragement [*Ten Reasons*] to the two Universities [Oxford and Cambridge], but as yet it has not come to our hands. See, Father, whether or not they push the work for ward. I have some time ago sent them the letter of Fr. General. May the Lord send many such laborers into His vineyard! At least 30 priests have entered England since Easter [March 26], not one of whom was hindered on landing, or has since been taken, blessed be the Lord. This year (I hope) will be every way a happy one for us. We sow in tears, but I trust in the Lord that we shall carry our sheaves with joy [*Ps.* 125], through God, and this [Pope] Gregory, our true father.

With me at present is the most generous companion and benefactor of the Fathers and priests in England, Mr. George Gilbert, who on their account has suffered the confiscation of almost all his goods and estates. And since the heretics have personally persecuted him more than the rest (knowing that the Fathers of the Society were kept and sustained by him), he has come here into France by the advice of Rev. Fr. Robert and others, in order to keep himself for that time. God willing, he will go to Rome in the autumn, and will dispose of himself according to the advice of Rev. Father General and yourself. He tells me that more Fathers are very much wanted, if it were only to assist Father Robert, who, he says, bears an incredible burden. He [Fr. Persons] wrote those two very beautiful booklets himself [*A Brief Discourse; A Brief Censure*], one of which we had hitherto supposed to be Campion's work or another's; he preaches continually, he resolves cases of con science for innumerable persons. The Catholics in the midst of persecutions have more[120] scrupulous consciences than anywhere else (that I know of), and have such an opinion of the [Jesuit] Fathers that they will not easily acquiesce in the judgment of any ordinary priest, unless it is confirmed by Fr. Robert. He has seven men continually at work at a press that he has, set up outside of London [Stonor Park], lest the noise of that machine be heard in the city. He is continually appealed to by gentle men, and by some of the [Queen's] Council, for necessary advice; so this Mr. Gilbert tells me, who has been his inseparable companion for this whole year, and who at his departure left Fr. Robert seven horses for the necessary journeys and affairs of the Fathers and priests, and a large sum of money to procure needful things, namely, paper, press, types, ink, and the like. For great things can only be done at great expense, and for the success of such works we must have men who are not only supreme despisers of money, but rich into the bargain.

Fr. Campion is no less industrious in his own province, and it is supposed that there are 20,000 more Catholics this year than last. Nor has God in this age anywhere given to the preachers of the word more power or success. Blessed be His name for ever.

Our *Apology* [defense of the Seminaries] (as I hear) is read both by enemies and friends, and the chief of the French mission, the Prince Dauphin, has given it to the Queen herself to read.

Christ Jesus preserve you for us. Rheims, June 23, 1581.

Your reverend Father's perpetual confrère, as I hope, in the Lord, on earth and in heaven,

William Allen[121]

The Heroic George Gilbert

To this account of Gilbert we may add a few more particulars of him. Gilbert, whose early life is described earlier,[122] is described in a government report as a man

> of reasonable tall stature, broad-shouldered, with a big leg, bending somewhat in the knees, short visaged, fair-complexioned, reasonably well-colored, little hair on his face, and short if he have any, thick of speech, and about twenty-four years of age. . . . In the country he resorts to his tenants' houses in Bucks, for thereabouts his mother, Grace Gilbert, a widow, dwells . . . His most familiar friends be one Mr. Pierrepoint, lying in Nottingham. Also one Mr. Peter Basset, who lies much at Mr. Roper's [Basset was great-grandson of Sir Thomas More, and therefore Roper's great-nephew], . . . one [Stephen] Brinkley, and divers others.[123]

About Midsummer 1580, Gilbert was taken before the Bishop of London by Norris the pursuivant, but discharged on Norris's declaring him an honest gentleman. Norris might well say so, for Gilbert paid him liberally, and hired his house to be a kind of sanctuary for hunted recusants.

As soon as Gilbert's rents came in, they were usually distributed in charity. His labors for souls were such, that he made as many conversions as any priest. A friend of his declared that the names of the wavering whom he had confirmed, the lapsed whom he had restored, the cold whom he had warmed (chiefly youths of his own age and condition), would fill a volume. He eluded his pursuers by a continual change of dress; going now as a gentleman, now as a servant. His sole anxiety was for Persons; for himself he never feared.

Fr. Hicks remarks, "The pursuit of him by the government, indeed, was so hot that it became greater labor and anxiety to take care of him than of themselves, so finally he was persuaded not without difficulty to cross the seas."[124] When he was sent to France, he had to conceal himself in a cave till the ship came in sight. He crossed over in April 1581, bearing a letter of Persons, leaving Persons seven horses and a large sum of money. He visited Allen at Rheims, and gave him 800 crowns. Thence he went to live at the English College at Rome, where he had the pictures of the English martyrs painted.[125] In the English seminary, he was a model to the seminarians of humility, obedience, chastity, penance, and prayer. Bombino records (no doubt from Fr. Persons's recollections) that Gilbert, having a "greed for afflicting his body, perpetually attached a cilice to his bare flesh, was ravenous for fasts, a father to the poor, an outstanding practitioner of obedience to his spiritual directors" and "spent two hours in the middle of the night in the contemplation of divine things."[126]

He presented himself to the Jesuit General, Claudio Acquaviva, who would not immediately receive him into the Society, nor yet allow him to put on the ecclesiastical habit in the college, as the pope and cardinals wished to employ him on English affairs.

In 1583, as he was about to start for France (and possibly England thence) on a commission of the pope, he was seized with a fever, which killed him on the seventh day. In his agony he held in his hands the cross that Alexander Briant had carved in the Tower, and began to talk to Campion as if he were present, lamenting that he had not been dragged with him on his hurdle to Tyburn. Just before he died, he was allowed to take vows as a Jesuit. He entered the next life on the night of October 6, 1583.[127]

CHAPTER 13

Controversy Erupts

The Preparation of *Rationes Decem: Ten Reasons*

CAMPION FINISHED his book about Easter, March 26, 1581, and
sent it by one Robinson, who delivered it to the home of Mr. Cleesby
in Yorkshire.[1] From there Fr. Richard Norris (also known as Richardson)
took it to London for Persons's approval.

Fr. Persons saw that the title was not that settled at Uxbridge and
that the margin swarmed with references to Fathers and Protestant writers, which for lack of books he was not able to verify. Knowing that the
enemy would closely scan every one of them and leap at any inaccuracy,

> Persons wrote to Campion [says Bombino] and asked him if he was
> quite sure that the authors cited were quoted faithfully. Campion
> answered that nothing had been alleged therein, except what was
> plain and obvious, and very carefully verified. When this reply
> was received, Persons, who was diffident only about this point and
> admired all the rest, not only approved, but ordered the book to
> be published. Campion, however, took the further precaution of
> getting friends to check his words carefully with the authors who
> were being quoted. Amongst these, Thomas Fitzherbert . . . most
> diligently exerted himself for Campion, at Persons's request. He
> researched in all the London libraries,[2] examining, at the sources,
> the places cited by Campion, for, being of good birth and a noted
> scholar, he could do so in safety. And, finally, having found that all
> was exceptionally accurate, he brought the good news to Persons,
> and urged on the publication of the work.[3]

Fitzherbert—then a young man just married, afterwards a Jesuit[4] was
later to recall how Fr. Persons gave him Campion's hand-written original

to check the references, and "after it was printed, Father Campion himself gave me one of the first printed copies as his own work."[5]

Printing books was not so easy as it had been. Though the works printed at Mr. Brokesby's bore the name "Doway" (Douay) on their title page, experts like Norton, who examined them for the government, reported: "The print is done in England." Undaunted, Brinkley, as we saw, continued to provide the press, now located at Stonor Park.

Persons desired that Campion should see to the printing of his own book, and so ordered him to return to London, without visiting Catholic homes on the way, but staying only at inns, in order to evade surveillance, for Catholic homes were being closely watched, and to avoid delays, for wherever Edmund went, the word would go round and people would congregate.[6] People were entranced and strengthened when he spoke; he confirmed the weak and lifted up the fallen. He seemed, Bombino says, "overwhelmed with a sense of most chaste pleasure as he regularly had to interrupt his speech with tears of joy streaming down his cheeks."[7]

Jesuit Fr. Philip Caraman gathers that, "from the care he [Campion] took over the printing of his *Decem Rationes* it is likely that he acquired some knowledge of type-setting from his father [a bookseller] since at the time booksellers were frequently also printers."[8]

Providential Escapes

Whilst riding to London he was once very nearly captured. A contemporary letter records:

> The Fathers of the Society in England have been delivered many times, and thrice almost miraculously, from the enemies' hands. One of them, Campion, on his way from York to London was watched by a certain fellow in hope of reward, to see where he stayed, and whither he was going. When they had come to a certain town thirty miles from London, the rascal gave information to a magistrate, telling the name of his fellow traveller, describing his appearance, and giving other signs by which he might be known. A boy heard the man dealing with the magistrate about the Jesuit, and noted all that took place. But as the word "Jesuit" was quite strange and unknown to him, he ran off at once to the inn, where the Father had put up, called him by his proper name, and also by that of "Jesuit,"

and advised him to save himself by flight. And so he providentially escaped. Similar adventures have happened at other times.[9]

Providence intervened in Robert Persons's favor too. Once, on his way to a meeting of Lancashire Catholics at the *Red Lion* hotel at Holborn, London,

> to reconcile to the bosom of the Church a nobleman coming from a great distance, and, though he was perfectly familiar with the place and had been there three days before, yet on the way his powers of perception were so altered that, when he came to the house, he failed to recognize it and was now unable to find it for all his careful efforts, in spite of his searching for it for a long time and making frequent inquiries of people about it; and so he was forced to go sorrowfully away.[10]

When Walsingham's men descended on the inn and arrested the group of seven—including Fr. Edward Rishton and his brother—Robert was not with them.

A contemporary Jesuit chronicle records: "Another time, when Father Persons was spending the night in the house of a priest, at daybreak he became disquieted by a strong impulse, urging him to depart as quickly as possible. Scarcely had he put his foot out of the door when the heretics, entering the house, arrested the [other] priest."[11]

On other occasions, escape owed less to divine intervention than to Jesuit shrewdness. One evening, the house in which Fr. Persons had sought refuge was suddenly surrounded by a noisy band in pursuit of him. Resistance or concealment was impossible. Persons at once determined on what he would do. He went to the door, opened it, and calmly asked what they wanted. "The Jesuit," was the reply (for his face was not known to them). "Very well, come in," he said, "and search for him, but do so quietly"—and as they entered, he went out, and made his escape.[12]

Reunion in London

While the things for printing were being readied, Campion quit Lancashire to rejoin his religious superior, Fr. Persons, in London. He departed for the south after Pentecost, that is, after May 14, 1581, since we know he spent that Feast-Day in the north.

On June 3, they were reunited. On that very day Persons received a letter from the new Father General Acquaviva in Rome and later wrote a reply in which he expressed what a joy it was to receive it:

> With what sentiments we read this letter I can not tell you! (Providentially we were gathered together at that time. I had called my father [Campion] from distant parts; I had not seen him for eight whole months). I will say only: we read it; re-read it; a third and a fourth time we read it; we showed it to our friends; we were exultant, delighted. May God thank you for so great a consolation.[13]

Fr. Bartoli says on this period:

> So they were in London for some twelve days, in which time they made a general confession to each other and, according to the custom of the Society, renewed their vows with solemnity in private, but not without great encouragement and consolation of spirit, which was made twofold for them by the most delightful letter they received then from the General, Claudio Acquaviva.[14]

Campion Contemplates the Future and Prays

Naturally enough, the recent torture of Alexander Briant was also a grim subject of conversation when Campion joined Persons in London, and they discussed with each other how they should conduct themselves if they fell into the enemies' hands. "For almost the whole of one night," Persons relates, "Campion and I sat up talking of what we should do, if we were taken—a fate which befell him soon after."[15] Bombino adds: "Persons told me, when I was writing this, that Campion spent these two days in almost continuous prayer, without taking any rest even at night."[16]

Visits in and around London

From arrival onwards, Campion was constantly employed in preaching either in London or in the outlying suburbs.[17]

One place which Campion and Persons frequently visited was Uxenden Hall, near Harrow-on-the-Hill, a spacious house on the property of William Bellamy and his wife Catherine, who, with their family, were converts of the two Fathers. The home had a well-endowed library where the Fathers could enjoy some spiritual recollection after their busy engagements.[18] Fr. William Weston S.J. would later write that Persons "had done much of his work and writing"[19] there. It was a thickly wooded retreat, nine miles from London, ideal for the purpose.

Campion at this time lodged sometimes at:

- Mrs. Brideman's in Westminster.
- White Friars, London, at Lady Babington's.[20] Born Margaret Croker, the wife of Sir William Babington was a leading recusant of Oxfordshire, where she had another house. Her son was Anthony, of the famous "Babington plot" to kill the queen.[21]
- Mr. Barnes's in Tothill Street, Westminster. This may be Robert Barnes, the intrepid Catholic gentleman who used various aliases (Winkfield, Strange, Mapledurham, Hynde) and served as courier and guide for missionary priests as they slipped in and out of England. After imprisonment, and much harassment from Topcliffe, he was banished from England in 1603.[22] Not long after his providential escape at Holborn, told above,[23] Persons had another close call at Mr. Barnes's house. The Justice came to search the house late at night and Persons escaped to the hayloft.[24]

There is another assistant to Campion listed as one-time prisoner in the Counter Prison in Wood St: a Mr. Richard Davies, who used the aliases Winkfield and Foster. He was arrested May 12, 1586. The prison records say he passed as a layman, was a notable corruptor (i.e., converted people to the Catholic religion) and conducted Campion, Persons, and "Edmonds" (Fr. Weston) through England. It is possible he was a priest.[25]

Campion at Tyburn

The road from these places to Harrow would generally lead Campion by Tyburn, a spot now marked by a stone which is erected at a place where "Tyburn-gate" once closed the great western road out of London, a few yards beyond the present Marble Arch. Just outside of this, probably within the garden of the house at the corner of the Edgeware Road, stood the famous gallows, three posts in a triangle, connected at the top by three cross bars, where the weekly batch of murderers, thieves, coiners, vagrants, traitors, or priests, were led out to suffer. It had been put

up anew in 1571 for the execution of Dr. Storey, whose blood had consecrated it. "Tyburn tree," as it came to be called, reminded Campion of the
wood of the Lord's Cross. Persons tells us "Campion would always pass
with his hat off and with a profound bow, both because of the sign of the
Cross, and in honor of some martyrs who had suffered there, and also
because he used to say that he would have his combat there."[26]

The Printing of *Ten Reasons*

The Privy Council ordered bookbinder Roland Jenks[27] to be sent to
London on April 28.[28] This settles approximately the date of the beginning of the printing at Stonor Park.[29] The book was finished near the end
of June. So the work lasted about nine weeks—a fairly long period, considering the smallness of the book itself. It will, however, be shown from
intrinsic evidence that the stock of type was very small.

The volume is, considering the printing of that time, distinctly well
done. Knowing that its publication had been a matter of much difficulty
and danger, when one scrutinizes every page with care, one finds it bears
some traces of the unusual circumstances of its production.

A Greek font was evidently lacking. Campion was fond, after the
fashion of scholars of that day, of throwing into his Latin letters a word
or two of Greek, which he wrote with the facility of one familiar with the
language. Here, Greek words are cited but spelt using the Roman alphabet. Certainly Greek letters would have been used if available.

A further indication of the difficulties under which type had been
procured is seen in the use of the "Black-letter" (Gothic script) question mark which differs somewhat from the Roman one in use then and
today. This is more readily understood when we remember that English
prose was then still generally printed in Gothic character. Campion's volume, however, being in Latin, it was necessary to procure Roman type.
The type, the printing, and the monogram or design on the title page are
precisely those used in Persons's *Reasons why Catholics refuse to go to
church*. Hence it cannot be doubted to be a work of Brinkley's press.

Another trace of the difficulty in finding type is found in the signs
for the a-e diphthong (æ), which is common in Latin. After using the
small stock they had, we find them using the Italian o-e diphthong (œ),
and then another medieval substitute for œ. It is noticed that these substitutions become increasingly frequent as we approach the end of each

printing section. At the start of each section, the proper or preferable characters are in use again, but only for as long as they last.[30]

The printers, then, could only set up a few pages at a time, correct them at once, and print off their four hundred copies or so, before they could go any further. Then they redistributed the type, and began again. When all was finished, they stabbed and bound their sheets. Considering the fewness of the workmen and the unforeseen delays which so often occur during printing, the nine weeks taken over the production do not seem unduly long.

The Release of *Ten Reasons*

By great industry, the five printers[31] managed to have Campion's book finished, and a certain number of copies bound, in time for the "commencement" at Oxford (twenty miles away) on June 27, the Tuesday next before the Feast of Sts. Peter and Paul, when those who were present found the benches of St. Mary's church strewed with the publication. Upwards of four hundred copies were distributed by Fr. William Hartley, partly in this way, and partly as gifts to individuals.[32] He was helped by Fr. John Curry, a native of Bodmin, Cornwall.[33]

The choice of such an occasion for the distribution was a bold and cheeky move that could have been suggested by any one of Persons, Campion, or Hartley, who all knew the routine of Oxford. They must have thrilled at the prospect of what would happen when it was discovered and read.

Indeed, the audience was more employed in reading the new book than in listening to the *responsions* (Oxford examinations) of the students. It was the reading, not the speaking, which so strangely moved them and held them in thoughtful silence. Some were furious, others amused, some exultant, others frightened or perplexed; but all agreed that the essay was a model of eloquence, elegance, and good taste.

There was a delicious irony in the fact that, whereas, back in 1569, Campion had failed to post two theological propositions on the door of St. Mary's in preparation for the Bachelor of Divinity degree,[34] in 1581 he posted ten on the pews inside![35]

Oxford had already caused some anxiety to the government. Lord Chancellor Bromley and the Earl of Leicester, Chancellor of the University, wrote on June 12, 1581,[36] to correct their loving friends, the students of

Christ Church, for being of late undutiful to the dean and sub-dean, slack in resorting to prayers and religious exercises, and so disorderly and insolent as to impair the service of God, the increase of learning and the husbandry of the house. After Campion's capture, the Privy Council ordered a letter to be written to the Vice-Chancellor and Heads of Houses to inform them that three Masters of Arts had been found in his company and that most of the seminary priests who at that time disturbed the Church had been heretofore scholars of that University. The Vice-Chancellor was therefore directed to search diligently through all the colleges after all persons suspected in religion, to report them to the Council and in the meantime to use the best means they could to bring them back to conformity.[37]

The young Oxonians were as tinder, and Campion's book was just the sort of spark to set them in a blaze. He had written, he says, not published, a challenge to disputation; this had been taken "atrociously," as if he were the most conceited man in the world. It was answered; but how? Not in the simple way, "We accept your challenge; the queen allows it; come," but with cries of "Jesuit, sedition, arrogance, traitor." He sees then that the only platform he will be allowed is the gallows; hence he gives the heads of his intended argument, a syllabus, as it were, of the lectures he was not allowed to deliver, to show that it was not his own strength, but the inherent strength of his cause and the native luster of truth that gave him courage to stand one against all. In a cause like this, he may be killed, he cannot be conquered.

Ten Reasons Summarized

The full title is *Rationes Decem: quibus fretus, certamen adversariis obtulit in causa fidei, Edmundus Campianus, e 'Societate Nominis Iesu presbyter allegatae ad clarissimos viros, nostrates academicos.* Translated: "Ten Reasons: presented to the illustrious men, our academics, relying on which Edmund Campion, priest of the Society of the name of Jesus, proposed to his adversaries disputation in the cause of the faith." The title has varied somewhat from edition to edition, but that given is copied exactly from the title-page of the original edition. It is usually named after its first two words ("Ten Reasons"), in either order: *Rationes Decem* or *Decem Rationes*. In the original, after the list of contents (the ten reasons's headings), the book's title is modified: *Rationes Oblati Certaminis Redditae Academicis Angliae* ("Reasons offered for the challenge made to the academics of England"). The running title (at the top, across each two pages) is *Rationes Redditae Academicis* ("Reasons put to the academics").

Ten Reasons is not a long work but a concise work covering many things pungently. The complete Latin text is 9,071 words. It has: a title page; a page of *errata* at the end; a five-page preface; a page listing the ten reasons; and the text itself occupying seventy-seven pages. A 1588 reprint of preface and text on the larger pages of *Concertatio*[38] occupies only thirty-three pages. A 1914 Latin edition has only fifty-eight small pages. In size, too, the original was a small book: 6 ½ x 4 inches.

For a long time, up to 1864, no original copy was publicly known to have survived. In 1863, a copy was found to be in the possession of a Mr. Godwin, a bookseller of Oxford—where else should it be found? He showed it to Mr. Thomas Edward Stonor, a residing family member of Stonor Park, who wrote a description of it in the *Miscellanies* of the Philobiblon Society for 1864 with a photograph of the title page.[39]

Fr. John Bridgewater, an older contemporary of Campion at Oxford,[40] gave a copy to the English Carthusian monastery "Sheen Anglorum" at Nieuport, France, whence it passed to the Carmelites of the same town in 1746. It was not heard of until it became known among the other copies that came to light in the 20th century. The Marquess of Bute possessed two (one was Bridgewater's copy) and munificently presented one of them to Stonyhurst College. In 1909 Canon Luke Gunning of St. Peter's Catholic parish, Winchester, found a copy.[41] Another original was discovered in 1936 in the six-penny box of a second-hand bookshop and is now in the library of Campion Hall, Oxford.

In his preface, Campion refers to his *Challenge*, which had been ignored or execrated, but not taken up. He had hoped for a public disputation with the scholars of his time, and a chance to argue the case for the Catholic position. Since this offer had not been accepted, he now sets down the main points of the arguments that he would have used in a public debate. After this preface, Campion expounds ten reasons, or topics of argument, on any of which he is ready to prove the falsity of Protestantism and the truth of the Catholic religion.

The ten reasons are:

1. Sacred Scripture
2. The Sense of Sacred Scripture

3. The Nature of the Church
4. Councils
5. Fathers
6. The Grounds Assumed by the Fathers
7. History
8. Absurdities
9. Sophisms
10. All Manner of Witness

1. *The Canon of the Scriptures.* All the old heretics, he says, in sheer despair of making the Bible speak their language, mutilated it. The Lutherans, Calvinists, and Anglicans have done the same with those parts of it which gave too clear a witness against them. They have deleted certain books from the Bible—on nothing but their own authority.

> What induced the Manichees to tear out the Gospel of Matthew and the Acts of the Apostles? Despair. . . . What induced the Ebionites to reject all St. Paul's Epistles? Despair. . . . What induced that crime-laden apostate Luther to call the Epistle of James "contentious," "turgid," "arid," "a thing of straw," and to judge it "unworthy of the Apostolic spirit"? Despair. For by this writing the wretched man's argument of righteousness consisting in faith alone was stabbed through and rent asunder. What induced Luther's whelps to expunge off-hand from the genuine canon of Scripture, Tobias, Ecclesiasticus, Maccabees, and, for hatred of these, several other books involved in the same false charge? Despair. For by these Oracles they are most manifestly confuted whenever they argue about the patronage of Angels, about free will, about the faithful departed, about the intercession of Saints.

2. *The sense of Sacred Scripture.* Protestants elude the force and meaning of the texts which tell plainly against them. Any subterfuge is used, for example, to deny the real Presence of Christ in the Holy Eucharist:

> Compare the Scriptures, they say, one with another. By all means. The Gospels agree, Paul concurs. The words, the clauses, the whole sentence reverently repeat living bread, signal miracle, heavenly food, flesh, body, blood. There is nothing enigmatic, nothing befogged

with a mist of words. Still our adversaries hold on and make no end of altercation. What are we to do? I presume, Antiquity should be heard; and what we two parties, suspicious of one another, cannot settle, let it be settled by the decision of venerable ancient men of all past ages, as being nearer Christ and further removed from this contention. They cannot stand that, they protest that they are being betrayed, they appeal to the word of God pure and simple, they turn away from the comments of men. Treacherous and fatuous excuse. We urge the Word of God; they darken the meaning of it. We appeal to the witness of the Saints as interpreters, they withstand them. In short their position is that there shall be no trial, unless you stand by the judgment of the accused party. And so they behave in every controversy which we start.

3. *The nature of the Church.* Protestants confess its authority in words, and then escape it by a definition; for their invisible Church is equally inaudible, and is incapable of bearing testimony to the truth.

> At hearing the name of the Church the enemy has turned pale. . . . He was well aware that in the Scriptures, as well of Prophets as of Apostles, everywhere there is made honorable mention of the Church: that it is called the holy City, the fruitful vine, the high mountain, the straight way, the only dove, the Kingdom of Heaven, the Spouse and Body of Christ, the ground of truth, the multitude to whom the Spirit has been promised and into whom He breathes all truths that make for salvation; her on whom, taken as a whole, the devil's jaws are never to inflict a deadly bite. . . . Such a loud pronouncement he dared not contradict; he would not seem rebellious against a Church of which the Scriptures make such frequent mention: so he cunningly kept the name, while by his definition he utterly abolished the thing, He has depicted the Church with such properties as altogether hide her away, and leave her open to the secret gaze of a very few men, as though she were removed from the senses, like a Platonic Idea. Only they can discern her who by a singular inspiration have the faculty of grasping with their intelligence this aerial body, and with keen eye regarding the members of such a company.

Campion continues in the spirit of the age, where no holds were barred in argument:

Throughout the whole course of fifteen centuries these men find neither town, village nor household professing their doctrine, until an unhappy monk [Luther] by an incestuous marriage had deflowered a virgin vowed to God [Catherine Bora], or a Swiss gladiator [Zwingli] had conspired against his country, or a branded runaway[42] [Calvin] had occupied Geneva. These people, if they want to have a Church at all, are compelled to crack up a Church all hidden away; and to claim parents whom they themselves have never known, and no mortal has ever set eyes on, Perhaps they glory in the ancestry of men whom everyone knows to have been heretics, such as Aerius, Jovinianus, Vigilantius, Helvidius, Berengarius, the Waldensians, the Lollards, Wycliffe, Huss, of whom they have begged sundry poisonous fragments of dogmas. Wonder not that I have no fear of their empty talk: once I can meet them in the noon-day, I shall have no trouble in dispelling such vaporings.

Our conversation with them would take this line:

Tell me, do you subscribe to the Church which flourished in bygone ages?

"Certainly."

Let us traverse, then, different countries and periods. What Church?

"The assembly of the faithful."

What faithful?

"Their names are unknown, but it is certain that there have been many of them."

Certain? To whom is it certain?

"To God Who says so!"

We, who have been taught of God—stuff and nonsense, how am I to believe it? . . . To think that all Christians should be bidden to join the Church; to beware of being cut down by the spiritual sword; to keep peace in the house of God; to trust their soul to the Church as to the pillar of truth; to lay all their complaints before the Church; to hold as heathen all who are cast out of the Church; and that nevertheless so many men for so many centuries should not know where the Church is or who belongs to it!

4. *The General Councils.* The English Church accepts the first four General Councils, and if so, she must admit their doctrines: the

supremacy of the See of Peter, the sacrifice of Christ on the altar, the intercession and invocation of saints, the celibacy of the clergy—and if the first four Councils are admitted, Campion engages to prove, on the same reasoning, that the Council of Trent (1545–63) must be admitted too.

> But if there shall be any one found so stark mad as to set his single self up as a match for the senators of the world, men whose greatness, holiness, learning and antiquity is beyond all exception, I shall be glad to look upon that face of impudence; and when I have shown it to you, I will leave the rest to your own thoughts. Meanwhile I will say thus much: The man who refuses consideration and weight to a General Council, brought to a conclusion in due and orderly fashion, seems to me witless, brainless, a dullard in theology, and a fool in politics. If ever the Spirit of God has shone upon the Church, then surely is the time for the sending of divine aid, when the most manifest religiousness, ripeness of judgment, science, wisdom, dignity of all the Churches on earth have flocked together in one city, and with employment of all means, divine and human, for the investigation of truth, implore the promised Spirit that they may make wholesome and prudent decrees.... There was found a Luther to say that he preferred to Councils the opinions of two good and learned men (I suppose himself and Philip Melanchthon) when they agreed in the name of Christ. Oh what quackery!

5. *The early Fathers.* We Catholics read and revere the Fathers, for these lights of the ancient Church teach the same doctrines we teach today. Protestants, finally realizing this, have therefore poured the most arrogant scorn upon the Fathers. Campion quotes the sneering comments of Luther and other writers who have pronounced against Dionysius, Ignatius, Irenaeus, Clement, Hippolytus, Cyprian, Chrysostom, and others.

> Ambrose was "under the spell of an evil demon." Jerome is "as damnable as the devil, injurious to the Apostle, a blasphemer, a wicked wretch." To Gregory Massow: "Calvin alone is worth more than a hundred Augustines." A hundred is a small number: Luther "reckons nothing of having against him a thousand Augustines, a thousand Cyprians, a thousand Churches." ...
>
> However, if we grant any just defense of an unjust cause, I do

not deny that the Fathers wherever you light upon them, afford the party of our opponents matter they needs must disagree with, so long as they are consistent with themselves. . . . Men who have sold their souls for gold, lust, drunkenness and ambitious display, can they be other than most hostile to Basil, Chrysostom, Jerome, Augustine, whose excellent books are in the hands of all, treating of the institute, rule, and virtues of monks? Men who have carried the human will into captivity, who have abolished Christian funerals, who have burnt the relics of Saints, can they possibly be reconciled to Augustine, who has composed three books on *Free Will*, one on *Care for the Dead*, besides sundry sermons and a long chapter in a noble work on the miracles wrought at the basilicas and monuments of the martyrs? . . .

They sing in their churches the Athanasian Creed. Do they stand by him? That grave anchorite who has written an elaborate book in praise of the Egyptian hermit Anthony, and who with the Synod of Alexandria suppliantly appealed to the judgment of the Apostolic See, the See of St. Peter. . . .

Jerome writes against Vigilantius in defense of the relics of the Saints and the honors paid to them; as also against Jovinian for the rank to be allowed to virginity. Will they endure him? Ambrose honored his patron saints Gervase and Protase with a most glorious solemnity by way of putting the Arians to shame. This action of his was praised by most godly Fathers, and God honored it with more than one miracle. Are they going to take a kindly view off Ambrose here? Gregory the Great, our Apostle [he sent to England St. Augustine of Canterbury], is most manifestly with us, and therefore is a hateful personage to our adversaries. Calvin, in his rage, says that he was not brought up in the school of the Holy Spirit, seeing that he had called holy images the books of the illiterate.

Those who turn aside from the ancient way are obliged to renounce the Fathers; and while the Fathers are read in England, it will be vain to proscribe the recent Catholic writers:

Time would fail me were I to try to count up the Epistles, Sermons, Homilies, Orations, Opuscula and dissertations of the Fathers, in which they have laboriously, earnestly and with much learning supported the doctrines of us Catholics. As long as these works are for sale at the booksellers' shops, it will be vain to prohibit the writings

of our controversialists; vain to keep watch at the ports and on the
sea-coast; vain to search houses, boxes, desks, and book-chests; vain
to set up so many threatening notices at the gates. No Harding, nor
Sanders, nor Allen, nor Stapleton, nor Bristow, attack these new-
fangled fancies with more vigor than do the Fathers whom I have
enumerated. . . .

Let him admit the Fathers, he is caught: let him shut them out,
he is undone.

Here too Campion mentions Bishop Jewel's famous challenge at
St. Paul's Cross, the alacrity with which it was accepted by the English
doctors at Louvain, and the immediate prohibition of their replies being
imported into England. He mentions Laurence Humphrey, who praises
Jewel in all else, but admits that he was imprudent in making this challenge. Campion also narrates a reply that Tobie Mathew once gave him at
Oxford about reading the Fathers but not believing them (both incidents
are related in ch. 1).[43]

6. *The grounds assumed by the Fathers.* Campion praises the extraordinary love and care for the Holy Scriptures shown by the Fathers.
They transcribed them, read them, meditated upon them, drank in
their contents and expounded them in every detail.

And if they also frequently have argued from the Authority of the
Ancients, from the Practice of the Church, from the Succession of
Pontiffs, from Ecumenical Councils, from Apostolic Traditions,
from the Blood of Martyrs, from the decrees of Bishops, from
Miracles, yet most persistently of all and most willingly do they set
forth in close array the testimonies of Sacred Scripture.

Wherefore I do all the more wonder at that haughty and famous
objection of the adversary, who, like one looking for water in a running stream, takes exception to the lack of Scripture texts—in writings crowded with Scripture texts. He says he will agree with the
Fathers so long as they keep close to Holy Scripture. . . .

The texts that they bring, we [Catholics] will bring: the texts
they confer, we will confer: what they infer, we will infer. Are you
agreed? Out with it and say so, please. "Not a bit of it," he says,
"unless they expound rightly." What is this "rightly"? At your discretion. Are you not ashamed of the vicious circle?

Hopeful as I am that in flourishing Universities there will be gathered together a good number, who will be no dull spectators, but acute judges of these controversies and who will weigh for what they are worth the frivolous answers of our adversaries, I will gladly await this meeting-day.

7. *The history of the Church*, which exhibits for so many centuries the progress, the vicissitudes, the enemies, and the contests of the Catholic Church, not of the Protestants. This is its positive side; the other is negative. It is admitted that the Roman Church was once holy, catholic, and so on. History ought to show how and when this once pure faith and practice were altered.

> Therefore this much is clear, that the articles of our belief are what History, manifold and various, History the messenger of antiquity, and life of memory, utters and repeats in abundance; while no narrative penned in human times records that the doctrines foisted in by our opponents ever had any footing in the Church. It is clear, I say, that the historians are mine, and that the adversary's raids upon history are utterly without point. No impression can they make unless the assertion be first received, that all Christians of all ages had lapsed into gross infidelity and gone down to the abyss of hell, until such time as Luther entered into an unholy union with Catherine Bora.

8. *Paradoxes:* what today we would call "absurdities" or "outrageous statements." It is a collection of the most offensive sayings of the Reformers: Zwingli, Luther, Calvin, Bucer, and others. The texts were well-known, and at every point the reference is accurately given to the author's original work:

> God is the author and cause of evil, willing it, suggesting it, effecting it, commanding it, working it out, and guiding the guilty counsels of the wicked to this end. As the call of Paul, so the adultery of David, and the wickedness of the traitor Judas, was God's own work. (Calvin; praised by Luther)
>
> My soul hates this word, *homousion* [consubstantial, from the Nicene Creed]. (Luther)
>
> When Christ Crucified exclaimed, "My God, my God, why hast Thou forsaken me," He was on fire with the flames of hell, He

uttered a cry of despair, He felt exactly as if nothing were before Him but to perish in everlasting death. (Calvin)

The image of God is utterly blotted out in man, not the slightest spark of good is left: his whole nature in all the parts of his soul is so thoroughly overturned that, even after he is born again and sanctified in baptism, there is nothing whatever within him but mere corruption and contagion. (Calvin)

Grace is neither infused into our hearts, nor strong enough to resist sin, but lies wholly outside of us, and consists in the mere favor of God—a favor which does not amend the wicked, nor cleanse, nor illuminate, nor enrich them, but, leaving still the old stinking odor of their sin, dissembles it by God's connivance, that it be not counted unsightly and hateful. And with this their invention they are so delighted that, with them, even Christ is called full of grace and truth for no other reason than that God the Father has borne wonderful favor to Him. (Luther, Bucer, and Brent)

Righteousness is only a relation. It is not made up of faith, hope and charity, vesting the soul in their splendor; it is only a hiding away of guilt. (Bucer and Calvin)

A Christian cannot lose his salvation, even if he wanted, except by refusing to believe. (Luther)

Baptism is not a wave of salvation, it is not a channel of grace, it does not apply to us the merits of Christ, it is a mere token of salvation. (Calvin)

And after plenty more, Campion says:

There remain the sayings of the heretics concerning life and morals, the noxious goblets which Luther has vomited on his pages, that out of the filthy hovel of his one breast he might breathe pestilence upon his readers. Listen patiently, and blush, and pardon me the recital.

And with this introduction, he gives a few more for measure—all from Luther:

If the wife will not, or cannot, summon the maid-servant. (Sermon on Marriage!)

Christ and Paul dissuaded men from virginity.

The more wicked you are, the nearer you are to grace.

All good actions are sins, in God's judgment, mortal sins; in God's mercy, venial.

No one thinks evil of his own volition.

The Ten Commandments are nothing to Christians.

God cares nothing at all about our works.

They alone rightly partake of the Lord's Supper who bear consciences that are sad, afflicted, troubled, confused and erring.

Sins are to be confessed, but to anyone you like; and if he absolves you even in jest, provided you believe, you are absolved.[44]

I think [says Campion] I have stirred up this puddle sufficiently. I now finish. Nor must you think me unfair for having turned my argument against Lutherans and Zwinglians indiscriminately. For, remembering their common parentage, they wish to be brothers and friends to one another; and they take it as a grave affront whenever any distinction is drawn between them ...

I am not weighty enough to claim for myself so much as an ordinary place among the select theologians who at this day have declared war on heresies. But this I know, that, puny as I am, supported by the grace of Christ, I run no risk while I do battle, with the aid of heaven and earth, against sayings such as these, so odious, so tasteless, so stupid.

9. *Sophisms:* the utter weakness of the Protestant arguments, as evidenced by four defects in Logic:

It is a shrewd saying that a one-eyed man may be king among the blind. With uneducated people, a mock-proof has force which a school of philosophers dismisses with scorn. Many are the offenses of the adversary under this head; but this case is made out chiefly by four fallacies, which I would rather unravel in the University than in a popular audience.

i. Their *skiamachia,* or *fighting with shadows,* as when they argue against celibacy with the text "marriage is honorable."

ii. Their *logomachia, taking words for things,* leaving the sense and wrangling over the word instead—as when they say, "You cannot find 'Mass' or 'Purgatory' in the Bible." [Nor, says Campion, can you find "Trinity" or "Person" in the Bible.]

iii. Their *homonumia* or *confusion of meanings,* as when they say, "Why priests, when John says we are all priests?" They may as well ask, "Why have kings, when we are all kings?"

iv. Their *circulatio* or *arguing in circles:*

Catholic: Give me the notes of the Church.

Protestant: The word of God and pure sacraments.

C: Have you them?

P: Who doubts it?

C: I deny it.

P: Consult the word of God.

C: I have already consulted it, and I am less friendly to you than before.

P: Yet it is plain.

C: Prove it to me.

P: Because we do not budge an inch from the word of God.

Campion then says, in exasperation:

Where is your understanding? Will you forever go on taking for an argument the very point that is called into question?

10. *All Manner of Witness.* Campion concludes the work with a dramatic peroration. He begins with Heaven—Who are the saints? He surveys Hell—Who are the damned, and why? And he answers with all Dante's positiveness. Then he returns to earth: the succession of the Apostolic See; the successions of all the bishoprics scattered over the world. Then he turns to the kings of the Christian world and cries out to Elizabeth herself.

Here is most of this glorious final chapter:

Let us put before our eyes the theatre of the universe: let us wander everywhere: all things supply us with an argument. Let us go to heaven: let us contemplate roses and lilies, Saints empurpled with martyrdom or white with innocence: Roman Pontiffs, I say, three and thirty in a continuous line put to death: Pastors all the world over, who have pledged their blood for the name of Christ: Flocks of faithful, who have followed in the footsteps of their Pastors: all the Saints of heaven, who as shining lights in purity and holiness have gone before the crowd of mankind. You will find that these were ours when they lived on earth, ours when they passed away from this world.

To cull a few instances, ours was that Ignatius, who in Church matters put no one, not even the Emperor, on a level with the Bishop; who committed to writing, that they might not be lost, certain Apostolic traditions of which he himself had been witness. Ours was that anchorite Telesphorus, who ordered the more strict observance of the fast of Lent established by the Apostles. Ours was Irenaeus, who declared the Apostolic faith by the Roman succession and chair. Ours was Pope Victor, who by an edict brought to order the whole of Asia; and though this proceeding seemed to some minds, and even to that holy man Irenaeus, somewhat harsh, yet no one made light of it as coming from a foreign power. Ours was Polycarp, who went to Rome on the question of Easter, whose burnt relics Smyrna gathered, and honored her Bishop with an anniversary feast and appointed ceremony. Ours were Cornelius and Cyprian, a golden pair of Martyrs, both great Bishops, but greater he, the Roman, who had rescinded the African error; while the latter was ennobled by the obedience which he paid to the elder, his very dear friend. Ours was Sixtus, to whom, as he offered solemn sacrifice at the altar, seven men of the clergy ministered. Ours was his Archdeacon Lawrence, whom the adversaries cast out of their calendar . . .

Ours are those highly-blest maids, Cecilia, Agatha, Anastasia, Barbara, Agnes, Lucy, Dorothy, Catherine, who held fast against the violent assault of men and devils the virginity they had resolved upon. Ours was Helen, celebrated for the finding of the Lord's Cross. Ours was Monica, who in death most piously begged prayers and sacrifices to be offered for her at the altar of Christ. Ours was Paula, who, leaving her City palace and her rich estates, hastened on a long journey a pilgrim to the cave at Bethlehem, to hide herself by the cradle of the Infant Christ. Ours were Paul, Hilarion, Antony, those dear ancient solitaries. Ours was Satyrus, own brother to Ambrose, who, when shipwrecked, jumped into the ocean, carrying about his neck in a napkin the Sacred Host, and full of faith swam to shore.

Ours are the Bishops Martin and Nicholas, exercised in watchings, clad in the military garb of hair cloths, fed with fasts. Ours is Benedict, father of so many monks. I should not run through their thousands in ten years. . . . Whoever wills, may seek these further details, not only from the copious histories of the ancients, but even much more from the grave authors who have bequeathed to memory almost one man one Saint. Let the reader report to me his judgment concerning those ancient blessed Christians, to what doctrine they adhered, the Catholic or the Lutheran. I call to witness the throne of God, and that Tribunal at which I shall stand to render reason for these Reasons, of everything I have said and done, that either there is no heaven at all, or heaven belongs to our people. The former position we abhor, we therefore fix upon the latter. . . .

Let us look down on heretics, the filth and fans and fuel of hell. The first that meets our gaze is Simon Magus. What did he do? He endeavored to snatch away free will from man: he prated of faith alone. After him, Novatian. Who was he? An Anti-pope, rival to the Roman Pontiff Cornelius, an enemy of the Sacraments, of Penance and Chrism. Then Manes the Persian. He taught that baptism did not confer salvation. After him the Arian Aerius. He condemned prayers for the dead: he confounded priests with bishops, and was surnamed "the atheist" no less than Lucian. There follows Vigilantius, who would not have the Saints prayed to; and Jovinian, who put marriage on a level with virginity; finally, a whole mess of nastiness, Macedonius, Pelagius, Nestorius, Eutyches, the Monothelites, the Iconoclasts, to whom posterity will aggregate Luther and Calvin. What of them? All blackcrows, born of the same egg, they revolted from the Prelates of our Church, and by, them were rejected and made void.

Let us leave the lower regions and return to earth. Wherever I cast my eyes and turn my thoughts, whether I regard the Patriarchates and the Apostolic Sees, or the Bishops of other lands, or meritorious Princes, Kings, and Emperors, or the origin of Christianity in any nation, or any evidence of antiquity, or light of reason, or beauty of virtue, all things serve and support our faith. I call to witness the Roman Succession, in which Church, to speak with Augustine, the Primacy of the Apostolic

Chair has ever flourished. I call to witness those other Apostolic Sees, to which this name eminently belongs, because they were erected by the Apostles themselves, or by their immediate disciples. I call to witness the Pastors of the nations, separate in place, but united in our religion: Ignatius and Chrysostom at Antioch; Peter, Alexander, Athanasius, Theophilus, at Alexandria; Macarius and

Cyril at Jerusalem; Proclus at Constantinople; Gregory and Basil in Cappadocia; Thaumaturgus in Pontus; at Smyrna, Polycarp; Justin at Athens; Dionysius at Corinth; Gregory at Nyssa; Methodius at Tyre; Ephrem in Syria; Cyprian, Optatus, Augustine in Africa; Epiphanius in Cyprus; Andrew in Crete; Ambrose, Paulinus, Gaudentius, Prosper, Faustus, Vigilius, in Italy; Irenaeus, Martin, Hilary, Eucherius, Gregory, Salvianus, in Gaul; Vincent, Orosius, Ildephonse, Leander, Isidore, in Spain; in Britain, Fugatius, Damian, Justus, Mellitus, Bede. Finally, not to appear to be making a vain display of names, whatever works, or fragments of works, are still extant of those who sowed the Gospel seed in distant lands, all exhibit to us one faith, that which we Catholics profess today. O Christ, what cause can I allege to Thee why Thou shouldst not banish me from Thine own, if to so many lights of the Church I should have preferred mannikins, dwellers in darkness, few, unlearned, split into sects, and of bad moral character!

I call to witness likewise Princes, Kings, Emperors, and their Commonwealths, whose own piety, and the people of their realms, and their established discipline in war and peace, were altogether founded on this our Catholic doctrine. What Theodosiuses here might I summon from the East, what Charleses from the West, what Edwards from England, what Louises from France, what Hermenegilds from Spain, Henries from Saxony, Wenceslauses from Bohemia, Leopolds from Austria, Stephens from Hungary, Josaphats from India, Dukes and Counts from all the world over, who by example, by arms, by laws, by loving care, by outlay of money, have nourished our Church! For so Isaiah foretold: Kings shall be thy foster-fathers, and queens thy nurses (49:23).

Hearken, Elizabeth, most powerful Queen, for thee this great prophet [Isaiah 49:23] utters this prophecy, and therein teaches thee thy part. I tell thee: one and the same heaven cannot hold Calvin and the Princes I have named. With these Princes then associate thyself, and so make thee worthy of thy ancestors, worthy of thy genius, worthy of thy excellence in letters, worthy of thy praises, worthy of thy fortune. To this effect alone do I labor about thy person, and will labor, whatever shall befall me, for whom these adversaries so often augur the gallows, as though I were an enemy of thy life. Hail, good Cross. The day shall come, Elizabeth, the day that will show thee clearly who has loved thee, the Society of Jesus or the brood of Luther. . . .

Conclusion: You have from me, Gentlemen of the University, this little present, put together by the labor of such leisure as I could snatch on the road. My purpose was to clear myself in your judgment of the charge of arrogance, and to show just cause for my confidence, and meanwhile, until such time as along with me you are invited by the adversaries to the disputations in the Schools, to give you a sort of foretaste of what is to come there. If you think it a just, safe, and virtuous choice for Luther or Calvin to be taken for the Canon of Scripture, the Mind of the Holy Spirit, the Standard of the Church, the Pedagogue of Councils and Fathers, in short, the God of all witnesses and ages, I have nothing to hope of your reading or hearing me. But if you are such as I have pictured you in my mind, philosophers, keen-sighted, lovers of the truth, of simplicity, of modesty, enemies of temerity, of trifles and sophisms, you will easily see daylight in the open air, seeing that you already see the peep of day through a narrow chink. I will say freely what my love of you, and your danger, and the importance of the matter requires. The devil is not unaware that you will see this light of day, if ever you raise your eyes to it. For what a piece of stupidity it would be to prefer Hanmers and Charkes[45] to Christian antiquity! But there are certain Lutheran enticements whereby the devil extends his kingdom, delicate snares whereby that hooker of men has caught with his baits already many of your rank and station. What are they! Gold, glory, pleasures, lusts. Despise them. What are they but bowels of earth, high-sounding air, a banquet of worms, airy dunghills. Scorn them. Christ is rich, who will maintain you; He is a King, who will provide for you; He is a sumptuous entertainer, who will feast you; He is beautiful, who will give in abundance all that can make you happy. Enrol yourselves in His service, that with Him you may gain triumphs, and show yourselves men truly most learned, truly most illustrious. Farewell.

At Cosmopolis, City of all the World, 1581

In short, Campion argues, Catholicism is the Christianity of history and fact, and his readers well know on which side truth lies, but are kept from confessing it by gold, glory, and pleasure.

Campion no doubt wrote these words in perfect good faith but when Persons gave the book his *imprimatur* he may have laughed to himself at the idea of Elizabeth changing religion. There was this *salvo*, however: the Jesuits wished to save Elizabeth's soul at the expense of her fortunes;

her friends wished to secure her fortunes and leave her soul to shift for itself.

The schema and content of this Catholic apologetics are not purely philosophical or logical—but the work of a preacher and rhetorician who also knows philosophy and logic and theology.

There is a formal order in the six first topics. They treat of the general and then of the particular, three times in a row. He takes the *Scriptures* as a whole, then the texts as the actual teaching of the Scriptures. He takes the *Church* as a whole, then the Councils, as it were the texts, the formal propositions enunciated by the Church. Next the *Fathers* are taken as a body of theologians, and then their consensus of teaching.

The seventh reason is a survey of *History*.

This was the order of things he had enunciated in his *Challenge*, article 5: "Scriptures, Councils, Fathers, History."

The eighth (the crowning *Absurdities* of the Protestants) and ninth (the four *Sophisms* by which they fail in Logic) launch bombshells at the Protestant position and blow it apart.

The tenth is a ringing peroration, gathering together, as he calls it, *All Manner of Witness*.

The Book's Popularity

To put it mildly, it was a book that succeeded. One may suspect the partisan prejudices of the Catholics when they repeated to one another the words of the greatest scholar of the day, the Frenchman, Marc Antoine Muret (1526–1585), *libellum aureum, vere digito Dei scriptum* (a golden booklet, truly written by the finger of God),[46] but it is impossible to misinterpret the anxious letters which the Anglican authorities wrote to one another on the subject, the orders of the Council that the book should be refuted, the terms of unmeasured abuse in which it was answered, the monstrous iniquity of the few disputations which its author was allowed to hold upon it, and the anxiety of the bishops to have even these conferences stopped; the tortures and death that were inflicted on the writer, and lastly, the voluminous mass of literature to which this little volume gave birth (see Simpson's bibliography, section 4: "Publications connected with *Rationes Decem*").

The spark may have been a little one, but it kindled a great fire. And the style of the book was such as to captivate the lover of learning of those days.

Its quality was praised, as its effect was lamented, by William Fulke, a Protestant controversialist who would be chosen to confront Campion in the debates in the Tower. Fulke said, "he set forth his *Ten Reasons* so purely for Latin, so plainly and pithily penned, that they were very taking, and fetched over many (neutral before) to his persuasion."[47]

From its first appearance until today, *Ten Reasons* has aroused intense interest. Within a few years, it was translated into Czech, Dutch, English, Flemish, French, German, Hungarian, and Polish. In Latin or in translation, separately or with other works, it has appeared in print 123 times—on average, once every three-and-a-half years, from 1581 to the present day, including six times in English already this century. (For details of these editions, see Simpson's bibliography, no. 91.)

Stonor Lodge today, four-and-a-half miles north of Henley-on-Thames, has a room set aside for a permanent exhibition on the life and work of Campion, open to the public on visiting days.

Campion and Persons Continue Visitation

While the book was being printed, Campion and Persons generally remained in the neighborhood of Stonor Park. Campion occasionally made excursions to the houses of:

- Mr. Robert Price (Apreece, Ap-rice; originally "ap Rhys," a Welsh name). He lived at Washingley Hall, Huntingdonshire, but had a second house at Newport Pagnall, Buckinghamshire, thirty-five miles from Stonor.[48] Price's name is constantly found in the Recusant Rolls, and he suffered greatly for the Faith. He was imprisoned for recusancy at Ely, March 25, 1594. In a monument to him at his parish church in Luton, Northamptonshire, he is depicted with a long white beard and praised for his virtues. The inscription records that he married Johanna Wilford, that they had nine sons and six daughters, and that he died aged ninety in the odor of sanctity, 1622. His sons also were imprisoned for aiding three priests to escape from Wisbeach Castle in March 1600. His grandson, Robert Price, was shot dead in cold blood by a soldier in 1644, purely for hatred of the Catholic religion.[49]

Burghley's notes say Mr. Price was absent when Campion visited.

- Mr. and Mrs. William and Jane Griffith,[50] at Southland, near Uxbridge, Buckinghamshire. Mrs. Griffith (Griffin), with her husband's brother, Mr. Ambrose Griffith (Griffyth, Gryffyth), was tried in the Star-Chamber on November 15, 1581, for being "a great receiver of Campion and Persons, and many the like, as one of her husband's brothers [not Ambrose][51] hath confessed, sometimes by the name of Foster, Colt, etc."[52] She and Ambrose were fined 500 marks apiece.[53] Burghley's notes say Persons and Campion met up here, as well as at Lady Stonor's. Mrs. Griffith had been arrested not long before, by order of a letter from the Council, to arrest her and her husband, after "information has been given unto their Lordships that William Griffith, esquire, dwelling at Southland in the county of Bucks, has been heretofore a receiver and harborer of Campion, Persons and others of that confederacy, by means of one Norris, by whom they have been at sundry times brought unto the house of the said Griffith."[54] William Griffith was not put on trial with his wife because he eluded discovery when his house was searched and people arrested.[55]

- Mr. Edwin (Edward) East, of Bledlow, Buckinghamshire (also of Cockthorpe, Oxfordshire): his only daughter Dorothy was married to one of the Gilbert group of helpers, Thomas Fitzherbert, who checked the references in Ten Reasons.

- Lady Babington,[56] at Twyford, Buckinghamshire (about a dozen miles from Stonor), where Campion seems to have spent St. John the Baptist's day, June 24, the first anniversary of his crossing to England.

- Robert Dormer (knighted in 1591) and his wife Elizabeth Montague, at Wing (Wynge), Buckinghamshire, where Campion said Mass and preached.[57] He was brought there by Fr. William Harris, and introduced as "Mr. Foster."[58]

- Mrs. Phillipe Pollard, a widow, of Little Haddon, Oxfordshire.[59]

- Mr. Yeates.[60]

During the three weeks that elapsed between the publication of his book and his capture, he wrote a letter to Claudio Acquaviva, the

General of the Order, of which we have only a paragraph. It was dated July 9, 1581, and written under an assumed name of Alexander Striber. Campion wrote:

> Our adversaries were never more monstrously cruel than now; and nevertheless the Catholic religion never in better condition, or in more security. For we are pressed with no other arguments than those whose premisses are the rack, shackles, starvation, insults; this has already broken down the dignity of our enemies, and turned the eyes and ears of the whole realm towards the Catholics. Nothing else was lacking to this cause than that to our books written with ink should succeed those others which are daily being published, written in blood.[61]

Fr. Hartley

Father William Hartley, who has the great credit of having distributed *Ten Reasons*, was born at Wyn, Derbyshire, about 1557. At eighteen he matriculated at St. John's, Oxford, where he became a chaplain. Expelled for his religion by Vice-Chancellor Tobie Mathew in 1579, he went to the seminary at Rheims, was ordained at Châlons, and returned to England in June 1580—the same month as Campion, in a separate band. He used Stonor Park as the basis for his missionary work. He was of great service to Frs. Persons and Campion in printing and distributing their books, but was eventually apprehended at Stonor Park about August 4, 1581, imprisoned in the Tower for a year and then sent to Marshalsea Prison. Caught saying Mass in a cell before Lord Vaux, he was laid in irons, December 5, 1583. He was indicted and tried for high treason in 1584, but for some unknown reason, not executed. In January 1585 he was sent into exile. He then spent a little time at Rheims, recovering his health, and made a pilgrimage to Rome, before returning to his perilous mission. In 1587 he was arrested in London and, as his friend Father William Warford said, "being beset by the deceits of the heretics, incurred the suspicion of having apostatized. But the event showed how unjust that suspicion was, for when he suffered at Tyburn, he won the greatest credit for constancy, and everyone testified to his loyalty towards all Catholics. . . . He was a man of the meekest disposition and naturally virtuous, modest and grave, with a sober and peaceful look."[62] He was executed October 5, 1588, and was beatified in 1929 by Pope Pius XI. After he was put to death, his mother, we are told, who witnessed his execution, made a great feast to which she called her neighbors and friends as to a marriage, bidding them rejoice with her, for she was the mother of a martyr of God.[63]

CHAPTER 14

Capture

C AMPION HAD now been laboring a year in England, and his time
was almost come. Many a spy was abroad who hoped to catch him,
many a false brother was ready to betray him, and the traitor who was to
set him in his enemies' hands was already at work.

George "Judas" Eliot

There was a certain George Eliot, formerly servant to Mr. Thomas
Roper (St. Thomas More's grandson) of Orpington in Kent, and later at
Ingatestone, Essex, in the service of the Dowager Lady Petre, the widow
of Sir William and mother of Sir John Petre. Eliot was a Catholic; but
either through avarice, or, as Campion's Catholic biographers assert, in
order to free himself by court favor from a charge of murder (which he
afterwards confessed to be true), he obtained access to Dudley, Earl of
Leicester, and communicated to him all that he knew, and much that
he invented, about Catholics. He wrote several letters to the earl, two of
which, seemingly written from prison, were thought to contain information worth laying before the Council. They were accordingly sent to Lord
Burghley, and are now in a volume of his papers in the British Museum.[1]

The first paper contains a list of thirty priests, followed by a list
of the chief lay Catholics known to him, or reported to him, listed
under Yorkshire, Derbyshire, Staffordshire, Lincolnshire, Berkshire,
Oxfordshire, London, Kent, and Essex.

He then goes further and adds detailed information about Sir John
Petre and his mother, and about a plot to assassinate the queen, which
he said was communicated to him at Christmas 1579 by John Payne
(Paine), a priest in the house of his old master, Thomas Roper. The plot is
described in this letter nearly in the words of Eliot's subsequent deposition

at Campion's trial, which will be given in its place. The informer goes on
to enumerate the persons who were named by Fr. Payne as accomplices
in this plot: Mr. Talbot, and his man Robert Eliot; another Robert Eliot,
servant to Lady Paulet; Robert Tunster, servant to Sir John Petre; and
Philip Lowe, servant to the old Lady Petre.

It is unlikely that Leicester believed such an outlandish story, but it *was*
helpful to learn new names of active Catholics, especially if they might
know where Campion was—and here the next letter is more important.

In the second letter, George Eliot informs Leicester of several matters:
the merely political conformity of Sir John Petre, who was a "schismatic
Catholic" attending the Protestant church, but refusing Communion; the
resolute character of Robert Tunster; the threats of vengeance against
Leicester by Ludovic Greville, who had married Sir John Petre's sister; the
high favor which the Queen of Scots bore to Mr. Rolleston; the likelihood
of getting some information about Campion and Persons from Francis
Browne or Charles Basset (Thomas Roper's nephew) or from Humphrey
Eyton (Roper's servant, who was imprisoned in the Gatehouse and
examined by Norton and Hammond);[2] the books published by Persons
and Campion; and two bookbinders in St Paul's Church yard, named
Gawood and Holden, whom Eliot supposes to have bound the said books.
Then he tells how Thompson, one of Roper's priests,[3] took these books to
his house, and how Payne, his other priest, had said Mass on Sunday, July
2 at Mr William Moore's house at Haddon, Oxfordshire, at which Mass
Eliot himself was present. (Mr. Moore's wife was Anne More, a grand-
daughter of Sir Thomas More.)

This shows that Eliot at that time was going about the country as a
fervent Catholic, making his observations so as to reap afterwards the
reward of a spy. Perhaps he was following Fr. Payne; for the same persons
who tell us of Eliot's crime of murder, tell us that he had a personal quarrel with Payne about some maid of Mr. Roper's household, with whom
he had eloped to London, in hopes that the priest would marry him to
her, and on this being refused, had resolved on revenge. Several of the
persons named in the letters were apprehended after Eliot's success in
taking Campion had given value to his information, which was at first
received with little credit.

Campion and Persons Part

After the thrilling adventure of the release of *Ten Reasons*, Persons was not one to let success go to his head. He naturally feared for the safety of his press at Stonor Lodge. He judged it prudent that they should part; and so on Tuesday, July 11, after the usual mutual confession and renewal of vows, he appointed Campion to proceed to Norfolk; first, however, returning to Lancashire, where he had left the greater part of his books and papers in the care of Richard Hoghton at Hoghton Tower, between Preston and Blackburn.

Persons, however, ordered him to make no stay there, and especially to avoid lodging at gentlemen's houses during his journey [4]—since some of them were under constant observation, and capture was more likely there than at inns.[5] As well, Persons recalls, "In order to get there [Norfolk] sooner, it was decided that he should avoid, as much as possible, the houses of the Catholic gentry on the way, who would have detained him."[6]

After all was settled, they waited till daylight, when they mounted their horses, Campion and Ralph Emerson riding north, Persons and his man towards Kent. They exchanged hats—as, on leaving Prague, Campion and Campana the Rector had exchanged habits—and bade one another farewell with the most tender embraces and tears, sensing this was the last time they would see each other in this life.[7]

But it was not so. They had not long been parted before Persons heard Campion galloping after him, to ask his per mission to turn off the northern route to visit the house of Mr. Yate, at Lyford Grange, some twenty miles to the west, near Wantage. Persons granted the permission—and then Campion departed from his friend forever.

The End of Fr. Persons's Mission in England

It was indeed the last time the famous duo saw each other.

Less than four weeks later, on Friday, August 4, the Privy Council ordered Sir Henry Neville to search Stonor Lodge for the printing-press and for any books by Campion and Persons, and to examine anyone there regarding Masses said in the house and their conformity to the established religion.[8] Neville and his agents surrounded the house. The press was seized, along with John Stonor, Fr. William Hartley, Stephen

Brinkley and his four assistants: John Harris, John Harvey, John Tucker and John Compton.[9] Indeed they were busy in printing another Catholic work. On August 13, they were sent to the Tower of London.

Fortunately, Persons happened to be in a house at Windsor Forest at the time of the raid. So he escaped it just in time and took up residence at Henley Park, a house belonging to Francis Browne (brother of Anthony Browne, Viscount Montague). Soon afterwards he moved to Mitchelgrove, West Sussex, home of William Shelley (then in the Fleet prison).[10] Intending to return to London, he heard of a group of priests and laymen who were going to France, and they offered to take him with them.

It was not an easy decision for Persons: on the one hand, escape could look like cowardice and desertion; the heretics might rejoice at his departure; returning to England might become well-nigh impossible; the chance of martyrdom would be lost. On the other hand, he needed a new press overseas to print his books from now on; he should give a report in person to Dr. Allen and his Jesuit superiors; he wished to confer with Scottish exiles with a view to a mission in their country too.[11] In the end, he chose to make the voyage.

At midnight, the group left for the sea-coast, to embark the ship in secrecy, but when they arrived, the wind had changed and the ship was far out from port. It was too dangerous for a numerous group to travel back together in broad daylight to Mitchelgrove; they would arouse suspicion. In fear of discovery, they took shelter in a barn in a field and waited for a favorable wind, which came after two or three days.[12] Some time between August 12 and 21, the party sailed for Rouen.[13] Persons then went to Rheims to see Dr. Allen.[14] Persons intended to return soon, but he was never to see England again.

The Jesuit General saw that there was no point in sending Persons back; it would be tantamount to handing him over to the Elizabethan government, since the search for him had become so keen, and anyone who knew him was being tortured to extract information about him. His presence had become therefore a source of the greatest danger to anyone who received him. Since he, with Dr. Allen, had been declared a rebel and traitor, anyone who sheltered him or even conversed with him would be liable to the death penalty.[15]

On the Continent, in the years following, Persons was engaged in several important political and educational enterprises. He wrote and plotted in favor of armed intervention to liberate English Catholics. He was instrumental in starting new seminaries and colleges at Valladolid, Seville, and Madrid to educate English youths in exile. He founded a school for boys at Eu, Normandy, later transferred to St. Omer, and now at Stonyhurst—where some of his manuscripts are now kept.

He engaged in Catholic controversy with vigor and intelligence. He has been called the writer of the best prose of his day; and his style and content are remarkably modern, when compared to his coevals. He has been reckoned "one of the most effective controversialists of his day,"[16] as a man who wrote lucid and forceful prose of simplicity, brevity, and clarity.[17] His manner of writing was both expressive and succinct, and he always had apt analogies to hand. Jonathan Swift praised his clarity and intelligibility, in contrast to his Elizabethan contemporaries.[18]

His greatest written work was a spiritual book, *The Christian Directory* (1582), which went through many editions and translations, right up to the end of the 20th century.[19] It also received the unexpected acclaim of Protestants by their plagiarism and imitation of it. Edmund Bunny, a Calvinist rector of Bolton Percy, Yorkshire, pirated the work, purged it of Catholicism, and put out a Protestant version. He gave due credit to the "R.P." who wrote the original work—but Persons would have none of it; he wrote a virulent rebuke of the piracy and bowdlerization.[20] In addition to *The Christian Directory*, Persons wrote more than twenty other books or pamphlets after leaving England.[21]

In 1588, for one year, he was made Rector of the English College in Rome, a post he held again in the years 1597–1609,[22] which took him up to his peaceful death there in 1610 at the age of sixty-four. At his desire he was buried in the College chapel next to Cardinal William Allen, but their tombs and others' were violated when French Revolutionary soldiers occupied Rome in 1798. According to Cardinal Wiseman's *Recollections of the Last Four Popes and of Rome in their Times*, when he arrived in Rome in December 1818 the old College chapel was in a derelict state; he saw "piled on one side, the skulls and bones of, perhaps, Cardinal Allen, Fr. Persons, and others, whose coffins had been dragged up from the vaults below, and converted into munitions of war."[23] These bones were eventually reburied in the crypt, but the exact resting place of Allen and Persons is not known.

Historians have often judged Fr. Persons unkindly—but it can safely be said that, unlike his political enemies, he had nothing personal to gain and never sought anything for himself. His cause all along was only the cause of Christ and the Church. He had the courage to take on a seemingly lost cause—the practice of the Catholic faith in England—and give it his utter best, risking prison, torture, and execution. He employed every spiritual and didactic means to maintain the faith—and political means too when this became necessary. In the judgment of J. H. Pollen S.J., "Persons was a man of great parts, eloquent, influential, zealous, spiritual, disinterested, fearless. Yet he had some of the defects of his qualities. . . . Though his services in the mission field, and in the education of the clergy were priceless, his participation in politics and in clerical feuds cannot be justified except in certain aspects."[24] His biographer, Francis Edwards S.J., says, "No Norman bishop or Knight Templar could have combined more readily than Fr. Robert the roles of priest and warrior," and "perhaps he could already be regarded as deserving of a place in the calendar of warrior saints. Certainly his cause never had a doughtier fighter or a supporter more single-minded in his devotion."[25] Anglican historian, Professor John Bossy, comments: "Yes, Persons was no angel, he got his hands dirty, he was touched with the sin of the world; but if he had kept himself as clean as Campion perhaps nothing would have got done at all."[26]

Was Persons a traitor to England, along with Dr. Allen, as many Protestant writers have claimed? Did he not seek the subjugation of England to Spain when he appealed to Philip for armed intervention? Rather, he sought only the freedom of Catholics to practice their faith, by the only means possible—a change of regime, as a final resort, which meant supporting schemes to overthrow Elizabeth. He had been kept in ignorance of the Papal and Spanish designs upon Ireland, and was greatly annoyed when he first heard of Sanders's expedition. He was *afterwards* forced to become a "traitor": "beaten for loyalty," says one of Shakespeare's characters, "excited me to treason" (*Cymbeline*, Act 5, sc. v, 418–9). Persecuted for doing his duty, he naturally wished to destroy the power of his persecutors. Fr. McCoog S.J. remarks on Persons's change of focus: "The quartering of Campion exploded unrealistic expectations for a quick conversion of England through the sheer irresistibility of Catholic truth."[27]

Fr. Hughes asks: "Is Allen to be condemned as un-English for refusing to acknowledge that a minority was England simply because the minority controlled the government?"[28]

E. E. Reynolds puts the issue in historical perspective:

> It is easy to condemn them [Persons and Allen] and the many English exiles who thought as they did. Perhaps we can gain a less prejudiced attitude if we consider an historical parallel. In June 1688 a letter signed by, among others, Bishop Compton of London, was sent to William of Orange [in France] asking him to intervene to protect the Protestant religion and succession. William landed on Guy Fawkes's Day with an army of which two-thirds were foreign mercenaries. He succeeded in forcing James II to leave the country and the Glorious Revolution was over. Were Bishop Compton and the other signatories traitors when they signed that letter? Perhaps the answer may be found in one of the epigrams of Sir John Harrington, the godson of Queen Elizabeth.
>
> > Treason doth never prosper: what's the reason?
> > For if it prosper, none dare call it treason.[29]

Campion Invited to Lyford

But let us return to Campion's request to visit the house of Mr. Francis Yate, at Lyford, Berkshire (now in Oxfordshire). Mr. Yate himself (c. 1545–1588) was at the time a prisoner for religion in Reading,[30] forty miles from his home, but he had written to Campion, beseeching him to visit his family. Campion had more than once refused; but now that he was in the region, he thought he could find no excuse.[31]

The moated grange at Lyford was an attractive place for a Catholic priest. Mrs. Yate had under her protection eight Brigittine nuns who had migrated into Belgium at the beginning of Elizabeth's reign, but had been compelled by the tumults in the Low Countries to return, and were committed by the queen to the custody of various non-Catholic persons, where they suffered many miseries till some gentlemen, in pity for them, begged the queen to transfer their custody to themselves.[32] They had been there now for several years, and Mr. Yate's widowed mother had joined their community.

It was natural that these women should desire to see and hear Fr. Campion; but it was scarcely necessary, as there were two Douay priests always in the house to supply their spiritual needs, Frs. Thomas Ford and John Collington (Colleton). "A great desire to hear Campion had so fired all these virgins and the mother, having heard so much about him," says Bombino, "they were all yearning exceedingly to confess their sins to *him*, and take the Eucharist from *his* hands."[33] Campion himself, besides his natural courtesy, seems to have had a special liking to the kind of spiritual conference which he might expect at Lyford; and his importunity at last overcame the prudence of Persons, who at first withheld consent. The house was notorious. The second son of the family, John Yate, was a priest of the Society of Jesus, a missionary in Brazil. In 1574 he had accompanied Robert Persons to Louvain, to be admitted into the Society there.[34] There would be a great concourse when Campion was heard to be there, and this would be perilous for himself and fatal to his expedition into Norfolk. Further, it was too close to Oxford, only about ten miles away. "I know," said Persons, "your easy temper; you are too soft to refuse anything that is requested of you. I know the ardent affection of the Yates and the whole family for the Society and the Catholic cause. Once they get hold of you, there will be no way out."[35]

Campion said he would stay exactly as long as Persons ordered him. Persons asked him what security he could give for that. Campion offered Br. Ralph Emerson as his bail—at which Persons made him Campion's superior on the journey and told Campion to obey him. Then he told them not to tarry at Lyford more than one day, or one night and morning, and bade Ralph to take care that this command was executed. They then once more separated. Campion was happy; he was able to satisfy the nuns, and he had received a delightful humiliation in being put under the obedience of a lay-brother.

What a happy surprise their visit brought the house, so desired but so unexpected! At Lyford, Campion found everything in order: the nuns were virtually living a monastic life in a section of the house given over to them. They were in such fervor and excitement that they fell on their knees at his arrival and would not rise until he had pronounced a blessing over them. He told them at once how short a time he had to stay with them, and they understood there was no time to be lost. The night was spent in confessions and conferences. With the earliest dawn, Campion said Mass and then preached.

Campion Leaves and Returns

After breakfast, in obedience to Persons's orders, he and Br. Ralph took horse and rode away, accompanied by Fr. Collington. This was on Wednesday, July 12.

It happened that in the afternoon of the same day a large party of Catholics visited Lyford to see the nuns. Nothing could exceed their mortification when they found what a treasure they had only just missed. It was useless to tell them that Campion had gone in obedience to the strict injunctions of his superior. They must send after him. Fr. Ford took horse and rode after him, and in the evening caught up with him at an inn not far from Oxford, where he found him with a number of students and masters of the University round him—for it was quite out of Campion's power or even will to keep himself concealed. Here Ford whispered his message to Collington, but the message was passed round the table and the whole company learnt his errand.

They had already tried to make Campion preach, but he had refused to perform any public act of religion at so dangerous a time and place; and they saw that if they could prevail on him to return to Lyford, they should have him all to themselves. Ford therefore began the assault. Attracted by his passionate tones and gestures, the rest of the party chimed in and begged Campion not to resist the prayers of so godly a company. Seeing that everybody was against him, Campion declared that he was simply acting under obedience.

Commands are not to be taken literally, they said; Persons never thought such a company would be gathered, or he would never have forbidden his preaching to them. Campion had devoted a day to a few nuns, and he could never refuse another to so many persons, all thirsting for the waters of life. It was nearly Thursday; on Friday he might ride back to Lyford, remain there on Saturday and Sunday morning, and then he might go.

Campion, the gentlest of men, was moved almost to tears. He would do nothing contrary to obedience, but then, after all, he was in Brother Ralph Emerson's hands. Such an excuse was too ridiculous; so he had to explain that Ralph was made his superior for this expedition, and that he would do whatever Ralph ordered him. This turned the tide; the assault was now against Ralph. The "little man" was at first quite

fierce in his refusals; but when they came to reasons, he was soon overwhelmed. He found that he could spare Campion a deal of trouble and
even danger if he left him at Lyford, while he fetched Campion's books
from Mr. Hoghton's in Lancashire. From Lyford, Campion could easily ride to a Catholic gentleman's house on the borders of Norfolk after
lunch on Sunday and there wait for Br. Ralph and the books. So said, so
done. Campion was ordered back to Lyford; and Ralph rode on towards
Lancashire.[36]

Reynolds comments on this scenario:

> There are one or two unexplained aspects of this matter. What was
> Campion doing near Oxford? The obvious route north was through
> Burford and Chipping Campden. And how did it come about that a
> group of Oxonians was gathered at this particular inn? The records
> give no clue to the answers to these questions. It may be that a
> student from Oxford was at Lyford and had there suggested that
> Campion should meet some of his friends at this inn. Another pos-
> sibility is that one of the priests, Ford or Colleton, had arranged this
> meeting soon after Campion's arrival for a few students who they
> knew were having doubts about Protestantism. This might explain
> why Colleton accompanied Campion from Lyford as he would
> know of the rendezvous; there was no need for him to act as a guide
> save in courtesy. Parsons was certainly right in fearing Campion's
> susceptibility to any Catholic appeal; he would go anywhere at any
> time, completely oblivious of his own safety if he could bring spiri-
> tual comfort to those in need. The Oxonians asked for a sermon, but
> this he refused to give as even he felt that proximity to the university
> was a serious risk.[37]

Oxford at the time was a hotbed of Catholicism. In recent years, Mass
had been celebrated in some inns in Oxford and in the immediate vicinity, including the Mitre, the Swan, the Star, and the Catherine Wheel.[38]

There is some variation in the records, and so some uncertainty as
to the exact chronology or location of these days, or at least of one day.
If July 11 and 12 are clear, then it is not clear where Campion was on
Thursday July 13. He was probably at the same inn that night, or a nearby
inn on the way to Lyford.[39] In any case, on Friday, July 14, the party
returned to Lyford.

Eliot at Large

Eliot, on the other hand, who had been at Haddon in Oxfordshire on July 3–4, had been in trouble at London, where he explained to the Earl of Leicester, first, his knowledge of Catholics and their hiding-places, and his willingness to tell all in the queen's service, and next, the danger in which he stood because of the impending charge of murder.[40] The motives of his having recourse to Leicester may be understood from the objections which Payne on his trial brought against the insufficiency of Eliot to be witness:[41] he declared him guilty of oppression of the poor, even unto death; of a rape and other notorious lewdness; of breach of contract, and defrauding Lady Petre; of changing his religion often; of malice against Payne himself; adding that he was also arrested for murder, and was a notorious dissembler.

Fr. Thompson, one of Roper's "servants," was arrested and committed to the Marshalsea on July 30, 1581.[42]

After saying Mass in Haddon, Fr. Payne was betrayed by Eliot and arrested at Warwickshire. He was then taken to Greenwich, to be examined by Walsingham there on July 14.[43]

On August 14, the Council ordered him to be put to the torture in the Tower.[44] He was violently racked at least twice.[45] On September 8, Eliot received a reward of £100 from the government for his betrayal of Fr. Payne.[46] St. John Payne, one of the Forty Martyrs of England and Wales, was hanged at Chelmsford on April 2, 1582. After he forgave all, including Eliot by name, his last words were, "Jesus, Jesus, Jesus." Thus, as Dr. Allen's contemporary account says, he "most constantly, Catholicly, patiently and meekly ended this mortal life."[47]

Whatever his exact movements, it is certain that Eliot was in Oxfordshire during the week that Campion spent at Lyford. Perhaps Eliot, as well as the students and masters of Oxford, had heard of his presence in the neighborhood. As it appears, by his letter to Leicester, that Moore's house at Oxford, and Yate's at Lyford, were the only two Catholic houses that he knew in Oxfordshire and Berkshire, it was natural that he should search first one and then the other for his victim. I suppose that it was for this reason he heard Mass at Haddon on Sunday, July 2, and again on Tuesday, July 4; and then denounced the priests who celebrated, Thompson and Godsalve, to Leicester. It was with this dangerous man in the neighborhood, furnished with full powers, with letters to all sheriffs and constables, and with an experienced pursuivant, David Jenkins, to attend him (and to watch him) that Campion went back into the trap from which he had just escaped.

Eliot at Lyford

Of course, Fr. Campion was received with exceeding joy on Friday, July 14, and for two days he, the nuns, and the Catholics of the neighborhood felt they were in Paradise. On Sunday, July 16, more than sixty Catholics and Oxford students were assembled to hear him preach (or thirty-seven lay people, if Eliot's account is right).[48]

That Sunday, Eliot came to the house, with his attendant pursuivant, on commission to catch any Jesuits and priests he could find. He knew, he said, that "Master Yate was a very earnest Papist, and one that gave great entertainment to any of that sect."[49] Eliot thought that if he and his companion arrived about eight o'clock on a Sunday morning, they were sure to find a Mass. He had a way in, via his friendship with the cook of the house, Thomas Cooper, an old fellow-servant of his at Mr. Roper's, who knew him to be a Catholic. On arriving, Eliot asked for the cook, who came out of the house and on to the drawbridge. Eliot then talked with him, saying simply he had come to see his old friend while on his way to Derbyshire. After a good chat together, Eliot said he must be going, but Cooper insisted he stay for lunch. After feigned reluctance, Eliot stayed on: "in truth I was as willing to stay as he to have me."

After a drink in the pantry, Eliot was asked about his companion Jenkins, and said he was not Catholic but well-disposed. The cook asked Eliot: "Will you go up?"—by which he meant to invite him to Mass. The cook whispered to Eliot how lucky he was—luckier than he thought— for he was to hear the famed Fr. Campion preach. Eliot had not seen Campion before. Jenkins stayed behind and Eliot was conducted upstairs, through the hall and other rooms, to a large chamber where Fr. Ford (alias Saltwell) was saying Mass. Two other priests were kneeling by: Fr. Collington and Fr. Campion, along with three nuns and thirty-seven other people. When "Fr. Saltwell" finished, Fr. Campion vested for Mass. Eliot remained to attend it.

Campion's Final Sermon

After Mass, Campion, seated, gave a sermon, "very nigh an hour long," says Eliot, which he preached upon the Gospel of the day, the Ninth Sunday after Pentecost: "When Jesus drew near to Jerusalem, He wept over it" (*Lk.* 19:41). The text was apt in its application to England England, once the most faithful of nations, now so changed as to be the subject of the most bitter tears of the Church. The preacher passed also to the passage, "Jerusalem, Jerusalem, thou that killest the prophets" (*Lk.* 13:34). He "applied the same [text] to this our country of England for the pope's authority and doctrine did not so flourish here as the same Campion desired." Every part of the passage conspired with the circumstances of the day and his own sentiments to raise the eloquence of the preacher to its highest pitch, and his congregation, shedding tears in abundance, had never heard or imagined such preaching. It was his swan song. The text of the Lord's lament over Jerusalem before entering upon His Passion applied also to the preacher, now about to enter upon his own, as England was about to kill *its* prophet.

During the Mass and sermon, Eliot had contemplated pulling out the queen's warrant and arresting Campion then and there.[50]

After the sermon, there was probably time for prayer, for Edmund and the other priests to pray more of their Divine Office.[51] Perhaps around 12 o'clock lunch was served. Following that, as he had settled with Emerson, Campion was to ride off towards Norfolk. Eliot did not stay for the meal but went down to Jenkins, still in the pantry below or the hall, oblivious to anything of note until Eliot told him. Eliot's sudden departure aroused some suspicion in Mrs. Yate but not enough to make her do more than place a watchman on one of the turrets to give notice of approach of danger.[52]

It seems that Campion lingered at lunch, for had he been speedy, he would have left before the events that followed.

Eliot and Jenkins went off to fetch the nearest sheriff, John Fettiplace of Denchworth,[53] two miles away. When he saw the warrant, he quickly convoked a band of forty or fifty men to assist him. The law required every able-bodied man to help a magistrate quell a riot or make an arrest.

It was about one o'clock in the afternoon. Lunch was not over at

Lyford Grange before a servant rushed in to announce the arrival at the gates of a band of armed men.

The company broke up in confusion. Some ran hither and thither distractedly, others stood stricken with fear. Campion was the first to speak, Bombino relates:

> "This is a matter that needs no long deliberation. I am the one sought by the armed magistrates. I am willing to meet them as they come. This way the house will be delivered from vexation, and the family and guests from the present peril." Having said this with a cheerful voice and an intrepid face, he began to leave.[54]

But they forced him to stay. "It is not one man's peril alone. Our spirits depend upon your safety," they told him.[55] The walls of the house had galleries and hiding-holes; he would have a much better chance stowed away in one of these.

There was no time to discuss. Campion, Ford, and Collington were hurried away to a hidden room where there was a narrow bed on which they stowed themselves, lying side by side, with their hands crossed over their breasts or lifted up in prayer. After mutual confession and absolution, there they lay all that afternoon, expecting every minute that the wall would be broken in by the maces of the searchers.

Surrounded

While the priests were being hidden, the men-at-arms surrounded the moat and set a guard at every outlet. The sheriff demanded admission into the house. Mrs. Yate kept the sheriff waiting half an hour before opening the gates, which were fast shut, as usual, with a moat between them and the home itself.

A chosen number, led by Eliot—Judas Eliot, as he was thenceforth called by Catholics and Protestants—entered. Mrs. Yate directed one of her servants to attend upon Eliot, ostensibly to serve him, really to give the household every possible warning of what he was about to do next.[56]

Eliot, Jenkins, and Fettiplace went into every chamber, sought in every angle, turned everything upside-down, found lots of secret corners, but could not find any priest. All signs of vestments, altar, and all else for Mass, were already concealed. Eliot noticed that the nuns at Mass were now dressed as gentlewomen.

> Continuing the search, although with no small toil, in the orchards,
> hedges and ditches, within the moat and other diverse places, at the
> last we found out Master Edward Yate, brother to the good man
> of the house, and two countrymen called Weblin [Webley] and
> Mansfield, fast locked together in a pigeon-house; but we could not
> find, at that time, Campion and the other two Priests whom we spe-
> cially sought for.[57]

The searchers, all Berkshire men and quiet neighbors, who had no
taste for this kind of work, were disgruntled. The whole afternoon was
spent, the walls had been sounded, the men were tired and they gave up
their search. Before going, they humbly begged pardon of Mrs. Yate for
the needless disturbance to her home, which they were forced to inflict
when the queen's letters were presented before them.

Bombino's account says that at this point the Catholics inside
rejoiced at their deliverance, summoned the priests out of hiding, and
all congratulated and embraced one another, giving heartfelt thanks to
Almighty God.[58]

Outside the house, the men were free to tell Eliot what they thought
of him for having spoiled their Sunday's holiday, and their credit both
with their neighbor Yate and with the rest of the county, who would
laugh at them for their fool's errand. Eliot was roused; the fault was not
his, but theirs; he would report to the Council their remissness in the
search and the marked favor they had shown to the notorious Papists.
They had not broken through the walls or searched for hiding holes. Did
they imagine they would catch Campion in an open space, or presenting
himself to them? The magistrate replied that he had no warrant to break
down or destroy. "But I have," said Eliot, as he drew out the warrant from
his bosom, and proceeded to read it. One of the men, suspecting he was
inventing rather than reading, went behind and looked over his shoulder.
He soon detected Eliot's fraud; and Eliot, infuriated, ordered him to be
arrested as a supporter of the Jesuits. This decided act frightened the rest,
and made them more readily submit to Eliot's order for a renewal of the
search.[59]

The excitement and relief in the Yate household were short-lived;
the magistrate was back again demanding entrance. Then indeed the
Catholics' fear and grief were greater than before. "One man, Campion

himself, whom the danger most concerned, showed cheerfulness in his countenance, piety in his words, and constancy in all his deportment."[60]

Mrs. Yate used her womanly dignity, indignation, and grief to plead with Fettiplace for relief from yet further disturbance to her family home, when she was not well and her husband was in prison. Fettiplace begged her not to blame him for Eliot's unkindness; he must obey the queen's warrant, though a zealot had been charged to execute it. He would, however, try to moderate what he could not prevent. He therefore allowed Mrs. Yate to choose a room where she might sleep in peace, which he promised should not be disturbed by any of his men.

Eliot saw that John Fettiplace was reluctant to continue, so, as evening approached, he sent for a second Justice of the Peace, Edmund Wiseman of Steventon, six miles away. He also summoned Humphrey Foster, High Sheriff of Berkshire, for further help and reinforcements. Foster could not be found, but Wiseman came promptly that evening with ten or twelve of his own men.

It was now evening, and Mrs. Yate had her bed made up in the part of the house where the priests were hidden. She was conducted there with all honor, while the rest of the house was examined, the walls sounded, and broken in where they seemed hollow. The search was continued till late at night, when she ordered the men to be well fed. The long excitement, the work, the despair of success, the food, and especially the beer, soon had their effect, and the sheriff's men all settled down to sleep.[61]

Eliot planned to sit out the night, with the help of seventy armed men inside and outside the house.

When Mrs. Yate was assured that all were asleep, she called the priests once more from their hiding-place, and with an importunity which seemed implausible to historian Fr. Bartoli,[62] she insisted on Fr. Campion preaching one more sermon to her community. Her servants were opposed to this perilous piety but were summoned and forced to obey. Campion was brought to her bedside, and had to preach then and there. She knew, she said, she would never hear him again.

Excited by his eloquence, the audience forgot the caution needed in such a beleaguered place. As the congregation broke up, one of the priests tumbled down. The noise awoke the sentinels placed at Mrs. Yate's door. They gave the alarm; the Jesuits had been in the room; they were almost seen; they were just missed. Mrs. Yate's bedroom was forthwith searched,

all the walls sounded and every closet explored. Again, all was to no purpose. The priests had glided away through the secret passages and left no
trace of their path.

Caught

Day broke. It was Monday, July 17.

An afternoon and night spent in fruitless destruction had reduced
not only the sheriff's men, but Eliot himself, to despair. Once more,
men began to depart, not without reproaches and jeers against the mad-
man who had led them into such a labyrinth. But their departure was
made good by the arrival that morning of another Justice of the Peace,
Christopher Lydcot, with another great company of men.

Eliot reports the moment of success:

> The same morning began a fresh search for the said Priests, which
> continued with very great labor until about ten o'clock in the fore-
> noon of the same day; but the said priests could not be found, and
> every man was almost persuaded that they were not there.
>
> Yet still searching, although in effect clean void of any hope for
> finding of them, the said David Jenkins, by God's great goodness,
> espied a certain secret place, which he quickly found to be hollow;
> and with a pin of iron which he had in his hand much like unto
> a harrow tine [spike], he forthwith did break a hole into the said
> place, where then presently he perceived the said Priests lying all
> close together upon a bed, of purpose there laid for them; where they
> had bread, meat and drink sufficient to have relieved them three or
> four days together.
>
> The said Jenkins then called very loudly, and said, "I have found
> the traitors!"; and presently company enough was with him; who
> there saw the said Priests, when there was no remedy for them but
> *nolens volens* [willing or not] courteously yielded themselves.[63]

The three priests, Campion, Ford, and Collington, had been lying
side by side, their faces and hands raised towards heaven. They had confessed their sins to one another, and had received for their penance to
say once *fiat voluntas tua* (Thy will be done), and to invoke St. John the
Baptist three times. For St. John had once before saved Campion from a
similar danger.[64]

Bombino's account differs. He says Eliot had vented all the ill-humor of his disappointment upon the man assigned by Mrs. Yate to accompany him, and he was now descending the stairs by his side, on the verge of departure. Suddenly, he turned to the servant and, pointing to the wall over the stairs, exclaimed, "We have not broken through here, have we?" The servant, who knew that it was precisely there that the priests were hidden, turned deadly pale, and stammered out that he thought enough walls had been smashed already. Eliot marked his distress and immediately asked for a crow-bar. He smashed in the wall, and there, in a little close cell, on a narrow bed, were the three priests.[65]

Bombino got his account of the whole search and capture from the notes and oral reports of Fr. Persons, who received the account from the man directed by Mrs. Yate to wait upon Eliot.[66] Some of the details of these last days are known also from Eliot's own pamphlet, published a few months later, perhaps November: *A very true Report of the apprehension and taking of that arch-papist Edmund Campion . . . with three other lewd Jesuit priests, and diverse other lay people, most seditious persons of like sort.*[67] While he wanted recognition for his own role in it all, there is no reason to doubt the basic accuracy of the narrative, especially when he credits Jenkins with the actual discovery of the priests. But "lewd" or not, the "three other lewd Jesuit priests" were not Jesuits but secular priests. (He says "three" others, by including Fr. Filby who was taken later the same day.) In due course, Eliot and Jenkins each received £10 for the capture.[68]

Eliot's account, as the full title shows,[69] contradicts Anthony Munday's version of the discovery, who wrote the following, saying it was in an upper chamber:

> A chamber near the top of the house, which was but very simple, having in it a large great shelf with divers tools and instruments both upon it, and hanging by it; which they judged to belong to some cross-bow maker. The simpleness of the place caused them to use small suspicion in it; and they were departing out again; but one in the company, by good hap [luck], espied a chink in the wall of boards whereto this shelf was fastened, and through the same he perceived some light. Drawing his dagger, he smit a great hole in it, and saw there was a room behind it; whereat the rest stayed, searching for some entrance into it, which by pulling down a shelf they found, being a little hole for one to creep in at. There they entered

and found Edmund Campion the Jesuit, and John Peters and Thomas Saltwell [aliases of Collington and Ford], priests, standing up very closely.[70]

With Campion and the two priests were arrested:

- John Cotton: an Oxford student of the Catholic family of Cottons of Warblington; he was to suffer a year's confinement in the dungeons of the Tower, and under James I was cast into the Tower again, for five years.
- William Hildesley of Beenham, Berkshire (his mother was a Stonor).
- Humphrey and Edward (James) Keynes, sons of a Justice of the Peace in Somerset.[71]
- Philip Lowe—he was imprisoned.
- two yeomen: William Webley and Henry (John) Mansfield of Taplow, Berkshire—they would be held and released.[72]
- John Jacob (John James), an Oxford musician.[73]
- three gentlewomen: Gilliam Harman, Katherine Kingsmill, and Mrs. Keynes (wife of Edward).
- Mrs. Yate and her brother-in-law Edward.[74]

Mrs. Yate was sent to jail. A sick woman already, she died later this very year. The other three women were released under heavy sureties.

Nearly six years later, two of the servants, John Doe and Richard Buckley, were also arrested and questioned, and confessed to being at Campion's Mass and of being reconciled to Rome when he was there.[75]

As for John Jacob: in 1583 he would be in the Marshalsea when Fr. John Gerard S.J. was sent there. Within the next twelve months Fr. Gerard saw him again at "the loathsome Bridewell prison":

I found him chained up because he had let fall some words in praise of the Father [Campion]. He had fetters on his legs and used to wear a rough hair-shirt which he never took off; he was very meek and full of kindness—once I saw a jailer strike him repeatedly in the face without this good man uttering a word.... When I visited him (John was his name), he was wasted to a skeleton and in a state of exhaustion from grinding at the treadmill, a most pitiful sight. There was nothing left of him except skin and bones and I cannot remember having seen anything like it—lice swarmed on him like ants on a mole-hill—but he was patient.[76]

After this, John Jacob is unheard of, and we presume he died there from ill-treatment and malnutrition.[77]

The priests were found but not all the Catholic materials. Recusant historian Tony Hadland records:

> In 1959 electricians working in the roof void found a wooden box about eight inches in diameter and of similar depth nailed to a joist. It had been there for 378 years. Inside the box was ancient vellum, still soft and pliable, on which was written a list of indulgences. Wrapped inside the vellum was an *Agnus Dei* (Latin for Lamb of God), a wax medallion issued by the Pope, so-called because it bore a picture of the Lamb of God. In Elizabeth's reign it was a criminal offense to import or possess such a medallion. The owner of Lyford Grange at the time of this remarkable find was a Miss Whiting who, with her companion Miss Morrell, had the *Agnus Dei* framed in gold. They presented it, together with its box and vellum wrapping, to the Jesuits of Campion Hall in Brewer Street, Oxford. There it is kept with a copy of a commentary on Aristotle's *Physics* containing several specimens of Fr. Campion's signature.[78]

In recent times, and up to the present, thanks to the good-will of the Anglican owner of Lyford Grange, every summer a commemorative Mass is celebrated at the scene of Campion's arrest.

No words or actions of Campion at this time are recorded. Dr. Allen says that, though made a spectacle and matter of mockery to the unwise and ungodly multitude, Campion "showed such remarkable modesty, mildness, patience and Christian humility in all his speeches and doings, that the good were exceedingly edified and the enemies much astonished."[79] Bishop Yepes tells us that he spoke so gracefully and looked so cheerfully that he disarmed the malice of his captors.[80]

Humphrey Forster of Aldermaston Court, the sheriff of Berkshire, was absent when Eliot summoned the *posse comitatus* (county force) of Abingdon to assist him. If Forster had been there, the proceedings would not have been so violent. When the news of the capture reached him, he hurried to Lyford, twenty-five miles away. He had no wish to be jailer to a man whose eloquence he had admired at Oxford, and the fame of whose sanctity had given him a secret inclination towards the Catholic religion.

When he arrived at Lyford he sent a messenger to London to learn the will of the Privy Council in the matter. In the meantime, Campion was treated as an old friend rather than as a prisoner, except that he could not have his liberty. He had the place of honor in the house and at the table. Indeed, his own winning ways had conciliated his keepers quite as much as the orders and example of the sheriff. Some of them began to wait upon him as if he were their master rather than their prisoner. Campion, ever a priest, "either forgetting or neglecting his own state, did not cease to admonish, exhort, inflame them, one by one, or all together, to all manner of integrity, both of faith and morals."[81]

Campion was held thus at Lyford from Monday to Wednesday, July 17–19, that is, for the three days they had to wait at Lyford for the answer of the Council. On the fourth, the sheriff received a letter ordering him to send his prisoners under strong guard to London.

The Procession to London
Thursday, July 20.

It was a sad parting for the women at Lyford, and a proud day for Eliot, who rode at the head of the company, not daunted by the nickname, "Judas Eliot," which the people pretty freely used to him, nor by the mocking query they made: is his name "Eliot" or "Iscariot"?

The company made three stops on the way to London. One was at Abingdon, where, amongst others, several scholars of Oxford (seven miles away) came to see the famous champion. Told this by Justice of the Peace, Christopher Lydcot, Campion said he was very glad, as he was once a member of that University, and asked whether they would hear a sermon.[82]

At dinner, Eliot said to him, "Mr. Campion, you look cheerfully upon everybody but me. I know you are angry with me in your heart for this work." "God forgive thee, Eliot," said he, "for so judging of me. I forgive thee, and in token thereof I drink to thee. Yea, and if thou wilt repent and come to confession, I will absolve thee; but large penance thou must have."[83]

The next break was at Henley. Possibly at this point the party was committed to the charge of Sir Thomas Heneage, the queen's treasurer, one of her most trusted servants. He received £33 "for bringing up of one Edmund Campion, a Jesuit, three other Popish priests and eight other persons taken."[84]

Fr. Filby's Nightmare

One of the prisoners was Fr. William Filby (Filbie), a young, recently ordained priest who had helped with the press at Stonor. He was the son of George Filby, a leather-worker, who kept open house to Catholic priests at his home in the parish of St. Mary Magdalen, Oxford. Eliot says he was arrested by chance on July 17, after the other priests were caught, when coming to Lyford to see Fr. Collington.

Eliot records:

> We went that day [July 20] to Henley upon Thames, where we lodged that night. And about midnight we were put into great fear by reason of a very great cry and noise that the said Filby made in his sleep; which wakened the most that were that night in the house, and that in such sort that every man almost thought that some of the prisoners had been broken from us and escaped; although there was in and about the same house a very strong watch appointed and charged for the same. The aforesaid Master [Justice of the Peace, Christopher] Lydcot was the first that came unto them; and when the matter was examined, it was found no more but that the said Filby was in a dream; and, as he said, he verily thought one to be a ripping down his body and taking out his bowels.[85]

This dream came true when Blessed William Filby suffered at Tyburn, May 30, 1582.

Robert Persons was then staying at Henley Park, in a house of Francis Browne, only a quarter of a mile from Henley. He longed to see Campion but his friends restrained him from going, so he sent his man Robert Alfield to observe how Campion bore himself.[86] Campion spotted Persons's servant but did nothing that would betray him to the guard. "Though Campion was not able to speak to him, he showed by signs his constancy, joy and contentment to suffer."[87] Persons was much comforted by the report.[88]

To London and the Tower

The third stop was at Colebrook (now Colnbrook), Friday, July 21, some fifteen miles from London, where they were bound by letters of the Council, which bade them to remain there the rest of the day, so as to make a public entry into London at noon, on Saturday, market-day, when the streets would be thronged with people. The crowds collected to see Campion, and his companions at Colebrook gave him a foretaste of what he had to expect the next day in London. Only at Colebrook a great number of Catholic and other gentlemen sought to speak with him; and Campion made a curious exhibition of versatility and dramatic ability in keeping the sentinels off their guard by his amusing talk, while he conversed by signs with the gentlemen who pressed around him, or gave his conversation with his keeper such a turn, as to make it serve the double purpose of amusing the one and instructing the others. At this place the instructions of the Council caused the treatment of the prisoners to be thoroughly altered.

The sheriff of Berkshire had treated them like gentlemen; the cue now was to render them ridiculous. They were to have their elbows tied behind them, their hands in front, and their legs under their horses' bellies. Campion was on a very tall horse. On each side of him were two guards close by, lest he should speak to anyone, or anyone to him. The total guard comprised fifty lancers. Campion was placed first in this mock triumph, and was further decorated in the way that perjurers were marked in those days, with a paper stuck into his hat, going round his head, with his title written in big capital letters: EDMUND CAMPION THE SEDITIOUS JESUIT. They were to be thus paraded through the whole length of the city on Saturday, July 22, especially through the places where, by reason of the markets of that day, was the greatest concourse of the common people.

These commands were executed to the letter; all London beheld the spectacle, the mob gazing with delight; but the wiser sort lamenting to see the land fallen to such barbarism as to abuse in this manner a gentleman famous throughout Europe for his scholarship and his innocence of life, and this before any trial, or any proof against him; his case being prejudged, and he paraded as if already condemned. A large crowd followed, some on horseback, some on foot.[89]

"A good many of these related to me," says Fr. Persons, "with how fearless and glad a countenance Fr. Edmund and the others endured that ignominy. They wore at all times a look full of peace, and smiled also at times."[90]

When the cavalcade reached the cross in Cheapside (the lower images of which had been defaced during the night of June 21 by Puritans, about whom a reward of forty crowns failed to procure information),[91] Campion made a low reverence to the cross, which still remained on the top, and tried to cross himself with his hands tied.

At last they reached the Tower. Before they were delivered over to the custody of Sir Owen Hopton, the governor, Campion turned to the guards who had brought him, thanked them and said a polite farewell.

Then the gloomy gates of the Tower of London closed behind him.

CHAPTER 15

The Tower of London

ONCE CAMPION was captured and brought to the Tower, it was time for his captors to decide what to do with him.

The Priests' Spiritual Purpose

At the council of priests which met in Southwark in July 1581, Campion and Persons, in their own names and in those of all the priests who had come with them, solemnly declared "that their coming only was apostolical, to treat matters of religion in truth and simplicity, and to attend to the gaining of souls, without any knowledge or intention in the world of matters of State."[1]

The Queen and Council's Knowledge of the Same

The Queen and her Council knew well that the missionaries were for the most part honest in their repudiation of interference in matters of State. Camden, whose *Annals* are said to have been read over by the queen herself and allowed by her, declared in the *Annals* of 1581 (quoted below)[2] that she did not believe in the treason of the greater part of those condemned with Campion, but that they were merely tools of their superiors, to whom they had vowed obedience.

It was, however, almost an avowed principle of the Tudors that if the real culprit could not be caught or dealt with, punishment must be inflicted on the first substitute that could be found: Achan's wife and children must be burnt for Achan's sacrilege (*Joshua* 7:1–25). It was a principle of her government to transform tools into traitors, and to reward them for their suppleness with the gallows. For every offence she gave or received, she made someone suffer. As she could not catch Sanders or Allen or the pope, she was willing to hang Campion instead of them, though she did not believe that he was in the secret of their designs against her. There can be little doubt that the English government seized Campion and all the priests it could catch, to make them answer for the rebellion in Ireland.[3]

Disunity within the Government

The Privy Council, however, was not united in one plan of policy with regard to the punishment of Catholic missionaries. There were some who, in spite of their Machiavellian use of means, were earnestly religious in their end, and, either from conviction or from policy, were determined to establish the new religion, cost what it might. Such a man was Walsingham; such, too, was Burghley.

Leicester was now, for his own political ends, with this party, but he seems not to have forgotten his former relations with the Catholics—of which we read obscurely in *Leicester's Commonwealth*, and of which the Earl of Westmoreland, when he was out of credit and a fugitive in France, used to make no secret. "They all might curse the Earl of Leicester," he said, "for he, being one of the chiefest of their conspiracy [in 1569], craved pardon, and disclosed all their 'pretense,'"[4] so that the two Earls of Northumberland and Westmoreland were left in the lurch. For which, and for other betrayals, Westmoreland hoped one day "to meet him in the field . . . and to lend him a lance in his breast for his labor."[5] But now, besides coveting the temporalities of the English bishops, Leicester was secretly jealous of Anjou (the queen's prospective husband),[6] whom he supported openly, and so was aligned against the Puritans in this matter. He had an eye to the future as well as to the past; he forecasted the possible toleration of Catholics if the marriage with Anjou took place. He was careful to watch the changes of his mistress' will, and he was more or less influenced by Sir Philip Sidney and others, who, hating the Spanish faction, were not at all disposed to force all Catholics into it by an indiscriminate persecution.

Burghley and Walsingham made no such distinction. With Bacon they might nominally divide the priests into the two categories, and call the Marian priests, priests of superstition; and the Seminary priests, priests of sedition; but the distinction was artificial and geographical, not substantial and real. Really they held with Philip II that all English Catholics were, if not open traitors, at least persons who held principles which would turn into open treason when priestly exhortation gave them practical application. Hence, while carefully avoiding the open and avowed persecution for religion which had made Queen Mary's reign odious and had rendered the Protestant reaction possible, they were determined to make a distinction without a difference and to repress Catholicism under the name of treason as effectually as Mary's government had repressed Protestantism under the name of heresy.

Elizabeth herself was, as usual, irresolute and many-minded. She had to profess to the French court the tolerant principles which France first reduced to form. She had at the same time to guard against a Puritan excitement on account of her potential marriage with a Catholic duke. The first consideration would lead her to lenient dealing with Campion and his companions; the second would lead her to treat him barbarously, or even to sacrifice him to the bloodthirsty bishops and preachers who demanded his death.

As for the nation itself, though perhaps the majority of Englishmen would still have gladly been Catholics, if they could have been so securely and without changing their politics, yet the circumstances of the time were such as to give the Puritans the place of power. There were among the people plenty who would justify any severity against conspirators with the pope or the Spaniard, and who were prepared to connive at injustice when its object was to terrify so dangerous a party. Public opinion was quite as much divided as the Council chamber was about the doom that ought to be pronounced on Campion.

Campion Unable to Communicate with Outsiders

Though there was this divergence on the ultimate punishment which should be inflicted on Campion, there could be no doubt that it was the Council's part to discredit him with both Catholics and Protestants, to make it appear that his big "Brag" had nothing but wind for foundation, that he was a coward, hardly secure in his own religion, and therefore untrustworthy as a pillar of others, a man so inconsiderate and cowardly that he would not scruple to purchase his own ease by telling everything he knew about Catholics who had received him into their houses, and by making them suffer instead of himself.

Again, they considered that it would not be good to let his *Challenge* and *Ten Reasons* remain unanswered. They therefore charged Bishop

Aylmer of London with the task of replying to his book, while another set
of theologians was to afford him the opportunity of controversy which
he had requested, but so biased in its conduct as to make it either useless
or unfavorable to the Catholic side. This was the first care of the Council.

Henceforth there are two lives of Campion: one his real life in the
Tower, the other the false published life, which represented him as his
enemies wished him to be perceived.

As for his real life, he was from the first committed as "a close prisoner,"
meaning he was not allowed visitors and was in solitary confinement. His
friends outside could learn nothing of him except what the authorities
chose to publish, or what could be known by bribing the officers.

The rules for the close prisoners are on record.[7] All their windows
were blocked up, and light and air conveyed to them by a "slope tunnel," slanting upwards so that nothing might be seen but the sky, glazed
or latticed at the top so that no thing might be thrown in or out. The
windows were closed also at the bottom with a casement made fast and
not to open, except, if need be, one diamond pane with its leaden bolt.
These openings were examined daily to see whether any glass was broken or board removed, and especially whether any of the pieces of lead
with which the glass was tied were taken away to write with. No one was
allowed to pass by the Tower wharf without cause, and watchmen were
on the look-out to observe whether any of the passengers made any stay,
or cast his eyes up to the prison windows. The same watch was also kept
over passengers by Tower-hill. The lieutenant himself was always to be
present when a keeper held communication with a close prisoner, and
the key of his cell was always to be in the lieutenant's own custody. Any
servant kept by such a prisoner was subject to the same regulations as his
master. Everything sent to him was to be searched, his clothes examined,
pies opened, bread cut across, and bottles decanted. The strictest rules
were made about admitting strangers, and every keeper and servant in
the place was bound by oath not to carry any message. This system of
secrecy was, however, tempered with bribery. Much of the lieutenant's
income was derived from the prisoners in his custody, and those who
paid liberally were treated with some consideration. Nor was it always
possible to make the watch so strict as to keep the keepers and servants to
the letter of the regulations. Bribery or pity or favor would often modify
an intolerable strictness.

The lieutenant had in his hands terrors as well as palliatives. It is peculiar to the Tower, says Fr. Hart in his journal, that each prisoner is confined in a separate cell, where under the eye of his own keeper he is continually immured, excluded from the sight and conversation of his fellow-captives, and cut off from every means of communication with others, either by letters or messengers. It is from this cell that he is led forth to the various scenes of his sufferings—to the punishments which the caprice of his persecutors is permitted to inflict on him, to his examinations, and to the rack where his confessions are extorted.

Tortures in the Tower

There were seven means of torture in the Tower:

"The Pit" was an underground cave, twenty feet deep, entirely without light.

"Little-ease" was a cell where the prisoner could not stand or lie at full length.

The rack was a wooden frame, with rollers at each end, to which the prisoner's ankles and wrists were attached by cords, gradually tightened by turning the rollers, till the bones were ready to start from their sockets.

The "scavenger's daughter" was a broad iron hoop, consisting of two parts hinged together, which was fastened round the victim, one part between his legs, the other over his head, in order to compress him, hands, feet, head and all, into a tightly packed ball; the parts forced together till they could be fastened.

The iron gauntlets, after being put on the hands, were contracted by screws, by which the wrists were compressed. Sometimes the prisoner was suspended by them from two distant points of a beam.

The sixth and seventh tortures were manacles for the hands, and fetters for the feet.

According to Tanner, the prisoner was tied to the rack either by the thumbs and big toes, or by twenty small strings, each tied to a finger or toe.[8] Campion, however, was tied by his ankles and by the wrists, so as to leave him able to write.

Campion's Secret Meeting with Privy Councilors

Sir Owen Hopton, seeing Campion brought with such derision to his custody, thought he could do nothing more acceptable to his masters than to thrust his prisoner into the narrow dungeon of Little-ease, in the White Tower.[9] Here Campion remained till the fourth day, July 25, when he was in great secrecy and under a strong guard put on board a boat, and rowed to York House, the residence of the Lord Chancellor. Here he was received with all honor and courtesy by three members of the Privy Council: Sir Thomas Bromley, the Lord Chancellor; Sir Christopher Hatton, Vice-Chamberlain of the royal household; and Campion's one-time patron, Robert Dudley, Earl of Leicester—whom he had not seen for eleven years, since leaving England for Ireland in 1570.

Bromley, Hatton, and Dudley told Campion they had sent for him to know the plain truth—why he and Persons had come into England and what commission they had brought from Rome. He gave them a sincere and truthful account of all matters, and then answered their questions one by one with such readiness, that he seemed to have convinced them that his only purpose was the propagation of the Catholic faith and the salvation of souls, and that he had no intention or desire to stir up rebellion against the government or queen. Seeing, as they said, he had done ill with good intentions, they pitied him, especially the Earl of Leicester, who had known and admired him in his youth at London and in Oxford. They told him that they found no fault with him, except that he was a Papist—"Which," he replied, "is my greatest glory."[10] He spoke with such modesty and generosity that Dudley sent word to Hopton to give him better accommodation and treat him more amiably.[11] Nothing more was known at the time concerning this interview, but at the trial it came out that the queen herself had directed them to ask if Campion thought her really Queen of England. To which he replied Yes, as he relates in his trial.[12] Whereupon they offered him his life, liberty, riches, and honors, but under conditions which he could not in conscience accept.

Did Edmund Meet with Elizabeth?

Based on Fathers More and Bartoli, and on a letter of Dr. Allen mistaken in small details,[13] the earlier editions of this book were wrong in a few particulars of the above meeting: they named the place as Leicester's house, included as present the Earl of Bedford, and omitted Hatton. More importantly, Simpson followed Frs. More and Bartoli[14] (and others, such as Evelyn Waugh and E. E. Reynolds, followed Simpson) in affirming that Queen Elizabeth herself was also present at this meeting. This seemed confirmed on the basis of a statement by Campion at his trial:

> Not long since, it pleased her Majesty to demand of me whether I
> did acknowledge her to be my queen or no. . . . and being further
> required of her Majesty whether I thought the Pope might lawfully
> excommunicate her or no . . .

A letter of Lord Burghley, quoted below[15]—whose accurate original
has only come to light since Simpson's time—names the venue and the
parties, but makes no mention of the queen. Her questions to Campion
therefore were put *via* the Privy Councilors. Since Burghley's letter is
closer to the source—in this case, the lure of Elizabethan drama must
cede to the demands of historical accuracy: the dramatic encounter
between the queen and the Jesuit did not take place.[16]

Campion's Change of Religion Announced

When Hopton was told to treat Campion better, it effected a speedy
revolution in his conduct. No man was more anxious to please. He saw
that Campion was a man of account, and it came into his fancy that he
might cover himself with glory if the famous Jesuit, the best mind that the
Papists had in England, could be brought to confess as Nichols had done,
that he had yielded to Hopton's arguments, and had embraced his religion. Knowing also that sunshine was more likely to make a man throw
off his cloak than wind, he exhibited extraordinary affection and made
promises which today, he said, were only words, but tomorrow should
be deeds: the queen's favor, an ample pension, a place at Court, or if
he liked it better, a rich benefice—even a major See, the archbishopric
of Canterbury![17] Hopton, who had neither consciousness nor imagination of a religion which could stand against such temptations, probably
believed that he had prevailed or would soon do so—and said so publicly.

The report exactly suited the intentions of the Council, which were
to undo in any way the work that the Jesuits had done, either by making
their persons despicable or by using their influence in favor of what they
had hitherto condemned. So Hopton declared, and the Court believed
or affected to believe, and committed the good news to the four winds
to carry.

Campion was at this moment the talk of all England. When the
queen's ministers declared that he had denied his religion and was on the

point of making a public recantation, the news flew, and grew as it flew. Before the end of July, it was declared by the preacher at Paul's Cross and by the clergy of nearly all the London churches that Campion was yielding and was almost sure to become a Protestant. Sir Owen Hopton had said so. Every preacher in London announced from the pulpit that Campion was shortly to make his appearance at Paul's Cross, where he would preach Protestantism and burn his own book with his own hands.

Walsingham—who, as we shall see further on, well knew the truth—just at this time (July 25) was sent on a mission to Paris. There he told the Court that the Jesuit Campion, after his capture, was soon convinced and brought back from his errors, had made solemn retractation and become Protestant, to the great content of the queen—and there was even talk of his having a bishopric.

After a few days, however, when Hopton openly proposed to his prisoner to go over to the Protestant Church, his proposal was received with such disdain that he saw that there was no probability of succeeding by the new method, and so, with the consent of the Council, he returned to the old one.

The Priests Racked

Campion had been just a week in the Tower when the Lords of the Council came to this decision to treat him severely.

On Sunday, July 30, they ordered a letter to be written to: Sir Owen Hopton, Lieutenant of the Tower; Dr. John Hammond, Chancellor of the Diocese of London and a member of the court of high commission; Robert Beale, clerk to the Council; and Thomas Norton, who earned the nickname of "Rackmaster-General"—advising them on how further to proceed. First, they were to demand of him whether he acknowledged himself to be her Majesty's subject or not. Upon confessing himself to be so, they were to administer an oath upon a Bible of St. Jerome's translation to avoid loss of time and further cavil (in other words, not a Protestant Bible, lest a Catholic quibble over its authenticity), to answer truly and directly all that is demanded of him. Then, they were to question him further on such points as he refused to answer in his former examinations, together with some others now added by the Council. They said—omitting the "not" with a slip of the pen—"in case he continue wilfully [not] to tell the truth, then to deal with him by the rack."[18] They were also required to record his answers to the questions enclosed on his relations with one Rochfort, an Irishman (one of the Irish rebels).[19]

Frs. Ford and Collington were similarly to be examined touching their allegiance to the Crown, the places where they had lain and whether a Mass had been said at Mr. Yate's when they were last there. If they hesitated, they were to be put "in fear of the torture"[20] and then remanded to the Marshalsea.

Instructions were added regarding Webley and Mansfield, two of the men taken at Lyford,[21] who had offered to conform. They were to be dealt with by some godly and learned preachers, who were to persuade them to make open renunciation of popery and to receive the Anglican sacraments, and then to release them on bonds for their good behavior.[22]

A postscript to the letter, addressed to Dr. Hammond in particular, told him to question Campion and the other priests on their allegiance to the queen, using the points he had drawn out of Dr. Sanders's book *De Visibili Monarchia Ecclesiae* (The visible monarchy of the Church, 1571), and Fr. Bristow's *Motives Inducing to the Catholic Faith* (1574). "We think it good that you propound the same to Campion and the priests, requiring their direct answer to the same."[23]

The First Racking of Campion

Dr. Allen notes as one of the refinements of the English Council that they tortured the priests on Sundays or other great Catholic feasts.[24] Campion's first racking was either on Sunday, July 30, or the next day, a great one even then to a Jesuit, as it was the anniversary of Ignatius of Loyola's death, but not yet a feast, since he was not beatified till 1609. The next day was the feast of St. Peter in Chains. It was on one of these days that Campion was led to the rack-chamber, where he knelt down at the door, crossed himself at the breast, and while he was being stripped and bound to the rack invoked the names of Jesus and Mary. The function for which the Council in mockery chose a holy day was, to him, a function of religion, a glorious confession, which was to win his eternal crown.

Campion was examined on the rack by the four men named above: Hopton, Norton, Beale, and the churchman Hammond.

The first points upon which he was interrogated during this first torture pointed to no suspicion beyond the general treason of his religion: "Who sent you to England? By whose counsel did you come? At whose houses were you received? Who comforted and assisted you? Whom have you reconciled, and how? At whose houses have you said Mass? Whose confessions have you heard, where did they live, and what did you talk to them about?"

Then came the questions on *Ten Reasons:* "Where was your book printed, and to whom have you given it?"

Then, as the pressure was increased, that "dangerous and ensnaring question": "What think you of the Bull of Pius V against Elizabeth?"

Lastly, the articles about Rochfort the Irishman indicated a wish to implicate Campion in Dr. Sanders's expedition, to attribute to him a political or military act of treason. At some time during his imprisonment, Campion told a friend that he had been examined on whether he had sent £30,000 to the rebels in Ireland, and (after denying it, of course) was racked, to know where the money was collected, to whom it was paid, and how and when it was conveyed into Ireland.[25]

There is no eye-witness account of what Campion said or did at this racking, nor at the others in August, October, and November. From his private life in the Tower, I am therefore obliged to pass over to his public life, such as the Lords of the Council gave it out to be, and such as it was during the month of August believed to be both by Catholics and Protestants.

A Series of Arrests

By August 2, the Council had somehow acquired a flood of light about Campion's doings.[26] They knew where he had lodged in Lancashire, and where he had left his books.[27] It was clear that they might damage his character by giving out that they had acquired all this information by his own confession.

Two days after, on August 4, they wrote to:

- The Earl of Huntingdon, to search the houses in Yorkshire where Campion "upon his examination here taken confessed that he has been at."[28]
- Alderman Martin, to apprehend one Nash, of St. Lawrence Lane, London,[29] and John Eden, who lived near Uxbridge, a former attorney in Guildhall, dismissed for recusancy—"in whose houses Edmund Campion has confessed that he was lodged at his being in London."[30]

- Sir Walter Mildmay, to search the house of Mr. Robert Price in Huntingdonshire, "where Edmund Campion has confessed that he appointed his man, Ralph Emerson, who attended on him, to bring certain books and papers which he left at the house of one Richard Hoghton in the county of Lancaster."[31]
- The keepers of Wisbeach prison, where Thomas Pounde was then lodged, "that whereupon the examination of Edmund Campion he has confessed that he delivered a copy of his challenge to one [Richard] Norris, a priest, commonly remaining about London [probably the man called Richardson by Laing[32] and Allen]; and that he delivered it to one Pounde, then prisoner in the Marshalsea, who is thought to have dispersed the same abroad; and that one Stephens brought the said Pounde to speak with Campion at Throckmorton House in London, and further, that Pounde directed Campion by a token to one [Thomas] Dimmock to speak with [Henry Wriothesley] the [second] Earl of Southampton"[33]—the said keepers were to examine Pounde on the matter. Dimmock (Dymock) was the servant to the Catholic Earl, but we know not if Campion met the Earl. The Stephens mentioned was Fr. Richard Stephens, former secretary to Bishop John Jewel.[34]

Then they wrote on August 4 to:

- Sir Henry Neville and another, telling them "to repair [go] unto the Lady Stonor's house and to enter into the same, and there to make diligent search and enquire for certain Latin books dispersed abroad in Oxford at the last Commencement, which Edmund Campion upon his examination has confessed to have been there printed in a wood, and also for such other English books as of late have been published for the maintenance of popery, printed also there, as it is thought, by one Parsons, a Jesuit, and others; and further, for the press and other instruments of printing, etc., thought also to be there remaining."[35]

Two days afterwards (August 6) another letter was sent to

- Sir Walter Mildmay, ordering him to apprehend Lord Vaux,

"at whose house Edmund Campion has upon his examination confessed that he has been";[36] to deal likewise with Sir Thomas Tresham, Sir William Catesby,[37] and Mr. Edward Griffin of Dingley and Braybrook, Northamptonshire.[38]

Next day (August 7) letters were written to:

- The Earl of Shrewsbury, to apprehend Mr. Henry Sacheverell of Morley, Derbyshire.[39]
- Sir Thomas Lucy, to apprehend Sir William Catesby (in case he were at his house in Warwickshire, and not at the other one in Northampton shire).
- Robert Drury, to examine Mr. Edwin (Edward) East, of Wickham (in Berkshire), and Mr. John Penn of Penn, Buckinghamshire.[40]
- Lord Norris, to examine Lady Babington,[41] Mrs. Phillipe Pollard (a widow),[42] and Mrs. Anne Morris, in Oxfordshire, "in whose houses the said Campion has also confessed that he has been."[43]
- Sir Francis Hastings, to examine Mrs. Anne Beaumont of Gracedieu Priory, Charnwood Forest, Leicestershire (sister to the Pierrepoint brothers who conducted Campion; she was put under house arrest. On August 30, the Council sent for the books and writings found at Gracedieu and ordered the "Massing stuff" to be defaced).
- Sir Henry Clarke, to examine Mr. Griffin of South Mimms, Mid dlesex (now Hertfordshire).[44]
- The Bishop of Lichfield, to examine one Worseley of Staffordshire.[45]
- Fleetwood, the Recorder of London, to examine Mrs. Brideman, "at whose house in Westminster Campion has confessed to have been,"[46] and to apprehend Mr. Barnes of Tothill Street, Westminster,[47] and Fr. John Biar,[48] "whom the said Campion has also confessed to have repaired [gone] to the said Mrs. Brideman's house."[49]

Lastly, there was a letter to Sir Owen Hopton, Dr. Hammond, and Thomas Norton, indicating to them that their Lordships, having perused the examinations of Campion, had thought good to return them for review, and for additional examinations upon matters which Robert

Beale had orders to indicate to them. Upon these points, then, "they might examine him [Campion] and certain of his fellows upon such points wherein their Lordships are desirous they should make a more plain and direct answer."[50]

Not all stood fast. When Mrs. Phillipe Pollard of Little Haddon, county of Oxford, was arrested (a widow, named above) she was questioned by her Majesty's Attorney and Solicitor-general on December 15, 1581, and promised to conform in religion and attend the services of the Established church—and was dismissed without charge.[51] The same concession was made by Bartholomew Hesketh, Richard Hoghton, and Edward Griffin.[52]

In a letter of August 7, the Lords of the Council, Burghley's signature heading the list, directed the Earl of Huntingdon, concerning Campion's harborers in Yorkshire, to appoint some trusty persons to go to every one

> of the said places and to apprehend the parties and diligently to search their houses for books and other superstitious stuff.... [They are to] give order that straight enquiry and examination be made both of them and others of their families and neighborhood, how often and at what times they and every one of them have been in the said Campion's company, or of any other Jesuit or priest, in what places and in what company; how long he continued in their said houses, or of any other; from whence he came, whither he went and with whom; how often he or any other Jesuit or priest said any Mass in their houses or in any other places to their knowledge; whether they themselves or any other have heard Mass or been reconciled or confessed; what relief in money, apparel or otherwise was given by them, or what may become of them [i.e., where they are now], together with such other particularities which your Lordships and the Commissioners . . . by you appointed shall think fit to be ministered unto them and every one of them so as the whole truth may be understood . . . And for the said parties named in the schedule, or such other as shall be besides found to have been offenders in this case, we think it meet that after their examination taken they were committed to the charge of the sheriff, or another, to remain under his custody unless they shall enter into bonds with two good sureties to her Majesty's use not to depart their houses without before they shall understand from us her Majesty's further pleasure therein [i.e., house arrest].

Postscript. In the questions both before specified and such other as shall be expounded unto the parties: We pray you to have a special regard unto the tenor and times of her Majesty's proclamation published the 10th of January last concerning Jesuits and seminary priests.

On August 6, the day before, Lord Burghley had written a private letter to Lord Shrewsbury:

There was this week a massing priest named Everard Duckett [Blessed Everard Hanse, *alias* Duckett, an Anglican minister for some time before his conversion], that, being apprehended, was charged with traitorous words and thereof convicted, maintaining the Pope's action to be lawful in publishing against her Majesty an excommunication and a sentence that she was not lawful queen, nor her subjects bound to obey her, for which fact he was condemned and suffered as a traitor [July 31, 1581]. If any of these late apprehended Papists shall do the like, the law is like to correct them. For their actions are not matters of religion, but merely [purely] of State, tending directly to the deprivation of her Majesty from the crown. . . .

I think your lordship has heard how Campion the Jesuit was taken in Berkshire at one Yate's house and 3 other massing priests with him. He is in the Tower and stiffly denieth to answer any question of moment, having been corrected before my Lord Chancellor, my Lord of Leicester and Mr. Vice-Chamberlain at my Lord Chancellor's house.[53]

What Did Campion Reveal?

Two things should be noted in this letter of August 6. First, the only charge against Campion at present believed by Lord Burghley was his presumed submission to the Bull of Pius V, which Burghley assures Shrewsbury is not a matter of religion but of State. Secondly, up to this date, four days after the Council had been despatching letters to magistrates and sheriffs all over the kingdom to apprehend parties at whose houses Campion had confessed that he had been, Burghley assures the Earl that Campion firmly refused "to answer any question of moment." At the same time it is evident by the letter to Hopton, Hammond, and Norton, that not only Campion, but "certain of his fellows,"[54] had been examined; and it is quite possible that the confessions may have been extorted from these "fellows" and then imputed to Campion to serve a purpose—namely, to blacken his name and demoralize Catholics. On the same day, Burghley wrote to Walsingham in Paris about "the discovery of a number of Popish subjects . . . a number of choice persons."[55] He does not say that Campion revealed their names, though Walsingham in his reply assumes that Campion did so.

All these letters of the Council were effectual. In county after county, gentlemen were apprehended, as having, by Campion's own confession, given lodging to Campion since the proclamation of January 10, 1581, against hosting Jesuits.

Indeed some of the councilors themselves were kept in the dark about the fraud; and Lord Huntingdon, the president of the north, wrote to Burghley on August 18: "What I may be able to perform touching those things that Campion has confessed, your lordship shall have so soon as may be. I dare assure you that some things which I see he has confessed be true; and if my hap [luck] had been good, I had taken him here in this country; but it may be I shall meet with his fellow Persons." Then he suggests another place where Campion may have been. "I would be glad to understand whether he were at Sir W. Colthorpe's house whilst he lived, or since his death. Of the conditions of that man your lordship is not ignorant, and I think the place is not mended since his death."[56]

On August 14, the Council had acquired some fresh information which they deemed sufficiently important to make them summon the Bishops of Salisbury and Rochester, and the Deans of St. Paul's and Windsor.[57]

At the same time, they wrote to:

- the Vice-Chancellor of Oxford, directing him to weed out popery from the colleges, and informing him that three Masters of Arts, Russell, Stubbs, and Yate, had been with Campion at Lyford, and that one John Jacob, a musician, taken with Campion, had been tolerated at the University many years without going to church.[58]
- the Bishop of London, who had transferred Thomas Pounde from the Marshalsea to Stortford, and thence to Wisbeach, ordering him to send his prisoner to the Tower.
- Sir Gervase Clifton, ordering him to send the Pierrepoint brothers, at whose house "Campion has upon his examination

confessed to have been at Christmas last by the space of fourteen days."[59]

Gervase Pierrepoint was arrested on August 14,[60] and he and his brother Henry, says Strype,[61] gave some information about their travels with Campion. In June 1586, Gervase was questioned about some recent suspicious travels he had made within England.[62]

The same day, August 14, the Council sent another letter to Hopton, Hammond, and Beale, "thanking them for their pains taken in the examination taken of Campion," and further ordering them again to examine Campion, Peters (meaning Collington), and Ford,

> who refuse to confess whether they have said any Masses or no, whom they have confessed, and where Persons and the other priests be, touching these points, and to put them in fear of the torture, if they shall refuse to answer directly thereto. And touching Keynes, Hildesley, and Cotton, who have confessed hearing Mass at Mr. Yate's, to understand from them what other persons were present in their company. Touching Payne [the priest accused by Eliot of conspiracy against the queen's life], since there are vehement presumptions that he is guilty of the fact wherewith he is charged, they are to proceed to the torture with him and to examine him thereupon.[63]

About August 15, therefore, Campion was interrogated for a third time, after that of July 30 or 31, and that of August 1 (related below).[64]

Also, the persons apprehended in Lady Cecilia Stonor's house were to be interrogated upon the questions enclosed, and Hopton was to receive Pounde into his custody at the Tower to be "jointly examined upon such interrogatories as in Campion's examinations he is charged with."

On Friday, August 18, Lord William Vaux and Sir Thomas Tresham were summoned and required to make oath whether Campion had been at their houses. They refused to swear. On Monday, August 21, Sir William Catesby in like manner refused the oath. All three were committed as close prisoners to the Fleet. Catesby, it is said, had put up Campion at his house, at Bushwood, in Lapworth, only twelve miles from Stratford.[65] According to Burghley's notes, Campion confessed to being in all three men's houses in the summer of 1580, but he did not say which specific residences. It seems the Privy Council was fishing for information: the Council never claimed that Campion said he was at Catesby's.

Accordingly Catesby was summoned for questioning, "if he shall be repaired [gone] into that [Northampton] shire"[66]—in other words, they did not know from Campion where (nor if) Catesby had met Campion.

Vaux, Tresham, and Catesby denied the charges; in their cases, they were vague enough to deny, or to demand evidence for them. (It is also possible, despite sources quoted elsewhere in this biography, that Vaux and Catesby, at least, only hosted Fr. Persons and not Fr. Campion;[67] or that Campion stayed at their houses in their absence.)

At the same time, another letter was sent to the Bishops of London and Rochester and the Dean of St. Paul's, to direct them to meet Hammond and Beale, who would inform them of things confessed by Campion and his fellows, and to desire them to devise some good means to redress the inconveniences late grown to the hindrance of the Church and disquieting of the State. Another letter directed Hammond to go to the Tower, and there examine Thomas Pounde, who had now arrived from Wisbeach.

Campion's Apostolate Summarized

We can divide Campion's apostolate into six periods:

1. June 25–July 18, 1580: arrival; the initial period in and around London.
2. July 19–October 1580: beginning from Hoxton, Middlesex, the first journey: through the south midlands: Berkshire, Oxfordshire, Northampton shire.
3. October–November 15, 1580: a respite, beginning with a meeting with Fr. Persons at Uxbridge, Buckinghamshire, then unknown local activity.
4. November 16, 1580–mid-May 1581: beginning from Uxbridge, the second journey: through northern counties: Warwickshire, Huntingdonshire, Leicestershire, Nottinghamshire, Derbyshire, Staffordshire, Yorkshire, Lancashire.
5. Mid-May–July 10, 1581: return trip from Lancashire to London (arrival June 3); then to Stonor Park to supervise printing of *Ten Reasons*, and visits around there.
6. July 11–17, 1581: beginning from Stonor Park, the third journey: northwards, to Norfolk via Lancashire; first stop Lyford Grange, Berkshire, where Campion is captured, July 17.

In all, Campion had visited Catholics in thirteen counties: Middlesex, Berkshire, Oxfordshire, Northamptonshire, Buckinghamshire, Huntingdonshire, Leicestershire, Warwickshire, Staffordshire, Derbyshire, Nottinghamshire, Yorkshire, and Lancashire.

What Did Burghley Know?

Leaving aside the point of capture—of periods 1–5, Burghley knew nothing of part 1, a vague bit of part 2, nothing of part 3, four of the six months of part 4, and several names of part 5 (Nash, Eden, Stonor, Babington, Pollard, Morris, Brideman, Barnes).[68]

Campion's Reputation Destroyed

The government's scheme to destroy Campion's reputation was very successful in the short-term. Bombino recounts:

> Meanwhile, lest they waste their effort at their first meeting, they openly fabricated that Campion under torture had given out all his own secrets and those of his accomplices; and slanders were spread abroad to this effect, namely, that he had confessed in whose company he had associated, in whose houses he had been welcomed, who had maintained him, and who had supported him—and that he had not even refrained from disclosing secrets, that he had not kept confidential whose sins and what manner of sins he had heard in Confession.
>
> Though disseminated by assiduous lying, at first these things found credit with scarcely any; yet when they were confirmed by the voice of preachers, by the vehement assertion of noblemen, and by the oaths of magistrates, they caused even among Catholics, if nothing else, at least a doubtful wavering of mind. Afterward, in fact, certain men of the leading nobility of England, Campion's closest friends, Lord Vaux, Sir Thomas Tresham and Sir William Catesby, were cast into prison, and the constant report was that they had suffered through his information. Then, indeed, great was the fear that came over Catholics, many openly complaining among their friends and acquaintances that there was no place anymore for fidelity, for where might it be, if not in Campion's breast?[69]

"Come Rack, Come Rope": Campion's Reply to Pounde's Letter

Thirty-two people were arrested on the charge of harboring Campion.

When Pounde, now in the Tower, heard of the long list of interrogatories drawn up, as they purported to be, from Campion's confessions, he was wounded to the heart. Could it be that the man whom he had taken for the great champion of Catholicism had turned out to be, after Eliot, the greatest traitor among them—the one who had furnished the government with the most names and the best proofs upon which convictions under the penal statutes could be secured? He who had suggested the writing of the *Brag* as a precaution against false reports issued by the government against close prisoners,[70] himself fell for the official lies spread against Campion. So the same zeal which had before led him to disperse Campion's *Challenge* prematurely, now led the impulsive, sanguine Pounde to another imprudence, equally grave in its consequences.

Some time between August 17 and 20, he wrote a letter to Campion.[71] After commending Christian fortitude at length and urging the priest to be mindful of his own dignity and the cause he upheld, and to "look towards Jesus, the author and perfecter of faith" (*Heb.* 12:2), he told him how much he grieved to see the priest's reputation suffer from so injurious a report that he had, through frailty, revealed many things which, considering the Christian cause, had better remain concealed. He gave particulars of rumors that were repulsive to hear, and besought Campion, in the name of God, the Author of all truth, to tell him whether these stories were true or false. This letter he gave to his keeper, who promised, for a fee of four marks, to have it privately delivered to Campion.

The man took the money and kept it, but the letter he gave to Hopton, who opened and read it, and closed it again as if it had never been tampered with, and told the keeper to deliver it to Campion and bring back the reply. Campion, ever hasty at such matters, and now urged by the treacherous keeper, scribbled off a note to his friend, no authentic copy of which is preserved. The most likely record of it occurs in the reports of the trial of Vaux, Tresham, Catesby, and others, in the Star-Chamber, November 15, 1581;[72] and the trial of Campion himself, where there was:

a letter produced, said to be intercepted, which Mr. Campion should seem to write to a fellow prisoner of his, namely, Mr. Pounde; wherein he did take notice that by frailty he had confessed of some houses where he had been, which now he repented him, and desired Mr. Pounde to beg him pardon of the Catholics therein, saying that in this he rejoiced, that he had discovered [revealed] no things of secret, nor would he, come rack, come rope.[73]

No Betrayal of Anything Unknown

What the real meaning of this letter was can only be guessed. Pounde's letter, to which it was a reply, was never produced, and the sketch of Pounde's that I have given was probably a guess of Persons.[74] The natural meaning of Campion's words is that he revealed nothing not already known by other persons' confessions. And I am disposed to believe this, in spite of the report of what he said on the scaffold, when he desired all to forgive him whose names he had confessed upon the rack—"for upon the commissioners' oaths that no harm should come unto them, he uttered some persons with whom he had been"; and he declared the phrase in his letter, that "he would not disclose the secrets of some houses where he had been entertained," to refer only to "saying of Mass, hearing of confessions, preaching and suchlike duties and functions of priesthood," and not, "as it was misconstrued by the enemy, treason or conspiracy or any matter else any way intended against her Majesty or the State."[75]

I believe that this speech was a mere interpretation of Campion's real words, turned by the author into the best apology he could then think of for excusing the universally credited report of Campion's weakness and even treachery. The unknown author of the French account of his death (afterwards translated into Latin by Dr. Laing)[76]—by one who knew him well—declares that to all the questions Campion answered little or nothing, except that he had sent his book to Mr. Richardson (alias of the priest Richard Norris) and to Mr. Pounde. He attributes the knowledge that the Council had obtained concerning Campion's lodging-places to the confessions of his companions.[77]

That this was so, there is the irrefragable evidence of the book, *A true report of the Disputation, or rather private Conference, had in the Tower of London with Ed. Campion, Jesuit, the last of August 1581. Set down by the Reverend learned men themselves that dealt therein,*[78] published by authority, January 1, 1583. We read there, on the second page, how Campion declared

> he was punished for religion himself, and had been twice on the rack, and that racking was more grievous than hanging, and that he had rather choose to be hanged than racked.

To which Sir Owen Hopton replied

> that he had no cause to complain of racking, who had rather seen than felt the rack; and admonished him to use good speech, that he give not cause to be used with more severity. For although you were put to the rack, yet notwithstanding you were so favorably used [treated] therein, as being taken off, you could and did presently go thence to your lodging without help, and use your hands in writing, and all other parts of your body, which you could not have done if you had been put to that punishment with any such extremity as you speak of.

Then Beale, clerk of the Privy Council, asked if he had been examined on any point of religion. Campion answered

> that he was not indeed directly examined of religion, but moved to confess in what places he had been conversant since his repair [coming] into the realm.

Beale replied that

> this was required of him because many of his fellows, and by likelihood he himself also, had reconciled divers of her Highness's subjects to the Romish Church, and had attempted to withdraw them from their obedience due to their natural Prince and Sovereign.

This Protestant account continues:

> Whereunto he answered, that forasmuch as the Christians in old time, being commanded to deliver up the books of their religion to such as persecuted them, refused to do so, and misliked with them that did so, calling them *traditores* [traitors], he might not betray his Catholic brethren, which were (as he said) the temples of the Holy Ghost.[79]

Catholic Sir Thomas Tresham's notes of the first Tower debate likewise say that Campion

> showed that his punishment was for that he would not betray the
> places and persons with whom he had conversed and dealt with as
> concerning the Catholic cause . . . Much more said he: I ought to suf-
> fer anything rather than to betray the bodies of those that ministered
> necessaries to supply my lack.[80]

Now I hold that if he had betrayed his Catholic brethren, as the
Council's letters had insinuated, Hopton and Beale and Hammond and
Norton, who were all present at this conference, and who had also been
at his racking, would at once have retorted: "But you have betrayed them,
and we have your confessions, signed with your own hand, where you
declare at whose houses you have been." For instance, here is one used at
Lord Vaux's trial, the content of which was:

> that he had been at the house of Lord Vaux sundry times; at Sir
> Thomas Tresham's house; at Mr. [Edward] Griffin's of Northampton,
> where also the Lady Tresham then was; and at the house of Sir W.
> Catesby, where Sir T. Tresham and his lady then were. Also at one
> time when he was at Lord Vaux's, he said that Lord Compton was
> there.[81]

However, when he said he would not be a traitor to his Catholic
brethren, not a voice was raised against him; the matter was let drop, lest
perchance he make a public denial of the authenticity of all his pretended
confessions.

Significantly, Bombino's account of the reply to Pounde's letter
urging Campion to "take up spirits worthy of himself and worthy of so
great a Captain,"[82] makes no mention of having named names, but says
Campion was prompt in replying

> that he grieved greatly the constancy of Catholics was, by reason of
> him, so unworthily shaken. He had lived hitherto, and did now live,
> mindful of Jesus, not only as his Captain, but also as his spectator
> and encourager, and no bitterness of torments ["come rack, come
> rope"] would ever constrain him to reveal anything that might be
> detrimental to the Church of God.[83]

Later, Bombino says, Campion was tortured to reveal the secrets
that this letter implied he withheld, but he swore that his letter had

no reference to plots but simply meant that no pains would make him endanger his friends who had liberally maintained him or hosted him.[84]

It was only after his death that his relentless enemy Charke ventured to call him

> a well-known, vain, light, runagate person . . . an arrant traitor . . . the Queen's open enemy . . . a lusty champion . . . a glorious Thraso [braggart] . . . [of] shameful ignorance in the learned tongues, which he sought most ridiculously to cover and hide . . . yet the glorious fool, partly to boast of his sufferings, partly to excuse his impatience and pusillanimity—which for fear rather than feeling of the rack, had discovered [revealed] many of his friends and accomplices with his own handwriting—immediately after his racking, was not ashamed on the day of the first conference to complain of his grievous torments, until by testimony of Master Lieutenant of the Tower, and others that were present, his impudence was so restrained for that time, that he thought it not best to brag any more of his intolerable racking.[85]

Despite Charke's claim, there was no "handwriting" by Campion naming anyone. It is all written in the hands of his torturers. Burghley in his *Declaration of the favorable dealing of her Majesty's Commissioners appointed for the examination of certain Traitors* (1583) says:

> Campion, I say, before the conference had with him by learned men in the Tower . . . was . . . racked, but . . . he was presently able to walk and to write, and did presently write and subscribe [sign] all his confessions, as by the originals thereof may appear.[86]

That "subscribe" was a lie. We have Burghley's handwriting but no confession signed by Campion. The significant point for us is that Burghley dates all the "confessions" before August 31—*before* this debate at which Edmund said he betrayed no fellow-Catholic.

Burghley also says there, speaking of the commissioners' dealings with the priests:

> But if he [a priest] said that his answer, in delivering truth, should hurt a Catholic, and so be an offense against charity, which they said to be sin, and that the Queen could not command them to sin, and therefore, howsoever the Queen commanded, they would not tell

the truth which they were known to know, or to such effect; they
were then put to the torture, or else not.[87]

The Council never allowed Campion to be publicly interrogated
about his confessions, nor let anyone see the record of the interrogations.
On trial for harboring Campion, Mr. Walter Powdrell[88] expressly asked
to see them before swearing, and was refused.[89] Now, if it were part of the
government's policy to discredit Campion—and it was—then certainly
anything embarrassing to Campion would gladly have been exhibited.

When Sir Thomas Tresham, required to make oath that Campion
had never been at his house, asked first to "see Mr. Campion, or hear him
speak, where by his face or speech I might call him to remembrance,"
he was told by the Lord Chancellor that his demand lacked discretion.
Tresham replied:

> If by seeing him I could call to memory that he had been at my house,
> then would I have deposed . . . as your lordship did say, [Campion]
> stayed little with me, came much disguised in apparel, and altering
> his name. All which made me refuse to swear to my knowledge, lest
> haply he might have been in my house, and in my company both, I
> not knowing him; and yet that the same should be referred to a jury
> . . . to judge whether I were perjured or no. Wherefore, as I have said,
> my desire was that by means of seeing him or hearing him that I the
> better might remember him.

To which the Chancellor again replied: "I can see no reason why it
should be granted you."[90] Yet even under Tudor law the accused had a
right to be brought face to face with his accuser.

The suspicion that Campion's confessions were forgeries was so fortified by this constant refusal to confront him with those whom he was
said to have accused, that these persons at last came entirely to disbelieve
in them. Thus, in the same trial, Tresham gives another reason for refusing to swear: "I should greatly sin uncharitably to belie him, to make him
and myself both guilty by my oath, who to my knowledge are most innocent."[91] He also said to the Chancellor: "I hear nothing of him [Campion]
(myself being close prisoner), but what I hear reported by you."

Moreover, most interestingly, Tresham's private papers contain his
refutation of the charge that Campion had betrayed his hosts.[92] In anticipation of his trial, Tresham prepared for himself a written statement of

defense that indirectly testifies to Campion's holiness. No one can call a traitor a man who "fasted thrice a week with bread and water, or that has been occupied whole nights in prayer, or has done alms-deeds, or in execution of those mysteries of religion which in my soul I think absolutely good."[93]

Fr. Persons also expressed his opinion that Campion's "confessions" were as false as the recantations of faith attributed to him, and as false as the denials that he had been tortured:

> For twice [four times][94] recently Campion was tortured on the rack: and what enemy did not utterly deny it? Yet at length the truth became known, when Campion himself said it before a crowd of people [at the first debate] . . .
>
> But they have also another stratagem, familiar in this Tower: to fabricate whatever they please about a prisoner and publish it to his shame, and so to deceive other Catholics. The matter is plainly evident and examples abound, but in order to be brief, we will touch on one or two only.
>
> When Campion had been caught, and afflicted with torments, it was being said that he had confessed whatsoever they had demanded of him, especially at whose houses and in what places he had been. And to make the lie complete, it was even added that he had made a guarantee of a [public] recantation of I know not what. But that tale no one thought probable; yet there were some who began to doubt, because of the enemies' most vehement assertions. For many gentlemen and noblemen were summoned from their homes to London, and charged on a confession of Campion, although in reality (as it later became apparent), he never yielded one word to his torments.[95]

Such are some of the difficulties that stand in the way of our supposing Campion's alleged confessions to be real.

We can only wonder who was the source of the supposed confession about Lord Vaux, Tresham, and the rest. No one can be named with certainty.[96] Back in December 1580, Sir George Peckham was called before the Privy Council, "charged with harboring and entertaining of Campion, the Jesuit, and one [George] Gilbert, a notorious practicer" (of the Catholic religion). For having "received the said Campion and Gilbert into his house, their Lordships . . . did commit him unto the Marshalsea [prison], there to remain a close [secluded] prisoner and without conference with any person." This followed the "examination of certain persons," not named.[97] Any one of these unknown persons, or the one who informed on Peckham himself, may have known or heard that Campion had recently (in "summer") visited these three men (Vaux, Tresham, Catesby) in Northamptonshire. Sir George's houses in London and Buckinghamshire were searched by order of the Privy Council, December 1580,[98] and Mrs. Peckham was later detained in the Fleet prison.[99]

When Campion wrote that he had confessed nothing secret, he probably meant he had confessed nothing which had not been previously wormed out of others. When a list of the places where he has been is shown to a man upon the rack, and he sees that the compiler of the list had access to authentic information, it is either folly or superhuman strength of will to refuse to acknowledge the truth of it.

That Campion's confessions were merely his acknowledgment of the truth of matters which he perceived were known by his examiners, may be inferred from a paper, partly in Burghley's handwriting,[100] containing a list of the places where Campion had been, founded on the joint confession of himself and others. Thus, to all the places where he was taken by Gervase Pierrepoint there is appended a note that either Pierrepoint or someone else had confessed the matter; but then as soon as Pierrepoint hands over his charge to Tempest, Campion "will confess no place of their being but at inns." (This is not to say that Gervase, his conductor through Derbyshire, was the *first* to tell; he was not arrested until August 14.)[101]

Again, if Campion had been the first to reveal the places where he had been, he probably would have mentioned all of them and not singled out special cases for delation. The list that the examiners made out is full of gaps, which were from time to time filled up by fresh information over the next two or three years.

In October 1581, Lord Norris was told to apprehend Mr. Edmunds in Oxfordshire, "which Edmunds is by Campion *and others* detected [revealed] to have been a receiver and harborer of the said Campion and other of the Jesuits and Seminary Priests."[102] It is clear that the "others" named Mr. Edmunds—for if Campion had named him, an order for the arrest of Mr. Edmunds would have gone out *in August* with all the other orders. Similarly, in 1584, an Anglican minister, Ralph Bentham,[103] declares that he was present at Lady Dormer's in Buckinghamshire, when Campion said Mass there about mid-summer 1581.[104]

Fr. Anstruther argues well from this very randomness and incompleteness of the confessions that it makes no sense to say they came from Campion:

> This list shows that Burghley was in possession of detailed information as to Campion's movements from January 10, 1581, till about Whitsuntide [May 14]. Outside that period his knowledge was vague and fragmentary. For the first six months of Campion's apostolate [July–December 1580] the only names given are those of the three Northamptonshire men [Vaux, Tresham, Catesby], and the time is only vaguely known ["summer 1580"]. Of his tour through the south midlands in [July–September] 1580 not a single definite detail of time or place had come to light. About his return journey from Lancashire [mid-May 1581 onwards] Burghley is equally in the dark, until he reaches Lyford where he was captured [July 17]. If all these facts were confessed by Campion, why should some be so detailed and others so vague? The proclamation against Jesuits, making it a crime to harbor them, was issued on January 10, 1581. Before that date it was dangerous of course, but not illegal to harbor them. If all this data came from Campion, why should he be so reticent as to where he was in 1580, and so forthcoming regarding his movements as soon as the proclamation was published? This document [of Burghley] is more intelligible on the supposition that the information contained in it was supplied in the first place by spies who picked up the trial only when Campion set out for the north. Campion, if he confessed anything on the rack, may have acknowledged the truth of these reports, but he can hardly have added anything that was not already known.[105]

Anstruther also observes:

> Equally suspicious is the monotonous frequency with which these letters from the Privy Council stress the fact that the information leading to the arrests was confessed by Campion; every letter has at least one reference to his confession, in striking contrast with the normal letters which never mention the source of the information supplied to the Council. From the very start it was Burghley's main object to discredit this popular hero by branding him as a coward.[106]

There are other suspicious statements of over-kill. In letters from the Privy Council, twice it is said that Campion's visits to the homes of four people, "*at sundry times* has been confessed by him."[107] Now if he truly gave out names, there was no reason for him to say them again and again at different interrogations.

Another obviously fabricated "confession" occurs in the summons of John Pollard, Esquire, of Baldon, Oxfordshire, "for it was confessed by Campion that he [Pollard] was present when he [Campion] was at the house of Mrs. Pollard, widow, in the said county."[108] As mentioned above, Mrs. Phillipe Pollard, under arrest, gave in and promised to attend the Established Church.[109] It is more plausible that she was the one who named John, her son or relative, rather than that Campion singled him out.[110]

We find phrases in *Acts of the Privy Council* which show that Campion did not tell all. George Gilbert was sought in a letter of the Council of August 4, and the wording is significant. Two men, "in whose houses Edmund Campion has confessed that he was lodged," are to be asked, "what is become of Gilbert, *who is said* to have brought Campion unto them."[111] Campion, then, did not specify Gilbert; otherwise, the wording would have been definite. The Council pretends he named his hosts but not his guide, whereas, clearly, he named no parties. On the same day, another letter orders a search of Stonor Park for Catholic books in English, "printed also there, *as it is thought*, by one Parsons, a Jesuit, and others."[112] Again, why would Campion confess all about his own book but give no information about other books Persons printed? The Council's uncertainty shows Campion gave no new information. Further, Campion was interrogated on July 30 or 31.[113] Now, since capturing the printing-press was a matter of urgency, why would the Council wait at least four days after learning about its location to send a letter to seize it? The information must have come from someone else just before August 4.

As said above, it looks very much like certain of Campion's companions or conductors in this four-month period gave way under torture or threat thereof, and then this information was ascribed to Campion. The Council says in a letter that Hammond and Beale can go to the Bishops of London and Rochester, and the Dean of St. Paul's, to "inform them touching things confessed by Campion *and his fellows*."[114] Armed with this information, it is possible that Campion was told that if *he* did not confess the fact of his visits, his hosts would be arrested and tortured to make *them* confess to the same. In other words, if Campion thought the Council knew already, he judged it dishonest and pointless to deny it, incriminating of his hosts by implication to remain silent, and a deliverance from torture for them if he admitted it—for as an early account says: "upon the commissioners' oaths that no harm should come to them, he uttered some persons with whom he had been."[115] He *confirmed* names known, but *revealed* none.

A list of Burghley begins: "Campion confesseth his being in their houses." One could argue: "It does not say Campion confessed to saying Mass or hearing confessions (both illegal activities) in any houses. It was not yet a statutory crime to harbor a Jesuit or to be visited by one. In saying he *visited* certain people, Campion was admitting to no crime of his or theirs. Further, he traveled in disguise and under an assumed name." In reply: this is a valid argument but only for visits *before* January 10, 1581, when the "Proclamation . . . against the retaining of Jesuits" made it illegal even to host a Jesuit. Burghley's notes make a point that certain people received Campion *after* the Proclamation. Still, there may be significance in the fact that these notes say Campion gave names only—whilst any mentions of Mass or confession come under the names of *other* people being interrogated. This comes back to the point that Campion may have given names (and nothing more about Mass, etc.) on the basis of oaths that no harm would come to them.

It is important to keep in mind the dates, as pointed out above ("A Series of Arrests"). On August 4, a man was directed to go to "Lady Stonor's house . . . and there to make diligent search . . . for certain Latin books dispersed abroad in Oxford at the last Commencement, which Edmund Campion upon his examination has confessed to have been there printed"[116]—but two days later, on August 4, Burghley writes privately that Campion "is in the Tower and stiffly denieth to answer any question of moment." The printing-press and the printing of *Ten Reasons* were certainly matters of moment! This can only mean the information came from someone else but was publicly ascribed to Campion to discredit him.

As we saw above, on August 14, the Council ordered a re-examination of Campion and the others, "who *refuse to confess* whether they have said any Masses or no, whom they have confessed, and where Persons and the other priests be,"[117] etc. Why this directive nearly two weeks after he had told all?[118]

I do not deny that Campion may have been deceived by the wily officers. "Some men," says Selden, "before they come to their trial are cozened to confess upon examination. Upon this trick, they are made to believe somebody has confessed before them; and then they think it a piece of honor to be clear and ingenuous, and that destroys them."[119] That this cozenage was familiar to Burghley, we may see by a letter of his relating to the treatment of Fr. James Younger, who had revealed all he knew of Catholics, and through whom the Council hoped to find out more. "The Queen," says Burghley, "would have those charged by him to be apprehended, and charged with some other things, and not with relieving of Younger, of whom she would have a general opinion conceived that nothing can be had of himself. So as he may retain his former credit with his complices."[120] Younger's treachery was to be studiously disguised, because they wished to save his credit for future use. The same men wished to destroy Campion's credit and therefore would studiously exaggerate or invent stories that seemed to prove his treachery.

This falls in exactly with Shakespeare's picture of Polonius—by whom he may have intended to represent Burghley in his dotage—instructing Reynaldo how to spy out the truth about Laertes's behavior at Paris:

> Your bait of falsehood takes this carp of truth:
> And thus do we of wisdom and of reach
> With windlasses and with assays of bias,
> By indirections find directions out.
>
> —*Hamlet*, Act II, sc. i, 63

"Windlass" (a hoisting machine) as a device for discovering men's secrets, is probably a metaphor borrowed from the rack.

The Case for the Authenticity of the Confessions

J. H. Pollen S.J., on the other hand, believes the confessions attributed to Campion are authentic. Here is a summary of his arguments.[121]

After some preliminaries, the serious examination of Campion at the rack about his activities began under the orders of the Privy Council of July 30, 1581. The rack was freely used, and two days later (August 2) the

Register shows that the Councilors had before them a list of Campion's hosts in Lancashire, said to be confessed by him. On August 4, a similar list occurs for Yorkshire; about August 6, one for Northants; about August 7–14, lists for Derbyshire, and some counties nearer London.

Through these lists, about thirty-two persons were summoned, of whom eight strongly denied having given hospitality, and six confessed it.[122] Their subsequent fortunes, so far as we can follow them, varied a good deal. Those who conformed and went to church, were freed. Those who remained steadfast were punished mercilessly for their constancy; but I cannot find that anyone was mulcted purely on the score of hospitality, and this confirms Dr. Allen's story that Campion only confessed after obtaining a promise that no one should suffer for entertaining him.

All these details are taken from the contemporary register of the Privy Council, and they leave us with some convictions, but some doubts. There are some real confessions from Campion behind the prosecutions. Though many details are not clear, some are. Simpson suggested that where a second confession is sometimes alleged as confirming Campion's, the truth might be that the second confession really came first; and that Campion's words were in fact only its endorsement. However, in these cases the register proves that Campion's confession came before even the arrest of the second party. So that defense will not hold.

We have also four letters from Lord Burghley which touch on the subject but again do not settle the problem. He was not the chief prosecutor at this moment, and his words sometimes understate, sometimes overstate the facts. At first he says Campion "denieth to answer any question of moment." In the last letter he writes, "We have gotten from Campion the knowledge of his peregrinations." There is something true in both cases, and difficult to reconcile. Campion's own statements, however, afford a solution, and their validity, when appreciated, can hardly be gainsaid.

They are three in number, and the first, it must be admitted, appears at first sight to go against us, and to support Simpson.

1. On August 31, the first debate was held. Among the preliminary scoffs and sneers, Campion was told that he was a traitor and that his claim to suffer for religion was quite erroneous. Campion promptly replied that he had been tortured, "for that he would not betray the places and persons with whom he had conversed and dealt with . . . I ought to

suffer anything rather than to betray the bodies of those that ministered necessaries to supply my lack."[123] The Protestant account equally says, "he answered, that forasmuch as the Christians in old time, being commanded to deliver up the books of their religion to such as persecuted them, refused to do so ... he might not betray his Catholic brethren, which were (he said) the temples of the Holy Ghost."[124] Simpson makes much of the silence which greeted this claim, when they could have denounced his betrayals of other Catholics. But the silence by the Protestants did not necessarily mean they had no ready answer—but could simply mean that they had no desire to pursue a side-issue, and wanted to get on with the debate. Further, it was of no interest to them directly whether he was a "traitor" to his fellow-Catholics; they charged him with being a "traitor" to the queen. (Reply: Pollen gives another reason for the silence but has not explained why Campion would needlessly assert his steadfastness before people who could openly refute it with concrete evidence, including the torturers present at the debate: Hopton, Beale, and Norton.)

2. Campion, when first brought out from his solitary cell in the Tower, would not have been aware of the reports that the government had been circulating about his confessions. His statements quoted above confirm this, but he was soon after acquainted with the rumors by a surreptitious note from Mr. Thomas Pounde, and wrote back an answer full of grief and concern:

> It grieveth me much to have offended the Catholic cause so highly as to confess the names of some gentlemen and friends in whose houses I had been entertained; yet in this I greatly cherish and comfort myself that I never discovered [revealed] any secrets there declared, and that I will not, come rack, come rope.

Now for this letter, the frankest of his confessions, we have very strong evidence indeed. The original text included is lost, but the above words are copied from the Catholic report of Campion's trial—a document of the highest value.[125] Words of exactly the same meaning are also given in the Protestant report and a third time in the trial of Lord Vaux in the Star-Chamber[126]—three independent contemporaries, whose exact agreement leave us no possible room for doubt. (Reply: Pollen's argument here partly depends upon a wrong chronology through an oversight. Pollen forgets that Pounde was at the first debate on August 31, where he would have heard Campion say he betrayed no one. His letter to Campion, then, must have been *before* that debate, after the arrests in early August of Campion's helpers and hosts. [See above: "*Come rack, come rope:* Campion's reply to Pounde's letter".] It is clear that one purpose of Campion's open claim not to have betrayed fellow-Catholics was to contradict publicly the rumors he learnt of through Pounde's letter to him.)

3. In his scaffold speech, Campion spoke again and in very similar words. In Dr. Allen's *Brief History* we read, "He desired all to forgive him, whose names he had confessed upon the rack, for upon the Commissioners' oaths, that no harm should come to them, he had uttered some names." The Protestant version again supports this exactly, and with two such witnesses the fact must surely be admitted.[127]

In conclusion, Pollen's arguments are rightly based on evidence beyond government propaganda, but the evidence to the contrary is stronger.[128]

Pollen above summarizes the information "given" by Campion (on August 2, a list of Campion's hosts in Lancashire; on August 4, a similar list for Yorkshire; about August 6, one for Northants; about August 7–14, lists for Derbyshire, and some counties nearer London). But he seems not to notice the strange way in which the Council's information grew neatly according to counties, as if Campion nicely confessed different counties on different days. The more likely explanation is a series of interrogations of several people from different counties.

Neither Simpson nor Pollen nor any other writer pays any attention to the *jail-keeper's* declarations that Campion confessed the names of his hosts and helpers—for such government stooges also asserted just as baldly (and patently falsely, as events showed) that Campion had never been tortured, and had recanted his religion. Mr. Cruse, a jail-keeper of Campion, told manifest lies to Sir Thomas Tresham to trick him into admitting he had harbored Campion, but Tresham could not be fooled into believing the lies or disclosing anything incriminating.[129] For which reason, Gerard Kilroy concludes, "we can be certain that the idea of Campion betraying those in whose houses he had stayed was as false as most of such official information."[130]

A Contemporary Defense of Campion's Confessions

Fr. Gibbons's *Concertatio* contains an account of Campion's life, with a passage on the controversy worth quoting in full. It is by an unknown priest who knew Campion well, and was present at both the Tower debates and the execution:

> On two days they tortured and maltreated and stretched him on the rack with such cruelty and savagery, that he afterwards secretly declared to a certain friend that he really thought they meant to kill him by the punishment; at the same time he revealed what questions had been put to him. They were: what financial aid had been given to the Irish rebels; what conspiracy there was to kill the queen; about the invasion of the realm of England; and about the meaning of the letter which he had written to the esteemed Mr. Pounde. To all these interrogations, Campion answered nothing or very little; he only confessed that he had sent his book [*Ten Reasons*] to Mr. Richardson [Fr. Richard Norris], and that he had sent a copy . . . to Mr. Pounde. Now he confessed this, because he saw clearly enough that by the grace of God these men were put beyond the assaults of further adversity, so that no harm could come to them by this confession of his. [They were already in prison, openly confessing their Catholic faith, and probably the books had been found on them.][131]

After Fr. Edmund had been questioned in this fashion, his companions, confined in separate places, were soon likewise examined with the greatest subtlety; and not just once, but over and over again, with repeated interrogations. If a single word could be extracted from them, which could be twisted in any way on any slight basis or inference so as to compromise any Catholic gentleman, it was enormously exaggerated, and publicized here and there, the false accusers spreading it all round that it had come from a confession of Campion wrested under interrogation.

In this matter the impudence of the persecutors was such, that one of them, a most distinguished member of the queen's Council, declared to a certain knight, who is still being held in prison [probably Sir Thomas Tresham] . . . that Campion under interrogation had confessed many things about him . . . Anyway, that knight easily dismissed that deception from his mind, both because he was sure and well aware of such things regarding himself, and because he had no doubt about Fr. Edmund's discretion and steadfastness.

Nevertheless, that abominable lie, namely, that Fr. Edmund had been tortured into betraying certain noblemen, had such an impact on the public, on account of the enormous authority of a Privy Councilor, that it was seriously and earnestly believed—so that even a certain Catholic nobleman affirmed before several people that he had it on certain authority that Campion under examination had confessed all he knew. But this same man soon afterwards openly admitted to some friend that he had been too credulous in allowing himself to be so easily deceived by the persecutors.[132] The same thought and fear tormented other Catholics also, through that false rumor indiscriminately broadcasted and accepted—to the point that the imprisonment of Lord Vaux, Sir Thomas Tresham, and Sir William Catesby was being imputed to Campion. As a result, the cunning of these malicious men caused this excellent man not only to lose his good name among the enemies of religion, but to suffer the same harm to his reputation among Catholics.

And this was the reason Mr. Pounde, who was in prison at the same time, exhorted him by letter to constancy, and devoutly encouraged him to be a true and strong confessor of Christ; he hinted that he was somewhat troubled at the reports [of his treachery] which had reached him, and begged him to tell him whether he had under torture done as the public rumor said he had. . . .

Edmund wrote a short answer, saying that no tortures of any kind will ever force him to reveal anything that could harm the Church of God. This answer,

> committed to writing, came into the hands of the Queen's Council, which, when they read it, made them suspect him to have suppressed something under questioning, which might perhaps contain something of great importance to the state of the whole Realm . . . and they would not neglect any means to obtain the information.[133]

This editor regards this passage as exonerating Campion definitively. There remains only one difficulty, and that is: on the day of his execution, why did Campion ask forgiveness of those he named? The answer is because, despite the commissioners' oaths no harm would come to them, harm *did* come to them: they were arrested and questioned and some were imprisoned.[134] But at the same time, the heroically holy Campion was not going to blame someone else for being the informant, nor claim he confirmed only what was known about them when they were going to be arrested anyway; nor was he going to say defiantly that he concealed all other names—a provocation to the government to arrest more people and harass Catholics more thoroughly. His humility and charity determined the apology, and he let go of any desire to vindicate his heroic fortitude.

This quotation from *Concertatio* enables us to close the discussion. It makes no sense to say Campion revealed some names—but not others; made a confession—but did not sign it; chose to betray names from a four-month period—but none from the other nine months; gave names and dates of many hosts—but names only and no dates for some others. This passage shows he was willing to suffer the rack unto what he thought was impending death upon it—and, knowing that he had betrayed nothing unknown, would remain steadfast as he had been hitherto, "come rack, come rope." The defiance in this phrase cannot come from a man who has already informed on thirty-two people. Other tortures too were inflicted upon Edmund[135]—precisely because he would not speak. Had he spoken, they would not have taken place.

In the popular verses that circulated afterwards, Campion was held to have remained steadfast:

> Not rack nor rope could daunt his dreadless mind,
> no hope nor hap could move him where he stood,
> he wrote the truth as in his books we find,
> which to confirm he sealed with his blood.[136]

More Questioning and Racking

The Council-book records that on August 21, Hopton and Hammond were directed to re-examine Campion on certain points.[137] Shortly after this date, then, Campion was stretched on the rack for the second time,[138] and this was no doubt occasioned by his written message to Pounde, for they wished to discover what secrets he would not betray, "come rack, come rope."

On August 30, the Earl of Derby and other magistrates of Lancashire were thanked for apprehending Thomas Southworth, Richard Hoghton, and Bartholomew Hesketh, with certain papers, in Hoghton House. If the parties persisted in denying Campion to have been at their houses, "which at sundry times has been confessed by him,"[139] they were to be kept in prison. Hoghton and his wife were to be re-examined concerning Campion's visit there, as well as about Br. Ralph Emerson, his books, and the books sent by Fr. Rishton and dispersed in that shire.[140] Lord Norris was charged to confine Lady Babington to her house on bond, "since by Campion it has been confessed sundry times that he has been both in her house at Oxford, and in the Whitefriars in London."[141] Also Francis Morris (husband of Anne Morris named above)[142] was to be sent up, if he would not confess that Campion had been at his house. Later this year, 1581, he was sent to the Fleet for having sheltered Fr. Campion.[143] He died three years later.

Also on August 30, a letter was written to Sir Henry Neville, to thank him for apprehending the printers at Stonor's Lodge, and requiring him to deface the "Massing stuff" and give the proceeds to the poor, and to send the press, books, and papers to London. He was to look out diligently for "Hartwell, a priest" (possibly they meant Hartley), Father Persons and his servant, and Robert Seely, servant to John Stonor, "if happily he shall light upon them or any others of their disposition."[144]

Another letter to Robert Drury told him, as Mr. John Penn, "seeing he obstinately persists in the denial of Campion's being with him,"[145] to examine Mrs. Penn and others of the family, and to search "Mrs. [Jane] Griffith's house, not far from Uxbridge,[146] where Campion was also once or twice."[147]

Cecily Stonor Defiant

Lady Cecily Stonor herself was also arrested. When rebuked by her judges at Oxford for recusancy in 1581, she boldly answered:

> I was born in such a time when Holy Mass was in great reverence, and brought up in the same faith. In King Edward's time, this reverence was neglected and reproved by such as governed. In Queen Mary's time, it was restored with much applause; and now in this time it pleaseth the State to question them, as now they do me, who continue in this Catholic profession. The State would have these several changes, which I have seen with mine eyes, good and laudable.

Whether it can be so, I refer it to your Lordships' consideration. I hold me still to that wherein I was born and bred; and find nothing taught in it but great virtue and sanctity; and so by the grace of God I will live and die in it.[148]

CHAPTER 16

Debates in the Tower

I N THE last chapter I traced the means used by the government to discredit Campion's moral superiority. In the present I will show how they tried to disparage his intellect. In their own hearts, perhaps their fear caused them to overrate his powers; but publicly they ludicrously contemned him as a fool.

Campion Must Be Refuted

When *Decem Rationes* was dispersed, the Establishment was in a flutter. Burghley wrote about it to Aylmer, Bishop of London, who replied:

I have not Campion's book, and yet have I sent to Oxford and searched

> in other places for it. And if I had it, yet my ague being now so sore fallen down to my leg, I am not able to travail in study with out great danger. Nevertheless if I can get the book, I will do what my health will suffer me. But I guess that the things wherewith he reproacheth our ancient learned men are nothing else but such railing accusations as are gathered against them by the apostate Staphilus.[1]

This note was answered by Burghley the same day; and Aylmer wrote again:

> Since I received your letters, I gave thought of those reproaches which the Jesuit objecteth against our learned men, and know there be divers *noevi* [novelties] in them, as lightly be in all men's writings; as some things spoke of Luther hyperbolically, and some of Calvin.[2]

Then he retorts that the same blots may be found in Catholic divines (theologians); then, after a compliment to Burghley, on whom comes the care of all the churches as well as that of the State, he proposes

443

to have a letter sent from the Lords of the Council to my Lord of Canterbury or to me, to enjoin the deans, archdeacons, and doctors to make some collections for these matters. For such as have not great dealings in the Church, as they have not—yea and some bishops also—might, having that leisure, help well to this building: wherefore else have they their livings? And for books, it were not amiss to point such a number as should serve for that purpose.

Then he annexes a schedule of the divines whom he would commission to reply to Campion. They are: the Deans of St. Paul's (Mr. Nowell), Winton, York, Christ Church, Windsor (Mr. Day), Sarum, Ely, Worcester, and Canterbury; the Archdeacons of Canterbury, London, Middlesex, Essex (Dr. Walker), Lincoln, Coventry (Dr. James), Sudbury (Dr. Styll); and three more to be "doers in writing," Dr. Fulke, Dr. Goade, and Dr. Some.

After this portentous list of people to answer Campion, it is amusing to find two of them, Nowell and Day, opining that *Ten Reasons* was written by a team of Jesuits before Campion had arrived in England! Their experience showed:

> we found him not to be that man that we looked for, and went away with that opinion, that the book which was so suddenly after his bragging challenge put in print, was none of his writing, much less penned by him as he was in his journey, as he reported himself; but that it was elaborated before, by the common and long study of all the best learned Jesuits, to serve at all opportunities.[3]
>
> ... We said it was more credible, that he brought the said book over with him [from Europe], ready framed by the common and long conference of himself, and his fellow Jesuits at convenient opportunity suddenly to be published, rather than that he did write it in his travels, having so much besides to do, and being destitute of his library as he said ...[4]

In their preface "To the reader" they repeat their judgment that *Ten Reasons* was not by Campion:

> we verily thought the book published in his name, to have been none of his.[5]

The same unintended compliment would be paid five years later to another Jesuit, St. Robert Bellarmine: when the first volume of

Bellarmine's *Controversies of the Christian Faith* was issued in 1586, a French Calvinist divine, François du Jon (Junius), overwhelmed with the erudition of the work—which exhibited such extraordinary knowledge of the Scriptures, Fathers, Councils, theologians, historians, philosophers, humanists, and Protestant writers—charged that "Bellarmine" was not a real man at all, but a pen-name used by a team of scholars: "Methinks it is not one Bellarmine who speaks in these pages," said the man in his panic. "It is the whole Jesuit phalanx, the entire legion of them mustered for our destruction."[6]

> Two days after the date of Aylmer's last letter, he writes again to thank Burghley for Campion's pamphlet. He promises to read it and set some others to work. For his collections in the chapter *Paradoxa* ["Absurdities," reason 8] I think none of our Church mean to defend Luther's hyperboles, or all things that have passed the pens of Calvin and Beza.[7]

Similar collections might be made from Catholic divines, he said (but this claim was not followed up).

Campion follows the Septuagint Greek version of the Old Testament, and not the Hebrew, so "his credit will be small." (Yet none of Campion's arguments depended upon a disputed translation of any passage).

Then a text is quoted to suggest to Burghley the proper treatment for his prisoner:

> *Ambitio ligata est in corde pueri, sed virga disciplinae fugabit eam.* [Ambition is bound up in the heart of a child, but the rod of discipline shall drive it away: cf. *Prov.* 22:15] . . . It is the property of a spider to gather the worst and leave the best. If this toil of mine were not, I could gladly occupy myself in searching out of his vanities. Truly, my lord, you shall find them but arrogant vanities of a Porphyrian or a Julian.

Besides the committee named above, Aylmer wrote to the Regius Professors of Divinity at the two Universities to reply at once to Campion. Whitaker did so in a Latin pamphlet, of which Aylmer wrote to Burghley, September 29, 1581: "The translating of Whitaker's book and the publishing thereof I mean to stay [stop], if it come to my hands."[8] Perhaps it was too abusive (which was not his normal style), for two years later, on occasion of the publication of his book against Fr. Dury S.J., Whitaker wrote to Burghley that he had followed his advice in sticking to his theme and avoiding personalities.[9] Humphrey, the Oxford divine, was slower; he published the first part of his *Jesuitry* only in 1582, and in it excused himself for his tardiness:

> It was a matter of time and difficulty to get Campion's book; it was late in August when I received the letter which laid this task on me; I was in the country, away from books and studies and University friends ... and laboring under an illness for some weeks. I was long in doubt whether to answer, for it is my instinct and preference to go for more pleasant studies, and I do not willingly get involved in strife and quarrels; and I would not have entered into these lively and passionate debates, if I had not been called by those whom I was obliged to obey, and more than once spurred on by those whom I would not displease. . . .
>
> While I was hard at work, behold, I was summoned by a new letter to a debate with Campion and other Jesuits . . .
>
> Among others, I too was summoned by a letter of the Most Rev. John Aylmer, Bishop of London, to dispute with Campion on October 13th. This somewhat retarded my writing; and I was ready to start out for the trip, when, behold, another letter countermanded my journey. It was then, perhaps, sniffed out that a different course was to be taken with these Jesuits and the others, and that they would have to plead no longer for religion but for life, not answering in a theological school before academics, but in Westminster Hall before judges, and the whole question was to be decided not so much by words as by law, since they were not to be charged with heresy, but the crime of *lèse majesté* [crime against the sovereign] was to be proved.[10]

While Bishop Aylmer was thus tasking the best pens at his command to answer Campion, he thought it good policy to speak slightingly of him in public. For which the Catholics reprehended his folly, in that he,

> a man of known wisdom and judgment, notwithstanding the known learning of Campion, was not ashamed at a sessions at Newgate to say openly that Mr. Campion was unlearned, and that a note-book or two of his fellows, being taken from him, he had nothing in him ... and much more to the discredit of Mr. Campion.[11]

Ten Reasons Feared and Commended

The anxiety of ministers and bishops about the effects of Campion's book was not without some justification.

There is a letter from Dr. John Reynolds of Corpus Christi College to his pupil, George Cranmer, a rising Englishmen of the late 16th century, which affords curious evidence of the enthusiasm excited by the style of *Rationes Decem*. Cranmer had written to Reynolds comparing Scotus with Aquinas, and Cicero with Campion. Reynolds replies:

> In your second parallel, wherein you join Campion with Cicero, I much more dissent from you, nor can I admit that I think either your affection therein is sober, or your judgment sound. For when you say you always have him at hand when you write, and praise him as a new son of Aesculapius, and (as though it were a little thing to rank him next to Cicero) declare him absolute in words, sentences, metaphors, figures, and indeed in every branch of eloquence, I cannot deny that you seem to me to study more industriously than decently a most virulent enemy of religion, and to admire more vehemently than justly a barbered and dandified rhetorician (*calamistratum rhetorculum*). But I judge not your judgment. Grant him to be terser than Isocrates, more pointed than Hyperides, more nervous than Demosthenes, more subtle than Lysias, more copious than Plato—grant that our age has produced one greater than Lactantius, whom antiquity called the Christian Cicero—yet your affection pleases me not, my George, in reading with such pleasure a writer who covers truth with falsehood, piety with reproaches, religion with slanders, and the votaries of truth, piety, and religion with evil speaking and bitter contumely. But you will say, "Suppose he is impure in his matter; I will drain out the dirt, and drink the pure water." But from that dirt there rises a pestilential smell, noxious to health, specially to those weak in body. Are you so sure of your strength as to have no fear of perils? Your uncle, when he asked me as usual what George was about, and I showed him your letter, groaned. Perhaps he feared more than he needed, for love is ever anxious and afraid; but still he groaned. God grant that the event may prove him to have been too fearful, not you too imprudent! But you should remember Cicero's sage saying, "when I walk in the sun. . ."[12] you know the rest [. . . I naturally get a tan]. I think Fabius [Quintillius] did quite rightly in forbidding boys to read the immoral poets.[13] Why

so, Fabius?—"Because I set a good life above even the best speech."
He only valued good life; do you think less of right faith?[14]

And so he goes on for a page more of polished phrases, in which he
clearly strives to rival Campion and to compete with him for Cranmer's
admiration. Cranmer is warned not to be too fond of Campion's style, lest
in listening to his words he be captured by his arguments, like Augustine
the Manichean, who, while he only wished to take a lesson from the honeyed rhetoric of St. Ambrose, was caught by the truth which underlay the
words. After the admiration of Cranmer, we can hardly wonder at that
of Muret (mentioned above),[15] who, according to Sir William Hamilton,
wrote Latin as well as Virgil himself. Muret called Campion's book, "a
golden one, really written by the finger of God." A contemporary Jesuit,
the immensely learned Fr. Antonio Possevino,[16] marvelled that, while it
was compendious as an index, it was eloquent as an oration, and called it
a gem, which the Calvinists had in vain endeavored to bury out of sight.[17]
Neither, again, can we wonder at the frantic attempts of the contrary
party to discredit both the writer and his writing.

The Council seems to have felt that it would not suit its purpose to
treat the author of such a book with the same lordly superiority with
which they had treated the replies of Harding and Stapleton to Jewel.
These books, written in the old scholastic style, had no attractions for
the new scholars. They had been blocked at the frontiers and no one but
the odd diligent student had read them. The absent are always wrong;
and a book that nobody reads is easily discredited, especially when it is a
misdemeanor to express any doubt of the validity of the refutation. But
Campion's book was in too many hands and appealed too loudly to all the
lovers of the new learning, to be exploded with inarticulate arguments.
Moreover, the courtiers, always on the lookout for some new intellectual
excitement, and already becoming exquisite critics of artistic exercises,
vehemently desired to hear the renowned author speak. To this wish the
Bishop of London opposed himself in vain. Some higher will, possibly
the queen's, ruled Burghley and the Council. Campion was to be allowed
the public disputation he had demanded.

A Public Debate Is Planned

It belongs to the highest authority to command, to the inferior agents to execute. The Bishop of London obeyed but gave no more than a literal compliance. He ordered that on the last day of August a public conference should be held in the chapel of St. Peter ad Vincula (St. Peter in Chains) in the Tower, and deputed Alexander Nowell (Dean of St. Paul's) and William Day (Dean of Windsor) to be the disputants. Both had Calvinist leanings. They were probably chosen for they had previously written and circulated in manuscript a reply to Campion's *Challenge*.[18] "In the guidelines drawn up before the first debate by either the debaters or the Bishop of London, it was agreed that they would abstain from angry words and *ad hominem* [personal] arguments, ground their case firmly in Scripture, and insist that Campion's was rooted in human tradition."[19]

Every advantage was to be taken to secure victory to the right side. The two Deans were to be the attacking parties; Campion was to reply to their objections, but forbidden to give any of his own. They were to have all the time and all the assistance and books they required for preparation; Campion was to be apprised neither that there was to be a conference, nor of the time of it, nor of the subjects in dispute, till an hour or two before he was led, under strong guard, to the chapel. No allowance was to be made for his racked and tortured body and distressed mind; no comfortable chair to rest in, not even a table to lean against; no books to refresh his memory were to be provided for him; no equal notary for his side.

The conference was to be public, but there were restrictions upon entrants. A contemporary account, after describing the unfair conditions, says: "Such was the disputation in the Tower with Mr. Campion and others where men were prohibited with bills and tipstaves [writs and court messengers] to enter. And many a knock on the head received for offering to hear; and much money spent to get places."[20]

Lake and Questier remark:

> What is really remarkable is the fact that this extraordinary event should have been allowed to take place at all. That it was allowed was a sure sign of the polemical discomfort inflicted on the regime by the Jesuits' tactics. It shows, in short, how effective Campion's campaign for a "fair" hearing had been, for having failed definitively

to break or turn him the regime clearly now felt constrained to con-
cede him at least the appearance of such a hearing. Evidently, with
Campion now in their grasp, some people thought that it was essential to address the questions that Campion's polemicizing had raised
and popularized.[21]

Persons records: some Catholics, once inside the Tower "to hear the
disputations, finding opportunity stepped aside unto the holes of some
secluded priests, to visit and salute those servants of Christ."[22]

The program of the conferences, debaters, subjects, and notaries
eventuated as follows, although at the start it was not known exactly how
many sessions there would be in all:[23]

Morning Session: 8:00 – 11:00
Afternoon Session: 2:00 – 5:00

1. August 31: Alexander Nowell and William Day
    Morning topic: The Canon of the Bible (Nowell)
    Afternoon topic: Faith alone (Day)
    Notaries: William Charke and William Whitaker
2. September 18: Roger Goade and William Fulke
    Morning topic: The invisible Church
    Afternoon topic: The fallibility of the Church
    Notaries: William Charke and John Field
3. September 23: Roger Goade and William Fulke
    Morning topic: Christ's presence in the Eucharist
    Afternoon topic: Transubstantiation
    Notary: John Field
4. September 27: John Walker and William Charke
    Morning topics: The Canon of the Bible. The Bible alone.
    Afternoon topic: Faith alone
    Notary: Thomas Norton
5. October 13: Laurence Humphrey and another—canceled at late
    notice.

Possibly William Whitaker was the second choice for October 13,
since he and Humphrey were the two asked by Bishop Aylmer to write
against *Ten Reasons*, which they did.[24]

We see that by the fourth debate they were going round in circles:
Walker and Charke returned to the topics of the first debate. Possibly this
decided the debates' discontinuance.

Apart from the major topics listed, several other issues were briefly raised and disputed, e.g., prayer for the dead, invocation of the saints, the efficacy of Baptism, Communion under one kind, the possibility of keeping the Commandments, the authority of Church Councils, and others. These "side issues" were all intimately linked with the major topics from the Protestant point of view. Prayer for the dead was linked with the dogma of Purgatory, which undermined the all-sufficiency of Christ's Passion if the soul had to undergo anything more after death to enter Heaven. Invocation of saints competed with Christ the one Mediator. Baptism challenged the all-sufficiency of faith which was alone necessary for salvation, while the authority of Councils threatened *sola Scriptura* (Bible alone).

Doctrinal Context of the Debates

The *Thirty-Nine Articles of Religion* represent the doctrinal position of the Church of England that emerged from the Church in Convocation in 1563. By an Act of Parliament in 1571 the clergy of the Church of England were required to subscribe to them. The *Articles* were composed to exclude Roman Catholics and Anabaptists, clarifying the limits of belief within England. This compromise became the standard of doctrine against which dissent was to be judged, remembering that, even within the State Church, Protestants were not always in agreement. The articles were strongly influenced by the confessions of Augsburg and Wurttemberg and, to a lesser degree, the teachings of the Calvinists.[25]

The debates between Campion and the State have to be understood against the backdrop of the Elizabethan Settlement and in relation to the doctrine contained within the *Thirty-Nine Articles of Religion*.

The First Debate

Thursday, August 31. When the day came, some Catholic prisoners— Fr. Ralph Sherwin, Fr. James Bosgrave, Fr. John Hart,[26] Mr. Thomas Pounde, and others—were conducted with Campion to the venue, the chapel of St. Peter ad Vincula.[27] They found the place as full as it would hold.[28]

Strict silence was imposed upon all of them, except Campion and Sherwin.[29]

The two sides of the chapel were fitted out for the tournament. At one side were two seats for the two Deans, in front of them a table covered with books; to their right and left a quantity of lower seats for the assistants of the principal combatants, each of whom held a copy of *Ten Reasons*. At the opposite side, a stage of some grandeur was erected for the ministers, nobles, and peers, present in large numbers. Between the two was another table, likewise covered with books, with seats for the two notaries: William Charke, the preacher of Gray's Inn, and William Whitaker, the Regius Professor of Divinity at Cambridge. Charke had answered Campion's *Challenge*, and Whitaker his *Rationes Decem*. In the middle of the chapel were a number of little stools, with a strong guard of soldiers around them, for the Catholic prisoners. All eyes were upon Campion. He was the one they had so eagerly come to see.

Behind the guards, the people were allowed to find what room they could. Among them were Catholics who were bold enough to take notes of this and of the other conferences. Some of their accounts survive today. A friend of Bombino had access to them at the English College in Rome and translated them into Latin to be printed within Bombino's biography. Portions of others appeared in print centuries later. These manuscript accounts, along with Bombino's and Bartoli's accounts, were gathered together into one book for the first time in 1999.[30] Among them are manuscript accounts of the second, third, and fourth debates, given to John Foxe, the Protestant martyrologist, by Topcliffe, the priest-catcher, who found them in the house of William Carter, the recusant printer hanged in 1584.

There was another Catholic present, who wrote a life of Campion, afterwards translated at Paris.[31] He noticed Campion's sickly face and mental weariness: "worn with the rack, his memory confused, and his force of mind almost extinguished."[32] Yet for all this, he says, "They heard Father Edmund reply to the subtleties of the adversaries so easily and readily . . . and bear so patiently all their contumely, abuse and derision . . . that a good part of the audience, even those ill-affected towards him for religious reasons, quite admired this virtue in him."[33] The second remark (about ready replies) contradicts the first ("memory confused"), for, as is confirmed by reading the various transcripts, one cannot say Edmund's memory was even affected. What is remarkable is that he had an answer "so easily and readily" for *every* objection that was levelled at him, from Scripture or Councils or Fathers or theology—and this without any warning or preparation.

Nowell opened the conferences. They had come to seek the truth—not for themselves, for they had found it—but to help Campion and his fellows, and to do them good, if God permitted. Not that they had much hope of a man so proudly impudent as, like a new Goliath, to challenge all the divines of England—a challenge which he clearly thought ever to avoid, for he could never be found; but the *miles gloriosus* [vain-glorious soldier] had been caught, and now had to make good his boast. He need not complain of being unprepared, because the matter of disputation would be taken from the beginning of his bragging book which he had just written. They asked him first, then, how he dared (in the preface to *Decem Rationes*) to charge the queen's most merciful government with *inusitata supplicia* (strange cruelty), and the bishops with preparing for him *tormenta non scholas* (tortures instead of conference), when the greater cruelties of Mary's reign were still remembered by all English men.

Campion, in his reply, first answered the objection to his modesty, by reciting a passage from his preface to *Ten Reasons:* "If it were confidence in my own talents, erudition, art, reading, memory, that led me to challenge all the skill that could be brought against me, then I were the vainest and proudest of mortals, not having considered either myself or my opponents. But if, with my cause before my eyes, I thought myself competent to show that the sun here shines at noon-day," my fervor may be pardoned. As to his hiding, everyone knew it was not for fear of arguments. As to the conditions of the discussion, though they were clearly most unjust, yet he accepted them. He had challenged them; they had met him on the field he had indicated, but they had taken care to deprive him of his arms, for the arms of the debater are books and preparation. He had not been given time for thought. As for books, even his notes had been taken from him. Was it an answer to his challenge to rack him first, then to deprive him of all books and set him to dispute? When life was in question, with the gallows before and the rack behind, the mind was hardly free for philosophy. He did not compare the cruelty of the English with that of others; he only complained of the positive tortures inflicted. He never persecuted, and it was folly to make distinctions when there was no difference, for the Elizabethan racks were as bad as the Marian executions. He had experience, and he had rather be hanged than racked.

Upon this ensued the conversation which I quoted in the last chapter, to show the impossibility of believing the confessions ascribed to Campion. The account quoted by Bombino adds a few touches. Campion told Hopton he did not complain of what he had suffered, he only deplored the sufferings of Catholics, who were daily treated in the prisons like thieves and murderers.[34] The audience was sensibly moved at this, when Beale interposed, and said that the racking and torture was not for religion, but for treason; whereupon Campion rose, and with indignation, rose up and cried out:

> If anyone, setting aside my religion, dare charge me with any crime whatsoever, I make no plea; inflict on me all the extreme examples of your cruelties.[35]

On this a significant silence ensued, and Campion went on to say what questions had been put to him on the rack, and why he had refused to answer them, as quoted in the last chapter.

The Canon of the Bible

In the opening debate Campion's opponents were Alexander Nowell and William Day who began by referring to a specific point in dispute. Behind this specific point—what books are to be counted as part of the Canon—lay important parts of the Protestant agenda. The Protestants believed in salvation by faith alone, but that doctrine seemed to be contradicted by the "faith without works is dead" passages in chapter two of the *Epistle of James*. There was evidence that Luther dealt with this inconvenience by rejecting the *Epistle of James* as an "epistle of straw" and casting doubts on its place within the Canon. The Protestants also rejected prayers for the dead because, in their view, at the moment of death the die is cast. We have been saved by faith. The practice of prayers for the dead was useless and dangerous because it implicitly, if not explicitly, denied the all-sufficiency of faith. The problem for the Protestants was that the *Second Book of Maccabees* explicitly commended prayers for the dead on the basis of the pharisaic belief in the resurrection: "For if he were not expecting that those who had fallen would rise again, it would have been superfluous and foolish to pray for the dead. But if he was looking to the splendid reward that is laid up for those who fall asleep in godliness, it was a holy and pious thought. Therefore he made atonement for the dead, that they might be delivered from their sin" (12:43–45).

In short there was motive behind this debate. Luther was the originator of the *sola fides* (faith alone) doctrine. If it could be shown he wanted to manipulate the Canon of Scripture to safeguard this innovation, then it would undermine the doctrine itself. The Protestants, then, had two tasks. They needed to show that, either he said no such thing about the *Epistle of James* and that Campion was guilty of misrepresenting Luther, or that, if he did, it was no different from the doubts raised about the Epistle by the early Fathers. They began by denying outright that Luther had rejected the *Epistle of James*.

We have seen that Campion was denied any books. His adversaries crudely took advantage of this to lead the disputation to a question of correctness of quotation. Campion had written: "What made that crime-laden apostate Luther call the *Epistle of St. James* 'contentious, turgid, arid, a thing of straw, and unworthy of the Apostolic spirit'?[36] Desperation. (*Ten Reasons*, reason no. 1). According to Tresham's account of the first debate, a copy of Luther's book, *The Babylonian Captivity*, was brought to Campion. After a few cavils, he was bidden to find the places he had referred to, and he was only able to show a passage where Luther doubted the apostolic origins of the Epistle. He could find nothing nearer than this: "some affirm that the Epistle of James is unworthy of the Apostolic spirit." But this, he said, indicated Luther's mind. The quotations he had made were taken from the editions printed in Jena (Thüringen, Germany). The editions used in England were those of Wittenburg or Strasburg, which had been purged, for, after his death in 1546, Luther's scholars and supporters, ashamed of his shameless errors, had pruned and purged many things he left in writing. If he might be allowed to send to Germany for copies, he would show the places cited. The Emperor and the Duke of Bavaria would take care to send the editions he sought. On this they unceremoniously called him a liar, falsifier, and forger, and laughed at him for talking of emperors and dukes, as if they cared for him and his controversies. Nowell finished his little tirade in Latin: *Ergo, impudentissime mentiris, Campiane.* (Therefore, you are lying most shamefully, Campion.)[37] Campion's only resource was to appeal to the Catholics around him, whether it was not notorious that Luther had written what he had alleged; and their unanimous assent was all he could oppose to the dishonest triumph of the two Deans. Despite his weak state of body, Campion, if they are to be believed, rose up from his seat, cast up and flung about his hands and arms, knocked and beat upon the book, with loud voice and sharp countenance affirming that all their printed books were false, whereupon Nowell broke out with an insult in Latin: *Os impudens* (You impudent mouther).[38]

Nowell and Day later defended the rudeness by saying it was provoked by the bad behavior of Pounde and Campion:

> Truth it is, but upon his often and fierce affirmation that all the printed books of Luther in England were false; and upon Pounde's odious interpellations [interjections] (as, "We know you to be a good Terence man") [i.e., "Mr. Nowell, we know you are very knowledgeable in the Roman poet Terence—but not so in theology"] and his most scornful looks through his fingers, staring upon him continually while he was reasoning with Master Campion, to put him out of his memory; he [Nowell] being offended both with Pounde's mockings, words and looks, and with Campion's shameless sayings, brake out with *Os impudens*, as he thinks, most deservedly on their parts.[39]

Of course, Campion's Catholic apologists exposed the dishonesty over Luther, who had written: "*The Epistle of James*, I count as the writing of no Apostle"; "truly an epistle of straw . . . with no evangelical character"; "wholly inferior to the apostolic majesty"; "unworthy of an apostolic spirit"; and so on.[40] Campion had not unfairly cited an offhand remark given once—for Luther's opinion was notorious; he had attacked the *Epistle of James* in no less than four printed works.

Fr. Bartoli says an original unexpurgated copy of Luther's works ("the virgin text of the Jena edition") was found not long afterward in London. Campion's opponents were confronted with the material and "the unfortunate men were obliged in spite of themselves to put on a good countenance."[41] Yet they ignored this inconvenient fact in their later published account, and stuck to their denial of Luther's statements. In spite of their defiance, Campion had been vindicated.

Campion's challengers now proceeded to justify Luther's expressed doubt about the Epistle of James's rightful inclusion in the Canon. First they called to their side the historian Eusebius, bishop of Caesarea (314–40 A.D.). Campion responded that Eusebius was not of this view but was simply reporting the view of a minority of people. Moreover, since the Canon had not yet been defined by the Church, it was not offensive to canvas such views. However, after the Church had determined that the *Epistle of James* was, in fact, canonical, it was blasphemous for Luther or anyone else to doubt its authenticity. In Bartoli's account, Father Campion did more. He showed that the *Epistle of James* had always been held by the Fathers of the Church to be canonical Scripture, and so accepted by the Church for all those centuries up to the present time.

Campion's adversaries called to their witness two epistles of St. Jerome, and especially his *Prologus Galeatus* which was printed in the front of all Bibles. This towering Biblical authority left out of the Canon the two *Books of the Maccabees* as well as other books deemed to be apocryphal. To this Fr. Campion pointed out that the prologue of St. Jerome referred only to the books of the Old Testament and not to the Epistle of James which is in the New Testament. It was true that Jerome did not include *Maccabees* and certain other books because he was referring to the Old Testament as recognized by the Jews. Jerome was not intending to exclude those other books from the Canon. Campion then went on the offensive. In *The City of God*, St. Augustine, a contemporary of St. Jerome, "expressly writeth this that the Jews receive not the Maccabees in their canon, but that the Church doth." Campion then really went on the attack. He pointed out that St. Augustine in his *De Doctrina Christiana* listed all the books of canonical Scripture. That list included the *Epistle of James*, the *Books of the Maccabees*, and the other contested books. Not only that, but the Canon was confirmed by the Third Council held in Carthage and again by the General Council held in Trullo.

The Protestant response to these facts was to make a distinction between books meant for faith, and these other books which were meant for the reform of manners. This view is expressed in the *Thirty-Nine Articles* at Article 6. Here all the books and letters of the New Testament (including James), together with the books of the Old Testament (which are specifically named), are accepted as canonical. The other books are also named and dealt with thus: "And the other Books (as Jerome saith) the Church doth read for example of life and instruction of manners; but yet doth it not apply them to establish any doctrine."

This equivocal attitude to the Canon of Scripture was rejected by Campion who argued that no such distinction was in the mind of St.

Augustine or the bishops in Council. The Council declared all these books to be the true Word of God and so arguments of faith can be determined from them. At this point the debate degenerated into personal abuse by the Protestants (*Impudentissime quamtes!*—"Most impudent as you are!"), but not by the Catholics, although Father Sherwin did at one point retort to Nowell: "I would not be of your religion one quarter of an hour to gain the value of the whole world."[42] In the afternoon session, Sherwin was on fire, defending the Catholic Faith with all zeal, so much so that his opponents tried to shout him down.

> Their protests not sufficing to make him be quiet, they raised their voices higher in an imperious manner used there, saying, "Keep your tongue to yourself." To this he replied: "I shall keep my tongue to myself, and my faith too."[43]

After this riposte they decided that, on account of his irascibility, Father Sherwin should not be allowed to attend any of the subsequent days. From now on, Father Campion would be on his own.

Mr. Nowell then recapitulated his arguments. When Father Campion asked for the same privilege, it was denied.

So ended the morning session.

Faith Alone

The crowd that came to the afternoon session was much greater.[44] The chapel was already full; hence many must have stayed outside.

This session focused largely on two themes, the authority of Scripture and the doctrine of justification by faith alone.

Mr. Day led the afternoon case for the Protestants. He referred to remarks made by Pope Leo IV in which he said that the authority of the Evangelists came first, then Councils, then chief Pastors, and then the Doctors of the Church who interpreted Scripture "indifferently" (impartially). What could the word "indifferently" be taken to mean? The Catholics pointed out the problem with this: who is to judge which Doctors are impartial or even what being impartial really means? Citing St. Matthew's Gospel, 18:17, the Catholics referred to the words Christ spoke to the twelve disciples when He said that the Church was the arbiter of disputes between Christians: "If he refuses to listen even to the Church, let him be to you as a Gentile and a tax collector." Jesus then said to His disciples: "Truly, I say to you, whatever you bind on earth shall be bound in heaven, and whatever you loose on earth will be loosed in heaven" (Matthew 18:18), and "He who hears you hears me" (Luke 10:16). The Protestant response was to push the argument further by insisting that Councils had no promise of the assistance of the Holy Spirit and so can make mistakes. The Catholics responded again by an appeal to Scripture: chapter 15 of the Acts of the Apostles. In that chapter, the circumcision controversy, the first major doctrinal dispute in the Church, was decided by the Council of Jerusalem. The conclusion of the Council and its definition began with the words: "For it has seemed good to the Holy Spirit and to us" (*Acts* 15:28).

This matter having been exhausted, the doctrine of justification by faith alone was then addressed. This doctrine lay at the heart of the Protestant account, a doctrine which Campion had excoriated in his writings and for which he was now to be held accountable.

Article 11 of the *Thirty-Nine Articles* says this about "the Justification of Man":

> We are accounted righteous before God, only for the merit of our Lord and Saviour Jesus Christ by faith, and not for our own works or deservings. Wherefore that we are justified by faith only is a most wholesome doctrine, and very full of comfort; as more largely is expressed in the *Homily of Justification*.

Added to this is Article 12 on "Good Works":

> Albeit that good works, which are the fruits of faith and follow after justification, cannot put away our sins and endure the severity of God's judgment, yet are they pleasing and acceptable to God in Christ, and do spring out necessarily of a true and lively faith, insomuch that by them a lively faith may be as evidently known as a tree discerned by the fruit.

The Protestants acknowledged that the word *sola* (alone) was not to be found in the Scripture, but they argued that the ancient Fathers of the Church interpreted Scripture in that precise manner. They said that St. Basil, St. Hilary, and one other (unnamed) Father had the same view as Luther.

Father Campion responded by saying that the Fathers were making a comparison between the Law (as understood by the Jews) and faith in the atoning works of Christ. But the Fathers' understanding of faith only was not Luther's. On the contrary, he argued, the Fathers were speaking of the words of St. Paul to be found in the Letter to the Galatians: "For in Christ Jesus neither circumcision nor uncircumcision is of any avail, but faith working through love" (*Galatians* 5:6). Since St. Paul linked together both faith and love, then faith alone cannot justify. The Protestants found difficulty in responding to the logic of this argument and so Father Campion followed up with a further appeal to St. Paul: "If I have all faith, so as to remove mountains, but have not love, I am nothing" (*1 Corinthians* 13:2). St. Paul goes on to say what love is, and how it is manifested in the way we do good works.

> *Protestants.* Unto which the Protestants said that he [St. Paul] spoke of the faith of miracles.
>
> *Catholics.* But reply was made by the Catholic, Mr. Sherwin, that whereas St. Paul said "if I have all faith," of necessity their only faith whereof they boast and brag of so much must be contained in that clause or else they must have no faith.
>
> *Protestants.* And unto this silence was their answer.[45]

The Catholics then concluded their case with reference to the Epistle of St. James, especially at the end of the second chapter where the Apostle says, "For as the body apart from the spirit is dead, so faith apart from works is dead." For the Catholics, "works were to faith that which the soul is to the body." The life of faith is good works (especially referred to as charity and hope), they said, and so together are the cause of our salvation. Moreover, St. Augustine in chapter 15 of his *De Fide et Operibus* (On faith and works) said that justification by faith alone was heresy, that this heretical doctrine dated back to the time of the Apostles, and that Saints John, Peter, Jude, and James wrote their epistles to confound this heresy.

The Protestants conceded that good works were in fact necessary, but the individual derived no personal merit for them because the word *merit* could not be found in the Scriptures. In other words, we should do good works as an expression of our faith, but these good works earn us no credit and especially so in terms of salvation. The Catholics responded by saying that the absence of the word "merit" meant nothing, that this was the clear meaning of Scripture, and that in any case a lot of other key words which by common consent encapsulate fundamental doctrines, such as *Trinity* and *consubstantial*, were not in Scripture either.

Perhaps Campion, who never had much reason to think that the object of this debate was to sift the truth, conceived some scruple about his earlier impatience in this encounter and resolved to embrace the next humiliation that offered itself. It was not long in coming.

A text was in dispute; they offered him the Greek Testament. Finding the print too small, he put it away from him. The Deans nodded at one another, *Graecum est, non legitur.* (It is Greek; he cannot read it.) Campion only smiled, and accepted the rebuff, thus allowing it to be imagined that he was no Greek scholar. I have myself copied his own letters from the Stonyhurst manuscripts, wherein are sundry apposite Greek quotations, written in a scholarly hand, which leaves no doubt of his familiarity with Greek. Yet when, in the subsequent parts of the conference, the Deans handed to him the texts of St. Basil and St. Gregory of Nazianzus, it seems he only read them in a whisper, audible to Mr. Stollard, who held the books for him, whom he called on to witness that he could read. Mr. Stollard did not refuse at the time, but after Campion's death he authorized the Deans to quote him as saying: "If he did read at all, he read the worst that ever I heard."[46] Perhaps he read as they read at Prague, with the Bohemian pronunciation. Anyhow, Campion rested quietly under this childish imputation of ignorance.

The result was not unfavorable. Campion's meekness was, perhaps, more effectual than his logic. The two Deans later complained in print that when they tried to assure people of the outcome of the debate, "divers gentlemen and others, neither unlearned nor of themselves evil affected, gave not much credit to our sayings"[47] and even considered that Campion had the best of the argument. This opinion they aimed to correct by their publication, though they suspected some "will cavil at this, as our biting of a dead man, whom being alive, they will say, we could not all match."[48]

Philip Howard

One of the illustrious converts that Campion made on this occasion was Philip Howard, Earl of Arundel, born in 1557. Eldest son of the Duke of Norfolk, he was at that time a Protestant and a courtier, quite immersed in pleasures and extravagance. He was the queen's favorite when he made his appearance at court at the age of eighteen. Yet, attending this debate at the age of twenty-four, the holy Jesuit's words made a deep impression on him: "by what he saw and heard then, he easily perceived on which side the truth and true religion was, though at that time, nor till a year or two after, he neither did, nor intended to, embrace and follow it; and after he did intend it, a good while passed before he did execute it."[49] He was converted, and finally received into the Church in 1584. As he was about to flee to the Continent, he was captured and thrown into prison. He spent eleven long years there, reading, praying, and meditating. He was condemned to death, but the sentence was postponed by the queen's intervention. He fell seriously ill and died in prison in 1595. The following inscription carved by him can still be read in the Tower of London, in one of the cells in which he was detained: *Quanto plus afflictionis pro Christo in hoc saeculo, tanto plus gloriae in futuro* (the more suffering for Christ in this life, the more glory in the future). St. Philip Howard is one of the Forty Martyrs of England and Wales.

Peace at No Price

Campion's conduct in this controversy is completely in accordance with the view of his character which I have given above (chapter 4). To him the foremost question was ever, not the settlement of controversy, but the peace of his own soul.

In spite of the eloquent·confidence of his *Rationes Decem*, and his trenchant condemnation of all Protestant doctrines, there was in him a conciliatory vein, and he would have been one of the first to hold out the olive-branch if he could have found any desire of peace in his opponents. The two Deans declare that, at the end of the conference, Master Campion and they had "now come to a very near point of agreement in the question of justification"[50]—for Campion's line was not to quarrel about words, but to see whether an inaccurate formula might not cover an honest sense. He really saw the root of the evil. It was the party spirit which divided men into factions who were determined to quarrel and to erect any question into a matter of dispute. Samuel Butler characterizes such men as "so perverse and opposite as if they worshipped God for spite."[51] They scanned their opponents' words with the benevolence of a barrister cross-examining a hostile witness.

Controversy was a passion. The sermons at Paul's Cross were attended by prince and court, the magistrates of the city, and a vast conflux of common people. The women and shopkeepers argued of predestination and church-government, and determined perplexed cases of conscience. At the sermons in the Temple, where Canterbury was preached in the morning and Geneva in the afternoon (in 1585), there were almost as many writers as hearers.[52] All this controversial bias took its complexion from an ingrained political animosity to the pope, who must be the Antichrist, and if not wrong in one point, must be so in another. "No peace with Rome" was a principle of faith and morals. Campion did nothing towards eradicating this false idea, which really turned "religion into rebellion and faith into faction";[53] his *eirenikon* (peace-proposal), on the matter of justification, was construed into a confession of defeat, his meekness was mere ignorance covering a colossal pride. For he had to do with a religion, the first dogma of which was that all its opponents were the brood of the devil and that their very virtues were a snare of the Evil One transforming himself into an angel of light.

> Nowell and Day record the end of the first day: Indeed when we had continued very long, and the sun shining upon our faces in at the South windows, and the throng being very great, and by occasion of both, the heat so intolerable, that some of us were fain to go out of the chancel to take breath, and to return again; and Master Campion and we being now come to a very near point of agreement in the question of justification (as is afore noted in the end of our conference) we turning to Master Lieutenant, said, "If it shall so please you, let us here make an end." "With a good will," said he; and so we broke off.[54]

In Nowell and Day's book it is made to appear that the only parties aggrieved by the reports which were made of this first day's disputation were the Protestants, whom everybody for some days after supposed to have got the worst of it. Under this imputation they rested quite contentedly for two years or more after Campion's death, when they published their own account, in which they said:

> We trust that all those Catholics . . . that have any spark of shamefulness left, may blush for Master Campion's sake, being so manifestly

deprehended [caught] in so many lies so braggingly avouched, and
in print in the Latin tongue published to the world.[55]

Unfortunately, these Catholic pamphlet accounts of the first disputation, against which Nowell and Day wrote, have not survived. The single
extant manuscript account, found among the papers of Campion's friend,
Thomas Tresham, was not discovered until 1828 and remained unpublished until it was transcribed by Sophia Crawford Lomas and printed by
the Historical Manuscript Commission in 1903–4. It is in English, the
language of the debate. However, it must have been printed (or at least
circulated), wholly or partly, some time in 1581 or 1582, for Nowell and
Day quote and rebut two passages of it.[56]

> The Catholics planned to publish them. In 1582, Dr. Allen recorded:
> But these disputations are to be published, and long since should
> have been; but, having but hard means to print, and few presses and
> many other books in hand, it could not yet be done.[57]

I have used the Tresham account as my main text for the first debate.
For additional Catholic accounts of the first day, one must turn to such
secondary sources as contemporary or near contemporary biographical
and historical accounts by authors who apparently had access to these
pamphlets and other sources. Of the secondary sources dealing with
Campion, the two fullest accounts of the disputations were written by Fr.
Bombino and Fr. Bartoli. The accounts of the debates by both Catholics
and Protestants agree on the order and substance of the arguments
presented.[58]

The Second Debate

No other conference was held till Monday, September 18. These eighteen days must have presented to Campion a wonderful contrast to the
turmoil of the previous month. Whether it was merely the monotony
of the prison, or whether his memory was impaired through sickness,
he had lost track of time, and the eighteen days had been but a week
to him: "about a sennight [seven nights: a week] past," he said, "there
came hither some who disputed with me about the first part of my book,
they being thereunto prepared, and I brought hither altogether unprovided." Then he went on to make the same complaint as Nowell and Day

had done, but in a contrary sense: "There were at that time such as did note, and afterwards reported our conference. But I understand there be many things published thereof more than truth is, and that I am belied in print."[59] He therefore demanded a notary on his own part. In the report published by authority, this complaint is made much more general, so as seemingly to apply to everything that had been reported of his acts in the prison: "I have been ill dealt withal already, and things heretofore spoken by me have been mistaken, and published in print otherwise than I ever meant."[60]

Bartoli says that, after the first debate, one of the noble ladies of court, who listened to Fr. Edmund most attentively right to the end, and observed with admiration his knowledge and virtue, and how he had beaten two theologians at once, openly said what a great imprudence it would be if the queen were to grant that man his wish to be heard freely in public: "All the world would follow him and we would all become Papists," she said.[61]

The Privy Council agreed with her. The first debate was held in a chapel, but this and the remaining ones were held in the hall of Lieutenant Hopton's house at the Tower,[62] so that the people might be more easily excluded than they could be from a public church. Only twenty-nine persons were present.[63] Among them were Sir Owen Hopton, Lord Clanricard, Sir William Gorge, Sir Thomas Heneage, Sir Nicholas Poynds, and others.[64] No Catholic prisoners accompanied Campion this time.

New disputants were chosen: Dr. Roger Goade (Goad, Goode), Provost of King's College, Oxford, and Dr. William Fulke, Master of Pembroke College, Cambridge. Fulke, a noted controversialist, was a Radical Protestant, or Puritan. He had been at school with Campion at Christ's Hospital, London, nearly thirty years before.[65] They were seated at a table, and had certain books about them. Charke (as before) and John Field (replacing Whitaker) sat as notaries. Opposite them, on a stool, sat Campion, having only a Bible. Fulke began. "Let us pray," he said, and he and the whole audience knelt. Fulke prayed that the solemn act might confirm the faithful and convert or confound the blind. When that prayer was over, Campion knelt and prayed by himself. When seated again, he made the sign of the cross on his forehead and breast, saying the words aloud in Latin.

The official Protestant report relates:

> After Master Dr. Fulke had made a godly prayer for direction in that
> action, that it would please God to confirm the faithful, and to con-
> found the obstinate and willful, and Campion, denying to pray with
> them, had superstitiously . . . becrossed himself, Master Dr. Fulke
> began with this preface in effect:
> "Whereas there hath been some proceeding with you before,
> and we are come by order to the third chapter of your book, where
> you slander our Church of England and the whole Church of God,
> for the definition of the Catholic Church, for we define it so, as it
> should be invisible: we come to prove both by the Scriptures and
> Fathers, that it is invisible. But this I would have known unto you,
> that our purpose is not to deal by discourse, but briefly by logical
> arguments, according to the order of schools."[66]

Then, not to avoid the conference, but to make the audience
understand the conditions of it, Campion complained of his want of
preparation:

> I wish you would consider it to be God's cause which we have in
> handling, and I would you would dispute to have the truth known,
> rather than to have victory. And if you did so, the better I came pro-
> vided for the disputations, the better the truth should be sifted and
> discussed. But I hope the truth is so plain that it will suffice at this
> time to defend itself.[67]

Not only was Campion refused opportunity to question his foes as
they questioned him; while his foes had many books in front of them, he
was allowed only a Bible as a source. That was all they gave him; he had
no books, no writing materials and no freedom to consult with anyone.
Campion remonstrated with his disputants about the unfairness of the
way the debate was structured, the misrepresentation of the first debate
in the official published record,[68] and the fact that he was given very short
notice to prepare. (This time, as a show of good manners, the heretics
had informed him two days before the debate what part of his book he
should be ready to defend next time.)[69] Fulke suggested that Campion
was given as much notice as they, to which Campion sharply responded,
"The contrary doth appear by your heap of books ready prepared before
you."[70]

The Invisible Church

The dispute was whether the Church was visible or invisible. The first part of no. 19 of the *Thirty-Nine Articles* states:

> The visible Church of Christ is a congregation of faithful men, in which the pure word of God is preached and the Sacraments be duly ministered according to Christ's ordinance in all those things that of necessity are requisite to the same.

The Reformers held that the Church could then at various times be invisible when there was no congregation of men faithful to the Gospel in the sense that they, the Protestants, understood fidelity to the Gospel. Moreover, and this was the crucial point, if the Church was at times invisible, Rome could not claim the primacy in teaching authority that it did claim. For Catholics, the true Church, i.e., the Church set up by Christ as reported in the Gospels, was always visible, its continuity throughout the ages being one of its essential qualities.

To the Catholic notion of a visible Church, Fulke objected that the Church in Heaven is invisible. Campion explained that since this is obviously so, when he said that the Church was visible, he was only speaking of the Church militant, on earth. Fulke told him that this was quibbling, eating his own words, and so on. Finally, they did agree the debate was over the Church on earth.

Dr. Fulke began his case by referring to the People of God in the Old Testament which he refers to as the true Church. The prophet Elijah was being persecuted by King Ahab and his wife Jezebel for exposing the god Baal as no god at all, and then killing the prophets of Baal. Elijah then fled as the King's wrath was turned against him and in a cave he complains to the God of Israel how his faithfulness to God by destroying the Baals had brought him undone. He believes he is the only faithful man left (1 Kings 19:10). Campion responded by pointing out that Elijah was in Samaria which was only a part of the true religion. Elijah would have known the people of Judah, for example, who were governed by a good king and so "the true religion was professed and the true Church known and visible."

Fulke tried again. Referring to the reigns of the Kings Ahaz (*2 Kings* 16) and Manasseh (*2 Kings* 21), when the Temple of the Lord was defiled by pagan practices, Fulke argued that the Church was not then visible because sacrifice could not be offered. Campion acknowledged that

sacrifice could not be offered in the Temple at that time but said that
made no difference since men of faith could identify each other. In any
case, there is a difference between the Jewish Church and the Church of
Christ. Jews could only offer sacrifice in one place.

> *Campion.* But the Church of Christ hath many places, and lawful
> for the administration of their Sacraments and rites; for it is lawful,
> and so used in times of persecution, to administer the Sacraments
> abroad in the field, in chambers, and in secret places. And I doubt
> not but that there be many in England that would run twenty miles
> to hear a Mass.

Fulke then proposed arguments using the style of syllogistic logic to
prove his own case and to limit Campion's opportunities to expand on
his case. Even here, Fulke did not carry the day, such dry argumentation
being about as interesting to many observers as watching wet paint dry.
And so Dr. Goade took over.

Goade strongly emphasized the notion of the Church as being made
up of the elect, i.e., those specially chosen by God to be His faithful. Since
God alone knows who are the real believers, the Church is not visible.
Campion's riposte was clear and direct. He agreed with the proposition
that God alone knows who are really faithful. But, in a clear reference to
Article 19, Campion referred to the Protestants' definition of the Church
as "a congregation of faithful men." That is, the elect keep company in
the congregation of the faithful which, as the Article says, is "the visible
Church of Christ." So the logic of Goade's position is that the Church is
in fact visible. Since Goade was left speechless, Campion goaded Fulke to
help him.

> *Fulke.* The Church is a congregation of the elected.

> *Campion.* Can you say any one man to be elected? This man, or that
> man? Which if you can not so say, then cannot you show any one
> man to be of your Church. How then, I pray you, answer you the
> Scripture, or can you say with the Scriptures: *Dic Ecclesiae*? [tell it to
> the Church: *Matthew* 18:17]

> Whereupon Mr. Goade somewhat pausing, Mr. Campion said: "Mr.
> Doctor Fulke, now help him with an answer if you can."

Later, Goade took up Campion's invitation to discuss St. Matthew's Gospel, 18:15–20, where Christ instructed His disciples to settle disputes between them by referring to the Church for the ultimate decision. Since this must always be done, the Church must always be visible. Goade responded with reference to times when the Church is under persecution and the faithful are not known to each other. He urged Campion to say how the rule *Dic Ecclesiae*, "Tell it to the Church," can be observed in such times. Campion answered that the remedy of arbitration is always available even if access to it is restricted in a particular place by persecution: "although persecution be in one place, yet this complaint may be done in divers other places, as the Protestants in Queen Mary's time being persecuted in England, yet they might have this remedy in Germany where their religion was used." This certainly seemed to justify the appeal of Allen and Persons to Philip and Gregory to avenge their brethren in England. Indeed, the difficulty was inseparable from the idea of Church-government as then conceived. During this debate, many thorny points about persecution were mooted.

The debate ended with Campion having the last word. Fulke had argued that belief in the Church was an article of faith, and that since faith is invisible the Church must be invisible. Faith might be invisible, Campion said, but not the object of faith.

> *Campion.* Although faith be invisible, yet the *obiectum fidei* [object of faith] is visible. And to believe in Christ is an article of our faith. Will you conclude, therefore, that Christ could not be seen when He was here on earth in His natural body?
>
> Mr. Campion urging them to reply against these answers, Mr. Fulke and Mr. Goade said that he vaunted himself too much and hath deceived them of the opinion of modesty, which they conceived and heard of him.

Campion's response to this *ad hominem* attack silenced the opposition. He said that

> For humility I would be contented to kiss your feet; but in the truth of Christ I must not by humility give you place; for the Scripture saith: *Non sis humilis in sapientia tua* [be not humble in your wisdom: *Ecclesiasticus* 13:11].

In the manuscript report there are many homely illustrations, telling
and rhetorical, used by Campion, and much winning speech; as when he
said to Goade, who had been quoting Jerome, "I would, Mr. Goade, that
you and I might shake hands together of St. Jerome's religion, that we
might meet together with him in Heaven." No, said the other, "I will not
be of man's religion, further than he is of Christ's."[71]

The session concluded, they adjourned until the afternoon.

The Fallibility of the Church

The audience at the afternoon assembly doubled to sixty persons.[72] It
was a rambling session, and the two doctors asserted dogmatically the
extremest Puritan tenets, whereat Campion marvelled.

The matter under discussion was "whether the Church Militant of
Christ may err in matters of Faith." The Protestant answer was *Yes*, the
second half of Article 19 saying:

> As the Church of Jerusalem, Alexandria, and Antioch have erred,
> so also the Church of Rome hath erred, not only in their living and
> manner of ceremonies, but also in matters of faith.

And Article 21, concerning the authority of General Councils, stated:

> General Councils may not be gathered together without the com-
> mandment and will of princes. And when they be gathered together,
> forasmuch as they be an assembly of men, whereof all be not gov-
> erned with the Spirit and Word of God, they may err and sometimes
> have erred, even in things pertaining unto God. Wherefore things
> ordained by them as necessary to salvation have neither strength
> nor authority, unless it may be declared that they be taken out of
> Holy Scripture.

So Fulke began with an argument based upon the assertion that
"what is incident to every member is incident unto the whole." In modern English, he means that what appertains to an individual, in this case
being in error at least some of the time, must apply to the whole community. So if individuals err, as they do, the Church as a whole can err.
Campion denies the truth of the original assertion but then goes on to
argue that even if it were normally the case, the fact is that Christ promised the Apostles the special assistance of the Holy Spirit to lead them

into all truth (*John* 16:13) This promise was not directed to all members of the Church, but only to the Apostles and their successors.

Dr. Goade, taking over, announced a new argument. Was it not true that the Church in Corinth was in error and had to be rebuked by St. Paul? So also the Church in Galatia? That being the case, did it not follow, then, that the whole Church could err? Campion responds by reference to *1 Corinthians* 4:18: "certain" or "some" of the Corinthian Christians had erred, and "some" does not mean "all." Where the Galatians are concerned, said Campion, St. Paul was speaking generally, as a preacher does, without meaning every individual in the assembly, when he said: "O foolish Galatians, who has bewitched you?" (*Galatians* 3:1)

Goade then went straight to the real issue, the authority of the Church of Rome in matters of faith. If, he said, the Church of Rome has erred in matters of faith, then the true Church has and may err. Campion made great play with Goade's seeming admission that the Church of Rome is the true Church. Goade responded by saying that he would suppose it for the sake of the argument. Then, said Campion, you must prove error in the true Church. I prove it thus, said Goade: the Council of Trent's erroneous teaching on justification. So arose a side-debate on the nature of justification and the possibility of keeping the Commandments. At this point, their Puritanism came to the fore and stunned Edmund with its inherent absurdity. Contrary to Trent, Fulke said, it "is not possible for any man to perform" the law of Christ.

> *Campion.* The law may be fulfilled by this means: in loving God above all things, and thy neighbor as thyself, which a man may well do by the grace of God.

> *Goade.* Note this absurdity, for no man can keep these commandments.

At this, there was a hiss at Campion's position.

> *Campion.* Because there was a hiss given in that I said the commandments might be performed, I beseech you give me leave to explain my mind how the commandments may be performed, and that is: to love God with all his heart so far forth as it is required at his hands, that is, to love Him above all things, to prefer Him before all other riches, to forsake all things for His sake, so that he would

renounce the world and also his life, to cleave and stick to God. And the other, to love his neighbor, that is to be understood to prefer him before any riches, and withal to be ready to please him in that that lieth in him. And in vain was it commanded to be performed, if it were impossible to be performed. And all this may be performed by the special assistance of Almighty God. And, I pray you, let this be noted.

Fulke. It was not Christ's meaning in giving these commandments that they should be performed, but that we, seeing our own infirmities by them, might be still [always] moved to call for mercy.

Campion. Then might Christ as well tell us that we might *not* perform them, and so bid us call for mercy, as to command us *to* perform them, seeing by your reason we may not. But the contrary doth appear in that He commanded it must be performed. For unjust were that father which would command his sons to do certain things which they cannot perform, and withal meaneth that they should not perform it, being plain contrary to his commandment. For how can his will be known but by his express words?

Fulke. No, that cannot be the meaning; but as I have alleged it before, seeing that it is impossible to perform them, every . . . temptation being a sin.

Campion. That is strange, that every temptation is a sin, whereas the Scripture saith: *Beatus vir qui suffert tentationem* [blessed is the man who suffers temptation: *James* 1:12], and by your reason he is *maledictus* [cursed]. And withal it followeth of your position that if one come to the Queen's jewel house and is tempted to steal, if he do resist the temptation, he doth offend in resisting—which is strange in my conceit.

Fulke. It may be strange among the Jesuits, but nothing strange among the servants of God.[73]

Goade then went on to produce several instances in which he claimed Councils had erred, and he was rebutted in kind by Campion. In two cases, despite all their books and preparation, his antagonists were not able to cite their sources except from their own note-book. Campion rejected the authority of note-books and thereby rejected as untrue certain assertions they attributed to St. Augustine or Nicaea II.

Goade charged the Council of Constantinople to have erred in for-bidding the chalice to the laity at Communion. Edmund replied that "it is no matter of faith whether the laity do receive under both kinds." He said, "I do allow that both kinds may be received, so that a man do it with humility and by licence; for so have I seen myself." (It was the custom in Bohemia.) "And I confess that in the primitive Church it hath been said to have been received sometimes under one kind, and sometimes under both; and so may be received again at the appointment and discretion of the Church."[74]

The last of the arguments heralded what would be a center-piece for the opposition when in the third debate they disputed the doctrine of transubstantiation. Goade and Fulke argued that the Church had erred because it had taken away one of the articles of faith to be found in the Creed. This article of faith, they said, was the Ascension of Christ into Heaven. Since the Church taught that Jesus was truly present in the Sacrament, He could not also be in Heaven. Therefore the Church had erred by denying, in effect, the Ascension.

Campion's response is one to which he will frequently return. You cannot limit Christ to the condition of a natural body as the miracle of the Ascension bears witness. It is perfectly possible for Christ, even in His natural body, to do things which no other natural bodied human being can do. For his proofs he referred to Christ walking on water (*Matthew* 14:22–27). He then referred to Christ, in His resurrected body, being able to enter a room even though the doors were shut (*John* 20:19). There followed a dispute over the meaning of the Greek and Latin texts as to whether this event was a miracle or not, Fulke suggesting that it was a "miracle of divine operation that the doors yielded unto our Savior Christ." In other words the doors opened in a way similar to the doors opening for St. Peter when the angel rescued him from prison (*Acts* 12:5–11). Campion's response is strong and to the point.

> And by these words, *clausis ianuis* [the doors being shut: *John* 20:19],
> it is manifest that the doors were not open but shut; and therefore
> He must needs come through the doors or walls. You will not say
> that He came in by a juggling trick. Luther, who was as great an
> enemy to me as you are, thought it a very strange and monstrous
> opinion to say that Christ was not really in the Sacrament.[75]

In referring to Luther, Campion was effectively making clear that Protestants of the Lutheran school, and Protestants of the Calvinist and Zwinglian schools, were in significant disagreement among themselves over the presence of Christ in the Eucharist. Goade made a weak response to Campion: that Luther believed in consubstantiation and not transubstantiation. The English Protestants had earlier used Luther as the paragon of Christian orthodoxy, rescuing Christians from the errors of Catholicism. Luther clearly believed in the Real Presence, however it might be argued that his understanding was faulty.

So Goade quickly changed the direction of the debate to an assertion that St. Augustine thought that there was no miracle wrought in the Sacrament. However, Goade could not say where St. Augustine had said this and Campion averred that he had said no such thing. St. Augustine knew there was no *visible* miracle to astound the human senses, he said, but that was another thing. The miracle was of a spiritual kind not visible to the eyes but only to the eyes of faith. And had not St. Chrysostom used the immortal words, "O great Mystery," of the Sacrament of the Altar, thereby affirming that at the time of the celebration the angels were present.

Earlier, Goade asserted that the Second Council of Nicaea had decreed that angels had bodies. Campion answered that the opinion was no matter of salvation, therefore no matter of faith. Goade held it to be a matter of faith, though not of salvation. "That is strange," said Campion, "show me one such matter of faith," and he went on to class this assertion with the other oddities he had heard:

> Here hath been many strange paradoxes granted this day. I would they were noted: That a thing may be a matter of faith, and no matter of salvation. That baptism taketh not away Original Sin. That if a man be once of the Church, he shall never be out of the Church, and so fall from the Church. That every temptation is sin. That David in committing adultery and murder was not in that act the servant of sin.[76]

On the other hand, we find Campion calling a Greek tense by a wrong name, re-affirming some of his old Oxonian physics, and offering to prove that the heavens are hard as crystal.[77]

The debate concluded with Campion seeking an opportunity to

oppose *their* positions, that is, to question *them* in the way they had spent two days questioning *him*. Fulke responded as one having no say in the matter: "We are therein to be directed by others. Wherefore if it please them to so appoint, we shall be well content." No such opportunity would be offered to Campion, fairness in debate not being on the State's agenda.

When John Field, the notary, published his report of this conference, he had the impudence to say in his preface: "If Campion's answers be thought shorter than they were, thou must know that he had much waste speech, which being impertinent, is now omitted."[78]

The Third Debate

Christ's Presence in the Eucharist

On Saturday, September 23, Campion had another conference with the same two, Fulke and Goade, on the Real Presence and on Transubstantiation, and he complained often that he was only allowed to solve objections and not to prove his point. He was told that at the former conference he had been allowed to use a multitude of words, similitudes, comparisons, and definitions, but that now he was to be cut shorter. He begged, if he was not allowed to dispute in words, to be allowed to controvert in writing, but Fulke refused to refer any request to the Council for any such man as he.

The chief characteristic of this debate was the way in which Fulke and Goade consistently used the technical language of logic to present their objections to Catholic doctrine. They did this because the more discursive approach allowed Campion too much latitude to expound Catholic teaching rather than restrict himself to brief answers to their questions. After all, they saw this debate more as an inquisition and less of a debate as Campion had requested. They were also concerned that the way things were going Campion seemed to be a winner, and they found it difficult to control the direction of the debate. So the theological matters in dispute were, as far as possible, to be argued within the restrictions and, to many, the aridity of philosophical logic.

Fulke and Goade used the first part of the morning session to attempt to recover the ground they had clearly lost in the disputation about the visibility of the Church. In this they seemed to be unsuccessful. So now they moved to the question as to whether or not Christ were really present in the Sacrament of the Eucharist.

The approach taken by Fulke and Goade rested upon the idea that Christ could not be both in Heaven and on earth in the Sacrament. This position was, to say the least, contentious within Anglicanism itself and in reality an unsafe basis upon which they should have proceeded. It indicated that both men were in the extremely Protestant group within the Established Church. Why is this so?

After the death of King Henry VIII, King Edward VI reigned. He and his protectors represented extreme Protestantism. In this reign, two new Prayer Books were published, one in 1549 and the other in 1552. The 1552 Book steered the Church of England to the most extreme Protestant position it would ever take in its entire history. The virulently anti-Roman stance of this new Prayer-Book was made clear in one of the petitions in the *Litany*, asking for deliverance "from the tyranny of the Bishop of Rome."

Moreover, the 1552 Prayer-Book contained the so-called "Black Rubric" at the end of the Communion Service, the purpose of which was to explain the kneeling for Holy Communion. Strictly speaking, it was not a rubric (ceremonial directive), but a theological explanation:

> Lest yet the same kneeling might be thought or taken otherwise, we do declare that it is not meant thereby that any adoration is done, or ought to be done, either unto the Sacramental bread or wine there bodily received, or unto any real and essential presence there being of Christ's natural flesh and blood. For as concerning the Sacramental bread and wine, they remain still in their very natural substances, and therefore may not be adored, for that were idolatry to be abhorred of all faithful Christians. And as concerning the natural body and blood of our saviour Christ, they are in heaven and not here. For it is against the truth of Christ's true natural body to be in more places than in one, at one time.

Here is a complete rejection of any kind of belief in the Real Presence on the basis that since Christ has ascended into Heaven, and His natural body and blood cannot be in more than one place at any one time, He cannot be present in the species of bread and wine.

Following the death of Edward VI, Queen Mary abolished the 1552 Prayer-Book and restored the old religion. Upon the accession to the throne of Queen Elizabeth I in November 1558, Protestantism again became the religion of England. In 1559, the Prayer-Book of 1552 was reissued, but with significant modifications to make it less Protestant and thus more inclusive. This 1559 Prayer-Book omitted the "Black Rubric," to appease the more Catholic-minded of the English people and to set up the compromise we now know as Anglicanism. It seems that Queen Elizabeth, while rejecting "transubstantiation," seemed to approve of some kind of doctrine of the Real Presence. A verse attributed to her authorship said:

> 'Twas God the Word that spake it,
> He took the bread and brake it,
> And what the Word doth make it,
> That I believe and take it.

The queen disliked extreme Protestantism and did not subscribe to the view that described the Eucharistic elements as "bare signs." The Elizabethan settlement of 1559 represented a retreat from the Puritanism of the 1552 Prayer-Book, and recaptured more of a Catholic sense. The point here is that Fulke and Goade were employing an argument which was no longer part of the official religion but one which was characteristic of the Puritans. The *Thirty-Nine Articles* certainly rejected transubstantiation but were not hostile to at least some senses of the Real Presence. For example, Article 25:

> The Sacraments were not ordained of Christ to be gazed upon or to be carried about, but that we should duly use them. And in such only as worthily receive the same, they have a wholesome effect or operation; but they that receive them unworthily purchase to themselves damnation, as St. Paul saith.

But even here the Article is ambiguous. All it says is that Christ did not "ordain" the Sacraments for the purpose of elevation, processions and adoration. But it does not say that it is prohibited. And Article 28:

> Transubstantiation (or the change of the substance of bread and wine) in the Supper of the Lord, cannot be proved by Holy Writ, but is repugnant to the plain words of Scripture, overthroweth the nature of a Sacrament, and hath given occasion to many superstitions.
>
> The Body of Christ is given, taken and eaten in the Supper, only after an heavenly and spiritual manner. And the mean whereby the

Body of Christ is received and eaten in the Supper is faith.

The Sacrament of the Lord's Supper was not by Christ's ordinance reserved, carried about, lifted up or worshipped.

Here again the studied ambiguity of the text, as John Henry Newman pointed out,[79] is capable of a Catholic interpretation. "Transubstantiation" is condemned, but the Article really does not describe what it is condemning. The Article does not condemn all belief in a spiritual presence, but affirms that what is "given, taken and eaten" is the body of Christ. The observation that reservation of the Blessed Sacrament and other specified practices were not introduced out of obedience to "Christ's ordinance" is no more than a statement of the obvious.

That Fulke and Goade adopted the now rejected theological position from which they would launch their attack on Campion's Eucharistic doctrine is a curiosity. No account of this background is provided in the Protestant account of these debates, but we note it here as a matter of considerable historical significance. Campion's antagonists were going well beyond the faith as described in the 1559 Prayer-Book and the *Thirty-Nine Articles of Religion*, that is, the faith prescribed by law in the Acts of Supremacy and Uniformity of 1559.

Notwithstanding the fact that they were not arguing from the legal position of the State but from their personal commitments to extreme Protestantism, Fulke and Goade began the debate.

The first argument was over the meaning of Scripture. Dr. Fulke referred to the passage where Christ says "this cup is the new testament in my blood." In the Catholic account of the debate, Campion intervened by saying that the passage really comes from Luke 22:20, and then disputing the translation. Fulke, clearly irritated, rebuked Father Campion: "You may not appoint me my place, Mr. Campion. My place is out of the first to the Corinthians, chapter 10, verse 16." Unfortunately for Dr. Fulke, he cited the wrong verse. In the Protestant account, Fulke does not prescribe the verse from chapter 10, which is in fact verse 25, and so is not wrong. In any case, the Pauline text is the same version as St. Luke to which Campion referred. The words in question are these: "This cup is the new testament in my blood." In Latin: *Hic calix novum testamentum est in meo sanguine.* Campion translated it: "This is the cup, the new testament in my blood."

Fulke described his argument from Scripture in these terms:

> The cup is the new testament.
> But the natural blood of Christ is not the new testament.
> *Ergo* [therefore] the natural blood of Christ is not the cup.

Campion rightly pointed out that Fulke's argument is not logically coherent, because, having four terms, it is not a syllogism, which has only three terms. Fulke had used the word "cup" in two senses in the same argument. Initially he uses the word "cup" figuratively for Christ's blood, and then in a literal sense meaning the chalice.

Goade quickly intervened to rescue the situation by proposing different scriptural arguments, again using the syllogism as the preferred mode of arguing. Goade referred to the Israelites' eating *manna* (bread from heaven) as also receiving Christ spiritually as we do in the Eucharist. Goade cited in support of his position the words of St. Paul in 1 Corinthians 10:4: "And did all eat the same spiritual meat, and did all drink the same spiritual drink, for they drank of the spiritual rock that followed them, and the rock was Christ."

In the Protestant account, the argument went like this:

> *Campion.* They did eat *eandem escam spiritualem, the same spiritual grace,* but not the same substance.

> *Goade.* They received the same that we do touching the substance; you can not so avoid the force of this place. Spiritual is added in respect of the corporal signs, which differ between them and us, as shall after appear, but the same spiritual substance in both, as the circumstance of that place enforceth.

> *Campion.* Why, Christ had yet received no substance of flesh, and therefore could not then be present to them substantially in His natural body.

> *Goade.* You reason well for me. Therefore He was present unto them spiritually, as the words are, *eandem escam spiritualem:* And so He is to us present, and not carnally, because Christ had not then taken flesh, and the Fathers did then eat Christ in substance as well as we, therefore the presence and eating in both must needs be spiritual.

> *Campion.* I answer they had the same in a mystery and figure.

Goade. This is no answer. I will easily take it away both by the words following in the text, and also by the manifest circumstance of the place, both which proveth to be clearly the same in substance. They had the same Christ, who is the substance of our Sacraments: *ergo* [therefore] the same substance that we have.

Campion. They had not the same Christ in substance, in their Sacrament.

Goade. The words following are plain to expound the Apostle's meaning: *Et omnes eundem potum biberunt, etc. Petra autem erat Christus. They did all drink the same spiritual drink, for they drunk of the spiritual rock that followed them, which rock was Christ:* Therefore they eating and drinking the same Christ, did eat and drink the same substance. *Campion.* There is a fallacy in [your use of] the word, *eandem, the same.* In a mystery and in signification the same, but in substance, great difference.[80]

Later in the debate, Fr. Campion tried to get Fulke and Goade to understand that they were using the words "natural body of Christ" and "substance" in different ways. Campion was referring to the natural body of Christ after His Resurrection, a body that was not constrained as our bodies are. By way of comparison, he referred to the three children of God in the burning fiery furnace who did not burn even though the property of a natural body in flames is to burn. (*Daniel* 3:23–27). Yet his adversaries continued as if he had not spoken. How could Christ be both in Heaven and in the Sacrament? It was simply not possible, they said, echoing the argument of the Black Rubric. Christ's place was circumscribed and He could not be in two places at one and the same time, they insisted. Campion responded forcefully:

It is not necessary that Christ's body being in the Sacrament miraculously should suffer circumscription, and you might as well jest at the Ascension of Christ and deny it, for if it had the properties of a true body, it should *petere deorsum* [fall downward].[81]

All Goade could do at this point was to suggest that if Christ was bodily present in the Sacrament, He must have two bodies. Campion retorted that Christ had one body in two places, and that the problem with Goade was that he was arguing from the constraints of human philosophy. He was not arguing theologically, engaging all of the data of Revelation as to the nature of Christ's natural body after the Resurrection.

The rest of the morning concentrated on conclusions that Goade and Fulke said flowed from the idea of the Real Presence, conclusions, they said, which were clearly nonsense. For example, Goade argued that if Christ is really bodily present then the wicked could eat His body and so be saved. But this is not possible, since St. Augustine said the wicked do not eat the body of Christ. That being the case, Christ's body is not in the Sacrament.

> Whosoever eateth Christ, the thing or substance of the Sacrament, shall live for ever.
> But none of the wicked or unfaithful shall live for ever.
> *Ergo* [therefore] none of the wicked can eat Christ, being the substance of the Sacrament.

Goade was no doubt relying on no. 29 of the *Thirty-Nine Articles*:

> The wicked and such as be void of a lively faith, although they do carnally and visibly press with their teeth (as S. Augustine saith) the Sacrament of the body and blood of Christ, yet in no wise are they partakers of Christ, but rather to their condemnation do eat and drink the sign or Sacrament of so great a thing.

Campion's response to this kind of argument, a response not included in the Protestant account, was to make a distinction between the objective eating of Christ's body and the effect of that eating on the person who eats it, that effect being dependent upon the person's spiritual state:

> [St. Augustine's] meaning is that the wicked receive not his body to salvation because they receive it unworthily, as when a Jew receiveth baptism for money, or some other filthy lucre or gain and not for the love of Christ. He receiveth true and perfect baptism but to his damnation, except he afterwards repent and believe, which if he do, he shall not again be baptized, but the first baptism shall now work in grace. So as he may be said to believe, though he have received the Sacrament of baptism, not to have received baptism, because he hath not received the effect of baptism, but damnation instead of salvation. So the wicked receive Christ, not with faith, but to their damnation. That is, they receive not worthily or in grace.[82]

Transubstantiation

The afternoon session was more of the same, it becoming clear that the philosophical and theological differences between Campion, on the one hand, and Goade and Fulke on the other, would militate against any agreement being found. Goade and Fulke did not accept the Aristotelian distinction between substance and accidents, the distinction employed by Aquinas and the Council of Trent to define the meaning of transubstantiation. Goade and Fulke would not admit to any idea of a miraculous event occurring at the time of consecration of bread and wine such that Christ's body and blood were truly present even though the elements had all the physical and material properties of bread and wine. They wanted to know if the Sacrament had sensible feelings, as Christ had sensible feelings. Campion responded by saying that Christ, in His resurrected body which could appear and disappear, presented His body to the Apostles so they could verify it was He, physically speaking. The Apostles had doubts about the Resurrection, doubts which were put to rest by His giving His body to be felt by them. But, Campion went on, the Apostles had no such doubt about the Eucharist, having been thoroughly instructed by Christ. They accepted that His true body was present even though "it be not seen nor felt."

The Fourth Debate

The fourth contest was just four days later, on Wednesday, September 27. This time the disputants were Dr. John Walker, Archdeacon of Essex and a preacher of Radical Protestant opinions, with William Charke, who had been reporter at the first two debates. Norton ("Rackmaster-General") acted as notary. These men treated Campion more harshly than any of the former disputants. Unlike their predecessors at the previous three debates, Walker and Charke were not generally considered to be among the most distinguished English divines. Neither had risen to prominent positions in the Church or government or universities. Except for their association with Campion, neither had established a scholarly reputation as a controversialist. Rather, they were known primarily for their preaching and for their rigid Puritan views.[83] Indeed, their opinions were not always those of the Church of England, as Campion pointed out.[84] Walker, indeed, so claimed to be above any non-Biblical source as to declare: "But as for me, I will neither defend Luther, nor Calvin, nor Beza, nor Zwingli. For I am neither a Lutheran, a Calvinist, a Bezian, nor Zwinglian."[85]

The Canon of the Bible

In the morning session, Charke and Walker began aggressively. According to the Protestant account, Charke prayed, "we are here assembled to maintain thy truth against the error and superstition of Antichrist." And Walker, in his opening speech, as the Catholic account relates, went even further:

> This man, having departed this realm, hath joined himself to the man of Rome, our common enemy Antichrist, and now hath returned again into this realm, where he hath wandered from place to place through the greatest part thereof; and in the north country he hath sown such sedition that they now cry out of him and curse him; and now he hath proceeded further, and hath charged us most impudently and falsely with mangling and cutting of the Scriptures.[86]

The Protestant account gives more or less the same from Walker. It sounds much like the formal indictment made against Campion at his trial:

> Gentlemen, ye shall understand that we be sent hither by authority, to talk and confer with one called *Campion*, an Englishman born and brought up in this realm in schools and places where good learning hath been taught, so that he might have been a good instrument in this commonwealth and God's Church; but contrary to his bringing up, his friends' expectation, and hope that this Church might have conceived of him, like an unnatural man to his country, degenerated from an Englishman, an apostate in religion, a fugitive from this realm, unloyal to his Prince, hath not only fled to the man of Rome, an adversary to Christ and his doctrine, but hath gotten a courage from that Romanist with certain other [of] his sectaries, to come into this realm again, to undermine the Gospel of Christ, to seduce God's people, and withdraw her Majesty's lawful subjects to disobedience and sedition, and hath been (disguised in ruffian's apparel) in divers places of this realm, to plant secretly that blasphemous Mass and other Popery, whereunto it appeareth he hath allured many unstable fools; and in Yorkshire where his sectaries

and disciples are apprehended and justly imprisoned, now they rage (as I hear say) and curse him that ever he came there. So ye see what manner of man we are to talk withal. What good we shall do with him, the Lord doth know, other manner of men than we are, and of another calling, were more meet to talk with him than we; notwithstanding we will do our best that we can.[87]

With this preface they began their dispute about the Canon and the sufficiency of Scripture. Dr. Walker, who later in the day protested that he had long left the University, and was no longer dexterous in using his logic and philosophy,[88] did not make a very good figure when, because Campion would not accept his caricature of Catholic doctrine as a good exposition thereof, he bitterly declared:

I have been these two or three days turning and seeking of books to prove that all things necessary to salvation are contained in the Scriptures; and now by this subtle shift and distinction [Campion had agreed to the proposition, with the condition "subject to the interpretation of the Catholic Church"] he hath avoided all; for it is the practice of them to preach and teach one thing; and when they come to defend it, to deny it and maintain another thing.[89]

No. 6 of the *Thirty-Nine Articles* made it clear that the Church of England accepted all twenty-seven books of the New Testament: "All the books of the New Testament, as they are commonly received, we do receive, and account them canonical." It was not open to Luther, Charke, or anyone else to question their canonicity, such disputes having been settled many centuries ago.

Following the Protestant disputants' stated desire to deal once again with the question of which books were canonical Scripture, Campion reminded them of their letter to him last Sunday, saying they were to discuss the authority of the authentic Scriptures. Charke and Walker were determined, however, to go over old ground which need not be reported here.

However, it did become clear that the Protestant objection to the books of the Maccabees was all about prayers for the dead, described as a "holy and pious thought" (*2 Maccabees* 12:45). Charke and Walker contended that this book was, by its own admission, an imperfect work that stood in need of correction and the author in need of God's pardon.

In this they were referring to the final verses of *2 Maccabees* where the author says:

> So I too will here end my story. If it is well told and to the point, that is what I myself desired; if it is poorly done and mediocre, that was the best I could do. (15:37–38)

Campion's response is clear. Look at the next verse, he says. It establishes that what the author, in his humility, is referring to, is his style, not the content. Moreover, said Campion, St. Paul exhibited the same modesty in *2 Corinthians* 11:6 when he, too, apologized for his speaking style ("even if I am unskilled in speaking"), but not for the content of his speeches ("I am not [unskilled] in knowledge").

Then follows an attack on the character of Judith, whose book is one of the disputed books. Campion easily saw off this ill-advised attack, calling to his aid St. Jerome who had praised her highly for her great chastity.

The odd thing here is that the Church of England included the *Book of Judith* as one of the Apocryphal books which, according to Article 6, "the Church doth read for example of life and instruction of manners." How can that be if the principal character in the book is such an unworthy person? Said Charke:

> What think you therefore of the story of Judith, touching the dressing and decking of herself with apparel and ornaments fittest to deceive Holofernes's eyes? And what say you to her lies and prayer that he might be taken with the snare of his eyes looking upon her? The speeches untrue, and the action unchaste in outward appearance, were they (think you) of the Holy Ghost?

Charke despises both the book and Judith herself. He presents a case contrary to the *Thirty-Nine Articles*, the State religion, which he is meant to be defending against Campion's popery. Clearly more leniency was shown by Elizabeth to Protestant dissenters than to Catholic dissenters.

The Bible Alone

The disputants finally move on to the question as to whether or not the Bible contains all teachings necessary for salvation. Campion denies this proposition which is to be found in Article 6:

Holy Scripture containeth all things necessary to salvation: so that whatsoever is not read therein, nor may be proved thereby, is not to be required of any man, that it should be believed as an article of the faith, or be thought requisite or necessary to salvation.

Campion challenged his adversaries to prove from Scripture alone the procession of the Holy Spirit from the Son, and the baptism of babies. (The former is in the Nicene Creed used by Anglicans, and the latter is a practice in the parishes.) They appeared unable to do this, while agreeing that these things were part of the Christian faith. Campion's point is that the Apostles did not write down everything Christ taught them. Charke and Walker maintained that the Apostles did write down everything necessary for salvation. This, of course, cannot be proved. Campion has as his witness St. Ignatius who studied under the Apostle, St. John. The Protestant account records the debate in these terms:

Walker. You have granted that all things are written in the Word, and that such traditions as can not manifestly be gathered out of the Canonical Scriptures are not to be received. Thereupon I reason thus:

The same that the Apostles wrote, the same they delivered in tradition. But they have written and delivered the same things that they read in the Canonical Scripture.

Ergo [therefore] their writings and traditions be all one and the same, *Campion.* The same, that is to say, nothing contrary.

Walker. The same and no other is needful to salvation. Hear the Apostle's words. *1 Cor. 4 . . . Who is my beloved son and faithful in the Lord, who will put you in mind of my ways which are in the Lord, even as I teach everywhere in every Church.* That he wrote and taught in one Church, he wrote and taught in another, and therefore *2 Cor.* 1 he saith . . . *For this is our glory, even the testimony of our conscience, etc. For we write no other things unto you, than which you read and know in deed.* Again, *2 Cor. 2 . . . The same that we are in speech by our Epistles, when we are absent, such we are also when we are present.*

Campion. The same, no contrariety. For there were afterwards many Scriptures that were not then written. How therefore could they teach all things? This Epistle was not then written, and divers others.

The meaning is, they taught one Faith, one Christ, one doctrine; but he speaketh not of the Scriptures.[90]

The argument went back and forth between the players like a tennis ball on a court.

Campion. Christ did teach all, and therefore the Apostles wrote all that Christ taught? *Nego argumentum. I deny the argument.*

Walker. Why, *Haec scripta sunt ut vitam habeamus: These things are written that we may have life* [*John* 20:31]: what need we more?

Campion. Enough is written, but in such sort as was said before, either in general words or special; either discoursed, or touched.[91]

In the Catholic account of this debate, Campion called the Doctor of Grace as his witness:

St. Augustine, writing against one Cresconius, saith that it cannot be vouched out of Scriptures by plain words that heretics' children should not be rebaptized; and many more things in like manner may be added, as that infants should be baptized before they believed, the proceeding of the Holy Ghost from the Father and the Son, that baptism is a Sacrament, and preaching is not, and yet commanded at one time, and that the Eucharist is a Sacrament, and washing of feet is none, and yet both commanded to us at one time. These and such like cannot be proved expressively by Scripture, not by express words; but for these we are referred by the Scriptures unto the Church as in that place where it is said: "let him hear the Church" [*Matt.* 18:17], "obey the pastors" [*Heb.* 13:17]; "if he do not hear the Church, let him be to thee as a heretic" [*Matt.* 18:17], and many such like places. And by this means all things necessary to salvation are contained in Scriptures.[92]

Campion's argument, then, is that in one sense the Scriptures do contain everything necessary for salvation, in that the Scriptures point us to the Church as the ultimate arbiter of what the Gospel is and how it should be received. It does not contain everything necessary for salvation in the way Protestants believe, that one can prove all doctrines necessary from the words contained in the Bible.

Faith Alone

The afternoon session was a rehash of the arguments over justification by faith alone. While the disputants were large on zeal, their arguments lacked the penetration of the disputants in the earlier debates and, in any case, Father Campion simply reiterated the Catholic response.

Walker began the afternoon session by questioning Campion as a parish cleric might drill a child at a catechism lesson. What is the etymology of "faith"? What is the subject of faith? What are the parts of man? In what part is faith? When Campion suggested that they were wasting time,[93] Walker assured him that the questions were leading to a point. What is the subject of hope? In what place of the soul is hope? What was the object of Abraham's hope? However, at the end of a score of questions posed by Walker, the unknown writer of the Catholic account observes that nothing had been concluded. Walker's point is equally elusive in the Protestant version. Apparently to save his colleague, Charke took over:[94]

> *Charke.* If there be anything specially labored and therewithal plain and evident in all the Scriptures, it is this profession: *sola fides justificat* [faith alone justifies]. And here I protest in the Lord that in the behalf of this audience to whom, as Campion lately said but feignedly to the doctors, I am ready in the Lord God to do all the service I may. I will allege 11 places out of the Scripture which do manifestly prove it to be the plain and true sense of God's Word that faith only doth justify.
>
> *Campion.* This position, that faith only doth justify, is not in all the Word of God.
>
> *Charke.* There are eleven places negative that works do not justify. [Which he then enumerated].[95]
>
> *Campion.* Of all your places there is none that doth probably [probatively] prove your position. And because you do generally vouch them, I will answer them generally. The cause why St. Paul urgeth faith so much was because he was troubled with two kind of people, the Jews and the Gentiles. The Jews thought they might not be justified without the performance of the ceremonies of the Old Law, and the performance thereof was the cause of their election. And likewise the Gentiles attributed so much to the moralities [the natural moral law], thinking them to be the cause of their election, to

avoid which errors was the scope of that epistle to the Romans, and to exclude works going *before* faith, and not to exclude works done in grace *after* faith. And this is my answer generally to those places alleged, reserving their several answers to every place incidently as they are alleged.[96]

The point may be obscure to the reader who has not studied the exact terms of the argument—but Campion's answer is as perfect and concise as possible.

On this day Campion was as successful as a man can be who has to follow the lead of two illogical bunglers, answering their miscellaneous and disjointed objections, but never allowed to build up any harmonious defense of his own system.

No more need be said except a reminder that Campion was being subject to inquisition but not allowed to cross-examine his critics, that his opponents were empowered to direct the course of the debates and their subject matter, that Campion had been seriously inconvenienced by the tortures he had endured before the debates, and was given no access to the books which his adversaries had used in abundance and at leisure. Yet it must have seemed obvious to all the observers that Campion had the better of the argument.

Fr. Persons on the Debates

It was at this fourth conference that Persons tells us how Charke outfaced Campion by his "high place, gay apparel, great words, assistance of friends, countenance of authority, applause of Protestants standing by."[97] Persons reminds Charke of his uncivil words against Campion in his earlier pamphlet:

> But that was nothing to the contemptuous usage of so learned a man in open audience, with barbarous threatening of that further cruelty, which then you had in mind, and now have put in execution upon him. But above all other things, that was most ridiculous, and fit for a stage, which you thought was excellent, and became you well: and that was your often turning to the people and requesting them to rejoice, and thank the Lord, that he had given you such an argument against the Papists, as now you had to propose. And then when great expectation was moved, and the argument came forth, it proved not worth three eggs in May: for Mr. Campian dispatched it

oftentimes in less than half three words. These are the comedies that
you exercise to get applause of the people withal. For which cause
also, you had Mr. Norton the Rack-master at your elbow, to repeat
and urge your argument for you to the purpose. Surely it is pity that
you durst not make these few disputations public, where more men
might have laughed, and been witnesses of your folly, especially of
that in the end; when being now brought to a *non plus* in arguing,
and thereupon the people beginning to depart, you (Mr. Charke)
caused the doors to be shut, and no man to be let out, until with one
consent they had joined with you in prayer to thank the Lord for
your victory that day gotten upon Mr. Campian.[98]

Many of the audience were laughing in their sleeves;[99] and it was the
common opinion that if the Protestant debaters had fancied they had
got the best of it, they would immediately put their triumph in print. Dr.
Fulke had visited Wisbeach Castle the year before, and framed to himself
the imagination of a victory because the prisoners refused conference,
and, behold, he presently printed a pamphlet in his own praise. What,
then, would Charke and Fulke and Walker and Goade and Nowell and
Day have done about their debates with Campion, if they had thought
them any way able to bear public scrutiny?[100]

Persons reproves them:

And yet (as I said) you know the inequality, whereby you dealt
with that man, being but one, unbooked, unprovided, wearied with
imprisonment, and almost dismembered with the rack, threatened
and terrified with death to come, appointed only to answer, and
never to oppose. All this you know, and the world both knoweth
and marvelleth at it abroad. Mary, we marvel not, who know your
purses. For we are sure, and dare avow to your faces, that you will
never deal with us at even hand, or upon equal conditions, while
you live.[101]

The Debates Discontinued

After the experience, the Council had come round to the opinion of
Bishop Aylmer, that these conferences did no good to the Protestant
cause.[102] The bishop wrote to Burghley on September 29:

> Touching [regarding] the conference with Campion in the Tower,
> I wrote unto Mr. Lieutenant of my misliking that so many were
> admitted to it, whose authority is not to be directed there by me, but
> by her Majesty and your lordships. And for the ill opinion that I had
> of it, I sent to stay [stop] it.[103]

Here upon the Council deliberated; and Norton, who had been notary at the last conference, was told to send in his report, which he did September 30, with his observations on the amendment of the order used with that Jesuit:

> I think the course hitherto taken, either by lack of aid [Campion
> being without books and preparation] or moderation [on the third
> day Hopton wanted to let any learned man present moderate, but
> none would undertake it][104] or convenient respect of admitting men
> to be hearers, hath been both fruitless and hurtful, and subject to
> great harm by reports.[105]

And he says that on the fourth day he took down each question and answer, and then read it over to the disputant, to avoid all quibbling. It does not appear, however in the *True report of the Disputation*, where Norton's name is not mentioned in connection with the fourth conference. The result of the Council's deliberation was that the conferences were discontinued, and the divines who had been summoned to dispute for a fifth debate in October were bidden to remain where they were.

Campion's Reputation Restored

Now the popular voice began to make itself heard. All through August, Campion was only known as the betrayer of his friends, the man whose faith was hardly secure, who might perhaps one day appear at Paul's Cross to make his recantation. All these ideas were totally overthrown by his public appearances at the four conferences.

Catholics who attended the debates (and perhaps waverers, and fair-minded and disillusioned Protestants also) spread the report that—far from being discredited—Campion, in a blatantly unfair contest, had proved the abler advocate.

When these voices were suppressed, the voice of the people was heard in ballads, which were effectual despite their lack of melody and grammar.

The first little poem seems to be by a disappointed Protestant. At the time of Campion's trial, the Privy Council ordered copies of this popular ballad to be seized.[106]

I

Campion is a champion,
Him once to overcome,
The rest be well drest
The sooner to mumm.
He looks for his life,
They say, to dispute,
And doubts not our doctrine
He brags to confute.
If instead of good argument,
We deal by the rack,
The Papists may think
That learning we lack.
Come forth, my fine darlings,
And make him a dolt;
You have him full fast,
And that in strong holt.

II

A Jesuit, a Jebusite? wherefore, I you pray?
Because he doth teach you the only right way?
He proferreth the same by learning to prove,
And shall we from learning to rack him remove?
His reasons were ready, his grounds were most sure,
The enemy cannot his force long endure;
Campion, in camping on spiritual field,
In God's cause his life is ready to yield.
Our preachers have preached in pastime and pleasure,
And now they be hated far passing all measure;
Their wives and their wealth have made them so mute,
They cannot nor dare not with Campion dispute.

III

Let reason rule, and racking cease,
Or else for ever hold your peace;
You cannot withstand God's power and His grace,
No, not with the Tower nor the racking-place.

The long poem attributed to St. Henry Walpole "Why do I use my paper, ink and pen?" has one stanza on the debates:[107]

> From rack in Tower they brought him to dispute,
> Bookless, alone, to answer all that came,
> Yet Christ gave grace, he did them all confute
> So sweetly there in glory of His name,
> That even the adverse part are forced to say
> That Campion's cause did bear the bell away.

Nowell and Day, in the preface to their printed account, report what Catholics were circulating in writing and in print:[108] "The Catholics, by the judgment of those that were not wedded wholly to will [prejudice], did get the goal." And: "In my soul I protest that in any indifferent [impartial] judgment, the adverse Protestants were quite confounded; and if I were not a Catholic already, just the hearing of that conference would have made me one."[109] The Protestants must have been smarting under the humiliation for a long time: it was two years and three months before "the relatively belated and almost embarrassed appearance of the "official" [doctored] account of the proceedings."[110]

They also complained of Catholic pamphlets protesting the injustice of the conditions:

> They leave no circumstances of Master Campion's imprisonment, his racking, sickness, lack of his notebooks, of his library, our sudden coming upon him, etc., untouched.[111]

Such libels were clearly intolerable: the replies given to Campion were to be held as sufficient, whether they would endure proof or not. Those who thought otherwise did so at their peril. A Mr. Cawood, who "talked very liberally, extolling Campion's learning, and attributing the victory to him: and for his confident and slanderous reports was brought before the Bishop [Aylmer], who gave him the punishment of confinement in the Clink."[112] "There was also another, named Oliver Plucket (another of the crowd of common auditors), who openly commended the said Campion, saying that he heard him dispute, and thought, in his conscience, that Campion was discreet and learned, and spoke very well, and that he would have convinced them that opposed him if he might have been heard with indifferency [impartiality]. Which words were laid to his charge by the foreman of the Wardmote-inquest of the parish of St. Andrew's, Holborn; which he owned [admitted]."[113] The case was reported to Fleetwood the Recorder; the outcome was that he was also committed to custody.[114] In June 1582, John Hamerton of Hellifield Peel, Yorkshire, was arrested for treasonous words, and was "also suspected of traitorous speeches in Wm. Ardington's house, in Craven, as that Campion, and those that suffered with him, were wrongfully condemned."[115] In October 1583, Fr. Robert Holmes (alias John Finche), a prisoner in the Fleet, was reported to Walsingham for saying, among other things, that "Campion and others were executed for treason and not for religion."[116] I shall later record a still more vindictive punishment inflicted on Stephen Vallenger, who printed some poetry on Campion's life and death—and in whose handwriting we have copies of notes of the debates, which seem to have been prepared for a printing that did not eventuate.

Persons, who was kept informed through his contacts, wrote of their good effect in a letter, written, it is thought, in London, on November 22, 1581, two days after Campion had been declared guilty and condemned:

> The [four][117] debates held with the heretics greatly stirred the souls of all here, such was the bearing of Fr. Campion, accompanied by Sherwin. After the first disputations, however, the heretics would not tolerate the presence of Sherwin, because they said he was too choleric, and so Fr. Campion had to debate alone. And truly it can scarcely be told how much good these disputations have done, and are doing every day. And if he dies for that cause they will certainly do still more good. For they are the common talk and subject of conversation of everybody, not only of Catholics, but of our enemies also, and always to the great honor of Father Campion, such was the charm God gave him in the eyes of all that day.[118]

CHAPTER 17

Preparations for the Trial

FOR THE seven-week period, from the conclusion of the fourth debate on September 27, until his arraignment at Westminster Hall on November 14, little is known about Campion, other than that on October 31 he was tortured on the rack for a third time, and again on November 2.

All attempts to disparage his religious and moral character, or his talents and learning, having thus failed, only one course was left—to disparage his patriotism, and to hold him up as a traitor to the scorn of his countrymen.

The Charge of Treason

John Nichols was an opportune "insider" who afforded grounds for the notion that all seminary priests were really traitors. In his recantation sermon preached before the priests in the Tower, February 5, 1581, he gave information concerning the re-publication of the Bull of Pius V, and the usual treasonable utterances of seminary lecturers and students.

> One of your readers in divinity positive, before two hundred scholars at least, said that it was lawful for any man of worship in England to give authority to the vilest wretch to seek the queen's death. . . .
>
> Father Pais, reader in scholastic theology in the Roman College, said: "The good will of the Pope is manifest, and his purse ready; but King Philip is either turned aside by fear, or prevented by want of means, and dares not lead his army into England."[1]

According to Nichols, the students used to say they would burn their sovereign's bones and those of her Council that opposed their attempts, alive or dead. He gave a long list of those against whom the threats were uttered—among them Lord Burghley, the Earl of Huntingdon; Knowles,

Walsingham, and a long list of bishops, deans, and doctors of divinity. Moreover, he said they wished their country to be destroyed with fire, sword, and famine, so as to bring back the Catholic religion. The belief even in an anti-Elizabethan oath was widespread: Francis Bacon in 1580 had spoken of "the seminaries, where none are now admitted, but those who take the oath against her Majesty."[2]

Plots against the Queen

It was nearly half a year after this that George Eliot gave his information about a plot of fifty men to murder the queen, Leicester, Burghley and Walsingham.[3] It was probably on this or some similar information that on July 14 Walsingham was set to work by the queen:

> I have been all this day by her Majesty's express commandment set at work about the examinations of certain persons charged to have conspired to attempt somewhat against her own person. But as far as I can gather by these examinations that I have already taken I think it will prove nothing. And yet it is happy that the parties charged are taken, for they be runagate priests, such as have been bred up in Rome and Douay, and seek to corrupt her Majesty's good subjects within this realm.[4]

The intention was to connect all the seminary priests with the Irish rebellion, which the pope stirred up not only with men and money, but specially through Dr. Sanders, who did better in a professor's chair than in charge of an army. The English ministers had obtained a copy of his letter to the Irish wherein Sanders tells the "Catholic lords and worshipful gentlemen of Ireland" that Elizabeth is a reproach to the crown, and they poltroons for abetting her. Her successor must be a Catholic, for the pope will require that the crown rest in none but Catholics; and he will punish them for having supported her.

The law recently enacted gave the government full power to treat any Jesuits or seminary priests whom they could catch in England as *ipso facto* traitors. There was no need of any laborious endeavor to connect this or that individual with the great Spanish-Papal scheme. On the other hand, public opinion did not altogether run with the statute. It was easier to say, than to make men believe, that the Catholic Faith was not really a religion but merely a political institution; that the Mass was not a sacrifice to God but a treasonable practice against the queen; that confession was not a means of cleansing the conscience from sin but only of enrolling oneself in a secret association, pledged to support the pope when his invasion of England came off. It was public caution that gave the Council pause and made them argue the case for and against putting their prisoners to death.[5]

The Case for and against Execution of Priests

All the arguments on both sides were raised. On one side, the breath of all such priests was contagious; the other, some of them might be amended. One, it was foolish to make severe laws and not execute them; the other, the law need not be repealed, but only the execution thereof mitigated. One, such pity would be interpreted to be either fear of vengeance, or an acknowledgment that the law was wicked; the other, that no one should be frightened by scarecrows from what is honorable, that it was better to be abused for leniency than for cruelty. One, Jesuitism could be best extirpated by the gallows; the other, to make martyrs would be to propagate their opinions. One, dead men cannot bite, but that men in prison are a standing provocation to a rescue; the other, the greater penalty will move greater revenge, and sharpen zeal. One asserted that no priest or Jesuit was ever converted by imprisonment; the other, that some had been so, and more had been half-converted, and had renounced the treasonable part of their profession. Finally, the one declared that if they were put to death, it would be not for religion but for rebellion; the other, that if their death was the child of their rebellion, it was the grandchild of their religion; for their obedience to their superiors put them on the propagation of their religion, and thus made them offenders to the State.

Elizabeth herself was inclined to the side of mercy, but among her Council were several of that peculiar sour leaven of Puritanism which was always biased towards cruelty and blood, and made the sincerest men the severest and bitterest. These men naturally had their senses most sharpened to the dangers that were gathering round Protestantism, and were willing to protect it by the most decisive measures. They were in terror lest the French match should bring about toleration of popery, and toleration lead to supremacy. Religiously, they were opposed to all toleration, to any compromise with Belial. Their aim was the extirpation of popery. A carefully secured toleration of Catholics was to them almost as abominable as a restoration of their supremacy. Yet, they could not afford to renounce the French match, for that would be to throw France into the arms of Spain. Indeed, Sir Henry Cobham, ambassador in France, wrote that the Queen-mother there was persuading Anjou to give up all idea of Elizabeth, and to marry one of Philip's daughters.[6] In this dilemma the priests in prison were a great commodity to them.

William Camden, the annalist of the time, records:

> These things were done presently after the Duke of Anjou's coming into England. Now while he abode here, the queen—to take away the fear which had possessed many men's minds that Religion would be altered and Popery tolerated—overcome by importunate pleas, permitted that the aforesaid Edmund Campion, of the Society of Jesus, Ralph Sherwin, Luke Kirby, and Alexander Briant, priests, should be arraigned . . . and charged with plotting the destruction of the queen and realm . . . and had come into England to disturb the quiet state of that realm, and to gather forces . . .[7]

If the marriage was to take place, the queen might be persuaded to sacrifice these men, in order to show that in marrying she had no intention to bring about a change of religion or a toleration of popery. On the other hand, if the cruelty could be carried far enough to shock the tolerant policy of the French court, or the feelings of the French people, there was a secret hope that it might delay, if not altogether prevent the marriage.[8]

By a combination of circumstances, Campion and his companions were deprived of all protection. The Spanish ambassador could not aid them, without exciting more suspicion of their complicity with the Spanish-Papal designs; the French ambassador could not, for fear of proving that the French match tended towards toleration of popery— and would not, because he suspected the Jesuits of a design to traverse the French alliance in favor of Spain.

The continual fears of a Spanish invasion stopped the mouths of those moderate men who in other circumstances would have counseled moderation. Hence it was that Walsingham and the others who wished to put Campion to death had not a very difficult part to play. They had merely to persuade the queen and people that he and his fellows had really conspired against her, had been guilty of particular treasons, besides the general one of their reconciling her Majesty's subjects to the pope, and then they might be hanged with general approbation. Walsingham doubtless thought it unlucky that just at this time, indeed the very day that Campion was paraded through London (July 22), he was sent to France on a special mission connected with the marriage match. The first letter that he wrote from Paris to Burghley testified his anxiety: "I pray she [the queen] may take profit of Campion's discovery by severely punishing the offenders, for nothing has done more harm than the overmuch lenity [leniency] that has been used in that behalf."[9] Perhaps these men had already satisfied their consciences that Campion and the rest might justly be hanged on the late statute, and that policy required them to be put to death. Hence it would be no murder if they used false pretenses to cajole the reluctant queen into allowing them to be hanged.

Three such pretenses suggested themselves: a confession of disloyalty against the sovereign; involvement with the Irish rebellion; an imaginary plot hatched in Europe.

Campion on the Queen's Title

The first was due to Dr. Hammond. Let the prisoners be asked what they thought of diverse treasonable passages collected out of the works of Sanders, Allen, and Bristow—three Catholic theologians whom it would be equally difficult for them to defend or to condemn. And let them be asked what they thought of the validity of Pius V's Bull, and of the queen's title to the crown, and (afterwards) what they would do in the event of the pope invading England. The passages that Hammond collected were published in 1582, with the replies of Campion and the rest, in a tract entitled *A particular Declaration or Testimony of the undutiful and traitorous affection borne against her Majesty by Edmund Campion, Jesuit, and other condemned priests, witnessed by their own confessions*, which has been often reprinted.[10] The theologians' passages refer in terms of praise to the mission of Dr. Morton and to the rebels of 1569, to the Bull of Pius V, to the excommunication of the queen, and to the martyrs Felton and Storey. We first hear of them in the letter of Council, of July 30, which consigned Campion to his first racking:

> Whereas we are given to understand that the Mr. Dr. Hammond
> has, out of [Rev. Dr.] Sanders's book *De Monarchia Ecclesiae* [The

monarchy of the Church], and [Fr.] Bristow's *Motives*, drawn certain points touching the acknowledgment of their allegiance towards her Majesty, we think it good that you propound the same to Campion and the priests, requiring their direct answer to the same.[11]

The reply, dated and testified by Hopton, Beale, Hammond, and Norton, is published in the tract named *A particular Declaration:*

August 1, 1581

Edmund Campion, being demanded
    [1] whether he would acknowledge the publishing of these things, before re cited, by Sanders, Bristow, and Allen, to be wicked in the whole or any part;
    [2] and whether he doth at this present acknowledge her Majesty to be a true and lawful queen, or a pretended queen, and deprived, and in possession of her crown only *de facto* [as a matter of fact, but not lawfully]; he answereth to the first, "That he meddleth neither to nor fro [will not say anything one way or the other], and will not further answer, but requireth that they [the authors themselves] may answer."
    To the second he saith, "That this question dependeth upon the fact [deed] of Pius V, whereof he is not to judge, and therefore refuseth further to answer."

Edmund Campion

This was thus answered and subscribed by Edmund Campion, the day and year above written, in the presence of us,

Owen Hopton,   John Hammond,
Robert Beale,   Thomas Norton.

The answers show how resolutely he refused to enter the field of politics. He would not answer for the opinions of other writers. He could not satisfy his conscience either of the pope's right to depose the queen, or of his own right to judge the pope. He decided therefore to confine himself to the merely religious aspect of the controversy, and refused to make himself umpire between two high contending parties so far above him as pope and queen. He would commit himself to neither side, even under duress.

Ay, but I fear you speak upon the rack,
Where men enforcèd do speak any thing.
—*Merchant of Venice*, Act III, sc. ii, 34–5

His was not a dogmatic, but a practical mind. He was in himself the demonstration that the political theories of Catholics need have no influence on their practice; but to condemn those theories as wicked in themselves was a thing that he felt he had no right to do, and no racking could force his conscience.

There is a subtle point behind Campion's non-answer which may escape the reader. At first sight, one may wonder why on August 1 he was silent about the queen's authority, when on July 25 he told the Privy Councilors at a private meeting (as he repeated at his future trial):

> I did acknowledge Her Highness not only as my queen, but also as my most lawful governess.[12]

The reason is that the question he refused to answer in August mixed *two* things, namely, the queen's lawful reign in itself, and the Papal concession granted to Catholics because of the situation *de facto*. If the pope truly had authority to depose her (and Campion was not sure he did), then she was deposed, because the Bull still applied to her, and the mitigation applied to Catholics only, who were allowed to acknowledge her as queen in the meantime.

Had he been asked simply: "Is she your queen?"—he would have answered Yes, meaning: "She is to me and I am allowed to acknowledge her as such."

But they asked, in effect: "Is she queen lawfully, or only because you are allowed by the pope to ignore her dethronement?"[13]

Briant and Sherwin gave very similar answers to Campion's under interrogation. Briant's answer makes the distinction just mentioned:

> He is content to affirm that the queen is his sovereign lady, but he will not affirm that she is so lawfully, and ought to be so, and to be obeyed by him as her subject, if the Pope declare or command the contrary. And he saith, that that question is too high and dangerous for him to answer. . . . Whether the Pope have authority to withdraw from obedience to her Majesty, he knoweth not. —Alexander Briant, May 7, 1581

> Being asked whether the Pope's Bull of deprivation of the queen
> were a lawful sentence or no, he refuseth to answer. Being asked
> whether the queen be his lawful sovereign, and so ought to con-
> tinue, notwithstanding any sentence that the Pope can give, he doth
> not answer. Being again asked whether the queen be his sovereign,
> notwithstanding any sentence that the Pope can give, he prayeth to
> be asked no such question as may touch his life. —Ralph Sherwin,
> November 12, 1580

Campion Not Involved in the Irish Rebellion

But when the Council had this "confession" of Campion, they had not
advanced matters: it was not treason to refuse to qualify others as traitors.
He was therefore to be examined about his dealings with one Rochfort,
an Irishman. When the Spaniards and Italians were massacred by Lord
Grey, at Smerwick in Kerry, the letters taken in their baggage discovered that the Bishops of Spain and Italy had contributed the money for
the expedition.[14] Laing's life of Campion[15] tells us that he was examined
at the rack about the conveyance of £30,000 into Ireland; probably the
Irishman Rochfort was the carrier of the sum, and the Council determined to rack out of Campion some confession that he knew the man;
perhaps, if they were lucky, that he was the very man, under a different
name. For they knew, and it was one of the accusations against him, that
he had often changed his name and dress. But though all the ingenuity of
the rack-masters was employed to involve him in this real rebellion; and
though, according to Laing, an indictment was drawn up on the strength
of their suspicions, it was allowed to fall through, because not a shadow
of proof could be vouched for it.[16] We shall see, when we come to the
trial, with what shadowy proof Campion's judges were contented.

The Resort to False Witnesses

Having failed to implicate Campion in any real conspiracy, it remained
still possible to suborn false witnesses to prove him to have engaged in an
imaginary one.

Campion was the man for whose sake this policy was invented. Says
Dr. Allen:

> These subtle machinations and figments of conspiracies were not
> invented by the ingenious councilors, till they had Rev. Fr. Campion

in their power, whose blood they singularly thirsted for and were determined to shed, if they could possibly find any other occasion (apart from the crime of religion) and extort a confession of that crime by torture, or any other way.[17]

The contemporary Protestant historian Camden, in effect, says the same thing, when he admits:

Yet the greater part of these silly priests, she [the queen] did not believe to be guilty of devising the destruction of their country.[18]

The charge does not rest on the mere authority of Allen or on a statement from Camden. It is quite clear from documents in the State Paper Office that Walsingham busied himself at Paris searching for plots which might involve Catholics, and when he could not find any to suit his purpose, inventing them and suborning false witnesses to swear to them. Lord Burghley seems to have been his accomplice in this proceeding. Walsingham writes to him from Paris on August 20: "I am by secret intelligence given most assuredly to understand that about two months ago there was a plot [plan] sent out of Spain to the pope, showing him upon the alienation of religion what way is to be taken for the conquest of Scotland,"[19] which the pope approved and earnestly recommended. Out of this, Walsingham probably hoped to get some matter with which to accuse Campion—but after a conversation with the giver of the intelligence he found that it would not suit his purpose, whereupon he threw discredit upon this first information and suggested another which would serve his turn better and for which he offered his man twenty crowns if he would testify to it in a court of justice. This may be gathered from a letter of this anonymous informer, who by his style of ending seems to be a Catholic—probably one of those unstable brethren like John Nichols, with whom the English seminaries abroad were occasionally infested. This letter Walsingham had the effrontery to pass on to Burghley and the Council, to prove their complicity in the conspiracy. The informer wrote:

Touching the plot: be out of doubt I would it were but false and sophistical . . . The last part of your letter you answered not in effect as you did in words. Believe me, it is not 20 crowns that shall make me a bondman, or make me say a false tale. But to what end these words? But only that you may, and as I think do, learn [know] them that for less will be well content to sell their country and all that is in it.[20]

The informer ends his letter by hinting to Walsingham the danger that all his spies ran. Walsingham, he says, is surrounded by "eyes of a lynx," so that everybody that goes near him is marked.

It is clear that at this period, when Campion's fate was hanging in the balance, Walsingham was not only throwing all his influence into the scale of death, but was also forging "false tales" of Catholic conspiracies, and trying to suborn false witnesses to prove them.

I do not think that all the Council were guilty of this. The following letter from Sir Francis Knowles to Leicester and Burghley, the two Chancellors of the Universities, proves that though he was an advocate of severity, he would have acted openly and honestly, without losing himself in the Machiavellian labyrinth of Walsingham. He is comparing the Anabaptists and the Family of Love with the Catholics:

> This difference is between the Papists and these sectaries, touching their practices here in England. These sectaries are more hypocritical, and will sooner deny their doctrine and assertions to avoid punishment than the Papists will; but the Papists' secret practices, by these Jesuits, in going from house to house to withdraw men from the obedience of the queen to that of the false Catholic Church of Rome, hath and will endanger her person and state more than all the sects of the world, if no execution shall follow upon the traitorous practicers that are for the same apprehended; or, at the least, if execution shall not follow upon such of them as will not openly and plainly recant.[21]

The Death Sentence

I believe that the final decision to put Campion to death was not made until the end of October, when the coming of the Duke of Anjou, who arrived on November 1, seemed to require the blood of a few Catholics to reassure the Puritans; but before putting him on trial they decided, if possible, to rack out of him and his fellows some evidence on which they might be hanged without too great a show of iniquity.

Accordingly, on Sunday, October 29, the Council ordered a letter to be written "to the Attorney and Solicitor-General, the Lieutenant of the Tower, Dr. Hammond, Thomas Wilkes, and Thomas Norton, for the examining of Edmund Campion, Thomas Ford, and others, prisoners in the Tower, upon certain matters, and to put them unto the rack."[22]

Campion Racked a Third and Fourth Time

This order took effect with all barbarity on Tuesday, October 31. Fr. John Hart's diary of the Tower records on this day: "Edmund Campion for the third time tortured upon the rack after the debates, and this time the worst of all."[23] With him, Fr. Payne, the priest accused by Eliot of conspiring against the queen's life, was also tortured most cruelly.[24] The Council wished to make it appear that they were both in the same boat. This time Campion "was so cruelly torn and rent upon the torture . . . that he told a secret friend of his that found means to speak with him, that he thought they meant to make him away in that sort,"[25] i.e., kill him then and there by racking.

> Dr. Allen records: He used to fall down at the rack-house door upon both knees to commend himself to God's mercy, and to crave His grace of patience in his pains. As also being upon the rack he cried continually with much mildness upon God and the holy name of Jesus.[26]

Fr. Persons was told that Campion was racked both on October 31 and November 2:

> Fr. Edmund Campion after his debates underwent most cruel tortures, both on the day before and the day after the Feast of All Saints, which by the help of God and of all the Saints he bore with a constancy almost unbelievable; and when these torments were scarcely ended, he recited in an earnest voice the *Te Deum Laudamus* ["We praise Thee as God": an ancient Latin hymn in praise of the Holy Trinity] so that all marvelled greatly.[27]

A Jesuit document records that Dr. Allen said that

> he was present at a sermon in which the preacher affirmed that he met Father Campian on All Saints' Day, in the prison, with both arms in a sling, from the effects of the previous day's racking, and that he spoke with such joy of heart that it appeared to strengthen others. He also added that Father Campian was again most cruelly

tortured on the following day, so that when taken down from the rack he was scarcely alive.[28]

When his keeper asked him the next day how his hands and feet felt, he answered, "Not ill, because not at all."[29] Èven when he was brought to the bar, November 22, he could not lift his hand.[30]

Those who managed to talk to Campion or speak to his keeper testified that he remained heroically happy and jovial, even after the two last, worst rackings. Disabled by the torture, he jested by comparing himself to an awkward elephant trying to lift his body off the ground. When, later, some feeling returned to his hands and joints and he was able to feed himself in a primitive fashion by joining both hands to food in-between, he asked his onlookers if they had ever seen a more refined ape.[31]

It is also possible that Campion was racked five times in all. Thomas Pounde says Campion was racked three times before the end of August.[32] Moreover, Bombino's account of the first Tower debate quotes Campion as saying he has "borne the rack three times."[33] This extra racking, if true, was most likely around August 15, when Campion was interrogated on when and where he said Mass, whom he confessed, and where Fr. Persons and other priests were.[34]

Other Tortures

Previously, in August, two ambassadors gave details of Edmund's mal-treatment in their despatches.

The Venetian ambassador wrote on August 5:

> They have inflicted torture on Campion, and not the ordinary torture; thrusting irons between his flesh and his nails, and have torn the nails off.[35]

A week later the Spanish ambassador reported:

> The priests they succeed in capturing are treated with a variety of terrible tortures: among others is one torment that people in Spain imagine to be that which will be wrought by the Antichrist, as the most dreadfully cruel of them all. This is to drive iron spikes between the nails and the quick; and two priests in the Tower have been tortured in this way, one of them being Campion, of the Society of Jesus, who was recently captured with the other [probably

Alexander Briant]. I am assured that when they would not confess under this torture, the nails of their fingers and toes were turned back, all of which they suffered with great patience and humility.[36]

These statements are confirmed by witnesses at Campion's trial and execution. They noticed that his finger nails had been torn out.[37] Persons writes that for that reason Campion came

> to the bar with his hands folded in linen cloth, and with that feebleness, as he was neither able to . . . lift a cup of drink to his mouth without help, may well show how he had been handled.[38]

But Puritan theologian Dr. Humphrey explained it was all a ruse to give credit to the lies about being tortured,[39] and, besides, it was his own fault:

> because he refused to use the ointment which the Lieutenant of the Tower, of his kind concern and pure mercy, beyond that of others, is wont to supply. . . . In fact, these [Catholic prisoners] in the Tower and elsewhere have all that is necessary, perhaps more than they ought to have, for their enjoyment . . .[40]

The Puritans certainly believed in "faith alone." No one ever had reason to accuse them of practising charity in order to enter the Kingdom of Heaven.

Baron Huns don (Henry Carey, first cousin to the queen), who witnessed Campion's torture, said, "You can pluck out his heart more easily than we can find words to express what religion meant to this man."[41]

After Campion's death these cruelties excited indignation in Europe, and Burghley defended them in a tract which he called *A Declaration of the favorable dealing of her Majesty's Commissioners appointed for the examination of certain Traitors, and of tortures unjustly reported to be done upon them for matters of Religion* (1583). "Those who revere the memory of lord Burleigh," says Protestant legal historian Hallam, "must blush for this pitiful apology."[42] The passages which Hallam quotes were transcribed by Burghley from Norton's letters in defense of his conduct. In conformity with Elizabethan practice, Norton was disgraced, to make it seem that the subordinates, not the principals, were answerable for all that was cruel and illegal in these proceedings.

In truth, it is difficult to revere the memory of Burghley at all, and

it is not just for his shameful words in that pamphlet. He was deceit-
ful, hypocritical, and cruel. He and Walsinghman used to send "agents-
provocateurs" among Catholics to instigate sham plots; and once they
gathered names of prominent Catholics involved, they would then self-
righteously denounce them as shameless traitors and sentence them to
death.[43] Queen Elizabeth was thus carefully manipulated for their own
purposes. Burghley had practiced as a Catholic under Queen Mary and
then enforced a cruel persecution of Catholics under Queen Elizabeth—
for which Protestant historian Lord Macaulay wrote: "The great stain on
his memory is that for differences of opinion, for which he would risk
nothing himself, in the day of his power he took away without scruple
the lives of others."[44]

In all this, one may say he differed not from his sovereign, who began
her reign without scruple. Within weeks of taking the Coronation Oath
to uphold the freedom of the Church, she set about violating it so as to
establish herself as tyrannical governor over the Church.[45]

In 1583, Robert Beale, the clerk of the Council, who had himself
been one of Campion's rack-masters, wrote a book vehemently against
the ecclesiastical system, in which he condemned, without exception, all
racking of offenders as cruel, barbarous, contrary to law and to English
liberties. Archbishop Whitgift of Canterbury thought this condemnation reprehensible.[46] The torture-chamber was one of the institutions on
which Anglicanism seemed to rely most securely.

Heresy was in despair.

CHAPTER 18

The Trial

THE DOCUMENTS connected with Campion's trial would, by themselves, be sufficient evidence of the vacillation of the Council about the grounds on which they would make him guilty.

The First Indictment

At first it was proposed to try Edmund Campion alone, before the others imprisoned in the Tower. So the first draft of the indictment against him said (with blank spaces to be filled in with a date, a place, and an informer):

> On the ___ day of June, in the 23rd year of the Queen, at ___ in Oxfordshire, he [Edmund Campion] did traitorously pretend to have power to absolve the subjects of the said Queen from their natural obedience to her majesty, and with the intention to withdraw the said subjects of the said Queen from the religion now by her supreme authority established within this realm of England to the Roman religion, and to move the same subjects of the said Queen to promise obedience to the pretended authority of the Roman See to be used within the dominions of the said Queen.
>
> Also, that the same Edmund Campion did, with the intention of withdrawing a certain ___, being a subject of the said Queen, and born within this realm of England, from his natural obedience, then and there wickedly, falsely, and traitorously persuade the same ___ from the religion now established; and did then and there wickedly, falsely, and traitorously move the same ___ to promise obedience to the pretended authority, etc., against the form of a statute in this case made and provided, and to the evil example of all other subjects in such wise offending.[1]

509

This indictment was based on the 1581 Act of Persuasions which made it treason to receive anyone "by any ways or means" into the Catholic Church, as it withdrew subjects from "their natural obedience" to the sovereign. For this crime of Campion, based on religion, the facts were certain and so too was a conviction—but if they hanged Campion on such an indictment, they could never clear themselves of the charge of putting him to death for religion and not for treason. So they forged a plot.

In accordance with their forgery, they drew up a new indictment based on political action—a plot to overthrow and kill the queen. It was impossible to prove, and very awkward even to fabricate; yet this was the course chosen. A single man could hardly plot such a course of action— so this required the trial of a number of traitors together.

A New Indictment

The second indictment was based on the Edward III Act of Treason of 1351. In that Act, the chief grounds were compassing the king's death, levying war against him and adhering to his enemies. So evidence had to be found and witnesses produced, to testify that rebellion and assassination were plotted by Campion and the other defendants. The new indictment read:

> The jury present in behalf of the Queen, that William Allen, D.D., Nicholas Morton, D.D., Robert Persons, and Edmund Campion . . .

—these were all whom they first thought of accusing; but on second thoughts they determined that the plot was quite capacious enough to include all the priests whom they then happened to have in confinement, so they added thirteen more names in the margin—

> James Bosgrave, William Filby, Thomas Ford, Thomas Cottam, Lawrence Richardson [real name Johnson], John Collyton [Collington], Ralph Sherwin, Luke Kirby, Robert Johnson, Edward Rishton, Alexander Briant, Henry Orton a civilian, and [John] Short,
>   that being traitors against the Queen, not having the fear of God in their hearts, nor weighing their due allegiance, but led astray by the devil, intending altogether to withdraw, blot out, and extinguish the hearty love and true and due obedience which true and faithful subjects should bear and are bound to bear towards the Queen,

did, on the last day of March, in the 22nd year [of Elizabeth's reign, 1580], at Rome in Italy, in parts beyond the sea, and on the last day of April in the same year at Rheims in Champagne,

and on diverse other days and occasions before and after, both at Rome and Rheims, and in diverse other places in parts beyond the seas,

falsely, maliciously, and traitorously conspire, imagine, contrive, and compass, not only to deprive, cast down, and disinherit the said Queen from her royal state, title, power, and rule of her realm of England, but also to bring and put the same Queen to death and final destruction,

and to excite, raise, and make sedition in the said realm,

and also to beget and cause miserable slaughter among the subjects of the said Queen throughout the realm, and to procure and set up insurrection and rebellion against the said Queen, their supreme and natural lady,

and to change and alter according to their will and pleasure the government of the said realm, and the pure religion there rightly and religiously established, and totally to subvert and destroy the state of the whole commonwealth of the realm,

and to invite, procure, and induce diverse strangers and aliens, not being subjects of the said Queen, to invade the realm, and to raise, carry on, and make war against the said Queen;

and in order to bring to pass the said wicked and traitorous designs, the said Allen, Morton, Persons, and Campion did, on the last day of March at home, and on the last day of April at Rheims, and on other days, falsely and traitorously conspire, treat, and debate by what ways and means they could compass the death of the said Queen and raise a sedition in the realm;

and with the said intent and purpose the said Allen, Morton, Persons, and Campion did afterwards, on the 20th of May 1580 at Rome aforesaid, and on diverse other days before and after, both by persuasions and letters, move, exhort, and comfort diverse strangers and aliens to invade the realm and raise war against the Queen.

And further, that the same Allen, Morton, Persons, and Campion did, on the 20th day of May at Rome, and on the last of the same month at Rheims, traitorously agree that the said Persons and Campion should go into England, there to move and persuade such subjects of the Queen as they could come at to aid and assist such strangers and aliens as they should traitorously bring into the realm to make war and rebellion against the Queen, and to change and alter the religion established.

And that the said Persons and Campion did after, to wit on the first day of June 1580, by the treason, procurance, comfort, and command of Allen and Morton at Rheims, set out to come into England to perform their aforesaid treasonable intents against their due allegiance, and against the peace of the said Queen, her crown and dignity, and in manifest contempt of the laws of this realm, and against the form of diverse statutes in this case made and provided.[2]

According to this indictment: Allen, Morton, Persons, Campion, and the thirteen others were together in Rome, March 31, 1580, were together in Rheims, April 30, were back again in Rome, May, 20 and again at Rheims, May 31, with Persons and Campion starting from Rheims on June 1, 1580.

Of course, it was impossible to prove a tale so clumsily constructed, but the law officers of the Crown were directed to obtain a conviction by any means necessary—packing the jury, suborning false witnesses, over-ruling evidence adduced for the defendants, confounding all the cases into one, and general bullying and unfairness in the conduct of the case.

Waugh comments on the extra thirteen names:

> This addition removes any possibility of believing in the sincerity of the prosecution. It is conceivable that some of the Council believed in the guilt of Allen, Morton, Persons and Campion. That Ford and Collington, who had been in England for the last four or five years, whose only connection with Campion was that they had been serving a handful of nuns at the house where he was arrested, and Filby, who had dropped in to call, had been dodging about Europe in his company—at Rome on March 31st, at Rheims on April 30th, back at Rome again on May 20th—was a charge which the most cursory investigation must instantly disprove.[3]

The final text of the indictment added three more names, to bring the number up to twenty: Fr. John Hart (arrested already), Dr. Humphrey Ely (a layman and professor of law, imprisoned for a time and later released),[4] and Fr. George Osclyffe (Oscliffe or Ostcliff, of the diocese of York).

Of these twenty men, four or five were not put on trial: Allen and Morton were not in England; Persons was not caught; Ely not tried; Osclyffe arrested but perhaps not tried.[5]

The Trial Procedures

E. E. Reynolds sums up the trial procedures of the Elizabethan period:

> A trial for treason at that period was a political act, and, though it had all the trappings of judicial procedure, it bore little resemblance to what we should consider an equitable trial; there was no nonsense about assuming a defendant to be innocent until proved guilty. The prisoner was not given a copy of the indictment until he came before the Grand Jury, nor was he allowed counsel to defend him except to argue a point of law, nor could he call witnesses in his support; the prisoner had in fact to defend himself as best he could, and the trial really resolved itself into a verbal duel between him and the prosecutor. He could challenge the jurors but this right was of small value as he was not given a list of them before he came into court. Juries were not the independent bodies we know today; they were often packed and were not incorruptible. They lacked the careful guidance of the judge in weighing up the evidence. Unless, as was usual, they gave their verdict at once in open court, and it was tacitly assumed they would find for the Crown, they were locked up without food, drink or heating, until they "came to their senses," as a judge of the time might have said. The verdict had to be unanimous. After the verdict, the prisoner was allowed to argue why sentence should not be passed upon him; this was seldom effective in gaining any mitigation but it gave the prisoner a chance to speak his mind, as Sir Thomas More did at his trial. Execution usually followed as soon as possible after the death sentence had been passed.[6]

Unlike the summary record of the trial of Sir Thomas More, we are blessed with a very full record of Campion's trial. It can be found in the first volume of Howell's *State Trials*.[7] The full text, which includes a bit of narrative and commentary from the unknown chronicler, is reproduced below [with this editor's additions and explanations in brackets]. There are indications that the transcripts we have omit some parts: the additional recollections of Walpole and others [added to the trial account below][8] show that not literally everything was recorded but some things were summarized.

Arraignment at Westminster Hall

The prisoners were divided into two groups. On Tuesday, November 14, 1581, Campion, Sherwin, Kirby, Bosgrave, Cottam, Robert Johnson, Orton, and Rishton were taken to Westminster Hall, and arraigned before the grand jury. After the indictment Campion said:

> I protest before God and His angels, by heaven and earth, and before this tribunal, which I pray God may be a mirror of the judgment to come, that I am Not Guilty of the treasons contained in the Indictment, or of any other whatsoever; and to prove these things against me it is merely [utterly] impossible.

Then, while the jury was being impaneled for the next Monday, he lifted up his voice and added:

> Is it possible to find twelve men so wicked and void of all con science in this city or land that will find us guilty together of this one crime, divers of us never meeting or knowing one the other before our bringing to this bar?

Sherwin added:

> The plain reason of our standing here is religion and not treason.

On this, Sir Christopher Wray, the chief-justice of the Queen's Bench, said:

> The time is not yet come wherein you shall be tried, and therefore you must now spare speech, and reserve it till then, at which time you shall have full liberty of defense, and me to sit indifferent between her Majesty and yourself; wherefore now plead to the indictment whether you be guilty or not.

They were then commanded, as the custom is, to hold up their hands; but both Campion's arms being pitifully benumbed by his often cruel racking before, and having them wrapped in a furred cuff, he was not able to lift his hand so high as the rest did, and was required of him; but one of his companions, kissing his hand so abused for the confession of Christ, took off his cuff, and so he lifted up Campion's arm as high as he could, and pleaded "Not guilty," as all the rest did. They were then conducted back to the prisons whence they came.

The same group of eight was brought to court again on Thursday, November 16, and remanded.[9]

Two days later, Thursday, November 16,[10] in like manner, were arraigned Collington, Lawrence Johnson (alias Richardson), Hart, Ford, Filby, Briant, and Short, and similarly remanded to their respective prisons. This group of seven was brought to court again on Friday, November 17, and remanded.[11]

The Trial Commences

On Monday, November 20, following, Campion was again put into a boat under a strong guard and taken up the river from the Tower to Westminster Hall to be tried, where,

> notwithstanding what commandment soever or order taken to the contrary, there was such a presence of people, and that of the more honorable, wise, learned, and best sort, as was never seen or heard of in that court in our or our fathers' memories before us. So wonderful an expectation there was of some to see the end of this marvelous tragedy, containing so many strange and divers acts of examining, racking, disputing, subornations of false witnesses, and the like; of others to behold whether the old honor of law and justice, wherein our nation hath of all the world had the praise, could or durst now stand its ground, notwithstanding any violent impression of power and authority to the contrary. Whether there were any Markhams [a proverbially just judge[12]] left in the land that would yield up coif, office, and life, rather than give sentence against such as they knew in conscience to be innocent, and, in truth, not touched by any evidence whatsoever. But this one day gave that assembly and all the world full proof of the sad fall of equity, law, conscience, and justice, together with the Catholic faith in our poor country.[13]

Dr. Allen and Bishop Challoner who wrote thus were doubtless partisans, but Henry Hallam, a Protestant, and no partisan therefore, confirms them:

> Of those brought to trial the most eminent was Campion, formerly a Protestant, but long known as the boast of Douay for his learning and virtues. This man, so justly respected, was put to the rack, and revealed through torture the names of some Catholic gentlemen with whom he had conversed. He appears to have been indicted, along

with several other priests, not on the recent statutes [against Mass or any Catholic activity], but on that of 25 Edw. 3. [Edward III's Act of Treason, 1351] for compassing and imagining the queen's death. Nothing that I have read affords the slightest proof of Campion's concern in treasonable practices . . .

If we may confide in the published trial, the prosecution was as unfairly conducted, and supported by as slender evidence, as any perhaps which can be found in our books.[14]

The Jury

The first indication of the kind of judgment they were to expect was to be found in the constitution of the jury.

On the previous Wednesday, the panel that was called included three esquires, who, "doubting that justice should have no free course that day, but that conscience were likely to be put to silence in these men's case, whose blood was so earnestly thirsted after, those three, I say, appeared not"[15] when the day came. The rest of the panel consisted of a set of men whom the prisoners did not challenge, only because they did not know them. One William Lee was foreman. He was a man of wealth. As may be seen by his letters to the government,[16] he was also an informer and a Calvinist fanatic who doubtless well understood his duty. The names of the others remain unknown.

The Judges

The presiding judge, at the grand jury and at the trial, was Sir Christopher Wray, chief-justice of the Queen's Bench since 1572, with a reputation for fairness and impartiality. In criminal proceedings he exhibited calmness and forbearance, and abstained from all show of intemperance and impartiality; an appearance of virtue, Lord Campbell suggests, dexterously assumed by him for the purpose of obtaining convictions against the parties arraigned. He was considered in his day to be a Catholic at heart, unwillingly performing a hateful task, which is said to have embittered all his remaining days and even to have brought him prematurely with sorrow to the grave in 1592. Dr. Allen described him as "a Catholic at heart, but in his outward behavior, as you see a Pilate."[17]

The other judges of the court were Thomas Gawdy and William Ayloff. Another was John Southcote, who is not likely to have been on the bench at this trial, since he was on the list that Hopton dictated to John Nichols to write down as those he knew to be Papists.[18]

The prosecution was conducted by Edmund Anderson, the queen's sergeant-at-law, who was made chief baron of the Common Pleas in May 1582 and held the post till his death in 1605. He was assisted by John Popham, the attorney-general, afterwards (in 1592) chief-justice of the Queen's Bench, and by the solicitor-general, Sir Thomas Egerton (a recusant in 1577—but now turned Protestant)[19] who was to become Lord Chancellor in 1609 under James I.

Edward (Edmund) Plowden, a famous lawyer, himself a Catholic, had come with the rest to see the trial, but one of the judges, ashamed that such an eminent figure should report or even witness their wicked proceedings, sent word to him to leave the court. As he was himself in question for religion, he thought it prudent to obey.[20]

When the prisoners were at the bar and the jury in their box, the clerk of the crown read the indictment and declared the charge to the jurors, which was, that if they found the parties here indicted guilty of the treasons, or to have fled for any of them (this of course referred to Allen, Morton, and Persons), they should then inquire what lands, tenements, goods, and chattels they had at the time of the treasons committed, or at any time since; and if they found them not guilty, then to say so, and no more.

As said above, the law of the time allowed no defense lawyer for the accused, and gave no provision for the accused to summon witnesses on their behalf.

Campion Complains of the Collective Trial

Campion was the first to speak.[21]

> CAMPION: My lord, forasmuch as our surmised offenses are several, so that the one is not to be tainted with the crime of the other, the offense of one not being the offense of all—I could have wished likewise that, for the avoidance of confusion, we might also have been severally indicted, and that our accusations carrying so great importance, and tending so nearly unto us as our lives, each one might have had one day for his trial. For albeit I acknowledge the jurors to be wise men and much experienced in such cases, yet all evidence being given or rather handled at once, must needs breed

a confusion in the jury, and perhaps such a misprision of matters, as they may take evidence against one to be against all, and consequently the crime of the one for the crime of the other, and finally the guilty to be saved and the guiltless to be condemned; wherefore I would it had pleased your lordship that the indictments had been several, and that we might have had several days of trial.

HUDSON [another Queen's Counsel]: It seemeth well, Campion, that you have had your counsel.

CAMPION: No counsel but a pure conscience.

LORD CHIEF-JUSTICE: Although, if many be indicted at once, the indictment in respect of them all containing all their names be joint, yet in itself being framed against several persons, it cannot be but several at the trial, whereof evidence shall be particularly given against every one, and to the matters objected every one shall have his particular answer, so that the jury shall have all things orderly; notwithstanding I could have wished also that every one should have had his special day assigned him, had the time so permitted; but since it cannot be otherwise, we must take it as it is.

The Queen's Counsel Accuses Them of Treason

Whereupon the queen's Counsel, Mr. Anderson, Mr. Popham (attorney general), and Mr. Egerton (solicitor-general), prepared to give in evidence, and first Mr. Anderson spake in effect as followeth:

ANDERSON: With how good and gracious a prince the Al mighty hath blessed this island, continuing the space of twenty-three years; the peace, the tranquility, the riches, and abundant supplies, but especially the light and success of the Gospel, wherewith since her Majesty's first reign this realm hath flourished above all other, most evidently doth manifest; the which, notwithstanding they ought to have stirred us up into a most dutiful affection and zealous love unto her crown, for whose sake and by whose means, next under God, we enjoy these prosperities; yet hath there not, from time to time, been wanting amongst us mischievous and evil-disposed enemies of her felicity, which, either by insolent and open denouncing of war, or by secret and privy practices of sinister devices, have ambitiously and most disloyally attempted to spoil her of her right, and us of these blessings. Yet such hath been God's incomparable puissance [power] against them, so tender His care over her, so favorable His mercy towards us, that neither they thereby have been bettered, nor her estate impaired, nor our quiet diminished; for who knoweth not of the rebellions and uproars in the North, who remembereth not the tragical pageant of Storey [Dr. Storey, tried and martyred in 1571], who still seeth not the traitorous practices of Felton? [John Felton, hanged in 1570 for nailing up the Bull of Pius V to the door of the Bishop of London's palace]. Prevailed they against her? Was not their strength vanquished? Were not their policies frustrated? And did not God detect [expose] them and protect her, to her safety and their perdition? The matter is fresh in remembrance. Their quarters are yet scarce consumed; they were discovered, they were convicted, they suffered; we saw it. If you ask from whence these treasons and seditious conspiracies had their first offspring, I ask from whence they could have it but from the well itself—the Pope? For if we inspect the Northern seditions, he it was that was not only the encouragement, but also, being put to flight, was their refuge. If we mean Storey, he it was that was the sworn liege and lord of so perjured a subject; if we look to Felton, he it was that excommunicated the queen and all the commonalty that did her obedience. Finally, if we recount all the treasons and rebellions that have been conspired since the first hour of her coronation, he it was, and principally he, that suborned them. What, then, are we to think these latest and present conspiracies to have been done either unwitting or unwilling the Pope? Shall we deny either Campion or his companions, without the Pope's assent or consent, to have con spired these matters beyond the seas themselves? Why? Had they no entertainment at his hands? Did he bestow nothing upon them for their maintenance? Was there no cause which he should either do for them, or they for him—they Papists, he Pope; they flying their country, he receiving them; they Jesuits, he their founder; he supreme head, they sworn members; he their chief provost, they his dearest subjects; how can it be but he was privy—privy! nay, the author and onsetter? We see that other treasons have been squared to his platforms, and yielded he no direction in this? Came all the rest from him, and came not this near him? It is impossible. An enemy to the Crown, a professed scourge to the Gospel, envying the tranquillity of the one, impatient of the success of the other, what would he not do to subvert them both? He hath been always like to himself—never liker in aught than in

this. He knew well enough no foreign hostility was convenient. The
Spaniard would be discovered; the Frenchman would be suspected;
the Roman not believed. How then? Forsooth, men bred and born in
our own nation, perfect in our own tongue and language, instructed
in our own Universities—they, and only they, must endeavor our
overthrow. In what order? They must come secretly into the realm;
they must change their habit and names; they must dissemble their
vocation; they must wander unknown. To what ends? To dissuade
the people from their allegiance to their prince, to reconcile them to
the Pope, to plant the Romish religion, to supplant both prince and
province. By what means? By saying of Mass, by administering the
Sacrament, by hearing confessions. When all these things were purposed, endeavored, and practiced by them, whether were they guilty
of these treasons or not? If not, then add this further: they were privy
and parties to the rebellion in the North, they were instruments to
the practices of Storey, they were ministers to execute the Bull sent
from Pius V against her Majesty. How appeareth that? How? How
should it appear better than by your own speeches and examinations? They highly commended the rebellion in the North; they
greatly rejoiced in the constancy of Storey; divers of their counsel
and conferences was required for the Bull. Yea, and which is more,
and yet sticketh in our stomachs, they afforded so large commendations to Sanders, liking and extolling his late proceedings in Ireland,
that it cannot be otherwise intended [understood] but that thereof
they also have been partakers. To conclude: what loyalty may we
hope for from the Pope; what fidelity from their hands that have
vowed themselves unto him; what trust may the country repose in
them that have fled and renounced their country? How can their
return be without danger, whose departure was so perilous? Note all
circumstances, note all probabilities, not one amongst all but notes
them for traitorous; and so being, it is reason they should have the
law and the due punishment ordained for traitors, the which, in her
Majesty's behalf, we pray that they may have, and that the jury, upon
our allegation, may pass [give a verdict] for the trial.

The chronicler of the trial records: "This speech, very vehemently pronounced and gestured, with a grim and austere countenance, dismayed
them all, and made them very impatient and troublesomely affected; for
it seemed by their distemperature that it sounded very grievously to their

trial; and therefore, utterly denying all that was alleged, they protested themselves true and faithful subjects; only Campion bore it out best, and yet, somewhat amazed, demanded of Mr. Anderson whether he came as an orator to accuse them, or as a pleader to give in evidence."

> LORD CHIEF-JUSTICE: You must have patience with him, and the rest likewise; for, they being of the Queen's Council, they speak of no other intent than of duty to her Majesty; and I cannot but marvel that men of your profession should upon any such occasion be so much distempered; for as concerning the matters which my brother Anderson hath alleged, they be but inducements [introductory statements] to the point itself, and thereto everyone shall have his several answer.

Campion Opens the Defense

Whereupon Campion, for himself and his companions, answered unto Mr. Anderson's speech as followeth:

> CAMPION: The wisdom and providence of the laws of England, as I take it, is such as proceedeth not to the trial of any man for life and death by shifts of probabilities and conjectural surmises, without proof of the crime by sufficient evidence and substantial witness; for otherwise it had been very unequally provided that upon the descant and flourishes of affected speeches a man's life should be brought into danger and extremity, or that, upon the persuasion of any orator or vehement pleader without witness *viva voce* [live speech] testifying the same, a man's offense should be judged or reputed mortal. If so, I see not to what end Mr. Sergeant's oration tended, or if I see an end, I see it but frustrate; for be the crime but in trifles, the law hath his passage [process]; be the theft but of a half-penny, witnesses are produced; so that probabilities, aggravations, invectives, are not the balance wherein justice must be weighed, but witnesses, oaths, and apparent guiltiness. Whereto, then, appertaineth these objections of treason? He barely [simply] affirmeth; we flatly deny them. But let us examine them; how will they urge us? We fled our country; what of that? The Pope gave us entertainment; how then? We are Catholics; what is that to the purpose? We persuaded the people; what followeth? We are therefore traitors. We deny the sequel; this is no more necessary than if a sheep had been stolen, and to accuse me you should frame this reason [reasoning]: my parents

are thieves, my companions suspected persons, myself an evil liver, and one that loveth mutton; therefore I stole the sheep. Who seeth not but these be odious circumstances to bring a man in hatred with the jury, and no necessary matter to conclude him guilty? Yea, but we seduced the queen's subjects from their allegiance to her majesty! What can be more unlikely? We are dead men to the world, we only traveled for souls; we touched neither state nor policy, we had no such commission. Where was, then, our seducing? Nay, but we reconciled them to the Pope. Nay, then, what reconciliation can there be to him, since reconciliation is only due to God? This word soundeth not to a lawyer's usage, and therefore is wrested against us inaptly. The reconciliation that we endeavored was only to God, and, as Paul saith, *reconciliamini Domino* [be reconciled to the Lord[22]]. What resteth, then, against us? That we were privy to the re bellion in the North, instruments to Storey, ministers to Felton, partakers with Sanders. How so? Forsooth, it must be presumed. Why, because we commended some, some we rejoiced at, concerning some we gave counsel and conference.

How appeareth that? By our own speeches, nothing less. God is our witness we never meant it, we dreamed it not. These matters ought to be proved and not urged, declared by evidence and not surmised by fancy. Notwithstanding it ought to be so, yet must all circumstances note us for traitors. Indeed, all yet that is laid against us be but bare circumstances, and no sufficient arguments to prove us traitors, insomuch that we think ourselves somewhat hardly dealt with, that for want of proof we must answer to circumstances. Well, circumstances or other, as I remember, this was all; and if this were all, all this were nothing. Wherefore, in God's behalf, we pray that better proof may be used, and that our lives be not brought in prejudice by conjectures.

*   *   *

Says Anthony Munday in his hostile account of the trial:

This answer so smoothly delivered, and with such coy looks and protestation of action gestured, that all the slanders by gave perfect notice of the man, both of his nature and disposition, as also of his prompt and ingenious wit, to shadow an absolute truth with a show of great wisdom and learning. For this he knew right well, that before he came to that place, he had won a marvelous goodly report, to be such a man as his like was not to be found, either for life, learning, or any other quality that might beautify a man. So that by his favorers and friends it was blown abroad, that we had neither doctors, nor others that were worthy to enter disputation with him, he was so far above them all, that they might not deal with him. Hereto do the great titles which they adorn him withal give credit . . . [he then quotes "from a certain famous pamphlet" some lines of Latin poetry written in praise of Campion's learning, saying he scarce had any equal].

Now being brought unto a public trial, it stood him upon to argue somewhat of the praise that had been given him: wherefore in very quaint and familiar eloquent glosses he stood upon quirks and fine device of speech . . .[23]

One could not ask an enemy of that period to give higher praise than this.

The Accusation of Disloyalty Renewed

When the case was thus opened, the evidence for the prosecution was given.

QUEEN'S COUNSEL: It is the use [practice] of all seminary men, at the first entrance into their seminaries, to make two personal oaths, the one unto a book called Bristow's *Motives*[24] for the fulfilling of all matters therein contained; the other unto the Pope, to be true to him and to his successors, of the which oaths there is neither but is traitorous; for how can a man be faithful to our State, and swear performance to those *Motives;* a true liege to his sovereign, and swear fealty to the Pope, forasmuch as the one is quite contrary to our laws and government, the other the most mortal enemy her majesty hath?

CAMPION: What oaths seminary men do take at their first entrance, or whether Bristow's *Motives* be repugnant to our laws or no, is not anything material to our indictment, for we are neither seminary men nor sworn at our entrance to any such *Motives*. But were it so that any seminary men stood here for trial, this matter could prove no great evidence against them, for none are sworn to such articles as Bristow's but young striplings that be under tuition; whereas unto men of riper years and better grounded in points of religion (as most

of England are before they pass the seas) that oath is never administered; and then many a study else flourisheth in Rome, wherein
both seminary men and others are far better employed than they
otherwise could be in reading English pamphlets.

KIRBIE: I think of my conscience there be not four books of those
Bristow's *Motives* in all the seminaries.

Campion Demonstrates Their Crime Is Religion

Thereupon they all cried, that whereas they were indicted of treason, they
feared lest under vizard [mask] of that they should be condemned of religion; and, to prove that, Campion framed a reason [reasoning] in manner
following:

CAMPION: There was offer made unto us, that if we would come
to the church to hear sermons and the Word preached, we should
be set at large and at liberty; so Paschal and Nichols [two Catholics
who had given in],[25] otherwise as culpable in all offenses as we, upon
coming to the church and acceptance of that offer, were received to
grace and had their pardon granted; whereas, if they had been so
happy as to have persevered to the end, they had been partakers of
our calamities. Wherefore, if liberty were offered to us on condition
to come to church and hear sermons—and that could we not do by
professing our religion—then, to change our religion and to become
Protestants, that, forsooth, was that that should purchase us liberty.
So that our religion was cause of our imprisonment, and, *ex conse-
quenti* [consequently], of our condemnation.

ATTORNEY-GENERAL POPHAM: All these matters at the time
of Nichols' enlargement [release] were altogether unknown, and not
once suspected; neither can we now conjecture that he was guilty of
any such drift or purpose, in that he stood not, as you do, stubbornly
in that religion which might be any cloak or color of such treasons.

More Evidence of Money and Vows

QUEEN'S COUNSEL: All you jointly and severally have received
money of the Pope to spend in your journeys. Some two hundred
crowns, some more, some less, according to your degrees and conditions. Was such liberality of the Pope's without cause? No, it had an

end; and what end should that be but by your privy inveiglings and persuasions to set on foot his devices and treacheries?

CAMPION: We received of him according to the rate he thought best to bestow it. We saw neither cause why to re fuse it, nor means how to come hither penniless; it was his liberality, it supplied our need. What would you have us do? We took it; was that treason? But it was to an end: I grant; had it been to no end, it had been in vain; and what end should that be? Merely to preach the Gospel; no treachery, no such end was intended.

Caddy's Testimony on the Vow

There was a witness produced, named H. CADDY or H. CADDOCKE,[26] who deposed, generally, against them all, that being beyond the seas he heard of the holy vow made between the pope and the English priests for the restoring and establishing of religion in England; for the which purpose two hundred priests should come into the realm, the which matter was declared to Sir Ralph [Richard] Shelley, an English knight, and captain to the pope, and that he should conduct an army into England, for the subduing of the realm unto the pope, and the destroying of the heretics. Whereto Sir Ralph made answer, that he would rather drink poison with Themistocles[27] than see the overthrow of his country; and added further, that he thought the Catholics in England would first stand in arms against the pope before they would join in such an enterprise.

[The Catholic account of the trial in Laing[28] says that Caddy deposed that while he was in prison in Rome he was visited by an Englishman who told him he was lucky to be out of his own country where soon there would be great tumult and much bloodshed and slaughter.]

QUEEN'S COUNSEL: The matter is flat [plain]: the holy vow was made, two hundred priests had their charge appointed, the captain-general was mentioned, our destruction purposed. If, then, we confer all likelihoods together, what is more apparent than that of those two hundred priests you made up a number, and therefore be parties and privy to the treason?

CAMPION: Two hundred priests made an holy vow to labor for restoring of religion. It seemeth, by all likelihood, that we made up the number, and therefore privy and parties to the treason: here is a conclusion without any jot of affinity to the premises; first, an holy vow, then an establishing of religion. What color is there here left for treason? All the treason rehearsed was imputed to Sir Ralph [Richard] Shelley; not one syllable thereof was referred to the priests. But granting, and which the witnesses have not deposed, namely, that we are some of the two hundred priests; you see Sir Ralph [Richard] Shelley, a Catholic, the Pope's captain, a layman, would rather drink poison than agree to such treason; is it like[29] that priests, devotaries and dead men to the world, would in any wise consent unto it? This deposition is more for us than against us.

*   *   *

Then was order taken that every man's evidence should be particularly read against himself, and everyone to have his several answer; and first against Campion.

The Bull of Pius V Discussed

QUEEN'S COUNSEL: About ten years since, you, Campion, were received into conference with the Cardinal of St. Cecilia [Cardinal Gesualdi: see chapter 4] concerning the Bull wherein Pius V did excommunicate the queen, the nobility, and commonalty of this realm; discharging such of them as were Papists from their obedience to her Majesty, the which conference cannot otherwise be referred than to the putting in execution of the Bull; so that the Bull containing manifest treason, whereto you were privy, doth flat prove you a traitor.

CAMPION: You, men of the jury, I pray you listen. This concerneth me only, and thereto this I answer. True it is that at my first arrival into Rome (which is now about ten years past) it was my hap [fortune] to have access to the said Cardinal, who, having some liking of me, would have been the means to prefer me to any place of service whereunto I should have most fancy; but I, being resolved what course to take, answered that I meant not to serve any man but to enter into the Society of Jesus, thereof to vow and to be professed. Then, being demanded further, what opinion I had conceived of the Bull, I said it procured much severity in England, and the heavy hand of her Majesty against the Catholics. Where unto the Cardinal replied that he doubted not it should be mitigated in such sort as the

Catholics should acknowledge her highness as their queen without danger of excommunication. And this was all the speech I had with the Cardinal, which can in nowise be construed as an offense, much less as the least point of treason.

QUEEN'S COUNSEL: We can impute no more by your words than a mitigation of the Bull against the Catholics only; so that the principal, which was the excommunication of her Majesty, was still left in force, not detected [reported to the authorities] by you, and there fore your privity [knowledge] thereto concludeth you a traitor.

CAMPION: My privity thereto enforceth not my consenting; nay, rather, it proved my disagreement, in that I said it procured much severity; and therefore, being here published before I could detect [report] it (for who knew not that the Queen of England was excommunicated?), it excused my privity and exempted me from treason.

[So absurd is the accusation, the reader may wonder if he has understood it aright. The charge is that Campion in Rome did not report to the English authorities that the pope had excommunicated Elizabeth, and therefore was a traitor for being in the know of this attack upon the queen. Campion is then forced to state the obvious: I was not in favor of the effect of the Bull, and, besides, everyone knew the Bull had been issued, so why should I report a well-known fact?]

QUEEN'S COUNSEL: You had conference with the Bishop of Ross [Catholic Bishop John Leslie, a supporter of Mary Queen of Scots], a professed Papist and a mortal enemy to the state and crown of England; and to what end should any such communication be had, but for the practising of such treasons as had been conspired?

CAMPION: What the Bishop of Ross is, either for religion or affection, I think little pertinent to me, much less to this purpose; but as for the conference passed between him and me, I utterly deny that ever there was any, and therefore let that be proved.

Dr. Allen's Military Plans for England

The Clerk of the Crown read a letter sent from Dr. Allen unto Dr. Sanders in Ireland,[30] wherein Allen showeth why the insurrection in the North prevailed not, was in two respects: either that God reserved England for a greater plague, or that the Catholics in other places had not intelligence of the purpose; for otherwise that could not so badly have succeeded. In this letter, moreover, was contained, that "[the King of Spain] feared the war as a child doth the rod," and that "[the pope] at all times will be ready with 2,000 [soldiers] to aid him."[31]

> QUEEN'S COUNSEL: What an army and host of men the Pope, by the aid of the King of Spain and the Duke of Florence, had levied for the overthrow of this realm, the destruction of her Majesty, and the placing of the Scottish Queen as governess in England, could not any ways have escaped your know ledge; for being sent from Prague, where your abode was, to Rome, and then being by the Pope charged presently to wards England, what other drift could this such a sudden ambassage [commission] portend than the practicing and execution of such a conspiracy? Whereof you are also the more to be suspected forasmuch as in your coming from Rome towards England, you entered into a certain privy conference with Dr. Allen at Rheims, to whose letters above mentioned, touching the estate, it cannot be but by means of that conference you were privy, for the furtherance of which platforms and devices yourself came as procurator from the Pope and Dr. Allen to break these matters to the English Papists, to withdraw the people from their due allegiance, and to prepare men ready to receive those foreign powers.

[This above-mentioned alliance, the Papal League of 1580, did not in fact exist.][32]

Campion's Only Concern and Labors Were for the Gospel

> CAMPION: When I was first received into the Order of Jesuits, I vowed three things incident to my calling—chastity, poverty, and obedience: chastity, in abstaining from all fleshly appetites and concupiscences; poverty, in despising all worldly wealth, living upon the devotion of others; obedience, in dutifully executing the commandments of my superiors. In respect of which vow enjoining obedience, I came, being sent for, from Prague to Rome, having not so much as the smallest inkling of those supposed armies, nor the least inclination to put any such thing in practice; but there rested for eight days attending the pleasure of my provost [Father General], who at last, according to my vow (which, by the grace of God, I will in no case violate), appointed me to undertake this journey into

England, the which accordingly I enterprised, being commanded thereto, not as a traitor to conspire the subversion of my country, but as a priest to minister the sacraments and to hear confessions; the which ambassage [commission] I protest before God I would as gladly have executed, and was as ready and willing to discharge, had I been sent to the Indians or uttermost regions in the world, as I was being sent into my native country.

In the which voyage I cannot deny but that I dined with Dr. Allen at Rheims, with whom also after dinner I walked in his garden, spending a time in speeches referred to our old familiarity and acquaintance; during the whole course thereof (I take God to witness) not one jot of our talk glanced to the crown or state of England; neither had I the least notice of any letters sent to Sanders, nor the smallest glimmering of these objected platforms.

Then, as for being procurator from the Pope and Dr. Allen, I must needs say there could no one thing have been inferred more contrary; for as concerning the one, he flatly [clearly] with charge and commandment excused me from matters of state and regiment; the other I owed no such duty and obedience unto, as to execute matters repugnant to my charge. But admitting (as I protest he did not) that Dr. Allen had communicated such affairs unto me, yet for that he was not my superior, it would have been full apostasy in me to obey him. Dr. Allen, for his learning and good religion, I reverence; but neither was I his subject or inferior, nor he the man at whose commandment I rested.

QUEEN'S COUNSEL: Were it not that your dealing afterwards had fully bewrayed [betrayed] you, your present speech had been more credible; but all afterclaps [unexpected aftermath] make those excuses but shadows, and your deeds and actions prove your words but forged; for what meaning had that changing of your name? Whereto be longed your disguising in apparel [clothing]? Can these alterations be wrought without suspicion? Your name being Campion, why were you called Hastings? You a priest and dead to the world, what pleasure had you to royst it [bluster]? A velvet hat and a feather, a buff leather jerkin, velvet Venetians [breeches], are they weeds for dead men? Can that beseem a professed man of religion which hardly becometh a layman of gravity? No, there was a further matter intended; your lurking and lying hid in secret places concludeth with the rest a mischievous meaning. Had you come hither for love of your country, you would never have wrought a hugger-mugger [concealment]; had your intent been to have done well, you would never have hated the light; and therefore this budging [sneaking] deciphereth your treason.

CAMPION: At what time the primitive Church was persecuted, and that Paul labored in the propagation and increase of the Gospel, it is not unknown to what straits and pinches he and his fellows were diversely driven; wherein, though in purpose he were already resolved rather to yield himself to martyrdom than to shrink an inch from the truth which he preached, yet if any hope or means appeared to escape, and that living he might benefit the Church more than dying, we read of sundry shifts whereto he betook him to increase God's number and to shun persecution; but especially the changing of his name was very oft and familiar, whereby, as opportunity and occasion was ministered, he termed himself now Paul, now Saul;[33] neither was he of opinion always to be known, but sometimes thought it expedient to be hidden, lest being discovered, persecution should ensue, and thereby the Gospel greatly forestalled. Such was his meaning, so was his purpose, when, being in durance [prison] for points of religion, he secretly stole out of prison in a basket. If these shifts were then approved in Paul, why are they now reproved in me?—he an Apostle, I a Jesuit. Were they commended in him, are they condemned in me? The same cause was common to us both; and shall the effect be peculiar to the one? I wished earnestly the planting of the Gospel; I knew a contrary religion professed; I saw if I were known I should be apprehended; I changed my name; I kept secretly; I imitated Paul. Was I therein a traitor? But the wearing of a buff jerkin, a velvet hat, and such like, is much forced against me, as though the wearing of any apparel were treason, or that I in so doing were ever the more a traitor. I am not indicted upon the Statute of Apparel, neither is it any part of this present arraignment; indeed, I acknowledge an offense to God for so doing, and thereof it did grievously repent me, and therefore do now penance as you see me. (He was newly shaven, in a rug-gown, and a great black nightcap[34] covering half his face).

[There was in fact a Statute of Apparel, of 1515, amended in Elizabeth's time, designed to stop Italian fashions spreading in England.]

Campion's Letter to Pounde Cited

The Clerk of the Crown read a letter sent from Campion unto one [Thomas] Pounde, a Catholic, part of the contents whereof was this:

> It grieveth me much to have offended the Catholic cause so highly as to confess the names of some gentlemen and friends in whose houses I had been entertained; yet in this I greatly cherish and comfort myself that I never discovered [revealed] any secrets there declared, and that I will not, come rack, come rope.

QUEEN'S COUNSEL: What can sound more suspiciously or nearer unto treason than this letter? It grieveth him to have bewrayed [betrayed] his favouers the Catholics; and therein he thinketh to have wrought prejudice to religion. What, then, may we think of that he concealeth? It must needs be some grievous matter, and very pernicious, that neither the rack nor the rope can wring from him. For his conscience being not called in question, nor sifted in any point of religion, no doubt if there had not been further devices intended, and affairs of the state and the commonwealth attempted, we should as well have discovered the matter as the person; wherefore it were well these hidden secrets were revealed, and then would appear the very face of these treasons.

CAMPION: As I am by profession and calling a priest, so I have singly vowed all conditions and covenants to such a charge and vocation belonging, whereby I sustain one office and duty of priesthood that consisteth in shriving and hearing confessions, in respect whereof, at my first consecration (as all other priests so accepted must do) I solemnly took and vowed to God never to disclose any secrets confessed; the force and effect of which vow is such as whereby every priest is bound, and endangered under pain of perpetual curse and damnation, never to disclose any offense opened nor infirmity whatsoever committed to his hearing. By virtue of this profession, and due execution of my priesthood, I was accustomed to be privy unto divers men's secrets, and those not such as concerned state or commonwealth, whereunto my authority was not extended, but such as surcharged the grieved soul and conscience, whereof I had power to proffer absolution.[35] These were the hidden matters, these were the secrets, in concealing of which I so greatly rejoiced, to the revealing whereof I cannot nor will not be brought, come rack, come rope.

Oaths against Her Majesty

Thereupon the Clerk of the Crown read certain papers containing in them oaths to be administered to the people for the renouncing their obedience to her Majesty, and the swearing of allegiance to the pope, acknowledging him for their supreme head and governor; the which papers were found in divers houses where Campion had lurked, and for religion been entertained.

[These may be nothing more than copies of the spiritual *Testament*, a profession of Catholic faith, given out by Persons and Campion, received originally from Cardinal Borromeo.][36]

> QUEEN'S COUNSEL: What can be more apparent [plain] than this? These oaths, if we went no further, are of themselves sufficient to convince [convict] you of treason; for what may be imagined more traitorous than to alien [alienate] the hearts of the subjects from her Majesty, renouncing their obedience to her, and swearing their subjection to the Pope? And therefore these papers thus found in houses where you were do clearly prove that for ministering such oaths you are a traitor.
>
> CAMPION: Neither is there, neither can there be anything imagined more directly contrary or repugnant to my calling than upon any occasion to minister an oath; neither had I any power or authority so to do; neither would I commit an offense so thwart [opposed] to my profession for all the substance and treasure in the world. But, admit I were authorised, what necessity importeth that reason, that neither being set down by my handwriting nor otherwise derived by any proof from myself, but only found in places where I resorted, therefore I should be he by whom they were ministered? This is but a naked presumption (who seeth it not?) and nothing vehement nor of force against me.
>
> ANDERSON: It could not otherwise be intended [understood] but that you ministered these oaths; and that being found behind you, it was you that left them. For if a poor man and a rich man come both to one house, and that after their departure a bag of gold be found hidden, forasmuch as the poor man had no such plenty, and therefore could leave no such bag behind him, by common presumption it is to be intended that the rich man only, and no other, did hide the bag. So you, a professed Papist, coming to a house, and there such

relics found after your departure, how can it otherwise be implied but that you did both bring them and leave them there? So it is flat [plain] they came there by means of a Papist, *ergo* [therefore] by your means.

CAMPION: Your conclusion had been necessary if you had also showed that none came into the house of my profession but I; but there you urge your conclusion before you frame your minor, whereby your reason [reasoning] is imperfect; *ergo* it proveth not.

ANDERSON: If here, as you do in schools, you bring in your minor and conclusion, you will prove yourself but a fool: but minor or conclusion, I will bring it to purpose anon.[37]

Campion Silent on Whether the Pope Can Depose

QUEEN'S COUNSEL: You refuse to swear to the supremacy, a notorious token of an evil willer to the crown, insomuch as, being demanded by the commissioners whether the Bull wherein Pius V had excommunicated her Majesty were in your opinion of force, and the excommunication of effect or no, you would answer nothing but that these were bloody questions, and that they which sought these sought your life: also resembling [likening] the commissioners unto the Pharisees, who to entrap Christ propounded a dilemma, whether tribute were to be paid to Caesar or no; so that in your examination you would come to no issue, but sought your evasions and made answers aloof, which vehemently argueth a guiltiness of conscience, in that the truth would never have sought corners [hiding places].

The two commissioners, Mr. [Thomas] Norton and Mr. [John] Hammond,[38] were present, and verified the matter as the queen's Counsel had urged.

CAMPION: Not long since [ago], it pleased her Majesty to demand of me whether I did acknowledge her to be my queen or no.[39] I answered that I did acknowledge Her Highness not only as my queen, but also as my most lawful governess; and being further required of her Majesty whether I thought the Pope might lawfully excommunicate her or no, I answered, I confess my self an insufficient umpire between her Majesty and the Pope for so high a controversy, whereof neither the certainty is as yet known, nor the best divines [theologians] in Christendom stand fully resolved.

[Campion says, rightly, that theologians were then divided on the question of whether a pope can directly depose a ruler—in addition to his undisputed power to excommunicate. "Excommunication" as an ecclesiastical penalty meant then what it means now, but in the context of Christendom—that is, a society, culture and State based explicitly on Christian faith and communion—the practical effect of the "greater excommunication" (cf. 1917 *Code of Canon Law*, canons 2257–67) was to render a Christian ruler incapable of exercising authority, so a sentence of deposition was a logical consequence. Today, theologians are agreed that the pope cannot by decree directly remove from office a temporal ruler of another country—but he can order Catholics not to obey in matters contrary to the law of God.]

> Albeit I thought that if the Pope should do it, yet it might be insufficient; for it is agreed, *clavis errare potest* [the key (of Peter) can err]; but the divines of the Catholic Church do distinguish of the Pope's authority, attributing unto him *ordinata et inordinata potestas* [ordinary and extraordinary power]: *ordinata* [ordinary], whereby he proceedeth in matters merely spiritual and pertinent to the Church, and by that he cannot excommunicate any prince or potentate; *inordinata* [extraordinary],[40] when he passeth by [bypasses] order of law, as by appeals and such like, and so, some think, he may excommunicate and depose princes.
>
> The self-same articles were required of me by the commissioners, but much more urged to the point of supremacy, and to further supposals than I could think of. I said, indeed, they were bloody questions, and very pharisaical, undermining of my life; whereunto I answered as Christ did to the dilemma, "Give unto Caesar that which is due to Caesar, and to God that to God belongeth": I acknowledged her Highness as my governess and sovereign; I acknowledged her Majesty both *facto et jure* [in fact and in law] to be queen; I confessed an obedience due to the crown as to my temporal head and primate. This I said then, so I say now. If, then, I failed in aught, I am now ready to supply it. What would you more? I will willingly pay to her Majesty what is hers, yet I must pay to God what is His. Then, as for excommunicating her Majesty, it was exacted of me—admitting that excommunication were of effect, and that the Pope had sufficient authority so to do—whether then I thought myself discharged of my allegiance or no? I said this was

a dangerous question, and they that demanded this demanded my blood. Admitting—why admitting? *ex admissis et concessis quid non sequitur* [what does not follow from the points admitted and conceded]—if I would admit his authority, and then he should excommunicate her, I would then do as God should give me grace.

But I never admitted any such matter, neither ought I to be wrested with any such suppositions. What then, say they, because I would not answer flatly [plainly] to that which I could not, forsooth I sought corners [refuges]; mine answers were aloof. Well, since once more it must needs be answered, I say generally that these matters be merely spiritual points of doctrine and disputable in schools, no part of mine indictment, not to be given in evidence, and unfit to be discussed at the King's Bench. To conclude: they are no matters of fact; they be not in the trial of the country; the jury ought not to take any notice of them; for although I doubt not but they are very discreet men and trained up in great use and experience of controversies and debates pertinent to their callings, yet are they laymen, they are temporal, and unfit judges to decide so deep a question.

Eliot Testifies

Eliot, a witness, deposed against Campion that he made a sermon in Berkshire [at Lyford Grange], his text being of Christ weeping over Jerusalem, wherein Campion showed many vices and enormities here abounding in England, and namely heresies, wherewith he was sorry that his countrymen were so blinded; but hoped shortly there would hap [happen] a day of change comfortable to the Catholics, now shaken and dispersed, and terrible to the heretics here flourishing in the land. Eliot added that in his sermon Campion had persuaded his audience to obedience to the pope; but on being urged by Campion he confessed that he did not remember the pope being named once in the sermon.[41]

[Henry Walpole here adds this detail on the exchange:[42]

CAMPION: Pray tell me, Eliot, did I mention the Pope's name in my sermon, or not?

ELIOT: I don't remember.

CAMPION: Then, my lords [the judges], and you, sirs [of the jury], I beg you to notice what a conscience this man has, and how he should be trusted in the rest of his story, seeing that after he has sworn that I exhorted him to abandon the Queen and obey the Pope, he now says that he does not remember what I said.

ELIOT: I told you so. If you will listen he has a pestilent tongue.]

QUEEN'S COUNSEL: Lo, what would you wish more manifest? The great day is threatened, comfortable to them, and terrible to us; and what day should that be but that wherein the Pope, the King of Spain, and the Duke of Florence have appointed to invade this realm?

CAMPION: O Judas, Judas! [so naming Eliot]. No other day was in my mind, I protest, than that wherein it should please God to make a restitution of faith and religion. For as in all other Christian commonwealths, so in England, many vices and iniquities do abound, neither is there any realm so godly, no people so devout, nowhere so religious, but that in the same very places many enormities do flourish, and evil men bear sway and regiment. Whereupon, as in every pulpit every Protestant doth, I pronounced a great day, not where in any temporal potentate should minister, but wherein the terrible Judge should reveal all men's consciences, and try every man of each kind of religion. This is the day of change, this is the great day which I threatened; comfort able to the well-believing, and terrible to all heretics. Any other day than this, God He knows I meant not.

Munday Testifies

Munday, a witness, deposed that he heard the Englishmen, as the doctors and others, talk, and conspire of these treasons against England, and that Campion and others afterwards had conference with Dr. Allen.

CAMPION: Here is nothing deposed against me directly; and as for my conference with Dr. Allen, it hath appeared when and what it was.

Charges against Sherwin

Evidence was next given against Sherwin, who before the commissioners had refused to swear to the supremacy, neither would answer plainly what he thought of the pope's Bull, but confessed that his coming into England was to persuade the people to the Catholic religion.

QUEEN'S COUNSEL: You well knew that it was not lawful for you to persuade the queen's subjects to any other religion than by her Highness's injunctions is already professed; and therefore, if there had not been a further matter in your meaning, you would have kept your conscience to yourself, and yourself where you were.

SHERWIN: We read that the Apostles and Fathers in the primitive Church have taught and preached in the dominions and empires of ethnic and heathen rulers, and yet not deemed worthy of death. The sufferance, and perhaps the like toleration, I well hope for in such a commonwealth as where open Christianity and godliness is pretended [claimed]; and albeit in such a diversity of religion it was to be feared lest I might not discharge my conscience without fear of danger, yet ought I not therefore to surcease in my functions, although that conscience is very wavering and unsteady, which with fear of danger draweth from duty.

ONE OF THE JUSTICES [forgetting his role as judge, and assuming the part of prosecutor]: But your case differeth from theirs in the primitive Church, for those Apostles and preachers never conspired the death of those emperors and rulers in whose dominions they so taught and preached.

THE CLERK OF THE CROWN read a letter, which showed that, by the fireside in the English seminary beyond the seas, Sherwin should say that if he were in England he could compass many things, and that there was one Arundell in Cornwall, who at an instant could levy a great power; and that if an army were to be sent into England, the best landing would be at St. Michael's Mount.

SHERWIN: I never spake any such matter, God is my record; neither was it ever the least part of my meaning.

Charges against Bosgrave

Bosgrave's opinion was read, wherein he had denied the supremacy, and staggered [hesitated] without any perfect answer to the Bull; but said that he came into England to persuade and teach, acknowledging her Majesty his queen and temporal head. In the which examination he confessed that beyond the seas he heard it reported how the pope, the King of Spain, and the Duke of Florence, would send a great army into England to deprive the queen's majesty both of life and dignity, for the restitution of the Catholic religion.

> QUEEN'S COUNSEL: The keeping close and not detecting of treason maketh the hearer of it to become a traitor; and therefore, inasmuch as you concealed what you heard, and made not information of it to her Majesty, the Council, nor the commonwealth of this realm, you became thereby privy and party unto it, and therefore in these respects you are a traitor.

> BOSGRAVE: What! Am I a traitor because I heard it spoken?

But Campion, perceiving Bosgrave merely [utterly] daunted with the matter, spake to excuse him in manner as followeth:

> CAMPION: My lord, it is not unknown to your Honor how brittle and slippery ground fame and reports are wont to be built on; the which, as for the most part they are more false than credible, so ought they always to ·make men wary and fearful to deal with them, insomuch as the broacher of rumors and news is he that getteth commonly least credit or thanks for his labor. The cause is the property and nature of fame, which is never but uncertain, and sometimes but forged; for who findeth it not by daily experience, how that in every city, every village, yea and in most barbers' shops, in all England, many speeches, both of states and common wealths be tossed, which were never meant nor determined of in the court. If it be so in England, shall we not look for the like in Italy, Flanders, France and Spain? Yes, truly; for though the countries do differ, yet the nature of the men remaineth the same, namely, always desirous and greedy of news. Many things there be diversely reported and diversely canvassed by the common sort, which were never intended [regarded] by the bearers of rule and principality. Were it not, then, a great point of credulity for a man divided from England by many seas and lands, upon a matter only blazed among the vulgar people, either by journey or letter to certify the queen's Council or commonalty of things never purposed, much less put in practice? I rather think Mr. Bosgrave's discretion to have been greater in passing [over] such dangerous occasions with themselves, than otherwise it had been in using means to bewray [expose] them. But, supposing he had done as you would have had him, and what he heard there he had signified here, what had come of it? Marry, then,

greater danger for slandering the realm, and how little thanks for his false information? So that, if he would deal either wisely or safely, how could he deal better than to do as he did?

ATTORNEY-GENERAL: There is no cloth so coarse but Campion can cast a color upon it. But what, was it not Bosgrave's own confession that he arrived into England to teach and persuade the people, and what persuasions should they be but to prepare a readiness for these wars?

CAMPION: These be but faint and bare implications, which move but urge not, affirm but prove not; whereas you ought not to amplify and gather upon words when a matter concerneth and toucheth a man's life.

Charges against Cottam

Cottam, in his examination, would neither agree to the supremacy, nor answer directly concerning the pope's authority.

QUEEN'S COUNSEL: You came into England at or near the time that the rest came; so that it must needs be intended [understood] a match made between you, for the furtherance of those affairs which were then a-brewing; and how answer you thereunto?

COTTAM: It was neither my purpose nor my message to come into England; neither would I have come had not God otherwise driven me; for my journey was appointed to the Indians, and thither had I gone had my health been thereto answerable; but in the meanwhiles it pleased God to visit me with sickness, and being counseled by the physicians for my health's sake to come into England—for otherways, as they said, either remaining there or going elsewhere, I should not recover it, I came upon that occasion, and upon no other, into this realm.

CAMPION: Indeed, the physicians in Rome do hold for a certainty that, if an Englishman shall fall sick amongst them, there is no better nor scant any other way for his health than to repair [go] into England, there to take his natural air, which agreeth best with his complexion.

COTTAM: And that only was the cause of my coming, and not any determinate intent either to persuade or dissuade, being otherwise

by my provost charged to the Indians. Neither after my arrival
here did I hide myself, nor dealt otherwise than might beseem any
man that meddled no more than I did. I lay for the most part in
Southwark; I walked daily in Paul's; I refrained no place, which
betokened my innocency.

QUEEN'S COUNSEL: Did you neither persuade nor dissuade? Was
there not a book found in your budget [bag], the contents whereof
tended to no other purpose? The which book was made by one
Azpilcueta,[43] entitled *Tractatus Conscientiæ* [Tract on Conscience],
containing certain answers to the supremacy, and how sophisti-
cally to frustrate any kinds of demands [questions]; with a further
method how you ought to demean yourself in every sort of company, whether it were of Protestants or Puritans, and what speeches
you should use to convert them both; as unto the Protestants highly
commending them and showing that they are far nearer the right
way than the Puritans, and whom you should utterly dispraise unto
the Puritans; likewise in commending the Protestants and persuading them to the obedience of the Pope. To what end, then, should
you carry this book about you, if you were not purposed to do as it
prescribeth?

COTTAM: I protest before God I knew nothing of that book, neither how nor when it came to me.

Then Campion, seeing him driven to so narrow an exigent [neces-
sity] as to deny that which was manifest, answered for him to this effect
following:

CAMPION: Many casualties and events may happen where by a
man may be endangered ere he beware by the carrying of a thing
he knoweth not, as either the malice of others that privily convey
it amongst other his provisions, or his own negligence or oversight
which marked not attentively what he took with him; whereof both
are to be judged errors, yet not deemed an offense; and therefore this
cannot be maintained to be done by Mr. Cottam on purpose which
we see flatly [plainly] to be out of his knowledge. But suppose that
purposely he brought the book with him, yet what can that make
against him for treason? It treateth of conscience; it toucheth good
demeanor; it showeth how to make the unbelieving faithful: matters wholly spiritual, points of edification, preparing to Godwards;

where is, then, the treason? But were these reasons impertinent, yet it is a custom with all students beyond the seas, when any man learned or well thought of draweth a treatise touching either conscience or good behavior, to copy it out and to carry it about with them, not thereby aiming at any faction or conspiracy, but for their own proper knowledge and private instruction.

Charges against Johnson

[Robert] Johnson would neither grant to the supremacy, neither yield any resolute opinion of the pope's authority in his Bull and excommunication.

Eliot, a witness, deposed against [Fr. Robert] Johnson, that at Christ's Nativity come two years [1579], being at my Lady Petre's house, he fell into acquaintance with one [John] Payne, a priest that exercised the office of a steward in the house,[44] who by reason that he was appointed to be his bed-fellow grew into a further familiarity with him, insomuch that at length he ventured to dissuade him from his allegiance to her Majesty and to become subject to the Pope; affirming that her Highness could not live for ever, and that shortly after her days the Catholic religion should be restored; for the furtherance whereof the Catholics beyond seas had already devised a practice, which is this: that fifty of them (whereof either should know other) should come to the court furnished with privy coats, pocket dags [pistols],[45] and two-handed swords, attending [waiting] until her Majesty should take the air or go on some petty progress [trip], and then some of them should set upon her Majesty, some upon the Lord-treasurer [Burghley], some upon the Earl of Leicester, some upon Sir Francis Walsingham, and others upon others the favorers of this heretical religion, there to kill her Majesty and to tie her by the hair of the head unto a horse, to be lugged and haled up and down to the joy of all Catholics and distress of all heretics; of the which, so Payne offered this deponent, if he would, he should be one, adding further, that if he had place and opportunity convenient, he should stab her Majesty with a dagger himself, for he thought it no more unlawful to kill her than to kill a horned beast.[46] After which communication, Payne, finding this deponent not so conformable unto him as he hoped, and receiving a bitter and flat refusal of his ungracious proffer, conveyed himself away, and was no more to be heard of. Whereupon this Johnson, now arraigned, came to the deponent, and inquired what was become of Payne, to whom he answered that he knew not. Then said Johnson, "He is gone beyond the seas, fearing lest you would discover his secrets; and therefore I forewarn and conjure you not to disclose anything that Payne hath told you; for if you do, you stand in state of damnation."

JOHNSON: I never in my life had any such talk with him, nor uttered any such speeches tending to any such matter.

Charges against Rishton

Rishton's[47] examination was read, wherein he had acknowledged her Majesty his lawful queen and governess, and that notwithstanding aught that the pope had done or could do, she was his supreme head.

QUEEN'S COUNSEL: What was, then, the cause of your coming into this realm? For it seemeth by your sudden arrival and journeying with the rest that you were also a party and furtherer of their purpose.

RISHTON: I have to my mother a poor widow, who besides had one other son, with the company of whom during his life she was well appayed [satisfied]; but it pleased God afterwards to dispose him at His mercy, and to deprive my mother of his further succor. She, taking the matter very heavily, used what means she could possibly for my return. She sent letters after letters, and those so importunate, that, will I nill I, I must needs come home; the which was the only cause of my arrival, and not any other, God is my witness.

Anthony Munday deposed against Rishton that he should say he was cunning in fireworks and that shortly he would make a confection of wildfire, wherewith he would burn her Majesty when she were on the Thames in her barge; and the deponent swore further that he heard it spoken beyond the seas that whosoever had not the watch word, which was "Jesus Maria," should be slain.

RISHTON: I call God to witness I never suffered [experienced] such thoughts, nor never had any such cunning in fireworks; and therefore he sweareth the greatest untruth that may be.

Sledd's Evidence against Kirbie

Kirbie, in his examination for the supremacy and the pope's authority, was of no other opinion than was Campion.

> Sledd,[48] a witness, deposed against Kirbie, that being sick beyond the seas, this Kirbie came unto his bedside and counseled him to beware how he dealt with any matters in England; for there would come a great day wherein the Pope, the King of Spain, and the Duke of Florence should make as great an alteration as ever was. He deposed that Kirbie was at a sermon of Dr. Allen's, who then persuaded the priests and seminary men to take their journey into England, to remove the Englishmen from their obedience to her Highness, and to persuade them to aid the Pope and his confederates. He deposed, moreover, that beyond the seas he spake with one [Father William] Tedder, a familiar friend of Kirbie's, of whom he, deponent, demanded whether he were of kin to her Majesty [Elizabeth Tudor], for his name was Tedder; whereunto he answered that if he knew himself to be kin to that Whore of Babylon, that Jezebel of England [Elizabeth], he would think the worse of himself as long as he lived; but one day he would make a journey into England, and, if it were possible, despatch her out of the way.
>
> KIRBIE: As I hope to be saved at the last doom, there is not one word of this deposition that concerneth me either true or credible; neither at any time made I the least mention of that alleged day; neither was I present at any sermon so preached; but I always bore as true and faithful heart to her Majesty as any subject whatsoever did in England, insomuch that I never heard her Majesty evil spoken of but I defended her cause, and always spake the best of her Highness. It is not unknown that I saved English mariners from hanging only for the duty I bore to her Majesty, with the love and goodwill which I bore to my country.[49] But you that have thus deposed, when was then this sermon that you talk of so preached? At what time of the day?

The witness answered that the same day there were three philosophical disputations, after the which the sermon was preached.

Munday Testifies against Orton

Orton would neither agree to the supremacy, nor openly affirm what authority the pope had, nor whether he thought the excommunication of Pope Pius V to be of force or no.

Anthony Munday deposed against Orton, that he being at Lyons in France, said unto this deponent, that her Majesty was not lawful queen of England, and that he owed her no kind of obedience. The deponent said further that this Orton made suit unto Dr. Allen that he might be one of the pope's pensioners, whereunto Dr. Allen would not agree unless Orton would become a priest or seminary man, which he refused.

> ORTON: I utterly deny that I ever had any speech with the witness, either at Lyons or elsewhere; but he manifestly forsweareth [perjures] himself, as one that having neither honesty nor religion, careth for neither.
>
> The same ALL THE PARTIES indicted did affirm, and that he was an atheist; for beyond the seas he went on pilgrimage, and received the Sacrament, making himself a Catholic, and here he taketh a new face, and playeth the Protestant; and there fore is an unfit and unworthy witness to give in evidence or to depose against life.
>
> MUNDAY, the witness, answered, that in France and other places he seemed to favor their religion, because he might thereby undermine them and sift out their purposes.
>
> THE PRISONERS took exception to another of the witnesses [Eliot, no doubt], which of them I know not, for he was a murderer and had slain two men, already well known by his own confession and acknowledgment; for which reason he was no sufficient nor allowable witness.

The Final Direction to the Jury

These matters thus sifted, and that the jury should pass [give a verdict],

> ONE OF THE JUSTICES said to the jurors: All the matter resteth in this, either to believe the prisoners that speak for their lives, or the witnesses that come freely to depose as they are demanded; the witnesses affirm sufficient proof against them; they deny whatsoever is alleged.

LORD CHIEF-JUSTICE: You that be here indicted, you see what is alleged against you. In discharge whereof, if you have any more to say, speak, and we will hear you till to morrow morning. We would be loath you should have any occasion to complain on the court; and therefore, if aught rest behind that is untold, that is available for you, speak, and you shall be heard with indifference [impartiality].

Campion's Closing Speech to the Jury

They all thanked his lordship, and said they could not otherwise affirm but that they had found of the Court both in difference and justice. Whereupon Campion made this speech to the jurors:

CAMPION: *[The gravity of the issue]:* What charge this day you sustain, and what accompt [account] you are to render at the dreadful Day of Judgment, whereof I would wish this also were a mirror, I trust there is not one of you but knoweth. I doubt not but in like manner you forecast [have before you] how dear the innocent is to God, and at what price He holdeth man's blood. Here we are accused and impleaded [prosecuted] to the death; here you do receive our lives into your custody; here must be your choice, either to restore them or condemn them. We have no whither to appeal but to your consciences; we have no friends to make there but your heeds and discretions. Take heed, I beseech you, let no colors nor inducements deceive you; let your ground be substantial, for your building is weighty. All this you may do sufficiently, we doubt not, if you will mark intentively [attentively] what things have been treated, in three distinct and several points.

The speech and discourse of this whole day consisteth, first, in presumptions and probabilities; secondly, in matters of religion; lastly, in oaths and testimonies of witnesses.

[Mere presumptions]: The weak and forceless proof that proceedeth from conjectures is neither worthy to carry the verdict of so many, nor sufficient evidence for trial of man's life. The constitutions of the realm exact a necessity and will that no man should totter upon the hazard of likelihoods; and albeit the strongest reasons of our accusers have been but in bare and naked probabilities, yet are they no matters for you to rely upon, who ought only to regard what is apparent. Set circumstances aside, set presumptions apart, set that reason for your rule which is warranted for certainty.

[Disputed doctrines]: But probabilities were not the only matters which impertinently have been discussed; there were also points of doctrine and religion, as excommunications, books, and pamphlets, wherein a great part of the day hath been as unfitly con sumed. Insomuch as this very day you have heard not only us, but also the Pope, the King of Spain, the Duke of Florence, Allen, Sanders, Bristow, Azpilcueta, and many more arraigned. What force excommunications be of, what authority is due to the Bishop of Rome, how men's consciences must be instructed, are no matters of fact, nor triable by jurors, but points yet disputed and not resolved in schools; how then can they be determined by you, though wise, laymen otherwise experienced, yet herein ignorant? Yet were it so, that for your knowledge and skill in divinity ye might seem approved censurers [judges] of so high a controversy, yet are they no part of all our indictments, and therefore not to be respected by the jury. You perchance would ask of me, "If these prove naught against us, what then should you inquire of?"—for those set aside, the rest is almost nothing.

[Lying witnesses]: Pardon me, I pray you, our innocency is such, that if all were cut off that have been objected either weakly or untruly against us, there would in deed rest nothing that might prove us guilty; but I answer unto you, that what remaineth be oaths, and those not to rest as proofs unto you, but to be duly examined and fully considered, whether they be true and their deposers of credit. In common matters we often see witnesses impealed[50] [contested], and if at any time their credit be little, it ought then to be less when they swear against life. Call, I pray you, to your remembrance how faintly some have deposed, how coldly others, how untruly the rest; especially two who have testified most. What truth may you expect from their mouths? The one hath confessed himself a murderer [Eliot], the other well known a detestable atheist [Munday]—a profane heathen—a destroyer of two men already. On your consciences, would you believe them—they that have betrayed both God and man, nay, that have left nothing to swear by, neither religion nor honesty? Though you would believe them, can you? I know your wisdom is greater, your consciences uprighter; esteem of them as they be. Examine the other two [Caddy and Sledd], you shall find neither of them precisely to affirm that we or any of us have

practised aught that might be prejudicial to this state, or dangerous to this commonwealth.

God give you grace to weigh our causes aright, and have respect to your own consciences; and so I will keep the jury no longer. I commit the rest to God, and our convictions to your good discretions.

CHAPTER 19

The Witnesses and the Verdict

The three principal accusers—Caddy, Munday, and Sledd—were young men who had at one time been in Rome.

The Witness Caddy

Caddocke, or "H. Caddy" as the trial record calls him, was actually Laurence Caddy, dismissed for bad conduct from the English College, Rome.[1] Like Sledd, he gathered his information in Rome, but it is confused and only loosely founded on fact.

He talks of the "holy vow" between the pope and the English priests. This clearly refers to the Irish invasion, of which the General of the Jesuits had told the Archbishop of Glasgow, and which the pope had approved, ordering it to be called "the sacred expedition." That the pope intended the great mission of priests into England to subserve the purposes of this invasion there can be little doubt—but there is not the least evidence that this purpose was known to any of the priests except Persons and Holt. Indeed, as such knowledge would only be an encumbrance to them, they would naturally be kept in ignorance of it, especially since the opinion in Rome was that all Catholics would naturally take the pope's part when it came to war. Caddy, then, may have been right in saying that two hundred priests were to be sent into England.

His examination before Sir Richard Shelly is very probable, as the Prior and Bishop Goldwell seem to have been employed in investigating the characters of the Englishmen who arrived in Rome in 1579 and 1580.[2]

His information about the command of the army having been offered to Sir Richard is probably correct. Negotiations were pending with the Knights of Malta for the transference of their order into Ireland, and though they did not agree to the whole proposal, they promised in 1581 to send some of their best men to that country. That Sir Richard would have been the chief, I have no doubt. He had been Turcopolier, the highest military officer in the order. In spite of his advanced age, he was held in such estimation by the King of Spain as to be named his ambassador to the Shah of Persia in 1581.[3] Moreover, that he would have refused such a command is clear from his character. Shelly himself, in his own letters to Burghley and Walsingham,[4] boasts of his fidelity to the queen during an exile of twenty-three years and of his having constantly refused to receive any pension from the King of Spain, which it was always in his power to have.

Caddy afterwards repented, in February 1583, and like John Nichols, his confessions were published.[5] The reason for his fall, he explains, was that, returning from Rome, he wanted to visit his parents and friends, but feared that they would not want to see him on account of the anti-Catholic penal laws. So he feigned to be a Protestant and went freely to Bishop Aylmer of London, who imprisoned him in the Gatehouse and coerced him by threats of punishment to make a public recantation against his conscience.

The Witness Munday

The two witnesses whom Campion impeached—one as an atheist, the other as a murderer—were Anthony Munday and George Eliot.

The charge of atheism against Munday rested on his confession that he had feigned himself a Catholic abroad in order to discover the secrets of the Catholics, and now claimed to be a Protestant. This seemed to imply an indifference to all religion and at least a practical atheism. Further, he told lies under oath. Fr. Alfield described him as "cogging [dishonest] Munday."[6] Vallenger spoke of him as one:

> who first was a stage player (no doubt a calling of some credit) after an apprenticeship, which time he well served with deceiving of his master; then wandering towards Italy, by his own report became a cozener [cheat] in his journey. Coming to Rome, in his short abode there, was charitably relieved, but never admitted in the seminary, as he pleaseth to lie in the title of his book [*The English Roman Life*];[7] and being weary of well doing, returned home to his first vomit again [*Prov.* 26:11]. I omit to declare how this scholar new come out of Italy did play extempore; those gentlemen and others which were

present can best give witness of his dexterity, who, being weary of his folly, hissed him from his stage. Then, being thereby discouraged, he set forth a ballad against plays; but yet (O constant youth!) he now begins again to ruffle upon the stage. I omit, among other places, his behavior in Barbican with his good mistress, and mother, from whence our superintendent [Anglican bishop] might fetch him to his court, were it not for love (I would say slander) to their gospel.[8]

Munday did not know Campion personally and had never seen him until the day of the trial, but it seems he had a personal animus against Campion, for he wrote three pamphlets[9] against him in 1581–82 and testified against him with the accusations repeated in his *English Roman Life*, published a few months later.

Munday attended the executions of the three priests, and disturbed them in their deaths as much as he could. An employee of Leicester,[10] he was the chief reporter of their executions. It is his story of the death of Campion which Holinshed printed in his *Chronicles* and which (Protestant) Hallam condemns for "a savageness and bigotry which, I am very sure, no scribe for the Inquisition could have surpassed."[11] Another commentator says, "He describes the sufferings of Fr. Campion with a savage exultation which makes the most nauseous reading."[12]

He afterwards attached himself to the arch priest-catcher Topcliffe, who employed him to guard and to take bonds of recusants. Topcliffe spoke of him as "a man who wants [lacks] no wit"; and indeed he was one of the best dramatists of the day, perhaps the best inventor of plots. He was dishonest in his account of Campion's capture, which "was disproved by George (I was about to say) Judas Eliot, who, writing against him, proved that those things he did were for very lucer's sake only, and not for the truth, although he himself be a person of the same predicament."[13]

The following description of Munday's way of dealing with recusants is from a report of one of Francis Walsingham's men, who signs himself PHS:

He hath been in divers places where I have passed; whose dealing hath been very rigorous, and yet done very small good, but rather much hurt; for in one place, under pretense to seek for *Agnus Deis* [wax images of the "Lamb of God" blessed by the pope] and hallowed grains, he carried from a widow £40, which he took out of a chest. A few of these matches will either raise a rebellion, or cause your officers to be murdered.[14]

The Witness Sledd

Charles Sledd used his service at the English College, Rome, to be an active and effective betrayer of priests. At Rome and Rheims he was a daily communicant, while making his observations with the intention of betraying his companions. Even when he started for England to put his design into execution, he duly made his confession first.[15] He communicated his observations in France to the English ambassador at Paris, who sent over his in formation to the Council. His treachery became known to Catholics in July 1580 when he informed against Orton, as told earlier.[16] Like Munday, he had never seen Campion until the trial.[17] Persons had written to Fr. Agazzari on June 16, 1581 (before Campion's capture):

> Sledd is on our track more than others, for he has authority from the Royal Council to break into all men's houses as he wills and to search all places, which he does diligently, wherever there is a gleam of hope of booty. It is incredible how much we are harassed by these traitors.[18]

The Witness Eliot

Of George Eliot and the charge of murder against him I have already spoken.[19] That charge had, however, now been entirely wiped out by his good service. He had captured Campion, and had been the means of taking nine other priests; he had been made a yeoman of her Majesty's guard, and had come flaunting into court with his red coat. He had shown too well how intimate he was with the secrets of priests, and his testimony, though evidently forged, was too valuable to lose. Campion gained nothing by impeaching the evidence of this man who had never seen him before that fateful day at Lyford.[20] We will hear again of Eliot when he speaks to Campion in the Tower one last time.

The Crown's Case

In all, the evidence was too paltry to convict a group of men of a capital crime. The Crown did not produce any convincing form of evidence of treason.

The main points of "evidence" were:

- The pope had paid the expenses of some priests.
- Campion and Allen had met and talked at Rheims.
- Campion had spoken to the Bishop of Ross.
- Campion had used an alias and various disguises.
- Campion had once been where copies of an oath renouncing allegiance were found.
- Cottam had a book on how to deal with Protestants.
- Rishton was alleged to be skilled in fireworks.[21]

Each informant then told his lying story, sometimes with no regard for even a smattering of credibility. None brought corroborative evidence. All the defendants declared their loyalty to the queen but answered nothing on the pope's authority, which was not part of the 1351 Statute against treason in any case.

Campion had said at the trial, and it was not denied by the prosecutors: "There was offer made unto us, that if we would come to the church to hear sermons and the Word preached, we should be set at large and at liberty."[22] This offer of life and liberty if they would act as Protestants was proof itself that they were condemned for their religion and that the queen and Council did not believe them to be conspirators or potential murderers of the sovereign. Traitors and would-be assassins are not let loose if they agree to go once to church!

Campion's Method of Defense

It would be rash to admit as true all that Campion in his pleadings refrained from denying. It is plain, by the line of defense he adopted for Cottam and Bosgrave, that his cue was not to deny allegations but to show their irrelevance. Thus he did not deny the story about the manuscript oaths found in the houses where he had been. He only showed that there was not any proof that he had left them there or had administered them. (Even Camden's *Annals*, printed in 1625, speak at A.D. 1584 of the practice of counterfeit letters being planted in the houses of Catholics in order to incriminate them.)[23]

He did likewise in his explanation of his letter to Pounde. If he had explained it then, according to his declaration in the Tower chapel on August 31, that he had not betrayed any Catholic, that he had revealed no secret, that is, had told of no one who was not already found out, he would only have provoked a stricter search. He therefore allowed it to be understood that he had confessed all their names, that nothing remained untold except the confessions which they had made, and those, "come rack, come rope," he would never reveal. It would have been an act of careless cruelty to his fellow-Catholics on his part to say, "You think that you got out of me the names of all who gave me hospitality. You are mistaken; I only told what I saw you already knew. The names unknown to you, I did not tell, nor will I." Such a declaration would have opened a vista for informers and pursuivants, and would have subjected the whole Catholic society to endless harassment.

A Foregone Conclusion

Father Persons's commentary on the trial was as follows:

> Many things were objected against them as they stood at the bar, but principally that they had conspired with the Pope, the Catholic King [of Spain], and the Duke of Florence to invade England: which never entered their heads even as a dream. They defended themselves well on every count. The chief accusers were three young men who had been for a time at Rome—Munday, Sledd, and Caddy— whose youth and insignificance were such as would have been an effectual bar against any such thing being communicated to them even had it been true. But the prisoners' answers and actions, and the event itself, proved that no such action was projected; and the three men acted exactly as false witnesses do, confining themselves to generalities, or to things which had no reference to the accusation: for instance, that the Pope had favored them, that some of them had had conversations with certain Cardinals, and the like. All this showed that it was either for fear or for money that they appeared as witnesses. It seemed, however, a predetermined matter that all were to be condemned; and so no defense could avail, but after some hours of exchanges sentence of death was passed upon all of them.[24]

A Cup to a Disciple

The pleadings had taken about three hours,[25] and the jury of nine[26] consulted for nearly an hour. In this interval, a descendant of Sir Thomas More brought Campion a glass of beer to refresh him after his labors. Bartoli records:

I would not want to omit here what was, in a small deed, no small sign of Christian kindness shown by a nobleman of the house of Roper. Since Fr. Edmund had the joints of both his arms manhandled on the rack, and so lacked the strength to be able to bring his hands to his mouth, this nobleman came forward and, wanting the honor of giving him to drink with his own hands, held the cup to the other's lips with such a beautiful act of reverence and love that even the Protestants blessed him for it.[27]

Blood on His Hands

As the jury considered of their verdict, there happened a thing which Catholics of the time, whose eyes were ever on the watch for divine signs, relate as a miracle. When Judge William Ayloff, "who, sitting to keep the place when the other judges retired, while the jury consulted about the condemnation of Father Campion and his company, and pulling off his glove, found all his hand and his seal of arms bloody, without any token of wrong, pricking, or hurt; and being dismayed therewith, wiping, it went not away, but still returned; he showed it to the gentlemen that sat before him, who can be witnesses of it till this day, and have some of them upon their faiths and credits avouched it to be true."[28]

The Verdict: Guilty

November 21. The trial account records: "The Jury departed under their Warden's custody, where they stayed an hour, and then returned and pronounced all Guilty."

Following Dr. Allen, Challoner says Fr. Campion's

innocence, in particular, was so plain in all men's sight, that what color soever might be made for the condemnation of the others, yet for Father Campion's none at all; insomuch, that whilst the jury were gone forth, divers wise and well-learned lawyers, and others, conjecturing and conferring one with another what should be the verdict, they all agreed, that whatever might be concluded as to some of the rest, it was impossible to condemn Father Campion. But it was Father Campion that especially was designed to die, and for his sake, the rest, and therefore no defense could serve; and the poor jury did that which they understood was looked for at their hands, and brought them in all guilty; Mr. Popham, the Attorney-general, having plainly signified to them, that it was the Queen's will it should be so.

The most unjust verdict that ever I think was given up in this land, whereat already [1582] not only England, but all the Christian world, doth wonder, and which our posterity shall lament and be ashamed of.[29]

One of the jurymen, according to Laing and Bombino, afterwards defended himself by saying that if he had not found the prisoners guilty, he had been no friend of Caesar.[30] The consultation, then, was a mere blind to put a decent veil on a foregone conclusion, but it did not avail to deceive the public, who in their ballads accused the foreman (William Lee) and jury of undue haste:

> Yet packed a Jury that cried guilty straight.
> You bloody jury, Lee and all th'eleven,
> Take heed your verdict, which was given in haste,
> Do not exclude you from the joys of heaven.

These last lines are from the long poem attributed to St. Henry Walpole.[31] Lee himself, in 1595, being "a prisoner [in the Fleet] restrained from bodily travel," wrote to Lord Keeper Puckering, "I have been persecuted by them [Catholics] for my verdict, given in haste (as Vallenger rhymed) against Campion and his traitorous companions."[32]

Campion's Impression upon the Observers

Fr. Thomas Fitzherbert S.J., who knew Campion at Oxford and was in London at the time of his trial, wrote in his "Recollections of Father Campion":

> Father Campion so substantially pleaded for himself and the rest, that a gentleman of good account, a lawyer, and an earnest Protestant, yet a friend of mine, who was present at the arraignment, told me the day after, that in truth the evidences that were given against Father Campion were so weak, and his answers so sufficient and clear, that he could not persuade himself that he should be condemned, until he heard the chief Judge give the sentence of death. And when I asked him how it could stand with conscience to condemn innocent men, he answered that it was necessary for the State. And the like I heard credibly reported of another of the judges,

who being asked afterwards by a familiar friend of his, with what conscience he could condemn Campion and the rest upon that evidence, he answered that he could do no less, for otherwise he should not be taken for a friend to Caesar.[33]

Fr. Henry Walpole S.J., perhaps ten years after the event,[34] also wrote his own recollections, restricting himself to things not recorded elsewhere. He was a Protestant at the time of the trial:

I was present during his arraignment in Court and indictment, and stood near him when sentence was passed. . . . On the second day he, with seven companions, stood at the bar from eight in the morning till seven in the evening,[35] during all which time the Queen's Solicitor and Attorney kept heaping up odious presumptions against them. A witness deposed, etc. To which Campion replied in his own behalf as well as that of the rest. (As well as I remember Mr. Cottam said: "For the love of God let Campion answer for us all.") Campion's speech was entirely unprepared, yet carefully adapted to meet their calumnies. So complete was his reply that some, who came from curiosity to see what passed, and to set down the speeches of the opposite side, were astonished at his remarkable talent and presence of mind in this predicament. Others, again, considering the merits of the case, were amazed, thinking that one and all, and especially Campion, were innocent, and quite beyond the reach of the law. It was really a wonder that men such as they . . . should have made such able answers to arguments on legal subjects, and that, too, with an unassuming grace of manner which reflected much credit on their cause and themselves. Here indeed our Lord's promises were wonderfully fulfilled: "I will give you a mouth and wisdom, which all your adversaries shall not be able to resist and gainsay." [Lk. 21:15].

Accordingly, in proof of all this, I may point to the conduct of Lord Chief Justice Wray. He addressed Campion with greater courtesy, calling him Master Campion, and afterwards, taking someone to task for not speaking in his turn or to the point, said: "Look you, imitate the good example of Mr. Campion." In fact he was, like Pilate, desirous of liberating him, but for fear of Caesar, upon the verdict of the jury, condemned him to death.

A certain Mr. Hewes, a heretical doctor, who had been engaged by the Earl of Warwick to take notes of everything that happened, promised me a copy of them, if his master would allow of their publication. When the Earl saw the notes, as the aforesaid Hewes told me, he asked him whether Campion really answered as well as he was reported to have done. "Yes, my lord," said he, " and better too, if I could have understood or remembered all." "God's will," replied the Earl, "he is a rare fellow." . . .

Thus the whole day passed, and the jury retired to consider whether they should find a verdict of guilty or of not guilty. I asked a lawyer called Strickland, a friend of mine, who stood near me, if he thought they would be condemned, and what he thought of Campion. "As far as he is concerned," was the answer, "he surely cannot be touched, his answers to all that has been laid to his charge have been so excellent. I should say the same of all the rest, except of one or two, who may be found guilty on the insinuations against them." As this man is known to be a heretic, he cannot be suspected of partiality. What the Catholics felt, I can conjecture from my own impressions. Never before or since did I listen to any one with so much pleasure, and I am well assured from the testimony of others that his words and his bearing gave strength to the faithful who heard and saw him, and converted many who were not blinded with passion and prejudice.[36]

Campion's Final Oration

When the verdict was given, the queen's Counsel prosecuting spoke:

ANDERSON: Forasmuch as these prisoners here indicted and arraigned undertook to be tried by God and their country, and by the verdict of a whole jury, directly and by most sufficient and manifest evidence, are found guilty of the said treasons and conspiracies, we pray your lordships to accept of the verdict, and in her Majesty's behalf to give judgment against them as traitors.

LORD CHIEF-JUSTICE: Campion and the rest, what can you say, why you should not die?

CAMPION: It was not our death that ever we feared. We knew that we were not lords of our own lives, and therefore for want of answer would not be guilty of our own deaths. The only thing that we have now to say is, that if our Religion do make us traitors, we are worthy to be condemned; but otherwise are and have been as true subjects as ever the Queen had.

In condemning us you condemn all your own ancestors—all
the ancient priests, bishops, and kings—all that was once the glory
of England, the island of saints, and the most devoted child of the
See of Peter. For what have we taught, however you may qualify it
with the odious name of treason, that they did not uniformly teach?
To be condemned with these old lights—not of England only, but
of the world—by their degenerate descendants, is both gladness and
glory to us. God lives; posterity will live: their judgment is not so
liable to corruption as that of those who are now going to sentence
us to death.[37]

Never, says Fitzherbert, was Campion's face more noble; his conduct
during the day had been full of calm and dignity, and his arguments of
point and conclusiveness; but in this last speech he surpassed himself.
His eloquence made his fellow-prisoners confront with boldness the fate
that hung over them. Cottam, on his return to the Tower, told Briscoe
that now he was quite willing to die, after hearing Campion speak so
gloriously.

The Sentence

The sentence was pronounced straightaway:

> LORD CHIEF-JUSTICE: You must go to the place from whence
> you came [prison], there to remain until ye shall be drawn through
> the open city of London upon hurdles to the place of execution, and
> there be hanged and let down alive, and your privy parts cut off, and
> your entrails taken out and burnt in your sight; then your heads to
> be cut off, and your bodies to be divided in four parts, to be disposed
> of at her Majesty's pleasure. And God have mercy on your souls.

All the prisoners, says the reporter of the trial, after this judgment,
stormed in countenance, crying, they were as true and faithful subjects
as ever the queen had any. Only Campion suppressed his affection, and
cried aloud, in the words of the ancient hymn: *Te Deum lau damus, Te
Dominum confitemur* (We praise Thee as God, we acknowledge Thee
to be the Lord). Sherwin took up the song, *Haec est dies quam fecit
Dominus, exultemus et laetemur in illa* (This is the day that the Lord has
made, let us rejoice and exult in it: *Ps.* 118:24). The rest expressed their
contentment and joy, some in one phrase of Scripture, some in another.
The multitude in the hall was visibly astonished and affected.

Campion Addresses the Crowd

Four accounts say that at this point, before being led out, Campion stopped to address the crowd, who listened in silence:

> You have heard us condemned as if we were guilty of *lèse majesté* [crime against the sovereign], but how deserving is the case, consider for yourselves. If I had offended Her Majesty in so many ways, never would she and the Royal Council have so bountifully offered me, not only life, but also liberty and an abundant living, if only I were to comply with them in matters of no great moment. In fact, the lieutenant of the Tower, standing here next to me [Sir Owen Hopton], promised the same, and more, if I would attend Protestant church only once. Now indeed, he would not have dared promise such immense favors, nor would the rulers of England have permitted it, if they had established me as guilty of any such thing. Therefore, gentlemen, it is not treason, but zeal for true religion, that has brought us to our condemnation to death.[38]

Campion was then taken to the barge and rowed back to the Tower. The rest were sent back to their own prisons, where, being laid up in irons for the rest of their time, they awaited God's mercy and the queen's pleasure.

It was the feast of Edmund's patron: St. Edmund, King of East Anglia, tortured to death on November 20 in the year 870.

Condemnation of the Other Priests

The next day, Tuesday, November 21,[39] the remaining priests—Collington, Lawrence Johnson (alias Richard son), Hart, Ford, Filby, Briant, and Short—were similarly tried and sentenced.[40] Only Collington was acquitted, for a Mr. Thomas Lancaster[41] gave witness that he was in company with him in Gray's Inn the very day that he was charged with plotting at Rheims, where indeed he had never been in his life, as he had been sent from Douay. Collington was afterwards banished.[42]

Among the spectators there was a priest named Nicholson, who, seeing the success of Lancaster's testimony about Collington, and being able to give similar witness about Ford, offered his evidence, but he—such was the caprice of English "justice"—was apprehended by the judge's order and sent to prison where he was well-nigh starved to death.

Although the collective trials resulted, not unexpectedly, in collective condemnations, the sentences were not carried out uniformly.

It is fitting here to summarize the various fortunes of the fourteen other men put on trial with Campion that day, or the next:

1. Fr. John Collington, of Milverton, Somerset, ordained in 1576, caught with Campion at Lyford, was kept in the Tower and the Marshalsea until banished in 1585. He returned to England in 1587 and for the rest of his life ministered in London and Kent, with various terms of imprisonment. He died at the Ropers' house at Eltham, Kent, in 1635, aged eighty-seven.[43]

2. Blessed Thomas Ford of Devonshire, ordained in 1573, sent to England 1576, caught with Campion at Lyford, was hanged on May 28, 1582. He was beatified under Pope Leo XIII in 1886.

3. Blessed William Filby, of Magdalen parish, Oxford, ordained a priest in 1581, and sent to England the same year, was arrested at Lyford, as related above.[44] He was hanged on May 30, 1582, and was beatified in 1886.

4. Blessed Fr. Thomas Cottam, of Lancashire, ordained in 1580, had given himself up to the law, lest Dr. Ely get into trouble for his sake.[45] He may have been re-admitted into the Society of Jesus in prison. He was hanged on May 30, 1582, and beatified in 1886.

5. Saint Ralph Sherwin, of Rodsley, Derbyshire, the first student and proto-martyr of the English College, Rome, was ordained in 1577. He was a member of the English mission of 1580. He was martyred with Campion on December 1, 1581. He was canonized as one of the Forty Martyrs of England and Wales in 1970.

6. Saint Alexander Briant, a pupil of Fr. Persons at Oxford, was ordained in 1578 and came to England the following year, first working in Somerset where he reconciled the father of Robert Persons. He was arrested in London, March 1581. While prisoner, he asked, and was granted, to be received into the Society of Jesus, which he esteemed so highly, especially through his close association with Frs. Persons and Campion. He was martyred with Campion on December 1, 1581, and is one of the Forty Martyrs.

7. Saint Luke Kirby, of Bedale, Yorkshire, ordained in 1577, a

member of the 1580 mission, was caught before the end of the year. In December 1580 he was transferred from prison to the Tower and was tortured in the "scavenger's daughter."[46] He was hanged on May 30, 1582, and is one of the Forty Martyrs.

8. Blessed Lawrence Johnson (alias Richardson),[47] of Sefton, Lancashire, ordained in 1577, was arrested in Lancashire in 1581. He was hanged on May 30, 1582, and beatified in 1886.

9. Blessed Robert Johnson, of Shropshire, ordained in 1576, came to England in 1580. As told already,[49] he was arrested with Henry Orton two months later in London at the instigation of Charles Sledd. Transferred to the Tower in December 1580, he was hanged on May 28, 1582, and was beatified in 1886.

10. Mr. Henry Orton, a young layman and student of jurisprudence in Rome, was arrested with Fr. Robert Johnson,[49] tried and condemned, but banished with a group of priests in 1585.

11. Blessed John Short (or Shert), of Cheshire, ordained about 1578, went to serve in England in 1578. He was arrested in July 1581 and hanged on May 28, 1582. He was beatified in 1886.

12. Fr. Edward Rishton, of Lancashire, ordained in 1577, a member of the 1580 mission, arrested in or before December 1580, was kept in prison until his banishment from England in 1585. Abroad, he edited and updated Dr. Sanders's book, *The Rise and Growth of the Anglican Schism.*

13. Fr. James Bosgrave S.J. was imprisoned and later banished, as related earlier.[50]

14. Fr. John Hart, of Eynsham Ferry, near Oxford, ordained in 1578, sent to England in June 1580, was first arrested upon arrival at Dover. He was in the second group of priests tried and condemned. However, before being taken to the hurdle to drag him to Tyburn for execution, fear overcame him and he recanted. Back in the Tower, he wrote to Walsingham a complete act of apostasy, now in the State Papers,[51] even suggesting he be sent to Rheims as a spy! But not much later he re-asserted his faith and in January 1582 was kept in irons for twenty days for not yielding to a Protestant minister. He was also racked, as he himself relates, until his limbs were so disabled that he could not rise from his bed for fifteen days. The reason for his change of heart

is told by Dr. Allen to Fr. Agazzari. Hart had been visited by someone close and ardent: "The mother of John Hart animated her son keenly to martyrdom."[52] He is the author of the well-known *Diary of a Priest in the Tower*, which gives, among other things, some valuable details of Campion's time there. In prison, he was received into the Society of Jesus. He was banished from England in 1585.[53]

In summary, then, of fifteen convicted: three, including Campion, were executed promptly; seven were hanged nearly six months after; four were kept in prison and later banished; one recanted to avoid execution, repented, and was later banished.

In 1585, seventy priests were banished in batches, including Fr. Jasper Heywood S.J. who took Persons's place in England.[54] The government put it out that they had all agreed to the condition of swearing never to return—something they had all refused to do. The deportation was, in part, an act of propaganda, to slander the priests in the eyes of the Catholic public, by showing they had renounced their missionary oath and had preferred their lives to apostolic labor.[55]

The Final Fate of the Fourteen Missionaries

Of the original band of fourteen[56] who left Rome in 1580, three (Campion, Kirby, Rishton) were part of this trial just related. The final outcome for the band was:

- Two did not enter England: Bishop Goldwell and Fr. Morton.
- One died soon after entering England: Fr. Bromborough.
- One labored and then escaped: Fr. Crayne, "being a very aged man, came over to Rouen after some time of his labor in England, and there died most godly."[57]
- Six were imprisoned—Mr. Briscoe[58] and Rev. Frs. Kemp, Rishton, Sherwin, Kirby, Campion—of whom the last three would soon be martyred. Rishton would be deported. Fr. Kemp was still in prison "to this day" (in 1594) when Persons was writing. Briscoe would survive to become a priest.
- Mr. Paschal had retired through fear.
- Three were still at large: Fr. Giblet, Fr. Persons and Br. Emerson.

Fr. Giblet "was apprehended [some time after Christmas 1581] after many godly and fruitful labors in England, and cast into banishment"[59] in 1585, and died five years afterwards in Rome.

Fr. Persons's future history has been told.[60]

On Thomas Briscoe, Persons tell us that he was a layman and student aged twenty-six when he went to England, that he went mad, but recovered, and that he eventually became a priest.[61] As mentioned,[62] he was caught by December 1580, and imprisoned in the Tower for eight years, including sixteen straight weeks in the Pit.[63] By a friend's help, he got out, left England, went to Rheims in 1592, and thence to Douay where he matriculated at the University in 1593. He went thence to the English College at Valladolid, Spain, was ordained priest, and returned to England in 1594.[64] He was twice banished as a priest, but returned, and was alive as late as 1620.

And what about "the little man," Brother Ralph Emerson? He had been Edmund's companion until the day they parted at the inn outside Oxford—he to fetch Campion's books from Hoghton Tower, while the other returned to Lyford. After Campion was captured, Ralph left England and rejoined Persons in France. Thereafter he was engaged in various missions, chiefly for the importation of Catholic books. He assisted Fr. William Crichton S.J. and Fr. William Holt S.J. in Scotland, and Fr. William Weston S.J in England.[65] In 1584, he was arrested while on the way to collect a shipment of books. He was imprisoned, and was transferred from one jail to another—as was done with long-term prisoners to foil their escape plots.

By the summer of 1594 he was in the Clink next to the cell of Fr. John Gerard S.J. who records the fact in his fascinating autobiography:

> Had I been given a choice I would have chosen just the neighbor I had. Next door to me was Ralph Emerson, the Brother, who was referred to by Father Campion in a letter to Father General as "My little man and I."[66] He was a very little man in build, but in endurance and sturdiness of spirit he was as great as you could wish anyone to be. Through many long years of imprisonment, he was always the same devout and good man, a true son of the Society [of Jesus]. He stayed on in the Clink six or seven years after my arrival there, and was finally taken off to Wisbeach Castle with the other confessors. There he was attacked by paralysis, losing control of half of his

body, and he could not move about or do the smallest thing to help himself. But he lived on and heaped up great merit by his patience. Eventually, with the same priest companions, he was sent into exile [in 1603] and came to St. Omers where he died [in 1604].[67]

What a blessed, joyous reunion it must have been in the Kingdom of Heaven when "the little man" Emerson met up again with the great martyr Campion!

CHAPTER 20

Martyrdom

WHEN CAMPION was carried back to the Tower after his condemnation, he was put into irons, and otherwise hardly used.
But he showed such patience, and spoke so gently to those who had to
deal with him, that his keeper, Mr. Delahays, having afterwards Thomas
Norton the rack-master in his custody, and comparing the two prisoners' behavior, declared that, where he had a saint in his keeping before,
he now had a devil.[1]

Campion Visited by His Sister and Offered Liberty

It was not yet too late for the Protestants to tempt their victim with
proffers of life and liberty if he would go over to them, or at least take
some steps towards them. Hopton, the Lieutenant of the Tower, sent
Campion's younger sister to her brother, on November 28, three days
before his death, with a message, that if he would but yield to change his
religion he should have a benefice of a hundred pounds a year.[2]

Visited by Eliot

He received also a visitor of another kind. "Judas" Eliot, when he saw
that he was condemned, came to him and said, "If I had thought that you
would have had to suffer aught [anything] but imprisonment through my
accusing of you, I would never have done it, however I might have lost by
it." "If that is the case," replied Campion, "I beseech you, in God's name,
to do penance, and confess your crime, to God's glory and your own
salvation." Then Eliot said he was in great danger and fear lest Catholics
slay him for his treachery. "You are much deceived," said Campion, "if
you think that the Catholics push their detestation and wrath so far as
revenge. Yet to make you quite safe, I will, if you please, recommend

567

you to a Catholic duke in Germany, where you may live in perfect security."[3]

Fr. Bartoli comments: "Such was the vendetta that Fr. Edmund wished to make upon his traitor: that of the Saints, to return good for evil."[4]

This interview had such an effect on Mr. Delahays, Campion's keeper, who was present, that he afterwards became a Catholic.[5]

Discussion over the Wisdom of the Execution

Outside the prison walls there were various conjectures how the affair would end. Many thought that the Duke of Anjou, then visiting England (from November 1) as a suitor for the queen's hand in marriage, would intercede, and that the prisoners' lives would be spared. Others, with more knowledge of the man, said that the Duke was occupied in quite other affairs, and had not a thought to bestow on Campion. Others, again, spread the report that Campion had killed himself in despair.

In the Council-chamber itself there was still indecision. Some of the councilors considered that a man of Campion's genius, knowledge, scholarship, European reputation, gentleness of manner, and integrity of life could not be executed without rousing the indignation of Europe, without wantonly sacrificing one of the ornaments of the English name, or without disgracing the fair fame of English justice, since the trial had been public, and had convinced everybody except the jury that he was innocent of treason. As for the pretense of the queen wishing him to be put to death, it was notoriously untrue; she wished to save him, especially for the sake of the Duke of Anjou, whom she did not wish to disgust by this exhibition of fury against the teachers of his own religion. Then, it was said, instead of Campion's death being propitiatory to her Majesty, it would probably bring down her anger on those who had contrived it. On the other hand, the advocates of the execution urged the ridicule of first spending so much care on securing a sentence, and then being afraid to carry it out; it would be a tacit confession of his innocence and their own guilt; they would have to meet the disgrace of having kept an innocent man so long in prison, and of having subjected him to illegal tortures. As for the indignation of Europe, that had been already incurred by his condemnation; they were now only to look at home, and consider how they could expect to find the judges again so pliable, if they failed to support them in this instance. As for the queen and Anjou, they were too much occupied in their amusements to make a great issue of who was hanged. In the end, firmness even in a questionable course was better than hesitation and instability. Lord Burghley took this side, and clenched the matter by saying that Campion and Sanders were in the same boat; and as they could not catch Sanders, they must hang Campion instead. The attorney-general had said nearly the same thing at the trial. Robert Persons says that he was "told by one that heard with his own ears the consultation about the matter" that Burghley "with his voice in Council persuaded his death, when others of his fellow-councilors were of contrary opinion."[6]

Timing of the Execution

When the Council had settled that Campion should be executed, there still remained the question of the time. Some were for putting it off till Anjou had gone away, for fear of the offense the French king might take at the manifest insult to his brother visiting England. Others thought that Anjou's presence was a reason for carrying out the sentence now, as a public statement that the marriage would bring no change in the government's religious policy. Besides, they said, any delay in the execution will give time for the most influential of the English nobles and gentry and for the foreign courts to intercede for the prisoners' lives, and the queen would never resist their united pleas. Moreover it was an excellent occasion for striking terror into the seditious Catholics, who fancied themselves secure under the protection either of Spain or of France. Such were the reasons alleged: the secret reason was, that all the puritanical part of the Council, together with Hatton who aspired to Anjou's place, wished to put an insult upon the French duke, and by some means or other to stop the marriage for which they pretended to be so anxious. Burghley, therefore, again carried the Council with him when he fixed on the following Saturday, November 25, for the execution. In order to make the lesson more complete, he selected two other victims from the condemned priests; Sherwin to represent the seminary at Rheims, and Briant to represent the English College of Rome. And in order to throw still greater disgrace on Campion's cause, he had already tried, on November 15, Vaux, Tresham, Catesby, the Powdrells, Edward Griffin, and others, before the Star-Chamber,[7] for giving Campion hospitality, and had inflicted upon them fines varying from 500 marks to £1,000.

The uncertainty of the Council was once more exhibited in deferring the execution till the next Wednesday, November 29. When this decision was announced to the prisoners, they congratulated each other that they were to die on the vigil of the Feast of Andrew the Apostle; and they comforted one another with the Apostle's salutation to his cross—*O bona crux!* (O good cross!). When this came to the ears of the Council, they once more changed the day, and fixed Friday, December 1st, for the execution. Campion had long esteemed himself dead to the world, and it would seem difficult to die to it more perfectly than he had hitherto done; but from the Saturday when he was at first appointed to die, he seems to have found means to increase his mortifications; for then must have begun, as Fr. Alfield writes,[8] "by report of some very near to him, his five days' fast from temporal and bodily sustenance"; and then, again, on the Wednesday he must have begun "his abstinence from sleep and ordinary rest, which was before his death, by credible report of some, continued two nights, bestowed in meditation and prayer."

In the meantime, the Catholics had been busy with Anjou, imploring him to use his influence with the queen to stay the execution of the sentence. He willingly promised everything, and is supposed to have made some attempts at performance. When the day was at last fixed, the Catholics again besieged his doors. He was just about to begin a game of tennis. His confessor, a French priest, came out to speak with the petitioners; they presented their case; the martyr would only suffer in body, but the duke's fame and honor would be lost if he permitted this foul tragedy to proceed. The Abbé went to the duke and delivered his message. The duke stood hesitating, like a man just awakened from deep sleep, stroking his face with his left hand. After a while he raised his right hand with the racquet in it, and said to his companion, "Play!" That was all the answer the petitioners could get from him.[9]

Earlier attempts to save Campion via appeals to French ambassador Castelnau and Spanish ambassador Mendoza were to no avail.

Hanging, Drawing, and Quartering

The full sentence passed upon those convicted of High Treason, which remained on the books up to 1870, was pronounced by the chief-justice as recorded above:

> You must go to the place from whence you came, there to remain
> until ye shall be drawn through the open city of London upon hur-
> dles to the place of execution, and there be hanged and let down
> alive, and your privy parts cut off, and your entrails taken out and
> burnt in your sight; then your heads to be cut off, and your bodies to
> be divided in four parts, to be disposed of at her Majesty's pleasure.

From the sentence it should properly be called "drawing, hanging
and quartering," as the condemned was first tied to a hurdle *drawn* by
a horse to the place of execution, as seen in contemporary illustrations.
This drawing remained part of the sentence for High Treason long after
the disembowelling and dismemberment had ceased. In itself, it was a
painful way to travel, as the hurdle (like a rack, or piece of fencing laying
on its side) was placed on the ground and the prisoner, exposed to the
mud and laying feet-up, felt the jolting in his head and body through the
trip. Once there, the convict was *hanged* without a sudden drop, thus
ensuring the neck was not broken. In most cases, he was not left hanging long enough to bring about death, but only for a very few seconds
as the noose tightened round his neck. Then he was cut down while still
conscious; the genitals were cut off and the stomach was slit open. The
intestines and heart were removed and burnt before his eyes. The other
organs were torn out and finally the head was cut off and the body divided
into four parts—*quartered*. In some older books this form of execution
was called "hanging, bowelling and quartering." The head and quarters
were parboiled to prevent them rotting too quickly and then displayed
as a grim warning to all: the head on London Bridge and the quarters
upon the city-gates. At some point in this agonizing process the prisoner inevitably died of strangulation or hemorrhage or shock and harm
to vital organs. It has to be one of the most sadistic forms of execution
ever invented—as it was in 1241, specifically to punish William Maurice,
convicted of piracy.[10] Sometimes at executions, Catholics would come
forward to heave down the suspended man, to make him die from hanging and so spare him the agony of dismemberment. At other times, the
crowd would ask the executioner to leave him hanging until he was dead,
before proceeding to the next grisly step.

Protestants tried, sometimes unsuccessfully, to prevent Catholics
from taking relics at these executions. After his beheading in 1535, St.

Thomas More's head was displayed over London Bridge for a month and was retrieved by his daughter, Margaret Roper. The skull is now in the Roper Vault of the Anglican church of St. Dunstan in Canterbury.

Tyburn, the place of Campion's execution, near Marble Arch, was the site of "The King's Gallows" for the execution of all kinds of criminals from 1196–1783. In the reign of Elizabeth I, the Triple Gallows was set up, which became known by a variety of names, including "Tyburn Tree." The way from the Tower of London to Tyburn, about three-and-a-half miles, ran west through the city of London and then via Holborn (Howlbourne).

The Day of Martyrdom

An eye-witness account was written at the time by Thomas Alfield,[11] a Douay priest, ordained March 4, last, and on the mission only since the end of March.

It opens with a declaration of purpose to preempt false reports:

> The divers and contrary reports falsely and maliciously bruted [reported] and published of [Rev.] Mr. Everard Hanse directly executed [July 31, 1581] for cause of Religion, after his late martyrdom, gave just fear of the like practice towards those three glorious Martyrs, learned, meek, stout, and constant Priests, Mr. Edmund Campion, Jesuit, Mr. Rodulph Sherwin, and Mr. Alexander Bryan, priests, who upon the first day of December last past were under pretense of high treason most injuriously to the great lamentation generally of all good men, martyred for the Catholic faith and religion. Upon which occasion many good Catholic gentlemen desirous to be eye-witnesses of that which might happen in the speech, demeanor, and passage of those three rare patterns of piety, virtue, and innocence, presented themselves at the place of execution, and myself a Catholic priest pressed to that bloody spectacle, no doubt a lively sacrifice unto God, and a sweet savor unto his Angels, with mind upon occasion to refer [recount] sincerely and truly to my power this tragedy, with such accidents [incidents] as did happen in the manner, course, and end thereof.

Thomas Dolman, a law student of Gray's Inn, was with Fr. Alfield and also took notes.[12] They promptly took these notes to a printer, an Oxford scholar with a secret press in Smithfield, London, named Richard

Verstegan (alias Richard Rowlands), who printed the account the following year.[13] (All our quotations below are from this, but for a few indicated.)[14] Later, when his press was seized, Verstegan managed to escape
abroad. Blessed Fr. Thomas Alfield would himself be tortured on the rack
in the Tower[15] and martyred at Tyburn in 1585.

In the splash and mud of a rainy morning, Friday, December 1,
Campion was brought forth from his cell, clad in the same gown of Irish
frieze which he had worn at his trial, and was taken to the Coleharbour
(an open spot on the south-west of the White Tower), where he found
Sherwin and Briant waiting for him. Here they embraced one another
and had some respite for spiritual conversation; for Hopton, wishing
to throw as much ridicule and disgrace upon Campion as was possible,
caused search to be made for the buff jerkin (an oiled leather waist-coat,
as worn by soldiers) which had been objected to Campion at his trial as
a military and highly unbecoming disguise, and which was stowed away
somewhere in the Tower. Much time was spent in the fruitless search,
and the morning was fast slipping away, when Hopton determined that
he should go as he was; so the three were brought out to be tied on their
hurdles.[16]

Another more probable explanation for the delay is that they were
kept waiting by the Privy Council as it discussed Fr. John Hart's letter of
apostasy, written to Walsingham that very morning, to escape execution.
(But he did later recover his courage.)[17] The Council decided to leave
Campion to occupy his hurdle alone.

Outside the Tower a vast crowd was already collected. Campion,
undaunted, looked cheerfully around and saluted them: "God save you
all! God bless you, and make you all good Catholics!" Then he knelt
and prayed, with his face towards the east, concluding with the words,
In manus tuas, Domine, commendo spiritum meum (Into Thy hands, O
Lord, I commend my spirit).[18] There were two hurdles in waiting, each
tied to the tails of two horses. On one Sherwin and Briant were laid and
bound, Campion alone on the other. As they were dragged through the
gutters and filth, each hurdle was followed by a rabble of ministers and
fanatics, calling upon them by the way for their defection. One preacher
addressed the Jesuit, "Take care to die well," and he replied, "And you to
live well, beginning with its sole principle, believing rightly."[19] William
Charke, as a conqueror, followed Campion "with big looks, stern

countenance, proud words, and merciless behavior . . . so fierce and violent upon God's Saints at home, in death and torments, and so pompous in gait and speech unto the people, for gathering or retaining some credit unto his cause."[20]

But even Charke's vigor was not proof against the mud and the rain and the pace of the horses. There were intervals during which various Catholics spoke to Campion of matters of religion and conscience, and received comfort, or asked him to remember them in Heaven.[21] One gentleman, like Veronica in another *via dolorosa*, "either for pity or affection wiped his face defiled with dirt, as he was drawn most miserably through thick and thin, as the saying is, to the place of execution; for which charity, and happily some sudden-moved affection, God reward him, and bless him."[22]

The procession took the usual route "through the open city," as the sentence said:[23] this would mean it ran by Tower Street, Cheapside, Newgate, Snow Hill, High Holborn, St. Giles, Oxford Street, to Tyburn in the fork of Edgware and Bayswater Roads.[24] A crowd of men followed it, and the women stood at their doors to see it pass by. "Helen Allen, wife of William Allen, linen-draper and citizen of London (she and Ralph Sherwin being brothers' children), the same day that Sherwin was executed, and passing on the hurdle by Helen's house, hard by St. Martin's (le Grand), Helen being at that time great with child and sore dismayed with the sight of her kinsman, after the throng of people were gone by, she went over the way to one of her neighbors' houses called Richard Amyas, who presently said unto her, 'I am sorry for the heaviness you take for your cousin Sherwin,' and she answered, 'Indeed I am sorrowful; but it is for that he hath led so evil a life as to deserve this death.' And Amyas said, 'Hold you content; for they that have procured their deaths will come to a worse end. And she that is the cause of it, one mischief or other will happen unto her; and then the world will amend, and until then it will not.'"[25]

A little farther, and the hurdles were dragged under the arch of Newgate, which crossed the street where the prison now stands. In a niche over the gate stood an image of the Blessed Virgin, that was yet untouched with the axes and hammers of the iconoclasts. Campion, as he passed beneath, with a great effort raised himself upon his hurdle and saluted the Queen of Heaven, whom he so soon hoped to see.

Mr. Christopher Issam (Isham),[26] who saw the martyrs on their way, always declared that they had a smile on their faces, and as they drew near Tyburn actually laughed. There was a cry raised among the people, "But they laugh; they don't care for death."[27]

There was throng on Tower-hill, there was throng through all the streets; but the throng at the place of execution at Tyburn exceeded all that anyone could remember. The Spanish ambassador's secretary in London said, "There were more than three thousand horses and an infinite number of souls present at the execution."[28] Anthony Munday's account says there were "divers of her Majesty's honorable Council, with many honorable personages, and gentlemen of worship and good account, beside a multitude of people, not here to be numbered."[29] They had been gathering all the morning in spite of the rain and wind; and now, when the hurdles were driven up, the clouds divided, and the sun shone out brightly. There were present many good Catholic gentlemen, as Alfield said above, who desired to be eye-witnesses of what might occur in the speech, conduct, and passing of those three rare patterns of virtue, with a mind to recount it accurately. Fr. Alfield says he himself got up very near the gallows, close by Sir Francis Knowles (Knollys, Treasurer of the Household), Lord Howard, Sir Henry Lee, and other gentlemen who were officially present.

Campion's Last Moments

After slowly working through the press and innumerable multitude, Campion was first put into the cart under the gallows, and was ordered to put his head into the halter, which he did with all obedience; and then, after some small pause, while he waited for the mighty murmur of so many people to be somewhat stilled, with grave countenance and sweet voice stoutly spake out:

> Spectaculum facti sumus Deo, angelis, et hominibus [1 Cor. 4:9]. These are the words of St. Paul, Englished thus: "We are made a spectacle or a sight unto God, unto His angels, and unto men;" verified this day in me, who am here a spectacle unto my Lord God, a spectacle unto His angels, and unto you men.[30]

Here he was interrupted by Sir Francis Knowles (an extreme Puritan) and the sheriffs, earnestly urging him: "Confess your treason against the queen; acknowledge yourself guilty." He answered: For the treasons which have been laid to my charge and which I am come here to suffer for, I desire you all to bear witness with me that thereof I am altogether innocent.

On this, one of the Council replied: "You are denying the things objected against you that have been proved so manifestly to your face, both by sufficient witness and evidence."

> Well, my lord, I am a Catholic man and a priest. In that faith have I
> lived hitherto, and in that faith I do intend to die; and if you esteem
> my religion treason, then of force I must grant unto you [then of
> course I must admit it].[31] As for any other treason, I never com-
> mitted any; God is my judge. But you have now what you desire. I
> beseech you to have patience, and suffer [let] me to speak a word or
> two for discharge of my conscience.

But not being allowed to continue, he was forced to speak only to that point which they always urged,

> I protest that I am guiltless, and innocent of all treason and conspir-
> acy; and I crave credit to be given to this answer, as to my last answer
> made upon my death and soul. The jury might be easily deceived,
> and more also put in the evidence than was true, but I forgive all, as I
> wish to be forgiven; and I desire all them to forgive me whose names
> I confessed upon the rack.

Dr. Allen explains: "for upon the commissioners' oaths that no harm should come unto them, he uttered [the names of] some persons with whom he had been."[32]

> Further, the meaning of the letter that I sent, in time of my impris-
> onment, to Mr. Pounde, himself also then a prisoner in the Tower,
> wherein I wrote that "I would not disclose the secrets of some
> houses where I had been entertained," I affirm, upon my soul, that
> the secrets I meant in that letter were not, as the enemy construed
> them, treason or conspiracy, or any matter else in any way intended
> against her Majesty or the State, but saying of Mass, hearing of con-
> fessions, preaching, and such-like duties and functions of priests.
> This I protest to be true, as I will answer before God.

Then Campion tried to save his fellow-defendant, Fr. Lawrence Johnson (who was using the alias Richardson). Campion said he desired

Sir Francis Knowles and some others of the nobility to hear him concerning one "Richardson," condemned about a book of his, and earnestly besought them to have consideration for that man, saying he was not that Richardson who delivered his book *(Ten Reasons);* and this he affirmed with vehement protestation upon his death.[33] (It was Fr. Richard Norris who also called himself Richardson. The appeal was unavailing.)

Then a schoolmaster, Mr. Hearne, stood forth, and with a loud voice read to the people *An Advertisement and Defense for Truth against her backbiters, and specially against the whispering favorers and colorers of Campion's and the rest of his confederates' treasons.*[34] This new advertisement was "a notable and most infamous libel . . . published there, and openly read . . . a pamphlet, false, impudent, and farssed [stuffed] with lies and untruths, only to color and shadow with some face of equity those strange proceedings." It declared in the queen's name that the men were executed not for religion, but for treason. To quote the *Advertisement:* "Their facts [deeds], whereof they were arraigned and condemned, were such as were in truth high treasons committed against her Majesty's most royal person and against the ancient laws and statutes of this realm, which many hundred years past were in force against like traitors, and not for facts [deeds] of doctrine or religion, nor yet for offenses against any late or new statutes." It was an eleven-hundred-word piece of the now customary drivel, in long rambling sentences.[35] The people, however, were not much moved, but seemed rather to conceive some suspicion at this new and unusual course. Campion all the while was devoutly praying.

Notwithstanding this advertisement in defense of their policy, the Lords of the Council, both because they distrusted their wisdom in taking such a novel step as this publication was held to be, and because they desired some better mask for their proceedings, pressed him:

"Declare your opinion of Pius V's Bull concerning the excommunication of our sovereign and queen."

Campion would give no answer. (Here, as at all times, he absolutely refused to give any answer about the pope's right to issue the Bull. All that he did was to use the liberty given to him by the mitigation which had suspended the Bull so far as Catholics were concerned, and had made it for the time as though it had never been issued, so to recognize Elizabeth as lawful queen.)

They next asked: "Do you renounce the Pope?" He answered,

> I am a Catholic.

—whereupon one inferred, saying, "In your Catholicism all treason is contained." At length, when he was preparing himself to drink the last draught of Christ's cup, he was interrupted in his prayer by a minister, wishing him to say, "Christ, have mercy upon me," or some such prayer, with him; unto whom, looking back with mild countenance, he humbly said,

> You and I are not one in religion, wherefore I pray you content yourself. I bar none of prayer; only I desire them of the household of faith to pray with me, and in my agony to say one Creed.

—to signify that he died for the confession of the Catholic and apostolic faith. Many uncovered their heads (a customary act of reverence before prayer) and prayed a Creed.[36]

Then he again turned to his prayers; he said an *Our Father* in Latin,[37] and some called out to him: "Pray in English!"—for it had grown to be quite a superstition in those days that prayer in a foreign language was a mockery of God; but he pleasantly answered,

> I will pray in a language that I well understand.

(A smarter reply, but not found in any early biography, is sometimes given: "I will pray God in a language that He and I both well understand.")[38]

Once more he was interrupted, and bidden: "Ask the queen's forgiveness, and pray for her." He meekly answered,

> Where in have I offended her? In this I am innocent. This is my last speech; in this give me credit. I have and do pray for her.

Then Lord Charles Howard asked of him: "For which queen do you pray? Elizabeth the queen?" (He meant to ascertain it was not Mary Queen of Scots.) Campion answered him,

> Yea, for Elizabeth, your queen and my queen, unto whom I wish a long quiet reign with all prosperity.

While he was speaking these last words the cart was drawn away, and he, amid the tears and groans of the vast multitude, meekly and sweetly yielded his soul unto his Savior, professing his faith, in a loud voice, in his last words:

> I die a true Catholic.[39]

When he had hung a few moments, the hangman was about to cut him down, but was bidden by Lord Charles Howard to hold till Edmund was dead, which he did.[40] Then his body was cut down and stripped, and the butchery proceeded with. Persons adds the detail that Howard made sure that Campion died from hanging by driving the executioner away in anger and threatening to kill him if he cut down Campion when still breathing.[41]

While Campion was being chopped to pieces, the Catholic gentlemen who stood around were contriving in some manner to procure a few relics of him; but the greatest precautions were taken to prevent it. A young man who dropped his hand kerchief into the blood on the ground was taken and imprisoned. In the tumult that ensued, another was quick enough to cut off a finger (or thumb) and carry it away. The loss was presently discovered, but the thief could not be found. Another young man, finding that nothing could be stolen, offered £20 for a single joint of a finger; but the hangman reluctantly refused; he was afraid. Large sums were offered for the clothes; but when Persons wrote, nothing had been gotten, and it was supposed that everything was to be burnt to prevent Catholics obtaining any relics.[42] What relics did eventually come to light are mentioned in the next chapter.[43]

Sherwin

When he had done with Campion, the hangman, with his hands and bare arms all bloody, seized hold on the next victim, saying to him, "Come, Sherwin, take thou also thy wages." But Sherwin, nothing dismayed, reverently kissed the martyr's blood on the man's hands, and climbed up into the cart, where he stood some moments in prayer, with his eyes shut and hands lifted up to heaven. Then he asked: "Do the people expect that I should speak?" When many of the people and some of the nobility cried out, "Yes, yes," he began, with a manly courage and loud voice, "Then first I thank the omnipotent and most merciful God the Father for my creation, my sweet and loving Savior, Christ Jesus, for my redemption, and the Holy Ghost for my sanctification, three Persons and one God." Then, as he was about to give an account of his faith, Sir Francis Knowles and the sheriffs interrupted him and bade him come to the point and confess his treason and disloyalty. "I am innocent and guiltless" was his reply. Being further pressed, he said, "I will not belie myself, for so should I condemn my own soul. And although I have confusion [tribulation] in this world yet I doubt not of my salvation in Christ Jesus, in whom only I look to be saved, and in whose death, Passion, and blood only I trust."

Upon this, the ministers present said he was a Protestant (for some were so misinformed about Catholic doctrine as to hold that Catholics hoped for salvation by their own merits apart from Christ's). Sherwin took no notice of them, but went on with his prayer, acknowledging the imperfection, misery, and sinful wickedness of his own nature, and still protesting his innocence of all traitorous practices. When Sir Francis Knowles again interrupted him, he said, "Tush, tush! You and I shall answer this before another Judge, where my innocence shall be known, and you will see that I am guiltless of this." Where upon Sir Francis said, "We know you are no contriver or doer of this treason, for you are no man of arms; but you are a traitor by consequence." Fr. Sherwin boldly answered, "If to be a Catholic only, if to be a perfect Catholic, be to be a traitor, then am I a traitor." Being debarred further speech, he only added, "I forgive all who, either by general presumption or particular error, have procured my death."

Then, after a devout prayer to Jesus, he was asked his opinion of the Bull of Pius V, but gave no answer.

Then, being willed to pray for the queen, he said, "I have and do." "For which queen, Queen Elizabeth?" said Lord Charles Howard again. To whom Sherwin said, somewhat smiling, "Yea, for Elizabeth, Queen, I now at this instant pray my Lord God to make her His servant in this life, and after this life co-heir with Christ Jesus." To this some objected that he meant to make her a Papist; to whom he replied, "God forbid otherwise!" and so recollecting himself in prayer he put his head into the halter, and "died patiently, stoutly, and mildly," repeating the aspiration, *Jesus, Jesus, Jesus, esto mihi Jesus!* (Jesus . . . be to me a Jesus!), the multitude crying out to him, "Good Mr. Sherwin, the Lord God receive your soul!" And this they kept crying out, and could not be stopped even after the cart had been drawn away, and he had been some time dead.[44]

Briant

After his butchery it was Briant's turn, "a man although in learning and knowledge inferior to them, yet equal in patience, constancy and humility." A secular priest, he entered the Society of Jesus in prison. He spoke little, to say only how he had been reared in the Catholic faith, and was at Oxford—but was interrupted to be told, "What have we to do with Oxford? Come to the purpose, and confess thy treason." Whereupon he answered, "I am not guilty of any such death. I was never at Rome, nor then at Rheims when Dr. Sanders came into Ireland" (the time of the pretended conspiracy). He spoke thus and protested that this was the truth as he would answer before God.

He was a very fair young man, not more than twenty-eight years of age. With his innocent and angelic face—at university he had been known as "the handsome boy of Oxford"—he greatly affected all who saw him, especially when he said that he rejoiced exceedingly that God had chosen him and made him worthy to suffer death for the Catholic faith in the same Society as Father Campion, whom he revered with all his heart. Indeed, it was only his intimacy with the Jesuit Fathers, and his refusal, amidst the most extreme tortures, to reveal anything about them, that was the real cause of his death.[45] He protested that he died a true Catholic, and as he was saying, *Miserere mei, Deus* (Have mercy on me, O God: *Ps.* 50), he was delivered from the cart, with more pain, by negligence of the hangman, than either of the others. Alfield adds, "upon report of others, not mine own sight," that "after his beheading, himself dismembered, his heart, bowels and entrails burned, to the great admiration of some, being laid upon the block, his belly downward, lifted up his whole body then remaining from the ground."

Walpole

There was standing beside the block where Campion was being cut into quarters another law student of Gray's Inn—a young man named Henry Walpole; he was still a Protestant, and had gone merely to see. He had been at the debates in the Tower and at the trial in Westminster Hall. As the hangman was throwing the quarters into the cauldron of boiling water, a drop of the mixture of water and martyr's blood splashed out upon Walpole's coat[46]—who at once felt he must become a Catholic, as he afterwards declared to Fr. Ignatius Basselier S.J. Upon his conversion, Walpole entered the seminary at Rheims. Later he joined the Society of Jesus, was ordained priest in 1588, and was sent into England in 1593, where he was apprehended. He was sent to the Tower, where he was frequently and severely racked, and again like Campion, condemned and executed as a traitor, in 1595. He too is one of the Forty Martyrs of England and Wales. Before leaving England it was he (most probably) who composed a long poem in honor of Edmund Campion: thirty stanzas of six lines each.[47] It was included, with other poems, in Fr. Thomas Alfield's account of the martyrdom.[48]

The Queen's Reaction

Lord Charles Howard, named above, who was in name a Protestant, must have been impressed by the martyrs' acknowledgement of Queen Elizabeth—for at the point of death they were free to speak whatever sedition or disloyalty they liked; it could not make their sentence any worse. Persons records what he told the queen:

> When a nobleman of high rank at Court had come back from the slaughter to the Queen, the Queen asked him publicly where he had come from. He answered: "From the death of the three papists." "And what," said she, "do you think of them?" "I think them," he said, "very learned and steadfast men and innocently put to death; for they prayed God for your Majesty, they pardoned all, and protested under pain of eternal perdition of their souls that they had never conspired against the commonwealth or against your Majesty." "Is that so?" said the Queen when she heard it. "Well, that is not our concern. Let the ones who condemned them look to it."[49]

Munday's Description of Campion

Not everyone in the vast crowd looked upon these events in the same light as the Catholic writers I have followed. Most of those present were Protestants; and they, in their endeavor to reconcile the behavior of the victims with the justice of their sentence, must have thought in the same puzzled and inconsistent guise as Anthony Munday writes:

> This man [he says of Campion], always directing the course of his life to a vain glorious imagination, and always covetous to make

himself famous, at this instant made a perfect discovery [exposure] of himself; for being somewhat learned . . . all matters whatsoever he bore away with a majestic countenance, the visor of vanity aptly fitting the face of only hypocrisy. . . . He set a courageous countenance on every slight reason, whereby he perverted many, deceived more, and was thought such a champion as the Pope never had the like. But now behold the man, whom neither rope nor rack would alter, whose faith was such as he boasted invincible, fear had caught hold on this brave boaster, and terror entered his thoughts, whereby was discovered [revealed] his impudent dissimulations. . . .

The outward protestations of this man urged some there present to tears, not entering into conceit of his inward hypocrisy. . . . Edmund Campion, as it is by men of sufficient credit reported, . . . was always addicted to a marvelous suppose [opinion] of himself: of ripe judgment, prompt audacity, and cunning conveyance in his school-points, wherethrough he fell into a proud and vainglorious judgment, practicing to be eloquent in phrase, and so fine in his quirks and fantastical conjectures, that the ignorant he won by his smooth devices; some other, affecting his pleasant imaginations, he charmed with subtlety and choked with sophistry. The learned, . . . pitying his folly, . . . loathed his manners; yet loved the man because Christian charity willed them so to do.

Now this glorious Thraso [braggart], having by his libels made himself famous, and under show and pose of great learning (though indeed being approved, found very simple in the speeches given by him) subdued many to affect him very much, when he was taken he knew it stood him upon not to lose the credit openly which he had won secretly. Wherefore, in his former ridiculous manner, both in prison, at his arraignment, yea, and at his death, he continued the same in all points, which the foulness of his treasons blemished every way. . . . To many, seeing the gifts of God so well bestowed on the man, and by him applied to so great abuse, through natural kindness bemoaned his case, wishing he had not fallen into so traitorous a cause.[50]

In this sketch, by a heartless scribbler, false witness, perjurer, and apostate, we can read the true character of the victim: we see there Campion's simple truth miscalled simplicity; his modesty, and his refusal to pronounce judgment in a case which his conscience could not decide, misnamed invincible fear; his confidence in his cause and in God mistaken for self-confidence and boastfulness; his gentleness misinterpreted into smooth device and subtle affectation; and his unconquerable constancy construed as hypocrisy. And we find the efficacy of his genius and the ascendancy of his character fully conceded, though only to be explained away.

Prodigies of Nature

Fr. Fitzherbert, in his recollections of Campion, mentions a prodigy of the Thames' standing still:

> As concerning his death I can say nothing but by report of others, because I was not present at it, only I think good to relate that the same day the River of Thames, which daily floweth and ebbeth with the sea, did change his course, ceasing to flow or ebb all that day; which was so notorious that some poets employed their pens to make sonnets thereupon to celebrate the wonder, applying it to the martyrdom of Father Campion.[51] When all the eye-witnesses, Catholic or Protestant, whom Campion had moved to tears, returned home from the pitiful spectacle, and were told of the wonderful tide of that morning, they naturally enough considered that Nature had sympathized with the tragedy, as it had once with the Passion on Calvary, and that the river Thames had in some obscure way felt and uttered its protest against the injustice that day committed by the city which sat as a queen on its waters.

One poem of the time (possibly by Vallenger)[52] eulogised Campion in two of its stanzas as it pointed to heaven and earth lamenting and vindicating the sacred victim:

> The scowling skies did storm and puff apace,
>   they could not bear the wrongs that malice wrought;
> the sun drew in his shining purple face,
>   the moistened clouds shed brinish tears for thought;
> the river Thames awhile astonished stood
>   to count the drops of Campion's sacred blood.
> Nature with tears bewailed her heavy loss;
>   Honesty feared herself should shortly die;
> Religion saw her Champion on the cross;
>   Angels and Saints desired leave to cry;

even Heresy, the eldest child of Hell,
  began to blush, and thought she did not well.

Bombino says:

> Afterwards, the wits of almost all the Catholics, yea, even of some
> heretics, were aroused to interpret this great portent, to the great
> honor of many of them. I myself saw and heard the perspicacious
> compositions in this kind of no mean poets, expounded in elegant
> verse, as they drew this prodigy, abundantly testified to the whole
> kingdom, to the praise of Campion or the shame of his enemies.[53]

One of the writers Bombino may have had in mind was the
Elizabethan poet, St. Robert Southwell, one of the Forty Martyrs of
England and Wales, a Jesuit priest and Tyburn martyr (1595), horribly
tortured on the rack over and over. Southwell recounts some stories in
his classic *Epistle of Comfort*, penned in 1587. They appear in its fifteenth
chapter, "A Warning to the Persecutors"—a collection of various anecdotes of divine judgment visited upon persecutors, judges, juries, and
witnesses; and among them he talks about:

> the wonderful stay and standing of the Thames the same day that
> Father Campion and his company were martyred, to the great mar-
> vel of the citizens and mariners. I omit the like stay of the river Trent
> about the same time. Although some will impute these accidents to
> other causes, yet as they happened at such special times when so
> open and unnatural injustice was done, they cannot but be inter-
> preted as tokens of God's indignation.[54]

CHAPTER 21

"Champions Have Swarmed"

Fathers Persons and Bombino somberly relate how the perpetrators and agents of the rank injustice against Campion came to a bad end. But it is safer to recall, as the Lord said, that those whom the tower of Siloam crushed were no worse sinners than their companions (*Lk.* 13:24). In any case, if a few of the instruments in this iniquity fell into misery, the chief agents in it not only lived in prosperity, but triumphantly established the cause for which they had sinned so boldly.

Misery and Conversions

If Norton the sadistic rack-master, and Hopton the lieutenant, fell into disgrace and poverty, this was only the Tudor policy, which always threw away or broke its tools after they were used. After serving as Campion's rack-master, Norton—the barrister, poet, politician, and Puritan—was himself placed in the Tower in December 1581, for intriguing against the queen's proposed marriage to Anjou.[1] He was released through the intercession of a friend but a second time was imprisoned there, under a charge of treason. Dr. Allen records an additional irony: "Norton was then in the Tower for treason, in the same chamber Fr. Campion was kept in."[2] Walsingham presently liberated him, but Norton's health was undermined, and not long after, in 1584 (if we may believe Persons) he died mad. His wife became mad before him: Alice Cranmer, who was hopelessly insane by 1582. At the time of her husband's death, she was living in the care of her eldest daughter Ann; she never recovered her reason but lived on for at least another twenty years.[3]

George Eliot, expecting to find himself in good favor with the heretics to whom he had fled for refuge, found himself neglected and hated by them. He fell into all manner of brazen wickedness. His life was ended when a bad fellow, with whom he had quarreled in his cups, knocked his brains out with an amphora.[4]

William Lee, foreman of the jury, himself ended up in jail, as related above.[5] According to Bombino, although well-monied at the time, he was inexplicably reduced to extreme poverty, passed many years amid the squalor of the common prisons and spent his miserable old age as a beggar.[6]

The reign of terror and of penal laws that began in 1580 was successful in stamping out the public face of the Catholic religion from England, and in erecting on its ruins the Establishment that usurped its place. But divine irony, and the law of unintended consequences, will relate how the daughters of Hopton and Walsingham, who must have seen close-up the policy of their fathers, both became Catholics.

Cecilia Hopton was converted by John Stonor, whom she met (and fell in love with) in the Tower where he was sent for having helped to print Campion's book. Stonor's life was spared, strangely, and he regained his freedom later and went to live abroad. While her father's rule lasted, Cecilia was ever ready to give her secret assistance to the Catholic prisoners, and in 1584 she was denounced to the government for conveying letters and messages between the prisoners of the Tower and the Marshalsea.[7] Her conversion, indeed, was one cause of her father's disgrace and subsequent misery. Cecilia was implicated, rightly or wrongly, in Francis Throgmorton's conspiracy to overthrow the queen, for which Throgmorton was executed in 1584. In addition, Hopton's son Ralph was apparently found to be a Catholic at Antwerp.

By his second wife, Walsingham had a daughter Frances, who in 1583 married Campion's friend, Sir Philip Sidney. After Sidney's death only three years later, she married Robert Devereux in 1590, the second Earl of Essex, who was executed in 1601 after participating in an attempted coup against the queen. Two years later Frances became a Catholic.

Tobie Mathew[8] lived on to become Archbishop of York. His son, Sir Tobie Mathew, however, disgraced him, in his turn, by not only reading the Fathers—as his father had done—but believing them:[9] he became a Catholic and was ordained a priest in 1614 by Jesuit Cardinal Saint Robert Bellarmine.[10]

We have already seen how Mr. Delahays, Campion's keeper in the Tower, afterwards became a Catholic.[11]

Another man who guarded Campion in the Tower became a Catholic and a priest. He was Samuel Kennet, converted by Fr. John Hart. He is described as "the man who guarded Campion, a most terrible Puritan, who was won over and is now [April 1583] firmly resolved to suffer martyrdom if necessary."[12] He went to Rheims in 1582 to study for the priesthood, was ordained in 1589 and sent back to England.

Another keeper in the Tower, Mr. Gaskin, gave testimony to a Catholic prisoner who had just been racked: "There were two things that did very much move me touching Papists: the first was the death of Father Campion, who died so patiently after all his racking and torments; the second, the fact of Sherwin kissing the hand of the executioner all wet with Campion's blood."[13]

"Campion Dead Bites with His Friends' Teeth"

To turn to the direct and immediate consequences of Campion's death: Henry Walpole, in the fervor of his own conversion, estimated that the martyrdom converted ten thousand persons on the spot.[14] A like statement was made in the Catholic work, *Ecclesiae Anglicanae Trophaea* (Trophies of the English Church, 1584) by G. B. Cavalleri (Cavalieri), where three plates refer to Campion: his racking, his drawing to Tyburn, and his and his companions' martyrdom.[15] There is a note to this third plate: *Horum constanti morte aliquot hominum millia ad Romanam ecclesiam conversa sunt.* (By the steadfast death of these, several thousand men were converted to the Roman Church.) Whatever the exact figure—God alone knows—it is clear that a very large number experienced a great revulsion of feeling, and consequent mitigation of prejudice.

The first consequences were felt by Campion's clerical assailants, to whose clamors his death was generally attributed. Humphrey, the Oxford Regius Professor of Divinity, wrote to Leicester:

> This I can say with truth, that the ghost of Campion dead has given me more trouble than the *Ten Reasons* of the man alive[16]—not only because he has left the poison of his doctrine behind him as he departed, like the beast Bonasus, which in its flight burns its pursuers with its dung, but much more because his friends dig up his corpse, defend his cause, and write his epitaph in English, French and Latin. It is an old proverb, "Dead men bite not"; and yet Campion dead bites with his friends' teeth.[17] This is monstrous

according to all experience and the old proverb. For as fresh heads grow on the Hydra when the old are cut off, as wave succeeds wave, as a harvest of new men arose from the seed of the dragon's teeth, so one labor of ours only begets another, and still another; and in the place of the single Campion, champions upon champions have swarmed to pester us.[18]

Published Accounts of the Martyrs

As the Catholics had made great exertions to publish Campion's controversy, they were no less silent on his death, which was more eloquent than any words he could speak. England and the Continent were inundated (as Humphrey lamented) with accounts of the martyrs.

Fr. Persons wrote:

> Countless is the number of books, dialogues, discourses, poems and witticisms, which have been composed and published, some in print and some in manuscript, in praise of these martyrs and in condemnation of their foes. In these, everything that happened to them has been dealt with: their arrests, imprisonments, tortures, debates, trials, defense, condemnations and deaths. The enemies rage, but in vain; even mere boys resist them to their face and reproach them for their cruelties to the servants of God. Two were lately found in the University of Oxford, in age little more than boys, who had published poems. One was flogged; the other escaped.[19]

The first account to be published was in French, anonymously, in Lyons.[20] The author is still unknown. By January 4, 1582, it had appeared; and on the 14th of that month the ambassador Cobham wrote to Walsingham:

> I sent you a small book of the death of Campion. They have been crying these books in the streets with outcries, naming them to be cruelties used by the Queen in England. Whereon I used [French Chancellor] Mr. Brulart's means to move his Majesty [Henry III of France] to give order that such untruths might be stayed and forbidden, which seemed to prejudice her Majesty's good fame. The king has now given order to his Procurer-fiscal that there shall be a prohibition of the further sale of such books, and those punished who have used such unworthy outcries; which I cause to be followed to the execution.[21]

But the sale was not stopped; only it proceeded without outcries. In its stead, a book against the cruelties of the Spaniards was cried in the streets. Cobham was disappointed in his designs of punishing the criers. He complained, "The Jesuits do very much enlarge their practices to advance the pope's credit and theirs, by teaching with their ceremonious sacrifices; through their spials, intelligences; as also in seeking slyly to win opinion by the distributing of their sacred trifles; whose practices will grow most dangerous to all princes' estates if it be not considered on, and they abolished." This incoherent nonsense reveals the terror in which statesmen stood of this active Society; its influence seemed to them pure magic, and they regarded anything that passed through its hands, a medal or a pair of beads, as a political engine of unknown power.

In the same year, 1582, an enlarged edition (thirty pages) of this unknown writer's work appeared in Paris: *L'Histoire de la Mort que le R. P. Edmonde Campion prestre de la Compagnie du nom de Jesus et autres ont souffert en Angleterre pour la foy Catholique et Romaine, le premier jour de Decembre 1581. Traduit d'Anglois en François* (An account of the death which Rev. Fr. Edmund Campion, priest of the Company of the name of Jesus, and others suffered in England for the Catholic and Roman faith, the first day of December 1581. Translated from English into French.) It was published four times in Italian, thrice in French, twice in Latin, and once in German.[22]

In the previous chapter,[23] we mentioned the eye-witness account by Fr. Thomas Alfield, edited by Stephen Vallenger, and printed in London by Richard Verstegan (alias Richard Rowlands) in February 1582.[24]

Dr. Allen substantially adopted Alfield's account and used it for his little book printed in Rheims later the same year, August or September: *A Brief History of the Glorious Martyrdom of Twelve Reverend Priests*, and this became the standard account for the next two centuries. Bishop Challoner used it in 1741 (not knowing Allen to be its author)[25] in a large collection of English martyrs' accounts, *Memoirs of Missionary Priests*. Fr. Pollen S.J. re-edited and reprinted Dr. Allen's book in 1908, and did the same for Dr. Challoner's book in 1924.

At Louvain in 1582, Dutch scholar Gulielmus Estius (Fr. Willem Hessels van Est) published a Latin version of the first French account (named above), *L'Histoire de la Mort.*[26]

In 1582 alone, accounts of Campion's life and martyrdom appeared in London, Paris, Lyons, Rheims, Rouen, Louvain, Rome, Brescia, Milan, Turin, and Venice—in English, French, Italian, and Latin. The year after, accounts appeared also in Spanish and German. The reader is directed to Simpson's bibliography, section 7, which lists these various accounts of Campion's martyrdom, which were printed in abundance.

English Justice Defended

All these provocations obliged the English government to defend themselves as they best might.

Their first publication was in 1582: *A particular Declaration or Testimony of the undutiful and traitorous affection borne against her Majesty by Edmund Campion, Jesuit, and other condemned Priests, witnessed by their own Confessions; in reproof of those slanderous books and libels delivered out to the contrary by such as are maliciously affected towards her Majesty and the State.* In this paper the pretended plot of Rheims and Rome is prudently forgotten; and the only justification of Campion's death is that he refused to enter into the question of whether Sanders, Bristow, and Allen's opinions were wicked or not, and declared himself incompetent to judge concerning "the fact of Pius V" and his Bull.

This paper was followed by Burghley's *Declaration of the favorable dealing of her Majesty's Commissioners* with the priests at the rack (1583), which disgusted Hallam exceedingly.[27] In short, Burghley said that the torture was not as severe or rigorous as claimed by Catholics, and that Campion was tortured justly and reluctantly only to extricate information about his treasonous activity, for he had entered England to prepare rebels for action.

Shortly after came Burghley's *Execution of Justice in England*,[28] which provoked Allen's remarkable reply, *A true, sincere and modest defense of English Catholics*.[29] But such replies were not to be read in England: Fr. Alfield was hanged for distributing them; Stephen Vallenger was put away for the rest of his life. Vallenger, who edited the abovementioned account of Campion's death, with poems on his life by various writers, had his home raided by government authorities in 1582. He was sentenced by the Star-Chamber to have his ears cut off in the pillory, to be fined £100, and be imprisoned in the Fleet during the queen's pleasure.[30] He died there, after nine years in prison, in November 1591.

It became a crime not only to print anything but even to give out one's opinion. One of the articles of accusation against John Hamerton, Esquire, of Yorkshire, is that he "is vehemently suspected of certain most traitorous speeches—that he should say that Campion was wrongfully condemned, and did not deserve death."[31] Even before Campion was put on trial, John Brenton, Esquire, of Stratton, Hereford, was arrested, and punished at the insistence of the Privy Council, for having spoken in Campion's favor at the table of Hereford city's mayor.[32]

All these books, to anyone who takes the trouble to discount the vehement rhetoric and the unproved assertions, reveal the consciousness of the writers that they had wrought a terrible injustice. Yet, on the principle, "tell a lie and stick to it," they morosely adhered to their policy, and hanged, batch by batch, nearly all the priests who had been condemned on the same indictment with Campion.

A history of the controversies which took their rise from Campion's *Rationes Decem* would be outside our scope, but the reader is directed to Simpson's bibliography (sections 3–7) at the end of this book where we read a fascinating list of the series of writings for and against Campion at each step of his way: namely, after his *Brag;* his *Ten Reasons;* his capture; his debates in the Tower; and his trial and execution. All the early controversial pamphlets, biographies, and accounts are there listed. It is enough here to say that his death added a point to his rhetoric, and consecrated his *Ten Reasons* in such a way that abler theologians were glad to take it as their text-book, to adopt its divisions, and to give their works the shape of commentaries and apologetics upon its assertions and arguments.

The Blood of Martyrs

Burghley, Walsingham, and the fanatics could not see the practical lesson of the effects; but Francis Bacon was a cooler counselor, and in 1583 he wrote a memoir to dissuade the queen from imposing on Catholics the oath of supremacy which they would never take, and against hanging them for their religion; for, all their protestations to the contrary notwithstanding, they knew and acknowledged to themselves that they did put men to death for religion.

> Their number will easily be lessened by the means of careful and diligent preachers in each parish to that end appointed, and especially

by good schoolmasters and bringers up of their youth; the former by
converting them after their fall, the later by preventing the same.[33]

... for no way do I account death to lessen or diminish them,
since we find by experience that death works no such effects, but
that, like Hydra's heads, upon one cut off, seven grow up; persecution being ever accounted as the badge of the Church; and therefore
they should never have the honor to take any pretense of martyrdom,
especially in England, where the fullness of blood and greatness of
heart is such that they will even for shameful things go bravely to
death, much more when they think they climb heaven; and that vice
of obstinacy, *proximitate boni* [by its proximity to goodness], seems
to the common people a divine constancy.[34]

Sir Robert Cotton, without any special reference to Campion, but to
the warfare in which Campion was one of the first to fall, laughs at all the
vulgar reasons given for the increase of popery, such as the royal clemency, or the slack execution of the laws:

If we will with a better insight behold how this great quantity of
[Popish] spawn is multiplied, we must especially ascribe the cause
thereof to their priests, who by their deaths prepare and assure more
to their sect than by their lives they could ever persuade. The number of priests which nowadays [1613] come to make a tragical conclusion is not great; yet as with one seal many patents are sealed, so
with the loss of few lives numbers of wavering spirits may be gained.
Sanguis martyrum semen ecclesiae.[35] [The blood of martyrs is the
seed of the Church: cf. Tertullian, A.D. 197, *Apology*, 50].

And this fruit of their deaths, which seemed so soon to force itself
on the experience of the enlightened Protestant laity (the clergy were
too passionate to see the effects of their thirst for blood) was only that
which was anticipated with all confidence by their friends. Thus Persons,
in his *Defense of the Censure*, addresses Charke and Hanmer, describing
Campion and his companions' Christian deaths, how

also they forgave most frankly, from the very bottom of their hearts,
all their unjust accusers, condemners, tormentors, executioners,
and also you ministers, who were the only or principal instigators of
their death and torments'. . . Whose blood, I doubt not but will fight
against your errors and impiety many hundred years after both you
are passed from this world altogether. And albeit if they had lived

(especially two of them), being endued with such gifts and rare parts as they were (which with you were great causes of hastening their deaths), they might (no doubt) have done much service in God's Church, and hurt to your cause, yet could they never have done it so strongly as they have, and do, and will do, by their deaths—the cry whereof worketh more forcibly both with God and man than any books or sermons that ever they could have made. Wherefore, I can say no more but that they were well bestowed upon you. You have used them to the best. Our Lord and His holy name be blessed therefore. And I beseech Him of His infinite mercy to pardon your great offenses in the pouring out of their blood.[36]

In the State Paper Office may be seen letters written by Catholics about the time of Campion's death. I will quote some passages, for they exhibit the temper and the feeling with which it was received. Persons writes to a friend five days before the execution:

I understand of the late advancement and exaltation of my dear brother Mr. Campion and his fellows, Our Lord be blessed for it; it is the joyfullest news in one respect that ever came to my heart since I was born. I call him brother for once God made me worthy of so great preferment, now I take him rather for my patron than for my brother, whose steps I beseech Christ I may be worthy to follow. There is nothing happened to him which he looked not for before, and whereof he made not oblation to God before he ever set foot to go towards England. I looked for this end of his disputation also; and surely also when I heard how prosperously God turned them to the glory of His cause, I suspected that He would have his life also; for it was like the adversaries would never put up with so great a blow without revengement upon his blood.

His impertinent and malicious witnesses God will judge, but yet I beseech His Divine Majesty (if it be His will) to pardon them and give them grace to repent, and to prevent His great wrath due to their most grievous iniquities. There be men in the world which drink blood as easily as beasts do water; and because the earth doth not open and presently swallow them down, they think all is well . . . The pretended dust of feigned treason wherewith they go out to cover his blood is blown away with every little air of consideration that cometh near it. Your conscience and mine, and the knowledge of God Almighty with all the Saints of heaven are privy and shall bear witness of his pure innocence in all such matters and meanings, either by fact [deed], word, or cogitation. This hath he protested, and will protest (I know) upon the perdition of his soul at his death (for I am not yet certified that he is dead) [rumors abounded about his death]; and we protest the same before God and man and angels in heaven; and all that ever we have dealt withal in England shall testify the same both living and dying, upon their salvation and damnation in the life to come. All which, seeing it serveth not in Westminster Hall, we are content quietly to leave it in God's hands and to refer it only to the tribunal of Christ. *Qui cum tempus accederit discernet causam nostram* [Who when the time comes, will vindicate our cause].[37] That I am so far touched in the same matter [Persons was named in the indictment] as Mr. Criss. [Mr. Arthur Creswell] telleth me, I can not but take it most thankfully at my good Lord's hands who vouchsafeth to lend me a portion *in sorte sanctorum* [in the lot of the Saints]. Free I am for any thought of such matters as were objected, God and my conscience and my friends with whom I do converse do know and rejoice.[38]

Persons had not yet entered into his career of conspiracy, and he could not consider his designs for the conversion of Scotland and the delivery of the Queen of Scots from prison to be any treason against England. One of the last paragraphs in Persons's letter to Agazzari, December 23, 1581, draws this conclusion from a narrative of the trial and death of Campion and his companions:

From this you may see with what preparation of mind our brethren ought to come to us; with what humility, what patience, what firm resolution, and, above all, what fervent charity to God, their neighbor, and one another, according to the law of brotherly love. . . . Let them come, then, joyfully and cheerfully—anyone, that is, who particularly wants to bear the martyr's distinctive palm. God will see to it that they get their desire.[39]

There is another letter, of one Francis Eyerman, to his brother, who was imprisoned for distributing copies of Allen's *Apology* for the seminaries. It chiefly turns on the providential signs of the goodness and truth of the cause. Campion's disputations and martyrdom hold the chief place. If the adversaries had not known they were in the wrong, they would not all have refused to justify their doctrine against this one man as they did, saving that, to their perpetual and damnable shame, they had some secret speeches with him in the Tower; where they received so many shameful foils as they never durst deal with him openly, but sought his most innocent blood and death by those treasons which were coined and made in their own forge of detestable deceit, lying, and falsehood. . . .

We have lost the chief pearl of Christendom, yet we are to hope that by the shedding of his innocent blood God will the sooner appease His wrath against us; and all men are of that opinion, that the offense and negligence of our forefathers were so great, and our own sins so many, as they must needs be redeemed by the blood of martyrs.[40]

As Dr. Allen sent some advance sheets of his coming publication of the martyrs' ordeals, he commented: "I do not believe the martyrs of the early Church were put to greater trial than these."[41] Writing to Fr. Agazzari, he spoke of the effects of the martyrdoms in favor of the Catholic cause:

Here you will see in all respects the constancy of the martyrs of old; and the effect has been to move and to change the minds of men marvelously: the good or the indifferent to penitence, the bad and the hostile to wonder. Truly the shedding of so much innocent blood makes a strong appeal. Many thousands of sermons could not have revealed the splendor of the faith and of the apostolic religion as the savor of these has done, holy sacrifices, sweet-smelling to God and to men. The rest of the confessors become more fervent, our own people here become keener, the harvest becomes more abundant. With God as our leader, by labor and constancy we shall conquer; moreover, our enemies are angrier than ever, for they wholly despair.[42]

Fr. Persons had written with the same ideas to Fr. Agazzari, exactly three months after the martyrdoms:

The persecution is severer at this time than it has been hitherto. Our adversaries seem quite beside themselves with rage at the great blow that their cause has sustained on occasion of the death of these last martyrs [Campion and companions]. . . . In short, it cannot be told, much less believed, unless we see it with our own eyes, how much good their death has brought about. Both our enemies and our own people all declare with one voice that even had the lives of these men been prolonged to a hundred years they could not have done such good to their cause as has been effected by their brief but glorious death-agony.

Many who had been timid before have come to stand out intrepid and constant; some have joined the Catholic Church; a countless multitude has begun to have doubts about the opposite side. All Catholics in prison and under persecution are so full of joy and gladness as to be insensible to their sufferings. Never were Masses in London so frequent, so abundant, so devout, as are now celebrated in almost every corner. The Catholic people confront danger fearlessly; and when the officers and pursuivants arrive on the scene, those who can, make their escape from one house, and at once have their Masses in another. When they are dragged to prison, there also they find means of offering the holy Sacrifice, till their persecutors are ready to burst with indignation and rage. . . .

He who was the private jailer of Father Campion in the Tower of London is now a most zealous Catholic, who before was obstinate in heresy. The jailers of others are wonderfully changed. Every day many things come out to the praise and honor of those who are dead.[43]

It is reported that when the great Oxford philosopher, Dr. John Case, on a visit to London some months after their execution, saw the martyrs' heads and quarters (including Campion's) on long poles over a City gate (as a warning to others), he commented that "their dead bodies preach to this day, even to this instant."[44]

One contemporary poem lamented this defilement of Campion's relics:[45]

O God, from sacred throne behold
    our secret sorrows here,
Regard with grace our helpless grief,
    amend our mournful cheer.
The bodies of thy Saints abroad
    are set for fowls to feed,
And brutish birds devour the flesh
    of faithful folk indeed.

So many of the martyrs openly forgave Queen Elizabeth and prayed for her even upon the scaffold. Did these martyrs' prayers ever avail for her? This is a secret known to God alone. But if she died unrepentant, she went to judgment with the blood of 123 priests, one friar (not yet ordained), and fifty-nine lay people, brutally executed in her reign for their religion. At least fifty-two of the priests were converts to the Catholic faith, nine of them formerly Protestant ministers.[46]

Newman on the English Martyrs

Father John Henry Newman was asked by the restored Catholic hierarchy of England to preach at the first Provincial Synod of Westminster, July 13, 1852, in St. Mary's, Oscott. In this famous sermon, *The Second Spring*, he evoked the history of the Church in England, the memory of the English martyrs, their powerful intercession and the long-desired fruit of their sacrifice:

> The English Church was, and the English Church was not, and the English Church is once again. This is the portent, worthy of a cry. It is the coming in of a Second Spring; it is a restoration in the moral world, such as that which yearly takes place in the physical.
>
> Three centuries ago, and the Catholic Church, that great creation of God's power, stood in this land in pride of place. It had the honors of near a thousand years upon it; it was enthroned on some twenty sees up and down the broad country; it was based in the will of a faithful people; it energized through ten thousand instruments of power and influence; and it was ennobled by a host of Saints and Martyrs. The churches, one by one, recounted and rejoiced in the line of glorified intercessors, who were the respective objects of their grateful homage. Canterbury alone numbered perhaps some sixteen, from St. Augustine to St. Dunstan and St. Elphege, from St. Anselm and St. Thomas down to St. Edmund. York had its St. Paulinus, St. John, St. Wilfrid, and St. William; London, its St. Erconwald; Durham, its St. Cuthbert; Winton, its St. Swithun. Then there were St. Aidan of Lindisfarne, and St. Hugh of Lincoln, and St. Chad of Lichfield, and St. Thomas of Hereford, and St. Oswald and St. Wulstan of Worcester, and St. Osmund of Salisbury, and St. Birinus of Dorchester, and St. Richard of Chichester. And then, too, its religious orders, its monastic establishments, its universities, its wide relations all over Europe, its high prerogatives in the temporal

state, its wealth, its dependencies, its popular honors,—where was there in the whole of Christendom a more glorious hierarchy? Mixed up with the civil institutions, with kings and nobles, with the people, found in every village and in every town,—it seemed destined to stand, so long as England stood, and to outlast, it might be, England's greatness.

But it was the high decree of heaven, that the majesty of that presence should be blotted out. It is a long story, my Fathers and Brothers—you know it well. I need not go through it. The vivifying principle of truth, the shadow of St. Peter, the grace of the Redeemer, left it. That old Church in its day became a corpse (a marvellous, an awful change!); and then it did but corrupt the air which once it refreshed, and cumber the ground which once it beautified. So all seemed to be lost; and there was a struggle for a time, and then its priests were cast out or martyred. There were sacrileges innumerable. Its temples were profaned or destroyed; its revenues seized by covetous nobles, or squandered upon the ministers of a new faith. The presence of Catholicism was at length simply removed,—its grace disowned,—its power despised,—its name, except as a matter of history, at length almost unknown. It took a long time to do this thoroughly; much time, much thought, much labor, much expense; but at last it was done. Oh, that miserable day, centuries before we were born! What a martyrdom to live in it and see the fair form of Truth, moral and material, hacked piecemeal, and every limb and organ carried off, and burned in the fire, or cast into the deep! But at last the work was done. Truth was disposed of, and shovelled away, and there was a calm, a silence, a sort of peace;—and such was about the state of things when we were born into this weary world. . . .

Shall the grave open? Shall the Saxons live again to God? Shall the shepherds, watching their poor flocks by night, be visited by a multitude of the heavenly army, and hear how their Lord has been new-born in their own city? Yes; for grace can, where nature cannot. The world grows old, but the Church is ever young. She can, in any time, at her Lord's will, "inherit the Gentiles, and inhabit the desolate cities." "Arise, Jerusalem, for thy light is come, and the glory of the Lord is risen upon thee. Behold, darkness shall cover the earth, and a mist the people; but the Lord shall arise upon thee, and His glory shall be seen upon thee. Lift up thine eyes round about, and see; all these are gathered together, they come to thee; thy sons shall come from afar, and thy daughters shall rise up at thy side." "Arise, make haste, my love, my dove, my beautiful one, and come. For the winter is now past, and the rain is over and gone. The flowers have appeared in our land . . . the fig-tree hath put forth her green figs; the vines in flower yield their sweet smell. Arise, my love, my beautiful one, and come." [*Is.* 54:3; 60:1–4; *Cant.* 2:10–13]. It is the time for thy Visitation. Arise, Mary, and go forth in thy strength into that north country, which once was thine own, and take possession of a land which knows thee not. Arise, Mother of God, and with thy thrilling voice, speak to those who labor with child, and are in pain, till the babe of grace leaps within them! Shine on us, dear Lady, with thy bright countenance, like the sun in his strength, O *stella matutina* [morning star], O harbinger of peace, till our year is one perpetual May. From thy sweet eyes, from thy pure smile, from thy majestic brow, let ten thousand influences rain down, not to confound or overwhelm, but to persuade, to win over thine enemies. O Mary, my hope, O Mother undefiled, fulfill to us the promise of this Spring. A second temple rises on the ruins of the old. Canterbury has gone its way, and York is gone, and Durham is gone, and Winchester is gone. It was sore to part with them. We clung to the vision of past greatness, and would not believe it could come to nought; but the Church in England has died, and the Church lives again. Westminster and Nottingham, Beverley and Hexham, Northampton and Shrewsbury, if the world lasts, shall be names as musical to the ear, as stirring to the heart, as the glories we have lost; and Saints shall rise out of them, if God so will, and Doctors once again shall give the law to Israel, and Preachers call to penance and to justice, as at the beginning.

Yes, my Fathers and Brothers, and if it be God's blessed will, not Saints alone, not Doctors only, not Preachers only, shall be ours—but Martyrs, too, shall reconsecrate the soil to God. We know not what is before us, ere we win our own; we are engaged in a great, a joyful work, but in proportion to God's grace is the fury of His enemies. They have welcomed us as the lion greets his prey. Perhaps they may be familiarized in time with our appearance, but perhaps they may be irritated the more. To set up the Church again in England is too great an act to be done in a corner. We have had reason to expect that such a boon would not be given to us without a cross. It is not God's way that great blessings should descend without the sacrifice first of great sufferings. If the truth is to be spread to any wide extent among this people, how can we dream, how can we hope, that trial and trouble shall not accompany its going forth? And we have already, if it may be said without presumption, to commence our work withal, a large store of merits. We have no slight outfit for our opening warfare. Can we religiously suppose that the blood of our martyrs, three centuries ago and since, shall never receive its recompense? Those priests, secular and regular, did they suffer for no end? or rather, for an end which is not yet accomplished? The long imprisonment, the fetid dungeon, the weary suspense, the tyrannous trial, the barbarous sentence, the savage execution, the rack, the gibbet, the knife, the cauldron, the numberless tortures of those holy victims, O my God, are they to have no reward? Are Thy martyrs to cry from under Thine altar for their loving vengeance on this guilty people, and to cry in vain? Shall they lose life, and not gain a better life for the children of those who persecuted them? Is this Thy way, O my God, righteous and true? Is it according to Thy promise, O King of saints, if I may dare talk to Thee of justice? Did not Thou Thyself pray for Thine enemies upon the cross, and convert them? Did not Thy first Martyr win Thy great Apostle, then a persecutor, by his loving prayer? And in that day of trial and desolation for England, when hearts were pierced through and through with Mary's woe, at the crucifixion of Thy body mystical, was not every tear that flowed, and every drop of blood that was shed, the seeds of a future harvest, when they who sowed in sorrow were to reap in joy?

Relics of Campion

At the executions, "The Catholics piously vied with each other in taking away relics of the martyrs. Many dipped handkerchiefs in the dismembered bodies; others carefully collected the blood-stained straw from off the ground; while some snatched from the flames the intestines, which, as usual, had been thrown into the cauldron, and carried them home."[47] Sometimes it was the executioner who sold the blood-stained garments to Catholics.[48]

At Stonyhurst is a piece of linen stained by Campion's blood.[49] This may be the one described in Fr. Persons's letter:

While these martyrs were being torn asunder, the Catholics did their best to retrieve at least a few of their remains. But their enemies exercised great care to prevent this. One young gentleman, however, pushing through the people round him, let his handkerchief fall in order to get it soaked in Campion's blood, or at least that it might collect a few drops. But his attempt was instantly noticed, and he was seized and put in jail.[50]

At Campion's execution, at the quartering, a youth secured a thumb, which was eventually handed over to the Society of Jesus, and is probably the relic treasured at the Gesù Church in Rome.[51] It was divided late in the 19th century, and half the bone is in the sacristy of St. Joseph's Church, Roehampton.

These may be the same items mentioned in a letter from Paris sent by one Mr. Thomas Covert to Fr. Agazzari, saying that some men and women were thrown into prison for dipping cloths into the blood of martyrs at executions. One was in jail because he bought a garment of Campion; another because by pleading or paying he obtained a finger for himself.[52]

Dr. Allen spoke of three first-class relics: a bone, a rib, and some skin:

> There is a nobleman who has come recently [to Rheims] from the court of England who has a small piece of a bone of Fr. Campion, but it is so small that he cannot conveniently hand over any of it to us; but the Catholics in England for a price redeemed from the hangman one of his ribs, a part of which I hope to possess soon, and then I will send some of its blessing for our [English] College [at Rome] and for Fr. General.[53]

Dr. Allen obtained some of the rib, and three months later wrote from Rheims to George Gilbert in Rome:

> I send you here enclosed a little piece of Father Campion's holy rib. Take half to yourself and give the other half to Father Rector [Agazzari].[54]

The following year he mentions that Fr. George Birket[55] brought to Rheims a significant piece of Campion's skin, treated for preservation.[56] That was a bonus, for he had previously written to Fr. Agazzari, "With difficulty will you receive more relics of the martyr Edmund Campion."[57]

Father Persons at one time told of the frustrated desire of Catholics to obtain relics of Campion. After he had written, he was more fortunate than before. One of the martyr's arms was stolen from the gate where it was nailed up; and Persons managed to get for a large sum the rope that tied Edmund Campion to the hurdle on which he was dragged to Tyburn. It was smuggled out of England. Persons always wore it about his waist, right up to his death at the English College at Rome in 1610. It was then kept at the College, but is now at Stonyhurst, the continuation of the College founded abroad by Persons in 1594.[58] A number of writers say this rope is the halter with which his dear friend was hanged, but this seems to be a mistake.[59]

Alternatively, it was ropes from the rack whereon Campion was stretched. The English College of Rome's annual letter of 1584 announced that Stephen Brinkley brought the College "a great treasure, viz. the ropes wherewith this blessed martyr [Campion] had been racked."[60] As with the halter, of which nothing is known, this racking rope is probably a confusion with the hurdle's rope.

In any case, there is only one rope, apart from an inch or so which was cut from it and presented to Pope Paul VI in 1970 at Campion's canonization.

Dr. Allen relates that a certain friend of his, a nobleman, credits his deliverance from peril at sea to a relic of Fr. Campion that he had on him.[61]

Fr. Bartoli relates that Jesuit Father Jacques Salès, born in 1556, an admirer of Edmund, obtained a very small piece of a bone of his and hung it at his breast. He commended himself to Fr. Edmund's intercession to obtain the grace of a death like his—which prayer was answered when he was slain by Calvinists in hatred for the faith, in Aubenas, in the diocese of Viviers, France, in 1593.[62] Fr. Possoz S.J., in his biography of Campion, says: "Fr. Salès also kept carefully a letter that Fr. Campion had written him, and in which he spoke to him of the merit that obedience gives to the most lowly works: "If even by feeding the dogs I can render some service to my Lord, who am I, or what is my Father's house, that I can refuse?"[63] Fr. Salès, a great devotee and defender of the Real Presence of Jesus in the Holy Eucharist, was beatified under Pope Pius XI in 1926.

Under the main altar of the *Venerabile College Inglese*, the English College, via Monserrato, Rome, is a collection of martyrs' relics, including some of St. Edmund Campion.

I have been told of a reliquary, said to have belonged to Mary Queen of Scots, and (in 1867) in the possession of H. Darell, Esq., of Cale Hill, which contains, among several others, relics of "B. Campianus, M." (Blessed Campion, Martyr). If this reliquary was ever Mary Stuart's, relics must have been added afterwards, for it contains those of St. Henry Walpole, martyred 1595, and Fr. Henry Garnet, martyred 1606.

There is a story of a Mr. Anderton, a 17th-century Lancashire gentleman, cured of the stone by relics of Father Campion, and afterwards raised to life by the help of the martyr's flesh laid on his body when laid out for dead due to another disease.[64]

At Claughton Hall (Claughton-on-Brock, Lancashire) is a pre-Reformation chalice from Mains, the ancient seat of the Hesketh family, no doubt used by Campion in his visit to Mains on his missionary journey in Lancashire in Easter-tide 1581.[65]

At the shrine of Ladyewell (Our Lady's well), in the Diocese of Lancaster, is a beautiful wooden bureau which folds out to become an altar. It dates from 1560 and was used by Campion at Easter-tide 1581, and by St. Edmund Arrowsmith in 1622 and by Blessed John Woodcock.

At the Jesuit house in Farm St, London, there is a rosary ring, consisting of a hoop, with ten knobs to count the *Hail Mary's*, said to be Campion's.[66]

Campion's linen cincture (worn at Mass) plays a great part in an exorcism by Fr. Weston described in his (unpublished) *Book of Miracles* (by "Edmunds," Weston's alias),[67] as referred to in Bishop Harsnett's *Declaration of Egregious Popish Impostures*.[68]

At St. Joseph's, Roehampton, is a piece of the hat Campion wore when paraded through the streets of London in mockery after capture.[69] That hat had belonged previously to Fr. Persons—for he and Campion had exchanged hats on the day they parted for the last time, July 11, 1581.[70] Stephen Brinkley, when in the Tower, begged Fr. Campion to let him have the hat he wore when wearing the sign, "Campion the seditious Jesuit."[71] Brinkley took the thick, dark-colored felt hat to Belgium and put it into a reliquary four years after Campion's martyrdom. In the first half of the 17th century a fragment was cut from it, and in the second half of the 19th century that piece was brought from Belgium and is now preserved at Roehampton. By that time, the original hat's location was unknown.[72] Another hat of Campion, made of black felt, is divided: a large piece is at Erdington Abbey, Birmingham, and the greater portion at the old Jesuit College, now the Episcopal Seminary at Prague.[73]

I have already mentioned Edmund's copy of Aquinas' *Summa Theologica*, with his handwritten notes in the margins.[74]

Campion Hall, Oxford, has a copy of a commentary on Aristotle's *Physics* containing several specimens of Fr. Campion's signature.[75]

Many manuscripts of Campion are preserved at Stonyhurst College, Lancashire, some of which are on display in the library there, and some are among the archives of the Archbishop of Westminster at the London Oratory.

Veneration of Campion

A Protestant writer says that when the news of Campion's execution reached Rome, the Rector of the English College, Fr. Agazzari, "caused the organs to be sounded and all the students to come to the chapel, and then and there he himself, pulling on his back a white surplice, and the stole about his neck, sang a *Collect* of martyrs, so after his manner canonizing Campion the rebel as a saint. It is usual among the English Papists to keep the relics of Campion, Sherwin, and the rest."[76]

In the same chapel is the large picture of the Holy Trinity, painted by Durante Alberti in 1581. It became customary at the College for the students to gather at this picture and sing the *Te Deum* as an act of thanks and glory to God whenever word arrived that a onetime student of the College had been martyred in England. This custom continues today (2010) when the *Te Deum* is sung in front of the painting on December 1, *Martyrs' Day* in the College. The College boasts forty-one martyrs over the years 1581–1678.

Well-known are the frescoes of martyrdoms by Niccolò Circignani ("Il Pomarancio"), added to the English College chapel in 1583, and the prints made shortly afterwards by Giovanni Battista Cavalleri, mentioned above,[77] that record them. "The original ones at the English College perished during the neglect the college suffered in the French occupation in the 19th century. Copies were made from the engravings of G.B. Cavalleri by the Italian artist Capparoni in 1893 for the tribune of the new church."[78]

Campion's picture was hung over altars, his name was assumed by religious persons in their novitiate,[79] and his aid was implored by persons in affliction even in Bohemia.[80] Pope Gregory XIII and his court acknowledged him as a martyr, and allowed his passion to be painted on the walls of the English College in 1583, and his relics (with those of the others) to be employed in the consecration of altars. Those who wrote his life, like Bombino, or collected his works, like Robert Turner, closed their labors with an invocation or hymn in his honor. The cell which he inhabited at Prague was venerated as a sanctuary.[81] An altar was erected in it, with his picture above.[82] Those who entered it knelt down on the pavement that his feet had trodden. His confessors there, Fr. Francis Anthony, and Fr. John Paul Campana, the Rector of the college, bore public testimony to his sanctity, his purity of conscience, and the unstained virginity of his life; and one who had known him in the college wrote upon the copy of his tragedy on St. Ambrose which he left behind him, *auctore beato Edmundo Campiano, Graeco, Latino, Poeta, Oratore, Philosopho, Theologo, Virgine, et Martyre* (by the author, the blessed Edmund Campion, a poet in Greek and Latin, an orator, philosopher, theologian, virgin and martyr).[83]

A few years ago, at the Strahov Monastery, Prague, Gerard Kilroy found a eulogy addressed to Campion by twenty-one fellow academics: *Literarum et Virtutum Studiosus; Poeta et Rhetor Eximius; Theologus Subtilis, Philosophus Excellens; Martyrio, Velut Doctorali Lauro, Insignis* (Ardent in his love of literature and virtue, an outstanding poet and orator, a subtle theologian, an excellent philosopher, and as distinguished for his wreath of erudition as for his martyrdom). The same eulogy says, "He excelled at Prague in every facet of Poetry to such an extent that he had few equals, and no one greater."[84]

Bombino says his name became a synonym for eloquence, and was given to any one of the scholars of the seminary who was an especially good preacher. Thus Fr. William Hart, martyred at York in 1583, was called another Campion.[85]

In a learned work on Latin writing style, teaching how to emulate the best Latin and Greek authors, Belgian Jesuit Fr. Jacques Masen (1606–81) praises Campion unreservedly as a second Cicero to be followed by all who would write eloquently.[86]

In his classic work, *The Practice of Christian and Religious Perfection* (1609), Spanish Jesuit Fr. Alphonsus Rodriguez names Campion as a model to emulate for his Jesuit readers.[87]

Fr. Francisco de Peralta, the first Rector of the English College in
Seville in 1592, records that there was a common saying among Catholics
at the beginning of the 17th century:

> If I spoke with the tongue of Fr. Campion and wrote with the pen of
> Fr. Persons and led the austere life of Fr. Weston and had not char-
> ity, it would avail me nothing.[88]

Named after Campion are countless churches and chapels, schools
and colleges, halls and auditoria, Catholic clubs and societies, university
associations and academic fraternities, scholarships and awards.

Each year now there is a pilgrimage retracing the footsteps of
St. Edmund, from Lyford to the Tower of London, and then Tyburn,
the place of execution, concluding at Tyburn Priory nearby. A relic of
Campion is carried from parish to parish, closely following the original route. Lyford is within the parish boundaries of St. John Vianney,
Wantage. At the local Anglican church of St. Mary the Virgin, Mass was
recently celebrated for the first time in over 400 years.

"The Flower of Oxford"

Fr. Alfield's account[89] contains a eulogy of Campion, with a phrase oft
since repeated: "the flower of Oxford."

> It is not unknown that Mr. Edmund Campion, Jesuit and Priest, a
> man reputed and taken, and by divers his co-equals plainly confessed
> the flower of Oxford for that time he studied there, and since abode
> in foreign countries one in whom our country hath had great honor,
> the fruit of his learning, virtue, and rare gifts, which as they were in
> his childhood here among us wonderful, so they were abroad, as in
> Italy, Germany, and Bohemia an honor to our country, a glass and
> mirror, a light and lantern, a pattern and example to youth, to age,
> to learned, to unlearned, to religious, and to the laity of all sort, state
> and condition, of modesty, gravity, eloquence, knowledge, virtue,
> and piety of which just and due commendation some of our adver-
> saries can give true and certain testimony, who after diligent sifting
> and enquiring of his life, manners, and demeanor, found nothing
> faulty, nothing worthy of blame. This man (Mr. Campion I say) hast
> meekly yielded himself and his carcass to this butchery, with such
> humility and courage as moved most beholders to compassion and
> pity.[90]

Celebration in Poetry

We have already mentioned the verses that appeared and did the rounds after the Tower debates.[91] After the execution, more verses appeared, in English, Latin, and Greek.[92] Fr. Pollen remarks: "Among the most remarkable results of Campion's death were the numerous pieces of verse which it occasioned. No other of our martyrs evoked the enthusiasm which these lines, when considered in their circumstances, so strikingly manifest."[93]

Morfill's edition of *Ballads from Manuscripts—Ballads Relating Chiefly to the Reign of Queen Elizabeth* contains twelve poems on Campion, friendly and hostile—but that is not a complete list.[94] Some others of the time, mentioned here below, he does not print.

In *A True Report* (1582) appeared four poems, probably by Walpole, Verstegan, and Vallenger. The best-known one is "Why do I use my paper, ink and pen"—the long poem attributed to St. Henry Walpole.[95] It appeared in print, anonymously for safety,[96] once in 1582; it was circulated secretly in manuscript until 1657, and was not seen publicly again until 1872 when printed in the English Jesuit journal *The Month*, under the title *A Contemporary Elegy on Edmund Campion*.[97] The full poem is at the end of this book: "St. Henry Walpole's elegy on Campion." Here are numbers 1, 6, 7, 24, and 25 of its thirty stanzas:

> Why do I use my paper, ink and pen,
> and call my wits to counsel what to say?
> Such memories were made for mortal men;
> I speak of Saints whose names can not decay.
> an Angel's trump were fitter for to sound
> their glorious death, if such on earth were found.
> With tongue and pen the truth he taught and wrote,
> by force whereof they came to Christ apace,
> but when it pleasèd God, it was his lot
> he should be thralled, He lent him so much grace,
> his patience then did work as much or more,
> as had his heavenly speeches done before.
> His fare was hard, yet mild and sweet his cheer;
> his prison close, yet free and loose his mind;
> his torture great, yet small or none his fear;
> his offers large, but nothing could him blind.

O constant man, O mind, O virtue strange,
whom want, nor woe, nor fear, nor hope could change.
His prison now the City of the King,
his rack and torture, joys and heavenly bliss;
for men's reproach, with angels he doth sing,
a sacred song which everlasting is;
for shame but short, and loss of small renown
he purchased hath an ever-during crown
His quartered limbs shall join with joy again,
and rise a body brighter than the sun,
your blinded malice tortured him in vain,
for every wrench some glory hath him won,
and every drop of blood which he did spend
hath reaped a joy which never shall have end.

In 1588, the famous Catholic composer William Byrd (1543–1623), organist of Elizabeth's Chapel Royal, took the first stanza of Walpole's poem, added two more stanzas, set it to music, and published it as part of his *Psalms, Sonnets and Songs*. The title was as the original poem, "Why do I use my paper, ink and pen."

Another very long poem, written early 1582, is found among Laud's manuscripts in the Bodleian Library, Oxford. It is entitled *A Brief of the Life and Death of Sir Edmund Campion of the Blessed Society of the Name of Jesus*.[98] It is not as elegant as Walpole's poem, but is just as sincere and ardent. Here is its conclusion:

For learning passing rare, for life and learning like,
The banks of Brute possess no peer, if equal there she seek.
Of Emperor beloved, and for him princes strive:
And yet not thought a worthy man, among us here to live.
A Solomon for wit, a Solon for his will,
A Cato for his public care, a Tully [Cicero] for his skill.
A Socrates for mind, that feared no loss of breath,
A mirror for his godly life, a martyr for his death.
A Joseph to forgive, a Joshua to guide,
As far from malice every way, as prudence is from pride. . . .
No sooner Truth had said, than Fame began to sound
With such a blast unto the world as it did large rebound.
Which pierced the cheerful skies and made the angels glad,
And those were then the words of Fame which full in force she had:

"If virtue ever live, if valor never die,
If learned arts for ever stand with grace eternally,
If perfect life get fame, if perfect fame endure,
If endless durance make us live, and set our honor sure;
If constance earn a crown, if conquest join the gain,
If learning armed with godly life do evermore remain;
If ardent thirst for souls, if aged acts in youth,
If for to sweat and die the death for the Eternal truth,
If martyrs purchase life, if meekness last in praise,
If charity of highest degree do flourish green always,
If mind invincible do ever blaze and bide,
If all the gifts of manly mind, and virtues therein tried:
Then is not Edmund dead, but gone to bliss before,
He lives among the sacred saints, and reigns for evermore."
When I had heard this Fame that Truth had sounded out,
And that indeed he was not dead: then, being void of doubt,
I cast mine eyes to heaven, I feared none annoy,
I wiped mine eyes, and thankèd God, and clapt my hands for joy.

Even the hostile account of the execution in Holinshed's *Chronicles* quotes Latin verse in praise of Campion's learning,[99] and another in celebration and vindication of the three martyrs. Among the latter we find:[100]

And for a brief death they rejoice with eternal crowns,
These are the gifts prepared for the devout martyrs. . . .
Religion, not an evil life, was the crime.

I have already given the epigram in verse in praise of the author of *Ambrosia*.[101]

At the end of his Latin version of Alfield's account in 1582, Dutch scholar Gulielmus Estius (Fr. Willem Hessels van Est), mentioned above,[102] put some savage lines against English justice in Latin poetry.[103]

Italian humanist Ianus Nicius Erythraeus (*nom de plume* of Gian Vittorio Rossi) wrote some eloquent lines in prose in favor of Campion, within a eulogy he wrote on Dr. Allen. Of the brutal racking and execution of Campion, he said, "Our age has seen nothing more foul than that crime, from the sight of which the sun herself should not more fittingly withdraw."[104]

In Dr. Allen's *Brief History* and in the compilation *Concertatio* (1583), an unnamed "friend and fellow-student of his when he [Campion] studied at Oxford"[105] (whom all take to be Gregory Martin) eulogizes him in eighty-six lines of Latin poetry, tracing the steps of his life from beginning to end. Here are a few lines:

> You were the first, and the prince of the flock;
> the rest of the crowd ceded first place and the palm to you. . . .
> O happy course of life, and blessed end:
> to die courageously in the Lord and for the Lord.
> Be to me, I beseech, a favorable patron to your student,
> and neglect not to pray God often for me.[106]

Regrettably, an ode on Edmund Campion by Gerard Manley Hopkins S.J. is lost. He alludes to it in correspondence, after writing at least a few stanzas.[107] It must have been in his room in Dublin, among the papers destroyed soon after his death in 1889.

Modern Biographies

In the 20th century, lives of Campion were written in English by Dom Bede Camm O.S.B. (1905), L.I. Guiney (1908), Evelyn Waugh (1935, 2nd ed. 1947), E.E. Reynolds (1980), and a small one for young people by Harold Gardiner S.J. (*Edmund Campion: Hero of God's Underground*, 1957). All of these, except Reynolds, were basically condensations of Simpson's biography.

In the last 150 years, full biographies of Campion have also appeared in Czech, Dutch, French, German, Italian, Slovak, and Spanish.[108]

In addition, Waugh's biography was translated into German, Dutch, French, Spanish, Slovak, and frequently reprinted.[109]

Numerous pamphlets have also told his story (Denys Jackson; Jesuit Fathers Goldie, Martindale, Basset, Caraman; and others).[110] Campion appears in many collections of saints' lives.

Monsignor Robert Hugh Benson's historical novels, *By What Authority?* (1904) and *Come Rack! Come Rope!* (1912), feature Campion as a character, accurately drawn.[111] So too does Lady Georgiana Fullerton's novel, *Constance Sherwood: an Autobiography of the Sixteenth Century* (1865).[113]

In recent fiction Campion appears: as a character in *Chesapeake* by James A. Michener (1978) and as a hot topic of discussion in *My Name is Will*, a novel about Shakespeare by Jess Winfield (2008).

Numerous plays have been written and performed to depict Campion's story.[113] No doubt, many have been written by Jesuit schoolmasters and played at Jesuit schools, but not published.

A Tyburn Prophecy Fulfilled

On June 8, 1585, an old Marian priest and venerable Confessor of the Faith, Father Gregory Gunnes, of Norfolk,[114] was reported to the Privy Council for traitorous speech in favor of Edmund Campion.

Gunnes had been educated at Magdalen College, Oxford,[115] and ordained priest in 1558, the last year of Queen Mary's reign and of the last Catholic bishop of Norwich, John Hopton. In the years 1562–67, he was a chaplain at Magdalen,[116] then, in 1567, appointed Anglican Rector of the tiny parish of Elford (now Yelford) near Witney in Oxfordshire. Finally, in 1579, he gave up this living to follow his faith and conscience, and was reconciled to the Catholic Church. He became a vagrant priest, ministering here and there, using the alias of "Stone."

On June 7, 1585, at the Bell Inn, Henley, around 6:00 p.m., Fr. Gunnes fell into conversation with a man called Evan Arden, a member of Sir Francis Knowles's household, and betrayed himself by praising Father Campion. The conversation was continued in a lane outside. "How can you praise Campion?," Arden asked. Gunnes replied, "He was the only [i.e., best] man in all England." Arden, in disbelief, asked again, "How can you praise Campion, being so arrant a traitor as he was?" Gunnes answered, "Say not so, for the day will come, and I hope to see it, and so may you too, that there shall be an offering where Campion did suffer." Then said Arden, "What? Shall we offer unto the gallows?" "No, not so," said Gunnes, "but you shall see a religious house built there for an offering."[117]

Another man, William Wheatley, affirmed the record of this conversation. Gunnes was arrested on June 8 and sent to the Marshalsea jail at Southwark on June 10.[118] Nothing more is known of his life thereafter.

Before daylight on Good Friday in 1624 there was a penitential procession of Catholics from Holborn to Tyburn,[119] which for a long time seemed the nearest approach to the accomplishment of Fr. Gunnes's prediction.[120]

The prophecy was finally fulfilled, 316 years after it was made, when in 1901 an anonymous French lady was the recipient of 35,000 francs (about £10,000 at the time) and promised the Sacred Heart to employ it for His glory. She offered it to Mother Marie-Adele Garnier to purchase a house for sale at Tyburn for her "Adorers of the Sacred Heart." In March 1903, the community moved from Basset Road, Notting Hill, into 6 Hyde Park Place.[121] Thus was Tyburn Priory founded.

Where Tyburn Tree once stood, there is now a small, cobbled, triangular traffic island, at the corner of Edgware and Bayswater Roads, with a round plaque on the ground, bearing a cross in the middle, encircled by the words: "The Site of Tyburn Tree." It is opposite Hyde Park, a few hundred paces east of Tyburn Priory, between the Priory in Bayswater Rd and Marble Arch tube-station.

On Earth as in Heaven

The Greek word *martyr* means witness. Martyrdom may be defined as the endurance of death in witness to the Christian religion. For a person to be declared a martyr by the Church, it must be demonstrated that he or she died through murder or execution or lethal sufferings; that death occurred in witness to the Christian faith or a Christian virtue; and that the persecutor or killer acted out of opposition to the Catholic religion.[122] All these three conditions must be met.

Having satisfied these criteria, Edmund Campion was beatified (declared "Blessed") on December 29, 1886, by decree of the Sacred Congregation of Rites,[123] Rome, under Pope Leo XIII.

An Office and Mass in honor of Edmund Campion, Ralph Sherwin, and Alexander Briant was approved by the Sacred Congregation of Rites, Rome, for use in the Society of Jesus in 1887, and for use in the diocese of Portsmouth in 1889.[124]

Not before, but once he is beatified, a *Beatus* may have a church named after him, his name may appear in the prayers of Mass or in the Litany of the Saints or any other public prayers, he may appear in art with a halo around his head to signify heavenly glory, or be depicted carrying a palm to indicate martyrdom, and so forth. Beatification, then, gives permission for a local and restricted public veneration—generally limited to the Blessed's region or country of origin or work, or to the houses of his religious congregation if he belonged to one.

Canonization, on the other hand, mandates a universal veneration by the Church. A canonization is a solemn declaration that a member of the Church is now in Heaven and is enrolled in the "canon" (official list) of saints, for public veneration and invocation by all the faithful.[125]

In the 19th and 20th centuries, in presenting to the Holy See the cause of the martyrs of England and Wales, the postulators or presenters had to demonstrate that the deaths were endured for religion and not for any political or worldly motive, and that the candidates had enjoyed a public reputation and veneration among Catholics as martyrs.

The introduction to the 1968 collection of documents regarding martyrdom and cult concludes:

> From the documents as a whole there emerges in the case of each martyr, a clear picture of the circumstances in which persecution was undergone, the religious motive behind denunciation to the civil authorities, the arraignment before a court or the refusal to accept the Act of Supremacy (which declared the King supreme head of the Church in England and consequently denied the primacy of the Roman Pontiff), the clear and deliberate acceptance of condemnation to death rather than renounce Catholic doctrine, the carrying out of the capital sentence amid unspeakable and heartrending tortures, and, finally, the international reaction, attested by unexceptionable documents which confirm the religious nature of the motive for which sentence was inflicted and death undergone.[126]

In 1960, the hierarchy of England and Wales chose 40 of the 199 martyrs declared Blessed under Popes Leo XIII and Pius XI, for promotion to Sainthood, and this was the group canonized in 1970: a representative group of Catholics martyred in England and Wales in the years 1535–1679. The Postulator General for the cause was Italian Jesuit, Fr. Paolo Molinari, assisted by the research of his fellow Jesuits Fr. James Walsh, Fr. Philip Caraman (author and translator of various books on Campion's time and beyond), Fr. Clement Tigar; also Mr. Patrick Barry.

The conditions of martyrdom already more than sufficiently demonstrated in his case, Edmund Campion was canonized (declared "Saint") as one of the Forty Martyrs of England and Wales by Pope Paul VI in 1970 on October 25, which is now their feast day. But Campion's own feast day, shared with his martyr-companions Briant and Sherwin, is December 1, the day of his martyrdom.

In the imagination of English-speaking Catholics, Campion holds a unique place among the Forty Martyrs, and indeed, among all the English martyrs. German Lutheran historian, Arnold Meyer, remarks:

> When Campion, after ten years' absence, returned to England with the greatest secrecy, he was already well disciplined in the virtues of fortitude and purity, and had attained to a gentleness of disposition which nothing could embitter, and to a greatness of mind which rose above all pettiness—qualities which give a winning majesty to his personality and place him on a level with the martyrs of Christian antiquity. No other of the missionaries working in England had the power of calling forth enthusiastic admiration and commanding unselfish devotion to the same extent as this proto-martyr of the English Jesuits.[127]

It is said that in the long run the world judges rightly. We may conclude with the world's judgment in the words of American poet and essayist, Louise Imogen Guiney:[128]

> Historians of all schools are agreed that the charges against Campion were wholesale sham. They praise his high intelligence, his beautiful gaiety, his fiery energy, his most chivalrous gentleness. He had renounced all opportunity for a dazzling career in a world of master men. Every tradition of Edmund Campion, every remnant of his written words, and not least his unstudied golden letters, show us that he was nothing less than a man of genius; truly one of the great Elizabethans, but holy as none other of them all.

St. Henry Walpole's Elegy on Campion

The following verses are attributed to St. Henry Walpole, who witnessed Campion's execution close-up while still a Protestant. (See chapter 20: "Walpole"; chapter 21: "Celebration in poetry"; Simpson's bibliography, no. 46). The text below is of the first printed edition, of 1582, with spelling and punctuation modernized. Other versions vary a little. The stanza numbers are added here. Notes* are given below to explain some references or meaning.

Upon the Death of Mr. Edmund Campion, One of the Society of the Holy Name of Jesus

1. Why do I use my paper, ink and pen,
   and call my wits to counsel what to say?
   Such memories were made for mortal men;
   I speak of Saints whose names can not decay.
   An Angel's trump were fitter for to sound
   their glorious death, if such on earth were found.

2. Pardon my want, I offer nought but will,
   their register remaineth safe above.
   Campion exceeds the compass of my skill,
   yet let me use the measure of my love,
   and give me leave in low and homely verse,
   his high attempts in England to rehearse.

3. He came by vow, the cause to conquer sin,
   his armor prayer; the word his targe* and shield,
   his comfort Heaven, his spoil our souls to win,
   the devil his foe, the wicked world the field,
   his triumph joy, his wage eternal bliss,
   his captain Christ, which ever blessed is.

4. From ease to pain, from honor to disgrace,
   from love to hate, to danger, being well,
   from safe abode to fears in every place,
   contemning death to save our souls from Hell,
   our new Apostle coming to restore
   the faith which Austin* planted here before.

5. His nature's flowers were mixed with herbs of grace,
   his mild behavior tempered well with skill,
   a lowly mind possessed a learned place,
   a sugared speech, a rare and virtuous will.
   A saint-like man was set on earth below,
   the seed of truth in erring hearts to sow.

6. With tongue and pen the truth he taught and wrote,
   by force whereof they came to Christ apace,
   but when it pleasèd God, it was his lot
   he should be thralled,* He lent him so much grace,
   his patience then did work as much or more,
   as had his heavenly speeches done before.

7. His fare was hard, yet mild and sweet his cheer;
   his prison close, yet free and loose his mind;
   his torture great, yet small or none his fear;
   his offers large, but nothing could him blind.
   O constant man, O mind, O virtue strange,
   whom want, nor woe, nor fear, nor hope could change.

8. From rack in Tower they brought him to dispute,
   bookless, alone, to answer all that came,
   yet Christ gave grace, he did them all confute
   so sweetly there in glory of His name,
   that even the adverse part are forced to say
   that Campion's cause did bear the bell away.

9. This foil enraged the minds of some so far,
   they thought it best to take his life away,
   because they saw he would their matter mar,
   and leave them shortly nought at all to say.
   Traitor he was with many and seely* slight,
   yet packed a jury that cried guilty straight.

10. Religion there was treason to the queen,
    preaching of penance war against the land,
    priests were such dangerous men as have not been,
    prayers and beads were fight and force of hand,
    cases of conscience bane unto the State,
    so blind is error, so false a witness hate.

11. And yet behold these lambs be drawn to die,
    treason proclaimed, the queen is put in fear,
    out upon Satan, fie malice, fie,
    speakest thou to them that did the guiltless hear?
    Can humble souls departing now to Christ,
    protest untrue? Avaunt,* foul fiend, thou liest.

12. My Sovereign Liege, behold your subjects' end,
    your secret foes do misinform Your Grace;
    who in your cause their holy lives would spend,
    as traitors die, a rare and monstrous case.
    The bloody wolf condemns the harmless sheep,
    before the dog, the while the shepherds sleep.

13. England, look up, thy soil is stained with blood,
    thou hast made martyrs many of thine own.
    If thou hast grace, their deaths will do thee good,
    the seed will take, which in such blood is sown,
    and Campion's learning fertile so before,
    thus watered too, must needs of force be more.

14. Repent thee, Eliot,* of thy Judas kiss,
    I wish thy penance, not thy desperate end.
    Let Norton* think, which now in prison is,
    to whom was said he was not Caesar's friend,
    and let the judge consider well in fear,
    that Pilate washed his hands, and was not clear.

15. The witness false, Sledd, Munday* and the rest,
    which had your slanders noted in your book,
    confess your fault beforehand, it were best,
    lest God do find it written when He doth look
    in dreadful doom upon the souls of men,
    it will be late, alas, to mend it then.

16. You bloody jury, Lee,* and all the 'leven,
    take heed your verdict which was given in haste,
    do not exclude you from the joys of heaven,
    and cause you rue it when the time is past;
    and everyone whose malice caused him say
    "Crucifige,"* let him dread the terror of that day.

17. Fond Elderton,* call in thy foolish rhyme,
    thy scurrile* ballads are too bad to sell,
    let good men rest, and mend thyself in time,
    confess in prose thou has not metered well.
    Or if thy folly can not choose but fain,
    write alehouse toys, blaspheme not in thy vein.

18. Remember you that would oppress the cause,
    the Church is Christ's, His honor cannot die,
    though Hell herself revest* her grisly jaws,
    and join in league with schism and heresy,
    though craft devise, and cruel rage oppress,
    yet skill will write and martyrdom confess.

19. You thought perhaps when learned Campion dies,
    his pen must cease, his sugared tongue be still;
    but you forgot how loud his death it cries,
    how far beyond the sound of tongue and quill.
    You did not know how rare and great a good
    it was to write his precious gifts in blood.

20. Living he spake to them that present were,
    His writings took their censure of the view.
    Now fame reports his learning far and near,
    and now his death confirms his doctrine true.
    His virtues are now written in the skies
    and often read with holy inward eyes.

21. All Europe wonders at so rare a man,
    England is filled with rumor of his end,
    London must needs, for it was present then,
    when constantly three saints* their lives did spend.
    The streets, the stones, the steps you hailed them by,
    proclaim the cause for which these martyrs die.

22. The Tower saith the truth he did defend,
    the bar bears witness of his guiltless mind,
    Tyburn doth tell he made a patient end,
    on every gate his martyrdom we find.
    In vain you wrought, that would obscure his name
    for Heaven and earth will still record the same.

23. Your sentence wrong pronounced of him here,
    exempts him from the judgments for to come.
    O happy he that is not judged there!
    God grant me too to have an earthly doom.
    Your witness false and lewdly taken in,
    doth cause he is not now accused of sin.

24. His prison now the City of the King,
    his rack and torture joys and heavenly bliss;
    for men's reproach with angels he doth sing,
    a sacred song which everlasting is.
    For shame but short, and loss of small renown
    he purchased hath an ever-during crown.

25. His quartered limbs shall join with joy again,
    and rise a body brighter than the sun,
    your blinded malice tortured him in vain,
    for every wrench some glory hath him won,
    and every drop of blood which he did spend
    hath reaped a joy which never shall have end.

26. Can dreary death then daunt our faith, or pain?
    Is't lingering life we fear to lose, or ease?
    No, no, such death procureth life again,
    'tis only God we tremble to displease,
    who kills but once, and ever still we die,
    whose hot revenge torments eternally.

27. We cannot fear a mortal torment, we,
    this martyr's blood hath moistened all our hearts,
    whose parted quarters when we chance to see,*
    we learn to play the constant Christian parts.
    His head doth speak, and heavenly precepts give,
    how we that look should frame ourselves to live.

28. His youth instructs us how to spend our days,
    his flying bids us how to banish sin,
    his straight profession shows the narrow ways
    which they must walk that look to enter in.
    His home return by danger and distress,
    emboldens us our conscience to profess.

29. His hurdle draws us with him to the cross,
    his speeches there provoke us for to die,
    his death doth say this life is but a loss,
    his martyred blood from heaven to us doth cry.
    His first and last, and all conspire in this,
    to show the way that leadeth unto bliss.

30. Blessed be God which lent him so much grace,
    thanked be Christ which blessed His martyr so,
    happy is he which sees his Master's face,
    cursed are they that thought to work him woe,
    bounden be we to give eternal praise,
    to Jesus' name which such a man did raise.
    Amen.

Notes

Stanza number:
3. *targe:* shield, buckler
4. *Austin:* St. Augustine of Canterbury who evangelized England
6. *thralled:* bound (when arrested)
9. *seely:* closed, hoodwinked
11. *avaunt:* begone!
14. *Eliot:* betrayed Campion
    Norton: tortured Campion on the rack, himself was imprisoned
    for a short period from December 1581—a reference which dates
    this poem as very close in time to Campion's death.
15. *Sledd, Munday:* two of the perjurers testifying against Campion
16. *Lee:* William Lee, foreman of the jury
    "Crucifige": "Crucify (him)!" *Luke* 23:21

17. *Elderton:* Willam Elderton wrote some verses against Campion (see Simpson's bibliography, nos. 13, 27, 44, 50).
 scurril: scurrilous
18. *revest:* put on again
21. *three saints:* Campion and the two executed with him
27. *parted quarters when we chance to see:* a martyr's head and quarters were put on city gates as a warning to the people.

Endnotes

In some endnotes, the more common or important works are given an added reference to the two bibliographies at the end of the book. For example:

E.B., no. 5 = Editor's Bibliography, 5th item
S.B., no. 41 = Simpson's Bibliography, 41st item

Chapter 1—London and Oxford

1. Letter of Fr. Robert Persons S.J. to Campion, Nov. 28, 1578, mentioning, "2 of them are your countrymen born in Paternoster Row": *Letters and Memorials of Father Robert Persons S.J., 1578–1588*, ed. Leo Hicks S.J., Catholic Record Society (vol. 39, London 1942) p. 2. "Countrymen" here means from the very same place, since he names five Englishmen but deems only two "countrymen." Full letter in ch. 5: "The situation in England; Persons to Campion."

2. Some older books say Campion was born "1539/40," since Jan. 25 was 1539 according to the English calendar of the time, but 1540 by later reckoning when Jan. 1 replaced March 25 as the start of the new year.

3. Leslie Campion, *The Family of Edmund Campion* (Research Publishing Co., London 1975) gives the possible family background of Campion. Gaps in the surviving records prevent certainty.

4. Michael F. J. McDonnell, "Edmund Campion, S.J., and St. Paul's School" *Notes and Queries* 194 (Oxford 1949) pp. 46–49, 67–70, 90–92, at p. 91 records that in 1549, Anne, wife of "Edmond Campion," witnessed a will of Richard Jones, a master at St. Paul's School.

5. Michael McDonnell, pp. 90–1, says a search of the surviving records of the local parishes has not produced a record of Edmund's baptism.

6. Fr. Robert Persons S.J., *Of the Life and Martyrdom of Father Edmond*

Campian, chapter 1 (hereafter Persons's *Life of Campion* will be Persons's *L. of C.*). Archives of Stonyhurst College, England. Manuscript written in 1594. Printed in *Letters and Notices* (Manresa Press, Roehampton, U.K.) vol. 11 (1877) pp. 219–42, 308–39; vol. 12 (1878) pp. 1–68. See S.B., no. 2. It is in two "books." Book 1 has 24 chapters. Book 2, unfinished, has 4 chapters only. Any reference to book 1 will give the chapter no. only; if from book 2, it will give both book and chapter no.

7.   Autograph of Campion quoted in ch 5: "Transfer to Brünn."

8.   Autograph of Campion at Jesuit College, Prague, in Fr. Bohuslav Balbin S.J., *Miscellanea Historica Regni Bohemiae Decadis I, lib. 4* ("Historical Miscellanea of the Kingdom of Bohemia, 1st Decade, book 4," Georgij Czernoch Press, Prague 1682). Leslie Campion, p. 55, suggests that there were four boys in Edmund's family and no girl, and surmises, p. 54, that Balbin, thinking a male name to be a female one, substituted a girl for a boy—but this is impossible, given the autograph of Edmund himself, which says: "I have two brothers and one sister," quoted in ch 5: "Transfer to Brünn."

9.   Carl I. Hammer, "Robert Campion: Edmund Campion's Brother?" *Recusant History*, 1980, p. 153

10.   W. H. Stevenson and H.E. Salter, *The Early History of St. John's College, Oxford* (Oxford University Press 1939) p. 180, n. 2

11.   Persons says, "the whole company of merchant adventurers (as I take it)": *L. of C.*, ch. 1. Simpson said he thinks it was the Grocers Company instead (who will in fact appear later), but Michael McDonnell, p. 47, judges this an arbitrary change and points out the Merchant Adventurers' link with the Mercers' Company who governed St. Paul's School.

12.   Persons's *L. of C.*, ch. 1

13.   London then had four grammar-schools: the three mentioned, and St. Thomas of Acons in Cheapside.

14.   Page ii of the introductory "Biographical Account of William Fulke" in William Fulke D.D., *A Defense of the Sincere and True Translations of the Holy Scriptures against the cavils of Gregory Martin* (ed. Rev. Charles H. Hartshorne, for the Parker Society, Cambridge 1843)

15.   See ch. 16: "The second debate" and through the same chapter. McDonnell, pp. 69–70, shows Fulke was at St. Paul's, not at Christ's Hospital, thus correcting a statement by Hartshorne in the biography of Fulke just cited.

16.   Persons's *L. of C.*, ch. 1, implies he went to more than one grammar school. McDonnell, p. 69.

17.   Rev. William Trollope, *A History of the Royal Foundation of Christ's*

Hospital (William Pickering, London 1834) p. 212. Says Leslie Campion, p. 16: "Edmund's connection with Christ's Hospital was another problem, as there are no records of the name in either the admission registers or the minute books. The Clerk to the Hospital thinks it probable that he was a private pupil of one of the masters." But Trollope, pp. 203, 212, mentions the imperfect or defective state of the registers preceding the great fire of London of 1666; and McDonnell, p. 47, says, "there is ample evidence, into which it is unnecessary to enter here, that this was one of the schools which he attended."

18. Her pre-coronation procession of Sept. 30, rather than, as Simpson says, her solemn entry into London on August 3—for that route did not include St. Paul's: McDonnell, p. 67. Persons says Edmund made the oration before the queen at St. Paul's "though at that time he were no scholar of the School." McDonnell, p. 69, explains that Persons, in saying "at that time," means "no longer" at St. Paul's.

19. McDonnell, pp. 47, 49

20. H. F. M. Prescott, *Mary Tudor—The Spanish Tudor* (Eyre and Spottiswoode, G. B. 1952. Reprint: Phoenix, London 2003) p. 249

21. Agnes Strickland, *Lives of the Queens of England from the Norman conquest* (Longman 1848) pp. 209–10 (Reprint: Chivers, Bath 1972); Herbert Norris, *Tudor Costume and Fashion* (1938. Reprint: Dover Publications, N.Y. 1997) p. 439

22. "Vox dulcis, lenis, plena, sonora, gravis." Fr. Gregory Martin, in *Concertatio Ecclesiae Catholicae in Anglia adversus Calvino-Papistas et Puritanos* ("The Struggle of the Catholic Church in England against the Calvinist-Papists and Puritans," 1st ed. Hatot, Trèves 1583/4). See S.B., no. 59. Reprint of 1588 ed.: John Gibbons, *Concertatio ecclesiae catholicae* (Gregg Press, Farnborough 1970) p. 67. In referring to this book, I will say "page" [rather than "folio" (leaf) and then "recto" (right leaf of an open book) or "verso" (back side; turned leaf)]. "Page" will mean the no. at the top right of the 2 pages visible when the book is open, and will refer to that page or the one opposite.

23. *Concertatio*, p. 67, the line preceding the lines cited in the previous note: from the same verses in Campion's honor by Fr. Martin.

24. Foundation deed of College, May 29, 1555, in Stevenson and Salter, pp. 378. Cf. p. 118 on 1557 as the first operational year.

25. Thomas M. McCoog S.J. (ed.), *The Reckoned Expense: Edmund Campion and the Early English Jesuits* (Boydell Press, Suffolk 1996) p. xvi, and Philip Caraman S.J., "Campion at St. John's" *Letters and Notices* 92 (1995) pp.

212–24, at p. 213, say 1558, but I say 1557 because the second Foundation charter of St. John's College, issued March 5, 1558, names Edmund Campion and others, apparently as freshmen—which means he and they must have entered in the previous calendar year, 1557, c. Sept. 29, when the academic year began: cf. Stevenson and Salter, pp. 119, 412.

26. Persons's *L. of C.*, ch. 1

27. L. Campion, *The Family of Edmund Campion*, p. 39

28. L. Campion, p. 39, says either Hussey or the estate of Abbot Gabriel Donne, the last Cistercian Abbot of Buckfast. McDonnell, p. 90, quotes this disposition of Hussey's will.

29. S. and Salter, p. 146

30. Kilroy, *Edmund Campion: Memory and Transcription* (Ashgate Publishing Ltd., U.K. 2005) p. 42

31. Kilroy, p. 45

32. S. and Salter, pp. 123, 424

33. S. and Salter, pp. 126–7, 130

34. S. and Salter, pp. 131, 330–1. On pp. 140, 322, 331 they correct the idea in Anthony à Wood, *Athenae Oxonienses: an Exact History of all the Writers and Bishops who have had their Education in the University of Oxford from 1500 to 1690* (2 vols, London 1691–2), that the 1st and 3rd presidents were deprived for refusing the oath of supremacy. It was for other reasons, decided by Thomas White. E. E. Reynolds, *Campion and Parsons: The Jesuit Mission of 1580–1* (Sheed and Ward, London 1980; Catholic Book Club, London 1982) p. 37, relies upon Anthony à Wood's information; his history of St. John's, and Campion's dates at St. John's, show that he did not see Stevenson and Salter's book.

35. S. and Salter, pp. 131, 192, 336

36. Robert Lemon (ed.), *Calendar of State Papers, Domestic Series, of the Reigns of Edward VI, Mary, Elizabeth 1547–1580* (Longman, London 1856) July 1571, nos. 11–3, p. 417. S. and Salter, p. 129.

37. Philip Caraman S.J., p. 213

38. Fr. Paolo Bombino S.J., *Vita et martyrium Edmundi Campiani* ("Life and Martyrdom of Edmund Campion," Mantua 1620) ch. 2, p. 6. S.B., no. 1.

39. T. McCoog S.J., introduction to *The Reckoned Expense*, p. xv

40. James McConica in *The Reckoned Expense*, p. 52

41. *Recollections of Father Campion* by Fr. Thomas Fitzherbert S.J., in J. H. Pollen S.J., *Acts of English Martyrs hitherto unpublished* (Burns and Oates, London 1891) p. 35

42. *Athenae Oxonienses* (3rd ed., London 1813, ed. Philip Bliss; facsimile

reprint 1967) vol. 1, columns 473–8 on Campion, at 473. Simpson corrects *dominare* to *dominari*. Wood is quoting Tobie's *Concio Apologetica*, given against Campion, p. 61: see below, this chapter: "Fathers of the Church."

43. Manuscript collections of the Society of Jesus, at Stonyhurst College, Lancashire, vol. 1, p. 149. But on another occasion Persons took the oath: ch. 6: "Campion and Persons compared."

44. C. W. Boase and Andrew Clark, *Register of the University of Oxford: 1449–1622* (Clarendon Press, Oxford 1885) vol. 1, p. 244. S. and Salter, p. 181, say "he determined as B.A. in Lent [Feb.–Mar.] 1561" but on p. 416, "in the spring of 1561."

45. S. and Salter, pp. 131, 181, 417

46. Campion in Balbin, *Misc. Historica*, book 4. The same autograph of Campion is fully quoted in Fr. Schmidl S.J. in ch 5: "Transfer to Brünn."

47. He is called "Edmund Campion, M.A." in the records of the Grocers' Company of Sept. 28, 1566 when the Company first granted him an exhibition.

48. In the autograph quoted in ch 5: "Transfer to Brünn."

49. "qui stilum meum, prius disjectum et libere effluentem extra oram artis et rationis, redegit in quadrum, aut aptius ad normam hanc rectam exegit." See S.B., no. 68.

50. The accusation is mentioned early in the pages of the anonymous *Leicester's Commonwealth* (1584) but was widespread before that.

51. Persons's *L. of C.*, ch. 2

52. Simpson narrated it as a fact, as did Dr. Allen in 1582 (ed. Pollen, p. 5: see S.B., nos. 52, 52a) and Wood in *Athenae Oxonienses* (1813 ed.) vol. 1, col. 476, but A.F. Vossen, *Two Bokes of the Histories of Ireland—compiled by Edmunde Campion* (Van Gorcum, Assen, The Netherlands 1963) p. 3, judges it "improbable" that, as an undergraduate, Campion made this oration, noting that Bombino's biography (1618, rev. ed. 1620) makes no mention of it, despite his dependence upon Persons who mentions itbut not as an eye-witness, since Persons was not yet at Oxford himself. Other writers, Stephenson and Salter, and Philip Caraman S.J., among them, disallow the oration.

53. S. and Salter, p. 404

54. Persons's *L. of C.*, ch. 2

55. Persons's *L. of C.*, ch. 2

56. S. and Salter give the full text of the oration, pp. 407–11. On p. 406 they mention four manuscripts of the oration: one at Westminster Cathedral, printed at pp. 165–72 of the work named in S.B., no. 100); three at the

Bodleian Library, Oxford, among the Rawlinson Mss. which also include another Ms. of extracts from it. 57 S. and Salter, p. 427. Original is English, spelling here modified.

58. Persons's *L. of C.*, ch. 2

59. Peter Heylyn, *Ecclesia restaurata* ["The Church Restored"], *or the History of the Reformation* (1661) vol. 2, p. 174

60. *Calendar of State Papers . . . 1547–1580*, Dec. 28, 1566, nos. 54–6, pp. 284–5. E.B., no. 1.

61. "the chick that sytteth next the henne": *Calendar of State Papers . . . 1547–1580*, Feb. 21, 1570, no. 43, p. 363, enclosure 4.

62. Castelnau, letter of Nov. 1580: Harlay deposit in the Paris Imperial Library, Ms. no. 223, vol. 1, p. 368

63. He re-appears in our story: ch. 7 "George Gilbert"; ch. 12: "Fr. Ralph Sherwin captured." The debaters are listed in John Nichols, *The Progresses and Public Processions of Queen Elizabeth* (John Nichols and Son, London 1823) p. 231; Charles Plummer (ed.), *Elizabethan Oxford* (Clarendon Press, Oxford 1887) pp. 174, 201; Harleian Mss. 7033, folio 142.

64. "litteratae Principi cum principe litterarum": *Edmundi Campiani . . . Decem Rationes . . . et opuscula eius selecta* ("Edmund Campion's . . . "Ten Reasons" . . . and select small works of his," Balthasar Moretus, Antwerp 1631) p. 330. See S.B., no. 97. *Beati Edmundi Campiani e Societate Iesu martyris in Anglia opuscula* ("Small works of Blessed Edmund Campion of the Society of Jesus, martyr in England") Franciscus Rosalius, Barcelona 1888) p. 71. See S.B., no. 100. Hereafter both works will be designated: *Camp. Opusc.* Hereon, where two page references are given to a work of Campion, the first is from the 1631 edition, and the second (in parentheses) is the reference, where it exists, to the most recent edition of Campion's works, 1888.

65. *Camp. Opusc.* (1888 ed.) p. 73 has "Te quae sic facis, te qui sic mones," but other Mss have "haec . . . haec" instead of "sic . . . sic."

66. Bodleian Rawlinson Mss. D. 272. The debate, found in several (somewhat varying) Mss, is printed in Thomas Hearne, *Historia vitæ et regni Ricardi II* ("History of the life and kingdom of Richard II," Oxford 1729) pp. 251–96. Campion's speech is in *Camp. Opusc.*, pp. 330–40 (pp. 71–5).

67. *Leicester's Commonwealth* (Antwerp 1584, ed. Nina Green 2002) pp. 8–9

68. Bombino, ch. 2, p. 7

69. Eleanor Rosenberg, *Leicester, Patron of Letters* (Columbia University Press, N.Y. 1955) p. 84

70. "Prince" here means generically a "sovereign" – in this case, Elizabeth,

whose accession occurred "thirteen years" before. Fr. Caraman mistakenly says Campion "thanks him [Leicester] fulsomely for his favors over thirteen years" ("Campion at St. John's" p. 223) but Campion's involvement with Leicester began only five years before, in 1566 (and he was not a prince!). "Prince" then could mean "queen": e.g., Allen (ed. Pollen, 1908) p. 35 (S.B., no. 52a).

71. *Narratio Divortii Henrici VIII* ("An Account of the Divorce of Henry VIII," c. 1570), *Camp. Opusc.*, pp. 165–70 (pp. 57–9)

72. In book 2, ch. 9. The open attack upon Henry VIII is not there—only the cynical remark that he is "now called Founder [of Wolsey's college at Oxford] because he let it stand."

73. S. and Salter, p. 181

74. See in this chapter: "Deacon in the Church of England."

75. L. Campion, *The Family of Edmund Campion*, pp. 36, 38–9

76. *Athenae Oxonienses* (ed. Bliss) vol. 1, col. 475

77. Persons's *L. of C.*, ch. 2

78. Persons, ch. 2

79. Persons, ch. 2

80. Persons, ch. 2: changed by me from oblique speech to direct speech.

81. Persons, ch. 2. See this book's ch. 20: "Discussion over the wisdom of the execution."

82. P. Caraman S.J., p. 216, with reference to Strickland Gibson (ed.), *Statuta antiqua universitatis Oxoniensis* ("Ancient statutes of Oxford University," Clarendon Press, Oxford 1931) p. 396

83. Among the Rawlinson Mss. at Oxford (D. 272) is a speech delivered by Campion at the Act of 1568 as Junior Proctor: S. and Salter, p. 406. Simpson adds here that Campion was "public orator," but S. and Salter simply deny it, p. 180.

84. T. McCoog S.J., *The Reckoned Expense*, introduction, p. xvii, with reference to *Statuta antiqua universitatis Oxoniensis*, p. lxxv

85. Fr. Godfrey Anstruther O.P., *Vaux of Harrowden – A Recusant Family* (R.H. Johns, Newport 1953) p. 100, followed by his trans. of Campion's letter, pp. 100–2, modified here a little. Latin original: *Camp. Opusc.*, pp. 341–7 (pp. 11–4).

86. Anstruther, p. 102

87. Vaux family members appear in ch. 10: "Organisation and precautions"; "The Jesuits' success"; ch. 11: "Reunion, review and plans at Uxbridge"; "Campion travels to the north, end of 1580"; "Campion in the north, start of 1581"; ch. 13: "Fr. Hartley"; ch. 15: "A series of arrests"; "What did

Campion reveal?"; "No betrayal of anything unknown"; ch. 20: "Timing of the execution."

88. Persons's *L. of C.*, ch. 3. I retain Simpson's reading, "pregnant" (which makes more sense), where Br. Foley's ed. of Persons has "frequent." The rest of this paragraph paraphrases Persons's account of Campion's conscience.

89. Persons's *L. of C.*, ch. 3

90. *Piissimi et eminentissimi viri, D. Tobiæ Matthoei Archiepiscopi olim Eboracensis Concio Apologetica adversus Campianum* ("Speech of defense against Campion of the most pious and most eminent man, Dr. Tobie Mathew, one-time archbishop of York," Leonard Lichfield, Oxford 1638) pp. 56–7. I revised Simpson's more eloquent translation of the passage cited, to remove his own phrases added to the Latin.

91. *Concio Apologetica*, pp. 59–60

92. Persons's *L. of C.*, ch. 4

93. *A Catalogue of the Manuscripts Preserved in the Library of the University of Cambridge* (Vol. 5, Cambridge University Press 1867) p. 582

94. Simpson calls him "Tarleton"; Foley's ed. of Persons has "Tarelson": obviously the Ms. is unclear. Whatever Persons wrote may have been wrong anyway, for he gives the name and then says, "if I remember not amiss his name." But Persons's designation of him (*L. of C.*, ch. 4) as (the first) "tutor and master" to Philip Sidney enables us to identify him as Thomas Thornton.

95. Persons's *L. of C.*, ch. 4

96. *Calendar of State Papers . . . 1547–1580*, Oct. 15 and 20, 1568, nos. 16, 22, p. 320. E.B., no. 1.

97. John Strype (d. 1737), *Annals of the Reformation and Establishment of Religion and other Various Occurrences in the Church of England during Queen Elizabeth's Happy Reign* (4 vols. Oxford 1824) vol. 1, part 2, ch. 52, p. 279. (Facsimile reprint of orig. ed. 1708–9: Burt Franklin, New York 1968)

98. *Contra Arianos vel Auxentium Mediolanensem* ("Against the Arians or Auxentius of Milan," A.D. 365), 12

99. Cf. *Calendar of State Papers . . . 1547–1580*, Oct. 24, 1577, no. 12, p. 560.

100. *Calendar of State Papers . . . 1547–1580*, Nov. 20, 1577, no. 32, p. 566

101. Ch. 9: "The rise of the Recusants."

102. S. and Salter, p. 181

103. Vossen, p. 7. E.E. Reynolds, *Campion and Parsons*, p. 41, says March 1569. Fr. McCoog, *Reckoned Expense*, p. xv (2nd ed. p. xxii), says, "late spring of 1569."

104. Based on the earliest biographers (Persons, Bombino, Allen, *Concertatio*, More), Vossen, pp. 3–11, concludes that Campion was definitely a Catholic when he arrived in Dublin, and that his ordination was shortly before this retreat to Ireland:

1. Fr. Persons's *L. of C.*, ch. 4, says "he ever fully minded to leave both the University and his country, whereunto he was greatly hastened by one thing [the Anglican diaconate]." Ch. 5 says "Mr. . Campian, having received once this order of Deaconship . . . took presently such a remorse of conscience . . . as he could never be quiet nor have rest with himself until he had broken off wholly from them, and left . . . the University and England itself." Persons's earlier notes say, however: "—his modesty—and his devotion in Ireland was very singular though yet he was not in the church." *Collectanea P*, vol. 1, folio 150: Fr. Grene's transcript of Persons's notes, to be exactwhich means it might be Grene's summary in English of Persons's Latin; quoted in J. H. Pollen, S.J., "Edmund Campion's History of Ireland," p. 566; and Vossen, p. 9, who at p. 10 explains "not in the church," rather than meaning not a Catholic, could mean he was not yet a cleric, and in any case, these are notes of Persons corrected in the later *Life*. The *Life*, ch. 6, seems to have the equivalent passage where it says, "his life even, this time being yet neither priest nor religious man, was so full of piety and edification"which fits in with Vossen's interpretation.

2. Fr. Bombino, ch. 5, p. 17, says Edmund was reconciled speedily ("propere") to the Catholic Church before going to Ireland.

3. Fr. Allen's account says "*after* [my emphasis] he had passed with all commendation through such exercises, degrees and offices, as the university yieldeth . . . he suffered himself to be made deacon": ed. Pollen, pp. 5–6 (see S.B., nos. 52, 52a).

4. *Concertatio's* equivalent life, p. 52, says God recalled him "suddenly" ("subito") after ordination.

5. Fr. More, *History Eng. Province*, book 2, no. 4, says "After setting his conscience at rest through a Catholic priest . . . he made a discreet withdrawal to Ireland" (see S.B., no. 3).

(6.) Further, Fr. Bartoli (not mentioned here by Vossen), vol. 3, bk 2, ch. 3, pp. 25–6, says an intense repentance came soon after ordination, he confessed to a priest, was reconciled to the Church and went to Ireland (see S.B., no. 4).

105. Vossen, p. 7

106. S. and Salter, p. 189

107. S. and Salter, p. 185, quoted again below, this chapter: "Gregory Martin and the end of Oxford."

108. S. and Salter, pp. 164, 329. They say Dec. 5 *and* Dec. 15.

109. Full letter in ch. 5: "Seven letters of Campion," letter no. 7.

110. Anstruther, *Vaux of Harrowden*, p. 102. He adds, "He held it nominally till March 1571." On p. 529 he gives the reference: Exchequer 334/8, folio 69. J. H. Pollen S.J. says "He compounded for the first fruits of this, March 3 . . . 1569. R.O., *Composition Books*, 1560–1566, Series iii." *The English Catholics in the Reign of Queen Elizabeth: A Study of their Politics, Civil Life, and Government, 1558–1580* (Longmans, Green and Co., London 1920) p. 253. *A History of the County of Gloucester*, ed. C. R. Elrington, volume 6 (Dawsons of Pall Mall, London 1965) in "Parishes: Sherborne," pp. 120–7, says "For a short time between 1568 and 1569 the benefice was held by Edmund Campion." Perhaps here 1568 means the year under the older method of counting, i.e., it was still 1568 until March 25, when the new year 1569 started.

111. Persons's *L. of C.*, ch. 5

112. Persons's *L. of C.*, ch. 5

113. Fr. Bombino, ch. 5, p. 17; ch. 9, p. 38. Persons's *L. of C.*, ch. 5: "the abomination of this character of the beast, as he was wont to term it."

114. Persons's *L. of C.*, ch. 11

115. Persons's *L. of C.*, chs. 11, 10. Simpson had "mark," which I keep in preference to "mask" in Foley's ed. of Persons.

116. All quotations from the Grocers' Company in L. Campion, *The Family of Edmund Campion*, pp. 36–38. The words and awkward expressions are retained exactly but the spelling is modernised.

117. Grocers Hall website: www.grocershall.co.uk/chu.html

118. Vossen, p. 4, suggests Campion told them of this reason, among the "divers reasons" as to why he could not preach, in his letter resigning his exhibition (below). But this makes no sense: it is in itself a sufficient and decisive reason, excluding the need to give others; further, he would not finally admit his non-ordination when, by resigning, he was not bound anymore to explain anything.

119. The wording of the summons to preach, with a proviso about what would happen if he refused, implies he had been ordained quite some time before April 1568—making even 1567 a possible year in their minds. Perhaps for this reason (not thinking Edmund was still a layman), Fr. Caraman says Campion was ordained "not later than Trinity Term [Apr.–Jun] 1566": p. 217.

120. S. and Salter, pp. 184–5. On p. 185, College records are cited to show that Campion left Oxford at the time said, close to Sept. 29, 1570. He was still in the College on Aug. 7 but gone by Sept. 30.

121. S. and Salter, p. 185
122. S. and Salter, p. 189
123. S. and Salter, p. 186
124. S. and Salter, p. 186
125. S. and Salter, pp. 188–9
126. S. and Salter, p. 187
127. So Martin was eulogized in an address to the Duke of Norfolk at St. John's.
128. *The Lives of Philip Howard, Earl of Arundel and Ann Dacres, his Wife* ed. from the original [contemporary] MSS [Manuscripts] by [H.G. Fitzalan] the [14th] Duke of Norfolk (Hurst and Blackett 1857) p. 9. Reprint: *The Life of Philip Howard, Earl of Arundel, Saint and Martyr, edited from the Original Mss by the Duke of Norfolk, E.M. London*, adapted by T.L. Griffin CFC (Treacy Centre, Parkville, Australia 1998)
129. Gregory Martin to Campion, being quoted back to him in a reply. Full letter in ch. 5: "seven letters of Campion," letter no. 7.
130. Bombino, ch. 5, p. 18
131. Kilroy, pp. 54–5; Bombino, ch. 1, p. 5. However, Bombino's phrase here about Campion's uncertainty refers to an earlier period. Bombino, ch. 5, p. 18, says Edmund was reconciled to the Catholic Church before going to Ireland.
132. S. and Salter, pp. 184–5, quoted above. Vossen, pp. 11–2, says, "The date of Campion's departure is uncertain. He was in residence at St. John's until March 1570, as appears from the lists of battels. . . . There is no documentary evidence that from April to September 1570 he was in residence throughout. . . . the battels of the Fellows for the terms April–September 1570 have not been entered. . . . He was, however, at the College on July 26–28 and on August 7, 1570." The bursar entered his name on lists up to Michaelmas (Sept.) 1571, thereby indicating he thought Campion could return at any time up to then: Vossen, p. 12, who says, p. 13, it is probable Campion arrived in Ireland on August 25—the date given in Persons's *Life*, ch. 5.

Chapter 2—Ireland

1. Simpson's free translation of Campion to Henry Vaux, *Camp. Opusc.*, pp. 343–4 (p. 12). Full letter given in ch. 1: "Tutor to Henry Vaux."
2. *Harmonia, seu catena dialectica in Porphyrianas institutiones* (Reyner Wolfe, London 1570)
3. *Camp. Opusc.*, p. 348 (p. 14), Dec. 1, 1570.
4. *Camp. Opusc.*, pp. 349–50 (pp. 14–5). Campion's letter is also printed in the preface to Stanihurst's *Harmonia*, p. xvi.

5. See S.B., nos. 19, 22.

6. Persons says Campion arrived in Ireland on August 25, 1569, but we now know this date is definitely a year too early. See Chronology at the end of this book for the various dates given by biographers.

7. Daniello Bartoli S.J., *Dell'Istoria della Compania di Gesu. L'Inghilterra parte dell'Europa* ("History of the Society of Jesus: England, part of Europe," Rome 1667): reprinted in *Opere del Padre Daniello Bartoli* ("Some works of Fr. D. Bartoli," Giacinto Marietti, Turin 1825) vol. 3, bk 2, ch. 3, p. 26. See S.B., no. 4.

8. Ch. 3: "His ideal Christian student"

9. The university is mentioned below: "Selections from the History's speeches."

10. Stevenson and Salter; the entry for "Campion" in the *Dictionary of National Biography;* Waugh; and others.

11. His intro., pp. 14–6, 20, to Campion's *Two Bokes of the Histories of Ireland.*

12. Persons's *L. of C.*, ch. 5

13. Persons's *L. of C.*, ch. 5

14. Bertrand Salignac de La Mothe Fénelon (French ambassador in England 1568–75) dépêches [dispatches] 158, 159: Feb. 6 and 12, 1571: A. Teulet (ed.), *Correspondance diplomatique de Bertrand de Salignac de La Mothe Fénelon*, vol. 3 (Paris and London 1840) pp. 458–9, 470–1.

15. State Papers Office, Ireland, Feb. 12, 1571

16. Vossen, p. 47

17. End of Campion's *History of Ireland*

18. *Camp. Opusc.*, pp. 351–6 (pp. 15–7). Following the 1888 ed., I put March 20, not 19 as Simpson had. Here, as elsewhere, the dates of letters may be changed, to follow the 1888 edition of Campion's works. In most cases, the date of a letter makes no difference to the biography.

19. *Camp. Opusc.*, pp. 357–60 (pp. 18–9)

20. So says Campion himself in the Preface to Leicester: "I had not in all the space of ten weeks." Holinshed repeats it in the dedicatory epistle to Sir Henry Sidney: *Holinshed's Chronicles* (Henry Denham, London 1587) vol. 2, p. 3.

21. As mentioned in ch. 1: "Campion receives patronage"

22. Stanihurst's preface to Campion's *History*, in *Holinshed's Chronicles* (1587) vol. 2, p. 7

23. Rosenberg, *Leicester, Patron of Letters*, p. 86, n. 37; Vossen, pp. 107, 122

24. A. C. Southern, *Elizabethan Recusant Prose, 1559–1582* (Sands and Co., London 1950) p. 287

25. The details of all these editions are in S.B., no. 82.

26. *Two Bokes of the Histories of Ireland—compiled by Edmunde Campion, feloe of St. John Baptistes College in Oxforde, Edited from MS Jones 6 Bodleian Library Oxford* (ed. Alphonsus Franciscus Vossen: Van Gorcum, Assen, The Netherlands 1963). A.F. Vossen, the youngest of sixteen children, was born on June 2, 1920 and died April 26, 2002.

27. Vossen, p. 86

28. "Historiam Hibernicam suspicor periisse; iustum volumen et absolutum: Inquisitores Hæretici rapuere." The only surviving sentence of an undated letter quoted in bk 2, no. 4, of Fr. Henry More S.J., *Historia Provinciae Anglicanae Societatis Jesu, collectore Henrico Moro, eiusdem Societatis, sacerdote* (Thomæ Gevbels, Audomari 1660: "History of the English Province of the Society of Jesus, compiled by Henry More, priest, of the same Society," Th. Geubels, St. Omer 1660). Eng. trans. of the Elizabethan part, namely, books 1–6: Francis Edwards S.J., *The Elizabethan Jesuits: Historia Missionis Anglicanae Societatis Jesu (1660) of Henry More* ["History of the Mission of the English Society of Jesus"] (Phillimore, London 1981). Hereon this will be cited as More, *History Eng. Province*. As pointed out by Vossen, pp. 22–3, More took the sentence from Nicholas Harpsfield's *Historia Anglicana Ecclesiastica* ("English Ecclesiastical History," ed. Fr. Richard Gibbons S.J., Douay 1622) p. i.

29. Gerard Kilroy, *Edmund Campion: Memory and Transcription*, p. 55. Simpson assumed Campion's manuscript of his *History* was seized on the ship at Drogheda, but it is now clear that it was confiscated at this later time; the officers would hardly seize a signed manuscript but not the man sought.

30. Lansdowne Mss. 15, no. 46, quoted in Stevenson and Salter, p. 190; Vossen, p. 129; Kilroy, p. 55 (with variant readings): spelling modernised. The same letter is mentioned in Rosenberg, p. 87, but she follows Simpson's assumption about the time of the seizure.

31. Recounted in ch. 5: "Seven letters of Campion" – straight after letter no. 2.

32. Vossen, p. 61

33. J. H. Pollen, S.J., "Edmund Campion's History of Ireland" *The Month*, Dec. 1905, pp. 561–76; Feb. 1906, pp. 156–69, at p. 159

34. "The Place of Allen, Campion and Parsons in the Development of English Prose," *The Review of English Studies*, vol. 20, no. 80, Oct. 1944, pp. 272–85, at p. 278

35. Preface to *Ireland*, in *Holinshed's Chronicles*, vol. 2, p. 7

36. Letter to Fr. Coster of Jan. 1577: quoted in full in ch. 5: "Seven letters of

Campion"—letter no. 1. See the endnote there explaining this quotation from Campion.

37.   "Edmund Campion's History of Ireland" p. 160
38.   "Edmund Campion's History of Ireland" pp. 161, 162
39.   *Edmund Campion*, 2nd ed. (Hollis and Carter, London 1947) ch. 1, pp. 35–6
40.   Start of the book
41.   Book 1, ch. 3
42.   Book 1, ch. 5
43.   Book 1, ch. 6
44.   Book 1, ch. 6
45.   Book 1, ch. 6
46.   Book 1, ch. 6
47.   Book 1, ch. 6
48.   Book 1, ch. 6
49.   Book 1, ch. 6
50.   Pollen, "Edmund Campion's History of Ireland" p. 169\
51.   Book 1, ch. 14
52.   Book 1, ch. 10
53.   Book 1, ch. 15
54.   Book 2, ch. 9
55.   Stanihurst's preface, Holinshed, vol. 2, p. 7
56.   Stanihurst's preface, vol. 2, p. 7
57.   S.B., no. 45. See ch. 19: "The witness Munday."
58.   A.D. 1320, Campion's *History of Ireland*, book 2, ch. 5
59.   Book 2, ch. 10
60.   Book 2, ch. 10
61.   Katherine Duncan-Jones in *Reckoned Expense*, p. 89
62.   End of the book
63.   Popularly then called *Tredagh;* also spelt Tredah or Tredake. In Latin, *Pontana:* Vossen, p. 21.
64.   A phrase adapted from Stanihurst's preface, quoted above.
65.   Quoted partly in ch. 1: "Campion receives patronage."
66.   S. and Salter, p. 189
67.   See ch. 1: "Deacon in the Church of England" and its longer endnotes.
68.   *History of Ireland*, book 1, ch. 13
69.   Book 2, ch. 9
70.   Book 2, ch. 9. Henry is "now called Founder [of Wolsey's college] because he let it stand." Cf. above, ch. 1: "Campion speaks and debates before

Queen Elizabeth."

71. Pollen, "Edmund Campion's History of Ireland" pp. 163–4
72. Book 1, ch. 6
73. Book 2, ch. 9
74. Book 1, ch. 13. These last two quotes are in the Jones Ms. given in Vossen, but lack their clear Catholic wording in earlier printed editions: e.g., Ware, 1633, omits "blessed" before "Queen Mary."
75. I insert this phrase for Campion asserts Papal authority over Ireland at least in the past, but not over England: see ch. 4: "The temporal power of the Popes," especially the last paragraph.
76. But Henry VIII is the object of a sarcastic remark by Campion, quoted above, ch. 1: "Campion speaks and debates before the Queen."
77. Rosenberg, pp. 87–8
78. *Camp. Opusc.*, p. 393 (p. 25). Campion's letter, here cited, is in ch. 5: "Seven letters of Campion"—letter no. 7.
79. Persons's *L. of C.*, ch. 6
80. Also called Meyler Hussey. Campion mentions him in his Irish history, bk 2, ch. 10.
81. Persons's *L. of C.*, ch. 7, paraphrased
82. *History Eng. Province*, book 2, no. 4
83. *L. of C.*, ch. 7, where he says it twice.
84. Simpson thus tries to reconcile the two pieces of evidence: one from Persons, the other from Campion's dating. Vossen, p. 24, says, "As the case now stands, no decisive arguments can be adduced for believing Persons or distrusting him" on this point of Campion's attending Dr. Storey's trial. He suggests, p. 24, note 105, the possibility of a copyist's error changing May to June by writing "VI" instead of "V": "The autograph may have said 'Drogheda. 9.V.1571.'" But this possibility is discounted by the date at the end of the Preface to Leicester: "Dublin May 27, 1571." It is too much to claim a copyist made such an error twice, or to say Campion post-dated *two* things.
85. *Holinshed's Chronicles* (1587) A.D. 1559, vol. 2, p. 1180
86. Persons's *L. of C.*, ch. 7, paraphrased
87. *Holinshed's Chronicles*, A.D. 1571, vol. 3, p. 1225
88. Persons's *L. of C.*, ch. 7, says Campion left England on the very day of Storey's execution.
89. Persons's *L. of C.*, ch. 7

Chapter 3—Seminarian at Douay

1. Bishop Challoner (1691–1781) completely re-did the translation, for it was already archaic and obscure by his time, but it misleadingly kept the name "Douay-Rheims" Bible. Dr. Challoner's version became the standard Bible for English-speaking Catholics for the next two centuries. The original Douay-Rheims of the 1500's would be unreadable to most people today, the word-order and vocabulary being so different. It is unfounded, therefore, to say, "it is difficult not to believe that during his [Campion's] stay at Douay . . . he did not contribute in some measure to his friend's [Martin's] achievement.": Philip Caraman S.J., "Campion at St. John's" p. 215. The original stilted translation of Douay, necessary for those times, shows no signs of Campion's flourish and literary elegance.

2. Full title: *A briefe treatise of diverse plaine and sure wayes to finde out the truthe in this doubtful and dangerous time of heresie: conteyning sundry worthy motives unto the Catholike faith* (John Fowler, Antwerp 1574). Reprint: *A briefe treatise of diverse plaine and sure wayes, 1574* (Scolar Press, Menston, England 1974).

3. Dr. Allen, *An Apology for the English Seminaries* (Mounts in Henault, France, 1581). Of course, in 16th cent. English, "apology for" meant "defense of." The full title was *An apologie and true declaration of the institution and endevors of the two English colleges, the one in Rome, the other now resident in Rhemes against certaine sinister informations giuen up against the same* (Jean de Foigny, "Mounts in Henault" [in reality at Rheims] 1581. Reprint: Scolar Press, U.K. 1971).

4. Letter of Sept. 16, 1578 in T.F. Knox (ed.) *The Letters and Memorials of William Cardinal Allen (1532–1594)* (D. Nutt, London 1882. The Gregg Press, Farnborough 1965) p. 59.

5. *Reckoned Expense*, p. 122

6. *Letters and Memorials of Cardinal Allen*, p. 65

7. Figures and years vary a little: others say the first priests arrived in 1574, and that by 1578, 52 of the 74 priests ordained were sent to England. Since many missionaries used aliases, the exact number of seminary priests sent to England is uncertain.

8. Ludwig von Pastor, *The History of the Popes*, vol. 19 (Kegan Paul, London 1930) p. 378

9. Simpson wrote, "On Campion's arrival in 1571, the foundation already numbered some 150 members, of whom eight or nine were doctors or licentiates in theology"—but Fr. John Morris S.J., "Blessed Edmund Campion at Douay" *The Month*, September 1887, pp. 30–46, at p. 33,

points out that this figure is far too big for that early year and gives the correct figure, making use of T. F. Knox (ed.), *The First and Second Diaries of the English College, Douay* (David Nutt, London 1878. Reprint: The Gregg Press, Ridgewood, N.J., 1965 and Farnborough 1969), popularly known as *Douay Diaries*, which also include the stint in Rheims, 1578–93.

10. *Apology for the English Seminaries*, ch. 3

11. *L. of C.*, ch. 10

12. John Strype (1711) *Life and Acts of Matthew Parker, Archbishop of Canterbury* (3 vols. Clarendon Press 1821) Appendix

13. Caroline Litzenberger, "Richard Cheyney, Bishop of Gloucester: An Infidel in Religion?" *Sixteenth Century Journal*, Vol. 25, No. 3 (Autumn 1994) p. 567. On the content of these Articles, see ch. 9: "*The Thirty-Nine Articles.*"

14. Convocation Journal, in *Records of Convocation* [complete set], ed. Gerald Bray (Boydell and Brewer, U.K. 2006)

15. J. Collier, *History of the Church of England* (London 1708–9) book 6, p. 531. *Ecclesiastical History of Great Britain* [to 1685], ed. T. Lathbury (9 vols., William Straker, London 1852) vol. 6, p. 492

16. Anthony à Wood, *Athenae Oxonienses* (1813 ed.) vol. 2, col. 791. Goodman's Ms. is in *The Court of King James the First. By Dr. Godfrey Goodman, Bishop of Gloucester. To which are added Letters illustrative. Now first published from the Original MSS.* by J.S. Brewer (Bentley 1839). Cf. Strype, *Annals of the Reformation*, vol. 1, p. 421.

17. *Rationes Decem* ("Ten Reasons"), Reason no. 8

18. T. Fuller, *Church History* [to 1648] vol. 4, ed. J.S. Brewer (Oxford 1845) p. 404

19. Strype, *Annals of the Reformation*, vol. 1, p. 422

20. William Camden, at A.D. 1559, in *Annales Rerum Gestarum Angliae et Hiberniae Regnante Elizabetha* ("Annals of the events of England and Ireland in the reign of Elizabeth," London 1615 and 1625)

21. The full original Latin text is in Bombino, ch. 7, pp. 30–38; *Edmundi Campiani, Societatis Iesu, martyris in Anglia, Orationes, Epistolae, tractatus de imitatione rhetorica* ("Orations, letters, tract on rhetorical imitation, of Edmund Campion of the Society of Jesus, martyr in England," ed. Robert Turner: Georg Wil ler, Ingoldstadt 1602) pp. 56–64; *Camp. Opusc.*, pp. 360–79 (1888 ed., pp. 36–43). The trans. above, a revision of Simpson's, is of Bombino's text with the addition of the last phrase and naming of year ("1571 . . . salvation)" not in Bombino but in others (e.g., *Camp. Opusc.*, 1631 ed., p. 379). Persons's *L. of C.*, ch. 10, dates the letter at

the *end* of Campion's time at Douay—but he mistakenly says in ch. 10 also that Campion was there only "somewhat more than a year." Simpson had put 1572, but 1571 fits in with Campion's urgent ardour and the recent events of Cheney's life. Also, a date of Nov. 1571 is in accord with his reference in the letter to meeting with Cheney at Dutton's home "three years ago"—meaning about Nov. 1568, *before* ordination—a more likely date than Nov. 1569, since by that later date he was thoroughly ashamed of his Anglican diaconate and was not likely to be visiting his parishioners in the place where he held a benefice received with an ordination he regretted; nor investigating doctrine with Cheney when he (Campion) was now resolutely Catholic.

22. Three Puritans who had accused Cheney of false doctrine: Bishop Thomas Cooper of Lincoln; Laurence Humphrey of Magdalen College, a theologian who later wrote against Campion; Thomas Sam(p)son, dean of Christ Church. Strype, *Annals of the Reformation* (Oxford 1824) vol. 2, part 1, bk 1, ch. 12 (Anno 1571) p. 158

23. Simpson had, "to hit the bird in the eye." The Latin, "cornicum oculos configere" (Cicero, *Pro Murena*, 25), means literally to pierce the crows' eyes, i.e., to outdo the sharp-eyed, to beat the expert.

24. "Baptism of heretics" (as in the Latin in Bombino, p. 34; *Camp. Opusc.*, 1631 ed., p. 371)—not "baptism of infants" as Simpson put, following another Ms., as in *Camp. Opusc.*, 1888 ed., p. 40. St. Cyprian and the Synod of Carthage had erred in saying that heretics' baptisms were invalid, even when done properly.

25. Following "Patrunculorum quorundam": Bombino, p. 35. This reading and trans. of the phrase above is in *Lives of the English Martyrs, Volume II: Martyrs under Queen Elizabeth* (Burns and Oates, London 1905) p. 288. E.B., no. 42. Alternative reading: "Latrunculorum quorumdam," *Camp. Opusc.*, 1631 ed., p. 372 and 1888 ed., p. 40—"of certain thieves and robbers," followed by Simpson.

26. *Misc. Historica*, book 4, p. 196: see S.B., no. 5.

27. *Douay Diaries*, p. 273; cf. Stevenson and Salter, p. 189. Fr. Henry Sebastian Bowden and Fr. J. H. Pollen S.J. in Dom Bede Camm O.S.B. (ed.), *Lives of the English Martyrs, Volume II: Martyrs under Queen Elizabeth* (Burns and Oates, London 1905) on p. 292 say he "took the degree of Bachelor of Divinity, in acts held on March the 21st, and the 27th of November, 1572, and the 21st of June, 1573." The last date is a misprint: "June" should read "January"; Pollen says January in "Edmund Campion's History of Ireland" *The Month*, December 1905, pp. 561–76; February 1906, pp. 156–69, at

p. 156. E.E. Reynolds, *Campion and Parson*, p. 49, without reference to any document, gives the date of the B.D. degree as Jan. 21, 1572, but that should read 1573. The fact of his B.D. is certain: Campion mentions it himself: "I graduated as . . . Bachelor of Theology at Douay," quoted below in ch. 5: "Transfer to Brünn."

28. Fr. Morris, "Blessed Edmund Campion at Douay" p. 40

29. Louise Imogen Guiney, *Blessed Edmund Campion* (Macdonald and Evans, London 1914) p. 55

30. Dom Bede Camm O.S.B., *Forgotten Shrines—f relics and memorials of the English martyrs* (Macdonald and Evans, London 1910. Facsimile reprint: Gracewing, U.K. 2004) p. 378.

31. Morris, "Blessed Edmund Campion at Douay" pp. 42–3

32. *Summa Theologica*, part III, question 68, article 2: objection 2 and reply 2

33. Annals of Douay, by Alban Butler, Brussels Ms. 15594

34. Simpson says we know he taught at Douay, for Campion speaks of (St) Cuthbert Mayne (1544–77), the proto-martyr of Douay, as having been his pupil (ch. 5: "More letters of Campion"). But, to be exact, Campion does not say *where* he taught Mayne. Cuthbert went to Douay in 1573, and perhaps only overlapped with Campion for a month or two, before Campion left in Spring that year (or missed him altogether). More likely, Edmund means Cuthbert was his pupil at St. John's when he was lecturer in Rhetoric from 1564–70, and Cuthbert was a pupil there. Cf. Helen Whelan, *Snow on the Hedges: A Life of Cuthbert Mayne* (Fowler Wright Books, Herefordshire 1984) pp. 50, 57, 59. See ch. 5: "Presentiment of martyrdom" and "More letters of Campion."

35. Persons's *L. of C.*, ch. 8

36. *Camp. Opusc.*, pp. 262–97 (pp. 103–17). On p. 297 (p. 117) Campion refers specifically to his audience: students in a "seminary," i.e., Douay. First printed in 1602 on pp. 29–44 of the book named in S.B., no. 92. Latin text with facing Eng. trans. in John F. Quirk S.J., *A Patron for Scholars— Eulogy on the Blessed Edmund Campion, S.J. with his Oration on "The Model College Student" done into English* (St. John's College, Fordham, N.Y. 1896): S.B., no. 81. In this section, "His ideal Christian student," I have omitted Simpson's personal commentary, added further quotations from the oration itself and removed some of the references obscure to the modern reader.

37. Campion expresses the same thought in his own person in *Ten Reasons*, Reason no. 8: "I am not weighty enough to claim for myself so much as an ordinary place among the select theologians who at this day have declared

war on heresies. But this I know, that, puny as I am, supported by the grace of Christ, I run no risk while I do battle, with the aid of heaven and earth, against sayings such as these, so odious, so tasteless, so stupid." Quoted in ch. 13: "*Ten Reasons* summarized" at the end of Reason 8.

38.   *Edmund Campion,* 2nd ed. (1947) ch. 1, p. 34

39.   *Narratio Divortii Henrici VIII* ("An Account of the Divorce of Henry VIII," c. 1570): *Camp. Opusc.,* p. 140 (p. 47)

40.   *Satires,* bk 2, no. 3, line 248: "equitare in arundine longa."

41.   *Camp. Opusc.,* pp. 310–29 (pp. 185–93)

42.   *Camp. Opusc.,* pp. 318–9 (pp. 188–9)

43.   *Camp. Opusc.,* pp. 328–9 (p. 193). The same story and description is told in his *History of Ireland,* bk 1, ch. 14, whence for this translation Simpson took some phrases.

44.   Persons's *L. of C.,* ch. 10, twice says he decided to join the Jesuits *before* leaving Douay.

45.   Bombino, ch. 9, p. 39; Bartoli, vol. 3, bk 2, ch. 4, p. 31

46.   Allen: (1) Eng. orig., *Letter written by M. Doctor Allen concerning the Yielding up of the City of Daventrie, unto his Catholic Majesty, by Sir William Stanley Knight* (Joachim Trognæsius, Antwerp 1587. Reprinted by the Chetham Society 1851, ed. Thomas Heywood, Esq.). Latin trans., *Epistola de Civitate Deventriensi reddita suo legitimo regi per illustrem virum Gul. Stanleium* (Cracow 1588). (2) *An Admonition to the Nobility and People of England and Ireland concerning the present wars made for the execution of His Holiness' sentence, by the high and mighty King Catholic of Spain. By the Cardinal of England.* (Antwerp 1588)

47.   Bombino, ch. 9, p. 39

48.   Persons's *L. of C.,* ch. 10

Chapter 4—Pilgrim to Rome

1.   See end of ch. 3: "He leaves for Rome."

2.   The group travelling by foot from Rome to Rheims took 44 days (Apr 18–May 31: ch. 7: "The band of fourteen departs from Rome"). If we deduct the various delays (four of the priests in their 50's and 60's; a stop of some days at Bologna when Fr. Persons's leg was bad; a stay of 8 days at Milan; avoidance of the most direct routes when dangerous; a pilgrimage to a shrine of St. Clovis; tardiness through sickness near the end)—they actually *walked* on about 28 days. So it is conceivable that Campion, if he escaped all delays, walked from Douay to Rome (c. 200 km farther) in 25 days (Mar 22–Apr 15), since he was only 32 and travelling alone. But if not

March 22, then perhaps Campion left a week or so earlier.

3. This we know from a letter to Bavand, quoted in full in ch. 5: "Seven letters of Campion," letter no. 5.

4. Also called "Gesualdo." Karlheinz Riedel S.J., *Sieger im Tod: Die Lebensgeschichte Edmund Campions, eines Kämpfers für Christus* ("Victor in death: the biography of E. Campion, a warrior for Christ," Verlag Herder, Freiburg 1953) p. 37, says Gesualdi was Protector of England, but this is a mistake; it was Cardinal John Moroni: J. M. Rigg, *Calendar of State Papers relating to English affairs . . . in the Vatican archives* (vol. 2) *1572–1578* (Hereford Times, London 1926) p. 141.

5. Campion said "*about* ten years past"—for an exact ten years would place his arrival in Rome in 1571, which is definitely too early; and all biographers date it 1572 or 1573. The quote re-appears at the trial in ch. 18: "The Bull of Pius V discussed."

6. *History of Ireland*, book 2, ch. 10: pp. [141–2] in Vossen's ed.

7. *History of Ireland*, book 2, ch. 9: pp. [129–30] in Vossen.

8. *History of Ireland*, book 2, ch. 2. The same ideas and almost same words are in book 2, ch. 1: Vossen, p. [72].

9. *History of Ireland*, book 2, ch. 1

10. *History of Ireland*, book 2, ch. 1

11. *History of Ireland*, book 2, ch. 3. The reference is to Thomas More's *The Supplication of Souls* (Newman Press, Maryland 1950) p. 29.

12. *Camp. Opusc.*, pp. 187–8 (p. 66): "excelsa propeque divina sapientia."

13. The Bull says: "1569, on the fifth of the Kalends of March." Since at that time the new year began on March 25, it was still 1569, but by later reckoning, 1570.

14. Fr. Nicholas Sanders [Nicolas Sander], *De Visibili Monarchia Ecclesiae* ("On the Visible Monarchy of the Church," Reynerus Velpius [Reynier Velpen], Louvain, Belgium 1571) p. 730

15. Fr. William Watson, *Quodlibets of Religion and State* (Richard Field, London 1602) p. 262. Full title: *A decacordon of ten quodlibetical questions concerning religion and state wherein the author framing himself a quilibet to every quodlibet, decides an hundred cross interrogatory doubts, about the general contentions betwixt the seminary priests and Jesuits at this present.* Fr. John Morris S.J., in 1891, called this book "notorious": his intro. to J. H. Pollen S.J., *Acts of English Martyrs hitherto unpublished* (Burns and Oates, London 1891) p. xxi, but the same book, p. 312, says Watson expressed his sorrow for this work on the scaffold. Watson also wrote *Important considerations, which ought to move all true and sound Catholics, who are*

not wholly Jesuited, to acknowledge without all equivocations, ambigui-
ties, or shiftings, that the proceedings of her Majesty, and of the state with
them, since the beginning of her Highness' reign, have been both mild and
merciful. Published by sundry . . . secular priests, in dislike of many trea-
tises, letters, and reports . . . to the contrary: together with our opinions of a
better course hereafter, for the promoting of the Catholic faith in England
(Richard Field, London 1601). Watson was so passionately opposed to the
Jesuits as to say that Englishmen trained under them "become traitors or
favorers of conspiracies against their Prince, country and dearest friends."
Quodlibets, pp. 141–2.

16. The Bull is printed in Nicolas Sanders, *De Origine ac Progressu Schismatis*
Anglicani ("On the Origin and Progress of the Anglican Schism," Rheims
1585) book 4, ch. 8. S.B., no. 75: Sander, *Rise and Growth of the Anglican*
Schism (1585 ed., trans. David Lewis: Burns and Oates, London 1877; Tan
Books, Illinois 1988) pp. 301–4; Fr. Philip Hughes, *The Reformation in*
England (rev. ed., 3 vols in one, Burns and Oates, London 1963) vol. 3, pp.
418–20. E.B., no. 55.

17. Henry's defense of the Pope's Primacy will be found in his *Assertio Septem*
Sacramentorum [Defense of the Seven Sacraments], London 1521, sig. B.
(Pollen's note).

18. J. H. Pollen S.J., "Religious Persecution under Queen Elizabeth" *The*
Month, November 1904, pp. 501–17, at p. 514.

19. Sanders, *The Anglican Schism*, book 4, ch. 9, opening paragraphs

20. Vol. 1, p. 186

21. *Edmund Campion* (1935), in the second half of ch. II: "The Priest." A.O.
Meyer probably refers to this opinion at p. 136 n. 1 of *England and the*
Catholic Church Under Queen Elizabeth (Kegan Paul, Trench, Trübner
and Co., London 1916. Trans. Rev. J.R. McKee. Reprints: Barnes and
Noble, N.Y. 1967; Routledge and Kegan Paul, London 1967 and 1969).
Fr. Edwards S.J., *Robert Persons*, p. 28, and Fr. McCoog S.J., *The Society of*
Jesus in Ireland, Scotland, and England 1541–1588 (E. J. Brill, N.Y. 1996)
pp. 134–5, n. 18, judge that this document records questions addressed to
Pope Gregory XIII by Persons and Campion on April 14 ,1580. McCoog,
p. 134: "During the audience eighteen questions were addressed to
Gregory XIII." Without doubting the audience, it is not the practice for
priests to submit a series of tangled questions to the Pope for immediate
resolution—and if the answers were authoritative, they would have been
publicized as such.

22. Simpson's date of Sept. 1572 for arrival in Rome is far too early, on
account of two pieces of evidence. Campion says he did nearly two years

of theology at Douay, from (June) 1571: see his autograph quoted in ch. 5: "Transfer to Brünn"; and in ch. 3: "His activities at Douay," we record an academic act of Campion on Jan. 21, 1573.

23. Also called Maggi, Magius or Mayer. He was born c. 1531 in Brescia, Italy, entered the Society in Rome in 1555, was ordained priest in 1556, and had been Provincial since 1566: Ladislaus [László] Lukács S.J., *Catalogi personarum et officiorum provinciae Austriae S.I.* ("Catalogues of persons and assignments of the Austrian province of the Society of Jesus," Institutum Historicum S.I. [Historical Institute of the Society of Jesus], Rome 1978) pp. 375–6, 724.

24. Persons's *L. of C.*, ch. 10

Chapter 5—Jesuit at Prague and Brünn

1. T. McCoog S.J., *Reckoned Expense* (2nd ed.) p. xxvi
2. Persons's *L. of C.*, ch. 11
3. "Nihil unquam pertinaciter defendi." See p. 563 of Pollen (E.B., no. 102).
4. Joannes Schmidl S.J., *Historiae Societatis Jesu Provinciae Bohemiae, Pars I: 1555–1592* (Typis Univ. Carolo Ferdinandeae, Pragae 1747: "History of the Society of Jesus of the Province of Bohemia. Part 1," Charles Ferdinand University Press, Prague) vol. 1, at A.D. 1573 (S.B., no. 6), pp. 338–9: "Sua manu . . . In Libro Examinum Pro bationis Brunensis, Capite 3" ("In the book of the examens of the probation of Brünn, at chapter 3 in his own hand") quotes Campion (all translated in the text):

"Vocor Edmundus Campianus, Anglus Londinensis, annum natus 34, ex legitimo matrimonio, et parentibus ab antiquo Christianis, et in Catho lica fide, ut speratur, defunctis. Pater vocatur Edmundus, conditione civis et bibliopola, mediocri fortuna. Fratres duos habeo, sororem unam. Frater major natu uxorem habet, vivit in militia, ut audio; minor vero studet. Habeo deliberatum propositum vivendi et moriendi in hac Societate Jesu; idque nunc primum hic statuo, si antea non statuissem, nullo impellente, sed proprio motu."

Capite 5 ("At chapter 5"):

"Primum in patria humanioribus literis: deinde Oxonii philosophiae septennium, theologiae sexennium circiter operam dedi; Aristoteli, theologiae positivae, et Patribus: deinde prope biennium scholasticae theologie Duaci. Oxonii in Magistrum Artium promotus, in Baccalaureum theologiae Duaci. Memoria utcunque felici, intellectu etiam satis perspicaci, animoque in studia propenso, ad quae suppetunt utcunque vires, ut et ad reliqua So cietatis munia.

"Haec ille, die 26 Augusti."

5.   He was born in Reggio Emilia; his original Italian name is Giovanni Paolo
       Campana. Simpson used a Latin form "Campanus," but in the Jesuit Latin
       lists he is called "Ioannes Paulus Campana": Ladislaus [László] Lukács
       S.J., *Monumenta antiquae Hungariae 1593–1600* ("Records of ancient
       Hungary," Institutum historicum S.I. [Historical Institute of the Society
       of Jesus], Rome 1987) pp. 16, 17, 31; L. Lukács, *Catalogi*, pp. 282, 285, 641.
       Simpson, and Schmidl, p. 346, name John Vivarius [Aquensis] as *socius*
       (assistant to the Novice-master) but he, born 1550, entered the Society in
       1571 (Lukács, *Monumenta*, pp. 41, 319; *Catalogi*, pp. 308, 341) and is not
       listed as *socius*—although ordained very soon, 1573 (*Catalogi*, p. 811).

6.   All these particulars are from Fr. Schmidl's *History of the Society of Jesus of
       the Province of Bohemia*, or from Fr. Balbin's *Historical Miscellanea of the
       Kingdom of Bohemia, 1st Decade*, book 4, no. 118, pp. 189–96 (S.B., no. 5).

7.   St. Ignatius of Loyola, *The Constitutions of the Society of Jesus* (intro., com-
       mentary and trans. George E. Ganss S.J., Institute of Jesuit Sources, St.
       Louis 1970) General Examen, chapter 4 [65–69]. Fr. Ganss divides the
       entire text into continuous paragraphs numbered [1] to [827].

8.   The surnames are added in brackets to Campion's text by Schmidl, A.D.
       1575, no. 77, p. 370, who says he took them from the novices' entry
       book (his note 1 on p. 370). He adds to Charles: "Benedictus Tinensis
       Bohemus." Drnoczky he says is Slav; Nagy is Hungarian; Rous is from
       Speyer. They appear, but differently, in Alexis Possoz S.J., *Le Premier
       Jésuite Anglais Martyrisé en Angleterre, ou Vie et Mort du Père Edmond
       Campian* ("The first English Jesuit martyred in England, or the Life and
       death of Fr. E. Campion," Charles Douniol, Paris 1864) pp. 60, 349. In
       Lukács, *Monumenta*, are found: Cantensis, a Pole, p. 642; Meinhart, a
       Bohemian, p. 394. The Latin name "Cantensis," used as a surname, prob-
       ably means here, "of Kenty," a town in the diocese of Cracow, Poland.

9.   This Charles we presume is not Charles van Tienen, named above, for he
       and Cantensis were still "so young that they can spend their childhood
       with the Child Jesus"—unable then to take life-long vows. In the first 25
       years of the Society of Jesus, 107 students joined who were aged 11–15 (G.
       Ganss S.J., *The Constitutions of the Society of Jesus*, note on p. 130) but one
       had to be 14 to enter probation, which meant one was 16 at least when
       taking first vows (*Constitutions*, p. 129).

10.   His [other] names are given in Lukács, *Monumenta*, p. 132; *Catalogi*, p.
       811. "Aquensis" was a Latin rendition of "Van Aken."

11.   Balbin, pp. 190–2; Schmidl, pp. 369–71, at A.D. 1575

12.   Balbin, p. 194, names Hoffaeus in the marginal note. Fr. Paul Hoffaeus, c.

1530–1608, was born in Westphalia: Lukács, *Catalogi*, p. 692.

13. Balbin, pp. 192–4; Schmidl, pp. 371–4; *Camp. Opusc.*, pp. 380–9 (pp. 19–23). Simpson had the date Feb. 19.

14. Here and elsewhere I give no exact references to the *Spiritual Exercises;* quotations from it can be found easily, it being only a short work, readily available in many editions and online.

15. Quoted in *Catechism of the Catholic Church*, no. 795.

16. *The Constitutions of the Society of Jesus*, General Examen, chapter 1 [3]

17. *Constitutions*, part 3, chapter 1 [263]. The selections following are from this chapter: respectively [277, 250, 251, 265, 275, 288], except for *Discretion in penances*, from part 3, ch. 2 [300]. The headings in italics, added here, are not part of St. Ignatius's text.

18. *Constitutions*, part 10 [817]

19. *Constitutions*, part 6, chapter 1 [547]

20. Persons's *L. of C.*, ch. 6. Cf. Bombino, ch. 58, p. 296; Schmidl, p. 463.

21. *Constitutions*, part 6, chapter 1 [547]. Fr. Ganss's trans. slightly modified.

22. In chapter 22, no. 5, of *Constitutiones monachorum* ("Constitutions of the monks"), St. Basil (if he is the author) speaks of blind obedience and likens the subject who obeys to a craftsman's tool. Other early Fathers say the same thing without the exact phrase "blind obedience." St. John Climacus speaks of iron in the hands of a blacksmith, in his *Scala Paradisi* ("The Ladder of Heaven," Step 4, Obedience: PG 88:689). In the same chapter of the same work, Climacus also uses the simile of a corpse (PG 88:680). St. Bonaventure's *Legend of St. Francis* (chapter 6) says St. Francis proposed a corpse as an example of true obedience.

23. Fr. McCoog says, "In 1574 or 1575 Campion returned to Prague . . . Because the Jesuit catalogues for these years are not extant, we do not know the precise year of Campion's return. . . . He had left Brno [Brünn] by February 26, 1575, the date of his first letter to the novices there." *Reckoned Expense*, p. xx. I take the date of Oct. 7, 1574 from Bartoli, vol. 3, bk 2, ch. 4, p. 33. Balbin, p. 190, says he was "summoned to Prague in September 1574," citing *Historia Collegii S.J. Pragensis*, 1620 ("History of the Jesuit College of Prague") by G. Ware S.J. (S.B., no. 2f).

24. Denzinger-Schönmetzer, 1179

25. *Rationes Decem* ("Ten Reasons," 1581), Reason no. 4

26. J. Dobneck (Cochlaeus), *Historia Hussitarum* ("History of the Hussites," Mainz 1549) book 1, p. 15

27. Schmidl, bk 4, no. 67, p. 367

28. Oration on St. Wenceslaus, A.D. 1576, *Camp. Opusc.*, pp. 260–1 (p. 102)

29. Oskar Garstein, *Rome and the Counter-Reformation in Scandinavia—Jesuit educational strategy 1553-1622* (E.J. Brill, Netherlands 1992) pp. 136, 138

30. Balbin, p. 190; cf. Schmidl, Part 1, p. 366.

31. "Edmundus Campianus . . . florebat tum Pragae doctrinae, ae praesertim eloquentiae gloria, easque cum orationes, tum comœdias dedit, quae justum volumen conficiunt." Part 1, bk 4, no. 75, p. 369. Balbin says the same, p. 190.

32. Schmidl, Part 1, p. 390. The oration is in *Camp. Opusc.*, pp. 221-61 (pp. 86102).

33. *L. of C.*, ch. 11

34. Balbin, pp. 194-5. Persons's ch. 11 and Bombino's ch. 11, p. 45, say exactly the same thing.

35. From his letter below: "Seven letters of Campion"—letter no. 3, in a differing trans.

36. "Multa doces, scribis, loqueris; Rectore iubente, / Omnia tam facile, quam iubet ille, facile." *Concertatio*, p. 67: S.B., no. 59.

37. *L. of C.*, ch. 11

38. Bombino, ch. 11, p. 48; cf. ch. 58, p. 296.

39. *Camp. Opusc.*, pp. 420-60 (pp. 263-81): at the end, dated Feb. 1, 1578. The tract is said to be taken "from the Compendium of Rhetoric propounded by Edmund" to his students at Prague (p. 263).

40. Miguel A. Bernad S.J., "The *Treatise on Imitation* of Blessed Edmund Campion" *Folia* 6 (1952) pp. 100–114; 7 (1953) pp. 20–29, at p. 101. I use Fr. Bernad's translation and modify it to be closer to the Latin, since, as he says, he aims to give the sense but not follow the letter.

41. *De Imitatione Rhetorica*, Ch. 2

42. *Europae Speculum* ["A Survey of Europe"] Or, *A view or survey of the state of religion in the western parts of the world. Wherein the Roman religion, and the pregnant policies of the Church of Rome to support the same, are notably displayed* (S. Waterson, London 1605; Thomas Basset, London 1673) p. 81

43. *De Dignitate et Augmentis Scientiarum*, vi, 4 (1623 trans., with additions, of his *Advancement of Learning*, 1605)

44. *The Table Talk of John Selden* (John Russell Smith, London 1856) p. 85, under heading, "Learning."

45. *L. of C.*, ch. 11

46. Steuart A. Pears, *Correspondence of Sir P. Sidney and Hubert Languet* (William Pickering, London 1845) p. 92

47. James Osborn, *Young Philip Sidney, 1572–1577* (Yale University Press, New Haven 1972) pp. 281–2

48. Sidney came to Christ Church as an undergraduate early in 1568: Katherine Duncan-Jones, *Sir Philip Sidney: Courtier Poet* (Yale University Press, New Haven 1991) p. 39

49. Duncan-Jones, *Sir Philip Sidney*, p. 55

50. I moderate (Persons's and) Simpson's judgment here who simply said Sidney professed himself convinced. Below, in Campion's letter, we read Sidney described as "wavering": letter no. 5 in "Seven letters of Campion."

51. Bombino, ch. 59, pp. 308–9

52. Katherine Duncan-Jones in *Reckoned Expense*, pp. 95–7. "Recusants" and "recusant fines" are explained in ch. 9: "The rise of the Recusants."

53. Sidney to Burghley, Oct. 10, 1581, in William Murdin, *A Collection of State Papers relating to affairs in the reign of Queen Elizabeth from the year 1571 to 1596* (William Bowyer, London 1759); Malcolm William Wallace, *The Life of Sir Philip Sidney* (Cambridge University Press 1915) p. 270

54. K. Duncan-Jones in *Reckoned Expense*, pp. 93–4

55. Letter no. 5 below in "Seven letters of Campion."

56. Letter to Walsingham, May 3, 1577: *The Complete Works of Sir Philip Sidney* (ed. Albert Feuillerat, vol. 3, Cambridge University Press 1923. Reprint 1962) p. 111

57. *L. of C.*, ch. 11

58. "Nobilem sub haec actionem in theatrum dedit Campianus, qua Abrahami sacrificium in filio Isaaco, inter patris secum ipso pugnantis miros affectus, ingeniose exhibuit." Schmidl, Part 1, p. 369. *Historia Collegii S.J. Pragensis . . . P. Georgio Varo, Anglo et aliis,* 1620 ("History of the Jesuit College of Prague, by Englishman Fr. George Ware and others," an unpublished Ms.). The "others" include Fr. B. Balbin S.J. Fr. Ware received a letter from Campion, given below: "More letters of Campion."

59. Schmidl, Part 1, p. 419. The Ms. of the play says at the start it was performed in October 1578. Gregory Martin's poem on Campion in *Concertatio*, p. 67, refers to the applause which made the whole theatre shake: lines 39–40.

60. Johannes Bolte, *Bellum grammaticale, Andrea Guarnas, und seine Nachahmungen* ("The *Grammatical War* of Andrea Guarna and its imitations," A. Hofmann, Berlin 1908) p. 48

61. Schmidl, p. 462. Philippe Alegambe S.J., *Mortes illustres et gesta eorum de Societate Iesu qui in odium fidei . . . necati . . . sunt* ("The illustrious deaths and deeds of those of the Society of Jesus put to death out of hatred of the faith," ed. J. Nadasi, Rome 1657) p. 100

62. Philippe Alegambe S.J., *Bibliotheca Scriptorum Societatis Iesu* ("Library of writers of the Society of Jesus," J. van Meurs, Antwerp 1643) p. 98. So too it is named in W. Carew Hazlitt, *A Manual for the Collector and Amateur of Old English Plays* (Pickering and Chatto, London 1892) p. 164.

63. In 1773, when the Jesuits left their college and university at Ingolstadt, possibly Campion's Ms. was brought to Dillingen, not far away. His Ms. (codex 221, folios 135–69, Studienbibliothek, Dillingen) is first mentioned in modern times in a book on early Jesuit dramas by Anton Dürrwaechter, printed 1896.

64. *Ambrosia: A Neo-Latin Drama by Edmund Campion, S.J.* (ed. and trans. Joseph Simons: Van Gorcum, Assen, The Netherlands 1969–70) 106 pp.

65. "docere, delectare, movere" (to teach, delight and move): cf. Petr Polehla, *Edmund Campion o vzde`lání, rétorice a jeho drama Ambrosia* ("Edmund Campion on Education, Rhetoric and his Drama *Ambrosia*," Masaryk University, Brno, Czech Republic 2009) p. 12. See also Lubomír Konec`n", "Edmund Campion, S.J., as Emblematist," in *The Jesuits and the Emblem Tradition*, ed. Marc van Vaeck and John Manning (Imago Figurata Studies, vol. 1A) Brepols, Turnhout, Belgium 1999, pp. 147–59.

66. A summary of the judgment of Joseph Simons's introduction to *Ambrosia*, p. xviii

67. Alison Shell in *Reckoned Expense*, p. 105

68. Latin orig. in *Ambrosia*, p. 2

69. Dennis Flynn in *Reckoned Expense*, p. 182. Letter of March 4, 1577: Jesuit Archives, Rome: German 138/I, folio 128

70. Persons's *L. of C.*, ch. 11

71. Persons's *L. of C.*, ch. 11

72. So Bombino describes him, ch. 11, p. 47: "parcissimus epistolarum."

73. Printed in T.F. Knox (ed.), *Douay Diaries*, p. 308.

74. Stevenson and Salter, p. 339. Godfrey Anstruther O.P., *The Seminary Priests* (vol. 1) p. 172.

75. Letter of Gregory Martin, May 21, 1578, printed in *Douay Diaries*, p. 317; cf. letter of Aug. 22, 1578, p. 318; letter of Feb. 13, 1579, p. 318; letter of Oct. 16, 1579, p. 320. I follow Anstruther, *Seminary Priests*, p. 173, which says Thomas Cox married Henry Holland's sister—not his p. 2, which mistakenly says, "Cox had a sister in Glos., who stored Campion's books."

76. Mentioned in ch. 16: "*Ten Reasons* feared and commended"

77. Simpson's translation of this sentence, dependent upon a false reading of one word of the autograph, is changed slightly, following Fr. Pollen, "Edmund Campion's History of Ireland" p. 158. *Camp. Opusc.* (1888 ed.) last line of p. 319, change "non" (not) to "nr," short for "noster" (ours).

78. *Camp. Opusc.* (1888 ed., pp. 319–20). No date is given on the letter but there is a date on the other side.

79. *Camp. Opusc.* (1888 ed., pp. 317–8). Simpson's July 12 is changed to 16.

80. John Morris S.J., *The Troubles of Our Catholic Forefathers Related by Themselves* (Burns and Oates, London: 2nd Series 1875) p. 236. B.A. at St. John's 1566. He visited Rheims Nov. 1577–March 1578. Anstruther, *Seminary Priests*, p. 380: "Wiggs, William."

81. Pollen, "Edmund Campion's History of Ireland" pp. 157–8

82. Ch. 6: "Campion and Persons compared"

83. Simpson had the misreading, "Ursnar," followed by many others since. Fr. Ursmar Goisson S.J. (1524–1578), born in Beaumont, Belgium, was the founding Rector of the Jesuit College in Prague, 1556. He had worked beside St. Ignatius himself in Rome. In 1558 he was sent to work again in Rome. Lukács, *Catalogi*, pp. 6, 13, 18, 676.

84. A sentence follows, illegible because worm-eaten.

85. Stevenson and Salter, pp. 130, 321. The original Latin letter to Bavand is in Stonyhurst, Anglia I/4a. Bavand is mentioned in ch. 1: "Sir Thomas White and the character of St. John's."

86. Reynolds, *Campion and Parsons*, pp. 38, 51, 59

87. See the start of ch. 6.

88. *Camp. Opusc.* (1888 ed., pp. 322–5). No date is given, but I say above "mid-1577," because in it Campion says Sidney's visit (of April) was "a few months ago." It could be written some time June–August.

89. *Camp. Opusc.* (1888 ed., pp. 318–9). Simpson's date was July 14.

90. Letter of Dr. Sanders from Madrid to Dr. Allen, in *Letters and Memorials of Cardinal Allen*, p. 38. *Calendar of State Papers . . . 1547–1580*, Nov. 6, 1577, no. 13, p. 565. E.B., no. 1. This letter was cited at Campion's trial; see ch 18: "Dr. Allen's military plans for England."

91. This sentence contains a Greek phrase: literally "owls to Athens," i.e., "carrying coals to Newcastle."

92. *Camp. Opusc.*, pp. 389–95 (pp. 23–6). Simpson had July 3.

93. Campion mentions his own ordination by the Archbishop in Reason 4 of his little book, *Ten Reasons*. Mohelnice, in Moravia, in its German form is Müglitz.

94. Balbin, p. 195

95. Not, as some books say, the parish church of St. Clement, which was not (re)built until the 1700's.

96. Schmidl at A.D. 1578, p. 419. *Camp. Opusc.* (1888 ed., pp. 117–35) where it is dated 1575, but very unlikely: Campion was not yet even a deacon.

97.   *Camp. Opusc.* (1888 ed., p. 135)

98.   *Camp. Opusc.* (1888 ed., pp. 172–9)

99.   *Camp. Opusc.*, pp. 196–221 (1888 ed., pp. 76–86). In the 1631 ed., it says at the start, "recited by Balthasar Jugel."

100.   Balbin, p. 195

101.   Catholic Record Society (hereafter "C.R.S.") vol. 39 (London 1942) pp. 1–2

102.   Persons's *L. of C.*, ch. 11

103.   As we remarked in an endnote above (ch. 3: "His activities at Douay"), Campion might have taught Mayne at Douay (for a very short time), but more likely over some years at St. John's when lecturer in Rhetoric, 1564–70, when Cuthbert was there. Cf. H. Whelan, *Snow on the Hedges*, pp. 50, 57, 59.

104.   Latin, "scriptiunculas"—jottings.

105.   See second paragraph above of "Seven letters of Campion."

106.   The reference to Sheldon is unexplained, but he must have helped in this matter of looking after Campion's books.

107.   *Camp. Opusc.*, pp. 396–400 (pp. 26–8)

108.   *Camp. Opusc.* (1888 ed., p. 320). Simpson's date of Jan. 22 is changed to 26.

109.   *Camp. Opusc.* (1888 ed., p. 321). Simpson's date was May 6.

110.   *Camp. Opusc.*, pp. 297–310 (pp. 180–5)

111.   Schmidl, bk 4, no. 5, p. 336, at A.D. 1573. Schmidl is Simpson's chief authority for Campion's life at Prague. Cf. also James Harrison, *Edmund Campion and Bohemia* (Université de Montréal, Canada 1960).

112.   See ch. 9: "The Act of Supremacy, 1559."

113.   Calendar of Court of Requests, Chapter House, in the time of Elizabeth, no. 315. Order in Exchequer. Lands in Cornwall, late of Francis Tregian, attainted, conveyed to Sir George Carey.

114.   Schmidl, pp. 361–2. Identical story in Bartoli, vol. 3, bk 2, ch. 4, p. 37.

115.   Latin original in *Letters and Memorials of Cardinal Allen*, pp. 84–5. Simpson followed Henry More who put Dec. 9 instead of 5: Francis Edwards S.J., *The Elizabethan Jesuits*, note 28 on p. 367. Fr. Bombino, ch. 12, prints nearly all the letter; Fr. More prints a part.

116.   *L. of C.*, ch. 10

117.   Fr. McCoog in *Reckoned Expense*, p. 123

118.   Bombino, ch. 12, p. 51

119.   Bombino, ch. 14, pp. 59–60; Schmidl, Part 1, p. 437; Balbin, p. 195. Also recounted by Persons in his Memoir III, C.R.S., vol. 2 (Arden Press,

London 1906) p. 195. Persons was told it by Campion's spiritual director, Portuguese Jesuit, Francis Anthony. James S. Gall, b. 1552, Glogów, Silesia (Glogau, Poland), entered the Jesuits in Prague, June 12, 1570, died Nov. 15, 1580, Vienna: Lukács, *Catalogi*, pp. 284, 286, 672. He was a scholastic (in religious vows but not yet ordained)—not a priest as often said by mistake. Fr. Francis Anthony was born in Lisbon: *Catalogi*, p. 620.

120. Bombino, ch. 58, p. 299, tells the story, and in a Ms. addition to that page of his own book names the man who did it, using a Latin form, Vitzumbius, since it was also spelt Vitz(t)umb and Fiztum. Vitztumb, of Olomouc, b. 1547, entered the Jesuits, June 20, 1570, and is named in Lukács's *Catalogi*, pp. 284, 286, 341 et al. Bartoli tells the stories of Gall and Vitztumb, without naming them: vol. 3, bk 3, ch. 8, p. 146.

121. *L. of C.*, ch. 14

122. K. Riedel S.J., *Sieger im Tod* ("Victor in death") p. 41

123. Balbin, p. 195

124. McCoog, *Reckoned Expense*, p. 125

125. McCoog says he left "early March" and arrived in Rome April 9: *Reckoned Expense*, p. 125. He quotes a letter of the Prague Rector of March 8 saying Campion had departed a few days earlier. Simpson's date of departure, March 25 (in Schmidl, p. 437), is thus seen to be a mistake, but has been repeated by many writers. Even without the Rector's letter of March 8, the 25th would leave too little time to arrive in Rome by April 9, considering that the trip from Innsbruck to Padua was by foot. It also contradicts Simpson's own statement that on the way, at Munich, Campion preached "on the feast of St. Thomas Aquinas" (March 7: 18 days earlier). Persons gives no departure date, and names Holy Week as the time of arrival.

126. Campion in a letter of April 30, 1580, given in ch. 7: "Bologna." *Camp. Opusc.* (1888 ed., p. 30)

Chapter 6—Rome and the English Mission

1. J. H. Pollen, S.J., *The English Catholics in the Reign of Queen Elizabeth*, pp. 271–2

2. Letter of Oct. 26, 1578 in T.F. Knox (ed.) *Letters and Memorials of Cardinal Allen*, p. 69

3. Fr. McCoog in *Reckoned Expense*, pp. 122–3; cf. Dennis Flynn, p. 180.

4. Fr. McCoog, *The Society of Jesus in Ireland, Scotland, and England 1541-1588*, pp. 101–2

5. Fr. Augustin Theiner, *Annals*, vol. 3 (Typ. Tiberina, Rome 1856) pp. 219, 700, 701. Fr. Theiner was 19th cent. Vatican archivist and historian.

His *Annals* of Church history are a continuation of those by 16th cent. Cardinal Baronius.

6.   Royal Archives, Brussels: Inventaire des Archives du Province des Jésuites, no. 1085. For the context of Father General Mercurian's change of mind and agreement to send Jesuits, see T. M. McCoog S.J., "The English Jesuit Mission and the French Match, 1579–1581" *The Catholic Historical Review* 87, April 2001, pp. 185–213. See also ch. 9: "Hopes for a royal Catholic marriage."

7.   *The Constitutions of the Society of Jesus*, part 7, chapters 1 and 2 [612, 629–30]

8.   The instructions, twenty-one small paragraphs, most a few lines only, are printed in C.R.S., vol. 39, Latin, then Eng. trans., pp. 316–21.

9.   J. H. Pollen, S.J., "The Politics of the English Catholics during the Reign of Queen Elizabeth. Part 3: Revival of Spiritual Life and of Political Aspiration, 1580–1582" *The Month*, March 1902, pp. 290–305, at p. 293; *English Catholics in the Reign of Queen Elizabeth*, pp. 292–3.

10.   Faculties granted by Pope Gregory XIII, April 14, 1580, to Persons and Campion, § 11, in A.O. Meyer, *England and the Catholic Church Under Queen Elizabeth*, p. 487. Burghley quoted this Papal mitigation in *The Execution of Justice* (1583), in *The Harleian Miscellany* (Robert Dutton, London 1808) vol. 1, pp. 499–500; *"The Execution of Justice in England"* *by William Cecil, and "A True, Sincere, and Modest Defense of English Catholics" by William Allen* (ed. Robert M. Kingdon, Cornell University Press, Ithaca, N.Y. 1965) p. 18. Copies of the Jesuits' special faculties are in the Public Record Office of London: mentioned in *Calendar of State Papers . . . 1547–1580*, April 14, 1580, nos. 26–8, p. 651. E.B., no. 1.

11.   Ch. 4: "Meeting with Cardinal Gesualdi"

12.   Fr. McCoog, *The Society of Jesus in Ireland, Scotland, and England 1541–1588*, p. 134, says: "On the 14th [April] Campion and Parsons, with Oliver Mannaerts [S.J.], had an audience with Pope Gregory XIII"—but he links it to the faculties granted, which could easily have been granted without an audience. The above-mentioned document of their special faculties does not say the Pope gave them in person to the priests.

13.   Faculties granted by Pope Gregory XIII, § 12, in A. O. Meyer, pp. 487–8

14.   Faculties, § 1, in Meyer, p. 486

15.   Faculties, § 2, in Meyer, p. 486

16.   Faculties, § 3, in Meyer, p. 486

17.   Faculties, § 10, in Meyer, p. 487

18.   Faculties, § 8, in Meyer, p. 487. See ch. 12: "Persons's printing press in Greenstreet" for details.

19. *Calendar of State Papers . . . 1547–1580*, April 14, 1580, nos. 26–8, p. 651
20. Faculties, § 17, in Meyer, p. 488
21. See ch. 5, paragraph preceding the last of Campion's seven letters.
22. Francis Edwards S.J., *Robert Persons: The Biography of an Elizabethan Jesuit, 1546–1610* (Institute of Jesuit Sources, St. Louis, U.S.A. 1995) p. 30, n. 31
23. *Seminary Priests*, p. 299
24. Pollen, *The English Catholics in the Reign of Queen Elizabeth*, p. 232
25. Persons's *L. of C.*, ch. 17
26. *The English Catholics in the Reign of Queen Elizabeth*, p. 331
27. Persons's *L. of C.*, ch. 15. Persons had 1584; Goldwell died April 3, 1585.
28. Persons's memoirs in C.R.S., vol. 2, p. 196
29. C.R.S., vol. 39, pp. 52, 59
30. Persons, *A Briefe Apologie, or Defense of the Catholike Ecclesiastical Hierarchie* (St. Omer 1601) p. 101. Reprint: Scolar Press, Menston, England 1975
31. C. Dodd, *Church History of England* [to 1625], ed. M.A. Tierney (5 vols., London 1839–1843) vol. 3, p. 47
32. Theiner, *Annals*, vol. 3, p. 700
33. See Dodd (ed. Tierney) vol. 3, p. 3, note.
34. He was Proctor in 1568, listed before Campion who was Junior Proctor, i.e., listed as second Proctor: *Fasti ecclesiae Anglicanae* ["Calendar of the Church of England"] *or A calendar of the principal ecclesiastical dignitaries in England and Wales, and of the chief officers in the Universities of Oxford and Cambridge* (Oxford University Press 1854) p. 489.
35. C.R.S., vol. 2, p. 19. Translation modified slightly in accordance with Latin original, p. 15.
36. Ch. 1: "Oxford University"
37. Fr. Edwards, *Robert Persons*, pp. 1–14
38. *English Catholics in the Reign of Queen Elizabeth*, p. 290
39. *Constitutions*, part 7, chapter 2 [624 j]
40. Persons's life after 1581 is treated briefly in ch. 14: "The end of Fr. Persons's mission in England."

Chapter 7—The Journey from Rome to England

1. *L. of C.*, ch. 14. Fr. Pollen S.J. supplies the three words [missing] from the Ms., in "The Journey of Blessed Edmund Campion from Rome to England, March–June, 1580" *The Month*, September 1897, pp. 243–55 at p. 246.

2. Ludwig von Pastor, *The History of the Popes*, vol. 19, p. 384

3. Campion mentions, "my stay in Rome, which was about eight days": letter of April 30, quoted below in: "Bologna." Bombino, ch. 14, p. 60, says "only eight days."

4. Persons's *L. of C.*, ch. 14

5. Persons's *L. of C.*, ch. 14

6. Lemon (ed.), *Calendar of State Papers . . . 1547–1580*, April 18, 1580, no. 38, p. 651. E.B., no. 1. The English College diary gives the same date, quoted in *Douay Diaries*, p. 297.

7. Lemon (ed.), *Calendar of State Papers, Domestic Series, of the Reign of Elizabeth, 1581–1590* (Longman, London 1865) April 1581, no. 61, p. 15

8. Reynolds, *Campion and Parsons*, pp. 62–3. See below, ch. 19: "The witness Munday"; "The witness Sledd."

9. More, *History Eng. Province*, bk 3, no. 32

10. C.R.S., vol. 45 (1950) p. 27

11. E. E. Reynolds lists 15, but I omit one: Fr. Lawrence Vaux, the deprived Warden of Manchester, aged 61. I suspect he joined the same mission from Louvain and so did not travel from Rome. He was imprisoned for the faith not long after arriving in England, and died in the Clink through starvation in 1585. Speaking of the last 6 listed, Reynolds says they were all aging and "do not appear to have entered England." *Campion and Parsons*, p. 33. This contradicts the account by Persons who mentions the fate of the 4 Marian priests in England (his ch. 15) and says only Goldwell pulled out (his chs 15, 17). In his life of Campion, Persons makes no mention of Vaux at all, nor of Morton as a member of the band, but in other memoirs he does mention Morton's advance trip to Rheims with Goldwell (C.R.S., vol. 2, p. 196).

12. Persons's *L. of C.*, ch. 15

13. Bombino, ch. 15, p. 68

14. Persons's *L. of C.*, ch. 14

15. Persons's *L. of C.*, ch. 14

16. Persons's *L. of C.*, ch. 16

17. Persons's *L. of C.*, ch. 16

18. Pollen, "The Journey of Blessed Edmund Campion from Rome to England" p. 250. Colle di Val d'Elsa as a port of call is mentioned in Campion's letter at the end of this chapter.

19. Lorenzo Cardella, *Memorie storiche de' cardinali della Santa Romana Chiesa* ("Historical memoirs of the cardinals of the holy Roman Church," Pagliarini, Rome 1792) tome 5, p. 102

20. Persons's *L. of C.*, ch. 16

21. On March 7, he preached in Munich—end of ch. 5: "Arrival in Rome."

22. End of ch. 5: "Arrival in Rome."

23. Ziffel of Bavaria, b. about 1536, is named in Lukács, *Catalogi*, pp. 285, 307, 340, 826.

24. Troger of Bohemia, b. about 1551, is named in Lukács, *Catalogi*, pp. 386, 801.

25. *Camp. Opusc.*, pp. 400–7 (pp. 28–31)

26. Pollen, "The Journey of Blessed Edmund Campion from Rome to England" p. 253

27. Persons's *L. of C.*, ch. 16

28. A 17th cent. copy is among the Mss. of Stonyhurst College (Grene, *Collectanea P*, vol. 2, p. 574), says Pollen, who gives the original Italian text: "The Journey of Blessed Edmund Campion from Rome to England" p. 254. Also printed in *Douay Diaries*, pp. 339–40.

29. Pollen, "The Journey of Blessed Edmund Campion from Rome to England" pp. 257–8; Fr. Edward S. Keogh and Dom Bede Camm O.S.B., *The Blessed Ralph Sherwin* in *Lives of the English Martyrs, Volume II: Martyrs under Queen Elizabeth* (Burns and Oates, London 1905) p. 367

30. Precisely because of its antiquity, they claimed it. The term "Catholic Church" was used by St. Ignatius of Antioch (d. 107) in his *Letter to the Smyrneans*, 8: "Where the bishop appears, there let the people be, just as where Jesus Christ is there is the Catholic Church."

31. Sherwin's letter, quoted in Camm, *Blessed Ralph Sherwin*, p. 368.

32. Persons in 1594 says Englishmen; they were obviously English speakers, but Sherwin says "three or four Irishmen more" in his letter written soon after, on June 11, 1580: *Blessed Ralph Sherwin*, p. 369.

33. Jamieson's *Scottish Dictionary* (1825): "a feeble, diminutive, half-distorted person."

34. Letter of June 4, quoted in *Blessed Ralph Sherwin*, pp. 374–5.

35. *Douay Diaries*, p. 166

36. Pollen, "The Journey of Blessed Edmund Campion from Rome to England" p. 261

37. See start of ch. 3.

38. Ch. 6: "The military mission to Ireland."

39. Persons's *L. of C.*, ch. 17, punctuation changed; "towards of England" I changed to "towards England."

40. *A Briefe Historie of the Glorious Martyrdom of Twelve Reverend Priests, Father Edmund Campion and his Companions, by William Cardinal*

Allen, With Contemporary Verses by the Venerable Henry Walpole, and the Earliest Engravings of the Martyrdom, Reprinted from the (probably unique) Copy in the British Museum, and edited by the Rev. J. H. Pollen S.J. (Burns and Oates, London 1908; facsimile reprint: The Neumann Press, Minnesota 2000) p. 7, spelling and punctuation changed. S.B., nos. 52, 52a.

41. Bombino, ch. 19, p. 88, says it was on the text of *Lk.* 12:49, but Louise Imogen Guiney, *Blessed Edmund Campion* (1908) p. 91, points out that the text of Isaiah, rather, fits the content of the sermon below, for the "fire" of the Gospel text is not a destructive one to be put out!

42. Persons's *L. of C.*, ch. 11. Persons's text has gaps in Foley's ed. The missing words at two points [in brackets] I supply as a guess.

43. Bombino, ch. 19, p. 88

44. Daniello Bartoli S.J., vol. 3, book 2, p. 60. See S.B., no. 4.

45. C.R.S., vol. 1 (1905) p. 27

46. See ch. 5: "Visit of Philip Sidney."

47. So says Simpson, but Sherwin in his letter, *Blessed Ralph Sherwin*, p. 371, says he is planning to leave on June 10 with "Dr. Brombrecke," a variant spelling of Bromborough. It is possible the plans changed; the date of departure did. Of the whole group of 12, who went with whom, when and where, is not certain; the accounts vary.

48. Persons's memoirs, C.R.S., vol. 2, p. 199

49. Knox (ed.), *Douay Diaries*, p. 166. Part of the Latin original, describing their skills and characters, reads: "summus uterque philosophus variisque et Latinis et Graecis doctrinis non mediocriter eruditus, magnus item uterque theologus; Campianus ita comptus sermone et disertus, ut non multos pares, Parsonus ita prudens, ut vix aliquos, ea qua is est aetate, habeat prudentia superiores." Simpson had June 6 as departure date, as Sherwin wrote in his letter, *Blessed Ralph Sherwin*, p. 371, but the College Diary entry has June 7, quoted above. Either is possible; College diaries also contain mistakes, especially when so many people, as here, are coming and going, and their entries are written some days after the events themselves, as they clearly are sometimes in the Douay diaries.

50. *Blessed Ralph Sherwin*, p. 376. Campion says the same in his letter given below: "Campion prepares to cross."

51. Persons's *L. of C.*, ch. 17

52. Ch. 12: "The press moved to Stonor Park"

53. Persons's *L. of C.*, ch. 18

54. Persons's *L. of C.*, ch. 18. Cf. Matt 13:46.

55. Arrival June 16: Leo Hicks S.J., C.R.S., vol. 39, p. xv. Some modern writers

give an earlier date for Persons's arrival in Dover. E.g., McCoog, *Reckoned Expense* (2nd ed.) p. 176, says June 12, but I follow the dates in Campion's letter at the end of this chapter.

56. McCoog, *The Society of Jesus in Ireland, Scotland, and England 15411588*, p. 142

57. *Campion and Parsons*, p. 69

58. This prison was disused by 1800. A second Marshalsea Prison was then built on another site altogether.

59. Quoted in More, *History Eng. Province*, bk 2, no. 15. This letter's date is certain, but the dates of Pounde's birth and death, etc., are not so certain, and vary among writers.

60. McCoog, *The Society of Jesus in Ireland, Scotland, and England 15411588*, p. 142. Fr. McCoog's article, "Sparrows on the Rooftop: "How We Live Where We Live" in Elizabethan England" in Thomas M. Lucas S.J. (ed.), *Spirit, Style, Story: Essays Honoring John W. Padberg, S.J.* (Loyola Press, Chicago 2002) p. 332, says "He had rented this large house . . . from the chief pursuivant."

61. Henry Foley S.J., *Jesuits in Conflict: or Historic Facts Illustrative of the Labors and Sufferings of the English Mission and Province of the Society of Jesus in the Times of Queen Elizabeth and Her Successors* (Burns and Oates, London 1873) pp. 149–50

62. Simpson calls him Robert, but Foley, *Jesuits in Conflict*, calls him Thomas throughout.

63. Persons's memoirs, C.R.S., vol. 2, p. 201. More on his life in ch 12: "The heroic George Gilbert."

64. Fr. Edwards S.J., *Robert Persons*, p. 8

65. "Sparrows on the Rooftop" in *Spirit, Style, Story*, p. 358.

66. Fr. Sabolini is named in Pietro Nencini (ed.), *Colle di Val d'Elsa: diocesi e città tra '500 e '600* (Società storica della Valdelsa, Florence 1994) p. 392. In the Ambrosian Library of Milan are two letters he sent to Cardinal Borromeo in 1572. Colle di Val d'Elsa is a town about 15 miles past Siena, on the pilgrims' way to Florence. Simpson, and later Edwards (*Elizabethan Jesuits*, p. 79), left this town in its Latin form, "Collensis," missing its meaning and treating it as the archpriest's surname. In 1580, Colle di Val d'Elsa was led by an archpriest, before becoming a diocese in 1592, led by a bishop. The original Latin version of Fr. More's *History of the English Province* (*Historia Provinciae Anglicanae Societatis Jesu*, 1660, bk 3, no. 2, p. 63) has a marginal note, "forte Comensis" (perhaps Como)—but Colle di Val d'Elsa was on their way, whereas Como was not; it is north of Milan, whence they turned west for Turin.

67.   More, *History Eng. Province*, bk 3, no. 2

68.   In the first sentence of "Persons crosses to Dover."

69.   Reynolds, *Campion and Parsons*, p. 74

70.   Leo Hicks S.J., C.R.S., vol. 39, p. xiv, presumed he joined them at Rheims itself, but the College diary says they arrived together, by saying George and they arrived "from Rome": *Douay Diaries*, May 31, p. 166. George did not travel with them from Rome, but from the viewpoint of a resident at Rheims his arrival *with* them would give the impression he came from Rome. At some unknown point, he joined the travelling band.

71.   *Douay Diaries*, p. 187

72.   Bombino, ch. 21, p. 94. McCoog, *Reckoned Expense* (2nd ed.) p. 176, says the night of June 25, but I presume this is a misprint: in the same book he says June 24 (p. xxvii), and in its 1st ed. he says June 24 (p. xxi).

Chapter 8—The Mission Begins

1.   Persons's *L. of C.*, ch. 19; Bombino, ch. 21, p. 95.

2.   Bombino, ch. 21, p. 96

3.   From Campion's own account in his letter given at the end of ch. 10: "Campion's account to the Jesuit General."

4.   Persons's *L. of C.*, ch. 19; Bombino, ch. 22, p.100.

5.   Persons's *L. of C.*, ch. 19

6.   *Douay Diaries*, Sept. 18, 1580, p. 171

7.   Persons's *L. of C.*, ch. 19

8.   Persons's *L. of C.*, ch. 21

9.   *L. of C.*, ch. 20

10.   *History Eng. Province*, book 3, no. 11\

11.   I date the synod July 12 since Orton and Johnson were committed to the Poultry Counter on that day: C.R.S., vol. 1, p. 67; vol. 2, p. 27; and Persons's memoirs specifically say they were on the way to this meeting: vol. 2, p. 27. His *De Vita Campiani* ("Of the life of Campion": hereafter *Draft life of Campion*), ch. 10, and Bombino (whom Persons helped), ch. 25, pp. 111–3, say the same. Persons's letter of August 1581 says Orton was on his way to an inn where Campion, Persons and Gilbert were together, which sounds like the same meeting: C.R.S., vol. 39, pp. 80, 88. – But once he places Orton and Johnson's arrest earlier than the meeting (*L. of C.*, ch. 22). Pollen, *The English Catholics in the Reign of Queen Elizabeth*, p. 339.

12.   Persons's memoirs, C.R.S., vol. 2. pp. 27, 176. Persons wrote "Edward" Mettam; Pollen says he probably means Thomas Metham: *English Catholics in the Reign of Queen Elizabeth*, p. 334. He is listed in Anstruther,

Seminary Priests, p. 229. Metham was born in Yorkshire, 1532, and matriculated in the licentiate at the University of Louvain, 1566.

13. Fr. Nicholas Sanders, *De Visibili Monarchia Ecclesiae* ("On the Visible Monarchy of the Church" 1571), quoted by Lord Burghley, *The Execution of Justice in England, not for Religion, but for Treason* (1583), 1675 reprint, p. 18

14. Persons's *L. of C.*, ch. 22

15. Persons's *L. of C.*, ch. 22

16. *Letters and Memorials of Cardinal Allen*, note on p. 303 gives his Christian name.

17. Persons's memoirs, C.R.S., vol. 2, pp. 177–8

18. *Edmund Campion. Jesuit and Martyr* (1935; 2nd ed. Hollis and Carter, London 1947) ch. III: The Hero.

19. His imprisonment there is mentioned in J.R. Dasent (ed.), *Acts of the Privy Council of England: New Series* (Eyre and Spottiswoode, London 1896) vol. 12 (1580–1581) p. 294: Dec. 24, 1580.

20. See ch. 7: "The party splits up" and ch. 19: "Condemnation of the other priests."

21. See ch. 18: "A new indictment," 2nd–last paragraph. The exact sequence or timing of the events of the Cottam-Ely story is not certain, but the basic facts are clear.

22. A. F. Allison, D.M. Rogers and W. Lottes, *The Contemporary Printed Literature of the English Counter-Reformation between 1558 and 1640: an annotated catalogue. Vol. 1: Works in Languages other than English* (Scolar Press, Aldershot, England 1989) Items 336, 336.1, 336.2 ("Missals for use in England")

23. "Salisbury or Sarum, Use of," in F. L. Cross (ed.), *The Oxford Dictionary of the Christian Church* (O.U.P. 1983)

24. Acknowledgements to Bishop Geoffrey Jarrett of Lismore, New South Wales, for the section on the Sarum Rite, and for communicating his transcription of the words in the Missal inspected in 2001 (here put in modern spelling). So far nothing more is known of Bartholomew Hussey: cf. Frederick Bussby, *Winchester Cathedral, 1079–1979* (Paul Cave Publications, Southampton 1979) p. 110.

Chapter 9—The Religious Situation in 1580

1. I have re-written and enlarged this chapter of Simpson, and deleted portions. Many of its facts, and some (modified) paragraphs, now come from chs 1–3 of E. E. Reynolds, *Campion and Parsons* (1980). Reynolds himself

at one part drew upon the article "English Recusants" in the *Catholic Encyclopedia* (1911). Other material was originally in Simpson or is taken from books and articles named in the endnotes or other books of history. Naturally, in this summary presentation for the average reader, there is no room for a comprehensive survey, scholarly qualifications or fine points.

2. Pollen, *The English Catholics in the Reign of Queen Elizabeth*, p. 94. *A Letter from Mary Queen of Scots to the Duke of Guise, January 1562* (T. and A. Constable, Scottish History Society 1904) p. xvi.

3. Under Henry VIII, he had, however, repudiated Papal primacy, later repenting. His signature is seen on the document reproduced in Fr. Philip Hughes, *The Reformation in England* (1963) frontispiece and p. xvii. E.B., no. 55.

4. Hughes, *The Reformation in England* (1963) vol. 3, pp. 245–6

5. 1573 martyr Fr. Thomas Woodhouse was "denying the female papacy of Elizabeth": *Concertatio*, p. 49. This phrase was in circulation in Elizabeth's time; it was used, e.g., by another Catholic of the time, James Leyborne, Esq., put to death for religion: Richard Hollingworth, d. 1656, *Mancuniensis; Or, an History of the Towne of Manchester* (William Willis, Manchester 1839, Original Ms. c. 1650) p. 92.

6. Ch. 1: "Oxford University"

7. John J. LaRocca S.J. in *Reçkoned Expense*, p. 256

8. A term first used in print in 1582: Alexandra Walsham, *Church Papists: Catholicism, Conformity and Confessional Polemic in Early Modern England* (Boydell Press, Suffolk 1993) 1999 ed., p. 9

9. John LaRocca, p. 257

10. LaRocca, p. 251

11. LaRocca, p. 255

12. Reynolds, *Campion and Parsons*, p. 9

13. Hughes, *The Reformation in England*, vol. 3, p. 35

14. Text of the rubric and more details are in ch. 16: "The third debate: *Christ's presence in the Eucharist*."

15. Hughes, vol. 3, pp. 96, 102–5, 110, 112

16. Hughes, vol. 3, pp. 114–5

17. Hughes, vol. 3, pp. 117–32

18. *An Admonition to Parliament* (1572) by two young Puritan preachers, John Field and Thomas Wilcox. Field was to be notary at Campion's second debate in the Tower and editor of a book recording the debates (see ch. 16).

19. Cf. (Protestant Reformer) Peter Martyr Vermigli to Thomas Sampson,

July 15, 1559; Edmund Grindal (Archbishop of Canterbury from 1576) to H. Bullinger, June 11, 1568: *The Zurich Letters, or the Correspondence of Several English Bishops and Others with some of the Helvetian ["Swiss"] Reformers, During the Reign of Queen Elizabeth* (Parker Society, trans. and ed. by Rev. Hastings Robinson, Cambridge University Press, 2nd ed. 1846) pp. 52, 314; cf. Bishop Jewel, Feb. 8, 1566, p. 208.

20. P. M. Vermigli to Sampson, Feb. 1, 1560: *The Zurich Letters*, p. 85; cf. p. 258.

21. Reynolds, p. 20. Reynolds says Puritans came later than Radical Protestants, but I use the terms interchangeably since, even in 1583, "Puritans" was a term used in the title of the well-known Catholic book *Concertatio . . . adversus . . . Puritanos* ("The struggle against Puritans").

22. Lansdowne Mss. 27, art. 20

23. Lansdowne Mss. 30, art. 77

24. *Certain Observations Made Upon a Libel* (1592), in Spedding (ed.), *The Letters and the Life of Francis Bacon including all his occasional works* (Longman, London 1861) vol. 1, p. 178. Cf. Juliet Gardiner (ed.), *Who's Who in British History* (Collins and Brown, London 2000) p. 295. This lovely and dishonest remark about the queen's leaving her people free in conscience is quoted in the second of the anti-Catholic propaganda films, *Elizabeth: The Golden Age* (2007). One blog has sought to redress the imbalance with a portrait entitled: "Elizabeth I: Heretic, Usurper, Tyrant."

25. Strype, *Annals of the Reformation*, vol. 1, part 2, ch. 57, pp. 371–2

26. Strype, p. 371

27. Thomas Rymer (d. 1713), *Foedera, Conventiones, Literae, et Cujuscunque Generis Acta Publica, inter reges Angliae Foedera, conventiones, litterae, et cujuscunque generis acta publica inter reges Angliae et alios quosvis imperatores, reges, pontifices, principes, vel communitates* ("Treaties, agreements, letters and public deeds of all sorts between the monarchs of England and all other emperors, kings, pontiffs, princes or communities," J. Tonson, London 1704–35) vol. 15, pp. 518, 519

28. Strype, *Life and Acts of Matthew Parker, Archbishop of Canterbury* (1711) (3 vols. Clarendon Press, Oxford 1821) vol. 1, p. 125; Peter Heylyn, *Ecclesia restaurata ["The Church Restored"], or the History of the Reformation* (1661) vol. 2, p. 174.

29. Rymer, pp. 546, 547

30. *Calendar of State Papers . . . 1547–1580*, Dec. 1559, no. 79, p. 145. E.B., no. 1.

31. Henry Norbert Birt O.S.B., *The Elizabethan Religious Settlement: A Study of Contemporary Documents* (George Bell and Sons, London 1907) p. 219

32. Hughes, vol. 3, p. 40
33. *Calendar of State Papers . . . 1547–1580*, June 30, 1559, no. 72, p. 133
34. British Library, Lansdowne Mss. 109, p. 17
35. John Strype, *Life and Acts of Matthew Parker*, vol. 1, p. 125
36. Percival Wiburn, Report on the state of the Church of England: *The Zurich Letters (second series), Comprising the Correspondence of Several English Bishops and Others with some of the Helvetian ["Swiss"] Reformers, During the Reign of Queen Elizabeth* (Parker Society, trans. and ed. by Rev. Hastings Robinson, Cambridge University Press 1845) p. 358, no. 6
37. Archdeacon George Withers, *The Zurich Letters (second series)* 1845, p. 163
38. Robert Persons S.J., *A Treatise of the Three Conversions of England from Paganism to Christian Religion* (St. Omer 1603–4) part 2, ch. 12 (ed. 1608) p. 206
39. Sanders-Rishton, *The Anglican Schism*, bk 4, ch. 4 (Eng. trans., p. 267)
40. *Acts of the Privy Council*, vol. 13, p. 56: May 18, 1581
41. *The Reformation in England* (1963) vol. 3, p. 38
42. *Campion and Parsons*, p. 10
43. *English Catholics in the Reign of Queen Elizabeth*, pp. 39–40. On the estimate of 8,000, see his p. 46. A.O. Meyer, *England and the Catholic Church under Elizabeth*, p. 29, has the same estimate.
44. A. Walsham, *Church Papists*, p. 15
45. *The Theology and Spirituality of Mary Tudor's Church* (Ashgate, U.K. 2006) p. 13
46. Meyer, *England and the Catholic Church under Elizabeth*, p. 29
47. The three quotes, respectively, from *Catechism of the Catholic Church* (A.D. 1992), nos. 1113, 1210, 1127.
48. Walsham, *Church Papists*, p. 81
49. *Church Papists* (1999) pp. xiii–xiv. E.B., no. 74.
50. Meyer, p. 68, says the approach was made via the Portuguese ambassadors at London and Trent.
51. Henry More S.J., *Historia Provinciae Anglicanae Societatis Jesu* (History of the English Province of the Society of Jesus, 1660) bk 3, no. 9. Nos. 6–10 give the full original Latin reply, omitted in Fr. Edwards's English ed. of More's *History*). Cf. Pollen, *English Catholics in the Reign of Queen Elizabeth*, pp. 100–2. Pollen says the English gentlemen asked the Portuguese ambassador to present their question to the Council of Trent, p. 100. The original document of the reply has never been found but Fr. Henry Garnet S.J. printed it at the end of his *Treatise of Christian Renunciation* (1593).

52. Letter of Fr. Lawrence Vaux, *Calendar of State Papers . . . 1547–1580*, Nov. 2. 1566, no. 1, p. 281; Hughes, *The Reformation in England*, vol. 3, p. 249; Lansdowne Mss. 951, p. 118.

53. Ch. 8: "The question of attending Protestant church"

54. More, *History Eng. Province*, bk 3, no. 5; bk 8, no. 3; Cardinal Allen, State Papers Office, Domestic, Dec. 12, 1592

55. More detail on the 1581 penal laws in ch. 12: "The passing of the penal laws."

56. Harleian Mss. 7042, folios 211–2

57. LaRocca in *Reckoned Expense*, p. 255

58. The last few paragraphs, with small changes, are mostly from *Francis Tregian—Cornish Recusant* by P.A. Boyan and G.R. Lamb (Sheed and Ward, N.Y. 1955) pp. 95, 97.

59. Meyer, p. 168

60. LaRocca, p. 254

61. Holleran, *A Jesuit Challenge*, p. 10, has some details of these studies. See E.B., no. 14.

62. H. Whelan, *Snow on the Hedges*, p. 104

63. *Annals*, book 1, p. 544

64. A letter of Sept. 16, 1578 (or 1580): Latin text in *Letters and Memorials of Cardinal Allen*, p. 56

65. *Letters and Memorials of Cardinal Allen*, p. 57, n. 1

66. Rev. George Andrew Beck A.A., *The Elizabethan Apostasy* (C.T.S., London 1947)

67. *Calendar of State Papers . . . 1547–1580*, Feb. 21, 1568, no. 32, p. 307; *Letters and Memorials of Cardinal Allen*, p. 21

68. Start of ch. 3: "Campion at the English seminary of Douay."

69. Meyer, p. 94

70. Ludwig von Pastor, *History of the Popes*, vol. 19, p. 377. A.O. Meyer says the same, p. 94.

71. Morris, "Blessed Edmund Campion at Douay" pp. 33–4. See also *Douay Diaries*.

72. Figures and years vary a little: others say the first priests arrived in 1574 (L. von Pastor, vol. 19, p. 378); and that by 1578, 52 of the 74 priests ordained were sent to England. Since many missionaries used aliases, the exact number of seminary priests sent to England is uncertain.

73. Lord Burghley, *The Execution of Justice in England, not for Religion, but for Treason* (1583), 1675 reprint, p. 7.

74. Quoted from Dr. Allen's trans. of Campion's letter, last lines of ch.10— though the trans. there differs somewhat.

75. Fr. Pollen's intro. to *A Briefe Historie . . . by William Cardinal Allen*, pp. vii–viii

76. *History of the Popes*, vol. 19, p. 386

77. Eng. orig. Letter of Aug. 10, 1577 in *Letters and Memorials of Cardinal Allen*, p. 36.

78. Quoted in Pastor, p. 386.

79. Letter of March 14, 1583 in *Letters and Memorials of Cardinal Allen*, pp. 181–2. Last sentence: "neque enim expectanda sunt meliora tempora sed facienda meliora."

80. Ch. 7: "The remarkable Thomas Pounde."

81. Meyer, p. 212

82. Letter of March 16, 1583 in *Letters and Memorials of Cardinal Allen*, p. 183

83. Meyer, pp. 58–65, espec. p. 62

84. *The Later Tudors—England 1547-1603* (Oxford Uni. Press 1998) p. 469. He had "5" million, which I change to conform to his p. 2 which says, "By 1603 the population of England had reached 4 million."

85. *Seminary Priests*, p. 395. In addition, he says, there were 35 priests abroad or unknown.

86. Meyer, p. 163

87. Meyer, pp. 165–6

88. Meyer, p. 184. For a Catholic tied to a tread-mill, see below, ch. 14: "Caught."

89. *Souls Departed—Being a Defense and Declaration of the Catholic Church's Doctrine touching Purgatory and Prayer for the Dead* (Burns and Oates, London 1886) 402 pp. Edited with modern spelling by T.E. Bridgett C.SS.R. It was in reply to Jewel's challenge to Catholics made in 1559.

90. Southern, *Elizabethan Recusant Prose*, pp. 3, 31

91. McCoog, *The Society of Jesus in Ireland, Scotland, and England 15411588*, p. 70

92. John Guy, *Queen of Scots – The True Life of Mary Stuart* (Houghton Mifflin Co., Boston 2004)

93. *English Catholics in the Reign of Queen Elizabeth*, p. 304

94. Ch. 6: "The military mission to Ireland"

95. See in ch. 4: "The temporal power of the Popes," "The Bull of Pius V" and "Catholics' reaction to the Bull."

96. Pollen, *English Catholics in the Reign of Queen Elizabeth*, pp. 157–8

97. *English Catholics in the Reign of Queen Elizabeth*, p. 156

98. T. McCoog S.J., "Sparrows on the Rooftop: 'How We Live Where We Live' in Elizabethan England" in Thomas M. Lucas S.J. (ed.), *Spirit, Style, Story:*

Essays Honoring John W. Padberg, S.J. (Loyola Press, Chicago 2002) pp. 328–9.

99. Pollen, *English Catholics in the Reign of Queen Elizabeth*, p. 361

100. Meyer, pp. 174–5

101. Meyer, pp. 170–1

102. J. R. Dasent (ed.), *Acts of the Privy Council of England* (Eyre and Spottiswoode, London 1896) vol. 10, p. 426; vol. 12, p. 198

103. See ch. 12: "More anti-Catholic penal laws" and "The passing of the penal laws."

104. See T. M. McCoog S.J., "The English Jesuit Mission and the French Match, 1579–1581." 105 *Calendar of State Papers . . . 1581–1590*, 1581, p. 38, nos. 42–3. E.B., no. 2.

106. Castelnau, dispatch of Sept. 8, 1578

107. Edward Nares (1762–1841), *Memoirs of the life and administration of the Right Honourable William Cecil, Lord Burghley* (Saunders and Otley; Colburn and Bentley, 3 vols. London 1828–31) vol. 2, pp. 240, 241; Strype, *Annals*, book 1, p. 405; Strype, *Life and Acts of Matthew Parker*, vol. 1, p. 212

108. Paolo Alessandro Maffei, *Vita di S. Pio Quinto* ("Life of St. Pius V," Francesco Gonzaga, Rome 1712) p. 47. Cf. Joseph Mendham, *The Life and Pontificate of Saint Pius the Fifth* (James Duncan, London 1832) p. 22.

109. *The Chronicles of England from Brute unto this present Year of Christ, collected by John Stowe, Citizen of London* (1580). The passages were expunged in the 1592 edition: *The Annals of England faithfully collected out of the most authentic Authors, Records, and other Monuments of Antiquity from the first inhabitation until 1592.*

110. Persons's *L. of C.*, ch. 20

111. Peter Marshall, *The Mercurial Emperor – The Magic Circle of Rudolf II in Renaissance Prague* (Pimlico, London 2007)

112. Benjamin Woolley, *The Queen's Conjurer: The Science and Magic of Dr. John Dee, Adviser to Queen Elizabeth I* (Henry Holt, New York 2001)

113. Cf. *Calendar of State Papers . . . 1547–1580*, Dec. 12, 1580, no. 48, p. 690. I cannot find any contemporary prominent name beginning with "I," who can mean "*I* will stand."

114. Last sentence paraphrased from Persons's *L. of C.*, ch. 20.

Chapter 10—Campion's *Brag*

1. *English Catholics in the Reign of Queen Elizabeth*, p. 343

2. Ch. 7: "George Gilbert." Mathias Tanner S.J., *Societas Jesu apostolorum*

imitatrix ("The Society of Jesus, imitator of the apostles," Charles Ferdinand University Press, Prague 1694) pp. 180–1.

3.   Simpson said it was, but Fr. Pollen S.J. corrects this notion in "An Error in Simpson's *Campion*" *The Month*, June 1905, pp. 592–9; again in his book, *English Catholics in the Reign of Queen Elizabeth*, pp. 345–6.

4.   Cf. ch. 6: "Instructions for the spiritual mission."

5.   Cf. ch. 6: "Faculties from the Pope" for the blessing the Pope gave to such co-workers of the priests.

6.   Some of the above phrases are from Walsingham's spies; others from Watson, *Quodlibets of Religion and State*, p. 113; and John Gee, *The Foot out of the Snare with a detection of sundry late practices and impostures of the priests and Iesuits in England. Whereunto is added a catalogue of such bookes as in this authors knowledge haue been vented within two yeeres last past in London, by the priests and their agents* (Robert Milbourne, London 1624) p. 66. Reprint: Cicero Press, Nijmegen 1992. Cf. Fr. Pollen, "An Error in Simpson's *Campion*," p. 595 n. 2.

7.   Persons's *L. of C.*, ch. 21

8.   Persons's *L. of C.*, ch. 21

9.   See ch. 1: "Tutor to Henry Vaux."

10.   Persons's *L. of C.*, ch. 21

11.   See ch. 12: "Persons's printing press in Greenstreet."

12.   Printed in 1581. See first section of ch. 13: "The preparation of *Rationes Decem: Ten Reasons.*"

13.   See start of ch. 13: "The preparation of *Rationes Decem: Ten Reasons.*"

14.   More on him in ch. 21: "Misery and conversions."

15.   Some attribute this 1584 work to Fr. Robert Persons—but this is unfounded. His priestly vocation, and devotion to religion over all else, preclude him as a possible author of such a scurrilous and gossipy work of such length (nearly 60,000 words), whose content clearly came from inside the Court.

      It is out of character; no other work of Persons is like it; his straightforward prose style is not in it; and most importantly—from this fearless and honest man who admitted his role in conspiracies and invasion attempts where relevant—he repudiated authorship. Cf. Fr. Edwards, *Robert Persons*, pp. 112, 227–8, for some references to relevant articles and Persons's denial. The first to impute it to Persons was his relentless Catholic opponent, Charles Paget, in 1598, as part of an attempt to discredit him: Victor Houliston, *Catholic Resistance in Elizabethan England: Robert Persons's Jesuit Polemic, 1580–1610* (Ashgate, U.K. and U.S.A and

Institutum Historicum Societatis Iesu [Historical Institute of the Society of Jesus] Rome 2007) pp. 12–3.

16. Mentioned by Bombino, ch. 23, p. 104, but not by Persons.

17. C.R.S., vol. 4, pp. 70–1

18. Albert J. Loomie S.J. (ed.), Joseph Cresswell [S.J.], *English Polemics at the Spanish Court* (Fordham University Press, N.Y. 1993) p. 6

19. See ch. 12: "Fr. Ralph Sherwin captured" and "The treatment of Catholic prisoners."

20. On Thomas Tresham, see ch. 11: "Reunion, review and plans at Uxbridge."

21. See the opening paragraphs of ch. 2.

22. C.R.S., vol. 4, p. 121. Also spelt elsewhere Fuljames, Foliambe. There are a few of the same name, leading to confusion by some historians. Simpson adds of him, "who afterwards did very little credit to the society"—probably because he "was a sympathizing correspondent of Mary queen of Scots" (Cooper, *Athenae Cantabrigienses*, vol. 2, 1861, p. 274), but I find no evidence of his involvement in assassination plots or any personal vice. Persons names him in a group of "gentlemen of quality and very zealous for religion for which they had suffered in England." C.R.S., vol. 4, p. 121.

23. Ch. 8: "Arrival in London"

24. McCoog, *The Society of Jesus in Ireland, Scotland, and England 15411588*, p. 143

25. 1558–1586. His two names are spelt variously. He wrote a beautiful and poignant elegy in the Tower the night before his execution; search internet for: Chidiock Tichborne's elegy.

26. Persons and Campion's visits to the Bellamy family are mentioned in ch. 13: "Reunion in London."

27. Donna B. Hamilton, *Anthony Munday and the Catholics, 1560–1633* (Ashgate, U.K. 2005) p. 3

28. Bombino, ch. 26, p. 113

29. Simpson said Pierrepoint (Pierpoint) was Campion's companion. Leo Hicks S.J. thought "possibly Charles Basset": *Letters and Memorials of Father Robert Persons, S.J., 1578–1588* (ed. L. Hicks S.J., London 1942) C.R.S., vol. 39, p. xxii. Br. Ralph Emerson is not mentioned in this trip, and we hear nothing of him again until Nov. 16.

30. Fr. Hicks, C.R.S., vol. 39, p. xxii

31. Persons's *L. of C.*, ch. 23, says a "gentleman who at that time was no Catholic though his wife were"—which fits in with Catesby. Fr. Edwards S.J., *Robert Persons*, p. 36, says probably the Treshams. Sir Thomas Tresham, married to Muriel Throgmorton, also had a house at Hoxton.

32. Persons's autobiographical notes in C.R.S., vol. 2, p. 27

33. *History Eng. Province*, bk 3, no. 12

34. Based on Fr. Pollen's introduction to *Campion's Ten Reasons* (trans. J. Rickaby S.J., Manresa Press, London 1914) p. 5.

35. Archdiocese of Westminster, *Cause of the Canonization of Blessed Martyrs ... Edmund Campion, Alexander Briant, Ralph Sherwin ... Put to Death in England in Defense of the Catholic Faith (1535–1582)* (Sacred Congregation of Rites, Vatican Polyglot Press 1968) p. 326, says less than an hour-and-a-half. If "less I suppose than half an hour" is right, as Persons recollects (*L. of C.*, ch. 24), this is very remarkable, even for a man of Campion's talents. He certainly had more than half an hour, since he and Persons stayed together while Persons wrote a declaration twice as long—needing more than thirty minutes.

36. Persons's *L. of C.*, ch. 24

37. I have headed it "A Letter to the Lords of the Privy Council," as J.H. Pollen S.J. says Campion headed it: "Blessed Edmund Campion's *Challenge*" *The Month*, January 1910, pp. 50–65, at p. 57. We can date the *Brag* July 19 with certainty, since it was the day following the evening they arrived at Hoxton, on which arrival: "Writing on the 5th of August, Persons says it was eighteen days ago." Pollen, *English Catholics in the Reign of Queen Elizabeth*, p. 346. To Fr. Pollen is due the credit of the *Brag's* exact dating, July 19: cf. pp. 346, 348. The letter of Aug. 5 is in Rome, Ms. *Vallicelliana*, no. 23, folio 179, only partly known to Simpson: J.H. Pollen, "Blessed Edmund Campion's *Challenge*" p. 50, n. 2. Persons's chronology in his life of Campion, written 14 years after this, is occasionally wrong. For example, he says that he and Campion met up in Oct. 1580 after not seeing one another since "they both departed London about the beginning of July" (*L. of C.*, ch. 24; a date repeated in book 2, ch. 2: "they departed from London in the beginning of July")—whereas they left on July 18. Another example of his confused dates: at the start of ch. 24, he says they prepared for their journey from London, "Hilary term being ended"—but Hilary term finishes mid-March, a date before even their entry into England. Perhaps Persons meant the end of "Trinity term," c. June 20. Simpson's ch. 8 (my ch. 10) unthinkingly began with this reference to Hilary term.

38. Here, and at a few more points, the text has "ye," an old way of writing "the" ("y" = "th"). I have put "the" in its stead.

39. *Elizabethan Recusant Prose*, p. 153

40. The text above (except where Roman numerals are replaced by Arabic; "ye" has been replaced by "the"; and spelling is updated, e.g., "Jesus"

instead of "Jhesus," "country" in place of "countrie," etc.) is from the article "Blessed Edmund Campion's *Challenge*" by Fr. J. H. Pollen S.J. in *The Month*, January 1910, reproduced in the introduction to Fr. Rickaby's translation of *Ten Reasons;* Evelyn Waugh's biography; E. E. Reynolds, and others. It differs here and there in small ways from the version that Simpson printed in 1867; and both differ from that of Br. Henry Foley S.J. in *Jesuits in Conflict* (1873) pp. 96–101. The three principal early texts are: Public Record Office, London, State Papers 12/142, no. 20 (A.D. 1580); British Museum, London, Harleian Mss. 422, folio 12 and 13; Archives of Stonyhurst College, Lancashire, Fr. C. Grene's *Collectanea P*, ii, 583 (also cited as Ms. A.IV.2, folios 593–4). Plus there are early printed versions in booklets by Charke and Hanmer, listed in S.B., nos. 8a and 9. Br. Foley, p. 96, says his version is transcribed from the copy in the State Papers Office, "the original being in some parts scarcely readable"—the copy sent to the Council by the Sheriff of Wilts: H. Foley S.J., *Records of the English Province of the Society of Jesus* (vol. 3, Burns and Oates, London 1878) p. 629, n. 53. Campion's original two copies, one given to Pounde, one kept on himself, are lost.

41. A contemporary Latin copy of the original (or translation from Englishthe original language of composition is not certain) is preserved among the Mss. at Stonyhurst. Edwards, *Robert Persons*, p. 36, n. 51, refers to a Latin copy or translation in the Jesuit archives in the Generalate, Rome. Latin original (or trans.), then Eng. trans., in C.R.S., vol. 39, pp. 28–41.

42. Edwards, *Robert Persons*, pp. 36–7

43. E.g., Edwards, *Robert Persons*, p. 36, but on p. 45 he says "perhaps" it was disseminated.

44. C.R.S., vol. 9 (1911) p. 31

45. *Douay Diaries*, p. 177

46. Foley, *Records of the English Province*, vol. 3, pp. 633–42, has the full text of Pounde's: Petition to the Privy Council; Six Reasons against Scripture alone (Sept. 8 addressed to Mr. Tripp); 2 letters to Tripp (and Tripp's reply to the 1st); letter to the Bishop of London.

47. For example, Sir Edwin Sandys in his *Europae Speculum* ["A Survey of Europe" 1605], p. 94: "Of their offers of disputation." Reprint: Ottawa, Canada 2002.

48. Ch. 8: "Campion says Mass"

49. "santa invero, e degna d'ogni spirituale consolazione; ma per l'età e per lo con ceputo fervore, più generosa che cauta": Daniello Bartoli S.J. (ed. 1825) vol. 3, bk 2, ch. 8, p. 73

50. Fr. Pollen, "Blessed Edmund Campion's *Challenge*," p. 56, n. 1, shows that Pounde's transfer from Marshalsea to Stortford was decided *before* he issued his challenge in imitation of Campion—not the other way round as Simpson said.

51. Ch. 15: "What did Campion reveal?" and *"Come rack, come rope:* Campion's reply to Pounde's letter."

52. Cf. *Calendar of State Papers . . . 1547–1580*, Nov. 18, 1580, no. 31, p. 688; Sept. 18, 1580, no. 20, p. 676. E.B., no. 1.

53. See State Papers Office, Ireland, Feb. 17, 1581.

54. Cf. Fr. Pollen, "Blessed Edmund Campion's *Challenge*," p. 63.

55. "Blessed Edmund Campion's *Challenge*," p. 57

56. McCoog, "The English Jesuit Mission and the French Match, 1579–1581" p. 202

57. "Blessed Edmund Campion's *Challenge*," p. 65

58. In 1994, Michael L. Carrafiello, reverted to pre-20th-century anti-Catholicism and argued in "English Catholicism and the Jesuit Mission of 1580–1581," according to the Abstract: "Beginning with A.O. Meyer in 1916 and continuing through John Bossy and Christopher Haigh in the 1970s and 1980s, historians have mistakenly characterized this mission as essentially pastoral. . . . But in fact the mission was fundamentally political in nature" ("English Catholicism and the Jesuit Mission of 1580–81" *The Historical Journal*, vol. 37, Dec. 1994, pp. 761–74). Carrafiello seems to have read and totally believed the mendacious Lord Burghley's *Execution of Justice* (1583). Naturally, if you regard all religion as a political thing, then Persons and Campion's instructing people in the Catholic faith, administering the Sacraments, praying the Breviary and meditation daily, willingness to suffer imprisonment and torture, observance of an austere life, spending hours in prayer, renouncing careers and honours offered to them if they attend Protestant church, and Campion's praying for the queen and forgiving enemies even when tortured and about to be executed—are all manifestations of a political mission! They must be the first and only political rebels in history to be offered life and liberty if they will but go to a Protestant church service!—At times, a distinction needs to be made between history and bigotry. Christ, too, was denounced as an enemy of Caesar. Fr. McCoog comments: "Contrary to Michael L. Carrafiello's assertion that Persons focussed on Scotland from the start of the mission, Persons first became interested in Scotland as a refuge for English Catholics and only gradually as a base for a more militant type of conversion of England." *Reckoned Expense*, p. 139; "Michael

L. Carrafiello argues that "the forcible conversion of England" through Scotland was among the original intentions of the English mission. . . . Dr. Carrafiello, however, fails to note Mercurian's reluctance to approve the mission and his strong aversion to political involvement. He also fails to explain how Scotland could have been considered a secure base for Catholic intrigues while the Earl of Morton was alive." *The Society of Jesus in Ireland, Scotland, and England 1541-1588*, p. 178; cf. p. 266: "Nor can we claim with Michael Carrafiello that Robert Parsons arrived in England with a clearly delineated political programme. Parsons only became interested in more political means for the restoration of Catholicism after the failure of the original mission and the opening of Scotland."

59. H. S. Bennett, *English Books and Readers 1558 to 1603: Being a Study in the History of the Book Trade in the Reign of Elizabeth I* (Vol. II in a series. Cambridge University Press 1965. Reprint 1989) p. 117

60. First page of Persons's *Brief Censure*, mentioned a few lines below in the text.

61. Their characters as described in E. Waugh, *Edmund Campion*, ch. III: The Hero.

62. Persons quotes this and refutes it in his *Brief Censure*. See ch 12: "Persons defends Campion in print."

63. Persons's *L. of C.*, book 2, ch. 1

64. Letter of Council to Cox, Bishop of Ely, March 1572: Bishop White Kennet's collection, vol. 48; Lansdowne Mss. 982, folio 6

65. Lord Burghley, *The Execution of Justice in England, not for Religion, but for Treason* (1583), 1675 reprint, p. 11

66. British Library: Harleian Mss. 360, folio 65

67. Harleian Mss. 360, folio 5

68. C.R.S., vol. 39, pp. 79, 87

69. Harleian Mss. 360, folio 65

70. Mentioned again in ch. 12: "The press is moved to Southwark."

71. Harleian Mss. 360, art. 1

72. Reynolds, *Campion and Parsons*, p. 86

73. *Letters and Memorials of Cardinal Allen*, pp. 89–91

74. Theiner, vol. 3, p. 217. "News from Ireland" early in Aug. 1580.

75. Persons's *L. of C.*, book 2, ch. 2

76. *L. of C.*, book 2, ch. 2

77. *L. of C.*, book 2, ch. 2

78. More on this book in ch. 14: "The end of Fr. Persons's mission in England."

79. Letter of August 1581: C.R.S., vol. 39, pp. 73, 83

80. Letter of August 1581: C.R.S., vol. 39, pp. 77–8, 85–7

81. C.R.S., vol. 39, pp. 48, 56

82. Says Hughes in *The Reformation in England*, vol. 3, pp. 363–4.

83. Fr. Hicks's note, C.R.S., vol. 39, p. 52

84. Letter of August 1581: C.R.S., vol. 39, pp. 81, 89. She is mentioned again by Fr. Persons and named as "Mistresse Tomson" in a marginal note of *An epistle of the persecution of catholickes in Englande* (Eng. trans. 1582 of Latin orig. 1581. Eng. reprint: Scolar Press, Menston, U.K. 1973) p. 79. S.B., no. 54. On the 25th page (unnumbered) of his preface to his *Jesuitismi pars prima* ("The first part of Jesuitry," Henry Middleton, London 1582), Laurence Humphrey said the story was a fabrication, defended Aylmer, "a most prudent and most strong Bishop" and said Miss Thomson was sent to Bridewell "not for conscience but for remarkable impudence and pertness." S.B., no. 19.

85. C.R.S., vol. 39, pp. 46–56, 56–62; pp. 46–7 explain the dating of Nov. 17. More, *History Eng. Province*, bk 3, no. 15, has some of the letter, with additional phrases; see Fr. Edwards's note, *The Elizabethan Jesuits*, p. 370. Simpson used Theiner, vol. 3, p. 216, an abbreviated version with slight variations from the original Latin.

86. C.R.S., vol. 2, p. 78

87. Marie B. Rowlands, "Recusant Women 1560–1640" in Mary Prior (ed.), *Women in English Society* (Routledge, N.Y. 1985) pp. 149–80

88. Mentioned above, this chapter: "The network of Catholic gentry."

89. Adam Hamilton O.S.B., *The Chronicle of the English Augustinian Canonesses Regular of the Lateran, at St. Monica's in Louvain* (vol. 2, Sands, Edinburgh 1906) pp. 165–6

90. "homulus meus et ego": "my little man and I."

91. "Ad maiorem Dei gloriam," "For the greater glory of God": a motto of St. Ignatius, often abbreviated to "A.M.D.G."

92. The letter is in *Camp. Opusc.*, pp. 408–19 (pp. 31–6); *Concertatio*, pp. 3–4; Cardinal William Allen, *A Briefe Historie* (ed. Pollen 1908) pp. 21–6 (trans. here revised, and missing phrases added, using the text in *Concertatio*). Minus some sentences, it is in Mary Anne Everett Green (ed.), *Calendar of State Papers, Domestic Series, of the Reigns of Elizabeth and James I, Addenda, 1580–1625* (Longman, London 1872) no. 60, pp. 24–5. It was probably written on the same day as Persons's letter, five months (as he says at the start of the letter) after arriving in England, reckoning from June 25. This would agree with Nov. 17, 1580, as mentioned in the note above, at the end of Persons's letter.

93.　McCoog in *Reckoned Expense*, p. 129. His surname is also given as "Manare."

Chapter 11—Campion's Progress

1.　Letter to Fr. Agazzari of Aug. 5, 1580: C.R.S., vol. 39, pp. 41, 44
2.　Persons's *L. of C.*, book 2, chs. 3 and 4, and his memoirs, C.R.S., vol. 2, p. 27. No date is given in October. Bombino, ch. 28, p. 125, says "they returned from the country in the beginning of October."
3.　Persons's *L. of C.*, book 2, ch. 3
4.　This house is mentioned again in ch. 13: "Campion and Persons continue visitation"; ch. 15: "More questioning and racking."
5.　Persons's *L. of C.*, book 2, ch. 2. However, he heard nothing of Campion for the first 17 days: his letter of Aug. 5 says, "we have neither seen nor heard anything of one another since" July 19.
6.　Persons's memoirs, C.R.S., vol. 2, p. 27
7.　The one whose office is to ride up to Westminster Hall on Coronation Day and challenge anyone who disputes the right of succession—an office established by William the Conqueror.
8.　*Lincolnshire Notes and Queries - A Quarterly Journal* (1893) p. 156; *The Catholic Encyclopedia* (1911) art. "Lacy, William"
9.　See below: "Shakespeare."
10.　These are the places given by Leo Hicks S.J., C.R.S., vol. 39, p. xxiii. Fr. More S.J. wrote: "Campion went with Ralph to undertake work in the remoter districts in the North": *History Eng. Province*, bk 3, no. 12; Eng. trans. pp. 86–7—but that must refer to a later period, the end of 1580. Cf. McCoog in *Spirit, Style, Story*, p. 334. The indictments mentioned in the text, in the next few lines, relating to July 30, show that Campion went to counties closer to London in his first, eleven-week, excursion.
11.　County boundaries were changed in 1972.
12.　King's Bench 9/654, no. 58: quoted in Anstruther, *Vaux of Harrowden*, p. 115.
13.　Anstruther, *Vaux of Harrowden*, p. 112
14.　Reynolds, p. 83
15.　Cobham to Walsingham, Nov. 27, 1580
16.　Persons's *L. of C.*, book 2, ch. 3
17.　"Blessed Edmund Campion's *Challenge*" p. 58
18.　*L. of C.*, book 2, ch. 3
19.　Persons's *L. of C.*, book 2, ch. 3
20.　In a letter to Fr. Agazzari, Nov. 17, Persons says Campion went north

yesterday: C.R.S., vol. 39, pp. 52, 59.

21.   Paraphrased from Persons's *L. of C.*, book 2, ch. 4.

22.   It is difficult to explain what Campion did in Uxbridge for so long from October some time till Nov. 16. Perhaps this is why Pollen ignores Persons's repeated statement that he and Campion met up in October (Persons's *L. of C.*, book 2, chs. 3 and 4, and his memoirs, C.R.S., vol. 2, p. 27; also Bombino, ch. 28, p. 125, quoted above) and says Persons "made him [Campion] stop in Uxbridge, and rode out there . . . perhaps early in November." *English Catholics in the Reign of Queen Elizabeth*, p. 368. November 16 is a sure date for the *end* of the period: in his letter to Fr. Agazzari of Nov. 17, 1580, Persons wrote: "When summer was over, we withdrew to London, meeting up in fixed places, and as soon as we had carried out the duties of the Society we separated again, and yesterday [Nov. 16] Father Edmund set out with Ralph for the counties assigned to him." C.R.S. vol. 39, pp. 52, 59. The "duties" were not lengthy: "prayer and some exhortations, mutual Confession, and renewal of their vows according to the custom of their Society" (Persons's *L. of C.*, book 2, ch. 3). In short, certain statements imply a stay of a few weeks before parting again on Nov. 16, but another statement implies brief reunions and meetings. Fr. McCoog in *Reckoned Expense* (2nd ed.), p. 177, says "Persons left London for Uxbridge circa October 20" but he merely cites a letter, p. 178, written by Persons in London on Oct. 20 without anything specific in the letter to say where he was going. See also ch. 13: "Reunion in London" and its first endnote, for another statement of Persons implying that October was the time of reunion.

23.   McCoog in *Spirit, Style, Story*, p. 336

24.   Lansdowne Mss. 30, no. 78

25.   Harleian Mss. 859. The full text of the trial is in Richard Simpson, "A Morning at the Star-Chamber" *The Rambler*, Jan. 1857, pp. 15–36. Extracts in Anstruther, *Vaux of Harrowden*, pp. 120–7. Different books vary as to the date of this trial: November 15 or 18 or 20. For convenience only, I choose Nov. 15 when mentioning the trial in this book.

26.   "A Morning at the Star-Chamber," p. 32

27.   Persons's *Memoirs*, C.R.S., vol. 4 (Arden Press, London 1907) pp. 114–5

28.   Named in ch. 10: "The network of Catholic gentry" and start of ch. 13: "The preparation of *Rationes Decem: Ten Reasons*."

29.   Philip Caraman S.J., *Henry Morse – Priest of the Plague and Martyr of England* (Fontana Books, Glasgow 1962) p. 25, says, without giving dates, that Fitzherbert hosted Persons and Campion at Swynnerton.

30. Lansdowne Mss. 30, no. 78, folios 201–2. For the period from Christmas to Jan. 16, I gain much precision and improvement upon Simpson from Michael Hodgetts's article, "Campion in Staffordshire and Derbyshire 1581" *Midland Catholic History* 7 (2000) pp. 52–54, which goes carefully through Burghley's notes. Hodgetts is the author of *Secret Hiding-Places* (Veritas, Dublin 1989), a study of hiding-holes made for priests in these times and after.

31. Hodgetts dates the visit as "probably the 10th," to fit between the visits to Pierrepoint and Longford, although Powdrell himself on trial insisted it was the 8th: "A Morning at the Star-Chamber" p. 28—because that was before the more repressive legislation of the 10th, which specifically forbade harboring Jesuits, mentioned below: "More anti-Catholic penal laws." *Acts of the Privy Council,* vol. 13, p. 170, mentions "the house of one Pierrepoint, where Campion has upon his examination confessed to have been at Christmas last by the space of 14 days." 14 days there from Christmas fits in with Powdrell's claim as to Jan. 8th. But after only "a night's lodging" (Sunday night) as Powdrell confesses, we have a gap on Monday and Tuesday.

32. "A Morning at the Star-Chamber," p. 28

33. *Collins's Peerage of England* (Rivington, London 1812) p. 95

34. Derbyshire Archaeological Journal (Derbyshire Archaeological Society 1961) p. 76

35. John Charles Cox, *Tourist's guide to Derbyshire* (Stanford, London 1878) p. 89

36. Joseph Foster, *Alumni Oxonienses 1500–1714* ["Students of Oxford"] vol. 4 (Parker and Co., Oxford 1891) p. 1297

37. Ch. 20: "Campion's last moments"

38. Agnes Strickland, *Lives of the Queens of Scotland and English Princesses Connected with the Regal Succession of Great Britain* (vol. 6. Blackwood, London 1856) p. 339

39. Doreen M. Rosman, *The Evolution of the English Churches, 1500–2000* (Cambridge University Press 2003) p. 68

40. Rosamond Meredith, "The Eyres of Hassop 1470–1640" [part 2], *Derbyshire Archaeological Journal* (Derbyshire Archaeological Society 1965) pp. 4491, at p. 54: "The 'Mr. . Ayers' [Ayre, Eyre, Eyres] in question was undoubtedly Robert Eyre of Spital, Chesterfield . . . a convicted recusant." Strype's *Annals* of 1581 spelt the place as "Stiple" (Oxford 1824, p. 359). Following the same notes of Burghley, Simpson put "The Stipte." But Michael Hodgetts's article says there is no such place as "The Stipte";

so it must be a misreading, he explains why, for either "Hasope" (now Hassop) or "the Hurst." Campion, he says, went to Hassop, two miles north of Bakewell—or, if not, to the same man eight miles away, at Nether Hurst, a mile from Hathersage. Both houses are in Derbyshire, close to the Yorkshire border. *Acts of the Privy Council*, vol. 13, p. 257, mentions a letter to the "Earle of Sallope" (Salop, today Shropshire) to summon "Langford" (named in this section) and "Ayre."

41.   John Wilson, *Verses and Notes: topographical, historical, antiquarian, miscellaneous* (A. Hill, Chorley, U.K. 1903) p. 150

42.   Burghley papers: British Library, Lansdowne Mss. 30, no. 78. Simpson wrote that "Burghley is at fault" for saying Campion was then nine days at inns; so Simpson says that, "However," a man was found whose home was visited by Campion on Jan. 28. If the dates (given by Burghley) are correct, there is no problem with Jan. 28—it does not interrupt, but comes after, the nine days in inns. Anstruther, *Vaux of Harrowden*, p. 137 says "six days": the Ms. is unclear at this and other points.

43.   C.R.S., vol. 12 (1913) p. 103. Fr. Aveling says the Privy Council said he was of Yeafford (Yafforth), but judges that this was from a confusion with the nearby house of Cleasby, mentioned below: Hugh Aveling O.S.B., *Northern Catholics - The Catholic Recusants of the North Riding of Yorkshire 1558-1790* (Geoffrey Chapman, Melbourne 1966) p. 60.

44.   *Acts of the Privy Council*, vol. 12, p. 108: July 17, 1580. York commission: *Calendar of State Papers . . . 1547-1580*, Aug. 16, 1580, no. 28, p. 671. E.B., no. 1. Hughes, *The Reformation in England*, vol. 3, p. 435. Dennis Flynn, *John Donne and the Ancient Catholic Nobility* (Indiana University Press 1995) p. 113, says, however, he was arrested in 1581 for harboring Campion and held in solitary confinement in the castle at Hull. Gatehouse imprisonment 1583 mentioned in *Calendar of State Papers . . . 1581-1590*, nos. 19-20, p. 145. E.B., no. 2

45.   Aveling, *Northern Catholics*, p. 60. She is named (spelt "Bulwer") among Catholics in *Calendar of State Papers . . . 1581-1590*, May 1582, no. 78, p. 57. E.B., no. 2.

46.   Dom Bede Camm O.S.B., *Forgotten Shrines* (Macdonald and Evans, London 1910. Facsimile reprint: Gracewing, U.K. 2004) p. 135. I replaced the word, "rogueing" with "roving," following Hughes, *The Reformation in England*, vol. 3, p. 433.

47.   Aveling, *Northern Catholics*, pp. 59-60, 95, 117

48.   C.R.S., vol. 13 (1913) p. 106

49.   Aveling, *Northern Catholics*, p. 60

50. He appears in the opening lines of ch. 12. Aveling, *Northern Catholics*, pp. 60, 65.

51. Foley, *Records of the English Province*, vol. 3, p. 670, says Tempest was Harrington's brother-in-law. Burghley's notes say instead Smyth was brother of Mrs. Harrington.

52. Or a whole month, if Campion spent Easter there, March 26, as Burghley's notes once say. His notes contain contradictory information on this point: (a) twice they say fourteen days, and once "about twelve days," the figure confessed by Mr. Harrington in the same series of notes; (b) elsewhere, he records that Campion was at Harrington's at Easter, which would mean two weeks longer. – If a choice has to be made, it is better to accept three equivalent statements, and discard (b) the one saying "at Easter." The reason for the gap of two weeks is explained in the next section of the text.

53. J. Morris S.J., *The Troubles of Our Catholic Forefathers* (3rd Series, 1877) p. 111; Aveling, *Northern Catholics*, p. 58.

54. Aveling, *Northern Catholics*, p. 105

55. Burghley's notes say that at Harrington's, "There he was busy at his study, and made a good piece of his Latin book."

56. A phrase in the full title of *Ten Reasons*.

57. Caraman, *Henry Morse – Priest of the Plague*, p. 40

58. Morris, *Troubles of Our Catholic Forefathers* (1877) p. 111, making specific reference to this gap passed over by Simpson.

59. But McCoog in *Spirit, Style, Story*, p. 337, says Mr. Price, a Yorkshireman and former pupil. Burghley's notes place "Price, Esquire" in the list after "More . . . in Yorkshire and his wife." I put Mr. Price in the list in ch. 13: "Campion and Persons continue visitation."

60. Henry Hawkes Spink, *The Gunpowder Plot and Lord Mounteagle's letter* (Simpkin and Co., London 1902) p. 396

61. See S.B., no. 3.

62. *Letter written by M. Doctor Allen concerning the Yielding up of the City of Daventrie, unto his Catholic Majesty, by Sir William Stanley Knight* (Chetham Society 1851) note on pp. xliv–v. Anstruther, *Seminary Priests*, p. 387.

63. Joseph Gillow, *The Haydock Papers: A Glimpse into English Catholic Life* (Burns and Oates, London 1888) p. 32

64. *Acts of the Privy Council*, vol. 13, pp. 184, 257, names [Thomas] Talbot with some others of the present list of eight in the text. Burghley's list has "Talbot" but no Christian name, as with many names he recorded.

65. John Harland (ed.), *The Lancashire Lieutenancy under the Tudors and*

Stuarts (Chetham Society 1859) pp. 46, 73. He is named for assisting priests in *Calendar of State Papers . . . 1547–1580*, July 13, 1568, no. 12 i, p. 312. E.B., no. 1

66. C.R.S., vol. 4, pp. 182, 185
67. C.R.S., vol. 4, pp. 180–1
68. Gillow, *Haydock Papers*, p. 23
69. Letter of Sir Francis Walsingham to the Bishop of Chester, May 2, 1584
70. She is named as a victim of injustice from the Lancashire sheriff in *Calendar of State Papers . . . 1581–1590*, Jan. 23, 1584, no. 42, p. 155. E.B., no. 2
71. Dom Bede Camm, *Forgotten Shrines*, p. 186
72. Richard Wilson and Randall Martin in *Theatre and Religion* (Manchester University Press, Manchester 2004) pp. 22, 108
73. Dom Bede Camm, *Forgotten Shrines*, pp. 304, 306; Gillow, *Haydock Papers*, pp. 18–9. Southworth, Hoghton and Hesketh are named again in ch. 15: "More questioning and racking."
74. Dom Bede Camm, *Forgotten Shrines*, p. 34. Burghley's notes have "Weston."
75. J. H. Pollen S.J., "Religious Persecution under Queen Elizabeth" *The Month*, November 1904, pp. 501–17, at p. 517, n. 1. The quote is a marginal note in Dr. Allen's own book next to where he says, "How many wander in places . . . into waters, to save themselves from . . . cruelty." Final chapter of Dr. Allen, *A true, sincere and modest defense of English Catholics that suffer for their faith both at home and abroad, against a false, seditious and slanderous libel entitled "The Execution of Justice in England"* (Rouen 1584). Reprint: Manresa Press (2 vols. London 1914) vol. 2, p. 100. Other reprints: Cornell Uni. Press 1965; Scolar Press, Yorkshire 1971.
76. Gillow, *Haydock Papers*, p. 32
77. C.R.S., vol. 4, p. 170
78. Simpson added here: "but according to Persons at Worthington's and Mrs. Allen's"—but provides no reference for this statement he attributes to Persons, says McCoog in *Spirit, Style, Story*, p. 337.
79. Lansdowne Mss. 30, no. 78
80. Ch. 13: "Visits in and around London"; "Campion and Persons continue visitation." Ch. 14: "Campion invited to Lyford." Ch. 15: "A series of arrests."
81. Bombino, ch. 27, p. 124
82. Related above, this chapter: "Campion travels to the north, end of 1580."
83. See ch. 7: "Cardinal Borromeo at Milan."

84. Mr. Shakespeare's copy is lost but we have the text from another copy signed by a nun in exile in 1638. See also Samuel Schoenbaum, *William Shakespeare—A Compact Documentary Life* (Oxford University Press 1987) pp. 50–3.

85. Schoenbaum, *Shakespeare*, p. 66. Cf. Hildegard Hammerschmidt-Hummel, *Die verborgene Existenz des William Shakespeare. Dichter und Rebell im katholischen Untergrund* ("The hidden existence of William Shakespeare. Poet and rebel in the Catholic underground," Herder, Freiburg im Breisgau 2001).

86. C. Richard Desper, "Allusions to Edmund Campion in *Twelfth Night*" Elizabethan Review, Spring/Summer 1995

87. See ch. 16: "The third debate." Desper says Sept. 24 by mistake, instead of 23.

88. From the Protestant account in print: John Field, *A true report of the Disputation, or rather private Conference, had in the Tower of London with Ed. Campion, Jesuit* (1583), 31st page of the report of the 3rd debate: S.B., no. 36. The Catholic account of the same scene is in Holleran, p. 129: S.B., no. 41.

89. Cf. "Edmund Campion and William Shakespeare: *Much Ado About Nothing?*" by T. McCoog S.J. and Peter Davidson in *Reckoned Expense* (2nd ed. 2007) pp. 165–85, wherein they admit even less than I have.

90. *Forgotten Shrines*, p. 186. The chronology of this part from Dom Camm does not match the order found in Burghley, but the names are the same.

91. More, *History Eng. Province*, bk 3, no. 14

Chapter 12—The Progress of the Mission

1. Letter of Nov. 17, 1580: C.R.S., vol. 39, pp. 54, 61: quoted in ch. 10: "Persons's letter to Rome" in a slightly different trans.

2. Francis Edwards S.J., *Robert Persons*, p. 40. T. McCoog S.J., "The English Jesuit Mission and the French Match, 1579–1581" p. 203, poses the question: "Parsons's first recorded contact with Mendoza was on October 19, 1580, around the time of the release of the "Brag." Are the two events connected?"

3. Edwards, *Robert Persons*, p. 46, based on a letter of Persons to Fr. Agazzari, Nov. 17, 1580.

4. C.R.S., vol. 39, pp. 42–3, 45

5. Persons's *Draft life of Campion*, ch. 15, Latin orig., partly quoted in C.R.S., vol. 39, p. 73; cf. C.R.S., vol. 2, p. 27.

6. Persons wrote "six whole months," not knowing that when they left

Rheims about the same time (ch. 7: "The party splits up"), Sherwin was delayed by Paschal's sickness and did not leave Rouen till August 1st: E.S. Keogh, *Blessed Ralph Sherwin*, pp. 378–80.

7.   C.R.S., vol. 39, pp. 82–3, 90

8.   C.R.S., vol. 2, p. 181, Persons says Kent, but in his *L. of C.*, ch. 15, he says Essex. His family was of Much Baddow, Essex: *Notes and Queries* (Oxford 1974) p. 302; cf. John Morris S.J., *The Troubles of Our Catholic Forefathers Related by Themselves* (2nd Series, 1875) p. 294.

9.   Mentioned in *Acts of the Privy Council*, vol. 12, p. 294.

10.   Persons's memoirs, C.R.S., vol. 4, p. 11

11.   Persons's *L. of C.*, ch. 15

12.   Persons's *L. of C.*, ch. 15, which also records the fate of all of them, in summary. He says Fr. Kemp is imprisoned "to this day" (1594) but gives no time of arrest.

13.   N. P. Brown in *Reckoned Expense*, pp. 193–4.

14.   Persons's *Draft life of Campion*, ch. 17: reference given by Fr. Hicks in C.R.S., vol. 39, p. xxxi. Blackwell was later named "Archpriest" (Superior) of the secular clergy of England. Maurice is mentioned again next paragraph. Tirwhit is also spelt Tyrwhit. Birkett is named again in ch. 21: "Relics of Campion." If Persons remembers his name aright, Fr. Chambers must be a Marian priest (pre-Nov. 1558) and so is not named in Godfrey Anstruther O.P., *The Seminary Priests – A Dictionary of the Secular Clergy of England and Wales 1558–1850* (vol. 1. Elizabethan 1558–1603. Ushaw College, Durham 1968) nor in Dominic Aidan Bellenger O.S.B, *English and Welsh Priests 1558–1800 – A Working List* (Downside Abbey, Bath, England 1984).

15.   Ch. 6: "Faculties from the Pope"

16.   C.R.S., vol. 2, p. 29. Mr. Brokesby was either "Thomas" or "Robert."

17.   C.R.S., vol. 2, p. 182

18.   Fr. Persons calls Fr. Maurice "a learned and resourceful [or practical] man": C.R.S., vol. 4, pp. 16–7.

19.   Bombino, ch. 30, p. 139, calls him Richard Maurice and says he went into exile and lived with Dr. Allen first at Rheims, and later at Rome, where he died in the English College.

20.   Persons's memoirs, C.R.S., vol. 2, p. 29

21.   C.R.S., vol. 4, pp. 16–7

22.   C.R.S., vol. 39, pp. 74, 84

23.   John Morris S.J., "Blessed Edmund Campion and his *Ten Reasons*" *The Month*, July 1889, pp. 372–83, at p. 374; Reynolds, *Campion and Parsons*, p. 88.

24. C.R.S., vol. 2, p. 228

25. Hart and Bosgrave are named as sent to the Tower, in *Acts of the Privy Council*, vol. 12, p. 294: Dec. 24, 1580.

26. Council of Trent: "Decree on the edition and use of sacred books," April 8, 1546, which also deals with the printing and examination of Catholic literature in general. Eng. trans. in *The Canons and Decrees of the Council of Trent* (trans. H. J. Schroeder O.P., Herder Book Co. 1941. Reprint: TAN Books, Illinois 1978) pp. 18–20.

27. Latin text in Meyer, p. 487. Copies of the Jesuits' special faculties are in the Public Record Office of London: *Calendar of State Papers . . . 1547–1580*, April 14, 1580, nos. 26–8, p. 651. E.B., no. 1

28. A. C. Southern, *Elizabethan Recusant Prose:* pp. 356–8, 464–5; cf. pp. 393–4, 428.

29. Several editions survive in the British Library: the first of 1580; and 1599, 1601. Reprinted 1621. Reprinted in 1972 by Scolar Press from the 1580 edition at Ushaw: cf. Edwards, *Robert Persons*, p. 41.

30. Southern, pp. 353, 460, 462

31. Persons's *Draft life of Campion*, ch. 17, cited in C.R.S., vol. 39, p. xxxii.

32. Southern, p. 141

33. This sentence and its place in the text are modified in accordance with Southern, pp. 464–5, who says Simpson had written *Censure* where he meant *Brief Discourse*.

34. Letter to Fr. Agazzari, C.R.S. vol 39, pp. xxxii, 77, 85

35. Charke, *An Answer to a seditious pamphlet lately cast abroad by a Jesuit* (C. Barker, London 1580). Hanmer, *The great Brag and Challenge of M. Champion a Jesuit, commonly called Edmund Campion, lately arrived in England, containing nine articles here severally laid down, directed by him to the Lords of the Council, confuted and answered by Meredith Hanmer, M. of Art, and Student in Divinity* (T. Marsch, London 1581). See ch. 10: "The *Brag* is publicised." Charke's book was licensed for printing on Dec. 20, Hanmer's on Jan. 3: Edward Arber (ed.), *A Transcript of the Registers of the Company of Stationers of London; 1554–1640, A.D.* (5 vols. Privately printed. London and Birmingham 1875–77, 1894. Reprint: Martino Publishing, Mansfield Centre, MA 2007) vol. 2, p. 176.

36. Michael C. Questier, *Catholicism and Community in Early Modern England: Politics, Aristocratic Patronage and Religion, c.1550–1640* (Cambridge University Press 2006) p. 155

37. C.R.S., vol. 39, p. 63, with reference to Persons's *Draft life of Campion*, ch. 18.

38. Persons's memoirs, C.R.S., vol. 2, p. 183

39. *Douay Diaries*, at March 20, 1581, p. 177

40. See S.B., no. 8a.

41. 2nd page of *A Brief Censure*. The book has no page nos.

42. A paraphrase and summary of the 3rd page of *A Brief Censure*.

43. *A Brief Censure*, 1st paragraph of the 2nd section, entitled: "Touching the man."

44. *Brief Censure*, last page of: "Touching the man."

45. *Brief Censure*, in the 3rd section, entitled: "Touching the matter."

46. Southern, p. 467

47. Edwards, *Robert Persons*, p. 42

48. *A Defense of the Censure:* S.B., no. 14.

49. C.R.S., vol. 39, pp. 72–6, 83–5. Along with editor Fr. Hicks, p. 72, Fr. Edwards, *Robert Persons*, p. 43, attributes this letter to Persons and dates it August 1581. It was printed in Sanders's *De Schismate Anglicano* ("The Anglican Schism," ed. Fr. Persons 1586) pp. 446–62, where the date was wrongly given as July 1582.

50. See above, this chapter: "Persons's printing press in Greenstreet."

51. *Apology and true declaration of the institution and endeavors of the two English Colleges, the one in Rome, the other now resident in Rheims, against certain sinister informations given up against the same* (Rheims 1581). Allen addressed a copy of the book to Cobham who sent it to Walsingham, June 15, 1581.

52. *A Defense and Declaration of . . . Purgatory*, mentioned in ch. 9: "English Catholic writers abroad." Fulke authored *Two Treatises written against the Papists* (1577).

53. *Apology to William Fulk, heretical Minister, in defense of Allen's book of Purgatory* (Louvain 1580). Brussels Mss. no. 15594.

54. This chapter: "Catholic attempts to compromise"

55. John Nichols, *A declaration of the recantation of John Nichols (for the space almost of two years the Pope's scholar in the English seminary or college at Rome): which desireth to be reconciled and received as a member into the true Church of Christ in England* (Christopher Barker, London Feb. 14, 1581)

56. *A discoverie of I. Nicols minister, misreported a Jesuite, latelye recanted in the Tower of London. Wherin besides the declaration of the man, is contayned a ful answere to his recantation, with a confutation of his slaunders, and proofe of the contraries, in the Pope, cardinals, clergie, students, and private men of Rome. There is also added a reproofe of an oratiuon and sermon, falsely presented by the sayd Nicols to be made in Rome, and presented*

to the Pope in his consistorye. Wherto is annexed a late information from Rome touchng [sic] *the aute[n]tical copie of Nicols recantation* (Brinkley's press 1581. Reprint: Scolar Press, Menston, U.K. 1971). Southern, p. 465, says it was printed at "Greenstreet House Press (now lodged in the house of Francis Browne)," but Fr. Edwards thinks Stonor Park: *Robert Persons*, p. 42. April 1581 seems the likely month (before April 2 is impossible: cf. Southern, p. 467), so Stonor Park is the likely place.

57. C.R.S., vol. 39, pp. 76–7, 85

58. John Strype (1710), *The History of the Life and Acts of the Most Reverend Father in God, Edmund Grindal* (Oxford 1821) part 2, ch. 12. Broached in *Acts of the Privy Council*, vol. 13, pp. 39–40: May 6, 1581.

59. *Acts of the Privy Council*, vol. 13, p. 200: Sept. 9, 1581.

60. C.R.S., vol. 39, pp. 127, 132; cf. vol. 4, pp. 41–3.

61. *Concertatio:* Nichols, pp. 231–4; Luke Kirby's letter, p. 92; Persons's memoirs, C.R.S., vol. 4, pp. 6–9

62. Edwards, *Robert Persons*, p. 53

63. C.R.S., vol. 4, p. 51; on pp. 48–55 Persons tells the whole story of Alfield; also in C.R.S., vol. 39, pp. 136–9, 139–41.

64. But Fr. Pollen's note in C.R.S., vol. 4, p. 30, says, with reference to R.O., Dom. Eliz. 248, no. 29, "To judge from the State Papers, the Venerable Thomas Alfield was betrayed by John Davis, the navigator." Anstruther, *Seminary Priests*, p. 3, says his father betrayed Alfield.

65. Martin Haile, *An Elizabethan Cardinal: William Allen* (Isaac Pitman and Sons, London 1914) pp. 250–1

66. C.R.S., vol. 2, p. 27

67. Simpson said Briant came to the Tower from the Marshalsea prison on March 27, but Fr. John Morris S.J. explains that Rishton's Diary (as it was then called) is wrong here on both place and date: it was the *Counter* prison, after *May 3*, the day of the Council's order to write a letter to arrange the transfer (Lansdowne Mss. 1162, folio 7b: *Acts of the Privy Council*, vol. 13, p. 37): "Blessed Edmund and Companions, Martyrs" *The Month*, December 1887, pp. 457–70, at p. 467. Later, Morris himself fell into the original mistake of saying the Marshalsea about March 25: "Blessed Edmund Campion and his *Ten Reasons*" p. 373.

68. Stonyhurst Mss. P. folio 155

69. B. A. Harrison (ed. and trans.), *A Tudor Journal: The Diary of a Priest in the Tower, 1580–1585* (Daughters of St. Paul, London 2000): entries at March 27 and April 6, 1581, but see endnote 67 above to correct these dates. The wording of the second paragraph cited here shows that some

diary entries were written some time after the events occurred; hence the mistaken dates. The translation of the passages cited is by Simpson. Once known as Rishton's or *Rushton's Diary*, when attributed to Fr. Edward Rishton, this Latin diary of a priest in the Tower is now known to be by Fr. John Hart. It was first published in the 2nd edition of Sanders's work *De Schismate Anglicano* ("The Anglican Schism"), Rome 1586.

70. *A Briefe Historie* (ed. Pollen) p. 49. The same text, slightly modified, is in Bishop Richard Challoner, *Memoirs of Missionary Priests as well Secular as Regular, and of other Catholics of both Sexes, that have suffered Death in England on Religious Accounts from the Year of our Lord 1577 to 1684, gathered, partly from Printed Accounts . . . and partly from Manuscript Relations. A new edition, revised and corrected by J. H. Pollen S.J.* (Burns Oates and Washbourne, London 1924) p. 36. Cf. *Concertatio*, pp. 73–4.

71. *Calendar of State Papers . . . 1581–1590*, March 27, 1582, no. 72, p. 48. E.B., no. 2.

72. Persons, *An epistle of the persecution of catholickes in Englande* (Eng. trans. 1582) p. 183 (unnumbered: 2nd–last page in original, as Norton says): S.B., no. 54. Norton's notorious statement is also given by Persons in *Concertatio*, p. 78 (pp. 76–8 have the same content as the *Epistle of persecution*, Eng. trans., pp. 171–2; 180–4).

73. Cf. *Calendar of State Papers . . . 1581–1590*, March 27, 1582, no. 72, p. 48.

74. C.R.S., vol. 39, pp. 130, 134–5

75. From a letter of Dec. 4, 1581 by Pedro Serrano, secretary to Spanish ambassador Bernardino de Mendoza, translated by John Morris S.J., in "A new Witness about Blessed Edmund Campion" *The Month*, August 1893, pp. 457–65, at pp. 459–60. Narrated also in *Concertatio*, p. 74.

76. Persons in C.R.S., vol. 2, p. 182. *Acts of the Privy Council*, vol. 13, pp. 34–5. Foley, *Records of the English Province* (vol. 4, Burns and Oates, London 1878) pp. 346–7. C.R.S., vol. 39, p. xxxvii. Bombino, ch. 32, p. 144.

77. Bombino, ch. 32, pp. 145–6. We can presume the distressed woman exaggerated the number of guards!

78. Persons in C.R.S., vol. 2, pp. 182–3; vol 4, p. 17; vol. 39, pp. 80–1, 88.

79. Persons in C.R.S., vol. 2, p. 182; some details taken from Bombino, ch. 30, p. 138.

80. Cf. Southern, pp. 353–5, 460–5. We do not know the exact dates the press spent at each place. Fr. Persons's accounts are inconsistent: he mentions its second location, Browne's house, in his *Draft life of Campion*, ch. 18 (quoted by Southern, p. 355), but later he mistakenly says it went from Greenstreet to Stonor Park (C.R.S. vol. 2, p. 182; followed by Bombino, ch.

30, p. 138).

81. As mentioned below, this chapter: "A letter of Dr. Allen to Rome." *Letters and Memorials of Cardinal Allen*, p. 98.

82. *Campion and Parsons*, p. 84. Cf. end of ch. 10: "Campion's account to the Jesuit General."

83. *Spirit, Style, Story*, p. 346. McCoog recommends, for what *is* known, Patrick McGrath and Joy Rowe, "The Marian Priests under Elizabeth I" *Recusant History* 17 (1984) pp. 103–20.

84. Nancy Pollard Brown in *Reckoned Expense*, p. 193, says 100, citing a work of Humphrey Ely (1580). She says 4 led the way from Douay in 1574 [Frs.. R. Bristowe, T. Ford, G. Martin, Th. Robinson]; 7 in 1575; 18 in 1576; 15 in 1577. Reynolds, *Campion and Parsons*, p. 84, says that by 1580 there were probably at least 150 priests on the mission, but gives no reference.

85. See ch. 12: "A letter of Dr. Allen to Rome."

86. C.R.S., vol. 39, pp. 43, 45–6

87. *A Tudor Journal: The Diary of a Priest in the Tower, 1580–1585*

88. Cf. *Calendar of State Papers . . . 1581–1590*, no. 97, p. 9; no. 61, p. 22.

89. Dr. Allen, *A true, sincere and modest defense of English Catholics*, vol. 1, p. 22

90. Cf. *Calendar of State Papers . . . 1581–1590*, Jan. 14, 1581, no. 8, p. 2.

91. Lansdowne Mss. 33, no. 14

92. Jean de Foigny, Rheims 1581

93. Persons's memoirs, C.R.S., vol 4, p. 25

94. Daniello Bartoli S.J.,vol. 3, book 2, p. 123. S.B., no. 4. It is not certain Langdale authored it: Walsham, *Church Papists*, p. 51, names other possible authors, including Clithero, mentioned next sentence above. E.B., no. 74. However, Persons's account, given below, leads to the presumption it was Langdale, or someone who used Langdale's books.

95. Anstruther, *Seminary Priests*, p. 81. St. Margaret is mentioned in ch. 11: "Campion in Yorkshire."

96. The letter to "Mr. Roberts" (= Fr. Robert Persons) is printed in Persons's memoirs: C.R.S., vol. 2, pp. 179–80. Chambers is named above: "Persons's printing press in Greenstreet."

97. *Calendar of State Papers . . . 1547–1580*, Dec. 31, 1581, no. 69, p. 691. E.B., no. 1. Portions of it are printed in Robert S. Miola (ed.), *Early Modern Catholicism - An Anthology of Primary Sources* (Oxford University Press 2007) pp. 72–5.

98. Persons tells the story of this tract and its effect in his memoirs, C.R.S., vol. 2, pp. 178–81, and again, vol. 4, pp. 4–5.

99.   Southern, pp. 139, 437, 460–2. Simpson gave the impression that Persons's *Brief Discourse* answered Langdale, but Southern says that Persons's book came first. His reply to Langdale was a different work, not printed, only copied. Cf. Walsham, *Church Papists*, p. 25, n. 13.

100. Sir Simonds D'Ewes, *Journals of all the Parliaments during the Reign of Queen Elizabeth* (London 1682) p. 285

101. *Campion and Parsons*, pp. 109–10

102. Fr. Pollen, "Religious Persecution under Queen Elizabeth," p. 511

103. Dr. Godfrey Goodman, Bishop of Gloucester, *The Court of King James the First* (Richard Bentley, London 1839) vol. 1, p. 100. For more on Goodman, see ch. 3: "The fate of Cheney."

104. *Campion and Parsons*, pp. 111–2. Some more basic facts on these threats to England are given in ch. 9: "Elizabeth's dangers at home" and "Dangers from abroad."

105. Persons to Agazzari: C.R.S., vol. 39, pp. 74, 83

106. End of ch. 6: "Campion and Persons compared"

107. Campion's letter to Pope Gregory XIII, no longer extant, mentioned by Fr. Ignaz Agricola S.J., *Historia Provinciae Societatis Jesu Germaniae Superioris* ("History of the province of the Society of Jesus of Upper Germany," 4 vols, G. Schlüter and M. Happach, Augsburg 1727–46) vol. 1, p. 244. Cf. Dennis Flynn in *Reckoned Expense*, p. 183.

108. D. Flynn, *John Donne and the Ancient Catholic Nobility*, p. 78. But in *Reckoned Expense*, p. 182, Flynn says Campion "possibly" met Heywood then. I presume Campion met him if he specifically requested him.

109. End of ch. 5: "Arrival in Rome."

110. D. Flynn in *Reckoned Expense*, p. 191

111. Theiner, *Annals*, vol. 3, p. 300. Not that it matters, but Flynn says the letter was May 9: *Reckoned Expense*, p. 183. McCoog, as Simpson, says May 27: *The Society of Jesus in Ireland, Scotland, and England 1541–1588*, p. 161.

112. C.R.S., vol 4, pp. 90–1

113. Cf. M. Tanner S.J., *Societas Jesu apostolorum imitatrix* ("The Society of Jesus, imitator of the apostles") p. 297; D. Flynn in *Reckoned Expense*, p. 188.

114. William Weston, *The Autobiography of an Elizabethan*, trans. Philip Caraman S.J. (Longmans, London 1955) p. 10

115. D. Flynn in *Reckoned Expense*, p. 189

116. McCoog, *The Society of Jesus in Ireland, Scotland, and England*, pp. 160, 180, 242

117. C.R.S., vol. 39, pp. 64–6, 66–7; p. 64 explains the true date is June 14, not 24.

118. In Latin, two readings: "Irisonus," "Frisonus." There is no other record of "Irison," "Ireson" or "Frison." Allen puts "D." at the start of his name which can mean "Dominus" (Mister) as for Mr. George Gilbert, below; or "D" can be short for "Doctor," often a title for a priest.

119. See ch. 11: "Shakespeare" regarding Spiritual Testaments. But Southern, p. 235, and McCoog in *Reckoned Expense* (2nd ed.) p. 175, say "English Testaments" means the New Testament translated into English at Rheims, to be printed next year, 1582, and condemned in *Calendar of State Papers . . . 1581–1590*, June 25, 1582, no. 16, p. 59; cf. July 5, 1582, no. 48, p. 62. E.B., no. 2.

120. Simpson had "less," following a different version, obviously mistaken here. See note following.

121. Cf. *Calendar of State Papers . . . 1581–1590*, June 23, 1581, nos. 51–2, p. 21. *Letters and Memorials of Cardinal Allen*, pp. 95–8. These two copies vary somewhat. I follow no one fully, but alternate according to what makes better sense at each point. Hughes says, "The original is lost, and both copies are evidently imperfect." *The Reformation in England*, vol. 3, p. 310

122. Ch. 7: "George Gilbert"

123. Cf. *Calendar of State Papers . . . 1547–1580*, Dec. 26, 1580, no. 62, p. 691.

124. C.R.S., vol. 39, p. xxxviii. The same remark would apply to Fr. Persons when he also decided to go abroad.

125. See ch. 21: "Veneration of Campion."

126. Bombino, ch. 22, pp. 102–3, part of an extended passage in praise of Gilbert.

127. Foley, *Jesuits in Conflict*, pp. 200–3

Chapter 13—Controversy Erupts

1. Burghley's notes: Lansdowne Mss. 30, no. 78. Probably Mr. Askulph Cleesby mentioned in ch. 11: "Campion in the north, start of 1581." Burghley spells his name "Claisbye."

2. Some time in early June, says McCoog in *Spirit, Style, Story*, p. 337. His basis for that date, I presume, is because Campion was summoned from the north to supervise its printing, and he only reached London early June. But that checking seems too late if the book was finished c. March 26 and then dispatched to Persons. Even supposing 20 days to deliver the book and exchange letters between Persons and Campion: given the ever-present dangers, Persons would not have delayed the printing for such a long time by holding on to it for another 6 weeks before having it checked. Further, if the manuscript was checked in early June (a task requiring a

few days), then it means 400 copies were printed within three weeks, for distribution on June 26—an unlikely swiftness, given the difficulties in printing, mentioned below. Pollen says the printing began roughly April 28 and took nine weeks (Introduction to *Campion's Ten Reasons*: Manresa Press, London 1914, p. 17). His reason for that starting date is that he links it to the summons of Jenks on April 28 (see below: "The printing of *Ten Reasons*" and endnotes). I adopt the same date by giving them all one month from March 26 to dispatch the book, exchange letters, and get the book's references checked. Father Persons's book against John Nichols could have been printed at Stonor Park either before or after *Ten Reasons*. See ch. 12: "Persons defends Campion in print."

3.   End of ch. 29, pp. 132–3

4.   Named in ch. 10: "The network of Catholic gentry."

5.   *Recollections of Father Campion* by Fr. Thomas Fitzherbert S.J., in Pollen, *Acts of English Martyrs hitherto unpublished*, p. 37. Original Ms., Westminster Archives, vol. 2, p. 185.

6.   Bombino, ch. 30, p. 134

7.   Ch. 30, p. 135

8.   Philip Caraman S.J., "Campion at St. John's" p. 212

9.   J. H. Pollen S.J. quotes this for the first time in print in his article, "Blessed Edmund Campion's *Decem Rationes*" *The Month*, January 1905, pp. 1126 at p. 17. Reference: Vatican Archives, Castel S. Angelo, caps. xiv. ii. 36, undated (April? 1581). The story, with less detail, is in Foley, *Records of the English Province*, vol. 3, pp. 40–1, quoting the Annual Letters of the Society of Jesus, 1580–81. Willem Frederik van Nieuwenhoff S.J., *Edmond Campion: eene bladzijde uit de geschiedenis van koningin Elisabeth* ("E. Campion, a separate page in the history of Queen Elizabeth," Borg, Amsterdam 1888) ch. 7, adds that it was a Protestant man, going the same way, who accompanied Campion and after three days realised who his companion was—but I cannot find this detail in any other source.

10.   Persons's letter of Aug. 1581, speaking of himself in the third person: C.R.S., vol. 39, pp. 80, 88. Also his memoirs, C.R.S., vol. 2, pp. 28–9, 182; More, *History Eng. Province*, bk 3, no. 18. It was the *Red Rose* or *Red Lion*, says Persons. *Red Lion* is the correct name: Br. Foley, *Records of the English Province*, vol. 3, p. 439, cites a letter to Walsingham naming this inn as a haunt of Catholics.

11.   Foley, *Records of the English Province*, vol. 3, p. 40, quoting the Annual Letters of 1580–81.

12.   Giovanni Battista Nicolini, *History of the Jesuits* (Henry G. Bohn, London

1854) p. 160, citing the Jesuits' Annual Letters of 1580-1 (not 1583 as he says); Foley, *Records of the English Province*, vol. 3, p. 40.

13. Letter written June 16, 1581, quoted in McCoog in *Spirit, Style, Story*, p. 360-1. Persons's statement, referring to the day he got the letter, i.e., June 3, "I had not seen him for eight whole months," means not since c. October 3, 1580. Now, Oct. 3 is a possible date for their reunion in Uxbridge (see start of ch. 11: "Reunion, review and plans at Uxbridge"), but Persons's other account implies they saw each other just before Campion left again for Lancashire on November 16 (see ch. 11: "Campion goes north for his second journey"). Perhaps Persons meant "*seven* whole months." Persons's memory was excellent; he could relate many details years after events; but he was not always right on dates. (C.R.S., vol. 39, pp. 73-4, n. 4, has an example of Persons giving three different dates for one event).

14. Vol. 3, bk 2, ch. 13, p. 140

15. Persons's *Draft life of Campion*, quoted (varying trans.) in C.R.S., vol. 39, p. xxxviii, and in Pollen's intro. to *Campion's Ten Reasons* (1914) p. 17.

16. Bombino, ch. 32, p. 147

17. Persons's *Draft life of Campion*, Collectanea P., folio 155: cited by Pollen in his intro. to *Campion's Ten Reasons* (1914) p. 21. Cf. Bombino, ch. 30, p. 135.

18. Bombino, ch. 30, p. 135

19. W. Weston, *The Autobiography of an Elizabethan*, p. 3. C.R.S., vol. 4, p. 161.

20. Dasent, *Acts of the Privy Council*, vol. 13, pp. 164, 185: Aug. 7 and 30, 1581.

21. The plot of 1586 to murder Queen Elizabeth, mentioned in passing in ch. 10: "Organisation and precautions."

22. His career is summarised in Frank Walsh Brownlow, *Shakespeare, Harsnett, and the Devils of Denham* (University of Delaware 1993) p. 21. Challoner, *Memoirs of Missionary Priests*, p. 268, records his banishment.

23. In this chapter: "Providential escapes."

24. Persons's memoirs, C.R.S., vol. 2, p. 29; mentioned briefly in his letter of Aug. 1581: C.R.S., vol. 39, pp. 80, 88.

25. Also spelt Davys or Davis. C.R.S., vol. 2, pp. 274-5. Brownlow, *Shakespeare, Harsnett, and the Devils of Denham*, p. 166, says he was probably a layman in minor orders (i.e., below diaconate) and that while Challoner calls him an "ancient missioner" (implying pre-Elizabethan activity), it is not so in his case. Anstruther, *Seminary Priests*, p. 97, and Bellenger, p. 53, list him as a priest from Rheims seminary, ordained 1578, although documentation is lacking of his priesthood.

26. Persons's *Draft life of Campion:* Collectanea P., folio 155: cited in a differing trans. in Pollen's intro. to *Campion's Ten Reasons*, p. 21. Cf. Bombino, ch. 30, pp. 135–6. Pollen adds a 2nd reference, to Fr. Persons's Memoirs, I, ch. 24—but this is a mistake; the Memoirs have nothing there or anywhere on Campion's passing by Tyburn.

27. Cf. ch. 12: "Persons's house raided."

28. J. R. Dasent (ed.), *Acts of the Privy Council*, vol. 13, pp. 34–5

29. This is the dating given by J.H. Pollen S.J. in his article, "Blessed Edmund Campion's *Decem Rationes*" p. 20, and in his Introduction to *Campion's Ten Reasons* (Manresa Press, London 1914) p. 17. Cf. ch. 12: "The press moved to Stonor Park." I follow this date for my own reasons given in endnote 2 above.

30. This description of the characters used is from Pollen, "Blessed Edmund Campion's *Decem Rationes*" pp. 22–23, and in his intro. to *Campion's Ten Reasons*.

31. Named in ch. 14: "The end of Fr. Persons's mission in England."

32. Bombino, ch. 31, p. 141

33. Philip Caraman S.J., *Henry Garnet 1555–1606 and the Gunpowder Plot* (Longmans, London 1964) pp. 96–7. Persons's *Draft life of Campion*, Collectanea P, folio 157. Anstruther, *Seminary Priests*, p. 95.

34. See ch. 1: "Gregory Martin and the end of Oxford."

35. Pointed out by Fr. McCoog in *Reckoned Expense*, p. xxi.

36. Cf. *Calendar of State Papers . . . 1581–1590*, June 12, 1581, no. 38, p. 18.

37. J. R. Dasent (ed.), *Acts of the Privy Council*, vol. 13, p. 170: Aug. 14, 1581

38. S.B., no. 59

39. Pollen, "Blessed Edmund Campion's *Decem Rationes*" p. 21. Thomas Edward Stonor, Baron Richard Monckton Milnes Houghton, *Description of a Copy of "Rationes Decem Campiani,"* printed at Stonor, 1581 (Philobiblon Society, Whittingham and Wilkins, London 1865–6) pp. 3–6. T.E. Stonor was a member of the Philobiblon Society: *Miscellanies of the Philobiblon Society* (Whittingham and Wilkins, London 1863–4) vol. 8, p. 7, who died a few days after sending his small article.

40. For a long time he was erroneously regarded as a Jesuit and one of the compilers or editors of *Concertatio* (S.B., no. 59), but D.M. Rogers shows: that Fr. Bridgewater was a secular priest, not a Jesuit; that he was always named "Bridgewaterus" in Latin; and that "Joannes Aquapontanus" (Latin for John Bridgewater) was a Latin pen-name of Jesuit Fr. John Gibbons of Somerset: *Concertatio* (1970 facsimile reprint), intro., p. 4. Pollen, "Campion's *Decem Rationes*" p. 21, says Bridgewater's name is on the

original copy of *Decem Rationes* that he describes in his article. If, he means, however, the name on it is "Aquapontanus," then Fr. John Gibbons was the owner of that copy.

41. Fr. Gunning, educated for the priesthood at the English College, Lisbon, was ordained in 1867. He was assigned to Winchester in 1869.

42. "stigmaticus perfuga" "branded runaway." As early biographers record, Calvin, convicted of sodomy, was sentenced to be branded on the shoulder with a lily: Debora K. Shuger, *Censorship and Cultural Sensibility: The Regulation of Language in Tudor-Stuart England* (Uni. of Pennsylvania Press 2006) pp. 20–1. Robert Persons mentions it in *A Defense of the Censure given upon two books of William Charke and Meredith Hammer, ministers, which they wrote against Mr. Edmond Campian, Priest of the Society of Jesus, and against his offer of disputation: taken in hand since the death of the said Mr. Campian* (Rouen 1582) pp. 77–8.

43. Ch. 1: "The Fathers of the Church."

44. Campion was not the first to gather outrageous statements of the Protestant Reformers; Fr. Persons gives nine of Luther's in *A Brief Censure* (Jan. 1581; see ch. 12: "Persons defends Campion in print"), in the 1st section, entitled "Touching the Society," wherein he compares the lives of Ignatius Loyola and Martin Luther.

45. Hanmer and Charke had rebutted Campion's *Brag* in print.

46. Bombino, ch. 29, p. 132, quotes the famous dictum, although he gives the other Latin form, "libellus aureus."

47. Thomas Wright ed., *Queen Elizabeth and her Times—A Series of Original Letters* (Henry Colburn, London 1838. Reprint: Elibron Classics, Adamant Media, 2005) vol. 2, p. 132

48. Bede Camm, *Forgotten Shrines*, p. 328, realising that Huntingdonshire is too far for an excursion from Stonor Park, places Campion's visit to Washingley Hall there "in the winter of 1580–1." So also says C.R.S., vol. 22, p. 274. But Burghley's schedule dates his visit to Price not in Dec.–Jan., but "since Whitsunday" (Pentecost), i.e., after May 14. It is clear, then, that Price had two houses, as many of the gentry; and this fits in with Price's absence when Campion visited. This residence at Newport, of a Robert Price, which I presume to be the same man, is mentioned in C.R.S., vol. 12, p. 126.

49. All information on the Price family is from Camm, *Forgotten Shrines*. Mr. and Mrs. Price of Huntingdonshire are named for their religion in *Acts of the Privy Council*, vol. 13, pp. 153, 238–9: Aug. 4 and Oct. 17, 1581.

50. Douglas Walthew Rice, *The Life and Achievements of Sir John Popham*

1531-1607 (Fairleigh Dickinson University Press 2005) p. 58. Mr. Griffith is mentioned above in ch. 11: "Reunion, review and plans at Uxbridge."

51. Possibly Richard, named in ch. 10: "The network of Catholic gentry."

52. Harleian Mss. 859: from p. 29 of the full text of the trial in Richard Simpson, "A Morning at the Star-Chamber."

53. "A Morning at the Star-Chamber" p. 32

54. *Acts of the Privy Council*, vol. 13, pp. 252–3: Nov. 7, 1581. I changed "Morris" to "Norris," because p. 187 speaks of the same Mrs. "Griffin" (= Griffith) having a servant or regular visitor, "Norris"—and this fits in with Campion's helper, Fr. Richard Norris, alias Richardson (see opening lines of this chapter). Anstruther, *Seminary Priests*, p. 255, also has "Norris," without comment.

55. *Calendar of State Papers . . . 1581-1590*, Nov. 12, 1581, no. 61, p. 30. E.B., no. 2.

56. Mentioned above at "Visits in and around London." She had more than one house.

57. Cf. *Calendar of State Papers . . . 1581-1590*, Feb. 24, 1584, no. 25 ii, p. 160. Mentioned again in ch. 15: "No betrayal of anything unknown."

58. Anstruther, *Seminary Priests*, p. 254; Questier, *Catholicism and Community in Early Modern England*, p. 187. Or Campion was there in summer 1580: Anstruther, *Vaux of Harrowden*, p. 115.

59. She appears again in ch 15: "A series of arrests."

60. This list of names, plus Lady Stonor, minus Robert Dormer (not known until Feb. 1584: see the note at his name), is in Burghley's notes: Lansdowne Mss. 30, no. 78. "Yeates" may or may not be Yate of Lyford Grange (ch. 14: "Campion and Persons part").

61. Fr. Francesco Sacchini S.J., *Historiae Societatis Iesu* ("Of the history of the Society of Jesus," Rome 1661) part 5, tome 1, book 1, no. 219, p. 34, who dates it "the sixth day before he was captured," i.e., July 11. Only the last sentence of this extract from Campion's letter is in Bartoli, vol. 3, bk 2, p. 149, who dates it July 9 and, as Sacchini, gives the pseudonym used. Before the passage from the letter, Simpson had a summary statement, also in quotation marks ("Lamenting his former letters which he had miscarried . . . he added"), but that paragraph is not in Bartoli or Sacchini.

62. Pollen, *Acts of English Martyrs hitherto unpublished*, p. 272

63. Dom Camm, *Forgotten Shrines*, pp. 101–2

Chapter 14—Capture

1. Lansdowne Library: vol. 33, no. 60, folios 145–9. This deposition of Eliot is partly reproduced in Archdiocese of Westminster, *Cause of the Canonization*, pp. 192–4.
2. *Acts of the Privy Council*, vol. 13, pp. 177–8: Aug. 21, 1581
3. This is not Christopher Thom(p)son, named in Anstruther, *Seminary Priests*, p. 350.
4. Bombino, ch. 32, p. 147. Bartoli, vol. 3, bk 3, ch. 1, p. 7
5. Henry Foley S.J., *Records of the English Province*, vol. 3, p. 25
6. C.R.S., vol. 4, p. 17
7. Bombino, ch. 32, p. 148. Bartoli, vol. 3, bk 3, ch. 1, p. 7
8. *Acts of the Privy Council*, vol. 13, p. 154. C.R.S., vol. 4, p. 18, says "The search at Stonor began Sunday, July 15"—but that should read "The search at *Lyford* began Sunday, July 16."
9. Named in Pollen, "Blessed Edmund Campion's *Decem Rationes*" p. 20. The first three are named in *Acts of the Privy Council*, vol. 13, p. 177; Brinkley at p. 264.
10. Edwards, *Robert Persons*, pp. 52–4
11. These are among the reasons he himself gives in his memoirs: C.R.S., vol. 4, pp. 26–9, and in a letter to his General in Oct. 1581: C.R.S., vol. 39, pp. 96–7, 107.
12. Persons's memoirs, C.R.S., vol. 4, p. 29
13. C.R.S. vol. 2, p. 30; vol. 4, p. 27. The date is unknown. Fr. Edwards says "Persons left England about August 12 to 15": *The Elizabethan Jesuits*, note on p. 374. Fr. Hicks says Aug. 13 to 21: C.R.S., vol. 39, p. 95.
14. Persons's memoirs, C.R.S., vol. 4, p. 31
15. Fr. Hicks, C.R.S., vol. 39, pp. 172–3
16. Southern, *Elizabethan Recusant Prose*, p. 157, with the other commendations of Persons's style in the text.
17. These are the praises given by Dom Hilary Steuert, "The Place of Allen, Campion and Parsons in the Development of English Prose" (1944), who quotes other writers of note also in praise of Persons's style: E.B., no. 93.
18. *The Tatler*, no. 230: Sept. 28, 1710
19. The title has varied: the first one was *The first book of the Christian exercise, appertaining to resolution* (George L'Oyselet, Rouen 1582). Persons's enlarged, revised version was *A Christian directory guiding men to their salvation* (Rouen 1585). It was translated into Latin, French, Italian, German and Welsh. The most recent edition is *The Christian Directory of Robert Persons, S.J.* (ed. Victor Houliston. Leiden, Boston 1998).

20. V. Houliston in *Reckoned Expense*, pp. 159–60
21. Listed in V. Houliston, *Catholic Resistance in Elizabethan England: Robert Persons's Jesuit Polemic, 1580–1610* (Ashgate, U.K. and U.S.A and Institutum Historicum Societatis Iesu [Historical Institute of the Society of Jesus] Rome 2007) pp. 183–4.
22. Anstruther, *Seminary Priests*, p. xi
23. Hurst and Blackett, London 1858, p. 12
24. *Catholic Encyclopedia* (1913): article "Persons, Robert"
25. F. Edwards S.J., *Robert Persons*, pp. 119, 395
26. In *Reckoned Expense*, p. 141
27. *The Society of Jesus in Ireland, Scotland, and England 1541–1588*, p. 219
28. *The Reformation in England*, vol. 3, p. 316
29. *Campion and Parsons*, p. 210. The same argument and parallel is presented by Fr. Edwards in *Robert Persons*, pp. ix–x; cf. also Edwards, pp. 57–8, on the attempt to solve the English problem of persecution by force of arms.
30. *Tudor Tracts*, intro. by A.F. Pollard (Archibald Constable and Co., London 1903) p. 473; marginal notes on pp. 461, 470.
31. Had Edmund visited the Yate family during his 1st journey (July–Sept. 1580)? "Yeates" is last in Burghley's list in ch. 13: "Campion and Persons continue visitation." If so, this would be Campion's first visit *after* the imprisonment of Mr. Yate. Another possibility is that his brother, Edward Yate, named below in "Caught," is the one meant in Burghley's list. Or it is another person altogether.
32. Bombino, ch. 33, pp. 149–50. A petition in their favor is in the State Papers Office.
33. Bombino, ch. 33, p. 150
34. W. van Nieuwenhoff S.J., *Edmond Campion*, ch. 9. Persons's trip to Louvain is mentioned in ch.6: "Fr. Campion and Fr. Persons compared."
35. Bombino, ch. 33, p. 151: 3rd person rendered into direct speech.
36. Bombino, ch. 34, pp. 154–7, gives all the details of the scene at the Oxford inn.
37. *Campion and Parsons*, p. 116
38. James McConica in *Reckoned Expense*, pp. 50–55
39. E. E. Reynolds, *Campion and Parsons*, tries to work out the chronology carefully, but his pp. 113 and 120 contradict p. 119. On p. 119, in his table of dates, he says Campion and Emerson arrive at Lyford July 10, stay there July 11, leave July 12. The arrival on July 10 must be a mistake, since, as Reynolds insists (pp. 113, 120), July 11 is the sure date they left

Stonor in the morning and arrived at Lyford later the same day. To correct Reynolds's misprint or mistake, delete "July 10" on p. 119, and refer the first two righthand phrases to July 11. His chronology from July 12–22 is helpful and carefully thought out. I follow it below. Bombino, ch. 34, p. 156, places the Oxford inn meeting on Thursday (July 13) but that is one day too late: after the night of July 11 at Lyford, they left on July 12, and were found at an inn later that day.

40. Bombino, ch. 35, pp. 163–5, and ch. 59, p. 307, says that Walsingham was the minister to whom he went. But Eliot's extant letters (Lansdowne Library: vol. 33, no. 60, folios 145–9) are addressed to Leicester, and the earliest account of Campion's capture—the one translated from the French by James Laing of the Sorbonne, published in 1585 (S.B., no. 70)—calls the man *totius regni fere maximus princeps* (almost the greatest lord in the entire realm), which clearly means Leicester. *Concertatio*, p. 55, has the same phrase in a differing translation: "one of the number . . . who held prime authority in the realm."

41. Dr. Allen, *A Briefe Historie* (ed. Pollen) p. 91. Bishop Richard Challoner (1741), *Memoirs of Missionary Priests* (ed. 1924), p. 41

42. Named above, this chapter: "George 'Judas' Eliot." Not Fr. Christopher Thom(p)son.

43. Letter of Walsingham to Burghley, July 14, 1581: Public Record Office, London, State Papers 12/149, no. 69. Bombino, ch. 35, p. 164, and Bartoli, vol. 3, bk 2, p. 147, make out that Eliot first of all betrayed Payne on July 13, and then pretending to fear revenge from Catholics, obtained a guard and was sent out of London to look for other priests before the news of his betrayal could be broadcast.

44. Mentioned in ch. 15: "What did Campion reveal?." *Acts of the Privy Council*, vol. 13, pp. 171–2.

45. Archdiocese of Westminster, *Cause of the Canonization*, p. 180

46. Public Record Office, London: E. 404/124, box 3. Cited in Westminster, *Cause of the Canonization*, p. 195

47. *A Briefe Historie* (ed. Pollen) p. 96

48. The account is named below under "Caught." *Tudor Tracts*, intro. by A.F. Pollard, p. 460. Dr. Allen in a letter to Fr. Agazzari, Aug. 8, 1581, *Letters and Memorials of Cardinal Allen*, p. 101, says about 70 were at Mass, many of them noble persons. The unreferenced quotations in the following paragraphs are from Eliot.

49. *Tudor Tracts*, p. 458

50. *Tudor Tracts*, p. 460, marginal note by Eliot.

51. The *Breviary, Divine Office,* or *Liturgy of the Hours* contains the cycle of Psalms and prayers for each day recited by clerics over the year.

52. Bombino, ch. 37, p. 172

53. Sir John Fettiplace was Sheriff. Eliot does not give his Christian name, and calls him "Justice of the Peace." Bombino, ch. 36, p. 169, says he knows not whether Eliot sent his companion off straightaway (before attending Campion's Mass himself), or after the sermon finished. Simpson said before Mass. I follow Eliot, who says he and Jenkins went off together after the sermon, skipping lunch. Since the armed men arrived during lunch, Eliot's account seems right. If Jenkins had left for a two-mile trip on horseback before Mass, the band of men would have arrived much earlier.

54. Bombino, ch. 37, p. 172. Cf. Bartoli, vol. 3, bk 3, pp. 16–7.

55. Bombino, ch. 37, p. 172

56. Bombino, ch. 39, p. 180

57. Eliot in *Tudor Tracts*, p. 462

58. Bombino, ch. 38, p. 176

59. Bombino, ch. 38, pp. 174–6

60. Bombino, ch. 38, p. 176

61. Bombino, ch. 38, pp. 177–8

62. Vol. 3, bk 3, p. 20. The account following of the sermon and noise is in Bombino, ch. 38, pp. 178–9. See S.B., no. 4, for Bartoli's comments on this nocturnal sermon.

63. Eliot in *Tudor Tracts*, p. 462

64. Bombino, ch. 39, p. 181

65. Bombino, ch. 39, pp. 180–1

66. Bombino, ch. 39, p. 183. I have incorporated elements from both Bombino's and Eliot's accounts of the search and capture, and in doing so have revised Simpson's account, which, following Bombino, attributed the actual discovery to Eliot—but, if that were true, Eliot's own account would surely have said so.

67. S.B., no. 30. *Tudor Tracts*, p. 452, gives the date as possibly November, since there is no reference to the final fate of Campion in December, and on p. 465 Eliot says he has been "silent so long" about Munday's untrue account to which it is a reply.

68. *Acts of the Privy Council*, vol. 13, p. 398: April 25, 1582

69. *A very true Report of the apprehension and taking of that arch-papist Edmund Campion, the Pope's right hand, with three other lewd Jesuit priests, and diverse other lay people, most seditious persons of like sort. Containing also a controulment* [critique] *of a most untrue former book set*

out by A. M. [Anthony Munday] *concerning the same, as is to be proved and justified by Geo. Ellyot, one of the ordinary yeomen of her Majesty's chamber, author of this book, and chiefest cause of the finding of the said lewd and seditious people, great enemies to God, their loving prince and country* (Thomas Dawson, London 1581) 28 pp. Full text in *Tudor Tracts*, pp. 451–74.

70. *A brief Discourse of the taking of Edmund Campion, the seditious Jesuit and divers other Papists in Barkshire . . . gathered by A. M.* [Anthony Munday] (William Wright, London 1581)

71. *Acts of the Privy Council*, vol. 13, p. 205

72. Mentioned again in ch. 15: "The priests racked."

73. *John Gerard—The Autobiography of an Elizabethan*, trans. Philip Caraman S.J. (Longmans, London 1951. Facsimile reprint: Family Publications, Oxford 2006) pp. 5, 216

74. W. Nieuwenhoff S.J., *Edmond Campion*, ch. 9, says Edward was the eldest son of Mrs. Yate.

75. *Calendar of State Papers . . . 1581–1590*, Feb. 12, 1587, no. 12, pp. 384–5. E.B., no. 2. They were arrested when a search was made at Lyford Grange in 1587 for escaped prisoners.

76. *John Gerard—The Autobiography of an Elizabethan*, pp. 4–5; note on p. 216

77. *John Gerard*, note on p. 216. Jacob is named below in ch. 15: "What did Campion reveal?"

78. *Thomas Valley Papists* in chapter, *The Press at Stonor (1581)*

79. *Briefe Historie* (ed. Pollen) p. 10

80. Bishop Diego de Yepes, *Historia particular de la persecucion de Inglaterra, y de los Martirios mas insignes que en ella ha avido desde el año del Señor 1570 . . . Recogida por el Padre Fray Diego de Yepes . . . Opispo de Taraçona* ("A particular history of the persecution in England and of the most noteworthy martyrdoms which have occurred in it since the year of the Lord 1570, gathered by the Father, Friar Diego de Yepes, Bishop of Saragossa," Madrid 1599. Reprint: Gregg International, Farnborough, England 1971. 949 pp.) p. 317, par. 5. See S.B., no. 77.

81. Bombino, ch. 41, pp. 185–6

82. *Concertatio*, p. 56

83. Allen's *Briefe Historie*, p. 11

84. *Acts of the Privy Council*, vol. 13, p. 136

85. *Tudor Tracts*, p. 464. *Concertatio*, p. 56. In agreement with Eliot, Dr. Allen, following the *Douay Diaries*, Aug. 27, 1581, p. 181, and an account of Filby

by an eye-witness, printed in 1582, says Filby was taken at Lyford, and dreamt at Henley: *A Briefe Historie* (ed. Pollen) p. 11; Challoner, *Memoirs of Missionary Priests*, pp. 51–2. An alternative account says: In the crowd of Henley townspeople was Fr. William Filby who broke his cover to speak to Fr. Campion, swapped hats with him, was arrested and added to the company of prisoners. According to local tradition this took place at the top of the Fair Mile, the road that leads north-west out of Henley towards Stonor: Tony Hadland, *Thomas Valley Papists: from Reformation to Emancipation 1534–1829* (Privately printed, 1992) in chapter, *The Press at Stonor (1581).* Bombino, ch. 42, p. 189, has substantially this (unlikely) version, and dates the dream "a few nights before."

86. Bombino, ch. 42, pp. 189–90
87. Persons's memoirs, C.R.S., vol. 4, p. 19. See also vol. 2, p. 30.
88. Bombino, ch. 42, p. 190
89. The details of this procession are in a letter of Persons to his General, Fr. Aquaviva, in Rome, Aug. 30, 1581: C.R.S., vol. 39, pp. 91–2, 92–3.
90. C.R.S., vol. 39, pp. 92, 93 .
91. *Holinshed's Chronicles*, A.D. 1581, vol. 3, p. 1321

Chapter 15—The Tower of London

1.   Persons's *L. of C.*, ch. 22, cited above in ch. 8: "The purely spiritual mission."
2.   In ch. 17: "The resort to false witnesses."
3.   Ch. 6: "The military mission to Ireland" and ch. 9: "Dangers from abroad."
4.   H. B. to Burghley, Aug. 18, 1580, in A.J. Butler (ed.), *Calendar of State Papers, Foreign Series, of the Reign of Elizabeth, 1579–1580* (Mackie and Co., London 1904) p. 389. The word "chief" is changed to "chiefest" by me.
5.   Ibid., p. 389
6.   Ch. 9: "Hopes for a royal Catholic marriage"
7.   Cf. *Calendar of State Papers . . . 1581–1590*, 1582, no. 53, p. 85.
8.   Mathias Tanner S.J., *Societas Jesu usque ad sanguinis et vitae profusionem militans* ("The Society of Jesus, doing battle unto the shedding of blood and life," Charles Ferdinand University Press, Prague 1675) p. 12. Eng. ed., *The Society of Jesus battling even to the outpouring of its life and blood in Europe, Asia, Africa and America* (trans. Joseph W. Riordan S.J., Los Angeles 1935)
9.   Bartoli, vol. 3, bk 3, ch. 2, p. 30, who refers to several letters of Dr. Allen.
10. Letter to Fr. Agazzari, Aug. 8, 1581, *Letters and Memorials of Cardinal Allen*, p. 102; Bartoli, vol. 3, bk 3, ch. 2, p. 31

11. *Letters and Memorials of Cardinal Allen*, p. 102
12. See next paragraph, and ch. 18: "Campion silent on whether the Pope can depose."
13. The meeting is described in a letter of Dr. Allen to Fr. Agazzari, Aug. 8, 1581: *Letters and Memorials of Cardinal Allen*, pp. 101–3, all described briefly on p. 102.
14. More, bk 3, no. 26; Bartoli, vol. 3, bk 3, ch. 2, p. 31
15. At the end of: "A series of arrests."
16. I follow here M. Colthorpe, "Edmund Campion's Alleged Interview with Queen Elizabeth in 1581" *Recusant History*, 1984, pp. 197–200. Westminster Archdiocese, *Cause of the Canonization of Blessed Martyrs* (1968) p. 234, in the biographical conspectus of Campion, mentions this meeting but not the queen's presence. Colthorpe points out, p. 199, that on July 30, i.e., *after* this meeting, they were ordered to ask him if he regarded himself as the queen's subject or not (see below: "The priests racked"). In More, bk 3, no. 26, Campion himself is quoted as saying that, "the queen ... wished to see me." But this is from a Latin version of the English original of the trial, that does not say that.
17. Bombino, ch. 43, pp. 195, 196
18. *Acts of the Privy Council*, vol. 13, p. 144
19. *Acts of the Privy Council*, vol. 13, pp. 144–5. The mention of Rochfort as early as this letter of July 30 shows Simpson was wrong to say the idea to link Campion to the Irish rebellion was a much later idea, conceived after August or September.
20. *Acts of the Privy Council*, vol. 13, p. 145
21. Ch. 14: "Caught"
22. *Acts of the Privy Council*, vol. 13, p. 145\
23. More details on Campion's replies in ch. 17: "Campion on the queen's title."
24. His preface to his *Briefe Historie* (1582: not in Pollen's 1908 ed.) p. 19 (a handwritten page no.); *Apologia Martyrum* (Defense of the Martyrs, 1583) in *Concertatio*, p. 223; *A True, Sincere and Modest Defense of English Catholics* (1584) ch. 1 (1914 ed., vol. 1, p. 26)
25. *Concertatio*, p. 60
26. *Acts of the Privy Council*, vol. 13, pp. 152–4: Aug. 4, 1581
27. *Acts of the Privy Council*, vol. 13, p. 149: Aug. 2, 1581; p. 153: Aug. 4.
28. *Acts of the Privy Council*, vol. 13, p. 152
29. *Acts of the Privy Council*, vol. 13, p. 152, 172
30. *Acts of the Privy Council*, vol. 13, pp. 152, cf. p. 188; vol. 15, p. 21.

31. *Acts of the Privy Council*, vol. 13, p. 153. On Price and Hoghton, see ch. 13: "Campion and Persons continue visitation" and ch. 11: "Campion in Lancashire."

32. S.B., no. 70; same in *Concertatio*, p. 66: S.B., no. 59. Bombino, ch. 43, pp. 202–3, also speaks of this man "Richardson."

33. *Acts of the Privy Council*, vol. 13, p. 153

34. Simpson suggests this is Pounde's great friend, Fr. Thomas Stevens: More, *History Eng. Province*, bk 2, no. 15—but he was sent to India in 1578 and reached Goa in 1579, before Campion came to London.

35. *Acts of the Privy Council*, vol. 13, p. 154

36. *Acts of the Privy Council*, vol. 13, p. 155

37. On Tresham and Catesby, see ch. 11: "Reunion, review and plans at Uxbridge."

38. *Vaux of Harrowden*, p. 117. E. Griffin is named in *Acts of the Privy Council*, vol. 13, pp. 196, 219–20, 249, 260–1; also p. 156 when spelt "Griffith"; and below: "No betrayal of anything unknown"; ch. 20: "Timing of the execution."

39. Mentioned in ch. 13: "Campion and Persons continue visitation." "A Morning at the Star-Chamber" p. 28 refers to an answer of his under questioning.

40. *Acts of the Privy Council*, vol. 13, Penn: pp. 164, 186, 248, 260; East pp. 164, 250, and ch. 13: "Campion and Persons continue visitation," where I say East lived in Bledlowe, Buckinghamshire. He evidently had two residences: *Privy Council*, p. 164, says he is "besides Wickham [in Berkshire]"; p. 250 says "dwelling in the county of Bucks [Buckinghamshire]."

41. Mentioned in ch. 13: "The preparation of *Rationes Decem: Ten Reasons*."

42. See ch 13: "Campion and Persons continue visitation."

43. *Acts of the Privy Council*, vol. 13, p. 164

44. He is named in *Acts of the Privy Council*, vol. 13, p. 164. No Christian name is given. There are a number of Griffins, Griffiths, etc. mentioned in this biography:

    (1) Ambrose, Richard and William Griffen (Griffin, Griffith)—brothers. William lived at Southland, near Uxbridge, and was married to Jane: ch. 10: "The network of Catholic gentry"; ch. 11: "Reunion, review and plans at Uxbridge"; ch. 13: "Campion and Persons continue visitation"; ch. 15: "More questioning and racking."

    (2) Edward Griffin of Dingley and Braybrook: ch. 15: "A series of arrests"; "No betrayal of anything unknown"; ch. 20: "Timing of the execution."

(3) Mr. Griffin of South Mims, Mid dlesex: ch. 15: "A series of arrests" (twice).

45. Among those (north of London) named in letters of August 7, three are not found in Burghley's schedule of Campion's visits: Penn, Beaumont and Worseley. These might be names on unreadable parts of the Ms.

46. *Acts of the Privy Council*, vol. 13, p. 164

47. Barnes is mentioned in ch. 13: "Reunion in London."

48. Anstruther, *Seminary Priests*, p. 34, says he was of the diocese of Lincoln, ordained 1579, sent to England May 2, 1580, but nothing is known of him after this order for his arrest.

49. *Acts of the Privy Council*, vol. 13, p. 164

50. *Acts of the Privy Council*, vol. 13, p. 165: Aug. 7, 1581

51. *Acts of the Privy Council*, vol. 13, pp. 267–8, 285–6, 290

52. *Acts of the Privy Council*, vol. 13, pp. 196, 290; p. 260 names three other men who gave in. The first two above are named in ch. 11: "Campion in Lancashire." E. Griffin is named above: "A series of arrests."

53. Geraint Dyfnallt Owen, ed., *Calendar of the Manuscripts . . . at Longleat, Vol. 5, Talbot, Dudley and Devereux Papers* (Her Majesty's Stationery Office, London 1980) p. 35. This original corrects an inaccurate copy of Burghley's letter used by Simpson.

54. *Acts of the Privy Council*, vol. 13, p. 165: Aug. 7, 1581; cf. p. 177: Aug. 21, 1581.

55. Harleian Mss. 6265, folio 292

56. Lansdowne Mss. 33, no. 8

57. *Acts of the Privy Council*, vol. 13, p. 169

58. John Jacob's fate is told in ch. 14: "Caught."

59. *Acts of the Privy Council*, vol. 13, p. 170

60. Reynolds, p. 83

61. *Annals of the Reformation*, vol. 2, part 2, bk 2, ch. 22 (Anno 1580) pp. 358–9

62. Questier, *Catholicism and Community in Early Modern England*, p. 81. *Calendar of State Papers . . . 1581–1590*, April 6, 1585, no. 11, p. 236, says he was "late in the Tower." There is also a reference to an "examination of Gervase Pierrepoint," May 10, 1600, in M.A.E. Green (ed.), *Calendar of State Papers, Domestic Series, of the Reign of Elizabeth 1598–1601* (Longman, London 1869) p. 434. It seems he was arrested and imprisoned a number of times.

63. Quoted in David Jardine, *A Reading on the Use of Torture in the Criminal Law of England* (Baldwin and Cradock, London 1837) appendix no. 27, pp. 88–9.

64. In ch. 17: "Campion on the queen's title."

65. Schoenbaum, *Shakespeare*, p. 51

66. *Acts of the Privy Council*, vol. 13, p. 156

67. *Vaux of Harrowden*, pp. 133, 138–9. See below, "No betrayal of anything unknown," where Tresham testifies that Edmund "fasted thrice a week with bread and water," etc. Such evidence surely came from hosting Edmund.

68. These eight are named above in this chapter: "A series of arrests."

69. Ch. 44, pp. 204–5

70. Ch. 10: "Meeting at Hoxton"

71. We have no exact dates for the exchange of letters between Pounde and Campion, but we can narrow it down to August 17–20. On August 14, a letter of the Council ordered Pounde's transfer from Wisbeach to the Tower, a distance of nearly 100 miles ("What did Campion reveal?," above). The letter would have arrived on the 16th at the earliest. Hence, by late on the 17th, at the earliest, Pounde arrived at the Tower where he wrote his letter. He was definitely there by the 18th, the date of a letter directing Hammond to go to the Tower to examine Pounde ("What did Campion reveal?"). It was written (and answered) before August 21, the day the Council ordered Campion's second racking (see last section of this chapter, "More questioning and racking"). The letter cannot possibly be after August 31, the day of the first debate, at which Pounde was present to hear Campion say he had betrayed no fellow–Catholic. See ch. 16: "The first debate," where Pounde's presence is mentioned; and this chapter's next section, "No betrayal of anything unknown" for Edmund's declaration to have been steadfast.

72. Harleian Mss. 859, reproduced in Richard Simpson, "A Morning at the Star-Chamber." As mentioned in ch. 11, dates for this trial vary: Nov. 15, 18 or 20 are three dates given. For convenience, I choose Nov. 15.

73. "A Morning at the Star-Chamber" p. 18

74. Bombino, ch. 44, pp. 206–7

75. Dr. Allen, *A Briefe Historie* (ed. Pollen) p. 3; Challoner, *Memoirs of Missionary Priests*, p. 29. The additional explanatory words about the commissioners' oaths are in Laing, reproduced in *Concertatio*, pp. 65–6, but are not in *A True Report of the Death and Martyrdom of M. Campion, Jesuit and priest, and M. Sherwin and M. Bryan, priests, at Tiborne, the 1st of December, 1581* (Richard Verstegan, London 1582. Facsimile reprint: Scolar Press, Menston, U.K. 1970): S.B., no. 46.

76. S.B., nos. 48, 70. It is quoted at length below: "A contemporary defense of Campion's confessions."

77. Details below: "A contemporary defense of Campion's confessions"

78. S.B., no. 36.

79. The whole exchange is on the 2nd and 3rd pages of the 1st day's debate in: *A True Report*, by the Protestant disputants. A part of it is quoted in James V. Holleran, *A Jesuit Challenge: Edmund Campion's Debates at the Tower of London in 1581* (Fordham Uni. Press, N.Y. 1999) p. 39.

80. Quoted in Holleran, *A Jesuit Challenge*, pp. 83–4.

81. "A Morning at the Star-Chamber" p. 18. Edward Griffin is named above: "A series of arrests."

82. Bombino, ch. 44, p. 206

83. Ch. 44, p. 207

84. Ch. 44, p. 209

85. Charke (or possibly Fulke), *A Treatise against the Defense of Censure given upon the books of Wm. Charke and Mer. Hanmer by an unknown Popish traitor* (1586) pp. 6–8: S.B., no. 16.

86. *The Harleian Misellany* (Robert Dutton, London 1808) vol. 1, p. 515; *"The Execution of Justice in England" by William Cecil, and "A True, Sincere, and Modest Defense of English Catholics" by William Allen* (ed. Robert M. Kingdon, Cornell University Press, Ithaca, N.Y. 1965) p. 46. The full sentence may deceive the modern reader: "Campion . . .in the Tower, wherein he was charitably used [treated], was never so racked, but that he was presently able to walk and to write"—meaning: "he was racked, but not so badly that he could not walk or write straight after."

87. *The Harleian Misellany*, vol. 1, p. 517; Kingdon's ed. (1965) p. 49

88. Ch. 11: "Campion in the north, start of 1581"

89. "A Morning at the Star-Chamber" pp. 18, 29

90. "Star-Chamber" pp. 30–1

91. "Star-Chamber" p. 22

92. In Tresham's book "Of Things Contingent": Gerard Kilroy, *Edmund Campion: Memory and Transcription*, pp. 15, 125.

93. Anstruther, *Vaux of Harrowden*, p. 129

94. See the Chronology near the end of this book for the dates of these rackings.

95. *De Persecutione Anglicana epistola* ("A letter on the English persecution," Latin orig. 1581), trans. from *Concertatio*, p. 28. Another trans. in *An epistle of the persecution of catholickes in Englande* (Eng. trans. 1582) pp. 87–9. S.B., no. 54.

96. Simpson had suggested Henry Tuke; he had written, "For instance, all the facts contained in his supposed confession about Lord Vaux, Tresham, and the rest, may easily have been obtained from Henry Tuke . . . servant

to Lord Vaux, who was committed to the Counter in the Poultry, Feb. 23, 1581, and discharged July 8, 1582," citing State Papers Office, Domestic, undated, 1583: "Lists of prisoners for religion"—but Fr. Anstruther says this cannot be, for Tuke was not arrested till Feb. 1582: *Vaux of Harrowden*, p. 133.

97. All three quotations under Dec. 18, 1580, *Acts of the Privy Council*, vol. 12, p. 282.

98. *Acts of the Privy Council*, vol. 12, p. 291: Dec. 21, 1580

99. *Acts of the Privy Council*, vol. 12, p. 325

100. Lansdowne Mss. 30, art. 78

101. Simpson's wording allowed Gervase to be the source, but Anstruther, *Vaux of Harrowden*, p. 133, corrects the suggestion, pointing out that Gervase was not arrested until Aug. 14 and so cannot be the *first* source of the information.

102. *Acts of the Privy Council*, vol. 13, p. 250; italics added.

103. *Calendar of State Papers . . . 1581–1590*, Feb. 24, 1584, no. 25 ii, p. 160

104. Named in ch. 13: "Campion and Persons continue visitation." "Midsummer" means he visited this home during the printing of *Ten Reasons* (5th period of "Campion's apostolate summarised": above).

105. *Vaux of Harrowden*, p. 138

106. *Vaux of Harrowden*, p. 133

107. *Acts of the Privy Council*, vol. 13, p. 184; "by Campion it has been confessed sundry times": p. 185

108. *Acts of the Privy Council*, vol. 13, p. 200; italics added: Sept. 10, 1581; cf. p. 164. See ch 13: "Campion and Persons continue visitation."

109. In: "A series of arrests."

110. Generally the Council does not say he named other guests present in houses he visited, but two other exceptions are in *Acts of the Privy Council*, vol. 13, pp. 164; 170–1.

111. *Acts of the Privy Council*, vol. 13, p. 152; italics added: the two men being Nash and Eden, mentioned above: "A series of arrests."

112. *Acts of the Privy Council*, vol. 13, p. 154; italics added.

113. That of August 1 was about the writings of Sanders, etc., not about his activities.

114. *Acts of the Privy Council*, vol. 13, p. 177: Aug. 21, 1581; italics added. Cf. p. 165: Aug. 7, 1581, for another reference to "his fellows," cited below.

115. *Concertatio*, pp. 65–6

116. *Acts of the Privy Council*, vol. 13, p. 154

117. *Acts of the Privy Council*, vol. 13, p. 172; italics added.

118. The last few paragraphs (from "Moreover, most interestingly . . .") are by me, except for the two by Simpson, starting "Such are some . . ." and "When Campion wrote . . ." The preceding paragraphs denying the authenticity of the confessions are by Simpson, with my modifications and additions. Below, I add Fr. Pollen's differing opinion, plus a section by me: "A contemporary defense of Campion's confessions," with a quotation from *Concertatio* found in Simpson, "Campion's Alleged Confessions" *The Rambler*, Feb. 1858, pp. 100–13, at pp. 101–2, trans. modified and citation enlarged.

119. *The Table Talk of John Selden* (John Russell Smith, London 1856) p. 158, under heading, "Trial."

120. Letter to Puckering, August 30, 1592: Strype, *Annals of the Reformation*, vol. 4, p. 147. Cf. Anstruther, *Seminary Priests*, p. 392.

121. "Blessed Edmund Campion's Confessions" *The Month*, July–December 1919, pp. 258–61

122. Anstruther, however, says only three denied it (Vaux, Tresham, Catesby): *Vaux of Harrowden*, p. 133.

123. Quoted in Holleran, pp. 83–4, from the account by the Catholic, Tresham.

124. *A True Report*, p. 2, by the Protestant disputants; cf. Holleran's introduction, p. 39.

125. A "Catholic" report because of the pro-Catholic comments and quotations at the end of it.

126. "A Morning at the Star-Chamber" p. 18, plus a reference to these letters on p. 29.

127. I must add that Bombino, ch. 57, p. 291, gives it differently: he quotes Campion as saying at the scaffold that in his letter to Pounde, "he had written that whatever had been entrusted to him secretly, he would never declare to any man, whatever the torture." There is no mention of naming names.

128. Simpson's arguments are presented more emphatically and with more detail in his article, "Was Campion a Traitor to his Brethren?" *The Rambler*, November 1857, pp. 322–31, and "Campion's Alleged Confessions" *Rambler*, Feb. 1858, pp. 100–13. See also ch. 19: "Campion's method of defense." Other writers also discuss the evidence for and against: Henry Foley S.J., *Records of the English Province*, vol. 3, pp. 649–52; Evelyn Waugh, *Edmund Campion*, ch. IV: The Martyr, pp. 165–73 (Hollis and Carter, London 1947); Godfrey Anstruther O.P., *Vaux of Harrowden – A Recusant Family*, pp. 133–9; E. E. Reynolds, *Campion and Parsons*, pp. 133–38; James Holleran, *A Jesuit Challenge*, pp. 36–41; Gerard Kilroy,

Edmund Campion: Memory and Transcription, pp. 125–32. The confessions' authenticity is definitively rejected by Foley, p. 649 (following
Simpson); Waugh, pp. 165–73; Anstruther, p. 138; and Kilroy, p. 132.

129. Kilroy, p. 128
130. *Edmund Campion: Memory and Transcription*, p. 132
131. Bombino says the same regarding the naming of Pounde and Richardson:
ch. 43, pp. 202–3. So too Bartoli, vol. 3, bk 3, ch. 2, p. 38. Bartoli says
"Laurence Johnson" was also called "Richardson." It is difficult now to be
certain about the identity and aliases of some of these priests.
132. Bombino above, "Campion's reputation destroyed," gives the same account
of a prominent man who believed, then disbelieved, in the "confessions."
133. *Concertatio*, pp. 57–8. See S.B., nos. 48, 59, 70. The argument is coherent, except that the opening sentence of the long passage quoted is out
of sequence. It seems to refer to the later two, worst rackings, of Oct. 31
and Nov. 2, which were long after the earlier racking and long after the
arrests, early August, of many hosts and helpers of Campion. No friend or
enemy of Campion ever connected the later torture with new information
to betray anyone. See this book's Chronology to review the sequence of
events in these months.
134. *Acts of the Privy Council*, vol. 13, pp. 267–8, says Rooksby, Harrington and
Morris were committed to the Fleet prison after confessing under oath
that Campion had been in their houses. The first two are named in ch.
11: "Campion in Yorkshire," and Morris is below, "More questioning and
racking."
135. E.g., the torture to his nails in ch. 17: "Campion racked a third and fourth
time."
136. Some lines of the 7th stanza of the 3rd poem, "A Dialogue between a
Catholic and Consolation," in Fr. Thomas Alfield, *A True Report of the
Death and Martyrdom of Mr. Campion* (1582): see S.B., no. 46. W.R.
Morfill (ed.), *Ballads from Manuscripts, Vol. II, Part I. . . . Part II. Ballads
Relating Chiefly to the Reign of Queen Elizabeth* (Printed for the Ballad
Society by Stephen Austin and Sons, Hertford 1873) p. 176; also p. 191
with slight variations.
137. *Acts of the Privy Council*, vol. 13, p. 178
138. This one is deemed the second because that of October 31 was named as
the third. See ch. 17: "Campion racked a third and fourth time."
139. *Acts of the Privy Council*, vol. 13, p. 184
140. These people are named in ch. 11: "Campion in Lancashire."
141. *Acts of the Privy Council*, vol. 13, p. 185

142. "A series of arrests"
143. *Acts of the Privy Council*, vol. 13, pp. 267–8
144. *Acts of the Privy Council*, vol. 13, p. 186
145. *Acts of the Privy Council*, vol. 13, p. 186. Penn is named above: "A series of arrests."
146. Mentioned in ch. 11: "Reunion, review and plans at Uxbridge"; ch 13: "Campion and Persons continue visitation."
147. *Acts of the Privy Council*, vol. 13, pp. 186–7
148. Margaret P. Hannay, *Philip's Phoenix: Mary Sidney, Countess of Pembroke* (Oxford University Press, New York 1990) p. 14. We do not know the years of Cecily's birth or death. Her husband Francis was born 1520. If about the same age, she was about 60 when saying this.

Chapter 16—Debates in the Tower

1. Lansdowne Mss. 33, art. 17, dated Fulham, July 25, 1581. Staphilus, a scholar of Luther and Melanchthon at Wittenberg, then Professor of Theology at Königsberg till 1553, when he became a Catholic and was made Councillor of the Empire and of the Duke of Bavaria, and Inspector of the University of Ingolstadt, where he died 1564. The works to which Aylmer alludes are *Epitome Martini Lutheri Theologiae trimem bris* and *Defensio pro trimembri Martino Lutheri Theologia contra aedificatores turris Babylonicae, Phil. Melancthonem, And. Musculum.*
2. Lansdowne Mss. 33, art. 18, Fulham, July 25, 1581
3. 6th page of "A brief recital of certain untruths" by Nowell and Day, at the end of the 1st day's debate in: John Field, *A true report of the Disputation, or rather private Conference, had in the Tower of London with Ed. Campion, Jesuit, the last of August 1581. Set down by the Reverend learned men themselves that dealt therein* [Nowell and Day]. *Whereunto is joined also a true report of the other three days' conferences had there with the same Jesuit. Which now are thought meet to be published in print by authority* (Christopher Barker, London 1583): S.B., no. 36. (The work has no page numbers, so I cite exact pages by referring to the debate or section, and the ordinal page no. within that part cited).
4. Field, *A true report*, 8th page of the report of the 1st day's debate
5. Field, preface "To the reader"
6. James Brodrick S.J., *Robert Bellarmine – Saint and Scholar* (Newman Press, Maryland 1961) p. 76
7. Lansdowne Mss. 33, art. 19: July 27, 1581
8. Lansdowne Mss. 33, art. 24

9.   Cf. *Calendar of State Papers . . . 1581–1590*, Aug. 13, 1583, no. 6, p. 117.

10. Laurence Humphrey, *Jesuitismi pars prima* ("The first part of Jesuitry") 49th, 51st pages (unnumbered) of his Preface to the Earl of Leicester; and pp. 95–6 of main text: S.B., no. 19.

11. *A True Report of the Death and Martyrdom of Mr. Campion, Jesuit and priest* (London 1582): S.B., no. 46.

12. *De Oratore* ("The Orator") book 2, part 14

13. Quintillian (c. 35–95 A.D.), *Institutio Oratoria* ("Education in rhetoric") book 1

14. Reynolds's letter is printed in Keble's *Works of Hooker* (Clarendon, Oxford 1888) vol. 1, p. 106.

15. Ch. 13: a few paragraphs before the section: "Campion and Persons continue visitation."

16. "Immensely learned" is no exaggeration for a man who knew many languages and wrote, among several other works, *Apparatus sacer ad scriptores veteris et novi testamenti* ("Holy apparatus for writers on the Old and New Testament," Venice 1603–06), wherein he records and analyses more than 8,000 books dealing with the Bible.

17. *Bibliotheca selecta de ratione studiorum* ("Select library of a plan of studies," Venice 1603) p. 345. On p. 380, he repeats the judgment it is "a golden book."

18. A copy is in the Har leian Mss. 1732.

19. McCoog in *Reckoned Expense*, p. 135

20. In a printed marginal note on p. 29 of the epistle by "G.T.," preceding his 1582 translation of Robert Persons, *An epistle of the persecution of catholickes in Englande* (Latin orig. 1581). S.B., no. 54.

21. Peter Lake and Michael Questier, "Puritans, Papists, and the 'Public Sphere' in Early Modern England: The Edmund Campion Affair in Context," *Journal of Modern History* 72 (September 2000) pp. 587–627, at p. 622

22. Persons, *An epistle of the persecution*, p. 171 (an unnumbered page in original). The same statement he makes in *Concertatio*, p. 76.

23. James V. Holleran, *A Jesuit Challenge: Edmund Campion's Debates at the Tower of London in 1581* (Fordham Uni. Press, N.Y. 1999) p. 42, says each debate was for three hours, as does Fr. Bartoli, quoted at pp. 200, 204. Fr. Bombino, quoted at pp. 190, 191, said each debate was four hours long. Bartoli, vol. 3, bk 3, ch. 3, p. 43, corrects this in a footnote saying, "not four, as others have written, contrary to the memories of that time, which all expressly say three."

24. Humphrey mentions this, quoted above: "Campion must be refuted": *Jesuitismi pars prima* ("The first part of Jesuitry") p. 95 of main text. His comments there on Whitaker suggest Whitaker was a contender: S.B., no. 19.

25. See ch. 9: "The Thirty-Nine Articles."

26. Field twice quotes a "Hart" (no Christian name) as giving an argument for the Catholic side in the first debate. We presume it is Fr. John Hart, who was in the Tower by Dec. 24, 1580: *Acts of the Privy Council*, vol. 12, p. 294. For more on him, see ch. 19: "Condemnation of the other priests," no. 14 of the list.

27. Holleran, *A Jesuit Challenge*, p. 41, says the manuscripts refer to both a *chapel* (implying the small royal chapel in the Tower, St. John's) and a *parish church* (St. Peter's); but, he says, "The large number of people present, however, suggests that the first debate was held in St. Peter's."

28. Bombino, ch. 46, p. 216

29. Bombino, ch. 46, p. 216

30. The details and full texts of these manuscripts are in James V. Holleran, *A Jesuit Challenge*, named above. See also Simpson's bibliography, section 6, and espec. no. 41 where I note what Holleran contains and excludes. Being accessible in Holleran, not every quotation from the debates will be given an exact reference. As Holleran modernised the text and punctuation, I also alter his spelling and punctuation a little.

31. S.B., nos. 48, 70. That life, or most of it, is printed in *Concertatio*.

32. *Concertatio*, p. 59

33. *Concertatio*, p. 59

34. Bombino, ch. 47, p. 226

35. Translated from Bombino, ch. 47, p. 227 (ch. 46 in Bombino's 1618 ed., given in Holleran, p. 187). Tresham's Ms. and Bartoli's account have the equivalent statement, in different words, quoted in Holleran, pp. 83, 202–3. The equivalent statement is quoted at an earlier date in Dr. Allen's letter to Fr. Agazzari, Aug. 8, 1581: *Letters and Memorials of Cardinal Allen*, p. 102.

36. *Preface to the Epistle of James* (Jena edition, 1529)

37. Holleran, p. 188

38. Field, 1st–2nd pages of "A brief recital of certain untruths" by Nowell and Day, at the end of the 1st day's debate, and partly on the 6th page of that debate.

39. 2nd page of "A brief recital of certain untruths"

40. The four quotes are found, respectively, in: Luther's Preface to the Epistle

of James, 1522; Fragmentary preface to N.T., 1524; Seventh thesis against
Eck, 1519; chapter on Extreme Unction in *Babylonian Captivity*, 1520.
Holleran, pp. 46–7, mistakenly says that in a 1606 English translation
of Whitaker's reply to *Ten Reasons* (S.B., no. 23), in a marginal note on
p. 29, Whitaker (d. 1595) reluctantly admits (after denying it earlier),
that Campion's quotation from Luther (on the Epistle of St. James) was
right. But p. 29's note says, "Whit[aker] p. 22 [of what work is not said]. I
acknowledge that Luther in a most ancient preface published by himself at
Wittenberg 1525 called it a strawen Epistle in comparison of the Epistles of
Saint Peter and Saint Paul." In other words, Whitaker still denied Luther
said the Epistle was strawen absolutely, without comparison—whereas
Luther had done so in the Jena edition of 1529, of which Whitaker seemingly remained ignorant, even after Fr. Dury (1582) had pointed the fact
out, as the marginal note on the same p. 29 mentions. However, Bombino,
ch. 47, p. 231, says Whitaker later openly admitted these statements were
in Luther's original works.

41.   Holleran, p. 204. Bartoli goes further and mistakenly says the Protestants
      cancelled their error from their printed account of the debate.

42.   Cf. Holleran, p. 87.

43.   Cf. Holleran, p. 207; same exchange recorded also on pp. 90, 195.

44.   Bombino, ch. 48, p. 332. Tresham's Ms. says, "In the afternoon greater
      recourse was made unto the place": Holleran, p. 87.

45.   Holleran, p. 90

46.   5th page of "A brief recital of certain untruths"

47.   Nowell and Day's preface "To the reader" in Field

48.   Nowell and Day, preface "To the reader"

49.   *The Lives of Philip Howard, Earl of Arundel and Ann Dacres, his Wife*, ed.
      by the Duke of Norfolk (1857) p. 19. Reprint: *The Life of Philip Howard*
      (Treacy Centre, Parkville, Australia 1998)

50.   Quoted more fully below, this section.

51.   From part 1 of his poem *Hudibras* (1660), a satire of Puritanism

52.   T. Fuller (1662), *The Worthies of England* (ed. 1840) p. 264, and *Church
      History*, vol. 9, p. 216

53.   A phrase from *A Form of Prayer with Thanksgiving* for the deliverance
      from the 1605 Gunpowder Plot, added to the Anglican *Book of Common
      Prayer* in 1606 and removed in 1859.

54.   Last page, the 9th, of "A brief recital of certain untruths"

55.   Nowell and Day's preface "To the reader"

56.   On the 4th page of "A brief recital of certain untruths," Nowell and Day

quote at length a Catholic pamphlet vindicating Campion's ability to read and translate Greek. Apart from a few words, the quotation is identical to Tresham's account in Holleran, pp. 90–1, from "It happened in process" to "another time for him to speak." On the 7th page is another almost identical quotation from Tresham, in Holleran, p. 90, from "Unto this was added" to "doctrine of good works." In his otherwise magnificent introduction and commentary, Holleran, pp. 51–2, 223–4, seems not to notice that Tresham's Ms. account was mentioned among Catholic "Pamphleteers" and quoted twice in Field's *True report* on Jan. 1, 1583—citations which supply a few words missing from Tresham's torn Ms.

57. *Briefe Historie* (ed. Pollen) p. 15. Spelling and punctuation changed; a superfluous "that" removed.

58. This background is in Holleran's introduction, p. 51.

59. Holleran, p. 95

60. Field, 2nd page of the 2nd day's debate

61. Bartoli, vol. 3, bk 3, ch. 4, p. 72

62. McCoog says the first three were in the chapel of St. Peter ad Vincula, and only the last in the Lieutenant's house: *Reckoned Expense*, p. 135. The text above follows Holleran, pp. 41, 43, who says, as Simpson did, that only the first was in St. Peter's. From the surviving accounts, it is difficult to know the sites for sure. Bombino, ch. 49, p. 239, says the second debate was held in Hopton's home.

63. Bartoli, vol. 3, bk 3, ch. 4, p. 59. Bombino, ch. 49, p. 240, says the listeners "did not reach thirty heads" and that Campion had no other Catholic prisoner with him. Strangely, p. 240, he gives October 14 as the date of this debate.

64. One Ms. specifically names these five noble spectators, "besides others" (Holleran, p. 94), without giving a total of attendants. Simpson says "only about thirteen persons were present." I think he got that number by guessing there were five or so others (plus Campion and the two notaries) along with the five named.

65. Mentioned in ch. 1: "First schooling."

66. Field, 1st–2nd pages of the 2nd day's debate

67. Holleran, p. 96

68. As Holleran, p. 95, notes, this means an official account of the 1st debate "was first circulated and later republished in *A true report*." I am not aware of any surviving manuscripts or pamphlets from before 1584, but it is interesting to see how well-informed Campion was.

69. Bombino, ch. 49, p. 240. Campion says the same in Holleran, pp. 95–6.

70.   Holleran, p. 96

71.   Holleran, p. 103

72.   Bartoli, vol. 3, bk 3, ch. 4, p. 64. Holleran, p. 105.

73.   Holleran, pp. 110-1. Bombino, ch. 50, pp. 246-8, records the same exchange in much the same words.

74.   Holleran, p. 113

75.   Holleran, p. 120

76.   Holleran, p. 116

77.   Holleran, pp. 119, 120

78.   Preface to the 2nd day's debate

79.   *Tracts for the Times* – Tract 90 (1841)

80.   13–14th pages of the 3rd day's debate

81.   Holleran, pp. 130-1

82.   Holleran, pp. 131-2

83.   Holleran, p. 72

84.   In this fourth debate: Holleran, p. 146

85.   Holleran, pp. 144-5

86.   Holleran, p. 144

87.   2nd page of the 4th day's debate

88.   Holleran, p. 158

89.   Holleran, p. 154

90.   20th–21st pages of the 4th day's debate (ignoring duplicate pages)

91.   22nd–23rd pages of the 4th day's debate (ignoring duplicate pages)

92.   Holleran, pp. 152-3

93.   Holleran, p. 159

94.   Summarized by Holleran, p. 77

95.   *Romans* 3:20, 3:28; 3:21; 4:6; 4:13; 9:11; 11:6; *Galatians* 2:16; *Ephesians* 2:8-9; *2 Timothy* 1:9; and *Titus* 3:5

96.   Holleran, pp. 160-1

97.   Persons, *A Defense of the Censure* (Rouen 1582) p. 5

98.   *Defense of the Censure*, p. 8. Cf. Holleran, p. 168.

99.   *Defense of the Censure*, p. 8

100.   This paragraph is paraphrased from *A Defense of the Censure*, p. 9.

101.   *Defense of the Censure*, p. 9

102.   Lansdowne Mss. 33, art. 24

103.   Thomas Wright ed., *Queen Elizabeth and her Times—A Series of Original Letters* (Henry Colburn, London 1838) vol. 2, p. 155

104.   Field, 2nd page of the 3rd day's debate

105.   Lansdowne Mss. 33, art. 61

106. *Calendar of State Papers . . . 1581–90*, Nov. 1581, no. 72, p. 31. E.B., no. 2. Nos. I–III following are in W.R. Morfill (ed.), *Ballads from Manuscripts*, pp. 164–5. E.B., no. 21.

107. Stanza 8. Full poem at end of this book: "St. Henry Walpole's elegy on Campion." Also reproduced in Allen (ed. Pollen, 1908) pp. 26–31: S.B., no. 52a.

108. Nothing survives printed by Catholics on the debates back then, save in Nowell and Day's rebuttal of passages cited by them, Persons's comments in *A Defense of the Censure*, and the materials used by Bombino and Bartoli.

109. "To the reader" in Field. I changed the original wording, "the onely hearing" to, "just the hearing."

110. Lake and Questier, "Puritans, Papists, and . . . The Edmund Campion Affair in Context" p. 622: E.B., no. 84. Field's *True report of the Disputation* is dated on the front page, Jan. 1, 1583, but that is the first day of the new year 1584 by modern reckoning (when March 25th ceased being its start). From the end of Sept. 1581 (last of the 4 debates) to Jan. 1584 is 2 years, 3 months.

111. 1st page of "A brief recital of certain untruths"

112. John Strype, *Historical collections of the life and acts of the Right Reverend Father in God, John Aylmer, Lord Bishop of London in the reign of Queen Elizabeth* (W. Bowyer, London 1701. New ed. Clarendon Press, Oxford 1821) ch. 3, p. 36

113. Strype, *Historical collections of . . . John Aylmer*, addition no. 2, p. 200. Lansdowne Mss. 33, art. 63: Dec. 28, 1581

114. Lansdowne Mss; Strype, *Aylmer*, p. 200

115. *Calendar of State Papers . . . Addenda, 1580–1625*, no. 93, p. 63. E.B., no. 3

116. *Calendar of State Papers . . . 1581–1590*, no. 2, p. 123; cf. Aug. 27, 1584, no. 111, p. 198. E.B., no. 2. Named in Bellenger, pp. 72, 232: E.B., no. 40.

117. Persons said *three* debates here by mistake; earlier he had mentioned four debates in a letter to the General on Oct. 21: C.R.S., vol. 39, pp. 95, 107. 118 C.R.S., vol. 39, pp. 118–9, 119

Chapter 17—Preparations for the Trial

1. J. Nichols, *A declaration of the recantation of John Nichols* (1581). See ch. 12: "The sad figure of John Nichols."

2. In his short piece, *Of the State of Europe*, in *The Works of Francis Bacon* (Parry and McMillan, Philadelphia 1859) p. 388

3. Lansdowne Library: vol. 33, no. 60, folios 145–9

4.   *Calendar of State Papers . . . 1581–1590*, July 14, 1581, no. 69, p. 23

5.   Fuller, *Church History* (Oxford 1845) vol. 4, p. 459

6.   State Papers Office, France, August 9, 1581

7.   Camden's *Annals*, at A.D. 1581

8.   See ch. 9: "Hopes for a royal Catholic marriage."

9.   A. J. Butler (ed.), *Calendar of State Papers, Foreign Series, of the Reign of Elizabeth, January 1581–April 1582* (Mackie and Co., London 1907), Aug. 11, 1581, no. 294, p. 289

10.   See S.B., no. 51.

11.   *Acts of the Privy Council*, vol. 13, p. 145. See ch. 15: "The priests racked."

12.   Quoted in ch. 18: "Campion silent on whether the Pope can depose."

13.   Ch 6: "Faculties from the Pope"

14.   Baldwin to Shrewsbury, Dec. 22, 1580; Edmund Lodge, *Illustrations of British History* (1791) p. 185

15.   S.B., no. 70. Cf. *Concertatio*, pp. 57, 60, for the relevant passages.

16.   *Concertatio*, p. 60

17.   *Apologia Martyrum* ("Defense of the Martyrs" 1583) in *Concertatio*, p. 223.

18.   Camden's *Annals*, at A.D. 1581: "Plerosque tamen ex misellis his sacerdotibus exitii in patriam conflandi conscios fuisse non credidit."

19.   *Calendar of State Papers . . . January 1581–April 1582*, Aug. 20, 1581, no. 311, pp. 298–9

20.   *Calendar of State Papers . . . January 1581–April 1582*, Sept. 19, 1581, no. 341, pp. 318–9

21.   Ellis, *Original Letters*, 3rd series, vol. 4, p. 36

22.   *Acts of the Privy Council*, vol. 13, p. 249

23.   "Edmundus Campianus tertio equuleo torquetur post disputationes, hocque omnium gravissime." *A Tudor Journal: The Diary of a Priest in the Tower, 1580–1585*: entry at Oct. 31, 1581. The second occasion was, we presume, at the "re-examining of Campion upon certain points" ordered in a letter of Aug. 21 of the Council: *Acts of the Privy Council*, vol. 13, p. 178; see ch. 15: "More questioning and racking."

24.   *A Tudor Journal*: entry at Oct. 31.

25.   Allen, *A Briefe Historie of the Glorious Martyrdom of Twelve Reverend Priests, Father Edmund Campion and his Companions* (ed. Pollen) p. 13: S.B., no. 52a. Bishop Challoner (1741), *Memoirs of Missionary Priests* (ed. 1924) p. 23. Cf. Bombino, ch. 44, p. 208.

26.   *A Briefe Historie* (ed. Pollen) p. 13

27.   C.R.S., vol. 39, pp. 118, 119. Bartoli, vol. 3, bk 3, ch. 5, pp. 77–8, relates

the hymn's being sung and also says the rack was used on both days, as Persons says.

28. Foley, *Records of the English Province*, vol. 3, p. 41, quoting the Annual Letters of 1580–81. This fits in with Fr. Rishton's continuation of Sanders's *De Schismate Anglicano* ("On the Anglican Schism"): he says Campion "was subject to interrogation three or four times to the dislocation of all his members" ("Quaestioni ter aut quarter ad luxationem omnium membrorum subjicitur."), in book 3, Elizabeth (Wolfgang Eder, Ingolstadt 1587) p. 345. The number "three or four" is not in earlier editions of the work, where no number is given.

29. Dr. Allen, *A Briefe Historie*, p. 14; Allen, *A true, sincere and modest defense of English Catholics*, ch. 1 (1914 ed., vol. 1, p. 27); *Concertatio*, p. 58. Cf. Bartoli, vol. 3, bk 3, ch. 5, p. 78.

30. *A Briefe Historie* (ed. Pollen) p. 17. Challoner, *Memoirs of Missionary Priests*, p. 25

31. Bombino, ch. 45, pp. 211–2. Cf. Allen's *Briefe Historie* (ed. Pollen) p. 14.

32. Bodleian Library, Oxford: Rawlinson Mss., D. 320, folio 1

33. Ch. 47, p. 224; quoted, varying trans., in Holleran, p. 186.

34. See ch. 15: "What did Campion reveal?" See this book's Chronology where the rackings are listed in order.

35. Public Record Office, Rome transcripts, 31/9, no. 78, Sept. 30

36. Calendar of Spanish State Papers, vol. 3, p. 153; cf. p. 231.

37. *Concertatio*, p. 77; Pedro Serrano, secretary to Spanish Ambassador, Bernardino de Mendoza, in a letter written in London, Dec. 4, 1581, says, "they had torn off his nails": John Morris S.J., "A new Witness about Blessed Edmund Campion" p. 459. This letter's statement about the nails' torture is cited in Bartoli, vol. 3, bk 3, ch. 5, p. 79.

38. *An epistle of the persecution of catholickes in Englande* (Eng. trans. 1582), p. 183 (unnumbered page in original). S.B., no. 54. Persons says the same in *Concertatio*, p. 78.

39. See next note.

40. Laurence Humphrey, *pars prima* ("The first part of Jesuitry" 1582) 23rd page (unnumbered) of the preface

41. More, *History Eng. Province*, bk 3, no. 38. Cf. Bartoli, vol. 3, bk 3, ch. 3, p. 54.

42. Henry Hallam, *The Constitutional History of England from the Accession of Henry VII to the Death of George II* (John Murray, London 1827) vol. 1, p. 161. See S.B., no. 61. Some now attribute *A Declaration of the favorable dealing of her Majesty's Commis sioners* to Norton: Michael A.R. Graves,

Thomas Norton: The Parliament Man (Oxford 1994) pp. 276–8.

43. Pollen, *English Catholics*, pp. 344–5, says there is a case that even the Babington plot to kill the queen was all an entrapment initiated by Walsingham.

44. Thomas Babington Macaulay, *Nares's Memoirs of Lord Burghley* (Edinburgh Review 1832) in *Essays Critical and Miscellaneous* (Phillips, Sampson, and Co., Boston 1858) p. 172

45. Pollen, *English Catholics*, pp. 24–5

46. John Strype, *The Life and Acts of John Whitgift D.D.* (Oxford 1822) vol. 1, p. 402   .

Chapter 18—The Trial

1. Lansdowne Mss. 33, no. 64

2. Lansdowne Mss. 33, no. 65. This was not a mere rough draft, but a copy kept as a record, as shown by the note to Collyton's name: "quited" (acquitted)- which must have been added after the trial. See ch. 19: "Condemnation of the other priests." I have broken the text into paragraphs, to help the reader follow the prolix sentences. The full and final Latin original is given in Archdiocese of Westminster, *Cause of the Canonization of Blessed Martyrs*, pp. 293–8, taken from King's Bench 27/1279, Crown side, rota [roll] 2, kept in the Public Record Office, London. The King's (Queen's) Bench at Westminster, London, was the highest court of common law in England. "Crown side" was the side for criminal cases "Coram Rege" ("before the King," as opposed to the "Plea side" for private plaintiffs), including those removed from lower courts. The translation in the text above is from the Lansdowne Ms., which differs only by being less wordy than the final indictment in King's Bench, and having three fewer names of defendants, mentioned soon in the text above.

3. *Edmund Campion*, ch. IV

4. Reynolds, pp. 66–7, 151. See ch. 8: "Fr. Cottam."

5. Ely and Osclyffe are not named in the summary of the trials in King's Bench 27/1279, Crown side, rolls 2 and 3: Archdiocese of Westminster, *Cause of the Canonization*, pp. 297–8. But Fr. Anstruther, *Seminary Priests*, p. 262, says Fr. "George Ostcliff," ordained 1579, was sent to England in Jan. 1580, was imprisoned by August, tried and condemned with Campion but not executed, spent five years in prison and was exiled June 1586. He is mentioned as a prisoner in *Acts of the Privy Council*, vol. 13, p. 184: Aug. 22, 1581.

6. *Campion and Parsons*, p. 164

7. T. B. Howell (compiler), *A Complete Collection of State Trials and Proceedings for High Treason and Other Crimes and Misdemeanors from the Earliest Period to the Year 1783* (21 vols, London 1816–1828). The record of Campion's trial is in vol. 1 (Hansard, London 1816) columns 1049–72. (Some books say col. 1049–84, but 1073–84 are not part of the trial but a separate work attacking Campion and others as traitors, and giving their answers to interrogations about the queen's authority and the Bull of Pius V, and so on). See S.B., nos. 42, 51. The trial record manuscript is no. 1014 of the Cotton Library (Bib. Cott. 1014) collected by Sir Robert Bruce Cotton (1571–1631), and housed in the British Museum, London, since 1753. It was printed first, it seems, by Joseph Morgan, *Phoenix Britannicus* [British Phoenix], *being a miscellaneous Collection of scarce and curious Tracts . . . interspersed with choice pieces from original MSS* (printed for the compiler and T. Edlin. J. Wilford, London 1732): first published as a periodical, six numbers appearing at irregular intervals from January 1731 to March 1732; then collected in one volume.

Simpson reproduces another record of the trial: British Library, Lansdowne Mss. 33, no. 65. I have retained that text but blended in more suitable words from Howell. There are only small differences between the two records. Howell's text (Cotton Ms.) has some minor mistakes, e.g., a reference to the "cardinal of Sicily" (col. 1057), which should read "cardinal of St. Cecilia." But at other points the Lansdowne text can be improved by following the Cotton text. Most difficulties in each one can be overcome by consulting the other. Overall, the Lansdowne Ms. is superior, has fewer obvious mistakes, and has as well a few lines not in the other.

8. In ch. 19: "Campion's impression upon the observers"

9. Westminster Archdiocese, *Cause of the Canonization*, p. 292

10. Simpson and Reynolds say Nov. 15. Westminster Archdiocese, *Cause of the Canonization*, pp. 235, 292, says this second group was indicted "two days later, on November 16, 1581," as seen in the King's Bench 27/1279, Crown side, roll 3.

11. *Cause of the Canonization*, p. 292

12. Markham (died 1479) was the just judge who tried the London merchant accused of treason for saying that he would make his son heir to the crown. Edward IV wanted the merchant's money, and the judge was overruled for directing an acquittal in 1469.

13. Challoner, *Memoirs of Missionary Priests*, p. 26, which he adapted from Allen's *Briefe Historie* (ed. Pollen) pp. 18–9.

14. *The Constitutional History of England* (1827) vol. 1, pp. 156–7

15. Dr. Allen, *Briefe Historie* (ed. Pollen) p. 18 (adapted in Challoner, *Missionary Priests*, p. 25). *Concertatio*, p. 62, says the same. Bombino, ch. 58, p. 301, says two jurymen.

16. Harleian Mss. 6998, folio 182

17. Letter of Feb. 7, 1582 in *Letters and Memorials of Cardinal Allen*, p. 112

18. In John Nichols's recantation, written to Dr. Allen: *Concertatio*, p. 233

19. *John Gerard—The Autobiography of an Elizabethan*, p. 66, note

20. In 1569, he refused to subscribe to the Protestant Divine Service, and was in trouble again for matters of religion in Dec. 1580: *Calendar of State Papers . . . 1547–1580*, nos. 47, p. 355; nos. 45–6, p. 689. E.B., no. 1.

21. We have already quoted from the trial record above, in the section, "Arraignment at Westminster Hall"—but hereon to the end of the chapter is all straight quotation from the same record [except for my additions in square brackets]. The following chapter quotes the original record also at "The verdict: guilty" and "Campion's final oration."

22. 2 Cor. 5:20. The Ms. had "Peter" instead of "Paul." The error is probably the notary's.

23. *Holinshed's Chronicles* at A.D. 1581 (1587 ed.) p. 1323. The wording is slightly different in *A Discovery of Edmund Campion and his Confederates, their most horrible and traitorous practices against her Majesty's most royal person and the realm. Wherein may be seen, how through the whole course of their arraignment they were notably convicted of every cause. Whereto is added the execution of Edmund Campion, Ralph Sherwin, and Alexander Briant, executed at Tyburn the 1. of December. Published by A. M.* [Anthony Munday] *sometime the Pope's scholar, allowed in the seminary at Rome amongst them: a discourse needful to be read of every man, to beware how they deal with such secret seducers* (John Charlewood, London 1582). S.B., no. 45.

24. Richard Bristow authored the apologetical work, *Motives Inducing to the Catholic faith*, first published in 1574. See ch. 3: "Campion at the English seminary of Douay."

25. For Paschal, see ch. 12: "Fr. Ralph Sherwin captured." For Nichols, see ch. 12: "The sad figure of John Nichols."

26. In Howell (col. 1056): "J. Caddy, or Cradocke."

27. Athenian soldier and statesman (d. 459 B.C.) who, according to one account, took poison to escape having to attack his country while in the service of the Persian king.

28. S.B., no. 70. Same in *Concertatio*, p. 62: S.B., no. 59.

29. Both Mss. say "it is like." Perhaps Campion is speaking in irony. To make

the meaning clearer, I made it a question. Campion is expressing how "unlikely" it is that priests would fight a military battle when a military captain refuses to.

30. From Sanders to Allen, rather. See ch. 6: "The military mission to Ireland."
31. This letter is quoted in ch 5: "Seven letters of Campion," before the 7th letter.
32. Reynolds, pp. 177, 197. Pollen, *The English Catholics*, p. 233–43.
33. As Reynolds comments, p. 197, "This explanation of Paul/Saul is not now accepted."
34. Howell here has "a great blacking strap."
35. Both Mss have "pray for absolution," which is not Catholic terminology, so I substitute what they probably misheard: "proffer absolution"—a phrase sometimes used in the past when transliterating the equivalent phrase in Latin.
36. See ch. 11: "Shakespeare."
37. See *Imago primi saeculi Societatis Jesu* ("An image of the first century of the Society of Jesus") by Jacobus Wallius S.J. (Balthasar Moretus, Antwerp 1640) p. 341, where many other examples of the Protestant protest against the determination of religious questions by logic are given.
38. Howell has "Hamon."
39. See ch. 15: "Campion's secret meeting with Privy Councillors" and "Did Edmund meet with Elizabeth?"
40. I changed the Latin forms from the Accusative to Nominative case. The meaning is the same.
41. Allen, *Apologia Martyrum* ("Defense of the Martyrs") in *Concertatio*, p. 220
42. His recollections of Campion's trial and martyrdom in J.H Pollen, *Acts of English Martyrs hitherto unpublished*, p. 46.
43. The manuscript has "D'Espigneta," but there is no such writer. Reynolds, p. 198, says that "Another record of the trial" gives "Dr. Navarre," so certainly Martin Azpilcueta is meant, a Spanish theologian at the university of Navarre, who became known as "Navarrus." The book title mentioned in the trial is unknown; it may have been his *Manuale confessariorum et poenitentium* ("Manual for confessors and penitents"). Below, in the record, the wrong name was used again; I correct it there also.
44. See ch. 14: "George 'Judas' Eliot."
45. The two Mss. say "poggets, daggs": text amended as suggested by Reynolds, p. 198.
46. Munday's account of the trial reports this same mad accusation of Eliot: *A Discovery of Edmund Campion and his Confederates*, S.B., no. 45. A paper

signed by "G.E." (George Eliot) says the same thing, among Burghley's papers: Lansdowne Mss. 33, no. 60.

47. Here and hereon a few times both Mss. say "Bristow" (the writer mentioned in the trial a few times already) but Reynolds points out (*Campion and Parsons*, p. 198) that they should read "Rishton," the only one not questioned hitherto. Bristow was never arrested or questioned; Rishton *is* named in the indictment. The similarity between the names may have led to the confusion. Reynolds's helpful amendment enables us to overcome Anstruther's difficulty (*Seminary Priests*, pp. 52–3) regarding the fate of Bristow. However, at another point, Anstruther, p. 51, took this "Bristow" to be "Briscow"; so too does Malcolm H. South, *The Jesuits and the Joint Mission to England During 1580–1581* (E. Mellen Press, N.Y. 1999) pp. 105, 154—but that is impossible, for Thomas Briscow/Briscoe (one of our missionaries, ch. 7: "The band of fourteen departs from Rome") was not named in the indictment.

48. In Howell, col. 1068, he is called "Sleidon."

49. This incident is unknown.

50. This is a rare word, not found in dictionaries, even of obsolete words. "Impealed" with reference to legislation means repealed. I have guessed the meaning, probably equivalent to "appealed against," "challenged" or even "impugned."

Chapter 19—The Witnesses and the Verdict

1. C.R.S., vol. 2, p. 134; vol. 4, p. 9; vol. 39, pp. 115–7. Cf. *Reckoned Expense*, p. 292.

2. *Calendar of State Papers . . . 1581–1590*, Jan. 1581, nos. 38–41, p. 4: information of Robert Barret

3. State Papers Office, Spain, January 22, 1582: Mendoza to Yaxley

4. Harleian Mss. 6992 and 6993

5. In *Concertatio* (S.B., no. 59): Nichols at pp. 231–4; Caddy at pp. 235–8

6. In the main text of *A True Report*, after the account of the execution: S.B., no. 46.

7. Munday's book about, among other things, the English College in Rome: *The English Roman life. Discovering* [exposing] *the lives of the Englishmen at Rome, the orders of the English Seminary . . . and a number of other matters . . . Thereunto is added the cruel tyranny used on an English man* [Richard Atkins] *at Rome. Written by A.M., sometime the Pope's scholar in the seminary among them* (John Charlewoode, London 1582. Rev. ed. 1590). Facsimile reprint: *The English Romayne Lyfe 1582* (E. P. Dutton

and Co., New York 1925). Other editions: 1966, 1972, 1980. Southern, p. 282, says it appears that Munday did enter the Roman seminary but under another name. Persons's *L. of C.*, ch. 15, says Munday was only 17 or 18 when he arrived in Rome and went to the English College initially as a poor pilgrim.

8.   From "A caveat to the reader touching A. M.'s *Discovery*" (A. Munday's *Discovery of Edmund Campion*), just before the verses at the end of *A True Report* (S.B., no. 46). Simpson attributes the caveat to Pounde, possibly because Pounde, a former performer, refers favorably to stageplayers, and perhaps also because he always called the Anglican bishops "superintendents" (a term they used themselves for a while). But Southern, p. 280, thinks the author not Pounde, but possibly Vallenger, and points out, p. 378, that Pounde's imprisonment in the Tower from Aug. 1581 makes it most unlikely he was connected with the book.

9.   Named in S.B., nos. 29, 45, 50.

10.   Rosenberg, *Leicester, Patron of Letters*, p. 90

11.   Henry Hallam, *The Constitutional History of England* (1827) vol. 1, p. 157. Hallam is also quoted in ch. 17: "Other tortures" and ch. 18: "The trial commences."

12.   G. B. Harrison's introduction, p. viii, to Munday, *The English Romayne Lyfe 1582* (New York 1925).

13.   From "A caveat to the reader" in *A True Report*. Munday and Eliot's booklets are in S.B., nos. 29 and 30.

14.   Topcliffe to Puckering, Sept. 20, 1592: Harleian Mss. 6998, folio 31; and PHS to Walsingham, State Papers Office, Domestic, 1590, undated papers, 138A. Morfill (ed.), *Ballads from Manuscripts*, vol. II, p. 159, asks if PHS means (Thomas) "Phellippes" (1556–1625) who cracked codes for Elizabeth's spymaster Walsingham.

15.   Dr. Allen, in his preface to his *Briefe Historie* of 1582 (not included in Pollen's 1908 ed.) p. 17, a handwritten page no.

16.   In ch. 8: "Danger in London"

17.   Dr. Allen's preface to his *Briefe Historie*, p. 12

18.   C.R.S., vol. 4, p. 9; vol. 39, pp. 68, 69

19.   Ch. 14: "George 'Judas' Eliot"; "Eliot at large"

20.   Dr. Allen's preface to his *Briefe Historie*, p. 12

21.   As summarized by Reynolds, pp. 195–6.

22.   Ch. 18: "Campion demonstrates their crime is religion."

23.   Latin ed. (1625) p. 377, anno 27, A.D. 1584–5; 1635 ed., p. 261

24.   Letter to Fr. Agazzari, Dec. 23, 1581, in More, *History Eng. Province*, bk 3, no. 35

25. Fr. Persons in a letter to Fr. Agazzari, Dec. 23, 1581, quoted in More, bk 3, no. 36. Others give a longer period. As said in ch. 18, it is possible the transcripts we have omit some parts.

26. Not wanting to share in a blatant injustice, three did not appear on the day: ch. 18: "The jury."

27. Vol. 3, bk 3, ch. 6, p. 111. Dr. Allen relates the same in a letter: C.R.S., vol. 9 (1911) p. 101. W. van Nieuwenhoff S.J., *Edmond Campion*, ch. 12, says his name was Dominic Roper—a name I cannot find among Roper's relations. The section's title is inspired by Matthew 10:42.

28. Ayloff is also spelt Alliffe, Alephe. Quoted, with spelling modernised, from Edward Foss, *The Judges of England* (vol. 5. Longman, London 1857. Reprint: Kessinger, U.S.A. 2006) p. 446. Foss attributes the account (while spurning it) to *An Epistle of Comfort to the Reverend Priests*—which first appeared anonymously in Paris, undated, now known to be the work of English Jesuit Saint and martyr, Robert Southwell (1561–95), finished late 1587: Robert Southwell, S.J., *An Epistle of Comfort to the Reverend Priests, and to the Honourable, Worshipful, and Other of the Lay Sort, Restrained in Durance for the Catholic Faith* (Burns and Oates, London 1966. Margaret Waugh, ed., foreword by Philip Caraman S.J.) p. 234. Simpson had attributed the book to Fr. Persons, as did Anstruther and others. M. Waugh's intro., pp. x–xi, settles its authorship and date. The editor's note on p. 234 says Southwell, in relating the blood on the judge, "is here quoting verbatim from a contemporary account." The story is not in all versions of the *Epistle*. See also the very end of ch. 20 below and its last endnote. Bombino, p. 318, in his final chapter, ch. 60: "Prodigies by which God adorned both the life and death of Campion," relates the story as well-known in England. The story is told in the briefest terms and said to be "constantly reported and very famous" in Thomas Fitzherbert S.J.'s recollections of Campion: Pollen, *Acts of English Martyrs hitherto unpublished*, p. 39. Bartoli relates it also: vol. 3, bk 3, ch. 6, p. 115; also Bishop Diego de Yepes, *Historia particular de la persecucion de Inglaterra* ("A particular history of the persecution in England," 1599) p. 91 (bk 2, ch. 11, no. 28): S.B., no. 77.

29. Challoner, *Missionary Priests*, pp. 26–7, adapted from Allen's *Briefe Historie* (ed. Pollen) p. 19.

30. Laing, *Historia de Morte Rev. P. Edm. Campiani Sac. de Soc. Jesu, et aliorum qui in Anglia propter fidem Catholicam Apostolicam atque Roma nam crudelissimam passi sunt mortem* ("An account of the death which Rev. Fr. Edmund Campion, priest of the Society Jesus, and others who suffered a most cruel death in England for the Catholic, Apostolic and Roman faith")

Paris 1585: S.B., no. 70. The passage from Laing is in *Concertatio*, p. 63. Bombino has the same words in ch. 58, p. 301.

31. Stanzas 9 and 16. Full poem at end of this book, and in Allen's *Briefe Historie* (ed. Pollen) pp. 26–31: S.B., no. 52a.

32. Harleian Mss. 6998, folio 182: Ruth Hughey (ed.), *The Arundel Harington Manuscript of Tudor Poetry* (Ohio State University Press, Columbus, Ohio 1960) vol. 2, p. 174

33. *Acts of English Martyrs hitherto unpublished*, pp. 38–39. Editor Fr. Pollen S.J. suggests that Fr. Fitzherbert S.J. wrote his recollections shortly before 1618 for Fr. Bombino S.J. who uses them in his life of Campion published in 1618.

34. Walpole went to serve as a priest in England in 1593, so we presume he wrote his recollections before then.

35. Eleven hours—in contrast to Fr. Persons's "about three hours" (at the start of "A foregone conclusion" above, this chapter). One might estimate a length of 3 hours simply from the written record, but it is possible some portions were not recorded, because not heard clearly. For example, Walpole's recollections enlarge upon the little exchange between Campion and Eliot recorded at ch. 18: "England's religious state lamented" (inserted there), and Walpole himself says: "I could not hear all, because of the noise.": Pollen, *Acts of English Martyrs hitherto unpublished*, p. 45. Munday's *Discovery of Edmund Campion and his Confederates*, relates that a (Catholic) tract was read out in court, on how to convert different classes of people—but that is missing from our trial record.

36. Walpole in Pollen, *Acts*, pp. 41–4.

37. Howell's *State Trials*, vol. 1, col. 1072, gives this speech only up to the words, "as ever the Queen had." The style and eloquence are undoubtedly Campion's.

38. Translated from *Concertatio*, p. 63. Similar wording in Bartoli, vol. 3, bk 3, ch. 6, pp. 117–8. Same ideas in More, bk 3, no. 28, and some of the ideas in Bombino, ch. 53, p. 275. Luis de Granada O.P. has the same as the text above: *Introduction del symbolo de la fe* ("Introduction to the creed," Salamanca 1583) part 5, ch. 23. The trial record does not have this little speech.

39. Westminster Archdiocese, *Cause of the Canonization*, p. 292. Simpson had Nov. 22.

40. Howell does not give the record of this group's trial, but a summary record is in King's Bench 27/1279, Crown Side, roll 3: original Latin in Westminster Archdiocese, *Cause of the Canonization*, pp. 298–300.

41. Alexis Possoz S.J., *Le Premier Jésuite Anglais Martyrisé en Angleterre, ou Vie et Mort du Père Edmond Campian* ("The first English Jesuit martyred in England, or the life and death of Fr. E. Campion," Charles Douniol, Paris 1864) p. 273 gives his Christian name.

42. Challoner, *Memoirs of Missionary Priests*, p. 27. John Morris S.J., "A new Witness about Blessed Edmund Campion," p. 462, corrects Simpson here who said Collington was acquitted "after the verdict was given."

43. Reynolds, pp. 151–2; Anstruther, *Seminary Priests*, p. 82 ("Colleton")

44. Ch. 14: "The procession to London"

45. Ch. 8: "Fr. Cottam"

46. See ch. 15: "Tortures in the Tower."

47. *Douay Diaries*, p. 188; Allen, *A True, Sincere, and Modest Defense of English Catholics*, ch. 2; Anstruther, *Seminary Priests*, p. 190

48. Ch. 8: "Danger in London"

49. Ch. 8: "Danger in London"

50. Ch. 8: "The example of Fr. Bosgrave"

51. *Calendar of State Papers . . . 1581–1590*, Dec. 1, 1581, no. 80, p. 32. Anstruther, *Seminary Priests*, p. 154.

52. Letter of Feb. 7, 1582 in *Letters and Memorials of Cardinal Allen*, p. 113: "Mater Joannis Harti insigniter animavit filium suum ad martyrium."

53. Reynolds, p. 152. Fr. Hart is named in Howell's *State Trials*, vol. 1, col. 1081, along with Campion and others, and his answers to questions are given.

54. Reynolds, p. 150

55. Hughes, *The Reformation in England*, vol. 3, p. 347

56. They are listed by name in ch. 7: "The band of fourteen departs from Rome." For an earlier summary of how the original band of fourteen was faring, see ch. 12: "The fate of the fourteen."

57. Persons's *L. of C.*, ch. 15

58. See ch. 12: "Persons's printing press in Greenstreet."

59. Persons's *L. of C.*, ch. 15

60. Ch. 14: "The end of Fr. Persons's mission in England"

61. C.R.S., vol. 2, pp. 133, 196, but without dates for these events.

62. See ch. 12: "Persons's printing press in Greenstreet."

63. Persons's *L. of C.*, ch. 15. For "the Pit," see ch. 15: "Tortures in the Tower."

64. Pollen, "The Journey of Blessed Edmund Campion from Rome to England" p. 249. C.R.S., vol. 30 (1930) p. 27. Anstruther, *Seminary Priests*, pp. 51–2.

65. Fr. Weston wrote his memoirs: William Weston, *The Autobiography of anElizabethan*, trans. Philip Caraman S.J. (Longmans, London 1955).

66. Letter in ch. 10: "Campion's account to the Jesuit General"
67. *John Gerard—The Autobiography of an Elizabethan*, pp. 78-9

Chapter 20—Martyrdom

1. Dr. Allen's preface to his *Briefe Historie*, p. 17; *Concertatio*, p. 222
2. Bombino, ch. 55, pp. 281-2; Allen's *Briefe Historie* (ed. Pollen) p. 20; *Concertatio*, p. 64; Bartoli, vol. 3, bk 3, ch. 7, p. 123. We do not know her name.
3. William Allen, *Apologia Martyrum* ("Defense of the Martyrs") in *Concertatio*, p. 224
4. Vol. 3, bk 3, ch. 6, p. 117
5. More, *History Eng. Province*, bk 3, no. 30
6. Persons's *L. of C.*, ch. 2
7. This trial is mentioned above in ch. 11: "Campion travels to the north, end of 1580"; "Campion in the north, start of 1581"; ch. 13: "Campion and Persons continue visitation." Edward Griffin is named in ch. 15: "A series of arrests"; "No betrayal of anything unknown."
8. *A True Report of the Death and Martyrdom of Mr. Campion* (1582): S.B., no. 46. All but three quotations in this chapter are from Alfield. At endnote 14 below, I list the others from Dr. Allen.
9. Bombino, Ms. additions to p. 311. See S.B., no. 1.
10. All background on this form of execution is from H. Thomas Milhorn, *Crime* (Universal Publishers, Florida 2005) p. 414.
11. Southern, pp. 377-8, shows it was certainly Alfield, whereas past writers were not so sure and used to say "attributed to."
12. The two are mentioned in *Acts of the Privy Council*, vol. 13, pp. 432-3, and *Calendar of State Papers . . . 1581-1590*, May 1582, no. 78, p. 57.
13. Lisa McClain, *Lest We Be Damned—Practical Innovation and Lived Experience Among Catholics in Protestant England, 1559-1642* (Routledge, N.Y. and London 2004) p. 151. Dolman can also be spelt Dolmen. For the account and its contents, see S.B., no. 46.
14. Except that indirect quotes of words of Campion, and others resent at his last moments, I have changed to direct speech. The following quotes in the text below are not in Alfield (nor Bombino) but are added from Allen's *Briefe Historie* (ed. Pollen) pp. 2-3 (they are also in *Concertatio*, p. 65, and repeated in Challoner, who modifies the English expression slightly):

    (1) "For the treasons which have been laid to my charge, and which I am come here to suffer for, I desire you all to bear witness with me that thereof I am altogether innocent."

(2) "One of the Council replied: 'You are denying the things objected against you . . .' [This objector's words are put into direct speech and modified slightly]. 'Well, my lord, I am a Catholic man and a priest. In that faith have I lived hitherto, and in that faith I do intend to die; and if you esteem my religion treason, then of force I must grant unto you. As for any other treason, I never committed any; God is my Judge.'"

(3) "For, upon the commissioners' oaths that no harm should come unto them, he uttered some persons with whom he had been."

15. *Acts of the Privy Council*, vol. 13, p. 401: Apr. 29, 1582
16. Bombino, ch. 57, pp. 287–8
17. Morris, "A new Witness about Blessed Edmund Campion" at p. 462. Fr. Hart's final fate is given in ch. 19: "Condemnation of the other priests," no. 14 in the list.
18. Our Lord on the Cross: *Luke* 23:46, quoting Psalm 31:5 (30:5)
19. Bartoli, vol. 3, bk 3, ch. 7, p. 126
20. Persons, *A Defense of the Censure* (1582) p. 2. I changed the second-last word from "your" to "his" in Persons's text; he is addressing Charke at this point.
21. Bombino, ch. 57, p. 289; Bartoli, vol. 3, bk 3, ch. 7, p. 126
22. Alfield, *True Report*. Cf. Allen, *Briefe Historie* (ed. Pollen) p. 2; *Concertatio*, p. 65; Bombino, ch. 57, p. 289; Challoner, *Missionary Priests*, p. 28.
23. Ch. 19: "The sentence"
24. Fr. Pollen, intro., p. xv, to Allen's *Briefe Historie*.
25. *Calendar of State Papers . . . 1581–1590*, May 1584, no. 95, p. 178
26. Simpson called him a priest, but Anstruther, *Seminary Priests*, p. 184, says Mr. Isham was a layman who suffered much for the Faith and his son William became a priest in 1602. He was a prisoner in the Clink in 1586: C.R.S., vol. 2, p. 260; cf. *Calendar of State Papers . . . 1581–1590*, Sept. 25, 1586, no. 66, p. 356.
27. Bombino, Ms. additions to p. 289. "Ex diversorum auctariis, sunt apud me." (From additions of divers people; they are with me).
28. In a letter of Dec. 4, 1581, translated by John Morris S.J., in "A new Witness about Blessed Edmund Campion" p. 459.
29. *A Discovery of Edmund Campion and his Confederates* (S.B., no. 45)
30. St. Paul's text has spectacle to the world, angels, men. Campion has put "God" in place of "world."
31. Challoner, p. 28, who modifies Allen's English a little, puts simply: "then am I guilty."

32. *Briefe Historie* (ed. Pollen) p. 3; *Concertatio,* pp. 65–6. The question of whether he did give names or not is discussed at length in ch. 15 above.

33. See the opening lines of ch. 13. Fr. L. Johnson is no. 8 in the list in ch. 19: "Condemnation of the other priests."

34. Anon. Christopher Barker, London 1581. S.B., no. 43. Reprinted in *Holinshed's Chronicles* at A.D. 1581 (1587 ed.) p. 1328, and as an appendix to Anthony Munday, *John a Kent and John a Cumber – A Comedy* (intro. and notes J. P. Collier, The Shakespeare Society, London 1851. Facsimile reprint: Elibron, Massachusetts 2001) pp. 133–6. Alfield's account names this, and gives its full title, as the Advertisement "published there, and openly read." I mention this, because Simpson had said this "must have been" the thing read out, implying it was a deduction, rather than something directly known by report.

35. In *John a Kent and John a Cumber,* editor J.P. Collier says, p. xxxviii, "It is a singular specimen of authorship, consisting of only two long, rambling, incoherent, and, in some places, almost unintelligible sentences. The object of the writer was to vindicate the execution of justice upon Campion and his associates, and it is very possible that Archbishop Grindal [who received such Mss. for censorship or approval] thought the case stronger without, than with, this uncouth species of advocacy, and therefore directed that the tract should not be published." The original work is in Lambeth librarybut it was published, as mentioned above, in Holinshed's *Chronicles.*

36. This act of many in the crowd is recorded in the Memories of Fr. Campion's martyrdom by Fr. Henry Walpole S.J., in Fr. Pollen, *Acts of English Martyrs hitherto unpublished,* p. 48.

37. Munday's *Discovery of Edmund Campion and his Confederates,* and his account in Holinshed, say, "he said his *Pater Noster* [Our Father] in Latin": *Holinshed's Chronicles* at A.D. 1581 (1587 ed.) p. 1328. Munday's account, less informative and exact than Alfield's, agrees with it in the basic sequence of events and words spoken.

38. The first of the two quotes in the text is in: Alfield; Allen (ed. Pollen) p. 4; *Concertatio,* p. 66; Challoner, p. 29. – Simpson, and others after him (Nieuwenhoff, Camm, Waugh, Guiney, Chanthann, Gardiner), give the cleverer reply but no reference. The quip may come from Dr. Allen: next to the words, "he would pray in a language he well understood," Allen's marginal note of 1582 says, "And God too."

39. Henry Walpole in Pollen, *Acts*, p. 48, specifically says these were his last words. Alfield uses the phrase "a perfect Catholic." "Perfect" here means complete or true.

40. "There he hanged till he was dead" says *Holinshed* at A.D. 1581 (1587 ed.) p. 1329.

41. C.R.S., vol. 4, pp. 44–7

42. All the points in this paragraph are from the letter of Persons to Fr. Agazzari, Dec. 23, 1581, in More, *History Eng. Province*, bk 3, no. 37.

43. Ch. 21: "Relics of Campion"

44. Sherwin's words and martyrdom I take from Alfield's account, with little bits added from Allen's *Briefe Historie*. Challoner here combines and paraphrases Alfield and Allen.

45. The points in this paragraph up to here are from the letter of Persons to Fr. Agazzari, Dec. 23, 1581, in More, *History Eng. Province*, bk 3, no. 36.

46. Register of the Jesuit novitiate at Malines, Belgium, p. 557. Ms. collection known as the "Bibliothèque de Bourgogne" (now at Brussels), no. 2167. The same story is referred to in other Mss. of the same collection, e.g., no. 3166, part 2, and no. 4554. Memories of Campion's martyrdom by Walpole, in Pollen, *Acts of English Martyrs hitherto unpublished*, p. 40

47. See ch. 16: "Campion's reputation restored." The poem: "Why do I use my paper, ink and pen" is in Allen (ed. Pollen, 1908) p. 26–31. The first printed copy is reproduced near the end of this book: "St. Henry Walpole's elegy on Campion." A critical edition of the poem, using the 5 Mss and 1 printed copy, is found in Gerard Kilroy, *Edmund Campion: Memory and Transcription*, pp. 198–207.

48. See S.B., no. 46.

49. C.R.S., vol. 4, pp. 44–5, original Latin with Eng. trans., modified a little.

50. From his account in *Holinshed*, p. 1327. The wording differs slightly from the same passage in Munday's *Discovery of Edmund Campion and his Confederates* (S.B., no. 45).

51. *Acts of English Martyrs hitherto unpublished*, p. 39. Also told by Bombino, ch. 60, p. 319, and Bartoli, vol. 3, bk 3, ch. 8, p. 156. It is mentioned (only to be denied) in *Holinshed*, p. 1329.

52. Stanzas 3 and 4 are given of the nine stanzas of the 2nd poem printed at the end of Thomas Alfield, *A True Report of the Death and Martyrdom of Mr. Campion* (1582): S.B., no. 46. With modernized spelling and punctuation, this is the text I follow. *Upon Campion, Sherwine and Brian*, reproduced in Allen (ed. Pollen, 1908) pp. 55–6: S.B., no. 52a.

53. Bombino, ch. 60, p. 319: "perspicacious": "acuta." Instead, he has the Latin adverb "acute" which must be a misprint.

54. Robert Southwell, S.J., *An Epistle of Comfort* (1587 orig., Burns and Oates, London 1966) p. 235. See ch. 19: "Blood on his hands" and my endnote there for another story told in the book. These stories of divine wrath are not in all versions of the *Epistle*.

Chapter 21—"Champions have Swarmed"

1. Pollen, *The English Catholics*, p. 327

2. Preface to his *Briefe Historie*, p. 17, marginal note

3. Herbert F. Seversmith, "George Norton of Salem Massachusetts" *The American Genealogist*, XV (April 1939) p. 108. See Fleetwood's account of her in Strype, *Annals of the Reformation*, vol. 3, ch. 92.

4. Bombino, ch. 59: "What sort of end they had who were noted to be most hostile to Campion," p. 304

5. Ch. 19: "The verdict: guilty"

6. Ch. 59, p. 305

7. *Calendar of State Papers . . . 1581–1590*, Feb. 20, 1584, no. 21, p. 160; cf. May 1584, no. 103, p. 178; Dec. 14, 1583, no. 27, p. 136.

8. His career is mentioned in Cardinal Pell's *Foreword* to this book, and also in ch. 1: "Sir Thomas White and the character of St. John's"; "Oxford University"; "The Fathers of the Church."

9. Tobie Mathew said he read them but without believing them: ch. 1: "The Fathers of the Church."

10. See A. H. Mathew and A. Calthrop, *The Life of Sir Tobie Matthew* (E. Mathews, London 1907) p. 72; David Mathew, *Sir Tobie Mathew* (Max Parrish, London 1950) p. 67.

11. Ch. 20: "Visited by Eliot"

12. Quoted in Anstruther, *Seminary Priests*, p. 195

13. Stonyhurst Mss. M. folio 191e: "Relations of Mr. George Stoker and Mr. Heath concerning martyrs" in J. Morris S.J., "Blessed Edmund and Companions, Martyrs" p. 470, quoting a manuscript note. Which of them related Gaskin's statement is not said. Also in Pollen, *Acts*, p. 310.

14. Register of the Jesuit novitiate at Malines

15. Printed by Bartolomeo Grassi, Rome 1584. The book reproduced Cavalleri's frescoes painted in the chapel of the English College in Rome in 1583 depicting the history of Christianity in England and Wales.

16. "Id vere dicere possum mortui Campiani Manes quam viventis Rationes plus mihi exhibuisse molestiæ."

17. "et tamen Campianus in ore suorum mordet mortuus."
18. *Jesuitismi pars prima* ("The first part of Jesuitry" 1582) 52nd page (unnumbered) of his Preface: S.B., no. 19
19. Letter of March 1, 1582: C.R.S., vol. 39, p. 133; also in memoirs, C.R.S., vol. 4, pp. 44–5.
20. Named in S.B., no. 47.
21. *Calendar of State Papers . . . January 1581–April 1582*, Jan. 14, 1582, no. 508, p. 454. E.B., no. 4.
22. Fr. T. McCoog S.J. in Ethan Shagan (ed.), *Catholics and the "Protestant Nation": Religious Politics and Identity in Early Modern England* (Manchester University Press, N.Y. 2005) p. 104
23. Ch. 20: "The day of martyrdom"
24. See S.B., no. 46. Southern, p. 379, quotes the Star Chamber's proceedings of May 16, 1582 saying the book was printed in February.
25. Says Fr. Pollen, p. xi, intro. to *A Briefe Historie . . . by William Cardinal Allen* (London 1908): E.B., no. 6. Dr. Challoner was probably unaware of the author because of the inconsistency of person in the work: Allen refers to himself in the third person as "Dr. Allen" (p. 7) but at other times, even in the same paragraph, uses the first person "I" (pp. 7, 8), when that speaker cannot be Dr. Allen but someone else, unnamed. Pollen says Simpson and Gillow did not know Allen was the author, and no one knew it until Allen's letters were published in 1882.
26. See S.B., no. 57, for details. He lived 1542–1613. In later years, this exegete, theologian and hagiographer was Chancellor of Douay University.
27. See the end of ch. 17: "Other tortures." Some now attribute *A Declaration of the favorable dealing* to Norton: M. Graves, *Thomas Norton*, pp. 2768. Even so, there is still enough in Burghley's life and output to disgust anyone exceedingly.
28. See S.B., nos. 63–64d.
29. See S.B., no. 65.
30. Proceedings of the Star-Chamber, May 16, 1582: Harleian Mss. 6265, folio 373
31. *Calendar of State Papers . . . Addenda, 1580–1625*, June 1582, no. 93, p. 63. E.B., no. 3. Harleian Mss. 6265, folio 373; see also *Calendar of State Papers . . . 1581–1590*, Jan. 7, 1584, no. 8, p. 150.
32. *Acts of the Privy Council*, vol. 13, p. 193
33. Spedding (ed.), *The Letters and the Life of Francis Bacon*, vol. 1, p. 49. Henry Hallam, *The Constitutional History of England* (1827) vol. 1, p. 163, attributes the paper to Burghley, but Simpson says that Spedding (vol. 1, pp. 43–6) rightly ascribes it to Bacon.

34. Spedding (ed.), *Bacon*, vol. 1, pp. 50–1
35. James Howell (ed.), *Cottoni Posthuma* ("Posthumous things of Cotton," Richard Lowndes, London 1672) p. 132
36. *A Defense of the Censure*, p. 4 (orig. ed.): S.B., no. 14. Word order and punctuation changed slightly. Reprint in: *Rationes Decem 1581 by Edmund Campion and A brief censure 1581; and A defense of the censure 1582 by Robert Persons* (Scolar Press, Menston, England 1971).
37. Cf. start of Psalm 43 (42). To make sense, I changed "acceperit" to "accederit."
38. *Calendar of State Papers . . . 1581–1590*, Nov. 26, 1581, no. 67, p. 31. E.B., no. 2. Eng. orig. C.R.S., vol. 39, p. 120. Fr. Hicks's note on p. 184 says Arthur Creswell, later called Joseph Creswell, entered the Jesuits on Oct. 10, 1583 with William Brokesby. The two are named in ch. 10: "The network of Catholic gentry."
39. Quoted in More, *History Eng. Province*, bk 3, no. 37
40. *Calendar of State Papers . . . 1581–1590*, Feb. 6, 1582, no. 39, p. 45
41. Letter of Aug. 16, 1582 to Fr. Agazzari in *Letters and Memorials of Cardinal Allen*, p. 156
42. Letter of July 17, 1582 informing Fr. Agazzari in Rome of the progress of his martyrs' accounts: *Letters and Memorials of Cardinal Allen*, p. 148
43. Letter of March 1, 1582: C.R.S., vol. 39, pp. 128–9, 133–4; also in C.R.S., vol. 4, pp. 44–5.
44. *Campian Englished. Or A translation of the ten reasons in which Edmund Campian (of the Society of Jesus) priest, insisted in his challenge, to the Universities of Oxford and Cambridge, Made by a priest of the Catholic and Roman Church* (Rouen 1632) pp. 19–20, in the translator's "Epistle to the Reader." Case's words in Latin, as given: "Concionantur et adhuc et adhuc."
45. "The complaint of a Catholic for the death of M. Edmund Campion," Allen's *Brief Historie* (ed. Pollen, 1908) p. 44: S.B., no. 52a. In line 5, instead of Pollen's "our," I put "thy" as the original 1582 edition has.
46. Hughes, *The Reformation in England*, vol. 3, pp. 338, 340
47. Pollen, *Acts*, p. 343
48. Meyer, p. 213
49. Dom Bede Camm, *Forgotten Shrines*, p. 377
50. Letter to Fr. Agazzari, Dec. 23, 1581, in More, *History Eng. Province*, bk 3, no. 37
51. Mentioned by Pedro Serrano in his letter of Dec. 4, 1581: Morris, "A new Witness about Blessed Edmund Campion" p. 460.
52. Letter of Jan. 16, 1582 in *Douay Diaries*, p. 347

53. Letter of Feb. 7, 1582 to Fr. Agazzari in *Letters and Memorials of Cardinal Allen*, p. 111

54. Letter of May 12, 1582 in *Letters and Memorials*, p. 135. Eng. orig.

55. Named in ch. 12: "Persons's printing press in Greenstreet"

56. Letter of Aug. 8, 1583 in *Letters and Memorials*, p. 202

57. Letter of July 18, 1582 in *Letters and Memorials*, p. 151

58. Mentioned in ch. 14: "The end of Fr. Persons's mission in England"

59. Simpson said halter; so did Dom Camm, *Forgotten Shrines*, pp. 363, 375. Mrs. Jan Graffius, Curator at Stonyhurst College, in 2007 gave me the origin and history of the rope there, now given in the text above.

60. Foley, *Records of the English Province*, vol. 6 (Burns and Oates, London 1880) p. 111. Scott R. Pilarz S.J., *Robert Southwell and the Mission of Literature, 1561–1595: Writing Reconciliation* (Ashgate, U.K. 2004) p. 201, says it was Stephen Brinkley; the Annual Letter says "a certain gentleman who had been a long time in prison for religion. He had been arrested for printing Catholic books, and was confined in the same gaol with Father Campion." Bartoli, vol. 3, bk 3, ch. 8, p. 152, says Persons's rope was from the ropes on the rack torturing Campion.

61. Letter of March 2, 1583 in *Letters and Memorials*, p. 177

62. Vol. 3, bk 3, ch. 8, p. 153

63. A. Possoz S.J., *Le Premier Jésuite Anglais Martyrisé en Angleterre* ("The first English Jesuit martyred in England," 1864) pp. 290–1: "si vel canibus alendis fœnerari possim Domino meo: quis sum, aut quæ est domus patris mei ut recusem."

64. Mentioned in the anti-Catholic work by John Gee, *The Foot out of the Snare with a detection of sundry late practices and impostures of the priests and Jesuits in England* (1624) pp. 47–8, citing a book he calls *Apology* by Fr. Richard Conway, who may be the Irish Jesuit, born 1572, who entered the Society, 1592: Foley, *Records of the English Province*, vol. 7 (Burns and Oates, London 1882) pp. 161–2.

65. See ch. 11: "Campion in Lancashire." *Forgotten Shrines*, p. 379

66. *Forgotten Shrines*, p. 375

67. Or "Edmonds." The book was found during a search of a recusant's house before 1590: Peter Milward S.J., *Religious Controversies of the Elizabethan Age: A Survey of Printed Sources* (Uni. of Nebraska Press, Lincoln; Scolar Press, London 1977) p. 171.

68. Samuel Harsnett, *A Declaration of Egregious Popish Impostures, to withdraw the hearts of her Majesty's Subjects from their allegiance, and from the truth of Christian Religion professed in England, under pretence of casting*

out devils. Practised by Edmunds, alias Weston a Jesuit, and divers Romish Priests, his wicked associates (James Roberts, London 1603) p. 84. Harsnett was Vicar of Chigwell, later Archbishop of York. See F. W. Brownlow, *Shakespeare, Harsnett, and the Devils of Denham*, pp. 267–8.

69. *Forgotten Shrines*, pp. 363, 378
70. Ch. 14: "Campion and Persons part"
71. Ch. 14: "To London and the Tower"
72. Fr. Morris S.J., "Blessed Edmund Campion and his *Ten Reasons*" p. 377
73. *Forgotten Shrines*, pp. 378–9. Dom Camm says the hat was given to Edmund by St. Francis Borgia S.J., but that is impossible: Campion arrived in Rome in 1573, after Borgia's death (1572).
74. See ch. 3: "His activities at Douay."
75. Mentioned in ch. 14: "Caught."
76. Thomas Bell, *The Anatomie of Popish Tyrannie* (John Harison, London 1603. Facsimile reprint: Amsterdam, Norwood, N.J. 1975) p. 97
77. In this chapter, at start of section: "Campion dead bites with his friends' teeth."
78. Fr. Michael E. Williams in *Reckoned Expense*, p. 293
79. Brussels Ms. 3349
80. *Literae annuae Collegii Graecensis* ("Annual records of the College of Graz" [Austria]), A.D. 1606
81. Mathias Tanner S.J., *Societas Jesu usque ad sanguinis et vitae profusionem militans* ("The Society of Jesus, doing battle unto the shedding of blood and life," 1675) pp. 13–4
82. Balbin, p. 195
83. Schmidl, *History of the Society of Jesus of the Province of Bohemia*, bk 1, at A.D. 1581, p. 462; Bombino, ch. 58, p. 296
84. Original Latin, with differing Eng. trans. in Gerard Kilroy, *Edmund Campion: Memory and Transcription*, p. 6
85. Bombino, Ms. additions to his own book; Challoner, *Missionary Priests*, p. 73
86. *Palaestra Styli Romani, Quae Artem and praesidia Latine ornateque quovis styli genere scribendi complectitur, cum brevi Graecarum and Romanarum antiquitatum compendio, Et Praeceptis Ad Dialogos, Epistolas, and Historias scribendas legendasque necessariis* ("Training in Roman style which includes the art and means of writing Latin ornately in any kind of style, with a brief compendium of Greek and Roman antiquities, and with precepts necessary for writing dialogues, epistles, histories and legends," Johannes Busaeus [John Buys], Cologne 1659) pp. 4, 88, 93, 102, 108–9, 258

87. Vol. 1, treatise 1, chapter 8. Facsimile reprint of the Eng. ed. of 1882: St. Athanasius Press, Wisconsin 2006, vol. 1, p. 35. The author is a priest, not the Jesuit Brother, St. Alphonsus Rodriguez.

88. William Weston, *The Autobiography of an Elizabethan* (trans. Philip Caraman S.J.), introduction, p. xv. Based on St. Paul, 1 Cor 13:1–3.

89. S.B., no. 46.

90. The meaning is clear even if the expression is awkward for lack of a few connecting words. Only spelling is here modified; the words remain the same. This has been copied from the original; some books quoting this have slight mistakes.

91. Ch. 16: "Campion's reputation restored." For other verses on Campion, cf. ch. 1: "First schooling"; ch. 5: "Playwright"; ch. 15, end of section: "A contemporary defense of Campion's confessions"; ch. 20: "Prodigies of nature"; ch. 21: "The blood of martyrs," and below, this chapter.

92. Letter of March 3, 1582 to Fr. Agazzari: *Letters and Memorials of Cardinal Allen*, p. 122

93. Intro. p. xviii, to Allen's *Brief Historie* (ed. Pollen, 1908): S.B., no. 52a. For verses, see also nos. 46, 77a.

94. Stephen Austin and Sons, Hertford 1873: E.B., no. 21. The verses on pp. 164–5 are really three separate pieces. See S.B., no. 77a, for a poem in twelve cantos written between 1582–92, not published till 1938.

95. See ch. 20: "Walpole." Full poem is at the end of this book: "St. Henry Walpole's elegy on Campion." See S.B., nos. 46, 52a.

96. See S.B., no. 46.

97. *The Month*, Jan.–Feb. 1872, p. 118. It appeared again in a book of 1878 (2nd ed. 1879): Kilroy, *Edmund Campion: Memory and Transcription*, p. 67. Kilroy prints a critical edition of the poem, from the varying surviving Mss., pp. 199–204. Also reproduced, with small variations, in Allen's *Brief Historie* (ed. Pollen, 1908) pp. 26–31: see S.B., no. 52a. Here and elsewhere in this book I quote the text of the first printed edition of 1582, with spelling and punctuation modified.

98. Full text in Pollen, *Acts of English Martyrs hitherto unpublished*, pp. 23–34. In the north of England for some centuries, "Sir" was a title for priests.

99. *Holinshed* at A.D. 1581 (1587 ed.) p. 1323; p. 1325 quotes another two lines of this verse from a pamphlet now lost.

100. At the end of the account, p. 1329. "Aeternisque brevi gaudent pro morte coronis / Haec sunt martyribus dona parata piis." "Religio crimen non mala vita fuit."

101. Ch. 5: "Playwright"

102. This chapter: "Published accounts of the martyrs"
103. S.B., no. 57. I omit the seven lines of poetry, given by Simpson in Latin but said by him to be "more savage than poetical."
104. Rossi lived 1577–1647. The eulogy is in his 1642 collection of eulogies, *Pinacotheca Imaginum* ("Picture-gallery of portraits," J. F. Gleditsch, Leipzig 1692) p. 92: "quo scelere nullum aetas nostra tetrius vidit, neque dignius cuius a conspectu sol ipse recederet."
105. *Concertatio* (1588 ed.) p. 67: S.B., no. 59. The verses were first printed at pp. 92–4 (handwritten page nos on the original) of Dr. Allen's *Briefe Historie* (1582): S.B., no. 52. In *Concertatio*, only one change: in line 62 (not quoted here) "parva" is changed to "magna."
106. "Primus eras, princepsque gregis, cessere priores / Partes, and palmam cætera turba tibi. . . . O fœlix vitae cursus, finisque beatus: / Fortiter in Domino, pro Dominoque mori. / Sis mihi quæso tuo facilis patronus alumno, / Nec cesses pro me sæpe rogare Deum." *Concertatio*, pp. 67–8. Another verse of the same poem is cited in ch. 1: "First schooling."
107. Letter of Sept. 16, 1881, *The Letters of Gerard Manley Hopkins to Robert Bridges* (Oxford 1955) pp. 135–6
108. They are listed towards the end of the Editor's Bibliography.
109. German 1938; Dutch 1947; French 1950; Spanish 1960; Slovak 1991
110. The latest is *Edmund Campion* by Alexander Haydon (88 pp. Catholic Truth Society, Saints of the Isles Series, London 2003)
111. In the latter novel, Campion appears, but some of Campion's recorded words are also put in the mouth of fictional hero, Fr. Robin Audrey, at Tyburn. Benson's novels are regularly reprinted.
112. Bernhard Tauchnitz, Leipzig 1865. A novel, despite the title.
113. Recent examples are listed at the end of the Editor's Bibliography. In 2009, the first film was made on his life, a one-hour narrative and enacted documentary: *Saint Edmund Campion—A Hero Returns*, produced by Mary's Dowry Productions, based in West Sussex. 114 Augustus Jessopp, *One Generation of a Norfolk House—A Contribution to Elizabethan History* (Miller and Leavins, Norwich 1878) p. 239. Also spelt "Gunnis." Simpson spelt it "Gunne," as in the original State Papers recording his examination and arrest.
115. *Calendar of State Papers . . . 1581–1590*, June 8, 1585, no.7, p. 244, where it also mentions "Gunnes's speeches in favor of Edmond Campion." E.B., no. 2
116. J. Foster, *Alumni Oxonienses 1500–1714* ("Students of Oxford") p. 619
117. The original Acts of the Privy Council from June 26, 1582 to Feb. 19,

1586 are lost and do not appear in J. R. Dasent, volumes 13–19 (Eyre and Spottiswoode, London 1896–9). All quotations from the State Papers are given in Charles A. Newdigate, "The Tyburn prophecy of Gregory Gunnes," *The Month* (July 1934) pp. 56–62, at pp. 59–60.

118. Tony Hadland, *Thomas Valley Papists* in chapter, *The Mission Becomes Established (1582–1588).*

119. J. Gee, *The Foot out of the Snare*, p. 86. Holborn is mentioned in the margin of the page.

120. Which is probably why Simpson mentioned it. The 1907 edition of this book had no update to say the prophecy had been fulfilled.

121. *Tyburn Hill of Glory* by the Nuns of Tyburn Convent (Catholic Book Club, London 1953) pp. 72–6

122. See the section on martyrdom in the *Catechism of the Catholic Church,* nos. 2471–74.

123. In the decree, *Anglia Sanctorum insula* ("England, the isle of Saints"), eleven were beatified on that date: five martyred under Henry VIII: the Carthusians John Houghton, Robert Lawrence and Augustine Webster; the Bridgettine Richard Reynolds, and the Augustinian John Stone; and six martyred under Elizabeth I: the Jesuits Edmund Campion and Alexander Briant; the secular priests Cuthbert Mayne, Ralph Sherwin, John Paine and Luke Kirby. Archdiocese of Westminster, *Cause of the Canonization of Blessed Martyrs*, pp. vi, xiii–xiv, 45–7, 344. Except for the years 1971–2004, Popes have not presided at beatification ceremonies, but beatifications have been performed by a Cardinal or delegated Bishop; hence the use of the phrase in the text, "*under* Pope Leo XIII." Since the year 1000, canonisations have been reserved to Popes.

124. Archdiocese of Westminster, *Cause of the Canonization*, pp. xliii, 344–7

125. See *Catechism of the Catholic Church*, no. 828.

126. Archdiocese of Westminster, *Cause of the Canonization of Blessed Martyrs . . . Edmund Campion, Alexander Briant, Ralph Sherwin . . . Put to Death in England in Defense of the Catholic Faith (1535–1582)* (Sacred Congregation of Rites, Vatican Polyglot Press 1968) p. xx

127. *England and the Catholic Church Under Queen Elizabeth*, p. 193

128. *The Catholic Encyclopedia* (1913) article, "Campion, Edmund." Guiney wrote *Blessed Edmund Campion* (Macdonald and Evans, London 1908.183 pp.).

On the Revision of *Edmund Campion*

The Original Work

ALONG WITH his bibliography and endnotes, Richard Simpson's original preface bears witness to the thoroughness of his research:

> The first eight chapters of the following Life were printed off from time to time, as they appeared in the *Rambler* in the years 1861 [January, March, May, July, September] and 1862 [May]. When the *Rambler* changed into the *Home and Foreign Review* this work was dropped, and was only resumed in November 1866.
>
> Campion has had so many biographers that a new one may be expected to state his reasons for telling again a tale so often told. They are very simple. In the course of my researches among different archives, I found a quantity of unpublished matter that had never been seen by the former biographers; and in reading over the earliest and most authentic memoirs I found so many points obscured by phrase-making, misunderstood through ignorance of England, or misrepresented through the one-sidedness of those whose information was depended upon, that there seemed ample room for another book on the same subject.
>
> I have to express my obligations to the Jesuit Fathers at Stonyhurst, who had the kindness to send the MSS. relating to Campion to London for my convenience; to Charles Weld, Esq., who took the trouble to copy from a MS. at [the Jesuit church] the Gesù in Rome the whole of Bombinus's unpublished additions and corrections for his biography; and lastly, to Father Victor de Buck, Bollandist, of Brussels, for several references to rare books, and for encouragement, without which the work would never have been resumed.

The Bibliographical Appendix and the references in the notes
will be a sufficient indication of the authorities which I have followed.
Clapham [London], Dec. 21, 1866

The revision of *Edmund Campion*

Well-written and thoroughly researched, Simpson's original work of 1867
only needed some revision and updating in the light of further research
on St. Edmund's life made since the time of its writing. In 1896, it was
"Reprinted from a copy corrected by the learned Author before his death,"
says the title page—and it appeared for the third time a century ago, in
1907.

Additions, Changes, and Corrections

Small additions on Campion's family and his dealings with the Grocers'
Company come from the research of Leslie Campion, published in his
book *The Family of Edmund Campion* (1975).

Precise dates and details regarding Campion's time at St. John's
College were gleaned from Stevenson and Salter's *The Early History of St.
John's College, Oxford* (1939).

The research of John Hungerford Pollen S.J. (1858–1925) furnished
further background on Campion's journey from Rome to England, his
Brag and the printing of his *Ten Reasons*.

Much more detail on Campion's debates in the Tower has been
added, from James Holleran's fascinating book *A Jesuit Challenge:
Edmund Campion's Debates at the Tower of London in 1581* (1999)—
which contains transcripts of the debates made at the time by Catholics
in attendance. Simpson gave summaries of the topics and issues, with
some arguments of these debates, but I provide full outlines of the arguments themselves (written by Fr. John Fleming) and some quotations
from the lively exchanges.

The publications of the volumes of the Catholic Record Society in
the 20th century made accessible many valuable documents, letters,
memoirs, and so on, of the period, which at one time were seen only
by very few. For this biography, the C.R.S. volumes 2, 4 and 39, in particular, furnished much original material. The C.R.S. editors from the
beginning most wisely and helpfully added translations of original texts
not in English, many of which were in Latin and Italian. For this reason,

a reference to a C.R.S. volume sometimes gives two sets of page numbers: one for the original text, one for the translation following. This biography's translations sometimes vary from the C.R.S. for the sake of greater accuracy or because Simpson's earlier translation is retained (or modified), or simply as a matter of style or wording. Other translations by Simpson of Latin letters by Campion, Allen and others have been checked, and modified a little, in order to make them closer to the original and to restore phrases omitted without notice. At other times, it seems Simpson worked from a manuscript copy of a letter differing from one published later, for he has small phrases and even sentences not in the later one. In those cases, I alternate between his version and the later one, to give the best version overall. T. F. Knox's *Douay Diaries*, and his *Letters and Memorials of Cardinal Allen*, were another source of original materials. Jesuit catalogues and histories enabled me to correct misspelt names of Jesuits contemporary with Campion, or to give their full names where Simpson or a document gave a Christian name or surname only.

With the help of these and other modern studies listed in the Editor's Bibliography, small factual errors were corrected, numerous new facts added, obscure points clarified, and there is further precision with names, dates and places. I used these studies to improve or fill out the narrative, but not to bog the reader down in useless details, tangled discussions on chronology, or comparisons of all alternative accounts. Whether a man was born on this day or the next is not so important; the main thing is that he was born.

Being a Catholic, a priest and a Jesuit, Campion based his life on Catholic doctrine and piety. For this reason, I included a few brief explanations of Catholic issues that arose in his life and times. I also added background on his Jesuit formation by outlining St. Ignatius's *Spiritual Exercises*, by quoting the Jesuit *Constitutions*, especially on religious obedience, and by summarizing the content and import of the three religious vows which Campion lived by. Without the Catholic basis and context, a Saint's life cannot be understood, and will be misunderstood.

On occasion, I added to the text brief biographical asides about people who came into Campion's life, especially if they are recognized martyrs or confessors of the faith. I think it interests a reader to know the fate of some important players: for instance, what the fate was of the priest who secretly distributed Campion's *Ten Reasons*, and the effect upon the young Protestant man at Campion's execution who was spattered by some of his blood. Both are now martyrs of the Catholic Church, and this is mentioned at the relevant places.

The biography has also been enhanced with additional quotations from *The Life and Martyrdom of Edmund Campion* written in 1594 by his close Jesuit colleague, Fr. Robert Persons. On several occasions, Simpson placed phrases or sentences in quotation marks without giving their source: these were nearly all from Persons. In some cases, I found that Simpson had kept passages from Persons's life of Campion (or other contemporary pieces) in quotation marks even after re-writing them to make the English more modern and readable—but, this being unaccept-able, I restored the original words, or if the expression was too awkward to understand easily, I kept the paraphrase and named the source, with-out quotation marks.

All the early biographies of Campion (by Bombino, Persons, More, Bartoli, Balbin and Schmidl) have been used and quoted more abundantly.

Simpson's chapter 7, now chapter 9, a presentation of the histori-cal situation in 1580, was judged out-of-date and so was completely re-written and much enlarged, using chapters 1–3 of *Campion and Parsons* by E.E. Reynolds (1980) as a guide.

Altogether, the text (chs 1–21) is much larger (from 156,000 words to 239,000). Over a quarter of the additions are in chapters 9 (histori-cal background) and 16 (Tower debates). There are nearly four times as many end-notes, although many of these are cross-references. Two maps are added.

There is a plethora of new and old studies of the Elizabethan age. This book is not a study of the period but a biography of one man in it. Hence the Editor's Bibliography lists only a few titles on that period, which were used merely to provide accurate historical background to the events in Campion's life.

Omissions

A few passages, short or long, giving historical background or asides or opinions were abridged or left out, but nothing biographical of St. Edmund was omitted. The longest deletion is of most of Simpson's final chapter, in which he gave the text of a military report of Dr. Allen, a sur-vey of subsequent history, and his own reflections on the Bull of Pius V that excommunicated and deposed Queen Elizabeth, and its effect upon Catholics then and thereafter. At earlier places, I omitted similar passages by Simpson criticizing Pius V and his Bull, and I shortened discussions of the whole question of the Popes' temporal power—a big issue in the 19th century but not so now.

Order of Material

Simpson's chapter divisions have been modified and increased. There are now twenty-one chapters where there were seventeen. Some material has been re-ordered, so as to treat of certain topics fully in one place, rather than in a number of separate places. Simpson regularly interrupted his narrative of Campion's life with stories of related people and events. Relevant as they were, the trail of Edmund's life was sometimes obscured. To overcome this, many of these are gathered together in chapter 12. Although the original book had running titles (at the top of the page), it had no chapter headings or sub-titles—now supplied, along with a chronology.

Language, References, and Quotations

In some places I modified Simpson's 19th century English: "one and the other" is changed to "one another"; "used hardly" is now "treated harshly"; "reduced"—"brought back"; "repaired thither"—"went there"; "Pius Quintus" is rendered "Pius V," and so on. Some wordy expressions are simplified. In Campion's time, and Simpson's, diocesan priests were entitled "Mister," and religious priests often, but not always, "Father." To avoid uncertainty, all priests in this book are called "Reverend" or "Father," except in contemporary quotation or book titles.

Without changing the words or grammar, Simpson had in most cases modified the spelling of the 16th century English to conform to that of his time. This has been retained and updated. For most people this is a necessity; otherwise the unusual spelling is such a distraction that they lose the meaning. It also gives a false impression of quaintness or semi-literacy.

In chapters 2 and 4, the quotations from Campion's *History of Ireland* are now taken—but with modernized spelling—from Vossen's critical edition of 1963, which prints for the first time the manuscript closest to the missing original.

Contemporary quotations are always given accurately, but not pedantically: the words are retained, but sometimes punctuation is simplified, or spelling modified to prevent confusion, as said. The only changes to wording are: "hath" is now "has," "doth" now "does" (and other equivalents, most of the time); once or twice "which" is changed to "who"; "for that" is now simply "for"; and, once, "valor" was changed to "value." Where a word is obsolete or has changed meaning, I add a modern equivalent or explanation [in square brackets] after it. Abbreviations may be changed too, for example, "F." is changed to "Fr."; "M." to "Mr."; "D." to "Dr."; the ampersand (and) to the word "and," usually. Sometimes I kept old spelling for book titles mentioned.

All Latin, Greek and Italian is now followed by a translation (in brackets) or simply translated. Obscure words or terms are explained (usually in brackets). When an explanation or translation is inserted [within a quotation], square brackets are used. Where Simpson refers to a quotation or writer or event well-known in his own time, but obscure today, I add the reference or a brief explanation for the benefit of the modern reader. At times he presumed much historical, literary and religious knowledge of the reader, but I prefer to spell things out and explain them, and give people's full names and titles and positions, so as to introduce them to the average reader who does not know every player or event in Elizabethan history. Of course, not every position is defined and explained; I presume the reader knows what a bishop or queen is, but I did outline the difference between a priest and a brother, since that is less known today. For the benefit of readers outside England, I added more details regarding distances or places.

Spelling of Names

In the 16th century, personal names were often spelt with great variety. To prevent uncertainty, generally a name is spelt one way only, both in the text and in quotation. Where there is no likelihood of confusion (e.g., Mathew or Matthew, Kirby or Kirbie), an original spelling has been left.

Apart from book titles in the Bibliographies, or a few quotations, I have uniformly spelt the names "Campion" and (Fr. Robert) "Persons," instead of "Campian" and "Parsons."

Edmund signed his name both "Campian" and "Campion," but the latter is the only form used now. In Latin it was usually "Campianus" but in the Latin foundation deed of St. John's College, it was written "Campyon."

"Parsons" or "Persons": both are correct. I chose "Persons," because it is more commonly used, and, according to his biographer, Fr. Francis Edwards S.J. (1995), the man himself consistently wrote it that way. Probably it was pronounced with something of an Irish lilt: the first syllable as the Italian *e*, as in *hair, pear, hare.* Hence the modern spelling of the name Pearson, where, however, the old pronunciation is lost. Today the name of "Persons" is simply pronounced "parsons."

Endnotes

The endnotes contain cross-references, points of chronology, alternative possibilities—but for the most part references to documents, books, articles and archival sources, some of which are also listed in the Bibliographies.

Some of Simpson's reference numbers were placed at wrong points in the text, or omitted, and so at times his endnote numbers and notes did not correspond. These have all been re-assigned correctly.

The original endnotes had many, almost cryptic, abbreviations. These have all been filled out, to remove obscurity and to furnish the full titles of books or documents cited, along with an English translation of original titles, many in Latin.

Where a note contained extra *information*, this was transferred to the main text, so that the narrative not be interrupted by having to turn to the endnotes. Some superfluous or irrelevant historical information and references were removed from the notes, as adding nothing to the biography.

*   *   *

All these changes have been incorporated into the text at the appropriate places, generally without notification. In the endnotes, I usually declare any factual change made to the text of Simpson and sometimes the basis for it. In the narrative and in Simpson's Bibliography, the personal pronoun "I" refers always to Simpson. In the endnotes it refers to the current editor. Any references to contemporary time are updated: "today" always means the year A.D. 2010.

In place of Simpson's rather dismal ending, I chose to conclude his

excellent account of a glorious life on a note of triumph and inspiration—
the purpose of all hagiography. Not that hagiography should involve suppression or fabrication; on the contrary. The facts, especially in this story,
are too good to change, and need no embellishment. And if martyrdom
is a victory, then Campion's life—already full of drama, controversy and
heroism—concluded in the most triumphant fashion possible.

Possibly the difficult situation of English Catholics in Simpson's time
led him to conclude on a dreary note. The full and lasting effect of the
"Second Spring" (1852) and the *Apologia Pro Vita Sua* (1864) of Father
John Henry Newman had not yet been felt, and still in the future lay the
20th century English Catholic revival, with its abundance of literary converts who would change the face of the Catholic Church in England, Our
Lady's Dowry—Campion's beloved homeland, which had once been, in
his own words, "the island of saints and the most devoted child of the See
of Peter."

P. J.

Editor's Bibliography

This bibliography does not name every work cited but only the more important ones or those cited a number of times.

Government Papers

1. Robert Lemon (ed.), *Calendar of State Papers, Domestic Series, of the Reigns of Edward VI, Mary, Elizabeth 1547–1580* (Longman, London 1856)
2. R. Lemon (ed.), *Calendar of State Papers, Domestic Series, of the Reign of Elizabeth, 1581–1590* (Longman, London 1865)
   Mary Anne Everett Green (ed.), *Calendar of State Papers, Domestic Series, of the Reign of Elizabeth 1598–1601* (Longman, London 1869)
3. M.A.E. Green (ed.), *Calendar of State Papers, Domestic Series, of the Reigns of Elizabeth and James I, Addenda, 1580–1625* (Longman, London 1872)
4. Arthur John Butler (ed.), *Calendar of State Papers, Foreign Series, of the Reign of Elizabeth, 1579–1580* (Mackie and Co., London 1904)
   A. J. Butler (ed.), *Calendar of State Papers, Foreign Series, of the Reign of Elizabeth, January 1581–April 1582* (Mackie and Co., London 1907)
5. J. R. Dasent (ed.), *Acts of the Privy Council of England: New Series* (Eyre and Spottiswoode, London 1896) vol. 12 (1580–1581); vol. 13 (1581–1582) Primary works and documents (originals or later editions)
6. Cardinal William Allen, *A Briefe Historie of the Glorious Martyrdom of Twelve Reverend Priests, Father Edmund Campion and his Companions, by William Cardinal Allen, With Contemporary Verses by the Venerable Henry Walpole, and the Earliest Engravings of the Martyrdom, Reprinted from the (probably unique) Copy in the British Museum, and edited by the Rev. J.H. Pollen S.J.* (First published 1582. Burns and Oates, London 1908. Facsimile reprint: Neumann Press, Minnesota 2000). See also Simpson's bibliography, nos. 52 and 52a, for this work.
7. Cardinal William Allen, *The Letters and Memorials of William Cardinal*

Allen (1532–1594), ed. T.F. Knox (David Nutt, London 1882. Reprint: The Gregg Press, Farnborough 1965)

8.   William Camden, *The Historie of the Most Renowned and Victorious Princesse Elizabeth* (Benjamin Fisher, London 1630)

9.   William Camden, *Annales Rerum Gestarum Angliae et Hiberniae Regnante Elizabetha* ("Annals of the events of England and Ireland in the reign of Elizabeth," London 1615 and 1625)

10. Edmund Campion, *Campion's Ten Reasons* (Manresa Press, London 1914. Loome Booksellers and Ignatius Press, U.S.A. 2002). The original Latin text, with an English trans. by Joseph Rickaby S.J.

11. Bishop Richard Challoner, *Memoirs of Missionary Priests as well Secular as Regular, and of other Catholics of both Sexes, that have suffered Death in England on Religious Accounts from the Year of our Lord 1577 to 1684, gathered, partly from Printed Accounts . . . and partly from Manuscript Relations. A new edition, revised and corrected by J. H. Pollen S.J.* (Burns Oates and Washbourne, London 1924). The original was first printed in 1741.

12. John Gerard S.J., *The Autobiography of an Elizabethan*, trans. Philip Caraman S.J. (Longmans, London 1951. Reprint: Family Publications, Oxford 2006). Same work but reduced notes: *Autobiography of a Hunted Priest* (Image Books, N.Y. 1955); *The Hunted Priest – Autobiography of John Gerard* (Fontana, G.B. 1959). The work is highly recommended as a piece of accurate history, full of lively anecdotes and personal recollections of a Jesuit priest's ministry amid danger and excitement. It depicts an active priestly life in England in the years 1588–94, much as St. Edmund Campion must have experienced it in England from June 1580.

13. Fr. John Gibbons S.J. (ed.), *Concertatio Ecclesiae Catholicae in Anglia adversus Calvino-Papistas et Puritanos, a paucis annis singulari studio quorundam hominum doctrina et sanctitate illustrium renovata* ("The Struggle of the Catholic Church in England against the Calvinist-Papists and the Puritans, renewed in recent years by the special effort of certain men illustrious for learning and sanctity," 1st ed. 1583/4. Reprint of the 1588 edition with an Introduction by D. M. Rogers: Gregg Press, Farnborough 1970). A collection of Latin and English texts already published—but all of them appear in Latin or Latin translation. See Simpson's bibliography, no. 59, for more details of this important work. For a long time the book was mistakenly ascribed to Fr. John Bridgewater, since his surname corresponds to the Latin penname used by Gibbons: "Aquapontanus." Rogers's introduction explains the true authorship.

14. James V. Holleran, *A Jesuit Challenge: Edmund Campion's Debates at the Tower of London in 1581* (Fordham Uni. Press, N.Y. 1999). Contains, for the first time in print, the detailed, at times almost *verbatim*, reports on Campion's four debates in the Tower made at the time by Catholics who were present. A very helpful bibliography is on pp. 231–40. Well-researched biographical material on Campion (apart from the debates) is on pp. 16–41, 79–81, 208–19. See also Simpson's bibliography, no. 41.

15. T. B. Howell (compiler), *A Complete Collection of State Trials and Proceedings for High Treason and Other Crimes and Misdemeanors from the Earliest Period to the Year 1783* (21 vols, London 1816–1828). Often known as Cobbett's *State Trials;* William Cobbett employed Thomas Howell as editor. The record of Campion's trial is in Howell's *State Trials* (Hansard, London 1816) vol. 1, columns 1049–72.

16. T. F. Knox (ed.), *The First and Second Diaries of the English College, Douay* (David Nutt, London 1878. Reprints: The Gregg Press, Ridgewood, N.J., 1965; Kessinger Publishing, U.S.A. 2006). Popularly known as the *Douay Diaries*, it includes the fifteen years spent at Rheims also.

17. Ladislaus [László] Lukács, *Catalogi personarum et officiorum provinciae Austriae S.I., I (1551–1600)* ("Catalogues of persons and assignments of the Austrian province of the Society of Jesus," Institutum Historicum S.I. [Historical Institute of the Society of Jesus], Rome 1978, 828 pp.). Campion is not named in this volume since the catalogues of some years and places are not extant, but it is relevant for his other Jesuit companions and superiors.

18. Ladislaus Lukács S.J., *Monumenta antiquae Hungariae 1593–1600* ("Records of ancient Hungary," Institutum historicum S.I. [Historical Institute of the Society of Jesus], Rome 1987). See no. 17 for its usefulness.

19. Robert S. Miola (ed.), *Early Modern Catholicism – An Anthology of Primary Sources* (Oxford University Press 2007)

20. Henry More S.J. (ed. and trans., Francis Edwards S.J.), *The Elizabethan Jesuits: Historia Missionis Anglicanae Societatis Jesu (1660) of Henry More* ["History of the Mission of the English Society of Jesus"] (Phillimore, London 1981). This is an English trans. of (most of) the Elizabethan part, namely books 1–6, of Henry More S.J., *Historia Provinciae Anglicanae Societatis Jesu, collectore Henrico Moro, eiusdem Societatis Sacerdote* (Audomari 1660). ("History of the English Province of the Society of Jesus, compiled by Henry More, priest of the same Society," St. Omer 1660). Fr. Edwards's endnotes are invaluable. See also Simpson's Bibliography, no. 3.

21. W. R. Morfill (ed.), *Ballads from Manuscripts, Vol. II, Part I. . . . Part II.*

Ballads Relating Chiefly to the Reign of Queen Elizabeth (Printed for the Ballad Society by Stephen Austin and Sons, Hertford 1873). The editor says that, "For the Introduction and Notes on the Campion poems I am indebted to Mr. . Richard Simpson." Chapter V: "Poems Relating to Campion" occupies pp. 157–91 and contains twelve poems.

22. John Morris S.J., *The Troubles of Our Catholic Forefathers Related by Themselves* (Burns and Oates, London: First Series 1872; Second Series 1875; Third Series 1877)

23. John Morris S.J., "A new Witness about Blessed Edmund Campion," *The Month*, August 1893, pp. 457–65. Trans. with commentary of a Spanish letter written by the Spanish Ambassador's secretary, Dec. 4, 1581, with a postscript by Spanish Ambassador Bernardino de Mendoza, describing the martyrdom of Campion and companions.

24. Geraint Dyfnallt Owen, ed., *Calendar of the Manuscripts . . . at Longleat, Vol. 5, Talbot, Dudley and Devereux Papers* (Her Majesty's Stationery Office, London 1980)

25. Robert Persons S.J., *Memoirs* (ed. J.H. Pollen), among other useful materials, in Volumes 2 (Arden Press, London 1906) and 4 (Arden 1907) of the Publications of the Catholic Record Society.

26. Robert Persons S.J., *Letters and Memorials of Father Robert Persons S.J., Vol. I, 1578–1588*, Catholic Record Society, vol. 39, ed. Leo Hicks S.J. (John Whitehead and Son, Leeds 1942)

27. John Hungerford Pollen S.J. (ed.), *Acts of English Martyrs hitherto unpublished* (Burns and Oates, London 1891)

28. John F. Quirk S.J., *A patron for scholars: eulogy on the Blessed Edmund Campion, S.J. with his Oration on "The Model College Student"* (St. John's College, Fordham, N.Y. 1896). Includes the Latin text with facing Eng. trans. of Campion's *De Juvene Academico* ("The young student").

29. Hyder E. Rollins, *Old English Ballads 1553–1625 Chiefly from Manuscripts* (Cambridge University Press 1920)

30. Nicolas Sander, *The Rise and Growth of the Anglican Schism* (trans. of 1585 ed. by David Lewis: Burns and Oates, London 1877; TAN Books, Rockford 1988, 380 pp.). Latin original, *De Origine ac Progressu Schismatis Anglicani* ("On the Origin and Progress of the Anglican Schism"), written in 1576, was published after the author's death, and updated by Fr. Edward Rishton to his own time, in 1585. It re-appeared several times more, with additions and updates, in Latin and translation, over the next few decades. See also Simpson's bibliography, no. 75.

31. Joseph Simons (ed. and trans.), *Ambrosia: A Neo-Latin Drama by Edmund*

Campion S.J. (Van Gorcum, Assen, The Netherlands 1969–70). Contains the original Latin text and a trans.

32. Richard Simpson, "A Morning at the Star-Chamber," *The Rambler*, January 1857, pp. 15–37. The full text (with a brief intro. and conclusion) of the trial of Lord Vaux, Sir Thomas Tresham, Sir William Catesby and others, Nov. 1581, all charged with hosting Campion.

33. John Strype, M.A., *Annals of the Reformation and Establishment of Religion and Other Various Occurrences in the Church of England During Queen Elizabeth's Happy Reign, together with an appendix of original Papers of State, Records, and Letters* (Oxford 1824)

34. Alphonsus F. Vossen (ed.), *Two Bokes of the Histories of Ireland – compiled by Edmunde Campion, feloe of St. John Baptistes College in Oxforde, Edited from MS Jones 6 Bodleian Library Oxford* (Van Gorcum, Assen, The Netherlands 1963). Vossen's intro. examines very thoroughly, among other things, Campion's dates and religion in Ireland.

Modern Studies

35. A. F. Allison, D.M. Rogers and W. Lottes, *The Contemporary Printed Literature of the English Counter-Reformation between 1558 and 1640: an annotated catalogue* (Vol. 1: Works in Languages other than English, 1989. Vol. 2: Works in English, 1994. Scolar Press, Aldershot, England)

36. Godfrey Anstruther O.P., *Vaux of Harrowden – A Recusant Family* (R.H. Johns, Newport 1953)

37. Godfrey Anstruther O.P., *The Seminary Priests – A Dictionary of the Secular Clergy of England and Wales 1558–1850* (vol. 1. Elizabethan 1558–1603. Ushaw College, Durham 1968). An alphabetical catalogue with summary facts and biography of each priest. Naturally, in an invaluable work amassing thousands of facts, there are a few mistakes and internal contradictions.

38. Archdiocese of Westminster, *Cause of the Canonization of Blessed Martyrs . . . Edmund Campion, Alexander Briant, Ralph Sherwin . . . Put to Death in England in Defense of the Catholic Faith (1535–1582)* (Sacred Congregation of Rites, Vatican Polyglot Press 1968). 422 pp. Eleven martyrs are named in the full title. Contains much historical and biographical documentation collated in preparation for the canonization of Campion and others.

39. Hugh Aveling O.S.B., *Northern Catholics—The Catholic Recusants of the North Riding of Yorkshire 1558–1790* (Geoffrey Chapman, Melbourne 1966)

40. Dominic Aidan Bellenger O.S.B, *English and Welsh Priests 1558–1800—A*

Working List (Downside Abbey, Bath, England 1984). He lists all known priests, both secular and religious (Anstruther has only secular), with their year of birth, ordination, place of training, and other basic data.

41.   P. A. Boyan and G.R. Lamb, *Francis Tregian – Cornish Recusant* (Sheed and Ward, N.Y. 1955)

42.   Dom Bede Camm O.S.B. (ed.), *Lives of the English Martyrs, Volume II: Martyrs under Queen Elizabeth* (Burns and Oates, London 1905). Campion's life is related on pp. 266–353, co-authored by "H.S.B. and J.H.P" (Fr. Henry Sebastian Bowden, 1836–1920, of the Oratory, London; and Fr. John Hungerford Pollen S.J., named below at no. 97). Ralph Sherwin's life is on pp. 358–95 by "E.S.K. and Ed." (Fr. Edward S. Keogh and the Editor, Fr. Camm).

43.   Dom Bede Camm O.S.B., *Forgotten Shrines* (Macdonald and Evans, London 1910. Reprint: Gracewing, U.K. 2005). Fr. Camm (1864–1942) was a Church of England minister until his reception into the Catholic Church in 1890. Thereafter he became a Benedictine monk and priest, and very interested in English martyrs and recusants.

44.   Leslie Campion, *The Family of Edmund Campion* (Research Publishing Co., London 1975)

45.   Katherine Duncan-Jones, *Sir Philip Sidney: Courtier Poet* (Yale University Press, New Haven 1991). The same writer has a chapter in *The Reckoned Expense* (ed. McCoog), listed below, giving a balanced and careful account of the relations between Campion and Sidney.

46.   Francis Edwards S.J., *The Jesuits in England: From 1580 to the Present Day* (Burns and Oates, Great Britain 1985)

47.   Francis Edwards S.J., *Robert Persons: The Biography of an Elizabethan Jesuit, 1546–1610* (Institute of Jesuit Sources, St. Louis, U.S.A. 1995). The first full biography of this important figure, by the late archivist and historian of the British Province of the Society of Jesus.

48.   Henry Foley S.J., *Jesuits in Conflict: or Historic Facts Illustrative of the Labors and Sufferings of the English Mission and Province of the Society of Jesus in the Times of Queen Elizabeth and Her Successors* (Burns and Oates, London 1873). This book, intended as the first of a series, relates the lives of Thomas Pounde, George Gilbert and Fr. Thomas Darbyshire. Pages 91–143 relate Pounde's connection with Campion and Persons, who both feature also in the other lives.

49.   Henry Foley S.J., *Records of the English Province of the Society of Jesus* (7 vols, Burns and Oates, London 1877–82. Reprint: Johnson Reprint Collection, New York 1966). The early volumes are a major source for

Jesuit activities in 16th century England. Foley was a holy Jesuit Brother and painstaking historian. Vol. 3 (1878) contains the contents of his *Jesuits in Conflict*, plus much other matter.

50. Joseph Gillow, *The Haydock Papers: A Glimpse into English Catholic Life* (Burns and Oates, London 1888)

51. Louise Imogen Guiney, *Blessed Edmund Campion* (Macdonald and Evans, London 1908)

52. Tony Hadland, *Thomas Valley Papists: from Reformation to Emancipation 1534–1829* (Privately printed, 1992: ISBN 0 950743143). Has a chapter each on the missionaries of 1581 and on the Stonor Park press.

53. Alice Hogge, *God's Secret Agents: Queen Elizabeth's Forbidden Priests and the Hatching of the Gunpowder Plot* (Harper Collins Publishers, N.Y. 2005)

54. Victor Houliston, *Catholic Resistance in Elizabethan England: Robert Persons's Jesuit Polemic, 1580–1610* (Ashgate, U.K. and U.S.A and Institutum Historicum Societatis Iesu [Historical Institute of the Society of Jesus] Rome 2007)

55. Philip Hughes, *The Reformation in England—revised edition, three volumes in one* (Burns and Oates, London 1963) 1,200 pp. in all. A thoroughly researched, carefully documented and balanced history of the period 1517–1605.

56. Gerard Kilroy, *Edmund Campion: Memory and Transcription* (Ashgate, U.K. 2005)

57. Thomas M. Lucas S.J. (ed.), *Spirit, Style, Story: Essays Honoring John W. Padberg, S.J.* (Loyola Press, Chicago 2002). Fr. McCoog S.J. contributes a chapter on the Jesuits' mode of life in Elizabethan England.

58. Thomas M. McCoog S.J. (ed.), *The Reckoned Expense: Edmund Campion and the Early English Jesuits* (Boydell Press, Suffolk 1996. 2nd ed., Institutum Historicum Societatis Iesu [Historical Institute of the Society of Jesus] Rome 2007). A collection of relevant, scholarly and up-to-date articles by various historians. From it I garnered valuable facts, references and background. The 2nd edition is a revision with additional material. All citations are from the 1st ed., unless otherwise noted.

59. Thomas M. McCoog S.J., *The Society of Jesus in Ireland, Scotland, and England 1541–1588* (E.J. Brill, N.Y. 1996). Historian Fr. McCoog is archivist of the British Province of the Society of Jesus and editor-in-chief of all publications of the Jesuit Historical Institute, Rome.

60. Arnold O. Meyer, *England and the Catholic Church Under Queen Elizabeth* (Kegan Paul, Trench, Trübner and Co., London 1916. Trans. Rev. J. R.

McKee. Reprints: Barnes and Noble, N.Y. 1967; Routledge and Kegan Paul, London 1967 and 1969, with intro. by John Bossy). A classic and balanced study by a German Lutheran historian: German. orig. 1911. Bossy's intro. points out its shortcomings. Fr. Philip Hughes, *The Reformation in England*, vol. 3 (1963) corrects some errors of fact in Meyer and some credence given to Elizabethan government false propaganda.

61.   Peter Milward S.J., *Religious Controversies of the Elizabethan Age: A Survey of Printed Sources* (Uni. of Nebraska Press, Lincoln; Scolar Press, London 1977). Pp. 55–63 cover the literature connected specifically with Campion.

62.   Petr Polehla, *Edmund Campion o vzde'lání, rétorice a jeho drama Ambrosia* ("Edmund Campion on Education, Rhetoric and his Drama Ambrosia," Masaryk University, Brno, Czech Republic 2009)

63.   Arnold Pritchard, *Catholic Loyalism in Elizabethan England* (Uni. of North Carolina Press 1979)

64.   Michael C. Questier, *Catholicism and Community in Early Modern England: Politics, Aristocratic Patronage and Religion, c. 1550–1640* (Cambridge University Press 2006)

65.   E. E. Reynolds, *Campion and Parsons: The Jesuit Mission of 1580–1* (Sheed and Ward, London 1980; Catholic Book Club, London 1982). A well-researched work by a noted historian, making use of the Catholic Record Society's volumes. From it I have adopted several points of explanation and new facts. Much of his biographical material is taken from Simpson, but suitably updated. The only shortcomings, apart from occasional misprints affecting dates or facts, are in the dates and information regarding Campion at St. John's College, through not having seen Stevenson and Salter, no. 70 below.

66.   Eleanor Rosenberg, *Leicester, Patron of Letters* (Columbia University Press, N.Y. 1955). Pp. 80–93 recount Leicester's patronage of Campion, and Campion's *History of Ireland*.

67.   Samuel Schoenbaum, *William Shakespeare – A Compact Documentary Life* (Oxford University Press 1987)

68.   Malcolm H. South, *The Jesuits and the Joint Mission to England During 1580–1581* (E. Mellen Press, N.Y. 1999)

69.   A. C. Southern, *Elizabethan Recusant Prose, 1559–1582* (Sands and Co., London 1950). Pp. 148–60 cover the literature connected with Campion's *Brag*; much other pertinent literature is listed with instructive comments and background.

70.   W. H. Stevenson and H.E. Salter, *The Early History of St. John's College, Oxford* (Oxford University Press 1939). Gives a number of precise dates

and details regarding Campion's time there, from documents not seen by Simpson and other biographers before 1939.

71. R. J. Stonor O.S.B., *Stonor: A Catholic Sanctuary in the Chilterns from the Fifth Century Till Today* (2nd ed., R.H. Johns, Newport 1952). Gives a full account of the Stonor family's involvement in the printing of Campion's *Rationes Decem*.

72. Ceri Sullivan, *Dismembered Rhetoric: English Recusant Writing, 1580 to 1603* (Fairleigh Dickinson University Press, N.J. 1995)

73. Ludwig von Pastor, *The History of the Popes*, vol. 19, Gregory XIII (1572-1585) (Kegan Paul, London 1930). Chapter 10 is on England.

74. Alexandra Walsham, *Church Papists: Catholicism, Conformity and Confessional Polemic in Early Modern England* (Boydell Press, Suffolk 1993, 1999)

75. Evelyn Waugh, *Edmund Campion. Jesuit and Martyr* (1935. 2nd ed., Hollis and Carter, London 1947). A popular and well-written biography, reprinted many times. Despite assistance received from Fr. Leo Hicks S.J., it has some historical errors and imprecision. Page numbers of this book vary so much from one publisher to another, I usually give only the chapter number when citing it.

Articles

76. Miguel A. Bernad S.J., "The *Treatise on Imitation* of Blessed Edmund Campion," *Folia* 6 (1952) pp. 100–114; 7 (1953) pp. 20–29. Latin text and Eng. trans. with brief historical intro. Fr. Bernad of Berchmans College, Novaliches, Manila, says his trans. conveys the sense and is not meant to be literal.

77. Philip Caraman S.J., "Campion at St. John's," *Letters and Notices* 92 (1995) pp. 212–24

78. Marion Colthorpe, "Edmund Campion's Alleged Interview with Queen Elizabeth in 1581," *Recusant History*, 1984, pp. 197–200. Shows that Campion had no private audience with the queen after capture.

79. C. Richard Desper, "Allusions to Edmund Campion in *Twelfth Night*," Elizabethan Review, Spring/Summer 1995

80. Carl I. Hammer, "Robert Campion: Edmund Campion's Brother?," *Recusant History*, 1980, p. 153

81. Michael Hodgetts, "Campion in Staffordshire and Derbyshire 1581," *Midland Catholic History* 7 (2000) pp. 52–54. Hodgetts goes carefully through Lord Burghley's notes on Campion's trips from Christmas 1580 to Easter 1581.

82. Denys G.M. Jackson, "Campion the Martyr," Advocate Press, Melbourne 1946, 31 pp.

83. Lubomír Konec'n," "Edmund Campion, S.J., as Emblematist," in *The Jesuits and the Emblem Tradition*, ed. Marc van Vaeck and John Manning (Imago Figurata Studies, vol. 1A) Brepols, Turnhout, Belgium 1999, pp. 147–59   .

84. Peter Lake and Michael Questier, "Puritans, Papists, and the 'Public Sphere' in Early Modern England: The Edmund Campion Affair in Context," *Journal of Modern History* 72 (September 2000) pp. 587–627

85. Thomas M. McCoog S.J., "The English Jesuit Mission and the French Match, 1579–1581," *The Catholic Historical Review* 87 (April 2001) pp. 185–213   ·

86. Michael F.J. McDonnell, "Edmund Campion, S.J., and St. Paul's School," *Notes and Queries* 194 (Oxford 1949) pp. 46–49, 67–70, 90–92 John Morris S.J., three articles:

87. "Blessed Edmund Campion at Douay," *The Month*, September 1887, pp. 30–46

88. "Blessed Edmund and Companions, Martyrs," *The Month*, December 1887, pp. 457–70

89. "Blessed Edmund Campion and his *Ten Reasons*," *The Month*, July 1889, pp. 372–83

90. Charles A. Newdigate, "The Tyburn Prophecy of Gregory Gunnes," *The Month*, July 1934, pp. 56–62. Prints for the first time in full the reports of Fr. Gunnes's statements of 1585. See ch. 21: "A Tyburn prophecy fulfilled."

91. Richard Simpson, "Was Campion a Traitor to his Brethren?" *The Rambler*, November 1857, pp. 322–31

92. Richard Simpson, "Campion's Alleged Confessions," *The Rambler*, February 1858, pp. 100–13

93. Dom Hilary Steuert, "The Place of Allen, Campion and Parsons in the Development of English Prose," *The Review of English Studies*, vol. 20, no. 80, October 1944, pp. 272–85

94. Rafael E. Tarrago, "Bloody Bess: The Persecution of Catholics in Elizabethan England," *Logos: A Journal of Catholic Thought and Culture*, Winter 2004, pp. 117–33

95. Carol Z. Weiner, "The Beleaguered Isle: A Study of Elizabethan and Early Jacobean Anti-Catholicism," *Past and Present*, 51 (May 1971) pp. 27–62

96. *Recusant History—A journal of research in post-reformation Catholic history in the British Isles*. A biennial journal founded in 1951 containing fascinating and scholarly articles on Campion's era and beyond. Works by John Hungerford Pollen S.J. (1858–1925)

97. "The Journey of Blessed Edmund Campion from Rome to England, March–June, 1580," *The Month*, September 1897, pp. 243–55. Reprinted with additions, Roehampton, U.K. 1897.

98. "The Politics of the English Catholics during the Reign of Queen Elizabeth:
    I. The First Period, 1558–1568
    II. The Second Period, 1568–1579
    III. Revival of Spiritual Life and of Political Aspiration, 1580–1582
    IV. The Political Crisis, 1583–1588
    V. Plots and Sham Plots (in 2 parts)
    VI. After the Armada"
    All are in *The Month*, respectively: vol. 99 (1902) pp. 43–60; 131–48; 290–305; 394–411; 600–18 and vol. 100 (1902) pp. 71–87; 176–88.

99. "Religious Persecution under Queen Elizabeth," *The Month*, November 1904, pp. 501–17

100. "Blessed Edmund Campion's *Decem Rationes*," *The Month*, January 1905, pp. 11–26

101. "An Error in Simpson's *Campion*," *The Month*, June 1905, pp. 592599. Corrects Simpson's notion that there was a formally constituted association of missionary helpers in England.

102. "Edmund Campion's History of Ireland," *The Month*, December 1905, pp. 561–76; February 1906, pp. 156–69

103. "Mr. . Herbert Paul on Campion," *The Month*, January 1906, pp. 89–91

104. "The Mission of Fathers Persons and Campion," *The Month*, February 1906, pp. 207–11

105. "Campion's *Decem Rationes*," *The Month*, July 1909, p. 80. Relates simply a discovery of a third copy of an original print of the work.

106. "Blessed Edmund Campion's *Challenge*," *The Month*, January 1910, pp. 50–65

107. Introduction to *Campion's Ten Reasons* (trans. J. Rickaby S.J., Manresa Press, London 1914) pp. 1–29

108. "Blessed Edmund Campion's Confessions," *The Month*, July–December 1919, pp. 258–61

109. "The Elizabethan Act that made Martyrs," *The Month*, March 1922, pp. 236–45

110. *The English Catholics in the Reign of Queen Elizabeth: A Study of their Politics, Civil Life, and Government, 1558–1580* (Longmans, Green and Co., London 1920. Reprint: Ayer, N.Y. 1971)
    Memoirs of Father Robert Persons, ed. J.H. Pollen: see no. 25
    Acts of English Martyrs hitherto unpublished, ed. J.H. Pollen: see no. 27
    See also no. 42

Foreign Biographies of Campion (chronological order)

Alexis Possoz S.J., *Le Premier Jésuite Anglais Martyrisé en Angleterre, ou Vie et Mort du Père Edmond Campian* ("The first English Jesuit martyred in England, or the life and death of Fr. E. Campion," French 1864)

Willem Frederik van Nieuwenhoff S.J., *Edmond Campion: eene bladzijde uit de geschiedenis van koningin Elisabeth* ("E. Campion, a separate page in the history of Queen Elizabeth," Dutch 1888; French trans. 1896)

Jaime Nonell, *Vida de los beatos Edmundo Campion y sus cuatro companeros martires* ("Life of Blessed E. Campion and his four martyr companions," Spanish 1888)

Antonín Rejzek S.J., *Blahoslaven" Edmund Kampian, kne˘ z z Tovaryšstva Ježíšova* ("Blessed E. Campion, priest of the Society of Jesus," Czech 1889)

Giovanni Berselli S.J., *Vita del Beato Edmondo Campion* ("Life of Blessed E. Campion," Italian 1889)

Karlheinz Riedel S.J., *Edmund Campion. Das Leben eines Kämpfers für Christus* ("E. Campion. The life of a warrior for Christ," German 1940)

2nd ed. *Sieger im Tod: Die Lebensgeschichte Edmund Campions, eines Kämpfers für Christus* ("Victor in death: the biography of E. Campion, a warrior for Christ," 1953; Slovak trans. 1995).

X. Chanthann, *Le grain sous la meule: Le bienheureux Edmond Campion* ("The grain under the grindstone: Blessed E. Campion," French 1946)

Except for Rejzek, none of these compares to Simpson in size, or depth of research, and in most cases their free use of Simpson is obvious.

Dramas about Campion

Henry Browne, *A tragedy of Queen Elizabeth: a religious drama of three acts with epilogue, relating to the life and martyrdom of the Blessed Edmund Campion* (62 pp. Burns, Oates and Washbourne, London 1932)

Richard Breen and Harry Schnibbe, *Who Ride on White Horses—the story of Edmund Campion* (1940), performed 1940 at the Heckscher Theatre, New York, by the Mimes and Mummers of Fordham University, Campion being played by Robert Speaight. Performed in 1941 at the Ateneo de Manila University, directed by two Jesuit scholastics, Rev. James Reuter and Horacio de la Costa.

Dunstan Thompson, an American poet, living in Holt, Norfolk, in the 1960's wrote an unpublished 3-act play on Campion, 118 typed pages, entitled *The Bright One.*

Christopher Buckley and James MacGuire, *Campion: A Play in Two Acts* (Ignatius Press, San Francisco, 1990)

Champion (Club Milites production, Dublin 2006)—performed at Dublin Oak Academy

Simpson's Bibliography

Revised, enlarged and updated (2010)

1. Early biographies and accounts of Campion
2. Manuscript sources
3. *Brag*
4. *Rationes Decem*
5. Publications connected with Campion's capture
6. Publications connected with the debates in the Tower
7. Publications connected with Campion's trial and execution
8. Campion's own works: Individual works
                                              Collected or selected works
                                              Unpublished miscellanea

Spelling of old titles is modernized except for recent facsimile reprints. This bibliography lists works by both Catholics and Protestants. For quick distinction in sections 1–7:
Catholic works are listed from the outer left margin, whilst -
    Protestant works are indented thus.

1. Early Biographies and Accounts of Campion

1. **Paolo Bombino S.J.**, *Vita et Martyrium Edmundi Campiani, Martyris Angli e Societate Jesu, auctore R. P. Paulo Bombino, ejusdem Societatis* (Joannes Meursius, Antwerpiae 1618) 260 pp. ("Life and Martyrdom of Edmund Campion, English Martyr of the Society of Jesus, by author Rev. Fr. Paolo Bombino of the same Society," J. van Meurs, Antwerp 1618).

The earliest detailed biography to be published. 59 chapters. Bombino (also known as Bombinus) consulted Fr. Persons about it. The Bodleian Library, Oxford, has a copy. This work was reprinted more than once in the next year or two, but Bombino repudiated all these editions. In an "Admonitio ad Lectorem" (A caution to the reader) of the Mantuan edition of 1620, he says, "They all have proceeded from the first Antwerp edition, which in its progress through the press, and in my absence, received from too benevolent an editor a cast and features which I cannot acknowledge as mine. And indeed it is not commendable that other men's books, like children, should by certain arbitrary critics, and without the consent of their parents, be mutilated, or branded with strange marks, without being granted an opportunity of defense."

2nd edition: *Vita et Martyrium Edmundi Campiani Martyris Angli e Societate Iesu. Editio posterior, ab auctore multis aucta partibus and emendata* (Apud Fratres Osannas, Ducales Impressores, Mantuae 1620) 333 pp. ("Life and Martyrdom of Edmund Campion, English Martyr of the Society of Jesus. A later edition, much expanded by the author and amended," Duke's Press, at the Osanna brothers [Aurelio and Lodovico Osanna], Mantua 1620). 60 chapters. Several copies are extant today in libraries and private possession. All citations of Bombino in this present biography are from this edition. Reprinted Paris 1626, Naples 1627—but these have not been found by modern scholars.

At the Bodleian Library, Oxford, is an unpublished 17th century manuscript, an anonymous accurate English translation of the 1618 edition, once the possession of the antiquarian Archbishop Sancroft. It is incomplete: chs 4–6, 22, 49–56, 58, and other portions, are not done. Its rendition of chapters 46 and 47 (47 and 48 in the 1620 ed.), recounting the first debate in the Tower, are in Holleran, pp. 182–95 (see no. 41 below).

In the library of Il Gesù church at Rome there is a copy of the Mantuan edition, full of notes, corrections and additions, in Bombino's handwriting, apparently intended for a third edition, which never saw the light, but I (Simpson) was given a hand-written copy of them all. Some of these were suggested by Persons or his writings, some by others who had known Campion. Thus he has an addition at p. 45 "Ex commentariis P. Personii tunc apud me" (from *Commentaries* of Fr. Persons with me at the time). These notes of Fr. Persons are mentioned in the next item. The history of Campion's stay at Prague is much enlarged "ex animadversionibus Monachiensibus" (from observations from Munich). Another remark on the trial at p. 273 is "ex exceptis ex apologia Thomae Fitzerberti" (from excerpts of T. Fitzherbert's defense) who became a priest and Jesuit in Rome, and again at p. 289 "ex diversorum auctariis, sunt apud me" (from additions of divers people; they are with me). He must have been engaged many years in writing his book: at ch. 32, p. 147, he says, "narrabat mihi, cum haec scriberem, Personius" (Persons was telling me when I was writing this). Now Fr. Persons died in 1610, eight years before the book was first published. As may be seen from Bombino's dedication to the Duke of Mantua, it was the main occupation of his life, the fruit of years of patience.

It was considered a book "castae et emendatae dictionis, et exquisitae ele gantiae" ("of pure and refined expression, and exquisite elegance": commendation by German scholar Gaspar Schoppe before the Contents). It is quite truthful and honest, though uncritical; and its great fault is that which its author thought its great virtue—its elegance. Bombino's bombastic style was tedious to the good sense of the learned Jesuits at Antwerp in 1618, who liked to tell stories in plain words and preserve the flavor of the age, instead of translating everything into a Ciceronian style. He had a right to his own views, though his literary criticism will not bear scrutiny; for, he says in the *Admonitio*, of all Campion's alleged works he accepts none as authentic, "but the small book *Ten Reasons* and two or three epistles." "Many things have come out recently under his name which either the style or the content clearly show not to be his. Anyone with a taste for style and of Campion's, will see that for himself." The other pieces "circulating under his name," he says, "I deem spurious, as only exercises of his students, excerpted from his lessons . . . or corrected by him." Homer may nod, and Campion too.

This opinion of Simpson immediately above is shared by the Jesuit editors of the documents presented to the Holy See in 1968: "Bombino wrote long complex Latin sentences, and his chapters are, for the most part, continuous diffuse narrative, not broken into paragraphs and only poorly indexed. Hence it is very difficult to quote briefly from him regarding particular events." Archdiocese of Westminster, *Cause of the Canonization of Blessed Martyrs*, p. 336 (see editor's bibliography no. 38 for full title).

2. Robert Persons S.J., *Of the Life and Martyrdom of Father Edmond Campian*, printed for the first time in *Letters and Notices* (Manresa Press, Roehampton, U.K.) vol. 11 (1877), pp. 219–42, 308–39; vol. 12 (1878), pp. 1–68. *Letters and Notices* is not found in libraries; it was for private circulation in the English Province of the Society of Jesus. The editor Br. H. Foley S.J. says, p. 242, "modern spelling and a little fuller punctuation have been introduced, but no change has been made in the text."

The original manuscript of 1594 was begun on July 5 that year. A 1689 transcript of it, by archivist of the English College, Rome, Fr. Christopher Grene S.J. (1629–97), is in the archives of Stonyhurst College, Lancashire, in Grene's *Collectanea P*, vol. 1, folios 76–146 (Ms. A.IV.2). Printed, as above, it occupies 124 pages. It is very full, clear, lively, well-written—and valuable, since Persons knew Campion closely—but incomplete, stopping at November 1580, and at times faulty on dates. The last (and incomplete) chapter is "Of Fr. Campian's

journey to Lancashire, and the letter he wrote to the General of all his affairs."
From Rome, Persons's Ms. may have been conveyed to Liège, Belgium, after the
suppression of the Society of Jesus in 1773, and thence to Stonyhurst.

There is a series of notes by the same hand, arranged as headings or analyses
of the chapters of a whole life: these are the *Commentaria* by Persons that were
lent to Fr. Bombino who follows them implicitly (e.g., ch. 39, p. 183, Bombino
says "these *Commentaria* were my guides"), even when Persons's memory failed
him, and Bombino is therefore criticised for carelessness by Fr. Bartoli (no. 4).
These still unpublished *Commentaria*, or "draft Life" as Pollen calls them, are
in *Collectanea P*, vol. 1, folios 147–59. These seem to be the start of a life of
Campion, in Latin, in Persons's hand (Ms. A.II.14, dated Sunday October 20,
1595 says Fr. Edwards in his edition of More, *Elizabethan Jesuits*, note on p.
372), which Fr. Hicks (C.R.S., vol. 39, p. xiii) calls *De Vita Campiani* ("Of the life
of Campion"), begun Dec. 1593 (Southern, p. 355). It is cited in this biography
as "Persons's *Draft life of Campion.*"

Persons planned the biography in three "Books" (as he says at the end of
Book 1). Book 1, in 24 chapters, goes from Campion's birth up to and including the *Brag* (July 1580). He wrote only 4 chapters of Book 2 (going up to Nov.
1580); and this is as far as he got.

There are other particulars on Campion in Persons's *Memoirs*, ed. by J.H.
Pollen S.J., among other materials, in volumes 2 (Arden Press, London 1906) and
4 (Arden 1907) of the Publications of the Catholic Record Society. In them, he
often gives names, dates and details touching on the English mission not given
elsewhere. The same is true of the valuable collection, *Letters and Memorials of
Father Robert Persons S.J., Vol. I (to 1588)*, ed. Leo Hicks S.J. (Catholic Record
Society, vol. 39, London 1942).

3. Henry More S.J., *Historia Provinciae Anglicanae Societatis Jesu, collectore
Henrico Moro, eiusdem Societatis, sacerdote* (Thomæ Gevbels, Audomari 1660)
("History of the English Province of the Society of Jesus, compiled by Henry
More, priest, of the same Society," Th. Geubels, St. Omer 1660). Eng. trans. of
the Elizabethan part, namely, books 1–6: Francis Edwards S.J., *The Elizabethan
Jesuits: Historia Missionis Anglicanae Societatis Jesu (1660) of Henry More*
["History of the Mission of the English Society of Jesus"] (Phillimore, London
1981).

Fr. More was a great-grandson of St. Thomas More. In 1622 he was sent
to work among Catholics in the London districts. He was arrested in 1628 and
imprisoned until 1633. His history of Campion, though taken in the main from
Bom bino, has additions and corrections from independent sources, especially
concerning the trial. He prints several of Persons's letters.

4. **Daniello Bartoli S.J.**, *Dell'Istoria della Compagnia di Gesù. L'Inghil terra parte dell'Europa* (Roma 1667) ("History of the Society of Jesus: England, part of Europe," Rome 1667).

Reprint in *Delle Opere del Padre Daniello Bartoli* ("Some works of Fr. D. Bartoli") vol. III [England, books 1–4] and vol. IV [England, books 5–6] (Giacinto Marietti, Torino [Turin] 1825). Biographical material on Campion is in books 2 and 3, which in the 1825 ed. occupy 311 pages on Persons, Campion and the English mission.

Bartoli's description of the first debate in the Tower, in book 3, chapter 3, is reprinted in English translation in Holleran, pp. 196–207 (no. 41).

Bartoli had the advantage of consulting all the Mss. in the Gesù, and his margins are full of references to letters which he must have read there. He made special use of Persons's Mss. there and at the English College at Rome, and carried his criticism so far as to omit much that Bombino tells, because it was not found in Persons's me moirs. Bombino finishes his account of Campion's capture thus: "I am aware that many things, especially of the capture of Campion, are related differently to that here set forth by us, even in printed books. . . . But I find that history is like a summer torrent—the water at first . . . is foul with dirt; but let it stand for a time, and it clears itself. So the first accounts of things are disfigured by passion . . . but what was at first unknown gradually creeps out . . . and everything is seen in its proper light. I certainly have sufficient witnesses of the rest that I tell; and in the story of this capture I follow not light rumours or muddy report (as is usual at the start), but things now long settled and I have Persons's own most sure authority, who had the whole story from the man whom Mrs. Yate ordered to accompany Eliot [see ch. 14: "Surrounded"], and wrote it all in his notes, which he gave me as guides when I was writing this book at Rome." (1620 ed., pp. 182–3). To which Bartoli (who omits all mention of Campion's nocturnal sermon in Mrs. Yate's room) says: "quanto a certi strani accidenti, che pur'altri ne conta, a me par che sentano dell'incredibile; nè ve n'è fiato in tante lettere del Personio, nè in niuna delle fresche memorie d'allora, o di poscia; onde non mi pajono degni di nè pur mentovarsi." (As to certain strange incidents, which, though others recount, I regard as not credible; they are neither in the numerous letters of Persons, nor in any of the fresh recollections of that time or later; hence I think them not even worthy of mention. 1825 ed., vol. 3, bk 3, ch. 2, p. 20). The fact is that Bombino followed Persons's notes now at Stonyhurst, while Bartoli had only the collection of Persons's letters at Rome and the printed lives of Campion to refer to.

5. **Bohuslav Balbin S.J.**, *Miscellanea Historica Regni Bohemiae Decadis I* (Typis Georgij Czernoch, Pragae 1682) ("Historical Miscellanea of the Kingdom of

Bohemia, the First Decade," George Czernoch Press, Prague 1682).

Part of the larger work *Miscellanea Historica Regni Bohemiae* (Pragae 1679-88), 13 vols. ("Historical Miscellanea of the Kingdom of Bohemia," Prague).

Balbin is also called Balbino and Balbinus. In "Decade 1": Book 4 *Liber hagiographicus* ("Hagiographical book") recounts the lives of 134 saints of Bohemia; in its part 1, no. 118, pp. 189–96, it recounts Campion's activities at Brünn and Prague. Gives also a few useful particulars, which I have adopted.

6. Johann Schmidl S.J., *Historiae Societatis Jesu Provinciae Bohemiae, Pars I: 1555–1592* (Typis Univ. Carolo Ferdinandeae, Pragae 1747) ("History of the Society of Jesus of the Province of Bohemia, Part 1," Charles Ferdinand University Press, Prague 1747).

The *History* is a 4-part work. This first part (1555–92) contains a chronicle of Campion's life at Prague, with some details not found elsewhere. These were taken from the archives of the Jesuit College at Prague.

These are all the original printed sources for Campion's life. The following accounts of him are all second-hand:

Richard Verstegan [alias Richard Rowlands], *Thea trum Crudelitatum Haereticorum nostri temporis* ("Theatre of the cruelties of the heretics of our time," Antwerp 1587). French trans. *Théatre des cruautés des hérétiques au seizième siècle* (Desclée, Lille 1883); *Théâtre des cruautés des hérétiques de notre temps* (Editions Chandeigne, Paris 1995). Campion is mentioned only once, in a list of martyrs; the book is mainly drawings of tortures and martyrdoms, with verses.

Luis de Granada O.P., *Introduction del symbolo de la fe* ("Introduction to the creed," Salamanca 1583) part 5, ch. 23. This book was translated into Italian and Latin, and frequently reprinted.

Jacques-Auguste Thou (Thuanus), *Historiarum Sui Temporis, pars quarta* ("Of the history of his own time, part 4," Paris 1609) pp. 462–3

Henri Spondanus, *Annals* (Paris 1637)

Joannes Fabritius, *Edmundus Campianus coelesti lauro insignis* ("E. Campion, marked with a heavenly laurel," Prague 1651)

Philippe Alegambe S.J., *Mortes illustres et gesta eorum de Societate Iesu qui in odium fidei . . . necati . . . sunt* ("The illustrious deaths and deeds of those of the Society of Jesus put to death out of hatred of the faith," ed. J. Nadasi, Rome 1657) p. 79

Francesco Sacchini S.J., *Historiae Societatis Iesu* ("Of the history of the Society of Jesus") *Part 4* (Rome 1652) book 8, pp. 263 ff., *Part 5* (Rome 1661) book 1, pp. 31ff. He has a fragment of a letter of Campion not found elsewhere.

Cornelius Hazart S.J., *Kerkelycke Historie van de Gheheele Werelt*

("Universal Church history," Antwerp 1669): at vol. 3, p. 247, begins the history of England, illustrated with fine portraits of More, Fisher, Pole, Queen Mary, Persons, Campion, Henry Garnet, Charles I, Henry Morse, et al.

Mathias Tanner S.J., *Societas Jesu usque ad sanguinis et vitae profusionem militans* ("The Society of Jesus, doing battle unto the shedding of blood and life," Prague 1675) pp. 7–14. Eng. ed., *The Society of Jesus battling even to the outpouring of its life and blood in Europe, Asia, Africa and America* (trans. Joseph W. Riordan S.J., Los Angeles 1935)

—Other early accounts are listed at nos. 68–77.

2. Manuscript sources

The Ms. sources for Campion's life which I have used in the foregoing pages:

a. The Stonyhurst Mss., containing the biography by Father Persons, listed above (printed after Simpson's death), and several letters, the first copies of them in Campion's own handwriting, all of which may be found in their proper places in the fore going pages.

b. An abundance of documents in the British Museum, the State Paper Office (abbreviated as "S.P.O." in the endnotes), and the Privy-Council Books, to all which I have referred when I have quoted them.—Many of these, published since Simpson's time, are cited from printed books.

c. I have also consulted the correspondence of the French ambassador in London, now in the imperial library at Paris; but I failed to find the letter wherein, according to Persons, he informed his court that no such scene as Campion's martyrdom had happened since the apostolic age (Bombino, ch. 58, p. 303).

d. I have found a few papers in the Archives and Burgundian library at Brussels (e.g. Ms. no. 15594); but the Spanish ambassador's letters from London for the year 1581 are not there in the proper series. Mendoza certainly wrote about Campion; but in all that I have seen of his writings at the period of Campion's imprisonment, trial, and death, there is not a word about him—no protest, no expression of indignation, nothing, in fact, which we should have anticipated from his known relations with Persons. – After Simpson's death, one of these became known to John Morris S.J. who printed it in *The Month*, Aug. 1893 (see editor's bibliography, no. 23).

e. In the archives of the Grocers' Company of London are some notices of Campion—now quoted fully and accurately in ch. 1: "Trouble from the Grocers' Company," thanks to the book of Leslie Campion, 1975 (see editor's bibliography, no. 44).

f. The documents printed by Balbin and Schmidl still exist in Ms. at Prague, in the album of the Novitiate, and in a manuscript kept today at the National Library of the Czech Republic, Prague: *Historia Collegii S.J. Pragensis . . . P. Georgio Varo, Anglo et aliis*, 1620 ("History of the Jesuit College of Prague, by Englishman Fr. George Ware and others." The "others" include Fr. Balbin S.J.). The Ms. has not been published; pp. 21–156 cover the years 1555–81.

In addition to the more important sources listed here are many others named in the endnotes.

3. Publications Connected with the *Brag*

7. Campion's *Letter to the Lords of the Privy Council* ("The Brag," July 19, 1580; see ch. 10: "Campion writes his *Brag*" and its endnote) was not printed by Campion, but circulated extensively in Ms., which accounts for the variations among the surviving copies.

The Brag called forth two replies:

> 8. William Charke. *An Answer to a seditious pamphlet lately cast abroad by a Jesuit, with a discovery* [exposure] *of that blasphemous sect. By W. Charke* (Christopher Barker, Lon don [Dec. 20] 1580)

Another enlarged edition the next year:

> 8a. *An answer to a seditious pamphlet lately cast abroad by a Jesuit: containing ix articles here inserted and set down at large, with a discovery of that blasphemous sect. By William Charke* (Christopher Barker, London 1581). Includes Campion's "Nine articles directed to the Lords of the PrivyCouncil" ("The Brag"), integrated with Charke's answer. This work printed the *Brag* for the first time. Charke also issued, separately, a translation of Christian Francken's *Colloquium Jesuiticum* ("Jesuitical dialogue" 1580) entitled *A conference or dialogue discovering* [exposing] *the sect of Jesuits.*

> 9. Meredith Hanmer. *The great Brag and Challenge of Mr. Champion a Jesuit, commonly called Edmund Campion, lately arrived in England, containing nine articles here severally laid down, directed by him to the Lords of the Council, confuted and answered by Meredith Hanmer, Master of Art, and Student in Divinity* (Thomas Marsh, London [Jan. 3] 1581)

Father Persons confuted both these books at once in his book:

10. *A Brief Censure upon two books written in answer to Mr. Edmond Campion's*

offer of disputation (John Lyon, Doway 1581). It was not really printed at Douay but at Browne's house in Southwark, near London, by Brinkley with his secret press. In the custom of the time, Persons found an apposite Biblical quotation to put on the title page: "Deut 5:5: You feared the fire, and therefore you ascended not up the mountain"! Reprint: see no. 14.

Charke and Hanmer made separate replies to this *Censure*:

11. *A Reply to a Censure written against the two answers to a Jesuit's seditious pamphlet, by Wm. Charke* (Christopher Barker, London 1581)

12. *The Jesuits' Banner: displaying their origin and success; their vow and oath; their hypocrisy and superstition; their doctrine and positions; with*

a confutation of a late pamphlet secretly imprinted, and entitled "A brief Censure. . . ." Compiled by Meredith Hanmer, Master of Art and student in divinity (Thomas Dawson and Richard Vernon, London 1581).

13. *A Ballad entitled A Gentle Jerk for the Jesuit* (Anon., possibly by the Smithfield anti-Catholic balladist, William Elderton, "rhyming Elderton," as the Catholics called him. Printed by Richard Jones, London Feb. 13, 1581). Not extant.

Shortly after Campion's death, Persons went over to Rouen, France, where, among other works, he printed:

14. *A Defense of the Censure given upon two books of William Charke and Meredith Hammer, ministers, which they wrote against Mr. Edmond Campian, Priest of the Society of Jesus, and against his offer of disputa tion: taken in hand since the death of the said Mr. Campian* (George L'Oyselet, Rouen 1582)

The *Censure* is fully reprinted, and each paragraph defended in detail. 173 pp. It rebuts nos. 11 and 12. Reprint in: *Rationes Decem 1581 by Edmund Campion and A brief censure 1581; and A defense of the censure 1582 by Robert Persons* (Scolar Press, Menston, England 1971) 396 pp. Nos. 17, 10, 14 together.

A year elapsed before any notice was taken of this able rejoinder; then

Charke, it seems (or possibly Fulke), published for the interim a portion of his reply:

15. *An Answer for the time unto that foul and wicked Defense of the Censure that was given upon Mr. Charke's book and Mere dith Hanmer's. Containing a maintenance of the credit and persons of all those worthy men: namely, of Mr. Luther, Calvin, Bucer, Beza, and the rest of those*

godly ministers of God's word, whom he, with a shameless pen most slanderously hath sought to deface: finished sometime since: and now published for the stay of the Christian reader till Mister Charke's book come forth (Thomas Dawson and Tobie Smith, London 1583) 107 pp.

After three years' more study, Charke (or possibly Fulke) gave to the world his completed treatise:

16. *A Treatise against the Defense of the Censure given upon the books of Wm. Charke and Mer. Hanmer by an unknown Popish traitor, in maintenance of the seditious challenge of Edm. Campion, lately condemned and executed for high treason. In which the reader shall wonder to see the impudent falsehood of the Popish defender in abusing the names and writings of the doctors old and new to blind the ignorant. Hereunto are adjoined two treatises written by Dr. Fulke: the one against Allen's book of the Authority of the Priesthood to remit sins, etc.; the other against the railing declamation of P. Frarine* (T. Thomas, Cambridge 1586). Three tracts with three title-pages. 359 + 531 + 54 pp.

This was a rejoinder to Allen's book, *A treatise made in defense of the lauful power and authoritie of priesthod to remitte sinnes* (John Fowler, Louvain 1567. Facsimile reprint of 1st edition: Scolar Press, Menston, England 1972). The book of Frarine was *Harangue of Peter Frarin of Antwerp, against the seditious motions excited by the Protestants on pretence of reforming religion* (trans. from Latin into English by John Fowler: Antwerp 1566).

4. Publications Connected with *Rationes Decem*

17. Edmund Campion, *Rationes Decem: quibus fretus certamen adversariis obtulit in causa fidei Edmundus Campianus, e Societate Nominis Iesu presbyter allegatae ad clarissimos viros, nostrates academicos* ("Ten Reasons: presented to the illustrious men, our academics, on the basis of which Edmund Campion, priest of the Society of the name of Jesus, proposed to his adversaries disputation in the name of the faith") Privately printed, Stonor Park, near Henley, 1581. The full title has varied somewhat from edition to edition, but that given here is copied from the title-page of the original edition. For the many editions of this work, see no. 91. The Latin original can be seen online at Project Gutenberg and other websites.

The Bishop of London (Aylmer) ordered the two Regius Professors of Divinity at Oxford and Cambridge to answer this book. The Cambridge divine William Whitaker (1548–1595) was the first to reply and did so while Campion was still alive:

18. *Ad Rationes Decem Edmundi Campiani Iesuitae . . . Responsio Guilielmi Whitakeri Theologiae in Academia Cantabrigiensi professoris regii* ("Reply of William Whitaker, Regius Professor of Theology at Cambridge university to *Rationes Decem* of Jesuit Edmund Campion") Thomas Vautrollier, London 1581. This work included Campion's full text and was reprinted in 1592 and 1617, and also within Whitaker's collected works at Geneva, 1610.

Cardinal (St. Robert) Bellarmine, who had crossed theological swords with Whitaker, procured a picture of Whitaker from England, and hung it up in his study, much admiring him for his singular learning; and being asked by a Jesuit, why he would let a picture of that heretic hang there, answered, "Though he is a heretic, and my adversary, yet he is a learned adversary." (Brodrick's *Bellarmine*, 1961, p. 84). In the dedication of his *Disputatio de Sacra Scriptura* ("A Disputation on Holy Scripture," 1588), Whitaker paid compliment to Bellarmine: "I deemed him a man unquestionably learned, possessed of a happy genius, a penetrating judgment, and multifarious reading; one, moreover, who was wont to deal more plainly and honestly than is the custom of other papists, to press his arguments more home, and to keep more closely to the question." Bellarmine and Whitaker were alike in being learned, and in arguing calmly and objectively about doctrines, without adding torrents of abuse or personal attacks (although Southern, p. 255, says his pamphlet against *Ten Reasons* is "somewhat abusive"). The difference can be seen even in the titles of Whitaker's books, compared to Humphrey's:

The Oxford theologian Laurence Humphrey (c. 1527–1590) put out half his elaborate reply the next year (2nd part below at no. 22):

19. *Jesuitismi pars prima: sive de Praxi Romanae Curiae contra respub licas et principes, et de nova legatione Jesuitarum in Angliam, προθεραπεια et praemonitio ad Anglos; cui adjuncta est concio ejusdem argumenti, cujus titulus est Pharisaismus vetus et novus, sive de fermento Pharisaeorum et Jesuitarum: authore Laurentio Humfredo* ("The first part of Jesuitry: namely, on the praxis of the Roman curia against governments and princes, and on the new mission of Jesuits into England, a forewarning and alert to the English; to which is added a defense of the same argument, whose title is Pharisaism new and old, or the ferment of the Pharisees and Jesuits; by author Laurence Humphrey") Henry Middleton, London 1582 twice. Dedicated to the Chancellor of the University, Robert Dudley, Earl of Leicester.

The same year, 1582, Father John Dury published his crushing reply to Whitaker:

20. *Confutatio Responsionis Gulielmi Whitakeri in Academia Cantabri gensi Professoris Regii ad Rationes Decem, quibus fretus Edmondus Campianus, Anglus, Societatis Jesu theologus, certamen Anglicanae Ecclesiae ministris obtulit in causa fidei. Authore Joanne Duraeo Scoto, Soc. Iesu presbytero* ("Confutation of the reply of William Whitaker, Regius Professor at Cambridge University, to the Ten Reasons, trusting in which, Englishman E. Campion, theologian of the Society of Jesus, proffered for a debate to the ministers of the Anglican Church for the cause of the faith, by author John Dury, Scot, priest of the Society of Jesus") Thomas Brumen, Paris 1582. 466 leaves, i.e., 932 pp. Incorporates the text of *Decem Rationes.* Reprinted with additions by D. Sartorius, Ingoldstadt 1585. 856 pp.

Whitaker was again quicker than his Oxford brother in replying:

21. *Responsionis ad Decem illas Rationes... Defensio contra Confu tationem Joannis Duraei, Scoti, presbyteri, Jesuitae. Authore Guil. Whitakero* ("Of the reply to those *Decem Rationes.* A defense against the rebuttal of John Dury, Scot, priest, Jesuit. By author Wm. Whitaker") Henry Middleton, London 1583. 887 pp.

Last comes Humphrey, part two:

22. *Jesuitismi pars secunda: Puritano-Papismi, seu doctrinae Jesuiticae aliquot rationibus ab Edm. Campiano comprehensae, et a Joanne Duraeo defensae, confutatio, et ex iisdem fundamentis reformatae religionis assertio: autore Lau. Humfredio s. theologiæ in Acad. Oxoniensi professore regio* ("Of the second part of Jesuitry: a rebuttal of Puritan-Papistry, or the Jesuitical doctrine summed up in several arguments by E. Campion, and defended by John Dury, and on the same basis a defense of the reformed religion, by author Laurence Humphrey, Regius Professor of sacred theology at Oxford University") Henry Middleton, London 1584.

Because of the Jesuits' evangelical emphasis on conversion and one's personal spiritual life, etc., the Anglicans derisively called them "Puritans"! There was some resemblance, superficially, in methods and spiritual doctrine, for which reason Persons's *Christian Directory* could be purloined by a Calvinist minister, Edmund Bunny, purged of Catholicism, and re-presented to a Protestant audience in 1584!

In 1585, the two authors' works were joined:

Responsionis ₐₐ decem illas rationes . . . Defensio contra Confu tationem Joannis Duraei . . . Pharisaismus vetus et novus L. Humfredi concio (La Rochelle, France 1585)

And here this particular controversy seems to have ended for the time, so far as England is concerned. Nearly a quarter of a century after, how ever, it revived for a moment:

William Whitaker's reply to Campion was first translated by Protestant Richard Stocke, who also translated Campion's book and included it at the start:

> 23. *An answer to the Ten Reasons of Edmund Campian the Jesuit: in confidence whereof he offered disputation to the ministers of the Church of England, in the controversy of faith. Whereunto is added in brief marginal notes, the sum of the defense of those reasons by John Duraeus the Scot, being a priest and a Jesuit, with a reply unto it. Written first in the Latin tongue by . . . William Whitaker . . . And now faithfully translated for the benefit of the unlearned (at the appointment and desire of some in authority) into the English tongue; by Richard Stocke, preacher in London.* 326 pp. (Felix Kyngston, London 1606). Bodleian Library, Oxford.

> 24. William Whitaker and Thomas Dawson (trans.), *A Seasonable Preservative against Popish delusions: or, an answer to Edmund Campian, the Jesuit's Ten Reasons for Popery; which he sent as a Challenge to the Two Universities of Oxford and Cambridge, 1580* (J. Batley, London 1732)

A German Socinian (of the Polish Unitarian Church) also authored a reply:

> 25. Thomas Pisecius (Pisecki), *Responsio ad decem rationes Edmundi Campiani Jesuitae* ("A reply to Ten Reasons of E. Campion, Jesuit") Rakow, Poland 1610

Tobie Matthew's *Concio Apologetica* (see ch. 1: "The Fathers of the Church") was printed as late as 1638:

> 26. *Piissimi et eminentissimi viri, D. Tobiæ Matthæi Archiepiscopi olim Eboracensis Concio apologetica adversus Campianum* ("Speech of defense against Campion of the most pious and most eminent man, Dr. Tobie Matthew, one-time archbishop of York") Leonard Lichfield, Oxford 1638.

5. Publications Connected with Campion's Capture

This section's entries are all hostile to Campion:

27. *Mr. Campion, the seditious Jesuit, is welcome to London* (Richard Jones, London, July 24, 1581). A poem, Anon., possibly William Elderton (see no. 13). Not extant.

28. Randall Hurlestone, *News from Rome concerning the blasphemous sacrifice of Papistical Mass; with divers other treatises, very godly and profitable. Canterbury, imprinted by John Mychell for E. Churton* [i.e., Campion] *the Jesuit.* No date.

29. *A brief Discourse of the taking of Edmund Campion, the seditious Jesuit and divers other Papists in Berkshire . . '. gathered by A. M.* [Anthony Munday] (William Wright, London 1581). It was submitted for publication on July 24, only a week after Campion's arrest. It was therefore written hurriedly, and mainly from information from Humphrey Foster, High Sheriff of Berkshire, who was not a witness of the search and discovery but came late on the scene, since as a Catholic he had no desire to help.

This pamphlet called forth a contradiction from George Eliot:

30. *A very true Report of the apprehension and taking of that arch-papist Edmund Campion, the Pope's right hand; with Three other lewd Jesuit Priests, and divers other Lay people, most seditious persons of like sort. Containing also a controlment* [critique] *of a most untrue former book set out by A. M., alias, Anthony Munday, concerning the same: as is to be proved and justified by George Elliot, one of the Ordinary Yeomen of Her Majesty's Chamber, Author of this Book, and chiefest cause of the finding of the said lewd and seditious people, great enemies to God, their loving Prince, and country* (Thomas Dawson, London 1581) 28 pp. Reprinted in *An English Garner,* ed. Edward Arber (vol. 8. Archibald Constable and Co., London 1896, pp. 203–26. Facsimile reprint: BiblioLife, Charleston 2009); *An English Garner: Tudor Tracts 1532–1588,* intro. A. F. Pollard (Archibald Constable and Co., London 1903, pp. 451–74).

6. Publications Connected with the Debates in the Tower

Out of the controversy of Campion's *Brag*, Campion's four days' debates in the Tower took their rise; and reports of these were immediately dispersed by the Catholics, "partly in print, but in written pamphlets much more dispersed" (says the intro. to no. 36). Still today nothing is known of the printed reports. The first five items following contain detailed, at times almost *verbatim*, manuscript reports of the debates, made at the time by Catholics who were present:

31. A Ms. report of the *1st day's debate* was in the library of the English College at Rome, and extracts of it are given in Latin translation by Bombino (1618 ed.), chapters 46 and 47 (47 and 48 in the 1620 ed.). See nos. 1, 41. 32. A Ms. found among the papers of Sir Thomas Tresham (c. 1543–1605) also has an account of the *1st day's debate*. The reporter is unknown. Sir Thomas was a famous recusant who had at one time harbored Edmund Campion. The Ms. was discovered in 1828 at Rushton Hall, Northamptonshire, when the removal of a partition revealed a secret closet containing some bundles of Tresham family papers. It was finally published in 1904 in Historical Manuscript Commission, *Various Collections*, vol. 3, pp. 8–16. See no. 41. See ch. 16: "Peace at no price."

33. Among the Mss. of Robert Harley (1661–1724) in the British Museum, Harleian Mss. 422, 433 have reports of the *2nd, 3rd and 4th days' debates* (the second one in duplicate, with only slight differences). They are in the handwriting of Stephen Vallenger (1541–91), and were found by Richard Topcliffe (1532–1604), the priest-catcher and priest-torturer, in the house of William Carter the printer (who was hanged in 1584), and were given to Foxe the martyrologist, who gave them to ecclesiastical historian John Strype, who sold them to the librarian of Robert Harley. Holleran (no. 41) judges these to be notes made in preparation for publication. See no. 41.

Alban Butler, in a Ms. account of the writers of the English College of Douay, now at Brussels (Royal Library, Ms. no. 15594), enumerates among Ralph Sherwin's writings one of these reports: *Collatio inter hereticos et Campianum in Turri Londinensi habita. Disputationes in castro Wisbecensi inter Fulkum ministrum et Catholicos* ("Conference held between heretics and Campion in the Tower of London. Debates in Wisbech Castle between the minister Fulke and Catholics").

34. Rawlinson Ms. D. 353 contains an account of the *2nd, 3rd and 4th days' debates*, among the collection of papers once belonging to Thomas Rawlinson (1681–1725), now at the Bodleian Library, Oxford. The author and copyist are unknown. See no. 41.

35. Additional Scudamore Ms. 11055, part of the Scudamore papers acquired by the British Library in 1837, contains an anonymous account of the *afternoon of the 2nd day's debate; and the 4th day's debate, morning and afternoon.* See no. 41.

It was not till Jan. 1 ,1583 (1584 by modern reckoning of Jan. 1st as new year; in other words, 2 years, 3 months after the debates) that the Protestant disputants pub lished their report of these conferences—a single volume in parts, with separate titles:

36. John Field, *A true report of the Disputation, or rather private Conference, had in the Tower of London with Ed. Campion, Jesuit, the last of August 1581. Set down by the Reverend learned men themselves that dealt therein* [Nowell and Day]. *Whereunto is joined also a true report of the other three days' conferences had there with the same Jesuit. Which now are thought meet to be published in print by authority* (Christopher Barker, London, Jan. 1, 1583)

37. *The three last days' Conferences had in the Tower with Edmund Campion Jesuit, the 18th, 23rd and 27th of September 1581, collected and faithfully set down by Mr. John Feilde* [Field], *Student in Divinity. Now perused by the learned men themselves, and thought meet to be published. A remembrance of the conference, had in the Tower with Edmunde Campion Jesuit, by William Fulke, and Roger Goade Doctors in Divinity, the 18, of September, 1581, as followeth* (C. Barker, Jan. 1, 1583)

This second part seems to have been struck off by itself. In the Faculty of Advocates' Library, Edinburgh, vol. 2, 1776, p. 172, is the following entry:

38. *Feilde (John). True report of the whole substance of the Conference had in the Tower of London between Wm. Charke, Wm. Fulke, Roger Goade, Dr. Walker, and Edward* [sic] *Campion the Jesuite, on the 18, 23, and 27 of Sept. 1581* (London 1583)

An opinion on faith and good works put forward by Campion at a debate was attacked by "H.D.," possibly the poet Henry Dod:

39. *A Godly and fruitful Treatise of Faith and works. Wherein is confuted a certain opinion of merit by works, which an adversary to the Gospel of Christ Jesus, held in the conference, had in the Tower of London* (Gregory Seton, London 1583)

40. Daniello Bartoli S.J., "History of the Society of Jesus," Rome 1667, has a summary description of the *1st day's debate* in bk 3, ch. 3, and the *2nd day's debate* in ch. 4. See nos. 4, 41.

41. James V. Holleran, *A Jesuit Challenge: Edmund Campion's Debates at the Tower of London in 1581* (Fordham Uni. Press, N.Y. 1999) contains the texts of nos. 32–35 (collating them where suitable, i.e., not giving every repetition), plus English translations of two relevant chapters of Bombino (see nos. 1, 31) and one of Bartoli's chapters (see nos. 4, 40). He omits Bombino's thin accounts of the

2nd and 3rd days' debates (1620 ed., 2nd debate, chs 49–50; 3rd debate, ch. 51) and Bartoli's adequate account of the *2nd day's debate.*

7. Campion's Trial and Execution Occasioned a Flood of Publications

42. There are two records of Campion's trial: British Library: Lansdowne Manuscripts 33, no. 65; and British Museum, London: Manuscript no. 1014 of the Cotton Library (Bib. Cott. 1014). There are small differences between the two records. The latter version was printed, for the first time, it seems, by Joseph Morgan, in a periodical, whose six numbers were collected in: *Phoenix Britannicus* [or *Britanniens*, British Phoenix], *being a miscellaneous Collection of scarce and curious Tracts . . . interspersed with choice pieces from original MSS* (J. Wilford, London 1732). More accessibly, it is reprinted in vol. 1, columns 1049–72, of T.B. Howell (compiler), *A Complete Collection of State Trials and Proceedings for High Treason and Other Crimes and Misdemeanors from the Earliest Period to the Year 1783* (21 vols, London 18161828). In Howell, this is immediately followed by the work named at no. 51. The only quotation from Campion within this second work is at column 1078: his answers to two questions put to him in the Tower on August 1st, 1581.

Simpson quoted the Lansdowne version. This text is retained but any additions found in Howell have been inserted. The trial record is in Howell's *State Trials* (Hansard, London 1816) vol. 1, columns 1049–72.

> 43. *An Advertisement and Defense for Truth against her backbiters, and specially against the whispering favorers and colorers of Campion's and the rest of his confederates' treasons* (Anon. Christopher Barker, London 1581). 1,100 words. One sheet of four leaves, the last page blank. Reprinted in *Holinshed's Chronicles* at A.D. 1581 (1587 ed., p. 1328) and as an appendix, pp. 133–6, to Anthony Munday, *John a Kent and John a Cumber—A Comedy* (intro. and notes J.P. Collier, The Shakespeare Society, London 1851. Facsimile reprint: Elibron, Massachusetts 2001). This was the advertisement read out at the execution by schoolmaster Hearne, mentioned in ch. 20: "Campion's last moments."

> 44. *A triumph for true subjects, and a terror unto all traitors: By the example of the late death of Edmund Campion, Ralph Sherwin, and Alexander Briant, Jesuits and seminary priests* (Richard Jones, London 1581). A ballad of fifteen 8-line stanzas, prob. by William Elderton: see no. 13), printed shortly after Dec. 1. The opening lines:

> > "Good subjects of England, rejoice and be glad;

Give glory to God—with humble knees down -
That Campion, the traitor, his hire [reward] hath now had.
Who sought for to spoil our queen and her Crown;
And all under color of Jesuits' profession,
To persuade the Queen's subjects to their own destruction.
Therefore unto God for our Queen let us pray,
That the Lord may preserve her life many a day."
—H.E. Rollins, *Old English Ballads 1553–1625 Chiefly from Manuscripts* (Cambridge Uni. Press 1920) p. 64

45. *A Discovery of Edmund Campion and his Confederates, their most horrible and traitorous practices against her Majesty's most royal person and the realm. Wherein may be seen, how through the whole course of their arraignment they were notably convicted of every cause. Whereto is added the execution of Edmund Campion, Ralph Sherwin, and Alexander Briant, executed at Tyburn the 1. of December. Pub lished by A. M.* [Anthony Munday] *sometime the Pope's scholar, allowed in the seminary at Rome amongst them: a discourse needful to be read of every man, to beware how they deal with such secret seducers* (John Charlewood, London 1582) 55 leaves, i.e., 110 pp. This pamphlet was entered in the Stationers' Register within two days of the execution, and published Jan. 29, and again on June 21, 1582. The same account, with small differences, is in *Holinshed's Chronicles* at A.D. 1581 (1587 ed., pp. 1322–9).

This called forth a little book by Fr. Thomas Alfield, printed by Richard Verstegan and edited by Stephen Vallenger, for printing which Vallenger was condemned in the Star-Chamber to lose his ears in the pillory and spend the rest of his life in prison:

46. *A True Report of the Death and Martyrdom of Mr. Campion, Jesuit and priest, and Mr. Sherwin and Mr. Briant, priests, at Tyburn, the first of December 1581. Observed and written by a Catholic priest, which was present thereat. Whereunto is annexed certain verses made by sundry persons* (Richard Verstegan [alias Richard Rowlands], Smithfield, London, Feb. 1582). 26 leaves. 49 pp., not numbered. Facsimile reprint: Scolar Press, Menston, U.K. 1970. Contents: 4 parts: A preface to the reader: 3/ pp.; the martyrdom account itself: 25 pp., ending with "God save the Queen"; a caveat to the reader concerning A. Munday's *Discovery of Edmund Campion* (no. 45), probably by Vallenger: 3 pp.; four poems, probably by Henry Walpole, Verstegan and Vallenger: 17 pp.; they are found in Pollen's edition of Allen's *Brief History* (no. 52a), the best-known one being,

"Why do I use my paper, ink and pen." There are three known copies: British Museum, London; Bodleian Library, Oxford; Oscott College, Sutton Coldfield, Warwickshire. The *True Report's* author and witness was (Blessed) Fr. Thomas Alfield, himself martyred at Tyburn in 1585. A copy is in the British Museum. Another contemporary long poem, "A Brief of the Life and Death of Sir Edmund Campion," is printed by Pollen, *Acts of the English Martyrs* (Burns and Oates London 1891) pp. 23–34. For some centuries in the north of England, "Sir" was a title sometimes used for priests.

But before this, the first printed account (says Southern, p. 377) of Campion's martyrdom appeared in Lyons, anonymously:

47. *L'Histoire de la mort que le R. P. Edmund Campion, et autres ont souffert en Angleterre pour la foy Catholique and Romaine, le premier iour de Decembre 1581. Traduit d'Anglois en François* ("An account of the death which Rev. Fr. Edmund Campion and others suffered in England for the Catholic and Roman faith, the first day of Dec. 1581. Translated from English into French") Jean Pillehotte, Lyons 1582. Only one copy of this is known. Translated from an English original now lost, and written by an unknown eye-witness to Campion's Tower debates. Not the same work as no. 46 (say Allison and Rogers, vol. 1, no. 196, correcting Southern, p. 273). The *Privilegium* (copyright) is dated Dec. 30, 1581. It appeared by Jan. 4, 1582.

An enlarged edition appeared in Paris:

48. *L'Histoire de la Mort que le R. P. Edmonde Campion prestre de la Compagnie du nom de Jesus et autres ont souffert en Angleterre pour la foy Catholique et Romaine, le premier jour de Decembre 1581. Traduit d'Anglois en François* ("An account of the death which Rev. Fr. Edmund Campion, priest of the Company of the name of Jesus, and others suffered in England for the Catholic and Roman faith, the first day of Dec. 1581. Translated from English into French") Guilluame Chaudiere, Paris 1582. 30 pp. It was thrice published in French, twice in Latin, four times in Italian, and once in German. At the end of the original text are further details of the three priests, plus a short account of the execution of Fr. Everard Hanse on July 31, 1581. See nos. 59, 69, 70.

49. *Discours des cruautés et tirannyes qua faict la Royne d'Angleterre, à l'endroict des Catholicques, Anglois,* . . . ("A discourse of the cruelties and tyranny that the Queen of England has done in regards to Catholics, English, . . .") Pierre le Sage, Paris 1582. Includes the additions in no. 48. While claiming to be a copy of a work printed at London, no such original is known.

Munday answered nos. 46 and 47 together:

50. *A brief Answer made unto two seditious pamphlets; the one printed in French, and the other in English; containing a defense of Edmund Campion and his complices, their most horrible and unnatural treasons against her Majesty and the realm. By A. M.* [Anthony Munday] (Edward White, London 1582). Printed March 12, 1582, and again same year. It also contains some verses on Campion's death, written, I suppose, by William Elderton (see no. 13). It also took some verses of no. 46 and changed them into reproofs of Campion (printed in Morfill, pp. 180–90: see editor's bibliog.). We have listed other anti-Campion verses at nos. 13, 27, 44.

Shortly afterwards the Council caused a paper to be drawn up, entitled:

51. *A particular Declaration or Testimony of the undutiful and traitorous affection borne against her Majesty by Edmund Campion, Jesuit, and other condemned Priests, witnessed by their own Confessions; in reproof of those slanderous books and libels delivered out to the contrary by such as are maliciously affected towards her Majesty and the State* (Christopher Barker, London 1582) 14 leaves, 28 pp. It contains the extracts from Sanders, Allen and Bristow that were submitted to Campion and his fellows, and their answers. The paper is printed in J. Morgan, *Phoenix Britannicus* (London 1732) 481; Howell's *State Trials*, vol. 1 (Hansard, London 1816) columns 1073–84; C. Dodd, *Church History of England* [to 1625] ed. M.A. Tierney (5 vols., London 1839–1843) vol. 3, Appendix 3.

Then came the executions of the rest of those who were condemned with Campion, which called forth:

52. William Allen, *A Brief History of the Glorious Martyrdom of XII Reverend Priests executed within these twelve months, for confession and defense of the Ca tholic Faith, but under the false pretence of treason. With a note of sun dry things that befell them in their life and imprisonment, and a preface declaring their innocence. Set forth by such as were much conversant with them in their life, and present at their arraignment and death* (Jean de Foigny, Rheims [Aug. or early Sept.] 1582). Reprint: Scolar Press, U.K. 1970. The 12 priests are Campion, Sherwin, Briant, Ford, Shert, Robert Johnson, Filby, Kirby, Lawrence Richardson (real name Johnson), Cottam, Paine, Hanse—all executed 1581-2 (plus earlier martyrs Maine, Nelson and layman Sherwood). Pages 92–4 contain Gregory Martin's Latin verses in honor of Campion.

52a. Reprint: *A Briefe Historie of the Glorious Martyrdom of Twelve Reverend*

Priests, Father Edmund Campion and his Companions, by William Cardinal Allen, With Contemporary Verses by the Venerable Henry Walpole, and the Earliest Engravings of the Martyrdom, Reprinted from the (probably unique) Copy in the British Museum, and edited by the Rev. J. H. Pollen S.J. (Burns and Oates, London 1908; facsimile reprint: Neumann Press, Minnesota 2000). Fr. Persons was one source of the account. Pollen says (p. xviii), "Dr. Allen's book may, in a certain way, be regarded as a second edition of the *True Report* [no. 46], in so far as he faithfully takes over, verbatim, or nearly so, the whole of Vallenger's history, omitting the introductory and apologetic paragraphs." Pollen took the verses from Alfield's *True Report*, no. 46, and the engravings depicting the road to martyrdom from the first Italian trans. of this *Brief History*, no. 62.

The following work, finished in late 1587, printed anonymously in Paris, undated, is by Jesuit St. Robert Southwell. I place it here because it mentions two prodigies of 1581 connected with Campion (see ch. 19: "Blood on his hands"; ch. 20: "Prodigies of nature"; and their endnotes):

> 53. St. Robert Southwell S.J., *An Epistle of Comfort to the Reverend Priests, and to the Honourable, Worshipful, and Other of the Lay Sort, Restrained in Durance for the Catholic Faith* (Paris 1587). Reprint with modern spelling: Burns and Oates, London 1966.

> 54. Robert Persons S.J., *De Persecutione Anglicana libellus (epistola), quo (qua) explicantur afflictiones, calamitates, cruciatus et acerbissima martyria quae Angli Catholici nunc ob fidem patiuntur* ("A booklet/epistle on the English persecution in which are set forth the afflictions, calamities, tortures, and most bitter martyrdom which English Catholics are now suffering for the faith") "Bologna" [but in reality at Rouen] 1581; Paris 1582; Rome 1582 [thrice]; and others. The Roman edition is 117 pp. with six pages of engravings that include Campion's capture and death. Within two years of its first publication there appeared, as listed, several editions in Latin, and German, Italian, French and English translations. See Catholic Record Society, vol. 39, p. xliii. An Italian ed. was printed in 1582 in Bologna, "by order of Cardinal Paleotti, Bishop of Bologna" says the title page (see ch. 7: "Bologna"). It was also printed (abridged) in *Concertatio* (no. 59). Eng. trans., *An epistle of the persecution of catholickes in Englande* ("Douay" but in reality Rouen 1582. Reprint: Scolar Press, Menston, U.K. 1973).

> 55. *Historia della Morte del R. P. Edm. Campiano della Comp. di Gesu ed altri due che han patito in Inghilterra per la fede Catholica Romana il primo di Dicembre, MDLXXXI, tradotto d'Inglese in Franchese, e di*

Franchese in Italiano ("An account of the death of Rev. Fr. E. Campion, of the Company of Jesus, and two others who suffered in England for the Roman Catholic faith, the first of December 1581, translated from English into French, and from French into Italian") Giacomo Piccaria, Milan 1582. 14 leaves. A trans. of no. 48.

56. *Martirio del Reverendo P. Edm. Campiano della Comp. di Gesu, patito in Inghilterra per la fede Cattolica di Roma, 1 Dec. 1581 tradotto d'Inglese in Francese, and poi dal Francese in Italiano* ("Martyrdom of Rev. Fr. E. Campion of the Company of Jesus, suffered in England for the Catholic faith of Rome, Dec. 1, 1581, translated from English into French, and then from French into Italian") Bevilacqua, Torino [Turin] 1582. Reprint: D. and G.-B. Guerra, Venezia [Venice] 1582. A trans. of no. 48.

57. *Martyrium R. P. Edmundi Campiani qui cum duobus aliis presbyteris . . . in Anglia propter constantem Romanae et Catholicae fidei confessionem mortis supplicio affectus est, e Gallico in Latinum versum per Gul. Estium* ("Martyrdom of Rev. Fr. Edmund Campion who with two other priests in England was dealt the death sentence for constant confession of the Roman and Catholic faith, translated from French into Latin by Gulielmus Estius [Willem Hessels van Est]") J. Masius, Louvain 1582. A trans. of no. 47.

58. *Lettere venute d'Inghilterra tradotte in Italiano, dove si hanno alcuni avisi della crudel persecutione di quel Regno verso i Catholici, et della morte d'alcuni che per la Fede sono stati martirizati* ("Letters come from England translated into Italian which contain news of the cruel persecution· of that Kingdom against Catholics, and of the death of some who have been martyred for the Faith") Vincenzo Sabbio, Brescia, Italy 1582. Includes translations of a letter of Fr. Anthony Tyrrell written in prison in London, July 18, 1581, one of Dr. Allen at Rheims, and others from France and England, ending with an account of the martyrdom of Campion and his two companions. A Spanish version, not now found, was printed in 1583.

The first edition of the book *Concertatio Ecclesiae Catholicae* was compiled in 1582 by Fr. John Gibbons S.J., assisted by Fr. Persons. Fr. John Fenn assisted with translation (see Fr. More's History of the English Province, Latin ed., p. 20; Eng. ed. p. 30 and note on p. 364; and D. M. Rogers's important intro. to the 1970 ed.). For a long time the book was mistakenly ascribed to another priest, Fr.

John Bridgewater (because Gibbons's Latin pen-name "Joannes Aquapontanus" means "John Bridgewater"). The full title:

59. *Concertatio Ecclesiae Catholicae in Anglia adversus Calvino-Papistas et Puritanos, a paucis annis singulari studio quorundam hominum doctrina et sanctitate illustrium renovata* ("The Struggle of the Catholic Church in England against the Calvinist-Papists and the Puritans, renewed in recent years by the special effort of certain men illustrious for learning and sanctity") Edmund Hatot, Trèves 1583 (or 1584) 369 pp. It was a collection, in Latin, of Latin and English texts already published elsewhere.

Republished with large addi tions (Heinrich Bock, Trèves 1588) 413 numbered leaves (= 826 pp.), plus others unnumbered: about 876 pp. in all. The 1589 and 1594 editions contain no new material.

Reprint of the 1588 edition: John Gibbons, *Concertatio ecclesiae catholicae in Anglia*, Intro. by D.M. Rogers (Gregg Press, Farnborough 1970) c. 876 pp.

In all it has appeared five times: 1583, 1588, 1589, 1594, 1970.

"Calvino-Papists" in the title was a term of derision for Anglicans, who retained a Roman Catholic structure and ceremonial, with bishops, liturgy, and other Catholic practices, but adopted Calvinist doctrine. The other Protestants, the "Puritans," were, in a sense, more logical and consistent.

Concertatio contained texts (most) already published: Campion's *Challenge* to the Council and a letter of his to the Jesuit General; his *Decem Rationes;* an abridgement of Persons's *De Persecutione Anglicana Epistola* (known in English as "An Epistle of the Persecution of Catholics in England" no. 54) 1582; the Lives and Martyrdoms of 80 martyrs (including Campion, Sherwin, Briant, with some of their letters, i.e., 2 works conflated and rearranged in chronological order, namely, Allen's *Brief History*, trans. it seems by Fr. John Gibbons S.J., plus material from the anonymous French work above, no. 48); *Ad persecutores Anglos* ("To the English persecutors," a Latin trans. of *A True, Sincere and Modest Defense of English Catholics:* see no. 65)—an answer to Cecil's *Execution of Justice* (nos. 63-4); several other things; and Allen's *Apologia Martyrum* ("Defense of the Martyrs") which must be considered a distinct work:

60. Allen, *Apologia Martyrum, qua ipsorum innocentia variis rationibus demonstratur; eosque solius religionis Catholicae causa, quam susceperant propagandam et propugnandam, crudelissime enecatos fuisse* ("A Defense of the Martyrs, by which their innocence is shown by various reasons; and that they were put to death most cruelly for the cause only of the Catholic religion which they maintained propagating and defending") 1583

These various attacks on the administration of justice in England in duced
Lord Burghley (William Cecil, Lord High Treasurer and principal minister to
Queen Elizabeth) to draw up from rack-master Norton's notes (or possibly
Norton himself wrote):

> 61. *A Declaration of the favorable dealing of her Majesty's Commissioners
> appointed for the examination of certain Traitors, and of tortures
> unjustly reported to be done upon them for matters of Religion* (1583) 6
> pp. A Latin edition was issued in 1584.

Reprint in Baron John Somers Somers, *A collection of scarce and valuable
tracts . . . from . . . public, as well as private libraries; particularly that of the late
Lord Somers* (popularly known as *Somers Tracts*, ed. Sir Walter Scott) (T. Cadell,
et al., 13 vols. 2nd ed. London 1809–15) vol. 1, p. 209.

But still, as each new priest was martyred, a fresh edition of the growing
Martyrology was put out, not only in English and French, but in Italian and
Latin also; for instance:

62. *Historia del glorioso Martirio di sedici sacerdoti martirizati in In ghilterra per
la confessione e difesa della fede Cattolica l'anno 1581, 2 e 3* ("Account of the glorious martyrdom of sixteen priests martyred in England for the confession and
defense of the Catholic faith, the year 1581-2-3") Macerata, Italy 1583. With six
plates. A translation, with updating, of no. 52.

Burghley therefore composed and anonymously published a much longer
tract (than no. 61):

> 63. *The execution of justice in England for maintenance of public and
> Christian peace, against certain stirrers of sedition, and adherents to the
> traitors and enemies of the Realm, without any persecution of them for
> questions of Religion, as is falsely reported and published by the fautors
> [favorers] and fosterers of their treasons* (London, Dec. 17, 1583)

The following year he made either a reprint or enlargement:

64. *The execution of justice in England* . . . (Christopher Barker, London
    1584)
This or the previous one was reprinted separately or in collections of works
by Burghley and others in 1675, 1677, 1688, 1809, 1936, 1965.

Burghley also had his tract translated and published in Latin, French, Dutch
(not German as some say) and Italian—Spanish being notably omitted:

64a. Latin: *Justitia Britannica* . . . ("British Justice") Thomas Vautroullier,
    London 1584. Ingoldstadt 1584.

64b. French: *L'execution de iustice faict en Angleterre* . . . *Traduite en langue Françoise* ("The execution of justice done in England, translated into the French language") Thomas Vautroullier, London 1584

64c. Dutch: *D'executie van iustitie: tot onderhoudinge vande publicke en christelicke vrede in Engelandt ghedaen* . . . ("Of the execution of justice, done in England for maintenance of the public and Christian peace") R. Schilders, Middelburgh 1584

64d. Italian: *Atto della Giustitia d'Inghilterra, esseguito, per la coseruatione della commune [e] christiana pace: contra alcuni seminatori di discordie, [e] seguaci de ribelli, [e] denemici del reame, [e] non per niuna persecutione* . . . *Traslatato d'inglese in vulgare* ("Act of justice in England, executed for maintenance of the public and Christian peace, against certain stirrers of sedition and adherents to the rebels and enemies of the realm, and not for any persecution . . . translated from English into the vulgar tongue") Giovanni Wolfio [John Wolfe], London 1584

The work called forth a rejoinder from Allen, residing at Rheims:

65. *A true, sincere and modest defense of English Catholics that suffer for their faith both at home and abroad, against a false, seditious and slanderous libel entitled "The Execution of Justice in England"* (Rouen 1584). Reprints: Manresa Press, 2 vols (262 pp. in toto) London 1914; Scolar Press, Yorkshire 1971. Allen also translated his reply, with the title *Justitiae Britannicae de sacerdotibus morte plectendis, confutatio* ("Of British Justice, concerning punishing priests by death: a rebuttal") 1583: Brussels Ms. no. 15594. But the published version was the translation into Latin by William Reynolds, with a long title beginning *Ad persecutores Anglos* ("To the English persecutors"), added to *Concertatio* (no. 59) in 1588.

Reprint of both together: *"The Execution of Justice in England" by William Cecil, and "A True, Sincere, and Modest Defense of English Catholics" by William Allen* (ed. Robert M. Kingdon, Cornell University Press, Ithaca, N.Y. 1965)

According to Strype, *Annals of the Reformation and Establishment of Religion and other Various Occurrences in the Church of England during Queen Elizabeth's Happy Reign* (Clarendon Press 1824, vol. 2, part 2, book 2, ch. 19. pp. 305–6), John Stubbs, the same man who had his right hand cut off for writing against the queen's possible marriage to Anjou, wrote an answer to Allen, at the request of Burghley himself. It was entitled *Vindication of the English Justice* (1587) but was never published.

Another official rebuttal of Allen's reply was by Thomas Bilson, Warden (later Bishop) of Winchester:

> 66. *Of the true difference between Christian Subjection and unchristian Rebellion; wherein the Prince's lawful power to command and bear the sword are* [sic] *defended against the Pope's censure and Jesuits' sophisms in their apology and defense of English Catholics; also a demonstration that the things reformed in the Church of England by the laws of this realm are truly Catholic; against the late Rhemish Testament* (Oxford 1585. London 1586)

Though reputed the most moderate of Anglican controversialists, Bilson here habitually uses the word "Jesuit" to mean simply "conscientious Catholic." It is noted by Belgian historian Paquot (Rector of Louvain University from 1735) that this book was used by the Puritans to justify their execution of Charles I. It is clear that the controversy was becoming generalised, and no longer had any special reference to Campion's history. So I return now to what was written about him in particular.

67. *Ecclesiae Anglicanae Trophaea* ("Trophies of the English Church") Bartolomeo Grassi, Rome 1584, reproducing the 1583 frescoes by G.B. Cavalleri (or Cavalieri), where three plates refer to Campion: his racking, his draw ing to Tyburn, and the martyrdom of him and his companions.

68. Robert Turner, *Vita et Martyrium Edm. Campiani sui quondam praeceptoris* ("Life and martyrdom of Edmund Campion, his former tutor") D. Sartorius, Ingoldstadt 1584 (prefixed to *Rationes Decem*)

69. Robert Turner, *Narratio de morte, quam in Anglia pro fide Romana Catholica Edmundus Campianus . . . ex Italica sermone facta Latine* ("An account of the death which Edmund Campion in England for the Roman Catholic faith . . . done into Latin from the Italian tongue") within the volume *Panegyrici duo* . . . ("Two panegyrics") A. Sartorius, Ingoldstadt 1599. A translation of no. 48. Printed also within nos. 94, 95, 96. Another edition 1609.

70. James Laing, *Historia de Morte Rev. P. Edm. Campiani Sac. de Soc. Jesu, et aliorum qui in Anglia propter fidem Catholicam Apostolicam atque Romanam crudelissimam passi sunt mortem. Traducta ex sermone Gallica in Latinum, interprete Jacobo Laingaeo Scoto, Doctore Sorbonico* ("An account of the death which Rev. Fr. Edmund Campion, priest of the Society Jesus, and others who suffered a most cruel death in England for the Catholic, Apostolic and Roman faith. Translated from French into Latin by James Laing, a Scot, Doctor at the Sorbonne") Paris 1585 (appended to the same author's treatise on Theodore Beza) 30 pp. A trans. of no. 48.

71. *Edmundi Campiani, eines Jesuites Leben und Leiden, welcher zu London in seinem Vaterland, anno 1581, den 17 Julii, gefänglich angenom men, nachmals den 1 Dec. gemartert worden* ("Life and suffering of Edmund Campion, Jesuit, who at London in his homeland in 1581 was captured July 17, thereafter martyred Dec. 1") Dilingen 1588

Robert Turner's *Vita et Martyrium* (no. 68) was translated into German:

72. *Leben und Leyden deß martyrers der Societet Jesu Priestern Edmundi Campiani* ("Life and suffering of E. Campion, martyr, priest of the Society of Jesus") Ingoldstadt 1583. J. Mayer, Dilingen 1588.

73. *De morte Edmundi Campiani S.J. . . . Maria Stuarta, Regina Scotiae . . . martyr ecclesiae* ("Of the death of E. Campion S.J. . . . Mary Stuart, Queen of Scots . . . martyr of the Church") Ingolstadt 1588.

A tract by Fr. Persons about Catholic martyrs in England and other matters was translated into Castilian Spanish about the same time:

74. *Relacion de algvnos martyrios, que de nueno han hecho los hereges en Inglaterra* ("Account of certain martyrdoms, which the heretics recently carried out in England") Pedro Madrigal, Madrid 1590. 76 leaves. A copy is kept in the special collection of the library of Siena College, Loudonville, N.Y.

From this time forth (and even earlier) an account of Campion occurs in all works that profess to give a narrative either of English Catholic affairs, or of the illus trious members of the Society of Jesus. For instance:

75. Rev. Dr. Nicolas Sanders, *De Origine ac Progressu Schismatis Anglicani* ("On the Origin and Progress of the Anglican Schism") Rheims 1585. It was written in 1576 and published after the author's death, updated by Fr. Edward Rishton to his own time, in 1585. Often called *De Schismate Anglicano* ("The Anglican Schism"). The publisher's details say Cologne but it was really at Rheims. Republished with many additions by Fr. Persons in Rome, 1586. From 1585–1628, it appeared in six Latin editions and was translated into French, German, Italian, Polish, Portuguese and Spanish—a popular work by reason of its sensational political content and easy narrative style. Eng. version: Sander, *The Rise and Growth of the Anglican Schism* (trans. of 1585 ed. by David Lewis: Burns and Oates, London 1877; Tan Books, Illinois 1988, 380 pp.).

76. Girolamo Pollini O.P., *Historia Ecclesiastica della rivoluzione d'Inghilterra* ("Ecclesiastical history of the revolution of England") Rome 1594. The Italian account of Campion occupies 40 pages, translated and enlarged from the Latin version in *Concertatio* (no. 59).

77. Bishop Diego de Yepes, *Historia particular de la persecucion de Inglaterra, y de los Martirios mas insignes que en ella ha avido desde el año del Señor 1570 . . . Recogida por el Padre Fray Diego de Yepes . . . Opispo de Taraçona* ("A particular history of the persecution in England and of the most noteworthy martyrdoms which have occurred in it since the year of the Lord 1570, gathered by the Father, Friar Diego de Yepes, Bishop of Saragossa") Madrid 1599. Reprint: Gregg International, Farnborough, England 1971. 949 pp. Pages 310–37 are a complete chapter on Campion, translated into Spanish (and enlarged) from the Latin of Cardinal Allen (no. 52).

77a. Fr. Francisco de Herrera Alemán S.J., *Historia del glorioso martirio de Edmundo Campiano y Thomas Cotamo . . .* ("History of the glorious martyrdom of E. Campion and T. Cottam," Ms. 513, Bodleian Library, Oxford), a poem in twelve cantos written between 1582–92, and published in Manila in 1938 in *Los mártires de la reforma en Inglaterra* ("The martyrs of the Reformation in England") ed. E. Gómez O.P. and H. Muñoz O.P., Islas filipinas, Librería de la Universidad de Sto. Tomás.

Many other annals and histories reprinted in whole or in part, or copied or recast, the above works, and contain nothing new. Many lists or catalogues of martyrs were also printed in various languages over the same years.

8. Campion's Own Works

Individual works

78. Campion's oration on Sir Thomas White, Feb. 1567 (see ch. 1: "Campion orates"), is printed in Stevenson and Salter's *Early History of St. John's College,* pp. 407–11 (see editor's bibliography).

79. A Christian epic poem of 821 lines, *Nascentis ecclesiae generatio prima* (c. 1567-9, "The first generation of the new-born Church"), in the style of Virgil, tracing the Church's history from Christ's Resurrection to the martyrdoms of Sts. Peter and Paul; in two manuscript copies, only recently rediscovered and recognised (Gerard Kilroy 2005, p. 4: see editor's bibliography): printed, translated and examined in Kilroy.

80. *Narratio Divortii Henrici VIII, Regis Angliae, ab Uxore Catherina, and ab Eccle sia Catholic Romana discessione* (c. 1570, "An account of the divorce of Henry VIII, king of England, from his wife Catherine and his split from the Roman Catholic Church")

First printed at p. 733 of Nicholas Harpsfield's *Historia Anglicana Ecclesiastica* ("English Ecclesiastical History") Marc Wyon, Douay 1622, ed. Richard Gibbons S.J., where it occupies 8 pages. Reprints in *Opuscula* ("Small works") nos. 94–100. Facsimile reprint of Harpsfield's *Historia:* Gregg International, Farnborough, England; Nieuwkoop, Netherlands, 1971. 804 pp.

81. The discourse *De Homine Academico* ("The university man"), composed at Dublin, 1570–1. The original is lost but it was probably re-presented with refinements as an oration at Douay, 1571–2, as *De Juvene Academico* ("The young student"), printed with facing Eng. trans. in John F. Quirk S.J., *A Patron for Scholars—Eulogy on the Blessed Edmund Campion, S.J. with his Oration on 'The Model College Student' done into English* (St. John's College, Fordham, N.Y. 1896).

82. *The History of Ireland*, written in 1571.

The original Ms. is lost. The work was first published, with many changes, by Richard Stanihurst in Raphael Holinshed's *Chronicles*, 1577; again in volume 2 of Holinshed, 1587; then in its original form by Sir James Ware in his *Historie of Ireland, collected by three learned authors viz. Meredith Hanmer Doctor in Divinitie: Edmund Campion sometime fellow of St. Johns Colledge in Oxford: and Edmund Spenser Esq.* Printed by the Societie of Stationers, printers to the Kings most excellent Majestie, Dublin [and Thomas Harper, London] 1633. Reprint of ed. of 1633: *Ancient Irish Histories*, 2 vols, Hibernia Press, Dublin

1809. Facsimile reprints: *A History of Ireland (1571) by Edmund Campion* (ed. Rudolf B. Gottfried: Scholars' Facsimiles and Reprints, N.Y. 1940, a reprint of 1633; Kennikat Press, New York 1970; Da Capo Press, N.Y. 1971; Lightning Source Inc., Tennessee 2009) and *A Historie of Ireland (1633)* (Carefree, Scholars' Facsimiles and Reprints, Arizona 2000).

A new and better edition: *Two Bokes of the Histories of Ireland – compiled by Edmunde Campion, feloe of St. John Baptistes College in Oxforde, Edited from MS Jones 6 Bodleian Library Oxford* (ed. Alphonsus Franciscus Vossen: Van Gorcum, Assen, The Netherlands 1963). Vossen, p. 86, shows that all other transcripts are copied from Ms. Jones 6 in the Bodleian, and that one probably from the original.

83. *Tractatus de imitatione rhetorica* ("Tract on rhetorical imitation") by Campion, 1577–8, first appeared in print in 1602 (see no. 92). It appears in *Roberti Turneri viri doctissimi oratoris et professoris in Academia Ingolstadiensi. Orationum volumen secundum* ("Second volume of orations, of the most learned man, Robert Turner, orator and professor in the Academy of Ingolstadt") John Kinckhes, Cologne 1625. Vol. 1 was printed 1615. Latin text and free Eng. trans. with short historical introduction by Miguel A. Bernad S.J., "The *Treatise on Imitation* of Blessed Edmund Campion" Folia 6 (1952), pp. 100–114; 7 (1953), pp. 20–29.

84. A play on the sacrifice of Abraham (1577), in which the pathos of Abraham's part was much admired (Fr. G. Ware's *History of the Jesuit College of Prague*: see Section 2f. above, and ch. 5: "Playwright"). The Ms. is lost.

85. A six-hour play on King Saul (1577). (See ch. 5: "Playwright"). Ms. lost.

86. *Ambrosia: A Neo-Latin Drama by Edmund Campion, S.J.* (ed. and trans. Joseph Simons: Van Gorcum, Assen, The Netherlands 1969 and 1970, 106 pp). This is the famous *Tragedia Am brosiana*, 1578 (see ch. 5: "Playwright"), the manuscript of which was expected to be among the archives of his college at Prague, but was discovered c. 1896 at Dillingen (on the Danube in Bavaria). This only known manuscript copy is in codex 221, folios 135–69, of the *Studienbibliothek* (study-library) at Dillingen.

87. *Oratio beati Patris Edmundi Campiani Donae Mariae a Cardona – Leichenrede mit einem Kommentar von* (1579 "Oration of Blessed Fr. Edmund Campion on Lady Mary Cardona—Funeral oration with a commentary by") *Richard Hofmann* (Munich 1991).

88. *Litaniæ Deiparae Virginis Mariae ex Patribus et script[oribus] a RR. PP. Edmondo Campiano . . . et Laurentio Maggio Soc. Jesu sacerdotibus et ab iisdem per singulos hebdomadae dies distributæ* ("Litany of the Virgin Mary Mother of God taken from the Fathers and writers by Rev. Frs.. Edmund Campion and Lawrence Maggio [Campion's Austrian Provincial] and allocated by the same through each day of the week") Sebastian Cramoisy, Paris 1633. Now lost. Reprint: E. Cagniard, Rothomagi [Rouen] 1887.

89. A *Chronologia Universalis* is listed among his works (W. Trollope, *A History of the Royal Foundation of Christ's Hospital*, Pickering, London 1834, p. 211; H. J. Rose, *A New General Biographical Dictionary*, Parker, Oxford 1857, p. 479; *The English Journal of Education*, Dec. 1, 1859, London, p. 392). J.N. Stoeger S.J., *Historiographi* (Ratisbon 1851) p. 27 lists it as "Dublin 1533"—a misprint for 1633, we presume, and since 1633 is the date of the first appearance of the *History of Ireland*, one wonders if there is a confusion somewhere, especially since the same man lists *Commentaria de Insula Hibernia* (Commentary on the island Ireland), London 1586, as a work of Campion, which can only mean the Irish *History*, referenced incorrectly. Vossen, p. 92, explains that some unused "Latin notes on Irish history may have given rise to the belief that Campion had also written a "Chronologia Universalis," which is mentioned in verses on Campion's life in the *Concertatio*, and of which no trace is left." His reference is to *Concertatio* (1583 ed.) p. 205—but in the 1582 ed. of those verses in Dr. Allen's *Briefe Historie* (no. 52 above) and the 1588 ed., p. 66 (no. 59 above), this editor finds no reference to it.

90. Letter to the Privy Council: The Challenge (*The Brag*, 1580).
Widely circulated in manuscript, and then printed when rebutted, e.g., in the 2nd ed. of William Charke, *An answer to a seditious pamphlet lately cast abroad by a Jesuit* (1581), and in Meredith Hanmer, *The great Brag and Challenge of Mr. Champion a Jesuit* (1581). See nos. 8a, 9.

91. *Rationes Decem* ("Ten Reasons," 1581). Full title given at no. 17.

A. Editions in Latin

- Original (Latin), printer Stephen Brinkley, Stonor Park, Henley-on-Thames, 1581
- Francesco Zanetti, Rome 1582
- Aegidius Radaeus [Gillis van den Rade], Antwerp 1582, with Whitaker's reply, no. 18
- 1582, 1585 in John Dury's *Confutatio* (no. 20)
- Pacificus Pontius [Pacifico Ponzio], Milan 1582
- Martin Mercator, Pont-à-Mousson, France 1582
- David Sartorius, Ingoldstadt 1583
- David Sartorius, Ingoldstadt 1584, with an account of his life and martyrdom by his pupil Robert Turner (no. 68)
- B. Bonfadini and T. Diani, Rome 1584
- M. K. Radziwiła, Vilnius, c. 1585
- Georgius Vuidmanstadius [Georg Widmanstetter], Graz, Austria 1588, with a preface by Abbot Peter Muchitsch
- Henricus Aquensis [Heinrich von Aich], Herbipolis [Würzburg, Germany] 1589
- Michael Peterle, Prague 1592
- Franz Kolb, Vienna 1594
- Wolgangus Kezelius, Lich, Germany 1601, with Whitaker's reply, no. 18. The title is *Rabsaces romanus: id est, Edmundi Campiani Jesuitae Rationes decem . . . and ad eas Guilielmi Whitakeri . . . Responsio* ('A Roman Rabsaces [2 Kings 18: the revolt led by Rabsaces or Rabshakeh], that is the Ten Reasons of Edmund Campion the Jesuit . . . and the "Answer to them of William Whitaker"). Reprint 1604.
- François Rezé, Paris 1600
- Jacques (François) Rezé, Paris 1601
- Melchior Bernard, Pont-à-Mousson, France 1605
- Andreas Petricovius, Cracow 1605
- Maurice Leuez, Bourges 1607
- Nicolai Constant, Rheims 1615

- Adam Cavelier, Cadonii [Caen, France] 1616
- J. K. Unckel, Frankfurt 1617, with Whitaker's reply, no. 18.
- Louis Hebert, La Flèche, France 1620, with De imitatione rhetorica ("On rhetorical imitation")
- Johann Christopher CoseMr. ov, Vienna, Austria 1676
- Percle, Prague 1692
- Martinus Szent-Ivany, Quinquaginta Rationes et Motiva . . . authore Edmundo Campiano ("Fifty reasons and motives," William Stryckwant, Louvain 1708; again at Louvain 1708; Wilhelm Metternich, Cologne 1710) (J. Gillow, A Literary and Biographical History, Or Bibliographical Dictionary, of the English Catholics [vol. 5, Burns and Oates, London
- 1902] p. 388)
- Limprecht, Erfordiae [Erfurt, Germany] 1718
- Joannes Engelert, Cologne 1731

B. "Rationes Decem" Appears also in the Following Collections in Latin

- Concertatio Ecclesiae Catholicae (1583, 1588, 1589, 1594, 1970: see no. 59)
- Doctrinae Jesuiticae praecipua capita ("Chief points of Jesuit teaching") Regius, Rupellae [La Rochelle] 1585, Tome 2, part 1
- Tres gravissimi perpetuae Catholicae fidei constantiae testes. Tertullianus . . . Vincentius Lirinensis . . . Edm. Campianus . . . rationes decem . . . quibus accessit brevis auctoris vita et epistolae ("Three most weighty witnesses to the constancy of the perpetual Catholic faith. Tertullian. Vincent of Lerins. E. Campion, Ten Reasons, to which is added a brief life and letters of the author") Arnold Mylius, Cologne 1594. Reprints 1600, 1613, 1622
- The same work, under a new title, Trium Nobilium Auctorum ("Of three noble authors") Bartholomew Schnell, Rorschach, Switzerland, 1606
- The same, without Tertullian: Arnold Mylius, Birckmann, Cologne 1600
- Antonio Possevino S.J., Bibliotheca selecta de ratione studiorum ("Select library of a plan of studies") Domenico Basa, Rome 1593. New editions: Venice 1603, Cologne 1607
- A similar collection of works by Tertullian, Vincent of Lerins, Leonard Lessius, with Campion's Ten Reasons: Claudius Landry, Lugduni [Lyons] 1622
- With a work of St. V. of Lerins: Jean de Fampoux, Douay 1632
- Praescriptionum adversus hereticos tractata viii edit. a Johanne Calvino ("8 tracts of prescriptions against heretics, edited by Jean Calvin") John Albin, Moguntiae [Mainz] 1602. Reprint 1605.

- St. Peter Canisius, *Institutio Christiana sive parvus catechismus . . . Rationes decem fortissimi martyris Edmundi Campiani* ("Christian instruction or a small catechism . . . Ten Reasons of the most courageous martyr E. Campion") Lambert Ratsfeld, Münster 1613
- In a volume of collected theological works, *Gründliches Gutachten . . .* ("Thorough experts") Molaus, Leipzig 1679
- In a collection of theological works, *Ex praelectionibus . . . (ed.* Joseph Haverlik), J. George Schneider, Prague 1764
- Also in the various editions of Campion's works, listed below.

C. Translations

FRENCH

Jean Bogard, Douay 1582 (trans. Rev. Baulduin Deglen)
Jean Pillehotte, Lyons 1584 (trans. Mr. Pierre Madur)
Regnauld Chaudiere, Paris 1601 (trans. Gabriel Chappuis)
M. Guillemot and S. Thiboust, Paris 1612
Nicolas Loyselet, Rouen 1654 (trans. Bernard Meynier)
Boudot, Trevoux and Paris 1701 (trans. Jean Brignon S.J.)
Delusseux, Paris 1725, 1728, 1731, 1737
Marc Bordelet 1743
Abbé Migne, *Démonstrations Evangéliques* (1842–52)

GERMAN

David Sartorius, Ingoldstadt 1583 (trans. Johann Christoff Hueber)
Casparus Behem, Mainz 1589 (trans. Vitus Miletus Canno) with a work of St. V. of Lerins
Andreas Reinheckel 1594 with a work of St. V. of Lerins
Elisabeth Ederin, Ingoldstadt 1598 (trans. Conrad Vetter S.J.)
Andreas Angermaier, Ingoldstadt 1599
Franz Kolb, Vienna 1599 (trans. C. Vetter S.J.)
Johann Gymnich, Cologne 1600, with other authors
Andreas Angermaier, Ingoldstadt 1602, within a collection of authors
Bartholomew Albert F., Brünn 1610 (trans. C. Vetter S.J.)

POLISH

M. K. Radz´iwiła, Vilnius 1584 (trans. Piotr Skarga S.J.)
M. K. Radz´iwiła, Vilnius 1584, with additional material (trans. possibly Kasper Wilkowski)

FLEMISH

Hieronymus [Jerome] Verdůssen, De Thien Redenen van Edmondus Campianus
  ... ("The Ten Reasons of Edmund Campion," trans. Laevinius Torrentius,
  Bishop of Antwerp) Antwerp 1591, 1592
Jan Maes, Leuven (Louvain) 1609, 1622 (same Flemish trans.)

CZECH

Gıˇrˊika Nygrina, Prague 1601 (trans. Ondreˇj Modestin S.J.)
J. Handle, Olomouc 1602
V. Praze, Prokopa, Moravia 1888 (trans. Antonín Rejzek S.J.)
Reprint: G. Francl, Prague 1894

SLOVAK

Academic Press of the Society of Jesus, Tyrnaviae [Trnava, Tyrnau: Slovakia]
  1700, 1742) prefaced by a life of Campion

HUNGARIAN

Margaret Formica, Vienna 1607 (trans. by Balassi Bálint S.J. of 7 reasons, completed by Dobokay Sándor S.J., says the dedicatory epistle)
Reprint: Universitas, Budapest 1994

DUTCH

Marten Iansz Brandt, Amsterdam 1624, with Whitaker's reply, no. 18. Thien
  Redenen van Edmundus Campianus Jesuwyt ... ("Ten Reasons of Edmund
  Campion, Jesuit," trans. Jacobus Triglandius)
Same work with Whitaker's reply is in Opuscula Iacobi Triglandij ("Small works
  of J. Triglandius") Amsterdam 1640
Cornelis du Jardin, Münster (Netherlands) 1646, 1660
  Italian
Giovanni Fassi-Como, Le "dieci ragioni" per provare la verità della nostra reli-
  gione ss. ("The Ten Reasons to prove the truth of our most holy religion")
  Genoa 1854

PORTUGUESE

Dez Razões www.literariolibros.org with J. H. Pollen's introduction to the Eng.
  version of 1914. Seems to be an online version only, not printed.

ENGLISH

i   *An answer to the Ten reasons of Edmund Campian the Jesuit*, London 1606 (trans. Richard Stocke, followed by his trans. of Whitaker's reply, no. 18)

ii   *Campian Englished. Or A translation of the ten reasons in which Edmund Campian (of the Society of Jesus) priest, insisted in his challenge, to the Universities of Oxford and Cambridge, Made by a priest of the Catholic and Roman Church* (Rouen 1632). The trans. is not by Laurence Anderton or any Jesuit, say Allison and Rogers (see editor's bibliog.). Reprint in: *Relatio . . . 1601 . . . Bagshaw . . . 1599; Campian englished, 1632, by Edmund Campion* (Scolar Press, Menston, U.K. 1971).

iii   *Reasons of a challenge sent to the universities of England, in matters of religion by Edmund Campion* (Mat. Turner, London 1687. Trans. from Meynier's French version above)

iv   *An appeal to the members of the two universities: presenting ten reasons for renouncing the Protestant and embracing the Catholic religion* (A. J. Valpy, London 1827. Trans. Fr. John Fletcher). Reprint: Battersby's Catholic tracts, W. J. Battersby, 1845. 56 pp.

v   *Campion's Ten Reasons*, London 1914 (for six 21st cent. reprints, see below)

RECENT LATIN REPRINTS

- *Rationes Decem 1581 by Edmund Campion and A brief censure . . .* (Scolar Press 1971)
- *Campion's Ten Reasons*, Edmund Campion (Manresa Press, London 1914. Orig. Latin text with Eng. trans. by Fr. Joseph Rickaby S.J.). Facsimile reprint: Loome Booksellers and Ignatius Press, U.S.A. 2002. Same text reset: Hard Press, N.Y. 2006; Echo Library, Cirencester, U.K. 2007; BiblioBazaar, U.K. 2007, 2008, 2009
- J. C. CoseMr. ov, Vienna 1676: facsimile reprint, Kessinger, U.S.A. 2009

Fr. J. H. Pollen's informative 30-page introduction says Rickaby's translation is the fifth into English, and the forty-seventh edition of *Ten Reasons*—but there were other editions not known to Pollen. Some seem impossible to find today (e.g., the Italian one). This editor would be pleased to hear of any other editions or translations printed before the 21st century.

Counting each print and reprint of the original or translations listed above under no. 91 (and nos. 18, 20, 23–4, 93–100), as well as printings of it in collections, selections or refutations of Campion's works, we have listed 123 times *Ten Reasons* has appeared, including several since Pollen's time. On average, therefore, the work has appeared in print, in one form or another, once every 3fi years from 1581 to 2010.

COLLECTED OR SELECTED WORKS

92. *Edmundi Campiani, Societatis Iesu, martyris in Anglia, Orationes, Epistolae, tractatus de imitatione rhetorica* ("Orations, letters, tract on rhetorical imitation, of Edmund Campion of the Society of Jesus, martyr in England") ed. Robert Turner: Andreas Angermaier, Ingoldstadt 1602. This book also contains works of Turner; and among other works of Campion, it "contains the oration of Campian before Elizabeth in 1566 and four of his orations delivered on the Continent, but is without his two other Oxford orations." (Stevenson and Salter, p. 406: see editor's bibliography).

93. *P. Edmundi Campiani, Orationes, Epistolae, Tractatus de imitatione rhetorica* ("Orations, letters, tract on rhetorical imitation, of Fr. Edmund Campion," ed. Robert Turner) Joannes Kinckhes, Cologne 1615 twice. Another edition, with additions, incl. *Decem Rationes*, same details, 1625.

94. *Opuscula omnia, nunc primum e Ms. edita* ("All small works, now published for the first time from manuscript") Sebastian Cramoisy, Paris 1618. 476 pp. An enlargement of no. 92 with *Rationes Decem* and a 100-page Life trans. from Latin by Robert Turner. Reprint: Sebastian Cramoisy, Pont-à-Mousson, France 1622. 476 pp. (*Opuscula*, Pisa 1618, listed by Simpson, but unknown to Allison and Rogers, is perhaps a misprint, and "Pisa 1618" should perhaps read "Paris 1618").

95. *Opuscula omnia: nunc primum e Ms. in lucem edita* ("All small works, now brought to light for the first time from manuscript") Pierre Charlot, Lyons 1619

96. *Edmundi Campiani Societatis Jesu, Martyris in Anglia, Opuscula omnia nunc primum e M.S. edita* ("All small works of Edmund Campion of the Society of Jesus, martyr in England, now edited for the first time from manuscript") G. Battista Bidellio, Milan 1625

97. *Edmundi Campiani, Angli e Soc. Iesu, "Decem Rationes" propositae in causa fidei, et opuscula eius selecta* ("Edmund Campion, Englishman of the Society of Jesus, his Ten Reasons presented in the cause of the faith, and selected small works of his," ed. Fr. Silvester Petra-Sancta S.J. [Silvestro da Pietrasanta]) Balthasar Moretus, Antwerp 1631, 460 pp.

This is an ample and correct edition, containing:

Decem Rationes; Nar ratio Divortii; Oratio de B.V.M.; Oratio de S. Wenceslao; Oratio de Juvene Academico; Oratio in funere Mariae Cardonae; Oratio de laudibus Scripturae S.; Oratio habita Oxonii coram Regina Eliz. ("Ten Reasons, Oration on [respectively] the Blessed Virgin Mary, St. Wenceslaus [given at Prague], the young student [given at Douay], at the funeral of Mary Cardona, the praises of Sacred Scripture; held at Oxford before Queen Elizabeth"); Letters to: Henry Vaux, Oxford, July 28, 1570; Richard Stanihurst, Oxford, Dec. 1, 1570; James Stanihurst, Turvey, March 20, 1571; Richard Stanihurst, same date; Richard Cheney, Bishop of Gloucester, Nov. 1, 1571; Novices of the Society of Jesus at Brünn, Feb. 20, 1577; Gregory Martin, July 10, 1577; to same, July 17, 1579; a Father of the Society of Jesus, April 30, 1580; Fr. Everardus Mercurian, Jesuit General, Nov. 1581; *Tractatus de Imitatione Rhetorica* ("Tract on rhetorical imitation") 1574. The dates given, not necessarily accurate, are those of the editor, Fr. Silvester.

98. *Trias . . . and R. P. Edmundi Campiani Opuscula* ("Three [letters of three Church Fathers] and small works of Rev. Fr. Edmund Campion") ed. Philippe Labbe S.J., Paris 1646

99. *R. P. Edmvndi Campiani Societatis Iesv in Anglia martyris opera omnia: orationes, epistolae, rationes, rhetorica* ("Complete works of Rev. Fr. Edmund Campion of the Society of Jesus, martyr in England: orations, letters, [Ten] reasons, oratory") Gaspar Meturas, Paris 1648

100. *Beati Edmundi Campiani e Societate Iesu martyris in Anglia opuscula* ("Small works of Blessed Edmund Campion of the Society of Jesus, martyr in England") Franciscus Rosalius, Barcelona 1888. 332 pp.

It includes all the works in no. 97, but through Fr. J. Morris S.J. there are a few additions printed for the first time, from manuscripts in the Archbishop of Westminster's archives at the London Oratory (incl. the oration at Thomas White's funeral), and from some manuscripts, some of them autographs, preserved at Stonyhurst College. It contains, among other things: 16 letters and a fragment of one; 12 orations (incl. one on the adorable Eucharist); *Tractatus de Imitatione Rhetorica* ("Tract on rhetorical imitation"); ten *Carmina* (hymns and verses) printed for the first time, plus a draft of one. Among those printed under *Carmina:* a Latin dramatic poem of 54 lines, *In festo Corporis Christi* ("On the Feast of Corpus Christi"); *Litaniae B. Virginis* ("Litany of the Bl. Virgin"), a dozen penta meter lines of phrases taken or adapted from the Litany of Loreto; *Dialogus mutus* ("Silent dialogue"), comprising five miniature acts with four choruses; a conference between Doctor Ironicus and Discipulus ("Ironic Teacher and Pupil"), something in the manner of Swift's advice to servants; a *Dialogue* between Stratocles discipulus ("student") and Eubulus praeceptor ("instructor"). "There is nothing much in the [last] piece," says Simpson, "but it illustrates the charming relations which existed between Campion and his pupils, and gives us a glimpse of one of the reasons why he was so much beloved." Simpson provided an English trans. of the opening monologue of Stratocles, which I have not reproduced in this book.

UNPUBLISHED MISCELLANEA

Among the Stonyhurst Mss. may be found:

- some fragments of dramatic poems (A.V.1 [N11] Grene *Collectanea)* for he seems to have written several plays or educational dialogues for his students at Prague.

- a folio volume of *Loci Communes Theologici* ("Common theological sources"), said to be in his handwriting.

In a book entitled B*ohuslai Balbini . . . Opus Posthumum* (ed. Fr. Candidus of St. Teresa, "A posthumous work of Bohuslav Balbin") J. C. Hraba, Prague 1777, there is a list in tract 2, pp. 44–9, of certain manuscripts at the Jesuit Clementine College, Prague. On p. 48, it lists "Concionale MS. scilicet Conciones latine habitae a R.P. Edmundo Campiano Pragae" ("Conference [or sermon] manuscript, namely conferences [or sermons] given in Latin by Rev. Fr. E. Campion at Prague"). It could be that no. 100 prints these things, for it contains some orations and pieces pronounced at Prague.

Portions of Campion's handwritten note-books may be seen today in the library displays at Stonyhurst College.

It seems unlikely other writings will be found in Prague: Prof. Konec̆n" at Charles University there says that the combined efforts of himself and several colleagues in Prague failed to find a particularly sought Ms. of Campion—and he does not mention anything new found in their searches: Lubomír Konec̆n", "Edmund Campion, S.J., as Emblematist," p. 148 (full reference in E.B., no. 83).

Chronology of St. Edmund Campion's Life

1540–1581

1540–1556—Early Years and Education

Jan. 25, 1540   Edmund Campion born in Paternoster Row, London, the second of three boys and one girl. His father is a bookseller.

1547–1553   Reign of Edward VI. Protestantism becomes the State religion.

c. 1549–1556   Campion is educated in London at St. Paul's grammar-school, and then at Christ Church, Newgate Street.

1553–1558   Reign of Queen Mary Tudor who repeals all anti-Catholic legislation and seeks to crush heresy in her realm. England is reconciled to the Holy See, Nov. 30, 1554.

Aug. 3, 1553   Campion makes a complimentary speech at a public visit to London by Queen Mary.

1557–1571—Scholar in England and Ireland

1557–1570   As a student of St. John's College, Oxford University, Campion studies seven years of philosophy and six years of theology.

Nov. 1558   Death of Queen Mary and Cardinal Pole. In the same month, Elizabeth Tudor, a Protestant, accedes to the throne, which she will hold till her death in 1603.

1559   The Act of Supremacy makes Queen Elizabeth supreme governor over the Church in England, punishes any who refuse to take the Oath of Supremacy, and makes it treason to maintain the Pope's authority. The Act of Uniformity prohibits Mass, restores the *Book of Common Prayer*, and makes attendance at the services of the Established Church compulsory.

1563	The Act of Supremacy's provisions are extended, and the penalties made more severe.
1564	Campion takes the Oath of Supremacy on the occasion of his Bachelor of Arts degree. He becomes a Fellow of St. John's and lectures in Rhetoric.
1566	Campion obtains the Master of Arts degree. Sept. 3, 1566 At Oxford, Campion is the main speaker in a public debate held before Queen Elizabeth. She recommends him to the patronage of Robert Dudley (Earl of Leicester) and her chief minister, William Cecil (Lord Burghley).
Sept. 28, 1566	Campion receives an annual exhibition of £5.13.4 from the Company of Grocers, which continues for two-and-a-half years.
April–August 1568	The Company of Grocers several times summons Campion to preach publicly but he stalls and avoids all preaching.
April 1568–April 1569	Campion holds the office of junior proctor at Oxford University.
1568	Rev. Dr. William Allen founds a seminary at Douay to train priests for England.
c. March 1569	Influenced by Richard Cheney, Bishop of Gloucester, Campion is ordained an Anglican deacon, but he soon repents of this step as his heart is in the Catholic Faith.
Nov. 1569	The unsuccessful Catholic Rising of the northern Earls of Northumberland and Westmoreland who seek to place Mary Stuart, Queen of Scots, on the English throne.
Feb. 25, 1570	Pope Pius V issues the Bull *Regnans in excelsis* excommunicating Queen Elizabeth and releasing her subjects from their obligation of obedience to her.
c. Sept. 29, 1570	Campion's position at Oxford becoming untenable, since he avoids open adherence to the Established Church, he leaves Oxford to retreat to Dublin, for academic pursuits, where he enjoys the protection of Sir Henry Sidney and Sir James Stanihurst. He will spend eight months in Ireland.
c. March 17, 1571	To escape arrest for his Catholic religion, Campion leaves James Stanihurst's home in Dublin for Sir Christopher Barnewall's, at Turvey, twelve miles away.

Mid-March– May 1571	While in hiding for three months, pursued for suspected Catholic opinions, he writes, in ten weeks, a *History of Ireland.*
April– May 1571	In response to Pius V's Bull, the Treason Act and the Act against Bulls from Rome make it an act of high treason, punishable by death, to bring into England "any bull, writing, or instrument obtained from the Bishop of Rome" or "to absolve or reconcile" any of the Queen's subjects to the Catholic Church, or to be absolved or reconciled. In the years following, further laws will prohibit and punish any Catholic activity or worship.
End of May 1571	After returning to Dublin, Campion flees it again for Drogheda and thence, in disguise, returns to England in time to see (or hear of) the trial of Catholic martyr, Dr. John Storey, held May 26.

1571–1579—Douay, Entrance into the Jesuits and the Priesthood

June 1, 1571	Campion leaves England for the English College, Douay (in modern France), conducted by Fr. William Allen, and is publicly reconciled to the Catholic Church. He spends nearly two years there, completing his studies of theology and preparing for the priesthood; perhaps also teaching. He receives the minor orders, including Subdiaconate.
May 1, 1572	Death of Pius V. On May 13, Pope Gregory XIII is elected.
Jan. 21, 1573	Campion receives his degree of Bachelor of Divinity from Douay's university.
March 1573	Probably in March, Campion leaves Douay College for Rome, to join the Society of Jesus.
Spring 1573 (mid-April)	He is received into the Society under the newly-elected Fr. General Mercurian and assigned to the Jesuit Province of Austria.
June 1573	After the Jesuit General Congregation ends on June 16, Campion leaves Rome with a group of Jesuit priests.
Aug. 26, 1573	Having travelled from Rome to Vienna, Campion arrives in Prague, capital of Bohemia, to begin his two-year Jesuit novitiate.
Oct. 10, 1573	The novitiate moves to Brünn, Moravia.

1574–5	The English missionary priests trained in Douay begin to arrive in England.
Oct. 7, 1574	Campion is re-assigned to Prague, while still a novice.
Oct. 1574	He becomes Professor of Rhetoric at the *Clementinum*, the new Jesuit college in Prague.
Aug. 1575	Campion completes his novitiate and takes the three religious vows.
1574–1580	Campion works in Prague, visiting prisons and hospitals, and teaching Christian doctrine, Latin, rhetoric and philosophy.
1578	Campion is ordained deacon and later priest by the Archbishop of Prague.
Sept. 8, 1578	Father Campion says Mass for the first time.
1578	Thomas Stukely's abortive attempt to invade Ireland with a Spanish Catholic force; he never arrives.
1579	July 18, Nicholas Sanders arrives in Ireland to assist the Catholic rebels. He eventually dies in Ireland as a fugitive. The invading Catholic forces are defeated.
	The English College in Rome is established to train priests for England.
Dec. 1579	William Allen informs Campion that he will soon be summoned to Rome by his superior and sent to England.

1580—The Secret English Mission and the Public Challenge

March	Campion receives the official notice calling him to Rome, in preparation for his mission to return to England to minister to English Catholics.
c. March 4	Campion leaves Prague for Rome. Prince Ferdinand's carriage takes him to the court of Bavaria.
March 7	He preaches on St. Thomas Aquinas's feast in Munich, Bavaria.
April 9	Having continued in Ferdinand's carriage to Innsbruck, and walked to Padua, Italy, where he took a horse, Campion arrives in Rome. In April, Campion and Fr. Robert Persons meet Jesuit General Fr. Mercurian and later Pope Gregory XIII to discuss their mission.

April 18	Disguised as a servant, Campion leaves Rome by foot for England, with eleven other missionaries, including Jesuits Fr. Persons (his immediate superior) and Brother Ralph Emerson; and secular priest Ralph Sherwin.
April–May	They visit Cardinal Paleotto at Bologna, and Cardinal (St.) Charles Borromeo at Milan, pass through Turin, and proceed to Geneva, where they dispute with Calvinist theologian, Theodore Beza. They enter France and continue to Rheims.
May 31	They arrive and meet up with William Allen at Rheims, France, new site of the English seminary once at Douay.
June 7	For safety—since they learn the English government is expecting them—they split into small groups. Campion, Persons and Emerson leave Rheims for the Jesuit house at St. Omer.
June 11–16	Fr. Persons leaves for England: he goes to Calais, sails to Dover, arrives in London, makes contact with Catholics and sends for Campion.
June 24	Campion and Emerson sail from Calais in the evening.
June 25	They arrive at Dover in the morning, and move on to London next day where Fr. Persons will meet them in early July upon his return to London.
June 25, 1580– July 17, 1581	Campion ministers in England. Starting from London, Middlesex, Campion in disguise travels through Berkshire, Oxfordshire, Buckinghamshire, Northamptonshire, Huntingdonshire, Leicestershire, Nottinghamshire, Derbyshire, Staffordshire, Yorkshire, Lancashire and Warwickshire, passing via an underground network of English Catholics— preaching, instructing, offering Mass, hearing Confessions, receiving converts and reconciling people to the Church.
June 29, 1580	Campion preaches to a large congregation in a home rented by Lord Paget at Smithfield, London.
c. July 8	Persons returns and meets up with Campion in a house in Southwark.

July 12	In Southwark, Persons, with Campion, conducts a meeting of priests and laymen to adopt common policy on some practical matters. 15 July Royal Proclamation against "Jesuits and Massing priests," calling, among other things, for the banishment of all Jesuits and seminary priests from England, and the punishment of any who assist them.
July 18	Campion and Persons meet at Hoxton, Middlesex, a village outside London, to plan their respective activities.
July 19	There, at the suggestion of recusant Thomas Pounde, Campion writes his *Challenge (The Brag)*, to be released in the event of his capture. It is soon copied and circulated, however, and by September is already well-known. Campion and Persons go their respective ways.
July 19–end of Sept.	Campion's 1st journey: from Middlesex to Berkshire, Oxfordshire and Northampton shire.
August 1	Death of Jesuit General Fr. Mercurian.
September	A second expedition, of 600 Spaniards and Italians, arrives to help the Irish Catholic rebels. They are defeated by November.
c. Oct. 4	Campion meets up with Persons in a house in Southland, near Uxbridge, outside London, to review their work and plan their next steps.
Nov. 16	After Campion and Persons have met up near Uxbridge, in October–November, Persons directing Campion to write a small book, Campion leaves with Br. Emerson for Lancaster.
Christmas 1580 to Mid-May 1581	Campion's 2nd journey: he visits Catholic homes in northern counties: Buckinghamshire, Warwickshire, Huntingdonshire, Leicestershire, Nottinghamshire, Derbyshire, Staffordshire, Yorkshire and Lancaster.

1581—Controversy, Capture, Torture, Debates, Trial, Martyrdom

| Jan. 10 | Royal Proclamation "Ordering Return of Seminarians, Arrest of Jesuits." |
| Feb. 19 | Election of Jesuit General Fr. Acquaviva. |

March 18	In the Act of Persuasions, Parliament passes further strict anti-Catholic legislation raising the fines for recusants, punishing more severely the saying or hearing of Mass, and outlawing as treason any attempt to convert anyone to the Catholic faith.
March	In Yorkshire, Campion finishes his polemical work *Rationes Decem* ("Ten Reasons") and sends it to Fr. Persons in London for checking.
Mid-May	Campion leaves Lancaster for the south to meet Persons.
June 3	Campion meets up with Persons in London and works in London and surroundings.
c. April 28– late June	*Ten Reasons* is printed in Stonor Park, Henley, Oxfordshire, over several weeks, while Campion visits there regularly and other nearby places.
June 27	Placed there by Fr. William Hartley, up to 400 copies of *Ten Reasons* are discovered on the benches of St. Mary's, Oxford, at the Commencement. Others are distributed privately. The book causes a sensation, and the pursuit for Campion is intensified.
July 11	Outside Stonor, early morning, Campion takes leave of Persons for the last time as he asks permission to visit the Yate family at Lyford Grange. Campion's 3rd journey: on their way to Norfolk, via Lancashire, Campion and Emerson stop at the town of Lyford (then in Berkshire).
July 12	Campion preaches and says Mass at the house of Mr. Yate. Campion and Emerson set off. At an inn near Oxford, Campion is persuaded to return to Lyford for the sake of other Catholics who had missed him.
July 14–15	Campion is back in the same house at Lyford.
Sunday July 16	Campion says Mass and preaches to a large congregation including one-time Catholic, George Eliot, turned informer. Eliot summons a band of men who surround the house and search it through.
Monday July 17	Campion is discovered in the house, with Frs.. Thomas Ford and John Collington, arrested, and held under guard in Lyford for three days.
July 20–21	The prisoners are conveyed to London, stopping on the way at Abingdon, Henley and Colebrook.

Saturday July 22	The prisoners arrive in London, are paraded through the city streets, and imprisoned in the Tower.
July 25	In the evening, Campion is taken secretly by boat to a meeting with Sir Thomas Bromley (Lord Chancellor), at his house, Sir Christopher Hatton (Vice-Chamberlain), and Robert Dudley (Earl of Leicester). On behalf of the Queen, they ask Campion his position on her authority and the Papal excommunication. He is offered liberty and preferment if he recants his religion.
July 30 or 31	Campion is tortured on the rack to extort details of his activities, his involvement in the Irish rebellion, and the names of his helpers and hosts in England.
August 1	He is asked whether he agrees with the "treasonous" passages in the works of Catholic theologians, Sanders, Bristow and Allen, and whether he acknowledges Elizabeth as queen.
August 4–7	The Queen's Council sends a series of letters ordering the arrest of many of Campion's helpers and hosts. The report goes out that Campion has betrayed their names.
c. August 15	Campion is interrogated (possibly on the rack) on when and where he said Mass, whom he confessed, and where Persons and other priests are.
August 17–20	Answering a letter sent by Thomas Pounde, fellow-prisoner in the Tower, Campion assures him he will betray no secret, "come rack, come rope."
c. August 22	Campion is racked a second time, regarding the "secrets" mentioned in his letter to Pounde.
August 31, September 18, 23, 27	In the morning and afternoon of these four days, Campion has debates with Protestant theologians in the Tower and emerges the victor.
Oct. 31	Campion is racked a third time.
Nov. 2	Campion is racked a fourth time.
Nov. 14	At Westminster Hall, Campion, with seven others, is arraigned and charged with treason for having conspired at Rome and Rheims to raise sedition and overthrow the Queen.
Nov. 20	At Westminster, Campion and the other seven are put on trial collectively. A verdict of guilty is given by the jury before Lord Chief-Justice Wray, who sentences them to death.

Nov. 28	Sent by the Lieutenant of the Tower, Edmund's sister visits him in the Tower to say a life-long benefice is offered him if he would recant his religion.
Friday Dec. 1, 1581	Fathers Edmund Campion, Ralph Sherwin and Alexander Briant, in that order, are executed by drawing, hanging and quartering at Tyburn, London.
Dec. 29, 1886	Campion is beatified under Pope Leo XIII.
Oct. 25, 1970	St. Edmund Campion is canonized by Pope Paul VI as one of the Forty Martyrs of England and Wales. His Feast-day is December 1st.

A Note on chronology

There is confusion regarding some dates of the events of Campion's life from 1569–73. Thus some things are placed in one year by some writers, and in the following year by others:

	Robert Persons 1594	Simpson 1867	Pollen and Bowden 1905
1. Leaves Oxford	August 1, 1569	August 1, 1570	August 1, 1569
			December 1570 says Pollen later
2. Arrives in Ireland	August 25, 1569	1570, August 25?	May 1571
3. Returns to England	May 1571	May 1571	May 1571
4. Time at Douay	June 1571 and somewhat more than a year[1]	June 1571– summer 1572	nearly 2 years [to April 1573 at latest]
			receives B.D. January 21, 1573[2]
5. Arrives in Rome	April 1573[1]	September 1572	September 1572
6. Joins Jesuits			

The full titles of these biographies are given in the bibliographies of this book. I have collected all the variations here rather than refer to them regularly through the biography. Any change to a date given in the original Simpson is always on the basis of a strong argument or new evidence. The dates I have adopted in this table are in the text and the Chronology above.

The most reliable Oxford dates are in Stevenson and Salter (1939) who cite records not seen by authors before them. It seems Reynolds did not see their book, since he dates Campion's departure from Oxford in 1569, a year earlier than they say: end of Sept. 1570.

Despite difficulties, I place Campion's return to England in May

Waugh 1935	Reynolds 1980	Westminster 1968, Holleran 1999	Simpson revised 2010
finishes work at Oxford August 1, 1569	1569	end of September 1570	end of September 1570
	Late 1569[4] (p. 46)	1570 (Holleran only)	end of September 1570
	1570[4] (p. 44)		
end of May 1572[3]	May 1571	end of May 1572	end of May 1571
May 1571[3]– c. February 1573	June 1571–1573	June 1572– spring 1573	June 1571– spring 1573
end of February 1573	early 1573	spring 1573	spring 1573
All say April 1573			

1. Persons' chronology leaves a big gap. He says Campion arrived in Rome "some days" before the election of the new Jesuit General, Fr. Mercurian (elected April 23, 1573). Thus I put April 1573 as the month he is implicitly stating for both arrival in Rome and entrance into the Society of Jesus. As can be seen, Campion's stay at Douay, said by Persons to be for "somewhat more than a year" must be corrected.

2. Pollen and Bowden had June 21, 1573, probably a misprint. I amend it here to January 21, as given in the Douay Diary. Otherwise they contradict their own dates.

3. Waugh's chronology here is inconsistent. He covers it up by not mentioning the date of Dr. Storey's trial (May 1571) which he says was attended by Campion.

4. Reynolds' chronology here is inconsistent.

1571 because Persons twice says Campion attended the trial of Dr. Storey (held that month), and that was probably from Campion's relating it to him. But if not May, then definitely June, and certainly 1571.

I then place Campion at Douay for nearly 2 years, since he himself says he did "nearly a biennium at Douay" (ch. 5: "Transfer to Brünn"). This indisputable quote from Campion himself is overlooked by Simpson, Westminster and Holleran who give him only a year or so there (probably because Persons says that; as did Allen, ed. Pollen, p. 6: Simpson's bibliography, no. 52a).

A Map of Europe

Showing places in the life of Campion
(with today's European borders)

A Map of England

showing the 13 counties visited by Edmund Campion

Scotland

Yorkshire

Lancashire

Derbyshire

Nottinghamshire

Staffordshire

Leicestershire

Wales

Warwickshire

Huntingdonshire

Northamptonshire

Oxfordshire

Buckinghamshire

Berkshire

Middlesex

Lyford

Kent

Dover

○○○○○ **1st** Journey ●●●●● **2nd** Journey —— **3rd** Journey
Starting from Middlesex Starting from Buckinghamshire Starting from Stonor Park
19 July - October 1580 16 Nov. 1580 - 3 June 1581 11 - 17 July 1581

The borders are of the historic counties, i.e., before the 1972 redistribution.
The routes are indicative only of counties visited (not specific towns) and do not show the return journeys.

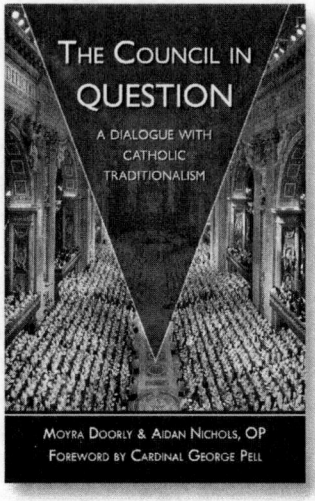

 **TAN·BOOKS**

TAN Books was founded in 1967 to preserve the spiritual, intellectual and liturgical traditions of the Catholic Church. At a critical moment in history TAN kept alive the great classics of the Faith and drew many to the Church. In 2008 TAN was acquired by Saint Benedict Press. Today TAN continues its mission to a new generation of readers.

From its earliest days TAN has published a range of booklets that teach and defend the Faith. Through partnerships with organizations, apostolates, and mission-minded individuals, well over 10 million TAN booklets have been distributed.

More recently, TAN has expanded its publishing with the launch of Catholic calendars and daily planners—as well as Bibles, fiction, and multimedia products through its sister imprints Catholic Courses (CatholicCourses.com) and Saint Benedict Press (SaintBenedictPress.com).

Today TAN publishes over 500 titles in the areas of theology, prayer, devotions, doctrine, Church history, and the lives of the saints. TAN books are published in multiple languages and found throughout the world in schools, parishes, bookstores and homes.

For a free catalog, visit us online at
TANBooks.com

Or call us toll-free at
(800) 437-5876

Spread the Faith with . . .

TAN·BOOKS

A Division of Saint Benedict Press, LLC

TAN books are powerful tools for evangelization. They lift the mind to God and change lives. Millions of readers have found in TAN books and booklets an effective way to teach and defend the Faith, soften hearts, and grow in prayer and holiness of life.

Throughout history the faithful have distributed Catholic literature and sacramentals to save souls. St. Francis de Sales passed out his own pamphlets to win back those who had abandoned the Faith. Countless others have distributed the Miraculous Medal to prompt conversions and inspire deeper devotion to God. Our customers use TAN books in that same spirit.

If you have been helped by this or another TAN title, share it with others. Become a TAN Missionary and share our life changing books and booklets with your family, friends and community. We'll help by providing special discounts for books and booklets purchased in quantity for purposes of evangelization. Write or call us for additional details.

TAN Books
Attn: TAN Missionaries Department
PO Box 410487
Charlotte, NC 28241

Toll-free (800) 437-5876
missionaries@TANBooks.com

Aldolase

SYNONYM/ACRONYM: ALD.

COMMON USE: To assist in the diagnosis of muscle-wasting diseases such as muscular dystrophy or other diseases that cause muscle and cellular damage such as hepatitis and cirrhosis of the liver.

SPECIMEN: Serum (1 mL) collected in a red- or tiger-top tube.

NORMAL FINDINGS: (Method: Spectrophotometry)

Age	Conventional & SI Units
Newborn–30 d	6.0–32.0 units/L
1 mo–2 yr	3.4–11.8 units/L
3–6 yr	2.7–8.8 units/L
7–17 yr	3.3–9.7 units/L
Adult	Less than 8.1 units/L

POTENTIAL DIAGNOSIS

Increased in

ALD is released from any damaged cell in which it is stored, so diseases of skeletal muscle, cardiac muscle, pancreas, red blood cells, and liver that cause cellular destruction demonstrate elevated ALD levels.

- Carcinoma (lung, breast, and genitourinary tract and metastasis to liver)
- Dermatomyositis
- Duchenne's muscular dystrophy
- Hepatitis (acute viral or toxic)
- Limb girdle muscular dystrophy
- Myocardial infarction
- Pancreatitis (acute)
- Polymyositis
- Severe crush injuries
- Tetanus
- Trichinosis *(related to myositis)*

Decreased in

- Hereditary fructose intolerance *(evidenced by hereditary deficiency of the aldolase B enzyme)*
- *Late stages of muscle-wasting diseases in which muscle mass has significantly diminished*

CRITICAL FINDINGS: N/A

Find and print out the full monograph at DavisPlus (http://davisplus.fadavis.com, keyword Van Leeuwen).

A

Aldosterone

SYNONYM/ACRONYM: N/A.

COMMON USE: To assist in the diagnosis of primary hyperaldosteronism disorders such as Conn's syndrome and Addison's disease. Blood levels fluctuate with dehydration and fluid overload. This test can be used in evaluation of hypertension.

SPECIMEN: Serum (1 mL) collected in a red- or tiger-top tube. Plasma (1 mL) collected in a green-top (heparin) or lavender-top (EDTA) tube is also acceptable.

NORMAL FINDINGS: (Method: Radioimmunoassay)

Age	Conventional Units	SI Units (Conventional Units × 0.0277)
Cord blood	40–200 ng/dL	1.11–5.54 nmol/L
3 days–1 wk	7–184 ng/dL	0.19–5.10 nmol/L
1 mo–1 yr	5–90 ng/dL	0.14–2.49 nmol/L
13–23 mo	7–54 ng/dL	0.19–1.50 nmol/L
2–10 yr		
Supine	3–35 ng/dL	0.08–0.97 nmol/L
Upright	5–80 ng/dL	0.14–2.22 nmol/L
11–15 yr		
Supine	2–22 ng/dL	0.06–0.61 nmol/L
Upright	4–48 ng/dL	0.11–1.33 nmol/L
Adult		
Supine	3–16 ng/dL	0.08–0.44 nmol/L
Upright	7–30 ng/dL	0.19–0.83 nmol/L
Older Adult	Levels decline with age	

These values reflect a normal-sodium diet. Values for a low-sodium diet are three to five times higher.

DESCRIPTION: Aldosterone is a mineralocorticoid secreted by the zona glomerulosa of the adrenal cortex in response to decreased serum sodium, decreased blood volume, and increased serum potassium. When needed, aldosterone also acts to increase sodium reabsorption in the renal tubules, resulting in potassium excretion and increased water retention, blood volume, and blood pressure. Changes in renal blood flow trigger or suppress release of renin from the glomeruli. The presence of circulating renin stimulates the liver to produce angiotensin I. Angiotensin I is converted by the lung and kidney into angiotensin II, a potent trigger for the release of aldosterone. Aldosterone and the renin-angiotensin system work together to regulate sodium and potassium levels. This test is of little diagnostic value in differentiating primary and secondary aldosteronism unless plasma renin activity is measured simultaneously (see monograph titled "Renin"). A variety of factors influence serum aldosterone levels, including sodium

intake, certain medications, and activity. Secretion of aldosterone is also affected by ACTH, a pituitary hormone that primarily stimulates secretion of glucocorticoids and minimally affects secretion of mineralocorticosteroids. Patients with serum potassium less than 3.6 mEq/L and 24-hour urine potassium greater than 40 mEq/L fit the general criteria to test for aldosteronism. Renin is low in primary aldosteronism and high in secondary aldosteronism. A ratio of plasma aldosterone to plasma renin activity greater than 50 is significant. Ratios greater than 20 obtained after unchallenged screening may indicate the need for further evaluation with a sodium-loading protocol. A captopril protocol can be substituted for patients who may not tolerate the sodium-loading protocol.

INDICATIONS

- Evaluate hypertension of unknown cause, especially with hypokalemia not induced by diuretics
- Investigate suspected hyperaldosteronism, as indicated by elevated levels
- Investigate suspected hypoaldosteronism, as indicated by decreased levels

POTENTIAL DIAGNOSIS

Increased in

Increased With Decreased Renin Levels

Primary hyperaldosteronism (evidenced by overproduction related to abnormal adrenal gland function):
- Adenomas (Conn's syndrome)
- Bilateral hyperplasia of the aldosterone-secreting zona glomerulosa cells

Increased With Increased Renin Levels

Secondary hyperaldosteronism (related to conditions that increase renin levels, which then stimulate aldosterone secretion):
- Bartter's syndrome *(related to excessive loss of potassium by the kidneys, leading to release of renin and subsequent release of aldosterone)*
- Cardiac failure *(related to diluted concentration of sodium by increased blood volume)*
- Chronic obstructive pulmonary disease
- Cirrhosis with ascites formation *(related to diluted concentration of sodium by increased blood volume)*
- Diuretic abuse *(related to direct stimulation of aldosterone secretion)*
- Hypovolemia *(secondary to hemorrhage and transudation)*
- Laxative abuse *(related to direct stimulation of aldosterone secretion)*
- Nephrotic syndrome *(related to excessive renal protein loss, development of decreased oncotic pressure, fluid retention, and diluted concentration of sodium)*
- Starvation (after 10 days) *(related to diluted concentration of sodium by development of edema)*
- Thermal stress *(related to direct stimulation of aldosterone secretion)*
- Toxemia of pregnancy *(related to diluted concentration of sodium by increased blood volume evidenced by edema; placental corticotropin-releasing hormone stimulates production of maternal adrenal hormones that can also contribute to edema)*

A

Decreased in

Without Hypertension
- Addison's disease *(related to lack of function in the adrenal cortex)*
- Hypoaldosteronism *(secondary to renin deficiency)*
- Isolated aldosterone deficiency

With Hypertension
- Acute alcohol intoxication *(related to toxic effects of alcohol on adrenal gland function and therefore secretion of aldosterone)*
- Diabetes *(related to impaired conversion of prerenin to renin by damaged kidneys, resulting in decreased aldosterone)*
- Excess secretion of deoxycorticosterone *(related to suppression of ACTH production by cortisol, which in turn affects aldosterone secretion)*
- Turner's syndrome (25% of cases) *(related to congenital adrenal hyperplasia resulting in underproduction of aldosterone and overproduction of androgens)*

CRITICAL FINDINGS: N/A

INTERFERING FACTORS
- Drugs that may increase aldosterone levels include amiloride, ammonium chloride, angiotensin, angiotensin II, dobutamine, dopamine, endralazine, fenoldopam, hydralazine, hydrochlorothiazide, laxatives (abuse), metoclopramide, nifedipine, opiates, potassium, spironolactone, and zacopride.
- Drugs that may decrease aldosterone levels include atenolol, captopril, carvedilol, cilazapril, enalapril, fadrozole, glycyrrhiza (licorice), ibuprofen, indomethacin, lisinopril, nicardipine, NSAIDs, perindopril, ranitidine, saline, sinorphan, and verapamil. Prolonged heparin therapy also decreases aldosterone levels.

- Upright body posture, stress, strenuous exercise, and late pregnancy can lead to increased levels.
- Recent radioactive scans or radiation within 1 wk before the test can interfere with test results when radioimmunoassay is the test method.
- Diet can significantly affect results. A low-sodium diet can increase serum aldosterone, whereas a high-sodium diet can decrease levels. Decreased serum sodium and elevated serum potassium increase aldosterone secretion. Elevated serum sodium and decreased serum potassium suppress aldosterone secretion.

NURSING IMPLICATIONS AND PROCEDURE

PRETEST:
- Positively identify the patient using at least two unique identifiers before providing care, treatment, or services.
- *Patient Teaching:* Inform the patient this test evaluates dehydration and can assist in identification of the causes of muscle weakness or high blood pressure.
- Obtain a history of the patient's complaints, including a list of known allergens, especially allergies or sensitivities to latex.
- Obtain a history of known or suspected fluid or electrolyte imbalance, hypertension, renal function, or stage of pregnancy. Note the amount of sodium ingested in the diet over the past 2 wk.
- Obtain a history of the patient's endocrine and genitourinary systems, symptoms, and results of previously performed laboratory tests and diagnostic and surgical procedures. Note any recent procedures that can interfere with test results.
- Obtain a list of the patient's current medications, including herbs, nutritional supplements, and nutraceuticals (see Appendix F).
- Review the procedure with the patient. Inform the patient that specimen

collection takes approximately 5 to 10 min. Inform the patient that multiple specimens may be required. Address concerns about pain and explain that there may be some discomfort during the venipuncture. Aldosterone levels may also be collected directly from the left and right adrenal veins. This procedure is performed by a radiologist via catheterization and takes approximately 1 hr.

▶ *Sensitivity to social and cultural issues,* as well as concern for modesty, is important in providing psychological support before, during, and after the procedure. Inform the patient that the required position, supine/lying down or upright/sitting up, must be maintained for 2 hr before specimen collection.

▶ The patient should be on a normal-sodium diet (1 to 2 g of sodium per day) for 2 to 4 wk before the test. Protocols may vary among facilities. Under medical direction, the patient should avoid diuretics, antihypertensive drugs and herbals, and cyclic progestogens and estrogens for 2 to 4 wk before the test. The patient should also be advised to avoid consuming anything that contains licorice for 2 wk before the test. Licorice inhibits short-chain dehydrogenase/reductase enzymes. These enzymes normally prevent cortisol from binding to aldosterone receptor sites in the kidney. In the absence of these enzymes, cortisol acts on the kidney and triggers the same effects as aldosterone, which include increased potassium excretion, sodium retention, and water retention. Aldosterone levels are not affected by licorice ingestion, but the simultaneous measurements of electrolytes may provide misleading results.

INTRATEST:

▶ Ensure that the patient has complied with dietary, medication, and pretesting preparations regarding activity.

▶ If the patient has a history of allergic reaction to latex, avoid the use of equipment containing latex.

▶ Instruct the patient to cooperate fully and to follow directions. Direct the patient to breathe normally and to avoid unnecessary movement.

▶ Observe standard precautions, and follow the general guidelines in Appendix A. Positively identify the patient, and label the appropriate tubes with the corresponding patient demographics, date, time of collection, patient position (upright or supine), and exact source of specimen (peripheral versus arterial). Perform a venipuncture after the patient has been in the upright (sitting or standing) position for 2 hr. If a supine specimen is requested on an inpatient, the specimen should be collected early in the morning before rising.

▶ Remove the needle, and apply direct pressure with dry gauze to stop bleeding. Observe/assess venipuncture site for bleeding or hematoma formation and secure gauze with adhesive bandage.

▶ Promptly transport the specimen on ice to the laboratory for processing and analysis.

POST-TEST:

▶ A report of the results will be made available to the requesting health-care provider (HCP), who will discuss the results with the patient.

▶ Instruct the patient to resume usual diet, medication, and activity as directed by the HCP.

▶ Instruct the patient to notify the HCP of any signs and symptoms of dehydration or fluid overload related to elevated aldosterone levels or compromised sodium regulatory mechanisms.

▶ *Nutritional Considerations:* Aldosterone levels are involved in the regulation of body fluid volume. Educate patients about the importance of proper water balance. The Institute of Medicine's Food and Nutrition Board suggests 3.7 L for males and 2.7 L for females as the daily intake goal of total dietary water for adults age 19 to greater than 70 yr; 3 L/d for pregnant females age 14 to 51 yr; 3.8 L/d for lactating females age 14 to 51 yr; 3.3 L/d for male and 2.3 L/d for female children age 14 to 18 yr; 2.4 L/d for male and 2.1 L/d for female children age 9 to 13 yr; 1.7 L/d for children age 4 to 8 yr; 1.3 L/d for children age 1 to 3 yr; 0.8 L/d for children age 7 to 12 mo; and 0.7 L/d (assumed to be from human milk) for children 0 to 6 mo. Reprinted with permission from the National Academies Press, copyright 2013, National Academy of Sciences.Tap water may also contain other nutrients. Water-softening systems replace minerals (e.g., calcium, magnesium, iron) with sodium, so caution should be used if a low-sodium diet is prescribed. *Nutritional Considerations:* Because aldosterone levels affect sodium levels, some consideration may be given to dietary adjustment if sodium allowances need to be regulated. The Institute of Medicine's Food and Nutrition Board suggests 1,200 mg as an adequate daily intake goal of dietary sodium for adult males and females greater than age 70 yr; 1,300 mg/d for adult males and females age 51 to 70 yr; 1,500 mg/d for adult males and females age 19 to 50 yr; 1,500 mg/d for pregnant and lactating females age 18 to 50 yr; 1,500 mg/d for children age 9 to 18 yr; 1,200 mg/d for children age 4 to 8 yr; 1,000 mg/d for children age 1 to 3 yr; 370 mg/d for children age 7 to 12 mo; and 120 mg/d for children age 0 to 6 mo. Reprinted with permission from the National Academies Press, copyright 2013, National Academy of Sciences. Educate patients with low sodium levels that the major source of dietary sodium is table salt. Many foods, such as milk and other dairy products, are also good sources of dietary sodium. Most other dietary sodium is available through consumption of processed foods. Patients who need to follow low-sodium diets should avoid beverages such as colas, ginger ale, Gatorade, lemon-lime sodas, and root beer. Many over-the-counter medications, including antacids, laxatives, analgesics, sedatives, and antitussives, contain significant amounts of sodium. The best advice is to emphasize the importance of reading all food, beverage, and medicine labels. The Institute of Medicine's Food and Nutrition Board suggests 4,700 mg as the daily intake goal of dietary potassium for adults age 19 to greater than 70 yr; 4,700 mg/d for pregnant females under age 18 to 51 yr; 5,100 mg/d for lactating females under age 18 to 51 yr; 4,700 mg/d for children age 14 to 18 yr; 4,500 mg/d for children age 9 to 13 yr; 3,800 mg/d for children age 4 to 8 yr; 3,000 mg/d for children age 1 to 3 yr; 700 mg/d for children age 7 to 12 mo; and 400 mg/d for children 0 to 6 mo. Reprinted with permission from the National Academies Press, copyright 2013, National Academy of Sciences. Potassium is present in all plant and animal cells, making dietary replacement simple. An HCP or nutritionist should be consulted before considering the use of salt substitutes. Reinforce information given by the patient's HCP regarding further testing, treatment, or referral to another HCP. Answer any questions or address any concerns voiced by the patient or family. Depending on the results of this procedure, additional testing may be performed to evaluate or monitor progression of the disease process and determine the need for a change in therapy. Evaluate test results in relation to the patient's symptoms and other tests performed.

RELATED MONOGRAPHS:

Related tests include adrenal gland scan, biopsy kidney, BUN, catecholamines, cortisol, creatinine, glucose, magnesium, osmolality, potassium, protein urine, renin, sodium, and UA. See the Endocrine and Genitourinary systems tables at the end of the book for related tests by body system.

Alkaline Phosphatase and Isoenzymes

SYNONYM/ACRONYM: Alk Phos, ALP and fractionation, heat-stable ALP.

COMMON USE: To assist in the diagnosis of liver cancer and cirrhosis, or bone cancer and bone fracture.

SPECIMEN: Serum (1 mL) collected in a red- or tiger-top tube. Plasma (1 mL) collected in a green-top (heparin) tube is also acceptable.

NORMAL FINDINGS: (Method: Spectrophotometry for total alkaline phosphatase, inhibition/electrophoresis for fractionation)

Total ALP	Conventional & SI Units	Bone Fraction	Liver Fraction
0–30 d			
Male	75–375 units/L		
Female	65–350 units/L		
1–11 mo			
Male	70–350 units/L		
Female	80–330 units/L		
1–5 yr			
Male	56–350 units/L	39–308 units/L	Less than 8–101 units/L
Female	73–378 units/L	56–300 units/L	Less than 8–53 units/L
6–7 yr			
Male	70–364 units/L	50–319 units/L	Less than 8–76 units/L
Female	73–378 units/L	56–300 units/L	Less than 8–53 units/L
8 yr			
Male	70–364 units/L	50–258 units/L	Less than 8–62 units/L
Female	98–448 units/L	78–353 units/L	Less than 8–62 units/L
9–12 yr			
Male	112–476 units/L	78–339 units/L	Less than 8–81 units/L
Female	98–448 units/L	78–353 units/L	Less than 8–62 units/L
13 yr			
Male	112–476 units/L	78–389 units/L	Less than 8–48 units/L
Female	56–350 units/L	28–252 units/L	Less than 8–50 units/L
14 yr			
Male	112–476 units/L	78–389 units/L	Less than 8–48 units/L
Female	56–266 units/L	31–190 units/L	Less than 8–48 units/L
15 yr			
Male	70–378 units/L	48–311 units/L	Less than 8–39 units/L
Female	42–168 units/L	20–115 units/L	Less than 8–53 units/L
16 yr			
Male	70–378 units/L	48–311 units/L	Less than 8–39 units/L
Female	28–126 units/L	14–87 units/L	Less than 8–50 units/L
17 yr			
Male	56–238 units/L	34–190 units/L	Less than 8–39 units/L
Female	28–126 units/L	17–84 units/L	Less than 8–53 units/L
18 yr			
Male	56–182 units/L	34–146 units/L	Less than 8–39 units/L
Female	28–126 units/L	17–84 units/L	Less than 8–53 units/L
19 yr			
Male	42–154 units/L	25–123 units/L	Less than 8–39 units/L
Female	28–126 units/L	17–84 units/L	Less than 8–53 units/L
20 yr			
Male	45–138 units/L	25–73 units/L	Less than 8–48 units/L
Female	33–118 units/L	17–56 units/L	Less than 8–50 units/L

(table continues on page 28)

A

Total ALP	Conventional & SI Units	Bone Fraction	Liver Fraction
21 yr and older			
Male	35–142 units/L	11–73 units/L	0–93 units/L
Female	25–125 units/L	11–73 units/L	0–93 units/L

Values may be slightly elevated in older adults.

DESCRIPTION: Alkaline phosphatase (ALP) is an enzyme found in the liver; in Kupffer cells lining the biliary tract; and in bones, intestines, and placenta. Additional sources of ALP include the proximal tubules of the kidneys, pulmonary alveolar cells, germ cells, vascular bed, lactating mammary glands, and granulocytes of circulating blood. ALP is referred to as alkaline because it functions optimally at a pH of 9.0. This test is most useful for determining the presence of liver or bone disease.

Isoelectric focusing methods can identify 12 isoenzymes of ALP. Certain cancers produce small amounts of distinctive Regan and Nagao ALP isoenzymes. Elevations in three main ALP isoenzymes, however, are of clinical significance: ALP_1 of liver origin, ALP_2 of bone origin, and ALP_3 of intestinal origin (normal elevations are present in Lewis antibody positive individuals with blood types O and B). ALP levels vary by age and gender. Values in children are higher than in adults because of the level of bone growth and development. An immunoassay method is available for measuring bone-specific ALP as an indicator of increased bone turnover and estrogen deficiency in postmenopausal women.

INDICATIONS

• Evaluate signs and symptoms of various disorders associated with elevated ALP levels, such as biliary obstruction, hepatobiliary disease, and bone disease, including malignant processes
• Differentiate obstructive hepatobiliary tract disorders from hepatocellular disease; greater elevations of ALP are seen in the former
• Determine effects of renal disease on bone metabolism
• Determine bone growth or destruction in children with abnormal growth patterns

POTENTIAL DIAGNOSIS

Increased in
Related to release of alkaline phosphatase from damaged bone, biliary tract, and liver cells
• Liver disease:
  Biliary atresia
  Biliary obstruction (acute cholecystitis, cholelithiasis, intrahepatic cholestasis of pregnancy, primary biliary cirrhosis)
  Cancer
  Chronic active hepatitis
  Cirrhosis
  Diabetes (diabetic hepatic lipidosis)
  Extrahepatic duct obstruction
  Granulomatous or infiltrative liver diseases (sarcoidosis, amyloidosis, TB)
  Infectious mononucleosis
  Intrahepatic biliary hypoplasia
  Toxic hepatitis
  Viral hepatitis

- Bone disease:
  Healing fractures
  Metabolic bone diseases (rickets, osteomalacia)
  Metastatic tumors in bone
  Osteogenic sarcoma
  Osteoporosis
  Paget's disease (osteitis deformans)
- Other conditions:
  Advanced pregnancy *(related to additional sources: placental tissue and new fetal bone growth; marked decline is seen with placental insufficiency and imminent fetal demise)*
  Cancer of the breast, colon, gallbladder, lung, or pancreas
  Congestive heart failure
  Familial hyperphosphatemia
  Hyperparathyroidism
  Perforated bowel
  Pneumonia
  Pulmonary and myocardial infarctions
  Pulmonary embolism
  Ulcerative colitis

Decreased in
- Anemia (severe)
- Celiac disease
- Folic acid deficiency
- HIV-1 infection
- Hypervitaminosis D
- Hypophosphatasia *(related to insufficient phosphorus source for ALP production; congenital and rare)*
- Hypothyroidism (characteristic in infantile and juvenile cases)
- Nutritional deficiency of zinc or magnesium
- Pernicious anemia
- Scurvy *(related to vitamin C deficiency)*
- Whipple's disease
- Zollinger-Ellison syndrome

CRITICAL FINDINGS: N/A

INTERFERING FACTORS
- Drugs that may increase ALP levels by causing cholestasis include anabolic steroids, erythromycin, ethionamide, gold salts, imipramine, interleukin-2, isocarboxazid, nitrofurans, oral contraceptives, phenothiazines, sulfonamides, and tolbutamide.
- Drugs that may increase ALP levels by causing hepatocellular damage include acetaminophen (toxic), amiodarone, anticonvulsants, arsenicals, asparaginase, bromocriptine, captopril, cephalosporins, chloramphenicol, enflurane, ethionamide, foscarnet, gentamicin, indomethacin, lincomycin, methyldopa, naproxen, nitrofurans, probenecid, procainamide, progesterone, ranitidine, tobramycin, tolcapone, and verapamil.
- Drugs that may cause an overall decrease in ALP levels include alendronate, azathioprine, calcitriol, clofibrate, estrogens with estrogen replacement therapy, and ursodiol.
- Hemolyzed specimens may cause falsely elevated results.
- Elevations of ALP may occur if the patient is nonfasting, usually 2 to 4 hr after a fatty meal, and especially if the patient is a Lewis-positive secretor of blood group B or O.

NURSING IMPLICATIONS AND PROCEDURE

PRETEST:

▸ Positively identify the patient using at least two unique identifiers before providing care, treatment, or services.
▸ *Patient Teaching:* Inform the patient this test can assist with determining the presence of liver or bone disease.
▸ Obtain a history of the patient's complaints, including a list of known allergens, especially allergies or sensitivities to latex.
▸ Obtain a history of the patient's hepatobiliary and musculoskeletal systems, symptoms, and results of previously performed laboratory

tests and diagnostic and surgical procedures.

- Obtain a list of the patient's current medications, including herbs, nutritional supplements, and nutraceuticals (see Appendix F).
- Review the procedure with the patient. Inform the patient that specimen collection takes approximately 5 to 10 min. Address concerns about pain and explain that there may be some discomfort during the venipuncture.
- *Sensitivity to social and cultural issues,* as well as concern for modesty, is important in providing psychological support before, during, and after the procedure.
- There are no food, fluid, or medication restrictions unless by medical direction.

INTRATEST:

- If the patient has a history of allergic reaction to latex, avoid the use of equipment containing latex.
- Instruct the patient to cooperate fully and to follow directions. Direct the patient to breathe normally and to avoid unnecessary movement.
- Observe standard precautions, and follow the general guidelines in Appendix A. Positively identify the patient, and label the appropriate specimen container with the corresponding patient demographics, initials of the person collecting the specimen, date, and time of collection. Perform a venipuncture.
- Remove the needle and apply direct pressure with dry gauze to stop bleeding. Observe/assess venipuncture site for bleeding and hematoma formation and secure gauze with adhesive bandage.
- Promptly transport the specimen to the laboratory for processing and analysis.

POST-TEST:

- A report of the results will be made available to the requesting health-care provider (HCP), who will discuss the results with the patient.
- *Nutritional Considerations:* Increased ALP levels may be associated with liver disease. Dietary recommendations may be indicated and vary depending on the severity of the condition. A

low-protein diet may be in order if the patient's liver has lost the ability to process the end products of protein metabolism. A diet of soft foods may be required if esophageal varices have developed. Ammonia levels may be used to determine whether protein should be added to or reduced from the diet. Patients should be encouraged to eat simple carbohydrates and emulsified fats (as in homogenized milk or eggs) rather than complex carbohydrates (e.g., starch, fiber, and glycogen [animal carbohydrates]) and complex fats, which require additional bile to emulsify them so that they can be used.

The cirrhotic patient should be carefully observed for the development of ascites, in which case fluid and electrolyte balance requires strict attention.

- Reinforce information given by the patient's HCP regarding further testing, treatment, or referral to another HCP. Answer any questions or address any concerns voiced by the patient or family.
- Depending on the results of this procedure, additional testing may be performed to evaluate or monitor progression of the disease process and determine the need for a change in therapy. Evaluate test results in relation to the patient's symptoms and other tests performed.

RELATED MONOGRAPHS:

- Related tests include acetaminophen, ALT, albumin, ammonia, anti-DNA antibodies, AMA/ASMA, ANA, α_1-antitrypsin, α_1-antitrypsin phenotyping, AST, bilirubin, biopsy bone, biopsy liver, bone scan, BMD, calcium, ceruloplasmin, collagen cross-linked telopeptides, C3 and C4, complements, copper, ERCP, GGT, hepatitis antigens and antibodies, hepatobiliary scan, KUB studies, magnesium, MRI abdomen, osteocalcin, PTH, phosphorus, potassium, protein, protein electrophoresis, PT/INR, salicylate, sodium, US abdomen, US liver, vitamin D, and zinc.
- See the Hepatobiliary and Musculoskeletal systems tables at the end of the book for related tests by body system.

Allergen-Specific Immunoglobulin E

A

SYNONYM/ACRONYM: Allergen profile, radioallergosorbent test (RAST), ImmunoCAP® Specific IgE.

COMMON USE: To assist in identifying environmental allergens responsible for causing allergic reactions.

SPECIMEN: Serum (2 mL per group of six allergens, 0.5 mL for each additional individual allergen) collected in a red- or tiger-top tube.

NORMAL FINDINGS: (Method: Radioimmunoassay or fluorescence enzyme immunoassay)

RAST Scoring Method (Radioimmunoassay)	Specific IgE	ImmunoCAP® Scoring Guide (Fluorescence Enzyme Immunoassay)	Specific IgE	
Specific IgE Antibody Level	International Units/L	Class	kU/L	
Absent or undetectable	Less than 0.35	0	Negative	Less than 0.10
Low	0.35–0.70	0/1	Equivocal	0.10–0.34
Moderate	0.71–3.50	1	Low positive	0.35–0.69
High	3.51–17.50	2	Moderate positive	0.70–3.4
Very high	Greater than 17.50	3	High positive	3.5–17.4
		4	Very high positive	17.5–49.9
		5	Very high positive	50.0–99.9
		6	Very high positive	Greater than 100

DESCRIPTION: Allergen-specific immunoglobulin E (IgE) is generally requested for groups of allergens commonly known to incite an allergic response in the affected individual. The test is based on the use of a radiolabeled or non-radiolabeled anti-IgE reagent to detect IgE in the patient's serum, produced in response to specific allergens. The panels include allergens such as animal dander, antibiotics, dust, foods, grasses, insects, trees, mites, molds, venom, and weeds. Allergen testing is useful for evaluating the cause of hay fever, extrinsic asthma, atopic eczema, respiratory allergies, and potentially fatal reactions to insect venom, penicillin, and other drugs or

A

chemicals. RAST and non-radiolabeled methods are alternatives to skin test anergy and provocation procedures, which can be inconvenient, painful, and potentially hazardous to patients. ImmunoCAP® FEIA is a newer, nonradioactive technology with minimal interference from nonspecific binding to total IgE versus allergen-specific IgE.

INDICATIONS
• Evaluate patients who refuse to submit to skin testing or who have generalized dermatitis or other dermatopathic conditions
• Monitor response to desensitization procedures
• Test for allergens when skin testing is inappropriate, such as in infants
• Test for allergens when there is a known history of allergic reaction to skin testing
• Test for specific allergic sensitivity before initiating immunotherapy or desensitization shots
• Test for specific allergic sensitivity when skin testing is unreliable (patients taking long-acting antihistamines may have false-negative skin test)

POTENTIAL DIAGNOSIS
Different scoring systems are used in the interpretation of RAST results.

Increased in
Related to production of IgE, the antibody that primarily responds to conditions that stimulate an allergic response
• Allergic rhinitis
• Anaphylaxis
• Asthma (exogenous)
• Atopic dermatitis
• *Echinococcus* infection
• Eczema
• Hay fever
• Hookworm infection
• Latex allergy

• Schistosomiasis
• Visceral larva migrans

Decreased in
• Asthma (endogenous)
• Pregnancy
• Radiation therapy

CRITICAL FINDINGS: N/A

INTERFERING FACTORS
• Recent radioactive scans or radiation within 1 wk of the test can interfere with test results when radioimmunoassay is the test method.

NURSING IMPLICATIONS AND PROCEDURE

PRETEST:

Positively identify the patient using at least two unique identifiers before providing care, treatment, or services.
Patient Teaching: Inform the patient this test can assist in identification of causal factors related to allergic reaction.
Obtain a history of the patient's complaints, including a list of known allergens, especially allergies or sensitivities to latex.
Obtain a history of the patient's immune and respiratory systems, symptoms, and results of previously performed laboratory tests and diagnostic and surgical procedures. Note any recent procedures that can interfere with test results.
Obtain a list of the patient's current medications, including herbs, nutritional supplements, and nutraceuticals (see Appendix F).
Review the procedure with the patient. Inform the patient that specimen collection takes approximately 5 to 10 min. Address concerns about pain and explain that there may be some discomfort during the venipuncture.
There are no food, fluid, or medication restrictions unless by medical direction.

INTRATEST:

If the patient has a history of allergic reaction to latex, avoid the use of equipment containing latex.

Instruct the patient to cooperate fully and to follow directions. Direct the patient to breathe normally and to avoid unnecessary movement.

Observe standard precautions, and follow the general guidelines in Appendix A. Positively identify the patient, and label the appropriate specimen container with the corresponding patient demographics, initials of the person collecting the specimen, date, and time of collection. Inform the laboratory of the specific allergen group to be tested. Perform a venipuncture.

Remove the needle and apply direct pressure with dry gauze to stop bleeding. Observe/assess venipuncture site for bleeding and hematoma formation and secure gauze with adhesive bandage.

Promptly transport the specimen to the laboratory for processing and analysis.

POST-TEST:

A report of the results will be made available to the requesting health-care provider (HCP), who will discuss the results with the patient.

Nutritional Considerations: Should be given to diet if food allergies are present. Lifestyle adjustments may be necessary depending on the specific allergens identified.

Recognize anxiety related to test results. Administer allergy treatment if ordered.

As appropriate, educate the patient in the proper technique for administering their own treatments as well as safe handling and maintenance of treatment materials. Treatments may include eye drops, inhalers, nasal sprays, oral medications, or shots. Remind the patient of the importance of avoiding triggers and of being in compliance with the recommended therapy, even if signs and symptoms disappear.

Reinforce information given by the patient's HCP regarding further testing, treatment, or referral to another HCP. Answer any questions or address any concerns voiced by the patient or family.

Depending on the results of this procedure, additional testing may be performed to evaluate or monitor progression of the disease process and determine the need for a change in therapy. Evaluate test results in relation to the patient's symptoms and other tests performed.

RELATED MONOGRAPHS:

Related tests include arterial/alveolar oxygen ratio, blood gases, CBC, eosinophil count, fecal analysis, hypersensitivity pneumonitis, IgE, and PFT.

See the Immune and Respiratory systems tables at the end of the book for related tests by body system.

Alveolar/Arterial Gradient and Arterial/Alveolar Oxygen Ratio

SYNONYM/ACRONYM: Alveolar-arterial difference, A/a gradient, a/A ratio.

COMMON USE: To assist in assessing oxygen delivery and diagnosing causes of hypoxemia such as pulmonary edema, acute respiratory distress syndrome, and pulmonary fibrosis.

SPECIMEN: Arterial blood (1 mL) collected in a heparinized syringe. Specimen should be transported tightly capped and in an ice slurry.

NORMAL FINDINGS: (Method: Selective electrodes that measure Po_2 and Pco_2)

Alveolar/arterial gradient	Less than 10 mm Hg at rest (room air)
	20–30 mm Hg at maximum exercise activity (room air)
Arterial/alveolar oxygen ratio	Greater than 0.75 (75%)

A

DESCRIPTION: A test of the ability of oxygen to diffuse from the alveoli into the lungs is of use when assessing a patient's level of oxygenation. This test can help identify the cause of hypoxemia (low oxygen levels in the blood) and intrapulmonary shunting that might result from one of the following three situations: ventilated alveoli without perfusion, unventilated alveoli with perfusion, or collapse of alveoli and associated blood vessels. Information regarding the alveolar/arterial (A/a) gradient can be estimated indirectly using the partial pressure of oxygen (Po_2) (obtained from blood gas analysis) in a simple mathematical formula:

A/a gradient = Po_2 in alveolar air (estimated from the alveolar gas equation) – Po_2 in arterial blood (measured from a blood gas).

An estimate of alveolar Po_2 is accomplished by subtracting the water vapor pressure from the barometric pressure, multiplying the resulting pressure by the fraction of inspired oxygen (Fio_2; percentage of oxygen the patient is breathing), and subtracting this from 1.25 times the arterial partial pressure of carbon dioxide (Pco_2). The gradient is obtained by subtracting the patient's arterial Po_2 from the calculated alveolar Po_2:

Alveolar Po_2 = [(barometric pressure – water vapor pressure) × Fio_2] – [1.25 × Pco_2].

The arterial/alveolar (a/A) ratio reflects the percentage of alveolar Po_2 that is contained in arterial Po_2. It is calculated by dividing the arterial Po_2 by the alveolar Po_2:

a/A = Pao_2/PAo_2

The A/a gradient increases as the concentration of oxygen the patient inspires increases. If the gradient is abnormally high, either there is a problem with the ability of oxygen to pass across the alveolar membrane or oxygenated blood is being mixed with nonoxygenated blood. The a/A ratio is not dependent on Fio_2; it does not increase with a corresponding increase in inhaled oxygen. For patients on a mechanical ventilator with a changing Fio_2, the a/A ratio can be used to determine if oxygen diffusion is improving.

INDICATIONS
- Assess intrapulmonary or coronary artery shunting
- Assist in identifying the cause of hypoxemia

POTENTIAL DIAGNOSIS

Increased in
- Acute respiratory distress syndrome (ARDS) *(related to thickened edematous alveoli)*
- Atelectasis *(related to mixing oxygenated and unoxygenated blood)*
- Arterial-venous shunts *(related to mixing oxygenated and unoxygenated blood)*
- Bronchospasm *(related to decrease in the diameter of the airway)*
- Chronic obstructive pulmonary disease *(related to decrease in the elasticity of lung tissue)*
- Congenital cardiac septal defects *(related to mixing oxygenated and unoxygenated blood)*
- Underventilated alveoli *(related to mucus plugs)*
- Pneumothorax *(related to collapsed lung, shunted air, and subsequent decrease in arterial oxygen levels)*

- Pulmonary edema *(related to thickened edematous alveoli)*
- Pulmonary embolus *(related to obstruction of blood flow to alveoli)*
- Pulmonary fibrosis *(related to thickened edematous alveoli)*

CRITICAL FINDINGS: N/A

INTERFERING FACTORS
- Specimens should be collected before administration of oxygen therapy or antihistamines.
- The patient's temperature should be noted and reported to the laboratory if significantly elevated or depressed so that measured values can be corrected to actual body temperature.
- Exposure of sample to room air affects test results.
- Values normally increase with increasing age (see monograph titled "Blood Gases").
- ❖ Samples for A/a gradient evaluation are obtained by arterial puncture, which carries a risk of bleeding, especially in patients with bleeding disorders or who are taking medications for a bleeding disorder.
- Prompt and proper specimen processing, storage, and analysis are important to achieve accurate results. Specimens should always be transported to the laboratory as quickly as possible after collection. Delay in transport of the sample or transportation without ice may affect test results.

NURSING IMPLICATIONS AND PROCEDURE

PRETEST:
- Positively identify the patient using at least two unique identifiers before providing care, treatment, or services.
- *Patient Teaching:* Inform the patient this test can help to assess respiratory status and identify the cause of respiratory problems.

- Obtain a history of the patient's complaints, including a list of known allergens, especially allergies or sensitivities to latex or anesthetics.
- Obtain a history of the patient's cardiovascular and respiratory systems, especially any bleeding disorders and other symptoms, as well as results of previously performed laboratory tests and diagnostic and surgical procedures. Note any recent procedures that can interfere with test results.
- Obtain a list of the patient's current medications, including anticoagulants, aspirin and other salicylates, herbs, nutritional supplements, and nutraceuticals (see Appendix F). Note the last time and dose of medication taken.
- Indicate the type of oxygen, mode of oxygen delivery, and delivery rate as part of the test requisition process. Wait 30 min after a change in type or mode of oxygen delivery or rate for specimen collection.
- Review the procedure with the patient, and advise rest for 30 min before specimen collection. Address concerns about pain and explain that an arterial puncture may be painful. The site may be anesthetized with 1% to 2% lidocaine before puncture. Inform the patient that specimen collection usually takes 10 to 15 min. The person collecting the specimen should be notified beforehand if the patient is receiving anticoagulant therapy or taking aspirin or other natural products that may prolong bleeding from the puncture site.
- If the sample is to be collected by radial artery puncture, perform an Allen test before puncture to ensure that the patient has adequate collateral circulation to the hand. The modified Allen test is performed as follows: extend the patient's wrist over a rolled towel. Ask the patient to make a fist with the hand extended over the towel. Use the second and third fingers to locate the pulses of the ulnar and radial arteries on the palmar surface of the wrist. (The thumb should not be used to locate these arteries because it has a pulse.) Compress both arteries, and ask the patient to open and close the fist several times until the palm turns pale. Release pressure on the

ulnar artery only. Color should return to the palm within 5 sec if the ulnar artery is functioning. This is a positive Allen test, and blood gases may be drawn from the radial artery site. The Allen test should then be performed on the opposite hand. The hand to which color is restored fastest has better circulation and should be selected for specimen collection.

Sensitivity to social and cultural issues, as well as concern for modesty, is important in providing psychological support before, during, and after the procedure. There are no food, fluid, or medication restrictions unless by medical direction. Prepare an ice slurry in a cup or plastic bag to have ready for immediate transport of the specimen to the laboratory.

INTRATEST:

If the patient has a history of allergic reaction to latex, avoid the use of equipment containing latex.

Instruct the patient to cooperate fully and to follow directions. Direct the patient to breathe normally and to avoid unnecessary movement.

Observe standard precautions, and follow the general guidelines in Appendix A. Positively identify the patient, and label the appropriate specimen container with the corresponding patient demographics, initials of the person collecting the specimen, date, and time of collection. Perform an arterial puncture.

Perform an arterial puncture, and collect the specimen in an air-free heparinized syringe. There is no demonstrable difference in results between samples collected in plastic syringes and samples collected in glass syringes. It is very important that no room air be introduced into the collection container, because the gases in the room and in the sample will begin equilibrating immediately. The end of the syringe must be stoppered immediately after the needle is withdrawn from the puncture site. Apply a pressure dressing over the puncture site. Samples should be mixed by gentle rolling of the syringe to ensure proper mixing of the heparin with the sample, which will prevent the formation of small clots leading to rejection

of the sample. The tightly capped sample should be placed in an ice slurry immediately after collection. Information on the specimen label should be protected from water in the ice slurry by first placing the specimen in a protective plastic bag. Promptly transport the specimen to the laboratory for processing and analysis.

POST-TEST:

A report of the results will be made available to the requesting health-care provider (HCP), who will discuss the results with the patient.

Pressure should be applied to the puncture site for at least 5 min in the unanticoagulated patient and for at least 15 min in a patient receiving anticoagulant therapy. Observe/assess puncture site for bleeding or hematoma formation. Apply pressure bandage.

Teach the patient breathing exercises to assist with the appropriate exchange of oxygen and carbon dioxide.

Administer oxygen, if appropriate.

Teach the patient how to properly use incentive spirometry or nebulizer, if ordered.

Intervene appropriately for hypoxia and ventilatory disturbances.

Reinforce information given by the patient's HCP regarding further testing, treatment, or referral to another HCP. Answer any questions or address any concerns voiced by the patient or family.

Depending on the results of this procedure, additional testing may be performed to evaluate or monitor progression of the disease process and determine the need for a change in therapy. Evaluate test results in relation to the patient's symptoms and other tests performed.

RELATED MONOGRAPHS:

Related tests include allergen-specific IgE, α_1-antitrypsin, α_1-antitrypsin phenotyping, blood gases, chest x-ray, D-dimer, echocardiography, eosinophil count, fibrinogen, hypersensitivity pneumonitis, IgE, potassium, PFT, and sodium.

See the Cardiovascular and Respiratory systems tables at the end of the book for related tests by body system.

Alzheimer's Disease Markers

SYNONYM/ACRONYM: CSF tau protein and β-amyloid-42, AD, APP, PS-1, PS-2, Apo E4.

COMMON USE: To assist in diagnosing Alzheimer's disease and monitoring the effectiveness of therapy.

SPECIMEN: Cerebrospinal fluid (CSF) (2 mL) collected in a plain plastic conical tube for tau protein and β-amyloid-42; whole blood from one full lavender-top (EDTA) tube for apolipoprotein E4 (ApoE4) genotyping, β-amyloid precursor protein, presenilin 1, and presenilin 2.

NORMAL FINDINGS: (Method: Enzyme-linked immunosorbent assay) Simultaneous tau protein and β-amyloid-42 measurements in CSF are used in conjunction with detection of apolipoprotein E4 alleles (restriction fragment length polymorphism) and identification of mutations in the β-amyloid precursor protein (APP), presenilin 1 (PS-1) and presenilin 2 (PS-2) genes (polymerase chain reaction and DNA sequencing) as biochemical and genetic markers of Alzheimer's disease (AD). Scientific studies indicate that a combination of elevated tau protein and decreased β-amyloid-42 protein levels are consistent with the presence of AD. The testing laboratory should be consulted for interpretation of results.

DESCRIPTION: AD is the most common cause of dementia in the elderly population. AD is a disorder of the central nervous system (CNS) that results in progressive and profound memory loss followed by loss of cognitive abilities and death. It may follow years of progressive formation of β-amyloid plaques and brain tangles, or it may appear as an early-onset form of the disease. Two recognized pathologic features of AD are neurofibrillary tangles and amyloid plaques found in the brain. Abnormal amounts of the phosphorylated microtubule-associated tau protein are the main component of the classic neurofibrillary tangles found in patients with AD. Tau protein concentration is believed to reflect the number of neurofibrillary tangles and may be an indication of the severity of the disease. β-Amyloid-42 is a free-floating protein normally present in CSF. It is believed to accumulate in the CNS of patients with AD, causing the formation of amyloid plaques on brain tissue. The result is that these patients have lower CSF values than age-matched healthy control participants. The study of genetic markers of AD has led to an association between an inherited autosomal dominant mutation in the APP, PS-1, and PS-2 genes and overproduction of amyloid proteins. Mutations in these genes are believed to be responsible for some cases of early-onset AD. An association also exists between a gene that codes for the production of ApoE4 and development of late-onset AD. Diagnosis of AD includes a thorough physical examination,

A

a complete medical history, neurological examination, tests of mental status, blood tests, and brain imaging procedures.

INDICATIONS
• Assist in establishing a diagnosis of AD

POTENTIAL DIAGNOSIS

Increased in
Tau protein is increased in AD.
Presence of ApoE4 alleles is a genetic risk factor for AD.
Identification of mutations in the APP, PS-1, and PS-2 genes is associated with forms of AD.

Decreased in
β-Amyloid-42 is decreased in up to 50% of healthy control participants.
• AD *(related to accumulation in the brain with a corresponding decrease in CSF)*
• Creutzfeldt-Jakob disease

CRITICAL FINDINGS: N/A

INTERFERING FACTORS
• Some patients with AD may have normal levels of tau protein because of an insufficient number of neurofibrillary tangles.

NURSING IMPLICATIONS AND PROCEDURE

PRETEST:
▸ Positively identify the patient using at least two unique identifiers before providing care, treatment, or services.
▸ *Patient Teaching:* Inform the patient this test can assist in diagnosing AD and/or evaluating the effectiveness of medication used to treat AD.
▸ Obtain a history of the patient's complaints, including a list of known allergens, especially allergies or sensitivities to latex or anesthetics.

▸ Obtain a history of the patient's neurological system, symptoms, and results of previously performed laboratory tests and diagnostic and surgical procedures.
▸ Obtain a list of the patient's current medications, including herbs, nutritional supplements, and nutraceuticals (see Appendix F).
▸ Review the procedure with the patient. Inform the patient that the procedure will be performed by a health-care provider (HCP) trained to perform the procedure and takes approximately 20 min. Address concerns about pain and explain that there may be some discomfort during the lumbar puncture. Inform the patient that a stinging sensation may be felt as the local anesthetic is injected. Instruct the patient to report any pain or other sensations that may require repositioning of the spinal needle.
▸ Inform the patient that the position required for the lumbar puncture may be awkward but that someone will assist. Stress the importance of remaining still and breathing normally throughout the procedure.
▸ *Sensitivity to social and cultural issues,* as well as concern for modesty, is important in providing psychological support before, during, and after the procedure.
▸ There are no food, fluid, or medication restrictions unless by medical direction.
▸ *Make sure a written and informed consent has been signed prior to the procedure and before administering any medications.*

INTRATEST:
▸ If the patient has a history of allergic reaction to latex, avoid the use of equipment containing latex.
▸ Instruct the patient to cooperate fully and to follow directions. Direct the patient to breathe normally and to avoid unnecessary movement.
▸ Observe standard precautions, and follow the general guidelines in Appendix A. Positively identify the patient, and label the appropriate specimen container with the corresponding patient demographics, initials of the person collecting the specimen, date, and time of collection.

Record baseline vital signs, and assess neurological status. Protocols may vary among facilities.

To perform a lumbar puncture, position the patient in the knee-chest position at the side of the bed. Provide pillows to support the spine or for the patient to grasp. The sitting position is an alternative. In this position, the patient must bend the neck and chest to the knees.

Prepare the site (usually between L3 and L4 or L4 and L5) with povidone-iodine, and drape the area.

A local anesthetic is injected. Using sterile technique, the HCP inserts the spinal needle through the spinous processes of the vertebrae and into the subarachnoid space. The stylet is removed. CSF drips from the needle if it is properly placed.

Attach the stopcock and manometer, and measure initial CSF pressure. Normal pressure for an adult in the lateral recumbent position is 60–200 mm H_2O, and 10–100 mm H_2O for children less than 8 yr. These values depend on the body position and are different in a horizontal or sitting position.

If the initial pressure is elevated, the HCP may perform Queckenstedt's test. To perform this test, apply pressure to the jugular vein for about 10 sec. CSF pressure usually rises in response to the occlusion, then rapidly returns to normal within 10 sec after the pressure is released. Sluggish response may indicate CSF obstruction.

Obtain CSF, and place in specimen tubes. Take a final pressure reading, and remove the needle. Clean the puncture site with an antiseptic solution, and apply a small bandage.

Promptly transport the specimen to the laboratory for processing and analysis.

POST-TEST:

A report of the results will be made available to the requesting HCP, who will discuss the results with the patient.

After lumbar puncture, monitor vital signs and neurologic status every 15 min for 1 hr, then every 2 hr for 4 hr, and as ordered. Take the temperature every 4 hr for 24 hr. Compare with baseline values. Protocols may vary among facilities.

Administer fluids, if permitted, to replace lost CSF and help prevent or relieve headache, which is a side effect of lumbar puncture.

Observe/assess the puncture site for leakage, and frequently monitor body signs, such as temperature and blood pressure.

Position the patient flat, either on the back or abdomen, although some HCPs allow 30 degrees of elevation. Maintain this position for 8 hr. Changing position is acceptable as long as the body remains horizontal.

Observe/assess the patient for neurological changes, such as altered level of consciousness, change in pupils, reports of tingling or numbness, and irritability.

Recognize anxiety related to test results, and be supportive of perceived loss of independence and fear of shortened life expectancy. Discuss the implications of abnormal test results on the patient's lifestyle. Provide teaching and information regarding the clinical implications of the test results, as appropriate.

Educate the patient and family members regarding access to counseling and other supportive services. Provide contact information, if desired, for the Alzheimer's Association (www.alz.org).

Reinforce information given by the patient's HCP regarding further testing, treatment, or referral to another HCP. Answer any questions or address any concerns voiced by the patient or family.

Depending on the results of this procedure, additional testing may be performed to evaluate or monitor progression of the disease process and determine the need for a change in therapy. Evaluate test results in relation to the patient's symptoms and other tests performed.

RELATED MONOGRAPHS:

Related tests include CT brain, evoked brain potentials, MRI brain, and FDG-PET scan.

See the Musculoskeletal System table at the end of the book for related tests by body system.

A

Amino Acid Screen, Blood

SYNONYM/ACRONYM: N/A.

COMMON USE: To assist in diagnosing congenital metabolic disorders in infants, typically homocystinuria, maple syrup urine disease, phenylketonuria (PKU) tyrosinuria, and unexplained mental retardation.

SPECIMEN: Plasma (1 mL) collected in a green-top (heparin) tube.

NORMAL FINDINGS: (Method: Liquid chromatography/mass spectrometry) There are numerous amino acids. Values vary, and the testing laboratory should be consulted for corresponding ranges.

POTENTIAL DIAGNOSIS

Increased in
Increased amino acid accumulation (total amino acids) occurs when a specific enzyme deficiency prevents its catabolism, with liver disease, or when there is impaired clearance by the kidneys:
- Aminoacidopathies *(usually related to an inherited disorder; specific amino acids are implicated)*
- Burns *(related to increased protein turnover)*
- Diabetes *(related to gluconeogenesis, where protein is broken down as a means to generate glucose)*
- Fructose intolerance *(related to hereditary enzyme deficiency)*
- Malabsorption *(related to lack of transport and opportunity for catabolism)*
- Renal failure (acute or chronic) *(related to impaired clearance)*
- Reyes syndrome *(related to liver damage)*
- Severe liver damage *(related to decreased production of amino acids by the liver)*
- Shock *(related to increased protein turnover from tissue death and decreased deamination due to impaired liver function)*

Decreased in
Decreased (total amino acids) in conditions that result in increased renal excretion or insufficient protein intake or synthesis:
- Adrenocortical hyperfunction *(related to excess cortisol, which assists in conversion of amino acids into glucose)*
- Carcinoid syndrome *(related to increased consumption of amino acids, especially tryptophan, to form serotonin)*
- Fever *(related to increased consumption)*
- Glomerulonephritis *(related to increased renal excretion)*
- Hartnups disease *(related to increased renal excretion)*
- Huntingtons chorea *(related to increased consumption due to muscle tremors; possible insufficient intake)*
- Malnutrition *(related to insufficient intake)*
- Nephrotic syndrome *(related to increased renal excretion)*
- Pancreatitis (acute) *(related to increased consumption as part of the inflammatory*

process and increased ureagenesis)
- Polycystic kidney disease *(related to increased renal excretion)*

- Rheumatoid arthritis *(related to insufficient intake evidenced by lack of appetite)*

CRITICAL FINDINGS: N/A

Find and print out the full monograph at DavisPlus (http://davisplus.fadavis .com, keyword Van Leeuwen).

Amino Acid Screen, Urine

SYNONYM/ACRONYM: N/A.

COMMON USE: To assist in diagnosing congenital metabolic disorders in infants, typically homocystinuria, maple syrup urine disease, phenylketonuria (PKU), tyrosinuria, and unexplained mental retardation.

SPECIMEN: Urine (10 mL) from a random or timed specimen collected in a clean plastic collection container with hydrochloric acid as a preservative.

NORMAL FINDINGS: (Method: Chromatography) There are numerous amino acids. Values vary, and the testing laboratory should be consulted for corresponding ranges.

POTENTIAL DIAGNOSIS

Increased in

Increased amino acid accumulation (total amino acids) occurs when a specific enzyme deficiency prevents its catabolism or when there is impaired clearance by the kidneys:

- Primary causes *(inherited):*
  Aminoaciduria (specific)
  Cystinosis *(may be masked because of decreased glomerular filtration rate, so values may be in normal range)*
  Fanconi's syndrome
  Fructose intolerance
  Galactosemia
  Hartnup's disease
  Lactose intolerance
  Lowe's syndrome
  Maple syrup urine disease
  Tyrosinemia type I

  Tyrosinosis
  Wilson's disease
- Secondary causes *(noninherited):*
  Acute leukemia
  Chronic renal failure *(reduced glomerular filtration rate)*
  Chronic renal failure
  Diabetic ketosis
  Epilepsy *(transient increase related to disturbed renal function during grand mal seizure)*
  Folic acid deficiency
  Hyperparathyroidism
  Liver necrosis and cirrhosis
  Multiple myeloma
  Muscular dystrophy (progressive)
  Osteomalacia *(secondary to parathyroid hormone excess)*
  Pernicious anemia
  Thalassemia major
  Vitamin deficiency *(B, C, and D; vitamin D–deficiency rickets, vitamin D–resistant rickets)*

Viral hepatitis *(related to the degree of hepatic involvement)*

CRITICAL FINDINGS: N/A

Decreased in: N/A

Find and print out the full monograph at DavisPlus (http://davisplus.fadavis.com, keyword Van Leeuwen).

δ-Aminolevulinic Acid

SYNONYM/ACRONYM: δ-ALA.

COMMON USE: To assist in diagnosing lead poisoning in children, or porphyria, a disorder that disrupts heme synthesis, primarily affecting the liver.

SPECIMEN: Urine (25 mL) from a timed specimen collected in a dark plastic container with glacial acetic acid as a preservative.

NORMAL FINDINGS: (Method: Spectrophotometry)

Conventional Units	SI Units (Conventional Units × 7.626)
1.5–7.5 mg/24 hr	11.4–57.2 micromol/24 hr

DESCRIPTION: δ-Aminolevulinic acid (δ-ALA) is involved in the formation of porphyrins, which ultimately leads to hemoglobin synthesis. Toxins including alcohol, lead, and other heavy metals can inhibit porphyrin synthesis. Accumulated δ-ALA is excreted in urine. Symptoms of the acute phase of intermittent porphyrias include abdominal pain, nausea, vomiting, neuromuscular signs and symptoms, constipation, and occasionally psychotic behavior. Hemolytic anemia may also exhibit during the acute phase. δ-ALA is a test of choice in the diagnosis of acute intermittent porphyria. Although lead poisoning can cause increased urinary excretion, the measurement of δ-ALA is not useful to indicate lead toxicity because it is not detectable in the urine until the blood lead level approaches and exceeds 40 mcg/dL, the level at which children should be evaluated to determine the need for chelation therapy.

INDICATIONS
• Assist in the diagnosis of porphyrias

POTENTIAL DIAGNOSIS

Increased in
Related to inhibition of the enzymes involved in porphyrin synthesis; results in accumulation of δ-ALA and is evidenced by exposure to medications, toxins, diet, or infection that can precipitate an attack
• Acute porphyrias
• Aminolevulinic acid dehydrase deficiency *(related to the inability to convert δ-ALA to porphobilinogen, leading to accumulation of δ-ALA)*

- Hereditary tyrosinemia
- Lead poisoning

Decreased in: N/A

CRITICAL FINDINGS

Conventional Units	SI Units (Conventional Units × 7.62)
Greater than 20 mg/24 hr	Greater then 152.4 micromol/24 hr

Note and immediately report to the health-care provider (HCP) abnormal results and associated symptoms. Timely notification of critical values for lab or diagnostic studies is a role expectation of the professional nurse. Notification processes will vary among facilities. Upon receipt of the critical value the information should be read back to the caller to verify accuracy. Most policies require immediate notification of the primary HCP, Hospitalist, or on-call HCP. Reported information includes the patient's name, unique identifiers, critical value, name of the person giving the report, and name of the person receiving the report. Documentation of notification should be made in the medical record with the name of the HCP notified, time and date of notification, and any orders received. Any delay in a timely report of a critical value may require completion of a notification form with review by Risk Management. Signs and symptoms of an acute porphyria attack include pain (commonly in the abdomen, arms, and legs), nausea, vomiting, muscle weakness, rapid pulse, and high blood pressure. Possible interventions include medication for pain, nausea, and vomiting and, if indicated, respiratory support. Initial treatment following a moderate to severe attack may include identification and cessation of harmful drugs the patient may be taking, IV infusion of carbohydrates, and IV heme therapy (Panhematin) if indicated by markedly elevated urine δ-ALA and porphyrins.

INTERFERING FACTORS

- Drugs that may increase δ-ALA levels include penicillins.
- Cimetidine may decrease δ-ALA levels.
- Numerous drugs are suspected as potential initiators of attacks of acute porphyria, but those classified as unsafe for high-risk individuals include aminopyrine, apronalide, barbiturates, chlordiazepoxide, chlorpropamide, diazepam, dichloralphenazone, ergot preparations, glutethimide, griseofulvin, hydantoin derivatives, isopropyl dipyrone, meprobamate, methyldopa, methylsulfonal, methyprylone, oral contraceptives, pentazocine, phenytoin, progestogens, succinimide, sulfonmethane, and tolbutamide.

NURSING IMPLICATIONS AND PROCEDURE

PRETEST:

Positively identify the patient using at least two unique identifiers before providing care, treatment, or services.
Patient Teaching: Inform the parent/patient this test can assist with identification of poisoning from lead or other toxins.
Obtain a history of the patient's complaints, including a list of known allergens, especially allergies or sensitivities to latex.
Obtain a history of the patient's hematopoietic system, symptoms, and results of previously performed laboratory tests and diagnostic and surgical procedures.
Obtain a list of the patient's current medications, including herbs, nutritional supplements, and nutraceuticals (see Appendix F).
Review the procedure with the patient. Provide a nonmetallic urinal, bedpan, or toilet-mounted collection device. Address concerns about pain and explain that there should be no discomfort during the procedure.
Usually a 24-hr time frame for urine collection is ordered. Inform the patient that all urine must be saved during that 24-hr period. Instruct the patient not to void directly into the laboratory collection container. Instruct the patient to avoid defecating in the collection device and to keep toilet tissue out of the collection device to prevent contamination of the specimen. Place a sign in the bathroom to remind the patient to save all urine.
Instruct the patient to void all urine into the collection device and then to pour the urine into the laboratory collection container. Alternatively, the specimen can be left in the collection device for a health-care staff member to add to the laboratory collection container.

Sensitivity to social and cultural issues, as well as concern for modesty, is important in providing psychological support before, during, and after the procedure.

There are no food, fluid, or medication restrictions unless by medical direction.

INTRATEST:

If the patient has a history of allergic reaction to latex, avoid the use of equipment containing latex.

Instruct the patient to cooperate fully and to follow directions.

Observe standard precautions, and follow the general guidelines in Appendix A. Positively identify the patient, and label the appropriate specimen container with the corresponding patient demographics, initials of the person collecting the specimen, date, and time of collection.

Timed Specimen

Obtain a clean 3-L urine specimen container, toilet-mounted collection device, and plastic bag (for transport of the specimen container). The specimen must be refrigerated or kept on ice throughout the entire collection period. If an indwelling urinary catheter is in place, the drainage bag must be kept on ice.

Begin the test between 6 and 8 a.m. if possible. Collect first voiding and discard. Record the time the specimen was discarded as the beginning of the timed collection period. The next morning, ask the patient to void at the same time the collection was started, and add this last voiding to the container. Urinary output should be recorded throughout the collection time.

If an indwelling catheter is in place, replace the tubing and container system at the start of the collection time. Keep the container system on ice during the collection period, or empty the urine into a larger container periodically during the collection period. Monitor to ensure continued drainage, and conclude the test the next morning at the same hour the collection was begun.

At the conclusion of the test, compare the quantity of urine with the urinary output record for the collection. If the specimen contains less than what was recorded as output, some urine may have been discarded, invalidating the test.

Include on the specimen collection container's label the amount of urine as well as test start and stop times. Note the ingestion of any medications that may affect test results.

Promptly transport the specimen to the laboratory for processing and analysis.

POST-TEST:

A report of the results will be made available to the requesting HCP, who will discuss the results with the patient

Nutritional Considerations: Increased δ-ALA levels may be associated with an acute porphyria attack. Patients prone to attacks should eat a normal or high-carbohydrate diet. Dietary recommendations may be indicated and will vary depending on the condition and its severity; however, restrictions of or wide variations in dietary carbohydrate content should be avoided, even for short periods of time. After recovering from an attack, the patient's daily intake of carbohydrates should be 300 g or more per day.

Recognize anxiety related to test results Discuss the implications of abnormal test results on the patient's lifestyle. Provide teaching and information regarding the clinical implications of the test results, as appropriate. Provide contact information, if desired, for the American Porphyria Foundation (www. porphyriafoundation.com).

Reinforce information given by the patient's HCP regarding further testing, treatment, or referral to another HCP. Answer any questions or address any concerns voiced by the patient or family

Depending on the results of this procedure, additional testing may be performed to evaluate or monitor progression of the disease process and determine the need for a change in therapy. Evaluate test results in relation to the patient's symptoms and other tests performed.

RELATED MONOGRAPHS:

Related tests include CBC, erythrocyte protoporphyrin (free), lead, and porphyrins urine.

See the Hematopoietic System table at the end of the book for related tests by body system.

Ammonia

SYNONYM/ACRONYM: NH_3.

COMMON USE: To assist in diagnosing liver disease such as hepatitis and cirrhosis and evaluating the effectiveness of treatment modalities. Specifically used to assist in diagnosing infant Reye's syndrome.

SPECIMEN: Plasma (1 mL) collected in completely filled lavender- (EDTA) or green-top (Na or Li heparin) tube. Specimen should be transported tightly capped and in an ice slurry.

NORMAL FINDINGS: (Method: Spectrophotometry)

Age	Conventional Units	SI Units (Conventional Units × 0.714)
Newborn	90–150 mcg/dL	64–107 micromol/L
1–12 mo	24–95 mcg/dL	17–68 micromol/L
1–18 yr	31–92 mcg/dL	22–66 micromol/L
Adult male	27–102 mcg/dL	19–73 micromol/L
Adult female	19–87 mcg/dL	14–62 micromol/L

DESCRIPTION: Blood ammonia (NH_3) comes from two sources: deamination of amino acids during protein metabolism and degradation of proteins by colon bacteria. The liver converts ammonia in the portal blood to urea, which is excreted by the kidneys. When liver function is severely compromised, especially in situations in which decreased hepatocellular function is combined with impaired portal blood flow, ammonia levels rise. Ammonia is potentially toxic to the central nervous system.

INDICATIONS

- Evaluate advanced liver disease or other disorders associated with altered serum ammonia levels
- Identify impending hepatic encephalopathy with known liver disease
- Monitor the effectiveness of treatment for hepatic encephalopathy, indicated by declining levels
- Monitor patients receiving hyperalimentation therapy

POTENTIAL DIAGNOSIS

Increased in

- Gastrointestinal hemorrhage *(related to decreased blood volume, which prevents ammonia from reaching the liver to be metabolized)*
- Genitourinary tract infection with distention and stasis *(related to decreased renal excretion; levels accumulate in the blood)*
- Hepatic coma *(related to insufficient functioning liver cells to metabolize ammonia; levels accumulate in the blood)*
- Inborn enzyme deficiency *(evidenced by inability to metabolize ammonia)*

A

- Liver failure, late cirrhosis *(related to insufficient functioning liver cells to metabolize ammonia)*
- Reye's syndrome *(related to insufficient functioning liver cells to metabolize ammonia)*
- Total parenteral nutrition *(related to ammonia generated from protein metabolism)*

Decreased in: N/A

CRITICAL FINDINGS: N/A

INTERFERING FACTORS
- Drugs that may increase ammonia levels include asparaginase, chlorthiazide, chlorthalidone, fibrin hydrolysate, furosemide, hydroflumethiazide, isoniazid, levoglutamide, mercurial diuretics, oral resins, thiazides, and valproic acid.
- Drugs/organisms that may decrease ammonia levels include diphenhydramine, kanamycin, monoamine oxidase inhibitors, neomycin, tetracycline, and *Lactobacillus acidophilus*.
- Hemolysis falsely increases ammonia levels because intracellular ammonia levels are three times higher than plasma.
- Prompt and proper specimen processing, storage, and analysis are important to achieve accurate results. The specimen should be collected on ice; the collection tube should be filled completely and then kept tightly stoppered. Ammonia increases rapidly in the collected specimen, so analysis should be performed within 20 min of collection.

NURSING IMPLICATIONS AND PROCEDURE

PRETEST:
- Positively identify the patient using at least two unique identifiers before providing care, treatment, or services.

- *Patient Teaching:* Inform the patient this test can assist with the evaluation of liver function related to processing protein waste. May be used to assist in diagnosis of Reye's syndrome in infants.
- Obtain a history of the patient's complaints, including a list of known allergens, especially allergies or sensitivities to latex.
- Obtain a history of the patient's gastrointestinal, genitourinary, and hepatobiliary systems; symptoms; and results of previously performed laboratory tests and diagnostic and surgical procedures.
- Obtain a list of the patient's current medications, including herbs, nutritional supplements, and nutraceuticals (see Appendix F).
- Review the procedure with the patient. Inform the patient that specimen collection takes approximately 5 to 10 min. Address concerns about pain and explain that there may be some discomfort during the venipuncture.
- *Sensitivity to social and cultural issues,* as well as concern for modesty, is important in providing psychological support before, during, and after the procedure.
- There are no food, fluid, or medication restrictions unless by medical direction

INTRATEST:
- If the patient has a history of allergic reaction to latex, avoid the use of equipment containing latex.
- Instruct the patient to cooperate fully and to follow directions. Direct the patient to breathe normally and to avoid unnecessary movement.
- Observe standard precautions, and follow the general guidelines in Appendix A. Positively identify the patient, and label the appropriate specimen container with the corresponding patient demographics, initials of the person collecting the specimen, date, and time of collection. Perform a venipuncture.
- Remove the needle and apply direct pressure with dry gauze to stop bleeding. Observe/assess the venipuncture site for bleeding or hematoma formation and secure the gauze with adhesive bandage.

A

Promptly transport the specimen to the laboratory for processing and analysis. The tightly capped sample should be placed in an ice slurry immediately after collection. Information on the specimen label should be protected from water in the ice slurry by first placing the specimen in a protective plastic bag.

POST-TEST:

A report of the results will be made available to the requesting health-care provider (HCP), who will discuss the results with the patient.

Nutritional Considerations: Increased ammonia levels may be associated with liver disease. Dietary recommendations may be indicated, depending on the severity of the condition. A low-protein diet may be in order if the patient's liver has lost the ability to process the end products of protein metabolism. A diet of soft foods may be required if esophageal varices have developed. Ammonia levels may be used to determine whether protein should be added to or reduced from the diet. Patients should be encouraged to eat simple carbohydrates and emulsified fats (as in homogenized milk or eggs) rather than complex carbohydrates (e.g., starch, fiber, and glycogen [animal carbohydrates]) and complex fats, which would require additional bile to emulsify them so that they could be used. The cirrhotic patient should be carefully observed for the development of ascites, in which case fluid and electrolyte balance requires strict attention.

Reinforce information given by the patient's HCP regarding further testing, treatment, or referral to another HCP. Answer any questions or address any concerns voiced by the patient or family.

Depending on the results of this procedure, additional testing may be performed to evaluate or monitor progression of the disease process and determine the need for a change in therapy. Evaluate test results in relation to the patient's symptoms and other tests performed.

RELATED MONOGRAPHS:

Related tests include ALT, albumin, analgesic, anti-inflammatory, and anti-pyretic drugs (acetaminophen and acetylsalicylic acid), anion gap, AST, bilirubin, biopsy liver, blood gases, BUN, blood calcium, CBC, CT biliary tract and liver, CT pelvis, cystometry, cystoscopy, EGD, electrolytes, GI blood loss scan, glucose, IVP, MRI pelvis, ketones, lactic acid, Mecke's scan, osmolality, protein, PT/INR, uric acid, and US pelvis.

See the Gastrointestinal, Genitourinary, and Hepatobiliary systems tables at the end of the book for related tests by body system.

Amniotic Fluid Analysis

SYNONYM/ACRONYM: N/A.

COMMON USE: To assist in identification of fetal gender, genetic disorders such as hemophilia, chromosomal disorders such as Down syndrome, anatomical abnormalities such as spina bifida, and hereditary metabolic disorders such as cystic fibrosis.

SPECIMEN: Amniotic fluid (10 to 20 mL) collected in a clean amber glass or plastic container.

A

NORMAL FINDINGS: (Method: Macroscopic observation of fluid for color and appearance, immunochemiluminometric assay [ICMA] for α_1-fetoprotein, electrophoresis for acetylcholinesterase, spectrophotometry for creatinine and bilirubin, chromatography for lecithin/sphingomyelin [L/S] ratio and phosphatidylglycerol, tissue culture for chromosome analysis, dipstick for leukocyte esterase, and automated cell counter for white blood cell count and lamellar bodies)

Test	Reference Value
Color	Colorless to pale yellow
Appearance	Clear
α_1-Fetoprotein	Less than 2.0 MoM*
Acetylcholinesterase	Absent
Creatinine	1.8–4.0 mg/dL at term
Bilirubin	Less than 0.075 mg/dL in early pregnancy
	Less than 0.025 mg/dL at term
Bilirubin ΔA_{450}	Less than 0.048 ΔOD in early pregnancy
	Less than 0.02 ΔOD at term
L/S ratio	Greater than 2:1 at term
Phosphatidylglycerol	Present at term
Chromosome analysis	Normal karyotype
White blood cell count	None seen
Leukocyte esterase	Negative
Lamellar bodies	Findings and interpretive ranges vary depending on the type of instrument used

*MoM = Multiples of the median.

DESCRIPTION: Amniotic fluid is formed in the membranous sac that surrounds the fetus. The total volume of fluid at term is 500 to 2,500 mL. In amniocentesis, fluid is obtained by ultrasound-guided needle aspiration from the amniotic sac. This procedure is generally performed between 14 and 16 weeks' gestation for accurate interpretation of test results, but it also can be done between 26 and 35 weeks' gestation if fetal distress is suspected. Amniotic fluid is tested to identify genetic and neural tube defects, hemolytic diseases of the newborn, fetal infection, fetal renal malfunction, or maturity of the fetal lungs (see monograph titled "Lecithin/Sphingomyelin Ratio"). Several rapid tests are also used to differentiate amniotic fluid from other body fluids in a vaginal specimen when premature rupture of membranes (PROM) is suspected. A vaginal swab obtained from the posterior vaginal pool can be used to perform a rapid, waived procedure to aid in the assessment of PROM. Nitrazine paper impregnated with an indicator dye will produce a color change indicative of vaginal pH. Normal vaginal pH is acidic (4.5 to 6.0) and the color of the paper will not change. Amniotic fluid has an alkaline pH (7.1 to 7.3) and the paper will turn a blue color. False-positive results occur in the presence of semen, blood, alkaline urine, vaginal infection, or if the patient is receiving antibiotics. The amniotic fluid crystallization or

Fern test is based on the observation of a fern pattern when amniotic fluid is placed on a glass slide and allowed to air dry. The fern pattern is due to the protein and sodium chloride content of the amniotic fluid. False-positive results occur in the presence of blood urine or cervical mucus. Both of these tests can produce false-negative results if only a small amount of fluid is leaked. The reliability of results is also significantly diminished with the passage of time (greater than 24 hr). AmniSure is an immunoassay that can be performed on a vaginal swab sample. It is a rapid test that detects placental alpha microglobulin-1 protein (PAMG-1), which is found in high concentrations in amniotic fluid. AmniSure does not demonstrate the high frequency of false-positive and false-negative results inherent with the pH and fern tests.

INDICATIONS

- Assist in the diagnosis of (in utero) metabolic disorders, such as cystic fibrosis, or errors of lipid, carbohydrate, or amino acid metabolism
- Detect infection secondary to ruptured membranes
- Detect fetal ventral wall defects
- Determine fetal maturity when preterm delivery is being considered; fetal maturity is indicated by an L/S ratio of 2:1 or greater (see monograph titled "Lecithin/Sphingomyelin Ratio")
- Determine fetal gender when the mother is a known carrier of a sex-linked abnormal gene that could be transmitted to male offspring, such as hemophilia or Duchenne's muscular dystrophy
- Determine the presence of fetal distress in late-stage pregnancy

- Evaluate fetus in families with a history of genetic disorders, such as Down syndrome, Tay-Sachs disease, chromosome or enzyme anomalies, or inherited hemoglobinopathies
- Evaluate fetus in mothers of advanced maternal age (some of the aforementioned tests are routinely requested in mothers age 35 and older)
- Evaluate fetus in mothers with a history of miscarriage or stillbirth
- Evaluate known or suspected hemolytic disease involving the fetus in an Rh-sensitized pregnancy, indicated by rising bilirubin levels, especially after the 30th week of gestation
- Evaluate suspected neural tube defects, such as spina bifida or myelomeningocele, as indicated by elevated α_1-fetoprotein (see monograph titled "α_1-Fetoprotein" for information related to triple-marker testing)

POTENTIAL DIAGNOSIS

- Yellow, green, red, or brown fluid *indicates the presence of bilirubin, blood (fetal or maternal), or meconium, which indicate fetal distress or death, hemolytic disease, or growth retardation.*
- Elevated bilirubin levels *indicate fetal hemolytic disease or intestinal obstruction. Measurement of bilirubin is not usually performed before 20 to 24 weeks' gestation because no action can be taken before then. The severity of hemolytic disease is graded by optical density (OD) zones: A value of 0.28 to 0.46 OD at 28 to 31 weeks' gestation indicates mild hemolytic disease, which probably will not affect the fetus; 0.47 to 0.90 OD indicates a moderate effect on the fetus; and 0.91 to 1.0 OD indicates a significant effect on the fetus. A trend of increasing values with serial*

measurements may indicate the need for intrauterine transfusion or early delivery, depending on the fetal age. After 32 to 33 weeks' gestation, early delivery is preferred over intrauterine transfusion, because early delivery is more effective in providing the required care to the neonate.

- Creatinine concentration greater than 2.0 mg/dL *indicates fetal maturity (at 36 to 37 wk) if maternal creatinine is also within the expected range. This value should be interpreted in conjunction with other parameters evaluated in amniotic fluid and especially with the L/S ratio, because normal lung development depends on normal kidney development.*

- An L/S ratio less than 2:1 and absence of phosphatidylglycerol at term *indicate fetal lung immaturity and possible respiratory distress syndrome. The expected L/S ratio for the fetus of an insulin-dependent diabetic mother is higher (3.5:1). (See monograph titled "Lecithin/Sphingomyelin Ratio.")*

- *Lamellar bodies are specialized alveolar cells in which lung surfactant is stored.* They are approximately the size of platelets. Their presence in sufficient quantities is an indicator of fetal lung maturity.

- Elevated α_1-fetoprotein levels and presence of acetylcholinesterase *indicate a neural tube defect (see monograph titled "α_1-Fetoprotein"). Elevation of acetylcholinesterase is also indicative of ventral wall defects.*

- Abnormal karyotype *indicates genetic abnormality (e.g., Tay-Sachs disease, mental retardation, chromosome or enzyme anomalies, and inherited hemoglobinopathies).* (See monograph titled "Chromosome Analysis, Blood.")

- Elevated white blood cell count and positive leukocyte esterase *are indicators of infection.*

CRITICAL FINDINGS: N/A

INTERFERING FACTORS

- Bilirubin may be falsely elevated if maternal hemoglobin or meconium is present in the sample; fetal acidosis may also lead to falsely elevated bilirubin levels.

- Bilirubin may be falsely decreased if the sample is exposed to light or if amniotic fluid volume is excessive.

- Maternal serum creatinine should be measured simultaneously for comparison with amniotic fluid creatinine for proper interpretation. Even in circumstances in which the maternal serum value is normal, the results of the amniotic fluid creatinine may be misleading. A high fluid creatinine value in the fetus of a diabetic mother may reflect the increased muscle mass of a larger fetus. If the fetus is big, the creatinine may be high, and the fetus may still have immature kidneys.

- Contamination of the sample with blood or meconium or complications in pregnancy may yield inaccurate L/S ratios.

- α_1-Fetoprotein and acetylcholinesterase may be falsely elevated if the sample is contaminated with fetal blood.

- Karyotyping cannot be performed under the following conditions: (1) failure to promptly deliver samples for chromosomal analysis to the laboratory performing the test or (2) improper incubation of the sample, which causes cell death.

- Amniocentesis is contraindicated in women with a history of premature labor or incompetent cervix. It is also contraindicated in the presence of placenta previa or abruptio placentae.

NURSING IMPLICATIONS AND PROCEDURE

PRETEST:

Positively identify the patient using at least two unique identifiers before providing care, treatment, or services.

Patient Teaching: Inform the parent this procedure/test can assist in providing a sample of fluid that will allow for evaluation of fetal well-being.

Obtain a history of the patient's complaints, including a list of known allergens, especially allergies or sensitivities to latex or anesthetics.

Obtain a history of the patient's reproductive system, previous pregnancies, symptoms, and results of previously performed laboratory tests and diagnostic and surgical procedures. Include any family history of genetic disorders such as cystic fibrosis, Duchenne's muscular dystrophy, hemophilia, sickle cell disease, Tay-Sachs disease, thalassemia, and trisomy 21. Obtain maternal Rh type. If Rh-negative, check for prior sensitization. A standard dose of $Rh_1(D)$ immune globulin RhoGAM IM or Rhophylac IM or IV is indicated after amniocentesis; repeat doses should be considered if repeated amniocentesis is performed.

Note any recent procedures that can interfere with test results.

Record the date of the last menstrual period and determine the pregnancy weeks' gestation and expected delivery date.

Obtain a list of the patient's current medications, including herbs, nutritional supplements, and nutraceuticals (see Appendix F).

Review the procedure with the patient. Warn the patient that normal results do not guarantee a normal fetus. Assure the patient that precautions to avoid injury to the fetus will be taken by localizing the fetus with ultrasound. Address concerns about pain and explain that during the transabdominal procedure, any discomfort associated with a needle biopsy will be minimized with local anesthetics. If the patient is less than 20 weeks' gestation, instruct her to drink extra fluids 1 hr before the test and to refrain from urination. The full bladder assists in raising the uterus up and out of the way to provide better visualization during the ultrasound procedure. Patients who are at 20 weeks' gestation or beyond do not need to drink extra fluids and should void before the test, because an empty bladder is less likely to be accidentally punctured during specimen collection. Encourage relaxation and controlled breathing during the procedure to aid in reducing any mild discomfort. Inform the patient that specimen collection is performed by a healthcare provider (HCP) specializing in this procedure and usually takes approximately 20 to 30 min to complete.

Sensitivity to social and cultural issues, as well as concern for modesty, is important in providing psychological support before, during, and after the procedure.

There are no food, fluid, or medication restrictions unless by medical direction.

Make sure a written and informed consent has been signed prior to the procedure and before administering any medications.

INTRATEST:

Ensure that the patient has a full bladder before the procedure if gestation is 20 wk or less; have patient void before the procedure if gestation is 21 wk or more.

Positively identify the patient, and label the appropriate collection containers with the corresponding patient demographics, date, time of collection, and site location.

Have patient remove clothes below the waist. Assist the patient to a supine position on the examination table with the abdomen exposed. Drape the patient's legs, leaving the abdomen exposed. Raise her head or legs slightly to promote comfort and to relax the abdominal muscles. If the uterus is large, place a pillow or rolled blanket under the patient's right side to prevent hypertension caused by great-vessel compression. Instruct the patient to cooperate fully and to follow directions. Direct the patient to breathe normally and to avoid unnecessary movement during the local anesthetic and the procedure.

Record maternal and fetal baseline vital signs, and continue to monitor throughout the procedure. Monitor for uterine contractions. Monitor fetal vital signs using ultrasound. Protocols may vary among facilities.

▸ Have emergency equipment readily available.

▸ Observe standard precautions, and follow the general guidelines in Appendix A. Positively identify the patient, and label the appropriate specimen container with the corresponding patient demographics, initials of the person collecting the specimen, date, and time of collection.

▸ Assess the position of the amniotic fluid, fetus, and placenta using ultrasound.

▸ Assemble the necessary equipment, including an amniocentesis tray with solution for skin preparation, local anesthetic, 10- or 20-mL syringe, needles of various sizes (including a 22-gauge, 5-in. spinal needle), sterile drapes, sterile gloves, and foil-covered or amber-colored specimen collection containers.

▸ Cleanse suprapubic area with an antiseptic solution, and protect with sterile drapes. A local anesthetic is injected. Explain that this may cause a stinging sensation.

▸ A 22-gauge, 5-in. spinal needle is inserted through the abdominal and uterine walls. Explain that a sensation of pressure may be experienced when the needle is inserted. Explain to the patient how to use focused and controlled breathing for relaxation during the procedure.

▸ After the fluid is collected and the needle is withdrawn, apply slight pressure to the site. If there is no evidence of bleeding or other drainage, apply a sterile adhesive bandage to the site.

▸ Monitor the patient for complications related to the procedure (e.g., premature labor, allergic reaction, anaphylaxis).

POST-TEST:

▸ A report of the results will be made available to the requesting HCP, who will discuss the results with the patient.

▸ After the procedure, fetal heart rate and maternal life signs (i.e., heart rate, blood pressure, pulse, and respiration) should be compared with baseline values and closely monitored every 15 min for 30 to 60 min after the amniocentesis procedure. Protocols may vary among facilities.

▸ Observe/assess for delayed allergic reactions, such as rash, urticaria, tachycardia, hyperpnea, hypertension, palpitations, nausea, or vomiting. Immediately report symptoms to the appropriate HCP.

▸ Observe/assess the amniocentesis site for bleeding, inflammation, or hematoma formation.

▸ Instruct the patient in the care and assessment of the amniocentesis site.

▸ Instruct the patient to report any redness, edema, bleeding, or pain at the amniocentesis site.

▸ Instruct the patient to expect mild cramping, leakage of small amounts of amniotic fluid, and vaginal spotting for up to 2 days following the procedure. Instruct the patient to report moderate to severe abdominal pain or cramps, change in fetal activity, increased or prolonged leaking of amniotic fluid from abdominal needle site, vaginal bleeding that is heavier than spotting, and either chills or fever.

▸ Instruct the patient to rest until all symptoms have disappeared before resuming normal levels of activity.

▸ Administer standard RhoGAM dose to maternal Rh-negative patients to prevent maternal Rh sensitization should the fetus be Rh-positive.

▸ Recognize anxiety related to test results. Discuss the implications of abnormal test results on the patient's lifestyle. Provide teaching and information regarding the clinical implications of the test results, as appropriate. Encourage the family to seek appropriate counseling if concerned with pregnancy termination and to seek genetic counseling if a chromosomal abnormality is determined. Decisions regarding elective abortion should take place in the presence of both parents. Provide a nonjudgmental, nonthreatening atmosphere for discussing the risks and difficulties of delivering and raising a developmentally challenged infant as well as for exploring other options (termination of pregnancy or adoption). It is also important to discuss problems the mother and father may experience (guilt, depression, anger) if fetal abnormalities are detected

▸ Reinforce information given by the patient's HCP regarding further testing, treatment, or referral to another HCP. Inform the patient that it may be 2 to

4 wk before all results are available. Answer any questions or address any concerns voiced by the patient or family. Instruct the patient in the use of any ordered medications. Explain the importance of adhering to the therapy regimen. As appropriate, instruct the patient in significant side effects and systemic reactions associated with the prescribed medication. Encourage her to review corresponding literature provided by a pharmacist.

Depending on the results of this procedure, additional testing may be performed to evaluate or monitor progression of the disease process

and determine the need for a change in therapy. Evaluate test results in relation to the patient's symptoms and other tests performed.

RELATED MONOGRAPHS:

Related tests include α_1-fetoprotein, antibodies anticardiolipin, blood groups and antibodies, chromosome analysis, fetal fibronectin, Kleihauer-Betke test, L/S ratio, lupus anticoagulant antibodies, newborn screening, and US biophysical profile obstetric.

Refer to the Reproductive System table at the end of the book for related tests by body system.

Amylase

SYNONYM/ACRONYM: N/A.

COMMON USE: To assist in diagnosis and evaluation of the treatment modalities used for pancreatitis.

SPECIMEN: Serum (1 mL) collected in a red- or tiger-top tube. Plasma (1 mL) collected in a green-top (heparin) tube is also acceptable.

NORMAL FINDINGS: (Method: Enzymatic)

	Conventional & SI Units
3–90 d	0–30 units/L
3–6 mo	6–40 units/L
7–11 mo	6–70 units/L
1–3 yr	11–80 units/L
4–9 yr	16–91 units/L
10–18 yr	19–76 units/L
Adult–older adult	30–110 units/L

Values may be slightly elevated in older adults due to the effects of medications and the presence of multiple chronic or acute diseases with or without muted symptoms.

DESCRIPTION: Amylase, a digestive enzyme, splits starch into disaccharides. Although many cells (e.g., liver, small intestine, ovaries, skeletal muscles) have amylase

activity, circulating amylase is derived from the parotid glands and the pancreas. Amylase is a sensitive indicator of pancreatic acinar cell damage and pancreatic

A

obstruction. Newborns and children up to 2 years old have little measurable serum amylase. In the early years of life, most of this enzyme is produced by the salivary glands. Amylase can be separated into pancreatic (P_1, P_2, P_3) and salivary (S_1, S_2, S_3) isoenzymes. Isoenzyme patterns are useful in identifying the organ source. Requests for amylase isoenzymes are rare because of the expense of the procedure and limited clinical utility of the result. Isoenzyme analysis is primarily used to assess decreasing pancreatic function in children 5 years and older who have been diagnosed with cystic fibrosis and who may be candidates for enzyme replacement. Cyst fluid amylase levels with isoenzyme analysis is useful in differentiating pancreatic neoplasms (low enzyme concentration) and pseudocysts (high enzyme concentration). Lipase is usually ordered in conjunction with amylase because lipase is more sensitive and specific to conditions affecting pancreatic function.

INDICATIONS

- Assist in the diagnosis of early acute pancreatitis; serum amylase begins to rise within 6 to 24 hr after onset and returns to normal in 2 to 7 days
- Assist in the diagnosis of macroamylasemia, a disorder seen in alcoholism, malabsorption syndrome, and other digestive problems
- Assist in the diagnosis of pancreatic duct obstruction, which causes serum amylase levels to remain elevated
- Detect blunt trauma or inadvertent surgical trauma to the pancreas
- Differentiate between acute pancreatitis and other causes of abdominal pain that require surgery

POTENTIAL DIAGNOSIS

Increased in

Amylase is released from any damaged cell in which it is stored, so conditions that affect the pancreas and parotid glands and cause cellular destruction demonstrate elevated amylase levels.

- Acute appendicitis *(related to enzyme release from damaged pancreatic tissue)*
- Administration of some drugs (e.g., morphine) is known to increase amylase levels *(related to increased biliary tract pressure as evidenced by effect of narcotic analgesic drugs)*
- Afferent loop syndrome *(related to impaired pancreatic duct flow)*
- Aortic aneurysm *(elevated amylase levels following rupture are associated with a poor prognosis; both S and P subtypes have been identified following rupture. The causes for elevation are mixed and difficult to state as a generalization)*
- Abdominal trauma *(related to release of enzyme from damaged pancreatic tissue)*
- Alcoholism *(related to increased secretion; salivary origin most likely)*
- Biliary tract disease *(related to impaired pancreatic duct flow)*
- Burns and traumatic shock
- Carcinoma of the head of the pancreas (advanced) *(related to enzyme release from damaged pancreatic tissue)*
- Common bile duct obstruction, common bile duct stones *(related to impaired pancreatic duct flow)*
- Diabetic ketoacidosis *(related to increased secretion; salivary origin most likely)*
- Duodenal obstruction *(accumulation in the blood as evidenced by leakage from the gut)*
- Ectopic pregnancy *(related to ectopic enzyme production by the fallopian tubes)*

- Extrapancreatic tumors (especially esophagus, lung, ovary)
- Gastric resection *(accumulation in the blood as evidenced by leakage from the gut)*
- Hyperlipidemias (etiology is unclear, but there is a distinct association with amylasemia)
- Hyperparathyroidism (etiology is unclear, but there is a distinct association with amylasemia)
- Intestinal obstruction *(related to impaired pancreatic duct flow)*
- Intestinal infarction *(related to impaired pancreatic duct flow)*
- Macroamylasemia *(related to decreased ability of renal glomeruli to filter large molecules as evidenced by accumulation in the blood)*
- Mumps *(related to increased secretion from inflamed tissue; salivary origin most likely)*
- Pancreatic ascites *(related to release of pancreatic fluid into the abdomen and subsequent absorption into the circulation)*
- Pancreatic cyst and pseudocyst *(related to release of pancreatic fluid into the abdomen and subsequent absorption into the circulation)*
- Pancreatitis *(related to enzyme release from damaged pancreatic tissue)*
- Parotitis *(related to increased secretion from inflamed tissue; salivary origin most likely)*
- Perforated peptic ulcer whether the pancreas is involved or not *(related to enzyme release from damaged pancreatic tissue; involvement of the pancreas may be unnoticed upon gross examination yet be present as indicated by elevated enzyme levels)*
- Peritonitis *(accumulation in the blood as evidenced by leakage from the gut)*
- Postoperative period *(related to complications of the surgical procedure)*

- Pregnancy *(related to increased secretion; salivary origin most likely related to hyperemesis or hyperlipidemia induced pancreatitis related to increased estrogen levels)*
- Renal disease *(related to decreased renal excretion as evidenced by accumulation in blood)*
- Some tumors of the lung and ovaries *(related to ectopic enzyme production)*
- Tumor of the pancreas or adjacent area *(related to release of enzyme from damaged pancreatic tissue)*

Decreased in
- Hepatic disease (severe) *(may be due to lack of amino acid production necessary for enzyme manufacture)*
- Pancreatectomy
- Pancreatic insufficiency

CRITICAL FINDINGS: N/A

INTERFERING FACTORS
- Drugs and substances that may increase amylase levels include acetaminophen, aminosalicylic acid, amoxapine, asparaginase, azathioprine, bethanechol, calcitriol, cholinergics, chlorthalidone, clozapine, codeine, corticosteroids, corticotropin, desipramine, dexamethasone, diazoxide, felbamate, fentanyl, fluvastatin, glucocorticoids, hydantoin derivatives, hydrochlorothiazide, hydroflumethiazide, meperidine, mercaptopurine, methacholine, methyclothiazide, metolazone, minocycline, morphine, nitrofurantoin, opium alkaloids, pegaspargase, pentazocine, potassium iodide, prednisone, procyclidine, tetracycline, thiazide diuretics, valproic acid, zalcitabine, and zidovudine.
- Drugs that may decrease amylase levels include anabolic steroids, citrates, and fluorides.

A

NURSING IMPLICATIONS AND PROCEDURE

PRETEST:

- Positively identify the patient using at least two unique identifiers before providing care, treatment, or services.
- *Patient Teaching:* Inform the patient this test can assist in evaluating pancreatic health and/or the effectiveness of medical treatment for pancreatitis.
- Obtain a history of the patient's complaints, including a list of known allergens, especially allergies or sensitivities to latex.
- Obtain a history of the patient's gastrointestinal and hepatobiliary systems, symptoms, and results of previously performed laboratory tests and diagnostic and surgical procedures.
- Obtain a list of the patient's current medications, including herbs, nutritional supplements, and nutraceuticals (see Appendix F).
- Review the procedure with the patient. Inform the patient that specimen collection takes approximately 5 to 10 min. Address concerns about pain and explain that there may be some discomfort during the venipuncture.
- *Sensitivity to social and cultural issues,* as well as concern for modesty, is important in providing psychological support before, during, and after the procedure.
- There are no food, fluid, or medication restrictions unless by medical direction.

INTRATEST:

- If the patient has a history of allergic reaction to latex, avoid the use of equipment containing latex.
- Instruct the patient to cooperate fully and to follow directions. Direct the patient to breathe normally and to avoid unnecessary movement.
- Observe standard precautions, and follow the general guidelines in Appendix A. Positively identify the patient, and label the appropriate specimen container with the corresponding patient demographics, initials of the person collecting the specimen, date, and time of collection. Perform a venipuncture.
- Remove the needle and apply direct pressure with dry gauze to stop bleeding. Observe/assess venipuncture site

for bleeding or hematoma formation and secure gauze with adhesive bandage.
- Promptly transport the specimen to the laboratory for processing and analysis.

POST-TEST:

- A report of the results will be made available to the requesting health-care provider (HCP), who will discuss the results with the patient.
- *Nutritional Considerations:* Increased amylase levels may be associated with gastrointestinal disease or alcoholism. Small, frequent meals work best for patients with gastrointestinal disorders. Consideration should be given to dietary alterations in the case of gastrointestinal disorders. Usually after acute symptoms subside and bowel sounds return, patients are given a clear liquid diet, progressing to a low-fat, high-carbohydrate diet. Vitamin B_{12} may be ordered for parenteral administration to patients with decreased levels, especially if their disease prevents adequate absorption of the vitamin. The alcoholic patient should be encouraged to avoid alcohol and to seek appropriate counseling for substance abuse.
- Reinforce information given by the patient's HCP regarding further testing, treatment, or referral to another HCP. Answer any questions or address any concerns voiced by the patient or family.
- Depending on the results of this procedure, additional testing may be performed to evaluate or monitor progression of the disease process and determine the need for a change in therapy. Evaluate test results in relation to the patient's symptoms and other tests performed.

RELATED MONOGRAPHS:

- Related tests include ALT, ALP, AST, bilirubin, cancer antigens, calcium, C-peptide, CBC WBC count and differential, CT pancreas, ERCP, fecal fat, GGT, lipase, magnesium, MRI pancreas, mumps serology, peritoneal fluid analysis, triglycerides, US abdomen, and US pancreas.
- See the Gastrointestinal and Hepatobiliary systems tables at the end of the book for related tests by body system.

Analgesic, Anti-inflammatory, and Antipyretic Drugs: Acetaminophen, Acetylsalicylic Acid

A

SYNONYM/ACRONYM: *Acetaminophen* (Acephen, Aceta, Apacet, APAP 500, Aspirin Free Anacin, Banesin, Cetaphen, Dapa, Datril, Dorcol, Exocrine, FeverALL, Genapap, Genebs, Halenol, Little Fevers, Liquiprin, Mapap, Myapap, Nortemp, Pain Eze, Panadol, Paracetamol, Redutemp, Ridenol, Silapap, Tempra, Tylenol, Ty-Pap, Uni-Ace, Valorin); *Acetylsalicylic acid* (salicylate, aspirin, Anacin, Aspergum, Bufferin, Easprin, Ecotrin, Empirin, Measurin, Synalgos, ZORprin, ASA).

COMMON USE: To assist in monitoring therapeutic drug levels and detect toxic levels of acetaminophen and salicylate in suspected overdose and drug abuse.

SPECIMEN: Serum (1 mL) collected in a red-top tube.

NORMAL FINDINGS: (Method: Immunoassay)

Drug	Therapeutic Range*	SI Units	Half-Life	Volume of Distribution	Protein Binding	Excretion
(SI = Conventional Units × 6.62)						
Acetamino-phen	5–20 mcg/mL	33–132 micromol/L	1–3 hr	0.95 L/kg	20%–50%	85%–95% hepatic, metabolites, renal
(SI = Conventional Units × 0.073)						
Salicylate	10–30 mg/dL	0.7–2.2 mmol/L	2–3 hr	0.1–0.3 L/kg	90%–95%	1° hepatic, metabolites, renal

*Conventional units.

DESCRIPTION: Acetaminophen is used for headache, fever, and pain relief, especially for individuals unable to take salicylate products or who have bleeding conditions. It is the analgesic of choice for children less than 13 yr old; salicylates are avoided in this age group because of the association between aspirin and Reye's syndrome. Acetaminophen is rapidly absorbed from the gastrointestinal tract and reaches peak concentration within 30 to 60 min after administration of a therapeutic dose. It can be a silent killer because, by the time symptoms of intoxication appear 24 to 48 hr after ingestion, the antidote is ineffective.

Acetylsalicylic acid (ASA) is also used for headache, fever, inflammation, and pain relief. Some patients with cardiovascular disease take small prophylactic doses. The main site of toxicity for both drugs is the liver, particularly in the presence of liver disease or decreased drug metabolism and excretion. Other medications indicated for use in controlling neuropathic pain include amitriptyline and nortriptyline. Detailed information is found in the monograph titled "Antidepressant Drugs (Cyclic): Amitriptyline, Nortriptyline, Protriptyline, Doxepin, Imipramine, Desipramine."

Many factors must be considered in interpreting drug levels, including patient age, patient weight, interacting medications, electrolyte balance, protein levels, water balance, conditions that affect absorption and excretion, and the ingestion of substances (e.g., foods, herbals, vitamins, and minerals) that can potentiate or inhibit the intended target concentration.

INDICATIONS

• Suspected overdose
• Suspected toxicity
• Therapeutic monitoring

POTENTIAL DIAGNOSIS

Increased in

• Acetaminophen
Alcoholic cirrhosis *(related to inability of damaged liver to metabolize the drug)*
Liver disease *(related to inability of damaged liver to metabolize the drug)*
Toxicity
• ASA
Toxicity

Decreased in

• Noncompliance with therapeutic regimen

CRITICAL FINDINGS

Note: The adverse effects of subtherapeutic levels are also important. Care should be taken to investigate signs and symptoms of too little and too much medication. Note and immediately report to the requesting health care provider (HCP) any critically increased or subtherapeutic values and related symptoms. Timely notification of critical values for lab or diagnostic studies is a role expectation of the professional nurse. Notification processes will vary among facilities. Upon receipt of the critical value the information should be read back to the caller to verify accuracy. Most policies require immediate notification of the primary HCP, Hospitalist, or on-call HCP. Reported information includes the patient's name, unique identifiers, critical value, name of the person giving the report, and name of the person receiving the report. Documentation of notification should be made in the medical record with the name of the HCP notified, time and date of notification, and any orders received. Any delay in a timely report of a critical value may require completion of a notification form with review by Risk Management.

Acetaminophen: Greater Than 200 mcg/mL (4 hr postingestion): (SI Greater Than 1,324 micromol/L [4 hr postingestion])

Signs and symptoms of acetaminophen intoxication occur in stages over a period of time. In stage I (0 to 24 hr after ingestion), symptoms may include gastrointestinal irritation, pallor, lethargy, diaphoresis, metabolic acidosis, and possibly coma. In stage II (24 to 48 hr after ingestion), signs and symptoms may include right upper quadrant abdominal pain; elevated liver enzymes aspartate aminotransferase (AST), and alanine aminotransferase (ALT); and possible decreased renal function. In stage III (72 to 96 hr after ingestion), signs and symptoms may include nausea, vomiting, jaundice, confusion, coagulation disorders, continued elevation of AST and ALT, decreased renal function, and coma. Intervention may include gastrointestinal decontamination (stomach pumping) if the patient presents within 6 hr of ingestion or administration of N-acetylcysteine (Mucomyst) in the case of an acute intoxication in which the patient presents more than 6 hr after ingestion.

ASA: Greater Than 40 mg/dL: (SI Greater Than 2.9 mmol/L)

Signs and symptoms of salicylate intoxication include ketosis, convulsions, dizziness, nausea, vomiting, hyperactivity, hyperglycemia, hyperpnea, hyperthermia, respiratory arrest, and tinnitus. Possible interventions include administration of activated charcoal as vomiting ceases, alkalinization of the urine with bicarbonate, and a single dose of vitamin K (for rare instances of hypoprothrombinemia).

INTERFERING FACTORS

* Blood drawn in serum separator tubes (gel tubes).
* Contraindicated in patients with liver disease, and caution advised in patients with renal impairment.
* Drugs that may increase acetaminophen levels include diflunisal, metoclopramide, and probenecid.
* Drugs that may decrease acetaminophen levels include carbamazepine, cholestyramine, iron, oral contraceptives, and propantheline.
* Drugs that increase ASA levels include choline magnesium trisalicylate, cimetidine, furosemide, and sulfinpyrazone.
* Drugs and substances that decrease ASA levels include activated charcoal, antacids (aluminum hydroxide), corticosteroids, and iron.

NURSING IMPLICATIONS AND PROCEDURE

PRETEST:

▶ Positively identify the patient using at least two unique identifiers before providing care, treatment, or services.
▶ *Patient Teaching:* Inform the patient this test can assist with evaluation of how much medication is in his or her system.
▶ Obtain a complete history of the time and amount of drug ingested by the patient.
▶ Obtain a history of the patient's complaints, including a list of known allergens, especially allergies or sensitivities to latex.
▶ Review results of previously performed laboratory tests and diagnostic and surgical procedures.
▶ These medications are metabolized and excreted by the kidneys and liver. Obtain a history of the patient's genitourinary and hepatobiliary systems, symptoms, and results of previously performed laboratory tests and diagnostic and surgical procedures.
▶ Obtain a list of the patient's current medications, including herbs, nutritional supplements, and nutraceuticals (see Appendix F).
▶ Review the procedure with the patient. Inform the patient that specimen collection takes approximately 5 to 10 min. Address concerns about pain and explain that there may be some discomfort during the venipuncture.
▶ *Sensitivity to social and cultural issues,* as well as concern for modesty, is important in providing psychological support before, during, and after the procedure.
▶ There are no food, fluid, or medication restrictions unless by medical direction.

INTRATEST:

▶ If the patient has a history of allergic reaction to latex, avoid the use of equipment containing latex.
▶ Instruct the patient to cooperate fully and to follow directions. Direct the patient to breathe normally and to avoid unnecessary movement.
▶ Observe standard precautions, and follow the general guidelines in

Appendix A. Consider recommended collection time in relation to the dosing schedule. Positively identify the patient, and label the appropriate specimen container with the corresponding patient demographics, initials of the person collecting the specimen, date, and time of collection, noting the last dose of medication taken. Perform a venipuncture.

▶ Remove the needle and apply direct pressure with dry gauze to stop the bleeding. Observe/assess the venipuncture site for bleeding and hematoma formation and secure gauze with adhesive bandage.

▶ Promptly transport the specimen to the laboratory for processing and analysis.

Explain to the patient the importance of following the medication regimen and instructions regarding food and drug interactions. Answer any questions or address any concerns voiced by the patient or family.

▶ Instruct the patient to be prepared to provide the pharmacist with a list of other medications he or she is already taking in the event that the requesting HCP prescribes a medication.

▶ Depending on the results of this procedure, additional testing may be performed to evaluate or monitor progression of the disease process and determine the need for a change in therapy. Evaluate test results in relation to the patient's symptoms and other tests performed.

POST-TEST:

▶ A report of the results will be made available to the requesting HCP, who will discuss the results with the patient. *Nutritional Considerations:* Include avoidance of alcohol consumption. Reinforce information given by the patient's HCP regarding further testing, treatment, or referral to another HCP.

RELATED MONOGRAPHS:

▶ Related tests include ALT, AST, bilirubin, biopsy liver, BUN, CBC, creatinine, electrolytes, glucose, lactic acid, aPTT, and PT/INR.

▶ See the Genitourinary and Hepatobiliary systems tables at the end of the book for related tests by body system.

Angiography, Abdomen

SYNONYM/ACRONYM: Abdominal angiogram, abdominal arteriography.

COMMON USE: To visualize and assess abdominal organs/structure for tumor infection, or aneurysm.

AREA OF APPLICATION: Abdomen.

CONTRAST: Iodine based

DESCRIPTION: Angiography allows x-ray visualization of the large and small arteries, veins, and associated branches of the abdominal vasculature and organ parenchyma after contrast medium injection. This visualization is accomplished by the injection of contrast medium through a catheter, which most commonly has been inserted into the femoral artery and advanced through the iliac artery and aorta into the organ-specific artery. Images of the organ under study and associated vessels are displayed on a monitor and recorded or stored electronically for future viewing and evaluation. Patterns of circulation, organ function, and changes in vessel wall appearance can be viewed to help diagnose the presence of vascular abnormalities, aneurysm, tumor, trauma, or lesions. The catheter used to administer the contrast medium to confirm the diagnosis of organ lesions may be used to deliver chemotherapeutic drugs or different types of materials used to stop bleeding. Catheters with attached inflatable balloons and wire mesh stents are used to widen areas of stenosis and to keep vessels open, frequently replacing surgery. Angiography is one of the definitive tests for organ disease and may be used to evaluate chronic disease and organ failure, treat arterial stenosis, differentiate a vascular cyst from hypervascular cancers, and evaluate the effectiveness of medical or surgical treatment.

INDICATIONS

- Aid in angioplasty, atherectomy, or stent placement
- Allow infusion of thrombolytic drugs into an occluded artery
- Detect arterial occlusion, which may be evidenced by a transection of the artery caused by trauma or penetrating injury
- Detect artery stenosis, evidenced by vessel dilation, collateral vessels, or increased vascular pressure
- Detect nonmalignant tumors before surgical resection
- Detect thrombosis, arteriovenous fistula, aneurysms, or emboli in abdominal vessels
- Detect tumors and arterial supply, extent of venous invasion, and tumor vascularity

- Detect peripheral artery disease (PAD)
- Differentiate between tumors and cysts
- Evaluate organ transplantation for function or organ rejection
- Evaluate placement of a shunt or stent
- Evaluate tumor vascularity before surgery or embolization
- Evaluate the vascular system of prospective organ donors before surgery

POTENTIAL DIAGNOSIS

Normal findings in
- Normal structure, function, and patency of abdominal organ vessels
- Contrast medium normally circulates throughout abdomen symmetrically and without interruption
- No evidence of obstruction, variations in number and size of vessels, malformations, cysts, or tumors

Abnormal findings in
- Abscess or inflammation
- Arterial aneurysm
- Arterial stenosis, dysplasia, or organ infarction
- Arteriovenous fistula or other abnormalities
- Congenital anomalies
- Cysts or tumors
- PAD
- Trauma causing tears or other disruption

CRITICAL FINDINGS
- Abscess
- Aneurysm

It is essential that critical diagnoses be communicated immediately to the appropriate health-care provider (HCP). A listing of these diagnoses varies among facilities. Note and immediately report to the HCP abnormal results and related symptoms. Timely notification of critical values for lab or diagnostic studies is a role expectation of the professional nurse. Notification processes will vary among facilities. Upon receipt of the critical value the information should be read back to the caller to verify accuracy. Most policies require immediate notification of the primary HCP, Hospitalist, or on-call HCP. Reported information includes the patient's name, unique identifiers, critical value, name of the person giving the report, and name of the person receiving the report. Documentation of notification should be made in the medical record with the name of the HCP notified, time and date of notification, and any orders received. Any delay in a timely report of a critical value may require completion of a notification form with review by Risk Management.

INTERFERING FACTORS

This procedure is contraindicated for

- Patients with allergies to shellfish or iodinated contrast medium. The contrast medium used may cause a life-threatening allergic reaction. Patients with a known hypersensitivity to contrast medium may benefit from premedication with corticosteroids or the use of nonionic contrast medium.
- Patients with bleeding disorders.
- Patients who are pregnant or suspected of being pregnant, unless the potential benefits of the procedure far outweigh the risk of radiation exposure to the fetus.
- Elderly and compromised patients who are chronically dehydrated before the test, because of their risk of contrast-induced renal failure.
- Patients who are in renal failure.

Factors that may impair clear imaging

- Gas or feces in the gastrointestinal tract resulting from inadequate cleansing or failure to restrict food intake before the study.
- Retained barium from a previous radiological procedure.

- Metallic objects within the examination field (e.g., jewelry, body rings), which may inhibit organ visualization and can produce unclear images.
- Inability of the patient to cooperate or remain still during the procedure because of age, significant pain, or mental status.

Other considerations

- Consultation with an HCP should occur before the procedure for radiation safety concerns regarding younger patients or patients who are lactating.
- Risks associated with radiation overexposure can result from frequent x-ray procedures. Personnel in the room with the patient should wear a protective lead apron, stand behind a shield, or leave the area while the examination is being done. Personnel working in the examination area should wear badges to record their level of radiation exposure.
- Failure to follow dietary restrictions and other pretesting preparations may cause the procedure to be canceled or repeated.

NURSING IMPLICATIONS AND PROCEDURE

PRETEST:

- Positively identify the patient using at least two unique identifiers before providing care, treatment, or services.
- *Patient Teaching:* Inform the patient this procedure can assist with the evaluation of abdominal organs.
- Obtain a history of the patient's complaints, including a list of known allergens, especially allergies or sensitivities to latex, iodine, seafood, contrast medium, or anesthetics.
- Obtain a history of the patient's cardiovascular system, symptoms, and results of previously performed laboratory tests and diagnostic and surgical procedures. Ensure results of coagulation testing are obtained and recorded prior to the procedure;

BUN and creatinine results are also needed because contrast medium is to be used.

Note any recent procedures that can interfere with test results, including examinations using iodine-based contrast medium or barium. Ensure that barium studies were performed more than 4 days before angiography.

Record the date of the last menstrual period and determine the possibility of pregnancy in perimenopausal women.

Obtain a list of the patient's current medications, including anticoagulants, aspirin and other salicylates, herbs, nutritional supplements, and nutraceuticals, especially those known to affect coagulation (see Appendix F). Such products should be discontinued by medical direction for the appropriate number of days prior to a surgical procedure. Note the last time and dose of medication taken.

If contrast medium is scheduled to be used, patients receiving metformin (Glucophage) for non-insulin-dependent (type 2) diabetes should discontinue the drug on the day of the test and continue to withhold it for 48 hr after the test. Failure to do so may result in lactic acidosis.

Review the procedure with the patient. Address concerns about pain and explain that there may be moments of discomfort and some pain experienced during the test. Inform the patient that the procedure is usually performed in a radiology or vascular suite by an HCP and takes approximately 30 to 60 min.

Sensitivity to social and cultural issues, as well as concern for modesty, is important in providing psychological support before, during, and after the procedure.

Explain that an IV line may be inserted to allow infusion of IV fluids, contrast medium, dye, or sedatives. Usually normal saline is infused.

Inform the patient that a burning and flushing sensation may be felt throughout the body during injection of the contrast medium. After injection of the contrast medium, the patient may experience an urge to cough, flushing, nausea, or a salty or metallic taste.

Instruct the patient to remove jewelry and other metallic objects from the area to be examined.

Instruct the patient to fast and restrict fluids for 2 to 4 hr prior to the procedure. Protocols may vary among facilities.

This procedure may be terminated if chest pain, severe cardiac arrhythmias, or signs of a cerebrovascular accident occur.

Make sure a written and informed consent has been signed prior to the procedure and before administering any medications.

INTRATEST:

Observe standard precautions, and follow the general guidelines in Appendix A. Positively identify the patient.

Ensure the patient has complied with dietary and fluid restrictions for 2 to 4 hr prior to the procedure.

Ensure the patient has removed all external metallic objects from the area to be examined.

If the patient has a history of allergic reactions to any substance or drug, administer ordered prophylactic steroids or antihistamines before the procedure. Use nonionic contrast medium for the procedure.

Have emergency equipment readily available.

Instruct the patient to void prior to the procedure and to change into the gown, robe, and foot coverings provided.

Instruct the patient to cooperate fully and to follow directions. Instruct the patient to remain still throughout the procedure because movement produces unreliable results.

Record baseline vital signs, and assess neurological status. Protocols may vary among facilities.

Establish an IV fluid line for the injection of emergency drugs and of sedatives.

Administer an antianxiety agent, as ordered, if the patient has claustrophobia. Administer a sedative to a child or to an uncooperative adult, as ordered.

Place electrocardiographic electrodes on the patient for cardiac monitoring. Establish a baseline rhythm; determine if the patient has ventricular arrhythmias.

Using a pen, mark the site of the patient's peripheral pulses before angiography; this allows for quicker and more consistent assessment of the pulses after the procedure.

Place the patient in the supine position on an examination table. Cleanse the selected area, and cover with a sterile drape.

A local anesthetic is injected at the site, and a small incision is made or a needle inserted under fluoroscopy.

The contrast medium is injected, and a rapid series of images is taken during and after the filling of the vessels to be examined. Delayed images may be taken to examine the vessels after a time and to monitor the venous phase of the procedure.

Instruct the patient to inhale deeply and hold his or her breath while the images are taken, and then to exhale after the images are taken.

Instruct the patient to take slow, deep breaths if nausea occurs during the procedure.

Monitor the patient for complications related to the procedure (e.g., allergic reaction, anaphylaxis, bronchospasm).

The needle or catheter is removed, and a pressure dressing is applied over the puncture site.

Observe/assess the needle/catheter insertion site for bleeding, inflammation, or hematoma formation.

POST-TEST:

A report of the results will be made available to the requesting HCP, who will discuss the results with the patient.

Instruct the patient to resume usual diet, fluids, medications, or activity, as directed by the HCP. Renal function should be assessed before metformin is resumed.

Monitor vital signs and neurological status every 15 min for 1 hr, then every 2 hr for 4 hr, and as ordered. Take temperature every 4 hr for 24 hr.

Monitor intake and output at least every 8 hr. Compare with baseline values. Protocols may vary among facilities.

Observe for delayed allergic reactions, such as rash, urticaria, tachycardia, hyperpnea, hypertension, palpitations, nausea, or vomiting.

Instruct the patient to immediately report symptoms such as fast heart rate, difficulty breathing, skin rash, itching, chest pain, persistent right shoulder pain, or abdominal pain.

Immediately report symptoms to the appropriate HCP.

Assess extremities for signs of ischemia or absence of distal pulse caused by a catheter-induced thrombus.

Observe/assess the needle/catheter insertion site for bleeding, inflammation, or hematoma formation.

Instruct the patient in the care and assessment of the site.

Instruct the patient to apply cold compresses to the puncture site as needed, to reduce discomfort or edema.

Instruct the patient to maintain bedrest for 4 to 6 hr after the procedure or as ordered.

Recognize anxiety related to test results, and be supportive of perceived loss of independent function. Discuss the implications of abnormal test results on the patient's lifestyle. Provide teaching and information regarding the clinical implications of the test results, as appropriate.

Reinforce information given by the patient's HCP regarding further testing, treatment, or referral to another HCP. Answer any questions or address any concerns voiced by the patient or family. Provide contact information, if desired, for the American Heart Association (www.americanheart.org), or the National Heart, Lung, and Blood Institute (www.nhlbi.nih.gov), or the Legs for Life (www.legsforlife.org).

Depending on the results of this procedure, additional testing may be performed to evaluate or monitor progression of the disease process and determine the need for a change in therapy. Evaluate test results in relation to the patient's symptoms and other tests performed.

RELATED MONOGRAPHS:

Related tests include angiography renal, BUN, CT abdomen, CT angiography, CT brain, CT spleen, CT thoracic, creatinine, KUB, MRA, MRI abdomen, MRI brain, MRI chest, MRI pelvis, aPTT, PT/INR, renogram, US abdomen, and US lower extremity.

See the Cardiovascular System table at the end of the book for related tests by body system.

Angiography, Adrenal

A

SYNONYM/ACRONYM: Adrenal angiogram, adrenal arteriography.

COMMON USE: To visualize and assess the adrenal gland for cancer or other tumors or masses.

AREA OF APPLICATION: Adrenal gland.

CONTRAST: Iodine based.

DESCRIPTION: Adrenal angiography evaluates adrenal dysfunction by allowing x-ray visualization of the large and small arteries of the adrenal gland vasculature and parenchyma. This visualization is accomplished by the injection of contrast medium through a catheter that has been inserted into the femoral artery for viewing the artery (arteriography) or into the femoral vein for viewing the veins (venography). After the catheter is in place, a blood sample may be taken from the vein of each gland to assess cortisol levels in determining a diagnosis of Cushing's syndrome or the presence of pheochromocytoma. After injection of the contrast medium through the catheter, images of the adrenal glands and associated vessels surrounding the adrenal tissue are displayed on a monitor and are recorded on film or electronically. Patterns of circulation, adrenal function, and changes in vessel wall appearance can be viewed to help diagnose the presence of vascular abnormalities, trauma, or lesions. This definitive test for adrenal disease may be used to evaluate chronic adrenal disease, evaluate arterial or venous stenosis, differentiate an adrenal cyst from adrenal tumors, and evaluate medical therapy or surgery of the adrenal glands.

INDICATIONS
- Assist in the infusion of thrombolytic drugs into an occluded artery
- Assist with the collection of blood samples from the vein for laboratory analysis
- Detect adrenal hyperplasia
- Detect and determine the location of adrenal tumors evidenced by arterial supply, extent of venous invasion, and tumor vascularity
- Detect arterial occlusion, evidenced by a transection of the artery caused by trauma or a penetrating injury
- Detect arterial stenosis, evidenced by vessel dilation, collateral vessels, or increased vascular pressure
- Detect nonmalignant tumors before surgical resection
- Detect thrombosis, arteriovenous fistula, aneurysms, or emboli in vessels
- Differentiate between adrenal tumors and adrenal cysts
- Evaluate tumor vascularity before surgery or embolization
- Perform angioplasty, perform atherectomy, or place a stent

POTENTIAL DIAGNOSIS

Normal findings in
- Normal structure, function, and patency of adrenal vessels

A

- Contrast medium circulating throughout the adrenal gland symmetrically and without interruption
- No evidence of obstruction, variations in number and size of vessels and organs, malformations, cysts, or tumors

Abnormal findings in
- Adrenal adenoma
- Adrenal carcinoma
- Bilateral adrenal hyperplasia
- Pheochromocytoma

CRITICAL FINDINGS: N/A

INTERFERING FACTORS

This procedure is contraindicated for
- ◆ Patients with allergies to shellfish or iodinated dye. The contrast medium used may cause a life-threatening allergic reaction. Patients with a known hypersensitivity to contrast medium may benefit from premedication with corticosteroids or the use of nonionic contrast medium.
- Patients with bleeding disorders.
- Patients who are pregnant or suspected of being pregnant, unless the potential benefits of the procedure far outweigh the risks to the fetus and mother.
- ◆ Elderly and other patients who are chronically dehydrated before the test, because of their risk of contrast-induced renal failure.
- ◆ Patients who are in renal failure.

Factors that may impair clear imaging
- Gas or feces in the gastrointestinal tract resulting from inadequate cleansing or failure to restrict food intake before the study.
- Retained barium from a previous radiological procedure.
- Metallic objects within the examination field (e.g., jewelry,

body rings), which may inhibit organ visualization and can produce unclear images.
- Inability of the patient to cooperate or remain still during the procedure because of age, significant pain, or mental status.

Other considerations
- Consultation with a health-care provider (HCP) should occur before the procedure for radiation safety concerns regarding younger patients or patients who are lactating.
- Risks associated with radiation overexposure can result from frequent x-ray procedures. Personnel in the examination room with the patient should wear a protective lead apron, stand behind a shield, or leave the area while the examination is being done. Personnel working in the examination area should wear badges to record their level of radiation exposure.
- Failure to follow dietary restrictions and other pretesting preparations may cause the procedure to be canceled or repeated.

NURSING IMPLICATIONS AND PROCEDURE

PRETEST:

▶ Positively identify the patient using at least two unique identifiers before providing care, treatment, or services.
▶ *Patient Teaching:* Inform the patient this procedure can assist with evaluation of the adrenal gland (located near the kidney).
▶ Obtain a history of the patient's complaints, including a list of known allergens (especially allergies or sensitivities to latex, iodine, seafood, anesthetics, or contrast medium).
▶ Obtain a history of the patient's endocrine system, symptoms, and results of previously performed laboratory tests and diagnostic and surgical procedures. Ensure results of coagulation testing are obtained and

recorded prior to the procedure; BUN and creatinine results are also needed if contrast medium is to be used.

▶ Note any recent procedures that can interfere with test results, including examinations using iodine-based contrast medium or barium. Ensure that barium studies were performed more than 4 days before angiography.

▶ Record the date of the last menstrual period and determine the possibility of pregnancy in perimenopausal women.

▶ Obtain a list of the patient's current medications, including anticoagulants, aspirin and other salicylates, herbs, nutritional supplements, and nutraceuticals, especially those known to affect coagulation (see Appendix F). Such products should be discontinued by medical direction for the appropriate number of days prior to a surgical procedure. Note the last time and dose of medication taken.

▶ If contrast medium is scheduled to be used, patients receiving metformin (Glucophage) for non-insulin-dependent (type 2) diabetes should discontinue the drug on the day of the test and continue to withhold it for 48 hr after the test. Failure to do so may result in lactic acidosis.

▶ Review the procedure with the patient. Address concerns about pain and explain that there may be moments of discomfort and some pain experienced during the test. Inform the patient that the procedure is usually performed in a radiology or vascular suite by an HCP and takes approximately 30 to 60 min. *Sensitivity to social and cultural issues,* as well as concern for modesty, is important in providing psychological support before, during, and after the procedure.

▶ Explain that an IV line may be inserted to allow infusion of IV fluids, contrast medium, dye, or sedatives. Usually normal saline is infused.

▶ Inform the patient that a burning and flushing sensation may be felt throughout the body during injection of the contrast medium. After injection of the contrast medium, the patient may experience an urge to cough, flushing, nausea, or a salty or metallic taste.

▶ Instruct the patient to remove jewelry and other metallic objects from the area to be examined.

▶ Instruct the patient to fast and restrict fluids for 2 to 4 hr prior to the procedure. Protocols may vary among facilities.

▶ This procedure may be terminated if chest pain, severe cardiac arrhythmias, or signs of a cerebrovascular accident occur.

▶ *Make sure a written and informed consent has been signed prior to the procedure and before administering any medications.*

INTRATEST:

▶ Observe standard precautions, and follow the general guidelines in Appendix A. Positively identify the patient.

▶ Ensure the patient has complied with dietary, fluid, and medication restrictions and pretesting preparations.

▶ Ensure the patient has removed all external metallic objects from the area to be examined.

▶ If the patient has a history of allergic reactions to any substance or drug, administer ordered prophylactic steroids or antihistamines before the procedure. Use nonionic contrast medium for the procedure.

▶ Have emergency equipment readily available.

▶ Instruct the patient to void prior to the procedure and to change into the gown, robe, and foot coverings provided.

▶ Instruct the patient to cooperate fully and to follow directions. Instruct the patient to remain still throughout the procedure because movement produces unreliable results.

▶ Record baseline vital signs, and continue to monitor throughout the procedure. Protocols may vary among facilities.

▶ Establish an IV fluid line for the injection of emergency drugs and of sedatives.

▶ Administer an antianxiety agent, as ordered, if the patient has claustrophobia. Administer a sedative to a child or to an uncooperative adult, as ordered.

▶ Place electrocardiographic electrodes on the patient for cardiac monitoring. Establish a baseline rhythm; determine if the patient has ventricular arrhythmias.

▶ Using a pen, mark the site of the patient's peripheral pulses before angiography; this allows for quicker

A

and more consistent assessment of the pulses after the procedure.

- Place the patient in the supine position on an examination table. Cleanse the selected area, and cover with a sterile drape.
- A local anesthetic is injected at the site, and a small incision is made or a needle inserted under fluoroscopy.
- The contrast medium is injected, and a rapid series of images is taken during and after the filling of the vessels to be examined. Delayed images may be taken to examine the vessels after a time and to monitor the venous phase of the procedure.
- Instruct the patient to inhale deeply and hold his or her breath while the x-ray images are taken, and then to exhale after the images are taken.
- Instruct the patient to take slow, deep breaths if nausea occurs during the procedure.
- Monitor the patient for complications related to the procedure (e.g., allergic reaction, anaphylaxis, bronchospasm).
- The needle or catheter is removed, and a pressure dressing is applied over the puncture site.
- Observe/assess the needle/catheter insertion site for bleeding, inflammation, or hematoma formation.

POST-TEST:

- A report of the results will be made available to the requesting HCP, who will discuss the results with the patient.
- Instruct the patient to resume usual diet, fluids, medications, or activity, as directed by the HCP. Renal function should be assessed before metformin is resumed.
- Monitor vital signs and neurological status every 15 min for 1 hr, then every 2 hr for 4 hr, and as ordered. Take temperature every 4 hr for 24 hr. Monitor intake and output at least every 8 hr. Compare with baseline values. Protocols may vary among facilities.
- Observe for delayed allergic reactions, such as rash, urticaria, tachycardia, hyperpnea, hypertension, palpitations, nausea, or vomiting.
- Instruct the patient to immediately report symptoms such as fast heart

rate, difficulty breathing, skin rash, itching, chest pain, persistent right shoulder pain, or abdominal pain. Immediately report symptoms to the appropriate HCP.

- Assess extremities for signs of ischemia or absence of distal pulse caused by a catheter-induced thrombus.
- Observe/assess the needle/catheter insertion site for bleeding, inflammation, or hematoma formation.
- Instruct the patient in the care and assessment of the site.
- Instruct the patient to apply cold compresses to the puncture site as needed, to reduce discomfort or edema.
- Instruct the patient to maintain bed rest for 4 to 6 hr after the procedure or as ordered.
- Recognize anxiety related to test results, and be supportive of perceived loss of independent function. Discuss the implications of abnormal test results on the patient's lifestyle. Provide teaching and information regarding the clinical implications of the test results, as appropriate.
- Reinforce information given by the patient's HCP regarding further testing, treatment, or referral to another HCP. Answer any questions or address any concerns voiced by the patient or family.
- Depending on the results of this procedure, additional testing may be performed to evaluate or monitor progression of the disease process and determine the need for a change in therapy. Evaluate test results in relation to the patient's symptoms and other tests performed.

RELATED MONOGRAPHS:

- Related tests include ACTH and challenge tests, adrenal gland scan, BUN, catecholamines, cortisol and challenge tests, creatinine, CT abdomen, HVA, KUB study, metanephrines, MRI abdomen, aPTT, PT/INR, renin, and VMA.
- Refer to the Endocrine System table at the end of the book for related tests by body system.

Angiography, Carotid

A

SYNONYM/ACRONYM: Carotid angiogram, carotid arteriography.

COMMON USE: To visualize and assess the carotid arteries and surrounding tissues for abscess, tumors, aneurysm, and evaluate for atherosclerotic disease related to stroke risk.

AREA OF APPLICATION: Neck/cervical area.

CONTRAST: Iodine based.

DESCRIPTION: The test evaluates blood vessels in the neck carrying arterial blood. This visualization is accomplished by the injection of contrast material through a catheter that has been inserted into the femoral artery for viewing the artery (arteriography). The angiographic catheter is a long tube about the size of a strand of spaghetti. After the injection of contrast media through the catheter, x-ray images of the carotid artery and associated vessels in surrounding tissue are displayed on a monitor and are recorded on film or electronically. The x-ray equipment is mounted on a C-shaped bed with the x-ray device beneath the table on which the patient lies. Over the patient is an image intensifier that receives the x-rays after they pass through the patient. Patterns of circulation or changes in vessel wall appearance can be viewed to help diagnose the presence of vascular abnormalities, disease, narrowing, enlargement, blockage, trauma, or lesions. This definitive test for arterial disease may be used to evaluate chronic vascular disease, arterial or venous stenosis, and medical therapy or surgery of the vasculature.

Catheter angiography still is used in patients who may undergo surgery, angioplasty, or stent placement.

INDICATIONS
- Aid in angioplasty, atherectomy, or stent placement
- Allow infusion of thrombolytic drugs into an occluded artery
- Detect arterial occlusion, which may be evidenced by a transection of the artery caused by trauma or penetrating injury
- Detect artery stenosis, evidenced by vessel dilation, collateral vessels, or increased vascular pressure
- Detect nonmalignant tumors before surgical resection
- Detect tumors and arterial supply, extent of venous invasion, and tumor vascularity
- Detect thrombosis, arteriovenous fistula, aneurysms, or emboli in vessels
- Evaluate placement of a stent
- Differentiate between tumors and cysts
- Evaluate tumor vascularity before surgery or embolization
- Evaluate the vascular system of prospective organ donors before surgery

A

POTENTIAL DIAGNOSIS

Normal findings in

- Normal structure, function, and patency of carotid arteries
- Contrast medium normally circulates throughout neck symmetrically and without interruption
- No evidence of obstruction, variations in number and size of vessels, malformations, cysts, or tumors

Abnormal findings in

- Abscess or inflammation
- Arterial stenosis or dysplasia
- Aneurysms
- Arteriovenous fistula or other abnormalities
- Congenital anomalies
- Cysts or tumors
- Trauma causing tears or other disruption
- Vascular blockage or other disruption

CRITICAL FINDINGS: N/A

INTERFERING FACTORS

This procedure is contraindicated for

- Patients with allergies to shellfish or iodinated contrast medium. The contrast medium used may cause a life-threatening allergic reaction. Patients with a known hypersensitivity to contrast medium may benefit from premedication with corticosteroids or the use of nonionic contrast medium.
- Patients with bleeding disorders.
- Patients who are pregnant or suspected of being pregnant, unless the potential benefits of the procedure far outweigh the risk of radiation exposure to the fetus.
- Elderly and compromised patients who are chronically dehydrated before the test, because of their risk of contrast-induced renal failure.
- Patients who are in renal failure.

Factors that may impair clear imaging

- Gas or feces in the gastrointestinal tract resulting from inadequate cleansing or failure to restrict food intake before the study.
- Retained barium from a previous radiological procedure.
- Metallic objects within the examination field (e.g., jewelry, body rings), which may inhibit organ visualization and can produce unclear images.
- Inability of the patient to cooperate or remain still during the procedure because of age, significant pain, or mental status.

Other considerations

- Consultation with a health-care provider (HCP) should occur before the procedure for radiation safety concerns regarding younger patients or patients who are lactating.
- Risks associated with radiation overexposure can result from frequent x-ray procedures. Personnel in the room with the patient should wear a protective lead apron, stand behind a shield, or leave the area while the examination is being done. Personnel working in the examination area should wear badges to record their level of radiation exposure.
- Failure to follow dietary restrictions and other pretesting preparations may cause the procedure to be canceled or repeated.

NURSING IMPLICATIONS AND PROCEDURE

PRETEST:

▸ Positively identify the patient using at least two unique identifiers before providing care, treatment, or services.

▸ *Patient Teaching:* Inform the patient this procedure can assist with evaluation of the cardiovascular system.

Obtain a history of the patient's complaints, including a list of known allergens, especially allergies or sensitivities to latex, iodine, seafood, contrast medium, anesthetics, or contrast medium.

Obtain a history of the patient's cardiovascular system, symptoms, and results of previously performed laboratory tests and diagnostic and surgical procedures. Ensure results of coagulation testing are obtained and recorded prior to the procedure; BUN and creatinine results are also needed since contrast medium is to be used.

Note any recent procedures that can interfere with test results, including examinations using iodine-based contrast medium or barium.

Ensure that barium studies were performed more than 4 days before angiography.

Record the date of the last menstrual period and determine the possibility of pregnancy in perimenopausal women.

Obtain a list of the patient's current medications, including anticoagulants, aspirin and other salicylates, herbs, nutritional supplements, and nutraceuticals, especially those known to affect coagulation (see Appendix F). Such products should be discontinued by medical direction for the appropriate number of days prior to a surgical procedure. Note the last time and dose of medication taken.

If contrast medium is scheduled to be used, patients receiving metformin (Glucophage) for non-insulin-dependent (type 2) diabetes should discontinue the drug on the day of the test and continue to withhold it for 48 hr after the test. Failure to do so may result in lactic acidosis.

Review the procedure with the patient. Address concerns about pain and explain that there may be moments of discomfort and some pain experienced during the test.

Inform the patient that the procedure is usually performed in a radiology or vascular suite by an HCP and takes approximately 30 to 60 min.

Sensitivity to social and cultural issues, as well as concern for modesty, is important in providing psychological support before, during, and after the procedure.

Explain that an IV line may be inserted to allow infusion of IV fluids, contrast medium, dye, or sedatives. Usually normal saline is infused.

Inform the patient that a burning and flushing sensation may be felt throughout the body during injection of the contrast medium. After injection of the contrast medium, the patient may experience an urge to cough, flushing, nausea, or a salty or metallic taste.

Instruct the patient to remove jewelry and other metallic objects from the area to be examined.

Instruct the patient to fast and restrict fluids for 2 to 4 hr prior to the procedure. Protocols may vary among facilities.

This procedure may be terminated if chest pain, severe cardiac arrhythmias, or signs of a cerebrovascular accident occur.

Make sure a written and informed consent has been signed prior to the procedure and before administering any medications.

INTRATEST:

Observe standard precautions, and follow the general guidelines in Appendix A. Positively identify the patient.

Ensure the patient has complied with dietary, fluid, and medication restrictions and pretesting preparations.

Ensure the patient has removed all external metallic objects from the area to be examined.

If the patient has a history of allergic reactions to any substance or drug, administer ordered prophylactic steroids or antihistamines before the procedure. Use nonionic contrast medium for the procedure.

Have emergency equipment readily available.

Instruct the patient to void prior to the procedure and to change into the gown, robe, and foot coverings provided.

Instruct the patient to cooperate fully and to follow directions. Instruct the patient to remain still throughout the procedure because movement produces unreliable results.

‣ Record baseline vital signs, and assess neurological status. Protocols may vary among facilities.

‣ Establish an IV fluid line for the injection of emergency drugs and sedatives.

‣ Administer an antianxiety agent, as ordered, if the patient has claustro-phobia. Administer a sedative to a child or to an uncooperative adult, as ordered.

‣ Place electrocardiographic electrodes on the patient for cardiac monitoring. Establish a baseline rhythm; determine if the patient has ventricular arrhythmias.

‣ Using a pen, mark the site of the patient's peripheral pulses before angiography; this allows for quicker and more consistent assessment of the pulses after the procedure.

‣ Place the patient in the supine position on an examination table. Cleanse the selected area, and cover with a sterile drape.

‣ A local anesthetic is injected at the site, and a small incision is made or a needle is inserted under fluoroscopy.

‣ The contrast medium is injected, and a rapid series of images is taken during and after the filling of the vessels to be examined. Delayed images may be taken to examine the vessels after a time and to monitor the venous phase of the procedure.

‣ Instruct the patient to inhale deeply and hold his or her breath while the images are taken, and then to exhale after the images are taken.

‣ Instruct the patient to take slow, deep breaths if nausea occurs during the procedure.

‣ Monitor the patient for complications related to the procedure (e.g., allergic reaction, anaphylaxis, bronchospasm).

‣ The needle or catheter is removed, and a pressure dressing is applied over the puncture site.

‣ Observe/assess the needle/catheter insertion site for bleeding, inflammation, or hematoma formation.

POST-TEST:

‣ A report of the results will be made available to the requesting HCP, who will discuss the results with the patient.

‣ Instruct the patient to resume usual diet, fluids, medications, or activity, as directed by the HCP. Renal function should be assessed before metformin is resumed.

‣ Monitor vital signs and neurological status every 15 min for 1 hr, then every 2 hr for 4 hr, and as ordered. Take temperature every 4 hr for 24 hr. Monitor intake and output at least every 8 hr. Compare with baseline values. Protocols may vary from facility to facility.

‣ Observe for delayed allergic reactions, such as rash, urticaria, tachycardia, hyperpnea, hypertension, palpitations, nausea, or vomiting.

‣ Instruct the patient to immediately report symptoms such as fast heart rate, difficulty breathing, skin rash, itching, chest pain, persistent right shoulder pain, or abdominal pain. Immediately report symptoms to the appropriate HCP.

‣ Assess extremities for signs of ischemia or absence of distal pulse caused by a catheter-induced thrombus.

‣ Observe/assess the needle/catheter insertion site for bleeding, inflammation, or hematoma formation.

‣ Instruct the patient in the care and assessment of the site.

‣ Instruct the patient to apply cold compresses to the puncture site as needed, to reduce discomfort or edema.

‣ Instruct the patient to maintain bedrest for 4 to 6 hr after the procedure or as ordered.

‣ Recognize anxiety related to test results, and be supportive of perceived loss of independent function. Discuss the implications of abnormal test results on the patient's lifestyle. Provide teaching and information regarding the clinical implications of the test results, as appropriate.

‣ Reinforce information given by the patient's HCP regarding further testing, treatment, or referral to another HCP. Answer any questions or address any concerns voiced by the patient or family.

‣ Instruct the patient in the use of any ordered medications. Explain the importance of adhering to the therapy regimen. As appropriate, instruct the patient in significant side effects and systemic reactions associated with the prescribed medication. Encourage him or her to review corresponding literature provided by a pharmacist. Depending on the results of this procedure, additional testing may be performed to evaluate or monitor progression of the disease process and determine the need for a change in therapy. Evaluate test results in relation to the patient's symptoms and other tests performed.

RELATED MONOGRAPHS:

Related tests include angiography abdomen, BUN, CT angiography, CT brain, creatinine, ECG, exercise stress test, MRA, MRI brain, PT/INR, plethysmography, US arterial Doppler lower extremities, and US peripheral Doppler.

See the Cardiovascular System table at the end of the book for related tests by body system.

Angiography, Coronary

SYNONYM/ACRONYM: Angiography of heart, angiocardiography, cardiac angiography, cardiac catheterization, cineangiocardiography, coronary angiography, coronary arteriography.

COMMON USE: To visualize and assess the heart and surrounding structure for abnormalities, defects, aneurysm, and tumors.

AREA OF APPLICATION: Heart.

CONTRAST: Intravenous or intra-arterial iodine based.

DESCRIPTION: Angiography allows x-ray visualization of the heart, aorta, inferior vena cava, pulmonary artery and vein, and coronary arteries after injection of contrast medium. Contrast medium is injected through a catheter, which has been inserted into a peripheral vein for a right heart catheterization or an artery for a left heart catheterization; through the same catheter, cardiac pressures are recorded. Images of the heart and associated vessels are displayed on a monitor and are recorded on film or electronically. Patterns of circulation, cardiac output, cardiac functions, and changes in vessel wall appearance can be viewed to help diagnose the presence of vascular abnormalities or lesions. Pulmonary artery abnormalities are seen with right heart views, and coronary artery and thoracic aorta abnormalities are seen with left heart views. Coronary angiography is a definitive test for coronary artery disease, and it is useful for evaluating other types of cardiac abnormalities.

INDICATIONS

• Allow infusion of thrombolytic drugs into an occluded coronary
• Detect narrowing of coronary vessels or abnormalities of the great vessels in patients with

angina, syncope, abnormal electro-cardiogram, hypercholesteremia with chest pain, and persistent chest pain after revascularization
- Evaluate cardiac muscle function
- Evaluate cardiac valvular and septal defects
- Evaluate disease associated with the aortic arch
- Evaluate previous cardiac surgery or other interventional procedures
- Evaluate peripheral artery disease (PAD)
- Evaluate peripheral vascular disease (PVD)
- Evaluate ventricular aneurysms
- Monitor pulmonary pressures and cardiac output
- Perform angioplasty, perform atherectomy, or place a stent
- Quantify the severity of atherosclerotic, occlusive coronary artery disease

POTENTIAL DIAGNOSIS

Normal findings in
- Normal great vessels and coronary arteries

Abnormal findings in
- Aortic atherosclerosis
- Aortic dissection
- Aortitis
- Aneurysms
- Cardiomyopathy
- Congenital anomalies
- Coronary artery atherosclerosis and degree of obstruction
- Graft occlusion
- PAD
- PVD
- Pulmonary artery abnormalities
- Septal defects
- Trauma causing tears or other disruption
- Tumors
- Valvular disease

CRITICAL FINDINGS
- Aneurysm
- Aortic dissection

It is essential that critical diagnoses be communicated immediately to the appropriate health-care provider (HCP). A listing of these diagnoses varies among facilities. Note and immediately report to the HCP abnormal results and related symptoms. Timely notification of critical values for lab or diagnostic studies is a role expectation of the professional nurse. Notification processes will vary among facilities. Upon receipt of the critical value the information should be read back to the caller to verify accuracy. Most policies require immediate notification of the primary HCP, Hospitalist, or on-call HCP. Reported information includes the patient's name, unique identifiers, critical value, name of the person giving the report, and name of the person receiving the report. Documentation of notification should be made in the medical record with the name of the HCP notified, time and date of notification, and any orders received. Any delay in a timely report of a critical value may require completion of a notification form with review by Risk Management.

INTERFERING FACTORS

This procedure is contraindicated for
- Patients with allergies to shellfish or iodinated contrast medium. The contrast medium used may cause a life-threatening allergic reaction. Patients with a known hypersensitivity to contrast medium may benefit from premedication with corticosteroids or the use of nonionic contrast medium.
- Patients with bleeding disorders.

- Patients who are pregnant or suspected of being pregnant, unless the potential benefits of the procedure far outweigh the risk of radiation exposure to the fetus.
- ✦ Elderly and compromised patients who are chronically dehydrated before the test, because of their risk of contrast-induced renal failure.
- ✦ Patients who are in renal failure.

Factors that may impair clear imaging

- Gas or feces in the gastrointestinal tract resulting from inadequate cleansing or failure to restrict food intake before the study.
- Retained barium from a previous radiological procedure.
- Metallic objects within the examination field (e.g., jewelry, body rings), which may inhibit organ visualization and can produce unclear images.
- Inability of the patient to cooperate or remain still during the procedure because of age, significant pain, or mental status.

Other considerations

- Consultation with an HCP should occur before the procedure for radiation safety concerns regarding younger patients or patients who are lactating.
- Risks associated with radiation overexposure can result from frequent x-ray procedures. Personnel in the room with the patient should wear a protective lead apron, stand behind a shield, or leave the area while the examination is being done. Personnel working in the examination area should wear badges to record their level of radiation exposure.
- Failure to follow dietary restrictions and other pretesting preparations may cause the procedure to be canceled or repeated.

NURSING IMPLICATIONS AND PROCEDURE

PRETEST:

▶ Positively identify the patient using at least two unique identifiers before providing care, treatment, or services.
▶ *Patient Teaching:* Inform the patient this procedure can assist with assessment of cardiac function and check for heart disease.
▶ Obtain a history of the patient's complaints, including a list of known allergens (especially allergies or sensitivities to latex, iodine, seafood, anesthetics or contrast medium).
▶ Obtain a history of results of the patient's cardiovascular system, symptoms, and results of previously performed laboratory tests and diagnostic and surgical procedures. Ensure results of coagulation testing are obtained and recorded prior to the procedure; BUN and creatinine results are also needed if contrast medium is to be used.
▶ Note any recent procedures that can interfere with test results, including examinations using iodine-based contrast medium or barium. Ensure that barium studies were performed more than 4 days before angiography.
▶ Record the date of last menstrual period and determine the possibility of pregnancy in perimenopausal women.
▶ Obtain a list of the patient's current medications, including anticoagulants, aspirin and other salicylates, herbs, nutritional supplements, and nutraceuticals, especially those known to affect coagulation (see Appendix F). Such products should be discontinued by medical direction for the appropriate number of days prior to a surgical procedure. Note the last time and dose of medication taken.
▶ If contrast medium is scheduled to be used, patients receiving metformin (Glucophage) for non-insulin dependent (type 2) diabetes should be instructed as ordered to discontinue the drug on the day of the test and continue to withhold it for 48 hr after the test. Failure to do so may result in lactic acidosis.
▶ Review the procedure with the patient. Address concerns about pain and explain that there may be moments of

discomfort and some pain experienced during the test. Inform the patient that the procedure is usually performed in a radiology or vascular suite by an HCP and takes approximately 30 to 60 min. *Sensitivity to social and cultural issues,* as well as concern for modesty, is important in providing psychological support before, during, and after the procedure.

Explain that an IV line may be inserted to allow infusion of IV fluids, anesthetics, or sedatives. Usually normal saline is infused.

Inform the patient that a burning and flushing sensation may be felt throughout the body during injection of the contrast medium. After injection of the contrast medium, the patient may experience an urge to cough, flushing, nausea, or a salty or metallic taste.

Instruct the patient to remove jewelry and other metallic objects from the area to be examined.

Instruct the patient to fast and restrict fluids for 2 to 4 hr prior to the procedure. Protocols may vary among facilities.

This procedure may be terminated if chest pain, severe cardiac arrhythmias, or signs of a cerebrovascular accident occur.

Make sure a written and informed consent has been signed prior to the procedure and before administering any medications.

INTRATEST:

Observe standard precautions, and follow the general guidelines in Appendix A. Positively identify the patient.

Ensure the patient has complied with dietary and fluid restrictions for 2 to 4 hr prior to the procedure.

Ensure that the patient has removed external metallic objects from the area to be examined prior to the procedure.

If the patient has a history of allergic reactions to any substance or drug, administer ordered prophylactic steroids or antihistamines before the procedure. Use nonionic contrast medium for the procedure.

Have emergency equipment readily available.

Instruct the patient to void prior to the procedure and to change into the gown, robe, and foot coverings provided.

Instruct the patient to cooperate fully and to follow directions. Instruct the patient to remain still throughout the procedure because movement produces unreliable results.

Record baseline vital signs, and continue to monitor throughout the procedure. Protocols may vary among facilities.

Establish an IV fluid line for the injection of emergency drugs and of sedatives.

Administer an antianxiety agent, as ordered, if the patient has claustrophobia. Administer a sedative to a child or to an uncooperative adult, as ordered.

Place electrocardiographic electrodes on the patient for cardiac monitoring. Establish a baseline rhythm; determine if the patient has ventricular arrhythmias.

Using a pen, mark the site of the patient's peripheral pulses before angiography; this allows for quicker and more consistent assessment of the pulses after the procedure.

Place the patient in the supine position on an examination table. Cleanse the selected area, and cover with a sterile drape.

A local anesthetic is injected at the site, and a small incision is made or a needle is inserted under fluoroscopy. The contrast medium is injected, and a rapid series of images is taken during and after the filling of the vessels to be examined. Delayed images may be taken to examine the vessels after a time and to monitor the venous phase of the procedure.

Instruct the patient to inhale deeply and hold his or her breath while the x-ray images are taken, and then to exhale after the images are taken.

Instruct the patient to take slow, deep breaths if nausea occurs during the procedure.

Monitor the patient for complications related to the procedure (e.g., allergic reaction, anaphylaxis, bronchospasm).

The needle or catheter is removed, and a pressure dressing is applied over the puncture site.

Observe/assess the needle/catheter insertion site for bleeding, inflammation, or hematoma formation.

POST-TEST:

▶ A report of the results will be made available to the requesting HCP, who will discuss the results with the patient.

▶ Instruct the patient to resume usual diet, fluids, medications, or activity as directed by the HCP. Renal function should be assessed before metformin is resumed.

▶ Monitor vital signs and neurological status every 15 min for 1 hr, then every 2 hr for 4 hr, and then as ordered by the HCP. Take temperature every 4 hr for 24 hr. Monitor intake and output at least every 8 hr. Compare with baseline values. Protocols may vary from facility to facility.

▶ Observe for delayed allergic reactions, such as rash, urticaria, tachycardia, hyperpnea, hypertension, palpitations, nausea, or vomiting.

▶ Instruct the patient to immediately report symptoms such as fast heart rate, difficulty breathing, skin rash, itching, chest pain, persistent right shoulder pain, or abdominal pain. Immediately report symptoms to the appropriate HCP.

▶ Assess extremities for signs of ischemia or absence of distal pulse caused by a catheter-induced thrombus.

▶ Observe/assess the needle/catheter insertion site for bleeding, inflammation, or hematoma formation.

▶ Instruct the patient in the care and assessment of the site and to observe for bleeding, hematoma formation, bile leakage, and inflammation. Any pleuritic pain, persistent right shoulder pain, or abdominal pain should be reported to the appropriate HCP.

▶ Instruct the patient to apply cold compresses to the puncture site as needed, to reduce discomfort or edema.

▶ Instruct the patient to maintain bedrest for 4 to 6 hr after the procedure or as ordered.

▶ *Nutritional Considerations:* A low-fat, low-cholesterol, and low-sodium diet should be consumed to reduce current disease processes and/or decrease risk of hypertension and coronary artery disease.

▶ Recognize anxiety related to test results. Discuss the implications of abnormal test results on the patient's lifestyle. Provide teaching and information regarding the clinical implications of the test results, as appropriate. Provide contact information, if desired, for the American Heart Association (www.americanheart.org), the National Heart, Lung, and Blood Institute (www.nhlbi.nih.gov), and the Legs for Life (www.legsforlife.org).

▶ Reinforce information given by the patient's HCP regarding further testing, treatment, or referral to another HCP. Answer any questions or address any concerns voiced by the patient or family.

▶ Instruct the patient in the use of any ordered medications. Explain the importance of adhering to the therapy regimen. As appropriate, instruct the patient in significant side effects and systemic reactions associated with the prescribed medication. Encourage him or her to review corresponding literature provided by a pharmacist.

▶ Depending on the results of this procedure, additional testing may be needed to evaluate or monitor progression of the disease process and determine the need for a change in therapy. Evaluate test results in relation to the patient's symptoms and other tests performed.

RELATED MONOGRAPHS:

▶ Related tests include angiography carotid, blood pool imaging, BNP, BUN, chest x-ray, CT abdomen, CT angiography, CT biliary tract and liver, CT cardiac scoring, CT spleen, CT thoracic, CK, creatinine, CRP, electrocardiography, electrocardiography transesophageal, Holter monitor, homocysteine, MR angiography, MRI abdomen, MRI chest, myocardial perfusion heart scan, plethysmography, aPTT, PT/INR, troponin, and US arterial Doppler carotid.

▶ Refer to the Cardiovascular System table at the end of the book for related tests by body system.

A

Angiography, Pulmonary

SYNONYM/ACRONYM: Pulmonary angiography, pulmonary arteriography.

COMMON USE: To visualize and assess the lungs and surrounding structure for abscess, tumor, cancer, defects, tuberculosis, and pulmonary embolism.

AREA OF APPLICATION: Pulmonary vasculature.

CONTRAST: Intravenous iodine based.

DESCRIPTION: Pulmonary angiography allows x-ray visualization of the pulmonary vasculature after injection of an iodinated contrast medium into the pulmonary artery or a branch of this great vessel. Contrast medium is injected through a catheter that has been inserted into the vascular system, usually through the femoral vein. It is one of the definitive tests for pulmonary embolism, but it is also useful for evaluating other types of pulmonary vascular abnormalities. It is definitive for peripheral pulmonary artery stenosis, anomalous pulmonary venous drainage, and pulmonary fistulae. Hemodynamic measurements during pulmonary angiography can assist in the diagnosis of pulmonary hypertension and cor pulmonale.

INDICATIONS

- Detect acute pulmonary embolism
- Detect arteriovenous malformations or aneurysms
- Detect tumors; aneurysms; congenital defects; vascular changes associated with emphysema, blebs, and bullae; and heart abnormalities
- Determine the cause of recurrent or severe hemoptysis
- Evaluate pulmonary circulation

POTENTIAL DIAGNOSIS

Normal findings in

- Normal pulmonary vasculature; radiopaque iodine contrast medium should circulate symmetrically and without interruption through the pulmonary circulatory system.

Abnormal findings in

- Aneurysms
- Arterial hypoplasia or stenosis
- Arteriovenous malformations
- Bleeding caused by tuberculosis, bronchiectasis, sarcoidosis, or aspergilloma
- Inflammatory diseases
- Pulmonary embolism (PE) acute or chronic
- Pulmonary sequestration
- Tumors

CRITICAL FINDINGS ❖

- PE

It is essential that critical diagnoses be communicated immediately to the appropriate health-care provider (HCP). A listing of these diagnoses varies among facilities. Note and immediately report to the HCP abnormal results and related symptoms. Timely notification of critical values for lab or diagnostic studies is a role expectation of the professional nurse. Notification processes will vary among facilities. Upon receipt of the critical value the information should be read back to the caller to verify accuracy. Most policies require immediate notification of the primary HCP, Hospitalist, or on-call HCP. Reported information includes the patient's name, unique identifiers, critical value, name of the person giving the report, and name of the person receiving the report. Documentation of notification should be made in the medical record with the name of the HCP notified, time and date of notification, and any orders received. Any delay in a timely report of a critical value may require completion of a notification form with review by Risk Management.

INTERFERING FACTORS

This procedure is contraindicated for

- ❖ Patients with allergies to shellfish or iodinated contrast medium. The contrast medium used may cause a life-threatening allergic reaction. Patients with a known hypersensitivity to contrast medium may benefit from premedication with corticosteroids or the use of nonionic contrast medium.
- Patients with bleeding disorders.
- Patients who are pregnant or suspected of being pregnant, unless the potential benefits of the procedure far outweigh the risks to the fetus and mother.
- ❖ Elderly and other patients who are chronically dehydrated before the test, because of their risk of contrast-induced renal failure.
- ❖ Patients who are in renal failure.

Factors that may impair clear imaging

- Retained barium from a previous radiological procedure.
- Metallic objects within the examination field (e.g., jewelry, body rings), which may inhibit organ visualization and can produce unclear images.
- Inability of the patient to cooperate or remain still during the procedure

because of age, significant pain, or mental status.

Other considerations

- Consultation with an HCP should occur before the procedure for radiation safety concerns regarding younger patients or patients who are lactating.
- Risks associated with radiation overexposure can result from frequent x-ray procedures. Personnel in the room with the patient should wear a protective lead apron, stand behind a shield, or leave the area while the examination is being done. Personnel working in the examination area should wear badges to record their level of radiation exposure.
- Failure to follow dietary restrictions and other pretesting preparations may cause the procedure to be canceled or repeated.

NURSING IMPLICATIONS AND PROCEDURE

PRETEST:

- Positively identify the patient using at least two unique identifiers before providing care, treatment, or services.
- *Patient Teaching:* Inform the patient this procedure can assist with assessment of lung function and check for disease.
- Obtain a history of the patient's complaints, including a list of known allergens, especially allergies or sensitivities to latex, iodine, seafood, contrast medium, or anesthetics.
- Obtain a history of the patient's cardiovascular and respiratory systems, symptoms, and results of previously performed laboratory tests and diagnostic and surgical procedures. Ensure results of coagulation testing are obtained and recorded prior to the procedure; BUN and creatinine results are also needed if contrast medium is to be used.
- Note any recent procedures that can interfere with test results, including examinations using iodine-based contrast medium or barium. Ensure that

barium studies were performed more than 4 days before angiography.

▸ Record the date of the last menstrual period and determine the possibility of pregnancy in perimenopausal women.

▸ Obtain a list of the patient's current medications, including anticoagulants, aspirin and other salicylates, herbs, nutritional supplements, and nutraceuticals, especially those known to affect coagulation (see Appendix F). Such products should be discontinued by medical direction for the appropriate number of days prior to a surgical procedure. Note the last time and dose of medication taken.

▸ If contrast medium is scheduled to be used, patients receiving metformin (Glucophage) for non-insulin-dependent (type 2) diabetes should discontinue the drug on the day of the test and continue to withhold it for 48 hr after the test. Failure to do so may result in lactic acidosis.

▸ Review the procedure with the patient. Address concerns about pain and explain that there may be moments of discomfort and some pain experienced during the test. Inform the patient that the procedure is usually performed in a radiology or vascular suite by an HCP and takes approximately 30 to 60 min.

▸ *Sensitivity to social and cultural issues,* as well as concern for modesty, is important in providing psychological support before, during, and after the procedure.

▸ Explain that an IV line may be inserted to allow infusion of IV fluids, contrast medium, or sedatives. Usually normal saline is infused.

▸ Inform the patient that a burning and flushing sensation may be felt throughout the body during injection of the contrast medium. After injection of the contrast medium, the patient may experience an urge to cough, flushing, nausea, or a salty or metallic taste.

▸ Instruct the patient to remove jewelry and other metallic objects from the area to be examined.

▸ Instruct the patient to fast and restrict fluids for 2 to 4 hr prior to the procedure. Protocols may vary among facilities.

▸ This procedure may be terminated if chest pain, severe cardiac arrhythmias, or signs of a cerebrovascular accident occur.

▸ *Make sure a written and informed consent has been signed prior to the procedure and before administering any medications.*

INTRATEST:

▸ Observe standard precautions, and follow the general guidelines in Appendix A. Positively identify the patient.

▸ Ensure the patient has complied with dietary, fluid, and medication restrictions and pretesting preparations for 2 to 4 hr prior to the procedure.

▸ Ensure the patient has removed all external metallic objects from the area to be examined.

▸ If the patient has a history of allergic reactions to any substance or drug, administer ordered prophylactic steroids or antihistamines before the procedure. Use nonionic contrast medium for the procedure.

▸ Have emergency equipment readily available.

▸ Instruct the patient to void prior to the procedure and to change into the gown, robe, and foot coverings provided.

▸ Instruct the patient to cooperate fully and to follow directions. Instruct the patient to remain still throughout the procedure because movement produces unreliable results.

▸ Record baseline vital signs, and continue to monitor throughout the procedure. Protocols may vary among facilities.

▸ Establish an IV fluid line for the injection of emergency drugs and of sedatives.

▸ Administer an antianxiety agent, as ordered, if the patient has claustrophobia. Administer a sedative to a child or to an uncooperative adult, as ordered.

▸ Place electrocardiographic electrodes on the patient for cardiac monitoring. Establish a baseline rhythm; determine if the patient has ventricular arrhythmias.

▸ Using a pen, mark the site of the patient's peripheral pulses before angiography; this allows for quicker and more consistent assessment of the pulses after the procedure.

- Place the patient in the supine position on an examination table. Cleanse the selected area, and cover with a sterile drape.
- A local anesthetic is injected at the site, and a small incision is made or a needle is inserted under fluoroscopy.
- The contrast medium is injected, and a rapid series of images is taken during and after the filling of the vessels to be examined.
- Instruct the patient to inhale deeply and hold his or her breath while the images are taken, and then to exhale after the images are taken.
- Instruct the patient to take slow, deep breaths if nausea occurs during the procedure.
- Monitor the patient for complications related to the procedure (e.g., allergic reaction, anaphylaxis, bronchospasm).
- The needle or catheter is removed, and a pressure dressing is applied over the puncture site.
- Observe/assess the needle/catheter insertion site for bleeding, inflammation, or hematoma formation.

POST-TEST:

- A report of the results will be made available to the requesting HCP, who will discuss the results with the patient.
- Instruct the patient to resume usual diet, fluids, medications, or activity, as directed by the HCP. Renal function should be assessed before metformin is resumed.
- Monitor vital signs and neurological status every 15 min for 1 hr, then every 2 hr for 4 hr, and as ordered. Take the temperature every 4 hr for 24 hr. Monitor intake and output at least every 8 hr. Compare with baseline values. Protocols may vary from facility to facility.
- Observe for delayed allergic reactions, such as rash, urticaria, tachycardia, hyperpnea, hypertension, palpitations, nausea, or vomiting.
- Instruct the patient to immediately report symptoms such as fast heart rate, difficulty breathing, skin rash, itching, chest pain, persistent right shoulder pain, or abdominal pain. Immediately report symptoms to the appropriate HCP.
- Assess extremities for signs of ischemia or absence of distal pulse caused by a catheter-induced thrombus.
- Observe/assess the needle/catheter insertion site for bleeding, inflammation, or hematoma formation.
- Instruct the patient in the care and assessment of the site.
- Instruct the patient to apply cold compresses to the puncture site as needed, to reduce discomfort or edema.
- Instruct the patient to maintain bedrest for 4 to 6 hr after the procedure or as ordered.
- Recognize anxiety related to test results, and be supportive of perceived loss of independent function. Discuss the implications of abnormal test results on the patient's lifestyle. Provide teaching and information regarding clinical implications of the test results, as appropriate.
- Reinforce information given by the patient's HCP regarding further testing, treatment, or referral to another HCP. Answer any questions or address any concerns voiced by the patient or family.
- Depending on the results of this procedure, additional testing may be performed to evaluate or monitor progression of the disease process and determine the need for a change in therapy. Evaluate test results in relation to the patient's symptoms and other tests performed.

RELATED MONOGRAPHS:

- Related tests include alveolar/arterial gradient, blood gases, BUN, chest x-ray, creatinine, CT angiography, CT thoracic, ECG, FDP, lactic acid, lung perfusion scan, lung ventilation scan, MRA, MRI chest, aPTT, and PT/INR.
- Refer to the Cardiovascular and Respiratory systems tables at the end of the book for related tests by body system.

A

Angiography, Renal

SYNONYM/ACRONYM: Renal angiogram, renal arteriography.

COMMON USE: To visualize and assess the kidneys and surrounding structure for tumor, cancer, absent kidney, and level of renal disease.

AREA OF APPLICATION: Kidney.

CONTRAST: Intra-arterial iodine based.

DESCRIPTION: Renal angiography allows x-ray visualization of the large and small arteries of the renal vasculature and parenchyma or the renal veins and their branches. Contrast medium is injected through a catheter that has been inserted into the femoral artery or vein and advanced through the iliac artery and aorta into the renal artery or the inferior vena cava into the renal vein. Images of the kidneys and associated vessels are displayed on a monitor and recorded on film or electronically. Patterns of circulation, renal function, or changes in vessel wall appearance can be viewed to help diagnose the presence of vascular abnormalities, trauma, or lesions. This definitive test for renal disease may be used to evaluate chronic renal disease, renal failure, and renal artery stenosis; differentiate a vascular renal cyst from hypervascular renal cancers; and evaluate renal transplant donors, recipients, and the kidney after transplantation.

INDICATIONS

- Aid in angioplasty, atherectomy, or stent placement
- Allow infusion of thrombolytic drugs into an occluded artery
- Assist with the collection of blood samples from renal vein for renin analysis
- Detect arterial occlusion as evidenced by a transection of the renal artery caused by trauma or a penetrating injury
- Detect nonmalignant tumors before surgical resection
- Detect renal artery stenosis as evidenced by vessel dilation, collateral vessels, or increased renovascular pressure
- Detect renal tumors as evidenced by arterial supply, extent of venous invasion, and tumor vascularity
- Detect small kidney or absence of a kidney
- Detect thrombosis, arteriovenous fistulae, aneurysms, or emboli in renal vessels
- Differentiate between renal tumors and renal cysts
- Evaluate placement of a stent
- Evaluate postoperative renal transplantation for function or organ rejection
- Evaluate renal function in chronic renal failure or end-stage renal disease or hydronephrosis
- Evaluate the renal vascular system of prospective kidney donors before surgery
- Evaluate tumor vascularity before surgery or embolization

POTENTIAL DIAGNOSIS

Normal findings in
- Normal structure, function, and patency of renal vessels
- Contrast medium circulating throughout the kidneys symmetrically and without interruption
- No evidence of obstruction, variations in number and size of vessels and organs, malformations, cysts, or tumors

Abnormal findings in
- Abscess or inflammation
- Arterial stenosis, dysplasia, or infarction
- Arteriovenous fistula or other abnormalities
- Congenital anomalies
- Intrarenal hematoma
- Renal artery aneurysm
- Renal cysts or tumors
- Trauma causing tears or other disruption

CRITICAL FINDINGS: N/A

INTERFERING FACTORS

This procedure is contraindicated for
- Patients with allergies to shellfish or iodinated contrast medium. The contrast medium used may cause a life-threatening allergic reaction. Patients with a known hypersensitivity to contrast medium may benefit from premedication with corticosteroids or the use of nonionic contrast medium.
- Patients with bleeding disorders.
- Patients who are pregnant or suspected of being pregnant, unless the potential benefits of the procedure far outweigh the risks to the fetus and mother.
- Elderly and other patients who are chronically dehydrated before the test, because of their risk of contrast-induced renal failure.
- Patients who are in renal failure.

Factors that may impair clear imaging
- Gas or feces in the gastrointestinal tract resulting from inadequate cleansing or failure to restrict food intake before the study.
- Retained barium from a previous radiological procedure.
- Metallic objects within the examination field (e.g., jewelry, body rings), which may inhibit organ visualization and can produce unclear images.
- Inability of the patient to cooperate or remain still during the procedure because of age, significant pain, or mental status.

Other considerations
- Consultation with a health-care provider (HCP) should occur before the procedure for radiation safety concerns regarding younger patients or patients who are lactating.
- Risks associated with radiation overexposure can result from frequent x-ray procedures. Personnel in the room with the patient should wear a protective lead apron, stand behind a shield, or leave the area while the examination is being done. Personnel working in the examination area should wear badges to record their level of radiation exposure.
- Failure to follow dietary restrictions and other pretesting preparations may cause the procedure to be canceled or repeated.

NURSING IMPLICATIONS AND PROCEDURE

PRETEST:
- Positively identify the patient using at least two unique identifiers before providing care, treatment, or services.
- *Patient Teaching:* Inform the patient this procedure can assist in assessment of kidney function and check for disease.

Obtain a history of the patient's complaints, including a list of known allergens (especially allergies or sensitivities to latex, iodine, seafood, anesthetics or contrast medium).

Obtain a history of the patient's genitourinary system, symptoms, and results of previously performed laboratory tests and diagnostic and surgical procedures. Ensure results of coagulation testing are obtained and recorded prior to the procedure; BUN and creatinine results are also needed since contrast medium is to be used.

Note any recent procedures that can interfere with test results, including examinations using iodine-based contrast medium or barium. Ensure that barium studies were performed more than 4 days before angiography.

Record the date of the last menstrual period and determine the possibility of pregnancy in perimenopausal women.

Obtain a list of the patient's current medications, including anticoagulants, aspirin and other salicylates, herbs, nutritional supplements, and nutraceuticals (see Appendix F). Such products should be discontinued by medical direction for the appropriate number of days prior to a surgical procedure. Note the last time and dose of medication taken.

If contrast medium is scheduled to be used, patients receiving metformin (Glucophage) for non–insulin–dependent (type 2) diabetes should discontinue the drug on the day of the test and continue to withhold it for 48 hr after the test. Failure to do so may result in lactic acidosis.

Review the procedure with the patient. Address concerns about pain and explain that there may be moments of discomfort and some pain experienced during the test. Inform the patient that the procedure is usually performed in a radiology or vascular suite by an HCP and takes approximately 30 to 60 min.

Sensitivity to social and cultural issues, as well as concern for modesty, is important in providing psychological support before, during, and after the procedure.

Explain that an IV line may be inserted to allow infusion of IV fluids, contrast medium, or sedatives. Usually normal saline is infused.

Inform the patient that a burning and flushing sensation may be felt throughout the body during injection of the contrast medium. After injection of the contrast medium, the patient may experience an urge to cough, flushing, nausea, or a salty or metallic taste.

Instruct the patient to remove jewelry, and other metallic objects from the area to be examined.

Instruct the patient to fast and restrict fluids for 2 to 4 hr prior to the procedure. Protocols may vary among facilities.

This procedure may be terminated if chest pain, severe cardiac arrhythmias, or signs of a cerebrovascular accident occur.

Make sure a written and informed consent has been signed prior to the procedure and before administering any medications.

INTRATEST:

Observe standard precautions, and follow the general guidelines in Appendix A. Positively identify the patient.

Ensure the patient has complied with dietary, fluid, and medication restrictions for 2 to 4 hr prior to the procedure.

Ensure the patient has removed all external metallic objects from the area to be examined.

If the patient has a history of allergic reactions to any substance or drug, administer ordered prophylactic steroids or antihistamines before the procedure. Use nonionic contrast medium for the procedure.

Have emergency equipment readily available.

Instruct the patient to void prior to the procedure and to change into the gown, robe, and foot coverings provided.

Instruct the patient to cooperate fully and to follow directions. Instruct the patient to remain still throughout the procedure because movement produces unreliable results.

Record baseline vital signs, and continue to monitor throughout the procedure. Protocols may vary among facilities.

Establish an IV fluid line for the injection of emergency drugs and of sedatives.

Administer an antianxiety agent, as ordered, if the patient has claustrophobia. Administer a sedative to a child or to an uncooperative adult, as ordered.

Place electrocardiographic electrodes on the patient for cardiac monitoring. Establish a baseline rhythm; determine if the patient has ventricular arrhythmias.

Using a pen, mark the site of the patient's peripheral pulses before angiography; this allows for quicker and more consistent assessment of the pulses after the procedure.

Place the patient in the supine position on an examination table. Cleanse the selected area, and cover with a sterile drape.

A local anesthetic is injected at the site, and a small incision is made or a needle is inserted under fluoroscopy.

The contrast medium is injected, and a rapid series of images is taken during and after the filling of the vessels to be examined. Delayed images may be taken to examine the vessels after a time and to monitor the venous phase of the procedure.

Instruct the patient to inhale deeply and hold his or her breath while the images are taken, and then to exhale after the images are taken.

Instruct the patient to take slow, deep breaths if nausea occurs during the procedure.

Monitor the patient for complications related to the procedure (e.g., allergic reaction, anaphylaxis, bronchospasm).

The needle or catheter is removed, and a pressure dressing is applied over the puncture site.

Observe/assess the needle/catheter insertion site for bleeding, inflammation, or hematoma formation.

POST-TEST:

A report of the results will be made available to the requesting HCP, who will discuss the results with the patient.

Instruct the patient to resume usual diet, fluids, medications, or activity, as directed by the HCP. Renal function should be assessed before metformin is resumed.

Monitor vital signs and neurological status every 15 min for 1 hr, then every 2 hr for 4 hr, and as ordered. Take temperature every 4 hr for 24 hr. Monitor intake and output at least every 8 hr. Compare with baseline values. Protocols may vary among facilities.

Observe for delayed allergic reactions, such as rash, urticaria, tachycardia, hyperpnea, hypertension, palpitations, nausea, or vomiting.

Instruct the patient to immediately report symptoms such as fast heart rate, difficulty breathing, skin rash, itching, chest pain, persistent right shoulder pain, or abdominal pain. Immediately report symptoms to the appropriate HCP.

Assess extremities for signs of ischemia or absence of distal pulse caused by a catheter-induced thrombus.

Observe/assess the needle/catheter insertion site for bleeding, inflammation, or hematoma formation.

Instruct the patient in the care and assessment of the site.

Instruct the patient to apply cold compresses to the puncture site as needed, to reduce discomfort or edema.

Instruct the patient to maintain bedrest for 4 to 6 hr after the procedure or as ordered.

Recognize anxiety related to test results, and be supportive of perceived loss of independent function. Discuss the implications of abnormal test results on the patient's lifestyle. Provide teaching and information regarding the clinical implications of the test results, as appropriate.

Reinforce information given by the patient's HCP regarding further testing, treatment, or referral to

A

another HCP. Answer any questions or address any concerns voiced by the patient or family.

Depending on the results of this procedure, additional testing may be needed to evaluate or monitor progression of the disease process and determine the need for a change in therapy. Evaluate test results in relation to the patient's symptoms and other tests performed.

RELATED MONOGRAPHS:

Related tests include biopsy kidney, BUN, creatinine, CT abdomen, CT angiography, culture urine, cytology urine, KUB study, IVP, MRA, MRI abdomen, aPTT, PT/INR, renin, renogram, US kidney, and UA.

Refer to the Genitourinary System table at the end of the book for related tests by body system.

Angiotensin-Converting Enzyme

SYNONYM/ACRONYM: Angiotensin I–converting enzyme (ACE).

COMMON USE: To assist in diagnosing, evaluating treatment, and monitoring the progression of sarcoidosis, a granulomatous disease that primarily affects the lungs.

SPECIMEN: Serum (1 mL) collected in a red- or tiger-top tube.

NORMAL FINDINGS: (Method: Spectrophotometry)

Age	Conventional Units	SI Units (Conventional Units × 0.017)
0–2 yr	5–83 units/L	0.09–1.41 microKat/L
3–7 yr	8–76 units/L	0.14–1.29 microKat/L
8–14 yr	6–89 units/L	0.10–1.51 microKat/L
Greater than 14 yr	12–68 units/L	0.20–1.16 microKat/L

POTENTIAL DIAGNOSIS

Increased in

- Bronchitis (acute and chronic) *(related to release of ACE from damaged pulmonary tissue)*
- Connective tissue disease *(related to release of ACE from scarred and damaged pulmonary tissue)*
- Gaucher's disease *(related to release of ACE from damaged pulmonary tissue; Gaucher's disease is due to the hereditary deficiency of an enzyme that results in accumulation of a fatty substance that damages pulmonary tissue)*
- Hansen's disease (leprosy)
- Histoplasmosis and other fungal diseases
- Hyperthyroidism (untreated) *(related to possible involvement of thyroid hormones in regulation of ACE)*
- Pulmonary fibrosis *(related to release of ACE from damaged pulmonary tissue)*

- Rheumatoid arthritis *(related to development of interstitial lung disease, pulmonary fibrosis, and release of ACE from damaged pulmonary tissue)*
- Sarcoidosis *(related to release of ACE from damaged pulmonary tissue)*

Decreased in
- Advanced pulmonary carcinoma *(related to lack of functional cells to produce ACE)*
- The period following corticosteroid therapy for sarcoidosis *(evidenced by cessation of effective therapy)*

CRITICAL FINDINGS: N/A

Find and print out the full monograph at DavisPlus (http://davisplus.fadavis.com, keyword Van Leeuwen).

Anion Gap

SYNONYM/ACRONYM: Agap.

COMMON USE: To assist in diagnosing metabolic disorders that result in metabolic acidosis and electrolyte imbalance such as severe dehydration.

SPECIMEN: Serum (1 mL) for electrolytes collected in a red- or tiger-top tube. Plasma (1 mL) collected in a green-top (heparin) tube is also acceptable.

NORMAL FINDINGS: (Method: Anion gap is derived mathematically from the direct measurement of sodium, chloride, and total carbon dioxide.) There are differences between serum and plasma values for some electrolytes. The reference ranges listed are based on serum values.

Age	Conventional and SI Units
Child or adult	8–16 mmol/L

DESCRIPTION: The anion gap is used most frequently as a clinical indicator of metabolic acidosis. The most common causes of an increased gap are lactic acidosis and ketoacidosis. The concept of estimating electrolyte disturbances in the extracellular fluid is based on the principle of electrical neutrality. The formula includes the major cation (sodium) and anions (chloride and bicarbonate) found in extracellular fluid. The anion gap is calculated as follows:

$$\text{anion gap} = \text{sodium} - (\text{chloride} + HCO_3^-)$$

Because bicarbonate (HCO_3^-) is not directly measured on most chemistry analyzers, it is estimated by substitution of the total carbon dioxide (Tco_2) value in the calculation. Some laboratories may include potassium in the calculation of the anion gap. Calculations including potassium can be invalidated because minor amounts of hemolysis can contribute significant levels of potassium leaked into the serum as a result of cell rupture. The anion gap is also widely used as a laboratory quality-control measure because low gaps usually indicate a reagent, calibration, or instrument error.

INDICATIONS
• Evaluate metabolic acidosis
• Indicate the presence of a disturbance in electrolyte balance
• Indicate the need for laboratory instrument recalibration or review of electrolyte reagent preparation and stability

POTENTIAL DIAGNOSIS

Increased in
Metabolic acidosis that results from the accumulation of unmeasured anionic substances like proteins, phosphorus, sulfates, ketoacids, or other organic acid waste products of metabolism
• Dehydration (severe)
• Ketoacidosis *caused by starvation, high-protein/low-carbohydrate diet, diabetes, and alcoholism*
• Lactic acidosis *(shock, excessive exercise, some malignancies)*
• Poisoning (salicylate, methanol, ethylene glycol, or paraldehyde)
• Renal failure
• Uremia

Decreased in
Conditions that result in metabolic alkalosis
• Chronic vomiting or gastric suction *(related to alkalosis due to net loss of acid)*
• Excess alkali ingestion
• Hypergammaglobulinemia *(related to an increase in measurable anions relative to the excessive production of unmeasured cationic M proteins)*
• Hypoalbuminemia *(related to decreased levels of unmeasured anionic proteins relative to stable and measurable cation concentrations)*
• Hyponatremia *(related to net loss of cations)*
Significant acidosis or alkalosis can result from increased levels of unmeasured cations like ionized calcium and magnesium or unmeasured anions like proteins, phosphorus, sulfates, or other organic acids, the effects of which may not be accurately reflected by the calculated anion gap.

CRITICAL FINDINGS: N/A

INTERFERING FACTORS
• Drugs that can increase or decrease the anion gap include those listed in the individual electrolyte (i.e., sodium, chloride, calcium, magnesium, and total carbon dioxide), total protein, lactic acid, and phosphorus monographs.
• Specimens should never be collected above an IV line because of the potential for dilution when the specimen and the IV solution combine in the collection container, falsely decreasing the result. There is also the potential of contaminating the sample with the substance of interest if it is present in the IV solution, falsely increasing the result.

NURSING IMPLICATIONS AND PROCEDURE

PRETEST:

▶ Positively identify the patient using at least two unique identifiers before providing care, treatment, or services.

▶ *Patient Teaching:* Inform the patient this test can assist in the evaluation of electrolyte balance.

▶ Obtain a history of the patient's complaints, including a list of known allergens, especially allergies or sensitivities to latex.

▶ Obtain a history of the patient's cardiovascular, endocrine, gastrointestinal, genitourinary, hematopoietic, immune, and respiratory systems; symptoms; and results of previously performed laboratory tests and diagnostic and surgical procedures.

▶ Obtain a list of the patient's current medications, including herbs, nutritional supplements, and nutraceuticals (see Appendix F).

▶ Review the procedure with the patient. Inform the patient that specimen collection takes approximately 5 to 10 min. Address concerns about pain and explain that there may be some discomfort during the venipuncture.

▶ *Sensitivity to social and cultural issues*, as well as concern for modesty, is important in providing psychological support before, during, and after the procedure.

▶ There are no food, fluid, or medication restrictions unless by medical direction.

INTRATEST:

▶ If the patient has a history of allergic reaction to latex, avoid the use of equipment containing latex.

▶ Instruct the patient to cooperate fully and to follow directions. Direct the patient to breathe normally and to avoid unnecessary movement.

▶ Observe standard precautions, and follow the general guidelines in Appendix A. Positively identify the patient, and label the appropriate specimen container with the corresponding patient demographics, initials of the person collecting the specimen, date, and time of collection. Perform a venipuncture.

▶ Remove the needle and apply direct pressure with dry gauze to stop bleeding. Observe/assess venipuncture site for bleeding and hematoma formation and secure gauze with adhesive bandage.

▶ Promptly transport the specimen to the laboratory for processing and analysis.

POST-TEST:

▶ A report of the results will be made available to the requesting health-care provider (HCP), who will discuss the results with the patient.

▶ *Nutritional Considerations:* Specific dietary considerations are listed in the monographs on individual electrolytes (i.e., sodium, chloride, calcium, magnesium, and potassium), total protein, and phosphorus.

▶ *Nutritional Considerations:* The anion gap can be used to indicate the presence of dehydration. Evaluate the patient for signs and symptoms of dehydration. Dehydration is a significant and common finding in geriatric patients.

▶ Reinforce information given by the patient's HCP regarding further testing, treatment, or referral to another HCP. Answer any questions or address any concerns voiced by the patient or family.

▶ Depending on the results of this procedure, additional testing may be performed to evaluate or monitor progression of the disease process and determine the need for a change in therapy. Evaluate test results in relation to the patient's symptoms and other tests performed.

RELATED MONOGRAPHS:

▶ Related tests include albumin, blood gases, BUN, creatinine, electrolytes, ethanol (drugs of abuse), glucose, ketones, lactic acid, osmolality, protein and fractions, salicylate, and UA.

▶ See the Cardiovascular, Endocrine, Gastrointestinal, Genitourinary, Hematopoietic, Immune, and Respiratory systems tables at the end of the book for related tests by body system.

A

Antiarrhythmic Drugs: Amiodarone Digoxin, Disopyramide, Flecainide, Lidocaine, Procainamide, Quinidine

SYNONYM/ACRONYM: *Amiodarone* (Cordarone); *Digoxin* (Digitek, Lanoxicaps, Lanoxin); *disopyramide* (Norpace, Norpace CR); *flecainide* (flecainide acetate, Tambocor); *lidocaine* (Xylocaine); *procainamide* (Procanbid, Pronestyl, Pronestyl SR); *quinidine* (Quinidex Extentabs, quinidine sulface SR, quinidine gluconate SR).

COMMON USE: To evaluate specific drugs for subtherapeutic, therapeutic, or toxic levels in treatment of heart failure and cardiac arrhythmias.

SPECIMEN: Serum (1 mL) collected in a red-top tube.

Drug	Route of Administration	Recommended Collection Time
Amiodarone	Oral	Trough: immediately before next dose
Digoxin	Oral	Trough: 12–24 hr after dose Never draw peak samples
Disopyramide	Oral	Trough: immediately before next dose Peak: 2–5 hr after dose
Flecainide	Oral	Trough: immediately before next dose Peak: 3 hr after dose
Lidocaine	IV	15 min, 1 hr, then every 24 hr
Procainamide	IV	15 min; 2, 6, 12 hr; then every 24 hr
Procainamide	Oral	Trough: immediately before next dose Peak: 75 min after dose
Quinidine sulfate	Oral	Trough: immediately before next dose Peak: 1 hr after dose
Quinidine gluconate	Oral	Trough: immediately before next dose Peak: 5 hr after dose
Quinidine polygalacturonate	Oral	Trough: immediately before next dose Peak: 2 hr after dose

NORMAL FINDINGS: (Method: Immunoassay)

A

Drug (Indication)	Therapeutic Range*	SI Units	Half-Life (hr)	Volume of Distribution (L/kg)	Protein Binding (%)	Excretion
(SI = Conventional Units × 1.60)						
Amiodarone	1.0–2.5 mcg/mL	1.6–4.0 micromol/L	250–1200	20–100	95–97	1° hepatic
(SI = Conventional Units × 1.28)						
Digoxin	0.5–2.0 ng/mL	0.6–2.6 nmol/L	20–60	7	20–30	1° renal
(SI = Conventional Units × 2.95)						
Disopyramide (atrial arrhythmias)	2.8–3.2 mcg/mL	8.3–9.4 micromol/L	4–10	0.7–0.9	20–60	1° renal
Disopyramide (ventricular arrhythmias)	3.3–5.0 mcg/mL	9.7–14.8 micromol/L				1° renal
(SI = Conventional Units × 2.41)						
Flecainide	0.2–1.0 mcg/mL	0.5–2.4 micromol/L	7–19	5–13	40–50	1° renal
(SI = Conventional Units × 4.27)						
Lidocaine	1.5–5.0 mcg/mL	6.4–21.4 micromol/L	1.5–2	1–1.5	60–80	1° hepatic
(SI = Conventional Units × 4.23)						
Procainamide	4–10 mcg/mL	17–42 micromol/L	2–6	2–4	10–20	1° renal
N-acetyl procainamide	10–20 mcg/mL	42–85 micromol/L	8			1° renal
(SI = Conventional Units × 3.08)						
Quinidine	2–5 mcg/mL	6–15 micromol/L	6–8	2–3	70–90	Renal and hepatic

*Conventional units.

A

DESCRIPTION: Cardiac glycosides are used in the prophylactic management and treatment of heart failure and ventricular and atrial arrhythmias. Because these drugs have narrow therapeutic windows, they must be monitored closely. The signs and symptoms of toxicity are often difficult to distinguish from those of cardiac disease. Patients with toxic levels may show gastrointestinal, ocular, and central nervous system effects and disturbances in potassium balance.

Many factors must be considered in effective dosing and monitoring of therapeutic drugs, including patient age, patient ethnicity, patient weight, interacting medications, electrolyte balance, protein levels, water balance, conditions that affect absorption and excretion, and the ingestion of substances (e.g., foods, herbals, vitamins, and minerals) that can either potentiate or inhibit the intended target concentration. Peak and trough collection times should be documented carefully in relation to the time of medication administration.

IMPORTANT NOTE
This information must be communicated clearly and accurately to avoid misunderstanding of the dose time in relation to the collection time. Miscommunication between the individual administering the medication and the individual collecting the specimen is the most frequent cause of subtherapeutic levels, toxic levels, and misleading information used in the calculation of future doses. If administration of the drug is delayed, notify the appropriate department(s) to reschedule the blood draw and notify the requesting health-care provider (HCP) if the delay has caused any real or perceived therapeutic harm.

INDICATIONS
- Assist in the diagnosis and prevention of toxicity
- Monitor compliance with therapeutic regimen
- Monitor patients who have a pacemaker, who have impaired renal or hepatic function, or who are taking interacting drugs

POTENTIAL DIAGNOSIS

Level	Response
Normal levels	Therapeutic effect
Subtherapeutic levels	Adjust dose as indicated
Toxic levels	Adjust dose as indicated
Amiodarone	Hepatic impairment, older results
Digoxin	Renal impairment, CHF,* older adults
Disopyramide	Renal impairment
Flecainide	Renal impairment, CHF
Lidocaine	Hepatic impairment, CHF
Procainamide	Renal impairment
Quinidine	Renal and hepatic impairment, CHF, older adults

*CHF = congestive heart failure.

CRITICAL FINDINGS

Adverse effects of subtherapeutic levels are important. Care should be taken to investigate the signs and symptoms of too little and too much medication. Note and immediately report to the HCP any critically increased or subtherapeutic values and related symptoms. Timely notification of critical values for lab or diagnostic studies is a role expectation of the professional nurse. Notification processes will vary among facilities. Upon receipt of the critical value the information should be read back to the caller to verify accuracy. Most policies require immediate notification of the primary HCP, Hospitalist, or on-call HCP. Reported information includes the patient's name, unique identifiers, critical value, name of the person giving the report, and name of the person receiving the report. Documentation of notification should be made in the medical record with the name of the HCP notified, time and date of notification, and any orders received. Any delay in a timely report of a critical value may require completion of a notification form with review by Risk Management.

Amiodarone: Greater Than 2.5 mcg/mL (SI: Greater Than 4.0 micromol/L)

Signs and symptoms of pulmonary damage related to amiodarone toxicity include bronchospasm, wheezing, fever, dyspnea, cough, hemoptysis, and hypoxia. Possible interventions include discontinuing the medication, monitoring pulmonary function with chest x-ray, monitoring liver function tests to assess for liver damage, monitoring thyroid function tests to assess for thyroid damage (related to the high concen-

tration of iodine contained in the medication), and electrocardiographic (ECG) monitoring for worsening of arrhythmia.

Digoxin: Greater Than 2.5 ng/mL (SI: Greater Than 3.2 nmol/L)

Signs and symptoms of digoxin toxicity include arrhythmias, anorexia, hyperkalemia, nausea, vomiting, diarrhea, changes in mental status, and visual disturbances (objects appear yellow or have halos around them). Possible interventions include discontinuing the medication, continuous ECG monitoring (prolonged P-R interval, widening QRS interval, lengthening Q-Tc interval, and atrioventricular block), transcutaneous pacing, administration of activated charcoal (if the patient has a gag reflex and central nervous system function), support and treatment of electrolyte disturbance, and administration of Digibind (digoxin immune Fab). The amount of Digibind given depends on the level of digoxin to be neutralized. Digoxin levels must be measured before the administration of Digibind. Digoxin levels should not be measured for several days after administration of Digibind in patients with normal renal function (1 wk or longer in patients with decreased renal function). Digibind cross-reacts in the digoxin assay and may provide misleading elevations or decreases in values depending on the particular assay in use by the laboratory.

Disopyramide: Greater Than 7 mcg/mL (SI: Greater Than 20.6 micromol/L)

Signs and symptoms of disopyramide toxicity include prolonged Q-T interval, ventricular tachycardia, hypotension, and heart failure.

Possible interventions include discontinuing the medication, airway support, and ECG and blood pressure monitoring.

Flecainide: Greater Than 1 mcg/mL (SI: Greater Than 2.41 micromol/L)
Signs and symptoms of flecainide toxicity include exaggerated pharmacological effects resulting in arrhythmia. Possible interventions include discontinuing the medication as well as continuous ECG, respiratory, and blood pressure monitoring.

Lidocaine: Greater Than 6 mcg/mL (SI: Greater Than 25.6 micromol/L)
Signs and symptoms of lidocaine toxicity include slurred speech, central nervous system depression, cardiovascular depression, convulsions, muscle twitches, and possible coma. Possible interventions include continuous ECG monitoring, airway support, and seizure precautions.

Procainamide: Greater Than 10 mcg/mL (SI: Greater Than 42.3 micromol/L); N-Acetyl Procainamide: Greater Than 40 mcg/mL (SI: Greater Than 169.2 micromol/L)
The active metabolite of procainamide is N-acetyl procainamide (NAPA). Signs and symptoms of procainamide toxicity include torsade de pointes (ventricular tachycardia), nausea, vomiting, agranulocytosis, and hepatic disturbances. Possible interventions include airway protection, emesis, gastric lavage, and administration of sodium lactate.

Quinidine: Greater Than 6 mcg/mL (SI: Greater Than 18.5 micromol/L)
Signs and symptoms of quinidine toxicity include ataxia, nausea, vomiting, diarrhea, respiratory system depression, hypotension, syncope, anuria, arrhythmias (heart block, widening of QRS and Q-T intervals), asystole, hallucinations, paresthesia, and irritability. Possible interventions include airway support, emesis, gastric lavage, administration of activated charcoal, administration of sodium lactate, and temporary transcutaneous or transvenous pacemaker.

INTERFERING FACTORS
- Blood drawn in serum separator tubes (gel tubes).
- Contraindicated in patients with liver disease, and caution advised in patients with renal impairment.
- Drugs that may increase amiodarone levels include cimetidine.
- Drugs that may decrease amiodarone levels include cholestyramine and phenytoin.
- Drugs that may increase digoxin levels or increase risk of toxicity include amiodarone, amphotericin B, diclofenac, diltiazem, erythromycin, ibuprofen, indomethacin, nifedipine, nisoldipine, propafenone, propantheline, quinidine, spironolactone, tetracycline, tiapamil, troleandomycin, and verapamil.
- Drugs that may decrease digoxin levels include albuterol, aluminum hydroxide (antacids), carbamazepine, cholestyramine, colestipol, digoxin immune Fab, hydralazine, hydroxychloroquine, iron, kaolin-pectin, magnesium hydroxide, magnesium trisilicate, metoclopramide, neomycin, nitroprusside, paroxetine, phenytoin, rifabutin, sulfasalazine, and ticlopidine.
- Drugs that may increase disopyramide levels or increase risk of

toxicity include amiodarone, atenolol, ritonavir, and troleandomycin.

- Drugs that may decrease disopyramide levels include phenobarbital, phenytoin, rifabutin, and rifampin.
- Drugs that may increase flecainide levels or increase risk of toxicity include amiodarone and cimetidine.
- Drugs that may decrease flecainide levels include carbamazepine, charcoal, phenobarbital, and phenytoin.
- Drugs that may increase lidocaine levels or increase risk of toxicity include beta blockers, cimetidine, metoprolol, nadolol, propranolol, and ritonavir.
- Drugs that may decrease lidocaine levels include phenytoin.
- Drugs that may increase procainamide levels or increase risk of toxicity include amiodarone, cimetidine, quinidine, ranitidine, and trimethoprim.
- Drugs that may increase quinidine levels or increase risk of toxicity include acetazolamide, amiodarone, cimetidine, itraconazole, mibefradil, nifedipine, nisoldipine, quinidine, ranitidine, thiazide diuretics, and verapamil.
- Drugs that may decrease quinidine levels include kaolin-pectin, ketoconazole, phenobarbital, phenytoin, rifabutin, and rifampin.
- Concomitant administration of amiodarone with other medications may result in toxic levels of the other medications related to the suppression of enzyme activity required to metabolize many other medications by amiodarone. It may also potentiate the anticoagulating effects of warfarin, resulting in increased PT values.

- Digitoxin cross-reacts with digoxin; results are falsely elevated if digoxin is measured when the patient is taking digitoxin.
- Digitalis-like immunoreactive substances are found in the serum of some patients who are not taking digoxin, causing false-positive results. Patients whose serum contains digitalis-like immunoreactive substances usually have a condition related to salt and fluid retention, such as renal failure, hepatic failure, low-renin hypertension, and pregnancy.
- Unexpectedly low digoxin levels may be found in patients with thyroid disease.
- Disopyramide may cause a decrease in glucose levels. It may also potentiate the anticoagulating effects of warfarin, resulting in increased PT values.
- Long-term administration of procainamide can cause false-positive antinuclear antibody results and development of a lupuslike syndrome in some patients.
- Quinidine may potentiate the effects of neuromuscular blocking medications and warfarin anticoagulants.
- Concomitant administration of quinidine and digoxin can rapidly raise digoxin to toxic levels. If both drugs are to be given together, the digoxin level should be measured before the first dose of quinidine and again in 4 to 6 days.

NURSING IMPLICATIONS AND PROCEDURE

PRETEST:

- Positively identify the patient using at least two unique identifiers before providing care, treatment, or services.

▸ *Patient Teaching:* Inform the patient this test can assist in monitoring for subtherapeutic, therapeutic, or toxic drug levels.

▸ Obtain a history of the patient's complaints, including a list of known allergens, especially allergies or sensitivities to latex.

▸ Obtain a history of the patient's cardiovascular system, symptoms, and results of previously performed laboratory tests and diagnostic and surgical procedures.

▸ These medications are metabolized and excreted by the kidneys and liver.

▸ Obtain a list of the patient's current medications, including herbs, nutritional supplements, and nutraceuticals (see Appendix F). Note the last time and dose of medication taken.

▸ Review the procedure with the patient. Inform the patient that specimen collection takes approximately 5 to 10 min. Address concerns about pain and explain that there may be some discomfort during the venipuncture.

▸ *Sensitivity to social and cultural issues,* as well as concern for modesty, is important in providing psychological support before, during, and after the procedure.

▸ There are no food, fluid, or medication restrictions unless by medical direction.

INTRATEST:

▸ If the patient has a history of allergic reaction to latex, avoid the use of equipment containing latex.

▸ Instruct the patient to cooperate fully and to follow directions. Direct the patient to breathe normally and to avoid unnecessary movement.

▸ Observe standard precautions, and follow the general guidelines in Appendix A. Consider recommended collection time in relation to the dosing schedule. Positively identify the patient, and label the appropriate specimen container with the corresponding patient demographics, initials of the person collecting the specimen, date, and time of collection, noting the last dose of medication taken. Perform a venipuncture.

▸ Remove the needle and apply direct pressure with dry gauze to stop bleeding. Observe/assess venipuncture site for bleeding or hematoma formation and secure gauze with adhesive bandage.

▸ Promptly transport the specimen to the laboratory for processing and analysis.

POST-TEST:

▸ A report of the results will be made available to the requesting HCP, who will discuss the results with the patient.

▸ *Nutritional Considerations:* Include avoidance of alcohol consumption.

▸ Reinforce information given by the patient's HCP regarding further testing, treatment, or referral to another HCP. Explain to the patient the importance of following the medication regimen and instructions regarding drug interactions. Instruct the patient to immediately report any unusual sensations (e.g., dizziness, changes in vision, loss of appetite, nausea, vomiting, diarrhea, weakness, or irregular heartbeat) to his or her HCP. Instruct the patient not to take medicine within 1 hr of food high in fiber. Answer any questions or address any concerns voiced by the patient or family.

▸ Instruct the patient to be prepared to provide the pharmacist with a list of other medications he or she is already taking in the event that the requesting HCP prescribes a medication.

▸ Depending on the results of this procedure, additional testing may be performed to evaluate or monitor progression of the disease process and determine the need for a change in therapy. Testing for aspirin responsiveness/resistance may be a consideration for patients, especially women, on low-dose aspirin therapy. Evaluate test results in relation to the patient's symptoms and other tests performed.

RELATED MONOGRAPHS:

Related tests include ALT; albumin; ALP; apolipoproteins A, B, and E; AST; atrial natriuretic peptide; BNP; blood gases; BUN; CRP; calcium; calcium ionized; chest x-ray; cholesterol (total, HDL, and LDL); CBC platelet count; CK and isoenzymes; creatinine; ECG; glucose; glycated hemoglobin; homocysteine; ketones; LDH and isoenzymes; magnesium; myoglobin; potassium; triglycerides; and troponin.

See the Cardiovascular System table at the end of the book for related tests by body system.

Antibodies, Anti-Cyclic Citrullinated Peptide

SYNONYM/ACRONYM: Anti-CCP antibodies, ACPA.

COMMON USE: To assist in diagnosing and monitoring rheumatoid arthritis.

SPECIMEN: Serum (1 mL) collected in a red- or tiger-top tube.

NORMAL FINDINGS: IgG Ab (Method: Immunoassay, enzyme-linked immunosorbent assay [ELISA])

Negative	Less than 20 units
Weak positive	20–39 units
Moderate positive	40–59 units
Strong positive	60 units or greater

DESCRIPTION: Rheumatoid arthritis (RA) is a chronic, systemic autoimmune disease that damages the joints. Inflammation caused by autoimmune responses can affect other organs and body systems. The current American Academy of Rheumatology criteria focuses on earlier diagnosis of newly presenting patients who have at least one swollen joint unrelated to another condition. The current criteria includes four determinants: joint involvement (number and size of joints involved), serological test results (rheumatoid factor [RF] and/or ACPA), indications of acute inflammation (CRP and/or ESR), and duration of symptoms. A score of 6 or greater defines the presence of RA. Patients with longstanding RA, whose condition is inactive, or whose prior history would have satisfied the

A

previous classification criteria by having four of seven findings—morning stiffness, arthritis of three or more joint areas, arthritis of hand joints, symmetric arthritis, rheumatoid nodules, abnormal amounts of rheumatoid factor, and radiographic changes—should remain classified as having RA. The study of RA is complex, and it is believed that multiple genes may be involved in the manifestation of RA. Scientific research has revealed an unusual peptide conversion from arginine to citrulline that results in formation of antibodies whose presence provides the basis for this test. Studies show that detection of antibodies formed against citrullinated peptides is specific and sensitive in detecting RA in both early and established disease. Anti-CCP assays have 96% specificity and 78% sensitivity for RA, compared to the traditional IgM RF marker with a specificity of 60% to 80% and sensitivity of 75% to 80% for RA. Anti-CCP antibodies are being used as a marker for erosive disease in RA, and the antibodies have been detected in healthy patients years before the onset of RA symptoms and diagnosed disease. Some studies have shown that as many as 40% of patients seronegative for RF are anti-CCP positive. The combined presence of RF and anti-CCP has a 99.5% specificity for RA. Women are two to three times more likely than men to develop RA. Although RA is most likely to affect people aged 35 to 50, it can affect all ages.

INDICATIONS

- Assist in the diagnosis of RA in both symptomatic and asymptomatic individuals
- Assist in the identification of erosive disease in RA
- Assist in the diagnostic prediction of RA development in undifferentiated arthritis

POTENTIAL DIAGNOSIS

Increased in
- RA *(The immune system produces antibodies that attack the joint tissues. Inflammation of the synovium, membrane that lines the joint, begins a process called synovitis. If untreated, the synovitis can expand beyond the joint tissue to surrounding ligaments, tissues, nerves, and blood vessels.)*

Decreased in: N/A

CRITICAL FINDINGS: N/A

INTERFERING FACTORS: N/A

NURSING IMPLICATIONS AND PROCEDURE

PRETEST:

- *Patient Teaching:* Inform the patient this test can assist in identifying the cause of joint inflammation.
- Obtain a history of the patient's complaints, including a list of known allergens, especially allergies or sensitivities to latex.
- Obtain a history of the patient's immune and musculoskeletal systems, symptoms, and results of previously performed laboratory tests and diagnostic and surgical procedures.
- Obtain a list of the patient's current medications, including herbs,

nutritional supplements, and nutraceuticals (see Appendix F).
- Review the procedure with the patient. Inform the patient that specimen collection takes approximately 5 to 10 min. Address concerns about pain and explain that there may be some discomfort during the venipuncture.
- *Sensitivity to social and cultural issues,* as well as concern for modesty, is important in providing psychological support before, during, and after the procedure.
- There are no food, fluid, or medication restrictions unless by medical direction.

INTRATEST:

- If the patient has a history of allergic reaction to latex, avoid the use of equipment containing latex.
- Instruct the patient to cooperate fully and to follow directions. Direct the patient to breathe normally and to avoid unnecessary movement.
- Observe standard precautions, and follow the general guidelines in Appendix A. Positively identify the patient, and label the appropriate specimen container with the corresponding patient demographics, initials of the person collecting the specimen, date, and time of collection. Perform a venipuncture.
- Remove the needle and apply direct pressure with dry gauze to stop bleeding. Observe/assess venipuncture site for bleeding or hematoma formation and secure gauze with adhesive bandage.
- Promptly transport the specimen to the laboratory for processing and analysis.

POST-TEST:

- A report of the results will be made available to the requesting health-care provider (HCP), who will discuss the results with the patient.

- Recognize anxiety related to test results, and be supportive of impaired activity related to anticipated chronic pain resulting from joint inflammation, impairment in mobility, muscular deformity, and perceived loss of independence. Discuss the implications of abnormal test results on the patient's lifestyle. Provide teaching and information regarding the clinical implications of the test results as appropriate. Explain the importance of physical activity in the treatment plan. Educate the patient regarding access to physical therapy, occupational therapy, and counseling services. Provide contact information, if desired, for the American College of Rheumatology (www.rheumatology.org) or for the Arthritis Foundation (www.arthritis.org). Encourage the patient to take medications as ordered. Treatment with disease-modifying antirheumatic drugs (DMARDs) and biologic response modifiers may take as long as 2 to 3 mo to demonstrate their effects.
- Reinforce information given by the patient's HCP regarding further testing, treatment, or referral to another HCP. Answer any questions or address any concerns voiced by the patient or family.
- Depending on the results of this procedure, additional testing may be performed to evaluate or monitor progression of the disease process and determine the need for a change in therapy.

RELATED MONOGRAPHS:

- Related tests include ANA, arthroscopy, BMD, bone scan, CBC, CRP, ESR, MRI musculoskeletal, radiography bone, RF, synovial fluid analysis, and uric acid.
- Refer to the Immune and Musculoskeletal systems tables at the end of the book for related tests by body system.

A

Antibodies, Anti-Glomerular Basement Membrane

SYNONYM/ACRONYM: Goodpasture's antibody, anti-GBM.

COMMON USE: To assist in differentiating Goodpasture's syndrome (an autoimmune disease) from renal dysfunction.

SPECIMEN: Serum (1 mL) collected in a red- or tiger-top tube. Lung or kidney tissue also may be submitted for testing. Refer to related biopsy monographs for specimen-collection instructions.

NORMAL FINDINGS: (Method: Enzyme immunoassay) Less than 20 units/mL = negative.

DESCRIPTION: Glomerulonephritis or inflammation of the kidney is initiated by an immune response, usually to an infection. It can be classified as either antibody-mediated or cell-mediated glomerulonephritis. Goodpasture's syndrome is a rare hypersensitivity condition characterized by the presence of circulating anti-glomerular basement membrane (GBM) antibodies in the blood and the deposition of immunoglobulin and complement in renal basement membrane tissue. Severe and progressive glomerulonephritis can lead to the development of pulmonary hemorrhage and idiopathic pulmonary hemosiderosis. The presence of anti-GBM antibodies can also be demonstrated in renal biopsy tissue cells of affected patients. Autoantibodies may also be directed to act against lung tissue in Goodpasture's syndrome.

INDICATIONS
- Differentiate glomerulonephritis caused by anti-GBM from glomerulonephritis from other causes
- Monitor therapy for glomerulonephritis caused by anti-GBM

POTENTIAL DIAGNOSIS

Increased in
- Glomerulonephritis *(of autoimmune origin as evidenced by the presence of anti-GBM antibodies)*
- Goodpasture's syndrome *(related to nephritis of autoimmune origin)*
- Idiopathic pulmonary hemosiderosis

Decreased in: N/A

CRITICAL FINDINGS: N/A

INTERFERING FACTORS: N/A

NURSING IMPLICATIONS AND PROCEDURE

PRETEST:
- Positively identify the patient using at least two unique identifiers before providing care, treatment, or services.
- *Patient Teaching:* Inform the patient this test can assist in diagnosing a disease that can affect the kidneys or lungs.
- Obtain a history of the patient's complaints, including a list of known allergens, especially allergies or sensitivities to latex.
- Obtain a history of the patient's genitourinary, immune, and respiratory systems; symptoms; and results of previously performed laboratory tests and diagnostic and surgical procedures.

Obtain a list of the patient's current medications, including herbs, nutritional supplements, and nutraceuticals (see Appendix F).

Review the procedure with the patient. Inform the patient that specimen collection takes approximately 5 to 10 min. Address concerns about pain and explain that there may be some discomfort during the venipuncture. *Sensitivity to social and cultural issues,* as well as concern for modesty, is important in providing psychological support before, during, and after the procedure. There are no food, fluid, or medication restrictions unless by medical direction.

INTRATEST:

If the patient has a history of allergic reaction to latex, avoid the use of equipment containing latex.

Instruct the patient to cooperate fully and to follow directions. Direct the patient to breathe normally and to avoid unnecessary movement.

Observe standard precautions, and follow the general guidelines in Appendix A. Positively identify the patient, and label the appropriate specimen container with the corresponding patient demographics, initials of the person collecting the specimen, date, and time of collection.

Perform a venipuncture.

Remove the needle and apply direct pressure with dry gauze to stop bleeding. Observe/assess venipuncture site for bleeding or hematoma formation and secure gauze with adhesive bandage.

Promptly transport the specimen to the laboratory for processing and analysis.

POST-TEST:

A report of the results will be made available to the requesting health-care provider (HCP), who will discuss the results with the patient.

Recognize anxiety related to test results, and be supportive of perceived loss of independence and fear of shortened life expectancy. Discuss the implications of abnormal test results on the patient's lifestyle. Provide teaching and information regarding the clinical implications of the test results, as appropriate. Educate the patient regarding access to counseling services.

Reinforce information given by the patient's HCP regarding further testing, treatment, or referral to another HCP. Answer any questions or address any concerns voiced by the patient or family.

Depending on the results of this procedure, additional testing may be performed to evaluate or monitor progression of the disease process and determine the need for a change in therapy. Evaluate test results in relation to the patient's symptoms and other tests performed.

RELATED MONOGRAPHS:

Related tests include ANCA, biopsy kidney, biopsy lung, IVP, renogram, US kidney, and UA.

See the Genitourinary, Immune, and Respiratory systems tables at the end of the book for related tests by body system.

Antibodies, Actin (Smooth Muscle) and Mitochondrial M2

SYNONYM/ACRONYM: Antiactin antibody, ASMA; mitochondrial M2 antibody, M2 antibody, AMA.

COMMON USE: To assist in the differential diagnosis of chronic liver disease, typically biliary cirrhosis.

SPECIMEN: Serum (1 mL) collected in a red-top tube.

NORMAL FINDINGS: (Method: Immunoassay, enzyme-linked immunosorbent [ELISA])

A

Actin smooth muscle antibody, IgG

Negative	Less than 20 units
Weak positive	20–30 units
Positive	Greater than 30 units

DESCRIPTION: Primary biliary cirrhosis (PBC) is a disease in which the small bile ducts of the liver are destroyed by an inflammatory process. Antimitochondrial antibodies are found in 90% of patients with PBC. Mitochondrial M2 antibody has a higher degree of specificity than any of the other three types of detectable mitochondrial antibodies (M1, M5, M6) for PBC. PBC is identified most frequently in women aged 35 to 60. Testing is useful in the differential diagnosis of chronic liver disease because antimitochondrial antibodies are rarely detected in extrahepatic biliary obstruction, various forms of hepatitis, and cirrhosis. Antismooth muscle antibodies are autoantibodies found in high titers in the sera of patients with autoimmune diseases of the liver and bile duct. Smooth muscle antibodies are directed against the F-actin subunits present in all smooth muscle fibers and are therefore not organ specific. Simultaneous testing for antimitochondrial antibodies can be useful in the differential diagnosis of chronic liver disease.

INDICATIONS

Actin antibodies (ASMA)
• Differential diagnosis of liver disease

Mitochondrial M2 antibodies (AMA)
• Assist in the diagnosis of PBC
• Assist in the differential diagnosis of chronic liver disease

Mitochondrial M2 antibody, IgG

Negative	Less than 20 units
Weak positive	20.1–24.9 units
Positive	Greater than 25 units

POTENTIAL DIAGNOSIS

Increased in
The exact cause of PBC is unknown. There is a high degree of correlation between the presence of actin smooth muscle antibodies (ASMA) and mitochodrial M2 antibodies (AMA) with PBC, and PBC therefore is thought to be an autoimmune disease. The antibodies have been identified in the sera of patients with other autoimmune diseases.

Actin antibodies (ASMA)
• Autoimmune hepatitis
• Chronic active viral hepatitis
• Infectious mononucleosis
• PBC
• Primary sclerosing cholangitis

Mitochondrial M2 antibodies (AMA)
• Hepatitis (alcoholic, viral)
• PBC
• Rheumatoid arthritis (occasionally)
• Systemic lupus erythematosus (occasionally)
• Thyroid disease (occasionally)

Decreased in: N/A

CRITICAL FINDINGS: N/A

INTERFERING FACTORS
• Drugs and substances that may increase mitochondrial M2 (AMA) levels include labetalol (liver damage).
• Drugs and substances that may decrease mitochondrial M2 (AMA) levels include cyclosporine and ursodiol

NURSING IMPLICATIONS AND PROCEDURE

PRETEST:

- Positively identify the patient using at least two unique identifiers before providing care, treatment, or services.
- *Patient Teaching:* Inform the patient this test can assist in the diagnosis of liver disease.
- Obtain a history of the patient's complaints, including a list of known allergens, especially allergies or sensitivities to latex.
- Obtain a history of the patient's hepatobiliary and immune systems, symptoms, and results of previously performed laboratory tests and diagnostic and surgical procedures.
- Obtain a list of the patient's current medications, including herbs, nutritional supplements, and nutraceuticals (see Appendix F).
- Review the procedure with the patient. Inform the patient that specimen collection takes approximately 5 to 10 min. Address concerns about pain and explain that there may be some discomfort during the venipuncture. *Sensitivity to social and cultural issues,* as well as concern for modesty, is important in providing psychological support before, during, and after the procedure. There are no food, fluid, or medication restrictions unless by medical direction.

INTRATEST:

- If the patient has a history of allergic reaction to latex, avoid the use of equipment containing latex.
- Instruct the patient to cooperate fully and to follow directions. Direct the patient to breathe normally and to avoid unnecessary movement.
- Observe standard precautions, and follow the general guidelines in Appendix A. Positively identify the patient, and label the appropriate specimen container with the corresponding patient demographics, initials of the person collecting the specimen, date, and time of collection.
- Perform a venipuncture.
- Remove the needle and apply direct pressure with dry gauze to stop bleeding. Observe/assess venipuncture site for bleeding or hematoma formation and secure gauze with adhesive bandage.
- Promptly transport the specimen to the laboratory for processing and analysis.

POST-TEST:

- A report of the results will be made available to the requesting health-care provider (HCP), who will discuss the results with the patient.
- *Nutritional Considerations:* The presence of antimitochondrial or antismooth muscle antibodies may be associated with liver disease. Dietary recommendations may be indicated and vary depending on the severity of the condition. A low-protein diet may be in order if the liver cannot process the end products of protein metabolism. A diet of soft foods may be required if esophageal varices have developed. Ammonia levels may be used to determine whether protein should be added to or reduced from the diet. Patients should be encouraged to eat simple carbohydrates and emulsified fats (as in homogenized milk or eggs) rather than complex carbohydrates (e.g., starch, fiber, and glycogen [animal carbohydrates]) and complex fats, which require additional bile to emulsify them so that they can be used. Observe the cirrhotic patient carefully for the development of ascites; if ascites develops, pay strict attention to fluid and electrolyte balance.
- Reinforce information given by the patient's HCP regarding further testing, treatment, or referral to another HCP. Answer any questions or address any concerns voiced by the patient or family.
- Depending on the results of this procedure, additional testing may be performed to evaluate or monitor progression of the disease process and determine the need for a change in therapy. Evaluate test results in relation to the patient's symptoms and other tests performed.

RELATED MONOGRAPHS:

- Related tests include albumin, ALP, ammonia, ANCA, ANA, bilirubin, biopsy liver, electrolytes, and GGT.
- See the Hepatobiliary and Immune systems tables at the end of the book for related tests by body system.

A

Antibodies, Antineutrophilic Cytoplasmic

SYNONYM/ACRONYM: Cytoplasmic antineutrophil cytoplasmic antibody (c-ANCA), perinuclear antineutrophil cytoplasmic antibody (p-ANCA).

COMMON USE: To assist in diagnosing and monitoring the effectiveness of therapeutic interventions for Wegener's syndrome.

SPECIMEN: Serum (1 mL) collected in a red-top tube.

NORMAL FINDINGS: (Method: Indirect immunofluorescence) Negative.

DESCRIPTION: Antineutrophil cytoplasmic autoantibodies (ANCA) are associated with vasculitis and glomerulonephritis. There are two types of cytoplasmic neutrophil antibodies, identified by their cellular staining characteristics. c-ANCA (cytoplasmic) is specific for proteinase 3 in neutrophils and monocytes and is found in the sera of patients with Wegener's granulomatosis (WG). Wegener's syndrome includes granulomatous inflammation of the upper and lower respiratory tract and vasculitis. Systemic necrotizing vasculitis is an inflammation of the blood vessels. p-ANCA (perinuclear) is specific for myeloperoxidase, elastase, and lactoferrin, as well as other enzymes in neutrophils. p-ANCA is present in the sera of patients with pauci-immune necrotizing glomerulonephritis.

INDICATIONS
- Assist in the diagnosis of WG and its variants
- Differential diagnosis of ulcerative colitis
- Distinguish between biliary cirrhosis and sclerosing cholangitis
- Distinguish between vasculitic disease and the effects of therapy

POTENTIAL DIAGNOSIS

Increased in
The exact mechanism by which ANCA are developed is unknown. One theory suggests colonization with bacteria capable of expressing microbial superantigens. It is thought that the superantigens may stimulate a strong cellular autoimmune response in genetically susceptible individuals. Another theory suggests the immune system may be stimulated by an accumulation of the antigenic targets of ANCA due to ineffective destruction of old neutrophils or ineffective removal of neutrophil cell fragments containing proteinase, myeloperoxidase, elastase, lactoferrin, or other proteins.

- c-ANCA
  WG and its variants
- p-ANCA
  Alveolar hemorrhage
  Angiitis and polyangiitis
  Autoimmune liver disease
  Capillaritis
  Churg-Strauss syndrome
  Crescentic glomerulonephritis
  Felty's syndrome
  Glomerulonephritis
  Inflammatory bowel disease
  Kawasaki's disease
  Leukocytoclastic skin vasculitis
  Microscopic polyarteritis
  Rheumatoid arthritis
  Vasculitis

Decreased in: N/A

CRITICAL FINDINGS: N/A

INTERFERING FACTORS: N/A

NURSING IMPLICATIONS AND PROCEDURE

PRETEST:

- Positively identify the patient using at least two unique identifiers before providing care, treatment, or services.
- *Patient Teaching:* Inform the patient this test can assist in identifying the cause of inflammatory activity.
- Obtain a history of the patient's complaints, including a list of known allergens, especially allergies or sensitivities to latex.
- Obtain a history of the patient's gastrointestinal, genitourinary, hepatobiliary, immune, and musculoskeletal systems; symptoms; and results of previously performed laboratory tests and diagnostic and surgical procedures.
- Obtain a list of the patient's current medications, including herbs, nutritional supplements, and nutraceuticals (see Appendix F).
- Review the procedure with the patient. Inform the patient that specimen collection takes approximately 5 to 10 min. Address concerns about pain and explain that there may be some discomfort during the venipuncture.
- There are no food, fluid, or medication restrictions unless by medical direction.

INTRATEST:

- If the patient has a history of allergic reaction to latex, avoid the use of equipment containing latex.
- Instruct the patient to cooperate fully and to follow directions. Direct the patient to breathe normally and to avoid unnecessary movement.
- Observe standard precautions, and follow the general guidelines in Appendix A. Positively identify the patient, and label the appropriate specimen container with the corresponding patient demographics,

initials of the person collecting the specimen, date, and time of collection. Perform a venipuncture.
- Remove the needle and apply direct pressure with dry gauze to stop bleeding. Observe/assess venipuncture site for bleeding or hematoma formation and secure the gauze with adhesive bandage.
- Promptly transport the specimen to the laboratory for processing and analysis.

POST-TEST:

- A report of the results will be made available to the requesting health-care provider (HCP), who will discuss the results with the patient.
- Recognize anxiety related to test results, and be supportive of perceived loss of independence and fear of shortened life expectancy. Discuss the implications of abnormal test results on the patient's lifestyle. Provide teaching and information regarding the clinical implications of the test results, as appropriate. Educate the patient regarding access to counseling services.
- Reinforce information given by the patient's HCP regarding further testing, treatment, or referral to another HCP. Answer any questions or address any concerns voiced by the patient or family.
- Depending on the results of this procedure, additional testing may be performed to evaluate or monitor progression of the disease process and determine the need for a change in therapy. Evaluate test results in relation to the patient's symptoms and other tests performed.

RELATED MONOGRAPHS:

- Related tests include ALT, ALKP, antibodies anti-glomerular basement membrane, antibodies AMA/ASMA, antibodies ANA, AST, bilirubin and fractions, biopsy kidney, BUN, CBC, chest x-ray, creatinine, echocardiography, eosinophil count, ESR, MRA, RF, and UA.
- See the Gastrointestinal, Genitourinary, Hepatobiliary, Immune, and Musculoskeletal systems tables at the end of the book for related tests by body system.

Antibodies, Antinuclear, Anti-DNA, Anticentromere, Antiextractable Nuclear Antigen, Anti-Jo, and Antiscleroderma

SYNONYM/ACRONYM: Antinuclear antibodies (ANA), anti-DNA (anti-ds DNA), antiextractable nuclear antigens (anti-ENA, ribonucleoprotein [RNP], Smith [Sm], SS-A/Ro, SS-B/La), anti-Jo (antihistidyl transfer RNA [tRNA] synthase), and antiscleroderma (progressive systemic sclerosis [PSS] antibody, Scl-70 antibody, topoisomerase I antibody).

COMMON USE: To diagnose multiple systemic autoimmune disorders; primarily used for diagnosing systemic lupus erythematosus (SLE).

SPECIMEN: Serum (3 mL) collected in a red-top tube.

NORMAL FINDINGS: (Method: Indirect fluorescent antibody for ANA and anticentromere; Immunoassay multiplex flow for anti-DNA, ENA, Scl-70, and Jo-1).
ANA and anticentromere: Titer of 1:40 or less. Anti-ENA, Jo-1, and anti-Scl-70: Negative. Reference ranges for anti-DNA, anti-ENA, anti-Scl-70, and anti-Jo-1 vary widely due to differences in methods and the testing laboratory should be consulted directly.

Anti-DNA

Negative	Less than 5 international units
Indeterminate	5–9 international units
Positive	Greater than 9 international units

DESCRIPTION: Antinuclear antibodies (ANA) are autoantibodies mainly located in the nucleus of affected cells. The presence of ANA indicates SLE, related collagen vascular diseases, and immune complex diseases. Antibodies against cellular DNA are strongly associated with SLE. Anticentromere antibodies are a subset of ANA. Their presence is strongly associated with CREST syndrome (*c*alcinosis, *R*aynaud's phenomenon, *e*sophageal dysfunction, *s*clerodactyly, and *t*elangiectasia). Women are much more likely than men to be diagnosed with SLE. Jo-1 is an autoantibody found in the sera of some ANA-positive patients. Compared to the presence of other autoantibodies, the presence of Jo-1 suggests a more aggressive course and a higher risk of mortality. The clinical effects of this autoantibody include acute onset fever, dry and crackled skin on the hands, Raynaud's phenomenon, and arthritis. The extractable nuclear antigens (ENAs) include ribonucleoprotein (RNP), Smith (Sm), SS-A/Ro, and SS-B/La antigens. ENAs and antibodies to them are found in various combinations in individuals with combinations of overlapping rheumatologic symptoms. The American College of Rheumatology's current criteria includes a list of 11 signs and/or symptoms to assist in differentiating lupus from similar diseases. The patient should have four or more of these to establish suspicion of lupus; the symptoms do not have to manifest at the same time: malar rash (rash over the cheeks), discoid rash (red raised patches), photosensitivity (exposure resulting in development of or increase in skin rash), oral ulcers, nonerosive arthritis involving two or more peripheral joints, pleuritis or pericarditis, renal disorder (as evidenced by excessive protein in urine or the presence of casts in the urine), neurological disorder (seizures or psychosis in the absence of drugs known to cause these effects), hematological disorder (hemolytic anemia, leukopenia, lymphopenia, thrombocytopenia where the leukopenia or lymphopenia occurs on more than two occasions and the thrombocytopenia occurs in the absence of drugs known to cause it), positive ANA in the absence of a drug known to induce lupus, or immunological disorder (evidenced by positive anti-ds DNA, positive anti-Sm, positive antiphospholipid such as anticardiolipin antibody, positive lupus anticoagulant test, or a false-positive serological syphilis test, known to be positive for at least 6 months and confirmed to be falsely positive by a negative *Treponema pallidum* immobilization or FTA-ABS).

INDICATIONS
- Assist in the diagnosis and evaluation of SLE
- Assist in the diagnosis and evaluation of suspected immune disorders, such as rheumatoid arthritis, systemic sclerosis, polymyositis, Raynaud's syndrome, scleroderma, Sjögren's syndrome, and mixed connective tissue disease
- Assist in the diagnosis and evaluation of idiopathic inflammatory myopathies

POTENTIAL DIAGNOSIS

ANA Pattern*	Associated Antibody	Associated Condition
Rim and/or homogeneous	Double-stranded DNA	SLE
	Single- or double-stranded DNA	
Homogeneous	Histones	SLE
Speckled	Sm (Smith) antibody	SLE, mixed connective tissue disease, Raynaud's scleroderma, Sjögren's syndrome
	RNP*	Mixed connective tissue disease, various rheumatoid conditions
	SS-B/La, SS-A/Ro	Various rheumatoid conditions

A

ANA Pattern*	Associated Antibody	Associated Condition
Diffuse speckled with positive mitotic figures	Centromere	PSS with CREST, Raynaud's
Nucleolar	Nucleolar, RNP	Scleroderma, CREST

*ANA patterns are helpful in that certain conditions are frequently associated with specific patterns. RNP = ribonucleoprotein.

Increased in
- Anti-Jo-1 *is associated with dermatomyositis, idiopathic inflammatory myopathies, and polymyositis*
- ANA *is associated with drug-induced lupus erythematosus*
- ANA *is associated with lupoid hepatitis*
- ANA *is associated with mixed connective tissue disease*
- ANA *is associated with polymyositis*
- ANA *is associated with progressive systemic sclerosis*
- ANA *is associated with Raynaud's syndrome*
- ANA *is associated with rheumatoid arthritis*
- ANA *is associated with Sjögren's syndrome*
- ANA and anti-DNA *are associated with SLE*
- Anti-RNP *is associated with mixed connective tissue disease*
- Anti-Scl 70 *is associated with progressive systemic sclerosis and scleroderma*
- Anti-SS-A and anti-SS-B *are helpful in antinuclear antibody (ANA)–negative cases of SLE*
- Anti-SS-A/ANA–positive, anti-SS-B–negative patients *are likely to have nephritis*
- Anti-SS-A/anti-SS-B–positive sera *are found in patients with neonatal lupus*
- Anti-SS-A–positive patients *may also have antibodies associated with antiphospholipid syndrome*
- Anti-SS-A/La *is associated with primary Sjögren's syndrome*
- Anti-SS-A/Ro *is a predictor of congenital heart block in neonates born to mothers with SLE*
- Anti-SS-A/Ro–positive patients *have photosensitivity*

Decreased in: N/A

CRITICAL FINDINGS: N/A

INTERFERING FACTORS
- Drugs that may cause positive ANA results include acebutolol (diabetics), anticonvulsants (increases with concomitant administration of multiple antiepileptic drugs), carbamazepine, chlorpromazine, ethosuximide, hydralazine, isoniazid, methyldopa, oxyphenisatin, penicillins, phenytoin, primidone, procainamide, quinidine, and trimethadione.
- A patient can have lupus and test ANA-negative.
- Inability of the patient to cooperate or remain still during the procedure because of age, significant pain, or mental status may interfere with the test results.

NURSING IMPLICATIONS AND PROCEDURE

PRETEST:
Positively identify the patient using at least two unique identifiers before providing care, treatment, or services.
Patient Teaching: Inform the patient this test can assist in evaluating immune system function.

- Obtain a history of the patient's complaints, including a list of known allergens, especially allergies or sensitivities to latex.
- Obtain a history of the patient's immune and musculoskeletal systems, symptoms, and results of previously performed laboratory tests and diagnostic and surgical procedures.
- Obtain a list of the patient's current medications, including herbs, nutritional supplements, and nutraceuticals (see Appendix F). Review the procedure with the patient. Inform the patient that specimen collection takes approximately 5 to 10 min. Address concerns about pain and explain that there may be some discomfort during the venipuncture. *Sensitivity to social and cultural issues,* as well as concern for modesty, is important in providing psychological support before, during, and after the procedure.
- There are no food, fluid, or medication restrictions unless by medical direction.

INTRATEST:

If the patient has a history of allergic reaction to latex, avoid the use of equipment containing latex.

Instruct the patient to cooperate fully and to follow directions. Direct the patient to breathe normally and to avoid unnecessary movement.

Observe standard precautions, and follow the general guidelines in Appendix A. Positively identify the patient, and label the appropriate specimen container with the corresponding patient demographics, initials of the person collecting the specimen, date, and time of collection. Perform a venipuncture.

Remove the needle and apply direct pressure with dry gauze to stop bleeding. Observe/assess venipuncture site for bleeding or hematoma formation and secure gauze with adhesive bandage.

Promptly transport the specimen to the laboratory for processing and analysis.

POST-TEST:

A report of the results will be made available to the requesting health-care provider (HCP), who will discuss the results with the patient.

- Recognize anxiety related to test results, and be supportive of perceived loss of independence and fear of shortened life expectancy. Collagen and connective tissue diseases are chronic and, as such, they must be addressed on a continuous basis. Discuss the implications of abnormal test results on the patient's lifestyle. Provide teaching and information regarding the clinical implications of the test results, as appropriate. Educate the patient regarding access to counseling services. Provide contact information, if desired, for the American College of Rheumatology (www.rheumatology.org), the Lupus Foundation of America (www.lupus .org), or the Arthritis Foundation (www.arthritis.org).
- Educate the patient, as appropriate, regarding the importance of preventing infection, which is a significant cause of death in immunosuppressed individuals.
- Reinforce information given by the patient's HCP regarding further testing, treatment, or referral to another HCP. Answer any questions or address any concerns voiced by the patient or family.
- Depending on the results of this procedure, additional testing may be performed to evaluate or monitor progression of the disease process and determine the need for a change in therapy. Evaluate test results in relation to the patient's symptoms and other tests performed.

RELATED MONOGRAPHS:

- Related tests include antibodies anticyclic citrullinated peptide, arthroscopy, biopsy kidney, biopsy skin, BMD, bone scan, chest x-ray, complement C3 and C4, complement total, CRP, ESR, EMG, MRI musculoskeletal, procainamide, radiography bone, RF, and synovial fluid analysis.
- See the Immune and Musculoskeletal systems tables at the end of the book for related tests by body system.

A

Antibodies, Antisperm

SYNONYM/ACRONYM: Infertility screen.

COMMON USE: To evaluate testicular fertility and identify causes of infertility such as congenital defects, cancer, and torsion.

SPECIMEN: Serum (1 mL) collected in a red-top tube.

NORMAL FINDINGS: (Method: Immunoassay)

Result	Sperm Bound by Immunobead (%)
Negative	0–15
Weak positive	16–30
Moderate positive	31–50
Strong positive	51–100

DESCRIPTION: Normally sperm develop in the seminiferous tubules of the testes separated from circulating blood by the blood-testes barrier. Any situation that disrupts this barrier can expose sperm to detection by immune response cells in the blood and subsequent antibody formation against the sperm. Antisperm antibodies attach to the head, midpiece, or tail of the sperm, impairing motility and ability to penetrate the cervical mucosa. The antibodies can also cause clumping of sperm, which may be noted on a semen analysis. A major cause of infertility in men is blocked efferent testicular ducts. Reabsorption of sperm from the blocked ducts may also result in development of sperm antibodies. Another more specific and sophisticated method than measurement of circulating antibodies is the immunobead sperm antibody test used to identify antibodies directly attached to the sperm. Semen and cervical mucus can also be tested for antisperm antibodies.

INDICATIONS
• Evaluation of infertility

POTENTIAL DIAGNOSIS

Increased in
Conditions that affect the integrity of the blood-testes barrier can result in antibody formation.
• Blocked testicular efferent duct *(related to absorption of sperm by blocked vas deferens)*
• Congenital absence of the vas deferens *(related to absorption of sperm by blocked vas deferens)*
• Cryptorchidism *(related to disruption in the integrity of the blood-testes barrier)*
• Infection (orchitis, prostatitis) *(related to disruption in the integrity of the blood-testes barrier)*
• Inguinal hernia repair prior to puberty *(related to disruption in the integrity of the blood-testes barrier)*
• Testicular biopsy *(related to disruption in the integrity of the blood-testes barrier)*

- Testicular cancer *(related to disruption in the integrity of the blood-testes barrier)*
- Testicular torsion *(related to disruption in the integrity of the blood-testes barrier)*
- Varicocele *(related to disruption in the integrity of the blood-testes barrier)*
- Vasectomy *(related to absorption of sperm by blocked vas deferens)*
- Vasectomy reversal *(related to interaction between sperm and autoantibodies developed after vasectomy)*

Decreased in: N/A

CRITICAL FINDINGS: N/A

INTERFERING FACTORS

The patient should not ejaculate for 3 to 4 days before specimen collection if semen will be evaluated.

Sperm antibodies have been detected in pregnant women and in women with primary infertility.

NURSING IMPLICATIONS AND PROCEDURE

PRETEST:

Positively identify the patient using at least two unique identifiers before providing care, treatment, or services.

Patient Teaching: Inform the patient this test can assist in the evaluation of infertility and provide guidance through assistive reproductive techniques.

Obtain a history of the patient's complaints, including a list of known allergens, especially allergies or sensitivities to latex.

Obtain a history of the patient's reproductive system, symptoms, and results of previously performed laboratory

tests and diagnostic and surgical procedures.

Obtain a list of the patient's current medications, including herbs, nutritional supplements, and nutraceuticals (see Appendix F).

Review the procedure with the patient. Inform the patient that specimen collection takes approximately 5 to 10 min and that additional specimens may be required. Address concerns about pain and explain that there may be some discomfort during the venipuncture.

Sensitivity to social and cultural issues, as well as concern for modesty, is important in providing psychological support before, during, and after the procedure.

There are no food, fluid, or medication restrictions unless by medical direction.

INTRATEST:

If the patient has a history of allergic reaction to latex, avoid the use of equipment containing latex.

Instruct the patient to cooperate fully and to follow directions. Direct the patient to breathe normally and to avoid unnecessary movement.

Observe standard precautions, and follow the general guidelines in Appendix A. Positively identify the patient, and label the appropriate specimen container with the corresponding patient demographics, initials of the person collecting the specimen, date, and time of collection. Perform a venipuncture.

Remove the needle and apply direct pressure with dry gauze to stop bleeding. Observe/assess venipuncture site for bleeding or hematoma formation and secure gauze with adhesive bandage.

Promptly transport the specimen to the laboratory for processing and analysis.

POST-TEST:

A report of the results will be made available to the requesting health-care provider (HCP), who will discuss the results with the patient.

Recognize anxiety related to test results. Discuss the implications of abnormal test results on the patient's lifestyle. Educate the patient regarding access to counseling services. Provide a supportive, nonjudgmental environment when assisting a patient through the process of fertility testing. Educate the patient regarding access to counseling services, as appropriate.

Reinforce information given by the patient's HCP regarding further testing, treatment, or referral to another HCP. Answer any questions or address any concerns voiced by the patient or family.

Depending on the results of this procedure, additional testing may be performed to evaluate or monitor progression of the disease process and determine the need for a change in therapy. Evaluate test results in relation to the patient's symptoms and other tests performed.

RELATED MONOGRAPHS:

Related tests include HCG, LH, progesterone, semen analysis, testosterone, and US scrotal.

See the Reproductive System tables at the end of the book for related tests by body system.

Antibodies, Antistreptolysin *O*

SYNONYM/ACRONYM: Streptozyme, ASO.

COMMON USE: To assist in the diagnosis of streptococcal infection.

SPECIMEN: Serum (1 mL) collected in a red-top tube.

NORMAL FINDINGS: (Method: Immunoturbidimetric) Adult/older adult: Less than 200 international units/mL; 17 yr and younger: Less than 150 international units/mL

DESCRIPTION: Group A β-hemolytic streptococci secrete the enzyme streptolysin *O*, which can destroy red blood cells. The enzyme acts as an antigen and stimulates the immune system to develop streptolysin *O* antibodies. These antistreptolysin *O* (ASO) antibodies occur within 1 wk after the onset of a streptococcal infection and peak 2 to 3 wk later. Detection of the antibody over several weeks strongly suggests exposure to group A β-hemolytic streptococci. The ASO titer usually returns to preinfection levels within 6 to 12 mo, assuming reinfection has not occurred.

Up to 95% of patients with acute glomerulonephritis and up to 85% of patients with rheumatic fever demonstrate a rise in titer. ASO titer may not become elevated in some patients who experience sequelae involving the skin or kidneys, and the antideoxyribonuclease-B, streptococcal test may a better test for these patients.

INDICATIONS

• Assist in establishing a diagnosis of streptococcal infection
• Evaluate patients with streptococcal infections for the development

of acute rheumatic fever or nephritis
• Monitor response to therapy in streptococcal illnesses

POTENTIAL DIAGNOSIS

Increased in
Presence of antibodies, especially a rise in titer, is indicative of exposure.
• Endocarditis
• Glomerulonephritis
• Rheumatic fever
• Scarlet fever

Decreased in: N/A

CRITICAL FINDINGS: N/A

INTERFERING FACTORS
• Drugs that may decrease ASO titers include antibiotics and corticosteroids because therapy suppresses antibody response.
• False-positive ASO titers can be caused by elevated levels of serum β-lipoprotein (observed in liver disease)

NURSING IMPLICATIONS AND PROCEDURE

PRETEST:
▸ Positively identify the patient using at least two unique identifiers before providing care, treatment, or services.
▸ *Patient Teaching:* Inform the patient this test can assist in documenting exposure to streptococcal bacteria.
▸ Obtain a history of the patient's complaints, including a list of known allergens, especially allergies or sensitivities to latex.
▸ Obtain a history of the patient's immune system, symptoms, and results of previously performed laboratory tests and diagnostic and surgical procedures.
▸ Obtain a list of the patient's current medications, including herbs, nutritional supplements, and nutraceuticals (see Appendix F).
▸ Review the procedure with the patient. Inform the patient that specimen collection takes approximately 5 to 10 min. Address concerns about pain and explain that there may be some discomfort during the venipuncture.
▸ Sensitivity to social and cultural issues, as well as concern for modesty, is important in providing psychological support before, during, and after the procedure.
▸ There are no food, fluid, or medication restrictions unless by medical direction.

INTRATEST:
▸ If the patient has a history of allergic reaction to latex, avoid the use of equipment containing latex.
▸ Instruct the patient to cooperate fully and to follow directions. Direct the patient to breathe normally and to avoid unnecessary movement.
▸ Observe standard precautions, and follow the general guidelines in Appendix A. Positively identify the patient, and label the appropriate specimen container with the corresponding patient demographics, initials of the person collecting the specimen, date, and time of collection. Perform a venipuncture.
▸ Remove the needle and apply direct pressure with dry gauze to stop bleeding. Observe/assess venipuncture site for bleeding or hematoma formation and secure gauze with adhesive bandage.
▸ Promptly transport the specimen to the laboratory for processing and analysis.

POST-TEST:
▸ A report of the results will be made available to the requesting health-care provider (HCP), who will discuss the results with the patient.
▸ Administer antibiotics as ordered. Remind the patient of the importance of completing the entire course of antibiotic therapy even if signs and symptoms disappear before completion of therapy.
▸ Reinforce information given by the patient's HCP regarding further testing,

A

treatment, or referral to another HCP. Answer any questions or address any concerns voiced by the patient or family.

▶ Depending on the results of this procedure, additional testing may be performed to evaluate or monitor progression of the disease process and determine the need for a change in therapy. Evaluate test results in relation to the patient's symptoms and other tests performed.

RELATED MONOGRAPHS:

▶ Related tests include culture throat, group A streptococcal screen, and antideoxyribonuclease-B streptococcal.
▶ See the Immune System table at the end of the book for related tests by body system.

Antibodies, Antithyroglobulin, and Antithyroid Peroxidase

SYNONYM/ACRONYM: Thyroid antibodies, antithyroid peroxidase antibodies (thyroid peroxidase [TPO] antibodies were previously called thyroid antimicrosomal antibodies).

COMMON USE: To assist in diagnosing hypothyroid and hyperthyroid disease.

SPECIMEN: Serum (1 mL) collected in a red-top tube.

NORMAL FINDINGS: (Method: Immunoassay)

Antibody	Conventional Units
Antithyroglobulin antibody	Less than 20 international units/mL
Antiperoxidase antibody	
Newborn–3 days	0–9 international units/mL
4–30 days	0–26 international units/mL
1–12 mo	0–13 international units/mL
13 mo–19 yr	0–20 international units/mL
20 yr–older adult	0–34 international units/mL

DESCRIPTION: Thyroid antibodies are mainly immunoglobulin G–type antibodies. Antithyroid peroxidase antibodies (anti-TPO antibodies) bind with microsomal antigens on cells lining the microsomal membrane of thyroid tissue. They are thought to destroy thyroid tissue as a result of stimulation by lymphocytic killer cells. These antibodies are present in hypothyroid and hyperthyroid conditions.

Anti-TPO antibodies are present in Hashimoto's autoimmune thyroiditis, a major cause of hypothyroidism. Hypothyroidism in women of childbearing age is a significant concern because of the deleterious effects of insufficient thyroxine levels on fetal brain development. Anti-TPO antibodies are also demonstrable in Graves' disease, a major cause of hyperthyroidism. Graves' disease is the most common type of thyrotoxicosis in women of childbearing age, impairing fertility and increasing risk of miscarriage to 26%. Transplacental passage of anti-TPO antibodies in pregnant patients may affect the developing fetus or lead to thyroid disease in the neonate. Mild depression is more common in postpartum women with anti-TPO antibodies. Antithyroglobulin antibodies are autoantibodies directed against thyroglobulin. The function of these antibodies is unclear. Both tests are normally requested together.

INDICATIONS

- Assist in confirming suspected inflammation of thyroid gland
- Assist in the diagnosis of suspected hypothyroidism caused by thyroid tissue destruction
- Assist in the diagnosis of suspected thyroid autoimmunity in patients with other autoimmune disorders

POTENTIAL DIAGNOSIS

Increased in
The presence of these antibodies differentiates the autoimmune origin of these disorders from non-autoimmune causes, which may influence treatment decisions.

- Autoimmune disorders
- Graves' disease
- Goiter
- Hashimoto's thyroiditis
- Idiopathic myxedema
- Pernicious anemia
- Thyroid carcinoma

Decreased in: N/A

CRITICAL FINDINGS: N/A

INTERFERING FACTORS

- Lithium may increase thyroid antibody levels.

NURSING IMPLICATIONS AND PROCEDURE

PRETEST:
- Positively identify the patient using at least two unique identifiers before providing care, treatment, or services.
- *Patient Teaching:* Inform the patient this test can assist in evaluating thyroid gland function.
- Obtain a history of the patient's complaints, including a list of known allergens, especially allergies or sensitivities to latex.
- Obtain a history of the patient's endocrine and immune systems, symptoms, and results of previously performed laboratory tests and diagnostic and surgical procedures.
- Obtain a list of the patient's current medications, including herbs, nutritional supplements, and nutraceuticals (see Appendix F).
- Note any recent procedures that can interfere with test results.
- Review the procedure with the patient. Inform the patient that specimen collection takes approximately 5 to 10 min. Address concerns about pain and explain that there may be some discomfort during the venipuncture.
- There are no food, fluid, or medication restrictions unless by medical direction.

INTRATEST:
- If the patient has a history of allergic reaction to latex, avoid the use of equipment containing latex.
- Instruct the patient to cooperate fully and to follow directions. Direct the patient to breathe normally and to avoid unnecessary movement.
- Observe standard precautions, and follow the general guidelines in Appendix A. Positively identify the patient, and label the appropriate specimen container with the corresponding patient demographics, initials of the person collecting the specimen, date, and time of collection. Perform a venipuncture.
- Remove the needle and apply direct pressure with dry gauze to stop bleeding. Observe/assess venipuncture site for bleeding or hematoma

A

formation and secure gauze with adhesive bandage.
Promptly transport the specimen to the laboratory for processing and analysis.

POST-TEST:

A report of the results will be made available to the requesting health-care provider (HCP), who will discuss the results with the patient.
Reinforce information given by the patient's HCP regarding further testing, treatment, or referral to another HCP. Answer any questions or address any concerns voiced by the patient or family.

Depending on the results of this procedure, additional testing may be performed to evaluate or monitor progression of the disease process and determine the need for a change in therapy. Evaluate test results in relation to the patient's symptoms and other tests performed.

RELATED MONOGRAPHS:

Related tests include biopsy thyroid, CBC, FT_3, FT_4, RAIU, T4, thyroid scan, thyroglobulin, TSH, TT3, and US thyroid.
See the Endocrine and Immune systems tables at the end of the book for related tests by body system.

Antibodies, Cardiolipin, Immunoglobulin A, Immunoglobulin G, and Immunoglobulin M

SYNONYM/ACRONYM: Antiphospholipid antibody, lupus anticoagulant, LA, ACA.

COMMON USE: To detect the presence of antiphospholipid antibodies, which can lead to the development of blood vessel problems and complications including stroke, heart attack, and miscarriage.

SPECIMEN: Serum (1 mL) collected in a red-top tube.

NORMAL FINDINGS: (Method: Immunoassay, enzyme-linked immunosorbent assay [ELIS])

IgA (APL = 1 unit IgA phospholipid)	IgG (GPL = 1 unit IgG phospholipid)	IgM (MPL = 1 unit IgM phospholipid)
Negative: 0–11 APL	Negative: 0–14 GPL	Negative: 0–12 MPL
Indeterminate: 12–19 APL	Indeterminate: 15–19 GPL	Indeterminate: 13–19 MPL
Low-medium positive: 20–80 APL	Low-medium positive: 20–80 GPL	Low-medium positive: 20–80 MPL
Positive: Greater than 80 APL	Positive: Greater than 80 GPL	Greater than 80 MPL

DESCRIPTION: Anticardiolipin (ACA) is one of several identified antiphospholipid antibodies. ACAs are of IgG, IgM, and IgA subtypes, which react with proteins in the

blood that are bound to phospholipid and interfere with normal blood vessel function. The two primary types of problems they cause are narrowing and

A

irregularity of the blood vessels and blood clots in the blood vessels. ACAs are found in individuals with lupus erythematosus, lupus-related conditions, infectious diseases, drug reactions, and sometimes fetal loss. ACAs are often found in association with lupus anticoagulant. Increased antiphospholipid antibody levels have been found in pregnant women with lupus who have had miscarriages. β_2 Glycoprotein 1, or apolipoprotein H, is an important facilitator in the binding of antiphospholipid antibodies like ACA. A normal level of β_2 glycoprotein 1 is 19 units or less when measured by ELISA assays. β_2Glycoprotein 1 measurements are considered to be more specific than ACA because they do not demonstrate nonspecific reactivity as do ACA in sera of patients with syphilis or other infectious diseases. The combination of noninflammatory thrombosis of blood vessels, low platelet count, and history of miscarriage is termed *antiphospholipid antibody syndrome* and is documented as present if at least one of the clinical and one of the laboratory criteria are met.

CLINICAL CRITERIA
- Vascular thrombosis confirmed by histopathology or imaging studies
- Pregnancy morbidity defined as either one or more unexplained deaths of a morphologically normal fetus at or beyond the 10th week of gestation
- One or more premature births of a morphologically normal neonate before the 34th week of gestation due to eclampsia or severe pre-eclampsia
- Three or more unexplained consecutive spontaneous abortions before the 10th week of gestation

LABORATORY CRITERIA (all measured by a standardized ELISA, according to recommended procedures)
- ACA IgG, or IgM, detectable at greater than 40 units on two or more occasions at least 12 wk apart
- Lupus anticoagulant (LA) detectable on two or more occasions at least 12 wk apart
- Anti-$\beta_2$glycoprotein 1 antibody, IgG, or IgM detectable on two or more occasions at least 12 wk apart

INDICATIONS
- Assist in the diagnosis of antiphospholipid antibody syndrome

POTENTIAL DIAGNOSIS

Increased in
While ACAs are observed in specific diseases, the exact mechanism of these antibodies in disease is unclear. In fact, the production of ACA can be induced by bacterial, treponemal, and viral infections. Development of ACA under this circumstance is transient and not associated with an increased risk of antiphospholipid antibody syndrome. Patients who initially demonstrate positive ACA levels should be retested after 6 to 8 wk to rule out transient antibodies that are usually of no clinical significance.

- Antiphospholipid antibody syndrome
- Chorea
- Drug reactions
- Epilepsy
- Infectious diseases
- Mitral valve endocarditis
- Patients with lupuslike symptoms (often antinuclear antibody–negative)
- Placental infarction
- Recurrent fetal loss (strong association with two or more occurrences)
- Recurrent venous and arterial thromboses
- SLE

Decreased in: N/A

CRITICAL FINDINGS: N/A

INTERFERING FACTORS
- Drugs that may increase anticardiolipin antibody levels include chlorpromazine, penicillin, procainamide, phenytoin, and quinidine.
- Cardiolipin antibody is partially cross-reactive with syphilis reagin antibody and lupus anticoagulant. False-positive rapid plasma reagin results may occur.

NURSING IMPLICATIONS AND PROCEDURE

PRETEST:
▶ Positively identify the patient using at least two unique identifiers before providing care, treatment, or services.
▶ *Patient Teaching:* Inform the patient this test can assist in evaluating the amount of potentially harmful circulating antibodies.
▶ Obtain a history of the patient's complaints, including a list of known allergens, especially allergies or sensitivities to latex.
▶ Obtain a history of the patient's hematopoietic, immune, and reproductive systems; symptoms; and results of previously performed laboratory tests and diagnostic and surgical procedures.
▶ Obtain a list of the patient's current medications, including herbs, nutritional supplements, and nutraceuticals (see Appendix F).
▶ Review the procedure with the patient. Inform the patient that specimen collection takes approximately 5 to 10 min. Address concerns about pain and explain that there may be some discomfort during the venipuncture.
▶ *Sensitivity to social and cultural issues,* as well as concern for modesty, is important in providing psychological support before, during, and after the procedure.

▶ There are no food, fluid, or medication restrictions unless by medical direction.

INTRATEST:
▶ If the patient has a history of allergic reaction to latex, avoid the use of equipment containing latex.
▶ Instruct the patient to cooperate fully and to follow directions. Direct the patient to breathe normally and to avoid unnecessary movement.
▶ Observe standard precautions, and follow the general guidelines in Appendix A. Positively identify the patient, and label the appropriate specimen container with the corresponding patient demographics, initials of the person collecting the specimen, date, and time of collection. Perform a venipuncture. Remove the needle and apply direct pressure with dry gauze to stop bleeding. Observe/assess venipuncture site for bleeding or hematoma formation and secure gauze with adhesive bandage.
▶ Promptly transport the specimen to the laboratory for processing and analysis.

POST-TEST:
▶ A report of the results will be made available to the requesting health-care provider (HCP), who will discuss the results with the patient.
▶ Recognize anxiety related to test results, and be supportive of fear of shortened life expectancy. Discuss the implications of abnormal test results on the patient's lifestyle. Provide teaching and information regarding the clinical implications of the test results, as appropriate. Educate the patient regarding access to counseling services. Provide contact information, if desired, for the Lupus Foundation of America (www.lupus.org).
▶ Reinforce information given by the patient's HCP regarding further testing, treatment, or referral to another HCP. Answer any questions or address any concerns voiced by the patient or family.

Depending on the results of this procedure, additional testing may be performed to evaluate or monitor progression of the disease process and determine the need for a change in therapy. Evaluate test results in relation to the patient's symptoms and other tests performed.

RELATED MONOGRAPHS:

Related tests include ANA, CBC, CBC platelet count, fibrinogen, lupus anticoagulant antibodies, protein C, protein S, and syphilis serology.

See the Hematopoietic, Immune, and Reproductive systems tables at the end of the book for related tests by body system.

Antibodies, Gliadin (Immunoglobulin G and Immunoglobulin A), Endomysial (Immunoglobulin A), Tissue Transglutaminase (Immunoglobulin A)

SYNONYM/ACRONYM: Endomysial antibodies (EMA), gliadin (IgG and IgA) antibodies, tTG.

COMMON USE: To assist in the diagnosis and monitoring of gluten-sensitive enteropathies that may damage intestinal mucosa.

SPECIMEN: Serum (1 mL) collected in a red-top tube.

NORMAL FINDINGS: (Method: Enzyme linked immunosorbent assay [ELISA] for gliadin antibody and tissue transglutaminase antibody; indirect immunofluorescence for endomysial antibodies)

IgA and IgG Gliadin Antibody	Conventional Units
Age	
0–2 yr	Less than 20 units/mL
2 yr–adult	Less than 25 units/mL
Tissue transglutaminase antibody	Negative
Endomysial antibodies	Negative

DESCRIPTION: Gliadin is a water-soluble protein found in the gluten of wheat, rye, oats, and barley. The intestinal mucosa of certain individuals does not digest gluten, allowing a toxic buildup of gliadin and intestinal inflammation. The inflammatory response interferes with intestinal absorption of nutrients and damages the intestinal mucosa. In severe cases, intestinal mucosa can be lost. Immunoglobulin G (IgG) and immunoglobulin A (IgA) gliadin antibodies are detectable in the serum of patients with gluten-sensitive enteropathy.

A

Endomysial antibodies and tissue transglutaminase (tTG) antibody are two other serological tests commonly used to investigate gluten-sensitive enteropathies. Gliadin IgA tests are the most sensitive for celiac disease (CD). However, it is also recognized that a significant percentage of patients with CD are also IgA deficient, meaning false-negative IgA results may be misleading in some cases. Estimates of up to 98% of individuals susceptible to CD carry either the DQ2 or DQ8 HLA cell surface receptors, which initiate formation of antibodies to gliadin. While it appears there is a strong association between CD and these gene markers, up to 40% of individuals without CD also carry the DQ2 or DQ8 markers. Molecular testing is available to establish the absence or presence of these susceptibility markers. CD is an inherited condition with significant impact on quality of life for the affected individual. The use of serological markers is useful in disease monitoring because research has established a relationship between amount of gluten in the diet and degree of intestinal damage as reflected by the level of detectable antibodies. CD shares an association with a number of other conditions such as type 1 diabetes, Down's syndrome, and Turner's syndrome.

INDICATIONS
- Assist in the diagnosis of asymptomatic gluten-sensitive enteropathy in some patients with dermatitis herpetiformis
- Assist in the diagnosis of gluten-sensitive enteropathies
- Assist in the diagnosis of nontropical sprue
- Monitor dietary compliance of patients with gluten-sensitive enteropathies

POTENTIAL DIAGNOSIS

Increased in
Evidenced by the combination of detectable gliadin or endomysial antibodies and improvement with a gluten-free diet.
- Asymptomatic gluten-sensitive enteropathy
- Celiac disease
- Dermatitis herpetiformis *(etiology of this skin manifestation is unknown, but there is an association related to gluten-sensitive enteropathy)*
- Nontropical sprue

Decreased in
- IgA deficiency *(related to an inability to produce IgA and evidenced by decreased IgA levels and false-negative IgA gliadin tests)*
- Children under the age of 18 mo *(related to immature immune system and low production of IgA)*

CRITICAL FINDINGS: N/A

INTERFERING FACTORS
- Conditions other than gluten-sensitive enteropathy can result in elevated antibody levels without corresponding histological evidence. These conditions include Crohn's disease, postinfection malabsorption, and food protein intolerance.
- A negative IgA gliadin result, especially with a positive IgG gliadin result in an untreated patient, does not rule out active gluten-sensitive enteropathy.

NURSING IMPLICATIONS AND PROCEDURE

PRETEST:

‣ Positively identify the patient using at least two unique identifiers before providing care, treatment, or services.

‣ *Patient Teaching:* Inform the patient this test can assist with evaluating the ability to digest gluten foods such as wheat, rye, and oats.

‣ Obtain a history of the patient's complaints, including a list of known allergens, especially allergies or sensitivities to latex.

‣ Obtain a history of the patient's gastrointestinal and immune systems, symptoms, and results of previously performed laboratory tests and diagnostic and surgical procedures.

‣ Obtain a list of foods and the patient's current medications, including herbs, nutritional supplements, and nutraceuticals (see Appendix F).

‣ Review the procedure with the patient. Inform the patient that specimen collection takes approximately 5 to 10 min. Address concerns about pain and explain that there may be some discomfort during the venipuncture.

‣ *Sensitivity to social and cultural issues,* as well as concern for modesty, is important in providing psychological support before, during, and after the procedure.

‣ There are no food, fluid, or medication restrictions unless by medical direction.

INTRATEST:

‣ If the patient has a history of allergic reaction to latex, avoid the use of equipment containing latex.

‣ Instruct the patient to cooperate fully and to follow directions.

‣ Direct the patient to breathe normally and to avoid unnecessary movement.

‣ Observe standard precautions, and follow the general guidelines

in Appendix A. Positively identify the patient, and label the appropriate specimen container with the corresponding patient demographics, initials of the person collecting the specimen, date, and time of collection. Perform a venipuncture.

‣ Remove the needle and apply direct pressure with dry gauze to stop bleeding. Observe/assess venipuncture site for bleeding or hematoma formation and secure gauze with adhesive bandage.

‣ Promptly transport the specimen to the laboratory for processing and analysis.

POST-TEST:

‣ A report of the results will be made available to the requesting health-care provider (HCP), who will discuss the results with the patient.

‣ *Nutritional Considerations:* Encourage the patient with abnormal findings to consult with a qualified nutritionist to plan a gluten-free diet. This dietary planning is complex because patients are often malnourished and have other related nutritional problems.

‣ Recognize anxiety related to test results, and offer support. Discuss the implications of abnormal test results on the patient's lifestyle. Provide teaching and information regarding the clinical implications of the test results, as appropriate. Educate the patient regarding access to appropriate counseling services. Provide contact information, if desired, for the Celiac Disease Foundation (www.celiac.org) or Children's Digestive Health and Nutrition Foundation (www.cdhnf.org).

‣ Reinforce information given by the patient's HCP regarding further testing, treatment, or referral to another HCP. Answer any questions or address any concerns voiced by the patient or family.

‣ Depending on the results of this procedure, additional testing may be performed to evaluate or monitor

A

progression of the disease process and determine the need for a change in therapy. Evaluate test results in relation to the patient's symptoms and other tests performed.

RELATED MONOGRAPHS:

Related tests include albumin, biopsy intestine, biopsy skin, calcium, capsule endoscopy, colonoscopy, D-xylose tolerance test, electrolytes, fecal analysis, fecal fat, folic acid, immunoglobulins (IgA), iron, and lactose tolerance test.

See the Gastrointestinal and Immune systems tables at the end of the book for related tests by body system.

Anticonvulsant Drugs: Carbamazepine, Ethosuximide, Lamotrigine, Phenobarbital, Phenytoin, Primidone, Valproic Acid

SYNONYM/ACRONYM: *Carbamazepine* (Carbamazepinum, Carbategretal, Carbatrol, Carbazep, CBZ, Epitol, Tegretol, Tegretol XR); *ethosuximide* (Suxinutin, Zarontin, Zartalin); *lamotrigine* (Lamictal) *phenobarbital* (Barbita, Comizial, Fenilcal, Gardenal, Phenemal, Phenemalum, Phenobarb, Phenobarbitone, Phenylethylmalonylurea, Solfoton, Stental Extentabs); *phenytoin* (Antisacer, Dilantin, Dintoina, Diphenylan Sodium, Diphenylhydantion, Ditan, Epanutin, Epinat, Fenitoina, Fenytoin, Fosphenytoin); *primidone* (Desoxyphenobarbital, Hexamidinum, Majsolin, Mylepsin, Mysoline, Primaclone, Prysolin); *valproic acid* (Depacon, Depakene, Depakote, Depakote XR, Depamide, Dipropylacetic Acid, Divalproex Sodium, Epilim, Ergenyl, Leptilan, 2–Propylpentanoic Acid, 2–Propylvaleric Acid, Valkote, Valproate Semisodium, Valproate Sodium).

COMMON USE: To monitor specific drugs for subtherapeutic, therapeutic, or toxic levels in evaluation of treatment.

SPECIMEN: Serum (1 mL) collected in a red-top tube.

Drug*	Route of Administration
Carbamazepine	Oral
Ethosuximide	Oral
Lamotrigine	Oral
Phenobarbital	Oral
Phenytoin	Oral
Primidone	Oral
Valproic Acid	Oral

*Recommended collection time = trough: immediately before next dose (at steady state) or at a consistent sampling time.

NORMAL FINDINGS: (Method: Immunoassay for all except lamotrigine; liquid chromatography/tandem mass spectrometry for lamotrigine)

Drug	Therapeutic Range*	SI Units	Half-Life (hr)	Volume of Distribution (L/kg)	Protein Binding (%)	Excretion
(SI = Conventional Units × 4.23)						
Carbamazepine	4–12 mcg/mL	17–51 micromol/L	15–40	0.8–1.8	60–80	Hepatic
(SI = Conventional Units × 7.08)						
Ethosuximide	40–100 mcg/mL	283–708 micromol/L	25–70	0.7	0–5	Renal
(SI = Conventional Units × 3.905)						
Lamotrigine	1–4 mcg/mL**	4–16 micromol/L	25–33	0.9–1.3	50–5	Hepatic
(SI = Conventional Units × 4.31)						
Phenobarbital	Adult: 15–40 mcg/mL	Adult: 65–172 micromol/L	Adult: 50–140	0.5–1	40–50	80% Hepatic
	Child: 15–30 mcg/mL	Child: 65–129 micromol/L	Child: 40–70			20% Renal
(SI = Conventional Units × 3.96)						
Phenytoin	10–20 mcg/mL	40–79 micromol/L	20–40	0.6–0.7	85–95	Hepatic
(SI = Conventional Units × 4.58)						
Primidone	Adult: 5–12 mcg/mL	Adult: 23–55 micromol/L	4–12	0.5–1	0–20	Hepatic
	Child: 7–10 mcg/mL	Child: 32–46 micromol/L				
(SI = Conventional Units × 6.93)						
Valproic acid	50–125 mcg/mL	347–866 micromol/L	8–15	0.1–0.5	85–95	Hepatic

*Conventional units.

A

DESCRIPTION: Anticonvulsants are used to reduce the frequency and severity of seizures for patients with epilepsy. Carbamazepine is also used for controlling neurogenic pain in trigeminal neuralgia and diabetic neuropathy and for treating for bipolar disease and other neurological and psychiatric conditions. Valproic acid is also used for some psychiatric conditions like bipolar disease and for prevention of migraine headache.

Many factors must be considered in effective dosing and monitoring of therapeutic drugs, including patient age, patient weight, interacting medications, electrolyte balance, protein levels, water balance, conditions that affect absorption and excretion, and the ingestion of substances (e.g., foods, herbals, vitamins, and minerals) that can either potentiate or inhibit the intended target concentration. Peak and trough collection times should be documented carefully in relation to the time of medication administration.

The metabolism of many commonly prescribed medications is driven by the cytochrome P450 (CYP450) family of enzymes. Genetic variants can alter enzymatic activity that results in a spectrum of effects ranging from the total absence of drug metabolism to ultrafast metabolism. Impaired drug metabolism can prevent the intended therapeutic effect or even lead to serious adverse drug reactions. Poor metabolizers (PM) are at increased risk for drug-induced side effects due to accumulation of drug in the blood, while ultra-rapid metabolizers (UM) require a higher than normal dosage because the drug is metabolized over a shorter duration than intended. In the case of pro-drugs, which require activation prior to metabolism, the opposite occurs: PM may require a higher dose because the activated drug becomes available more slowly than intended, and UM requires less because the activated drug becomes available sooner than intended. Other genetic phenotypes used to report CYP450 results are intermediate metabolizer (IM) and extensive metabolizer (EM). Genetic testing can be performed on blood samples submitted to a laboratory. The test method commonly used is polymerase chain reaction. Counseling and informed written consent are generally required for genetic testing. CYP2C9 is a gene in the CYP450 family that metabolizes pro-drugs like phenytoin as well as other drugs like phenobarbital; the anticoagulant warfarin; and opioid analgesics like codeine, hydrocodone, dihydrocodeine, oxycodone, and tramadol. Testing for the most common genetic variants of CYP2C9 is used to predict altered enzyme activity and anticipate the most effective therapeutic plan. Incidence of the PM phenotype is estimated to be less than 0.04% of African Americans and less than 0.1% of Caucasians and Asians.

IMPORTANT NOTE

This information must be clearly and accurately communicated to avoid misunderstanding of the dose time in relation to the collection time. Miscommunication between the individual administering the medication and the individual collecting the specimen is the most frequent cause of subtherapeutic levels, toxic levels, and misleading information used in calculation of future doses. If administration of the drug is delayed, notify the appropriate department(s) to reschedule the blood draw and notify the requesting healthcare provider (HCP) if the delay has caused any real or perceived therapeutic harm.

INDICATIONS
- Assist in the diagnosis of and prevention of toxicity
- Evaluate overdose, especially in combination with ethanol
- Monitor compliance with therapeutic regimen

POTENTIAL DIAGNOSIS

Level	Response
Normal levels	Therapeutic effect
Subtherapeutic levels	Adjust dose as indicated
Toxic levels	Adjust dose as indicated
Carbamazepine	Hepatic impairment
Ethosuximide	Renal impairment
Lamotrigine	Hepatic impairment
Phenobarbital	Hepatic or Renal impairment
Phenytoin	Hepatic impairment
Primidone	Hepatic impairment
Valproic acid	Hepatic impairment

CRITICAL FINDINGS

It is important to note the adverse effects of toxic and subtherapeutic levels. Care must be taken to investigate signs and symptoms of not enough medication and too much medication. Note and immediately report to the HCP any critically increased or subtherapeutic values and related symptoms. Timely notification of critical values for lab or diagnostic studies is a role expectation of the professional nurse. Notification processes will vary among facilities. Upon receipt of the critical value the information should be read back to the caller to verify accuracy. Most policies require immediate notification of the primary HCP, Hospitalist, or on-call HCP. Reported information includes the patient's name, unique identifiers, critical value, name of the person giving the report, and name of the person receiving the report. Documentation of notification should be made in the medical record with the name of the HCP notified, time and date of notification, and any orders received. Any delay in a timely report of a critical value may require completion of a notification form with review by Risk Management.

Carbamazepine: Greater Than 20 mcg/mL (SI: Greater Than 84.6 micromol/L)

Signs and symptoms of carbamazepine toxicity include respiratory depression, seizures, leukopenia, hyponatremia, hypotension, stupor, and possible coma. Possible interventions include gastric lavage (contraindicated if ileus is present); airway protection; administration of fluids and vasopressors for hypotension; treatment of seizures with diazepam, phenobarbital, or phenytoin; cardiac monitoring; monitoring of vital signs; and discontinuing the medication. Emetics are contraindicated.

Ethosuximide: Greater Than 200 mcg/mL (SI: Greater Than 1416 micromol/L)

Signs and symptoms of ethosuximide toxicity include nausea, vomiting, and lethargy. Possible interventions include administration of activated charcoal, administration of saline cathartic and gastric lavage (contraindicated if ileus is present), airway protection, hourly assessment of neurologic function, and discontinuing the medication.

Lamotrigine: Greater Than 20 mcg/mL (SI: Greater Than 78.1 micromol/L)

Signs and symptoms of lamotrigine toxicity include severe skin rash, nausea, vomiting, ataxia, decreased levels of consciousness, coma, increased seizures, nystagmus. Possible interventions include administration of activated charcoal, administration of saline cathartic and gastric lavage (contraindicated if ileus is present), airway protection, hourly assessment of neurologic function, and discontinuing the medication

Phenobarbital: Greater Than 60 mcg/mL (SI: Greater Than 258.6 micromol/L)

Signs and symptoms of phenobarbital toxicity include cold, clammy skin; ataxia; central nervous system (CNS) depression; hypothermia; hypotension; cyanosis; Cheyne-Stokes respiration; tachycardia; possible coma; and possible renal impairment. Possible interventions include gastric lavage, administration of activated charcoal with cathartic, airway protection, possible intubation and mechanical ventilation (especially during gastric lavage if there is no gag reflex), monitoring for hypotension, and discontinuing the medication.

Phenytoin (adults): Greater Than 40 mcg/mL (SI: Greater Than 158.4 micromol/L)

Signs and symptoms of phenytoin toxicity include double vision, nystagmus, lethargy, CNS depression, and possible coma. Possible interventions include airway support, electrocardiographic monitoring, administration of activated charcoal, gastric lavage with warm saline or tap water, administration of saline or sorbitol cathartic, and discontinuing the medication.

Primidone: Greater Than 15 mcg/mL (SI: Greater Than 68.7 micromol/L)

Signs and symptoms of primidone toxicity include ataxia, anemia, CNS depression, lethargy, somnolence, vertigo, and visual disturbances. Possible interventions include airway protection, treatment of anemia with vitamin B_{12} and folate, and discontinuing the medication.

Valproic Acid: Greater Than 200 mcg/mL (SI: Greater Than 1386 micromol/L)

Signs and symptoms of valproic acid toxicity include loss of appetite, mental changes, numbness, tingling, and weakness. Possible interventions include administration of activated charcoal and naloxone and discontinuing the medication.

INTERFERING FACTORS

• Blood drawn in serum separator tubes (gel tubes).
• Contraindicated in patients with liver disease, and caution advised in patients with renal impairment.
• Drugs that may increase carbamazepine levels or increase risk of toxicity include acetazolamide, azithromycin, bepridil, cimetidine, danazol, diltiazem, erythromycin, felodipine, fluoxetine, flurithromycin, fluvoxamine, gemfibrozil, isoniazid, itraconazole, josamycin,

ketoconazole, loratadine, macro-lides, niacinamide, nicardipine, nifedipine, nimodipine, nisoldipine, propoxyphene, ritonavir, terfenadine, troleandomycin, valproic acid, verapamil, and viloxazine.

- Drugs that may decrease carbamazepine levels include phenobarbital, phenytoin, and primidone.
- Carbamazepine may affect other body chemistries as seen by a decrease in calcium, sodium, T_3, T_4 levels, and WBC count and increase in ALT, alkaline phosphatase, ammonia, AST, and bilirubin levels.
- Drugs that may increase ethosuximide levels include isonia-zid, ritonavir, and valproic acid.
- Drugs that may decrease ethosuxi-mide levels include phenobarbital, phenytoin, and primidone.
- Drugs that may increase lamotri-gine levels include valproic acid.
- Drugs that may decrease lamotrigine levels include acetaminophen, carbamazepine, hydantoins (e.g., phenytoin), oral contraceptives, orlistat, oxcarbazepine, phenobarbital, primidone, protease inhibitors (e.g., ritonavir), rifamycins (e.g., rifampin), and succinimides (e.g., ethosuximide).
- Drugs that may increase phenobar-bital levels or increase risk of toxicity include barbital drugs, furosemide, primidone, salicylates, and valproic acid.
- Phenobarbital may affect the metabolism of other drugs, increasing their effectiveness, such as β-blockers, chloramphenicol, corticosteroids, doxycycline, griseofulvin, haloperidol, methylphenidate, phenothiazines, phenylbutazone, propoxyphene, quinidine, theophylline, tricyclic antidepressants, and valproic acid.

- Phenobarbital may affect the metabolism of other drugs, decreas-ing their effectiveness, such as chloramphenicol, cyclosporine, ethosuximide, oral anticoagulants, oral contraceptives, phenytoin, theophylline, vitamin D, and vitamin K.
- Phenobarbital is an active metabolite of primidone, and both drug levels should be monitored while the patient is receiving primidone to avoid either toxic or subtherapeutic levels of both medications.
- Phenobarbital may affect other body chemistries as seen by a decrease in bilirubin and calcium levels and increase in alkaline phosphatase, ammonia, and gamma glutamyl transferase levels.
- Drugs that may increase phenytoin levels or increase the risk of phenytoin toxicity include amiodarone, azapropazone, carbamazepine, chloramphenicol, cimetidine, disulfiram, ethanol, fluconazole, halothane, ibuprofen, imipramine, levodopa, metronida-zole, miconazole, nifedipine, phenylbutazone, sulfonamides, trazodone, tricyclic antidepressants, and trimethoprim. Small changes in formulation (i.e., changes in brand) also may increase phenytoin levels or increase the risk of phenytoin toxicity.
- Drugs that may decrease phenyto-in levels include bleomycin, carbamazepine, cisplatin, disulfi-ram, folic acid, intravenous fluids containing glucose, nitrofurantoin, oxacillin, rifampin, salicylates, and vinblastine.
- Primidone decreases the effective-ness of carbamazepine, ethosuxi-mide, felbamate, lamotrigine, oral anticoagulants, oxcarbazepine, topiramate, and valproate.
- Primidone may affect other body chemistries as seen by a decrease

in calcium levels and increase in alkaline phosphatase levels.

- Drugs that may increase valproic acid levels or increase risk of toxicity include dicumarol, phenylbutazone, and high doses of salicylate.
- Drugs that may decrease valproic acid levels include carbamazepine, phenobarbital, phenytoin, and primidone.

NURSING IMPLICATIONS AND PROCEDURE

PRETEST:

▸ Positively identify the patient using at least two unique identifiers before providing care, treatment, or services.

▸ *Patient Teaching:* Inform the patient this test can assist with monitoring for subtherapeutic, therapeutic, or toxic drug levels.

▸ Obtain a history of the patient's complaints, including a list of known allergens, especially allergies or sensitivities to latex.

▸ These medications are metabolized and excreted by the kidneys and liver. Obtain a history of the patient's genitourinary and hepatobiliary systems, symptoms, and results of previously performed laboratory tests and diagnostic and surgical procedures.

▸ Obtain a list of the patient's current medications, including herbs, nutritional supplements, and nutraceuticals (see Appendix F). Note the last time and dose of medication taken.

▸ Review the procedure with the patient. Inform the patient that specimen collection takes approximately 5 to 10 min. Address concerns about pain and explain that there may be some discomfort during the venipuncture.

▸ *Sensitivity to social and cultural issues,* as well as concern for modesty, is important in providing psychological support before, during, and after the procedure.

▸ There are no food, fluid, or medication restrictions unless by medical direction.

INTRATEST:

▸ If the patient has a history of allergic reaction to latex, avoid the use of equipment containing latex.

▸ Direct the patient to breathe normally and to avoid unnecessary movement.

▸ Observe standard precautions, and follow the general guidelines in Appendix A. Consider recommended collection time in relation to the dosing schedule. Positively identify the patient and label the appropriate specimen container with the corresponding patient demographics, initials of the person collecting the specimen, date, and time of collection, noting the last dose of medication taken. Perform a venipuncture.

▸ Remove the needle and apply direct pressure with dry gauze to stop bleeding. Observe/assess venipuncture site for bleeding or hematoma formation and secure gauze with adhesive bandage.

▸ Promptly transport the specimen to the laboratory for processing and analysis.

POST-TEST:

▸ A report of the results will be made available to the requesting HCP, who will discuss the results with the patient.

▸ *Nutritional Considerations:* Antiepileptic drugs antagonize folic acid, and there is a corresponding slight increase in the incidence of fetal malformations in children of epileptic mothers. Women of childbearing age who are taking carbamazepine, phenobarbital, phenytoin, primadone, and/or valproic acid should also be prescribed supplemental folic acid to reduce the incidence of neural tube defects. Neonates born to epileptic mothers taking antiseizure medications during pregnancy may experience a temporary drug-induced deficiency of vitamin K–dependent coagulation factors. This can be avoided by administration of vitamin K to the mother in the last few weeks of pregnancy and to the infant at birth.

▸ Reinforce information given by the patient's HCP regarding further testing, treatment, or referral to another HCP.

A

Explain to the patient the importance of following the medication regimen and instructions regarding drug interactions. Instruct the patient to immediately report any unusual sensations (e.g., ataxia, dizziness, dyspnea, lethargy, rash, tremors, mental changes, weakness, or visual disturbances) to his or her HCP. Answer any questions or address any concerns voiced by the patient or family.

Instruct the patient to be prepared to provide the pharmacist with a list of other medications he or she is already taking in the event that the requesting HCP prescribes a medication.

Depending on the results of this procedure, additional testing may be performed to evaluate or monitor progression of the disease process and determine the need for a change in therapy. Evaluate test results in relation to the patient's symptoms and other tests performed.

RELATED MONOGRAPHS:

Related tests include ALT, albumin, AST, bilirubin, BUN, CBC, creatinine, electrolytes, GGT, and protein blood total and fractions.

See the Genitourinary and Hepatobiliary systems tables at the end of the book for related tests by body system.

Antideoxyribonuclease-B, Streptococcal

SYNONYM/ACRONYM: ADNase-B, AntiDNase-B titer, antistreptococcal DNase-B titer, streptodornase.

COMMON USE: To assist in assessing the cause of recent infection, such as streptococcal exposure, by identification of antibodies.

SPECIMEN: Serum (1 mL) collected in a red-top tube.

NORMAL FINDINGS: (Method: Nephelometry)

Age	Normal Results
1–6 yr	Less than 70 units/mL
7–17 yr	Less than 170 units/mL
18 yr and older	Less than 120 units/mL

DESCRIPTION: The presence of streptococcal deoxyribonuclease (DNase)-B antibodies is an indicator of recent group A, beta hemolytic streptococcal infection, especially if a rise in antibody titer can be shown. This test is more sensitive than the antistreptolysin O (ASO) test. Anti-DNase B titers rise more slowly than ASO titers, peaking 4 to 8 wk after infection. They also decline much more slowly, remaining elevated for several months. A rise in titer of two or more dilution increments between acute and convalescent specimens is clinically significant.

A

INDICATIONS

- Investigate the presence of streptococcal antibodies as a source of recent infection

POTENTIAL DIAGNOSIS

Increased in

Presence of antibodies, especially a rise in titer, is indicative of exposure.

- Post streptococcal glomerulonephritis
- Rheumatic fever
- Streptococcal infections (systemic)

Decreased in: N/A

CRITICAL FINDINGS: N/A

INTERFERING FACTORS: N/A

NURSING IMPLICATIONS AND PROCEDURE

PRETEST:

- Positively identify the patient using at least two unique identifiers before providing care, treatment, or services.
- *Patient Teaching:* Inform the patient this test can assist in documenting recent streptococcal infection.
- Obtain a history of the patient's complaints, including a list of known allergens, especially allergies or sensitivities to latex.
- Obtain a history of the patient's immune system, symptoms, and results of previously performed laboratory tests and diagnostic and surgical procedures.
- Obtain a list of the patient's current medications, including herbs, nutritional supplements, and nutraceuticals (see Appendix F).
- Review the procedure with the patient. Inform the patient that specimen collection takes approximately 5 to 10 min. Address concerns about pain and explain that there may be some discomfort during the venipuncture.
- *Sensitivity to social and cultural issues,* as well as concern for modesty, is important in providing psychological support before, during, and after the procedure.
- There are no food, fluid, or medication restrictions unless by medical direction.

INTRATEST:

- If the patient has a history of allergic reaction to latex, avoid the use of equipment containing latex.
- Instruct the patient to cooperate fully and to follow directions. Direct the patient to breathe normally and to avoid unnecessary movement.
- Observe standard precautions, and follow the general guidelines in Appendix A. Positively identify the patient, and label the appropriate specimen container with the corresponding patient demographics, initials of the person collecting the specimen, date, and time of collection. Perform a venipuncture.
- Remove the needle and apply direct pressure with dry gauze to stop bleeding. Observe/assess venipuncture site for bleeding or hematoma formation and secure gauze with adhesive bandage.
- Promptly transport the specimen to the laboratory for processing and analysis.

POST-TEST:

- A report of the results will be made available to the requesting health-care provider (HCP), who will discuss the results with the patient.
- Administer analgesics and antibiotics if ordered. Remind the patient of the importance of completing the entire course of antibiotic therapy, even if signs and symptoms disappear before completion of therapy.
- Reinforce information given by the patient's HCP regarding further testing treatment, or referral to another HCP. Inform the patient that a convalescent

specimen may be requested in 7 to 10 days. Answer any questions or address any concerns voiced by the patient or family.

Depending on the results of this procedure, additional testing may be performed to evaluate or monitor progression of the disease process and determine the need for a change in therapy. Evaluate test results in relation to the patient's symptoms and other tests performed.

RELATED MONOGRAPHS:
- Related tests include antibodies antistreptolysin O, culture throat, and group A streptococcal screen.
- See the Immune System table at the end of the book for related tests by body system.

Antidepressant Drugs (Cyclic): Amitriptyline, Nortriptyline, Protriptyline, Doxepin, Imipramine

SYNONYM/ACRONYM: *Cyclic antidepressants: amitriptyline* (Elavil, Endep, Etrafon, Limbitrol, Triavil); *nortriptyline* (Allegron, Aventyl HCL, Nortrilen, Norval, Pamelor); *protriptyline* (Aventyl, Sinequan, Surmontil, Tofranil, Vivactil); *doxepin* (Adapin, Co-Dax, Novoxapin, Sinequan, Triadapin); *imipramine* (Berkomine, Dimipressin, Iprogen, Janimine, Pentofrane, Presamine, SK-Pramine, Tofranil PM).

COMMON USE: To monitor subtherapeutic, therapeutic, or toxic drug levels in evaluation of effective treatment modalities.

SPECIMEN: Serum (1 mL) collected in a red-top tube.

Drug	Route of Administration	Recommended Collection Time
Amitriptyline	Oral	Trough: immediately before next dose (at steady state)
Nortriptyline	Oral	Trough: immediately before next dose (at steady state)
Protriptyline	Oral	Trough: immediately before next dose (at steady state)
Doxepin	Oral	Trough: immediately before next dose (at steady state)
Imipramine	Oral	Trough: immediately before next dose (at steady state)

NORMAL FINDINGS: (Method: Chromatography for amitriptyline, nortriptyline, protriptyline, and doxepin; immunoassay for imipramine)

Drug	Therapeutic Range*	SI Units	Half-Life (h)	Volume of Distribution (L/kg)	Protein Binding (%)	Excretion
(SI = Conventional Units × 3.61) Amitriptyline	125–250 ng/mL	451–902 nmol/L	20–40	10–36	85–95	Hepatic
(SI = Conventional Units × 3.8) Nortriptyline	50–150 ng/mL	190–570 nmol/L	20–60	15–23	90–95	Hepatic
(SI = Conventional Units × 3.8) Protriptyline	70–250 ng/mL	266–950 nmol/L	60–90	15–31	91–93	Hepatic
(SI = Conventional Units × 3.58) Doxepin	110–250 ng/mL	394–895 nmol/L	10–25	10–30	75–85	Hepatic
(SI = Conventional Units × 3.57) Imipramine	180–240 ng/mL	643–857 nmol/L	6–18	9–23	60–95	Hepatic

*Conventional units.

DESCRIPTION: Cyclic antidepressants are used in the treatment of major depression. They have also been used effectively to treat bipolar disorder, panic disorder, attention deficit-hyperactivity disorder (ADHD), obsessive-compulsive disorder (OCD), enuresis, eating disorders (bulimia nervosa in particular), nicotine dependence (tobacco), and cocaine dependence. Numerous drug interactions occur with the cyclic antidepressants.

Many factors must be considered in effective dosing and monitoring of therapeutic drugs, including patient age, patient ethnicity, patient weight, interacting medications, electrolyte balance, protein levels, water balance, conditions that affect absorption and excretion, and the ingestion of substances (e.g., foods, herbals, vitamins, and minerals) that can either potentiate or inhibit the intended target concentration. Trough collection times should be documented carefully in relation to the time of medication administration.

The metabolism of many commonly prescribed medications is driven by the cytochrome P450 (CYP450) family of enzymes. Genetic variants can alter enzymatic activity that results in a spectrum of effects ranging from the total absence of drug metabolism to ultrafast metabolism. Impaired drug metabolism can prevent the intended therapeutic effect or even lead to serious adverse drug reactions. Poor metabolizers (PM) are at increased risk for drug-induced side effects due to accumulation of drug in the blood, while ultra-rapid metabolizers (UM) require a higher than normal dosage because the drug is metabolized over a shorter duration than intended. Other genetic phenotypes used to report CYP450 results are intermediate metabolizer (IM) and extensive metabolizer (EM). Genetic testing can be performed on blood samples submitted to a laboratory. The test method commonly used is polymerase chain reaction. Counseling and informed written consent are generally required for genetic testing. CYP2D6 is a gene in the CYP450 family that metabolizes drugs such as tricyclic antidepressants like nortriptyline, antipsychotics like haloperidol, and beta blockers. Testing for the most common genetic variants of CYP2D6 is used to predict altered enzyme activity and anticipate the most effective therapeutic plan. Incidence of the PM phenotype is estimated to be 10% of Caucasians and Hispanics, 2% of African Americans, and 1% of Asians.

IMPORTANT NOTE

This information must be clearly and accurately communicated to avoid misunderstanding of the dose time in relation to the collection time. Miscommunication between the individual administering the medication and the individual collecting the specimen is the most frequent cause of subtherapeutic levels, toxic levels, and misleading information used in calculation of future doses. If administration of the drug is delayed, notify the appropriate department(s) to reschedule the blood draw and notify the requesting health-care

A

provider (HCP) if the delay has caused any real or perceived therapeutic harm.

INDICATIONS
- Assist in the diagnosis and prevention of toxicity
- Evaluate overdose, especially in combination with ethanol (*Note*: Doxepin abuse is unusual.)
- Monitor compliance with therapeutic regimen

POTENTIAL DIAGNOSIS

Level	Response
Normal levels	Therapeutic effect
Subtherapeutic levels	Adjust dose as indicated
Toxic levels	Adjust dose as indicated
Amitriptyline	Hepatic impairment
Nortriptyline	Hepatic impairment
Protriptyline	Hepatic impairment
Doxepin	Hepatic impairment
Imipramine	Hepatic impairment

CRITICAL FINDINGS ✦
It is important to note the adverse effects of toxic and subtherapeutic levels of antidepressants. Care must be taken to investigate signs and symptoms of too little and too much medication. Note and immediately report to the HCP any critically increased or subtherapeutic values and related symptoms. Timely notification of critical values for lab or diagnostic studies is a role expectation of the professional nurse. Notification processes will vary among facilities. Upon receipt of the critical value the information should be read back to the caller to verify accuracy. Most policies require immediate notification of the primary HCP, Hospitalist, or on-call HCP. Reported information includes the patient's name, unique identifiers, critical value, name of the person giving the report, and name of the person receiving the report. Documentation of notification should be made in the medical record with the name of the HCP notified, time and date of notification, and any orders received. An delay in a timely report of a critical value may require completion of a notification form with review by Risk Management.

Cyclic antidepressants
- Amitriptyline: Greater Than 500 ng/ mL (SI: Greater Than 1805 nmol/L)
- Nortriptyline: Greater Than 500 ng/ mL (SI: Greater Than 1900 nmol/L)
- Protriptyline: Greater Than 500 ng/ mL (SI: Greater Than 1900 nmol/L)
- Doxepin: Greater Than 500 ng/mL (SI: Greater Than 1790 nmol/L)
- Imipramine: Greater Than 500 ng/ mL (SI: Greater Than 1785 nmol/L)

Signs and symptoms of cyclic antidepressant toxicity include agitation, drowsiness, hallucinations, confusion, seizures, arrhythmias, hyperthermia, flushing, dilation of the pupil, and possible coma. Possible interventions include administration of activated charcoal; emesis; gastric lavage with saline; administration of physostigmine to counteract seizures, hypertension, or respiratory depression; administration of bicarbonate, propranolol, lidocaine, or phenytoin to counteract arrhythmias; and electrocardiographic monitoring.

INTERFERING FACTORS
- Blood drawn in serum separator tubes (gel tubes).
- Contraindicated in patients with liver disease, and caution advised in patients with renal impairment.
- Cyclic antidepressants may potentiate the effects of oral anticoagulants.

NURSING IMPLICATIONS AND PROCEDURE

PRETEST:

- Positively identify the patient using at least two unique identifiers before providing care, treatment, or services.
- *Patient Teaching:* Inform the patient this test can assist in monitoring subtherapeutic, therapeutic, or toxic drug levels.
- Obtain a history of the patient's complaints, including a list of known allergens, especially allergies or sensitivities to latex.
- These medications are metabolized and excreted by the kidneys and liver. Obtain a history of the patient's genitourinary and hepatobiliary systems, symptoms, and results of previously performed laboratory tests and diagnostic and surgical procedures.
- Obtain a list of the patient's current medications, including herbs, nutritional supplements, and nutraceuticals (see Appendix F). Note the last time and dose of medication taken.
- Review the procedure with the patient. Inform the patient that specimen collection takes approximately 5 to 10 min. Address concerns about pain and explain that there may be some discomfort during the venipuncture.
- *Sensitivity to social and cultural issues,* as well as concern for modesty, is important in providing psychological support before, during, and after the procedure.
- There are no food, fluid, or medication restrictions unless by medical direction.

INTRATEST:

- If the patient has a history of allergic reaction to latex, avoid the use of equipment containing latex.
- Instruct the patient to cooperate fully and to follow directions. Direct the patient to breathe normally and to avoid unnecessary movement.
- Observe standard precautions, and follow the general guidelines in Appendix A. Consider recommended collection time in relation to the dosing schedule. Positively identify the patient, and label the appropriate specimen container with the corresponding patient demographics, initials of the person collecting the specimen, date, and time of collection, noting the last dose of medication taken. Perform a venipuncture.
- Remove the needle and apply direct pressure with dry gauze to stop bleeding. Observe/assess venipuncture site for bleeding or hematoma formation and secure gauze with adhesive bandage.
- Promptly transport the specimen to the laboratory for processing and analysis.

POST-TEST:

- A report of the results will be made available to the requesting HCP, who will discuss the results with the patient.
- *Nutritional Considerations:* Include avoidance of alcohol consumption.
- Reinforce information given by the patient's HCP regarding further testing, treatment, or referral to another HCP. Explain to the patient the importance of following the medication regimen and instructions regarding drug interactions. Instruct the patient to immediately report any unusual sensations (e.g., severe headache, vomiting, sweating, visual disturbances) to his or her HCP. Blood pressure should be monitored regularly. Answer any questions or address any concerns voiced by the patient or family.
- Instruct the patient to be prepared to provide the pharmacist with a list of other medications he or she is already taking in the event that the requesting HCP prescribes a medication.
- Depending on the results of this procedure, additional testing may be performed to evaluate or monitor progression of the disease process and determine the need for a change in therapy. Evaluate test results in relation to the patient's symptoms and other tests performed.

RELATED MONOGRAPHS:

- Related tests include ALT, albumin, AST, bilirubin, BUN, creatinine, CBC, electrolytes, GGT, and protein blood total and fractions.
- See the Genitourinary and Hepatobiliary systems tables at the end of the book for related tests by body system.

A

Antidiuretic Hormone

SYNONYM/ACRONYM: Vasopressin, arginine vasopressin hormone, ADH.

COMMON USE: To evaluate disorders that affect urine concentration related to fluctuations of ADH secretion, such as diabetes insipidus.

SPECIMEN: Plasma (1 mL) collected in a lavender-top (EDTA) tube.

NORMAL FINDINGS: (Method: Radioimmunoassay) Normally hydrated adults: 0 to 5 pg/mL; normally hydrated children (1 day to 18 yr): 0.5 to 1.7.

Age	Antidiuretic Hormone	SI Units (Conventional Units × 0.926)
Neonates	Less than 1.5 pg/mL	Less than 1.4 pmol/L
1 day–18 yr	0.5–1.5 pg/mL	Less than 0.5–1.4 pmol/L
Adult	0–5 pg/mL	0–4.6 pmol/L

*Conventional units.

Recommendation
This test should be ordered and interpreted with results of a serum osmolality

Serum Osmolality*	Antidiuretic Hormone	SI Units (Conventional Units × 0.926)
270–280 mOsm/kg	Less than 1.5 pg/mL	Less than 1.4 pmol/L
280–285 mOsm/kg	Less than 2.5 pg/mL	Less than 2.3 pmol/L
285–290 mOsm/kg	1–5 pg/mL	0.9–4.6 pmol/L
290–295 mOsm/kg	2–7 pg/mL	1.9–6.5 pmol/L
295–300 mOsm/kg	4–12 pg/mL	3.7–11.1 pmol/L

DESCRIPTION: Antidiuretic hormone (ADH) is formed by the hypothalamus and stored in the posterior pituitary gland. ADH is released in response to increased serum osmolality or decreased blood volume. When the hormone is active, water is reabsorbed by the kidneys into the circulating plasma instead of being excreted, and small amounts of concentrated urine are produced; in its absence, large amounts of dilute urine are produced. Although a 1% change in serum osmolality stimulates ADH secretion, blood volume must decrease by approximately 10% for ADH secretion to be induced. Psychogenic stimuli, such as stress, pain, and anxiety, may also stimulate ADH release, but the mechanism is unclear.

INDICATIONS
• Assist in the diagnosis of known or suspected malignancy associated with syndrome of inappropriate ADH secretion (SIADH), such as oat cell lung cancer, thymoma, lymphoma, leukemia, pancreatic carcinoma

prostate gland carcinoma, and intestinal carcinoma; elevated ADH levels indicate the presence of this syndrome

Assist in the diagnosis of known or suspected pulmonary conditions associated with SIADH, such as tuberculosis, pneumonia, and positive-pressure mechanical ventilation

Detect central nervous system trauma, surgery, or disease that may lead to impaired ADH secretion

Differentiate neurogenic (central) diabetes insipidus from nephrogenic diabetes insipidus by decreased ADH levels in neurogenic diabetes insipidus or elevated levels in nephrogenic diabetes insipidus if normal feedback mechanisms are intact

Evaluate polyuria or altered serum osmolality to identify possible alterations in ADH secretion as the cause

POTENTIAL DIAGNOSIS

Increased in

Acute intermittent porphyria *(speculated to be related to the release of ADH from damaged cells in the hypothalamus and effect of hypovolemia; the mechanisms are unclear)*

Brain tumor *(related to ADH production from the tumor or release from damaged cells in an adjacent affected area)*

Disorders involving the central nervous system, thyroid gland, and adrenal gland *(numerous conditions influence the release of ADH)*

Ectopic production *(related to ADH production from a systemic neoplasm)*

Guillain-Barré; syndrome *(relationship to SIADH is unclear)*

- Hypovolemia *(potent instigator of ADH release)*
- Nephrogenic diabetes insipidus *(related to lack of renal system response to ADH stimulation; evidenced by increased secretion of ADH)*
- Pain, stress, or exercise *(all are potent instigators of ADH release)*
- Pneumonia *(related to SIADH)*
- Pulmonary tuberculosis *(related to SIADH)*
- SIADH *(numerous conditions influence the release of ADH)*
- Tuberculous meningitis *(related to SIADH)*

Decreased in

Decreased production or secretion of ADH in response to changes in blood volume or pressure

- Hypervolemia *(related to increased blood volume, which inhibits secretion of ADH)*
- Nephrotic syndrome *(related to destruction of pituitary cells that secrete ADH)*
- Pituitary (central) diabetes insipidus *(related to destruction of pituitary cells that secrete ADH)*
- Pituitary surgery *(related to destruction or removal of pituitary cells that secrete ADH)*
- Psychogenic polydipsia *(evidenced by decreased osmolality, which inhibits secretion of ADH)*

CRITICAL FINDINGS

Effective treatment of SIADH depends on identifying and resolving the cause of increased ADH production. Signs and symptoms of SIADH are the same as those for hyponatremia, including irritability, tremors, muscle spasms, convulsions, and neurologic changes. The patient has enough sodium, but it is diluted in excess retained water.

A

INTERFERING FACTORS

• Drugs that may increase ADH levels include cisplatin, ether, furosemide, hydrochlorothiazide, lithium, methyclothiazide, and polythiazide.
• Drugs that may decrease ADH levels include chlorpromazine, clonidine, demeclocycline, ethanol, and phenytoin.
• Recent radioactive scans or radiation within 1 week before the test can interfere with test results when radioimmunoassay is the test method.
• ADH exhibits diurnal variation, with highest levels of secretion occurring at night; first morning collection is recommended.
• ADH secretion is also affected by posture, with higher levels measured while upright.

NURSING IMPLICATIONS AND PROCEDURE

PRETEST:

▶ Positively identify the patient using at least two unique identifiers before providing care, treatment, or services.
▶ *Patient Teaching:* Inform the patient this test can assist in providing information about effective urine concentration.
▶ Obtain a history of the patient's complaints, including a list of known allergens, especially allergies or sensitivities to latex.
▶ Obtain a history of the patient's endocrine and genitourinary systems, symptoms, and results of previously performed laboratory tests and diagnostic and surgical procedures.
▶ Note any recent procedures that can interfere with test results.
▶ Obtain a list of the patient's current medications, including herbs, nutritional supplements, and nutraceuticals (see Appendix F).
▶ Review the procedure with the patient. Inform the patient that specimen collection takes approximately 5 to 10 min. Address concerns about pain and explain that there may be some discomfort during the venipuncture.

▶ *Sensitivity to social and cultural issues,* as well as concern for modesty, is important in providing psychological support before, during, and after the procedure.
▶ There are no food, fluid, or medication restrictions unless by medical direction
▶ Prepare an ice slurry in a cup or plastic bag to have ready for immediate transport of the specimen to the laboratory. Pre-chill the lavender-top tube in the ice slurry.

INTRATEST:

▶ If the patient has a history of allergic reaction to latex, avoid the use of equipment containing latex.
▶ Instruct the patient to cooperate fully and to follow directions. The patient should be encouraged to be calm and in a sitting position for specimen collection. Direct the patient to breathe normally and to avoid unnecessary movement.
▶ Observe standard precautions, and follow the general guidelines in Appendix A. Positively identify the patient, and label the appropriate specimen container with the corresponding patient demographics, initials of the person collecting the specimen, date, and time of collection. Perform a venipuncture.
▶ Remove the needle and apply direct pressure with dry gauze to stop bleeding. Observe/assess venipuncture site for bleeding or hematoma formation and secure gauze with adhesive bandage.
▶ The sample should be placed in an ice slurry immediately after collection. Information on the specimen label should be protected from water in the ice slurry by first placing the specimen in a protective plastic bag. Promptly transport the specimen to the laboratory for processing and analysis.

POST-TEST:

▶ A report of the results will be made available to the requesting health-care provider (HCP), who will discuss the results with the patient.
▶ Reinforce information given by the patient's HCP regarding further testing, treatment, or referral to another HCP. Inform the patient, as appropriate, that treatment may include diuretic therapy and fluid restriction to successfully eliminate the excess water. Answer any

questions or address any concerns voiced by the patient or family. Depending on the results of this procedure, additional testing may be performed to evaluate or monitor pro-gression of the disease process and determine the need for a change in therapy. Evaluate test results in relation to the patient's symptoms and other tests performed.

RELATED MONOGRAPHS:
- Related tests include BUN, chest x-ray, chloride, osmolality, phosphorus, potassium, sodium, TSH, uric acid, and UA.
- See the Endocrine and Genitourinary systems tables at the end of the book for related tests by body system.

Antimicrobial Drugs—Aminoglycosides: Amikacin, Gentamicin, Tobramycin; Tricyclic Glycopeptide: Vancomycin

SYNONYM/ACRONYM: *Amikacin* (Amikin); *gentamicin* (Garamycin, Genoptic, Gentacidin, Gentafair, Gentak, Gentamar, Gentrasul, G-myticin, Oco-Mycin, Spectro-Genta); *tobramycin* (Nebcin, Tobrex); *vancomycin* (Lyphocin, Vancocin, Vancoled).

COMMON USE: To evaluate specific drugs for subtherapeutic, therapeutic, or toxic levels in treatment of infection.

SPECIMEN: Serum (1 mL) collected in a red-top tube.

Drug	Route of Administration	Recommended Collection Time*
Amikacin	IV, IM	Trough: immediately before next dose Peak: 30 min after the end of a 30-min IV infusion
Gentamicin	IV, IM	Trough: immediately before next dose Peak: 30 min after the end of a 30-min IV infusion
Tobramycin	IV, IM	Trough: immediately before next dose Peak: 30 min after the end of a 30-min IV infusion
Tricyclic glycopeptide and vancomycin	IV, PO	Trough: immediately before next dose Peak: 30–60 min after the end of a 60-min IV infusion

*Usually after fifth dose if given every 8 hr or third dose if given every 12 hr.
IM = intramuscular; IV = intravenous; PO = by mouth.

NORMAL FINDINGS: (Method: Immunoassay)

Drug	Therapeutic Range*	SI Units	Half-Life (hr)	Distribution (L/kg)	Volume of Binding (%)	Protein Excretion
(SI = Conventional Units × 1.71) Amikacin						
Peak	15–30 mcg/mL	26–51 micromol/L	4–8	0.4–1.3	50	1° renal
Trough	4–8 mcg/mL	7–14 micromol/L				
(SI = Conventional Units × 2.09) Gentamicin (Standard dosing)						
Peak	6–10 mcg/mL	12–21 micromol/L	4–8	0.4–1.3	50	1° renal
Trough	0.5–1.5 mcg/mL	1–3 micromol/L				
(SI = Conventional Units × 2.09) Tobramycin (Standard dosing)						
Peak	4–8 mcg/mL	8.4–16.7 micromol/L	4–8	0.4–1.3	50	1° renal
Trough	Less than 1 mcg/mL	Less than 2.1 micromol/L				
Tobramycin (Once daily dosing)						
Peak	8–12 mcg/mL	16.7–25.1 micromol/L	4–8	0.4–1.3	50	1° renal
Trough	Less than 0.5 mcg/mL	Less than 1 micromol/L				
(SI = Conventional Units × 0.69) Vancomycin Trough (General) Values vary with indication	10–15 mcg/mL	7–10.4 micromol/L				

DESCRIPTION: The aminoglycoside antibiotics amikacin, gentamicin, and tobramycin are used against many gram-negative (*Acinetobacter, Citrobacter, Enterobacter, Escherichia coli, Klebsiella, Proteus, Providencia, Pseudomonas, Raoultella, Salmonella, Serratia, Shigella,* and *Stenotrophomonas*) and some gram-positive (*Staphylococcus aureus*) pathogenic microorganisms. Aminoglycosides are poorly absorbed through the gastro-intestinal tract and are most frequently administered IV.

Vancomycin is a tricyclic glycopeptide antibiotic used against many gram-positive microorganisms, such as staphylococci, *Streptococcus pneumoniae*, group A β-hemolytic streptococci, enterococci, *Corynebacterium*, and *Clostridium*. Vancomycin has also been used in an oral form for the treatment of pseudo-membranous colitis resulting from *Clostridium difficile* infection. This approach is less frequently used because of the emergence of vancomycin-resistant enterococci (VRE).

Many factors must be considered in effective dosing and monitoring of therapeutic drugs, including patient age, patient weight, interacting medications, electrolyte balance, protein levels, water balance, conditions that affect absorption and excretion, and ingestion of substances (e.g., foods, herbals, vitamins, and minerals) that can either potentiate or inhibit the intended target concentration. The most serious side effects of the aminoglycosides and vancomycin are nephrotoxicity and irreversible ototoxicity (uncommon). Peak and trough collection times should be documented carefully in relation to the time of medication admini-stration. Creatinine levels should be monitored every 2 to 3 days to detect renal impairment due to toxic drug levels.

IMPORTANT NOTE

This information must be clearly and accurately communicated to avoid misunderstanding of the dose time in relation to the collection time. Miscommunication between the individual administering the medication and the individual collecting the specimen is the most frequent cause of subtherapeutic levels, toxic levels, and misleading information used in the calculation of future doses. Some pharmacies use a computerized pharmacokinetics approach to dosing that eliminates the need to be concerned about peak and trough collections; random specimens are adequate. If administration of the drug is delayed, notify the appropriate department(s) to re-schedule the blood draw and notify the requesting health-care provider (HCP) if the delay has caused any real or perceived therapeutic harm.

INDICATIONS

- Assist in the diagnosis and prevention of toxicity
- Monitor renal dialysis patients or patients with rapidly changing renal function
- Monitor therapeutic regimen

A

POTENTIAL DIAGNOSIS

Level	Response
Normal levels	Therapeutic effect
Subtherapeutic levels	Adjust dose as indicated
Toxic levels	Adjust dose as indicated
Amikacin	Renal, hearing impairment
Gentamicin	Renal, hearing impairment
Tobramycin	Renal, hearing impairment
Vancomycin	Renal, hearing impairment

CRITICAL FINDINGS

The adverse effects of subtherapeutic levels are important. Care should be taken to investigate signs and symptoms of too little and too much medication. Note and immediately report to the health-care provider (HCP) any critically increased or subtherapeutic values and related symptoms. Timely notification of critical values for lab or diagnostic studies is a role expectation of the professional nurse. Notification processes will vary among facilities. Upon receipt of the critical value the information should be read back to the caller to verify accuracy. Most policies require immediate notification of the primary HCP, Hospitalist, or on-call HCP. Reported information includes the patient's name, unique identifiers, critical value, name of the person giving the report, and name of the person receiving the report. Documentation of notification should be made in the medical record with the name of the HCP notified, time and date of notification, and any orders received. Any delay in timely report of a critical value may require completion of a notification form with review by Risk Management.

Signs and symptoms of toxic levels of these antibiotics are similar and include loss of hearing and decreased renal function. Suspected hearing loss can be evaluated by audiometry testing. Impaired renal function may be identified by monitoring BUN and creatinine levels as well as intake and output. The most important intervention is accurate therapeutic drug monitoring so the medication can be discontinued before irreversible damage is done.

Drug Name	Toxic Levels Conventional Units	Toxic Levels SI Units
Amikacin	Greater than 10 mcg/mL	Greater than 17.1 micromol/L
Gentamicin	Peak greater than 12 mcg/mL, trough greater than 2 mcg/mL	Peak greater than 25.1 micromol/L, trough greater than 4.2 micromol/L
Tobramycin	Peak greater than 12 mcg/mL, trough greater than 2 mcg/mL	Peak greater than 25.1 micromol/L, trough greater than 4.2 micromol/L
Vancomycin	Trough greater than 30 mcg/mL	Trough greater than 20.7 micromol/L

INTERFERING FACTORS

• Blood drawn in serum separator tubes (gel tubes).
• Contraindicated in patients with liver disease, and caution advised in patients with renal impairment.
• Drugs that may decrease aminoglycoside efficacy include penicillins (e.g., carbenicillin, piperacillin).

Obtain a culture before and after the first dose of aminoglycosides. The risks of ototoxicity and nephrotoxicity are increased by the concomitant administration of aminoglycosides.

NURSING IMPLICATIONS AND PROCEDURE

RETEST:

Positively identify the patient using at least two unique identifiers before providing care, treatment, or services. *Patient Teaching:* Inform the patient this test can assist in monitoring for subtherapeutic, therapeutic, or toxic drug levels used in treatment of infection. Obtain a history of the patient's complaints, including a list of known allergens, especially allergies or sensitivities to latex. Obtain a history of the patient's immune system, symptoms, and results of previously performed laboratory tests and diagnostic and surgical procedures. Nephrotoxicity is a risk associated with administration of aminoglycosides. Obtain a history of the patient's genitourinary system, symptoms, and results of previously performed laboratory tests and diagnostic and surgical procedures. Ototoxicity is a risk associated with administration of aminoglycosides. Obtain a history of the patient's known or suspected hearing loss, including type and cause; ear conditions with treatment regimens; ear surgery; and other tests and procedures to assess and diagnose auditory deficit. Obtain a list of the patient's current medications, including herbs, nutritional supplements, and nutraceuticals (see Appendix F). Note the last time and dose of medication taken. Review the procedure with the patient. Inform the patient that specimen collection takes approximately 5 to 10 min. Address concerns about pain and explain that there may be some discomfort during the venipuncture. Obtain a culture, if ordered, before the first dose of aminoglycosides. *Sensitivity to social and cultural issues,* as well as concern for modesty, is

important in providing psychological support before, during, and after the procedure.
There are no food, fluid, or medication restrictions unless by medical direction.

INTRATEST:

If the patient has a history of allergic reaction to latex, avoid the use of equipment containing latex.
Instruct the patient to cooperate fully and to follow directions. Direct the patient to breathe normally and to avoid unnecessary movement.
Observe standard precautions, and follow the general guidelines in Appendix A. Consider recommended collection time in relation to the dosing schedule. Positively identify the patient, and label the appropriate specimen container with the corresponding patient demographics, initials of the person collecting the specimen, date, and time of collection, noting the last dose of medication taken. Perform a venipuncture.
Remove the needle and apply direct pressure with dry gauze to stop bleeding. Observe/assess venipuncture site for bleeding or hematoma formation and secure gauze with adhesive bandage.
Promptly transport the specimen to the laboratory for processing and analysis.

POST-TEST:

A report of the results will be made available to the requesting HCP, who will discuss the results with the patient.
Instruct the patient receiving aminoglycosides to immediately report any unusual symptoms (e.g., hearing loss, decreased urinary output) to his or her HCP.
Nutritional Considerations: Include avoidance of alcohol consumption.
Administer antibiotic therapy if ordered. Remind the patient of the importance of completing the entire course of antibiotic therapy, even if signs and symptoms disappear before completion of therapy.
Reinforce information given by the patient's HCP regarding further testing, treatment, or referral to another HCP. Explain to the patient the importance of following the medication regimen and instructions regarding food and drug interactions. Answer any questions or

A

address any concerns voiced by the patient or family.
▸ Instruct the patient to be prepared to provide the pharmacist with a list of other medications he or she is already taking in the event that the requesting HCP prescribes a medication.
▸ Depending on the results of this procedure, additional testing may be performed to evaluate or monitor progression of the disease process and determine the need for a change in therapy. Evaluate test results in relation to the patient's symptoms and other tests performed.

RELATED MONOGRAPHS:
▸ Related tests include albumin, audiometry hearing loss, BUN, creatinine, creatinine clearance, cultures bacterial (ear, eye, skin, wound, blood, stool, sputum, urine), otoscopy, potassium, spondee speech recognition test, tuning fork tests, and UA.
▸ See the Auditory, Genitourinary, and Immune systems tables at the end of the book for related tests by body system.

Antipsychotic Drugs and Antimanic Drugs: Haloperidol, Lithium

SYNONYM/ACRONYM: *Antipsychotic drugs: haloperidol* (Dozic, Fortunan, Haldo Haldol Decanoate, Haloneural, Serenace); *antimanic drugs: lithium* (Cibalith-Eskalith, Lithane, Lithobid, Lithonate, Lithotabs, PFI-Lith, Phasal).

COMMON USE: To assist in monitoring subtherapuetic, therapeutic, or toxic dru levels related to medical interventions.

SPECIMEN: Serum (1 mL) collected in a red-top tube.

Drug	Route of Administration	Recommended Collection Time
Haloperidol	Oral	Peak: 3–6 hr
Lithium	Oral	Trough: at least 12 hr after last dose; steady state occurs at 90–120 hr

NORMAL FINDINGS: (Method: Chromatography for haloperidol; ion-selectiv electrode for lithium)

Drug	Therapeutic Range*	SI Units	Half-Life (hr)	Volume of Distribution (L/kg)	Protein Binding (%)	Excretion
(SI = Conventional Units × 2)						
Haloperidol	5–20 ng/mL	10–40 nmo/L	15–40	18–30	90	Hepatic
(SI = Conventional Units × 1)						
Lithium	0.6–1.4 mEq/L	0.6–1.4 mmol/L	18–24	0.7–1	0	Renal

*Conventional units.

DESCRIPTION: Haloperidol is an antipsychotic tranquilizer used for treatment of acute and chronic psychotic disorders, Tourette's syndrome, and hyperactive children with severe behavioral problems. Frequent monitoring is important due to the unstable relationship between dosage and circulating steady-state concentration. Lithium is used in the treatment of manic depression. Daily monitoring of lithium levels is important until the proper dosage is achieved. Lithium is cleared and reabsorbed by the kidney. Clearance is increased when sodium levels are increased and decreased in conditions associated with low sodium levels; therefore, patients receiving lithium therapy should try to maintain a balanced daily intake of sodium. Lithium levels affect other organ systems. A high incidence of pulmonary complications is associated with lithium toxicity. Lithium can also affect cardiac conduction, producing T-wave depressions. These electrocardiographic (ECG) changes are usually insignificant and reversible and are seen in 10% to 20% of patients on lithium therapy. Chronic lithium therapy has been shown to result in enlargement of the thyroid gland in a small percentage of patients. Other medications indicated for use as mood stabilizers include carbamazepine, lamotrigine, and valproic acid. Detailed information is found in the monograph titled "Anticonvulsant Drugs."

Many factors must be considered in effective dosing and monitoring of therapeutic drugs, including patient age, patient weight, interacting medications, electrolyte balance, protein levels, water balance, conditions that affect absorption and excretion, and the ingestion of substances (e.g., foods, herbals, vitamins, and minerals) that can either potentiate or inhibit the intended target concentration. Peak collection times should be documented carefully in relation to the time of medication administration.

The metabolism of many commonly prescribed medications is driven by the cytochrome P450 (CYP450) family of enzymes. Genetic variants can alter enzymatic activity that results in a spectrum of effects ranging from the total absence of drug metabolism to ultrafast metabolism. Impaired drug metabolism can prevent the intended therapeutic effect or even lead to serious adverse drug reactions. Poor metabolizers (PM) are at increased risk for drug-induced side effects due to accumulation of drug in the blood, while ultra-rapid metabolizers (UM) require a higher than normal dosage because the drug is metabolized over a shorter duration than intended. Other genetic phenotypes used to report CYP450 results are intermediate metabolizer (IM) and extensive metabolizer (EM). Genetic testing can be performed on blood samples submitted to a laboratory. The test method commonly used is polymerase chain reaction. Counseling and informed written consent are generally required for genetic testing. CYP2D6 is a gene in the CYP450 family that metabolizes drugs such as antipsychotics like haloperidol, tricyclic antidepressants like nortriptyline, and beta blockers. Testing for the most common genetic variants of CYP2D6 is used to predict altered enzyme activity and anticipate the most effective therapeutic plan. Incidence of the PM Phenotype is

A

estimated to be 10% of Caucasians and Hispanics, 2% of African Americans, and 1% of Asians.

IMPORTANT NOTE

This information must be clearly and accurately communicated to avoid misunderstanding of the dose time in relation to the collection time. Miscommunication between the individual administering the medication and the individual collecting the specimen is the most frequent cause of subtherapeutic levels, toxic level and misleading information used i calculation of future doses. If admi istration of the drug is delayed, notif the appropriate department(s) t reschedule the blood draw and noti the requesting health-care (HCP) the delay has caused any real or pe ceived therapeutic harm.

INDICATIONS
• Assist in the diagnosis and prevention of toxicity
• Monitor compliance with therapeutic regimen

POTENTIAL DIAGNOSIS

Level	Response
Normal levels	Therapeutic effect
Subtherapeutic levels	Adjust dose as indicated
Toxic levels	Adjust dose as indicated
Haloperidol	Hepatic impairment
Lithium	Renal impairment

CRITICAL FINDINGS

It is important to note the adverse effects of toxic and subtherapeutic levels. Care must be taken to investigate signs and symptoms of not enough medication and too much medication. Note and immediately report to the HCP any critically increased or subtherapeutic values and related symptoms. Timely notification of critical values for lab or diagnostic studies is a role expectation of the professional nurse. Notification processes will vary among facilities. Upon receipt of the critical value the information should be read back to the caller to verify accuracy. Most policies require immediate notification of the primary HCP, Hospitalist, or on-call HCP. Reported information includes the patient's name, unique identifiers, critical value, name of the person giving the report, and name of the person receiving the report. Documentation of notification should be made in the medical record with the name of the HCP notified, time an date of notification, and any orde received. Any delay in a timely repo of a critical value may require compl tion of a notification form with revie by Risk Management.

Haloperidol: Greater Than 42 ng/m (SI: Greater Than 84 nmol/L)
Signs and symptoms of haloperid toxicity include hypotension, myoca dial depression, respiratory depre sion, and extrapyramidal neuromu cular reactions. Possible interventior include emesis (contraindicated i the absence of gag reflex or centr nervous system depression or excit tion) and gastric lavage followed b administration of activated charcoal

Lithium: Greater Than 2 mEq/L (SI: Greater Than 2 mmol/L)
Signs and symptoms of lithium toxici include ataxia, coarse tremors, musc rigidity, vomiting, diarrhea, confusio convulsions, stupor, T-wave flattenin

loss of consciousness, and possible coma. Possible interventions include administration of activated charcoal, gastric lavage, and administration of intravenous fluids with diuresis.

INTERFERING FACTORS

• Blood drawn in serum separator tubes (gel tubes).
• Contraindicated in patients with liver disease, and caution advised in patients with renal impairment.
• Haloperidol may increase levels of tricyclic antidepressants and increase the risk of lithium toxicity.
• Drugs that may increase lithium levels include angiotensin-converting enzyme inhibitors, some NSAIDs, and thiazide diuretics.
• Drugs and substances that may decrease lithium levels include acetazolamide, osmotic diuretics, theophylline, and caffeine.

NURSING IMPLICATIONS AND PROCEDURE

PRETEST:

▶ Positively identify the patient using at least two unique identifiers before providing care, treatment, or services.
Patient Teaching: Inform the patient this test can assist in monitoring subtherapeutic, therapeutic, or toxic drug levels. Obtain a history of the patient's complaints, including a list of known allergens, especially allergies or sensitivities to latex.
These medications are metabolized and excreted by the kidneys and liver. Obtain a history of the patient's genitourinary and hepatobiliary systems, symptoms, and results of previously performed laboratory tests and diagnostic and surgical procedures.
Obtain a list of the patient's current medications, including herbs, nutritional supplements, and nutraceuticals (see Appendix F). Note the last time and dose of medication taken.
Review the procedure with the patient. Inform the patient that specimen

collection takes approximately 5 to 10 min. Address concerns about pain and explain that there may be some discomfort during the venipuncture. *Sensitivity to social and cultural issues,* as well as concern for modesty, is important in providing psychological support before, during, and after the procedure.
▶ There are no food, fluid, or medication restrictions unless by medical direction.

INTRATEST:

▶ If the patient has a history of allergic reaction to latex, avoid the use of equipment containing latex.
▶ Instruct the patient to cooperate fully and to follow directions. Direct the patient to breathe normally and to avoid unnecessary movement.
▶ Observe standard precautions, and follow the general guidelines in Appendix A. Consider recommended collection time in relation to the dosing schedule. Positively identify the patient, and label the appropriate specimen container with the corresponding patient demographics, initials of the person collecting the specimen, date, and time of collection, noting the last dose of medication taken. Perform a venipuncture.
▶ Remove the needle and apply direct pressure with dry gauze to stop bleeding. Observe/assess venipuncture site for bleeding or hematoma formation and secure gauze with adhesive bandage.
▶ Promptly transport the specimen to the laboratory for processing and analysis.

POST-TEST:

▶ A report of the results will be made available to the requesting HCP, who will discuss the results with the patient. *Nutritional Considerations:* Include avoidance of alcohol consumption.
▶ Reinforce information given by the patient's HCP regarding further testing, treatment, or referral to another HCP. Explain to the patient the importance of following the medication regimen and instructions regarding drug interactions. Instruct the patient receiving haloperidol to immediately report any unusual symptoms (e.g., arrhythmias, blurred vision, dry eyes, repetitive uncontrolled movements) to his or her HCP. Instruct

A

the patient receiving lithium to immediately report any unusual symptoms (e.g., anorexia, nausea, vomiting, diarrhea, dizziness, drowsiness, dysarthria, tremor, muscle twitching, visual disturbances) to his or her HCP. Answer any questions or address any concerns voiced by the patient or family.

Instruct the patient to be prepared to provide the pharmacist with a list of other medications he or she is already taking in the event that the requesting HCP prescribes a medication.

Depending on the results of this procedure, additional testing may be performed to evaluate or monitor progression of the disease process and determine the need for a change in therapy. Evaluate test results in relation to the patient's symptoms and other tests performed.

RELATED MONOGRAPHS:

Related laboratory tests include albumin, BUN, calcium, creatinine, ECG, glucose, magnesium, osmolality urine, potassium, sodium, T_4, and TSH.

See the Genitourinary and Hepatobiliary systems tables at the end of the book for related tests by body system.

Antithrombin III

SYNONYM/ACRONYM: Heparin cofactor assay, AT-III.

COMMON USE: To assist in diagnosing heparin resistance or disorders resulting from a hypercoagulable state such as thrombus.

SPECIMEN: Plasma (1 mL) collected in a completely filled blue-top (3.2% sodium citrate) tube. If the patient's hematocrit exceeds 55%, the volume of citrate in the collection tube must be adjusted.

NORMAL FINDINGS: (Method: Chromogenic Immunoturbidimetric)

Age	Conventional Units
1–4 days	39–87%
5–29 days	41–93%
1–3 mo	48–108%
3–6 mo	73–121%
6–12 mo	84–124%
1–5 yr	82–139%
6–17 yr	90–131%
18 yr-older adult	80–120%

DESCRIPTION: Antithrombin III (AT-III) can inhibit thrombin (factor IIa) and factors IX, X, XI, and XII. It is a heparin cofactor, produced by the liver, interacting with heparin and thrombin. AT-III acts to increase the rate at which thrombin is neutralized or inhibited, and it decreases the total quantity of thrombin inhibited. Patients with low levels of AT-III show some level of resistance to heparin therapy and are at risk for venous thrombosis. AT III deficiency can be acquired (most common) or congenital.

INDICATIONS

- Investigate tendency for thrombosis

POTENTIAL DIAGNOSIS

Increased in

- Acute hepatitis
- Renal transplantation *(Some studies have demonstrated high levels of AT III in proximal tubule epithelial cells at the time of renal transplant. The exact relationship between the kidneys and AT III levels is unknown. It is believed the kidneys may play a role in maintaining plasma levels of AT III as evidenced by the correlation between renal disease and low AT III levels.)*
- Vitamin K deficiency *(decreased consumption related to impaired coagulation factor function)*

Decreased in

- Carcinoma *(related to decreased synthesis)*
- Chronic liver failure *(related to decreased synthesis)*
- Cirrhosis *(related to decreased synthesis)*
- Congenital deficiency
- Disseminated intravascular coagulation *(related to increased consumption)*
- Liver transplantation or partial hepatectomy *(related to decreased synthesis)*
- Nephrotic syndrome *(related to increased protein loss)*
- Pulmonary embolism *(related to increased consumption)*
- Septic shock *(related to increased consumption and decreased synthesis due to hepatic impairment)*
- Venous thrombosis *(related to increased consumption)*

CRITICAL FINDINGS: N/A

INTERFERING FACTORS

- Drugs that may increase AT-III levels include anabolic steroids, gemfibrozil, and warfarin (Coumadin).
- Drugs that may decrease AT-III levels include asparaginase, estrogens, heparin, and oral contraceptives.
- Hematocrit greater than 55% may cause falsely prolonged results because of anticoagulant excess relative to plasma volume.
- Incompletely filled collection tubes, specimens contaminated with heparin, clotted specimens, or unprocessed specimens not delivered to the laboratory within 1 to 2 hr of collection should be rejected.
- Placement of the tourniquet for longer than 1 min can result in venous stasis and changes in the concentration of the plasma proteins to be measured. Platelet activation may also occur under these conditions, resulting in erroneous measurements.

NURSING IMPLICATIONS AND PROCEDURE

PRETEST:

- Positively identify the patient using at least two unique identifiers before providing care, treatment, or services.
- *Patient Teaching:* Inform the patient this test can assist in diagnosing clotting disorders.
- Obtain a history of the patient's complaints, including a list of known allergens, especially allergies or sensitivities to latex.
- Obtain a history of the patient's hematopoietic system, symptoms, and results of previously performed laboratory tests and diagnostic and surgical procedures.
- Obtain a list of the patient's current medications, including herbs, nutritional supplements, and nutraceuticals (see Appendix F).
- Review the procedure with the patient. Inform the patient that specimen collection takes approximately 5 to 10 min.

Address concerns about pain and explain that there may be some discomfort during the venipuncture.

Sensitivity to social and cultural issues, as well as concern for modesty, is important in providing psychological support before, during, and after the procedure.

There are no food, fluid, or medication restrictions unless by medical direction.

INTRATEST:

If the patient has a history of allergic reaction to latex, avoid the use of equipment containing latex.

Instruct the patient to cooperate fully and to follow directions. Direct the patient to breathe normally and to avoid unnecessary movement.

Observe standard precautions, and follow the general guidelines in Appendix A. Positively identify the patient, and label the appropriate specimen container with the corresponding patient demographics, initials of the person collecting the specimen, date, and time of collection. Perform a venipuncture. Fill tube completely. *Important note:* Two different concentrations of sodium citrate preservative are currently added to blue-top tubes for coagulation studies: 3.2% and 3.8%. The Clinical and Laboratory Standards Institute/CLSI (formerly the National Committee for Clinical Laboratory Standards/NCCLS) guideline for sodium citrate is 3.2%. Laboratories establish reference ranges for coagulation testing based on numerous factors, including sodium citrate concentration, test equipment, and test reagents. It is important to ask the laboratory which concentration it recommends, because each concentration will have its own specific reference range. When multiple specimens are drawn, the blue-top tube should be collected after sterile (i.e., blood culture) tubes. Otherwise, when using a standard vacutainer system, the blue top is the first tube collected. When a butterfly is used, due to the added tubing, an extra red-top tube should be collected before the blue-top tube to ensure complete filling of the blue-top tube.

Remove the needle and apply direct pressure with dry gauze to stop bleeding. Observe/assess venipuncture site for bleeding or hematoma

formation and secure gauze with adhesive bandage.

Promptly transport the specimen to the laboratory for processing and analysis. The CLSI recommendation for processed and unprocessed samples stored in unopened tubes is that testing should be completed within 1 to 4 hr of collection. If the patient has a known hematocrit above 55%, adjust the amount of anticoagulant in the collection tube before drawing the blood according to the CLSI guidelines:

$$\text{Anticoagulant vol } [x] =$$
$$(100 - \text{hematocrit})/(595 - \text{hematocrit})$$
$$\times \text{ total vol of anticoagulated blood required}$$

Example:

$$\text{Patient hematocrit} = 60\%$$
$$= [(100 - 60)/(595 - 60) \times 5.0]$$
$$= 0.37 \text{ mL sodium citrate for a 5-mL standard drawing tube}$$

POST-TEST:

A report of the results will be made available to the requesting health-care provider (HCP), who will discuss the results with the patient.

Reinforce information given by the patient's HCP regarding further testing, treatment, or referral to another HCP. Answer any questions or address any concerns voiced by the patient or family.

Depending on the results of this procedure, additional testing may be performed to evaluate or monitor progression of the disease process and determine the need for a change in therapy. Evaluate test results in relation to the patient's symptoms and other tests performed.

RELATED MONOGRAPHS:

Related tests include antibodies cardiolipin, echocardiography, lung perfusion scan, aPTT, procalcitonin, protein C, protein S, US venous Doppler extremity studies, venography lower extremities, and vitamin K.

See the Hematopoietic System table a the end of the book for related tests by body system.

α₁-Antitrypsin and α₁-Antitrypsin Phenotyping

A

SYNONYM/ACRONYM: α₁-antitrypsin: A₁AT, α₁-AT, AAT; α₁-antitrypsin phenotyping: A₁AT phenotype, α₁-AT phenotype, AAT phenotype, Pi phenotype.

COMMON USE: To assist in the identification of chronic obstructive pulmonary disease (COPD) and liver disease associated with α₁-antitrypsin (α₁-AT) deficiency.

SPECIMEN: Serum (1 mL) for α₁-AT and serum (2 mL) for α₁-AT phenotyping collected in a red- or tiger-top tube.

NORMAL FINDINGS: (Method: Rate nephelometry for α₁-AT, isoelectric focusing/high-resolution electrophoresis for α₁-AT phenotyping)

α₁-Antitrypsin

Age	Conventional Units	SI Units (Conventional Units × 0.01)
0–1 mo	124–348 mg/dL	1.24–3.48 g/L
2–6 mo	111–297 mg/dL	1.11–2.97 g/L
7 mo–2 yr	95–251 mg/dL	0.95–2.51 g/L
3–19 yr	110–279 mg/dL	1.10–2.79 g/L
Adult	126–226 mg/dL	1.26–2.26 g/L

α₁-Antitrypsin Phenotyping

There are three major protease inhibitor phenotypes:

- MM—Normal
- SS—Intermediate; heterozygous
- ZZ—Markedly abnormal; homozygous

The total level of measurable α₁-AT varies with genotype. The effects of α₁-AT deficiency depend on the patient's personal habits but are most severe in patients who smoke tobacco.

DESCRIPTION: α₁-AT is the main glycoprotein produced by the liver. Its inhibitory function is directed against proteolytic enzymes, such as trypsin, elastin, and plasmin, released by alveolar macrophages and bacteria. In the absence of α₁-AT, functional tissue is destroyed by proteolytic enzymes and replaced with excessive connective tissue. Emphysema develops at an earlier age in α₁-AT–deficient emphysema patients than in other emphysema patients. α₁-AT deficiency is passed on as an autosomal recessive trait. Inherited deficiencies are associated early in life with development of lung and liver disorders. In the pediatric population, the ZZ phenotype usually presents as liver disease, cholestasis, and cirrhosis. Greater than 80% of ZZ-deficient individuals ultimately develop chronic lung or liver disease. It is important to identify inherited deficiencies early in life. Typically, α₁-AT–deficient patients have circulating

A

levels less than 50 mg/dL. Patients who have α_1-AT values less than 140 mg/dL should be phenotyped. Elevated levels are found in normal individuals when an inflammatory process, such as rheumatoid arthritis, bacterial infection, neoplasm, or vasculitis, is present. Decreased levels are found in affected patients with COPD and in children with cirrhosis of the liver. Deficiency of this enzyme is the most common cause of liver disease in the pediatric population. Decreased α_1-AT levels also may be elevated into the normal range in heterozygous α_1-AT–deficient patients during concurrent infection, pregnancy, estrogen therapy, steroid therapy, cancer, and postoperative periods. Homozygous α_1-AT–deficient patients do not show such an elevation.

INDICATIONS
- Assist in establishing a diagnosis of COPD
- Assist in establishing a diagnosis of liver disease
- Detect hereditary absence or deficiency of α_1-AT

POTENTIAL DIAGNOSIS

Increased in
- Acute and chronic inflammatory conditions *(related to rapid, non-specific response to inflammation)*
- Carcinomas *(related to rapid, non-specific response to inflammation)*
- Estrogen therapy
- Postoperative recovery *(related to rapid, nonspecific response to inflammation or stress)*
- Pregnancy *(related to rapid, non-specific response to stress)*
- Steroid therapy
- Stress (extreme physical) *(related to rapid, nonspecific response to stress)*

Decreased in
- COPD *(related to malnutrition and evidenced by decreased protein synthesis)*
- Homozygous α_1-AT–deficient patients *(related to decreased protein synthesis)*
- Liver disease (severe) *(related to decreased protein synthesis)*
- Liver cirrhosis (infant or child) *(related to decreased protein synthesis)*
- Malnutrition *(related to insufficient protein intake)*
- Nephrotic syndrome *(related to increased protein loss from diminished renal function)*

CRITICAL FINDINGS: N/A

INTERFERING FACTORS
- α_1-AT is an acute-phase reactant protein, and any inflammatory process elevates levels. If a serum C–reactive protein is performed simultaneously and is positive, the patient should be retested for α_1-AT in 10 to 14 days.
- Rheumatoid factor causes false-positive elevations.
- Drugs that may increase serum α_1-AT levels include aminocaproic acid, estrogen therapy, oral contraceptives (high-dose preparations), oxymetholone, streptokinase, tamoxifen, and typhoid vaccine.

NURSING IMPLICATIONS AND PROCEDURE

PRETEST:
- Positively identify the patient using at least two unique identifiers before providing care, treatment, or services.
- *Patient Teaching:* Inform the patient this test can assist in identifying lung and liver disease.
- Obtain a history of the patient's complaints, including a list of known allergens, especially allergies or sensitivities to latex.

Obtain a history of the patient's hepatobiliary and respiratory systems, symptoms, and results of previously performed laboratory tests and diagnostic and surgical procedures. Obtain a list of the patient's current medications, including herbs, nutritional supplements, and nutraceuticals (see Appendix F). Oral contraceptives should be withheld 24 hr before the specimen is collected, although this restriction should first be confirmed with the health-care provider (HCP) ordering the test.

Review the procedure with the patient. Inform the patient that specimen collection takes approximately 5 to 10 min. Address concerns about pain and explain to the patient that there may be some discomfort during the venipuncture.

Sensitivity to social and cultural issues, as well as concern for modesty, is important in providing psychological support before, during, and after the procedure. There are no food, fluid, or medication restrictions unless by medical direction.

If the patient has a history of allergic reaction to latex, avoid the use of equipment containing latex. Instruct the patient to cooperate fully and to follow directions. Direct the patient to breathe normally and to avoid unnecessary movement. Observe standard precautions, and follow the general guidelines in Appendix A. Positively identify the patient, and label the appropriate specimen container with the corresponding patient demographics, initials of the person collecting the specimen, date, and time of collection. Perform a venipuncture. Remove the needle and apply direct pressure with dry gauze to stop bleeding. Observe/assess venipuncture site for bleeding or hematoma formation and secure gauze with adhesive bandage. Promptly transport the specimen to the laboratory for processing and analysis.

A report of the results will be made available to the requesting HCP, who will discuss the results with the patient.

Instruct the patient to resume usual medication as directed by the HCP.

Nutritional Considerations: Malnutrition is commonly seen in α_1-AT–deficient patients with severe respiratory disease for many reasons, including fatigue, lack of appetite, and gastrointestinal distress. Research has estimated that the daily caloric intake required for respiration in patients with COPD is 10 times higher than that required in normal individuals. Inadequate nutrition can result in hypophosphatemia, especially in the respirator-dependent patient. During periods of starvation, phosphorus leaves the intracellular space and moves outside the tissue, resulting in dangerously decreased phosphorus levels. Adequate intake of vitamins A and C is important to prevent pulmonary infection and to decrease the extent of lung tissue damage. The importance of following the prescribed diet should be stressed to the patient and caregiver.

Nutritional Considerations: Water balance must be closely monitored in α_1-AT–deficient patients with COPD. Fluid retention can lead to pulmonary edema. Educate the patient with abnormal findings in preventive measures for protection of the lungs (e.g., avoid contact with persons who have respiratory or other infections; avoid the use of tobacco; avoid areas having highly polluted air; and avoid work environments with hazards such as fumes, dust, and other respiratory pollutants). Instruct the affected patient in deep breathing and pursed-lip breathing to enhance breathing patterns as appropriate. Inform the patient of smoking cessation programs, as appropriate. Recognize anxiety related to test results, and be supportive of fear of shortened life expectancy. Discuss the implications of abnormal test results on the patient's lifestyle. Provide teaching and information regarding the clinical implications of the test results, as appropriate. Because decreased α_1-AT can be an inherited disorder, it may be appropriate to recommend resources for genetic counseling if levels less than 140 mg/dL are reported. It may also be appropriate to inform the patient that α_1-AT phenotype testing can be performed on family members

A

to determine the homozygous or heterozygous nature of the deficiency.

Reinforce information given by the patient's HCP regarding further testing, treatment, or referral to another HCP. Inform the patient of the importance of medical follow-up, and suggest ongoing support resources to assist the patient in coping with chronic illness and possible early death. Answer any questions or address any concerns voiced by the patient or family.

Depending on the results of this procedure, additional testing may be performed to evaluate or monitor progression of the disease process and determine the need for a change in therapy. Evaluate test results in relation to the patient's symptoms and other tests performed.

RELATED MONOGRAPHS:

Related tests include ACE, anion gap, arterial/alveolar oxygen ratio, biopsy lung, blood gases, blood pool imaging, bronchoscopy, electrolytes, lung perfusion scan, lung ventilation scan, osmolality, PET heart, phosphorus, PFTs, plethysmography, and pulse oximetry if COPD is suspected. ALT, albumin, ALP, ammonia, bilirubin and fractions, biopsy liver, cholangiography percutaneous transhepatic, cholangiography postop, CT biliary tract and liver, ERCP, GGT, hepatobiliary scan, liver and spleen scan, protein and fractions, PT/INR, and US liver if liver disease is suspected.

See the Hepatobiliary and Respiratory systems tables at the end of the book for related tests by body system.

Apolipoproteins: A, B, and E

SYNONYM/ACRONYM: Apo A (Apo A1), Apo B (Apo B100), and Apo E.

COMMON USE: To identify levels of circulating lipoprotein to evaluate the risk of coronary artery disease.

SPECIMEN: Serum (1 mL) collected in a red- or tiger-top tube or plasma collected in a green- (heparin) or lavender-top (EDTA) tube for Apo A and Apo B. Plasma (1mL) collected in a lavender-top (EDTA) tube.

NORMAL FINDINGS: (Method: Immunonephelometry for Apo A and Apo B; PCR with restriction length enzyme digestion and polyacrylamide gel electrophoresis for Apo E)

Apolipoprotein A

Age	Conventional Units	SI Units (Conventional Units × 0.01)
Newborn		
Male	41–93 mg/dL	0.41–0.93 g/L
Female	38–106 mg/dL	0.38–1.06 g/L
6 mo–4 yr		
Male	67–163 mg/dL	0.67–1.63 g/L
Female	60–148 mg/dL	0.60–1.48 g/L
Adult		
Male	81–166 mg/dL	0.81–1.66 g/L
Female	80–214 mg/dL	0.80–2.14 g/L

Apolipoprotein B

Age	Conventional Units	SI Units (Conventional Units × 0.01)
Newborn–5 yr	11–31 mg/dL	0.11–0.31 g/L
5–17 yr		
Male	47–139 mg/dL	0.47–1.39 g/L
Female	41–96 mg/dL	0.41–0.96 g/L
Adult		
Male	46–174 mg/dL	0.46–1.74 g/L
Female	46–142 mg/dL	0.46–1.42 g/L

Normal Apo E: Homozygous phenotype for e3/e3.

DESCRIPTION: Apolipoproteins assist in the regulation of lipid metabolism by activating and inhibiting enzymes required for this process. The apolipoproteins also help keep lipids in solution as they circulate in the blood and direct the lipids toward the correct target organs and tissues in the body. A number of types of apolipoproteins have been identified (A, B, C, D, E, H, J), each of which contain subgroups. Apolipoprotein A (Apo A), the major component of high-density lipoprotein (HDL), is synthesized in the liver and intestines. Apo A-I activates the enzyme lecithin-cholesterol acyltransferase (LCAT), whereas Apo A-II inhibits LCAT. It is believed that Apo A measurements may be more important than HDL cholesterol measurements as a predictor of coronary artery disease (CAD). There is an inverse relationship between Apo A levels and risk for developing CAD. Because of difficulties with method standardization, the above-listed reference ranges should be used as a rough guide in assessing abnormal conditions. Values for African Americans are 5 to 10 mg/dL higher than values for whites. Apolipoprotein B (Apo B), the major component of the low-density lipoproteins (chylomicrons, low-density lipoprotein [LDL], and very-low-density lipoprotein), is synthesized in the liver and intestines. Apolipoprotein E is found in most lipoproteins, except LDL, and is synthesized in a variety of cell types including liver, brain astrocytes, spleen, lungs, adrenals, ovaries, kidneys, muscle cells, and in macrophages. The largest amount is produced by the liver; the next significant amount is produced by the brain. There are three forms of Apo E: apo-E 2, apo-E 3, and apo-E 4, and six possible combinations; of these, Apo E 3 (e3/3e) is the fully functioning form. The varied roles of Apo E include removal of chylomicrons and very-low-density lipoprotein (VLDL) from the circulation by binding to LDL. The Apo E2 isoform demonstrates significantly less LDL receptor binding, which results in impaired clearance of chylomicrons, VLDL, and triglyceride remnants. The presence of Apo E isoforms E2 and E4 is associated with high cholesterol levels, high triglyceride levels, and the premature development of atherosclerosis. The presence of the E2 isoform is associated with type III hyperlipidemia, a familial dyslipidemia,

A

which is important to distinguish from other causes of hyperlipidemia to determine the correct treatment regimen. Apo E4 is being used in association with studies of predisposing factors in the development of Alzheimer's disease. Detailed information is found in the monograph titled "Alzheimer's Disease Markers."

INDICATIONS
• Evaluation for risk of CAD

POTENTIAL DIAGNOSIS
Apolipoproteins are the protein portion of lipoproteins. Their function is to transport and to assist in cell surface receptor recognition and cellular absorption of lipoproteins to be used as energy. While studies of the exact role of apolipoproteins in health and disease continue, there is a very strong association between Apo A and HDL "good" cholesterol and Apo B and LDL "bad" cholesterol.

Apolipoprotein A

Increased in
• Familial hyper-α-lipoproteinemia
• Pregnancy
• Weight reduction

Decreased in
• Abetalipoproteinemia
• Cholestasis
• Chronic renal failure
• Coronary artery disease
• Diabetes (uncontrolled)
• Diet high in carbohydrates or polyunsaturated fats
• Familial deficiencies of related enzymes and lipoproteins (e.g., Tangier's disease)
• Hemodialysis
• Hepatocellular disorders
• Hypertriglyceridemia
• Nephrotic syndrome
• Premature coronary heart disease
• Smoking

Apolipoprotein B

Increased in
• Anorexia nervosa
• Biliary obstruction
• Coronary artery disease
• Cushing's syndrome
• Diabetes
• Dysglobulinemia
• Emotional stress
• Hemodialysis
• Hepatic disease
• Hepatic obstruction
• Hyperlipoproteinemias
• Hypothyroidism
• Infantile hypercalcemia
• Nephrotic syndrome
• Porphyria
• Pregnancy
• Premature CAD
• Renal failure
• Werner's syndrome

Decreased in
• Acute stress (burns, illness)
• Chronic anemias
• Chronic pulmonary disease
• Familial deficiencies of related enzymes and lipoproteins (e.g., Tangier's disease)
• Hyperthyroidism
• Inflammatory joint disease
• Intestinal malabsorption
• α-Lipoprotein deficiency (Tangier's disease)
• Malnutrition
• Myeloma
• Reye's syndrome
• Weight reduction

CRITICAL FINDINGS: N/A

INTERFERING FACTORS
• Drugs and substances that may increase Apo A levels include anticonvulsants, beclobrate, bezafibrate ciprofibrate, estrogens, furosemide, lovastatin, pravastatin, prednisolone simvastatin, and ethanol (abuse).
• Drugs that may decrease Apo A levels include androgens, β-blockers, diuretics, and probucol.

- Drugs that may increase Apo B levels include amiodarone, androgens, β-blockers, catecholamines, cyclosporine, diuretics, ethanol (abuse), etretinate, glucogenic corticosteroids, oral contraceptives, and phenobarbital.
- Drugs that may decrease Apo B levels include beclobrate, captopril, cholestyramine, fibrates, ketanserin, lovastatin, niacin, nifedipine, pravastatin, prazosin, probucol, and simvastatin.
- Drugs that may decrease Apo E levels include bezafibrate, fluvastatin, gemfibrozil, ketanserin, lovastatin, niacin, nifedipine, oral contraceptives, pravastatin, probucol, and simvastatin.
- Failure to follow dietary restrictions before the procedure may cause the procedure to be canceled or repeated.

NURSING IMPLICATIONS AND PROCEDURE

PRETEST:

▸ Positively identify the patient using at least two unique identifiers before providing care, treatment, or services.
▸ *Patient Teaching:* Inform the patient this test can assist in assessing and monitoring risk for coronary artery (heart) disease.
▸ Obtain a history of the patient's complaints, including a list of known allergens, especially allergies or sensitivities to latex.
▸ Obtain a history of the patient's cardiovascular system, symptoms, and results of previously performed laboratory tests and diagnostic and surgical procedures.
▸ Obtain a list of the patient's current medication, including herbs, nutritional supplements, and nutraceuticals (see Appendix F).
▸ Review the procedure with the patient. Inform the patient that specimen collection takes approximately 5 to

10 min. Address concerns about pain and explain that there may be some discomfort during the venipuncture. *Sensitivity to social and cultural issues,* as well as concern for modesty, is important in providing psychological support before, during, and after the procedure.
▸ The patient should abstain from food for 6 to 12 hr before specimen collection.
▸ There are no fluid or medication restrictions unless by medical direction.

INTRATEST:

▸ Ensure that the patient has complied with dietary or activity restrictions, and pretesting preparations; assure that food has been restricted for at least 6 to 12 hr prior to the procedure.
▸ If the patient has a history of allergic reaction to latex, avoid the use of equipment containing latex.
▸ Instruct the patient to cooperate fully and to follow directions. Direct the patient to breathe normally and to avoid unnecessary movement.
▸ Observe standard precautions, and follow the general guidelines in Appendix A. Positively identify the patient, and label the appropriate specimen container with the corresponding patient demographics, initials of the person collecting the specimen, date, and time of collection. Perform a venipuncture.
▸ Remove the needle and apply direct pressure with dry gauze to stop bleeding. Observe/assess venipuncture site for bleeding or hematoma formation and secure gauze with adhesive bandage.
▸ Promptly transport the specimen to the laboratory for processing and analysis.

POST-TEST:

▸ A report of the results will be made available to the requesting health-care provider (HCP), who will discuss the results with the patient.
▸ Instruct the patient to resume usual diet as directed by the HCP.

A

Nutritional Considerations: Decreased Apo A and/or increased Apo B levels may be associated with CAD. The American Heart Association and National Heart, Lung, and Blood Institute (NHLBI) recommend nutritional therapy for individuals identified to be at high risk for developing CAD or individuals who have specific risk factors and/or existing medical conditions (e.g., elevated LDL cholesterol levels, other lipid disorders, insulin-dependent diabetes, insulin resistance, or metabolic syndrome). If overweight, the patient should be encouraged to achieve a normal weight. Guidelines for the Therapeutic Lifestyle Changes (TLC) diet are outlined in the Third Report of the Expert Panel on Detection, Evaluation, and Treatment of High Blood Cholesterol in Adults (Adult Treatment Panel III [ATP III]). The TLC diet emphasizes a reduction in foods high in saturated fats and cholesterol. Red meats, eggs, and dairy products are the major sources of saturated fats and cholesterol. If triglycerides also are elevated, the patient should be advised to eliminate or reduce alcohol and simple carbohydrates from the diet. The TLC approach also includes the use of plant stanols or sterols and increased dissolved fiber as an option for lowering LDL cholesterol levels; nutritional recommendations for daily total caloric intake; recommendations for allowable percentage of calories derived from fat (saturated and unsaturated), carbohydrates, protein, and cholesterol; as well as recommendations for daily expenditure of energy.

Nutritional Considerations: Overweight patients with high blood pressure should be encouraged to achieve a normal weight. Other changeable risk factors warranting patient education include strategies to safely decrease sodium intake, increase physical activity, decrease alcohol consumption, eliminate tobacco use, and decrease cholesterol levels.

Social and Cultural Considerations: Numerous studies point to the prevalence of excess body weight in American children and adolescents. Experts estimate that obesity is present in 25% of the population ages 6 to 11. The medical, social, and emotional consequences of excess body weight are significant. Special attention should be given to instructing the child and caregiver regarding health risks and weight-control education.

▶ Recognize anxiety related to test results, and be supportive of fear of shortened life expectancy. Discuss the implications of abnormal test results on the patient's lifestyle. Provide teaching and information regarding the clinical implications of the test results, as appropriate. Educate the patient regarding access to counseling services. Provide contact information, if desired, for the American Heart Association (www.americanheart.org) or the NHLBI (www.nhlbi.nih.gov).

▶ Reinforce information given by the patient's HCP regarding further testing, treatment, or referral to another HCP. Answer any questions or address any concerns voiced by the patient or family.

▶ Depending on the results of this procedure, additional testing may be performed to evaluate or monitor progression of the disease process and determine the need for a change in therapy. Evaluate test results in relation to the patient's symptoms and other tests performed.

RELATED MONOGRAPHS:

▶ Related tests include Alzheimer's disease markers, antiarrhythmic drugs, AST, ANP, BNP, blood gases, CRP, calcium and ionized calcium, cholesterol (total, HDL, and LDL), CK and isoenzymes, CT scoring, echocardiography, glucose, glycated hemoglobin, Holter monitor, homocysteine, ketones, LDH and isoenzymes, lipoprotein electrophoresis, magnesium, MRI chest, myocardial infarct scan, myocardial perfusion heart scan, myoglobin, PET heart, potassium, triglycerides, and troponin.

▶ See the Cardiovascular System table at the end of the book for related tests by body system.

Arthrogram

SYNONYM/ACRONYM: Joint study.

COMMON USE: To assess and identify the cause of persistent joint pain and monitor the progression of joint disease.

AREA OF APPLICATION: Shoulder, elbow, wrist, hip, knee, ankle, temporomandibular joint.

CONTRAST: Iodinated or gadolinium.

DESCRIPTION: An arthrogram evaluates the cartilage, ligaments, and bony structures that compose a joint. After local anesthesia is administered to the area of interest, a fluoroscopically guided small-gauge needle is inserted into the joint space. Fluid in the joint space is aspirated and sent to the laboratory for analysis. Contrast medium is inserted into the joint space to outline the soft tissue structures and the contour of the joint. After brief exercise of the joint, radiographs or magnetic resonance images (MRIs) are obtained. Arthrograms are used primarily for assessment of persistent, unexplained joint discomfort.

INDICATIONS
- Evaluate pain, swelling, or dysfunction of a joint
- Monitor disease progression

POTENTIAL DIAGNOSIS

Normal findings in
- Normal bursae, menisci, ligaments, and articular cartilage of the joint (note: the cartilaginous surfaces and menisci should be smooth, without evidence of erosion, tears, or disintegration)

Abnormal findings in
- Arthritis
- Cysts
- Diseases of the cartilage (chondromalacia)
- Injury to the ligaments
- Joint derangement
- Meniscal tears or laceration
- Muscle tears
- Osteochondral fractures
- Osteochondritis dissecans
- Synovial tumor
- Synovitis

CRITICAL FINDINGS: N/A

INTERFERING FACTORS

This procedure is contraindicated for
- Patients with allergies to shellfish or iodinated dye. The contrast medium used may cause a life-threatening allergic reaction. Patients with a known hypersensitivity to the medium may benefit from premedication with corticosteroids or the use of a nonionic contrast medium.
- Patients with metal in their body, such as shrapnel or ferrous metal in the eye.
- Patients with cardiac pacemakers, because the pacemaker can be deactivated by MRI.
- Use of gadolinium-based contrast agents (GBCAs) is contraindicated

A

in patients with acute or chronic severe renal insufficiency (glomerular filtration rate less than 30 mL/min/1.73 m^2). Patients should be screened for renal dysfunction prior to administration. The use of GBCAs should be avoided in these patients unless the benefits of the studies outweigh the risks and if essential diagnostic information is not available using non–contrast-enhanced diagnostic studies.

- Patients who are pregnant or suspected of being pregnant, unless the potential benefits of the procedure far outweigh the risks to the fetus and mother.
- Patients with bleeding disorders, active arthritis, or joint infections.

Factors that may impair clear imaging

- Metallic objects within the examination field which may inhibit organ visualization and can produce unclear images
- Inability of the patient to cooperate or remain still during the procedure because of age, significant pain, or mental status

Other considerations

- Consultation with a health-care provider (HCP) should occur before the procedure for radiation safety concerns regarding younger patients or patients who are lactating.
- Risks associated with radiation overexposure can result from frequent x-ray procedures. Personnel in the examination room with the patient should wear a protective lead apron, stand behind a shield, or leave the area while the examination is being done. Personnel working in the examination area should wear badges to record their level of radiation exposure.

NURSING IMPLICATIONS AND PROCEDURE

PRETEST:

▶ Positively identify the patient using at least two unique identifiers before providing care, treatment, or services.

▶ *Patient Teaching:* Inform the patient this procedure can assist in assessing the joint being examined.

▶ Obtain a history of the patient's complaints, including a list of known allergens, especially allergies or sensitivities to latex, iodine, seafood, contrast medium, anesthetics and dyes.

▶ Obtain a history of the patient's musculoskeletal system, symptoms, and previously performed laboratory tests and diagnostic and surgical procedures. Ensure that the results of blood tests are obtained and recorded before the procedure, especially coagulation tests, BUN, and creatinine, if contrast medium is to be used. Obtain a history of renal dysfunction if the use of GBCA is anticipated.

▶ Ensure the results of BUN, creatinine, and eGFR (estimated glomerular filtration rate) are obtained if GBCA is to be used.

▶ Record the date of the last menstrual period and determine the possibility of pregnancy in perimenopausal women.

▶ Obtain a list of the patient's current medications, including anticoagulants, aspirin and other salicylates, herbs, nutritional supplements, and nutraceuticals (see Appendix F). Such products should be discontinued by medical direction for the appropriate number of days prior to a surgical procedure. Note the last time and dose of medication taken.

▶ Review the procedure with the patient. Address concerns about pain and explain that there may be moments of discomfort and some pain experienced during the test. Inform the patient that the procedure is usually performed in the radiology department by an HCP and takes approximately 30 to 60 min.

▶ *Sensitivity to social and cultural issues,* as well as concern for modesty, is important in providing psychological support before, during, and after the procedure.

There are no food, fluid, or medication restrictions unless by medical direction.

Make sure a written and informed consent has been signed prior to the procedure and before administering any medications.

INTRATEST:

Observe standard precautions, and follow the general guidelines in Appendix A. Positively identify the patient.

Ensure that the patient has removed all external metallic objects prior to the procedure.

Have emergency equipment readily available.

If the patient has a history of allergic reactions to any substance or drug, administer ordered prophylactic steroids or antihistamines before the procedure.

Have emergency equipment readily available.

Instruct the patient to void prior to the procedure and to change into the gown, robe, and foot coverings provided.

Place the patient on the table in a supine position.

The skin surrounding the joint is aseptically cleaned and anesthetized.

A small-gauge needle is inserted into the joint space.

Any fluid in the space is aspirated and sent to the laboratory for analysis.

Contrast medium is inserted into the joint space with fluoroscopic guidance.

The needle is removed, and the joint is exercised to help distribute the contrast medium.

X-rays or MRIs are taken of the joint.

Instruct the patient to cooperate fully and to follow directions. Instruct the patient to remain still throughout the procedure because movement produces unreliable results.

During x-ray imaging, lead protection is placed over the gonads to prevent their irradiation.

If MRI images are taken, supply earplugs to the patient to block out the loud, banging sounds that occur during the test. Instruct the patient to communicate with the technologist during the examination via a microphone within the scanner.

POST-TEST:

A report of the results will be made available to the requesting HCP, who will discuss the results with the patient.

Observe/assess the joint for swelling after the test. Apply ice as needed.

Instruct the patient to use a mild analgesic (aspirin, acetaminophen), as ordered, if there is discomfort.

Advise the patient to avoid strenuous activity until approved by the HCP.

Instruct the patient to notify the HCP if fever, increased pain, drainage, warmth, edema, or swelling of the joint occurs.

Inform the patient that noises from the joint after the procedure are common and should disappear 24 to 48 hr after the procedure.

Recognize anxiety related to test results, and be supportive of impaired activity related to anticipated chronic pain resulting from joint inflammation, impairment in mobility, musculoskeletal deformity, and loss of independence. Discuss the implications of abnormal test results on the patient's lifestyle. Provide teaching and information regarding the clinical implications of the test results, as appropriate. Educate the patient regarding access to counseling services, as appropriate. Provide contact information, if desired, for the American College of Rheumatology (www.rheumatology.org) or for the Arthritis Foundation (www.arthritis.org).

Reinforce information given by the patient's HCP regarding further testing, treatment, or referral to another HCP. Answer any questions or address any concerns voiced by the patient or family.

Depending on the results of this procedure, additional testing may be needed to evaluate or monitor progression of the disease process and determine the need for a change in therapy. Evaluate test results in relation to the patient's symptoms and other tests performed.

A

RELATED MONOGRAPHS:

Related tests include antibodies anticyclic citrullinated peptide, ANA, arthroscopy, BMD, bone scan, BUN, CBC, CRP, creatinine, ESR, MRI musculoskeletal, PT/INR, radiography bone, RF, synovial fluid analysis, and uric acid.

Refer to the Musculoskeletal System table at the end of the book for related tests by body system.

Arthroscopy

SYNONYM/ACRONYM: N/A.

COMMON USE: To obtain direct visualization of a specific joint to assist in diagnosis of joint disease.

AREA OF APPLICATION: Joints.

CONTRAST: None.

DESCRIPTION: Arthroscopy provides direct visualization of a joint through the use of a fiberoptic endoscope. The arthroscope has a light, fiberoptics, and lenses; it connects to a monitor, and the images are recorded for future study and comparison. This procedure is used for inspection of joint structures, performance of a biopsy, and surgical repairs to the joint. Meniscus removal, spur removal, and ligamentous repair are some of the surgical procedures that may be performed. This procedure is most commonly performed to diagnose athletic injuries and acute or chronic joint disorders. Because arthroscopy allows direct visualization, degenerative processes can be accurately differentiated from injuries. A local anesthetic allows the arthroscope to be inserted through the skin with minimal discomfort. This procedure may also be done under a spinal or general anesthetic, especially if surgery is anticipated.

INDICATIONS
- Detect torn ligament or tendon
- Evaluate joint pain and damaged cartilage
- Evaluate meniscal, patellar, condylar extrasynovial, and synovial injuries or diseases of the knee
- Evaluate the extent of arthritis
- Evaluate the presence of gout
- Monitor effectiveness of therapy
- Remove loose objects

POTENTIAL DIAGNOSIS

Normal findings in
- Normal muscle, ligament, cartilage, synovial, and tendon structures of the joint

Abnormal findings in
- Arthritis
- Chondromalacia

- Cysts
- Degenerative joint changes
- Ganglion or Baker's cyst
- Gout or pseudogout
- Joint tumors
- Loose bodies
- Meniscal disease
- Osteoarthritis
- Osteochondritis
- Rheumatoid arthritis
- Subluxation, fracture, or dislocation
- Synovitis
- Torn cartilage
- Torn ligament
- Torn rotator cuff
- Trapped synovium

CRITICAL FINDINGS: N/A

INTERFERING FACTORS

This procedure is contraindicated for
- Patients with bleeding disorders, active arthritis, or cardiac conditions.
- Patients with joint infection or skin infection near proposed arthroscopic site.
- Patients who have had an arthrogram within the last 14 days.

Factors that may impair clear imaging
- Inability of the patient to cooperate or remain still during the procedure because of age, significant pain, or mental status.
- Fibrous ankylosis of the joint preventing effective use of the arthroscope.
- Joints with flexion of less than 50°.

Other considerations
- Failure to follow dietary restrictions before the procedure may cause the procedure to be canceled or repeated.

NURSING IMPLICATIONS AND PROCEDURE

PRETEST:

▶ Positively identify the patient using at least two unique identifiers before providing care, treatment, or services.

▶ *Patient Teaching:* Inform the patient this procedure can assist in assessing the joint being examined.

▶ Obtain a history of the patient's complaints, including a list of known allergens, especially allergies or sensitivities to latex and anesthetics.

▶ Obtain a history of the patient's musculoskeletal system, symptoms, and results of previously performed laboratory tests and diagnostic and surgical procedures.

▶ Record the date of the last menstrual period and determine the possibility of pregnancy in perimenopausal women.

▶ Obtain a list of the patient's current medications including anticoagulants, aspirin and other salicylates, herbs, nutritional supplements, and nutraceuticals (see Appendix F). Such products should be discontinued by medical direction for the appropriate number of days prior to a surgical procedure. Note the last time and dose of medication taken.

▶ Review the procedure with the patient. Address concerns about pain, and explain that some discomfort and pain may be experienced during the test. Inform the patient that the procedure is performed by a health-care provider (HCP), usually in the surgery department, and takes approximately 30 to 60 min.

▶ Explain that a preprocedure sedative may be administered to promote relaxation, as ordered.

▶ Crutch walking should be taught before the procedure if it is anticipated postoperatively.

▶ The joint area and areas 5 to 6 in. above and below the joint are shaved and prepared for the procedure.

▶ *Sensitivity to social and cultural issues,* as well as concern for modesty, is important in providing psychological support before, during, and after the procedure.

A

Instruct the patient to refrain from food and fluids for 6 to 8 hr before the test. Protocols may vary among facilities.
Make sure a written and informed consent has been signed prior to the procedure and before administering any medications.

INTRATEST:

Observe standard precautions, and follow the general guidelines in Appendix A. Positively identify the patient.

Ensure the patient has complied with food and fluid restrictions for at least 6 to 8 hr prior to the procedure.

Resuscitation equipment and patient monitoring equipment must be available.

Instruct the patient to void prior to the procedure and to change into the gown, robe, and foot coverings provided.

The extremity is scrubbed, elevated, and wrapped with an elastic bandage from the distal portion of the extremity to the proximal portion to drain as much blood from the limb as possible.

A pneumatic tourniquet placed around the proximal portion of the limb is inflated, and the elastic bandage is removed.

As an alternative to a tourniquet, a mixture of lidocaine with epinephrine and sterile normal saline may be instilled into the joint to help reduce bleeding.

The joint is placed in a 45° angle, and a local anesthetic is administered.

A small incision is made in the skin in the lateral or medial aspect of the joint.

The arthroscope is inserted into the joint spaces. The joint is manipulated as it is visualized. Added puncture sites may be needed to provide a full view of the joint.

Biopsy or treatment can be performed at this time, and photographs should be taken for future reference.

After inspection, specimens may be obtained for cytological and microbiological study. All specimens are placed in appropriate containers, labeled with the corresponding patient demographics, date and time of collection, site location, and promptly sent to the laboratory.

The joint is irrigated, and the arthroscope is removed. Manual pressure is applied to the joint to remove remaining irrigation solution.

The incision sites are sutured, and a pressure dressing is applied.

Sterile gloves and gowns are worn throughout the procedure.

POST-TEST:

A report of the results will be made available to the requesting HCP, who will discuss the results with the patient.

Advise the patient to avoid strenuous activity involving the joint until approved by the HCP.

Instruct the patient to resume normal diet and medications, as directed by the HCP.

Monitor the patient's circulation and sensations in the joint area.

Instruct the patient to immediately report symptoms such as fever, excessive bleeding, difficulty breathing, incision site redness, swelling, and tenderness.

Instruct the patient to elevate the joint when sitting and to avoid overbending of the joint to reduce swelling.

Instruct the patient to take an analgesic for joint discomfort after the procedure; ice bags may be used to reduce postprocedure swelling.

Inform the patient to shower after 48 hr but to avoid a tub bath until after his or her appointment with the HCP.

Recognize anxiety related to test results, and be supportive of impaired activity related to anticipated chronic pain resulting from joint inflammation, impairment in mobility, musculoskeletal deformity, and loss of independence. Discuss the implications of abnormal test results on the patient's lifestyle. Provide teaching and information regarding the clinical implications of the test results, as appropriate. Educate the patient regarding access to counseling services, as appropriate. Provide contact information, if desired, for the American College of Rheumatology (www.rheumatology.org) or for the Arthritis Foundation (www.arthritis.org).

Reinforce information given by the patient's HCP regarding further testing, treatment, or referral to another HCP. Answer any questions or address any concerns voiced by the patient or family. Depending on the results of this procedure, additional testing may be needed to evaluate or monitor progression of the disease process and determine the need for a change in therapy. Evaluate test results in relation to the patient's symptoms and other tests performed.

RELATED MONOGRAPHS:

Related tests include anti-cyclic citrullinated peptide, ANA, arthrogram, BMD, bone scan, CBC, CRP, ESR, MRI musculoskeletal, radiography of the bone, RF, synovial fluid analysis, and uric acid.
Refer to the Musculoskeletal System table at the end of the book for related tests by body system.

Aspartate Aminotransferase

SYNONYM/ACRONYM: Serum glutamic-oxaloacetic transaminase, AST, SGOT.

COMMON USE: Considered an indicator of cellular damage in liver disease, such as hepatitis or cirrhosis; and in heart disease, such as myocardial infarction.

SPECIMEN: Serum (1 mL) collected in a red- or tiger-top tube.

NORMAL FINDINGS: (Method: Spectrophotometry, enzymatic at 37°C)

Age	Conventional Units	SI Units (Conventional Units × 0.017)
Newborn	25–75 units/L	0.43–1.28 micro kat/L
10 days–23 mo	15–60 units/L	0.26–1.02 micro kat/L
2–3 yr	10–56 units/L	0.17–0.95 micro kat/L
4–6 yr	20–39 units/L	0.34–0.66 micro kat/L
7–19 yr	12–32 units/L	0.20–0.54 micro kat/L
20–49 yr		
Male	20–40 units/L	0.34–0.68 micro kat/L
Female	15–30 units/L	0.26–0.51 micro kat/L
Greater than 50 yr (older adult)		
Male	10–35 units/L	0.17–0.60 micro kat/L
Greater than 45 yr (older adult)		
Female	10–35 units/L	0.17–0.60 micro kat/L

Values may be slightly elevated in older adults due to the effects of medications and the presence of multiple chronic or acute diseases with or without muted symptoms.

DESCRIPTION: Aspartate aminotransferase (AST) is an enzyme that catalyzes the reversible transfer of an amino group between aspartate and α-ketoglutaric acid.

It was formerly known as serum glutamic-oxaloacetic transaminase (SGOT). AST exists in large amounts in liver and myocardial cells and in smaller but significant amounts in skeletal muscle, kidneys, pancreas, red blood cells, and the brain. Serum AST rises when there is cellular damage to the tissues where the enzyme is found. AST values greater than 500 units/L are usually associated with hepatitis and other hepatocellular diseases in an acute phase. AST levels are very elevated at birth, decrease with age to adulthood, and increase slightly in elderly adults. *Note:* Measurement of AST in evaluation of myocardial infarction has been replaced by more sensitive tests, such as creatine kinase–MB fraction (CK-MB) and troponin.

INDICATIONS

- Assist in the diagnosis of disorders or injuries involving the tissues where AST is normally found
- Assist (formerly) in the diagnosis of myocardial infarction (*Note:* AST rises within 6 to 8 hr, peaks at 24 to 48 hr, and declines to normal within 72 to 96 hr of a myocardial infarction if no further cardiac damage occurs)
- Compare serially with alanine aminotransferase levels to track the course of hepatitis
- Monitor response to therapy with potentially hepatotoxic or nephrotoxic drugs
- Monitor response to treatment for various disorders in which AST may be elevated, with tissue repair indicated by declining levels

POTENTIAL DIAGNOSIS

Increased in

AST is released from any damaged cell in which it is stored, so conditions that affect the liver, kidneys, heart, pancreas, red blood cells, or skeletal muscle, and cause cellular destruction demonstrate elevated AST levels.

Significantly Increased in (greater than five times normal levels)

- Acute hepatitis (*AST is very elevated in acute viral hepatitis*)
- Acute hepatocellular disease (*especially related to chemical toxicity or drug overdose; moderate doses of acetaminophen have initiated severe hepatocellular disease in alcoholics*)
- Acute pancreatitis
- Shock

Moderately Increased in (three to five times normal levels)

- Alcohol abuse (chronic)
- Biliary tract obstruction
- Cardiac arrhythmias
- Cardiac catheterization, angioplasty, or surgery
- Cirrhosis
- Chronic hepatitis
- Congestive heart failure
- Infectious mononucleosis
- Liver tumors
- Muscle diseases (e.g., dermatomyositis, dystrophy, gangrene, polymyositis, trichinosis)
- Myocardial infarct
- Reye's syndrome
- Trauma (*related to injury or surgery of liver, head, and other sites where AST is found*)

Slightly Increased in (two to three times normal)

- Cerebrovascular accident
- Cirrhosis, fatty liver (*related to obesity, diabetes, jejunoileal bypass, administration of total parenteral nutrition*)
- Delirium tremens
- Hemolytic anemia
- Pericarditis
- Pulmonary infarction

Decreased in

- Hemodialysis (*presumed to be related to a corresponding deficiency of vitamin B$_6$ observed in hemodialysis patients*)

A

- Uremia *(related to a buildup of toxins which modify the activity of coenzymes required for transaminase activity)*
- Vitamin B_6 deficiency *(related to the lack of vitamin B_6, a required cofactor for the transaminases)*

CRITICAL FINDINGS: N/A

INTERFERING FACTORS

- Drugs that may increase AST levels by causing cholestasis include amitriptyline, anabolic steroids, androgens, benzodiazepines, chlorothiazide, chlorpropamide, dapsone, erythromycin, estrogens, ethionamide, gold salts, imipramine, mercaptopurine, nitrofurans, oral contraceptives, penicillins, phenothiazines, progesterone, propoxyphene, sulfonamides, tamoxifen, and tolbutamide.
- Drugs that may increase AST levels by causing hepatocellular damage include acetaminophen, acetylsalicylic acid, allopurinol, amiodarone, anabolic steroids, anticonvulsants, asparaginase, azithromycin, bromocriptine, captopril, cephalosporins, chloramphenicol, clindamycin, clofibrate, danazol, enflurane, ethambutol, ethionamide, fenofibrate, fluconazole, fluoroquinolones, foscarnet, gentamicin, indomethacin, interferon, interleukin-2, levamisole, levodopa, lincomycin, low-molecular-weight heparin, methyldopa, monoamine oxidase inhibitors, naproxen, nifedipine, nitrofurans, oral contraceptives, probenecid, procainamide, quinine, ranitidine, retinol, ritodrine, sulfonylureas, tetracyclines, tobramycin, and verapamil.
- Drugs that may decrease AST levels include allopurinol, cyclosporine, interferon alpha, naltrexone, progesterone, trifluoperazine, and ursodiol.
- Hemolysis falsely increases AST values.
- Hemodialysis falsely decreases AST values.

NURSING IMPLICATIONS AND PROCEDURE

PRETEST:

- Positively identify the patient using at least two unique identifiers before providing care, treatment, or services.
- *Patient Teaching:* Inform the patient this test can assist in assessing liver function.
- Obtain a history of the patient's complaints, including a list of known allergens, especially allergies or sensitivities to latex.
- Obtain a history of the patient's cardiovascular and hepatobiliary systems, symptoms, and results of previously performed laboratory tests and diagnostic and surgical procedures.
- Obtain a list of the patient's current medications, including herbs, nutritional supplements, and nutraceuticals (see Appendix F).
- Review the procedure with the patient. Inform the patient that specimen collection takes approximately 5 to 10 min. Address concerns about pain, and explain to the patient that there may be some discomfort during the venipuncture.
- *Sensitivity to social and cultural issues,* as well as concern for modesty, is important in providing psychological support before, during, and after the procedure.
- There are no food, fluid, or medication restrictions unless by medical direction.

INTRATEST:

- If the patient has a history of allergic reaction to latex, avoid the use of equipment containing latex.
- Instruct the patient to cooperate fully and to follow directions. Direct the patient to breathe normally and to avoid unnecessary movement.
- Observe standard precautions, and follow the general guidelines in Appendix A. Positively identify the patient, and label the appropriate specimen container with the corresponding patient demographics, initials of the person collecting the specimen, date, and time of collection. Perform a venipuncture.

A

Remove the needle and apply direct pressure with dry gauze to stop bleeding. Observe/assess venipuncture site for bleeding or hematoma formation and secure gauze with adhesive bandage.

Promptly transport the specimen to the laboratory for processing and analysis.

POST-TEST:

A report of the results will be made available to the requesting health-care provider (HCP), who will discuss the results with the patient.

Nutritional Considerations: Increased AST levels may be associated with liver disease. Dietary recommendations may be indicated and will vary depending on the condition and its severity. Currently, there are no specific medications that can be given to cure hepatitis, but elimination of alcohol ingestion and a diet optimized for convalescence are commonly included in the treatment plan. A high-calorie, high-protein, moderate-fat diet with a high fluid intake is often recommended for patients with hepatitis. Treatment of cirrhosis is different; a low-protein diet may be in order if the patient's liver can no longer process the end products of protein metabolism. A diet of soft foods may be required if esophageal varices have developed. Ammonia levels may be used to determine whether protein should be added to or reduced from the diet. Patients should be encouraged to eat simple carbohydrates and emulsified fats (as in homogenized milk or eggs) rather than complex carbohydrates (e.g., starch, fiber, and glycogen [animal carbohydrates]) and complex fats, which require additional bile to emulsify them so that they can be used. The cirrhotic patient should be observed carefully for the development of ascites, in which case fluid and electrolyte balance requires strict attention.

Nutritional Considerations: Increased AST levels may be associated with coronary artery disease (CAD). The American Heart Association and National Heart, Lung, and Blood Institute (NHLBI) recommend

nutritional therapy for individuals identified to be at high risk for developing CAD or individuals who have specific risk factors and/or existing medical conditions (e.g., elevated low-density lipoprotein LDL cholesterol levels, other lipid disorders, insulin-dependent diabetes, insulin resistance, or metabolic syndrome). If overweight, the patient should be encouraged to achieve a normal weight. Guidelines for the Therapeutic Lifestyle Changes (TLC) diet are outlined in the Third Report of the Expert Panel on Detection, Evaluation, and Treatment of High Blood Cholesterol in Adults (Adult Treatment Panel III [ATP III]). The TLC diet emphasizes a reduction in foods high in saturated fats and cholesterol. Red meats, eggs, and dairy products are the major sources of saturated fats and cholesterol. If triglycerides also are elevated, the patient should be advised to eliminate or reduce alcohol and simple carbohydrates from the diet. The TLC approach also includes the use of plant stanols or sterols and increased dissolved fiber as an option for lowering LDL cholesterol levels; nutritional recommendations for daily total caloric intake; recommendations for allowable percentage of calories derived from fat (saturated and unsaturated), carbohydrates, protein, and cholesterol; as well as recommendations for daily expenditure of energy.

Nutritional Considerations: Overweight patients with high blood pressure should be encouraged to achieve a normal weight. Other changeable risk factors warranting patient education include strategies to safely decrease sodium intake, increase physical activity, decrease alcohol consumption, eliminate tobacco use, and decrease cholesterol levels.

Social and Cultural Considerations: Numerous studies point to the prevalence of excess body weight in American children and adolescents. Experts estimate that obesity is present in 25% of the population ages 6 to 11. The medical, social, and emotional consequences of excess body weight are significant. Special attention should be given to instructing the child and caregiver regarding health risks and weight-control education.

▸ Recognize anxiety related to test results, and be supportive of fear of shortened life expectancy. Discuss the implications of abnormal test results on the patient's lifestyle. Provide teaching and information regarding the clinical implications of the test results, as appropriate. Educate the patient regarding access to counseling services. Provide contact information, if desired, for the American Heart Association (www.americanheart.org) or the NHLBI (www.nhlbi.nih.gov).

▸ Instruct the patient to immediately report chest pain and changes in breathing pattern to the HCP.

▸ Reinforce information given by the patient's HCP regarding further testing, treatment, or referral to another HCP. Answer any questions or address any concerns voiced by the patient or family.

▸ Depending on the results of this procedure, additional testing may be performed to evaluate or monitor progression of the disease process and determine the need for a change in therapy. Evaluate test results in relation to the patient's symptoms and other tests performed.

RELATED MONOGRAPHS:

▸ Related tests include acetaminophen, ALT, albumin, ALP, ammonia, AMA/ASMA, α_1-antitrypsin/phenotyping, bilirubin and fractions, biopsy liver, cholangiography percutaneous transhepatic, cholangiography post-op, CT biliary tract and liver, ERCP, ethanol, ferritin, GGT, hepatitis antigens and antibodies, hepatobiliary scan, iron/total iron-binding capacity, liver and spleen scan, protein and fractions, PT/INR, US abdomen, and US liver if liver disease is suspected; and antiarrhythmic drugs, apolipoprotein A and B, ANP, BNP, blood gases, CRP, calcium/ionized calcium, CT scoring, cholesterol (total, HDL, and LDL), CK, echocardiography, Holter monitor, homocysteine, LDH, MRI chest, myocardial infarct scan, myocardial perfusion heart scan, myoglobin, PET heart, potassium, triglycerides, and troponin if myocardial infarction is suspected.

▸ See the Cardiovascular and Hepatobiliary systems tables at the end of the book for related tests by body system.

Atrial Natriuretic Peptide

SYNONYM/ACRONYM: Atrial natriuretic hormone, atrial natriuretic factor, ANF, ANH.

COMMON USE: To assist in diagnosing and monitoring congestive heart failure (CHF) and to differentiate CHF from other causes of dyspnea.

SPECIMEN: Plasma (1 mL) collected in a chilled, lavender-top tube. Specimen should be transported tightly capped and in an ice slurry.

NORMAL FINDINGS: (Method: Radioimmunoassay)

Conventional Units	SI Units (Conventional Units × 1)
20–77 pg/mL	20–77 ng/L

A

POTENTIAL DIAGNOSIS

Increased in

ANP is secreted in response to increased hemodynamic load caused by physiological stimuli as with atrial stretch or endocrine stimuli from the aldosterone/renin system.

- Asymptomatic cardiac volume overload
- CHF
- Elevated cardiac filling pressure
- Paroxysmal atrial tachycardia

Decreased in: N/A

CRITICAL FINDINGS: N/A

Find and print out the full monograph at DavisPlus (http://davisplus.fadavis.com, keyword Van Leeuwen).

Audiometry, Hearing Loss

SYNONYM/ACRONYM: N/A.

COMMON USE: To evaluate hearing loss in school-age children but can be used for all ages.

AREA OF APPLICATION: Ears.

CONTRAST: N/A.

DESCRIPTION: Tests to estimate hearing ability can be performed on patients of any age (e.g., at birth before discharge from a hospital or birthing center, as part of a school screening program, or as adults if indicated). Hearing loss audiometry includes quantitative testing for a hearing deficit. An audiometer is used to measure and record thresholds of hearing by air conduction and bone conduction tests. The test results determine if hearing loss is conductive, sensorineural, or a combination of both. An elevated air-conduction threshold with a normal bone-conduction threshold indicates a conductive hearing loss. An equally elevated threshold for both air and bone conduction indicates a sensorineural hearing loss. An elevated threshold of air conduction that is greater than an elevated threshold of bone conduction indicates a composite of both types of hearing loss. A conductive hearing loss is caused by an abnormality in the external auditory canal or middle ear, and a sensorineural hearing loss by an abnormality in the inner ear or of the VIII (auditory) nerve. Sensorineural hearing loss can be further differentiated clinically by sensory (cochlear) or neural (VIII nerve) lesions. Sensorineural hearing loss is permanent. Additional information for comparing and differentiating between conductive and sensorineural hearing loss can be obtained from hearing loss tuning fork tests. Every state and territory in the United States has a newborn screening program that includes early hearing loss detection and intervention (EHDI). The goal of EHDI is to assure that permanent hearing loss is identified before 3 mo of age, appropriate and timely intervention services are provided before 6 mo of age, families of infants with hearing loss receive culturally competent support, and tracking and data management systems for newborn hearing screens are linked with other relevant public health information systems.

INDICATIONS

- Determine the need for a type of hearing aid and evaluate its effectiveness
- Determine the type and extent of hearing loss and if further radiological, audiological, or vestibular procedures are needed to identify the cause
- Evaluate communication disabilities and plan for rehabilitation interventions
- Evaluate degree and extent of preoperative and postoperative hearing loss following stapedectomy in patients with otosclerosis
- Screen for hearing loss in infants and children and determine the need for a referral to an audiologist

POTENTIAL DIAGNOSIS

ASHA Category	Pure Tone Averages
Normal range or no impairment	−10–15 dB*
Slight loss	16–25 dB
Mild loss	26–40 dB
Moderate loss	41–55 dB
Moderately severe loss	56–70 dB
Severe loss	71–90 dB
Profound loss	Greater than 91 dB

*dB = decibel.

Normal findings in
- Normal pure tone average of −10 to 15 dB for infants, children, or adults

Abnormal findings in
- Causes of conductive hearing loss
Impacted cerumen
Hole in eardrum
Malformed outer ear, ear canal, or middle ear
Obstruction of external ear canal (related to presence of a foreign body)
Otitis externa (related to infection in ear canal)
Otitis media (related to poor eustachian tube function or infection)

Otitis media serous (related to fluid in middle ear due to allergies or a cold)
Otosclerosis
- Causes of sensorineural hearing loss
Congenital damage or malformations of the inner ear
Ménière's disease
Ototoxic drugs administered orally, topically, as otic drops, by IV, or passed to the fetus in utero (aminoglycoside antibiotics, e.g., gentamicin or tobramycin, and chemotherapeutic drugs, e.g., cisplatin and carboplatin, are known to cause permanent hearing loss; quinine, loop diuretics, and salicylates, e.g., aspirin are known to cause temporary hearing loss; other categories of drugs

known to be ototoxic include anesthetics, cardiac medications, mood altering
medications, and glucocorticosteroids,
e.g. cortisone, steroids)

Presbycusis *(gradual hearing loss experienced in advancing age related to
degeneration of the cochlea)*

Serious infections *(meningitis, measles,
mumps, other viral, syphilis)*

Trauma to the inner ear *(related to exposure to noise in excess of 90 dB or as
a result of physical trauma)*

Tumor *(e.g., acoustic neuroma, cerebellopontine angle tumor, meningioma)*

Vascular disorders

CRITICAL FINDINGS: N/A

INTERFERING FACTORS

*Factors that may impair the
results of the examination*

• Effects of ototoxic medications can
cause temporary, intermittent, or
permanent hearing loss.

• Failure to follow pretesting preparations before the procedure may
cause the procedure to be canceled
or repeated.

• Improper earphone fit or audiometer calibration can affect results.

• Inability of the patient to cooperate
or remain still during the procedure
because of age, language barriers,
significant pain, or mental status
may interfere with the test results.

• Noisy environment or extraneous
movements can affect results.

• Tinnitus or other sensations can
cause abnormal responses.

NURSING IMPLICATIONS AND PROCEDURE

PRETEST:

▶ Positively identify the patient using at
least two unique identifiers before
providing care, treatment, or services.

▶ *Patient Teaching:* Inform the patient/
caregiver this procedure can assist in
detecting hearing loss.

▶ Obtain a history of the patient's
complaints, including a list of known
allergens.

▶ Obtain a history of the patient's known
or suspected hearing loss, including
type and cause; ear conditions with
treatment regimens; ear surgery; and
other tests and procedures to assess
and diagnose auditory deficit.

▶ Obtain a history of the patient's symptoms and results of previously performed laboratory tests and diagnostic
and surgical procedures.

▶ Obtain a list of the patient's current
medications, including herbs, nutritional supplements, and nutraceuticals
(see Appendix F).

▶ Review the procedure with the patient.
Address concerns about pain and
explain that no discomfort will be
experienced during the test. Inform
the patient that an audiologist or
health-care provider (HCP) specializing
in this procedure performs the test in a
quiet, soundproof room, and that the
test can take up to 20 min to evaluate
both ears. Explain that each ear will be
tested separately by using earphones
and/or a device placed behind the ear
to deliver sounds of varying intensities.
Address concerns about claustrophobia, as appropriate. Explain and
demonstrate to the patient how to
communicate with the audiologist and
how to exit from the room.

▶ *Sensitivity to social and cultural issues,*
as well as concern for modesty, is
important in providing psychological
support before, during, and after the
procedure.

▶ There are no food, fluid, or medication
restrictions unless by medical direction.

▶ Ensure that the external auditory canal
is clear of impacted cerumen.

▶ *Make sure a written and informed
consent has been signed prior to the
procedure and before administering
any medications.*

INTRATEST:

▶ Observe standard precautions, and
follow the general guidelines in
Appendix A. Positively identify the
patient.

▶ Instruct the patient to cooperate fully
and to follow directions. Instruct the

patient to remain still during the procedure because movement produces unreliable results.

▶ Perform otoscopy examination to ensure that the external ear canal is free from any obstruction (see monograph titled "Otoscopy").

▶ Test for closure of the canal from the pressure of the earphones by compressing the tragus. Tendency for the canal to close (often the case in children and elderly patients) can be corrected by the careful insertion of a small stiff plastic tube into the anterior canal.

▶ Place the patient in a sitting position in comfortable proximity to the audiometer in a soundproof room. The ear not being tested is masked to prevent crossover of test tones, and the earphones are positioned on the head and over the ear canals. Infants and children may be tested using earphones that are inserted into the ear, unless contraindicated. An oscillating probe may be placed over the mastoid process behind the ear or on the forehead if bone conduction testing is to be performed as part of the hearing assessment.

▶ Start the test by providing a trial tone of 15 to 20 dB above the expected threshold to the ear for 1 to 2 sec to familiarize the patient with the sounds. Instruct the patient to press the button each time a tone is heard, no matter how loudly or faintly it is perceived. If no response is indicated, the level is increased until a response is obtained and then raised in 10-dB increments or until the audiometer's limit is reached for the test frequency. The test results are plotted on a graph called an audiogram using symbols that indicate the ear tested and responses using earphones (air conduction) or oscillator (bone conduction).

Air Conduction

▶ Air conduction is tested first by starting at 1,000 Hz and gradually decreasing the intensity 10 dB at a time until the patient no longer presses the button, indicating that the tone is no longer heard. The intensity is then increased 5 dB at a time until the tone is heard again. The tone is delivered to an infant

through insert earphones or ear muffs, and the auditory response is measured through electrodes placed on the infant's scalp. This is repeated until the same response is achieved at a 50% response rate at the same hertz level. The threshold is derived from the lowest decibel level at which the patient correctly identifies three out of six responses to a tone at that hertz level. The test is continued for each ear, testing the better ear first, with tones delivered at 1,000 Hz; 2,000 Hz; 4,000 Hz; and 8,000 Hz; and then again at 1,000 Hz; 500 Hz; and 250 Hz to determine a second threshold. Results are recorded on a graph called an audiogram. Averaging the air conduction thresholds at the 500-Hz; 1,000-Hz; and 2,000-Hz levels reveals the degree of hearing loss and is called the pure tone average (PTA).

Bone Conduction

▶ Bone conduction testing is performed in a similar manner to air conduction testing; a vibrator placed on the skull is used to deliver tones to an infant. The raised and lowered tones are delivered as in air conduction using 250 Hz; 500 Hz; 1,000 Hz; 2,000 Hz; and 4,000 Hz to determine the thresholds. An analysis of thresholds for air and bone conduction tones is done to determine the type of hearing loss (conductive, sensorineural, or mixed).

▶ In children between 6 mo and 2 yr of age, minimal response levels can be determined by behavioral responses to test tone. In the child 2 yr and older, play audiometry that requires the child to perform a task or raise a hand in response to a specific tone is performed. In children 12 yr and older, the child is asked to follow directions in identifying objects; response to speech of specific intensities can be used to evaluate hearing loss that is affected by speech frequencies.

POST-TEST:

▶ A report of the results will be made available to the requesting HCP, who will discuss the results with the patient.

▶ Instruct the patient to resume usual activity, as directed by the HCP.

Recognize anxiety related to test results, and be supportive of impaired activity related to hearing loss or perceived loss of independence. Discuss the implications of abnormal test results on the patient's lifestyle. Provide teaching and information regarding the clinical implications of the test results, as appropriate. Educate the patient regarding access to counseling services. Provide contact information, if desired, for the National Center for Hearing Assessment and Management (www.infanthearing.org) or for the American Speech-Language-Hearing Association (www.asha.org) or for assistive technology at ABLEDATA (sponsored by the National Institute on Disability and Rehabilitation Research, www.abledata.com).

Reinforce information given by the patient's HCP regarding further testing, treatment, or referral to another HCP. As appropriate, instruct the patient in the use, cleaning, and storing of a hearing aid. Answer any questions or address any concerns voiced by the patient or family.

Depending on the results of this procedure, additional testing may be performed to evaluate or monitor progression of the disease process and determine the need for a change in therapy. Evaluate test results in relation to the patient's symptoms and other tests performed.

RELATED MONOGRAPHS:

Related tests include analgesic and antipyretic drugs, antibiotic drugs, cultures bacterial (ear), evoked brain potential studies for hearing loss, gram stain, newborn screening, otoscopy, spondee speech reception threshold, and tuning fork tests (Webber, Rinne).

Refer to the table of tests associated with the Auditory System at the end of the book.

β₂-Microglobulin, Blood and Urine

SYNONYM/ACRONYM: β_2-M, BMG.

COMMON USE: To assist in diagnosing malignancy such as lymphoma, leukemia, or multiple myeloma. Also valuable in assessing for chronic severe inflammatory and renal diseases.

SPECIMEN: Serum (1 mL) collected in a red-top tube or 5 mL urine from a timed collection in a clean plastic container with 1 N NaOH as a preservative.

NORMAL FINDINGS: (Method: Immunochemiluminometric assay)

Sample	Conventional & SI Units
Serum	
Newborn–1 mo	1.6–4.8 mg/L
2–6 mo	1.0–3.8 mg/L
7–11 mo	0.9–3.1 mg/L
1–6 yr	0.6–2.4 mg/L
7–18 yr	0.7–2.0 mg/L
Adult	0.6–2.4 mg/L
Urine	0–300 mcg/L

DESCRIPTION: β_2-Microglobulin (BMG) is an amino acid peptide component of human leukocyte antigen (HLA) complexes. BMG is on the surface of most cells and is therefore a useful indicator of cell death or unusually high levels of cell production. BMG is a small protein and is readily reabsorbed by kidneys with normal function. BMG increases in inflammatory conditions and when lymphocyte turnover increases, such as in lymphocytic leukemia or when T-lymphocyte helper (OKT4) cells are attacked by HIV. Serum BMG becomes elevated with malfunctioning glomeruli but decreases with malfunctioning tubules because it is metabolized by the renal tubules. Conversely, urine BMG decreases with malfunctioning glomeruli but becomes elevated with malfunctioning tubules.

INDICATIONS

- Detect aminoglycoside toxicity
- Detect chronic lymphocytic leukemia, multiple myeloma, lung cancer, hepatoma, or breast cancer
- Detect HIV infection (*Note*: levels do not correlate with stages of infection)
- Evaluate renal disease to differentiate glomerular from tubular dysfunction
- Evaluate renal transplant viability and predict rejection
- Monitor antiretroviral therapy

POTENTIAL DIAGNOSIS

Increased in

- AIDS *(related to increased lymphocyte turnover)*
- Aminoglycoside toxicity *(related to renal damage; urine BMG becomes elevated before creatinine)*
- Amyloidosis *(related to chronic inflammatory conditions associated with increased BMG and other acute-phase reactant proteins; also related to deposition of amyloid in joints and tissues of patients receiving long-term hemodialysis)*
- Autoimmune disorders *(related to increased lymphocyte turnover)*
- Breast cancer *(related to increased lymphocyte turnover; serum BMG indicates tumor growth rate, size, and response to treatment)*
- Crohn's disease *(related to chronic inflammatory conditions*

B

associated with increased BMG
and other acute-phase reactant
proteins)
- Felty's syndrome *(related to
chronic inflammatory conditions
associated with increased BMG
and other acute-phase reactant
proteins)*
- Heavy metal poisoning
- Hepatitis *(related to increased
lymphocyte turnover in response
to viral infection)*
- Hepatoma *(related to increased
lymphocyte turnover; serum BMG
indicates tumor growth rate,
size, and response to treatment)*
- Hyperthyroidism *(related to
increased lymphocyte turnover in
immune thyroid disease)*
- Leukemia (chronic lymphocytic)
*(related to increased lymphocyte
turnover; serum BMG indicates
tumor growth rate, size, and
response to treatment)*
- Lung cancer *(related to increased
lymphocyte turnover; serum BMG
indicates tumor growth rate,
size, and response to treatment)*
- Lymphoma *(related to increased
lymphocyte turnover; serum BMG
indicates tumor growth rate,
size, and response to treatment)*
- Multiple myeloma *(related to
increased lymphocyte turnover)*
- Poisoning with heavy metals, such
as mercury or cadmium *(related to
renal damage that decreases
BMG absorption)*
- Renal dialysis *(related to ability of
renal tubule to reabsorb BMG)*
- Renal disease (glomerular): serum
only *(related to ability of renal
tubule to reabsorb BMG)*
- Renal disease (tubular): urine only
*(related to ability of renal tubule
to reabsorb BMG)*
- Sarcoidosis
- Sjögren's disease
- Systemic lupus erythematosus
*(related to chronic inflammatory
conditions associated with*

increased BMG and other acute
phase reactant proteins)
- Vasculitis *(related to chronic
inflammatory conditions associated with increased BMG and other
acute phase reactant proteins)*
- Viral infections (e.g., cytomegalovirus)
*(related to increased lymphocyte
turnover)*

Decreased in
- Renal disease (glomerular):
urine only
- Renal disease (tubular): serum only
- Response to zidovudine (AZT)
*(related to decreased viral
replication and lymphocyte
destruction)*

CRITICAL FINDINGS: N/A

INTERFERING FACTORS
- Drugs and proteins that may
increase serum BMG levels include
cyclosporin A, gentamicin, interferon alfa, and lithium.
- Drugs that may decrease serum
BMG levels include zidovudine.
- Drugs that may increase urine
BMG levels include azathioprine,
cisplatin, cyclosporin A, furosemide,
gentamicin, iodixanol, iopentol,
mannitol, nifedipine, sisomicin, and
tobramycin.
- Urinary BMG is unstable at pH less
than 5.5.

**NURSING IMPLICATIONS
AND PROCEDURE**

PRETEST:
▶ Positively identify the patient using at
least two unique identifiers before
providing care, treatment, or services.
▶ *Patient Teaching:* Inform the patient that
the test is used to evaluate renal disease, AIDS, and certain malignancies.
▶ Obtain a history of the patient's complaints, including a list of known allergens, especially allergies or sensitivities
to latex.

Obtain a history of the patient's genitourinary and immune systems, symptoms, and results of previously performed laboratory tests and diagnostic and surgical procedures.

Note any recent procedures that can interfere with test results.

Obtain a list of the patient's current medications, including herbs, nutritional supplements, and nutraceuticals (see Appendix F).

Sensitivity to social and cultural issues, as well as concern for modesty, is important in providing psychological support before, during, and after the procedure.

There are no food, fluid, or medication restrictions unless by medical direction.

Blood

Review the procedure with the patient. Inform the patient that specimen collection takes approximately 5 to 10 min. Address concerns about pain and explain that there may be some discomfort during the venipuncture.

Urine

Review the procedure with the patient. Provide a nonmetallic urinal, bedpan, or toilet-mounted collection device. Usually a 24-hr urine collection is ordered. Inform the patient that all urine over a 24-hr period must be saved; instruct the patient to avoid defecating in the collection device and to keep toilet tissue out of the collection device to prevent contamination of the specimen. Place a sign in the bathroom as a reminder to save all urine.

Instruct the patient to void all urine into the collection device and then pour the urine into the laboratory collection container. Alternatively, the specimen can be left in the collection device for a health care staff member to add to the laboratory collection container.

INTRATEST:

Instruct the patient to cooperate fully and to follow directions. Direct the patient to breathe normally and to avoid unnecessary movement during the venipuncture.

Observe standard precautions, and follow the general guidelines in Appendix A. Positively identify the patient, and label the appropriate specimen container with the corresponding patient demographics, initials of the person collecting the specimen, date, and time of collection. Perform a venipuncture as appropriate.

Blood

If the patient has a history of allergic reaction to latex, avoid the use of equipment containing latex.

Perform a venipuncture.

Remove the needle and apply direct pressure with dry gauze to stop bleeding. Observe/assess venipuncture site for bleeding or hematoma formation and secure gauze with adhesive bandage.

Urine

Obtain a clean 3-L urine specimen container, toilet-mounted collection device, and plastic bag (for transport of the specimen container). The specimen must be refrigerated or kept on ice throughout the entire collection period. If an indwelling urinary catheter is in place, the drainage bag must be kept on ice.

If possible, begin the test between 6 and 8 a.m. Collect first voiding and discard. Record the time the specimen was discarded as the beginning of the timed collection period. At the same time the next morning, ask the patient to void and add this last voiding to the container. Urinary output should be recorded throughout the collection time.

If an indwelling catheter is in place, replace the tubing and container system at the start of the collection time. Keep the container system on ice during the collection period, or empty the urine into a larger container periodically during the collection period; monitor to ensure continued drainage, and conclude the test the next morning at the same hour the collection started.

At the conclusion of the test, compare the quantity of urine with the urinary output record for the collection. If the specimen contains less than what was recorded as output, some urine may have been discarded, thus invalidating the test.

Blood or Urine

▸ Promptly transport the specimen to the laboratory for processing and analysis. Include on the urine specimen label the amount of urine and ingestion of any medications that can affect test results.

POST-TEST:

▸ A report of the results will be made available to the requesting health-care provider (HCP), who will discuss the results with the patient.

▸ Educate the patient regarding the risk of infection related to immunosuppressed inflammatory response and fatigue related to decreased energy production.

▸ *Nutritional Considerations:* Stress the importance of good nutrition, and suggest that the patient meet with a nutritional specialist. Also, stress the importance of following the care plan for medications and follow-up visits.

▸ *Social and Cultural Considerations:* Recognize anxiety related to test results, and be supportive of impaired activity related to weakness, perceived loss of independence, and fear of shortened life expectancy. Discuss the implications of abnormal test results on the patient's lifestyle. Provide teaching and information regarding the clinical implications of the test results, as appropriate. Educate the patient regarding access to counseling services. Provide contact information, if desired, for AIDS information provided by the National Institutes of Health (www.aidsinfo.nih.gov).

▸ *Social and Cultural Considerations:* Counsel the patient, as appropriate, regarding risk of transmission and proper prophylaxis, and reinforce the importance of strict adherence to the treatment regimen.

▸ *Social and Cultural Considerations:* Offer support, as appropriate, to patients who may be the victims of rape or sexual assault. Educate the patient regarding access to counseling services. Provide a nonjudgmental, nonthreatening atmosphere for a discussion during which risks of sexually transmitted diseases are explained. It is also important to discuss problems the patient may experience (e.g., guilt, depression, anger).

▸ Reinforce information given by the patient's HCP regarding further testing, treatment, or referral to another HCP. Inform the patient that retesting may be necessary. Answer any questions or address any concerns voiced by the patient or family.

▸ Depending on the results of this procedure, additional testing may be performed to evaluate or monitor progression of the disease process and determine the need for a change in therapy. Evaluate test results in relation to the patient's symptoms and other tests performed.

RELATED MONOGRAPHS:

▸ Related tests include antibiotic drugs, ANA, barium enema, biopsy (bone marrow, biopsy breast, biopsy liver, biopsy lung, biopsy lymph node), BUN, capsule endoscopy, CD4/CD8 enumeration, colonoscopy, CRP, cancer antigens, CBC, creatinine, cultures (mycobacteria, sputum, viral), cytology sputum, CMV, ESR, gallium scan, GGT, hepatitis antigens and antibodies (A, B, C), HIV-1/HIV-2 serology, immunofixation electrophoresis, immunoglobulins (A, G, and M), liver and spleen scan, lymphangiogram, MRI breast, mammogram, microalbumin, osmolality, protein total and fractions, renogram, RF, stereotactic breast biopsy, TB tests, US (breast, liver, lymph node), and UA.

▸ Refer to the Genitourinary and Immune systems tables at the end of the book for related tests by body system.

Barium Enema

SYNONYM/ACRONYM: Air-contrast barium enema, double-contrast barium enema, lower GI series, BE.

COMMON USE: To assist in diagnosing bowel disease in the colon such as tumors and polyps.

AREA OF APPLICATION: Colon.

CONTRAST: Barium sulfate, air, iodine mixture.

DESCRIPTION: This radiological examination of the colon, distal small bowel, and occasionally the appendix follows instillation of barium using a rectal tube inserted into the rectum or an existing ostomy. The patient must retain the barium while a series of radiographs are obtained. Visualization can be improved by using air or barium as the contrast medium (double-contrast study). A combination of x-ray and fluoroscopy techniques is used to complete the study. This test is especially useful in the evaluation of patients experiencing lower abdominal pain, changes in bowel habits, or the passage of stools containing blood or mucus, and for visualizing polyps, diverticula, and tumors. A barium enema may be therapeutic; it may reduce an obstruction caused by intussusception, or telescoping of the intestine. Barium enema should be performed before an upper gastrointestinal (GI) study or barium swallow.

INDICATIONS
- Determine the cause of rectal bleeding, blood, pus, or mucus in feces
- Evaluate suspected inflammatory process, congenital anomaly, motility disorder, or structural change
- Evaluate unexplained weight loss, anemia, or a change in bowel pattern
- Identify and locate benign or malignant polyps or tumors

POTENTIAL DIAGNOSIS

Normal findings in
- Normal size, filling, shape, position, and motility of the colon
- Normal filling of the appendix and terminal ileum

Abnormal findings in
- Appendicitis
- Colorectal cancer
- Congenital anomalies
- Crohn's disease
- Diverticular disease
- Fistulas
- Gastroenteritis
- Granulomatous colitis
- Hirschsprung's disease
- Intussusception
- Perforation of the colon
- Polyps
- Sarcoma
- Sigmoid torsion
- Sigmoid volvulus
- Stenosis
- Tumors
- Ulcerative colitis

CRITICAL FINDINGS: N/A

INTERFERING FACTORS

This procedure is contraindicated for

- Patients with allergies to shellfish or iodinated dye, when iodinated contrast medium is used. The contrast medium, when used, may cause life-threatening allergic reaction. Patients with a known hypersensitivity to contrast medium may benefit from premedication with corticosteroids or the use of nonionic contrast medium.
- Patients who are pregnant or suspected of being pregnant, unless the potential benefits of the procedure far outweigh the risks to the fetus and mother.
- Patients with intestinal obstruction, acute ulcerative colitis, acute diverticulitis, megacolon, or suspected rupture of the colon.

Factors that may impair clear imaging

- Gas or feces in the GI tract resulting from inadequate cleansing or failure to restrict food intake before the study.
- Retained barium from a previous radiological procedure.
- Metallic objects within the examination field (e.g., jewelry, body rings).
- Improper adjustment of the radiographic equipment to accommodate obese or thin patients.
- Incorrect patient positioning, which may produce poor visualization of the area to be examined.
- Inability of the patient to cooperate or remain still during the procedure because of age, significant pain, or mental status.
- Spasm of the colon, which can mimic the radiographic signs of cancer. (*Note*: The use of intravenous glucagon minimizes spasm.)
- Inability of the patient to tolerate introduction of or retention of barium, air, or both in the bowel.

Other considerations

- Complications of the procedure may include hemorrhage and cardiac arrhythmias.
- The procedure may be terminated if chest pain or severe cardiac arrhythmias occur.
- Failure to follow dietary restrictions and other pretesting preparations may cause the procedure to be canceled or repeated.
- Consultation with a health-care provider (HCP) should occur before the procedure for radiation safety concerns regarding younger patients or patients who are lactating.
- Risks associated with radiation overexposure can result from frequent x-ray procedures. Personnel in the room with the patient should wear a protective lead apron, stand behind a shield, or leave the area while the examination is being done. Personnel working in the area during the examination should wear badges to record their level of radiation exposure.

NURSING IMPLICATIONS AND PROCEDURE

PRETEST:

▶ Positively identify the patient using at least two unique identifiers before providing care, treatment, or services.
Patient Teaching: Inform the patient this procedure can assist in assessing the colon.

▶ Obtain a history of the patient's complaints, including a list of known allergens, especially allergies or sensitivities to latex, iodine, seafood, anesthetics, or contrast mediums.

▶ Obtain a history of the patient's gastrointestinal system, symptoms, and results of previously performed laboratory tests and diagnostic and surgical procedures.

▶ Verify that this procedure is performed before an upper GI study or barium swallow.

▶ Record the date of the last menstrual period and determine the possibility of pregnancy in perimenopausal women.

▶ Obtain a list of the patient's current medications including anticoagulants, aspirin and other salicylates, herbs, nutritional supplements, and nutraceuticals (see Appendix F). Note the last time and dose of medication taken.

▶ Review the procedure with the patient. Address concerns about pain and explain that there may be moments of discomfort and some pain experienced during the test. Inform the patient that the procedure is performed in a radiology department, by an HCP specializing in this procedure, with support staff, and takes approximately 30 min. *Sensitivity to social and cultural issues,* as well as concern for modesty, is important in providing psychological support before, during, and after the procedure.

▶ Patients with a colostomy will be ordered special preparations and colostomy irrigation.

▶ Inform the patient that a laxative and cleansing enema may be needed the day before the procedure, with cleansing enemas on the morning of the procedure, depending on the institution's policy.

▶ Instruct the patient to remove all metallic objects from the area of the procedure.

▶ Instruct the patient to eat a low-residue diet for several days before the procedure and to consume only clear liquids the evening before the test. The patient should fast and restrict fluids for 8 hr prior to the procedure. Protocols may vary among facilities.

INTRATEST:

▶ Observe standard precautions, and follow the general guidelines in Appendix A. Positively identify the patient.

▶ Ensure the patient has complied with dietary, fluid, and medication restrictions and pretesting preparations.

▶ Ensure the patient has removed all external metallic objects from the area to be examined.

▶ Assess for completion of bowel preparation according to the institution's procedure.

▶ Have emergency equipment readily available.

▶ Instruct the patient to void prior to the procedure and to change into the gown, robe, and foot coverings provided.

▶ Instruct the patient to cooperate fully and to follow directions. Instruct the patient to remain still throughout the procedure because movement produces unreliable results.

▶ Place the patient in the supine position on an examination table and take an initial image.

▶ Instruct the patient to lie on his or her left side (Sims' position). A rectal tube is inserted into the anus and an attached balloon is inflated after it is situated against the anal sphincter.

▶ Barium is instilled into the colon by gravity, and its movement through the colon is observed by fluoroscopy.

▶ For patients with a colostomy, an indwelling urinary catheter is inserted into the stoma and barium is administered.

▶ Images are taken with the patient in different positions to aid in the diagnosis.

▶ If a double-contrast barium enema has been ordered, air is then instilled in the intestine and additional images are taken.

▶ The patient is helped to the bathroom to expel the barium or placed on a bedpan if unable to ambulate.

▶ After expulsion of the barium, a post-evacuation image is taken of the colon.

POST-TEST:

▶ A report of the results will be made available to the requesting HCP, who will discuss the results with the patient.

▶ Instruct the patient to resume usual diet, medications, or activity, as directed by the HCP.

▶ Instruct the patient to take a mild laxative and increase fluid intake (four 8-oz glasses) to aid in elimination of barium, unless contraindicated.

▶ Carefully monitor the patient for fatigue and fluid and electrolyte imbalance.

▶ Instruct the patient that stools will be white or light in color for 2 to 3 days. If the patient is unable to eliminate the barium, or if stools do not return to normal color, the patient should notify the HCP.

B

▸ Advise patients with a colostomy that tap water colostomy irrigation may aid in barium removal.

▸ Recognize anxiety related to test results. Discuss the implications of abnormal test results on the patient's lifestyle. Provide teaching and information regarding the clinical implications of the test results, as appropriate.

▸ Reinforce information given by the patient's HCP regarding further testing, treatment, or referral to another HCP. Decisions regarding the need for and frequency of occult blood testing, colonoscopy, or other cancer screening procedures should be made after consultation between the patient and HCP. The most current guidelines for colon cancer screening of the general population as well as individuals with increased risk are available from the American Cancer Society (www.cancer.org) and the American College of Gastroenterology (www.gi.org). Answer any questions or address any concerns voiced by the patient or family.

▸ Depending on the results of this procedure, additional testing may be performed to evaluate or monitor progression of the disease process and determine the need for a change in therapy. Evaluate test results in relation to the patient's symptoms and other tests performed.

RELATED MONOGRAPHS:

▸ Related tests include cancer antigens, colonoscopy, colposcopy, CT abdomen, fecal analysis, MRI abdomen, PET pelvis, and proctosigmoidoscopy. Refer to the Gastrointestinal System table at the end of the book for related tests by body system.

Barium Swallow

SYNONYM/ACRONYM: Esophagram, video swallow, esophagus x-ray, swallowing function, esophagraphy.

COMMON USE: To assist in diagnosing disease of the esophagus such as stricture or tumor.

AREA OF APPLICATION: Esophagus.

CONTRAST: Barium sulfate, water-soluble iodinated contrast.

DESCRIPTION: This radiological examination of the esophagus evaluates motion and anatomic structures of the esophageal lumen by recording images of the lumen while the patient swallows a barium solution of milkshake consistency and chalky taste. The procedure uses fluoroscopic and cineradiographic techniques. The barium swallow is often performed as part of an upper gastrointestinal (GI) series or cardiac series and is indicated for patients with a history of dysphagia and gastric reflux. The study may identify reflux of the barium from the stomach back into the esophagus. Muscular abnormalities such as achalasia, as well as diffuse esophageal spasm, can be easily detected with this procedure.

INDICATIONS

- Confirm the integrity of esophageal anastomoses in the postoperative patient
- Detect esophageal reflux, tracheoesophageal fistulas, and varices
- Determine the cause of dysphagia or heartburn
- Determine the type and location of foreign bodies within the pharynx and esophagus
- Evaluate suspected esophageal motility disorders
- Evaluate suspected polyps, strictures, Zenker's diverticula, tumor, or inflammation

POTENTIAL DIAGNOSIS

Normal findings in

- Normal peristalsis through the esophagus into the stomach with normal size, filling, patency, and shape of the esophagus

Abnormal findings in

- Achalasia
- Acute or chronic esophagitis
- Benign or malignant tumors
- Chalasia
- Diverticula
- Esophageal ulcers
- Esophageal varices
- Hiatal hernia
- Perforation of the esophagus
- Strictures or polyps

CRITICAL FINDINGS: N/A

INTERFERING FACTORS

This procedure is contraindicated for

- Patients who are pregnant or suspected of being pregnant, unless the potential benefits of the procedure far outweigh the risks to the fetus and mother.
- Patients with intestinal obstruction or suspected esophageal rupture,
unless water-soluble iodinated contrast medium is used.
- Patients with suspected tracheo-esophageal fistula, unless barium is used.

Factors that may impair clear imaging

- Metallic objects within the examination field.
- Improper adjustment of the radiographic equipment to accommodate obese or thin patients, which can cause overexposure or underexposure.
- Incorrect patient positioning, which may produce poor visualization of the area to be examined.
- Inability of the patient to cooperate or remain still during the procedure because of age, significant pain, or mental status.

Other considerations

- Failure to follow dietary restrictions and other pretesting preparations may cause the procedure to be canceled or repeated.
- A potential complication of a barium swallow is barium-induced fecal impaction.
- Ensure that the procedure is done after cholangiography and barium enema.
- Consultation with a health-care provider (HCP) should occur before the procedure for radiation safety concerns regarding younger patients or patients who are lactating.
- Risks associated with radiation overexposure can result from frequent x-ray procedures. Personnel in the room with the patient should wear a protective lead apron, stand behind a shield, or leave the area while the examination is being done. Personnel working in the examination area should wear badges to record their level of radiation exposure.

NURSING IMPLICATIONS AND PROCEDURE

PRETEST:

▶ Positively identify the patient using at least two unique identifiers before providing care, treatment, or services.
Patient Teaching: Inform the patient this procedure can assist in assessing the esophagus.

▶ Obtain a history of the patient's complaints, including a list of known allergens, especially allergies or sensitivities to latex, iodine, seafood, anesthetics, or contrast medium.

▶ Obtain a history of the patient's gastrointestinal system, symptoms, and results of previously performed laboratory tests and diagnostic and surgical procedures.

▶ Ensure that this procedure is performed before an upper GI study or video swallow.

▶ Record the date of the last menstrual period and determine the possibility of pregnancy in perimenopausal women.

▶ Obtain a list of the patient's current medications, including herbs, nutritional supplements, and nutraceuticals (see Appendix F).

▶ Explain to the patient that some pain may be experienced during the test, and there may be moments of discomfort. Review the procedure with the patient and explain the need to swallow a barium contrast medium. Inform the patient that the procedure is performed in a radiology department by a HCP and takes approximately 15 to 30 min.

▶ *Sensitivity to social and cultural issues,* as well as concern for modesty, is important in providing psychological support before, during, and after the procedure.

▶ Instruct the patient to remove all external metallic objects from the area to be examined.

▶ Instruct the patient to fast and restrict fluids for 8 hr prior to the procedure. Protocols may vary among facilities.

INTRATEST:

▶ Observe standard precautions, and follow the general guidelines in Appendix A. Positively identify the patient.

▶ Ensure the patient has complied with dietary and fluid restrictions for 8 hr prior to the procedure.

▶ Ensure the patient has removed all external metallic objects from the area to be examined.

▶ Instruct the patient to void prior to the procedure and to change into the gown, robe, and foot coverings provided.

▶ Instruct the patient to cooperate and follow directions. Instruct the patient to remain still throughout the procedure because movement produces unreliable results.

▶ Instruct the patient to stand in front of the x-ray fluoroscopy screen. Place the patient supine on the radiographic table if he or she is unable to stand.

▶ An initial image is taken, and the patient is asked to swallow a barium solution with or without a straw.

▶ Multiple images at different angles may be taken.

▶ The patient may be asked to drink additional barium to complete the study. Swallowing the additional barium evaluates the passage of barium from the esophagus into the stomach.

POST-TEST:

▶ A report of the results will be made available to the requesting HCP, who will discuss the results with the patient.

▶ Instruct the patient to resume usual diet, fluids, medications, and activity, as directed by the HCP.

▶ Carefully monitor the patient for fatigue and fluid and electrolyte imbalance.

▶ Instruct the patient to take a mild laxative and increase fluid intake (four 8-oz glasses) to aid in elimination of barium, unless contraindicated.

▶ Instruct the patient that stools will be white or light in color for 2 to 3 days. If the patient is unable to eliminate the barium, or if stools do not return to normal color, the patient should notify the requesting HCP.

▶ Recognize anxiety related to test results. Discuss the implications of abnormal test results on the patient's lifestyle. Provide teaching and information regarding the clinical implications of the test results, as appropriate.

Reinforce information given by the patient's HCP regarding further testing, treatment, or referral to another HCP. Answer any questions or address any concerns voiced by the patient or family.

Depending on the results of this procedure, additional testing may be performed to evaluate or monitor progression of the disease process and determine the need for a change in therapy. Evaluate test results in relation to the patient's symptoms and other tests performed.

RELATED MONOGRAPHS:

Related tests include capsule endoscopy, chest x-ray, CT thoracic, endoscopy, esophageal manometry, gastroesophageal reflux scan, MRI chest, and thyroid scan.

Refer to the Gastrointestinal System table at the end of the book for related tests by body system.

Bilirubin and Bilirubin Fractions

SYNONYM/ACRONYM: Conjugated/direct bilirubin, unconjugated/indirect bilirubin, delta bilirubin, TBil.

COMMON USE: A multipurpose lab test that acts as an indicator for various diseases of the liver or for disease that affects the liver.

SPECIMEN: Serum (1 mL) collected in a red- or tiger-top tube. Plasma (1 mL) collected in green-top (heparin) tube or in a heparinized microtainer is also acceptable. Protect sample from direct light.

NORMAL FINDINGS: (Method: Spectrophotometry) Total bilirubin levels in infants should decrease to adult levels by day 10 as the development of the hepatic circulatory system matures. Values in breastfed infants may take longer to reach normal adult levels. Values in premature infants may initially be higher than in full-term infants and also take longer to decrease to normal levels.

Bilirubin	Conventional Units	SI Units (Conventional Units × 17.1)
Total bilirubin		
Newborn–1 day	Less than 5.8 mg/dL	Less than 99 micromol/L
1–2 days	Less than 8.2 mg/dL	Less than 140 micromol/L
3–5 days	Less than 11.7 mg/dL	Less than 200 micromol/L
6–7 days	Less than 8.4 mg/dL	Less than 144 micromol/L
8–9 days	Less than 6.5 mg/dL	Less than 111 micromol/L
10–11 days	Less than 4.6 mg/dL	Less than 79 micromol/L
12–13 days	Less than 2.7 mg/dL	Less than 46 micromol/L
14–30 days	Less than 0.8 mg/dL	Less than 14 micromol/L
1 mo–older adult	Less than 1.2 mg/dL	Less than 21 micromol/L
Unconjugated bilirubin	Less than 1.1 mg/dL	Less than 19 micromol/L

(table continues on page 186)

B

Bilirubin	Conventional Units	SI Units (Conventional Units × 17.1)
Conjugated bilirubin		
Neonate	Less than 0.6 mg/dL	Less than 10 micromol/L
29 days–older adult	Less than 0.3 mg/dL	Less than 5 micromol/L
Delta bilirubin	Less than 0.2 mg/dL	Less than 3 micromol/L

DESCRIPTION: Bilirubin is a by-product of heme catabolism from aged red blood cells (RBCs). Bilirubin is primarily produced in the liver, spleen, and bone marrow. Total bilirubin is the sum of unconjugated or indirect bilirubin, monoglucuronide and diglucuronide, conjugated or direct bilirubin, and albumin-bound delta bilirubin. Unconjugated bilirubin is carried to the liver by albumin, where it becomes conjugated. In the small intestine, conjugated bilirubin converts to urobilinogen and then to urobilin. Urobilin is then excreted in the feces. Increases in bilirubin levels can result from prehepatic, hepatic, and/or posthepatic conditions, making fractionation useful in determining the cause of the increase in total bilirubin levels. Delta bilirubin has a longer half-life than the other bilirubin fractions and therefore remains elevated during convalescence after the other fractions have decreased to normal levels. Delta bilirubin can be calculated using the formula:

Delta bilirubin = Total bilirubin − (Indirect bilirubin + Direct bilirubin)

When bilirubin concentration increases, the yellowish pigment deposits in skin and sclera. This increase in yellow pigmentation is termed *jaundice* or *icterus*. Bilirubin levels can also be checked using noninvasive methods. Hyperbilirubinemia in neonates can be reliably evaluated using transcutaneous measurement devices. Defects in bilirubin excretion can be identified in a routine urinalysis.

INDICATIONS
- Assist in the differential diagnosis of obstructive jaundice
- Assist in the evaluation of liver and biliary disease
- Monitor the effects of drug reactions on liver function
- Monitor the effects of phototherapy on jaundiced newborns
- Monitor jaundice in newborn patients

POTENTIAL DIAGNOSIS

Increased in
- Prehepatic (hemolytic) jaundice *(related to excessive amounts of heme released from RBC destruction. Heme is catabolized to bilirubin in concentrations that exceed the liver's conjugation capacity, and indirect bilirubin accumulates)*
  Erythroblastosis fetalis
  Hematoma
  Hemolytic anemia
  Pernicious anemia
  Physiological jaundice of the newborn
  The post blood transfusion period, when a number of units are rapidly infused or in the case of a delayed transfusion reaction
  RBC enzyme abnormalities (i.e., glucose-6-phosphate dehydrogenase, pyruvate kinase, spherocytosis)

- Hepatic jaundice *(related to bilirubin conjugation failure)*
  Crigler-Najjar syndrome
- Hepatic jaundice *(related to disturbance in bilirubin transport)*
  Dubin-Johnson syndrome *(related to preconjugation transport failure)*
  Gilbert's syndrome *(related to postconjugation transport failure)*
- Hepatic jaundice *(evidenced by liver damage or necrosis that interferes with excretion into bile ducts either by physical obstruction or drug inhibition and bilirubin accumulates)*
  Alcoholism
  Cholangitis
  Cholecystitis
  Cholestatic drug reactions
  Cirrhosis
  Hepatitis
  Hepatocellular damage
  Infectious mononucleosis
- Posthepatic jaundice *(evidenced by blockage that interferes with excretion into bile ducts, resulting in accumulated bilirubin)*
  Advanced tumors of the liver
  Biliary obstruction
- Other conditions
  Anorexia or starvation *(related to liver damage)*
  Hypothyroidism *(related to effect on the liver whereby hepatic enzyme activity for formation of conjugated or direct bilirubin is enhanced in combination with decreased flow of bile and secretion of bile acids; results in accumulation of direct bilirubin)*
  Premature or breastfed infants *(evidenced by diminished hepatic function of the liver in premature infants; related to inability of neonate to feed in sufficient quantity. Insufficient breast milk intake results in weight loss, decreased stool formation, and decreased elimination of bilirubin)*

Decreased in: N/A

CRITICAL FINDINGS

Adults and children
- Greater than 15 mg/dL (Greater than 257 micromol/L)

Newborns
- Greater than 13 mg/dL (Greater than 222 micromol/L)

Note and immediately report to the health-care provider (HCP) any critically increased values and related symptoms. Timely notification of critical values for lab or diagnostic studies is a role expectation of the professional nurse. Notification processes will vary among facilities. Upon receipt of the critical value, the information should be read back to the caller to verify accuracy. Most policies require immediate notification of the primary HCP, hospitalist, or on-call HCP. Reported information includes the patient's name, unique identifiers, critical value, name of the person giving the report, and name of the person receiving the report. Documentation of notification should be made in the medical record with the name of the HCP notified, time and date of notification, and any orders received. Any delay in a timely report of a critical value may require completion of a notification form with review by Risk Management.

Sustained hyperbilirubinemia can result in brain damage. Kernicterus refers to the deposition of bilirubin in the basal ganglia and brainstem nuclei. There is no exact level of bilirubin that puts infants at risk for developing kernicterus. Symptoms of kernicterus in infants include lethargy, poor feeding, upward deviation of the eyes, and seizures. Intervention for infants may include early frequent feedings to stimulate gastrointestinal motility, phototherapy, and exchange transfusion.

INTERFERING FACTORS
- Drugs that may increase bilirubin levels by causing cholestasis include

B

anabolic steroids, androgens, buta-perazine, chlorothiazide, chlorprom-azine, chlorpropamide, cinchophen, dapsone, dienoestrol, erythromycin, estrogens, ethionamide, gold salts, hydrochlorothiazide, icterogenin, imipramine, iproniazid, isocarboxa-zid, isoniazid, meprobamate, mercap-topurine, meropenem, methandriol, nitrofurans, norethandrolone, nor-triptyline, oleandomycin, oral contra-ceptives, penicillins, phenothiazines, prochlorperazine, progesterone, pro-mazine, promethazine, propoxy-phene, protriptyline, sulfonamides, tacrolimus, thiouracil, tolazamide, tolbutamide, thiacetazone, trifluo-perazine, and trimeprazine.

• Drugs that may increase bilirubin levels by causing hepatocellular damage include acetaminophen (toxic), acetylsalicylic acid, allopuri-nol, aminothiazole, anabolic steroids, asparaginase, azathioprine, azithro-mycin, carbamazepine, carbutamide, chloramphenicol, clindamycin, clofi-brate, chlorambucil, chlorampheni-col, chlordane, chloroform, chlorzoxazone, clonidine, colchicine, coumarin, cyclophosphamide, cyclo-propane, cycloserine, cyclosporine, dactinomycin, danazol, desipramine, dexfenfluramine, diazepam, diethyl-stilbestrol, dinitrophenol, enflurane, ethambutol, ethionamide, ethoxa-zene, factor IX complex, felbamate, flavaspidic acid, flucytosine, fusidic acid, gentamicin, glycopyrrolate, gua-noxan, haloperidol, halothane, hycanthone, hydroxyacetamide, ibuprofen, interferon, interleukin-2, isoniazid, kanamycin, labetalol, levamisole, lincomycin, melphalan, mesoridazine, metahexamide, metax-alone, methotrexate, methoxsalen, methyldopa, nitrofurans, oral contra-ceptives, oxamniquine, oxyphenisat-in, pemoline, penicillin, perphen-azine, phenazopyridine, phenelzine, phenindione, pheniprazine,

phenothiazines, piroxicam, probenecid, procainamide, pyrazin-amide, quinine, sulfonylureas, thiothix-ene, timolol, tobramycin, tolcapone, tretinoin, trimethadione, urethan, and verapamil.

• Drugs that may increase bilirubin levels by causing hemolysis include aminopyrine, amphotericin B, car-bamazepine, cephaloridine, cepha-lothin, chloroquine, dimercaprol, dipyrone, furadaltone, furazolidone, mefenamic acid, melphalan, mephe-nytoin, methylene blue, nitrofurans, nitrofurazone, pamaquine, penicil-lins, pentaquine, phenylhydrazine, piperazine, pipobroman, prima-quine, procainamide, quinacrine, quinidine, quinine, stibophen, streptomycin, sulfonamides, triethyl-enemelamine, tyrothricin, and vitamin K.

• Drugs that may decrease bilirubin levels include anticonvulsants, bar-biturates (newborns), chloropheno-thane, cyclosporine, flumecinolone (newborns), and salicylates.

• Bilirubin is light sensitive. Therefore, the collection container should be suitably covered to protect the specimen from light between the time of collection and analysis.

PRETEST:

▶ Positively identify the patient using at least two unique identifiers before providing care, treatment, or services.
▶ *Patient Teaching:* Inform the patient this test can assist in assessing liver function.
▶ Obtain a history of the patient's complaints, including a list of known allergens, especially allergies or sensitivities to latex.
▶ Obtain a history of the patient's hepa-tobiliary system, symptoms, and results of previously performed labora-tory tests and diagnostic and surgical procedures.

- Obtain a list of the patient's current medication, including herbs, nutritional supplements, and nutraceuticals (see Appendix F).
- Review the procedure with the patient. Inform the patient that specimen collection takes approximately 5 to 10 min. Address concerns about pain and explain that there may be some discomfort during the venipuncture. *Sensitivity to social and cultural issues,* as well as concern for modesty, is important in providing psychological support before, during, and after the procedure.
- There are no food, fluid, or medication restrictions unless by medical direction.

INTRATEST:

- If the patient has a history of allergic reaction to latex, avoid the use of equipment containing latex.
- Instruct the patient to cooperate fully and to follow directions. Direct the patient to breathe normally and to avoid unnecessary movement.
- Observe standard precautions, and follow the general guidelines in Appendix A. Positively identify the patient, and label the appropriate specimen container with the corresponding patient demographics, initials of the person collecting the specimen, date, and time of collection. Perform a venipuncture.
- Remove the needle and apply direct pressure with dry gauze to stop bleeding. Observe/assess venipuncture site for bleeding or hematoma formation and secure gauze with adhesive bandage.
- Protect the specimen from light and promptly transport the specimen to the laboratory for processing and analysis.

POST-TEST:

- A report of the results will be made available to the requesting HCP, who will discuss the results with the patient.
- *Nutritional Considerations:* Increased bilirubin levels may be associated with liver disease. Dietary recommendations

may be indicated depending on the condition and severity of the condition. Currently, for example, there are no specific medications that can be given to cure hepatitis, but elimination of alcohol consumption and a diet optimized for convalescence are commonly included in the treatment plan. A high-calorie, high-protein, moderate-fat diet with a high fluid intake is often recommended for the patient with hepatitis. Treatment of cirrhosis is different because a low-protein diet may be in order if the patient's liver has lost the ability to process the end products of protein metabolism. A diet of soft foods may also be required if esophageal varices have developed. Ammonia levels may be used to determine whether protein should be added to or reduced from the diet. Patients should be encouraged to eat simple carbohydrates and emulsified fats (as in homogenized milk or eggs) rather than complex carbohydrates (e.g., starch, fiber, and glycogen [animal carbohydrates]) and complex fats, which require additional bile to emulsify them so that they can be used. The cirrhotic patient should be carefully observed for the development of ascites, in which case fluid and electrolyte balance requires strict attention. The alcoholic patient should be encouraged to avoid alcohol and also to seek appropriate counseling for substance abuse.
- Intervention for hyperbilirubinemia in the neonatal patient may include early frequent feedings (to stimulate gastrointestinal motility), phototherapy, and exchange transfusion.
- Reinforce information given by the patient's HCP regarding further testing, treatment, or referral to another HCP. Answer any questions or address any concerns voiced by the patient or family.
- Depending on the results of this procedure, additional testing may be performed to evaluate or monitor progression of the disease process and determine the need for a change in therapy. Evaluate test results in relation to the patient's symptoms and other tests performed.

B

RELATED MONOGRAPHS:

Related tests include ALT, albumin, ALP, ammonia, amylase, AMA/ASMA, α_1-antitrypsin/phenotyping, AST, biopsy liver, cholesterol, coagulation factor assays, CBC, cholangiography percutaneous transhepatic, cholangiography post-op, CT biliary tract and liver, copper, ERCP, GGT, hepatobiliary scan, hepatitis serologies, infectious mononucleosis screen, lipase, liver and spleen scan, protein total and fractions, PT/INR, US abdomen, US liver, and UA. See the Hepatobiliary System table at the end of the book for related tests by body system.

Biopsy, Bladder

SYNONYM/ACRONYM: N/A.

COMMON USE: To assist in diagnosing bladder cancer.

SPECIMEN: Bladder tissue or cells.

NORMAL FINDINGS: (Method: Macroscopic and microscopic examination of tissue) No abnormal tissue or cells.

DESCRIPTION: Biopsy is the excision of a sample of tissue that can be analyzed microscopically to determine cell morphology and the presence of tissue abnormalities. This test is used to assist in confirming the diagnosis of cancer when clinical symptoms or other diagnostic findings are suspicious. A urologist performs a biopsy of the bladder during cystoscopic examination. The procedure can be performed in the urologist's office with local anesthesia or in the operating room under general anesthesia. Samples can be obtained by fine-needle aspiration of fluid and tumor cells from the tumor site. Needle biopsies are often performed using guidance by CT scan or ultrasound. If the cystoscopic or other diagnostic imaging examinations indicate the cancer has spread outside the bladder, confirmatory samples can be obtained by surgical biopsy. After the bladder is filled with saline for irrigation, the bladder and urethra are examined by direct and lighted visualization using a cystoscope. A sample of suspicious bladder tissue is then excised and examined macroscopically and microscopically to determine the presence of cell morphology and tissue abnormalities.

INDICATIONS
- Assist in confirmation of malignant lesions of the bladder or ureter, especially if tumor is seen by radiological examination
- Assist in the evaluation of cases in which symptoms such as hematuria persist after previous treatment (e.g., removal of polyps or kidney stones)
- Monitor existing recurrent benign lesions for malignant changes

POTENTIAL DIAGNOSIS
- Positive findings in neoplasm of the bladder or ureter

CRITICAL FINDINGS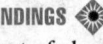
- Assessment of clear margins after tissue excision
- Classification or grading of tumor
- Identification of malignancy

It is essential that critical diagnoses be communicated immediately to the requesting health-care provider (HCP). A listing of these diagnoses varies among facilities. Timely notification of critical values for lab or diagnostic studies is a role expectation of the professional nurse. Notification processes will vary among facilities. Upon receipt of the critical value, the information should be read back to the caller to verify accuracy. Most policies require immediate notification of the primary HCP, hospitalist, or on-call HCP. Reported information includes the patient's name, unique identifiers, critical value, name of the person giving the report, and name of the person receiving the report. Documentation of notification should be made in the medical record with the name of the HCP notified, time and date of notification, and any orders received. Any delay in a timely report of a critical value may require completion of a notification form with review by Risk Management.

INTERFERING FACTORS
- This test is contraindicated in patients with an acute infection of the bladder, urethra, or prostate.
- This procedure is contraindicated in patients with bleeding disorders.
- Failure to follow dietary restrictions before the procedure may cause the procedure to be canceled or repeated.

NURSING IMPLICATIONS AND PROCEDURE

PRETEST:

- Positively identify the patient using at least two unique identifiers before providing care, treatment, or services.
- *Patient Teaching:* Inform the patient this procedure can assist in establishing a diagnosis of bladder disease.
- Obtain a history of the patient's complaints, including a list of known allergens, especially allergies or sensitivities to latex or anesthetics.
- Obtain a history of the patient's genitourinary system, any bleeding disorders or other symptoms, and results of previously performed laboratory tests and diagnostic and surgical procedures.
- Record the date of the last menstrual period and determine the possibility of pregnancy in perimenopausal women.
- Note any recent procedures that can interfere with test results.
- Obtain a list of the patient's current medications including anticoagulants, aspirin and other salicylates, herbs, nutritional supplements, and nutraceuticals (see Appendix F). Such products should be discontinued by medical direction for the appropriate number of days prior to a surgical procedure.
- Review the procedure with the patient. Inform the patient that it may be necessary to remove hair from the site before the procedure. Inform the patient that back pain and burning or pressure in the genital area may be experienced after the procedure. Instruct the patient that prophylactic antibiotics may be administered before the procedure. Address concerns about pain and explain that a sedative and/or analgesia will be administered before the percutaneous biopsy to promote relaxation and reduce discomfort; general anesthesia will be administered before the open biopsy. Explain to the patient that no pain will be experienced during the test when general anesthesia is used but that any discomfort with a needle biopsy will be minimized with local anesthetics and systemic analgesics. Inform

B

the patient that the biopsy is performed under sterile conditions by an HCP specializing in this procedure. The procedure usually takes about 30 to 45 min to complete.

Sensitivity to social and cultural issues, as well as concern for modesty, is important in providing psychological support before, during, and after the procedure.

Explain that an IV line will be inserted to allow infusion of IV fluids, antibiotics, anesthetics, and analgesics.

Instruct the patient that nothing should be taken by mouth for 8 hr prior to a general anesthetic, or that only clear liquids may be taken for 2 hr prior to the procedure if local anesthesia is to be used to reduce the risk of nausea and vomiting. Patients on beta blockers before the surgical procedure should be instructed to take their medication as ordered during the perioperative period. Protocols may vary among facilities.

Make sure a written and informed consent has been signed prior to the procedure and before administering any medications.

INTRATEST:

Ensure that the patient has complied with dietary restrictions; ensure that food and liquids have been restricted for at least 8 hr and clear liquids have been restricted for at least 2 hr prior to the procedure depending on the anesthetic chosen for the procedure.

Ensure that anticoagulant therapy has been withheld for the appropriate number of days prior to the procedure. Number of days to withhold medication is dependent on the type of anticoagulant. Notify the HCP if patient anticoagulant therapy has not been withheld. Ensure that patients on beta-blocker therapy have continued their medication regimen as ordered.

Have emergency equipment readily available.

Have the patient void before the procedure.

Observe standard precautions, and follow the general guidelines in Appendix A. Positively identify the patient, and label the appropriate specimen containers with the corresponding patient demographics, initials of the person collecting the specimen, date and time of collection, and site location.

Assist the patient to the desired position depending on the test site to be used, and direct the patient to breathe normally during the beginning of the general anesthetic. Instruct the patient to cooperate fully and to follow directions. For the patient undergoing local anesthesia, direct him or her to breathe normally and to avoid unnecessary movement during the procedure.

Record baseline vital signs, and continue to monitor throughout the procedure. Protocols may vary among facilities.

Cystoscopy

After administration of local or general anesthesia, place the patient in a lithotomy position on the examination table (with the feet up in stirrups). Drape the patient's legs. Clean the external genitalia with a suitable antiseptic solution and drape the area with sterile towels.

Once the cystoscope is inserted, the bladder is irrigated with saline. A tissue sample is removed using a cytology brush or biopsy forceps. Catheters may be used to obtain samples from the ureter.

Open Biopsy

Adhere to Surgical Care Improvement Project (SCIP) quality measures. Administer ordered prophylactic antibiotics 1 hr before incision, use antibiotics that are consistent with current guidelines specific to the procedure, and use clippers to remove hair from the surgical site if appropriate.

After administration of general anesthesia and surgical preparation are completed, an incision is made, suspicious areas are located, and tissue samples are collected.

General

Monitor the patient for complications related to the procedure (e.g., allergic reaction, anaphylaxis).

▸ Place tissue samples in properly labeled specimen container containing formalin solution, and promptly transport the specimen to the laboratory for processing and analysis.

POST-TEST:

▸ A report of the results will be made available to the requesting HCP, who will discuss the results with the patient.
▸ Instruct the patient to resume preoperative diet, as directed by the HCP. Assess the patient's ability to swallow before allowing the patient to attempt liquids or solid foods.
▸ Monitor vital signs and neurological status every 15 min for 1 hr, then every 2 hr for 4 hr, and then as ordered by the HCP. Monitor temperature every 4 hr for 24 hr. Monitor intake and output at least every 8 hr. Compare with baseline values. Notify the HCP if temperature is elevated. Discontinue prophylactic antibiotics within 24 hr after the conclusion of the procedure. Protocols may vary among facilities.
▸ Instruct the patient on intake and output recording and provide appropriate measuring containers.
▸ Encourage fluid intake of 3,000 mL in 24 hr unless contraindicated.
▸ Observe for delayed allergic reactions, such as rash, urticaria, tachycardia, hyperpnea, hypertension, palpitations, nausea, or vomiting.
▸ Instruct the patient to immediately report pain, chills, or fever. Assess for infection, hemorrhage, or perforation of the bladder.
▸ Inform the patient that blood may be seen in the urine after the first or second postprocedural voiding.
▸ Instruct the patient to report any further changes in urinary pattern, volume, or appearance.

Open Biopsy

▸ Observe/assess the biopsy site for bleeding, inflammation, or hematoma formation.
▸ Instruct the patient in the care and assessment of the site.
▸ Instruct the patient to report any redness, edema, bleeding, or pain at the biopsy site.

General

▸ Assess for nausea, pain, and bladder spasms. Administer antiemetic, analgesic, and antispasmodic medications as needed and as directed by the HCP.
▸ Administer antibiotic therapy if ordered. Remind the patient of the importance of completing the entire course of antibiotic therapy, even if signs and symptoms disappear before completion of therapy.
▸ Recognize anxiety related to test results. Discuss the implications of abnormal test results on the patient's lifestyle. Provide teaching and information regarding the clinical implications of the test results, as appropriate. Educate the patient regarding access to counseling services.
▸ Reinforce information given by the patient's HCP regarding further testing, treatment, or referral to another HCP. Answer any questions or address any concerns voiced by the patient or family.
▸ Instruct the patient in the use of any ordered medications. Explain the importance of adhering to the therapy regimen. As appropriate, instruct the patient in significant side effects and systemic reactions associated with the prescribed medication. Encourage him or her to review corresponding literature provided by a pharmacist.
▸ Depending on the results of this procedure, additional testing may be performed to evaluate or monitor progression of the disease process and determine the need for a change in therapy. Evaluate test results in relation to the patient's symptoms and other tests performed.

RELATED MONOGRAPHS:

▸ Related tests include calculus kidney stone panel, CT renal, cystometry, cystoscopy, cystourethrography voiding, IVP, KUB studies, MRI bladder, retrograde ureteropyelography, US bladder, UA, and urine bladder cancer markers.
▸ Refer to the Genitourinary System table at the end of the book for related tests by body system.

Biopsy, Bone

SYNONYM/ACRONYM: N/A.

COMMON USE: To assist in diagnosing bone cancer.

SPECIMEN: Bone tissue.

NORMAL FINDINGS: (Method: Microscopic study of bone samples) No abnormal tissue or cells.

DESCRIPTION: Biopsy is the excision of a sample of tissue that can be analyzed microscopically to determine cell morphology and the presence of tissue abnormalities. This test is used to assist in confirming the diagnosis of cancer when clinical symptoms or x-rays are suspicious. After surgical biopsy by incision to reveal the affected area, a bone biopsy is obtained. An alternative collection method is needle biopsy. There are two types of needle biopsy: fine-needle biopsy in which fluid and tumor cells are aspirated from the tumor site and core-needle biopsy in which a plug of bone is removed using a special serrated needle. The choice of biopsy method is based on the type of tumor expected, whether the tumor is benign or malignant, and the surgeon's anticipated plan regarding removal of the tumor.

INDICATIONS
- Differentiation of a benign from a malignant bone lesion
- Radiographic evidence of a bone lesion

POTENTIAL DIAGNOSIS
Abnormal findings in
- Ewing's sarcoma
- Multiple myeloma
- Osteoma
- Osteosarcoma

CRITICAL FINDINGS
- Classification or grading of tumor
- Identification of malignancy

It is essential that critical diagnoses be communicated immediately to the requesting health-care provider (HCP). A listing of these diagnoses varies among facilities. Timely notification of critical values for lab or diagnostic studies is a role expectation of the professional nurse. Notification processes will vary among facilities. Upon receipt of the critical value, the information should be read back to the caller to verify accuracy. Most policies require immediate notification of the primary HCP, hospitalist, or on-call HCP. Reported information includes the patient's name, unique identifiers, critical value, name of the person giving the report, and name of the person receiving the report. Documentation of notification should be made in the medical record with the name of the HCP notified, time and date of notification, and any orders received. Any delay in a timely report of a critical value may require completion of a notification form with review by Risk Management.

INTERFERING FACTORS
- ❖ This procedure is contraindicated in patients with bleeding disorders.

- **Failure to follow dietary restrictions before the procedure may cause the procedure to be canceled or repeated.**

NURSING IMPLICATIONS AND PROCEDURE

PRETEST:

Positively identify the patient using at least two unique identifiers before providing care, treatment, or services.

Patient Teaching: Inform the patient this procedure can assist to establish a diagnosis of bone disease.

Obtain a history of the patient's complaints, including a list of known allergens, especially allergies or sensitivities to latex or anesthetics.

Obtain a history of the patient's immune and musculoskeletal systems, especially any bleeding disorders and other symptoms, and results of previously performed laboratory tests and diagnostic and surgical procedures.

Record the date of the last menstrual period and determine the possibility of pregnancy in perimenopausal women.

Note any recent procedures that can interfere with test results.

Obtain a list of the patient's current medications, including anticoagulants, aspirin and other salicylates, herbs, nutritional supplements, and nutraceuticals (see Appendix F). Such products should be discontinued by medical direction for the appropriate number of days prior to a surgical procedure.

Review the procedure with the patient. Inform the patient that it may be necessary to remove hair from the site before the procedure. Instruct the patient that prophylactic antibiotics may be administered before the procedure. Address concerns about pain and explain that a sedative and/or analgesia will be administered to promote relaxation and reduce discomfort prior to the percutaneous biopsy; general anesthesia will be administered prior to the open biopsy. Explain to the patient that no pain will be experienced during the test when general anesthesia is used but that any discomfort with a needle biopsy will be minimized with local anesthetics and systemic analgesics. Inform the patient that the biopsy is performed under sterile conditions by an HCP specializing in this procedure. The surgical procedure usually takes about 30 min to complete, and sutures may be necessary to close the site. A needle biopsy usually takes about 20 min to complete.

Sensitivity to social and cultural issues, as well as concern for modesty, is important in providing psychological support before, during, and after the procedure.

Explain that an IV line will be inserted to allow infusion of IV fluids, anesthetics, analgesics, or IV sedation.

Instruct the patient that, to reduce the risk of nausea and vomiting, nothing should be taken by mouth for 8 hr before a general anesthetic or only clear liquids may be taken for 2 hr before the procedure if local anesthesia is to be used. Patients on beta blockers before the surgical procedure should be instructed to take their medication as ordered during the perioperative period. Protocols may vary among facilities.

Make sure a written and informed consent has been signed prior to the procedure and before administering any medications.

INTRATEST:

Ensure that the patient has complied with dietary restrictions; ensure that food and liquids have been restricted for at least 8 hr and clear liquids have been restricted for at least 2 hr before the procedure depending on the anesthetic chosen for the procedure.

Ensure that anticoagulant therapy has been withheld for the appropriate number of days prior to the procedure. Number of days to withhold medication is dependent on the type of anticoagulant. Notify the HCP if patient anticoagulant therapy has not been withheld. Ensure that patients on beta-blocker therapy have continued their medication regimen as ordered.

Have emergency equipment readily available.

Have the patient void before the procedure.

Observe standard precautions, and follow the general guidelines in Appendix A. Positively identify the patient, and label the appropriate specimen containers with the corresponding patient demographics, initials of the person collecting the specimen, date and time of collection, and site location.

Assist the patient to the desired position depending on the test site to be used, and direct the patient to breathe normally at the beginning of the general anesthetic. Instruct the patient to cooperate fully and to follow directions. For the patient undergoing local anesthesia, direct him or her to breathe normally and to avoid unnecessary movement during the procedure.

Record baseline vital signs, and continue to monitor throughout the procedure. Protocols may vary among facilities.

After the administration of general or local anesthesia cleanse the site with an antiseptic solution and drape the area with sterile towels.

Open Biopsy

Adhere to Surgical Care Improvement Project (SCIP) quality measures. Administer ordered prophylactic antibiotics 1 hr before incision, use antibiotics that are consistent with current guidelines specific to the procedure, and use clippers to remove hair from the surgical site if appropriate.

After administration of general anesthesia and surgical preparation are completed, an incision is made, suspicious area(s) are located, and tissue samples are collected.

Needle Biopsy

Instruct the patient to take slow, deep breaths when the local anesthetic is injected. Protect the site with sterile drapes. A small incision is made and the biopsy needle is inserted to remove the specimen. Pressure is applied to the site for 3 to 5 min, then a sterile pressure dressing is applied.

General

Monitor the patient for complications related to the procedure (e.g., allergic reaction, anaphylaxis).

Place tissue samples in properly labeled specimen container containing formalin solution, and promptly transport the specimen to the laboratory for processing and analysis.

POST-TEST:

A report of the results will be made available to the requesting HCP, who will discuss the results with the patient.

Instruct the patient to resume preoperative diet, as directed by the HCP. Assess the patient's ability to swallow before allowing the patient to attempt liquids or solid foods.

Monitor vital signs and neurological status every 15 min for 1 hr, then every 2 hr for 4 hr, and then as ordered by the HCP. Monitor temperature every 4 hr for 24 hr. Monitor intake and output at least every 8 hr. Compare with baseline values. Notify the HCP if temperature is elevated. Discontinue prophylactic antibiotics within 24 hr after the conclusion of the procedure. Protocols may vary among facilities.

Observe/assess for delayed allergic reactions, such as rash, urticaria, tachycardia, hyperpnea, hypertension, palpitations, nausea, or vomiting.

Observe/assess the biopsy site for bleeding, inflammation, or hematoma formation.

Instruct the patient in the care and assessment of the site.

Instruct the patient to report any redness, edema, bleeding, or pain at the biopsy site. Instruct the patient to immediately report chills or fever.

Assess for nausea and pain. Administer antiemetic and analgesic medications as needed and as directed by the HCP.

Administer antibiotic therapy if ordered. Remind the patient of the importance of completing the entire course of antibiotic therapy, even if signs and symptoms disappear before completion of therapy.

Recognize anxiety related to test results. Discuss the implications of abnormal test results on the patient's lifestyle. Provide teaching and information regarding the clinical implications of the test results, as appropriate. Educate the patient regarding access to counseling services.

Reinforce information given by the patient's HCP regarding further testing, treatment, or referral to another HCP. Inform the patient of a follow-up appointment for removal of sutures, if indicated. Answer any questions or address any concerns voiced by the patient or family.

Instruct the patient in the use of any ordered medications. Explain the importance of adhering to the therapy regimen. As appropriate, instruct the patient in significant side effects and systemic reactions associated with the prescribed medication. Encourage him or her to review corresponding literature provided by a pharmacist.

Depending on the results of this procedure, additional testing may be performed to evaluate or monitor progression of the disease process and determine the need for a change in therapy. Evaluate test results in relation to the patient's symptoms and other tests performed.

RELATED MONOGRAPHS:

Related tests include ALP, biopsy bone marrow, bone scan, calcium, CBC, cortisol, CT spine, immunofixation electrophoresis, immunoglobulins (A, G, and M), β_2-microglobulin, MRI musculoskeletal, PTH, phosphorus, total protein and fractions, radiography bone, UA, and vitamin D.

See the Immune and Musculoskeletal systems tables at the end of the book for related tests by body system.

Biopsy, Bone Marrow

SYNONYM/ACRONYM: N/A.

COMMON USE: To assist in diagnosing hematological diseases and in identifying and staging cancers such as leukemia.

SPECIMEN: Bone marrow aspirate, bone core biopsy, marrow and peripheral smears.

NORMAL FINDINGS: (Method: Microscopic study of bone and bone marrow samples, flow cytometry) Reference ranges are subject to many variables, and therefore the laboratory should be consulted for their specific interpretation. Some generalities may be commented on regarding findings as follows:

- Ratio of marrow fat to cellular elements is related to age, with the amount of fat increasing with increasing age.
- Normal cellularity, cellular distribution, presence of megakaryocytes, and absence of fibrosis or tumor cells.
- The myeloid-to-erythrocyte ratio (M:E) is 2:1 to 4:1 in adults. It may be slightly higher in children.

B

Differential Parameter	Conventional Units
Erythrocyte precursors	18–32%
Myeloblasts	0–2%
Promyelocytes	2–6%
Myelocytes	9–17%
Metamyelocytes	7–25%
Bands	10–16%
Neutrophils	18–28%
Eosinophils and precursors	1–5%
Basophils and precursors	0–1%
Monocytes and precursors	1–5%
Lymphocytes	9–19%
Plasma cells	0–1%

DESCRIPTION: This test involves the removal of a small sample of bone marrow by aspiration, needle biopsy, or open surgical biopsy for a complete hematological analysis. The marrow is a suspension of blood, fat, and developing blood cells, which is evaluated for morphology and examined for all stages of maturation; iron stores; and myeloid-to-erythrocyte ratio (M:E). Sudan black B and periodic acid–Schiff (PAS) stains can be performed for microscopic examination to differentiate the types of leukemia, although flow cytometry and cytogenetics have become more commonly used techniques for this purpose. Immunophenotyping by flow cytometry uses markers directed at specific antigens on white blood cell membranes to provide rapid enumeration and identification of white blood cell types as well as detection of abnormal increases or decreases in specific cell lines. Cytogenetics is a specialization within the area of genetics that includes chromosome analysis or karyotyping. Bone marrow cells are incubated in culture media to increase the number of cells available for study and to allow for hybridization of the cellular DNA with fluorescent DNA probes in a technique called fluorescence in situ hybridization (FISH). The probes are designed to target areas of the chromosome known to correlate with genetic risk for a particular disease. When a suitable volume of hybridized sample is achieved, cell growth is chemically inhibited during the prophase and metaphase stages of mitosis (cell division) and cellular DNA is examined to detect fluorescence, which represents chromosomal abnormalities, in the targeted areas.

INDICATIONS

- Determine marrow differential (proportion of the various types of cells present in the marrow) and M:E
- Evaluate abnormal results of complete blood count or white blood cell count with differential showing increased numbers of leukocyte precursors
- Evaluate hepatomegaly or splenomegaly

- Identify bone marrow hyperplasia or hypoplasia
- Identify infectious organisms present in the bone marrow (histoplasmosis, mycobacteria, cytomegalovirus, parvovirus inclusions)
- Monitor effects of exposure to bone marrow depressants
- Monitor bone marrow response to chemotherapy or radiation therapy

POTENTIAL DIAGNOSIS

Increased Reticulocytes
- Compensated red blood cell (RBC) loss
- Response to vitamin B_{12} therapy

Decreased Reticulocytes
- Aplastic crisis of sickle cell anemia or hereditary spherocytosis

Increased Leukocytes
- *General associations include compensation for infectious process, leukemias, or leukemoid drug reactions*

Decreased Leukocytes
- *General associations include reduction in the marrow space as seen in metastatic neoplasm or myelofibrosis, lack of production of cells as seen in the elderly, or following suppressive therapy such as chemotherapy or radiation*

Increased Neutrophils (total)
- Acute myeloblastic leukemia
- Myeloid (chronic) leukemias

Decreased Neutrophils (total)
- Aplastic anemia
- Leukemias (monocytic and lymphoblastic)

Increased Lymphocytes
- Aplastic anemia
- Lymphatic leukemia
- Lymphomas

- Lymphosarcoma
- Mononucleosis
- Viral infections

Increased Plasma Cells
- Cancer
- Cirrhosis of the liver
- Connective tissue disorders
- Hypersensitivity reactions
- Infections
- Macroglobulinemia
- Ulcerative colitis

Increased Megakaryocytes
- Hemorrhage
- Increasing age
- Infections
- Megakaryocytic myelosis
- Myeloid leukemia
- Pneumonia
- Polycythemia vera
- Thrombocytopenia

Decreased Megakaryocytes
- Agranulocytosis
- Cirrhosis of the liver
- Pernicious aplastic anemia
- Radiation therapy
- Thrombocytopenic purpura

Increased M:E
- Bone marrow failure
- Infections
- Leukemoid reactions
- Myeloid leukemia

Decreased M:E
- Anemias
- Hepatic disease
- Polycythemia vera
- Posthemorrhagic hematopoiesis

Increased Normoblasts
- Anemias
- Chronic blood loss
- Polycythemia vera

Decreased Normoblasts
- Aplastic anemia
- Folic acid or vitamin B_{12} deficiency
- Hemolytic anemia

Increased Eosinophils
• Bone marrow cancer
• Lymphadenoma
• Myeloid leukemia

CRITICAL FINDINGS
• Classification or grading of tumor
• Identification of malignancy

It is essential that critical diagnoses be communicated immediately to the requesting health-care provider (HCP). A listing of these diagnoses varies among facilities. Timely notification of critical values for lab or diagnostic studies is a role expectation of the professional nurse. Notification processes will vary among facilities. Upon receipt of the critical value, the information should be read back to the caller to verify accuracy. Most policies require immediate notification of the primary HCP, hospitalist, or on-call HCP. Reported information includes the patient's name, unique identifiers, critical value, name of the person giving the report, and name of the person receiving the report. Documentation of notification should be made in the medical record with the name of the HCP notified, time and date of notification, and any orders received. Any delay in a timely report of a critical value may require completion of a notification form with review by Risk Management.

INTERFERING FACTORS
• Recent blood transfusions, iron therapy, or administration of cytotoxic agents may alter test results.
• ✸ This procedure is contraindicated in patients with known bleeding disorders.
• Failure to follow dietary restrictions before the procedure may cause the procedure to be canceled or repeated.

NURSING IMPLICATIONS AND PROCEDURE

PRETEST:

▶ Positively identify the patient using at least two unique identifiers before providing care, treatment, or services.

▶ *Patient Teaching:* Inform the patient this procedure can assist in establishing a diagnosis of bone marrow and immune system disease.

▶ Obtain a history of the patient's complaints, including a list of known allergens, especially allergies or sensitivities to latex or anesthetics.

▶ Obtain a history of the patient's hematopoietic and immune systems, especially any bleeding disorders and other symptoms, and results of previously performed laboratory tests and diagnostic and surgical procedures.

▶ Record the date of the last menstrual period and determine the possibility of pregnancy in perimenopausal women.

▶ Note any recent procedures that can interfere with test results.

▶ Obtain a list of the patient's current medications, including anticoagulants, aspirin and other salicylates, herbs, nutritional supplements, and nutraceuticals (see Appendix F). Such products should be discontinued by medical direction for the appropriate number of days prior to a surgical procedure.

▶ Review the procedure with the patient. Inform the patient that it may be necessary to remove hair from the site before the procedure. Address concerns about pain and explain that a sedative and/or analgesia will be administered to promote relaxation and reduce discomfort prior to the percutaneous biopsy. Explain to the patient that any discomfort with the needle biopsy will be minimized with local anesthetics and systemic analgesics. Explain that the patient may feel some pain when the lidocaine is injected and some discomfort at the stage in the procedure when the specimen is aspirated. Inform the patient that the biopsy is performed under sterile conditions by an HCP specializing in this procedure. A needle biopsy usually takes about 20 min to complete.

Sensitivity to social and cultural issues, as well as concern for modesty, is important in providing psychological support before, during, and after the procedure.

▸ Explain that an IV line may be inserted to allow infusion of IV fluids, anesthetics, or sedatives.

▸ Instruct the patient that, to reduce the risk of nausea and vomiting, only clear liquids may be taken for 2 hr before the procedure if local anesthesia is to be used. Protocols may vary among facilities.

▸ *Make sure a written and informed consent has been signed prior to the procedure and before administering any medications.*

INTRATEST:

▸ Ensure that the patient has complied with dietary restrictions; ensure that clear liquids have been restricted for at least 2 hr before the procedure depending on the anesthetic chosen for the procedure.

▸ Ensure that anticoagulant therapy has been withheld for the appropriate number of days prior to the procedure. Number of days to withhold medication is dependent on the type of anticoagulant. Notify the HCP if patient anticoagulant therapy has not been withheld.

▸ Have emergency equipment readily available.

▸ Have the patient void before the procedure.

▸ Observe standard precautions, and follow the general guidelines in Appendix A. Positively identify the patient, and label the appropriate specimen containers with the corresponding patient demographics, initials of the person collecting the specimen, date and time of collection, and site location.

▸ Assist the patient to the desired position depending on the test site to be

used. In young children, the most frequently chosen site is the proximal tibia. Vertebral bodies T10 through L4 are preferred in older children. In adults, the sternum or iliac crests are the preferred sites. Place the patient in the prone, sitting, or side-lying position for the vertebral bodies; the side-lying position for iliac crest or tibial sites; or the supine position for the sternum. Instruct the patient to cooperate fully and to follow directions. Direct the patient to breathe normally and to avoid unnecessary movement during the local anesthetic and the procedure.

▸ Record baseline vital signs, and continue to monitor throughout the procedure. Protocols may vary among facilities.

▸ After the administration of local anesthesia, use clippers to remove hair from the biopsy site if appropriate, cleanse the site with an antiseptic solution, and drape the area with sterile towels.

Needle Aspiration

▸ The HCP will anesthetize the site with procaine or lidocaine, and then insert a needle with stylet into the marrow. The stylet is removed, a syringe attached, and a 0.5-mL aliquot of marrow withdrawn. The needle is removed, and pressure is applied to the site. The aspirate is applied to slides, and, when dry, a fixative is applied.

Needle Biopsy

▸ Instruct the patient to take slow deep breaths when the local anesthetic is injected. Protect the site with sterile drapes.

▸ Local anesthetic is introduced deeply enough to include periosteum. A cutting biopsy needle is introduced through a small skin incision and bored into the marrow cavity. A core needle is introduced through the cutting needle, and a plug of marrow is removed. The needles are withdrawn, and the specimen is placed in a preservative solution. Pressure is applied to the site for 3 to 5 min, and then a pressure dressing is applied.

General

▶ Monitor the patient for complications related to the procedure (e.g., allergic reaction, anaphylaxis).

▶ Place tissue samples in properly labeled specimen container containing formalin solution, and promptly transport the specimen to the laboratory for processing and analysis.

POST-TEST:

▶ A report of the results will be made available to the requesting HCP, who will discuss the results with the patient.

▶ Instruct the patient to resume preoperative diet, as directed by the HCP.

▶ Monitor vital signs and neurological status every 15 min for 1 hr, then every 2 hr for 4 hr, and then as ordered by the HCP. Monitor temperature every 4 hr for 24 hr. Monitor intake and output at least every 8 hr. Compare with baseline values. Notify the HCP if temperature is elevated. Protocols may vary among facilities.

▶ Observe for delayed allergic reactions, such as rash, urticaria, tachycardia, hyperpnea, hypertension, palpitations, nausea, or vomiting.

▶ Observe/assess the biopsy site for bleeding, inflammation, or hematoma formation.

▶ Instruct the patient in the care and assessment of the site.

▶ Instruct the patient to report any redness, edema, bleeding, or pain at the biopsy site. Instruct the patient to immediately report chills or fever.

▶ Assess for nausea and pain. Administer antiemetic and analgesic medications as needed and as directed by the HCP.

▶ Administer antibiotic therapy if ordered. Remind the patient of the importance of completing the entire course of antibiotic therapy, even if signs and symptoms disappear before completion of therapy.

▶ Recognize anxiety related to test results. Discuss the implications of abnormal test results on the patient's lifestyle. Provide teaching and information regarding the clinical implications of the test results, as appropriate. Educate the patient and family members regarding access to counseling and other supportive services. Provide contact information, if desired, for the National Marrow Donor Program (www.marrow.org).

▶ Reinforce information given by the patient's HCP regarding further testing, treatment, or referral to another HCP. Inform the patient of a follow-up appointment for removal of sutures, if indicated. Answer any questions or address any concerns voiced by the patient or family.

▶ Instruct the patient in the use of any ordered medications. Explain the importance of adhering to the therapy regimen. As appropriate, instruct the patient in significant side effects and systemic reactions associated with the prescribed medication. Encourage him or her to review corresponding literature provided by a pharmacist.

▶ Depending on the results of this procedure, additional testing may be performed to evaluate or monitor progression of the disease process and determine the need for a change in therapy. Evaluate test results in relation to the patient's symptoms and other tests performed.

RELATED MONOGRAPHS:

▶ Related tests include biopsy lymph node, CBC, LAP, immunofixation electrophoresis, mediastinoscopy, and vitamin B_{12}.

▶ Refer to the Hematopoietic and Immune systems tables at the end of the book for related tests by body system.

Biopsy, Breast

SYNONYM/ACRONYM: N/A.

COMMON USE: To assist in establishing a diagnosis of breast disease; in the presence of breast cancer, this test is also used to assist in evaluating prognosis and management of response to therapy.

SPECIMEN: Breast tissue or cells.

NORMAL FINDINGS: (Method: Macroscopic and microscopic examination of tissue for biopsy; cytochemical or immunohistochemical for estrogen and progesterone receptors, Ki67, PCNA, P53; flow cytometry for DNA ploidy and S-phase fraction; immunohistochemical or FISH for Her-2/neu) Fluorescence in situ hybridization (FISH) is a cytogenic technique that uses fluorescent-labeled DNA probes to detect specific chromosome abnormalities. Favorable findings:

- Biopsy: no abnormal cells or tissue
- DNA ploidy: majority diploid cell population
- SPF: low fraction of replicating cells in total cell population
- Her-2/neu, Ki67, PCNA, and P53: negative to low percentage of stained cells
- Estrogen and progesterone receptors: high percentage of stained cells

DESCRIPTION: Breast cancer is the most common newly diagnosed cancer in American women. It is the second leading cause of cancer-related death. Biopsy is the excision of a sample of tissue that can be analyzed microscopically to determine cell morphology and the presence of tissue abnormalities. Fine-needle and open biopsies of the breast have become more commonly ordered in recent years as increasing emphasis on early detection of breast cancer has become stronger. Breast biopsies are used to assist in the identification and prognosis of breast cancer. A number of tests can be performed on breast tissue to assist in identification and management of breast cancer. *Estrogen and progesterone receptor assays (ER and PR)* are used to identify patients with a type of breast cancer that may be more responsive than other types of tumors to estrogen-deprivation (antiestrogen) therapy or removal of the ovaries. Patients with these types of tumors generally have a better prognosis. *DNA ploidy* testing by flow cytometry may also be performed on suspicious tissue. Cancer is the unchecked proliferation of tumor cells that contain abnormal amounts of DNA. The higher the grade of tumor cells, the more likely abnormal DNA will be detected. The *ploidy* (number of chromosome sets in the nucleus) is an indication of the speed of cell replication and tumor growth. Cells synthesize DNA in the S phase of mitosis. *S-phase fraction (SPF)* is an indicator of the number of cells undergoing replication. Normal tissue has a higher percentage of resting diploid cells, or cells containing two chromosomes. Aneuploid cells contain multiple chromosomes. Genes on the chromosomes are coded to produce specific proteins. *Ki67 and proliferating cell nuclear antigen (PCNA)* are examples of proteins that can be measured to indicate the degree of cell proliferation in biopsied tissue. Overexpression of a protein called *human epidermal growth factor receptor 2* (HER-2/neu oncoprotein) is helpful in establishing histological evidence of metastatic breast cancer. Metastatic breast cancer patients with high levels of HER-2/neu oncoprotein have a poor prognosis. They have rapid tumor progression, increased rate of recurrence, poor response to standard therapies, and a lower survival rate. Herceptin (trastuzumab) is indicated for treatment of HER-2/neu overexpression. *P53* is a suppressor protein that normally prevents cells with abnormal DNA from multiplying. Mutations in the P53 gene cause the loss of P53 functionality; the checkpoint is lost, and cancerous cells are allowed to proliferate.

INDICATIONS
- Evidence of breast lesion by palpation, mammography, or ultrasound
- Identify patients with breast or other types of cancer that may respond to hormone or antihormone therapy
- Monitor responsiveness to hormone or antihormone therapy
- Observable breast changes such as "peau d'orange" skin, scaly skin of the areola, drainage from the nipple, or ulceration of the skin

POTENTIAL DIAGNOSIS

Positive findings in
- Carcinoma of the breast
- Hormonal therapy (ER and PR)
- Receptor-positive tumors (ER and PR)

CRITICAL FINDINGS
- Assessment of clear margins after tissue excision
- Classification or grading of tumor
- Identification of malignancy

It is essential that critical diagnoses be communicated immediately to the requesting health-care provider (HCP). A listing of these diagnoses varies among facilities. Timely notification of critical values for lab or diagnostic studies is a role expectation of the professional nurse. Notification processes will vary among facilities. Upon receipt of the critical value, the information should be read back to the caller to verify accuracy. Most policies require immediate notification of the primary HCP, hospitalist, or on-call HCP. Reported information includes the patient's name, unique identifiers, critical value, name of the person giving the report, and name of the person receiving the report. Documentation of notification should be made in the medical record with the name of the HCP notified, time and date of notification, and any orders received. Any delay in a timely report of a critical value may require completion of a notification form with review by Risk Management.

INTERFERING FACTORS
- This procedure is contraindicated in patients with bleeding disorders.
- Antiestrogen preparations (e.g., tamoxifen) ingested 2 mo before tissue sampling will affect test results (ER and PR).
- Pretesting preservation of the tissue is method and test dependent. The testing laboratory should be consulted for proper instructions prior to the biopsy procedure.
- Failure to transport specimen to the laboratory immediately can

result in degradation of tissue. Prompt and proper specimen processing, storage, and analysis are important to achieve accurate results.

• Massive tumor necrosis or tumors with low cellular composition falsely decrease results.

• Failure to follow dietary restrictions before the procedure may cause the procedure to be canceled or repeated.

NURSING IMPLICATIONS AND PROCEDURE

PRETEST:

▶ Positively identify the patient using at least two unique identifiers before providing care, treatment, or services.

▶ *Patient Teaching:* Inform the patient this procedure can assist in evaluating breast health.

▶ Obtain a history of the patient's complaints, including a list of known allergens, especially allergies or sensitivities to latex or anesthetics.

▶ Obtain a history of the patient's reproductive system, especially any bleeding disorders and other symptoms, and results of previously performed laboratory tests and diagnostic and surgical procedures.

▶ Record the date of the last menstrual period and determine the possibility of pregnancy in perimenopausal women.

▶ Note any recent procedures that can interfere with test results. Ensure that the patient has not received antiestrogen therapy within 2 mo of the test.

▶ Obtain a list of the patient's current medications, including anticoagulants, aspirin and other salicylates, herbs, nutritional supplements, and nutraceuticals (see Appendix F). Such products should be discontinued by medical direction for the appropriate number of days prior to a surgical procedure.

▶ Review the procedure with the patient. Inform the patient that it may be necessary to remove hair from the site before the procedure. Instruct that prophylactic antibiotics may be administered prior to the procedure. Address concerns about pain and explain that a sedative and/or analgesia will be administered to promote relaxation and reduce discomfort prior to the percutaneous biopsy; a general anesthesia will be administered prior to the open biopsy. Explain to the patient that no pain will be experienced during the test when general anesthesia is used but that any discomfort with a needle biopsy will be minimized with local anesthetics and systemic analgesics. Inform the patient that the biopsy is performed under sterile conditions by an HCP specializing in this procedure. The surgical procedure usually takes about 20 to 30 min to complete, and sutures may be necessary to close the site. A needle biopsy usually takes about 15 min to complete.

▶ *Sensitivity to social and cultural issues,* as well as concern for modesty, is important in providing psychological support before, during, and after the procedure.

▶ Explain that an IV line may be inserted to allow infusion of IV fluids, anesthetics, analgesics, or IV sedation.

▶ Instruct the patient that, to reduce the risk of nausea and vomiting, nothing should be taken by mouth for 8 hr before a general anesthetic or only clear liquids may be taken for 2 hr before the procedure if local anesthesia is to be used. Patients on beta blockers before the surgical procedure should be instructed to take their medication as ordered during the perioperative period. Protocols may vary among facilities.

▶ *Make sure a written and informed consent has been signed prior to the procedure and before administering any medications.*

INTRATEST:

▶ Ensure that the patient has complied with dietary restrictions; ensure that food and liquids have been restricted for at least 8 hr and clear liquids have been restricted for at least 2 hr before the procedure depending on the anesthetic chosen for the procedure. Ensure that the patient has not received antiestrogen therapy within 2 mo of the test.

Ensure that anticoagulant therapy has been withheld for the appropriate number of days prior to the procedure. Number of days to withhold medication is dependent on the type of anticoagulant. Notify the HCP if patient anticoagulant therapy has not been withheld. Ensure that patients on beta-blocker therapy have continued their medication regimen as ordered.

Have emergency equipment readily available.

Have the patient void before the procedure.

Observe standard precautions, and follow the general guidelines in Appendix A. Positively identify the patient, and label the appropriate specimen containers with the corresponding patient demographics, initials of the person collecting the specimen, date and time of collection, and site location, especially right or left breast.

Assist the patient to the desired position depending on the test site to be used, and direct the patient to breathe normally during the beginning of the general anesthetic. Instruct the patient to cooperate fully and to follow directions. For the patient undergoing local anesthesia, direct him or her to breathe normally and to avoid unnecessary movement during the procedure.

Open Biopsy

Adhere to Surgical Care Improvement Project (SCIP) quality measures. Administer ordered prophylactic antibiotics 1 hr before incision, use antibiotics that are consistent with current guidelines specific to the procedure, and use clippers to remove hair from the surgical site if appropriate.

After administration of general anesthesia and surgical preparation are completed, an incision is made, suspicious area(s) are located, and tissue samples are collected.

Record baseline vital signs, and continue to monitor throughout the procedure. Protocols may vary among facilities.

Needle Biopsy

Direct the patient to take slow deep breaths when the local anesthetic is injected. Protect the site with sterile drapes. Instruct the patient to take a deep breath, exhale forcefully, and hold the breath while the biopsy needle is inserted and rotated to obtain a core of breast tissue. Once the needle is removed, the patient may breathe. Pressure is applied to the site for 3 to 5 min, then a sterile pressure dressing is applied.

General

Monitor the patient for complications related to the procedure (e.g., allergic reaction, anaphylaxis).

Place tissue samples in formalin solution. Label the specimen, indicating site location, and promptly transport the specimen to the laboratory for processing and analysis.

POST-TEST:

A report of the results will be made available to the requesting HCP, who will discuss the results with the patient.

Instruct the patient to resume preoperative diet, as directed by the HCP. Assess the patient's ability to swallow before allowing the patient to attempt liquids or solid foods.

Monitor vital signs and neurological status every 15 min for 1 hr, then every 2 hr for 4 hr, and then as ordered by the HCP. Monitor temperature every 4 hr for 24 hr. Monitor intake and output at least every 8 hr. Compare with baseline values. Notify the HCP if temperature is elevated. Discontinue prophylactic antibiotics within 24 hr after the conclusion of the procedure. Protocols may vary among facilities.

Observe/assess for delayed allergic reactions, such as rash, urticaria, tachycardia, hyperpnea, hypertension, palpitations, nausea, or vomiting.

Observe/assess the biopsy site for bleeding, inflammation, or hematoma formation.

Instruct the patient in the care and assessment of the site.

Instruct the patient to report any redness, edema, bleeding, or pain at the biopsy site. Instruct the patient to immediately report chills or fever.

Assess for nausea and pain. Administer antiemetic and analgesic medications as needed and as directed by the HCP.

Administer antibiotic therapy if ordered. Remind the patient of the importance of completing the entire course of antibiotic therapy, even if signs and symptoms disappear before completion of therapy.

▶ Recognize anxiety related to test results. Discuss the implications of abnormal test results on the patient's lifestyle. Provide teaching and information regarding the clinical implications of the test results, as appropriate. Educate the patient regarding access to counseling services. Provide contact information, if desired, for the American Cancer Society (www.cancer.org).

▶ Reinforce information given by the patient's HCP regarding further testing, treatment, or referral to another HCP. Inform the patient of a follow-up appointment for removal of sutures, if indicated. Decisions regarding the need for and frequency of breast self-examination, mammography, magnetic resonance imaging (MRI) breast, or other cancer screening procedures should be made after consultation between the patient and HCP. The most current guidelines for breast cancer screening of the general population as well as of individuals with increased risk are available from the American Cancer Society (www.cancer.org), the American College of Obstetricians and Gynecologists (ACOG) (www.acog.org), and the American College of Radiology (www.acr.org). Answer any questions or address any concerns voiced by the patient or family.

▶ Instruct the patient in the use of any ordered medications. Explain the importance of adhering to the therapy regimen. As appropriate, instruct the patient in significant side effects and systemic reactions associated with the prescribed medication. Encourage the patient to review corresponding literature provided by a pharmacist.

▶ Depending on the results of this procedure, additional testing may be performed to evaluate or monitor progression of the disease process and determine the need for a change in therapy. Evaluate test results in relation to the patient's symptoms and other tests performed.

RELATED MONOGRAPHS:

▶ Related tests include cancer antigens, ductography, mammogram, MRI breast, stereotactic biopsy breast, and US breast.

▶ Refer to the Reproductive System table at the end of the book for related tests by body system.

Biopsy, Cervical

SYNONYM/ACRONYM: Cone biopsy, LEEP.

COMMON USE: To assist in diagnosing and staging cervical cancer.

SPECIMEN: Cervical tissue.

NORMAL FINDINGS: (Method: Microscopic examination of tissue cells) No abnormal cells or tissue.

DESCRIPTION: Biopsy is the excision of a sample of tissue that can be analyzed microscopically to determine cell morphology and the presence of tissue abnormalities. The cervical biopsy is used to assist in confirmation of cancer when screening tests are positive. Cervical biopsy is obtained using an instrument that punches into the tissue and retrieves a tissue sample. Schiller's test entails applying an iodine solution to the cervix. Normal cells pick up the iodine and stain brown. Abnormal cells do not pick up any color. Punch biopsy results may indicate the need for a cone biopsy of the cervix. Cone biopsy involves removing a wedge of tissue from the cervix by using a surgical knife, a carbon dioxide laser, or a loop electrosurgical excision procedure (LEEP). LEEP can be performed by placing the patient under a general anesthetic; by a regional anesthesia, such as a spinal or epidural; or by a cervical block whereby a local anesthetic is injected into the cervix. The patient is given oral or IV pain medicine in conjunction with the local anesthetic when this method is used. Following colposcopy or cervical biopsy, LEEP can be used to treat abnormal tissue identified on biopsy.

INDICATIONS
• Follow-up to abnormal Papanicolaou (Pap) smear, Schiller's test, or colposcopy
• Suspected cervical malignancy

POTENTIAL DIAGNOSIS

Positive findings in
• Carcinoma in situ
• Cervical dysplasia
• Cervical polyps

CRITICAL FINDINGS
• Assessment of clear margins after tissue excision
• Classification or grading of tumor
• Identification of malignancy

It is essential that critical diagnoses be communicated immediately to the requesting health-care provider (HCP). A listing of these diagnoses varies among facilities. Timely notification of critical values for lab or diagnostic studies is a role expectation of the professional nurse. Notification processes will vary among facilities. Upon receipt of the critical value, the information should be read back to the caller to verify accuracy. Most policies require immediate notification of the primary HCP, hospitalist, or on-call HCP. Reported information includes the patient's name, unique identifiers, critical value, name of the person giving the report, and name of the person receiving the report. Documentation of notification should be made in the medical record with the name of the HCP notified, time and date of notification, and any orders received. Any delay in a timely report of a critical value may require completion of a notification form with review by Risk Management.

INTERFERING FACTORS
• ◈ The test is contraindicated in cases of acute pelvic inflammatory disease or bleeding disorders.
• This test should not be performed while the patient is menstruating.
• Failure to follow dietary restrictions before the procedure may cause the procedure to be canceled or repeated.

NURSING IMPLICATIONS AND PROCEDURE

PRETEST:
▸ Positively identify the patient using at least two unique identifiers before providing care, treatment, or services.
Patient Teaching: Inform the patient this procedure can assist in establishing a diagnosis of cervical disease.
▸ Obtain a history of the patient's complaints, including a list of known allergens, especially allergies or sensitivities to latex, iodine, or anesthetics.
▸ Obtain a history of the patient's reproductive system, especially any bleeding

disorders and other symptoms, and results of previously performed laboratory tests and diagnostic and surgical procedures.

Record the date of the last menstrual period and determine the possibility of pregnancy in perimenopausal women.

Obtain a list of the patient's current medications, including herbs, nutritional supplements, and nutraceuticals (see Appendix F). Such products should be discontinued by medical direction for the appropriate number of days prior to a surgical procedure.

Review the procedure with the patient. Inform the patient that it may be necessary to remove hair from the site before the procedure. Instruct the patient that prophylactic antibiotics may be administered before the procedure. Address concerns about pain and explain that a sedative and/or analgesia will be administered to promote relaxation and reduce discomfort prior to the percutaneous biopsy; general anesthesia will be administered prior to the open biopsy. Explain that no pain will be experienced during the test when general anesthesia is used but that any discomfort with a needle biopsy will be minimized with local anesthetics and systemic analgesics. Inform the patient the biopsy is performed under sterile conditions by an HCP specializing in this procedure. The biopsy can be performed in the HCP's office and takes approximately 5 to 10 min to complete. The open biopsy is performed in a surgical suite, usually takes about 20 to 30 min to complete, and sutures may be necessary to close the site.

Sensitivity to social and cultural issues, as well as concern for modesty, is important in providing psychological support before, during, and after the procedure.

Explain that an IV line may be inserted to allow infusion of IV fluids, anesthetics, analgesics, or IV sedation.

Instruct the patient that, to reduce the risk of nausea and vomiting, nothing should be taken by mouth for 8 hr before a general anesthetic or only clear liquids may be taken for 2 hr before the procedure if local anesthesia

is to be used. Patients on beta blockers before the surgical procedure should be instructed to take their medication as ordered during the perioperative period. Protocols may vary among facilities.

Make sure a written and informed consent has been signed prior to the procedure and before administering any medications.

INTRATEST:

Ensure that the patient has complied with dietary restrictions; ensure that food and liquids have been restricted for at least 8 hr and clear liquids have been restricted for at least 2 hr before the procedure depending on the anesthetic chosen for the procedure.

Ensure that anticoagulant therapy has been withheld for the appropriate number of days prior to the procedure. Number of days to withhold medication is dependent on the type of anticoagulant. Notify HCP if patient anticoagulant therapy has not been withheld. Ensure that patients on beta-blocker therapy have continued their medication regimen as ordered.

Have emergency equipment readily available.

Have the patient void before the procedure.

Observe standard precautions, and follow the general guidelines in Appendix A. Positively identify the patient, and label the appropriate specimen containers with the corresponding patient demographics, initials of the person collecting the specimen, date and time of collection, and site location.

Have the patient remove clothes below the waist. Assist the patient into a lithotomy position on a gynecological examination table (with feet in stirrups). Drape the patient's legs. Instruct the patient to cooperate fully and to follow directions. Direct the patient to breathe normally and to avoid unnecessary movement during the local or general anesthetic and the procedure.

Punch Biopsy

Iodine solution is used to cleanse the cervix and distinguish normal from abnormal tissue. Local anesthesia, analgesics, or both, are administered to minimize discomfort.

A small, round punch is rotated into the skin to the desired depth. The cylinder of skin is pulled upward with forceps and separated at its base with a scalpel or scissors.

LEEP in the HCP's Office

A speculum is inserted into the vagina and is opened to gently spread apart the vagina for inspection of the cervix.

Iodine solution is used to cleanse the cervix and distinguish normal from abnormal tissue. Local anesthesia, analgesics, or both, are administered to minimize discomfort.

The diseased tissue is removed along with a small amount of healthy tissue along the margins of the biopsy to ensure that no diseased tissue is left in the cervix after the procedure.

Open Biopsy

Adhere to Surgical Care Improvement Project (SCIP) quality measures. Administer ordered prophylactic antibiotics 1 hr before incision, use antibiotics that are consistent with current guidelines specific to the procedure, and use clippers to remove hair from the surgical site if appropriate.

After administration of general anesthesia and surgical preparation are completed, the procedure is carried out as noted above.

General

Monitor the patient for complications related to the procedure (e.g., allergic reaction, anaphylaxis).

Place tissue samples in properly labeled specimen container containing formalin solution, and promptly transport the specimen to the laboratory for processing and analysis.

POST-TEST:

A report of the results will be made available to the requesting HCP, who will discuss the results with the patient.

Instruct the patient to resume preoperative diet, as directed by the HCP.

Assess the surgical patient's ability to swallow before allowing the patient to attempt liquids or solid foods.

Monitor vital signs and neurological status every 15 min for 1 hr, then every 2 hr for 4 hr, and then as ordered by the HCP. Monitor temperature every 4 hr for 24 hr. Monitor intake and output at least every 8 hr. Compare with baseline values. Notify the HCP if temperature is elevated. Discontinue prophylactic antibiotics within 24 hr after the conclusion of the procedure. Protocols may vary among facilities.

Observe/assess for delayed allergic reactions, such as rash, urticaria, tachycardia, hyperpnea, hypertension, palpitations, nausea, or vomiting.

Advise the patient to expect a gray-green vaginal discharge for several days, that some vaginal bleeding may occur for up to 1 wk but should not be heavier than a normal menses, and that some pelvic pain may occur. Instruct the patient to wear a sanitary pad, and advise the patient that tampons should not be used for 1 to 3 wk.

Patients who have undergone a simple cervical punch biopsy can usually resume normal activities immediately following the procedure. Instruct patients who have undergone LEEP or open biopsy to avoid strenuous activity for 8 to 24 hr; to avoid douching or intercourse for 2 to 4 wk or as instructed; and to report excessive bleeding, chills, fever, or any other unusual findings to the HCP.

Assess for nausea and pain. Administer antiemetic and analgesic medications as needed and as directed by the HCP.

Administer antibiotic therapy if ordered. Remind the patient of the importance of completing the entire course of antibiotic therapy, even if signs and symptoms disappear before completion of therapy.

Recognize anxiety related to test results, and offer support. Discuss the implications of abnormal test results on the patient's lifestyle. Provide teaching and information regarding the clinical implications of the test results, as appropriate. Educate the patient regarding access to counseling services.

Reinforce information given by the patient's HCP regarding further testing, treatment, or referral to another HCP. Decisions regarding the need for and frequency of conventional or liquid-based Pap tests or other cancer screening procedures should be made after consultation between the patient and HCP. The most current guidelines for cervical cancer screening of the general population as well as of individuals with increased risk are available from the American Cancer Society (www.cancer.org) and the American College of Obstetricians and Gynecologists (ACOG) (www.acog.org). Answer any questions or address any concerns voiced by the patient or family.

Instruct the patient in the use of any ordered medications. Explain the importance of adhering to the therapy regimen. As appropriate, instruct the patient in significant side effects and systemic reactions associated with the prescribed medication. Encourage her to review corresponding literature provided by a pharmacist.

Depending on the results of this procedure, additional testing may be performed to evaluate or monitor progression of the disease process and determine the need for a change in therapy. Evaluate test results in relation to the patient's symptoms and other tests performed.

RELATED MONOGRAPHS:

Related tests include *Chlamydia* group antibodies, colposcopy, culture anal/genital, culture viral, Pap smear, and syphilis serology.

See the Reproductive System table at the end of the book for related tests by body system.

B

Biopsy, Chorionic Villus

SYNONYM/ACRONYM: N/A.

COMMON USE: To assist in diagnosing genetic fetal abnormalities such as Down syndrome.

SPECIMEN: Chorionic villus tissue.

NORMAL FINDINGS: (Method: Tissue culture) Normal karyotype.

DESCRIPTION: This test is used to detect fetal abnormalities caused by numerous genetic disorders. The advantage over amniocentesis is that it can be performed as early as the 8th week of pregnancy, permitting earlier decisions regarding termination of pregnancy. However, unlike amniocentesis, this test will not detect neural tube defects.

INDICATIONS

• Assist in the diagnosis of in utero metabolic disorders such as cystic fibrosis or other errors of lipid, carbohydrate, or amino acid metabolism

• Detect abnormalities in the fetus of women of advanced maternal age

• Determine fetal gender when the mother is a known carrier of a sex-linked abnormal gene that

could be transmitted to male offspring, such as hemophilia or Duchenne's muscular dystrophy
• Evaluate fetus in families with a history of genetic disorders, such as Down syndrome, Tay-Sachs disease, chromosome or enzyme anomalies, or inherited hemoglobinopathies

POTENTIAL DIAGNOSIS

Abnormal karyotype: *Numerous genetic disorders. Generally, the laboratory provides detailed interpretive information regarding the specific chromosome abnormality detected.*

CRITICAL FINDINGS ✦

• Identification of abnormalities in chorionic villus tissue.
• It is essential that critical diagnoses be communicated immediately to the requesting health-care provider (HCP). A listing of these diagnoses varies among facilities. Timely notification of critical values for lab or diagnostic studies is a role expectation of the professional nurse. Notification processes will vary among facilities. Upon receipt of the critical value, the information should be read back to the caller to verify accuracy. Most policies require immediate notification of the primary HCP, hospitalist, or on-call HCP. Reported information includes the patient's name, unique identifiers, critical value, name of the person giving the report, and name of the person receiving the report. Documentation of notification should be made in the medical record with the name of the HCP notified, time and date of notification, and any orders received. Any delay in a timely report of a critical value may require completion of a notification form with review by Risk Management.

INTERFERING FACTORS

• ✦ The test is contraindicated in the patient with a history of or in the presence of incompetent cervix.
• Failure to follow dietary restrictions before the procedure may cause the procedure to be canceled or repeated.

NURSING IMPLICATIONS AND PROCEDURE

PRETEST:

▸ Positively identify the patient using at least two unique identifiers before providing care, treatment, or services.
▸ *Patient Teaching:* Inform the patient this procedure can assist in establishing a diagnosis of in utero genetic disorders.
▸ Obtain a history of the patient's complaints, including a list of known allergens, especially allergies or sensitivities to latex or anesthetics.
▸ Obtain a history of the patient's reproductive system, symptoms, and results of previously performed laboratory tests and diagnostic and surgical procedures. Include any family history of genetic disorders such as cystic fibrosis, Duchenne's muscular dystrophy, hemophilia, sickle cell anemia, Tay-Sachs disease, thalassemia, and trisomy 21. Obtain maternal Rh type. If Rh-negative, check for prior sensitization.
▸ Record the date of the last menstrual period and determine that the pregnancy is in the first trimester between the 10th and 12th weeks.
▸ Obtain a history of intravenous drug use, high-risk sexual activity, or occupational exposure.
▸ Obtain a list of the patient's current medications, including herbs, nutritional supplements, and nutraceuticals (see Appendix F).
▸ Review the procedure with the patient. Warn the patient that normal results do not guarantee a normal fetus. Assure the patient that precautions to avoid injury to the fetus will be taken by locating the fetus with ultrasound.

Address concerns about pain related to the procedure. Explain that during the transabdominal procedure, any discomfort with a needle biopsy will be minimized with local anesthetics. Explain that during the transvaginal procedure, some cramping may be experienced as the catheter is guided through the cervix. Encourage relaxation and controlled breathing during the procedure to aid in reducing any mild discomfort. Inform the patient that specimen collection is performed by an HCP specializing in this procedure and usually takes approximately 10 to 15 min to complete.

Sensitivity to social and cultural issues, as well as concern for modesty, is important in providing psychological support before, during, and after the procedure.

There are no food, fluid, or medication restrictions unless by medical direction.

Instruct the patient to drink a glass of water about 30 min prior to testing so that the bladder is full. This elevates the uterus higher in the pelvis. The patient should not void before the procedure.

Make sure a written and informed consent has been signed prior to the procedure and before administering any medications.

INTRATEST:

Ensure that the patient has a full bladder before the procedure.

Have emergency equipment readily available.

Observe standard precautions, and follow the general guidelines in Appendix A. Positively identify the patient, and label the appropriate specimen containers with the corresponding patient demographics, initials of the person collecting the specimen, date and time of collection, and site location.

Have the patient remove clothes below the waist. *Transabdominal:* Assist the patient into a supine position on the examination table with abdomen exposed. Drape the patient's legs, leaving abdomen exposed.

Transvaginal: Assist the patient into a lithotomy position on a gynecologic examination table (with feet in stirrups). Drape the patient's legs. Instruct the patient to cooperate fully and to follow directions. Direct the patient to breathe normally and to avoid unnecessary movement during the local anesthetic and the procedure.

Record maternal and fetal baseline vital signs, and continue to monitor throughout the procedure. Monitor for uterine contractions. Monitor fetal vital signs using ultrasound. Protocols may vary among facilities.

After the administration of local anesthesia, use clippers to remove hair from the surgical site if appropriate, cleanse the site with an antiseptic solution, and drape the area with sterile towels.

Transabdominal Biopsy

Assess the position of the amniotic fluid, fetus, and placenta using ultrasound.

A needle is inserted through the abdomen into the uterus, avoiding contact with the fetus. A syringe is connected to the needle, and the specimen of chorionic villus cells is withdrawn from the uteroplacental area. Pressure is applied to the site for 3 to 5 min, and then a sterile pressure dressing is applied.

Transvaginal Biopsy

Assess the position of the fetus and placenta using ultrasound.

A speculum is inserted into the vagina and is opened to gently spread apart the vagina for inspection of the cervix. The cervix is cleansed with a swab of antiseptic solution.

A catheter is inserted through the cervix into the uterus, avoiding contact with the fetus. A syringe is connected to the catheter, and the specimen of chorionic villus cells is withdrawn from the uteroplacental area.

General

Monitor the patient for complications related to the procedure (e.g., premature labor, allergic reaction, anaphylaxis).

Place tissue samples in formalin solution. Label the specimen, indicating site location, and promptly transport the specimen to the laboratory for processing and analysis.

B

POST-TEST:

A report of the results will be made available to the requesting HCP, who will discuss the results with the patient.

After the procedure, the patient is placed in the left side-lying position, and both maternal and fetal vital signs are monitored for at least 30 min. Protocols may vary among facilities.

Observe/assess for delayed allergic reactions, such as rash, urticaria, tachycardia, hyperpnea, hypertension, palpitations, nausea, or vomiting.

Observe/assess the biopsy site for bleeding, inflammation, or hematoma formation.

Instruct the patient in the care and assessment of the site.

Instruct the patient to report any redness, edema, bleeding, or pain at the biopsy site.

Advise the patient to expect mild cramping, leakage of small amount of amniotic fluid, and vaginal spotting for up to 2 days following the procedure. Instruct the patient to report moderate to severe abdominal pain or cramps, increased or prolonged leaking of amniotic fluid from vagina or abdominal needle site, vaginal bleeding that is heavier than spotting, and either chills or fever.

Administer Rh$_o$(D) immune globulin (RhoGAM IM or Rhophylac IM or IV) to maternal Rh-negative patients to prevent maternal Rh sensitization should the fetus be Rh-positive.

Administer mild analgesic and antibiotic therapy as ordered. Remind the patient of the importance of completing the entire course of antibiotic therapy, even if signs and symptoms disappear before completion of therapy.

Recognize anxiety related to test results. Discuss the implications of abnormal test results on the patient's lifestyle. Provide teaching and information regarding the clinical implications of the test results, as appropriate. Encourage family to seek counseling if concerned with pregnancy termination or to seek genetic counseling if chromosomal abnormality is determined. Decisions regarding elective abortion should take place in the presence of both parents. Provide a nonjudgmental, nonthreatening atmosphere for a discussion during which risks of delivering a developmentally challenged infant are discussed with options (termination of pregnancy or adoption). It is also important to discuss problems the mother and father may experience (guilt, depression, anger) if fetal abnormalities are detected.

Reinforce information given by the patient's HCP regarding further testing, treatment, or referral to another HCP. Answer any questions or address any concerns voiced by the patient or family.

Instruct the patient in the use of any ordered medications. Explain the importance of adhering to the therapy regimen. As appropriate, instruct the patient in significant side effects and systemic reactions associated with the prescribed medication. Encourage her to review corresponding literature provided by a pharmacist.

Depending on the results of this procedure, additional testing may be performed to evaluate or monitor progression of the disease process and determine the need for a change in therapy. Evaluate test results in relation to the patient's symptoms and other tests performed.

RELATED MONOGRAPHS:

Related tests include amniotic fluid analysis, chromosome analysis, α_1 fetoprotein, HCG, hexosaminidase A and B, L/S ratio, newborn screening, US biophysical profile, and US obstetric.

Refer to the Reproductive System table at the end of the book for related tests by body system.

Biopsy, Intestinal

SYNONYM/ACRONYM: N/A.

COMMON USE: To assist in confirming a diagnosis of intestinal cancer or disease.

SPECIMEN: Intestinal tissue or cells.

NORMAL FINDINGS: (Method: Macroscopic and microscopic examination of tissue) No abnormal tissue or cells.

DESCRIPTION: Intestinal biopsy is the excision of a tissue sample from the small intestine for microscopic analysis to determine cell morphology and the presence of tissue abnormalities. This test assists in confirming the diagnosis of cancer or intestinal disorders. Biopsy specimen is usually obtained during endoscopic examination.

INDICATIONS

- Assist in the diagnosis of various intestinal disorders, such as lactose and other enzyme deficiencies, celiac disease, and parasitic infections
- Confirm suspected intestinal malignancy
- Confirm suspicious findings during endoscopic visualization of the intestinal wall

POTENTIAL DIAGNOSIS

Abnormal findings in
- Cancer
- Celiac disease
- Lactose deficiency
- Parasitic infestation
- Tropical sprue

CRITICAL FINDINGS

- Assessment of clear margins after tissue excision

- Classification or grading of tumor
- Identification of malignancy

It is essential that critical diagnoses be communicated immediately to the requesting health-care provider (HCP). A listing of these diagnoses varies among facilities. Timely notification of critical values for lab or diagnostic studies is a role expectation of the professional nurse. Notification processes will vary among facilities. Upon receipt of the critical value, the information should be read back to the caller to verify accuracy. Most policies require immediate notification of the primary HCP, hospitalist, or on-call HCP. Reported information includes the patient's name, unique identifiers, critical value, name of the person giving the report, and name of the person receiving the report. Documentation of notification should be made in the medical record with the name of the HCP notified, time and date of notification, and any orders received. Any delay in a timely report of a critical value may require completion of a notification form with review by Risk Management.

INTERFERING FACTORS

- Barium swallow within 48 hr of small intestine biopsy affects results.
- This procedure is contraindicated in patients with bleeding disorders and aortic arch aneurysm.

B

• Failure to follow dietary restrictions before the procedure may cause the procedure to be canceled or repeated.

NURSING IMPLICATIONS AND PROCEDURE

PRETEST:

▶ Positively identify the patient using at least two unique identifiers before providing care, treatment, or services.

▶ *Patient Teaching:* Inform the patient this procedure can assist in establishing a diagnosis of intestinal disease.

▶ Obtain a history of the patient's complaints, including a list of known allergens, especially allergies or sensitivities to latex or anesthetics.

▶ Obtain a history of the patient's gastrointestinal and immune systems, any bleeding disorders, symptoms, and results of previously performed laboratory tests and diagnostic and surgical procedures.

▶ Record the date of the last menstrual period and determine the possibility of pregnancy in perimenopausal women.

▶ Note any recent procedures that can interfere with test results.

▶ Obtain a list of the patient's current medications including anticoagulants, aspirin and other salicylates, herbs, nutritional supplements, and nutraceuticals (see Appendix F). Such products should be discontinued by medical direction for the appropriate number of days prior to a surgical procedure.

▶ Review the procedure with the patient. Address concerns about pain and explain that a sedative may be administered to promote relaxation during the procedure. Inform the patient that the procedure is performed by an HCP specializing in this procedure and usually takes about 60 min to complete.

▶ *Sensitivity to social and cultural issues,* as well as concern for modesty, is important in providing psychological support before, during, and after the procedure.

▶ Explain that an IV line will be inserted to allow infusion of IV fluids, anesthetics, and analgesics.

▶ Explain that a clear liquid diet is to be consumed 1 day prior to the procedure. Instruct the patient that, to reduce the risk of nausea and vomiting, nothing should be taken by mouth for 8 hr before a general anesthetic. Protocols may vary among facilities.

▶ Provide the patient with a gown, robe, and foot coverings and instruct him or her to void prior to the procedure.

▶ Instruct the patient to remove dentures. Inform the HCP if the patient has any crowns or caps on the teeth.

▶ *Make sure a written and informed consent has been signed prior to the procedure and before administering any medications.*

INTRATEST:

▶ Ensure that the patient has complied with dietary restrictions; ensure that food has been restricted for 8 hr prior to the procedure if general anesthesia will be used.

▶ Ensure that anticoagulant therapy has been withheld for the appropriate number of days prior to the procedure. Number of days to withhold medication is dependent on the type of anticoagulant. Notify the HCP if patient anticoagulant therapy has not been withheld.

▶ Have emergency equipment readily available.

▶ Observe standard precautions, and follow the general guidelines in Appendix A. Positively identify the patient, and label the appropriate specimen containers with the corresponding patient demographics, initials of the person collecting the specimen, date and time of collection, and site location.

▶ Assist the patient into a semireclining position. Instruct the patient to cooperate fully and to follow directions. Direct the patient to breathe normally and to avoid unnecessary movement.

▶ Record baseline vital signs, and continue to monitor throughout the procedure. Protocols may vary among facilities.

Esophagogastroduodenoscopy (EGD) Biopsy

A local anesthetic is sprayed into the throat. A protective tooth guard and a bite block may be placed in the mouth. The flexible endoscope is passed into and through the mouth, and the patient is asked to swallow. Once the endoscope passes into the esophagus, assist the patient into the left lateral position. A suction device is used to drain saliva.

The esophagus, stomach, and duodenum are visually examined as the endoscope passes through each section. A biopsy specimen can be taken from any suspicious sites.

Tissue samples are obtained by inserting a cytology brush or biopsy forceps through the endoscope.

When the examination and tissue removal are complete, the endoscope and suction device are withdrawn and the tooth guard and bite block are removed.

Monitor the patient for complications related to the procedure (e.g., allergic reaction, anaphylaxis).

Place tissue samples in formalin solution. Label the specimen, indicating site location, and promptly transport the specimen to the laboratory for processing and analysis.

POST-TEST:

A report of the results will be made available to the requesting HCP, who will discuss the results with the patient.

Instruct the patient to resume usual diet, as directed by the HCP. Assess the patient's ability to swallow before allowing the patient to attempt liquids or solid foods.

Monitor vital signs and neurological status every 15 min for 1 hr, then every 2 hr for 4 hr, and then as ordered by the HCP. Monitor temperature every 4 hr for 24 hr. Monitor intake and output at least every 8 hr. Compare with baseline values. Notify the HCP if temperature is elevated. Protocols may vary among facilities.

Observe/assess for delayed allergic reactions, such as rash, urticaria, tachycardia, hyperpnea, hypertension, palpitations, nausea, or vomiting.

Instruct the patient to report any chest pain, upper abdominal pain, pain on swallowing, difficulty breathing, or expectoration of blood. Report these to the HCP immediately.

Administer mild analgesic and antibiotic therapy as ordered. Remind the patient of the importance of completing the entire course of antibiotic therapy, even if signs and symptoms disappear before completion of therapy.

Recognize anxiety related to test results. Discuss the implications of abnormal test results on the patient's lifestyle. Provide teaching and information regarding the clinical implications of the test results, as appropriate. Educate the patient regarding access to counseling services.

Reinforce information given by the patient's HCP regarding further testing, treatment, or referral to another HCP. Answer any questions or address any concerns voiced by the patient or family.

Instruct the patient in the use of any ordered medications. Explain the importance of adhering to the therapy regimen. As appropriate, instruct the patient in significant side effects and systemic reactions associated with the prescribed medication. Encourage him or her to review corresponding literature provided by a pharmacist.

Depending on the results of this procedure, additional testing may be performed to evaluate or monitor progression of the disease process and determine the need for a change in therapy. Evaluate test results in relation to the patient's symptoms and other tests performed.

RELATED MONOGRAPHS:

Related tests include albumin, antibodies gliadin, calcium, cancer antigens, capsule endoscopy, colonoscopy, D-xylose tolerance, fecal analysis, fecal fat, folic acid, iron/TIBC, LTT, ova and parasite, potassium, PT/INR, sodium, US abdomen, vitamin B_{12}, and vitamin D.

Refer to the Gastrointestinal and Immune systems tables at the end of the book for related tests by body system.

Biopsy, Kidney

B

SYNONYM/ACRONYM: Renal biopsy.

COMMON USE: To assist in diagnosing cancer and other renal disorders.

SPECIMEN: Kidney tissue or cells.

NORMAL FINDINGS: (Method: Macroscopic and microscopic examination of tissue) No abnormal cells or tissue.

DESCRIPTION: Kidney or renal biopsy is the excision of a tissue sample from the kidney for microscopic analysis to determine cell morphology and the presence of tissue abnormalities. This test assists in confirming a diagnosis of cancer found on x-ray or ultrasound or to diagnose certain inflammatory or immunological conditions. Biopsy specimen is usually obtained either percutaneously or after surgical incision.

INDICATIONS

• Assist in confirming suspected renal malignancy
• Assist in the diagnosis of the cause of renal disease
• Determine extent of involvement in systemic lupus erythematosus or other immunological disorders
• Monitor progression of nephrotic syndrome
• Monitor renal function after transplantation

POTENTIAL DIAGNOSIS

Positive findings in
• Acute and chronic poststreptococcal glomerulonephritis
• Amyloidosis infiltration
• Cancer
• Disseminated lupus erythematosus
• Goodpasture's syndrome
• Immunological rejection of transplanted kidney
• Nephrotic syndrome
• Pyelonephritis
• Renal venous thrombosis

CRITICAL FINDINGS

• Assessment of clear margins after tissue excision
• Classification or grading of tumor
• Identification of malignancy

It is essential that critical diagnoses be communicated immediately to the requesting health-care provider (HCP). A listing of these diagnoses varies among facilities. Timely notification of critical values for lab or diagnostic studies is a role expectation of the professional nurse. Notification processes will vary among facilities. Upon receipt of the critical value, the information should be read back to the caller to verify accuracy. Most policies require immediate notification of the primary HCP, hospitalist, or on-call HCP. Reported information includes the patient's name, unique identifiers, critical value, name of the person giving the report, and name of the person receiving the report. Documentation of notification should be made in the medical record with the name of the HCP notified, time and date of notification, and any orders received. Any delay in a timely report of a critical value may require completion of a notification form with review by Risk Management.

B

INTERFERING FACTORS

- ◈ This procedure is contraindicated in bleeding disorders, advanced renal disease, uncontrolled hypertension, or solitary kidney (except transplanted kidney).
- Obesity and severe spinal deformity can make percutaneous biopsy impossible.
- Failure to follow dietary restrictions before the procedure may cause the procedure to be canceled or repeated.

NURSING IMPLICATIONS AND PROCEDURE

PRETEST:

- Positively identify the patient using at least two unique identifiers before providing care, treatment, or services.
- *Patient Teaching:* Inform the patient this procedure can assist in establishing a diagnosis of kidney disease.
- Obtain a history of the patient's complaints, including a list of known allergens, especially allergies or sensitivities to latex or anesthetics.
- Obtain a history of the patient's genitourinary and immune systems, especially any bleeding disorders or other symptoms, and results of previously performed laboratory tests and diagnostic and surgical procedures.
- Record the date of the last menstrual period and determine the possibility of pregnancy in perimenopausal women.
- Note any recent procedures that can interfere with test results.
- Obtain a list of the patient's current medications, including anticoagulants, aspirin and other salicylates, herbs, nutritional supplements, and nutraceuticals (see Appendix F). Such products should be discontinued by medical direction for the appropriate number of days prior to a surgical procedure.
- Review the procedure with the patient. Inform the patient that it may be necessary to remove hair from the site before the procedure. Instruct the patient that prophylactic antibiotics may be administered before the procedure. Address

concerns about pain and explain that a sedative and/or analgesia will be administered before the percutaneous biopsy to promote relaxation and reduce discomfort; general anesthesia will be administered before the open biopsy. Explain to the patient that no pain will be experienced during the test when general anesthesia is used but that any discomfort with a needle biopsy will be minimized with local anesthetics and systemic analgesics. Inform the patient that the biopsy is performed under sterile conditions by an HCP specializing in this procedure. The surgical procedure usually takes about 60 min to complete, and sutures may be necessary to close the site. A needle biopsy usually takes about 40 min to complete.

- *Sensitivity to social and cultural issues,* as well as concern for modesty, is important in providing psychological support before, during, and after the procedure.
- Explain that an IV line will be inserted to allow infusion of IV fluids, antibiotics, anesthetics, analgesics, or IV sedation.
- Instruct the patient that, to reduce the risk of nausea and vomiting, nothing should be taken by mouth for 8 hr before a general anesthetic or only clear liquids may be taken for 2 hr before the procedure if local anesthesia is to be used. Patients on beta blockers before the surgical procedure should be instructed to take their medication as ordered during the perioperative period. Protocols may vary among facilities.
- *Make sure a written and informed consent has been signed prior to the procedure and before administering any medications.*

INTRATEST:

- Ensure that the patient has complied with dietary restrictions; ensure that food and liquids have been restricted for at least 8 hr and clear liquids have been restricted for at least 2 hr before the procedure depending on the anesthetic chosen for the procedure.
- Ensure that anticoagulant therapy has been withheld for the appropriate

number of days prior to the procedure. Number of days to withhold medication is dependent on the type of anticoagulant. Notify the HCP if patient anticoagulant therapy has not been withheld. Ensure that patients on beta-blocker therapy have continued their medication regimen as ordered.

Have emergency equipment readily available.

Have the patient void before the procedure.

Observe standard precautions, and follow the general guidelines in Appendix A. Positively identify the patient, and label the appropriate specimen containers with the corresponding patient demographics, initials of the person collecting the specimen, date and time of collection, and site location, especially right or left kidney.

Assist the patient to the desired position depending on the test site to be used, and direct the patient to breathe normally during the beginning of the general anesthetic. Instruct the patient to cooperate fully and to follow directions. Direct the patient to avoid unnecessary movement.

Record baseline vital signs, and continue to monitor throughout the procedure. Protocols may vary among facilities.

After the administration of general or local anesthesia, use clippers to remove hair from the surgical site if appropriate, cleanse the site with an antiseptic solution, and drape the area with sterile towels.

Open Biopsy

Adhere to Surgical Care Improvement Project (SCIP) quality measures. Administer ordered prophylactic antibiotics 1 hr before incision, and use antibiotics that are consistent with current guidelines specific to the procedure.

After administration of general anesthesia and surgical preparation are completed, an incision is made, suspicious area(s) are located, and tissue samples are collected.

Needle Biopsy

A sandbag may be placed under the abdomen to aid in moving the kidneys to the desired position. Direct the patient to take slow deep breaths when the local anesthetic is injected. Protect the site with sterile drapes. Instruct the patient to take a deep breath, exhale forcefully, and hold the breath while the biopsy needle is inserted and rotated to obtain a core of renal tissue. Once the needle is removed, the patient may breathe. Pressure is applied to the site for 5 to 20 min, then a sterile pressure dressing is applied.

General

Monitor the patient for complications related to the procedure (e.g., allergic reaction, anaphylaxis).

Place tissue samples in formalin solution. Label the specimen, indicating site location, and promptly transport the specimen to the laboratory for processing and analysis.

POST-TEST:

A report of the results will be made available to the requesting HCP, who will discuss the results with the patient.

Instruct the patient to resume preoperative diet, as directed by the HCP. Assess the patient's ability to swallow before allowing the patient to attempt liquids or solid foods.

Monitor vital signs and neurological status every 15 min for 1 hr, then every 2 hr for 4 hr, and then as ordered by the HCP. Monitor temperature every 4 hr for 24 hr. Monitor intake and output at least every 8 hr. Compare with baseline values. Notify the HCP if temperature is elevated. Discontinue prophylactic antibiotics within 24 hr after the conclusion of the procedure. Protocols may vary among facilities.

Observe/assess for delayed allergic reactions, such as rash, urticaria, tachypnea, hyperpnea, hypertension, palpitations, nausea, or vomiting.

Instruct the patient to immediately report symptoms such as fast heart rate, difficulty breathing, skin rash, itching, chest pain, persistent right shoulder pain, or abdominal pain. Immediately report symptoms to the appropriate HCP.

Observe/assess the biopsy site for bleeding, inflammation, or hematoma formation.

Instruct the patient in the care and assessment of the site.

Instruct the patient to report any redness, edema, bleeding, or pain at the biopsy site. Instruct the patient to immediately report chills or fever. Observe/assess the biopsy site for bleeding, inflammation, or hematoma formation.

Inform the patient that blood may be seen in the urine after the first or second postprocedural voiding.

Monitor fluid intake and output for 24 hr. Instruct the patient on intake and output recording and provide appropriate measuring containers.

Instruct the patient to report any changes in urinary pattern or volume or any unusual appearance of the urine. If urinary volume is less than 200 mL in the first 8 hr, encourage the patient to increase fluid intake unless contraindicated by another medical condition.

Assess for nausea and pain. Administer antiemetic and analgesic medications as needed and as directed by the HCP.

Administer antibiotic therapy if ordered. Remind the patient of the importance of completing the entire course of antibiotic therapy, even if signs and symptoms disappear before completion of therapy.

Recognize anxiety related to test results. Discuss the implications of abnormal test results on the patient's lifestyle. Provide teaching and information regarding the clinical implications of the test results, as appropriate.

Educate the patient regarding access to counseling services.

Reinforce information given by the patient's HCP regarding further testing, treatment, or referral to another HCP. Inform the patient of a follow-up appointment for removal of sutures, if indicated. Answer any questions or address any concerns voiced by the patient or family.

Instruct the patient in the use of any ordered medications. Explain the importance of adhering to the therapy regimen. As appropriate, instruct the patient in significant side effects and systemic reactions associated with the prescribed medication. Encourage him or her to review corresponding literature provided by a pharmacist.

Depending on the results of this procedure, additional testing may be performed to evaluate or monitor progression of the disease process and determine the need for a change in therapy. Evaluate test results in relation to the patient's symptoms and other tests performed.

RELATED MONOGRAPHS:

Related tests include albumin, aldosterone, angiography renal, antibodies antiglomerular basement membrane, β_2-microglobulin, BUN, CT renal, creatinine, creatinine clearance, cytology urine, cystoscopy, IVP, KUB studies, osmolality, PTH, potassium, protein, renin, renogram, sodium, US kidney, and UA.

Refer to the Genitourinary and Immune systems tables at the end of the book for related tests by body system.

Biopsy, Liver

SYNONYM/ACRONYM: N/A.

COMMON USE: To assist in diagnosing liver cancer, and other liver disorders such as cirrhosis and hepatitis.

SPECIMEN: Liver tissue or cells.

NORMAL FINDINGS: (Method: Macroscopic and microscopic examination of tissue) No abnormal cells or tissue.

B

DESCRIPTION: Liver biopsy is the excision of a tissue sample from the liver for microscopic analysis to determine cell morphology and the presence of tissue abnormalities. This test is used to assist in confirming a diagnosis of cancer or certain disorders of the hepatic parenchyma. Biopsy specimen is usually obtained either percutaneously or after surgical incision.

INDICATIONS
• Assist in confirming suspected hepatic malignancy
• Assist in confirming suspected hepatic parenchymal disease
• Assist in diagnosing the cause of persistently elevated liver enzymes, hepatomegaly, or jaundice

POTENTIAL DIAGNOSIS

Positive findings in
• Benign tumor
• Cancer
• Cholesterol ester storage disease
• Cirrhosis
• Galactosemia
• Hemochromatosis
• Hepatic involvement with systemic lupus erythematosus, sarcoidosis, or amyloidosis
• Hepatitis
• Parasitic infestations (e.g., amebiasis, malaria, visceral larva migrans)
• Reye's syndrome
• Wilson's disease

CRITICAL FINDINGS
• Assessment of clear margins after tissue excision
• Classification or grading of tumor
• Identification of malignancy

It is essential that critical diagnoses be communicated immediately to the requesting health-care provider (HCP).

A listing of these diagnoses varies among facilities. Timely notification of critical values for lab or diagnostic studies is a role expectation of the professional nurse. Notification processes will vary among facilities. Upon receipt of the critical value, the information should be read back to the caller to verify accuracy. Most policies require immediate notification of the primary HCP, hospitalist, or on-call HCP. Reported information includes the patient's name, unique identifiers, critical value, name of the person giving the report, and name of the person receiving the report. Documentation of notification should be made in the medical record with the name of the HCP notified, time and date of notification, and any orders received. Any delay in a timely report of a critical value may require completion of a notification form with review by Risk Management.

INTERFERING FACTORS
• This procedure is contraindicated in patients with bleeding disorders, suspected vascular tumor of the liver, ascites that may obscure proper insertion site for needle biopsy, subdiaphragmatic or right hemothoracic infection, or biliary tract infection.
• Failure to follow dietary restrictions before the procedure may cause the procedure to be canceled or repeated.

NURSING IMPLICATIONS AND PROCEDURE

PRETEST:
▶ Positively identify the patient using at least two unique identifiers before providing care, treatment, or services.
▶ *Patient Teaching:* Inform the patient this procedure can assist in establishing a diagnosis of liver disease.
▶ Obtain a history of the patient's complaints, especially fatigue and pain related to inflammation and swelling of the

liver. Include a list of known allergens, especially allergies or sensitivities to latex or anesthetics.

Obtain a history of the patient's hepatobiliary and immune systems, especially any bleeding disorders and other symptoms, and results of previously performed laboratory tests and diagnostic and surgical procedures.

Record the date of the last menstrual period and determine the possibility of pregnancy in perimenopausal women.

Note any recent procedures that can interfere with test results.

Obtain a list of the patient's current medications including anticoagulants, aspirin and other salicylates, herbs, nutritional supplements, and nutraceuticals (see Appendix F). Such products should be discontinued by medical direction for the appropriate number of days prior to a surgical procedure.

Review the procedure with the patient. Inform the patient that it may be necessary to remove hair from the site before the procedure. Instruct the patient that prophylactic antibiotics may be administered before the procedure. Address concerns about pain and explain that a sedative and/or analgesia will be administered before the percutaneous biopsy to promote relaxation and reduce discomfort; general anesthesia will be administered before the open biopsy. Explain to the patient that no pain will be experienced during the test when general anesthesia is used but that any discomfort with a needle biopsy will be minimized with local anesthetics and systemic analgesics. Inform the patient that the biopsy is performed under sterile conditions by an HCP specializing in this procedure. The surgical procedure usually takes about 90 min to complete, and sutures may be necessary to close the site. A needle biopsy usually takes about 15 min to complete.

Sensitivity to social and cultural issues, as well as concern for modesty, is important in providing psychological support before, during, and after the procedure.

Explain that an IV line will be inserted to allow infusion of IV fluids, antibiotics, anesthetics, analgesics, or IV sedation.

Instruct the patient that, to reduce the risk of nausea and vomiting, nothing should be taken by mouth for 8 hr before a general anesthetic or only clear liquids may be taken for 2 hr before the procedure if local anesthesia is to be used. Patients on beta blockers before the surgical procedure should be instructed to take their medication as ordered during the perioperative period. Protocols may vary among facilities.

Make sure a written and informed consent has been signed prior to the procedure and before administering any medications.

INTRATEST:

Ensure that the patient has complied with dietary restrictions; ensure that food and liquids have been restricted for at least 8 hr and clear liquids have been restricted for at least 2 hr before the procedure depending on the anesthetic chosen for the procedure.

Ensure that anticoagulant therapy has been withheld for the appropriate number of days prior to the procedure. Number of days to withhold medication is dependent on the type of anticoagulant. Notify the HCP if patient anticoagulant therapy has not been withheld. Ensure that patients on beta-blocker therapy have continued their medication regimen as ordered.

Have emergency equipment readily available.

Have the patient void before the procedure.

Observe standard precautions, and follow the general guidelines in Appendix A. Positively identify the patient, and label the appropriate specimen containers with the corresponding patient demographics, initials of the person collecting the specimen, date and time of collection, and site location.

Assist the patient to the desired position depending on the test site to be used and direct the patient to breathe normally during the beginning of the general anesthetic. Instruct the patient to cooperate fully and to follow directions. For the patient undergoing local anesthesia, direct him or her to breathe normally and to avoid unnecessary movement during the procedure. Instruct the patient to avoid coughing or straining, which may increase intra-abdominal pressure.

Record baseline vital signs, and continue to monitor throughout the procedure. Protocols may vary among facilities.

After the administration of general or local anesthesia, use clippers to remove hair from the surgical site if appropriate, cleanse the site with an antiseptic solution, and drape the area with sterile towels.

Open Biopsy

Adhere to Surgical Care Improvement Project (SCIP) quality measures. Administer ordered prophylactic antibiotics 1 hr before incision, and use antibiotics that are consistent with current guidelines specific to the procedure.

After administration of general anesthesia and surgical preparation are completed, an incision is made, suspicious area(s) are located, and tissue samples are collected.

Needle Biopsy

Direct the patient to take slow deep breaths when the local anesthetic is injected. Protect the site with sterile drapes. Instruct the patient to take a deep breath, exhale forcefully, and hold the breath while the biopsy needle is inserted and rotated to obtain a core of liver tissue. Once the needle is removed, the patient may breathe. Pressure is applied to the site for 3 to 5 min, then a sterile pressure dressing is applied.

General

Monitor the patient for complications related to the procedure (e.g., allergic reaction, anaphylaxis).

Place tissue samples in formalin solution. Label the specimen, indicating site location, and promptly transport the specimen to the laboratory for processing and analysis.

POST-TEST:

A report of the results will be made available to the requesting HCP, who will discuss the results with the patient.

Instruct the patient to resume preoperative diet, as directed by the HCP. Assess the patient's ability to swallow before allowing the patient to attempt liquids or solid foods.

Monitor vital signs and neurological status every 15 min for 1 hr, then every 2 hr for 4 hr, and then as ordered by the HCP. Monitor temperature every 4 hr for 24 hr. Monitor intake and output at least every 8 hr. Compare with baseline values. Notify the HCP if temperature is elevated. Discontinue prophylactic antibiotics within 24 hr after the conclusion of the procedure. Protocols may vary among facilities.

Observe/assess for delayed allergic reactions, such as rash, urticaria, tachycardia, hyperpnea, hypertension, palpitations, nausea, or vomiting.

Instruct the patient to immediately report symptoms such as fast heart rate, difficulty breathing, skin rash, itching, chest pain, persistent right shoulder pain, or abdominal pain. Immediately report symptoms to the appropriate HCP.

Observe/assess the biopsy site for bleeding, inflammation, or hematoma formation.

Instruct the patient in the care and assessment of the site.

Instruct the patient to report any redness, edema, bleeding, or pain at the biopsy site. Instruct the patient to immediately report chills or fever.

Assess for nausea and pain.

Administer antiemetic and analgesic medications as needed and as directed by the HCP.

Administer antibiotic therapy if ordered. Remind the patient of the importance of completing the entire course of antibiotic therapy, even if signs and symptoms disappear before completion of therapy.

Recognize anxiety related to test results. Discuss the implications of abnormal test results on the patient's lifestyle. Provide teaching and information regarding the clinical implications of the test results, as appropriate.

Educate the patient regarding access to counseling services.

Reinforce information given by the patient's HCP regarding further testing, treatment, or referral to another HCP. Inform the patient of a follow-up appointment for removal of sutures, if indicated. Answer any questions or address any concerns voiced by the patient or family.

Instruct the patient in the use of any ordered medications. Explain the importance of adhering to the therapy regimen. As appropriate, instruct the patient in significant side effects and systemic reactions associated with the prescribed medication. Encourage him or her to review corresponding literature provided by a pharmacist.

Depending on the results of this procedure, additional testing may be performed to evaluate or monitor progression of the disease process and determine the need for a change in therapy. Evaluate test results in relation to the patient's symptoms and other tests performed.

RELATED MONOGRAPHS:

Related tests include ALT, albumin, ALP, ammonia, amylase, AMA/ASMA, α_1-antitrypsin/phenotyping, AST, bilirubin, cholesterol, coagulation factors, CBC, copper, GGT, hepatitis antigens and antibodies, infectious mononucleosis screen, laparoscopy abdominal, lipase, liver and spleen scan, MRI liver, PT/INR, radiofrequency ablation liver, UA, US abdomen, and US liver.

Refer to the Hepatobiliary and Immune systems tables at the end of the book for related tests by body system.

Biopsy, Lung

SYNONYM/ACRONYM: Transbronchial lung biopsy, open lung biopsy.

COMMON USE: To assist in diagnosing lung cancer and other lung tissue disease.

SPECIMEN: Lung tissue or cells.

NORMAL FINDINGS: (Method: Macroscopic and microscopic examination of tissue) No abnormal tissue or cells; no growth in culture.

DESCRIPTION: A biopsy of the lung is performed to obtain lung tissue for examination of pathological features. The specimen can be obtained transbronchially or by open lung biopsy. In a transbronchial biopsy, forceps pass through the bronchoscope to obtain the specimen. In a transbronchial needle aspiration biopsy, a needle passes through a bronchoscope to obtain the specimen. In a transcatheter bronchial brushing, a brush is inserted through the bronchoscope. In an open lung biopsy, the chest is opened and a small thoracic incision is made to remove tissue from the chest wall. Lung biopsies are used to differentiate between infection and other sources of disease indicated by initial radiology studies, computed tomography scans, or sputum analysis. Specimens are cultured to detect pathogenic organisms or directly examined for the presence of malignant cells.

B

INDICATIONS
- Assist in the diagnosis of lung cancer
- Assist in the diagnosis of fibrosis and degenerative or inflammatory diseases of the lung
- Assist in the diagnosis of sarcoidosis

POTENTIAL DIAGNOSIS

Abnormal findings in
- Amyloidosis
- Cancer
- Granulomas
- Infections caused by *Blastomyces, Histoplasma, Legionella* spp., and *Pneumocystis jiroveci* (formerly *P. carinii*)
- Sarcoidosis
- Systemic lupus erythematosus
- Tuberculosis

CRITICAL FINDINGS ◈
- Any postprocedural decrease in breath sounds noted at the biopsy site should be reported immediately.
- Assessment of clear margins after tissue excision
- Classification or grading of tumor
- Identification of malignancy
- Shortness of breath, cyanosis, or rapid pulse during the procedure must be reported immediately

It is essential that critical diagnoses be communicated immediately to the requesting health-care provider (HCP). A listing of these diagnoses varies among facilities. Timely notification of critical values for lab or diagnostic studies is a role expectation of the professional nurse. Notification processes will vary among facilities. Upon receipt of the critical value, the information should be read back to the caller to verify accuracy. Most policies require immediate notification of the primary HCP, hospitalist, or on-call HCP. Reported information includes the patient's name, unique identifiers, critical value, name of the person giving the report, and name of the person receiving the report. Documentation of notification should be made in the medical record with the name of the HCP notified, time and date of notification, and any orders received. Any delay in a timely report of a critical value may require completion of a notification form with review by Risk Management.

INTERFERING FACTORS
- ◈ Conditions such as vascular anomalies of the lung, bleeding abnormalities, or pulmonary hypertension may increase the risk of bleeding.
- ◈ Conditions such as bullae or cysts and respiratory insufficiency increase the risk of pneumothorax.
- Failure to follow dietary restriction before the procedure may cause the procedure to be canceled or repeated.

NURSING IMPLICATIONS AND PROCEDURE

PRETEST:

> Positively identify the patient using at least two unique identifiers before providing care, treatment, or services.
> *Patient Teaching:* Inform the patient this procedure can assist in establishing a diagnosis of lung disease.
> Obtain a history of the patient's complaints, including a list of known allergens, especially allergies or sensitivities to latex or anesthetics.
> Obtain a history of the patient's immune and respiratory systems, any bleeding disorders or other symptoms and results of previously performed laboratory tests and diagnostic and surgical procedures.
> Note any recent procedures that can interfere with test results.
> Record the date of the last menstrual period and determine the possibility of pregnancy in perimenopausal women.
> Obtain a list of the patient's current medications including anticoagulants, aspirin and other salicylates, herbs, nutritional supplements, and nutraceuticals

(see Appendix F). Such products should be discontinued by medical direction for the appropriate number of days prior to a surgical procedure. Review the procedure with the patient. Inform the patient that it may be necessary to remove hair from the site before the procedure. Instruct the patient that prophylactic antibiotics may be administered before the procedure. Address concerns about pain and explain that a sedative and/or analgesia will be administered before the percutaneous biopsy to promote relaxation and reduce discomfort; general anesthesia will be administered before the open biopsy. Explain to the patient that no pain will be experienced during the test when general anesthesia is used but that any discomfort with a needle biopsy will be minimized with local anesthetics and systemic analgesics. Atropine is usually given before bronchoscopy examinations to reduce bronchial secretions and prevent vagally induced bradycardia. Meperidine (Demerol) or morphine may be given as a sedative. Lidocaine is sprayed in the patient's throat to reduce discomfort caused by the presence of the tube. Inform the patient that the biopsy is performed under sterile conditions by an HCP specializing in this procedure. The surgical procedure usually takes about 30 min to complete, and sutures may be necessary to close the site. A needle biopsy usually takes about 15 to 30 min to complete.

Sensitivity to social and cultural issues, as well as concern for modesty, is important in providing psychological support before, during, and after the procedure.

Explain that an IV line will be inserted to allow infusion of IV fluids, antibiotics, anesthetics, and analgesics.

Instruct the patient that, to reduce the risk of nausea and vomiting, nothing should be taken by mouth for 8 hr before a general anesthetic or only clear liquids may be taken for 2 hr before the procedure if local anesthesia is to be used. Patients on beta blockers before the surgical procedure should be instructed to take their medication as ordered during the perioperative period. Protocols may vary among facilities.

Have the patient void before the procedure.

Make sure a written and informed consent has been signed prior to the procedure and before administering any medications.

INTRATEST:

Ensure that the patient has complied with dietary restrictions; ensure that food and liquids have been restricted for at least 8 hr and clear liquids have been restricted for at least 2 hr before the procedure depending on the anesthetic chosen for the procedure.

Ensure that anticoagulant therapy has been withheld for the appropriate number of days prior to the procedure. Number of days to withhold medication is dependent on the type of anticoagulant. Notify the HCP if patient anticoagulant therapy has not been withheld. Ensure that patients on beta-blocker therapy have continued their medication regimen as ordered.

Have emergency equipment readily available. Keep resuscitation equipment on hand in the case of respiratory impairment or laryngospasm after the procedure.

Avoid using morphine sulfate in those with asthma or other pulmonary disease. This drug can further exacerbate bronchospasms and respiratory impairment.

Observe standard precautions, and follow the general guidelines in Appendix A. Positively identify the patient, and label the appropriate specimen containers with the corresponding patient demographics, initials of the person collecting the specimen, date and time of collection, and site location, especially right or left lung.

Have patient remove dentures and notify the HCP if the patient has permanent crowns on teeth. Have the patient remove clothing and change into a gown for the procedure.

Assist the patient to a comfortable position and direct the patient to breathe normally during the beginning of the general anesthetic. Instruct the patient to cooperate fully and to follow directions. For the patient undergoing local anesthesia, direct him or her to breathe normally and to avoid unnecessary movement during the procedure.

▶ Record baseline vital signs and continue to monitor throughout the procedure. Protocols may vary among facilities.

▶ After the administration of general or local anesthesia, use clippers to remove hair from the surgical site if appropriate, cleanse the site with an antiseptic solution, and drape the area with sterile towels.

Open Biopsy

▶ Adhere to Surgical Care Improvement Project (SCIP) quality measures. Administer ordered prophylactic antibiotics 1 hr before incision, and use antibiotics that are consistent with current guidelines specific to the procedure.

▶ The patient is prepared for thoracotomy under general anesthesia in the operating room. Tissue specimens are collected from suspicious sites. Place specimen from needle aspiration or brushing on clean glass microscope slides. Place tissue or aspirate specimens in appropriate sterile container for culture or appropriate fixative container for histological studies.

▶ Carefully observe/assess the patient for any signs of respiratory distress during the procedure.

▶ A chest tube is inserted after the procedure.

Needle Biopsy

▶ Instruct the patient to take slow, deep breaths when the local anesthetic is injected. Protect the site with sterile drapes. Assist patient to a sitting position with arms on a pillow over a bed table. Instruct patient to avoid coughing during the procedure. The needle is inserted through the posterior chest wall and into the intercostal space. The needle is rotated to obtain the sample and then withdrawn. Pressure is applied to the site with a petroleum jelly gauze, and a pressure dressing is applied over the petroleum jelly gauze.

Bronchoscopy

▶ Provide mouth care to reduce oral bacterial flora.

▶ After administration of general anesthesia, position the patient in a supine position with the neck hyperextended. If local anesthesia is used, the patient is seated while the tongue and oropharynx are sprayed and swabbed with anesthetic. Provide an emesis basin for the increased saliva and encourage the patient to spit out the saliva because the gag reflex may be impaired. When loss of sensation is adequate, the patient is placed in a supine or side-lying position. The fiberoptic scope can be introduced through the nose, the mouth, an endotracheal tube, a tracheostomy tube, or a rigid bronchoscope. Most common insertion is through the nose. Patients with copious secretions or massive hemoptysis, or in whom airway complications are more likely, may be intubated before the bronchoscopy. Additional local anesthetic is applied through the scope as it approaches the vocal cords and the carina, eliminating reflexes in these sensitive areas. The fiberoptic approach allows visualization of airway segments without having to move the patient's head through various positions.

▶ After visual inspection of the lungs, tissue samples are collected from suspicious sites by bronchial brush or biopsy forceps to be used for cytological and microbiological studies.

▶ After the procedure, the bronchoscope is removed. Patients who had local anesthesia are placed in a semi-Fowler's position to recover.

General

▶ Monitor the patient for complications related to the procedure (e.g., allergic reaction, anaphylaxis).

▶ Place tissue samples in properly labeled specimen containers containing formalin solution, and promptly transport the specimen to the laboratory for processing and analysis.

POST-TEST:

▶ A report of the results will be made available to the requesting HCP, who will discuss the results with the patient

Instruct the patient to resume preoperative diet, as directed by the HCP. Assess the patient's ability to swallow before allowing the patient to attempt liquids or solid foods.

Inform the patient that he or she may experience some throat soreness and hoarseness. Instruct patient to treat throat discomfort with lozenges and warm gargles when the gag reflex returns.

Monitor vital signs and neurological status every 15 min for 1 hr, then every 2 hr for 4 hr, and then as ordered by the HCP. Monitor temperature every 4 hr for 24 hr. Monitor intake and output at least every 8 hr. Compare with baseline values. Notify the HCP if temperature is elevated. Discontinue prophylactic antibiotics within 24 hr after the conclusion of the procedure. Protocols may vary among facilities.

Emergency resuscitation equipment should be readily available if the vocal cords become spastic after intubation.

Observe/assess for delayed allergic reactions, such as rash, urticaria, tachycardia, hyperpnea, hypertension, palpitations, nausea, or vomiting.

Observe/assess the biopsy site for bleeding, inflammation, or hematoma formation.

Instruct the patient in the care and assessment of the biopsy site.

Instruct the patient to report any redness, edema, bleeding, or pain at the biopsy site.

Observe/assess the patient for hemoptysis, difficulty breathing, cough, air hunger, excessive coughing, pain, or absent breath sounds over the affected area. Monitor chest tube patency and drainage after a thoracotomy.

Evaluate the patient for symptoms indicating the development of pneumothorax, such as dyspnea, tachypnea, anxiety, decreased breathing sounds, or restlessness. A chest x-ray may be ordered to check for the presence of this complication.

Evaluate the patient for symptoms of empyema, such as fever, tachycardia, malaise, or elevated white blood cell count.

Observe/assess the patient's sputum for blood if a biopsy was taken, because large amounts of blood may indicate the development of a problem; a small amount of streaking is expected. Evaluate the patient for signs of bleeding, such as tachycardia, hypotension, or restlessness.

Instruct the patient to remain in a semi-Fowler's position after bronchoscopy or fine-needle aspiration to maximize ventilation. Semi-Fowler's position is a semisitting position with the knees flexed and supported by pillows on the bed or examination table. Instruct the patient to stay in bed lying on the affected side for at least 2 hr with a pillow or rolled towel under the site to prevent bleeding. The patient will also need to remain on bedrest for 24 hr.

Assess for nausea and pain. Administer antiemetic and analgesic medications as needed and as directed by the HCP.

Administer antibiotic therapy if ordered. Remind the patient of the importance of completing the entire course of antibiotic therapy, even if signs and symptoms disappear before completion of therapy.

Recognize anxiety related to test results. Discuss the implications of abnormal test results on the patient's lifestyle. Provide teaching and information regarding the clinical implications of the test results, as appropriate. Educate the patient regarding access to counseling services.

Reinforce information given by the patient's HCP regarding further testing, treatment, or referral to another HCP. Instruct the patient to use lozenges or gargle for throat discomfort. Inform the patient of smoking cessation programs as appropriate. Malnutrition is commonly seen in patients with severe respiratory disease for numerous reasons, including fatigue, lack of appetite, and gastrointestinal distress. Adequate intake of vitamins A and C are also important to prevent pulmonary infection and to decrease the extent of lung tissue damage. The importance of following the prescribed diet should be stressed to the patient/caregiver. Educate the patient regarding access to counseling services, as appropriate. Answer any questions or

B

address any concerns voiced by the patient or family.

Instruct the patient in the use of any ordered medications. Explain the importance of adhering to the therapy regimen. As appropriate, instruct the patient in significant side effects and systemic reactions associated with the prescribed medication. Encourage him or her to review corresponding literature provided by a pharmacist.

Depending on the results of this procedure, additional testing may be performed to evaluate or monitor progression of the disease process and determine the need for a change in therapy. Evaluate test results in relation to the patient's symptoms and other tests performed.

RELATED MONOGRAPHS:

Related tests include arterial/alveolar oxygen ratio, antibodies antiglomerular basement membrane, blood gases, bronchoscopy, chest x-ray, CBC, CT thoracic, culture sputum, cytology sputum, gallium scan, gram/acid fast stain, lung perfusion scan, lung ventilation scan, MRI chest, mediastinoscopy, pleural fluid analysis, PFT, and TB skin tests.

Refer to the Immune and Respiratory systems tables at the end of the book for related tests by body system.

Biopsy, Lymph Node

SYNONYM/ACRONYM: N/A.

COMMON USE: To assist in diagnosing cancer such as lymphoma and leukemia as well as other systemic disorders.

SPECIMEN: Lymph node tissue or cells.

NORMAL FINDINGS: (Method: Macroscopic and microscopic examination of tissue). No abnormal tissue or cells.

DESCRIPTION: Lymph node biopsy is the excision of a tissue sample from one or more lymph nodes for microscopic analysis to determine cell morphology and the presence of tissue abnormalities. This test assists in confirming a diagnosis of cancer, diagnosing disorders causing systemic illness, or determining the stage of metastatic cancer. A biopsy specimen is usually obtained either by needle biopsy or after surgical incision. Biopsies are most commonly performed on the following types of lymph nodes: cervical nodes, which drain the face and scalp; axillary nodes, which drain the arms, breasts, and upper chest; and inguinal nodes, which drain the legs, external genitalia, and lower abdominal wall.

INDICATIONS
- Assist in confirming suspected fungal or parasitic infections of the lymphatics
- Assist in confirming suspected malignant involvement of the lymphatics

- Determine the stage of metastatic cancer
- Differentiate between benign and malignant disorders that may cause lymph node enlargement
- Evaluate persistent enlargement of one or more lymph nodes for unknown reasons

POTENTIAL DIAGNOSIS

Abnormal findings in
- Chancroid
- Fungal infection (e.g., cat scratch disease)
- Immunodeficiency
- Infectious mononucleosis
- Lymph involvement of systemic diseases (e.g., systemic lupus erythematosus, sarcoidosis)
- Lymphangitis
- Lymphogranuloma venereum
- Malignancy (e.g., lymphomas, leukemias)
- Metastatic disease
- Parasitic infestation (e.g., pneumoconiosis)

CRITICAL FINDINGS

- Assessment of clear margins after tissue excision
- Classification or grading of tumor
- Identification of malignancy

It is essential that critical diagnoses be communicated immediately to the requesting health-care provider (HCP). A listing of these diagnoses varies among facilities. Timely notification of critical values for lab or diagnostic studies is a role expectation of the professional nurse. Notification processes will vary among facilities. Upon receipt of the critical value, the information should be read back to the caller to verify accuracy. Most policies require immediate notification of the primary HCP, hospitalist, or on-call HCP. Reported information includes the patient's name, unique identifiers, critical value, name of the person giving the report,

and name of the person receiving the report. Documentation of notification should be made in the medical record with the name of the HCP notified, time and date of notification, and any orders received. Any delay in a timely report of a critical value may require completion of a notification form with review by Risk Management.

INTERFERING FACTORS

- This procedure is contraindicated in patients with bleeding disorders.
- Failure to follow dietary restrictions before the procedure may cause the procedure to be canceled or repeated.

NURSING IMPLICATIONS AND PROCEDURE

PRETEST:

- Positively identify the patient using at least two unique identifiers before providing care, treatment, or services.
- *Patient Teaching:* Inform the patient this procedure can assist in establishing a diagnosis of lymph node disease.
- Obtain a history of the patient's complaints, including a list of known allergens, especially allergies or sensitivities to latex or anesthetics.
- Obtain a history of the patient's immune system, any bleeding disorders or other symptoms, and results of previously performed laboratory tests and diagnostic and surgical procedures.
- Record the date of the last menstrual period and determine the possibility of pregnancy in perimenopausal women.
- Note any recent procedures that can interfere with test results.
- Obtain a list of the patient's current medications including anticoagulants, aspirin and other salicylates, herbs, nutritional supplements, and nutraceuticals (see Appendix F). Such products should be discontinued by medical direction for the appropriate number of days prior to a surgical procedure.

Review the procedure with the patient. Inform the patient that it may be necessary to remove hair from the site before the procedure. Instruct the patient that prophylactic antibiotics may be administered before the procedure. Address concerns about pain and explain that a sedative and/or analgesia will be administered before the percutaneous biopsy to promote relaxation and reduce discomfort; general anesthesia will be administered before the open biopsy. Explain to the patient that no pain will be experienced during the test when general anesthesia is used but that any discomfort with a needle biopsy will be minimized with local anesthetics and systemic analgesics. Inform the patient that the biopsy is performed under sterile conditions by an HCP, with support staff, specializing in this procedure. The surgical procedure usually takes about 30 min to complete, and sutures may be necessary to close the site. A needle biopsy usually takes about 15 min to complete.

Sensitivity to social and cultural issues, as well as concern for modesty, is important in providing psychological support before, during, and after the procedure.

Explain that an IV line will be inserted to allow infusion of IV fluids, antibiotics, anesthetics, analgesics, or IV sedation.

Instruct the patient that, to reduce the risk of nausea and vomiting, nothing should be taken by mouth for 8 hr before a general anesthetic or only clear liquids may be taken for 2 hr before the procedure if local anesthesia is to be used. Patients on beta blockers before the surgical procedure should be instructed to take their medication as ordered during the perioperative period. Protocols may vary among facilities.

Make sure a written and informed consent has been signed prior to the procedure and before administering any medications.

INTRATEST:

Ensure that the patient has complied with dietary restrictions; ensure that food and liquids have been restricted for at least 8 hr and clear liquids have been restricted for at least 2 hr before the procedure depending on the anesthetic chosen for the procedure.

Ensure that anticoagulant therapy has been withheld for the appropriate number of days prior to the procedure. Number of days to withhold medication is dependent on the type of anticoagulant. Notify the HCP if patient anticoagulant therapy has not been withheld. Ensure that patients on beta-blocker therapy have continued their medication regimen as ordered.

Have emergency equipment readily available.

Have the patient void before the procedure.

Observe standard precautions, and follow the general guidelines in Appendix A. Positively identify the patient, and label the appropriate specimen containers with the corresponding patient demographics, initials of the person collecting the specimen, date and time of collection, and site location.

Assist the patient to the desired position depending on the test site to be used, and direct the patient to breathe normally during the beginning of the general anesthetic. Instruct the patient to cooperate fully and to follow directions. For the patient undergoing local anesthesia, direct him or her to breathe normally and to avoid unnecessary movement during the procedure.

Record baseline vital signs, and continue to monitor throughout the procedure. Protocols may vary among facilities.

After the administration of general or local anesthesia, use clippers to remove hair from the surgical site if appropriate, cleanse the site with an antiseptic solution, and drape the area with sterile towels.

Open Biopsy

Adhere to Surgical Care Improvement Project (SCIP) quality measures. Administer ordered prophylactic antibiotics 1 hr before incision, and use antibiotics that are consistent with current guidelines specific to the procedure.

After administration of general anesthesia and surgical preparation are completed, an incision is made, suspicious area(s) are located, and tissue samples are collected.

Needle Biopsy

Instruct the patient to take slow, deep breaths when the local anesthetic is injected. Protect the site with sterile drapes. The node is grasped with sterile gloved fingers, and a needle (with attached syringe) is inserted directly into the node. The node is aspirated to collect the specimen. Pressure is applied to the site for 3 to 5 min, then a sterile dressing is applied.

General

Monitor the patient for complications related to the procedure (e.g., allergic reaction, anaphylaxis).

Place tissue samples in formalin solution. Label the specimen, indicating site location, and promptly transport the specimen to the laboratory for processing and analysis.

POST-TEST:

A report of the results will be made available to the requesting HCP, who will discuss the results with the patient.

Instruct the patient to resume preoperative diet, as directed by the HCP. Assess the patient's ability to swallow before allowing the patient to attempt liquids or solid foods.

Monitor vital signs and neurological status every 15 min for 1 hr, then every 2 hr for 4 hr, and then as ordered by the HCP. Monitor temperature every 4 hr for 24 hr. Monitor intake and output at least every 8 hr. Compare with baseline values. Notify the HCP if temperature is elevated. Discontinue prophylactic antibiotics within 24 hr after the conclusion of the procedure. Protocols may vary among facilities.

Observe/assess for delayed allergic reactions, such as rash, urticaria, tachycardia, hyperpnea, hypertension, palpitations, nausea, or vomiting.

Observe/assess the biopsy site for bleeding, inflammation, or hematoma formation.

Instruct the patient in the care and assessment of the site.

Instruct the patient to report any redness, edema, bleeding, or pain at the biopsy site.

Assess for nausea and pain. Administer antiemetic and analgesic medications as needed and as directed by the HCP.

Administer antibiotic therapy if ordered. Remind the patient of the importance of completing the entire course of antibiotic therapy, even if signs and symptoms disappear before completion of therapy.

Recognize anxiety related to test results. Discuss the implications of abnormal test results on the patient's lifestyle. Provide teaching and information regarding the clinical implications of the test results, as appropriate. Educate the patient regarding access to counseling services.

Reinforce information given by the patient's HCP regarding further testing, treatment, or referral to another HCP. Inform the patient of a follow-up appointment for removal of sutures, if indicated. Answer any questions or address any concerns voiced by the patient or family.

Instruct the patient in the use of any ordered medications. Explain the importance of adhering to the therapy regimen. As appropriate, instruct the patient in significant side effects and systemic reactions associated with the prescribed medication. Encourage him or her to review corresponding literature provided by a pharmacist.

Depending on the results of this procedure, additional testing may be performed to evaluate or monitor progression of the disease process and determine the need for a change in therapy. Evaluate test results in relation to the patient's symptoms and other tests performed.

RELATED MONOGRAPHS:

Related tests include biopsy bone marrow, CD4/CD8 enumeration, cerebrospinal fluid analysis, *Chlamydia* serology, CBC, CT pelvis, CT thoracic, culture for bacteria/fungus, CMV, Gram stain, HIV-1/HIV-2 serology, immunofixation electrophoresis, immunoglobulins (A, G, and M), infectious mononucleosis screen, lymphangiography, mammogram, mediastinoscopy, PET

pelvis, RF, total protein and fractions, toxoplasmosis serology, and US lymph nodes.

Refer to the Immune System table at the end of the book for related tests by body system.

Biopsy, Muscle

SYNONYM/ACRONYM: N/A.

COMMON USE: To assist in diagnosing muscular disease such as Duchenne's muscular dystrophy as well as other neuropathies and parasitic infections.

SPECIMEN: Muscle tissue or cells.

NORMAL FINDINGS: (Method: Macroscopic and microscopic examination of tissue) No abnormal tissue or cells.

DESCRIPTION: Muscle biopsy is the excision of a muscle tissue sample for microscopic analysis to determine cell morphology and the presence of tissue abnormalities. This test is used to confirm a diagnosis of neuropathy or myopathy and to diagnose parasitic infestation. A biopsy specimen is usually obtained from the deltoid or gastrocnemius muscle after a surgical incision.

INDICATIONS

- Assist in confirming suspected fungal infection or parasitic infestation of the muscle
- Assist in diagnosing the cause of neuropathy or myopathy
- Assist in the diagnosis of Duchenne's muscular dystrophy

POTENTIAL DIAGNOSIS

Abnormal findings in
- Alcoholic myopathy

- Amyotrophic lateral sclerosis
- Duchenne's muscular dystrophy
- Fungal infection
- Myasthenia gravis
- Myotonia congenita
- Parasitic infestation
- Polymyalgia rheumatica
- Polymyositis

CRITICAL FINDINGS

- Assessment of clear margins after tissue excision
- Classification or grading of tumor
- Identification of malignancy

It is essential that critical diagnoses be communicated immediately to the requesting health-care provider (HCP). A listing of these diagnoses varies among facilities. Timely notification of critical values for lab or diagnostic studies is a role expectation of the professional nurse. Notification processes will vary among facilities. Upon receipt of the critical value, the information should be read back to the caller to verify accuracy. Most policies equire immediate notification of the primary HCP, hospitalist, or on-call ICP. Reported information includes the patient's name, unique identifiers, critical value, name of the person giving the report, and name of the person receiving the report. Documentation of notification should be made in the medical record with the name of the ICP notified, time and date of notification, and any orders received. Any delay in a timely report of a critical value may require completion of a notification form with review by Risk Management.

INTERFERING FACTORS

If electromyography is performed before muscle biopsy, residual inflammation may lead to false-positive biopsy results.

◆ This procedure is contraindicated in patients with bleeding disorders.

Failure to follow dietary restrictions before the procedure may cause the procedure to be canceled or repeated.

NURSING IMPLICATIONS AND PROCEDURE

PRETEST:

Positively identify the patient using at least two unique identifiers before providing care, treatment, or services.
Patient Teaching: Inform the patient this procedure can assist in establishing a diagnosis of musculoskeletal disease.
Obtain a history of the patient's complaints, including a list of known allergens, especially allergies or sensitivities to latex or anesthetics.
Obtain a history of the patient's immune and musculoskeletal systems, any bleeding disorders or other symptoms, and results of previously performed laboratory tests and diagnostic and surgical procedures.
Record the date of the last menstrual period and determine the possibility of pregnancy in perimenopausal women.

▶ Note any recent procedures that can interfere with test results.
▶ Obtain a list of the patient's current medications including anticoagulants, aspirin and other salicylates, herbs, nutritional supplements, and nutraceuticals (see Appendix F). Such products should be discontinued by medical direction for the appropriate number of days prior to a surgical procedure.
▶ Review the procedure with the patient. Inform the patient that it may be necessary to remove hair from the site before the procedure. Instruct the patient that prophylactic antibiotics may be administered before the procedure. Address concerns about pain and explain that a sedative and/or analgesia will be administered before the percutaneous biopsy to promote relaxation and reduce discomfort; general anesthesia will be administered before the open biopsy. Explain to the patient that no pain will be experienced during the test when general anesthesia is used but that any discomfort with a needle biopsy will be minimized with local anesthetics and systemic analgesics. Inform the patient that the biopsy is performed under sterile conditions by an HCP specializing in this procedure. The surgical procedure usually takes about 20 min to complete, and sutures may be necessary to close the site. A needle biopsy usually takes about 15 min to complete.
▶ *Sensitivity to social and cultural issues,* as well as concern for modesty, is important in providing psychological support before, during, and after the procedure.
▶ Explain that an IV line may be inserted to allow infusion of IV fluids, antibiotics, anesthetics, or sedatives.
▶ Instruct the patient that, to reduce the risk of nausea and vomiting, nothing should be taken by mouth for 8 hr before a general anesthetic or only clear liquids may be taken for 2 hr before the procedure if local anesthesia is to be used. Patients on beta blockers before the surgical procedure should be instructed to take their medication as ordered during the perioperative period. Protocols may vary among facilities.

Make sure a written and informed consent has been signed prior to the procedure and before administering any medications.

INTRATEST:

- Ensure that the patient has complied with dietary restrictions; ensure that food and liquids have been restricted for at least 8 hr and clear liquids have been restricted for at least 2 hr before the procedure depending on the anesthetic chosen for the procedure.
- Ensure that anticoagulant therapy has been withheld for the appropriate number of days prior to the procedure. Number of days to withhold medication is dependent on the type of anticoagulant. Notify the HCP if patient anticoagulant therapy has not been withheld. Ensure that patients on beta-blocker therapy have continued their medication regimen as ordered.
- Have emergency equipment readily available.
- Have the patient void before the procedure.
- Observe standard precautions, and follow the general guidelines in Appendix A. Positively identify the patient, and label the appropriate specimen containers with the corresponding patient demographics, initials of the person collecting the specimen, date and time of collection, and site location.
- Assist the patient to a comfortable position: a supine position (for deltoid biopsy) or prone position (for gastrocnemius biopsy). Instruct the patient to cooperate fully and to follow directions. Direct the patient to breathe normally and to avoid unnecessary movement during the local anesthetic and the procedure.
- Record baseline vital signs, and continue to monitor throughout the procedure. Protocols may vary among facilities.
- After the administration of general or local anesthesia, use clippers to remove hair from the surgical site if appropriate, cleanse the site with an antiseptic solution, and drape the area with sterile towels.

Open Biopsy
- Adhere to Surgical Care Improvement Project (SCIP) quality measures. Administer ordered prophylactic antibiotics 1 hr before incision, and use antibiotics that are consistent with current guidelines specific to the procedure.
- After administration of general anesthesia and surgical preparation are completed, an incision is made, suspicious areas are located, and tissue samples are collected.

Needle Biopsy
- Instruct the patient to take slow deep breaths when the local anesthetic is injected. Protect the site with sterile drapes.
- After infiltration of the site with local anesthetic, a cutting biopsy needle is introduced through a small skin incision and bored into the muscle. A core needle is introduced through the cutting needle, and a plug of muscle is removed. The needles are withdrawn, and the specimen is placed in a preservative solution. Pressure is applied to the site for 3 to 5 min, and then a pressure dressing is applied.

General
- Monitor the patient for complications related to the procedure (e.g., allergic reaction, anaphylaxis).
- Place tissue samples in properly labeled specimen container containing formalin solution, and promptly transport the specimen to the laboratory for processing and analysis.

POST-TEST:

- A report of the results will be made available to the requesting HCP, who will discuss the results with the patient.
- Instruct the patient to resume preoperative diet, as directed by the HCP.
- Monitor vital signs and neurological status every 15 min for 1 hr, then every 2 hr for 4 hr, and then as ordered by the HCP. Monitor temperature every 4 hr for 24 hr. Compare with baseline values. Notify the HCP if temperature is elevated. Discontinue prophylactic antibiotics within 24 hr after the conclusion of the procedure. Protocols may vary among facilities.

◗ Observe/assess for delayed allergic reactions, such as rash, urticaria, tachycardia, hyperpnea, hypertension, palpitations, nausea, or vomiting.

◗ Observe/assess the biopsy site for bleeding, inflammation, or hematoma formation.

◗ Instruct the patient in the care and assessment of the site.

◗ Instruct the patient to report any redness, edema, bleeding, or pain at the biopsy site.

◗ Assess for nausea and pain. Administer antiemetic and analgesic medications as needed and as directed by the HCP.

◗ Administer antibiotic therapy if ordered. Remind the patient of the importance of completing the entire course of antibiotic therapy, even if signs and symptoms disappear before completion of therapy.

◗ Recognize anxiety related to test results. Discuss the implications of abnormal test results on the patient's lifestyle. Provide teaching and information regarding the clinical implications of the test results, as appropriate. Educate the patient regarding access to counseling services.

◗ Reinforce information given by the patient's HCP regarding further testing, treatment, or referral to another HCP.

Inform the patient of a follow-up appointment for removal of sutures, if indicated. Answer any questions or address any concerns voiced by the patient or family.

◗ Instruct the patient in the use of any ordered medications. Explain the importance of adhering to the therapy regimen. As appropriate, instruct the patient in significant side effects and systemic reactions associated with the prescribed medication. Encourage him or her to review corresponding literature provided by a pharmacist.

◗ Depending on the results of this procedure, additional testing may be performed to evaluate or monitor progression of the disease process and determine the need for a change in therapy. Evaluate test results in relation to the patient's symptoms and other tests performed.

RELATED MONOGRAPHS:

◗ Related tests include AChR, aldolase, ANA, antibody Jo-1, antithyroglobulin antibodies, CK and isoenzymes, EMG, ENG, myoglobin, and RF.

◗ Refer to the Immune and Musculoskeletal systems tables at the end of the book for related tests by body system.

Biopsy, Prostate

SYNONYM/ACRONYM: N/A.

COMMON USE: To assist in diagnosing prostate cancer.

SPECIMEN: Prostate tissue.

NORMAL FINDINGS: (Method: Microscopic examination of tissue cells) No abnormal cells or tissue.

B

DESCRIPTION: Biopsy of the prostate gland is performed to identify cancerous cells, especially if serum prostate-specific antigen (PSA) is increased. New technology makes it possible to combine data such as analysis of molecular biomarkers and cellular structure specific to the individual's biopsy tissue, standard tissue biopsy results, Gleason's score, number of positive tumor cores, tumor stage, presurgical and postsurgical PSA levels, and postsurgical margin status with computerized mathematical programs to create a personalized report that predicts the likelihood of postprostatectomy disease progression. Serial measurements of PSA in the blood are often performed before and after surgery. Approximately 15% to 40% of patients who have had their prostate removed will encounter an increase in PSA. Patients treated for prostate cancer and who have had a PSA recurrence can still develop a metastasis as much as 8 yr after the postsurgical PSA level increased. The majority of tumors develop slowly and require minimal intervention, but patients with an increase in PSA greater than 2.0 ng/mL in a year are more likely to have an aggressive form of prostate cancer with a greater risk of death. Personalized medicine provides a technology to predict the progression of prostate cancer, likelihood of recurrence, or development of related metastatic disease.

INDICATIONS
- Evaluate prostatic hypertrophy of unknown etiology
- Investigate suspected cancer of the prostate

POTENTIAL DIAGNOSIS
Positive findings in prostate cancer

	Gleason Grading
1	Simple round glands, closely packed rounded masses with well-defined edges. Closely resemble normal prostate tissue.
2	Simple round glands, loosely packed in vague, rounded masses with loosely packed edges. Closely resemble normal prostate tissue.
3	Discrete glands of varying size and shape interposed among nonneoplastic cells.
4	Small, medium, or large ill-defined glands fused into cords, chains, or ragged infiltrating masses; glands may be perforated or have a hypernephromatoid pattern.
5	No glandular differentiation, solid sheets, cords, single cells with central necrosis.

Gleason's score is the sum of two grades assigned by the pathologist during microscopic examination of the biopsy samples. The score ranges from 1 to 10 with 10 being the worst. The first number assigned is the primary grade (1 to 5), which indicates where the cancer is the most prominent. The second number is the secondary grade (1 to 5), which indicates

where the cancer is next most prominent. It is important to have the
breakdown in grading as well as the
total score. For example, Patient A's
Gleason's score is 4 + 3 = 7, and
Patient B's Gleason's score is 3 + 4 = 7.
Even though both patients have the
same Gleason's score, Patient B has a
slightly better prognosis because the
primary area is graded a 3.

B

TNM Classification of Tumors	
T refers to the size of the primary tumor	
T_0	No evidence of primary tumor
T_{IS}	Carcinoma in situ
T_{1-4}	Increasing degrees in tumor size and involvement
N refers to lymph node involvement	
N_0	No evidence of disease in lymph nodes
N_{1-4}	Increasing degrees in lymph node involvement
N_X	Regional lymph nodes unable to be assessed clinically
M refers to distant metastases	
M_0	No evidence of distant metastases
M_{1-4}	Increasing degrees of distant metastatic involvement, including distant nodes

CRITICAL FINDINGS

- Assessment of clear margins after
  tissue excision
- Classification or grading of tumor
- Identification of malignancy

It is essential that critical diagnoses be
communicated immediately to the
requesting health-care provider (HCP).
A listing of these diagnoses varies
among facilities. Timely notification of
critical values for lab or diagnostic
studies is a role expectation of the
professional nurse. Notification processes will vary among facilities. Upon
receipt of the critical value, the information should be read back to the
caller to verify accuracy. Most policies
require immediate notification of the
primary HCP, hospitalist, or on-call
HCP. Reported information includes
the patient's name, unique identifiers,
critical value, name of the person giving the report, and name of the person
receiving the report. Documentation
of notification should be made in the
medical record with the name of the
HCP notified, time and date of notification, and any orders received. Any
delay in a timely report of a critical
value may require completion of a
notification form with review by Risk
Management.

INTERFERING FACTORS

- This procedure is
  contraindicated in patients
  with bleeding disorders.
- Failure to follow dietary restrictions before the procedure
  may cause the procedure to be canceled or repeated.
- The various sampling approaches
  have individual drawbacks that
  should be considered: Transurethral
  sampling does not always ensure
  that malignant cells will be included
  in the specimen, whereas transrectal
  sampling carries the risk of
  perforating the rectum and creating
  a channel through which malignant
  cells can seed normal tissue.

B

NURSING IMPLICATIONS AND PROCEDURE

PRETEST:

▶ Positively identify the patient using at least two unique identifiers before providing care, treatment, or services.

▶ *Patient Teaching:* Inform the patient this procedure can assist in establishing a diagnosis of prostate disease.

▶ Obtain a history of the patient's complaints, including a list of known allergens, especially allergies or sensitivities to latex or anesthetics.

▶ Obtain a history of the patient's genitourinary system, any bleeding disorders or other symptoms, and results of previously performed laboratory tests and diagnostic and surgical procedures.

▶ Note any recent procedures that can interfere with test results.

▶ Obtain a list of the patient's current medications including anticoagulants, aspirin and other salicylates, herbs, nutritional supplements, and nutraceuticals (see Appendix F). Such products should be discontinued by medical direction for the appropriate number of days prior to a surgical procedure.

▶ Review the procedure with the patient. Inform the patient that it may be necessary to remove hair from the site before the procedure. Instruct the patient that prophylactic antibiotics may be administered before the procedure. Address concerns about pain and explain that a sedative and/or analgesia will be administered to promote relaxation and reduce discomfort before the percutaneous biopsy; general anesthesia will be administered before the open biopsy. Explain to the patient that no pain will be experienced during the test when general anesthesia is used but that any discomfort with a needle biopsy will be minimized with local anesthetics and systemic analgesics. Inform the patient that the biopsy is performed under sterile conditions by an HCP, with support staff, specializing in this procedure. The surgical procedure usually takes about 30 min to complete, and sutures may be necessary to close the site. A needle biopsy usually takes about 20 min to

complete. Instructions regarding the appropriate transport container for molecular diagnostic studies should be obtained from the laboratory prior to the procedure.

▶ *Sensitivity to social and cultural issues,* as well as concern for modesty, is important in providing psychological support before, during, and after the procedure.

▶ Explain that an IV line will be inserted to allow infusion of IV fluids, antibiotics, anesthetics, and analgesics.

▶ Instruct the patient that, to reduce the risk of nausea and vomiting, nothing should be taken by mouth for 8 hr before a general anesthetic or only clear liquids may be taken for 2 hr before the procedure if local anesthesia is to be used. Patients on beta blockers before the surgical procedure should be instructed to take their medication as ordered during the perioperative period. Protocols may vary among facilities.

▶ *Make sure a written and informed consent has been signed prior to the procedure and before administering any medications.*

INTRATEST:

▶ Ensure that the patient has complied with dietary restrictions; ensure that food and liquids have been restricted for at least 8 hr and clear liquids have been restricted for at least 2 hr before the procedure depending on the anesthetic chosen for the procedure.

▶ Ensure that anticoagulant therapy has been withheld for the appropriate number of days before the procedure. The number of days to withhold medication depends on the type of anticoagulant. Notify the HCP if patient anticoagulant therapy has not been withheld. Ensure that patients on beta-blocker therapy have continued their medication regimen as ordered.

▶ Have emergency equipment readily available.

▶ Have the patient void before the procedure. Administer enemas if ordered.

▶ Observe standard precautions, and follow the general guidelines in Appendix A. Positively identify the

patient, and label the appropriate specimen containers with the corresponding patient demographics, initials of the person collecting the specimen, date and time of collection, and site location.
- Assist the patient to a comfortable position, and direct the patient to breathe normally during the beginning of the general anesthesia.
- Cleanse the biopsy site with an antiseptic solution, use clippers to remove hair from the surgical site if appropriate, and drape the area with sterile towels.
- Record baseline vital signs, and continue to monitor throughout the procedure. Protocols may vary among facilities.

Transurethral Approach
- After administration of general anesthesia, position the patient on a urological examination table with the feet in stirrups. The endoscope is inserted into the urethra. The tissue is excised with a cutting loop and is placed in formalin solution.

Transrectal Approach
- Adhere to Surgical Care Improvement Project (SCIP) quality measures. Administer ordered prophylactic antibiotics 1 hr before incision, and use antibiotics that are consistent with current guidelines specific to the procedure.
- After administration of general anesthesia, position the patient in the Sims' position. A rectal examination is performed to locate suspicious nodules. A biopsy needle guide is placed at the biopsy site, and the biopsy needle is inserted through the needle guide. The cells are aspirated, the needle is withdrawn, and the sample is placed in formalin solution.

Perineal Approach
- Adhere to Surgical Care Improvement Project (SCIP) quality measures. Administer ordered prophylactic antibiotics 1 hr before incision, and use antibiotics that are consistent with current guidelines specific to the procedure.
- After administration of general anesthesia, position the patient in the lithotomy

position. Clean the perineum with an antiseptic solution, and protect the biopsy site with sterile drapes. A small incision is made, and the sample is removed by needle biopsy or biopsy punch and placed in formalin solution.

General
- Monitor the patient for complications related to the procedure (e.g., allergic reaction, anaphylaxis).
- Apply digital pressure to the biopsy site. If there is no bleeding after the perineal approach, place a sterile dressing on the biopsy site. Immediately notify the HCP if there is significant bleeding.
- Place tissue samples for standard biopsy examination in properly labeled specimen containers containing formalin solution, place tissue samples for molecular diagnostic studies in properly labeled specimen containers, and promptly transport the specimen to the laboratory for processing and analysis.

POST-TEST:
- A report of the results will be made available to the requesting HCP, who will discuss the results with the patient.
- Instruct the patient to resume preoperative diet, as directed by the HCP. Assess the patient's ability to swallow before allowing the patient to attempt liquids or solid foods.
- *Nutritional Considerations:* There is growing evidence that inflammation and oxidation play key roles in the development of numerous diseases, including prostate cancer. Research also shows that diets containing dried beans, fresh fruits and vegetables, nuts, spices, whole grains, and smaller amounts of red meats can increase the amount of protective antioxidants. Regular exercise, especially in combination with a healthy diet, can bring about changes in the body's metabolism that decrease inflammation and oxidation.
- Monitor vital signs and neurological status every 15 min for 1 hr, then every 2 hr for 4 hr, and then as ordered by

the HCP. Monitor temperature every 4 hr for 24 hr. Monitor intake and output at least every 8 hr. Compare with baseline values. Notify the HCP if temperature is elevated. Discontinue prophylactic antibiotics within 24 hr after the conclusion of the procedure. Protocols may vary among facilities.

▸ Instruct the patient on intake and out-put recording and provide appropriate measuring containers.

▸ Encourage fluid intake of 3,000 mL unless contraindicated.

▸ Observe/assess for delayed allergic reactions, such as rash, urticaria, tachycardia, hyperpnea, hypertension, palpitations, nausea, or vomiting.

▸ Instruct the patient in the care and assessment of the site.

▸ Instruct the patient to report any chills, fever, redness, edema, bleeding, or pain at the biopsy site.

▸ Assess for infection, hemorrhage, or perforation of the urethra or rectum.

▸ Inform the patient that blood may be seen in the urine after the first or second postprocedural voiding.

▸ Instruct the patient to report any further changes in urinary pattern, volume, or appearance.

▸ Assess for nausea, pain, and bladder spasms. Administer antiemetic, analgesic, and antispasmodic medica-tions as needed and as directed by the HCP.

▸ Administer antibiotic therapy if ordered. Remind the patient of the importance of completing the entire course of antibiotic therapy, even if signs and symptoms disappear before comple-tion of therapy.

▸ Recognize anxiety related to test results. Discuss the implications of abnormal test results on the patient's lifestyle. Provide teaching and informa-tion regarding the clinical implications of the test results, as appropriate. Educate the patient regarding access to counseling services. Provide

contact information, if desired, for the National Cancer Institute (www.cancer.gov).

▸ Reinforce information given by the patient's HCP regarding further testing, treatment, or referral to another HCP. Decisions regarding the need for and frequency of routine PSA testing or other cancer screen-ing procedures should be made after consultation between the patient and HCP. The most current guidelines for prostate cancer screening of the gen-eral population as well as of individu-als with increased risk are available from the American Cancer Society (www.cancer.org) and the American Urological Association (www.aua.org) Counsel the patient, as appropriate, that sexual dysfunction related to altered body function, drugs, or radiation may occur. Answer any questions or address any concerns voiced by the patient or family.

▸ Instruct the patient in the use of any ordered medications. Explain the importance of adhering to the therapy regimen. As appropriate, instruct the patient in significant side effects and systemic reactions associated with the prescribed medication. Encourage him to review corresponding literature provided by a pharmacist.

▸ Depending on the results of this procedure, additional testing may be performed to evaluate or monitor pro-gression of the disease process and determine the need for a change in therapy. Evaluate test results in relation to the patient's symptoms and other tests performed.

RELATED MONOGRAPHS:

▸ Related tests include cystoscopy, cystourethrography voiding, PAP, PSA, retrograde ureteropyelography, semen analysis, and US prostate.

▸ Refer to the Genitourinary System table at the end of the book for related tests by body system.

Biopsy, Skin

SYNONYM/ACRONYM: N/A.

COMMON USE: To assist in diagnosing skin cancer.

SPECIMEN: Skin tissue or cells.

NORMAL FINDINGS: (Method: Macroscopic and microscopic examination of tissue) No abnormal tissue or cells.

DESCRIPTION: Skin biopsy is the excision of a tissue sample from suspicious skin lesions. The microscopic analysis can determine cell morphology and the presence of tissue abnormalities. This test assists in confirming the diagnosis of malignant or benign skin lesions. A skin biopsy can be obtained by any of these four methods: curettage, shaving, excision, or punch. A Tzanck smear may be prepared from vesicles (blisters) present on the skin. Skin cells in the vesicles can be evaluated microscopically to indicate the presence of certain viruses, especially herpes, that cause cells to become enlarged and otherwise abnormal in appearance.

INDICATIONS

- Assist in the diagnosis of keratoses, warts, moles, keloids, fibromas, cysts, or inflamed lesions
- Assist in the diagnosis of inflammatory process of the skin, especially herpes infection
- Assist in the diagnosis of skin cancer
- Evaluate suspicious skin lesions

POTENTIAL DIAGNOSIS

Abnormal findings in

- Basal cell carcinoma
- Cysts
- Dermatitis
- Dermatofibroma
- Keloids
- Malignant melanoma
- Neurofibroma
- Pemphigus
- Pigmented nevi
- Seborrheic keratosis
- Skin involvement in systemic lupus erythematosus, discoid lupus erythematosus, and scleroderma
- Squamous cell carcinoma
- Viral infection (herpes, varicella)
- Warts

CRITICAL FINDINGS

- Assessment of clear margins after tissue excision
- Classification or grading of tumor
- Identification of malignancy

It is essential that critical diagnoses be communicated immediately to the requesting health-care provider (HCP). A listing of these diagnoses varies among facilities. Timely notification of critical values for lab or diagnostic studies is a role expectation of the professional nurse. Notification processes will vary among facilities. Upon receipt of the critical value, the information should be read back to the caller to verify accuracy. Most policies require immediate notification of the primary HCP, hospitalist, or on-call HCP. Reported information includes the patient's name, unique identifiers, critical value, name of the person giving the report,

B

B

and name of the person receiving the report. Documentation of notification should be made in the medical record with the name of the HCP notified, time and date of notification, and any orders received. Any delay in a timely report of a critical value may require completion of a notification form with review by Risk Management.

INTERFERING FACTORS

- ❖ This procedure is contraindicated in patients with bleeding disorders.
- Failure to follow dietary restrictions before the procedure may cause the procedure to be canceled or repeated.

NURSING IMPLICATIONS AND PROCEDURE

PRETEST:

▶ Positively identify the patient using at least two unique identifiers before providing care, treatment, or services.

▶ *Patient Teaching:* Inform the patient this procedure can assist in establishing a diagnosis of skin disease.

▶ Obtain a history of the patient's complaints, including a list of known allergens, especially allergies or sensitivities to latex or anesthetics.

▶ Obtain a history of the patient's immune and musculoskeletal systems, any bleeding disorders or other symptoms, and results of previously performed laboratory tests and diagnostic and surgical procedures.

▶ Record the date of the last menstrual period and determine the possibility of pregnancy in perimenopausal women.

▶ Note any recent procedures that can interfere with test results.

▶ Obtain a list of the patient's current medications including anticoagulants, aspirin and other salicylates, herbs, nutritional supplements, and nutraceuticals (see Appendix F). Such products should be discontinued by medical

direction for the appropriate number of days prior to a surgical procedure.

▶ Review the procedure with the patient. Inform the patient that it may be necessary to remove hair from the site before the procedure. Instruct that prophylactic antibiotics may be administered before the procedure. Address concerns about pain and explain that a sedative and/or analgesia will be administered before the punch biopsy to promote relaxation and reduce discomfort. Explain that any discomfort will be minimized with local anesthetics and systemic analgesics. Inform the patient the biopsy is performed under sterile conditions by an HCP, with support staff, specializing in this procedure. The procedure usually takes about 20 min to complete, and sutures may be necessary to close the site.

▶ *Sensitivity to social and cultural issues,* as well as concern for modesty, is important in providing psychological support before, during, and after the procedure.

▶ Explain that an IV line may be inserted to allow infusion of IV fluids, anesthetics, or sedatives, depending on the type of biopsy.

▶ There are no food, fluid, or medication restrictions unless by medical direction.

▶ *Make sure a written and informed consent has been signed prior to the procedure and before administering any medications.*

INTRATEST:

▶ Ensure that the patient has complied with dietary restrictions if ordered by the HCP.

▶ Ensure that anticoagulant therapy has been withheld for the appropriate number of days prior to the procedure. Number of days to withhold medication is dependent on the type of anticoagulant. Notify the HCP if patient anticoagulant therapy has not been withheld.

▶ Have emergency equipment readily available.

▶ Have the patient void before the procedure.

▶ Observe standard precautions, and follow the general guidelines in

Appendix A. Positively identify the patient, and label the appropriate specimen containers with the corresponding patient demographics, initials of the person collecting the specimen, date and time of collection, and site location.

Assist the patient to the desired position depending on the test site to be used, and direct the patient to breathe normally during the local anesthetic and the procedure. Instruct the patient to cooperate fully, follow directions, and avoid unnecessary movement.

Record baseline vital signs, and continue to monitor throughout the procedure. Protocols may vary among facilities.

After the administration of local anesthesia, use clippers to remove hair from the site if appropriate, cleanse the site with an antiseptic solution, and drape the area with sterile towels.

Curettage
The skin is scraped with a curette to obtain specimen.

Shaving or Excision
A scalpel is used to remove a portion of the lesion that protrudes above the epidermis. If the lesion is to be excised, the incision is made as wide and as deep as needed to ensure that the entire lesion is removed. Bleeding is controlled with external pressure to the site. Large wounds are closed with sutures. An adhesive bandage is applied when excision is complete.

Punch Biopsy
A small, round punch about 4 to 6 mm in diameter is rotated into the skin to the desired depth. The cylinder of skin is pulled upward with forceps and separated at its base with a scalpel or scissors. If needed, sutures are applied. A sterile dressing is applied over the site.

Monitor the patient for complications related to the procedure (e.g., allergic reaction, anaphylaxis).

Place tissue samples in properly labeled specimen container containing formalin solution, and promptly transport the specimen to the laboratory for processing and analysis.

POST-TEST:
A report of the results will be made available to the requesting HCP, who will discuss the results with the patient.

Monitor vital signs and neurological status every 15 min for 1 hr, then every 2 hr for 4 hr, and then as ordered by the HCP. Monitor temperature every 4 hr for 24 hr. Compare with baseline values. Notify the HCP if temperature is elevated. Protocols may vary among facilities.

Observe/assess for delayed allergic reactions, such as rash, urticaria, tachycardia, hyperpnea, hypertension, palpitations, nausea, or vomiting.

Observe/assess the biopsy site for bleeding, inflammation, or hematoma formation.

Instruct the patient in the care and assessment of the site.

Instruct the patient to report any redness, edema, bleeding, or pain at the biopsy site.

Assess for nausea and pain. Administer antiemetic and analgesic medications as needed and as directed by the HCP.

Administer antibiotic therapy if ordered. Remind the patient of the importance of completing the entire course of antibiotic therapy, even if signs and symptoms disappear before completion of therapy.

Recognize anxiety related to test results. Discuss the implications of abnormal test results on the patient's lifestyle. Provide teaching and information regarding the clinical implications of the test results, as appropriate. Educate the patient regarding access to counseling services.

Reinforce information given by the patient's HCP regarding further testing, treatment, or referral to another HCP. Inform the patient of a follow-up appointment for the removal of sutures, if indicated. Answer any questions or address any concerns voiced by the patient or family.

Instruct the patient in the use of any ordered medications. Explain the importance of adhering to the therapy regimen. As appropriate, instruct the patient in significant side effects and systemic reactions associated with the prescribed medication. Encourage him or her to review corresponding literature provided by a pharmacist. Depending on the results of this procedure, additional testing may be performed to evaluate or monitor progression of the disease process and determine the need for a change in therapy. Evaluate test results in relation to the patient's symptoms and other tests performed.

RELATED MONOGRAPHS:

- Related tests include allergen-specific IgE, ANA, culture skin, eosinophil count, ESR, and IgE.
- Refer to the Immune and Musculoskeletal systems tables at the end of the book for related tests by body system.

Biopsy, Thyroid

SYNONYM/ACRONYM: N/A.

COMMON USE: To assist in diagnosing thyroid cancer.

SPECIMEN: Thyroid gland tissue or cells.

NORMAL FINDINGS: (Method: Macroscopic and microscopic examination of tissue) No abnormal tissue or cells.

DESCRIPTION: Thyroid biopsy is the excision of a tissue sample for microscopic analysis to determine cell morphology and the presence of tissue abnormalities. This test assists in confirming a diagnosis of cancer or determining the cause of persistent thyroid symptoms. A biopsy specimen can be obtained by needle aspiration or by surgical excision.

INDICATIONS

- Assist in the diagnosis of thyroid cancer or benign cysts or tumors
- Determine the cause of inflammatory thyroid disease
- Determine the cause of hyperthyroidism
- Evaluate enlargement of the thyroid gland

POTENTIAL DIAGNOSIS

Positive findings in

- Benign thyroid cyst
- Granulomatous thyroiditis
- Hashimoto's thyroiditis
- Nontoxic nodular goiter
- Thyroid cancer

CRITICAL FINDINGS

- Assessment of clear margins after tissue excision
- Classification or grading of tumor
- Identification of malignancy

It is essential that critical diagnoses be communicated immediately to the requesting health-care provider (HCP). A listing of these diagnoses varies among facilities. Timely notification of critical values for lab or diagnostic studies is a role expectation of the professional nurse. Notification processes will vary among facilities.

Upon receipt of the critical value, the information should be read back to the caller to verify accuracy. Most policies require immediate notification of the primary HCP, hospitalist, or on-call HCP. Reported information includes the patient's name, unique identifiers, critical value, name of the person giving the report, and name of the person receiving the report. Documentation of notification should be made in the medical record with the name of the HCP notified, time and date of notification, and any orders received. Any delay in a timely report of a critical value may require completion of a notification form with review by Risk Management.

INTERFERING FACTORS

- ⬥ This procedure is contraindicated in patients with bleeding disorders.
- Failure to follow dietary restrictions before the procedure may cause the procedure to be canceled or repeated.

NURSING IMPLICATIONS AND PROCEDURE

PRETEST:

- Positively identify the patient using at least two unique identifiers before providing care, treatment, or services.
- *Patient Teaching:* Inform the patient this procedure can assist in establishing a diagnosis of thyroid disease.
- Obtain a history of the patient's complaints, including a list of known allergens, especially allergies or sensitivities to latex or anesthetics.
- Obtain a history of the patient's endocrine and immune systems, any bleeding disorders or other symptoms, and results of previously performed laboratory tests and diagnostic and surgical procedures.
- Record the date of the last menstrual period and determine possibility of pregnancy in perimenopausal women.
- Note any recent procedures that can interfere with test results.
- Obtain a list of the patient's current medications including anticoagulants, aspirin and other salicylates, herbs, nutritional supplements, and nutraceuticals (see Appendix F). Such products should be discontinued by medical direction for the appropriate number of days prior to a surgical procedure.
- Review the procedure with the patient. Inform the patient that it may be necessary to remove hair from the site before the procedure. Instruct the patient that prophylactic antibiotics may be administered before the procedure. Address concerns about pain and explain that a sedative and/or analgesia will be administered before the percutaneous biopsy to promote relaxation and reduce discomfort; general anesthesia will be administered before the open biopsy. Explain to the patient that no pain will be experienced during the test when general anesthesia is used but that any discomfort with a needle biopsy will be minimized with local anesthetics and systemic analgesics. Inform the patient that the biopsy is performed under sterile conditions by an HCP, with support staff, specializing in this procedure. The surgical procedure usually takes about 30 min to complete, and sutures may be necessary to close the site. A needle biopsy usually takes about 15 min to complete.
- *Sensitivity to social and cultural issues,* as well as concern for modesty, is important in providing psychological support before, during, and after the procedure.
- Explain that an IV line will be inserted to allow infusion of IV fluids, antibiotics, anesthetics, analgesics, or IV sedation.
- Instruct the patient that, to reduce the risk of nausea and vomiting, nothing should be taken by mouth for 8 hr before a general anesthetic or only clear liquids may be taken for 2 hr before the procedure if local anesthesia is to be used. Patients on beta blockers before the surgical procedure should be instructed to take their medication as ordered during the perioperative period. Protocols may vary among facilities.
- Have the patient void before the procedure.

B

Make sure a written and informed consent has been signed prior to the procedure and before administering any medications.

INTRATEST:

Ensure that the patient has complied with dietary restrictions; ensure that food and liquids have been restricted for at least 8 hr and clear liquids have been restricted for at least 2 hr before the procedure depending on the anesthetic chosen for the procedure.

Ensure that anticoagulant therapy has been withheld for the appropriate number of days prior to the procedure. Number of days to withhold medication is dependent on the type of anticoagulant. Notify HCP if patient anticoagulant therapy has not been withheld. Ensure that patients on beta-blocker therapy have continued their medication regimen as ordered.

Have emergency equipment readily available.

Observe standard precautions, and follow the general guidelines in Appendix A. Positively identify the patient, and label the appropriate specimen containers with the corresponding patient demographics, initials of the person collecting the specimen, date and time of collection, and site location.

Assist the patient to the desired position depending on the test site to be used, and direct the patient to breathe normally during the beginning of the general anesthetic. Instruct the patient to cooperate fully and to follow directions. For the patient undergoing local anesthesia, direct him or her to breathe normally and to avoid unnecessary movement during the procedure.

Record baseline vital signs and continue to monitor throughout the procedure. Protocols may vary among facilities.

After the administration of general or local anesthesia, use clippers to remove hair from the surgical site if appropriate, cleanse the site with an antiseptic solution, and drape the area with sterile towels.

Open Biopsy

Adhere to Surgical Care Improvement Project (SCIP) quality measures.

Administer ordered prophylactic antibiotics 1 hr before incision, use antibiotics that are consistent with current guidelines specific to the procedure.

After administration of general anesthesia and surgical preparation is completed, an incision is made, suspicious area(s) are located, and tissue samples are collected.

Needle Biopsy

Direct the patient to take slow, deep breaths when the local anesthetic is injected. Protect the site with sterile drapes. Instruct the patient to take a deep breath, exhale forcefully, and hold the breath while the biopsy needle is inserted and rotated to obtain a core of thyroid tissue. Once the needle is removed, the patient may breathe. Pressure is applied to the site for 3 to 5 min, then a sterile pressure dressing is applied.

General

Monitor the patient for complications related to the procedure (e.g., allergic reaction, anaphylaxis).

Place tissue samples in properly labeled specimen container containing formalin solution, and promptly transport the specimen to the laboratory for processing and analysis.

POST-TEST:

A report of the results will be made available to the requesting HCP, who will discuss the results with the patient

Instruct the patient to resume preoperative diet, as directed by the HCP. Assess the patient's ability to swallow before allowing the patient to attempt liquids or solid foods.

Monitor vital signs and neurological status every 15 min for 1 hr, then every 2 hr for 4 hr, and then as ordered by the HCP. Monitor temperature every 4 hr for 24 hr. Monitor intake and output at least every 8 hr. Compare with baseline values. Notify the HCP if temperature is elevated. Discontinue prophylactic antibiotics within 24 hr after the conclusion of the procedure. Protocols may vary among facilities.

Observe/assess for delayed allergic reactions, such as rash, urticaria,

tachycardia, hyperpnea, hypertension, palpitations, nausea, or vomiting.
- Observe/assess the biopsy site for bleeding, inflammation, or hematoma formation.
- Instruct the patient in the care and assessment of the site.
- Instruct the patient to report any redness, edema, bleeding, or pain at the biopsy site.
- Assess for nausea and pain. Administer antiemetic and analgesic medications as needed and as directed by the HCP.
- Administer antibiotic therapy if ordered. Remind the patient of the importance of completing the entire course of antibiotic therapy, even if signs and symptoms disappear before completion of therapy.
- Recognize anxiety related to test. Discuss the implications of the abnormal test results on the patient's lifestyle. Provide teaching and information regarding the clinical implications of the test results, as appropriate. Educate the patient regarding access to counseling services.
- Reinforce information given by the patient's HCP regarding further testing, treatment, or referral to another HCP. Inform the patient of a follow-up appointment for removal of sutures,

if indicated. Answer any questions or address any concerns voiced by the patient or family.
- Instruct the patient in the use of any ordered medications. Explain the importance of adhering to the therapy regimen. As appropriate, instruct the patient in significant side effects and systemic reactions associated with the prescribed medication. Encourage him or her to review corresponding literature provided by a pharmacist.
- Depending on the results of this procedure, additional testing may be performed to evaluate or monitor progression of the disease process and determine the need for a change in therapy. Evaluate test results in relation to the patient's symptoms and other tests performed.

RELATED MONOGRAPHS:
- Related tests include antibodies, antithyroglobulin, calcitonin and stimulation tests, parathyroid scan, radioactive iodine uptake, thyroid-binding inhibitory immunoglobulin, thyroid scan, TSH, free thyroxine, and US thyroid.
- Refer to the Endocrine and Immune systems tables at the end of the book for related tests by body system.

Bladder Cancer Markers, Urine

SYNONYM/ACRONYM: Nuclear matrix protein (NMP) 22, BTA, cytogenic marker for bladder cancer.

COMMON USE: To assist in diagnosing bladder cancer.

SPECIMEN: Urine (5 mL), unpreserved random specimen collected in a clean plastic collection container for NMP22 and Bard BTA; urine (30 mL), first void specimen collected in fixative specific for FISH testing.

NORMAL FINDINGS: (Method: Enzyme immunoassay for NMP22 and bladder tumor antigen (BTA), fluorescence in situ hybridization [FISH] for cytogenic marker)
NMP22: Negative: Less than 6 units/mL, borderline: 6 to 10 units/mL, positive: Greater than 10 units/mL
BTA: Negative
Cytogenic Marker: Negative

B

DESCRIPTION: Cystoscopy is still considered the gold standard for detection of bladder cancer, but other noninvasive tests have been developed, including several urine assays approved by the U.S. Food and Drug Administration. Compared to cytological studies, these assays are believed to be more sensitive but less specific for detecting transitional cell carcinoma. FISH is a cytogenic technique that uses fluorescent-labeled DNA probes to detect specific chromosome abnormalities. The FISH bladder cancer assay specifically detects the presence of aneuploidy for chromosomes 3, 7, and 17 and absence of the 9p21 loci, findings associated with transitional cell cancer of the bladder.

NMP22: Nuclear matrix proteins (NMPs) are involved in the regulation and expression of various genes. The NMP identified as NuMA is abundant in bladder tumor cells. The dying tumor cells release the soluble NMP into the urine. This assay is quantitative.

Bladder tumor antigen (BTA): A human complement factor H-related protein (hCFHrp) is thought to be produced by bladder tumor cells as protection from the body's natural immune response. BTA is released from tumor cells into the urine. This assay is qualitative.

INDICATIONS
• Detection of bladder carcinoma
• Management of recurrent bladder cancer

POTENTIAL DIAGNOSIS
Increased in bladder carcinoma.

CRITICAL FINDINGS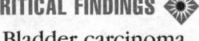
• Bladder carcinoma

It is essential that critical diagnoses be communicated immediately to the requesting health-care provider (HCP). A listing of these diagnoses varies among facilities. Timely notification of critical values for lab or diagnostic studies is a role expectation of the professional nurse. Notification processes will vary among facilities. Upon receipt of the critical value, the information should be read back to the caller to verify accuracy. Most policies require immediate notification of the primary HCP, hospitalist, or on-call HCP. Reported information includes the patient's name, unique identifiers, critical value, name of the person giving the report, and name of the person receiving the report. Documentation of notification should be made in the medical record with the name of the HCP notified, time and date of notification, and any orders received. Any delay in a timely report of a critical value may require completion of a notification form with review by Risk Management.

INTERFERING FACTORS
• *NMP22:* Any condition that results in inflammation of the bladder or urinary tract may cause falsely elevated values.
• *BTA:* Recent surgery, biopsy, or other trauma to the bladder or urinary tract may cause falsely elevated values. Bacterial overgrowth from active urinary tract infection, renal or bladder calculi, gross contamination from blood, and positive leukocyte dipstick may also cause false-positive results.
• *Cytogenic marker:* Incorrect fixative, gross contamination from blood, bacterial overgrowth from active urinary tract infection, inadequate number of bladder cells in specimen.

B

NURSING IMPLICATIONS AND PROCEDURE

PRETEST:

- Positively identify the patient using at least two unique identifiers before providing care, treatment, or services.
- *Patient Teaching:* Inform the patient this procedure can assist in establishing a diagnosis of bladder disease.
- Obtain a history of the patient's complaints, including a list of known allergens.
- Obtain a history of the patient's genitourinary system, symptoms, and results of previously performed laboratory tests and diagnostic and surgical procedures.
- Note any recent procedures that can interfere with test results.
- Obtain a list of the patient's current medications including herbs, nutritional supplements, and nutraceuticals (see Appendix F).
- Review the procedure with the patient. Address concerns about pain and explain that there should be no discomfort during the procedure. Inform the patient that specimen collection takes approximately 5 min, depending on the cooperation and ability of the patient.
- *Sensitivity to social and cultural issues,* as well as concern for modesty, is important in providing psychological support before, during, and after the procedure.
- There are no food, fluid, or medication restrictions unless by medical direction.

INTRATEST:

- Instruct the patient to cooperate fully and to follow directions.
- Observe standard precautions, and follow the general guidelines in Appendix A. Positively identify the patient, and label the appropriate specimen containers with the corresponding patient demographics, initials of the person collecting the specimen, date and time of collection.
- Obtain urine specimen in a clean plastic collection container.
- Promptly transport the specimen to the laboratory for processing and analysis.

POST-TEST:

- A report of the results will be made available to the requesting HCP, who will discuss the results with the patient.
- Recognize anxiety related to test results, and be supportive of fear of shortened life expectancy. Discuss the implications of abnormal test results on the patient's lifestyle. Provide teaching and information regarding the clinical implications of the test results, as appropriate. Educate the patient regarding access to counseling services. Provide contact information, if desired, for the American Cancer Society (www.cancer.org) or the National Cancer Institute (www.cancer.gov).
- Reinforce information given by the patient's HCP regarding further testing, treatment, or referral to another HCP. The greatest risk factor for bladder cancer is smoking. Inform the patient of smoking cessation programs as appropriate. Answer any questions or address any concerns voiced by the patient or family.
- Depending on the results of this procedure, additional testing may be performed to evaluate or monitor progression of the disease process and determine the need for a change in therapy. Evaluate test results in relation to the patient's symptoms and other tests performed.

RELATED MONOGRAPHS:

- Related tests include biopsy bladder, cytology urine, cystoscopy, IVP, and US bladder.
- Refer to the Genitourinary System table at the end of the book for related tests by body system.

Bleeding Time

B

SYNONYM/ACRONYM: Mielke bleeding time, Simplate bleeding time, template bleeding time, Surgicutt bleeding time, Ivy bleeding time.

COMMON USE: To evaluate platelet function.

SPECIMEN: Whole blood.

NORMAL FINDINGS: (Method: Timed observation of incision)
Template: 2.5 to 10 min
Ivy: 2 to 7 min
Slight differences exist in the disposable devices used to make the incision. Although the Mielke or template bleeding time is believed to offer greater standardization to a fairly subjective procedure, both methods are thought to be of equal sensitivity and reproducibility.

POTENTIAL DIAGNOSIS

This test does not predict excessive bleeding during a surgical procedure.

Prolonged In

- Bernard-Soulier syndrome *(evidenced by a rare hereditary condition in which platelet glycoprotein GP1b is deficient and platelet aggregation is decreased)*
- Fibrinogen disorders *(related to the role of fibrinogen to help platelets link together)*
- Glanzmann's thrombasthenia *(evidenced by a rare hereditary condition in which platelet glycoprotein IIb/IIIa is deficient and platelet aggregation is decreased)*
- Hereditary telangiectasia *(evidenced by fragile blood vessels that do not permit adequate constriction to stop bleeding)*
- Liver disease *(related to decreased production of coagulation proteins that affect bleeding time)*
- Some myeloproliferative disorders *(evidenced by disorders of decreased platelet production)*

- Renal disease *(related to abnormal platelet function)*
- Thrombocytopenia *(evidenced by insufficient platelets to stop bleeding)*
- von Willebrand's disease *(evidenced by deficiency of von Willebrand factor, necessary for normal platelet adhesion)*

Decreased in: N/A

CRITICAL FINDINGS

Greater than 14 min
Note and immediately report to the health-care provider (HCP) any critically increased values and related symptoms. Timely notification of critical values for lab or diagnostic studies is a role expectation of the professional nurse. Notification processes will vary among facilities. Upon receipt of the critical value, the information should be read back to the caller to verify accuracy. Most policies require immediate notification of the primary HCP, hospitalist, or on-call HCP. Reported information includes the patient's name, unique identifiers, critical value, name of the person giving the report, and name of the person receiving the

report. Documentation of notification should be made in the medical record with the name of the HCP notified, time and date of notification, and any orders received. Any delay in a timely report of a critical value may require completion of a notification form with review by Risk Management.

Find and print out the full monograph at DavisPlus (http://davisplus.fadavis .com, keyword Van Leeuwen).

B

Blood Gases

SYNONYM/ACRONYM: Arterial blood gases (ABGs), venous blood gases, capillary blood gases, cord blood gases.

COMMON USE: To assess oxygenation and acid base balance.

SPECIMEN: Whole blood. Specimen volume and collection container may vary with collection method. See Intratest section for specific collection instructions. Specimen should be tightly capped and transported in an ice slurry.

NORMAL FINDINGS: (Method: Selective electrodes for pH, Pco_2 and Po_2)

Blood Gas Value (pH)	Arterial	Venous	Capillary
Scalp			7.25–7.35
Birth, cord, full term	7.11–7.36	7.25–7.45	7.32–7.49
Adult/child	7.35–7.45	7.32–7.43	7.35–7.45

Note: SI units (conversion factor × 1).

Pco_2	Arterial	SI Units (Conventional Units × 0.133)	Venous	SI Units (Conventional Units × 0.133)	Capillary	SI Units (Conventional Units × 0.133)
Scalp	–	–	–	–	40–50 mm Hg	5.3–6.6 kPa
Birth, cord, full term	32–66 mm Hg	4.3–8.8 kPa	27–49 mm Hg	3.6–6.5 kPa	–	–
Newborn–adult	35–45 mm Hg	4.7–6 kPa	41–51 mm Hg	5.4–6.8 kPa	26–41 mm Hg	3.5–5.4 kPa

Po_2	Arterial	SI Units (Conventional Units × 0.133)	Venous	SI Units (Conventional Units × 0.133)	Capillary	SI Units (Conventional Units × 0.133)
Scalp	–	–	–	–	20–30 mm Hg	2.7–4 kPa
Birth, cord, full term	8–24 mm Hg	1.1–3.2 kPa	17–41 mm Hg	2.3–5.4 kPa	–	–
0–1 hr	33–85 mm Hg	4.4–11.3 kPa	–	–	–	–
Greater than 1 hr–adult	80–95 mm Hg	10.6–12.6 kPa	20–49 mm Hg	2.7–6.5 kPa	80–95 mm Hg	10.6–12.6 kPa

HCO$_3^-$	Arterial Conventional & SI Units	Venous Conventional & SI Units	Capillary Conventional & SI Units
Birth, cord, full term	17–24 mmol/L	17–24 mmol/L	N/A
2 mo–2 yr	16–23 mmol/L	24–28 mmol/L	18–23 mmol/L
Adult	22–26 mmol/L	24–28 mmol/L	18–23 mmol/L

O$_2$ Sat	Arterial	Venous	Capillary
Birth, cord, full term	40–90%	40–70%	—
Adult/child	95–99%	70–75%	95–98%

Tco$_2$	Arterial Conventional & SI Units mmol/L	Venous Conventional & SI Units mmol/L
Birth, cord, full term	13–22 mmol/L	14–22 mmol/L
Adult/child	22–29 mmol/L	25–30 mmol/L

Base Excess Arterial	Conventional & SI Units
Birth, cord, full term	(−10) – (−2) mmol/L
Adult/child	(−2) – (+3) mmol/L

DESCRIPTION: Blood gas analysis is used to evaluate respiratory function and provide a measure for determining acid-base balance. Respiratory, renal, and cardiovascular system functions are integrated in order to maintain normal acid-base balance. Therefore, respiratory or metabolic disorders may cause abnormal blood gas findings. The blood gas measurements commonly reported are pH, partial pressure of carbon dioxide in the blood (Pco$_2$), partial pressure of oxygen in the blood (Po$_2$), bicarbonate (HCO$_3^-$), O$_2$ saturation, and base excess (BE) or base deficit (BD). pH reflects the number of free hydrogen ions (H$^+$) in the body. A pH less than 7.35 indicates acidosis. A pH greater than 7.45

indicates alkalosis. Changes in the ratio of free H$^+$ to HCO$_3$ will result in a compensatory response from the lungs or kidneys to restore proper acid-base balance.

Pco$_2$ is an important indicator of ventilation. The level of Pco$_2$ is controlled primarily by the lungs and is referred to as the respiratory component of acid-base balance. The main buffer system in the body is the bicarbonate–carbonic acid system. Bicarbonate is an important alkaline ion that participates along with other anions, such as hemoglobin, proteins, and phosphates, to neutralize acids. For the body to maintain proper balance, there must be a ratio of 20 parts bicarbonate to one part carbonic acid (20:1). Carbonic acid level is indirectly measured by P_{CO_2}. Bicarbonate level is indirectly measured by the total carbon dioxide content (T_{CO_2}). The carbonic acid level is not measured directly but can be estimated because it is 3% of the P_{CO_2}. Bicarbonate can also be calculated from these numbers once the carbonic acid value has been obtained because of the 20:1 ratio. For example, if the P_{CO_2} were 40, the carbonic acid would be calculated as (3% × 40) or 1.2, and the HCO_3^- would be calculated as (20 × 1.2) or 24. The main acid in the acid-base system is carbonic acid. It is the metabolic or nonrespiratory component of the acid-base system and is controlled by the kidney. Bicarbonate levels can either be measured directly or estimated from the T_{CO_2} in the blood. BE/BD reflects the number of anions available in the blood to help buffer changes in pH. A BD (negative BE) indicates metabolic acidosis, whereas a positive BE indicates metabolic alkalosis.

Extremes in acidosis are generally more life threatening than alkalosis. Acidosis can develop either very quickly (e.g., cardiac arrest) or over a longer period of time (e.g., renal failure). Infants can develop acidosis very quickly if they are not kept warm and given enough calories. Children with diabetes tend to go into acidosis more quickly than do adults who have been dealing with the disease over a longer period of time. In many cases, a venous or capillary specimen is satisfactory to obtain the necessary information regarding acid-base balance without subjecting the patient to an arterial puncture with its associated risks.

As seen in the table of reference ranges, P_{O_2} is lower in infants than in children and adults owing to the respective level of maturation of the lungs at birth. P_{O_2} tends to trail off after age 30, decreasing by approximately 3 to 5 mm Hg per decade as the organs age and begin to lose elasticity. The formula used to approximate the relationship between age and P_{O_2} is:

$$P_{O_2} = 104 - (age \times 0.27)$$

Like carbon dioxide, oxygen is carried in the body in a dissolved and combined (oxyhemoglobin) form. Oxygen content is the sum of the dissolved and combined oxygen. The oxygen-carrying capacity of the blood indicates how much oxygen could be carried if all the hemoglobin were saturated with oxygen. Percentage of oxygen saturation is [oxyhemoglobin concentration ÷ (oxyhemoglobin concentration + deoxyhemoglobin concentration)] × 100.

Testing on specimens other than arterial blood is often ordered when oxygen measurements are not needed or when the information regarding oxygen can be obtained by noninvasive techniques such as pulse oximetry. Capillary blood is satisfactory for most purposes for pH and P_{CO_2}; the use of capillary P_{O_2} is limited to the exclusion of hypoxia. Measurements involving oxygen are usually not useful when performed on venous samples; arterial blood is required to accurately measure P_{O_2} and oxygen saturation. Considerable evidence indicates that prolonged exposure to high levels of oxygen can result in injury, such as retinopathy of prematurity in infants or the drying of airways in any patient. Monitoring P_{O_2} from blood gases is especially appropriate under such circumstances.

INDICATIONS

This group of tests is used to assess conditions such as asthma, chronic obstructive pulmonary disease (COPD), embolism (e.g., fatty or other embolism) during coronary arterial bypass surgery, and hypoxia. It is also used to assist in the diagnosis of respiratory failure, which is defined as a Po_2 less than 50 mm Hg and Pco_2 greater than 50 mm Hg. Blood gases can be valuable in the management of patients on ventilators or being weaned from ventilators. Blood gas values are used to determine acid-base status, the type of imbalance, and the degree of compensation as summarized in the following section. Restoration of pH to near-normal values is referred to as fully compensated balance. When pH values are moving in the same direction (i.e., increasing or decreasing) as the Pco_2 or HCO_3^-, the imbalance is metabolic. When the pH values are moving in the opposite direction from the Pco_2 or HCO_3^-, the imbalance is caused by respiratory disturbances. To remember this concept, the following mnemonic can be useful: MeTRO = **Metabolic Together, Respiratory Opposite.**

Acid-Base Disturbance	pH	Pco_2	Po_2	HCO_3^-
Respiratory Acidosis				
Uncompensated	Decreased	Increased	Normal	Normal
Compensated	Normal	Increased	Increased	Increased
Respiratory Alkalosis				
Uncompensated	Increased	Decreased	Normal	Normal
Compensated	Normal	Decreased	Decreased	Decreased
Uncompensated	Decreased	Normal	Decreased	Decreased
Compensated	Normal	Decreased	Decreased	Decreased
Metabolic (Nonrespiratory) Acidosis				
Uncompensated	Increased	Normal	Increased	Increased
Compensated	Normal	Increased	Increased	Increased

POTENTIAL DIAGNOSIS

Acid-base imbalance is determined by evaluating pH, Pco_2, and HCO_3^- values. pH less than 7.35 reflects an acidic state, whereas pH greater than 7.45 reflects alkalosis. Pco_2 and HCO_3^- determine whether the imbalance is respiratory or nonrespiratory (metabolic). Because a patient may have more than one imbalance and may also be in the process of compensating, the interpretation of blood gas values may not always seem straightforward.

Respiratory conditions that interfere with normal breathing cause CO_2 *to be retained in the blood. This results in an increase of circulating carbonic acid and a corresponding decrease in pH (respiratory acidosis). Acute respiratory acidosis can occur in acute pulmonary edema, severe respiratory infections, bronchial obstruction, pneumothorax, hemothorax, open chest wounds, opiate poisoning, respiratory depressant drug therapy, and inhalation of air with a high CO_2 content. Chronic respiratory acidosis can be seen in patients with asthma, pulmonary fibrosis, emphysema, bronchiectasis, and* *respiratory depressant drug therapy. Respiratory conditions that increase the breathing rate cause CO_2 to be removed from the alveoli more rapidly than it is being produced. This results in an alkaline pH. Acute respiratory alkalosis may be seen in anxiety, hysteria, hyperventilation, and pulmonary embolus and with an increase in artificial ventilation. Chronic respiratory alkalosis may be seen in high fever, administration of drugs (e.g., salicylate and sulfa) that stimulate the respiratory system, hepatic coma, hypoxia of high altitude, and central nervous system (CNS) lesions or injury that result in stimulation of the respiratory center.*

Metabolic (nonrespiratory) conditions that cause the excessive formation or decreased excretion of organic or inorganic acids result in metabolic acidosis. Some of these conditions include ingestion of salicylates, ethylene glycol, and methanol, as well as uncontrolled diabetes, starvation, shock, renal disease, and biliary or pancreatic fistula. Metabolic alkalosis results from conditions that increase pH, as can be seen in excessive intake of antacids to treat gastritis or peptic ulcer, excessive administration of HCO_3^-, loss of stomach acid caused by protracted vomiting, cystic fibrosis, or potassium and chloride deficiencies.

Respiratory Acidosis
- Decreased pH
- Decreased O_2 saturation
- Increased P_{CO_2}:
  Acute intermittent porphyria
  Anemia (severe)
  Anorexia
  Anoxia

  Asthma
  Atelectasis
  Bronchitis
  Bronchoconstriction
  Carbon monoxide poisoning
  Cardiac disorders
  Congenital heart defects
  Congestive heart failure
  COPD
  Cystic fibrosis
  Depression of respiratory center
  Drugs depressing the respiratory system
  Electrolyte disturbances (severe)
  Emphysema
  Fever
  Head injury
  Hypercapnia
  Hypothyroidism (severe)
  Near drowning
  Pleural effusion
  Pneumonia
  Pneumothorax
  Poisoning
  Poliomyelitis
  Pulmonary edema
  Pulmonary embolism
  Pulmonary tuberculosis
  Respiratory distress syndrome (adult and neonatal)
  Respiratory failure
  Sarcoidosis
  Smoking
  Tumor
- A decreased P_{O_2} that increases P_{CO_2}:
  Decreased alveolar gas exchange: cancer, compression or resection of lung, respiratory distress syndrome (newborns), sarcoidosis
  Decreased ventilation or perfusion: asthma, bronchiectasis, bronchitis, cancer, croup, cystic fibrosis (mucoviscidosis), emphysema, granulomata, pneumonia, pulmonary infarction, shock

B

Hypoxemia: anesthesia, carbon monoxide exposure, cardiac disorders, high altitudes, near drowning, presence of abnormal hemoglobins

Hypoventilation: cerebrovascular incident, drugs depressing the respiratory system, head injury

Right-to-left shunt: congenital heart disease, intrapulmonary venoarterial shunting

Compensation
- Increased Po_2:
  Hyperbaric oxygenation
  Hyperventilation
- Increased base excess:
  Increased HCO_3^- to bring pH to (near) normal

Respiratory Alkalosis
- Increased pH
- Decreased Pco_2:
  Anxiety
  CNS lesions or injuries that cause stimulation of the respiratory center
  Excessive artificial ventilation
  Fever
  Head injury
  Hyperthermia
  Hyperventilation
  Hysteria
  Salicylate intoxication

Compensation
- Decreased Po_2:
  Rebreather mask
- Decreased base excess:
  Decreased HCO_3^- to bring pH to (near) normal

Metabolic Acidosis
- Decreased pH
- Decreased HCO_3^-
- Decreased base excess
- Decreased Tco_2:
  Decreased excretion of H^+: acquired (e.g., drugs, hypercalcemia), Addison's disease, diabetic ketoacidosis, Fanconi's syndrome, inherited (e.g.,

cystinosis, Wilson's disease), renal failure, renal tubular acidosis

Increased acid intake

Increased formation of acids: diabetic ketoacidosis, high-fat/low-carbohydrate diets

Increased loss of alkaline body fluids: diarrhea, excess potassium, fistula

Renal disease

Compensation
- Decreased Pco_2:
  Hyperventilation

Metabolic Alkalosis
- Increased pH
- Increased HCO_3^-
- Increased base excess
- Increased Tco_2:
  Alkali ingestion (excessive)
  Anoxia
  Gastric suctioning
  Hypochloremic states
  Hypokalemic states
  Potassium depletion: Cushing's disease, diarrhea, diuresis, excessive vomiting, excessive ingestion of licorice, inadequate potassium intake, potassium-losing nephropathy, steroid administration
  Salicylate intoxication
  Shock
  Vomiting

Compensation
- Increased Tco_2:
  Hypoventilation

CRITICAL FINDINGS

Note and immediately report to the health-care provider (HCP) any critically increased or decreased values and related symptoms. Timely notification of critical values for lab or diagnostic studies is a role expectation of the professional nurse. Notification processes will vary among facilities. Upon receipt of the critical value, the information should be read back to the caller to verify accuracy. Most policies require immediate notification of the primary HCP, hospitalist, or on-call HCP. Reported information includes the patient's name, unique identifiers, critical value, name of the person giving the report, and name of the person receiving the report. Documentation of notification should be made in the medical record with the name of the HCP notified, time and date of notification, and any orders received. Any delay in a timely report of a critical value may require completion of a notification form with review by Risk Management.

	Arterial Blood Gas Parameter	Less Than	Greater Than
Adult/child	pH	7.20	7.60
Adult/child	HCO_3^-	10 mmol/L	40 mmol/L
Adult/child	Pco_2	20 mm Hg (SI: 2.7 kPa)	67 mm Hg (SI: 8.9 kPa)
Adult/child	Po_2	45 mm Hg (SI: 6 kPa)	
Newborns	Po_2	37 mm Hg (SI: 4.9 kPa)	92 mm Hg (SI: 12.2 kPa)

INTERFERING FACTORS

• Drugs that may cause an increase in HCO_3^- include acetylsalicylic acid (initially), antacids, carbenicillin, carbenoxolone, ethacrynic acid, glycyrrhiza (licorice), laxatives, mafenide, and sodium bicarbonate.

• Drugs that may cause a decrease in HCO_3^- include acetazolamide, acetylsalicylic acid (long term or high doses), citrates, dimethadione, ether, ethylene glycol, fluorides, mercury compounds (laxatives), methylenedioxyamphetamine, paraldehyde, and xylitol.

• Drugs that may cause an increase in Pco_2 include acetylsalicylic acid, aldosterone bicarbonate, carbenicillin, carbenoxolone, corticosteroids, dexamethasone, ethacrynic acid, laxatives (chronic abuse), and x-ray contrast agents.

• Drugs that may cause a decrease in Pco_2 include acetazolamide, acetylsalicylic acid, ethamivan, neuromuscular relaxants (secondary to postoperative hyperventilation), NSD 3004 (arterial long-acting carbonic anhydrase inhibitor), theophylline, tromethamine, and xylitol.

• Drugs that may cause an increase in Po_2 include theophylline and urokinase.

• Drugs that may cause a decrease in Po_2 include althesin, barbiturates, granulocyte-macrophage colony-stimulating factor, isoproterenol, and meperidine.

• Samples for blood gases are obtained by arterial puncture, which carries a risk of bleeding, especially in patients who have bleeding disorders or are taking anticoagulants or other blood thinning medications.

• Recent blood transfusion may produce misleading values.

• Specimens with extremely elevated white blood cell counts will undergo misleading decreases in pH resulting from cellular metabolism, if transport to the laboratory is delayed.

• Specimens collected soon after a change in inspired oxygen has occurred will not accurately reflect the patient's oxygenation status.

- Specimens collected within 20 to 30 min of respiratory passage suctioning or other respiratory therapy will not be accurate.
- Excessive differences in actual body temperature relative to normal body temperature will not be reflected in the results. Temperature affects the amount of gas in solution. Blood gas analyzers measure samples at 37°C (98.6°F); therefore, if the patient is hyperthermic or hypothermic, it is important to notify the laboratory of the patient's actual body temperature at the time the specimen was collected. Fever will increase actual Po_2 and Pco_2 values; therefore, the uncorrected values measured at 37°C will be falsely decreased. Hypothermia decreases actual Po_2 and Pco_2 values; therefore, the uncorrected values measured at 37°C will be falsely increased.
- A falsely increased O_2 saturation may occur because of elevated levels of carbon monoxide in the blood.
- O_2 saturation is a calculated parameter based on an assumption of 100% hemoglobin A. Values may be misleading when hemoglobin variants with different oxygen dissociation curves are present. Hemoglobin S will cause a shift to the right, indicating decreased oxygen binding. Fetal hemoglobin and methemoglobin will cause a shift to the left, indicating increased oxygen binding.
- Excessive amounts of heparin in the sample may falsely decrease pH, Pco_2, and Po_2.
- Citrates should never be used as an anticoagulant in evacuated collection tubes for venous blood gas determinations because citrates will cause a marked analytic decrease in pH.
- Air bubbles or blood clots in the specimen are cause for rejection.

Air bubbles in the specimen can falsely elevate or decrease the results depending on the patient's blood gas status. If an evacuated tube is used for venous blood gas specimen collection, the tube must be removed from the needle before the needle is withdrawn from the arm or else the sample will be contaminated with room air.

- Specimens should be placed in ice slurry immediately after collection because blood cells continue to carry out metabolic processes in the specimen after it has been removed from the patient. These natural life processes can affect pH, Po_2, Pco_2, and the other calculated values in a short period of time. The cold temperature provided by the ice slurry will slow down, but not completely stop, metabolic changes occurring in the sample over time. Iced specimens not analyzed within 60 min of collection should be rejected for analysis. Electrolyte analysis from iced specimens should be carried out within 30 min of collection to avoid falsely elevated potassium values.

NURSING IMPLICATIONS AND PROCEDURE

PRETEST:

- Positively identify the patient using at least two unique identifiers before providing care, treatment, or services.
- *Patient Teaching:* Inform the patient this test can assist in assessing blood oxygen balance and oxygenation level.
- Obtain a history of the patient's complaints, including a list of known allergens, especially allergies or sensitivities to latex and anesthetics.
- Obtain a history of the patient's cardiovascular, genitourinary, and respiratory systems, any bleeding disorders or other symptoms, and results of previously performed laboratory tests and diagnostic and surgical procedures.

Note any recent procedures that can interfere with test results.

Obtain a list of the patient's current medications, including anticoagulants, aspirin and other salicylates, herbs, nutritional supplements, and nutraceuticals (see Appendix F).

Record the patient's temperature.

Indicate the type of oxygen, mode of oxygen delivery, and delivery rate as part of the test requisition process. Wait 30 min after a change in type or mode of oxygen delivery or rate for specimen collection.

Review the procedure with the patient and advise rest for 30 min before specimen collection. Explain to the patient that an arterial puncture may be painful. The site may be anesthetized with 1% to 2% lidocaine before puncture. Inform the patient that specimen collection and postprocedure care of the puncture site usually take 10 to 15 min. The person collecting the specimen should be notified beforehand if the patient is receiving anticoagulant therapy or taking aspirin or other natural products that may prolong bleeding from the puncture site.

If the sample is to be collected by radial artery puncture, perform an Allen test before puncture to ensure that the patient has adequate collateral circulation to the hand if thrombosis of the radial artery occurs after arterial puncture. The modified Allen test is performed as follows: Extend the patient's wrist over a rolled towel. Ask the patient to make a fist with the hand extended over the towel. Use the second and third fingers to locate the pulses of the ulnar and radial arteries on the palmar surface of the wrist. (The thumb should not be used to locate these arteries because it has a pulse.) Compress both arteries and ask the patient to open and close the fist several times until the palm turns pale. Release pressure on the ulnar artery only. Color should return to the palm within 5 sec if the ulnar artery is functioning. This is a positive Allen test, and blood gases may be drawn from the radial artery site. The Allen test should then be performed on the opposite hand. The hand to which color is restored fastest has better

circulation and should be selected for specimen collection.

Sensitivity to social and cultural issues, as well as concern for modesty, is important in providing psychological support before, during, and after the procedure.

There are no food, fluid, or medication restrictions unless by medical direction.

Prepare an ice slurry in a cup or plastic bag to have ready for immediate transport of the specimen to the laboratory.

INTRATEST:

If the patient has a history of allergic reaction to latex, avoid the use of equipment containing latex.

Instruct the patient to cooperate fully and to follow directions. Direct the patient to breathe normally and to avoid unnecessary movement.

Observe standard precautions, and follow the general guidelines in Appendix A. Positively identify the patient, and label the appropriate specimen container with the corresponding patient demographics, initials of the person collecting the specimen, date, and time of collection. Perform an arterial puncture.

Arterial

Perform an arterial puncture and collect the specimen in an air-free heparinized syringe. There is no demonstrable difference in results between samples collected in plastic syringes and samples collected in glass syringes. It is very important that no room air be introduced into the collection container because the gases in the room and in the sample will begin equilibrating immediately. The end of the syringe must be stoppered immediately after the needle is withdrawn and removed. Apply a pressure dressing over the puncture site. Samples should be mixed by gently rolling the syringe to ensure proper mixing of the heparin with the sample, which prevents the formation of small clots leading to rejection of the sample. The tightly capped sample should be placed in an ice slurry immediately after collection. Information on the specimen label

B

should be protected from water in the ice slurry by first placing the specimen in a protective plastic bag. Promptly transport the specimen to the laboratory for processing and analysis.

Venous
Central venous blood is collected in a heparinized syringe.

Venous blood is collected percutaneously by venipuncture in a 5-mL green-top (heparin) tube (for adult patients) or a heparinized Microtainer (for pediatric patients). The vacuum collection tube must be removed from the needle before the needle is removed from the patient's arm. Apply a pressure dressing over the puncture site. Samples should be mixed by gently rolling the syringe to ensure proper mixing of the heparin with the sample, which prevents the formation of small clots leading to rejection of the sample. The tightly capped sample should be placed in an ice slurry immediately after collection. Information on the specimen label should be protected from water in the ice slurry by first placing the specimen in a protective plastic bag. Promptly transport the specimen to the laboratory for processing and analysis.

Capillary
Perform a capillary puncture and collect the specimen in two 250-μL heparinized capillaries (scalp or heel for neonatal patients) or a heparinized Microtainer (for pediatric patients). Observe standard precautions and follow the general guidelines in Appendix A. The capillary tubes should be filled as much as possible and capped on both ends. Some hospitals recommend that metal "fleas" be added to the capillary tube before the ends are capped. During transport, a magnet can be moved up and down the outside of the capillary tube to facilitate mixing and prevent the formation of clots, which would cause rejection of the sample. It is important to inform the laboratory or respiratory therapy staff of the number of fleas used so the fleas can be accounted for and removed before the sample is introduced into the blood gas analyz-

ers. Fleas left in the sample may damage the blood gas equipment if allowed to enter the analyzer. Microtainer samples should be mixed by gently rolling the capillary tube to ensure proper mixing of the heparin with the sample, which prevents the formation of small clots leading to rejection of the sample. Promptly transport the specimen to the laboratory for processing and analysis.

Cord Blood
The sample may be collected immediately after delivery from the clamped cord, using a heparinized syringe. The tightly capped sample should be placed in an ice slurry immediately after collection. Information on the specimen label should be protected from water in the ice slurry by first placing the specimen in a protective plastic bag. Promptly transport the specimen to the laboratory for processing and analysis.

Scalp Sample
Samples for scalp pH may be collected anaerobically before delivery in special scalp-sample collection capillaries and transported immediately to the laboratory for analysis. The procedure takes approximately 5 min. Place the patient on her back with her feet in stirrups. The cervix must be dilated at least 3 to 4 cm. A plastic cone is placed in the vagina and fit snugly against the scalp of the fetus. The cone provides access for visualization using an endoscope and to cleanse the site. The site is pierced with a sharp blade. Containment of the blood droplet can be aided by smearing a small amount of silicone cream on the fetal skin site. The blood sample is collected in a thin, heparinized tube. Some hospitals recommend that small metal fleas be added to the scalp tube before the ends are capped. See preceding section on capillary collection for discussion of fleas.

POST-TEST:
A report of the results will be made available to the requesting HCP, who will discuss the results with the patient.

B

▸ Pressure should be applied to the puncture site for at least 5 min in the unanticoagulated patient and for at least 15 min in the case of a patient receiving anticoagulant therapy. Observe/assess puncture site for bleeding or hematoma formation. Apply pressure bandage.

▸ Observe/assess the patient for signs or symptoms of respiratory acidosis, such as dyspnea, headache, tachycardia, pallor, diaphoresis, apprehension, drowsiness, coma, hypertension, or disorientation.

▸ Teach the patient breathing exercises to assist with the appropriate exchange of oxygen and carbon dioxide.

▸ Administer oxygen, if appropriate.

▸ Teach the patient how to properly use the incentive spirometer device or mininebulizer if ordered.

▸ Observe/assess the patient for signs or symptoms of respiratory alkalosis, such as tachypnea, restlessness, agitation, tetany, numbness, seizures, muscle cramps, dizziness, or tingling fingertips.

▸ Instruct the patient to breathe deeply and slowly; performing this type of breathing exercise into a paper bag decreases hyperventilation and quickly helps the patient's breathing return to normal.

▸ Observe/assess the patient for signs or symptoms of metabolic acidosis, such as rapid breathing, flushed skin, nausea, vomiting, dysrhythmias, coma, hypotension, hyperventilation, and restlessness.

▸ Observe/assess the patient for signs or symptoms of metabolic alkalosis, such as shallow breathing, weakness, dysrhythmias, tetany, hypokalemia, hyperactive reflexes, and excessive vomiting.

▸ *Nutritional Considerations:* Abnormal blood gas values may be associated with diseases of the respiratory system. Malnutrition is commonly seen in patients with severe respiratory disease for reasons including fatigue, lack of appetite, and gastrointestinal distress. Research has estimated that the daily caloric intake required for respiration of patients with COPD is 10 times higher than that of normal individuals. Inadequate nutrition can result in hypophosphatemia, especially in the respirator-dependent patient. During periods of starvation, phosphorus leaves the intracellular space and moves outside the tissue, resulting in dangerously decreased phosphorus levels. Adequate intake of vitamins A and C is also important to prevent pulmonary infection and to decrease the extent of lung tissue damage. The importance of following the prescribed diet should be stressed to the patient and/or caregiver.

▸ Water balance needs to be closely monitored in COPD patients. Fluid retention can lead to pulmonary edema.

▸ Reinforce information given by the patient's HCP regarding further testing, treatment, or referral to another HCP. Answer any questions or address any concerns voiced by the patient or family.

▸ Depending on the results of this procedure, additional testing may be performed to evaluate or monitor progression of the disease process and determine the need for a change in therapy. Evaluate test results in relation to the patient's symptoms and other tests performed.

RELATED MONOGRAPHS:

▸ Related tests include α_1-AT, anion gap, arterial/alveolar oxygen ratio, biopsy lung, bronchoscopy, carboxyhemoglobin, chest x-ray, chloride sweat, CBC hemoglobin, CBC WBC and diff, culture and smear for mycobacteria, culture bacterial sputum, culture viral, cytology sputum, electrolytes, gram stain, IgE, lactic acid, lung perfusion scan, lung ventilation scan, osmolality, phosphorus, plethysmography, pleural fluid analysis, pulse oximetry, PFT, and TB skin tests.

▸ Refer to the Cardiovascular, Genitourinary, and Respiratory systems tables at the end of the book for related tests by body system.

Blood Groups and Antibodies

SYNONYM/ACRONYM: ABO group and Rh typing, blood group antibodies, type and screen, type and crossmatch.

COMMON USE: To identify ABO blood group and Rh type, typically for transfusion purposes.

SPECIMEN: Serum (2 mL) collected in a red-top tube or whole blood (2 mL) collected in a lavender-top (EDTA) tube.

NORMAL FINDINGS: (Method: FDA-approved reagents with glass slides, glass tubes, gel, or automated systems) Compatibility (no clumping or hemolysis).

DESCRIPTION: Blood typing is a series of tests that include the ABO and Rh blood-group system performed to detect surface antigens on red blood cells (RBCs) by an agglutination test and compatibility tests to determine antibodies against these antigens. The major antigens in the ABO system are A and B, although AB and O are also common phenotypes. The patient with A antigens has group A blood; the patient with B antigens has group B blood. The patient with both A and B antigens has group AB blood (universal recipient); the patient with neither A nor B antigens has group O blood (universal donor). Blood group and type is genetically determined. After 6 mo of age, individuals develop serum antibodies that react with A or B antigen absent from their own RBCs. These are called *anti-A* and *anti-B* antibodies.

In ABO blood typing, the patient's RBCs mix with anti-A and anti-B sera, a process known as *forward grouping*. The process then reverses, and the patient's serum mixes with type A and B cells in *reverse grouping*.

Generally, only blood with the same ABO group and Rh type as the recipient is transfused because the anti-A and anti-B antibodies are strong agglutinins that cause a rapid, complement-mediated destruction of incompatible cells. However, blood donations have decreased nationwide, creating shortages in the available supply. Safe substitutions with blood of a different group and/or Rh type may occur depending on the inventory of available units. Many laboratories require consultation with the requesting health-care provider (HCP) prior to issuing Rh-positive units to an Rh-negative individual.

ABO and Rh testing is also performed as a prenatal screen in pregnant women to identify the risk of hemolytic disease of the newborn. Although most of the anti-A and anti-B activity resides in the immunoglobulin M (IgM) class of immunoglobulins, some activity rests with immunoglobulin G (IgG). Anti-A and anti-B antibodies of the IgG class coat the RBCs without immediately affecting their viability and can readily cross the placenta, resulting in hemolytic disease of the newborn. Individuals with type O blood frequently have more IgG anti-A and anti-B than other people; thus, ABO hemolytic disease of the newborn will affect infants of type O mothers almost exclusively (unless the newborn is also type O).

Major antigens of the Rh system are D (or Rh_o), C, E, c, and e. Individuals whose RBCs possess D antigen are called Rh-positive; those who lack D antigen are called Rh-negative, no matter what other Rh antigens are present. Individuals who are Rh-negative produce anti-D antibodies when exposed to Rh-positive cells by either transfusions or pregnancy. These anti-D antibodies cross the placenta to the fetus and can cause hemolytic disease of the newborn or transfusion reactions if Rh-positive blood is administered.

The type and screen (T&S) procedure is performed to determine the ABO/Rh and identify any antibodies that may react with transfused blood products. The T&S may take from 30 to 45 min or longer to complete depending on whether unexpected or unusual antibodies are detected. Every unit of product must be crossmatched against the intended recipient's serum and red blood cells for compatibility before transfusion. Knowing the ABO/Rh and antibody status saves time when the patient's sample is crossmatched against units of donated blood products. There are three crossmatch procedures. If no antibodies are identified in the T&S, it is permissible to use either an immediate spin crossmatch or an electronic crossmatch, either of which may take 5 to 10 min to

complete. If antibodies are detected, the antiglobulin crossmatch procedure is performed, along with antibody identification testing, or the process is repeated, beginning with the selection of other units for compatibility testing. Typically, specimens for T&S can be held for 72 hr from the time of collection for use in future crossmatch procedures. This timeframe may be extended for up to 14 days for patients with a reliably known history of no prior transfusions or pregnancy within the previous 3 months. Donated blood products are tested for ABO type, Rh factor, blood group antibodies, and transmissible infectious diseases to include hepatitis B surface antigen, hepatitis B core antibody, hepatitis C antibody (by the nucleic acid test [NAT]), ALT, HTLV I and II antibody, HIV 1 and 2 antibody, syphilis, West Nile virus (by the nucleic acid test [NAT]), and *Trypanosoma cruzi*.

INDICATIONS

- Determine ABO and Rh compatibility of donor and recipient before transfusion (type and screen or crossmatch).
- Determine anti-D antibody titer of Rh-negative mothers after sensitization by pregnancy with an Rh-positive fetus.
- Determine the need for a microdose of immunosuppressive therapy (e.g., with RhoGAM) during the first 12 wk of gestation or a standard dose after 12 wk of gestation for complications such as abortion, miscarriage, vaginal hemorrhage, ectopic pregnancy, or abdominal trauma.
- Determine Rh blood type and perform antibody screen of prenatal

patients on initial visit to determine maternal Rh type and to indicate whether maternal RBCs have been sensitized by any antibodies known to cause hemolytic disease of the newborn, especially anti-D antibody. Rh blood type, antibody screen, and antibody titration (if an antibody has been identified) will be rechecked at 28 wk of gestation and prior to injection of prophylactic standard dose of $Rh_o(D)$ immune globulin RhoGAM IM or Rhophylac IM or IV for Rh-negative mothers. These tests will also be repeated after delivery of an Rh-positive fetus to an Rh-negative mother and prior to injection of prophylactic standard dose of $Rh_o(D)$ immune globulin (if maternal Rh-negative blood has not been previously sensitized with Rh-positive cells resulting in a positive anti-D antibody titer). A postpartum blood sample must be evaluated for fetal-maternal bleed on all Rh-negative mothers to determine the need for additional doses of Rh immune globulin. One in 300 cases will demonstrate

hemorrhage greater than 15 mL of blood and require additional $Rh_o(D)$ immune globulin.

- Identify donor ABO and Rh blood type for stored blood.
- Identify maternal and infant ABO and Rh blood types to predict risk of hemolytic disease of the newborn.
- Identify the patient's ABO and Rh blood type, especially before a procedure in which blood loss is a threat or blood replacement may be needed.
- Identify any unusual transfusion related antibodies in the patient's blood, especially before a procedure in which blood replacement may be needed.

POTENTIAL DIAGNOSIS

- ABO system: A, B, AB, or O specific to person
- Rh system: positive or negative specific to person
- Crossmatching: compatibility between donor and recipient
- Incompatibility indicated by clumping (agglutination) of red blood cells

Group and Type	Incidence (%)	Alternative Transfusion Group and Type of Packed Cell Units in Order of Preference If Patient's Own Group and Type Not Available
O positive	37.4	O negative
O negative	6.6	O positive*
A positive	35.7	A negative, O positive, O negative
A negative	6.3	O negative, A positive,* O positive*
B positive	8.5	B negative, O positive, O negative
B negative	1.5	O negative, B positive,* O positive*
AB positive	3.4	AB negative, A positive, B positive, A negative, B negative, O positive, O negative
AB negative	0.6	A negative, B negative, O negative, AB positive,* A positive,* B positive,* O positive*

(*table continues on page 268*)

B

Group and Type	Incidence (%)	Alternative Transfusion Group and Type of Packed Cell Units in Order of Preference If Patient's Own Group and Type Not Available
Rh Type		
Rh positive	85–90	
Rh negative	10–15	

*If blood units of exact match to the patient's group and type are not available, a switch in ABO blood group is preferable to a change in Rh type. However, in extreme circumstances, Rh-positive blood can be issued to an Rh-negative recipient. It is very likely that the recipient will develop antibodies as the result of receiving Rh-positive red blood cells. Rh antibodies are highly immunogenic, and, once the antibodies are developed, the recipient can only receive Rh-negative blood for subsequent red blood cell transfusion.

CRITICAL FINDINGS ✦

Note and immediately report to the HCP any signs and symptoms associated with a blood transfusion reaction. Timely notification of critical values for lab or diagnostic studies is a role expectation of the professional nurse. Notification processes will vary among facilities. Upon receipt of the critical value, the information should be read back to the caller to verify accuracy. Most policies require immediate notification of the primary HCP, hospitalist, or on-call HCP. Reported information includes the patient's name, unique identifiers, critical value, name of the person giving the report, and name of the person receiving the report. Documentation of notification should be made in the medical record with the name of the HCP notified, time and date of notification, and any orders received. Any delay in a timely report of a critical value may require completion of a notification form with review by Risk Management.

Signs and symptoms of blood transfusion reaction range from mildly febrile to anaphylactic and may include chills, dyspnea, fever, headache, nausea, vomiting, palpitations and tachycardia, chest or back pain, apprehension, flushing, hives, angio-edema, diarrhea, hypotension, oliguria, hemoglobinuria, renal failure, sepsis, shock, and jaundice. Complications from disseminated intravascular coagulation (DIC) may also occur.

Possible interventions in mildly febrile reactions include slowing the rate of infusion, then verifying and comparing patient identification, transfusion requisition, and blood bag label. The patient should be monitored closely for further development of signs and symptoms. Administration of epinephrine may be ordered.

Possible interventions in a more severe transfusion reaction may include immediate cessation of infusion, notification of the HCP, keeping the IV line open with saline or lactated Ringer's solution, collection of red- and lavender-top tubes for posttransfusion work-up, collection of urine, monitoring vital signs every 5 min, ordering additional testing if DIC is suspected, maintaining patent airway and blood pressure, and administering mannitol. See Appendix D for a more detailed description of transfusion reactions and potential nursing interventions.

INTERFERING FACTORS

• Drugs, including levodopa, methyldopa, methyldopate hydrochloride, and cephalexin, may cause a false-positive result in Rh typing and in antibody screens.

- Recent administration of blood, blood products, dextran, or IV contrast medium causes cellular aggregation resembling agglutination in ABO typing.
- Contrast material such as iodine, barium, and gadolinium may interfere with testing.
- Abnormal proteins, cold agglutinins, and bacteremia may interfere with testing.
- Testing does not detect every antibody and may miss the presence of a weak antibody.
- History of bone marrow transplant, cancer, or leukemia may cause discrepancy in ABO typing.

NURSING IMPLICATIONS AND PROCEDURE

PRETEST:

Positively identify the patient using at least two unique identifiers before providing care, treatment, or services.
Patient Teaching: Inform the patient this test can assist in identification of blood type.

Obtain a history of the patient's complaints, including a list of known allergens, especially allergies or sensitivities to latex.

Obtain a history of the patient's immune and hematopoietic systems, symptoms, and results of previously performed laboratory tests and diagnostic and surgical procedures.

Note any recent or past procedures, especially blood or blood product transfusion or bone marrow transplantation, that could complicate or interfere with test results.

Obtain a list of the patient's current medications including herbs, nutritional supplements, and nutraceuticals (see Appendix F).

Review the procedure with the patient. Inform the patient that specimen collection takes approximately 5 to 10 min. Address concerns about pain

and explain that there may be some discomfort during the venipuncture.
Sensitivity to social and cultural issues, as well as concern for modesty, is important in providing psychological support before, during, and after the procedure.

There are no food, fluid, or medication restrictions unless by medical direction.
Make sure a written and informed consent has been signed prior to any transfusion of ABO- and Rh-compatible blood products.

INTRATEST:

If the patient has a history of allergic reaction to latex, avoid the use of equipment containing latex.

Instruct the patient to cooperate fully and to follow directions. Direct the patient to breathe normally and to avoid unnecessary movement.

Observe standard precautions, and follow the general guidelines in Appendix A. Positively identify the patient, and label the appropriate specimen container with the corresponding patient demographics, initials of the person collecting the specimen, date, and time of collection. Perform a venipuncture.

Although correct patient identification is important for test specimens, it is crucial when blood is collected for type and crossmatch because clerical error is the most frequent cause of life-threatening ABO incompatibility. Therefore, additional requirements are necessary, including the verification of two unique identifiers that could include any two unique patient demographics such as name, date of birth, Social Security number, hospital number, date, or blood bank number on requisition and specimen labels; completing and applying a wristband on the arm with the same information; and placing labels with the same information and blood bank number on blood sample tubes.

Remove the needle and apply direct pressure with dry gauze to stop bleeding. Observe/assess venipuncture site for bleeding or hematoma formation and secure gauze with adhesive bandage.

B

Promptly transport the specimen to the laboratory for processing and analysis.

POST-TEST:

A report of the results will be made available to the requesting HCP, who will discuss the results with the patient.

Inform the patient of ABO blood and Rh type, and advise him or her to record the information on a card or other document routinely carried.

Inform women who are Rh-negative to inform the HCP of their Rh-negative status if they become pregnant or need a transfusion.

Reinforce information given by the patient's HCP regarding further testing, treatment, or referral to another HCP. Answer any questions or address any concerns voiced by the patient or family.

Depending on the results of this procedure, additional testing may be performed to evaluate or monitor progression of the disease process and determine the need for a change in therapy. Evaluate test results in relation to the patient's symptoms and other tests performed.

RELATED MONOGRAPHS:

Related tests include Coomb's antiglobulin, bilirubin, CBC, CBC hematocrit, CBC hemoglobin, CBC platelet count, CBC RBC count, cold agglutinin, FDP, fecal analysis, GI blood loss scan, haptoglobin, IgA, iron, Kleihauer-Betke, laparoscopy abdominal, Meckel's diverticulum scan, and UA.

Refer to Appendix D for further information regarding laboratory studies used in the investigation of transfusion reactions, findings, and potential nursing interventions associated with types of transfusion reactions.

Refer to the Immune and Hematopoietic systems tables at the end of the book for related tests by body system.

Blood Pool Imaging

SYNONYM/ACRONYM: Cardiac blood pool scan, ejection fraction study, gated cardiac scan, radionuclide ventriculogram, wall motion study, MUGA.

COMMON USE: To evaluate cardiac function after a myocardial infarction.

AREA OF APPLICATION: Heart.

CONTRAST: Intravenous radioactive material.

DESCRIPTION: Multigated blood pool imaging (MUGA; also known as *cardiac blood pool scan*) is used to diagnose cardiac abnormalities involving the left ventricle and myocardial wall abnormalities by imaging the blood within the cardiac chamber rather than the myocardium. The ventricular blood pool can be imaged during the initial transit of a peripherally injected, intravenous bolus of radionuclide (first-pass technique) or when the radionuclide has reached equilibrium concentration. The patient's electrocardiogram

(ECG) is synchronized to the gamma camera imager and computer and therefore termed "gated." For multigated studies, technetium-99m (Tc-99m) pertechnetate is injected after an injection of pyrophosphate, allowing the labeling of circulating red blood cells;Tc-99m sulfur colloid is used for first-pass studies. Studies detect abnormalities in heart wall motion at rest or with exercise, ejection fraction, ventricular dilation, stroke volume, and cardiac output. The MUGA procedure, performed with the heart in motion, is used to obtain multiple images of the heart in contraction and relaxation during an R-to-R cardiac cycle. The resulting images can be displayed in a cinematic mode to visualize cardiac function. Repetitive data acquisitions are possible during graded levels of exercise, usually a bicycle ergometer or handgrip, to assess ventricular functional response to exercise.

After the administration of sublingual nitroglycerin, the MUGA scan can evaluate the effectiveness of the drug on ventricular function. Heart shunt imaging is done in conjunction with a resting MUGA scan to obtain ejection fraction and assess regional wall motion.

First-pass cardiac flow study is done to study heart chamber disorders, including left-to-right and right-to-left shunts, determine both right and left ventricular ejection fractions, and assess blood flow through the great vessels. The study uses a jugular or antecubital vein injection of the radionuclide.

INDICATIONS

- Aid in the diagnosis of myocardial infarction
- Aid in the diagnosis of true or false ventricular aneurysms
- Aid in the diagnosis of valvular heart disease and determining the optimal time for valve replacement surgery
- Detect left-to-right shunts and determine pulmonary-to-systemic blood flow ratios, especially in children
- Determine cardiomyopathy
- Determine drug cardiotoxicity to stop therapy before development of congestive heart failure
- Determine ischemic coronary artery disease
- Differentiate between chronic obstructive pulmonary disease and left ventricular failure
- Evaluate ventricular size, function, and wall motion after an acute episode or in chronic heart disease
- Quantitate cardiac output by calculating global or regional ejection fraction

POTENTIAL DIAGNOSIS

Normal findings in
- Normal wall motion, ejection fraction (55% to 65%), coronary blood flow, ventricular size and function, and symmetry in contractions of the left ventricle

Abnormal findings in
- Abnormal wall motion (akinesia or dyskinesia)
- Cardiac hypertrophy
- Cardiac ischemia
- Enlarged left ventricle
- Infarcted areas are akinetic
- Ischemic areas are hypokinetic
- Myocardial infarction

CRITICAL FINDINGS ✦
- Myocardial infarction

It is essential that critical diagnoses be communicated immediately to the appropriate health-care provider (HCP). A listing of these diagnoses varies among facilities. Note and immediately report to the HCP abnormal results and related symptoms. Timely notification of critical values for diagnostic studies is a role expectation of the professional nurse. Notification processes will vary among facilities. Upon receipt of the critical value, the information should be read back to the caller to verify accuracy. Most policies require immediate notification of the primary HCP, hospitalist, or on-call HCP. Reported information includes the patient's name, unique identifiers, critical value, name of the person giving the report, and name of the person receiving the report. Documentation of notification should be made in the medical record with the name of the HCP notified, time and date of notification, and any orders received. Any delay in a timely report of a critical value may require completion of a notification form with review by Risk Management.

INTERFERING FACTORS

This procedure is contraindicated for

• Patients who are pregnant or suspected of being pregnant, unless the potential benefits of the procedure far outweigh the risks to the fetus and mother.
• Dipyridamole testing is not performed in patients with anginal pain at rest or in patients with severe atherosclerotic coronary vessels.
• Chemical stress with vasodilators should not be done to patients having asthma; bronchospasm can occur.

Factors that may impair clear imaging

• Inability of the patient to cooperate or remain still during the procedure because of age, significant pain, or mental status.
• Metallic objects within the examination field (e.g., jewelry, body rings), which may inhibit organ visualization and can produce unclear images.

Other considerations

• Conditions such as chest wall trauma, cardiac trauma, angina that is

difficult to control, significant cardiac arrhythmias, or a recent cardioversion procedure may affect test results.
• Atrial fibrillation and extrasystoles invalidate the procedure.
• Suboptimal cardiac stress or patient exhaustion, preventing maximum heart rate testing, will affect results when the procedure is done in conjunction with exercise testing.
• Consultation with an HCP should occur before the procedure for radiation safety concerns regarding younger patients or patients who are lactating.
• Risks associated with radiation overexposure can result from frequent x-ray or radionuclide procedures. Personnel working in the examination area should wear badges to record their level of radiation.

NURSING IMPLICATIONS AND PROCEDURE

PRETEST:

▶ Positively identify the patient using at least two unique identifiers before providing care, treatment, or services.
▶ *Patient Teaching:* Inform the patient this procedure can assist in assessing the pumping action of the heart.
▶ Obtain a history of the patient's complaints, including a list of known allergens, especially allergies or sensitivities to latex, iodine, seafood, contrast medium, anesthetics, or dyes.
▶ Obtain a history of the patient's cardiovascular system, symptoms, and results of previously performed laboratory tests and diagnostic and surgical procedures.
▶ Note any recent procedures that can interfere with test results, including examinations using iodine-based contrast medium.
▶ Record the date of the last menstrual period and determine the possibility of pregnancy in perimenopausal women.

Obtain a list of the patient's current medications including herbs, nutritional supplements, and nutraceuticals (see Appendix F).

Review the procedure with the patient. Address concerns about pain related to the procedure and explain that some pain may be experienced during the test, or there may be moments of discomfort. Reassure the patient that the radionuclide poses no radioactive hazard and rarely produces side effects. Inform the patient that the procedure is performed in a nuclear medicine department by an HCP specializing in this procedure and takes approximately 60 min.

Sensitivity to social and cultural issues, as well as concern for modesty, is important in providing psychological support before, during, and after the procedure.

Instruct the patient to wear walking shoes for the treadmill or bicycle exercise. Emphasize to the patient the importance of reporting fatigue, pain, or shortness of breath.

Instruct the patient to remove external metallic objects from the area to be examined prior to the procedure.

The patient should fast and restrict fluids for 4 hr prior to the procedure. Instruct the patient to withhold medications for 24 hr before the test as ordered by the HCP. Protocols may vary among facilities.

Make sure a written and informed consent has been signed prior to the procedure and before administering any medications.

Observe standard precautions, and follow the general guidelines in Appendix A. Positively identify the patient.

Ensure that the patient has complied with dietary and medication restrictions.

Ensure that the patient has removed external metallic objects from the area to be examined prior to the procedure.

If the patient has a history of allergic reactions to any substance or drug, administer ordered prophylactic steroids or antihistamines before the procedure.

Have emergency equipment readily available.

Record baseline vital signs and assess neurological status. Protocols may vary among facilities.

Instruct the patient to cooperate fully and to follow directions. Instruct the patient to remain still throughout the procedure because movement produces unreliable results.

The patient is placed at rest in the supine position on the scanning table. Expose the chest and attach the ECG leads. Record baseline readings.

IV radionuclide is administered and the heart is scanned with images taken in various positions over the entire cardiac cycle.

When the scan is to be done under exercise conditions, the patient is assisted onto the treadmill or bicycle ergometer and is exercised to a calculated 80% to 85% of the maximum heart rate as determined by the protocol selected. Images are done at each exercise level and begun immediately after injection of the radionuclide.

If nitroglycerin is given, an HCP assessing the baseline MUGA scan injects the medication. Additional scans are repeated until blood pressure reaches the desired level. Patients who cannot exercise are given dipyridamole before the radionuclide is injected.

Monitor the patient for complications related to the procedure (e.g., allergic reaction, anaphylaxis, bronchospasm).

Remove the needle or catheter and apply a pressure dressing over the puncture site.

Observe/assess the needle/catheter site for bleeding, hematoma formation, or inflammation.

A report of the results will be made available to the requesting HCP, who will discuss the results with the patient.

Unless contraindicated, advise patient to drink increased amounts of fluids for 24 to 48 hr to eliminate the radionuclide from the body. Inform the patient that radionuclide is eliminated from the body within 6 to 24 hr.

- No other radionuclide tests should be scheduled for 24 to 48 hr after this procedure.
- Evaluate the patient's vital signs. Monitor vital signs and neurological status every 15 min for 1 hr, then every 2 hr for 4 hr, and then as ordered by HCP. Monitor intake and output at least every 8 hr. Compare with baseline values. Protocols may vary among facilities.
- Instruct the patient to resume usual dietary, medication, and activity, as directed by the HCP.
- Observe for delayed allergic reactions, such as rash, urticaria, tachycardia, hyperpnea, hypertension, palpitations, nausea, or vomiting.
- Instruct the patient to immediately report symptoms such as fast heart rate, difficulty breathing, skin rash, itching, chest pain, persistent right shoulder pain, or abdominal pain. Immediately report symptoms to the appropriate HCP.
- Monitor ECG tracings and compare with baseline readings until stable.
- Observe/assess the needle/catheter site for bleeding, hematoma formation, or inflammation.
- Instruct the patient in the care and assessment of the injection site.
- If a woman who is breastfeeding must have a nuclear scan, she should not breastfeed the infant until the radionuclide has been eliminated. This could take as long as 3 days. She should be instructed to express the milk and discard it during the 3-day period to prevent cessation of milk production.
- Instruct the patient to immediately flush the toilet and to meticulously wash hands with soap and water after each voiding for 24 hr after the procedure.
- Instruct all caregivers to wear gloves when discarding urine for 24 hr after the procedure. Wash gloved hands with soap and water before removing gloves. Then wash hands after the gloves are removed.
- *Nutritional Considerations:* Abnormal findings may be associated with cardiovascular disease. The American Heart Association and National Heart, Lung, and Blood Institute (NHLBI) recommend nutritional therapy for individuals

identified to be at high risk for developing coronary artery disease (CAD) or individuals who have specific risk factors and/or existing medical conditions (e.g., elevated low-density lipoprotein [LDL] cholesterol levels, other lipid disorders, insulin-dependent diabetes, insulin resistance, or metabolic syndrome). If overweight, the patient should be encouraged to achieve a normal weight. Guidelines for the Therapeutic Lifestyle Changes (TLC) diet are outlined in the Third Report of the Expert Panel on Detection, Evaluation, and Treatment of High Blood Cholesterol in Adults (Adult Treatment Panel III [ATP III]). The TLC diet emphasizes a reduction in foods high in saturated fats and cholesterol. Red meats, eggs, and dairy products are the major sources of saturated fats and cholesterol. If triglycerides also are elevated, the patient should be advised to eliminate or reduce alcohol and simple carbohydrates from the diet. The TLC approach also includes the use of plant stanols or sterols and increased dissolved fiber as an option for lowering LDL cholesterol levels; nutritional recommendations for daily total caloric intake; recommendations for allowable percentage of calories derived from fat (saturated and unsaturated), carbohydrates, protein, and cholesterol; as well as recommendations for daily expenditure of energy.

- *Nutritional Considerations:* Overweight patients with high blood pressure should be encouraged to achieve a normal weight. Other changeable risk factors warranting patient education include strategies to safely decrease sodium intake, increase physical activity, decrease alcohol consumption, eliminate tobacco use, and decrease cholesterol levels.
- *Social and Cultural Considerations:* Numerous studies point to the prevalence of excess body weight in American children and adolescents. Experts estimate that obesity is present in 25% of the population ages 6 to 11 yr. The medical, social, and emotional consequences of excess body weight are significant. Special attention should be given to instructing the child and

caregiver regarding health risks and weight control education.

Recognize anxiety related to test results, and be supportive of fear of shortened life expectancy. Discuss the implications of abnormal test results on the patient's lifestyle. Provide teaching and information regarding the clinical implications of the test results, as appropriate. Educate the patient regarding access to counseling services. Provide contact information, if desired, for the American Heart Association (www.americanheart.org) or the NHLBI (www.nhlbi.nih.gov).

Recognize anxiety related to test results, and be supportive of perceived loss of independent function. Discuss the implications of abnormal test results on the patient's lifestyle. Provide teaching and information regarding the clinical implications of the test results, as appropriate.

Reinforce information given by the patient's HCP regarding further testing, treatment, or referral to another HCP. Answer any questions or address any concerns voiced by the patient or family.

Depending on the results of this procedure, additional testing may be needed to evaluate and determine the need for a change in therapy or progression of the disease process. Evaluate test results in relation to the patient's symptoms and other tests performed.

RELATED MONOGRAPHS:

Related tests include antiarrhythmic drugs, apolipoprotein A and B, AST, ANP, blood gases, BNP, calcium, ionized calcium, cholesterol (total, HDL, and LDL), CRP, CT cardiac scoring, CK and isoenzymes, culture viral, echocardiography, echocardiography transesophageal, ECG, exercise stress test, glucose, glycated hemoglobin, Holter monitor, homocysteine, ketones, LDH and isoenzymes, lipoprotein electrophoresis, magnesium, MRI chest, MI infarct scan, myocardial perfusion heart scan, myoglobin, pericardial fluid analysis, PET heart scan, potassium, triglycerides, and troponin.

Refer to the Cardiovascular System table at the end of the book for related tests by body system.

Bone Mineral Densitometry

SYNONYM/ACRONYM: DEXA, DXA, SXA, QCT, RA, ultrasound densitometry.

Dual-energy x-ray absorptiometry (DEXA, DXA): Two x-rays of different energy levels measure bone mineral density and predict risk of fracture.

Single-energy x-ray absorptiometry (SXA): A single-energy x-ray measures bone density at peripheral sites.

Quantitative computed tomography (QCT): QCT is used to examine the lumbar vertebrae. It measures trabecular and cortical bone density. Results are compared to a known standard. This test is the most expensive and involves the highest radiation dose of all techniques.

Radiographic absorptiometry (RA): A standard x-ray of the hand. Results are compared to a known standard.

Ultrasound densitometry: Studies bone mineral content in peripheral densitometry sites such as the heel or wrist. It is not as precise as x-ray techniques but is less expensive than other techniques.

COMMON USE: To evaluate bone density related to osteoporosis.

AREA OF APPLICATION: Lumbar spine, heel, hip, wrist, whole body.

CONTRAST: None.

B

DESCRIPTION: Bone mineral density (BMD) can be measured at any of several body sites, including the spine, hip, wrist, and heel. Machines to measure BMD include computed tomography (CT), radiographic absorptiometry, ultrasound, SXA, and most commonly, DEXA. The radiation exposure from SXA and DEXA machines is approximately one-tenth that of a standard chest x-ray.

The BMD values measured by the various techniques cannot be directly compared. Therefore, they are stated in terms of standard deviation (SD) units. The patient's T-score is the number of SD units above or below the average BMD in young adults. A Z-score is the number of SD units above or below the average value for a person of the same age as the measured patient. For most BMD readings, 1 SD is equivalent to 10% to 12% of the average young-normal BMD value. A T-score of −2.5 is therefore equivalent to a bone mineral loss of 30% when compared to a young adult.

INDICATIONS

Osteoporosis is a condition characterized by low BMD, which results in increased risk of fracture. The National Osteoporosis Foundation estimates that 4 to 6 million postmenopausal women in the United States have osteoporosis, and an additional 13 to 17 million (30% to 50%) have low bone density at the hip. It is estimated that one of every two women will experience a fracture as a result of low bone mineral content in her lifetime. The measurement of BMD gives the best indication of risk for a fracture. The lower the BMD, the greater the risk of fracture. The most common fractures are those of the hip, vertebrae, and distal forearm. Bone mineral loss is a disease of the entire skeleton and not restricted to the areas listed. The effect of the fractures has a wide range, from complete recovery to chronic pain, disability, and possible death.

- Determine the mineral content of bone
- Determine a possible cause of amenorrhea
- Establish a diagnosis of osteoporosis
- Estimate the actual fracture risk compared to young adults
- Evaluate bone demineralization associated with chronic renal failure
- Evaluate bone demineralization associated with immobilization
- Monitor changes in BMD due to medical problems or therapeutic intervention
- Predict future fracture risk

POTENTIAL DIAGNOSIS

Normal findings in
- Normal bone mass with T-score value not less than −1.

Abnormal findings in
- Osteoporosis is defined as T-score value less than −2.5.
- Low bone mass or osteopenia has T-scores from −1 to −2.5.
- Fracture risk increases as BMD declines from young-normal levels (low T-scores).
- Low Z-scores in older adults can be misleading because low BMD is very common.

• Z-scores estimate fracture risk compared to others of the same age (versus young-normal adults).

CRITICAL FINDINGS: N/A

INTERFERING FACTORS (or factors associated with increased risk of osteoporosis)

This procedure is contraindicated for
• Patients who are pregnant or suspected of being pregnant, unless the potential benefits of the procedure far outweigh the risks to the fetus and mother.

Factors that may impair clear imaging
• Inability of the patient to cooperate or remain still during the procedure because of age, significant pain, or mental status.
• Metallic objects within the examination field (e.g., jewelry, earrings, and/or dental amalgams), which may inhibit organ visualization and can produce unclear images.

Other considerations
• The use of anticonvulsant drugs, cytotoxic drugs, tamoxifen, glucocorticoids, lithium, or heparin, as well as increased alcohol intake, increased aluminum levels, excessive thyroxin, renal dialysis, or smoking, may affect the test results by either increasing or decreasing the bone mineral content.
• Consultation with a health-care provider (HCP) should occur before the procedure for radiation safety concerns regarding younger patients or patients who are lactating.
• Risks associated with radiation overexposure can result from frequent x-ray or radionuclide procedures. Personnel in the room with the patient should stand behind a shield, or leave the area while the examination is being done. Personnel working in the examination area should wear badges to record their radiation exposure level.

Other considerations as a result of altered BMD, not the BMD testing process
• Vertebral fractures may cause complications including back pain, height loss, and kyphosis.
• Limited activity, including difficulty bending and reaching, may result.
• Patient may have poor self-esteem resulting from the cosmetic effects of kyphosis.
• Potential restricted lung function may result from fractures.
• Fractures may alter abdominal anatomy, resulting in constipation, pain, distention, and diminished appetite.
• Potential for a restricted lifestyle may result in depression and other psychological symptoms.
• Possible increased dependency on family for basic care may occur.

NURSING IMPLICATIONS AND PROCEDURE

PRETEST:

▶ Positively identify the patient using at least two unique identifiers before providing care, treatment, or services.
▶ *Patient Teaching:* Inform the patient this procedure can assist in assessing bone density.
▶ Obtain a history of the patient's complaints, including a list of known allergens, especially allergies or sensitivities to latex, iodine, seafood, contrast medium, anesthetics, or dyes.
▶ Obtain a history of the patient's musculoskeletal system, symptoms, and results of previously performed laboratory tests and diagnostic and surgical procedures

B

▶ Note any recent procedures that can interfere with test results, including examinations using iodine-based contrast medium.

▶ Record the date of the last menstrual period and determine the possibility of pregnancy in perimenopausal women.

▶ Obtain a list of the patient's current medications, including herbs, nutritional supplements, and nutraceuticals (see Appendix F).

▶ Review the procedure with the patient. Address concerns about pain related to the procedure and explain that some pain may be experienced during the test, or there may be moments of discomfort. Inform the patient that the procedure is usually performed in a radiology department by a HCP, and staff, specializing in this procedure and takes approximately 60 min.

▶ Instruct the patient to remove jewelry and other metallic objects from the area to be examined.

▶ There are no food, fluid, or medication restrictions unless by medical direction.

▶ *Sensitivity to social and cultural issues,* as well as concern for modesty, is important in providing psychological support before, during, and after the procedure.

INTRATEST:

▶ Observe standard precautions, and follow the general guidelines in Appendix A. Positively identify the patient.

▶ Ensure that the patient has removed all external metallic objects from the area to be examined prior to the procedure.

▶ Instruct the patient to void prior to the procedure and to change into the gown, robe, and foot coverings provided. Patient's clothing may not need to be removed unless it contains metal that would interfere with the test.

▶ Instruct the patient to cooperate fully and to follow directions. Instruct the

patient to remain still throughout the procedure because movement produces unreliable results.

▶ Place the patient in a supine position on a flat table with foam wedges, which help maintain position and immobilization.

POST-TEST:

▶ A report of the results will be made available to the requesting HCP, who will discuss the results with the patient.

▶ Recognize anxiety related to test results, and be supportive of perceived loss of independent function. Discuss the implications of abnormal test results on the patient's lifestyle. Provide teaching and information regarding the clinical implications of the test results, as appropriate.

▶ Reinforce information given by the patient's HCP regarding further testing, treatment, or referral to another HCP. Answer any questions or address any concerns voiced by the patient or family.

▶ Depending on the results of this procedure, additional testing may be needed to evaluate or monitor progression of the disease process and determine the need for a change in therapy. Evaluate test results in relation to the patient's symptoms, previous BMD values, and other tests performed.

RELATED MONOGRAPHS:

▶ Related tests include ALP, antibodies anticyclic citrullinated peptide, ANA, arthrogram, arthroscopy, biopsy bone, bone scan, calcium, CRP, collagen cross-linked telopeptides, CT pelvis, CT spine, ESR, MRI musculoskeletal, MRI pelvis, osteocalcin, PTH, phosphorus, radiography bone, RF, synovial fluid analysis, and vitamin D.

▶ Refer to the Musculoskeletal System table at the end of the book for related tests by body system.

Bone Scan

SYNONYM/ACRONYM: Bone imaging, radionuclide bone scan, bone scintigraphy, whole-body bone scan.

COMMON USE: To assist in diagnosing bone disease such as cancer or other degenerative bone disorders.

AREA OF APPLICATION: Bone/skeleton.

CONTRAST: Intravenous radioactive material (diphosphonate compounds), usually combined with technetium-99m.

DESCRIPTION: This nuclear medicine scan assists in diagnosing and determining the extent of primary and metastatic bone disease and bone trauma and monitors the progression of degenerative disorders. Abnormalities are identified by scanning 1 to 3 hr after the intravenous injection of a radionuclide such as technetium-99m methylene diphosphonate. Areas of increased uptake and activity on the bone scan represent abnormalities unless they occur in normal areas of increased activity, such as the sternum, sacroiliac, clavicle, and scapular joints in adults, and growth centers and cranial sutures in children. The radionuclide mimics calcium physiologically and therefore localizes in bone with an intensity proportional to the degree of metabolic activity. Gallium, magnetic resonance imaging (MRI), or white blood cell scanning can follow a bone scan to obtain a more sensitive study if acute inflammatory conditions such as osteomyelitis or septic arthritis are suspected. In addition, bone scan can detect fractures in patients who continue to have pain even though x-rays have proved negative. A gamma camera detects the radiation emitted from the injected radioactive material. Whole-body or representative images of the skeletal system can be obtained.

INDICATIONS
- Aid in the diagnosis of benign tumors or cysts
- Aid in the diagnosis of metabolic bone diseases
- Aid in the diagnosis of osteomyelitis
- Aid in the diagnosis of primary malignant bone tumors (e.g., osteogenic sarcoma, chondrosarcoma, Ewing's sarcoma, metastatic malignant tumors)
- Aid in the detection of traumatic or stress fractures
- Assess degenerative joint changes or acute septic arthritis
- Assess suspected child abuse
- Confirm temporomandibular joint derangement
- Detect Legg-Calvé-Perthes disease
- Determine the cause of unexplained bone or joint pain
- Evaluate the healing process following fracture, especially if an underlying bone disease is present

B

- Evaluate prosthetic joints for infection, loosening, dislocation, or breakage
- Evaluate tumor response to radiation or chemotherapy
- Identify appropriate site for bone biopsy, lesion excision, or débridement

POTENTIAL DIAGNOSIS

Normal findings in
- No abnormalities, as indicated by homogeneous and symmetric distribution of the radionuclide throughout all skeletal structures

Abnormal findings in
- Bone necrosis
- Degenerative arthritis
- Fracture
- Legg-Calvé-Perthes disease
- Metastatic bone neoplasm
- Osteomyelitis
- Paget's disease
- Primary metastatic bone tumors
- Renal osteodystrophy
- Rheumatoid arthritis

CRITICAL FINDINGS: N/A

INTERFERING FACTORS

This procedure is contraindicated for
- Patients who are pregnant or suspected of being pregnant, unless the potential benefits of the procedure far outweigh the risks to the fetus and mother.

Factors that may impair clear imaging
- Inability of the patient to cooperate or remain still during the procedure because of age, significant pain, or mental status.
- Metallic objects within the examination field (e.g., jewelry, earrings, and/or dental amalgams), which may inhibit organ visualization and can produce unclear images.

- Retained barium from a previous radiological procedure may affect the image.
- A distended bladder may obscure pelvic detail.
- Other nuclear scans done within the previous 24 to 48 hr may alter image.

Other considerations
- The existence of multiple myeloma or thyroid cancer can result in a false-negative scan for bone abnormalities.
- Improper injection of the radionuclide may allow the tracer to seep deep into the muscle tissue, producing erroneous hot spots.
- Consultation with a health-care provider (HCP) should occur before the procedure for radiation safety concerns regarding younger patients or patients who are lactating.
- Risks associated with radiation overexposure can result from frequent x-ray or radionuclide procedures. Personnel working in the examination area should wear badges to record their level of radiation exposure.

NURSING IMPLICATIONS AND PROCEDURE

PRETEST:
- Positively identify the patient using at least two unique identifiers before providing care, treatment, or services.
- *Patient Teaching:* Inform the patient this procedure can assist in identification of bone disease before it can be detected with plain x-ray images.
- Obtain a history of the patient's complaints, including a list of known allergens, especially allergies or sensitivities to latex, iodine, seafood, contrast medium, anesthetics, or dyes.
- Obtain a history of results of the patient's musculoskeletal systems, symptoms, and results of previously performed laboratory tests and diagnostic and surgical procedures.

- Note any recent procedures that can interfere with test results, including examinations using iodine-based contrast medium.
- Record the date of the last menstrual period and determine the possibility of pregnancy in perimenopausal women.
- Obtain a list of the patient's current medications, including herbs, nutritional supplements, and nutraceuticals (see Appendix F).
- Review the procedure with the patient. Address concerns about pain related to the procedure and explain to the patient that some pain may be experienced during the test, or there may be moments of discomfort. Reassure the patient that the radionuclide poses no radioactive hazard and rarely produces side effects. Inform the patient the procedure is performed in a nuclear medicine department by an HCP specializing in this procedure, and takes approximately 30 to 60 min.
- *Sensitivity to social and cultural issues,* as well as concern for modesty, is important in providing psychological support before, during, and after the procedure.
- There are no food, fluid, or medication restrictions unless by medical direction.
- Instruct the patient to remove jewelry and other metallic objects in the area to be examined.
- *Make sure a written and informed consent has been signed prior to the procedure and before administering any medications.*

INTRATEST:

- Observe standard precautions, and follow the general guidelines in Appendix A. Positively identify the patient.
- Ensure that the patient has removed all external metallic objects from the area to be examined prior to the procedure.
- If the patient has a history of allergic reactions to any substance or drug, administer ordered prophylactic steroids or antihistamines before the procedure.
- Have emergency equipment readily available.
- Instruct the patient to void prior to the procedure and to change into the gown, robe, and foot coverings provided.

- Instruct the patient to cooperate fully and to follow directions. Instruct the patient to remain still throughout the procedure because movement produces unreliable results.
- Administer sedative to a child or to an uncooperative adult, as ordered.
- Place the patient in a supine position on a flat table with foam wedges to help maintain position and immobilization.
- IV radionuclide is administered and images are taken immediately to assess blood flow to the bones.
- After a delay of 2 to 3 hr to allow the radionuclide to be taken up by the bones, multiple images are obtained over the complete skeleton. Delayed views may be taken up to 24 hr after the injection.
- The needle or catheter is removed, and a pressure dressing is applied over the puncture site.
- Observe/assess the needle/catheter insertion site for bleeding, inflammation, or hematoma formation.
- The patient may be imaged by single-photon emission computed tomography (SPECT) techniques to further clarify areas of suspicious radionuclide localization.

POST-TEST:

- A report of the results will be made available to the requesting HCP, who will discuss the results with the patient.
- Unless contraindicated, advise patient to drink increased amounts of fluids for 24 to 48 hr to eliminate the radionuclide from the body. Inform the patient that radionuclide is eliminated from the body within 6 to 24 hr.
- No other radionuclide tests should be scheduled for 24 to 48 hr after this procedure.
- Instruct the patient to resume medication and activity as directed by the HCP.
- Observe/assess the needle/catheter insertion site for bleeding, inflammation, or hematoma formation.
- Instruct the patient in the care and assessment of the injection site.
- If a woman who is breastfeeding must have a nuclear scan, she should not breastfeed the infant until the radionuclide has been eliminated. This could

B

take as long as 3 days. She should be instructed to express the milk and discard it during the 3-day period to prevent cessation of milk production.

Instruct the patient to immediately flush the toilet and to meticulously wash hands with soap and water after each voiding for 24 hr after the procedure.

Instruct all caregivers to wear gloves when discarding urine for 24 hr after the procedure. Wash gloved hands with soap and water before removing gloves. Then wash ungloved hands after the gloves are removed.

Recognize anxiety related to test results, and be supportive of perceived loss of independent function. Discuss the implications of abnormal test results on the patient's lifestyle. Provide teaching and information regarding the clinical implications of the test results, as appropriate. Provide contact information, if desired, for the American College of Rheumatology (www.rheumatology.org) or for the Arthritis Foundation (www.arthritis.org).

Reinforce information given by the patient's HCP regarding further testing, treatment, or referral to another HCP. Answer any questions or address any concerns voiced by the patient or family.

Depending on the results of this procedure, additional testing may be needed to evaluate or monitor progression of the disease process and determine the need for a change in therapy. Evaluate test results in relation to the patient's symptoms and other tests performed.

RELATED MONOGRAPHS:

Related tests include antibodies, anti-cyclic citrullinated peptide, ANA, arthroscopy, BMD, calcium, CRP, collagen cross-linked telopeptide, CT pelvis, CT spine, culture blood, ESR, MRI musculoskeletal, MRI pelvis, osteocalcin, radiography bone, RF, synovial fluid analysis, and white blood cell scan.

Refer to the Musculoskeletal System table at the end of the book for related tests by body system.

Bronchoscopy

SYNONYM/ACRONYM: Flexible bronchoscopy.

COMMON USE: To visualize and assess bronchial structure for disease such as cancer and infection.

AREA OF APPLICATION: Bronchial tree, larynx, trachea.

CONTRAST: None.

DESCRIPTION: This procedure provides direct visualization of the larynx, trachea, and bronchial tree by means of either a rigid or a flexible bronchoscope. A fiber-optic bronchoscope with a light incorporated is guided into the tracheobronchial tree. A local anesthetic may be used to allow the scope to be inserted through the mouth or nose into the trachea and into the bronchi. The patient must breathe during insertion and with the scope in place. The purpose of the procedure is both diagnostic and therapeutic.

The rigid bronchoscope allows visualization of the larger

airways, including the lobar, segmental, and subsegmental bronchi, while maintaining effective gas exchange. Rigid bronchoscopy is preferred when large volumes of blood or secretions need to be aspirated, foreign bodies are to be removed, large-sized biopsy specimens are to be obtained, and for most bronchoscopies in children.

The flexible fiberoptic bronchoscope has a smaller lumen that is designed to allow for visualization of all segments of the bronchial tree. The accessory lumen of the bronchoscope is used for tissue biopsy, bronchial washings, instillation of anesthetic agents and medications, and to obtain specimens with brushes for cytological examination. In general, fiberoptic bronchoscopy is less traumatic to the surrounding tissues than the larger rigid bronchoscopes. Fiberoptic bronchoscopy is performed under local anesthesia; patient tolerance is better for fiber-optic bronchoscopy than for rigid bronchoscopy.

INDICATIONS

• Detect end-stage bronchogenic cancer
• Detect lung infections and inflammation
• Determine etiology of persistent cough, hemoptysis, hoarseness, unexplained chest x-ray abnormalities, and/or abnormal cytological findings in sputum
• Determine extent of smoke-inhalation or other traumatic injury
• Evaluate airway patency; aspirate deep or retained secretions
• Evaluate endotracheal tube placement or possible adverse sequelae to tube placement
• Evaluate possible airway obstruction in patients with known or suspected sleep apnea
• Evaluate respiratory distress and tachypnea in an infant to rule out tracheoesophageal fistula or other congenital anomaly
• Identify bleeding sites and remove clots within the tracheobronchial tree
• Identify hemorrhagic and inflammatory changes in Kaposi's sarcoma
• Intubate patients with cervical spine injuries or massive upper airway edema
• Remove foreign body
• Treat lung cancer through instillation of chemotherapeutic agents, implantation of radioisotopes, or laser palliative therapy

POTENTIAL DIAGNOSIS

Normal findings in
• Normal larynx, trachea, bronchi, bronchioles, and alveoli

Abnormal findings in
• Abscess
• Bronchial diverticulum
• Bronchial stenosis
• Bronchogenic cancer
• Coccidioidomycosis, histoplasmosis, blastomycosis, phycomycosis
• Foreign bodies
• Inflammation
• Interstitial pulmonary disease
• Opportunistic lung infections (e.g., pneumocystitis, nocardia, cytomegalovirus)
• Strictures
• Tuberculosis
• Tumors

CRITICAL FINDINGS: N/A

INTERFERING FACTORS

This procedure is contraindicated for
• Patients with bleeding disorders, especially those associated with uremia and cytotoxic chemotherapy.

- Patients with pulmonary hypertension.
- Patients with cardiac conditions or dysrhythmias.
- Patients with disorders that limit extension of the neck.
- Patients with severe obstructive tracheal conditions.
- Patients with or having the potential for respiratory failure; introduction of the bronchoscope alone may cause a 10 to 20 mm Hg drop in Pao_2.

Factors that may impair the results of the examination

- Inability of the patient to cooperate or remain still during the procedure because of age, significant pain, or mental status.
- Metallic objects within the examination field (e.g., jewelry, earrings, and/or dental amalgams), which may inhibit organ visualization and can produce unclear images.

Other considerations

- Hypoxemic or hypercapnic states require continuous oxygen administration.
- Failure to follow dietary restrictions before the procedure may cause the procedure to be canceled or repeated.

NURSING IMPLICATIONS AND PROCEDURE

PRETEST:

▸ Positively identify the patient using at least two unique identifiers before providing care, treatment, or services.

▸ *Patient Teaching:* Inform the patient this procedure can assess the lungs and respiratory system.

▸ Obtain a history of the patient's complaints or symptoms, including a list of known allergens, especially allergies or sensitivities to latex, iodine, seafood, contrast medium, and anesthetics.

▸ Obtain a history of the patient's immune and respiratory systems, symptoms, and results of previously performed laboratory tests and diagnostic and surgical procedures.

▸ Note any recent procedures that can interfere with test results. Ensure that this procedure is performed before an upper gastrointestinal study or barium swallow.

▸ Record the date of the last menstrual period and determine the possibility of pregnancy in perimenopausal women.

▸ Obtain a list of the patient's current medications including anticoagulants, aspirin and other salicylates, herbs, nutritional supplements, and nutraceuticals (see Appendix F). Such products should be discontinued by medical direction for the appropriate number of days prior to a surgical procedure. Note the last time and dose of medication taken.

▸ Review the procedure with the patient. Instruct that prophylactic antibiotics may be administered prior to the procedure. Address concerns about pain related to the procedure and explain that some pain may be experienced during the test, and there may be moments of discomfort. Explain that a sedative and/or analgesia may be administered to promote relaxation and reduce discomfort prior to the bronchoscopy. Atropine is usually given before bronchoscopy examinations to reduce bronchial secretions and prevent vagally induced bradycardia. Meperidine (Demerol) or morphine may be given as a sedative. Lidocaine is sprayed in the patient's throat to reduce discomfort caused by the presence of the tube. Inform the patient that the procedure is performed in a gastrointestinal laboratory or radiology department, under sterile conditions, by a health-care provider (HCP) specializing in this procedure. The procedure usually takes about 30 to 60 min to complete.

▸ *Sensitivity to social and cultural issues,* as well as concern for modesty, is important in providing psychological

support before, during, and after the procedure.

- Explain that an IV line will be inserted to allow infusion of IV fluids, antibiotics, anesthetics, and analgesics.
- The patient should fast and restrict fluids for 8 hr prior to the procedure. Instruct the patient to avoid taking anticoagulant medication or to reduce dosage as ordered prior to the procedure. Number of days to withhold medication is dependent on the type of anticoagulant. Protocols may vary among facilities.
- *Make sure a written and informed consent has been signed prior to the procedure and before administering any medications.*

INTRATEST:

- Ensure that the patient has complied with food, fluid, and medication restrictions for 8 hr prior to the procedure.
- Ensure that the patient has removed dentures, jewelry, and external metallic objects in the area to be examined prior to the procedure.
- Have emergency equipment readily available.
- Instruct the patient to void prior to the procedure and change into the gown, robe, and foot coverings provided.
- Avoid using morphine sulfate in those with asthma or other pulmonary disease. This drug can further exacerbate bronchospasms and respiratory impairment.
- Observe standard precautions, and follow the general guidelines in Appendix A. Positively identify the patient, and label the appropriate specimen container with the corresponding patient demographics, initials of the person collecting the specimen, date and time of collection, and site location, especially right or left lung.
- Assist the patient to a comfortable position, and direct the patient to breathe normally during the beginning of the general anesthesia. Instruct the patient to cooperate fully and to follow directions. Direct the patient to breathe normally and to avoid unnecessary movement during the local anesthetic and the procedure.

- Record baseline vital signs and continue to monitor throughout the procedure. Protocols may vary among facilities.

Rigid Bronchoscopy

- The patient is placed in the supine position and a general anesthetic is administered. The patient's neck is hyperextended, and the lightly lubricated bronchoscope is inserted orally and passed through the glottis. The patient's head is turned or repositioned to aid visualization of various segments.
- After inspection, the bronchial brush, suction catheter, biopsy forceps, laser, and electrocautery devices are introduced to obtain specimens for cytological or microbiological study or for therapeutic procedures.
- If a bronchial washing is performed, small amounts of solution are instilled into the airways and removed.
- After the procedure, the bronchoscope is removed and the patient is placed in a side-lying position with the head slightly elevated to promote recovery.

Fiberoptic Bronchoscopy

- Provide mouth care to reduce oral bacterial flora.
- The patient is placed in a sitting position while the tongue and oropharynx are sprayed or swabbed with local anesthetic. Provide an emesis basin for the increased saliva and encourage the patient to spit out the saliva because the gag reflex may be impaired. When loss of sensation is adequate, the patient is placed in a supine or side-lying position. The fiberoptic scope can be introduced through the nose, the mouth, an endotracheal tube, a tracheostomy tube, or a rigid bronchoscope. Most common insertion is through the nose. Patients with copious secretions or massive hemoptysis, or in whom airway complications are more likely, may be intubated before the bronchoscopy. Additional local anesthetic is applied through the scope as it approaches the vocal cords and the carina, eliminating reflexes in these sensitive areas. The fiberoptic approach allows visualization of airway segments without having to move the patient's head through various positions.

After visual inspection of the lungs, tissue samples are collected from suspicious sites by bronchial brush or biopsy forceps to be used for cytological and microbiological studies. After the procedure, the bronchoscope is removed. Patients who had local anesthesia are placed in a semi-Fowler's position to recover.

General

Monitor the patient for complications related to the procedure (e.g., allergic reaction, anaphylaxis).

Place tissue samples in properly labeled specimen containers containing formalin solution, and promptly transport the specimen to the laboratory for processing and analysis.

POST-TEST:

A report of the results will be made available to the requesting HCP, who will discuss the results with the patient.

Instruct the patient to resume preoperative diet, as directed by the HCP. Assess the patient's ability to swallow before allowing the patient to attempt liquids or solid foods.

Inform the patient that he or she may experience some throat soreness and hoarseness. Instruct patient to treat throat discomfort with lozenges and warm gargles when the gag reflex returns.

Monitor vital signs and neurological status every 15 min for 1 hr, then every 2 hr for 4 hr, and then as ordered by the HCP. Monitor temperature every 4 hr for 24 hr. Monitor intake and output at least every 8 hr. Compare with baseline values. Notify the HCP if temperature changes. Protocols may vary among facilities.

Emergency resuscitation equipment should be readily available if the vocal cords become spastic after intubation.

Observe for delayed allergic reactions, such as rash, urticaria, tachycardia, hyperpnea, hypertension, palpitations, nausea, or vomiting.

Observe the patient for hemoptysis, difficulty breathing, cough, air hunger, excessive coughing, pain, or absent breathing sounds over the affected area. Immediately report symptoms to the appropriate HCP.

Evaluate the patient for symptoms indicating the development of pneumothorax, such as dyspnea, tachypnea, anxiety, decreased breathing sounds, or restlessness. A chest x-ray may be ordered to check for the presence of this complication.

Evaluate the patient for symptoms of empyema, such as fever, tachycardia, malaise, or elevated white blood cell count.

Observe the patient's sputum for blood if a biopsy was taken, because large amounts of blood may indicate the development of a problem; a small amount of streaking is expected. Evaluate the patient for signs of bleeding such as tachycardia, hypotension, or restlessness.

Assess for nausea and pain. Administer antiemetic and analgesic medications as needed and as directed by the HCP.

Administer antibiotic therapy if ordered. Remind the patient of the importance of completing the entire course of antibiotic therapy even if signs and symptoms disappear before completion of therapy.

Recognize anxiety related to test results. Discuss the implications of abnormal test results on the patient's lifestyle. Provide teaching and information regarding the clinical implications of the test results, as appropriate. Educate the patient regarding access to counseling services.

Instruct the patient to use lozenges or gargle for throat discomfort. Inform the patient of smoking cessation programs as appropriate. Malnutrition is commonly seen in patients with severe respiratory disease for numerous reasons, including fatigue, lack of appetite, and gastrointestinal distress. Adequate intake of vitamins A and C is also important to prevent pulmonary infection and to decrease the extent of lung tissue damage. The importance of following the prescribed diet should be stressed to the patient/caregiver. Educate the patient regarding access to counseling services, as appropriate.

Reinforce information given by the patient's HCP regarding further testing, treatment, or referral to another HCP.

Answer any questions or address any concerns voiced by the patient or family. Depending on the results of this procedure, additional testing may be needed to evaluate or monitor progression of the disease process and determine the need for a change in therapy. Evaluate test results in relation to the patient's symptoms and other tests performed.

RELATED MONOGRAPHS:

Related tests include arterial/alveolar oxygen ratio, antibodies, anti-glomerular basement membrane, biopsy lung, blood gases, chest x-ray, complete blood count, CT thorax, culture and smear mycobacteria, culture sputum, culture viral, cytology sputum, Gram stain, lung perfusion scan, lung ventilation scan, MRI chest, mediastinoscopy, and pulse oximetry.

▶ Refer to the Immune and Respiratory systems tables at the end of the book for related tests by body system.

B-Type Natriuretic Peptide and Pro-B-Type Natriuretic Peptide

SYNONYM/ACRONYM: BNP and proBNP.

COMMON USE: To assist in diagnosing congestive heart failure.

SPECIMEN: Plasma (1 mL) collected in a plastic, lavender-top (EDTA) tube.

NORMAL FINDINGS: (Method: Chemiluminescent immunoassay for BNP; electrochemiluminescent immunoassay for proBNP).

BNP	Conventional Units	SI Units (Conventional Units × 1)
Male & Female proBNP (N-terminal)	Less than 100 pg/mL	Less than 100 ng/L
0–74 yr	Less than 125 pg/mL	Less than 125 ng/mL
Greater than 75 yr	Less than 449 pg/mL	Less than 449 ng/mL

BNP levels are increased in elderly adults.

Two primary systems are used to classify heart failure (HF) presentation by stage or class. The American College of Cardiology and American Heart Association (ACC/AHA) collaborated to develop a staging system focused on the development and progression of HF based on symptoms. The ACC/AHA is unique in that it includes pre-heart failure as the initial stage. The New York Heart Association (NYHA) Functional Classification System focuses on classification of HF based on activity tolerance.

B

ACC/AHA	NYHA
Stage A—at risk for developing heart failure; at-risk groups are people with diabetics, coronary artery disease, hypertension; no structural heart disease; no symptoms of HF	Class I—participates in ordinary physical activity; no undue fatigue, dyspnea, or angina
Stage B—some structural changes; no symptoms of HF; at-risk groups are those with history of myocardial infarction, valve regurgitation, ventricular hypertrophy	Class II—slight limitation of activity; asymptomatic at rest; ordinary physical activity causes dyspnea, fatigue, palpations, and angina
Stage C—structural changes are noted; HF symptoms are noted	Class III—marked limitation of physical activity; asymptomatic at rest; less than ordinary activity causes fatigue, dyspnea, palpations, and angina
Stage D—refractory HF present; requires mechanical or pharmaceutical support; may require a heart transplant; may require end-of-life counseling	Class IV—cannot perform any activity without discomfort; symptoms present at rest; discomfort increases with any activity; may require heart transplant, mechanical or pharmaceutical support; may require end-of-life counseling

DESCRIPTION: The peptides B-type natriuretic peptide (BNP) and atrial natriuretic peptide (ANP) are antagonists of the renin-angiotensin-aldosterone system, which assist in the regulation of electrolytes, fluid balance, and blood pressure. BNP, proBNP, and ANP are useful markers in the diagnosis of congestive heart failure (CHF). BNP or brain natriuretic peptide, first isolated in the brain of pigs, is a neurohormone synthesized primarily in the ventricles of the human heart in response to increases in ventricular pressure and volume. Circulating levels of BNP and proBNP increase in proportion to the severity of heart failure. A rapid BNP point-of-care immunoassay may be performed, in which a venous blood sample is collected, placed on a strip, and inserted into a device that measures BNP. Results are completed in 10 to 15 min.

INDICATIONS
- Assist in determining the prognosis and therapy of patients with heart failure
- Assist in the diagnosis of heart failure
- Assist in differentiating heart failure from pulmonary disease
- Cost-effective screen for left ventricular dysfunction; positive findings would point to the need for echocardiography and further assessment

POTENTIAL DIAGNOSIS

Increased in
BNP is secreted in response to increased hemodynamic load caused by physiological stimuli, as with ven

ricular stretch or endocrine stimuli rom the aldosterone/renin system.

Cardiac inflammation (myocarditis, cardiac allograft rejection)
Cirrhosis
Cushing's syndrome
Heart failure
Kawasaki's disease
Left ventricular hypertrophy
Myocardial infarction
Primary hyperaldosteronism
Primary pulmonary hypertension
Renal failure
Ventricular dysfunction

Decreased in: N/A

CRITICAL FINDINGS: N/A

INTERFERING FACTORS

Nesiritide (Natrecor) is a recombinant form of BNP that may be given therapeutically by IV to patients in acutely decompensated heart failure; with some assays, BNP levels may be transiently elevated at the time of administration and must be interpreted with caution. The testing laboratory should be consulted to verify whether test measurements are affected by Natrecor.

NURSING IMPLICATIONS AND PROCEDURE

PRETEST:

Positively identify the patient using at least two unique identifiers before providing care, treatment, or services.
Patient Teaching: Inform the patient this test can assist in diagnosing congestive heart failure.
Obtain a history of the patient's complaints, including a list of known allergens, especially allergies or sensitivities to latex.
Obtain a history of the patient's cardiovascular system, symptoms, and results of previously performed labora-

tory tests and diagnostic and surgical procedures.
Obtain a list of the patient's current medications, including herbs, nutritional supplements, and nutraceuticals (see Appendix F).
Review the procedure with the patient. Inform the patient that specimen collection takes approximately 5 to 10 min. Address concerns about pain and explain to the patient that there may be some discomfort during the venipuncture.
Sensitivity to social and cultural issues, as well as concern for modesty, is important in providing psychological support before, during, and after the procedure.
There are no food, fluid, or medication restrictions unless by medical direction.

INTRATEST:

If the patient has a history of allergic reaction to latex, avoid the use of equipment containing latex.
Instruct the patient to cooperate fully and to follow directions. Direct the patient to breathe normally and to avoid unnecessary movement.
Observe standard precautions, and follow the general guidelines in Appendix A. Positively identify the patient, and label the appropriate specimen container with the corresponding patient demographics, initials of the person collecting the specimen, date, and time of collection. Perform a venipuncture.
Remove the needle and apply direct pressure with dry gauze to stop bleeding. Observe/assess venipuncture site for bleeding or hematoma formation and secure gauze with adhesive bandage.
Promptly transport the specimen to the laboratory for processing and analysis.

POST-TEST:

A report of the results will be made available to the requesting health-care provider (HCP), who will discuss the results with the patient.
Treatment Considerations for CHF: Ensure that the patient (if not currently taking)

is placed on an angiotensin-converting enzyme inhibitor, β-blocker, and diuretic and is monitored with daily weights.

▸ *Nutritional Considerations:* Instruct patients to consume a variety of foods within the basic food groups, eat foods high in potassium when taking diuretics, eat a diet high in fiber (25 to 35 g/day), maintain a healthy weight, be physically active, limit salt intake to 2,000 mg/day, limit alcohol intake, and be a nonsmoker.

▸ *Nutritional Considerations:* Foods high in potassium include fruits such as bananas, strawberries, oranges; cantaloupes; green leafy vegetables such as spinach and broccoli; dried fruits such as dates, prunes, and raisins; legumes such as peas and pinto beans; nuts and whole grains.

▸ Reinforce information given by the patient's HCP regarding further testing, treatment, or referral to another HCP.

Answer any questions or address any concerns voiced by the patient or family.

▸ Depending on the results of this procedure, additional testing may be performed to evaluate or monitor progression of the disease process and determine the need for a change in therapy. Evaluate test results in relation to the patient's symptoms and other tests performed.

RELATED MONOGRAPHS:

▸ Related tests include AST, ANF, calcium and ionized calcium, CRP, CK and isoenzymes, CT scoring, echocardiography, glucose, homocysteine, Holter monitor, LDH and isoenzymes, magnesium, MRI chest, MI scan, myocardial perfusion heart scan, myoglobin, PET heart, potassium, and troponin.

▸ Refer to the Cardiovascular System table at the end of the book for related tests by body system.

Calcitonin and Calcitonin Stimulation Tests

SYNONYM/ACRONYM: Thyrocalcitonin, hCT.

COMMON USE: To diagnose and monitor the effectiveness of treatment for medullary thyroid cancer.

SPECIMEN: Serum (3 mL) collected in a red- or tiger-top tube.

NORMAL FINDINGS: (Method: Chemiluminescent immunoassay)

Procedure	Medication Administered	Recommended Collection Times
Calcium and pentagastrin stimulation	Calcium, 2 mg/kg IV for 1 min, followed by pentagastrin 0.5 mcg/kg	4 calcitonin levels—baseline immediately before bolus; and 1 min, 2 min, and 5 min postbolus
Calcium stimulation	Calcium, 2 mg/kg IV for 1 min or 2.4 mg/kg IV push	4 calcitonin levels—baseline immediately before bolus; and 1 min, 2 min, and 5 min postbolus
Pentagastrin stimulation	Pentagastrin 0.5 mcg/kg	4 calcitonin levels—baseline immediately before bolus; and 1 min, 2 min, and 5 min postbolus

IV = intravenous.

	Conventional Units	SI Units (Conventional Units × 1)
Calcitonin Baseline		
Male	Less than 10 pg/mL	Less than 10 ng/L
Female	Less than 5 pg/mL	Less than 5 ng/L
Maximum Response		
5 min after calcium and pentagastrin stimulation		
Male	8–343 pg/mL	8–343 ng/L
Female	Less than 39 pg/mL	Less than 39 ng/L
5 min after calcium stimulation		
Male	Less than 190 pg/mL	Less than 190 ng/L
Female	Less than 130 pg/mL	Less than 130 ng/L
5 min after pentagastrin stimulation		
Male	Less than 110 pg/mL	Less than 110 ng/L
Female	Less than 30 pg/mL	Less than 30 ng/L

DESCRIPTION: Calcitonin, also called thyrocalcitonin, is secreted by the parafollicular or C cells of the thyroid gland in response to elevated serum calcium levels. Calcitonin antagonizes the effects of parathyroid hormone and vitamin D so that calcium continues to be laid down in bone rather than reabsorbed into the blood. Calcitonin also increases renal clearance of magnesium and inhibits tubular reabsorption of phosphates. The net result is that calcitonin decreases the serum calcium level. The pentagastrin (Peptavlon) provocation test and the calcium pentagastrin provocation test are useful for diagnosing medullary thyroid cancer.

INDICATIONS

- Assist in the diagnosis of hyperparathyroidism
- Assist in the diagnosis of medullary thyroid cancer
- Evaluate altered serum calcium levels
- Monitor response to therapy for medullary thyroid carcinoma
- Predict recurrence of medullary thyroid carcinoma
- Screen family members of patients with medullary thyroid carcinoma (20% have a familial pattern)

POTENTIAL DIAGNOSIS

Increased in

- Alcoholic cirrhosis *(related to release of calcium from body stores associated with acute instances of malnutrition)*
- Cancer of the breast, lung, and pancreas *(related to metastasis of calcitonin-producing cells to other organs)*
- Carcinoid syndrome *(related to calcitonin-producing tumor cells)*
- C-cell hyperplasia *(related to increased production due to hyperplasia)*
- Chronic renal failure *(related to increased excretion of calcium and retention of phosphorus resulting in release of calcium*

from body stores; C cells respond to an increase in serum calcium levels)

- Ectopic secretion *(especially neuroendocrine origins)*
- Hypercalcemia (any cause) *(related to increased production by C cells in response to increased calcium levels)*
- Medullary thyroid cancer *(related to overproduction by cancerous cells)*
- MEN type II *(related to calcitonin-producing tumor cells)*
- Pancreatitis *(related to alcoholism or hypercalcemia)*
- Pernicious anemia *(related to hypergastrinemia)*
- Pheochromocytoma *(related to calcitonin-producing tumor cells)*
- Pregnancy (late) *(related to increased maternal loss of circulating calcium to developing fetus; release of calcium from maternal stores stimulates increased release of calcitonin)*
- Pseudohypoparathyroidism *(related to release of calcium from body stores initiates feedback response from C cells)*
- Thyroiditis *(related to calcitonin-producing tumor cells)*
- Zollinger-Ellison syndrome *(related to hypergastrinemia)*

Decreased in: N/A

CRITICAL FINDINGS: N/A

INTERFERING FACTORS

- Drugs that may increase calcitonin levels include calcium, epinephrine, estrogens, glucagon, oral contraceptives, pentagastrin, and sincalide.
- Failure to follow dietary restrictions before the procedure may cause the procedure to be canceled or repeated.

NURSING IMPLICATIONS AND PROCEDURE

PRETEST:

- Positively identify the patient using at least two unique identifiers before providing care, treatment, or services.
- *Patient Teaching:* Inform the patient this test can assist in assessing the thyroid gland for disease or can monitor effectiveness of therapy.
- Obtain a history of the patient's complaints, including a list of known allergens, especially allergies or sensitivities to latex.
- Obtain a history of the patient's endocrine system, as well as results of previously performed laboratory tests and diagnostic and surgical procedures. Note any recent procedures that can interfere with test results.
- Obtain a list of the patient's current medications, including herbs, nutritional supplements, and nutraceuticals (see Appendix F).
- Review the procedure with the patient. Inform the patient that specimen collection takes approximately 5 to 10 min; a few extra minutes are required to administer the stimulation tests. Address concerns about pain and explain that there may be some discomfort during the venipuncture. *Sensitivity to social and cultural issues,* as well as concern for modesty, is important in providing psychological support before, during, and after the procedure.
- The patient should fast for 10 to 12 hr before specimen collection. Protocols may vary among facilities.
- There are no fluid or medication restrictions unless by medical direction.
- Prepare an ice slurry in a cup or plastic bag to have ready for immediate transport of the specimen to the laboratory. Prechill the collection tube in the ice slurry.

INTRATEST:

- Ensure that the patient has complied with dietary restrictions and pretesting preparations; ensure that food has been restricted for at least 10 to 12 hr prior to the procedure.

- If the patient has a history of allergic reaction to latex, avoid the use of equipment containing latex.
- Instruct the patient to cooperate fully and to follow directions. Direct the patient to breathe normally and to avoid unnecessary movement.
- Observe standard precautions, and follow the general guidelines in Appendix A. Positively identify the patient, and label the appropriate tubes with the corresponding patient demographics, initials of the person collecting the specimen, date, and time of collection. Perform a venipuncture; collect the specimen in a prechilled tube.
- Remove the needle and apply direct pressure with dry gauze to stop bleeding. Observe/assess venipuncture site for bleeding or hematoma formation and secure gauze with adhesive bandage.
- The sample should be placed in an ice slurry immediately after collection. Information on the specimen label should be protected from water in the ice slurry by first placing the specimen in a protective plastic bag. Promptly transport the specimen to the laboratory for processing and analysis.

POST-TEST:

- A report of the results will be made available to the requesting health-care provider (HCP), who will discuss the results with the patient.
- Instruct the patient to resume usual diet as directed by the HCP.
- Reinforce information given by the patient's HCP regarding further testing, treatment, or referral to another HCP. Answer any questions or address any concerns voiced by the patient or family.
- Depending on the results of this procedure, additional testing may be performed to evaluate or monitor progression of the disease process and determine the need for a change in therapy. Evaluate test results in relation to the patient's symptoms and other tests performed.

C

RELATED MONOGRAPHS:

Related tests include ACTH, biopsy thyroid, calcium, cancer antigens, catecholamines, CBC, gastrin stimulation test, magnesium, metanephrines, PTH, parathyroid scan, phosphorus, thyroglobulin, thyroid scan, TSH, US thyroid and parathyroid, and vitamin D.

Refer to the Endocrine System table at the end of the book for related tests by body system.

Calcium, Blood

SYNONYM/ACRONYM: Total calcium, Ca.

COMMON USE: To investigate various conditions related to abnormally increased or decreased calcium levels.

SPECIMEN: Serum (1 mL) collected in a red- or tiger-top tube. Plasma (1 mL) collected in a green-top (heparin) tube is also acceptable.

NORMAL FINDINGS: (Method: Spectrophotometry)

Age	Conventional Units	SI Units (Conventional Units × 0.25)
Cord	8.2–11.2 mg/dL	2.1–2.8 mmol/L
0–10 days	7.6–10.4 mg/dL	1.9–2.6 mmol/L
11 days–2 yr	9–11 mg/dL	2.2–2.8 mmol/L
3–12 yr	8.8–10.8 mg/dL	2.2–2.7 mmol/L
13–18 yr	8.4–10.2 mg/dL	2.1–2.6 mmol/L
Adult	8.2–10.2 mg/dL	2.1–2.6 mmol/L
Adult older than 90 yr	8.2–9.6 mg/dL	2.1–2.4 mmol/L

DESCRIPTION: Calcium, the most abundant cation in the body, participates in almost all of the vital processes. Calcium concentration is largely regulated by the parathyroid glands and by the action of vitamin D. Of the body's calcium reserves, 98% to 99% is stored in the teeth and skeleton. Calcium values are higher in children because of growth and active bone formation. About 45% of the total amount of blood calcium circulates as free ions that participate in coagulation, neuromuscular conduction, intracellular regulation, glandular secretion, and control of skeletal and cardiac muscle contractility. The remaining calcium is bound to circulating proteins (40% bound mostly to albumin) and anions (15% bound to anions such as bicarbonate, citrate, phosphate, and lactate) and plays no physiological role. Calcium values can be adjusted up or down by 0.8 mg/dL for every 1 g/dL that albumin is greater than or less than 4 g/dL. Calcium and phosphorus levels are inversely proportional.

C

Fluid and electrolyte imbalances are often seen in patients with serious illness or injury; in these clinical situations, the normal homeostatic balance of the body is altered. During surgery or in the case of a critical illness, bicarbonate, phosphate, and lactate concentrations can change dramatically. Therapeutic treatments may also cause or contribute to electrolyte imbalance. This is why total calcium values can sometimes be misleading. Abnormal calcium levels are used to indicate general malfunctions in various body systems. Ionized calcium is used in more specific conditions (see monograph titled "Calcium, Ionized").

Calcium values should be interpreted in conjunction with results of other tests. Normal calcium with an abnormal phosphorus value indicates impaired calcium absorption (possibly because of altered parathyroid hormone level or activity). Normal calcium with an elevated urea nitrogen value indicates possible hyperparathyroidism (primary or secondary). Normal calcium with decreased albumin value is an indication of hypercalcemia (high calcium levels). The most common cause of hypocalcemia (low calcium levels) is hypoalbuminemia. The most common causes of hypercalcemia are hyperparathyroidism and cancer (with or without bone metastases).

INDICATIONS

Detect parathyroid gland loss after thyroid or other neck surgery, as indicated by decreased levels

- Evaluate cardiac arrhythmias and coagulation disorders to determine if altered serum calcium level is contributing to the problem
- Evaluate the effects of various disorders on calcium metabolism, especially diseases involving bone
- Monitor the effectiveness of therapy being administered to correct abnormal calcium levels, especially calcium deficiencies
- Monitor the effects of renal failure and various drugs on calcium levels

POTENTIAL DIAGNOSIS

Increased in
- Acidosis *(related to imbalance in electrolytes; longstanding acidosis can result in osteoporosis and release of calcium into circulation)*
- Acromegaly *(related to alteration in vitamin D metabolism, resulting in increased calcium)*
- Addison's disease *(related to adrenal gland dysfunction; decreased blood volume and dehydration occur in the absence of aldosterone)*
- Cancers (bone, Burkitt's lymphoma, Hodgkin's lymphoma, leukemia, myeloma, and metastases from other organs)
- Dehydration *(related to a decrease in the fluid portion of blood, causing an overall increase in the concentration of most plasma constituents)*
- Hyperparathyroidism *(related to increased parathyroid hormone [PTH] and vitamin D levels, which increase circulating calcium levels)*
- Idiopathic hypercalcemia of infancy
- Lung disease (tuberculosis, histoplasmosis, coccidioidomycosis, berylliosis) *(related to activity by macrophages in the epithelium that interfere with vitamin D regulation by converting it to its*

active form; vitamin D increases circulating calcium levels)

- Malignant disease without bone involvement *(some cancers [e.g., squamous cell carcinoma of the lung and kidney cancer] produce PTH-related peptide that increases calcium levels)*
- Milk-alkali syndrome (Burnett's syndrome) *(related to excessive intake of calcium-containing milk or antacids, which can increase calcium levels)*
- Paget's disease *(related to calcium released from bone)*
- Pheochromocytoma *(hyperparathyroidism related to multiple endocrine neoplasia type 2A [MEN2A] syndrome associated with some pheochromocytomas; PTH increases calcium levels)*
- Polycythemia vera *(related to dehydration; decreased blood volume due to excessive production of red blood cells)*
- Renal transplant *(related to imbalances in electrolytes; a common post-transplant issue)*
- Sarcoidosis *(related to activity by macrophages in the granulomas that interfere with vitamin D regulation by converting it to its active form; vitamin D increases circulating calcium levels)*
- Thyrotoxicosis *(related to increased bone turnover and release of calcium into the blood)*
- Vitamin D toxicity *(vitamin D increases circulating calcium levels)*

Decreased in

- Acute pancreatitis *(complication of pancreatitis related to hypoalbuminemia and calcium binding by excessive fats)*
- Alcoholism *(related to insufficient nutrition)*
- Alkalosis *(increased blood pH causes intracellular uptake of calcium to increase)*

- Chronic renal failure *(related to decreased synthesis of vitamin D)*
- Cystinosis *(hereditary disorder of the renal tubules that results in excessive calcium loss)*
- Hepatic cirrhosis *(related to impaired metabolism of vitamin D and calcium)*
- Hyperphosphatemia *(phosphorus and calcium have an inverse relationship)*
- Hypoalbuminemia *(related to insufficient levels of albumin, an important carrier protein)*
- Hypomagnesemia *(lack of magnesium inhibits PTH and thereby decreases calcium levels)*
- Hypoparathyroidism (congenital, idiopathic, surgical) *(related to lack of PTH)*
- Inadequate nutrition
- Leprosy *(related to increased bone retention)*
- Long-term anticonvulsant therapy *(these medications block calcium channels and interfere with calcium transport)*
- Malabsorption (celiac disease, tropical sprue, pancreatic insufficiency) *(related to insufficient absorption)*
- Massive blood transfusion *(related to the presence of citrate preservative in blood product that chelates or binds calcium and removes it from circulation)*
- Neonatal prematurity
- Osteomalacia (advanced) *(bone loss is so advanced there is little calcium remaining to be released into circulation)*
- Renal tubular disease *(related to decreased synthesis of vitamin D)*
- Vitamin D deficiency (rickets) *(related to insufficient amounts of vitamin D, resulting in decreased calcium metabolism)*

CRITICAL FINDINGS

Less than 7 mg/dL (SI: Less than 1.8 mmol/L)
Greater than 12 mg/dL (SI: Greater than 3 mmol/L) (some patients can tolerate higher concentrations)

Note and immediately report to the health-care provider (HCP) any critically increased or decreased values and related symptoms. Timely notification of critical values for lab or diagnostic studies is a role expectation of the professional nurse. Notification processes will vary among facilities. Upon receipt of the critical value, the information should be read back to the caller to verify accuracy. Most policies require immediate notification of the primary HCP, hospitalist, or on-call HCP. Reported information includes the patient's name, unique identifiers, critical value, name of the person giving the report, and name of the person receiving the report. Documentation of notification should be made in the medical record with the name of the HCP notified, time and date of notification, and any orders received. Any delay in a timely report of a critical value may require completion of a notification form with review by Risk Management.

Observe the patient for symptoms of critically decreased or elevated calcium levels. Hypocalcemia is evidenced by convulsions, arrhythmias, changes in electrocardiogram (ECG) in the form of prolonged ST segment and Q-T interval, facial spasms (positive Chvostek's sign), tetany, muscle cramps, numbness in extremities, tingling, and muscle twitching (positive Trousseau's sign). Possible interventions include seizure precautions, increased frequency of ECG monitoring, and administration of calcium or magnesium.

Severe hypercalcemia is manifested by polyuria, constipation, changes in ECG (shortened ST segment), lethargy, muscle weakness, apathy, anorexia, headache, and nausea and ultimately may result in coma. Possible interventions include the administration of normal saline and diuretics to speed up excretion or administration of calcitonin or steroids to force the circulating calcium into the cells.

INTERFERING FACTORS

- Drugs that may increase calcium levels include anabolic steroids, some antacids, calcitriol, calcium salts, danazol, diuretics (long-term), ergocalciferol, isotretinoin, lithium, oral contraceptives, parathyroid extract, parathyroid hormone, prednisone, progesterone, tamoxifen, vitamin A, and vitamin D.
- Drugs that may decrease calcium levels include albuterol, alprostadil, aminoglycosides, anticonvulsants, calcitonin, diuretics (initially), gastrin, glucagon, glucocorticoids, glucose, insulin, laxatives (excessive use), magnesium salts, methicillin, phosphates, plicamycin, sodium sulfate (given IV), tetracycline (in pregnancy), trazodone, and viomycin.
- Calcium exhibits diurnal variation; serial samples should be collected at the same time of day for comparison.
- Venous hemostasis caused by prolonged use of a tourniquet during venipuncture can falsely elevate calcium levels.
- Patients on ethylenediaminetetra-acetic acid (EDTA) therapy (chelation) may show falsely decreased calcium values.
- Hemolysis and icterus cause false-positive results because of interference from biological pigments.
- Specimens should never be collected above an IV line because of the potential for dilution when the specimen and the IV solution

C

combine in the collection container, falsely decreasing the result. There is also the potential of contaminating the sample with the substance of interest if it is present in the IV solution, falsely increasing the result.

C

NURSING IMPLICATIONS AND PROCEDURE

PRETEST:

▶ Positively identify the patient using at least two unique identifiers before providing care, treatment, or services.
▶ *Patient Teaching:* Inform the patient this test can assist as a general indicator in diagnosing health concerns.
▶ Obtain a history of the patient's complaints, including a list of known allergens, especially allergies or sensitivities to latex.
▶ Obtain a history of the patient's cardiovascular, gastrointestinal, genitourinary, hematopoietic, hepatobiliary, and musculoskeletal systems, as well as results of previously performed laboratory tests and diagnostic and surgical procedures.
▶ Note any recent procedures that can interfere with test results.
▶ Obtain a list of the patient's current medications, including herbs, nutritional supplements, and nutraceuticals (see Appendix F).
▶ Review the procedure with the patient. Inform the patient that specimen collection takes approximately 5 to 10 min. Address concerns about pain and explain that there may be some discomfort during the venipuncture.
▶ *Sensitivity to social and cultural issues,* as well as concern for modesty, is important in providing psychological support before, during, and after the procedure.
▶ There are no food, fluid, or medication restrictions unless by medical direction.

INTRATEST:

▶ If the patient has a history of allergic reaction to latex, avoid the use of equipment containing latex.

▶ Instruct the patient to cooperate fully and to follow directions. Direct the patient to breathe normally and to avoid unnecessary movement.
▶ Observe standard precautions, and follow the general guidelines in Appendix A. Positively identify the patient, and label the appropriate specimen container with the corresponding patient demographics, initials of the person collecting the specimen, date, and time of collection. Perform a venipuncture.
▶ Remove the needle and apply direct pressure with dry gauze to stop bleeding. Observe/assess venipuncture site for bleeding or hematoma formation and secure gauze with adhesive bandage.
▶ Promptly transport the specimen to the laboratory for processing and analysis.

POST-TEST:

▶ A report of the results will be made available to the requesting HCP, who will discuss the results with the patient.
▶ *Nutritional Considerations:* Patients with abnormal calcium values should be informed that daily intake of calcium is important even though body stores in the bones can be called on to supplement circulating levels. The Institute of Medicine's Food and Nutrition Board suggests 1,200 mg as an adequate daily intake goal of dietary calcium for adult males and females age 51 to greater than 70 yr; 1,000 mg/d for adult males and females age 19 to 50 yr; 1,000 mg/d for pregnant and lactating females age 19 to 50 yr; 1,300 mg/d for pregnant and lactating females under age 19 yr; 1,300 mg/d for children age 9 to 18 yr; 800 mg/d for children age 4 to 8 yr; 500 mg/d for children age 1 to 3 yr; 270 mg/d for children age 7 to 12 mo; and 210 mg/d for children age 0 to 6 mo. Reprinted with permission from the National Academies Press, copyright 2013, National Academy of Sciences. Dietary calcium can be obtained from animal or plant sources. Milk and milk products, sardines, clams, oysters, salmon, rhubarb, spinach, beet greens, broccoli, kale, tofu, legumes, and fortified orange juice are

high in calcium. Milk and milk products also contain vitamin D and lactose, which assist calcium absorption. Cooked vegetables yield more absorbable calcium than raw vegetables. Patients should be informed of the substances that can inhibit calcium absorption by irreversibly binding to some of the calcium, making it unavailable for absorption, such as oxalates, which naturally occur in some vegetables (e.g., beet greens, collards, leeks, okra, parsley, quinoa, spinach, Swiss chard) and are found in tea; phytic acid, found in some cereals (e.g., wheat bran, wheat germ); phosphoric acid, found in dark cola; and insoluble dietary fiber (in excessive amounts). Excessive protein intake can also negatively affect calcium absorption, especially if it is combined with foods high in phosphorus and in the presence of a reduced dietary calcium intake. Reinforce information given by the patient's HCP regarding further testing, treatment, or referral to another HCP. Answer any questions or address any concerns voiced by the patient or family. Educate the patient regarding access to nutritional counseling services. Provide contact information, if desired, for the Institute of Medicine

of the National Academies (www.iom.edu).

▶ Depending on the results of this procedure, additional testing may be performed to evaluate or monitor progression of the disease process and determine the need for a change in therapy. Evaluate test results in relation to the patient's symptoms and other tests performed.

RELATED MONOGRAPHS:

▶ Related tests include ACTH, albumin, aldosterone, ALP, biopsy bone marrow, BMD, bone scan, calcitonin, calcium ionized, urine calcium, calculus kidney stone analysis, catecholamines, chloride, collagen cross-linked telopeptides, CBC, CT pelvis, CT spine, cortisol, CK and isoenzymes, DHEA, fecal fat, glucose, HVA, magnesium, metanephrines, osteocalcin, PTH, phosphorus, potassium, protein total, radiography bone, renin, sodium, thyroid scan, thyroxine, US abdomen, US thyroid and parathyroid, UA, and vitamin D.

▶ Refer to the Cardiovascular, Gastrointestinal, Genitourinary, Hematopoietic, Hepatobiliary, and Musculoskeletal systems tables at the end of the book for related tests by body system.

C

Calcium, Ionized

SYNONYM/ACRONYM: Free calcium, unbound calcium, Ca^{++}, Ca^{2+}.

COMMON USE: To investigate various conditions related to altered levels of ionized calcium such as hypocalcemia and hypercalcemia.

SPECIMEN: Serum (1 mL) collected in a red- or tiger-top tube. Specimen should be transported tightly capped and remain unopened until testing. Exposure of serum to room air changes the pH of the specimen due to the release of carbon dioxide and can cause erroneous results.

NORMAL FINDINGS: (Method: Ion-selective electrode)

C

Age	Conventional Units	SI Units (Conventional Units × 0.25)
Whole blood		
0–11 mo	4.2–5.84 mg/dL	1.05–1.46 mmol/L
1 yr-Adult	4.6–5.08 mg/dL	1.12–1.32 mmol/L
Plasma		
Adult	4.12–4.92 mg/dL	1.03–1.23 mmol/L
Serum		
1–18 yr	4.8–5.52 mg/dL	1.2–1.38 mmol/L
Adult	4.64–5.28 mg/dL	1.16–1.32 mmol/L

DESCRIPTION: Calcium is the most abundant cation in the body and participates in almost all vital body processes (see other calcium monographs). Circulating calcium is found in the free or ionized form; bound to organic anions such as lactate, phosphate, or citrate; and bound to proteins such as albumin. Ionized calcium is the physiologically active form of circulating calcium. About half of the total amount of calcium circulates as free ions that participate in blood coagulation, neuromuscular conduction, intracellular regulation, glandular secretion, and control of skeletal and cardiac muscle contractility. Calcium levels are regulated largely by the parathyroid glands and by vitamin D. Compared to total calcium level, ionized calcium is a better measurement of calcium metabolism. Ionized calcium levels are not influenced by protein concentrations, as seen in patients with chronic renal failure, nephrotic syndrome, malabsorption, and multiple myeloma. Levels are also not affected in patients with metabolic acid-base balance disturbances. Elevations in ionized calcium may be seen when the total calcium is normal. Measurement of ionized calcium is useful to monitor patients undergoing cardiothoracic surgery or organ transplantation. It is also useful in the evaluation of patients in cardiac arrest.

INDICATIONS
• Detect ectopic parathyroid hormone (PTH)–producing neoplasms
• Evaluate the effect of protein on calcium levels
• Identify individuals with hypocalcemia
• Identify individuals with toxic levels of vitamin D
• Investigate suspected hyperparathyroidism
• Monitor patients with renal failure or organ transplantation in whom secondary hyperparathyroidism may be a complication
• Monitor patients with sepsis or magnesium deficiency

POTENTIAL DIAGNOSIS

Increased in
• Hyperparathyroidism *(related to increased PTH)*
• PTH-producing neoplasms *(PTH increases calcium levels)*
• Vitamin D toxicity *(related to increased absorption of calcium)*

Decreased in
• Burns, severe *(related to increased amino acid release)*
• Hypoparathyroidism (primary) *(related to decreased PTH)*

- Magnesium deficiency *(inhibits release of PTH)*
- Multiple organ failure
- Pancreatitis *(associated with saponification or binding of calcium to fats in tissue surrounding the pancreas)*
- The postdialysis period *(result of low-calcium dialysate administration)*
- The postsurgical period (i.e., major surgeries) *(related to decreased PTH)*
- The post-transfusion period *(result of the use of citrated blood product preservative [calcium chelator])*
- Premature infants with hypoproteinemia and acidosis *(related to alterations in transport protein levels)*
- Pseudohypoparathyroidism *(related to decreased PTH)*
- Sepsis *(related to decreased PTH)*
- Trauma *(related to decreased PTH)*
- Vitamin D deficiency *(related to decreased absorption of calcium)*

CRITICAL FINDINGS ❖

- Less than 3.2 mg/dL (SI: Less than 0.8 mmol/L)
- Greater than 6.2 mg/dL (SI: Greater than 1.6 mmol/L)

Note and immediately report to the health-care provider (HCP) any critically increased or decreased values and related symptoms. Timely notification of critical values for lab or diagnostic studies is a role expectation of the professional nurse. Notification processes will vary among facilities. Upon receipt of the critical value, the information should be read back to the caller to verify accuracy. Most policies require immediate notification of the primary HCP, hospitalist, or on-call HCP. Reported information includes the patient's name, unique identifiers, critical value, name of the person giving the report, and name of the person receiving the report. Documentation of notification should be made in the medical record with the name of the HCP notified, time and date of notification, and any orders received. Any delay in a timely report of a critical value may require completion of a notification form with review by Risk Management.

Observe the patient for symptoms of critically decreased or elevated calcium levels. Hypocalcemia is evidenced by convulsions, arrhythmias, changes in electrocardiogram (ECG) in the form of prolonged ST segment and Q-T interval, facial spasms (positive Chvostek's sign), tetany, muscle cramps, numbness in extremities, tingling, and muscle twitching (positive Trousseau's sign). Possible interventions include seizure precautions, increased frequency of ECG monitoring, and administration of calcium or magnesium.

Severe hypercalcemia is manifested by polyuria, constipation, changes in ECG (shortened ST segment), lethargy, muscle weakness, apathy, anorexia, headache, and nausea and ultimately may result in coma. Possible interventions include the administration of normal saline and diuretics to speed up excretion or administration of calcitonin or steroids to force the circulating calcium into the cells.

INTERFERING FACTORS

- Drugs that may increase calcium levels include antacids (some), calcitriol, and lithium.
- Drugs that may decrease calcium levels include calcitonin, citrates, foscarnet, and pamidronate (initially).
- Calcium exhibits diurnal variation; serial samples should

be collected at the same time of day for comparison.

- Venous hemostasis caused by prolonged use of a tourniquet during venipuncture can falsely elevate calcium levels.
- Patients on ethylenediaminetetraacetic acid (EDTA) therapy (chelation) may show falsely decreased calcium values.
- Specimens should never be collected above an IV line because of the potential for dilution when the specimen and the IV solution combine in the collection container, falsely decreasing the result. There is also the potential of contaminating the sample with the substance of interest if it is present in the IV solution, falsely increasing the result.

NURSING IMPLICATIONS AND PROCEDURE

PRETEST:

▶ Positively identify the patient using at least two unique identifiers before providing care, treatment, or services.
▶ *Patient Teaching:* Inform the patient this test can assist in evaluating the level of blood calcium.
▶ Obtain a history of the patient's complaints, including a list of known allergens, especially allergies or sensitivities to latex.
▶ Obtain a history of the patient's cardiovascular, gastrointestinal, genitourinary, hematopoietic, hepatobiliary, and musculoskeletal systems, as well as results of previously performed laboratory tests and diagnostic and surgical procedures.
▶ Note any recent procedures that could interfere with test results.
▶ Obtain a list of the patient's current medications, including herbs, nutritional supplements, and nutraceuticals (see Appendix F).
▶ Review the procedure with the patient. Inform the patient that specimen collection takes approximately 5 to

10 min. Address concerns about pain and explain that there may be some discomfort during the venipuncture.
▶ *Sensitivity to social and cultural issues,* as well as concern for modesty, is important in providing psychological support before, during, and after the procedure.
▶ There are no food, fluid, or medication restrictions unless by medical direction.

INTRATEST:

▶ If the patient has a history of allergic reaction to latex, avoid the use of equipment containing latex.
▶ Instruct the patient to cooperate fully and to follow directions. Direct the patient to breathe normally and to avoid unnecessary movement.
▶ Observe standard precautions, and follow the general guidelines in Appendix A. Positively identify the patient, and label the appropriate specimen container with the corresponding patient demographics, initials of the person collecting the specimen, date, and time of collection. Perform a venipuncture and, without using a tourniquet, collect the specimen.
▶ Remove the needle and apply direct pressure with dry gauze to stop bleeding. Observe/assess venipuncture site for bleeding or hematoma formation and secure gauze with adhesive bandage.
▶ The specimen should be stored under anaerobic conditions after collection to prevent the diffusion of gas from the specimen. Falsely decreased values result from unstoppered specimens. Promptly transport the specimen to the laboratory for processing and analysis.

POST-TEST:

▶ A report of the results will be made available to the requesting HCP, who will discuss the results with the patient.
▶ *Nutritional Considerations:* Patients with abnormal calcium values should be informed that daily intake of calcium is important even though body stores in the bones can be called on to supplement circulating levels. The Institute of Medicine's Food and Nutrition Board suggests 1,200 mg as an adequate

daily intake goal of dietary calcium for adult males and females age 51 to greater than 70 yr; 1,000 mg/d for adult males and females age 19 to 50 yr; 1,000 mg/d for pregnant and lactating females age 19 to 50 yr; 1,300 mg/d for pregnant and lactating females under age 19 yr; 1,300 mg/d for children age 9 to 18 yr; 800 mg/d for children age 4 to 8 yr; 500 mg/d for children age 1 to 3 yr; 270 mg/d for children age 7 to 12 mo; and 210 mg/d for children age 0 to 6 mo. Reprinted with permission from the National Academies Press, copyright 2013, National Academy of Sciences. Dietary calcium can be obtained from animal or plant sources. Milk and milk products, sardines, clams, oysters, salmon, rhubarb, spinach, beet greens, broccoli, kale, tofu, legumes, and fortified orange juice are high in calcium. Milk and milk products also contain vitamin D and lactose, which assist calcium absorption. Cooked vegetables yield more absorbable calcium than raw vegetables. Patients should be informed of the substances that can inhibit calcium absorption by irreversibly binding to some of the calcium, making it unavailable for absorption, such as oxalates, which naturally occur in some vegetables (e.g., beet greens, collards, leeks, okra, parsley, quinoa, spinach, Swiss chard) and are found in tea; phytic acid, found in some cereals (e.g., wheat bran, wheat germ);

phosphoric acid, found in dark cola; and insoluble dietary fiber (in excessive amounts). Excessive protein intake can also negatively affect calcium absorption, especially if it is combined with foods high in phosphorus and in the presence of a reduced dietary calcium intake.

▸ Reinforce information given by the patient's HCP regarding further testing, treatment, or referral to another HCP. Answer any questions or address any concerns voiced by the patient or family.

▸ Depending on the results of this procedure, additional testing may be performed to evaluate or monitor progression of the disease process and determine the need for a change in therapy. Evaluate test results in relation to the patient's symptoms and other tests performed.

RELATED MONOGRAPHS:

▸ Related tests include albumin, ALP, calcitonin, calcium, calculus kidney stone panel, gastrin and gastrin stimulation, magnesium, PTH, parathyroid scan, phosphorus, potassium, protein total, sodium, thyroglobulin, US thyroid and parathyroid, UA, and vitamin D.

▸ Refer to the Cardiovascular, Gastrointestinal, Genitourinary, Hematopoietic, Hepatobiliary, and Musculoskeletal systems tables at the end of the book for related tests by body system.

Calcium, Urine

SYNONYM/ACRONYM: N/A.

COMMON USE: To indicate sufficiency of dietary calcium intake and rate of absorption. Urine calcium levels are also used to assess bone resorption, renal stones, and renal loss of calcium.

SPECIMEN: Urine (5 mL) from an unpreserved random or timed specimen collected in a clean plastic collection container.

NORMAL FINDINGS: (Method: Spectrophotometry)

Age	Conventional Units*	SI Units (Conventional Units × 0.025)*
Infant and child	Up to 6 mg/kg per 24 hr	Up to 0.15 mmol/kg per 24 hr
Adult on average diet	100–300 mg/24 hr	2.5–7.5 mmol/24 hr

*Values depend on diet.

DESCRIPTION: Regulating electrolyte balance is a major function of the kidneys. In normally functioning kidneys, urine levels increase when serum levels are high and decrease when serum levels are low to maintain homeostasis. Analyzing urinary electrolyte levels can provide important clues to the functioning of the kidneys and other major organs. Tests for calcium in urine usually involve timed urine collections during a 12- or 24-hr period. Measurement of random specimens may also be requested. Urinary calcium excretion may also be expressed as calcium-to-creatinine ratio: In a healthy individual with constant muscle mass, the ratio is less than 0.14.

INDICATIONS
- Assist in establishing the presence of kidney stones
- Evaluate bone disease
- Evaluate dietary intake and absorption
- Evaluate renal loss
- Monitor patients on calcium replacement

POTENTIAL DIAGNOSIS

Increased in
- Acromegaly *(related to imbalance in vitamin D metabolism)*
- Diabetes *(related to increased loss from damaged kidneys)*
- Fanconi's syndrome *(evidenced by hereditary or acquired disorder of the renal tubules that results in excessive calcium loss)*
- Glucocorticoid excess *(related to action of glucocorticoids, which is to decrease the gastrointestinal absorption of calcium and increase urinary excretion)*
- Hepatolenticular degeneration (Wilson's disease) *(related to excessive electrolyte loss due to renal damage)*
- Hyperparathyroidism *(related to increased levels of PTH which result in increased calcium levels)*
- Hyperthyroidism *(related to increased bone turnover; excess circulating calcium is excreted by the kidneys)*
- Idiopathic hypercalciuria
- Immobilization *(related to disruption in calcium homeostasis and bone loss)*
- Kidney stones *(evidenced by excessive urinary calcium; contributes to the formation of kidney stones)*
- Leukemia and lymphoma (some instances)
- Myeloma *(calcium is released from damaged bone; excess circulating calcium is excreted by the kidneys)*
- Neoplasm of the breast or bladder *(some cancers secrete PTH or PTH-related peptide that increases calcium levels)*
- Osteitis deformans *(calcium is released from damaged bone; excess circulating calcium is excreted by the kidneys)*

- Osteolytic bone metastases (carcinoma, sarcoma) *(calcium is released from damaged bone; excess circulating calcium is excreted by the kidneys)*
- Osteoporosis *(calcium is released from damaged bone; excess circulating calcium is excreted by the kidneys)*
- Paget's disease *(calcium is released from damaged bone; excess circulating calcium is excreted by the kidneys)*
- Renal tubular acidosis *(metabolic acidosis resulting in loss of calcium by the kidneys)*
- Sarcoidosis *(macrophages in the granulomas interfere with vitamin D regulation by converting it to its active form; vitamin D increases circulating calcium levels, and excess is excreted by the kidneys)*
- Schistosomiasis
- Thyrotoxicosis *(increased bone turnover; excess circulating calcium is excreted by the kidneys)*
- Vitamin D intoxication *(increases calcium metabolism; excess is excreted by the kidneys)*

Decreased in

- Hypocalcemia (other than renal disease)
- Hypocalciuric hypercalcemia (familial, nonfamilial)
- Hypoparathyroidism *(PTH instigates release of calcium; if PTH levels are low, calcium levels will be decreased)*
- Hypothyroidism
- Malabsorption (celiac disease, tropical sprue) *(related to insufficient levels of calcium)*
- Malignant bone neoplasm
- Nephrosis and acute nephritis *(related to decreased synthesis of vitamin D)*
- Osteoblastic metastases
- Osteomalacia *(related to vitamin D deficiency)*

- Pre-eclampsia
- Pseudohypoparathyroidism
- Renal osteodystrophy
- Rickets *(related to deficiency in vitamin D)*
- Vitamin D deficiency *(deficiency in vitamin D results in decreased calcium levels)*

CRITICAL FINDINGS: N/A

INTERFERING FACTORS

- Drugs that can increase urine calcium levels include acetazolamide, ammonium chloride, asparaginase, calcitonin, corticosteroids, corticotropin, dexamethasone, dihydroxycholecalciferol, diuretics (initially), ergocalciferol, ethacrynic acid, glucocorticoids, mannitol (initially), meralluride, mercaptomerin, mersalyl, metolazone, nandrolone, parathyroid extract, parathyroid hormone, plicamycin, prednisolone, sodium sulfate, sulfates, torsemide, triamcinolone, triamterene, viomycin, and vitamin D.
- Drugs that can decrease urine calcium levels include angiotensin, bicarbonate, calcitonin, cellulose phosphate, citrates, diuretics (chronic), lithium, mestranol, methyclothiazide, neomycin, oral contraceptives, parathyroid extract, polythiazide, sodium phytate, spironolactone, thiazides, trichlormethiazide, and vitamin K.
- Failure to collect all the urine and store the specimen properly during the 24-hr test period invalidates the results.

NURSING IMPLICATIONS AND PROCEDURE

PRETEST:

- Positively identify the patient using at least two unique identifiers before providing care, treatment, or services.

Patient Teaching: Inform the patient this test can assist in evaluating the effectiveness of the body's absorption of calcium.

Obtain a history of the patient's complaints, including a list of known allergens, especially allergies or sensitivities to latex.

Obtain a history of the patient's endocrine, genitourinary, and musculoskeletal systems and results of previously performed laboratory tests and diagnostic and surgical procedures.

Obtain a list of the patient's current medications, including herbs, nutritional supplements, and nutraceuticals (see Appendix F).

Review the procedure with the patient. Provide a nonmetallic urinal, bedpan, or toilet-mounted collection device. Address concerns about pain and explain that there should be no discomfort during the procedure.

Sensitivity to social and cultural issues, as well as concern for modesty, is important in providing psychological support before, during, and after the procedure.

Usually a 24-hr time frame for urine collection is ordered. Inform the patient that all urine must be saved during that 24-hr period. Instruct the patient not to void directly into the laboratory collection container. Instruct the patient to avoid defecating in the collection device and to keep toilet tissue out of the collection device to prevent contamination of the specimen. Place a sign in the bathroom to remind the patient to save all urine.

Instruct the patient to void all urine into the collection device and then to pour the urine into the laboratory collection container. Alternatively, the specimen can be left in the collection device for a health care staff member to add to the laboratory collection container.

There are no fluid or medication restrictions unless by medical direction.

Instruct the patient to follow a normal calcium diet for at least 4 days before test. Protocols may vary among facilities.

INTRATEST:

Ensure that the patient has complied with dietary restrictions; ensure that a normal calcium diet has been followed for at least 4 days prior to the procedure.

If the patient has a history of allergic reaction to latex, avoid the use of equipment containing latex.

Instruct the patient to cooperate fully and to follow directions.

Observe standard precautions, and follow the general guidelines in Appendix A. Positively identify the patient, and label the appropriate specimen container with the corresponding patient demographics, initials of the person collecting the specimen, date, and time of collection.

Random Specimen (collect in early morning)

Obtain urine specimen in a properly labeled plastic collection container and immediately transport urine. If an indwelling catheter is in place, it may be necessary to clamp off the catheter for 15 to 30 min before specimen collection. Cleanse specimen port with antiseptic swab, and then aspirate 5 mL of urine with a 21- to 25-gauge needle and syringe. Transfer urine to a plastic container.

Timed Specimen

Obtain a clean 3-L urine specimen container, toilet-mounted collection device, and plastic bag (for transport of the specimen container). The specimen must be refrigerated or kept on ice throughout the collection period. If an indwelling urinary catheter is in place, the drainage bag must be kept on ice.

Begin the test between 6 and 8 a.m. if possible. Collect first voiding and discard. Record the time the specimen was discarded as the beginning of the timed collection period. The next morning, ask the patient to void at the same time the collection was started, and add this last voiding to the container. Urinary output should be recorded throughout the collection time.

If an indwelling catheter is in place, replace the tubing and container system at the start of the collection time. Keep the container system on ice during the collection period or empty the urine into a larger container periodically during the collection period; monitor to ensure continued drainage, and conclude the test the next morning at the same hour the collection began.

- At the conclusion of the test, compare the quantity of urine with the urinary output record for the collection; if the specimen contains less than the recorded output, some urine may have been discarded, invalidating the test.
- Include on the collection container's label the amount of urine collected and test start and stop times. Promptly transport the specimen to the laboratory for processing and analysis.

POST-TEST:

- A report of the results will be sent to the requesting health-care provider (HCP), who will discuss the results with the patient.
- Instruct the patient to resume usual diet as directed by the HCP.
- *Nutritional Considerations:* Increased urine calcium levels may be associated with kidney stones. Educate the patient, if appropriate, as to the importance of drinking a sufficient amount of water when kidney stones are suspected.
- Recognize anxiety related to test results. Discuss the implications of abnormal test results on the patient's lifestyle.

Provide teaching and information regarding the clinical implications of the test results, as appropriate.

- Reinforce information given by the patient's HCP regarding further testing, treatment, or referral to another HCP. Answer any questions or address any concerns voiced by the patient or family.
- Depending on the results of this procedure, additional testing may be performed to evaluate or monitor progression of the disease process and determine the need for a change in therapy. Evaluate test results in relation to the patient's symptoms and other tests performed.

RELATED MONOGRAPHS:

- Related tests include ACTH, albumin, aldosterone, ALP, biopsy bone marrow, BMD, bone scan, calcitonin, calcium ionized, calculus kidney stone analysis, catecholamines, chloride, collagen cross-linked telopeptides, CBC, CT pelvis, CT spine, cortisol, CK and iso-enzymes, DHEA, fecal fat, glucose, HVA, magnesium, metanephrines, osteocalcin, oxalate, PTH, phosphorus, potassium, protein total, radiography bone, renin, sodium, thyroid scan, thyroxine, US thyroid and parathyroid, UA, uric acid, and vitamin D.
- Refer to the Endocrine, Genitourinary, and Musculoskeletal systems tables at the end of the book for related tests by body system.

Calculus, Kidney Stone Panel

SYNONYM/ACRONYM: Kidney stone analysis, nephrolithiasis analysis.

COMMON USE: To identify the presence of kidney stones.

SPECIMEN: Kidney stones.

NORMAL FINDINGS: (Method: Infrared spectrometry) None detected.

DESCRIPTION: Renal calculi (kidney stones) are formed by the crystallization of calcium oxalate (most common), magnesium ammonium phosphate, calcium phosphate, uric acid, and cystine. Formation of stones may be hereditary, related to diet or poor hydration, urinary tract infections caused by urease-producing bacteria, conditions resulting in reduced urine flow, or excessive amounts of the previously mentioned insoluble substances due to other predisposing conditions. The presence of stones is confirmed by diagnostic visualization or passing of the stones in the urine. The chemical nature of the stones is confirmed qualitatively. Analysis also includes a description of color, size, and weight.

INDICATIONS
• Identify substances present in renal calculi

POTENTIAL DIAGNOSIS
Positive findings in

Presence of calcium calculi (75–85%)
• Decreased levels of citric acid, which creates an imbalance of mineral salts *(related to conditions such as enteric hyperoxaluria, enterocystoplasty, or small bowel resection)*
• Distal renal tubular acidosis *(related to accumulation of calcium in the kidneys)*
• Etiology unknown
• Increased levels of calcium with or without alkaline pH, which creates an imbalance of mineral salts *(related to conditions such as Cushing's disease, Dent's disease, enterocystoplasty, ileostomy,*
immobilization, medullary sponge kidney, metabolic syndrome, milk alkali syndrome, primary biliary cirrhosis, primary hyperparathyroidism, sarcoidosis, Sjörgren's syndrome, use of calcium carbonate–containing antacids, use of corticosteroids, or vitamin D intoxication)
• Increased levels of oxalic acid, which creates an imbalance of mineral salts *(related to conditions such as bariatric surgery, enteric hyperoxaluria, enterocystoplasty, hereditary hyperoxaluria, hypomagnesemia, jejunal-ileal bypass, metabolic syndrome, pancreatitis, or small bowel resection)*
• Increased levels of uric acid, which creates an imbalance of mineral salts (uric acid crystals sometimes provide the base upon which calcium oxalate crystals grow)

Presence of magnesium ammonium phosphate (struvite or triple phosphate) calculi (10–15%)
• Urinary tract infection *(related to chronic indwelling catheter, neurogenic bladder dysfunction, obstruction, or urinary diversion)*
• Gram-positive bacteria associated with development of struvite calculi include *Bacillus* species, *Corynebacterium* species, *Peptococcus asaccharolyticus*, *Staphylococcus aureus*, and *Staphylococcus epidermidis*
• Gram-negative bacteria associated with development of struvite calculi include *Bacteroides corrodens*, *Flavobacterium* species, *Klebsiella* species, *Pasteurella* species, *Proteus* species, *Providencia stuartii*, *Pseudomonas aeruginosa*, *Serratia marcescens*, *Ureaplasma urealyticum*, and *Yersinia enterocolitica*
• Yeast associated with development of struvite calculi include *Candida humicola*, *Cryptococcus* species, *Rhodotorula* species,

Sporobolomyces species, and
Trichosporon cutaneum

Presence of uric acid calculi (5–8%)
- Increased levels of uric acid or increased urinary excretion of uric acid
- Anemias (pernicious, lead poisoning) *(related to cellular destruction and turnover)*
- Chemotherapy and radiation therapy *(related to high cell turnover)*
- Gout *(usually related to excess dietary intake)*
- Glycogen storage disease type I (von Gierke's disease) *(related to a genetic deficiency of the enzyme G-6-P-D, ultimately resulting in hyperuricemia, increased production of uric acid via the pentose phosphate pathway, and increased purine catabolism)*
- Hemoglobinopathies (sickle cell anemia, thalassemias) *(related to cellular destruction and turnover)*
- Ileostomy *(related to imbalances in mineral salts)*
- Lesch-Nyhan syndrome *(related to a disorder of uric acid metabolism)*
- Metabolic syndrome *(elevated uric acid levels are associated with metabolic syndrome; there is evidence that uric acidemia is a risk factor for cardiovascular and renal disease)*
- Polycythemia *(related to increased cellular destruction)*
- Psoriasis *(related to increased skin cell turnover)*
- Tumors *(related to high cell turnover)*

Presence of cystine calculi (approximately 1%)
- Fanconi's syndrome (hereditary hypercistinuria) *(related to increased excretion of cystine)*

Negative findings in: N/A

CRITICAL FINDINGS: N/A

INTERFERING FACTORS
- Drugs and substances that may increase the formation of urine calculi include probenecid and vitamin D.
- Adhesive tape should not be used to attach stones to any transportation or collection container, because the adhesive interferes with infrared spectrometry.

NURSING IMPLICATIONS AND PROCEDURE

PRETEST:

- Positively identify the patient using at least two unique identifiers before providing care, treatment, or services.
- *Patient Teaching:* Inform the patient this test can assist in identification of the presence of kidney stones.
- Obtain a history of the patient's complaints, especially hematuria, recurrent urinary tract infection, and abdominal pain. Also, obtain a list of known allergens.
- Obtain a history of the patient's genitourinary system and results of previously performed laboratory tests and diagnostic and surgical procedures.
- Obtain a list of the patient's current medications, including herbs, nutritional supplements, and nutraceuticals (see Appendix F).
- Review the procedure with the patient. Address concerns about pain and explain that there may be some discomfort during the procedure.
- *Sensitivity to social and cultural issues,* as well as concern for modesty, is important in providing psychological support before, during, and after the procedure.
- There are no food, fluid, or medication restrictions unless by medical direction.

INTRATEST:

- Instruct the patient to cooperate fully and to follow directions.
- Observe standard precautions, and follow the general guidelines in Appendix A. Positively identify the patient, and label the appropriate

specimen container with the corresponding patient demographics, initials of the person collecting the specimen, date, and time of collection.

▸ The patient presenting with symptoms indicating the presence of kidney stones may be provided with a device to strain the urine. The patient should be informed to transfer any particulate matter remaining in the strainer into the specimen collection container provided. Stones removed by the health-care provider (HCP) should be placed in the appropriate collection container.

▸ Promptly transport the specimen to the laboratory for processing and analysis.

POST-TEST:

▸ A report of the results will be made available to the requesting HCP, who will discuss the results with the patient.

▸ Inform the patient with kidney stones that the likelihood of recurrence is high. Educate the patient regarding risk factors that contribute to the likelihood of kidney stone formation, including family history, osteoporosis, urinary tract infections, gout, magnesium deficiency, Crohn's disease with prior resection, age, gender (males are two to three times more likely than females to develop stones), race (whites are three to four times more likely than African Americans to develop stones), and climate.

▸ *Nutritional Considerations:* Nutritional therapy is indicated for individuals identified as being at high risk for developing kidney stones. Educate the

patient that diets rich in protein, salt, and oxalates increase the risk of stone formation. Adequate fluid intake should be encouraged.

▸ Recognize anxiety related to test results. Discuss the implications of abnormal test results on the patient's lifestyle. Provide teaching and information regarding the clinical implications of the test results, as appropriate.

▸ Reinforce information given by the patient's HCP regarding further testing, treatment, or referral to another HCP. Follow-up testing of urine may be requested, but usually not for 1 mo after the stones have passed or been removed. Answer any questions or address any concerns voiced by the patient or family.

▸ Depending on the results of this procedure, additional testing may be performed to evaluate or monitor progression of the disease process and determine the need for a change in therapy. Evaluate test results in relation to the patient's symptoms and other tests performed.

RELATED MONOGRAPHS:

▸ Related tests include CT abdomen, calcium, creatinine clearance, culture bacterial urine, cystoscopy, IVP, KUB, magnesium, oxalate, phosphorus, potassium, renogram, retrograde ureteropyelography, US abdomen, US kidney, uric acid, and UA.

▸ Refer to the Genitourinary System table at the end of the book for related tests by body system.

Cancer Antigens: CA 15-3, CA 19-9, CA 125, and Carcinoembryonic

SYNONYM/ACRONYM: Carcinoembryonic antigen (CEA), cancer antigen 125 (CA 125), cancer antigen 15-3 (CA 15-3), cancer antigen 19-9 (CA 19-9), cancer antigen 27.29 (CA 27.29).

COMMON USE: To identify the presence of various cancers, such as breast and ovarian, as well as to evaluate the effectiveness of cancer treatment.

SPECIMEN: Serum (1 mL) collected in a red-top tube. Care must be taken to use the same assay method if serial measurements are to be taken.

NORMAL FINDINGS: (Method: Electrochemiluminometric immunoassay)

Smoking Status	Conventional Units	SI Units (Conventional Units × 1)
CEA		
Smoker	Less than 5.0 ng/mL	Less than 5.0 mcg/L
Nonsmoker	Less than 2.5 ng/mL	Less than 2.5 mcg/L

Conventional Units	SI Units (Conventional Units × 1)
CA 125	
Less than 35 units/mL	Less than 35 kU/L
CA 15-3	
Less than 25 units/mL	Less than 25 kU/L
CA 19-9	
Less than 35 units/mL	Less than 35 kU/L
CA 27.29	
Less than 38.6 units/mL	Less than 38.6 kU/L

DESCRIPTION: Carcinoembryonic antigen (CEA) is a glycoprotein normally produced only during early fetal life and rapid multiplication of epithelial cells, especially those of the digestive system. CEA also appears in the blood of chronic smokers. Although the test is not diagnostic for any specific disease and is not useful as a screening test for cancer, it is very useful for monitoring response to therapy in breast, liver, colon, and gastrointestinal cancer. Serial monitoring is also a useful indicator of recurrence or metastasis in colon or liver carcinoma.

CA 125, a glycoprotein present in normal endometrial tissue, appears in the blood when natural endometrial protective barriers are destroyed, as occurs in cancer or endometriosis.

Persistently rising levels indicate a poor prognosis, but absence of the tumor marker does not rule out tumor presence. Levels may also rise in pancreatic, liver, colon, breast, and lung cancers. CA 125 is most useful in monitoring the progression or recurrence of known ovarian cancer. It is not useful as a screening test when used alone.

CA 15-3 monitors patients for recurrence or metastasis of breast carcinoma.

CA 19-9 is a carbohydrate antigen used for post-therapeutic monitoring of patients with gastrointestinal, pancreatic, liver, and colorectal cancer.

CA 27.29 is a glycoprotein product of the muc-1 gene. It is most useful as a serial monitor for response to therapy or recurrence of breast carcinoma.

INDICATIONS
CEA
* Determine stage of colorectal cancer and test for recurrence or metastasis
* Monitor response to treatment of breast and gastrointestinal cancers

CA 125
* Assist in the diagnosis of carcinoma of the cervix and endometrium
* Assist in the diagnosis of ovarian cancer
* Monitor response to treatment of ovarian cancer

CA 15-3 and CA 27.29
* Monitor recurrent carcinoma of the breast

CA 19-9
* Monitor effectiveness of therapy
* Monitor gastrointestinal, head and neck, and gynecological carcinomas
* Predict recurrence of cholangiocarcinoma
* Predict recurrence of stomach, pancreatic, colorectal, gallbladder, liver, and urothelial carcinomas

POTENTIAL DIAGNOSIS
Increased in
CEA
* Benign tumors, including benign breast disease
* Chronic tobacco smoking
* Cirrhosis
* Colorectal, pulmonary, gastric, pancreatic, breast, head and neck, esophageal, ovarian, and prostate cancer
* Inflammatory bowel disease
* Pancreatitis
* Radiation therapy (transient)

CA 125
* Breast, colon, endometrial, liver, lung, ovarian, and pancreatic cancer
* Endometriosis
* First-trimester pregnancy
* Menses

* Ovarian abscess
* Pelvic inflammatory disease
* Peritonitis

CA 15-3 and CA 27.29
* Recurrence of breast carcinoma

CA 19-9
* Gastrointestinal, head and neck, and gynecologic carcinomas
* Recurrence of stomach, pancreatic, colorectal, gallbladder, liver, and urothelial carcinomas
* Recurrence of cholangiocarcinoma

Decreased in
* Effective therapy or removal of the tumor

CRITICAL FINDINGS: N/A

INTERFERING FACTORS: N/A

NURSING IMPLICATIONS AND PROCEDURE

PRETEST:
▸ Positively identify the patient using at least two unique identifiers before providing care, treatment, or services.
▸ *Patient Teaching:* Inform the patient this test can assist in monitoring the progress of various types of disease and evaluate response to therapy.
▸ Obtain a history of the patients complaints, including a list of known allergens, especially allergies or sensitivities to latex.
▸ Obtain a history of the patients gastrointestinal, immune, and reproductive systems, as well as results of previously performed laboratory tests and diagnostic and surgical procedures.
▸ Note any recent radiology procedures that can interfere with test results.
▸ Obtain a list of the patients current medications, including herbs, nutritional supplements, and nutraceuticals (see Appendix F).
▸ Determine if the patient smokes, because smokers may have false elevations of CEA.

Review the procedure with the patient. Inform the patient that specimen collection takes approximately 5 to 10 minutes. Address concerns about pain and explain that there may be some discomfort during the venipuncture. *Sensitivity to social and cultural issues,* as well as concern for modesty, is important in providing psychological support before, during, and after the procedure.

There are no food, fluid, or medication restrictions unless by medical direction.

INTRATEST:

If the patient has a history of allergic reaction to latex, avoid the use of equipment containing latex.

Instruct the patient to cooperate fully and to follow directions. Direct the patient to breathe normally and to avoid unnecessary movement.

Observe standard precautions, and follow the general guidelines in Appendix A. Positively identify the patient, and label the appropriate specimen container with the corresponding patient demographics, initials of the person collecting the specimen, date, and time of collection. Perform a venipuncture.

Remove the needle and apply direct pressure with dry gauze to stop bleeding. Observe/assess venipuncture site for bleeding or hematoma formation and secure gauze with adhesive bandage.

Promptly transport the specimen to the laboratory for processing and analysis.

POST-TEST:

A report of the results will be made available to the requesting health-care provider (HCP), who will discuss the results with the patient.

Recognize anxiety related to test results, and be supportive of perceived loss of independence and fear of shortened life expectancy. Discuss the implications of abnormal test results on the patients lifestyle. Provide teaching and information regarding the clinical implications of the test results, as appropriate. Educate the patient regarding access to counseling services. Provide contact information, if desired, for the American Cancer Association (www.cancer.org).

Reinforce information given by the patients HCP regarding further testing, treatment, or referral to another HCP. Decisions regarding the need for and frequency of breast self-examination, mammography, MRI breast, or other cancer screening procedures should be made after consultation between the patient and HCP. The most current guidelines for breast cancer screening of the general population as well as of individuals with increased risk are available from the American Cancer Society (www.cancer.org), the American College of Obstetricians and Gynecologists (ACOG) (www.acog.org), and the American College of Radiology (www.acr.org). Answer any questions or address any concerns voiced by the patient or family.

Decisions regarding the need for and frequency of occult blood testing, colonoscopy, or other cancer screening procedures should be made after consultation between the patient and HCP. The most current guidelines for colon cancer screening of the general population as well as of individuals with increased risk are available from the American Cancer Society (www.cancer.org) and the American College of Gastroenterology (www.gi.org).

Depending on the results of this procedure, additional testing may be performed to evaluate or monitor progression of the disease process and determine the need for a change in therapy. Evaluate test results in relation to the patients symptoms and other tests performed.

RELATED MONOGRAPHS:

Related tests include barium enema, biopsy breast, biopsy cervical, biopsy intestinal, biopsy liver, capsule endoscopy, colonoscopy, colposcopy, fecal analysis, HCG, liver and spleen scan, MRI breast, MRI liver, mammogram, stereotactic breast biopsy, proctosigmoidoscopy, radiofrequency ablation liver, US abdomen, US breast, and US liver.

Refer to the Gastrointestinal, Immune, and Reproductive systems tables at the end of the book for related tests by body system.

Capsule Endoscopy

SYNONYM/ACRONYM: Pill GI endoscopy.

COMMON USE: To assist in visualization of the GI tract to identify disease such as tumor and inflammation.

AREA OF APPLICATION: Esophagus, stomach, upper duodenum, and small bowel.

CONTRAST: None.

DESCRIPTION: This outpatient procedure involves ingesting a small (size of a large vitamin pill) capsule that is wireless and contains a small video camera that will pass naturally through the digestive system while taking pictures of the intestine. The capsule is 11 mm by 30 mm and contains a camera, light source, radio transmitter, and battery. The patient swallows the capsule, and the camera takes and transmits two images per second. The images are transmitted to a recording device, which saves all images for review later by a health-care provider (HCP). This device is approximately the size of a personal compact disk player. The recording device is worn on a belt around the patient's waist, and the video images are transmitted to aerials taped to the body and stored on the device. After 8 hr, the device is removed and returned to the HCP for processing. Thousands of images are downloaded onto a computer for viewing by an HCP specialist. The capsule is disposable and will be excreted naturally in the patient's bowel movements. In the rare case that it is not excreted naturally, it will need to be removed endoscopically or surgically.

INDICATIONS

- Assist in differentiating between benign and neoplastic tumors
- Detect gastric or duodenal ulcers
- Detect gastrointestinal tract (GI) inflammatory disease
- Determine the presence and location of GI bleeding and vascular abnormalities
- Evaluate the extent of esophageal injury after ingestion of chemicals
- Evaluate stomach or duodenum after surgical procedures
- Evaluate suspected gastric obstruction
- Identify Crohn's disease, infectious enteritis, and celiac sprue
- Identify source of chronic diarrhea
- Investigate the cause of abdominal pain, celiac syndrome, and other malabsorption syndromes

POTENTIAL DIAGNOSIS

Normal findings in

- Esophageal mucosa is normally yellow-pink. At about 9 in. from the incisor teeth, a pulsation indicates the location of the aortic arch. The gastric mucosa is orange-red and contains rugae. The proximal duodenum is reddish and contains a few longitudinal folds, whereas the distal duodenum has circular folds lined with villi. No abnormal structures or functions are observed in the esophagus, stomach, or duodenum.

Abnormal findings in
- Achalasia
- Acute and chronic gastric and duodenal ulcers
- Crohn's disease, infectious enteritis, and celiac sprue
- Diverticular disease
- Duodenal cancer, diverticula, and ulcers
- Duodenitis
- Esophageal or pyloric stenosis
- Esophageal varices
- Esophagitis or strictures
- Gastric cancer, tumors, and ulcers
- Gastritis
- Hiatal hernia
- Mallory-Weiss syndrome
- Perforation of the esophagus, stomach, or small bowel
- Polyps
- Small bowel tumors
- Strictures
- Tumors (benign or malignant)

CRITICAL FINDINGS: N/A

INTERFERING FACTORS

This procedure is contraindicated for
- Patients who have had surgery involving the stomach or duodenum, which can make locating the duodenal papilla difficult.
- Patients with a bleeding disorder.
- Patients with unstable cardiopulmonary status, blood coagulation defects, or cholangitis, unless the patient received prophylactic antibiotic therapy before the test (otherwise, the examination must be rescheduled).
- Patients with unstable cardiopulmonary status, blood coagulation defects, known aortic arch aneurysm, large esophageal Zenker's diverticulum, recent GI

surgery, esophageal varices, or known esophageal perforation.

Factors that may impair clear imaging
- Gas or feces in the GI tract resulting from inadequate cleansing or failure to restrict food intake before the study.
- Retained barium from a previous radiological procedure.

Other considerations
- The patient should not be near any electromagnetic source, such as magnetic resonance imaging (MRI) or amateur (ham) radio equipment.
- Undergoing an MRI during the procedure may result in serious damage to the patient's intestinal tract or abdomen. The patient should contact his or her HCP for evaluation prior to any other procedure.
- Delayed capsule transit times may be a result of narcotic use, somatostatin use, gastroparesis, or psychiatric illness.

NURSING IMPLICATIONS AND PROCEDURE

PRETEST:
- Positively identify the patient using at least two unique identifiers before providing care, treatment, or services.
- *Patient Teaching:* Inform the patient this procedure can assist in assessing the esophagus, stomach, and upper intestines for disease.
- Obtain a history of the patient's complaints, including a list of known allergens, especially allergies or sensitivities to latex, iodine, seafood, contrast medium, anesthetics, and dyes.
- Obtain a history of the patient's gastrointestinal system, symptoms, and results of previously performed laboratory tests and diagnostic and surgical procedures.
- Ensure that this procedure is performed before an upper GI series or barium swallow.

▶ Record the date of the last menstrual period and determine the possibility of pregnancy in perimenopausal women.

▶ Obtain a list of the patient's current medications, including anticoagulants, aspirin and other salicylates, herbs, nutritional supplements, and nutraceuticals (see Appendix F). Such products should be discontinued by medical direction for the appropriate number of days prior to a surgical procedure. Note time and date of last dose.

▶ Review the procedure with the patient. Address concerns about pain and explain that no pain will be experienced during the procedure. Inform the patient that the procedure is begun in a GI laboratory or office, usually by an HCP or support staff, and that it takes approximately 30 to 60 min to begin the procedure.

▶ *Sensitivity to social and cultural issues,* as well as concern for modesty, is important in providing psychological support before, during, and after the procedure.

▶ Instruct the patient to stop taking medications that have a coating effect, such as sucralfate and Pepto-Bismol, 3 days before the procedure.

▶ Instruct the patient to abstain from the use of tobacco products for 24 hr prior to the procedure.

▶ Instruct the patient to start a liquid diet on the day before the procedure. From 10 p.m. the evening before the procedure, the patient should not eat or drink except for necessary medication with a sip of water. Instruct the patient to take a standard bowel prep the night before the procedure. Protocols may vary among facilities.

▶ Instruct the patient not to take any medication for 2 hr prior to the procedure.

▶ Inform the patient that there is a chance of intestinal obstruction associated with the procedure.

▶ Instruct the patient to wear loose, two-piece clothing on the day of the procedure. This assists with the placement of the sensors on the patient's abdomen.

▶ *Make sure a written and informed consent has been signed prior to the procedure.*

INTRATEST:

▶ Observe standard precautions, and follow the general guidelines in Appendix A. Positively identify the patient.

▶ Ensure that the patient has complied with dietary and medication restrictions and pretesting preparations for at least 8 hr prior to the procedure.

▶ Obtain accurate height, weight, and abdominal girth measurements prior to beginning the examination.

▶ Instruct the patient to cooperate fully and to follow directions.

▶ Ask the patient to ingest the capsule with a full glass of water. The water may have simethicone in it to reduce gastric and bile bubbles.

▶ After ingesting the capsule, the patient should not eat or drink for at least 2 hr. After 4 hr, the patient may have a light snack.

▶ After ingesting the capsule and until it is excreted, the patient should not be near any source of powerful electromagnetic fields, such as MRI or amateur (ham) radio equipment.

▶ The procedure lasts approximately 8 hr.

▶ Instruct the patient not to disconnect the equipment or remove the belt at any time during the test.

▶ If the data recorder stops functioning, instruct the patient to record the time and the nature of any event such as eating or drinking.

▶ Instruct the patient to keep a timed diary for the day detailing the food and liquids ingested and symptoms during the recording period.

▶ Instruct the patient to avoid any strenuous physical activity, bending, or stooping during the test.

POST-TEST:

▶ Instruct the patient to resume normal activity, medication, and diet after the test is ended or as tolerated after the examination, as directed by the HCP.

▶ Instruct the patient to remove the recorder and return it to the HCP.

▶ Patients are asked to verify the elimination of the capsule but not to retrieve the capsule.

Inform the patient that the capsule is a single-use device that does not harbor any environmental hazards.

Emphasize that any abdominal pain, fever, nausea, vomiting, or difficulty breathing must be immediately reported to the HCP.

A report of the results will be made available to the requesting HCP, who will discuss the results with the patient.

Recognize anxiety related to test results. Discuss the implications of abnormal test results on the patient's lifestyle. Provide teaching and information regarding the clinical implications of the test results, as appropriate.

Reinforce information given by the patient's HCP regarding further testing, treatment, or referral to another HCP. Decisions regarding the need for and frequency of occult blood testing, colonoscopy, or other cancer screening procedures should be made after consultation between the patient and HCP. The most current guidelines for colon cancer screening of the general population as well as individuals with increased risk are available from the American Cancer Society (www.cancer.org)

and the American College of Gastroenterology (www.gi.org). Answer any questions or address any concerns voiced by the patient or family.

Depending on the results of this procedure, additional testing may be needed to evaluate or monitor progression of the disease process and determine the need for a change in therapy. Evaluate test results in relation to the patient's symptoms and other tests performed.

RELATED MONOGRAPHS:

Related tests include barium enema, barium swallow, biopsy intestinal, cancer antigens, colonoscopy, CT abdomen, CT colonoscopy, esophageal manometry, esophagogastroduodenoscopy, fecal analysis, folate, gastric acid emptying scan, gastric acid stimulation test, gastrin, Helicobacter pylori, KUB studies, MRI abdomen, PET pelvis, proctosigmoidoscopy, upper GI and small bowel series, US abdomen, and vitamin B_{12}.

Refer to the Gastrointestinal System table at the end of the book for related tests by body system.

Carbon Dioxide

SYNONYM/ACRONYM: CO_2 combining power, CO_2, Tco_2.

COMMON USE: To assess the effect of total carbon dioxide levels on respiratory and metabolic acid-base balance.

SPECIMEN: Serum (1 mL) collected in a red- or tiger-top tube, plasma (1 mL) collected in a green-top (lithium or sodium heparin) tube; or whole blood (1 mL) collected in a green-top (lithium or sodium heparin) tube or heparinized syringe.

NORMAL FINDINGS: (Method: Colorimetry, enzyme assay, or Pco_2 electrode)

Carbon Dioxide	Conventional & SI Units
Plasma or serum (venous)	
Infant–2 yr	13–29 mmol/L
2 yr–older adult	23–29 mmol/L
Whole blood (venous)	
Infant–2 yr	18–28 mmol/L
2 yr–older adult	22–26 mmol/L

DESCRIPTION: Serum or plasma carbon dioxide (CO_2) measurement is usually done as part of an electrolyte panel. Total CO_2 (Tco_2) is an important component of the body's buffering capability, and measurements are used mainly in the evaluation of acid-base balance. It is important to understand the differences between Tco_2 (CO_2 content) and CO_2 gas (Pco_2). *Total CO_2* reflects the majority of CO_2 in the body, mainly in the form of bicarbonate (HCO_3^-); is present as a base; and is regulated by the kidneys. CO_2 gas contributes little to the Tco_2 level, is acidic, and is regulated by the lungs (see monograph titled "Blood Gases").

CO_2 provides the basis for the principal buffering system of the extracellular fluid system, which is the bicarbonate–carbonic acid buffer system. CO_2 circulates in the body either bound to protein or physically dissolved. Constituents in the blood that contribute to Tco_2 levels are bicarbonate, carbamino compounds, and carbonic acid (carbonic acid includes undissociated carbonic acid and dissolved CO_2). Bicarbonate is the second largest group of anions in the extracellular fluid (chloride is the largest). Tco_2 levels closely reflect bicarbonate levels in the blood, because 90% to 95% of CO_2 circulates as HCO_3^-.

INDICATIONS
- Evaluate decreased venous CO_2 in the case of compensated metabolic acidosis
- Evaluate increased venous CO_2 in the case of compensated metabolic alkalosis
- Monitor decreased venous CO_2 as a result of compensated respiratory alkalosis
- Monitor increased venous CO_2 as a result of compensation for respiratory acidosis secondary to significant respiratory system infection or cancer; decreased respiratory rate

POTENTIAL DIAGNOSIS

Increased in
- *Interpretation requires clinical information and evaluation of other electrolytes*
- Acute intermittent porphyria *(related to severe vomiting associated with acute attacks)*
- Airway obstruction *(related to impaired elimination from weak breathing responses)*
- Asthmatic shock *(related to impaired elimination from abnormal breathing responses)*
- Brain tumor *(related to abnormal blood circulation)*
- Bronchitis (chronic) *(related to impaired elimination from weak breathing responses)*
- Cardiac disorders *(related to lack of blood circulation)*

- Depression of respiratory center *(related to impaired elimination from weak breathing responses)*
- Electrolyte disturbance (severe) *(response to maintain acid-base balance)*
- Emphysema *(related to impaired elimination from weak breathing responses)*
- Hypothyroidism *(related to impaired elimination from weak breathing responses)*
- Hypoventilation *(related to impaired elimination from weak breathing responses)*
- Metabolic alkalosis *(various causes; excessive vomiting)*
- Myopathy *(related to impaired ventilation)*
- Pneumonia *(related to impaired elimination from weak breathing responses)*
- Poliomyelitis *(related to impaired elimination from weak breathing responses)*
- Respiratory acidosis *(related to impaired elimination)*
- Tuberculosis (pulmonary) *(related to impaired elimination from weak breathing responses)*

Decreased in
- *Interpretation requires clinical information and evaluation of other electrolytes*
- Acute renal failure *(response to buildup of ketoacids)*
- Anxiety *(related to hyperventilation; too much CO_2 is exhaled)*
- Dehydration *(response to metabolic acidosis that develops)*
- Diabetic ketoacidosis *(response to buildup of ketoacids)*
- Diarrhea (severe) *(acidosis related to loss of base ions like HCO_3; most of CO_2 content is in this form)*
- High fever *(response to neutralize acidosis present during fever)*
- Metabolic acidosis *(response to neutralize acidosis)*

- Respiratory alkalosis *(hyperventilation; too much CO_2 is exhaled)*
- Salicylate intoxication *(response to neutralize related metabolic acidosis)*
- Starvation *(CO_2 buffer system used to neutralize buildup of ketoacids)*

CRITICAL FINDINGS
- Less than 15 mmol/L (SI: Less than 15 mmol/L)
- Greater than 40 mmol/L (SI: Greater than 40 mmol/L)

Note and immediately report to the health-care provider (HCP) any critically increased or decreased values and related symptoms. Timely notification of critical values for lab or diagnostic studies is a role expectation of the professional nurse. Notification processes will vary among facilities. Upon receipt of the critical value, the information should be read back to the caller to verify accuracy. Most policies require immediate notification of the primary HCP, hospitalist, or on-call HCP. Reported information includes the patient's name, unique identifiers, critical value, name of the person giving the report, and name of the person receiving the report. Documentation of notification should be made in the medical record with the name of the HCP notified, time and date of notification, and any orders received. Any delay in a timely report of a critical value may require completion of a notification form with review by Risk Management.

Observe the patient for signs and symptoms of excessive or insufficient CO_2 levels, and report these findings to the HCP. If the patient has been vomiting for several days and is breathing shallowly, or if the patient has had gastric suctioning and is breathing shallowly, this may indicate elevated CO_2 levels. Decreased CO_2

levels are evidenced by deep, vigorous breathing and flushed skin.

INTERFERING FACTORS

- Drugs that may cause an increase in Tco_2 levels include acetylsalicylic acid, aldosterone, bicarbonate, carbenicillin, carbenoxolone, corticosteroids, dexamethasone, ethacrynic acid, laxatives (chronic abuse), and x-ray contrast agents.
- Drugs that may cause a decrease in Tco_2 levels include acetazolamide, acetylsalicylic acid (initially), amiloride, ammonium chloride, fluorides, metformin, methicillin, nitrofurantoin, NSD 3004 (long-acting carbonic anhydrase inhibitor), paraldehyde, tetracycline, triamterene, and xylitol.
- Prompt and proper specimen processing, storage, and analysis are important to achieve accurate results. The specimen should be stored under anaerobic conditions after collection to prevent the diffusion of CO_2 gas from the specimen. Falsely decreased values result from uncovered specimens. It is estimated that CO_2 diffuses from the sample at the rate of 6 mmol/hr.

NURSING IMPLICATIONS AND PROCEDURE

PRETEST:

▶ Positively identify the patient using at least two unique identifiers before providing care, treatment, or services.
▶ *Patient Teaching:* Inform the patient this test can assist in measuring the amount of carbon dioxide in the body.
▶ Obtain a history of the patient's complaints, including a list of known allergens, especially allergies or sensitivities to latex.

▶ Obtain a history of the patient's cardiovascular, genitourinary, and respiratory systems, as well as results of previously performed laboratory tests and diagnostic and surgical procedures.
▶ Note any recent procedures that can interfere with test results.
▶ Obtain a list of the patient's current medications, including herbs, nutritional supplements, and nutraceuticals (see Appendix F).
▶ Review the procedure with the patient. Inform the patient that specimen collection takes approximately 5 to 10 min. Address concerns about pain and explain that there may be some discomfort during the venipuncture.
▶ *Sensitivity to social and cultural issues,* as well as concern for modesty, is important in providing psychological support before, during, and after the procedure.
▶ There are no food, fluid, or medication restrictions unless by medical direction.

INTRATEST:

▶ If the patient has a history of allergic reaction to latex, avoid the use of equipment containing latex.
▶ Instruct the patient to cooperate fully and to follow directions. Direct the patient to breathe normally and to avoid unnecessary movement.
▶ Observe standard precautions, and follow the general guidelines in Appendix A. Positively identify the patient, and label the appropriate specimen container with the corresponding patient demographics, initials of the person collecting the specimen, date, and time of collection. Perform a venipuncture.
▶ Remove the needle and apply direct pressure with dry gauze to stop bleeding. Observe/assess venipuncture site for bleeding or hematoma formation and secure gauze with adhesive bandage.
▶ Promptly transport the specimen to the laboratory for processing and analysis.

POST-TEST:

A report of the results will be made available to the requesting HCP, who will discuss the results with the patient.
Nutritional Considerations: Abnormal CO_2 values may be associated with diseases of the respiratory system. Malnutrition is commonly seen in patients with severe respiratory disease for reasons including fatigue, lack of appetite, and gastrointestinal distress. Research has estimated that the daily caloric intake required for respiration of patients with chronic obstructive pulmonary disease is 10 times higher than that of normal individuals. Adequate intake of vitamins A and C is also important to prevent pulmonary infection and to decrease the extent of lung tissue damage. The importance of following the prescribed diet should be stressed to the patient and/or caregiver.

Reinforce information given by the patient's HCP regarding further testing, treatment, or referral to another HCP. Answer any questions or address any concerns voiced by the patient or family.

Depending on the results of this procedure, additional testing may be performed to evaluate or monitor progression of the disease process and determine the need for a change in therapy. Evaluate test results in relation to the patient's symptoms and other tests performed.

RELATED MONOGRAPHS:

Related tests include anion gap, arterial/alveolar oxygen ratio, biopsy lung, blood gases, chest x-ray, chloride, cold agglutinin titer, CBC white blood cell count and differential, culture bacterial blood, culture bacterial sputum, culture mycobacterium, culture viral, cytology sputum, eosinophil count, ESR, gallium scan, Gram stain, IgE, ketones, lung perfusion scan, osmolality, phosphorus, plethysmography, pleural fluid analysis, potassium, PFT, pulse oximetry, salicylate, and US abdomen.

Refer to the Cardiovascular, Genitourinary, and Respiratory systems tables at the end of the book for related tests by body system.

Carboxyhemoglobin

SYNONYM/ACRONYM: Carbon monoxide, CO, COHb, COH.

COMMON USE: To identify the amount of carbon monoxide in the blood related to poisoning, toxicity from smoke inhalation, or exhaust from cars.

SPECIMEN: Whole blood (1 mL) collected in a green-top (heparin) or lavender-top (EDTA) tube, depending on laboratory requirement. Specimen should be transported tightly capped (anaerobic) and in an ice slurry if blood gases are to be performed simultaneously. Carboxyhemoglobin is stable at room temperature.

NORMAL FINDINGS: (Method: Spectrophotometry, co-oximetry)

	% Saturation of Hemoglobin
Newborns	10–12%
Nonsmokers	Up to 2%
Smokers	Up to 10%

DESCRIPTION: Exogenous carbon monoxide (CO) is a colorless, odorless, tasteless by-product of incomplete combustion derived from the exhaust of automobiles, coal and gas burning, and tobacco smoke. Endogenous CO is produced as a result of red blood cell catabolism. CO levels are elevated in newborns as a result of the combined effects of high hemoglobin turnover and the inefficiency of the infant's respiratory system. CO binds tightly to hemoglobin with an affinity 250 times greater than oxygen, competitively and dramatically reducing the oxygen-carrying capacity of hemoglobin. The increased percentage of bound CO reflects the extent to which normal transport of oxygen has been negatively affected. Overexposure causes hypoxia, which results in headache, nausea, vomiting, vertigo, collapse, or convulsions. Toxic exposure causes anoxia, increased levels of lactic acid, and irreversible tissue damage, which can result in coma or death. Acute exposure may be evidenced by a cherry red color to the lips, skin, and nail beds; this observation may not be apparent in cases of chronic exposure. A direct correlation has been implicated between carboxyhemoglobin levels and symptoms of atherosclerotic disease, angina, and myocardial infarction.

INDICATIONS
* Assist in the diagnosis of suspected CO poisoning
* Evaluate the effect of smoking on the patient
* Evaluate exposure to fires and smoke inhalation

POTENTIAL DIAGNOSIS

Increased in
* CO poisoning
* Hemolytic disease *(CO released during red blood cell catabolism)*
* Tobacco smoking

Decreased in: N/A

CRITICAL FINDINGS ✸

Percent of Total Hemoglobin	Symptoms
10%–20%	Asymptomatic
10%–30%	Disturbance of judgment, headache, dizziness
30%–40%	Dizziness, muscle weakness, vision problems, confusion, increased heart rate, increased breathing rate
50%–60%	Loss of consciousness, coma
Greater than 60%	Death

Note and immediately report to the health-care provider (HCP) any critically increased or decreased values and related symptoms. Timely notification of critical values, for lab or diagnostic studies is a role expectation of the professional nurse. Notification processes will vary among facilities. Upon receipt of the critical value, the information should be read back to the caller to verify accuracy. Most policies require immediate notification of the primary HCP, hospitalist, or on-call HCP. Reported information includes the patient's name, unique identifiers, critical value, name of the person giving the report, and name of the person receiving the report. Documentation of notification should be made in the medical record with the name of the HCP notified, time and date of notification, and any orders received. Any delay in a timely report of a critical value may require completion of a notification form with review by Risk Management.

Women and children may suffer more severe symptoms of carbon monoxide poisoning at lower levels of carbon monoxide than men because women and children usually have lower red blood cell counts.

A possible intervention in moderate CO poisoning is the administration of supplemental oxygen given at atmospheric pressure. In severe CO poisoning, hyperbaric oxygen treatments may be used.

INTERFERING FACTORS

Specimen should be collected before administration of oxygen therapy.

NURSING IMPLICATIONS AND PROCEDURE

PRETEST:

▶ Positively identify the patient using at least two unique identifiers before providing care, treatment, or services.

▶ *Patient Teaching:* Inform the patient this test can assist in evaluating the extent of carbon monoxide poisoning or toxicity.

▶ Obtain a history of the patient's complaints, including a list of known allergens, especially allergies or sensitivities to latex.

▶ Obtain a history of the patient's respiratory system and results of previously performed laboratory tests and diagnostic and surgical procedures.

▶ Note any recent procedures that can interfere with test results.

▶ Obtain a list of the patient's current medications, including herbs, nutritional supplements, and nutraceuticals (see Appendix F).

▶ Review the procedure with the patient. Explain to the patient or family members that the cause of the headache, vomiting, dizziness, convulsions, or coma could be related to CO exposure. Inform the patient that specimen collection takes approximately 5 to 10 min. Address concerns about pain and explain to the patient that there may be some discomfort during the venipuncture.

▶ *Sensitivity to social and cultural issues,* as well as concern for modesty, is important in providing psychological support before, during, and after the procedure.

▶ If carboxyhemoglobin measurement will be performed simultaneously with arterial blood gases, prepare an ice slurry in a cup or plastic bag and have it on hand for immediate transport of the specimen to the laboratory.

▶ There are no food, fluid, or medication restrictions unless by medical direction.

INTRATEST:

▶ If the patient has a history of allergic reaction to latex, avoid the use of equipment containing latex.

▶ Instruct the patient to cooperate fully and to follow directions. Direct the patient to breathe normally and to avoid unnecessary movement. Observe standard precautions, and follow the general guidelines in Appendix A. Positively identify the patient, and label the appropriate

specimen container with the corresponding patient demographics, initials of the person collecting the specimen, date, and time of collection. Perform a venipuncture. The tightly capped sample should be placed in an ice slurry immediately after collection. Information on the specimen label should be protected from water in the ice slurry by first placing the specimen in a protective plastic bag.
▸ Remove the needle and apply direct pressure with dry gauze to stop bleeding. Observe/assess venipuncture site for bleeding or hematoma formation and secure gauze with adhesive bandage.
▸ Promptly transport the specimen to the laboratory for processing and analysis.

POST-TEST:

▸ A report of the results will be made available to the requesting HCP, who will discuss the results with the patient.
▸ Recognize anxiety related to test results, and be supportive of impaired activity related to fear of shortened life expectancy. Discuss the implications of abnormal test results on the patient's lifestyle. Provide teaching and information regarding the clinical implications of the test results, as appropriate. Educate the patient

regarding access to counseling services. Educate the patient regarding avoiding gas heaters and indoor cooking fires without adequate ventilation and the need to have gas furnaces checked yearly for CO leakage. Inform the patient of smoking cessation programs, as appropriate.
▸ Reinforce information given by the patient's HCP regarding further testing, treatment, or referral to another HCP. Answer any questions or address any concerns voiced by the patient or family.
▸ Depending on the results of this procedure, additional testing may be performed to evaluate or monitor progression of the disease process and determine the need for a change in therapy. Evaluate test results in relation to the patient's symptoms and other tests performed.

RELATED MONOGRAPHS:

▸ Related tests include angiography pulmonary, arterial/alveolar oxygen ratio, blood gases, carbon dioxide, CBC, lung perfusion scan, lung ventilation scan, plethysmography, and PFT.
▸ Refer to the Respiratory System table at the end of the book for related tests by body system.

Catecholamines, Blood and Urine

SYNONYM/ACRONYM: Epinephrine, norepinephrine, dopamine.

COMMON USE: To assist in diagnosing catecholamine-secreting tumors, such as those found in the adrenal medulla, and in the investigation of hypertension. The urine test is used to assist in diagnosing pheochromocytoma and as a work-up of neuroblastoma.

SPECIMEN: Plasma (2 mL) collected in green-top (heparin) tube. Urine (25 mL) from a timed specimen collected in a clean, plastic, amber collection container with 6N hydrochloric acid as a preservative.

NORMAL FINDINGS: (Method: High-performance liquid chromatography)

Blood	Conventional Units	SI Units
		(Conventional Units × 5.46)
Epinephrine		
Newborn–1 yr	0–34 pg/mL	0–186 pmol/L
1–18 yr	0–80 pg/mL	0–437 pmol/L
Adult		
Supine, 30 min	0–110 pg/mL	0–600 pmol/L
Standing, 30 min	0–140 pg/mL	0–764 pmol/L
		(Conventional Units × 5.91)
Norepinephrine		
Newborn–1 yr	0–659 pg/mL	0–3,895 pmol/L
1–18 yr	0–611 pg/mL	0–3,611 pmol/L
Adult		
Supine, 30 min	70–750 pg/mL	414–4,432 pmol/L
Standing, 30 min	200–1,700 pg/mL	1,182–10,047 pmol/L
		(Conventional Units × 6.53)
Dopamine		
Newborn–1 yr	0–42 pg/mL	0–274 pmol/L
1–18 yr	0–32 pg/mL	0–209 pmol/L
Adult		
Supine or standing	0–48 pg/mL	0–313 pmol/L

Urine	Conventional Units	SI Units
		(Conventional Units × 5.46)
Epinephrine		
Newborn–9 yr	0–11.0 mcg/24 hr	0–60.1 nmol/24 hr
10–19 yr	0–18.0 mcg/24 hr	0–98.3 nmol/24 hr
20 yr–older adult	0–20 mcg/24 hr	0–109 nmol/24 hr
		(Conventional Units × 5.91)
Norepinephrine		
Newborn–9 yr	0–59 mcg/24 hr	0–349 nmol/24 hr
10–19 yr	0–90 mcg/24 hr	0–532 nmol/24 hr
20 yr–older adult	0–135 mcg/24 hr	0–798 nmol/24 hr
		(Conventional Units × 6.53)
Dopamine		
Newborn–9 yr	0–414 mcg/24 hr	0–2,703 nmol/24 hr
10–19 yr	0–575 mcg/24 hr	0–3,755 nmol/24 hr
20 yr–older adult	0–510 mcg/24 hr	0–3,330 nmol/24 hr

C

DESCRIPTION: Catecholamines are produced by the chromaffin tissue of the adrenal medulla. They also are found in sympathetic nerve endings and in the brain. The major catecholamines are epinephrine, norepinephrine, and dopamine. They prepare the body for the fight-or-flight stress response, help regulate metabolism, and are excreted from the body by the kidneys. Levels are affected by diurnal variations, fluctuating in response to stress, postural changes, diet, smoking, drugs, and temperature changes. As a result, blood measurement is not as reliable as a 24-hr timed urine test. For test results to be valid, all of the previously mentioned environmental variables must be controlled when the test is performed. Results of blood specimens are most reliable when the specimen is collected during a hypertensive episode. Catecholamines are measured when there is high suspicion of pheochromocytoma but urine results are normal or borderline. Use of a clonidine suppression test with measurement of plasma catecholamines may be requested. Failure to suppress production of catecholamines after administration of clonidine supports the diagnosis of pheochromocytoma. Elevated homovanillic acid levels rule out pheochromocytoma because this tumor primarily secretes epinephrine. Elevated catecholamines without hypertension suggest neuroblastoma or ganglioneuroma. Findings should be compared with metanephrines and vanillylmandelic acid, which are the metabolites of epinephrine and norepinephrine.

Findings should also be compared with homovanillic acid, which is the product of dopamine metabolism.

INDICATIONS
- Assist in the diagnosis of neuroblastoma, ganglioneuroma, or dysautonomia
- Assist in the diagnosis of pheochromocytoma
- Evaluate acute hypertensive episode
- Evaluate hypertension of unknown origin
- Screen for pheochromocytoma among family members with an autosomal dominant inheritance pattern for Lindau–von Hippel disease or multiple endocrine neoplasia

POTENTIAL DIAGNOSIS

Increased in
- Diabetic acidosis (epinephrine and norepinephrine) *(related to metabolic stress; are released to initiate glycogenolysis, gluconeogenesis, and lipolysis)*
- Ganglioblastoma (epinephrine, slight increase; norepinephrine, large increase) *(related to production by the tumor)*
- Ganglioneuroma (all are increased; norepinephrine, largest increase) *(related to production by the tumor)*
- Hypothyroidism (epinephrine and norepinephrine) *(possibly related to interactions among the immune, endocrine, and nervous systems)*
- Long-term manic-depressive disorders (epinephrine and norepinephrine) *(some studies indicate a relationship between decreased catecholamine levels and manic*

depressive illnesses; the pathophysiology is not well understood)
• Myocardial infarction (epinephrine
and norepinephrine) *(related to
physical stress)*
• Neuroblastoma (all are increased;
norepinephrine and dopamine, largest increase) *(related to production by the tumor)*
• Pheochromocytoma (epinephrine,
continuous or intermittent increase;
norepinephrine, slight increase)
*(related to production by the
tumor)*
• Shock (epinephrine and norepinephrine) *(related to physical
stress)*
• Strenuous exercise (epinephrine
and norepinephrine) *(related to
physical stress)*

Decreased in
• Autonomic nervous system dysfunction (norepinephrine)
• Orthostatic hypotension caused by
central nervous system disease (norepinephrine) *(related to inability
of sympathetic nervous system to
activate postganglionic neuron)*
• Parkinson's disease (dopamine)
*(some studies indicate a relation-
ship between decreased catecholamine levels and Parkinson's disease; the pathophysiology is not
well understood)*

CRITICAL FINDINGS: N/A

INTERFERING FACTORS
• Drugs that may increase plasma
catecholamine levels include ajmaline, chlorpromazine, cyclopropane, diazoxide, ether, monoamine
oxidase inhibitors, nitroglycerin,
pentazocine, perphenazine,
phenothiazine, promethazine,
and theophylline.
• Drugs that may decrease plasma
catecholamine levels include
captopril, and reserpine.

• Drugs that may increase urine
catecholamine levels include
atenolol, isoproterenol,
methyldopa, niacin, nitroglycerin,
prochlorperazine, rauwolfia,
reserpine, syrosingopine, and
theophylline.
• Drugs that may decrease urine catecholamine levels include bretylium
tosylate, clonidine, decaborane, guanethidine, guanfacine, methyldopa,
ouabain, radiographic substances,
and reserpine.
• Stress, hypoglycemia, smoking, and
drugs can produce elevated catecholamines.
• Secretion of catecholamines exhibits diurnal variation, with the lowest levels occurring at night.
• Secretion of catecholamines varies
during the menstrual cycle, with
higher levels excreted during the
luteal phase and lowest levels during ovulation.
• Diets high in amines (e.g., bananas,
avocados, beer, aged cheese, chocolate, cocoa, coffee, fava beans,
grains, tea, vanilla, walnuts, Chianti
wine) can produce elevated catecholamine levels.
• Failure to collect all urine and store
24-hr specimen properly will yield
a falsely low result.
• Failure to follow dietary restrictions
before the procedure may cause
the procedure to be canceled or
repeated.

NURSING IMPLICATIONS AND PROCEDURE

PRETEST:
▸ Positively identify the patient using
at least two unique identifiers before
providing care, treatment, or
services.
▸ *Patient Teaching:* Inform the patient this
test can assist in the diagnosis of a
type of tumor that produces excessive

amounts of hormones related to physical and emotional stress.

▸ Obtain a history of the patient's complaints, including a list of known allergens, especially allergies or sensitivities to latex.

▸ Obtain a history of the patient's endocrine system, as well as results of previously performed laboratory tests and diagnostic and surgical procedures.

▸ Record the date of the patient's last menstrual period.

▸ Obtain a list of the patient's current medications, including herbs, nutritional supplements, and nutraceuticals (see Appendix F).

▸ Review the procedure with the patient.

Blood

▸ Inform the patient that he or she may be asked to keep warm and to rest for 45 to 60 min before the test. Inform the patient that multiple specimens may be required. Inform the patient that specimen collection takes approximately 5 to 10 min. Address concerns about pain and explain that there may be some discomfort during the venipuncture. Inform the patient that a saline lock may be inserted before the test because the stress of repeated venipunctures may increase catecholamine levels.

Urine

▸ Provide a nonmetallic urinal, bedpan, or toilet-mounted collection device. Address concerns about pain related to the procedure. Explain to the patient that there should be no discomfort during the procedure. Usually a 24-hr time frame for urine collection is ordered. Inform the patient that all urine over a 24-hr period must be saved; if a preservative has been added to the container, instruct the patient not to discard the preservative. Instruct the patient not to void directly into the laboratory collection container. Instruct the patient to avoid defecating in the collection device and to keep toilet tissue out of the collection device to prevent contamination of the specimen. Place a sign in the bathroom as a reminder to save all urine. Instruct the patient to void all urine into the collection device, then pour the urine into the laboratory collection container. Alternatively, the specimen can be left in the collection device for a health care staff member to add to the laboratory collection container.

Blood and Urine

▸ *Sensitivity to social and cultural issues,* as well as concern for modesty, is important in providing psychological support before, during, and after the procedure.

▸ Instruct the patient to follow a normal-sodium diet for 3 days before testing, abstain from smoking tobacco for 24 hr before testing, and avoid consumption of foods high in amines for 48 hr before testing.

▸ Instruct the patient to avoid self-prescribed medications for 2 wk before testing (especially appetite suppressants and cold and allergy medications, such as nose drops, cough suppressants, and bronchodilators).

▸ Instruct the patient to withhold prescribed medication (especially methyldopa, epinephrine, levodopa, and methenamine mandelate) if directed by the health-care provider (HCP).

▸ Instruct the patient to withhold food and fluids for 10 to 12 hr before the test. Protocols may vary from facility to facility.

▸ Instruct the patient collecting a 24-hr urine specimen to avoid excessive stress and exercise during the test collection period.

▸ Prior to blood specimen collection, prepare an ice slurry in a cup or plastic bag to have ready for immediate transport of the specimen to the laboratory. Prechill the collection tube in the ice slurry.

INTRATEST:

▸ Ensure that the patient has complied with dietary, medication, and activity restrictions and with pretesting preparations; ensure that food and fluids have been restricted for at least 10 to 12 hr prior to the procedure, and that excessive exercise and stress have been avoided prior to the procedure. Instruct the patient to continue to avoid excessive exercise and stress during the 24-hr collection of urine.

If the patient has a history of allergic reaction to latex, care should be taken to avoid the use of equipment containing latex.

Instruct the patient to cooperate fully and to follow directions.

Observe standard precautions, and follow the general guidelines in Appendix A. Positively identify the patient, and label the appropriate specimen container with the corresponding patient demographics, initials of the person collecting the specimen, date, and time of collection. Perform a venipuncture as appropriate.

Blood

Perform a venipuncture between 6 and 8 a.m.; collect the specimen in a prechilled tube.

Remove the needle and apply direct pressure with dry gauze to stop bleeding. Observe/assess venipuncture site for bleeding or hematoma formation and secure gauze with adhesive bandage.

Ask the patient to stand for 10 min, and then perform a second venipuncture and obtain a sample as previously described.

Each sample should be placed in an ice slurry immediately after collection. Information on the specimen labels should be protected from water in the ice slurry by first placing the specimens in a protective plastic bag. Promptly transport the specimens to the laboratory for processing and analysis.

Urine

Obtain a clean 3-L urine specimen container, toilet-mounted collection device, and plastic bag (for transport of the specimen container). The specimen must be refrigerated or kept on ice throughout the collection period. If an indwelling urinary catheter is in place, the drainage bag must be kept on ice.

Begin the test between 6 and 8 a.m. if possible. Collect first voiding and discard. Record the time the specimen was discarded as the beginning of the timed collection period. The next morning, ask the patient to void at the same time the collection was started and add this last voiding to the container.

If an indwelling catheter is in place, replace the tubing and container system at the start of the collection time. Keep the container system on ice during the collection period or empty the urine into a larger container periodically during the collection period; monitor to ensure continued drainage, and conclude the test the next morning at the same hour the collection was begun.

At the conclusion of the test, compare the quantity of urine with the urinary output record for the collection; if the specimen contains less than what was recorded as output, some urine may have been discarded, invalidating the test.

Blood and Urine

Include on the collection container's label the amount of urine, test start and stop times, and ingestion of any foods or medications that can affect test results.

Promptly transport the specimen to the laboratory for processing and analysis.

POST-TEST:

A report of the results will be made available to the requesting HCP, who will discuss the results with the patient.

Instruct the patient to resume usual diet, fluids, medications, and activity, as directed by the HCP.

Recognize anxiety related to test results. Discuss the implications of abnormal test results on the patient's lifestyle. Provide teaching and information regarding the clinical implications of the test results, as appropriate.

Reinforce information given by the patient's HCP regarding further testing,

treatment, or referral to another HCP. Answer any questions or address any concerns voiced by the patient or family.

▶ Depending on the results of this procedure, additional testing may be performed to evaluate or monitor progression of the disease process and determine the need for a change in therapy. Evaluate test results in relation to the patient's symptoms and other tests performed.

RELATED MONOGRAPHS:

▶ Related tests include angiography adrenal, calcitonin, CT renal, HVA, metanephrines, renin, and VMA.
▶ Refer to the Endocrine System table at the end of the book for related tests by body system.

CD4/CD8 Enumeration

SYNONYM/ACRONYM: T-cell profile.

COMMON USE: To monitor HIV disease progression and the effectiveness of retroviral therapy.

SPECIMEN: Whole blood (1 mL) collected in a green-top (heparin) tube.

NORMAL FINDINGS: (Method: Flow cytometry)

Age	Mature T cells (CD3)		Helper T cells (CD4)		Suppressor T cells (CD8)	
	Absolute (cells/mm^3)	%	Absolute (cells/mm^3)	%	Absolute (cells/mm^3)	%
0–2 mo	2,500–5,500	53–84	1,600–4,000	35–64	560–1,700	12–28
3–5 mo	2,500–5,600	51–77	1,800–4,000	35–56	590–1,600	12–23
6–11 mo	1,900–5,900	49–76	1,400–4,300	31–56	500–1,700	12–24
12–23 mo	2,100–6,200	53–75	1,300–3,400	32–51	620–2,000	14–30
2–5 yr	1,400–3,700	56–75	700–2,200	28–47	490–1,300	16–30
6–11 yr	1,200–2,600	60–76	650–1,500	31–47	370–1100	18–35
12–17 yr	1,000–2,200	56–84	530–1,300	31–52	330–920	18–35
Adult	527–2,846	49–81	332–1,642	28–51	170–811	12–38

DESCRIPTION: Enumeration of lymphocytes, identification of cell lineage, and identification of cellular stage of development are used to diagnose and classify malignant myeloproliferative diseases and to plan treatment. T-cell enumeration is also useful in the evaluation and management of immunodeficiency and autoimmune disease. The CD4 count is a reflection of immune status. It is used to make decisions regarding initiation of antiretroviral therapy (ART) and is also an excellent predictor of imminent opportunistic infection. A sufficient response for patients receiving ART is defined as an increase of 50 to 150 cells/mm^3 per year with rapid response during the first 3 mo of treatment followed by an annual increase of 50 to 100 cells/mm^3 until stabilization is achieved. HIV viral load is another important test used to establish a baseline for viral activity when a person is first diagnosed with HIV and then afterward to monitor response to ART. Viral load testing, also called plasma HIV RNA, is performed on plasma from a whole blood sample. The viral load demonstrates how actively the virus is reproducing and helps determine whether treatment is necessary. Optimal viral load is considered to be less than 20 to 75 copies/mL or below the level of detection, but the actual level of detection varies somewhat by test method. Methods commonly used to perform viral load testing include branched DNA (bDNA) or reverse transcriptase polymerase chain reaction (RT-PCR). Results are not interchangeable from method to method. Therefore, it is important to use the same viral load method for serial testing. Public health guidelines recommend CD4 counts and viral load testing upon initiation of care for HIV; 3 to 4 mo before commencement of ART; every 3 to 4 mo, but no later than 6 mo, thereafter; and if treatment failure is suspected or otherwise when clinically indicated. Additionally, viral load testing should be requested 2 to 4 wk, but no later than 8 wk, after initiation of ART to verify success of therapy. In clinically stable patients, CD4 testing may be recommended every 6 to 12 mo rather than every 3 to 6 mo. Guidelines also state that treatment of asymptomatic patients should begin when CD4 count is less than 350/mm^3; treatment is recommended when the patient is symptomatic regardless of test results or when the patient is asymptomatic and CD4 count is between 350 and 500/mm^3. Failure to respond to therapy is defined as a viral load greater than 200 copies/mL. Increased viral load may be indicative of viral mutations, drug resistance, or noncompliance to the therapeutic regimen. Testing for drug resistance is recommended if viral load is greater than 1,000 copies/mL.

INDICATIONS
- Assist in the diagnosis of AIDS and plan treatment
- Evaluate malignant myeloproliferative diseases and plan treatment
- Evaluate thymus-dependent or cellular immunocompetence

POTENTIAL DIAGNOSIS

Increased in
- Malignant myeloproliferative diseases (e.g., acute and chronic lymphocytic leukemia, lymphoma)

Decreased in
- AIDS
- Aplastic anemia
- Hodgkins disease

CRITICAL FINDINGS: N/A

INTERFERING FACTORS
- Drugs that may increase T-cell count include interferon-γ.
- Drugs that may decrease T-cell count include chlorpromazine and prednisone.
- Specimens should be stored at room temperature.
- Recent radioactive scans or radiation can decrease T-cell counts.
- Values may be abnormal in patients with severe recurrent illness or after recent surgery requiring general anesthesia.

NURSING IMPLICATIONS AND PROCEDURE

PRETEST:

Positively identify the patient using at least two unique identifiers before providing care, treatment, or services.

Patient Teaching: Inform the patient this test can assist in diagnosing disease and monitoring the effectiveness of disease therapy.

Obtain a history of the patient's complaints, including a list of known allergens, especially allergies or sensitivities to latex.

Obtain a history of the patient's hematopoietic and immune systems and results of previously performed laboratory tests and diagnostic and surgical procedures.

Note any recent procedures that can interfere with test results.

Obtain a list of the patient's current medications, including herbs, nutritional supplements, and nutraceuticals (see Appendix F).

Review the procedure with the patient. Inform the patient that specimen collection takes approximately 5 to 10 min. Address concerns about pain and explain that there may be some discomfort during the venipuncture.

Sensitivity to social and cultural issues, as well as concern for modesty, is important in providing psychological

support before, during, and after the procedure.

There are no food, fluid, or medication restrictions unless by medical direction.

INTRATEST:

If the patient has a history of allergic reaction to latex, avoid the use of equipment containing latex.

Instruct the patient to cooperate fully and to follow directions. Direct the patient to breathe normally and to avoid unnecessary movement.

Observe standard precautions, and follow the general guidelines in Appendix A. Positively identify the patient, and label the appropriate specimen container with the corresponding patient demographics, initials of the person collecting the specimen, date, and time of collection. Perform a venipuncture.

Remove the needle and apply direct pressure with dry gauze to stop bleeding. Observe/assess venipuncture site for bleeding or hematoma formation and secure gauze with adhesive bandage.

Promptly transport the specimen to the laboratory for processing and analysis.

POST-TEST:

A report of the results will be made available to the requesting health-care provider (HCP), who will discuss the results with the patient.

Nutritional Considerations: As appropriate, stress the importance of good nutrition and suggest that the patient meet with a nutritional specialist. Stress the importance of following the care plan for medications and follow-up visits. Inform the patient that subsequent requests for follow-up blood work at regular intervals should be anticipated.

Recognize anxiety related to test results, and be supportive of impaired activity related to perceived loss of independence and fear of shortened life expectancy. Discuss the implications of abnormal test results on the patient's lifestyle. Provide teaching and information regarding the clinical implications of the test results, as appropriate. Educate the patient as to the risk of infection related to immunosuppressed inflammatory response and fatigue related to decreased energy production. Educate the patient regarding access to counseling services.

Counsel the patient, as appropriate, regarding risk of transmission and proper prophylaxis, and reinforce the importance of strict adherence to the treatment regimen, including consultation with a pharmacist. Reinforce information given by the patient's HCP regarding further testing, treatment, or referral to another HCP. Provide contact information, if desired, for the Centers for Disease Control and Prevention (www.cdc.org). Answer any questions or address any concerns voiced by the patient or family.

Depending on the results of this procedure, additional testing may be performed to evaluate or monitor progression of the disease process and determine the need for a change in therapy. Evaluate test results in relation to the patient's symptoms and other tests performed.

RELATED MONOGRAPHS:

Related tests include biopsy bone marrow, bronchoscopy, CBC, CBC platelet count, CBC WBC count and differential, culture and smear mycobacteria, culture viral, cytology sputum, gallium scan, HIV-1/HIV-2 antibodies, laparoscopy abdominal, LAP, lymphangiogram, MRI musculoskeletal, mediastinoscopy, and β_2-microglobulin.

Refer to the Hematopoietic and Immune systems tables at the end of the book for related tests by body system.

Cerebrospinal Fluid Analysis

SYNONYM/ACRONYM: CSF analysis.

COMMON USE: To assist in the differential diagnosis of infection or hemorrhage of the brain. Also used in the evaluation of other conditions with significant neuromuscular effects, such as multiple sclerosis.

SPECIMEN: CSF (1 to 3 mL) collected in three or four separate plastic conical tubes. Tube 1 is used for chemistry and serology testing, tube 2 is used for microbiology, tube 3 is used for cell count, and tube 4 is used for miscellaneous testing.

NORMAL FINDINGS: (Method: Macroscopic evaluation of appearance; spectrophotometry for glucose, lactic acid, and protein; immunoassay for myelin basic protein; nephelometry for immunoglobulin G [IgG]; electrophoresis for oligoclonal banding; Gram stain, India ink preparation, and culture for microbiology; microscopic examination of fluid for cell count; flocculation for Venereal Disease Research Laboratory [VDRL])

C

Lumbar Puncture	Conventional Units	SI Units
Color and appearance	Crystal clear	
		(Conventional Units × 10)
Protein		
0–1 mo	Less than 150 mg/dL	Less than 1,500 mg/L
1–6 mo	30–100 mg/dL	300–1,000 mg/L
7 mo–adult	15–45 mg/dL	150–450 mg/L
Older adult	15–60 mg/dL	150–600 mg/L
		(Conventional Units × 0.0555)
Glucose		
Infant or child	60–80 mg/dL	3.3–4.4 mmol/L
Adult/older adult	40–70 mg/dL	2.2–3.9 mmol/L
		(Conventional Units × 0.111)
Lactic acid		
Neonate	10–60 mg/dL	1.1–6.7 mmol/L
3–10 days	10–40 mg/dL	1.1–4.4 mmol/L
Adult	Less than 25.2 mg/dL	Less than 2.8 mmol/L
		(Conventional Units × 1)
Myelin basic protein		
	Less than 4.0 ng/mL	Less than 4.0 mcg/L
Oligoclonal bands	Absent	
		(Conventional Units × 10)
IgG	Less than 3.4 mg/dL	Less than 34 mg/L
Gram stain	Negative	
India ink	Negative	
Culture	No growth	
RBC count	0	0
		(Conventional Units × 1)
WBC count		
Neonate–1 mo	0–30 cells/mm^3	0–30 × 10^9/L
1 mo–1 yr	0–10 cells/mm^3	0–10 × 10^9/L
1–5 yr	0–8 cells/mm^3	0–8 × 10^9/L
5 yr–adult	0–5 cells/mm^3	0–5 × 10^9/L
VDRL	Nonreactive	
Cytology	No abnormal cells seen	

CSF glucose should be 60%–70% of plasma glucose level.
RBC = red blood cell; VDRL = Venereal Disease Research Laboratory; WBC = white blood cell.
Color should be assessed after sample is centrifuged.

WBC Differential	Adult	Children
Lymphocytes	40%–80%	5%–13%
Monocytes	15%–45%	50%–90%
Neutrophils	0%–6%	0%–8%

C

DESCRIPTION: Cerebrospinal fluid (CSF) circulates in the subarachnoid space and has a twofold function: to protect the brain and spinal cord from injury and to transport products of cellular metabolism and neurosecretion. The total volume of CSF is 90 to 150 mL in adults and 60 mL in infants. CSF analysis helps determine the presence and cause of bleeding and assists in diagnosing cancer, infections, and degenerative and autoimmune diseases of the brain and spinal cord. Specimens for analysis are most frequently obtained by lumbar puncture and sometimes by ventricular or cisternal puncture. Lumbar puncture can also have therapeutic uses, including injection of drugs and anesthesia.

INDICATIONS

- Assist in the diagnosis and differentiation of subarachnoid or intracranial hemorrhage
- Assist in the diagnosis and differentiation of viral or bacterial meningitis or encephalitis
- Assist in the diagnosis of diseases such as multiple sclerosis, autoimmune disorders, or degenerative brain disease
- Assist in the diagnosis of neurosyphilis and chronic central nervous system (CNS) infections
- Detect obstruction of CSF circulation due to hemorrhage, tumor, or edema
- Establish the presence of any condition decreasing the flow of oxygen to the brain
- Monitor for metastases of cancer into the CNS
- Monitor severe brain injuries

POTENTIAL DIAGNOSIS

Increased in

Color and appearance *(xanthochromia is any pink, yellow, or orange color; bloody—hemorrhage; xanthochromic—old hemorrhage, red blood cell [RBC] breakdown, methemoglobin, bilirubin [greater than 6 mg/dL], increased protein [greater than 150 mg/dL], melanin [meningeal melanosarcoma], carotene [systemic carotenemia]; hazy—meningitis; pink to dark yellow—aspiration of epidural fat; turbid—cells, microorganisms, protein, fat, or contrast medium)*

- Protein *(related to alterations in blood-brain barrier that allow permeability to proteins)*: meningitis, encephalitis
- Lactic acid *(related to cerebral hypoxia and correlating anaerobic metabolism)*: bacterial, tubercular, fungal meningitis
- Myelin basic protein *(related to accumulation as a result of nerve sheath demyelination)*: trauma, stroke, tumor, multiple sclerosis, subacute sclerosing panencephalitis
- IgG and oligoclonal banding *(related to autoimmune or inflammatory response)*: multiple sclerosis, CNS syphilis, and subacute sclerosing panencephalitis
- Gram stain: *Meningitis due to Escherichia coli, Streptococcus agalactiae, Streptococcus pneumoniae, Haemophilus influenzae, Mycobacterium avium-intracellulare, Mycobacterium leprae, Mycobacterium tuberculosis, Neisseria meningitidis, Cryptococcus neoformans*
- India ink preparation: *Meningitis due to C. neoformans*
- Culture: *Encephalitis or meningitis due to herpes simplex virus, S. pneumoniae, H. influenzae, N. meningitidis, C. neoformans*
- RBC count: *Hemorrhage*
- White blood cell (WBC) count: *General increase—injection of contrast media or anticancer drugs in subarachnoid space; CSF infarct;*

metastatic tumor in contact with CSF; reaction to repeated lumbar puncture
Elevated WBC count with a predominance of neutrophils indicative of bacterial meningitis
Elevated WBC count with a predominance of lymphocytes indicative of viral, tubercular, parasitic, or fungal meningitis; multiple sclerosis
Elevated WBC count with a predominance of monocytes indicative of chronic bacterial meningitis, amebic meningitis, multiple sclerosis, toxoplasmosis
Increased plasma cells indicative of acute viral infections, multiple sclerosis, sarcoidosis, syphilitic meningoencephalitis, subacute sclerosing panencephalitis, tubercular meningitis, parasitic infections, Guillain-Barré syndrome
Presence of eosinophils indicative of parasitic and fungal infections, acute polyneuritis, idiopathic hypereosinophilic syndrome, reaction to drugs or a shunt in CSF

- VDRL: ***Syphilis***

Positive findings in
- Cytology: ***Malignant cells***

Decreased in
- Glucose: ***Bacterial and tubercular meningitis***

CRITICAL FINDINGS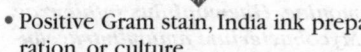

- Positive Gram stain, India ink preparation, or culture
- Presence of malignant cells or blasts
- Elevated WBC count
- Adults: Glucose less than 37 mg/dL (SI: Less than 2.1 mmol/L); greater than 440 mg/dL (SI: Greater than 24.4 mmol/L)
- Children: Glucose less than 31 mg/dL (SI: Less than 1.7 mmol/L); greater than 440 mg/dL (SI: Greater than 24.4 mmol/L)

Note and immediately report to the health-care provider (HCP) any positive or critically increased results and

related symptoms. Timely notification of critical values for lab or diagnostic studies is a role expectation of the professional nurse. Notification processes will vary among facilities. Upon receipt of the critical value, the information should be read back to the caller to verify accuracy. Most policies require immediate notification of the primary HCP, hospitalist, or on-call HCP. Reported information includes the patient's name, unique identifiers, critical value, name of the person giving the report, and name of the person receiving the report. Documentation of notification should be made in the medical record with the name of the HCP notified, time and date of notification, and any orders received. Any delay in a timely report of a critical value may require completion of a notification form with review by Risk Management.

INTERFERING FACTORS

This procedure is contraindicated for
- This procedure is contraindicated if infection is present at the needle insertion site.
- It may also be contraindicated in patients with degenerative joint disease or coagulation defects and in patients who are uncooperative during the procedure.
- Use with extreme caution in patients with increased intracranial pressure because overly rapid removal of CSF can result in herniation.

Other considerations
- Drugs that may decrease CSF protein levels include cefotaxime and dexamethasone.
- Interferon-β may increase myelin basic protein levels.
- Drugs that may increase CSF glucose levels include cefotaxime and dexamethasone.
- RBC count may be falsely elevated with a traumatic spinal tap.

Delays in analysis may present a false positive appearance of xanthochromia due to RBC lysis that begins within 4 hr of a bloody tap.

NURSING IMPLICATIONS AND PROCEDURE

PRETEST:

Positively identify the patient using at least two unique identifiers before providing care, treatment, or services.

Patient Teaching: Inform the patient this procedure can assist in evaluating health by providing a sample of fluid from around the spinal cord to be tested for disease and infection.

Obtain a history of the patient's complaints, including a list of known allergens, especially allergies or sensitivities to latex or anesthetics.

Obtain a history of the patient's immune and musculoskeletal systems and results of previously performed laboratory tests and diagnostic and surgical procedures.

Obtain a list of the patient's current medications, including herbs, nutritional supplements, and nutraceuticals (see Appendix F).

Review the procedure with the patient. Inform the patient that the position required may be awkward but that someone will assist during the procedure. Stress the importance of remaining still and breathing normally throughout the procedure. Inform the patient that specimen collection takes approximately 20 min. Address concerns about pain and explain that a stinging sensation may be felt when the local anesthetic is injected.

Instruct the patient to report any pain or other sensations that may require repositioning the spinal needle.

Explain that there may be some discomfort during the procedure. Inform the patient the procedure will be performed by an HCP.

Sensitivity to social and cultural issues, as well as concern for modesty, is important in providing psychological support before, during, and after the procedure.

There are no food, fluid, or medication restrictions unless by medical direction.

Make sure a written and informed consent has been signed prior to the procedure and before administering any medications.

INTRATEST:

If the patient has a history of allergic reaction to latex, avoid the use of equipment containing latex.

Ensure that anticoagulant therapy has been withheld for the appropriate number of days prior to the procedure. Number of days to withhold medication is dependent on the type of anticoagulant. Notify HCP if patient anticoagulant therapy has not been withheld.

Have emergency equipment readily available.

Instruct the patient to cooperate fully and to follow directions. Direct the patient to breathe normally and to avoid unnecessary movement.

Observe standard precautions, and follow the general guidelines in Appendix A. Positively identify the patient, and label the appropriate tubes with the corresponding patient demographics, date, and time of collection. Collect the specimen in four plastic conical tubes.

Record baseline vital signs.

To perform a lumbar puncture, position the patient in the knee-chest position at the side of the bed. Provide pillows to support the spine or for the patient to grasp. The sitting position is an alternative. In this position, the patient must bend the neck and chest to the knees.

Prepare the site—usually between L3 and L4, or between L4 and L5—with povidone-iodine and drape the area.

A local anesthetic is injected. Using sterile technique, the HCP inserts the spinal needle through the spinous processes of the vertebrae and into the subarachnoid space. The stylet is removed. If the needle is properly placed, CSF drips from the needle.

Attach the stopcock and manometer, and measure initial pressure. Normal pressure for an adult in the lateral recumbent position is 60–200 mm H_2O, and 10–100 mm H_2O for children less than 8 yr. These values depend on the body position and are different in a horizontal than in a sitting position.

▶ CSF pressure may be elevated if the patient is anxious, holding his or her breath, or tensing muscles. It may also be elevated if the patient's knees are flexed too firmly against the abdomen. CSF pressure may be significantly elevated in patients with intracranial tumors. If the initial pressure is elevated, the HCP may perform Queckenstedt's test. To perform this test, pressure is applied to the jugular vein for about 10 sec. CSF pressure usually rises rapidly in response to the occlusion and then returns to the pretest level within 10 sec after the pressure is released. Sluggish response may indicate CSF obstruction.

▶ Obtain four (or five) vials of fluid, according to the HCP's request, in separate tubes (1 to 3 mL in each), and label them numerically (1 to 4 or 5) in the order they were filled.

▶ A final pressure reading is taken, and the needle is removed. Clean the puncture site with an antiseptic solution and apply direct pressure with dry gauze to stop bleeding or CSF leakage. Observe/assess puncture site for bleeding, CSF leakage, or hematoma formation and secure gauze with adhesive bandage.

▶ Promptly transport the specimen to the laboratory for processing and analysis.

POST-TEST:

▶ A report of the results will be made available to the requesting HCP, who will discuss the results with the patient.

▶ Monitor vital signs and neurological status and for headache every 15 min for 1 hr, then every 2 hr for 4 hr, and then as ordered by the HCP. Monitor temperature every 4 hr for 24 hr. Compare with baseline values. Notify the HCP if temperature is elevated. Protocols may vary among facilities.

▶ If permitted, administer fluids to replace lost CSF and help prevent or relieve headache—a side effect of lumbar puncture.

▶ Position the patient flat in the supine position with head of bed at not more than a 30° elevation, following the HCP's instructions. Maintain position for 8 hr. Changing position is acceptable as long as the body remains horizontal.

▶ Recognize anxiety related to test results. Discuss the implications of abnormal test results on the patient's lifestyle. Provide teaching and information regarding the clinical implications of the test results, as appropriate.

▶ Reinforce information given by the patient's HCP regarding further testing, treatment, or referral to another HCP. Provide information regarding vaccine-preventable diseases when indicated (encephalitis, influenza, meningococcal diseases). Answer any questions or address any concerns voiced by the patient or family.

▶ Instruct the patient in the use of any ordered medications. Explain the importance of adhering to the therapy regimen. As appropriate, instruct the patient in significant side effects and systemic reactions associated with the prescribed medication. Encourage him or her to review corresponding literature provided by a pharmacist.

▶ Depending on the results of this procedure, additional testing may be performed to evaluate or monitor progression of the disease process and determine the need for a change in therapy. Evaluate test results in relation to the patient's symptoms and other tests performed.

RELATED MONOGRAPHS:

▶ Related tests include CBC, CT brain, culture for appropriate organisms (blood, fungal, mycobacteria, sputum, throat, viral, wound), EMG, evoked brain potentials, Gram stain, MRI brain, PET brain, and syphilis serology.

▶ Refer to the Immune and Musculoskeletal systems tables at the end of the book for related tests by body system.

Ceruloplasmin

SYNONYM/ACRONYM: Copper oxidase, Cp.

COMMON USE: To assist in the evaluation of copper intoxication and liver disease, especially Wilson's disease.

SPECIMEN: Serum (1 mL) collected in a red- or tiger-top tube.

NORMAL FINDINGS: (Method: Nephelometry)

Age	Conventional Units	SI Units (Conventional Units × 10)
Newborn–3 mo	5–18 mg/dL	50–180 mg/L
6–12 mo	33–43 mg/dL	330–430 mg/L
1–3 yr	26–55 mg/dL	260–550 mg/L
4–5 yr	27–56 mg/dL	270–560 mg/L
6–7 yr	24–48 mg/dL	240–480 mg/L
8 yr–older adult	20–54 mg/dL	200–540 mg/L

DESCRIPTION: Ceruloplasmin is an α_2-globulin produced by the liver that binds copper for transport in the blood after it is absorbed from the gastrointestinal system. Decreased production of this globulin causes copper to be deposited in body tissues such as the brain, liver, corneas, and kidneys.

INDICATIONS

Assist in the diagnosis of Menkes' (kinky hair) disease

Assist in the diagnosis of Wilson's disease

Determine genetic predisposition to Wilson's disease

Monitor patient response to total parenteral nutrition (hyperalimentation)

POTENTIAL DIAGNOSIS

Increased in

Ceruloplasmin is an acute-phase reactant protein and will be increased in many inflammatory conditions, including cancer

- Acute infections
- Biliary cirrhosis
- Cancer of the bone, lung, stomach
- Copper intoxication
- Hodgkin's disease
- Leukemia
- Pregnancy (last trimester) (estrogen increases copper levels)
- Rheumatoid arthritis
- Tissue necrosis

Decreased in

- Menkes' disease (severe X-linked defect causing failed transport to the liver and tissues)
- Nutritional deficiency of copper
- Wilson's disease (genetic defect causing failed transport to the liver and tissues)

CRITICAL FINDINGS: N/A

INTERFERING FACTORS

- Drugs that may increase ceruloplasmin levels include anticonvulsants,

C

norethindrone, oral contraceptives, and tamoxifen.
- Drugs that may decrease ceruloplasmin levels include asparaginase and levonorgestrel (Norplant).
- Excessive therapeutic intake of zinc may interfere with intestinal absorption of copper.

NURSING IMPLICATIONS AND PROCEDURE

PRETEST:

▶ Positively identify the patient using at least two unique identifiers before providing care, treatment, or services.

▶ *Patient Teaching:* Inform the patient this test can determine copper levels in the blood.

▶ Obtain a history of the patient's complaints, including a list of known allergens, especially allergies or sensitivities to latex.

▶ Obtain a history of the patient's hepatobiliary system and results of previously performed laboratory tests and diagnostic and surgical procedures.

▶ Obtain a list of the patient's current medications, including herbs, nutritional supplements, and nutraceuticals (see Appendix F).

▶ Review the procedure with the patient. Inform the patient that specimen collection takes approximately 5 to 10 min. Address concerns about pain and explain that there may be some discomfort during the venipuncture.

▶ *Sensitivity to social and cultural issues,* as well as concern for modesty, is important in providing psychological support before, during, and after the procedure.

▶ There are no food, fluid, or medication restrictions unless by medical direction.

INTRATEST:

▶ If the patient has a history of allergic reaction to latex, avoid the use of equipment containing latex.

▶ Instruct the patient to cooperate fully and to follow directions. Direct the patient to breathe normally and to avoid unnecessary movement.

▶ Observe standard precautions, and follow the general guidelines in Appendix A. Positively identify the patient, and label the appropriate specimen container with the corresponding patient demographics, initials of the person collecting the specimen, date, and time of collection. Perform a venipuncture.

▶ Remove the needle and apply direct pressure with dry gauze to stop bleeding. Observe/assess venipuncture site for bleeding or hematoma formation and secure gauze with adhesive bandage.

▶ Promptly transport the specimen to the laboratory for processing and analysis.

POST-TEST:

▶ A report of the results will be made available to the requesting health-care provider (HCP), who will discuss the results with the patient.

▶ *Nutritional Considerations:* Instruct the patient with copper deficiency to increase intake of foods rich in copper, as appropriate. Organ meats, shellfish, nuts, and legumes are good sources of dietary copper. High intake of zinc, iron, calcium, and manganese interferes with copper absorption. Copper deficiency does not normally occur in adults; however, patients receiving long-term total parenteral nutrition should be evaluated if signs and symptoms of copper deficiency appear, such as jaundice or eye color changes. Kayser-Fleischer rings (green-gold rings) in the cornea and a liver biopsy specimen showing more than 250 mcg of copper per gram confirms Wilson's disease.

▶ Reinforce information given by the patient's HCP regarding further testing, treatment, or referral to another HCP. Answer any questions or address any concerns voiced by the patient or family.

▶ Depending on the results of this procedure, additional testing may be performed to evaluate or monitor progression of the disease process and determine the need for a change in therapy. Evaluate test results in relation to the patient's symptoms and other tests performed.

RELATED MONOGRAPHS:
▶ Related tests include biopsy liver, copper, and zinc.
▶ Refer to the Hepatobiliary System table at the end of the book for related tests by body system.

Chest X-Ray

SYNONYM/ACRONYM: Chest radiography, CXR, lung radiography.

COMMON USE: To assist in the evaluation of cardiac, respiratory, and skeletal structure within the lung cavity and diagnose multiple diseases such as pneumonia and congestive heart failure.

AREA OF APPLICATION: Heart, mediastinum, lungs.

CONTRAST: None.

DESCRIPTION: Chest radiography, commonly called chest x-ray, is one of the most frequently performed radiological diagnostic studies. This study yields information about the pulmonary, cardiac, and skeletal systems. The lungs, filled with air, are easily penetrated by x-rays and appear black on chest images. A routine chest x-ray includes a posteroanterior (PA) projection, in which x-rays pass from the posterior to the anterior, and a left lateral projection. Additional projections that may be requested are obliques, lateral decubitus, or lordotic views. Portable x-rays, done in acute or critical situations, can be done at the bedside and usually include only the anteroposterior (AP) projection with additional images taken in a lateral decubitus position if the presence of free pleural fluid or air is in question. Chest images should be taken on full inspiration and erect when possible to minimize heart

magnification and demonstrate fluid levels. Expiration images may be added to detect a pneumothorax or locate foreign bodies. Rib detail images may be taken to delineate bone pathology, useful when chest radiographs suggest fractures or metastatic lesions. Fluoroscopic studies of the chest can also be done to evaluate lung and diaphragm movement. In the beginning of the disease process of tuberculosis, asthma, and chronic obstructive pulmonary disease, the results of a chest x-ray may not correlate with the clinical status of the patient and may even be normal.

INDICATIONS
• Aid in the diagnosis of diaphragmatic hernia, lung tumors, intravenous devices, and metastasis
• Evaluate known or suspected pulmonary disorders, chest trauma, cardiovascular disorders, and skeletal disorders

- Evaluate placement and position of an endotracheal tube, tracheostomy tube, nasogastric feeding tube, pacemaker wires, central venous catheters, Swan-Ganz catheters, chest tubes, and intra-aortic balloon pump
- Evaluate positive purified protein derivative (PPD) or Mantoux tests
- Monitor resolution, progression, or maintenance of disease
- Monitor effectiveness of the treatment regimen

POTENTIAL DIAGNOSIS

Normal findings in
- Normal lung fields, cardiac size, mediastinal structures, thoracic spine, ribs, and diaphragm

Abnormal findings in
- Atelectasis
- Bronchitis
- Curvature of the spinal column (scoliosis)
- Enlarged heart
- Enlarged lymph nodes
- Flattened diaphragm
- Foreign bodies lodged in the pulmonary system
- Fractures of the sternum, ribs, and spine
- Lung pathology, including tumors
- Malposition of tubes or wires
- Mediastinal tumor and pathology
- Pericardial effusion
- Pericarditis
- Pleural effusion
- Pneumonia
- Pneumothorax
- Pulmonary bases, fibrosis, infiltrates
- Tuberculosis
- Vascular abnormalities

CRITICAL FINDINGS ◈
- Foreign body
- Malposition of tube, line, or postoperative device (pacemaker)
- Pneumonia
- Pneumoperitoneum
- Pneumothorax
- Spine fracture

It is essential that critical diagnoses be communicated immediately to the appropriate health-care provider (HCP). A listing of these diagnoses varies among facilities. Note and immediately report to the HCP abnormal results and related symptoms.

Timely notification of critical values for lab or diagnostic studies is a role expectation of the professional nurse. Notification processes will vary among facilities. Upon receipt of the critical value, the information should be read back to the caller to verify accuracy. Most policies require immediate notification of the primary HCP, hospitalist or on-call HCP. Reported information includes the patient's name unique identifiers, critical value name of the person giving the report, and name of the person receiving the report. Documentation of notification should be made in the medical record with the name of the HCP notified, time and date of notification, and any orders received. Any delay in a timely report of a critical value may require completion of a notification form with review by Risk Management.

INTERFERING FACTORS

This procedure is contraindicated for
- Patients who are pregnant or suspected of being pregnant, unless the potential benefits of the procedure far outweigh the risks to the fetus and mother.

Factors that may impair the results of the examination
- Metallic objects within the examination field.
- Improper adjustment of the radiographic equipment to accommodate obese or thin patients, which can cause overexposure or underexposure.

Incorrect positioning of the patient, which may produce poor visualization of the area to be examined. Inability of the patient to cooperate or remain still during the procedure because of age, significant pain, or mental status.

Other considerations
The procedure may be terminated if chest pain or severe cardiac arrhythmias occur.
Consultation with an HCP should occur before the procedure for radiation safety concerns regarding younger patients or patients who are lactating.
Risks associated with radiation overexposure can result from frequent x-ray procedures. Personnel in the examination room with the patient should wear a protective lead apron, stand behind a shield, or leave the area while the examination is being done. Personnel working in the examination area should wear badges to record their level of radiation exposure.

NURSING IMPLICATIONS AND PROCEDURE

PRETEST:

Positively identify the patient using at least two unique identifiers before providing care, treatment, or services.
Patient Teaching: Inform the patient this procedure can assist in assessing the heart and lungs for disease.
Obtain a history of the patient's complaints, including a list of known allergens.
Obtain a history of the patient's cardiovascular and respiratory systems, symptoms, and results of previously performed laboratory tests and diagnostic and surgical procedures.
Record the date of the last menstrual period and determine the possibility of pregnancy in perimenopausal women.
Obtain a list of the patient's current medications, including herbs, nutrition-

al supplements, and nutraceuticals (see Appendix F).
Review the procedure with the patient. Address concerns about pain and explain that no pain will be experienced during the test. Inform the patient that the procedure is performed in the radiology department or at the bedside by a registered radiological technologist, and takes approximately 5 to 15 min.
Sensitivity to social and cultural issues, as well as concern for modesty, is important in providing psychological support before, during, and after the procedure.
Instruct the patient to remove all metallic objects from the area to be examined.
There are no food, fluid, or medication restrictions unless by medical direction.

INTRATEST:

Observe standard precautions, and follow the general guidelines in Appendix A. Positively identify the patient.
Ensure that the patient has removed all external metallic objects from the area to be examined.
Patients are given a gown, robe, and foot coverings to wear.
Instruct the patient to cooperate fully and to follow directions. Instruct the patient to remain still throughout the procedure because movement produces unreliable results.
Place the patient in the standing position facing the cassette or image detector, with hands on hips, neck extended, and shoulders rolled forward.
Position the chest with the left side against the image holder for a lateral view.
For portable examinations, elevate the head of the bed to the high Fowler's position.
Ask the patient to inhale deeply and hold his or her breath while the x-ray images are taken, and then to exhale after the images are taken.

POST-TEST:

A report of the results will be made available to the requesting HCP, who will discuss the results with the patient.
Recognize anxiety related to test results and be supportive of impaired activity related to respiratory capacity

and perceived loss of physical activity. Discuss the implications of abnormal test results on the patient's lifestyle. Provide teaching and information regarding the clinical implications of the test results, as appropriate.

Reinforce information given by the patient's HCP regarding further testing, treatment, or referral to another HCP. Answer any questions or address any concerns voiced by the patient or family.

Depending on the results of this procedure, additional testing may be performed to evaluate and determine the need for a change in therapy or progression of the disease process.

Evaluate test results in relation to the patient's symptoms and other tests performed.

RELATED MONOGRAPHS:

Related tests include biopsy lung, blood gases, bronchoscopy, CT thoracic, CBC, culture mycobacteria, culture sputum, culture viral, electrocardiogram, Gram stain, lung perfusion scan, MRI chest, pulmonary function study, pulse oximetry, and TB tests.

Refer to the Cardiovascular and Respiratory systems tables at the end of the book for related tests by body system.

Chlamydia Group Antibody, IgG and IgM

SYNONYM/ACRONYM: N/A.

COMMON USE: To diagnose some of the more common chlamydia infections such as community-acquired pneumonia transmitted by *C. pneumoniae* and chlamydia disease that is sexually transmitted by *Chlamydia trachomatis*.

SPECIMEN: Serum (1 mL) collected in a red-top tube.

NORMAL FINDINGS: (Method: Enzyme immunofluorescent assay)

IgG	IgM
Less than 1:64	Less than 1:20

DESCRIPTION: Chlamydia, one of the most common sexually transmitted diseases, is caused by *Chlamydia trachomatis*. These gram-negative bacteria are called *obligate cell parasites* because they require living cells for growth. There are three serotypes of *C. trachomatis*. One group causes lymphogranuloma venereum, with symptoms of the first phase of the disease appearing 2 to 6 wk after infection; another causes a genital tract infection different from lymphogranuloma venereum, in which symptoms in men appear 7 to 28 days after intercourse (women are generally asymptomatic); and the third causes the ocular disease trachoma (incubation period, 7 to 10 days). *C. psittaci* is the cause of psittacosis in birds and humans. It is increasing in prevalence as a pathogen responsible for other significant diseases of the respiratory system. The incubation period for *C. psittaci* infections in humans is 7 to 15 days and is followed by chills, fever, and a persistent nonproductive cough. *C. pneumoniae* is a common cause of community-acquired pneumonia. It is also less commonly associated with meningoencephalitis, arthritis, myocarditis, and Guillain-Barré syndrome.

Chlamydia is difficult to culture and grow, so antibody testing has become the technology of choice. A limitation of antibody screening is that positive results may not distinguish past from current infection. The antigen used in many screening kits is not species specific and can confirm only the presence of *Chlamydia* species. Newer technology using nucleic acid amplification and DNA probes can identify the species. Assays that can specifically identify *C. trachomatis* require special collection and transport kits. They also have specific collection instructions, and the specimens are collected on swabs. The laboratory performing this testing should be consulted before specimen collection.

INDICATIONS

Establish Chlamydia as the cause of atypical pneumonia
Establish the presence of chlamydial infection

POTENTIAL DIAGNOSIS

Positive findings in
Chlamydial infection
Community-acquired pneumonia
Infantile pneumonia *(related to transmission at birth from an infected mother)*
Infertility *(related to scarring of ovaries or fallopian tubes from untreated chlamydial infection)*

- Lymphogranuloma venereum
- Ophthalmia neonatorum *(related to transmission at birth from an infected mother)*
- Pelvic inflammatory disease
- Urethritis

CRITICAL FINDINGS: N/A

INTERFERING FACTORS
- Hemolysis or lipemia may interfere with analysis.
- Positive results may demonstrate evidence of past infection and not necessarily indicate current infection.

NURSING IMPLICATIONS AND PROCEDURE

PRETEST:
- Positively identify the patient using at least two unique identifiers before providing care, treatment, or services.
- *Patient Teaching:* Inform the patient this test can assist in diagnosing chlamydial infection.
- Obtain a history of the patient's complaints, including a list of known allergens, especially allergies or sensitivities to latex.
- Obtain a history of the patient's immune and reproductive systems, as well as results of previously performed laboratory tests and diagnostic and surgical procedures.
- Obtain a list of the patient's current medications, including herbs, nutritional supplements, and nutraceuticals (see Appendix F).
- Review the procedure with the patient. Inform the patient that specimen collection takes approximately 5 to 10 min. Address concerns about pain and explain that there may be some discomfort during the venipuncture.
- *Sensitivity to social and cultural issues,* as well as concern for modesty, is important in providing psychological support before, during, and after the procedure.
- Inform the patient that several tests may be necessary to confirm diagnosis.

Any individual positive result should be repeated in 7 to 10 days to monitor a change in titer.

▶ There are no food, fluid, or medication restrictions unless by medical direction.

INTRATEST:

▶ If the patient has a history of allergic reaction to latex, avoid the use of equipment containing latex.

▶ Instruct the patient to cooperate fully and to follow directions. Direct the patient to breathe normally and to avoid unnecessary movement.

▶ Observe standard precautions, and follow the general guidelines in Appendix A. Positively identify the patient, and label the appropriate specimen container with the corresponding patient demographics, initials of the person collecting the specimen, date, and time of the collection. Perform a venipuncture.

▶ Remove the needle and apply direct pressure with dry gauze to stop bleeding. Observe/assess venipuncture site for bleeding or hematoma formation and secure gauze with adhesive bandage.

▶ Promptly transport the specimen to the laboratory for processing and analysis.

POST-TEST:

▶ A report of the results will be made available to the requesting health-care provider (HCP), who will discuss the results with the patient.

▶ Recognize anxiety related to test results, and be supportive. Discuss the implications of abnormal test results on the patient's lifestyle. Provide teaching and information regarding the clinical implications of the test results, as appropriate. Emphasize the need to return to have a convalescent blood sample taken in 7 to 14 days. Educate the patient regarding access to counseling services.

▶ *Social and Cultural Considerations:* Counsel the patient, as appropriate, as to the risk of sexual transmission and

educate the patient regarding proper prophylaxis. Reinforce the importance of strict adherence to the treatment regimen.

▶ *Social and Cultural Considerations:* Inform the patient with positive *C. trachomatis* that findings must be reported to a local health department official, who will question the patient regarding his or her sexual partners.

▶ *Social and Cultural Considerations:* Offer support, as appropriate, to patients who may be the victim of rape or sexual assault. Educate the patient regarding access to counseling services. Provide a nonjudgmental, nonthreatening atmosphere for a discussion during which you explain the risks of sexually transmitted diseases. It is also important to discuss emotions the patient may experience (guilt, depression, anger) as a victim of rape or sexual assault.

▶ Provide emotional support if the patient is pregnant and if results are positive. Inform the patient that chlamydial infection during pregnancy places the newborn at risk for pneumonia and conjunctivitis.

▶ Reinforce information given by the patient's HCP regarding further testing, treatment, or referral to another HCP. Answer any questions or address any concerns voiced by the patient or family.

▶ Depending on the results of this procedure, additional testing may be performed to evaluate or monitor progression of the disease process and determine the need for a change in therapy. Evaluate test results in relation to the patient's symptoms and other tests performed.

RELATED MONOGRAPHS:

▶ Related tests include culture bacterial (anal, genital), culture viral, Gram stain, Pap smear, and syphilis serology.

▶ Refer to the Immune and Reproductive systems tables at the end of the book for related tests by body system.

Chloride, Blood

SYNONYM/ACRONYM: Cl^-.

COMMON USE: To evaluate electrolytes, acid-base balance, and hydration level.

SPECIMEN: Serum (1 mL) collected in a red- or tiger-top tube. Plasma (1 mL) collected in a green-top (heparin) tube is also acceptable.

NORMAL FINDINGS: (Method: Ion-selective electrode)

Age	Conventional & SI Units
Premature	95–110 mmol/L
0–1 mo	98–113 mmol/L
2 mo–older adult	97–107 mmol/L

DESCRIPTION: Chloride is the most abundant anion in the extracellular fluid. Its most important function is in the maintenance of acid-base balance, in which it competes with bicarbonate for sodium. Chloride levels generally increase and decrease proportionally to sodium levels and inversely proportional to bicarbonate levels. Chloride also participates with sodium in the maintenance of water balance and aids in the regulation of osmotic pressure. Chloride contributes to gastric acid (hydrochloric acid) for digestion and activation of enzymes. The chloride content of venous blood is slightly higher than that of arterial blood because chloride ions enter red blood cells in response to absorption of carbon dioxide into the cell. As carbon dioxide enters the blood cell, bicarbonate leaves and chloride is absorbed in exchange to maintain electrical neutrality within the cell.

Chloride is provided by dietary intake, mostly in the form of sodium chloride. It is absorbed by the gastrointestinal system, filtered out by the glomeruli, and reabsorbed by the renal tubules. Excess chloride is excreted in the urine. Serum values normally remain fairly stable. A slight decrease may be detectable after meals because chloride is used to produce hydrochloric acid as part of the digestive process. Measurement of chloride levels is not as essential as measurement of other electrolytes such as sodium or potassium. Chloride is usually included in standard electrolyte panels to detect the presence of unmeasured anions via calculation of the anion gap. Chloride levels are usually not interpreted apart from sodium, potassium, carbon dioxide, and anion gap.

The patient's clinical picture needs to be considered in the evaluation of electrolytes. Fluid and electrolyte imbalances are often seen in patients with serious illness or injury because in these cases the clinical situation has affected the normal homeostatic balance of the body. It is also possible that therapeutic treatments being administered are causing or contributing to the electrolyte imbalance. Children and adults are at high risk for fluid and electrolyte imbalances when chloride levels are depleted. Children are considered to be at high risk during chloride imbalance because a positive serum chloride balance is important for expansion of the extracellular fluid compartment. Anemia, the result of decreased hemoglobin levels, is a frequent issue for elderly patients. Because hemoglobin participates in a major buffer system in the body, depleted hemoglobin levels affect the efficiency of chloride ion exchange for bicarbonate in red blood cells, which in turn affects acid-base balance. Elderly patients are also at high risk because their renal response to change in pH is slower, resulting in a more rapid development of electrolyte imbalance.

INDICATIONS

- Assist in confirming a diagnosis of disorders associated with abnormal chloride values, as seen in acid-base and fluid imbalances
- Differentiate between types of acidosis (hyperchloremic versus anion gap)
- Monitor effectiveness of drug therapy to increase or decrease serum chloride levels

POTENTIAL DIAGNOSIS

Increased in
- Acute renal failure *(related to decreased renal excretion)*
- Cushing's disease *(related to sodium retention as a result of increased levels of aldosterone; typically, chloride levels follow sodium levels)*

- Dehydration *(related to hemoconcentration)*
- Diabetes insipidus *(hemoconcentration related to excessive urine production)*
- Excessive infusion of normal saline *(related to excessive intake)*
- Head trauma with hypothalamic stimulation or damage
- Hyperparathyroidism (primary) *(high chloride-to-phosphate ratio is used to assist in diagnosis)*
- Metabolic acidosis *(associated with prolonged diarrhea)*
- Renal tubular acidosis *(acidosis related to net retention of chloride ions)*
- Respiratory alkalosis (e.g., hyperventilation) *(related to metabolic exchange of intracellular chloride replaced by bicarbonate; chloride levels increase)*
- Salicylate intoxication *(related to acid-base imbalance resulting in a hyperchloremic acidosis)*

Decreased in
- Addison's disease *(related to insufficient production of aldosterone; potassium is retained while sodium and chloride are lost)*
- Burns *(dilutional effect related to sequestration of extracellular fluid)*
- Congestive heart failure *(related to dilutional effect of fluid buildup)*
- Diabetic ketoacidosis *(related to acid-base imbalance with accumulation of ketone bodies and increased chloride)*
- Excessive sweating *(related to excessive loss of chloride without replacement)*
- Gastrointestinal loss from vomiting (severe), diarrhea, nasogastric suction, or fistula
- Metabolic alkalosis *(related to homeostatic response in which*

intracellular chloride increases to reduce alkalinity of extracellular fluid)
- Overhydration *(related to dilutional effect)*
- Respiratory acidosis (chronic)
- Salt-losing nephritis *(related to excessive loss)*
- Syndrome of inappropriate antidiuretic hormone secretion *(related to dilutional effect)*
- Water intoxication *(related to dilutional effect)*

CRITICAL FINDINGS
- Less than 80 mmol/L (SI: Less than 80 mmol/L)
- Greater than 115 mmol/L (SI: Greater than 115 mmol/L)

Note and immediately report to the health-care provider (HCP) any critically increased or decreased values and related symptoms. Timely notification of critical values for lab or diagnostic studies is a role expectation of the professional nurse. Notification processes will vary among facilities. Upon receipt of the critical value, the information should be read back to the caller to verify accuracy. Most policies require immediate notification of the primary HCP, hospitalist, or on-call HCP. Reported information includes the patient's name, unique identifiers, critical value, name of the person giving the report, and name of the person receiving the report. Documentation of notification should be made in the medical record with the name of the HCP notified, time and date of notification, and any orders received. Any delay in a timely report of a critical value may require completion of a notification form with review by Risk Management. Observe the patient for symptoms of critically decreased or elevated chloride levels. Proper interpretation of chloride values must be made within the context of other electrolyte values and requires clinical knowledge of the patient.

The following may be seen in hypochloremia: twitching or tremors, which may indicate excitability of the nervous system; slow and shallow breathing; and decreased blood pressure as a result of fluid loss. Possible interventions relate to treatment of the underlying cause.

Signs and symptoms associated with hyperchloremia are weakness; lethargy; and deep, rapid breathing. Proper interventions include treatments that correct the underlying cause.

INTERFERING FACTORS
- Drugs that may cause an increase in chloride levels include acetazolamide, acetylsalicylic acid, ammonium chloride, androgens, bromide, chlorothiazide, cholestyramine, cyclosporine, estrogens, guanethidine, hydrochlorothiazide, lithium, methyldopa, NSAIDs, oxyphenbutazone, phenylbutazone, and triamterene.
- Drugs that may cause a decrease in chloride levels include aldosterone, bicarbonate, corticosteroids, corticotropin, cortisone, diuretics, ethacrynic acid, furosemide, hydroflumethiazide, laxatives (if chronic abuse occurs), mannitol, meralluride, mersalyl, methyclothiazide, metolazone, and triamterene. Many of these drugs can cause a diuretic action that inhibits the tubular reabsorption of chloride. *Note*: Triamterene has nephrotoxic and azotemic effects, and when organ damage has occurred, increased serum chloride levels result. Potassium chloride (found in salt substitutes) can lower blood chloride

levels and raise urine chloride levels.

- Elevated triglyceride or protein levels may cause a volume-displacement error in the specimen, reflecting falsely decreased chloride values when chloride measurement methods employing predilution specimens are used (e.g., indirect ion-selective electrode, flame photometry).

- Specimens should never be collected above an IV line because of the potential for dilution when the specimen and the IV solution combine in the collection container, falsely decreasing the result. There is also the potential of contaminating the sample with the normal saline contained in the IV solution, falsely increasing the result.

NURSING IMPLICATIONS AND PROCEDURE

PRETEST:

▶ Positively identify the patient using at least two unique identifiers before providing care, treatment, or services.

▶ *Patient Teaching:* Inform the patient this test can assist in evaluating the amount of chloride in the blood.

▶ Obtain a history of the patient's complaints, including a list of known allergens, especially allergies or sensitivities to latex.

▶ Obtain a history of the patient's cardio-vascular, endocrine, gastrointestinal, genitourinary, and respiratory systems, as well as results of previously performed laboratory tests and diagnostic and surgical procedures. Specimens should not be collected during hemodialysis.

▶ Obtain a list of the patient's current medications, including herbs, nutritional supplements, and nutraceuticals (see Appendix F).

▶ Review the procedure with the patient. Inform the patient that specimen collection takes approximately 5 to 10 min. Address concerns about pain and explain that there may be some discomfort during the venipuncture.

▶ *Sensitivity to social and cultural issues,* as well as concern for modesty, is important in providing psychological support before, during, and after the procedure.

▶ There are no food, fluid, or medication restrictions unless by medical direction.

INTRATEST:

▶ If the patient has a history of allergic reaction to latex, avoid the use of equipment containing latex.

▶ Instruct the patient to cooperate fully and to follow directions. Direct the patient to breathe normally and to avoid unnecessary movement. Instruct the patient not to clench and unclench fist immediately before or during specimen collection.

▶ Observe standard precautions, and follow the general guidelines in Appendix A. Positively identify the patient, and label the appropriate specimen container with the corresponding patient demographics, initials of the person collecting the specimen, date, and time of collection. Perform a venipuncture.

▶ Remove the needle and apply direct pressure with dry gauze to stop bleeding. Observe/assess venipuncture site for bleeding or hematoma formation and secure gauze with adhesive bandage.

▶ Promptly transport the specimen to the laboratory for processing and analysis.

POST-TEST:

▶ A report of the results will be made available to the requesting HCP, who will discuss the results with the patient.

▶ Observe the patient on saline IV fluid replacement therapy for signs of over-hydration, especially in cases in which there is a history of cardiac or renal disease. Signs of overhydration include constant, irritable cough; chest rales; dyspnea; or engorgement of neck and hand veins.

Evaluate the patient for signs and symptoms of dehydration. Check the patient's skin turgor, mucous membrane moisture, and ability to produce tears. Dehydration is a significant and common finding in geriatric and other patients in whom renal function has deteriorated.

Monitor daily weights as well as intake and output to determine whether fluid retention is occurring because of sodium and chloride excess. Patients at risk for or with a history of fluid imbalance are also at risk for electrolyte imbalance.

Nutritional Considerations: Careful observation of the patient on IV fluid replacement therapy is important. A patient receiving a continuous 5% dextrose solution (D_5W) may not be taking in an adequate amount of chloride to meet the body's needs. The patient, if allowed, should be encouraged to drink fluids such as broths, tomato juice, or colas and to eat foods such as meats, seafood, or eggs, which contain sodium and chloride. The use of table salt may also be appropriate.

Nutritional Considerations: Instruct patients with elevated chloride levels to avoid eating or drinking anything containing sodium chloride salt. The patient or caregiver should also be encouraged to read food labels to determine which products are suitable for a low-sodium diet.

Nutritional Considerations: Instruct patients with low chloride levels that a decrease in iron absorption may occur as a result of less chloride available to form gastric acid, which is essential for iron absorption. In prolonged periods of chloride deficit, iron-deficiency anemia could develop.

Nutritional Considerations: The Institute of Medicine's Food and Nutrition Board suggests 1,800 mg/d as the daily intake goal of dietary chloride for adult males and females age greater than 70 yr; 2,000 mg/d as the daily intake goal of dietary chloride for adult males and females age 51 to 70 yr; 2,300 mg/d as the daily intake goal of dietary chloride for adult males and females age 19 to 50 yr; 2,300 mg/d for pregnant and lactating females age 18 to 50 yr; 2,300 mg/ day for children age 9 to 18 yr; 1,900 mg/d for children age 4 to 8 yr; 1,500 mg/d for children age 1 to 3 yr; 570 mg/d for children age 7 to 12 mo; 180 mg/d for children age 0 to 6 mo. Reprinted with permission from the National Academies Press, copyright 2013, National Academy of Sciences.

Reinforce information given by the patient's HCP regarding further testing, treatment, or referral to another HCP. Answer any questions or address any concerns voiced by the patient or family. Educate the patient regarding access to nutritional counseling services. Provide contact information, if desired, for the Institute of Medicine of the National Academies (www.iom.edu).

Depending on the results of this procedure, additional testing may be performed to evaluate or monitor progression of the disease process and determine the need for a change in therapy. Evaluate test results in relation to the patient's symptoms and other tests performed.

RELATED MONOGRAPHS:

Related tests include ACTH, anion gap, blood gases, carbon dioxide, CBC hematocrit, CBC hemoglobin, osmolality, potassium, protein total and fractions, sodium, and US abdomen.

Refer to the Cardiovascular, Endocrine, Gastrointestinal, Genitourinary, and Respiratory systems tables at the end of the book for related test by body system.

Chloride, Sweat

SYNONYM/ACRONYM: Sweat test, pilocarpine iontophoresis sweat test, sweat chloride.

COMMON USE: To assist in diagnosing cystic fibrosis.

SPECIMEN: Sweat (0.1 mL minimum) collected by pilocarpine iontophoresis.

NORMAL FINDINGS: (Method: Ion-specific electrode or titration)

	Conventional & SI Units
Normal	0–40 mmol/L
Borderline	41–60 mmol/L
Consistent with the diagnosis of CF	Greater than 60 mmol/L

DESCRIPTION: Cystic fibrosis (CF) is a genetic disease that affects normal functioning of the exocrine glands, causing them to excrete large amounts of electrolytes. Patients with CF have sweat electrolyte levels two to five times normal. Sweat test values, with family history and signs and symptoms, are required to establish a diagnosis of CF. CF is transmitted as an autosomal recessive trait and is characterized by abnormal exocrine secretions within the lungs, pancreas, small intestine, bile ducts, and skin. Clinical presentation may include chronic problems of the gastrointestinal and/or respiratory system. CF is more common in Caucasians. Sweat conductivity is a screening method that estimates chloride levels. Sweat conductivity values greater than or equal to 50 mmol/L should be referred for quantitative analysis of sweat chloride. Testing of stool samples for decreased trypsin activity has been used as a screen for CF in infants and children, but this is a much less reliable method than the sweat test. The American College of Obstetricians and Gynecologists (ACOG) suggests that carrier screening be discussed as an option to patients (and couples) who are pregnant or are considering pregnancy. Laboratories generally offer a panel of the current and most common cystic fibrosis mutations recommended by ACOG and the American College of Medical Genetics. Some states include CF in the neonatal screening performed at birth. Genetic testing can also be reliably performed on DNA material harvested from whole blood, amniotic fluid (submitted with maternal blood sample), chorionic villus samples (submitted with maternal blood sample), or buccal swabs to screen for genetic mutations associated with CF and can assist in confirming a diagnosis of CF, but the sweat electrolyte test is still considered the gold standard diagnostic for CF.

The sweat test is a noninvasive study done to assist in the diagnosis of CF when considered with other test results and physical assessments. This test is usually performed on children, although adults may also be tested; it is not usually ordered on adults because results can be highly variable and should be interpreted with caution. Sweat for specimen collection is induced by a small electrical current carrying the drug pilocarpine. The test measures the concentration of chloride produced by the sweat glands of the skin. A high concentration of chloride in the specimen indicates the presence of CF. The sweat test is used less commonly to measure the concentration of sodium ions for the same purpose.

INDICATIONS

- Assist in the diagnosis of CF
- Screen for CF in individuals with a family history of the disease
- Screen for suspected CF in children with recurring respiratory infections
- Screen for suspected CF in infants with failure to thrive and infants who pass meconium late
- Screen for suspected CF in individuals with malabsorption syndrome

POTENTIAL DIAGNOSIS

Increased in
Conditions that affect electrolyte distribution and excretion may produce false-positive sweat test results.

- Addison's disease
- Alcoholic pancreatitis *(dysfunction of CF gene is linked to pancreatic disease susceptibility)*
- CF
- Chronic pulmonary infections *(related to undiagnosed CF)*

- Congenital adrenal hyperplasia
- Diabetes insipidus
- Familial cholestasis
- Familial hypoparathyroidism
- Fucosidosis
- Glucose-6-phosphate dehydrogenase deficiency
- Hypothyroidism
- Mucopolysaccharidosis
- Nephrogenic diabetes insipidus
- Renal failure

Decreased in
Conditions that affect electrolyte distribution and retention may produce false-negative sweat test results.

- Edema
- Hypoaldosteronism
- Hypoproteinemia
- Sodium depletion

CRITICAL FINDINGS ◈

- 20 yr or younger: greater than 60 mmol/L considered diagnostic of CF
- Older than 20 years: greater than 70 mmol/L considered diagnostic of CF

Note and immediately report to the health-care provider (HCP) any critically increased values and related symptoms. Values should be interpreted with consideration of family history and clinical signs and symptoms. Timely notification of critical values for lab or diagnostic studies is a role expectation of the professional nurse. Notification processes will vary among facilities. Upon receipt of the critical value, the information should be read back to the caller to verify accuracy. Most policies require immediate notification of the primary HCP, hospitalist, or on-call HCP. Reported information includes the patient's name, unique identifiers, critical value, name of the person giving the report, and name of the person receiving the report. Documentation of notification should be made in the medical record with the name of the HCP notified, time and date of notification, and any orders received. Any delay in a timely report of a critical value may require completion of a notification form with review by Risk Management.

The validity of the test result is affected tremendously by proper specimen collection and handling. Before proceeding with appropriate patient education and counseling, it is important to perform duplicate testing on patients whose results are in the diagnostic or intermediate ranges. A negative test should be repeated if test results do not support the clinical picture.

INTERFERING FACTORS

- An inadequate amount of sweat may produce inaccurate results.
- ❖ This test should not be performed on patients with skin disorders (e.g., rash, erythema, eczema).
- Improper cleaning of the skin or improper application of gauze pad or filter paper for collection affects test results.
- Hot environmental temperatures may reduce the sodium chloride concentration in sweat; cool environmental temperatures may reduce the amount of sweat collected.
- If the specimen container that stores the gauze or filter paper is handled without gloves, the test results may show a false increase in the final weight of the collection container.

NURSING IMPLICATIONS AND PROCEDURE

PRETEST:

▸ Positively identify the patient using at least two unique identifiers before providing care, treatment, or services.

Patient Teaching: Inform the patient this test can assist in diagnosing an inherited disease that affects the lungs.

▸ Obtain a history of the patient's complaints, including a list of known allergens, especially allergies or sensitivities to latex.

▸ Obtain a history of the patient's endocrine and respiratory systems, especially failure to thrive or CF in other family members, as well as results of previously performed laboratory tests and diagnostic and surgical procedures.

▸ Obtain a list of the patient's current medications, including herbs, nutritional supplements, and nutraceuticals (see Appendix F).

▸ Review the procedure with the patient and caregiver. Encourage the caregiver to stay with and support the child during the test. The iontophoresis and specimen collection usually takes approximately 75 to 90 min. Address concerns about pain and explain that there is no pain associated with the test, but a stinging sensation may be experienced when the low electrical current is applied at the site.

▸ *Sensitivity to social and cultural issues,* as well as concern for modesty, is important in providing psychological support before, during, and after the procedure.

▸ There are no food, fluid, or medication restrictions unless by medical direction.

INTRATEST:

▸ Instruct the patient to cooperate fully and to follow directions.

▸ Observe standard precautions, and follow the general guidelines in Appendix A. Positively identify the patient, and label the appropriate specimen container with the corresponding patient demographics, initials of the person collecting the specimen, date, and time of collection.

▸ ❖ The test should not be performed if the patient is receiving oxygen by means of an open system related to the remote possibility of explosion from an electrical spark. If the patient can temporarily receive oxygen via a facemask or nasal cannula, then sweat testing can be done.

The patient is placed in a position that will allow exposure of the site on the forearm or thigh. To ensure collection of an adequate amount of sweat in a small infant, two sites (right forearm and right thigh) can be used. The patient should be covered to prevent cool environmental temperatures from affecting sweat production. The site selected for iontophoresis should never be the chest or left side because of the risk of cardiac arrest from the electrical current.

The site is washed with distilled water and dried. A positive electrode is attached to the site on the right forearm or right thigh and covered with a pad that is saturated with pilocarpine, a drug that stimulates sweating. A negative electrode is covered with a pad that is saturated with bicarbonate solution. Iontophoresis is achieved by supplying a low (4 to 5 mA) electrical current via the electrode for 12 to 15 min. Battery-powered equipment is preferred over an electrical outlet to supply the current.

The electrodes are removed, revealing a red area at the site, and the site is washed with distilled water and dried to remove any possible contaminants on the skin.

Preweighed disks made of filter paper are placed on the site with a forceps; to prevent evaporation of sweat collected at the site, the disks are covered with paraffin or plastic and sealed at the edges. The disks are left in place for about 1 hr. Distract the child with books or games to allay fears.

After 1 hr, the paraffin covering is removed, and disks are placed in a preweighed container with a forceps. The container is sealed and sent immediately to the laboratory for weighing and analysis of chloride content. At least 100 mg of sweat is required for accurate results.

Terminate the test if the patient complains of burning at the electrode site. Reposition the electrode before the test is resumed.

Promptly transport the specimen to the laboratory for processing and analysis. Do not directly handle the preweighed specimen container or filter paper.

POST-TEST:

A report of the results will be made available to the requesting HCP, who will discuss the results with the patient/caregiver.

Observe/assess the site for unusual color, sensation, or discomfort.

Inform the patient and caregiver that redness at the site fades in 2 to 3 hr.

Instruct the patient to resume usual diet, fluids, medications, and activity, as directed by the HCP.

Nutritional Considerations: If appropriate, instruct the patient and caregiver that nutrition may be altered because of impaired digestive processes associated with CF. Increased viscosity of exocrine gland secretion may lead to poor absorption of digestive enzymes and fat-soluble vitamins, necessitating oral intake of digestive enzymes with each meal and calcium and vitamin (A, D, E, and K) supplementation. Malnutrition also is seen commonly in patients with chronic, severe respiratory disease for many reasons, including fatigue, lack of appetite, and gastrointestinal distress. Research has estimated that the daily caloric intake needed for children with CF between 4 and 7 yr may be 2,000 to 2,800 and for teens 3,000 to 5,000. Tube feeding may be necessary to supplement regular high-calorie meals. To prevent pulmonary infection and decrease the extent of lung tissue damage, adequate intake of vitamins A and C is also important. Excessive loss of sodium chloride through the sweat glands of a patient with CF may necessitate increased salt intake, especially in environments where increased sweating is induced. The importance of following the prescribed diet should be stressed to the patient and caregiver.

If appropriate, instruct the patient and caregiver that ineffective airway clearance related to excessive production of mucus and decreased ciliary action may result. Chest physical therapy and the use of aerosolized antibiotics and mucus-thinning drugs are an important part of the daily treatment regimen.

Recognize anxiety related to test results, and be supportive of impaired activity related to perceived loss of independence and fear of shortened life expectancy. Discuss the implications of abnormal test results on the patient's lifestyle. Provide teaching and information regarding the clinical implications of the test results, as appropriate. Educate the patient regarding access to counseling services. Help the patient and caregiver to cope with long-term implications. Recognize that anticipatory anxiety and grief related to potential lifestyle changes may be expressed when someone is faced with a chronic disorder. Provide information regarding genetic counseling and possible screening of other family members if appropriate. Provide contact information, if desired, for the Cystic Fibrosis Foundation (www.cff.org). Reinforce information given by the patient's HCP regarding further testing, treatment, or referral to another HCP. Explain that a positive sweat test alone is not diagnostic of CF; repetition of

borderline and positive tests is generally recommended. Answer any questions or address any concerns voiced by the patient or family.
Depending on the results of this procedure, additional testing may be performed to evaluate or monitor progression of the disease process and determine the need for a change in therapy. Evaluate test results in relation to the patient's symptoms and other tests performed.

RELATED MONOGRAPHS:

Related tests include α_1-antitrypsin/phenotype, amylase, anion gap, biopsy chorionic villus, blood gases, fecal analysis, fecal fat, newborn screening, osmolality, phosphorus, potassium, and sodium.
Refer to the Endocrine and Respiratory systems tables at the end of the book for related tests by body system.

Cholangiography, Percutaneous Transhepatic

SYNONYM/ACRONYM: Percutaneous cholecystogram, PTC, PTHC.

COMMON USE: To visualize and assess biliary ducts for causes of obstruction and jaundice, such as cancer or stones.

AREA OF APPLICATION: Biliary system.

CONTRAST: Radiopaque iodine-based contrast medium.

DESCRIPTION: Percutaneous transhepatic cholangiography (PTC) is a test used to visualize the biliary system in order to evaluate persistent upper abdominal pain after cholecystectomy and to determine the presence and cause of obstructive jaundice. The liver is punctured with a thin needle under fluoroscopic guidance, and

contrast medium is injected as the needle is slowly withdrawn. This test visualizes the biliary ducts without depending on the gallbladder's concentrating ability. The intrahepatic and extrahepatic biliary ducts, and occasionally the gallbladder, can be visualized to determine possible obstruction. In obstruction of the extrahepatic ducts, a catheter can be placed in the duct to allow external drainage of bile. Endoscopic retrograde cholangiopancreatography (ERCP) and PTC are the only methods available to view the biliary tree in the presence of jaundice. ERCP poses less risk and is probably done more often. PTC is an invasive procedure and has potential risks, including bleeding, septicemia, bile peritonitis, and extravasation of the contrast medium.

INDICATIONS

- Aid in the diagnosis of obstruction caused by gallstones, benign strictures, malignant tumors, congenital cysts, and anatomic variations
- Determine the cause, extent, and location of mechanical obstruction
- Determine the cause of upper abdominal pain after cholecystectomy
- Distinguish between obstructive and nonobstructive jaundice

POTENTIAL DIAGNOSIS

Normal findings in

- Biliary ducts are normal in diameter, with no evidence of dilation, filling defects, duct narrowing, or extravasation.
- Contrast medium fills the ducts and flows freely.
- Gallbladder appears normal in size and shape.

Abnormal findings in

- Anatomic biliary or pancreatic duct variations
- Biliary sclerosis
- Cholangiocarcinoma
- Cirrhosis
- Common bile duct cysts
- Gallbladder carcinoma
- Gallstones
- Hepatitis
- Nonobstructive jaundice
- Pancreatitis

- Sclerosing cholangitis
- Tumors, strictures, inflammation, or gallstones of the common bile duct

CRITICAL FINDINGS: N/A

INTERFERING FACTORS

This procedure is contraindicated for

- ❖ Patients with allergies to shellfish or iodinated dye. The contrast medium used may cause a life-threatening allergic reaction. Patients with a known hypersensitivity to the medium may benefit from premedication with corticosteroids or the use of nonionic contrast medium.
- Patients who are pregnant or suspected of being pregnant, unless the potential benefits of the procedure far outweigh the risks to the fetus and mother.
- ❖ Patients with cholangitis. The injection of the contrast medium can increase biliary pressure, leading to bacteremia, septicemia, and shock.
- Patients with postoperative wound sepsis, hypersensitivity to iodine, or acute renal failure.
- ❖ Patients with bleeding disorders, massive ascites, or acute renal failure.

Factors that may impair clear imaging

- Gas or feces in the gastrointestinal (GI) tract resulting from inadequate cleansing or failure to restrict food intake before the study.
- Retained barium from a previous radiological procedure.
- Metallic objects within the examination field, which may inhibit organ visualization and cause unclear images.
- Inability of the patient to cooperate or remain still during the procedure because of age, significant pain, or mental status.

Other considerations

- The procedure may be terminated if chest pain or severe cardiac arrhythmias occur.
- Failure to follow dietary restrictions and other pretesting preparations may cause the procedure to be canceled or repeated.
- Peritonitis may occur as a result of bile extravasation.
- Consultation with a health-care provider (HCP) should occur before the procedure for radiation safety concerns regarding younger patients or patients who are lactating.
- Risks associated with radiation over-exposure can result from frequent x-ray procedures. Personnel in the examination room with the patient should wear a protective lead apron stand behind a shield, or leave the area while the examination is being done. Personnel working in the examination area should wear badges to record their level of radiation exposure.

NURSING IMPLICATIONS AND PROCEDURE

PRETEST:

▸ Positively identify the patient using at least two unique identifiers before providing care, treatment, or services.

▸ *Patient Teaching:* Inform the patient this procedure can assist in assessing the bile ducts of the gallbladder and pancreas.

▸ Obtain a history of the patient's complaints, including a list of known allergens, especially allergies or sensitivities to latex, iodine, seafood, contrast medium, anesthetics, and dyes.

▸ Obtain a history of the patient's gastrointestinal and hepatobiliary systems, symptoms, and results of previously performed laboratory tests and diagnostic and surgical procedures.

▸ Ensure that this procedure is performed before an upper GI study or barium swallow.

▸ Record the date of the last menstrual period and determine the possibility of pregnancy in perimenopausal women.

▸ Obtain a list of the patient's current medications, including anticoagulants, aspirin and other salicylates, herbs, nutritional supplements, and nutraceuticals (see Appendix F). Such products should be discontinued by medical direction for the appropriate number of days prior to a surgical procedure. Note time and date of last dose.

▸ If contrast medium is scheduled to be used, patients receiving metformin (Glucophage) for non-insulin-dependent (type 2) diabetes should discontinue the drug on the day of the test and continue to withhold it for 48 hr after the test. Failure to do so may result in lactic acidosis.

▸ Review the procedure with the patient. Address concerns about pain and explain that there may be moments of discomfort and some pain experienced during the test. Inform the patient that the procedure is usually performed in the radiology department by an HCP, with support staff, and takes approximately 30 to 60 min.

▸ *Sensitivity to social and cultural issues,* as well as concern for modesty, is important in providing psychological support before, during, and after the procedure.

▸ Explain that an IV line may be inserted to allow infusion of IV fluids, anesthetics, or sedatives.

▸ Type and screen the patient's blood for possible transfusion.

▸ Inform the patient that a laxative and cleansing enema may be needed the day before the procedure, with cleansing enemas on the morning of the procedure depending on the institution's policy.

▸ Instruct the patient to remove all external metallic objects from the area to be examined.

▸ The patient should fast and restrict fluids for 8 hr prior to the procedure. Instruct the patient to avoid taking anticoagulant medication or to reduce dosage as ordered prior to the procedure. Protocols may vary among facilities.

▸ *Make sure a written and informed consent has been signed prior to the*

*procedure and before administering
any medications.*

INTRATEST:

- Observe standard precautions, and follow the general guidelines in Appendix A. Positively identify the patient.
- Ensure that the patient has complied with dietary, fluid, and medication restrictions for 8 hr prior to the procedure.
- Ensure the patient has removed all external metallic objects from the area to be examined.
- Assess for completion of bowel preparation according to the institution's procedure.
- If the patient has a history of allergic reactions to any relevant substance or drug, administer ordered prophylactic steroids or antihistamines before the procedure. Use nonionic contrast medium for the procedure.
- Have emergency equipment readily available.
- Instruct the patient to void prior to the procedure and to change into the gown, robe, and foot coverings provided.
- Instruct the patient to cooperate fully and to follow directions. Instruct the patient to remain still throughout the procedure because movement produces unreliable results.
- Record baseline vital signs, and continue to monitor throughout the procedure. Protocols may vary among facilities.
- Place the patient in the supine position on an examination table.
- A kidney, ureter, and bladder (KUB) or plain film is taken to ensure that no barium or stool will obscure visualization of the biliary system.
- An area over the abdominal wall is anesthetized, and the needle is inserted and advanced under fluoroscopic guidance. Contrast medium is injected when placement is confirmed by the free flow of bile.
- A specimen of bile may be sent to the laboratory for culture and cytological analysis.
- At the end of the procedure, the contrast medium is aspirated from the biliary ducts, relieving pressure on the dilated ducts.
- If an obstruction is found during the procedure, a catheter is inserted into the bile duct to allow drainage of bile.
- Maintain pressure over the needle insertion site for several hours if bleeding is persistent.
- Observe/assess the needle site for bleeding, inflammation, or hematoma formation.
- Establish a closed and sterile drainage system if a catheter is left in place.

POST-TEST:

- A report of the results will be made available to the requesting HCP, who will discuss the results with the patient.
- Instruct the patient to resume usual diet, fluids, medications, and activity, as directed by the HCP. Renal function should be assessed before metformin is restarted.
- Monitor vital signs and neurological status every 15 min for 1 hr, then every 2 hr for 4 hr, and as ordered. Take temperature every 4 hr for 24 hr. Monitor intake and output at least every 8 hr. Compare with baseline values. Notify the HCP if temperature is elevated. Protocols may vary among facilities.
- Monitor for reaction to iodinated contrast medium, including rash, urticaria, tachycardia, hyperpnea, hypertension, palpitations, nausea, or vomiting.
- Observe/assess the puncture site for signs of bleeding, hematoma formation, ecchymosis, or leakage of bile. Notify the HCP if any of these is present.
- Advise the patient to watch for symptoms of infection, such as pain, fever, increased pulse rate, and muscle aches.
- Recognize anxiety related to test results. Discuss the implications of abnormal test results on the patient's lifestyle. Provide teaching and information regarding the clinical implications of the test results, as appropriate.
- Reinforce information given by the patient's HCP regarding further testing, treatment, or referral to another HCP. Answer any questions or address any concerns voiced by the patient or family.

C

▶ Depending on the results of this procedure, additional testing may be needed to evaluate or monitor progression of the disease process and determine the need for a change in therapy. Evaluate test results in relation to the patient's symptoms and other tests performed.

RELATED MONOGRAPHS:

▶ Related tests include ALT, amylase, AMA, AST, biopsy liver, cancer antigens, cholangiography postoperative, cholangiopancreatography endoscopic retrograde, CT abdomen, GGT, hepatitis antigens and antibodies (A, B, C), hepatobiliary scan, KUB studies, laparoscopy abdominal, lipase, MRI abdomen, peritoneal fluid analysis, pleural fluid analysis, and US liver and biliary tract.

▶ Refer to the Gastrointestinal and Hepatobiliary systems tables at the end of the book for related tests by body system.

Cholangiography, Postoperative

SYNONYM/ACRONYM: T-tube cholangiography.

COMMON USE: A postoperative evaluation to provide ongoing assessment of the effectiveness of bile duct or gall bladder surgery.

AREA OF APPLICATION: Gallbladder, bile ducts.

CONTRAST: Iodinated contrast medium.

DESCRIPTION: After cholecystectomy, a self-retaining, T-shaped tube may be inserted into the common bile duct. Postoperative (T-tube) cholangiography is a fluoroscopic and radiographic examination of the biliary tract that involves the injection of a contrast medium through the T-tube inserted during surgery. This test may be performed at the time of surgery and again 7 to 10 days after cholecystectomy to assess the patency of the common bile duct and to detect any remaining calculi. T-tube placement may also be done after a liver transplant because biliary duct obstruction or anastomotic leakage is possible. This test should be performed before any gastrointestinal (GI) studies using barium and after any studies involving the measurement of iodinated compounds.

INDICATIONS
• Determine biliary duct patency before T-tube removal
• Identify the cause, extent, and location of obstruction after surgery

POTENTIAL DIAGNOSIS

Normal findings in
• Biliary ducts are normal in size.
• Contrast medium fills the ductal system and flows freely.

Abnormal findings in
• Appearance of channels of contrast medium outside of the biliary ducts, indicating a fistula

- Filling defects, dilation, or shadows within the biliary ducts, indicating calculi or neoplasm

CRITICAL FINDINGS: N/A

INTERFERING FACTORS

This procedure is contraindicated for

- ◈ Patients with allergies to shellfish or iodinated dye. The contrast medium used may cause a life-threatening allergic reaction. Patients with a known hypersensitivity to the medium may benefit from premedication with corticosteroids or the use of nonionic contrast medium.
- Patients who are pregnant or suspected of being pregnant, unless the potential benefits of the procedure far outweigh the risks to the fetus and mother.
- ◈ Patients with cholangitis. The injection of the contrast medium can increase biliary pressure, leading to bacteremia, septicemia, and shock.
- ◈ Patients with postoperative wound sepsis, hypersensitivity to iodine, or acute renal failure.

Factors that may impair clear imaging

- Gas or feces in the GI tract resulting from inadequate cleansing or failure to restrict food intake before the study.
- Retained barium from a previous radiological procedure.
- Metallic objects within the examination field, which may inhibit organ visualization and cause unclear images.
- Inability of the patient to cooperate or remain still during the procedure because of age, significant pain, or mental status.

Other considerations

- The procedure may be terminated if chest pain or severe cardiac arrhythmias occur.

- Air bubbles resembling calculi may be seen if there is inadvertent injection of air.
- Peritonitis may occur as a result of bile extravasation.
- Failure to follow dietary restrictions and other pretesting preparations may cause the procedure to be canceled or repeated.
- Consultation with a health-care provider (HCP) should occur before the procedure for radiation safety concerns regarding younger patients or patients who are lactating.
- Risks associated with radiation overexposure can result from frequent x-ray procedures. Personnel in the examination room with the patient should wear a protective lead apron, stand behind a shield, or leave the area while the examination is being done. Personnel working in the examination area should wear badges to record their radiation level.

NURSING IMPLICATIONS AND PROCEDURE

PRETEST:

▸ Positively identify the patient using at least two unique identifiers before providing care, treatment, or services.
▸ *Patient Teaching:* Inform the patient this procedure can assist in assessing the bile ducts of the gallbladder and pancreas.
▸ Obtain a history of the patient's complaints, including a list of known allergens, especially allergies or sensitivities to latex, iodine, seafood, contrast medium, anesthetics, and dyes.
▸ Obtain a history of results of the patient's gastrointestinal and hepatobiliary systems, symptoms, and previously performed laboratory tests and diagnostic and surgical procedures.
▸ Ensure that this procedure is performed before an upper GI study or barium swallow.

362 | Davis's Comprehensive Laboratory and Diagnostic Handbook—*with Nursing Implications*

Record the date of the last menstrual period and determine the possibility of pregnancy in perimenopausal women.

Obtain a list of the patient's current medications, including herbs, nutritional supplements, and nutraceuticals (see Appendix F).

If contrast medium is scheduled to be used, patients receiving metformin (Glucophage) for non-insulin-dependent (type 2) diabetes should discontinue the drug on the day of the test and continue to withhold it for 48 hr after the test. Failure to do so may result in lactic acidosis.

Review the procedure with the patient. Address concerns about pain and explain that there may be moments of discomfort and some pain experienced during the test. Inform the patient that the procedure is usually performed in the radiology department by an HCP and takes approximately 30 to 60 min.

Sensitivity to social and cultural issues, as well as concern for modesty, is important in providing psychological support before, during, and after the procedure.

Instruct the patient to remove jewelry and other metallic objects in the area to be examined.

Instruct the patient to fast and restrict fluids for 8 hr prior to the procedure. Protocols may vary among facilities.

Make sure a written and informed consent has been signed prior to the procedure and before administering any medications.

INTRATEST:

Observe standard precautions, and follow the general guidelines in Appendix A. Positively identify the patient.

Ensure that the patient has complied with dietary, fluid, and medication restrictions for 8 hr prior to the procedure.

Ensure that the patient has removed all external metallic objects from the area to be examined prior to the procedure.

If the patient has a history of allergic reactions to any relevant substance or drug, administer ordered prophylactic steroids or antihistamines before the procedure.

Have emergency equipment readily available.

Instruct the patient to void prior to the procedure and to change into the gown, robe, and foot coverings provided.

Instruct the patient to cooperate fully and to follow directions. Instruct the patient to remain still throughout the procedure because movement produces unreliable results.

Record baseline vital signs, and continue to monitor throughout the procedure. Protocols may vary among facilities.

Clamp the T-tube 24 hr before and during the procedure, if ordered, to help prevent air bubbles from entering the ducts.

An x-ray of the abdomen is obtained to determine if any residual contrast medium is present from previous studies.

The patient is placed on an examination table in the supine position.

The area around the T-tube is draped; the end of the T-tube is cleansed with 70% alcohol. If the T-tube site is inflamed and painful, a local anesthetic (e.g., lidocaine) may be injected around the site. A needle is inserted into the open end of the T-tube, and the clamp is removed.

Contrast medium is injected, and fluoroscopy is performed to visualize contrast medium moving through the duct system.

The patient may feel a bloating sensation in the upper right quadrant as the contrast medium is injected. The tube is clamped, and images are taken. A delayed image may be taken 15 min later to visualize passage of the contrast medium into the duodenum.

For procedures done after surgery, the T-tube is removed if findings are normal; a dry, sterile dressing is applied to the site.

If retained calculi are identified, the T-tube is left in place for 4 to 6 wk until the tract surrounding the T-tube is healed to perform a percutaneous removal.

POST-TEST:

A report of the results will be made available to the requesting HCP, who will discuss the results with the patient.

▶ Instruct the patient to resume usual diet, fluids, medications, and activity, as directed by the HCP. Renal function should be assessed before metformin is resumed, if contrast was used.

▶ Monitor vital signs and neurological status every 15 min for 1 hr, then every 2 hr for 4 hr, and as ordered. Take temperature every 4 hr for 24 hr. Monitor intake and output at least every 8 hr. Compare with baseline values. Notify the HCP if temperature is elevated. Protocols may vary among facilities.

▶ Monitor T-tube site and change sterile dressing, as ordered.

▶ Instruct the patient on the care of the site and dressing changes.

▶ Monitor for reaction to iodinated contrast medium, including rash, urticaria, tachycardia, hyperpnea, hypertension, palpitations, nausea, or vomiting.

▶ Instruct the patient to immediately report symptoms such as fast heart rate, difficulty breathing, skin rash, itching, chest pain, persistent right shoulder pain, or abdominal pain. Immediately report symptoms to the appropriate HCP.

▶ Carefully monitor the patient for fatigue and fluid and electrolyte imbalance.

▶ Recognize anxiety related to test results. Discuss the implications of abnormal test results on the patient's lifestyle. Provide teaching and information regarding the clinical implications of the test results, as appropriate.

▶ Reinforce information given by the patient's HCP regarding further testing, treatment, or referral to another HCP. Answer any questions or address any concerns voiced by the patient or family.

▶ Depending on the results of this procedure, additional testing may be needed to evaluate or monitor progression of the disease process and determine the need for a change in therapy. Evaluate test results in relation to the patient's symptoms and other tests performed.

RELATED MONOGRAPHS:

▶ Related tests include CT abdomen, hepatobiliary scan, KUB, MRI abdomen, and US liver and biliary system.

▶ Refer to the Gastrointestinal and Hepatobiliary systems tables at the end of the book for tests by related body systems.

Cholangiopancreatography, Endoscopic Retrograde

SYNONYM/ACRONYM: ERCP.

COMMON USE: To visualize and assess the pancreas and common bile ducts for occlusion or stricture.

AREA OF APPLICATION: Gallbladder, bile ducts, pancreatic ducts.

CONTRAST: Iodinated contrast medium.

C

DESCRIPTION: Endoscopic retrograde cholangiopancreatography (ERCP) allows direct visualization of the pancreatic and biliary ducts with a flexible endoscope and, after injection of contrast material, with x-rays. It allows the physician to view the pancreatic, hepatic, and common bile ducts and the ampulla of Vater. ERCP and percutaneous transhepatic cholangiography (PTC) are the only procedures that allow direct visualization of the biliary and pancreatic ducts. ERCP is less invasive and has less morbidity than PTC. It is useful in the evaluation of patients with jaundice, because the ducts can be visualized even when the patient's bilirubin level is high. (In contrast, oral cholecystography and IV cholangiography cannot visualize the biliary system when the patient has high bilirubin levels.) By endoscopy, the distal end of the common bile duct can be widened, and gallstones can be removed and stents placed in narrowed bile ducts to allow bile to be drained in jaundiced patients. During endoscopy, specimens of suspicious tissue can be taken for pathological review, and manometry pressure readings can be obtained from the bile and pancreatic ducts. ERCP is used in the diagnosis and follow-up of pancreatic disease.

INDICATIONS
- Assess jaundice of unknown cause to differentiate biliary tract obstruction from liver disease
- Collect specimens for cytology
- Identify obstruction caused by calculi, cysts, ducts, strictures, stenosis, and anatomic abnormalities
- Retrieve calculi from the distal common bile duct and release strictures

- Perform therapeutic procedures, such as sphincterotomy and placement of biliary drains

POTENTIAL DIAGNOSIS

Normal findings in
- Normal appearance of the duodenal papilla
- Patency of the pancreatic and common bile ducts

Abnormal findings in
- Duodenal papilla tumors
- Pancreatic cancer
- Pancreatic fibrosis
- Pancreatitis
- Sclerosing cholangitis

CRITICAL FINDINGS: N/A

INTERFERING FACTORS

This procedure is contraindicated for
- Patients who are pregnant or suspected of being pregnant, unless the potential benefits of the procedure far outweigh the risks to the fetus and mother.
- Patients with allergies to shellfish or iodinated dye. The contrast medium used may cause a life-threatening allergic reaction. Patients with a known hypersensitivity to the medium may benefit from premedication with corticosteroids or the use of nonionic contrast medium.

Factors that may impair clear imaging
- Gas or feces in the gastrointestinal (GI) tract resulting from inadequate cleansing or failure to restrict food intake before the study.
- Retained barium from a previous radiological procedure.
- Previous surgery involving the stomach or duodenum, which can make locating the duodenal papilla difficult.

- A patient with Zenker's diverticulum involving the esophagus, who may be unable to undergo ERCP.
- A patient with unstable cardiopulmonary status, blood coagulation defects, or cholangitis (test may have to be rescheduled unless the patient received antibiotic therapy before the test).
- A patient with known acute pancreatitis.
- Incorrect positioning of the patient, which may produce poor visualization of the area to be examined.
- Inability of the patient to cooperate or remain still during the procedure because of age, significant pain, or mental status.

Other considerations

- The procedure may be terminated if chest pain or severe cardiac arrhythmias occur.
- Failure to follow dietary restrictions and other pretesting preparations may cause the procedure to be canceled or repeated.
- Consultation with a health-care provider (HCP) should occur before the procedure for radiation safety concerns regarding younger patients or patients who are lactating.
- Risks associated with radiation overexposure can result from frequent x-ray procedures. Personnel in the examination room with the patient should wear a protective lead apron, stand behind a shield, or leave the area while the examination is being done. Personnel working in the examination area should wear badges to record their level of radiation exposure.

NURSING IMPLICATIONS AND PROCEDURE

PRETEST:

▶ Positively identify the patient using at least two unique identifiers before providing care, treatment, or services.

▶ *Patient Teaching:* Inform the patient this procedure can assist in assessing the bile ducts of the gallbladder and pancreas.

▶ Obtain a history of the patient's complaints, including a list of known allergens, especially allergies or sensitivities to latex, iodine, seafood, contrast medium, anesthetics, and dyes.

▶ Obtain a history of the patient's gastrointestinal and hepatobiliary systems, symptoms, and results of previously performed laboratory tests and diagnostic and surgical procedures.

▶ Ensure that this procedure is performed before an upper GI study or barium swallow.

▶ Record the date of the last menstrual period and determine the possibility of pregnancy in perimenopausal women.

▶ Obtain a list of the patient's current medications including anticoagulants, aspirin and other salicylates, herbs, nutritional supplements, and nutraceuticals (see Appendix F). Note the last time and dose of medication taken.

▶ If contrast medium is scheduled to be used, patients receiving metformin (Glucophage) for non-insulin-dependent (type 2) diabetes should discontinue the drug on the day of the test and continue to withhold it for 48 hr after the test. Failure to do so may result in lactic acidosis.

▶ Review the procedure with the patient. Address concerns about pain and explain that some pain may be experienced during the test, and there may be moments of discomfort. Inform the patient that the procedure is performed in a GI lab or radiology department, usually by an HCP, with support staff, and takes approximately 30 to 60 min.

▶ *Sensitivity to social and cultural issues,* as well as concern for modesty, is important in providing psychological support before, during, and after the procedure.

▶ Explain that an IV line may be inserted to allow infusion of IV fluids, anesthetics, or sedatives.

▶ Instruct the patient to remove jewelry and other metallic objects from the area to be examined.

▶ The patient should fast and restrict fluids for 8 hr prior to the procedure. Instruct the patient to avoid taking anticoagulant

C

medication or to reduce dosage as ordered prior to the procedure. Protocols may vary among facilities.

Make sure a written and informed consent has been signed prior to the procedure and before administering any medications.

INTRATEST:

- Observe standard precautions, and follow the general guidelines in Appendix A. Positively identify the patient, and label the appropriate specimen container with the corresponding patient demographics, initials of the person collecting the specimen, date, and time of collection.
- Ensure the patient has complied with dietary, fluid, and medication restrictions for 8 hr prior to the procedure.
- Ensure the patient has removed all external metallic objects from the area to be examined.
- Assess for completion of bowel preparation according to the institution's procedure.
- If the patient has a history of allergic reactions to any relevant substance or drug, administer ordered prophylactic steroids or antihistamines before the procedure. Use nonionic contrast medium for the procedure.
- Have emergency equipment readily available.
- Instruct the patient to void prior to the procedure and to change into the gown, robe, and foot coverings provided.
- Instruct the patient to cooperate fully and to follow directions. Instruct the patient to remain still throughout the procedure because movement produces unreliable results.
- Record baseline vital signs, and continue to monitor throughout the procedure. Protocols may vary among facilities.
- Insert an IV line for administration of drugs, as needed.
- Administer ordered sedation.
- An x-ray of the abdomen is obtained to determine if any residual contrast medium is present from previous studies.
- The oropharynx is sprayed or swabbed with a topical local anesthetic.

The patient is placed on an examination table in the left lateral position with the left arm behind the back and right hand at the side with the neck slightly flexed. A protective guard is inserted into the mouth to cover the teeth. A bite block can also be inserted to maintain adequate opening of the mouth.

- The endoscope is passed through the mouth with a dental suction device in place to drain secretions. A side-viewing flexible fiberoptic endoscope is passed into the duodenum, and a small cannula is inserted into the duodenal papilla (ampulla of Vater).
- The patient is placed in the prone position. The duodenal papilla is visualized and cannulated with a catheter. Occasionally the patient can be turned slightly to the right side to aid in visualization of the papilla.
- IV glucagon or anticholinergics can be administered to minimize duodenal spasm and to facilitate visualization of the ampulla of Vater.
- ERCP manometry can be done at this time to measure the pressure in the bile duct, pancreatic duct, and sphincter of Oddi at the papilla area via the catheter as it is placed in the area before the contrast medium is injected.
- When the catheter is in place, contrast medium is injected into the pancreatic and biliary ducts via the catheter, and fluoroscopic images are taken. Biopsy specimens for cytological analysis may be obtained.
- Place specimens in appropriate containers, label them properly, and promptly transport them to the laboratory.

POST-TEST:

- A report of the results will be made available to the requesting HCP, who will discuss the results with the patient.
- Do not allow the patient to eat or drink until the gag reflex returns, after which the patient is permitted to eat lightly for 12 to 24 hr.
- Instruct the patient to resume usual diet, fluids, medications, and activity after 24 hr, or as directed by the HCP. Renal function should be assessed before metformin is resumed, if contrast was used.

Monitor vital signs and neurological status every 15 min for 1 hr, then every 2 hr for 4 hr, and as ordered. Take temperature every 4 hr for 24 hr. Monitor intake and output at least every 8 hr. Compare with baseline values. Notify the HCP if temperature is elevated. Protocols may vary among facilities.

Monitor for reaction to iodinated contrast medium, including rash, urticaria, tachycardia, hyperpnea, hypertension, palpitations, nausea, or vomiting.

Tell the patient to expect some throat soreness and possible hoarseness. Advise the patient to use warm gargles, lozenges, ice packs to the neck, or cool fluids to alleviate throat discomfort.

Inform the patient that any belching, bloating, or flatulence is the result of air insufflation.

Instruct the patient to immediately report symptoms such as fast heart rate, difficulty breathing, skin rash, itching, chest pain, persistent right shoulder pain, or abdominal pain. Immediately report symptoms to the appropriate HCP.

Recognize anxiety related to test results. Discuss the implications of abnormal test results on the patient's lifestyle. Provide teaching and information regarding the clinical implications of the test results, as appropriate.

Reinforce information given by the patient's HCP regarding further testing, treatment, or referral to another HCP. Answer any questions or address any concerns voiced by the patient or family.

Depending on the results of this procedure, additional testing may be needed to evaluate or monitor progression of the disease process and determine the need for a change in therapy. Evaluate test results in relation to the patient's symptoms and other tests performed.

RELATED MONOGRAPHS:

Related tests include amylase, CT abdomen, hepatobiliary scan, KUB studies, lipase, MRI abdomen, peritoneal fluid analysis, pleural fluid analysis, and US liver and biliary system.

Refer to the Gastrointestinal and Hepatobiliary systems tables at the end of the book for related tests by body system.

Cholesterol, HDL and LDL

SYNONYM/ACRONYM: α_1-Lipoprotein cholesterol, high-density cholesterol, HDLC, and β-lipoprotein cholesterol, low-density cholesterol, LDLC.

COMMON USE: To assess risk and monitor for coronary artery disease.

SPECIMEN: Serum (2 mL) collected in a red- or tiger-top tube.

NORMAL FINDINGS: (Method: Spectrophotometry)

HDLC	Conventional Units	SI Units (Conventional Units × 0.0259)
Birth	6–56 mg/dL	0.16–1.45 mmol/L
Children, adults, and older adults		
Desirable	Greater than 60 mg/dL	Greater than 1.56 mmol/L
Acceptable	40–60 mg/dL	0.9–1.56 mmol/L
Low	Less than 40 mg/dL	Less than 0.9 mmol/L

LDLC	Conventional Units	SI Units (Conventional Units × 0.0259)
Optimal	Less than 100 mg/dL	Less than 2.59 mmol/L
Near optimal	100–129 mg/dL	2.59–3.34 mmol/L
Borderline high	130–159 mg/dL	3.37–4.11 mmol/L
High	160–189 mg/dL	4.14–4.90 mmol/L
Very high	Greater than 190 mg/dL	Greater than 4.92 mmol/L

	NMR LDLC Particle Number	NMR LDLC Small Particle Size
High-risk CAD	Less than 1,000 nmol/L	Less than 850 nmol/L
Moderately high-risk CAD	Less than 1,300 nmol/L	Less than 850 nmol/L

CAD, coronary artery disease; NMR = nuclear magnetic resonance.

DESCRIPTION: High-density lipoprotein cholesterol (HDLC) and low-density lipoprotein cholesterol (LDLC) are the major transport proteins for cholesterol in the body. It is believed that HDLC may have protective properties in that its role includes transporting cholesterol from the arteries to the liver. LDLC is the major transport protein for cholesterol to the arteries from the liver. LDLC can be calculated using total cholesterol, total triglycerides, and HDLC levels. Beyond the total cholesterol, HDL and LDL cholesterol values, other important risk factors must be considered. The Framingham algorithm can assist in estimating the risk of developing coronary artery disease (CAD) within a 10-yr period. The National Cholesterol Education Program (NCEP) also provides important guidelines. The latest NCEP guidelines for target lipid levels, major risk factors, and therapeutic interventions are outlined in Adult Treatment Panel III (ATP III) (www.nhlbi.nih.gov/guidelines/cholesterol/index.htm).

Studies have shown that CAD is inversely related to LDLC particle number and size. The nuclear magnetic resonance (NMR) lipid profile uses NMR imaging spectroscopy to determine LDLC particle number and size in addition to measurement of the traditional lipid markers.

HDLC levels less than 40 mg/dL in men and women represent a coronary risk factor. There is an inverse relationship between HDLC and risk of CAD (i.e., lower HDLC levels represent a higher risk of CAD). Levels of LDLC in terms of risk for CAD are directly proportional to risk and vary by age group. The LDLC can be estimated using the Friedewald formula:

$$LDLC = (Total\ Cholesterol) - (HDLC) - (VLDLC)$$

Very-low-density lipoprotein cholesterol (VLDLC) is estimated by dividing the triglycerides (conventional units) by 5. Triglycerides in SI units would be divided by 2.18 to estimate VLDLC. It is important to note that the formula is valid only if the triglycerides are less than 400 mg/dL or 4.52 mmol/L.

INDICATIONS
- Determine the risk of cardiovascular disease
- Evaluate the response to dietary and drug therapy for hypercholesterolemia
- Investigate hypercholesterolemia in light of family history of cardiovascular disease

POTENTIAL DIAGNOSIS
Although the exact pathophysiology is unknown, cholesterol is required for many functions at the cellular and organ levels. Elevations of cholesterol are associated with conditions caused by an inherited defect in lipoprotein metabolism, liver disease, kidney disease, or a disorder of the endocrine system. Decreases in cholesterol levels are associated with conditions caused by enzyme deficiencies, malnutrition, malabsorption, liver disease, and sudden increased utilization.

HDLC increased in
- Alcoholism
- Biliary cirrhosis
- Chronic hepatitis
- Exercise
- Familial hyper-α-lipoproteinemia

HDLC decreased in
- Abetalipoproteinemia
- Cholestasis
- Chronic renal failure
- Fish-eye disease
- Genetic predisposition or enzyme/cofactor deficiency
- Hepatocellular disorders
- Hypertriglyceridemia
- Nephrotic syndrome
- Obesity
- Premature CAD
- Sedentary lifestyle
- Smoking
- Tangier's disease
- Syndrome X (metabolic syndrome)
- Uncontrolled diabetes

LDLC increased in
- Anorexia nervosa
- Chronic renal failure
- Corneal arcus
- Cushing's syndrome
- Diabetes
- Diet high in cholesterol and saturated fat
- Dysglobulinemias
- Hepatic disease
- Hepatic obstruction
- Hyperlipoproteinemia types IIA and IIB
- Hypothyroidism
- Nephrotic syndrome
- Porphyria
- Pregnancy
- Premature CAD
- Syndrome X (metabolic syndrome)
- Tendon and tuberous xanthomas

LDLC decreased in
- Acute stress (severe burns, illness)
- Chronic anemias
- Chronic pulmonary disease
- Genetic predisposition or enzyme/cofactor deficiency
- Hyperthyroidism
- Hypolipoproteinemia and abetalipoproteinemia
- Inflammatory joint disease
- Myeloma
- Reye's syndrome
- Severe hepatocellular destruction or disease
- Tangier disease

CRITICAL FINDINGS: N/A

INTERFERING FACTORS
- Drugs that may increase HDLC levels include albuterol, anticonvulsants, cholestyramine, cimetidine, clofibrate and other fibric acid derivatives, estrogens, ethanol (moderate use), lovastatin, niacin, oral contraceptives, pindolol, pravastatin, prazosin, and simvastatin.
- Drugs that may decrease HDLC levels include acebutolol, atenolol,

danazol, diuretics, etretinate, interferon, isotretinoin, linseed oil, metoprolol, neomycin, nonselective β-adrenergic blocking agents, probucol, progesterone, steroids, and thiazides.

- Drugs that may increase LDLC levels include androgens, catecholamines, chenodiol, cyclosporine, danazol, diuretics, etretinate, glucogenic corticosteroids, and progestins.

- Drugs that may decrease LDLC levels include aminosalicylic acid, cholestyramine, colestipol, estrogens, fibric acid derivatives, interferon, lovastatin, neomycin, niacin, pravastatin, prazosin, probucol, simvastatin, terazosin, and thyroxine.

- Some of the drugs used to lower total cholesterol and LDLC or increase HDLC may cause liver damage.

- Grossly elevated triglyceride levels invalidate the Friedewald formula for mathematical estimation of LDLC; if the triglyceride level is greater than 400 mg/dL, the formula should not be used.

- Fasting before specimen collection is highly recommended. Ideally, the patient should be on a stable diet for 3 wk and fast for 12 hr before specimen collection.

- Failure to follow dietary restrictions before the procedure may cause the procedure to be canceled or repeated.

NURSING IMPLICATIONS AND PROCEDURE

PRETEST:

- Positively identify the patient using at least two unique identifiers before providing care, treatment, or services.
- *Patient Teaching:* Inform the patient this test can assist with evaluation of cholesterol level.
- Obtain a history of the patient's complaints, including a list of known allergens, especially allergies or sensitivities to latex.
- Obtain a history of the patient's cardiovascular system and results of previously performed laboratory tests and diagnostic and surgical procedures. The presence of other risk factors, such as family history of heart disease, smoking, obesity, diet, lack of physical activity, hypertension, diabetes, previous myocardial infarction, and previous vascular disease, should be investigated.
- Obtain a list of the patient's current medications, including herbs, nutritional supplements, and nutraceuticals (see Appendix F).
- Review the procedure with the patient. Inform the patient that specimen collection takes approximately 5 to 10 min. Address concerns about pain and explain that there may be some discomfort during the venipuncture.
- Sensitivity to social and cultural issues, as well as concern for modesty, is important in providing psychological support before, during, and after the procedure.
- Instruct the patient to fast for 12 hr before specimen collection. Protocols may vary among facilities.
- Confirm with the requesting health-care provider (HCP) that the patient should withhold medications known to influence test results, and instruct the patient accordingly.
- There are no fluid restrictions unless by medical direction.

INTRATEST:

- Ensure that the patient has complied with dietary and medication restrictions as well as other pretesting preparations; ensure that food has been restricted for at least 12 hr prior to the procedure.
- If the patient has a history of allergic reaction to latex, avoid the use of equipment containing latex.
- Instruct the patient to cooperate fully and to follow directions. Direct the patient to breathe normally and to avoid unnecessary movement.
- Observe standard precautions, and follow the general guidelines in Appendix A. Positively identify the

patient, and label the appropriate specimen container with the corresponding patient demographics, initials of the person collecting the specimen, date, and time of collection. Perform a venipuncture.

▸ Remove the needle and apply direct pressure with dry gauze to stop bleeding. Observe/assess venipuncture site for bleeding or hematoma formation and secure gauze with adhesive bandage.

▸ Promptly transport the specimen to the laboratory for processing and analysis.

POST-TEST:

▸ A report of the results will be made available to the requesting HCP, who will discuss the results with the patient.

▸ Instruct the patient to resume usual diet, fluids, and medications, as directed by the HCP.

▸ *Nutritional Considerations:* Decreased HDLC level and increased LDLC level may be associated with CAD. Nutritional therapy is recommended for the patient identified to be at high risk for developing CAD. The American Heart Association and National Heart, Lung, and Blood Institute (NHLBI) recommend nutritional therapy for individuals identified to be at high risk for developing CAD or individuals who have specific risk factors and/or existing medical conditions (e.g., elevated LDL cholesterol levels, other lipid disorders, insulin-dependent diabetes, insulin resistance, or metabolic syndrome). If overweight, the patient should be encouraged to achieve a normal weight. Guidelines for the Therapeutic Lifestyle Changes (TLC) diet are outlined in the Third Report of the Expert Panel on Detection, Evaluation, and Treatment of High Blood Cholesterol in Adults (Adult Treatment Panel III [ATP III]). The TLC diet emphasizes a reduction in foods high in saturated fats and cholesterol. Red meats, eggs, and dairy products are the major sources of saturated fats and cholesterol. If triglycerides also are elevated, the patient should be advised to eliminate or reduce alcohol and simple carbohydrates from the diet. The TLC approach also includes the use of plant stanols or sterols and increased dissolved fiber as an option for lowering LDL cholesterol levels; nutritional recommendations for daily total caloric intake; recommendations for allowable percentage of calories derived from fat (saturated and unsaturated), carbohydrates, protein, and cholesterol; as well as recommendations for daily expenditure of energy.

▸ *Nutritional Considerations:* Overweight patients with high blood pressure should be encouraged to achieve a normal weight. Other changeable risk factors warranting patient education include strategies to safely decrease sodium intake, increase physical activity, decrease alcohol consumption, eliminate tobacco use, and decrease cholesterol levels.

▸ *Social and Cultural Considerations:* Numerous studies point to the prevalence of excess body weight in American children and adolescents. Experts estimate that obesity is present in 25% of the population ages 6 to 11 yr. The medical, social, and emotional consequences of excess body weight are significant. Special attention should be given to instructing the child and caregiver regarding health risks and weight-control education.

▸ Recognize anxiety related to test results, and be supportive of fear of shortened life expectancy. Discuss the implications of abnormal test results on the patient's lifestyle. Provide teaching and information regarding the clinical implications of the test results, as appropriate. Educate the patient regarding access to counseling services. Provide contact information, if desired, for the American Heart Association (www.americanheart.org) or the NHLBI (www.nhlbi.nih.gov).

▸ Reinforce information given by the patient's HCP regarding further testing, treatment, or referral to another HCP. Answer any questions or address any concerns voiced by the patient or family.

▸ Depending on the results of this procedure, additional testing may be performed to evaluate or monitor progression of the disease process and determine the need for a change in therapy. Evaluate test results in relation to the patient's symptoms and other tests performed.

RELATED MONOGRAPHS:

▶ Related tests include antiarrhythmic drugs, apolipoprotein A and B, AST, ANP, blood gases, BNP, calcium (total and ionized), cholesterol total, CT cardiac scoring, CRP, CK and iso-enzymes, echocardiography, glucose, glycated hemoglobin, Holter monitor, homocysteine, ketones, LDH and iso-enzymes, lipoprotein electrophoresis, magnesium, MRI chest, MI scan, myocardial perfusion heart scan, myoglobin, PET heart, potassium, triglycerides, and troponin.

▶ Refer to the Cardiovascular System table at the end of the book for related tests by body system.

Cholesterol, Total

SYNONYM/ACRONYM: N/A.

COMMON USE: To assess and monitor risk for coronary artery disease.

SPECIMEN: Serum (1 mL) collected in a red- or tiger-top tube. Plasma (1 mL) collected in a green-top (heparin) tube is also acceptable. It is important to use the same tube type when serial specimen collections are anticipated for consistency in testing.

NORMAL FINDINGS: (Method: Spectrophotometry)

Risk	Conventional Units	SI Units (Conventional Units × 0.0259)
Children and adolescents (less than 20 yr)		
Desirable	Less than 170 mg/dL	Less than 4.4 mmol/L
Borderline	170–199 mg/dL	4.4–5.2 mmol/L
High	Greater than 200 mg/dL	Greater than 5.2 mmol/L
Adults and older adults		
Desirable	Less than 200 mg/dL	Less than 5.18 mmol/L
Borderline	200–239 mg/dL	5.18–6.19 mmol/L
High	Greater than 240 mg/dL	Greater than 6.22 mmol/L

Plasma values may be 10% lower than serum values.

DESCRIPTION: Cholesterol is a lipid needed to form cell membranes and a component of the materials that render the skin waterproof. It also helps form bile salts, adrenal corticosteroids, estrogen, and androgens. Cholesterol is obtained from the diet (exogenous cholesterol) and also synthesized in the body (endogenous cholesterol). Although most body cells can form some cholesterol, it is produced mainly by the liver and intestinal mucosa. Cholesterol is an integral component in cell membrane maintenance and hormone production. Very low cholesterol values, as are sometimes seen in critically ill patients, can be as life-threatening as very high levels.

According to the National Cholesterol Education Program, maintaining cholesterol levels less than 200 mg/dL significantly reduces the risk of coronary heart disease. Beyond the total cholesterol and high-density lipoprotein cholesterol (HDLC) values, other important risk factors must be considered. The Framingham algorithm can assist in estimating the risk of developing coronary artery disease (CAD) within a 10-yr period. Many myocardial infarctions occur even in patients whose cholesterol levels are considered to be within acceptable limits or who are in a moderate-risk category. The combination of risk factors and lipid values helps identify individuals at risk so that appropriate interventions can be taken. If the cholesterol level is greater than 200 mg/dL, repeat testing after a 12- to 24-hr fast is recommended. Another predictor of CAD is lipoprotein (a) or Lp(a). Lp(a) is considered an independent risk factor for CAD and cerebral infarction at levels greater than 30 mg/dL.

- Evaluate the response to dietary and drug therapy for hypercholesterolemia
- Investigate hypercholesterolemia in light of family history of cardiovascular disease

POTENTIAL DIAGNOSIS

Increased in

Although the exact pathophysiology is unknown, cholesterol is required for many functions at the cellular and organ level. Elevations of cholesterol are associated with conditions caused by an inherited defect in lipoprotein metabolism, liver disease, kidney disease, or a disorder of the endocrine system.

- Acute intermittent porphyria
- Alcoholism
- Anorexia nervosa
- Cholestasis
- Chronic renal failure
- Diabetes (with poor control)
- Diets high in cholesterol and fats
- Familial hyperlipoproteinemia
- Glomerulonephritis
- Glycogen storage disease (von Gierke's disease)
- Gout
- Hypothyroidism (primary)
- Ischemic heart disease
- Nephrotic syndrome
- Obesity
- Pancreatic and prostatic malignancy
- Pregnancy
- Syndrome X (metabolic syndrome)
- Werner's syndrome

Decreased in

Although the exact pathophysiology is unknown, cholesterol is required for many functions at the cellular and organ level. Decreases in cholesterol levels are associated with conditions caused by malnutrition, malabsorption, liver disease, and sudden increased utilization.

INDICATIONS

Assist in determining risk of cardiovascular disease

Assist in the diagnosis of nephrotic syndrome, hepatic disease, pancreatitis, and thyroid disorders

- Burns
- Chronic myelocytic leukemia
- Chronic obstructive pulmonary disease
- Hyperthyroidism
- Liver disease (severe)
- Malabsorption and malnutrition syndromes
- Myeloma
- Pernicious anemia
- Polycythemia vera
- Severe illness
- Sideroblastic anemias
- Tangier disease
- Thalassemia
- Waldenström's macroglobulinemia

CRITICAL FINDINGS: N/A

INTERFERING FACTORS

- Drugs that may increase cholesterol levels include amiodarone, androgens, β-blockers, calcitriol, cortisone, cyclosporine, danazol, diclofenac, disulfiram, fluoxymesterone, glucogenic corticosteroids, ibuprofen, isotretinoin, levodopa, mepazine, methyclothiazide, miconazole (owing to castor oil vehicle, not the drug), nafarelin, nandrolone, some oral contraceptives, oxymetholone, phenobarbital, phenothiazine, prochlorperazine, sotalol, thiabendazole, thiouracil, tretinoin, and trifluoperazine.
- Drugs that may decrease cholesterol levels include acebutolol, amiloride, aminosalicylic acid, androsterone, ascorbic acid, asparaginase, atenolol, atorvastatin, beclobrate, bezafibrate, carbutamide, cerivastatin, cholestyramine, ciprofibrate, clofibrate, clonidine, colestipol, dextrothyroxine, doxazosin, enalapril, estrogens, fenfluramine, fenofibrate, fluvastatin, gemfibrozil, haloperidol, hormone replacement therapy, hydralazine, hydrochlorothiazide, interferon, isoniazid, kanamycin, ketoconazole, lincomycin, lisinopril, lovastatin,

metformin, nafenopin, nandrolone, neomycin, niacin, nicotinic acid, nifedipine, oxandrolone, paromomycin, pravastatin, probucol, simvastatin, tamoxifen, terazosin, thyroxine, trazodone, triiodothyronine, ursodiol, valproic acid, and verapamil.
- Ingestion of alcohol 12 to 24 hr before the test can falsely elevate results.
- Ingestion of drugs that alter cholesterol levels within 12 hr of the test may give a false impression of cholesterol levels, unless the test is done to evaluate such effects.
- Positioning can affect results; lower levels are obtained if the specimen is from a patient who has been supine for 20 min.
- Failure to follow dietary restriction before the procedure may cause the procedure to be canceled or repeated.

NURSING IMPLICATIONS AND PROCEDURE

PRETEST:

- Positively identify the patient using at least two unique identifiers before providing care, treatment, or services.
- *Patient Teaching:* Inform the patient this test can assist with evaluation of cholesterol level.
- Obtain a history of the patient's complaints, including a list of known allergens, especially allergies or sensitivities to latex.
- Obtain a history of the patient's cardiovascular, gastrointestinal, and hepatobiliary systems, as well as results of previously performed laboratory tests and diagnostic and surgical procedures. The presence of other risk factors, such as family history of heart disease, smoking, obesity, diet, lack of physical activity, hypertension, diabetes, previous myocardial infarction, and previous vascular disease, should be investigated.

Obtain a list of the patient's current medications, including herbs, nutritional supplements, and nutraceuticals (see Appendix F).

Review the procedure with the patient. Inform the patient that specimen collection takes approximately 5 to 10 min. Address concerns about pain and explain that there may be some discomfort during the venipuncture. *Sensitivity to social and cultural issues,* as well as concern for modesty, is important in providing psychological support before, during, and after the procedure.

Instruct the patient to withhold alcohol and drugs known to alter cholesterol levels for 12 to 24 hr before specimen collection, at the direction of the health-care provider (HCP).

There are no fluid or medication restrictions unless by medical direction. Fasting 6 to 12 hr before specimen collection is required if triglyceride measurements are included; it is recommended if cholesterol levels alone are measured for screening. Protocols may vary among facilities.

INTRATEST:

Ensure that the patient has complied with dietary restrictions and pretesting preparations; ensure that food has been restricted for at least 6 to 12 hr prior to the procedure if triglycerides are to be measured.

If the patient has a history of allergic reaction to latex, avoid the use of equipment containing latex.

Instruct the patient to cooperate fully and to follow directions. Direct the patient to breathe normally and to avoid unnecessary movement.

Observe standard precautions, and follow the general guidelines in Appendix A. Positively identify the patient, and label the appropriate specimen container with the corresponding patient demographics, initials of the person collecting the specimen, date, and time of collection. Perform a venipuncture.

Remove the needle and apply direct pressure with dry gauze to stop bleeding. Observe/assess venipuncture site for bleeding or hematoma formation

and secure gauze with adhesive bandage.

Promptly transport the specimen to the laboratory for processing and analysis.

POST-TEST:

A report of the results will be made available to the requesting HCP, who will discuss the results with the patient.

Instruct the patient to resume usual diet as directed by the HCP.

Secondary causes for increased cholesterol levels should be ruled out before therapy to decrease levels is initiated by use of drugs.

Nutritional Considerations: Increases in total cholesterol levels may be associated with CAD. Nutritional therapy is recommended for patients identified to be at high risk for developing CAD. If overweight, the patient should be encouraged to achieve a normal weight. The American Heart Association and National Heart, Lung, and Blood Institute (NHLBI) recommend nutritional therapy for individuals identified to be at high risk for developing CAD or individuals who have specific risk factors and/or existing medical conditions (e.g., elevated LDL cholesterol levels, other lipid disorders, insulin-dependent diabetes, insulin resistance, or metabolic syndrome). If overweight, the patient should be encouraged to achieve a normal weight. Guidelines for the Therapeutic Lifestyle Changes (TLC) diet are outlined in the Third Report of the Expert Panel on Detection, Evaluation, and Treatment of High Blood Cholesterol in Adults (Adult Treatment Panel III [ATP III]). The TLC diet emphasizes a reduction in foods high in saturated fats and cholesterol. Red meats, eggs, and dairy products are the major sources of saturated fats and cholesterol. If triglycerides also are elevated, the patient should be advised to eliminate or reduce alcohol and simple carbohydrates from the diet. The TLC approach also includes the use of plant stanols or sterols and increased dissolved fiber as an option for lowering LDL cholesterol levels; nutritional recommendations for daily total caloric intake; recommendations for allowable percentage of calories derived from fat (saturated and unsaturated), carbohydrates, protein, and cholesterol; as well as recommendations for daily expenditure of energy.

Nutritional Considerations: Overweight patients with high blood pressure should be encouraged to achieve a normal weight. Other changeable risk factors warranting patient education include strategies to safely decrease sodium intake, increase physical activity, decrease alcohol consumption, eliminate tobacco use, and decrease cholesterol levels.

Social and Cultural Considerations: Numerous studies point to the prevalence of excess body weight in American children and adolescents. Experts estimate that obesity is present in 25% of the population ages 6 to 11 yr. The medical, social, and emotional consequences of excess body weight are significant. Special attention should be given to instructing the child and caregiver regarding health risks and weight-control education.

Recognize anxiety related to test results, and be supportive of fear of shortened life expectancy. Discuss the implications of abnormal test results on the patient's lifestyle. Provide teaching and information regarding the clinical implications of the test results, as appropriate. Educate the patient regarding access to counseling services. Provide contact information,

if desired, for the American Heart Association (www.americanheart.org) or the NHLBI (www.nhlbi.nih.gov).

Reinforce information given by the patient's HCP regarding further testing, treatment, or referral to another HCP. Answer any questions or address any concerns voiced by the patient or family.

Depending on the results of this procedure, additional testing may be performed to evaluate or monitor progression of the disease process and determine the need for a change in therapy. Evaluate test results in relation to the patient's symptoms and other tests performed.

RELATED MONOGRAPHS:

Related tests include antiarrhythmic drugs, apolipoprotein A and B, AST, ANP, blood gases, BNP, calcium, cholesterol (HDL and LDL), CT cardiac scoring, CRP, CK and isoenzymes, echocardiography, glucose, glycated hemoglobin, Holter monitor, homocysteine, ketones, LDH and isoenzymes, lipoprotein electrophoresis, MRI chest, magnesium, MI scan, myocardial perfusion heart scan, myoglobin, PET heart, potassium, triglycerides, and troponin.

Refer to the Cardiovascular, Gastrointestinal, and Hepatobiliary systems tables at the end of the book for related tests by body system.

Chromosome Analysis, Blood

SYNONYM/ACRONYM: N/A.

COMMON USE: To test for suspected chromosomal disorders that result in birth defects such as Down's syndrome.

SPECIMEN: Whole blood (2 mL) collected in a green-top (sodium heparin) tube

NORMAL FINDINGS: (Method: Tissue culture and microscopic analysis) No chromosomal abnormalities identified.

DESCRIPTION: Cytogenetics is a specialization within the area of genetics that includes chromosome analysis or karyotyping. Chromosome analysis or karyotyping involves comparison of test samples against normal chromosome patterns of number and structure. A normal karyotype consists of 22 pairs or autosomal chromosomes and one pair sex chromosomes, XX for female and XY for male. Variations in number or structure can be congenital or acquired. Variations can range from a small, single-gene mutation to abnormalities in an entire chromosome or set of chromosomes due to duplication, deletion, substitution, translocation, or other rearrangement. Molecular probe techniques are used to detect smaller, more subtle changes in chromosomes. Cells are incubated in culture media to increase the number of cells available for study and to allow for hybridization of the cellular DNA with fluorescent DNA probes in a technique called fluorescence in situ hybridization (FISH). The probes are designed to target areas of the chromosome known to correlate with genetic risk for a particular disease. When a suitable volume of hybridized sample is achieved, cell growth is chemically inhibited during the prophase and metaphase stages of mitosis (cell division), and cellular DNA is examined to detect fluorescence, which represents chromosomal abnormalities, in the targeted areas. Amniotic fluid, chorionic villus sampling, and cells from fetal tissue or products of conception can also be evaluated for chromosomal abnormalities.

INDICATIONS
- Evaluate conditions related to cryptorchidism, hypogonadism, primary amenorrhea, and infertility
- Evaluate congenital anomaly, delayed development (physical or mental), mental retardation, and ambiguous sexual organs
- Investigate the carrier status of patients or relatives with known genetic abnormalities
- Investigate the cause of still birth or multiple miscarriages
- Investigate types of solid tumor or hematologic malignancies
- Provide prenatal care or genetic counseling

POTENTIAL DIAGNOSIS
The following tables list some common genetic defects.

Syndrome	Autosomal Chromosome Defect	Features
Beckwith-Wiedemann	Duplication 11p15	Macroglossia, omphalocele, earlobe creases
Cat's eye	Trisomy 2q11	Anal atresia, coloboma
Cri du chat	Deletion 5p	Catlike cry, microcephaly, hypertelorism, mental retardation, retrognathia
Down	Trisomy 21	Epicanthal folds, simian crease of palm, flat nasal bridge, mental retardation, congenital heart disease

Syndrome	Autosomal Chromosome Defect	Features
Edwards	Trisomy 18	Micrognathia, clenched third/fourth fingers with the fifth finger overlapping, rocker-bottom feet, mental retardation, congenital heart disease
Pallister-Killian	Trisomy 12p	Psychomotor delay, sparse anterior scalp hair, micrognathia, hypotonia
Patau	Trisomy 13	Microcephaly, cleft palate or lip, polydactyly, mental retardation, congenital heart disease
Warkam	Mosaic trisomy 8	Malformed ears, bulbous nose, deep palm creases, absent or hypoplastic patellae
Wolf-Hirschhorn	Deletion 4p	Microcephaly, growth retardation, mental retardation, carp mouth

Syndrome	Sex-Chromosome Defect	Features
XYY	47,XYY	Tall, increased risk of behavior problems
Klinefelter	47,XXY	Hypogonadism, infertility, underdeveloped secondary sex characteristics, learning disabilities
Triple X	47,XXX	Increased risk of infertility and learning disabilities
Ullrich-Turner	45,X	Short, gonadal dysgenesis, webbed neck, low posterior hairline, renal and cardiovascular abnormalities

CRITICAL FINDINGS: N/A

INTERFERING FACTORS: N/A

NURSING IMPLICATIONS AND PROCEDURE

PRETEST:

▶ Positively identify the patient using at least two unique identifiers before providing care, treatment, or services.

▶ *Patient Teaching:* Inform the patient this test can assist in identification of potential birth defects.

▶ Obtain a history of the patient's complaints, including a list of known allergens, especially allergies or sensitivities to latex.

▶ Obtain a history of the patient's reproductive system, family history of known or suspected genetic disorders, and results of previously performed laboratory tests and diagnostic and surgical procedures.

▶ Obtain a list of the patient's current medications, including herbs, nutritional supplements, and nutraceuticals (see Appendix F).

▶ Review the procedure with the patient. Inform the patient that specimen collection takes approximately 5 to 10 min. Address concerns about pain and explain that there may be some discomfort during the venipuncture. *Sensitivity to social and cultural issues,* as well as concern for modesty, is important in providing psychological support before, during, and after the procedure.

There are no food, fluid, or medication restrictions unless by medical direction.

INTRATEST:

If the patient has a history of allergic reaction to latex, avoid the use of equipment containing latex.

Instruct the patient to cooperate fully and to follow directions. Direct the patient to breathe normally and to avoid unnecessary movement.

Observe standard precautions, and follow the general guidelines in Appendix A. Positively identify the patient, and label the appropriate specimen container with the corresponding patient demographics, initials of the person collecting the specimen, date, and time of collection. Perform a venipuncture.

Remove the needle and apply direct pressure with dry gauze to stop bleeding. Observe/assess venipuncture site for bleeding or hematoma formation and secure gauze with adhesive bandage.

Promptly transport the specimen to the laboratory for processing and analysis.

POST-TEST:

A report of the results will be made available to the requesting health-care provider (HCP), who will discuss the results with the patient.

Recognize anxiety related to test results, and be supportive of the sensitive nature of the testing. Discuss the implications of abnormal test results on the patient's lifestyle. Provide teaching and information regarding the clinical implications of the test results, as appropriate. Educate the patient regarding access to counseling services.

Social and Cultural Considerations: Encourage the family to seek counseling if they are contemplating pregnancy termination or to seek genetic counseling if a chromosomal abnormality is determined. Decisions regarding elective abortion should occur in the presence of both parents. Provide a nonjudgmental, nonthreatening atmosphere for discussing the risks and difficulties of delivering and raising a developmentally challenged infant, as well as exploring other options (termination of pregnancy or adoption). It is also important to discuss feelings the mother and father may experience (e.g., guilt, depression, anger) if fetal abnormalities are detected. Educate the patient and family regarding access to counseling services, as appropriate.

Reinforce information given by the patient's HCP regarding further testing, treatment, or referral to another HCP. Answer any questions or address any concerns voiced by the patient or family.

Depending on the results of this procedure, additional testing may be performed to evaluate or monitor changes in health status and determine the need for a change in therapy. Evaluate test results in relation to the patient's symptoms and other tests performed.

RELATED MONOGRAPHS:

Related tests include α_1-fetoprotein, amniotic fluid analysis, biopsy chorionic villus, newborn screening, and US biophysical profile obstetric.

Refer to the Reproductive System table at the end of the book for related tests by body system.

Clot Retraction

SYNONYM/ACRONYM: N/A.

COMMON USE: To assist in the diagnosis of bleeding disorders.

SPECIMEN: Whole blood collected in a full 5-mL red-top tube.

NORMAL FINDINGS: (Method: Macroscopic observation of sample) A normal clot gently separated from the side of the test tube and incubated at 37°C, shrinks to about half of its original size within 1 hr. The result is a firm, cylindrical fibrin clot that contains red blood cells and is sharply demarcated from the clear serum. Complete clot retraction can take 6 to 24 hr.

POTENTIAL DIAGNOSIS

Increased in

- Anemia (severe) *(related to inadequate numbers of red blood cells (RBCs) that quickly produce a clot)*
- Hypofibrinogenemia, dysfibrinogenemia, disseminated intravascular coagulation (DIC) *(evidenced by rapid formation of a small, loosely formed clot; absence of functional fibrinogen reduces fibrinolysis)*
- Medications like aspirin *(related to effect of acetylsalicylic acid as a potentiator of platelet aggregation)*

Decreased in

- Glanzmann's thrombasthenia *(related to autosomal recessive abnormality of platelet glycoprotein IIb–IIIa required for platelet aggregation)*
- Polycythemia *(related to excessive numbers of RBCs that physically limit the extent to which the clot can retract)*
- Thrombocytopenia *(related to inadequate numbers of platelets to produce a well-formed clot)*
- von Willebrand disease *(related to deficiency of von Willebrand factor required for platelet aggregation)*
- Waldenström's macroglobulinemia *(related to excessive production of paraproteins that physically obstruct platelet aggregation)*

CRITICAL FINDINGS: N/A

Find and print out the full monograph at DavisPlus (http://davisplus.fadavis.com, keyword Van Leeuwen).

Coagulation Factors

SYNONYM/ACRONYM: See table.

COMMON USE: To detect factor deficiencies and related coagulopathies such as found in disseminated intravascular coagulation (DIC).

SPECIMEN: Whole blood collected in a completely filled blue-top (3.2% sodium citrate) tube. If the patient's hematocrit exceeds 55%, the volume of citrate in the collection tube must be adjusted.

NORMAL FINDINGS: (Method: Photo-optical clot detection) Activity from 50% to 150%.

	Preferred Name	Synonym	Role in Modern Coagulation Cascade Model	Coagulation Test Responses in the Presence of Factor Deficiency
Factor I	Fibrinogen	–	Assists in the formation of the fibrin clot	PT prolonged, aPTT prolonged
Factor II	Prothrombin	Prethrombin	Assists factor Xa in formation of trace thrombin in the initiation phase and assists factors VIIIa, IXa, Xa, and Va to form thrombin in the propagation phase of hemostasis	PT prolonged, aPTT prolonged
Tissue factor (formerly known as factor III)	Tissue factor	Tissue thromboplastin	Assists factor VII and Ca^{2+} in the activation of factors IX and X during the initiation phase of hemostasis	PT prolonged, aPTT prolonged
Calcium (formerly known as factor IV)	Calcium	Ca^{2+}	Essential to the activation of multiple clotting factors	N/A
Factor V	Proaccelerin	Labile factor, accelerator globulin (AcG)	Assists factors VIIIa, IXa, Xa, and II in the formation of thrombin during the amplification and propa-gation phases of hemostasis	PT prolonged, aPTT prolonged

(table continues on page 382)

	Preferred Name	Synonym	Role in Modern Coagulation Cascade Model	Coagulation Test Responses in the Presence of Factor Deficiency
Factor VII	Proconvertin	Stabile factor, serum prothrombin conversion accelerator, autoprothrombin I	Assists tissue factor and Ca^{2+} in the activation of factors IX and X	PT prolonged, aPTT normal
Factor VIII	Antihemophilic factor (AHF)	Antihemophilic globulin (AHG), antihemophilic factor A, platelet cofactor 1	Activated by trace thrombin during the initiation phase of hemostasis to amplify formation of additional thrombin	aPTT prolonged, PT normal
Factor IX	Plasma thromboplastin component (PTC)	Christmas factor, antihemophilic factor B, platelet cofactor 2	Assists factors Va and VIIIa in the amplification phase and factors VIIIa, Xa, Va, and II to form thrombin in the propagation phase	aPTT prolonged, PT normal
Factor X	Stuart-Prower factor	Autoprothrombin III, thrombokinase	Assists with formation of trace thrombin in the initiation phase and acts with factors VIIIa, IXa, Va, and II to form thrombin in the propagation phase	PT prolonged, aPTT prolonged

Preferred Name	Synonym	Role in Modern Coagulation Cascade Model	Coagulation Test Responses in the Presence of Factor Deficiency
Factor XI	Plasma thrombo-plastin antecedent (PTA)	Antihemophilic factor C	Activated by thrombin produced in the extrinsic path-way to enhance production of additional thrombin inside the fibrin clot via the intrinsic path-way; this factor also participates in slowing down the process of fibrinolysis	aPTT pro-longed, PT normal
Factor XII	Hageman factor	Glass factor, contact factor	Contact activator of the kinin system (e.g., prekallikrein, and high-mole-cular-weight kininogen)	aPTT pro-longed, PT normal
Factor XIII	Fibrin-stabilizing factor (FSF)	Laki-Lorand factor (LLF), fibrinase, plasma transglu-taminase	Activated by thrombin and assists in formation of bonds between fibrin strands to complete secondary hemostasis	PT normal, aPTT normal
von Wille brand factor	von Willebrand factor	vWF	Assists in platelet adhesion and thrombus formation	Ristocetin cofactor decreased

C

C

DESCRIPTION: Hemostasis involves three components: blood vessel walls, platelets, and plasma coagulation proteins. Primary hemostasis has three major stages involving platelet adhesion, platelet activation, and platelet aggregation. Platelet adhesion is initiated by exposure of the endothelium as a result of damage to blood vessels. Exposed tissue factor–bearing cells trigger the simultaneous binding of von Willebrand factor to exposed collagen and circulating platelets. Activated platelets release a number of procoagulant factors, including thromboxane, a very potent platelet activator, from storage granules. These factors enter the circulation and activate other platelets, and the cycle continues. The activated platelets aggregate at the site of vessel injury, and at this stage of hemostasis, the glycoprotein IIb/IIIa receptors on the activated platelets bind fibrinogen, causing the platelets to stick together and form a plug. There is a balance in health between the prothrombotic or clot formation process and the antithrombotic or clot disintegration process. Simultaneously, the coagulation process or secondary hemostasis occurs. In secondary hemostasis, the coagulation proteins respond to blood vessel injury in an overlapping chain of events. The contact activation (formerly known as the intrinsic pathway) and tissue factor (formerly known as the extrinsic pathway) pathways of secondary hemostasis are a series of reactions involving the substrate protein fibrinogen, the coagulation factors (also known as *enzyme precursors* or *zymogens*), nonenzymatic cofactors (Ca^2+), and phospholipids. The factors were assigned Roman numerals in the order of their discovery, not their place in the coagulation sequence. Factor VI was originally thought to be a separate clotting factor. It was subsequently proved to be the same as a modified form of factor Va, and therefore the number is no longer used. The antithrombotic process includes tissue factor pathway inhibitor (TFPI), antithrombin, protein C, and fibrinolysis.

The coagulation factors are formed in the liver. They can be divided into three groups based on their common properties:

1. The contact group is activated in vitro by a surface such as glass and is activated in vivo by collagen. The contact group includes factor XI, factor XII, prekallikrein, and high-molecular-weight kininogen.
2. The prothrombin or vitamin K–dependent group includes factors II, VII, IX, and X.
3. The fibrinogen group includes factors I, V, VIII, and XIII. They are the most labile of the factors and are consumed during the coagulation process. The factors listed in the table are the ones most commonly measured.

For many years it was believed that the intrinsic and extrinsic pathways operated equally, in parallel. A more modern concept of the coagulation process has replaced the traditional model (formerly called the coagulation cascade) and is presented on the next page. The cellular based model includes four overlapping phases in the formation of thrombin: initiation, amplification, propagation, and termination. It is now known that the tissue factor pathway is the primary pathway for the initiation of blood coagulation. Tissue factor (TF) bearing cells (e.g., endothelial cells, smooth muscle cells, monocytes) can be induced to express TF and are the primary initiators of the coagulation cascade either by contact activation or trauma. The contact activation pathway is more related to inflammation, and although it plays an important role in the body's reaction to damaged endothelial surfaces, a deficiency in factor XII does not result in development of a bleeding disorder, which demonstrates the minor role of the intrinsic pathway in the process of blood coagulation. Substances such as endotoxins, tumor necrosis factor alpha, and lipoproteins can also stimulate expression of TF. TF, in combination with factor VII and calcium, forms a complex that then activates factors IX and X in the initiation phase. Activated factor X in the presence of factor II (prothrombin) leads to the formation of thrombin. TFPI quickly inactivates this stage of the pathway so that limited or trace amounts of thrombin are produced and which results in the activation of factors VIII and V. Activated factor IX, assisted by activated factors V

and VIII, initiate amplification and propagation of thrombin in the cascade. Thrombin activates factor XIII and begins converting fibrinogen into fibrin monomers, which spontaneously polymerize and then become cross-linked into a stable clot by activated factor XIII.

Qualitative and quantitative factor deficiencies can affect the function of the coagulation pathways. Factor V and factor II (prothrombin) mutations are examples of qualitative deficiencies and are the most common inherited predisposing factors for blood clots. Approximately 5% to 7% of Caucasians, 2% of Hispanics, 1% of African Americans and Native American, and 0.5% of Asians have the factor V Leiden mutation, and 2% to 3% of Caucasians and 0.3% of African Americans have a prothrombin mutation. Hemophilia A is an inherited deficiency of factor VIII and occurs at a prevalence of about 1 in 5,000 to 10,000 male births. Hemophilia B is an inherited deficiency of factor IX and occurs at a prevalence of about 1 in about 20,000 to 34,000 male births.

The PT/INR measures the function of the extrinsic and common pathways of coagulation and is used to monitor patients receiving warfarin or coumarin-derivative anticoagulant therapy. The aPTT measures the function of the intrinsic and common pathways of coagulation and is used to monitor patients receiving heparin anticoagulant therapy.

C

Coagulation Process

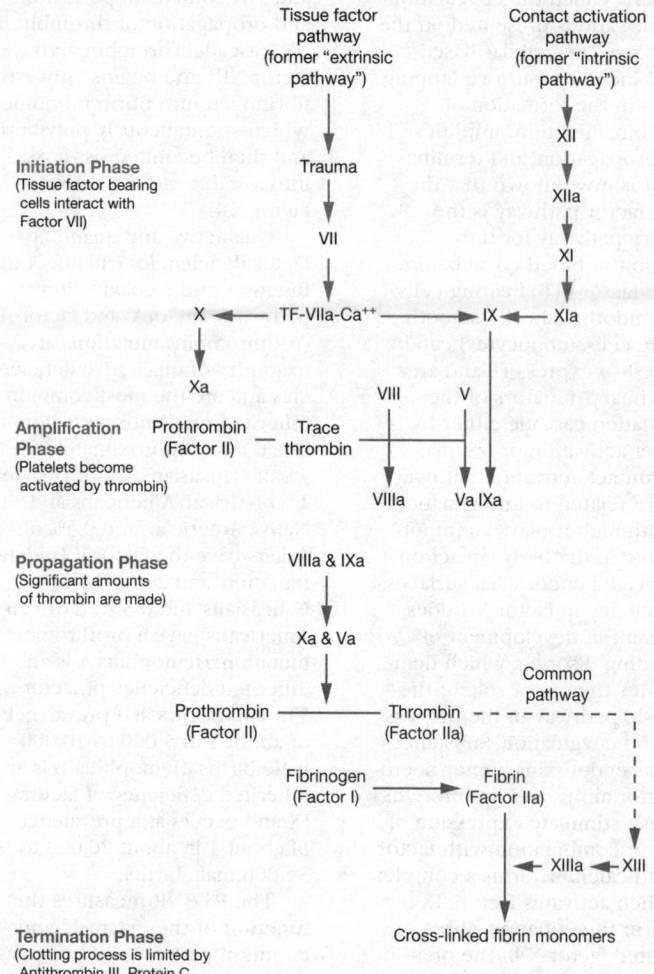

Initiation Phase
(Tissue factor bearing cells interact with Factor VII)

Tissue factor pathway (former "extrinsic pathway")

Contact activation pathway (former "intrinsic pathway")

Trauma → VII → TF-VIIa-Ca++ → X → Xa

XII → XIIa → XI → XIa → IX

Amplification Phase
(Platelets become activated by thrombin)

Prothrombin (Factor II) — Trace thrombin — VIII, V → VIIIa, Va IXa

Propagation Phase
(Significant amounts of thrombin are made)

VIIIa & IXa → Xa & Va

Prothrombin (Factor II) — Thrombin (Factor IIa)

Common pathway

Fibrinogen (Factor I) → Fibrin (Factor IIa)

XIIIa ← XIII

Termination Phase
(Clotting process is limited by Antithrombin III, Protein C, Protein S, thrombomodulin, and TF pathway inhibitor in order to prevent occlusion of the vessel)

Cross-linked fibrin monomers

INDICATIONS

- Identify the presence of inherited bleeding disorders
- Identify the presence of qualitative or quantitative factor deficiency

POTENTIAL DIAGNOSIS

Increased in: N/A

Decreased in

- Congenital deficiency
- Disseminated intravascular coagulation *(related to consumption of factors as part of the coagulation cascade)*
- Liver disease *(related to inability of damaged liver to synthesize coagulation factors)*

CRITICAL FINDINGS: N/A

INTERFERING FACTORS

• Drugs that may increase factor II levels include fluoxymesterone, methandrostenolone, nandrolone, and oxymetholone.
• Drugs that may decrease factor II levels include warfarin.
• Drugs that may increase factor V, VII, and X levels include anabolic steroids, fluoxymesterone, methandrostenolone, nandrolone, oral contraceptives, and oxymetholone.
• Drugs that may decrease factor V levels include streptokinase.
• Drugs that may decrease factor VII levels include acetylsalicylic acid, asparaginase, cefamandole, ceftriaxone, dextran, dicumarol, gemfibrozil, oral contraceptives, and warfarin.
• Drugs that may increase factor VIII levels include chlormadinone.
• Drugs that may decrease factor VIII levels include asparaginase.
• Drugs that may increase factor IX levels include chlormadinone and oral contraceptives.
• Drugs that may decrease factor IX levels include asparaginase and warfarin.
• Drugs that may decrease factor X levels include chlormadinone, dicumarol, oral contraceptives, and warfarin.
• Drugs that may increase factor XI levels include asparaginase and captopril.
• Drugs that may decrease factor XII levels include captopril.
• Test results of patients on anticoagulant therapy are unreliable.
• Placement of tourniquet for longer than 1 min can result in venous stasis and changes in the concentration of plasma proteins to be measured. Platelet activation may also occur under these conditions, causing erroneous results.
• Vascular injury during phlebotomy can activate platelets and coagulation factors, causing erroneous results.
• Hemolyzed specimens must be rejected because hemolysis is an indication of platelet and coagulation factor activation.
• Icteric or lipemic specimens interfere with optical testing methods, producing erroneous results.
• Incompletely filled collection tubes, specimens contaminated with heparin, clotted specimens, or unprocessed specimens not delivered to the laboratory within 1 to 2 hr of collection should be rejected.

NURSING IMPLICATIONS AND PROCEDURE

PRETEST:

▸ Positively identify the patient using at least two unique identifiers before providing care, treatment, or services.
▸ *Patient Teaching:* Inform the patient this test can assist in evaluating the effectiveness of blood clotting and identify deficiencies in blood factor levels.
▸ Obtain a history of the patient's complaints, including a list of known allergens, especially allergies or sensitivities to latex.
▸ Obtain a history of the patient's hematopoietic and hepatobiliary systems, any bleeding disorders, and results of previously performed laboratory tests and diagnostic and surgical procedures.
▸ Obtain a list of the patient's current medications. Include anticoagulants, aspirin and other salicylates, herbs, nutritional supplements, and nutraceuticals (see Appendix F). Such products should be discontinued by medical direction for the appropriate number of days prior to a surgical procedure.
▸ Review the procedure with the patient. Inform the patient that specimen collection takes approximately 5 to 10 min. Address concerns about pain and

explain that there may be some discomfort during the venipuncture.

▸ *Sensitivity to social and cultural issues,* as well as concern for modesty, is important in providing psychological support before, during, and after the procedure.

▸ There are no food, fluid, or medication restrictions unless by medical direction.

C

INTRATEST:

▸ If the patient has a history of allergic reaction to latex, avoid the use of equipment containing latex.

▸ Instruct the patient to cooperate fully and to follow directions. Direct the patient to breathe normally and to avoid unnecessary movement.

▸ Observe standard precautions, and follow the general guidelines in Appendix A. Positively identify the patient, and label the appropriate specimen container with the corresponding patient demographics, initials of the person collecting the specimen, date, and time of collection. Perform a venipuncture. When multiple specimens are drawn, the blue-top tube should be collected after sterile (i.e., blood culture) tubes. Otherwise, when using a standard vacutainer system, the blue top is the first tube collected. When a butterfly is used and due to the added tubing, an extra red-top tube should be collected before the blue-top tube to ensure complete filling of the blue top tube.

▸ Remove the needle and apply direct pressure with dry gauze to stop bleeding. Observe/assess venipuncture site for bleeding or hematoma formation and secure gauze with adhesive bandage.

▸ Promptly transport the specimen to the laboratory for processing and analysis. The Clinical Laboratory Standards Institute (CLSI) recommends that processed and unprocessed samples stored in unopened tubes is that testing should be completed within 1 to 4 hr of collection. If the patient has a known hematocrit above 55%, adjust the amount of anticoagulant in the collection tube

before drawing the blood according to the CLSI guidelines:

Anticoagulant vol. [x] = (100 – hematocrit)/(595 – hematocrit) × total vol. of anticoagulated blood required

Example:

Patient hematocrit = 60%
= [(100 – 60)/(595 – 60) × 5.0]
= 0.37 mL sodium citrate for a 5-mL standard drawing tube

POST-TEST:

▸ A report of the results will be made available to the requesting health-care provider (HCP), who will discuss the results with the patient.

▸ Instruct the patient to report immediately any signs of unusual bleeding or bruising.

▸ Inform the patient with decreased factor levels of the importance of taking precautions against bruising and bleeding. These precautions may include the use of a soft bristle toothbrush, use of an electric razor, avoidance of constipation, avoidance of acetylsalicylic acid and similar products, and avoidance of intramuscular injections.

▸ Reinforce information given by the patient's HCP regarding further testing, treatment, or referral to another HCP. Answer any questions or address any concerns voiced by the patient or family.

▸ Depending on the results of this procedure, additional testing may be performed to evaluate or monitor progression of the disease process and determine the need for a change in therapy. Evaluate test results in relation to the patient's symptoms and other tests performed.

RELATED MONOGRAPHS:

▸ Related tests include aPTT, ALT, ALP, AT-III, AST, clot retraction, CBC platelet count, copper, fibrinogen, FDP, plasminogen, procalcitonin, protein C, protein S, PT/INR, and vitamin K.

▸ Refer to the Hematopoietic and Hepatobiliary systems tables at the end of the book for related tests by body system.

Cold Agglutinin Titer

SYNONYM/ACRONYM: Mycoplasma serology.

COMMON USE: To identify and confirm the presence of viral infections such as found in atypical pneumonia.

SPECIMEN: Serum (2 mL) collected in a red-top tube. The tube must be placed in a water bath or heat block at 37°C for 1 hr and allowed to clot before the serum is separated from the red blood cells (RBCs).

NORMAL FINDINGS: (Method: Patient serum containing autoantibodies titered against type O RBCs at 2°C to 8°C. Type O cells are used because they have no antigens on the cell membrane surface. Agglutination with patient sera would not occur because of reaction between RBC blood type antigens and patient blood type antibodies.) Negative: Single titer less than 1:32 or less than a fourfold increase in titer over serial samples.

DESCRIPTION: Cold agglutinins are antibodies that cause clumping or agglutination of RBCs at cold temperatures in individuals with certain conditions or who are infected by particular organisms. Cold agglutinins are associated with *Mycoplasma pneumoniae* infection. *M. pneumoniae* has I antigen specificity to human RBC membranes. Fetal cells largely contain i antigens, but by 18 mo most cells carry the I antigen. The agglutinins are usually immunoglobulin M (IgM) antibodies and cause agglutination of cells at temperatures in the range of 0°C to 10°C. The temperature of circulating blood in the extremities may be lower than core temperatures. RBCs of affected individuals may agglutinate and obstruct blood vessels in fingers, toes, and ears, or they may initiate the complement cascade. Affected cells may be lysed immediately within the capillaries and blood vessels as a result of the action of complement on the cell wall, or they may return to the circulatory system and be lysed in the spleen by macrophages.

The titer endpoint is the highest dilution of serum that shows a specific antigen-antibody reaction. Single titers greater than 1:64, or a fourfold increase in titer between specimens collected 5 or more days apart, are clinically significant. Patients affected with primary atypical viral pneumonia exhibit a rise in titer 8 to 10 days after the onset of illness. IgM antibodies peak in 12 to 25 days and begin to diminish 30 days after onset.

INDICATIONS
- Assist in the confirmation of primary atypical pneumonia, influenza, or pulmonary embolus
- Provide additional diagnostic support for cold agglutinin disease associated with viral infections or lymphoreticular cancers

POTENTIAL DIAGNOSIS

Increased in
Mycoplasma infection stimulates production of antibodies against specific RBC antigens in affected individuals

- Cirrhosis
- Gangrene

- Hemolytic anemia
- Infectious diseases (e.g., staphylococcemia, influenza, tuberculosis)
- Infectious mononucleosis
- Malaria
- *M. pneumoniae* (primary atypical pneumonia)
- Multiple myeloma
- Pulmonary embolism
- Raynaud's disease (severe)
- Systemic lupus erythematosus
- Trypanosomiasis

Decreased in: N/A

CRITICAL FINDINGS: N/A

INTERFERING FACTORS
- Antibiotic use may interfere with or decrease antibody production.
- A high antibody titer may interfere with blood typing and crossmatching procedures.
- High titers may appear spontaneously in elderly patients and persist for many years.
- Prompt and proper specimen processing, storage, and analysis are important to achieve accurate results. Specimens should always be transported to the laboratory as quickly as possible after collection. The specimen must clot in a 37°C water bath for 1 hr before separation. Refrigeration of the sample before serum separates from the RBCs may falsely decrease the titer.

NURSING IMPLICATIONS AND PROCEDURE

PRETEST:

▶ Positively identify the patient using at least two unique identifiers before providing care, treatment, or services.
▶ *Patient Teaching:* Inform the patient this test can assist in diagnosing primary atypical pneumonia versus other infectious diseases or immune related conditions.

▶ Obtain a history of the patient's complaints, including a list of known allergens, especially allergies or sensitivities to latex.
▶ Obtain a history of the patient's immune and respiratory systems, as well as results of previously performed laboratory tests and diagnostic and surgical procedures.
▶ Obtain a list of the patient's current medications, including herbs, nutritional supplements, and nutraceuticals (see Appendix F).
▶ Note any recent medications that can interfere with test results.
▶ Review the procedure with the patient. Inform the patient that multiple specimens may be required. Inform the patient that specimen collection takes approximately 5 to 10 min. Address concerns about pain and explain that there may be some discomfort during the venipuncture.
▶ *Sensitivity to social and cultural issues,* as well as concern for modesty, is important in providing psychological support before, during, and after the procedure.
▶ There are no food, fluid, or medication restrictions (except antibiotics) unless by medical direction.

INTRATEST:

▶ Ensure that the patient has complied with medication restrictions prior to the procedure.
▶ If the patient has a history of allergic reaction to latex, avoid the use of equipment containing latex.
▶ Instruct the patient to cooperate fully and to follow directions. Direct the patient to breathe normally and to avoid unnecessary movement.
▶ Observe standard precautions, and follow the general guidelines in Appendix A. Positively identify the patient, and label the appropriate specimen container with the corresponding patient demographics, initials of the person collecting the specimen, date, and time of collection. Perform a venipuncture.
▶ Remove the needle and apply direct pressure with dry gauze to stop

bleeding. Observe/assess venipuncture site for bleeding or hematoma formation and secure gauze with adhesive bandage.
Promptly transport the specimen to the laboratory for processing and analysis.
Inform the laboratory if the patient is receiving antibiotics.

POST-TEST:
A report of the results will be made available to the requesting health-care provider (HCP), who will discuss the results with the patient.
Instruct the patient to resume antibiotics as directed by the HCP.
Instruct the patient in the importance of completing the entire course of antibiotic therapy even if no symptoms are present.
Reinforce information given by the patient's HCP regarding further testing, treatment, or referral to another HCP. Emphasize the need for the patient to return in 7 to 14 days

for a convalescent blood sample. Answer any questions or address any concerns voiced by the patient or family.
Depending on the results of this procedure, additional testing may be performed to evaluate or monitor progression of the disease process and determine the need for a change in therapy. Evaluate test results in relation to the patient's symptoms and other tests performed.

RELATED MONOGRAPHS:
Related tests include arterial/alveolar oxygen ratio, blood gases, chest x-ray, CBC, CBC WBC count, Coombs' antiglobulin, culture viral, ESR, gallium scan, infectious mono-nucleosis screen, lung perfusion scan, plethysmography, and pleural fluid analysis.
Refer to the Immune and Respiratory systems tables at the end of the book for related tests by body system.

Collagen Cross-Linked N-Telopeptide

SYNONYM/ACRONYM: NT_x.

COMMON USE: To evaluate the effectiveness of treatment for osteoporosis.

SPECIMEN: Urine (2 mL) from a random specimen collected in a clean plastic container.

NORMAL FINDINGS: (Method: Immunoassay)

Adult male 18–29 yr	Less than 100 mmol bone collagen equivalents (BCE)/mmol creatinine
Adult male 30–59 yr	Less than 65 mmol BCE/mmol creatinine
Adult female (premenopausal)	Less than 65 mmol BCE/mmol creatinine

Tanner Stage	Male	Female
I	55–508 (mmol BCE/mmol creatinine)	6–662 (mmol BCE/mmol creatinine)
II	21–423 (mmol BCE/mmol creatinine)	193–514 (mmol BCE/mmol creatinine)
III	27–462 (mmol BCE/mmol creatinine)	13–632 (mmol BCE/mmol creatinine)
IV	Less than 609 (mmol BCE/ mmol creatinine)	Less than 389 (mmol BCE/ mmol creatinine)
V	Less than 240 (mmol BCE/ mmol creatinine)	Less than 132 (mmol BCE/ mmol creatinine)

Values are higher in children.

DESCRIPTION: Osteoporosis is the most common bone disease in the West. It is often called the "silent disease" because bone loss occurs without symptoms. The formation and maintenance of bone mass is dependent on a combination of factors that include genetics, nutrition, exercise, and hormone function. Normally, the rate of bone formation is equal to the rate of bone resorption. After midlife, the rate of bone loss begins to increase. Osteoporosis is more commonly identified in women than in men. Other risk factors include thin, small-framed body structure; family history of osteoporosis; diet low in calcium; white or Asian race; excessive use of alcohol; cigarette smoking; sedentary lifestyle; long-term use of corticosteroids, thyroid replacement medications, or antiepileptics; history of bulimia, anorexia nervosa, chronic liver disease, or malabsorption disorders; and postmenopausal state. Osteoporosis is a major consequence of menopause in women owing to the decline of estrogen production. Osteoporosis is rare in premenopausal women. Estrogen replacement therapy (after menopause) is one strategy that has been commonly employed to prevent osteoporosis, although its exact protective mechanism is unknown. Results of some recently published studies indicate that there may be significant adverse side effects to estrogen replacement therapy; more research is needed to understand the long-term effects (positive and negative) of this therapy. Other treatments include raloxifene (selectively modulates estrogen receptors), calcitonin (interacts directly with osteoclasts), and bisphosphates (inhibit osteoclast-mediated bone resorption).

A noninvasive test to detect the presence of collagen cross-linked N-telopeptide (NT_x) is used to follow the progress of patients who have begun treatment for osteoporosis. NT_x is formed when collagenase acts on bone. Small NT_x fragments are excreted in the urine after bone resorption. A desirable response, 2 to 3 mo after therapy is initiated, is a 30% reduction in NT_x and a reduction of 50% below baseline by 12 mo.

INDICATIONS
- Assist in the evaluation of osteoporosis
- Assist in the management and treatment of osteoporosis

Monitor effects of estrogen replacement therapy

POTENTIAL DIAGNOSIS

Increased in

Conditions that reflect increased bone resorption are associated with increased levels of N-telopeptide in the urine

Alcoholism *(related to inadequate nutrition)*

Chronic immobilization

Chronic treatment with anticonvulsants, corticosteroids, gonadotropin releasing hormone agonists, heparin, or thyroid hormone

Conditions that include hypercortisolism, hyperparathyroidism, hyperthyroidism, and hypogonadism

Gastrointestinal disease *(related to inadequate dietary intake or absorption of minerals required for bone formation and maintenance)*

Growth disorders (acromegaly, growth hormone deficiency, osteogenesis imperfecta)

Hyperparathyroidism *(related to imbalance in calcium and phosphorus that affects the rate of bone resorption)*

Multiple myeloma and metastatic tumors

Osteomalacia *(related to defective bone mineralization)*

Osteoporosis

Paget's disease

Postmenopausal women *(related to estrogen deficiency)*

Recent fracture

Renal insufficiency *(related to excessive loss through renal dysfunction)*

Rheumatoid arthritis and other connective tissue diseases *(related to inadequate diet due to loss of appetite)*

Decreased in

• Effective therapy for osteoporosis

CRITICAL FINDINGS: N/A

INTERFERING FACTORS

• NT$_x$ levels are affected by urinary excretion, and values may be influenced by the presence of renal impairment or disease.

NURSING IMPLICATIONS AND PROCEDURE

PRETEST:

▶ Positively identify the patient using at least two unique identifiers before providing care, treatment, or services.

▶ *Patient Teaching:* Inform the patient this test can assist in diagnosing osteoporosis and evaluating the effectiveness of therapy.

▶ Obtain a history of the patient's complaints, including a list of known allergens.

▶ Obtain a history of the patient's musculoskeletal system and results of previously performed laboratory tests and diagnostic and surgical procedures.

▶ Obtain a list of the patient's current medications, including herbs, nutritional supplements, and nutraceuticals (see Appendix F).

▶ Review the procedure with the patient. Inform the patient that specimen collection takes approximately 5 to 10 min. Address concerns about pain and explain that there should be no discomfort during the procedure.

▶ *Sensitivity to social and cultural issues,* as well as concern for modesty, is important in providing psychological support before, during, and after the procedure.

▶ There are no food, fluid, or medication restrictions unless by medical direction.

C

INTRATEST:

▶ Instruct the patient to cooperate fully and to follow directions.

▶ Observe standard precautions, and follow the general guidelines in Appendix A. Positively identify the patient, and label the appropriate specimen container with the corresponding patient demographics, initials of the person collecting the specimen, date, and time of collection.

▶ Instruct the patient to collect a second-void morning specimen as follows: (1) void and then drink a glass of water; (2) wait 30 min, and then try to void again.

▶ Promptly transport the specimen to the laboratory for processing and analysis.

POST-TEST:

▶ A report of the results will be made available to the requesting health-care provider (HCP), who will discuss the results with the patient.

▶ Instruct the patient to resume usual diet, fluids, medications, and activity, as directed by the HCP.

▶ *Nutritional Considerations:* Increased NT_x levels may be associated with osteoporosis. Nutritional therapy may be indicated for patients identified as being at high risk for developing osteoporosis. Educate the patient about the National Osteoporosis Foundation's guidelines regarding a regular regimen of weight-bearing exercises, limited alcohol intake, avoidance of tobacco products, and adequate dietary intake of vitamin D and calcium. The Institute of Medicine's Food and Nutrition Board suggests 1,200 mg as an adequate daily intake goal of dietary calcium for adult males and females age 51 to greater than 70 yr; 1,000 mg/d for adult males and females age 19 to 50 yr; 1,000 mg/d for pregnant and lactating females age 19 to 50 yr; 1,300 mg/d for pregnant and lactating females under age 19 yr; 1,300 mg/d for children age 9 to 18 yr; 800 mg/d for children age 4 to 8 yr; 500 mg/dL for children age 1 to 3 yr; 270 mg/d for children age 7 to 12 mo; and

210 mg/d for children age 0 to 6 mo. Reprinted with permission from the National Academies Press, copyright 2013, National Academy of Sciences. Dietary calcium can be obtained in animal or plant sources. Milk and milk products, sardines, clams, oysters, salmon, rhubarb, spinach, beet greens, broccoli, kale, tofu, legumes, and fortified orange juice are high in calcium. Milk and milk products also contain vitamin D and lactose to assist in absorption. Cooked vegetables yield more absorbable calcium than raw vegetables. Patients should also be informed of the substances that can inhibit calcium absorption by irreversibly binding to some of the calcium and making it unavailable for absorption, such as oxalates, which naturally occur in some vegetables (e.g., beet greens, collards, leeks, okra, parsley, quinoa, spinach, Swiss chard) and are found in tea; phytic acid, found in some cereals (e.g., wheat bran, wheat germ); phosphoric acid, found in dark cola; and excessive intake of insoluble dietary fiber (in excessive amounts). Excessive protein intake also can affect calcium absorption negatively, especially if it is combined with foods high in phosphorus. The Institute of Medicine's Food and Nutrition Board suggests 50 mcg/d as the daily intake goal of dietary Vitamin D for males and females age 1 to greater than 70 yr; 50 mcg/d for pregnant and lactating females age 18 to 50 yr; 25 mcg/d for children age 0 to 12 mo. Reprinted with permission from the National Academies Press, copyright 2013, National Academy of Sciences. Vitamin D is synthesized by the skin and is available in fortified dairy foods and cod liver oil.

▶ Recognize anxiety related to test results, and be supportive of impaired activity related to lack of muscular control, perceived loss of independence, and fear of shortened life expectancy. Discuss the implications of abnormal test results on the patient's lifestyle. Provide teaching and information regarding the clinical implications of the test results, as appropriate.

Educate the patient regarding access to counseling services. Provide contact information, if desired, for the American College of Rheumatology (www.rheumatology.org), the Institute of Medicine of the National Academies (www.iom.edu), or the National Osteoporosis Foundation (www.nof.org). Reinforce information given by the patient's HCP regarding further testing, treatment, or referral to another HCP. Answer any questions or address any concerns voiced by the patient or family. Depending on the results of this procedure, additional testing may

be performed to evaluate or monitor progression of the disease process and determine the need for a change in therapy. Evaluate test results in relation to the patient's symptoms and other tests performed.

RELATED MONOGRAPHS:

- Related tests include ALP, BMD, calcitonin, calcium, creatinine, creatinine clearance, osteocalcin, PTH, phosphorus, radiography bone, and vitamin D.
- Refer to the Musculoskeletal System table at the end of the book for related tests by body system.

Colonoscopy

SYNONYM/ACRONYM: Full colonoscopy, lower endoscopy, lower panendoscopy.

COMMON USE: To visualize and assess the lower colon for tumor, cancer, and infection.

AREA OF APPLICATION: Colon.

CONTRAST: Air.

DESCRIPTION: Colonoscopy allows inspection of the mucosa of the entire colon, ileocecal valve, and terminal ileum using a flexible fiberoptic colonoscope inserted through the anus and advanced to the terminal ileum. The colonoscope is a multichannel instrument that allows viewing of the gastrointestinal (GI) tract lining, insufflation of air, aspiration of fluid, obtaining of tissue biopsy samples, and passage of a laser beam for obliteration of tissue and control of bleeding. Mucosal surfaces of the lower GI tract are examined for ulcerations, polyps, chronic diarrhea, hemorrhagic

sites, neoplasms, and strictures. During the procedure, tissue samples may be obtained for cytology, and some therapeutic procedures may be performed, such as excision of small tumors or polyps, coagulation of bleeding sites, and removal of foreign bodies.

INDICATIONS
- Assess GI function in a patient with a personal or family history of colon cancer, polyps, or ulcerative colitis
- Confirm diagnosis of colon cancer and inflammatory bowel disease

- Detect Hirschsprung's disease and determine the areas affected by the disease
- Determine cause of lower GI disorders, especially when barium enema and proctosigmoidoscopy are inconclusive
- Determine source of rectal bleeding and perform hemostasis by coagulation
- Evaluate postsurgical status of colon resection
- Evaluate stools that show a positive occult blood test, lower GI bleeding, or change in bowel habits
- Follow up on previously diagnosed and treated colon cancer
- Investigate iron-deficiency anemia of unknown origin
- Reduce volvulus and intussusception in children
- Remove colon polyps
- Remove foreign bodies and sclerosing strictures by laser

POTENTIAL DIAGNOSIS

Normal findings in

- Normal intestinal mucosa with no abnormalities of structure, function, or mucosal surface in the colon or terminal ileum

Abnormal findings in

- Benign lesions
- Bleeding sites
- Bowel distention
- Bowel infection or inflammation
- Colitis
- Colon cancer
- Crohn's disease
- Diverticula
- Foreign bodies
- Hemorrhoids
- Polyps
- Proctitis
- Tumors
- Vascular abnormalities

CRITICAL FINDINGS: N/A

INTERFERING FACTORS

This procedure is contraindicated for

- Patients with bleeding disorders or cardiac conditions.
- Patients with bowel perforation, acute peritonitis, acute colitis, ischemic bowel necrosis, toxic colitis, recent bowel surgery, advanced pregnancy, severe cardiac or pulmonary disease, recent myocardial infarction, known or suspected pulmonary embolus, and large abdominal aortic or iliac aneurysm.
- Patients who have had a colon anastomosis within the past 14 to 21 days, because an anastomosis may break down with gas insufflation.

Factors that may impair clear imaging

- Gas or feces in the GI tract resulting from inadequate cleansing or failure to restrict food intake before the study.
- Retained barium from a previous radiological procedure.
- Metallic objects (e.g., jewelry, body rings) within the examination field, which may inhibit organ visualization and cause unclear images.
- Patients who are very obese or who may exceed the weight limit for the equipment.
- Inability of the patient to cooperate or remain still during the procedure because of age, significant pain, or mental status.
- Severe lower GI bleeding or the presence of feces, barium, blood, or blood clots, which can interfere with visualization.
- Spasm of the colon, which can mimic the radiographic signs of

cancer. (*Note:* The use of IV glucagon minimizes spasm.)

• Inability of the patient to tolerate introduction of or retention of barium, air, or both in the bowel.

Other considerations

• Complications of the procedure may include hemorrhage and cardiac arrhythmias.

• The procedure may be terminated if chest pain or severe cardiac arrhythmias occur.

• Failure to follow dietary restrictions and other pretesting preparations may cause the procedure to be canceled or repeated.

• Bowel preparations that include laxatives or enemas should be avoided in pregnant patients or patients with inflammatory bowel disease unless specifically directed by a health-care provider (HCP).

• Consultation with an HCP should occur before the procedure for radiation safety concerns regarding younger patients or patients who are lactating.

• Risks associated with radiation overexposure can result from frequent x-ray procedures. Personnel in the examination room with the patient should wear a protective lead apron, stand behind a shield, or leave the area while the examination is being done. Personnel working in the examination area should wear badges to record their level of radiation exposure.

NURSING IMPLICATIONS AND PROCEDURE

PRETEST:

▸ Positively identify the patient using at least two unique identifiers before providing care, treatment, or services.

Patient Teaching: Inform the patient this procedure can assist in assessing the colon for disease.

▸ Obtain a history of the patient's complaints, including a list of known allergens, especially allergies or sensitivities to latex, iodine, seafood, anesthetics, or contrast medium.

▸ Obtain a history of patient's gastrointestinal system, symptoms, and results of previously performed laboratory tests and diagnostic and surgical procedures.

▸ Note any recent procedures that can interfere with test results, including examinations using barium- or iodine-based contrast medium. Ensure that barium studies were performed more than 4 days before the CT scan.

▸ Ensure that this procedure is performed before an upper GI study or barium swallow.

▸ Record the date of the last menstrual period and determine the possibility of pregnancy in perimenopausal women.

▸ Obtain a list of the patient's current medications including anticoagulants, aspirin and other salicylates, herbs, nutritional supplements, and nutraceuticals (see Appendix F). Such products should be discontinued by medical direction for the appropriate number of days prior to a surgical procedure. Note the last time and dose of medication taken.

▸ Note intake of oral iron preparations within 1 wk before the procedure because these cause black, sticky feces that are difficult to remove with bowel preparation.

▸ Review the procedure with the patient. Address concerns about pain and explain that some pain may be experienced during the test, and there may be moments of discomfort. Inform the patient that the procedure is performed in a GI lab, by an HCP, with support staff, and takes approximately 30 to 60 min.

Sensitivity to social and cultural issues, as well as concern for modesty, is important in providing psychological

support before, during, and after the procedure.

Inform the patient that it is important that the bowel be cleaned thoroughly so that the physician can visualize the colon. Inform the patient that a laxative and cleansing enema may be needed the day before the procedure, with cleansing enemas on the morning of the procedure, depending on the institution's policy.

Instruct the patient to remove all external metallic objects from the area to be examined.

Instruct the patient to eat a low-residue diet for several days before the procedure and to consume only clear liquids the evening before the test. The patient should fast and restrict fluids for 8 hr prior to the procedure. Protocols may vary among facilities.

Make sure a written and informed consent has been signed prior to the procedure and before administering any medications.

INTRATEST:

Observe standard precautions, and follow the general guidelines in Appendix A. Positively identify the patient, and label the appropriate specimen container with the corresponding patient demographics, initials of the person collecting the specimen, date, and time of collection.

Ensure that the patient has complied with dietary, fluid and medication restrictions, and pretesting preparations for at least 8 hr prior to the procedure.

Ensure that ordered laxatives were administered late in the afternoon of the day before the procedure.

Assess for completion of bowel preparation according to the institution's procedure.

Instruct the patient to remove all external metallic objects from the area to be examined.

Have emergency equipment readily available.

Instruct the patient to void prior to the procedure and to change into the gown, robe, and foot coverings provided.

Instruct the patient to cooperate fully and to follow directions. Instruct the patient to remain still throughout the procedure because movement produces unreliable results.

Obtain and record baseline vital signs.

An IV line may be started to allow infusion of a sedative or IV fluids.

Administer medications, as ordered, to reduce discomfort and to promote relaxation and sedation.

Place the patient on an examination table in the left lateral decubitus position and drape with the buttocks exposed.

The HCP performs a visual inspection of the perianal area and a digital rectal examination.

Instruct the patient to bear down as if having a bowel movement as the fiberoptic tube is inserted through the rectum.

The scope is advanced through the sigmoid. The patient's position is changed to supine to facilitate passage into the transverse colon. Air is insufflated through the tube during passage to aid in visualization.

Instruct the patient to take deep breaths to aid in movement of the scope downward through the ascending colon to the cecum and into the terminal portion of the ileum.

Air is insufflated to distend the GI tract, as needed. Biopsies, cultures, or any endoscopic surgery is performed.

Foreign bodies or polyps are removed and placed in appropriate specimen containers, labeled, and sent to the laboratory.

Photographs are obtained for future reference.

At the end of the procedure, excess air and secretions are aspirated through the scope, and the colonoscope is removed.

POST-TEST:

- A report of the results will be made available to the requesting health-care provider (HCP), who will discuss the results with the patient.
- Monitor the patient for signs of respiratory depression.
- Monitor vital signs and neurological status every 15 min for 1 hr, then every 2 hr for 4 hr, or as ordered. Take temperature every 4 hr for 24 hr. Monitor intake and output at least every 8 hr. Compare with baseline values. Notify the HCP if temperature is elevated. Protocols may vary among facilities.
- Observe the patient until the effects of the sedation have worn off.
- Instruct the patient to resume usual diet, fluids, medications, and activity, as directed by the HCP.
- Monitor for any rectal bleeding. Instruct the patient to expect slight rectal bleeding for 2 days after removal of polyps or biopsy specimens but that an increasing amount of bleeding or sustained bleeding should be reported to the HCP immediately.
- Instruct the patient to immediately report symptoms such as fast heart rate, difficulty breathing, skin rash, itching, chest pain, persistent right shoulder pain, or abdominal pain. Immediately report symptoms to the appropriate HCP.
- Inform the patient that belching, bloating, or flatulence is the result of air insufflation.
- Encourage the patient to drink several glasses of water to help replace fluids lost during the preparation for the test.
- Carefully monitor the patient for fatigue and fluid and electrolyte imbalance.
- Recognize anxiety related to test results. Discuss the implications of abnormal test results on the patient's lifestyle. Provide teaching and information regarding the clinical implications of the test results, as appropriate.
- Reinforce information given by the patient's HCP regarding further testing, treatment, or referral to another HCP. Decisions regarding the need for and frequency of occult blood testing, colonoscopy or other cancer screening procedures should be made after consultation between the patient and HCP. The most current guidelines for colon cancer screening of the general population as well as individuals with increased risk are available from the American Cancer Society (www.cancer.org) and the American College of Gastroenterology (www.gi.org). Answer any questions or address any concerns voiced by the patient or family.
- Depending on the results of this procedure, additional testing may be needed to evaluate or monitor progression of the disease process and determine the need for a change in therapy. Evaluate test results in relation to the patient's symptoms and other tests performed.

RELATED MONOGRAPHS:

- Related tests include barium enema, biopsy intestinal, capsule endoscopy, carcinoembryonic and cancer antigens, CT abdomen, CT colonoscopy, fecal analysis, KUB, MRI abdomen, and proctosigmoidoscopy.
- Refer to the Gastrointestinal System table at the end of the book for related tests by body system.

Color Perception Test

SYNONYM/ACRONYM: Color blindness test, Ishihara color perception test, Ishihara pseudoisochromatic plate test.

C

COMMON USE: To assist in the diagnosis of color blindness.

AREA OF APPLICATION: Eyes.

CONTRAST: N/A.

DESCRIPTION: Defects in color perception can be hereditary or acquired. The congenital defect for color blindness is carried by the female, who is generally unaffected, and is expressed dominantly in males. Color blindness occurs in 8% of males and 0.4% of females. It may be partial or complete. The partial form is the hereditary form, and in the majority of patients the color deficiency is in the red-green area of the spectrum. Acquired color blindness may occur as a result of diseases of the retina or optic nerve. Color perception tests are performed to determine the acuity of color discrimination. The most common test uses pseudoisochromic plates with numbers or letters buried in a maze of dots. Misreading the numbers or letters indicates a color perception deficiency and may indicate color blindness, a genetic dysfunction, or retinal pathology.

INDICATIONS
- Detect deficiencies in color perception
- Evaluate because of family history of color visual defects

- Investigate suspected retinal pathology affecting the cones

POTENTIAL DIAGNOSIS

Normal findings in
- Normal visual color discrimination; no difficulty in identification of color combinations

Abnormal findings in
- Identification of some but not all colors

CRITICAL FINDINGS: N/A

INTERFERING FACTORS
- Inability of the patient to cooperate or remain still during the procedure because of age, significant pain, or mental status.
- Inability of the patient to read.
- Poor visual acuity or poor lighting.
- Failure of the patient to wear corrective lenses (glasses or contact lenses).
- Damaged or discolored test plates.

NURSING IMPLICATIONS AND PROCEDURE

PRETEST:

▸ Positively identify the patient using at least two unique identifiers before providing care, treatment, or services.

Patient Teaching: Inform the patient or parent/child this procedure can assist in detection of color vision impairment.

Obtain a history of the patient's complaints, including a list of known allergens.

Obtain a history of the patient's known or suspected vision loss; changes in visual acuity, including type and cause; use of glasses or contact lenses; eye conditions with treatment regimens; eye surgery; and other tests and procedures to assess and diagnose visual deficit.

Obtain a history of symptoms and results of previously performed laboratory tests and diagnostic and surgical procedures.

Obtain a list of the patient's current medications, including herbs, nutritional supplements, and nutraceuticals (see Appendix F).

Review the procedure with the patient. Ask the patient if he or she wears corrective lenses; also inquire about the importance of color discrimination in his or her work, as applicable. Address concerns about pain and explain that no discomfort will be experienced during the test. Inform the patient that a health-care provider (HCP) performs the test in a quiet, darkened room, and that to evaluate both eyes, the test can take 5 to 15 or up to 30 min, depending on the complexity of testing required.

Sensitivity to social and cultural issues, as well as concern for modesty, is important in providing psychological support before, during, and after the procedure.

There are no food, fluid, or medication restrictions unless by medical direction.

INTRATEST:

Observe standard precautions, and follow the general guidelines in Appendix A. Positively identify the patient.

Instruct the patient to cooperate fully and to follow directions.

Seat the patient comfortably. Occlude one eye and hold test booklet 12 to 14 in. in front of the exposed eye.

Ask the patient to identify the numbers or letters buried in the maze of dots or to trace the objects with a handheld pointed object.

Repeat on the other eye.

POST-TEST:

A report of the results will be made available to the requesting HCP, who will discuss the results with the patient.

Recognize anxiety related to test results and be supportive of impaired activity related to color vision loss. Discuss the implications of abnormal test results on the patient's lifestyle. Provide teaching and information regarding the clinical implications of the test results, as appropriate. Provide contact information regarding vision aids for people with impaired color perception, if desired: ABLEDATA (sponsored by the National Institute on Disability and Rehabilitation Research [NIDRR], available at www.abledata.com).

Reinforce information given by the patient's HCP regarding further testing, treatment, or referral to another HCP. Answer any questions or address any concerns voiced by the patient or family.

Depending on the results of this procedure, additional testing may be performed to evaluate or monitor progression of the disease process and determine the need for a change in therapy. Evaluate test results in relation to the patient's symptoms and other tests performed.

RELATED MONOGRAPHS:

Related tests include refraction and slit-lamp biomicroscopy.

Refer to the Ocular System table at the end of the book for related tests by body system.

Colposcopy

SYNONYM/ACRONYM: Cervical biopsy, endometrial biopsy.

COMMON USE: To visualize and assess the cervix and vagina related to suspected cancer or other disease.

AREA OF APPLICATION: Vagina and cervix.

CONTRAST: None.

DESCRIPTION: In this procedure, the vagina and cervix are viewed using a colposcope, a special binocular microscope and light system that magnifies the mucosal surfaces. Colposcopy is usually performed after suspicious Papanicolaou (Pap) test results or when suspected lesions cannot be visualized fully by the naked eye. The procedure is useful for identifying areas of cellular dysplasia and diagnosing cervical cancer because it provides the best view of the suspicious lesion, ensuring that the most representative area of the lesion is obtained for cytological analysis to confirm malignant changes. Colposcopy is also valuable for assessing women with a history of exposure to diethylstilbestrol (DES) in utero. The goal is to identify precursor changes in cervical tissue before the changes advance from benign or atypical cells to cervical cancer. Photographs (cervicography) can also be taken of the cervix.

INDICATIONS

- Evaluate the cervix after abnormal Pap smear
- Evaluate vaginal lesions

- Localize the area from which cervical biopsy samples should be obtained because such areas may not be visible to the naked eye
- Monitor conservatively treated cervical intraepithelial neoplasia
- Monitor women whose mothers took DES during pregnancy

POTENTIAL DIAGNOSIS

Normal findings in
- Normal appearance of the vagina and cervix
- No abnormal cells or tissues

Abnormal findings in
- Atrophic changes
- Cervical erosion
- Cervical intraepithelial neoplasia
- Infection
- Inflammation
- Invasive carcinoma
- Leukoplakia
- Papilloma, including condyloma

CRITICAL FINDINGS: N/A

INTERFERING FACTORS

This procedure is contraindicated for
- Patients who are pregnant or suspected of being pregnant, unless the potential benefits of the procedure far outweigh the risks to the fetus and mother.

- Patients with cardiac conditions.
- Patients with bleeding disorders, especially if cervical biopsy specimens are to be obtained.
- Women who are currently menstruating.

Factors that may impair clear imaging
- Inadequate cleansing of the cervix of secretions and medications.
- Scarring of the cervix.
- Inability of the patient to cooperate or remain still during the procedure because of age, significant pain, or mental status.
- Severe bleeding or the presence of feces, blood, or blood clots, which can interfere with visualization.

Other considerations
- Complications of the procedure may include hemorrhage and cardiac arrhythmias.
- The procedure may be terminated if chest pain or severe cardiac arrhythmias occur.

NURSING IMPLICATIONS AND PROCEDURE

PRETEST:

▶ Positively identify the patient using at least two unique identifiers before providing care, treatment, or services.

▶ *Patient Teaching:* Inform the patient this procedure can assist in assessing the uterus and cervix for disease.

▶ Obtain a history of the patient's complaints including a list of known allergens, especially allergies or sensitivities to latex, iodine, or anesthetics.

▶ Obtain a history of the patient's reproductive system, symptoms, and results of previously performed laboratory tests and diagnostic and surgical procedures.

▶ Record the date of the last menstrual period and determine the possibility of pregnancy in perimenopausal women.

▶ Obtain a list of the patient's current medications, including anticoagulants, aspirin and other salicylates, herbs, nutritional supplements, and nutraceuticals (see Appendix F). Such products should be discontinued by medical direction for the appropriate number of days prior to a surgical procedure. Note the last time and dose of medication taken.

▶ Review the procedure with the patient. Address concerns about pain related to the procedure and explain that some pain may be experienced during the test, and there may be moments of discomfort. Inform the patient that the procedure is performed by a healthcare provider (HCP), with support staff, and takes approximately 30 to 60 min.

▶ *Sensitivity to social and cultural issues,* as well as concern for modesty, is important in providing psychological support before, during, and after the procedure.

▶ Explain to the patient that if a biopsy is performed, she may feel menstrual-like cramping during the procedure and experience a minimal amount of bleeding.

▶ There are no food, fluid, or medication restrictions unless by medical direction.

▶ *Make sure a written and informed consent has been signed prior to the procedure and before administering any medications.*

INTRATEST:

▶ Observe standard precautions, and follow the general guidelines in Appendix A. Positively identify the patient, and label the appropriate specimen container with the corresponding patient demographics, initials of the person collecting the specimen, date, and time of collection.

▶ Have emergency equipment readily available.

▶ Instruct the patient to void prior to the procedure and to change into the gown, robe, and foot coverings provided.

▶ Instruct the patient to cooperate fully and to follow directions. Instruct the patient to remain still throughout the procedure because movement produces unreliable results.

▶ Obtain and record baseline vital signs.

An IV line may be started to allow infusion of a sedative or IV fluids.

Administer medications, as ordered, to reduce discomfort and to promote relaxation and sedation.

Place the patient in the lithotomy position on the examining table and drape her. Cleanse the external genitalia with an antiseptic solution.

If a Pap smear is performed, the vaginal speculum is inserted, using water as a lubricant.

The cervix is swabbed with 3% acetic acid to remove mucus or any cream medication and to improve the contrast between tissue types. The scope is positioned at the speculum and is focused on the cervix. The area is examined carefully, using light and magnification. Photographs can be taken for future reference.

Tissues that appear abnormal or atypical undergo biopsy using a forceps inserted through the speculum. Bleeding, which is common after cervical biopsy, may be controlled by cautery, suturing, or application of silver nitrate or ferric subsulfate (Monsel's solution) to the site.

The vagina is rinsed with sterile saline or water to remove the acetic acid and prevent burning after the procedure. If bleeding persists, a tampon may be inserted after removal of the speculum.

Biopsy samples are placed in appropriately labeled containers with special preservative solution, and promptly transported to the laboratory.

POST-TEST:

A report of the results will be made available to the requesting HCP, who will discuss the results with the patient.

Monitor the patient for signs of respiratory depression.

Monitor vital signs and neurological status every 15 min for 1 hr, then every 2 hr for 4 hr, and as ordered. Take temperature every 4 hr for 24 hr. Monitor intake and output at least every 8 hr. Compare with baseline values. Notify the HCP if temperature is elevated. Protocols may vary among facilities.

Observe the patient until the effects of the sedation, if ordered, have worn off.

Instruct the patient to remove the vaginal tampon, if inserted, within 8 to 24 hr; after that time, the patient should wear pads if there is bleeding or drainage.

If a biopsy was performed, inform the patient that a discharge may persist for a few days to a few weeks.

Advise the patient to avoid strenuous exercise 8 to 24 hr after the procedure and to avoid douching and intercourse for about 2 wk or as directed by the HCP.

Monitor for any bleeding.

Instruct the patient to expect slight bleeding for 2 days after removal of biopsy specimens, but emphasize that persistent vaginal bleeding or abnormal vaginal discharge, an increasing amount of bleeding, abdominal pain, and fever must be reported to the HCP immediately.

Instruct the patient to immediately report symptoms such as fast heart rate, difficulty breathing, skin rash, itching, chest pain, persistent right shoulder pain, or abdominal pain. Immediately report symptoms to the appropriate HCP.

Recognize anxiety related to test results. Discuss the implications of abnormal test results on the patient's lifestyle. Provide teaching and information regarding the clinical implications of the test results, as appropriate.

Reinforce information given by the patient's HCP regarding further testing, treatment, or referral to another HCP. Answer any questions or address any concerns voiced by the patient or family.

Depending on the results of this procedure, additional testing may be needed to evaluate or monitor progression of the disease process and determine the need for a change in therapy. Evaluate test results in relation to the patient's symptoms and other tests performed.

RELATED MONOGRAPHS:

Related tests include biopsy cervical, CT abdomen, culture viral, MRI abdomen, Pap smear, and US pelvis.

Refer to the Reproductive System table at the end of the book for related tests by body system.

Complement C3 and Complement C4

SYNONYM/ACRONYM: C3 and C4.

COMMON USE: To assist in the diagnosis of immunological diseases, such as rheumatoid arthritis, and systemic lupus erythematosus (SLE), in which complement is consumed at an increased rate, or to detect inborn deficiency.

SPECIMEN: Serum (1 mL) collected in a red-top tube.

NORMAL FINDINGS: (Method: Immunoturbidimetric)

C3

Age	Conventional Units	SI Units (Conventional Units × 10)
Newborn	57–116 mg/dL	570–1,160 mg/L
6 mo–adult	74–166 mg/dL	740–1,660 mg/L
Adult	83–177 mg/dL	830–1,770 mg/L

C4

Age	Conventional Units	SI Units (Conventional Units × 10)
Newborn	10–31 mg/dL	100–310 mg/L
6 mo–6 yr	15–52 mg/dL	150–520 mg/L
7–12 yr	19–40 mg/dL	190–400 mg/L
13–15 yr	19–57 mg/dL	190–570 mg/L
16–18 yr	19–42 mg/dL	190–420 mg/L
Adult	12–36 mg/dL	120–360 mg/L

DESCRIPTION: Complement is a system of 25 to 30 distinct cell membrane and plasma proteins, numbered C1 through C9. Once activated, the proteins interact with each other in a specific sequence called the complement cascade. The classical pathway is triggered by antigen-antibody complexes and includes participation of all complement proteins C1 through C9. The alternate pathway occurs when C3,

C5, and C9 are activated without participation of C1, C2, and C4 or the presence of antigen-antibody complexes. Complement proteins act as enzymes that aid in the immunological and inflammatory response. The complement system is an important mechanism for the destruction and removal of foreign materials. Serum complement levels are used to detect autoimmune diseases. C3 and C4 are the most frequently

C

assayed complement proteins, along with total complement.

Circulating C3 is synthesized in the liver and comprises 70% of the complement system, but cells in other tissues can also produce C3. C3 is an essential activating protein in the classic and alternate complement cascades. It is decreased in patients with immunological diseases, in whom

it is consumed at an increased rate. C4 is produced primarily in the liver but can also be produced by monocytes, fibroblasts, and macrophages. C4 participates in the classic complement pathway.

INDICATIONS
• Detect genetic deficiencies
• Evaluate immunological diseases

POTENTIAL DIAGNOSIS

Normal C4 and decreased C3	Acute glomerulonephritis, membranous glomerulonephritis, immune complex diseases, SLE, C3 deficiency
Decreased C4 and normal C3	Immune complex diseases, cryoglobulinemia, C4 deficiency, hereditary angioedema
Decreased C4 and decreased C3	Immune complex diseases

Increased in
Response to sudden increased demand
• C3 and C4
  Acute-phase reactions
• C3
  Amyloidosis
  Cancer
  Diabetes
  Myocardial infarction
  Pneumococcal pneumonia
  Pregnancy
  Rheumatic disease
  Thyroiditis
  Viral hepatitis
• C4
  Certain malignancies

Decreased in
Related to overconsumption during immune response
• C3 and C4
  Hereditary deficiency *(insufficient production)*
  Liver disease *(insufficient production related to damaged liver cells)*
  SLE

• C3
  Chronic infection (bacterial, parasitic, viral)
  Post-membranoproliferative glomerulonephritis
  Post–streptococcal infection
  Rheumatic arthritis
• C4
  Angioedema *(hereditary and acquired)*
  Autoimmune hemolytic anemia
  Autoimmune thyroiditis
  Cryoglobulinemia
  Glomerulonephritis
  Juvenile dermatomyositis
  Meningitis (bacterial, viral)
  Pneumonia
  Streptococcal or staphylococcal sepsis

CRITICAL FINDINGS: N/A

INTERFERING FACTORS
• Drugs that may increase C3 levels include cimetidine and cyclophosphamide.
• Drugs that may decrease C3 levels include danazol and phenytoin.

- Drugs that may increase C4 levels include cimetidine, cyclophosphamide, and danazol.
- Drugs that may decrease C4 levels include dextran and penicillamine.

NURSING IMPLICATIONS AND PROCEDURE

PRETEST:

- Positively identify the patient using at least two unique identifiers before providing care, treatment, or services.
- *Patient Teaching:* Inform the patient this test can assist in diagnosing diseases of the immune system.
- Obtain a history of the patient's complaints, including a list of known allergens, especially allergies or sensitivities to latex.
- Obtain a history of the patient's immune system and results of previously performed laboratory tests and diagnostic and surgical procedures.
- Obtain a list of the patient's current medications, including herbs, nutritional supplements, and nutraceuticals (see Appendix F).
- Review the procedure with the patient. Inform the patient that specimen collection takes approximately 5 to 10 min. Address concerns about pain and explain that there may be some discomfort during the venipuncture.
- *Sensitivity to social and cultural issues,* as well as concern for modesty, is important in providing psychological support before, during, and after the procedure.
- There are no food, fluid, or medication restrictions unless by medical direction.

INTRATEST:

- If the patient has a history of allergic reaction to latex, avoid the use of equipment containing latex.

- Instruct the patient to cooperate fully and to follow directions. Direct the patient to breathe normally and to avoid unnecessary movement.
- Observe standard precautions, and follow the general guidelines in Appendix A. Positively identify the patient, and label the appropriate specimen container with the corresponding patient demographics, initials of the person collecting the specimen, date, and time of collection. Perform a venipuncture.
- Remove the needle and apply direct pressure with dry gauze to stop bleeding. Observe/assess venipuncture site for bleeding or hematoma formation and secure gauze with adhesive bandage.
- Promptly transport the specimen to the laboratory for processing and analysis.

POST-TEST:

- A report of the results will be made available to the requesting health-care provider (HCP), who will discuss the results with the patient.
- Reinforce information given by the patient's HCP regarding further testing, treatment, or referral to another HCP. Answer any questions or address any concerns voiced by the patient or family.
- Depending on the results of this procedure, additional testing may be performed to evaluate or monitor progression of the disease process and determine the need for a change in therapy. Evaluate test results in relation to the patient's symptoms and other tests performed.

RELATED MONOGRAPHS:

- Related tests include anticardiolipin antibody, ANA, complement total, cryoglobulin, and ESR.
- Refer to the Immune System table at the end of the book for related tests by body system.

Complement, Total

SYNONYM/ACRONYM: Total hemolytic complement, CH_{50}, CH_{100}.

COMMON USE: To evaluate immune diseases related to complement activity and follow up on a patient's response to therapy such as treatment for systemic lupus erythematosus (SLE).

SPECIMEN: Serum (1 mL) collected in a red-top tube.

NORMAL FINDINGS: (Method: Quantitative hemolysis)

Conventional Units	SI Units (Conventional Units × 1)
25–110 CH_{50} units/mL	25–110 CH_{50} kU/L

DESCRIPTION: The complement system comprises proteins that become activated and interact in a sequential cascade. The complement system is an important part of the body's natural defense against allergic and immune reactions. It is activated by plasmin and is interrelated with the coagulation and fibrinolytic systems. Activation of the complement system results in cell lysis, release of histamine, chemotaxis of white blood cells, increased vascular permeability, and contraction of smooth muscle. The activation of this system can sometimes occur with uncontrolled self-destructive effects on the body. In the serum complement assay, a patient's serum is mixed with sheep red blood cells coated with antibodies. If complement is present in sufficient quantities, 50% of the red blood cells are lysed. Lower amounts of lysed cells are associated with decreased complement levels.

INDICATIONS
- Assist in the diagnosis of hereditary angioedema
- Evaluate complement activity in autoimmune disorders
- Evaluate and monitor therapy for systemic lupus erythematosus (SLE)
- Screen for complement deficiency

POTENTIAL DIAGNOSIS

Increased in
- Acute-phase immune response *(related to sudden response to increased demand)*

Decreased in
- Autoimmune diseases *(related to continuous demand)*
- Autoimmune hemolytic anemia *(related to consumption during hemolytic process)*
- Burns *(related to increased consumption from initiation of complement cascade)*
- Cryoglobulinemia *(related to increased consumption)*
- Hereditary deficiency *(related to insufficient production)*
- Infections *(bacterial, parasitic, viral; related to increased*

consumption during immune response)
- Liver disease *(related to decreased production by damaged liver cells)*
- Malignancy *(related to consumption during cellular immune response)*
- Membranous glomerulonephritis *(related to consumption during cellular immune response)*
- Rheumatoid arthritis *(related to consumption during immune response)*
- SLE *(related to consumption during immune response)*
- Trauma *(related to consumption during immune response)*
- Vasculitis *(related to consumption during cellular immune response)*

CRITICAL FINDINGS: N/A

INTERFERING FACTORS
- Drugs that may increase total complement levels include cyclophosphamide and oral contraceptives.
- Specimen should not remain at room temperature longer than 1 hr.

NURSING IMPLICATIONS AND PROCEDURE

PRETEST:
- Positively identify the patient using at least two unique identifiers before providing care, treatment, or services.
- *Patient Teaching:* Inform the patient this test can assist in evaluating response to treatment for infection or disease.
- Obtain a history of the patient's complaints, including a list of known allergens, especially allergies or sensitivities to latex.
- Obtain a history of the patient's immune system and results of previously performed laboratory tests and diagnostic and surgical procedures.
- Obtain a list of the patient's current medications, including herbs,

nutritional supplements, and nutraceuticals (see Appendix F).
- Review the procedure with the patient. Inform the patient that specimen collection takes approximately 5 to 10 min. Address concerns about pain and explain that there may be some discomfort during the venipuncture.
- *Sensitivity to social and cultural issues,* as well as concern for modesty, is important in providing psychological support before, during, and after the procedure.
- There are no food, fluid, or medication restrictions unless by medical direction.

INTRATEST:
- If the patient has a history of allergic reaction to latex, avoid the use of equipment containing latex.
- Instruct the patient to cooperate fully and to follow directions. Direct the patient to breathe normally and to avoid unnecessary movement.
- Observe standard precautions, and follow the general guidelines in Appendix A. Positively identify the patient, and label the appropriate specimen container with the corresponding patient demographics, initials of the person collecting the specimen, date, and time of collection. Perform a venipuncture.
- Remove the needle and apply direct pressure with dry gauze to stop bleeding. Observe/assess venipuncture site for bleeding or hematoma formation and secure gauze with adhesive bandage.
- Promptly transport the specimen to the laboratory for processing and analysis.

POST-TEST:
- A report of the results will be made available to the requesting health-care provider (HCP), who will discuss the results with the patient.
- Reinforce information given by the patient's HCP regarding further testing, treatment, or referral to another HCP. Answer any questions or

address any concerns voiced by the patient or family.

▶ Depending on the results of this procedure, additional testing may be performed to evaluate or monitor progression of the disease process and determine the need for a change in therapy. Evaluate test results in relation to the patient's symptoms and other tests performed.

RELATED MONOGRAPHS:

▶ Related tests include antibody anticytoplasmic neutrophilic, ANA, Coombs' antiglobulin, complement C3 and C4, cryoglobulin, ESR, G6PD, Ham's test, osmotic fragility, PK, and RF.

▶ Refer to the Immune System table at the end of the book for related tests by body system.

Complete Blood Count

SYNONYM/ACRONYM: CBC.

COMMON USE: To evaluate numerous conditions involving red blood cells, white blood cells, and platelets. This test is also used to indicate inflammation, infection, and response to chemotherapy.

SPECIMEN: Whole blood from one full lavender-top (EDTA) tube or Microtainer. Whole blood from a green-top (lithium or sodium heparin) tube may be submitted, but the following automated values may not be reported: white blood cell (WBC) count, WBC differential, platelet count, immature platelet fraction (IPF), and mean platelet volume.

NORMAL FINDINGS: (Method: Automated, computerized, multichannel analyzers. Many of these analyzers are capable of determining a five- or six-part WBC differential.) This battery of tests includes hemoglobin, hematocrit, red blood cell (RBC) count, RBC morphology, RBC indices, RBC distribution width index (RDWCV and RDWSD), platelet count, platelet size, IPF, WBC count, and WBC differential. The six-part automated WBC differential identifies and enumerates neutrophils, lymphocytes, monocytes, eosinophils, basophils, and immature granulocytes (IG), where IG represents the combined enumeration of promyelocytes, metamyelocytes, and myelocytes as both an absolute number and a percentage. The five-part WBC differential includes all but the IG parameters.)

Hemoglobin

Age	Conventional Units	SI Units (Conventional Units × 10)
Cord blood	13.5–20.7 g/dL	135–207 mmol/L
0–1 wk	15.2–23.6 g/dL	152–236 mmol/L
2–3 wk	12.7–18.7 g/dL	127–187 mmol/L

Age	Conventional Units	SI Units (Conventional Units × 10)
1–2 mo	9.7–17.3 g/dL	97–173 mmol/L
3–11 mo	9.3–13.3 g/dL	93–133 mmol/L
1–5 yr	10.4–13.6 g/dL	104–136 mmol/L
6–8 yr	10.9–14.5 g/dL	109–145 mmol/L
9–14 yr	11.5–15.5 g/dL	115–155 mmol/L
15 yr–adult		
Male	13.2–17.3 g/dL	132–173 mmol/L
Female	11.7–15.5 g/dL	117–155 mmol/L
Older adult		
Male	12.6–17.4 g/dL	126–174 mmol/L
Female	11.7–16.1 g/dL	117–161 mmol/L

Note: See "Complete Blood Count, Hemoglobin" monograph for more detailed information.

Hematocrit

Age	Conventional Units (%)	SI Units (Conventional Units × 0.01)
Cord blood	42–62	0.42–0.62
0–1 wk	46–68	0.46–0.68
2–3 wk	40–56	0.41–0.56
1–2 mo	32–54	0.32–0.54
3 mo–5 yr	31–43	0.31–0.43
6–8 yr	33–41	0.33–0.41
9–14 yr	33–45	0.33–0.45
15 yr–adult		
Male	38–51	0.38–0.51
Female	33–45	0.33–0.45
Older adult		
Male	36–52	0.36–0.52
Female	34–46	0.34–0.46

Note: See "Complete Blood Count, Hematocrit" monograph for more detailed information.

White Blood Cell Count and Differential

Age	Conventional Units WBC × 10³/microL	Neutrophils			Lymphocytes	Monocytes	Eosinophils	Basophils
		Total Neutrophils (Absolute) and %	Bands (Absolute) and %	Segments (Absolute) and %	(Absolute) and %	(Absolute) and %	(Absolute) and %	(Absolute) and %
Birth	9.1–30.1	(5.5–18.3) 61%	(0.8–2.7) 9.1%	(4.7–15.6) 52%	(2.8–9.3) 31%	(0.5–1.7) 5.8%	(0.02–0.7) 2.2%	(0.1–0.2) 0.6%
1–23 mo	6.1–17.5	(1.9–5.4) 31%	(0.2–0.5) 3.1%	(1.7–4.9) 28%	(3.7–10.7) 61%	(0.3–0.8) 4.8%	(0.2–0.5) 2.6%	(0–0.1) 0.5%
2–10 yr	4.5–13.5	(2.4–7.3) 54%	(0.1–0.4) 3.0%	(2.3–6.9) 51%	(1.7–5.1) 38%	(0.2–0.6) 4.3%	(0.1–0.3) 2.4%	(0–0.1) 0.5%
11 yr–older adult	4.5–11.1	(2.7–6.5) 59%	(0.1–0.3) 3.0%	(2.5–6.2) 56%	(1.5–3.7) 34%	(0.2–0.4) 4.0%	(0.05–0.5) 2.7%	(0–0.1) 0.5%

*SI Units (Conventional Units × 1 or WBC × 10⁹/L).

Note: See "Complete Blood Count, WBC Count and Differential" monograph for more detailed information.

White Blood Cell Count and Differential

Age	Immature Granulocytes (Absolute) (10³/microL)	Immature Granulocyte Fraction (IGF) (%)
Birth–9 yr	0–0.03	0–0.4%
10 yr–older adult	0–0.09	0–0.9%

Red Blood Cell Count

Age	Conventional Units (10^6 cells/microL)	SI Units (10^{12} cells/L) (Conventional Units × 1)
Cord blood	3:61–5.81	3.61–5.81
0–1 wk	4.51–7.01	4.51–7.01
2–3 wk	3.71–6.11	3.71–6.11
1–2 mo	3.11–5.11	3.11–5.11
3–11 mo	3.01–5.01	3.01–5.01
1–5 yr	3.81–5.01	3.81–5.01
6–8 yr	3.91–5.11	3.91–5.11
9–14 yr	3.91–5.61	3.91–5.61
15 yr–adult		
Male	5.21–5.81	5.21–5.81
Female	3.91–5.11	3.91–5.11
Older adult		
Male	3.81–5.81	3.81–5.81
Female	3.71–5.31	3.71–5.31

Note: See "Complete Blood Count, RBC Count" monograph for more detailed information.

Red Blood Cell Indices

Age	MCV (fl)	MCH (pg/cell)	MCHC (g/dL)	RDW	RDWSD
Cord blood	107–119	35–39	31–35	14.9–18.7	51–66
0–1 wk	104–116	29–45	24–36	14.9–18.7	51–66
2–3 wk	95–117	26–38	26–34	14.9–18.7	51–66
1–2 mo	81–125	25–37	26–34	14.9–18.7	44–55
3–11 mo	78–110	22–34	26–34	14.9–18.7	35–46
1–5 yr	74–94	24–32	30–34	11.6–14.8	35–42
6–8 yr	73–93	24–32	32–36	11.6–14.8	35–42
9–14 yr	74–94	25–33	32–36	11.6–14.8	37–44
15 yr–adult					
Male	77–97	26–34	32–36	11.6–14.8	38–48
Female	78–98	26–34	32–36	11.6–14.8	38–48
Older adult					
Male	79–103	27–35	32–36	11.6–14.8	38–48
Female	78–102	27–35	32–36	11.6–14.8	38–48

MCH = mean corpuscular hemoglobin; MCHC = mean corpuscular hemoglobin concentration; MCV = mean corpuscular volume; RDWCV = coefficient of variation in RBC distribution width index; RDWSD = standard deviation in RBC distribution width index.
Note: See "Complete Blood Count, RBC Indices" monograph for more detailed information.

Red Blood Cell Morphology

Morphology	Within Normal Limits	1+	2+	3+	4+
Size					
Anisocytosis	0–5	5–10	10–20	20–50	Greater than 50
Macrocytes	0–5	5–10	10–20	20–50	Greater than 50
Microcytes	0–5	5–10	10–20	20–50	Greater than 50
Shape					
Poikilocytes	0–2	3–10	10–20	20–50	Greater than 50
Burr cells	0–2	3–10	10–20	20–50	Greater than 50
Acanthocytes	Less than 1	2–5	5–10	10–20	Greater than 20
Schistocytes	Less than 1	2–5	5–10	10–20	Greater than 20
Dacryocytes (teardrop cells)	0–2	2–5	5–10	10–20	Greater than 20
Codocytes (target cells)	0–2	2–10	10–20	20–50	Greater than 50
Spherocytes	0–2	2–10	10–20	20–50	Greater than 50
Ovalocytes	0–2	2–10	10–20	20–50	Greater than 50
Stomatocytes	0–2	2–10	10–20	20–50	Greater than 50
Drepanocytes (sickle cells)	Absent	Reported as present or absent			
Helmet cells	Absent	Reported as present or absent			
Agglutination	Absent	Reported as present or absent			
Rouleaux	Absent	Reported as present or absent			
Hemoglobin Content					
Hypochromia	0–2	3–10	10–50	50–75	Greater than 75
Polychromasia					
Adult	Less than 1	2–5	5–10	10–20	Greater than 20
Newborn	1–6	7–15	15–20	20–50	Greater than 50

Note: See "Complete Blood Count, RBC Morphology and Inclusions" monograph for more detailed information.

Red Blood Cell Inclusions

Inclusions	Within Normal Limits	1+	2+	3+	4+
Cabot's rings	Absent	Reported as present or absent			
Basophilic stippling	0–1	1–5	5–10	10–20	Greater than 20
Howell-Jolly bodies	Absent	1–2	3–5	5–10	Greater than 10
Heinz bodies	Absent	Reported as present or absent			
Hemoglobin C crystals	Absent	Reported as present or absent			
Pappenheimer bodies	Absent	Reported as present or absent			
Intracellular parasites (e.g., *Plasmodium, Babesia,* trypanosomes)	Absent	Reported as present or absent			

Note: See "Complete Blood Count, RBC Morphology and Inclusions" monograph for more detailed information.

Platelet Count

Age	Conventional Units	SI Units (Conventional Units × 1)	MPV (fl)	IPF (%)
Newborn				
Male	150–350 × 10³/microL	150–350 × 10⁹/L	7.1–10.2	1.1–7.1
Female	235–345 × 10³/microL	235–345 × 10⁹/L	7.3–10.2	1.1–7.1
1–2 mo				
Male	275–565 × 10³/microL	275–565 × 10⁹/L	7.1–11.3	1.1–7.1
Female	295–615 × 10³/microL	295–615 × 10⁹/L	7.4–9.7	1.1–7.1
3–6 mo				
Male	275–565 × 10³/microL	275–565 × 10⁹/L	6.8–9.1	1.1–7.1
Female	288–598 × 10³/microL	288–598 × 10⁹/L	7.2–8.9	1.1–7.1
7–23 mo				
Male	220–450 × 10³/microL	220–450 × 10⁹/L	7.1–9.3	1.1–7.1
Female	230–465 × 10³/microL	230–465 × 10⁹/L	7.1–9.3	1.1–7.1
2–6 yr				
Male & Female	205–405 × 10³/microL	205–405 × 10⁹/L	7.1–9.3	1.1–7.1
7–12 yr				
Male	195–365 × 10³/microL	195–365 × 10⁹/L	7.2–9.4	1.1–7.1
Female	185–370 × 10³/microL	185–370 × 10⁹/L	7.1–9.2	1.1–7.1
12–18 yr				
Male	165–332 × 10³/microL	165–332 × 10⁹/L	7.3–9.7	1.1–7.1
Female	185–335 × 10³/microL	185–335 × 10⁹/L	7.5–9.3	1.1–7.1
Adult/Older adult				
Male & Female	150–450 × 10³/microL	150–450 × 10⁹/L	7.1–10.2	1.1–7.1

Note: See "Complete Blood Count, Platelet Count" monograph for more detailed information. Platelet counts may decrease slightly with age.

DESCRIPTION: A complete blood count (CBC) is a group of tests used for basic screening purposes. It is probably the most widely ordered laboratory test. Results provide the enumeration of the cellular elements of the blood, measurement of red blood cell (RBC) indices, and determination of cell morphology by automation and evaluation of stained smears. The results can provide valuable diagnostic information regarding the overall health of the patient and the patient's response to disease and treatment. Detailed information is found in monographs titled "Complete Blood Count, Hemoglobin"; "Complete Blood Count, Hematocrit"; "Complete Blood Count, RBC Indices"; "Complete Blood Count, RBC Morphology and Inclusions"; "Complete Blood Count, RBC Count"; "Complete Blood Count, Platelet Count"; and "Complete Blood Count, WBC Count and Cell Differential."

INDICATIONS
- Detect hematological disorder, neoplasm, leukemia, or immunological abnormality
- Determine the presence of hereditary hematological abnormality
- Evaluate known or suspected anemia and related treatment
- Monitor blood loss and response to blood replacement
- Monitor the effects of physical or emotional stress
- Monitor fluid imbalances or treatment for fluid imbalances
- Monitor hematological status during pregnancy
- Monitor progression of nonhematological disorders, such as chronic obstructive pulmonary disease, malabsorption syndromes, cancer, and renal disease

- Monitor response to chemotherapy and evaluate undesired reactions to drugs that may cause blood dyscrasias
- Provide screening as part of a general physical examination, especially on admission to a health-care facility or before surgery

POTENTIAL DIAGNOSIS
- See monographs titled "Complete Blood Count, Hemoglobin"; "Complete Blood Count, Hematocrit"; "Complete Blood Count, RBC Indices"; "Complete Blood Count, RBC Morphology and Inclusions"; "Complete Blood Count, RBC Count"; "Complete Blood Count, Platelet Count"; and "Complete Blood Count, WBC Count and Differential."

Increased in
- See above-listed monographs.

Decreased in
- See above-listed monographs.

CRITICAL FINDINGS
Hemoglobin
Adults & children
- Less than 6.6 g/dL (SI: Less than 66 mmol/L)
- Greater than 20 g/dL (SI: Greater than 200 mmol/L)

Newborns
- Less than 9.5 g/dL (SI: Less than 95 mmol/L)
- Greater than 22.3 g/dL (SI: Greater than 223 mmol/L)

Hematocrit
Adults & children
- Less than 19.8% (SI: Less than 0.2 L/L)
- Greater than 60% (SI: Greater than 0.6 L/L)

Newborns
- Less than 28.5% (SI: Less than 0.28 L/L)
- Greater than 66.9% (SI: Greater than 0.67 L/L)

WBC Count (on Admission)
- Less than 2.5 × 10³/microL (SI: Less than 2.5 × 10⁹/L)
- Greater than 30 × 10³/microL (SI: Greater than 30 × 10⁹/L)

Platelet Count
- Less than 50 × 10³/microL (SI: Less than 50 × 10⁹/L)
- Greater than 1,000 × 10³/microL (SI: Greater than 1,000 × 10⁹/L)

Note and immediately report to the health-care provider (HCP) any critically increased or decreased values and related symptoms. Timely notification of critical values for lab or diagnostic studies is a role expectation of the professional nurse. Notification processes will vary among facilities. Upon receipt of the critical value, the information should be read back to the caller to verify accuracy. Most policies require immediate notification of the primary HCP, hospitalist, or on-call HCP. Reported information includes the patient's name, unique identifiers, critical value, name of the person giving the report, and name of the person receiving the report. Documentation of notification should be made in the medical record with the name of the HCP notified, time and date of notification, and any orders received. Any delay in a timely report of a critical value may require completion of a notification form with review by Risk Management.

The presence of abnormal cells, other morphological characteristics, or cellular inclusions may signify a potentially life-threatening or serious health condition and should be investigated. Examples are the presence of sickle cells, moderate numbers of spherocytes, marked schistocytosis, oval macrocytes, basophilic stippling, eosinophil count greater than 10%, monocytosis greater than 15%, nucleated RBCs (if patient is not an infant), malarial organisms, hypersegmented neutrophils, agranular neutrophils, blasts or other immature cells, Auer rods, Döhle bodies, marked toxic granulation, or plasma cells.

INTERFERING FACTORS
- Failure to fill the tube sufficiently (less than three-fourths full) may yield inadequate sample volume for automated analyzers and may be a reason for specimen rejection.
- Hemolyzed or clotted specimens should be rejected for analysis.
- Elevated serum glucose or sodium levels may produce elevated mean corpuscular volume values because of swelling of erythrocytes.
- Recent transfusion history should be considered when evaluating the CBC.

NURSING IMPLICATIONS AND PROCEDURE

PRETEST:
▶ Positively identify the patient using at least two unique identifiers before providing care, treatment, or services.
▶ *Patient Teaching:* Inform the patient this test can assist in evaluating general health and the body's response to illness.
▶ Obtain a history of the patient's complaints, including a list of known allergens, especially allergies or sensitivities to latex.
▶ Obtain a history of the patient's gastrointestinal, hematopoietic, immune, and respiratory systems as well as results of previously performed laboratory tests and diagnostic and surgical procedures.
▶ Obtain a list of the patient's current medications, including herbs, nutritional supplements, and nutraceuticals (see Appendix F).
▶ Review the procedure with the patient. Inform the patient that specimen

collection takes approximately 5 to 10 min. Address concerns about pain and explain that there may be some discomfort during the venipuncture.

Sensitivity to social and cultural issues, as well as concern for modesty, is important in providing psychological support before, during, and after the procedure.

There are no food, fluid, or medication restrictions unless by medical direction.

INTRATEST:

If the patient has a history of allergic reaction to latex, avoid the use of equipment containing latex.

Instruct the patient to cooperate fully and to follow directions. Direct the patient to breathe normally and to avoid unnecessary movement.

Observe standard precautions, and follow the general guidelines in Appendix A. Positively identify the patient, and label the appropriate specimen container with the corresponding patient demographics, initials of the person collecting the specimen, date, and time of collection. Perform a venipuncture. An EDTA Microtainer sample may be obtained from infants, children, and adults for whom venipuncture may not be feasible. The specimen should be analyzed within 24 hr when stored at room temperature or within 48 hr if stored at refrigerated temperature. If it is anticipated the specimen will not be analyzed within 24 hr, two blood smears should be made immediately after the venipuncture and submitted with the blood sample. Smears made from specimens older than 24 hr may contain an unacceptable number of misleading artifactual abnormalities of the RBCs, such as echinocytes and spherocytes, as well as necrobiotic white blood cells.

Remove the needle and apply direct pressure with dry gauze to stop bleeding. Observe/assess venipuncture site for bleeding or hematoma formation and secure gauze with adhesive bandage.

Promptly transport the specimen to the laboratory for processing and analysis.

POST-TEST:

A report of the results will be made available to the requesting HCP, who will discuss the results with the patient.

Nutritional Considerations: Instruct patients to consume a variety of foods within the basic food groups, maintain a healthy weight, be physically active, limit salt intake, limit alcohol intake, and avoid use of tobacco.

Reinforce information given by the patient's HCP regarding further testing, treatment, or referral to another HCP. Answer any questions or address any concerns voiced by the patient or family.

Depending on the results of this procedure, additional testing may be performed to evaluate or monitor progression of the disease process and determine the need for a change in therapy. Evaluate test results in relation to the patient's symptoms and other tests performed.

RELATED MONOGRAPHS:

Related tests include alveolar arterial ratio, biopsy bone marrow, blood gases, blood groups and antibodies, erythropoietin, ferritin, CBC hematocrit, CBC hemoglobin, CBC platelet count, CBC RBC count, CBC RBC indices, CBC RBC morphology, CBC WBC count and cell differential, iron/TIBC, lead, pulse oximetry, reticulocyte count, and US abdomen.

Refer to the Gastrointestinal, Hematopoietic, Immune, and Respiratory systems tables at the end of the book for related tests by body system.

C

Complete Blood Count, Hematocrit

SYNONYM/ACRONYM: Packed cell volume (PCV), Hct.

COMMON USE: To evaluate anemia, polycythemia, and hydration status and to monitor therapy.

SPECIMEN: Whole blood from one full lavender-top (EDTA) tube, Microtainer, or capillary. Whole blood from a green-top (lithium or sodium heparin) tube may also be submitted.

NORMAL FINDINGS: (Method: Automated, computerized, multichannel analyzers)

Age	Conventional Units (%)	SI Units (Conventional Units × 0.01)
Cord blood	42–62	0.42–0.62
0–1 wk	46–68	0.46–0.68
2–3 wk	40–56	0.41–0.56
1–2 mo	32–54	0.32–0.54
3 mo–5 yr	31–43	0.31–0.43
6–8 yr	33–41	0.33–0.41
9–14 yr	33–45	0.33–0.45
15 yr–adult		
Male	38–51	0.38–0.51
Female	33–45	0.33–0.45
Older adult		
Male	36–52	0.36–0.52
Female	34–46	0.34–0.46

DESCRIPTION: Blood consists of a fluid portion (plasma) and a solid portion that includes red blood cells (RBCs), white blood cells, and platelets. The hematocrit, or packed cell volume, is the percentage of RBCs in a volume of whole blood. For example, a hematocrit (Hct) of 45% means that a 100-mL sample of blood contains 45 mL of packed RBCs. Although the Hct depends primarily on the number of RBCs, the average size of the RBCs plays a role. Conditions that cause the RBCs to swell, such as when the serum sodium concentration is elevated, may increase the Hct level.

Hct level is included in the complete blood count (CBC) and is generally tested together with hemoglobin (Hgb). These levels parallel each other and are the best determinant of the degree of anemia or polycythemia. *Polycythemia* is a term used in conjunction with conditions resulting from an abnormal increase in Hgb, Hct, and RBC counts. *Anemia* is a term associated with conditions resulting from

C

an abnormal decrease in Hgb, Hct, and RBC counts. Results of the Hgb, Hct, and RBC counts should be evaluated simultaneously because the same underlying conditions affect this triad of tests similarly. The RBC count multiplied by 3 should approximate the Hgb concentration. The Hct should be within 3 times the Hgb if the RBC population is normal in size and shape. The Hct plus 6 should approximate the first two figures of the RBC count within 3 (e.g., Hct is 40%; therefore 40 + 6 = 46, and the RBC count should be 4.6 or in the range of 4.3 to 4.9). There are some cultural variations in Hgb and Hct (H&H) values. After the first decade of life, the mean Hgb in African Americans is 0.5 to 1.0 g lower than in whites. Mexican Americans and Asian Americans have higher H&H values than whites.

INDICATIONS

Detect hematological disorder, neoplasm, or immunological abnormality

Determine the presence of hereditary hematological abnormality

Evaluate known or suspected anemia and related treatment, in combination with Hgb

Monitor blood loss and response to blood replacement, in combination with Hgb

Monitor the effects of physical or emotional stress on the patient

Monitor fluid imbalances or their treatment

Monitor hematological status during pregnancy, in combination with Hgb

Monitor the progression of nonhematological disorders such as chronic obstructive pulmonary disease, malabsorption syndromes, cancer, and renal disease

• Monitor response to drugs or chemotherapy, and evaluate undesired reactions to drugs that may cause blood dyscrasias

• Provide screening as part of a CBC in a general physical examination, especially upon admission to a health-care facility or before surgery

POTENTIAL DIAGNOSIS

Increased in

• Burns *(related to dehydration; total blood volume is decreased, but RBC count remains the same)*

• Congestive heart failure *(when the underlying cause is anemia, the body responds by increasing production of RBCs with a corresponding increase in Hct)*

• Chronic obstructive pulmonary disease *(related to chronic hypoxia that stimulates production of RBC and a corresponding increase in Hct)*

• Dehydration *(total blood volume is decreased, but RBC count remains the same)*

• Erythrocytosis *(total blood volume remains the same, but RBC count is increased)*

• Hemoconcentration *(same effect as seen in dehydration)*

• High altitudes *(related to hypoxia that stimulates production of RBC and therefore increases Hct)*

• Polycythemia *(abnormal bone marrow response resulting in overproduction of RBC)*

• Shock

Decreased in

• Anemia *(overall decrease in RBC and corresponding decrease in Hct)*

- Blood loss (acute and chronic) *(overall decrease in RBC and corresponding decrease in Hct)*
- Bone marrow hyperplasia *(bone marrow failure that results in decreased RBC production)*
- Carcinoma *(anemia is often associated with chronic disease)*
- Cirrhosis *(related to accumulation of fluid)*
- Chronic disease *(anemia is often associated with chronic disease)*
- Fluid retention *(dilutional effect of increased blood volume while RBC count remains stable)*
- Hemoglobinopathies *(reduced RBC survival with corresponding decrease in Hgb)*
- Hemolytic disorders (e.g., hemolytic anemias, prosthetic valves) *(reduced RBC survival with corresponding decrease in Hct)*
- Hemorrhage (acute and chronic) *(related to loss of RBC that exceeds rate of production)*
- Hodgkin's disease *(bone marrow failure that results in decreased RBC production)*
- Incompatible blood transfusion *(reduced RBC survival with corresponding decrease in Hgb)*
- Intravenous overload *(dilutional effect)*
- Fluid retention *(dilutional effect of increased blood volume while RBC count remains stable)*
- Leukemia *(bone marrow failure that results in decreased RBC production)*
- Lymphomas *(bone marrow failure that results in decreased RBC production)*
- Nutritional deficit *(anemia related to dietary deficiency in iron, vitamins, folate needed to produce sufficient RBC; decreased RBC*

count with corresponding decrease in Hct)*
- Pregnancy *(related to anemia)*
- Renal disease *(related to decreased levels of erythropoietin, which stimulates production of RBCs)*
- Splenomegaly *(total blood volume remains the same, but spleen retains RBCs and Hct reflects decreased RBC count)*

CRITICAL FINDINGS

Adults & children
- Less than 19.8% (SI: Less than 0.2 L/L)
- Greater than 60% (SI: Greater than 0.6 L/L)

Newborns
- Less than 28.5% (SI: Less than 0.28 L/L)
- Greater than 66.9% (SI: Greater than 0.67 L/L)

Note and immediately report to the health-care provider (HCP) any critically increased or decreased values and related symptoms. Timely notification of critical values for lab or diagnostic studies is a role expectation of the professional nurse. Notification processes will vary among facilities. Upon receipt of the critical value, the information should be read back to the caller to verify accuracy. Most policies require immediate notification of the primary HCP, hospitalist, or on-call HCP. Reported information includes the patient's name, unique identifier, critical value, name of the person giving the report, and name of the person receiving the report. Documentation of notification should be made in the medical record with the name of the HCP notified, time and date of notification, and any orders received. Any delay in a timely report of a critical value may require completion of a notification form with review by Risk Management.

Low Hct leads to anemia. Anemia can be caused by blood loss, decreased blood cell production, increased blood cell destruction, and hemodilution. Causes of blood loss include menstrual excess or frequency, gastrointestinal bleeding, inflammatory bowel disease, and hematuria. Decreased blood cell production can be caused by folic acid deficiency, vitamin B_{12} deficiency, iron deficiency, and chronic disease. Increased blood cell destruction can be caused by a hemolytic reaction, chemical reaction, medication reaction, and sickle cell disease. Hemodilution can be caused by congestive heart failure, renal failure, polydipsia, and overhydration. Symptoms of anemia (due to these causes) include anxiety, dyspnea, edema, hypertension, hypotension, hypoxia, jugular venous distention, fatigue, pallor, rales, restlessness, and weakness. Treatment of anemia depends on the cause.

High Hct leads to polycythemia. Polycythemia can be caused by dehydration, decreased oxygen levels in the body, and an overproduction of RBCs by the bone marrow. Dehydration from diuretic use, vomiting, diarrhea, excessive sweating, severe burns, or decreased fluid intake decreases the plasma component of whole blood, thereby increasing the ratio of RBCs to plasma, and leads to a higher than normal Hct. Causes of decreased oxygen include smoking, exposure to carbon monoxide, high altitude, and chronic lung disease, which leads to a mild hemoconcentration of blood in the body to carry more oxygen to the body's tissues. An overproduction of RBCs by the bone marrow leads to polycythemia vera, which is a rare chronic myeloproliferative disorder that leads to a severe hemoconcentration of blood. Severe hemoconcentration can lead to thrombosis (spontaneous blood clotting). Symptoms of hemoconcentration include decreased pulse pressure and volume, loss of skin turgor, dry mucous membranes, headaches, hepatomegaly, low central venous pressure, orthostatic hypotension, pruritus (especially after a hot bath), splenomegaly, tachycardia, thirst, tinnitus, vertigo, and weakness. Treatment of polycythemia depends on the cause. Possible interventions for hemoconcentration due to dehydration include intravenous fluids and discontinuance of diuretics if they are believed to be contributing to critically elevated Hct. Polycythemia due to decreased oxygen states can be treated by removal of the offending substance, such as smoke or carbon monoxide. Treatment includes oxygen therapy in cases of smoke inhalation, carbon monoxide poisoning, and desaturating chronic lung disease. Symptoms of polycythemic overload crisis include signs of thrombosis, pain and redness in the extremities, facial flushing, and irritability. Possible interventions for hemoconcentration due to polycythemia include therapeutic phlebotomy and intravenous fluids.

INTERFERING FACTORS

- Drugs and substances that may cause a decrease in Hct include those that induce hemolysis due to drug sensitivity or enzyme deficiency and those that result in anemia (see monograph titled "Complete Blood Count, RBC Count").
- Some drugs may also affect Hct values by increasing the RBC count (see monograph titled "Complete Blood Count, RBC Count").
- The results of RBC counts may vary depending on the patient's position: Hct can decrease when the patient is recumbent as a result of hemodilution and can increase when the patient rises as a result of hemoconcentration.

- Leaving the tourniquet in place for longer than 60 sec can falsely increase Hct levels by 2% to 5%.
- Traumatic venipuncture and hemolysis may result in falsely decreased Hct values.
- Failure to fill the tube sufficiently (i.e., tube less than three-quarters full) may yield inadequate sample volume for automated analyzers and may be a reason for specimen rejection.
- Clotted or hemolyzed specimens must be rejected for analysis.
- Care should be taken in evaluating the Hct during the first few hours after transfusion or acute blood loss because the value may appear to be normal and may not be a reliable indicator of anemia.
- Abnormalities in the RBC size (macrocytes, microcytes) or shape (spherocytes, sickle cells) may alter Hct values, as in diseases and conditions including sickle cell anemia, hereditary spherocytosis, and iron deficiency.
- Elevated blood glucose or serum sodium levels may produce elevated Hct levels because of swelling of the erythrocytes.

NURSING IMPLICATIONS AND PROCEDURE

PRETEST:

▶ Positively identify the patient using at least two unique identifiers before providing care, treatment, or services.
▶ *Patient Teaching:* Inform the patient this test can assist in evaluating the body's blood cell volume status.
▶ Obtain a history of the patient's complaints, including a list of known allergens, especially allergies or sensitivities to latex.
▶ Obtain a history of the patient's cardiovascular, gastrointestinal, hematopoietic, hepatobiliary, immune,

and respiratory systems; symptoms; and results of previously performed laboratory tests and diagnostic and surgical procedures.
▶ Note any recent procedures that can interfere with test results.
▶ Obtain a list of the patient's current medications, including herbs, nutritional supplements, and nutraceuticals (see Appendix F).
▶ Review the procedure with the patient. Inform the patient that specimen collection takes approximately 5 to 10 min. Address concerns about pain and explain that there may be some discomfort during the venipuncture.
▶ *Sensitivity to social and cultural issues,* as well as concern for modesty, is important in providing psychological support before, during, and after the procedure.
▶ There are no food, fluid, or medication restrictions unless by medical direction.

INTRATEST:

▶ If the patient has a history of allergic reaction to latex, avoid the use of equipment containing latex.
▶ Instruct the patient to cooperate fully and to follow directions. Direct the patient to breathe normally and to avoid unnecessary movement.
▶ Observe standard precautions, and follow the general guidelines in Appendix A. Positively identify the patient, and label the appropriate tubes with the corresponding patient demographics, date, and time of collection. Perform a venipuncture; collect the specimen in a 5-mL lavender-top (EDTA) tube. An EDTA Microtainer sample may be obtained from infants, children, and adults for whom venipuncture may not be feasible. The specimen should be mixed gently by inverting the tube 10 times. The specimen should be analyzed within 24 hr when stored at room temperature or within 48 hr if stored at refrigerated temperature. If it is anticipated the specimen will not be analyzed within 24 hr, two blood smears should be made immediately after the venipuncture and submitted with the blood sample. Smears made from specimens older than 24 hr may contain an

unacceptable number of misleading artifactual abnormalities of the RBCs, such as echinocytes and spherocytes, as well as necrobiotic white blood cells.
- Remove the needle and apply direct pressure with dry gauze to stop bleeding. Observe/assess venipuncture site for bleeding or hematoma formation and secure gauze with adhesive bandage.
- Promptly transport the specimen to the laboratory for processing and analysis.

POST-TEST:

- A report of the results will be made available to the requesting HCP, who will discuss the results with the patient.
- *Nutritional Considerations:* Nutritional therapy may be indicated for patients with increased Hct if iron levels are also elevated. Educate the patient with abnormally elevated iron values, as appropriate, on the importance of reading food labels. Patients with hemochromatosis or acute pernicious anemia should be educated to avoid foods rich in iron. Iron absorption is affected by numerous factors that may enhance or decrease absorption regardless of the original content of the iron-containing dietary source (see monograph titled "Iron"). Iron levels in foods can be increased if foods are cooked in cookware containing iron. Consumption of large amounts of alcohol damages the intestine and allows increased absorption of iron. A high intake of calcium and ascorbic acid also increases iron absorption. Iron absorption after a meal is also increased by factors in meat, fish, and poultry.
- *Nutritional Considerations:* Nutritional therapy may be indicated for patients with decreased Hct. Iron deficiency is the most common nutrient deficiency in the United States. The Institute of Medicine's Food and Nutrition Board suggests 8 mg as the daily recommended dietary allowance of iron for adult males and females age 51 to greater than 70 yr; 18 mg/d for adult females age 19 to 50 yr;

8 mg/d for adult males age 19 to 50 yr; 27 mg/d for pregnant females under age 18 through 50 yr; 9 mg/d for lactating females age 19 to 50 yr; 10 mg/d for lactating females under age 18 yr; 15 mg/d for female children age 14 to 18 yr; 11 mg/d for male children age 14 to 18 yr; 8 mg/d for children age 9 to 13 yr; 10 mg/d for children age 4 to 8 yr; 7 mg/d for children age 1 to 3 yr; 11 mg/d for children age 7 to 12 mo; 0.27 mg/d for children age 0 to 6 mo (recommended adequate intake). Reprinted with permission from the National Academies Press, copyright 2013, National Academy of Sciences. Patients at risk (e.g., children, pregnant women, women of childbearing age, and low-income populations) should be instructed to include in their diet foods that are high in iron, such as meats (especially liver), eggs, grains, green leafy vegetables, and multivitamins with iron. Educate the patient with abnormally elevated iron values, as appropriate, on the importance of reading food labels. Iron absorption is affected by numerous factors, enhancing or decreasing absorption regardless of the original content of the iron containing dietary source (see monograph titled "Iron"). Iron absorption is affected by numerous factors, enhancing or decreasing absorption regardless of the original content of the iron containing dietary source (see monograph titled "Iron"). Iron absorption is decreased by the absence (gastric resection) or diminished presence (use of antacids) of gastric acid. Phytic acids from cereals; tannins from tea and coffee; oxalic acid from vegetables; and minerals such as copper, zinc, and manganese interfere with iron absorption.
- Reinforce information given by the patient's HCP regarding further testing, treatment, or referral to another HCP. Answer any questions or address any concerns voiced by the patient or family. Educate the patient regarding access to nutritional counseling services. Provide contact information, if desired, for the Institute

of Medicine of the National Academies (www.iom.edu).

▶ Depending on the results of this procedure, additional testing may be performed to evaluate or monitor progression of the disease process and determine the need for a change in therapy. Evaluate test results in relation to the patient's symptoms and other tests performed.

RELATED MONOGRAPHS:

▶ Related tests include biopsy bone marrow, CBC, CBC hemoglobin, CBC RBC indices, CBC RBC morphology, erythropoietin, ferritin, iron/TIBC, reticulocyte count, and US abdomen.

▶ Refer to the Cardiovascular, Gastrointestinal, Hematopoietic, Hepatobiliary, Immune, and Respiratory systems tables at the end of the book for related tests by body system.

Complete Blood Count, Hemoglobin

SYNONYM/ACRONYM: Hgb.

COMMON USE: To evaluate anemia, polycythemia, hydration status, and monitor therapy such as transfusion.

SPECIMEN: Whole blood from one full lavender-top (EDTA) tube, Microtainer, or capillary. Whole blood from a green-top (lithium or sodium heparin) tube may also be submitted.

NORMAL FINDINGS: (Method: Spectrophotometry)

Age	Conventional Units	SI Units (Conventional Units × 10)
Cord blood	13.5–20.7 g/dL	135–207 g/L
0–1 wk	15.2–23.6 g/dL	152–236 g/L
2–3 wk	12.7–18.7 g/dL	127–187 g/L
1–2 mo	9.7–17.3 g/dL	97–173 g/L
3–11 mo	9.3–13.3 g/dL	93–133 g/L
1–5 yr	10.4–13.6 g/dL	104–136 g/L
6–8 yr	10.9–14.5 g/dL	109–145 g/L
9–14 yr	11.5–15.5 g/dL	115–155 g/L
15 yr–adult		
Male	13.2–17.3 g/dL	132–173 g/L
Female	11.7–15.5 g/dL	117–155 g/L
Older adult		
Male	12.6–17.4 g/dL	126–174 g/L
Female	11.7–16.1 g/dL	117–161 g/L

DESCRIPTION: Hemoglobin (Hgb) is the main intracellular protein of erythrocytes. It carries oxygen (O_2) to and removes carbon dioxide (CO_2) from red blood cells (RBCs). It also serves as a buffer to maintain acid-base balance in the extracellular fluid. Each Hgb molecule consists of heme and globulin. Copper is a cofactor necessary for the enzymatic incorporation of iron molecules into heme. Heme contains iron and porphyrin molecules that have a high affinity for O_2. The affinity of Hgb molecules for O_2 is influenced by 2,3-diphosphoglycerate (2,3-DPG), a substance produced by anaerobic glycolysis to generate energy for the RBCs. When Hgb binds with 2,3-DPG, O_2 affinity decreases. The ability of Hgb to bind and release O_2 can be graphically represented by an oxyhemoglobin dissociation curve. The term *shift to the left* describes an increase in the affinity of Hgb for O_2. Conditions that can cause this leftward shift include decreased body temperature, decreased 2,3-DPG, decreased CO_2 concentration, and increased pH. Conversely, a *shift to the right* represents a decrease in the affinity of Hgb for O_2. Conditions that can cause a rightward shift include increased body temperature, increased 2,3-DPG levels, increased CO_2 concentration, and decreased pH.

Hgb levels are a direct reflection of the O_2-combining capacity of the blood. It is the combination of heme and O_2 that gives blood its characteristic red color. RBC counts parallel the O_2-combining capacity of Hgb, but because some RBCs contain more Hgb than others, the relationship is not directly proportional. As CO_2 diffuses into RBCs, an enzyme called carbonic anhydrase converts the CO_2 into

bicarbonate and hydrogen ions. Hgb that is not bound to O_2 combines with the free hydrogen ions, increasing pH. As this binding is occurring, bicarbonate is leaving the RBC in exchange for chloride ions. (For additional information about the relationship between the respiratory and renal components of this buffer system, see monograph titled "Blood Gases.")

Hgb is included in the complete blood count (CBC) and generally performed with a hematocrit (Hct). These levels parallel each other and are frequently used to evaluate anemia. *Polycythemia* is a condition resulting from an abnormal increase in Hgb, Hct, and RBC count. *Anemia* is a condition resulting from an abnormal decrease in Hgb, Hct, and RBC count. Results of the Hgb, Hct, and RBC count should be evaluated simultaneously because the same underlying conditions affect this triad of tests similarly. The RBC count multiplied by 3 should approximate the Hgb concentration. The Hct should be within three times the Hgb if the RBC population is normal in size and shape. The Hct plus 6 should approximate the first two figures of the RBC count within 3 (e.g., Hct is 40%; therefore 40 + 6 = 46, and the RBC count should be 4.6 or in the range of 4.3 to 4.9). There are some cultural variations in Hgb and Hct (H&H) values. After the first decade of life, the mean Hgb in African Americans is 0.5 to 1.0 g lower than in whites. Mexican Americans and Asian Americans have higher Hgb and H&H values than whites.

INDICATIONS

- Detect hematological disorder, neoplasm, or immunological abnormality
- Determine the presence of hereditary hematological abnormality
- Evaluate known or suspected anemia and related treatment, in combination with Hct
- Monitor blood loss and response to blood replacement, in combination with Hct
- Monitor the effects of physical or emotional stress on the patient
- Monitor fluid imbalances or their treatment
- Monitor hematological status during pregnancy, in combination with Hct
- Monitor the progression of nonhematological disorders, such as chronic obstructive pulmonary disease (COPD), malabsorption syndromes, cancer, and renal disease
- Monitor response to drugs or chemotherapy and evaluate undesired reactions to drugs that may cause blood dyscrasias
- Provide screening as part of a CBC in a general physical examination, especially upon admission to a health care facility or before surgery

POTENTIAL DIAGNOSIS

Increased in

- Burns *(related to dehydration; total blood volume is decreased, but RBC count remains the same)*
- Congestive heart failure *(when the underlying cause is anemia, the body will respond by increasing production of RBCs; with a responding increase in Hct)*
- COPD *(related to chronic hypoxia that stimulates production of RBCs and a corresponding increase in Hgb)*
- Dehydration *(total blood volume is decreased, but RBC count remains the same)*
- Erythrocytosis *(total blood volume remains the same, but RBC count is increased)*
- Hemoconcentration *(same effect as seen in dehydration)*
- High altitudes *(related to hypoxia that stimulates production of RBCs and therefore increases Hgb)*
- Polycythemia vera *(abnormal bone marrow response resulting in overproduction of RBCs)*
- Shock

Decreased in

- Anemias *(overall decrease in RBCs and corresponding decrease in Hgb)*
- Blood loss (acute and chronic) *(overall decrease in RBC and corresponding decrease in Hct)*
- Bone marrow hyperplasia *(bone marrow failure that results in decreased RBC production)*
- Carcinoma *(anemia is often associated with chronic disease)*
- Cirrhosis *(related to accumulation of fluid)*
- Chronic disease *(anemia is often associated with chronic disease*
- Fluid retention *(dilutional effect of increased blood volume while RBC count remains stable)*
- Hemoglobinopathies *(reduced RBC survival with corresponding decrease in Hgb)*
- Hemolytic disorders (e.g. hemolytic anemias, prosthetic valves) *(reduced RBC survival with corresponding decrease in Hct)*
- Hemorrhage (acute and chronic) *(overall decrease in RBCs and corresponding decrease in Hgb*
- Hodgkin's disease *(bone marrow failure that results in decreased RBC production)*
- Incompatible blood transfusion *(reduced RBC survival with corresponding decrease in Hgb)*
- Intravenous overload *(dilutional effect)*

Leukemia *(bone marrow failure that results in decreased RBC production)*

Lymphomas *(bone marrow failure that results in decreased RBC production)*

Nutritional deficit *(anemia related to dietary deficiency in iron, vitamins, folate needed to produce sufficient RBCs; decreased RBC count with corresponding decrease in Hgb)*

Pregnancy *(related to anemia)*

Renal disease*(related to decreased levels of erythropoietin, which stimulates production of RBCs)*

Splenomegaly *(total blood volume remains the same, but spleen retains RBCs and Hgb reflects decreased RBC count)*

CRITICAL FINDINGS ◈

Adults & children

Less than 6.6 g/dL (SI: Less than 66 g/L)

Greater than 20 g/dL (SI: Greater than 200 g/L)

Newborns

Less than 9.5 g/dL (SI: Less than 95 g/L)

Greater than 22.3 g/dL (SI: Greater than 223 g/L)

Note and immediately report to the health-care provider (HCP) any critically increased or decreased values and related symptoms. Timely notification of critical values for lab or diagnostic studies is a role expectation of the professional nurse. Notification processes will vary among facilities. Upon receipt of the critical value, the information should be read back to the caller to verify accuracy. Most policies require immediate notification of the primary HCP, hospitalist, or on-call HCP. Reported information includes the patient's name, unique identifiers, critical value, name of the person giving the report, and name of the person receiving the report. Documentation of notification should be made in the medical record with the name of the HCP notified, time and date of notification, and any orders received. Any delay in a timely report of a critical value may require completion of a notification form with review by Risk Management.

Low Hgb leads to anemia. Anemia can be caused by blood loss, decreased blood cell production, increased blood cell destruction, and hemodilution. Causes of blood loss include menstrual excess or frequency, gastrointestinal bleeding, inflammatory bowel disease, and hematuria. Decreased blood cell production can be caused by folic acid deficiency, vitamin B_{12} deficiency, iron deficiency, and chronic disease. Increased blood cell destruction can be caused by a hemolytic reaction, chemical reaction, medication reaction, and sickle cell disease. Hemodilution can be caused by congestive heart failure, renal failure, polydipsia, and overhydration. Symptoms of anemia (due to these causes) include anxiety, dyspnea, edema, fatigue, hypertension, hypotension, hypoxia, jugular venous distention, pallor, rales, restlessness, and weakness. Treatment of anemia depends on the cause.

High Hgb leads to polycythemia. Polycythemia can be caused by dehydration, decreased oxygen levels in the body, and an overproduction of RBCs by the bone marrow. Dehydration from diuretic use, vomiting, diarrhea, excessive sweating, severe burns, or decreased fluid intake decreases the plasma component of whole blood, thereby increasing the ratio of RBCs to plasma, and leads to a higher than normal Hgb. Causes of decreased oxygen include smoking, exposure to carbon monoxide, high altitude, and chronic lung disease, which leads to a mild hemo-concentration of blood in the body to carry more oxygen to the body's tissues. An overproduction of RBCs by the bone marrow leads to polycythemia vera, which is a rare chronic myeloproliferative disorder that leads to a severe hemoconcentration of blood. Severe hemoconcentration can lead to thrombosis (spontaneous blood clotting). Symptoms of hemoconcentration include decreased pulse pressure and volume, loss of skin turgor, dry mucous membranes, headaches, hepatomegaly, low central venous pressure, orthostatic hypotension, pruritus (especially after a hot bath), splenomegaly, tachycardia, thirst, tinnitus, vertigo, and weakness. Treatment of polycythemia depends on the cause. Possible interventions for hemoconcentration due to dehydration include intravenous fluids and discontinuance of diuretics if they are believed to be contributing to critically elevated Hgb. Polycythemia due to decreased oxygen states can be treated by removal of the offending substance, such as smoke or carbon monoxide. Treatment includes oxygen therapy in cases of smoke inhalation, carbon monoxide poisoning, and desaturating chronic lung disease. Symptoms of polycythemic overload crisis include signs of thrombosis, pain and redness in extremities, facial flushing, and irritability. Possible interventions for hemoconcentration due to polycythemia include therapeutic phlebotomy and intravenous fluids.

INTERFERING FACTORS

- Drugs and substances that may cause a decrease in Hgb include those that induce hemolysis due to drug sensitivity or enzyme deficiency and those that result in anemia (see monograph titled "Complete Blood Count, RBC Count").
- Some drugs may also affect Hgb values by increasing the RBC count (see monograph titled "Complete Blood Count, RBC Count").
- The results of RBC counts may vary depending on the patient's position: Hgb can decrease when the patient is recumbent as a result of hemodilution and can increase when the patient rises as a result of hemoconcentration.
- Use of the nutraceutical liver extract is strongly contraindicated in iron-storage disorders, such as hemochromatosis, because it is rich in heme (the iron-containing pigment in Hgb).
- A severe copper deficiency may result in decreased Hgb levels.
- Cold agglutinins may falsely increase the mean corpuscular Hgb concentration (MCHC) and decrease the RBC count, affecting Hgb values. This can be corrected by warming the blood or replacing the plasma with warmed saline and repeating the analysis.
- Leaving the tourniquet in place for longer than 60 sec can falsely increase Hgb levels by 2% to 5%.
- Failure to fill the tube sufficiently (i.e., tube less than three-quarters full) may yield inadequate sample volume for automated analyzers and may be a reason for specimen rejection.
- Clotted or hemolyzed specimens must be rejected for analysis.
- Care should be taken in evaluating the Hgb during the first few hours after transfusion or acute blood loss because the value may appear to be normal.
- Abnormalities in the RBC size (macrocytes, microcytes) or shape (spherocytes, sickle cells) may alter Hgb values, as in diseases and conditions including sickle cell anemia, hereditary spherocytosis, and iron deficiency.
- Lipemia will falsely increase the Hgb measurement, also affecting the mean corpuscular volume

(MCV) and MCHC. This can be corrected by replacing the plasma with saline, repeating the measurement, and manually correcting the Hgb, MCH, and MCHC using specific mathematical formulas.

NURSING IMPLICATIONS AND PROCEDURE

RETEST:

Positively identify the patient using at least two unique identifiers before providing care, treatment, or services.

Patient Teaching: Inform the patient this test can assist in evaluating the amount of hemoglobin in the blood to assist in diagnosis and monitor therapy.

Obtain a history of the patient's complaints, including a list of known allergens, especially allergies or sensitivities to latex.

Obtain a history of the patient's cardiovascular, gastrointestinal, hematopoietic, hepatobiliary, immune, and respiratory systems; symptoms; and results of previously performed laboratory tests and diagnostic and surgical procedures.

Note any recent procedures that can interfere with test results.

Obtain a list of the patient's current medications, including herbs, nutritional supplements, and nutraceuticals (see Appendix F).

Review the procedure with the patient. Inform the patient that specimen collection takes approximately 5 to 10 min. Address concerns about pain and explain that there may be some discomfort during the venipuncture.

Sensitivity to social and cultural issues, as well as concern for modesty, is important in providing psychological support before, during, and after the procedure.

There are no food, fluid, or medication restrictions unless by medical direction.

INTRATEST:

If the patient has a history of allergic reaction to latex, avoid the use of equipment containing latex.

Instruct the patient to cooperate fully and to follow directions. Direct the patient to breathe normally and to avoid unnecessary movement.

Observe standard precautions, and follow the general guidelines in Appendix A. Positively identify the patient, and label the appropriate tubes with the corresponding patient demographics, date, and time of collection. Perform a venipuncture; collect the specimen in a 5-mL lavender-top (EDTA) tube. An EDTA Microtainer sample may be obtained from infants, children, and adults for whom venipuncture may not be feasible. The specimen should be mixed gently by inverting the tube 10 times. The specimen should be analyzed within 24 hr when stored at room temperature or within 48 hr if stored at refrigerated temperature. If it is anticipated the specimen will not be analyzed within 24 hr, two blood smears should be made immediately after the venipuncture and submitted with the blood sample. Smears made from specimens older than 24 hr may contain an unacceptable number of misleading artifactual abnormalities of the RBCs, such as echinocytes and spherocytes, as well as necrobiotic white blood cells.

Remove the needle and apply direct pressure with dry gauze to stop bleeding. Observe/assess venipuncture site for bleeding or hematoma formation and secure gauze with adhesive bandage.

Promptly transport the specimen to the laboratory for processing and analysis.

POST-TEST:

A report of the results will be made available to the requesting HCP, who will discuss the results with the patient.

Nutritional Considerations: Nutritional therapy may be indicated for patients with increased Hgb if iron levels are also elevated. Educate the patient with abnormally elevated iron values, as appropriate, on the importance of reading food labels. Patients with hemochromatosis or acute pernicious anemia should be educated to avoid foods rich in iron. Iron absorption is affected by numerous factors that may enhance or decrease absorption regardless of the original content of the iron-containing dietary source (see monograph titled "Iron"). Iron levels in foods can be increased if foods are cooked in cookware containing iron. Consumption of large amounts of alcohol damages the intestine and allows increased absorption of iron. A high intake of calcium and ascorbic acid also increases iron absorption. Iron absorption after a meal is also increased by factors in meat, fish, and poultry.

Nutritional Considerations: Nutritional therapy may be indicated for patients with decreased Hgb. Iron deficiency is the most common nutrient deficiency in the United States. The Institute of Medicine's Food and Nutrition Board suggests 8 mg as the daily recommended dietary allowance of iron for adult males and females age 51 to greater than 70 yr; 18 mg/d for adult females age 19 to 50 yr; 8 mg/d for adult males age 19 to 50 yr; 27 mg/d for pregnant females under age 18 through 50 yr; 9 mg/d for lactating females age 19 to 50 yr; 10 mg/d for lactating females under age 18 yr; 15 mg/d for female children age 14 to 18 yr; 11 mg/d for male children age 14 to 18 yr; 8 mg/d for children age 9 to 13 yr; 10 mg/d for children age 4 to 8 yr; 7 mg/d for children age 1 to 3 yr; 11 mg/d for children age 7 to 12 mo; and 0.27 mg/d for children age 0 to 6 mo (recommended adequate intake). Reprinted with permission from the National Academies Press, copyright 2013, National Academy of Sciences. Patients at risk (e.g., children, pregnant women, women of childbearing age, and low-income populations) should be instructed to include in their diet foods that are high in iron, such as meats (especially liver), eggs, grains, green leafy vegetables, and

multivitamins with iron. Educate the patient with abnormally elevated iron values, as appropriate, on the importance of reading food labels. Iron absorption is affected by numerous factors, enhancing or decreasing absorption regardless of the original content of the iron containing dietary source (see monograph titled "Iron"). Iron absorption is decreased by the absence (gastric resection) or diminished presence (use of antacids) of gastric acid. Phytic acids from cereals; tannins from tea and coffee; oxalic acid from vegetables; and minerals such as copper, zinc, and manganese interfere with iron absorption.

Reinforce information given by the patient's HCP regarding further testing, treatment, or referral to another HCP. Answer any questions or address any concerns voiced by the patient or family. Educate the patient regarding access to nutritional counseling services. Provide contact information, if desired, for the Institute of Medicine of the National Academies (www.iom.edu).

Depending on the results of this procedure, additional testing may be performed to evaluate or monitor progression of the disease process and determine the need for a change in therapy. Evaluate test results in relation to the patient's symptoms and other tests performed.

RELATED MONOGRAPHS:

Related tests include biopsy bone marrow, biopsy lymph node, biopsy kidney, blood groups and antibodies, CBC, CBC hematocrit, Coombs' antiglobulin, CT thoracic, erythropoietin, fecal analysis (occult blood), ferritin, gallium scan, haptoglobin, hemoglobin electrophoresis, iron/TIBC, lymphangiogram, Meckel's diverticulum scan, reticulocyte count, sickle cell screen, and US abdomen.

Refer to the Cardiovascular, Gastrointestinal, Hematopoietic, Hepatobiliary, Immune, and Respiratory systems tables at the end of the book for related tests by body system.

Complete Blood Count, Platelet Count

SYNONYM/ACRONYM: Thrombocytes.

COMMON USE: To assist in diagnosing and evaluating treatment for blood disorders such as thrombocytosis and thrombocytopenia and to evaluate preprocedure or preoperative coagulation status.

SPECIMEN: Whole blood from one full lavender-top (EDTA) tube.

NORMAL FINDINGS: (Method: Automated, computerized, multichannel analyzers)

Age	Platelet Count*	SI Units (Conventional Units × 1)	MPV (fL)	IPF (%)
Newborn				
Male	150–350 × 10³/microL	150–350 × 10⁹/L	7.1–10.2	1.1–7.1
Female	235–345 × 10³/microL	235–345 × 10⁹/L	7.3–10.2	1.1–7.1
1–2 mo				
Male	275–565 × 10³/microL	275–565 × 10⁹/L	7.1–11.3	1.1–7.1
Female	295–615 × 10³/microL	295–615 × 10⁹/L	7.4–9.7	1.1–7.1
3–6 mo				
Male	275–565 × 10³/microL	275–565 × 10⁹/L	6.8–9.1	1.1–7.1
Female	288–598 × 10³/microL	288–598 × 10⁹/L	7.2–8.9	1.1–7.1
7–23 mo				
Male	220–450 × 10³/microL	220–450 × 10⁹/L	7.1–9.3	1.1–7.1
Female	230–465 × 10³/microL	230–465 × 10⁹/L	7.1–9.3	1.1–7.1
2–6 yr				
Male & Female	205–405 × 10³/microL	205–405 × 10⁹/L	7.1–9.3	1.1–7.1
7–12 yr				
Male	195–365 × 10³/microL	195–365 × 10⁹/L	7.2–9.4	1.1–7.1
Female	185–370 × 10³/microL	185–370 × 10⁹/L	7.1–9.2	1.1–7.1
12–18 yr				
Male	165–332 × 10³/microL	165–332 × 10⁹/L	7.3–9.7	1.1–7.1
Female	185–335 × 10³/microL	185–335 × 10⁹/L	7.5–9.3	1.1–7.1
Adult/Older adult				
Male & Female	150–450 × 10³/microL	150–450 × 10⁹/L	7.1–10.2	1.1–7.1

Note: Platelet counts may decrease slightly with age.
*Conventional units.
MPV = mean platelet volume.

C

DESCRIPTION: Primary hemostasis has three major stages involving platelet adhesion, platelet activation, and platelet aggregation. Platelet adhesion is initiated by exposure of the endothelium as a result of damage to blood vessels. Exposed tissue factor–bearing cells trigger the simultaneous binding of von Willebrand factor to exposed collagen and circulating platelets. *Platelets* are nonnucleated, cytoplasmic, round or oval disks formed by budding off of large, multinucleated cells (megakaryocytes). Platelets have an essential function in coagulation, hemostasis, and blood thrombus formation. Activated platelets release a number of procoagulant factors, including thromboxane, a very potent platelet activator, from storage granules. These factors enter the circulation and activate other platelets and the cycle continues. The activated platelets aggregate at the site of vessel injury, and at this stage of hemostasis the glycoprotein IIb/IIIa receptors on the activated platelets bind fibrinogen, causing the platelets to stick together and form a plug. Coagulation must be localized to the site of vessel wall injury, or the growing platelet plug would eventually occlude the affected vessel. The fibrinolytic system, under normal circumstances, begins to work, once fibrin begins to form, to ensure coagulation is limited to the appropriate site. *Thrombocytosis* is an increase in platelet count. In reactive thrombocytosis, the increase is transient and short-lived, and it usually does not pose a health risk. One exception may be reactive thrombocytosis

occurring after coronary bypass surgery. This circumstance has been identified as an important risk factor for postoperative infarction and thrombosis. The term *thrombocythemia* describes platelet increases associated with chronic myeloproliferative disorders; *thrombocytopenia* describes platelet counts of less than $140 \times 10^3/$microL. Decreased platelet counts occur whenever the body's need for platelets exceeds the rate of platelet production; this circumstance will arise if production rate decreases or platelet loss increases. The severity of bleeding is related to platelet count as well as platelet function. Platelet counts can be within normal limits, but the patient may exhibit signs of internal bleeding; this circumstance usually indicates an anomaly in platelet function. Abnormal findings by automated cell counters may indicate the need to review a smear of peripheral blood for platelet estimate. Abnormally large or giant platelets may result in underestimation of automated counts by 30% to 50%. A large discrepancy between the automated count and the estimate requires that a manual count be performed. Platelet clumping may result in the underestimation of the platelet count. Clumping may be detected by the automated cell counter or upon microscopic review of a blood smear. A citrated platelet count, performed on a specimen collected in a blue-top tube, can be performed to obtain an accurate platelet count from patients who demonstrate platelet clumping in EDTA-preserved samples.

Thrombopoiesis or platelet production is reflected by the measurement of the immature platelet fraction (IPF). This parameter can be correlated to the total platelet count in the investigation of platelet disorders. A low platelet count with a low IPF can indicate a disorder of platelet production (e.g., drug toxicity, aplastic anemia or bone marrow failure of another cause), whereas a low platelet count with an increased IPF might indicate platelet destruction or abnormally high platelet consumption (e.g., mechanical destruction, disseminated intravascular coagulation [DIC], idiopathic thrombocytopenic purpura [ITP], thrombotic thrombocytopenic purpura [TTP]).

Platelet size, reflected by mean platelet volume (MPV), and cellular age are inversely related; that is, younger platelets tend to be larger. An increase in MPV indicates an increase in platelet turnover. Therefore, in a healthy patient, the platelet count and MPV have an inverse relationship. Abnormal platelet size may also indicate the presence of a disorder. MPV and platelet distribution width (PDW) are both increased in ITP. MPV is also increased in May-Hegglin anomaly, Bernard-Soulier syndrome, myeloproliferative disorders, hyperthyroidism, and pre-eclampsia. MPV is decreased in Wiskott-Aldrich syndrome, septic thrombocytopenia, and hypersplenism.

Platelets have receptor sites that are essential for normal platelet function and activation. Drugs such as clopidogrel, abciximab (Reopro), eptifibatide (Integrilin), and tirofiban block these receptor sites and inhibit platelet function. Aspirin also can affect platelet function by the irreversible inactivation of a crucial cyclooxygenase (COX) enzyme. Medications like clopidogrel (Plavix) and aspirin are prescribed to prevent heart attack, stroke, and blockage of coronary stents. Studies have confirmed that up to 30% of patients receiving these medications may be nonresponsive. There are several commercial test systems that can assess platelet function and provide information that confirms platelet response. Platelet response testing helps ensure alternative or additional platelet therapy is instituted, if necessary. The test results can also be used preoperatively to determine whether antiplatelet medications have been sufficiently cleared from the patient's circulation such that surgery can safely be performed without risk of excessive bleeding. Thromboxane A2 is a potent stimulator of platelet activation. 11-dehydrothromboxane B2 is the stable, inactive product of thromboxane A2 metabolism, released by activated platelets. Urine levels of 11-dehydrothromboxane B2 can be used to monitor response to aspirin therapy.

The metabolism of many commonly prescribed medications is driven by the cytochrome P450 (CYP450) family of enzymes. Genetic variants can alter enzymatic activity that results in a spectrum of effects ranging from the total absence of drug metabolism to ultrafast metabolism. Impaired drug metabolism can prevent the intended therapeutic effect or even lead to serious adverse drug reactions. Poor metabolizers (PM) are at increased risk for drug-induced side effects due to accumulation of drug in the blood, while ultrarapid metabolizers (UM) require a higher than normal dosage because the drug is metabolized over a shorter duration than intended. Other genetic phenotypes used to report CYP450 results are intermediate metabolizer (IM) and extensive metabolizer (EM). CYP2C19 is a gene in the CYP450 family that metabolizes drugs such as clopidogrel (Plavix). Genetic testing can be performed on blood samples submitted to a laboratory. Testing for the most common genetic variants of CYP2C19 is used to predict altered enzyme activity and anticipate the most effective therapeutic plan. The test method commonly used is polymerase chain reaction. Counseling and informed written consent are generally required for genetic testing.

INDICATIONS

- Confirm an elevated platelet count (thrombocytosis), which can cause increased clotting
- Confirm a low platelet count (thrombocytopenia), which can be associated with bleeding
- Identify the possible cause of abnormal bleeding, such as epistaxis, hematoma, gingival bleeding, hematuria, and menorrhagia
- Provide screening as part of a complete blood count (CBC) in a general physical examination, especially upon admission to a health-care facility or before surgery

POTENTIAL DIAGNOSIS

Increased in
Conditions that involve inflammation activate and increase the number of circulating platelets:

- Acute infections
- After exercise (transient)

- Anemias (posthemorrhagic, hemolytic, iron-deficiency) *(bone marrow response to anemia; platelet formation is unaffected by iron deficiency)*
- Chronic heart disease
- Cirrhosis
- Essential thrombocythemia
- Leukemias (chronic)
- Malignancies (carcinoma, Hodgkin's, lymphomas)
- Pancreatitis (chronic)
- Polycythemia vera *(hyperplastic bone marrow response in all cell lines)*
- Rebound recovery from thrombocytopenia *(initial response)*
- Rheumatic fever (acute)
- Rheumatoid arthritis
- Splenectomy (2 mo postprocedure) *(normal function of the spleen is to cull aging cells from the blood; without the spleen, the count increases)*
- Surgery (2 wk postprocedure)
- Trauma
- Tuberculosis
- Ulcerative colitis

Decreased in

Decreased in (as a result of megakaryocytic hypoproliferation)
- Alcohol toxicity
- Aplastic anemia
- Congenital states (Fanconi's syndrome, May-Hegglin anomaly, Bernard-Soulier syndrome, Wiskott-Aldrich syndrome, Gaucher's disease, Chédiak-Higashi syndrome)
- Drug toxicity
- Prolonged hypoxia

Decreased in (as a result of ineffective thrombopoiesis)
- Ethanol abuse without malnutrition
- Iron-deficiency anemia
- Megaloblastic anemia (B_{12}/folate deficiency)
- Paroxysmal nocturnal hemoglobinuria

- Thrombopoietin deficiency
- Viral infection

Decreased in (as a result of bone marrow replacement)
- Lymphoma
- Granulomatous infections
- Metastatic carcinoma
- Myelofibrosis

Increased in

Increased destruction in (as a result of increased loss/consumption)
- Contact with foreign surfaces (dialysis membranes, artificial organs, grafts, prosthetic devices)
- Disseminated intravascular coagulation
- Extensive transfusion
- Severe hemorrhage
- Thrombotic thrombocytopenic purpura
- Uremia

Increased destruction in (as a result of immune reaction)
- Antibody/human leukocyte antigen reactions
- Hemolytic disease of the newborn *(target is platelets instead of RBCs)*
- Idiopathic thrombocytopenic purpura
- Refractory reaction to platelet transfusion

Increased destruction in (as a result of immune reaction secondary to infection)
- Bacterial infections
- Burns
- Congenital infections (cytomegalovirus, herpes, syphilis, toxoplasmosis)
- Histoplasmosis
- Malaria
- Rocky Mountain spotted fever

Increased destruction in (as a result of other causes)
- Radiation
- Splenomegaly caused by liver disease

CRITICAL FINDINGS
- Less than 50×10^3/microL (SI: Less than 50×10^9/L)
- Greater than $1,000 \times 10^3$/microL (SI: Greater than $1,000 \times 10^9$/L)

Note and immediately report to the health-care provider (HCP) any critically increased or decreased values and related symptoms. Timely notification of critical values for lab or diagnostic studies is a role expectation of the professional nurse. Notification processes will vary among facilities. Upon receipt of the critical value, the information should be read back to the caller to verify accuracy. Most policies require immediate notification of the primary HCP, hospitalist, or on-call HCP. Reported information includes the patient's name, unique identifiers, critical value, name of the person giving the report, and name of the person receiving the report. Documentation of notification should be made in the medical record with the name of the HCP notified, time and date of notification, and any orders received. Any delay in a timely report of a critical value may require completion of a notification form with review by Risk Management. Possible interventions for decreased platelet count may include transfusion of platelets.

INTERFERING FACTORS
- Drugs that may decrease platelet counts include acetohexamide, acetophenazine, amphotericin B, antazoline, anticonvulsants, antimony compounds, apronalide, arsenicals, azathioprine, barbiturates, benzene, busulfan, butaperazine, chlordane, chlorophenothane, chlortetracycline, dactinomycin, dextromethorphan, diethylstilbestrol, ethinamate, ethoxzolamide, floxuridine, hexachlorobenzene, hydantoin

derivatives, hydroflumethiazide, hydroxychloroquine, iproniazid, mechlorethamine, mefenamic acid, mepazine, miconazole, mitomycin, nitrofurantoin, novobiocin, nystatin, phenolphthalein, phenothiazine, pipamazine, plicamycin, procarbazine, pyrazolones, streptomycin, sulfonamides, tetracycline, thiabendazole, thiouracil, tolazamide, tolazoline, tolbutamide, trifluoperazine, and urethane.

- Drugs that may increase platelet counts include glucocorticoids.
- X-ray therapy may also decrease platelet counts.
- The results of blood counts may vary depending on the patient's position. Platelet counts can decrease when the patient is recumbent, as a result of hemodilution, and can increase when the patient rises, as a result of hemoconcentration.
- Platelet counts normally increase under a variety of stressors, such as high altitudes or strenuous exercise.
- Platelet counts are normally decreased before menstruation and during pregnancy.
- Leaving the tourniquet in place for longer than 60 sec can affect the results.
- Traumatic venipunctures may lead to erroneous results as a result of activation of the coagulation sequence.
- Failure to fill the tube sufficiently (i.e., tube less than three-quarters full) may yield inadequate sample volume for automated analyzers and may be a reason for specimen rejection.
- Hemolysis or clotted specimens are reasons for rejection.
- CBC should be carefully evaluated after transfusion or acute blood loss because the value may appear to be normal.

NURSING IMPLICATIONS AND PROCEDURE

PRETEST:

- Positively identify the patient using at least two unique identifiers before providing care, treatment, or services.
- *Patient Teaching:* Inform the patient this test can assist in diagnosing, evaluating, and monitoring bleeding disorders.
- Obtain a history of the patient's complaints, including a list of known allergens, especially allergies or sensitivities to latex.
- Obtain a history of the patient's hematopoietic and immune systems, especially any bleeding disorders and other symptoms, as well as results of previously performed laboratory tests and diagnostic and surgical procedures.
- Note any recent procedures that can interfere with test results.
- Obtain a list of the patient's current medications, including anticoagulants, aspirin and other salicylates, herbs, nutritional supplements, and nutraceuticals (see Appendix F).
- Review the procedure with the patient. Inform the patient that specimen collection takes approximately 5 to 10 min. Address concerns about pain and explain that there may be some discomfort during the venipuncture.
- *Sensitivity to social and cultural issues,* as well as concern for modesty, is important in providing psychological support before, during, and after the procedure.
- There are no food, fluid, or medication restrictions unless by medical direction.

INTRATEST:

- If the patient has a history of allergic reaction to latex, avoid the use of equipment containing latex.
- Instruct the patient to cooperate fully and to follow directions. Direct the patient to breathe normally and to avoid unnecessary movement.
- Observe standard precautions, and follow the general guidelines in Appendix A. Positively identify the patient, and label the appropriate specimen container with the corresponding patient demographics, initials of the person collecting the specimen,

date, and time of collection. Perform a venipuncture. The specimen should be mixed gently by inverting the tube 10 times. The specimen should be analyzed within 24 hr when stored at room temperature or within 48 hr if stored at refrigerated temperature. If it is anticipated the specimen will not be analyzed within 24 hr, two blood smears should be made immediately after the venipuncture and submitted with the blood sample.

Remove the needle and apply direct pressure with dry gauze to stop bleeding. Observe/assess venipuncture site for bleeding or hematoma formation and secure gauze with adhesive bandage. Promptly transport the specimen to the laboratory for processing and analysis.

OST-TEST:

A report of the results will be made available to the requesting HCP, who will discuss the results with the patient. Instruct the patient to report bleeding from any areas of the skin or mucous membranes.

Inform the patient with a decreased platelet count of the importance of taking precautions against bruising and bleeding, including the use of a soft bristle toothbrush, use of an electric razor, avoidance of constipation, avoidance of acetylsalicylic acid and similar products, and avoidance of intramuscular injections.

Inform the patient of the importance of periodic laboratory testing if he or she is taking an anticoagulant.

Nutritional Considerations: Instruct patients to consume a variety of foods within the basic food groups, maintain a healthy weight, be physically active, limit salt intake, limit alcohol intake, and avoid the use of tobacco.

Recognize anxiety related to test results. Discuss the implications of abnormal test results on the patient's lifestyle. Provide teaching and information regarding the clinical implications of the test results, as appropriate.

Reinforce information given by the patient's HCP regarding further testing, treatment, or referral to another HCP. Answer any questions or address any concerns voiced by the patient or family.

Depending on the results of this procedure, additional testing may be performed to evaluate or monitor progression of the disease process and determine the need for a change in therapy. Evaluate test results in relation to the patient's symptoms and other tests performed.

RELATED MONOGRAPHS:

Related tests include antiarrhythmic drugs (quinidine), biopsy bone marrow, bleeding time, blood groups and antibodies, clot retraction, coagulation factors, CBC, CBC RBC morphology and inclusions, CBC WBC count and differential, CT angiography, CT brain, FDP, fibrinogen, PTT, platelet antibodies, procalcitonin, PT/INR, and US pelvis.

Refer to the Hematopoietic and Immune systems tables at the end of the book for related tests by body system.

Complete Blood Count, RBC Count

SYNONYM/ACRONYM: RBC.

COMMON USE: To evaluate the number of circulating red cells in the blood toward diagnosing disease and monitoring therapeutic treatment. Variations in the number of cells is most often seen in anemias, cancer, and hemorrhage.

SPECIMEN: Whole blood (1 mL) collected in a lavender-top (EDTA) tube.

NORMAL FINDINGS: (Method: Automated, computerized, multichannel analyzers)

Age	Conventional Units (10^6 cells/microL)	SI Units (10^12 cells/L) (Conventional Units × 1)
Cord blood	3.61–5.81	3.61–5.81
0–1 wk	4.51–7.01	4.51–7.01
2–3 wk	3.71–6.11	3.71–6.11
1–2 mo	3.11–5.11	3.11–5.11
3–11 mo	3.01–5.01	3.01–5.01
1–5 yr	3.81–5.01	3.81–5.01
6–8 yr	3.91–5.11	3.91–5.11
9–14 yr	3.91–5.61	3.91–5.61
15 yr–adult		
Male	5.21–5.81	5.21–5.81
Female	3.91–5.11	3.91–5.11
Older adult		
Male	3.81–5.81	3.81–5.81
Female	3.71–5.31	3.71–5.31

DESCRIPTION: A component of the complete blood count (CBC), the red blood cell (RBC) count determines the number of RBCs per cubic millimeters (expressed as the number of RBCs per liter of blood according to the international system of units [SI]). Because RBCs contain hemoglobin (Hgb), which is responsible for the transport and exchange of oxygen, the number of circulating RBCs is important. Although the life span of the normal RBC is 120 days, other factors besides cell age and decreased production can cause decreased values; examples are abnormal destruction due to intravascular trauma caused by atherosclerosis or due to an enlarged spleen caused by leukemia. The main sites of RBC production in healthy adults include the bone marrow of the vertebrae, pelvis, ribs, sternum, skull, and proximal ends of the femur and humerus. The main sites of RBC destruction are the spleen and liver. Erythropoietin, a hormone produced by the kidneys, regulates RBC production. Normal RBC development and function are also dependent on adequate levels of vitamin B_{12}, folic acid, and iron. A deficiency in vitamin E (α-tocopherol), which is needed to protect the RBC membrane from oxidizers, can result in increased cellular destruction. *Polycythemia* is a condition resulting from an abnormal increase in Hgb, hematocrit (Hct), and RBC count. *Anemia* is a condition resulting from an abnormal decrease in Hgb, Hct, and RBC count. Results of the Hgb, Hct, and RBC count should be evaluated simultaneously because the same underlying conditions affect this triad of tests similarly. The RBC count multiplied by 3 should approximate the Hgb concentration. The Hct should be within three times the Hgb if the RBC population is normal in size and shape. The Hct plus 6 should approximate the first two figures of the RBC count within 3 (e.g., Hct is 40%; therefore 40 + 6 = 46, and the RBC count should be 4.6 or in the range 4.3 to 4.9). (See monographs titled "Complete

C

Blood Count, Hematocrit,"
"Complete Blood Count,
Hemoglobin," and "Complete
Blood Count, RBC Indices.")

INDICATIONS

- Detect a hematological disorder involving RBC destruction (e.g., hemolytic anemia)
- Determine the presence of hereditary hematological abnormality
- Monitor the effects of acute or chronic blood loss
- Monitor the effects of physical or emotional stress on the patient
- Monitor patients with disorders associated with elevated erythrocyte counts (e.g., polycythemia vera, chronic obstructive pulmonary disease [COPD])
- Monitor the progression of nonhematological disorders associated with elevated erythrocyte counts, such as COPD, liver disease, hypothyroidism, adrenal dysfunction, bone marrow failure, malabsorption syndromes, cancer, and renal disease
- Monitor the response to drugs or chemotherapy and evaluate undesired reactions to drugs that may cause blood dyscrasias
- Provide screening as part of a CBC in a general physical examination, especially upon admission to a health care facility or before surgery

POTENTIAL DIAGNOSIS

Increased in

- Anxiety or stress *(related to physiological response)*
- Bone marrow failure *(initial response is stimulation of RBC production)*
- COPD with hypoxia and secondary polycythemia *(related to chronic hypoxia that stimulates production of RBCs and a corresponding increase in RBCs)*
- Dehydration with hemoconcentration *(related to decrease in total blood volume relative to unchanged RBC count)*
- Erythremic erythrocytosis *(related to unchanged total blood volume relative to increase in RBC count)*
- High altitude *(related to hypoxia that stimulates production of RBCs)*
- Polycythemia vera *(related to abnormal bone marrow response resulting in overproduction of RBCs)*

Decreased in

- Chemotherapy *(related to reduced RBC survival)*
- Chronic inflammatory diseases *(related to anemia of chronic disease)*
- Hemoglobinopathy *(related to reduced RBC survival)*
- Hemolytic anemia *(related to reduced RBC survival)*
- Hemorrhage *(related to overall decrease in RBC count)*
- Hodgkin's disease *(evidenced by bone marrow failure that results in decreased RBC production)*
- Leukemia *(evidenced by bone marrow failure that results in decreased RBC production)*
- Multiple myeloma *(evidenced by bone marrow failure that results in decreased RBC production)*
- Nutritional deficit *(related to deficiency of iron or vitamins required for RBC production and/or maturation)*
- Overhydration *(related to increase in blood volume relative to unchanged RBC count)*
- Pregnancy *(related to anemia; normal dilutional effect)*
- Renal disease *(related to decreased production of erythropoietin)*
- Subacute endocarditis

CRITICAL FINDINGS

The presence of abnormal cells, other morphological characteristics, or cellular inclusions may signify a potentially life-threatening or serious health condition and should be investigated. Examples are the presence of sickle cells, moderate numbers of spherocytes, marked schistocytosis, oval macrocytes, basophilic stippling, nucleated RBCs (if the patient is not an infant), or malarial organisms.

Note and immediately report to the health-care provider (HCP) any critically increased or decreased values and related symptoms. Timely notification of critical values for lab or diagnostic studies is a role expectation of the professional nurse. Notification processes will vary among facilities. Upon receipt of the critical value, the information should be read back to the caller to verify accuracy. Most policies require immediate notification of the primary HCP, hospitalist, or on-call HCP. Reported information includes the patient's name, unique identifiers, critical value, name of the person giving the report, and name of the person receiving the report. Documentation of notification should be made in the medical record with the name of the HCP notified, time and date of notification, and any orders received. Any delay in a timely report of a critical value may require completion of a notification form with review by Risk Management.

Low RBC count leads to anemia. Anemia can be caused by blood loss, decreased blood cell production, increased blood cell destruction, or hemodilution. Causes of blood loss include menstrual excess or frequency, gastrointestinal bleeding, inflammatory bowel disease, or hematuria. Decreased blood cell production can be caused by folic acid deficiency, vitamin B_{12} deficiency, iron deficiency or chronic disease. Increased blood cell destruction can be caused by a hemolytic reaction, chemical reaction, medication reaction, or sickle cell disease. Hemodilution can be caused by congestive heart failure, renal failure, polydipsia, or overhydration. Symptoms of anemia (due to these causes) include anxiety, dyspnea, edema, hypertension, hypotension, hypoxia, jugular venous distention, fatigue, pallor, rales, restlessness, and weakness. Treatment of anemia depends on the cause.

High RBC count leads to polycythemia. Polycythemia can be caused by dehydration, decreased oxygen levels in the body, and an overproduction of RBCs by the bone marrow. Dehydration by diuretic use, vomiting, diarrhea, excessive sweating, severe burns, or decreased fluid intake decreases the plasma component of whole blood, thereby increasing the ratio of RBCs to plasma, and leads to a higher than normal Hct. Causes of decreased oxygen include smoking, exposure to carbon monoxide, high altitude, and chronic lung disease, which leads to a mild hemoconcentration of blood in the body to carry more oxygen to the body's tissues. An overproduction of RBCs by the bone marrow leads to polycythemia vera, which is a rare chronic myeloproliferative disorder that leads to a severe hemoconcentration of blood. Severe hemoconcentration can lead to thrombosis (spontaneous blood clotting). Symptoms of hemoconcentration include decreased pulse pressure and volume, loss of skin turgor, dry mucous membranes, headaches, hepatomegaly, low central venous pressure, orthostatic hypotension, pruritus (especially after a hot bath), splenomegaly, tachycardia, thirst, tinnitus, vertigo, and weakness. Treatment of polycythemia depends on the cause

Possible interventions for hemoconcentration due to dehydration include intravenous fluids and discontinuance of diuretics if they are believed to be contributing to critically elevated Hct. Polycythemia due to decreased oxygen states can be treated by removal of the offending substance, such as smoke or carbon monoxide. Treatment includes oxygen therapy in cases of smoke inhalation, carbon monoxide poisoning, and desaturating chronic lung disease. Symptoms of polycythemic overload crisis include signs of thrombosis, pain and redness in extremities, facial flushing, and irritability. Possible interventions for hemoconcentration due to polycythemia include therapeutic phlebotomy and intravenous fluids.

INTERFERING FACTORS

- Drugs and substances that may decrease RBC count by causing hemolysis resulting from drug sensitivity or enzyme deficiency include acetaminophen, aminopyrine, aminosalicylic acid, amphetamine, anticonvulsants, antipyrine, arsenicals, benzene, busulfan, carbenicillin, cephalothin, chemotherapy drugs, chlorate, chloroquine, chlorothiazide, chlorpromazine, colchicine, diphenhydramine, dipyrone, glucosulfone, gold, hydroflumethiazide, indomethacin, mephenytoin, nalidixic acid, neomycin, nitrofurantoin, penicillin, phenacemide, phenazopyridine, and phenothiazine.

- Drugs that may decrease RBC count by causing anemia include miconazole, penicillamine, phenylhydrazine, primaquine, probenecid, pyrazolones, pyrimethamine, quinines, streptomycin, sulfamethizole, sulfamethoxypyridazine, sulfisoxazole, suramin, thioridazine, tolbutamide, trimethadione, and tripelennamine.

- Drugs that may decrease RBC count by causing bone marrow suppression include amphotericin B, floxuridine, and phenylbutazone.

- Drugs and vitamins that may increase the RBC count include glucocorticosteroids, pilocarpine, and vitamin B_{12}.

- Use of the nutraceutical liver extract is strongly contraindicated in patients with iron-storage disorders such as hemochromatosis because it is rich in heme (the iron-containing pigment in Hgb).

- Hemodilution (e.g., excessive administration of intravenous fluids, normal pregnancy) in the presence of a normal number of RBCs may lead to false decreases in RBC count.

- Cold agglutinins may falsely increase the mean corpuscular volume (MCV) and decrease the RBC count. This can be corrected by warming the blood or diluting the sample with warmed saline and repeating the analysis.

- Excessive exercise, anxiety, pain, and dehydration may cause false elevations in RBC count.

- Care should be taken in evaluating the CBC after transfusion.

- RBC counts can vary depending on the patient's position, decreasing when the patient is recumbent as a result of hemodilution and increasing when the patient rises as a result of hemoconcentration.

- Venous stasis can falsely elevate RBC counts; therefore, the tourniquet should not be left on the arm for longer than 60 sec.

- Failure to fill the tube sufficiently (i.e., tube less than three-quarters full) may yield inadequate sample volume for automated analyzers and may be a reason for specimen rejection.

- Hemolyzed or clotted specimens must be rejected for analysis.

C

C

NURSING IMPLICATIONS AND PROCEDURE

PRETEST:

- Positively identify the patient using at least two unique identifiers before providing care, treatment, or services.
- *Patient Teaching:* Inform the patient this test can assist in assessing for anemia and disorders affecting the number of circulating RBCs.
- Obtain a history of the patient's complaints, including a list of known allergens, especially allergies or sensitivities to latex.
- Obtain a history of the patient's cardiovascular, gastrointestinal, genitourinary, hematopoietic, hepatobiliary, immune, and respiratory systems; symptoms; and results of previously performed laboratory tests and diagnostic and surgical procedures.
- Note any recent procedures that can interfere with test results.
- Obtain a list of the patient's current medications, including herbs, nutritional supplements, and nutraceuticals (see Appendix F).
- Review the procedure with the patient. Inform the patient that specimen collection takes approximately 5 to 10 min. Address concerns about pain and explain that there may be some discomfort during the venipuncture.
- *Sensitivity to social and cultural issues,* as well as concern for modesty, is important in providing psychological support before, during, and after the procedure.
- There are no food, fluid, or medication restrictions unless by medical direction.

INTRATEST:

- If the patient has a history of allergic reaction to latex, avoid the use of equipment containing latex.
- Instruct the patient to cooperate fully and to follow directions. Direct the patient to breathe normally and to avoid unnecessary movement.
- Observe standard precautions, and follow the general guidelines in Appendix A. Positively identify the patient, and label the appropriate specimen container with the corresponding patient demographics, initials of the person collecting the specimen, date, and time of collection. Perform a venipuncture. An EDTA Microtainer sample may be obtained from infants, children, and adults for whom venipuncture may not be feasible. The specimen should be mixed gently by inverting the tube 10 times. The specimen should be analyzed within 24 hr when stored at room temperature or within 48 hr if stored at refrigerated temperature. If it is anticipated the specimen will not be analyzed within 24 hr, two blood smears should be made immediately after the venipuncture and submitted with the blood sample. Smears made from specimens older than 24 hr will contain an unacceptable number of misleading artifactual abnormalities of the RBCs, such as echinocytes and spherocytes, as well as necrobiotic WBCs.
- Remove the needle and apply direct pressure with dry gauze to stop bleeding. Observe/assess venipuncture site for bleeding or hematoma formation and secure gauze with adhesive bandage.
- Promptly transport the specimen to the laboratory for processing and analysis.

POST-TEST:

- A report of the results will be made available to the requesting HCP, who will discuss the results with the patient.
- *Nutritional Considerations:* Nutritional therapy may be indicated for patients with decreased RBC count. Iron deficiency is the most common nutrient deficiency in the United States. Patients at risk (e.g., children, pregnant women and women of childbearing age, low-income populations) should be instructed to include foods that are high in iron in their diet, such as meats (especially liver), eggs, grains, green leafy vegetables, and multivitamins with iron. Iron absorption is affected by numerous factors (see monograph titled "Iron").

Nutritional Considerations: Patients at risk for vitamin B_{12} or folate deficiency include those with the following conditions: malnourishment (inadequate intake), pregnancy (increased need), infancy, malabsorption syndromes (inadequate absorption/increased metabolic rate), infections, cancer, hyperthyroidism, serious burns, excessive blood loss, and gastrointestinal damage. The Institute of Medicine's Food and Nutrition Board suggests 2.4 mcg as the daily recommended dietary allowance of vitamin B_{12} for adult males and females age 19 to greater than 70 yr; 2.6 mcg/d for pregnant females less than age 18 through 50 yr; 2.8 mcg/d for lactating females less than age 18 through 50 yr; 2.4 mcg/day for children age 14 to 18 yr; 1.8 mcg/d for children age 9 to 13 yr; 1.2 mcg/d for children age 4 to 8 yr; 0.9 mcg/d for children age 1 to 3 yr; 0.5 mcg/d for children age 7 to 12 mo (recommended adequate intake); 0.4 mcg/d for children age 0 to 6 mo (recommended adequate intake). Reprinted with permission from the National Academies Press, copyright 2013, National Academy of Sciences. Instruct the patient with vitamin B_{12} deficiency, as appropriate, in the use of vitamin supplements. Inform the patient, as appropriate, that the best dietary sources of vitamin B_{12} are meats, milk, cheese, eggs, and fortified soy milk products. The Institute of Medicine's Food and Nutrition Board suggests 400 mcg as the daily recommended dietary allowance of folate for adult males and females age 19 to greater than 70 yr; 600 mcg/d for pregnant females less than age 18 through 50 yr; 500 mcg/d for lactating females less than age 18 through 50 yr; 400 mcg/day for children age 14 to 18 yr; 300 mcg/d for children age 9 to 13 yr; 200 mcg/d for children age 4 to 8 yr; 150 mcg/d for children age 1 to 3 yr; 80 mcg/d for children age 7 to 12 mo (recommended adequate intake); 65 mcg/d for children age 0 to 6 mo (recommended adequate intake). Reprinted with permission from the National Academies Press, copyright 2013, National Academy of Sciences. Instruct the folate-deficient patient (especially pregnant women), as appropriate, to eat foods rich in folate, such as meats (especially liver), salmon, eggs, beets, asparagus, green leafy vegetables such as spinach, cabbage, oranges, broccoli, sweet potatoes, kidney beans, and whole wheat.

Nutritional Considerations: A diet deficient in vitamin E puts the patient at risk for increased RBC destruction, which could lead to anemia. Nutritional therapy may be indicated for these patients. The Institute of Medicine's Food and Nutrition Board suggests 15 mg/d as the daily recommended dietary allowance for dietary vitamin E for adult males and females age 14 to greater than 70 yr; 15 mg/d for pregnant females less than age 18 through 50 yr; 12 mg/day for pregnant females age 14 to 18 yr; 19 mg/d for lactating females less than age 18 through 50 yr; 11 mg/day for children age 9 to 13 yr; 7 mg/d for children age 4 to 8 yr; 6 mg/d for children age 1 to 3 yr; 5 mg/d for children age 7 to 12 mo; 4 mg/d for children age 0 to 6 mo. Reprinted with permission from the National Academies Press, copyright 2013, National Academy of Sciences. Educate the patient with a vitamin E deficiency, if appropriate, that the main dietary sources of vitamin E are vegetable oils including olive oil), whole grains, wheat germ, nuts, milk, eggs, meats, fish, and green leafy vegetables. Vitamin E is fairly stable at most cooking temperatures (except frying) and when exposed to acidic foods. Supplemental vitamin E may also be taken, but the danger of toxicity should be explained to the patient. Very large supplemental doses, in excess of 600 mg of vitamin E over a period of 1 yr, may result in excess bleeding. Vitamin E is heat stable but is very negatively affected by light.

Reinforce information given by the patient's HCP regarding further testing, treatment, or referral to another HCP. Answer any questions or address any concerns voiced by the patient or family. Educate the patient regarding access to nutritional counseling services. Provide contact information, if desired, for the Institute of Medicine of the National Academies (www.iom.edu). Depending on the results of this procedure, additional testing may be performed to evaluate or monitor progression of the disease process and determine the need for a change in therapy. Evaluate test results in relation to the patient's symptoms and other tests performed.

RELATED MONOGRAPHS:

Related tests include biopsy bone marrow, biopsy kidney, blood groups and antibodies, CBC, CBC hematocrit, CBC hemoglobin, CBC RBC morphology and inclusions, Coombs' antiglobulin, erythropoietin, fecal analysis, ferritin, folate, gallium scan, haptoglobin, iron/TIBC, lymphangiogram, Meckel's diverticulum scan, reticulocyte count, and vitamin B_{12}.

Refer to the Cardiovascular, Gastrointestinal, Genitourinary, Hematopoietic, Hepatobiliary, Immune, and Respiratory systems tables at the end of the book for related tests by body system.

Complete Blood Count, RBC Indices

SYNONYM/ACRONYM: Mean corpuscular hemoglobin (MCH), mean corpuscular volume (MCV), mean corpuscular hemoglobin concentration (MCHC), red blood cell distribution width (RDW).

COMMON USE: To evaluate cell size, shape, weight, and hemoglobin concentration. Used to diagnose and monitor therapy for diagnoses such as iron-deficiency anemia.

SPECIMEN: Whole blood (1 mL) collected in a lavender-top (EDTA) tube.

NORMAL FINDINGS: (Method: Automated, computerized, multichannel analyzers)

Age	MCV(fL)	MCH (pg/cell)	MCHC (g/dL)	RDWCV	RDWSD
Cord blood	107–119	35–39	31–35	14.9–18.7	51–66
0–1 wk	104–116	29–45	24–36	14.9–18.7	51–66
2–3 wk	95–117	26–38	26–34	14.9–18.7	51–66
1–2 mo	81–125	25–37	26–34	14.9–18.7	44–55
3–11 mo	78–110	22–34	26–34	14.9–18.7	35–46
1–5 yr	74–94	24–32	30–34	11.6–14.8	35–42
6–8 yr	73–93	24–32	32–36	11.6–14.8	35–42
9–14 yr	74–94	25–33	32–36	11.6–14.8	37–44
15 yr–adult					
Male	77–97	26–34	32–36	11.6–14.8	38–48
Female	78–98	26–34	32–36	11.6–14.8	38–48
Older adult					
Male	79–103	27–35	32–36	11.6–14.8	38–48
Female	78–102	27–35	32–36	11.6–14.8	38–48

MCV = mean corpuscular volume; MCH = mean corpuscular hemoglobin; MCHC = mean corpuscular hemoglobin concentration; RDWCV = coefficient of variation in red blood cell distribution width; RDWSD = standard deviation in RBC distribution width index.

C

DESCRIPTION: Red blood cell (RBC) indices provide information about the mean corpuscular volume (MCV), mean corpuscular hemoglobin (MCH), mean corpuscular hemoglobin concentration (MCHC), and RBC distribution width (RDWCV and RDWSD). The hematocrit, RBC count, and total hemoglobin tests are used to determine the RBC indices. MCV is determined by dividing the hematocrit by the total RBC count and is helpful in classifying anemias. MCH is determined by dividing the total hemoglobin concentration by the RBC count. MCHC is determined by dividing total hemoglobin by hematocrit. Hemoglobin content is indicated as normochromic, hypochromic, and hyperchromic. The RDW is a measurement of cell size distribution over the entire RBC population measured. It can indicate anisocytosis, or excessive variations in cell size. Cell size is indicated as normocytic, microcytic, and macrocytic. RDWCV is an indication of variation in cell size over the circulating RBC population. The RDWSD is also an indicator of RBC size, is not affected by the MCV as with the RDWCV index, and is a more accurate measurement of the degree of variation in cell size. (See monographs titled "Complete Blood Count, Hemoglobin," "Complete Blood Count, Hematocrit," "Complete Blood Count, RBC Count," and "Complete Blood Count, RBC Morphology and Inclusions.")

INDICATIONS

- Assist in the diagnosis of anemia
- Detect a hematological disorder, neoplasm, or immunological abnormality
- Determine the presence of a hereditary hematological abnormality
- Monitor the effects of physical or emotional stress
- Monitor the progression of non-hematological disorders such as chronic obstructive pulmonary disease, malabsorption syndromes, cancer, and renal disease
- Monitor the response to drugs or chemotherapy, and evaluate undesired reactions to drugs that may cause blood dyscrasias
- Provide screening as part of a complete blood count (CBC) in a general physical examination, especially upon admission to a health care facility or before surgery

POTENTIAL DIAGNOSIS

Increased in

MCV
- Alcoholism *(vitamin deficiency related to malnutrition)*
- Antimetabolite therapy *(the therapy inhibits vitamin B_{12} and folate)*
- Liver disease *(complex effect on RBCs that includes malnutrition, alterations in RBC shape and size, effects of chronic disease)*
- Pernicious anemia (vitamin B_{12}/folate anemia)

MCH
- Macrocytic anemias *(related to increased hemoglobin or cell size)*

MCHC
- Spherocytosis *(artifact in measurement caused by abnormal cell shape)*

RDW
- Anemias with heterogeneous cell size as a result of hemoglobinopathy, hemolytic anemia, anemia following acute blood loss, iron-deficiency anemia, vitamin- and

folate-deficiency anemia *(related to a mixture of cell sizes as the bone marrow responds to the anemia and/or to a mixture of cell shapes due to cell fragmentation as a result of the disease)*

Decreased in

MCV
- Iron-deficiency anemia *(related to low hemoglobin)*
- Thalassemias *(related to low hemoglobin)*

MCH
- Hypochromic anemias *(related to low hemoglobin)*
- Microcytic anemias *(related to low hemoglobin)*

MCHC
- Iron-deficiency anemia *(the amount of hemoglobin in the RBC is small relative to RBC size)*

RDW: N/A

CRITICAL FINDINGS: N/A

INTERFERING FACTORS
- Drugs and substances that may decrease the MCHC include styrene (occupational exposure).
- Drugs that may decrease the MCV include nitrofurantoin.
- Drugs that may increase the MCV include colchicine, pentamidine, pyrimethamine, and triamterene.
- Drugs that may increase the MCH and MCHC include oral contraceptives (long-term use).
- Diseases that cause agglutination of RBCs will alter test results.
- Cold agglutinins may falsely increase the MCV and decrease the RBC count. This can be corrected by warming the blood or diluting the sample with warmed saline and

then correcting the RBC count mathematically.
- RBC counts can vary depending on the patient's position, decreasing when the patient is recumbent as a result of hemodilution and increasing when the patient rises as a result of hemoconcentration.
- Care should be taken in evaluating the CBC after transfusion.
- Venous stasis can falsely elevate RBC counts; therefore, the tourniquet should not be left on the arm for longer than 60 sec.
- Failure to fill the tube sufficiently (i.e., tube less than three-quarters full) may yield inadequate sample volume for automated analyzers and may be a reason for specimen rejection.
- Hemolyzed or clotted specimens should be rejected.
- Lipemia will falsely increase the hemoglobin measurement, also affecting the MCV and MCH.

NURSING IMPLICATIONS AND PROCEDURE

PRETEST:
- Positively identify the patient using at least two unique identifiers before providing care, treatment, or services.
- *Patient Teaching:* Inform the patient this test can assist in assessing RBC shape and size.
- Obtain a history of the patient's complaints, including a list of known allergens especially allergies or sensitivities to latex.
- Obtain a history of the patient's gastrointestinal, hematopoietic, immune, and respiratory systems; symptoms; and results of previously performed laboratory tests and diagnostic and surgical procedures.
- Note any recent procedures that can interfere with test results.
- Obtain a list of the patient's current medications including herbs, nutritional

supplements, and nutraceuticals (see Appendix F).

Review the procedure with the patient. Inform the patient that specimen collection takes approximately 5 to 10 min. Address concerns about pain and explain that there may be some discomfort during the venipuncture.

Sensitivity to social and cultural issues, as well as concern for modesty, is important in providing psychological support before, during, and after the procedure.

There are no food, fluid, or medication restrictions unless by medical direction.

If the patient has a history of allergic reaction to latex, avoid the use of equipment containing latex.

Instruct the patient to cooperate fully and to follow directions. Direct the patient to breathe normally and to avoid unnecessary movement.

Observe standard precautions, and follow the general guidelines in Appendix A. Positively identify the patient, and label the appropriate specimen container with the corresponding patient demographics, initials of the person collecting the specimen, date, and time of collection. Perform a venipuncture. An EDTA Microtainer sample may be obtained from infants, children, and adults for whom venipuncture may not be feasible. The specimen should be mixed gently by inverting the tube 10 times. The specimen should be analyzed within 24 hr when stored at room temperature or within 48 hr if stored at refrigerated temperature. If it is anticipated the specimen will not be analyzed within 24 hr, two blood smears should be made immediately after the venipuncture and submitted with the blood sample. Smears made from specimens older than 24 hr may

contain an unacceptable number of misleading artifactual abnormalities of the RBCs, such as echinocytes and spherocytes, as well as necrobiotic white blood cells.

Remove the needle and apply direct pressure with dry gauze to stop bleeding. Observe/assess venipuncture site for bleeding or hematoma formation and secure gauze with adhesive bandage.

Promptly transport the specimen to the laboratory for processing and analysis.

POST-TEST:

A report of the results will be made available to the requesting HCP, who will discuss the results with the patient.

Reinforce information given by the patient's HCP regarding further testing, treatment, or referral to another HCP. Answer any questions or address any concerns voiced by the patient or family.

Depending on the results of this procedure, additional testing may be performed to evaluate or monitor progression of the disease process and determine the need for a change in therapy. Evaluate test results in relation to the patient's symptoms and other tests performed.

RELATED MONOGRAPHS:

Related tests include biopsy bone marrow, CBC, CBC hematocrit, CBC hemoglobin, CBC RBC count, CBC RBC morphology and inclusions, CBC WBC count and differential, erythropoietin, ferritin, folate, Hgb electrophoresis, iron/TIBC, lead, reticulocyte count, sickle cell screen, and vitamin B_{12}.

Refer to the Gastrointestinal, Hematopoietic, Immune, and Respiratory systems tables at the end of the book for related tests by body system.

Complete Blood Count, RBC Morphology and Inclusions

SYNONYM/ACRONYM: N/A.

COMMON USE: To make a visual evaluation of the red cell shape and/or size as a confirmation in assisting to diagnose and monitor disease progression.

SPECIMEN: Whole blood from one full lavender-top (EDTA) tube or Wright's-stained, thin-film peripheral blood smear. The laboratory should be consulted as to the necessity of thick-film smears for the evaluation of malarial inclusions.

NORMAL FINDINGS: (Method: Microscopic, manual review of stained blood smear)

Red Blood Cell Morphology	Within Normal Limits	1+	2+	3+	4+
Size					
Anisocytosis	0–5	5–10	10–20	20–50	Greater than 50
Macrocytes	0–5	5–10	10–20	20–50	Greater than 50
Microcytes	0–5	5–10	10–20	20–50	Greater than 50
Shape					
Poikilocytes	0–2	3–10	10–20	20–50	Greater than 50
Burr cells	0–2	3–10	10–20	20–50	Greater than 50
Acanthocytes	Less than 1	2–5	5–10	10–20	Greater than 20
Schistocytes	Less than 1	2–5	5–10	10–20	Greater than 20
Dacryocytes (teardrop cells)	0–2	2–5	5–10	20–50	Greater than 20
Codocytes (target cells)	0–2	2–10	10–20	20–50	Greater than 50
Spherocytes	0–2	2–10	10–20	20–50	Greater than 50
Ovalocytes	0–2	2–10	10–20	20–50	Greater than 50
Stomatocytes	0–2	2–10	10–20	20–50	Greater than 50
Drepanocytes (sickle cells)	Absent	Reported as present or absent			
Helmet cells	Absent	Reported as present or absent			
Agglutination	Absent	Reported as present or absent			

Red Blood Cell Morphology	Within Normal Limits	1+	2+	3+	4+
Rouleaux	Absent	Reported as present or absent			
Hemoglobin (Hgb) Content					
Hypochromia	0–2	3–10	10–50	50–75	Greater than 75
Polychromasia					
Adult	Less than 1	2–5	5–10	10–20	Greater than 20
Newborn	1–6	7–15	15–20	20–50	Greater than 50
Inclusions					
Cabot rings	Absent	Reported as present or absent			
Basophilic stippling	0–1	1–5	5–10	10–20	Greater than 20
Howell-Jolly bodies	Absent	1–2	3–5	5–10	Greater than 10
Heinz bodies	Absent	Reported as present or absent			
Hgb C crystals	Absent	Reported as present or absent			
Pappenheimer bodies	Absent	Reported as present or absent			
Intracellular parasites (e.g., *Plasmodium, Babesia, Trypanosoma*)	Absent	Reported as present or absent			

DESCRIPTION: The decision to manually review a peripheral blood smear for abnormalities in red blood cell (RBC) shape or size is made on the basis of criteria established by the reporting laboratory. Cues in the results of the complete blood count (CBC) will point to specific abnormalities that can be confirmed visually by microscopic review of the sample on a stained blood smear.

INDICATIONS
• Assist in the diagnosis of anemia
• Detect a hematological disorder, neoplasm, or immunological abnormality

- Determine the presence of a hereditary hematological abnormality
- Monitor the effects of physical or emotional stress on the patient
- Monitor the progression of nonhematological disorders, such as chronic obstructive pulmonary disease, malabsorption syndromes, cancer, and renal disease
- Monitor the response to drugs or chemotherapy, and evaluate undesired reactions to drugs that may cause blood dyscrasias
- Provide screening as part of a CBC in a general physical examination, especially upon admission to a health-care facility or before surgery

POTENTIAL DIAGNOSIS

Red Blood Cell Size

Increased in

Cell Size
- Alcoholism
- Aplastic anemia
- Chemotherapy
- Chronic hemolytic anemia
- Grossly elevated glucose (hyperosmotic)
- Hemolytic disease of the newborn
- Hypothyroidism
- Leukemia
- Lymphoma
- Metastatic carcinoma
- Myelofibrosis
- Myeloma
- Refractory anemia
- Sideroblastic anemia
- Vitamin B$_{12}$/folate deficiency *(related to impaired DNA synthesis and delayed cell division, which permits the cells to grow for a longer period than normal)*

Decreased in

Cell Size
- Hemoglobin C disease
- Hemolytic anemias

- Hereditary spherocytosis
- Inflammation
- Iron-deficiency anemia
- Thalassemias

Red Blood Cell Shape
Variations in cell shape are the result of hereditary conditions such as elliptocytosis, sickle cell anemia, spherocytosis, thalassemias, or hemoglobinopathies (e.g., hemoglobin C disease). Irregularities in cell shape can also result from acquired conditions, such as physical/mechanical cellular trauma, exposure to chemicals, or reactions to medications.

- Acquired spherocytosis can result from Heinz body hemolytic anemia, microangiopathic hemolytic anemia, secondary isoimmunohemolytic anemia, and transfusion of old banked blood.
- Acanthocytes are associated with acquired conditions such as alcoholic cirrhosis with hemolytic anemia, disorders of lipid metabolism, hepatitis of newborns, malabsorptive diseases, metastatic liver disease, the postsplenectomy period, and pyruvate kinase deficiency.
- Burr cells are commonly seen in acquired renal insufficiency, burns, cardiac valve disease, disseminated intravascular coagulation (DIC), hypertension, intravenous fibrin deposition, metastatic malignancy, normal neonatal period, and uremia.
- Codocytes are seen in hemoglobinopathies, iron-deficiency anemia, obstructive liver disease, and the postsplenectomy period.
- Dacryocytes are most commonly associated with metastases to the bone marrow, myelofibrosis, myeloid metaplasia, pernicious anemia, and tuberculosis.
- Schistocytes are seen in burns, cardiac valve disease, DIC, glomerulonephritis, hemolytic anemia,

microangiopathic hemolytic anemia, renal graft rejection, thrombotic thrombocytopenic purpura, uremia, and vasculitis.

Red Blood Cell Hemoglobin Content

• RBCs with a normal hemoglobin (Hgb) level have a clear central pallor and are referred to as *normochromic*.

• Cells with low Hgb and lacking in central pallor are referred to as *hypochromic*. Hypochromia is associated with iron-deficiency anemia, thalassemias, and sideroblastic anemia.

• Cells with excessive Hgb levels are referred to as *hyperchromic* even though they technically lack a central pallor. Hyperchromia is usually associated with an elevated mean corpuscular Hgb concentration as well as hemolytic anemias.

• Cells referred to as *polychromic* are young erythrocytes that still contain ribonucleic acid (RNA). The RNA is picked up by the Wright's stain. Polychromasia is indicative of premature release of RBCs from bone marrow secondary to increased erythropoietin stimulation.

Red Blood Cell Inclusions

RBC inclusions can result from certain types of anemia, abnormal Hgb precipitation, or parasitic infection.

• Cabot rings may be seen in megaloblastic and other anemias, lead poisoning, and conditions in which RBCs are destroyed before they are released from bone marrow.

• Basophilic stippling is seen whenever there is altered Hgb synthesis, as in thalassemias, megaloblastic anemias, alcoholism, and lead or arsenic intoxication.

• Howell-Jolly bodies are seen in sickle cell anemia, other hemolytic anemias, megaloblastic anemia, congenital absence of the spleen, and the postsplenectomy period.

• Pappenheimer bodies may be seen in cases of sideroblastic anemia, thalassemias, refractory anemia, dyserythropoietic anemias, hemosiderosis, and hemochromatosis.

• Heinz bodies are most often seen in the blood of patients who have ingested drugs known to induce the formation of these inclusion bodies. They are also seen in patients with hereditary glucose-6-phosphate dehydrogenase (G6PD) deficiency.

• Hgb C crystals can often be identified in stained peripheral smears of patients with hereditary hemoglobin C disease.

• Parasites such as *Plasmodium* (transmitted by mosquitoes and causing malaria) and *Babesia* (transmitted by ticks), known to invade human RBCs, can be visualized with Wright's stain and other special stains of the peripheral blood.

CRITICAL FINDINGS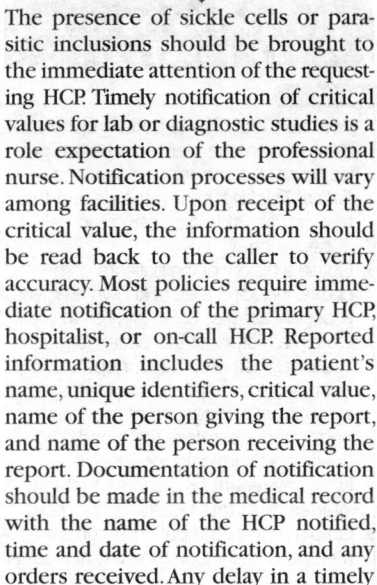

The presence of sickle cells or parasitic inclusions should be brought to the immediate attention of the requesting HCP. Timely notification of critical values for lab or diagnostic studies is a role expectation of the professional nurse. Notification processes will vary among facilities. Upon receipt of the critical value, the information should be read back to the caller to verify accuracy. Most policies require immediate notification of the primary HCP, hospitalist, or on-call HCP. Reported information includes the patient's name, unique identifiers, critical value, name of the person giving the report, and name of the person receiving the report. Documentation of notification should be made in the medical record with the name of the HCP notified, time and date of notification, and any orders received. Any delay in a timely report of a critical value may require completion of a notification form with review by Risk Management.

INTERFERING FACTORS

• Drugs and substances that may increase Heinz body formation as an initial precursor to significant hemolysis include acetanilid, acetylsalicylic acid, aminopyrine, antimalarials, antipyretics, furaltadone, furazolidone, methylene blue, naphthalene, and nitrofurans.

• Care should be taken in evaluating the CBC after transfusion.

• Leaving the tourniquet in place for longer than 60 sec can falsely affect the results.

• Morphology can be evaluated to some extent via indices; therefore, failure to fill the tube sufficiently (i.e., tube less than three-quarters full) may yield inadequate sample volume for automated analyzers and may be a reason for specimen rejection.

• Hemolyzed or clotted specimens should be rejected.

NURSING IMPLICATIONS AND PROCEDURE

PRETEST:

‣ Positively identify the patient using at least two unique identifiers before providing care, treatment, or services.

‣ *Patient Teaching:* Inform the patient this test can assist in assessing red cell appearance.

‣ Obtain a history of the patient's complaints, including a list of known allergens, especially allergies or sensitivities to latex.

‣ Obtain a history of the patient's gastrointestinal, hematopoietic, hepatobiliary, immune, and respiratory systems; symptoms; and results of previously performed laboratory tests and diagnostic and surgical procedures.

‣ Note any recent procedures that can interfere with test results.

‣ Obtain a list of the patient's current medications, including herbs, nutritional supplements, and nutraceuticals (see Appendix F).

‣ Review the procedure with the patient. Inform the patient that specimen collection takes approximately 5 to 10 min. Address concerns about pain and explain that there may be some discomfort during the venipuncture.

‣ *Sensitivity to social and cultural issues,* as well as concern for modesty, is important in providing psychological support before, during, and after the procedure.

‣ There are no food, fluid, or medication restrictions unless by medical direction.

INTRATEST:

‣ If the patient has a history of allergic reaction to latex, avoid the use of equipment containing latex.

‣ Instruct the patient to cooperate fully and to follow directions. Direct the patient to breathe normally and to avoid unnecessary movement.

‣ Observe standard precautions, and follow the general guidelines in Appendix A. Positively identify the patient, and label the appropriate specimen container with the corresponding patient demographics, initials of the person collecting the specimen, date, and time of collection. Perform a venipuncture. An EDTA Microtainer sample may be obtained from infants, children, and adults for whom venipuncture may not be feasible. The specimen should be mixed gently by inverting the tube 10 times. The specimen should be analyzed within 6 hr when stored at room temperature or within 24 hr if stored at refrigerated temperature. if it is anticipated the specimen will not be analyzed within 4 to 6 hr, two blood smears should be made immediately after the venipuncture and submitted with the blood sample. Smears made from specimens older than 6 hr will contain an unacceptable number of misleading artifactual abnormalities of the RBCs, such as echinocytes and spherocytes, as well as necrobiotic white blood cells.

‣ Remove the needle and apply direct pressure with dry gauze to stop bleeding. Observe/assess venipuncture site for bleeding or hematoma formation and secure gauze with adhesive bandage.

Promptly transport the specimen to the laboratory for processing and analysis.

A report of the results will be made available to the requesting HCP, who will discuss the results with the patient.

Nutritional Considerations: Instruct patients to consume a variety of foods within the basic food groups, maintain a healthy weight, be physically active, limit salt intake, limit alcohol intake, and avoid the use of tobacco.

Reinforce information given by the patient's HCP regarding further testing, treatment, or referral to another HCP. Answer any questions or address any concerns voiced by the patient or family.

Depending on the results of this procedure, additional testing may be performed to evaluate or monitor progression of the disease process and determine the need for a change in therapy. Evaluate test results in relation to the patient's symptoms and other tests performed.

Related tests include biopsy bone marrow, CBC, CBC hematocrit, CBC hemoglobin, CBC platelet count, CBC RBC count, CBC RBC indices, CBC WBC count with differential, δ-aminolevulinic acid, erythropoietin, ferritin, G6PD, hemoglobin electrophoresis, iron/TIBC, lead, and reticulocyte count.

Refer to the Gastrointestinal, Hematopoietic, Hepatobiliary, Immune, and Respiratory systems tables at the end of the book for related tests by body system.

Complete Blood Count, WBC Count and Differential

SYNONYM/ACRONYM: WBC with diff, leukocyte count, white cell count.

COMMON USE: To evaluate viral and bacterial infections and to assist in diagnosing and monitoring leukemic disorders.

SPECIMEN: Whole blood from one full lavender-top (EDTA) tube.

NORMAL FINDINGS: (Method: Automated, computerized, multichannel analyzers. Many analyzers can determine a five- or six-part WBC differential. The six-part automated WBC differential identifies and enumerates neutrophils, lymphocytes, monocytes, eosinophils, basophils, and immature granulocytes (IG), where IG represents the combined enumeration of promyelocytes, metamyelocytes, and myelocytes as both an absolute number and a percentage. The five-part WBC differential includes all but the immature granulocyte parameters.)

White Blood Cell Count and Differential

Age	Conventional Units WBC × 10³/microL	Total Neutrophils (Absolute) and %	Neutrophils Bands (Absolute) and %	Segments (Absolute) and %	Lymphocytes (Absolute) and %	Monocytes (Absolute) and %	Eosinophils (Absolute) and %	Basophils (Absolute) and %
Birth	9.1–30.1	(5.5–18.3) 61%	(0.8–2.7) 9.1%	(4.7–15.6) 52%	(2.8–9.3) 31%	(0.5–1.7) 5.8%	(0.02–0.7) 2.2%	(0.1–0.2) 0.6%
1–23 mo	6.1–17.5	(1.9–5.4) 31%	(0.2–0.5) 3.1%	(1.7–4.9) 28%	(3.7–10.7) 61%	(0.3–0.8) 4.8%	(0.2–0.5) 2.6%	(0–0.1) 0.5%
2–10 yr	4.5–13.5	(2.4–7.3) 54%	(0.1–0.4) 3.0%	(2.3–6.9) 51%	(1.7–5.1) 38%	(0.2–0.6) 4.3%	(0.1–0.3) 2.4%	(0–0.1) 0.5%
11 yr–older adult	4.5–11.1	(2.7–6.5) 59%	(0.1–0.3) 3.0%	(2.5–6.2) 56%	(1.5–3.7) 34%	(0.2–0.4) 4.0%	(0.05–0.5) 2.7%	(0–0.1) 0.5%

*SI Units (Conventional Units × 1 or WBC count × 10⁹/L).

White Blood Cell Count and Differential

Age	Immature Granulocytes (Absolute) (10^3/microL)	Immature Granulocyte Fraction (IGF) (%)
Birth–9 yr	0–0.03	0–0.4%
10 yr–older adult	0–0.09	0–0.9%

DESCRIPTION: White blood cells (WBCs) constitute the body's primary defense system against foreign organisms, tissues, and other substances. The life span of a normal WBC is 13 to 20 days. Old WBCs are destroyed by the lymphatic system and excreted in the feces. Reference values for WBC counts vary significantly with age. WBC counts vary diurnally, with counts being lowest in the morning and highest in the late afternoon. Other variables such as stress and high levels of activity or physical exercise can trigger transient increases of 2,000 to 5,000 mm^3. The main WBC types are neutrophils (band and segmented neutrophils), eosinophils, basophils, monocytes, and lymphocytes. WBCs are produced in the bone marrow. B-cell lymphocytes remain in the bone marrow to mature. T-cell lymphocytes migrate to and mature in the thymus. The WBC count can be performed alone with the differential cell count or as part of the complete blood count (CBC). The WBC differential can be performed by an automated instrument or manually on a slide prepared from a stained peripheral blood sample. Automated instruments provide excellent, reliable information, but the accuracy of the WBC count can be affected by the presence of circulating nucleated red blood cells (RBCs), clumped platelets, fibrin strands, cold agglutinins, cryoglobulins, intracellular parasitic organisms, or other significant blood cell inclusions and may not be identified in the interpretation of an automated blood count. The decision to report a manual or automated differential is based on specific criteria established by the laboratory. The criteria are designed to identify findings that warrant further investigation or confirmation by manual review. An increased WBC count is termed *leukocytosis*, and a decreased WBC count is termed *leukopenia*. A total WBC count indicates the degree of response to a pathological process, but a more complete evaluation for specific diagnoses for any one disorder is provided by the differential count. The WBCs in the count and differential are reported as an *absolute value* and as a percentage. The relative percentages of cell types are arrived at by basing the enumeration of each cell type on a 100-cell count. The absolute value is obtained by multiplying the relative percentage value of each cell type by the total WBC count. For example, on a CBC report, with a total WBC of 9×10^9 and WBC differential with 92% segmented neutrophils, 1% band neutrophils, 5% lymphocytes, and 1% monocytes the absolute values are calculated as follows: $92/100 \times 9 = 8.3$ segs, $1/100 \times 9 = 0.1$ bands, $5/100 \times 9 = 0.45$ lymphs, $1/100 \times 9 = 0.1$ monos for a total of 9.0 WBC count.

Acute leukocytosis is initially accompanied by changes in the WBC count population, followed by changes within the individual

WBCs. Leukocytosis usually occurs by way of increase in a single WBC family rather than a proportional increase in all cell types. Toxic granulation and vacuolation are commonly seen in leukocytosis accompanied by a *shift to the left*, or increase in the percentage of immature neutrophils to mature segmented neutrophils. An increased number or percentage of immature granulocytes, reflected by a shift to the left, represents production of WBCs and is useful as an indicator of infection. *Bandemia* is defined by the presence of greater than 6% band neutrophils in the total neutrophil cell population. These changes in the white cell population are most commonly associated with an infectious process, usually bacterial, but they can occur in healthy individuals who are under stress (in response to epinephrine production), such as women in childbirth and very young infants. The WBC count and differential of a woman in labor or of an actively crying infant may show an overall increase in WBCs with a shift to the left. Before initiating any kind of intervention, it is important to determine whether an increased WBC count is the result of a normal condition involving physiological stress or a pathological process. The use of multiple specimen types may confuse the interpretation of results in infants. Multiple samples from the same collection site (i.e., capillary versus venous) may be necessary to obtain an accurate assessment of the WBC picture in these young patients.

Neutrophils are normally found as the predominant WBC type in the circulating blood. Also called *polymorphonuclear cells*, they are the body's first line of defense through the process of phagocytosis. They also contain enzymes and pyogenes, which combat foreign invaders.

Lymphocytes are agranular, mononuclear blood cells that are smaller than granulocytes. They are found in the next highest percentage in normal circulation. Lymphocytes are classified as B cells and T cells. Both types are formed in the bone marrow, but B cells mature in the bone marrow and T cells mature in the thymus. Lymphocytes play a major role in the body's natural defense system. B cells differentiate into immunoglobulin-synthesizing plasma cells. T cells function as cellular mediators of immunity and comprise helper/inducer (CD4) lymphocytes, delayed hypersensitivity lymphocytes, cytotoxic (CD8 or CD4) lymphocytes, and suppressor (CD8) lymphocytes.

Monocytes are mononuclear cells similar to lymphocytes, but they are related more closely to granulocytes in terms of their function. They are formed in the bone marrow from the same cells as those that produce neutrophils. The major function of monocytes is phagocytosis. Monocytes stay in the peripheral blood for about 70 hr, after which they migrate into the tissues and become macrophages.

The function of eosinophils is phagocytosis of antigen-antibody complexes. They become active in the later stages of inflammation. Eosinophils respond to allergic and parasitic diseases: They have granules that contain histamine used to kill foreign cells in the body and proteolytic enzymes that damage parasitic worms (see monograph titled "Eosinophil Count").

Basophils are found in small numbers in the circulating blood. They have a phagocytic function and, similar to eosinophils, contain numerous specific granules. Basophilic granules contain heparin, histamines, and serotonin. Basophils may also be found in tissue and as such are classified as mast cells. Basophilia is noted in conditions such as leukemia, Hodgkin's disease, polycythemia vera, ulcerative colitis, nephrosis, and chronic hypersensitivity states.

INDICATIONS

* Assist in confirming suspected bone marrow depression
* Assist in determining the cause of an elevated WBC count (e.g., infection, inflammatory process)
* Detect hematological disorder, neoplasm, or immunological abnormality
* Determine the presence of a hereditary hematological abnormality
* Monitor the effects of physical or emotional stress
* Monitor the progression of non-hematological disorders, such as chronic obstructive pulmonary disease, malabsorption syndromes, cancer, and renal disease
* Monitor the response to drugs or chemotherapy and evaluate undesired reactions to drugs that may cause blood dyscrasias
* Provide screening as part of a CBC in a general physical examination, especially on admission to a healthcare facility or before surgery

POTENTIAL DIAGNOSIS

Increased in

Leukocytosis
* Normal physiological and environmental conditions:
  Early infancy *(increases are believed to be related to the physiological stress of birth and metabolic demands of rapid development)*

Emotional stress *(related to secretion of epinephrine)*
Exposure to extreme heat or cold *(related to physiological stress)*
Pregnancy and labor *(WBC counts may be modestly elevated due to increased neutrophils into the third trimester and during labor, returning to normal within a week postpartum)*
Strenuous exercise *(related to epinephrine secretion; increases are short in duration, minutes to hours)*
Ultraviolet light *(related to physiological stress and possible inflammatory response)*
* Pathological conditions:
Acute hemolysis, especially due to splenectomy or transfusion reactions *(related to leukocyte response to remove lysed RBC fragments)*
All types of infections *(related to an inflammatory or infectious response)*
Anemias *(bone marrow disorders affecting RBC production may result in elevated WBC count)*
Appendicitis
Collagen disorders *(related to an inflammatory or infectious response)*
Cushing's disease *(related to overproduction of cortisol, a corticosteroid, which stimulates WBC production)*
Inflammatory disorders *(related to an inflammatory or infectious response)*
Leukemias and other malignancies *(related to bone marrow disorders that result in abnormal WBC production)*
Parasitic infestations *(related to an inflammatory or infectious response)*
Polycythemia vera *(myeloproliferative bone marrow disorder causing an increase in all cell lines)*

Decreased in

Leukopenia
* Normal physiological conditions
  Diurnal rhythms (lowest in the morning)
* Pathological conditions
  Alcoholism *(related to WBC changes associated with nutritional deficiencies of vitamin B_{12} or folate)*

Anemias *(related to WBC changes associated with nutritional deficiencies of vitamin B$_{12}$ or folate, especially in megaloblastic anemias)*

Bone marrow depression *(related to decreased production)*

Malaria *(related to hypersplenism)*

Malnutrition *(related to WBC changes associated with nutritional deficiencies of vitamin B$_{12}$ or folate)*

Radiation *(related to physical cell destruction due to toxic effects of radiation)*

Rheumatoid arthritis *(related to side effect of medications used to treat the condition)*

Systemic lupus erythematosus (SLE) and other autoimmune disorders *(related to side effect of medications used to treat the condition)*

Toxic and antineoplastic drugs *(related to bone marrow suppression)*

Very low birth weight neonates *(related to bone marrow activity being diverted to develop RBCs in response to hypoxia)*

Viral infections *(leukopenia, lymphocytopenia, and abnormal lymphocytes may be present in the early stages of viral infections)*

Neutrophils Increased (neutrophilia)
- Acute hemolysis
- Acute hemorrhage
- Extremes in temperature
- Infectious diseases
- Inflammatory conditions (rheumatic fever, gout, rheumatoid arthritis, vasculitis, myositis)
- Malignancies
- Metabolic disorders (uremia, eclampsia, diabetic ketoacidosis, thyroid storm, Cushing's syndrome)
- Myelocytic leukemia
- Physiological stress (e.g., allergies, asthma, exercise, childbirth, surgery)
- Tissue necrosis (burns, crushing injuries, abscesses, myocardial infarction)

- Tissue poisoning with toxins and venoms

Neutrophils Decreased (neutropenia)
- Acromegaly
- Addison's disease
- Anaphylaxis
- Anorexia nervosa, starvation, malnutrition
- Bone marrow depression (viruses, toxic chemicals, overwhelming infection, radiation, Gaucher's disease)
- Disseminated SLE
- Thyrotoxicosis
- Viral infection (mononucleosis, hepatitis, influenza)
- Vitamin B$_{12}$ or folate deficiency

Lymphocytes Increased (lymphocytosis)
- Addison's disease
- Felty's syndrome
- Infections
- Lymphocytic leukemia
- Lymphomas
- Lymphosarcoma
- Myeloma
- Rickets
- Thyrotoxicosis
- Ulcerative colitis
- Waldenström's macroglobulinemia

Lymphocytes Decreased (lymphopenia)
- Antineoplastic drugs
- Aplastic anemia
- Bone marrow failure
- Burns
- Gaucher's disease
- Hemolytic disease of the newborn
- High doses of adrenocorticosteroids
- Hodgkin's disease
- Hypersplenism
- Immunodeficiency diseases
- Malnutrition
- Pernicious anemia
- Pneumonia
- Radiation
- Rheumatic fever
- Septicemia

- Thrombocytopenic purpura
- Toxic chemical exposure
- Transfusion reaction

Monocytes Increased (monocytosis)
- Carcinomas
- Cirrhosis
- Collagen diseases
- Gaucher's disease
- Hemolytic anemias
- Hodgkin's disease
- Infections
- Lymphomas
- Monocytic leukemia
- Polycythemia vera
- Radiation
- Sarcoidosis
- SLE
- Thrombocytopenic purpura
- Ulcerative colitis

CRITICAL FINDINGS
- Less than 2.5×10^3/microL (SI: Less than 2.5×10^9/L)
- Greater than 30×10^3/microL (SI: Greater than 30×10^9/L)

Note and immediately report to the requesting health-care provider (HCP) any critically increased or decreased values and related symptoms. Timely notification of critical values for lab or diagnostic studies is a role expectation of the professional nurse. Notification processes will vary among facilities. Upon receipt of the critical value, the information should be read back to the caller to verify accuracy. Most policies require immediate notification of the primary HCP, hospitalist, or on-call HCP. Reported information includes the patient's name, unique identifiers, critical value, name of the person giving the report, and name of the person receiving the report. Documentation of notification should be made in the medical record with the name of the HCP notified, time and date of notification, and any orders received. Any

delay in a timely report of a critical value may require completion of a notification form with review by Risk Management.

The presence of abnormal cells, other morphological characteristics, or cellular inclusions may signify a potentially life-threatening or serious health condition and should be investigated. Examples are hypersegmented neutrophils, agranular neutrophils, blasts or other immature cells, Auer rods, Döhle bodies, marked toxic granulation, or plasma cells.

INTERFERING FACTORS
- Drugs that may decrease the overall WBC count include acetyldigitoxin, acetylsalicylic acid, aminoglutethimide, aminopyrine, aminosalicylic acid, ampicillin, amsacrine, antazoline, anticonvulsants, antineoplastic agents (therapeutic intent), antipyrine, barbiturates, busulfan, carbutamide, carmustine, chlorambucil, chloramphenicol, chlordane, chlorophenothane, chlortetracycline, chlorthalidone, cisplatin, colchicine, colistimethate, cycloheximide, cyclophosphamide, cytarabine, dacarbazine, dactinomycin, Diaprim, diazepam, diethylpropion, digitalis, dipyridamole, dipyrone, fumagillin, glaucarubin, glucosulfone, hexachlorobenzene, hydroflumethiazide, hydroxychloroquine, iothiouracil, iproniazid, lincomycin, local anesthetics, mefenamic acid, mepazine, meprobamate, mercaptopurine, methotrexate, methylpromazine, mitomycin, paramethadione, parathion, penicillin, phenacemide, phenindione, phenothiazine, pipamazine, prednisone (by Coulter S method), primaquine, procainamide, procarbazine, prochlorperazine, promazine, promethazine, pyrazolones, quinacrine, quinines, radioactive compounds, razoxane, ristocetin, sulfa drugs, tamoxifen,

C

tetracycline, thenalidine, thioridazine, tolazamide, tolazoline, tolbutamide, trimethadione, and urethane.

- A significant decrease in basophil count occurs rapidly after intravenous injection of propanidid and thiopental.
- A significant decrease in lymphocyte count occurs rapidly after administration of corticotropin, mechlorethamine, methysergide, and x-ray therapy; and after megadoses of niacin, pyridoxine, and thiamine.
- Drugs that may increase the overall WBC count include amphetamine, amphotericin B, chloramphenicol, chloroform (normal response to anesthesia), colchicine (leukocytosis follows leukopenia), corticotropin, erythromycin, ether (normal response to anesthesia), fluroxene (normal response to anesthesia), isoflurane (normal response to anesthesia), niacinamide, phenylbutazone, prednisone, and quinine.
- Drug allergies may have a significant effect on eosinophil count and may affect the overall WBC count. Refer to the monograph titled "Eosinophil Count" for a detailed listing of interfering drugs.
- The WBC count may vary depending on the patient's position, decreasing when the patient is recumbent owing to hemodilution and increasing when the patient rises owing to hemoconcentration.
- Venous stasis can falsely elevate results; the tourniquet should not be left on the arm for longer than 60 sec.
- Failure to fill the tube sufficiently (i.e., tube less than three-quarters full) may yield inadequate sample volume for automated analyzers and may be reason for specimen rejection.
- Hemolyzed or clotted specimens should be rejected for analysis.

- The presence of nucleated red blood cells or giant or clumped platelets affects the automated WBC, requiring a manual correction of the WBC count.
- Care should be taken in evaluating the CBC during the first few hours after transfusion.
- Patients with cold agglutinins or monoclonal gammopathies may have a falsely decreased WBC count as a result of cell clumping.

NURSING IMPLICATIONS AND PROCEDURE

PRETEST:

- Positively identify the patient using at least two unique identifiers before providing care, treatment, or services.
- *Patient Teaching:* Inform the patient this test can assist in assessing for infection or monitoring leukemia.
- Obtain a history of the patient's complaints, including a list of known allergens, especially allergies or sensitivities to latex.
- Obtain a history of the patient's hematopoietic, immune, and respiratory systems; symptoms; and results of previously performed laboratory tests and diagnostic and surgical procedures.
- Note any recent procedures that can interfere with test results.
- Obtain a list of the patient's current medications, including herbs, nutritional supplements, and nutraceuticals (see Appendix F).
- Review the procedure with the patient. Inform the patient that specimen collection takes approximately 5 to 10 min. Address concerns about pain and explain that there may be some discomfort during the venipuncture.
- *Sensitivity to social and cultural issues,* as well as concern for modesty, is important in providing psychological support before, during, and after the procedure.
- There are no food, fluid, or medication restrictions unless by medical direction.

INTRATEST:

- If the patient has a history of allergic reaction to latex, avoid the use of equipment containing latex.
- Instruct the patient to cooperate fully and to follow directions. Direct the patient to breathe normally and to avoid unnecessary movement.
- Observe standard precautions, and follow the general guidelines in Appendix A. Positively identify the patient, and label the appropriate specimen container with the corresponding patient demographics, initials of the person collecting the specimen, date, and time of collection. Perform a venipuncture. The specimen should be mixed gently by inverting the tube 10 times. The specimen should be analyzed within 24 hr when stored at room temperature or within 48 hr if stored at refrigerated temperature. If it is anticipated the specimen will not be analyzed within 24 hr, two blood smears should be made immediately after the venipuncture and submitted with the blood sample. Smears made from specimens older than 24 hr may contain an unacceptable number of misleading artifactual abnormalities of the RBCs, such as echinocytes and spherocytes, as well as necrobiotic white blood cells.
- Remove the needle and apply direct pressure with dry gauze to stop bleeding. Observe/assess venipuncture site for bleeding or hematoma formation and secure gauze with adhesive bandage.
- Promptly transport the specimen to the laboratory for processing and analysis.

POST-TEST:

- A report of the results will be made available to the requesting HCP, who will discuss the results with the patient.
- *Nutritional Considerations:* Infection, fever, sepsis, and trauma can result in an impaired nutritional status. Malnutrition can occur for many reasons, including fatigue, lack of appetite, and gastrointestinal distress.

Nutritional Considerations: Adequate intake of vitamins A and C, and zinc are also important for regenerating body stores depleted by the effort exerted in fighting infections. Educate the patient or caregiver regarding the importance of following the prescribed diet.

Nutritional Considerations: The Institute of Medicine's Food and Nutrition Board suggests 900 mcg/d as the daily recommended dietary allowance for vitamin A for males age 14 to greater than 70 yr and 700 mcg/d for females age 14 to greater than 70 yr; 770 mcg/d for pregnant females age 19 to 50 yr; 750 mcg/day for pregnant females under age 19 yr; 1,300 mcg/d for lactating females age 19 to 50 yr; 1,200 mcg/d for lactating females under age 18 yr; 600 mcg/day for children age 9 to 13 yr; 400 mcg/d for children age 4 to 8 yr; 300 mcg/d for children age 1 to 3 yr; 500 mcg/d for children age 7 to 12 mo (recommended adequate intake); and 400 mcg/d for children age 0 to 6 mo (recommended adequate intake). Reprinted with permission from the National Academies Press, copyright 2013, National Academy of Sciences. Educate the patient with vitamin A deficiency, as appropriate, that the main dietary source of vitamin A comes from carotene, a yellow pigment noticeable in most fruits and vegetables, especially carrots, sweet potatoes, squash, apricots, and cantaloupe. It is also present in spinach, collards, broccoli, and cabbage. This vitamin is fairly stable at most cooking temperatures, but it is destroyed easily by light and oxidation.

Vitamin C
Nutritional Considerations: The Institute of Medicine's Food and Nutrition Board suggests 90 mg/d as the daily recommended dietary allowance for dietary vitamin C for adult males age 19 to greater than 70 yr and 75 mg/d for adult females age 19 to greater than 70 yr; 85 mg/d for pregnant females age 19 to 50 yr; 80 mg/day for pregnant females under age 19 yr; 120 mg/d for lactating females age 19 to 50 yr; 115 mg/d for lactating

females under age 19 yr; 75 mg/day for male children age 14 to 18 yr and 65 mg/d for female children age 14 to 18 yr; 45 mg/d for children age 9 to 13 yr; 25 mg/d for children age 4 to 8 yr; 15 mg/d for children age 1 to 3 yr; 50 mg/d for children age 7 to 12 mo (recommended adequate intake); 40 mg/d for children age 0 to 6 mo (recommended adequate intake). Reprinted with permission from the National Academies Press, copyright 2013, National Academy of Sciences. Educate the patient with vitamin C deficiency, as appropriate, that citrus fruits are excellent dietary sources of vitamin C. Other good sources are green and red peppers, tomatoes, white potatoes, cabbage, broccoli, chard, kale, turnip greens, asparagus, berries, melons, pineapple, and guava. Vitamin C is destroyed by exposure to air, light, heat, or alkalis. Boiling water before cooking eliminates dissolved oxygen that destroys vitamin C in the process of boiling. Vegetables should be crisp and cooked as quickly as possible.

Nutritional Considerations: Topical or oral supplementation may be ordered for patients with zinc deficiency. The Institute of Medicine's Food and Nutrition Board suggests 11 mg/d as the daily recommended dietary allowance for dietary zinc for males age 14 to greater than 50 yr; 8 mg/d for adult females age 19 to greater than 50 yr; 11 mg/d for pregnant females age 19 to 50 yr; 12 mg/day for pregnant females age 14 to 18 yr; 12 mg/d for lactating females age 19 to 50 yr; 13 mg/d for lactating females age 14 to 18 yr; 9 mg/d for females age 14 to 18 yr; 8 mg/day for children age 9 to 13 yr; 5 mg/d for children age 4 to 8 yr; 3 mg/d for children age 7 mo to 3 yr; 2 mg/d for children age 0 to 6 mo. Reprinted with permission from the National Academies Press, copyright 2013, National Academy of Sciences. Dietary sources high in zinc include shellfish, red meat, wheat germ, nuts, and processed foods such as canned pork and beans and canned chili. Patients should be informed that phytates (from whole grains, coffee, cocoa, or tea) bind zinc and prevent it from being absorbed. Decreases in zinc also can be induced by increased intake of iron, copper, or manganese. Vitamin and mineral supplements with a greater than 3:1 iron/zinc ratio inhibit zinc absorption.

‣ Recognize anxiety related to test results, and be supportive of fear of shortened life expectancy. Discuss the implications of abnormal test results on the patient's lifestyle. Provide teaching and information regarding the clinical implications of the test results, as appropriate. Educate the patient regarding access to counseling services. Provide contact information, if desired, for the National Cancer Institute (www.nci.nih.org) and for the Institute of Medicine of the National Academies (www.iom.edu).

‣ Reinforce information given by the patient's HCP regarding further testing, treatment, or referral to another HCP. Answer any questions or address any concerns voiced by the patient or family.

‣ Depending on the results of this procedure, additional testing may be performed to evaluate or monitor progression of the disease process and determine the need for a change in therapy. Evaluate test results in relation to the patient's symptoms and other tests performed.

RELATED MONOGRAPHS:

‣ Related tests include albumin, antibody, anti–neutrophilic cytoplasmic biopsy bone marrow, biopsy lymph node, CBC, CBC RBC count, CBC RBC indices, CBC RBC morphology, culture bacterial (see individually listed culture monographs), culture fungal, culture viral, eosinophil count, ESR, fecal analysis, Gram stain, infectious mononucleosis, LAP, procalcitonin, UA, US abdomen, and WBC scan.

‣ Refer to the Hematopoietic, Immune, and Respiratory systems tables at the end of the book for related tests by body system.

Computed Tomography, Abdomen

SYNONYM/ACRONYM: Computed axial tomography (CAT), computed transaxial tomography (CTT), abdominal CT, helical/spiral CT.

COMMON USE: To visualize and assess abdominal structures and to assist in diagnosing tumors, bleeding, and abscess. Used as an evaluation tool for surgical, radiation, and medical therapeutic interventions.

AREA OF APPLICATION: Abdomen.

CONTRAST: With or without oral or IV iodinated contrast medium.

DESCRIPTION: Abdominal computed tomography (CT) is a noninvasive procedure used to enhance certain anatomic views of the abdominal structures. It becomes invasive when contrast medium is used. During the procedure, the patient lies on a table and is moved in and out of a doughnut-like device called a *gantry*, which houses the x-ray tube and associated electronics. The scanner uses multiple x-ray beams and a series of detectors that rotate around the patient to produce cross-sectional views in a three-dimensional fashion. Differences in tissue density are detected and recorded and are viewable as computerized digital images. Slices or thin sections of certain anatomic views of the liver, biliary tract, pancreas, kidneys, spleen, intestines, and vascular system are reviewed to allow differentiations of solid, cystic, inflammatory, or vascular lesions, as well as identification of suspected hematomas and aneurysms. The procedure is repeated after intravenous injection of iodinated contrast medium for vascular evaluation or after oral ingestion of contrast medium for evaluation of bowel and adjacent structures. Images can be recorded on photographic or x-ray film or stored in digital format as digitized computer data. Cine scanning is used to produce a series of moving images of the area scanned. The CT scan can be used to guide biopsy needles into areas of abdominal tumors to obtain tissue for laboratory analysis and to guide placement of catheters for drainage of intra-abdominal abscesses. Tumors, before and after therapy, may be monitored with CT scanning.

INDICATIONS
- Assist in differentiating between benign and malignant tumors
- Detect aortic aneurysms
- Detect tumor extension of masses and metastasis into the abdominal area
- Differentiate aortic aneurysms from tumors near the aorta
- Differentiate between infectious and inflammatory processes
- Evaluate cysts, masses, abscesses, renal calculi, gastrointestinal (GI) bleeding and obstruction, and trauma

- Evaluate retroperitoneal lymph nodes
- Monitor and evaluate the effectiveness of medical, radiation, or surgical therapies

POTENTIAL DIAGNOSIS

Normal findings in
- Normal size, position, and shape of abdominal organs and vascular system

Abnormal findings in
- Abdominal abscess
- Abdominal aortic aneurysm
- Adrenal tumor or hyperplasia
- Appendicitis
- Bowel obstruction
- Bowel perforation
- Dilation of the common hepatic duct, common bile duct, or gallbladder
- GI bleeding
- Hematomas, diverticulitis, gallstones
- Hemoperitoneum
- Hepatic cysts or abscesses
- Pancreatic pseudocyst
- Primary and metastatic neoplasms
- Renal calculi
- Splenic laceration, tumor, infiltration, and trauma

CRITICAL FINDINGS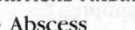

- Abscess
- Acute GI bleed
- Aortic aneurysm
- Appendicitis
- Aortic dissection
- Bowel perforation
- Bowel obstruction
- Mesenteric torsion
- Tumor with significant mass effect
- Visceral injury; significant solid organ laceration

It is essential that critical diagnoses be communicated immediately to the appropriate HCP. A listing of these diagnoses varies among facilities. Note and immediately report to the HCP abnormal results and relat-

ed symptoms. Timely notification of critical values for lab or diagnostic studies is a role expectation of the professional nurse. Notification processes will vary among facilities. Upon receipt of the critical value, the information should be read back to the caller to verify accuracy. Most policies require immediate notification of the primary HCP, hospitalist, or on-call HCP. Reported information includes the patient's name, unique identifiers, critical value, name of the person giving the report, and name of the person receiving the report. Documentation of notification should be made in the medical record with the name of the HCP notified, time and date of notification, and any orders received. Any delay in a timely report of a critical value may require completion of a notification form with review by Risk Management.

INTERFERING FACTORS

This procedure is contraindicated for
- Patients with allergies to shellfish or iodinated dye. The contrast medium used may cause a life-threatening allergic reaction. Patients with a known hypersensitivity to the medium may benefit from premedication with corticosteroids or the use of nonionic contrast medium.
- Patients who are claustrophobic.
- Patients who are pregnant or suspected of being pregnant, unless the potential benefits of the procedure far outweigh the risks to the fetus and mother.
- Elderly and other patients who are chronically dehydrated before the test, because of their risk of contrast-induced renal failure.
- Patients who are in renal failure.
- Young patients (17 yr and younger), unless the benefits of the x-ray diagnosis outweigh the risks

of exposure to high levels of radiation. Information on the Image Gently Campaign can be found at the Alliance for Radiation Safety in Pediatric Imaging (www.pedrad.org/associations/5364/ig/).

Factors that may impair clear imaging
- Gas or feces in the GI tract resulting from inadequate cleansing or failure to restrict food intake before the study.
- Retained barium from a previous radiological procedure.
- Metallic objects within the examination field (e.g., jewelry, body rings), which may inhibit organ visualization and cause unclear images.
- Patients with extreme claustrophobia unless sedation is given before the study.
- Inability of the patient to cooperate or remain still during the procedure because of age, significant pain, or mental status.

Other considerations
- Complications of the procedure may include hemorrhage, infection at the IV needle insertion site, and cardiac arrhythmias.
- The procedure may be terminated if chest pain or severe cardiac arrhythmias occur.
- Failure to follow dietary restrictions and other pretesting preparations may cause the procedure to be canceled or repeated.
- Consultation with an HCP should occur before the procedure for radiation safety concerns regarding younger patients or patients who are lactating.
- Risks associated with radiation overexposure can result from frequent x-ray procedures. Personnel in the room with the patient should wear a protective lead apron, stand behind a shield, or leave the area while the examination is being done. Personnel working in the examination area should wear badges to record their level of radiation exposure.

NURSING IMPLICATIONS AND PROCEDURE

PRETEST:

▶ Positively identify the patient using at least two unique identifiers before providing care, treatment, or services.

▶ *Patient Teaching:* Inform the patient this procedure can assist in assessing the abdominal organs.

▶ Obtain a history of the patient's complaints, including a list of known allergens, especially allergies or sensitivities to latex, iodine, seafood, anesthetics, or contrast medium.

▶ Obtain a history of the patient's gastrointestinal and hepatobiliary systems, symptoms, and results of previously performed laboratory tests and diagnostic and surgical procedures.

▶ Ensure results of coagulation testing are obtained and recorded prior to the procedure; BUN and creatinine results are also needed if contrast medium is to be used.

▶ Note any recent procedures that can interfere with test results, including examinations using barium- or iodine-based contrast medium. Ensure that barium studies were performed more than 4 days before the CT scan.

▶ Record the date of the last menstrual period and determine the possibility of pregnancy in perimenopausal women.

▶ Obtain a list of the patient's current medications including anticoagulants, aspirin and other salicylates, herbs, nutritional supplements, and nutraceuticals (see Appendix F). Note the last time and dose of medication taken.

- If contrast medium is scheduled to be used, patients receiving metformin (Glucophage) for non-insulin-dependent (type 2) diabetes should discontinue the drug on the day of the test and continue to withhold it for 48 hr after the test. Failure to do so may result in lactic acidosis.
- Review the procedure with the patient. Explain the purpose of the test and how the procedure is performed. Address concerns about pain and explain that there may be moments of discomfort and some pain experienced during the test. Inform the patient that the procedure is performed in a radiology suite, usually by an HCP, and takes approximately 30 to 60 min.
- *Sensitivity to social and cultural issues,* as well as concern for modesty, is important in providing psychological support before, during, and after the procedure.
- Explain that an IV line may be inserted to allow infusion of IV fluids, anesthetics, or sedatives.
- Inform the patient that he or she may experience nausea, a feeling of warmth, a salty or metallic taste, or a transient headache after injection of contrast medium, if given.
- The patient may be requested to drink approximately 450 mL of a dilute barium solution (approximately 1% barium) or a water soluble oral contrast beginning 1 hr before the examination. This is administered to distinguish GI organs from the other abdominal organs.
- Instruct the patient to remove jewelry and other metallic objects from the area to be examined.
- The patient should fast and restrict fluids for 8 hr prior to the procedure. Instruct the patient to avoid taking anticoagulant medication or to reduce dosage as ordered prior to the procedure. Protocols may vary among facilities.
- *Make sure a written and informed consent has been signed prior to the procedure and before administering any medications.*

INTRATEST:

- Observe standard precautions, and follow the general guidelines in Appendix A. Positively identify the patient.
- Ensure the patient has complied with dietary, fluids, and medication restrictions for 8 hr prior to the procedure.
- Ensure the patient has removed all external metallic objects from the area to be examined.
- If the patient has a history of allergic reactions to any substance or drug, administer ordered prophylactic steroids or antihistamines before the procedure. Use nonionic contrast medium for the procedure.
- Have emergency equipment readily available.
- Instruct the patient to void prior to the procedure and to change into the gown, robe, and foot coverings provided.
- Instruct the patient to cooperate fully and to follow directions. Instruct the patient to remain still throughout the procedure because movement produces unreliable results.
- Record baseline vital signs, and continue to monitor throughout the procedure. Protocols may vary among facilities.
- Establish an IV fluid line for the injection of contrast, emergency drugs, and sedatives.
- Administer an antianxiety agent, as ordered, if the patient has claustrophobia. Administer a sedative to a child or to an uncooperative adult, as ordered.
- Place the patient in the supine position on an examination table.
- If IV contrast media is used, during and after injection a rapid series of images is taken.
- Instruct the patient to inhale deeply and hold his or her breath while the x-ray images are taken, and then to exhale after the images are taken.
- Instruct the patient to take slow, deep breaths if nausea occurs during the procedure.
- Monitor the patient for complications related to the procedure (e.g., allergic

reaction, anaphylaxis, bronchospasm) if contrast is used.

▸ The needle is removed, and a pressure dressing is applied over the puncture site.

▸ Observe/assess the needle site for bleeding, inflammation, or hematoma formation.

POST-TEST:

▸ A report of the results will be made available to the requesting HCP, who will discuss the results with the patient.

▸ Instruct the patient to resume usual diet, fluids, medications, and activity, as directed by the HCP. Renal function should be assessed before metformin is resumed, if contrast was used.

▸ Monitor vital signs and neurological status every 15 min for 1 hr, then every 2 hr for 4 hr, and then as ordered by the HCP. Monitor temperature every 4 hr for 24 hr. Monitor intake and output at least every 8 hr. Compare with baseline values. Notify the HCP if temperature is elevated. Protocols may vary from facility to facility.

▸ If contrast was used, observe for delayed allergic reactions, such as rash, urticaria, tachycardia, hyperpnea, hypertension, palpitations, nausea, or vomiting.

▸ Instruct the patient to immediately report symptoms such as fast heart rate, difficulty breathing, skin rash, itching, chest pain, persistent right shoulder pain, or abdominal pain. Immediately report symptoms to the appropriate HCP.

▸ Observe/assess the needle insertion site for bleeding, inflammation, or hematoma formation.

▸ Instruct the patient in the care and assessment of the site.

▸ Instruct the patient to apply cold compresses to the insertion site as needed, to reduce discomfort or edema.

▸ Instruct the patient to increase fluid intake to help eliminate the contrast medium, if used.

▸ Inform the patient that diarrhea may occur after ingestion of oral contrast medium.

▸ Recognize anxiety related to test results. Discuss the implications of abnormal test results on the patient's lifestyle. Provide teaching and information regarding the clinical implications of the test results, as appropriate.

▸ Reinforce information given by the patient's HCP regarding further testing, treatment, or referral to another HCP. Answer any questions or address any concerns voiced by the patient or family.

▸ Depending on the results of this procedure, additional testing may be needed to evaluate or monitor progression of the disease process and determine the need for a change in therapy. Evaluate test results in relation to the patient's symptoms and other tests performed.

RELATED MONOGRAPHS:

▸ Related tests include ACTH and challenge tests, amylase, angiography abdomen, biopsy intestinal, BUN, calculus kidney stone panel, CBC, CBC hematocrit, CBC hemoglobin, cortisol and challenge tests, creatinine, cystoscopy, hepatobiliary scan, IVP, KUB studies, MRI abdomen, peritoneal fluid analysis, PT/INR, renogram, US abdomen, and US pelvis.

▸ Refer to the Gastrointestinal and Hepatobiliary systems tables at the end of the book for related tests by body system.

Computed Tomography, Angiography

SYNONYM/ACRONYM: Computed axial tomography (CAT) angiography, CTA.

COMMON USE: To visualize and assess the vascular structure to assist in the diagnosis of aneurysm, embolism, or stenosis.

AREA OF APPLICATION: Vessels.

CONTRAST: IV iodinated contrast medium.

DESCRIPTION: Computed tomography angiography (CTA) is a noninvasive procedure that enhances certain anatomic views of vascular structures. This procedure complements traditional angiography and allows reconstruction of the images in different planes and removal of surrounding structures, leaving only the vessels to be studied. While lying on a table, the patient is moved in and out of a doughnut-like device called a *gantry*, which houses the x-ray tube and associated electronics. The scanner uses multiple x-ray beams and a series of detectors that rotate around the patient to produce cross-sectional views in a three-dimensional fashion by detecting and recording differences in tissue density after having an x-ray beam passed through the tissues. CTA uses spiral CT technology and collects large amounts of data with each scan. Retrospectively, the data can be manipulated to produce the desired image without exposure to additional radiation or contrast medium. Multiplanar reconstruction images are reviewed by the health-care provider (HCP) at a computerized workstation. These images are helpful when there are heavily calcified vessels. The axial images give the most precise information regarding the true extent of stenosis, and they can also evaluate intracerebral aneurysms. Small ulcerations and plaque irregularity are readily seen with CTA; the degree of stenosis can be estimated better with CTA because of the increased number of imaging planes. Density measurements are sent to a computer that produces a digital image of the anatomy, enabling the HCP to look at slices or thin sections of certain anatomic views of the vessels. Iodinated contrast medium is given IV for vascular evaluation. Images can be recorded on photographic or x-ray film or stored in digital format as digitized computer data.

INDICATIONS

- Detect aneurysms
- Detect embolism or other occlusions
- Detect fistula
- Detect stenosis
- Detect peripheral artery disease (PAD)
- Differentiate aortic aneurysms from tumors near the aorta
- Differentiate between vascular and nonvascular tumors
- Evaluate atherosclerosis
- Evaluate hemorrhage or trauma
- Monitor and evaluate the effectiveness of medical or surgical therapies

POTENTIAL DIAGNOSIS

Normal findings in
- Normal size, position, and shape of vascular structures

Abnormal findings in
- Aortic aneurysm
- Cysts or abscesses
- Emboli
- Hemorrhage
- Neoplasm
- Occlusion
- PAD
- Shunting
- Stenosis

CRITICAL FINDINGS
- Brain or spinal cord ischemia
- Emboli
- Hemorrhage
- Leaking aortic aneurysm
- Occlusion
- Tumor with significant mass effect

It is essential that critical diagnoses be communicated immediately to the appropriate HCP. A listing of these diagnoses varies among facilities. Note and immediately report to the HCP abnormal results and related symptoms. Timely notification of critical values for lab or diagnostic studies is a role expectation of the professional nurse. Notification processes will vary among facilities. Upon receipt of the critical value the information should be read back to the caller to verify accuracy. Most policies require immediate notification of the primary HCP, hospitalist, or on-call HCP. Reported information includes the patient's name, unique identifiers, critical value, name of the person giving the report, and name of the person receiving the report. Documentation of notification should be made in the medical record with the name of the HCP notified, time and date of notification, and any orders received. Any delay in a timely report of a critical value may require completion of a notification form with review by Risk Management.

INTERFERING FACTORS

This procedure is contraindicated for
- Patients with allergies to shellfish or iodinated dye. The contrast medium used may cause a life-threatening allergic reaction. Patients with a known hypersensitivity to the medium may benefit from premedication with corticosteroids or the use of nonionic contrast medium.
- Patients who are claustrophobic.
- Patients who are pregnant or suspected of being pregnant, unless the potential benefits of the procedure far outweigh the risks to the fetus and mother.
- Elderly and other patients who are chronically dehydrated before the test, because of their risk of contrast-induced renal failure.
- Patients who are in renal failure.
- Young patients (17 yr and younger), unless the benefits of the x-ray diagnosis outweigh the risks of exposure to high levels of radiation. Information on the Image Gently Campaign can be found at the Alliance for Radiation Safety in Pediatric Imaging (www.pedrad.org/associations/5364/ig/).

Factors that may impair clear imaging
- Gas or feces in the gastrointestinal tract resulting from inadequate cleansing or failure to restrict food intake before the study.
- Retained barium from a previous radiological procedure.
- Metallic objects within the examination field (e.g., jewelry, body rings), which may inhibit organ visualization and cause unclear images.
- Patients who are very obese or who may exceed the weight limit for the equipment.
- Patients with extreme claustrophobia unless sedation is given before the study.

• Inability of the patient to cooperate or remain still during the procedure because of age, significant pain, or mental status.

Other considerations

• Complications of the procedure include hemorrhage, infection at the IV needle insertion site, and cardiac arrhythmias.

• The procedure may be terminated if chest pain or severe cardiac arrhythmias occur.

• Failure to follow dietary restrictions and other pretesting preparations may cause the procedure to be canceled or repeated.

• Consultation with the HCP should occur before the procedure for radiation safety concerns regarding younger patients or patients who are lactating.

• Risks associated with radiation overexposure can result from frequent x-ray procedures. Personnel in the room with the patient should wear a protective lead apron, stand behind a shield, or leave the area while the examination is being done. Personnel working in the examination area should wear badges to record their level of radiation exposure.

NURSING IMPLICATIONS AND PROCEDURE

PRETEST:

▶ Positively identify the patient using at least two unique identifiers before providing care, treatment, or services.

▶ *Patient Teaching:* Inform the patient this procedure can assist in assessing the cardiovascular system.

▶ Obtain a history of the patient's complaints or clinical symptoms, including a list of known allergens, especially allergies or sensitivities to latex, iodine, seafood, anesthetics, or contrast mediums.

▶ Obtain a history of patient's cardiovascular system, symptoms, and results of previously performed laboratory tests and diagnostic and surgical procedures.

▶ Ensure results of coagulation testing are obtained and recorded prior to the procedure; BUN and creatinine results are also needed if contrast medium is to be used.

▶ Note any recent procedures that can interfere with test results, including examinations using barium- or iodine-based contrast medium. Ensure that barium studies were performed more than 4 days before the CT scan.

▶ Record the date of the last menstrual period and determine the possibility of pregnancy in perimenopausal women.

▶ Obtain a list of the patient's current medications, including anticoagulants, aspirin and other salicylates, herbs, nutritional supplements, and nutraceuticals (see Appendix F). Such products should be discontinued by medical direction for the appropriate number of days prior to a surgical procedure. Note the last time and dose of medication taken.

▶ If contrast medium is scheduled to be used, patients receiving metformin (Glucophage) for non–insulin-dependent (type 2) diabetes should discontinue the drug on the day of the test and continue to withhold it for 48 hr after the test. Failure to do so may result in lactic acidosis.

▶ Review the procedure with the patient. Address concerns about pain and explain that there may be moments of discomfort and some pain experienced during the test. Inform the patient that the procedure is usually performed in a radiology suite by an HCP specializing in this procedure, with support staff, and takes approximately 30 to 60 min.

▶ *Sensitivity to social and cultural issues,* as well as concern for modesty, is important in providing psychological support before, during, and after the procedure.

▶ Explain that an IV line may be inserted to allow infusion of IV fluids, anesthetics, or sedatives.

▶ Inform the patient that a burning and flushing sensation may be felt throughout the body during injection of the contrast medium. After injection of the contrast medium, the patient may experience an urge to cough, flushing, nausea, or a salty or metallic taste.

- Instruct the patient to remove all external metallic objects from the area to be examined.
- The patient should fast and restrict fluids for 8 hr prior to the procedure.
- Instruct the patient to avoid taking anticoagulant medication or to reduce dosage as ordered prior to the procedure. Protocols may vary among facilities.
- *Make sure a written and informed consent has been signed prior to the procedure and before administering any medications.*

INTRATEST:

- Observe standard precautions, and follow the general guidelines in Appendix A. Positively identify the patient.
- Ensure that the patient has complied with dietary, fluid, and medication restrictions for 8 hr prior to the procedure.
- Ensure that the patient has removed all external metallic objects from the area to be examined.
- If the patient has a history of allergic reactions to any substance or drug, administer ordered prophylactic steroids or antihistamines before the procedure. Use nonionic contrast medium for the procedure.
- Have emergency equipment readily available.
- Instruct the patient to void prior to the procedure and to change into the gown, robe, and foot coverings provided.
- Instruct the patient to cooperate fully and to follow directions. Instruct the patient to remain still throughout the procedure because movement produces unreliable results.
- Establish an IV fluid line for the injection of contrast, emergency drugs, and sedatives.
- Administer an antianxiety agent, as ordered, if the patient has claustrophobia. Administer a sedative to a child or to an uncooperative adult, as ordered.
- Place the patient in the supine position on an examination table.
- The contrast medium is injected, and a rapid series of images is taken during and after the filling of the vessels to be examined. Delayed images may be

taken to examine the vessels after a time and to monitor the venous phase of the procedure.

- Ask the patient to inhale deeply and hold his or her breath while the x-ray images are taken, and then to exhale after the images are taken.
- Instruct the patient to take slow, deep breaths if nausea occurs during the procedure. Monitor and administer an antiemetic agent if ordered. Ready an emesis basin for use.
- Monitor the patient for complications related to the procedure (e.g., allergic reaction, anaphylaxis, bronchospasm).
- The needle is removed and a pressure dressing is applied over the puncture site.
- Observe/assess the needle site for bleeding, inflammation, or hematoma formation.

POST-TEST:

- A report of the results will be made available to the requesting HCP, who will discuss the results with the patient.
- Instruct the patient to resume pretesting diet, as directed by the HCP. Assess the patient's ability to swallow before allowing the patient to attempt liquids or solid foods. Renal function should be assessed before metformin is resumed.
- Monitor vital signs and neurological status every 15 min for 1 hr, then every 2 hr for 4 hr, and then as ordered by the HCP. Monitor temperature every 4 hr for 24 hr. Monitor intake and output at least every 8 hr. Compare with baseline values. Notify the HCP if temperature is elevated. Protocols may vary among facilities.
- If contrast was used, observe for delayed allergic reactions, such as rash, urticaria, tachycardia, hyperpnea, hypertension, palpitations, nausea, or vomiting.
- Instruct the patient to immediately report symptoms such as fast heart rate, difficulty breathing, skin rash, itching, chest pain, persistent right shoulder pain, or abdominal pain. Immediately report symptoms to the appropriate HCP.

- Assess extremities for signs of ischemia or absence of distal pulse caused by a catheter-induced thrombus.
- Observe/assess the needle insertion site for bleeding, inflammation, or hematoma formation.
- Instruct the patient to apply cold compresses to the insertion site as needed, to reduce discomfort or edema.
- Instruct the patient to increase fluid intake to help eliminate the contrast medium, if used.
- Inform the patient that diarrhea may occur after ingestion of oral contrast medium.
- Instruct the patient to maintain bed rest for 4 to 6 hr after the procedure.
- *Nutritional Considerations:* Abnormal findings may be associated with cardiovascular disease. The American Heart Association and National Heart, Lung, and Blood Institute (NHLBI) recommend nutritional therapy for individuals identified to be at high risk for developing coronary artery disease (CAD) or individuals who have specific risk factors and/or existing medical conditions (e.g., elevated LDL cholesterol levels, other lipid disorders, insulin-dependent diabetes, insulin resistance, or metabolic syndrome). If overweight, the patient should be encouraged to achieve a normal weight. Guidelines for the Therapeutic Lifestyle Changes (TLC) diet are outlined in the Third Report of the Expert Panel on Detection, Evaluation, and Treatment of High Blood Cholesterol in Adults (Adult Treatment Panel III [ATP III]). The TLC diet emphasizes a reduction in foods high in saturated fats and cholesterol. Red meats, eggs, and dairy products are the major sources of saturated fats and cholesterol. If triglycerides also are elevated, the patient should be advised to eliminate or reduce alcohol and simple carbohydrates from the diet. The TLC approach also includes the use of plant stanols or sterols and increased dissolved fiber as an option for lowering LDL cholesterol levels; nutritional recommendations for daily total caloric intake; recommendations for allowable percentage of calories derived from fat (saturated and unsaturated), carbohydrates, protein, and cholesterol; as well as recommendations for daily expenditure of energy.

- *Nutritional Considerations:* Overweight patients with high blood pressure should be encouraged to achieve a normal weight. Other changeable risk factors warranting patient education include strategies to safely decrease sodium intake, increase physical activity, decrease alcohol consumption, eliminate tobacco use, and decrease cholesterol levels.
- *Social and Cultural Considerations:* Numerous studies point to the prevalence of excess body weight in American children and adolescents. Experts estimate that obesity is present in 25% of the population ages 6 to 11 yr. The medical, social, and emotional consequences of excess body weight are significant. Special attention should be given to instructing the child and caregiver regarding health risks and weight control education.
- Recognize anxiety related to test results, and be supportive of fear of shortened life expectancy. Discuss the implications of abnormal test results on the patient's lifestyle. Provide teaching and information regarding the clinical implications of the test results, as appropriate. Educate the patient regarding access to counseling services. Provide contact information, if desired, for the American Heart Association (www.americanheart.org) or the NHLBI (www.nhlbi.nih.gov).
- Recognize anxiety related to test results. Discuss the implications of abnormal test results on the patient's lifestyle. Provide teaching and information regarding the clinical implications of the test results, as appropriate.
- Reinforce information given by the patient's HCP regarding further testing, treatment, or referral to another HCP. Answer any questions or address any concerns voiced by the patient or family.
- Instruct the patient in the use of any ordered medications. Explain the importance of adhering to the therapy regimen. As appropriate, instruct the patient in significant side effects and systemic reactions associated with the prescribed medication. Encourage him

or her to review corresponding literature provided by a pharmacist. Depending on the results of this procedure, additional testing may be needed to evaluate or monitor progression of the disease process and determine the need for a change in therapy. Evaluate test results in relation to the patient's symptoms and other tests performed.

RELATED MONOGRAPHS:

Related tests include angiography of the specific area (abdomen, adrenal, carotid, coronary, pulmonary, renal), blood pool imaging, BUN, chest x-ray, colonoscopy, CBC, CBC hematocrit, CBC hemoglobin, CT of the specific area (abdomen, biliary/liver, brain, pituitary, renal, spine, spleen, thoracic), creatinine echocardiography, echocardiography transesophageal, fluorescein angiography, fundus photography, MRA, MRI of the specific area (abdomen, brain, chest, pituitary), MRI venography, MI scan, plethysmography, PET (brain, heart), proctosigmoidoscopy, PT/INR, US carotid, and US venous Doppler extremity. Refer to the Cardiovascular System table at the end of the book for related tests by body system.

Computed Tomography, Biliary Tract and Liver

SYNONYM/ACRONYM: Computed axial tomography (CAT), computed transaxial tomography (CTT), abdominal CT, helical/spiral CT.

COMMON USE: To visualize and assess the structure of the liver and biliary tract toward the diagnosis of tumor, obstruction, bleeding, and infection. Used as an evaluation tool for surgical, radiation, and medical therapeutic interventions.

AREA OF APPLICATION: Liver, biliary tract, and adjacent structures.

CONTRAST: With or without IV iodinated contrast medium.

DESCRIPTION: Computed tomography (CT) of the liver and biliary tract is a noninvasive procedure that enhances certain anatomic views of these structures. It becomes invasive with the use of contrast medium. During the procedure, the patient lies on a table and is moved in and out of a doughnut-like device called a *gantry*, which houses the x-ray tube and associated electronics. The scanner uses multiple x-ray beams and a series of detectors that rotate around the patient to produce cross-sectional views in a three-dimensional fashion. Differences in tissue density are detected and recorded and are viewable as computerized digital images. Slices or thin sections of certain anatomic views of the kidneys and associated vascular system are reviewed to allow differentiation of solid, cystic, inflammatory, or vascular lesions,

C

as well as identification of suspected hematomas and aneurysms. The procedure is repeated after IV injection of iodinated contrast medium for vascular evaluation or after oral ingestion of contrast medium for evaluation of bowel and adjacent structures. Images can be recorded on photographic or x-ray film or stored in digital format as digitized computer data. Cine scanning produces a series of moving images of the scanned area. The CT scan can be used to guide biopsy needles into areas of liver and biliary tract masses to obtain tissue for laboratory analysis and for placement of needles to aspirate cysts or abscesses. CT scanning can monitor mass, cyst, or tumor growth and post-therapy response.

INDICATIONS

- Assist in differentiating between benign and malignant tumors
- Detect dilation or obstruction of the biliary ducts with or without calcification or gallstone
- Detect liver abnormalities, such as cirrhosis with ascites and fatty liver
- Detect tumor extension of masses and metastasis into the hepatic area
- Differentiate aortic aneurysms from tumors near the aorta
- Differentiate between obstructive and nonobstructive jaundice
- Differentiate infectious from inflammatory processes
- Evaluate hepatic cysts, masses, abscesses, and hematomas, or hepatic trauma
- Monitor and evaluate effectiveness of medical, radiation, or surgical therapies

POTENTIAL DIAGNOSIS

Normal findings in

- Normal size, position, and contour of the liver and biliary ducts

Abnormal findings in

- Dilation of the common hepatic duct, common bile duct, or gallbladder
- Gallstones
- Hematomas
- Hepatic cysts or abscesses
- Jaundice (obstructive or nonobstructive)
- Primary and metastatic neoplasms

CRITICAL FINDINGS: N/A

INTERFERING FACTORS

This procedure is contraindicated for

- ◆ Patients with allergies to shellfish or iodinated dye. The contrast medium used may cause a life-threatening allergic reaction. Patients with a known hypersensitivity to the medium may benefit from premedication with corticosteroids or the use of nonionic contrast medium.
- Patients who are claustrophobic.
- Patients who are pregnant or suspected of being pregnant, unless the potential benefits of the procedure far outweigh the risks to the fetus and mother.
- ◆ Elderly and other patients who are chronically dehydrated before the test, because of their risk of contrast-induced renal failure.
- ◆ Patients who are in renal failure.
- Young patients (17 yr and younger) unless the benefits of the x-ray diagnosis outweigh the risks of exposure to high levels of radiation. Information on the Image Gently Campaign can be found at the Alliance for Radiation Safety in Pediatric Imaging (www.pedrad.org/associations/5364/ig/).

Factors that may impair clear imaging

Gas or feces in the gastrointestinal (GI) tract resulting from inadequate cleansing or failure to restrict food intake before the study.

Retained barium from a previous radiological procedure.

Metallic objects (e.g., jewelry, body rings) within the examination field, which may inhibit organ visualization and cause unclear images.

Patients who are very obese or who may exceed the weight limit for the equipment.

Patients with extreme claustrophobia unless sedation is given before the study.

Inability of the patient to cooperate or remain still during the procedure because of age, significant pain, or mental status.

Other considerations

Complications of the procedure include hemorrhage, infection at the IV needle insertion site, and cardiac arrhythmias.

The procedure may be terminated if chest pain or severe cardiac arrhythmias occur.

Failure to follow dietary restrictions and other pretesting preparations may cause the procedure to be canceled or repeated.

Consultation with a health-care provider (HCP) should occur before the procedure for radiation safety concerns regarding younger patients or patients who are lactating.

Risks associated with radiation overexposure can result from frequent x-ray procedures. Personnel in the room with the patient should wear a protective lead apron, stand behind a shield, or leave the area while the examination is being done. Personnel working in the examination area should wear badges to record their level of radiation exposure.

NURSING IMPLICATIONS AND PROCEDURE

PRETEST:

> Positively identify the patient using at least two unique identifiers before providing care, treatment, or services.

> *Patient Teaching:* Inform the patient this procedure can assist in assessing the liver, biliary tract, and surrounding structures.

> Obtain a history of the patient's complaints or clinical symptoms, including a list of known allergens, especially allergies or sensitivities to latex, iodine, seafood, anesthetics, or contrast medium.

> Obtain a history of the patient's hepatobiliary system, symptoms, and results of previously performed laboratory tests and diagnostic and surgical procedures.

> Ensure results of coagulation testing are obtained and recorded prior to the procedure; BUN and creatinine results are also needed if contrast medium is to be used.

> Note any recent procedures that can interfere with test results, including examinations using barium- or iodine-based contrast medium. Ensure that barium studies were performed more than 4 days before the CT scan.

> Record the date of the last menstrual period and determine the possibility of pregnancy in perimenopausal women.

> Obtain a list of the patient's current medications, including anticoagulants, aspirin and other salicylates, herbs, nutritional supplements, and nutraceuticals (see Appendix F). Note the last time and dose of medication taken.

> If contrast medium is scheduled to be used, patients receiving metformin (Glucophage) for non–insulin-dependent (type 2) diabetes should discontinue the drug on the day of the test and continue to withhold it for 48 hr after the test. Failure to do so may result in lactic acidosis.

> Review the procedure with the patient. Address concerns about pain and explain that there are moments of discomfort and some pain experienced during the test. Inform the patient the

C

procedure is usually performed in a radiology suite by an HCP specializing in this procedure, with support staff, and takes approximately 30 to 60 min. *Sensitivity to social and cultural issues,* as well as concern for modesty, is important in providing psychological support before, during, and after the procedure.

Explain that an IV line may be inserted to allow infusion of IV fluids, anesthetics, or sedatives.

Inform the patient that he or she may experience nausea, a feeling of warmth, a salty or metallic taste, or a transient headache after injection of contrast medium, if given.

The patient may be requested to drink approximately 450 mL of a dilute barium solution (approximately 1% barium) or water soluble contrast beginning 1 hr before the examination. This is administered to distinguish GI organs from the other abdominal organs.

Instruct the patient to remove all external metallic objects from the area to be examined.

The patient should fast and restrict fluids for 8 hr prior to the procedure. Instruct the patient to avoid taking anticoagulant medication or to reduce dosage as ordered prior to the procedure. Protocols may vary among facilities.

Make sure a written and informed consent has been signed prior to the procedure and before administering any medications.

INTRATEST:

Observe standard precautions, and follow the general guidelines in Appendix A. Positively identify the patient.

Ensure the patient has complied with dietary, fluids, and medication restrictions and pretesting preparations for 8 hr prior to the procedure.

Ensure the patient has removed all external metallic objects from the area to be examined.

If the patient has a history of allergic reactions to any substance or drug, administer ordered prophylactic steroids or antihistamines before the procedure. Use nonionic contrast medium for the procedure.

Have emergency equipment readily available.

Instruct the patient to void prior to the procedure and to change into the gown, robe, and foot coverings provided.

Instruct the patient to cooperate fully and to follow directions. Instruct the patient to remain still throughout the procedure because movement produces unreliable results.

Record baseline vital signs, and continue to monitor throughout the procedure. Protocols may vary among facilities.

Establish an IV fluid line for the injection of contrast medium, emergency drugs, and sedatives.

Administer an antianxiety agent, as ordered, if the patient has claustrophobia. Administer a sedative to a child or to an uncooperative adult, as ordered.

Place the patient in the supine position on an examination table.

If IV contrast medium is used, a rapid series of images is taken during and after injection.

Instruct the patient to inhale deeply and hold his or her breath while the x-ray images are taken, and then to exhale after the images are taken.

Instruct the patient to take slow, deep breaths if nausea occurs during the procedure.

Monitor the patient for complications related to the procedure (e.g., allergic reaction, anaphylaxis, bronchospasm) if contrast is used.

The needle is removed, and a pressure dressing is applied over the puncture site.

Observe/assess the needle site for bleeding, inflammation, or hematoma formation.

POST-TEST:

A report of the results will be made available to the requesting HCP, who will discuss the results with the patient.

Instruct the patient to resume usual diet, fluids, medications, and activity, as directed by the HCP. Renal function should be assessed before metformin is resumed, if contrast was used.

Monitor vital signs and neurological status every 15 min for 1 hr, then ever

2 hr for 4 hr, and then as ordered by the HCP. Monitor temperature every 4 hr for 24 hr. Monitor intake and output at least every 8 hr. Compare with baseline values. Notify the HCP if temperature is elevated. Protocols may vary among facilities.

If contrast was used, observe for delayed allergic reactions, such as rash, urticaria, tachycardia, hyperpnea, hypertension, palpitations, nausea, or vomiting.

Instruct the patient to immediately report symptoms such as fast heart rate, difficulty breathing, skin rash, itching, chest pain, persistent right shoulder pain, or abdominal pain. Immediately report symptoms to the appropriate HCP.

Observe/assess the needle insertion site for bleeding, inflammation, or hematoma formation.

Instruct the patient in the care and assessment of the site.

Instruct the patient to apply cold compresses to the insertion site as needed, to reduce discomfort or edema.

Instruct the patient to increase fluid intake to help eliminate the contrast medium, if used.

Inform the patient that diarrhea may occur after ingestion of oral contrast media.

Recognize anxiety related to test results. Discuss the implications of abnormal test results on the patient's lifestyle. Provide teaching and information regarding the clinical implications of the test results, as appropriate.

Reinforce information given by the patient's HCP regarding further testing, treatment, or referral to another HCP. Answer any questions or address any concerns voiced by the patient or family.

Depending on the results of this procedure, additional testing may be needed to evaluate or monitor progression of the disease process and determine the need for a change in therapy. Evaluate test results in relation to the patient's symptoms and other tests performed.

RELATED MONOGRAPHS:

Related tests include ALT, AST, bilirubin, biopsy liver, BUN, CBC, CBC hematocrit, CBC hemoglobin, creatinine, GGT, hepatobiliary scan, KUB, liver and spleen scan, MRI abdomen, PT/INR, and US liver.

Refer to the Hepatobiliary System table at the end of the book for related tests by body system.

Computed Tomography, Brain

SYNONYM/ACRONYM: Computed axial tomography (CAT) of the head, computed transaxial tomography (CTT) of the head, brain CT, helical/spiral CT.

COMMON USE: To visualize and assess the brain to assist in diagnosing tumor, bleeding, infarct, infection, structural changes, and edema. Also valuable in evaluation of medical, radiation, and surgical interventions.

AREA OF APPLICATION: Brain.

CONTRAST: With or without IV iodinated contrast medium.

DESCRIPTION: Computed tomography (CT) of the brain is a noninvasive procedure used to assist in diagnosing abnormalities of the head, brain tissue, cerebrospinal fluid, and blood circulation. It becomes invasive if contrast medium is used. The patient lies on a table and is moved in and out of a doughnut-like device called a *gantry*, which houses the x-ray tube and associated electronics. The scanner uses multiple x-ray beams and a series of detectors that rotate around the patient to produce cross-sectional views in a three-dimensional fashion. Differences in tissue density are detected and recorded and are viewable as computerized digital images for the health-care provider (HCP) to look at. Slices or thin sections of certain anatomic views of the brain and associated vascular system are viewed to allow differentiations of solid, cystic, inflammatory, or vascular lesions, as well as identification of suspected hematomas or aneurysms. The procedure is repeated after intravenous injection of iodinated contrast medium for vascular evaluation. Images can be recorded on photographic or x-ray film or stored in digital format as digitized computer data. Cine scanning is used to produce a series of moving images of the area scanned. Tumor progression, before and after therapy, and effectiveness of medical interventions may be monitored by CT scanning.

INDICATIONS

- Detect brain infection, abscess, or necrosis, as evidenced by decreased density on the image
- Detect ventricular enlargement or displacement by increased cerebrospinal fluid
- Determine benign and cancerous intracranial tumors and cyst formation, as evidenced by changes in tissue densities
- Determine cause of increased intracranial pressure
- Determine presence and type of hemorrhage in infants and children experiencing signs and symptoms of intracranial trauma or congenital conditions such as hydrocephalus and arteriovenous malformations (AVMs)
- Determine presence of multiple sclerosis, as evidenced by sclerotic plaques
- Determine lesion size and location causing infarct or hemorrhage
- Differentiate hematoma location after trauma (e.g., subdural, epidural, cerebral) and determine extent of edema, as evidenced by higher blood densities
- Differentiate between cerebral infarction and hemorrhage
- Evaluate abnormalities of the middle ear ossicles, auditory nerve, and optic nerve
- Monitor and evaluate the effectiveness of medical, radiation, or surgical therapies

POTENTIAL DIAGNOSIS

Normal findings in
- Normal size, position, and shape of intracranial structures and vascular system

Abnormal findings in
- Abscess
- Alzheimer's disease
- Aneurysm
- AVMs
- Cerebral atrophy
- Cerebral edema
- Cerebral infarction
- Congenital abnormalities
- Craniopharyngioma
- Cysts
- Hematomas (e.g., epidural, subdural, intracerebral)
- Hemorrhage
- Hydrocephaly
- Increased intracranial pressure or trauma

- Infection
- Sclerotic plaques suggesting multiple sclerosis
- Tumor
- Ventricular or tissue displacement or enlargement

CRITICAL FINDINGS ◈

- Abscess
- Acute hemorrhage
- Aneurysm
- Infarction
- Infection
- Tumor with significant mass effect

It is essential that critical diagnoses be communicated immediately to the appropriate HCP. A listing of these diagnoses varies among facilities. Note and immediately report to the HCP abnormal results and related symptoms. Timely notification of critical values for lab or diagnostic studies is a role expectation of the professional nurse. Notification processes will vary among facilities. Upon receipt of the critical value, the information should be read back to the caller to verify accuracy. Most policies require immediate notification of the primary HCP, hospitalist, or on-call HCP. Reported information includes the patient's name, unique identifiers, critical value, name of the person giving the report, and name of the person receiving the report. Documentation of notification should be made in the medical record with the name of the HCP notified, time and date of notification, and any orders received. Any delay in a timely report of a critical value may require completion of a notification form with review by Risk Management.

INTERFERING FACTORS

This procedure is contraindicated for

- Patients with allergies to shellfish or iodinated dye. The contrast medium used may cause a life-threatening allergic reaction. Patients with a known hypersensitivity to the medium may benefit from premedication with corticosteroids or the use of nonionic contrast medium.
- Patients who are claustrophobic.
- Patients who are pregnant or suspected of being pregnant, unless the potential benefits of the procedure far outweigh the risks to the fetus and mother.
- ◈ Elderly and other patients who are chronically dehydrated before the test, because of their risk of contrast-induced renal failure.
- ◈ Patients who are in renal failure.
- Young patients (17 yr and younger), unless the benefits of the x-ray diagnosis outweigh the risks of exposure to high levels of radiation. Information on the Image Gently Campaign can be found at the Alliance for Radiation Safety in Pediatric Imaging (www.pedrad.org/associations/5364/ig/).

Factors that may impair clear imaging

- Metallic objects (e.g., jewelry, dentures, body rings) within the examination field, which may inhibit organ visualization and cause unclear images.
- Patients who are very obese or who may exceed the weight limit for the equipment.
- Patients with extreme claustrophobia unless sedation is given before the study.
- Inability of the patient to cooperate or remain still during the procedure because of age, significant pain, or mental status.

Other considerations

- Complications of the procedure may include hemorrhage, infection at the IV needle insertion site, and cardiac arrhythmias.
- The procedure may be terminated if chest pain or severe cardiac arrhythmias occur.

- Failure to follow dietary restrictions and other pretesting preparations may cause the procedure to be canceled or repeated.
- Consultation with the HCP should occur before the procedure for radiation safety concerns regarding younger patients or patients who are lactating.
- Risks associated with radiation overexposure can result from frequent x-ray procedures. Personnel in the room with the patient should wear a protective lead apron, stand behind a shield, or leave the area while the examination is being done. Personnel working in the examination area should wear badges to record their level of radiation exposure.

NURSING IMPLICATIONS AND PROCEDURE

PRETEST:

▶ Positively identify the patient using at least two unique identifiers before providing care, treatment, or services.

▶ *Patient Teaching:* Inform the patient this procedure can assist in assessing the brain.

▶ Obtain a history of the patient's complaints or clinical symptoms, including a list of known allergens, especially allergies or sensitivities to latex, iodine, seafood, anesthetics, or contrast medium.

▶ Obtain a history of the patient's musculoskeletal system, symptoms, and results of previously performed laboratory tests and diagnostic and surgical procedures.

▶ Ensure results of coagulation testing are obtained and recorded prior to the procedure; BUN and creatinine results are also needed if contrast medium is to be used.

▶ Note any recent procedures that can interfere with test results, including examinations using barium- or iodine-based contrast medium. Ensure that barium studies were performed more than 4 days before the CT scan.

▶ Record the date of the last menstrual period and determine the possibility of pregnancy in perimenopausal women.

▶ Obtain a list of the patient's current medications including anticoagulants, aspirin and other salicylates, herbs, nutritional supplements, and nutraceuticals (see Appendix F). Note the last time and dose of medication taken.

▶ If contrast media is scheduled to be used, patients receiving metformin (Glucophage) for non–insulin-dependent (type 2) diabetes should discontinue the drug on the day of the test and continue to withhold it for 48 hr after the test. Failure to do so may result in lactic acidosis.

▶ Review the procedure with the patient. Address concerns about pain and explain that there may be moments of discomfort and some pain experienced during the test. Inform the patient the procedure is usually performed in a radiology suite by an HCP specializing in this procedure, with support staff, and takes approximately 15 to 30 min.

▶ *Sensitivity to social and cultural issues,* as well as concern for modesty, is important in providing psychological support before, during, and after the procedure. Explain that an IV line may be inserted to allow infusion of IV fluids, contrast medium, dye, or sedatives. Usually contrast medium and normal saline are infused.

▶ Inform the patient that he or she may experience nausea, a feeling of warmth, a salty or metallic taste, or a transient headache after injection of contrast medium.

▶ Instruct the patient to remove dentures and jewelry and other metallic objects from the area to be examined.

▶ There are no food or fluid restrictions unless by medical direction. Instruct the patient to avoid taking anticoagulant medication or to reduce dosage as ordered prior to the procedure. Protocols may vary among facilities.

▶ *Make sure a written and informed consent has been signed prior to the procedure and before administering any medications.*

INTRATEST:

▶ Observe standard precautions, and follow the general guidelines in Appendix A. Positively identify the patient.

- Ensure the patient has complied with medication restrictions and pretesting preparations.
- Ensure the patient has removed dentures and all external metallic objects from the area to be examined prior to the procedure.
- If the patient has a history of allergic reactions to any substance or drug, administer ordered prophylactic steroids or antihistamines before the procedure. Use nonionic contrast medium for the procedure.
- Have emergency equipment readily available.
- Instruct the patient to cooperate fully and to follow directions. Instruct the patient to remain still throughout the procedure because movement produces unreliable results.
- Establish an IV fluid line for the injection of contrast medium, emergency drugs, and sedatives.
- Administer an antianxiety agent, as ordered, if the patient has claustrophobia. Administer a sedative to a child or to an uncooperative adult, as ordered.
- Place the patient in the supine position on an examination table.
- If contrast media is used, a rapid series of images is taken during and after injection.
- Instruct the patient to take slow, deep breaths if nausea occurs during the procedure.
- Monitor the patient for complications related to the procedure (e.g., allergic reaction, anaphylaxis, bronchospasm) if contrast is used.
- The needle is removed, and a pressure dressing is applied over the puncture site.
- Observe/assess the needle insertion site for bleeding, inflammation, or hematoma formation.

POST-TEST:

- A report of the results will be made available to the requesting HCP, who will discuss the results with the patient.
- Instruct the patient to resume medications and activity, as directed by the HCP. Renal function should be assessed before metformin is resumed, if contrast was used.

- Monitor vital signs and neurological status every 15 min for 1 hr, then every 2 hr for 4 hr, and then as ordered by the HCP. Monitor temperature every 4 hr for 24 hr. Monitor intake and output at least every 8 hr. Compare with baseline values. Notify the HCP if temperature is elevated. Protocols may vary among facilities.
- If contrast was used, observe for delayed allergic reactions, such as rash, urticaria, tachycardia, hyperpnea, hypertension, palpitations, nausea, or vomiting.
- Instruct the patient to immediately report symptoms such as fast heart rate, difficulty breathing, skin rash, itching, chest pain, persistent right shoulder pain, or abdominal pain. Immediately report symptoms to the appropriate HCP.
- Observe/assess the needle insertion site for bleeding, inflammation, or hematoma formation.
- Instruct the patient in the care and assessment of the site.
- Instruct the patient to apply cold compresses to the puncture site as needed, to reduce discomfort or edema.
- Instruct the patient to increase fluid intake to help eliminate the contrast medium, if used.
- Inform the patient that diarrhea may occur after ingestion of oral contrast medium.
- Recognize anxiety related to test results. Discuss the implications of abnormal test results on the patient's lifestyle. Provide teaching and information regarding the clinical implications of the test results, as appropriate.
- Reinforce information given by the patient's HCP regarding further testing, treatment, or referral to another HCP. Answer any questions or address any concerns voiced by the patient or family.
- Depending on the results of this procedure, additional testing may be needed to evaluate or monitor progression of the disease process and determine the need for a change in therapy. Evaluate test results in relation to the patient's symptoms and other tests performed.

RELATED MONOGRAPHS:
▸ Related tests include angiography carotid, audiometry hearing loss, BUN, CSF analysis, CBC, CBC hematocrit, CBC hemoglobin, CT angiography, creatinine, EEG, EMG, evoked brain potentials, MR angiography, MRI brain, nerve fiber analysis, otoscopy, PET brain, PT/INR, spondee speech reception threshold, and tuning fork tests.
▸ Refer to the Musculoskeletal System table at the end of the book for related tests by body system.

C

Computed Tomography, Cardiac Scoring

SYNONYM/ACRONYM: Computed axial tomography (CAT), computed transaxial tomography (CTT), heart vessel calcium CT, helical/spiral CT, cardiac plaque CT.

COMMON USE: To visualize and assess coronary artery status related to plaque buildup, associated with coronary artery disease and heart failure. Used as an evaluation tool for surgical, radiation, and medical therapeutic interventions.

AREA OF APPLICATION: Heart.

CONTRAST: None.

DESCRIPTION: Cardiac scoring is a noninvasive test for quantifying coronary artery calcium content. Coronary artery disease (CAD) occurs when the arteries that carry blood and oxygen to the heart muscle become clogged or built up with plaque. Plaque buildup slows the flow of blood to the heart muscle, causing ischemia and increasing the risk of heart failure. The procedure begins with a computed tomography (CT) scan of the heart. The patient lies on a table and is moved in and out of a doughnut-like device called a *gantry*, which houses the x-ray tube and associated electronics. The scanner uses multiple x-ray beams and a series of detectors that rotate around the patient to produce cross-sectional views in a three-dimensional fashion by detecting and recording differences in plaque density after having an x-ray beam passed through the tissues. The scanner takes an image of the beating heart while the patient holds his or her breath for approximately 20 sec. The procedure requires no contrast medium injections. These density measurements are sent to a computer that produces a digital analysis of the anatomy, enabling the health-care provider (HCP) to look at the quantified amount of calcium (cardiac plaque score) in the coronary arteries. The data can be recorded on photographic or x-ray film or stored in digital format as digitized computer data.

INDICATIONS
• Detect and quantify coronary artery calcium content
 CAD is the leading cause of death in most industrialized nations.

Cardiac scoring is a more powerful predictor of CAD than cholesterol screening.

Of all myocardial infarctions (MIs), 45% occur in people younger than age 65.

Of women who have had MIs, 44% will die within 1 yr after the attack.

Women are more likely to die of heart disease than of breast cancer.

- Family history of heart disease
- Screening for coronary artery calcium in patients with:
  Diabetes
  High blood pressure
  High cholesterol
  High-stress lifestyle
  Overweight by 20% or more
  Personal history of smoking
  Sedentary lifestyle
- Screening for coronary artery plaque in patients with chest pain of unknown cause

POTENTIAL DIAGNOSIS

Normal findings in
- If the score is 100 or less, the probability of having significant CAD is minimal or is unlikely to be causing a narrowing at the time of the examination.

Abnormal findings in
- If the score is between 101 and 400, a significant amount of calcified plaque was found in the coronary arteries. There is an increased risk of a future MI, and a medical assessment of cardiac risk factors needs to be done. Additional testing may be needed.
- If the score is greater than 400, the procedure has detected extensive calcified plaque in the coronary arteries, which may have caused a critical narrowing of the vessels. A full medical assessment is needed as soon as possible. Further testing may be needed, and treatment may be needed to reduce the risk of MI.

CRITICAL FINDINGS: N/A

INTERFERING FACTORS

This procedure is contraindicated for
- Patients who are claustrophobic.
- Patients who are pregnant or suspected of being pregnant, unless the potential benefits of the procedure far outweigh the risks to the fetus and mother.
- Young patients (17 yr and younger), unless the benefits of the x-ray diagnosis outweigh the risks of exposure to high levels of radiation. Information on the Image Gently Campaign can be found at the Alliance for Radiation Safety in Pediatric Imaging (www.pedrad.org/associations/5364/ig/).

Factors that may impair clear imaging
- Retained barium or radiological contrast from a previous radiological procedure.
- Metallic objects (e.g., jewelry, body rings) within the examination field, which may inhibit organ visualization and cause unclear images.
- Improper adjustment of the radiographic equipment to accommodate obese or thin patients, which can cause overexposure or underexposure and a poor-quality study.
- Patients with extreme claustrophobia unless sedation is given before the study.
- Inability of the patient to cooperate or remain still during the procedure because of age, significant pain, or mental status.

Other considerations
- The procedure may be terminated if chest pain or severe cardiac arrhythmias occur.
- Consultation with the HCP should occur before the procedure for radiation safety concerns regarding

younger patients or patients who are lactating.

• Risks associated with radiation overexposure can result from frequent x-ray procedures. Personnel in the room with the patient should wear a protective lead apron, stand behind a shield, or leave the area while the examination is being done. Personnel working in the examination area should wear badges to record their level of radiation exposure.

NURSING IMPLICATIONS AND PROCEDURE

PRETEST:

▶ Positively identify the patient using at least two unique identifiers before providing care, treatment, or services.

▶ *Patient Teaching:* Inform the patient this procedure can assist in assessing the coronary arteries.

▶ Obtain a history of the patient's complaints or clinical symptoms, including a list of known allergens, especially allergies or sensitivities to latex, iodine, seafood, anesthetics, or contrast medium.

▶ Obtain a history of patient's cardiovascular system, symptoms, and results of previously performed laboratory tests and diagnostic and surgical procedures.

▶ Ensure results of coagulation testing are obtained and recorded prior to the procedure; BUN and creatinine results are also needed if contrast medium is to be used.

▶ Note any recent procedures that can interfere with test results, including examinations using barium- or iodine-based contrast medium. Ensure that barium studies were performed more than 4 days before the CT scan.

▶ Record the date of the last menstrual period and determine the possibility of pregnancy in perimenopausal women.

▶ Obtain a list of the patient's current medications, including anticoagulants, aspirin and other salicylates, herbs, nutritional supplements, and nutraceuticals

(see Appendix F). Note the last time and dose of medication taken.

▶ If contrast medium is scheduled to be used, patients receiving metformin (Glucophage) for non–insulin-dependent (type 2) diabetes should discontinue the drug on the day of the test and continue to withhold it for 48 hr after the test. Failure to do so may result in lactic acidosis.

▶ Review the procedure with the patient. Address concerns about pain and explain that there may be moments of discomfort and some pain experienced during the test. Inform the patient the procedure is usually performed in a radiology suite by an HCP specializing in this procedure, with support staff, and takes approximately 30 to 60 min.

▶ *Sensitivity to social and cultural issues,* as well as concern for modesty, is important in providing psychological support before, during, and after the procedure.

▶ Explain that an IV line may be inserted to allow infusion of IV fluids, anesthetics, or sedatives.

▶ Inform the patient that he or she may experience nausea, a feeling of warmth, a salty or metallic taste, or a transient headache after injection of contrast medium, if given.

▶ The patient should not fast or restrict fluids prior to the procedure. Protocols may vary among facilities.

▶ Instruct the patient to remove all external metallic objects from the area to be examined.

INTRATEST:

▶ Observe standard precautions, and follow the general guidelines in Appendix A. Positively identify the patient.

▶ Ensure the patient has complied with pretesting preparations.

▶ Ensure that the patient has removed all external metallic objects from the area to be examined.

▶ If the patient has a history of allergic reactions to any substance or drug, administer ordered prophylactic steroids or antihistamines before the procedure. Use nonionic contrast medium for the procedure.

▶ Have emergency equipment readily available.

Instruct the patient to void prior to the procedure and to change into the gown, robe, and foot coverings provided.

Instruct the patient to cooperate fully and to follow directions. Instruct the patient to remain still throughout the procedure because movement produces unreliable results.

Record baseline vital signs, and continue to monitor throughout the procedure. Protocols may vary among facilities.

Establish an IV fluid line for the injection of contrast medium, emergency drugs, and sedatives.

Administer an antianxiety agent, as ordered, if the patient has claustrophobia. Administer a sedative to a child or to an uncooperative adult, as ordered.

Place the patient in the supine position on an examination table.

A rapid series of images is taken of the vessels to be examined.

Instruct the patient to inhale deeply and hold his or her breath while the x-ray images are taken, and then to exhale after the images are taken.

Instruct the patient to take slow, deep breaths if nausea occurs during the procedure.

Monitor the patient for complications related to the procedure (e.g., allergic reaction, anaphylaxis, bronchospasm) if contrast is used.

The needle is removed, and a pressure dressing is applied over the puncture site.

Observe/assess the needle site for bleeding, inflammation, or hematoma formation.

POST-TEST:

A report of the results will be made available to the requesting HCP, who will discuss the results with the patient.

Instruct the patient to resume usual diet, fluids, medications, and activity, as directed by the HCP. Renal function should be assessed before metformin is resumed, if contrast was used.

Monitor vital signs and neurological status every 15 min for 1 hr, then every 2 hr for 4 hr, and then as ordered by the HCP. Monitor temperature every 4 hr for 24 hr. Monitor intake and output at least every 8 hr. Compare with baseline values. Notify the HCP if temperature is elevated. Protocols may vary among facilities.

If contrast was used, observe for delayed allergic reactions, such as rash, urticaria, tachycardia, hyperpnea, hypertension, palpitations, nausea, or vomiting.

Instruct the patient to immediately report symptoms such as fast heart rate, difficulty breathing, skin rash, itching, chest pain, persistent right shoulder pain, or abdominal pain. Immediately report symptoms to the appropriate HCP.

Observe/assess the needle insertion site for bleeding, inflammation, or hematoma formation.

Instruct the patient in the care and assessment of the site.

Instruct the patient to apply cold compresses to the insertion site as needed, to reduce discomfort or edema.

Instruct the patient to increase fluid intake to help eliminate the contrast medium, if used.

Inform the patient that diarrhea may occur after ingestion of oral contrast media.

Recognize anxiety related to test results. Discuss the implications of abnormal test results on the patient's lifestyle. Provide teaching and information regarding the clinical implications of the test results, as appropriate.

Nutritional Considerations: Abnormal findings may be associated with cardiovascular disease. The American Heart Association and National Heart, Lung, and Blood Institute (NHLBI) recommend nutritional therapy for individuals identified to be at high risk for developing CAD or individuals who have specific risk factors and/or existing medical conditions (e.g., elevated LDL cholesterol levels, other lipid disorders, insulin-dependent diabetes, insulin resistance, or metabolic syndrome). If overweight, the patient should be encouraged to achieve a normal weight. Guidelines for the Therapeutic Lifestyle Changes (TLC) diet are outlined in the Third Report of the Expert Panel on Detection, Evaluation, and Treatment of High Blood Cholesterol in Adults (Adult Treatment Panel III [ATP III]). The TLC diet emphasizes a reduction in foods high in saturated fats and cholesterol. Red meats, eggs, and dairy products are the major sources of saturated fats and cholesterol. If triglycerides also are elevated, the patient should be advised to eliminate or reduce alcohol and simple carbohydrates from the diet. The TLC approach also includes the use of plant stanols or sterols and increased dissolved fiber as an option for lowering LDL cholesterol levels; nutritional recommendations for daily total caloric intake; recommendations for allowable percentage of calories derived from fat (saturated and unsaturated), carbohydrates, protein, and cholesterol; as well as recommendations for daily expenditure of energy.

Nutritional Considerations: Overweight patients with high blood pressure should be encouraged to achieve a normal weight. Other changeable risk factors warranting patient education include strategies to safely decrease sodium intake, increase physical activity, decrease alcohol consumption, eliminate tobacco use, and decrease cholesterol levels.

Social and Cultural Considerations: Numerous studies point to the prevalence of excess body weight in American children and adolescents. Experts estimate that obesity is present in 25% of the population ages 6 to 11 yr. The medical, social, and emotional consequences of excess body weight are significant. Special attention should be given to instructing the child and caregiver regarding health risks and weight control education.

Recognize anxiety related to test results, and be supportive of fear of shortened life expectancy. Discuss the implications of abnormal test results on the patient's lifestyle. Provide teaching and information regarding the clinical implications of the test results, as appropriate. Educate the patient regarding access to counseling services. Provide contact information, if desired, for the American Heart Association (www.americanheart.org) or the NHLBI (www.nhlbi.nih.gov).

Reinforce information given by the patient's HCP regarding further testing, treatment, or referral to another HCP. Answer any questions or address any concerns voiced by the patient or family.

Depending on the results of this procedure, additional testing may be needed to evaluate or monitor progression of the disease process and determine the need for a change in therapy. Evaluate test results in relation to the patient's symptoms and other tests performed.

RELATED MONOGRAPHS:

Related tests include antiarrhythmic drugs, apolipoprotein A and B, AST, atrial natriuretic peptide, BNP, BUN, calcium, chest x-ray, cholesterol (total, HDL, LDL), CRP, CBC, CBC hematocrit, CBC hemoglobin, coronary angiography, CT thorax, CK and isoenzymes, creatinine echocardiography, echocardiography transesophageal ECG, glucose, glycated hemoglobin, Holter monitor, homocysteine, ketones, LDH and isoenzymes lipoprotein electrophoresis, lung scan, magnesium, MRI chest, MI scan, myocardial perfusion heart scan, myoglobin, PET heart, potassium, PT/INR, triglycerides, and troponin.

Refer to the Cardiovascular System table at the end of the book for related tests by body system.

Computed Tomography, Colonoscopy

SYNONYM/ACRONYM: Computed axial tomography (CAT), computed transaxial tomography (CTT), CT colonography, CT virtual colonoscopy.

COMMON USE: To visualize and assess the rectum and colon related to identification and evaluation of large polyps, lesions, and tumors. Also used to assess the effectiveness of therapeutic interventions such as surgery. Primarily used for patients who cannot tolerate conventional colonoscopy.

AREA OF APPLICATION: Colon.

CONTRAST: Screening examinations are done without IV iodinated contrast medium. Examinations done to clarify questionable or abnormal areas may require IV iodinated contrast medium.

DESCRIPTION: Computed tomography (CT) colonoscopy is a noninvasive technique that involves examining the colon by taking multiple CT scans of the patient's colon and rectum and using computer software to create three-dimensional images. The procedure is used to detect polyps, which are growths of tissue in the colon or rectum. Some types of polyps increase the risk of colon cancer, especially if they are large or if a patient has several polyps. Compared to conventional colonoscopy, CT colonoscopy is less effective in detecting polyps smaller than 5 mm, more effective when the polyps are between 5 and 9.9 mm, and most effective when the polyps are 10 mm or larger. This test may be valuable for patients who have diseases rendering them unable to undergo conventional colonoscopy (e.g., bleeding disorders, lung or heart disease) and for patients who are unable to undergo the sedation required for traditional colonoscopy. The procedure is less invasive

than conventional colonoscopy, with little risk of complications and no recovery time. CT colonoscopy can be done as an outpatient procedure, and the patient may return to work or usual activities the same day.

CT colonoscopy and conventional colonoscopy require the bowel to be cleansed before the examination. The patient lies on a table and is moved in and out of a doughnut-like device called a *gantry*, which houses the x-ray tube and associated electronics. The scanner uses multiple x-ray beams and a series of detectors that rotate around the patient to produce cross-sectional views in a three-dimensional fashion by detecting and recording differences in densities in the colon after having an x-ray beam passed through it. The screening procedure requires no contrast medium injections, but if a suspicious area or abnormality is detected, a repeat series of images may be completed after IV contrast medium is given. These

C

density measurements are sent to a computer that produces a digital analysis of the anatomy, enabling a health-care provider (HCP) to look at slices or thin sections of certain anatomic views of the colon and vascular system. The data can be recorded on photographic or x-ray film or stored in digital format as digitized computer data. A drawback of CT colonoscopy is that polyp removal and biopsies of tissue in the colon must be done using conventional colonoscopy. Therefore, if polyps are discovered during CT colonoscopy and biopsy becomes necessary, the patient must undergo bowel preparation a second time.

INDICATIONS

- Detect polyps in the colon
- Evaluate the colon for metachronous lesions
- Evaluate the colon in patients with obstructing rectosigmoid disease
- Evaluate polyposis syndromes
- Evaluate the site of resection for local recurrence of lesions
- Examine the colon in patients with heart or lung disease, patients unable to be sedated, and patients unable to undergo colonoscopy
- Failure to visualize the entire colon during conventional colonoscopy
- Identify metastases
- Investigate cause of positive occult blood test
- Investigate further after an abnormal barium enema
- Investigate further when flexible sigmoidoscopy is positive for polyps

POTENTIAL DIAGNOSIS

Normal findings in
- Normal colon and rectum, with no evidence of polyps or growths

Abnormal findings in
- Abnormal endoluminal wall of the colon
- Extraluminal extension of primary cancer
- Mesenteric and retroperitoneal lymphadenopathy
- Metachronous lesions
- Metastases of cancer
- Polyps or growths in colon or rectum
- Tumor recurrence after surgery

CRITICAL FINDINGS: N/A

INTERFERING FACTORS

This procedure is contraindicated for

- Patients with allergies to shellfish or iodinated dye. The contrast medium used may cause a life-threatening allergic reaction. Patients with a known hypersensitivity to the medium may benefit from premedication with corticosteroids or the use of nonionic contrast medium, if contrast is used.
- Patients who are claustrophobic.
- Patients who are pregnant or suspected of being pregnant, unless the potential benefits of the procedure far outweigh the risks to the fetus and mother.
- Elderly and other patients who are chronically dehydrated before the test, because of their risk of contrast-induced renal failure, if contrast is used.
- Patients who are in renal failure, if contrast is used.
- Young patients (17 yr and younger) unless the benefits of the x-ray diagnosis outweigh the risks of exposure to high levels of radiation. Information on the Image Gently Campaign can be found at the Alliance for Radiation Safety in Pediatric Imaging (www.pedrad.org/associations/5364/ig/).

Factors that may impair clear imaging

Gas or feces in the gastrointestinal tract resulting from inadequate cleansing or failure to restrict food intake before the study.

Retained barium from a previous radiological procedure.

Metallic objects (e.g., jewelry, body rings) within the examination field, which may inhibit organ visualization and cause unclear images.

Patients who are very obese or who may exceed the weight limit for the equipment.

Patients with extreme claustrophobia unless sedation is given before the study.

Inability of the patient to cooperate or remain still during the procedure because of age, significant pain, or mental status.

Other considerations

Complications of the procedure may include hemorrhage, infection at the IV needle insertion site, and cardiac arrhythmias.

The procedure may be terminated if chest pain or severe cardiac arrhythmias occur.

Failure to follow dietary restrictions and other pretesting preparations may cause the procedure to be canceled or repeated.

Consultation with the HCP should occur before the procedure for radiation safety concerns regarding younger patients or patients who are lactating.

Risks associated with radiation overexposure can result from frequent x-ray procedures. Personnel in the room with the patient should wear a protective lead apron, stand behind a shield, or leave the area while the examination is being done. Personnel working in the examination area should wear badges to record their level of radiation exposure.

NURSING IMPLICATIONS AND PROCEDURE

PRETEST:

Positively identify the patient using at least two unique identifiers before providing care, treatment, or services.

Patient Teaching: Inform the patient this procedure can assist in assessing the colon.

Obtain a history of the patient's complaints or clinical symptoms, including a list of known allergens, especially allergies or sensitivities to latex, iodine, seafood, anesthetics, or contrast mediums.

Obtain a history of the patient's gastrointestinal system, symptoms, and results of previously performed laboratory tests and diagnostic and surgical procedures.

Ensure results of coagulation testing are obtained and recorded prior to the procedure; BUN and creatinine results are also needed if contrast medium is to be used.

Note any recent procedures that can interfere with test results, including examinations using barium- or iodine-based contrast medium. Ensure that barium studies were performed more than 4 days before the CT scan.

Record the date of the last menstrual period and determine the possibility of pregnancy in perimenopausal women.

Obtain a list of the patient's current medications, including anticoagulants, aspirin and other salicylates, herbs, nutritional supplements, and nutraceuticals (see Appendix F). Note the last time and dose of medication taken.

If contrast is scheduled to be used, patients receiving metformin (Glucophage) for non–insulin-dependent (type 2) diabetes should discontinue the drug on the day of the test and continue to withhold it for 48 hr after the test. Failure to do so may result in lactic acidosis.

Review the procedure with the patient. Address concerns about pain and explain that some pain may be experienced during the test, and there may be moments of discomfort. Inform the patient that the procedure is performed in a radiology department, usually by

C

an HCP specializing in this procedure, with support staff, and takes approximately 30 to 60 min.

Sensitivity to social and cultural issues, as well as concern for modesty, is important in providing psychological support before, during, and after the procedure.

▸ Explain that an IV line may be inserted to allow infusion of IV fluids, contrast medium, dye, or sedatives.

▸ Inform the patient that he or she may experience nausea, a feeling of warmth, a salty or metallic taste, or a transient headache after injection of contrast medium.

▸ Instruct the patient to remove jewelry and other metallic objects from the area to be examined.

▸ The patient should fast and restrict fluids for 6 to 8 hr prior to the procedure. Instruct the patient to avoid taking anticoagulant medication or to reduce dosage as ordered prior to the procedure. Protocols may vary among facilities.

Make sure a written and informed consent has been signed prior to the procedure and before administering any medications.

INTRATEST:

▸ Observe standard precautions, and follow the general guidelines in Appendix A. Positively identify the patient.

▸ Ensure that the patient has complied with dietary, fluids, and medication restrictions and pretesting preparations; ensure that food and fluids have been restricted for at least 6 hr prior to the procedure.

▸ Ensure that the patient has removed all external metallic objects from the area to be examined prior to the procedure.

▸ If the patient has a history of allergic reactions to any substance or drug, administer ordered prophylactic steroids or antihistamines before the procedure. Use nonionic contrast medium for the procedure.

▸ Have emergency equipment readily available.

▸ Instruct the patient to void prior to the procedure and to change into the gown, robe, and foot coverings provided.

▸ Instruct the patient to cooperate fully and to follow directions. Instruct the patient to remain still throughout the procedure because movement produces unreliable results.

▸ Record baseline vital signs, and continue to monitor throughout the procedure. Protocols may vary among facilities.

▸ Establish an IV fluid line for the injection of contrast (if used), emergency drugs, and sedatives.

▸ Administer an antianxiety agent, as ordered, if the patient has claustrophobia. Administer a sedative to a child or to an uncooperative adult, as ordered.

▸ Place the patient in the supine position on an examination table.

▸ The colon is distended with room air or carbon dioxide by means of a rectal tube and balloon retention device. Maximal colonic distention is guided by patient tolerance.

▸ If IV contrast is used, a rapid series of images is taken during and after injection.

▸ Instruct the patient to inhale deeply and hold his or her breath while the x-ray images are taken, and then to exhale after the images are taken.

▸ The sequence of images is repeated in the prone position.

▸ Instruct the patient to take slow, deep breaths if nausea occurs during the procedure.

▸ Monitor the patient for complications related to the procedure (e.g., allergic reaction, anaphylaxis, bronchospasm) if contrast is used.

▸ The needle is removed, and a pressure dressing is applied over the puncture site.

▸ Observe/assess the needle site for bleeding, inflammation, or hematoma formation.

POST-TEST:

▸ A report of the results will be made available to the requesting HCP, who will discuss the results with the patient.

▸ Instruct the patient to resume usual diet, fluids, medications, and activity, as directed by the HCP. Renal function should be assessed before metformin is resumed, if contrast was used.

▸ Monitor vital signs and neurological status every 15 min for 1 hr, then every 2 hr for 4 hr, and then as ordered by the HCP. Monitor temperature every

4 hr for 24 hr. Monitor intake and output at least every 8 hr. Compare with baseline values. Notify the HCP if temperature is elevated. Protocols may vary among facilities.

If contrast was used, observe for delayed allergic reactions, such as rash, urticaria, tachycardia, hyperpnea, hypertension, palpitations, nausea, or vomiting.

Instruct the patient to immediately report symptoms such as fast heart rate, difficulty breathing, skin rash, itching, chest pain, persistent right shoulder pain, or abdominal pain. Immediately report symptoms to the appropriate HCP.

Observe/assess the needle/catheter insertion site for bleeding, inflammation, or hematoma formation.

Instruct the patient in the care and assessment of the site.

Instruct the patient to apply cold compresses to the puncture site as needed, to reduce discomfort or edema.

Instruct the patient to increase fluid intake to help eliminate the contrast medium, if used.

Inform the patient that diarrhea may occur after ingestion of oral contrast media.

Recognize anxiety related to test results. Discuss the implications of abnormal test results on the patient's lifestyle. Provide teaching and information regarding the clinical implications of the test results, as appropriate.

Reinforce information given by the patient's HCP regarding further testing, treatment, or referral to another HCP. Decisions regarding the need for and frequency of occult blood testing, colonoscopy, or other cancer screening procedures should be made after consultation between the patient and HCP. The most current guidelines for colon cancer screening of the general population as well as individuals with increased risk are available from the American Cancer Society (www.cancer.org) and the American College of Gastroenterology (www.gi.org). Answer any questions or address any concerns voiced by the patient or family.

Depending on the results of this procedure, additional testing may be needed to evaluate or monitor progression of the disease process and determine the need for a change in therapy. Evaluate test results in relation to the patient's symptoms and other tests performed.

RELATED MONOGRAPHS:

Related tests include barium enema, BUN, cancer antigens, capsule endoscopy, colonoscopy, CBC, CBC hematocrit, CBC hemoglobin, CT abdomen, creatinine, fecal analysis, KUB studies, MRI abdomen, PET pelvis, proctosigmoidoscopy, PT/INR, and US pelvis.

Refer to the Gastrointestinal System table at the end of the book for related tests by body system.

Computed Tomography, Pancreas

SYNONYM/ACRONYM: Computed axial tomography (CAT), computed transaxial tomography (CTT, abdominal CT, helical/spiral CT).

COMMON USE: To visualize and assess the pancreas toward assisting in diagnosing tumors, masses, cancer, bleeding, infection, and abscess. Used as an evaluation tool for surgical, radiation, and medical therapeutic interventions.

AREA OF APPLICATION: Pancreas.

CONTRAST: With or without oral or IV iodinated contrast medium.

C

DESCRIPTION: Computed tomography (CT) is a noninvasive procedure used to enhance certain anatomic views of the abdominal structures. It becomes an invasive procedure when contrast medium is used. CT of the pancreas aids in the diagnosis or evaluation of pancreatic cysts, pseudocysts, inflammation, tumors, masses, metastases, abscesses, and trauma. In all but the thinnest or most emaciated patients, the pancreas is surrounded by fat that clearly defines its margins. During the procedure, the patient lies on a table and is moved in and out of a doughnut-like device called a *gantry*, which houses the x-ray tube and associated electronics. The scanner uses multiple x-ray beams and a series of detectors that rotate around the patient to produce cross-sectional views in a three-dimensional fashion. Differences in tissue density are detected and recorded and are viewable as computerized digital images. Slices or thin sections of certain anatomic views of the kidneys and associated vascular system are reviewed to allow differentiation of solid, cystic, inflammatory, or vascular lesions, as well as identification of suspected hematomas and aneurysms. The procedure is repeated after intravenous injection of iodinated contrast medium for vascular evaluation or after oral ingestion of contrast medium for evaluation of bowel and adjacent structures. Images can be recorded on photographic or x-ray film or stored in digital format as digitized computer data. Cine scanning produces a series of moving images of the scanned area. The CT scan can be used to guide biopsy needles into areas of pancreatic masses to obtain tissue for laboratory analysis and for placement of needles to aspirate cysts or abscesses. CT scanning can monitor mass, cyst, or tumor growth and post-therapy response.

INDICATIONS
- Detect dilation or obstruction of the pancreatic ducts
- Differentiate between pancreatic disorders and disorders of the retroperitoneum
- Evaluate benign or cancerous tumors or metastasis to the pancreas
- Evaluate pancreatic abnormalities (e.g., bleeding, pancreatitis, pseudocyst, abscesses)
- Evaluate unexplained weight loss, jaundice, and epigastric pain
- Monitor and evaluate effectiveness of medical or surgical therapies

POTENTIAL DIAGNOSIS

Normal findings in
- Normal size, position, and contour of the pancreas, which lies obliquely in the upper abdomen

Abnormal findings in
- Acute or chronic pancreatitis
- Obstruction of the pancreatic ducts
- Pancreatic abscesses
- Pancreatic carcinoma
- Pancreatic pseudocyst
- Pancreatic tumor

CRITICAL FINDINGS: N/A

INTERFERING FACTORS

This procedure is contraindicated for
- ❖ Patients with allergies to shellfish or iodinated dye. The contrast medium used may cause a life-threatening allergic reaction. Patients with a known hypersensitivity to the medium may benefit from premedication with corticosteroids or the use of nonionic contrast medium.
- Patients who are claustrophobic.

COMPUTED TOMOGRAPHY, PANCREAS | 495

- Patients who are pregnant or suspected of being pregnant, unless the potential benefits of the procedure far outweigh the risks to the fetus and mother.
- ❖ Elderly and other patients who are chronically dehydrated before the test, because of their risk of contrast-induced renal failure.
- ❖ Patients who are in renal failure.
- Young patients (17 yr and younger), unless the benefits of the x-ray diagnosis outweigh the risks of exposure to high levels of radiation. Information on the Image Gently Campaign can be found at the Alliance for Radiation Safety in Pediatric Imaging (www.pedrad.org/associations/5364/ig/).

Factors that may impair clear imaging

- Gas or feces in the gastrointestinal (GI) tract resulting from inadequate cleansing or failure to restrict food intake before the study.
- Retained barium from a previous radiological procedure.
- Metallic objects (e.g., jewelry, body rings) within the examination field, which may inhibit organ visualization and cause unclear images.
- Patients who are very obese or who may exceed the weight limit for the equipment.
- Patients with extreme claustrophobia unless sedation is given before the study.
- Inability of the patient to cooperate or remain still during the procedure because of age, significant pain, or mental status.

Other considerations

- Complications of the procedure include hemorrhage, infection at the IV needle insertion site, and cardiac arrhythmias.
- The procedure may be terminated if chest pain or severe cardiac arrhythmias occur.

- Failure to follow dietary restrictions and other pretesting preparations may cause the procedure to be canceled or repeated.
- Consultation with a health-care provider (HCP) should occur before the procedure for radiation safety concerns regarding younger patients or patients who are lactating.
- Risks associated with radiation overexposure can result from frequent x-ray procedures. Personnel in the room with the patient should wear a protective lead apron, stand behind a shield, or leave the area while the examination is being done. Personnel working in the examination area should wear badges to record their level of radiation exposure.

NURSING IMPLICATIONS AND PROCEDURE

PRETEST:

▸ Positively identify the patient using at least two unique identifiers before providing care, treatment, or services.
▸ *Patient Teaching:* Inform the patient this procedure can assist in assessing the abdomen and pancreatic area.
▸ Obtain a history of the patient's complaints, including a list of known allergens, especially allergies or sensitivities to latex, iodine, seafood, anesthetics, or other contrast medium.
▸ Obtain a history of the patient's gastrointestinal and hepatobiliary system, symptoms, and results of previously performed laboratory tests and diagnostic and surgical procedures.
▸ Ensure results of coagulation testing are obtained and recorded prior to the procedure; BUN and creatinine results are also needed if contrast medium is to be used.
▸ Note any recent procedures that can interfere with test results, including examinations using barium- or iodine-based contrast medium. Ensure that barium studies were performed more than 4 days before the CT scan.

Access additional resources at davisplus.fadavis.com

C

Record the date of the last menstrual period and determine the possibility of pregnancy in perimenopausal women.

Obtain a list of the patient's current medications, including anticoagulants, aspirin and other salicylates, herbs, nutritional supplements, and nutraceuticals (see Appendix F). Note the last time and dose of medication taken.

If contrast medium is scheduled to be used, patients receiving metformin (Glucophage) for non–insulin-dependent (type 2) diabetes should discontinue the drug on the day of the test and continue to withhold it for 48 hr after the test. Failure to do so may result in lactic acidosis.

Review the procedure with the patient. Address concerns about pain and explain that there may be moments of discomfort and some pain experienced during the test. Inform the patient the procedure is usually performed in a radiology suite by an HCP specializing in this procedure, with support staff, and takes approximately 30 to 60 min.

Sensitivity to social and cultural issues, as well as concern for modesty, is important in providing psychological support before, during, and after the procedure.

Explain that an IV line may be inserted to allow infusion of IV fluids, contrast medium, dye, or sedatives. Usually contrast medium and normal saline are infused.

Inform the patient that he or she may experience nausea, a feeling of warmth, a salty or metallic taste, or a transient headache after injection of contrast medium.

The patient should fast and restrict fluids for 2 to 4 hr prior to the procedure. Instruct the patient to avoid taking anticoagulant medication or to reduce dosage as ordered prior to the procedure. Protocols may vary among facilities.

The patient may be requested to drink approximately 450 mL of a dilute barium solution (approximately 1% barium) or a water soluble oral contrast beginning 1 hr before the examination. This is administered to distinguish GI organs from the other abdominal organs.

Instruct the patient to remove jewelry and other metallic objects from the area to be examined.

Make sure a written and informed consent has been signed prior to the procedure and before administering any medications.

INTRATEST:

Observe standard precautions, and follow the general guidelines in Appendix A. Positively identify the patient.

Ensure the patient has complied with dietary, fluids, and medication restrictions and pretesting preparations; ensure that food and fluids have been restricted for at least 2 to 4 hr prior to the procedure.

Ensure that the patient has removed all external metallic objects from the area to be examined prior to the procedure.

If the patient has a history of allergic reactions to any substance or drug, administer ordered prophylactic steroids or antihistamines before the procedure. Use nonionic contrast medium for the procedure.

Have emergency equipment readily available.

Instruct the patient to void prior to the procedure and to change into the gown, robe, and foot coverings provided.

Instruct the patient to cooperate fully and to follow directions. Instruct the patient to remain still throughout the procedure because movement produces unreliable results.

Establish an IV fluid line for the injection of contrast medium, emergency drugs, and sedatives.

Administer an antianxiety agent, as ordered, if the patient has claustrophobia. Administer a sedative to a child or to an uncooperative adult, as ordered.

Place the patient in the supine position on an examination table.

If IV contrast medium is used, a rapid series of images is taken during and after injection.

Instruct the patient to inhale deeply and hold his or her breath while the x-ray images are taken, and then to exhale after the images are taken.

Instruct the patient to take slow, deep breaths if nausea occurs during the procedure.

Monitor the patient for complications related to the procedure (e.g., allergic reaction, anaphylaxis, bronchospasm) if contrast is used.

The needle is removed, and a pressure dressing is applied over the puncture site.

Observe/assess the needle site for bleeding, inflammation, or hematoma formation.

POST-TEST:

A report of the results will be made available to the requesting HCP, who will discuss the results with the patient.

Instruct the patient to resume usual diet, fluids, medications, and activity, as directed by the HCP. Renal function should be assessed before metformin is resumed, if contrast was used.

Monitor vital signs and neurological status every 15 min for 1 hr, then every 2 hr for 4 hr, and then as ordered by the HCP. Monitor temperature every 4 hr for 24 hr. Monitor intake and output at least every 8 hr. Compare with baseline values. Notify the HCP if temperature is elevated. Protocols may vary among facilities.

If contrast was used, observe for delayed allergic reactions, such as rash, urticaria, tachycardia, hyperpnea, hypertension, palpitations, nausea, or vomiting.

Instruct the patient to immediately report symptoms such as fast heart rate, difficulty breathing, skin rash, itching, chest pain, persistent right shoulder pain, or abdominal pain. Immediately report symptoms to the appropriate HCP.

Observe/assess the needle site for bleeding, inflammation, or hematoma formation.

Instruct the patient in the care and assessment of the site.

Instruct the patient to apply cold compresses to the puncture site as needed, to reduce discomfort or edema.

Instruct the patient to increase fluid intake to help eliminate the contrast medium, if used.

Inform the patient that diarrhea may occur after ingestion of oral contrast medium.

Recognize anxiety related to test results. Discuss the implications of abnormal test results on the patient's lifestyle. Provide teaching and information regarding the clinical implications of the test results, as appropriate.

Reinforce information given by the patient's HCP regarding further testing, treatment, or referral to another HCP. Answer any questions or address any concerns voiced by the patient or family.

Depending on the results of this procedure, additional testing may be needed to evaluate or monitor progression of the disease process and determine the need for a change in therapy. Evaluate test results in relation to the patient's symptoms and other tests performed.

RELATED MONOGRAPHS:

Related tests include amylase, angiography of the abdomen, biopsy intestinal, BUN, cancer antigens, CBC hemoglobin, creatinine, ERCP, lipase, MRI abdomen, PT/INR, and US pancreas.

Refer to the Gastrointestinal and Hepatobiliary systems tables at the end of the book for related tests by body system.

Computed Tomography, Pelvis

SYNONYM/ACRONYM: Computed axial tomography (CAT), computed transaxial tomography (CTT), pelvis CT, helical/spiral CT.

COMMON USE: To visualize and assess pelvic structures and vascularities related to assisting in diagnosing bleeding, infection, masses, and cyst aspiration (needle-guided biopsy). Used to monitor the effectiveness of medical, radiation, and surgical therapeutic interventions.

AREA OF APPLICATION: Pelvis.

CONTRAST: With or without oral or IV iodinated contrast medium.

DESCRIPTION: Computed tomography (CT) of the pelvis is a noninvasive procedure used to enhance certain anatomic views of the pelvic structures. It becomes an invasive procedure when intravenous contrast medium is used. During the procedure, the patient lies on a table and is moved in and out of a doughnut-like device called a *gantry*, which houses the x-ray tube and associated electronics. The scanner uses multiple x-ray beams and a series of detectors that rotate around the patient to produce cross-sectional views in a three-dimensional fashion. Differences in tissue density are detected and recorded and are viewable as computerized digital images. Slices or thin sections of certain anatomic views of the pelvic structures and associated vascular system are reviewed to allow differentiation of solid, cystic, inflammatory, or vascular lesions, as well as identification of suspected hematomas and aneurysms. The procedure is repeated after intravenous injection of iodinated contrast medium for vascular evaluation or after oral ingestion of contrast medium for evaluation of bowel and adjacent structures. Images can be recorded on photographic or x-ray film or stored in digital format as digitized computer data. Cine scanning produces a series of moving images of the scanned area. The CT scan can be used to guide biopsy needles into areas of pelvic masses to obtain tissue for laboratory analysis and for placement of needles to aspirate cysts or abscesses. CT scanning can monitor mass, cyst, or tumor growth and post-therapy response.

INDICATIONS
- Assist in differentiating between benign and malignant tumors
- Detect tumor extension of masses and metastasis into the pelvic area
- Differentiate infectious from inflammatory processes
- Evaluate pelvic lymph nodes
- Evaluate cysts, masses, abscesses, ureteral and bladder calculi, gastrointestinal (GI) bleeding and obstruction, and trauma
- Monitor and evaluate effectiveness of medical, radiation, or surgical therapies

POTENTIAL DIAGNOSIS

Normal findings in
- Normal size, position, and shape of pelvic organs and vascular system

Abnormal findings in
- Bladder calculi
- Ectopic pregnancy
- Fibroid tumors
- Hydrosalpinx
- Ovarian cyst or abscess
- Primary and metastatic neoplasms

CRITICAL FINDINGS
- Ectopic pregnancy
- Tumor with significant mass effect

It is essential that critical diagnoses be communicated immediately to the appropriate HCP. A listing of these diagnoses varies among facilities. Note and immediately report to the HCP abnormal results and related symptoms. Timely notification of critical values for lab or diagnostic studies is a role expectation of the professional nurse. Notification processes will vary among facilities.

Upon receipt of the critical value, the information should be read back to the caller to verify accuracy. Most policies require immediate notification of the primary HCP, hospitalist, or on-call HCP. Reported information includes the patient's name, unique identifiers, critical value, name of the person giving the report, and name of the person receiving the report. Documentation of notification should be made in the medical record with the name of the HCP notified, time and date of notification, and any orders received. Any delay in a timely report of a critical value may require completion of a notification form with review by Risk Management.

INTERFERING FACTORS

This procedure is contraindicated for

- ◈ Patients with allergies to shellfish or iodinated dye. The contrast medium used may cause a life-threatening allergic reaction. Patients with a known hypersensitivity to the medium may benefit from premedication with corticosteroids or the use of nonionic contrast medium.
- Patients who are claustrophobic.
- Patients who are pregnant or suspected of being pregnant, unless the potential benefits of the procedure far outweigh the risks to the fetus and mother.
- ◈ Elderly and other patients who are chronically dehydrated before the test, because of their risk of contrast-induced renal failure.
- ◈ Patients who are in renal failure.
- Young patients (17 yr and younger), unless the benefits of the x-ray diagnosis outweigh the risks of exposure to high levels of radiation. Information on the Image Gently Campaign can be found at the Alliance for Radiation Safety in Pediatric Imaging (www.pedrad. org/associations/5364/ig/).

Factors that may impair clear imaging

- Gas or feces in the GI tract resulting from inadequate cleansing or failure to restrict food intake before the study.
- Retained barium from a previous radiological procedure.
- Metallic objects (e.g., jewelry, body rings) within the examination field, which may inhibit organ visualization and can produce unclear images.
- Patients who are very obese or who may exceed the weight limit for the equipment.
- Patients with extreme claustrophobia unless sedation is given before the study.
- Inability of the patient to cooperate or remain still during the procedure because of age, significant pain, or mental status.

Other considerations

- Complications of the procedure include hemorrhage, infection at the IV needle insertion site, and cardiac arrhythmias.
- The procedure may be terminated if chest pain or severe cardiac arrhythmias occur.
- Failure to follow dietary restrictions and other pretesting preparations may cause the procedure to be canceled or repeated.
- Consultation with an HCP should occur before the procedure for radiation safety concerns regarding younger patients or patients who are lactating.
- Risks associated with radiation overexposure can result from frequent x-ray procedures. Personnel in the room with the patient should wear a protective lead apron, stand behind a shield, or leave the area while the examination is being done. Personnel working in the examination area should wear badges to record their level of radiation exposure.

NURSING IMPLICATIONS AND PROCEDURE

PRETEST:

- Positively identify the patient using at least two unique identifiers before providing care, treatment, or services.
- *Patient Teaching:* Inform the patient this procedure can assist in assessing the pelvis and pelvic organs.
- Obtain a history of the patient's complaints or clinical symptoms, including a list of known allergens, especially allergies or sensitivities to latex, iodine, seafood, anesthetics, or contrast medium.
- Obtain a history of the patient's gastrointestinal, genitourinary, and reproductive systems; symptoms; and results of previously performed laboratory tests and diagnostic and surgical procedures.
- Ensure results of coagulation testing are obtained and recorded prior to the procedure; BUN and creatinine results are also needed if contrast medium is to be used.
- Note any recent procedures that can interfere with test results, including examinations using barium- or iodine-based contrast medium. Ensure that barium studies were performed more than 4 days before the CT scan.
- Record the date of the last menstrual period and determine the possibility of pregnancy in perimenopausal women.
- Obtain a list of the patient's current medications including anticoagulants, aspirin and other salicylates, herbs, nutritional supplements, and nutraceuticals (see Appendix F). Note the last time and dose of medication taken.
- If contrast medium is scheduled to be used, patients receiving metformin (Glucophage) for non–insulin-dependent (type 2) diabetes should discontinue the drug on the day of the test and continue to withhold it for 48 hr after the test. Failure to do so may result in lactic acidosis.
- Review the procedure with the patient. Address concerns about pain and explain that there may be moments of discomfort and some pain experienced during the test. Inform the patient the procedure is usually performed in a radiology suite by an HCP specializing in this procedure, with support staff, and takes approximately 30 to 60 min.
- *Sensitivity to social and cultural issues,* as well as concern for modesty, is important in providing psychological support before, during, and after the procedure.
- Explain that an IV line may be inserted to allow infusion of IV fluids, contrast medium, dye, or sedatives. Usually contrast medium and normal saline are infused.
- Inform the patient that he or she may experience nausea, a feeling of warmth, a salty or metallic taste, or a transient headache after injection of contrast medium.
- The patient should fast and restrict fluids for 2 to 4 hr prior to the procedure. Instruct the patient to avoid taking anticoagulant medication or to reduce dosage as ordered prior to the procedure. Protocols may vary among facilities.
- The patient may be requested to drink approximately 450 mL of a dilute barium solution (approximately 1% barium) or a water soluble oral contrast beginning 1 hr before the examination. This is administered to distinguish GI organs from the other abdominal organs.
- Instruct the patient to remove jewelry and other metallic objects from the area to be examined.
- *Make sure a written and informed consent has been signed prior to the procedure and before administering any medications.*

INTRATEST:

- Observe standard precautions, and follow the general guidelines in Appendix A. Positively identify the patient.
- Ensure the patient has complied with dietary, fluids, and medication restrictions and pretesting preparations; ensure that food and fluids have been restricted for at least 2 to 4 hr prior to the procedure.
- Ensure the patient has removed all external metallic objects from the area to be examined prior to the procedure.
- If the patient has a history of allergic reactions to any substance or drug,

administer ordered prophylactic steroids or antihistamines before the procedure. Use nonionic contrast medium for the procedure.

Have emergency equipment readily available.

Instruct the patient to void prior to the procedure and to change into the gown, robe, and foot coverings provided.

Instruct the patient to cooperate fully and to follow directions. Instruct the patient to remain still throughout the procedure because movement produces unreliable results.

Establish an IV fluid line for the injection of contrast, emergency drugs, and sedatives.

Administer an antianxiety agent, as ordered, if the patient has claustrophobia. Administer a sedative to a child or to an uncooperative adult, as ordered.

Place the patient in the supine position on an examination table.

If IV contrast medium is used, a rapid series of images is taken during and after injection.

Instruct the patient to inhale deeply and hold his or her breath while the x-ray images are taken, and then to exhale after the images are taken.

Instruct the patient to take slow, deep breaths if nausea occurs during the procedure.

Monitor the patient for complications related to the procedure (e.g., allergic reaction, anaphylaxis, bronchospasm) if contrast is used.

The needle is removed, and a pressure dressing is applied over the puncture site.

Observe/assess the needle site for bleeding, inflammation, or hematoma formation.

POST-TEST:

A report of the results will be made available to the requesting HCP, who will discuss the results with the patient.

Instruct the patient to resume usual diet, fluids, medications, and activity, as directed by the HCP. Renal function should be assessed before metformin is resumed, if contrast was used.

Monitor vital signs and neurological status every 15 min for 1 hr, then every 2 hr for 4 hr, and then as ordered by the HCP. Monitor temperature every 4 hr for 24 hr. Monitor intake and output at least every 8 hr. Compare with baseline values. Notify the HCP if temperature is elevated. Protocols may vary among facilities.

If contrast was used, observe for delayed allergic reactions, such as rash, urticaria, tachycardia, hyperpnea, hypertension, palpitations, nausea, or vomiting.

Instruct the patient to immediately report symptoms such as fast heart rate, difficulty breathing, skin rash, itching, chest pain, persistent right shoulder pain, or abdominal pain. Immediately report symptoms to the appropriate HCP.

Observe/assess the needle insertion site for bleeding, inflammation, or hematoma formation.

Instruct the patient in the care and assessment of the site.

Instruct the patient to apply cold compresses to the insertion site as needed, to reduce discomfort or edema.

Instruct the patient to increase fluid intake to help eliminate the contrast medium, if used.

Inform the patient that diarrhea may occur after ingestion of oral contrast medium.

Recognize anxiety related to test results. Discuss the implications of abnormal test results on the patient's lifestyle. Provide teaching and information regarding the clinical implications of the test results, as appropriate.

Reinforce information given by the patient's HCP regarding further testing, treatment, or referral to another HCP. Answer any questions or address any concerns voiced by the patient or family.

Depending on the results of this procedure, additional testing may be needed to evaluate or monitor progression of the disease process and determine the need for a change in therapy. Evaluate test results in relation to the patient's symptoms and other tests performed.

RELATED MONOGRAPHS:

Related tests include angiography pelvis, barium enema, BUN, calculus kidney stone panel, cancer antigens, CBC, CBC hematocrit, CBC hemoglobin, creatinine, HCG, IVP, KUB film, MRI abdomen, proctosigmoidoscopy, PT/INR, US pelvis, and UA.

Refer to the Gastrointestinal, Genitourinary, and Reproductive systems tables at the end of the book for related tests by body system.

C

Computed Tomography, Pituitary

SYNONYM/ACRONYM: Computed axial tomography (CAT), computed transaxial tomography (CTT), pituitary CT, helical/spiral CT.

COMMON USE: To visualize and assess portions of the brain and pituitary gland for cancer, tumor, and bleeding. Used as an evaluation tool for surgical, radiation, and medical therapeutic interventions.

AREA OF APPLICATION: Pituitary/brain.

CONTRAST: With or without IV iodinated contrast medium.

DESCRIPTION: Computed tomography (CT) of the pituitary is a noninvasive procedure that enhances certain anatomic views of the pituitary gland and perisellar region. It becomes invasive when a contrast medium is used. This procedure aids in the evaluation of pituitary adenoma, craniopharyngioma, meningioma, aneurysm, metastatic disease, exophthalmos, and cysts. Visualization of bony septa in the sphenoid sinus and evaluation for non-pneumatization of the sphenoid sinus are best performed with this procedure. During the procedure, the patient lies on a table and moves in and out of a doughnut-like device called a *gantry*, which houses the x-ray tube and associated electronics. The scanner uses multiple x-ray beams and a series of detectors that rotate around the patient to produce cross-sectional views in a three-dimensional fashion. Differences in tissue density are detected and recorded and are viewable as computerized digital images. Slices or thin sections of certain anatomic views of the pituitary and associated vascular system are reviewed to allow differentiations of solid, cystic, inflammatory, or vascular lesions, as well as identification of suspected hematomas and aneurysms. The procedure may be repeated after iodinated contrast medium is given IV for blood vessel and vascular evaluation. Images can be recorded on photographic or x-ray film or stored in digital format as digitized computer data. Cine scanning produces a series of moving images of the scanned area. Tumors, before and after therapy, may be monitored by CT scanning.

INDICATIONS

- Assist in differentiating between benign and malignant tumors
- Detect aneurysms and vascular abnormalities
- Detect congenital anomalies, such as partially empty sella
- Detect tumor extension of masses and metastasis
- Determine pituitary size and location in relation to surrounding structures
- Evaluate cysts, masses, abscesses, and trauma
- Monitor and evaluate effectiveness of medical, radiation, or surgical therapies

POTENTIAL DIAGNOSIS

Normal findings in

- Normal size, position, and shape of the pituitary fossa, cavernous sinuses, and vascular system

Abnormal findings in

- Abscess
- Adenoma
- Aneurysm
- Chordoma
- Craniopharyngioma
- Cyst
- Meningioma
- Metastasis
- Pituitary hemorrhage

CRITICAL FINDINGS: N/A

INTERFERING FACTORS

This procedure is contraindicated for

- ◈ Patients with allergies to shellfish or iodinated dye. The contrast medium used may cause a life-threatening allergic reaction. Patients with a known hypersensitivity to the medium may benefit from premedication with corticosteroids or the use of nonionic contrast medium.
- Patients who are claustrophobic.

- Patients who are pregnant or suspected of being pregnant, unless the potential benefits of the procedure far outweigh the risks to the fetus and mother.
- ◈ Elderly and other patients who are chronically dehydrated before the test, because of their risk of contrast-induced renal failure.
- ◈ Patients who are in renal failure.
- Young patients (17 yr and younger), unless the benefits of the x-ray diagnosis outweigh the risks of exposure to high levels of radiation. Information on the Image Gently Campaign can be found at the Alliance for Radiation Safety in Pediatric Imaging (www.pedrad.org/associations/5364/ig/).

Factors that may impair clear imaging

- Retained contrast from a previous radiological procedure.
- Metallic objects (e.g., jewelry, dentures, body rings) within the examination field, which may inhibit organ visualization and cause unclear images.
- Patients who are very obese or who may exceed the weight limit for the equipment.
- Patients with extreme claustrophobia unless sedation is given before the study.
- Inability of the patient to cooperate or remain still during the procedure because of age, significant pain, or mental status.

Other considerations

- Complications of the procedure may include hemorrhage, infection at the IV needle insertion site, and cardiac arrhythmias.
- The procedure may be terminated if chest pain or severe cardiac arrhythmias occur.
- Failure to follow pretesting preparations may cause the procedure to be canceled or repeated.

- Consultation with a health-care provider (HCP) should occur before the procedure for radiation safety concerns regarding younger patients or patients who are lactating.
- Risks associated with radiation overexposure can result from frequent x-ray procedures. Personnel in the room with the patient should wear a protective lead apron, stand behind a shield, or leave the area while the examination is being done. Personnel working in the examination area should wear badges to record their level of radiation exposure.

NURSING IMPLICATIONS AND PROCEDURE

PRETEST:

Positively identify the patient using at least two unique identifiers before providing care, treatment, or services.

Patient Teaching: Inform the patient this procedure can assist in assessing the brain and pituitary gland.

Obtain a history of the patient's complaints or clinical symptoms, including a list of known allergens, especially allergies or sensitivities to latex, iodine, seafood, anesthetics, or contrast medium.

Obtain a history of the patient's endocrine system, symptoms, and results of previously performed laboratory tests and diagnostic and surgical procedures.

Ensure results of coagulation testing are obtained and recorded prior to the procedure; BUN and creatinine results are also needed if contrast medium is to be used.

Note any recent procedures that can interfere with test results, including examinations using barium- or iodine-based contrast medium. Ensure that barium studies were performed more than 4 days before the CT scan.

Record the date of the last menstrual period and determine the possibility of pregnancy in perimenopausal women.

Obtain a list of the patient's current medications, including anticoagulants, aspirin and other salicylates, herbs, nutritional supplements, and nutraceuticals

(see Appendix F). Note the last time and dose of medication taken.

If contrast medium is scheduled to be used, patients receiving metformin (Glucophage) for non–insulin-dependent (type 2) diabetes should discontinue the drug on the day of the test and continue to withhold it for 48 hr after the test. Failure to do so may result in lactic acidosis.

Review the procedure with the patient. Address concerns about pain and explain that there may be moments of discomfort and some pain experienced during the test. Inform the patient the procedure is usually performed in a radiology suite by an HCP specializing in this procedure, with support staff, and takes approximately 30 to 60 min.

Sensitivity to social and cultural issues, as well as concern for modesty, is important in providing psychological support before, during and after the procedure.

Explain that an IV line may be inserted to allow infusion of IV fluids, contrast medium, dye, or sedatives. Usually contrast medium and normal saline are infused.

Inform the patient that he or she may experience nausea, a feeling of warmth, a salty or metallic taste, or a transient headache after injection of contrast medium.

Instruct the patient to remove dentures and other metallic objects from the area to be examined.

There are no food or fluid restrictions unless by medical direction. Instruct the patient to avoid taking anticoagulant medication or to reduce dosage as ordered prior to the procedure. Protocols may vary among facilities.

Make sure a written and informed consent has been signed prior to the procedure and before administering any medications.

INTRATEST:

Observe standard precautions, and follow the general guidelines in Appendix A. Positively identify the patient.

Ensure the patient has complied with medication restrictions and pretesting preparations.

Ensure the patient has removed dentures and all external metallic objects from the area to be examined prior to the procedure.

If the patient has a history of allergic reactions to any substance or drug, administer ordered prophylactic steroids or antihistamines before the procedure. Use nonionic contrast medium for the procedure.

Have emergency equipment readily available.

Instruct the patient to cooperate fully and to follow directions. Instruct the patient to remain still throughout the procedure because movement produces unreliable results.

Establish an IV fluid line for the injection of contrast medium, emergency drugs, and sedatives.

Administer an antianxiety agent, as ordered, if the patient has claustrophobia. Administer a sedative to a child or to an uncooperative adult, as ordered.

Place the patient in the supine position on an examination table.

If IV contrast medium is used, a rapid series of images is taken during and after injection.

Instruct the patient to take slow, deep breaths if nausea occurs during the procedure.

Monitor the patient for complications related to the procedure (e.g., allergic reaction, anaphylaxis, bronchospasm) if contrast medium is used.

The needle is removed, and a pressure dressing is applied over the puncture site.

Observe/assess the needle site for bleeding, inflammation, or hematoma formation.

POST-TEST:

A report of the results will be made available to the requesting HCP, who will discuss the results with the patient.

Instruct the patient to resume usual medications and activity, as directed by the HCP. Renal function should be assessed before metformin is resumed, if contrast was used.

Monitor vital signs and neurological status every 15 min for 1 hr, then every 2 hr for 4 hr, and then as ordered by the HCP. Monitor temperature every 4 hr for 24 hr. Monitor intake and output at least every 8 hr. Compare with baseline values. Notify the HCP if temperature is elevated. Protocols may vary among facilities.

If contrast was used, observe for delayed allergic reactions, such as rash, urticaria, tachycardia, hyperpnea, hypertension, palpitations, nausea, or vomiting.

Instruct the patient to immediately report symptoms such as fast heart rate, difficulty breathing, skin rash, itching, chest pain, persistent right shoulder pain, or abdominal pain. Immediately report symptoms to the appropriate HCP.

Observe/assess the needle insertion site for bleeding, inflammation, or hematoma formation.

Instruct the patient in the care and assessment of the site.

Instruct the patient to apply cold compresses to the insertion site as needed, to reduce discomfort or edema.

Instruct the patient to increase fluid intake to help eliminate the contrast medium, if used.

Inform the patient that diarrhea may occur after ingestion of oral contrast medium.

Recognize anxiety related to test results. Discuss the implications of abnormal test results on the patient's lifestyle. Provide teaching and information regarding the clinical implications of the test results, as appropriate.

Reinforce information given by the patient's HCP regarding further testing, treatment, or referral to another HCP. Answer any questions or address any concerns voiced by the patient or family.

Depending on the results of this procedure, additional testing may be needed to evaluate or monitor progression of the disease process and determine the need for a change in therapy. Evaluate test results in relation to the patient's symptoms and other tests performed.

RELATED MONOGRAPHS:

Related tests include ACTH and challenge tests, BUN, CT angiography, CBC, CBC hematocrit, CBC hemoglobin, CT brain, cortisol and challenge tests, creatinine, MRA, MRI brain, PET brain, and PT/INR.

Refer to the Endocrine System table at the end of the book for related tests by body system.

Computed Tomography, Renal

SYNONYM/ACRONYM: Computed axial tomography (CAT), computed transaxial tomography (CTT), kidney CT, helical/spiral CT.

C

COMMON USE: To visualize and assess the kidney and surrounding structures to assist in diagnosing cancer, tumor, infection, and congenital anomalies. Used to evaluate the success of therapeutic medical, surgical, and radiation interventions.

AREA OF APPLICATION: Kidney.

CONTRAST: With or without oral or IV iodinated contrast medium.

DESCRIPTION: Renal computed tomography (CT) is a noninvasive procedure used to enhance certain anatomic views of the renal structures. It becomes an invasive procedure when contrast medium is used. CT scanning is a safe, rapid method for renal evaluation that is independent of renal function. It provides unique cross-sectional anatomic information and is unsurpassed in evaluating lesions containing fat or calcium. During the procedure, the patient lies on a table and is moved in and out of a doughnut-like device called a *gantry*, which houses the x-ray tube and associated electronics. The scanner uses multiple x-ray beams and a series of detectors that rotate around the patient to produce cross-sectional views in a three-dimensional fashion. Differences in tissue density are detected and recorded and are viewable as computerized digital images. Slices or thin sections of certain anatomic views of the kidneys and associated vascular system are reviewed to allow differentiation of solid, cystic, inflammatory, or vascular lesions, as well as identification

of suspected hematomas and aneurysms. The procedure is repeated after IV injection of iodinated contrast medium for vascular evaluation or after oral ingestion of contrast medium for evaluation of bowel and adjacent structures. Images can be recorded on photographic or x-ray film or stored in digital format as digitized computer data. Cine scanning produces a series of moving images of the area scanned. The CT scan can be used to guide biopsy needles into areas of suspected tumors to obtain tissue for laboratory analysis and to guide placement of catheters for drainage of renal abscesses. Tumors, before and after therapy, may be monitored with CT scanning.

INDICATIONS
- Aid in the diagnosis of congenital anomalies, such as polycystic kidney disease, horseshoe kidney, absence of one kidney, or kidney displacement
- Aid in the diagnosis of perirenal hematomas and abscesses and assist in localizing for drainage

- Assist in differentiating between benign and malignant tumors
- Assist in differentiating between an infectious and an inflammatory process
- Detect aneurysms and vascular abnormalities
- Detect bleeding or hyperplasia of the adrenal glands
- Detect tumor extension of masses and metastasis into the renal area
- Determine kidney size and location in relation to the bladder in post-transplant patients
- Determine presence and type of adrenal tumor, such as benign adenoma, cancer, or pheochromocytoma
- Evaluate abnormal fluid accumulation around the kidney
- Evaluate cysts, masses, abscesses, renal calculi, obstruction, and trauma
- Evaluate spread of a tumor or invasion of nearby retroperitoneal organs
- Monitor and evaluate effectiveness of medical, radiation, or surgical therapies

POTENTIAL DIAGNOSIS

Normal findings in
- Normal size, position, and shape of kidneys and vascular system

Abnormal findings in
- Adrenal tumor or hyperplasia
- Congenital anomalies, such as polycystic kidney disease, horseshoe kidney, absence of one kidney, or kidney displacement
- Dilation of the common hepatic duct, common bile duct, or gallbladder
- Renal artery aneurysm
- Renal calculi and ureteral obstruction
- Renal cell carcinoma
- Renal cysts or abscesses
- Renal laceration, fracture, tumor, and trauma

- Perirenal abscesses and hematomas
- Primary and metastatic neoplasms

CRITICAL FINDINGS: N/A

INTERFERING FACTORS

This procedure is contraindicated for
- Patients with allergies to shellfish or iodinated dye. The contrast medium used may cause a life-threatening allergic reaction. Patients with a known hypersensitivity to the medium may benefit from premedication with corticosteroids or the use of nonionic contrast medium.
- Patients who are claustrophobic.
- Patients who are pregnant or suspected of being pregnant, unless the potential benefits of the procedure far outweigh the risks to the fetus and mother.
- Elderly and other patients who are chronically dehydrated before the test, because of their risk of contrast-induced renal failure.
- Patients who are in renal failure.
- Young patients (17 yr and younger), unless the benefits of the x-ray diagnosis outweigh the risks of exposure to high levels of radiation. Information on the Image Gently Campaign can be found at the Alliance for Radiation Safety in Pediatric Imaging (www.pedrad. org/associations/5364/ig/).

Factors that may impair clear imaging
- Gas or feces in the gastrointestinal (GI) tract resulting from inadequate cleansing or failure to restrict food intake before the study.
- Retained barium from a previous radiological procedure.
- Metallic objects (e.g., jewelry, body rings) within the examination field, which may inhibit organ visualization and cause unclear images.

- Patients who are very obese or who may exceed the weight limit for the equipment.
- Patients with extreme claustrophobia unless sedation is given before the study.
- Inability of the patient to cooperate or remain still during the procedure because of age, significant pain, or mental status.

Other considerations

- Complications of the procedure include hemorrhage, infection at the IV needle insertion site, and cardiac arrhythmias.
- The procedure may be terminated if chest pain or severe cardiac arrhythmias occur.
- Failure to follow dietary restrictions and other pretesting preparations may cause the procedure to be canceled or repeated.
- Consultation with a health-care provider (HCP) should occur before the procedure for radiation safety concerns regarding younger patients or patients who are lactating.
- Risks associated with radiation overexposure can result from frequent x-ray procedures. Personnel in the room with the patient should wear a protective lead apron, stand behind a shield, or leave the area while the examination is being done. Personnel working in the examination area should wear badges to record their level of radiation exposure.

NURSING IMPLICATIONS AND PROCEDURE

PRETEST:

▶ Positively identify the patient using at least two unique identifiers before providing care, treatment, or services.
▶ *Patient Teaching:* Inform the patient this procedure can assist in assessing the kidney.

▶ Obtain a history of the patient's complaints or clinical symptoms, including a list of known allergens, especially allergies or sensitivities to latex, iodine, seafood, anesthetics, or contrast mediums.
▶ Obtain a history of the patient's genitourinary system, symptoms, and results of previously performed laboratory tests and diagnostic and surgical procedures.
▶ Ensure results of coagulation testing are obtained and recorded prior to the procedure; BUN and creatinine results are also needed if contrast medium is to be used.
▶ Note any recent procedures that can interfere with test results, including examinations using barium- or iodine-based contrast medium. Ensure that barium studies were performed more than 4 days before the CT scan.
▶ Record the date of the last menstrual period and determine the possibility of pregnancy in perimenopausal women.
▶ Obtain a list of the patient's current medications including anticoagulants, aspirin and other salicylates, herbs, nutritional supplements, and nutraceuticals (see Appendix F). Note the last time and dose of medication taken.
▶ If contrast medium is scheduled to be used, patients receiving metformin (Glucophage) for non–insulin-dependent (type 2) diabetes should discontinue the drug on the day of the test and continue to withhold it for 48 hr after the test. Failure to do so may result in lactic acidosis.
▶ Review the procedure with the patient. Address concerns about pain and explain that there may be moments of discomfort and some pain experienced during the test. Inform the patient the procedure is usually performed in a radiology suite by an HCP specializing in this procedure, with support staff, and takes approximately 30 to 60 min.
▶ Explain that an IV line may be inserted to allow infusion of IV fluids, contrast medium, dye, or sedatives. Usually contrast medium and normal saline are infused.
▶ *Sensitivity to social and cultural issues,* as well as concern for modesty, is important in providing psychological

support before, during, and after the procedure.

- The patient may be requested to drink approximately 450 mL of a dilute barium solution (approximately 1% barium) or a water soluble oral contrast beginning 1 hr before the examination. This is administered to distinguish GI organs from the other abdominal organs.
- Inform the patient that he or she may experience nausea, a feeling of warmth, a salty or metallic taste, or a transient headache after injection of contrast medium.
- Instruct the patient to remove jewelry and other metallic objects from the area to be examined.
- The patient should fast and restrict fluids for 2 to 4 hr prior to the procedure. Instruct the patient to avoid taking anticoagulant medication or to reduce dosage as ordered prior to the procedure. Protocols may vary among facilities.

Make sure a written and informed consent has been signed prior to the procedure and before administering any medications.

INTRATEST:

- Observe standard precautions, and follow the general guidelines in Appendix A. Positively identify the patient.
- Ensure the patient has complied with dietary, fluids, and medication restrictions for 2 to 4 hr prior to the procedure.
- Ensure the patient has removed all external metallic objects from the area to be examined prior to the procedure.
- If the patient has a history of allergic reactions to any substance or drug, administer ordered prophylactic steroids or antihistamines before the procedure. Use nonionic contrast medium for the procedure.
- Have emergency equipment readily available.
- Instruct the patient to void prior to the procedure and to change into the gown, robe, and foot coverings provided.
- Instruct the patient to cooperate fully and to follow directions. Instruct the patient to remain still throughout the

procedure because movement produces unreliable results.

- Establish an IV fluid line for the injection of contrast, emergency drugs, and sedatives.
- Administer an antianxiety agent, as ordered, if the patient has claustrophobia. Administer a sedative to a child or to an uncooperative adult, as ordered.
- Place the patient in the supine position on an examination table.
- If IV contrast is used, a rapid series of images is taken during and after injection.
- Instruct the patient to inhale deeply and hold his or her breath while the x-ray images are taken, and then to exhale after the images are taken.
- Instruct the patient to take slow, deep breaths if nausea occurs during the procedure.
- Monitor the patient for complications related to the procedure (e.g., allergic reaction, anaphylaxis, bronchospasm) if contrast is used.
- The needle is removed, and a pressure dressing is applied over the puncture site.
- Observe/assess the needle site for bleeding, inflammation, or hematoma formation.

POST-TEST:

- A report of the results will be made available to the requesting HCP, who will discuss the results with the patient.
- Instruct the patient to resume usual diet, fluids, medications, and activity, as directed by the HCP. Renal function should be assessed before metformin is resumed, if contrast was used.
- Monitor vital signs and neurological status every 15 min for 1 hr, then every 2 hr for 4 hr, and then as ordered by the HCP. Monitor temperature every 4 hr for 24 hr. Monitor intake and output at least every 8 hr. Compare with baseline values. Notify the HCP if temperature is elevated. Protocols may vary among facilities.
- If contrast was used, observe for delayed allergic reactions, such as rash, urticaria, tachycardia, hyperpnea, hypertension, palpitations, nausea, or vomiting.

Instruct the patient to immediately report symptoms such as fast heart rate, difficulty breathing, skin rash, itching, chest pain, persistent right shoulder pain, or abdominal pain. Immediately report symptoms to the appropriate HCP.

Observe/assess the needle insertion site for bleeding, inflammation, or hematoma formation.

Instruct the patient in the care and assessment of the site.

Instruct the patient to apply cold compresses to the insertion site as needed, to reduce discomfort or edema.

Instruct the patient to increase fluid intake to help eliminate the contrast medium, if used.

Inform the patient that diarrhea may occur after ingestion of oral contrast medium.

Recognize anxiety related to test results. Discuss the implications of abnormal test results on the patient's lifestyle. Provide teaching and information regarding the clinical implications of the test results, as appropriate.

Reinforce information given by the patient's HCP regarding further testing, treatment, or referral to another HCP. Answer any questions or address any concerns voiced by the patient or family.

Depending on the results of this procedure, additional testing may be needed to evaluate or monitor progression of the disease process and determine the need for a change in therapy. Evaluate test results in relation to the patient's symptoms and other tests performed.

RELATED MONOGRAPHS:

Related tests include ACTH, angiography adrenal, renal biopsy, BUN, calculus/kidney stone panel, catecholamines, CBC, CBC hematocrit, CBC hemoglobin, creatinine, CT abdomen, homovanillic acid, IVP, KUB, MRI abdomen, PT/INR, US renal, and VMA.

Refer to the Genitourinary System table at the end of the book for related tests by body system.

Computed Tomography, Spine

SYNONYM/ACRONYM: Computed axial tomography (CAT), computed transaxial tomography (CTT), spine CT, CT myelogram.

COMMON USE: To visualize and assess spinal structure related to tumor, injury, bleeding, and infection. Used as an evaluation tool for surgical, radiation, and medical therapeutic interventions.

AREA OF APPLICATION: Spine.

CONTRAST: With or without oral or IV iodinated contrast medium.

DESCRIPTION: Computed tomography (CT) of the spine is a noninvasive procedure that enhances certain anatomic views of the spinal structures. CT scanning is more versatile than conventional radiography and can easily detect and identify tumors and their types.

During the procedure, the patient lies on a table and is moved in and out of a doughnut-like device called a *gantry*, which houses the x-ray tube and associated electronics. The scanner uses multiple x-ray beams and a series of detectors that rotate around the patient to produce cross-sectional views in a three-dimensional fashion. Differences in tissue density are detected and recorded and are viewable as computerized digital images. Slices or thin sections of certain anatomic views of the spine and associated vascular system are reviewed to allow differentiations of solid, cystic, inflammatory, or vascular lesions, as well as identification of suspected hematomas and aneurysms. The procedure may be repeated after intravenous injection of iodinated contrast medium for vascular evaluation. Images can be recorded on photographic or x-ray film or stored in digital format as digitized computer data. Cine scanning produces a series of moving images of the scanned area. CT scanning can be used to guide biopsy needles into areas of suspected tumor to obtain tissue for laboratory analysis and to guide placement of catheters for drainage of abscesses. Tumor size, progression, and pre- and post-therapy changes may be monitored with CT scanning.

INDICATIONS

- Assist in differentiating between benign and malignant tumors
- Detect congenital spinal anomalies, such as spina bifida, meningocele, and myelocele
- Detect herniated intervertebral disks
- Detect paraspinal cysts
- Detect vascular malformations
- Monitor and evaluate effectiveness of medical, radiation, or surgical therapies

POTENTIAL DIAGNOSIS

Normal findings in

- Normal density, size, position, and shape of spinal structures

Abnormal findings in

- Congenital spinal malformations, such as meningocele, myelocele, or spina bifida
- Herniated intervertebral disks
- Paraspinal cysts
- Spinal tumors
- Spondylosis (cervical or lumbar)
- Vascular malformations

CRITICAL FINDINGS

- Cord compression
- Fracture
- Tumor with significant mass effect

It is essential that critical diagnoses be communicated immediately to the appropriate HCP. A listing of these diagnoses varies among facilities. Note and immediately report to the HCP abnormal results and related symptoms. Timely notification of critical values for lab or diagnostic studies is a role expectation of the professional nurse. Notification processes will vary among facilities. Upon receipt of the critical value, the information should be read back to the caller to verify accuracy. Most policies require immediate notification of the primary HCP, hospitalist, or on-call HCP. Reported information includes the patient's name, unique identifiers, critical value, name of the person giving the report, and name of the person receiving the report. Documentation of notification should be made in the medical record with the name of the HCP notified, time and date of notification, and any orders received. Any delay in a timely report of a critical value may require completion of a notification form with review by Risk Management.

INTERFERING FACTORS

This procedure is contraindicated for

- Patients with allergies to shellfish or iodinated dye. The contrast medium used may cause a life-threatening allergic reaction. Patients with a known hypersensitivity to the

medium may benefit from premedication with corticosteroids or the use of nonionic contrast medium.
- Patients who are claustrophobic.
- Patients who are pregnant or suspected of being pregnant, unless the potential benefits of the procedure far outweigh the risks to the fetus and mother.
- Elderly and other patients who are chronically dehydrated before the test, because of their risk of contrast-induced renal failure.
- Patients who are in renal failure.
- Young patients (17 yr and younger), unless the benefits of the x-ray diagnosis outweigh the risks of exposure to high levels of radiation. Information on the Image Gently Campaign can be found at the Alliance for Radiation Safety in Pediatric Imaging (www.pedrad.org/associations/5364/ig/).

Factors that may impair clear imaging
- Gas or feces in the gastrointestinal tract resulting from inadequate cleansing or failure to restrict food intake before the study.
- Retained barium from a previous radiological procedure.
- Metallic objects (e.g., jewelry, body rings) within the examination field, which may inhibit organ visualization and cause unclear images.
- Patients who are very obese or who may exceed the weight limit for the equipment.
- Patients with extreme claustrophobia unless sedation is given before the study.
- Inability of the patient to cooperate or remain still during the procedure because of age, significant pain, or mental status.

Other considerations
- Complications of the procedure may include hemorrhage, infection at the IV needle insertion site, and cardiac arrhythmias.
- The procedure may be terminated if chest pain or severe cardiac arrhythmias occur.
- Failure to follow pretesting preparations may cause the procedure to be canceled or repeated.
- Consultation with an HCP should occur before the procedure for radiation safety concerns regarding younger patients or patients who are lactating.
- Risks associated with radiation overexposure can result from frequent x-ray procedures. Personnel in the room with the patient should wear a protective lead apron, stand behind a shield, or leave the area while the examination is being done. Personnel working in the examination area should wear badges to record their level of radiation exposure.

NURSING IMPLICATIONS AND PROCEDURE

PRETEST:
- Positively identify the patient using at least two unique identifiers before providing care, treatment, or services.
- *Patient Teaching:* Inform the patient this procedure can assist in assessing the spine.
- Obtain a history of the patient's complaints or clinical symptoms, including a list of known allergens, especially allergies or sensitivities to latex, iodine, seafood, anesthetics, or contrast medium.
- Obtain a history of the patient's musculoskeletal system, symptoms, and results of previously performed laboratory tests and diagnostic and surgical procedures.
- Ensure results of coagulation testing are obtained and recorded prior to the procedure; BUN and creatinine results are also needed if contrast medium is to be used.

Note any recent procedures that can interfere with test results, including examinations using barium- or iodine-based contrast medium. Ensure that barium studies were performed more than 4 days before the CT scan.

Record the date of the last menstrual period and determine the possibility of pregnancy in perimenopausal women.

Obtain a list of the patient's current medications including anticoagulants, aspirin and other salicylates, herbs and nutritional supplements, and nutraceuticals (see Appendix F). Note the last time and dose of medication taken.

If contrast medium is scheduled to be used, patients receiving metformin (Glucophage) for non–insulin-dependent (type 2) diabetes should discontinue the drug on the day of the test and continue to withhold it for 48 hr after the test. Failure to do so may result in lactic acidosis.

Review the procedure with the patient. Address concerns about pain and explain that there may be moments of discomfort and some pain experienced during the test. Inform the patient the procedure is usually performed in a radiology suite by an HCP specializing in this procedure, with support staff, and takes approximately 30 to 60 min. *Sensitivity to social and cultural issues,* as well as concern for modesty, is important in providing psychological support before, during, and after the procedure.

Explain that an IV line may be inserted to allow infusion of IV fluids, contrast medium, dye, or sedatives. Usually contrast medium and normal saline are infused.

Inform the patient that he or she may experience nausea, a feeling of warmth, a salty or metallic taste, or a transient headache after injection of contrast medium.

Instruct the patient to remove jewelry and other metallic objects from the area to be examined.

There are no food or fluid restrictions unless by medical direction. Instruct the patient to avoid taking anticoagulant medication or to reduce dosage as ordered prior to the procedure. Protocols may vary among facilities.

Make sure a written and informed consent has been signed prior to the procedure and before administering any medications.

INTRATEST:

Observe standard precautions, and follow the general guidelines in Appendix A. Positively identify the patient.

Ensure that the patient has complied with medication restrictions and pretesting preparations.

Ensure that the patient has removed all external metallic objects from the area to be examined prior to the procedure.

If the patient has a history of allergic reactions to any substance or drug, administer ordered prophylactic steroids or antihistamines before the procedure. Use nonionic contrast medium for the procedure.

Have emergency equipment readily available.

Instruct the patient to void prior to the procedure and to change into the gown, robe, and foot coverings provided.

Instruct the patient to cooperate fully and to follow directions. Instruct the patient to remain still throughout the procedure because movement produces unreliable results.

If ordered, establish an IV fluid line for the injection of contrast medium, emergency drugs, and sedatives.

Administer an antianxiety agent, as ordered, if the patient has claustrophobia. Administer a sedative to a child or to an uncooperative adult, as ordered.

Place the patient in the supine position on an examination table.

If IV contrast medium is used, a rapid series of images is taken during and after injection.

Instruct the patient to inhale deeply and hold his or her breath while the x-ray images are taken, and then to exhale after the images are taken.

Instruct the patient to take slow, deep breaths if nausea occurs during the procedure.

Monitor the patient for complications related to the procedure (e.g., allergic reaction, anaphylaxis, bronchospasm) if contrast is used.

The needle is removed, and a pressure dressing is applied over the puncture site.

Observe/assess the needle insertion site for bleeding, inflammation, or hematoma formation.

POST-TEST:

A report of the results will be made available to the requesting HCP, who will discuss the results with the patient.

Instruct the patient to resume usual medications and activity, as directed by the HCP. Renal function should be assessed before metformin is resumed, if contrast was used.

Monitor vital signs and neurological status every 15 min for 1 hr, then every 2 hr for 4 hr, and then as ordered by the HCP. Monitor temperature every 4 hr for 24 hr. Monitor intake and output at least every 8 hr. Compare with baseline values. Notify the HCP if temperature is elevated. Protocols may vary among facilities.

If contrast was used, observe for delayed allergic reactions, such as rash, urticaria, tachycardia, hyperpnea, hypertension, palpitations, nausea, or vomiting.

Instruct the patient to immediately report symptoms such as fast heart rate, difficulty breathing, skin rash, itching, chest pain, persistent right shoulder pain, or abdominal pain. Immediately report symptoms to the appropriate HCP.

Observe/assess the needle insertion site for bleeding, inflammation, or hematoma formation. Instruct the patient in the care and assessment of the site.

Instruct the patient to apply cold compresses to the insertion site as needed, to reduce discomfort or edema.

Instruct the patient to increase fluid intake to help eliminate the contrast medium, if used.

Recognize anxiety related to test results. Discuss the implications of abnormal test results on the patient's lifestyle. Provide teaching and information regarding the clinical implications of the test results, as appropriate.

Reinforce information given by the patient's HCP regarding further testing, treatment, or referral to another HCP. Answer any questions or address any concerns voiced by the patient or family.

Depending on the results of this procedure, additional testing may be needed to evaluate or monitor progression of the disease process and determine the need for a change in therapy. Evaluate test results in relation to the patient's symptoms and other tests performed.

RELATED MONOGRAPHS:

Related tests include ALP, BUN, bone scan, CBC, CBC hematocrit, CBC hemoglobin, creatinine, MRI bone, PT/INR, and radiography of the bones.

Refer to the Musculoskeletal System table at the end of the book for related tests by body system.

Computed Tomography, Spleen

SYNONYM/ACRONYM: Computed axial tomography (CAT), computed transaxial tomography (CTT), helical/spiral CT, splenic CT.

COMMON USE: To visualize and assess the spleen and surrounding structure for tumor, bleeding, infection, and trauma. Used to monitor the effectiveness of medical, surgical, and radiation therapeutic interventions.

AREA OF APPLICATION: Abdomen/spleen.

CONTRAST: With or without oral or IV iodinated contrast medium.

DESCRIPTION: Computed tomography (CT) of the spleen is a noninvasive procedure that enhances certain anatomic views of the splenic structures. It becomes an invasive procedure with the use of contrast medium. The spleen is not often the organ of interest when abdominal CT scans are obtained. However, a wide variety of splenic variations and abnormalities may be detected on abdominal scans designed to evaluate the liver, pancreas, or retroperitoneum. During the procedure, the patient lies on a table and is moved in and out of a doughnut-like device called a *gantry*, which houses the x-ray tube and associated electronics. The scanner uses multiple x-ray beams and a series of detectors that rotate around the patient to produce cross-sectional views in a three-dimensional fashion. Differences in tissue density are detected and recorded and are viewable as computerized digital images. Slices or thin sections of certain anatomic views of the spleen and associated vascular system are reviewed to allow differentiation of solid, cystic, inflammatory, or vascular lesions, as well as identification of suspected hematomas and aneurysms. The procedure is repeated after IV injection of iodinated contrast medium for vascular evaluation or after oral ingestion of contrast medium for evaluation of bowel and adjacent structures. Images can be recorded on photographic or x-ray film or stored in digital format as digitized computer data. Cine scanning produces a series of moving images of the scanned area. The CT scan can be used to guide biopsy needles into areas of splenic masses to obtain tissue for laboratory analysis and for placement of needles to aspirate cysts or abscesses. CT scanning can monitor mass, cyst, or tumor growth and post-therapy response.

INDICATIONS
- Assist in differentiating between benign and malignant tumors
- Detect tumor extension of masses and metastasis
- Differentiate infectious from inflammatory processes
- Evaluate cysts, masses, abscesses, and trauma
- Evaluate the presence of an accessory spleen, polysplenia, or asplenia
- Evaluate splenic vein thrombosis
- Monitor and evaluate effectiveness of medical, radiation, or surgical therapies

POTENTIAL DIAGNOSIS

Normal findings in
- Normal size, position, and shape of the spleen and associated vascular system

Abnormal findings in
- Abdominal aortic aneurysm
- Hematomas
- Hemoperitoneum
- Primary and metastatic neoplasms
- Splenic cysts or abscesses
- Splenic laceration, tumor, infiltration, and trauma

CRITICAL FINDINGS
- Abscess
- Hemorrhage
- Laceration

It is essential that critical diagnoses be communicated immediately to the appropriate HCP. A listing of these diagnoses varies among facilities. Note and immediately report to the HCP abnormal results and related symptoms. Timely notification of critical values for lab or diagnostic studies is a role expectation of the professional nurse. Notification processes will vary among facilities. Upon receipt of the critical value, the information should be read back to the caller to verify accuracy. Most policies require immediate notification of the primary HCP, hospitalist, or on-call HCP. Reported information includes the patient's name, unique identifiers, critical value, name of the person giving the report, and name of the person receiving the report. Documentation of notification should be made in the medical record with the name of the HCP notified, time and date of notification, and any orders received. Any delay in a timely report of a critical value may require completion of a notification form with review by Risk Management.

INTERFERING FACTORS

This procedure is contraindicated for

• Patients with allergies to shellfish or iodinated dye. The contrast medium used may cause a life-threatening allergic reaction. Patients with a known hypersensitivity to the medium may benefit from premedication with corticosteroids or the use of nonionic contrast medium.
• Patients who are claustrophobic.
• Patients who are pregnant or suspected of being pregnant, unless the potential benefits of the procedure far outweigh the risks to the fetus and mother.
• Elderly and other patients who are chronically dehydrated before the test, because of their risk of contrast-induced renal failure.
• Patients who are in renal failure.
• Young patients (17 yr and younger), unless the benefits of the x-ray diagnosis outweigh the risks of exposure to high levels of radiation. Information on the Image Gently Campaign can be found at the Alliance for Radiation Safety in Pediatric Imaging (www.pedrad.org/associations/5364/ig/).

Factors that may impair clear imaging

• Gas or feces in the gastrointestinal (GI) tract resulting from inadequate cleansing or failure to restrict food intake before the study.
• Retained barium from a previous radiological procedure.
• Metallic objects (e.g., jewelry, body rings) within the examination field, which may inhibit organ visualization and cause unclear images.
• Patients who are very obese or who may exceed the weight limit for the equipment.
• Patients with extreme claustrophobia unless sedation is given before the study.
• Inability of the patient to cooperate or remain still during the procedure because of age, significant pain, or mental status.

Other considerations

• Complications of the procedure include hemorrhage, infection at the IV needle insertion site, and cardiac arrhythmias.
• The procedure may be terminated if chest pain or severe cardiac arrhythmias occur.
• Failure to follow dietary restrictions and other pretesting preparations may cause the procedure to be canceled or repeated.
• Consultation with an HCP should occur before the procedure for radiation safety concerns regarding younger patients or patients who are lactating.
• Risks associated with radiation overexposure can result from frequent x-ray procedures. Personnel in the room with the patient should wear a protective lead apron, stand behind a shield, or leave the area while the examination is being done. Personnel working in the examination area should wear badges to record their level of radiation exposure.

NURSING IMPLICATIONS AND PROCEDURE

PRETEST:

- Positively identify the patient using at least two unique identifiers before providing care, treatment, or services.
- *Patient Teaching:* Inform the patient this procedure can assist in assessing the abdomen and spleen.
- Obtain a history of the patient's complaints, including a list of known allergens, especially allergies or sensitivities to latex, iodine, seafood, anesthetics, or contrast medium.
- Obtain a history of the patient's hematopoietic system, symptoms, and results of previously performed laboratory tests and diagnostic and surgical procedures.
- Ensure results of coagulation testing are obtained and recorded prior to the procedure; BUN and creatinine results are also needed if contrast medium is to be used.
- Note any recent procedures that can interfere with test results, including examinations using barium- or iodine-based contrast medium. Ensure that barium studies were performed more than 4 days before the CT scan.
- Record the date of the last menstrual period and determine the possibility of pregnancy in perimenopausal women.
- Obtain a list of the patient's current medications including anticoagulants, aspirin and other salicylates, herbs, nutritional supplements, and nutraceuticals (see Appendix F). Note the last time and dose of medication taken.
- If contrast medium is scheduled to be used, patients receiving metformin (Glucophage) for non–insulin-dependent (type 2) diabetes should discontinue the drug on the day of the test and continue to withhold it for 48 hr after the test. Failure to do so may result in lactic acidosis.
- Review the procedure with the patient. Address concerns about pain and explain that there may be moments of discomfort and some pain experienced during the test. Inform the patient the procedure is usually

performed in a radiology suite by an HCP specializing in this procedure, with support staff, and takes approximately 30 to 60 min.
- Explain that an IV line may be inserted to allow infusion of IV fluids, contrast medium, dye, or sedatives. Usually contrast medium and normal saline are infused.
- *Sensitivity to social and cultural issues,* as well as concern for modesty, is important in providing psychological support before, during, and after the procedure.
- The patient may be requested to drink approximately 450 mL of a dilute barium solution (approximately 1% barium) or a water soluble oral contrast beginning 1 hr before the examination. This is administered to distinguish GI organs from the other abdominal organs.
- Inform the patient that he or she may experience nausea, a feeling of warmth, a salty or metallic taste, or a transient headache after injection of contrast medium.
- Instruct the patient to remove jewelry and other metallic objects from the area to be examined.
- The patient should fast and restrict fluids for 2 to 4 hr prior to the procedure. Instruct the patient to avoid taking anticoagulant medication or to reduce dosage as ordered prior to the procedure. Protocols may vary among facilities.
- *Make sure a written and informed consent has been signed prior to the procedure and before administering any medications.*

INTRATEST:

- Observe standard precautions, and follow the general guidelines in Appendix A. Positively identify the patient.
- Ensure the patient has complied with dietary, fluids, and medication restrictions for 2 to 4 hr prior to the procedure.
- Ensure the patient has removed all external metallic objects from the area to be examined prior to the procedure.
- If the patient has a history of allergic reactions to any substance or drug,

administer ordered prophylactic steroids or antihistamines before the procedure. Use nonionic contrast medium for the procedure.

▸ Have emergency equipment readily available.

▸ Instruct the patient to void prior to the procedure and to change into the gown, robe, and foot coverings provided.

▸ Instruct the patient to cooperate fully and to follow directions. Instruct the patient to remain still throughout the procedure because movement produces unreliable results.

▸ Establish an IV fluid line for the injection of contrast medium, emergency drugs, and sedatives.

▸ Administer an antianxiety agent, as ordered, if the patient has claustrophobia. Administer a sedative to a child or to an uncooperative adult, as ordered.

▸ Place the patient in the supine position on an examination table.

▸ If IV contrast medium is used, a rapid series of images is taken during and after injection.

▸ Instruct the patient to inhale deeply and hold his or her breath while the x-ray images are taken, and then to exhale after the images are taken.

▸ Instruct the patient to take slow, deep breaths if nausea occurs during the procedure.

▸ Monitor the patient for complications related to the procedure (e.g., allergic reaction, anaphylaxis, bronchospasm) if contrast medium is used.

▸ The needle is removed, and a pressure dressing is applied over the puncture site.

▸ Observe/assess the needle site for bleeding, inflammation, or hematoma formation.

POST-TEST:

▸ A report of the results will be made available to the requesting HCP, who will discuss the results with the patient.

▸ Instruct the patient to resume usual diet, fluids, medications, and activity, as directed by the HCP. Renal function should be assessed before metformin is resumed, if contrast was used.

▸ Monitor vital signs and neurological status every 15 min for 1 hr, then every 2 hr for 4 hr, and then as ordered by the HCP. Monitor temperature every 4 hr for 24 hr. Monitor intake and output at least every 8 hr. Compare with baseline values. Notify the HCP if temperature is elevated. Protocols may vary among facilities.

▸ If contrast was used, observe for delayed allergic reactions, such as rash, urticaria, tachycardia, hyperpnea, hypertension, palpitations, nausea, or vomiting.

▸ Instruct the patient to immediately report symptoms such as fast heart rate, difficulty breathing, skin rash, itching, chest pain, persistent right shoulder pain, or abdominal pain. Immediately report symptoms to the appropriate HCP.

▸ Observe/assess the needle site for bleeding, inflammation, or hematoma formation.

▸ Instruct the patient in the care and assessment of the site.

▸ Instruct the patient to apply cold compresses to the puncture site as needed, to reduce discomfort or edema.

▸ Instruct the patient to increase fluid intake to help eliminate the contrast medium, if used.

▸ Inform the patient that diarrhea may occur after ingestion of oral contrast medium.

▸ Recognize anxiety related to test results. Discuss the implications of abnormal test results on the patient's lifestyle. Provide teaching and information regarding the clinical implications of the test results, as appropriate.

▸ Reinforce information given by the patient's HCP regarding further testing, treatment, or referral to another HCP. Answer any questions or address any concerns voiced by the patient or family.

▸ Depending on the results of this procedure, additional testing may be needed to evaluate or monitor progression of the disease process and determine the need for a change in therapy. Evaluate test results in relation to the patient's symptoms and other tests performed.

RELATED MONOGRAPHS:
▶ Related tests include angiography abdomen, BUN, CBC, CBC

hematocrit, CBC hemoglobin, creatinine, KUB film, MRI abdomen, PT/INR, and US liver.
▶ Refer to the Hematopoietic System table at the end of the book for related tests by body system.

Computed Tomography, Thoracic

SYNONYM/ACRONYM: Chest CT, computed axial tomography (CAT), computed transaxial tomography (CTT), helical/spiral CT.

COMMON USE: To visualize and assess structures within the thoracic cavity such as the heart, lungs, and mediastinal structures to evaluate for aneurysm, cancer, tumor, and infection. Used as an evaluation tool for surgical, radiation, and medical therapeutic interventions.

AREA OF APPLICATION: Thorax.

CONTRAST: With or without oral or IV iodinated contrast medium.

DESCRIPTION: Computed tomography (CT) of the thorax is more detailed than a chest x-ray. It is a noninvasive procedure used to enhance certain anatomic views of the lungs, heart, and mediastinal structures. It becomes invasive when a contrast medium is used. During the procedure, the patient lies on a table and is moved in and out of a doughnut-like device called a *gantry*, which houses the x-ray tube and associated electronics. The scanner uses multiple x-ray beams and a series of detectors that rotate around the patient to produce cross-sectional views in a three-dimensional fashion. Differences in tissue density are detected and recorded and are viewable as computerized digital images. Slices or thin sections of certain anatomic views of the spine, spinal cord, and lung areas are reviewed to allow differentiations of solid, cystic, inflammatory, or

vascular lesions. Images can be recorded on photographic or x-ray film or stored in digital format as digitized computer data. Cine scanning is used to produce moving images of the heart.

INDICATIONS
- Detect aortic aneurysms
- Detect bronchial abnormalities, such as stenosis, dilation, or tumor
- Detect lymphomas, especially Hodgkin's disease
- Detect mediastinal and hilar lymphadenopathy
- Detect primary and metastatic pulmonary, esophageal, or mediastinal tumors
- Detect tumor extension of neck mass to thoracic area
- Determine blood, fluid, or fat accumulation in tissues, pleuritic space, or vessels
- Differentiate aortic aneurysms from tumors near the aorta

- Differentiate between benign and malignant tumors
- Differentiate infectious from inflammatory processes
- Differentiate tumor from tuberculosis
- Evaluate cardiac chambers and pulmonary vessels
- Evaluate the presence of plaque in cardiac vessels
- Monitor and evaluate effectiveness of medical or surgical therapeutic regimen

POTENTIAL DIAGNOSIS

Normal findings in
- Normal size, position, and shape of thoracic organs, tissues, and structures

Abnormal findings in
- Aortic aneurysm
- Chest, mediastinal, spine, or rib lesions
- Cysts or abscesses
- Enlarged lymph nodes
- Esophageal pathology, including tumors
- Hodgkin's disease
- Pleural effusion
- Pneumonitis
- Pneumothorax
- Pulmonary embolism

CRITICAL FINDINGS ◈

- Aortic aneurysm
- Aortic dissection
- Pneumothorax
- Pulmonary embolism

It is essential that critical diagnoses be communicated immediately to the appropriate HCP. A listing of these diagnoses varies among facilities. Note and immediately report to the HCP abnormal results and related symptoms. Timely notification of critical values for lab or diagnostic studies is a role expectation of the professional nurse. Notification processes will vary among facilities. Upon receipt of the critical value, the information should be read back to the caller to verify accuracy. Most policies require immediate notification of the primary HCP, hospitalist, or on-call HCP. Reported information includes the patient's name, unique identifiers, critical value, name of the person giving the report, and name of the person receiving the report. Documentation of notification should be made in the medical record with the name of the HCP notified, time and date of notification, and any orders received. Any delay in a timely report of a critical value may require completion of a notification form with review by Risk Management.

INTERFERING FACTORS

This procedure is contraindicated for
- Patients with allergies to shellfish or iodinated dye. The contrast medium used may cause a life-threatening allergic reaction. Patients with a known hypersensitivity to the medium may benefit from premedication with corticosteroids or the use of nonionic contrast medium.
- Patients who are claustrophobic.
- Patients who are pregnant or suspected of being pregnant, unless the potential benefits of the procedure far outweigh the risks to the fetus and mother.
- Elderly and other patients who are chronically dehydrated before the test, because of their risk of contrast-induced renal failure.
- Patients who are in renal failure.
- Young patients (17 yr and younger) unless the benefits of the x-ray diagnosis outweigh the risks of exposure to high levels of radiation. Information on the Image Gently Campaign can be found at the Alliance for Radiation Safety in Pediatric Imaging (www.pedrad.org/associations/5364/ig/).

Factors that may impair clear imaging
- Metallic objects (e.g., jewelry, body rings) within the examination field,

which may inhibit organ visualization and cause unclear images.
- Patients who are very obese or who may exceed the weight limit for the equipment.
- Patients with extreme claustrophobia unless sedation is given before the study.
- Inability of the patient to cooperate or remain still during the procedure because of age, significant pain, or mental status.

Other considerations
- Complications of the procedure may include hemorrhage, infection at the IV needle insertion site, and cardiac arrhythmias.
- The procedure may be terminated if chest pain or severe cardiac arrhythmias occur.
- Failure to follow dietary restrictions and other pretesting preparations may cause the procedure to be canceled or repeated.
- Consultation with an HCP should occur before the procedure for radiation safety concerns regarding younger patients or patients who are lactating.
- Risks associated with radiation overexposure can result from frequent x-ray procedures. Personnel in the room with the patient should wear a protective lead apron, stand behind a shield, or leave the area while the examination is being done. Personnel working in the examination area should wear badges to record their level of radiation exposure.

NURSING IMPLICATIONS AND PROCEDURE

PRETEST:
- Positively identify the patient using at least two unique identifiers before providing care, treatment, or services.

Patient Teaching: Inform the patient this procedure can assist in assessing the chest.
- Obtain a history of the patient's complaints or clinical symptoms, including a list of known allergens, especially allergies or sensitivities to latex, iodine, seafood, anesthetics, or contrast medium.
- Obtain a history of the patient's respiratory system, symptoms, and results of previously performed laboratory tests and diagnostic and surgical procedures.
- Ensure results of coagulation testing are obtained and recorded prior to the procedure; BUN and creatinine results are also needed if contrast medium is to be used.
- Note any recent procedures that can interfere with test results, including examinations using barium- or iodine-based contrast medium. Ensure that barium studies were performed more than 4 days before the CT scan.
- Record the date of the last menstrual period and determine the possibility of pregnancy in perimenopausal women.
- Obtain a list of the patient's current medications, including anticoagulants, aspirin and other salicylates, herbs, nutritional supplements, and nutraceuticals (see Appendix F). Note the last time and dose of medication taken.
- If contrast medium is scheduled to be used, patients receiving metformin (Glucophage) for non–insulin-dependent (type 2) diabetes should discontinue the drug on the day of the test and continue to withhold it for 48 hr after the test. Failure to do so may result in lactic acidosis.
- Review the procedure with the patient. Address concerns about pain and explain that there may be moments of discomfort and some pain experienced during the test. Inform the patient the procedure is usually performed in a radiology suite by an HCP specializing in this procedure, with support staff, and takes approximately 30 to 60 min.
- Explain that an IV line may be inserted to allow infusion of IV fluids, contrast medium, dye, or sedatives. Usually contrast medium and normal saline are infused.

Sensitivity to social and cultural issues, as well as concern for modesty, is important in providing psychological support before, during, and after the procedure.

Inform the patient that he or she may experience nausea, a feeling of warmth, a salty or metallic taste, or a transient headache after injection of contrast medium.

Instruct the patient to remove jewelry and other metallic objects from the area to be examined.

The patient should fast and restrict fluids for 2 to 4 hr prior to the procedure. Instruct the patient to avoid taking anticoagulant medication or to reduce dosage as ordered prior to the procedure. Protocols may vary among facilities.

Make sure a written and informed consent has been signed prior to the procedure and before administering any medications.

INTRATEST:

Observe standard precautions, and follow the general guidelines in Appendix A. Positively identify the patient.

Ensure the patient has complied with dietary, fluid, and medication restrictions for 2 to 4 hr prior to the procedure.

Ensure the patient has removed all external metallic objects from the area to be examined prior to the procedure.

If the patient has a history of allergic reactions to any substance or drug, administer ordered prophylactic steroids or antihistamines before the procedure. Use nonionic contrast medium for the procedure.

Have emergency equipment readily available.

Instruct the patient to void prior to the procedure and to change into the gown, robe, and foot coverings provided.

Instruct the patient to cooperate fully and to follow directions. Instruct the patient to remain still throughout the procedure because movement produces unreliable results.

Establish an IV fluid line for the injection of contrast medium, emergency drugs, and sedatives.

Administer an antianxiety agent, as ordered, if the patient has claustrophobia. Administer a sedative to a child or to an uncooperative adult, as ordered.

Place the patient in the supine position on an examination table.

If IV contrast medium is used, a rapid series of images is taken during and after injection.

Ask the patient to inhale deeply and hold his or her breath while the x-ray images are taken, and then to exhale after the images are taken.

Instruct the patient to take slow, deep breaths if nausea occurs during the procedure. Monitor and administer an antiemetic agent if ordered. Ready an emesis basin for use.

Monitor the patient for complications related to the procedure (e.g., allergic reaction, anaphylaxis, bronchospasm) if contrast is used.

The needle is removed, and a pressure dressing is applied over the puncture site.

Observe/assess the needle insertion site for bleeding, inflammation, or hematoma formation.

POST-TEST:

A report of the results will be made available to the requesting HCP, who will discuss the results with the patient.

Instruct the patient to resume usual medications and activity, as directed by the HCP. Renal function should be assessed before metformin is resumed if contrast was used.

Monitor vital signs and neurological status every 15 min for 1 hr, then every 2 hr for 4 hr, and then as ordered by the HCP. Monitor temperature every 4 hr for 24 hr. Monitor intake and output at least every 8 hr. Compare with baseline values. Notify the HCP if temperature is elevated. Protocols may vary among facilities.

If contrast was used, observe for delayed allergic reactions, such as rash, urticaria, tachycardia, hyperpnea, hypertension, palpitations, nausea, or vomiting.

Instruct the patient to immediately report symptoms such as fast heart rate, difficulty breathing, skin rash, itching, chest pain, persistent right shoulder pain, or abdominal pain. Immediately report symptoms to the appropriate HCP.

Observe/assess the needle site for bleeding, inflammation, or hematoma formation.

Instruct the patient in the care and assessment of the site.

Instruct the patient to apply cold compresses to the insertion site as needed, to reduce discomfort or edema.

Instruct the patient to increase fluid intake to help eliminate the contrast medium, if used.

Recognize anxiety related to test results. Discuss the implications of abnormal test results on the patient's lifestyle. Provide teaching and information regarding the clinical implications of the test results, as appropriate. Reinforce information given by the patient's HCP regarding further testing, treatment, or referral to another HCP. Answer any questions or address any concerns voiced by the patient or family. Depending on the results of this procedure, additional testing may be needed to evaluate or monitor progression of the disease process and determine the need for a change in therapy. Evaluate test results in relation to the patient's symptoms and other tests performed.

RELATED MONOGRAPHS:

Related tests include biopsy bone marrow, BUN, chest x-ray, CBC, CBC hematocrit, CBC hemoglobin, creatinine, echocardiogram, gallium scan, lung scan, MRI chest, mediastinoscopy, pleural fluid analysis, and PT/INR.

Refer to the Respiratory System table at the end of the book for related tests by body system.

C

Coombs' Antiglobulin, Direct

SYNONYM/ACRONYM: Direct antiglobulin testing (DAT).

COMMON USE: To detect associated conditions or drug therapies that can result a cell hemolysis, such as found in hemolytic disease of newborns, and hemolytic transfusion reactions.

SPECIMEN: Serum (1 mL) collected in a red-top tube and whole blood (1 mL) collected in a lavender-top (EDTA) tube.

NORMAL FINDINGS: (Method: Agglutination) Negative (no agglutination).

DESCRIPTION: Direct antiglobulin testing (DAT) detects in vivo antibody sensitization of red blood cells (RBCs). Immunoglobulin G (IgG) produced in certain disease states or in response to certain drugs can coat the surface of RBCs, resulting in cellular damage and hemolysis. When DAT is performed, RBCs are taken from the patient's blood sample, washed with saline to remove residual globulins, and mixed with anti–human globulin reagent. If the anti–human globulin reagent causes agglutination of the patient's RBCs, specific antiglobulin reagents can be used to determine whether the patient's RBCs are coated with IgG, complement, or both. (See monograph titled "Blood Groups and Antibodies" and Appendix D for more information regarding transfusion reactions.)

INDICATIONS
• Detect autoimmune hemolytic anemia or hemolytic disease of the newborn
• Evaluate suspected drug-induced hemolytic anemia
• Evaluate transfusion reaction

POTENTIAL DIAGNOSIS

Positive findings in
Antibodies formed during these circumstances or conditions attach to the patient's RBCs, and hemolysis occurs.

• Anemia *(autoimmune hemolytic, drug-induced)*
• Hemolytic disease of the newborn *(related to ABO or Rh incompatibility)*
• Infectious mononucleosis
• Lymphomas
• Mycoplasma pneumonia
• Paroxysmal cold hemoglobinuria *(idiopathic or disease related)*
• Passively acquired antibodies from plasma products
• Post–cardiac vascular surgery *(increased incidence of positive DAT has been reported in patients following cardiac surgery, possibly related to mechanical RBC destruction while the patient is on cardiac bypass)*
• Systemic lupus erythematosus and other connective tissue immune disorders
• Transfusion reactions *(related to blood incompatibility)*

Negative findings in
• Samples in which sensitization of erythrocytes has not occurred

CRITICAL FINDINGS: N/A

INTERFERING FACTORS
• Drugs and substances that may cause a positive DAT include acetaminophen, aminopyrine, aminosalicylic acid, ampicillin, antihistamines, aztreonam, cephalosporins, chlorinated hydrocarbon insecticides, chlorpromazine, chlorpropamide, cisplatin, clonidine, dipyrone, ethosuximide, fenfluramine, hydralazine, hydrochlorothiazide, ibuprofen, insulin, isoniazid, levodopa, mefenamic acid, melphalan, methadone, methicillin, methyldopa, moxalactam, penicillin, phenytoin, probenecid, procainamide, quinidine, quinine, rifampin, stibophen, streptomycin, sulfonamides, and tetracycline.
• Wharton's jelly may cause a false-positive DAT.
• Cold agglutinins and large amounts of paraproteins in the specimen may cause false-positive results.
• Newborns' cells may give negative results in ABO hemolytic disease.
• Tube methods for DAT are less sensitive than gel methods, and false-negative findings are possible in cases where weak, incompletely developed antigen sites on newborns' RBCs may not allow detectable amounts of anti-A and/or anti-B to bind to the RBC membrane.

NURSING IMPLICATIONS AND PROCEDURE

PRETEST:
▶ Positively identify the patient using at least two unique identifiers before providing care, treatment, or services.
▶ *Patient Teaching:* Inform the patient/parent this test can assist in assessing for disorders that break down red blood cells.
▶ Obtain a history of the patient's complaints, including a list of known allergens, especially allergies or sensitivities to latex.
▶ Obtain a history of the patient's hematopoietic system as well as results of previously performed laboratory tests

and diagnostic and surgical procedures.

Obtain a list of the patient's current medications, including herbs, nutritional supplements, and nutraceuticals (see Appendix F).

Review the procedure with the patient. Inform the patient that specimen collection takes approximately 5 to 10 min. Address concerns about pain and explain that there may be some discomfort during the venipuncture. If a cord sample is to be taken from a newborn, inform parents that the sample will be obtained at the time of delivery and will not result in blood loss to the infant.

Sensitivity to social and cultural issues, as well as concern for modesty, is important in providing psychological support before, during, and after the procedure.

There are no food, fluid, or medication restrictions unless by medical direction.

NTRATEST:

If the patient has a history of allergic reaction to latex, avoid the use of equipment containing latex.

Instruct the patient to cooperate fully and to follow directions. Direct the patient to breathe normally and to avoid unnecessary movement.

Observe standard precautions, and follow the general guidelines in Appendix A. Positively identify the patient, and label the appropriate specimen container with the corresponding patient demographics, initials of the person collecting the specimen, date, and time of collection. Perform a venipuncture. Cord specimens are obtained by inserting a needle attached to a syringe into the umbilical vein. The specimen is drawn into the syringe and gently expressed into the appropriate collection container.

Remove the needle and apply direct pressure with dry gauze to stop bleeding. Observe/assess venipuncture site for bleeding or hematoma formation and secure gauze with adhesive bandage.

Promptly transport the specimen to the laboratory for processing and analysis.

POST-TEST:

A report of the results will be made available to the requesting health-care provider (HCP), who will discuss the results with the patient.

Note positive test results in cord blood of neonate; also assess newborn's bilirubin and hematocrit levels. Results may indicate the need for immediate exchange transfusion of fresh whole blood that has been typed and crossmatched with the mother's serum.

Inform the postpartum patient of the implications of positive test results in cord blood. Prepare the newborn for exchange transfusion, on medical direction.

Reinforce information given by the patient's HCP regarding further testing, treatment, or referral to another HCP. Answer any questions or address any concerns voiced by the patient or family.

Depending on the results of this procedure, additional testing may be performed to evaluate or monitor progression of the disease process and determine the need for a change in therapy. Evaluate test results in relation to the patient's symptoms and other tests performed.

RELATED MONOGRAPHS:

Related tests include bilirubin, blood groups and antibodies, CBC hematocrit, CBC hemoglobin, Coombs' indirect antiglobulin (IAT), Ham's test, and haptoglobin.

Refer to Appendix D at the end of the book for further information regarding laboratory studies used in the investigation of transfusion reactions, findings, and potential nursing interventions associated with types of transfusion reactions.

Refer to the Hematopoietic System table at the end of the book for related tests by body system.

C

Coombs' Antiglobulin, Indirect

SYNONYM/ACRONYM: Indirect antiglobulin test (IAT), antibody screen.

COMMON USE: To check recipient serum for antibodies prior to blood transfusion.

SPECIMEN: Serum (1 mL) collected in a red-top tube.

NORMAL FINDINGS: (Method: Agglutination) Negative (no agglutination).

DESCRIPTION: The indirect antiglobulin test (IAT) detects and identifies unexpected circulating complement molecules or antibodies in the patient's serum. The first use of this test was for the detection and identification of anti-D using an indirect method. The test is now commonly used to screen a patient's serum for the presence of antibodies that may react against transfused red blood cells (RBCs). During testing, the patient's serum is allowed to incubate with reagent RBCs. The reagent RBCs used are from group O donors and have most of the clinically significant antigens present (D, C, E, c, e, K, M, N, S, s, Fy^a, Fy^b, Jk^a, and Jk^b). Antibodies present in the patient's serum coat antigenic sites on the RBC membrane. The reagent cells are washed with saline to remove any unbound antibody. Antihuman globulin is added in the final step of the test. If the patient's serum contains antibodies, the antihuman globulin will cause the antibody-coated RBCs to stick together or agglutinate. (See monograph titled "Blood Groups and Antibodies" and Appendix D for more information regarding transfusion reactions.)

INDICATIONS

- Detect other antibodies in maternal blood that can be potentially harmful to the fetus
- Determine antibody titers in Rh-negative women sensitized by an Rh-positive fetus
- Screen for antibodies before blood transfusions
- Test for the weak Rh-variant antigen D^u.

POTENTIAL DIAGNOSIS

Positive findings in
Circulating antibodies or medications attach to the patient's RBCs and hemolysis occurs.

- Hemolytic anemia *(drug-induced or autoimmune)*
- Hemolytic disease of the newborn *(related to ABO or Rh incompatibility)*
- Incompatible crossmatch
- Infections (mycoplasma pneumonia, mononucleosis)

Negative findings in
- Samples in which the patient's antibodies exhibit dosage effects (i.e., stronger reaction with homozygous than with heterozygous expression of an antigen) and reagent erythrocyte antigens contain single-dose expressions of the corresponding antigen (heterozygous)

Samples in which reagent erythrocyte antigens are unable to detect low-prevalence antibodies
Samples in which sensitization of erythrocytes has not occurred (complete absence of antibodies)

CRITICAL FINDINGS: N/A

INTERFERING FACTORS

Drugs that may cause a positive IAT include meropenem, methyldopa, penicillin, phenacetin, quinidine, and rifampin.
Recent administration of dextran, whole blood or fractions, or IV contrast media can result in a false-positive reaction.

NURSING IMPLICATIONS AND PROCEDURE

PRETEST:

Positively identify the patient using at least two unique identifiers before providing care, treatment, or services.
Patient Teaching: Inform the patient this test can assist in assessing for blood compatibility prior to transfusion.
Obtain a history of the patient's complaints, including a list of known allergens, especially allergies or sensitivities to latex.
Obtain a history of the patient's hematopoietic system as well as results of previously performed laboratory tests and diagnostic and surgical procedures.
Note any recent procedures that can interfere with test results.
Obtain a list of the patient's current medications, including herbs, nutritional supplements, and nutraceuticals (see Appendix F).
Review the procedure with the patient. Inform the patient that specimen collection takes approximately 5 to 10 min. Address concerns about pain and explain that there may be some discomfort during the venipuncture.
Sensitivity to social and cultural issues, as well as concern for modesty, is important in providing psychological support before, during, and after the procedure.
There are no food, fluid, or medication restrictions unless by medical direction.

INTRATEST:

If the patient has a history of allergic reaction to latex, avoid the use of equipment containing latex.
Instruct the patient to cooperate fully and to follow directions. Direct the patient to breathe normally and to avoid unnecessary movement.
Observe standard precautions, and follow the general guidelines in Appendix A. Positively identify the patient, and label the appropriate specimen container with the corresponding patient demographics, initials of the person collecting the specimen, date, and time of collection. Perform a venipuncture.
Remove the needle and apply direct pressure with dry gauze to stop bleeding. Observe/assess venipuncture site for bleeding or hematoma formation and secure gauze with adhesive bandage.
Promptly transport the specimen to the laboratory for processing and analysis.

POST-TEST:

A report of the results will be made available to the requesting health-care provider (HCP), who will discuss the results with the patient.
Inform pregnant women that negative tests during the first 12 wk of gestation should be repeated at 28 wk to rule out the presence of an antibody.
Positive test results in pregnant women after 28 wk of gestation indicate the need for antibody identification testing.
Reinforce information given by the patient's HCP regarding further testing, treatment, or referral to another HCP. Answer any questions or address any concerns voiced by the patient or family.
Depending on the results of this procedure, additional testing may be performed to evaluate or monitor progression of the disease process and determine the need for a change in therapy. Evaluate test results in relation

to the patient's symptoms and other tests performed.

RELATED MONOGRAPHS:

Related tests include bilirubin, blood groups and antibodies, CBC hematocrit, CBC hemoglobin, Coombs' direct antiglobulin (DAT), and haptoglobin.

Refer to Appendix D at the end of the book for further information regarding laboratory studies used in the investigation of transfusion reactions, findings and potential nursing interventions associated with types of transfusion reactions.

Refer to the Hematopoietic System table at the end of the book for related tests by body system.

Copper

SYNONYM/ACRONYM: Cu.

COMMON USE: To evaluate and monitor exposure to copper and to assist in diagnosing Wilson's disease.

SPECIMEN: Serum (1 mL) collected in a royal blue-top, trace element–free tube.

NORMAL FINDINGS: (Method: Inductively coupled plasma-mass spectrometry)

Age	Conventional Units	SI Units (Conventional Units × 0.157)
Newborn–5 days	9–46 mcg/dL	1.4–7.2 micromol/L
1–5 yr	80–150 mcg/dL	12.6–23.6 micromol/L
6–9 yr	84–136 mcg/dL	13.2–21.4 micromol/L
10–14 yr	80–120 mcg/dL	12.6–18.8 micromol/L
15–19 yr	80–171 mcg/dL	12.6–26.8 micromol/L
Adult		
Male	71–141 mcg/dL	11.1–22.1 micromol/L
Female	80–155 mcg/dL	12.6–24.3 micromol/L
Pregnant female	118–302 mcg/dL	18.5–47.4 micromol/L

Values for African Americans are 8% to 12% higher. Values increase in older adults.

DESCRIPTION: Copper is an important cofactor for the enzymes that participate in the formation of hemoglobin and collagen. Copper is also a component of coagulation factor V and assists in the oxidation of glucose. It is required for melanin pigment formation and maintenance of myelin sheaths and is used to synthesize ceruloplasmin. Copper levels vary with intake. Levels vary diurnally and peak during morning hours. This mineral is absorbed in the stomach and duodenum, stored in the liver, and excreted in urine and in feces with bile salts. Copper deficiency results in neutropenia and a hypochromic, microcytic anemia that is not responsive to iron therapy. Other signs and symptoms of copper deficiency include osteoporosis, depigmentation of skin and hair, impaired immune system response, and possible neurological and cardiac abnormalities.

NDICATIONS

Assist in establishing a diagnosis of Menkes' disease

Assist in establishing a diagnosis of Wilson's disease

Monitor patients receiving long-term parenteral nutrition therapy

POTENTIAL DIAGNOSIS

Increased in

Ceruloplasmin is an acute-phase reactant protein and the main protein binder of copper; therefore, copper levels will be increased in many inflammatory conditions, including cancer. Estrogens increase levels of binding protein; therefore, copper is elevated in pregnancy and estrogen therapy.

- Anemias *(related to increased RBC production)*
- Ankylosing rheumatoid spondylitis
- Biliary cirrhosis *(related to release from damaged liver tissue)*
- Collagen diseases
- Complications of renal dialysis *(trace element disturbances related to contamination from dialysate fluid and the disease process itself can be significant and can compound over time)*
- Hodgkin's disease
- Infections
- Inflammation
- Leukemia
- Malignant neoplasms

- Myocardial infarction (MI) *(a correlation exists among copper levels, CK, and LDH in MI; the pathophysiology is unclear, but some studies indicate a relationship between trace metal levels and risk of acute MI)*
- Pellagra *(related to niacin deficiency; niacin is an essential cofactor in reactions involving copper)*
- Poisoning from copper-contaminated solutions or insecticides *(related to excessive accumulation due to environmental exposure)*
- Pregnancy
- Pulmonary tuberculosis
- Rheumatic fever
- Rheumatoid arthritis
- Systemic lupus erythematosus
- Thalassemias *(related to zinc deficiency of thalassemia and increased rate of release from hemolyzed RBCs; copper and zinc compete for the same binding sites so that a deficiency in one results in an increase of the other)*
- Thyroid disease (hypothyroid or hyperthyroid) *(related to stimulation of thyroid hormone production by copper)*
- Trauma
- Typhoid fever
- Use of copper intrauterine device *(related to copper leaching from the device)*

Decreased in

- Burns *(related to loss of stores in tissue and possibly to competitive inhibition of zinc-containing medications or vitamins administered as part of burn therapy)*
- Cystic fibrosis *(related to inadequate intake and absorption)*
- Dysproteinemia *(related to decreased transport to and from stores)*
- Infants *(related to inadequate intake of milk or consumption of*

C

milk deficient in copper;
especially premature infants)
- Iron-deficiency anemias (some)
*(related to decreased absorption
of iron from the intestines and
transfer from tissues to plasma;
it is essential to hemoglobin formation)*
- Long-term total parenteral nutrition
(related to inadequate intake)
- Malabsorption disorders (celiac disease, tropical sprue) *(related to
inadequate absorption)*
- Malnutrition *(related to inadequate intake)*
- Menkes' disease *(evidenced by a
severe genetic X-linked defect
causing failed transport to the
liver and tissues)*
- Nephrotic syndrome *(related to
loss of transport proteins)*
- Occipital horn syndrome (OHS)
*(evidenced by an inherited disor-
der of copper metabolism; similar to Menkes' disease)*
- Wilson's disease *(evidenced by a
genetic defect causing failed
transport to the liver and
tissues)*

CRITICAL FINDINGS: N/A

INTERFERING FACTORS
- Drugs that may increase copper
levels include anticonvulsants and
oral contraceptives.
- Drugs that may decrease copper
levels include citrates, penicillamine, and valproic acid.
- Excessive therapeutic intake of zinc
may interfere with intestinal
absorption of copper.

NURSING IMPLICATIONS AND PROCEDURE

PRETEST:
▸ Positively identify the patient using at
least two unique identifiers before providing care, treatment, or services.

Patient Teaching: Inform the patient this
test can assist in monitoring the
amount of copper in the body.
▸ Obtain a history of the patient's complaints, including a list of known allergens, especially allergies or sensitivities
to latex.
▸ Obtain a history of the patient's
hematopoietic, hepatobiliary, and
immune systems, as well as results of
previously performed laboratory tests
and diagnostic and surgical
procedures.
▸ Obtain a list of the patient's current
medications, including herbs, nutritional supplements, and nutraceuticals
(see Appendix F).
▸ Review the procedure with the patient.
Inform the patient that specimen collection takes approximately 5 to
10 min. Address concerns about pain
and explain that there may be some
discomfort during the venipuncture.
Sensitivity to social and cultural issues, as
well as concern for modesty, is important in providing psychological support
before, during, and after the procedure.
▸ There are no food, fluid, or medication restrictions unless by medical
direction.

INTRATEST:
▸ If the patient has a history of allergic
reaction to latex, avoid the use of
equipment containing latex.
▸ Instruct the patient to cooperate fully
and to follow directions. Direct the
patient to breathe normally and to
avoid unnecessary movement.
▸ Observe standard precautions, and
follow the general guidelines in
Appendix A. Positively identify the
patient, and label the appropriate
specimen container with the corresponding patient demographics, initials of the person collecting the specimen, date, and time of collection.
Perform a venipuncture.
▸ Remove the needle and apply direct
pressure with dry gauze to stop bleeding. Observe/assess venipuncture site
for bleeding or hematoma formation
and secure gauze with adhesive
bandage.
▸ Promptly transport the specimen to the
laboratory for processing and analysis.

POST-TEST:

A report of the results will be made available to the requesting health-care provider (HCP), who will discuss the results with the patient.

Nutritional Considerations: The Institute of Medicine's Food and Nutrition Board suggests 900 mcg as the daily recommended dietary allowance of copper for adult males and females age 19 to greater than 70 yr; 1,000 mcg/d for pregnant females less than age 18 through 50 yr; 1,300 mcg/d for lactating females less than age 18 through 50 yr; 890 mcg/d for children age 14 to 18 yr; 700 mcg/d for children age 9 to 13 yr; 440 mcg/d for children age 4 to 8 yr; 340 mcg/d for children age 1 to 3 yr; 220 mcg/d for children age 7 to 12 mo (recommended adequate intake); 200 mcg/d for children age 0 to 6 mo (recommended adequate intake). Reprinted with permission from the National Academies Press, copyright 2013, National Academy of Sciences. Instruct the patient with increased copper levels to avoid foods rich in copper and to increase intake of elements (zinc, iron, calcium, and manganese) that interfere with copper absorption, as appropriate. Copper deficiency does not normally occur in adults, but patients receiving long-term total parenteral nutrition should be evaluated if signs and symptoms of copper deficiency appear. These patients should be informed that organ meats, shellfish, nuts, and legumes are good sources of dietary copper.

Reinforce information given by the patient's HCP regarding further testing, treatment, or referral to another HCP. Answer any questions or address any concerns voiced by the patient or family. Educate the patient regarding access to nutritional counseling services. Provide contact information, if desired, for the Institute of Medicine of the National Academies (www.iom.edu).

Depending on the results of this procedure, additional testing may be performed to evaluate or monitor progression of the disease process and determine the need for a change in therapy. Evaluate test results in relation to the patient's symptoms and other tests performed.

RELATED MONOGRAPHS:

Related tests include biopsy liver, ceruloplasmin, CBC, and zinc.

Refer to the Hematopoietic, Hepatobiliary, and Immune systems tables at the end of the book for related tests by body system.

Cortisol and Challenge Tests

SYNONYM/ACRONYM: Hydrocortisone, compound F.

COMMON USE: To assist in diagnosing adrenocortical insufficiency such as found in Cushing's syndrome and Addison's disease.

SPECIMEN: Serum (1 mL) collected in a red- or tiger-top tube. Plasma (1 mL) collected in a green-top (heparin) tube is also acceptable. Care must be taken to use the same type of collection container if serial measurements are to be taken.

Procedure	Medication Administered	Recommended Collection Times
ACTH stimulation, rapid test	1 mcg (low-dose protocol) cosyntropin IM	3 cortisol levels: baseline immediately before bolus, 30 min after bolus, and 60 min after bolus
CRH stimulation	IV dose of 1 mg/kg ovine or human CRH	8 cortisol and 8 ACTH levels: baseline collected 15 min before injection, 0 min before injection, and then 5, 15, 30, 60, 120, and 180 min after injection
Dexamethasone suppression (overnight)	Oral dose of 1 mg dexamethasone (Decadron) at 11 p.m.	Collect cortisol at 8 a.m. on the morning after the dexamethasone dose
Metyrapone stimulation (overnight)	Oral dose of 30 mg/kg metyrapone with snack at midnight	Collect cortisol and ACTH at 8 a.m. on the morning after the metyrapone dose

ACTH = adrenocorticotropic hormone; CRH = corticotropin-releasing hormone; IM = intramuscular; IV = intravenous.

NORMAL FINDINGS: (Method: Immunochemiluminescent assay)

Cortisol

Time	Conventional Units	SI Units (Conventional Units × 27.6)
8 a.m.		
Birth–11 yr	10–340 mcg/dL	28–938 nmol/L
12–18 yr	10–280 mcg/dL	28–773 nmol/L
Adult/older adult	5–25 mcg/dL	138–690 nmol/L
4 p.m.		
Birth–11 yr	10–330 mcg/dL	28–910 nmol/L
12–18 yr	10–272 mcg/dL	28–750 nmol/L
Adult/older adult	3–16 mcg/dL	83–442 nmol/L

Long-term use of corticosteroids in patients, especially older adults, may be reflected by elevated cortisol levels.

ACTH Challenge Tests

ACTH (Cosyntropin) Stimulated, Rapid Test	Conventional Units	SI Units (Conventional Units × 27.6)
Baseline	Cortisol greater than 5 mg/dL	Greater than 138 nmol/L
30- or 60-min response	Cortisol 18–20 mcg/dL or incremental increase of 7 mcg/dL over baseline value	497–552 nmol/L

Corticotropin-Releasing Hormone Stimulated	Conventional Units	SI Units (Conventional Units × 27.6)
	Cortisol peaks at greater than 20 mcg/dL within 30–60 min	Greater than 552 nmol/L
		SI Units (Conventional Units × 0.22)
	ACTH increases twofold to fourfold within 30–60 min	Twofold to fourfold increase within 30–60 min

Dexamethasone Suppressed Overnight Test	Conventional Units	SI Units (Conventional Units × 27.6)
	Cortisol less than 1.8 mcg/dL next day	Less than 49.7 nmol/L

Metyrapone Stimulated Overnight Test	Conventional Units	SI Units (Conventional Units × 27.6)
	Cortisol less than 3 mcg/dL next day	Less than 83 nmol/L
		SI Units (Conventional Units × 0.22)
	ACTH greater than 75 pg/mL	Greater than 16.5 pmol/L
		SI Units (Conventional Units × 28.9)
	11-deoxycortisol greater than 7 mcg/dL	Greater than 202 nmol/L

DESCRIPTION: Cortisol (hydrocortisone) is the predominant glucocorticoid secreted in response to stimulation by the hypothalamus and pituitary adrenocorticotropic hormone (ACTH). Cortisol stimulates gluconeogenesis, mobilizes fats and proteins, antagonizes insulin, and suppresses inflammation. Measuring levels of cortisol in blood is the best indicator of adrenal function. Cortisol secretion varies diurnally, with highest levels occurring on awakening and lowest levels occurring late in the day. Bursts of cortisol excretion can occur at night. Cortisol and ACTH test results are evaluated together because they each control the other's concentrations (i.e., any change in one causes a change in the other). ACTH levels exhibit a diurnal variation, peaking between 6 and 8 a.m. and reaching the lowest point between 6 and 11 p.m. Evening levels are generally one-half to two-thirds lower than morning levels. (See monograph titled "Adrenocorticotropic Hormone [and Challenge Tests].")

INDICATIONS
- Detect adrenal hyperfunction (Cushing's syndrome)
- Detect adrenal hypofunction (Addison's disease)

POTENTIAL DIAGNOSIS
The dexamethasone suppression test is useful in differentiating the causes for increased cortisol levels. Dexamethasone is a synthetic steroid that suppresses secretion of ACTH. With this test, a baseline morning cortisol level is collected, and the patient is given a 1-mg dose of dexamethasone at bedtime. A second specimen is collected the following morning. If cortisol levels have not been suppressed, adrenal adenoma may be suspected. The dexamethasone suppression test also produces abnormal results in patients with psychiatric illnesses.

The corticotropin-releasing hormone (CRH) stimulation test works as well as the dexamethasone suppression test in distinguishing Cushing's disease from conditions in which ACTH is secreted ectopically. In this test, cortisol levels are measured after an injection of CRH. A fourfold increase in cortisol levels above baseline is seen in Cushing's disease. No increase in cortisol is seen if ectopic ACTH secretion is the cause.

The ACTH (cosyntropin)-stimulated rapid test is used when adrenal insufficiency is suspected. Cosyntropin is a synthetic form of ACTH. A baseline cortisol level is collected before the injection of cosyntropin. Specimens are subsequently collected at 30- and 60-min intervals. If the adrenal glands are functioning normally, cortisol levels rise significantly after administration of cosyntropin.

The metyrapone stimulation test is used to distinguish corticotropin dependent (pituitary Cushing's disease and ectopic Cushing's disease) from corticotropin-independent (carcinoma of the lung or thyroid) causes of increased cortisol levels. Metyrapone inhibits the conversion of 11-deoxycortisol to cortisol. Cortisol levels should decrease to less than 3 mcg/dL if normal pituitary stimulation by ACTH occurs after an oral dose of metyrapone. Specimen collection and administration of the medication are performed as with the overnight dexamethasone test.

Increased in
Conditions that result in excessive production of cortisol.

- Adrenal adenoma
- Cushing's syndrome
- Ectopic ACTH production
- Hyperglycemia
- Pregnancy
- Stress

Decreased in
Conditions that result in adrenal hypofunction and corresponding low levels of cortisol.

- Addison's disease
- Adrenogenital syndrome
- Hypopituitarism

CRITICAL FINDINGS: N/A

INTERFERING FACTORS

Drugs and substances that may increase cortisol levels include anticonvulsants, clomipramine, corticotropin, cortisone, CRH, ether, fenfluramine, gemfibrozil, hydrocortisone, insulin, lithium, methadone, metoclopramide, mifepristone, naloxone, opiates, oral contraceptives, ranitidine, tetracosactrin, and vasopressin.

Drugs and substances that may decrease cortisol levels include barbiturates, beclomethasone, betamethasone, clonidine, desoximetasone, dexamethasone, ephedrine, etomidate, fluocinolone, ketoconazole, levodopa, lithium, methylpredniso-lone, metyrapone, midazolam, morphine, nitrous oxide, oxazepam, phenytoin, ranitidine, and trimipramine.

Test results are affected by the time this test is done because cortisol levels vary diurnally.

Stress and excessive physical activity can produce elevated levels.

Normal values can be obtained in the presence of partial pituitary deficiency.

Recent radioactive scans within 1 wk of the test can interfere with test results.

◆ The metyrapone stimulation test is contraindicated in patients with suspected adrenal insufficiency.

◆ Metyrapone may cause gastrointestinal distress and/or confusion. Administer oral dose of metyrapone with milk and snack.

NURSING IMPLICATIONS AND PROCEDURE

PRETEST:

Positively identify the patient using at least two unique identifiers before providing care, treatment, or services.

Patient Teaching: Inform the patient this test can assist in assessing for the amount of cortisol in the blood.

Obtain a history of the patient's complaints, including a list of known allergens, especially allergies or sensitivities to latex.

Obtain a history of the patient's endocrine system, as well as results of previously performed laboratory tests and diagnostic and surgical procedures.

Obtain a list of the patient's current medications, including herbs, nutritional supplements, and nutraceuticals (see Appendix F).

Review the procedure with the patient. Inform the patient that multiple specimens may be required. Inform the patient that specimen collection takes approximately 5 to 10 min. Address concerns about pain and explain that there may be some discomfort during the venipuncture.

Sensitivity to social and cultural issues, as well as concern for modesty, is important in providing psychological support before, during, and after the procedure.

There are no food, fluid, or medication restrictions unless by medical direction.

Drugs that enhance steroid metabolism may be withheld by medical direction prior to metyrapone stimulation testing.

Instruct the patient to minimize stress to avoid raising cortisol levels.

INTRATEST:

Have emergency equipment readily available.

If the patient has a history of allergic reaction to latex, avoid the use of equipment containing latex.

Instruct the patient to cooperate fully and to follow directions. Direct the patient to breathe normally and to avoid unnecessary movement.

Observe standard precautions, and follow the general guidelines in Appendix A. Positively identify the patient, and label the appropriate specimen container with the corresponding patient demographics, initials of the person collecting the specimen, date, and time of collection.

Perform a venipuncture. Collect specimen between 6 and 8 a.m., when cortisol levels are highest.

C

Adverse reactions to metyrapone include nausea and vomiting (N/V), abdominal pain, headache, dizziness, sedation, allergic rash, decreased white blood cell count, or bone marrow depression. Signs and symptoms of overdose or acute adrenocortical insufficiency include cardiac arrhythmias, hypotension, dehydration, anxiety, confusion, weakness, impairment of consciousness, N/V, epigastric pain, diarrhea, hyponatremia, and hyperkalemia.

Remove the needle and apply direct pressure with dry gauze to stop bleeding. Observe/assess venipuncture site for bleeding or hematoma formation and secure gauze with adhesive bandage.

Promptly transport the specimen to the laboratory for processing and analysis.

POST-TEST:

A report of the results will be made available to the requesting health-care provider (HCP), who will discuss the results with the patient.

Instruct the patient to resume usual medications, as directed by the HCP.

Recognize anxiety related to test results. Discuss the implications of abnormal test results on the patient's lifestyle. Provide teaching and information regarding the clinical implications of the test results, as appropriate. Educate the patient regarding access to counseling services. Provide contact information, if desired, for the Cushing's Support and Research Foundation (www.csrf. net).

Reinforce information given by the patient's HCP regarding further testing, treatment, or referral to another HCP. Answer any questions or address any concerns voiced by the patient or family.

Depending on the results of this procedure, additional testing may be performed to evaluate or monitor progression of the disease process and determine the need for a change in therapy. Evaluate test results in relation to the patient's symptoms and other tests performed.

RELATED MONOGRAPHS:

Related tests include ACTH and challenge tests, angiography adrenal, chloride, CT abdomen, CT pituitary, DHEA, glucagon, glucose, glucose tolerance test, growth hormone, insulin, MRI abdomen, MRI pituitary, renin, sodium, testosterone, and US abdomen.

Refer to the Endocrine System table at the end of the book for related tests by body system.

C-Peptide

SYNONYM/ACRONYM: Connecting peptide insulin, insulin C-peptide, proinsulin C-peptide.

COMMON USE: To evaluate hypoglycemia, assess beta cell function, and distinguish between type 1 and type 2 diabetes.

SPECIMEN: Serum (1 mL) collected in a red-top tube.

NORMAL FINDINGS: (Method: Immunochemiluminometric assay, ICMA)

Age	Conventional Units	SI Units (Conventional Units × 0.333)
9 yr	0.0–3.3 ng/mL	0.0–1.1 nmol/L
10–16 yr	0.4–3.3 ng/mL	0.1–1.1 nmol/L
Greater than 16 yr	0.8–3.5 ng/mL	0.3–1.2 nmol/L
1 h response to glucose	2.3–11.8 ng/mL	0.8–3.9 nmol/L

DESCRIPTION: C-peptide is a biologically inactive peptide formed when beta cells of the pancreas convert proinsulin to insulin. Most of C-peptide is secreted by the kidneys. C-peptide levels usually correlate with insulin levels and provide a reliable indication of how well the beta cells secrete insulin. Release of C-peptide is not affected by exogenous insulin administration. C-peptide values double after stimulation with glucose or glucagon, and measurement of C-peptide levels are very useful in the evaluation of hypoglycemia. An insulin/C-peptide ratio less than 1 indicates endogenous insulin secretion, whereas a ratio greater than 1 indicates an excess of exogenous insulin. An elevated C-peptide level in the presence of plasma glucose less than 40 mg/dL supports a diagnosis of pancreatic islet cell tumor.

INDICATIONS
- Assist in the diagnosis of insulinoma: serum levels of insulin and C-peptide are elevated.
- Detect suspected factitious cause of hypoglycemia (excessive insulin administration): an increase in blood insulin from injection does not increase C-peptide levels.
- Determine beta cell function when insulin antibodies preclude accurate measurement of serum insulin production.
- Distinguish between insulin-dependent (type 1) and non–insulin-dependent (type 2) diabetes (with C-peptide–stimulating test): Patients with diabetes whose C-peptide stimulation level is greater than 18 ng/mL can be managed without insulin treatment.
- Evaluate hypoglycemia.
- Evaluate viability of pancreatic transplant.

POTENTIAL DIAGNOSIS

Increased in
- Islet cell tumor *(related to excessive endogenous insulin production)*
- Non–insulin-dependent (type 2) diabetes *(related to increased insulin production)*
- Pancreas or beta cell transplants *(related to increased insulin production)*
- Renal failure *(increase in circulating levels of C-peptide related to decreased renal excretion)*

Decreased in
- Factitious hypoglycemia *(related to decrease in blood glucose levels in response to insulin injection)*
- Insulin-dependent (type 1) diabetes *(evidenced by insufficient production of insulin by the pancreas)*
- Pancreatectomy *(evidenced by absence of the pancreas)*

CRITICAL FINDINGS: N/A

C

INTERFERING FACTORS

- Drugs that may increase C-peptide levels include beta-methasone, chloroquine, danazol, deferoxamine, ethinyl estradiol, glibenclamide, glimepiride, indapamide, oral contraceptives, piretanide, prednisone, and rifampin.
- Drugs that may decrease C-peptide levels include atenolol and calcitonin.
- C-peptide and endogenous insulin levels do not always correlate in obese patients.
- Failure to follow dietary restrictions before the procedure may cause the procedure to be canceled or repeated.

NURSING IMPLICATIONS AND PROCEDURE

PRETEST:

▶ Positively identify the patient using at least two unique identifiers before providing care, treatment, or services.
▶ *Patient Teaching:* Inform the patient this test can assist in assessing for low blood sugar.
▶ Obtain a history of the patient's complaints, including a list of known allergens, especially allergies or sensitivities to latex.
▶ Obtain a history of the patient's endocrine system, symptoms, and results of previously performed laboratory tests and diagnostic and surgical procedures.
▶ Obtain a list of the patient's current medications, including herbs, nutritional supplements, and nutraceuticals (see Appendix F).
▶ Review the procedure with the patient. Inform the patient that specimen collection takes approximately 5 to 10 min. Address concerns about pain and explain that there may be some discomfort during the venipuncture.
▶ *Sensitivity to social and cultural issues,* as well as concern for modesty, is important in providing psychological support before, during, and after the procedure.

▶ The patient should fast for at least 10 hr before specimen collection. Protocols may vary among facilities.
▶ There are no fluid or medication restrictions unless by medical direction.

INTRATEST:

▶ Ensure that the patient has complied with dietary restrictions and pretesting preparations; assure that food has been restricted for at least 10 hr prior to the procedure.
▶ If the patient has a history of allergic reaction to latex, avoid the use of equipment containing latex.
▶ Instruct the patient to cooperate fully and to follow directions. Direct the patient to breathe normally and to avoid unnecessary movement.
▶ Observe standard precautions, and follow the general guidelines in Appendix A. Positively identify the patient, and label the appropriate specimen container with the corresponding patient demographics, initials of the person collecting the specimen, date, and time of collection. Perform a venipuncture.
▶ Remove the needle and apply direct pressure with dry gauze to stop bleeding. Observe/assess venipuncture site for bleeding or hematoma formation and secure gauze with adhesive bandage.
▶ Promptly transport the specimen to the laboratory for processing and analysis.

POST-TEST:

▶ A report of the results will be made available to the requesting health-care provider (HCP), who will discuss the results with the patient.
▶ Instruct the patient to resume usual diet as directed by the HCP.
▶ *Nutritional Considerations:* Abnormal C-peptide levels may be associated with diabetes. There is no "diabetic diet"; however, many meal-planning approaches with nutritional goals are endorsed by the American Dietetic Association. Patients who adhere to dietary recommendations report a better general feeling of health, better weight management, greater control of glucose and lipid values, and improved use of insulin. Instruct the patient, as

appropriate, in nutritional management of diabetes. The American Heart Association's Therapeutic Lifestyle Changes (TLC) diet provides goals directed at people with specific risk factors and/or existing medical conditions (e.g., elevated low-density lipoprotein [LDL] cholesterol levels, other lipid disorders, coronary artery disease [CAD], insulin-dependent diabetes, insulin resistance, or metabolic syndrome). The dietary therapy includes nutritional recommendations for daily total caloric intake and recommendations for allowable percentage of calories derived from fat (saturated and unsaturated), carbohydrates, protein, and cholesterol, as well as recommendations for daily expenditure of energy. The nutritional needs of each diabetic patient need to be determined individually (especially during pregnancy) with the appropriate health care professionals, particularly professionals trained in nutrition.

▶ Instruct the patient and caregiver to report signs and symptoms of hypoglycemia (weakness, confusion, diaphoresis, rapid pulse) or hyperglycemia (thirst, polyuria, hunger, lethargy). Emphasize, as appropriate, that good control of glucose levels delays the onset and slows the progression of diabetic retinopathy, nephropathy, and neuropathy.

▶ Recognize anxiety related to test results, and be supportive of perceived loss of independence and fear of shortened life expectancy. Discuss the implications of abnormal test results on the patient's lifestyle. Provide teaching and information regarding the clinical implications of the test results, as appropriate. Emphasize, if indicated, that good glycemic control delays the onset and slows the progression of diabetic retinopathy, nephropathy, and neuropathy. Educate the patient regarding access to counseling services, as appropriate. Provide contact information, if desired, for the American Diabetes Association (www.diabetes.org) or the American Heart Association (www.americanheart.org).

▶ Reinforce information given by the patient's HCP regarding further testing, treatment, or referral to another HCP. Answer any questions or address any concerns voiced by the patient or family.

▶ Depending on the results of this procedure, additional testing may be performed to evaluate or monitor progression of the disease process and determine the need for a change in therapy. Evaluate test results in relation to the patient's symptoms and other tests performed.

RELATED MONOGRAPHS:

▶ Related tests include CT cardiac scoring, cortisol, creatinine, creatinine clearance, EMG, ENG, fluorescein angiography, fructose, fundus photography, glucagon, glucose, glucose tolerance tests, glycated hemoglobin, insulin, insulin antibodies, microalbumin, plethysmography, and visual fields test.

▶ Refer to the Endocrine System table at the end of the book for related tests by body system.

C-Reactive Protein

SYNONYM/ACRONYM: CRP.

COMMON USE: Indicates a nonspecific inflammatory response; this highly sensitive test is used to assess risk for cardiovascular and peripheral artery disease.

SPECIMEN: Serum (1 mL) collected in a red- or tiger-top tube.

NORMAL FINDINGS: (Method: Nephelometry)

High-sensitivity immunoassay (cardiac applications)	Conventional Units	SI Units (Conventional Units × 10)
Low risk	Less than 1 mg/dL	Less than 1 mg/L
Average risk	1–3 mg/dL	10–30 mg/L
High risk	Greater than 10 mg/dL (after repeat testing)	Greater than 100 mg/L (after repeat testing)

Conventional Assay	Conventional Units	SI Units (Conventional Units × 10)
Adult	0–0.8 mg/dL	0–8 mg/L

Values for infants are approximately half normal adult values.

DESCRIPTION: C-reactive protein (CRP) is a glycoprotein produced by the liver in response to acute inflammation. The CRP assay is a nonspecific test that determines the presence (not the cause) of inflammation; it is often ordered in conjunction with erythrocyte sedimentation rate (ESR). CRP assay is a more sensitive and rapid indicator of the presence of an inflammatory process than ESR. CRP disappears from the serum rapidly when inflammation has subsided. The inflammatory process and its association with atherosclerosis make the presence of CRP, as detected by highly sensitive CRP assays, a potential marker for coronary artery disease. It is believed that the inflammatory process may instigate the conversion of a stable plaque to a weaker one that can rupture and occlude an artery.

INDICATIONS

- Assist in the differential diagnosis of appendicitis and acute pelvic inflammatory disease
- Assist in the differential diagnosis of Crohn's disease and ulcerative colitis
- Assist in the differential diagnosis of rheumatoid arthritis and uncomplicated systemic lupus erythematosus (SLE)
- Assist in the evaluation of coronary artery disease
- Detect the presence or exacerbation of inflammatory processes
- Monitor response to therapy for autoimmune disorders such as rheumatoid arthritis

POTENTIAL DIAGNOSIS

Increased in
Conditions associated with an inflammatory response stimulate production of CRP.

- Acute bacterial infections
- Crohn's disease
- Inflammatory bowel disease
- Myocardial infarction *(inflammation of the coronary vessels is associated with increased CRP levels and increased risk for coronary vessel injury, which may result in distal vessel plaque occlusions)*
- Pregnancy (second half)
- Rheumatic fever
- Rheumatoid arthritis
- SLE
- Syndrome X (metabolic syndrome) *(inflammation of the*

coronary vessels is associated with increased CRP levels and increased risk for coronary vessel injury, which may result in distal vessel plaque occlusions)

Decreased in: N/A

CRITICAL FINDINGS: N/A

INTERFERING FACTORS

- Drugs that may increase CRP levels include chemotherapy, interleukin-2, oral contraceptives, and pamidronate.
- Drugs that may decrease CRP levels include aurothiomalate, dexamethasone, gemfibrozil, leflunomide, methotrexate, NSAIDs, oral contraceptives (progestogen effect), penicillamine, pentopril, prednisolone, prinomide, and sulfasalazine.
- NSAIDs, salicylates, and steroids may cause false-negative results because of suppression of inflammation.
- Falsely elevated levels may occur with the presence of an intrauterine device.
- Lipemic samples that are turbid in appearance may be rejected for analysis when nephelometry is the test method.

NURSING IMPLICATIONS AND PROCEDURE

PRETEST:

▶ Positively identify the patient using at least two unique identifiers before providing care, treatment, or services.
▶ *Patient Teaching:* Inform the patient this test can assist in assessing for inflammation.
▶ Obtain a history of the patient's complaints, including a list of known allergens, especially allergies or sensitivities to latex. The patient may complain of pain related to the inflammatory process in connective or other tissues.
▶ Obtain a history of the patient's cardiovascular and immune systems, symptoms, and results of previously performed laboratory tests and diagnostic and surgical procedures.
▶ Obtain a list of the patient's current medications, including herbs, nutritional supplements, and nutraceuticals (see Appendix F).
▶ Review the procedure with the patient. Inform the patient that specimen collection takes approximately 5 to 10 min. Address concerns about pain and explain that there may be some discomfort during the venipuncture.
▶ *Sensitivity to social and cultural issues,* as well as concern for modesty, is important in providing psychological support before, during, and after the procedure.
▶ There are no food, fluid, or medication restrictions unless by medical direction.

INTRATEST:

▶ If the patient has a history of allergic reaction to latex, avoid the use of equipment containing latex.
▶ Instruct the patient to cooperate fully and to follow directions. Direct the patient to breathe normally and to avoid unnecessary movement.
▶ Observe standard precautions, and follow the general guidelines in Appendix A. Positively identify the patient, and label the appropriate specimen container with the corresponding patient demographics, initials of the person collecting the specimen, date, and time of collection. Perform a venipuncture.
▶ Remove the needle and apply direct pressure with dry gauze to stop bleeding. Observe/assess venipuncture site for bleeding or hematoma formation and secure gauze with adhesive bandage.
▶ Promptly transport the specimen to the laboratory for processing and analysis.

C

POST-TEST:

> A report of the results will be made available to the requesting health-care provider (HCP), who will discuss the results with the patient.

> Answer any questions or address any concerns voiced by the patient or family.

> Depending on the results of this procedure, additional testing may be performed to evaluate or monitor progression of the disease process and determine the need for a change in therapy. Evaluate test results in relation to the patient's symptoms and other tests performed.

RELATED MONOGRAPHS:

> Related tests include antiarrhythmic drugs, antibodies anticyclic citrullinated peptide, ANA, apolipoprotein A and B, AST, arthroscopy, ANP, blood gases, BMD, bone scan, BNP, calcium (blood and ionized), cholesterol (total, HDL, and LDL), CBC, CBC WBC count and differential, CT, cardiac scoring, CK and isoenzymes, echocardiography, ESR, glucose, glycated hemoglobin, Holter monitor, homocysteine, ketones, LDH and isoenzymes, MRI chest, MRI musculoskeletal, MI scan, myocardial perfusion scan, myoglobin, PET heart, potassium, procalcitonin, radiography bone, RF, synovial fluid analysis, triglycerides, and troponin.

> Refer to the Cardiovascular and Immune systems tables at the end of the book for related tests by body system.

Creatine Kinase and Isoenzymes

SYNONYM/ACRONYM: CK and isoenzymes.

COMMON USE: To monitor myocardial infarction and some disorders of the musculoskeletal system such as Duchenne's muscular dystrophy.

SPECIMEN: Serum (1 mL) collected in a red- or tiger-top tube. Serial specimens are highly recommended. Care must be taken to use the same type of collection container if serial measurements are to be taken.

NORMAL FINDINGS: (Method: Enzymatic for CK, electrophoresis for isoenzymes; enzyme immunoassay techniques are in common use for CK-MB)

	Conventional & SI Units
Total CK	
Newborn–1 yr	Up to 2 × adult values
Male (children and adults)	50–204 units/L
Female (children and adults)	36–160 units/L
CK Isoenzymes by Electrophoresis	
CK-BB	Absent
CK-MB	04%
CK-MM	96–100%

	Conventional & SI Units
CK-MB by Immunoassay	0–3 ng/mL
CK-MB Index	0–2.5

CK = creatine kinase; CK-BB = CK isoenzyme in brain; CK-MB = CK isoenzyme in heart; CK-MM = CK isoenzyme in skeletal muscle.
The CK-MB index is the CK-MB (by immunoassay) divided by the total CK and then multiplied by 100. For example, a CK-MB by immunoassay of 25 ng/mL with a total CK of 250 units/L would have a CK-MB index of 10.
Elevations in total CK occur after exercise. Values in older adults may decline slightly related to loss of muscle mass.

DESCRIPTION: Creatine kinase (CK) is an enzyme that exists almost exclusively in skeletal muscle, heart muscle, and, in smaller amounts, in the brain and lungs. This enzyme is important in intracellular storage and energy release. Three isoenzymes, based on primary location, have been identified by electrophoresis: brain and lungs CK-BB, cardiac CK-MB, and skeletal muscle CK-MM. When injury to these tissues occurs, the enzymes are released into the bloodstream. Levels increase and decrease in a predictable time frame. Measuring the serum levels can help determine the extent and timing of the damage. Noting the presence of the specific isoenzyme helps determine the location of the tissue damage. Atypical forms of CK can be identified. Macro-CK, an immunoglobulin complex of normal CK isoenzymes, has no clinical significance. Mitochondrial-CK is sometimes identified in the sera of seriously ill patients, especially those with metastatic carcinoma.

Acute myocardial infarction (MI) releases CK into the serum within the first 48 hr; values return to normal in about 3 days. The isoenzyme CK-MB appears in the first 4 to 6 hr, peaks in 24 hr, and usually returns to normal in 72 hr. Recurrent elevation of CK suggests reinfarction or extension of ischemic damage. Significant elevations of CK are expected in early phases of muscular dystrophy, even before the clinical signs and symptoms appear. CK elevation diminishes as the disease progresses and muscle mass decreases. Differences in total CK with age and gender relate to the fact that the predominant isoenzyme is muscular in origin. Body builders have higher values, whereas older individuals have lower values because of deterioration of muscle mass.

Serial use of the mass assay for CK-MB with serial cardiac troponin I, myoglobin, and serial electrocardiograms in the assessment of MI has largely replaced the use of CK isoenzyme assay by electrophoresis. CK-MB mass assays are more sensitive and rapid than electrophoresis. Studies have demonstrated a high positive predictive value for acute MI when the CK-MB (by immunoassay) is greater than 10 ng/mL with a relative CK-MB index greater than 3.

Timing for Appearance and Resolution of Serum/Plasma Cardiac Markers in Acute MI

Cardiac Marker	Appearance (hr)	Peak (hr)	Resolution (days)
AST	6–8	24–48	3–4
CK (total)	4–6	24	2–3
CK-MB	4–6	15–20	2–3
LDH	12	24–48	10–14
Myoglobin	1–3	4–12	1
Troponin I	2–6	15–20	5–7

INDICATIONS

- Assist in the diagnosis of acute MI and evaluate cardiac ischemia (CK-MB)
- Detect musculoskeletal disorders that do not have a neurological basis, such as dermatomyositis or Duchenne's muscular dystrophy (CK-MM)
- Determine the success of coronary artery reperfusion after streptokinase infusion or percutaneous transluminal angioplasty, as evidenced by a decrease in CK-MB

POTENTIAL DIAGNOSIS

Increased in
CK is released from any damaged cell in which it is stored, so conditions that affect the brain, heart, or skeletal muscle and cause cellular destruction demonstrate elevated CK levels and correlating isoenzyme source CK-BB, CK-MB, CK-MM.

- Alcoholism *(CK-MM)*
- Brain infarction (extensive) *(CK-BB)*
- Congestive heart failure *(CK-MB)*
- Delirium tremens *(CK-MM)*
- Dermatomyositis *(CK-MM)*
- Head injury *(CK-BB)*
- Hypothyroidism *(CK-MM related to metabolic effect on and damage to skeletal muscle tissue)*
- Hypoxic shock *(CK-MM related to muscle damage from lack of oxygen)*
- Gastrointestinal (GI) tract infarction *(CK-MM)*
- Loss of blood supply to any muscle *(CK-MM)*
- Malignant hyperthermia *(CK-MM related to skeletal muscle injury)*
- MI *(CK-MB)*
- Muscular dystrophies *(CK-MM)*
- Myocarditis *(CK-MB)*
- Neoplasms of the prostate, bladder, and GI tract *(CK-MM)*
- Polymyositis *(CK-MM)*
- Pregnancy; during labor *(CK-MM)*
- Prolonged hypothermia *(CK-MM)*
- Pulmonary edema *(CK-MM)*
- Pulmonary embolism *(CK-MM)*
- Reye's syndrome *(CK-BB)*
- Rhabdomyolysis *(CK-MM)*
- Surgery *(CK-MM)*
- Tachycardia *(CK-MB)*
- Tetanus *(CK-MM related to muscle injury from injection)*
- Trauma *(CK-MM)*

Decreased in
- Small stature *(related to lower muscle mass than average stature)*
- Sedentary lifestyle *(related to decreased muscle mass)*

CRITICAL FINDINGS: N/A

INTERFERING FACTORS

- Drugs that may increase total CK levels include any intramuscularly injected preparations because of tissue trauma caused by injection.
- Drugs that may decrease total CK levels include dantrolene and statins.

NURSING IMPLICATIONS AND PROCEDURE

PRETEST:

▶ Positively identify the patient using at least two unique identifiers before providing care, treatment, or services.

▶ *Patient Teaching:* Inform the patient this test can assist in assessing for heart muscle cell damage.

▶ Obtain a history of the patient's complaints, including a list of known allergens, especially allergies or sensitivities to latex.

▶ Obtain a history of the patient's cardiovascular and musculoskeletal systems, symptoms, and results of previously performed laboratory tests and diagnostic and surgical procedures.

▶ Obtain a list of the patient's current medications, including herbs, nutritional supplements, and nutraceuticals (see Appendix F).

▶ Review the procedure with the patient. Inform the patient that a series of samples will be required. (Samples at time of admission and 2 to 4 hr, 6 to 8 hr, and 12 hr after admission are the minimal recommendations. Protocols may vary among facilities. Additional samples may be requested.) Inform the patient that specimen collection takes approximately 5 to 10 min. Address concerns about pain and explain that there may be some discomfort during the venipuncture.

▶ There are no food, fluid, or medication restrictions unless by medical direction.

INTRATEST:

▶ If the patient has a history of allergic reaction to latex, avoid the use of equipment containing latex.

▶ Instruct the patient to cooperate fully and to follow directions. Direct the patient to breathe normally and to avoid unnecessary movement.

▶ Observe standard precautions, and follow the general guidelines in Appendix A. Positively identify the patient, and label the appropriate specimen container with the corresponding patient demographics, initials of the person collecting the specimen, date, and time of collection. Perform a venipuncture.

▶ Remove the needle and apply direct pressure with dry gauze to stop bleeding. Observe/assess venipuncture site for bleeding or hematoma formation and secure gauze with adhesive bandage.

▶ Promptly transport the specimen to the laboratory for processing and analysis.

POST-TEST:

▶ A report of the results will be made available to the requesting health-care provider (HCP), who will discuss the results with the patient.

▶ *Nutritional Considerations:* Increased CK levels may be associated with coronary artery disease (CAD). The American Heart Association and National Heart, Lung, and Blood Institute (NHLBI) recommend nutritional therapy for individuals identified to be at high risk for developing CAD or individuals who have specific risk factors and/or existing medical conditions (e.g., elevated LDL cholesterol levels, other lipid disorders, insulin-dependent diabetes, insulin resistance, or metabolic syndrome). If overweight, the patient should be encouraged to achieve a normal weight. Guidelines for the Therapeutic Lifestyle Changes (TLC) diet are outlined in the Third Report of the Expert Panel on Detection, Evaluation, and Treatment of High Blood Cholesterol in Adults (Adult

Treatment Panel III [ATP III]). The TLC diet emphasizes a reduction in foods high in saturated fats and cholesterol. Red meats, eggs, and dairy products are the major sources of saturated fats and cholesterol. If triglycerides also are elevated, the patient should be advised to eliminate or reduce alcohol and simple carbohydrates from the diet. The TLC approach also includes the use of plant stanols or sterols and increased dissolved fiber as an option for lowering LDL cholesterol levels; nutritional recommendations for daily total caloric intake; recommendations for allowable percentage of calories derived from fat (saturated and unsaturated), carbohydrates, protein, and cholesterol; as well as recommendations for daily expenditure of energy.

Nutritional Considerations: Overweight patients with high blood pressure should be encouraged to achieve a normal weight. Other changeable risk factors warranting patient education include strategies to safely decrease sodium intake, increase physical activity, decrease alcohol consumption, eliminate tobacco use, and decrease cholesterol levels.

Social and Cultural Considerations: Numerous studies point to the prevalence of excess body weight in American children and adolescents. Experts estimate that obesity is present in 25% of the population ages 6 to 11 yr. The medical, social, and emotional consequences of excess body weight are significant. Special attention should be given to instructing the child and caregiver regarding health risks and weight-control education.

▶ Recognize anxiety related to test results, and be supportive of fear of shortened life expectancy. Discuss the implications of abnormal test results on the patient's lifestyle. Provide teaching and information regarding the clinical implications of the test results, as appropriate. Educate the patient regarding access to counseling services. Provide contact information, if desired, for the American Heart Association (www.americanheart.org) or the NHLBI (www.nhlbi.nih.gov).

▶ Reinforce information given by the patient's HCP regarding further testing, treatment, or referral to another HCP. Answer any questions or address any concerns voiced by the patient or family.

▶ Depending on the results of this procedure, additional testing may be performed to evaluate or monitor progression of the disease process and determine the need for a change in therapy. Evaluate test results in relation to the patient's symptoms and other tests performed.

RELATED MONOGRAPHS:

▶ Related tests include antiarrhythmic drugs, apolipoprotein A and B, AST, ANP, blood gases, BNP, calcium (blood and ionized), cholesterol (total, HDL and LDL), CRP, CT cardiac scoring, echocardiography, glucose, glycated hemoglobin, Holter monitor, homocysteine, ketones, LDH and isoenzymes, lipoprotein electrophoresis, magnesium, MRI chest, MI scan, myocardial perfusion scan, myoglobin, pericardial fluid, PET heart, potassium, triglycerides, and troponin.

▶ Refer to the Cardiovascular and Musculoskeletal systems tables at the end of the book for related tests by body system.

Creatinine, Blood

SYNONYM/ACRONYM: N/A.

COMMON USE: To assess kidney function found in acute and chronic renal failure, related to drug reaction and disease such as diabetes.

SPECIMEN: Serum (1 mL) collected in a red- or tiger-top tube. Plasma (1 mL) collected in a green-top (heparin) tube is also acceptable.

NORMAL FINDINGS: (Method: Spectrophotometry)

Age	Conventional Units	SI Units (Conventional Units × 88.4)
Newborn	0.31–1.21 mg/dL	27–107 micromol/L
Infant	0.31–0.71 mg/dL	27–63 micromol/L
1–5 yr	0.31–0.51 mg/dL	27–45 micromol/L
6–10 yr	0.51–0.81 mg/dL	45–72 micromol/L
Adult male	0.61–1.21 mg/dL	54–107 micromol/L
Adult female	0.51–1.11 mg/dL	45–98 micromol/L

Values in older adults remain relatively stable after a period of decline related to loss of muscle mass during the transition from adult to older adult.

The National Kidney Foundation recommends the use of two decimal places in reporting serum creatinine for use in calculating estimated glomerular filtration rate.

DESCRIPTION: Creatinine is the end product of creatine metabolism. Creatine resides almost exclusively in skeletal muscle, where it participates in energy-requiring metabolic reactions. In these processes, a small amount of creatine is irreversibly converted to creatinine, which then circulates to the kidneys and is excreted. The amount of creatinine generated in an individual is proportional to the mass of skeletal muscle present and remains fairly constant unless there is massive muscle damage resulting from crushing injury or degenerative muscle disease. Creatinine values also decrease with age owing to diminishing muscle mass. Blood urea nitrogen (BUN) is often ordered with creatinine for comparison. The BUN/creatinine ratio is also a useful indicator of disease. The ratio should be between 10:1 and 20:1. Creatinine is the ideal substance for determining renal clearance because a fairly constant quantity is produced within the body. The creatinine clearance test measures a blood sample and a urine sample to determine the rate at which the kidneys are clearing creatinine from the blood; this reflects the glomerular filtration rate, or GFR (see monograph titled "Creatinine, Urine, and Creatinine Clearance, Urine").

Chronic kidney disease (CKD) is a significant health concern worldwide. An international effort to standardize methods to identify and monitor CKD has been undertaken by the National Kidney Disease Education Program (NKDEP), the International Confederation of Clinical Chemistry and Laboratory Medicine, and the European Communities Confederation of Clinical Chemistry. International efforts have resulted in development of an isotope dilution mass spectrometry (IDMS) reference method for standardized measurement of creatinine. The National Kidney Foundation (NKF) has recommended use of an equation to estimate glomerular filtration rate (eGFR). The equation is based on factors identified in the NKF Modification of Diet in Renal Disease (MDRD) study. The equation includes four factors: serum or plasma creatinine value, age (in years), gender, and race. The equation is valid only for patients between the ages of 18 and 70. A correction factor is incorporated in the equation if the patient is African American because CKD is more prevalent in African Americans; results are approximately 20% higher. It is very important to know whether the creatinine has been measured using an IDMS traceable test method because the values will differ; results are lower. The equations have not been validated for pregnant women (GFR is significantly increased in pregnancy); patients younger than 18 or older than 70; patients with serious comorbidities; or patients with extremes in body size, muscle mass, or nutritional status. eGFR calculators can be found at the National Kidney Disease Education Program (www.nkdep.

nih.gov/professionals/gfr_calculators/index.htm).

The equation used for creatinine methods that are not traceable to IDMS reference method is:

- **If creatinine is reported in mg/L:**

$$[\text{eGFR (mL/min/1.73 m}^2) = 186 \times (\text{creat})^{-1.154} \times (\text{Age})^{-0.203} \times (0.742 \text{ if female}) \times (1.21 \text{ if African American})]$$

- **If creatinine is reported in (SI) micromol/L:**

$$[\text{eGFR (mL/min/1.73 m}^2) = 186 \times (\text{creat}/88.4)^{-1.154} \times (\text{Age})^{-0.203} \times (0.742 \text{ if female}) \times (1.21 \text{ if African American})]$$

The equation used for creatinine methods that *are* traceable to IDMS reference method is:

- **If creatinine is reported in mg/dL:**

$$[\text{eGFR (mL/min/1.73 m}^2) = 175 \times (\text{creat})^{-1.154} \times (\text{Age})^{-0.203} \times (0.742 \text{ if female}) \times (1.21 \text{ if African American})]$$

- **If creatinine is reported in (SI) micromol/L:**

$$[\text{eGFR (mL/min/1.73 m}^2) = 175 \times (\text{creat}/88.4)^{-1.154} \times (\text{Age})^{-0.203} \times (0.742 \text{ if female}) \times (1.21 \text{ if African American})]$$

- **Creatinine clearance can be estimated from a blood creatinine level:**

Creatinine clearance = [1.2 × (140 − age in years) × (weight in kg)]/blood creatinine level.

The result is multiplied by 0.85 if the patient is female; the result is multiplied by 1.18 if the patient is African American.

INDICATIONS
- Assess a known or suspected disorder involving muscles in the absence of renal disease
- Evaluate known or suspected impairment of renal function

POTENTIAL DIAGNOSIS

Increased in
- Acromegaly *(related to increased muscle mass)*
- Congestive heart failure *(related to decreased renal blood flow)*
- Dehydration *(related to hemoconcentration)*
- Gigantism *(related to increased muscle mass)*
- Poliomyelitis *(related to increased release from damaged muscle)*
- Renal calculi *(related to decreased renal excretion due to obstruction)*
- Renal disease, acute and chronic renal failure *(related to decreased urinary excretion)*
- Rhabdomyolysis *(related to increased release from damaged muscle)*
- Shock *(related to increased release from damaged muscle)*

Decreased in
- Decreased muscle mass *(related to debilitating disease or increasing age)*
- Hyperthyroidism *(related to increased GFR)*
- Inadequate protein intake *(related to decreased muscle mass)*
- Liver disease (severe) *(related to fluid retention)*
- Muscular dystrophy *(related to decreased muscle mass)*
- Pregnancy *(related to increased GFR and renal clearance)*
- Small stature *(related to decreased muscle mass)*

CRITICAL FINDINGS

Adults
Potential critical value is greater than 7.4 mg/dL (SI: 654.2 micromol/L) (nondialysis patient).

Children
Potential critical value is greater than 3.8 mg/dL (SI: 336 micromol/L) (nondialysis patient).

Note and immediately report to the health-care provider (HCP) any critically increased values and related symptoms. Timely notification of critical values for lab or diagnostic studies is a role expectation of the professional nurse. Notification processes will vary among facilities. Upon receipt of the critical value, the information should be read back to the caller to verify accuracy. Most policies require immediate notification of the primary HCP, hospitalist, or on-call HCP. Reported information includes the patient's name, unique identifiers, critical value, name of the person giving the report, and name of the person receiving the report. Documentation of notification should be made in the medical record with the name of the HCP notified, time and date of notification, and any orders received. Any delay in a timely report of a critical value may require completion of a notification form with review by Risk Management.

Chronic renal insufficiency is identified by creatinine levels between 1.5 and 3 mg/dL; chronic renal failure is present at levels greater than 3 mg/dL.

Possible interventions may include renal or peritoneal dialysis and organ transplant, but early discovery of the cause of elevated creatinine levels might avoid such drastic interventions.

C

INTERFERING FACTORS

- Drugs and substances that may increase creatinine levels include acebutolol, acetaminophen (overdose), acetylsalicylic acid, aldatense, amikacin, amiodarone, amphotericin B, arginine, arsenicals, ascorbic acid, asparaginase, barbiturates, capreomycin, captopril, carbutamide, carvedilol, cephalothin, chlorthalidone, cimetidine, cisplatin, clofibrate, colistin, corn oil (Lipomul), cyclosporine, dextran, doxycycline, enalapril, ethylene glycol, gentamicin, indomethacin, ipodate, kanamycin, levodopa, mannitol, methicillin, methoxyflurane, mitomycin, neomycin, netilmicin, nitrofurantoin, NSAIDs, oxyphenbutazone, paromomycin, penicillin, pentamidine, phosphorus, plicamycin, radiographic agents, semustine, streptokinase, streptozocin, tetracycline, thiazides, tobramycin, triamterene, vancomycin, vasopressin, viomycin, and vitamin D.
- Drugs that may decrease creatinine levels include citrates, dopamine, ibuprofen, and lisinopril.
- High blood levels of bilirubin and glucose can cause false decreases in creatinine.
- A diet high in meat can cause increased creatinine levels.
- Ketosis can cause a significant increase in creatinine.
- Hemolyzed specimens are unsuitable for analysis.

NURSING IMPLICATIONS AND PROCEDURE

PRETEST:

- Positively identify the patient using at least two unique identifiers before providing care, treatment, or services.
- *Patient Teaching:* Inform the patient this test can assist in assessing kidney function.
- Obtain a history of the patient's complaints, including a list of known allergens, especially allergies or sensitivities to latex.
- Obtain a history of the patient's genitourinary and musculoskeletal systems, symptoms, and results of previously performed laboratory tests and diagnostic and surgical procedures.
- Obtain a list of the patient's current medications, including herbs, nutritional supplements, and nutraceuticals (see Appendix F).
- Review the procedure with the patient. Inform the patient that specimen collection takes approximately 5 to 10 min. Address concerns about pain and explain that there may be some discomfort during the venipuncture.
- *Sensitivity to social and cultural issues,* as well as concern for modesty, is important in providing psychological support before, during, and after the procedure.
- There are no food, fluid, or medication restrictions unless by medical direction.
- Instruct the patient to refrain from excessive exercise for 8 hr before the test.

INTRATEST:

- Ensure that the patient has complied with activity restrictions; assure that activity has been restricted for at least 8 hr prior to the procedure.
- If the patient has a history of allergic reaction to latex, avoid the use of equipment containing latex.
- Instruct the patient to cooperate fully and to follow directions. Direct the patient to breathe normally and to avoid unnecessary movement.
- Observe standard precautions, and follow the general guidelines in Appendix A. Positively identify the patient, and label the appropriate specimen container with the corresponding patient demographics, initials of the person collecting the specimen, date, and time of collection. Perform a venipuncture.
- Remove the needle and apply direct pressure with dry gauze to stop bleeding. Observe/assess venipuncture site for bleeding or hematoma formation and secure gauze with adhesive bandage.
- Promptly transport the specimen to the laboratory for processing and analysis.

POST-TEST:

▶ A report of the results will be made available to the requesting HCP, who will discuss the results with the patient.

▶ Instruct the patient to resume usual activity as directed by the HCP.

▶ *Nutritional Considerations:* Increased creatinine levels may be associated with kidney disease. The nutritional needs of patients with kidney disease vary widely and are in constant flux. Anorexia, nausea, and vomiting commonly occur, prompting the need for continuous monitoring for malnutrition, especially among patients receiving long-term hemodialysis therapy.

▶ Recognize anxiety related to test results and be supportive of impaired activity related to fear of shortened life expectancy. Discuss the implications of abnormal test results on the patient's lifestyle. Provide teaching and information regarding the clinical implications of the test results, as appropriate. Educate the patient regarding access to counseling services. Help the patient to cope with long-term implications. Recognize that anticipatory anxiety and grief related to potential lifestyle changes may be expressed when someone is faced with a chronic disorder. Provide contact information, if desired, for the National Kidney Foundation (www.kidney.org) or the National Kidney Disease Education Program (www.nkdep.nih.gov).

▶ Reinforce information given by the patient's HCP regarding further testing, treatment, or referral to another HCP. Answer any questions or address any concerns voiced by the patient or family.

▶ Depending on the results of this procedure, additional testing may be performed to evaluate or monitor progression of the disease process and determine the need for a change in therapy. Evaluate test results in relation to the patient's symptoms and other tests performed.

RELATED MONOGRAPHS:

▶ Related tests include anion gap, antibiotic drugs, ANF, BNP, biopsy muscle, blood gases, BUN, calcium, calculus kidney stone panel, CT abdomen, CT renal, CK and isoenzymes, creatinine clearance, cystoscopy, echocardiography, echocardiography transesophageal, electrolytes, EMG, ENG, glucagon, glucose, glycolated hemoglobin, insulin, IVP, KUB studies, lung perfusion scan, MRI venography, microalbumin, osmolality, phosphorus, renogram, retrograde ureteropyelography, TSH, thyroxine, US abdomen, uric acid, and UA.

▶ Refer to the Genitourinary and Musculoskeletal systems tables at the end of the book for related tests by body system.

Creatinine, Urine, and Creatinine Clearance, Urine

SYNONYM/ACRONYM: N/A.

COMMON USE: To assess and monitor kidney function related to acute or chronic nephritis.

SPECIMEN: Urine (5 mL) from an unpreserved random or timed specimen collected in a clean plastic collection container.

NORMAL FINDINGS: (Method: Spectrophotometry)

Age	Conventional Units	SI Units
		Urine Creatinine (Conventional Units × 8.84)
2–3 yr	6–22 mg/kg/24 hr	53–194 micromol/kg/24 hr
4–18 yr	12–30 mg/kg/24 hr	106–265 micromol/kg/24 hr
Adult male	14–26 mg/kg/24 hr	124–230 micromol/kg/24 hr
Adult female	11–20 mg/kg/24 hr	97–177 micromol/kg/24 hr
		Creatinine Clearance (Conventional Units × 0.0167)
Children	70–140 mL/min/1.73 m²	1.17–2.33 mL/s/1.73 m²
Adult male	85–125 mL/min/1.73 m²	1.42–2.08 mL/s/1.73 m²
Adult female	75–115 mL/min/1.73 m²	1.25–1.92 mL/s/1.73 m²
For each decade after 40 yr	Decrease of 6–7 mL/min/1.73 m²	Decrease of 0.06–0.07 mL/s/1.73 m²

DESCRIPTION: Creatinine is the end product of creatine metabolism. Creatine resides almost exclusively in skeletal muscle, where it participates in energy-requiring metabolic reactions. In these processes, a small amount of creatine is irreversibly converted to creatinine, which then circulates to the kidneys and is excreted. The amount of creatinine generated in an individual is proportional to the mass of skeletal muscle present and remains fairly constant, unless there is massive muscle damage resulting from crushing injury or degenerative muscle disease. Creatinine values decrease with advancing age owing to diminishing muscle mass. Although the measurement of urine creatinine is an effective indicator of renal function, the creatinine clearance test is more precise. The creatinine clearance test measures a blood sample and a urine sample to determine the rate at which the kidneys are clearing creatinine from the blood; this reflects the glomerular filtration rate (GFR) and is based on an estimate of body surface.

Chronic kidney disease (CKD) is a significant health concern worldwide. An international effort to standardize methods to identify and monitor CKD has been undertaken by the National Kidney Disease Education Program (NKDEP), the International Confederation of Clinical Chemistry and Laboratory Medicine, and the European Communities Confederation of Clinical Chemistry. International efforts have resulted in development of an isotope dilution mass spectrometry (IDMS) reference method for standardized measurement of creatinine. The National Kidney Foundation (NKF) has recommended use of an equation to estimate glomerular filtration rate (eGFR). The equation is based on factors identified in the NKF Modification of Diet in Renal Disease (MDRD) study. The equation includes four factors: serum or plasma creatinine value, age in years, gender, and race. The equation is valid only for patients between the ages of 18 and 70. A correction factor is incorporated in the equation if the patient is African American because CKD is more prevalent in African Americans; results are approximately 20% higher. It is very important to know whether the creatinine has been measured using an IDMS traceable test method because the values will differ; results are lower. The equations have not been validated for pregnant women (GFR is significantly increased in pregnancy); patients younger than 18 or older than 70; patients with serious comorbidities; or patients with extremes in body size, muscle mass, or nutritional status. eGFR calculators can be found at the NKDEP (www.nkdep.nih.gov/professionals/gfr_calculators/index.htm).

The equation used for creatinine methods that are *not* traceable to IDMS reference method is:

- **If creatinine is reported in mg/dL:**

$$[eGFR (mL/min/1.73 m^2) = 186 \times (creat)^{-1.154} \times (Age)^{-0.203} \times (0.742 \text{ if female}) \times (1.21 \text{ if African American})]$$

- **If creatinine is reported in (SI) micromol/L:**

$$[eGFR (mL/min/1.73 m^2) = 186 \times (creat/88.4)^{-1.154} \times (Age)^{-0.203} \times (0.742 \text{ if female}) \times (1.21 \text{ if African American})]$$

The equation used for creatinine methods that *are* traceable to IDMS reference method is:

- **If creatinine is reported in mg/dL:**

$$[eGFR (mL/min/1.73 m^2) = 175 \times (creat)^{-1.154} \times (Age)^{-0.203} \times (0.742 \text{ if female}) \times (1.21 \text{ if African American})]$$

- **If creatinine is reported in (SI) micromol/L:**

$$[eGFR (mL/min/1.73 m^2) = 175 \times (creat/88.4)^{-1.154} \times (Age)^{-0.203} \times (0.742 \text{ if female}) \times (1.21 \text{ if African American})]$$

- **Creatinine clearance can be estimated from a blood creatinine level:**

Creatinine clearance = [1.2 × (140 − age in years) × (weight in kg)]/blood creatinine level.

The result is multiplied by 0.85 if the patient is female; the result is multiplied by 1.18 if the patient is African American.

INDICATIONS
- Determine the extent of nephron damage in known renal disease (at least 50% of functioning nephrons must be lost before values are decreased)
- Determine renal function before administering nephrotoxic drugs
- Evaluate accuracy of a 24-hr urine collection based on the constant level of creatinine excretion
- Evaluate glomerular function
- Monitor effectiveness of treatment in renal disease

POTENTIAL DIAGNOSIS

Increased in
- Acromegaly *(related to increased muscle mass)*
- Carnivorous diets *(related to increased intake of creatine, which is metabolized to creatinine and excreted by the kidneys)*
- Exercise *(related to muscle damage; increased renal blood flow)*
- Gigantism *(related to increased muscle mass)*

Decreased in

Conditions that decrease GFR, impair kidney function, or reduce renal blood flow will decrease renal excretion of creatinine

- Acute or chronic glomerulonephritis
- Chronic bilateral pyelonephritis
- Leukemia
- Muscle wasting diseases *(related to abnormal creatinine production; decreased production reflected in decreased excretion)*
- Paralysis *(related to abnormal creatinine production; decreased production reflected in decreased excretion)*
- Polycystic kidney disease
- Shock
- Urinary tract obstruction (e.g., from calculi)
- Vegetarian diets *(evidenced by diets that exclude intake of animal muscle, the creatine source metabolized to creatinine and excreted by the kidneys)*

CRITICAL FINDINGS

- Degree of impairment:
  Borderline: 62.5–80 mL/min/1.73 m²
  (SI: 1–1.3 mL/s/1.73 m²)
  Slight: 52–62.5 mL/min/1.73 m²
  (SI: 0.9–1 mL/s/1.73 m²)
  Mild: 42–52 mL/min/1.73 m²
  (SI: 0.7–0.9 mL/s/1.73 m²)
  Moderate: 28–42 mL/min/1.73 m²
  (SI: 0.5–0.7 mL/s/1.73 m²)
  Marked: Less than 28 mL/min/1.73 m²
  (SI: Less than 0.5 mL/s/1.73 m²)

Note and immediately report to the health-care provider (HCP) any critically increased values and related symptoms. Timely notification of critical values for lab or diagnostic studies is a role expectation of the professional nurse. Notification processes will vary among facilities. Upon receipt of the critical value, the information should be read back to the caller to verify accuracy. Most policies require immediate notification of the primary HCP, hospitalist, or on-call HCP. Reported information includes the patient's name, unique identifiers, critical value, name of the person giving the report, and name of the person receiving the report. Documentation of notification should be made in the medical record with the name of the HCP notified, time and date of notification, and any orders received. Any delay in a timely report of a critical value may require completion of a notification form with review by Risk Management.

INTERFERING FACTORS

- Drugs that may increase urine creatinine levels include ascorbic acid, cefoxitin, cephalothin, corticosteroids, fluoxymesterone, levodopa, methandrostenolone, methotrexate, methyldopa, nitrofurans (including nitrofurazone), oxymetholone, phenolphthalein, and prednisone.
- Drugs that may increase urine creatinine clearance include enalapril, oral contraceptives, prednisone, and ramipril.
- Drugs that may decrease urine creatinine levels include anabolic steroids, androgens, captopril, and thiazides.
- Drugs that may decrease the urine creatinine clearance include acetylsalicylic acid, amphotericin B, carbenoxolone, chlorthalidone, cimetidine, cisplatin, cyclosporine, guancidine, ibuprofen, indomethacin, mitomycin, oxyphenbutazone, probenecid (coadministered with digoxin), puromycin, and thiazides.
- Excessive ketones in urine may cause falsely decreased values.
- Failure to follow proper technique in collecting 24-hr specimen may invalidate test results.
- Failure to refrigerate specimen throughout urine collection period allows decomposition of creatinine, causing falsely decreased values.

- Consumption of large amounts of meat, excessive exercise, and stress should be avoided for 24 hr before the test. Protocols may vary among facilities.
- Failure to follow dietary restrictions before the procedure may cause the procedure to be canceled or repeated.

NURSING IMPLICATIONS AND PROCEDURE

PRETEST:

▸ Positively identify the patient using at least two unique identifiers before providing care, treatment, or services.

▸ *Patient Teaching:* Inform the patient this test can assist in assessing kidney function.

▸ Obtain a history of the patient's complaints, including a list of known allergens, especially allergies or sensitivities to latex.

▸ Obtain a history of the patient's genitourinary system, symptoms, and results of previously performed laboratory tests and diagnostic and surgical procedures.

▸ Obtain a list of the patient's current medications, including herbs, nutritional supplements, and nutraceuticals (see Appendix F).

▸ Review the procedure with the patient. Provide a nonmetallic urinal, bedpan, or toilet-mounted collection device. Address concerns about pain and explain to the patient that there should be no discomfort during the urine collection procedure. Inform the patient that a blood sample for creatinine will be required on the day urine collection begins or at some point during the 24 hr collection period (see monograph titled "Creatinine, Blood" for additional information).

▸ *Sensitivity to social and cultural issues,* as well as concern for modesty, is important in providing psychological support before, during, and after the procedure.

▸ Usually a 24-hr time frame for urine collection is ordered. Inform the patient

that all urine must be saved during that 24-hr period. Instruct the patient not to void directly into the laboratory collection container. Instruct the patient to avoid defecating in the collection device and to keep toilet tissue out of the collection device to prevent contamination of the specimen. Place a sign in the bathroom to remind the patient to save all urine.

▸ Instruct the patient to void all urine into the collection device and then to pour the urine into the laboratory collection container. Alternatively, the specimen can be left in the collection device for a health-care staff member to add to the laboratory collection container.

▸ There are no fluid or medication restrictions unless by medical direction.

▸ Instruct the patient to refrain from eating meat during the test. Protocols may vary among facilities.

INTRATEST:

▸ Ensure that the patient has complied with dietary and activity restrictions for 24 hr prior to the procedure; assure that ingestion of meat has been restricted during the test.

▸ If the patient has a history of allergic reaction to latex, avoid the use of equipment containing latex.

▸ Instruct the patient to cooperate fully and to follow directions.

▸ Observe standard precautions, and follow the general guidelines in Appendix A. Positively identify the patient, and label the appropriate specimen container with the corresponding patient demographics, initials of the person collecting the specimen, date, and time of collection. Perform a venipuncture as appropriate.

Random Specimen (collect in early morning) Clean-Catch Specimen

▸ Instruct the male patient to (1) thoroughly wash his hands, (2) cleanse the meatus, (3) void a small amount into the toilet, and (4) void directly into the specimen container.

▸ Instruct the female patient to (1) thoroughly wash her hands; (2) cleanse the labia from front to back; (3) while keeping the labia separated, void a small amount into the toilet; and (4) without interrupting the urine stream, void directly into the specimen container.

Pediatric Urine Collector

Put on gloves. Appropriately cleanse the genital area and allow the area to dry. Remove the covering over the adhesive strips on the collector bag and apply over the genital area. Diaper the child. When specimen is obtained, place the entire collection bag in a sterile urine container.

Indwelling Catheter

Put on gloves. Empty drainage tube of urine. It may be necessary to clamp off the catheter for 15 to 30 min before specimen collection. Cleanse specimen port with antiseptic swab, and then aspirate 5 mL of urine with a 21- to 25-gauge needle and syringe. Transfer urine to a sterile container.

Urinary Catheterization

Place female patient in lithotomy position or male patient in supine position. Using sterile technique, open the straight urinary catheterization kit and perform urinary catheterization. Place the retained urine in a sterile specimen container.

Suprapubic Aspiration

Place the patient in a supine position. Cleanse the area with antiseptic and drape with sterile drapes. A needle is inserted through the skin into the bladder. A syringe attached to the needle is used to aspirate the urine sample. The needle is then removed and a sterile dressing is applied to the site. Place the sterile sample in a sterile specimen container.

Do not collect urine from the pouch from the patient with a urinary diversion (e.g., ileal conduit). Instead, perform catheterization through the stoma.

Timed Specimen

Obtain a clean 3-L urine specimen container, toilet-mounted collection device, and plastic bag (for transport of the specimen container). The specimen must be refrigerated or kept on ice throughout the entire collection period. If an indwelling urinary catheter is in place, the drainage bag must be kept on ice.

Begin the test between 6 and 8 a.m. if possible. Collect first voiding and discard. Record the time the specimen was discarded as the beginning of the timed collection period. The next morning, ask the patient to void at the same time the collection was started and add this last voiding to the container. Urinary output should be recorded throughout the collection time.

If an indwelling catheter is in place, replace the tubing and container system at the start of the collection time. Keep the container system on ice during the collection period, or empty the urine into a larger container periodically during the collection period; monitor to ensure continued drainage, and conclude the test the next morning at the same time the collection was begun.

At the conclusion of the test, compare the quantity of urine with the urinary output record for the collection; if the specimen contains less than what was recorded as output, some urine may have been discarded, invalidating the test.

Include on the collection container's label the amount of urine, test start and stop times, and any foods or medications that can affect test results.

Promptly transport the specimen to the laboratory for processing and analysis.

POST-TEST:

A report of the results will be made available to the requesting HCP, who will discuss the results with the patient.

Instruct the patient to resume usual diet, medications, and activity, as directed by the HCP.

Recognize anxiety related to test results and be supportive of impaired activity related to fear of shortened life expectancy. Discuss the implications of abnormal test results on the patient's lifestyle. Provide teaching and information regarding the clinical implications of the test results, as appropriate. Educate the patient regarding access to counseling services. Help the patient to cope with long-term implications. Recognize that

anticipatory anxiety and grief related to potential lifestyle changes may be expressed when someone is faced with a chronic disorder. Provide contact information, if desired, for the NKF (www.kidney.org) or the NKDEP (www.nkdep.nih.gov).
▶ Reinforce information given by the patient's HCP regarding further testing, treatment, or referral to another HCP. Answer any questions or address any concerns voiced by the patient or family.
▶ Depending on the results of this procedure, additional testing may be performed to evaluate or monitor progression of the disease process and determine the need for a change in therapy. Evaluate test results in relation to the patient's symptoms and other tests performed.

RELATED MONOGRAPHS:
▶ Related tests include anion gap, antibiotic drugs, antibodies antiglomerular basement membrane, ANF, biopsy kidney, biopsy muscle, blood gases, BNP, BUN, calcium, calculus kidney stone analysis, C4, CT abdomen, CT renal, CK and isoenzymes, creatinine, culture urine, cytology urine, cystoscopy, echocardiography, echocardiography transesophageal, electrolytes, EMG, ENG, EPO, gallium scan, glucagon, glucose, haptoglobin, insulin, IVP, KUB studies, lung perfusion scan, microalbumin, osmolality, phosphorus, renogram, retrograde ureteropyelography, TSH, thyroxine, US kidney, uric acid, and UA.
▶ Refer to the Genitourinary System table at the end of the book for related tests by body system.

Cryoglobulin

SYNONYM/ACRONYM: Cryo.

COMMON USE: To assist in identifying the presence of certain immunological disorders such as Reynaud's phenomenon.

SPECIMEN: Serum (1 mL) collected in a red-top tube.

NORMAL FINDINGS: (Method: Visual observation for changes in appearance) Negative.

DESCRIPTION: Cryoglobulins are abnormal serum proteins that cannot be detected by protein electrophoresis. Cryoglobulins cause vascular problems because they can precipitate in the blood vessels of the fingers when exposed to cold, causing Raynaud's phenomenon. They are usually associated with immunological disease. The laboratory procedure to detect cryoglobulins is a two-step process. The serum sample is observed for cold precipitation after 72 hr of storage at 4°C. True cryoglobulins disappear on warming to room temperature, so in the second step of the procedure, the sample is rewarmed to confirm reversibility of the reaction.

INDICATIONS
• Assist in diagnosis of neoplastic diseases, acute and chronic infections, and collagen diseases

- Detect cryoglobulinemia in patients with symptoms indicating or mimicking Raynaud's disease
- Monitor course of collagen and rheumatic disorders

POTENTIAL DIAGNOSIS

Increased in
Cryoglobulins are present in varying degrees in associated conditions.

- Type I cryoglobulin (monoclonal)
- Chronic lymphocytic leukemia
- Lymphoma
- Multiple myeloma
- Type II cryoglobulin (mixtures of monoclonal immunoglobulin [Ig] M and polyclonal IgG)
- Autoimmune hepatitis
- Rheumatoid arthritis
- Sjögren's syndrome
- Waldenström's macroglobulinemia
- Type III cryoglobulin (mixtures of polyclonal IgM and IgG)
- Acute poststreptococcal glomerulo-nephritis
- Chronic infection (especially hepatitis C)
- Cirrhosis
- Endocarditis
- Infectious mononucleosis
- Polymyalgia rheumatica
- Rheumatoid arthritis
- Sarcoidosis
- Systemic lupus erythematosus

Decreased in: N/A

CRITICAL FINDINGS: N/A

INTERFERING FACTORS

- Testing the sample prematurely (before total precipitation) may yield incorrect results.
- Failure to maintain sample at normal body temperature before centrifugation can affect results.
- A recent fatty meal can increase turbidity of the blood, decreasing visibility.

NURSING IMPLICATIONS AND PROCEDURE

PRETEST:

- Positively identify the patient using at least two unique identifiers before providing care, treatment, or services.
- *Patient Teaching:* Inform the patient this test can assist in assessing for immune system disorders.
- Obtain a history of the patient's complaints, including a list of known allergens, especially allergies or sensitivities to latex.
- Obtain a history of the patient's immune system as well as results of previously performed laboratory tests and diagnostic and surgical procedures.
- Obtain a list of the patient's current medications, including herbs, nutritional supplements, and nutraceuticals (see Appendix F).
- Review the procedure with the patient. Inform the patient that specimen collection takes approximately 5 to 10 min. Address concerns about pain and explain that there may be some discomfort during the venipuncture.
- *Sensitivity to social and cultural issues,* as well as concern for modesty, is important in providing psychological support before, during, and after the procedure.
- There are no food, fluid, or medication restrictions unless by medical direction.

INTRATEST:

- If the patient has a history of allergic reaction to latex, avoid the use of equipment containing latex.
- Instruct the patient to cooperate fully and to follow directions. Direct the patient to breathe normally and to avoid unnecessary movement.
- Observe standard precautions, and follow the general guidelines in Appendix A. Positively identify the patient, and label the appropriate specimen container with the corresponding patient demographics, initials of the person collecting the specimen, date, and time of collection. Perform a venipuncture.

▶ Remove the needle and apply direct pressure with dry gauze to stop bleeding. Observe/assess venipuncture site for bleeding or hematoma formation and secure gauze with adhesive bandage.

▶ Promptly transport the specimen to the laboratory for processing and analysis.

POST-TEST:

▶ A report of the results will be made available to the requesting health-care provider (HCP), who will discuss the results with the patient.

▶ Reinforce information given by the patient's HCP regarding further testing, treatment, or referral to another HCP. Answer any questions or address any concerns voiced by the patient or family.

▶ Depending on the results of this procedure, additional testing may be performed to evaluate or monitor progression of the disease process and determine the need for a change in therapy. Evaluate test results in relation to the patient's symptoms and other tests performed.

RELATED MONOGRAPHS:

▶ Related tests include ALT, ANA, arthroscopy, AST, bilirubin, biopsy liver, bone scan, ceruloplasmin, copper, CRP, ESR, GGT, infectious mono screen, hepatitis C antibody, IgA, IgG, IgM, IFE, liver and spleen scan, protein, protein electrophoresis, RF, synovial fluid analysis, and US liver.

▶ Refer to the Immune System table at the end of the book for related tests by body system.

Culture and Smear, Mycobacteria

SYNONYM/ACRONYM: Acid-fast bacilli (AFB) culture and smear, tuberculosis (TB) culture and smear, *Mycobacterium* culture and smear.

COMMON USE: To assist in the diagnosis of tuberculosis.

SPECIMEN: Sputum (5 to 10 mL), bronchopulmonary lavage, tissue, material from fine-needle aspiration, bone marrow, cerebrospinal fluid (CSF), gastric aspiration, urine, and stool.

NORMAL FINDINGS: (Method: Culture on selected media, microscopic examination of sputum by acid-fast or auramine-rhodamine fluorochrome stain) Rapid methods include: chemiluminescent-labeled DNA probes that target ribosomal RNA of the *Mycobacterium* radiometric carbon dioxide detection from ^{14}C-labeled media, polymerase chain reaction/amplification techniques.

Culture: No growth
Smear: Negative for AFB

DESCRIPTION: A culture and smear test is used primarily to detect *Mycobacterium tuberculosis*, which is a tubercular bacillus. The cell wall of this mycobacterium contains complex lipids and waxes that do not take up ordinary stains. Cells that resist decolorization by acid alcohol are termed *acid-fast*. There are only a few groups of acid-fast bacilli (AFB); this characteristic is helpful in rapid identification so that therapy can be initiated in a timely manner. Smears may be negative 50% of the time even though the culture develops positive growth 3 to 8 wk later. AFB cultures are used to confirm positive and negative AFB smears. *M. tuberculosis* grows in culture slowly. Automated liquid culture systems, such as the Bactec and MGIT (Becton Dickinson and Company, 1 Becton Drive, Franklin Lakes, NJ, 07417), have a turnaround time of approximately 10 days. Results of tests by polymerase chain reaction culture methods are available in 24 to 72 hr. The QuantiFERON-TB Gold (QFT-G), QuantiFERON-TB Gold In-Tube (QFT-GIT), and T-SPOT interferon release blood tests are approved by the U.S. Food and Drug Administration for all applications in which the TB skin test is used. The blood test is a procedure in which a sample of whole blood from the patient is incubated with a reagent cocktail of peptides known to be present in individuals infected by *Mycobacterium tuberculosis* but not found in the blood of previously vaccinated individuals or individuals who do not have the disease. The blood test offers the advantage of eliminating many of the false reactions encountered with skin testing, only a single patient visit is required, and results can be available within 24 hr. The blood tests and skin tests are approved as indirect tests for *Mycobacterium tuberculosis*, and the Centers for Disease Control and Prevention (CDC) recommends their use in conjunction with risk assessment, chest x-ray, and other appropriate medical and diagnostic evaluations. Detailed information is found in the monograph titled "Tuberculosis: Skin and Blood Tests."

M. tuberculosis is transmitted via the airborne route to the lungs. It causes areas of granulomatous inflammation, cough, fever, and hemoptysis. It can remain dormant in the lungs for long periods. The incidence of tuberculosis has increased since the late 1980s in depressed inner-city areas, among prison populations, and among HIV-positive patients. Of great concern is the increase in antibiotic-resistant strains. HIV-positive patients often become ill from concomitant infections caused by *M. tuberculosis* and *Mycobacterium avium intracellulare. M. avium intracellulare* is acquired via the gastrointestinal tract through ingestion of contaminated food or water. The organism's waxy cell wall protects it from acids in the human digestive tract. Isolation of mycobacteria in the stool does not mean the patient has tuberculosis of the intestines because mycobacteria in stool are most often present in sputum that has been swallowed.

INDICATIONS
• Assist in the diagnosis of mycobacteriosis
• Assist in the diagnosis of suspected pulmonary tuberculosis secondary to AIDS
• Assist in the differentiation of tuberculosis from carcinoma or bronchiectasis
• Investigate suspected pulmonary tuberculosis
• Monitor the response to treatment for pulmonary tuberculosis

POTENTIAL DIAGNOSIS

Identified Organism	Primary Specimen Source	Condition
Mycobacterium avium intracellulare	CSF, lymph nodes, semen, sputum, urine	Opportunistic pulmonary infection
M. fortuitum	Bone, body fluid, sputum, surgical wound, tissue	Opportunistic infection (usually pulmonary)
M. leprae	CSF, skin scrapings, lymph nodes	Hanson's disease (leprosy)
M. kansasii	Joint, lymph nodes, skin, sputum	Pulmonary tuberculosis
M. marinum	Joint	Granulomatous skin lesions
M. tuberculosis	CSF, gastric washing, sputum, urine	Pulmonary tuberculosis
M. xenopi	Sputum	Pulmonary tuberculosis

CRITICAL FINDINGS

- *Smear:* Positive for AFB
- *Culture:* Growth of pathogenic bacteria

Note and immediately report to the health-care provider (HCP) positive results and related symptoms. Lists of specific organisms may vary among facilities; specific organisms are required to be reported to local, state, and national departments of health. Timely notification of critical values for lab or diagnostic studies is a role expectation of the professional nurse. Notification processes will vary among facilities. Upon receipt of the critical value, the information should be read back to the caller to verify accuracy. Most policies require immediate notification of the primary HCP, hospitalist, or on-call HCP. Reported information includes the patient's name, unique identifiers, critical value, name of the person giving the report, and name of the person receiving the report. Documentation of notification should be made in the medical record with the name of the HCP notified, time and date of notification, and any orders received. Any delay in a timely report of a critical value may require completion of a notification form with review by Risk Management.

INTERFERING FACTORS

- Specimen collection after initiation of treatment with antituberculosis drug therapy may result in inhibited or no growth of organisms.
- Contamination of the sterile container with organisms from an exogenous source may produce misleading results.
- Specimens received on a dry swab should be rejected: A dry swab indicates that the sample is unlikely to have been collected properly or unlikely to contain a representative quantity of significant organisms for proper evaluation.
- Inadequate or improper (e.g., saliva) samples should be rejected.
- Failure to follow dietary restrictions before the procedure may cause the procedure to be canceled or repeated.

NURSING IMPLICATIONS AND PROCEDURE

PRETEST:

- Positively identify the patient using at least two unique identifiers before providing care, treatment, or services.

Patient Teaching: Inform the patient this test can assist in diagnosing respiratory disease.

Obtain a history of the patient's complaints, including a list of known allergens, especially allergies or sensitivities to latex. Obtain a history of the patient's exposure to tuberculosis.

Obtain a history of the patient's immune and respiratory systems, symptoms, and results of previously performed laboratory tests and diagnostic and surgical procedures.

Obtain a list of the patient's current medications, including herbs, nutritional supplements, and nutraceuticals (see Appendix F).

Note any recent procedures that can interfere with test results.

Review the procedure with the patient. Reassure the patient that he or she will be able to breathe during the procedure if sputum specimen is collected via suction method. Ensure that oxygen has been administered 20 to 30 min before the procedure if the specimen is to be obtained by tracheal suction. Address concerns about pain related to the procedure. Atropine is usually given before bronchoscopy examinations to reduce bronchial secretions and prevent vagally induced bradycardia. Meperidine (Demerol) or morphine may be given as a sedative. Lidocaine is sprayed in the patient's throat to reduce discomfort caused by the presence of the tube.

Explain to the patient that the time it takes to collect a proper specimen varies according to the level of cooperation of the patient and the specimen collection site. Emphasize that sputum and saliva are not the same. Inform the patient that multiple specimens may be required at timed intervals. Inform the patient that the culture results will not be reported for 3 to 8 wk.

Sensitivity to social and cultural issues, as well as concern for modesty, is important in providing psychological support before, during, and after the procedure.

Bronchoscopy

Make sure a written and informed consent has been signed prior to the procedure and before administering any medications.

Other than antimicrobial drugs, there are no medication restrictions unless by medical direction.

The patient should fast and refrain from drinking liquids beginning at midnight the night before the procedure. Protocols may vary among facilities.

Expectorated Specimen

Additional liquids the night before may assist in liquefying secretions during expectoration the following morning.

Assist the patient with oral cleaning before sample collection to reduce the amount of sample contamination by organisms that normally inhabit the mouth.

Instruct the patient not to touch the edge or inside of the container with the hands or mouth.

Other than antimicrobial drugs, there are no medication restrictions unless by medical direction.

There are no food or fluid restrictions unless by medical direction.

Tracheal Suctioning

Assist in providing extra fluids, unless contraindicated, and proper humidification to decrease tenacious secretions. Inform the patient that increasing fluid intake before retiring on the night before the test aids in liquefying secretions and may make it easier to expectorate in the morning. Also explain that humidifying inspired air also helps liquefy secretions.

Other than antimicrobial drugs, there are no medication restrictions unless by medical direction.

There are no food or fluid restrictions unless by medical direction.

INTRATEST:

Ensure that the patient has complied with dietary and medication restrictions; assure that food and fluids have been restricted for at least 8 hr prior to the bronchoscopy procedure.

Have patient remove dentures, contact lenses, eyeglasses, and jewelry. Notify the HCP if the patient has permanent crowns on teeth. Have the patient remove clothing and change into a gown for the procedure.

▶ Have emergency equipment readily available. Keep resuscitation equipment on hand in case of respiratory impairment or laryngospasm after the procedure.

▶ Avoid using morphine sulfate in patients with asthma or other pulmonary disease. This drug can further exacerbate bronchospasms and respiratory impairment.

▶ If the patient has a history of allergic reaction to latex, avoid the use of equipment containing latex.

▶ Assist the patient to a comfortable position, and direct the patient to breathe normally during the beginning of the local anesthesia and to avoid unnecessary movement during the local anesthetic and the procedure. Instruct the patient to cooperate fully and to follow directions.

▶ Observe standard precautions, and follow the general guidelines in Appendix A. Positively identify the patient, and label the appropriate collection container with the corresponding patient demographics, date and time of collection, and any medication the patient is taking that may interfere with test results (e.g., antibiotics).

Bronchoscopy
▶ Record baseline vital signs.

▶ The patient is positioned in relation to the type of anesthesia being used. If local anesthesia is used, the patient is seated and the tongue and oropharynx are sprayed and swabbed with anesthetic before the bronchoscope is inserted. For general anesthesia, the patient is placed in a supine position with the neck hyperextended. After anesthesia, the patient is kept in supine or shifted to a side-lying position and the bronchoscope is inserted. After inspection, the samples are collected from suspicious sites by bronchial brush or biopsy forceps.

Expectorated Specimen
▶ Ask the patient to sit upright, with assistance and support (e.g., with an overbed table) as needed.

▶ Ask the patient to take two or three deep breaths and cough deeply. Any sputum raised should be expectorated directly into a sterile sputum collection container.

▶ If the patient is unable to produce the desired amount of sputum, several strategies may be attempted. One approach is to have the patient drink two glasses of water, and then assume the position for postural drainage of the upper and middle lung segments. Effective coughing may be assisted by placing either the hands or a pillow over the diaphragmatic area and applying slight pressure.

▶ Another approach is to place a vaporizer or other humidifying device at the bedside. After sufficient exposure to adequate humidification, postural drainage of the upper and middle lung segments may be repeated before attempting to obtain the specimen.

▶ Other methods may include obtaining an order for an expectorant to be administered with additional water approximately 2 hr before attempting to obtain the specimen. Chest percussion and postural drainage of all lung segments may also be employed. If the patient is still unable to raise sputum, the use of an ultrasonic nebulizer ("induced sputum") may be necessary; this is usually done by a respiratory therapist.

Tracheal Suctioning
▶ Obtain the necessary equipment, including a suction device, suction kit, and Lukens tube or in-line trap.

▶ Position the patient with head elevated as high as tolerated.

▶ Put on sterile gloves. Maintain the dominant hand as sterile and the non-dominant hand as clean.

▶ Using the sterile hand, attach the suction catheter to the rubber tubing of the Lukens tube or in-line trap. Then attach the suction tubing to the male adapter of the trap with the clean hand. Lubricate the suction catheter with sterile saline.

▶ Tell nonintubated patients to protrude the tongue and to take a deep breath as the suction catheter is passed through the nostril. When the catheter enters the trachea, a reflex cough is stimulated; immediately advance the catheter into the trachea and apply suction. Maintain suction for approximately 10 sec, but never longer than 15 sec. Withdraw the catheter without applying suction. Separate the suction catheter and suction tubing from the trap, and place the rubber tubing over the male adapter to seal the unit.

For intubated patients or patients with a tracheostomy, the previous procedure is followed except that the suction catheter is passed through the existing endotracheal or tracheostomy tube rather than through the nostril. The patient should be hyperoxygenated before and after the procedure in accordance with standard protocols for suctioning these patients.

Generally, a series of three to five early morning sputum samples are collected in sterile containers. If leprosy is suspected, obtain a smear from nasal scrapings or a biopsy specimen from lesions in a sterile container.

General

Monitor the patient for complications related to the procedure (e.g., allergic reaction, anaphylaxis, bronchospasm). Promptly transport the specimen to the laboratory for processing and analysis.

POST-TEST:

A report of the results will be made available to the requesting HCP, who will discuss the results with the patient.

Instruct the patient to resume preoperative diet, as directed by the HCP. Assess the patient's ability to swallow before allowing the patient to attempt liquids or solid foods.

Inform the patient that he or she may experience some throat soreness and hoarseness. Instruct patient to treat throat discomfort with lozenges and warm gargles when the gag reflex returns.

Monitor vital signs and compare with baseline values every 15 min for 1 hr, then every 2 hr for 4 hr, and then as ordered by the HCP. Monitor temperature every 4 hr for 24 hr. Notify the HCP if temperature is elevated. Protocols may vary among facilities.

Emergency resuscitation equipment should be readily available if the vocal cords become spastic after intubation.

Observe for delayed allergic reactions, such as rash, urticaria, tachycardia, hyperpnea, hypertension, palpitations, nausea, or vomiting.

Observe the patient for hemoptysis, difficulty breathing, cough, air hunger, excessive coughing, pain, or absent breathing sounds over the affected area. Report any symptoms to the HCP.

Evaluate the patient for symptoms indicating the development of pneumothorax, such as dyspnea, tachycardia, anxiety, decreased breathing sounds, or restlessness. A chest x-ray may be ordered to check for the presence of this complication.

Evaluate the patient for symptoms of empyema, such as fever, tachycardia, malaise, or elevated white blood cell count.

Administer antibiotic therapy if ordered. Remind the patient of the importance of completing the entire course of antibiotic therapy, even if signs and symptoms disappear before completion of therapy.

Nutritional Considerations: Malnutrition is commonly seen in patients with severe respiratory disease for numerous reasons, including fatigue, lack of appetite, and gastrointestinal distress. Adequate intake of vitamins A and C are also important to prevent pulmonary infection and to decrease the extent of lung tissue damage.

Recognize anxiety related to test results. Discuss the implications of abnormal test results on the patient's lifestyle. Provide teaching and information regarding the clinical implications of the test results, as appropriate.

Reinforce information given by the patient's HCP regarding further testing, treatment, or referral to another HCP. Instruct the patient to use lozenges or gargle for throat discomfort. Inform the patient of smoking cessation programs as appropriate. The importance of following the prescribed diet should be stressed to the patient/caregiver. Educate the patient regarding access to counseling services, as appropriate. Answer any questions or address any concerns voiced by the patient or family.

- Instruct the patient in the use of any ordered medications. Explain the importance of adhering to the therapy regimen. As appropriate, instruct the patient in significant side effects and systemic reactions associated with the prescribed medication. Encourage him or her to review corresponding literature provided by a pharmacist.
- Depending on the results of this procedure, additional testing may be needed to evaluate or monitor progression of the disease process and determine the need for a change in therapy. Evaluate test results in relation to the patient's symptoms and other tests performed.

RELATED MONOGRAPHS:

- Related tests include antibodies, antiglomerular basement membrane, arterial/alveolar oxygen ratio, blood gases, bronchoscopy, chest x-ray, complete blood count, CT thoracic, cultures (fungal, sputum, throat, viral), cytology sputum, gallium scan, Gram stain, lung perfusion scan, lung ventilation scan, MRI chest, mediastinoscopy, pleural fluid analysis, pulmonary function tests, and TB tests.
- Refer to the Immune and Respiratory systems tables at the end of the book for related tests by body system.

C

Culture, Bacterial, Anal/Genital, Ear, Eye, Skin, and Wound

SYNONYM/ACRONYM: N/A.

COMMON USE: To identify pathogenic bacterial organisms as an indicator for appropriate therapeutic interventions for multiple sites of infection.

SPECIMEN: Sterile fluid or swab from affected area placed in transport media tube provided by laboratory.

NORMAL FINDINGS: (Method: Culture aerobic and/or anaerobic on selected media; nucleic acid amplification and DNA probe assays [e.g., Gen-Probe] are available for identification of *Neisseria gonorrhoeae* and *Chlamydia trachomatis*.) Negative: no growth of pathogens.

DESCRIPTION: When indicated by patient history, anal and genital cultures may be performed to isolate the organism responsible for sexually transmitted disease. Group B streptococcus (GBS) is a significant and serious neonatal infection. The Centers for Disease Control and Prevention (CDC) recommends universal GBS screening for all pregnant women at 35 to 37 wk gestation. Rapid GBS test kits can provide results within minutes on vaginal or rectal fluid swab specimens submitted in a sterile red-top tube.

Ear and eye cultures are performed to isolate the organism responsible for chronic or acute infectious disease of the ear and eye.

Skin and soft tissue samples from infected sites must be collected carefully to avoid contamination from the surrounding normal skin flora. Skin and tissue infections may be caused by both aerobic and anaerobic organisms. Therefore, a portion of the sample should be placed in aerobic and a portion in anaerobic transport media. Care must be taken to use transport media that are approved by the laboratory performing the testing.

Sterile fluids can be collected from the affected site. Refer to related body fluid monographs (i.e., amniotic fluid, cerebrospinal fluid, pericardial fluid, peritoneal fluid, pleural fluid, synovial fluid) for specimen collection.

A wound culture involves collecting a specimen of exudates, drainage, or tissue so that the causative organism can be isolated and pathogens identified. Specimens can be obtained from superficial and deep wounds.

Optimally, specimens should be obtained before antibiotic use. The method used to culture and grow the organism depends on the suspected infectious organism. There are transport media specifically for bacterial agents. The laboratory will select the appropriate media for suspect organisms and will initiate antibiotic sensitivity testing if indicated by test results. Sensitivity testing identifies the antibiotics to which organisms are susceptible to ensure an effective treatment plan.

INDICATIONS

Anal/Genital
- Assist in the diagnosis of sexually transmitted diseases
- Determine the cause of genital itching or purulent drainage
- Determine effective antimicrobial therapy specific to the identified pathogen
- Routine prenatal screening for vaginal and rectal GBS colonization

Ear
- Isolate and identify organisms responsible for ear pain, drainage, or changes in hearing
- Isolate and identify organisms responsible for outer-, middle-, or inner-ear infection
- Determine effective antimicrobial therapy specific to the identified pathogen

Eye
- Isolate and identify pathogenic microorganisms responsible for infection of the eye
- Determine effective antimicrobial therapy specific to identified pathogen

Skin
- Isolate and identify organisms responsible for skin eruptions, drainage, or other evidence of infection
- Determine effective antimicrobial therapy specific to the identified pathogen

Sterile Fluids
- Isolate and identify organisms before surrounding tissue becomes infected
- Determine effective antimicrobial therapy specific to the identified pathogen

Wound
- Detect abscess or deep-wound infectious process
- Determine if an infectious agent is the cause of wound redness, warmth, or edema with drainage at a site
- Determine presence of infectious agents in a stage 3 and stage 4 decubitus ulcer
- Isolate and identify organisms responsible for the presence of pus or other exudate in an open wound

• Determine effective antimicrobial therapy specific to the identified pathogen

POTENTIAL DIAGNOSIS

Positive findings in

Anal/Endocervical/Genital

Infections or carrier states are caused by the following organisms: *C. trachomatis*, obligate intra-cellular bacteria without a cell wall, gram variable *Gardnerella vaginalis*, gram negative *N. gonorrhoeae, Treponema pallidum*, and toxin-producing strains of gram positive *Staphylococcus aureus*, and gram positive GBS.

Ear

Commonly identified gram negative organisms include *Escherichia coli, Proteus* spp., *Pseudomonas aeruginosa*, gram positive *S. aureus*, and β-hemolytic streptococci.

Eye

Commonly identified organisms include *C. trachomatis* (transmitted to newborns from infected mothers), gram negative *Haemophilus influenzae* (transmitted to newborns from infected mothers), *H. aegyptius, N. gonorrhoeae* (transmitted to newborns from infected mothers), *P. aeruginosa*, gram positive *S. aureus*, and *Streptococcus pneumoniae*.

Skin

Commonly identified gram negative organisms include *Bacteroides, Pseudomonas*, gram positive *Clostridium, Corynebacterium*, staphylococci, and group A streptococci.

Sterile Fluids

Commonly identified pathogens include gram negative *Bacteroides, E. coli, P. aeruginosa*, gram positive *Enterococcus* spp., and *Peptostreptococcus* spp.

Wound

Aerobic and anaerobic microorganisms can be identified in wound culture specimens. Commonly identified gram negative organisms include *Klebsiella, Proteus, Pseudomonas*, gram-positive *Clostridium perfringens, S. aureus*, and group A streptococci.

CRITICAL FINDINGS

• *Listeria* in genital cultures
• Methicillin-resistant *S. aureus* (MRSA) in skin or wound cultures

Note and immediately report to the health-care provider (HCP) positive results and related symptoms. Lists of specific organisms may vary among facilities; specific organisms are required to be reported to local, state, and national departments of health. Timely notification of critical values for lab or diagnostic studies is a role expectation of the professional nurse. Notification processes will vary among facilities. Upon receipt of the critical value, the information should be read back to the caller to verify accuracy. Most policies require immediate notification of the primary HCP, hospitalist, or on-call HCP. Reported information includes the patient's name, unique identifiers, critical value, name of the person giving the report, and name of the person receiving the report. Documentation of notification should be made in the medical record with the name of the HCP notified, time and date of notification, and any orders received. Any delay in a timely report of a critical value may require completion of a notification form with review by Risk Management.

INTERFERING FACTORS

• Failure to collect adequate specimen, improper collection or storage technique, and failure to transport specimen in a timely

C

fashion are causes for specimen rejection.

- Pretest antimicrobial therapy will delay or inhibit the growth of pathogens.
- Testing specimens more than 1 hr after collection may result in decreased growth or no growth of organisms.

NURSING IMPLICATIONS AND PROCEDURE

PRETEST:

Positively identify the patient using at least two unique identifiers before providing care, treatment, or services.

Patient Teaching: Inform the patient that test can assist in identification of the organism causing infection.

Obtain a history of the patient's complaints, including a list of known allergens.

Obtain a history of the patient's immune system, symptoms, and results of previously performed laboratory tests and diagnostic and surgical procedures. Obtain, as appropriate, a history of sexual activity.

Obtain a list of the patient's current medications, including herbs, nutritional supplements, and nutraceuticals (see Appendix F).

Note any recent medications that can interfere with test results.

Review the procedure with the patient. Inform the patient that specimen collection takes approximately 5 min. Address concerns about pain and explain that there may be some discomfort during the specimen collection. Instruct female patients not to douche for 24 hr before a cervical or vaginal specimen is to be obtained.

Sensitivity to social and cultural issues, as well as concern for modesty, is important in providing psychological support before, during, and after the procedure.

There are no food or fluid restrictions unless by medical direction.

INTRATEST:

Ensure that the patient has complied with medication restrictions prior to the procedure.

Instruct the patient to cooperate fully and to follow directions. Direct the patient to breathe normally and to avoid unnecessary movement.

Observe standard precautions, and follow the general guidelines in Appendix A. Positively identify the patient, and label the appropriate specimen containers with the corresponding patient demographics, specimen source (left or right as appropriate), patient age and gender, date and time of collection, and any medication the patient is taking that may interfere with the test results (e.g., antibiotics). Do not freeze the specimen or allow it to dry.

Anal

Place the patient in a lithotomy or side-lying position and drape for privacy. Insert the swab 1 in. into the anal canal and rotate, moving it from side to side to allow it to come into contact with the microorganisms. Remove the swab. Place the swab in the Culturette tube, and squeeze the bottom of the tube to release the transport medium. Ensure that the end of the swab is immersed in the medium. Repeat with a clean swab if the swab is pushed into feces.

Genital

Female Patient

Position the patient on the gynecological examination table with the feet up in stirrups. Drape the patient's legs to provide privacy and reduce chilling. Cleanse the external genitalia and perineum from front to back with towelettes provided in culture kit. Using a Culturette swab, obtain a sample of the lesion or discharge from the urethra or vulva. Place the swab in the Culturette tube, and squeeze the bottom of the tube to release the transport medium. Ensure that the end of the swab is immersed in the medium.

To obtain a vaginal and endocervical culture, insert a water-lubricated vaginal speculum. Insert the swab into the cervical orifice and rotate the swab to collect the secretions containing the microorganisms. Remove and place in the appropriate culture medium or Gen-Probe transport tube. Material from the vagina can be collected by moving a swab along the sides of the vaginal mucosa. The swab is removed and then placed in a tube of saline medium.

Male Patient
To obtain a urethral culture, cleanse the penis (retracting the foreskin), have the patient milk the penis to express discharge from the urethra. Insert a swab into the urethral orifice and rotate the swab to obtain a sample of the discharge. Place the swab in the Culturette or Gen-Probe transport tube, and squeeze the bottom of the tube to release the transport medium. Ensure that the end of the swab is immersed in the medium.

Ear
Cleanse the area surrounding the site with a swab containing cleaning solution to remove any contaminating material or flora that have collected in the ear canal. If needed, assist the appropriate HCP in removing any cerumen that has collected.
Insert a Culturette swab approximately 1/4 in. into the external ear canal. Rotate the swab in the area containing the exudate. Carefully remove the swab, ensuring that it does not touch the side or opening of the ear canal. Place the swab in the Culturette tube, and squeeze the bottom of the tube to release the transport medium. Ensure that the end of the swab is immersed in the medium.

Eye
Pass a moistened swab over the appropriate site, avoiding eyelid and eyelashes unless those areas are selected for study. Collect any visible pus or other exudate. Place the swab in the Culturette or Gen-Probe transport tube, and squeeze the bottom of the tube to release the transport medium. Ensure that the end of the swab is immersed in the medium. An appropriate HCP should perform procedures requiring eye culture.

Skin
Assist the appropriate HCP in obtaining a skin sample from several areas of the affected site. If indicated, the dark, moist areas of the folds of the skin and outer growing edges of the infection where microorganisms are most likely to flourish should be selected. Place the scrapings in a collection container or spread on a slide. Aspirate any fluid from a pustule or vesicle using a sterile needle and tuberculin syringe. The exudate will be flushed into a sterile collection tube. If the lesion is not fluid filled, open the lesion with a scalpel and swab the area with a sterile cotton-tipped swab. Place the swab in the Culturette tube, and squeeze the bottom of the tube to release the transport medium. Ensure that the end of the swab is immersed in the medium.

Sterile Fluid
Refer to related body fluid monographs (i.e., amniotic fluid, cerebrospinal fluid, pericardial fluid, peritoneal fluid, pleural fluid, synovial fluid) for specimen collection.

Wound
Place the patient in a comfortable position, and drape the site to be cultured. Cleanse the area around the wound to remove flora indigenous to the skin.
Place a Culturette swab in a superficial wound where the exudate is the most excessive without touching the wound edges. Place the swab in the Culturette tube, and squeeze the bottom of the tube to release the transport medium. Ensure that the end of the swab is immersed in the medium. Use more than one swab and Culturette tube to obtain specimens from other areas of the wound.
To obtain a deep wound specimen, insert a sterile syringe and needle into the wound and aspirate the drainage. Following aspiration, inject the material into a tube containing an anaerobic culture medium.

General
Promptly transport the specimen to the laboratory for processing and analysis.

POST-TEST:
Instruct the patient to resume usual medication as directed by the HCP.

C

Instruct the patient to report symptoms such as pain related to tissue inflammation or irritation.

Instruct the patient to begin antibiotic therapy, as prescribed. Instruct the patient in the importance of completing the entire course of antibiotic therapy even if no symptoms are present.

Inform the patient that a repeat culture may be needed in 1 wk after completion of the antimicrobial regimen.

Advise the patient that final test results may take 24 to 72 hr depending on the organism suspected but that antibiotic therapy may be started immediately.

Anal/Endocervical/Genital

Inform the patient that final results may take from 24 hr to 4 wk, depending on the test performed.

Advise the patient to avoid sexual contact until test results are available.

Instruct the patient in vaginal suppository and medicated cream installation and administration of topical medication to treat specific conditions, as indicated.

Inform infected patients that all sexual partners must be tested for the microorganism.

Inform the patient that positive culture findings for certain organisms must be reported to a local health department official, who will question him or her regarding sexual partners.

Social and Cultural Considerations: Offer support, as appropriate, to patients who may be the victims of rape or sexual assault. Educate the patient regarding access to counseling services. Provide a nonjudgmental, nonthreatening atmosphere for discussing the risks of sexually transmitted diseases. It is also important to address problems the patient may experience (e.g., guilt, depression, anger).

Wound

Instruct the patient in wound care and nutritional requirements (e.g., protein, vitamin C) to promote wound healing.

General

A report of the results will be made available to the requesting HCP,

who will discuss the results with the patient.

Recognize anxiety related to test results. Discuss the implications of abnormal test results on the patient's lifestyle. Provide teaching and information regarding the clinical implications of the test results, as appropriate.

Reinforce information given by the patient's HCP regarding further testing, treatment, or referral to another HCP. Emphasize the importance of reporting continued signs and symptoms of the infection. Provide information regarding vaccine-preventable diseases where indicated (e.g., anthrax, cervical cancer, diphtheria, encephalitis, hepatitis A and B, H1N1 flu, human papillomavirus, *Haemophilus influenza*, seasonal influenza, Lyme disease, measles, meningococcal disease, monkeypox, mumps, pertussis, pneumococcal disease, polio, rotavirus, rubella, shingles, smallpox, tetanus, typhoid fever, varicella, yellow fever). Provide contact information, if desired, for the CDC (www.cdc.gov/vaccines/vpd-vac). Answer any questions or address any concerns voiced by the patient or family.

Instruct the patient in the use of any ordered medications (oral, topical, drops). Instruct the patient in the proper use of sterile technique for cleansing the affected site and application of dressings, as directed. Explain the importance of adhering to the therapy regimen. As appropriate, instruct the patient in significant side effects and systemic reactions associated with the prescribed medication. Encourage him or her to review corresponding literature provided by a pharmacist.

Depending on the results of this procedure, additional testing may be performed to evaluate or monitor progression of the disease process and determine the need for a change in therapy. Evaluate test results in relation to the patient's symptoms and other tests performed.

RELATED MONOGRAPHS:

Related tests include relevant amniotic fluid analysis, audiometry hearing loss, biopsy site, CSF analysis, culture viral,

Gram stain, otoscopy, pericardial fluid analysis, Pap smear, peritoneal fluid analysis, pleural fluid analysis, procalcitonin, spondee speech reception threshold, synovial fluid analysis, syphilis serology, tuning fork tests, vitamin C, and zinc.

▶ Refer to the Immune System table at the end of the book for related tests by body system.

Culture, Bacterial, Blood

SYNONYM/ACRONYM: N/A.

COMMON USE: To identify pathogenic bacterial organisms in the blood as an indicator for appropriate therapeutic interventions for sepsis.

SPECIMEN: Whole blood collected in bottles containing standard aerobic and anaerobic culture media; 10 to 20 mL for adult patients or 1 to 5 mL for pediatric patients.

NORMAL FINDINGS: (Method: Growth of organisms in standard culture media identified by radiometric or infrared automation, or by manual reading of subculture.) Negative: no growth of pathogens.

DESCRIPTION: Blood cultures are collected whenever bacteremia or septicemia is suspected. Although mild bacteremia is found in many infectious diseases, a persistent, continuous, or recurrent bacteremia indicates a more serious condition that may require immediate treatment. Early detection of pathogens in the blood may aid in making clinical and etiological diagnoses.

Blood culture involves the introduction of a specimen of blood into artificial aerobic and anaerobic growth culture medium. The culture is incubated for a specific length of time, at a specific temperature, and under other conditions suitable for the growth of pathogenic microorganisms. Pathogens enter the bloodstream from soft-tissue infection sites, contaminated IV lines, or invasive procedures (e.g., surgery, tooth extraction, cystoscopy). A blood culture may also be done with an antimicrobial removal device (ARD). This involves transferring some of the blood sample into a special vial containing absorbent resins that remove antibiotics from the sample before the culture is performed. The laboratory will initiate antibiotic sensitivity testing if indicated by test results. Sensitivity testing identifies the antibiotics to which the organisms are susceptible to ensure an effective treatment plan.

INDICATIONS
• Determine sepsis in the newborn as a result of prolonged labor, early rupture of membranes, maternal infection, or neonatal aspiration

- Evaluate chills and fever in patients with infected burns, urinary tract infections, rapidly progressing tissue infection, postoperative wound sepsis, and indwelling venous or arterial catheter
- Evaluate intermittent or continuous temperature elevation of unknown origin
- Evaluate persistent, intermittent fever associated with a heart murmur
- Evaluate a sudden change in pulse and temperature with or without chills and diaphoresis
- Evaluate suspected bacteremia after invasive procedures
- Identify the cause of shock in the postoperative period

POTENTIAL DIAGNOSIS

Positive findings in
- Bacteremia or septicemia: Gram-negative organisms such as *Aerobacter, Bacteroides, Brucella, Escherichia coli* and other coliform bacilli, *Haemophilus influenzae, Klebsiella, Pseudomonas aeruginosa*, and *Salmonella*.
- Bacteremia or septicemia: Gram-positive organisms such as *Clostridium perfringens, Enterococci, Listeria monocytogenes, Staphylococcus aureus, S. epidermidis*, and β-hemolytic streptococci.
- Plague
- Malaria (by special request, a stained capillary smear would be examined)
- Typhoid fever

Note: *Candida albicans* is a yeast that can cause disease and can be isolated by blood culture.

CRITICAL FINDINGS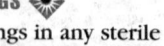

- Positive findings in any sterile body fluid such as blood

Note and immediately report to the health-care provider (HCP) positive results and related symptoms. Lists of specific organisms may vary among facilities; specific organisms are required to be reported to local, state and national departments of health Timely notification of critical values for lab or diagnostic studies is a role expectation of the professional nurse Notification processes will vary among facilities. Upon receipt of the critical value, the information should be read back to the caller to verify accuracy. Most policies require immediate notification of the primary HCP hospitalist, or on-call HCP. Reported information includes the patient's name, unique identifiers, critical value, name of the person giving the report, and name of the person receiving the report. Documentation of notification should be made in the medical record with the name of the HCP notified, time and date of notification, and any orders received. Any delay in a timely report of a critical value may require completion of a notification form with review by Risk Management.

INTERFERING FACTORS
- Pretest antimicrobial therapy will delay or inhibit growth of pathogens.
- Contamination of the specimen by the skin's resident flora may invalidate interpretation of test results.
- An inadequate amount of blood or number of blood specimens drawn for examination may invalidate interpretation of results.
- Testing specimens more than 1 hr after collection may result in decreased growth or no growth of organisms. Delay in transport of specimen to the laboratory may result in specimen rejection. Verify submission requirements with the laboratory prior to specimen collection.

- Collection of the specimen in an expired media tube will result in specimen rejection.
- Negative findings do not ensure the absence of infection.

NURSING IMPLICATIONS AND PROCEDURE

PRETEST:

- Positively identify the patient using at least two unique identifiers before providing care, treatment, or services.
- *Patient Teaching:* Inform the patient this test can assist in identification of the organism causing infection.
- Obtain a history of the patient's complaints, including a list of known allergens, especially allergies or sensitivities to iodine.
- Obtain a history of the patient's immune system, symptoms, and results of previously performed laboratory tests and diagnostic and surgical procedures.
- Obtain a list of the patient's current medications, including herbs, nutritional supplements, and nutraceuticals (see Appendix F).
- Note any recent medications that can interfere with test results.
- Review the procedure with the patient. Inform the patient that specimen collection takes approximately 5 min. Inform the patient that multiple specimens may be required at timed intervals. Address concerns about pain and explain to the patient that there may be some discomfort during the venipuncture.
- *Sensitivity to social and cultural issues,* as well as concern for modesty, is important in providing psychological support before, during, and after the procedure.
- There are no food or fluid restrictions unless by medical direction.

INTRATEST:

- Ensure that the patient has complied with medication restrictions prior to the procedure.
- If the patient has a history of severe allergic reaction to iodine, care should be taken to avoid the use of iodine.
- Instruct the patient to cooperate fully and to follow directions. Direct the patient to breathe normally and to avoid unnecessary movement.
- Observe standard precautions, and follow the general guidelines in Appendix A. Positively identify the patient, and label the appropriate specimen containers with the corresponding patient demographics, date and time of collection, and any medication the patient is taking that may interfere with test results (e.g., antibiotics). Perform a venipuncture; collect the specimen in the appropriate blood culture collection container.
- The high risk for infecting a patient by venipuncture can be decreased by using an aseptic technique during specimen collection.
- The contamination of blood cultures by skin and other flora can also be dramatically reduced by careful preparation of the puncture site and collection containers before specimen collection. Cleanse the rubber stoppers of the collection containers with the appropriate disinfectant as recommended by the laboratory, allow to air-dry, and cleanse with 70% alcohol. Once the vein has been located by palpation, cleanse the site with 70% alcohol followed by swabbing with an iodine solution. The iodine should be swabbed in a circular, concentric motion, moving outward or away from the puncture site. The iodine should be allowed to completely dry before the sample is collected. If the patient is sensitive to iodine, a double alcohol scrub or green soap may be substituted.
- If collection is performed by directly drawing the sample into a culture tube, fill the aerobic culture tube first.
- If collection is performed using a syringe, transfer the blood sample directly into each culture bottle.
- Remove the needle, and apply direct pressure with a dry gauze to stop bleeding. Observe/assess venipuncture site for bleeding and secure gauze with adhesive bandage.
- Promptly transport the specimen to the laboratory for processing and analysis.
- More than three sets of cultures per day do not significantly add to the

likelihood of pathogen capture. Capture rates are more likely affected by obtaining a sufficient volume of blood per culture.

- The use of ARDs or resin bottles is costly and controversial with respect to

their effectiveness versus standard culture techniques. They may be useful in selected cases, such as when septicemia or bacteremia is suspected after antimicrobial therapy has been initiated.

C

Disease Suspected	Recommended Collection
Bacterial pneumonia, fever of unknown origin, meningitis, osteomyelitis, sepsis	Two sets of cultures, each collected from a separate site, 30 min apart
Acute or subacute endocarditis	Three sets of cultures, each collected from a separate site, 30–40 min apart. If cultures are negative after 24–48 hr, repeat collections
Septicemia, fungal or mycobacterial infection in immunocompromised patient	Two sets of cultures, each collected from a separate site, 30–60 min apart (laboratory may use a lysis concentration technique to enhance recovery)
Septicemia, bacteremia after therapy has been initiated, or request to monitor effectiveness of antimicrobial therapy	Two sets of cultures, each collected from a separate site, 30–60 min apart (consider use of ARD to enhance recovery)

POST-TEST:

- A report of the results will be made available to the requesting HCP, who will discuss the results with the patient.
- Instruct the patient to resume usual medication as directed by the HCP.
- Cleanse the iodine from the collection site.
- Instruct the patient to report symptoms such as pain related to tissue inflammation or irritation.
- Instruct the patient to report fever, chills, and other signs and symptoms of acute infection to the HCP.
- Instruct the patient to begin antibiotic therapy, as prescribed. Instruct the patient in the importance of completing the entire course of antibiotic therapy even if no symptoms are present.
- Inform the patient that preliminary results should be available in 24 to 72 hr, but final results are not available for 5 to 7 days.
- Recognize anxiety related to test results. Discuss the implications of

abnormal test results on the patient's lifestyle. Provide teaching and information regarding the clinical implications of the test results, as appropriate.

- Reinforce information given by the patient's HCP regarding further testing, treatment, or referral to another HCP. Emphasize the importance of reporting continued signs and symptoms of the infection. Provide information regarding vaccine-preventable diseases where indicated (e.g., anthrax, cervical cancer, diphtheria, encephalitis, hepatitis A and B, H1N1 flu, human papillomavirus, *Haemophilus influenza*, seasonal influenza, Lyme disease, measles, meningococcal disease, monkeypox, mumps, pertussis, pneumococcal disease, polio, rotavirus, rubella, shingles, smallpox, tetanus, typhoid fever, varicella, yellow fever). Provide contact information, if desired, for the Centers for Disease Control and Prevention (www.cdc.gov/vaccines/vpd-vac).

Answer any questions or address any concerns voiced by the patient or family.
- Depending on the results of this procedure, additional testing may be performed to evaluate or monitor progression of the disease process and determine the need for a change in therapy. Evaluate test results in relation to the patient's symptoms and other tests performed.

RELATED MONOGRAPHS:

Related tests include bone scan, bronchoscopy, CBC, cultures (fungal, mycobacteria, throat, sputum, viral), CSF analysis, ESR, gallium scan, Gram stain, HIV-1/2 antibodies, MRI musculoskeletal, procalcitonin, PFT, radiography bone, and TB tests.
Refer to the Immune System table at the end of the book for related tests by body system.

C

Culture, Bacterial, Sputum

SYNONYM/ACRONYM: Routine culture of sputum.

COMMON USE: To identify pathogenic bacterial organisms in the sputum as an indicator for appropriate therapeutic interventions for respiratory infections.

SPECIMEN: Sputum (10 to 15 mL).

NORMAL FINDINGS: (Method: Aerobic culture on selective and enriched media; microscopic examination of sputum by Gram stain.) The presence of normal upper respiratory tract flora should be expected. Tracheal aspirates and bronchoscopy samples can be contaminated with normal flora, but transtracheal aspiration specimens should show no growth. Normal respiratory flora include *Neisseria catarrhalis*, *Candida albicans*, diphtheroids, α-hemolytic streptococci, and some staphylococci. The presence of normal flora does not rule out infection. A normal Gram stain of sputum contains polymorphonuclear leukocytes, alveolar macrophages, and a few squamous epithelial cells.

DESCRIPTION: This test involves collecting a sputum specimen so the pathogen can be isolated and identified. The test results will reflect the type and number of organisms present in the specimen as well as the antibiotics to which the identified pathogenic organisms are susceptible. Sputum collected by expectoration or suctioning with catheters and by bronchoscopy cannot be cultured for anaerobic organisms; instead, transtracheal aspiration or lung biopsy must be used. The laboratory will initiate antibiotic sensitivity testing if indicated by test results. Sensitivity testing identifies antibiotics to which the organisms are susceptible to ensure an effective treatment plan.

INDICATIONS

Culture
• Assist in the diagnosis of respiratory infections, as indicated by the presence or absence of organisms in culture

Gram Stain
• Assist in the differentiation of gram-positive from gram-negative bacteria in respiratory infection
• Assist in the differentiation of sputum from upper respiratory tract secretions, the latter being indicated by excessive squamous cells or absence of polymorphonuclear leukocytes

POTENTIAL DIAGNOSIS
• The major difficulty in evaluating results is in distinguishing organisms infecting the lower respiratory tract from organisms that have colonized but not infected the lower respiratory tract. Review of the Gram stain assists in this process. The presence of greater than 25 squamous epithelial cells per low-power field (lpf) indicates oral contamination, and the specimen should be rejected. The presence of many polymorphonuclear neutrophils and few squamous epithelial cells indicates that the specimen was collected from an area of infection and is satisfactory for further analysis.
• Bacterial pneumonia can be caused by *Streptococcus pneumoniae*, *Haemophilus influenzae*, staphylococci, and some gram-negative bacteria. Other pathogens that can be identified by culture are *Corynebacterium diphtheriae*, *Klebsiella pneumoniae*, and *Pseudomonas aeruginosa*. Some infectious agents, such as *C. diphtheriae*, are more fastidious in their growth requirements and cannot be cultured and identified without special treatment. Suspicion of infection by less commonly identified and/or fastidious organisms must be communicated to the laboratory to ensure selection of the proper procedure required for identification.

CRITICAL FINDINGS
• *C. diphtheriae*
• *Legionella*

Note and immediately report to the health-care provider (HCP) positive results and related symptoms. Lists of specific organisms may vary among facilities; specific organisms are required to be reported to local, state, and national departments of health. Timely notification of critical values for lab or diagnostic studies is a role expectation of the professional nurse. Notification processes will vary among facilities. Upon receipt of the critical value, the information should be read back to the caller to verify accuracy. Most policies require immediate notification of the primary HCP, hospitalist, or on-call HCP. Reported information includes the patient's name, unique identifiers, critical value, name of the person giving the report, and name of the person receiving the report. Documentation of notification should be made in the medical record with the name of the HCP notified, time and date of notification, and any orders received. Any delay in a timely report of a critical value may require completion of a notification form with review by Risk Management.

INTERFERING FACTORS
• Contamination with oral flora may invalidate results.
• Specimen collection after antibiotic therapy has been initiated may result in inhibited or no growth of organisms.

NURSING IMPLICATIONS AND PROCEDURE

PRETEST:

Positively identify the patient using at least two unique identifiers before providing care, treatment, or services.

Patient Teaching: Inform the patient this test can assist in identification of the organism causing infection.

Obtain a history of the patient's complaints, including a list of known allergens, especially allergies or sensitivities to latex.

Obtain a history of the patient's immune and respiratory systems, symptoms, and results of previously performed laboratory tests and diagnostic and surgical procedures.

Obtain a list of the patient's current medications, including herbs, nutritional supplements, and nutraceuticals (see Appendix F).

Note any recent medications that can interfere with test results.

Review the procedure with the patient. Reassure the patient that he or she will be able to breathe during the procedure if specimen collection is accomplished via suction method.

Ensure that oxygen has been administered 20 to 30 min before the procedure if the specimen is to be obtained by tracheal suctioning.

Address concerns about pain related to the procedure. Atropine is usually given before bronchoscopy examinations to reduce bronchial secretions and prevent vagally induced bradycardia. Meperidine (Demerol) or morphine may be given as a sedative. Lidocaine is sprayed in the patient's throat to reduce discomfort caused by the presence of the tube.

Explain to the patient that the time it takes to collect a proper specimen varies according to the level of cooperation of the patient and the specimen collection site. Emphasize that sputum and saliva are not the same. Inform the patient that multiple specimens may be required at timed intervals.

Sensitivity to social and cultural issues, as well as concern for modesty, is important in providing psychological support before, during, and after the procedure.

Bronchoscopy

Make sure a written and informed consent has been signed prior to the bronchoscopy/biopsy procedure and before administering any medications.

Other than antimicrobial drugs, there are no medication restrictions, unless by medical direction.

The patient should fast and refrain from drinking liquids beginning at midnight the night before the procedure. Protocols may vary among facilities.

Expectorated Specimen

Additional liquids the night before may assist in liquefying secretions during expectoration the following morning.

Assist the patient with oral cleaning before sample collection to reduce the amount of sample contamination by organisms that normally inhabit the mouth.

Instruct the patient not to touch the edge or inside of the container with the hands or mouth.

Other than antimicrobial drugs, there are no medication restrictions, unless by medical direction.

There are no food or fluid restrictions, unless by medical direction.

Tracheal Suctioning

Assist in providing extra fluids, unless contraindicated, and proper humidification to decrease tenacious secretions. Inform the patient that increasing fluid intake before retiring on the night before the test aids in liquefying secretions and may make it easier to expectorate in the morning. Also explain that humidifying inspired air also helps liquefy secretions.

Other than antimicrobial drugs, there are no medication restrictions, unless by medical direction.

There are no food or fluid restrictions, unless by medical direction.

If the specimen is collected by expectoration or tracheal suctioning, there are no food, fluid, or medication restrictions (except antibiotics), unless by medical direction.

INTRATEST:

Ensure that the patient has complied with dietary and medication restrictions; ensure that food and fluids have been restricted for at least 8 hr prior to the bronchoscopy procedure.

Have patient remove dentures, contact lenses, eyeglasses, and jewelry. Notify the HCP if the patient has permanent crowns on teeth. Have the patient remove clothing and change into a gown for the procedure.

Have emergency equipment readily available. Keep resuscitation equipment on hand in case of respiratory impairment or laryngospasm after the procedure.

Avoid using morphine sulfate in patients with asthma or other pulmonary disease. This drug can further exacerbate bronchospasms and respiratory impairment.

If the patient has a history of allergic reaction to latex, avoid the use of equipment containing latex.

Assist the patient to a comfortable position and direct the patient to breathe normally during the beginning of the general anesthesia and to avoid unnecessary movement during the local anesthetic and the procedure. Instruct the patient to cooperate fully and to follow directions.

Observe standard precautions and follow the general guidelines in Appendix A. Positively identify the patient, and label the appropriate tubes with the corresponding patient demographics, date and time of collection, and any medication the patient is taking that may interfere with test results (e.g., antibiotics). Collect the specimen in the appropriate sterile collection container.

Bronchoscopy

Record baseline vital signs.

The patient is positioned in relation to the type of anesthesia being used. If local anesthesia is used, the patient is seated and the tongue and oropharynx are sprayed and swabbed with anesthetic before the bronchoscope is inserted. For general anesthesia, the patient is placed in a supine position with the neck hyperextended. After anesthesia, the patient is kept in supine or shifted to a side-lying position and the bronchoscope is inserted. After inspection, the samples are collected from suspicious sites by bronchial brush or biopsy forceps.

Expectorated Specimen

Ask the patient to sit upright, with assistance and support (e.g., with an overbed table) as needed.

Ask the patient to take two or three deep breaths and cough deeply. Any sputum raised should be expectorated directly into a sterile sputum collection container.

If the patient is unable to produce the desired amount of sputum, several strategies may be attempted. One approach is to have the patient drink two glasses of water, and then assume the position for postural drainage of the upper and middle lung segments. Effective coughing may be assisted by placing either the hands or a pillow over the diaphragmatic area and applying slight pressure.

Another approach is to place a vaporizer or other humidifying device at the bedside. After sufficient exposure to adequate humidification, postural drainage of the upper and middle lung segments may be repeated before attempting to obtain the specimen.

Other methods may include obtaining an order for an expectorant to be administered with additional water approximately 2 hr before attempting to obtain the specimen. Chest percussion and postural drainage of all lung segments may also be employed. If the patient is still unable to raise sputum, the use of an ultrasonic nebulizer ("induced sputum") may be necessary; this is usually done by a respiratory therapist.

Tracheal Suctioning

Obtain the necessary equipment, including a suction device, suction kit, and Lukens tube or in-line trap.

Position the patient with head elevated as high as tolerated.

Put on sterile gloves. Maintain the dominant hand as sterile and the nondominant hand as clean.

Using the sterile hand, attach the suction catheter to the rubber tubing of the Lukens tube or in-line trap. Then attach the suction tubing to the male adapter of the trap with the clean hand. Lubricate the suction catheter with sterile saline.

Tell nonintubated patients to protrude the tongue and to take a deep breath as the suction catheter is passed through the nostril. When the catheter enters the trachea, a reflex cough is stimulated; immediately advance the catheter into the trachea and apply suction. Maintain suction for approximately 10 sec, but never longer than 15 sec. Withdraw the catheter without applying suction. Separate the suction catheter and suction tubing from the trap, and place the rubber tubing over the male adapter to seal the unit.

For intubated patients or patients with a tracheostomy, the previous procedure is followed except that the suction catheter is passed through the existing endotracheal or tracheostomy tube rather than through the nostril. The patient should be hyperoxygenated before and after the procedure in accordance with standard protocols for suctioning these patients.

Generally, a series of three to five early morning sputum samples are collected in sterile containers.

General

Monitor the patient for complications related to the procedure (e.g., allergic reaction, anaphylaxis, bronchospasm).

Promptly transport the specimen to the laboratory for processing and analysis.

POST-TEST:

A report of the results will be made available to the requesting HCP, who will discuss the results with the patient.

Instruct the patient to resume preoperative diet, as directed by the HCP. Assess the patient's ability to swallow before allowing the patient to attempt liquids or solid foods.

Inform the patient that he or she may experience some throat soreness and hoarseness. Instruct patient to treat throat discomfort with lozenges and warm gargles when the gag reflex returns.

Monitor vital signs and compare with baseline values every 15 min for 1 hr, then every 2 hr for 4 hr, and then as ordered by the HCP. Monitor temperature every 4 hr for 24 hr. Notify the HCP if temperature is elevated. Protocols may vary among facilities.

Emergency resuscitation equipment should be readily available if the vocal cords become spastic after intubation.

Observe for delayed allergic reactions, such as rash, urticaria, tachycardia, hyperpnea, hypertension, palpitations, nausea, or vomiting.

Observe the patient for hemoptysis, difficulty breathing, cough, air hunger, excessive coughing, pain, or absent breathing sounds over the affected area. Report any symptoms to the HCP.

Evaluate the patient for symptoms indicating the development of pneumothorax, such as dyspnea, tachypnea, anxiety, decreased breathing sounds, or restlessness. A chest x-ray may be ordered to check for the presence of this complication.

Evaluate the patient for symptoms of empyema, such as fever, tachycardia, malaise, or elevated white blood cell count.

Access additional resources at davisplus.fadavis.com

Administer antibiotic therapy if ordered. Remind the patient of the importance of completing the entire course of antibiotic therapy, even if signs and symptoms disappear before completion of therapy.

Nutritional Considerations: Malnutrition is commonly seen in patients with severe respiratory disease for numerous reasons including fatigue, lack of appetite, and gastrointestinal distress. Adequate intake of vitamins A and C are also important to prevent pulmonary infection and to decrease the extent of lung tissue damage.

Recognize anxiety related to test results. Discuss the implications of abnormal test results on the patient's lifestyle. Provide teaching and information regarding the clinical implications of the test results, as appropriate. Educate the patient regarding access to counseling services.

Reinforce information given by the patient's HCP regarding further testing, treatment, or referral to another HCP. Instruct the patient to use lozenges or gargle for throat discomfort. Inform the patient of smoking cessation programs as appropriate. The importance of following the prescribed diet should be stressed to the patient/caregiver. Educate the patient regarding access to counseling services, as appropriate. Provide information regarding vaccine preventable diseases where indicated (e.g., anthrax, cervical cancer, diphtheria, encephalitis, hepatitis A and B, H1N1 flu, human papillomavirus, *Haemophilus influenza,* seasonal influenza, Lyme disease, measles, meningococcal disease, monkeypox, mumps, pertussis, pneumococcal disease, polio, rotavirus, rubella, shingles, smallpox, tetanus, typhoid fever, varicella, yellow fever). Provide contact information, if desired, for the Centers for Disease Control and Prevention (www.cdc.gov/vaccines/vpd-vac). Answer any questions or address any concerns voiced by the patient or family.

Instruct the patient in the use of any ordered medications. Explain the importance of adhering to the therapy regimen. As appropriate, instruct the patient in significant side effects and systemic reactions associated with the prescribed medication. Encourage him or her to review corresponding literature provided by a pharmacist.

Depending on the results of this procedure, additional testing may be needed to evaluate or monitor progression of the disease process and determine the need for a change in therapy. Evaluate test results in relation to the patient's symptoms and other tests performed.

RELATED MONOGRAPHS:

Related tests include antibodies, anti–glomerular basement membrane, arterial/alveolar oxygen ratio, biopsy lung, blood gases, bronchoscopy, chest x-ray, CBC, CT thoracic, culture (fungal, mycobacterium, throat, viral), cytology sputum, gallium scan, Gram stain/acid-fast stain, HIV-1/2 antibodies, lung perfusion scan, lung ventilation scan, MRI chest, mediastinoscopy, pleural fluid analysis, PFT, and TB tests.

Refer to the Immune and Respiratory systems tables at the end of the book for related tests by body system.

Culture, Bacterial, Stool

SYNONYM/ACRONYM: N.A.

COMMON USE: To identify pathogenic bacterial organisms in the stool as an indicator for appropriate therapeutic interventions to treat organisms such as *Clostridium difficile* and *Escherichia coli*.

SPECIMEN: Fresh, random stool collected in a clean plastic container.

NORMAL FINDINGS: (Method: Culture on selective media for identification of pathogens usually to include *Salmonella. Shigella, Escherichia coli* O157:H7, *Yersinia enterocolitica*, and *Campylobacter*; latex agglutination or enzyme immunoassay for *Clostridium* A and B toxins) Negative: No growth of pathogens. Normal fecal flora is 96% to 99% anaerobes and 1% to 4% aerobes. Normal flora present may include *Bacteroides*, *Candida albicans*, *Clostridium*, *Enterococcus*, *E. coli*, *Proteus*, *Pseudomonas*, and *Staphylococcus aureus*.

DESCRIPTION: Stool culture involves collecting a sample of feces so that organisms present can be isolated and identified. Certain bacteria are normally found in feces. However, when overgrowth of these organisms occurs or pathological organisms are present, diarrhea or other signs and symptoms of systemic infection occur. These symptoms are the result of damage to the intestinal tissue by the pathogenic organisms. Routine stool culture normally screens for a small number of common pathogens, such as *S. aureus*, *Salmonella*, and *Shigella*. Identification of other bacteria is initiated by special request or upon consultation with a microbiologist when there is knowledge of special circumstances. The laboratory will initiate antibiotic sensitivity testing if indicated by test results. Sensitivity testing identifies the antibiotics to which organisms are susceptible to ensure an effective treatment plan. Life-threatening *C. difficile* infection of the bowel may occur in patients who are immunocompromised or are receiving broad-spectrum antibiotic therapy (e.g., clindamycin, ampicillin, cephalosporins). The bacteria release a toxin that causes necrosis of the colon tissue. The toxin can be more rapidly identified from a stool sample using an immunochemical method than from a routine culture. Appropriate interventions can be quickly initiated and might include IV replacement of fluid and electrolytes, cessation of broad-spectrum antibiotic administration, and institution of vancomycin or metronidazole antibiotic therapy.

INDICATIONS

- Assist in establishing a diagnosis for diarrhea of unknown etiology
- Identify pathogenic organisms causing gastrointestinal disease and carrier states

POTENTIAL DIAGNOSIS

Positive findings in

- Bacterial infection: Gram-negative organisms such as *Aeromonas* spp., *Campylobacter*, *E. coli* including serotype O157: H7, *Plesiomonas*

shigelloides, *Salmonella*, *Shigella*, *Vibrio*, and *Yersinia*.
- Bacterial infection: Gram-positive organisms such as *Bacillus cereus*, *C. difficile*, and *Listeria*. Isolation of *Staphylococcus aureus* may indicate infection or a carrier state
- Botulism: *Clostridium botulinum* (the bacteria must also be isolated from the food or the presence of toxin confirmed in the stool specimen)
- Parasitic enterocolitis

CRITICAL FINDINGS ✧
- Bacterial pathogens: *Campylobacter*, *C. difficile*, *E. coli* including 0157:H7, *Listeria*, *Rotavirus*, *Salmonella*, *Shigella*, *Vibrio*, *Yersinia*, or parasites *Acanthamoeba*, *Ascaris* (hookworm), *Cyclospora*, *Cryptosporidium*, *Entamoeba histolytica*, *Giardia*, and *Strongyloides* (tapeworm), parasitic ova, proglottid, and larvae.

Note and immediately report to the health-care provider (HCP) positive results for bacterial pathogens or parasites. Lists of specific organisms may vary among facilities; specific organisms are required to be reported to local, state, and national departments of health. Timely notification of critical values for lab or diagnostic studies is a role expectation of the professional nurse. Notification processes will vary among facilities. Upon receipt of the critical value, the information should be read back to the caller to verify accuracy. Most policies require immediate notification of the primary HCP, hospitalist, or on-call HCP. Reported information includes the patient's name, unique identifiers, critical value, name of the person giving the report, and name of the person receiving the report. Documentation of notification should be made in the medical record with the name of the HCP notified, time and date of notification, and any orders received. Any delay in a timely

report of a critical value may require completion of a notification form with review by Risk Management.

INTERFERING FACTORS
- A rectal swab does not provide an adequate amount of specimen for evaluating the carrier state and should be avoided in favor of a standard stool specimen.
- A rectal swab should never be submitted for *Clostridium* toxin studies. Specimens for *Clostridium* toxins should be refrigerated if they are not immediately transported to the laboratory because toxins degrade rapidly.
- A rectal swab should never be submitted for *Campylobacter* culture. Excessive exposure of the sample to air or room temperature may damage this bacterium so that it will not grow in the culture.
- Therapy with antibiotics before specimen collection may decrease the type and the amount of bacteria.
- Failure to transport the culture within 1 hr of collection or urine contamination of the sample may affect results.
- Barium and laxatives used less than 1 wk before the test may reduce bacterial growth.

NURSING IMPLICATIONS AND PROCEDURE

PRETEST:
▸ Positively identify the patient using at least two unique identifiers before providing care, treatment, or services.
▸ *Patient Teaching:* Inform the patient this test can assist in identification of the organism causing infection.
▸ Obtain a history of the patient's complaints, including a list of known allergens.
▸ Obtain a history of the patient's gastrointestinal and immune systems, symptoms, and results of previously performed laboratory tests and diagnostic and surgical procedures.
▸ Obtain a history of the patient's travel to foreign countries.

Obtain a list of the patient's current medications, including herbs, nutritional supplements, and nutraceuticals (see Appendix F).

Note any recent medications that can interfere with test results.

Review the procedure with the patient. Address concerns about pain and explain that there may be some discomfort during the specimen collection. Inform the patient that specimen collection takes approximately 5 min. *Sensitivity to social and cultural issues,* as well as concern for modesty, is important in providing psychological support before, during, and after the procedure. There are no food or fluid restrictions unless by medical direction.

INTRATEST:

Ensure that the patient has complied with medication restrictions prior to the procedure.

Instruct the patient to cooperate fully and to follow directions. Direct the patient to breathe normally and to avoid unnecessary movement.

Observe standard precautions, and follow the general guidelines in Appendix A. Positively identify the patient, and label the appropriate collection containers with the corresponding patient demographics, date and time of collection, and any medication the patient is taking that may interfere with test results (e.g., antibiotics).

Collect a stool specimen directly into a clean container. If the patient requires a bedpan, make sure it is clean and dry, and use a tongue blade to transfer the specimen to the container. Make sure representative portions of the stool are sent for analysis. Note specimen appearance on collection container label.

Promptly transport the specimen to the laboratory for processing and analysis.

POST-TEST:

A report of the results will be made available to the requesting HCP, who will discuss the results with the patient.

Instruct the patient to resume usual medication as directed by the HCP.

Instruct the patient to report symptoms such as pain related to tissue inflammation or irritation.

Advise the patient that final test results may take up to 72 hr but that antibiotic therapy may be started immediately. Instruct the patient about the importance of completing the entire course of antibiotic therapy even if no symptoms are present. Note: Antibiotic therapy is frequently contraindicated for Salmonella infection unless the infection has progressed to a systemic state.

Recognize anxiety related to test results. Discuss the implications of abnormal test results on the patient's lifestyle. Provide teaching and information regarding the clinical implications of the test results, as appropriate.

Reinforce information given by the patient's HCP regarding further testing, treatment, or referral to another HCP. Emphasize the importance of reporting continued signs and symptoms of the infection. Provide information regarding vaccine-preventable diseases where indicated (e.g., anthrax, cervical cancer, diphtheria, encephalitis, hepatitis A and B, H1N1 flu, human papillomavirus, *Haemophilus influenza,* seasonal influenza, Lyme disease, measles, meningococcal disease, monkeypox, mumps, pertussis, pneumococcal disease, polio, rotavirus, rubella, shingles, smallpox, tetanus, typhoid fever, varicella, yellow fever). Provide contact information, if desired, for the Centers for Disease Control and Prevention (www.cdc.gov/vaccines/vpd-vac). Answer any questions or address any concerns voiced by the patient or family.

Depending on the results of this procedure, additional testing may be performed to evaluate or monitor progression of the disease process and determine the need for a change in therapy. Evaluate test results in relation to the patient's symptoms and other tests performed.

RELATED MONOGRAPHS:

Related tests include capsule endoscopy, colonoscopy, fecal analysis, Gram stain, ova and parasites, and proctosigmoidoscopy.

Refer to the Gastrointestinal and Immune systems tables at the end of the book for related tests by body system.

C

Culture, Bacterial, Throat or Nasopharyngeal

SYNONYM/ACRONYM: Routine throat culture.

COMMON USE: To identify pathogenic bacterial organisms in the throat and nares as an indicator for appropriate therapeutic interventions. Treat infections such as pharyngitis, thrush, strep throat, and screen for methicillin-resistant *Staphylococcus aureus* (MRSA).

SPECIMEN: Throat or nasopharyngeal swab.

NORMAL FINDINGS: (Method: Aerobic culture) No growth.

DESCRIPTION: The routine throat culture is a commonly ordered test to screen for the presence of group A β-hemolytic streptococci. *Streptococcus pyogenes* is the gram-positive organism that most commonly causes acute pharyngitis. The more dangerous sequelae of scarlet fever, rheumatic heart disease, and glomerulonephritis are less frequently seen because of the early treatment of infection at the pharyngitis stage. There are a number of other bacterial agents responsible for pharyngitis. Specific cultures can be set up to detect other pathogens such as *Bordetella*, *Corynebacteria* (gram positive), *Haemophilus* (gram negative), or *Neisseria* (gram negative) if they are suspected or by special request from the health-care provider (HCP). *Corynebacterium diphtheriae* is the causative agent of diphtheria. *Neisseria gonorrhoeae* is a sexually transmitted pathogen. In children, a positive throat culture for *Neisseria* usually indicates sexual abuse. The laboratory will initiate antibiotic sensitivity testing if indicated by test results. Sensitivity testing identifies the antibiotics to which the organisms are susceptible to ensure an effective treatment plan.

INDICATIONS
- Assist in the diagnosis of bacterial infections such as tonsillitis, diphtheria, gonorrhea, or pertussis
- Assist in the diagnosis of upper respiratory infections resulting in bronchitis, pharyngitis, croup, and influenza
- Isolate and identify group A β-hemolytic streptococci as the cause of strep throat, acute glomerulonephritis, scarlet fever, or rheumatic fever

POTENTIAL DIAGNOSIS
Reports on cultures that are positive for group A β-hemolytic streptococci are generally available within 24 to 48 hr. Cultures that report on normal respiratory flora are issued after 48 hr. Culture results of no growth for *Corynebacterium* require 72 hr to report; 48 hr are required to report negative *Neisseria* cultures.

CRITICAL FINDINGS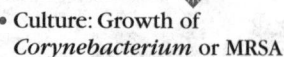
- Culture: Growth of *Corynebacterium* or MRSA

Note and immediately report to the HCP positive results and related symptoms. Lists of specific organisms may vary among facilities; specific organisms are required to be reported to local, state, and national departments of health. Timely notification of critical values for lab or diagnostic studies is a role expectation of the professional nurse. Notification processes will vary among facilities. Upon receipt of the critical value, the information should be read back to the caller to verify accuracy. Most policies require immediate notification of the primary HCP, hospitalist, or on-call HCP. Reported information includes the patient's name, unique identifiers, critical value, name of the person giving the report, and name of the person receiving the report. Documentation of notification should be made in the medical record with the name of the HCP notified, time and date of notification, and any orders received. Any delay in a timely report of a critical value may require completion of a notification form with review by Risk Management.

INTERFERING FACTORS
- Contamination with oral flora may invalidate results.
- Specimen collection after antibiotic therapy has been initiated may result in inhibited or no growth of organisms.

NURSING IMPLICATIONS AND PROCEDURE

PRETEST:
- Positively identify the patient using at least two unique identifiers before providing care, treatment, or services.
- *Patient Teaching:* Inform the patient this test can assist in identification of the organism causing infection.
- Obtain a history of the patient's complaints, including a list of known allergens, especially allergies or sensitivities to latex.
- Obtain a history of the patient's immune and respiratory systems, symptoms, and results of previously performed laboratory tests and diagnostic and surgical procedures.
- Obtain a list of the patient's current medications, including herbs, nutritional

supplements, and nutraceuticals (see Appendix F).
- Note any recent medications that can interfere with test results.
- Review the procedure with the patient. In cases of acute epiglottitis, do not swab the throat. This can cause a laryngospasm resulting in a loss of airway. A patient with epiglottitis will be sitting up and leaning forward in the tripod position with the head and jaw thrust forward to breathe. Address concerns about pain and explain that there may be some discomfort during the specimen collection. The time it takes to collect a proper specimen varies according to the level of cooperation of the patient. Inform the patient that specimen collection takes approximately 5 min.
- There are no food or fluid restrictions unless by medical direction.
- *Sensitivity to social and cultural issues,* as well as concern for modesty, is important in providing psychological support before, during, and after the procedure.

INTRATEST:
- Ensure that the patient has complied with medication restrictions prior to the procedure.
- Have emergency equipment readily available. Keep resuscitation equipment on hand in case of respiratory impairment or laryngospasm after the procedure.
- Instruct the patient to cooperate fully and to follow directions. Direct the patient to breathe normally and to avoid unnecessary movement.
- Observe standard precautions, and follow the general guidelines in Appendix A. Positively identify the patient, and label the appropriate collection containers with the corresponding patient demographics, date and time of collection, and any medication the patient is taking that may interfere with test results (e.g., antibiotics).
- To collect the throat culture, tilt the patient's head back. Swab both tonsillar pillars and oropharynx with the

sterile Culturette. A tongue depressor can be used to ensure that contact with the tongue and uvula is avoided.

A nasopharyngeal specimen is collected through the use of a flexible probe inserted through the nose and directed toward the back of the throat.

Place the swab in the Culturette tube and squeeze the bottom of the Culturette tube to release the liquid transport medium. Ensure that the end of the swab is immersed in the liquid transport medium.

Promptly transport the specimen to the laboratory for processing and analysis.

POST-TEST:

A report of the results will be made available to the requesting HCP, who will discuss the results with the patient.

Instruct the patient to resume usual medication as directed by the HCP.

Instruct the patient to notify the HCP immediately if difficulty in breathing or swallowing occurs or if bleeding occurs.

Instruct the patient to perform mouth care after the specimen has been obtained.

Provide comfort measures and treatment such as antiseptic gargles; inhalants; and warm, moist applications as needed. A cool beverage may aid in relieving throat irritation caused by coughing or suctioning.

Administer antibiotic therapy if ordered. Remind the patient of the importance of completing the entire course of antibiotic therapy, even if signs and symptoms disappear before completion of therapy.

Nutritional Considerations: Dehydration can been seen in patients with a bacterial throat infection due to pain with swallowing. Pain medications reduce patient's dysphagia and allow for adequate intake of fluids and foods.

Recognize anxiety related to test results. Discuss the implications of abnormal test results on the patient's lifestyle. Provide teaching and information regarding the clinical implications of the test results, as appropriate.

Reinforce information given by the patient's HCP regarding further testing, treatment, or referral to another HCP. Instruct the patient to use lozenges or gargle for throat discomfort. Inform the patient of smoking cessation programs as appropriate. Emphasize the importance of reporting continued signs and symptoms of the infection. Provide information regarding vaccine-preventable diseases where indicated (e.g., anthrax, cervical cancer, diphtheria, encephalitis, hepatitis A and B, H1N1 flu, human papillomavirus, *Haemophilus influenza*, seasonal influenza, Lyme disease, measles, meningococcal disease, monkeypox, mumps, pertussis, pneumococcal disease, polio, rotavirus, rubella, shingles, smallpox, tetanus, typhoid fever, varicella, yellow fever). Provide contact information, if desired, for the Centers for Disease Control and Prevention (www.cdc.gov/vaccines/vpd-vac). Answer any questions or address any concerns voiced by the patient or family.

Depending on the results of this procedure, additional testing may be performed to evaluate or monitor progression of the disease process and determine the need for a change in therapy. Evaluate test results in relation to the patient's symptoms and other tests performed.

RELATED MONOGRAPHS:

Related tests include CBC, Gram stain, and group A streptococcal (rapid) screen.

Refer to the Immune and Respiratory systems tables at the end of the book for related tests by body system.

Culture, Bacterial, Urine

SYNONYM/ACRONYM: Routine urine culture.

COMMON USE: To identify the pathogenic bacterial organisms in the urine as an indicator for appropriate therapeutic interventions to treat urinary tract infections.

SPECIMEN: Urine (5 mL) collected in a sterile plastic collection container. Transport tubes containing a preservative are highly recommended if testing will not occur within 2 hr of collection.

NORMAL FINDINGS: (Method: Culture on selective and enriched media) Negative: no growth.

DESCRIPTION: A urine culture involves collecting a urine specimen so that the organism causing disease can be isolated and identified. Urine can be collected by clean catch, urinary catheterization, or suprapubic aspiration. The severity of the infection or contamination of the specimen can be determined by knowing the type and number of organisms (colonies) present in the specimen. The laboratory will initiate sensitivity testing if indicated by test results. Sensitivity testing identifies the antibiotics to which the organisms are susceptible to ensure an effective treatment plan.

Commonly detected organisms are those normally found in the genitourinary tract, including gram negative *Enterococci, Escherichia coli, Klebsiella, Proteus,* and *Pseudomonas.* A culture showing multiple organisms indicates a contaminated specimen.

Colony counts of 100,000/mL or more indicate urinary tract infection (UTI).

Colony counts of 1,000/mL or less suggest contamination resulting from poor collection technique.

Colony counts between 1,000 and 10,000/mL may be significant depending on a variety of factors, including patient's age, gender, number of types of organisms present, method of specimen collection, and presence of antibiotics.

INDICATIONS
- Assist in the diagnosis of suspected UTI
- Determine the sensitivity of significant organisms to antibiotics
- Monitor the response to UTI treatment

POTENTIAL DIAGNOSIS

Positive findings in
- UTIs

Negative findings in: N/A

CRITICAL FINDINGS
- Gram negative extended spectrum beta lactamases (ESBL) *E. coli* or *Klebsiella*
- Gram negative *Legionella*
- Gram positive Vancomycin-resistant *Enterococci* (VRE)

Note and immediately report to the health-care provider (HCP) positive

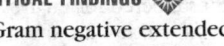

results and related symptoms. Lists of specific organisms may vary among facilities; specific organisms are required to be reported to local, state, and national departments of health. Timely notification of critical values for lab or diagnostic studies is a role expectation of the professional nurse. Notification processes will vary among facilities. Upon receipt of the critical value, the information should be read back to the caller to verify accuracy. Most policies require immediate notification of the primary HCP, hospitalist, or on-call HCP. Reported information includes the patient's name, unique identifiers, critical value, name of the person giving the report, and name of the person receiving the report. Documentation of notification should be made in the medical record with the name of the HCP notified, time and date of notification, and any orders received. Any delay in a timely report of a critical value may require completion of a notification form with review by Risk Management.

INTERFERING FACTORS

- Antibiotic therapy initiated before specimen collection may produce false-negative results.
- Improper collection techniques may result in specimen contamination.
- Specimen storage for longer than 2 hr at room temperature or 24 hr at refrigerated temperature may result in overgrowth of bacteria and false-positive results. Such specimens may be rejected for analysis.
- Results of urine culture are often interpreted along with routine urinalysis findings.
- Discrepancies between culture and urinalysis may be reason to re-collect the specimen.
- Specimens submitted in expired urine transport tubes will be rejected for analysis.

NURSING IMPLICATIONS AND PROCEDURE

PRETEST:

- Positively identify the patient using at least two unique identifiers before providing care, treatment, or services.
- *Patient Teaching:* Inform the patient this test can assist in identification of the organism causing infection.
- Obtain a history of the patient's complaints, including a list of known allergens.
- Obtain a history of the patient's genitourinary and immune systems, symptoms, and results of previously performed laboratory tests and diagnostic and surgical procedures.
- Obtain a list of the patient's current medications, including herbs, nutritional supplements, and nutraceuticals (see Appendix F).
- Note any recent medications that can interfere with test results.
- Review the procedure with the patient. Address concerns about pain and explain that there should be no discomfort during the specimen collection. Inform the patient that specimen collection depends on patient cooperation and usually takes approximately 5 to 10 min.
- *Sensitivity to social and cultural issues,* as well as concern for modesty, is important in providing psychological support before, during, and after the procedure.
- There are no food or fluid restrictions, unless by medical direction.
- Instruct the patient on clean-catch procedure and provide necessary supplies.

INTRATEST:

- Ensure that the patient has complied with medication restrictions prior to the procedure.
- Instruct the patient to cooperate fully and to follow directions. Direct the patient to breathe normally and to avoid unnecessary movement.
- Observe standard precautions, and follow the general guidelines in Appendix A. Positively identify the patient, and

label the appropriate collection containers with the corresponding patient demographics, date and time of collection, method of specimen collection, and any medications the patient has taken that may interfere with test results (e.g., antibiotics).

Clean-Catch Specimen

Instruct the male patient to (1) thoroughly wash his hands, (2) cleanse the meatus, (3) void a small amount into the toilet, and (4) void directly into the specimen container.

Instruct the female patient to (1) thoroughly wash her hands; (2) cleanse the labia from front to back; (3) while keeping the labia separated, void a small amount into the toilet; and (4) without interrupting the urine stream, void directly into the specimen container.

Pediatric Urine Collector

Put on gloves. Appropriately cleanse the genital area, and allow the area to dry. Remove the covering over the adhesive strips on the collector bag and apply over the genital area. Diaper the child. When specimen is obtained, place the entire collection bag in a sterile urine container.

Indwelling Catheter

Put on gloves. Empty drainage tube of urine. It may be necessary to clamp off the catheter for 15 to 30 min before specimen collection. Cleanse specimen port with antiseptic swab, and then aspirate 5 mL of urine with a 21- to 25-gauge needle and syringe. Transfer urine to a sterile container.

Urinary Catheterization

Place female patient in lithotomy position or male patient in supine position. Using sterile technique, open the straight urinary catheterization kit and perform urinary catheterization. Place the retained urine in a sterile specimen container.

Suprapubic Aspiration

Place the patient in supine position. Cleanse the area with antiseptic, and drape with sterile drapes. A needle is inserted through the skin into the bladder. A syringe attached to the needle is used to aspirate the urine sample. The needle is then removed and a

sterile dressing is applied to the site. Place the sterile sample in a sterile specimen container.

Do not collect urine from the pouch from a patient with a urinary diversion (e.g., ileal conduit). Instead, perform catheterization through the stoma.

General

Promptly transport the specimen to the laboratory for processing and analysis. If a delay in transport is expected, an aliquot of the specimen into a special tube containing a preservative is recommended. Urine transport tubes can be requested from the laboratory.

POST-TEST:

A report of the results will be made available to the requesting HCP, who will discuss the results with the patient.

Instruct the patient to resume usual medication as directed by the HCP.

Instruct the patient to report symptoms such as pain related to tissue inflammation, pain or irritation during void, bladder spasms, or alterations in urinary elimination.

Observe for signs of inflammation if the specimen is obtained by suprapubic aspiration.

Administer antibiotic therapy as ordered. Remind the patient of the importance of completing the entire course of antibiotic therapy, even if signs and symptoms disappear before completion of therapy.

Nutritional Considerations: Instruct the patient to increase water consumption by drinking 8 to 12 glasses of water to assist in flushing the urinary tract. Instruct the patient to avoid alcohol, caffeine, and carbonated beverages, which can cause bladder irritation.

Prevention of UTIs includes increasing daily water consumption, urinating when urge occurs, wiping the perineal area from front to back after urination/defecation, and urinating immediately after intercourse. Prevention also includes maintaining the normal flora of the body. Patients should avoid using spermicidal creams with diaphragms or condoms (when recommended by an

HCP), becoming constipated, douching, taking bubble baths, wearing tight-fitting garments, and using deodorizing feminine hygiene products that alter the body's normal flora and increase susceptibility to UTIs.

▶ Recognize anxiety related to test results. Discuss the implications of abnormal test results on the patient's lifestyle. Provide teaching and information regarding the clinical implications of the test results, as appropriate.

▶ Reinforce information given by the patient's HCP regarding further testing, treatment, or referral to another HCP. Emphasize the importance of reporting continued signs and symptoms of the infection. Instruct patient on the proper technique for wiping the perineal area (front to back) after a bowel movement. Answer any questions or address any concerns voiced by the patient or family.

▶ Depending on the results of this procedure, additional testing may be performed to evaluate or monitor progression of the disease process and determine the need for a change in therapy. Evaluate test results in relation to the patient's symptoms and other tests performed.

RELATED MONOGRAPHS:

▶ Related tests include CBC, CBC WBC count and differential, cystometry, cystoscopy, cystourethrography voiding, cytology urine, Gram stain, renogram, and UA.

▶ Refer to the Genitourinary and Immune systems tables at the end of the book for related tests by body system.

Culture, Fungal

SYNONYM/ACRONYM: N/A.

COMMON USE: To identify the pathogenic fungal organisms causing infection.

SPECIMEN: Hair, skin, nail, pus, sterile fluids, blood, bone marrow, stool, bronchial washings, sputum, or tissue samples collected in a sterile plastic, tightly capped container.

NORMAL FINDINGS: (Method: Culture on selective media; macroscopic and microscopic examination) No presence of fungi.

DESCRIPTION: Fungi, organisms that normally live in soil, can be introduced into humans through the accidental inhalation of spores or inoculation of spores into tissue through trauma. Individuals most susceptible to fungal infection usually are debilitated by chronic disease, are receiving prolonged antibiotic therapy, or have impaired immune systems. Fungal diseases may be classified according to the involved tissue type: dermatophytoses involve superficial and cutaneous tissue; there are also subcutaneous and systemic mycoses.

INDICATIONS

• Determine antimicrobial sensitivity of the organism
• Isolate and identify organisms responsible for nail infections or abnormalities

- Isolate and identify organisms responsible for skin eruptions, drainage, or other evidence of infection

POTENTIAL DIAGNOSIS

Positive findings in
- Blood
  Candida albicans
  Histoplasma capsulatum

- Cerebrospinal fluid
  Coccidioides immitis
  Cryptococcus neoformans
  Members of the order Mucorales
  Paracoccidioides brasiliensis
  Sporothrix schenckii

- Hair
  Epidermophyton
  Microsporum
  Trichophyton

- Nails
  C. albicans
  Cephalosporium
  Epidermophyton
  Trichophyton

- Skin
  Actinomyces israelii
  C. albicans
  C. immitis
  Epidermophyton
  Microsporum
  Trichophyton

- Tissue
  A. israelii
  Aspergillus
  C. albicans
  Nocardia
  P. brasiliensis

CRITICAL FINDINGS

- Positive findings in any sterile body fluid such as blood or cerebrospinal fluid

Note and immediately report to the health-care provider (HCP) positive results and related symptoms. Lists of specific organisms may vary among

facilities; specific organisms are required to be reported to local, state, and national departments of health. Timely notification of critical values for lab or diagnostic studies is a role expectation of the professional nurse. Notification processes will vary among facilities. Upon receipt of the critical value, the information should be read back to the caller to verify accuracy. Most policies require immediate notification of the primary HCP, hospitalist, or on-call HCP. Reported information includes the patient's name, unique identifiers, critical value, name of the person giving the report, and name of the person receiving the report. Documentation of notification should be made in the medical record with the name of the HCP notified, time and date of notification, and any orders received. Any delay in a timely report of a critical value may require completion of a notification form with review by Risk Management.

INTERFERING FACTORS
Prompt and proper specimen processing, storage, and analysis are important to achieve accurate results.

NURSING IMPLICATIONS AND PROCEDURE

PRETEST:
- Positively identify the patient using at least two unique identifiers before providing care, treatment, or services.
- *Patient Teaching:* Inform the patient this test can assist in identification of the organism causing infection.
- Obtain a history of the patient's complaints, including a list of known allergens.
- Obtain a history of the patient's immune system, symptoms, and results of previously performed laboratory tests and diagnostic and surgical procedures.
- Obtain a list of the patient's current medications, including herbs,

nutritional supplements, and nutraceuticals (see Appendix F).

- Note any recent medications that can interfere with test results.
- Review the procedure with the patient. Inform the patient that specimen collection takes approximately 5 min. Address concerns about pain and explain that there may be some discomfort during the specimen collection.
- *Sensitivity to social and cultural issues,* as well as concern for modesty, is important in providing psychological support before, during, and after the procedure.
- There are no food or fluid restrictions unless by medical direction.

INTRATEST:

- Instruct the patient to cooperate fully and to follow directions. Direct the patient to breathe normally and to avoid unnecessary movement.
- Observe standard precautions, and follow the general guidelines in Appendix A. Instructions regarding the appropriate transport materials for blood, bone marrow, bronchial washings, sputum, sterile fluids, stool, and tissue samples should be obtained from the laboratory. Positively identify the patient, and label the appropriate collection containers with the corresponding patient demographics, initials of the person collecting the specimen, date, and time of collection.
- Promptly transport the specimen to the laboratory for processing and analysis.

Skin

Clean the collection site with 70% alcohol. Scrape the peripheral margin of the collection site with a sterile scalpel or wooden spatula. Place the scrapings in a sterile collection container.

Hair

Fungi usually grow at the base of the hair shaft. Infected hairs can be identified by using a Wood's lamp in a darkened room. A Wood's lamp provides rays of ultraviolet light at a wavelength of 366 nm, or 3,660 Å. Infected hairs fluoresce a bright yellow-green when exposed to light from the Wood's lamp. Using tweezers, pluck hair from skin.

Nails

Ideally, softened material from the nailbed is sampled from beneath the nail plate. Alternatively, shavings from the deeper portions of the nail itself can be collected.

The potassium hydroxide (KOH) test is used to indicate the presence of mycelium, mycelial fragments, spores, or budding yeast cells. A portion of the specimen is mixed with 15% KOH on a glass slide, and then a cover slip is placed over the specimen on the slide. The slide is examined under a microscope for the presence of fungal elements.

POST-TEST:

- A report of the results will be made available to the requesting HCP, who will discuss the results with the patient.
- Instruct patient to begin antifungal therapy, as prescribed. Instruct the patient in the importance of completing the entire course of antifungal therapy even if no symptoms are present.
- Recognize anxiety related to test results. Discuss the implications of abnormal test results on the patient's lifestyle. Provide teaching and information regarding the clinical implications of the test results, as appropriate.
- Reinforce information given by the patient's HCP regarding further testing, treatment, or referral to another HCP. Emphasize the importance of reporting continued signs and symptoms of the infection. Answer any questions or address any concerns voiced by the patient or family.
- Depending on the results of this procedure, additional testing may be performed to evaluate or monitor progression of the disease process and determine the need for a change in therapy. Evaluate test results in relation to the patient's symptoms and other tests performed.

Related tests include relevant biopsies (lung, lymph node, skin), bronchoscopy, cultures (blood, mycobacteria, throat, sputum, viral), CSF analysis, gallium scan, HIV-1/2 antibodies, pulmonary function tests, and TB tests. Refer to the Immune System table at the end of the book for related tests by body system.

Culture, Viral

SYNONYM/ACRONYM: N/A.

COMMON USE: To identify infection caused by pathogenic viral organisms as evidenced by ocular, genitourinary, intestinal, or respiratory symptoms. Commonly identified are cytomegalovirus (CMV), Epstein-Barr virus, herpes simplex virus (HSV), HIV, human papillomavirus (HPV), respiratory syncytial virus (RSV), and varicella zoster virus.

SPECIMEN: Urine, semen, blood, body fluid, stool, tissue, or swabs from the affected site.

NORMAL FINDINGS: (Method: Culture in special media, enzyme-linked immunoassays, direct fluorescent antibody techniques, latex agglutination, immunoperoxidase techniques) No virus isolated.

DESCRIPTION: Viruses, the most common cause of human infection, are submicroscopic organisms that invade living cells. They can be classified as either RNA- or DNA-type viruses. Viral titers are highest in the early stages of disease before the host has begun to manufacture significant antibodies against the invader. Specimens need to be collected as early as possible in the disease process.

INDICATIONS
Assist in the identification of viral infection

POTENTIAL DIAGNOSIS

Positive findings in
- AIDS
  HIV

- Acute respiratory failure
  Hantavirus
- Anorectal infections
  HSV
  HPV
- Bronchitis
  Parainfluenza virus
  RSV
- Cervical cancer
  HPV
- Condylomata
  HPV
- Conjunctivitis/keratitis
  Adenovirus
  Epstein-Barr virus
  HSV
  Measles virus
  Parvovirus
  Rubella virus
  Varicella zoster virus
  (shingles)

- Croup
  Parainfluenza virus
  RSV

- Cutaneous infection with rash
  Enteroviruses
  HSV
  Varicella zoster virus

- Encephalitis
  Enteroviruses
  Flaviviruses
  HSV
  HIV
  Measles virus
  Rabies virus
  Togaviruses
  West Nile virus (mosquito-borne arbovirus)

- Febrile illness with rash
  Coxsackieviruses
  Echovirus

- Gastroenteritis
  Norwalk virus
  Rotavirus

- Genital herpes
  HSV-1
  HSV-2

- Genital warts
  HPV

- Hemorrhagic cystitis
  Adenovirus

- Hemorrhagic fever
  Ebola virus
  Hantavirus
  Lassa virus
  Marburg virus

- Herpangina
  Coxsackievirus (group A)

- Infectious mononucleosis
  CMV
  Epstein-Barr virus

- Meningitis
  Coxsackieviruses
  Echovirus
  HSV-2
  Lymphocytic choriomeningitis virus

- Myocarditis/pericarditis
  Coxsackievirus
  Echovirus

- Parotitis
  Mumps virus
  Parainfluenza virus

- Pharyngitis
  Adenovirus
  Coxsackievirus (group A)
  Epstein-Barr virus
  HSV
  H1N1 influenza virus (swine flu)
  Influenza virus
  Parainfluenza virus
  Rhinovirus

- Pleurodynia
  Coxsackievirus (group B)

- Pneumonia
  Adenovirus
  H1N1 influenza virus (swine flu)
  Influenza virus
  Parainfluenza virus
  RSV

- Upper respiratory tract infection
  Adenovirus
  Coronavirus
  H1N1 influenza virus (swine flu)
  Influenza virus
  Parainfluenza virus
  RSV
  Rhinovirus

CRITICAL FINDINGS ❖

Positive RSV, influenza, and varicella zoster cultures should be reported immediately to the requesting healthcare provider (HCP).

Note and immediately report to the HCP positive results and related symptoms. Lists of specific organisms may vary among facilities; specific organisms are required to be reported to local, state, and national departments of health. Timely notification of critical values for lab or diagnostic studies is a role expectation of the professional nurse. Notification processes will vary among facilities. Upon receipt of the critical value, the information should be read back to the caller to verify accuracy. Most policies require immediate notification of the primary HCP, hospitalist, or on-call HCP. Reported information includes the patient's name, unique identifiers, critical value, name of the person giving the report, and name of the person receiving the report. Documentation of notification should be made in the medical record with the name of the HCP notified, time and date of notification, and any orders received. Any delay in a timely report of a critical value may require completion of a notification form with review by Risk Management.

INTERFERING FACTORS

Viral specimens are unstable. Prompt and proper specimen processing, storage, and analysis are important to achieve accurate results.

NURSING IMPLICATIONS AND PROCEDURE

PRETEST:

▸ Positively identify the patient using at least two unique identifiers before providing care, treatment, or services.
▸ *Patient Teaching:* Inform the patient this test can assist in identification of the organism causing infection.
▸ Obtain a history of the patient's complaints, including a list of known allergens, especially allergies or sensitivities to latex.
▸ Obtain a history of the patient's gastrointestinal, genitourinary, immune, reproductive, and respiratory systems; symptoms; and results of previously performed laboratory tests and diagnostic and surgical procedures.
▸ Obtain a list of the patient's current medications, including herbs, nutritional supplements, and nutraceuticals (see Appendix F).
▸ Note any recent medications that can interfere with test results.

▸ Review the procedure with the patient. Inform the patient that specimen collection takes approximately 5 min. Address concerns about pain and explain that there may be some discomfort during the specimen collection.
▸ There are no food, fluid, or medication restrictions unless by medical direction.
▸ *Sensitivity to social and cultural issues,* as well as concern for modesty, is important in providing psychological support before, during, and after the procedure.

INTRATEST:

▸ Instruct the patient to cooperate fully and to follow directions. Direct the patient to breathe normally and to avoid unnecessary movement.
▸ Observe standard precautions, and follow the general guidelines in Appendix A. Positively identify the patient, and label the appropriate collection containers with the corresponding patient demographics, date and time of collection, exact site, contact person for notification of results, and other pertinent information (e.g., patient immunocompromised owing to organ transplant, radiation, or chemotherapy).
▸ Instructions regarding the appropriate transport materials for blood, bronchial washings, sputum, sterile fluids, stool, and tissue samples should be obtained from the laboratory. The type of applicator used to obtain swabs should be verified by consultation with the testing laboratory personnel.
▸ The appropriate viral transport material should be obtained from the laboratory. Nasopharyngeal washings or swabs for RSV testing should be immediately placed in cold viral transport media.
▸ Promptly transport the specimen to the laboratory for processing and analysis.

POST-TEST:

▸ A report of the results will be made available to the requesting HCP, who will discuss the results with the patient.
▸ *Nutritional Considerations:* Dehydration can been seen in patients with viral infections due to loss of fluids through fever, diarrhea, and/or vomiting.

Antipyretic medication includes acetaminophen to decrease fever and allow for adequate intake of fluids and foods. Do not give acetylsalicylic acid to pediatric patients with a viral illness because it increases the risk of Reye's syndrome. *Sensitivity to social and cultural issues:* Offer support, as appropriate, to patients who may be the victims of rape or sexual assault. Educate the patient regarding access to counseling services. Provide a nonjudgmental, nonthreatening atmosphere for discussing the risks of sexually transmitted diseases. It is also important to address problems the patient may experience (e.g., guilt, depression, anger).

Recognize anxiety related to test results. Discuss the implications of abnormal test results on the patient's lifestyle. Provide teaching and information regarding the clinical implications of the test results, as appropriate.

Reinforce information given by the patient's HCP regarding further testing, treatment, or referral to another HCP. Provide information regarding vaccine-preventable diseases where indicated (e.g., anthrax, cervical cancer, diphtheria, encephalitis, hepatitis A and B, H1N1 flu, HPV, *Haemophilus influenza*, seasonal influenza, Lyme disease, measles, meningococcal disease, monkeypox, mumps, pertussis, pneumococcal disease, polio, rotavirus, rubella, shingles, smallpox, tetanus, typhoid fever, varicella, yellow fever). Provide contact information, if desired, for the Centers for Disease Control and Prevention (www.cdc.gov/vaccines/vpd-vac). Answer any questions or address any concerns voiced by the patient or family.

Depending on the results of this procedure, additional testing may be performed to evaluate or monitor progression of the disease process and determine the need for a change in therapy. Evaluate test results in relation to the patient's symptoms and other tests performed.

RELATED MONOGRAPHS:

Related tests include alveolar/arterial gradient, β-2-microglobulin, barium enema, biopsy (cervical, intestinal, kidney, liver, lung, lymph node, muscle, skin), blood gases, bronchoscopy, CD4/CD8 ratio, CSF analysis, *Chlamydia* group antibody, chest x-ray, cultures (anal, blood, ear, eye, fungal, genital, mycobacteria, skin, sputum, stool, throat, urine, wound), CBC, cytology (sputum, urine), gallium scan, gastric emptying scan, lung perfusion scan, lung ventilation scan, Pap smear, pericardial fluid analysis, plethysmography, pulse oximetry, PFT, slit-lamp biomicroscopy, syphilis serology, TB tests, and viral serology tests (hepatitis, HIV, HTLV, infectious mononucleosis, mumps, rubella, rubeola, varicella).

Refer to the Gastrointestinal, Genitourinary, Immune, Reproductive, and Respiratory systems tables at the end of the book for related tests by body system.

Cystometry

SYNONYM/ACRONYM: CMG, urodynamic testing of bladder function.

COMMON USE: To assess bladder function related to obstruction, neurogenic pathology, and infection including evaluation of surgical, and medical management.

AREA OF APPLICATION: Bladder, urethra.

CONTRAST: None.

DESCRIPTION: Cystometry evaluates the motor and sensory function of the bladder when incontinence is present or neurological bladder dysfunction is suspected and monitors the effects of treatment for the abnormalities. This noninvasive manometric study measures the bladder pressure and volume characteristics in milliliters of water (cm H_2O) during the filling and emptying phases. The test provides information about bladder structure and function that can lead to uninhibited bladder contractions, sensations of bladder fullness and need to void, and ability to inhibit voiding. These abnormalities cause incontinence and other impaired patterns of micturition. Cystometry can be performed with cystoscopy and sphincter electromyography.

INDICATIONS

- Detect congenital urinary abnormalities
- Determine cause of bladder dysfunction and pathology
- Determine cause of recurrent urinary tract infections (UTIs)
- Determine cause of urinary retention
- Determine type of incontinence: *functional* (involuntary and unpredictable), *reflex* (involuntary when a specific volume is reached), *stress* (weak pelvic muscles), *total* (continuous and unpredictable), *urge* (involuntary when urgency is sensed), and *psychological* (e.g., dementia, confusion affecting awareness)
- Determine type of neurogenic bladder (motor or sensory)
- Evaluate the management of neurological bladder before surgical intervention
- Evaluate postprostatectomy incontinence

- Evaluate signs and symptoms of urinary elimination pattern dysfunction
- Evaluate urinary obstruction in male patients experiencing urinary retention
- Evaluate the usefulness of drug therapy on detrusor muscle function and tonicity and on internal and external sphincter function
- Evaluate voiding disorders associated with spinal cord injury

POTENTIAL DIAGNOSIS

Normal findings in

- Absence of residual urine (0 mL)
- Normal sensory perception of bladder fullness, desire to void, and ability to inhibit urination; appropriate response to temperature (hot and cold)
- Normal bladder capacity: 350 to 750 mL for men and 250 to 550 mL for women
- Normal functioning bladder pressure: 8 to 15 cm H_2O
- Normal sensation of fullness: 40 to 100 cm H_2O or 300 to 500 mL
- Normal bladder pressure during voiding: 30 to 40 cm H_2O
- Normal detrusor pressure: less than 10 cm H_2O
- Normal urge to void: 150 to 450 mL
- Normal filling pattern
- Urethral pressure that is higher than bladder pressure, ensuring continence

Abnormal findings in

- Flaccid bladder that fills without contracting
- Inability to perceive bladder fullness
- Inability to initiate or maintain urination without applying external pressure
- Sensory or motor paralysis of bladder
- Total loss of conscious sensation and vesical control or uncontrollable micturition (incontinence)

CRITICAL FINDINGS: N/A

INTERFERING FACTORS

This procedure is contraindicated for

- Patients with acute UTIs because the study can cause infection to spread to the kidneys.
- Patients who are pregnant or suspected of being pregnant, unless the potential benefits of the procedure far outweigh the risks to the fetus and mother.
- Patients with urethral obstruction.
- Patients with cervical cord lesions because they may exhibit autonomic dysreflexia, as seen by bradycardia, flushing, hypertension, diaphoresis, and headache.
- Inability to catheterize the patient.

Factors that may impair the results of the examination

- Inability of the patient to cooperate or remain still during the procedure because of age, significant pain, or mental status.
- Inability of the patient to void in a supine position or straining to void during the study.
- A high level of patient anxiety or embarrassment, which may interfere with the study, making it difficult to distinguish whether the results are due to stress or organic pathology.
- Administration of drugs that affect bladder function, such as muscle relaxants or antihistamines.

NURSING IMPLICATIONS AND PROCEDURE

PRETEST:

▶ Positively identify the patient using at least two unique identifiers before providing care, treatment, or services.
▶ *Patient Teaching:* Inform the patient this procedure can assist in assessing bladder function.
▶ Obtain a history of the patient's complaints including a list of known allergens, especially allergies or sensitivities

to latex, iodine, seafood, contrast medium, anesthetics, and dyes.
▶ Obtain a history of the patient's genitourinary system, symptoms, and results of previously performed laboratory tests and diagnostic and surgical procedures. Ensure results of coagulation and urinalysis testing are obtained and recorded prior to the procedure.
▶ Record the date of the last menstrual period and determine the possibility of pregnancy in perimenopausal women.
▶ Obtain a list of the patient's current medications, including anticoagulants, aspirin and other salicylates, herbs, nutritional supplements, and nutraceuticals (see Appendix F). Note the last time and dose of medication taken.
▶ Review the procedure with the patient. Address concerns about pain and explain that there may be moments of discomfort and some pain experienced during the test. Inform the patient that the procedure is performed in a special urology room or in a clinic setting by the health-care provider (HCP), with support staff, and takes approximately 30 to 45 min.
▶ *Sensitivity to social and cultural issues,* as well as concern for modesty, is important in providing psychological support before, during, and after the procedure.
▶ Instruct the patient to report pain, sweating, nausea, headache, and the urge to void during the study.
▶ Instruct the patient to remove jewelry and other metallic objects in the area to be examined.
▶ There are no food, fluid, or medication restrictions unless by medical direction.
▶ *Make sure a written and informed consent has been signed prior to the procedure and before administering any medications.*

INTRATEST:

▶ Observe standard precautions, and follow the general guidelines in Appendix A
▶ Positively identify the patient.
▶ Ensure that the patient has removed all external metallic objects from the area to be examined prior to the procedure.
▶ Instruct the patient to change into the gown, robe, and foot coverings provided, but not to void.

Position the patient in a supine or litho-tomy position on the examination table. If spinal cord injury is present, the patient can remain on a stretcher in a supine position and be draped appropriately.

Ask the patient to void. During voiding, note characteristics such as start time; force and continuity of the stream; volume voided; presence of dribbling, straining, or hesitancy; and stop time.

Instruct the patient to cooperate fully and to follow directions. Instruct the patient to remain still during the procedure.

A urinary catheter is inserted into the bladder under sterile conditions, and residual urine is measured and recorded. A test for sensory response to temperature is done by instilling 30 mL of room-temperature sterile water followed by 30 mL of warm sterile water. Sensations are assessed and recorded.

Fluid is removed from the bladder, and the catheter is connected to a cysto-meter that measures the pressure. Sterile normal saline, distilled water, or carbon dioxide gas is instilled in controlled amounts into the bladder. When the patient indicates the urge to void, the bladder is considered full. The patient is instructed to void, and urination amounts as well as start and stop times are then recorded.

Pressure and volume readings are recorded and graphed for response to heat, full bladder, urge to void, and ability to inhibit voiding. The patient is requested to void without straining, and pressures are taken and recorded during this activity.

After completion of voiding, the bladder is emptied of any other fluid, and the catheter is withdrawn, unless further testing is planned.

Further testing may be done to determine if abnormal bladder function is being caused by muscle incompetence or interruption in innervation; anticholinergic medication (e.g., atropine) or cholinergic medication (e.g., bethanechol [Urecholine]) can be injected and the study repeated in 20 or 30 min.

POST-TEST:

A report of the results will be made available to the requesting HCP, who will discuss the results with the patient.

Monitor fluid intake and urinary output for 24 hr after the procedure.

Monitor vital signs after the procedure every 15 min for 2 hr or as directed. Monitor intake and output at least every 8 hr. Elevated temperature may indicate infection. Notify the HCP if temperature is elevated. Protocols may vary among facilities.

Instruct the patient to immediately report symptoms such as fast heart rate, difficulty breathing, skin rash, itching, chest pain, persistent right shoulder pain, or abdominal pain. Immediately report symptoms to the appropriate HCP.

Inform the patient that he or she may experience burning or discomfort on urination for a few voidings after the procedure.

Persistent flank or suprapubic pain, fever, chills, blood in the urine, difficulty urinating, or change in urinary pattern must be reported immediately to the HCP.

Recognize anxiety related to test results. Discuss the implications of abnormal test results on the patient's lifestyle. Provide teaching and information regarding the clinical implications of the test results, as appropriate.

Reinforce information given by the patient's HCP regarding further testing, treatment, or referral to another HCP. Answer any questions or address any concerns voiced by the patient or family.

Depending on the results of this procedure, additional testing may be needed to evaluate or monitor progression of the disease process and determine the need for a change in therapy. Evaluate test results in relation to the patient's symptoms and other tests performed.

RELATED MONOGRAPHS:

Related tests include bladder cancer markers, calculus kidney stone panel, *Chlamydia* group antibody, CBC, CBC hematocrit, CBC hemoglobin, CT pelvis, culture urine, cytology urine, IVP, MRI pelvis, PT/INR, US pelvis, and UA.

Refer to the Genitourinary System table at the end of the book for related tests by body system.

Cystoscopy

SYNONYM/ACRONYM: Cystoureterography, prostatography.

COMMON USE: To assess the urinary tract for bleeding, cancer, tumor, and prostate health.

AREA OF APPLICATION: Bladder, urethra, ureteral orifices.

CONTRAST: None.

DESCRIPTION: Cystoscopy provides direct visualization of the urethra, urinary bladder, and ureteral orifices—areas not usually visible with x-ray procedures. This procedure is also used to obtain specimens and treat pathology associated with the aforementioned structures. Cystoscopy is accomplished by transurethral insertion of a cystoscope into the bladder. Rigid cystoscopes contain an obturator and a telescope with a lens and light system; there are also flexible cystoscopes, which use fiberoptic technology. The procedure may be performed during or after ultrasonography or radiography, or during urethroscopy or retrograde pyelography.

INDICATIONS
- Coagulate bleeding areas
- Determine the possible source of persistent urinary tract infections
- Determine the source of hematuria of unknown cause
- Differentiate, through tissue biopsy, between benign and cancerous lesions involving the bladder
- Dilate the urethra and ureters
- Evacuate blood clots and perform fulguration of bleeding sites within the lower urinary tract
- Evaluate changes in urinary elimination patterns

- Evaluate the extent of prostatic hyperplasia and degree of obstruction
- Evaluate the function of each kidney by obtaining urine samples via ureteral catheters
- Evaluate urinary tract abnormalities such as dysuria, frequency, retention, inadequate stream, urgency, and incontinence
- Identify and remove polyps and small tumors (including by fulguration) from the bladder
- Identify congenital anomalies, such as duplicate ureters, ureteroceles, urethral or ureteral strictures, diverticula, and areas of inflammation or ulceration
- Implant radioactive seeds
- Place ureteral catheters to drain urine from the renal pelvis or for retrograde pyelography
- Place ureteral stents and resect prostate gland tissue (transurethral resection of the prostate)
- Remove renal calculi from the bladder or ureters
- Resect small tumors

POTENTIAL DIAGNOSIS

Normal findings in
- Normal ureter, bladder, and urethral structure

Abnormal findings in
- Diverticulum of the bladder, fistula, stones, and strictures

- Inflammation or infection
- Obstruction
- Polyps
- Prostatic hypertrophy or hyperplasia
- Renal calculi
- Tumors
- Ureteral or urethral stricture
- Urinary tract malformation and congenital anomalies

CRITICAL FINDINGS: N/A

INTERFERING FACTORS

This procedure is contraindicated for

- Patients who are pregnant or suspected of being pregnant, unless the potential benefits of the procedure far outweigh the risks to the fetus and mother.
- Patients with bleeding disorders because instrumentation may lead to excessive bleeding from the lower urinary tract.
- Patients with acute cystitis or urethritis because instrumentation could allow bacteria to enter the bloodstream, resulting in septicemia.

Factors that may impair clear imaging

- Inability of the patient to cooperate or remain still during the procedure because of age, significant pain, or mental status.

Other considerations

- Failure to follow dietary restrictions before the procedure may cause the procedure to be canceled or repeated.

NURSING IMPLICATIONS AND PROCEDURE

PRETEST:

Positively identify the patient using at least two unique identifiers before providing care, treatment, or services.

Patient Teaching: Inform the patient this procedure can assist in assessing the urinary tract.

Obtain a history of the patient's complaints, including a list of known allergens, especially allergies or sensitivities to latex, iodine, seafood, contrast medium, anesthetics, and dyes.

Obtain a history of results of the patient's genitourinary system, symptoms, and previously performed laboratory tests and diagnostic and surgical procedures.

Record the date of the last menstrual period and determine the possibility of pregnancy in perimenopausal women.

Obtain a list of the patient's current medications, including anticoagulants, aspirin and other salicylates, herbs, nutritional supplements, and nutraceuticals (see Appendix F). Such products should be discontinued by medical direction for the appropriate number of days prior to a surgical procedure. Note the last time and dose of medication taken.

Review the procedure with the patient. Address concerns about pain and explain that there may be moments of discomfort and some pain experienced during the test. Inform the patient that the procedure is usually performed in a special cystoscopy suite near or in the surgery department by a health-care provider (HCP), with support staff, and takes approximately 30 to 60 min.

Sensitivity to social and cultural issues, as well as concern for modesty, is important in providing psychological support before, during, and after the procedure.

Restrict food and fluids for 8 hr if the patient is having general or spinal anesthesia. For local anesthesia, allow only clear liquids 8 hr before the procedure. Protocols may vary among facilities.

Obtain and record the patient's vital signs.

Make sure a written and informed consent has been signed prior to the procedure and before administering any medications.

INTRATEST:

Observe standard precautions, and follow the general guidelines in

Appendix A. Positively identify the patient, and label the appropriate specimen container with the corresponding patient demographics, initials of the person collecting the specimen, date, and time of collection.

Ensure that the patient has complied with dietary restrictions; ensure that food has been restricted for at least 8 hr depending on the anesthetic chosen for the procedure.

Administer ordered preoperative sedation.

Instruct the patient to void prior to the procedure and to change into the gown, robe, and foot coverings provided.

Position patient on the examination table, draped and with legs in stirrups. If general or spinal anesthesia is to be used, it is administered before positioning the patient on the table.

Cleanse external genitalia with antiseptic solution. If local anesthetic is used, it is instilled into the urethra and retained for 5 to 10 min. A penile clamp may be used for male patients to aid in retention of anesthetic.

The HCP inserts a cystoscope or a urethroscope to examine the urethra before cystoscopy. The urethroscope has a sheath that may be left in place, and the cystoscope is inserted through it, avoiding multiple instrumentations.

After insertion of the cystoscope, a sample of residual urine may be obtained for culture or other analysis. The bladder is irrigated via an irrigation system attached to the scope. The irrigation fluid aids in bladder visualization.

If a prostatic tumor is found, a biopsy specimen may be obtained by means of a cytology brush or biopsy forceps inserted through the scope. If the tumor is small and localized, it can be excised and fulgurated. This procedure is termed *transurethral resection of the bladder*. Polyps can also be identified and excised.

Ulcers or bleeding sites can be fulgurated using electrocautery.

Renal calculi can be crushed and removed from the ureters and bladder.

Ureteral catheters can be inserted via the scope to obtain urine samples from each kidney for comparative analysis and radiographic studies.

Ureteral and urethral strictures can also be dilated during this procedure.

Upon completion of the examination and related procedures, the cystoscope is withdrawn.

Place obtained specimens in proper containers, label them properly, and immediately transport them to the laboratory.

POST-TEST:

A report of the results will be made available to the requesting HCP, who will discuss the results with the patient.

Instruct the patient to resume his or her usual diet and medications, as directed by the HCP.

Encourage the patient to drink increased amounts of fluids (125 mL/hr for 24 hr) after the procedure.

Monitor vital signs and neurological status every 15 min for 1 hr, then every 2 hr for 4 hr, and then as ordered by the HCP. Take the temperature every 4 hr for 24 hr. Monitor intake and output at least every 8 hr. Compare with baseline values. Notify the HCP if temperature is elevated. Protocols may vary among facilities.

Instruct the patient to immediately report symptoms such as fast heart rate, difficulty breathing, skin rash, itching, chest pain, persistent right shoulder pain, or abdominal pain. Immediately report symptoms to the appropriate HCP.

Inform the patient that burning or discomfort on urination can be experienced for a few voidings after the procedure and that the urine may be blood-tinged for the first and second voidings after the procedure.

Persistent flank or suprapubic pain, fever, chills, blood in the urine, difficulty urinating, or change in urinary pattern must be reported immediately to the HCP.

Recognize anxiety related to test results. Discuss the implications of abnormal test results on the patient's lifestyle. Provide teaching and information regarding the clinical implications of the test results, as appropriate.

Reinforce information given by the patient's HCP regarding further testing,

treatment, or referral to another HCP. Answer any questions or address any concerns voiced by the patient or family. Depending on the results of this procedure, additional testing may be needed to evaluate or monitor progression of the disease process and determine the need for a change in therapy. Evaluate test results in relation to the patient's symptoms and other tests performed.

RELATED MONOGRAPHS:

Related tests include biopsy kidney, biopsy prostate, calculus kidney stone panel, *Chlamydia* group antibody, CT pelvis, culture urine, cytology urine, IVP, MRI pelvis, PSA, US pelvis, and UA.

Refer to the Genitourinary System table at the end of the book for related tests by body system.

Cystourethrography, Voiding

SYNONYM/ACRONYM: Voiding cystourethrography (VCU), voiding cystogram.

COMMON USE: To visualize and assess the bladder during voiding for evaluation of chronic urinary tract infections.

AREA OF APPLICATION: Bladder, urethra.

CONTRAST: Radiopaque iodine-based contrast medium.

DESCRIPTION: Voiding cystourethrography involves visualization of the bladder filled with contrast medium instilled through a catheter by use of a syringe or gravity, and, after the catheter is removed, the excretion of the contrast medium. Excretion or micturition is recorded electronically or on videotape for confirmation or exclusion of ureteral reflux and evaluation of the urethra. Fluoroscopic or plain images may also be taken to record bladder filling and emptying. This procedure is often used to evaluate chronic urinary tract infections (UTIs).

INDICATIONS

• Assess the degree of compromise of a stenotic prostatic urethra

• Assess hypertrophy of the prostate lobes
• Assess ureteral stricture
• Confirm the diagnosis of congenital lower urinary tract anomaly
• Evaluate abnormal bladder emptying and incontinence
• Evaluate the effects of bladder trauma
• Evaluate possible cause of frequent UTIs
• Evaluate the presence and extent of ureteral reflux
• Evaluate the urethra for obstruction and strictures

POTENTIAL DIAGNOSIS

Normal findings in
• Normal bladder and urethra structure and function

Abnormal findings in
• Bladder trauma
• Bladder tumors

- Hematomas
- Neurogenic bladder
- Pelvic tumors
- Prostatic enlargement
- Ureteral stricture
- Ureterocele
- Urethral diverticula
- Vesicoureteral reflux

CRITICAL FINDINGS: N/A

INTERFERING FACTORS

This procedure is contraindicated for

- Patients with allergies to shellfish or iodinated dye. The contrast medium used may cause a life-threatening allergic reaction. Patients with a known hypersensitivity to the contrast medium may benefit from premedication with corticosteroids or the use of nonionic contrast medium.
- Patients with bleeding disorders.
- Patients who are pregnant or suspected of being pregnant, unless the potential benefits of the procedure far outweigh the risks to the fetus and mother.
- Patients with UTI, obstruction, or injury.
- Elderly and other patients who are chronically dehydrated before the test, because of their risk of contrast-induced renal failure.
- Patients who are in renal failure.

Factors that may impair clear imaging

- Metallic objects within the examination field, which may inhibit organ visualization and cause unclear images.
- Inability of the patient to cooperate or remain still during the procedure because of age, significant pain, or mental status.
- Gas or feces in the gastrointestinal tract resulting from inadequate

cleansing or failure to restrict food intake before the study.
- Retained barium from a previous radiological procedure.

Other considerations
- Consultation with a health-care provider (HCP) should occur before the procedure for radiation safety concerns regarding younger patients or patients who are lactating.
- Risks associated with radiation overexposure can result from frequent x-ray procedures. Personnel in the room with the patient should wear a protective lead apron, stand behind a shield, or leave the area while the examination is being done. Personnel working in the examination area should wear badges to record their level of radiation exposure.

NURSING IMPLICATIONS AND PROCEDURE

PRETEST:
- Positively identify the patient using at least two unique identifiers before providing care, treatment, or services.
- *Patient Teaching:* Inform the patient this procedure can assist in assessing the urinary tract.
- Obtain a history of the patient's complaints, including a list of known allergens, especially allergies or sensitivities to latex, iodine, seafood, contrast medium, anesthetics, and dyes.
- Obtain a history of results of the patient's genitourinary system, symptoms, and previously performed laboratory tests and diagnostic and surgical procedures. Ensure that the results of blood tests are obtained and recorded before the procedure, especially coagulation tests, BUN, and creatinine if contrast medium is to be used.
- Ensure that this procedure is performed before an upper gastrointestinal study or barium swallow.

Record the date of the last menstrual period and determine the possibility of pregnancy in perimenopausal women.

Obtain a list of the patient's current medications, including anticoagulants, aspirin and other salicylates, herbs, nutritional supplements, and nutraceuticals (see Appendix F). Note the last time and dose of medication taken.

Review the procedure with the patient. Address concerns about pain and explain that there may be moments of discomfort and some pain experienced during the test. Inform the patient that the procedure is usually performed in the radiology department by an HCP, with support staff, and takes approximately 30 to 60 min.

Sensitivity to social and cultural issues, as well as concern for modesty, is important in providing psychological support before, during, and after the procedure.

Inform the patient that he or she may receive a laxative the night before the test or an enema or a cathartic the morning of the test, as ordered.

Instruct the patient to increase fluid intake the day before the test and to have only clear fluids 8 hr before the test.

Make sure a written and informed consent has been signed prior to the procedure and before administering any medications.

INTRATEST:

Observe standard precautions, and follow the general guidelines in Appendix A. Positively identify the patient.

Ensure that the patient has complied with dietary restrictions. Assess for completion of bowel preparation if ordered.

Ensure that the patient has removed all external metallic objects from the area to be examined prior to the procedure. If the patient has a history of allergic reactions to any substance or drug, administer ordered prophylactic steroids or antihistamines before the procedure.

Have emergency equipment readily available.

Instruct the patient to void prior to the procedure and to change into the gown, robe, and foot coverings provided.

Insert a Foley catheter before the procedure, if ordered. Inform the patient that he or she may feel some pressure when the catheter is inserted and when the contrast medium is instilled through the catheter.

Place the patient on the table in a supine or lithotomy position.

A kidney, ureter, and bladder radiograph (KUB) is taken to ensure that no barium or stool obscures visualization of the urinary system.

A catheter is filled with contrast medium to eliminate air pockets and is inserted until the balloon reaches the meatus if not previously inserted in the patient.

When three-fourths of the contrast medium has been injected, a radiographic exposure is made while the remainder of the contrast medium is injected.

When the patient is able to void, the catheter is removed and the patient is asked to urinate while images of the bladder and urethra are recorded.

Monitor the patient for complications related to the procedure (e.g., allergic reaction, anaphylaxis, bronchospasm).

POST-TEST:

A report of the results will be made available to the requesting HCP, who will discuss the results with the patient.

Instruct the patient to resume usual diet and medications, as directed by the HCP.

Monitor vital signs and neurological status every 15 min for 1 hr, then every 2 hr for 4 hr, and then as ordered by the HCP. Take the temperature every 4 hr for 24 hr. Monitor intake and output at least every 8 hr. Compare with baseline values. Notify the HCP if temperature is elevated. Protocols may vary among facilities.

Monitor for reaction to iodinated contrast medium, including rash, urticaria, tachycardia, hyperpnea, hypertension, palpitations, nausea, or vomiting.

Instruct the patient to immediately report symptoms such as fast heart rate, difficulty breathing, skin rash, itching, chest pain, persistent right shoulder pain, or abdominal pain. Immediately report symptoms to the appropriate HCP.

Maintain the patient on adequate hydration after the procedure. Encourage the patient to drink increased amounts of fluids (125 mL/hr for 24 hr) after the procedure to prevent stasis and bacterial buildup.

Recognize anxiety related to test results. Discuss the implications of abnormal test results on the patient's lifestyle. Provide teaching and information regarding the clinical implications of the test results, as appropriate.

Reinforce information given by the patient's HCP regarding further testing, treatment, or referral to another HCP. Answer any questions or address any concerns voiced by the patient or family.

Depending on the results of this procedure, additional testing may be needed to evaluate or monitor progression of the disease process and determine the need for a change in therapy. Evaluate test results in relation to the patient's symptoms and other tests performed.

RELATED MONOGRAPHS:

Related tests include biopsy prostate, bladder cancer markers, BUN, CT pelvis, creatinine cytology urine, IVP, MRI pelvis, PSA, PT/INR, and US pelvis.

Refer to the Genitourinary System table at the end of the book for related tests by body system.

Cytology, Sputum

SYNONYM/ACRONYM: N/A.

COMMON USE: To identify cellular changes associated with neoplasms or organisms that result in respiratory tract infections, such as *Pneumocystis jiroveci* (formerly *P. carinii*).

SPECIMEN: Sputum (10 to 15 mL) collected on three to five consecutive first-morning, deep-cough expectorations.

NORMAL FINDINGS: (Method: Macroscopic and microscopic examination) Negative for abnormal cells, fungi, ova, and parasites.

DESCRIPTION: Cytology is the study of the origin, structure, function, and pathology of cells. In clinical practice, cytological examinations are generally performed to detect cell changes resulting from neoplastic or inflammatory conditions. Sputum specimens for cytological examinations may be collected by expectoration alone, by suctioning, by lung biopsy, during bronchoscopy, or by expectoration after bronchoscopy.

A description of the method of specimen collection by bronchoscopy and biopsy is found in the monograph titled "Biopsy, Lung."

INDICATIONS
• Assist in the diagnosis of lung cancer
• Assist in the identification of *Pneumocystis jiroveci* (formerly *P. carinii*) in persons with AIDS
• Detect known or suspected fungal or parasitic infection involving the lung

- Detect known or suspected viral disease involving the lung
- Screen cigarette smokers for neoplastic (nonmalignant) cellular changes
- Screen patients with history of acute or chronic inflammatory or infectious lung disorders, which may lead to benign atypical or metaplastic changes

POTENTIAL DIAGNOSIS

(Method: Microscopic examination) The method of reporting results of cytology examinations varies according to the laboratory performing the test. Terms used to report results may include *negative* (no abnormal cells seen), *inflammatory, benign atypical, suspect for neoplasm, and positive for neoplasm*.

Positive findings in
- Infections caused by fungi, ova, or parasites
- Lipoid or aspiration pneumonia, as seen by lipid droplets contained in macrophages
- Neoplasms
- Viral infections and lung disease

CRITICAL FINDINGS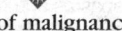
- Identification of malignancy

It is essential that critical diagnoses be communicated immediately to the requesting health-care provider (HCP). A listing of these diagnoses varies among facilities. Timely notification of critical values for lab or diagnostic studies is a role expectation of the professional nurse. Notification processes will vary among facilities. Upon receipt of the critical value, the information should be read back to the caller to verify accuracy. Most policies require immediate notification of the primary HCP, hospitalist, or on-call HCP. Reported information includes the patient's name, unique identifiers, critical value, name of the person giving

the report, and name of the person receiving the report. Documentation of notification should be made in the medical record with the name of the HCP notified, time and date of notification, and any orders received. Any delay in a timely report of a critical value may require completion of a notification form with review by Risk Management.

If the patient becomes hypoxic or cyanotic, remove catheter immediately and administer oxygen.

If patient has asthma or chronic bronchitis, watch for aggravated bronchospasms with use of normal saline or acetylcysteine in an aerosol.

INTERFERING FACTORS
- Improper specimen fixation may be cause for specimen rejection.
- Improper technique used to obtain bronchial washing may be cause for specimen rejection.
- Failure to follow dietary restrictions before the procedure may cause the procedure to be canceled or repeated.

NURSING IMPLICATIONS AND PROCEDURE

PRETEST:
- Positively identify the patient using at least two unique identifiers before providing care, treatment, or services.
- *Patient Teaching:* Inform the patient this test can assist in identification of the organism causing infection.
- Obtain a history of the patient's complaints, including a list of known allergens, especially allergies or sensitivities to latex.
- Obtain a history of the patient's immune and respiratory systems, symptoms, and results of previously performed laboratory tests and diagnostic and surgical procedures.
- Obtain a list of the patient's current medications, including herbs, nutritional supplements, and nutraceuticals (see Appendix F).

C

Note any recent procedures that can interfere with test results.

Review the procedure with the patient. If the laboratory has provided a container with fixative, instruct the patient that the fixative contents of the specimen collection container should not be ingested or otherwise removed. Instruct the patient not to touch the edge or inside of the specimen container with the hands or mouth. Inform the patient that three samples may be required, on three separate mornings, either by passing a small tube (tracheal catheter) and adding suction or by expectoration. The time it takes to collect a proper specimen varies according to the level of cooperation of the patient and the specimen collection procedure. Address concerns about pain related to the procedure. Atropine is usually given before bronchoscopy examinations to reduce bronchial secretions and to prevent vagally induced bradycardia. Meperidine (Demerol) or morphine may be given as a sedative. Lidocaine is sprayed in the patient's throat to reduce discomfort caused by the presence of the tube.

Reassure the patient that he or she will be able to breathe during the procedure if specimen is collected via suction method. Ensure that oxygen has been administered 20 to 30 min before the procedure if the specimen is to be obtained by tracheal suctioning.

Assist in providing extra fluids, unless contraindicated, and proper humidification to loosen tenacious secretions. Inform the patient that increasing fluid intake before retiring on the night before the test aids in liquefying secretions and may make it easier to expectorate in the morning. Also explain that humidifying inspired air also helps to liquefy secretions.

Assist with mouth care (brushing teeth or rinsing mouth with water), if needed, before collection so as not to contaminate the specimen by oral secretions.

Sensitivity to social and cultural issues, as well as concern for modesty, is important in providing psychological support before, during and after the procedure.

For specimens collected by suctioning or expectoration without bronchoscopy, there are no food, fluid, or medication restrictions unless by medical direction.

Instruct the patient to fast and refrain from taking liquids from midnight the night before if bronchoscopy or biopsy is to be performed. Protocols may vary among facilities.

Make sure a written and informed consent has been signed prior to the bronchoscopy or biopsy procedure and before administering any medications.

INTRATEST:

Ensure that the patient has complied with dietary restrictions; assure that food and liquids have been restricted for at least 6 to 8 hr prior to the procedure.

Have patient remove dentures, contact lenses, eyeglasses, and jewelry. Notify the HCP if the patient has permanent crowns on teeth. Have the patient remove clothing and change into a gown for the procedure.

Have emergency equipment readily available. Keep resuscitation equipment on hand in the case of respiratory impairment or laryngospasm after the procedure.

Avoid using morphine sulfate in those with asthma or other pulmonary disease. This drug can further exacerbate bronchospasms and respiratory impairment.

If the patient has a history of allergic reaction to latex, avoid the use of equipment containing latex.

Assist the patient to a comfortable position, and direct the patient to breathe normally during the beginning of the general anesthesia and to avoid unnecessary movement during the local anesthetic and the procedure. Instruct the patient to cooperate fully and to follow directions.

Observe standard precautions, and follow the general guidelines in Appendix A. Positively identify the patient, and label the appropriate collection container with the corresponding patient demographics, date and time of collection, and any medication the patient is taking that may interfere with test results (e.g., antibiotics). Cytology specimens may also be expressed onto a glass slide and sprayed with a fixative or 95% alcohol.

Bronchoscopy

▸ Record baseline vital signs.
▸ The patient is positioned in relation to the type of anesthesia being used. If local anesthesia is used, the patient is seated, and the tongue and oropharynx are sprayed and swabbed with anesthetic before the bronchoscope is inserted. For general anesthesia, the patient is placed in a supine position with the neck hyperextended. After anesthesia, the patient is kept in supine or shifted to side-lying position, and the bronchoscope is inserted. After inspection, the samples are collected from suspicious sites by bronchial brush or biopsy forceps.

Expectorated Specimen

▸ Ask the patient to sit upright, with assistance and support (e.g., with an overbed table) as needed.
▸ Ask the patient to take two or three deep breaths and cough deeply. Any sputum raised should be expectorated directly into a sterile sputum collection container.
▸ If the patient is unable to produce the desired amount of sputum, several strategies may be attempted. One approach is to have the patient drink two glasses of water, and then assume the position for postural drainage of the upper and middle lung segments. Effective coughing may be assisted by placing either the hands or a pillow over the diaphragmatic area and applying slight pressure.
▸ Another approach is to place a vaporizer or other humidifying device at the bedside. After sufficient exposure to adequate humidification, postural drainage of the upper and middle lung segments may be repeated before attempting to obtain the specimen.
▸ Other methods may include obtaining an order for an expectorant to be administered with additional water approximately 2 hr before attempting to obtain the specimen. Chest percussion and postural drainage of all lung segments may also be employed. If

the patient is still unable to raise sputum, the use of an ultrasonic nebulizer ("induced sputum") may be necessary; this is usually done by a respiratory therapist.

Tracheal Suctioning

▸ Obtain the necessary equipment, including a suction device, suction kit, and Lukens tube or in-line trap.
▸ Position the patient with head elevated as high as tolerated.
▸ Put on sterile gloves. Maintain the dominant hand as sterile and the non-dominant hand as clean.
▸ Using the sterile hand, attach the suction catheter to the rubber tubing of the Lukens tube or in-line trap. Then attach the suction tubing to the male adapter of the trap with the clean hand. Lubricate the suction catheter with sterile saline.
▸ Tell nonintubated patients to protrude the tongue and to take a deep breath as the suction catheter is passed through the nostril. When the catheter enters the trachea, a reflex cough is stimulated; immediately advance the catheter into the trachea and apply suction. Maintain suction for approximately 10 sec, but never longer than 15 sec. Withdraw the catheter without applying suction. Separate the suction catheter and suction tubing from the trap, and place the rubber tubing over the male adapter to seal the unit.
▸ For intubated patients or patients with a tracheostomy, the previous procedure is followed except that the suction catheter is passed through the existing endotracheal or tracheostomy tube rather than through the nostril. The patient should be hyperoxygenated before and after the procedure in accordance with standard protocols for suctioning these patients.
▸ Generally, a series of three to five early-morning sputum samples are collected in sterile containers.

General

▸ Monitor the patient for complications related to the procedure (e.g., allergic reaction, anaphylaxis, bronchospasm).
▸ Promptly transport the specimen to the laboratory for processing and analysis.

C

POST-TEST:

- A report of the results will be made available to the requesting HCP, who will discuss the results with the patient.
- Instruct the patient to resume usual diet, as directed by the HCP. Assess the patient's ability to swallow before allowing the patient to attempt liquids or solid foods.
- Inform the patient that he or she may experience some throat soreness and hoarseness. Instruct patient to treat throat discomfort with lozenges and warm gargles when the gag reflex returns.
- Monitor vital signs and compare with baseline values every 15 min for 1 hr, then every 2 hr for 4 hr, and then as ordered by the HCP. Monitor temperature every 4 hr for 24 hr. Notify the HCP if temperature is elevated. Protocols may vary among facilities.
- Emergency resuscitation equipment should be readily available if the vocal cords become spastic after intubation.
- Observe/assess for delayed allergic reactions, such as rash, urticaria, tachycardia, hyperpnea, hypertension, palpitations, nausea, or vomiting.
- Observe/assess the patient for hemoptysis, difficulty breathing, cough, air hunger, excessive coughing, pain, or absent breathing sounds over the affected area. Report any symptoms to the HCP.
- Evaluate the patient for symptoms indicating the development of pneumothorax, such as dyspnea, tachypnea, anxiety, decreased breathing sounds, or restlessness. A chest x-ray may be ordered to check for the presence of this complication.
- Evaluate the patient for symptoms of empyema, such as fever, tachycardia, malaise, or elevated white blood cell count.
- Administer antibiotic therapy if ordered. Remind the patient of the importance of completing the entire course of antibiotic therapy, even if signs and symptoms disappear before completion of therapy.
- *Nutritional Considerations:* Malnutrition is commonly seen in patients with severe respiratory disease for numerous rea-

sons including fatigue, lack of appetite, and gastrointestinal distress. Adequate intake of vitamins A and C are also important to prevent pulmonary infection and to decrease the extent of lung tissue damage.
- Recognize anxiety related to test results, and be supportive of impaired activity related to perceived loss of independence and fear of shortened life expectancy. Discuss the implications of abnormal test results on the patient's lifestyle. Provide teaching and information regarding the clinical implications of the test results, as appropriate. Educate the patient regarding access to counseling services. Provide contact information, if desired, for the American Lung Association (www.lungusa.org).
- Reinforce information given by the patient's HCP regarding further testing, treatment, or referral to another HCP. Inform the patient of smoking cessation programs, as appropriate. Inform the patient with abnormal findings of the importance of medical follow-up, and suggest ongoing support resources to assist in coping with chronic illness and possible early death. Answer any questions or address any concerns voiced by the patient or family.
- Instruct the patient in the use of any ordered medications. Explain the importance of adhering to the therapy regimen. As appropriate, instruct the patient in significant side effects and systemic reactions associated with the prescribed medication. Encourage him or her to review corresponding literature provided by a pharmacist.
- Depending on the results of this procedure, additional testing may be performed to evaluate or monitor progression of the disease process and determine the need for a change in therapy. Evaluate test results in relation to the patient's symptoms and other tests performed.

RELATED MONOGRAPHS:

- Related tests include arterial/alveolar oxygen ratio, biopsy lung, blood gases, bronchoscopy, CBC, CT thoracic, relevant cultures (fungal, mycobacteria, sputum, throat, viral), gallium scan, Gram/acid-fast stain, lung perfusion scan, lung ventilation scan, MRI chest, mediastinoscopy,

pleural fluid analysis, pulmonary function tests, and TB tests.
▶ Refer to the Immune and Respiratory systems tables at the end of the book for related tests by body system.

Cytology, Urine

SYNONYM/ACRONYM: N/A.

COMMON USE: To identify the presence of neoplasms of the urinary tract and assist in the diagnosis of urinary tract infections.

SPECIMEN: Urine (180 mL for an adult; at least 10 mL for a child) collected in a clean wide-mouth plastic container.

NORMAL FINDINGS: (Method: Microscopic examination) No abnormal cells or inclusions seen.

DESCRIPTION: Cytology is the study of the origin, structure, function, and pathology of cells. In clinical practice, cytological examinations are generally performed to detect cell changes resulting from neoplastic or inflammatory conditions. Cells from the epithelial lining of the urinary tract can be found in the urine. Examination of these cells for abnormalities is useful with suspected infection, inflammatory conditions, or malignancy.

INDICATIONS
• Assist in the diagnosis of urinary tract diseases, such as cancer, cytomegalovirus infection, and other inflammatory conditions

POTENTIAL DIAGNOSIS

Positive findings in
• Cancer of the urinary tract
• Cytomegalic inclusion disease
• Inflammatory disease of the urinary tract

Negative findings in: N/A

CRITICAL FINDINGS
• Identification of malignancy

It is essential that critical diagnoses be communicated immediately to the requesting health-care provider (HCP). A listing of these diagnoses varies among facilities. Timely notification of critical values for lab or diagnostic studies is a role expectation of the professional nurse. Notification processes will vary among facilities. Upon receipt of the critical value, the information should be read back to the caller to verify accuracy. Most policies require immediate notification of the primary HCP, hospitalist, or on-call HCP. Reported information includes the patient's name, unique identifiers, critical value, name of the person giving the report, and name of the person receiving the report. Documentation of notification should be made in the medical record with the name of the HCP notified, time and date of notification, and any orders received. Any delay in a timely report of a critical value may require completion of a notification form with review by Risk Management.

INTERFERING FACTORS: N/A

NURSING IMPLICATIONS AND PROCEDURE

PRETEST:

Positively identify the patient using at least two unique identifiers before providing care, treatment, or services.

Patient Teaching: Inform the patient this test can assist in identification of the organism causing infection or the presence of a tumor in the urinary tract.

Obtain a history of the patient's complaints, including a list of known allergens, especially allergies or sensitivities to latex.

Obtain a history of the patient's genitourinary and immune systems, symptoms, and results of previously performed laboratory tests and diagnostic and surgical procedures.

Obtain a list of the patient's current medications, including herbs, nutritional supplements, and nutraceuticals (see Appendix F).

Note any recent procedures that can interfere with test results.

Review the procedure with the patient. If a catheterized specimen is to be collected, explain this procedure to the patient and obtain a catheterization tray. Address concerns about pain and explain that there may be some discomfort during the catheterization.

Sensitivity to social and cultural issues, as well as concern for modesty, is important in providing psychological support before, during, and after the procedure.

There are no food, fluid, or medication restrictions, unless by medical direction.

INTRATEST:

If the patient has a history of allergic reaction to latex, avoid the use of equipment containing latex.

Instruct the patient to cooperate fully and to follow directions.

Observe standard precautions, and follow the general guidelines in Appendix A. Positively identify the patient, and label the appropriate tubes with the corresponding patient demographics, date and time of collection, method of specimen collection, and any medications the patient has taken that may interfere with test results (e.g., antibiotics).

Clean-Catch Specimen

Instruct the male patient to (1) thoroughly wash his hands, (2) cleanse the meatus, (3) void a small amount into the toilet, and (4) void directly into the specimen container.

Instruct the female patient to (1) thoroughly wash her hands; (2) cleanse the labia from front to back; (3) while keeping the labia separated, void a small amount into the toilet; and (4) without interrupting the urine stream, void directly into the specimen container.

Pediatric Urine Collector

Put on gloves. Appropriately cleanse the genital area, and allow the area to dry. Remove the covering over the adhesive strips on the collector bag and apply over the genital area. Diaper the child. After obtaining the specimen, place the entire collection bag in a sterile urine container.

Indwelling Catheter

Put on gloves. Empty drainage tube of urine. It may be necessary to clamp off the catheter for 15 to 30 min before specimen collection. Cleanse specimen port with antiseptic swab, and then aspirate 5 mL of urine with a 21- to 25-gauge needle and syringe. Transfer urine to a sterile container.

Urinary Catheterization

Place female patient in lithotomy position or male patient in supine position. Using sterile technique, open the straight urinary catheterization kit and perform urinary catheterization. Place the retained urine in a sterile specimen container.

Suprapubic Aspiration

Place the patient in supine position. Cleanse the area with antiseptic, and drape with sterile drapes. A needle is inserted through the skin into the bladder. A syringe attached to the needle is used to aspirate the urine sample. The needle is then removed and a sterile dressing is applied to the site. Place the sterile sample in a sterile specimen container.

Do not collect urine from the pouch from a patient with a urinary diversion (e.g., ileal conduit). Instead perform catheterization through the stoma.

General
Promptly transport the specimen to the laboratory for processing and analysis. If a delay in transport is expected, add an equal volume of 50% alcohol to the specimen as a preservative.

OST-TEST:

A report of the results will be made available to the requesting HCP, who will discuss the results with the patient. Instruct the patient to resume usual medication as directed by the HCP. Instruct the patient to report symptoms such as pain related to tissue inflammation, pain or irritation during void, bladder spasms, or alterations in urinary elimination.

Observe for signs of inflammation if the specimen is obtained by suprapubic aspiration.

Administer antibiotic therapy as ordered. Remind the patient of the importance of completing the entire course of antibiotic therapy, even if signs and symptoms disappear before completion of therapy.

Recognize anxiety related to test results, and be supportive of fear of shortened life expectancy. Discuss the implications of abnormal test results on the patient's lifestyle. Provide teaching and information regarding the clinical implications of the test results, as appropriate. Educate the patient regarding access to counseling services.

Reinforce information given by the patient's HCP regarding further testing, treatment, or referral to another HCP. Answer any questions or address any concerns voiced by the patient or family.

Depending on the results of this procedure, additional testing may be performed to evaluate or monitor progression of the disease process and determine the need for a change in therapy. Evaluate test results in relation to the patient's symptoms and other tests performed.

RELATED MONOGRAPHS:

Related tests include biopsy kidney, bladder cancer markers, cystoscopy, CMV IgG and IgM, Pap smear, UA, and US bladder.

Refer to the Genitourinary and Immune systems tables at the end of the book for related tests by body system.

Cytomegalovirus, Immunoglobulin G and Immunoglobulin M

SYNONYM/ACRONYM: CMV.

COMMON USE: To assist in diagnosing cytomegalovirus infection.

SPECIMEN: Serum (1 mL) collected in a plain red-top tube.

NORMAL FINDINGS: (Method: Enzyme immunoassay)

	IgM & IgG	Interpretation
Negative	0.9 index or less	No significant level of detectable antibody
Indeterminate	0.91–1.09 index	Equivocal results; retest in 10–14 d
Positive	1.1 index or greater	Antibody detected; indicative of recent immunization, current or recent infection

C

DESCRIPTION: Cytomegalovirus (CMV) is a double-stranded DNA herpesvirus. The Centers for Disease Control and Prevention (CDC) estimates that 50% to 85% of adults are infected by age 40. The incubation period for primary infection is 4 to 8 wk. Transmission may occur by direct contact with oral, respiratory, or venereal secretions and excretions. CMV infection is of primary concern in pregnant or immunocompromised patients or patients who have recently received an organ transplant. Blood units are sometimes tested for the presence of CMV if patients in these high-risk categories are the transfusion recipients. CMV serology is part of the TORCH (*t*oxoplasmosis, *o*ther [congenital syphilis and viruses], *r*ubella, *C*MV, and *h*erpes simplex type 2) panel used to test pregnant women. CMV, as well as these other infectious agents, can cross the placenta and result in congenital malformations, abortion, or stillbirth. The presence of immunoglobulin (Ig) M antibodies indicates acute infection. The presence of IgG antibodies indicates current or past infection. There are numerous methods for detection of CMV. The methodology selected is based on both the test purpose and specimen type. Other types of assays used to detect CMV include direct fluorescent assays used to identify CMV in tissue, sputum, and swab specimens; hemagglutination assays, cleared by the FDA for testing blood prior to transfusion; polymerase chain reaction (PCR), used to test a wide variety of specimen types, including amniotic fluid, plasma, urine, CSF, and whole blood; and cell tissue culture, which remains the gold standard for the identification of CMV.

INDICATIONS
• Assist in the diagnosis of congenital CMV infection in newborns
• Determine susceptibility, particularly in pregnant women, immunocompromised patients, and patients who recently have received an organ transplant
• Screen blood for high-risk-category transfusion recipients

POTENTIAL DIAGNOSIS

Positive findings in
• CMV infection

Negative findings in: N/A

CRITICAL FINDINGS: N/A

INTERFERING FACTORS
• False-positive results may occur in the presence of rheumatoid factor.
• False-negative results may occur if treatment was begun before antibodies developed or if the test was done less than 6 days after exposure to the virus.

NURSING IMPLICATIONS AND PROCEDURE

RETEST:

Positively identify the patient using at least two unique identifiers before providing care, treatment, or services. *Patient Teaching:* Inform the patient this test can assist in identification of the organism causing infection.

Obtain a history of the patient's complaints and history of exposure. Obtain a list of known allergens, especially allergies or sensitivities to latex.

Obtain a history of the patient's immune and reproductive systems, symptoms, and results of previously performed laboratory tests and diagnostic and surgical procedures.

Obtain a list of the patient's current medications, including herbs, nutritional supplements, and nutraceuticals (see Appendix F).

Review the procedure with the patient. Inform the patient that multiple specimens may be required. Any individual positive result should be repeated in 7 to 14 days to monitor a change in titer. Inform the patient that specimen collection takes approximately 5 to 10 min. Address concerns about pain and explain that there may be some discomfort during the venipuncture. *Sensitivity to social and cultural issues,* as well as concern for modesty, is important in providing psychological support before, during, and after the procedure.

There are no food, fluid, or medication restrictions, unless by medical direction.

NTRATEST:

If the patient has a history of allergic reaction to latex, avoid the use of equipment containing latex.

Instruct the patient to cooperate fully and to follow directions. Direct the patient to breathe normally and to avoid unnecessary movement.

Observe standard precautions, and follow the general guidelines in Appendix A. Positively identify the patient, and label the appropriate specimen container with the corresponding patient demographics, initials of the person collecting the specimen, date, and time of collection. Perform a venipuncture.

Remove the needle and apply direct pressure with dry gauze to stop bleeding. Observe/assess venipuncture site for bleeding or hematoma formation and secure gauze with adhesive bandage.

Promptly transport the specimen to the laboratory for processing and analysis.

POST-TEST:

A report of the results will be made available to the requesting health-care provider (HCP), who will discuss the results with the patient.

Instruct the patient in isolation precautions during time of communicability or contagion.

Emphasize the need to return to have a convalescent blood sample taken in 7 to 14 days.

Warn the patient that there is a possibility of false-negative or false-positive results.

Recognize anxiety related to test results if the patient is pregnant, and offer support. Discuss the implications of abnormal test results on the patient's lifestyle. Provide teaching and information regarding the clinical implications of the test results, as appropriate. Educate the patient regarding access to counseling services.

Reinforce information given by the patient's HCP regarding further testing, treatment, or referral to another HCP. Answer any questions or address any concerns voiced by the patient or family.

Depending on the results of this procedure, additional testing may be performed to evaluate or monitor progression of the disease process and determine the need for a change in therapy. Evaluate test results in relation to the patient's symptoms and other tests performed.

RELATED MONOGRAPHS:

Related tests include β_2-microglobulin, bronchoscopy, *Chlamydia* group antibody, culture viral, cytology urine, HIV-1/2 antibodies, Pap smear, rubella antibody, and *Toxoplasma* antibody.

Refer to the Immune and Reproductive systems tables at the end of the book for related tests by body system.

D-Dimer

SYNONYM/ACRONYM: Dimer, fibrin degradation fragment.

COMMON USE: To assist in diagnosing a diffuse state of hypercoagulation as seen in disseminated intravascular coagulation (DIC), acute myocardial infarction (MI), deep venous thrombosis (DVT), and pulmonary embolism (PE).

SPECIMEN: Plasma (1 mL) collected in a completely filled blue-top (3.2% sodium citrate) tube. If the patient's hematocrit exceeds 55%, the volume of citrate in the collection tube must be adjusted.

NORMAL FINDINGS: (Method: Immunoturbidimetric)

Conventional Units (FEU = Fibrinogen Equivalent Units)	SI Units (Conventional Units × 5.476)
0.5 mcg/mL FEU	0–3 nmol/L

Levels increase with age.

DESCRIPTION: The D-dimer is an asymmetric carbon compound formed by a cross-link between two identical fibrin molecules. The test is specific for secondary fibrinolysis because the cross-linkage occurs with fibrin and not fibrinogen. A positive test is presumptive evidence of disseminated intravascular coagulation (DIC) or pulmonary embolism (PE).

INDICATIONS
- Assist in the detection of DIC and deep venous thrombosis (DVT)
- Assist in the evaluation of myocardial infarction (MI) and unstable angina
- Assist in the evaluation of possible veno-occlusive disease associated with sequelae of bone marrow transplant
- Assist in the evaluation of pulmonary embolism

POTENTIAL DIAGNOSIS
The sensitivity and specificity of the assay varies among test kits and between test methods.

Increased in
D-Dimers are formed in inflammatory conditions where plasmin carries out its fibrinolytic action on a fibrin clot.
- Arterial or venous thrombosis
- DVT
- DIC
- Neoplastic disease
- Pre-eclampsia
- Pregnancy (late and postpartum)
- PE
- Recent surgery (within 2 days)
- Secondary fibrinolysis
- Thrombolytic or fibrinolytic therapy

Decreased in: N/A

CRITICAL FINDINGS: N/A

INTERFERING FACTORS
- High rheumatoid factor titers can cause a false-positive result.
- Increased CA 125 levels can cause a false-positive result; patients with cancer may demonstrate increased levels.
- Drugs that may cause an increase in plasma D-dimer include those administered for antiplatelet therapy.

- Drugs that may cause a decrease in plasma D-dimer include pravastatin and warfarin.
- Placement of tourniquet for longer than 1 min can result in venous stasis and changes in the concentration of plasma proteins to be measured. Platelet activation may also occur under these conditions, causing erroneous results.
- Vascular injury during phlebotomy can activate platelets and coagulation factors, causing erroneous results.
- Hemolyzed specimens must be rejected because hemolysis is an indication of platelet and coagulation factor activation.
- Hematocrit greater than 55% may cause falsely prolonged results because of anticoagulant excess relative to plasma volume.
- Incompletely filled collection tubes, specimens contaminated with heparin, clotted specimens, or unprocessed specimens not delivered to the laboratory within 1 to 2 hr of collection should be rejected.
- Icteric or lipemic specimens interfere with optical testing methods, producing erroneous results.

NURSING IMPLICATIONS AND PROCEDURE

PRETEST:

- Positively identify the patient using at least two unique identifiers before providing care, treatment, or services.
- *Patient Teaching:* Inform the patient this test can assist in diagnosing and evaluating conditions affecting normal blood clot formation.
- Obtain a history of the patient's complaints, including a list of known allergens, especially allergies or sensitivities to latex.
- Obtain a history of hematological diseases and recent surgery.
- Obtain a history of the patient's cardiovascular, hematopoietic, and respiratory systems; symptoms; and results of previously performed laboratory tests and diagnostic and surgical procedures.
- Obtain a list of the patient's current medications, including herbs, nutritional supplements, and nutraceuticals (see Appendix F).
- Review the procedure with the patient. Inform the patient that specimen collection takes approximately 5 to 10 min. Address concerns about pain and explain that there may be some discomfort during the venipuncture.
- *Sensitivity to social and cultural issues,* as well as concern for modesty, is important in providing psychological support before, during, and after the procedure.
- There are no food, fluid, or medication restrictions unless by medical direction.

INTRATEST:

- If the patient has a history of allergic reaction to latex, avoid the use of equipment containing latex.
- Instruct the patient to cooperate fully and to follow directions. Direct the patient to breathe normally and to avoid unnecessary movement.
- Observe standard precautions, and follow the general guidelines in Appendix A. Positively identify the patient, and label the appropriate specimen container with the corresponding patient demographics, initials of the person collecting the specimen, date, and time of collection. Perform a venipuncture. Fill tube completely. *Important note:* Two different concentrations of sodium citrate preservative are currently added to blue-top tubes for coagulation studies: 3.2% and 3.8%. The Clinical and Laboratory Standards Institute/CLSI (formerly the National Committee for Clinical Laboratory Standards/NCCLS) guideline for sodium citrate is 3.2%. Laboratories establish reference ranges for coagulation testing based on numerous factors, including sodium citrate concentration, test equipment, and test reagents. It is important to ask the laboratory which concentration it recommends, because each concentration will have its own

specific reference range. When multiple specimens are drawn, the blue-top tube should be collected after sterile (i.e., blood culture) tubes. Otherwise, when using a standard vacutainer system, the blue top is the first tube collected. When a butterfly is used and due to the added tubing, an extra red-top tube should be collected before the blue-top tube to ensure complete filling of the blue-top tube.

▶ Remove the needle and apply direct pressure with dry gauze to stop bleeding. Observe/assess venipuncture site for bleeding or hematoma formation and secure gauze with adhesive bandage.

▶ Promptly transport the specimen to the laboratory for processing and analysis. The CLSI recommendation for processed and unprocessed samples stored in unopened tubes is that testing should be completed within 1 to 4 hr of collection. If the patient has a known hematocrit above 55%, adjust the amount of anticoagulant in the collection tube before drawing the blood according to the CLSI guidelines:

Anticoagulant vol. [x] = (100 − hematocrit)/(595 − hematocrit) × total vol. of anticoagulated blood required

Example:
Patient hematocrit = 60% = [(100 − 60)/(595 − 60) × 5.0] = 0.37 mL sodium citrate for a 5-mL standard drawing tube

POST-TEST:
▶ A report of the results will be made available to the requesting health-care provider (HCP), who will discuss the results with the patient.
▶ Reinforce information given by the patient's HCP regarding further testing, treatment, or referral to another HCP. Answer any questions or address any concerns voiced by the patient or family.
▶ Depending on the results of this procedure, additional testing may be performed to evaluate or monitor progression of the disease process and determine the need for a change in therapy. Evaluate test results in relation to the patient's symptoms and other tests performed.

RELATED MONOGRAPHS:
▶ Related tests include aPTT, alveolar/arterial gradient, angiography pulmonary, antibodies anticardiolipin, AT-III, blood gases, coagulation factors, CBC platelet count, FDP, fibrinogen, lactic acid, lung perfusion scan, plasminogen, plethysmography, protein S, PT/INR, US venous Doppler extremity studies, and venography lower extremity studies.
▶ Refer to the Cardiovascular, Hematopoietic, and Respiratory systems tables at the end of the book for related tests by body system.

Dehydroepiandrosterone Sulfate

SYNONYM/ACRONYM: DHEAS.

COMMON USE: To assist in identifying the cause of infertility, amenorrhea, or hirsutism.

SPECIMEN: Serum (1 mL) collected in a red- or tiger-top tube. Plasma (1 mL) collected in a lavender-top (EDTA) tube is also acceptable.

NORMAL FINDINGS: (Method: Immunochemiluminometric assay [ICMA])

Age	Male Conventional Units mcg/dL	Male SI Units micromol/L (Conventional Units × 0.027)	Female Conventional Units mcg/dL	Female SI Units micromol/L (Conventional Units × 0.027)
Newborn	108–607	2.9–16.4	108–607	2.9–16.4
7–30 d	32–431	0.9–11.6	32–431	0.9–11.6
1–5 mo	3–124	0.1–3.3	3–124	0.1–3.3
6–35 mo	0–30	0–0.8	0–30	0–0.8
3–6 yr	0–50	0–1.4	0–50	0–1.4
7–9 yr	5–115	0.1–3.1	5–94	0.1–2.5
10–14 yr	22–332	0.6–9	22–255	0.6–6.9
15–19 yr	88–483	2.4–13	63–373	1.7–10
20–29 yr	280–640	7.6–17.3	65–380	1.8–10.3
30–39 yr	120–520	3.2–14	45–270	1.2–7.3
40–49 yr	95–530	2.6–14.3	32–240	0.9–6.5
50–59 yr	70–310	1.9–8.4	26–200	0.7–5.4
60–69 yr	42–290	1.1–7.8	13–130	0.4–3.5
70 yr and older	28–175	0.8–4.7	10–90	0.3–2.4

Tanner Stage	Male Conventional Units mcg/dL	Male SI Units micromol/L	Female Conventional Units mcg/dL	Female SI Units micromol/L
I	7–209	0.2–5.6	7–126	0.2–3.4
II	28–260	0.8–7	13–241	0.4–6.5
III	39–390	1.1–10.5	32–446	0.9–12
IV & V	81–488	2.2–13.2	65–371	1.8–10

DESCRIPTION: Dehydroepiandrosterone sulfate (DHEAS) is the major precursor of 17-ketosteroids. DHEAS is a metabolite of DHEA, the principal adrenal androgen. DHEAS is primarily synthesized in the adrenal gland, with a small amount secreted by the testes. DHEAS is a weak androgen and can be converted into more potent androgens (e.g., testosterone) as well as estrogens (e.g., estradiol). It is secreted in concert with cortisol, under the control of adrenocorticotropic hormone (ACTH) and prolactin. Excessive production causes masculinization in women and children. DHEAS has replaced measurement of urinary 17-ketosteroids in the estimation of adrenal androgen production.

INDICATIONS
• Assist in the evaluation of androgen excess, including congenital adrenal hyperplasia, adrenal tumor, and Stein-Leventhal syndrome
• Evaluate women with infertility, amenorrhea, or hirsutism

POTENTIAL DIAGNOSIS

Increased in
DHEAS is produced by the adrenal cortex and testis; therefore, any

condition stimulating these organs or associated feedback mechanisms will result in increased levels.

- Anovulation
- Cushing's syndrome
- Ectopic ACTH-producing tumors
- Hirsutism
- Hyperprolactinemia
- Polycystic ovary (Stein-Leventhal syndrome)
- Virilizing adrenal tumors

Decreased in

DHEAS is produced by the adrenal cortex and testis; therefore, any condition suppressing the normal function of these organs or associated feedback mechanisms will result in decreased levels.

- Addison's disease
- Adrenal insufficiency (primary or secondary)
- Aging adults *(related to natural decline in production with age)*
- Hyperlipidemia
- Pregnancy *(related to DHEAS produced by fetal adrenals and converted to estrogens in the placenta)*
- Psoriasis *(some potent topical medications used for long periods of time can result in chronic adrenal insufficiency)*
- Psychosis *(related to acute adrenal insufficiency)*

CRITICAL FINDINGS: N/A

INTERFERING FACTORS

- Drugs that may increase DHEAS levels include aloin, benfluorex, clomiphene, corticotropin, danazol, exemestane, gemfibrozil, metformin, mifepristone, and nitrendipine.
- Drugs that may decrease DHEAS levels include aspirin, carbamazepine, dexamethasone, exemestane, finasteride, ketoconazole, leuprolide, oral contraceptives, phenobarbital, phenytoin, and tamoxifen.

NURSING IMPLICATIONS AND PROCEDURE

PRETEST:

Positively identify the patient using at least two unique identifiers before providing care, treatment, or services. *Patient Teaching:* Inform the patient this test can assist in diagnosing the cause of hormonal fluctuations.

Obtain a history of the patient's complaints, including a list of known allergens, especially allergies or sensitivities to latex.

Obtain a history of the patient's endocrine system, symptoms, phase of menstrual cycle, and results of previously performed laboratory tests and diagnostic and surgical procedures.

Obtain a list of the patient's current medications, including herbs, nutritional supplements, and nutraceuticals (see Appendix F).

Review the procedure with the patient. Inform the patient that specimen collection takes approximately 5 to 10 min. Address concerns about pain and explain that there may be some discomfort during the venipuncture.

Sensitivity to social and cultural issues, as well as concern for modesty, is important in providing psychological support before, during, and after the procedure.

There are no food, fluid, or medication restrictions unless by medical direction.

INTRATEST:

If the patient has a history of allergic reaction to latex, avoid the use of equipment containing latex.

Instruct the patient to cooperate fully and to follow directions. Direct the patient to breathe normally and to avoid unnecessary movement.

Observe standard precautions, and follow the general guidelines in Appendix A. Positively identify the patient, and label the appropriate specimen container with the corresponding patient demographics, initials of the person collecting the specimen, date, and time of collection. Perform a venipuncture.

Remove the needle and apply direct pressure with dry gauze to stop bleeding. Observe/assess venipuncture site for bleeding or hematoma formation and secure gauze with adhesive bandage.
Promptly transport the specimen to the laboratory for processing and analysis.

OST-TEST:

A report of the results will be made available to the requesting health-care provider (HCP), who will discuss the results with the patient.
Reinforce information given by the patient's HCP regarding further testing, treatment, or referral to another HCP.

Answer any questions or address any concerns voiced by the patient or family.
Depending on the results of this procedure, additional testing may be performed to evaluate or monitor progression of the disease process and determine the need for a change in therapy. Evaluate test results in relation to the patient's symptoms and other tests performed.

RELATED MONOGRAPHS:

Related tests include ACTH, cortisol, prolactin, and testosterone.
Refer to the Endocrine System table at the end of the book for related tests by body system.

D

Drugs of Abuse

Amphetamines	Ethanol (Alcohol)
Cannabinoids	Opiates
Cocaine	Phencyclidine

SYNONYM/ACRONYM: Amphetamines, cannabinoids (THC), cocaine, ethanol (alcohol, ethyl alcohol, ETOH), phencyclidine (PCP), opiates (heroin).

COMMON USE: To assist in rapid identification of commonly abused drugs in suspected drug overdose or for workplace drug screening.

SPECIMEN: For ethanol, serum (1 mL) collected in a red-top tube; plasma (1 mL) collected in a gray-top (sodium fluoride/potassium oxalate) tube is also acceptable. For drug screen, urine (15 mL) collected in a clean plastic container. Gastric contents (20 mL) may also be submitted for testing.

Workplace drug-screening programs, because of the potential medico-legal consequences associated with them, require collection of urine and blood specimens using a *chain of custody protocol*. The protocol provides securing the sample in a sealed transport device in the presence of the donor and a representative of the donor's employer, such that tampering would be obvious. The protocol also provides a written document of specimen transfer from donor to specimen collection personnel, to storage, to analyst, and to disposal.

NORMAL FINDINGS: (Method: Spectrophotometry for ethanol; immunoassay for drugs of abuse)

Ethanol: None detected
Drug screen: None detected

DESCRIPTION: Drug abuse continues to be one of the most significant social and economic problems in the United States. The Substance Abuse and Mental Health Services Administration (SAMHSA) has identified opiates, cocaine, cannabinoids, amphetamines, and phencyclidines (PCPs) as the most commonly abused illicit drugs. Alcohol is the most commonly encountered legal substance of abuse. Chronic alcohol abuse can lead to liver disease, high blood pressure, cardiac disease, and birth defects.

INDICATIONS
- Differentiate alcohol intoxication from diabetic coma, cerebral trauma, or drug overdose
- Investigate suspected drug abuse
- Investigate suspected drug overdose
- Investigate suspected noncompliance with drug or alcohol treatment program
- Monitor ethanol levels when administered to treat methanol intoxication
- Routine workplace screening

	Screening Cutoff Concentrations for Drugs of Abuse Recommended by SAMHSA	Confirmatory Cutoff Concentrations for Drugs of Abuse Recommended by SAMHSA	Detectable Duration After Last Single-Use Dose	Detectable Duration After Last Dose: Prolonged Use
Hallucinogens				
Cannabinoids	50 ng/mL	15 ng/mL	2–7 days	1–2 mo
Phencyclidine	25 ng/mL	25 ng/mL	1 wk	2–4 wk
Opiates	2,000 ng/mL	2,000 ng/mL	1–3 days	1–3 days
6–Acetylmorphine	10 ng/mL	10 ng/mL	20 hr	1–7 days
Stimulants				
Amphetamines (either amphetamine or methamphetamine)[a]	500 ng/mL	250 ng/mL	48 hr	7–10 days
Cocaine	150 ng/mL	100 ng/mL	3 days	4 days
MDMA (either methylenedioxy-methamphetamine, methylenedioxyamphetamine, or meth-ylenedioxyethylamphetamine)	500 ng/mL	250 ng/mL	24 hr	24 hr

[a] To be reported as positive for methamphetamine, the specimen must also contain amphetamine at a concentration of 100 ng/mL or greater.

POTENTIAL DIAGNOSIS

A urine screen merely identifies the presence of these substances in urine; it does not indicate time of exposure, amount used, quality of the source used, or level of impairment. Positive screens should be considered presumptive. Drug-specific confirmatory methods should be used to investigate questionable results of a positive urine screen.

CRITICAL FINDINGS

Note and immediately report to the health-care provider (HCP) any critically increased values and related symptoms. Timely notification of critical values for lab or diagnostic studies is a role expectation of the professional nurse. Notification processes will vary among facilities. Upon receipt of the critical value the information should be read back to the caller to verify accuracy. Most policies require immediate notification of the primary HCP, hospitalist, or on-call HCP. Reported information includes the patient's name, unique identifiers, critical value, name of the person giving the report, and name of the person receiving the report. Documentation of notification should be made in the medical record with the name of the HCP notified, time and date of notification, and any orders received. Any delay in a timely report of a critical value may require completion of a notification form with review by Risk Management.

The legal limit for ethanol intoxication varies by state, but in most states, greater than 80 mg/dL (0.08 %) is considered impaired for driving. Levels greater than 300 mg/dL are associated with amnesia, vomiting, double vision, and hypothermia. Levels of 400 to 700 mg/dL are associated with coma and may be fatal. Possible interventions for ethanol toxicity include administration of tap water or 3% sodium bicarbonate lavage, breathing support, and hemodialysis (usually indicated only if levels exceed 300 mg/dL).

Amphetamine intoxication (greater than 1 mcg/mL) causes psychoses, tremors, convulsions, insomnia, tachycardia, dysrhythmias, impotence, cerebrovascular accident, and respiratory failure. Possible interventions include emesis (if orally ingested and if the patient has a gag reflex and normal central nervous system [CNS] function), administration of activated charcoal followed by magnesium citrate cathartic, acidification of the urine to promote excretion, and administration of liquids to promote urinary output.

Cocaine intoxication (greater than 1 mcg/mL) causes short-term symptoms of CNS stimulation, hypertension, tachypnea, mydriasis, and tachycardia. Possible interventions include emesis (if orally ingested and if the patient has a gag reflex and normal CNS function), gastric lavage (if orally ingested), whole-bowel irrigation (if packs of the drug were ingested), airway protection, cardiac support, and administration of diazepam or phenobarbital for convulsions. The use of beta blockers is contraindicated.

Heroin and morphine are opiates that at toxic levels (greater than 200 ng/mL) cause bradycardia, flushing, itching, hypotension, hypothermia, and respiratory depression. Possible interventions include airway protection and the administration of naloxone (Narcan).

PCP intoxication (greater than 1 mg/mL) causes a variety of symptoms depending on the stage of intoxication. Stage I includes psychiatric signs, muscle spasms, fever, tachycardia, flushing, small pupils, salivation, nausea, and vomiting. Stage II includes stupor, convulsions, hallucinations, increased heart rate, and increased blood pressure. Stage III includes further increases of heart rate and blood pressure that may culminate in cardiac and respiratory failure. Possible interventions may include providing respiratory support, administration of activated charcoal with a cathartic such as sorbitol, gastric lavage and suction, administration of IV nutrition and electrolytes, and acidification of the urine to promote PCP excretion.

INTERFERING FACTORS

- Codeine-containing cough medicines and antidiarrheal preparations, as well as ingestion of large amounts of poppy seeds, may produce a false-positive opiate result.
- Adulterants such as bleach or other strong oxidizers can produce erroneous urine drug screen results.
- Alcohol is a volatile substance, and specimens should be stored in a tightly stoppered containers to avoid falsely decreased values.

NURSING IMPLICATIONS AND PROCEDURE

PRETEST:

Positively identify the patient using at least two unique identifiers before providing care, treatment, or services.

Patient Teaching: Inform the patient this test can assist with identification of drugs in the body.

Obtain a history of the patient's complaints, including a list of known allergens, especially allergies or sensitivities to latex.

Obtain a history of the patient's symptoms and previously performed laboratory tests and diagnostic and surgical procedures.

Obtain a list of the patient's current medications, including herbs, nutritional supplements, and nutraceuticals (see Appendix F).

Review the entire procedure with the patient, especially if the circumstances require collection of urine and blood specimens using a chain-of-custody protocol. Inform the patient that specimen collection takes approximately 5 to

10 min but may vary depending on the level of patient cooperation. Address concerns about pain and explain that there may be some discomfort during the venipuncture, but there should be no discomfort during urine specimen collection.

Sensitivity to social and cultural issues, as well as concern for modesty, is important in providing psychological support before, during, and after the procedure.

There are no food, fluid, or medication restrictions unless by medical direction.

If appropriate or required: *Make sure a written and informed consent has been signed prior to the procedure.*

INTRATEST:

If the patient has a history of allergic reaction to latex, avoid the use of equipment containing latex.

Instruct the patient to cooperate fully and to follow directions. Direct the patient receiving venipuncture to breathe normally and to avoid unnecessary movement.

Observe standard precautions, and follow the general guidelines in Appendix A. Positively identify the patient, and label the appropriate collection containers with the corresponding patient demographics, initials of the person collecting the specimen, date, and time of collection. For alcohol level, use a non–alcohol-containing solution to cleanse the venipuncture site before specimen collection. Perform a venipuncture, as appropriate. Cadaver blood is taken from the aorta. For a urine drug screen, instruct the patient to obtain a clean-catch urine specimen.

Remove the needle and apply direct pressure with dry gauze to stop bleeding. Observe/assess venipuncture site for bleeding or hematoma formation and secure gauze with adhesive bandage.

Clean-Catch Specimen

Instruct the male patient to (1) thoroughly wash his hands, (2) cleanse the meatus, (3) void a small amount into the toilet, and (4) void directly into the specimen container.

Instruct the female patient to (1) thoroughly wash her hands; (2) cleanse the labia from front to back

(3) while keeping the labia separated, void a small amount into the toilet; and (4) without interrupting the urine stream, void directly into the specimen container. Follow the chain-of-custody protocol, if required. Monitor specimen collection, labeling, and packaging to prevent tampering. This protocol may vary by institution.

Promptly transport the specimen to the laboratory for processing and analysis.

OST-TEST:

A report of the results will be made available to the requesting HCP, who will discuss the results with the patient. Ensure that results are communicated to the proper individual, as indicated in the chain-of-custody protocol. Recognize anxiety related to test results. Discuss the implications of abnormal test results on the patient's lifestyle. Provide teaching and information regarding the clinical implications of the

test results, as appropriate. Educate the patient regarding access to counseling services. Provide support and information regarding detoxification programs, as appropriate. Provide contact information, if desired, for the National Institute on Drug Abuse (www.nida.nih.gov). Reinforce information given by the patient's HCP regarding further testing, treatment, or referral to another HCP. Answer any questions or address any concerns voiced by the patient or family. Depending on the results of this procedure, additional testing may be performed to evaluate or monitor progression of the disease process and determine the need for a change in therapy. Evaluate test results in relation to the patient's symptoms and other tests performed.

RELATED MONOGRAPHS:

Refer to the Therapeutic/Toxicology table at the end of the book for related tests.

Ductography

YNONYM/ACRONYM: Breast ductoscopy, fiberoptic ductoscopy, galactography.

OMMON USE: To visualize and assess the breast ducts for disease and malignancy in women with nipple discharge.

REA OF APPLICATION: Breast.

ONTRAST: Iodine-based contrast medium.

DESCRIPTION: Ductography is a procedure that outlines the ductal system and provides information on the reasons for production of a nipple discharge. It can locate the site within the duct where the nipple discharge is produced. Fiberoptic ductoscopy allows visualization of the breast ductal wall and sampling of the abnormal area for diagnostic purposes and provides specimens

that are generally cellular. The majority of both benign and malignant breast disease originates from the cells that line the ductal-lobular unit. In ductography, the lactiferous duct is cannulated and a small amount of contrast medium is injected into the duct. Mammographic radiographs are then taken. Ductography is not indicated in patients with bilateral discharge because this is generally caused by hormonal changes. Biopsy and ablation techniques can also be performed during ductoscopy with correlation between visual findings and histopathology.

INDICATIONS
- Breast cancer
- Normal breast examination with high risk of developing breast cancer
- Unilateral nipple discharge, bloody or clear and watery

POTENTIAL DIAGNOSIS

Normal findings in
- Normal breast tissue

Abnormal findings in
- Ductal thickening
- Papillary lesions

CRITICAL FINDINGS
- Ductal carcinoma in situ (DSIS)
- Invasive breast cancer

It is essential that critical diagnoses be communicated immediately to the appropriate health-care provider (HCP). A listing of these diagnoses varies among facilities. Note and immediately report to the HCP abnormal results and related symptoms. Timely notification of critical values for lab or diagnostic studies is a role expectation of the professional nurse. Notification processes will vary among facilities. Upon receipt of the critical value the information should be read back to the caller to verify accuracy. Most policies require immediate notification of the primary HCP, hospitalist, or on-call HCP. Reported information includes the patient's name, unique identifiers, critical value, name of the person giving the report, and name of the person receiving the report. Documentation of notification should be made in the medical record with the name of the HCP notified, time and date of notification, and any orders received. Any delay in a timely report of

a critical value may require completion of a notification form with review by Risk Management.

INTERFERING FACTORS

This procedure is contraindicated for
- Patients who are pregnant or suspected of being pregnant, unless the potential benefits of the procedure far outweigh the risks to the fetus and mother.
- Patients younger than age 25, because the density of the breast tissue is such that diagnostic x-rays are of limited value.

Factors that may impair clear imaging
- Inability of the patient to cooperate or remain still during the procedure because of age, significant pain, or mental status.
- Metallic objects within the examination field (e.g., jewelry, body rings), which may inhibit organ visualization and can produce unclear images.
- Application of substances such as talcum powder, deodorant, or cream to the skin of breasts or underarms, which may alter test results.
- Previous breast surgery, breast augmentation, or the presence of breast implants, which may decrease the readability of the examination.

Other considerations
- Consultation with an HCP should occur before the procedure for radiation safety concerns regarding younger patients or patients who are lactating.
- Risks associated with radiologic overexposure can result from frequent x-ray procedures. Personnel in the room with the patient should stand behind a shield or leave the area while the examination is being done. Personnel working in the examination area should wear badges to record their level of radiation exposure.

NURSING IMPLICATIONS AND PROCEDURE

PRETEST:

Positively identify the patient using at least two unique identifiers before providing care, treatment, or services.

Patient Teaching: Inform the patient this procedure can assist in evaluating the breast and mammary ducts for disease.

Obtain a history of the patient's complaints, including a list of known allergens, especially allergies or sensitivities to latex, iodine, seafood, contrast medium, or anesthetics.

Obtain a history of the patient's reproductive system, symptoms, and results of previously performed laboratory tests and diagnostic and surgical procedures. Record the date of last menstrual period and determine the possibility of pregnancy in perimenopausal women.

Obtain a list of the patient's current medications, including herbs, nutritional supplements, and nutraceuticals (see Appendix F).

Review the procedure with the patient. Address concerns about pain and explain that there may be moments of discomfort and some pain experienced during the test. Inform the patient that the procedure is usually performed in a mammography department by an HCP, with support staff, and takes approximately 30 min.

Sensitivity to social and cultural issues, as well as concern for modesty, is important in providing psychological support before, during, and after the procedure. There are no food, fluid, or medication restrictions unless by medical direction.

Inform the patient not to apply deodorant, body creams, or powders on the day of the procedure.

Instruct the patient to remove jewelry and other metallic objects in the area to be examined.

Make sure a written and informed consent has been signed prior to the procedure and before administering any medications.

INTRATEST:

Observe standard precautions, and follow the general guidelines in Appendix A. Positively identify the patient.

Ensure that the patient has removed external metallic objects prior to the procedure.

Ensure that the patient has removed any deodorant and talcum powder.

Have emergency equipment readily available for possible contrast reactions.

Instruct the patient to change into the gown, robe, and foot coverings provided.

Instruct the patient to cooperate fully and to follow directions. Instruct the patient to remain still throughout the procedure because movement produces unreliable results.

Place the patient in the supine position on an examination table.

Stroke the breast with firm pressure to discharge a small amount of fluid from the duct.

Cannulate the duct until it passes beyond the sphincter of the orifice.

Inject a small amount of contrast into the duct, allowing gravity to move it.

Tape the cannula to the breast and assist the patient to the mammography unit for two mammographic images.

Remove the cannula and apply a dressing over the nipple.

Observe/assess the cannula insertion site for bleeding, inflammation, or hematoma formation.

POST-TEST:

A report of the results will be made available to the requesting HCP, who will discuss the results with the patient.

Observe/assess the cannula insertion site for bleeding, inflammation, or hematoma formation.

Instruct the patient in the care and assessment of the injection site.

Recognize anxiety related to test results. Discuss the implications of abnormal test results on the patient's lifestyle. Provide teaching and information regarding the clinical implications of the test results, as appropriate. Educate the patient regarding access to counseling services.

Reinforce information given by the patient's HCP regarding further testing, treatment, or referral to another HCP. Decisions regarding the need for and frequency of breast self-examination, mammography, MRI breast, or other cancer screening procedures should be

D

made after consultation between the patient and HCP. The most current guidelines for breast cancer screening of the general population as well as individuals with increased risk are available from the American Cancer Society (www.cancer.org), the American College of Obstetricians and Gynecologists (ACOG) (www.acog.org), and the American College of Radiology (www.acr.org). Answer any questions or address any concerns voiced by the patient or family.

Instruct the patient in the use of any ordered medications. Explain the importance of adhering to the therapy regimen. As appropriate, instruct the patient in significant side effects and systemic reactions associated with the prescribed medication. Encourage the patient to review corresponding literature provided by a pharmacist.

Depending on the results of this procedure, additional testing may be needed to evaluate or monitor progression of the disease process and determine the need for a change in therapy. Evaluate test results in relation to the patient's symptoms and other tests performed.

RELATED MONOGRAPHS:

Related tests include biopsy breast, cancer antigens, mammography, MRI breast, stereotactic biopsy breast, and US breast.

Refer to the Reproductive System table at the end of the book for related tests by body system.

D-Xylose Tolerance Test

SYNONYM/ACRONYM: N/A.

COMMON USE: To assist in the differential diagnosis of small intestine malabsorption syndromes such as celiac, tropical sprue, and Crohn's diseases.

SPECIMEN: Plasma (1 mL) collected in a gray-top (fluoride/oxalate) tube and urine (10 mL from a 5-hr collection) in a clean amber plastic container.

NORMAL FINDINGS: (Method: Spectrophotometry)

Dose by Age	Conventional Units	SI Units (Conventional Units × 0.0666)
Plasma		
Adult dose		
25 g	Greater than 25 mg/dL	Greater than 1.7 mmol/L
5 g	Greater than 20 mg/dL	Greater than 1.3 mmol/L
Pediatric dose		
0.5 g/kg (max. 25 g)	Greater than 30 mg/dL	Greater than 2 mmol/L
Urine		
Adult dose		
25 g	Greater than 4 g/5-hr collection	Greater than 26.6 mmol/5 hr
5 g	Greater than 1.2 g/5-hr collection	Greater than 8 mmol/5 hr
Pediatric dose		
0.5 g/kg (max. 25 g)	Greater than 16%–40% of dose	Greater than 16%–40% of dose

DESCRIPTION: The D-xylose tolerance test is used to screen for intestinal malabsorption of carbohydrates. D-Xylose is a pentose sugar not normally present in the blood in significant amounts. It is partially absorbed when ingested and normally passes unmetabolized in the urine.

INDICATIONS

Assist in the diagnosis of malabsorption syndromes

POTENTIAL DIAGNOSIS

Increased in: N/A

Decreased in
Conditions that involve defective mucosal absorption of carbohydrates and other nutrients.

- Amyloidosis
- Bacterial overgrowth *(sugar is consumed by bacteria)*
- Eosinophilic gastroenteritis
- Lymphomá
- Nontropical sprue (celiac disease, gluten-induced enteropathy)
- Parasitic infestations (*Giardia*, schistosomiasis, hookworm)
- Postoperative period after massive resection of the intestine
- Radiation enteritis
- Scleroderma
- Small bowel ischemia
- Tropical sprue
- Whipple's disease
- Zollinger-Ellison syndrome

CRITICAL FINDINGS: N/A

INTERFERING FACTORS

- Drugs that may increase urine D-xylose levels include phenazopyridine.
- Drugs and substances that may decrease urine D-xylose levels include acetylsalicylic acid, aminosalicylic acid, arsenicals, colchicine, digitalis, ethionamide, gold, indomethacin, isocarboxazid, kanamycin, monoamine oxidase inhibitors, neomycin, and phenelzine.
- Poor renal function or vomiting may cause low urine values.

NURSING IMPLICATIONS AND PROCEDURE

PRETEST:

- Positively identify the patient using at least two unique identifiers before providing care, treatment, or services.
- *Patient Teaching:* Inform the patient this test can assist in assessing the ability of the small intestine to absorb carbohydrates.
- Obtain a history of the patient's complaints, including a list of known allergens, especially allergies or sensitivities to latex.
- Obtain a history of the patient's gastrointestinal system, symptoms, and results of previously performed laboratory tests and diagnostic and surgical procedures.
- Obtain a list of the patient's current medications, including herbs, nutritional supplements, and nutraceuticals (see Appendix F).
- Review the procedure with the patient. Inform the patient that activity will be restricted during the test. Obtain the pediatric patient's weight to calculate dose of D-xylose to be administered. Inform the patient that blood specimen collection takes approximately 5 to 10 min. Address concerns about pain and explain that there may be some discomfort during the venipuncture.
- *Sensitivity to social and cultural issues,* as well as concern for modesty, is important in providing psychological support before, during, and after the procedure.
- Ask the patient to void and discard the urine before the administration of the D-xylose. Inform the patient that once the test has begun, all urine for a 5-hr period must be saved. Provide a non-metallic urinal, bedpan, or toilet-mounted collection device.
- Instruct the patient not to void directly into the laboratory collection container. Instruct the patient to avoid defecating

in the collection device and to keep toilet tissue out of the collection device to prevent contamination of the specimen. Place a sign in the bathroom to remind the patient to save all urine.

Instruct the patient to void all urine into the collection device and then to pour the urine into the laboratory collection container. Alternatively, the specimen can be left in the collection device for a health-care staff member to add to the laboratory collection container.

Numerous medications (e.g., acetylsalicylic acid, indomethacin, neomycin) interfere with the test and should be withheld, by medical direction, for 24 hr before testing.

There are no fluid restrictions, unless by medical direction.

The patient should fast for at least 12 hr before the test. In addition, the patient should refrain from eating foods containing pentose sugars such as fruits, jams, jellies, and pastries. Protocols may vary among facilities.

INTRATEST:

Ensure that the patient has complied with dietary and medication restrictions; assure that food has been restricted for at least 12 hr prior to the procedure and medications have been withheld, by medical direction, for 24 hr prior to the procedure.

If the patient has a history of allergic reaction to latex, avoid the use of equipment containing latex.

Instruct the patient to cooperate fully and to follow directions. Direct the patient to breathe normally and to avoid unnecessary movement.

Observe standard precautions, and follow the general guidelines in Appendix A. Positively identify the patient, and label the appropriate specimen container with the corresponding patient demographics, initials of the person collecting the specimen, date, and time of collection. Perform a venipuncture.

Remove the needle and apply direct pressure with dry gauze to stop bleeding. Observe/assess venipuncture site for bleeding or hematoma formation and secure gauze with adhesive bandage.

Timed Specimen

Obtain a clean 3-L urine specimen container, toilet-mounted collection device, and plastic bag (for transport of the specimen container). The specimen must be refrigerated or kept on ice throughout the entire collection period. If an indwelling urinary catheter is in place, the drainage bag must be kept on ice.

Begin the test between 6 a.m. and 8 a.m., if possible. Remind the patient to remain supine and at rest throughout the duration of the test. Instruct the patient to collect all urine for a 5-hr period after administration of the D-xylose.

Adults are given a 25-g dose of D-xylose dissolved in 250 mL of water to take orally. The dose for pediatric patients is calculated by weight up to a maximum of 25 g. The patient should drink an additional 250 mL of water as soon as the D-xylose solution has been taken. Some adult patients with severe symptoms may be given a 5-g dose, but the test results are less sensitive at the lower dose.

If an indwelling catheter is in place, replace the tubing and container system at the start of the collection time. Keep the container system on ice during the collection period or empty the urine into a larger container periodically during the collection period; monitor to ensure continued drainage.

Blood samples are collected 1 hr postdose for pediatric patients and 2 hr postdose for adults.

Direct the patient to breathe normally and to avoid unnecessary movement. Perform a venipuncture, and collect the specimen in a 5-mL gray-top tube.

Include on the collection container's label the amount of urine, test start and stop times, and ingestion of any foods or medications that could affect test results.

Promptly transport the specimens to the laboratory for processing and analysis.

POST-TEST:

A report of the results will be made available to the requesting health-care provider (HCP), who will discuss the results with the patient.

Instruct the patient to resume usual medications, as directed by the HCP.

Nutritional Considerations: Decreased D-xylose levels may be associated with gastrointestinal disease. Nutritional therapy may be indicated in the presence of malabsorption disorders. Encourage the patient, as appropriate, to consult with a qualified nutrition specialist to plan a lactose- and gluten-free diet. This dietary planning is complex because patients are often malnourished and have related nutritional problems.

Recognize anxiety related to test results. Discuss the implications of abnormal test results on the patient's lifestyle. Provide teaching and information regarding the clinical implications of the test results, as appropriate. Offer support to help the patient and/or caregiver cope with the long-term implications of a chronic disorder and related lifestyle changes. Educate the patient regarding access to counseling services, as appropriate.

Reinforce information given by the patient's HCP regarding further testing, treatment, or referral to another HCP. Answer any questions or address any concerns voiced by the patient or family.

Depending on the results of this procedure, additional testing may be performed to evaluate or monitor progression of the disease process and determine the need for a change in therapy. Evaluate test results in relation to the patient's symptoms and other tests performed.

RELATED MONOGRAPHS:

Related tests include biopsy intestine, chloride sweat, fecal analysis, fecal fat, gastric emptying scan, lactose tolerance, ova and parasite, and RAIU.

Refer to the Gastrointestinal System table at the end of the book for related tests by body system.

Echocardiography

SYNONYM/ACRONYM: Doppler echo, Doppler ultrasound of the heart, echo.

COMMON USE: To assist in diagnosing cardiovascular disorders such as defec heart failure, tumor, infection, and bleeding.

AREA OF APPLICATION: Chest/thorax.

CONTRAST: Can be done with or without noniodinated contrast mediur (microspheres).

DESCRIPTION: Echocardiography, a noninvasive ultrasound (US) procedure, uses high-frequency sound waves of various intensities to assist in diagnosing cardiovascular disorders. The procedure records the echoes created by the deflection of an ultrasonic beam off the cardiac structures and allows visualization of the size, shape, position, thickness, and movement of all four valves, atria, ventricular and atria septa, papillary muscles, chordae tendineae, and ventricles. This study can also determine blood-flow velocity and direction and the presence of pericardial effusion during the movement of the transducer over areas of the chest. Electrocardiography and phonocardiography can be done simultaneously to correlate the findings with the cardiac cycle. These procedures can be done at the bedside or in a specialized department, health-care provider's (HPC's) office, or clinic.

Included in the study are the M-mode method, which produces a linear tracing of timed motions of the heart, its structures, and associated measurements over time; and the two-dimensional method, using real-time Doppler color-flow imaging with pulsed and continuous-wave Doppler spectral tracings, which produces a cross-section of the structures of the heart and their relationship to one another, including changes in the coronary vasculature, velocity and direction of blood flow, and areas of eccentric blood flow. Doppler color-flow imaging may also be helpful in depicting the function of biological and prosthetic valves.

Cardiac contrast medium is used to aid in the diagnosis of intracardiac shunt and tricuspid valve regurgitation. The contrast agent is injected IV and outlines the chambers of the heart.

INDICATIONS

- Detect atrial tumors (myxomas)
- Detect subaortic stenosis as evidenced either by displacement of the anterior atrial leaflet or by a reduction in aortic valve flow, depending on the obstruction
- Detect ventricular or atrial mural thrombi and evaluate cardiac wall motion after myocardial infarction
- Determine the presence of pericardi effusion, tamponade, and pericarditis
- Determine the severity of valvular abnormalities such as stenosis, prolapse, and regurgitation
- Evaluate congenital heart disorders
- Evaluate endocarditis
- Evaluate or monitor prosthetic valve function
- Evaluate the presence of shunt flow and continuity of the aorta and pulmonary artery
- Evaluate unexplained chest pain, electrocardiographic changes, and abnormal chest x-ray (e.g., enlarge cardiac silhouette)

Evaluate ventricular aneurysms and/or thrombus

Measure the size of the heart's chambers and determine if hypertrophic cardiomyopathy or congestive heart failure is present

OTENTIAL DIAGNOSIS

Normal findings in

Normal appearance in the size, position, structure, and movements of the heart valves visualized and recorded in a combination of ultrasound modes; and normal heart muscle walls of both ventricles and left atrium, with adequate blood filling. Established values for the measurement of heart activities obtained by the study may vary by HCP and institution.

Abnormal findings in

Aortic aneurysm

Aortic valve abnormalities

Cardiac neoplasm

Cardiomyopathy

Congenital heart defect

Congestive heart failure

Coronary artery disease (CAD)

Endocarditis

Mitral valve abnormalities

Myxoma

Pericardial effusion, tamponade, and pericarditis

Pulmonary hypertension

Pulmonary valve abnormalities

Septal defects

Ventricular hypertrophy

Ventricular or atrial mural thrombi

RITICAL FINDINGS ◈

Aortic aneurysm

Infection

Obstruction

Tumor with significant mass effect (rare)

It is essential that critical diagnoses be communicated immediately to the appropriate HCP. A listing of those diagnoses varies among facilities. Note and immediately report to the HCP abnormal results and related symptoms. Timely notification of critical values for lab or diagnostic studies is a role expectation of the professional nurse. Notification processes will vary among facilities. Upon receipt of the critical value the information should be read back to the caller to verify accuracy. Most policies require immediate notification of the primary HCP, hospitalist, or on-call HCP. Reported information includes the patient's name, unique identifiers, critical value, name of the person giving the report, and name of the person receiving the report. Documentation of notification should be made in the medical record with the name of the HCP notified, time and date of notification, and any orders received. Any delay in a timely report of a critical value may require completion of a notification form with review by Risk Management.

INTERFERING FACTORS

Factors that may impair clear imaging

- Incorrect placement of the transducer over the desired test site.
- Retained barium from a previous radiological procedure.
- Patients who are dehydrated, resulting in failure to demonstrate the boundaries between organs and tissue structures.
- Metallic objects (e.g., jewelry, body rings) within the examination field, which may inhibit organ visualization and cause unclear images.
- The presence of chronic obstructive pulmonary disease or use of mechanical ventilation, which increases the air between the heart and chest wall (hyperinflation) and can attenuate the ultrasound waves.
- The presence of arrhythmias.
- Inability of the patient to cooperate or remain still during the procedure because of age, significant pain, or mental status.

E

NURSING IMPLICATIONS AND PROCEDURE

PRETEST:

▶ Positively identify the patient using at least two unique identifiers before providing care, treatment, or services.

▶ *Patient Teaching:* Inform the patient this procedure can assist in assessing cardiac (heart) function.

▶ Obtain a history of the patient's symptoms, including a list of known allergens, especially allergies or sensitivities to latex, iodine, seafood, anesthetics, or contrast mediums.

▶ Obtain a history of the patient's cardiovascular system, symptoms, and results of previously performed laboratory tests and diagnostic and surgical procedures.

▶ Note any recent procedures that can interfere with test results (i.e., barium procedures, surgery, or biopsy). Ensure that barium studies were performed at least 24 hr before this test.

▶ Record the date of the last menstrual period and determine the possibility of pregnancy in perimenopausal women.

▶ Obtain a list of the patient's current medications, including herbs, nutritional supplements, and nutraceuticals (see Appendix F).

▶ Review the procedure with the patient. Address concerns about pain related to the procedure and explain that there should be no discomfort during the procedure. Inform the patient the procedure is performed in a US or cardiology department, usually by an HCP, and takes approximately 30 to 60 min.

▶ *Sensitivity to social and cultural issues,* as well as concern for modesty, is important in providing psychological support before, during, and after the procedure.

▶ Instruct the patient to remove jewelry, and other metallic objects from the area to be examined.

▶ There are no food or fluid restrictions unless by medical direction.

INTRATEST:

▶ Observe standard precautions, and follow the general guidelines in Appendix A. Positively identify the patient.

▶ Ensure the patient has removed all external metallic objects from the area to be examined prior to the procedure.

▶ Have emergency equipment readily available.

▶ Instruct the patient to void prior to the procedure and to change into the gown, robe, and foot coverings provided.

▶ Instruct the patient to cooperate fully and to follow directions. Instruct the patient to remain still throughout the procedure because movement produces unreliable results.

▶ Place the patient in a supine position on a flat table with foam wedges to help maintain position and immobilization.

▶ Expose the chest, and attach electrocardiogram leads for simultaneous tracings, if desired.

▶ Apply conductive gel to the chest. Place the transducer on the chest surface along the left sternal border, the subxiphoid area, suprasternal notch, and supraclavicular areas to obtain views and tracings of the portions of the heart. Scan the areas by systematically moving the probe in a perpendicular position to direct the ultrasound waves to each part of the heart.

▶ To obtain different views or information about heart function, position the patient on the left side and/or sitting up, or request that the patient breathe slowly or hold the breath during the procedure. To evaluate heart function changes, the patient may be asked to inhale amyl nitrate (vasodilator).

▶ Administer contrast medium, if ordered. A second series of images is obtained.

POST-TEST:

▶ A report of the results will be made available to the requesting HCP, who will discuss the results with the patient.

▶ When the study is completed, remove the gel from the skin.

▶ Recognize anxiety related to test results, and offer support. Discuss the implications of abnormal test results on the patient's lifestyle. Provide teaching and information regarding the clinical implications of the test results, as appropriate.

Nutritional Considerations: Abnormal findings may be associated with cardiovascular disease. The American Heart Association and National Heart, Lung, and Blood Institute (NHLBI) recommend nutritional therapy for individuals identified to be at high risk for developing CAD or individuals who have specific risk factors and/or existing medical conditions (e.g., elevated LDL cholesterol levels, other lipid disorders, insulin-dependent diabetes, insulin resistance, or metabolic syndrome). If overweight, the patient should be encouraged to achieve a normal weight. Guidelines for the Therapeutic Lifestyle Changes (TLC) diet are outlined in the Third Report of the Expert Panel on Detection, Evaluation, and Treatment of High Blood Cholesterol in Adults (Adult Treatment Panel III [ATP III]). The TLC diet emphasizes a reduction in foods high in saturated fats and cholesterol. Red meats, eggs, and dairy products are the major sources of saturated fats and cholesterol. If triglycerides also are elevated, the patient should be advised to eliminate or reduce alcohol and simple carbohydrates from the diet. The TLC approach also includes the use of plant stanols or sterols and increased dissolved fiber as an option for lowering LDL cholesterol levels; nutritional recommendations for daily total caloric intake; recommendations for allowable percentage of calories derived from fat (saturated and unsaturated), carbohydrates, protein, and cholesterol; as well as recommendations for daily expenditure of energy.

Nutritional Considerations: Overweight patients with high blood pressure should be encouraged to achieve a normal weight. Other changeable risk factors warranting patient education include strategies to safely decrease sodium intake, increase physical activity, decrease alcohol consumption, eliminate tobacco use, and decrease cholesterol levels.

Social and Cultural Considerations: Numerous studies point to the prevalence of excess body weight in American children and adolescents. Experts estimate that obesity is present in 25% of the population ages 6 to 11 yr. The medical, social, and emotional consequences of excess body weight are significant. Special attention should be given to instructing the child and caregiver regarding health risks and weight control education.

Recognize anxiety related to test results, and be supportive of fear of shortened life expectancy. Discuss the implications of abnormal test results on the patient's lifestyle. Provide teaching and information regarding the clinical implications of the test results, as appropriate. Educate the patient regarding access to counseling services. Provide contact information, if desired, for the American Heart Association (www.americanheart.org) or the NHLBI (www.nhlbi.nih.gov).

Reinforce information given by the patient's HCP regarding further testing, treatment, or referral to another HCP. Answer any questions or address any concerns voiced by the patient or family.

Depending on the results of this procedure, additional testing may be needed to evaluate or monitor progression of the disease process and determine the need for a change in therapy. Evaluate test results in relation to the patient's symptoms and other tests performed.

RELATED MONOGRAPHS:

Related tests include antiarrhythmic drugs, apolipoprotein A and B, AST, atrial natriuretic peptide, BNP, blood gases, blood pool imaging, calcium, chest x-ray, cholesterol (total, HDL, LDL), CT cardiac scoring, CT thorax, CRP, CK and isoenzymes, echocardiography, echocardiography transesophageal, electrocardiogram, exercise stress test, glucose, glycated hemoglobin, Holter monitor, homocysteine, ketones, LDH and isos, lipoprotein electrophoresis, lung perfusion scan, magnesium, MRI chest, MI infarct scan, myocardial perfusion heart scan, myoglobin, PET heart, potassium, pulse oximetry, sodium, triglycerides, and troponin.

Refer to the Cardiovascular System table at the end of the book for related tests by body system.

Echocardiography, Transesophageal

SYNONYM/ACRONYM: Echo, TEE.

COMMON USE: To assess and visualize cardiovascular structures toward diagnosing disorders such as tumors, congenital defects, valve disorders, chamber disorders, and bleeding.

AREA OF APPLICATION: Chest/thorax.

CONTRAST: Can be done with or without noniodinated contrast medium (microspheres).

DESCRIPTION: Transesophageal echocardiography (TEE) is performed to assist in the diagnosis of cardiovascular disorders when noninvasive echocardiography is contraindicated or does not reveal enough information to confirm a diagnosis. Noninvasive echocardiography may be an inadequate procedure for patients who are obese, have chest wall structure abnormalities, or have chronic obstructive pulmonary disease (COPD). TEE provides a better view of the posterior aspect of the heart, including the atrium and aorta. It is done with a transducer attached to a gastroscope that is inserted into the esophagus. The transducer and the ultrasound (US) instrument allow the beam to be directed to the back of the heart. The echoes are amplified and recorded on a screen for visualization and recorded on graph paper or videotape. The depth of the endoscope and movement of the transducer is controlled to obtain various images of the heart structures. TEE is usually performed during surgery; it is also used on patients who are in the intensive care unit, in whom the transmission of waves to and from the chest has been compromised and more definitive information is needed. The images obtained by TEE have better resolution than those obtained by routine transthoracic echocardiography because TEE uses higher frequency sound waves and offers closer proximity of the transducer to the cardiac structures. Cardiac contrast medium is used to improve the visualization of viable myocardial tissue within the heart.

INDICATIONS

- Confirm diagnosis if conventional echocardiography does not correlate with other findings
- Detect and evaluate congenital heart disorders
- Detect atrial tumors (myxomas)
- Detect or determine the severity of valvular abnormalities and regurgitation
- Detect subaortic stenosis as evidenced by displacement of the anterior atrial leaflet and reduction in aortic valve flow, depending on the obstruction
- Detect thoracic aortic dissection and coronary artery disease (CAD)

- Detect ventricular or atrial mural thrombi and evaluate cardiac wall motion after myocardial infarction
- Determine the presence of pericardial effusion
- Evaluate aneurysms and ventricular thrombus
- Evaluate or monitor biological and prosthetic valve function
- Evaluate septal defects
- Measure the size of the heart's chambers and determine if hypertrophic cardiomyopathy or congestive heart failure is present
- Monitor cardiac function during open heart surgery (most sensitive method for monitoring ischemia)
- Reevaluate after inadequate visualization with conventional echocardiography as a result of obesity, trauma to or deformity of the chest wall, or lung hyperinflation associated with COPD

POTENTIAL DIAGNOSIS

Normal findings in

- Normal appearance of the size, position, structure, movements of the heart valves and heart muscle walls, and chamber blood filling; no evidence of valvular stenosis or insufficiency, cardiac tumor, foreign bodies, or CAD. The established values for the measurement of heart activities obtained by the study may vary by health-care provider (HCP) and institution.

Abnormal findings in

- Aortic aneurysm
- Aortic valve abnormalities
- CAD
- Cardiomyopathy
- Congenital heart defects
- Congestive heart failure
- Mitral valve abnormalities
- Myocardial infarction
- Myxoma
- Pericardial effusion
- Pulmonary hypertension
- Pulmonary valve abnormalities
- Septal defects

- Shunting of blood flow
- Thrombus
- Ventricular hypertrophy
- Ventricular or atrial mural thrombi

CRITICAL FINDINGS

- Aortic aneurysm
- Aortic dissection

It is essential that critical diagnoses be communicated immediately to the appropriate HCP. A listing of those diagnoses varies among facilities. Note and immediately report to the HCP abnormal results and related symptoms. Timely notification of critical values for lab or diagnostic studies is a role expectation of the professional nurse. Notification processes will vary among facilities. Upon receipt of the critical value the information should be read back to the caller to verify accuracy. Most policies require immediate notification of the primary HCP, hospitalist, or on-call HCP. Reported information includes the patient's name, unique identifiers, critical value, name of the person giving the report, and name of the person receiving the report. Documentation of notification should be made in the medical record with the name of the HCP notified, time and date of notification, and any orders received. Any delay in a timely report of a critical value may require completion of a notification form with review by Risk Management.

INTERFERING FACTORS

This procedure is contraindicated for

- Patients with significant esophageal pathology (procedure may cause bleeding).

Factors that may impair clear imaging

- Incorrect placement of the transducer over the desired test site.
- Retained barium from a previous radiological procedure.

- Patients who are dehydrated, resulting in failure to demonstrate the boundaries between organs and tissue structures.
- Laryngospasm, dysrhythmias, or esophageal bleeding.
- Known upper esophageal pathology.
- Conditions such as esophageal dysphagia and irradiation of the mediastinum.
- The presence of COPD or use of mechanical ventilation, which increases the air between the heart and chest wall (hyperinflation) and can attenuate the US waves.
- The presence of arrhythmias.
- Inability of the patient to cooperate or remain still during the procedure because of age, significant pain, or mental status.

Other considerations

- Failure to follow dietary restrictions before the procedure may cause the procedure to be canceled or repeated.

NURSING IMPLICATIONS AND PROCEDURE

PRETEST:

Positively identify the patient using at least two unique identifiers before providing care, treatment, or services.
Patient Teaching: Inform the patient this procedure can assist in assessing cardiac (heart) function.
Obtain a history of the patient's complaints, including a list of known allergens, especially allergies or sensitivities to latex, iodine, seafood, anesthetics, or contrast mediums.
Obtain a history of the patient's cardiovascular system, symptoms, and results of previously performed laboratory tests and diagnostic and surgical procedures. Note any recent procedures that can interfere with test results (i.e., barium procedures, surgery, or biopsy). Ensure that barium studies were performed at least 24 hr before this test.
Record the date of the last menstrual period and determine the possibility

of pregnancy in perimenopausal women.
Obtain a list of the patient's current medications, including anticoagulants, aspirin and other salicylates, herbs, nutritional supplements, and nutraceuticals (see Appendix F). Note the last time and dose of medication taken.
Review the procedure with the patient. Address concerns about pain related to the procedure. Explain that some pain may be experienced during the test, and there may be moments of discomfort during insertion of the scope. Lidocaine is sprayed in the patient's throat to reduce discomfort caused by the presence of the endoscope. Inform the patient that the procedure is performed in a US or cardiology department, usually by an HCP, and takes approximately 30 to 60 min.
Explain that an IV line may be inserted to allow infusion of IV fluids, contrast medium, or sedatives.
Sensitivity to social and cultural issues, as well as concern for modesty, is important in providing psychological support before, during, and after the procedure.
Instruct the patient to remove jewelry and other metallic objects from the area to be examined.
The patient should avoid food and fluids for 8 hr prior to the procedure. Protocols may vary among facilities.
Make sure a written and informed consent has been signed prior to the procedure and before administering any medications.

INTRATEST:

Observe standard precautions, and follow the general guidelines in Appendix A. Positively identify the patient.
Ensure that the patient has complied with dietary and fluid restriction for at least 8 hr prior to the procedure.
Ensure the patient has removed all external metallic objects from the area to be examined prior to the procedure.
Have emergency equipment readily available.
Instruct the patient to void prior to the procedure and to change into the gown, robe, and foot coverings provided.
Obtain and record the patient's vital signs.

▶ Instruct the patient to cooperate fully and to follow directions. Instruct the patient to remain still throughout the procedure because movement produces unreliable results.

▶ Ask the patient, as appropriate, to remove his or her dentures.

▶ Monitor pulse oximetry to determine oxygen saturation in sedated patients.

▶ Expose the chest, and attach electrocardiogram leads for simultaneous tracings, if desired.

▶ Spray or swab the patient's throat with a local anesthetic, and place the oral bridge device in the mouth to prevent biting of the endoscope.

▶ Place the patient in a left side-lying position on a flat table with foam wedges to help maintain position and immobilization. The pharyngeal area is anesthetized, and the endoscope with the ultrasound device attached to its tip is inserted 30 to 50 cm to the posterior area of the heart, as in any esophagogastroduodenoscopy procedure.

▶ Ask the patient to swallow as the scope is inserted. When the transducer is in place, the scope is manipulated by controls on the handle to obtain scanning that provides real-time images of the heart motion and recordings of the images for viewing. Actual scanning is usually limited to 15 min or until the desired number of image planes is obtained at different depths of the scope.

▶ Administer contrast medium, if ordered. A second series of images is obtained.

POST-TEST:

▶ A report of the results will be made available to the requesting HCP, who will discuss the results with the patient.

▶ Monitor vital signs and neurological status every 15 min for 1 hr, then every 2 hr for 4 hr, and as ordered. Take temperature every 4 hr for 24 hr. Monitor intake and output at least every 8 hr. Compare with baseline values. Notify the HCP if temperature is elevated. Protocols may vary among facilities.

▶ Instruct the patient to resume usual diet and activity 4 to 6 hr after the test, as directed by the HCP.

▶ Instruct the patient to treat throat discomfort with lozenges and warm gargles when the gag reflex returns.

▶ Recognize anxiety related to test results, and offer support. Discuss the implications of abnormal test results on the patient's lifestyle. Provide teaching and information regarding the clinical implications of the test results, as appropriate.

▶ *Nutritional Considerations:* Abnormal findings may be associated with cardiovascular disease. The American Heart Association and National Heart, Lung, and Blood Institute (NHLBI) recommend nutritional therapy for individuals identified to be at high risk for developing CAD or individuals who have specific risk factors and/or existing medical conditions (e.g., elevated LDL cholesterol levels, other lipid disorders, insulin-dependent diabetes, insulin resistance, or metabolic syndrome). If overweight, the patient should be encouraged to achieve a normal weight. Guidelines for the Therapeutic Lifestyle Changes (TLC) diet are outlined in the Third Report of the Expert Panel on Detection, Evaluation, and Treatment of High Blood Cholesterol in Adults (Adult Treatment Panel III [ATP III]). The TLC diet emphasizes a reduction in foods high in saturated fats and cholesterol. Red meats, eggs, and dairy products are the major sources of saturated fats and cholesterol. If triglycerides also are elevated, the patient should be advised to eliminate or reduce alcohol and simple carbohydrates from the diet. The TLC approach also includes the use of plant stanols or sterols and increased dissolved fiber as an option for lowering LDL cholesterol levels; nutritional recommendations for daily total caloric intake; recommendations for allowable percentage of calories derived from fat (saturated and unsaturated), carbohydrates, protein, and cholesterol; as well as recommendations for daily expenditure of energy.

▶ *Nutritional Considerations:* Overweight patients with high blood pressure should be encouraged to achieve a normal weight. Other changeable risk factors warranting patient education include strategies to safely decrease sodium intake, increase physical activity, decrease alcohol consumption, eliminate tobacco use, and decrease cholesterol levels.

Social and Cultural Considerations:
Numerous studies point to the prevalence of excess body weight in American children and adolescents. Experts estimate that obesity is present in 25% of the population ages 6 to 11 yr. The medical, social, and emotional consequences of excess body weight are significant. Special attention should be given to instructing the child and caregiver regarding health risks and weight control education.

Recognize anxiety related to test results, and be supportive of fear of shortened life expectancy. Discuss the implications of abnormal test results on the patient's lifestyle. Provide teaching and information regarding the clinical implications of the test results, as appropriate. Educate the patient regarding access to counseling services. Provide contact information, if desired, for the American Heart Association (www.americanheart.org) or the NHLBI (www.nhlbi.nih.gov).

Reinforce information given by the patient's HCP regarding further testing, treatment, or referral to another HCP. Answer any questions or address any concerns voiced by the patient or family.

Depending on the results of this procedure, additional testing may be needed to evaluate or monitor progression of the disease process and determine the need for a change in therapy. Evaluate test results in relation to the patient's symptoms and other tests performed.

RELATED MONOGRAPHS:

Related tests include antiarrhythmic drugs, apolipoprotein A and B, AST, atrial natriuretic peptide, BNP, blood gases, blood pool imaging, calcium, chest x-ray, cholesterol (total, HDL, LDL), CT cardiac scoring, CT thorax, CRP, CK and isoenzymes, echocardiography, electrocardiogram, exercise stress test, glucose, glycated hemoglobin, Holter monitor, homocysteine, ketones, LDH and isos, lipoprotein electrophoresis, lung perfusion scan, magnesium, MRI chest, MI infarct scan, myocardial perfusion heart scan, myoglobin, PET heart, potassium, pulse oximetry, sodium, triglycerides, and troponin.

Refer to the Cardiovascular System table at the end of the book for related tests by body system.

Electrocardiogram

SYNONYM/ACRONYM: ECG, EKG.

COMMON USE: To evaluate the electrical impulses generated by the heart during the cardiac cycle to assist with diagnosis of cardiac arrhythmias, blocks, damage, infection, or enlargement.

AREA OF APPLICATION: Heart.

CONTRAST: None.

DESCRIPTION: The cardiac muscle consists of three layers of cells: the inner layer called the *endocardium*, the middle layer called the *myocardium*, and the outer layer called the *epicardium*. The systolic phase of the cardiac cycle reflects the contraction of the myocardium, whereas the diastolic phase takes place when the heart relaxes to allow blood to rush in. All muscle cells have a characteristic rate of contraction called *depolarization*. Therefore, the heart will maintain a predetermined heart rate unless other stimuli are received.

The monitoring of pulse and blood pressure evaluates only the mechanical activity of the heart. The electrocardiogram (ECG), a noninvasive study, measures the electrical currents or impulses that the heart generates during a cardiac cycle (see figure of a normal ECG at end of monograph). Electrical impulses travel through a conduction system beginning with the sinoatrial (SA) node and moving to the atrioventricular (AV) node via internodal pathways. From the AV node, the impulses travel to the bundle of His and onward to the right and left bundle branches. These bundles are located within the right and left ventricles. The impulses continue to the cardiac muscle cells by terminal fibers called *Purkinje fibers*. The ECG is a graphic display of the electrical activity of the heart, which is analyzed by time intervals and segments. Continuous tracing of the cardiac cycle activity is captured as heart cells are electrically stimulated, causing depolarization and movement of the activity through the cells of the myocardium.

The ECG study is completed by using 12 electrodes attached to the skin surface to obtain the total electrical activity of the heart. Each lead records the electrical potential between the limbs or between the heart and limbs. The ECG machine records and marks the 12 leads on the strip of paper in the machine in proper sequence, usually 6 in. of the strip for each lead. The ECG pattern, called a *heart rhythm*, is recorded by a machine as a series of waves, intervals, and segments, each of which pertains to a specific occurrence during the contraction of the heart. The ECG tracings are recorded on graph paper using vertical and horizontal lines for analysis and calculations of time, measured by the vertical lines (1 mm apart and 0.04 sec per line), and of voltage, measured by the horizontal lines (1 mm apart and 0.5 mV per 5 squares). A pulse rate can be calculated from the ECG strip to obtain the beats per minute. The P wave represents the depolarization of the atrial myocardium; the QRS complex represents the depolarization of the ventricular myocardium; the P-R interval represents the time from beginning of the excitation of the atrium to the beginning of the ventricular excitation; and the ST segment has no deflection from baseline, but in an abnormal state may be elevated or depressed. An abnormal rhythm is called an *arrhythmia*.

The ankle-brachial index (ABI) can also be assessed during this study. This noninvasive, simple comparison of blood pressure measurements in the arms and legs can be used to detect peripheral artery disease (PAD). A Doppler stethoscope is used to obtain the systolic pressure in either the dorsalis pedis or the posterior tibial artery. This ankle pressure is then divided by the highest brachial systolic pressure acquired after taking the blood pressure in both arms of the patient. This index should be greater than 1.00. When the index falls below 0.5, blood flow impairment is considered significant. Patients should be scheduled for a vascular consult for an abnormal ABI. Patients with diabetes or kidney disease, as well as some elderly patients, may have a falsely elevated ABI due to calcifications of the vessels in the ankle causing an increased systolic pressure. The ABI test approaches 95% accuracy in detecting PAD. However, a normal ABI value does not absolutely rule out the possibility of PAD for some individuals, and additional tests should be done to evaluate symptoms.

INDICATIONS

- Assess the extent of congenital heart disease
- Assess the extent of myocardial infarction (MI) or ischemia, as indicated by abnormal ST segment, interval times, and amplitudes
- Assess the function of heart valves
- Assess global cardiac function
- Detect arrhythmias, as evidenced by abnormal wave deflections
- Detect peripheral artery disease (PAD)
- Detect pericarditis, shown by ST segment changes or shortened P-R interval
- Determine electrolyte imbalances, as evidenced by short or prolonged Q-T interval
- Determine hypertrophy of the chamber of the heart or heart hypertrophy, as evidenced by P or R wave deflections
- Evaluate and monitor cardiac pacemaker function
- Evaluate and monitor the effect of drugs, such as digitalis, antiarrhythmics, or vasodilating agents
- Monitor ECG changes during an exercise test

- Monitor rhythm changes during the recovery phase after an MI

POTENTIAL DIAGNOSIS

Normal findings in

- Normal heart rate according to age: range of 60 to 100 beats/min in adults
- Normal, regular rhythm and wave deflections with normal measurement of ranges of cycle components and height, depth, and duration of complexes as follows:
  P wave: 0.12 sec or three small blocks with amplitude of 2.5 mm
  Q wave: less than 0.04 mm
  R wave: 5 to 27 mm amplitude, depending on lead
  T wave: 1 to 13 mm amplitude, depending on lead
  QRS complex: 0.1 sec or two and a half small blocks
  ST segment: 1 mm

Abnormal findings in

- Arrhythmias
- Atrial or ventricular hypertrophy
- Bundle branch block
- Electrolyte imbalances
- Heart rate of 40 to 60 beats/min in adults
- MI or ischemia
- PAD
- Pericarditis
- Pulmonary infarction
- P wave: An enlarged P wave deflection could indicate atrial enlargement; an absent or altered P wave could suggest that the electrical impulse did not come from the SA node
- P-R interval: An increased interval could imply a conduction delay in the AV node
- QRS complex: An enlarged Q wave may indicate an old infarction; an enlarged deflection could indicate ventricular hypertrophy; increased time duration may indicate a bundle branch block
- ST segment: A depressed ST segment indicates myocardial ischemia;

an elevated ST segment may indicate an acute MI or pericarditis; a prolonged ST segment (or prolonged QT) may indicate hypocalcemia. A shortened ST segment may indicate hypokalemia
- Tachycardia greater than 120 beats/min
- T wave: A flat or inverted T wave may indicate myocardial ischemia, infarction, or hypokalemia; a tall, peaked T wave with a shortened QT interval may indicate hyperkalemia

CRITICAL FINDINGS ◈

Adult
- Acute changes in ST elevation are usually associated with acute MI or pericarditis
- Asystole
- Heart block, second- and third-degree with bradycardia less than 60 beats/min
- Pulseless electrical activity
- Pulseless ventricular tachycardia
- Premature ventricular contractions (PVCs) greater than three in a row, pauses greater than 3 sec, or identified blocks
- Unstable tachycardia
- Ventricular fibrillation

Pediatric
- Asystole
- Bradycardia less than 60 beats/min
- Pulseless electrical activity
- Pulseless ventricular tachycardia
- Supraventricular tachycardia
- Ventricular fibrillation

It is essential that critical diagnoses be communicated immediately to the appropriate health-care provider (HCP). A listing of these diagnoses varies among facilities. Note and immediately report to the HCP abnormal results and related symptoms. Timely notification of critical values for lab or diagnostic studies is a role expectation of the professional nurse. Notification

processes will vary among facilities. Upon receipt of the critical value the information should be read back to the caller to verify accuracy. Most policies require immediate notification of the primary HCP, hospitalist, or on-call HCP. Reported information includes the patient's name, unique identifiers, critical value, name of the person giving the report, and name of the person receiving the report. Documentation of notification should be made in the medical record with the name of the HCP notified, time and date of notification, and any orders received. Any delay in a timely report of a critical value may require completion of a notification form with review by Risk Management.

INTERFERING FACTORS

Factors that may impair the results of the examination
- Anatomic variation of the heart (i.e., the heart may be rotated in both the horizontal and frontal planes).
- Distortion of cardiac cycles due to age, gender, weight, or a medical condition (e.g., infants, women [may exhibit slight ST segment depression], obese patients, pregnant patients, patients with ascites).
- High intake of carbohydrates or electrolyte imbalances of potassium or calcium.
- Improper placement of electrodes or inadequate contact between skin and electrodes because of insufficient conductive gel or poor placement, which can cause ECG tracing problems.
- ECG machine malfunction or interference from electromagnetic waves in the vicinity.
- Inability of the patient to remain still during the procedure, because movement, muscle tremor, or twitching can affect accurate test recording.

- Increased patient anxiety, causing hyperventilation or deep respirations.
- Medications such as barbiturates and digitalis.
- Strenuous exercise before the procedure.

NURSING IMPLICATIONS AND PROCEDURE

E

PRETEST:

Positively identify the patient using at least two unique identifiers before providing care, treatment, or services.

Patient Teaching: Inform the patient this procedure can assist in assessing cardiac (heart) function.

Obtain a history of the patient's complaints, including a list of known allergens, especially allergies or sensitivities to latex, iodine, seafood, anesthetics, or contrast mediums. Ask if the patient has had a heart transplant, implanted pacemaker, or internal cardiac defibrillator.

Obtain a history of the patient's cardiovascular system, symptoms, and results of previously performed laboratory tests and diagnostic and surgical procedures.

Obtain a list of the patient's current medications, including herbs, nutritional supplements, and nutraceuticals (see Appendix F).

Review the procedure with the patient. Address concerns about pain related to the procedure and explain that there should be no discomfort related to the procedure. Inform the patient that the procedure is performed by an HCP and takes approximately 15 min.

Sensitivity to social and cultural issues, as well as concern for modesty, is important in providing psychological support before, during, and after the procedure.

Instruct the patient to remove jewelry and other metallic objects from the area to be examined.

There are no food, fluid, or medication restrictions unless by medical direction.

INTRATEST:

Observe standard precautions, and follow the general guidelines in Appendix A. Positively identify the patient.

Ensure the patient has complied with pretesting preparations.

Ensure the patient has removed all external metallic objects from the area to be examined prior to the procedure.

Instruct the patient to void prior to the procedure and to change into the gown, robe, and foot coverings provided.

Instruct the patient to cooperate fully and to follow directions. Instruct the patient to remain still throughout he procedure because movement produces unreliable results.

Record baseline values.

Place patient in a supine position. Expose and appropriately drape the chest, arms, and legs.

Prepare the skin surface with alcohol and remove excess hair. Shaving may be necessary. Dry skin sites.

Apply the electrodes in the proper position. When placing the six unipolar chest leads, place V_1 at the fourth intercostal space at the border of the right sternum, V_2 at the fourth intercostal space at the border of the left sternum, V_3 between V_2 and V_4, V_4 at the fifth intercostal space at the midclavicular line, V_5 at the left anterior axillary line at the level of V_4 horizontally, and V_6 at the level of V_4 horizontally and at the left midaxillary line. The wires are connected to the matched electrodes and the ECG machine. Chest leads (V_1, V_2, V_3, V_4, V_5, and V_6) record data from the horizontal plane of the heart.

Place three limb bipolar leads (two electrodes combined for each) on the arms and legs. Lead I is the combination of two arm electrodes, lead II is the combination of right arm and left leg electrodes, and lead III is the combination of left arm and left leg electrodes. Limb leads (I, II, III, aVL, aVF, and aVR) record data from the frontal plane of the heart.

The machine is set and turned on after the electrodes, grounding, connections, paper supply, computer, and data storage device are checked.

If the patient has any chest discomfort or pain during the procedure, mark the ECG strip indicating that occurrence.

POST-TEST:

A report of the results will be made available to the requesting HCP, who will discuss the results with the patient.

When the procedure is complete, remove the electrodes and clean the skin where the electrode pads were applied.

Evaluate the results in relation to previously performed ECGs. Denote cardiac rhythm abnormalities on the strip.

Monitor vital signs and compare with baseline values. Protocols may vary among facilities.

Instruct the patient to immediately notify an HCP of chest pain, changes in pulse rate, or shortness of breath.

Recognize anxiety related to the test results and be supportive of perceived loss of independence and fear of shortened life expectancy. Discuss the implications of abnormal test results on the patient's lifestyle. Provide teaching and information regarding the clinical implications of the test results, as appropriate.

Nutritional Considerations: Abnormal findings may be associated with cardiovascular disease. The American Heart Association and National Heart, Lung, and Blood Institute (NHLBI) recommend nutritional therapy for individuals identified to be at high risk for developing coronary artery disease (CAD) or individuals who have specific risk factors and/or existing medical conditions (e.g., elevated LDL cholesterol levels, other lipid disorders, insulin-dependent diabetes, insulin resistance, or metabolic syndrome). If overweight, the patient should be encouraged to achieve a normal weight. Guidelines for the Therapeutic Lifestyle Changes (TLC) diet are outlined in the Third Report of the Expert Panel on Detection, Evaluation, and Treatment of High Blood Cholesterol in Adults (Adult Treatment Panel III [ATP III]). The TLC diet emphasizes a reduction in foods high in saturated fats and cholesterol. Red meats, eggs, and dairy products are the major sources of saturated fats and cholesterol. If triglycerides also are elevated, the patient should be advised to eliminate or reduce alcohol and simple carbohydrates from the diet. The TLC approach also includes the use of plant stanols or sterols and increased dissolved fiber as an option for lowering LDL cholesterol levels; nutritional recommendations for daily total caloric intake; recommendations for allowable percentage of calories derived from fat (saturated and unsaturated), carbohydrates, protein, and cholesterol; as well as recommendations for daily expenditure of energy.

Nutritional Considerations: Overweight patients with high blood pressure should be encouraged to achieve a normal weight. Other changeable risk factors warranting patient education include strategies to safely decrease sodium intake, increase physical activity, decrease alcohol consumption, eliminate tobacco use, and decrease cholesterol levels.

Social and Cultural Considerations: Numerous studies point to the prevalence of excess body weight in American children and adolescents. Experts estimate that obesity is present in 25% of the population ages 6 to 11 yr. The medical, social, and emotional consequences of excess body weight are significant. Special attention should be given to instructing the child and caregiver regarding health risks and weight control education.

Recognize anxiety related to test results, and be supportive of fear of shortened life expectancy. Discuss the implications of abnormal test results on the patient's lifestyle. Provide teaching and information regarding the clinical implications of the test results, as appropriate. Educate the patient regarding access to counseling services. Provide contact information, if desired, for the American Heart Association (www.americanheart.org), the NHLBI (www.nhlbi.nih.gov), or the Legs for Life (www.legsforlife.org).

Reinforce information given by the patient's HCP regarding further testing, treatment, or referral to another HCP. Answer any questions or address any

E

concerns voiced by the patient or family.

▶ Depending on the results of this procedure, additional testing may be performed to evaluate or monitor progression of the disease process and determine the need for a change in therapy. Evaluate test results in relation to the patient's symptoms and other tests performed.

RELATED MONOGRAPHS:

▶ Related tests include antiarrhythmic drugs, apolipoprotein A and B, AST, atrial natriuretic peptide, BNP, blood gases, blood pool imaging, calcium, chest x-ray, cholesterol (total, HDL, LDL), CT cardiac scoring, CT thorax, CRP, CK and isoenzymes, echocardiography, echocardiography transesophageal, exercise stress test, glucose, glycated hemoglobin, Holter monitor, homocysteine, ketones, LDH and isos, lipoprotein electrophoresis, lung perfusion scan, magnesium, MRI chest, MI infarct scan, myocardial perfusion heart scan, myoglobin, PET heart, potassium, pulse oximetry, sodium, triglycerides, and troponin.

▶ Refer to the Cardiovascular System table at the end of the book for related tests by body system.

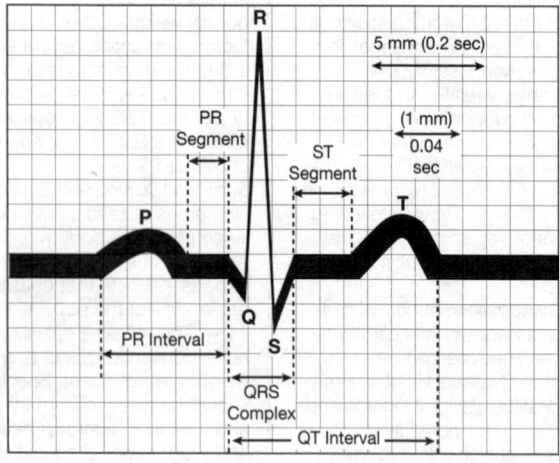

Electroencephalography

SYNONYM/ACRONYM: Electrical activity (for sleep disturbances), EEG.

COMMON USE: To assess the electrical activity in the brain toward assisting in diagnosis of brain death, injury, infection, and bleeding.

AREA OF APPLICATION: Brain.

CONTRAST: None.

DESCRIPTION: Electroencephalography (EEG) is a noninvasive study that measures the brain's electrical activity and records that activity on graph paper. These electrical impulses arise from the brain cells of the cerebral cortex. Electrodes, placed at 8 to 20 sites (or pairs of sites) on the patient's scalp, transmit the different frequencies and amplitudes of the brain's electrical activity to the EEG machine, which records the results in graph form on a moving paper strip. This procedure can evaluate responses to various stimuli, such as flickering light, hyperventilation, auditory signals, or somatosensory signals generated by skin electrodes. The procedure is usually performed in a room designed to eliminate electrical interference and minimize distractions. EEG can be done at the bedside, especially to confirm brain death. A health-care provider (HCP) analyzes the waveforms. The test is used to detect epilepsy, intracranial abscesses, or tumors; to evaluate cerebral involvement due to head injury or meningitis; and to monitor for cerebral tissue ischemia during surgery when cerebral vessels must be occluded. EEG is also used to confirm brain death, which can be defined as absence of electrical activity in the brain. To evaluate abnormal EEG waves further, the patient may be connected to an ambulatory EEG system similar to a Holter monitor for the heart. Patients keep a journal of their activities and any symptoms that occur during the monitoring period.

INDICATIONS
- Confirm brain death
- Confirm suspicion of increased intracranial pressure caused by trauma or disease
- Detect cerebral ischemia during endarterectomy
- Detect intracranial cerebrovascular lesions, such as hemorrhages and infarcts
- Detect seizure disorders and identify focus of seizure and seizure activity, as evidenced by abnormal spikes and waves recorded on the graph
- Determine the presence of tumors, abscesses, or infection
- Evaluate the effect of drug intoxication on the brain
- Evaluate sleeping disorders, such as sleep apnea and narcolepsy
- Identify area of abnormality in dementia

POTENTIAL DIAGNOSIS

Normal findings in
- Normal occurrences of alpha, beta, theta, and delta waves (rhythms varying depending on the patient's age)
- Normal frequency, amplitude, and characteristics of brain waves

Abnormal findings in
- Abscess
- Brain death
- Cerebral infarct
- Encephalitis
- Glioblastoma and other brain tumors
- Head injury
- Hypocalcemia or hypoglycemia
- Intracranial hemorrhage
- Meningitis
- Migraine headaches
- Narcolepsy
- Seizure disorders (grand mal, focal, temporal lobe, myoclonic, petit mal)
- Sleep apnea

CRITICAL FINDINGS ◈
- Abscess
- Brain death
- Head injury
- Hemorrhage
- Intracranial hemorrhage

It is essential that critical diagnoses be communicated immediately to the appropriate HCP. A listing of those diagnoses varies among facilities. Note and immediately report to the HCP abnormal results and related symptoms. Timely notification of critical values for lab or diagnostic studies is a role expectation of the professional nurse. Notification processes will vary among facilities. Upon receipt of the critical value the information should be read back to the caller to verify accuracy. Most policies require immediate notification of the primary HCP, hospitalist, or on-call HCP. Reported information includes the patient's name, unique identifiers, critical value, name of the person giving the report, and name of the person receiving the report. Documentation of notification should be made in the medical record with the name of the HCP notified, time and date of notification, and any orders received. Any delay in a timely report of a critical value may require completion of a notification form with review by Risk Management.

INTERFERING FACTORS

Factors that may impair the results of the examination

• Inability of the patient to cooperate or remain still during the procedure because of age, significant pain, or mental status.
• Drugs and substances such as sedatives, anticonvulsants, anxiolytics, alcohol, and stimulants such as caffeine and nicotine.
• Hypoglycemic or hypothermic states.
• Hair that is dirty, oily, or sprayed or treated with hair preparations.

NURSING IMPLICATIONS AND PROCEDURE

PRETEST:

‣ Positively identify the patient using at least two unique identifiers before providing care, treatment, or services.

‣ *Patient Teaching:* Inform the patient/family this procedure can assist in measuring the electrical activity in the brain.
‣ Obtain a history of the patient's complaints, including a list of known allergens, especially allergies or sensitivities to latex, iodine, seafood, anesthetics, or contrast mediums.
‣ Obtain a history of the patient's musculoskeletal system, symptoms, and results of previously performed laboratory tests and diagnostic and surgical procedures.
‣ Obtain a list of the patient's current medications, including herbs, nutritional supplements, and nutraceuticals (see Appendix F).
‣ Review the procedure with the patient. Address concerns about pain related to the procedure and assure the patient there is no discomfort during the procedure, but if needle electrodes are used, a slight pinch may be felt. Explain that electricity flows from the patient's body, not into the body, during the procedure. Explain that the procedure reveals brain activity only, not thoughts, feelings, or intelligence. Inform the patient the procedure is performed in a neurodiagnostic department, usually by an HCP and support staff, and takes approximately 30 to 60 min.
‣ Inform the patient that he or she may be asked to alter breathing pattern; be asked to follow simple commands such as opening or closing eyes, blinking, or swallowing; be stimulated with bright light; or be given a drug to induce sleep during the study.
‣ *Sensitivity to social and cultural issues,* as well as concern for modesty, is important in providing psychological support before, during, and after the procedure.
‣ Instruct the patient to clean the hair and to refrain from using hair sprays, creams, or solutions before the test.
‣ Instruct the patient to limit sleep to 5 hr for an adult and 7 hr for a child the night before the study. Young infants and children should not be allowed to nap before the study.
‣ Instruct the patient to eat a meal before the study and to avoid stimulants such as caffeine and nicotine for 8 hr prior to the procedure. Under medical direction, the patient should

avoid sedatives, anticonvulsants, anxiolytics, and alcohol for 24 to 48 hr before the test.

▸ *Make sure a written and informed consent has been signed prior to the procedure and before administering any medications.*

INTRATEST:

▸ Observe standard precautions, and follow the general guidelines in Appendix A. Positively identify the patient.

▸ Ensure the patient has complied with pretesting preparations. Ensure that caffeine-containing beverages were withheld for 8 hr before the procedure and that a meal was ingested before the study.

▸ Ensure that all substances with the potential to interfere with test results were withheld for 24 to 48 hr before the test.

▸ Ensure that the patient is able to relax; report any extreme anxiety or restlessness.

▸ Ensure that hair is clean and free of hair sprays, creams, or solutions.

▸ Place the patient in the supine position in a bed or in a semi-Fowler's position on a recliner in a special room protected from any noise or electrical interferences that could affect the tracings.

▸ Remind the patient to relax and not to move any muscles or parts of the face or head. The HCP should be able to observe the patient for movements or other interferences through a window into the test room.

▸ The electrodes are prepared and applied to the scalp. Electrodes are placed in as many as 20 locations over the frontal, temporal, parietal, and occipital areas, and amplifier wires are attached. An electrode is also attached to each earlobe as grounding electrodes. At this time, a baseline recording can be made with the patient at rest.

▸ Recordings are made with the patient at rest and with eyes closed. Recordings are stopped about every 5 min to allow the patient to move. Recordings are also made during a drowsy and sleep period, depending on the patient's clinical condition and symptoms.

▸ Procedures (e.g., stroboscopic light stimulation, hyperventilation to induce

alkalosis, and sleep induction by administration of sedative to detect abnormalities that occur only during sleep) may be done to bring out abnormal electrical activity or other brain abnormalities.

▸ Observations for seizure activity are carried out during the study, and a description and time of activity is noted by the HCP.

POST-TEST:

▸ A report of the results will be made available to the requesting HCP, who will discuss the results with the patient.

▸ When the procedure is complete, remove electrodes from the hair and remove paste by cleansing with oil or witch hazel.

▸ If a sedative was given during the test, allow the patient to recover. Bedside rails are put in the raised position for safety.

▸ Instruct the patient to resume medications, as directed by the HCP.

▸ Instruct the patient to report any seizure activity.

▸ Recognize anxiety related to test results, and be supportive of perceived loss of independent function. Discuss the implications of abnormal test results on the patient's lifestyle. Provide teaching and information regarding the clinical implications of the test results, as appropriate.

▸ Reinforce information given by the patient's HCP regarding further testing, treatment, or referral to another HCP. Answer any questions or address any concerns voiced by the patient or family.

▸ Depending on the results of this procedure, additional testing may be performed to evaluate or monitor progression of the disease process and determine the need for a change in therapy. Evaluate test results in relation to the patient's symptoms and other tests performed.

RELATED MONOGRAPHS:

▸ Related tests include CSF analysis, CT brain, evoked brain potentials (SER, VER), MRI brain, and PET brain.

▸ Refer to the Musculoskeletal System table at the end of the book for related tests by body system.

Electromyography

SYNONYM/ACRONYM: Electrodiagnostic study, EMG, neuromuscular junction testing.

COMMON USE: To assess the electrical activity within the skeletal muscles to assist in diagnosing diseases such as muscular dystrophy, Guillain-Barré, polio, and other myopathies.

AREA OF APPLICATION: Muscles.

CONTRAST: None.

DESCRIPTION: Electromyography (EMG) measures skeletal muscle activity during rest, voluntary contraction, and electrical stimulation. Percutaneous extracellular needle electrodes containing fine wires are inserted into selected muscle groups to detect neuromuscular abnormalities and measure nerve and electrical conduction properties of skeletal muscles. The electrical potentials are amplified, displayed on a screen in waveforms, and electronically recorded, similar to electrocardiography. Comparison and analysis of the amplitude, duration, number, and configuration of the muscle activity provide diagnostic information about the extent of nerve and muscle involvement in the detection of primary muscle diseases, including lower motor neuron, anterior horn cell, or neuromuscular junction diseases; defective transmission at the neuromuscular junction; and peripheral nerve damage or disease. Responses of a relaxed muscle are electrically silent, but spontaneous muscle movement such as fibrillation and fasciculation can be detected in a relaxed, denervated muscle.

Muscle action potentials are detected with minimal or maximal muscle contractions. The differences in the size and numbers of activity potentials during voluntary contractions determine whether the muscle weakness is a disease of the striated muscle fibers or cell membranes (myogenic) or a disease of the lower motor neuron (neurogenic). Nerve conduction studies (electroneurography) are commonly done in conjunction with electromyelography; the combination of the procedures is known as electromyoneurography. The major use of the examination lies in differentiating among the following disease classes: primary myopathy, peripheral motor neuron disease, and disease of the neuromuscular junction.

INDICATIONS
- Assess primary muscle diseases affecting striated muscle fibers or cell membrane, such as muscular dystrophy or myasthenia gravis
- Detect muscle disorders caused by diseases of the lower motor neuron involving the motor neuron on the

anterior horn of the spinal cord, such as anterior poliomyelitis, amyotrophic lateral sclerosis, amyotonia, and spinal tumors
• Detect muscle disorders caused by diseases of the lower motor neuron involving the nerve root, such as Guillain-Barré syndrome, herniated disk, or spinal stenosis
• Detect neuromuscular disorders, such as peripheral neuropathy caused by diabetes or alcoholism, and locate the site of the abnormality
• Determine if a muscle abnormality is caused by the toxic effects of drugs (e.g., antibiotics, chemotherapy) or toxins (e.g., *Clostridium botulinum*, snake venom, heavy metals)
• Differentiate between primary and secondary muscle disorders or between neuropathy and myopathy
• Differentiate secondary muscle disorders caused by polymyositis, sarcoidosis, hypocalcemia, thyroid toxicity, tetanus, and other disorders
• Monitor and evaluate progression of myopathies or neuropathies, including confirmation of diagnosis of carpal tunnel syndrome

POTENTIAL DIAGNOSIS

Normal findings in
• Normal muscle electrical activity during rest and contraction states

Abnormal findings in
• Evidence of neuromuscular disorders or primary muscle disease (*Note:* Findings must be correlated with the patient's history, clinical features, and results of other neurodiagnostic tests.):
Amyotrophic lateral sclerosis
Bell's palsy
Beriberi
Carpal tunnel syndrome
Dermatomyositis
Diabetic peripheral neuropathy
Eaton-Lambert syndrome
Guillain-Barré syndrome

Multiple sclerosis
Muscular dystrophy
Myasthenia gravis
Myopathy
Polymyositis
Radiculopathy
Traumatic injury

CRITICAL FINDINGS: N/A

INTERFERING FACTORS

This procedure is contraindicated for
• Patients with extensive skin infection.
• Patients receiving anticoagulant therapy.
• Patients with an infection at the sites of electrode placement.

Factors that may impair the results of the examination
• Inability of the patient to cooperate or remain still during the procedure because of age, significant pain, or mental status.
• Age-related decreases in electrical activity.
• Medications such as muscle relaxants, cholinergics, and anticholinergics.
• Improper placement of surface or needle electrodes.

NURSING IMPLICATIONS AND PROCEDURE

PRETEST:
▶ Positively identify the patient using at least two unique identifiers before providing care, treatment, or services.
▶ *Patient Teaching:* Inform the patient this procedure can assist in measuring the electrical activity of the muscles.
▶ Obtain a history of the patient's complaints, including a list of known allergens, especially allergies or sensitivities to latex, iodine, seafood, anesthetics, or contrast mediums.
▶ Obtain a history of the patient's musculoskeletal system, symptoms, and

results of previously performed laboratory tests and diagnostic and surgical procedures.

Obtain a list of the patient's current medications, including herbs, nutritional supplements, and nutraceuticals (see Appendix F).

Review the procedure with the patient. Address concerns about pain related to the procedure and warn the patient the procedure may be uncomfortable, but an analgesic or sedative will be administered. Inform the patient that as many as 10 electrodes may be inserted at various locations on the body. Inform the patient the procedure is performed in a special laboratory by a health-care provider (HCP) and takes approximately 1 to 3 hr to complete, depending on the patient's condition.

Sensitivity to social and cultural issues, as well as concern for modesty, is important in providing psychological support before, during, and after the procedure.

Assess for the ability to comply with directions given for exercising during the test.

Instruct the patient to remove jewelry and other metallic objects from the area to be examined.

Under medical direction, the patient should avoid muscle relaxants, cholinergics, and anticholinergics for 3 to 6 days before the test.

Instruct the patient to refrain from smoking and drinking caffeine-containing beverages for 3 hr before the procedure. Protocols may vary among facilities.

Make sure a written and informed consent has been signed prior to the procedure and before administering any medications.

INTRATEST:

Observe standard precautions, and follow the general guidelines in Appendix A. Positively identify the patient.

Ensure the patient has refrained from smoking and drinking caffeine-containing beverages for 3 hr before the procedure.

Ensure medications such as muscle relaxants, cholinergics, and anticholinergics have been withheld, as ordered.

Ensure the patient has removed all external metallic objects from the area to be examined prior to the procedure.

Instruct the patient to void prior to the procedure and to change into the gown, robe, and foot coverings provided.

Ask the patient to remain very still and relaxed and to cooperate with instructions given to contract muscles during the procedure.

Place the patient in a supine or sitting position depending on the location of the muscle to be tested. Ensure that the area or room is protected from noise or metallic interference that may affect the test results.

Administer mild analgesic (adult) or sedative (children), as ordered, to promote a restful state before the procedure.

Cleanse the skin thoroughly with alcohol pads, as necessary.

An electrode is applied on the skin to ground the patient, and then 24-gauge needles containing a fine-wire electrode are inserted into the muscle. The electrical potentials of the muscle are amplified, displayed on a screen, and electronically recorded.

During the test, muscle activity is tested while the patient is at rest, during incremental needle insertion, and during varying degrees of muscle contraction.

Ask the patient to alternate between a relaxed and a contracted muscle state or to perform progressive muscle contractions while the potentials are being measured.

POST-TEST:

A report of the results will be made available to the requesting HCP, who will discuss the results with the patient.

When the procedure is complete, remove the electrodes and clean the skin where the electrode was applied.

Monitor electrode sites for bleeding, hematoma, or inflammation.

If residual pain is noted after the procedure, instruct the patient to apply warm compresses and to take analgesics, as ordered.

Instruct the patient to resume usual diet, medication, and activity, as directed by the HCP.

Reinforce information given by the patient's HCP regarding further testing, treatment, or referral to another HCP. Answer any questions or address any concerns voiced by the patient or family.

Depending on the results of this procedure, additional testing may be performed to evaluate or monitor progression of the disease process and determine the need for a change in therapy. Evaluate test results in relation to the patient's symptoms and other tests performed.

RELATED MONOGRAPHS:

Related tests include acetylcholine receptor antibody, biopsy muscle, CSF analysis, CT brain, CK, ENG, evoked brain potentials (SER, VER), MRI brain, plethysmography, and PET brain.

Refer to the Musculoskeletal System table at the end of the book for related tests by body system.

Electromyography, Pelvic Floor Sphincter

SYNONYM/ACRONYM: Electrodiagnostic study, rectal electromyography.

COMMON USE: To assess urinary sphincter electrical activity to assist with diagnosis of urinary incontinence.

AREA OF APPLICATION: Sphincter muscles.

CONTRAST: None.

DESCRIPTION: Pelvic floor sphincter electromyography, also known as rectal electromyography, is performed to measure electrical activity of the external urinary sphincter. This procedure, often done in conjunction with cystometry and voiding urethrography as part of a full urodynamic study, helps to diagnose neuromuscular dysfunction and incontinence.

electromyographic signals during the filling of the urinary bladder and at the conclusion of voiding; absence of signals during the actual voiding; no incontinence

Abnormal findings in
• Neuromuscular dysfunction of lower urinary sphincter, pelvic floor muscle dysfunction of the anal sphincter

CRITICAL FINDINGS: N/A

INTERFERING FACTORS:

This procedure is contraindicated for
• Patients who are pregnant or suspected of being pregnant, unless the potential benefits of the procedure far outweigh the risks to the fetus and mother.

INDICATIONS
Evaluate neuromuscular dysfunction and incontinence

POTENTIAL DIAGNOSIS

Normal findings in
• Normal urinary and anal sphincter muscle function; increased

Factors that may impair the results of the examination

- Inability of the patient to cooperate or remain still during the procedure because of age, significant pain, or mental status.
- Age-related decreases in electrical activity.
- Medications such as muscle relaxants, cholinergics, and anticholinergics.

Other considerations

- Failure to follow dietary restrictions before the procedure may cause the procedure to be canceled or repeated.

NURSING IMPLICATIONS AND PROCEDURE

PRETEST:

Positively identify the patient using at least two unique identifiers before providing care, treatment, or services.

Patient Teaching: Inform the patient this procedure can assist in measuring the electrical activity of the pelvic floor muscles.

Obtain a history of the patient's complaints, including a list of known allergens, especially allergies or sensitivities to latex, iodine, seafood, anesthetics, or contrast mediums.

Obtain a history of the patient's genitourinary system, symptoms, and results of previously performed laboratory tests and diagnostic and surgical procedures.

Obtain a list of the patient's current medications, including herbs, nutritional supplements, and nutraceuticals (see Appendix F).

Review the procedure with the patient. Address concerns about pain related to the procedure. Warn the patient the procedure may be uncomfortable, but an analgesic or sedative will be administered. Assure the patient the pain is minimal during the catheter insertion. Inform the patient the procedure is performed in a special laboratory by a health-care provider (HCP) and takes about 30 min to complete.

Sensitivity to social and cultural issues, as well as concern for modesty, is important

in providing psychological support before, during, and after the procedure.

Instruct the patient to remove jewelry and other metallic objects from the area to be examined.

Assess for ability to comply with directions given for exercising during the test.

Under medical direction, the patient should avoid muscle relaxants, cholinergics, and anticholinergics for 3 to 6 days before the test.

Instruct the patient to refrain from smoking and drinking caffeine-containing beverages for 3 hr before the procedure. Protocols may vary among facilities.

Make sure a written and informed consent has been signed prior to the procedure and before administering any medications.

INTRATEST:

Observe standard precautions, and follow the general guidelines in Appendix A. Positively identify the patient.

Ensure the patient has complied with dietary, fluid, tobacco, and medication restrictions and pretesting preparations.

Record baseline vital signs.

Instruct the patient to void prior to the procedure and to change into the gown, robe, and foot coverings provided.

Place the patient in a supine position on the examining table and place a drape over the patient, exposing the perianal area.

Ask the patient to remain very still and relaxed and to cooperate when instructed to contract muscles during the procedure.

Two skin electrodes are positioned slightly to the left and right of the perianal area and a grounding electrode is placed on the thigh.

If needle electrodes are used, they are inserted into the muscle surrounding the urethra.

Muscle activity signals are recorded as waves, which are interpreted for number and configurations in diagnosing urinary abnormalities.

An indwelling urinary catheter is inserted, and the bulbocavernosus reflex is tested; the patient is instructed to cough while the catheter is gently pulled.

Voluntary control is tested by requesting the patient to contract and relax the muscle. Electrical activity is recorded during this period of relaxation with the bladder empty.

- The bladder is filled with sterile water at a rate of 100 mL/min while the electrical activity during filling is recorded.
- The catheter is removed; the patient is then placed in a position to void and is asked to urinate and empty the full bladder. This voluntary urination is then recorded until completed. The complete procedure includes recordings of electrical signals before, during, and at the end of urination.

POST-TEST:

- A report of the results will be made available to the requesting HCP, who will discuss the results with the patient.
- Instruct the patient to resume usual diet, fluids, medications, and activity, as directed by the HCP.
- Monitor vital signs and neurological status every 15 min for 1 hr, then every 2 hr for 4 hr, and as ordered. Take temperature every 4 hr for 24 hr. Monitor intake and output at least every 8 hr. Compare with baseline values. Protocols may vary among facilities.
- Instruct the patient to increase fluid intake unless contraindicated.
- If tested with needle electrodes, warn female patients to expect hematuria after the first voiding.

- Advise the patient to report symptoms of urethral irritation, such as dysuria, persistent or prolonged hematuria, and urinary frequency.
- Recognize anxiety related to test results, and be supportive of perceived loss of independent function. Discuss the implications of abnormal test results on the patient's lifestyle. Provide teaching and information regarding the clinical implications of the test results, as appropriate.
- Reinforce information given by the patient's HCP regarding further testing, treatment, or referral to another HCP. Answer any questions or address any concerns voiced by the patient or family.
- Depending on the results of this procedure, additional testing may be needed to evaluate or monitor progression of the disease process and determine the need for a change in therapy. Evaluate test results in relation to the patient's symptoms and other tests performed.

RELATED MONOGRAPHS:

- Related tests include CT pelvis, cystometry, cystoscopy, cystourethrography voiding, IVP, and US bladder.
- Refer to the Genitourinary System table at the end of the book for related tests by body system.

Electroneurography

SYNONYM/ACRONYM: Electrodiagnostic study, nerve conduction study, ENG.

COMMON USE: To assess peripheral nerve conduction to assist in the diagnosis of diseases such as diabetic neuropathy and muscular dystrophy.

AREA OF APPLICATION: Muscles.

CONTRAST: None.

DESCRIPTION: Electroneurography (ENG) is performed to identify peripheral nerve injury, to differen-

tiate primary peripheral nerve pathology from muscular injury, and to monitor response of the nerve injury to treatment. A stimulus is applied through a surface electrode over a nerve. After a nerve is electrically stimulated proximally, the time for the impulse to travel to a second or distal site is measured. Because the conduction study of a nerve can vary from nerve to nerve, it is important to compare the results of the affected side to those of the contralateral side. The results of the stimulation are shown on a monitor, but the actual velocity must be calculated by dividing the distance in meters between the stimulation point and the response point by the time between the stimulus and response. Traumatic nerve transection, contusion, or neuropathy will usually cause maximal slowing of conduction velocity in the affected side compared with that in the normal side. A velocity greater than normal does not indicate a pathological condition. This test is usually performed in conjunction with electromyography in a combined test called electromyoneurography.

INDICATIONS
Confirm diagnosis of peripheral nerve damage or trauma

POTENTIAL DIAGNOSIS

Normal findings in
• No evidence of peripheral nerve injury or disease. Variable readings depend on the nerve being tested. For patients age 3 yr and older, the maximum conduction velocity is 40 to 80 milliseconds; for infants and the elderly, the values are divided by 2.

Abnormal findings in
• Carpal tunnel syndrome
• Diabetic neuropathy
• Guillain-Barré syndrome
• Herniated disk disease
• Muscular dystrophy
• Myasthenia gravis
• Poliomyelitis
• Tarsal tunnel syndrome
• Thoracic outlet syndrome

CRITICAL FINDINGS: N/A

INTERFERING FACTORS

Factors that may impair the results of the examination
• Inability of the patient to cooperate or remain still during the procedure because of age, significant pain, or mental status.
• Age-related decreases in electrical activity.
• Poor electrode conduction or failure to obtain contralateral values for comparison.

NURSING IMPLICATIONS AND PROCEDURE

PRETEST:
▶ Positively identify the patient using at least two unique identifiers before providing care, treatment, or services.
▶ *Patient Teaching:* Inform the patient this procedure is performed to measure the electrical activity of the muscles.
▶ Obtain a history of the patient's complaints or symptoms, including a list of known allergens, especially allergies or sensitivities to latex, iodine, seafood, anesthetics, or contrast mediums.
▶ Obtain a history of the patient's neuromuscular system, symptoms, and results of previously performed laboratory tests and diagnostic and surgical procedures.
▶ Obtain a list of the patient's current medications, including herbs, nutritional supplements, and nutraceuticals (see Appendix F).
▶ Review the procedure with the patient. Address concerns about pain related to the procedure and inform the patient the procedure may be uncomfortable because of a mild electrical shock. Advise the patient that the electrical shock is brief and is not harmful. Inform the patient the procedure is performed

in a special laboratory by a health-care provider (HCP) and takes approximately 15 min to complete but can take longer depending on the patient's condition.

▶ Sensitivity to social and cultural issues, as well as concern for modesty, is important in providing psychological support before, during, and after the procedure.

▶ There are no food, fluid, or medication restrictions unless by medical direction.

▶ Instruct the patient to remove jewelry and other metallic objects from the area to be examined.

▶ *Make sure a written and informed consent has been signed prior to the procedure and before administering any medications.*

INTRATEST:

▶ Observe standard precautions, and follow the general guidelines in Appendix A. Positively identify the patient.

▶ Ensure the patient has removed all external metallic objects from the area to be examined prior to the procedure.

▶ Instruct the patient to void prior to the procedure and to change into the gown, robe, and foot coverings provided.

▶ Place the patient in a supine or sitting position, depending on the location of the muscle to be tested.

▶ Shave the extremity in the area to be stimulated, and cleanse the skin thoroughly with alcohol pads.

▶ Apply electrode gel and place a recording electrode at a known distance from the stimulation point. Measure the distance between the stimulation point and the site of the recording electrode in centimeters.

▶ Place a reference electrode nearby on the skin surface.

▶ The nerve is electrically stimulated by a shock-emitter device; the time between nerve impulse and electrical contraction, measured in milliseconds (distal latency), is shown on a monitor.

▶ The nerve is also electrically stimulated at a location proximal to the area of suspected injury or disease.

▶ The time required for the impulse to travel from the stimulation site to location of the muscle contraction (total latency) is recorded in milliseconds.

▶ Calculate the conduction velocity. The conduction velocity is converted to meters per second (m/sec) and computed using the following equation:

Conduction velocity (m/sec) = [distance (m)] / [total latency − distal latency]

POST-TEST:

▶ A report of the results will be made available to the requesting HCP, who will discuss the results with the patient.

▶ When the procedure is complete, remove the electrodes and clean the skin where the electrodes were applied.

▶ Monitor electrode sites for inflammation.

▶ If residual pain is noted after the procedure, instruct the patient to apply warm compresses and to take analgesics, as ordered.

▶ Instruct the patient to resume usual diet, medication, and activity, as directed by the HCP.

▶ Recognize anxiety related to test results, and be supportive of perceived loss of independent function. Discuss the implications of abnormal test results on the patient's lifestyle. Provide teaching and information regarding the clinical implications of the test results, as appropriate.

▶ Reinforce information given by the patient's HCP regarding further testing, treatment, or referral to another HCP. Answer any questions or address any concerns voiced by the patient or family.

▶ Depending on the results of this procedure, additional testing may be performed to evaluate or monitor progression of the disease process and determine the need for a change in therapy. Evaluate test results in relation to the patient's symptoms and other tests performed.

RELATED MONOGRAPHS:

▶ Related tests include acetylcholine receptor antibody, biopsy muscle, CK, EMG, evoked brain potentials (SER, VER), fluorescein angiography, fundus photography, glucose, glycated hemoglobin, insulin, microalbumin, and plethysmography.

▶ Refer to the Musculoskeletal System table at the end of the book for related tests by body system.

Endoscopy, Sinus

SYNONYM/ACRONYM: N/A.

COMMON USE: To facilitate diagnosis and treatment of recurring sinus infections or infections resulting from unresolved sinus infection, including incursion into the brain, eye orbit, or eyeball.

AREA OF APPLICATION: Sinuses.

CONTRAST: N/A.

E

DESCRIPTION: Sinus endoscopy, done with a narrow flexible tube, is used to help diagnose damage to the sinuses, nose, and throat. The tube contains an optical device with a magnifying lens with a bright light; the tube is inserted through the nose and threaded through the sinuses to the throat. A camera, monitor, or other viewing device is connected to the endoscope to record areas being examined. Sinus endoscopy helps to diagnose structural defects, infection, damage to the sinuses, or structures in the nose and throat. It allows visualization of polyps and growths in the sinuses and can be used to investigate causes of recurrent inflammation of the sinuses (sinusitis). The procedure is usually done in a health-care provider's (HCP's) office, but if done as a surgical procedure, the endoscope may be used to remove polyps from the nose or throat.

INDICATIONS
• Nasal obstruction
• Recurrent sinusitis

POTENTIAL DIAGNOSIS

Normal findings in
• Normal soft tissue appearance

Abnormal findings in
• Foreign bodies in the nose
• Growths in the nasal passages
• Polyps
• Sinusitis

CRITICAL FINDINGS: N/A

INTERFERING FACTORS
• Inability of the patient to cooperate or remain still during the test because of age, significant pain, or mental status may interfere with the test results.

NURSING IMPLICATIONS AND PROCEDURE

PRETEST:

▶ Positively identify the patient using at least two unique identifiers before providing care, treatment, or services.
▶ *Patient Teaching:* Inform the patient this procedure can assist in locating and treating infection of the sinus or surrounding areas.
▶ Obtain a history of the patient's complaints, including a list of known allergens, especially allergies or sensitivities to latex.
▶ Obtain a history of the patient's respiratory system, symptoms, and results of previously performed laboratory tests and diagnostic and surgical procedures.

Obtain a list of the patient's current medications, including herbs, nutritional supplements, and nutraceuticals (see Appendix F).

Instruct the patient to remove contact lenses or glasses, as appropriate.

Review the procedure with the patient. Inform the patient that the procedure is usually done with the patient awake and seated upright in a chair. Address concerns about pain and explain that a local anesthetic spray or liquid may be applied to the throat to ease with insertion of the endoscope. Inform the patient that the procedure is usually performed in the office of an HCP and takes about 10 minutes.

Sensitivity to social and cultural issues, as well as concern for modesty, is important in providing psychological support before, during, and after the procedure.

There are no food, fluid, or medication restrictions unless by medical direction.

Make sure a written and informed consent has been signed prior to the procedure and before administering any medications.

INTRATEST:

Instruct the patient to cooperate fully and to follow directions. Instruct the patient to remain still throughout the procedure because movement produces unreliable results.

Seat the patient comfortably. Instill ordered topical anesthetic in the throat, as ordered, and allow time for it to work.

Observe standard precautions, and follow the general guidelines in Appendix A. Positively identify the patient, and label the appropriate specimen

container with the corresponding patient demographics, initials of the person collecting the specimen, date, and time of collection, if cultures are to be obtained on aspirated sinus material.

POST-TEST:

A report of the results will be made available to the requesting HCP, who will discuss the results with the patient.

Instruct the patient to wait until the numbness in the throat wears off before attempting to eat or drink following the procedure.

Recognize anxiety related to test results. Discuss the implications of abnormal test results on the patient's lifestyle. Provide teaching and information regarding the clinical implications of the test results, as appropriate.

Reinforce information given by the patient's HCP regarding further testing, treatment, or referral to another HCP. Answer any questions or address any concerns voiced by the patient or family.

Depending on the results of this procedure, additional testing may be needed to evaluate or monitor progression of the disease process and determine the need for a change in therapy. Evaluate test results in relation to the patient's symptoms and other tests performed.

RELATED MONOGRAPHS:

Related tests include CT brain.

Refer to the Respiratory System table at the end of the book for related tests by body system.

Eosinophil Count

SYNONYM/ACRONYM: Eos count, total eosinophil count.

COMMON USE: To assist in diagnosing conditions related to immune response such as asthma, dermatitis, and hay fever. Also used to assist in identification of parasitic infections.

SPECIMEN: Whole blood (1 mL) collected in a lavender-top (EDTA) tube.

NORMAL FINDINGS: (Method: Manual count using eosinophil stain and hemocytometer or automated analyzer)
Absolute count: 50 to 500/mm^3
Relative percentage: 1% to 4%

DESCRIPTION: Eosinophils are white blood cells whose function is phagocytosis of antigen-antibody complexes and response to allergy-inducing substances and parasites. Eosinophils have granules that contain histamine used to kill foreign cells in the body. Eosinophils also contain proteolytic substances that damage parasitic worms. The binding of histamine to receptor sites on cells results in smooth muscle contraction in the bronchioles and upper respiratory tract, constriction of pulmonary vessels, increased mucus production, and secretion of acid by the cells that line the stomach. Eosinophil counts can increase to greater than 30% of normal in parasitic infections; however, a significant percentage of children with visceral larva migrans infestations have normal eosinophil counts.

INDICATIONS
Assist in the diagnosis of conditions such as allergies, parasitic infections, drug reactions, collagen diseases, and myeloproliferative disorders.

POTENTIAL DIAGNOSIS

Increased in
Eosinophils are released and migrate to inflammatory sites in response to numerous environmental, chemical/drug, or immune-mediated triggers. T cells, mast cells, and macrophages release cytokines like interlukin-3 (IL3), interlukin-5 (IL5), granulocyte/macrophage colony–stimulating factor, and chemokines like the eotaxins, which can result in the activation of eosinophils.

- Addison's disease *(most commonly related to autoimmune destruction of adrenal glands)*
- Allergy
- Asthma
- Cancer
- Dermatitis
- Drug reactions
- Eczema
- Hay fever
- Hodgkin's disease
- Hypereosinophilic syndrome (rare and idiopathic)
- Löffler's syndrome *(pulmonary eosinophilia due to allergic reaction or infection from a fungus or parasite)*
- Myeloproliferative disorders *(related to abnormal changes in the bone marrow)*
- Parasitic infection (visceral larva migrans)
- Rheumatoid arthritis *(possibly related to medications used in therapy)*
- Rhinitis
- Sarcoidosis
- Splenectomy
- Tuberculosis

Decreased in
- Aplastic anemia *(bone marrow failure)*
- Eclampsia *(shift to the left; relative to significant production of neutrophils)*

E

- Infections *(shift to the left; relative to significant production of neutrophils)*
- Stress *(release of cortisol suppresses eosinophils)*

CRITICAL FINDINGS: N/A

INTERFERING FACTORS

- Numerous drugs and substances can cause an increase in eosinophil levels as a result of an allergic response or hypersensitivity reaction. These include acetophenazine, allopurinol, aminosalicylic acid, ampicillin, butaperazine, capreomycin, carisoprodol, cephaloglycin, cephaloridine, cephalosporins, cephapirin, cephradine, chloramphenicol, clindamycin, cloxacillin, dapsone, epicillin, erythromycin, fluorides, gold, imipramine, iodides, kanamycin, mefenamic acid, methicillin, methyldopa, minocycline, nalidixic acid, niridazole, nitrofurans (including nitrofurantoin), NSAIDs, nystatin, oxamniquine, penicillin, penicillin G, procainamide, ristocetin, streptokinase, streptomycin, tetracycline, triamterene, tryptophan, and viomycin.
- Drugs that can cause a decrease in eosinophil levels include acetylsalicylic acid, amphotericin B, corticotropin, desipramine, glucocorticoids, hydrocortisone, interferon, niacin, prednisone, and procainamide.
- Clotted specimens should be rejected for analysis.
- Specimens more than 4 hr old should be rejected for analysis.
- There is a diurnal variation in eosinophil counts. The count is lowest in the morning and continues to rise throughout the day until midnight. Therefore, serial measurements should be performed at the same time of day for purposes of continuity.

NURSING IMPLICATIONS AND PROCEDURE

PRETEST:

- Positively identify the patient using at least two unique identifiers before providing care, treatment, or services.
- *Patient Teaching:* Inform the patient this test can assist in diagnosing immune response conditions and parasitic infections.
- Obtain a history of the patient's complaints, including a list of known allergens, especially allergies or sensitivities to latex.
- Obtain a history of the patient's hematopoietic, immune, and respiratory systems; symptoms; and results of previously performed laboratory tests and diagnostic and surgical procedures.
- Obtain a list of the patient's current medications, including herbs, nutritional supplements, and nutraceuticals (see Appendix F).
- Review the procedure with the patient. Inform the patient that specimen collection takes approximately 5 to 10 min. Address concerns about pain and explain that there may be some discomfort during the venipuncture.
- *Sensitivity to social and cultural issues,* as well as concern for modesty, is important in providing psychological support before, during, and after the procedure.
- There are no food, fluid, or medication restrictions unless by medical direction.

INTRATEST:

- If the patient has a history of allergic reaction to latex, avoid the use of equipment containing latex.
- Instruct the patient to cooperate fully and to follow directions. Direct the patient to breathe normally and to avoid unnecessary movement.
- Observe standard precautions, and follow the general guidelines in Appendix A. Positively identify the patient, and label the appropriate specimen container with the corresponding patient demographics, initials of the person collecting the specimen, date, and time of collection. Perform a venipuncture.

▶ Remove the needle and apply direct pressure with dry gauze to stop bleeding. Observe/assess venipuncture site for bleeding or hematoma formation and secure gauze with adhesive bandage.

▶ Promptly transport the specimen to the laboratory for processing and analysis.

POST-TEST:

▶ A report of the results will be made available to the requesting health-care provider (HCP), who will discuss the results with the patient.

▶ *Nutritional Considerations:* Consideration should be given to diet if food allergies are present.

▶ Instruct the patient with an elevated eosinophil count to report any signs or symptoms of infection, such as fever.

▶ Instruct the patient with an elevated count to rest and take medications as prescribed, to increase fluid intake as appropriate, and to monitor temperature.

▶ Reinforce information given by the patient's HCP regarding further testing, treatment, or referral to another HCP. Answer any questions or address any concerns voiced by the patient or family

▶ Depending on the results of this procedure, additional testing may be performed to evaluate or monitor progression of the disease process and determine the need for a change in therapy. Evaluate test results in relation to the patient's symptoms and other tests performed.

RELATED MONOGRAPHS:

▶ Related tests include allergen-specific immunoglobulin E, biopsy bone marrow, blood gases, CBC, culture stool, ESR, fecal analysis, hypersensitivity pneumonitis screen, IgE, lung perfusion scan, ova and parasites, plethysmography, and PFT.

▶ Refer to the Hematopoietic, Immune, and Respiratory systems tables at the end of the book for related tests by body system.

Erythrocyte Protoporphyrin, Free

SYNONYM/ACRONYM: Free erythrocyte protoporphyrin (FEP).

COMMON USE: To assist in diagnosing anemias related to chronic disease, hemolysis, iron deficiency, and lead toxicity.

SPECIMEN: Whole blood (1 mL) collected in a lavender-top (EDTA), royal blue top (EDTA), or a pink-top (EDTA) tube.

NORMAL FINDINGS: (Method: Fluorometry)

Conventional Units	SI Units (Conventional Units × 0.0178)
Adult	
Male	
Less than 30 mcg/dL	Less than 0.534 micromol/L
Female	
Less than 40 mcg/dL	Less than 0.712 micromol/L

DESCRIPTION: The free erythrocyte protoporphyrin (FEP) test measures the concentration of protoporphyrin in red blood cells. Protoporphyrin comprises the predominant porphyrin in red blood cells, which combines with iron to form the heme portion of hemoglobin. Protoporphyrin converts to bilirubin, combines with albumin, and remains unconjugated in the circulation after hemoglobin breakdown. Increased amounts of protoporphyrin can be detected in erythrocytes, urine, and stool in conditions interfering with heme synthesis. Protoporphyria is an autosomal dominant disorder in which increased amounts of protoporphyrin are secreted and excreted; the disorder is thought to be the result of an enzyme deficiency. Protoporphyria causes photosensitivity and may lead to cirrhosis of the liver and cholelithiasis as a result of protoporphyrin deposits. FEP is elevated in cases of lead toxicity or chronic exposure.

INDICATIONS
- Assist in the diagnosis of erythropoietic protoporphyrias
- Assist in the differential diagnosis of iron deficiency in pediatric patients
- Evaluate lead poisoning

POTENTIAL DIAGNOSIS

Increased in
- Anemia of chronic disease *(related to accumulation of protoporphyrin in the absence of available iron)*
- Conditions with marked erythropoiesis (e.g., hemolytic anemias) *(related to increased cell destruction)*
- Erythropoietic protoporphyria *(related to abnormal increased secretion)*
- Iron-deficiency anemias *(related to accumulation of protoporphyrin in the absence of available iron)*
- Lead poisoning *(possibly related to inactivation of enzymes involved in iron binding or transfer)*
- Some sideroblastic anemias

Decreased in: N/A

CRITICAL FINDINGS: N/A

INTERFERING FACTORS
- Drugs that may increase FEP levels include erythropoietin.
- The test is unreliable in infants less than 6 mo of age.

NURSING IMPLICATIONS AND PROCEDURE

PRETEST:

- Positively identify the patient using at least two unique identifiers before providing care, treatment, or services.
- *Patient Teaching:* Inform the patient this test can assist in diagnosing specific types of anemias and lead toxicity as well as monitor chronic lead exposure.
- Obtain a history of the patient's complaints, including a list of known allergens, especially allergies or sensitivities to latex.
- Obtain a history of the patient's hematopoietic system, symptoms, and results of previously performed laboratory tests and diagnostic and surgical procedures.
- Obtain a list of the patient's current medications, including herbs, nutritional supplements, and nutraceuticals (see Appendix F).
- Review the procedure with the patient. Inform the patient that specimen collection takes approximately 5 to 10 min. Address concerns about pain and explain that there may be some discomfort during the venipuncture.

Sensitivity to social and cultural issues, as well as concern for modesty, is important in providing psychological support before, during, and after the procedure.

There are no food, fluid, or medication restrictions unless by medical direction.

INTRATEST:

If the patient has a history of allergic reaction to latex, avoid the use of equipment containing latex.

Instruct the patient to cooperate fully and to follow directions. Direct the patient to breathe normally and to avoid unnecessary movement.

Observe standard precautions, and follow the general guidelines in Appendix A. Positively identify the patient, and label the appropriate specimen container with the corresponding patient demographics, initials of the person collecting the specimen, date, and time of collection. Perform a venipuncture. Specimens should be protected from light.

Remove the needle and apply direct pressure with dry gauze to stop bleeding. Observe/assess venipuncture site for bleeding or hematoma formation and secure gauze with adhesive bandage.

Promptly transport the specimen to the laboratory for processing and analysis.

POST-TEST:

A report of the results will be made available to the requesting health-care provider (HCP), who will discuss the results with the patient.

Recognize anxiety related to test results. Discuss the implications of abnormal test results on the patient's lifestyle. Provide teaching and information regarding the clinical implications of the test results, as appropriate. Provide contact information, if desired, for the American Porphyria Foundation (www.porphyriafoundation.org).

Reinforce information given by the patient's HCP regarding further testing, treatment, or referral to another HCP. Answer any questions or address any concerns voiced by the patient or family.

Depending on the results of this procedure, additional testing may be performed to evaluate or monitor progression of the disease process and determine the need for a change in therapy. Evaluate test results in relation to the patient's symptoms and other tests performed.

RELATED MONOGRAPHS:

Related tests include CBC hematocrit, CBC hemoglobin, iron/TIBC, lead, and urine porphyrins.

Refer to the Hematopoietic System table at the end of the book for related tests by body system.

Erythrocyte Sedimentation Rate

SYNONYM/ACRONYM: Sed rate, ESR.

COMMON USE: To assist in diagnosing acute infection in diseases such as tissue necrosis, chronic infection, and acute inflammation.

SPECIMEN: Whole blood (5 mL) collected in a lavender-top (EDTA) tube for the modified Westergren method or a gray-top (3.8% sodium citrate) tube for the original Westergren method.

NORMAL FINDINGS: (Method: Westergren or modified Westergren)

Age	Male	Female
Newborn	0–2 mm/hr	0–2 mm/hr
Less than 50 yr	0–15 mm/hr	0–25 mm/hr
50 yr and older	0–20 mm/hr	0–30 mm/hr

DESCRIPTION: The erythrocyte sedimentation rate (ESR) is a measure of the rate of sedimentation of red blood cells (RBCs) in an anticoagulated whole blood sample over a specified period of time. The basis of the ESR test is the alteration of blood proteins by inflammatory and necrotic processes that cause the RBCs to stick together, become heavier, and rapidly settle at the bottom of a vertically held, calibrated tube over time. The most common promoter of rouleaux is an increase in circulating fibrinogen levels. In general, relatively little settling occurs in normal blood because normal RBCs do not form rouleaux (which increases their mass and rate of sedimentation) and would not stack together. The sedimentation rate is proportional to the size or mass of the falling RBCs and is inversely proportional to plasma viscosity. The test is a nonspecific indicator of disease but is fairly sensitive and is frequently the earliest indicator of widespread inflammatory reaction due to infection or autoimmune disorders. Prolonged elevations are also present in malignant disease. The ESR can also be used to monitor the course of a disease and the effectiveness of therapy. The most commonly used method to measure the ESR is the Westergren (or modified Westergren) method.

INDICATIONS

- Assist in the diagnosis of acute infection, such as tuberculosis or tissue necrosis
- Assist in the diagnosis of acute inflammatory processes
- Assist in the diagnosis of chronic infections
- Assist in the diagnosis of rheumatoid or autoimmune disorders
- Assist in the diagnosis of temporal arthritis and polymyalgia rheumatica
- Monitor inflammatory and malignant disease

POTENTIAL DIAGNOSIS

Increased in

Increased rouleaux formation is associated with increased levels of fibrinogen and/or production of cytokines and other acute-phase reactant proteins in response to inflammation. Anemia of chronic disease as well as acute anemia influence the ESR because the decreased number of RBCs falls faster with the relatively increased plasma volume.

- Acute myocardial infarction
- Anemia *(RBCs fall faster with increased plasma volume)*
- Carcinoma
- Cat scratch fever (*Bartonella henselae*)
- Collagen diseases, including systemic lupus erythematosus (SLE)
- Crohn's disease *(due to anemia or related to acute-phase reactant proteins)*
- Elevated blood glucose *(hyperglycemia in older patients can*

induce production of cytokines responsible for the inflammatory response; hyperglycemia related to insulin resistance can cause hepatocytes to shift protein synthesis from albumin to production of acute-phase reactant proteins)
- Endocarditis
- Heavy metal poisoning *(related to anemia affecting size and shape of RBCs)*
- Increased plasma protein level *(RBCs fall faster with increased plasma viscosity)*
- Infections (e.g., pneumonia, syphilis)
- Inflammatory diseases
- Lymphoma
- Lymphosarcoma
- Multiple myeloma *(RBCs fall faster with increased plasma viscosity)*
- Nephritis
- Pregnancy *(related to anemia)*
- Pulmonary embolism
- Rheumatic fever
- Rheumatoid arthritis
- Subacute bacterial endocarditis
- Temporal arteritis
- Toxemia
- Tuberculosis
- Waldenström's macroglobulinemia *(RBCs fall faster with increased plasma viscosity)*

Normal findings in
- Congestive heart failure
- Glucose-6-phosphate dehydrogenase deficiency
- Hemoglobin C disease
- Hypofibrinogenemia
- Polycythemia
- Sickle cell anemia
- Spherocytosis

Decreased in
- Conditions resulting in high hemoglobin and RBC count

CRITICAL FINDINGS: N/A

INTERFERING FACTORS
- Some drugs cause an SLE-like syndrome that results in a physiological increase in ESR. These include anticonvulsants, hydrazine derivatives, nitrofurantoin, procainamide, and quinidine. Other drugs that may cause an increased ESR include acetylsalicylic acid, cephalothin, cephapirin, cyclosporin A, dextran, and oral contraceptives.
- Drugs that may cause a decrease in ESR include aurothiomalate, corticotropin, cortisone, dexamethasone, methotrexate, minocycline, NSAIDs, penicillamine, prednisolone, prednisone, quinine, sulfasalazine, tamoxifen, and trimethoprim.
- Menstruation may cause falsely increased test results.
- Prolonged tourniquet constriction around the arm may cause hemoconcentration and falsely low values.
- The Westergren and modified Westergren methods are affected by heparin, which causes a false elevation in values.
- Bubbles in the Westergren tube or pipette, or tilting the measurement column more than 3° from vertical, will falsely increase the values.
- Movement or vibration of the surface on which the test is being conducted will affect the results.
- Inaccurate timing will invalidate test results.
- Specimens that are clotted, hemolyzed, or insufficient in volume should be rejected for analysis.
- The test should be performed within 4 hr of collection when the specimen has been stored at room temperature; delays in testing may result in decreased values. If a delay in testing is anticipated, refrigerate the sample at 2°C to 4°C; stability at refrigerated temperature is reported to be extended up to 12 hr. Refrigerated specimens

should be brought to room temperature before testing.

NURSING IMPLICATIONS AND PROCEDURE

PRETEST:

Positively identify the patient using at least two unique identifiers before providing care, treatment, or services.

Patient Teaching: Inform the patient this test can assist in identification of inflammation.

Obtain a history of the patient's complaints, including a list of known allergens, especially allergies or sensitivities to latex.

Obtain a history of infectious, autoimmune, or neoplastic diseases.

Obtain a history of the patient's cardiovascular, hematopoietic, immune, and respiratory systems; symptoms; and results of previously performed laboratory tests and diagnostic and surgical procedures.

Obtain a list of the patient's current medications, including herbs, nutritional supplements, and nutraceuticals (see Appendix F).

Review the procedure with the patient. Inform the patient that specimen collection takes approximately 5 to 10 min. Address concerns about pain and explain that there may be some discomfort during the venipuncture. *Sensitivity to social and cultural issues,* as well as concern for modesty, is important in providing psychological support before, during, and after the procedure.

There are no food, fluid, or medication restrictions unless by medical direction.

INTRATEST:

If the patient has a history of allergic reaction to latex, avoid the use of equipment containing latex.

Instruct the patient to cooperate fully and to follow directions. Direct the patient to breathe normally and to avoid unnecessary movement.

Observe standard precautions, and follow the general guidelines in Appendix A. Positively identify the patient, and label the appropriate tubes with the corresponding patient demographics, date, and time of collection. Perform a venipuncture; collect the specimen in a 5-mL gray-top (sodium citrate) tube if the Westergren method will be used. Collect the specimen in a 5-mL purple-top (EDTA) tube if the modified Westergren method will be used.

Remove the needle and apply direct pressure with dry gauze to stop bleeding. Observe/assess venipuncture site for bleeding or hematoma formation and secure gauze with adhesive bandage.

Promptly transport the specimen to the laboratory for processing and analysis.

POST-TEST:

A report of the results will be made available to the requesting health-care provider (HCP), who will discuss the results with the patient.

Provide teaching and information regarding the clinical implications of the test results, as appropriate. Educate the patient regarding access to counseling services, as appropriate. Provide contact information, if desired, for the American College of Rheumatology (www.rheumatology .org) or for the Arthritis Foundation (www.arthritis.org).

Reinforce information given by the patient's HCP regarding further testing, treatment, or referral to another HCP. Answer any questions or address any concerns voiced by the patient or family.

Depending on the results of this procedure, additional testing may be performed to evaluate or monitor progression of the disease process and determine the need for a change in therapy. Evaluate test results in relation to the patient's symptoms and other tests performed.

RELATED MONOGRAPHS:

Related tests include antibodies, anti-cyclic citrullinated peptide, ANA, arthroscopy, arthrogram, blood pool imaging, BMD, bone scan, CBC, CBC hematocrit, CBC hemoglobin,

E

CBC RBC indices, CBC RBC morphology, CT cardiac scoring, copper, CRP, D-dimer, exercise stress test, fibrinogen, glucose, iron, lead, MRI musculoskeletal, microorganism-specific serologies and related cultures, myocardial perfusion heart scan, procalcitonin, radiography bone, RF, synovial fluid analysis, and troponin. Refer to the Cardiovascular, Hematopoietic, Immune, and Respiratory systems tables at the end of the book for related tests by body system.

E Erythropoietin

SYNONYM/ACRONYM: EPO.

COMMON USE: To evaluate the effectiveness of erythropoietin (EPO) administration as a treatment for anemia, especially related to chemotherapy and renal disease.

SPECIMEN: Serum (2 mL) collected in a red- or tiger-top tube.

NORMAL FINDINGS: (Method: Immunochemiluminometric assay).

Age	Conventional & SI Units	Conventional & SI Units
	Male	*Female*
0–3 yr	1.7–17.9 milli-International Units	2.1–15.9 milli-International Units
4–6 yr	3.5–21.9 milli-International Units	2.9–8.5 milli-International Units
7–9 yr	1.1–13.5 milli-International Units	2.1–8.2 milli-International Units
10–12 yr	1.1–14.1 milli-International Units	1.1–9.1 milli-International Units
13–15 yr	2.2–14.4 milli-International Units	3.8–20.5 milli-International Units
16–18 yr	1.5–15.2 milli-International Units	2.1–14.2 milli-International Units
Adult	4.2–27.8 milli-International Units	4.2–27.8 milli-International Units

Based on normal hemoglobin and hematocrit. Values may be decreased in older adults due to the effects of medications and the presence of multiple chronic or acute diseases with or without muted symptoms.

DESCRIPTION: Erythropoietin (EPO) is a glycoprotein produced mainly by the kidney. Its function is to stimulate the bone marrow to make red blood cells (RBCs). EPO levels fall after removal of the kidney but do not disappear completely. It is thought that small amounts of EPO may be produced by the liver.

Erythropoiesis is regulated by EPO and tissue Po_2. When Po_2 is normal, EPO levels decrease; when Po_2 falls, EPO secretion occurs and EPO levels increase.

INDICATIONS
• Assist in assessment of anemia of end-stage renal disease

Assist in the diagnosis of EPO-producing tumors

Evaluate the presence of rare anemias

Monitor patients receiving EPO therapy

POTENTIAL DIAGNOSIS

Increased in

After moderate bleeding in an otherwise healthy patient *(related to loss of RBCs, which stimulates production)*

AIDS *(related to anemia, which stimulates production)*

Anemias (e.g., hemolytic, iron deficiency, megaloblastic) *(related to low RBC count, which stimulates production)*

Hepatoma *(related to EPO-producing tumors)*

Kidney transplant rejection *(15% of cases respond with an exaggerated secretion of EPO and a transient post-transplantation erythrocytosis)*

Nephroblastoma *(related to EPO-producing tumors)*

Pheochromocytoma *(related to EPO-producing tumors)*

Polycystic kidney disease *(related to EPO-producing tumors or cysts)*

Pregnancy *(related to anemia of pregnancy, which stimulates production)*

Secondary polycythemia where low oxygen levels stimulate production *(high-altitude hypoxia, chronic obstructive pulmonary disease, pulmonary fibrosis)*

Decreased in

Chemotherapy *(related to therapy, which can be toxic to the kidney)*

Primary polycythemia *(related to feedback loop response to elevated RBC count)*

Renal failure *(related to decreased production and excessive loss through excretion by damaged kidneys)*

CRITICAL FINDINGS: N/A

INTERFERING FACTORS

- Drugs, hormones, and other substances that may increase EPO levels include adrenocorticotropic hormone (ACTH), anabolic steroids, androgens, angiotensin, epinephrine, daunorubicin, fenoterol, growth hormone, and thyroid-stimulating hormone (TSH).
- Phlebotomy may increase EPO levels.
- Drugs that may decrease EPO levels include amphotericin B, cisplatin, enalapril, estrogens, furosemide, and theophylline.
- Blood transfusions may also decrease EPO levels.

NURSING IMPLICATIONS AND PROCEDURE

PRETEST:

Positively identify the patient using at least two unique identifiers before providing care, treatment, or services.

Patient Teaching: Inform the patient this test can assist in evaluation of anemia.

Obtain a history of the patient's complaints, including a list of known allergens, especially allergies or sensitivities to latex.

Obtain a history of the patient's hematopoietic and genitourinary systems, symptoms, and results of previously performed laboratory tests and diagnostic and surgical procedures.

Note any recent procedures that can interfere with test results.

Obtain a list of the patient's current medications, including herbs, nutritional supplements, and nutraceuticals (see Appendix F).

Review the procedure with the patient. Inform the patient that specimen collection takes approximately 5 to 10 min. Address concerns about pain and explain to the patient that there may be some discomfort during the venipuncture.

Sensitivity to social and cultural issues, as well as concern for modesty, is important in providing psychological support before, during, and after the procedure.

There are no food, fluid, or medication restrictions unless by medical direction.

INTRATEST:

If the patient has a history of allergic reaction to latex, avoid the use of equipment containing latex.

Instruct the patient to cooperate fully and to follow directions. Direct the patient to breathe normally and to avoid unnecessary movement.

Observe standard precautions, and follow the general guidelines in Appendix A. Positively identify the patient, and label the appropriate specimen container with the corresponding patient demographics, initials of the person collecting the specimen, date, and time of collection. Perform a venipuncture.

Remove the needle and apply direct pressure with dry gauze to stop bleeding. Observe/assess venipuncture site for bleeding or hematoma formation and secure gauze with adhesive bandage.

Promptly transport the specimen to the laboratory for processing and analysis.

POST-TEST:

A report of the results will be made available to the requesting health-care provider (HCP), who will discuss the results with the patient.

Reinforce information given by the patient's HCP regarding further testing, treatment, or referral to another HCP. Answer any questions or address any concerns voiced by the patient or family.

Depending on the results of this procedure, additional testing may be performed to evaluate or monitor progression of the disease process and determine the need for a change in therapy. Evaluate test results in relation to the patient's symptoms and other tests performed.

RELATED MONOGRAPHS:

Related tests include biopsy bone marrow, BUN, CBC, CBC hematocrit, CBC hemoglobin, CBC RBC count, CBC RBC indices, CBC RBC morphology and inclusions, CT renal, creatinine, creatinine clearance, ferritin iron/TIBC, microalbumin, retrograde ureteropyelography, US kidney, and vitamin B_{12}.

Refer to the Hematopoietic and Genitourinary systems tables at the end of the book for related tests by body system.

Esophageal Manometry

SYNONYM/ACRONYM: Esophageal function study, esophageal acid study (Tuttl test), acid reflux test, Bernstein test (acid perfusion), esophageal motility stud

COMMON USE: To evaluate potential ineffectiveness of the esophageal muscl and structure in swallowing, vomiting, and regurgitation in diseases such a scleroderma, infection, and gastric esophageal reflux.

AREA OF APPLICATION: Esophagus.

CONTRAST: Done with or without noniodinated contrast medium.

DESCRIPTION: Esophageal manometry (EM) consists of a group of invasive studies performed to assist in diagnosing abnormalities of esophageal muscle function and esophageal structure. These studies measure esophageal pressure, the effects of gastric acid in the esophagus, lower esophageal sphincter pressure, and motility patterns that result during swallowing. EM can be used to document and quantify gastroesophageal reflux (GER). It is indicated when a patient is experiencing difficulty swallowing, heartburn, regurgitation, or vomiting or has chest pain for which no diagnosis has been found. Tests performed in combination with EM include the acid reflux, acid clearing, and acid perfusion (Bernstein) tests.

INDICATIONS

• Aid in the diagnosis of achalasia, evidenced by increased pressure in EM
• Aid in the diagnosis of chalasia in children, evidenced by decreased pressure in EM
• Aid in the diagnosis of esophageal scleroderma, evidenced by decreased pressure in EM
• Aid in the diagnosis of esophagitis, evidenced by decreased motility
• Aid in the diagnosis of GER, evidenced by low pressure in EM, decreased pH in acidity test, and pain in acid reflux and perfusion tests
• Differentiate between esophagitis or cardiac condition as the cause of epigastric pain
• Evaluate pyrosis and dysphagia to determine if the cause is GER or esophagitis

POTENTIAL DIAGNOSIS

Normal findings in
• Acid clearing: fewer than 10 swallows
• Acid perfusion: no GER
• Acid reflux: no regurgitation into the esophagus
• Bernstein test: negative
• Esophageal secretions: pH 5 to 6
• Esophageal sphincter pressure: 10 to 20 mm Hg

Abnormal findings in
• Achalasia (sphincter pressure of 50 mm Hg)
• Chalasia
• Esophageal scleroderma
• Esophagitis
• GER (sphincter pressure of 0 to 5 mm Hg, pH of 1 to 3)
• Hiatal hernia
• Progressive systemic sclerosis (scleroderma)
• Spasms

CRITICAL FINDINGS: N/A

INTERFERING FACTORS

This procedure is contraindicated for
• Patients with unstable cardiopulmonary status, blood coagulation defects, recent gastrointestinal surgery, esophageal varices, or bleeding.

Factors that may impair the results of the examination
• Inability of the patient to cooperate or remain still during the procedure because of age, significant pain, or mental status.
• Administration of medications (e.g., sedatives, antacids, anticholinergics, cholinergics, corticosteroids) that can change pH or relax the sphincter muscle, causing inaccurate results.

Other considerations
• Failure to follow dietary restrictions before the procedure may cause the procedure to be canceled or repeated.

E

NURSING IMPLICATIONS AND PROCEDURE

PRETEST:

▶ Positively identify the patient using at least two unique identifiers before providing care, treatment, or services.

▶ *Patient Teaching:* Inform the patient this procedure can assist in assessing the esophagus.

▶ Obtain a history of the patient's complaints, including a list of known allergens, especially allergies or sensitivities to latex, iodine, seafood, anesthetics, and contrast mediums.

▶ Obtain a history of the patient's gastrointestinal system, symptoms, and results of previously performed laboratory tests and diagnostic and surgical procedures.

▶ Note any recent barium or other radiological contrast procedures. Ensure that barium studies were performed more than 4 days before the EM.

▶ Record the date of the last menstrual period and determine the possibility of pregnancy in perimenopausal women.

▶ Obtain a list of the patient's current medications, including anticoagulants, aspirin and other salicylates, herbs, nutritional supplements, and nutraceuticals (see Appendix F). Note the last time and dose of medication taken.

▶ Review the procedure with the patient. Address concerns about pain related to the procedure and explain that some pain may be experienced during the test; there may be moments of discomfort and gagging when the scope is inserted, but there are no complications resulting from the procedure; and the throat will be anesthetized with a spray or swab. Inform the patient that he or she will not be able to speak during the procedure but breathing will not be affected. Inform the patient that the procedure is performed in an endoscopy suite by a health-care provider (HCP), under local anesthesia, and takes approximately 30 to 45 min.

▶ *Sensitivity to social and cultural issues,* as well as concern for providing modesty, is important in providing psychological support before, during, and after the procedure.

▶ Explain that an IV line may be started to allow for the infusion of a sedative or IV fluids.

▶ Instruct the patient to remove dentures and eyewear.

▶ Under medical direction, the patient should withhold medications for 24 hr before the study; special arrangements may be necessary for diabetic patients.

▶ Instruct the patient to fast and restrict fluids for 6 to 8 hr prior to the procedure. Protocols may vary among facilities.

▶ Obtain and record baseline vital signs.

▶ Make sure a written and informed consent has been signed prior to the procedure and before administering any medications.

INTRATEST:

▶ Observe standard precautions, and follow the general guidelines in Appendix A. Positively identify the patient.

▶ Ensure that the patient has complied with dietary, fluids, and medication restrictions and pretesting preparations for at least 6 to 8 hr prior to the procedure.

▶ Ensure the patient has removed dentures and eyewear prior to the procedure.

▶ Avoid using morphine sulfate in patients with asthma or other pulmonary disease. This drug can further exacerbate bronchospasms and respiratory impairment.

▶ Have emergency equipment readily available.

▶ Instruct the patient to void prior to the procedure and to change into the gown, robe, and foot coverings provided.

▶ Instruct the patient to cooperate fully and to follow directions. Instruct the patient to remain still throughout the procedure because movement produces unreliable results.

▶ Insert an IV line and inject ordered sedation.

▶ Spray or swab the oropharynx with a topical local anesthetic.

▶ Provide an emesis basin for the increased saliva and encourage the patient to spit out saliva since the gag reflex may be impaired.

Monitor the patient for complications related to the procedure (e.g., aspiration of stomach contents into the lungs, dyspnea, tachypnea, adventitious sounds).

Suction the mouth, pharynx, and trachea, and administer oxygen as ordered.

Esophageal Manometry

One or more small tubes are inserted through the nose into the esophagus and stomach.

A small transducer is attached to the ends of the tubes to measure lower esophageal sphincter pressure, intraluminal pressures, and regularity and duration of peristaltic contractions.

Instruct the patient to swallow small amounts of water or flavored gelatin.

Esophageal Acid and Clearing (Tuttle Test)

With the tube in place, a pH electrode probe is inserted into the esophagus with Valsalva maneuvers performed to stimulate reflux of stomach contents into the esophagus.

If acid reflux is absent, 100 mL of 0.1% hydrochloric acid is instilled into the stomach during a 3-min period, and the pH measurement is repeated.

To determine acid clearing, hydrochloric acid is instilled into the esophagus and the patient is asked to swallow while the probe measures the pH.

Acid Perfusion (Bernstein Test)

A catheter is inserted through the nose into the esophagus, and the patient is asked to inform the HCP when pain is experienced.

Normal saline solution is allowed to drip into the catheter at about 10 mL/min. Then hydrochloric acid is allowed to drip into the catheter.

Pain experienced when the hydrochloric acid is instilled determines the presence of an esophageal abnormality. If no pain is experienced, symptoms are the result of some other condition.

POST-TEST:

A report of the results will be made available to the requesting HCP, who will discuss the results with the patient.

Monitor the patient for signs of respiratory depression (less than 15 respirations/min) every 15 min for 2 hr. Resuscitation equipment should be available.

Observe the patient for indications of perforation: painful swallowing with neck movement, substernal pain with respiration, shoulder pain, dyspnea, abdominal or back pain, cyanosis, and fever.

Instruct the patient not to eat or drink until the gag reflex returns and then to eat lightly for 12 to 24 hr.

Instruct the patient to resume usual activity, medication, and diet 24 hr after the examination or as tolerated, as directed by the HCP.

Inform the patient to expect some throat soreness and possible hoarseness. Advise the patient to use warm gargles, lozenges, or ice packs to the neck and to drink cool fluids to alleviate throat discomfort.

Emphasize that any severe pain, fever, difficulty breathing, or expectoration of blood must be reported to the HCP immediately.

Recognize anxiety related to test results, and offer support. Discuss the implications of abnormal test results on the patient's lifestyle. Provide teaching and information regarding the clinical implications of the test results, as appropriate.

Reinforce information given by the patient's HCP regarding further testing, treatment, or referral to another HCP. Answer any questions or address any concerns voiced by the patient or family.

Depending on the results of this procedure, additional testing may be needed to evaluate or monitor progression of the disease process and determine the need for a change in therapy. Evaluate test results in relation to the patient's symptoms and other tests performed.

RELATED MONOGRAPHS:
▸ Related tests include ANA, barium swallow, biopsy skin, capsule endoscopy, chest x-ray, CT thoracic, esophagogastroduodenoscopy, fecal analysis, gastric emptying scan, GER scan, lung perfusion scan, mediastinoscopy, and upper GI series.
▸ Refer to the Gastrointestinal System table at the end of the book for related tests by body system.

Esophagogastroduodenoscopy

E

SYNONYM/ACRONYM: Esophagoscopy, gastroscopy, upper GI endoscopy, EGD.

COMMON USE: To visualize and assess the esophagus, stomach, and upper portion of the duodenum to assist in diagnosis of bleeding, ulcers, inflammation, tumor, and cancer.

AREA OF APPLICATION: Esophagus, stomach, and upper duodenum.

CONTRAST: Done without contrast.

DESCRIPTION: Esophagogastroduodenoscopy (EGD) allows direct visualization of the upper gastrointestinal (GI) tract mucosa, which includes the esophagus, stomach, and upper portion of the duodenum, by means of a flexible endoscope. The standard flexible fiberoptic endoscope contains three channels that allow passage of the instruments needed to perform therapeutic or diagnostic procedures, such as biopsies or cytology washings. The endoscope, a multichannel instrument, allows visualization of the GI tract linings, insufflation of air, aspiration of fluid, removal of foreign bodies by suction or by snare or forceps, and passage of a laser beam for obliteration of abnormal tissue or control of bleeding. Direct visualization yields greater diagnostic data than is possible through radiological procedures, and therefore EGD is rapidly replacing upper GI series as the diagnostic procedure of choice.

INDICATIONS

• Assist in differentiating between benign and neoplastic tumors
• Detect gastric or duodenal ulcers
• Detect upper GI inflammatory disease
• Determine the presence and location of acute upper GI bleeding
• Evaluate the extent of esophageal injury after ingestion of chemicals
• Evaluate stomach or duodenum after surgical procedures
• Evaluate suspected gastric outlet obstruction
• Identify tissue abnormalities and obtain biopsy specimens
• Investigate the cause of dysphagia, dyspepsia, and epigastric pain

POTENTIAL DIAGNOSIS

Normal findings in
• Esophageal mucosa is normally yellow-pink. At about 9 in. from the incisor teeth, a pulsation indicates the location of the aortic arch. The gastric mucosa is orange-red and contains rugae. The proximal duodenum is reddish and contains

a few longitudinal folds, whereas the distal duodenum has circular folds lined with villi. No abnormal structures or functions are observed in the esophagus, stomach, or duodenum.

Abnormal findings in
- Acute and chronic gastric and duodenal ulcers
- Diverticular disease
- Duodenitis
- Esophageal varices
- Esophageal or pyloric stenosis
- Esophagitis or strictures
- Gastritis
- Hiatal hernia
- Mallory-Weiss syndrome
- Tumors (benign or malignant)

CRITICAL FINDINGS
- Presence and location of acute GI bleed

It is essential that critical diagnoses be communicated immediately to the appropriate HCP. A listing of those diagnoses varies among facilities. Note and immediately report to the HCP abnormal results and related symptoms. Timely notification of critical values for lab or diagnostic studies is a role expectation of the professional nurse. Notification processes will vary among facilities. Upon receipt of the critical value the information should be read back to the caller to verify accuracy. Most policies require immediate notification of the primary HCP, Hospitalist, or on-call HCP. Reported information includes the patient's name, unique identifiers, critical value, name of the person giving the report, and name of the person receiving the report. Documentation of notification should be made in the medical record with the name of the HCP notified, time and date of notification, and any orders received. Any delay in a timely report of a critical value may require completion of a notification form with review by Risk Management.

INTERFERING FACTORS

This procedure is contraindicated for
- Patients who have had surgery involving the stomach or duodenum, which can make locating the duodenal papilla difficult.
- Patients with a bleeding disorder.
- Patients with unstable cardiopulmonary status, blood coagulation defects, or cholangitis, unless the patient received prophylactic antibiotic therapy before the test (otherwise the examination must be rescheduled).
- Patients with unstable cardiopulmonary status, blood coagulation defects, known aortic arch aneurysm, large esophageal Zenker's diverticulum, recent GI surgery, esophageal varices, or known esophageal perforation.

Factors that may impair clear imaging
- Gas or food in the GI tract resulting from inadequate cleansing or failure to restrict food intake before the study.
- Retained barium from a previous radiological procedure.
- Inability of the patient to cooperate or remain still during the procedure because of age, significant pain, or mental status.

Other considerations
- The procedure may be terminated if chest pain or severe cardiac arrhythmias occur.
- Failure to follow dietary restrictions and other pretesting preparations may cause the procedure to be canceled or repeated.

NURSING IMPLICATIONS AND PROCEDURE

PRETEST:
▸ Positively identify the patient using at least two unique identifiers before providing care, treatment, or services.

Patient Teaching: Inform the patient this procedure can assist in assessing the esophagus and gastrointestinal tract.

Obtain a history of the patient's complaints, including a list of known allergens, especially allergies or sensitivities to latex, iodine, seafood, anesthetics, or contrast mediums.

Obtain a history of the patient's gastrointestinal system, symptoms, and results of previously performed laboratory tests and diagnostic and surgical procedures.

Note any recent barium or other radiological contrast procedures ordered. Ensure that barium studies are performed after this study.

Record the date of the last menstrual period and determine the possibility of pregnancy in perimenopausal women.

Obtain a list of the patient's current medications including anticoagulants, aspirin and other salicylates, herbs, nutritional supplements, and nutraceuticals (see Appendix F). Note the last time and dose of medication taken.

Review the procedure with the patient. Address concerns about pain related to the procedure and explain that some pain may be experienced during the test, and there may be moments of discomfort, but the throat will be anesthetized with a spray or swab. Inform the patient that he or she will not be able to speak during the procedure, but breathing will not be affected. Inform the patient that the procedure is performed in a GI laboratory or radiology department, usually by an HCP and support staff, and takes approximately 30 to 60 min.

Sensitivity to social and cultural issues, as well as concern for modesty, is important in providing psychological support before, during, and after the procedure.

Explain that an IV line may be started to allow for the infusion of a sedative or IV fluids.

Inform the patient that a laxative and cleansing enema may be needed the day before the procedure, with cleansing enemas on the morning of the procedure, depending on the institution's policy.

Inform the patient that dentures and eyewear will be removed before the test.

Instruct the patient to remove jewelry and other metallic objects from the area to be examined.

Instruct the patient to fast and restrict fluids for 8 hr prior to the procedure. Protocols may vary among facilities. *Make sure a written and informed consent has been signed prior to the procedure and before administering any medications.*

INTRATEST:

Ensure the patient has complied with dietary and medication restrictions and pretesting preparations for at least 8 h prior to the procedure.

Ensure the patient has removed all external metallic objects from the area to be examined prior to the procedure.

Assess for completion of bowel preparation according to the institution's procedure.

Have emergency equipment readily available.

Instruct the patient to void prior to the procedure and to change into the gown, robe, and foot coverings provided.

Instruct the patient to cooperate fully and to follow directions. Instruct the patient to remain still throughout the procedure because movement produces unreliable results.

Observe standard precautions, and follow the general guidelines in Appendix A. Positively identify the patient, and label the appropriate specimen container with the corresponding patient demographics, initials of the person collecting the specimen, date, and time of collection.

Obtain and record baseline vital signs.

Start an IV line and administer ordered sedation.

Spray or swab the oropharynx with a topical local anesthetic.

Provide an emesis basin for the increased saliva and encourage the patient to spit out the saliva because the gag reflex may be impaired.

Place the patient on an examination table in the left lateral decubitus position with the neck slightly flexed forward.

The endoscope is passed through the mouth with a dental suction device in place to drain secretions. A side-viewing flexible, fiberoptic endoscope is advanced, and visualization of the GI tract is started.

▶ Air is insufflated to distend the upper GI tract, as needed. Biopsy specimens are obtained and/or endoscopic surgery is performed.

▶ Promptly transport the specimens to the laboratory for processing and analysis.

▶ At the end of the procedure, excess air and secretions are aspirated through the scope and the endoscope is removed.

▶ The needle or catheter is removed, and a pressure dressing is applied over the puncture site.

▶ Observe/assess the needle/catheter insertion site for bleeding, inflammation, or hematoma formation.

POST-TEST:

▶ A report of the results will be made available to the requesting HCP, who will discuss the results with the patient.

▶ Observe the patient for indications of esophageal perforation (i.e., painful swallowing with neck movement, substernal pain with respiration, shoulder pain or dyspnea, abdominal or back pain, cyanosis, or fever).

▶ Do not allow the patient to eat or drink until the gag reflex returns; then allow the patient to eat lightly for 12 to 24 hr.

▶ Monitor vital signs and neurological status every 15 min for 1 hr, then every 2 hr for 4 hr, and as ordered by the HCP. Take temperature every 4 hr for 24 hr. Monitor intake and output at least every 8 hr. Compare with baseline values. Notify the HCP if temperature is elevated. Protocols may vary among facilities.

▶ Instruct the patient to resume usual activity and diet in 24 hr or as tolerated after the examination, as directed by the HCP.

▶ Observe/assess the needle/catheter insertion site for bleeding, inflammation, or hematoma formation.

▶ Instruct the patient in the care and assessment of the injection site.

▶ Inform the patient that he or she may experience some throat soreness and hoarseness. Instruct patient to treat throat discomfort with lozenges and warm gargles when the gag reflex returns.

▶ Inform the patient that any belching, bloating, or flatulence is the result of air insufflation and is temporary.

▶ Instruct the patient to report any severe pain, fever, difficulty breathing, or expectoration of blood. Immediately report symptoms to the appropriate HCP.

▶ Recognize anxiety related to test results, and offer support. Discuss the implications of abnormal test results on the patient's lifestyle. Provide teaching and information regarding the clinical implications of the test results, as appropriate.

▶ Reinforce information given by the patient's HCP regarding further testing, treatment, or referral to another HCP. Answer any questions or address any concerns voiced by the patient or family.

▶ Depending on the results of this procedure, additional testing may be needed to evaluate or monitor progression of the disease process and determine the need for a change in therapy. Evaluate test results in relation to the patient's symptoms and other tests performed.

RELATED MONOGRAPHS:

▶ Related tests include barium enema, barium swallow, capsule endoscopy, colonoscopy, CT abdomen, esophageal manometry, fecal analysis, gastric acid emptying scan, gastric fluid analysis and gastric acid stimulation test, gastrin and gastrin stimulation test, GI blood loss scan, *Helicobacter pylori,* MRI abdomen, proctosigmoidoscopy, US pelvis, and upper GI series.

▶ Refer to the Gastrointestinal System table at the end of the book for related tests by body system.

Estradiol

SYNONYM/ACRONYM: E_2.

COMMON USE: To assist in diagnosing female fertility problems that may occur from tumor or ovarian failure.

SPECIMEN: Serum (1 mL) collected in a red- or tiger-top tube. Plasma (1 mL) collected in green-top (heparin) tube is also acceptable.

NORMAL FINDINGS: (Method: Immunoassay)

Age	Conventional Units	SI Units (Conventional Units × 3.67)
6 mo–10 yr		
Male and female	Less than 15 pg/mL	Less than 55 pmol/L
11–15 yr		
Male	Less than 40 pg/mL	Less than 147 pmol/L
Female	10–300 pg/mL	37–1,100 pmol/L
Adult male	10–50 pg/mL	37–184 pmol/L
Adult female		
Early follicular phase	20–150 pg/mL	73–551 pmol/L
Late follicular phase	40–350 pg/mL	147–1,285 pmol/L
Midcycle peak	150–750 pg/mL	551–2,753 pmol/L
Luteal phase	30–450 pg/mL	110–1,652 pmol/L
Postmenopause	Less than 20 pg/mL	Less than 73 pmol/L

POTENTIAL DIAGNOSIS

Increased in
- Adrenal tumors *(related to overproduction by tumor cells)*
- Estrogen-producing tumors
- Feminization in children *(related to increased production)*
- Gynecomastia *(newborns may demonstrate swelling of breast tissue in response to maternal estrogens; somewhat common and transient in pubescent males)*
- Hepatic cirrhosis *(accumulation occurs due to lack of liver function)*
- Hyperthyroidism *(related to primary increases in estrogen or response to increased levels of sex hormone–binding globulin)*

Decreased in
- Ovarian failure *(resulting in lack of estrogen synthesis)*
- Primary and secondary hypogonadism *(related to lack of estrogen synthesis)*
- Turner's syndrome *(genetic abnormality in females in which there is only one X chromosome, resulting in varying degrees of underdeveloped sexual characteristics)*

CRITICAL FINDINGS: N/A

Find and print out the full monograph at DavisPlus (http://davisplus.fadavis.com, keyword Van Leeuwen).

Evoked Brain Potentials

SYNONYM/ACRONYM: Brainstem auditory evoked potentials (BAEP), brainstem auditory evoked responses (BAER), EP studies.

COMMON USE: To assist in diagnosing sensory deficits related to nervous system lesions manifested by visual defects, hearing defects, neuropathies, and cognitive disorders.

AREA OF APPLICATION: Brain.

CONTRAST: None.

DESCRIPTION: Evoked brain potentials, also known as evoked potential (EP) responses, are electrophysiological studies performed to measure the brain's electrical responses to various visual, auditory, and somatosensory stimuli. EP studies help diagnose lesions of the nervous system by evaluating the integrity of the visual, somatosensory, and auditory nerve pathways. Three response types are measured: visual evoked response (VER), auditory brainstem response (ABR), and somatosensory evoked response (SER). The stimuli activate the nerve tracts that connect the stimulated (receptor) area with the cortical (visual and somatosensory) or midbrain (auditory) sensory area. A number of stimuli are given, and then responses are electronically displayed in waveforms, recorded, and computer analyzed. Abnormalities are determined by a delay in time, measured in milliseconds, between the stimulus and the response. This is known as *increased latency.* VER provides information about visual pathway function to identify lesions of the optic nerves, optic tracts, and demyelinating diseases such as multiple sclerosis. ABR provides information about auditory pathways to identify hearing loss and lesions of the brainstem. SER provides information about the somatosensory pathways to identify lesions at various levels of the central nervous system (spinal cord and brain) and peripheral nerve disease. EP studies are especially useful in patients with problems and those unable to speak or respond to instructions during the test, because these studies do not require voluntary cooperation or participation in the activity. This allows collection of objective diagnostic information about visual or auditory disorders affecting infants and children and allows differentiation between organic brain and psychological disorders in adults. EP studies are also used to monitor the progression of or the effectiveness of treatment for deteriorating neurological diseases such as multiple sclerosis.

E

INDICATIONS

VER (potentials)
- Detect cryptic or past retrobulbar neuritis
- Detect lesions of the eye or optic nerves
- Detect neurological disorders such as multiple sclerosis, Parkinson's disease, and Huntington's chorea
- Evaluate binocularity in infants
- Evaluate optic pathway lesions and visual cortex defects

ABR (potentials)
- Detect abnormalities or lesions in the brainstem or auditory nerve areas
- Detect brainstem tumors and acoustic neuromas
- Screen or evaluate neonates, infants, children, and adults for auditory problems
- EP studies may be indicated when a child falls below growth chart norms

SER (potentials)
- Detect multiple sclerosis and Guillain-Barré syndrome
- Detect sensorimotor neuropathies and cervical pathology
- Evaluate spinal cord and brain injury and function
- Monitor sensory potentials to determine spinal cord function during a surgical procedure or medical regimen

ERP (potentials)
- Detect suspected psychosis or dementia
- Differentiate between organic brain disorder and cognitive function abnormality

POTENTIAL DIAGNOSIS

Normal findings in
- *VER and ABR:* Normal latency in recorded cortical and brainstem waveforms depending on age, gender, and stature
- *ERP:* Normal recognition and attention span
- *SER:* No loss of consciousness or presence of weakness

Abnormal findings in
- VER (potentials):
  P100 latencies (extended) confined to one eye suggest a lesion anterior to the optic chiasm.
  Bilateral abnormal P100 latencies indicate multiple sclerosis, optic neuritis, retinopathies, spinocerebellar degeneration, sarcoidosis, Parkinson's disease, adrenoleukodystrophy, Huntington's chorea, or amblyopias.
- ABR (potentials):
  Normal response at high intensities; wave V may occur slightly later. Earlier wave distortions suggest cochlear lesion.
  Absent or late waves at high intensities; increased amplitude of wave V suggests retrocochlear lesion.
- SER (potentials):
  Abnormal upper limb latencies suggest cervical spondylosis or intracerebral lesions.
  Abnormal lower limb latencies suggest peripheral nerve root disease such as Guillain-Barré syndrome, multiple sclerosis, transverse myelitis, or traumatic spinal cord injuries.

CRITICAL FINDINGS: N/A

INTERFERING FACTORS

Factors that may impair the results of the examination
- Inability of the patient to cooperate or remain still during the procedure because of age, significant pain, or mental status. (*Note:* Significant behavioral problems may limit the ability to complete the test.)
- Improper placement of electrodes.
- Patient stress, which can affect brain chemistry, thus making it difficult to distinguish whether the

results are due to the patient's emotional reaction or to organic pathology.

- Extremely poor visual acuity, which can hinder accurate determination of VER.
- Severe hearing loss, which can interfere with accurate determination of ABR.

NURSING IMPLICATIONS AND PROCEDURE

PRETEST:

- Positively identify the patient using at least two unique identifiers before providing care, treatment, or services.
- *Patient Teaching:* Inform the patient this procedure measures electrical activity in the nervous system.
- Obtain a history of the patient's complaints or symptoms, including a list of known allergens, especially allergies or sensitivities to latex, iodine, seafood, anesthetics, or contrast mediums.
- Obtain a history of the patient's neuromuscular system, symptoms, and results of previously performed laboratory tests and diagnostic and surgical procedures.
- Obtain a list of the patient's current medications, including herbs, nutritional supplements, and nutraceuticals (see Appendix F).
- Review the procedure with the patient. Address concerns about pain related to the procedure and explain that the procedure is painless and harmless. Inform the patient that the procedure is performed in a special laboratory by a health-care provider (HCP) and takes approximately 30 min to 2 hr, depending on the type of studies required.
- *Sensitivity to social and cultural issues,* as well as concern for modesty, is important in providing psychological support before, during, and after the procedure.
- Instruct the patient to clean the hair and to refrain from using hair sprays, creams, or solutions before the test.
- Instruct the patient to remove jewelry and other metallic objects from the area to be examined.

- There are no food, fluid, or medication restrictions unless by medical direction.
- *Make sure a written and informed consent has been signed prior to the procedure and before administering any medications.*

INTRATEST:

- Observe standard precautions, and follow the general guidelines in Appendix A. Positively identify the patient.
- Ensure the patient is able to relax; report any extreme anxiety or restlessness.
- Ensure that hair is clean and free of hair sprays, creams, or solutions.
- Ensure the patient has removed all external metallic objects from the area to be examined prior to the procedure.

Visual Evoked Potentials

- Place the patient in a comfortable position about 1 m from the stimulation source. Attach electrodes to the occipital and vertex lobe areas and a reference electrode to the ear. A light-emitting stimulation or a checkerboard pattern is projected on a screen at a regulated speed. This procedure is done for each eye (with the opposite eye covered) as the patient looks at a dot on the screen without any change in the gaze while the stimuli are delivered. A computer interprets the brain's responses to the stimuli and records them in waveforms.

Auditory Evoked Potentials

- Place the patient in a comfortable position, and place the electrodes on the scalp at the vertex lobe area and on each earlobe. Earphones are placed on the patient's ears, and a clicking noise stimulus is delivered into one ear while a continuous tone is delivered to the opposite ear. Responses to the stimuli are recorded as waveforms for analysis.

Somatosensory Evoked Potentials

- Place the patient in a comfortable position, and place the electrodes at the nerve sites of the wrist, knee, and ankle and on the scalp at the sensory cortex of the hemisphere on the opposite side (the electrode that picks up the response and delivers it to the recorder). Additional electrodes can be positioned at the cervical or lumbar vertebrae for upper or lower limb stimulation. The rate at which the electric shock stimulus is delivered to the nerve electrodes and travels to the brain is measured, computer analyzed, and recorded in waveforms for analysis. Both sides of the area being examined can be tested by switching the electrodes and repeating the procedure.

Event-Related Potentials

Place the patient in a sitting position in a chair in a quiet room. Earphones are placed on the patient's ears and auditory cues administered. The patient is asked to push a button when the tones are recognized. Flashes of light are also used as visual cues, with the client pushing a button when cues are noted. Results are compared to normal EP waveforms for correct, incorrect, or absent responses.

POST-TEST:

A report of the results will be made available to the requesting HCP, who will discuss the results with the patient.
When the procedure is complete, remove the electrodes and clean the skin where the electrodes were applied.

Recognize anxiety related to test results, and be supportive of perceived loss of independent function. Discuss the implications of abnormal test results on the patient's lifestyle. Provide teaching and information regarding the clinical implications of the test results, as appropriate.
Reinforce information given by the patient's HCP regarding further testing, treatment, or referral to another HCP. Answer any questions or address any concerns voiced by the patient or family.
Depending on the results of this procedure, additional testing may be needed to evaluate or monitor progression of the disease process and determine the need for a change in therapy. Evaluate test results in relation to the patient's symptoms and other tests performed.

RELATED MONOGRAPHS:

Related tests include acetylcholine receptor antibody, Alzheimer's disease markers, biopsy muscle, CSF analysis, CT brain, CK, EEG, ENG, MRI brain, plethysmography, and PET brain.
Refer to the Musculoskeletal System table at the end of the book for related tests by body system.

Exercise Stress Test

SYNONYM/ACRONYM: Exercise electrocardiogram, ECG, EKG, graded exercise tolerance test, stress testing, treadmill test.

COMMON USE: To assess cardiac function in relation to increased workload evidenced by dysrhythmia or pain during exercise.

AREA OF APPLICATION: Heart.

CONTRAST: None.

DESCRIPTION: The exercise stress test is a noninvasive study to measure cardiac function during physical stress. Exercise electrocardiography is primarily useful in determining the extent of coronary artery occlusion by the heart's ability to meet the need for additional oxygen in response to the stress of exercising in a safe environment. The patient exercises on a treadmill or pedals a stationary bicycle to increase the heart rate to 80% to 90% of maximal heart rate determined by age and gender, known as the *target heart rate*. Every 2 to 3 min, the speed and/or grade of the treadmill is increased to yield an increment of stress. The patient's electrocardiogram (ECG) and blood pressure are monitored during the test. The test proceeds until the patient reaches the target heart rate or experiences chest pain or fatigue. The risks involved in the procedure are possible myocardial infarction (1 in 500) and death (1 in 10,000) in patients experiencing frequent angina episodes before the test. Although useful, this procedure is not as accurate as cardiac nuclear scans for diagnosing coronary artery disease (CAD).

For patients unable to complete the test, pharmacological stress testing can be done. Medications used to pharmacologically exercise the patient's heart include vasodilators such as dipyridamole and adenosine or dobutamine (which stimulates heart rate and pumping force). The patient's ECG and blood pressure are monitored during the test. The test proceeds until the stimulated exercise portion when a radiotracer, such as technetium-99m or sestamibi, is injected. Pictures are taken by a gamma camera during the stimulated portion and compared with images taken at rest.

INDICATIONS
- Detect dysrhythmias during exercising, as evidenced by ECG changes
- Detect peripheral artery disease (PAD), as evidenced by leg pain or cramping during exercising
- Determine exercise-induced hypertension
- Evaluate cardiac function after myocardial infarction or cardiac surgery to determine safe exercise levels for cardiac rehabilitation as well as work limitations
- Evaluate effectiveness of medication regimens, such as antianginals or antiarrhythmics
- Evaluate suspected CAD in the presence of chest pain and other symptoms
- Screen for CAD in the absence of pain and other symptoms in patients at risk

POTENTIAL DIAGNOSIS

Normal findings in
- Normal heart rate during physical exercise. Heart rate and systolic blood pressure rise in direct proportion to workload and to metabolic oxygen demand, which is based on age and exercise protocol. Maximal heart rate for adults is normally 150 to 200 beats/min.

Abnormal findings in
- Activity intolerance related to oxygen supply and demand imbalance
- Bradycardia
- CAD
- Chest pain related to ischemia or inflammation

- Decreased cardiac output
- Dysrhythmias
- Hypertension
- PAD
- ST segment depression of 1 mm (considered a positive test), indicating myocardial ischemia
- Tachycardia

CRITICAL FINDINGS: N/A

INTERFERING FACTORS

The following factors may impair interpretation of examination results because they create an artificial state that makes it difficult to determine true physiological function:

- Anxiety or panic attack.
- Drugs such as beta blockers, cardiac glycosides, calcium channel blockers, coronary vasodilators, and barbiturates.
- High food intake or smoking before testing.
- Hypertension, hypoxia, left bundle branch block, and ventricular hypertrophy.
- Improper electrode placement.
- Potassium or calcium imbalance.
- Viagra should not be taken in combination with nitroglycerin or other nitrates 24 hr prior to the procedure because it may result in a dangerously low blood pressure.
- Wolff-Parkinson-White syndrome (anomalous atrioventricular excitation).

NURSING IMPLICATIONS AND PROCEDURE

PRETEST:

▶ Positively identify the patient using at least two unique identifiers before providing care, treatment, or services.
▶ *Patient Teaching:* Inform the patient this procedure can assist in assessing the heart's ability to respond to an increasing workload.

▶ Obtain a history of the patient's cardiovascular system, symptoms, and results of previously performed laboratory tests and diagnostic and surgical procedures.
▶ Inquire if the patient has had any chest pain within the past 48 hr or has a history of anginal attacks; if either of these has occurred, inform the health-care provider (HCP) immediately because the stress test may be too risky and should be rescheduled in 4 to 6 wk.
▶ Obtain a list of the patient's current medications, including herbs, nutritional supplements, and nutraceuticals (see Appendix F).
▶ Review the procedure with the patient. Address concerns about pain related to the procedure and explain that some discomfort may be experienced during the stimulated portion of the test. Inform the patient that the procedure is performed in a special department by an HCP specializing in this procedure and takes approximately 30 to 60 min.
▶ *Sensitivity to social and cultural issues,* as well as concern for modesty, is important in providing psychological support before, during, and after the procedure.
▶ Record a baseline 12-lead ECG and vital signs.
▶ Instruct the patient to wear comfortable shoes and clothing for the exercise.
▶ Instruct the patient to fast, restrict fluids, and avoid tobacco products for 4 hr prior to the procedure. Protocols may vary among facilities.
▶ *Make sure a written and informed consent has been signed prior to the procedure and before administering any medications.*

INTRATEST:

▶ Observe standard precautions, and follow the general guidelines in Appendix A. Positively identify the patient.
▶ Ensure the patient has complied with dietary and tobacco restrictions for at least 4 hr prior to the procedure.
▶ An IV access may be established for emergency use.
▶ Have emergency equipment readily available.

Instruct the patient to void prior to the procedure and to change into the gown provided.

Place electrodes in appropriate positions on the patient and connect a blood pressure cuff to a monitoring device. If the patient's oxygen consumption is to be continuously monitored, connect the patient to a machine via a mouthpiece or to a pulse oximeter via a finger lead.

Instruct the patient to walk on a treadmill (most commonly used) and use the handrails to maintain balance or to peddle a bicycle. As stress is increased, inform the patient to report any symptoms, such as chest or leg pain, dyspnea, or fatigue.

Turn the treadmill on at a slow speed, and increase in speed and elevation to raise the patient's heart rate. Increase the stress until the patient's predicted target heart rate is reached.

Instruct the patient to report symptoms such as dizziness, sweating, breathlessness, or nausea, which can be normal, as speed increases. The test is terminated if pain or fatigue is severe; maximum heart rate under stress is attained; signs of ischemia are present; maximum effort has been achieved; or dyspnea, hypertension (systolic blood pressure greater than 200 mm Hg, diastolic blood pressure greater than 110 mm Hg, or both), tachycardia (greater than 200 beats/min minus person's age), new dysrhythmias, chest pain that begins or worsens, faintness, extreme dizziness, or confusion develops.

After the exercise period, allow a 3- to 15-min rest period with the patient in a sitting position. During this period, the ECG, blood pressure, and heart rate monitoring is continued.

Remove the electrodes and cleanse the skin of any remaining gel or ECG electrode adhesive.

POST-TEST:

A report of the results will be made available to the requesting HCP, who will discuss the results with the patient.

Instruct the patient to resume usual activity, as directed by the HCP.

Instruct the patient to contact the HCP to report any anginal pain or other discomforts experienced after the test.

Nutritional Considerations: Abnormal findings may be associated with cardiovascular disease. The American Heart Association and National Heart, Lung, and Blood Institute (NHLBI) recommend nutritional therapy for individuals identified to be at high risk for developing CAD or individuals who have specific risk factors and/or existing medical conditions (e.g., elevated LDL cholesterol levels, other lipid disorders, insulin-dependent diabetes, insulin resistance, or metabolic syndrome). If overweight, the patient should be encouraged to achieve a normal weight. Guidelines for the Therapeutic Lifestyle Changes (TLC) diet are outlined in the Third Report of the Expert Panel on Detection, Evaluation, and Treatment of High Blood Cholesterol in Adults (Adult Treatment Panel III [ATP III]). The TLC diet emphasizes a reduction in foods high in saturated fats and cholesterol. Red meats, eggs, and dairy products are the major sources of saturated fats and cholesterol. If triglycerides also are elevated, the patient should be advised to eliminate or reduce alcohol and simple carbohydrates from the diet. The TLC approach also includes the use of plant stanols or sterols and increased dissolved fiber as an option for lowering LDL cholesterol levels; nutritional recommendations for daily total caloric intake; recommendations for allowable percentage of calories derived from fat (saturated and unsaturated), carbohydrates, protein, and cholesterol; as well as recommendations for daily expenditure of energy.

Nutritional Considerations: Overweight patients with high blood pressure should be encouraged to achieve a normal weight. Other changeable risk factors warranting patient education include strategies to safely decrease sodium intake, increase physical activity, decrease alcohol consumption, eliminate tobacco use, and decrease cholesterol levels.

Social and Cultural Considerations: Numerous studies point to the prevalence of excess body weight in American children and adolescents. Experts estimate that obesity is present in 25% of the population ages 6 to 11 yr. The medical, social, and emotional consequences of excess body weight are significant. Special attention should be given to instructing the child and caregiver regarding health risks and weight control education.

Recognize anxiety related to test results, and be supportive of fear of shortened life expectancy. Discuss the implications of abnormal test results on the patient's lifestyle. Provide teaching and information regarding the clinical implications of the test results, as appropriate. Educate the patient regarding access to counseling services. Provide contact information, if desired, for the American Heart Association (www.americanheart.org), the NHLBI (www.nhlbi.nih.gov), or the Legs for Life (www.legsforlife.org).

Reinforce information given by the patient's HCP regarding further testing, treatment, or referral to another HCP. Answer any questions or address any concerns voiced by the patient or family.

Depending on the results of this procedure, additional testing may be performed to evaluate or monitor progression of the disease process and determine the need for a change in therapy. Evaluate test results in relation to the patient's symptoms and other tests performed.

RELATED MONOGRAPHS:

Related tests include antiarrhythmic drugs, apolipoprotein A and B, AST, atrial natriuretic peptide, BNP, blood gases, blood pool imaging, calcium, chest x-ray, cholesterol (total, HDL, LDL), CT cardiac scoring, CT thorax, CRP, CK and isoenzymes, echocardiography, echocardiography transesophageal, electrocardiogram, glucose, glycated hemoglobin, Holter monitor, homocysteine, ketones, LDH and isos, lipoprotein electrophoresis, lung perfusion scan, magnesium, MRI chest, MI infarct scan, myocardial perfusion heart scan, myoglobin, PET heart, potassium, pulse oximetry, sodium, triglycerides, and troponin.

Refer to the Cardiovascular System table at the end of the book for related tests by body system.

Fecal Analysis

SYNONYM/ACRONYM: N/A.

COMMON USE: To assess for the presence of blood in the stool toward diagnosing gastrointestinal bleeding, cancer, inflammation, and infection.

SPECIMEN: Stool.

NORMAL FINDINGS: (Method: Macroscopic examination, for appearance and color; microscopic examination, for cell count and presence of meat fibers; leukocyte esterase, for leukocytes; Clinitest [Bayer Corporation, Pittsburgh, Pennsylvania] for reducing substances; guaiac, for occult blood; x-ray paper, for trypsin.)

Characteristic	Normal Result
Appearance	Solid and formed
Color	Brown
Epithelial cells	Few to moderate
Fecal fat	See "Fecal Fat" monograph
Leukocytes (white blood cells)	Negative
Meat fibers	Negative
Occult blood	Negative
Reducing substances	Negative
Trypsin	2+ to 4+

DESCRIPTION: Feces consist mainly of cellulose and other undigested foodstuffs, bacteria, and water. Other substances normally found in feces include epithelial cells shed from the gastrointestinal (GI) tract, small amounts of fats, bile pigments in the form of urobilinogen, GI and pancreatic secretions, electrolytes, and trypsin. Trypsin is a proteolytic enzyme produced in the pancreas. The average adult excretes 100 to 300 g of fecal material per day, the residue of approximately 10 L of liquid material that enters the GI tract each day. The laboratory analysis of feces includes macroscopic examination (volume, odor, shape, color, consistency, presence of mucus), microscopic examination (leukocytes, epithelial cells, meat fibers), and chemical tests for specific substances (occult blood, trypsin, estimation of carbohydrate). Detection of occult blood is the most common test performed on stool. The prevalence of colorectal adenoma is greater than 30% in people aged 60 and older. Progression from adenoma to carcinoma occurs over a period of 5 to 12 yr; from carcinoma to metastatic disease in 2 to 3 yr.

INDICATIONS
- Assist in diagnosing disorders associated with GI bleeding or drug therapy that leads to bleeding
- Assist in the diagnosis of pseudomembranous enterocolitis after use of broad-spectrum antibiotic therapy
- Assist in the diagnosis of suspected inflammatory bowel disorder
- Detect altered protein digestion

- Detect intestinal parasitic infestation, as indicated by diarrhea of unknown cause
- Investigate diarrhea of unknown cause
- Monitor effectiveness of therapy for intestinal malabsorption or pancreatic insufficiency
- Screen for cystic fibrosis

POTENTIAL DIAGNOSIS

Unusual Appearance
- Bloody: *Excessive intestinal wall irritation or malignancy*
- Bulky or frothy: *Malabsorption*
- Mucous: *Inflammation of intestinal walls*
- Slender or ribbonlike: *Obstruction*

Unusual Color
- Black: *Bismuth (antacid) or charcoal ingestion, iron therapy, upper GI bleeding*
- Grayish white: *Barium ingestion, bile duct obstruction*
- Green: *Antibiotics, biliverdin, green vegetables*
- Red: *Beets and food coloring, lower GI bleed, phenazopyridine hydrochloride compounds, rifampin*
- Yellow: *Rhubarb*

Increased
- Carbohydrates/reducing substances: *Malabsorption syndromes*
- Epithelial cells: *Inflammatory bowel disorders*
- Leukocytes: *Bacterial infections of the intestinal wall, salmonellosis, shigellosis, and ulcerative colitis*
- Meat fibers: *Altered protein digestion*
- Occult blood: *Anal fissure, diverticular disease, esophageal varices, esophagitis, gastritis, hemorrhoids, infectious diarrhea, inflammatory bowel disease, Mallory-Weiss tears, polyps, tumors, ulcers*

Decreased
- Leukocytes: *Amebic colitis, cholera, disorders resulting from toxins, parasites, viral diarrhea*
- Trypsin: *Cystic fibrosis, malabsorption syndromes, pancreatic deficiency*

CRITICAL FINDINGS: N/A

INTERFERING FACTORS
- Drugs that can cause positive results for occult blood include acetylsalicylic acid, anticoagulants, colchicine, corticosteroids, iron preparations, and phenylbutazone.
- Ingestion of a diet high in red meat, certain vegetables, and bananas can cause false-positive results for occult blood.
- Large doses of vitamin C can cause false-negative occult blood.
- Constipated stools may not indicate any trypsin activity owing to extended exposure to intestinal bacteria.

NURSING IMPLICATIONS AND PROCEDURE

PRETEST:
- Positively identify the patient using at least two unique identifiers before providing care, treatment, or services.
- *Patient Teaching:* Inform the patient this test can assist in the diagnosis of intestinal disorders.
- Obtain a history of the patient's complaints, including a list of known allergens, especially allergies or sensitivities to latex.
- Obtain a history of the patient's gastrointestinal system, symptoms, and results of previously performed laboratory tests and diagnostic and surgical procedures.
- Obtain a list of the patient's current medications, including herbs, nutritional supplements, and nutraceuticals (see Appendix F).
- Review the procedure with the patient. Inform the patient of the procedure for collecting a stool sample, including the importance of good hand-washing techniques. The patient should place

the sample in a tightly covered container. Instruct the patient not to contaminate the specimen with urine, water, or toilet tissue. Address concerns about pain and explain that there should be no discomfort during the procedure.

▶ *Sensitivity to social and cultural issues,* as well as concern for modesty, is important in providing psychological support before, during, and after the procedure.

▶ Instruct the patient not to use laxatives, enemas, or suppositories for 3 days before the test.

▶ Instruct the patient to follow a normal diet. If the test is being performed to identify blood, instruct the patient to follow a special diet that includes small amounts of chicken, turkey, and tuna (no red meats), raw and cooked vegetables and fruits, and bran cereal for several days before the test. Foods to avoid with the special diet include beets, turnips, cauliflower, broccoli, bananas, parsnips, and cantaloupe, because these foods can interfere with the occult blood test.

INTRATEST:

▶ Ensure that the patient has complied with medication restrictions; assure laxatives, enemas, or suppositories have been restricted for at least 3 days prior to the procedure.

▶ Instruct the patient to cooperate fully and to follow directions.

▶ Observe standard precautions, and follow the general guidelines in Appendix A. Positively identify the patient, and label the appropriate specimen container with the corresponding patient demographics, initials of the person collecting the specimen, date and time of collection, and suspected cause of enteritis; note any current or recent antibiotic therapy.

▶ Collect a stool specimen in a half-pint waterproof container with a tight-fitting lid; if the patient is not ambulatory, collect it in a clean, dry bedpan. Use a tongue blade to transfer the specimen to the container, and include any mucoid and bloody portions. Collect specimen from the first, middle, and last portion of the stool. The specimen should be refrigerated if it will not be transported to the laboratory within 4 hr after collection.

▶ To collect specimen by rectal swab, insert the swab past the anal sphincter, rotate gently, and withdraw. Place the swab in the appropriate container.

▶ Promptly transport the specimen to the laboratory for processing and analysis.

POST-TEST:

▶ A report of the results will be made available to the requesting health-care provider (HCP), who will discuss the results with the patient.

▶ Recognize anxiety related to test results. Discuss the implications of abnormal test results on the patient's lifestyle. Provide teaching and information regarding the clinical implications of the test results, as appropriate.

▶ Reinforce information given by the patient's HCP regarding further testing, treatment, or referral to another HCP. Decisions regarding the need for and frequency of occult blood testing, colonoscopy, or other cancer screening procedures should be made after consultation between the patient and HCP. The most current guidelines for colon cancer screening of the general population as well as of individuals with increased risk are available from the American Cancer Society (www.cancer.org) and the American College of Gastroenterology (www.gi.org). Answer any questions or address any concerns voiced by the patient or family.

▶ Depending on the results of this procedure, additional testing may be performed to evaluate or monitor progression of the disease process and determine the need for a change in therapy. Evaluate test results in relation to the patient's symptoms and other tests performed.

RELATED MONOGRAPHS:

▶ Related tests include α_1-antitrypsin/phenotyping, barium enema, biopsy intestine, capsule endoscopy, CEA and cancer antigens, chloride sweat, colonoscopy, CT colonoscopy, culture stool, D-xylose tolerance, fecal fat, gliadin antibody, lactose tolerance test, ova and parasites, and proctosigmoidoscopy.

▶ Refer to the Gastrointestinal System table at the end of the book for related tests by body system.

F

Fecal Fat

SYNONYM/ACRONYM: Stool fat, fecal fat stain.

COMMON USE: To assess for the presence of fat in the stool toward diagnosing malabsorption disorders such as Crohn's disease and cystic fibrosis.

SPECIMEN: Stool (80 mL) aliquot from an unpreserved and homogenized 24- to 72-hr timed collection. Random specimens may also be submitted.

NORMAL FINDINGS: (Method: Stain with Sudan black or oil red O. Treatment with ethanol identifies neutral fats; treatment with acetic acid identifies fatty acids.)

	Random, Semiquantitative
Neutral fat	Less than 60 fat globules/hpf*
Fatty acids	Less than 100 fat globules/hpf
	72-hr, Quantitative
Age (normal diet)	
Infant (breast milk)	Less than 1 g/24 hr
0–6 yr	Less than 2 g/24 hr
Adult	2–7 g/24 hr; less than 20% of total solids
Adult (fat-free diet)	Less than 4 g/24 hr

*hpf = high-power field.

DESCRIPTION: Fecal fat primarily consists of triglycerides (neutral fats), fatty acids, and fatty acid salts. Through microscopic examination, the number and size of fat droplets can be determined as well as the type of fat present. Excretion of more than 7 g of fecal fat in a 24-hr period is abnormal but nonspecific for disease. Increases in excretion of neutral fats are associated with pancreatic exocrine insufficiency, whereas decreases are related to small bowel disease. An increase in triglycerides indicates that insufficient pancreatic enzymes are available to convert the triglycerides into fatty acids. Patients with malabsorption conditions have normal amounts of triglycerides but an increase in total fecal fat because the fats are not absorbed through the intestine. Malabsorption disorders (e.g., cystic fibrosis) cause blockage of the pancreatic ducts by mucus, which prevents the enzymes from reaching the duodenum and results in lack of fat digestion. Without digestion, the fats cannot be absorbed, and steatorrhea results. The appearance and odor of stool from patients with steatorrhea is typically foamy, greasy, soft, and foul-smelling. The semiquantitative test is used to screen for the presence of fecal fat. The quantitative method, which requires a 72-hr stool collection, measures the amount of fat present in grams.

INDICATIONS

- Assist in the diagnosis of malabsorption or pancreatic insufficiency, as indicated by elevated fat levels
- Monitor the effectiveness of therapy

POTENTIAL DIAGNOSIS

Increased in

- Abetalipoprotein deficiency *(related to lack of transport proteins for absorption)*
- Addison's disease *(related to impaired transport)*
- Amyloidosis *(increased rate of excretion related to malabsorption)*
- Bile salt deficiency *(related to lack of bile salts required for proper fat digestion)*
- Carcinoid syndrome *(increased rate of excretion related to malabsorption)*
- Celiac disease *(increased rate of excretion related to malabsorption)*
- Crohn's disease *(increased rate of excretion related to malabsorption)*
- Cystic fibrosis *(related to insufficient digestive enzymes)*
- Diabetes *(abnormal motility related to primary condition)*
- Enteritis *(increased rate of excretion related to malabsorption)*
- Malnutrition *(related to detrimental effects on organs and systems responsible for digestion, transport, and absorption)*
- Multiple sclerosis *(abnormal motility related to primary condition)*
- Pancreatic insufficiency or obstruction *(related to insufficient digestive enzymes)*
- Peptic ulcer disease *(related to improper digestion due to low pH)*
- Pernicious anemia *(related to bacterial overgrowth that decreases overall absorption and results in vitamin B_{12} deficiency)*
- Progressive systemic sclerosis *(abnormal motility related to primary condition)*
- Thyrotoxicosis *(abnormal motility related to primary condition)*
- Tropical sprue *(increased rate of excretion related to malabsorption)*
- Viral hepatitis *(related to insufficient production of digestive enzymes and bile)*
- Whipple's disease *(increased rate of excretion related to malabsorption)*
- Zollinger-Ellison syndrome *(related to improper digestion due to low pH)*

Decreased in: N/A

CRITICAL FINDINGS: N/A

INTERFERING FACTORS

- Cimetidine has been associated with decreased fecal fat in some patients with cystic fibrosis who are also receiving pancreatic enzyme therapy.
- Some drugs cause steatorrhea as a result of mucosal damage. These include colchicine, kanamycin, lincomycin, methotrexate, and neomycin. Other drugs that can cause an increase in fecal fat include aminosalicylic acid, bisacodyl and phenolphthalein (observed in laxative abusers), and cholestyramine (in high doses).
- Use of suppositories, oily lubricants, or mineral oil in the perianal area for 3 days before the test can falsely increase neutral fats.
- Use of herbals with laxative effects, including cascara, psyllium, and senna, for 3 days before the test can falsely increase neutral fats.
- Barium interferes with test results.
- Failure to collect all stools may reflect falsely decreased results.
- Ingestion of a diet too high or low in fats may alter the results.

NURSING IMPLICATIONS AND PROCEDURE

PRETEST:

‣ Positively identify the patient using at least two unique identifiers before providing care, treatment, or services.

‣ *Patient Teaching:* Inform the patient this test can assist in the diagnosis of intestinal disorders.

‣ Obtain a history of the patient's complaints that indicate a gastrointestinal (GI) disorder, diarrhea related to GI dysfunction, pain related to tissue inflammation or irritation, alteration in diet resulting from an inability to digest certain foods, or fluid volume deficit related to active loss. Obtain a history of known allergens.

‣ Obtain a history of the patient's gastrointestinal and respiratory systems, symptoms, and results of previously performed laboratory tests and diagnostic and surgical procedures.

‣ Note any recent procedures that can interfere with test results.

‣ Obtain a list of the patient's current medications, including herbs, nutritional supplements, and nutraceuticals (see Appendix F).

‣ Review the procedure with the patient. Stress the importance of collecting all stools for the quantitative test, including diarrhea, over the timed specimen-collection period. Inform the patient not to urinate in the stool-collection container and not to put toilet paper in the container. Address concerns about pain related to the procedure. Explain to the patient that there should be no discomfort during the procedure.

‣ *Sensitivity to social and cultural issues,* as well as concern for modesty, is important in providing psychological support before, during, and after the procedure.

‣ Instruct the patient not to use laxatives, enemas, or suppositories for 3 days before the test.

‣ There are no fluid restrictions unless by medical direction.

‣ Instruct the patient to ingest a diet containing 50 to 150 g of fat for at least 3 days before beginning specimen collection. This approach does not work well with children; instruct the

caregiver to record the child's dietary intake to provide a basis from which an estimate of fat intake can be made.

INTRATEST:

‣ Ensure that the patient has complied with dietary and other pretesting preparations prior to the procedure.

‣ Instruct the patient to cooperate fully and to follow directions.

‣ Observe standard precautions, and follow the general guidelines in Appendix A. Positively identify the patient, and label the appropriate specimen container with the corresponding patient demographics, initials of the person collecting the specimen, date, and the start and stop times of collection.

‣ Obtain the appropriate-sized specimen container, toilet-mounted collection container to aid in specimen collection, and plastic bag for specimen transport. A large, clean, preweighed container should be used for the timed test. A smaller, clean container can be used for the collection of the random sample.

‣ For the quantitative procedure, instruct the patient to collect each stool and place it in the 500-mL container during the timed collection period. Keep the container refrigerated in the plastic bag throughout the entire collection period.

‣ Promptly transport the specimen to the laboratory for processing and analysis.

POST-TEST:

‣ A report of the results will be made available to the requesting health-care provider (HCP), who will discuss the results with the patient.

‣ Instruct the patient to resume usual diet and medication, as directed by the HCP.

‣ Recognize anxiety related to test results, and be supportive of impaired activity related to perceived loss of independence and fear of shortened life expectancy. Discuss the implications of abnormal test results on the patient's lifestyle. Instruct the patient with abnormal values on the importance of fluid intake and proper diet specific to his or her condition. Provide teaching and information regarding the clinical implications of the test results, as appropriate. Educate the patient regarding access to counseling services. Help the patient and caregiver cope with long-term implications. Recognize that anticipatory anxiety and grief may be expressed when someone is faced with a chronic disorder. Provide contact information, if desired and as appropriate, for the American Diabetes Association (www.diabetes.org), the Celiac Disease Foundation (www.celiac.org), the Crohn's and Colitis Foundation of America (www.ccfa.org), or the Cystic Fibrosis Foundation (www.cff.org).

▶ Reinforce information given by the patient's HCP regarding further testing, treatment, or referral to another HCP. Answer any questions or address any concerns voiced by the patient or family.

Depending on the results of this procedure, additional testing may be performed to evaluate or monitor progression of the disease process and determine the need for a change in therapy. Evaluate test results in relation to the patient's symptoms and other tests performed.

RELATED MONOGRAPHS:

▶ Related tests include α_1-antitrypsin/phenotyping, biopsy intestine, chloride sweat, CBC, CBC RBC indices, CBC RBC morphology, D-xylose tolerance test, fecal analysis, folate, gastric acid stimulation test, gastric emptying scan, radioactive iodine uptake, and vitamin B_{12}.

▶ Refer to the Gastrointestinal and Respiratory systems tables at the end of the book for related tests by body system.

Ferritin

SYNONYM/ACRONYM: N/A.

COMMON USE: To assist in diagnosing and monitoring various forms of anemia related to ferritin levels such as iron-deficiency anemia, anemia of malnourishment related to alcoholism, hemolytic anemia, chronic anemia of inflammation, and anemia related to long-term kidney dialysis.

SPECIMEN: Serum (1 mL) collected in a red- or tiger-top tube.

NORMAL FINDINGS: (Method: Immunoassay)

Age	Conventional Units	SI Units (Conventional Units × 1)
Newborn	25–200 ng/mL	25–200 mcg/L
1 mo	200–600 ng/mL	200–600 mcg/L
2–5 mo	50–200 ng/mL	50–200 mcg/L
6 mo–15 yr	7–140 ng/mL	7–140 mcg/L
Adult		
Males	20–250 ng/mL	20–250 mcg/L
Females (18–39 yr)	10–120 ng/mL	10–120 mcg/L
Females (40 yr and older)	12–263 ng/mL	12–263 mcg/L

DESCRIPTION: Ferritin, a protein manufactured in the liver, spleen, and bone marrow, consists of a protein shell, apoferritin, and an iron core. The amount of ferritin in the circulation is usually proportional to the amount of stored iron (ferritin and hemosiderin) in body tissues. Levels vary according to age and gender, but they are not affected by exogenous iron intake or subject to diurnal variations. Compared to iron and total iron-binding capacity, ferritin is a more sensitive and specific test for diagnosing iron-deficiency anemia. Iron-deficiency anemia in adults is indicated at ferritin levels less than 10 ng/mL; hemochromatosis or hemosiderosis is indicated at levels greater than 400 ng/mL.

INDICATIONS

- Assist in the diagnosis of iron-deficiency anemia
- Assist in the differential diagnosis of microcytic, hypochromic anemias
- Monitor hematological responses during pregnancy, when serum iron is usually decreased and ferritin may be decreased
- Support diagnosis of hemochromatosis or other disorders of iron metabolism and storage

POTENTIAL DIAGNOSIS

Increased in

- Alcoholism *(active abuse, as evidenced by release of ferritin into the circulation from damaged hepatocytes and red blood cells [RBCs])*
- Breast cancer *(acute, related to release of ferritin as an acute-phase reactant protein; chronic, pathophysiology is uncertain)*
- Hemochromatosis *(related to increased iron deposits in the liver, which stimulate ferritin production)*
- Hemolytic anemia *(related to increased iron levels from hemolyzed RBCs, which stimulate ferritin production)*
- Hemosiderosis *(related to increased iron levels, which stimulate ferritin production)*
- Hepatocellular disease *(acute, related to release of ferritin as an acute-phase reactant protein; chronic, related to release of ferritin into the circulation from damaged hepatocytes)*
- Hodgkin's disease *(acute, related to release of ferritin as an acute-phase reactant protein; chronic, pathophysiology is uncertain)*
- Hyperthyroidism *(possibly related to the stimulating effect of thyroid-stimulating hormone on ferritin production)*
- Infection *(acute, related to release of ferritin as an acute-phase reactant protein; chronic, pathophysiology is uncertain)*
- Inflammatory diseases *(related to release of ferritin as an acute-phase reactant protein)*
- Leukemias *(acute, related to release of ferritin as an acute-phase reactant protein; chronic, pathophysiology is uncertain)*
- Oral or parenteral administration of iron *(evidenced by an increased circulating iron level, which stimulates ferritin production)*
- Thalassemia *(related to increased iron levels from hemolyzed RBCs, which stimulate ferritin production)*

Decreased in
Conditions that decrease iron stores result in corresponding low levels of ferritin.

- Hemodialysis
- Iron-deficiency anemia

CRITICAL FINDINGS: N/A

INTERFERING FACTORS

• Drugs that may increase ferritin levels include ethanol, ferric polymaltose, iron, and oral contraceptives.
• Drugs that may decrease ferritin levels include erythropoietin and methimazole.
• Recent transfusion can elevate serum ferritin.

NURSING IMPLICATIONS AND PROCEDURE

PRETEST:

▸ Positively identify the patient using at least two unique identifiers before providing care, treatment, or services.
▸ *Patient Teaching:* Inform the patient this test can assist in the diagnosis of anemia.
▸ Obtain a history of the patient's complaints, including a list of known allergens, especially allergies or sensitivities to latex.
▸ Obtain a history of the patient's hematopoietic system, symptoms, and results of previously performed laboratory tests and diagnostic and surgical procedures.
▸ Note any recent procedures that can interfere with test results.
▸ Obtain a list of the patient's current medications, including herbs, nutritional supplements, and nutraceuticals (see Appendix F).
▸ Review the procedure with the patient. Inform the patient that specimen collection takes approximately 5 to 10 min. Address concerns about pain and explain that there may be some discomfort during the venipuncture.
▸ *Sensitivity to social and cultural issues,* as well as concern for modesty is important in providing psychological support before, during, and after the procedure.
▸ There are no food, fluid, or medication restrictions unless by medical direction.

INTRATEST:

▸ If the patient has a history of allergic reaction to latex, avoid the use of equipment containing latex.
▸ Instruct the patient to cooperate fully and to follow directions. Direct the patient to breathe normally and to avoid unnecessary movement.
▸ Observe standard precautions, and follow the general guidelines in Appendix A. Positively identify the patient, and label the appropriate specimen container with the corresponding patient demographics, initials of the person collecting the specimen, date, and time of collection. Perform a venipuncture.
▸ Remove the needle and apply direct pressure with dry gauze to stop bleeding. Observe/assess venipuncture site for bleeding or hematoma formation and secure gauze with adhesive bandage.
▸ Promptly transport the specimen to the laboratory for processing and analysis.

POST-TEST:

▸ A report of the results will be made available to the requesting health-care provider (HCP), who will discuss the results with the patient.
▸ *Nutritional Considerations:* Nutritional therapy may be indicated for patients with decreased ferritin values because this may indicate corresponding iron deficiency. Instruct these patients in the dietary inclusion of iron-rich foods and in the administration of iron supplements, including side effects, as appropriate.
▸ Reinforce information given by the patient's HCP regarding further testing, treatment, or referral to another HCP. Answer any questions or address any concerns voiced by the patient or family.
▸ Depending on the results of this procedure, additional testing may be performed to evaluate or monitor progression of the disease process and determine the need for a change in therapy. Evaluate test results in relation to the patient's symptoms and other tests performed.

RELATED MONOGRAPHS:

Related tests include biopsy bone marrow, biopsy liver, complement, CBC, CBC hematocrit, CBC hemoglobin, CBC platelet count, CBC RBC count, CBC RBC indices, CBC RBC morphology and inclusions, CBC WBC count and differential, Coomb's

antiglobulin direct and indirect, erythropoietin, FEP, G6PD, Ham's test, Hgb electrophoresis, hemosiderin, iron/TIBC, osmotic fragility, PK, sickle cell screen, and transferrin.

Refer to the Hematopoietic System table at the end of the book for related tests by body system.

Fetal Fibronectin

SYNONYM/ACRONYM: fFN.

COMMON USE: To assist in assessing for premature labor.

SPECIMEN: Swab of vaginal secretions.

NORMAL FINDINGS: (Method: Immunoassay) Negative.

DESCRIPTION: Fibronectin is a protein found in fetal connective tissue, amniotic fluid, and the placenta of pregnant women. Placental fetal fibronectin (fFN) is concentrated in the area where the placenta and its membranes are in contact with the uterine wall. It is first secreted early in pregnancy and is believed to help implantation of the fertilized egg to the uterus. Fibronectin is not detectable again until just before delivery, at approximately 37 wk. If it is detected in vaginal secretions at 22 to 34 wk of gestation, delivery may happen prematurely. The test is a useful marker for impending membrane rupture within 7 to 14 days if the level rises to greater than 0.05 mcg/mL.

INDICATIONS
Investigate signs of premature labor

POTENTIAL DIAGNOSIS

Positive findings in
• Premature labor *(possibly initiated by mechanical or infectious processes, the membranes pull away from the uterine wall and amniotic fluid containing fFN leaks into endocervical fluid)*

CRITICAL FINDINGS: N/A

INTERFERING FACTORS
If signs and symptoms persist in light of negative test results, repeat testing may be necessary.

NURSING IMPLICATIONS AND PROCEDURE

PRETEST:

Positively identify the patient using at least two unique identifiers before providing care, treatment, or services.
Patient Teaching: Inform the patient this test can assess for risk of preterm delivery.

- Obtain a history of the patient's complaints, including a list of known allergens, especially allergies or sensitivities to latex.
- Obtain a history of the patient's reproductive system, symptoms, and results of previously performed laboratory tests and diagnostic and surgical procedures.
- Ensure that the patient knows the symptoms of premature labor, which include uterine contractions (with or without pain) lasting 20 sec or longer or increasing in frequency, menstrual-like cramping (intermittent or continuous), pelvic pressure, lower back pain that does not dissipate with a change in position, persistent diarrhea, intestinal cramps, changes in vaginal discharge, or a feeling that something is wrong.
- The health-care provider (HCP) should be informed if contractions occur more frequently than four times per hour.
- Obtain a list of the patient's current medications, including herbs, nutritional supplements, and neutraceuticals (see Appendix F).
- Review the procedure with the patient. Inform the patient that specimen collection takes approximately 5 to 10 min and will be performed by an HCP specializing in this branch of medicine. Address concerns about pain related to the procedure. Explain to the patient that there should be minimal to no discomfort during the procedure.
- *Sensitivity to social and cultural issues,* as well as concern for modesty, is important in providing psychological support before, during, and after the procedure.
- There are no food, fluid, or medication restrictions unless by medical direction.

INTRATEST:

- If the patient has a history of allergic reaction to latex, avoid the use of equipment containing latex.
- Instruct the patient to cooperate fully and to follow directions. Direct the patient to breathe normally and to avoid unnecessary movement.
- Observe standard precautions, and follow the general guidelines in Appendix A. Positively identify the patient, and label the appropriate specimen container with the corresponding patient demographics, initials of the person collecting the specimen, date, and time of collection.
- Position the patient on the gynecological examination table with the feet up in stirrups. Drape the patient's legs to provide privacy and to reduce chilling. Collect a small amount of vaginal secretion using a special swab from a fetal fibronectin kit.
- Promptly transport the specimen to the laboratory for processing and analysis.

F

POST-TEST:

- A report of the results will be made available to the requesting HCP, who will discuss the results with the patient.
- Recognize anxiety related to test results. Discuss the implications of abnormal test results on the patient's lifestyle. Provide teaching and information regarding the clinical implications of the test results, as appropriate. Educate the patient regarding access to counseling services.
- Reinforce information given by the patient's HCP regarding further testing, treatment, or referral to another HCP. Explain the possible causes and increased risks associated with premature labor and delivery. Reinforce education on signs and symptoms of labor, as appropriate. Inform the patient that hospitalization or more frequent prenatal checks may be ordered. Other therapies may also be administered, such as antibiotics, corticosteroids, and IV tocolytics. Instruct the patient in the importance of completing the entire course of antibiotic therapy, if ordered, even if no symptoms are present. Answer any questions or address any concerns voiced by the patient or family.
- Depending on the results of this procedure, additional testing may be performed to evaluate or monitor progression of the disease process and determine the need for a change in therapy. Evaluate test results in relation to the patient's symptoms and other tests performed.

RELATED MONOGRAPHS:
▶ Related tests include amniotic fluid analysis (nitrazine and fern test), biopsy chorionic villus, chromosome analysis, estradiol, α₁-fetoprotein, HCG, LS

ratio, progesterone, and US biophysical profile obstetric.
▶ Refer to the Reproductive System table at the back of the book for related tests by body system.

α₁-Fetoprotein

SYNONYM/ACRONYM: AFP.

COMMON USE: To assist in the evaluation of fetal health related to neural tube defects and some forms of liver cancer.

SPECIMEN: Serum (1 mL for tumor marker in men and nonpregnant women; 3 mL for maternal triple- or quad-marker testing), collected in a red- or tiger-top tube. For maternal triple- or quad-marker testing, include human chorionic gonadotropin and free estriol measurement.

NORMAL FINDINGS: (Method: Immunochemiluminometric assay)

α₁-Fetoprotein as a Tumor Marker: Males, Females, and Children

	Males (Conventional Units)	SI Units (Conventional Units × 1)	Females (Conventional Units)	SI Units (Conventional Units × 1)
Less than 1 mo	0.5–16,387 ng/mL	0.5–16,387 mcg/L	0.5–18,964 ng/mL	0.5–18,964 mcg/L
1–11 mo	0.5–28.3 ng/mL	0.5–28.3 mcg/L	0.5–77 ng/mL	0.5–77 mcg/L
1–3 yr	0.5–7.9 ng/mL	0.5–7.9 mcg/L	0.5–11.1 ng/mL	0.5–11.1 mcg/L
4 yr and older	Less than 6.1 ng/mL	Less than 6.1 mcg/L	Less than 6.1 ng/mL	Less than 6.1 mcg/L

Values may be higher for premature newborns.

	α₁-Fetoprotein (AFP) in Maternal Serum for Triple or Quad Marker			
	White AFP (Median)	Black AFP (Median)	Hispanic AFP (Median)	Asian AFP (Median)
Low risk	Less than 2 MoM	Less than 2 MoM	Less than 2 MoM	Less than 2 MoM

MoM = multiples of the median. Serum values vary with maternal race, weight, weeks of gestation, diabetic status, and number of fetuses, and variations exist between test methods. Serial testing should be determined using the same test method.

Gestational Age (wk)	HCG (Conventional Units)	SI Units (Conventional Units × 1)
2 wk	5–100 milli-international units/mL	5–100 international units/L
3 wk	200–3,000 milli-international units/mL	200–3,000 international units/L
4 wk	10,000–80,000 milli-international units/mL	10,000–80,000 international units/L
5–12 wk	90,000–500,000 milli-international units/mL	90,000–500,000 international units/L
13–24 wk	5,000–80,000 milli-international units/mL	5,000–80,000 international units/L
26–28 wk	3,000–15,000 milli-international units/mL	3,000–15,000 international units/L
	Pregnancy-associated plasma protein A (PAPP-A)	
8 wk	90–7,000 milli-international units/L	
9 wk	0–5,800 milli-international units/L	
10 wk	140–7,000 milli-international units/L	
11 wk	575–7,250 milli-international units/L	
12 wk	900–9,000 milli-international units/L	
13 wk	550–11,500 milli-international units/L	
14 wk	2,200–39,500 milli-international units/L	
	Unconjugated Estriol (E3) (Conventional Units)	**SI Units (Conventional Units × 3.467)**
30 wk	3.5–19 ng/mL	12.1–66.2 nmol/L
34 wk	5.3–18.3 ng/mL	18.4–63.5 nmol/L
35 wk	5.2–26.4 ng/mL	18–91.6 nmol/L
36 wk	8.2–28.1 ng/mL	28.4–97.5 nmol/L
37 wk	8–30.1 ng/mL	27.8–104.4 nmol/L
38 wk	8.6–38 ng/mL	29.8–131.9 nmol/L
39 wk	7.2–34.3 ng/mL	25–119 nmol/L
40 wk	9.6–28.9 ng/mL	33.3–100.3 nmol/L

Results vary widely among laboratories and methods.
HCG = human chorionic gonadotropin.

F

DESCRIPTION: Maternal blood screening for birth defects is optimally performed between 16 and 18 wk but may be done as early as 15 wk or as late as 22.9 wk. A number of serum and amniotic fluid markers can be used in collaboration to screen for Down syndrome, neural tube defects, and trisomy 18. These markers include α_1-fetoprotein (AFP), human chorionic gonadotropin (HCG), unconjugated estriol, dimeric inhibin-A (DIA), and pregnancy-associated plasma protein A (PAPP-A). Ultrasound (nuchal translucency [NT] ultrasound measurements of the fluid-filled space in the back of the fetus's neck, larger-than-normal NT measurements are found in Down syndrome), maternal age, race, weight, diabetic status, and number of fetuses are also factors used to calculate risk. The algorithm used to calculate risk depends on whether gestational age is based on ultrasound findings or date of last menstrual period. Diagnostic tests that include AFP, acetylcholinesterase, chromosome analysis, and fetal hemoglobin testing performed on amniotic fluid are discussed in the monographs titles "Amniotic Fluid Analysis" and "Biopsy, Chorionic Villus."

AFP is a glycoprotein produced in the fetal liver, gastrointestinal tract, and yolk sac. AFP is the major serum protein produced for 10 wk in early fetal life. (See "Amniotic Fluid Analysis" monograph for measurement of AFP levels in amniotic fluid.) After 10 wk of gestation, levels of fetal AFP can be detected in maternal blood, with peak levels occurring at 16 to 18 wk. Elevated maternal levels of AFP on two tests taken 1 wk apart suggest further investigation into fetal well-being by ultrasound or amniocentesis. HCG, a hormone secreted by the placenta, stimulates secretion of progesterone by the corpus luteum. (The use of HCG as a triple marker is also discussed in the monograph titled "Human Chorionic Gonadotropin.") During intrauterine development, the normal fetus and placenta produce estriol, a portion of which passes into maternal circulation. Decreased estriol levels are an independent indicator of neural tube defects. Dimeric inhibin-A (DIA) is the fourth biochemical marker used in prenatal quad screening. It is a glycoprotein secreted by the placenta. Maternal blood levels of DIA normally remain fairly stable during the 15th to 18th weeks of pregnancy. Blood levels are twice as high in the second trimester of pregnancies affected by Down syndrome. The incidence of Down syndrome is 1 in 750 live births. The triple screen detection rate for Down syndrome is 67%. The Down syndrome detection rate increases to 76% and maintains a false-positive rate of 5% when DIA is included. The incidence of neural tube defects is 1 in 1,300 pregnancies; anencephaly is almost always fatal at, or within a very short time after, birth. The incidence of trisomy 18 is 1 in 4,100 live births; most die within the first year after birth.

The presence of AFP in excessive amounts is abnormal in adults and children. AFP measurements are used as a tumor marker to assist in the diagnosis of cancer.

INDICATIONS

• Assist in the diagnosis of primary hepatocellular carcinoma or metastatic lesions involving the liver, as indicated by highly elevated levels (30% to 50% of Americans with liver cancer do not have elevated AFP levels)
• Investigate suspected hepatitis or cirrhosis, indicated by slightly to moderately elevated levels
• Monitor response to treatment for hepatic carcinoma, with successful treatment indicated by an immediate decrease in levels
• Monitor for recurrence of hepatic carcinoma, with elevated levels occurring 1 to 6 mo before the patient becomes symptomatic
• Investigate suspected intrauterine fetal death, as indicated by elevated levels
• Routine prenatal screening at 15 to 16 wk of pregnancy for fetal neural tube defects and other disorders, as indicated by elevated levels in maternal serum and amniotic fluid
• Support diagnosis of embryonal gonadal teratoblastoma, hepatoblastoma, and testicular or ovarian carcinomas

POTENTIAL DIAGNOSIS

Maternal serum AFP test results report actual values and multiples of the median (MoM) by gestational age (in weeks). MoM are calculated by dividing the patient's AFP by the midpoint (or median) of values expected for a large population of unaffected women at the same gestational age in weeks. MoM should be corrected for maternal weight. The MoM should also be corrected for maternal insulin requirement (achieved by dividing MoM by 1.1 for diabetic African American patients and by 0.8 for diabetic patients of other races) and multiple fetuses (multiply by 2.13 for twins). Some laboratories also provide additional statistical information regarding Down syndrome risk.

Increased in

• Pregnant women:
  Congenital nephrosis *(related to defective renal reabsorption)*
  Fetal abdominal wall defects *(related to release of AFP from open body wall defect)*
  Fetal distress
  Fetal neural tube defects (e.g., anencephaly, spina bifida, myelomeningocele) *(related to release of AFP from open body wall defect)*
  Low birth weight *(related to inaccurate estimation of gestational age)*
  Multiple pregnancy *(related to larger quantities from multiple fetuses)*
  Polycystic kidneys *(related to defective renal reabsorption)*
  Underestimation of gestational age *(related to the expectation of a lower value based on incorrect prediction of gestational age, i.e., AFP increases with age; therefore, if the age is believed to be less than it is actually, the expectation of the corresponding AFP value will be lower than it is actually, and the result appears to be elevated)*
• Men, nonpregnant women, and children (the cancer cells contain undifferentiated hepatocytes that produce glycoproteins of fetal origin):
  Cirrhosis
  Hepatic carcinoma
  Hepatitis
  Metastatic lesions involving the liver

Decreased in

• Pregnant women:
  Down syndrome (trisomy 21)
  Edwards' syndrome (trisomy 18)
  Fetal demise (undetected over a lengthy period of time) *(related to cessation of AFP production)*
  Hydatidiform moles *(partial mole may secrete some AFP)*
  Overestimation of gestational age *(related to the expectation of a higher value based on incorrect prediction of gestational age; i.e., AFP increases with age; therefore, if the age is believed to be greater than it actually is, the expectation*

of the corresponding AFP value will be
greater than it actually is, and the result
appears to be decreased)*
Pseudopregnancy *(there is no fetus to
produce AFP)*
Spontaneous abortion *(there is no fetus
to produce AFP)*

CRITICAL FINDINGS: N/A

INTERFERING FACTORS
- Drugs that may decrease AFP levels
  in pregnant women include acetaminophen, acetylsalicylic acid, and
  phenacetin.
- Multiple fetuses can cause increased
  levels.
- Gestational age must be between
  15 and 22 wk for initial and follow-
  up testing. The most common
  cause of an abnormal MoM is
  inaccurate estimation of gestational
  age (defined as weeks from the
  first day of the last menstrual
  period).
- Maternal AFP levels vary by race.

NURSING IMPLICATIONS AND PROCEDURE

PRETEST:
▶ Positively identify the patient using
  at least two unique identifiers before
  providing care, treatment, or
  services.
▶ *Patient Teaching:* Inform the patient this
  test can assist in evaluating fetal
  health.
▶ Obtain a history of the patient's complaints and known or suspected malignancy. Obtain a list of known allergens,
  especially allergies or sensitivities to
  latex.
▶ Obtain a history of the patient's immune
  and reproductive systems, gestational
  age, symptoms, and results of previously performed laboratory tests and
  diagnostic and surgical procedures.
▶ Note any recent procedures that can
  interfere with test results.
▶ Provide required information to laboratory for triple-marker testing, including

maternal birth date, weight, age, race,
calculated gestational age, gestational
age by ultrasound, gestational date by
physical examination, first day of last
menstrual period, estimated date of
delivery, and whether the patient has
insulin-dependent (type 1) diabetes.
▶ Obtain a list of the patient's current
  medications, including herbs, nutritional supplements, and nutraceuticals
  (see Appendix F).
▶ Review the procedure with the patient.
  Inform the patient that specimen collection takes approximately 5 to 10
  min. Address concerns about pain and
  explain that there may be some discomfort during the venipuncture.
▶ There are no food, fluid, or medication
  restrictions unless by medical direction.
▶ *Make sure a written and informed
  consent has been signed prior to the
  procedure and before administering
  any medications.*

INTRATEST:
▶ If the patient has a history of allergic
  reaction to latex, avoid the use of
  equipment containing latex.
▶ Instruct the patient to cooperate fully
  and to follow directions. Direct the
  patient to breathe normally and to
  avoid unnecessary movement.
▶ Observe standard precautions, and follow the general guidelines in Appendix A.
  Positively identify the patient, and label
  the appropriate specimen container with
  the corresponding patient demographics,
  initials of the person collecting the specimen, date, and time of collection.
  Perform a venipuncture.
▶ The sample may be collected directly
  from the cord using a syringe and
  transferred to a red-top tube.
▶ Remove the needle and apply direct
  pressure with dry gauze to stop bleeding. Observe/assess venipuncture site
  for bleeding or hematoma formation and
  secure gauze with adhesive bandage.
▶ Promptly transport the specimen to the
  laboratory for processing and analysis.

POST-TEST:
▶ A report of the results will be made
  available to the requesting health-care
  provider (HCP), who will discuss the
  results with the patient.

Nutritional Considerations: Hyperhomocysteinemia resulting from folate deficiency in pregnant women is believed to increase the risk of neural tube defects. Elevated levels of homocysteine are thought to chemically damage the exposed neural tissue of the developing fetus. As appropriate, instruct pregnant patients to eat foods rich in folate, such as liver, salmon, eggs, asparagus, green leafy vegetables, broccoli, sweet potatoes, beans, and whole wheat.

Social and Cultural Considerations: In pregnant patients, recognize anxiety related to test results, and encourage the family to seek counseling if concerned with pregnancy termination or to seek genetic counseling if a chromosomal abnormality is determined. Discuss the implications of abnormal test results on the patient's lifestyle. Provide teaching and information regarding the clinical implications of the test results, as appropriate. Decisions regarding elective abortion should take place in the presence of both parents. Provide a nonjudgmental, nonthreatening atmosphere for discussing the risks and difficulties of delivering and raising a developmentally challenged infant, as well as exploring other options (termination of pregnancy or adoption). It is also important to discuss feelings the mother and father may experience (e.g., guilt, depression, anger) if fetal abnormalities are detected. Educate the patient regarding access to counseling services.

In patients with carcinoma, recognize anxiety related to test results, and offer support. Discuss the implications of abnormal test results on the patient's lifestyle. Provide teaching and information regarding the clinical implications of the test results, as appropriate. Educate the patient regarding access to counseling services, as appropriate.

Reinforce information given by the patient's HCP regarding further testing, treatment, or referral to another HCP. Answer any questions or address any concerns voiced by the patient or family.

Depending on the results of this procedure, additional testing may be performed to evaluate or monitor progression of the disease process and determine the need for a change in therapy. Inform the pregnant patient that an ultrasound may be performed and AFP levels in amniotic fluid may be analyzed if maternal blood levels are elevated in two samples obtained 1 wk apart. Evaluate test results in relation to the patient's symptoms and other tests performed.

RELATED MONOGRAPHS:

Related tests include amniotic fluid analysis, biopsy chorionic villus, cancer antigens, estradiol, fetal fibronectin, folic acid, hexosaminidase, homocysteine, HCG, L/S ratio, and US biophysical profile obstetric.

Refer to the Immune and Reproductive systems tables at the end of the book for related tests by body system.

Fetoscopy

SYNONYM/ACRONYM: Endoscopic fetal surgery, fetal endoscopy.

COMMON USE: To facilitate diagnosis and treatment of the fetus. Evaluate for disorders such as neural tube defects and congenital blood disorders, and assist with fetal karyotyping.

AREA OF APPLICATION: Fetus, uterus.

CONTRAST: N/A.

DESCRIPTION: Fetoscopy is usually performed around the 18th week of pregnancy or later when the fetus is developed sufficiently for diagnosis of potential problems. It is done to evaluate or treat the fetus during pregnancy. Fetoscopy can be accomplished externally using a stethoscope with an attached headpiece, which is placed on the mother's abdomen to assess the fetal heart tones. Endoscopic fetoscopy is accomplished using an instrument called a fetoscope, a thin, 1-mm flexible scope, which is placed with the aid of sonography. The fetoscope is inserted into the uterus through a thin incision in the abdominal wall (transabdominally) or through the cervix (transcervically) in earlier stages of pregnancy. Fetal tissue and blood samples can be obtained through the fetoscope. In addition, fetal surgery can be performed for such procedures as the repair of a fetal congenital diaphragmatic hernia, enlarged bladder, and spina bifida.

INDICATIONS
• Pregnancy

POTENTIAL DIAGNOSIS

Normal findings in
• Absence of birth defects

Abnormal findings in
• Acardiac twin
• Congenital diaphragmatic hernia (CDH)
• Hemophilia
• Neural tube defects
• Spinal bifida

CRITICAL FINDINGS: N/A

INTERFERING FACTORS

Factors that may impair clear imaging
• Activity of fetus.
• Amniotic fluid that is extremely cloudy.
• Inability of patient to remain still during the procedure.
• Obesity or very overweight patient.

NURSING IMPLICATIONS AND PROCEDURE

PRETEST:

Positively identify the patient using at least two unique identifiers before providing care, treatment, or services.
Patient Teaching: Inform the patient this procedure can assist in locating and treating fetal abnormalities.
Obtain a history of the patient's complaints, including a list of known allergens, especially allergies or sensitivities to latex and anesthetics.
Obtain a history of the patient's reproductive system, symptoms, and results of previously performed laboratory tests and diagnostic and surgical procedures.
Note any recent procedures that can interfere with test results (i.e., barium procedures, surgery, or biopsy).
Record the date of last menstrual period and determine the age of the fetus.
Obtain a list of the patient's current medications, including herbs, nutritional supplements, and nutraceuticals (see Appendix F).
Instruct the patient to remove jewelry and other metallic objects in the area to be examined.
Review the procedure with the patient. Address concerns about pain and explain that a local anesthetic will be applied to the abdomen to ease with insertion of the fetoscope. Inform the patient that the procedure is performed in an ultrasound department, by a health-care provider (HCP) specializing

in this procedure, with support staff, and takes approximately 60 min.

▶ *Sensitivity to social and cultural issues,* as well as concern for modesty, is important in providing psychological support before, during, and after the procedure.

▶ Food and fluid should be withheld for 8 hr prior to the procedure. There are no medication restrictions unless by medical direction.

▶ *Make sure a written and informed consent has been signed prior to the procedure and before administering any medications.*

INTRATEST:

▶ Ensure that the patient has complied with dietary restrictions; ensure that food and fluid has been restricted for at least 8 hr prior to the procedure.

▶ Ensure that the patient has removed external metallic objects prior to the procedure.

▶ Instruct the patient to void prior to the procedure and to change into the gown, robe, and foot coverings provided.

▶ Instruct the patient to cooperate fully and to follow directions. Instruct the patient to remain still throughout the procedure because movement produces unreliable results.

▶ Instruct the patient to lie on her back. The lower abdomen area is cleaned, and a local anesthetic is administered in the area where the incision will be made.

▶ Observe standard precautions, and follow the general guidelines in Appendix A. Positively identify the patient, and label the appropriate specimen container with the corresponding patient demographics, initials of the person collecting the specimen, date, and time of collection if samples are to be obtained on aspirated amniotic fluid or fetal material.

▶ Conductive gel is applied to the skin, and a Doppler transducer is moved over the skin to locate the position of the fetus.

▶ Ask the patient to breathe normally during the examination. If necessary for better fetal visualization, ask the patient to inhale deeply and hold her breath.

POST-TEST:

▶ A report of the results will be made available to the requesting HCP, who will discuss the results with the patient.

▶ When the study is completed, remove the gel from the skin.

▶ Observe/assess the incision for redness or leakage of fluid or blood.

▶ Instruct the patient in the care of the incision and to contact her HCP immediately if she is experiencing chills, fever, dizziness, moderate or severe abdominal cramping, or fluid or blood loss from the vagina or incision.

▶ Inform the patient that a follow-up ultrasound will be completed the next day to assess the fetus and placenta.

▶ Recognize anxiety related to test results. Discuss the implications of abnormal test results on the patient's lifestyle. Provide teaching and information regarding the clinical implications of the test results, as appropriate.

▶ Reinforce information given by the patient's HCP regarding further testing, treatment, or referral to another HCP. Answer any questions or address any concerns voiced by the patient or family.

▶ Depending on the results of this procedure, additional testing may be needed to evaluate or monitor progression of the disease process and determine the need for a change in therapy. Evaluate test results in relation to the patient's symptoms and other tests performed.

RELATED MONOGRAPHS:

▶ Related tests include amniotic fluid analysis, biopsy chorionic villus, blood groups and antibodies, chromosome analysis, culture bacterial anal/genital, culture viral, fetal fibronectin, α_1-fetoprotein, hexosaminidase A and B, human chorionic gonadotropin, KUB, Kleihauer-Betke test, lecithin/sphingomyelin ratio, prolactin, MRI abdomen, and ultrasound biophysical profile obstetric.

▶ Refer to the Reproductive System table at the end of the book for related tests by body system.

F

Fibrinogen

SYNONYM/ACRONYM: Factor I.

COMMON USE: Commonly used to evaluate fibrinolytic activity as well as identify congenital deficiency, disseminated intravascular coagulation (DIC), and severe liver disease.

SPECIMEN: Plasma (1 mL) collected in a completely filled blue-top (3.2% sodium citrate) tube. If the patient's hematocrit exceeds 55%, the volume of citrate in the collection tube must be adjusted.

NORMAL FINDINGS: (Method: Photo-optical clot detection)

Age	Conventional Units	SI Units (Conventional Units × 0.0294)
Newborn	200–500 mg/dL	5.9–14.7 micromol/L
Adult	200–400 mg/dL	5.9–11.8 micromol/L

Values are higher in older adults.

DESCRIPTION: Fibrinogen (factor I) is synthesized in the liver. In the common final pathway of the coagulation sequence, thrombin converts fibrinogen to fibrin, which then clots blood as it combines with platelets. In healthy individuals, the serum should contain no residual fibrinogen after clotting has occurred.

INDICATIONS
• Assist in the diagnosis of suspected disseminated intravascular coagulation (DIC), as indicated by decreased fibrinogen levels
• Evaluate congenital or acquired dysfibrinogenemias
• Monitor hemostasis in disorders associated with low fibrinogen levels or elevated levels that can predispose patients to excessive thrombosis

POTENTIAL DIAGNOSIS

Increased in
Fibrinogen is an acute-phase reactant protein and will be increased in inflammatory conditions.

• Acute myocardial infarction
• Cancer
• Eclampsia
• Hodgkin's disease
• Inflammation
• Multiple myeloma
• Nephrotic syndrome
• Pregnancy
• Tissue necrosis

Decreased in
• Congenital fibrinogen deficiency (rare) *(related to deficient synthesis)*
• DIC *(related to rapid consumption as fibrinogen is converted to fibrin)*
• Dysfibrinogenemia *(related to an inherited abnormality in fibrinogen synthesis)*

- Liver disease (severe) *(related to decreased synthesis)*
- Primary fibrinolysis *(related to rapid conversion during fibrinolysis; plasmin breaks down fibrinogen and fibrin)*

CRITICAL FINDINGS

- Less than 80 mg/dL (SI: Less than 2.4 micromol/L)

Note and immediately report to the health-care provider (HCP) any critically decreased values and related symptoms. Signs and symptoms of microvascular thrombosis include cyanosis, ischemic tissue necrosis, hemorrhagic necrosis, tachypnea, dyspnea, pulmonary emboli, venous distention, abdominal pain, and oliguria. Possible interventions include identification and treatment of the underlying cause, support through administration of required blood products (platelets, cryoprecipitate, or fresh frozen plasma), and administration of heparin. Timely notification of critical values for lab or diagnostic studies is a role expectation of the professional nurse. Notification processes will vary among facilities. Upon receipt of the critical value the information should be read back to the caller to verify accuracy. Most policies require immediate notification of the primary HCP, hospitalist, or on-call HCP. Reported information includes the patient's name, unique identifiers, critical value, name of the person giving the report, and name of the person receiving the report. Documentation of notification should be made in the medical record with the name of the HCP notified, time and date of notification, and any orders received. Any delay in a timely report of a critical value may require completion of a notification form with review by Risk Management.

INTERFERING FACTORS

- Drugs that may increase fibrinogen levels include acetylsalicylic acid, norethandrolone, oral contraceptives, oxandrolone, and oxymetholone.
- Drugs that may decrease fibrinogen levels include anabolic steroids, asparaginase, bezafibrate, danazol, dextran, fenofibrate, fish oils, gemfibrozil, lovastatin, pentoxifylline, phosphorus, and ticlopidine.
- Transfusions of whole blood, plasma, or fractions within 4 wk of the test invalidate results.
- Placement of tourniquet for longer than 60 sec can result in venous stasis and changes in the concentration of plasma proteins to be measured. Platelet activation may also occur under these conditions, causing erroneous results.
- Vascular injury during phlebotomy can activate platelets and coagulation factors, causing erroneous results.
- Hemolyzed specimens must be rejected because hemolysis is an indication of platelet and coagulation factor activation.
- Hematocrit greater than 55% may cause falsely prolonged results because of anticoagulant excess relative to plasma volume.
- Incompletely filled collection tubes, specimens contaminated with heparin, clotted specimens, or unprocessed specimens not delivered to the laboratory within 1 to 2 hr of collection should be rejected.
- Icteric or lipemic specimens interfere with optical testing methods, producing erroneous results.
- Traumatic venipuncture and excessive agitation of the sample can alter test results.

NURSING IMPLICATIONS AND PROCEDURE

PRETEST:

▶ Positively identify the patient using at least two unique identifiers before providing care, treatment, or services.

▶ *Patient Teaching:* Inform the patient that this lab test can assist in diagnosing diseases associated with clotting disorders.

▶ Obtain a history of the patient's complaints, including a list of known allergens, especially allergies or sensitivities to latex.

▶ Obtain a history of the patient's hematopoietic and hepatobiliary systems, symptoms, and results of previously performed laboratory tests and diagnostic and surgical procedures.

▶ Note any recent procedures that can interfere with test results.

▶ Obtain a list of the patient's current medications, including herbs, nutritional supplements, and nutraceuticals (see Appendix F).

▶ Review the procedure with the patient. Inform the patient that specimen collection takes approximately 5 to 10 min. Address concerns about pain and explain that there may be some discomfort during the venipuncture.

▶ *Sensitivity to social and cultural issues,* as well as concern or modesty, is important in providing psychological support before, during, and after the procedure.

▶ There are no food, fluid, or medication restrictions unless by medical direction.

INTRATEST:

▶ If the patient has a history of allergic reaction to latex, avoid the use of equipment containing latex.

▶ Instruct the patient to cooperate fully and to follow directions. Direct the patient to breathe normally and to avoid unnecessary movement.

▶ Observe standard precautions, and follow the general guidelines in Appendix A. Positively identify the patient, and label the appropriate specimen container with the corresponding patient demographics, initials of the person collecting the specimen, date, and time of collection. Perform a venipuncture. Fill tube completely. *Important note:* Two different concentrations of sodium citrate preservative are currently added to blue-top tubes for coagulation studies: 3.2% and 3.8%. The Clinical and Laboratory Standards Institute (CLSI; formerly the National Committee for Clinical Laboratory Standards [NCCLS]) guideline for sodium citrate is 3.2%. Laboratories establish reference ranges for coagulation testing based on numerous factors, including sodium citrate concentration, test equipment, and test reagents. It is important to ask the laboratory which concentration it recommends, because each concentration will have its own specific reference range. When multiple specimens are drawn, the blue-top tube should be collected after sterile (i.e., blood culture) tubes. Otherwise, when using a standard vacutainer system, the blue-top tube is the first tube collected. When a butterfly is used, due to the added tubing, an extra red-top tube should be collected before the blue-top tube to ensure complete filling of the blue top tube.

▶ Remove the needle and apply direct pressure with dry gauze to stop bleeding. Observe/assess venipuncture site for bleeding or hematoma formation and secure gauze with adhesive bandage.

▶ Promptly transport the specimen to the laboratory for processing and analysis. The CLSI recommendation for processed and unprocessed samples stored in unopened tubes is that testing should be completed within 1 to 4 hr of collection. If the patient has a known hematocrit above 55%, adjust the amount of anticoagulant in the collection tube before drawing the blood according to the CLSI guidelines:

Anticoagulant vol. [x] =
(100 − hematocrit)/(595 − hematocrit)
× total vol. of anticoagulated blood
required

Example:

Patient hematocrit = 60% = (100 − 60)/ (595 − 60) × 5.0 = 0.37 mL sodium citrate for a 5-mL standard drawing tube

POST-TEST:

▶ A report of the results will be made available to the requesting HCP, who will discuss the results with the patient.

▶ Instruct the patient to report bruising, petechiae, and bleeding from mucous membranes, hematuria, and occult blood.

▶ Inform the patient with a decreased fibrinogen level of the importance of taking precautions against bruising and bleeding, including the use of a soft bristle toothbrush, use of an electric razor, avoidance of constipation, avoidance of acetylsalicylic acid and similar products, and avoidance of intramuscular injections.

▶ Reinforce information given by the patient's HCP regarding further testing, treatment, or referral to another HCP. Answer any questions or address any concerns voiced by the patient or family.

▶ Depending on the results of this procedure, additional testing may be performed to evaluate or monitor progression of the disease process and determine the need for a change in therapy. Evaluate test results in relation to the patient's symptoms and other tests performed.

RELATED MONOGRAPHS:

▶ Related tests include ALT, albumin, ALP, AT-III, AST, bilirubin, biopsy bone, biopsy bone marrow, biopsy liver, clot retraction, coagulation factors, CBC platelet count, CT cardiac scoring, CK and isoenzymes, CRP, D-dimer, echocardiography, echocardiography transesophageal, ECG, ESR, exercise stress test, FDP, GGT, Holter monitor, IFE, immunoglobulins, myocardial perfusion heart scan, aPTT, plasminogen, procalcitonin, protein S, and PT/INR.

▶ Refer to the Hematopoietic and Hepatobiliary systems tables at the end of the book for related tests by body system.

Fibrinogen Degradation Products

SYNONYM/ACRONYM: Fibrin split products, fibrin breakdown products, FDP, FSP, FBP.

COMMON USE: To evaluate conditions associated with abnormal fibrinolytic and fibrinogenolytic activity such as disseminated intravascular coagulation (DIC), deep vein thrombophlebitis (DVT), and pulmonary embolism (PE).

SPECIMEN: Plasma (1 mL) collected in a completely filled blue-top (3.2% sodium citrate) tube. If the patient's hematocrit exceeds 55%, the volume of citrate in the collection tube must be adjusted.

NORMAL FINDINGS: (Method: Latex agglutin: on)

Conventional Units	SI Units (Conventional Units × 1)
Less than 5 mcg/mL	Less than 5 mg/dL

DESCRIPTION: This coagulation test evaluates fibrin split products or fibrin/fibrinogen degradation products (FDPs) that interfere with normal coagulation and formation of the hemostatic platelet plug. After a fibrin clot has formed, the fibrinolytic system prevents excessive clotting. In the fibrinolytic system, plasmin digests fibrin. Fibrinogen also can be degraded if there is a disproportion among plasmin, fibrin, and fibrinogen. Seven substances labeled *A, B, C, D, E, X,* and *Y* result from this degradation, which can indicate abnormal coagulation. Under normal conditions, the liver and reticuloendothelial system remove fibrin split products from the circulation.

INDICATIONS

- Assist in the diagnosis of suspected DIC
- Evaluate response to therapy with fibrinolytic drugs
- Monitor the effects on hemostasis of trauma, extensive surgery, obstetric complications, and disorders such as liver or renal disease

POTENTIAL DIAGNOSIS

Increased in
- DIC *(FDP can be positive in a number of conditions in which the coagulation system has been excessively stimulated as a result of tissue injury and fibrin and/or fibrinogen is being degraded by plasmin)*
- Excessive bleeding *(clot formation related to depletion of platelets and clotting factors will stimulate fibrinolysis and increase circulation of fibrin breakdown products)*
- Liver disease *(related to decreased hepatic clearance)*

- Myocardial infarction *(FDP can be positive in a number of conditions in which the coagulation system has been excessively stimulated as a result of tissue injury and fibrin and/or fibrinogen is being degraded by plasmin)*
- Obstetric complications, such as pre-eclampsia, abruptio placentae, intrauterine fetal death *(excessive stimulation of the coagulation system; microthrombi are formed and plasminogen is released to dissolve the fibrin clots)*
- Post–cardiothoracic surgery period *(FDP can be positive in a number of conditions in which the coagulation system has been excessively stimulated as a result of tissue injury and fibrin and/or fibrinogen is being degraded by plasmin)*
- Pulmonary embolism *(FDP can be positive in a number of conditions in which the coagulation system has been excessively stimulated as a result of tissue injury and fibrin and/or fibrinogen is being degraded by plasmin)*
- Renal disease *(FDP can be positive in a number of conditions in which the coagulation system has been excessively stimulated as a result of tissue injury and fibrin and/or fibrinogen is being degraded by plasmin)*
- Renal transplant rejection

Decreased in: N/A

CRITICAL FINDINGS: N/A

INTERFERING FACTORS

- Traumatic venipunctures and excessive agitation of the sample can alter test results.
- Drugs that may increase fibrin degradation product levels include heparin and fibrinolytic drugs such as streptokinase and urokinase.
- The presence of rheumatoid factor may falsely elevate results with some test kits.

- The test should not be ordered on patients receiving heparin therapy.
- Hematocrit greater than 55% may cause falsely prolonged results because of anticoagulant excess relative to plasma volume.
- Incompletely filled collection tubes, specimens contaminated with heparin, clotted specimens, or unprocessed specimens not delivered to the laboratory within 1 to 2 hr of collection should be rejected.

NURSING IMPLICATIONS AND PROCEDURE

PRETEST:

- Positively identify the patient using at least two unique identifiers before providing care, treatment, or services.
- *Patient Teaching:* Inform the patient this test can assist in diagnosing diseases associated with clotting disorders.
- Obtain a history of the patient's complaints, including a list of known allergens, especially allergies or sensitivities to latex.
- Obtain a history of the patient's hematopoietic system, any bleeding disorders, symptoms, and results of previously performed laboratory tests and diagnostic and surgical procedures. Note any recent procedures that can interfere with test results.
- Obtain a list of the patient's current medications, including anticoagulants, aspirin and other salicylates, herbs, nutritional supplements, and nutraceuticals (see Appendix F). Note the last time and dose of medication taken.
- Review the procedure with the patient. Inform the patient that specimen collection takes approximately 5 to 10 min. Address concerns about pain and explain that there may be some discomfort during the venipuncture. *Sensitivity to social and cultural issues,* as well as concern for modesty, is important in providing psychological support before, during, and after the procedure.
- There are no food, fluid, or medication restrictions unless by medical direction.

INTRATEST:

- If the patient has a history of allergic reaction to latex, avoid the use of equipment containing latex.
- Instruct the patient to cooperate fully and to follow directions. Direct the patient to breathe normally and to avoid unnecessary movement.
- Observe standard precautions, and follow the general guidelines in Appendix A. Positively identify the patient, and label the appropriate specimen container with the corresponding patient demographics, initials of the person collecting the specimen, date, and time of collection. Perform a venipuncture. Fill tube completely. *Important note:* Two different concentrations of sodium citrate preservative are currently added to blue-top tubes for coagulation studies: 3.2% and 3.8%. The Clinical and Laboratory Standards Institute (CLSI; formerly the National Committee for Clinical Laboratory Standards [NCCLS]) guideline for sodium citrate is 3.2%. Laboratories establish reference ranges for coagulation testing based on numerous factors, including sodium citrate concentration, test equipment, and test reagents. It is important to ask the laboratory which concentration it recommends, because each concentration will have its own specific reference range. When multiple specimens are drawn, the blue-top tube should be collected after sterile (i.e., blood culture) tubes. Otherwise, when using a standard vacutainer system, the blue-top tube is the first tube collected. When a butterfly is used, due to the added tubing, an extra red-top tube should be collected before the blue-top tube to ensure complete filling of the blue top tube.
- Remove the needle and apply direct pressure with dry gauze to stop bleeding. Observe/assess venipuncture site for bleeding or hematoma formation and secure gauze with adhesive bandage.
- Promptly transport the specimen to the laboratory for processing and analysis. The CLSI recommendation for processed and unprocessed samples stored in unopened tubes is that testing should be completed within 1 to 4 hr of collection. If the patient has a known hematocrit above

55%, adjust the amount of anticoagulant in the collection tube before drawing the blood according to the CLSI guidelines:

Anticoagulant vol. [x] = (100 − hematocrit)/(595 − hematocrit) × total vol. of anticoagulated blood required

Example:

Patient hematocrit = 60% = (100 − 60)/(595 − 60) × 5.0 = 0.37 mL sodium citrate for a 5-mL standard drawing tube

POST-TEST:

A report of the results will be made available to the requesting HCP, who will discuss the results with the patient.

Instruct the patient to report bleeding from skin or mucous membranes, ecchymosis, petechiae, hematuria, and occult blood.

Inform the patient with increased levels of fibrin degradation products of the importance of taking precautions against bruising and bleeding, including the use of a soft bristle toothbrush, use of an electric razor, avoidance of constipation, avoidance of acetylsalicylic acid and similar products, and avoidance of intramuscular injections.

Reinforce information given by the patient's HCP regarding further testing, treatment, or referral to another HCP. Answer any questions or address any concerns voiced by the patient or family.

Depending on the results of this procedure, additional testing may be performed to evaluate or monitor progression of the disease process and determine the need for a change in therapy. Evaluate test results in relation to the patient's symptoms and other tests performed.

RELATED MONOGRAPHS:

Related tests include aPTT, ALT, alveolar/arterial gradient, angiography pulmonary, AT-III, AST, bilirubin, biopsy liver, blood pool imaging, BUN, coagulation factors, CT cardiac scoring, creatinine, CBC, CK and isoenzymes, CRP, D-dimer, exercise stress test, FDP, fibrinogen, GGT, lung perfusion scan, lung ventilation scan, myoglobin, plasminogen, platelet count, PET heart, procalcitonin, protein S, PT/INR, troponin, US venous Doppler extremity studies, and venography lower extremity studies.

Refer to the Hematopoietic System table at the end of the book for related tests by body system.

Fluorescein Angiography

SYNONYM/ACRONYM: FA.

COMMON USE: To assist in detecting vascular changes in the eyes affecting vision related to diseases such as diabetic retinopathy and macular degeneration.

AREA OF APPLICATION: Eyes.

CONTRAST: Fluorescein dye.

DESCRIPTION: Fluorescein angiography (FA) involves the color radiographic examination of the retinal vasculature following rapid IV injection of a sodium fluorescein contrast medium. A special camera allows images to be taken in sequence and manipulated by a computer to provide views of the retinal vessels during filling and emptying of the dye. The camera allows only light waves in the blue range to strike the fundus of the eye. When the fluorescein reaches the blood vessels in the eye, blue light excites the dye molecules to a higher state of activity and causes them to emit a greenish-yellow fluorescence that is recorded.

INDICATIONS
• Detect arterial or venous occlusion evidenced by the reduced, delayed, or absent flow of the contrast medium through the vessels or possible vessel leakage of the medium
• Detect possible vascular disorders affecting visual acuity
• Detect presence of microaneurysms caused by hypertensive retinopathy
• Detect the presence of tumors, retinal edema, or inflammation, as evidenced by abnormal patterns or degree of fluorescence
• Diagnose diabetic retinopathy
• Diagnose past reduced flow or patency of the vascular circulation of the retina, as evidenced by neovascularization
• Diagnose presence of macular degeneration and any other degeneration and any associated hemorrhaging
• Observe ocular effects resulting from the long-term use of high-risk medications

POTENTIAL DIAGNOSIS
Normal findings in
• No leakage of dye from retinal blood vessels
• Normal retina and retinal and choroidal vessels

• No evidence of vascular abnormalities, such as hemorrhage, retinopathy, aneurysms, or obstructions caused by stenosis and resulting in collateral circulation

Abnormal findings in
• Aneurysm
• Arteriovenous shunts
• Diabetic retinopathy
• Macular degeneration
• Neovascularization
• Obstructive disorders of the arteries or veins that lead to collateral circulation

CRITICAL FINDINGS: N/A

INTERFERING FACTORS
This procedure is contraindicated for
• Patients with a past history of hypersensitivity to radiographic dyes.
• Patients with narrow-angle glaucoma if pupil dilation is performed; dilation can initiate a severe and sight-threatening open-angle attack.
• Patients with allergies to mydriatics if pupil dilation using mydriatics is performed.

Factors that may impair the results of the examination
• Inability of the patient to cooperate or remain still during the test because of age, significant pain, or mental status may interfere with the test results.
• Presence of cataracts may interfere with fundal view.
• Ineffective dilation of the pupils may impair clear imaging.
• Allergic reaction to radiographic dye, including nausea and vomiting, may interrupt the procedure.
• Failure to follow medication restrictions before the procedure may cause the procedure to be canceled or repeated.

NURSING IMPLICATIONS AND PROCEDURE

PRETEST:

▶ Positively identify the patient using at least two unique identifiers before providing care, treatment, or services.

▶ *Patient Teaching:* Inform the patient this procedure can assist in detecting changes in the eye that affect vision.

▶ Obtain a history of the patient's complaints, including a list of known allergens, especially allergies or sensitivities to radiographic dyes, shellfish, and bee venom.

▶ Obtain a history of the patient's known or suspected vision loss; changes in visual acuity, including type and cause; use of glasses or contact lenses; and eye conditions with treatment regimens.

▶ Obtain a history of the patient's symptoms and results of previously performed laboratory tests and diagnostic and surgical procedures.

▶ Obtain a list of the patient's current medications, including herbs, nutritional supplements, and nutraceuticals (see Appendix F).

▶ Instruct the patient to remove contact lenses or glasses, as appropriate. Instruct the patient regarding the importance of keeping the eyes open for the test.

▶ Review the procedure with the patient. Explain that the patient will be requested to fixate the eyes during the procedure. Address concerns about pain and explain that mydriatics, if used, may cause blurred vision and sensitivity to light. There may also be a brief stinging sensation when the drop is put in the eye. Explain to the patient that some discomfort may be experienced during the insertion of the IV. Inform the patient that when fluorescein dye is injected, it may cause facial flushing or nausea and vomiting. Inform the patient that a health-care provider (HCP) performs the test, in a quiet, darkened room, and that to dilate and evaluate both eyes, the test can take up 60 min.

▶ *Sensitivity to social and cultural issues,* as well as concern for modesty, is important in providing psychological support before, during, and after the procedure.

▶ Explain that an IV line will be inserted to allow intermittent infusion of dye.

▶ There are no food or fluid restrictions unless by medical direction.

▶ The patient should avoid eye medications (particularly miotic eye drops which may constrict the pupil preventing a clear view of the fundus and mydriatic eyedrops in order to avoid instigation of an acute open angle attack in patients with narrow angle glaucoma) for at least 1 day prior to the test.

▶ Ensure that the patient understands that he or she must refrain from driving until the pupils return to normal (about 4 hr) after the test and has made arrangements to have someone else be responsible for transportation after the test.

▶ *Make sure a written and informed consent has been signed prior to the procedure and before administering any medications.*

INTRATEST:

▶ Observe standard precautions, and follow the general guidelines in Appendix A. Positively identify the patient.

▶ Ensure that the patient has complied with medication restrictions; ensure that eye medications, especially miotics and mydriatics, have been withheld for at least 1 day prior to the test.

▶ Have emergency equipment readily available.

▶ Instruct the patient to cooperate fully and to follow directions. Instruct the patient to remain still during the procedure because movement produces unreliable results.

▶ Seat the patient in a chair that faces the camera. Instruct the patient to look at a directed target while the eyes are examined.

▶ If dilation is to be performed, administer the ordered mydriatic to each eye and repeat in 5 to 15 min. Drops are placed in the eye with the patient looking up and the solution directed at the six o'clock position of the sclera (white of the eye) near the limbus (gray, semitransparent area of the eyeball where the cornea and sclera meet). Neither dropper nor bottle should touch the eyelashes.

- Insert an intermittent infusion device, as ordered, for subsequent injection of the contrast media or emergency medications.
- After the eyedrops are administered but before the dye is injected, color fundus photographs are taken.
- Instruct the patient to place the chin in the chin rest and gently press the forehead against the support bar. Instruct the patient to open his or her eyes wide and look at the desired target.
- Fluorescein dye is injected into the brachial vein using the intermittent infusion device, and a rapid sequence of photographs are taken and repeated after the dye has reached the retinal vascular system. Follow-up photographs are taken in 20 to 30 min.
- At the conclusion of the procedure, remove the IV needle and apply direct pressure with dry gauze to stop bleeding. Observe venipuncture site for bleeding or hematoma formation and secure gauze with adhesive bandage.
- Observe for hypersensitive reaction to the dye. The patient may become nauseous and vomit.

▶ **POST-TEST:**

- A report of the results will be made available to the requesting HCP, who will discuss the results with the patient.
- Instruct the patient to resume usual medications, as directed by the HCP.
- *Nutritional Considerations:* Increased glucose levels may be associated with diabetes. There is no "diabetic diet"; however, many meal-planning approaches with nutritional goals are endorsed by the American Dietetic Association. Patients who adhere to dietary recommendations report a better general feeling of health, better weight management, greater control of glucose and lipid values, and improved use of insulin. Instruct the patient, as appropriate, in nutritional management of diabetes. The American Heart Association's Therapeutic Lifestyle Changes (TLC) diet provides goals directed at people with specific risk factors and/or existing medical conditions (e.g., elevated LDL cholesterol levels, other lipid disorders, coronary artery disease, insulin-dependent diabetes, insulin resistance, or metabolic syndrome). The TLC approach also includes the use of plant stanols or sterols and increased dissolved fiber as an option for lowering LDL cholesterol levels; nutritional recommendations for daily total caloric intake; recommendations for allowable percentage of calories derived from fat (saturated and unsaturated), carbohydrates, protein, and cholesterol; as well as recommendations for daily expenditure of energy. The nutritional needs of each diabetic patient need to be determined individually (especially during pregnancy) with the appropriate HCPs, particularly professionals trained in nutrition.

- Recognize anxiety related to test results, and be supportive of impaired activity related to vision loss or anticipated loss of driving privileges. Discuss the implications of abnormal test results on the patient's lifestyle. Provide teaching and information regarding the clinical implications of the test results, as appropriate. Emphasize, as appropriate, that good glycemic control delays the onset of and slows the progression of diabetic retinopathy, nephropathy, and neuropathy. Provide education regarding smoking cessation, as appropriate. Provide contact information regarding vision aids, if desired, for ABLEDATA (sponsored by the National Institute on Disability and Rehabilitation Research [NIDRR], available at www.abledata. com). Information can also be obtained from the American Macular Degeneration Foundation (www.macular .org), the Glaucoma Research Foundation (www.glaucoma.org), the American Diabetes Association (www .diabetes.org), or the American Heart Association (www.americanheart.org).

- Reinforce information given by the patient's HCP regarding further testing, treatment, or referral to another HCP. Inform the patient that visual acuity and responses to light may change. Suggest that the patient wear dark glasses after the test until the pupils return to normal size. Inform the patient that yellow discoloration of the skin and urine from the radiographic dye is normally present for up to 2 days. Answer any questions or address any concerns voiced by the patient or family.

▶ Depending on the results of this procedure, additional testing may be performed to evaluate or monitor progression of the disease process and determine the need for a change in therapy. Evaluate test results in relation to the patient's symptoms and other tests performed.

RELATED MONOGRAPHS:

▶ Related tests include fructosamine, fundus photography, glucagon, glucose, glycated hemoglobin, gonioscopy, insulin, intraocular pressure, microalbumin, plethysmography, refraction, slit-lamp biomicroscopy, and visual field testing.

▶ Refer to the Ocular System table at the end of the book for related tests by body system.

F Folate

SYNONYM/ACRONYM: Folic acid, vitamin B_9.

COMMON USE: To assist in evaluation of diagnoses that are related to fluctuations in folate levels such as vitamin B_{12} deficiency and malabsorption.

SPECIMEN: Serum (1 mL) collected in a red- or tiger-top tube.

NORMAL FINDINGS: (Method: Immunochemiluminometric assay [ICMA])

	Conventional Units	SI Units (Conventional Units × 2.265)
Normal	Greater than 5.4 ng/mL	Greater than 12.2 nmol/L
Intermediate	3.4–5.4 ng/mL	7.7–12.2 nmol/L
Deficient	Less than 3.4 ng/mL	Less than 7.7 nmol/L

Values may be slightly decreased in older adults due to the effects of medications and the presence of multiple chronic or acute diseases with or without muted symptoms.

DESCRIPTION: Folate, a water-soluble vitamin, is produced by bacteria in the intestines and stored in small amounts in the liver. Dietary folate is absorbed through the intestinal mucosa and stored in the liver. Folate is necessary for normal red blood cell (RBC) and white blood cell function, DNA replication, and cell division. Folate levels are often measured in association with serum vitamin B_{12} determinations because vitamin B_{12} is required for folate to enter tissue cells. Folate is an essential coenzyme in the conversion of homocysteine to methionine. Hyperhomocysteinemia resulting from folate deficiency in pregnant women is believed to increase the risk of neural tube defects. Hyperhomocyteinemia related to low folic acid levels is also associated with increased risk for cardiovascular disease.

NDICATIONS

- Assist in the diagnosis of megaloblastic anemia resulting from deficient folate intake or increased folate requirements, such as in pregnancy and hemolytic anemia
- Monitor the effects of prolonged parenteral nutrition
- Monitor response to disorders that may lead to folate deficiency or decreased absorption and storage

POTENTIAL DIAGNOSIS

Increased in

- Blind loop syndrome *(related to malabsorption in a segment of the intestine due to competition for absorption of folate produced by bacterial overgrowth)*
- Excessive dietary intake of folate or folate supplements
- Pernicious anemia *(related to inadequate levels of vitamin B_{12}, due to impaired absorption, resulting in increased circulating folate levels)*
- Vitamin B_{12} deficiency *(related to vitamin B_{12} levels inadequate to metabolize folate, resulting in increased circulating folate levels)*

Decreased in

- Chronic alcoholism *(related to insufficient intake combined with malabsorption)*
- Crohn's disease *(related to malabsorption)*
- Exfoliative dermatitis *(related to increased demand)*
- Hemolytic anemias *(related to increased demand due to shortened RBC life span caused by folate deficiency)*
- Liver disease *(related to increased excretion)*
- Malnutrition *(related to insufficient intake)*
- Megaloblastic anemia *(related to folate deficiency, which affects development of RBCs and results in anemia)*
- Myelofibrosis *(related to increased demand)*
- Neoplasms *(related to increased demand)*
- Pregnancy *(related to increased demand possibly combined with insufficient dietary intake)*
- Regional enteritis *(related to malabsorption)*
- Scurvy *(related to insufficient intake)*
- Sideroblastic anemias *(evidenced by an acquired anemia resulting from folate deficiency; iron enters and accumulates in the RBCs but cannot become incorporated in hemoglobin)*
- Sprue *(related to malabsorption)*
- Ulcerative colitis *(related to malabsorption)*
- Whipple's disease *(related to malabsorption)*

CRITICAL FINDINGS: N/A

INTERFERING FACTORS

- Drugs that may decrease folate levels include aminopterin, ampicillin, antacids, anticonvulsants, barbiturates, chloramphenicol, chloroguanide, erythromycin, ethanol, glutethimide, lincomycin, metformin, methotrexate, nitrofurans, oral contraceptives, penicillin, pentamidine, phenytoin, pyrimethamine, tetracycline, and triamterene.
- Hemolysis may falsely increase folate levels.

NURSING IMPLICATIONS AND PROCEDURE

PRETEST:

- Positively identify the patient using at least two unique identifiers before providing care, treatment, or services.
- *Patient Teaching:* Inform the patient this test can assist in detecting folate deficiency and monitoring folate therapy.
- Obtain a history of the patient's complaints, including a list of known allergens,

especially allergies or sensitivities to latex.

▶ Obtain a history of the patient's gastrointestinal and hematopoietic systems, symptoms, and results of previously performed laboratory tests and diagnostic and surgical procedures.

▶ Obtain a list of the patient's current medications, including herbs, nutritional supplements, and nutraceuticals (see Appendix F).

▶ Review the procedure with the patient. Inform the patient that specimen collection takes approximately 5 to 10 min. Address concerns about pain and explain that there may be some discomfort during the venipuncture.

▶ *Sensitivity to social and cultural issues,* as well as concern for modesty, is important in providing psychological support before, during, and after the procedure.

▶ There are no food, fluid, or medication restrictions unless by medical direction.

INTRATEST:

▶ If the patient has a history of allergic reaction to latex, avoid the use of equipment containing latex.

▶ Instruct the patient to cooperate fully and to follow directions. Direct the patient to breathe normally and to avoid unnecessary movement.

▶ Observe standard precautions, and follow the general guidelines in Appendix A. Positively identify the patient, and label the appropriate specimen container with the corresponding patient demographics, initials of the person collecting the specimen, date, and time of collection. Perform a venipuncture. Protect the specimen from light.

▶ Remove the needle and apply direct pressure with dry gauze to stop bleeding. Observe/assess venipuncture site for bleeding or hematoma formation and secure gauze with adhesive bandage.

▶ Promptly transport the specimen to the laboratory for processing and analysis.

POST-TEST:

▶ A report of the results will be made available to the requesting health-care provider (HCP), who will discuss the results with the patient.

▶ *Nutritional Considerations:* The Institute of Medicine's Food and Nutrition Board

suggests 400 mcg as the daily recommended dietary allowance of folate for adult males and females age 19 to greater than 70 yr; 600 mcg/d for pregnant females under age 18 through 50 yr; 500 mcg/d for lactating females under age 18 through 50 yr; 400 mcg/day for children age 14 to 18 yr; 300 mcg/d for children age 9 to 13 yr; 200 mcg/d for children age 4 to 8 yr; 150 mcg/d for children age 1 to 3 yr; 80 mcg/d for children age 7 to 12 mo (recommended adequate intake); 65 mcg/d for children age 0 to 6 mo (recommended adequate intake). Reprinted with permission from the National Academies Press, copyright 2013, National Academy of Sciences. Instruct the folate-deficient patient (especially pregnant women), as appropriate, to eat foods rich in folate, such as liver, salmon, eggs, asparagus, green leafy vegetables, broccoli, sweet potatoes, beans, and whole wheat.

▶ Reinforce information given by the patient's HCP regarding further testing, treatment, or referral to another HCP. Answer any questions or address any concerns voiced by the patient or family. Educate the patient regarding access to nutritional counseling services. Provide contact information, if desired, for the Institute of Medicine of the National Academies (www.iom.edu).

▶ Depending on the results of this procedure, additional testing may be performed to evaluate or monitor progression of the disease process and determine the need for a change in therapy. Evaluate test results in relation to the patient's symptoms and other tests performed.

RELATED MONOGRAPHS:

▶ Related tests include antibodies antithyroglobulin, biopsy intestinal, capsule endoscopy, CBC, CBC RBC indices, complete blood count, RBC morphology, complete blood count, WBC count and differential, eosinophil count, fecal analysis, gastric acid emptying scan, gastric acid stimulation test, gastrin, G6PD, hemosiderin, homocysteine, intrinsic factor antibodies, thyroid, and vitamin B_{12}.

▶ Refer to the Gastrointestinal and Hematopoietic systems tables at the end of the book for related tests by body system.

Follicle-Stimulating Hormone

SYNONYM/ACRONYM: Follitropin, FSH.

COMMON USE: To distinguish primary causes of gonadal failure from secondary causes, evaluate menstrual disturbances, and assist in infertility evaluations.

SPECIMEN: Serum (1 mL) collected in a red- or tiger-top tube.

NORMAL FINDINGS: (Method: Immunoassay)

Age	Conventional Units and SI Units
Child	
Prepuberty	Less than 10 international units/mL
Adult	
Male	1.4–15.5 international units/mL
Female	
Follicular phase	1.4–9.9 international units/mL
Ovulatory peak	6.2–17.2 international units/mL
Luteal phase	1.1–9.2 international units/mL
Postmenopause	19–100 international units/mL

DESCRIPTION: Follicle-stimulating hormone (FSH) is produced and stored in the anterior portion of the pituitary gland. In women, FSH promotes maturation of the graafian (germinal) follicle, causing estrogen secretion and allowing the ovum to mature. In men, FSH partially controls spermatogenesis, but the presence of testosterone is also necessary. Gonadotropin-releasing hormone secretion is stimulated by a decrease in estrogen and testosterone levels. Gonadotropin-releasing hormone secretion stimulates FSH secretion. FSH production is inhibited by an increase in estrogen and testosterone levels. FSH production is pulsatile, episodic, and cyclic and is subject to diurnal variation. Serial measurement is often required.

INDICATIONS

- Assist in distinguishing between primary and secondary (pituitary or hypothalamic) gonadal failure
- Define menstrual cycle phases as a part of infertility testing
- Evaluate ambiguous sexual differentiation in infants
- Evaluate early sexual development in girls younger than age 9 or boys younger than age 10 (precocious puberty associated with elevated levels)
- Evaluate failure of sexual maturation in adolescence
- Evaluate testicular dysfunction
- Investigate impotence, gynecomastia, and menstrual disturbances

POTENTIAL DIAGNOSIS

Increased in

- Alcoholism *(related to suppressed secretion from the pituitary gland)*

- Castration *(oversecretion related to feedback mechanism involving decreased testosterone levels)*
- Gonadal failure *(oversecretion related to feedback mechanism involving decreased estrogen or testosterone levels)*
- Gonadotropin-secreting pituitary tumors *(related to oversecretion by tumor cells)*
- Klinefelter's syndrome *(oversecretion related to feedback mechanism involving decreased estrogen or testosterone levels)*
- Menopause *(oversecretion related to feedback mechanism involving decreased estrogen levels)*
- Orchitis *(oversecretion related to feedback mechanism involving decreased testosterone levels)*
- Precocious puberty in children *(related to oversecretion from the pituitary gland)*
- Primary hypogonadism *(oversecretion related to feedback mechanism involving decreased estrogen or testosterone levels; failure of testes or ovaries to produce sex hormones)*
- Reifenstein's syndrome *(oversecretion related to feedback mechanism involving familial partial resistance to testosterone levels)*
- Turner's syndrome *(oversecretion related to feedback mechanism involving decreased estrogen or testosterone levels)*

Decreased in
- Anorexia nervosa *(related to suppressive effects of severe caloric restriction on the hypothalamic-pituitary axis)*
- Anterior pituitary hypofunction *(underproduction resulting from dysfunctional pituitary gland)*
- Hemochromatosis *(hypogonadotropic hypogonadism related to absence of the gonadal stimulating pituitary hormones, estrogen, and testosterone; iron deposits in pituitary may affect normal production of FSH)*
- Hyperprolactinemia *(related to suppressive effect on estrogen production)*
- Hypothalamic disorders *(decreased production in response to lack of hypothalamic stimulators)*
- Polycystic ovary disease (Stein-Leventhal syndrome) *(suppressed secretion related to feedback mechanism involving increased estrogen levels)*
- Pregnancy *(related to elevated estrogen levels)*
- Sickle cell anemia *(although primary testicular dysfunction is mainly associated with sickle cell disease, related to testicular microinfarcts, hypogonadotropic hypogonadism has been reported in some men with sickle cell disease)*

CRITICAL FINDINGS: N/A

INTERFERING FACTORS
- Drugs that may increase FSH levels include bicalutamide, bombesin, cimetidine, clomiphene, digitalis, erythropoietin, exemestane, finasteride, gonadotropin-releasing hormone, ketoconazole, levodopa, metformin, nafarelin, naloxone, nilutamide, oxcarbazepine, pravastatin, and tamoxifen.
- Drugs that may decrease FSH levels include anabolic steroids, anticonvulsants, buserelin, estrogens, corticotropin-releasing hormone, danazol, diethylstilbestrol, goserelin, megestrol, mestranol, oral contraceptives, phenothiazine, pimozide, pravastatin, progesterone, stanozolol, tamoxifen, toremifene, and valproic acid.
- In menstruating women, values vary in relation to the phase of the menstrual cycle. Values are higher in postmenopausal women.

NURSING IMPLICATIONS AND PROCEDURE

PRETEST:

- Positively identify the patient using at least two unique identifiers before providing care, treatment, or services.
- *Patient Teaching:* Inform the patient this test can assist in evaluating disturbances in hormone levels.
- Obtain a history of the patient's complaints, including a list of known allergens, especially allergies or sensitivities to latex.
- Obtain a history of the patient's endocrine and reproductive systems, as well as phase of menstrual cycle, symptoms, and results of previously performed laboratory tests and diagnostic and surgical procedures.
- Obtain a list of the patient's current medications, including herbs, nutritional supplements, and nutraceuticals (see Appendix F).
- Review the procedure with the patient. Inform the patient that specimen collection takes approximately 5 to 10 min. Address concerns about pain and explain that there may be some discomfort during the venipuncture.
- *Sensitivity to social and cultural issues,* as well as concern for modesty, is important in providing psychological support before, during, and after the procedure.
- There are no food, fluid, or medication restrictions unless by medical direction.

INTRATEST:

- If the patient has a history of allergic reaction to latex, avoid the use of equipment containing latex.
- Instruct the patient to cooperate fully and to follow directions. Direct the patient to breathe normally and to avoid unnecessary movement.
- Observe standard precautions, and follow the general guidelines in Appendix A. Positively identify the patient, and label the appropriate specimen container with the corresponding patient demographics, initials of the person collecting the specimen, date, and time of collection. Perform a venipuncture.

- Remove the needle and apply direct pressure with dry gauze to stop bleeding. Observe/assess venipuncture site for bleeding or hematoma formation and secure gauze with adhesive bandage.
- Promptly transport the specimen to the laboratory for processing and analysis.

POST-TEST:

- A report of the results will be made available to the requesting health-care provider (HCP), who will discuss the results with the patient.
- Recognize anxiety related to test results and provide a supportive, nonjudgmental environment when assisting a patient through the process of fertility testing. Discuss the implications of abnormal test results on the patient's lifestyle. Provide teaching and information regarding the clinical implications of the test results, as appropriate. Educate the patient and partner regarding access to counseling services, as appropriate.
- Reinforce information given by the patient's HCP regarding further testing, treatment, or referral to another HCP. Inform the patient that multiple specimens may be required. Answer any questions or address any concerns voiced by the patient or family.
- Depending on the results of this procedure, additional testing may be performed to evaluate or monitor progression of the disease process and determine the need for a change in therapy. Evaluate test results in relation to the patient's symptoms and other tests performed.

RELATED MONOGRAPHS:

- Related tests include antibodies antisperm, BMD, *Chlamydia* group antibody, chromosome analysis, CT pituitary, estradiol, laparoscopy gynecologic, LH, MRI pituitary, prolactin, testosterone, semen analysis, and US scrotal.
- Refer to the Endocrine and Reproductive systems tables at the end of the book for related tests by body system.

Fructosamine

SYNONYM/ACRONYM: Glycated albumin.

COMMON USE: To assist in assessing long-term glucose control in diabetes.

SPECIMEN: Serum (1 mL) collected in a red- or tiger-top tube.

NORMAL FINDINGS: (Method: Spectrophotometry)

Status	Conventional Units	SI Units (Conventional Units × 0.01)
Normal	174–286 micromol/L	1.74–2.86 mmol/L
Diabetic (values vary with degree of control)	210–563 micromol/L	2.10–5.63 mmol/L

DESCRIPTION: Fructosamine is the result of a covalent linkage between glucose and albumin or other proteins. Similar to glycated hemoglobin, fructosamine can be used to monitor long-term control of glucose in diabetics. It has a shorter half-life than glycated hemoglobin and is thought to be more sensitive to short-term fluctuations in glucose concentrations. Some glycated hemoglobin methods are affected by hemoglobin variants. Fructosamine is not subject to this interference.

INDICATIONS
• Evaluate diabetic control

POTENTIAL DIAGNOSIS

Increased in
• Diabetic patients with poor glucose control

Decreased in
• Severe hypoproteinemia

CRITICAL FINDINGS: N/A

INTERFERING FACTORS
• Drugs that may increase fructosamine levels include bendroflumethiazide and captopril.
• Drugs that may decrease fructosamine levels include ascorbic acid, pyridoxine, and terazosin.
• Decreased albumin levels may result in falsely decreased fructosamine levels.

NURSING IMPLICATIONS AND PROCEDURE

PRETEST:

▶ Positively identify the patient using at least two unique identifiers before providing care, treatment, or services.
▶ *Patient Teaching:* Inform the patient this test can assist in evaluating blood sugar control.
▶ Obtain a history of the patient's complaints, especially related to diabetic control. Obtain a list of known allergens, especially allergies or sensitivities to latex.
▶ Obtain a history of the patient's endocrine and gastrointestinal systems, symptoms, and results of previously performed laboratory tests and diagnostic and surgical procedures.

- Obtain a list of the patient's current medications, including herbs, nutritional supplements, and nutraceuticals (see Appendix F).
- Review the procedure with the patient. Inform the patient that specimen collection takes approximately 5 to 10 min. Address concerns about pain and explain that there may be some discomfort during the venipuncture. *Sensitivity to social and cultural issues,* as well as concern for modesty, is important in providing psychological support before, during, and after the procedure.
- There are no food, fluid, or medication restrictions unless by medical direction.

INTRATEST:

- If the patient has a history of allergic reaction to latex, avoid the use of equipment containing latex.
- Instruct the patient to cooperate fully and to follow directions. Direct the patient to breathe normally and to avoid unnecessary movement.
- Observe standard precautions, and follow the general guidelines in Appendix A. Positively identify the patient, and label the appropriate specimen container with the corresponding patient demographics, initials of the person collecting the specimen, date, and time of collection. Perform a venipuncture.
- Remove the needle and apply direct pressure with dry gauze to stop bleeding. Observe/assess venipuncture site for bleeding or hematoma formation and secure gauze with adhesive bandage.
- Promptly transport the specimen to the laboratory for processing and analysis.

POST-TEST:

- A report of the results will be made available to the requesting health-care provider (HCP), who will discuss the results with the patient.
- *Nutritional Considerations:* Abnormal fructosamine levels may be associated with conditions resulting from poor glucose control. There is no "diabetic diet"; however, many meal-planning approaches with nutritional goals are endorsed by the American Dietetic Association. Patients who adhere to dietary recommendations report a better general feeling of health, better weight management, greater control of glucose and lipid values, and improved use of insulin. Instruct the patient, as appropriate, in nutritional management of diabetes. The American Heart Association's Therapeutic Lifestyle Changes (TLC) diet provides goals directed at people with specific risk factors and/or existing medical conditions (e.g., elevated LDL cholesterol levels, other lipid disorders, coronary artery disease, insulin-dependent diabetes, insulin resistance, or metabolic syndrome). The TLC approach also includes the use of plant stanols or sterols and increased dissolved fiber as an option for lowering LDL cholesterol levels; nutritional recommendations for daily total caloric intake; recommendations for allowable percentage of calories derived from fat (saturated and unsaturated), carbohydrates, protein, and cholesterol; as well as recommendations for daily expenditure of energy. The nutritional needs of each diabetic patient need to be determined individually (especially during pregnancy) with the appropriate HCPs, particularly professionals trained in nutrition.
- Instruct the patient and caregiver to report signs and symptoms of hypoglycemia (weakness, confusion, diaphoresis, rapid pulse) or hyperglycemia (thirst, polyuria, hunger, lethargy).
- Recognize anxiety related to test results, and be supportive of perceived loss of independence and fear of shortened life expectancy. Discuss the implications of abnormal test results on the patient's lifestyle. Provide teaching and information regarding the clinical implications of the test results, as appropriate. Emphasize, if indicated, that good glycemic control delays the onset and slows the progression of diabetic retinopathy, nephropathy, and neuropathy. Educate the patient regarding access to counseling services, as appropriate. Provide contact information, if desired, for the American Diabetes Association (www.diabetes.org) or the American Heart Association (www.americanheart.org).

F

▶ Reinforce information given by the patient's HCP regarding further testing, treatment, or referral to another HCP. Answer any questions or address any concerns voiced by the patient or family. Depending on the results of this procedure, additional testing may be performed to evaluate or monitor progression of the disease process and determine the need for a change in therapy. Evaluate test results in relation to the patient's symptoms and other tests performed.

RELATED MONOGRAPHS:

▶ Related tests include CT cardiac scoring, cortisol, C-peptide, fecal fat, fluorescein angiography, fundus photography, gastric emptying scan, glucagon, glucose, GTT, glycated hemoglobin, insulin, insulin antibodies, intraocular pressure, ketones, microalbumin, slit-lamp biomicroscopy, and visual fields testing.
▶ Refer to the Endocrine and Gastrointestinal systems tables at the end of the book for related tests by body system.

F

Fundus Photography

SYNONYM/ACRONYM: N/A.

COMMON USE: To evaluate vascular and structural changes in the eye in assessing the progression of diseases such as glaucoma, diabetic retinopathy, and macular degeneration.

AREA OF APPLICATION: Eyes.

CONTRAST: N/A.

DESCRIPTION: This test involves the photographic examination of the structures of the eye to document the condition of the eye, detect abnormalities, and assist in following the progress of treatment.

INDICATIONS
• Detect the presence of choroidal nevus
• Detect various types and stages of glaucoma
• Document the presence of diabetic retinopathy
• Document the presence of macular degeneration and any other degeneration and any associated hemorrhaging

• Observe ocular effects resulting from the long-term use of high-risk medications

POTENTIAL DIAGNOSIS

Normal findings in
• Normal optic nerve and vessels
• No evidence of other ocular abnormalities

Abnormal findings in
• Aneurysm
• Choroidal nevus
• Diabetic retinopathy
• Macular degeneration
• Obstructive disorders of the arteries or veins that lead to collateral circulation
• Retinal detachment or tear

CRITICAL FINDINGS
- Detached retina

Flashers, floaters, or a veil that moves across the field of vision may indicate detached retina or retinal tear. This condition requires immediate examination by an ophthalmologist. Untreated, full retinal detachment can result in irreversible and complete loss of vision in the affected eye.

It is essential that critical diagnoses be communicated immediately to the appropriate health-care provider (HCP). A listing of these diagnoses varies among facilities. Note and immediately report to the HCP abnormal results and related symptoms. Timely notification of critical values for lab or diagnostic studies is a role expectation of the professional nurse. Notification processes will vary among facilities. Upon receipt of the critical value the information should be read back to the caller to verify accuracy. Most policies require immediate notification of the primary HCP, hospitalist, or on-call HCP. Reported information includes the patient's name, unique identifiers, critical value, name of the person giving the report, and name of the person receiving the report. Documentation of notification should be made in the medical record with the name of the HCP notified, time and date of notification, and any orders received. Any delay in a timely report of a critical value may require completion of a notification form with review by Risk Management.

INTERFERING FACTORS

This procedure is contraindicated for
- Patients with narrow-angle glaucoma if pupil dilation is performed; dilation can initiate a severe and sight-threatening open-angle attack.
- Patients with allergies to mydriatics if pupil dilation using mydriatics is performed.

Factors that may impair the results of the examination
- Inability of the patient to cooperate or remain still during the test because of age, significant pain, or mental status may interfere with the test results.
- Presence of cataracts may interfere with fundal view.
- Ineffective dilation of the pupils may impair clear imaging.
- Rubbing or squeezing the eyes may affect results.
- Failure to follow medication restrictions before the procedure may cause the procedure to be canceled or repeated.

F

NURSING IMPLICATIONS AND PROCEDURE

PRETEST:

▸ Positively identify the patient using at least two unique identifiers before providing care, treatment, or services.
▸ *Patient Teaching:* Inform the patient this procedure assists in detecting changes in the eye that effect vision.
▸ Obtain a history of the patient's complaints, including a list of known allergens, especially mydriatics if dilation is to be performed.
▸ Obtain a history of the patient's known or suspected vision loss; changes in visual acuity, including type and cause; use of glasses or contact lenses; and eye conditions with treatment regimens.
▸ Obtain results of previously performed laboratory tests and diagnostic and surgical procedures.
▸ Obtain a list of the patient's current medications, including herbs, nutritional supplements, and nutraceuticals (see Appendix F).
▸ Instruct the patient to remove contact lenses or glasses, as appropriate.
▸ Instruct the patient regarding the importance of keeping the eyes open for the test.
▸ Review the procedure with the patient. Explain that the patient will be

requested to fixate the eyes during the procedure. Address concerns about pain and explain that mydriatics, if used, may cause blurred vision and sensitivity to light. There may also be a brief stinging sensation when the drop is put in the eye, but no discomfort will be experienced during the examination. Inform the patient that an HCP performs the test, in a quiet, darkened room, and that to dilate and evaluate both eyes, the test can take up to 60 min.

Sensitivity to social and cultural issues, as well as concern for modesty, is important in providing psychological support before, during, and after the procedure.

There are no food or fluid restrictions, unless by medical direction.

The patient should avoid eye medications (particularly miotic eye drops which may constrict the pupil preventing a clear view of the fundus and mydriatic eyedrops in order to avoid instigation of an acute open angle attack in patients with narrow angle glaucoma) for at least 1 day prior to the test.

Ensure that the patient understands that he or she must refrain from driving until the pupils return to normal (about 4 hr) after the test and has made arrangements to have someone else be responsible for transportation after the test.

INTRATEST:

Observe standard precautions, and follow the general guidelines in Appendix A. Positively identify the patient.

Ensure that the patient has complied with medication restrictions; ensure that eye medications, especially miotics and mydriatics, have been restricted for at least 1 day prior to the test.

Instruct the patient to cooperate fully and to follow directions. Instruct the patient to remain still during the procedure because movement produces unreliable results.

Seat the patient in a chair that faces the camera. Instruct the patient to look at a directed target while the eyes are examined.

If dilation is to be performed, administer the ordered mydriatic to each eye

and repeat in 5 to 15 min. Drops are placed in the eye with the patient looking up and the solution directed at the six o'clock position of the sclera (white of the eye) near the limbus (gray, semitransparent area of the eyeball where the cornea and sclera meet). Neither dropper nor bottle should touch the eyelashes.

Instruct the patient to place the chin in the chin rest and gently press the forehead against the support bar. Instruct the patient to open his or her eyes wide and look at desired target while a sequence of photographs are taken.

POST-TEST:

A report of the results will be made available to the requesting HCP, who will discuss the results with the patient.

Instruct the patient to resume usual medications, as directed by the HCP.

Nutritional Considerations: Increased glucose levels may be associated with diabetes. There is no "diabetic diet"; however, many meal-planning approaches with nutritional goals are endorsed by the American Dietetic Association. Patients who adhere to dietary recommendations report a better general feeling of health, better weight management, greater control of glucose and lipid values, and improved use of insulin. Instruct the patient, as appropriate, in nutritional management of diabetes. The American Heart Association's Therapeutic Lifestyle Changes (TLC) diet provides goals directed at people with specific risk factors and/or existing medical conditions (e.g., elevated LDL cholesterol levels, other lipid disorders, coronary artery disease, insulin-dependent diabetes, insulin resistance, or metabolic syndrome). The TLC approach also includes the use of plant stanols or sterols and increased dissolved fiber as an option for lowering LDL cholesterol levels; nutritional recommendations for daily total caloric intake; recommendations for allowable percentage of calories derived from fat (saturated and unsaturated), carbohydrates, protein, and cholesterol; as well as recommendations for daily expenditure of energy. The nutritional needs of each diabetic patient need to be determined individually (especially during pregnancy) with the appropriate HCPs, particularly professionals trained in nutrition.

Recognize anxiety related to test results, and be supportive of impaired activity related to vision loss or anticipated loss of driving privileges. Discuss the implications of abnormal test results on the patient's lifestyle. Provide teaching and information regarding the clinical implications of the test results, as appropriate. Emphasize, as appropriate, that good glycemic control delays the onset of and slows the progression of diabetic retinopathy, nephropathy, and neuropathy. Provide education regarding smoking cessation, as appropriate. Provide contact information regarding vision aids, if desired, for ABLEDATA (sponsored by the National Institute on Disability and Rehabilitation Research [NIDRR], available at www.abledata.com).

Information can also be obtained from the American Macular Degeneration Foundation (www.macular.org), the American Diabetes Association (www.diabetes.org), or the American Heart Association (www.americanheart.org).

Instruct the patient to avoid strenuous physical activities, like lifting heavy objects, that may increase pressure in the eye, as ordered.

Reinforce information given by the patient's HCP regarding further testing, treatment, or referral to another HCP. Inform the patient that visual acuity and responses to light may change. Suggest that the patient wear dark glasses after the test until the pupils return to normal size. Answer any questions or address any concerns voiced by the patient or family.

Depending on the results of this procedure, additional testing may be performed to evaluate or monitor progression of the disease process and determine the need for a change in therapy. Evaluate test results in relation to the patient's symptoms and other tests performed.

RELATED MONOGRAPHS:

Related tests include fluorescein angiography, fructosamine, glucagon, glucose, glycated hemoglobin, gonioscopy, insulin, intraocular pressure, microalbumin, plethysmography, refraction, slit-lamp biomicroscopy, and visual field testing.

Refer to the Ocular System table at the end of the book for related tests by body system.

F

Gallium Scan

SYNONYM/ACRONYM: Ga scan.

COMMON USE: To assist in diagnosing, evaluating, and staging tumors and in detecting areas of infection, inflammation, and abscess.

AREA OF APPLICATION: Whole body.

CONTRAST: IV radioactive gallium-67 citrate.

DESCRIPTION: Gallium imaging is a nuclear medicine study that assists in diagnosing neoplasm and inflammation activity. Gallium, which has 90% sensitivity for inflammatory disease, is readily distributed throughout plasma and body tissues. Gallium imaging is sensitive in detecting abscesses, pneumonia, pyelonephritis, active sarcoidosis, and active tuberculosis. In immunocompromised patients, such as patients with AIDS, gallium imaging can detect complications such as *Pneumocystis jiroveci* (formerly *P. carinii*) pneumonitis. Gallium imaging is useful but less commonly performed in the diagnosis and staging of some neoplasms, including Hodgkin's disease, lymphoma, melanoma, and leukemia. Imaging can be performed 6 to 72 hr after gallium injection. A gamma camera detects the radiation emitted from the injected radioactive material, and a representative image of the distribution of the radioactive material is obtained. The nonspecificity of gallium imaging requires correlation with other diagnostic studies, such as computed tomography, magnetic resonance imaging, and ultrasonography.

INDICATIONS
- Aid in the diagnosis of infectious or inflammatory diseases
- Evaluate lymphomas

- Evaluate recurrent lymphomas or tumors after radiation therapy or chemotherapy
- Perform as a screening examination for fever of undetermined origin

POTENTIAL DIAGNOSIS

Normal findings in
- Normal distribution of gallium; some localization of the radionuclide within the liver, spleen, bone, nasopharynx, lacrimal glands, breast, and bowel is expected

Abnormal findings in
- Abscess
- Infection
- Inflammation
- Lymphoma
- Tumor

CRITICAL FINDINGS: N/A

INTERFERING FACTORS

This procedure is contraindicated for
- Patients who are pregnant or suspected of being pregnant, unless the potential benefits of the procedure far outweigh the risks to the fetus and mother.

Factors that may impair clear imaging
- Inability of the patient to cooperate or remain still during the procedure because of age, significant pain, or mental status.
- Metallic objects (e.g., jewelry, body rings) within the examination field, which may inhibit organ

visualization and cause unclear images.

- Performance of other nuclear scans within the preceding 24 to 48 hr.
- Administration of certain medications (e.g., gastrin, cholecystokinin), which may interfere with gastric emptying.

Other considerations

- Improper injection of the radionuclide may allow the tracer to seep deep into the muscle tissue, producing erroneous hot spots.
- Consultation with a health-care provider (HCP) should occur before the procedure for radiation safety concerns regarding younger patients or patients who are lactating.
- Risks associated with radiation overexposure can result from frequent x-ray or radionuclide procedures. Personnel working in the examination area should wear badges to record their level of radiation.

NURSING IMPLICATIONS AND PROCEDURE

PRETEST:

- Positively identify the patient using at least two unique identifiers before providing care, treatment, or services.
- *Patient Teaching:* Inform the patient this procedure can assist in identifying infection or other disease.
- Obtain a history of the patient's complaints, including a list of known allergens, especially allergies or sensitivities to latex, iodine, seafood, contrast medium, anesthetics, or dyes.
- Obtain a history of the patient's immune system, symptoms, and results of previously performed laboratory tests and diagnostic and surgical procedures.
- Note any recent procedures that can interfere with test results, including examinations using iodine-based contrast medium.

- Record the date of the last menstrual period and determine the possibility of pregnancy in perimenopausal women. Obtain a list of the patient's current medications, including herbs, nutritional supplements, and nutraceuticals (see Appendix F).
- Review the procedure with the patient. Address concerns about pain related to the procedure and explain that some pain may be experienced during the test, or there may be moments of discomfort. Reassure the patient that the radionuclide poses no radioactive hazard and rarely produces side effects. Inform the patient that the procedure is performed in a nuclear medicine department by an HCP specializing in this procedure, with support staff, and takes approximately 60 min. *Sensitivity to social and cultural issues,* as well as concern for modesty, is important in providing psychological support before, during, and after the procedure.
- Instruct the patient to remove jewelry and other metallic objects from the area to be examined.
- There are no food, fluid, or medication restrictions unless by medical direction.
- *Make sure a written and informed consent has been signed prior to the procedure and before administering any medications.*

INTRATEST:

- Observe standard precautions, and follow the general guidelines in Appendix A. Positively identify patient.
- Ensure that the patient has removed all external metallic objects from the area to be examined prior to the procedure.
- If the patient has a history of allergic reactions to any substance or drug, administer ordered prophylactic steroids or antihistamines before the procedure.
- Have emergency equipment readily available.
- Instruct the patient to void prior to the procedure and to change into the gown, robe, and foot coverings provided.
- Instruct the patient to cooperate fully and to follow directions. Instruct the

G

patient to lie still during the procedure because movement produces unclear images.

▸ Administer a sedative to a child or to an uncooperative adult, as ordered.

▸ Place the patient in a supine position on a flat table with foam wedges, which help maintain position and immobilization.

▸ IV radionuclide is administered, and the patient is instructed to return for scanning at a designated time after injection. Typical scanning occurs at 6, 24, 48, 72, 96, and/or 120 hr postinjection depending on diagnosis.

▸ If an abdominal abscess or infection is suspected, laxatives or enemas may be ordered before imaging at 48 or 72 hr after the injection.

▸ Monitor the patient for complications related to the procedure (e.g., allergic reaction, anaphylaxis, bronchospasm).

▸ The needle or catheter is removed, and a pressure dressing is applied over the puncture site.

▸ Observe the needle/catheter insertion site for bleeding, inflammation, or hematoma formation.

POST-TEST:

▸ A report of the results will be made available to the requesting HCP, who will discuss the results with the patient.

▸ Unless contraindicated, advise patient to drink increased amounts of fluids for 24 to 48 hr to eliminate the radionuclide from the body. Inform the patient that radionuclide is eliminated from the body within 6 to 24 hr.

▸ Instruct the patient to resume usual medication or activity, as directed by the HCP.

▸ Instruct the patient in the care and assessment of the injection site.

▸ If a woman who is breastfeeding must have a nuclear scan, she should not breastfeed the infant until the radionuclide has been eliminated. This could take as long as 3 days. She should be instructed to express the milk and discard it during the 3-day period to prevent cessation of milk production.

▸ Instruct the patient to immediately flush the toilet and to meticulously wash hands with soap and water after each voiding for 24 hr after the procedure.

▸ Instruct all caregivers to wear gloves when discarding urine for 48 hr after the procedure. Wash gloved hands with soap and water before removing gloves. Then wash ungloved hands after removing the gloves.

▸ Recognize anxiety related to test results, and be supportive of perceived loss of independent function. Discuss the implications of abnormal test results on the patient's lifestyle. Provide teaching and information regarding the clinical implications of the test results, as appropriate.

▸ Reinforce information given by the patient's HCP regarding further testing, treatment, or referral to another HCP. Answer any questions or address any concerns voiced by the patient or family.

▸ Depending on the results of this procedure, additional testing may be needed to evaluate or monitor progression of the disease process and determine the need for a change in therapy. Evaluate test results in relation to the patient's symptoms and other tests performed.

RELATED MONOGRAPHS:

▸ Related tests include angiotensin converting enzyme, biopsy bone marrow, biopsy kidney, biopsy lung, blood gases, bronchoscopy, CBC, CBC WBC and differential, chest x-ray, CT abdomen, CT pelvis, CT thoracic, culture blood, culture and smear mycobacteria, culture viral, cytology sputum, cytology urine, ESR, HIV-1/2 antibodies, IVP, lung perfusion scan, MRI chest, MRI abdomen, mediastinoscopy, pleural fluid analysis, plethysmography, PFT, pulse oximetry, renogram, US kidney, and US lymph node.

▸ Refer to the Immune System table at the end of the book for related tests by body system.

γ-Glutamyltranspeptidase

SYNONYM/ACRONYM: Serum γ-glutamyltransferase, γ-glutamyl transpeptidase, GGT, SGGT.

COMMON USE: To assist in diagnosing and monitoring liver disease.

SPECIMEN: Serum (1 mL) collected in a red- or tiger-top tube. Plasma (1 mL) collected in a green-top (heparin) tube is also acceptable.

NORMAL FINDINGS: (Method: Enzymatic spectrophotometry)

	Conventional & SI Units
Newborn–6 mo	12–122 units/L
7 mo and older	
Male	0–30 units/L
Female	0–24 units/L

Values may be elevated in older adults due to the effects of medications and the presence of multiple chronic or acute diseases with or without muted symptoms.

DESCRIPTION: Glutamyltransferase (GGT) assists with the reabsorption of amino acids and peptides from the glomerular filtrate and intestinal lumen. Hepatobiliary, renal tubular, and pancreatic tissues contain large amounts of GGT. Other sources include the prostate gland, brain, and heart. GGT is elevated in all types of liver disease and is more responsive to biliary obstruction, cholangitis, or cholecystitis than any of the other enzymes used as markers for liver disease.

INDICATIONS
- Assist in the diagnosis of obstructive jaundice in neonates
- Detect the presence of liver disease
- Evaluate and monitor patients with known or suspected alcohol abuse (levels rise after ingestion of small amounts of alcohol)

POTENTIAL DIAGNOSIS

Increased in
GGT is released from any damaged cell in which it is stored, so conditions that affect the liver, kidneys, or pancreas and cause cellular destruction demonstrate elevated GGT levels.
- Cirrhosis
- Diabetes with hypertension
- Hepatitis
- Hepatobiliary tract disorders
- Hepatocellular carcinoma
- Hyperthyroidism *(there is a strong association with concurrent liver abnormalities)*
- Infectious mononucleosis
- Obstructive liver disease
- Pancreatitis
- Renal transplantation
- Significant alcohol ingestion

Decreased in
- Hypothyroidism *(related to decreased enzyme production by the liver)*

G

CRITICAL FINDINGS: N/A

INTERFERING FACTORS
- Drugs and substances that may increase GGT levels include acetaminophen, alcohol, aminoglutethimide, anticonvulsants, aurothioglucose, barbiturates, captopril, cetirizine, dactinomycin, dantrolene, dexfenfluramine, estrogens, flucytosine, halothane, labetalol, medroxyprogesterone, meropenem, methyldopa, naproxen, niacin, nortriptyline, oral contraceptives, pegaspargase, phenothiazines, piroxicam, probenecid, rifampin, streptokinase, tocainide, and trifluoperazine.
- Drugs that may decrease GGT levels include clofibrate conjugated estrogens and ursodiol.

NURSING IMPLICATIONS AND PROCEDURE

PRETEST:
- Positively identify the patient using at least two unique identifiers before providing care, treatment, or services.
- *Patient Teaching:* Inform the patient this test can assist in assessing liver function.
- Obtain a history of the patient's complaints, including a list of known allergens, especially allergies or sensitivities to latex.
- Obtain a history of the patient's hepatobiliary system, symptoms, and results of previously performed laboratory tests and diagnostic and surgical procedures.
- Obtain a history of IV drug use, alcohol use, high-risk sexual activity, and occupational exposure.
- Obtain a list of the patient's current medications, including herbs, nutritional supplements, and nutraceuticals (see Appendix F).
- Review the procedure with the patient. Inform the patient that specimen collection takes approximately 5 to 10 min. Address concerns about pain and explain that there may be some discomfort during the venipuncture.
- *Sensitivity to social and cultural issues,* as well as concern for modesty, is important in providing psychological support before, during, and after the procedure.
- There are no food, fluid, or medication restrictions unless by medical direction.

INTRATEST:
- If the patient has a history of allergic reaction to latex, avoid the use of equipment containing latex.
- Instruct the patient to cooperate fully and to follow directions. Direct the patient to breathe normally and to avoid unnecessary movement.
- Observe standard precautions, and follow the general guidelines in Appendix A. Positively identify the patient, and label the appropriate specimen container with the corresponding patient demographics, initials of the person collecting the specimen, date, and time of collection. Perform a venipuncture.
- Remove the needle and apply direct pressure with dry gauze to stop bleeding. Observe/assess venipuncture site for bleeding or hematoma formation and secure gauze with adhesive bandage.
- Promptly transport the specimen to the laboratory for processing and analysis.

POST-TEST:
- A report of the results will be sent to the requesting health-care provider (HCP), who will discuss the results with the patient.
- *Nutritional Considerations:* Increased GGT levels may be associated with liver disease. Dietary recommendations may be indicated and vary depending on the condition and its severity. Currently, there are no specific medications that can be given to cure hepatitis, but elimination of alcohol ingestion and a diet optimized for convalescence are commonly included in the treatment

plan. A high-calorie, high-protein, moderate-fat diet with a high fluid intake is often recommended for patients with hepatitis. Treatment of cirrhosis is different because a low-protein diet may be in order if the patient's liver has lost the ability to process the end products of protein metabolism. A diet of soft foods also may be required if esophageal varices have developed. Ammonia levels may be used to determine whether protein should be added to or reduced from the diet. The patient should be encouraged to eat simple carbohydrates and emulsified fats (as in homogenized milk or eggs) rather than complex carbohydrates (e.g., starch, fiber, and glycogen [animal carbohydrates]) and complex fats, which require additional bile to emulsify them so that they can be used. The cirrhotic patient should also be carefully observed for the development of ascites, in which case fluid and electrolyte balance requires strict attention. The alcoholic patient should be encouraged to avoid alcohol and to seek appropriate counseling for substance abuse.
▶ Recognize anxiety related to test results, and be supportive of impaired activity related to lack of neuromuscular control, perceived loss of independence, and fear of shortened life expectancy. Discuss the implications of abnormal test results on the patient's lifestyle. Provide teaching and information regarding the clinical implications of the test results, as appropriate. Educate the patient regarding access to counseling services.
▶ Reinforce information given by the patient's HCP regarding further testing, treatment, or referral to another HCP. Answer any questions or address any concerns voiced by the patient or family.
▶ Depending on the results of this procedure, additional testing may be performed to evaluate or monitor progression of the disease process and determine the need for a change in therapy. Evaluate test results in relation to the patient's symptoms and other tests performed.

RELATED MONOGRAPHS:

▶ Related tests include ALT, ALP ammonia, AST, bilirubin, cholangiography percutaneous transhepatic, electrolytes, HAV antibody, HBV antigen and antibody, HCV antibody, hepatobiliary scan, infectious mono screen, KUB studies, liver and spleen scan, MRI liver, TSH, US abdomen, and US liver.
▶ Refer to the Hepatobiliary System table at the end of the book for related tests by body system.

Gastric Analysis and Gastric Acid Stimulation Test

SYNONYM/ACRONYM: N/A.

COMMON USE: To evaluate gastric fluid and the amount of gastric acid secreted toward diagnosing gastrointestinal disorders such as ulcers, cancers, and inflammation.

SPECIMEN: Gastric fluid collected in eight plastic tubes at 15-min intervals.

NORMAL FINDINGS: (Method: Volume measurement and pH by ion-selective electrode)

Basal acid output (BAO)	Male: 0–10.5 mmol/hr
	Female: 0–5.6 mmol/hr
Peak acid output (PAO)	Male: 12–60 mmol/hr
	Female: 8–40 mmol/hr
Peak response time	Pentagastrin, intramuscular: 15–45 min
	Pentagastrin, subcutaneous: 10–30 min
BAO/PAO ratio	Less than 0.2

DESCRIPTION: Gastric fluid is evaluated macroscopically for general physical and chemical characteristics such as color, presence of mucus or blood, and pH; gastric fluid is also evaluated microscopically for the presence of organisms and abnormal cells. The normal appearance of gastric fluid is a translucent, pale gray, slightly viscous fluid containing some mucus but not usually blood. pH is usually less than 2 and not greater than 6. Organisms are usually absent in gastric fluid owing to the acidic pH.

The gastric acid stimulation test is performed to determine the response to substances administered to induce increased gastric acid production. Pentagastrin is the usual drug of choice to induce gastric secretion because it has no major side effects. The samples obtained from gastric acid stimulation tests are examined for volume, pH, and amount of acid secreted. First, basal acid output (BAO) is determined by averaging the results of gastric samples collected before the administration of a gastric stimulant. Then a gastric stimulant is administered and peak acid output (PAO) is determined by adding together the gastric acid output of the highest two consecutive 15-min stimulation samples. Finally, BAO and PAO are compared as a ratio, which is normally less than 0.2.

INDICATIONS

- Detect duodenal ulcer
- Detect gastric carcinoma
- Detect pernicious anemia
- Detect Zollinger-Ellison syndrome
- Evaluate effectiveness of vagotomy in the treatment of peptic ulcer disease

POTENTIAL DIAGNOSIS

Increased in

Any alteration in the balance between the digestive and protective functions of the stomach that increases gastric acidity, such as hypersecretion of gastrin, use of NSAIDs, or Helicobacter pylori infection.

Appearance
- Color
  Yellow to green indicates the presence of bile. *(related to obstruction in the small intestine distal to the ampulla of Vater)*
  Pink, red, brown indicates the presence of blood. *(related to some type of gastric lesion evidenced by ulcer, gastritis, or carcinoma)*
- Microscopic evaluation
  Red blood cells *(related to trauma or active bleeding)*
  White blood cells *(related to inflammation of the gastric mucosa, mouth, paranasal sinuses, or respiratory tract)*
  Epithelial cells *(related to inflammation of the gastric mucosa)*
  Malignant cells *(related to gastric carcinoma)*

Bacteria and yeast *(related to conditions such as pyloric obstruction, pulmonary tuberculosis)*

Parasites *(related to parasitic infestation such as* Giardia, H. pylori, **hookworm,** *or* Strongyloides*)*

Increased Gastric Acid Output

- BAO

Basophilic leukemia
Duodenal ulcer
G-cell hyperplasia
Recurring peptic ulcer
Retained antrum syndrome
Systemic mastocytosis
Vagal hyperfunction
Zollinger-Ellison syndrome

- PAO

Duodenal ulcer
Zollinger-Ellison syndrome

Decreased in

Conditions that result in the gradual loss of function of the antrum and G cells, where gastrin is produced, will reflect decreased gastrin levels.

Decreased Gastric Acid Output

- BAO

Gastric ulcer

- PAO

Chronic gastritis
Gastric cancers
Gastric polyps
Gastric ulcer
Myxedema
Pernicious anemia

CRITICAL FINDINGS: N/A

INTERFERING FACTORS

- Drugs that may increase gastric volume include atropine, diazepam, ganglionic blocking agents, and insulin.
- Drugs and substances that may increase gastric pH include caffeine, calcium salts, corticotropin, ethanol, rauwolfia, reserpine, and tolazoline.
- Drugs and substances that may decrease gastric pH include atropine, cimetidine, diazepam, famotidine, ganglionic blocking agents, glucagon, nizatidine, omeprazole, oxmetidine, propranolol, prostaglandin F_{2a}, ranitidine, and secretin.
- Gastric intubation is contraindicated in patients with esophageal varices, diverticula, stenosis, malignant neoplasm of the esophagus, aortic aneurysm, severe gastric hemorrhage, and congenital heart failure.
- The use of histamine diphosphate is contraindicated in patients with a history of asthma, paroxysmal hypertension, urticaria, or other allergic conditions.
- Failure to follow dietary restrictions may result in stimulation of gastric secretions.
- Failure to follow dietary restrictions before the procedure may cause the procedure to be canceled or repeated.
- Exposure to the sight, smell, or thought of food immediately before and during the test may result in stimulation of gastric secretions.

NURSING IMPLICATIONS AND PROCEDURE

PRETEST:

- Positively identify the patient using at least two unique identifiers before providing care, treatment, or services.
- *Patient Teaching:* Inform the patient this procedure can assist in diagnosing disease and inflammation in the stomach and upper intestine.
- Obtain a history of the patient's complaints, including a list of known allergens, especially allergies or sensitivities to latex.
- Obtain a history of the patient's gastrointestinal system, symptoms, and results of previously performed laboratory tests and diagnostic and surgical procedures.
- Obtain a list of the patient's current medications, including herbs,

G

nutritional supplements, and nutraceuticals (see Appendix F).

▶ Review the procedure with the patient. Inform the patient that specimen collection takes approximately 60 to 120 min. Address concerns about pain and explain that some discomfort is experienced from insertion of the nasogastric tube.

▶ *Sensitivity to social and cultural issues,* as well as concern for modesty, is important in providing psychological support before, during, and after the procedure.

▶ Drugs and substances that may alter gastric secretions (e.g., alcohol, histamine, nicotine, adrenocorticotropic steroids, insulin, parasympathetic agents, belladonna alkaloids, anticholinergic drugs, histamine receptor antagonists) should be restricted by medical direction for 72 hr before the test.

▶ Instruct the patient to fast from food after the evening meal the night before the test and not to drink water for 1 hr before the test. Instruct the patient to refrain from the use of chewing gum or tobacco products for at least 12 hr prior to and for the duration of the test. Protocols may vary among facilities.

▶ *Make sure a written and informed consent has been signed prior to the procedure and before administering any medications.*

INTRATEST:

▶ Ensure that the patient has complied with dietary restrictions and other pretesting preparations; ensure that food has been restricted for at least 12 hr prior to the procedure.

▶ If the patient has a history of allergic reaction to latex, avoid the use of equipment containing latex.

▶ Ensure that the patient does not have a history of asthma, paroxysmal hypertension, urticaria, or other allergic conditions if histamine diphosphate is being considered for use in the test.

▶ Record baseline vital signs.

▶ If the patient is wearing dentures, have him or her remove them.

▶ Ask the patient to sit, or help the patient recline on the left side.

▶ Instruct the patient to cooperate fully and to follow directions. Direct the

patient to breathe normally and to avoid unnecessary movement.

▶ Observe standard precautions, and follow the general guidelines in Appendix A. Positively identify the patient, and label the appropriate specimen container with the corresponding patient demographics, initials of the person collecting the specimen, date, and time of collection.

▶ A cold lubricated gastric (Levine) tube is inserted orally. Alternatively, if the patient has a hyperactive gag reflex, the tube can be inserted nasally. The tube must have a radiopaque tip.

▶ Fluoroscopy or x-ray is used to confirm proper position of the tube before the start of the test.

▶ Using a constant but gentle suction, gastric contents are collected. Do not use specimens obtained from the first 15 to 30 min of suctioning.

▶ The gastric stimulant is administered, and the peak basal specimens are collected over a 60-min period as four 15-min specimens. Number the specimen tubes in the order in which they were collected.

▶ Promptly transport the specimen to the laboratory for processing and analysis.

POST-TEST:

▶ A report of the results will be sent to the requesting health-care provider (HCP), who will discuss the results with the patient.

▶ Instruct the patient to resume usual diet and medication, as directed by the HCP.

▶ Monitor vital signs and neurological status every 15 min for 1 hr, then every 2 hr for 4 hr, and then as ordered by the HCP for evaluation. Protocols may vary among facilities.

▶ Instruct the patient to report any chest pain, upper abdominal pain, pain on swallowing, difficulty breathing, or expectoration of blood. Report these to the HCP immediately.

▶ Monitor for side effects of drugs administered to induce gastric secretion (e.g., flushing, headache, nasal stuffiness, dizziness, faintness, nausea).

▶ *Nutritional Considerations:* Nutritional support with calcium, iron, and vitamin B_{12} supplementation may be ordered, as appropriate. Dietary modifications may include encouraging liquids and low-residue foods, eating multiple small meals throughout the day, and avoidance of foods that slow digestion such as foods high in fat and fiber. Severe cases of gastroparesis may require temporary treatments that include total parenteral nutrition or use of jejunostomy tubes.

▶ Recognize anxiety related to test results. Discuss the implications of abnormal test results on the patient's lifestyle. Provide teaching and information regarding the clinical implications of the test results, as appropriate.

▶ Reinforce information given by the patient's HCP regarding further testing, treatment, or referral to another HCP. Answer any questions or address any concerns voiced by the patient or family.

▶ Instruct the patient in the use of any ordered medications. Explain the importance of adhering to the therapy regimen. As appropriate, instruct the patient in significant side effects and systemic reactions associated with the prescribed medication. Encourage him or her to review corresponding literature provided by a pharmacist.

▶ Depending on the results of this procedure, additional testing may be performed to evaluate or monitor progression of the disease process and determine the need for a change in therapy. Evaluate test results in relation to the patient's symptoms and other tests performed.

RELATED MONOGRAPHS:

▶ Related tests include capsule endoscopy, CBC, CBC RBC indices, CBC RBC morphology, CBC WBC count and differential, endoscopy sinus, esophagogastroduodenoscopy, fecal analysis, folate, gastric emptying scan, gastrin, *H. pylori* antibody, intrinsic factor antibodies, upper GI series, and vitamin B_{12}.

▶ Refer to the Gastrointestinal System table at the end of the book for related tests by body system.

Gastric Emptying Scan

SYNONYM/ACRONYM: Gastric emptying quantitation, gastric emptying scintigraphy.

COMMON USE: To visualize and assess the time frame for gastric emptying to assist in the diagnosis of diseases such as gastroenteritis and dumping syndrome.

AREA OF APPLICATION: Esophagus, stomach, small bowel.

CONTRAST: Oral radioactive technetium-99m sulfur colloid.

DESCRIPTION: A gastric emptying scan quantifies gastric emptying physiology. The procedure is indicated for patients with gastric motility symptoms, including diabetic gastroparesis, anorexia nervosa, gastric outlet obstruction syndromes, postvagotomy and postgastrectomy syndromes, and assessment of medical and surgical treatments for diseases known to affect gastric motility. A radionuclide is administered, and the clearance of solids and liquids may be evaluated. The images are recorded electronically, showing the gastric emptying function over time.

INDICATIONS
- Investigate the cause of rapid or slow rate of gastric emptying
- Measure gastric emptying rate

POTENTIAL DIAGNOSIS

Normal findings in
- Mean time emptying of liquid phase: 30 min (range, 11 to 49 min)
- Mean time emptying of solid phase: 40 min (range, 28 to 80 min)
- No delay in gastric emptying rate

Abnormal findings in
- Decreased rate:
  Dumping syndrome
  Duodenal ulcer
  Malabsorption syndromes
  Zollinger-Ellison syndrome
- Increased rate:
  Amyloidosis
  Anorexia nervosa
  Diabetes
  Gastric outlet obstruction
  Gastric ulcer
  Gastroenteritis
  Gastroesophageal reflux
  Hypokalemia, hypomagnesemia
  Post–gastric surgery period
  Postoperative ileus
  Post–radiation therapy period
  Scleroderma

CRITICAL FINDINGS: N/A

INTERFERING FACTORS

This procedure is contraindicated for
- Patients who are pregnant or suspected of being pregnant, unless the potential benefits of the procedure far outweigh the risks to the fetus and mother.
- Patients with esophageal motor disorders or swallowing difficulties.

Factors that may impair clear imaging
- Inability of the patient to cooperate or remain still during the procedure because of age, significant pain, or mental status.

- Metallic objects (e.g., jewelry, body rings) within the examination field, which may inhibit organ visualization and cause unclear images.
- Retained barium from a previous radiological procedure.
- Other nuclear scans done within the previous 24 to 48 hr.
- Administration of certain medications (e.g., gastrin, cholecystokinin), which may interfere with gastric emptying.

Other considerations
- Failure to follow dietary restrictions before the procedure may cause the procedure to be canceled or repeated.
- Consultation with a health-care provider (HCP) should occur before the procedure for radiation safety concerns regarding younger patients or patients who are lactating.
- Risks associated with radiation overexposure can result from frequent x-ray or radionuclide procedures. Personnel working in the examination area should wear badges to record their level of radiation.

NURSING IMPLICATIONS AND PROCEDURE

PRETEST:
▶ Positively identify the patient using at least two unique identifiers before providing care, treatment, or services.
▶ *Patient Teaching:* Inform the patient this procedure can assist in evaluating the time it takes for the stomach to empty.
▶ Obtain a history of the patient's complaints, including a list of known allergens, especially allergies or sensitivities to latex, iodine, seafood, contrast medium, anesthetics, or dyes.
▶ Obtain a history of the patient's gastrointestinal system, symptoms, and results of previously performed laboratory tests and diagnostic and surgical procedures.

- Note any recent procedures that can interfere with test results, including examinations using barium- or iodine-based contrast medium.
- Record the date of the last menstrual period and determine the possibility of pregnancy in perimenopausal women.
- Obtain a list of the patient's current medications, including herbs, nutritional supplements, and nutraceuticals (see Appendix F).
- Review the procedure with the patient. Address concerns about pain related to the procedure and explain that some pain may be experienced during the test, and there may be moments of discomfort. Reassure the patient that the radionuclide poses no radioactive hazard and rarely produces side effects. Inform the patient that the procedure is performed in a nuclear medicine department by an HCP specializing in this procedure, with support staff, and takes approximately 30 to 120 min.
- *Sensitivity to social and cultural issues,* as well as concern for modesty, is important in providing psychological support before, during and after the procedure.
- Instruct the patient to restrict food and fluids for 8 hr before the scan. Protocols may vary among facilities.
- Instruct the patient to remove jewelry and other metallic objects from the area to be examined.
- *Make sure a written and informed consent has been signed prior to the procedure and before administering any medications.*

INTRATEST:

- Observe standard precautions, and follow the general guidelines in Appendix A. Positively identify the patient.
- Ensure the patient has complied with dietary and fluid restrictions for 8 hr before the scan.
- Ensure that the patient has removed all external metallic objects from the area to be examined prior to the procedure.
- Instruct the patient to void prior to the procedure and to change into the gown, robe, and foot coverings provided.

- Record baseline vital signs and neurological status. Protocols may vary among facilities.
- Instruct the patient to cooperate fully and to follow directions. Instruct the patient to lie still during the procedure because movement produces unclear images.
- Administer sedative to a child or to an uncooperative adult, as ordered.
- Place the patient in an upright position in front of the gamma camera.
- Ask the patient to take the radionuclide mixed with water or other liquid orally, or combined with eggs for a solid study.
- Images are recorded over a period of time (30 to 60 min) and evaluated with regard to the amount of time the stomach takes to empty its contents.

POST-TEST:

- A report of the results will be made available to the requesting HCP, who will discuss the results with the patient.
- Advise the patient to drink increased amounts of fluids for 24 to 48 hr to eliminate the radionuclide from the body, unless contraindicated. Tell the patient that radionuclide is eliminated from the body within 6 to 24 hr.
- Monitor vital signs every 15 min for 1 hr, then every 2 hr for 4 hr, and then as ordered by the HCP. Monitor intake and output at least every 8 hr. Compare with baseline values. Protocols may vary among facilities.
- Instruct the patient to resume usual diet, fluids, medication, and activity, as directed by the HCP.
- If a woman who is breastfeeding must have a nuclear scan, she should not breastfeed the infant until the radionuclide has been eliminated. This could take as long as 3 days. She should be instructed to express the milk and discard it during the 3-day period to prevent cessation of milk production.
- Instruct the patient to immediately flush the toilet and to meticulously wash hands with soap and water after each voiding for 24 hr after the procedure.
- Instruct all caregivers to wear gloves when discarding urine for 24 hr after the procedure. Wash gloved hands with soap and water before removing

G

gloves. Then wash hands after removing the gloves.

- Recognize anxiety related to test results, and be supportive of perceived loss of independent function. Discuss the implications of abnormal test results on the patient's lifestyle. Provide teaching and information regarding the clinical implications of the test results, as appropriate.
- Reinforce information given by the patient's HCP regarding further testing, treatment, or referral to another HCP. Answer any questions or address any concerns voiced by the patient or family.
- Depending on the results of this procedure, additional testing may be needed to evaluate or monitor progression of the disease process and determine the need for a change

in therapy. Evaluate test results in relation to the patient's symptoms and other tests performed.

RELATED MONOGRAPHS:

- Related tests include barium swallow, biopsy kidney, biopsy liver, biopsy lung, calcitonin stimulation, calcium, capsule endoscopy, CT abdomen, esophageal manometry, EGD, fecal analysis, gastric fluid analysis and gastric acid stimulation test, gastrin and gastrin stimulation test, GI blood loss scan, glucose, glycated hemoglobin, *H. pylori* antibodies, liver and spleen scan, magnesium, PTH, UGI and small bowel series, and vitamin B_{12}.
- Refer to the Gastrointestinal System table at the end of the book for related tests by body system.

G

Gastrin and Gastrin Stimulation Test

SYNONYM/ACRONYM: N/A.

COMMON USE: To evaluate gastric production to assist in diagnosis of gastric disease such as Zollinger-Ellison syndrome and gastric cancer.

SPECIMEN: Serum (1 mL) collected in a red- or tiger-top tube.

NORMAL FINDINGS: (Method: Immunoassay)

Age	Conventional Units	SI Units (Conventional Units × 1)
0–1 mo	70–190 pg/mL	70–190 ng/L
2 mo–15 yr	55–185 pg/mL	55–185 ng/L
16 yr and older	Less than 100 pg/mL	Less than 100 ng/L

Values represent fasting levels.

Stimulation Tests

Gastrin stimulation test with secretin; 0.4 mcg/kg by IV bolus	No response or slight increase over baseline; increase of greater than 200 pg/ml above baseline is considered abnormal

Calcium may also be used as a stimulant.

DESCRIPTION: Gastrin is a hormone secreted by the stomach and duodenum in response to vagal stimulation; the presence of food, alcohol, or calcium in the stomach; and the alkalinity of gastric secretions. After its absorption into the circulation, gastrin returns to the stomach and acts as a stimulant for acid, insulin, pepsin, and intrinsic factor secretion. Gastrin stimulation tests can be performed after a test meal or IV infusion of calcium or secretin.

INDICATIONS
- Assist in the diagnosis of gastric carcinoma, pernicious anemia, or G-cell hyperplasia
- Assist in the diagnosis of Zollinger-Ellison syndrome
- Assist in the differential diagnosis of ulcers from other gastrointestinal (GI) peptic disorders

POTENTIAL DIAGNOSIS

Increased in
- Chronic gastritis *(related to hypersecretion of gastrin, use of NSAIDs, or Helicobacter pylori infection)*
- Chronic renal failure *(related to inadequate renal excretion)*
- Gastric and duodenal ulcers *(related to hypersecretion of gastrin, use of NSAIDs, or H. pylori infection)*
- Gastric carcinoma *(related to disturbance in pH favoring alkalinity, which stimulates gastrin production)*
- G-cell hyperplasia *(hyperplastic G cells produce excessive amounts of gastrin)*
- Hyperparathyroidism *(related to hypercalcemia; calcium is a potent stimulator for the release of gastrin)*
- Pernicious anemia *(related to antibodies against gastric intrinsic factor [66% of cases] and parietal cells [80% of cases that affect the stomach's ability to secrete acid; achlorhydria is a strong stimulator of gastrin production])*
- Pyloric obstruction *(related to gastric distention, which stimulates gastrin production)*
- Retained antrum *(remaining tissue stimulates gastrin production)*
- Zollinger-Ellison syndrome *(gastrin-producing tumor)*

Decreased in
- Hypothyroidism *(related to hypocalcemia)*
- Vagotomy *(vagus nerve impulses stimulate secretion of digestive secretions; interruptions in these nerve impulses result in decreased gastrin levels)*

CRITICAL FINDINGS: N/A

INTERFERING FACTORS
- Drugs and substances that may increase gastrin levels include amino acids, catecholamines, cimetidine, insulin, morphine, omeprazole, pantoprazole, sufotidine, terbutaline, calcium products, and coffee.
- Drugs that may decrease gastrin levels include atropine, enprostil, glucagon, secretin, streptozocin, and tolbutamide.
- In some cases, protein ingestion elevates serum gastrin levels.
- Failure to follow dietary and medication restrictions before the procedure may cause the procedure to be canceled or repeated.

NURSING IMPLICATIONS AND PROCEDURE

PRETEST:
Positively identify the patient using at least two unique identifiers before providing care, treatment, or services.

Patient Teaching: Inform the patient this test can assist in diagnosing stomach disease.

Obtain a history of the patient's complaints, including a list of known allergens, especially allergies or sensitivities to latex.

Obtain a history of the patient's endocrine and gastrointestinal systems, symptoms, and results of previously performed laboratory tests and diagnostic and surgical procedures.

Note any recent procedures that can interfere with test results.

Obtain a list of the patient's current medications, including herbs, nutritional supplements, and nutraceuticals (see Appendix F).

Review the procedure with the patient. Inform the patient that multiple specimens will be collected and that each specimen collection takes approximately 5 to 10 min. Explain that pretest samples will be collected at 10 min and 1 min before administration of the stimulant. Poststimulation samples will be collected at 2, 5, 10, 15, 20, and 30 min. Address concerns about pain and explain that there may be some discomfort during the venipuncture.

Sensitivity to social and cultural issues, as well as concern for modesty, is important in providing psychological support before, during, and after the procedure.

Instruct the patient to fast for 12 hr before the test. Instruct the patient to refrain from the use of chewing gum or tobacco products for at least 4 hr prior to and for the duration of the test. Protocols may vary among facilities.

Instruct the patient to withhold medications and alcohol for 12 to 24 hr, as ordered by the health-care provider (HCP).

There are no fluid restrictions unless by medical direction.

Make sure a written and informed consent has been signed prior to the procedure and before administering any medications.

INTRATEST:

Ensure that the patient has complied with dietary and medication restrictions and other pretesting preparations; ensure that food and medications have been withheld for at least 4 and 12 hr, respectively, prior to the procedure. The patient should be reminded to refrain from use of chewing gum or tobacco products during the test.

If the patient has a history of allergic reaction to latex, avoid the use of equipment containing latex.

Instruct the patient to cooperate fully and to follow directions. Direct the patient to breathe normally and to avoid unnecessary movement.

Administer gastrin stimulators as appropriate.

Observe standard precautions, and follow the general guidelines in Appendix A. Positively identify the patient, and label the appropriate specimen container with the corresponding patient demographics, initials of the person collecting the specimen, date, and time of collection. Perform a venipuncture.

Remove the needle and apply direct pressure with dry gauze to stop bleeding. Observe/assess venipuncture site for bleeding or hematoma formation and secure gauze with adhesive bandage.

Promptly transport the specimen to the laboratory for processing and analysis.

POST-TEST:

A report of the results will be made available to the requesting HCP, who will discuss the results with the patient.

Instruct the patient to resume usual diet and medications, as directed by the HCP.

Nutritional Considerations: Nutritional support with calcium, iron, and vitamin B_{12} supplementation may be ordered, as appropriate. Dietary modifications may include encouraging liquids and low-residue foods, eating multiple small meals throughout the day, and avoidance of foods that slow digestion such as foods high in fat and fiber. Severe cases of gastroparesis may require temporary treatments that include total parenteral nutrition or use of jejunostomy tubes.

Reinforce information given by the patient's HCP regarding further testing,

treatment, or referral to another HCP. Answer any questions or address any concerns voiced by the patient or family. Instruct the patient in the use of any ordered medications. Explain the importance of adhering to the therapy regimen. As appropriate, instruct the patient in the significant side effects and systemic reactions associated with the prescribed medication. Encourage him or her to review corresponding literature provided by a pharmacist.

Depending on the results of this procedure, additional testing may be performed to evaluate or monitor progression of the disease process and determine the need for a change in therapy. Evaluate test results in relation to the patient's symptoms and other tests performed.

RELATED MONOGRAPHS:

Related tests include capsule endoscopy, CBC, CBC RBC indices, CBC RBC morphology, CBC WBC count and differential, esophagogastroduodenoscopy, fecal analysis, folate, gastric acid stimulation test, gastric emptying scan, *H. pylori* antibody, intrinsic factor antibodies, upper GI series, and vitamin B_{12}.

Refer to the Endocrine and Gastrointestinal systems tables at the end of the book for related tests by body system.

G

Gastroesophageal Reflux Scan

SYNONYM/ACRONYM: Aspiration scan, GER scan, GERD scan.

COMMON USE: To assess for gastric reflux in relation to heartburn, difficulty swallowing, vomiting, and aspiration.

AREA OF APPLICATION: Esophagus and stomach.

CONTRAST: Oral radioactive technetium-99m sulfur colloid.

DESCRIPTION: The gastroesophageal reflux (GER) scan assesses gastric reflux across the esophageal sphincter. Symptoms of GER include heartburn, regurgitation, vomiting, dysphagia, and a bitter taste in the mouth. This procedure may be used to evaluate the medical or surgical treatment of patients with GER and to detect aspiration of gastric contents into the lungs. A radionuclide such as technetium-99m sulfur colloid is ingested orally in orange juice. Scanning studies are done immediately to assess the amount of liquid that has reached the stomach. An abdominal binder is applied and then tightened gradually to obtain images at increasing degrees of abdominal pressure: 0, 20, 40, 60, 80, and 100 mm Hg. Computer calculation determines the amount of reflux into the esophagus at each of these abdominal pressures as recorded on the images. For aspiration scans, images are taken over the lungs to detect tracheoesophageal aspiration of the radionuclide.

In infants, the study distinguishes between vomiting and reflux. Reflux occurs predominantly in infants younger than age 2 who are mainly on a milk diet. This procedure is indicated when an infant has symptoms such as failure to thrive, feeding problems, and episodes of wheezing with chest infection. The radionuclide is added to the infant's milk, images are obtained of the gastric and esophageal area, and the images are evaluated visually and by computer.

INDICATIONS

- Aid in the diagnosis of GER in patients with unexplained nausea and vomiting
- Distinguish between vomiting and reflux in infants with failure to thrive, feeding problems, and wheezing combined with chest infection

POTENTIAL DIAGNOSIS

Normal findings in
- Reflux less than or equal to 4% across the esophageal sphincter

Abnormal findings in
- Reflux of greater than 4% at any pressure level
- Pulmonary aspiration

CRITICAL FINDINGS: N/A

INTERFERING FACTORS

This procedure is contraindicated for
- Patients who are pregnant or suspected of being pregnant, unless the potential benefits of the procedure far outweigh the risks to the fetus and mother.
- Patients with hiatal hernia, esophageal motor disorders, or swallowing difficulties.

Factors that may impair clear imaging
- Inability of the patient to cooperate or remain still during the procedure because of age, significant pain, or mental status.
- Metallic objects (e.g., jewelry, body rings, dentures) within the examination field, which may inhibit organ visualization and cause unclear images.
- Retained barium from a previous radiological procedure.
- Other nuclear scans done within the previous 24 to 48 hr.

Other considerations
- Failure to follow dietary restrictions before the procedure may cause the procedure to be canceled or repeated.
- Consultation with a health-care provider (HCP) should occur before the procedure for radiation safety concerns regarding younger patients or patients who are lactating.
- Risks associated with radiation overexposure can result from frequent x-ray or radionuclide procedures. Personnel working in the examination area should wear badges to record their level of radiation.

NURSING IMPLICATIONS AND PROCEDURE

PRETEST:

- Positively identify the patient using at least two unique identifiers before providing care, treatment, or services.
- *Patient Teaching:* Inform the patient this procedure can assist in evaluating stomach reflux.
- Obtain a history of the patient's complaints, including a list of known allergens (especially allergies or sensitivities to latex, iodine, seafood, contrast medium, anesthetics, or dyes).
- Obtain a history of the patient's gastrointestinal system, symptoms, and results of previously performed

laboratory tests and diagnostic and surgical procedures.

‣ Note any recent procedures that can interfere with test results, including examinations using barium- or iodine-based contrast medium.

‣ Record the date of the last menstrual period and determine the possibility of pregnancy in perimenopausal women.

‣ Obtain a list of the patient's current medications, including herbs, nutritional supplements, and nutraceuticals (see Appendix F).

‣ Review the procedure with the patient. Address concerns about pain related to the procedure and explain that some pain may be experienced during the test, or there may be moments of discomfort. Reassure the patient that the radionuclide poses no radioactive hazard and rarely produces side effects. Inform the patient that the procedure is performed in a nuclear medicine department by an HCP specializing in this procedure, with support staff, and takes approximately 30 to 60 min.

‣ *Sensitivity to social and cultural issues,* as well as concern for modesty, is important in providing psychological support before, during, and after the procedure.

‣ Instruct the patient to remove jewelry and other metallic objects from the area to be examined.

‣ There are no food or fluid restrictions unless by medical direction.

‣ *Make sure a written and informed consent has been signed prior to the procedure and before administering any medications.*

INTRATEST:

‣ Observe standard precautions, and follow the general guidelines in Appendix A. Positively identify the patient.

‣ Ensure that the patient has removed all external metallic objects from the area to be examined prior to the procedure.

‣ Have emergency equipment readily available.

‣ Instruct the patient to void prior to the procedure and to change into the gown, robe, and foot coverings provided.

‣ Record baseline vital signs and assess neurological status. Protocols may vary among facilities.

‣ Instruct the patient to cooperate fully and to follow directions. Instruct the patient to remain still throughout the procedure because movement produces unreliable results.

‣ Administer a sedative to a child or to an uncooperative adult, as ordered.

‣ Place the patient in an upright position and instruct him or her to ingest the radionuclide combined with orange juice.

‣ Place the patient in a supine position on a flat table 15 min after ingestion

‣ An abdominal binder with an attached sphygmomanometer is applied, and scans are taken as the binder is tightened at various pressures.

‣ If reflux occurs at lower pressures, an additional 30 mL of water may be given to clear the esophagus.

‣ Instruct the patient to take slow, deep breaths if nausea occurs during the procedure. Monitor and administer an antiemetic agent if ordered. Ready an emesis basin for use.

‣ Monitor the patient for complications related to the procedure (e.g., allergic reaction, anaphylaxis, bronchospasm).

POST-TEST:

‣ A report of the results will be made available to the requesting HCP, who will discuss the results with the patient.

‣ Advise the patient to drink increased amounts of fluids for 24 to 48 hr to eliminate the radionuclide from the body unless contraindicated. Tell the patient that radionuclide is eliminated from the body within 6 to 24 hr.

‣ Monitor vital signs and neurological status every 15 min for 1 hr, then every 2 hr for 4 hr, and then as ordered by the HCP. Monitor intake and output at least every 8 hr. Compare with baseline values. Protocols may vary among facilities.

‣ Instruct the patient to resume usual diet, fluids, medication, and activity, as directed by the HCP.

‣ No other radionuclide tests should be scheduled for 24 to 48 hr after this procedure.

G

If a woman who is breastfeeding must have a nuclear scan, she should not breastfeed the infant until the radionuclide has been eliminated. This could take as long as 3 days. She should be instructed to express the milk and discard it during the 3-day period to prevent cessation of milk production.

Instruct the patient to immediately flush the toilet and to meticulously wash hands with soap and water after each voiding for 24 hr after the procedure.

Instruct all caregivers to wear gloves when discarding urine for 24 hr after the procedure. Wash gloved hands with soap and water before removing gloves. Then wash hands after the gloves are removed.

Nutritional Considerations: A low-fat, low-cholesterol, and low-sodium diet should be consumed to reduce current disease processes. High fat consumption increases the amount of bile acids in the colon and should be avoided.

Recognize anxiety related to test results, and be supportive of expected changes in lifestyle. Discuss the implications of abnormal test results on the patient's lifestyle. Provide teaching and information regarding the clinical implications of the test results, as appropriate.

Reinforce information given by the patient's HCP regarding further testing, treatment, or referral to another HCP. Answer any questions or address any concerns voiced by the patient or family.

Depending on the results of this procedure, additional testing may be needed to evaluate or monitor progression of the disease process and determine the need for a change in therapy. Evaluate test results in relation to the patient's symptoms and other tests performed.

RELATED MONOGRAPHS:

Related tests include CT abdomen, esophageal manometry, gastric emptying scan, and upper GI series.

Refer to the Gastrointestinal System table at the end of the book for related tests by body system.

Gastrointestinal Blood Loss Scan

SYNONYM/ACRONYM: Gastrointestinal bleed localization study, GI scintigram, GI bleed scintigraphy, lower GI blood loss scan.

COMMON USE: To detect areas of active gastrointestinal bleeding or hemorrhage to facilitate surgical intervention or medical treatment. Usefulness is limited in emergency situations because of time constraints in performing the scan.

AREA OF APPLICATION: Abdomen.

CONTRAST: IV radioactive technetium-99m-labeled red blood cells.

DESCRIPTION: Gastrointestinal (GI) blood loss scan is a nuclear medicine study that assists in detecting and localizing active GI tract bleeding (2 or 3 mL/min) for the purpose of better directing endoscopic or angiographic studies. This procedure can detect bleeding if the rate is greater than 0.5 mL/min, but it is not specific for site localization or cause of bleeding. Endoscopy is the procedure of choice for diagnosing upper GI bleeding. After injection of technetium-99m-labeled red blood cells, immediate and delayed images of various views of the abdomen are obtained. The radionuclide remains in the circulation long enough to extravasate and accumulate within the bowel lumen at the site of active bleeding. This procedure is valuable for the detection and localization of recent non-GI intra-abdominal hemorrhage. Images may be taken over an extended period to show intermittent bleeding.

INDICATIONS
- Diagnose unexplained abdominal pain and GI bleeding

POTENTIAL DIAGNOSIS

Normal findings in
- Normal distribution of radionuclide in the large vessels with no extravascular activity

Abnormal findings in
- Angiodysplasia
- Aortoduodenal fistula
- Diverticulosis
- GI bleeding
- Inflammatory bowel disease
- Polyps
- Tumor
- Ulcer

CRITICAL FINDINGS
- Acute GI bleed

It is essential that critical diagnoses be communicated immediately to the appropriate health-care provider (HCP). A listing of these diagnoses varies among facilities. Note and immediately report to the HCP abnormal results and related symptoms. Timely notification of critical values for lab or diagnostic studies is a role

expectation of the professional nurse. Notification processes will vary among facilities. Upon receipt of the critical value the information should be read back to the caller to verify accuracy. Most policies require immediate notification of the primary HCP, hospitalist, or on-call HCP. Reported information includes the patient's name, unique identifiers, critical value, name of the person giving the report, and name of the person receiving the report. Documentation of notification should be made in the medical record with the name of the HCP notified, time and date of notification, and any orders received. Any delay in a timely report of a critical value may require completion of a notification form with review by Risk Management.

INTERFERING FACTORS

This procedure is contraindicated for
- Patients who are pregnant or suspected of being pregnant, unless the potential benefits of the procedure far outweigh the risks to the fetus and mother.

Factors that may impair clear imaging
- Inability of the patient to cooperate or remain still during the procedure because of age, significant pain, or mental status.
- Retained barium from a previous radiological procedure.
- Metallic objects (e.g., jewelry, body rings) within the examination field, which may inhibit organ visualization and cause unclear images.
- Other nuclear scans done within the previous 24 to 48 hr.
- Inaccurate timing of imaging after the radionuclide injection.

Other considerations
- The examination detects only active or intermittent bleeding.

- The procedure is of little value in patients with chronic anemia or slowly decreasing hematocrit.
- The scan is less accurate for localization of bleeding sites in the upper GI tract.
- Improper injection of the radionuclide allows the tracer to seep deep into the muscle tissue, producing erroneous hot spots.
- The test is not specific, does not indicate the exact pathological condition causing the bleeding, and may miss small sites of bleeding (less than 0.5 mL/min) caused by diverticular disease or angiodysplasia.
- Physiologically unstable patients may be unable to be scanned over long periods or may need to go to surgery before the procedure is complete.
- Consultation with an HCP should occur before the procedure for radiation safety concerns regarding younger patients or patients who are lactating.
- Risks associated with radiation overexposure can result from frequent x-ray or radionuclide procedures. Personnel working in the examination area should wear badges to record their level of radiation exposure.

NURSING IMPLICATIONS AND PROCEDURE

PRETEST:

▶ Positively identify the patient using at least two unique identifiers before providing care, treatment, or services.
▶ *Patient Teaching:* Inform the patient this procedure can assist in evaluating for stomach and intestinal bleeding.
▶ Obtain a history of the patient's complaints, including a list of known allergens, especially allergies or sensitivities to latex, iodine, seafood, contrast medium, anesthetics, or dyes.
▶ Obtain a history of the patient's gastrointestinal system, symptoms,

and results of previously performed laboratory tests and diagnostic and surgical procedures.
▶ Note any recent procedures that can interfere with test results, including examinations using barium- or iodine-based contrast medium.
▶ Record the date of the last menstrual period and determine the possibility of pregnancy in perimenopausal women.
▶ Obtain a list of the patient's current medications, including herbs, nutritional supplements, and nutraceuticals (see Appendix F).
▶ Review the procedure with the patient. Address concerns about pain related to the procedure and explain that some pain may be experienced during the test, or there may be moments of discomfort. Reassure the patient that the radionuclide poses no radioactive hazard and rarely produces side effects. Inform the patient that the procedure is performed in a nuclear medicine department by an HCP specializing in this procedure, with support staff, and takes approximately 60 min to complete, with additional images taken periodically over 24 hr.
▶ Explain that an IV line may be inserted to allow infusion of IV fluids, contrast medium, or sedatives. Usually normal saline is infused.
▶ *Sensitivity to social and cultural issues,* as well as concern for modesty, is important in providing psychological support before, during, and after the procedure.
▶ Instruct the patient to remove jewelry and other metallic objects from the area to be examined.
▶ There are no food or fluid restrictions unless by medical direction.
▶ *Make sure a written and informed consent has been signed prior to the procedure and before administering any medications.*

INTRATEST:

▶ Observe standard precautions, and follow the general guidelines in Appendix A. Positively identify the patient.
▶ Ensure that the patient has removed all external metallic objects from the area to be examined prior to the procedure.

Instruct the patient to void prior to the procedure and to change into the gown, robe, and foot coverings provided.

Record baseline vital signs and assess neurological status. Protocols may vary among facilities.

Have emergency equipment readily available.

Instruct the patient to cooperate fully and to follow directions. Instruct the patient to remain still throughout the procedure because movement produces unreliable results.

Administer a sedative to a child or to an uncooperative adult, as ordered.

Establish IV fluid line for the injection of emergency drugs, radionuclide, and sedatives.

Place the patient in a supine position on a flat table with foam wedges to help maintain position and immobilization.

The radionuclide is administered IV, and images are recorded immediately and every 5 min over a period of 60 min in various positions.

The needle or catheter is removed, and a pressure dressing is applied over the puncture site.

Observe/assess the needle/catheter insertion site for bleeding, inflammation, or hematoma formation.

POST-TEST:

A report of the results will be made available to the requesting HCP, who will discuss the results with the patient.

Advise the patient to drink increased amounts of fluids for 24 to 48 hr to eliminate the radionuclide from the body, unless contraindicated. Tell the patient that radionuclide is eliminated from the body within 6 to 24 hr.

Monitor vital signs and neurological status every 15 min for 1 hr, then every 2 hr for 4 hr, and then as ordered by the HCP. Monitor intake and output at least every 8 hr. Compare with baseline values. Protocols may vary among facilities.

No other radionuclide tests should be scheduled for 24 to 48 hr after this procedure.

Instruct the patient to resume usual diet, fluids, medication, and activity, as directed by the HCP.

Instruct the patient in the care and assessment of the injection site.

If a woman who is breastfeeding must have a nuclear scan, she should not breastfeed the infant until the radionuclide has been eliminated. This could take as long as 3 days. She should be instructed to express the milk and discard it during the 3-day period to prevent cessation of milk production.

Instruct the patient to immediately flush the toilet and to meticulously wash hands with soap and water after each voiding for 24 hr after the procedure.

Instruct all caregivers to wear gloves when discarding urine for 24 hr after the procedure. Wash gloved hands with soap and water before removing gloves. Then wash hands after the gloves are removed.

Nutritional Considerations: A low-fat, low-cholesterol, and low-sodium diet should be consumed to reduce current disease processes. High fat consumption increases the amount of bile acids in the colon and should be avoided.

Recognize anxiety related to test results, and be supportive of perceived loss of independent function. Discuss the implications of abnormal test results on the patient's lifestyle. Provide teaching and information regarding the clinical implications of the test results, as appropriate.

Reinforce information given by the patient's HCP regarding further testing, treatment, or referral to another HCP. Answer any questions or address any concerns voiced by the patient or family.

Depending on the results of this procedure, additional testing may be needed to evaluate or monitor progression of the disease process and determine the need for a change in therapy. Evaluate test results in relation to the patient's symptoms and other tests performed.

RELATED MONOGRAPHS:

Related tests include antibodies antineutrophilic cytoplasmic, angiography abdomen, barium enema, barium swallow, cancer antigens, capsule endoscopy, colonoscopy, CBC, CBC hematocrit, CBC hemoglobin, CT abdomen, EGD, fecal analysis, IgA, MRI abdomen, Meckel's diverticulum scan, proctosigmoidoscopy, upper GI series, and WBC scan.

Refer to the Gastrointestinal System table at the end of the book for related tests by body system.

Glucagon

SYNONYM/ACRONYM: N/A.

COMMON USE: To evaluate the amount of circulating glucagon toward diagnosing diseases such as hypoglycemia, pancreatic cancer, or inflammation.

SPECIMEN: Plasma (1 mL) collected in chilled, lavender-top (EDTA) tube. Specimen should be transported tightly capped and in an ice slurry.

NORMAL FINDINGS: (Method: Radioimmunoassay)

Age	Conventional Units	SI Units (Conventional Units × 1)
Cord blood	0–215 pg/mL	0–215 ng/L
Newborn	0–1,750 pg/mL	0–1,750 ng/L
Child	0–148 pg/mL	0–148 ng/L
Adult	20–100 pg/mL	20–100 ng/L

DESCRIPTION: Glucagon is a hormone secreted by the alpha cells of the islets of Langerhans in the pancreas in response to hypoglycemia. This hormone acts primarily on the liver to promote glucose production from glycogen stores and to control glycogen storage. Glucagon also produces glucose from the oxidation of fatty acids like triglycerides to basic glycerol components. The coordinated release of insulin, glucagon, and somatostatin ensures an adequate fuel supply while maintaining stable blood glucose. Patients with glucagonoma have values greater than 500 ng/L. Values greater than 1,000 ng/L are diagnostic for this condition. Glucagonoma causes three different syndromes:

Syndrome 1: A characteristic skin rash, diabetes or impaired glucose tolerance, weight loss, anemia, and venous thrombosis
Syndrome 2: Severe diabetes
Syndrome 3: Multiple endocrine neoplasia

A dramatic increase in glucagon occurring soon after renal transplant may indicate organ rejection. In the case of kidney transplant rejection, glucagon levels increase several days before an increase in creatinine levels.

Glucagon deficiency can be confirmed by measuring glucagon

levels before and after IV infusion of arginine 0.5 g/kg. Glucagon deficiency is confirmed when levels fail to rise 30 to 60 min after infusion. Newborn infants of diabetic mothers have impaired glucagon secretion, which may play a role in their hypoglycemia.

INDICATIONS

* Assist in confirming glucagon deficiency
* Assist in the diagnosis of suspected glucagonoma (alpha islet-cell neoplastic tumor)
* Assist in the diagnosis of suspected renal failure or renal transplant rejection

POTENTIAL DIAGNOSIS

Increased in

Glucagon is produced in the pancreas and excreted by the kidneys; conditions that affect the pancreas and cause cellular destruction or conditions that impair the ability of the kidneys to remove glucagon from circulation will result in elevated glucagon levels.

* Acromegaly *(related to stimulated production of glucagon in response to growth hormone)*
* Acute pancreatitis *(related to decreased pancreatic function)*
* Burns *(related to stress-induced release of catecholamines, which stimulates glucagon production)*
* Cirrhosis *(pathophysiology is not well established)*
* Cushing's syndrome *(evidenced by overproduction of cortisol, which stimulates glucagon production)*
* Diabetes (uncontrolled) *(pathophysiology is not well established)*
* Glucagonoma *(related to excessive production by the tumor)*
* Hyperlipoproteinemia *(pathophysiology is not well established)*
* Hypoglycemia *(related to response to decreased glucose level)*
* Infection *(related to feedback loop in response to stress)*
* Kidney transplant rejection *(related to decreased renal excretion)*
* Pheochromocytoma *(excessive production of catecholamines stimulates increased glucagon levels)*
* Renal failure *(related to decreased renal excretion)*
* Stress *(related to stress-induced release of catecholamines, which stimulates glucagon production)*
* Trauma *(related to stress-induced release of catecholamines, which stimulates glucagon production)*

Decreased in

Low glucagon levels are related to decreased pancreatic function.
* Chronic pancreatitis
* Cystic fibrosis
* Postpancreatectomy period

CRITICAL FINDINGS: N/A

INTERFERING FACTORS

* Drugs that may increase glucagon levels include amino acids (e.g., arginine), cholecystokinin, danazol, gastrin, glucocorticoids, insulin, and nifedipine.
* Drugs that may decrease glucagon levels include atenolol, pindolol, propranolol, secretin, and verapamil.
* Recent radioactive scans or radiation within 1 wk before the test can interfere with test results when radioimmunoassay is the test method.
* Failure to follow dietary restrictions before the procedure may cause the procedure to be canceled or repeated.

NURSING IMPLICATIONS AND PROCEDURE

PRETEST:

- Positively identify the patient using at least two unique identifiers before providing care, treatment, or services.
- *Patient Teaching:* Inform the patient this test can assist in evaluating the hormone that participates in regulating blood sugar.
- Obtain a history of the patient's complaints, including a list of known allergens, especially allergies or sensitivities to latex.
- Obtain a history of the patient's endocrine system, symptoms, and results of previously performed laboratory tests and diagnostic and surgical procedures.
- Note any recent procedures that can interfere with test results.
- Obtain a list of the patient's current medications, including herbs, nutritional supplements, and nutraceuticals (see Appendix F).
- Review the procedure with the patient. Inform the patient that specimen collection takes approximately 5 to 10 min. Address concerns about pain and explain that there may be some discomfort during the venipuncture.
- *Sensitivity to social and cultural issues,* as well as concern for modesty, is important in providing psychological support before, during, and after the procedure.
- Instruct the patient to fast for at least 12 hr before specimen collection for baseline values. Diabetic patients should be in good glycemic control before testing.
- Prepare an ice slurry in a cup or plastic bag to have ready for immediate transport of the specimen to the laboratory. Prechill the lavender-top tube in the ice slurry.

INTRATEST:

- Ensure that the patient has complied with dietary restrictions; ensure that food has been restricted for at least 12 hr prior to the procedure.

- If the patient has a history of allergic reaction to latex, avoid the use of equipment containing latex.
- Instruct the patient to cooperate fully and to follow directions. Direct the patient to breathe normally and to avoid unnecessary movement.
- Observe standard precautions, and follow the general guidelines in Appendix A. Positively identify the patient, and label the appropriate specimen container with the corresponding patient demographics, initials of the person collecting the specimen, date, and time of collection. Perform a venipuncture; collect the specimen in a chilled tube. The sample should be placed in an ice slurry immediately after collection.
- Information on the specimen label should be protected from water in the ice slurry by first placing the specimen in a protective plastic bag.
- Remove the needle and apply direct pressure with dry gauze to stop bleeding. Observe/assess venipuncture site for bleeding or hematoma formation and secure gauze with adhesive bandage.
- Promptly transport the specimen to the laboratory for processing and analysis.

POST-TEST:

- A report of the results will be made available to the requesting health-care provider (HCP), who will discuss the results with the patient.
- Instruct the patient to resume usual diet, as directed by the HCP.
- *Nutritional Considerations:* Abnormal results may be associated with diabetes. There is no "diabetic diet"; however, many meal-planning approaches with nutritional goals are endorsed by the American Dietetic Association. Patients who adhere to dietary recommendations report a better general feeling of health, better weight management, greater control of glucose and lipid values, and improved use of insulin. Instruct the patient, as appropriate, in nutritional management of diabetes. The American Heart Association's Therapeutic Lifestyle Changes (TLC) diet provides goals

directed at people with specific risk factors and/or existing medical conditions (e.g., elevated LDL cholesterol levels, other lipid disorders, coronary artery disease, insulin-dependent diabetes, insulin resistance, or metabolic syndrome). The TLC approach also includes the use of plant stanols or sterols and increased dissolved fiber as an option for lowering LDL cholesterol levels; nutritional recommendations for daily total caloric intake; recommendations for allowable percentage of calories derived from fat (saturated and unsaturated), carbohydrates, protein, and cholesterol; as well as recommendations for daily expenditure of energy. The nutritional needs of each diabetic patient need to be determined individually (especially during pregnancy) with the appropriate HCPs, particularly professionals trained in nutrition. Increased glucagon levels may be associated with diabetes. Instruct the patient and caregiver to report signs and symptoms of hypoglycemia (weakness, confusion, diaphoresis, rapid pulse) or hyperglycemia (thirst, polyuria, hunger, lethargy).

Recognize anxiety related to test results, and be supportive of perceived loss of independence and fear of shortened life expectancy. Discuss the implications of abnormal test results on the patient's lifestyle. Provide teaching and information regarding the clinical implications of the test results, as appropriate. Emphasize, if indicated,

that good glycemic control delays the onset and slows the progression of diabetic retinopathy, nephropathy, and neuropathy. Educate the patient regarding access to counseling services, as appropriate. Provide contact information, if desired, for the American Diabetes Association (www.diabetes.org) or the American Heart Association (www.americanheart.org).

Reinforce information given by the patient's HCP regarding further testing, treatment, or referral to another HCP. Answer any questions or address any concerns voiced by the patient or family.

Depending on the results of this procedure, additional testing may be performed to evaluate or monitor progression of the disease process and determine the need for a change in therapy. Evaluate test results in relation to the patient's symptoms and other tests performed.

RELATED MONOGRAPHS:

Related tests include angiography adrenal, catecholamines, cholangio-pancreatography endoscopic retrograde, CT cardiac scoring, CT pancreas, CT renal, C peptide, gastric emptying scan, glucose, GTT, glycated hemoglobin, GH, HVA, insulin, insulin antibodies, MRI pancreas, metanephrines, microalbumin, peritoneal fluid analysis, and US pancreas.

Refer to the Endocrine System table at the end of the book for related tests by body system.

Glucose

SYNONYM/ACRONYM: Blood sugar, fasting blood sugar (FBS), postprandial glucose, 2-hr PC.

COMMON USE: To assist in the diagnosis of diabetes and to evaluate disorders of carbohydrate metabolism such as malabsorption syndrome.

SPECIMEN: Serum (1 mL) collected in a red- or tiger-top tube, although plasma is recommended for diagnosis of diabetes. Plasma (1 mL) collected in a gray-top (sodium fluoride) or a green-top (heparin) tube.

NORMAL FINDINGS: (Method: Spectrophotometry)

Age	Conventional Units	SI Units (Conventional Units × 0.0555)
Fasting		
Cord blood	45–96 mg/dL	2.5–5.3 mmol/L
Premature infant	20–80 mg/dL	1.1–4.4 mmol/L
Newborn 2 days–2 yr	30–100 mg/dL	1.7–5.6 mmol/L
Child	60–100 mg/dL	3.3–5.6 mmol/L
Adult-older adult	Less than 100 mg/dL	Less than 5.6 mmol/L
Prediabetes or impaired fasting glucose	100–125 mg/dL	5.6–6.9 mmol/L
2-hr postprandial	65–139 mg/dL	3.6–7.7 mmol/L
Prediabetes or impaired 2-hr sample	140–199 mg/dL	7.8–11 mmol/L
Random	Less than 200 mg/dL	Less than 11.1 mmol/L

The American Diabetes Association and National Institute of Diabetes and Digestive and Kidney Diseases consider a confirmed fasting blood glucose greater than 126 mg/dL to be consistent with a diagnosis of diabetes. Values tend to increase in older adults.

DESCRIPTION: Glucose, a simple six-carbon sugar (monosaccharide), enters the diet as part of the sugars sucrose, lactose, and maltose and as the major constituent of the complex polysaccharide called dietary starch. The body acquires most of its energy from the oxidative metabolism of glucose. Excess glucose is stored in the liver or in muscle tissue as glycogen.

Diabetes is a group of diseases characterized by hyperglycemia, or elevated glucose levels. Hyperglycemia results from a defect in insulin secretion (type 1 diabetes), a defect in insulin action, or a combination of defects in secretion and action (type 2 diabetes). The chronic hyperglycemia of diabetes may result over time in damage, dysfunction, and eventually failure of the eyes, kidneys, nerves, heart, and blood vessels. The American Diabetes Association and National Institute of Diabetes and Digestive and Kidney Disease have established criteria for diagnosing diabetes to include any combination of the following findings or confirmation of any of the individual findings by repetition on a subsequent day:

Symptoms of diabetes (e.g., polyuria, polydipsia, unexplained weight loss) in addition to a random glucose level greater than 200 mg/dL
Fasting blood glucose greater than 126 mg/dL after a minimum of an 8-hr fast
Glucose level greater than 200 mg/dL 2 hr after glucose challenge with standardized 75-mg load

Glucose measurements have been used for many years as an indicator of short-term glycemic control to identify diabetes and assist in management of the disease. Glycated hemoglobin, or hemoglobin A_{1c}, is used to indicate long-term glycemic control over a period of several months. The estimated average glucose (eAG) is a mathematical relationship between hemoglobin A_{1c} and glucose levels expressed by the formula eAG = $(28.7 \times$ hemoglobin A_{1c}) – 46.7. Studies have documented the need for markers that reflect intermediate glycemic control, or the period of time between 2 to 4 wk as opposed to hours or months. Many patients who appear to be well controlled according to glucose and A_{1c} values actually have significant postprandial hyperglycemia. 1,5 Anhydroglucitol is a naturally occurring monosaccharide found in most foods. It is not normally metabolized by the body and is excreted by the kidneys. During periods of normal glucose levels, there is an equilibrium between glucose and 1,5 anhydroglucitol concentrations. When blood glucose concentration rises above 180 mg/dL, the renal threshold for glucose, levels of circulating 1,5 anhydroglucitol decrease due to competitive inhibition of renal tubular absorption favoring glucose over 1,5 anhydroglucitol. As

glucose is retained in the circulating blood and levels of glucose increase, correspondingly higher amounts of 1,5 anhydroglucitol are excreted in the urine. The change in 1,5 anhydroglucitol levels is directly proportional to the severity and frequency of hyperglycemic episodes. 1,5 Anhydroglucitol concentration returns to normal after 2 wk with no recurrence of hyperglycemia. The GlycoMark assay measures 1,5 anhydroglucitol and can be used in combination with glucose and hemoglobin A_{1c} measurements to provide a more complete picture of glucose levels over time. Another indicator of intermediate glycemic control is glycated albumin; values of 0.8% to 1.4% are considered normal. Reports from the medical community indicate that over half of the U.S. population will have diabetes or prediabetes by 2020. The combined use of available markers of glycemic control will greatly improve the ability to achieve tighter, more timely glycemic control.

Comparison of Markers of Glycemic Control to Approximate Blood Glucose Concentration

1,5–Anhydroglucitol Measured Using the GlycoMark Assay	Hemoglobin A_{1c}	Estimated Blood Glucose (mg/dL)	Degree of Diabetic Control
14 mcg/mL or greater	4–5%	68–97 mg/dL	Normal/nondiabetic
10–12 mcg/mL	4–6%	68–126 mg/dL	Well controlled
5–10 mcg/mL	6–8%	126–183 mg/dL	Moderately well controlled
2–5 mcg/mL	8–10%	183–240 mg/dL	Poorly controlled
Less than 2 mcg/mL	Greater than 10% (11–14%)	269–355 mg/dL	Very poorly controlled

Assessment of medications used to manage diabetes is an important facet of controlling the disease and its health-related complications. Drug response is an active area of study to ensure that the medications prescribed are meeting the needs of the patients who are taking them. Insulin and metformin are two commonly prescribed medications for the treatment of diabetes. See the "Insulin Antibodies" monograph for more detailed information. The AccuType Metformin Assay is a genetic test that identifies individuals who may not respond appropriately or have a suboptimal response to metformin related to a genetic mutation in the proteins responsible for transporting metformin.

INDICATIONS
• Assist in the diagnosis of insulinoma
• Determine insulin requirements
• Evaluate disorders of carbohydrate metabolism
• Identify hypoglycemia
• Screen for diabetes

POTENTIAL DIAGNOSIS

Increased in
• Acromegaly, gigantism *(growth hormone [GH] stimulates the release of glucagon, which in turn increases glucose levels)*
• Acute stress reaction *(hyperglycemia is stimulated by the release of catecholamines and glucagon)*
• Cerebrovascular accident *(possibly related to stress)*
• Cushing's syndrome *(related to elevated cortisol)*
• Diabetes *(glucose intolerance and elevated glucose levels define diabetes)*
• Glucagonoma *(glucagon releases stored glucose; glucagon-secreting tumors will increase glucose levels)*
• Hemochromatosis *(related to iron deposition in the pancreas; subsequent damage to pancreatic tissue releases cell contents, including glucagon, resulting in hyperglycemia)*
• Liver disease (severe) *(damaged liver tissue releases cell contents, including stored glucose, into circulation)*
• Myocardial infarction *(related to stress and/or pre-existing diabetes)*
• Pancreatic adenoma *(damage to pancreatic tissue releases cell contents, including glucagon, resulting in hyperglycemia)*
• Pancreatitis (acute and chronic) *(damage to pancreatic tissue releases cell contents, including glucagon, resulting in hyperglycemia)*
• Pancreatitis due to mumps *(damage to pancreatic tissue releases cell contents, including glucagon, resulting in hyperglycemia)*
• Pheochromocytoma *(related to increased catecholamines, which increase glucagon; glucagon increases glucose levels)*
• Renal disease (severe) *(glucagon is degraded by the kidneys; when damaged kidneys cannot metabolize glucagon, glucagon levels in blood rise and result in hyperglycemia)*
• Shock, trauma *(hyperglycemia is stimulated by the release of catecholamines and glucagon)*
• Somatostatinoma *(somatostatin-producing tumor of pancreatic delta cells, associated with diabetes)*
• Strenuous exercise *(hyperglycemia is stimulated by the release of catecholamines and glucagon)*
• Syndrome X (metabolic syndrome) *(related to the development of diabetes)*
• Thyrotoxicosis *(related to loss of kidney function)*

- Vitamin B$_1$ deficiency *(thiamine is involved in the metabolism of glucose; deficiency results in accumulation of glucose)*

Decreased in

- Acute alcohol ingestion *(most glucose metabolism occurs in the liver; alcohol inhibits the liver from making glucose)*
- Addison's disease *(cortisol affects glucose levels; insufficient levels of cortisol result in diminished glucose levels)*
- Ectopic insulin production from tumors (adrenal carcinoma, carcinoma of the stomach, fibrosarcoma)
- Excess insulin by injection
- Galactosemia *(inherited enzyme disorder that results in accumulation of galactose in excessive proportion to glucose levels)*
- Glucagon deficiency *(glucagon controls glucose levels; hypoglycemia occurs in the absence of glucagon)*
- Glycogen storage diseases *(deficiencies in enzymes involved in conversion of glycogen to glucose)*
- Hereditary fructose intolerance *(inherited disorder of fructose metabolism; phosphates needed for intermediate steps in gluconeogenesis are trapped from further action by the enzyme deficiency responsible for fructose metabolism)*
- Hypopituitarism *(decreased levels of hormones such as adrenocorticotropin hormone [ACTH] and GH result in decreased glucose levels)*
- Hypothyroidism *(thyroid hormones affect glucose levels; decreased thyroid hormone levels result in decreased glucose levels)*
- Insulinoma *(the function of insulin is to decrease glucose levels)*
- Malabsorption syndromes *(insufficient absorption of carbohydrates)*

- Maple syrup urine disease *(inborn error of amino acid metabolism; accumulation of leucine is believed to inhibit the rate of gluconeogenesis, independently of insulin, and thereby diminish release of hepatic glucose stores)*
- Poisoning resulting in severe liver disease *(decreased liver function correlates with decreased glucose metabolism)*
- Postgastrectomy *(insufficient intake of carbohydrates)*
- Starvation *(insufficient intake of carbohydrates)*
- von Gierke's disease *(most common glycogen storage disease; G6PD deficiency)*

CRITICAL FINDINGS

Glucose
Adults & children
- Less than 40 mg/dL (SI: Less than 2.22 mmol/L)
- Greater than 400 mg/dL (SI: Greater than 22.2 mmol/L)
Newborns
- Less than 32 mg/dL (SI: Less than 1.8 mmol/L)
- Greater than 328 mg/dL (SI: Greater than 18.2 mmol/L)

Note and immediately report to the health-care provider (HCP) any critically increased or decreased values and related symptoms. Timely notification of critical values for lab or diagnostic studies is a role expectation of the professional nurse. Notification processes will vary among facilities. Upon receipt of the critical value the information should be read back to the caller to verify accuracy. Most policies require immediate notification of the primary HCP, hospitalist, or on-call HCP. Reported information includes the patient's name, unique identifiers, critical value, name of the person giving the report, and name of the person receiving the report. Documentation of notification should be made in the medical record with the name of the HCP notified, time and date of notification, and any orders received. Any delay in a timely report of a critical value may require completion of a notification form with review by Risk Management.

Glucose monitoring is an important measure in achieving tight glycemic control. The enzymatic GDH-PQQ test method may produce falsely elevated results in patients who are receiving products that contain other sugars (e.g., oral xylose, parenterals containing maltose or galactose, and peritoneal dialysis solutions that contain icodextrin). The GDH-NAD, glucose oxidase, and glucose hexokinase methods can distinguish between glucose and other sugars.

Symptoms of decreased glucose levels include headache, confusion, hunger, irritability, nervousness, restlessness, sweating, and weakness. Possible interventions include oral or IV administration of glucose, IV or intramuscular injection of glucagon, and continuous glucose monitoring.

Symptoms of elevated glucose levels include abdominal pain, fatigue, muscle cramps, nausea, vomiting, polyuria, and thirst. Possible interventions include subcutaneous or IV injection of insulin with continuous glucose monitoring.

INTERFERING FACTORS
- Drugs that may increase glucose levels include acetazolamide, alanine, albuterol, anesthetic agents, antipyrine, atenolol, betamethasone, cefotaxime, chlorpromazine, chlorprothixene, clonidine, clorexolone, corticotropin, cortisone, cyclic AMP, cyclopropane, dexamethasone, dextroamphetamine, diapamide, epinephrine, enflurane, ethacrynic acid, ether, fludrocortisone, fluoxymesterone, furosemide, glucagon, glucocorticoids, homoharringtonine, hydrochlorothiazide, hydroxydione, isoniazid, maltose, meperidine, meprednisone, methyclothiazide, metolazone, niacin, nifedipine, nortriptyline, octreotide, oral contraceptives, oxyphenbutazone, pancreozymin, phenelzine, phenylbutazone, piperacetazine, polythiazide, prednisone, quinethazone, reserpine, rifampin, ritodrine, salbutamol, secretin, somatostatin, thiazides, thyroid hormone, and triamcinolone.
- Drugs that may decrease glucose levels include acarbose, acetylsalicylic acid, acipimox, alanine, allopurinol, antimony compounds, arsenicals, ascorbic acid, benzene, buformin, cannabis, captopril, carbutamide, chloroform, clofibrate, dexfenfluramine, enalapril, enprostil, erythromycin, fenfluramine, gemfibrozil, glibornuride, glyburide, guanethidine, niceritrol, nitrazepam, oral contraceptives, oxandrolone, oxymetholone, phentolamine, phosphorus, promethazine, ramipril, rotenone, sulfonylureas, thiocarlide, tolbutamide, tromethamine, and verapamil.
- Elevated urea levels and uremia can lead to falsely elevated glucose levels.
- Extremely elevated white blood cell counts can lead to falsely decreased glucose values.
- Failure to follow dietary restrictions before the fasting test can lead to falsely elevated glucose values.
- Administration of insulin or oral hypoglycemic agents within 8 hr of a fasting blood glucose can lead to falsely decreased values.
- Specimens should never be collected above an IV line because of the potential for dilution when the specimen and the IV solution combine in the collection container, falsely decreasing the result.

There is also the potential of contaminating the sample with the substance of interest, if it is present in the IV solution, falsely increasing the result.

• Failure to follow dietary restrictions before the procedure may cause the procedure to be canceled or repeated.

NURSING IMPLICATIONS AND PROCEDURE

PRETEST:

▶ Positively identify the patient using at least two unique identifiers before providing care, treatment, or services.

▶ *Patient Teaching:* Inform the patient this test can assist in evaluating blood sugar levels.

▶ Obtain a history of the patient's complaints, including a list of known allergens, especially allergies or sensitivities to latex.

▶ Obtain a history of the patient's endocrine system, symptoms, and results of previously performed laboratory tests and diagnostic and surgical procedures.

▶ Obtain a list of medications the patient is taking, including herbs, nutritional supplements, nutraceuticals (see Appendix F), insulin, and any other substances used to regulate glucose levels.

▶ Review the procedure with the patient. Inform the patient that specimen collection takes approximately 5 to 10 min. Address concerns about pain and explain that there may be some discomfort during the venipuncture.

▶ *Sensitivity to social and cultural issues,* as well as concern for modesty, is important in providing psychological support before, during, and after the procedure.

▶ For the fasting glucose test, the patient should fast for at least 12 hr before specimen collection.

▶ The patient should follow the instructions given for 2-hr postprandial glucose test. Some HCPs may order administration of a standard glucose solution, whereas others may instruct the patient to eat a meal with a known carbohydrate composition.

INTRATEST:

▶ Ensure that the patient has complied with dietary restrictions and other pretesting preparations; assure that food has been restricted for at least 12 hr prior to the fasting procedure.

▶ If the patient has a history of allergic reaction to latex, avoid the use of equipment containing latex.

▶ Instruct the patient to cooperate fully and to follow directions. Direct the patient to breathe normally and to avoid unnecessary movement.

▶ Observe standard precautions, and follow the general guidelines in Appendix A. Positively identify the patient, and label the appropriate specimen container with the corresponding patient demographics, initials of the person collecting the specimen, date, and time of collection. Perform a venipuncture.

▶ Remove the needle and apply direct pressure with dry gauze to stop bleeding. Observe/assess venipuncture site for bleeding or hematoma formation and secure gauze with adhesive bandage.

▶ Promptly transport the specimen to the laboratory for processing and analysis.

POST-TEST:

▶ A report of the results will be made available to the requesting HCP, who will discuss the results with the patient.

▶ Instruct the patient to resume usual diet, as directed by the HCP.

▶ *Nutritional Considerations:* Increased glucose levels may be associated with diabetes. There is no "diabetic diet"; however, many meal-planning approaches with nutritional goals are endorsed by the American Dietetic Association. Patients who adhere to dietary recommendations report a better general feeling of health, better weight management, greater control of glucose and lipid values, and improved use of insulin. Instruct the patient, as appropriate, in nutritional management of diabetes. The American Heart Association's Therapeutic Lifestyle Changes (TLC) diet provides goals directed at people with specific risk factors and/or existing medical conditions (e.g., elevated LDL cholesterol levels, other lipid disorders, coronary artery disease, insulin-dependent diabetes, insulin resistance, or metabolic syndrome). The TLC approach also includes the use of plant stanols or sterols and increased dissolved fiber as an option for lowering LDL cholesterol levels; nutritional recommendations for daily total caloric intake; recommendations for allowable percentage of calories derived from fat (saturated and unsaturated), carbohydrates, protein, and cholesterol; as well as recommendations for daily expenditure of energy. The nutritional needs of each diabetic patient need to be determined individually (especially during pregnancy) with the appropriate HCPs, particularly professionals trained in nutrition.

Social and Cultural Considerations:
Numerous studies point to the prevalence of excess body weight in American children and adolescents. Experts estimate that obesity is present in 25% of the population ages 6 to 11 yr. The medical, social, and emotional consequences of excess body weight are significant. Special attention should be given to instructing the child and caregiver regarding health risks and weight control education.

▸ Instruct the patient and caregiver to report signs and symptoms of hypoglycemia (weakness, confusion, diaphoresis, rapid pulse) or hyperglycemia (thirst, polyuria, hunger, lethargy).

▸ Recognize anxiety related to test results, and be supportive of perceived loss of independence and fear of shortened life expectancy. Discuss the implications of abnormal test results on the patient's lifestyle. Provide teaching and information regarding the clinical implications of the test results, as appropriate. Emphasize, if indicated, that good glycemic control delays the onset and slows the progression of diabetic retinopathy, nephropathy, and neuropathy. Educate the patient regarding access to counseling services, as appropriate. Provide

contact information, if desired, for the American Diabetes Association (ADA; www.diabetes.org) or the American Heart Association (www.americanheart.org) or the NHLBI (www.nhlbi.nih.gov). The ADA recommends A_{1C} testing 4 times a year for insulin-dependent type 1 or type 2 diabetes and twice a year for non–insulin-dependent type 2 diabetes. The ADA also recommends that testing for diabetes commence at age 45 for asymptomatic individuals and continue every 3 yr in the absence of symptoms.

▸ Reinforce information given by the patient's HCP regarding further testing, treatment, or referral to another HCP. Instruct the patient in the use of home test kits approved by the U.S. Food and Drug Administration, if prescribed. Answer any questions or address any concerns voiced by the patient or family.

▸ Depending on the results of this procedure, additional testing may be performed to evaluate or monitor progression of the disease process and determine the need for a change in therapy. Evaluate test results in relation to the patient's symptoms and other tests performed.

RELATED MONOGRAPHS:

▸ Related tests include ACTH, angiography adrenal, BUN, calcium, catecholamines, cholesterol (HDL, LDL, total), cortisol, C-peptide, CT cardiac scoring, CRP, CK and isoenzymes, creatinine, DHEA, echocardiography, fecal analysis, fecal fat, fluorescein angiography, fructosamine, fundus photography, gastric emptying scan, GTT, glycated hemoglobin A_{1C}, gonioscopy, Holter monitor, HVA, insulin, insulin antibodies, ketones, LDH and isoenzymes, lipoprotein electrophoresis, MRI chest, metanephrines, microalbumin, myoglobin, MI infarct scan, myocardial perfusion heart scan, PET heart, renin, sodium, troponin, and visual fields test.

▸ Refer to the Endocrine System table at the end of the book for related tests by body system.

Glucose-6-Phosphate Dehydrogenase

SYNONYM/ACRONYM: G6PD.

COMMON USE: To identify an enzyme deficiency that can result in hemolytic anemia.

SPECIMEN: Whole blood (1 mL) collected in a lavender-top (EDTA) tube.

NORMAL FINDINGS: (Method: Fluorescent) Qualitative assay—enzyme activity detected; quantitative assay—the following table reflects enzyme activity in units per gram of hemoglobin:

Age	Conventional Units	SI Units (Conventional Units × 0.0645)
Newborn	7.8–14.4 international units/g hemoglobin	0.5–0.93 micro units/mol hemoglobin
Adult–older adult	5.5–9.3 international units/g hemoglobin	0.35–0.60 micro units/mol hemoglobin

DESCRIPTION: Glucose-6-phosphate dehydrogenase (G6PD) is a red blood cell (RBC) enzyme. It is involved in the hexose monophosphate shunt, and its function is to protect hemoglobin from oxidation. G6PD deficiency is an inherited X-linked abnormality; approximately 20% of female carriers are heterozygous. This deficiency results in hemolysis of varying degrees and acuity depending on the severity of the abnormality. There are three G6PD variants of high frequency in different ethnic groups. G6PD A–is more common in African Americans (10% of males) than in other populations. G6PD Mediterranean is especially common in Iraqis, Kurds, Sephardic Jews, and Lebanese and less common in Greeks, Italians, Turks, North Africans, Spaniards, Portuguese, and Ashkenazi Jews. G6PD Mahidol is common in Southeast Asians (22% of males). Polymerase chain reaction (PCR) methods that can detect gene mutations for the enzyme in whole blood are also available. Counseling and written, informed consent are recommended and sometimes required before genetic testing.

INDICATIONS
- Assist in identifying the cause of hemolytic anemia resulting from drug sensitivity, metabolic disorder, or infection
- Assist in identifying the cause of hemolytic anemia resulting from enzyme deficiency

POTENTIAL DIAGNOSIS

Increased in
The pathophysiology is not well understood but release of the

enzymes from hemolyzed cells increases blood levels.

- Chronic blood loss *(related to reticulocytosis; replacement of RBCs)*
- Hepatic coma *(pathophysiology is unclear)*
- Hyperthyroidism *(possible response to increased basal metabolic rate and role of G6PD in glucose metabolism)*
- Idiopathic thrombocytopenic purpura
- Megaloblastic anemia *(related to reticulocytosis; replacement of RBCs)*
- Myocardial infarction *(medications [e.g., salicylates] may aggravate or stimulate a hemolytic crisis in G6PD-deficient patients)*
- Pernicious anemia *(related to reticulocytosis; replacement of RBCs)*
- Viral hepatitis *(pathophysiology is unclear)*

Decreased in

- Congenital nonspherocytic anemia
- G6PD deficiency
- Nonimmunological hemolytic disease of the newborn

CRITICAL FINDINGS: N/A

INTERFERING FACTORS

- Drugs that may increase G6PD levels include fluorouracil.
- Drugs that may precipitate hemolysis in G6PD deficient individuals include acetanilid, acetylsalicylic acid, ascorbic acid, chloramphenicol (Chloromycetin), dapsone, doxorubicin, furazolidone, isobutyl nitrate, methylene blue, nalidixic acid, naphthalene, niridazole, nitrofurantoin, para-aminosalicylic acid, pentaquine, phenacetin, phenazopyridine, phenylhydrazine, primaquine, quinidine, quinine, sulfacetamide, sulfamethoxazole, sulfanilamide, sulfapyridine,

sulfisoxazole, thiazolsulfone, toluidine blue, trinitrotoluene, urate oxidase, and vitamin K.

- G6PD levels are increased in reticulocytes; the test results may be falsely positive when a patient is in a period of acute hemolysis. G6PD levels can also be affected by the presence of large numbers of platelets and white blood cells, which also contain significant amounts of the enzyme.

NURSING IMPLICATIONS AND PROCEDURE

PRETEST:

▸ Positively identify the patient using at least two unique identifiers before providing care, treatment, or services.
▸ *Patient Teaching:* Inform the patient this test can assist in diagnosing anemia.
▸ Obtain a history of the patient's complaints, including a list of known allergens, especially allergies or sensitivities to latex.
▸ Obtain a history of the patient's hematopoietic system, symptoms, and results of previously performed laboratory tests and diagnostic and surgical procedures.
▸ Obtain a list of the patient's current medications, including herbs, nutritional supplements, and nutraceuticals (see Appendix F).
▸ Review the procedure with the patient. Inform the patient that specimen collection takes approximately 5 to 10 min. Address concerns about pain and explain that there may be some discomfort during the venipuncture.
▸ *Sensitivity to social and cultural issues,* as well as concern for modesty, is important in providing psychological support before, during, and after the procedure.
▸ There are no food, fluid, or medication restrictions unless by medical direction.

INTRATEST:

▸ If the patient has a history of allergic reaction to latex, avoid the use of equipment containing latex.

Instruct the patient to cooperate fully and to follow directions. Direct the patient to breathe normally and to avoid unnecessary movement. Observe standard precautions, and follow the general guidelines in Appendix A. Positively identify the patient, and label the appropriate specimen container with the corresponding patient demographics, initials of the person collecting the specimen, date, and time of collection. Perform a venipuncture.

Remove the needle and apply direct pressure with dry gauze to stop bleeding. Observe/assess venipuncture site for bleeding or hematoma formation and secure gauze with adhesive bandage.

Promptly transport the specimen to the laboratory for processing and analysis.

POST-TEST:

A report of the results will be made available to the requesting health-care provider (HCP), who will discuss the results with the patient.

Nutritional Considerations: Educate the patient with G6PD deficiency, as appropriate, to avoid certain foods, vitamins, and drugs that may precipitate an acute episode of intravascular hemolysis, including fava beans, ascorbic acid (large doses), acetanilid, antimalarials, furazolidone, isobutyl nitrate, methylene blue, nalidixic acid, naphthalene, niridazole, nitrofurantoin, phenazopyridine, phenylhydrazine, primaquine, sulfacetamide, sulfamethoxazole, sulfanilamide, sulfapyridine, thiazolsulfone, toluidine blue, trinitrotoluene, and urate oxidase.

Reinforce information given by the patient's HCP regarding further testing, treatment, or referral to another HCP. Answer any questions or address any concerns voiced by the patient or family.

Depending on the results of this procedure, additional testing may be performed to evaluate or monitor progression of the disease process and determine the need for a change in therapy. Evaluate test results in relation to the patient's symptoms and other tests performed.

RELATED MONOGRAPHS:

Related tests include biopsy bone marrow, bilirubin, CBC, CBC RBC morphology (including examination of peripheral smear for the presence of Heinz bodies), direct antiglobulin test, folate, Ham's test, haptoglobin, hemosiderin, newborn screening, osmotic fragility, reticulocyte count, UA, and vitamin B_{12}.

Refer to the Hematopoietic System table at the end of the book for related tests by body system.

Glucose Tolerance Tests

SYNONYM/ACRONYM: Standard oral tolerance test, standard gestational screen, standard gestational tolerance test, GTT.

COMMON USE: To evaluate blood glucose levels to assist in diagnosing diseases such as diabetes.

SPECIMEN: Plasma (1 mL) collected in a gray-top (sodium fluoride) tube. Serum (1 mL) collected in a red- or tiger-top tube or plasma collected in a green-top (heparin) tube is also acceptable, but plasma is recommended for diagnosis.

It is important to use the same type of collection container throughout the entire test.

NORMAL FINDINGS: (Method: Spectrophotometry)

	Conventional Units	SI Units (Conventional Units × 0.0555)	
Standard Oral Glucose Tolerance (Up to 75-g Glucose Load)			
Fasting sample	Less than 100 mg/dL	Less than 5.6 mmol/L	
Prediabetes or impaired fasting sample	100–125 mg/dL	5.6–6.9 mmol/L	
2-hr sample	Less than 200 mg/dL	Less than 11.1 mmol/L	
Prediabetes or impaired 2-hr sample	140–199 mg/dL	7.8–11 mmol/L	
Tolerance Tests for Gestational Diabetes			
ACOG Standard gestational screen (50-g glucose load)	Less than 141 mg/dL	Less than 7.8 mmol/L	
Standard gestational tolerance	ADA Threshold Recommendations for Gestational Diabetes (2012) **(75-g glucose load)**	ACOG Threshold Recommendations for Gestational Diabetes (2011); either Carpenter and Coustan or National Diabetes Data Group **(100-g glucose load)**	
		Carpenter and Coustan	National Diabetes Data Group
Fasting sample	Less than 93 mg/dL (SI: Less than 5.2 mmol/L)	Less than 95 mg/dL (SI: Less than 5.3 mmol/L)	Less than 105 mg/dL (SI: Less than 5.8 mmol/L)
1-hr sample	Less than 181 mg/dL (SI: Less than 10 mmol/L)	Less 180 mg/dL (SI: Less than 10 mmol/L)	Less than 190 mg/dL (SI: Less than 10.5 mmol/L)
2-hr sample	Less than 154 mg/dL (SI: Less than 8.5 mmol/L)	Less than 155 mg/dL (SI: Less than 8.5 mmol/L)	Less than 165 mg/dL (SI: Less than 9.2 mmol/L)
3-hr sample	N/A	Less than 140 mg/dL (SI: Less than 7.8 mmol/L)	Less than 145 mg/dL (SI: Less than 8 mmol/L)

Plasma glucose values are reported to be 10% to 20% higher than serum values. According to recommendations of the ADA, the diagnosis of gestational diabetes is made if any of the four thresholds are met or exceeded. According to recommendations of the ACOG or National Diabetes Data Group, the diagnosis of gestational diabetes is made if any two of the four thresholds are met or exceeded. ACOG = American Congress of Obstetricians and Gynecologists; ADA = American Diabetes Association

DESCRIPTION: The glucose tolerance test (GTT) measures glucose levels after administration of an oral or IV carbohydrate challenge. Patients with diabetes are unable to metabolize glucose at a normal rate. The oral GTT is used for individuals who are able to eat and who are not known to have problems with gastrointestinal malabsorption. The IV GTT is used for individuals who are unable to tolerate oral glucose.

Diabetes is a group of diseases characterized by hyperglycemia or elevated glucose levels. Hyperglycemia results from a defect in insulin secretion (type 1 diabetes), a defect in insulin action, or a combination of dysfunction secretion and action (type 2 diabetes). The chronic hyperglycemia of diabetes over time results in damage, dysfunction, and eventually failure of the eyes, kidneys, nerves, heart, and blood vessels. The American Diabetes Association and National Institute of Diabetes and Digestive and Kidney Disease have established criteria for diagnosing diabetes to include any combination of the following findings or confirmation of any of the individual findings by repetition on a subsequent day:

Symptoms of diabetes (e.g., polyuria, polydipsia, and unexplained weight loss) in addition to a random glucose level greater than 200 mg/dL

Fasting blood glucose greater than 126 mg/dL after a minimum of an 8-hr fast

Glucose level greater than 200 mg/dL 2 hr after glucose challenge with standardized 75-mg load

Both the ADA and the American Congress of Obstetricians and Gynecologists (ACOG) recommend screening for all pregnant women at 24 to 28 wk of gestation using patient history, clinical risk factors, or carbohydrate challenge testing. Protocol recommendations may vary among requesting health care providers (HCPs).

INDICATIONS
- Evaluate abnormal fasting or postprandial blood glucose levels that do not clearly indicate diabetes
- Evaluate glucose metabolism in women of childbearing age, especially women who are pregnant and have (1) a history of previous fetal loss or birth of infants weighing 9 lb or more and/or (2) a family history of diabetes
- Identify abnormal renal tubular function if glycosuria occurs without hyperglycemia
- Identify impaired glucose metabolism without overt diabetes
- Support the diagnosis of hyperthyroidism and alcoholic liver disease, which are characterized by a sharp rise in blood glucose followed by a decline to subnormal levels

POTENTIAL DIAGNOSIS

Tolerance Increased in
- Decreased absorption of glucose: Adrenal insufficiency (Addison's disease, hypopituitarism)
  Hypothyroidism
  Intestinal diseases, such as celiac disease and tropical sprue
  Whipple's disease
- Increased insulin secretion: Pancreatic islet cell tumor

Tolerance Impaired in
- Increased absorption of glucose:
  Excessive intake of glucose
  Gastrectomy
  Gastroenterostomy
  Hyperthyroidism
  Vagotomy
- Decreased usage of glucose:
  Central nervous system lesions
  Cushing's syndrome
  Diabetes
  Hemochromatosis
  Hyperlipidemia
- Decreased glycogenesis:
  Hyperthyroidism
  Infections
  Liver disease (severe)
  Pheochromocytoma
  Pregnancy
  Stress
  Von Gierke disease

CRITICAL FINDINGS ✦

Glucose
Adults & Children
- Less than 40 mg/dL (SI: Less than 2.22 mmol/L)
- Greater than 400 mg/dL (SI: Greater than 22.2 mmol/L)

Note and immediately report to the HCP any critically increased or decreased values and related symptoms. Timely notification of critical values for lab or diagnostic studies is a role expectation of the professional nurse. Notification processes will vary among facilities. Upon receipt of the critical value the information should be read back to the caller to verify accuracy. Most policies require immediate notification of the primary HCP, hospitalist, or on-call HCP. Reported information includes the patient's name, unique identifiers, critical value, name of the person giving the report, and name of the person receiving the report. Documentation of notification should be made in the medical record with the name of the HCP notified, time and date of notification, and any orders received. Any delay in a timely report of a critical value may require completion of a notification form with review by Risk Management.

Symptoms of decreased glucose levels include headache, confusion, hunger, irritability, nervousness, restlessness, sweating, and weakness. Possible interventions include oral or IV administration of glucose, IV or intramuscular injection of glucagon, and continuous glucose monitoring.

Symptoms of elevated glucose levels include abdominal pain, fatigue, muscle cramps, nausea, vomiting, polyuria, and thirst. Possible interventions include subcutaneous or IV injection of insulin with continuous glucose monitoring.

INTERFERING FACTORS
- Drugs and substances that may increase GTT values include acetylsalicylic acid, atenolol, bendroflumethiazide, caffeine, clofibrate, fenfluramine, fluoxymesterone, glyburide, guanethidine, lisinopril, methandrostenolone, metoprolol, nandrolone, niceritrol, nifedipine, nitrendipine, norethisterone, phenformin, phenobarbital, prazosin, and terazosin.
- Drugs and substances that may decrease GTT values include acebutolol, beclomethasone, bendroflumethiazide, betamethasone, calcitonin, catecholamines, chlorothiazide, chlorpromazine, chlorthalidone, cimetidine, corticotropin, cortisone, danazol, deflazacort, dexamethasone, diapamide, diethylstilbestrol, ethacrynic acid, fludrocortisone, furosemide,

glucagon, glucocorticosteroids, heroin, hydrochlorothiazide, mephenytoin, mestranol, methadone, methandrostenolone, methylprednisolone, muzolimine, niacin, nifedipine, norethindrone, norethynodrel, oral contraceptives, paramethasone, perphenazine, phenolphthalein, phenothiazine, phenytoin, pindolol, prednisolone, prednisone, propranolol, quinethazone, thiazides, triamcinolone, triamterene, and verapamil.

The test should be performed on ambulatory patients. Impaired physical activity can lead to falsely increased values.

Excessive physical activity before or during the test can lead to falsely decreased values.

Failure of the patient to ingest a diet with sufficient carbohydrate content (e.g., 150 g/day) for at least 3 days before the test can result in falsely decreased values.

The patient may have difficulty drinking the extremely sweet glucose beverage and become nauseous. Vomiting during the course of the test will cause the test to be canceled.

Smoking before or during the test can lead to falsely increased values.

The patient should not be under recent or current physiological stress during the test. If the patient has had recent surgery (less than 2 wk previously), an infectious disease, or a major illness (e.g., myocardial infarction), the test should be delayed or rescheduled.

Failure to follow dietary restrictions before the procedure may cause the procedure to be canceled or repeated.

NURSING IMPLICATIONS AND PROCEDURE

PRETEST:

Positively identify the patient using at least two unique identifiers before providing care, treatment, or services.

Patient Teaching: Inform the patient this test can assist in evaluating blood sugar levels.

Obtain a history of the patient's complaints, including a list of known allergens, especially allergies or sensitivities to latex.

Obtain a history of the patient's endocrine system, symptoms, and results of previously performed laboratory tests and diagnostic and surgical procedures.

Obtain a list of the patient's current medications, including herbs, nutritional supplements, and nutraceuticals (see Appendix F).

Review the procedure with the patient. Inform the patient that specimen collection takes approximately 5 to 10 min. Inform the patient that multiple specimens may be required. Address concerns about pain and explain that there may be some discomfort during the venipuncture.

Sensitivity to social and cultural issues, as well as concern for modesty, is important in providing psychological support before, during, and after the procedure.

The patient should fast for at least 8 to 16 hr before the standard oral and standard gestational GTTs.

There are no fluid or medication restrictions unless by medical direction prior to the gestational screen.

INTRATEST:

Ensure that the patient has complied with dietary and activity restrictions as well as other pretesting preparations; ensure that food has been restricted for at least 8 to 12 hr prior to the procedure.

G

If the patient has a history of allergic reaction to latex, avoid the use of equipment containing latex.

Instruct the patient to cooperate fully and to follow directions. Direct the patient to breathe normally and to avoid unnecessary movement.

Observe standard precautions, and follow the general guidelines in Appendix A. Positively identify the patient, and label the appropriate specimen container with the corresponding patient demographics, initials of the person collecting the specimen, date, and time of collection. Perform a venipuncture.

Remove the needle and apply direct pressure with dry gauze to stop bleeding. Observe/assess venipuncture site for bleeding or hematoma formation and secure gauze with adhesive bandage.

Promptly transport the specimen to the laboratory for processing and analysis. Do not wait until all specimens have been collected to transport.

Standard Oral GTT

The standard oral GTT takes 2 hr. A fasting blood glucose is determined before administration of an oral glucose load. If the fasting blood glucose is less than 126 mg/dL, the patient is given an oral glucose load. An oral glucose load should not be administered before the value of the fasting specimen has been received. If the fasting blood glucose is greater than 126 mg/dL, the standard glucose load is not administered and the test is canceled. The laboratory will follow its protocol as far as notifying the patient of his or her glucose level and the reason why the test was canceled. The requesting HCP will then be issued a report indicating the glucose level and the cancellation of the test. A fasting glucose greater than 126 mg/dL indicates diabetes; therefore, the glucose load would never be administered before allowing the requesting HCP to evaluate the clinical situation. Adults receive 75 g and children receive 1.75 g/kg ideal weight, not to exceed 75 g. The glucose load should be consumed within 5 min, and time 0

begins as soon as the patient begins to ingest the glucose load. A second specimen is collected at 2 hr, concluding the test. The test is discontinued if the patient vomits before the second specimen has been collected.

Standard Gestational Screen

The standard gestational screen is performed on pregnant women. If results from the screen are abnormal, a full gestational GTT is performed. The gestational screen does not require a fast. The patient is given a 50-g oral glucose load. The glucose load should be consumed within 5 min, and time 0 begins as soon as the patient begins to ingest the glucose load. A specimen is collected 1 hr after ingestion. The test is discontinued if the patient vomits before the 1-hr specimen has been collected. If the result is normal, the test may be repeated between 24 and 28 wk gestation.

Standard Gestational GTT

The standard gestational GTT takes 3 hr. A fasting blood glucose is determined before administration of a 75-g or 100-g oral glucose load, depending on the order. If the fasting blood glucose is less than 126 mg/dL, the patient is given an oral glucose load.

An oral glucose load should not be administered before the value of the fasting specimen has been received. If the fasting blood glucose is greater than 126 mg/dL, the Glucola is not administered and the test is canceled (see previous explanation).

The glucose load should be consumed within 5 min, and time 0 begins as soon as the patient begins to ingest the glucose load. Subsequent specimens are collected at 1, 2, and 3 hr, concluding the test. The test is discontinued if the patient vomits before all specimens have been collected.

POST-TEST:

A report of the results will be made available to the requesting HCP, who will discuss the results with the patient.

Instruct the patient to resume usual diet and activity, as directed by the HCP.

Nutritional Considerations: Increased glucose levels may be associated with diabetes. There is no "diabetic diet"; however, many meal-planning approaches with nutritional goals are endorsed by the American Dietetic Association. Patients who adhere to dietary recommendations report a better general feeling of health, better weight management, greater control of glucose and lipid values, and improved use of insulin. Instruct the patient, as appropriate, in nutritional management of diabetes. The American Heart Association's Therapeutic Lifestyle Changes (TLC) diet provides goals directed at people with specific risk factors and/or existing medical conditions (e.g., elevated LDL cholesterol levels, other lipid disorders, coronary artery disease, insulin-dependent diabetes, insulin resistance, or metabolic syndrome). The TLC approach also includes the use of plant stanols or sterols and increased dissolved fiber as an option for lowering LDL cholesterol levels; nutritional recommendations for daily total caloric intake; recommendations for allowable percentage of calories derived from fat (saturated and unsaturated), carbohydrates, protein, and cholesterol; as well as recommendations for daily expenditure of energy. The nutritional needs of each diabetic patient need to be determined individually (especially during pregnancy) with the appropriate HCPs, particularly professionals trained in nutrition.

Impaired glucose tolerance may be associated with diabetes. Instruct the patient and caregiver to report signs and symptoms of hypoglycemia (weakness, confusion, diaphoresis, rapid pulse) or hyperglycemia (thirst, polyuria, hunger, lethargy).

Recognize anxiety related to test results, and be supportive of perceived loss of independence and fear of shortened life expectancy. Discuss the implications of abnormal test results on the patient's lifestyle.

Provide teaching and information regarding the clinical implications of the test results, as appropriate. Emphasize, if indicated, that good glycemic control delays the onset and slows the progression of diabetic retinopathy, nephropathy, and neuropathy. Educate the patient regarding access to counseling services, as appropriate. Provide contact information, if desired, for the American Diabetes Association (www.diabetes.org) or the American Heart Association (www.americanheart.org).

Reinforce information given by the patient's HCP regarding further testing, treatment, or referral to another HCP. Instruct the patient in the use of home test kits approved by the U.S. Food and Drug Administration, if prescribed. Answer any questions or address any concerns voiced by the patient or family.

Depending on the results of this procedure, additional testing may be performed to evaluate or monitor progression of the disease process and determine the need for a change in therapy. Evaluate test results in relation to the patient's symptoms and other tests performed.

RELATED MONOGRAPHS:

Related tests include ACTH, ALP, antibodies gliadin, angiography adrenal, biopsy intestinal, biopsy thyroid, BUN, C-peptide, capsule endoscopy, catecholamines, cholesterol (total and HDL), cortisol, creatinine, DHEAS, fecal fat, fluorescein angiography, folate, fructosamine, fundus photography, gastric acid stimulation, gastrin stimulation, glucagon, glucose, glycated hemoglobin, gonioscopy, 5-HIAA, insulin, insulin antibodies, ketones, metanephrines, microalbumin, oxalate, RAIU, thyroid scan, TSH, thyroxine, triglycerides, VMA, and visual fields test.

Refer to the Endocrine System table at the end of the book for related tests by body system.

G

Glycated Hemoglobin

SYNONYM/ACRONYM: Hemoglobin A_{1c}, A_{1c}.

COMMON USE: To monitor treatment in individuals with diabetes by evaluating their long-term glycemic control.

SPECIMEN: Whole blood (1 mL) collected in a lavender-top (EDTA) tube.

NORMAL FINDINGS: (Method: Chromatography)

A_{1c}	
	4.0–5.5%
Prediabetes	5.7–6.4%
ADA recommended treatment goal	6.5% or less

Values vary widely by method. American Diabetes Association (ADA).

DESCRIPTION: *Glycosylated* or *glycated hemoglobin* is the combination of glucose and hemoglobin into a ketamine; the rate at which this occurs is proportional to glucose concentration. The average life span of a red blood cell (RBC) is approximately 120 days; measurement of glycated hemoglobin is a way to monitor long-term diabetic management. The average plasma glucose can be estimated using the formula:

$$\text{Average plasma glucose (mg/dL)} = [(A_{1c} \times 28.7) - 46.7]$$

For example, an A_{1c} value of 6% would reflect an average plasma glucose of 125.5 mg/dL or $[(6 \times 28.7) - 46.7]$.

Diabetes is a group of diseases characterized by hyperglycemia or elevated glucose levels. Hyperglycemia results from a defect in insulin secretion (type 1 diabetes), a defect in insulin action, or a combination of dysfunctional secretion and action (type 2 diabetes). The chronic hyperglycemia of diabetes over time results in damage, dysfunction, and eventually failure of the eyes, kidneys, nerves, heart, and blood vessels. Hemoglobin A_{1c} levels are not age dependent and are not affected by exercise, diabetic medications, or nonfasting state before specimen collection. The hemoglobin A_{1c} assay would not be useful for patients with hemolytic anemia or abnormal hemoglobins (e.g., hemoglobin S) accompanied by abnormal RBC turnover. These patients would be screened, diagnosed, and managed using symptoms, clinical risk factors, short-term glycemic indicators (glucose), and intermediate glycemic indicators (1,5 anhydroglucitol or glycated albumin).

INDICATIONS
Assess long-term glucose control in individuals with diabetes

POTENTIAL DIAGNOSIS

Increased in

- Diabetes (poorly controlled or uncontrolled) *(related to and evidenced by elevated glucose levels)*
- Pregnancy *(evidenced by gestational diabetes)*
- Splenectomy *(related to prolonged RBC survival, which extends the amount of time hemoglobin is available for glycosylation)*

Decreased in

- Chronic blood loss *(related to decreased concentration of RBC-bound glycated hemoglobin due to blood loss)*
- Chronic renal failure *(low RBC count associated with this condition reflects corresponding decrease in RBC-bound glycated hemoglobin)*
- Conditions that decrease RBC life span *(evidenced by anemia and low RBC count, reflecting a corresponding decrease in RBC-bound glycated hemoglobin)*
- Hemolytic anemia *(evidenced by low RBC count due to hemolysis, reflecting a corresponding decrease in RBC-bound glycated hemoglobin)*
- Pregnancy *(evidenced by anemia and low RBC count, reflecting a corresponding decrease in RBC-bound glycated hemoglobin)*

CRITICAL FINDINGS: N/A

INTERFERING FACTORS

- Drugs that may increase glycated hemoglobin A_{1c} values include insulin and sulfonylureas.
- Drugs that may decrease glycated hemoglobin A_{1c} values include cholestyramine and metformin.
- Conditions involving abnormal hemoglobins (hemoglobinopathies) affect the reliability of glycated hemoglobin A_{1c} values, causing (1) falsely increased values, (2) falsely decreased values, or (3) discrepancies in either direction depending on the method.

NURSING IMPLICATIONS AND PROCEDURE

PRETEST:

- Positively identify the patient using at least two unique identifiers before providing care, treatment, or services.
- *Patient Teaching:* Inform the patient this test can assist in evaluating blood sugar control over approximately the past 3 mo.
- Obtain a history of the patient's complaints, including a list of known allergens, especially allergies or sensitivities to latex.
- Obtain a history of the patient's endocrine system, symptoms, and results of previously performed laboratory tests and diagnostic and surgical procedures.
- Obtain a list of the patient's current medications, including herbs, nutritional supplements, and nutraceuticals (see Appendix F).
- Review the procedure with the patient. Inform the patient that specimen collection takes approximately 5 to 10 min. Address concerns about pain and explain that there may be some discomfort during the venipuncture.
- *Sensitivity to social and cultural issues,* as well as concern for modesty, is important in providing psychological support before, during, and after the procedure.
- There are no food, fluid, or medication restrictions unless by medical direction.

INTRATEST:

- If the patient has a history of allergic reaction to latex, avoid the use of equipment containing latex.
- Instruct the patient to cooperate fully and to follow directions. Direct the patient to breathe normally and to avoid unnecessary movement.
- Observe standard precautions, and follow the general guidelines in

Appendix A. Positively identify the patient, and label the appropriate specimen container with the corresponding patient demographics, initials of the person collecting the specimen, date, and time of collection. Perform a venipuncture.

Remove the needle and apply direct pressure with dry gauze to stop bleeding. Observe/assess venipuncture site for bleeding or hematoma formation and secure gauze with adhesive bandage.

Promptly transport the specimen to the laboratory for processing and analysis.

POST-TEST:

A report of the results will be made available to the requesting health-care provider (HCP), who will discuss the results with the patient.

Nutritional Considerations: Increased glycated hemoglobin A_{1C} levels may be associated with diabetes. There is no "diabetic diet"; however, many meal-planning approaches with nutritional goals are endorsed by the American Dietetic Association. Patients who adhere to dietary recommendations report a better general feeling of health, better weight management, greater control of glucose and lipid values, and improved use of insulin. Instruct the patient, as appropriate, in nutritional management of diabetes. The American Heart Association's Therapeutic Lifestyle Changes (TLC) diet provides goals directed at people with specific risk factors and/or existing medical conditions (e.g., elevated LDL cholesterol levels, other lipid disorders, coronary artery disease, insulin-dependent diabetes, insulin resistance, or metabolic syndrome). The TLC approach also includes the use of plant stanols or sterols and increased dissolved fiber as an option for lowering LDL cholesterol levels; nutritional recommendations for daily total caloric intake; recommendations for allowable percentage of calories derived from fat (saturated and unsaturated), carbohydrates, protein, and cholesterol; as well as recommendations for daily expenditure of energy. The nutritional needs of each diabetic patient need to be determined individually (especially during pregnancy) with the appropriate HCPs, particularly professionals trained in nutrition.

Social and Cultural Considerations: Numerous studies point to the prevalence of excess body weight in American children and adolescents. Experts estimate that obesity is present in 25% of the population ages 6 to 11 yr. The medical, social, and emotional consequences of excess body weight are significant. Special attention should be given to instructing the child and caregiver regarding health risks and weight control education.

Instruct the patient and caregiver to report signs and symptoms of hypoglycemia (weakness, confusion, diaphoresis, rapid pulse) or hyperglycemia (thirst, polyuria, hunger, lethargy).

Recognize anxiety related to test results, and be supportive of perceived loss of independence and fear of shortened life expectancy. Discuss the implications of abnormal test results on the patient's lifestyle. Provide teaching and information regarding the clinical implications of the test results, as appropriate. Emphasize, if indicated, that good glycemic control delays the onset and slows the progression of diabetic retinopathy, nephropathy, and neuropathy. Educate the patient regarding access to counseling services, as appropriate. Provide contact information, if desired, for the American Diabetes Association (ADA; www.diabetes.org) or the American Heart Association (www.americanheart.org) or the NHLBI (www.nhlbi.nih.gov). The ADA recommends A_{1c} testing 4 times a year for patients whose treatment plan has changed or who are not meeting treatments goals and twice a year for patients who are meeting treatment goals and have stable, good glycemic control.

Reinforce information given by the patient's HCP regarding further testing, treatment, or referral to another HCP. Instruct the patient in the use of home test kits approved by the U.S. Food and Drug Administration, if prescribed. Answer any questions or address any concerns voiced by the patient or family.

Depending on the results of this procedure, additional testing may be performed to evaluate or monitor progression of the disease process and determine the need for a change in therapy. Evaluate test results in relation to the patient's symptoms and other tests performed.

Related tests include C-peptide, cholesterol (total and HDL), CT cardiac scoring, creatinine/eGFR, EMG, ENG, fluorescein angiography, fructosamine, fundus photography, gastric emptying scan, glucagon, glucose, glucose tolerance tests, insulin, insulin antibodies, ketones, microalbumin, plethysmography, slit-lamp biomicroscopy, triglycerides, and visual fields test.

Refer to the Endocrine System table at the end of the book for related tests by body system.

Gonioscopy

SYNONYM/ACRONYM: N/A.

COMMON USE: To detect abnormalities in the structure of the anterior chamber of the eye such as in glaucoma.

AREA OF APPLICATION: Eyes.

CONTRAST: N/A.

DESCRIPTION: Gonioscopy is a technique used for examination of the anterior chamber structures of the eye (i.e., the trabecular meshwork and the anatomical relationship of the trabecular meshwork to the iris). The trabecular meshwork is the drainage system of the eye, and gonioscopy is performed to determine if the drainage angle is damaged, blocked, or clogged. Gonioscopy in combination with biomicroscopy is considered to be the most thorough basis to confirm a diagnosis of glaucoma and to differentiate between open-angle and angle-closure glaucoma. The angle structures of the anterior chamber are normally not visible because light entering the eye through the cornea is reflected back into the anterior chamber.

Placement of a special contact lens (goniolens) over the cornea allows reflected light to pass back through the cornea and onto a reflective mirror in the contact lens. It is in this way that the angle structures can be visualized. There are two types of gonioscopy: indirect and direct. The more commonly used indirect technique employs a mirrored goniolens and biomicroscope. Direct gonioscopy is performed with a gonioscope containing a dome-shaped contact lens known as a gonioprism. The gonioprism eliminates internally reflected light, allowing direct visualization of the angle. Interpretation of visual examination is usually documented in a colored hand-drawn diagram. Scheie's classification is used to standardize definition of angles based on appearance by gonioscopy. Shaffer's classification is based on the angular width of the angle recess.

INDICATIONS
* Assessment of peripheral anterior synechiae (PAS)
* Conditions affecting the ciliary body
* Degenerative conditions of the anterior chamber
* Evaluation of glaucoma (confirmation of normal structures and estimation of angle width)
* Growth or tumor in the angle
* Hyperpigmentation
* Post-trauma evaluation for angle recession
* Suspected neovascularization of the angle
* Uveitis

POTENTIAL DIAGNOSIS

Scheie's Classification Based on Visible Angle Structures	
Classification	*Appearance*
Wide open	All angle structures seen
Grade I narrow	Difficult to see over the iris root
Grade II narrow	Ciliary band obscured
Grade III narrow	Posterior trabeculum hazy
Grade IV narrow	Only Schwalbe's line visible

Shaffer's Classification Based on Angle Width	
Classification	*Appearance*
Wide open (20°–45°)	Closure improbable
Moderately narrow (10°–20°)	Closure possible
Extremely narrow (less than 10°)	Closure possible
Partially/totally closed	Closure present

Normal findings in
* Normal appearance of anterior chamber structures and wide, unblocked, normal angle

Abnormal findings in
* Corneal endothelial disorders (Fuchs' endothelial dystrophy, iridocorneal endothelial syndrome)
* Glaucoma
* Lens disorders (cataract, displaced lens)
* Malignant ocular neoplasm in angle
* Neovascularization in angle
* Ocular hemorrhage
* PAS
* Schwartz's syndrome
* Trauma
* Tumors
* Uveitis

CRITICAL FINDINGS: N/A

INTERFERING FACTORS
* Inability of the patient to cooperate or remain still during the test because of age, significant pain, or mental status may interfere with the test results.

NURSING IMPLICATIONS AND PROCEDURE

RETEST:

Positively identify the patient using at least two unique identifiers before providing care, treatment, or services.

Patient Teaching: Inform the patient this procedure can assist in evaluating the eye for disease.

Obtain a history of the patient's complaints, including a list of known allergens, especially allergies or sensitivities to latex.

Obtain a history of the patient's known or suspected vision loss; changes in visual acuity, including type and cause, use of glasses or contact lenses, eye conditions with treatment regimens, and eye surgery; as well as results of previously performed laboratory tests and diagnostic and surgical procedures.

Obtain a list of the patient's current medications, including herbs, nutritional supplements, and nutraceuticals (see Appendix F).

Instruct the patient to remove contact lenses or glasses, as appropriate. Instruct the patient regarding the importance of keeping the eyes open for the test.

Review the procedure with the patient. Explain that the patient will be requested to fixate the eyes during the procedure. Address concerns about pain related to the procedure. Explain that no pain will be experienced during the test, but there may be moments of discomfort. Explain that some discomfort may be experienced after the test when the numbness wears off from anesthetic drops administered prior to the test. Inform the patient that the test is performed by a healthcare provider (HCP) or optometrist specially trained to perform this procedure and takes about 5 min to complete.

Sensitivity to social and cultural issues, as well as concern for modesty, is important in providing psychological support before, during, and after the procedure.

There are no food, fluid, or medication restrictions unless by medical direction.

INTRATEST:

Observe standard precautions, and follow the general guidelines in Appendix A. Positively identify the patient.

Instruct the patient to cooperate fully and to follow directions. Ask the patient to remain still during the procedure because movement produces unreliable results.

Seat the patient comfortably. Instill topical anesthetic in each eye, as ordered, and allow time for it to work. Topical anesthetic drops are placed in the eye with the patient looking up and the solution directed at the six o'clock position of the sclera (white of the eye) near the limbus (gray, semitransparent area of the eyeball where the cornea and sclera meet). Neither the dropper nor the bottle should touch the eyelashes.

Ask the patient to place the chin in the chin rest and gently press the forehead against the support bar. Ask the patient to open his or her eyes wide and look at desired target. Explain that the HCP or optometrist will place a lens on the eye while a narrow beam of light is focused on the eye.

POST-TEST:

A report of the results will be made available to the requesting HCP, who will discuss the results with the patient.

Recognize anxiety related to test results, and be supportive of impaired activity related to vision loss or anticipated loss of driving privileges. Discuss the implications of abnormal test results on the patient's lifestyle. Provide teaching and information regarding the clinical implications of the test results, as appropriate.

Reinforce information given by the patient's HCP regarding further testing, treatment, or referral to another HCP. Answer any questions or address any concerns voiced by the patient or family.

Depending on the results of this procedure, additional testing may be performed to evaluate or monitor progression of the disease process and determine the need for a change in therapy. Evaluate test results in relation to the patient's symptoms and other tests performed.

RELATED MONOGRAPHS:

▸ Related tests include fundus photography, pachymetry, slit-lamp biomicroscopy, and visual field testing.
▸ Refer to the Ocular System table at the end of the book for related tests by body system.

Gram Stain

SYNONYM/ACRONYM: N/A.

COMMON USE: To provide a quick reference for gram-negative or gram-positive organisms to assist in medical management.

SPECIMEN: Blood, biopsy specimen, or body fluid as collected for culture.

NORMAL FINDINGS: N/A.

DESCRIPTION: Gram stain is a technique commonly used to identify bacterial organisms on the basis of their specific staining characteristics. The method involves smearing a small amount of specimen on a slide, and then exposing it to gentian or crystal violet, iodine, alcohol, and safranin O. Gram-positive bacteria retain the gentian or crystal violet and iodine stain complex after a decolorization step and appear purple-blue in color. Gram-negative bacteria do not retain the stain after decolorization but can pick up the pink color of the safranin O counterstain. Gram stains provide information regarding the adequacy of a sample. For example, a sputum Gram stain showing greater than 25 squamous epithelial cells per low-power field, regardless of the number of polymorphonuclear white blood cells, indicates contamination of the specimen with saliva, and the specimen should be rejected for subsequent culture. Gram stains are reviewed over a number of fields for an impression of the quantity of organisms present, which reflects the extent of infection. For example, a Gram stain of unspun urine showing the occasional presence of bacteria per low-power field suggests a correlating colony count of 10,000 bacteria/mL, while the presence of bacteria in most fields is clinically significant and suggests greater than 100,000 bacteria/mL of urine. Gram stain results should be correlated with culture and sensitivity results to interpret the significance of isolated organisms and to select appropriate antibiotic therapy.

NDICATIONS

- Provide a rapid determination of the acceptability of the specimen for further analysis

- Provide rapid, presumptive information about the type of potential pathogen present in the specimen (i.e., gram-positive bacteria, gram-negative bacteria, or yeast)

POTENTIAL DIAGNOSIS

Gram Positive				
Actinomadura	Actinomyces	Bacillus	Clostridium	Corynebacterium
Enterococcus	Erysipelothrix	Lactobacillus	Listeria	Micrococcus
Mycobacterium (gram variable)	Peptostreptococcus	Propionibacterium	Rhodococcus	Staphylococcus
Streptococcus				

Gram Negative				
Acinetobacter	Aeromonas	Alcaligenes	Bacteroides	Bordetella
Borrelia	Brucella	Campylobacter	Citrobacter	Chlamydia
Enterobacter	Escherichia	Flavobacterium	Francisella	Fusobacterium
Gardnerella	Haemophilus	Helicobacter	Klebsiella	Legionella
Leptospira	Moraxella	Neisseria	Pasteurella	Plesiomonas
Porphyromonas	Prevotella	Proteus	Pseudomonas	Rickettsia
Salmonella	Serratia	Shigella	Vibrio	Xanthomonas
Yersinia				

Acid Fast or Partial Acid Fast	
Nocardia	Mycobacterium

Note: *Treponema* species are classified as gram-negative spirochetes, but they are most often visualized using dark-field or silver-staining techniques.

CRITICAL FINDINGS

- Any positive results in blood, cerebrospinal fluid, or any body cavity fluid.

Note and immediately report to the requesting health-care provider (HCP) any positive results and related symptoms. Timely notification of critical values for lab or diagnostic studies is a role expectation of the professional nurse. Notification processes will vary among facilities. Upon receipt of the critical value the information should be read back to the caller to verify accuracy. Most policies require immediate notification of the primary HCP, hospitalist, or on-call HCP. Reported information includes the patient's name, unique identifiers, critical value, name of the person giving the report, and name of the person receiving the report. Documentation of notification should be made in the medical record with the name of the HCP notified, time and date of notification, and any orders received. Any delay in a timely report of a critical value may require completion of a notification form with review by Risk Management.

INTERFERING FACTORS
• Very young, very old, or dead cultures may react atypically to the Gram stain technique.

NURSING IMPLICATIONS AND PROCEDURE

PRETEST:

▶ Positively identify the patient using at least two unique identifiers before providing care, treatment, or services.
▶ *Patient Teaching:* Inform the patient this test can assist in identifying the presence of pathogenic organisms.
▶ Obtain a history of the patient's complaints, including a list of known allergens, especially allergies or sensitivities to latex.
▶ Obtain a history of the patient's gastrointestinal, genitourinary, immune, reproductive, and respiratory systems; symptoms; and results of previously performed laboratory tests and diagnostic and surgical procedure.
▶ Obtain a list of the patient's current medications, including herbs, nutritional supplements, and nutraceuticals (see Appendix F).
▶ Review the procedure with the patient. Inform the patient that the time it takes to collect a proper specimen varies according to the patient's level of cooperation as well as the specimen collection site. Address concerns about pain and explain that there may be some discomfort during the procedure.
▶ *Sensitivity to social and cultural issues,* as well as concern for modesty, is important in providing psychological support before, during, and after the procedure.
▶ There are no food, fluid, or medication restrictions unless by medical direction.

INTRATEST:

▶ Instruct the patient to cooperate fully and to follow directions.
▶ Observe standard precautions, and follow the general guidelines in Appendix A. Positively identify the patient, and label the appropriate specimen container with the corresponding patient demographics, initials of the person collecting the specimen, date, and time of collection.
▶ Specific collection instructions are found in the associated culture monographs.
▶ Promptly transport the specimen to the laboratory for processing and analysis.

POST-TEST:

▶ A report of the results will be made available to the requesting HCP, who will discuss the results with the patient.
▶ Administer antibiotics as ordered, and instruct the patient in the importance of completing the entire course of antibiotic therapy even if no symptoms are present.
▶ Recognize anxiety related to test results. Discuss the implications of abnormal test results on the patient's lifestyle. Provide teaching and information regarding the clinical implications of the test results, as appropriate.
▶ Reinforce information given by the patient's HCP regarding further testing, treatment, or referral to another HCP. Answer any questions or address any concerns voiced by the patient or family.
▶ Depending on the results of this procedure, additional testing may be performed to evaluate or monitor progression of the disease process and determine the need for a change in therapy. Evaluate test results in relation to the patient's symptoms and other tests performed.

RELATED MONOGRAPHS:

▶ Related tests include amniotic fluid analysis, relevant biopsies, bronchoscopy, cultures bacterial and viral, CSF analysis, CBC, pericardial fluid analysis, peritoneal fluid analysis, pleural fluid analysis, procalcitonin, synovial fluid analysis, and UA.
▶ Refer to the Gastrointestinal, Genitourinary, Immune, Reproductive, and Respiratory systems tables at the end of the book for related tests by body system.

Group A Streptococcal Screen

SYNONYM/ACRONYM: Strep screen, rapid strep screen, direct strep screen.

COMMON USE: To detect a group A streptococcal infection such as strep throat.

SPECIMEN: Throat swab (two swabs should be submitted so that a culture can be performed if the screen is negative).

NORMAL FINDINGS: (Method: Enzyme immunoassay or latex agglutination) Negative.

DESCRIPTION: Rheumatic fever is a possible sequela to an untreated streptococcal infection. Early diagnosis and treatment appear to lessen the seriousness of symptoms during the acute phase and overall duration of the infection and sequelae. The onset of strep throat is sudden and includes symptoms such as chills, headache, sore throat, malaise, and exudative gray-white patches on the tonsils or pharynx. The group A streptococcal screen should not be ordered unless the results would be available within 1 to 2 hr of specimen collection to make rapid, effective therapeutic decisions. A positive result can be a reliable basis for the initiation of therapy. A negative result is presumptive for infection and should be backed up by culture results. In general, specimens showing growth of less than 10 colonies on culture yield negative results by the rapid screening method. Evidence of group A streptococci disappears rapidly after the initiation of antibiotic therapy. A nucleic acid probe method has also been developed for rapid detection of group A streptococci.

INDICATIONS
- Assist in the rapid determination of the presence of group A streptococci

POTENTIAL DIAGNOSIS

Positive findings in
- Rheumatic fever
- Scarlet fever
- Strep throat
- Streptococcal glomerulonephritis
- Tonsillitis

CRITICAL FINDINGS: N/A

INTERFERING FACTORS
- Polyester (rayon or Dacron) swabs are favored over cotton for best chance of detection. Fatty acids are created on cotton fibers during the sterilization process. Detectable target antigens on the streptococcal cell wall are destroyed without killing the organism when there is contact between the specimen and the fatty acids on the cotton collection swab. False-negative test results can be obtained on specimens collected with cotton tip swabs. Negative strep screens should always be followed with a traditional culture.
- Sensitivity of the method varies among manufacturers.

G

• Adequate specimen collection in children may be difficult to achieve, which explains the higher percentage of false-negative results in this age group.

NURSING IMPLICATIONS AND PROCEDURE

PRETEST:

▶ Positively identify the patient using at least two unique identifiers before providing care, treatment, or services.

Patient Teaching: Inform the patient this test can assist in identifying a streptococcal infection.

▶ Obtain a history of the patient's complaints, including a list of known allergens, especially allergies or sensitivities to latex.

▶ Obtain a history of the patient's immune and respiratory systems, symptoms, and results of previously performed laboratory tests and diagnostic and surgical procedures.

▶ Obtain a history of prior antibiotic therapy.

▶ Obtain a list of the patient's current medications, including herbs, nutritional supplements, and nutraceuticals (see Appendix F).

▶ Before specimen collection, verify with the laboratory whether wet or dry swabs are preferred for collection.

▶ Review the procedure with the patient. Inform the patient that specimen collection takes approximately 5 to 10 min. Address concerns about pain and explain that there may be some discomfort during the swabbing procedure.

Sensitivity to social and cultural issues, as well as concern for modesty, is important in providing psychological support before, during, and after the procedure.

▶ There are no food, fluid, or medication restrictions unless by medical direction.

INTRATEST:

▶ Instruct the patient to cooperate fully and to follow directions. Direct the patient to breathe normally and to avoid unnecessary movement.

▶ Observe standard precautions, and follow the general guidelines in Appendix A. Positively identify the patient, and label the appropriate specimen container with the corresponding patient demographics, initials of the person collecting the specimen, date, and time of collection. Vigorous swabbing of both tonsillar pillars and the posterior throat enhances the probability of streptococcal antigen detection.

▶ Promptly transport the specimen to the laboratory for processing and analysis.

POST-TEST:

▶ A report of the results will be made available to the requesting health-care provider (HCP), who will discuss the results with the patient.

▶ Administer antibiotics as ordered, and emphasize to the patient or caregiver the importance of completing the entire course of antibiotic therapy even if no symptoms are present.

▶ Reinforce information given by the patient's HCP regarding further testing, treatment, or referral to another HCP. Answer any questions or address any concerns voiced by the patient or family.

▶ Depending on the results of this procedure, additional testing may be performed to evaluate or monitor progression of the disease process and determine the need for a change in therapy. Evaluate test results in relation to the patient's symptoms and other tests performed.

RELATED MONOGRAPHS:

▶ Related laboratory tests include analgesic and antipyretic drugs, antibiotic drugs, ASO, chest x-ray, CBC, culture (throat, viral), and Gram stain.

▶ Refer to the Immune and Respiratory systems tables at the end of the book for related tests by body system.

Growth Hormone, Stimulation and Suppression Tests

SYNONYM/ACRONYM: Somatotropic hormone, somatotropin, GH, hGH.

COMMON USE: To assess pituitary function and evaluate the amount of secreted growth hormone to assist in diagnosing diseases such as giantism and dwarfism.

SPECIMEN: Serum (1 mL) collected in a red- or tiger-top tube.

NORMAL FINDINGS: (Method: Immunoassay)

Growth Hormone

Age	Conventional Units	SI Units (Conventional Units × 1)
Cord blood	8–40 ng/mL	8–40 mcg/L
1 day	5–50 ng/mL	5–50 mcg/L
1 wk	5–25 ng/mL	5–25 mcg/L
Child	2–10 ng/mL	2–10 mcg/L
Adult		
Male	0–5 ng/mL	0–5 mcg/L
Female	0–10 ng/mL	0–10 mcg/L
Male older than 60 yr	0–10 ng/mL	0–10 mcg/L
Female older than 60 yr	0–14 ng/mL	0–14 mcg/L
Stimulation Tests		
Rise above baseline	Greater than 5 ng/mL	Greater than 5 mcg/L
Peak response	Greater than 10 ng/mL	Greater than 10 mcg/L
Suppression Tests	0–2 ng/mL	0–2 mcg/L

DESCRIPTION: Human growth hormone (GH) is secreted in episodic bursts by the anterior pituitary gland; the highest level is usually secreted during deep sleep. Release of GH is modulated by three hypothalamic factors: GH-releasing hormone, GH-releasing peptide-6, and GH inhibitory hormone (also known as somatostatin). The effects of GH are carried out by insulin-like growth factors, formerly called somatomedins.

GH plays an integral role in growth from birth to puberty. GH promotes skeletal growth by stimulating hepatic production of proteins; it also affects lipid and glucose metabolism. Random levels are rarely useful because secretion of GH is episodic and pulsatile. Stimulation tests with arginine, glucagon, insulin, or L-dopa, as well as suppression tests with glucose, provide useful information.

INDICATIONS

* Assist in the diagnosis of acromegaly in adults
* Assist in establishing a diagnosis of dwarfism or growth retardation in children with decreased GH levels, indicative of a pituitary cause
* Assist in establishing a diagnosis of gigantism in children with GH increased levels, indicative of a pituitary cause
* Detect suspected disorder associated with decreased GH
* Monitor response to treatment of growth retardation

POTENTIAL DIAGNOSIS

Increased in

Production of GH is modulated by numerous factors, including stress, exercise, sleep, nutrition, and response to circulating levels of GH.

* Acromegaly
* Anorexia nervosa
* Cirrhosis
* Diabetes (uncontrolled)
* Ectopic GH secretion (neoplasms of stomach, lung)
* Exercise
* Gigantism (pituitary)
* Hyperpituitarism
* Laron dwarfism
* Malnutrition
* Renal failure
* Stress

Decreased in

* Adrenocortical hyperfunction *(inhibits secretion of GH)*
* Dwarfism (pituitary) *(related to GH deficiency)*
* Hypopituitarism *(related to lack of production)*

CRITICAL FINDINGS: N/A

INTERFERING FACTORS

* Drugs that may increase GH levels include alanine, anabolic steroids, angiotensin II, apomorphine, arginine, clonidine, corticotropin, cyclic AMP, desipramine, dexamethasone, dopamine, fenfluramine, galanin, glucagon, GH-releasing hormone, hydrazine, levodopa, methamphetamine, methyldopa, metoclopramide, midazolam, niacin, oral contraceptives, phenytoin, propranolol, and vasopressin.
* Drugs that may decrease GH levels include corticosteroids, corticotropin, hydrocortisone, octreotide, and pirenzepine.
* Failure to follow dietary and activity restrictions before the procedure may cause the procedure to be canceled or repeated.

NURSING IMPLICATIONS AND PROCEDURE

PRETEST:

▶ Positively identify the patient using at least two unique identifiers before providing care, treatment, or services.
▶ *Patient Teaching:* Inform the patient this test can assist in assessing the amount of GH secreted.
▶ Obtain a history of the patient's complaints, including a list of known allergens, especially allergies or sensitivities to latex.
▶ Obtain a history of the patient's endocrine system, symptoms, and results of previously performed laboratory tests and diagnostic and surgical procedures.
▶ Record pertinent information related to diet, sleep pattern, and activity at the time of the test.
▶ Note any recent procedures that can interfere with test results.
▶ Obtain a list of the patient's current medications, including herbs, nutritional supplements, and nutraceuticals (see Appendix F).
▶ Review the procedure with the patient. Protocols may vary depending on the type of induction used. Patients may be allowed to walk around, or they may be required to be recumbent. Inform the patient that multiple specimens may be required. Inform the patient that specimen collection takes

approximately 5 to 10 min. Address concerns about pain and explain that there may be some discomfort during the venipuncture. *Sensitivity to social and cultural issues,* as well as concern for modesty, is important in providing psychological support before, during, and after the procedure.

▸ The patient should fast and avoid strenuous exercise for 12 hr before specimen collection. Protocols may vary among facilities.

INTRATEST:

▸ Ensure that the patient has complied with dietary and activity restrictions; ensure that food and strenuous activity have been restricted for at least 12 hr prior to the procedure.

▸ If the patient has a history of allergic reaction to latex, avoid the use of equipment containing latex.

▸ Instruct the patient to cooperate fully and to follow directions. Direct the patient to breathe normally and to avoid unnecessary movement.

▸ Observe standard precautions, and follow the general guidelines in Appendix A. Positively identify the patient, and label the appropriate specimen container with the corresponding patient demographics, initials of the person collecting the specimen, date, and time of collection. Perform a venipuncture. Test samples may be requested at baseline and 30-, 60-, 90-, and 120-min intervals after stimulation and at baseline and 60- and 120-min intervals after suppression.

▸ Remove the needle and apply direct pressure with dry gauze to stop bleeding. Observe/assess venipuncture site for bleeding or hematoma formation and secure gauze with adhesive bandage.

▸ Promptly transport the specimen to the laboratory for processing and analysis.

POST-TEST:

▸ A report of the results will be made available to the requesting health-care provider (HCP), who will discuss the results with the patient.

▸ Instruct the patient to resume usual diet, fluids, medications, and activity, as directed by the HCP.

▸ Reinforce information given by the patient's HCP regarding further testing, treatment, or referral to another HCP. Answer any questions or address any concerns voiced by the patient or family.

▸ Depending on the results of this procedure, additional testing may be performed to evaluate or monitor progression of the disease process and determine the need for a change in therapy. Evaluate test results in relation to the patient's symptoms and other tests performed.

RELATED MONOGRAPHS:

▸ Related tests include ACTH and insulin.

▸ Refer to the Endocrine System table at the end of the book for related tests by body system.

Ham's Test for Paroxysmal Nocturnal Hemoglobinuria

SYNONYM/ACRONYM: Acid hemolysis test for PNH.

COMMON USE: To assist in diagnosing a rare condition called paroxysmal nocturnal hemoglobinuria (PNH), wherein red blood cells undergo lysis during and after sleep with hemoglobin excreted in the urine.

SPECIMEN: Whole blood (5 mL) collected in lavender-top (EDTA) tube and serum (3 mL) collected in red-top tube.

NORMAL FINDINGS: (Method: Acidified hemolysis) No hemolysis seen.

POTENTIAL DIAGNOSIS

Decreased in: N/A

Increased in
- Congenital dyserythropoietic anemia, type II
- PNH

CRITICAL FINDINGS: N/A

Find and print out the full monograph at DavisPlus (davisplus.fadavis .com, keyword Van Leeuwen).

H

Haptoglobin

SYNONYM/ACRONYM: Hapto, HP, Hp.

COMMON USE: To assist in evaluating for intravascular hemolysis related to transfusion reactions, chronic liver disease, hemolytic anemias, and tissue inflammation or destruction.

SPECIMEN: Serum (1 mL) collected in a red- or tiger-top tube.

NORMAL FINDINGS: (Method: Immunoturbidimetric)

Age	Conventional Units	SI Units (Conventional Units × 0.01)
Newborn	5–48 mg/dL	0.05–0.48 g/L
6 mo–16 yr	25–138 mg/dL	0.25–1.38 g/L
Adult	15–200 mg/dL	0.15–2 g/L

DESCRIPTION: Haptoglobin is an α_2-globulin produced in the liver. It binds with the free hemoglobin released when red blood cells (RBCs) are lysed. If left unchecked, free hemoglobin in the plasma can cause renal damage; haptoglobin prevents it from accumulating. In conditions such as hemolytic anemia, so many hemolyzed RBCs are available for binding that the liver cannot compensate by producing additional haptoglobin fast enough, resulting in low serum levels.

INDICATIONS
- Assist in the investigation of suspected transfusion reaction
- Evaluate known or suspected chronic liver disease, as indicated by decreased levels of haptoglobin
- Evaluate known or suspected disorders characterized by excessive RBC hemolysis, as indicated by decreased levels of haptoglobin
- Evaluate known or suspected disorders involving a diffuse inflammatory process or tissue destruction, as indicated by elevated levels of haptoglobin

POTENTIAL DIAGNOSIS

Increased in
Haptoglobin is an acute-phase reactant protein, and any condition that stimulates an acute-phase response will result in elevations of haptoglobin.

- Biliary obstruction
- Disorders involving tissue destruction, such as cancers, burns, and acute myocardial infarction
- Infection or inflammatory diseases, such as ulcerative colitis, arthritis, and pyelonephritis
- Neoplasms
- Steroid therapy

Decreased in
- Autoimmune hemolysis *(related to increased excretion rate of haptoglobin bound to free hemoglobin; rate of excretion exceeds the liver's immediate ability to replenish)*
- Hemolysis due to drug reaction *(related to increased excretion rate of haptoglobin bound to free hemoglobin; rate of excretion exceeds the liver's immediate ability to replenish)*

- Hemolysis due to mechanical destruction (e.g., artificial heart valves, contact sports, subacute bacterial endocarditis) *(related to increased excretion rate of haptoglobin bound to free hemoglobin; rate of excretion exceeds the liver's immediate ability to replenish)*
- Hemolysis due to RBC membrane or metabolic defects *(related to increased excretion rate of haptoglobin bound to free hemoglobin; rate of excretion exceeds the liver's immediate ability to replenish)*
- Hemolysis due to transfusion reaction *(related to increased excretion rate of haptoglobin bound to free hemoglobin; rate of excretion exceeds the liver's immediate ability to replenish)*
- Hypersplenism *(related to increased excretion rate of haptoglobin bound to free hemoglobin due to increased red blood cell destruction; rate of excretion exceeds the liver's immediate ability to replenish)*
- Ineffective hematopoiesis due to conditions such as folate deficiency or hemoglobinopathies *(related to decreased numbers of RBCs or dysfunctional binding in the presence of abnormal hemoglobins)*
- Liver disease *(related to decreased production)*
- Pregnancy *(related to effect of estrogen)*

CRITICAL FINDINGS: N/A

INTERFERING FACTORS
- Drugs that may increase haptoglobin levels include anabolic steroids, danazol, ethylestrenol, fluoxymesterone, methandrostenolone, norethandrolone, oxandrolone, oxymetholone, and stanozolol.
- Drugs that may decrease haptoglobin levels include acetanilid,

aminosalicylic acid, chlorpromazine, dapsone, dextran, diphenhydramine, furadaltone, furazolidone, isoniazid, nitrofurantoin, norethindrone, oral contraceptives, quinidine, resorcinol, stibophen, tamoxifen, thiazolsulfone, and tripelennamine.

NURSING IMPLICATIONS AND PROCEDURE

PRETEST:

Positively identify the patient using at least two unique identifiers before providing care, treatment, or services.
Patient Teaching: Inform the patient this test can assist with evaluating causes of red blood cell loss.
Obtain a history of the patient's complaints, including a list of known allergens, especially allergies or sensitivities to latex.
Obtain a history of the patient's hematopoietic, hepatobiliary, and immune systems; symptoms; and results of previously performed laboratory tests and diagnostic and surgical procedures.
Obtain a list of the patient's current medications, including herbs, nutritional supplements, and nutraceuticals (see Appendix F).
Review the procedure with the patient. Inform the patient that specimen collection takes approximately 5 to 10 min. Address concerns about pain and explain that there may be some discomfort during the venipuncture.
There are no food, fluid, or medication restrictions unless by medical direction.

INTRATEST:

If the patient has a history of allergic reaction to latex, avoid the use of equipment containing latex.
Instruct the patient to cooperate fully and to follow directions. Direct the patient to breathe normally and to avoid unnecessary movement.
Observe standard precautions, and follow the general guidelines in Appendix A. Positively identify the patient, and label the appropriate specimen container with the corresponding patient demographics, initials of the person collecting the specimen, date, and time of collection. Perform a venipuncture.
Remove the needle and apply direct pressure with dry gauze to stop bleeding. Observe/assess venipuncture site for bleeding or hematoma formation and secure gauze with adhesive bandage.
Promptly transport the specimen to the laboratory for processing and analysis.

POST-TEST:

A report of the results will be made available to the requesting health-care provider (HCP), who will discuss the results with the patient.
Instruct the patient to immediately report symptoms of hemolysis, including chills, fever, flushing, back pain, and fast heartbeat, to the HCP.
Reinforce information given by the patient's HCP regarding further testing, treatment, or referral to another HCP. Answer any questions or address any concerns voiced by the patient or family.
Depending on the results of this procedure, additional testing may be performed to evaluate or monitor progression of the disease process and determine the need for a change in therapy. Evaluate test results in relation to the patient's symptoms and other tests performed.

RELATED MONOGRAPHS:

Related tests include ALT, AST, bilirubin, blood group and type, CBC, CBC RBC count, CBC RBC indices, CBC RBC morphology, Coombs' antiglobulin, folate, G6PD, GGT, Ham's test, hepatobiliary scan, and osmotic fragility.
Refer to the Hematopoietic, Hepatobiliary, and Immune systems tables at the end of the book for related tests by body system.

Helicobacter Pylori Antibody

SYNONYM/ACRONYM: *H. pylori.*

COMMON USE: To test blood for findings that would indicate past or current *Helicobacter pylori* infection.

SPECIMEN: Serum (1 mL) collected in a plain red-top tube.

NORMAL FINDINGS: (Method: Enzyme-linked immunosorbent assay [ELISA]) Negative.

DESCRIPTION: There is a strong association between *Helicobacter pylori* infection and gastric cancer, duodenal and gastric ulcer, and chronic gastritis. Immunoglobulin G (IgG) antibodies can be detected for up to 1 yr after treatment. The presence of *H. pylori* can also be demonstrated by a positive urea breath test, positive stool culture, or positive endoscopic biopsy. Patients with symptoms and evidence of *H. pylori* infection are considered to be infected with the organism; patients who demonstrate evidence of *H. pylori* but are without symptoms are said to be colonized.

INDICATIONS

* Assist in differentiating between *H. pylori* infection and NSAID use as the cause of gastritis or peptic or duodenal ulcer
* Assist in establishing a diagnosis of gastritis, gastric carcinoma, or peptic or duodenal ulcer

POTENTIAL DIAGNOSIS

Positive findings in
* *H. pylori* infection
* *H. pylori* colonization

Negative findings in: N/A

CRITICAL FINDINGS: N/A

INTERFERING FACTORS: N/A

NURSING IMPLICATIONS AND PROCEDURE

PRETEST:

▶ Positively identify the patient using at least two unique identifiers before providing care, treatment, or services.
▶ Inform the patient that the test is used to assist in the diagnosis of *H. pylori* infection in patients with duodenal and gastric disease.
▶ Obtain a history of the patient's complaints, including a list of known allergens, especially allergies or sensitivities to latex.
▶ Obtain a history of the patient's gastrointestinal system, symptoms, and results of previously performed laboratory tests and diagnostic and surgical procedures.
▶ Obtain a list of the patient's current medications, including herbs, nutritional supplements, and nutraceuticals (see Appendix F).
▶ Review the procedure with the patient. Inform the patient that specimen collection takes approximately 5 to 10 min. Address concerns about pain and explain that there may be some discomfort during the venipuncture.

Sensitivity to social and cultural issues, as well as concern for modesty, is important in providing psychological support before, during, and after the procedure. There are no food, fluid, or medication restrictions unless by medical direction.

INTRATEST:

If the patient has a history of allergic reaction to latex, avoid the use of equipment containing latex.

Instruct the patient to cooperate fully and to follow directions. Direct the patient to breathe normally and to avoid unnecessary movement.

Observe standard precautions, and follow the general guidelines in Appendix A. Positively identify the patient, and label the appropriate specimen container with the corresponding patient demographics, initials of the person collecting the specimen, date, and time of collection. Perform a venipuncture.

Remove the needle and apply direct pressure with dry gauze to stop bleeding. Observe/assess venipuncture site for bleeding or hematoma formation and secure gauze with adhesive bandage.

Promptly transport the specimen to the laboratory for processing and analysis.

POST-TEST:

A report of the results will be made available to the requesting health-care provider (HCP), who will discuss the results with the patient.

Reinforce information given by the patient's HCP regarding further testing, treatment, or referral to another HCP. Inform the patient that a positive test result constitutes an independent risk factor for gastric cancer. Answer any questions or address any concerns voiced by the patient or family.

Depending on the results of this procedure, additional testing may be performed to evaluate or monitor progression of the disease process and determine the need for a change in therapy. Evaluate test results in relation to the patient's symptoms and other tests performed.

RELATED MONOGRAPHS:

Related tests include capsule endoscopy, EGD, gastric acid stimulation, gastric emptying scan, gastrin, and upper GI series.

Refer to the Gastrointestinal System table at the end of the book for related test by body system.

Hemoglobin Electrophoresis

SYNONYM/ACRONYM: N/A.

COMMON USE: To assist in evaluating hemolytic anemias and identifying hemoglobin variants, diagnose thalassemias, and sickle cell anemia.

SPECIMEN: Whole blood (1 mL) collected in a lavender-top (EDTA) tube.

NORMAL FINDINGS: (Method: Electrophoresis)

	Hgb A
Adult	Greater than 95%

	Hgb A$_2$
Adult	1.5–3.7%

	Hgb F
Newborns and infants	
1 day–3 wk	70–77%
6–9 wk	42–64%
3–4 mo	7–39%
6 mo	3–7%
8–11 mo	0.6–2.6%
Adult–older adult	Less than 2%

DESCRIPTION: Hemoglobin (Hgb) electrophoresis is a separation process used to identify normal and abnormal forms of Hgb. Electrophoresis and high-performance liquid chromatography as well as molecular genetics testing for mutations can also be used to identify abnormal forms of Hgb. Hgb A is the main form of Hgb in the normal adult. Hgb F is the main form of Hgb in the fetus, the remainder being composed of Hgb A_1 and A_2. Small amounts of Hgb F are normal in the adult. Hgb D, E, H, S, and C result from abnormal amino acid substitutions during the formation of Hgb and are inherited hemoglobinopathies.

INDICATIONS
• Assist in the diagnosis of Hgb C disease
• Assist in the diagnosis of thalassemia, especially in patients with a family history positive for the disorder
• Differentiate among thalassemia types
• Evaluate hemolytic anemia of unknown cause
• Evaluate a positive sickle cell screening test to differentiate sickle cell trait from sickle cell disease

POTENTIAL DIAGNOSIS

Increased in

Hgb A_2
• Hyperthyroidism
• Megaloblastic anemia
• β-Thalassemias
• Sickle trait

Hgb F
• Anemia (aplastic, associated with chronic disease or due to blood loss)
• Erythropoietic porphyria
• Hereditary elliptocytosis or spherocytosis
• Hereditary persistence of fetal Hgb
• Hyperthyroidism
• Leakage of fetal blood into maternal circulation
• Leukemia (acute or chronic)
• Myeloproliferative disorders
• Paroxysmal nocturnal hemoglobinuria
• Pernicious anemia
• Sickle cell disease
• Thalassemias
• Unstable hemoglobins

Hgb C
• Hgb C disease (second most common variant in the United States; has a higher prevalence among African Americans)

Hgb D
• Hgb D (rare hemoglobinopathy that may also be found in combination with Hgb S or thalassemia)

Hgb E

• Hgb E disease; thalassemia-like condition (second most common hemoglobinopathy in the world; occurs with the highest frequency in Southeast Asians and African Americans)

Hgb S

• Sickle cell trait or disease (most common variant in the United States; occurs with a frequency of about 8% among African Americans)

Hgb H

• α-Thalassemias
• Hgb Bart's hydrops fetalis syndrome

Decreased in

Hgb A$_2$

• Erythroleukemia
• Hgb H disease
• Iron-deficiency anemia (untreated)
• Sideroblastic anemia

CRITICAL FINDINGS: N/A

INTERFERING FACTORS

• High altitude and dehydration may increase values.
• Iron deficiency may decrease Hgb A$_2$, C, and S.
• In patients less than 3 mo of age, false-negative results for Hgb S occur in coincidental polycythemia.
• Red blood cell transfusion within 4 mo of test can mask abnormal Hgb levels.

NURSING IMPLICATIONS AND PROCEDURE

PRETEST:

▶ Positively identify the patient using at least two unique identifiers before providing care, treatment, or services.
Patient Teaching: Inform the patient this test can assist in diagnosing various types of anemias.

▶ Obtain a history of the patient's complaints, including a list of known allergens, especially allergies or sensitivities to latex.
▶ Obtain a history of the patient's hematopoietic system, symptoms, and results of previously performed laboratory tests and diagnostic and surgical procedures.
▶ Note any recent procedures that can interfere with test results.
▶ Obtain a list of the patient's current medications, including herbs, nutritional supplements, and nutraceuticals (see Appendix F).
▶ Review the procedure with the patient. Inform the patient that specimen collection takes approximately 5 to 10 min. Address concerns about pain and explain that there may be some discomfort during the venipuncture.
Sensitivity to social and cultural issues, as well as concern for modesty, is important in providing psychological support before, during, and after the procedure.
▶ There are no food, fluid, or medication restrictions unless by medical direction.

INTRATEST:

▶ If the patient has a history of allergic reaction to latex, avoid the use of equipment containing latex.
▶ Instruct the patient to cooperate fully and to follow directions. Direct the patient to breathe normally and to avoid unnecessary movement.
▶ Observe standard precautions, and follow the general guidelines in Appendix A. Positively identify the patient, and label the appropriate specimen container with the corresponding patient demographics, initials of the person collecting the specimen, date, and time of collection. Perform a venipuncture.
▶ Remove the needle and apply direct pressure with dry gauze to stop bleeding. Observe/assess venipuncture site for bleeding or hematoma formation and secure gauze with adhesive bandage.
▶ Promptly transport the specimen to the laboratory for processing and analysis.

▸ A report of the results will be made available to the requesting health-care provider (HCP), who will discuss the results with the patient.

▸ Reinforce information given by the patient's HCP regarding further testing, treatment, or referral to another HCP. Answer any questions or address any concerns voiced by the patient or family.

▸ Depending on the results of this procedure, additional testing may be performed to evaluate or monitor progression of the disease process and determine the need for a change in therapy. Evaluate test results in relation to the patient's symptoms and other tests performed.

RELATED MONOGRAPHS:

▸ Related tests include biopsy bone marrow, blood gases, CBC, CBC hematocrit, CBC hemoglobin, CBC RBC morphology, methemoglobin, newborn screening, osmotic fragility, and sickle cell screen.

▸ Refer to the Hematopoietic System table at the end of the book for related tests by body system.

Hemosiderin

SYNONYM/ACRONYM: Hemosiderin stain, Pappenheimer body stain, iron stain.

COMMON USE: To assist in investigating recent intravascular hemolysis and to assist in the diagnosis of unexplained anemias, hemochromatosis, and renal tube damage.

SPECIMEN: Urine (5 mL) from a random first morning sample, collected in a clean plastic collection container.

NORMAL FINDINGS: (Method: Microscopic examination of Prussian blue–stained specimen) None seen.

DESCRIPTION: Hemosiderin stain is used to indicate the presence of iron storage granules called *hemosiderin* by microscopic examination of urine sediment. Granules of hemosiderin stain blue when potassium ferrocyanide is added to the sample. Hemosiderin is normally found in the liver, spleen, and bone marrow, but not in the urine. Under normal conditions, hemosiderin is absorbed by the renal tubules; however, in extensive hemolysis, renal tubule damage, or an iron metabolism disorder, hemosiderin filters its way into the urine. The Prussian blue stain may also be used to identify siderocytes (iron-containing red blood cells [RBCs]) in peripheral blood. The presence of siderocytes in circulating RBCs is abnormal.

INDICATIONS
• Assist in the diagnosis of hemochromatosis (tissue damage caused by iron toxicity)
• Detect excessive RBC hemolysis within the systemic circulation
• Evaluate renal tubule dysfunction

POTENTIAL DIAGNOSIS

Increased in
Any condition that involves hemolysis will release hemoglobin from RBCs into circulation. Hemoglobin is converted to hemosiderin in the renal tubular epithelial cells.

- Burns
- Cold hemagglutinin disease
- Hemochromatosis
- Hemolytic transfusion reactions
- Mechanical trauma to RBCs
- Megaloblastic anemia
- Microangiopathic hemolytic anemia
- Paroxysmal nocturnal hemoglobinuria
- Pernicious anemia
- Sickle cell anemia
- Thalassemia major

Decreased in: N/A

CRITICAL FINDINGS: N/A

INTERFERING FACTORS: N/A

NURSING IMPLICATIONS AND PROCEDURE

PRETEST:

Positively identify the patient using at least two unique identifiers before providing care, treatment, or services.
Patient Teaching: Inform the patient this test can assist in diagnosing various types of anemias.
Obtain a history of the patient's complaints, including a list of known allergens, especially allergies or sensitivities to latex.
Obtain a history of the patient's hematopoietic system, especially a history of hemolytic anemia; symptoms; and results of previously performed laboratory tests and diagnostic and surgical procedures.
Obtain a list of the patient's current medications, including herbs, nutritional supplements, and nutraceuticals (see Appendix F).

Review the procedure with the patient. Inform the patient that specimen collection takes approximately 5 to 10 min. Address concerns about pain and explain that there should be no discomfort during the procedure.
Sensitivity to social and cultural issues, as well as concern for modesty, is important in providing psychological support before, during, and after the procedure.
There are no food, fluid, or medication restrictions unless by medical direction.

INTRATEST:

If the patient has a history of allergic reaction to latex, avoid the use of equipment containing latex.
Instruct the patient to cooperate fully and to follow directions.
Observe standard precautions, and follow the general guidelines in Appendix A. Positively identify the patient, and label the appropriate specimen container with the corresponding patient demographics, initials of the person collecting the specimen, date, and time of collection.

Clean-Catch Specimen
Instruct the male patient to (1) thoroughly wash his hands, (2) cleanse the meatus, (3) void a small amount into the toilet, and (4) void directly into the specimen container.
Instruct the female patient to (1) thoroughly wash her hands; (2) cleanse the labia from front to back; (3) while keeping the labia separated, void a small amount into the toilet; and (4) without interrupting the urine stream, void directly into the specimen container.

Indwelling Catheter
Put on gloves. Empty drainage tube of urine. It may be necessary to clamp off the catheter for 15 to 30 min before specimen collection. Cleanse specimen port with antiseptic swab, and then aspirate 5 mL of urine with a 21- to 25-gauge needle and syringe. Transfer urine to a collection container.

General
Promptly transport the specimen to the laboratory for processing and analysis.

POST-TEST:

A report of the results will be made available to the requesting health-care provider (HCP), who will discuss the results with the patient.

Recognize anxiety related to test results. Discuss the implications of abnormal test results on the patient's lifestyle. Provide teaching and information regarding the clinical implications of the test results, as appropriate.

Reinforce information given by the patient's HCP regarding further testing, treatment, or referral to another HCP. Answer any questions or address any concerns voiced by the patient or family.

Depending on the results of this procedure, additional testing may be performed to evaluate or monitor progression of the disease process and determine the need for a change in therapy. Evaluate test results in relation to the patient's symptoms and other tests performed.

RELATED MONOGRAPHS:

Related tests include biopsy bone marrow, biopsy kidney, BUN, CBC, CBC hematocrit, CBC hemoglobin, CBC RBC count, CBC RBC morphology, CBC WBC count and differential, CT renal, creatinine, creatinine clearance, D-dimer, ferritin, iron/total iron-binding capacity, lead, aPTT, PT/INR, and transferrin.

Refer to the Hematopoietic System table at the end of the book for related tests by body system.

Hepatitis A Antibody

SYNONYM/ACRONYM: HAV serology.

COMMON USE: To test blood for the presence of antibodies that would indicate a past or current hepatitis A infection.

SPECIMEN: Serum (1 mL) collected in a red- or tiger-top tube.

NORMAL FINDINGS: (Method: Enzyme immunoassay) Negative.

DESCRIPTION: The hepatitis A virus (HAV) is classified as a picornavirus. Its primary mode of transmission is by the fecal-oral route under conditions of poor personal hygiene or inadequate sanitation. The incubation period is about 28 days, with a range of 15 to 50 days. Onset is usually abrupt, with the acute disease lasting about 1 wk. Therapy is supportive, and there is no development of chronic or carrier states. Assays for total (immunoglobulin G and immunoglobulin M [IgM]) hepatitis A antibody and IgM-specific hepatitis A antibody assist in differentiating recent infection from prior exposure. If results from the IgM-specific or from both assays are positive, recent infection is suspected. If the IgM-specific test results are negative and the total antibody test results are positive, past infection is indicated. The clinically significant assay—IgM-specific antibody—is often the only test requested. Jaundice occurs in 70% to 80% of adult cases of HAV infection and in 70% of pediatric cases.

INDICATIONS

• Screen individuals at high risk of exposure, such as those in long-term residential facilities or correctional facilities
• Screen individuals with suspected HAV infection

POTENTIAL DIAGNOSIS

Positive findings in
• Individuals with current HAV infection
• Individuals with past HAV infection

CRITICAL FINDINGS: N/A

INTERFERING FACTORS: N/A

NURSING IMPLICATIONS AND PROCEDURE

PRETEST:

▶ Positively identify the patient using at least two unique identifiers before providing care, treatment, or services.
▶ *Patient Teaching:* Inform the patient this test can assist in evaluating for hepatitis infection.
▶ Obtain a history of the patient's complaints, including a list of known allergens, especially allergies or sensitivities to latex.
▶ Obtain a history of the patient's hepatobiliary and immune systems, symptoms, and results of previously performed laboratory tests and diagnostic and surgical procedures.
▶ Obtain a list of the patient's current medications, including herbs, nutritional supplements, and nutraceuticals (see Appendix F).
▶ Review the procedure with the patient. Inform the patient that specimen collection takes approximately 5 to

10 min. Address concerns about pain and explain that there may be some discomfort during the venipuncture.
▶ There are no food, fluid, or medication restrictions unless by medical direction.

INTRATEST:

▶ If the patient has a history of allergic reaction to latex, avoid the use of equipment containing latex.
▶ Instruct the patient to cooperate fully and to follow directions. Direct the patient to breathe normally and to avoid unnecessary movement.
▶ Observe standard precautions, and follow the general guidelines in Appendix A. Positively identify the patient, and label the appropriate specimen container with the corresponding patient demographics, initials of the person collecting the specimen, date, and time of collection. Perform a venipuncture.
▶ Remove the needle and apply direct pressure with dry gauze to stop bleeding. Observe/assess venipuncture site for bleeding or hematoma formation and secure gauze with adhesive bandage.
▶ Promptly transport the specimen to the laboratory for processing and analysis.

POST-TEST:

▶ A report of the results will be made available to the requesting health-care provider (HCP), who will discuss the results with the patient.
▶ *Nutritional Considerations:* Dietary recommendations may be indicated and will vary depending on the type and severity of the condition. Elimination of alcohol ingestion and a diet optimized for convalescence are commonly included in the treatment plan.
▶ *Social and Cultural Considerations:* Recognize anxiety related to test results, and offer support. Discuss the implications of abnormal test results on the patient's lifestyle. Provide teaching and information regarding the clinical implications of the test results, as appropriate. Counsel the patient, as appropriate, regarding risk of transmission and proper prophylaxis. Immune globulin can be given before

exposure (in the case of individuals who may be traveling to a location where the disease is endemic) or after exposure, during the incubation period. Prophylaxis is most effective when administered 2 wk after exposure. Reinforce information given by the patient's HCP regarding further testing, treatment, or referral to another HCP. Provide information regarding vaccine-preventable diseases where indicated (e.g., anthrax, cervical cancer, diphtheria, encephalitis, hepatitis A and B, H1N1 flu, human papillomavirus, *Haemophilus* influenza, seasonal influenza, Lyme disease, measles, meningococcal disease, monkeypox, mumps, pertussis, pneumococcal disease, polio, rotavirus, rubella, shingles, smallpox, tetanus, typhoid fever, varicella, yellow fever). Provide contact information, if desired, for the Centers for Disease Control and Prevention (www.cdc.gov/vaccines/vpd-vac). Answer any questions or address any concerns voiced by the patient or family. Depending on the results of this procedure, additional testing may be performed to evaluate or monitor progression of the disease process and determine the need for a change in therapy. Evaluate test results in relation to the patient's symptoms and other tests performed.

RELATED MONOGRAPHS:

Related tests include ALT, ALP, AST, bilirubin, GGT, and HBV, HBC, HBD, and HBE antigens and antibodies.
Refer to the Hepatobiliary and Immune systems tables at the end of the book for related tests by body system.

H

Hepatitis B Antigen and Antibody

SYNONYM/ACRONYM: HBeAg, HBeAb, HBcAb, HBsAb, HBsAg.

COMMON USE: To test blood for the presence of antibodies that would indicate a past or current hepatitis B infection.

SPECIMEN: Serum (1 mL) collected in a red- or tiger-top tube.

NORMAL FINDINGS: (Method: Enzyme immunoassay) Negative.

DESCRIPTION: The hepatitis B virus (HBV) is classified as a double-stranded DNA retrovirus of the Hepadnaviridae family. Its primary modes of transmission are parenteral, perinatal, and sexual contact. Serological profiles vary with different scenarios (i.e., asymptomatic infection, acute/resolved infection, coinfection, and chronic carrier state). The formation and detectability of markers is also dose dependent. The following description refers to HBV infection that becomes resolved. The incubation period is generally 6 to 16 wk. The hepatitis B surface antigen (HBsAg) is the first marker to appear after infection. It is detectable 8 to 12 wk after exposure and often precedes symptoms. At about the time liver enzymes fall back to normal levels, the HBsAg titer has fallen to nondetectable levels. If the HBsAg remains detectable after 6 mo, the patient will likely become a chronic carrier who can transmit the virus. Hepatitis Be antigen (HBeAg) appears in the serum 10 to 12 wk after exposure. HBeAg can be found in the serum of patients with acute or chronic HBV infection and is a sign of active viral replication and infectivity. Levels of hepatitis Be antibody (HBeAb) appear about 14 wk after exposure, suggesting resolution of the infection and reduction of the patient's ability to transmit the disease. The more quickly HBeAg disappears, the shorter the acute phase of the infection. Immunoglobulin M–specific hepatitis B core antibody (HBcAb) appears 6 to 14 wk after exposure to HBsAg and continues to be detectable either until the infection is resolved or over the life span in patients who are in a chronic carrier state. In some cases, HBcAb may be the only detectable marker; hence, its lone appearance has sometimes been referred to as the *core window.* HBcAb is not an indicator of recovery or immunity; however, it does indicate current or previous infection. Hepatitis B surface antibody (HBsAb) appears 2 to 16 wk after HBsAg disappears. Appearance of HBsAb represents clinical recovery and immunity to the virus.

Onset of HBV infection is usually insidious. Most children and half of infected adults are asymptomatic. During the acute phase of infection, symptoms range from mild to severe. Chronicity decreases with age. HBsAg and HBcAb tests are used to screen donated blood before transfusion. HBsAg testing is often part of the routine prenatal screen. Vaccination of infants, children, and young adults is becoming a standard of care and in some cases a requirement.

INDICATIONS
- Detect exposure to HBV
- Detect possible carrier status
- Pre- and postvaccination testing
- Routine prenatal testing
- Screen donated blood before transfusion
- Screen for individuals at high risk of exposure, such as hemodialysis patients, persons with multiple sex partners, persons with a history of other sexually transmitted diseases, IV drug abusers, infants born to infected mothers, individuals residing in long-term residential facilities or correctional facilities, recipients of blood- or plasma-derived products, allied health-care workers, and public service employees who come in contact with blood and blood products

POTENTIAL DIAGNOSIS

Positive findings in
- Patients currently infected with HBV
- Patients with a past HBV infection

CRITICAL FINDINGS: N/A

INTERFERING FACTORS
- Drugs that may decrease HBeAb and HBsAb include interferon.

NURSING IMPLICATIONS AND PROCEDURE

PRETEST:

▸ Positively identify the patient using at least two unique identifiers before providing care, treatment, or services.
▸ *Patient Teaching:* Inform the patient this test can assist in evaluating for hepatitis infection.
▸ Obtain a history of the patient's complaints, including a list of known allergens, especially allergies or sensitivities to latex.
▸ Obtain a history of the patient's hepatobiliary and immune systems,

symptoms, and results of previously performed laboratory tests and diagnostic and surgical procedures.

Obtain a history of IV drug use, high-risk sexual activity, or occupational exposure.

Obtain a list of the patient's current medications, including herbs, nutritional supplements, and nutraceuticals (see Appendix F).

Review the procedure with the patient. Inform the patient that specimen collection takes approximately 5 to 10 min. Address concerns about pain and explain that there may be some discomfort during the venipuncture.

Sensitivity to social and cultural issues, as well as concern for modesty, is important in providing psychological support before, during, and after the procedure.

There are no food, fluid, or medication restrictions unless by medical direction.

INTRATEST:

If the patient has a history of allergic reaction to latex, avoid the use of equipment containing latex.

Instruct the patient to cooperate fully and to follow directions. Direct the patient to breathe normally and to avoid unnecessary movement.

Observe standard precautions, and follow the general guidelines in Appendix A. Positively identify the patient, and label the appropriate specimen container with the corresponding patient demographics, initials of the person collecting the specimen, date, and time of collection. Perform a venipuncture.

Remove the needle and apply direct pressure with dry gauze to stop bleeding. Observe/assess venipuncture site for bleeding or hematoma formation and secure gauze with adhesive bandage.

Promptly transport the specimen to the laboratory for processing and analysis.

POST-TEST:

A report of the results will be made available to the requesting health-care provider (HCP), who will discuss the results with the patient.

Nutritional Considerations: Dietary recommendations may be indicated and will vary depending on the type and severity of the condition. Elimination of alcohol ingestion and a diet optimized for convalescence are commonly included in the treatment plan. A high-calorie, high-protein, moderate-fat diet with a high fluid intake is often recommended for patients with hepatitis.

Cultural and Social Considerations: Recognize anxiety related to test results, and be supportive of impaired activity related to lack of neuromuscular control, perceived loss of independence, and fear of shortened life expectancy. Discuss the implications of abnormal test results on the patient's lifestyle. Provide teaching and information regarding the clinical implications of the test results, as appropriate. Educate the patient regarding access to counseling services. Counsel the patient, as appropriate, regarding risk of transmission and proper prophylaxis. Hepatitis B immune globulin (HBIG) vaccination should be given immediately after situations in which there is a potential for HBV exposure (e.g., accidental needle stick, perinatal period, sexual contact) for temporary, passive protection. Some studies have indicated that interferon alfa may be useful in the treatment of chronic hepatitis B.

Counsel the patient and significant contacts, as appropriate, that HBIG immunization is available and has in fact become a requirement in many places as part of childhood immunization and employee health programs. Parents may choose to sign a waiver preventing their newborns from receiving the vaccine; they may choose not to vaccinate on the basis of philosophical, religious, or medical reasons. Vaccination regulations vary by state.

Inform the patient that positive findings must be reported to local health department officials, who will question him or her regarding sexual partners.

Cultural and Social Considerations: Offer support, as appropriate, to patients who may be the victims of rape or other forms of sexual assault, including children and elderly individuals. Educate the patient regarding access to counseling services. Provide a nonjudgmental, nonthreatening atmosphere for a discussion during which the risks of sexually transmitted diseases are explained. It is also important to discuss the problems that the patient may experience (e.g., guilt, depression, anger).

Reinforce information given by the patient's HCP regarding further testing, treatment, or referral to another HCP. Provide information regarding vaccine-preventable diseases where indicated (e.g., anthrax, cervical cancer, diphtheria, encephalitis, hepatitis A and B, H1N1 flu, human papillomavirus, *Haemophilus* influenza, seasonal influenza, Lyme disease, measles, meningococcal disease, monkeypox, mumps, pertussis, pneumococcal disease, polio, rotavirus, rubella, shingles, smallpox, tetanus, typhoid fever, varicella, yellow fever). Provide contact information, if desired, for the Centers for Disease Control and Prevention (www.cdc.gov/vaccines/vpd-vac). Answer any questions or address any concerns voiced by the patient or family.

Depending on the results of this procedure, additional testing may be performed to evaluate or monitor progression of the disease process and determine the need for a change in therapy. Evaluate test results in relation to the patient's symptoms and other tests performed.

RELATED MONOGRAPHS:

Related tests include ALT, ALP, antibodies, antimitochondrial, AST, bilirubin, biopsy liver, *Chlamydia* group antibody, cholangiography percutaneous transhepatic, culture anal, GGT, hepatitis C serology, HIV serology, liver and spleen scan, syphilis serology, and US liver.

Refer to the Hepatobiliary and Immune systems tables at the end of the book for related tests by body system.

Hepatitis C Antibody

SYNONYM/ACRONYM: HCV serology, hepatitis non-A/non-B.

COMMON USE: To test blood for the presence of antibodies that would indicate a past or current hepatitis C infection.

SPECIMEN: Serum (1 mL) collected in a red- or tiger-top tube.

NORMAL FINDINGS: (Method: Enzyme immunoassay, branched chain DNA [bDNA], polymerase chain reaction [PCR], recombinant immunoblot assay [RIBA]) Negative.

DESCRIPTION: The hepatitis C virus (HCV) causes the majority of bloodborne non-A/non-B hepatitis cases. Its primary modes of transmission are parenteral, perinatal, and sexual contact. The virus is thought to be a flavivirus and contains a single-stranded RNA core. The incubation period varies widely, from 2 to 52 wk. Onset is insidious, and the risk of chronic liver disease after infection is high. On average, antibodies to hepatitis C are detectable in approximately 45% of infected individuals within 6 wk of infection. The remaining 55% produce antibodies within the next 6 to 12 mo. Once infected with HCV, 50% of patients will become chronic carriers. Infected individuals and carriers have a high frequency of chronic liver diseases such as cirrhosis and chronic active hepatitis, and they have a higher risk of developing hepatocellular cancer. The transmission of hepatitis C by blood transfusion has decreased dramatically since it became part of the routine screening panel for blood donors. The possibility of prenatal transmission exists, especially in the presence of HIV coinfection. Therefore, this test is often included in prenatal testing packages. Currently, nucleic acid amplification testing (NAAT) is the only way to document the presence of ongoing infection. PCR and bDNA methods are recognized by the Centers for Disease Control and Prevention (CDC) as appropriate supplemental testing for the confirmation of anti-HCV antibody.

INDICATIONS
- Assist in the diagnosis of non-A/non-B viral hepatitis infection
- Monitor patients suspected of HCV infection but who have not yet produced antibody
- Routine prenatal testing
- Screen donated blood before transfusion

POTENTIAL DIAGNOSIS

Positive findings in
- Patients currently infected with HCV
- Patients with a past HCV infection

Negative findings in: N/A

CRITICAL FINDINGS: N/A

INTERFERING FACTORS
- Drugs that may decrease hepatitis C antibody levels include interferon.

NURSING IMPLICATIONS AND PROCEDURE

PRETEST:
- Positively identify the patient using at least two unique identifiers before providing care, treatment, or services.
- *Patient Teaching:* Inform the patient this test can assist in evaluating for hepatitis infection.
- Obtain a history of the patient's complaints, including a list of known allergens, especially allergies or sensitivities to latex.
- Obtain a history of the patient's hepatobiliary and immune systems, symptoms, and results of previously performed laboratory tests and diagnostic and surgical procedures.
- Obtain a history of IV drug use, high-risk sexual activity, and occupational exposure.
- Obtain a list of the patient's current medications, including herbs, nutritional supplements, and nutraceuticals (see Appendix F).
- Review the procedure with the patient. Inform the patient that specimen collection takes approximately 5 to 10 min. Address concerns about pain and explain that there may be some discomfort during the venipuncture.
- *Sensitivity to social and cultural issues,* as well as concern for modesty, is important in providing psychological support before, during, and after the procedure.
- There are no food, fluid, or medication restrictions unless by medical direction.

INTRATEST:
- If the patient has a history of allergic reaction to latex, avoid the use of equipment containing latex.
- Instruct the patient to cooperate fully and to follow directions. Direct the patient to breathe normally and to avoid unnecessary movement.

- Observe standard precautions, and follow the general guidelines in Appendix A. Positively identify the patient, and label the appropriate specimen container with the corresponding patient demographics, initials of the person collecting the specimen, date, and time of collection. Perform a venipuncture.
- Remove the needle and apply direct pressure with dry gauze to stop bleeding. Observe/assess venipuncture site for bleeding or hematoma formation and secure gauze with adhesive bandage.
- Promptly transport the specimen to the laboratory for processing and analysis.

POST-TEST:

- A report of the results will be made available to the requesting health-care provider (HCP), who will discuss the results with the patient.
- *Nutritional Considerations:* Dietary recommendations may be indicated and will vary depending on the type and severity of the condition. Currently, for example, there are no specific medications that can be given to cure hepatitis; however, bedrest, elimination of alcohol ingestion, and a diet optimized for convalescence are commonly included in the treatment plan. A high-calorie, high-protein, moderate-fat diet with a high fluid intake is often recommended for patients with hepatitis.
- *Cultural and Social Considerations:* Recognize anxiety related to test results, and be supportive of impaired activity related to lack of neuromuscular control, perceived loss of independence, and fear of shortened life expectancy. Discuss the implications of abnormal test results on the patient's lifestyle. Provide teaching and information regarding the clinical implications of the test results, as appropriate. Educate the patient regarding access to counseling services. Counsel the patient, as appropriate, regarding the risk of transmission and proper prophylaxis. Interferon alfa was approved in 1991 by the U.S. Food and Drug Administration for use as a therapeutic agent in the treatment of chronic HCV infection.
- Inform the patient that positive findings must be reported to local health department officials, who will question him or her regarding sexual partners.
- *Cultural and Social Considerations:* Offer support, as appropriate, to patients who may be the victims of rape or other forms of sexual assault, including children and elderly individuals. Educate the patient regarding access to counseling services. Provide a nonjudgmental, nonthreatening atmosphere for a discussion during which the risks of sexually transmitted diseases are explained. It is also important to discuss the problems that the patient may experience (e.g., guilt, depression, anger).
- Reinforce information given by the patient's HCP regarding further testing, treatment, or referral to another HCP. Provide information regarding vaccine-preventable diseases where indicated (e.g., anthrax, cervical cancer, diphtheria, encephalitis, hepatitis A and B, H1N1 flu, human papillomavirus, *Haemophilus* influenza, seasonal influenza, Lyme disease, measles, meningococcal disease, monkeypox, mumps, pertussis, pneumococcal disease, polio, rotavirus, rubella, shingles, smallpox, tetanus, typhoid fever, varicella, yellow fever). Provide contact information, if desired, for the CDC (www.cdc.gov/vaccines/vpd-vac). Answer any questions or address any concerns voiced by the patient or family.
- Depending on the results of this procedure, additional testing may be performed to evaluate or monitor progression of the disease process and determine the need for a change in therapy. Evaluate test results in relation to the patient's symptoms and other tests performed.

RELATED MONOGRAPHS:

- Related tests include ALT, ALP, antibodies, antimitochondrial, AST, bilirubin, biopsy liver, *Chlamydia* group antibody, cholangiography percutaneous transhepatic, culture anal, GGT, hepatitis B serology, hepatobiliary scan, HIV serology, liver and spleen scan, syphilis serology, and US liver.
- Refer to the Hepatobiliary and Immune systems tables at the end of the book for related tests by body system.

Hepatitis D Antibody

SYNONYM/ACRONYM: Delta hepatitis.

COMMON USE: To test blood for the presence of antibodies that would indicate a past or current hepatitis D infections.

SPECIMEN: Serum (1 mL) collected in a red- or tiger-top tube.

NORMAL FINDINGS: (Method: Enzyme immunoassay, EIA) Negative.

POTENTIAL DIAGNOSIS

Positive findings in
- Individuals currently infected with HDV
- Individuals with a past HDV infection

CRITICAL FINDINGS: N/A

Find and print out the full monograph at DavisPlus (davisplus.fadavis.com, keyword Van Leeuwen).

Hepatitis E Antibody

SYNONYM/ACRONYM: HEV.

COMMON USE: To test blood for the presence of antibodies that would indicate a past or current hepatitis E infection.

SPECIMEN: Serum (1 mL) collected in a red- or tiger-top tube.

NORMAL FINDINGS: (Method: Enzyme immunoassay) Negative.

DESCRIPTION: The hepatitis E virus is classified as a single-stranded RNA hepevirus with five separate genotypes. HEV is a major cause of enteric non-A hepatitis worldwide; about 20% of the U.S. population demonstrates presence of immunoglobulin G (IgG) antibody. Its primary mode of transmission is the fecal-oral route under conditions of poor personal hygiene or inadequate sanitation.

The incubation period is about 28 days. IgM and IgG are detectable within one month mo after infection. Onset is usually abrupt, with the acute disease lasting several weeks. Therapy is supportive, and patients usually recover, although the disease is quite debilitating during the acute phase. Hepatitis E infection can occasionally develop into a severe liver disease and may cause chronic infection in organ transplant or other immunocompromised patients. Assays for total (IgG and immunoglobulin M [IgM]) hepatitis E antibody and IgM-specific hepatitis E antibody help differentiate recent infection from prior exposure. If results from the IgM-specific or from both assays are positive, recent infection is suspected. If the IgM-specific test results are negative and the total antibody test results are positive, past infection is indicated. IgM remains detectable for about 2 mo; IgG levels persist for months to years after recovery.

INDICATIONS
• Screen individuals with suspected HEV infection

POTENTIAL DIAGNOSIS

Positive findings in
• Individuals with current HEV infection
• Individuals with past HEV infection

CRITICAL FINDINGS: N/A

INTERFERING FACTORS: N/A

NURSING IMPLICATIONS AND PROCEDURE

PRETEST:
▶ Positively identify the patient using at least two unique identifiers before providing care, treatment, or services.
▶ *Patient Teaching:* Inform the patient this test can assist in evaluating for hepatitis infection.
▶ Obtain a history of the patient's complaints, including a list of known allergens, especially allergies or sensitivities to latex.
▶ Obtain a history of the patient's hepatobiliary and immune systems, symptoms, and results of previously performed laboratory tests and diagnostic and surgical procedures.
▶ Obtain a list of the patient's current medications, including herbs, nutritional supplements, and nutraceuticals (see Appendix F).
▶ Review the procedure with the patient. Inform the patient that specimen collection takes approximately 5 to 10 min. Address concerns about pain and explain that there may be some discomfort during the venipuncture. There are no food, fluid, or medication restrictions unless by medical direction.

INTRATEST:
▶ If the patient has a history of allergic reaction to latex, avoid the use of equipment containing latex.
▶ Instruct the patient to cooperate fully and to follow directions. Direct the patient to breathe normally and to avoid unnecessary movement.
▶ Observe standard precautions, and follow the general guidelines in Appendix A. Positively identify the patient, and label the appropriate specimen container with the corresponding patient demographics, initials of the person collecting the specimen, date, and time of collection. Perform a venipuncture.
▶ Remove the needle and apply direct pressure with dry gauze to stop bleeding. Observe/assess venipuncture site for bleeding or hematoma formation and secure gauze with adhesive bandage.
▶ Promptly transport the specimen to the laboratory for processing and analysis.

POST-TEST:
▶ A report of the results will be made available to the requesting health-care provider (HCP), who will discuss the results with the patient.
▶ *Nutritional Considerations:* Dietary recommendations may be indicated and will vary depending on the type and severity of the condition. Elimination of alcohol ingestion and a diet optimized for convalescence are commonly included in the treatment plan.
▶ *Social and Cultural Considerations:* Recognize anxiety related to test results, and offer support. Discuss

the implications of abnormal test results on the patient's lifestyle. Provide teaching and information regarding the clinical implications of the test results, as appropriate. Counsel the patient, as appropriate, regarding risk of transmission and proper prophylaxis.

Reinforce information given by the patient's HCP regarding further testing, treatment, or referral to another HCP. Provide information regarding vaccine-preventable diseases where indicated (e.g., anthrax, cervical cancer, diphtheria, encephalitis, hepatitis A and B, H1N1 flu, human papillomavirus, *Haemophilus* influenza, seasonal influenza, Lyme disease, measles, meningococcal disease, monkeypox, mumps, pertussis, pneumococcal disease, polio, rotavirus, rubella, shingles, smallpox, tetanus, typhoid fever, varicella, yellow fever). Provide contact information, if desired, for the Centers for Disease Control and Prevention (www.cdc.gov/vaccines/vpd-vac). Answer any questions or address any concerns voiced by the patient or family. Depending on the results of this procedure, additional testing may be performed to evaluate or monitor progression of the disease process and determine the need for a change in therapy. Evaluate test results in relation to the patient's symptoms and other tests performed.

RELATED MONOGRAPHS:

Related tests include ALT, ALP, AST, bilirubin, GGT, and HAV, HBV, HBC, and HBD antigens and antibodies.

Refer to the Hepatobiliary and Immune systems tables at the end of the book for related tests by body system.

Hepatobiliary Scan

SYNONYM/ACRONYM: Biliary tract radionuclide scan, cholescintigraphy, hepatobiliary imaging, hepatobiliary scintigraphy, gallbladder scan, HIDA (a technetium-99m diisopropyl analogue) scan.

COMMON USE: To visualize and assess the cystic and common bile ducts of the gall bladder toward diagnosing obstructions, stones, inflammation, and tumor.

AREA OF APPLICATION: Bile ducts.

CONTRAST: IV contrast medium (iminodiacetic acid compounds), usually combined with technetium-99m.

DESCRIPTION: The hepatobiliary scan is a nuclear medicine study of the hepatobiliary excretion system. It is primarily used to determine the patency of the cystic and common bile ducts, but it can also be used to determine overall hepatic function, gallbladder function, presence of gallstones (indirectly), and sphincter of Oddi dysfunction. Technetium (Tc-99m) HIDA (tribromoethyl, an iminodiacetic acid) is injected IV and excreted into the bile duct system. A gamma camera detects the radiation emitted from the injected contrast medium, and a representative image of the duct system is obtained. The results are correlated with other diagnostic studies, such as IV cholangiography, computed tomography (CT) scan of the gallbladder, and ultrasonography. Gallbladder emptying or ejection fraction can be determined by administering a fatty meal or cholecystokinin to the patient. This procedure can be used before and after surgery to determine the extent of bile reflux.

INDICATIONS

- Aid in the diagnosis of acute and chronic cholecystitis
- Aid in the diagnosis of suspected gallbladder disorders, such as inflammation, perforation, or calculi
- Assess enterogastric reflux
- Assess obstructive jaundice when done in combination with radiography or ultrasonography
- Determine common duct obstruction caused by tumors or choledocholithiasis
- Evaluate biliary enteric bypass patency
- Postoperatively evaluate gastric surgical procedures and abdominal trauma

POTENTIAL DIAGNOSIS

Normal findings in
- Normal shape, size, and function of the gallbladder with patent cystic and common bile ducts

Abnormal findings in
- Cholecystitis (acalculous, acute, chronic)
- Common bile duct obstruction secondary to gallstones, tumor, or stricture
- Congenital biliary atresia or choledochal cyst
- Postoperative biliary leak, fistula, or obstruction
- Trauma-induced bile leak or cyst

CRITICAL FINDINGS: N/A

INTERFERING FACTORS

This procedure is contraindicated for
- Patients who are pregnant or suspected of being pregnant, unless the potential benefits of the procedure far outweigh the risks to the fetus and mother.

Factors that may impair clear imaging
- Inability of the patient to cooperate or remain still during the procedure because of age, significant pain, or mental status.
- Retained barium from a previous radiological procedure.
- Metallic objects (e.g., jewelry, body rings) within the examination field, which may inhibit organ visualization and cause unclear images.
- Bilirubin levels greater than or equal to 30 mg/dL, depending on the radionuclide used, which may decrease hepatic uptake.
- Other nuclear scans done within the previous 24 to 48 hr.
- Fasting for more than 24 hr before the procedure, total parenteral nutrition, and alcoholism.
- Ingestion of food or liquids within 2 to 4 hr before the scan.

Other considerations
- Failure to follow dietary restrictions before the procedure may cause the procedure to be canceled or repeated.
- Improper injection of the radionuclide that allows the tracer to seep deep into the muscle tissue can produce erroneous hot spots.
- Inaccurate timing of imaging after the radionuclide injection can affect the results.
- Consultation with a health-care provider (HCP) should occur before the procedure for radiation safety concerns regarding younger

patients or patients who are lactating.

Risks associated with radiation overexposure can result from frequent x-ray or radionuclide procedures. Personnel working in the examination area should wear badges to record their level of radiation exposure.

NURSING IMPLICATIONS AND PROCEDURE

PRETEST:

Positively identify the patient using at least two unique identifiers before providing care, treatment, or services.

Patient Teaching: Inform the patient this procedure can assist in detecting inflammation or obstruction of the gallbladder or ducts.

Obtain a history of the patient's complaints, including a list of known allergens, especially allergies or sensitivities to latex, iodine, seafood, contrast medium, anesthetics, or dyes.

Obtain a history of the patient's hepatobiliary system, symptoms, and results of previously performed laboratory tests and diagnostic and surgical procedures.

Note any recent procedures that can interfere with test results, including examinations using iodine-based contrast medium.

Record the date of the last menstrual period and determine the possibility of pregnancy in perimenopausal women.

Obtain a list of the patient's current medications, including herbs, nutritional supplements, and nutraceuticals (see Appendix F).

Review the procedure with the patient. Address concerns about pain and explain that some pain may be experienced during the test, or there may be moments of discomfort. Reassure the patient that the radionuclide poses no radioactive hazard and rarely produces side effects. Inform the patient the procedure is performed in a nuclear medicine department by an HCP specializing in this procedure, with support staff, and takes approximately 30 to 60 min.

Inform the patient that the HCP will place him or her in a supine position on a flat table.

Sensitivity to social and cultural issues, as well as concern for modesty, is important in providing psychological support before, during, and after the procedure.

Instruct the patient to remove jewelry and other metallic objects from the area to be examined prior to the procedure.

Instruct the patient to restrict food and fluids for 4 to 6 hr prior to the procedure. Protocols may vary among facilities.

Make sure a written and informed consent has been signed prior to the procedure and before administering any medications.

INTRATEST:

Observe standard precautions, and follow the general guidelines in Appendix A. Positively identify the patient.

Ensure that the patient has complied with dietary, fluids, and medication restrictions for 4 to 6 hr prior to the procedure.

Ensure that the patient has removed all external metallic objects prior to the procedure.

If the patient has a history of allergic reactions to any substance or drug, administer ordered prophylactic steroids or antihistamines before the procedure.

Have emergency equipment readily available.

Instruct the patient to void prior to the procedure and to change into the gown, robe, and foot coverings provided.

Instruct the patient to cooperate fully and to follow directions. Instruct the patient to lie still during the procedure because movement produces unclear images.

Administer sedative to a child or to an uncooperative adult, as ordered.

Place the patient in a supine position on a flat table with foam wedges to help maintain position and immobilization.

H

IV radionuclide is administered, and the upper right quadrant of the abdomen is scanned immediately, with images then taken every 5 min for the first 30 min and every 10 min for the next 30 min. If the gallbladder cannot be visualized, delayed views are taken in 2, 4, and 24 hr in order to differentiate acute from chronic cholecystitis or to detect the degree of obstruction.

IV morphine may be administered during the study to initiate spasms of the sphincter of Oddi, forcing the radionuclide into the gallbladder, if the organ is not visualized within 1 hr of injection of the radionuclide. Imaging is then done 20 to 50 min later to determine delayed visualization or nonvisualization of the gallbladder.

If gallbladder function or bile reflux is being assessed, the patient will be given a fatty meal or cholecystokinin 60 min after the injection.

Remove the needle or catheter and apply a pressure dressing over the puncture site.

Observe the needle/catheter insertion site for bleeding, inflammation, or hematoma formation.

POST-TEST:

A report of the results will be made available to the requesting HCP, who will discuss the results with the patient.

Unless contraindicated, advise patient to drink increased amounts of fluids for 24 to 48 hr to eliminate the radionuclide from the body. Inform the patient that radionuclide is eliminated from the body within 6 to 24 hr.

No other radionuclide tests should be scheduled for 24 to 48 hr after this procedure.

Instruct the patient to resume usual diet, fluids, medications, and activity as directed by the HCP.

Instruct the patient in the care and assessment of the injection site.

If a woman who is breastfeeding must have a nuclear scan, she should not breastfeed the infant until the radionuclide has been eliminated. This could take as long as 3 days. She should be instructed to express the milk and discard it during the 3-day period to prevent cessation of milk production.

Instruct the patient to immediately flush the toilet and to meticulously wash hands with soap and water after each voiding for 24 hr after the procedure.

Instruct all caregivers to wear gloves when discarding urine for 24 hr after the procedure. Wash gloved hands with soap and water before removing gloves. Then wash ungloved hands after the gloves are removed.

Recognize anxiety related to test results, and be supportive of perceived loss of independent function. Discuss the implications of abnormal test results on the patient's lifestyle. Provide teaching and information regarding the clinical implications of the test results, as appropriate.

Reinforce information given by the patient's HCP regarding further testing, treatment, or referral to another HCP. Answer any questions or address any concerns voiced by the patient or family.

Depending on the results of this procedure, additional testing may be needed to evaluate or monitor progression of the disease process and determine the need for a change in therapy. Evaluate test results in relation to the patient's symptoms and other tests performed.

RELATED MONOGRAPHS:

Related tests include amylase, bilirubin, CT abdomen, lipase, liver and spleen scan, MRI abdomen, radiofrequency ablation liver, US abdomen, and US liver and bile ducts.

Refer to the Hepatobiliary System table at the end of the book for related tests by body system.

Hexosaminidase A and B

SYNONYM/ACRONYM: N/A.

COMMON USE: To assist in diagnosing Tay-Sachs disease by identifying a hexosaminidase enzyme deficiency.

SPECIMEN: Serum (3 mL) collected in a red-top tube. After the specimen is collected, it must be brought immediately to the laboratory. Once in the laboratory, the specimen must be allowed to clot for 1 to 1.5 hr in the refrigerator. The serum should then be removed and frozen immediately.

NORMAL FINDINGS: (Method: Fluorometry)

Total Hexosaminidase	Conventional Units	SI Units (Conventional Units × 0.0167)
Noncarrier	589–955 nmol/hr/mL	9.83–15.95 units/L
Heterozygote	465–675 nmol/hr/mL	7.77–11.27 units/L
Tay-Sachs homozygote	Greater than 1,027 nmol/hr/mL	Greater than 17.15 units/L

Hexosaminidase A	Conventional Units	SI Units (Conventional Units × 0.0167)
Noncarrier	456–592 nmol/hr/mL	7.62–9.88 units/L
Heterozygote	197–323 nmol/hr/mL	3.29–5.39 units/L
Tay-Sachs homozygote	0 nmol/hr/mL	0 units/L

Hexosaminidase B	Conventional Units	SI Units (Conventional Units × 0.0167)
Noncarrier	12–32 nmol/hr/mL	0.2–0.54 units/L
Heterozygote	21–81 nmol/hr/mL	0.35–1.35 units/L
Tay-Sachs homozygote	Greater than 305 nmol/hr/mL	Greater than 5.09 units/L

DESCRIPTION: Hexosaminidase is a lysosomal enzyme. There are three predominant isoenzymes: hexosaminidase A, B, and S. Deficiency results in the accumulation of complex sphingolipids and gangliosides in the brain. There are more than 70 lysosomal enzyme disorders. Testing for hexosaminidase A is done to determine the presence of Tay-Sachs disease, a genetic autosomal recessive condition characterized by early and progressive retardation of physical and mental development. This enzyme deficiency is most common among Ashkenazi Jews, for whom the incidence is 1 in 3,000 and carrier rate is 1 in 30. Genetic testing by DNA polymerase chain reaction analysis can identify as many as 94% of the gene mutations associated with Tay-Sachs disease in persons with Ashkenazi Jewish heritage, 80% of the mutations in persons with French-Canadian ancestry, and 25% of mutations in non-Jewish Caucasians. Genetic testing combined with enzyme screening analysis and correlation of clinical information provides the most reliable means of determining carrier status. The American College of Medical genetics recommends routine preconceptual or prenatal screening for nine different hereditary diseases common to persons with Ashkenazi Jewish heritage. Counseling and written, informed consent are recommended and sometimes required before genetic testing. Patients who are homozygous for this trait have no hexosaminidase A and have greatly elevated levels of hexosaminidase B; signs and symptoms include red spot in the retina, blindness, and muscular weakness. Tay-Sachs disease results in early death, usually by age 3 or 4.

Hereditary Disease	Estimated Incidence in Ashkenazim	Estimated Carrier Rate in Ashkenazim
Bloom's syndrome	1:40,000	1 in 100
Canavan disease	1:10,000	1 in 50
Familial dysautonomia	1:3,600	1 in 32
Fanconi's anemia group C	1:32,000	1 in 89
Gaucher's disease	1:900	1 in 15
Mucolipidosis IV	1:63,000	1 in 127
Niemann-Pick disease type A	1:32,000	1 in 90
Tay-Sachs disease	1:3,000	1 in 30
Cystic fibrosis	1:3,000	1 in 25

INDICATIONS

- Assist in the diagnosis of Tay-Sachs disease
- Identify carriers with hexosaminidase deficiency

POTENTIAL DIAGNOSIS

Increased in
Alterations in lysosomal enzymes metabolism are associated with various conditions.

- Total
  Gastric cancer
  Hepatic disease
  Myeloma
  Myocardial infarction
  Pregnancy
  Symptomatic porphyria
  Vascular complications of diabetes
- Hexosaminidase A
  Diabetes
  Pregnancy
- Hexosaminidase B
  Tay-Sachs disease

Decreased in
- Total
  Sandhoff's disease *(inherited disorder of enzyme metabolism lacking both essential enzymes for metabolizing gangliosides)*

Hexosaminidase A
Tay-Sachs disease *(inherited disorder of enzyme metabolism lacking only the hexosaminidase A enzyme for metabolizing gangliosides)*
Hexosaminidase B
Sandhoff's disease

RITICAL FINDINGS: N/A

ITERFERING FACTORS

Drugs that may increase hexosaminidase levels include ethanol, isoniazid, oral contraceptives, and rifampin.

The serum specimen hexosaminidase assay should not be performed on women who are pregnant or who are taking oral contraceptives. Increases in enzyme activity during pregnancy occur in carriers and noncarriers of the Tay-Sachs gene. Enzyme activity is also notably increased in women taking oral contraceptives regardless of carrier status.

NURSING IMPLICATIONS AND PROCEDURE

RETEST:

Positively identify the patient using at least two unique identifiers before providing care, treatment, or services.
Patient Teaching: Inform the patient this test can assist in diagnosing or identifying carrier status for Tay-Sachs disease.
Obtain a history of the patient's complaints, including a list of known allergens, especially allergies or sensitivities to latex.
Obtain a history of the patient's reproductive system, symptoms, and results of previously performed laboratory tests and diagnostic and surgical procedures.
Obtain a list of the patient's current medications, including herbs, nutritional supplements, and nutraceuticals (see Appendix F).
Review the procedure with the patient. Inform the patient that specimen collection takes approximately 5 to 10 min. Address concerns about pain and explain that there may be some discomfort during the venipuncture.
Sensitivity to social and cultural issues, as well as concern for modesty, is important in providing psychological support before, during, and after the procedure.
There are no food, fluid, or medication restrictions unless by medical direction.

INTRATEST:

If the patient has a history of allergic reaction to latex, avoid the use of equipment containing latex.
Instruct the patient to cooperate fully and to follow directions. Direct the patient to breathe normally and to avoid unnecessary movement.
Observe standard precautions, and follow the general guidelines in Appendix A. Positively identify the patient, and label the appropriate specimen container with the corresponding patient demographics, initials of the person collecting the specimen, date, and time of collection. Perform a venipuncture.
Remove the needle and apply direct pressure with dry gauze to stop bleeding. Observe/assess venipuncture site for bleeding or hematoma formation and secure gauze with adhesive bandage.
Immediately transport the specimen to the laboratory for processing and analysis.

POST-TEST:

A report of the results will be made available to the requesting health-care provider (HCP), who will discuss the results with the patient.
Recognize anxiety related to test results, and be supportive of fear of shortened life expectancy. Discuss the implications of abnormal test results on the patient's lifestyle. Provide teaching and information regarding the clinical implications of the test results, as appropriate. Encourage the family to seek genetic counseling if results are abnormal. It is also important to discuss feelings the mother and father

H

may experience (e.g., guilt, depression, anger) if abnormalities are detected. Educate the patient regarding access to counseling services. Provide contact information, if desired, for the National Tay-Sachs and Allied Diseases Association (www.ntsad.org).

➤ Reinforce information given by the patient's HCP regarding further testing, treatment, or referral to another HCP. Answer any questions or address any concerns voiced by the patient or family.

➤ Depending on the results of this procedure, additional testing may be performed to evaluate or monitor

progression of the disease process and determine the need for a change in therapy. Evaluate test results in relation to the patient's symptoms and other tests performed.

RELATED MONOGRAPHS:

➤ Related tests include ALT, amniotic fluid analysis, bilirubin, biopsy chorionic villus, biopsy liver, chromosome analysis, GGT, liver and spleen scan, and protein total and fractions.

➤ Refer to the Reproductive System table at the end of the book for related tests by body system.

H Holter Monitor

SYNONYM/ACRONYM: Ambulatory electrocardiography, ambulatory monitoring, event recorder, Holter electrocardiography.

COMMON USE: To evaluate cardiac symptoms associated with activity to assist with diagnosis of arrhythmias and cardiomegaly.

AREA OF APPLICATION: Heart.

CONTRAST: None.

DESCRIPTION: The Holter monitor records electrical cardiac activity on a continuous basis for 24 to 48 hr. This noninvasive study includes the use of a portable device worn around the waist or over the shoulder that records cardiac electrical impulses on a magnetic tape. The recorder has a clock that allows accurate time markings on the tape. The patient is asked to keep a log or diary of daily activities and to record any occurrence of cardiac symptoms. When the client pushes a button indicating that symptoms (e.g., pain, palpitations, dyspnea,

syncope) have occurred, an event marker is placed on the tape for later comparison with the cardiac activity recordings and the daily activity log. Some recorders allow the data to be transferred to the physician's office by telephone, where the tape is interpreted by a computer to detect any significantly abnormal variations in the recorded waveform patterns.

INDICATIONS

• Detect arrhythmias that occur during normal daily activities and correlate them with symptoms experienced by the patient

Evaluate activity intolerance related to oxygen supply and demand imbalance

Evaluate chest pain, dizziness, syncope, and palpitations
Evaluate the effectiveness of antiarrhythmic medications for dosage adjustment, if needed

Evaluate pacemaker function
Monitor for ischemia and arrhythmias after myocardial infarction or cardiac surgery before changing rehabilitation and other therapy regimens

POTENTIAL DIAGNOSIS

Normal findings in
Normal sinus rhythm

Abnormal findings in
Arrhythmias such as premature ventricular contractions, brady-arrhythmias, tachyarrhythmias, conduction defects, and bradycardia
Cardiomyopathy
Hypoxic or ischemic changes
Mitral valve abnormality
Palpitations

CRITICAL FINDINGS: N/A

INTERFERING FACTORS

Factors that may impair the results of the examination
Improper placement of the electrodes or movement of the electrodes.
Failure of the patient to maintain a daily log of symptoms or to push the button to produce a mark on the strip when experiencing a symptom.

NURSING IMPLICATIONS AND PROCEDURE

PRETEST:

Positively identify the patient using at least two unique identifiers before providing care, treatment, or services.

Patient Teaching: Inform the patient this procedure can assist in evaluating the heart's response to exercise or medication.

Obtain a history of the patient's complaints or symptoms, including a list of known allergens, especially allergies or sensitivities to latex, iodine, seafood, anesthetics, or contrast mediums.

Obtain a history of the patient's cardiovascular system, symptoms, and results of previously performed laboratory tests and diagnostic and surgical procedures.

Obtain a list of the patient's current medications, including herbs, nutritional supplements, and nutraceuticals (see Appendix F).

Review the procedure with the patient. Address concerns about pain related to the procedure and explain that no electricity is delivered to the body during this procedure and no discomfort is experienced during monitoring. Inform the patient that the electrocardiography (ECG) recorder is worn for 24 to 48 hr, at which time the patient is to return to the laboratory with an activity log to have the monitor and strip removed for interpretation.

Sensitivity to social and cultural issues, as well as concern for modesty, is important in providing psychological support before, during, and after the procedure.

Instruct the patient to wear loose-fitting clothing over the electrodes and not to disturb or disconnect the electrodes or wires.

Advise the patient to avoid contact with electrical devices that can affect the strip tracings (e.g., shavers, toothbrush, massager, blanket) and to avoid showers and tub bathing.

Instruct the patient to perform normal activities, such as walking, sleeping, climbing stairs, sexual activity, bowel or urinary elimination, cigarette smoking, emotional upsets, and medications, and to record them in an activity log.

Instruct the patient regarding recording and pressing the button upon experiencing pain or discomfort.

Advise the patient to report a light signal on the monitor, which indicates

H

equipment malfunction or that an electrode has come off.

There are no food, fluid, or medication restrictions unless by medical direction.

INTRATEST:

Observe standard precautions, and follow the general guidelines in Appendix A. Positively identify the patient.

Instruct the patient to void prior to the procedure and to change into the gown, robe, and foot coverings provided.

Instruct the patient to cooperate fully and to follow directions.

Place the patient in a supine position.

Expose the chest. Shave excessive hair at the skin sites; cleanse thoroughly with alcohol and rub until red in color.

Apply electropaste to the skin sites to provide conduction between the skin and electrodes, or apply prelubricated disposable disk electrodes.

Apply two electrodes (negative electrodes) on the manubrium, one in the V_1 position (fourth intercostal space at the border of the right sternum), and one at the V_5 position (level of the fifth intercostal space at the midclavicular line, horizontally and at the left axillary line). A ground electrode is also placed and secured to the skin of the chest or abdomen.

After checking to ensure that the electrodes are secure, attach the electrode cable to the monitor and the lead wires to the electrodes.

Check the monitor for paper supply and battery, insert the tape, and turn on the recorder. Tape all wires to the chest, and place the belt or shoulder strap in the proper position.

POST-TEST:

After the patient has worn the monitor for the required 24 to 48 hr, gently remove the tape and other items securing the electrodes to him or her.

The activity log and tape recording are compared for changes during the monitoring period.

A report of the results will be made available to the requesting health-care provider (HCP), who will discuss the results with the patient.

Advise the patient to immediately report symptoms such as fast heart rate or difficulty breathing.

Recognize anxiety related to test results, and be supportive of perceived loss of independence and fear of shortened life expectancy. Discuss the implications of abnormal test results on the patient's lifestyle. Provide teaching and information regarding the clinical implications of the test results, as appropriate. Educate the patient regarding access to counseling services.

Reinforce information given by the patient's HCP regarding further testing, treatment, or referral to another HCP. Answer any questions or address any concerns voiced by the patient or family.

Depending on the results of this procedure, additional testing may be needed to evaluate or monitor progression of the disease process and determine the need for a change in therapy. Evaluate test results in relation to the patient's symptoms and other tests performed.

RELATED MONOGRAPHS:

Related tests include antiarrhythmic drugs, blood pool imaging, calcium, chest x-ray, echocardiography, echocardiography transesophageal, electrocardiogram, exercise stress test, magnesium, myocardial perfusion heart scan, PET heart, and potassium.

Refer to the Cardiovascular System table at the end of the book for related tests by body system.

Homocysteine and Methylmalonic Acid

SYNONYM/ACRONYM: N/A.

COMMON USE: To assist in evaluating increased risk for blood clots, plaque formation, and platelet aggregations associated with atherosclerosis and stroke risk.

SPECIMEN: Serum (4 mL) collected in a red- or tiger-top tube if methylmalonic acid and homocysteine are to be measured together. Alternatively, plasma collected in a lavender-top (EDTA) tube may be acceptable for the homocysteine measurement. The laboratory should be consulted before specimen collection because specimen type may be method dependent. Care must be taken to use the same type of collection container if serial measurements are to be taken.

NORMAL FINDINGS: (Method: Chromatography)

Homocysteine	4.6–11.2 micromol/L
Methylmalonic Acid	70–270 nmol/L

DESCRIPTION: Homocysteine is an amino acid formed from methionine. Normally, homocysteine is rapidly remetabolized in a biochemical pathway that requires vitamin B_{12} and folate, preventing the buildup of homocysteine in the blood. Excess levels damage the endothelial lining of blood vessels; change coagulation factor levels, increasing the risk of blood clot formation and stroke; prevent smaller arteries from dilating, increasing the risk of plaque formation; cause platelet aggregation; and cause smooth muscle cells lining the arterial wall to multiply, promoting atherosclerosis.

Approximately one-third of patients with hyperhomocystinuria have normal fasting levels. Patients with a heterozygous biochemical enzyme defect in cystathionine B synthase or with a nutritional deficiency in vitamin B_6 can be identified through the administration of a methionine challenge or loading test. Specimens are collected while fasting and 2 hr later. An increase in homocysteine after 2 hr is indicative of hyperhomocystinuria. In patients with vitamin B_{12} deficiency, elevated levels of methylmalonic acid and homocysteine develop fairly early in the course of the disease. Unlike vitamin B_{12} levels, homocysteine levels will remain elevated for at least 24 hr after the start of vitamin therapy. This may be useful if vitamin therapy is inadvertently begun before specimen collection. Patients with folate deficiency, for the most part, will only develop elevated homocysteine levels. A methylmalonic acid level can differentiate between vitamin B_{12} and folate deficiency, since it is increased in vitamin B_{12}

H

deficiency, but not in folate deficiency. Hyperhomocysteinemia due to folate deficiency in pregnant women is believed to increase the risk of neural tube defects. Elevated levels of homocysteine are thought to chemically damage the exposed neural tissue of the developing fetus.

INDICATIONS
• Evaluate inherited enzyme deficiencies that result in homocystinuria
• Evaluate the risk for cardiovascular disease
• Evaluate the risk for venous thrombosis

POTENTIAL DIAGNOSIS

Increased in
• Cerebrovascular disease (CVD) *(there is a relationship, but the pathophysiology is unclear)*
• Chronic renal failure *(pathophysiology is unclear)*
• Coronary artery disease (CAD) *(there is a relationship, but the pathophysiology is unclear)*
• Folic acid deficiency *(folate is required for completion of biochemical reactions involved in homocysteine metabolism)*
• Homocystinuria *(inherited disorder of methionine metabolism that results in accumulation of homocysteine)*
• Peripheral vascular disease *(related to vascular wall damage and formation of occlusive plaque)*
• Vitamin B_{12} deficiency *(vitamin B_{12} is required for completion of biochemical reactions involved in homocysteine metabolism)*

Decreased in: N/A

CRITICAL FINDINGS: N/A

INTERFERING FACTORS
• Drugs that may increase plasma homocysteine levels include anticonvulsants, cycloserine, hydralazine, isoniazid, methotrexate, penicillamine, phenelzine, and procarbazine.
• Drugs that may decrease plasma homocysteine levels include folic acid.
• Specimens should be kept at a refrigerated temperature and delivered immediately to the laboratory for processing.

NURSING IMPLICATIONS AND PROCEDURE

PRETEST:
Positively identify the patient using at least two unique identifiers before providing care, treatment, or services.
Patient Teaching: Inform the patient this test can assist in screening for risk of cardiovascular disease and stroke.
Obtain a history of the patient's complaints, including a list of known allergens, especially allergies or sensitivities to latex.
Obtain a history of the patient's cardiovascular and hematopoietic systems, symptoms, and results of previously performed laboratory tests and diagnostic and surgical procedures.
Obtain a list of the patient's current medications, including herbs, nutritional supplements, and nutraceuticals (see Appendix F).
Review the procedure with the patient. Inform the patient that specimen collection takes approximately 5 to 10 min. Address concerns about pain and explain that there may be some discomfort during the venipuncture.
Sensitivity to social and cultural issues, as well as concern for modesty, is important in providing psychological support before, during, and after the procedure.
There are no food, fluid, or medication restrictions unless by medical direction.

NTRATEST:

- If the patient has a history of allergic reaction to latex, avoid the use of equipment containing latex.
- Instruct the patient to cooperate fully and to follow directions. Direct the patient to breathe normally and to avoid unnecessary movement.
- Observe standard precautions, and follow the general guidelines in Appendix A. Positively identify the patient, and label the appropriate collection container with the corresponding patient demographics, initials of the person collecting the specimen, date, and time of collection. Perform a venipuncture; collect the specimen for combined methylmalonic acid and homocysteine studies in two 5-mL red-, green-, or tiger-top tubes. If only homocysteine is to be measured, a 5-mL lavender-top tube is acceptable.
- Remove the needle and apply direct pressure with dry gauze to stop bleeding. Observe/assess venipuncture site for bleeding or hematoma formation and secure gauze with adhesive bandage.
- Promptly transport the specimen to the laboratory for processing and analysis.

POST-TEST:

- A report of the results will be made available to the requesting health-care provider (HCP), who will discuss the results with the patient.
- *Nutritional Considerations:* Increased homocysteine levels may be associated with atherosclerosis and CAD. Nutritional therapy is recommended for individuals identified to be at high risk for developing CAD. The American Heart Association and National Heart, Lung, and Blood Institute (NHLBI) recommend nutritional therapy for individuals identified to be at high risk for developing CAD or individuals who have specific risk factors and/or existing medical conditions (e.g., elevated LDL cholesterol levels, other lipid disorders, insulin-dependent diabetes, insulin resistance, or metabolic syndrome). If overweight, the patient should be encouraged to achieve a normal weight. Guidelines for the

Therapeutic Lifestyle Changes (TLC) diet are outlined in the Third Report of the Expert Panel on Detection, Evaluation, and Treatment of High Blood Cholesterol in Adults (Adult Treatment Panel III [ATP III]). The TLC diet emphasizes a reduction in foods high in saturated fats and cholesterol. Red meats, eggs, and dairy products are the major sources of saturated fats and cholesterol. If triglycerides also are elevated, the patient should be advised to eliminate or reduce alcohol and simple carbohydrates from the diet. The TLC approach also includes the use of plant stanols or sterols and increased dissolved fiber as an option for lowering LDL cholesterol levels; nutritional recommendations for daily total caloric intake; recommendations for allowable percentage of calories derived from fat (saturated and unsaturated), carbohydrates, protein, and cholesterol; as well as recommendations for daily expenditure of energy.

- *Nutritional Considerations:* Overweight patients with high blood pressure should be encouraged to achieve a normal weight. Other changeable risk factors warranting patient education include strategies to safely decrease sodium intake, increase physical activity, decrease alcohol consumption, eliminate tobacco use, and decrease cholesterol levels.
- *Nutritional Considerations:* Diets rich in fruits, grains, and cereals, in addition to a multivitamin containing B_{12} and folate, may be recommended for patients with elevated homocysteine levels related to a dietary deficiency. Processed and refined foods should be kept to a minimum.
- *Nutritional Considerations:* The Institute of Medicine's Food and Nutrition Board suggests 400 mcg as the daily recommended dietary allowance of folate for adult males and females age 19 to greater than 70 yr; 600 mcg/d for pregnant females under age 18 through 50 yr; 500 mcg/d for lactating females under age 18 through 50 yr; 400 mcg/d for children age 14 to 18 yr; 300 mcg/d for children age 9 to 13 yr; 200 mcg/d for children age 4 to 8 yr; 150 mcg/d for children age 1 to 3 yr; 80 mcg/d for

children age 7 to 12 mo (recommended adequate intake); 65 mcg/d for children age 0 to 6 mo (recommended adequate intake). Reprinted with permission from the National Academies Press, copyright 2013, National Academy of Sciences. Instruct the folate-deficient patient (especially pregnant women), as appropriate, to eat foods rich in folate, such as liver, salmon, eggs, asparagus, green leafy vegetables, broccoli, sweet potatoes, beans, and whole wheat.

Nutritional Considerations: The Institute of Medicine's Food and Nutrition Board suggests 2.4 mcg as the daily recommended dietary allowance of vitamin B_{12} for adult males and females age 19 to greater than 70 yr; 2.6 mcg/d for pregnant females under age 18 through 50 yr; 2.8 mcg/d for lactating females under age 18 through 50 yr; 2.4 mcg/d for children age 14 to 18 yr; 1.8 mcg/d for children age 9 to 13 yr; 1.2 mcg/d for children age 4 to 8 yr; 0.9 mcg/d for children age 1 to 3 yr; 0.5 mcg/d for children age 7 to 12 mo (recommended adequate intake); 0.4 mcg/d for children age 0 to 6 mo (recommended adequate intake). Reprinted with permission from the National Academies Press, copyright 2013, National Academy of Sciences. Instruct the patient with vitamin B_{12} deficiency, as appropriate, in the use of vitamin supplements. Inform the patient, as appropriate, that the best dietary sources of vitamin B_{12} are meats, fish, poultry, eggs, and milk.

Social and Cultural Considerations: Numerous studies point to the prevalence of excess body weight in American children and adolescents. Experts estimate that obesity is present in 25% of the population ages 6 to 11 yr. The medical, social, and emotional consequences of excess body weight are significant. Special attention should be given to instructing the child and caregiver regarding health risks and weight-control education.

Recognize anxiety related to test results, and be supportive of fear of shortened life expectancy. Discuss the implications of abnormal test results on the patient's lifestyle. Provide teaching and information regarding the clinical implications of the test results, as appropriate. Educate the patient regarding access to counseling services. Provide contact information, if desired, for the American Heart Association (www.americanheart.org) or the NHLBI (www.nhlbi.nih.gov).

Reinforce information given by the patient's HCP regarding further testing, treatment, or referral to another HCP. Answer any questions or address any concerns voiced by the patient or family. Educate the patient regarding access to nutritional counseling services. Provide contact information, if desired, for the Institute of Medicine of the National Academies (www.iom.edu).

Depending on the results of this procedure, additional testing may be performed to evaluate or monitor progression of the disease process and determine the need for a change in therapy. Evaluate test results in relation to the patient's symptoms and other tests performed.

RELATED MONOGRAPHS:

Related tests include antiarrhythmic drugs, apolipoprotein A and B, AST, ANP, blood gases, BMD, BNP, BUN, calcitonin, calcium, cholesterol (total, HDL, and LDL), CBC, CBC RBC count, CBC RBC indices, CBC RBC morphology, CBC WBC count and differential, CRP, CK and isoenzymes, creatinine, folate, glucose, glycated hemoglobin, ketones, LDH and isoenzymes, lipoprotein electrophoresis, magnesium, myoglobin, osteocalcin, PTH, pericardial fluid analysis, potassium, prealbumin, renogram, triglycerides, troponin, US kidney, UA, and vitamin B_{12}.

Refer to the Cardiovascular and Hematopoietic systems tables at the end of the book for related tests by body system.

omovanillic Acid

NONYM/ACRONYM: HVA.

MMON USE: To assist in diagnosis of neuroblastoma, pheochromocytoma, and nglioblastoma and to monitor therapy.

ECIMEN: Urine (10 mL) from a timed specimen collected in a clean plastic llection container with 6N HCl as a preservative.

RMAL FINDINGS: (Method: Chromatography)

Age	Conventional Units	SI Units
Homovanillic Acid		*(Conventional Units × 5.49)*
3–6 yr	1.4–4.3 mg/24 hr	8–24 micromol/24 hr
7–10 yr	2.1–4.7 mg/24 hr	12–26 micromol/24 hr
11–16 yr	2.4–8.7 mg/24 hr	13–48 micromol/24 hr
Adult–older adult	1.4–8.8 mg/24 hr	8–48 micromol/24 hr
Vanillylmandelic Acid		*(Conventional Units × 5.05)*
3–6 yr	1–2.6 mg/24 hr	5–13 micromol/24 hr
7–10 yr	2–3.2 mg/24 hr	10–16 micromol/24 hr
11–16 yr	2.3–5.2 mg/24 hr	12–26 micromol/24 hr
Adult–older adult	1.4–6.5 mg/24 hr	7–33 micromol/24 hr

ESCRIPTION: Homovanillic acid (HVA) is the main terminal metabolite of dopamine. Vanillylmandelic acid is a major metabolite of epinephrine and norepinephrine. Both of these tests should be evaluated together for the diagnosis of neuroblastoma. Excretion may be intermittent; therefore, a 24-hr specimen is preferred. Creatinine is usually measured simultaneously to ensure adequate collection and to calculate an excretion ratio of metabolite to creatinine.

DICATIONS

Assist in the diagnosis of pheochromocytoma, neuroblastoma, and ganglioblastoma
Monitor the course of therapy

POTENTIAL DIAGNOSIS

Increased in

HVA is excreted in excessive amounts in the following conditions:
- Ganglioblastoma
- Neuroblastoma
- Pheochromocytoma
- Riley-Day syndrome

Decreased in
- Schizotypal personality disorders

CRITICAL FINDINGS: N/A

INTERFERING FACTORS
- Drugs that may increase HVA levels include acetylsalicylic acid, disulfiram, levodopa, pyridoxine, and reserpine.
- Drugs that may decrease HVA levels include moclobemide.

• All urine voided for the timed collection period must be included in the collection, or else falsely decreased values may be obtained. Compare output records with volume collected to verify that all voids were included in the collection.

NURSING IMPLICATIONS AND PROCEDURE

PRETEST:

▶ Positively identify the patient using at least two unique identifiers before providing care, treatment, or services.

▶ *Patient Teaching:* Inform the patient this test can assist in screening for presence of a tumor.

▶ Obtain a history of the patient's complaints, including a list of known allergens, especially allergies or sensitivities to latex.

▶ Obtain a history of the patient's endocrine system, symptoms, and results of previously performed laboratory tests and diagnostic and surgical procedures.

▶ Obtain a list of the patient's current medications, including herbs, nutritional supplements, and nutraceuticals (see Appendix F).

▶ Review the procedure with the patient. Provide a nonmetallic urinal, bedpan, or toilet-mounted collection device. Address concerns about pain and explain that there should be no discomfort during the procedure.

▶ Usually a 24-hr time frame for urine collection is ordered. Inform the patient that all urine must be saved during that 24-hr period. Instruct the patient not to void directly into the laboratory collection container. Instruct the patient to avoid defecating in the collection device and to keep toilet tissue out of the collection device to prevent contamination of the specimen. Place a sign in the bathroom to remind the patient to save all urine.

▶ Instruct the patient to void all urine into the collection device and then to pour the urine into the laboratory collection

container. Alternatively, the specimen can be left in the collection device for health-care staff member to add to the laboratory collection container.

▶ *Sensitivity to social and cultural issues,* as well as concern for modesty, is important in providing psychological support before, during, and after the procedure.

▶ If possible, and with medical direction patients should withhold acetylsalicylic acid, disulfiram, pyridoxine, and reserpine for 2 days before specimen collection. Levodopa should be withheld for 2 wk before specimen collection.

▶ There are no food or fluid restrictions unless by medical direction.

INTRATEST:

▶ Ensure that the patient has complied with medication restrictions; assure that specified medications, with medical direction, have been restricted for at least 2 days prior to the procedure.

▶ If the patient has a history of allergic reaction to latex, avoid the use of equipment containing latex.

▶ Instruct the patient to cooperate fully and to follow directions.

▶ Observe standard precautions, and follow the general guidelines in Appendix A. Positively identify the patient, and label the appropriate specimen container with the corresponding patient demographics, initial of the person collecting the specimen date, and time of collection.

Timed Specimen

▶ Obtain a clean 3-L urine specimen container, toilet-mounted collection device, and plastic bag (for transport of the specimen container). The specimen must be refrigerated or kept on ice throughout the entire collection period. If an indwelling urinary catheter is in place, the drainage bag must be kept on ice.

▶ Begin the test between 6 and 8 a.m. if possible. Collect first voiding and discard. Record the time the specimen was discarded as the beginning of the timed collection period. The next morning, ask the patient to void at the same time the collection was started and add this last voiding to the container. Urinary output should be recorded throughout the collection time.

If an indwelling catheter is in place, replace the tubing and container system at the start of the collection time. Keep the container system on ice during the collection period, or empty the urine into a larger refrigerated container periodically during the collection period; monitor to ensure continued drainage, and conclude the test the next morning at the same hour the collection was begun.

At the conclusion of the test, compare the quantity of urine with the urinary output record for the collection; if the specimen contains less than what was recorded as output, some urine may have been discarded, invalidating the test.

Include on the collection container's label the amount of urine, test start and stop times, and ingestion of any foods or medications that can affect test results.

Promptly transport the specimen to the laboratory for processing and analysis.

OST-TEST:

A report of the results will be made available to the requesting health-care provider (HCP), who will discuss the results with the patient.

▶ Instruct the patient to resume usual medications, as directed by the HCP.
▶ Recognize anxiety related to test results. Discuss the implications of abnormal test results on the patient's lifestyle. Provide teaching and information regarding the clinical implications of the test results, as appropriate. Educate the patient regarding access to counseling services.
▶ Reinforce information given by the patient's HCP regarding further testing, treatment, or referral to another HCP. Answer any questions or address any concerns voiced by the patient or family.
▶ Depending on the results of this procedure, additional testing may be performed to evaluate or monitor progression of the disease process and determine the need for a change in therapy. Evaluate test results in relation to the patient's symptoms and other tests performed.

RELATED MONOGRAPHS:

▶ Related tests include angiography adrenal, CEA, catecholamines, CT renal, metanephrines, renin, and VMA.
▶ Refer to the Endocrine System table at the end of the book for related tests by body system.

Human Chorionic Gonadotropin

YNONYM/ACRONYM: Chorionic gonadotropin, pregnancy test, HCG, hCG, -HCG, β-subunit HCG.

OMMON USE: To assist in verification of pregnancy, screen for neural tube efects, and evaluate human chorionic gonadotropin (HCG)–secreting tumors.

PECIMEN: Serum (1 mL) collected in a red- or tiger-top tube. Plasma (1 mL) ollected in a green-top (heparin) tube is also acceptable.

ORMAL FINDINGS: (Method: Immunoassay)

	Conventional Units	SI Units (Conventional Units × 1)
Males and nonpregnant females	Less than 5 milli international units/mL	Less than 5 international units/L
Pregnant females by week of gestation:		
2 wk	5–100 milli international units/mL	5–100 international units/L
3 wk	200–3,000 milli international units/mL	200–3,000 international units/L
4 wk	10,000–80,000 milli international units/mL	10,000–80,000 international units/L
5–12 wk	90,000–500,000 milli international units/mL	90,000–500,000 international units/L
13–24 wk	5,000–80,000 milli international units/mL	5,000–80,000 international units/L
26–28 wk	3,000–15,000 milli international units/mL	3,000–15,000 international units/L

H

DESCRIPTION: Human chorionic gonadotropin (HCG) is a hormone secreted by the placenta beginning 8 to 10 days after conception, which coincides with implantation of the fertilized ovum. It stimulates secretion of progesterone by the corpus luteum. HCG levels peak at 8 to 12 wk of gestation and then fall to less than 10% of first trimester levels by the end of pregnancy. By postpartum week 2, levels are undetectable. HCG levels increase at a slower rate in ectopic pregnancy and spontaneous abortion than in normal pregnancy; a low rate of change between serial specimens is predictive of a nonviable fetus. As assays improve in sensitivity over time, ectopic pregnancies are increasingly being identified before rupture. HCG is used along with α-fetoprotein, dimeric inhibin-A, and estriol in prenatal screening for neural tube defects. These prenatal measurements are also known as triple or quad markers, depending on which tests are included. Serial measurements are needed for an accurate estimate of gestational stage and determination of fetal viability. Triple- and quad-marker testing has also been used to screen for trisomy 21 (Down syndrome). (To compare HCG to other tests in the triple- and quad-marker screening procedure, see monograph titled "α_1-Fetoprotein.") HCG is also produced by some germ cell tumors. Most assays measure both the intact and free β-HCG subunit, but if HCG is to be used as a tumor marker, the assay must be capable of detecting both intact and free β-HCG.

INDICATIONS

• Assist in the diagnosis of suspected HCG-producing tumors, such as choriocarcinoma, germ cell tumors of the ovary and testes, or hydatidiform moles

• Confirm pregnancy, assist in the diagnosis of suspected ectopic

pregnancy, or determine threatened or incomplete abortion
• Determine adequacy of hormonal levels to maintain pregnancy
• Monitor effects of surgery or chemotherapy
• Monitor ovulation induction treatment
• Prenatally detect neural tube defects and trisomy 21 (Down syndrome)

POTENTIAL DIAGNOSIS

Increased in

• Choriocarcinoma *(related to HCG-producing tumor)*
• Ectopic HCG-producing tumors (stomach, lung, colon, pancreas, liver, breast) *(related to HCG-producing tumor)*
• Erythroblastosis fetalis *(hemolytic anemia as a result of fetal sensitization by incompatible maternal blood group antigens such as Rh, Kell, Kidd, and Duffy is associated with increased HCG levels)*
• Germ cell tumors (ovary and testes) *(related to HCG-producing tumors)*
• Hydatidiform mole *(related to HCG-secreting mole)*
• Islet cell tumors *(related to HCG-producing tumors)*
• Multiple gestation pregnancy *(related to increased levels produced by the presence of multiple fetuses)*
• Pregnancy *(related to increased production by placenta)*

Decreased in

Any condition associated with diminished viability of the placenta will reflect decreased levels.

• Ectopic pregnancy *(HCG levels increase slower than in viable intrauterine pregnancies, plateau, and then decrease prior to rupture)*

• Incomplete abortion
• Intrauterine fetal demise
• Spontaneous abortion
• Threatened abortion

CRITICAL FINDINGS: N/A

INTERFERING FACTORS

• Drugs that may decrease HCG levels include epostane and mifepristone.
• Results may vary widely depending on the sensitivity and specificity of the assay. Performance of the test too early in pregnancy may cause false-negative results. HCG is composed of an α and a β subunit. The structure of the α subunit is essentially identical to the β subunit of follicle-stimulating hormone, luteinizing hormone, and thyroid-stimulating hormone. The structure of the β subunit differentiates HCG from the other hormones. False-positive results can therefore be obtained if the HCG assay does not detect β subunit.

NURSING IMPLICATIONS AND PROCEDURE

PRETEST:

◆ Positively identify the patient using at least two unique identifiers before providing care, treatment, or services.
◆ *Patient Teaching:* Inform the patient this test can assist in screening for pregnancy, identifying tumors, and evaluating fetal health.
◆ Obtain a history of the patient's complaints, including a list of known allergens, especially allergies or sensitivities to latex.
◆ Obtain a history of the patient's endocrine, immune, and reproductive systems; symptoms; and results of previously performed laboratory tests and diagnostic and surgical procedures.
◆ Record the date of the last menstrual period and determine the possibility of pregnancy in perimenopausal women.

Obtain a list of the patient's current medications, including herbs, nutritional supplements, and nutraceuticals (see Appendix F).

Review the procedure with the patient. Inform the patient that specimen collection takes approximately 5 to 10 min. Address concerns about pain and explain that there may be some discomfort during the venipuncture.

Sensitivity to social and cultural issues, as well as concern for modesty, is important in providing psychological support before, during, and after the procedure.

There are no food, fluid, or medication restrictions unless by medical direction.

INTRATEST:

If the patient has a history of allergic reaction to latex, avoid the use of equipment containing latex.

Instruct the patient to cooperate fully and to follow directions. Direct the patient to breathe normally and to avoid unnecessary movement.

Observe standard precautions, and follow the general guidelines in Appendix A. Positively identify the patient, and label the appropriate specimen container with the corresponding patient demographics, initials of the person collecting the specimen, date, and time of collection. Perform a venipuncture.

Remove the needle and apply direct pressure with dry gauze to stop bleeding. Observe/assess venipuncture site for bleeding or hematoma formation and secure gauze with adhesive bandage.

Promptly transport the specimen to the laboratory for processing and analysis.

POST-TEST:

A report of the results will be made available to the requesting health-care provider (HCP), who will discuss the results with the patient.

Social and Cultural Considerations: Recognize anxiety related to abnormal test results, and encourage the family to seek counseling if concerned with pregnancy termination or to seek genetic counseling if a chromosomal

abnormality is determined. Provide teaching and information regarding the clinical implications of the test results, as appropriate. Decisions regarding elective abortion should take place in the presence of both parents. Provide a nonjudgmental, nonthreatening atmosphere for discussing the risks and difficulties of delivering and raising a developmentally challenged infant, as well as exploring other options (termination of pregnancy or adoption). It is also important to discuss feelings the mother and father may experience (e.g., guilt, depression, anger) if fetal abnormalities are detected.

Social and Cultural Considerations: Offer support, as appropriate, to patients who may be the victims of rape or sexual assault. Educate the patient regarding access to counseling services. Provide a nonjudgmental, nonthreatening atmosphere for a discussion during which risks of sexually transmitted diseases are explained. It is also important to discuss problems the victim of sexual assault may experience (e.g., guilt, depression, anger) if there is possibility of pregnancy related to the assault.

Social and Cultural Considerations: In patients with carcinoma, recognize anxiety related to test results and offer support. Provide teaching and information regarding the clinical implications of abnormal test results, as appropriate. Educate the patient regarding access to counseling services, as appropriate.

Reinforce information given by the patient's HCP regarding further testing, treatment, or referral to another HCP. Instruct the patient in the use of home test kits for pregnancy approved by the U.S. Food and Drug Administration, as appropriate. Answer any questions or address any concerns voiced by the patient or family.

Depending on the results of this procedure, additional testing may be performed to evaluate or monitor the patient's condition and determine the need for a change in therapy. Evaluate test results in relation to the patient's symptoms and other tests performed.

RELATED MONOGRAPHS:

Related laboratory tests include biopsy chorionic villus, *Chlamydia* group antibody, chromosome analysis, CMV, estradiol, fetal fibronectin, α_1-fetoprotein, CBC, hematocrit, CBC hemoglobin, CBC WBC count and differential,

progesterone, rubella antibody, rubeola antibody, syphilis serology, toxoplasma antibody, US abdomen, and US biophysical profile obstetric.

Refer to the Endocrine, Immune, and Reproductive systems tables at the end of the book for related tests by body system.

Human Immunodeficiency Virus Type 1 and Type 2 Antibodies

SYNONYM/ACRONYM: HIV-1/HIV-2.

COMMON USE: Test blood for the presence of antibodies that would indicate a human immunodeficiency virus (HIV) infection.

SPECIMEN: Serum (1 mL) collected in a red-top tube.

NORMAL FINDINGS: (Method: Enzyme immunoassay) Negative.

DESCRIPTION: HIV is the etiological agent of AIDS and is transmitted through bodily secretions, especially by blood or sexual contact. The virus preferentially binds to the T4 helper lymphocytes and replicates within the cells using viral reverse transcriptase, integrase and protease enzymes. Current assays detect antibodies to one or more of several viral proteins. Public health guidelines recommend CD4 counts and viral load testing upon initiation of care for HIV; 3 to 4 mo before commencement of ART; every 3 to 4 mo, but no later than 6 mo, thereafter; and if treatment failure is suspected or otherwise when clinically indicated. Additionally, viral load testing should be requested 2 to 4 wk, but no later than 8 wk, after initiation of ART to verify success of therapy. In clinically sta-

ble patients, CD4 testing may be recommended every 6 to 12 mo rather than every 3 to 6 mo. Guidelines also state that treatment of asymptomatic patients should begin when CD4 count is less than 350/mm^3; treatment is recommended when the patient is symptomatic regardless of test results or when the patient is asymptomatic and CD4 count is between 350 and 500/mm^3. Failure to respond to therapy is defined as a viral load greater than 200 copies/mL. Increased viral load may be indicative of viral mutations, drug resistance, or noncompliance to the therapeutic regimen. Testing for drug resistance is recommended if viral load is greater than 1,000 copies/mL. Initial screening is generally performed using a third-generation immunoassay for antibodies to HIV1/HIV2.

The antibody screening tests most commonly used do not distinguish between HIV1 and HIV2. A reactive screen result is followed by repeat testing in duplicate. Positive or indeterminate results should be confirmed by Western blot assay where positive is defined by the Centers for Disease Control and Prevention (CDC) as presence of two of the three viral proteins: gp41, gp120 (from the viral membrane), and p24 (from the viral core). The newest HIV testing algorithm was developed jointly by the Association of Public Health Laboratories and the CDC. This new algorithm provides for earlier detection of acute infection as well as identification of established infection. Recommendations for initial screening call for the use of a fourth-generation immunoassay capable of the simultaneous detection of HIV antigen and antibody. The fourth-generation assays demonstrate the ability to detect infection 7 days earlier than third-generation assays. Positive initial screens should be followed by a rapid immunoassay that differentiates between HIV1 and HIV2 antibody. A negative or indeterminate supplemental antibody result should be followed by a nucleic acid amplification test (NAAT), during the period after infection has occurred but before the development of antibodies to the virus, to determine if HIV viral RNA is present. The HIV screening test is routinely recommended as part of a prenatal work-up and is required for evaluating donated blood units before release for transfusion. The CDC has structured its recommendations to increase identification of HIV-infected patients as early as possible; early identification increases

treatment options, increases frequency of successful treatment, and can decrease further spread of disease. The CDC recommends the following:

- Include HIV testing in routine medical care; screening of all patients between the ages of 13 and 64 years of age as part of routine medical care, unless the patient requests to opt out.
- Implement new models to diagnose HIV infections outside medical settings; promote availability of rapid waived testing kits like OraQuick.
- Prevent new infections by working with persons diagnosed with HIV and their partners; adapt a voluntary opt-out approach that includes elimination of pretest counseling and written consent requirements.
- Further decrease prenatal transmission of HIV by incorporating HIV testing as a routine part of prenatal medical care and also perform third-trimester testing in areas with high rates of HIV infection among pregnant women.

HIV genotyping by polymerase chain reaction (PCR) methods may also be required to guide selection of medications for therapeutic regimens, assess potential for drug resistance, and monitor for transmission of drug resistant HIV. Genotyping is also useful to determine eligibility for new medications once resistance to conventional drugs has been identified.

INDICATIONS
- Evaluate donated blood units before transfusion
- Perform as part of prenatal screening

- Screen organ transplant donors
- Test individuals who have documented and significant exposure to other infected individuals
- Test exposed high-risk individuals for detection of antibody (e.g., persons with multiple sex partners, persons with a history of other sexually transmitted diseases, IV drug users, infants born to infected mothers, allied health-care workers, public service employees who have contact with blood and blood products)

POTENTIAL DIAGNOSIS

Positive findings in
- HIV1 or HIV2 infection

CRITICAL FINDINGS: N/A

INTERFERING FACTORS

- Drugs that may decrease HIV antibody levels include didanosine, dideoxycytidine, zalcitabine, and zidovudine.
- Nonreactive HIV test results occur during the acute stage of the disease, when the virus is present but antibodies have not sufficiently developed to be detected. It may take up to 6 mo for the test to become positive. During this stage, the test for HIV antigen may not confirm an HIV infection.
- Test kits for HIV are very sensitive. As a result, nonspecific reactions may occur, leading to a false-positive result.

NURSING IMPLICATIONS AND PROCEDURE

PRETEST:

▶ Positively identify the patient using at least two unique identifiers before providing care, treatment, or services.
▶ *Patient Teaching:* Inform the patient that this laboratory test can assist in evaluating for HIV infection.

▶ Obtain a history of the patient's complaints, including a list of known allergens, especially allergies or sensitivities to latex.
▶ Obtain a history of the patient's immune system, a history of high-risk behaviors, symptoms, and results of previously performed laboratory tests and diagnostic and surgical procedures.
▶ Obtain a list of the patient's current medications, including herbs, nutritional supplements, and nutraceuticals (see Appendix F).
▶ Review the procedure with the patient. Inform the patient that specimen collection takes approximately 5 to 10 min. Address concerns about pain and explain that there may be some discomfort during the venipuncture.
▶ There are no food, fluid, or medication restrictions unless by medical direction.

INTRATEST:

▶ If the patient has a history of allergic reaction to latex, avoid the use of equipment containing latex.
▶ Instruct the patient to cooperate fully and to follow directions. Direct the patient to breathe normally and to avoid unnecessary movement.
▶ Observe standard precautions, and follow the general guidelines in Appendix A. Positively identify the patient, and label the appropriate specimen container with the corresponding patient demographics, initials of the person collecting the specimen, date, and time of collection. Perform a venipuncture.
▶ Remove the needle and apply direct pressure with dry gauze to stop bleeding. Observe/assess venipuncture site for bleeding or hematoma formation and secure gauze with adhesive bandage.
▶ Promptly transport the specimen to the laboratory for processing and analysis.

POST-TEST:

▶ A report of the results will be made available to the requesting health-care provider (HCP), who will discuss the results with the patient.
▶ Warn the patient that false-positive results occur and that the absence of

antibody does not guarantee absence of infection, because the virus may be latent or may not have produced detectable antibody at the time of testing.

Social and Cultural Considerations: Recognize anxiety related to test results, and be supportive of impaired activity related to weakness, perceived loss of independence, and fear of shortened life expectancy. Discuss the implications of abnormal test results on the patient's lifestyle. Provide teaching and information regarding the clinical implications of the test results, as appropriate. Educate the patient regarding access to counseling services. Provide contact information, if desired, for AIDS information provided by the National Institutes of Health (www.aidsinfo.nih.gov) or the CDC (www.cdc.gov).

Social and Cultural Considerations: Counsel the patient, as appropriate, regarding risk of transmission and proper prophylaxis, and reinforce the importance of strict adherence to the treatment regimen, including consultation with a pharmacist.

Social and Cultural Considerations: Inform patient that positive findings must be reported to local health department officials, who will question him or her regarding sexual partners.

Social and Cultural Considerations: Offer support, as appropriate, to patients who may be the victims of rape or sexual assault. Educate the patient regarding access to counseling services. Provide a nonjudgmental, nonthreatening atmosphere for a discussion during which risks of sexually transmitted diseases are explained. It is also important to discuss problems the patient may experience (e.g., guilt, depression, anger).

Inform the patient that retesting may be necessary.

Reinforce information given by the patient's HCP regarding further

testing, treatment, or referral to another HCP. Provide information regarding vaccine-preventable diseases where indicated (e.g., anthrax, cervical cancer, diphtheria, encephalitis, hepatitis A and B, H1N1 flu, human papillomavirus, *Haemophilus* influenza, seasonal influenza, Lyme disease, measles, meningococcal disease, monkeypox, mumps, pertussis, pneumococcal disease, polio, rotavirus, rubella, shingles, smallpox, tetanus, typhoid fever, varicella, yellow fever). Provide contact information, if desired, for the CDC (www.cdc.gov/vaccines/vpd-vac). Instruct the patient in the use of home test kits approved by the U.S. Food and Drug Administration, if prescribed. Answer any questions or address any concerns voiced by the patient or family.

Depending on the results of this procedure, additional testing may be performed to evaluate or monitor progression of the disease process and determine the need for a change in therapy. Evaluate test results in relation to the patient's symptoms and other tests performed.

RELATED MONOGRAPHS:

Related tests include biopsy bone marrow, bronchoscopy, CD4/CD8 enumeration, *Chlamydia* group antibody, CBC, CBC platelet count, CBC WBC count and differential, culture and smear mycobacteria, culture viral, cytology sputum, CMV, culture skin, gallium scan, HBV antibody and antigen, HCV antibody, human T-cell lymphotropic virus types I and II, laparoscopy abdominal, LAP, lymphangiogram, MRI musculoskeletal, mediastinoscopy, β_2-microglobulin, newborn screening, and syphilis serology.

Refer to the Immune System table at the end of the book for related tests by body system.

Human Leukocyte Antigen B27

SYNONYM/ACRONYM: HLA-B27.

COMMON USE: To assist in diagnosing juvenile rheumatoid arthritis, psoriatic arthritis, ankylosing spondylitis, and Reiter's syndrome.

SPECIMEN: Whole blood (5 mL) collected in a green-top (heparin) or a yellow-top (acid-citrate-dextrose [ACD]) tube.

NORMAL FINDINGS: (Method: Flow cytometry) Negative (indicating absence of the antigen).

DESCRIPTION: The human leukocyte antigens (HLAs) are gene products of the major histocompatibility complex, derived from their respective loci on the short arm of chromosome 6. There are more than 27 identified HLAs. HLA-B27 is an allele (one of two or more genes for an inheritable trait that occupy the same location on each chromosome, paternal and maternal) of the HLA-B locus. The antigens are present on the surface of nucleated tissue cells as well as on white blood cells. HLA testing is used in determining histocompatibility for organ and tissue transplantation. Another application for HLA testing is in paternity investigations. The presence of HLA-B27 is associated with several specific autoimmune conditions including ankylosing spondylitis, rheumatoid arthritis, psoriatic arthritis, undifferentiated oligoarthritis, uveitis, and inflammatory bowel disease. Although less than 10% of the population are carriers of HLA B-27, 20% of carriers will develop an autoimmune condition.

INDICATIONS
- Assist in diagnosing ankylosing spondylitis and Reiter's syndrome
- Determine compatibility for organ and tissue transplantation

POTENTIAL DIAGNOSIS
Positive findings in
- Ankylosing spondylitis
- Inflammatory bowel disease
- Juvenile rheumatoid arthritis
- Psoriatic arthritis
- Reiter's syndrome
- Sacroiliitis
- Uveitis

CRITICAL FINDINGS: N/A

INTERFERING FACTORS
- The specimen should be stored at room temperature and should be received by the laboratory performing the assay within 24 hr of collection. It is highly recommended that the laboratory be contacted before specimen collection to avoid specimen rejection.

NURSING IMPLICATIONS AND PROCEDURE

PRETEST:

▶ Positively identify the patient using at least two unique identifiers before providing care, treatment, or services.

▶ *Patient Teaching:* Inform the patient this test can assist with investigation of specific leukocyte disorders and determine compatibility for organ and tissue transplantation.

▶ Obtain a history of the patient's complaints, including a list of known allergens, especially allergies or sensitivities to latex.

▶ Obtain a history of the patient's immune system, symptoms, and results of previously performed laboratory tests and diagnostic and surgical procedures.

▶ Obtain a list of the patient's current medications, including herbs, nutritional supplements, and nutraceuticals (see Appendix F).

▶ Review the procedure with the patient. Inform the patient that specimen collection takes approximately 5 to 10 min. Address concerns about pain and explain that there may be some discomfort during the venipuncture.

▶ *Sensitivity to social and cultural issues,* as well as concern for modesty, is important in providing psychological support before, during, and after the procedure.

▶ There are no food, fluid, or medication restrictions unless by medical direction.

INTRATEST:

▶ If the patient has a history of allergic reaction to latex, avoid the use of equipment containing latex.

▶ Instruct the patient to cooperate fully and to follow directions. Direct the patient to breathe normally and to avoid unnecessary movement.

▶ Observe standard precautions, and follow the general guidelines in Appendix A. Positively identify the patient, and label the appropriate specimen container with the corresponding patient demographics, initials of the person collecting the specimen,

date, and time of collection. Perform a venipuncture.

▶ Remove the needle and apply direct pressure with dry gauze to stop bleeding. Observe/assess venipuncture site for bleeding or hematoma formation and secure gauze with adhesive bandage.

▶ Promptly transport the specimen to the laboratory for processing and analysis.

POST-TEST:

▶ A report of the results will be made available to the requesting health-care provider (HCP), who will discuss the results with the patient.

▶ Recognize anxiety related to test results, and be supportive of perceived loss of independence and fear of shortened life expectancy. These diseases can be moderately to severely debilitating, resulting in significant lifestyle changes. Discuss the implications of abnormal test results on the patient's lifestyle. Provide teaching and information regarding the clinical implications of the test results, as appropriate. Educate the patient regarding access to counseling services.

▶ Reinforce information given by the patient's HCP regarding further testing, treatment, or referral to another HCP. Inform the patient that false-positive test results occur and that retesting may be required. Answer any questions or address any concerns voiced by the patient or family.

▶ Depending on the results of this procedure, additional testing may be performed to evaluate or monitor progression of the disease process and determine the need for a change in therapy. Evaluate test results in relation to the patient's symptoms and other tests performed.

RELATED MONOGRAPHS:

▶ Related tests include ANA, CBC, CT spine, ESR, MRI musculoskeletal, radiography bone, and RF.

▶ Refer to the Immune System table at the end of the book for related tests by body system.

Human T-Lymphotropic Virus Type I and Type II Antibodies

SYNONYM/ACRONYM: HTLV-I/HTLV-II.

COMMON USE: To test the blood for the presence of antibodies that would indicate past or current human T-lymphocyte virus (HTLV) infection. Helpful in diagnosing certain types of leukemia.

SPECIMEN: Serum (1 mL) collected in a red-top tube.

NORMAL FINDINGS: (Method: Enzyme immunoassay) Negative.

DESCRIPTION: Human T-lymphotropic virus type I (HTLV-I) and type II (HTLV-II) are two closely related retroviruses known to remain latent for extended periods before becoming reactive. The viruses are transmitted by sexual contact, contact with blood, placental transfer from mother to fetus, or ingestion of breast milk. As with HIV-1 and HIV-2, HTLV targets the T4 lymphocytes. HTLV-I has been associated with adult T-cell leukemia/lymphoma (ATL) and myelopathy/tropical spastic paraparesis (HAM/TSP). Although it is believed HTLV-II may affect the immune system, it has been not been associated clearly with any particular disease or condition. Retrospective studies conducted by the American Red Cross demonstrated that a small percentage of transfusion recipients became infected by HTLV-positive blood. The results of this study led to a requirement that all donated blood units be tested for HTLV-I/HTLV-II before release for transfusion.

INDICATIONS

- Distinguish HTLV-I/HTLV-II infection from spastic myelopathy
- Establish HTLV-I as the causative agent in adult lymphoblastic (T-cell) leukemia
- Evaluate donated blood units before transfusion
- Evaluate HTLV-II as a contributing cause of chronic neuromuscular disease

POTENTIAL DIAGNOSIS

Positive findings in
- HTLV-I/HTLV-II infection

CRITICAL FINDINGS: N/A

INTERFERING FACTORS: N/A

NURSING IMPLICATIONS AND PROCEDURE

PRETEST:

- Positively identify the patient using at least two unique identifiers before providing care, treatment, or services.
- *Patient Teaching:* Inform the patient this test can assist with indicating a past or present HTLV infection.
- Obtain a history of the patient's complaints, including a list of known

H

allergens, especially allergies or sensitivities to latex.

▸ Obtain a history of the patient's immune system, a history of high-risk behaviors, symptoms, and results of previously performed laboratory tests and diagnostic and surgical procedures.

▸ Obtain a list of the patient's current medications, including herbs, nutritional supplements, and nutraceuticals (see Appendix F).

▸ Review the procedure with the patient. Inform the patient that specimen collection takes approximately 5 to 10 min. Address concerns about pain and explain that there may be some discomfort during the venipuncture.

▸ *Sensitivity to social and cultural issues,* as well as concern for modesty, is important in providing psychological support before, during, and after the procedure.

▸ There are no food, fluid, or medication restrictions unless by medical direction.

INTRATEST:

▸ If the patient has a history of allergic reaction to latex, avoid the use of equipment containing latex.

▸ Instruct the patient to cooperate fully and to follow directions. Direct the patient to breathe normally and to avoid unnecessary movement.

▸ Observe standard precautions, and follow the general guidelines in Appendix A. Positively identify the patient, and label the appropriate specimen container with the corresponding patient demographics, initials of the person collecting the specimen, date, and time of collection. Perform a venipuncture.

▸ Remove the needle and apply direct pressure with dry gauze to stop bleeding. Observe/assess venipuncture site for bleeding or hematoma formation and secure gauze with adhesive bandage.

▸ Promptly transport the specimen to the laboratory for processing and analysis.

POST-TEST:

▸ A report of the results will be made available to the requesting health-care provider (HCP), who will discuss the results with the patient.

▸ Warn the patient that false-positive results occur and that the absence of antibody does not guarantee absence of infection, because the virus may be latent or not have produced detectable antibody at the time of testing.

▸ Recognize anxiety related to test results, and be supportive of impaired activity related to weakness, perceived loss of independence, and fear of shortened life expectancy. Discuss the implications of positive test results on the patient's lifestyle. Provide teaching and information regarding the clinical implications of the test results, as appropriate. Educate the patient regarding access to counseling services.

▸ *Social and Cultural Considerations:* Counsel the patient, as appropriate, regarding risk of transmission and proper prophylaxis, and reinforce the importance of strict adherence to the treatment regimen, including consultation with a pharmacist.

▸ Inform the patient that the presence of HTLV-I/HTLV-II antibodies precludes blood donation, but it does not mean that leukemia or a neurological disorder is present or will develop.

▸ Inform the patient that subsequent retesting may be necessary.

▸ Reinforce information given by the patient's HCP regarding further testing, treatment, or referral to another HCP. Provide information regarding vaccine-preventable diseases where indicated (e.g., anthrax, cervical cancer, diphtheria, encephalitis, hepatitis A and B, H1N1 flu, human papillomavirus, *Haemophilus* influenza, seasonal influenza, Lyme disease, measles, meningococcal disease, monkeypox, mumps, pertussis, pneumococcal disease, polio, rotavirus, rubella, shingles, smallpox, tetanus, typhoid fever, varicella, yellow fever). Provide contact information, if desired, for the Centers for Disease Control and Prevention (www.cdc.gov/vaccines/vpd-vac). Answer any questions or address any concerns voiced by the patient or family.

▶ Depending on the results of this procedure, additional testing may be performed to evaluate or monitor progression of the disease process and determine the need for a change in therapy. Evaluate test results in relation to the patient's symptoms and other tests performed.

RELATED MONOGRAPHS:
▶ Related tests include CBC; hepatitis B, C, and D antigens and antibodies; and HIV-1/HIV-2.
▶ Refer to the Immune System table at the end of the book for related tests by body system.

5-Hydroxyindoleacetic Acid

SYNONYM/ACRONYM: 5-HIAA.

COMMON USE: To assist in diagnosing carcinoid tumors.

SPECIMEN: Urine (10 mL) from a timed specimen collected in a clean plastic collection container with boric acid as a preservative.

NORMAL FINDINGS: (Method: High-pressure liquid chromatography)

Conventional Units	SI Units (Conventional Units × 5.23)
2–7 mg/24 hr	10.5–36.6 micromol/24 hr

DESCRIPTION: Because 5-hydroxy-indoleacetic acid (5-HIAA) is a metabolite of serotonin, 5-HIAA levels reflect plasma serotonin concentrations. 5-HIAA is excreted in the urine. Increased urinary excretion occurs in the presence of carcinoid tumors. This test, which replaces serotonin measurement, is most accurate when obtained from a 24-hr urine specimen.

INDICATIONS
Detect early, small, or intermittently secreting carcinoid tumors

POTENTIAL DIAGNOSIS

Increased in
Serotonin is produced by the entero-chromaffin cells of the small intestine and secreted ectopically by tumor cells. It is converted to 5-HIAA in the liver and excreted in the urine. Increased values are associated with malabsorption conditions, but the relationship is unclear.

• Celiac and tropical sprue
• Cystic fibrosis
• Foregut and midgut carcinoid tumors
• Oat cell carcinoma of the bronchus
• Ovarian carcinoid tumors
• Whipple's disease

Decreased in
The documented relationship between decreased levels of serotonin, defective amino acid metabolism, and mental illness is not well understood.

• Depressive illnesses
• Hartnup's disease

- Mastocytosis
- Phenylketonuria
- Renal disease *(related to decreased renal excretion)*
- Small intestine resection *(related to a decrease in enterochromaffin-producing cells)*

CRITICAL FINDINGS: N/A

INTERFERING FACTORS
- Drugs that may increase 5-HIAA levels include cisplatin, fluorouracil, cough syrups containing glyceryl guaiacolate, melphalan, rauwolfia alkaloids, and reserpine.
- Drugs that may decrease 5-HIAA levels include chlorophenylalanine, corticotropin, ethanol, imipramine, isocarboxazid, isoniazid, levodopa, methyldopa, monoamine oxidase inhibitors, and octreotide.
- Foods containing serotonin, such as avocados, bananas, chocolate, eggplant, pineapples, plantains, red plums, tomatoes, and walnuts, can falsely elevate levels if ingested within 4 days of specimen collection.
- Severe gastrointestinal disturbance or diarrhea can interfere with test results.
- Failure to collect all the urine and store the specimen properly during the 24-hr test period invalidates the results.
- Failure to follow dietary restrictions before the procedure may cause the procedure to be canceled or repeated.

NURSING IMPLICATIONS AND PROCEDURE

PRETEST:
- Positively identify the patient using at least two unique identifiers before providing care, treatment, or services.
- *Patient Teaching:* Inform the patient this test can assist in diagnosing tumor.
- Obtain a history of the patient's complaints, including a list of known allergens, especially allergies or sensitivities to latex.
- Obtain a history of the patient's endocrine, gastrointestinal, and immune systems; symptoms; and results of previously performed laboratory tests and diagnostic and surgical procedures.
- Obtain a list of the patient's current medications, including herbs, nutritional supplements, and nutraceuticals (see Appendix F).
- Review the procedure with the patient. Provide a nonmetallic urinal, bedpan, or toilet-mounted collection device. Address concerns about pain and explain to the patient that there should be no discomfort during the procedure.
- Inform the patient that all urine collected over a 24-hr period must be saved; if a preservative has been added to the container, instruct the patient not to discard the preservative. Instruct the patient not to void directly into the container. Instruct the patient to avoid defecating in the collection device and to keep toilet tissue out of the collection device to prevent contamination of the specimen. Place a sign in the bathroom as a reminder to save all urine.
- Instruct the patient to void all urine into the collection device, then pour the urine into the laboratory collection container. Alternatively, the specimen can be left in the collection device for a health-care staff member to add to the laboratory collection container.
- *Sensitivity to social and cultural issues,* as well as concern for modesty, is important in providing psychological support before, during, and after the procedure.
- There are no fluid restrictions unless by medical direction.
- Inform the patient that foods and medications listed under "Interfering Factors" should be restricted by medical direction for at least 4 days before specimen collection.

INTRATEST:
- Ensure that the patient has complied with dietary and medication restrictions; assure foods and medications

listed under "Interfering Factors" have been restricted for at least 4 days prior to the procedure.

- If the patient has a history of allergic reaction to latex, avoid the use of equipment containing latex.
- Instruct the patient to cooperate fully and to follow directions.
- Observe standard precautions, and follow the general guidelines in Appendix A. Positively identify the patient, and label the appropriate specimen container with the corresponding patient demographics, initials of the person collecting the specimen, date, and time of collection.

Timed Specimen

- Obtain a clean 3-L urine specimen container, toilet-mounted collection device, and plastic bag (for transport of the specimen container). The specimen must be refrigerated or kept on ice throughout the entire collection period. If an indwelling urinary catheter is in place, the drainage bag must be kept on ice.
- Begin the test between 6 and 8 a.m. if possible. Collect first voiding and discard. Record the time the specimen was discarded as the beginning of the timed collection period. The next morning, ask the patient to void at the same time the collection was started, and add this last voiding to the container. Urinary output should be recorded throughout the collection time.
- If an indwelling catheter is in place, replace the tubing and container system at the start of the collection time. Keep the container system on ice during the collection period, or empty the urine into a larger container periodically during the collection period; monitor to ensure continued drainage. Conclude the test the next morning at the same hour the collection was begun.
- At the conclusion of the test, compare the quantity of urine with the urinary output record for the collection; if the specimen contains less than what was recorded as output, some urine may have been discarded, invalidating the test.

- Include on the specimen collection container's label the amount of urine, test start and stop times, and ingestion of any foods or medications that can affect test results. Promptly transport the specimen to the laboratory for processing and analysis.

POST-TEST:

- A report of the results will be made available to the requesting health-care provider (HCP), who will discuss the results with the patient.
- Instruct the patient to resume usual diet, as directed by the HCP. Consideration may be given to niacin supplementation and increased protein, if appropriate, for patients with abnormal findings. In some cases, the tumor may divert dietary tryptophan to serotonin, resulting in pellagra.
- Recognize anxiety related to test results. Discuss the implications of abnormal test results on the patient's lifestyle. Provide teaching and information regarding the clinical implications of the test results, as appropriate.
- Reinforce information given by the patient's HCP regarding further testing, treatment, or referral to another HCP. Answer any questions or address any concerns voiced by the patient or family.
- Depending on the results of this procedure, additional testing may be performed to evaluate or monitor progression of the disease process and determine the need for a change in therapy. Evaluate test results in relation to the patient's symptoms and other tests performed.

RELATED MONOGRAPHS:

- Related tests include ALP, amino acid screen, antibodies gliadin, biopsy intestine, biopsy lung, calcium, cancer antigens, capsule endoscopy, chloride sweat, fecal fat, and folate.
- Refer to the Endocrine, Gastrointestinal, and Immune systems tables at the end of the book for related tests by body system.

Hypersensitivity Pneumonitis Serology

SYNONYM/ACRONYM: Farmer's lung disease serology, extrinsic allergic alveolitis.

COMMON USE: To assist in identification of pneumonia related to inhaled allergens containing *Aspergillus* or actinomycetes (dust, mold, or chronic exposure to moist organic materials).

SPECIMEN: Serum (2 mL) collected in a red-top tube.

NORMAL FINDINGS: (Method: Immunodiffusion) Negative.

POTENTIAL DIAGNOSIS

Increased in
• Hypersensitivity pneumonitis

CRITICAL FINDINGS: N/A

Find and print out the full monograph at DavisPlus (http://davisplus.fadavis.com, keyword Van Leeuwen).

Hysterosalpingography

SYNONYM/ACRONYM: Hysterogram, uterography, uterosalpingography.

COMMON USE: To visualize and assess the uterus and fallopian tubes to assess for obstruction, adhesions, malformations, or injuries that may be related to infertility.

AREA OF APPLICATION: Uterus and fallopian tubes.

CONTRAST: Iodinated contrast medium.

DESCRIPTION: Hysterosalpingography is performed as part of an infertility study to identify anatomical abnormalities of the uterus or occlusion of the fallopian tubes. The procedure allows visualization of the uterine cavity, fallopian tubes, and peritubal area after the injection of contrast medium into the cervix. The contrast medium should flow through the uterine cavity, through the fallopian tubes, and into the peritoneal cavity, where it is absorbed if no obstruction exists. Passage of the contrast medium through the tubes may clear mucous plugs, straighten kinked tubes, or break up adhesions, thus restoring fertility. This procedure is also used to evaluate the fallopian tubes after tubal ligation and to evaluate the results of reconstructive surgery. Risks include uterine perforation, exposure to radiation, infection, allergic reaction to contrast medium, bleeding, and pulmonary embolism.

INDICATIONS

- Confirm the presence of fistulas or adhesions
- Confirm tubal abnormalities such as adhesions and occlusions
- Confirm uterine abnormalities such as congenital malformation, traumatic injuries, or the presence of foreign bodies
- Detect bicornate uterus
- Evaluate adequacy of surgical tubal ligation and reconstructive surgery

POTENTIAL DIAGNOSIS

Normal findings in

- Contrast medium flowing freely into the fallopian tubes and from the uterus into the peritoneal cavity
- Normal position, shape, and size of the uterine cavity

Abnormal findings in

- Bicornate uterus
- Developmental abnormalities
- Extrauterine pregnancy
- Internal scarring
- Kinking of the fallopian tubes due to adhesions
- Partial or complete blockage of fallopian tube(s)
- Tumors
- Uterine cavity anomalies
- Uterine fistulas
- Uterine masses or foreign body
- Uterine fibroid tumors (leiomyomas)

CRITICAL FINDINGS: N/A

INTERFERING FACTORS

This procedure is contraindicated for

- Patients with allergies to shellfish or iodinated dye. The contrast medium used may cause a life-threatening allergic reaction. Patients with a known hypersensitivity to the contrast medium may benefit from premedication with corticosteroids or the use of nonionic contrast medium.
- Patients with bleeding disorders.
- Patients who are chronically dehydrated before the test, because of their risk of contrast-induced renal failure.
- Patients who are in renal failure.
- Patients with menses, undiagnosed vaginal bleeding, or pelvic inflammatory disease.
- Young patients (17 yr and younger), unless the benefits of the x-ray diagnosis outweigh the risks of exposure to high levels of radiation.

Factors that may impair clear imaging

- Gas or feces in the gastrointestinal tract resulting from inadequate cleansing or failure to restrict food intake before the study.
- Retained barium from a previous radiological procedure.
- Metallic objects (e.g., jewelry, body rings) within the examination field, which may inhibit organ visualization and cause unclear images.
- Inability of the patient to cooperate or remain still during the procedure because of age, significant pain, or mental status.
- Insufficient injection of contrast medium.
- Excessive traction during the test or tubal spasm, which may cause

the appearance of a stricture in an otherwise normal fallopian tube.

Other considerations
- Excessive traction during the test may displace adhesions, making the fallopian tubes appear normal.
- The procedure may be terminated if chest pain or severe cardiac arrhythmias occur.
- Failure to follow pretesting preparations may cause the procedure to be canceled or repeated.
- Risks associated with radiation overexposure can result from frequent x-ray procedures. Personnel in the room with the patient should wear a protective lead apron, stand behind a shield, or leave the area while the examination is being done. Personnel working in the examination area should wear badges to record their level of radiation exposure.

NURSING IMPLICATIONS AND PROCEDURE

PRETEST:

- Positively identify the patient using at least two unique identifiers before providing care, treatment, or services.
- *Patient Teaching:* Inform the patient this procedure can assist in assessing the uterus and fallopian tubes.
- Obtain a history of the patient's complaints, including a list of known allergens, especially allergies or sensitivities to latex, iodine, seafood, anesthetics, and contrast mediums.
- Obtain a history of the patient's reproductive system, symptoms, and results of previously performed laboratory tests and diagnostic and surgical procedures.
- Note any recent barium or other radiological contrast procedures.

- Ensure that barium studies were performed more than 4 days before the hysterosalpingography.
- Record the date of the last menstrual period and determine the possibility of pregnancy in perimenopausal women.
- Obtain a list of the patient's current medications, including anticoagulants, aspirin and other salicylates, herbs, nutritional supplements, and nutraceuticals, especially those known to affect coagulation (see Appendix F). Such products should be discontinued by medical direction for the appropriate number of days prior to a surgical procedure. Note the last time and dose of medication taken.
- Review the procedure with the patient. Address concerns about pain related to the procedure and explain that some pain may be experienced during the test, and there may be moments of discomfort. Explain to the patient that she may feel temporary sensations of nausea, dizziness, slow heartbeat, and menstrual-like cramping during the procedure, as well as shoulder pain from subphrenic irritation from the contrast medium as it spills into the peritoneal cavity. Inform the patient that the procedure is performed in a radiology department by a health-care provider (HCP), with support staff, and takes approximately 30 to 60 min.
- *Sensitivity to social and cultural issues,* as well as concern for modesty, is important in providing psychological support before, during and after the procedure.
- Instruct the patient to take a laxative or a cathartic, as ordered, on the evening before the examination.
- Instruct the patient to remove jewelry and other metallic objects from the area to be examined.
- There are no food, fluid, or medication restrictions unless by medical direction or department protocol.
- *Make sure a written and informed consent has been signed prior to the procedure and before administering any medications.*

INTRATEST:

▸ Observe standard precautions, and follow the general guidelines in Appendix A. Positively identify the patient.

▸ Ensure the patient has complied with pretesting preparations prior to the procedure.

▸ Ensure the patient has removed all external metallic objects from the area to be examined prior to the procedure.

▸ Assess for completion of bowel preparation according to the institution's procedure. Administer enemas or suppositories on the morning of the test, as ordered.

▸ Have emergency equipment readily available.

▸ Instruct the patient to void prior to the procedure and to change into the gown, robe, and foot coverings provided.

▸ Instruct the patient to cooperate fully and to follow directions. Instruct the patient to remain still throughout the procedure because movement produces unreliable results.

▸ Place the patient in a lithotomy position on the fluoroscopy table.

▸ A kidney, ureter, and bladder film is taken to ensure that no stool, gas, or barium will obscure visualization of the uterus and fallopian tubes.

▸ A speculum is inserted into the vagina, and contrast medium is introduced into the uterus through the cervix via a cannula, after which both fluoroscopic and radiographic images are taken.

POST-TEST:

▸ A report of the results will be made available to the requesting HCP, who will discuss the results with the patient.

▸ Instruct the patient to resume usual medications and activity, as directed by the HCP.

▸ Observe for delayed reaction to iodinated contrast medium, including rash, urticaria, tachycardia, hyperpnea, hypertension, palpitations, nausea, or vomiting.

▸ Instruct the patient to immediately report symptoms such as fast heart rate, difficulty breathing, skin rash, itching, chest pain, persistent right shoulder pain, or abdominal pain. Immediately report symptoms to the appropriate HCP.

▸ Inform the patient that a vaginal discharge is common and that it may be bloody, lasting 1 to 2 days after the test.

▸ Inform the patient that dizziness and cramping may follow this procedure, and that analgesia may be given if there is persistent cramping. Instruct the patient to contact the HCP in the event of severe cramping or profuse bleeding.

▸ Recognize anxiety related to test results. Discuss the implications of abnormal test results on the patient's lifestyle. Provide teaching and information regarding the clinical implications of the test results, as appropriate.

▸ Reinforce information given by the patient's HCP regarding further testing, treatment, or referral to another HCP. Answer any questions or address any concerns voiced by the patient or family.

▸ Depending on the results of this procedure, additional testing may be needed to evaluate or monitor progression of the disease process and determine the need for a change in therapy. Evaluate test results in relation to the patient's symptoms and other tests performed.

RELATED MONOGRAPHS:

▸ Related tests include CT abdomen, laparoscopy gynecological, MRI abdomen, US obstetric, US pelvis, and uterine fibroid embolization.

▸ Refer to the Reproductive System table at the end of the book for related tests by body system.

Hysteroscopy

SYNONYM/ACRONYM: N/A.

COMMON USE: To visualize and assess the endometrial lining of the uterus to assist in diagnosing disorders such as fibroids, cancer, and polyps.

AREA OF APPLICATION: Uterus.

CONTRAST: Carbon dioxide, saline.

DESCRIPTION: Hysteroscopy is a diagnostic or surgical procedure of the uterus done using a thin telescope (hysteroscope), which is inserted through the cervix with minimal or no dilation. Normal saline, glycine, or carbon dioxide is used to fill and distend the uterus. The inner surface of the uterus is examined, and laser beam or electrocautery can be accomplished during the procedure. Diagnostic hysteroscopy is used to diagnose uterine abnormalities and may be completed in conjunction with a dilatation and curettage (D & C). This minor surgical procedure is generally done to assess abnormal uterine bleeding or repeated miscarriages. An operative hysteroscopy is done instead of abdominal surgery to treat many uterine conditions such as septums or fibroids (myomas). A resectoscope (a hysteroscope that uses high-frequency electrical current to cut or coagulate tissue) may be used to remove any localized myomas. Local, regional, or general anesthesia can be used, but usually general anesthesia is needed. The procedure may done in a health-care practitioner's office, but if done as an outpatient surgical procedure, it is usually completed in a hospital setting.

INDICATIONS

POTENTIAL DIAGNOSIS

Normal findings in
• Normal uterine appearance

Abnormal findings in
• Areas of active bleeding
• Adhesions
• Displaced intrauterine devices
• Fibroid tumors
• Polyps
• Uterine septum

CRITICAL FINDINGS: N/A

INTERFERING FACTORS
• Inability of the patient to cooperate or remain still during the test because of age, significant pain, or mental status may interfere with the test results.
• Patients with bleeding disorders.
• Failure to follow dietary restrictions and other pretesting preparations may cause the procedure to be canceled or repeated.

NURSING IMPLICATIONS AND PROCEDURE

PRETEST:

▸ Positively identify the patient using at least two unique identifiers before providing care, treatment, or services.

Patient Teaching: Inform the patient that this procedure can assist in assessing uterine health.

Obtain a history of the patient's complaints, including a list of known allergens, especially allergies or sensitivities to latex.

Obtain a history of the patient's reproductive system, symptoms, and results of previously performed laboratory tests and diagnostic and surgical procedures.

Record the date of last menstrual period and determine the possibility of pregnancy in perimenopausal women.

Obtain a list of the patient's current medications, including herbs, nutritional supplements, and nutraceuticals (see Appendix F).

Review the procedure with the patient. Address concerns about pain and explain that a local anesthetic spray or liquid may be applied to the cervix to ease with insertion of the hysteroscope if general anesthesia is not used. Inform the patient that the procedure is usually performed in the office of a health-care provider (HCP) or a surgery suite and takes about 30–45 min.

Sensitivity to social and cultural issues, as well as concern for modesty, is important in providing psychological support before, during, and after the procedure.

Explain that an IV line may be inserted to allow infusion of IV fluids, anesthetics, or sedatives. Usually normal saline is infused.

Instruct the patient to fast and restrict fluids for 8 hr prior to the procedure. Protocols may vary among facilities.

Instruct the patient not to douche or use tampons or vaginal medications for 24 hr prior to the procedure.

Make sure a written and informed consent has been signed prior to the procedure and before administering any medications.

INTRATEST:

Observe standard precautions, and follow the general guidelines in Appendix A. Positively identify the patient.

Ensure the patient has complied with dietary and fluid restrictions for 8 hr prior to the procedure.

Instruct the patient to void prior to the procedure and to change into the gown, robe, and foot coverings provided.

Instruct the patient to cooperate fully and to follow directions.

Record baseline vital signs, and continue to monitor throughout the procedure. Protocols may vary among facilities.

Establish an IV fluid line for the injection of emergency drugs and of sedatives.

Place the patient in the supine position on an exam table. Cleanse the vaginal area, and cover with a sterile drape.

Monitor the patient for complications related to the procedure.

POST-TEST:

A report of the results will be made available to the requesting HCP, who will discuss the results with the patient.

Instruct the patient to resume usual diet, fluids, medications, and activity as directed by the HCP.

Instruct the patient to immediately report symptoms such as excessive uterine bleeding or fever.

Recognize anxiety related to test results. Discuss the implications of abnormal test results on the patient's lifestyle. Provide teaching and information regarding the clinical implications of the test results, as appropriate.

Reinforce information given by the patient's HCP regarding further testing, treatment, or referral to another HCP. Answer any questions or address any concerns voiced by the patient or family.

Depending on the results of this procedure, additional testing may be needed to evaluate or monitor progression of the disease process and determine the need for a change in therapy. Evaluate test results in relation to the patient's symptoms and other tests performed.

RELATED MONOGRAPHS:

Related tests include CBC hematocrit, CBC hemoglobin, CT abdomen, HCG, KUB, and US pelvis.

Refer to the Reproductive System table at the end of the book for related tests by body system.

Immunofixation Electrophoresis, Blood and Urine

SYNONYM/ACRONYM: IFE.

COMMON USE: To identify the individual types of immunoglobulins, toward diagnosing diseases such as multiple myeloma, and to evaluate effectiveness of chemotherapy.

SPECIMEN: Serum (1 mL) collected in a red-top tube. Urine (10 mL) from a random or timed collection in a clean plastic container.

NORMAL FINDINGS: (Method: Immunoprecipitation combined with electrophoresis) Test results are interpreted by a pathologist. Normal placement and intensity of staining provide information about the immunoglobulin bands.

DESCRIPTION: Immunofixation electrophoresis (IFE) is a qualitative technique that provides a detailed separation of individual immunoglobulins according to their electrical charges. Abnormalities are revealed by changes produced in the individual bands, such as displacement, color, or absence of color. Urine IFE has replaced the Bence Jones screening test for light chains. IFE has replaced immunoelectrophoresis because it is more sensitive and easier to interpret.

CRITICAL FINDINGS: N/A

INTERFERING FACTORS
- Drugs that may increase immunoglobulin levels include asparaginase, cimetidine, and narcotics.
- Drugs that may decrease immunoglobulin levels include dextran, oral contraceptives, methylprednisolone (high doses), and phenytoin.
- Chemotherapy and radiation treatments may alter the width of the bands and make interpretation difficult.

INDICATIONS
- Assist in the diagnosis of multiple myeloma and amyloidosis
- Assist in the diagnosis of suspected immunodeficiency
- Assist in the diagnosis of suspected immunoproliferative disorders, such as multiple myeloma and Waldenström's macroglobulinemia
- Identify biclonal or monoclonal gammopathies
- Identify cryoglobulinemia
- Monitor the effectiveness of chemotherapy or radiation therapy

POTENTIAL DIAGNOSIS
See monograph titled "Immunoglobulins A, D, G, and M."

NURSING IMPLICATIONS AND PROCEDURE

PRETEST:
- Positively identify the patient using at least two unique identifiers before providing care, treatment, or services.
- *Patient Teaching:* Inform the patient this test can assist in assessing the immune system.
- Obtain a history of the patient's complaints, including a list of known allergens, especially allergies or sensitivities to latex.
- Obtain a history of the patient's hematopoietic and immune systems, symptoms, and results of previously performed laboratory tests and diagnostic and surgical procedures.
- Note any recent procedures that can interfere with test results. Assess

whether the patient received any vaccinations or immunizations within the last 6 mo or any blood or blood components within the last 6 wk.

Obtain a list of the patient's current medications, including herbs, nutritional supplements, and nutraceuticals (see Appendix F).

Review the procedure with the patient. Inform the patient that specimen collection takes approximately 5 to 10 min. Address concerns about pain and explain that there may be some discomfort during the venipuncture.

Provide a nonmetallic urinal, bedpan, or toilet-mounted collection device. Usually a 24-hr time frame for urine collection is ordered. Inform the patient that all urine must be saved during that 24-hr period. Instruct the patient not to void directly into the laboratory collection container. Instruct the patient to avoid defecating in the collection device and to keep toilet tissue out of the collection device to prevent contamination of the specimen. Place a sign in the bathroom to remind the patient to save all urine.

Instruct the patient to void all urine into the collection device and then to pour the urine into the laboratory collection container. Alternatively the specimen can be left in the collection device for a health-care staff member to add to the laboratory collection container.

Sensitivity to social and cultural issues, as well as concern for modesty, is important in providing psychological support before, during, and after the procedure.

There are no food, fluid, or medication restrictions unless by medical direction.

INTRATEST:

If the patient has a history of allergic reaction to latex, avoid the use of equipment containing latex.

Instruct the patient to cooperate fully and to follow directions. Direct the patient to breathe normally and to avoid unnecessary movement.

Observe standard precautions, and follow the general guidelines in Appendix A. Positively identify the patient, and label the appropriate

specimen container with the corresponding patient demographics, initials of the person collecting the specimen, date, and time of collection. Perform a venipuncture as appropriate.

Blood

Perform a venipuncture.

Remove the needle and apply direct pressure with dry gauze to stop bleeding. Observe/assess venipuncture site for bleeding or hematoma formation and secure gauze with adhesive bandage.

Urine

Clean-Catch Specimen

Instruct the male patient to (1) thoroughly wash his hands, (2) cleanse the meatus, (3) void a small amount into the toilet, and (4) void directly into the specimen container.

Instruct the female patient to (1) thoroughly wash her hands; (2) cleanse the labia from front to back; (3) while keeping the labia separated, void a small amount into the toilet; and (4) without interrupting the urine stream, void directly into the specimen container.

Blood or Urine

Promptly transport the specimen to the laboratory for processing and analysis.

POST-TEST:

A report of the results will be made available to the requesting health-care provider (HCP), who will discuss the results with the patient.

Reinforce information given by the patient's HCP regarding further testing, treatment, or referral to another HCP. Answer any questions or address any concerns voiced by the patient or family.

Depending on the results of this procedure, additional testing may be performed to evaluate or monitor progression of the disease process and determine the need for a change in therapy. Evaluate test results in relation to the patient's symptoms and other tests performed.

RELATED MONOGRAPHS:

Related tests include anion gap, biopsy bone, biopsy bone marrow, biopsy liver, biopsy lymph node, cold agglutinin, CBC, CBC WBC count and differential, cryoglobulin, ESR, fibrinogen, quantitative immunoglobulin levels, LAP, liver and spleen scan, β-2-microglobulin, platelet antibodies, protein total and fractions, and UA. Refer to the Hematopoietic and Immune systems tables at the end of the book for related tests by body system.

Immunoglobulin E

SYNONYM/ACRONYM: IgE.

COMMON USE: To assess immunoglobulin E (IgE) levels in order to identify the presence of an allergic or inflammatory immune response.

SPECIMEN: Serum (1 mL) collected in a red- or tiger-top tube.

NORMAL FINDINGS: (Method: Immunoassay)

Age	Conventional Units
Newborn	Less than 12 kU/L
Less than 1 yr	Less than 50 kU/L
2–4 yr	Less than 200 kU/L
5–9 yr	Less than 300 kU/L
10 yr and older	Less than 100 kU/L

DESCRIPTION: Immunoglobulin E (IgE) is an antibody whose primary response is to allergic reactions and parasitic infections. Most of the body's IgE is bound to specialized tissue cells; little is available in the circulating blood. IgE binds to the membrane of special granulocytes called *basophils* in the circulating blood and *mast cells* in the tissues. Basophil and mast cell membranes have receptors for IgE. Mast cells are abundant in the skin and the tissues lining the respiratory and alimentary tracts. When IgE antibody becomes cross-linked with antigen/allergen, the release of histamine, heparin, and other chemicals from the granules in the cells is triggered. A sequence of events follows activation of IgE that affects smooth muscle contraction, vascular permeability, and inflammatory reactions. The inflammatory response allows proteins from the bloodstream to enter the tissues. Helminths (worm parasites) are especially susceptible to immunoglobulin-mediated cytotoxic chemicals. The inflammatory reaction proteins attract macrophages from the circulatory system and granulocytes, such as eosinophils, from circulation and bone marrow. Eosinophils also contain enzymes effective against the parasitic invaders.

INDICATIONS

Assist in the evaluation of allergy and parasitic infection

POTENTIAL DIAGNOSIS

Increased in

Conditions involving allergic reactions or infections that stimulate production of IgE.

- Alcoholism *(alcohol may play a role in the development of environmentally instigated IgE-mediated hypersensitivity)*
- Allergy
- Asthma
- Bronchopulmonary aspergillosis
- Dermatitis
- Eczema
- Hay fever
- IgE myeloma
- Parasitic infestation
- Rhinitis
- Sinusitis
- Wiskott-Aldrich syndrome

Decreased in

- Advanced carcinoma *(related to generalized decrease in immune system response)*
- Agammaglobulinemia *(related to decreased production)*
- Ataxia-telangiectasia *(evidenced by familial immunodeficiency disorder)*
- IgE deficiency

CRITICAL FINDINGS: N/A

INTERFERING FACTORS

- Drugs that may cause a decrease in IgE levels include phenytoin and tryptophan.
- Penicillin G has been associated with increased IgE levels in some patients with drug-induced acute interstitial nephritis.
- Normal IgE levels do not eliminate allergic disorders as a possible diagnosis.

NURSING IMPLICATIONS AND PROCEDURE

PRETEST:

- Positively identify the patient using at least two unique identifiers before providing care, treatment, or services.
- *Patient Teaching:* Inform the patient this test can assist in identification of an allergic or inflammatory response.
- Obtain a history of the patient's complaints, including a list of known allergens, especially allergies or sensitivities to latex.
- Obtain a history of the patient's immune and respiratory systems, symptoms, and results of previously performed laboratory tests and diagnostic and surgical procedures.
- Obtain a list of the patient's current medications, including herbs, nutritional supplements, and nutraceuticals (see Appendix F).
- Review the procedure with the patient. Inform the patient that specimen collection takes approximately 5 to 10 min. Address concerns about pain and explain that there may be some discomfort during the venipuncture.
- *Sensitivity to social and cultural issues,* as well as concern for modesty, is important in providing psychological support before, during, and after the procedure.
- There are no food, fluid, or medication restrictions unless by medical direction.

INTRATEST:

- If the patient has a history of allergic reaction to latex, avoid the use of equipment containing latex.
- Instruct the patient to cooperate fully and to follow directions. Direct the patient to breathe normally and to avoid unnecessary movement.
- Observe standard precautions, and follow the general guidelines in Appendix A. Positively identify the patient, and label the appropriate specimen container with the corresponding patient demographics, initials of the person collecting the specimen, date, and time of collection. Perform a venipuncture.

Remove the needle and apply direct pressure with dry gauze to stop bleeding. Observe/assess venipuncture site for bleeding or hematoma formation and secure gauze with adhesive bandage. Promptly transport the specimen to the laboratory for processing and analysis.

POST-TEST:

A report of the results will be made available to the requesting health-care provider (HCP), who will discuss the results with the patient.

Nutritional Considerations: Increased IgE levels may be associated with allergy. Consideration should be given to diet if the patient has food allergies.

Reinforce information given by the patient's HCP regarding further testing, treatment, or referral to another HCP. Answer any questions or address any concerns voiced by the patient or family.

Depending on the results of this procedure, additional testing may be performed to evaluate or monitor progression of the patient's condition and determine the need for a change in therapy. Evaluate test results in relation to the patient's symptoms and other tests performed.

RELATED MONOGRAPHS:

Related tests include allergen-specific IgE, alveolar/arterial gradient, biopsy intestine, biopsy liver, biopsy muscle, blood gases, carbon dioxide, CBC, CBC platelet count, CBC WBC count and differential, eosinophil count, fecal analysis, hypersensitivity pneumonitis, lung perfusion scan, and PFT.

Refer to the Immune and Respiratory systems tables at the end of the book for related tests by body system.

Immunoglobulins A, D, G, and M

SYNONYM/ACRONYM: IgA, IgD, IgG, and IgM.

COMMON USE: To quantitate immunoglobulins A, D, G, and M as indicators of immune system function, to assist in the diagnosis of immune system disorders such as multiple myeloma, and to investigate transfusion anaphylaxis.

SPECIMEN: Serum (1 mL) collected in a red-top tube.

NORMAL FINDINGS: (Method: Nephelometry)

Age	Conventional Units	SI Units
Immunoglobulin A		*(Conventional Units × 0.01)*
Newborn	1–4 mg/dL	0.01–0.04 g/L
1–9 mo	2–80 mg/dL	0.02–0.8 g/L
10–12 mo	15–90 mg/dL	0.15–0.9 g/L
2–3 yr	18–150 mg/dL	0.18–1.5 g/L
4–5 yr	25–160 mg/dL	0.25–1.6 g/L
6–8 yr	35–200 mg/dL	0.35–2 g/L
9–12 yr	45–250 mg/dL	0.45–2.5 g/L
Older than 12 yr	40–350 mg/dL	0.40–3.5 g/L

Age	Conventional Units	SI Units
Immunoglobulin D		*(Conventional Units × 10)*
Newborn	Greater than 2 mg/dL	Greater than 20 mg/L
Adult	Less than 15 mg/dL	Less than 150 mg/L
Immunoglobulin G		*(Conventional Units × 0.01)*
Newborn	650–1,600 mg/dL	6.5–16 g/L
1–9 mo	250–900 mg/dL	2.5–9 g/L
10–12 mo	290–1,070 mg/dL	2.9–10.7 g/L
2–3 yr	420–1,200 mg/dL	4.2–12 g/L
4–6 yr	460–1,240 mg/dL	4.6–12.4 g/L
Greater than 6 yr	650–1,600 mg/dL	6.5–16 g/L
Immunoglobulin M		*(Conventional Units × 0.01)*
Newborn	Less than 25 mg/dL	Less than 0.25 g/L
1–9 mo	20–125 mg/dL	0.2–1.25 g/L
10–12 mo	40–150 mg/dL	0.4–1.5 g/L
2–8 yr	45–200 mg/dL	0.45–2 g/L
9–12 yr	50–250 mg/dL	0.5–2.5 g/L
Greater than 12 yr	50–300 mg/dL	0.5–3 g/L

DESCRIPTION: Immunoglobulins A, D, E, G, and M are made by plasma cells in response to foreign particles. Immunoglobulins neutralize toxic substances, support phagocytosis, and destroy invading microorganisms. They are made up of heavy and light chains. Immunoglobulins produced by the proliferation of a single plasma cell (clone) are called *monoclonal*. Polyclonal increases result when multiple cell lines produce antibody. IgA is found mainly in secretions such as tears, saliva, and breast milk. It is believed to protect mucous membranes from viruses and bacteria. The function of IgD is not well understood. For details on IgE, see the monograph titled "Immunoglobulin E." IgG is the predominant serum immunoglobulin and is important in long-term defense against disease. It is the only antibody that crosses the placenta. IgM is the largest immunoglobulin, and it is the first antibody to react to an antigenic stimulus. IgM also forms natural antibodies, such as ABO blood group antibodies. The presence of IgM in cord blood is an indication of congenital infection.

INDICATIONS
- Assist in the diagnosis of multiple myeloma
- Evaluate humoral immunity status
- Monitor therapy for multiple myeloma
- IgA: Evaluate patients suspected of IgA deficiency prior to transfusion. Evaluate anaphylaxis associated with the transfusion of blood and blood products (anti-IgA antibodies may develop in patients with low levels of IgA, possibly resulting in anaphylaxis when donated blood is transfused)

POTENTIAL DIAGNOSIS

Increased in

IgA

Polyclonal
- Chronic liver disease *(pathophysiology is unclear)*
- Immunodeficiency states, such as Wiskott-Aldrich syndrome *(inherited condition of lymphocytes characterized by increased IgA and IgE)*
- Inflammatory bowel disease *(IgG and/or IgA antibody positive for Saccharomyces cerevisiae with negative perinuclear-antineutrophil cytoplasmic antibody is indicative of Crohn's disease)*
- Lower gastrointestinal (GI) cancer *(pathophysiology is unclear)*
- Rheumatoid arthritis *(pathophysiology is unclear)*

Monoclonal
- IgA-type multiple myeloma *(related to excessive production by a single clone of plasma cells)*

IgD

Polyclonal *(pathophysiology is unclear, but increases are associated with increases in IgM)*
- Certain liver diseases
- Chronic infections
- Connective tissue disorders

Monoclonal
- IgD-type multiple myeloma *(related to excessive production by a single clone of plasma cells)*

IgG

(Conditions that involve inflammation and/or development of an infection stimulate production of IgG.)

Polyclonal
- Autoimmune diseases, such as systemic lupus erythematosus, rheumatoid arthritis, and Sjögren's syndrome
- Chronic liver disease
- Chronic or recurrent infections

- Intrauterine devices *(the IUD creates a localized inflammatory reaction that stimulates production of IgG)*
- Sarcoidosis

Monoclonal
- IgG-type multiple myeloma *(related to excessive production by a single clone of plasma cells)*
- Leukemias
- Lymphomas

IgM

Polyclonal *(humoral response to infections and inflammation; both acute and chronic)*
- Active sarcoidosis
- Chronic hepatocellular disease
- Collagen vascular disease
- Early response to bacterial or parasitic infection
- Hyper-IgM dysgammaglobulinemia
- Rheumatoid arthritis
- Variable in nephrotic syndrome
- Viral infection (hepatitis or mononucleosis)

Monoclonal
- Cold agglutinin hemolysis disease
- Malignant lymphoma
- Neoplasms (especially in GI tract)
- Reticulosis
- Waldenström's macroglobulinemia *(related to excessive production by a single clone of plasma cells)*

Decreased in

IgA
- Ataxia-telangiectasia
- Chronic sinopulmonary disease
- Genetic IgA deficiency

IgD
- Genetic IgD deficiency
- Malignant melanoma of the skin
- Pre-eclampsia

IgG
- Burns
- Genetic IgG deficiency
- Nephrotic syndrome
- Pregnancy

IgM
- Burns
- Secondary IgM deficiency associated with IgG or IgA gammopathies

CRITICAL FINDINGS: N/A

INTERFERING FACTORS
- Drugs that may increase immunoglobulin levels include asparaginase, cimetidine, and narcotics.
- Drugs that may decrease immunoglobulin levels include dextran, oral contraceptives, methylprednisolone (high doses), and phenytoin.
- Chemotherapy, immunosuppressive therapy, and radiation treatments decrease immunoglobulin levels.
- Specimens with macroglobulins, cryoglobulins, or cold agglutinins tested at cold temperatures may give falsely low values.

NURSING IMPLICATIONS AND PROCEDURE

PRETEST:
- Positively identify the patient using at least two unique identifiers before providing care, treatment, or services.
- *Patient Teaching:* Inform the patient this test can assess the immune system by evaluating the levels of immunoglobulins in the blood.
- Obtain a history of the patient's complaints, including a list of known allergens, especially allergies or sensitivities to latex.
- Obtain a history of the patient's hematopoietic and immune systems, symptoms, and results of previously performed laboratory tests and diagnostic and surgical procedures.
- Obtain a list of the patient's current medications, including herbs, nutritional supplements, and nutraceuticals (see Appendix F).
- Note any recent procedures that can interfere with test results.
- Review the procedure with the patient. Inform the patient that specimen collection takes approximately 5 to 10 min. Address concerns about pain and explain to the patient that there may be some discomfort during the venipuncture.
- *Sensitivity to social and cultural issues,* as well as concern for modesty, is important in providing psychological support before, during, and after the procedure.
- There are no food, fluid, or medication restrictions unless by medical direction.

INTRATEST:
- If the patient has a history of allergic reaction to latex, avoid the use of equipment containing latex.
- Instruct the patient to cooperate fully and to follow directions. Direct the patient to breathe normally and to avoid unnecessary movement.
- Observe standard precautions, and follow the general guidelines in Appendix A. Positively identify the patient, and label the appropriate specimen container with the corresponding patient demographics, initials of the person collecting the specimen, date, and time of collection. Perform a venipuncture.
- Remove the needle and apply direct pressure with dry gauze to stop bleeding. Observe/assess venipuncture site for bleeding or hematoma formation and secure gauze with adhesive bandage.
- Promptly transport the specimen to the laboratory for processing and analysis.

POST-TEST:
- A report of the results will be made available to the requesting health-care provider (HCP), who will discuss the results with the patient.
- Reinforce information given by the patient's HCP regarding further testing, treatment, or referral to another HCP. Answer any questions or address any concerns voiced by the patient or family.
- Depending on the results of this procedure, additional testing may be performed to evaluate or monitor progression of the disease process and

determine the need for a change in therapy. Evaluate test results in relation to the patient's symptoms and other tests performed.

RELATED MONOGRAPHS:

▶ Related tests include ALT, anion gap, ANA, bilirubin, biopsy bone, biopsy bone marrow, biopsy liver, biopsy lymph node, blood groups and antibodies, cold agglutinin, CBC, CBC WBC count and differential, Coomb's antiglobulin (direct and indirect), cryoglobulin, ESR, fibrinogen, IFE, quantitative immunoglobulin levels, GGT, LAP, liver and spleen scan, beta-2-microglobulin, platelet antibodies, protein total and fractions, RF, and uric acid.

▶ Refer to the Hematopoietic and Immune systems tables at the end of the book for related tests by body system.

Immunosuppressants: Cyclosporine, Methotrexate, Everolimus, Sirolimus, and Tacrolimus

SYNONYM/ACRONYM: *Cyclosporine* (Sandimmune), *methotrexate* (MTX, amethopterin, Folex, Rheumatrex), methotrexate sodium (Mexate), *everolimus* (Afinitor, Certican, Zortress), *sirolimus* (Rapamycin), *tacrolimus* (Prograf).

COMMON USE: To monitor appropriate drug dosage of immunosuppressant related to organ transplant maintenance.

SPECIMEN: Whole blood (1 mL) collected in lavender-top tube for cyclosporine, everolimus; sirolimus; tacrolimus. Serum (1 mL) collected in a red-top tube for methotrexate; specimen must be protected from light.

Immunosuppressant	Route of Administration	Recommended Collection Time
Cyclosporine	Oral or intravenous	12 hr after dose or immediately prior to next dose
Methotrexate	Oral	Varies according to dosing protocol
	Intramuscular	Varies according to dosing protocol
Everolimus	Oral	Immediately prior to next dose
Sirolimus	Oral	Immediately prior to next dose
Tacrolimus	Oral	Immediately prior to next dose

Leucovorin therapy, also called leucovorin rescue, is used in conjunction with administration of methotrexate. Leucovorin, a fast-acting form of folic acid, protects healthy cells from the toxic effects of methotrexate.

Important note: This information must be clearly and accurately communicated to avoid misunderstanding of the dose time in relation to the collection time. Miscommunication between the individual administering the medication and the individual collecting the specimen is the most frequent cause of subtherapeutic levels, toxic levels, and misleading information used in calculation of future doses.

NORMAL FINDINGS: (Method: Immunoassay for cyclosporine and methotrexate; liquid chromatography with tandem mass spectrometry for everolimus, sirolimus, and tacrolimus)

	Therapeutic Dose		Half-Life (hr)	Volume of Distribution (L/kg)	Protein Binding (%)	Excretion
	Conventional Units	*SI Units (Conventional Units × 0.832)*				
Cyclosporine	100–300 ng/mL renal transplant	83–250 nmol/L	8–24	4–6	90	Renal
	200–350 ng/mL cardiac, hepatic, pancreatic transplant	166–291 nmol/L	8–24	4–6	90	Renal
	100–300 ng/mL bone marrow transplant	83–250 nmol/L	8–24	4–6	90	Renal
Methotrexate	Dependent on therapeutic approach Low dose: 0.5–1 micromol/L High dose: Less than 5 micromol/L at 24 h; less than 0.5 micromol/L at 48 h; less than 0.1 micromol/L at 72 h		5–9	0.4–1	50–70	Renal

(*table continues on page 850*)

	Therapeutic Dose		Half-Life (hr)	Volume of Distribution (L/kg)	Protein Binding (%)	Excretion
	Conventional Units	*SI Units (Conventional Units × 0.832)*				
Everolimus	Transplant: 3–8 ng/mL		18–35 (kidney); 30–35 (liver)	128–589	75	Biliary
	Oncology: 5–10 ng/mL		18–35	128–589	75	Biliary
Sirolimus	Maintenance phase: renal transplant: 4–12 ng/mL; liver transplant: 12–20 ng/mL		46–78	4–20	92	Biliary
Tacrolimus	Maintenance phase: renal transplant: 6–12 ng/mL; liver transplant: 4–10 ng/mL; pancreas transplant: 10–18 ng/mL; bone marrow transplant: 10–20 ng/mL		10–14	1.5	99	Biliary

Therapeutic targets for the initial phase post-transplantation are slightly higher than during the maintenance phase and are influenced by the specific therapy chosen for each patient with respect to coordination of treatment for other conditions and corresponding therapies. Therapeutic ranges for everolimus, sirolimus, and tacrolimus assume concomitant administration of cyclosporine and steroids.

DESCRIPTION: Cyclosporine is an immunosuppressive drug used in the management of organ rejection, especially rejection of heart, liver, pancreas, and kidney transplants. Its most serious side effect is renal impairment or renal failure. Cyclosporine is often administered in conjunction with corticosteroids (e.g., prednisone) for its anti-inflammatory or immune-suppressing properties and with other drugs (e.g., everolimus, sirolimus, tacrolimus) to reduce graft-versus-host disease. Methotrexate is a highly toxic drug that causes cell death by disrupting DNA synthesis. Methotrexate is also used in the treatment of rheumatoid arthritis, psoriasis, polymyositis, and Reiter's syndrome. These drugs are metabolized by the cytochrome enzyme, CYP3A4 of the CYP450 family of cytochrome enzymes. Careful management of all medications, especially concomitant administration of medications known to be either strong inducers or inhibitors of CYP3A4, is essential to achieve the desired therapeutic effect.

Many factors must be considered in effective dosing and monitoring of therapeutic drugs, including patient age; weight; interacting medications; electrolyte balance; protein levels; water balance; conditions that affect absorption and excretion; as well as foods, herbals, vitamins, and minerals that can either potentiate or inhibit the intended target concentration.

INDICATIONS

Cyclosporine, Sirolimus, Tacrolimus
• Assist in the management of treatments to prevent organ rejection
• Monitor for toxicity

Everolimus
• Assist in the management of treatments to prevent organ rejection
• Assist in the management of treatments for subependymal giant cell astrocytoma
• Monitor effectiveness of treatment of renal cell carcinoma
• Monitor for toxicity

Methotrexate
• Monitor effectiveness of treatment of cancer and some autoimmune disorders
• Monitor for toxicity

POTENTIAL DIAGNOSIS

Level	Response
Normal levels	Therapeutic effect
Toxic levels	Adjust dose as indicated
Cyclosporine	Renal impairment
Methotrexate	Renal impairment
Everolimus, sirolimus, tacrolimus	Hepatic impairment

CRITICAL FINDINGS

It is important to note the adverse effects of toxic and subtherapeutic levels. Care must be taken to investigate signs and symptoms of too little and too much medication.

Note and immediately report to the health-care provider (HCP) any critically increased values and related symptoms. Timely notification of critical values for lab or diagnostic studies is a role expectation of the professional nurse. Notification processes will vary among facilities. Upon receipt of the critical value the information should be read back to the caller to verify accuracy. Most policies require immediate notification of the primary HCP, Hospitalist, or on-call HCP. Reported information includes the patient's name, unique identifiers, critical value, name of the person giving the report, and name of the person receiving the report. Documentation of notification should be made in the medical record with the name of the HCP notified, time and date of notification, and any orders received. Any delay in a timely report of a critical value may require completion of a notification form with review by Risk Management.

Cyclosporine: Greater Than 400 ng/mL (SI: Greater Than 332.8 nmol/L)

Signs and symptoms of cyclosporine toxicity include increased severity of expected side effects, which include nausea, stomatitis, vomiting, anorexia, hypertension, infection, fluid retention, hypercalcemic metabolic acidosis, tremor, seizures, headache, and flushing. Possible interventions include close monitoring of blood levels to make dosing adjustments, inducing emesis (if orally ingested), performing gastric lavage (if orally ingested), withholding the drug, and initiating alternative therapy for a short time until the patient is stabilized.

Methotrexate: Greater Than 1 micromol/L After 48 Hr With High-Dose Therapy; Greater Than 0.02 micromol/L After 48 Hr With Low-Dose Therapy

Signs and symptoms of methotrexate toxicity include increased severity of expected side effects, which include nausea, stomatitis, vomiting, anorexia, bleeding, infection, bone marrow depression, and, over a prolonged period of use, hepatotoxicity. The effect of methotrexate on normal cells can be reversed by administration of 5-formyltetrahydrofolate (citrovorum or leucovorin). 5-Formyltetrahydrofolate allows higher doses of methotrexate to be given.

Everolimus: Greater Than 15 ng/mL

Signs and symptoms of everolimus pulmonary toxicity include hypoxia, pleural effusion, cough, and dyspnea. Possible interventions include dosing adjustments, administration of corticosteroids, and monitoring of pulmonary function with chest x-ray. Use of everolimus is contraindicated in patients with severe hepatic impairment. Concomitant administration of strong CYP3A4 inhibitors may significantly increase everolimus levels.

Sirolimus: Greater Than 20 ng/mL

Signs and symptoms of sirolimus pulmonary toxicity include cough, shortness of breath, chest pain, and rapid heart rate. Possible interventions include dosing adjustments, administration of corticosteroids, and monitoring of pulmonary function with chest x-ray.

Tacrolimus: Greater Than 25 ng/mL

Signs and symptoms of tacrolimus toxicity include tremors, seizures, headache, high blood pressure, hyperkalemia, tinnitus, nausea, and vomiting. Possible interventions include treatment of hypertension, administration of antiemetics for nausea and vomiting, and dosing adjustments.

INTERFERING FACTORS

- Numerous drugs interact with cyclosporine and either increase cyclosporine levels or increase the risk of toxicity. These drugs include acyclovir, aminoglycosides, amiodarone, amphotericin B, anabolic steroids, cephalosporins, cimetidine, danazol, erythromycin, furosemide, ketoconazole, melphalan, methylprednisolone, miconazole, NSAIDs, oral contraceptives, and trimethoprim-sulfamethoxazole.
- Drugs that may decrease cyclosporine levels include carbamazepine, ethotoin, mephenytoin, phenobarbital, phenytoin, primidone, and rifampin.
- Drugs that may increase methotrexate levels or increase the risk of toxicity include NSAIDs, probenecid, salicylate, and sulfonamides.
- Antibiotics may decrease the absorption of methotrexate.
- Drugs and foods that may increase everolimus levels include ketoconazole, amprenavir, aprepitant, atazanavir, clarithromycin, delavirdine, diltiazem, erythromycin, fluconazole, fosamprenavir, grapefruit juice, indinavir, itraconazole, nefazodone,

nelfinavir, ritonavir, saquinavir, telithromycin, verapamil, and voriconazole.

- Drugs and herbs that may decrease everolimus levels include carbamazepine, dexamethasone, phenobarbital, phenytoin, rifabutin, rifampin, and St. John's Wort.

- Drugs and foods that may increase sirolimus levels include bromocriptine, cimetidine, cisapride, clotrimazole, danazol, diltiazem, fluconazole, indinavir, metoclopramide, nicardipine, ritonavir, troleandomycin, and verapamil.

- Drugs and herbs that may increase sirolimus levels include carbamazepine, phenobarbital, phenytoin, rifapentine, and St. John's Wort.

- Drugs and foods that may increase tacrolimus levels include bromocriptine, chloramphenicol, cimetidine, cisapride, clarithromycin, clotrimazole, cyclosporine, danazol, diltiazem, erythromycin, fluconazole, grapefruit juice, itraconazole, ketoconazole, methylprednisolone, metoclopramide, nelfinavir, nicardipine, nifedipine, torinavir, troleandomycin, verapamil, and voriconazole.

- Drugs and herbs that may decrease tacrolimus levels include carbamazepine, ethotoin, mephenytoin, octreotide, phenobarbital, primidone, rifabutin, rifampin, sirolimus, and St. John's Wort.

NURSING IMPLICATIONS AND PROCEDURE

PRETEST:

- Positively identify the patient using at least two unique identifiers before providing care, treatment, or services.
- *Patient Teaching:* Inform the patient this test can assess in monitoring therapeutic and toxic drug levels.
- Obtain a history of the patient's complaints, including a list of known

allergens, especially allergies or sensitivities to latex.

- Obtain a history of the patient's genitourinary and immune systems, symptoms, and results of previously performed laboratory tests and diagnostic and surgical procedures. Some considerations prior to medication administration include documentation of adequate renal function with creatinine and BUN levels, documentation of adequate hepatic function with alanine aminotransferase (ALT) and bilirubin levels, and documentation of adequate hematological and immune function with platelet and white blood cell (WBC) count. Patients receiving methotrexate must be well hydrated and, depending on the therapy, may be treated with sodium bicarbonate for urinary alkalinization to enhance drug excretion. Leucovorin calcium rescue therapy may also be part of the protocol.

- Obtain a list of the patient's current medications, including herbs, nutritional supplements, and nutraceuticals (see Appendix F).

- Review the procedure with the patient. Inform the patient that specimen collection takes approximately 5 to 10 min. Address concerns about pain and explain that there may be some discomfort during the venipuncture.

- *Sensitivity to social and cultural issues,* as well as concern for modesty, is important in providing psychological support before, during, and after the procedure.

- There are no food, fluid, or medication restrictions unless by medical direction.

INTRATEST:

- If the patient has a history of allergic reaction to latex, avoid the use of equipment containing latex.
- Instruct the patient to cooperate fully and to follow directions. Direct the patient to breathe normally and to avoid unnecessary movement.
- Observe standard precautions, and follow the general guidelines in Appendix A. Consider recommended collection time in relation to the dosing schedule. Positively identify the patient, and label the appropriate specimen container with the corresponding

patient demographics, initials of the person collecting the specimen, date, and time of collection, noting the last dose of medication taken. Perform a venipuncture.

Remove the needle and apply direct pressure with dry gauze to stop bleeding. Observe/assess venipuncture site for bleeding or hematoma formation and secure gauze with adhesive bandage.

Promptly transport the specimen to the laboratory for processing and analysis.

POST-TEST:

A report of the results will be made available to the requesting HCP, who will discuss the results with the patient.

Nutritional Considerations: Patients taking immunosuppressant therapy tend to have decreased appetites due to the side effects of the medication. Instruct patients to consume a variety of foods within the basic food groups, maintain a healthy weight, be physically active, limit salt intake, limit alcohol intake, and be a nonsmoker.

Recognize anxiety related to test results, and offer support. Patients receiving these drugs usually have conditions that can be intermittently moderately to severely debilitating, resulting in significant lifestyle changes. Educate the patient regarding access to counseling services, as appropriate.

Reinforce information given by the patient's HCP regarding further testing, treatment, or referral to another HCP. Explain to the patient the importance of following the medication regimen and give instructions regarding drug interactions. Answer any questions or address any concerns voiced by the patient or family.

Instruct the patient to be prepared to provide the pharmacist with a list of other medications he or she is already taking in the event that the requesting HCP prescribes a medication.

Depending on the results of this procedure, additional testing may be performed to evaluate or monitor progression of the disease process and determine the need for a change in therapy. Evaluate test results in relation to the patient's symptoms and other tests performed.

RELATED MONOGRAPHS:

Related tests include ALT, AST, bilirubin, BUN, CBC platelet count, CBC WBC count and differential, and creatinine.

Refer to the Genitourinary and Immune systems tables at the end of the book for related tests by body system.

Infectious Mononucleosis Screen

SYNONYM/ACRONYM: Monospot, heterophil antibody test, IM serology.

COMMON USE: To assess for Epstein-Barr virus and assist with diagnosis of infectious mononucleosis.

SPECIMEN: Serum (1 mL) collected in a red-top tube.

NORMAL FINDINGS: (Method: Agglutination) Negative.

DESCRIPTION: Infectious mononucleosis is caused by the Epstein-Barr virus (EBV). The incubation period is 10 to 50 days, and the symptoms last 1 to 4 wk after the infection has fully developed. The hallmark of EBV infection is the presence of heterophil antibodies, also called Paul-Bunnell-Davidsohn antibodies, which are immunoglobulin M (IgM) antibodies that agglutinate sheep or horse red blood cells. The disease induces formation of abnormal lymphocytes in the lymph nodes; stimulates increased formation of heterophil antibodies; and is characterized by fever, cervical lymphadenopathy, tonsillopharyngitis, and hepatosplenomegaly. EBV is also thought to play a role in Burkitt's lymphoma, nasopharyngeal carcinoma, and chronic fatigue syndrome. If the results of the heterophil antibody screening test are negative and infectious mononucleosis is highly suspected, EBV-specific serology should be requested.

INDICATIONS
• Assist in confirming infectious mononucleosis

POTENTIAL DIAGNOSIS

Positive findings in
• Infectious mononucleosis

Negative findings in: N/A

CRITICAL FINDINGS: N/A

INTERFERING FACTORS
• False-positive results may occur in the presence of narcotic addiction, serum sickness, lymphomas, hepatitis, leukemia, cancer of the pancreas, and phenytoin therapy.

• A false-negative result may occur if treatment was begun before antibodies developed or if the test was done less than 6 days after exposure to the virus.

NURSING IMPLICATIONS AND PROCEDURE

PRETEST:

▸ Positively identify the patient using at least two unique identifiers before providing care, treatment, or services.

▸ *Patient Teaching:* Inform the patient this test can assist with diagnosing a mononucleosis infection.

▸ Obtain a history of the patient's complaints, including a list of known allergens, especially allergies or sensitivities to latex. Obtain a history of exposure.

▸ Obtain a history of the patient's hepatobiliary and immune systems, symptoms, and results of previously performed laboratory tests and diagnostic and surgical procedures.

▸ Note any recent therapies that can interfere with test results.

▸ Obtain a list of the patient's current medications, including herbs, nutritional supplements, and nutraceuticals (see Appendix F).

▸ Review the procedure with the patient. Inform the patient that specimen collection takes approximately 5 to 10 min. Address concerns about pain and explain that there may be some discomfort during the venipuncture.

▸ *Sensitivity to social and cultural issues,* as well as concern for modesty, is important in providing psychological support before, during, and after the procedure.

▸ There are no food, fluid, or medication restrictions unless by medical direction.

INTRATEST:

▸ If the patient has a history of allergic reaction to latex, avoid the use of equipment containing latex.

Instruct the patient to cooperate fully and to follow directions. Direct the patient to breathe normally and to avoid unnecessary movement.

Observe standard precautions, and follow the general guidelines in Appendix A. Positively identify the patient, and label the appropriate specimen container with the corresponding patient demographics, initials of the person collecting the specimen, date, and time of collection. Perform a venipuncture.

Remove the needle and apply direct pressure with dry gauze to stop bleeding. Observe/assess venipuncture site for bleeding or hematoma formation and secure gauze with adhesive bandage.

Promptly transport the specimen to the laboratory for processing and analysis.

POST-TEST:

A report of the results will be made available to the requesting health-care provider (HCP), who will discuss the results with the patient.

Inform the patient that approximately 10% of all results are false-negative or false-positive. Inform the patient that signs and symptoms of infection include fever, chills, sore throat, enlarged lymph nodes, and fatigue. Self-care while the disease runs its course includes adequate fluid and nutritional intake along with sufficient rest. Activities that cause fatigue or stress should be avoided.

Reinforce information given by the patient's HCP regarding further testing, treatment, or referral to another HCP. Advise the patient to refrain from direct contact with others because the disease is transmitted through saliva. Answer any questions or address any concerns voiced by the patient or family.

Depending on the results of this procedure, additional testing may be performed to evaluate or monitor progression of the disease process and determine the need for a change in therapy. Evaluate test results in relation to the patient's symptoms and other tests performed.

RELATED MONOGRAPHS:

Related tests include CBC with peripheral blood smear evaluation and US abdomen.

Refer to the Hepatobiliary and Immune systems tables at the end of the book for related tests by body system.

Insulin and Insulin Response to Glucose

SYNONYM/ACRONYM: N/A.

COMMON USE: To assess the amount of insulin secreted in response to blood glucose to assist in diagnosis of types of hypoglycemia and insulin resistant pathologies.

SPECIMEN: Serum (1 mL) collected in a red-top tube.

NORMAL FINDINGS: (Method: Immunoassay)

75-g Glucose Load	Insulin	SI Units (Conventional Units × 6.945)	Tolerance for Glucose (Hypoglycemia)
Fasting	Less than 17 micro international units/L	Less than 118.1 pmol/L	Less than 110 mg/dL
30 min	6–86 micro international units/L	41.7–597.3 pmol/L	Less than 200 mg/dL
1 hr	8–118 micro international units/L	55.6–819.5 pmol/L	Less than 200 mg/dL
2 hr	5–55 micro international units/L	34.7–382 pmol/L	Less than 140 mg/dL
3 hr	Less than 25 micro international units/L	Less than 174 pmol/L	65–120 mg/dL
4 hr	Less than 15 micro international units/L	Less than 104.2 pmol/L	65–120 mg/dL
5 hr	Less than 8 micro international units/L	Less than 55.6 pmol/L	65–115 mg/dL

DESCRIPTION: Insulin is secreted in response to elevated blood glucose, and its overall effect is to promote glucose use and energy storage. The insulin response test measures the rate of insulin secreted by the beta cells of the islets of Langerhans in the pancreas; it may be performed simultaneously with a 5-hr glucose tolerance test for hypoglycemia.

INDICATIONS
• Assist in the diagnosis of early or developing non–insulin-dependent (type 2) diabetes, as indicated by excessive production of insulin in relation to blood glucose levels (best shown with glucose tolerance tests or 2-hr postprandial tests)
• Assist in the diagnosis of insulino-ma, as indicated by sustained high levels of insulin and absence of blood glucose–related variations

• Confirm functional hypoglycemia, as indicated by circulating insulin levels appropriate to changing blood glucose levels
• Differentiate between insulin-resistant diabetes, in which insulin levels are high, and non–insulin-resistant diabetes, in which insulin levels are low
• Evaluate fasting hypoglycemia of unknown cause
• Evaluate postprandial hypoglycemia of unknown cause
• Evaluate uncontrolled insulin-dependent (type 1) diabetes

POTENTIAL DIAGNOSIS

Increased in
• Acromegaly *(related to excess production of growth hormone, which increases insulin levels)*
• Alcohol use *(related to stimulation of insulin production)*
• Cushing's syndrome *(related to overproduction of cortisol, which increases insulin levels)*
• Excessive administration of insulin
• Insulin- and proinsulin-secreting tumors (insulinomas)

- **Obesity** *(related to development of insulin resistance; body does not respond to insulin being produced)*
- Persistent hyperinsulinemic hypoglycemia *(collection of hypoglycemic disorders of infants and children)*
- Reactive hypoglycemia in developing diabetes
- Severe liver disease

Decreased in

- Beta cell failure *(pancreatic beta cells produce insulin; therefore, damage to these cells will decrease insulin levels)*
- Insulin-dependent diabetes *(related to lack of endogenous insulin)*

CRITICAL FINDINGS: N/A

INTERFERING FACTORS

- Drugs and substances that may increase insulin levels include acetohexamide, albuterol, amino acids, beclomethasone, betamethasone, broxaterol, calcium gluconate, cannabis, chlorpropamide, glibornuride, glipizide, glisoxepide, glucagon, glyburide, ibopamine, insulin, oral contraceptives, pancreozymin, prednisolone, prednisone, rifampin, terbutaline, tolazamide, tolbutamide, trichlormethiazide, and verapamil.
- Drugs that may decrease insulin levels include acarbose, calcitonin, cimetidine, clofibrate, dexfenfluramine, diltiazem, doxazosin, enalapril, enprostil, ether, hydroxypropyl methylcellulose, metformin (Glucophage), niacin, nifedipine, nitrendipine, octreotide, phenytoin, propranolol, and psyllium.
- Administration of insulin or oral hypoglycemic agents within 8 hr of the test can lead to falsely elevated levels.
- Hemodialysis destroys insulin and affects test results.

NURSING IMPLICATIONS AND PROCEDURE

PRETEST:

- Positively identify the patient using at least two unique identifiers before providing care, treatment, or services.
- *Patient Teaching:* Inform the patient this test can assist in the evaluation of low blood sugar.
- Obtain a history of the patient's complaints, including a list of known allergens, especially allergies or sensitivities to latex.
- Obtain a history of the patient's endocrine system, symptoms, and results of previously performed laboratory tests and diagnostic and surgical procedures. Note any recent procedures that can interfere with test results.
- Obtain a list of the patient's current medications, including herbs, nutritional supplements, and nutraceuticals (see Appendix F). Note the last time and dose of medication taken.
- Review the procedure with the patient. Inform the patient that multiple specimens may be required. Inform the patient that specimen collection takes approximately 5 to 10 min. Address concerns about pain and explain that there may be some discomfort during the venipuncture.
- *Sensitivity to social and cultural issues,* as well as concern for modesty, is important in providing psychological support before, during, and after the procedure.
- If a single sample is to be collected, the patient should have fasted and refrained, with medical direction, from taking insulin or other oral hypoglycemic agents for at least 8 hr before specimen collection. Protocols may vary among facilities.
- *Hypoglycemia:* Serial specimens for insulin levels are collected in conjunction with glucose levels after administration of a 75-g glucose load. The patient should be prepared as for a standard oral glucose tolerance test over a 5-hr period. Protocols may vary among facilities.
- There are no fluid restrictions unless by medical direction.

INTRATEST:

▸ Ensure that the patient has complied with dietary and medication restrictions and other pretesting preparations; assure that food or medications have been restricted as instructed prior to the specific procedure's protocol.

▸ If the patient has a history of allergic reaction to latex, avoid the use of equipment containing latex.

▸ Instruct the patient to cooperate fully and to follow directions. Direct the patient to breathe normally and to avoid unnecessary movement.

▸ Observe standard precautions, and follow the general guidelines in Appendix A. Positively identify the patient, and label the appropriate specimen container with the corresponding patient demographics, initials of the person collecting the specimen, date, and time of collection. Perform a venipuncture.

▸ Remove the needle and apply direct pressure with dry gauze to stop bleeding. Observe/assess venipuncture site for bleeding or hematoma formation and secure gauze with adhesive bandage.

▸ Promptly transport the specimen to the laboratory for processing and analysis.

POST-TEST:

▸ A report of the results will be made available to the requesting health-care provider (HCP), who will discuss the results with the patient.

▸ Instruct the patient to resume usual diet and medication, as directed by the HCP.

▸ *Nutritional Considerations:* Increased insulin levels may be associated with diabetes. There is no "diabetic diet"; however, many meal-planning approaches with nutritional goals are endorsed by the American Dietetic Association. Patients who adhere to dietary recommendations report a better general feeling of health, better weight management, greater control of glucose and lipid values, and improved use of insulin. Instruct the patient, as appropriate, in nutritional management of diabetes. The American Heart Association's Therapeutic Lifestyle Changes (TLC) diet provides goals directed at people with specific risk factors and/or existing medical conditions (e.g., elevated LDL cholesterol levels, other lipid disorders, coronary artery disease [CAD], insulin-dependent diabetes, insulin resistance, or metabolic syndrome). The TLC approach also includes the use of plant stanols or sterols and increased dissolved fiber as an option for lowering LDL cholesterol levels; nutritional recommendations for daily total caloric intake; recommendations for allowable percentage of calories derived from fat (saturated and unsaturated), carbohydrates, protein, and cholesterol; as well as recommendations for daily expenditure of energy. The nutritional needs of each diabetic patient need to be determined individually (especially during pregnancy) with the appropriate HCPs, particularly professionals trained in nutrition.

▸ Impaired glucose tolerance may be associated with diabetes. Instruct the patient and caregiver to report signs and symptoms of hypoglycemia (weakness, confusion, diaphoresis, rapid pulse) or hyperglycemia (thirst, polyuria, hunger, lethargy).

▸ *Social and Cultural Considerations:* Numerous studies point to the prevalence of excess body weight in American children and adolescents. Experts estimate that obesity is present in 25% of the population ages 6 to 11 yr. The medical, social, and emotional consequences of excess body weight are significant. Special attention should be given to instructing the child and caregiver regarding health risks and weight control education.

▸ Recognize anxiety related to test results, and be supportive of perceived loss of independence and fear of shortened life expectancy. Discuss the implications of abnormal test results on the patient's lifestyle. Provide teaching and information regarding the clinical implications of the test results, as appropriate. Emphasize, if indicated, that good glycemic control delays the onset and slows the progression of diabetic retinopathy, nephropathy, and neuropathy. Educate the patient regarding access to counseling services, as appropriate. Provide contact information, if desired, for the

American Diabetes Association (www .diabetes.org), the American Heart Association (www.americanheart.org), or the NHLBI (www.nhlbi.nih.gov). Reinforce information given by the patient's HCP regarding further testing, treatment, or referral to another HCP. Instruct the patient in the use of home test kits approved by the U.S. Food and Drug Administration, if prescribed. Answer any questions or address any concerns voiced by the patient or family. Depending on the results of this procedure, additional testing may be performed to evaluate or monitor progression of the disease process and determine the need for a change in therapy. Evaluate test results in relation to the patient's symptoms and other tests performed.

RELATED MONOGRAPHS:

Related tests include ACTH, ALT, angiography adrenal, bilirubin, BUN, calcium, catecholamines, cholesterol (HDL, LDL, total), cortisol, C-peptide, DHEA, creatinine, fecal analysis, fecal fat, fructosamine, GGT, gastric emptying scan, glucagon, glucose, GTT, glycated hemoglobin, GH, HVA, insulin antibodies, ketones, lipoprotein electrophoresis, metanephrines, microalbumin, and myoglobin.

Refer to the Endocrine System table at the end of the book for related tests by body system.

Insulin Antibodies

SYNONYM/ACRONYM: N/A.

COMMON USE: To assist in the prediction, diagnosis, and management of type 1 diabetes as well as insulin resistance and insulin allergy.

SPECIMEN: Serum (1 mL) collected in a red-top tube.

NORMAL FINDINGS: (Method: Radioimmunoassay) Less than 3%; includes binding of human, beef, and pork insulin to antibodies in patient's serum.

DESCRIPTION: The most common anti-insulin antibody is immunoglobulin (Ig) G, but IgA, IgM, IgD, and IgE antibodies also have anti-insulin properties. These antibodies usually do not cause clinical problems, but they may complicate insulin assay testing. IgM is thought to participate in insulin resistance and IgE in insulin allergy. Improvements in the purity of animal insulin and increased use of human insulin have resulted in a significant decrease in the incidence of insulin antibody formation.

INDICATIONS

- Assist in confirming insulin resistance
- Assist in determining if hypoglycemia is caused by insulin abuse
- Assist in determining insulin allergy

POTENTIAL DIAGNOSIS

Increased in

- Factitious hypoglycemia *(assists in differentiating lack of response due to the presence of insulin antibodies from secretive self-administration of insulin)*
- Insulin allergy or resistance *(antibodies bind to insulin and*

decrease amount of free insulin available for glucose metabolism)
- Polyendocrine autoimmune syndromes
- Steroid-induced diabetes *(a side effect of treatment for systemic lupus erythematosus)*

Decreased in: N/A

CRITICAL FINDINGS: N/A

INTERFERING FACTORS
Recent radioactive scans or radiation can interfere with test results when radioimmunoassay is the test method.

NURSING IMPLICATIONS AND PROCEDURE

PRETEST:

Positively identify the patient using at least two unique identifiers before providing care, treatment, or services.
Patient Teaching: Inform the patient this test can assist in the diagnosis and management of type 1 diabetes.
Obtain a history of the patient's complaints, including a list of known allergens, especially allergies or sensitivities to latex.
Obtain a history of the patient's endocrine and immune systems, symptoms, and results of previously performed laboratory tests and diagnostic and surgical procedures.
Note any recent procedures that can interfere with test results.
Obtain a list of the patient's current medications, including herbs, nutritional supplements, and nutraceuticals (see Appendix F). Note the last time and dose of medication taken.
Review the procedure with the patient. Inform the patient that specimen collection takes approximately 5 to 10 min. Address concerns about pain and explain that there may be some discomfort during the venipuncture.
Sensitivity to social and cultural issues, as well as concern for modesty, is important in providing psychological support before, during, and after the procedure.
There are no food, fluid, or medication restrictions unless by medical direction.

INTRATEST:

If the patient has a history of allergic reaction to latex, avoid the use of equipment containing latex.
Instruct the patient to cooperate fully and to follow directions. Direct the patient to breathe normally and to avoid unnecessary movement.
Observe standard precautions, and follow the general guidelines in Appendix A. Positively identify the patient, and label the appropriate specimen container with the corresponding patient demographics, initials of the person collecting the specimen, date, and time of collection. Perform a venipuncture.
Remove the needle and apply direct pressure with dry gauze to stop bleeding. Observe/assess venipuncture site for bleeding or hematoma formation and secure gauze with adhesive bandage.
Promptly transport the specimen to the laboratory for processing and analysis.

POST-TEST:

A report of the results will be made available to the requesting health-care provider (HCP), who will discuss the results with the patient.
Instruct the patient to resume usual diet and medication, as directed by the HCP.
Nutritional Considerations: Abnormal findings may be associated with diabetes. There is no "diabetic diet"; however, many meal-planning approaches with nutritional goals are endorsed by the American Dietetic Association. Patients who adhere to dietary recommendations report a better general feeling of health, better weight management, greater control of glucose and lipid values, and improved use of insulin. Instruct the patient, as appropriate, in nutritional management of diabetes. The American Heart Association's Therapeutic Lifestyle

Changes (TLC) diet provides goals directed at people with specific risk factors and/or existing medical conditions (e.g., elevated LDL cholesterol levels, other lipid disorders, coronary artery disease [CAD], insulin-dependent diabetes, insulin resistance, or metabolic syndrome). The TLC approach also includes the use of plant stanols or sterols and increased dissolved fiber as an option for lowering LDL cholesterol levels; nutritional recommendations for daily total caloric intake; recommendations for allowable percentage of calories derived from fat (saturated and unsaturated), carbohydrates, protein, and cholesterol; as well as recommendations for daily expenditure of energy. The nutritional needs of each diabetic patient need to be determined individually (especially during pregnancy) with the appropriate HCPs, particularly professionals trained in nutrition.

▶ Impaired glucose tolerance may be associated with diabetes. Instruct the patient and caregiver to report signs and symptoms of hypoglycemia (weakness, confusion, diaphoresis, rapid pulse) or hyperglycemia (thirst, polyuria, hunger, lethargy).

▶ Recognize anxiety related to test results, and be supportive of perceived loss of independence and fear of shortened life expectancy. Discuss the implications of abnormal test results on the patient's lifestyle.

Provide teaching and information regarding the clinical implications of the test results, as appropriate. Emphasize, if indicated, that good glycemic control delays the onset and slows the progression of diabetic retinopathy, nephropathy, and neuropathy. Educate the patient regarding access to counseling services, as appropriate. Provide contact information, if desired, for the American Diabetes Association (www.diabetes.org) or the American Heart Association (www.americanheart.org).

▶ Reinforce information given by the patient's HCP regarding further testing, treatment, or referral to another HCP. Answer any questions or address any concerns voiced by the patient or family.

▶ Depending on the results of this procedure, additional testing may be performed to evaluate or monitor progression of the disease process and determine the need for a change in therapy. Evaluate test results in relation to the patient's symptoms and other tests performed.

RELATED MONOGRAPHS:

▶ Related tests include C-peptide, glucose, GTT, glycated hemoglobin, and insulin.

▶ Refer to the Endocrine and Immune systems tables at the end of the book for related tests by body system.

Intraocular Muscle Function

SYNONYM/ACRONYM: IOM function.

COMMON USE: To assess the function of the extraocular muscle to assist with diagnosis of strabismus, amblyopia, and other ocular disorders.

AREA OF APPLICATION: Eyes.

CONTRAST: N/A.

DESCRIPTION: Evaluation of ocular motility is performed to detect and measure muscle imbalance in conditions classified as heterophorias or heterotropias. This evaluation is performed in a manner to assess fixation of each eye, alignment of both eyes in all directions, and the ability of both eyes to work together binocularly. Heterophorias are latent ocular deviations kept in check by the binocular power of fusion and made intermittent by disrupting fusion. Heterotropias are conditions that manifest constant ocular deviations. The prefixes *eso-* (tendency for the eye to turn in), *exo-* (tendency for the eye to turn out), and *hyper-* (tendency for one eye to turn up) indicate the direction in which the affected eye moves spontaneously. *Strabismus* is the failure of both eyes to spontaneously fixate on the same object because of a muscular imbalance (crossed eyes). *Amblyopia*, or lazy eye, is a term used for loss of vision in one or both eyes that cannot be attributed to an organic pathological condition of the eye or optic nerve. There are six extraocular muscles in each eye; their movement is controlled by three nerves. The actions of the muscles vary depending on the position of the eye when they become innervated. The cover test is commonly used because it is reliable, easy to perform, and does not require special equipment. The cover test method is described in this monograph. Another method for evaluation of ocular muscle function is the corneal light reflex test. It is useful with patients who cannot cooperate for prism cover testing or for patients who have poor fixation.

INDICATIONS

- Detection and evaluation of extraocular muscle imbalance

POTENTIAL DIAGNOSIS

The examiner should determine the range of ocular movements in all gaze positions, usually to include up and out, in, down and out, up and in, down and in, and out. Limited movements in gaze position can be recorded semiquantitatively as −1 (minimal), −2 (moderate), −3 (severe), or −4 (total).

Normal findings in
- Normal range of ocular movements in all gaze positions.

Abnormal findings in
- Amblyopia
- Heterophorias
- Heterotropias
- Strabismus

CRITICAL FINDINGS: N/A

INTERFERING FACTORS

Factors that may impair the results of the examination
- Inability of the patient to cooperate and remain still during the test because of age, significant pain, or mental status may interfere with the test results.
- Rubbing or squeezing the eyes may affect results.

NURSING IMPLICATIONS AND PROCEDURE

PRETEST:

▸ Positively identify the patient using at least two unique identifiers before providing care, treatment, or services.
▸ *Patient Teaching:* Inform the patient this procedure can assist in evaluating eye muscle function.
▸ Obtain a history of the patient's complaints, including a list of known allergens, especially latex.

Obtain a history of the patient's known or suspected vision loss, changes in visual acuity, including type and cause; use of glasses or contact lenses; eye conditions with treatment regimens; eye surgery; and other tests and procedures to assess and diagnose visual deficit.

Obtain a history of symptoms and results of previously performed laboratory tests and diagnostic and surgical procedures.

Obtain a list of the patient's current medications, including herbs, nutritional supplements, and nutraceuticals (see Appendix F).

Review the procedure with the patient. Address concerns about pain and explain that no discomfort will be experienced during the test. Inform the patient that a health-care provider (HCP) performs the test in a quiet room and that to evaluate both eyes, the test can take 2 to 4 min.

Instruct the patient to remove contact lenses or glasses, as appropriate. Instruct the patient regarding the importance of keeping the eyes open for the test.

Sensitivity to social and cultural issues, as well as concern for modesty, is important in providing psychological support before, during, and after the procedure.

There are no food, fluid, or medication restrictions unless by medical direction.

INTRATEST:

Observe standard precautions, and follow the general guidelines in Appendix A. Positively identify the patient.

Instruct the patient to cooperate fully and to follow directions. Ask the patient to remain still during the procedure because movement produces unreliable results.

One eye is tested at a time. The patient is given a fixation point, usually the testing personnel's index finger. An object, such as a small toy, can be used to ensure fixation in pediatric patients. The patient is asked to follow the fixation point with his or her gaze in the direction the fixation point moves.

When testing is completed, the procedure is repeated using the other eye. The procedure is performed at a distance and near, first with and then without corrective lenses.

POST-TEST:

A report of the results will be made available to the requesting HCP, who will discuss the results with the patient.

Recognize anxiety related to test results, and be supportive of impaired activity related to vision loss, anticipated loss of driving privileges, or the possibility of requiring corrective lenses (self-image).

Reinforce information given by the patient's HCP regarding further testing, treatment, or referral to another HCP. Educate the patient, as appropriate, that he or she may be referred for special therapy to correct the anomaly, which may include glasses, prisms, eye exercises, eye patches, or chemical patching with drugs that modify the focusing power of the eye. The patient and family should be educated that the chosen therapy involves a process of mental retraining. The mode of therapy in itself does not correct vision. It is the process by which the brain becomes readapted to accept, receive, and store visual images received by the eye that results in vision correction. Therefore, the patient must be prepared to be alert, cooperative, and properly motivated. Answer any questions or address any concerns voiced by the patient or family.

Depending on the results of this procedure, additional testing may be performed to evaluate or monitor progression of the disease process and determine the need for a change in therapy. Evaluate test results in relation to the patient's symptoms and other tests performed.

RELATED MONOGRAPHS:

Related tests include refraction and slit-lamp biomicroscopy.

Refer to the Ocular System table at the end of the book for related tests by body system.

Intraocular Pressure

SYNONYM/ACRONYM: IOP.

COMMON USE: To evaluate changes in ocular pressure to assist in diagnosis of disorders such as glaucoma.

AREA OF APPLICATION: Eyes.

CONTRAST: N/A.

DESCRIPTION: The intraocular pressure (IOP) of the eye depends on a number of factors. The two most significant are the amount of aqueous humor present in the eye and the circumstances by which it leaves the eye. Other physiological variables that affect IOP include respiration, pulse, and the degree of hydration of the body. Individual eyes respond to IOP differently. Some can tolerate high pressures (20 to 30 mm Hg), and some will incur optic nerve damage at lower pressures. With respiration, variations of up to 4 mm Hg in IOP can occur, and changes of 1 to 2 mm Hg occur with every pulsation of the central retinal artery. IOP is measured with a tonometer; normal values indicate the pressure at which no damage is done to the intraocular contents. The rate of fluid leaving the eye, or its ability to leave the eye unimpeded, is the most important factor regulating IOP. There are three primary conditions that result in occlusion of the outflow channels for fluid. The most common condition is open-angle glaucoma, in which the diameter of the openings of the trabecular meshwork becomes narrowed, resulting in an increased IOP due to an increased resistance of fluid moving out of the eye. In secondary glaucoma, the trabecular meshwork becomes occluded by tumor cells, pigment, red blood cells in hyphema, or other material. Additionally, the obstructing material may cover parts of the meshwork itself, as with scar tissue or other types of adhesions that form after severe iritis, an angle-closure glaucoma attack, or a central retinal vein occlusion. The third condition impeding fluid outflow in the trabecular channels occurs with pupillary block, most commonly associated with primary angle-closure glaucoma. In eyes predisposed to this condition, dilation of the pupil causes the iris to fold up like an accordion against the narrow-angle structures of the eye. Fluid in the posterior chamber has difficulty circulating into the anterior chamber; therefore, pressure in the posterior chamber increases, causing the iris to bow forward and obstruct the outflow channels even more. Angle-closure attacks occur quite suddenly and therefore do not give the eye a chance to adjust itself to the sudden increase in pressure. The eye becomes very red, the cornea edematous (patient may report seeing halos), and the pupil fixed and dilated, accompanied by a complaint of moderate pain. Pupil dilation can be initiated by emotional arousal or fear, conditions in which the eye must adapt to darkness (movie theaters), or mydriatics. Angle-closure glaucoma is an ocular emergency resolved by a peripheral iridectomy to allow movement of fluid between the anterior and posterior chambers. This procedure constitutes removal of a portion of the peripheral iris either by surgery or by use of an argon or yttrium-aluminum-garnet (YAG) laser.

INDICATIONS

- Diagnosis or ongoing monitoring of glaucoma
- Screening test included in a routine eye examination

POTENTIAL DIAGNOSIS

Normal findings in
- Normal IOP is between 13 and 22 mm Hg

Abnormal findings in
- Open-angle glaucoma
- Primary angle-closure glaucoma
- Secondary glaucoma

CRITICAL FINDINGS: N/A

INTERFERING FACTORS

- Inability of the patient to remain still and cooperative during the test may interfere with the test results.

NURSING IMPLICATIONS AND PROCEDURE

PRETEST:

▸ Positively identify the patient using at least two unique identifiers before providing care, treatment, or services.

Patient Teaching: Inform the patient this procedure can assist in measuring eye pressure.

▸ Obtain a history of the patient's complaints, including a list of known allergens, especially allergies or sensitivities to topical anesthetic eyedrops.

▸ Obtain a history of the patient's known or suspected vision loss, changes in visual acuity, including type and cause; use of glasses or contact lenses; eye conditions with treatment regimens; eye surgery; and other tests and procedures to assess and diagnose visual deficit.

▸ Obtain a history of symptoms and results of previously performed laboratory tests and diagnostic and surgical procedures.

▸ Obtain a list of the patient's current medications, including herbs, nutritional supplements, and nutraceuticals (see Appendix F).

▸ Review the procedure with the patient. Explain that the patient will be requested to fixate the eyes during the procedure. Address concerns about pain and explain that he or she may feel coldness or a slight sting when the anesthetic/fluorescein drops are instilled at the beginning of the procedure but that no discomfort will be experienced during the test. Instruct the patient as to what should be expected with the use of the tonometer. The patient will experience less anxiety if he or she understands that the tonometer tip will touch the tear film and not the eye directly. Inform the patient that a health-care provider (HCP) performs the test in a quiet, darkened room and that to evaluate both eyes, the test can take 1 to 3 min.

▸ Instruct the patient to remove contact lenses or glasses, as appropriate. Instruct the patient regarding the importance of keeping the eyes open for the test.

▸ *Sensitivity to social and cultural issues,* as well as concern for modesty, is important in providing psychological support before, during, and after the procedure.

▸ There are no food, fluid, or medication restrictions unless by medical direction.

INTRATEST:

▶ Observe standard precautions, and follow the general guidelines in Appendix A. Positively identify the patient.

▶ Instruct the patient to cooperate fully and to follow directions. Ask the patient to remain still during the procedure because any movement, such as coughing, breath-holding, or wandering eye movements, produces unreliable results.

▶ Seat the patient comfortably. Instruct the patient to look at directed target while the eyes are examined.

▶ Instill ordered topical anesthetic/fluorescein drops in each eye, as ordered, and allow time for it to work. Topical anesthetic/fluorescein drops are placed in the eye with the patient looking up and the solution directed at the six o'clock position of the sclera (white of the eye) near the limbus (gray, semitransparent area of the eyeball where the cornea and sclera meet). Neither dropper nor bottle should touch the eyelashes.

▶ Instruct the patient to look straight ahead, keeping the eyes open and unblinking.

▶ A number of techniques are used to measure IOP. It can be measured at the slit lamp or with a miniaturized, handheld applanation tonometer or an airpuff tonometer.

▶ When the applanation tonometer is positioned on the patient's cornea, the instrument's headrest is placed against the patient's forehead. The tonometer should be held at an angle with the handle slanted away from the patient's nose. The tonometer tip should not touch the eyelids.

▶ When the tip is properly aligned and in contact with the fluorescein-stained tear film, force is applied to the tip using an adjustment control to the desired endpoint. The tonometer is removed from the eye. The reading is taken a second time, and if the pressure is elevated, a third reading is taken. The procedure is repeated on the other eye.

▶ With the airpuff tonometer, an air pump blows air onto the cornea, and the time it takes for the air puff to flatten the cornea is detected by infrared light and photoelectric cells. This time is directly related to the IOP.

POST-TEST:

▶ A report of the results will be made available to the requesting HCP, who will discuss the results with the patient.

▶ Recognize anxiety related to test results, and be supportive of impaired activity related to vision loss or anticipated loss of driving privileges. Discuss the implications of abnormal test results on the patient's lifestyle. Provide teaching and information regarding the clinical implications of the test results, as appropriate. Provide contact information, if desired, for the Glaucoma Research Foundation (www.glaucoma.org).

▶ Reinforce information given by the patient's HCP regarding further testing, treatment, or referral to another HCP. Answer any questions or address any concerns voiced by the patient or family.

▶ Instruct the patient in the use of any ordered medications, usually eyedrops, that are intended to decrease IOP. Explain the importance of adhering to the therapy regimen, especially since increased IOP does not present symptoms. Instruct the patient in both the ocular side effects and systemic reactions associated with the prescribed medication. Encourage him or her to review corresponding literature provided by a pharmacist.

▶ Depending on the results of this procedure, additional testing may be performed to evaluate or monitor progression of the disease process and determine the need for a change in therapy. Evaluate test results in relation to the patient's symptoms and other tests performed.

RELATED MONOGRAPHS:

▶ Related tests include fundus photography, gonioscopy, nerve fiber analysis, pachymetry, slit-lamp biomicroscopy, and visual field testing.

▶ Refer to the Ocular System table at the end of the book for related tests by body system.

Intravenous Pyelography

SYNONYM/ACRONYM: Antegrade pyelography, excretory urography (EUG), intravenous urography (IVU, IUG), IVP.

COMMON USE: To assess urinary tract dysfunction or evaluate progression of renal disease such as stones, bleeding, and congenital anomalies.

AREA OF APPLICATION: Kidneys, ureters, bladder, and renal pelvis.

CONTRAST: IV radiopaque iodine-based contrast medium.

DESCRIPTION: Intravenous pyelography (IVP) is the most commonly performed test to determine urinary tract dysfunction or renal disease. IVP uses IV radiopaque contrast medium to visualize the kidneys, ureters, bladder, and renal pelvis. The contrast medium concentrates in the blood and is filtered out by the glomeruli; it passes out through the renal tubules and is concentrated in the urine. Renal function is reflected by the length of time it takes the contrast medium to appear and to be excreted by each kidney. A series of images is performed during a 30-min period to view passage of the contrast through the kidneys and ureters into the bladder. Tomography may be employed during the examination to permit the examination of an individual layer or plane of the organ that may be obscured by surrounding overlying structures.

INDICATIONS

- Aid in the diagnosis of renovascular hypertension
- Evaluate the cause of blood in the urine
- Evaluate the effects of urinary system trauma
- Evaluate function of the kidneys, ureters, and bladder
- Evaluate known or suspected ureteral obstruction
- Evaluate the presence of renal, ureter, or bladder calculi
- Evaluate space-occupying lesions or congenital anomalies of the urinary system

POTENTIAL DIAGNOSIS

Normal findings in
- Normal size and shape of kidneys, ureters, and bladder
- Normal bladder and absence of masses or renal calculi, with prompt visualization of contrast medium through the urinary system

Abnormal findings in
- Absence of a kidney (congenital malformation)
- Benign and malignant kidney tumors
- Bladder tumors
- Congenital renal or urinary tract abnormalities
- Glomerulonephritis
- Hydronephrosis
- Prostatic enlargement
- Pyelonephritis
- Renal cysts
- Renal hematomas
- Renal or ureteral calculi
- Soft tissue masses
- Tumors of the collecting system

CRITICAL FINDINGS: N/A

INTERFERING FACTORS

This procedure is contraindicated for

- Patients with allergies to shellfish or iodinated dye. The contrast medium used may cause a life-threatening allergic reaction. Patients with a known hypersensitivity to the contrast medium may benefit from pre-medication with corticosteroids or the use of nonionic contrast medium.
- Patients with bleeding disorders.
- Patients who are pregnant or suspected of being pregnant, unless the potential benefits of the procedure far outweigh the risks to the fetus and mother.
- ◆ Elderly and other patients who are chronically dehydrated before the test, because of their risk of contrast-induced renal failure.
- ◆ Patients who are in renal failure.
- Patients with renal insufficiency, indicated by a blood urea nitrogen (BUN) value greater than 40 mg/dL or creatinine value greater than 1.5 mg/dL, because contrast medium can complicate kidney function.
- Young patients (17 yr and younger), unless the benefits of the x-ray diagnosis outweigh the risks of exposure to high levels of radiation.
- Patients with multiple myeloma, who may experience decreased kidney function subsequent to administration of contrast medium.

Factors that may impair clear imaging

- Gas or feces in the gastrointestinal (GI) tract resulting from inadequate cleansing or failure to restrict food intake before the study.
- Retained barium from a previous radiological procedure.
- Metallic objects (e.g., jewelry, body rings) within the examination field,

which may inhibit organ visualization and cause unclear images.

- Inability of the patient to cooperate or remain still during the procedure because of age, significant pain, or mental status.

Other considerations

- The procedure may be terminated if chest pain or severe cardiac arrhythmias occur.
- Failure to follow dietary restrictions and other pretesting preparations may cause the procedure to be canceled or repeated.
- Consultation with a health-care provider (HCP) should occur before the procedure for radiation safety concerns regarding younger patients or patients who are lactating.
- Risks associated with radiation overexposure can result from frequent x-ray procedures. Personnel in the room with the patient should wear a protective lead apron, stand behind a shield, or leave the area while the examination is being done. Personnel working in the examination area should wear badges to record their level of radiation exposure.

NURSING IMPLICATIONS AND PROCEDURE

PRETEST:

- Positively identify the patient using at least two unique identifiers before providing care, treatment, or services.
- *Patient Teaching:* Inform the patient this procedure can assist in assessing the kidneys, ureters, and bladder.
- Obtain a history of the patient's complaints or symptoms, including a list of known allergens, especially allergies or sensitivities to latex, iodine, seafood, anesthetics, or contrast mediums.
- Obtain a history of the patient's genitourinary system, symptoms, and results of previously performed laboratory tests and diagnostic and surgical

procedures. Ensure that the results of blood tests, especially BUN and creatinine, are obtained and recorded before the procedure.

▸ Note any recent barium or other radiological contrast procedures. Ensure that barium studies were performed more than 4 days before the IVP.

▸ Record the date of the last menstrual period and determine the possibility of pregnancy in perimenopausal women.

▸ Obtain a list of the patient's current medications including anticoagulants, aspirin and other salicylates, herbs, nutritional supplements, and nutraceuticals (see Appendix F). Note the last time and dose of medication taken.

▸ If contrast media is scheduled to be used, patients receiving metformin (Glucophage) for non–insulin-dependent (type 2) diabetes should discontinue the drug on the day of the test and continue to withhold it for 48 hr after the test. Failure to do so may result in lactic acidosis.

▸ Review the procedure with the patient. Address concerns about pain related to the procedure and explain that some pain may be experienced during the test, and there may be moments of discomfort. Inform the patient that the procedure is performed in a radiology department by an HCP and takes approximately 30 to 60 min. *Sensitivity to social and cultural issues,* as well as concern for modesty, is important in providing psychological support before, during, and after the procedure.

▸ Instruct the patient to take a laxative or a cathartic, as ordered, on the evening before the examination.

▸ Instruct the patient to remove jewelry and other metallic objects from the area to be examined.

▸ Instruct the patient to fast and restrict fluids for 8 hr prior to the procedure. Protocols may vary among facilities.

▸ *Make sure a written and informed consent has been signed prior to the procedure and before administering any medications.*

INTRATEST:

▸ Observe standard precautions, and follow the general guidelines in Appendix A. Positively identify the patient.

▸ Ensure the patient has complied with dietary, fluid, and medication restrictions for 8 hr prior to the procedure.

▸ Ensure the patient has removed all external metallic objects from the area to be examined prior to the procedure.

▸ Assess for completion of bowel preparation according to the institution's procedure. Administer enemas or suppositories on the morning of the test, as ordered.

▸ If the patient has a history of allergic reactions to any substance or drug, administer ordered prophylactic steroids or antihistamines before the procedure. Use nonionic contrast medium for the procedure.

▸ Have emergency equipment readily available.

▸ Instruct the patient to void prior to the procedure and to change into the gown, robe, and foot coverings provided.

▸ Instruct the patient to cooperate fully and to follow directions. Instruct the patient to remain still throughout the procedure because movement produces unreliable results.

▸ Place the patient in the supine position on an examination table.

▸ A kidney, ureter, and bladder (KUB) or plain film is taken to ensure that no barium or stool obscures visualization of the urinary system.

▸ Insert an IV line, if one is not already in place, and inject the contrast medium.

▸ Instruct the patient to take slow, deep breaths if nausea occurs during the procedure.

▸ Monitor the patient for complications related to the procedure (e.g., allergic reaction, anaphylaxis, bronchospasm).

▸ Images are taken at 1, 5, 10, 15, 20, and 30 min following injection of the contrast medium into the urinary system. Instruct the patient to exhale deeply and to hold his or her breath while each image is taken.

▸ Remove the needle or catheter and apply a pressure dressing over the puncture site.

▸ Instruct the patient to void if a postvoiding exposure is required to visualize the empty bladder.

POST-TEST:

A report of the results will be made available to the requesting HCP, who will discuss the results with the patient.

Instruct the patient to resume usual diet, fluids, medications, and activity, as directed by the HCP. Renal function should be assessed before metformin is resumed if contrast was used.

Observe for delayed reaction to iodinated contrast medium, including rash, urticaria, tachycardia, hyperpnea, hypertension, palpitations, nausea, or vomiting.

Observe/assess the needle/catheter insertion site for bleeding, inflammation, or hematoma formation.

Instruct the patient in the care and assessment of the injection site.

Instruct the patient to apply cold compresses to the puncture site as needed, to reduce discomfort or edema.

Monitor urinary output after the procedure. Decreased urine output may indicate impending renal failure.

Recognize anxiety related to test results, and offer support. Discuss the implications of abnormal test results on the patient's lifestyle. Provide teaching and information regarding the clinical implications of the test results, as appropriate.

Reinforce information given by the patient's HCP regarding further testing, treatment, or referral to another HCP. Answer any questions or address any concerns voiced by the patient or family.

Depending on the results of this procedure, additional testing may be needed to evaluate or monitor progression of the disease process and determine the need for a change in therapy. Evaluate test results in relation to the patient's symptoms and other tests performed.

RELATED MONOGRAPHS:

Related tests include biopsy bladder, biopsy kidney, biopsy prostate, BUN, CT abdomen, CT pelvis, creatinine, cystometry, cystoscopy, gallium scan, KUB, MRI abdomen, renogram, retrograde ureteropyelography, US abdomen, US bladder, US kidney, US prostate, urine markers of bladder cancer, urinalysis, urine cytology, and voiding cystourethrography.

Refer to the Genitourinary System table at the end of the book for related tests by body system.

Intrinsic Factor Antibodies

SYNONYM/ACRONYM: IF antibodies, intrinsic factor blocking antibodies.

COMMON USE: To assist in the investigation of suspected pernicious anemia.

SPECIMEN: Serum (1 mL) collected in a red- or tiger-top tube.

NORMAL FINDINGS: (Method: Immunoassay) Negative.

DESCRIPTION: Intrinsic factor (IF) is produced by the parietal cells of the gastric mucosa and is required for the normal absorption of vitamin B_{12}. Intrinsic factor antibodies are found in 50% to 75% of adults and also in a high percentage of pediatric patients with juvenile pernicious anemia.

In some diseases, antibodies are produced that bind to the cobalamin-IF complex, prevent the complex from binding to ileum receptors, and prevent vitamin B_{12} absorption. There are two types of antibodies: type 1, the more commonly present blocking antibody, and type 2, the binding antibody. The blocking antibody inhibits uptake of vitamin B_{12} at the binding site of IF. Binding antibody combines with either free or complexed IF.

INDICATIONS
- Assist in the diagnosis of pernicious anemia
- Evaluate patients with decreased vitamin B_{12} levels

POTENTIAL DIAGNOSIS

Increased in

Conditions that involve the production of these blocking and binding autoantibodies
- Megaloblastic anemia
- Pernicious anemia
- Some patients with hyperthyroidism
- Some patients with insulin-dependent (type 1) diabetes

Decreased in: N/A

CRITICAL FINDINGS: N/A

INTERFERING FACTORS
- Recent treatment with methotrexate or another folic acid antagonist can interfere with test results.
- Vitamin B_{12} injected or ingested within 48 hr of the test invalidates results.
- Failure to follow dietary restrictions before the procedure may cause the procedure to be canceled or repeated.

NURSING IMPLICATIONS AND PROCEDURE

PRETEST:
- Positively identify the patient using at least two unique identifiers before providing care, treatment, or services.
- *Patient Teaching:* Inform the patient this test can assist in assessing for anemia.
- Obtain a history of the patient's complaints, including a list of known allergens, especially allergies or sensitivities to latex.
- Obtain a history of the patient's gastrointestinal and hematopoietic systems, symptoms, and results of previously performed laboratory tests and diagnostic and surgical procedures.
- Note any recent procedures that can interfere with test results.
- Obtain a list of the patient's current medications, including herbs, nutritional supplements, and nutraceuticals (see Appendix F).
- Review the procedure with the patient. Inform the patient that specimen collection takes approximately 5 to 10 min. Address concerns about pain and explain that there may be some discomfort during the venipuncture.
- *Sensitivity to social and cultural issues,* as well as concern for modesty, is important in providing psychological support before, during, and after the procedure.
- There are no food or fluid restrictions unless by medical direction. Administration of vitamin B_{12} should be withheld within 48 hr before testing.

INTRATEST:
- Ensure that vitamin B_{12} has been withheld within 48 hr before testing.
- If the patient has a history of allergic reaction to latex, avoid the use of equipment containing latex.
- Instruct the patient to cooperate fully and to follow directions. Direct the patient to breathe normally and to avoid unnecessary movement.
- Observe standard precautions, and follow the general guidelines in Appendix A. Positively identify the patient, and label the appropriate specimen container with the corresponding patient demographics, initials of the person collecting the specimen, date, and time of collection. Perform a venipuncture.
- Remove the needle and apply direct pressure with dry gauze to stop bleeding. Observe/assess venipuncture site for bleeding or hematoma formation and secure gauze with adhesive bandage.

Promptly transport the specimen to the laboratory for processing and analysis.

POST-TEST:

- A report of the results will be made available to the requesting health-care provider (HCP), who will discuss the results with the patient.
- Reinforce information given by the patient's HCP regarding further testing, treatment, or referral to another HCP. Answer any questions or address any concerns voiced by the patient or family.
- Depending on the results of this procedure, additional testing may be performed to evaluate or monitor

progression of the disease process and determine the need for a change in therapy. Evaluate test results in relation to the patient's symptoms and other tests performed.

RELATED MONOGRAPHS:

- Related tests include antibodies antithyroglobulin and antithyroid peroxidase, biopsy bone marrow, CBC, CBC RBC indices, folic acid, and vitamin B_{12}.
- Refer to the Gastrointestinal and Hematopoietic systems tables at the end of the book for related tests by body system.

Iron

SYNONYM/ACRONYM: Fe.

COMMON USE: To monitor and assess blood iron levels related to treatment, blood loss, metabolism, anemia, and storage disorders.

SPECIMEN: Serum (1 mL) collected in a red- or tiger-top tube.

NORMAL FINDINGS: (Method: Spectrophotometry)

Age	Conventional Units	SI Units (Conventional Units × 0.179)
Newborn	100–250 mcg/dL	17.9–44.8 micromol/L
Infant–9 yr	20–105 mcg/dL	3.6–18.8 micromol/L
10–14 yr	20–145 mcg/dL	3.6–26 micromol/L
Adult		
Male	65–175 mcg/dL	11.6–31.3 micromol/L
Female	50–170 mcg/dL	9–30.4 micromol/L

Values tend to decrease in older adults.

DESCRIPTION: Iron plays a principal role in erythropoiesis. Iron is necessary for the proliferation and maturation of red blood cells (RBCs) and is required for hemoglobin (Hgb) synthesis. Of the body's normal 4 g of iron,

approximately 65% resides in Hgb and 3% in myoglobin. A small amount is also found in cellular enzymes that catalyze the oxidation and reduction of iron. The remainder of iron is stored in the liver, bone marrow, and spleen as ferritin or hemosiderin. Any iron present in the serum is in transit among the alimentary tract, the bone marrow, and available iron storage forms. Iron travels in the bloodstream bound to transferrin, a protein manufactured by the liver. Normally, iron enters the body by oral ingestion; only 10% is absorbed, but up to 20% can be absorbed in patients with iron-deficiency anemia. Unbound iron is highly toxic, but there is generally an excess of transferrin available to prevent the buildup of unbound iron in the circulation. Iron overload is as clinically significant as iron deficiency, especially in the accidental poisoning of children caused by excessive intake of iron-containing multivitamins.

INDICATIONS

- Assist in the diagnosis of blood loss, as evidenced by decreased serum iron
- Assist in the diagnosis of hemochromatosis or other disorders of iron metabolism and storage
- Determine the differential diagnosis of anemia
- Determine the presence of disorders that involve diminished protein synthesis or defects in iron absorption
- Evaluate accidental iron poisoning
- Evaluate iron overload in dialysis patients or patients with transfusion-dependent anemias
- Evaluate thalassemia and sideroblastic anemia
- Monitor hematological responses during pregnancy, when serum iron is usually decreased
- Monitor response to treatment for anemia

POTENTIAL DIAGNOSIS

Increased in

- Acute iron poisoning (children) *(related to excessive intake)*
- Acute leukemia
- Acute liver disease *(possibly related to decrease in synthesis of iron storage proteins by damaged liver; iron accumulates and levels increase)*
- Aplastic anemia *(related to repeated blood transfusions)*
- Excessive iron therapy *(related to excessive intake)*
- Hemochromatosis *(inherited disorder of iron overload; the iron is not excreted in proportion to the rate of accumulation)*
- Hemolytic anemias *(related to release of iron from lysed RBCs)*
- Lead toxicity *(lead can biologically mimic iron, displace it, and release it into circulation where its concentration increases)*
- Nephritis *(related to decreased renal excretion; accumulation in blood)*
- Pernicious anemias (PA) *(achlorhydria associated with PA prevents absorption of dietary iron, and it accumulates in the blood)*
- Sideroblastic anemias *(enzyme disorder prevents iron from being incorporated into Hgb, and it accumulates in the blood)*
- Thalassemia *(treatment for some types of thalassemia include blood transfusions, which can lead to iron overload)*
- Transfusions (repeated)
- Vitamin B_6 deficiency *(this vitamin is essential to Hgb formation; deficiency prevents iron from being incorporated into Hgb, and it accumulates in the blood)*

Decreased in

- Acute and chronic infection *(iron is a nutrient for invading organisms)*
- Carcinoma *(related to depletion of iron stores)*

- Chronic blood loss (gastrointestinal, uterine) *(blood contains iron incorporated in Hgb)*
- Dietary deficiency
- Hypothyroidism *(pathophysiology is unclear)*
- Intestinal malabsorption
- Iron-deficiency anemia *(related to depletion of iron stores)*
- Nephrosis *(anemia is common in people with kidney disease; fewer RBCs are made because of a deficiency of erythropoietin related to the damaged kidneys, blood can be lost in dialysis, and iron intake may be lower due to lack of appetite)*
- Postoperative state
- Pregnancy *(related to depletion of iron stores by developing fetus)*
- Protein malnutrition (kwashiorkor) *(protein is required to form transport proteins, RBCs, and Hgb)*

CRITICAL FINDINGS ◈

- Mild toxicity: greater than 350 mcg/dL (SI: greater than 62.6 micromol/L)
- Serious toxicity: greater than 400 mcg/dL (SI: greater than 71.6 micromol/L)
- Lethal: greater than 1,000 mcg/dL (SI: greater than 179 micromol/L)

Note and immediately report to the health-care provider (HCP) any critically increased values and related symptoms. Timely notification of critical values for lab or diagnostic studies is a role expectation of the professional nurse. Notification processes will vary among facilities. Upon receipt of the critical value the information should be read back to the caller to verify accuracy. Most policies require immediate notification of the primary HCP, Hospitalist, or on-call HCP. Reported information includes the patient's name, unique identifiers, critical value, name of the person giving the report, and name of the person receiving the report. Documentation of notification should

be made in the medical record with the name of the HCP notified, time and date of notification, and any orders received. Any delay in a timely report of a critical value may require completion of a notification form with review by Risk Management. Intervention may include chelation therapy by administration of deferoxamine mesylate (Desferal).

INTERFERING FACTORS

- Drugs that may increase iron levels include blood transfusions, chemotherapy drugs, iron (intramuscular), iron dextran, iron-protein-succinylate, methimazole, methotrexate, oral contraceptives, and rifampin.
- Drugs that may decrease iron levels include acetylsalicylic acid, allopurinol, cholestyramine, corticotropin, cortisone, deferoxamine, and metformin.
- Gross hemolysis can interfere with test results.
- Failure to withhold iron-containing medications 24 hr before the test may falsely increase values.
- Failure to follow dietary restrictions before the procedure may cause the procedure to be canceled or repeated.

NURSING IMPLICATIONS AND PROCEDURE

PRETEST:

- Positively identify the patient using at least two unique identifiers before providing care, treatment, or services.
- *Patient Teaching:* Inform the patient this test can assist in evaluating the amount of iron in the blood.
- Obtain a history of the patient's complaints, including a list of known allergens, especially allergies or sensitivities to latex.
- Obtain a history of the patient's gastrointestinal and hematopoietic systems, symptoms, and results of previously performed laboratory tests and diagnostic and surgical procedures.

Note any recent therapies that can interfere with test results. Specimen collection should be delayed for several days after blood transfusion.

Obtain a list of the patient's current medications, including herbs, nutritional supplements, and nutraceuticals (see Appendix F).

Review the procedure with the patient. Inform the patient that specimen collection takes approximately 5 to 10 min. Address concerns about pain and explain that there may be some discomfort during the venipuncture.

Sensitivity to social and cultural issues, as well as concern for modesty, is important in providing psychological support before, during, and after the procedure.

Instruct the patient to fast for at least 12 hr before testing and, with medical direction, to refrain from taking iron-containing medicines before specimen collection. Protocols may vary among facilities.

There are no fluid restrictions unless by medical direction.

INTRATEST:

Ensure that the patient has complied with dietary and medication restrictions; ensure that food has been restricted for at least 12 hr prior to the procedure.

If the patient has a history of allergic reaction to latex, avoid the use of equipment containing latex.

Instruct the patient to cooperate fully and to follow directions. Direct the patient to breathe normally and to avoid unnecessary movement.

Observe standard precautions, and follow the general guidelines in Appendix A. Positively identify the patient, and label the appropriate specimen container with the corresponding patient demographics, initials of the person collecting the specimen, date, and time of collection. Perform a venipuncture.

Remove the needle and apply direct pressure with dry gauze to stop bleeding. Observe/assess venipuncture site for bleeding or hematoma formation and secure gauze with adhesive bandage.

Promptly transport the specimen to the laboratory for processing and analysis.

POST-TEST:

A report of the results will be made available to the requesting HCP, who will discuss the results with the patient.

Instruct the patient to resume usual diet, fluids, medications, or activity, as directed by the HCP.

Nutritional Considerations: Educate the patient with abnormally elevated iron values, as appropriate, on the importance of reading food labels. Foods high in iron include meats (especially liver), eggs, grains, and green leafy vegetables. It is also important to explain that iron levels in foods can be increased if foods are cooked in cookware containing iron.

Nutritional Considerations: The Institute o Medicine's Food and Nutrition Board suggests 8 mg as the daily recommended dietary allowance of iron for adult males and females age 51 to greater than 70 yr; 18 mg/d for adult females age 19 to 50 yr; 8 mg/d for adult males age 19 to 50 yr; 27 mg/d for pregnant females under age 18 through 50 yr; 9 mg/d for lactating females age 19 to 50 yr; 10 mg/d for lactating females under age 18 yr; 15 mg/d for female children age 14 to 18 yr; 11 mg/d for male children age 14 to 18 yr; 8 mg/d for children age 9 to 13 yr; 10 mg/d for children age 4 to 8 yr; 7 mg/d for children age 1 to 3 yr; 11 mg/d for children age 7 to 12 mo; and 0.27 mg/d for children age 0 to 6 mo (recommended adequate intake). Reprinted with permission from the National Academies Press, copyright 2013, National Academy of Sciences. Educate the patient with abnormal iron values that numerous factors affect the absorption of iron, enhancing or decreasing absorption regardless of the original content of the iron-containing dietary source. Patients must be educated to either increase or avoid intake of iron and iron-rich foods depending on their specific condition; for example, a patient with hemochromatosis or acute pernicious anemia should be educated to avoid foods rich in iron. Consumption of large amounts of alcohol damages the intestine and allows increased absorption of iron. A high intake of calcium and ascorbic acid also increases iron absorption. Iron absorption after a meal is also increased by factors in meat, fish, and poultry. Iron absorption is decreased by the absence (gastric resection) or diminished presence (use of antacids) of gastric acid. Phytic acids from cereals, tannins from tea and coffee, oxalic acid from vegetables, and minerals such as copper, zinc, and manganese interfere with iron absorption.

Reinforce information given by the patient's HCP regarding further testing, treatment, or referral to another HCP. Answer any questions or address any concerns voiced by the patient or family. Educate the patient regarding access to nutritional counseling services. Provide contact information, if desired, for the Institute of Medicine of the National Academies (www.iom.edu).

▶ Depending on the results of this procedure, additional testing may be performed to evaluate or monitor progression of the disease process and determine the need for a change in therapy. Evaluate test results in relation to the patient's symptoms and other tests performed.

RELATED MONOGRAPHS:

▶ Related tests include biopsy bone marrow, biopsy liver, CBC, CBC RBC count, CBC RBC indices, CBC RBC morphology, CBC WBC count and differential, erythropoietin, ferritin, folate, FEP, gallium scan, hemosiderin, iron binding/transferrin, lead, porphyrins, reticulocyte count, and vitamin B_{12}.

▶ Refer to the Gastrointestinal and Hematopoietic systems tables at the end of the book for related tests by body system.

Iron-Binding Capacity (Total), Transferrin, and Iron Saturation

SYNONYM/ACRONYM: TIBC, Fe Sat.

COMMON USE: To monitor iron replacement therapy and assess blood iron levels to assist in diagnosing types of anemia such as iron deficiency.

SPECIMEN: Serum (1 mL) collected in a red- or tiger-top tube.

NORMAL FINDINGS: (Method: Spectrophotometry for TIBC and nephelometry for transferrin)

Test	Conventional Units	SI Units
TIBC	250–350 mcg/dL	(Conventional Units × 0.179) 45–63 micromol/L
Transferrin	215–380 mg/dL	(Conventional Units × 0.01) 2.15–3.8 g/L
Iron saturation	20–50%	

TIBC = total iron-binding capacity.

DESCRIPTION: Iron plays a principal role in erythropoiesis. It is necessary for proliferation and maturation of red blood cells and for hemoglobin (Hgb) synthesis. Of the body's normal 4 g of iron (less in women), about 65% is present in Hgb and about 3% in myoglobin. A small amount is also found in cellular enzymes that catalyze the oxidation and reduction of iron. The remainder of iron is stored in the liver, bone marrow, and spleen as ferritin or hemosiderin. Any iron present in the serum is in transit among the alimentary tract, the bone marrow, and available iron storage forms. Iron travels in the bloodstream bound to transport proteins. Transferrin is the major iron-transport protein, carrying 60% to 70% of the body's iron. (See monograph titled "Transferrin" for more detailed information.) For this reason, total iron-binding capacity (TIBC) and transferrin are sometimes referred to interchangeably, even though other proteins carry iron and contribute to the TIBC. Unbound iron is highly toxic, but there is generally an excess of transferrin available to prevent the buildup of unbound iron in the circulation. The percentage of iron saturation is calculated by dividing the serum iron value by the TIBC value and multiplying by 100.

INDICATIONS

* Assist in the diagnosis of iron-deficiency anemia
* Differentiate between iron-deficiency anemia and anemia secondary to chronic disease
* Monitor hematological response to therapy during pregnancy and iron-deficiency anemias
* Provide support for diagnosis of hemochromatosis or diseases of iron metabolism and storage

POTENTIAL DIAGNOSIS

Increased in

* Acute liver disease
* Hypochromic (iron-deficiency) anemias *(insufficient circulating iron levels to saturate binding sites)*
* Late pregnancy

Decreased in

* Chronic infections *(transferrin is a negative acute-phase reactant protein and during periods of inflammation will demonstrate decreased levels)*
* Cirrhosis *(transferrin is a negative acute-phase reactant protein and during periods of inflammation will demonstrate decreased levels)*
* Hemochromatosis *(occurs early in the disease as intestinal absorption of iron available for binding increases)*
* Hemolytic anemias *(transferrin becomes saturated, and the iron-binding capacity is significantly decreased)*
* Neoplastic diseases *(transferrin is a negative acute-phase reactant protein and during periods of inflammation will demonstrate decreased levels)*
* Protein depletion *(transferrin contributes to the total protein concentration and will reflect a decrease in protein depletion)*
* Renal disease *(transferrin is a negative acute-phase reactant protein and during periods of inflammation will demonstrate decreased levels)*
* Sideroblastic anemias *(transferrin becomes saturated, and the iron-binding capacity is significantly decreased)*
* Thalassemia *(transferrin becomes saturated, and the iron-binding capacity is significantly decreased)*

CRITICAL FINDINGS: N/A

INTERFERING FACTORS

- Drugs that may increase TIBC levels include mestranol and oral contraceptives.
- Drugs that may decrease TIBC levels include asparaginase, chloramphenicol, corticotropin, cortisone, and testosterone.

NURSING IMPLICATIONS AND PROCEDURE

PRETEST:

Positively identify the patient using at least two unique identifiers before providing care, treatment, or services.

Patient Teaching: Inform the patient this test can assist in diagnosing anemia.

Obtain a history of the patient's complaints, including a list of known allergens, especially allergies or sensitivities to latex.

Obtain a history of the patient's hematopoietic system, symptoms, and results of previously performed laboratory tests and diagnostic and surgical procedures.

Obtain a list of the patient's current medications, including herbs, nutritional supplements, and nutraceuticals (see Appendix F).

Review the procedure with the patient. Inform the patient that specimen collection takes approximately 5 to 10 min. Address concerns about pain and explain that there may be some discomfort during the venipuncture.

Sensitivity to social and cultural issues, as well as concern for modesty, is important in providing psychological support before, during, and after the procedure.

There are no food, fluid, or medication restrictions unless by medical direction.

INTRATEST:

If the patient has a history of allergic reaction to latex, avoid the use of equipment containing latex.

Instruct the patient to cooperate fully and to follow directions. Direct the patient to breathe normally and to avoid unnecessary movement. Observe standard precautions, and follow the general guidelines in Appendix A. Positively identify the patient, and label the appropriate specimen container with the corresponding patient demographics, initials of the person collecting the specimen, date, and time of collection. Perform a venipuncture.

Remove the needle and apply direct pressure with dry gauze to stop bleeding. Observe/assess venipuncture site for bleeding or hematoma formation and secure gauze with adhesive bandage.

Promptly transport the specimen to the laboratory for processing and analysis.

POST-TEST:

A report of the results will be made available to the requesting health-care provider (HCP), who will discuss the results with the patient.

Reinforce information given by the patient's HCP regarding further testing, treatment, or referral to another HCP. Answer any questions or address any concerns voiced by the patient or family.

Depending on the results of this procedure, additional testing may be performed to evaluate or monitor progression of the disease process and determine the need for a change in therapy. Evaluate test results in relation to the patient's symptoms and other tests performed.

RELATED MONOGRAPHS:

Related tests include biopsy bone marrow, biopsy liver, CBC, CBC RBC count, CBC RBC indices, CBC RBC morphology, CBC WBC count and differential, erythropoietin, ferritin, folate, FEP, gallium scan, hemosiderin, lead, porphyrins, reticulocyte count, and vitamin B_{12}.

Refer to the Hematopoietic System table at the end of the book for related tests by body system.

Ketones, Blood and Urine

SYNONYM/ACRONYM: Ketone bodies, acetoacetate, acetone.

COMMON USE: To investigate diabetes as the cause of ketoacidosis and monitor therapeutic interventions.

SPECIMEN: Serum (1 mL) collected from red- or tiger-top tube. Urine (5 mL), random or timed specimen, collected in a clean plastic collection container.

NORMAL FINDINGS: (Method: Colorimetric nitroprusside reaction) Negative.

DESCRIPTION: Ketone bodies refer to the three intermediate products of metabolism: acetone, acetoacetic acid, and β-hydroxybutyrate. Even though β-hydroxybutyrate is not a ketone, it is usually listed with the ketone bodies. In healthy individuals, ketones are produced and completely metabolized by the liver so that measurable amounts are not normally present in serum. Ketones appear in the urine before a significant serum level is detectable. If the patient has excessive fat metabolism, ketones are found in blood and urine. Excessive fat metabolism may occur if the patient has impaired ability to metabolize carbohydrates, inadequate carbohydrate intake, inadequate insulin levels, excessive carbohydrate loss, or increased carbohydrate demand. A strongly positive acetone result without severe acidosis, accompanied by normal glucose, electrolyte, and bicarbonate levels, is strongly suggestive of isopropyl alcohol poisoning. A low-carbohydrate or high-fat diet may cause a positive acetone test. Ketosis in people with diabetes is usually accompanied by increased glucose and decreased bicarbonate and pH. Extremely elevated levels of ketone bodies can result in coma. This situation is particularly life threatening in children younger than 10 yr.

INDICATIONS

- Assist in the diagnosis of starvation, stress, alcoholism, suspected isopropyl alcohol ingestion, glycogen storage disease, and other metabolic disorders
- Detect and monitor treatment of diabetic ketoacidosis
- Monitor the control of diabetes
- Screen for ketonuria due to acute illness or stress in nondiabetic patients
- Screen for ketonuria to assist in the assessment of inborn errors of metabolism
- Screen for ketonuria to assist in the diagnosis of suspected isopropyl alcohol poisoning

POTENTIAL DIAGNOSIS

Increased in
Ketones are generated in conditions that involve the metabolism of carbohydrates, fatty acids, and protein.

- Acidosis
- Branched-chain ketonuria
- Carbohydrate deficiency
- Eclampsia
- Fasting or starvation
- Gestational diabetes
- Glycogen storage diseases
- High-fat or high-protein diet
- Hyperglycemia
- Ketoacidosis of alcoholism and diabetes
- Illnesses with marked vomiting and diarrhea
- Isopropyl alcohol ingestion
- Methylmalonic aciduria

- Postanesthesia period
- Propionyl coenzyme A carboxylase deficiency

Decreased in: N/A

CRITICAL FINDINGS

- Strongly positive test results for glucose and ketones

Note and immediately report to the health-care provider (HCP) strongly positive results in urine and related symptoms. An elevated level of ketone bodies is evidenced by fruity-smelling breath, acidosis, ketonuria, and decreased level of consciousness. Administration of insulin and frequent blood glucose measurement may be indicated. Timely notification of critical values for lab or diagnostic studies is a role expectation of the professional nurse. Notification processes will vary among facilities. Upon receipt of the critical value the information should be read back to the caller to verify accuracy. Most policies require immediate notification of the primary HCP, hospitalist, or on-call HCP. Reported information includes the patient's name, unique identifiers, critical value, name of the person giving the report, and name of the person receiving the report. Documentation of notification should be made in the medical record with the name of the HCP notified, time and date of notification, and any orders received. Any delay in a timely report of a critical value may require completion of a notification form with review by Risk Management.

INTERFERING FACTORS

- Drugs that may cause an increase in serum ketone levels include acetylsalicylic acid (if therapy results in acidosis, especially in children), albuterol, fenfluramine, nifedipine, and rimiterol.
- Drugs that may cause a decrease in serum ketone levels include acetylsalicylic acid and valproic acid.

Increases have been shown in hyperthyroid patients receiving propranolol and propylthiouracil.

- Drugs that may increase urine ketone levels include acetylsalicylic acid (if therapy results in acidosis, especially in children), ether, metformin, and niacin.
- Drugs that may decrease urine ketone levels include acetylsalicylic acid.
- Urine should be checked within 60 min of collection.
- Bacterial contamination of urine can cause false-negative results.
- Failure to keep reagent strip container tightly closed can cause false-negative results. Light and moisture affect the ability of the chemicals in the strip to perform as expected.
- False-negative or weakly false-positive test results can be obtained when β-hydroxybutyrate is the predominating ketone body in cases of lactic acidosis.

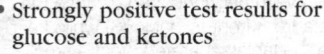

NURSING IMPLICATIONS AND PROCEDURE

PRETEST:

- Positively identify the patient using at least two unique identifiers before providing care, treatment, or services.
- *Patient Teaching:* Inform the patient this test can assist in diagnosing metabolic disorders such as diabetes.
- Obtain a history of the patient's complaints, including a list of known allergens, especially allergies or sensitivities to latex.
- Obtain a history of the patient's endocrine system, symptoms, and results of previously performed laboratory tests and diagnostic and surgical procedures.
- Obtain a list of the patient's current medications, including herbs, nutritional supplements, and nutraceuticals (see Appendix F).
- Review the procedure with the patient. Inform the patient that blood specimen collection takes approximately 5 to 10 min. The amount of time required to

collect a urine specimen depends on the level of cooperation from the patient. Address concerns about pain and explain that there may be some discomfort during the venipuncture. *Sensitivity to social and cultural issues,* as well as concern for modesty, is important in providing psychological support before, during, and after the procedure.

There are no food, fluid, or medication restrictions, unless by medical direction.

INTRATEST:

Observe standard precautions, and follow the general guidelines in Appendix A. Positively identify the patient, and label the appropriate specimen container with the corresponding patient demographics, initials of the person collecting the specimen, date, and time of collection. Perform a venipuncture as appropriate.

Blood

If the patient has a history of allergic reaction to latex, avoid the use of equipment containing latex.

Instruct the patient to cooperate fully and to follow directions. Direct the patient to breathe normally and to avoid unnecessary movement.

Positively identify the patient, and label the appropriate specimen container with the corresponding patient demographics, initials of the person collecting the specimen, date, and time of collection. Perform a venipuncture. Alternatively, a fingerstick or heel stick method of specimen collection can be used.

Remove the needle and apply direct pressure with dry gauze to stop bleeding. Observe/assess venipuncture site for bleeding or hematoma formation and secure gauze with adhesive bandage.

Urine

Review the procedure with the patient. Explain to the patient how to collect a second-voided midstream void, then drink a glass of water, wait 30 min, and then try to void again.

Instruct the patient to avoid excessive exercise and stress before specimen collection.

Clean-Catch Specimen

Instruct the male patient to (1) thoroughly wash his hands, (2) cleanse the meatus, (3) void a small amount into the toilet, and (4) void directly into the specimen container.

Instruct the female patient to (1) thoroughly wash her hands; (2) cleanse the labia from front to back; (3) while keeping the labia separated, void a small amount into the toilet; and (4) without interrupting the urine stream, void directly into the specimen container.

Blood or Urine

Promptly transport the specimen to the laboratory for processing and analysis.

POST-TEST:

A report of the results will be made available to the requesting HCP, who will discuss the results with the patient.

Nutritional Considerations: Increased levels of ketone bodies may be associated with diabetes. There is no "diabetic diet"; however, many meal-planning approaches with nutritional goals are endorsed by the American Dietetic Association. Patients who adhere to dietary recommendations report a better general feeling of health, better weight management, greater control of glucose and lipid values, and improved use of insulin. Instruct the patient, as appropriate, in nutritional management of diabetes. The American Heart Association's Therapeutic Lifestyle Changes (TLC) diet provides goals directed at people with specific risk factors and/or existing medical conditions, (e.g., elevated LDL cholesterol levels, other lipid disorders, coronary artery disease [CAD], insulin-dependent diabetes, insulin resistance, or metabolic syndrome). The TLC approach also includes the use of plant stanols or sterols and increased dissolved fiber as an option for lowering LDL cholesterol levels; nutritional recommendations for daily total caloric intake; recommendations for allowable percentage of calories derived from fat (saturated and unsaturated), carbohydrates, protein, and cholesterol; as well as recommendations for daily expenditure of energy. The nutritional needs of each diabetic

K

patient need to be determined individually (especially during pregnancy) with the appropriate HCPs, particularly professionals trained in nutrition.

Impaired glucose tolerance may be associated with diabetes. Instruct the patient and caregiver to report signs and symptoms of hypoglycemia (weakness, confusion, diaphoresis, rapid pulse) or hyperglycemia (thirst, polyuria, hunger, lethargy).

Nutritional Considerations: Increased levels of ketone bodies may be associated with poor carbohydrate intake; therefore, the body breaks down fat instead of carbohydrate for energy. Increasing carbohydrate intake in the patient's diet reduces the levels of ketone bodies. Carbohydrates can be found in starches and sugars. Starch is a complex carbohydrate that can be found in foods such as grains (breads, cereals, pasta, rice) and starchy vegetables (corn, peas, potatoes). Sugar is a simple carbohydrate that can be found in natural foods (fruits and natural honey) and processed foods (desserts and candy).

Recognize anxiety related to test results, and be supportive of perceived loss of independence and fear of shortened life expectancy. Discuss the implications of abnormal test results on the patient's lifestyle. Provide teaching and information regarding the clinical implications of the test results, as appropriate. Emphasize, if indicated, that good glycemic control delays the onset and slows the progression of diabetic retinopathy, nephropathy, and neuropathy. Educate the patient regarding access to counseling services, as appropriate. Provide contact information, if desired, for the American Diabetes Association (www.diabetes .org) or the American Heart Association (www.americanheart.org).

Reinforce information given by the patient's HCP regarding further testing, treatment, or referral to another HCP. Answer any questions or address any concerns voiced by the patient or family.

Depending on the results of this procedure, additional testing may be performed to evaluate or monitor progression of the disease process and determine the need for a change in therapy. Evaluate test results in relation to the patient's symptoms and other tests performed.

RELATED MONOGRAPHS:

Related tests include ACTH, angiography adrenal, anion gap, blood gases, BUN, calcium, catecholamines, cholesterol (HDL, LDL, total), cortisol, C-peptide, DHEA, electrolytes, fecal analysis, fecal fat, fluorescein angiography, fructosamine, fundus photography, gastric emptying scan, GTT, glycated hemoglobin A_{1C}, HVA, insulin, insulin antibodies, lactic acid, lipoprotein electrophoresis, metanephrines, microalbumin, osmolality, phosphorus, UA, and visual fields test.

Refer to the Endocrine System table at the end of the book for related tests by body system.

K

Kidney, Ureter, and Bladder Study

SYNONYM/ACRONYM: Flat plate of the abdomen, KUB, plain film of the abdomen.

COMMON USE: To visualize and assess the abdominal organs for obstruction or abnormality related to mass, trauma, bleeding, stones, or congenital anomaly.

AREA OF APPLICATION: Kidneys, ureters, bladder, and abdomen.

CONTRAST: None.

DESCRIPTION: A kidney, ureter, and bladder (KUB) x-ray examination provides information regarding the structure, size, and position of the abdominal organs; it also indicates whether there is any obstruction or abnormality of the abdomen caused by disease or congenital malformation. Calcifications of the renal calyces, renal pelvis, and any radiopaque calculi present in the urinary tract or surrounding organs may be visualized. Normal air and gas patterns are visualized within the intestinal tract. Perforation of the intestinal tract or an intestinal obstruction can be visualized on erect KUB images. KUB x-rays are among the first examinations done to diagnose intra-abdominal diseases such as intestinal obstruction, masses, tumors, ruptured organs, abnormal gas accumulation, and ascites.

INDICATIONS

* Determine the cause of acute abdominal pain or palpable mass
* Evaluate the effects of lower abdominal trauma, such as internal hemorrhage
* Evaluate known or suspected intestinal obstructions
* Evaluate the presence of renal, ureter, or other organ calculi
* Evaluate the size, shape, and position of the liver, kidneys, and spleen
* Evaluate suspected abnormal fluid, air, or metallic objects in the abdomen

POTENTIAL DIAGNOSIS

Normal findings in
* Normal size and shape of kidneys
* Normal bladder, absence of masses and renal calculi, and no abnormal accumulation of air or fluid

Abnormal findings in
* Abnormal accumulation of bowel gas
* Ascites
* Bladder distention
* Congenital renal anomaly
* Hydronephrosis
* Intestinal obstruction
* Organomegaly
* Renal calculi
* Renal hematomas
* Ruptured viscus
* Soft tissue masses
* Trauma to liver, spleen, kidneys, and bladder
* Vascular calcification

CRITICAL FINDINGS
* Bowel obstruction
* Ischemic bowel
* Visceral injury

It is essential that critical diagnoses be communicated immediately to the appropriate health care provider (HCP). A listing of these diagnoses varies among facilities. Note and immediately report to the HCP abnormal results and related symptoms. Timely notification of critical values for lab or diagnostic studies is a role expectation of the professional nurse. Notification processes will vary among facilities. Upon receipt of the critical value the information should be read back to the caller to verify accuracy. Most policies require immediate notification of the primary HCP, hospitalist, or on-call HCP. Reported information includes the patient's name, unique identifiers, critical value, name of the person giving the report, and name of the person receiving the report. Documentation of notification should be made in the medical record with the name of the HCP notified, time and date of notification, and any orders received. Any delay in a timely report of a critical value may require completion of a notification form with review by Risk Management.

INTERFERING FACTORS

This procedure is contraindicated for

• Patients who are pregnant or suspected of being pregnant, unless the potential benefits of the procedure far outweigh the risks to the fetus and mother.

Factors that may impair clear imaging

• Inability of the patient to cooperate or remain still during the procedure because of age, significant pain, or mental status.
• Metallic objects (e.g., jewelry, body rings) within the examination field, which may inhibit organ visualization and cause unclear images.
• Improper adjustment of the radiographic equipment to accommodate obese or thin patients, which can cause overexposure or underexposure and a poor-quality study.
• Incorrect positioning of the patient, which may produce poor visualization of the area to be examined, for images done by portable equipment.
• Retained barium from a previous radiological procedure.

Other considerations

• Consultation with an HCP should occur before the procedure for radiation safety concerns regarding patients younger than 17.
• Risks associated with radiation overexposure can result from frequent x-ray procedures. Personnel in the room with the patient should wear a protective lead apron, stand behind a shield, or leave the area while the examination is being done. Personnel working in the examination area should wear badges to record their level of radiation exposure.

NURSING IMPLICATIONS AND PROCEDURE

PRETEST:

▶ Positively identify the patient using at least two unique identifiers before providing care, treatment, or services.
▶ *Patient Teaching:* Inform the patient this procedure can assist in assessing the status of the abdomen.
▶ Obtain a history of the patient's complaints, including a list of known allergens, especially allergies and sensitivities to latex.
▶ Obtain a history of the patient's gastrointestinal and genitourinary systems, symptoms, and results of previously performed laboratory tests and diagnostic and surgical procedures.
▶ Record the date of the last menstrual period and determine the possibility of pregnancy in perimenopausal women.
▶ Obtain a list of the patient's current medications, including herbs, nutritional supplements, and nutraceuticals (see Appendix F).
▶ Review the procedure with the patient. Address concerns about pain and explain that little to no pain is expected during the test, but there may be moments of discomfort. Inform the patient that the procedure is performed in the radiology department or at the bedside by a registered radiologic technologist and takes approximately 5 to 15 min to complete.
▶ *Sensitivity to social and cultural issues,* as well as concern for modesty, is important in providing psychological support before, during, and after the procedure.
▶ Instruct the patient to remove all metallic objects from the area to be examined.
▶ There are no food, fluid, or medication restrictions unless by medical direction.

INTRATEST:

▶ Observe standard precautions, and follow the general guidelines in Appendix A. Positively identify the patient.
▶ Ensure the patient has removed all metallic objects from the area to be examined prior to the procedure.

K

- Instruct the patient to void prior to the procedure and to change into the gown, robe, and foot coverings provided.
- Instruct the patient to cooperate fully and follow directions. Instruct the patient to remain still throughout the procedure because movement produces unreliable results.
- Place the patient on the table in a supine position with hands relaxed at the side.
- Instruct the patient to inhale deeply and hold his or her breath while the x-ray images are taken, and then to exhale after the images are taken.

POST-TEST:

- A report of the results will be made available to the requesting HCP, who will discuss the results with the patient.
- Reinforce information given by the patient's HCP regarding further testing, treatment, or referral to another HCP.

- Answer any questions or address any concerns voiced by the patient or family.
- Depending on the results of this procedure, additional testing may be performed to evaluate or monitor progression of the disease process and determine the need for a change in therapy. Evaluate test results in relation to the patient's symptoms and other tests performed.

RELATED MONOGRAPHS:

- Related tests include angiography renal, calculus kidney stone panel, CT abdomen, CT pelvis, CT renal, IVP, and MRI abdomen, retrograde ureteropyelography, US abdomen, US kidney, US pelvis, and UA.
- Refer to the Gastrointestinal and Genitourinary systems tables at the end of the book for related tests by body system.

K

Kleihauer-Betke Test

SYNONYM/ACRONYM: Fetal hemoglobin, hemoglobin F, acid elution slide test.

COMMON USE: To assist in assessing occurrence and extent of fetal maternal hemorrhage and calculate the amount of Rh immune globulin to be administered.

SPECIMEN: Whole blood (1 mL) collected in a lavender-top (EDTA) tube. Freshly prepared blood smears are also acceptable. Cord blood may be requested for use as a positive control.

NORMAL FINDINGS: (Method: Microscopic examination of treated and stained peripheral blood smear) Less than 1% fetal cells present.

DESCRIPTION: The Kleihauer-Betke test is used to determine the degree of fetal-maternal hemorrhage (FMH) and to help calculate the dosage of Rh immune globulin (RhIG)—Rh$_o$(D) RhoGAM IM or Rhophylac IM or IV—to be given in some cases of Rh-negative mothers. Administration of RhIG inhibits formation of Rh antibodies in the mother to prevent Rh disease in future pregnancies with Rh-positive children. The test is also used to resolve the question of whether FMH was the cause of fetal death in the case of stillbirth.

A sample of maternal blood should be collected within 1 hr of delivery. A blood film of maternal red blood cells (RBCs) is prepared, treated with an acid buffer, and stained. The acid solution causes hemoglobin to be leached from the maternal cells, giving them a ghostlike appearance. Fetal cells containing hemoglobin F retain their hemoglobin and are stained bright red. Approximately 2,000 cells are examined microscopically and counted. The ratio between maternal cells and fetal cells is determined by dividing the number of fetal cells present by the total number of cells counted. The percentage of fetal cells is determined by multiplying the ratio by 100. For example if 12 fetal cells were identified in a total cell count of 2000, then $12/2000 = 0.006 \times 100 = 0.6\%$ fetal cells. The estimated number of fetal cells present in maternal circulation is used to calculate the quantity of fetal bleed in milliliters of fetal whole blood. FMH is calculated by dividing the percentage of fetal cells by 100 (to convert the percentage back to an absolute number) and then multiplying by 5000 (based on the assumption that maternal blood volume is 5 liters or 5000 mL). For example, if the percentage of fetal cells counted is 0.6%, then FMH = $(0.6/100) \times 5000 = 30$ mL. The fetal blood cell volume can also be used to calculate the quantity of fetal bleed in milliliters of fetal packed cells. For example, if the fetal blood cell volume is 30 mL the packed cell volume would be 15 mL, based on the assumption that the hematocrit of fetal whole blood is 50%. The FMH is used to estimate the dosage of RhIG needed. A commonly accepted recommendation is that one 300 mcg dose of RhIG will cover 30 mL of fetal whole blood or 15 mL fetal cells. In the example the FMH was determined to be 30 mL of whole blood. Therefore, 30 mL of fetal blood divided by 30 mL covered per dose indicates that a single dose of RhIG should be administered. In another example if the FMH was determined to be 55 mL then $55/30 = 1.8$. When the number after the decimal is 5 or greater the dose would be rounded up to the next whole number plus one, meaning 3 doses would be required. In a third example if the FMH was determined to be 40 mL then $40/30 = 1.3$. When the number after the decimal is less than 5 the dose would be rounded down to the next whole number plus one, meaning 2 doses would be required. Calculation of RhIG dosage is based on the calculated size of FMH and *should only be done after reviewing the information in the manufacturer's package insert*. Postpartum RhIG should be given within 72 hr of delivery. The test can also be used to distinguish some forms of thalassemia from the hereditary persistence of fetal hemoglobin, but hemoglobin electrophoresis and flow cytometry methods are more commonly used for this purpose.

INDICATIONS

- Assist in the diagnosis of certain types of anemia
- Calculating dosage of RhoGAM
- Determine whether FMH was a potential cause of death in stillborn delivery
- Screening postpartum maternal blood for the presence of FMH

POTENTIAL DIAGNOSIS

Positive findings in
- Fetal-maternal hemorrhage *(related to leakage of fetal RBCs into maternal circulation)*
- Hereditary persistence of fetal hemoglobin *(the test does not differentiate fetal hemoglobin from neonate and adult)*

Negative findings in: N/A

CRITICAL FINDINGS: N/A

INTERFERING FACTORS

Specimens must be obtained before transfusion.

NURSING IMPLICATIONS AND PROCEDURE

PRETEST:

- Positively identify the patient using at least two unique identifiers before providing care, treatment, or services.
- *Patient Teaching:* Inform the patient this test can assist in identifying how much medication should be given after delivery.
- Obtain a history of the patient's complaints, including a list of known allergens, especially allergies or sensitivities to latex.
- Obtain a history of the patient's hematopoietic and reproductive systems, symptoms, and results of previously performed laboratory tests and diagnostic and surgical procedures.
- Note any recent procedures that can interfere with test results.
- Obtain a list of the patient's current medications, including herbs, nutritional supplements, and nutraceuticals (see Appendix F).
- Review the procedure with the patient. Inform the patient that specimen collection takes approximately 5 to 10 min. Address concerns about pain and explain that there may be some discomfort during the venipuncture.
- *Sensitivity to social and cultural issues,* as well as concern for modesty, is important in providing psychological support before, during, and after the procedure.
- There are no food, fluid, or medication restrictions unless by medical direction.

INTRATEST:

- If the patient has a history of allergic reaction to latex, avoid the use of equipment containing latex.
- Instruct the patient to cooperate fully and to follow directions. Direct the patient to breathe normally and to avoid unnecessary movement.
- Observe standard precautions, and follow the general guidelines in Appendix A. Positively identify the patient, and label the appropriate specimen container with the corresponding patient demographics, initials of the person collecting the specimen, date, and time of collection. Perform a venipuncture.
- Remove the needle and apply direct pressure with dry gauze to stop bleeding. Observe/assess venipuncture site for bleeding or hematoma formation and secure gauze with adhesive bandage.
- Promptly transport the specimen to the laboratory for processing and analysis. Sample must be less than 6 hr old.

POST-TEST:

- A report of the results will be made available to the requesting health-care provider (HCP), who will discuss the results with the patient.
- Reinforce information given by the patient's HCP regarding further testing, treatment, or referral to another HCP. Answer any questions or address any concerns voiced by the patient or family.
- Depending on the results of this procedure, additional testing may be performed to evaluate or monitor progression of the disease process and determine the need for a change in therapy. Evaluate test results in relation to the patient's symptoms and other tests performed.

RELATED MONOGRAPHS:

- Related tests include amniotic fluid analysis, blood group and type, hemoglobin electrophoresis, and US biophysical profile obstetric.
- Refer to the Hematopoietic and Reproductive systems tables at the end of the book for related tests by body system.

Lactate Dehydrogenase and Isoenzymes

SYNONYM/ACRONYM: LDH and isos, LD and isos.

COMMON USE: To assess myocardial or skeletal muscle damage toward diagnosing disorders such as myocardial infarction or damage to brain, liver, kidneys, and skeletal muscle.

SPECIMEN: Serum (1 mL) collected in a red- or tiger-top tube.

NORMAL FINDINGS: (Method: Enzymatic [L to P] for lactate dehydrogenase, electrophoretic analysis for isoenzymes) Reference ranges are method dependent and may vary among laboratories.

Lactate Dehydrogenase

Age	Conventional & SI Units
0–2 yr	125–275 units/L
2–3 yr	166–232 units/L
4–6 yr	104–206 units/L
7–12 yr	90–203 units/L
13–14 yr	90–199 units/L
15–43 yr	90–156 units/L
Greater than 43 yr	90–176 units/L

LDH Fraction	% of Total	Fraction of Total
LDH_1	14–26	0.14–0.26
LDH_2	29–39	0.29–0.39
LDH_3	20–26	0.20–0.26
LDH_4	8–16	0.08–0.16
LDH_5	6–16	0.06–0.16

POTENTIAL DIAGNOSIS

Total LDH Increased In

LDH is released from any damaged cell in which it is stored so conditions that affect the heart, liver, kidneys, red blood cells, skeletal muscle, or other tissue source and cause cellular destruction demonstrate elevated LDH levels.

- Carcinoma of the liver
- Chronic alcoholism
- Cirrhosis
- Congestive heart failure
- Hemolytic anemias
- Hypoxia
- Leukemias
- Megaloblastic and pernicious anemia
- MI or pulmonary infarction
- Musculoskeletal disease
- Obstructive jaundice
- Pancreatitis
- Renal disease (severe)
- Shock
- Viral hepatitis

Total LDH Decreased In: N/A

LDH Isoenzymes

- LDH_1 fraction increased over LDH_2 can be seen in acute MI, anemias (pernicious, hemolytic, acute sickle cell, megaloblastic, hemolytic), and acute renal cortical injury due to

any cause. The LDH$_1$ fraction in particular is elevated in cases of germ cell tumors.
- Increases in the middle fractions are associated with conditions in which massive platelet destruction has occurred (e.g., pulmonary embolism, post-transfusion period) and in lymphatic system disorders

(e.g., infectious mononucleosis, lymphomas, lymphocytic leukemias).
- An increase in LDH$_5$ occurs with musculoskeletal damage and many types of liver damage (e.g., cirrhosis, cancer, hepatitis).

CRITICAL FINDINGS: N/A

Find and print out the full monograph at DavisPlus (davisplus.fadavis.com, keyword Van Leeuwen).

Lactic Acid

SYNONYM/ACRONYM: Lactate.

COMMON USE: To assess for lactic acid acidosis related to poor organ perfusion and liver failure. May also be used to differentiate between lactic acid acidosis and ketoacidosis by evaluating blood glucose levels.

SPECIMEN: Plasma (1 mL) collected in a gray-top (sodium fluoride) or a green-top (lithium heparin) tube. Specimen should be transported tightly capped and in an ice slurry.

NORMAL FINDINGS: (Method: Spectrophotometry/enzymatic analysis)

	Conventional Units	SI Units (Conventional Units × 0.111)
0–90 d	3–32 mg/dL	0.3–3.6 mmol/L
3–24 mo	3–30 mg/dL	0.3–3.3 mmol/L
2 yr–adult	3–23 mg/dL	0.3–2.6 mmol/L

DESCRIPTION: Lactic acid (present in blood as lactate) is a by-product of carbohydrate metabolism. Normally metabolized in the liver, lactate concentration is based on the rate of production and metabolism. Levels increase during strenuous exercise, which results in insufficient oxygen delivery to the tissues. Pyruvate, the normal end product of glucose metabolism, is converted to lactate in

emergency situations when energy is needed but there is insufficient oxygen in the system to favor the aerobic and customary energy cycle. When hypoxia or circulatory collapse increases production of lactate, or when the hepatic system does not metabolize lactate sufficiently, lactate levels become elevated. The lactic acid test can be performed in conjunction with pyruvic acid testing to monitor tissue oxygenation. Lactic acidosis can be differentiated from ketoacidosis by the absence of ketosis and grossly elevated glucose levels.

INDICATIONS
- Assess tissue oxygenation
- Evaluate acidosis

POTENTIAL DIAGNOSIS

Increased in
The liver is the major organ responsible for the breakdown of lactic acid. Any condition affecting normal liver function may also reflect increased blood levels of lactic acid.

- Cardiac failure *(decreased blood flow and insufficient oxygen in tissues result in accumulation of lactic acid from anaerobic glycolysis)*
- Diabetes *(inefficient aerobic glycolysis and decreased blood flow caused by diabetes result in accumulation of lactic acid from anaerobic glycolysis)*
- Hemorrhage *(decreased blood circulation and insufficient oxygen in tissues result in accumulation of lactic acid from anaerobic glycolysis)*
- Hepatic coma *(related to liver damage and decreased tissue oxygenation)*
- Ingestion of large doses of alcohol or acetaminophen *(related to liver damage)*
- Lactic acidosis *(related to strenuous exercise that results in accumulations in metabolic by-products of anaerobic breakdown of sugars for energy)*
- Pulmonary embolism *(decreased blood flow and insufficient oxygen in tissues result in accumulation of lactic acid from anaerobic glycolysis)*

- Pulmonary failure *(decreased blood flow and insufficient oxygen in tissues result in accumulation of lactic acid from anaerobic glycolysis)*
- Reye's syndrome *(related to liver damage)*
- Shock *(decreased blood flow and insufficient oxygen in tissues result in accumulation of lactic acid from anaerobic glycolysis)*
- Strenuous exercise *(related to lactic acidosis)*

Decreased in: N/A

CRITICAL FINDINGS
Adults
- Greater than 31 mg/dL (SI: Greater than 3.4 mmol/L)
Children
- Greater than 37 mg/dL (SI: Greater than 4.1 mmol/L)

Note and immediately report to the health-care provider (HCP) any critically increased values and related symptoms. Timely notification of critical values for lab or diagnostic studies is a role expectation of the professional nurse. Notification processes will vary among facilities. Upon receipt of the critical value the information should be read back to the caller to verify accuracy. Most policies require immediate notification of the primary HCP, hospitalist, or on-call HCP. Reported information includes the patient's name, unique identifiers, critical value, name of the person giving the report, and name of the person receiving the report. Documentation of notification should be made in the medical record with the name of the HCP notified, time and date of notification, and any orders received. Any delay in a timely report of a critical value may require completion of a notification form with review by Risk Management.

Observe the patient for signs and symptoms of elevated levels of lactate, such as Kussmaul's breathing and increased pulse rate. In general, there is an inverse relationship between critically elevated lactate levels and survival.

INTERFERING FACTORS

• Drugs that may increase lactate levels include albuterol, aspirin, anticonvulsants (long-term use), isoniazid, metformin (Glucophage), oral contraceptives, sodium bicarbonate, and sorbitol.

• Falsely low lactate levels are obtained in samples with elevated levels of the enzyme lactate dehydrogenase because this enzyme reacts with the available lactate substrate.

• Using a tourniquet or instructing the patient to clench his or her fist during a venipuncture can cause elevated levels.

• Engaging in strenuous physical activity (i.e., activity in which blood flow and oxygen distribution cannot keep pace with increased energy needs) before specimen collection can cause an elevated result.

• Delay in transport of the specimen to the laboratory must be avoided. Specimens not processed by centrifugation in a tightly stoppered collection container within 15 min of collection should be rejected for analysis. It is preferable to transport specimens to the laboratory in an ice slurry to further retard cellular metabolism that might shift lactate levels in the sample before analysis.

• Failure to follow dietary restrictions before the procedure may cause the procedure to be canceled or repeated.

NURSING IMPLICATIONS AND PROCEDURE

PRETEST:

▶ Positively identify the patient using at least two unique identifiers before providing care, treatment, or services.

Patient Teaching: Inform the patient this test can assist with assessing organ function.

▶ Obtain a history of the patient's complaints, including a list of known allergens, especially allergies or sensitivities to latex.

▶ Obtain a history of the patient's cardiovascular, endocrine, hepatobiliary, musculoskeletal, and respiratory systems; symptoms; and results of previously performed laboratory tests and diagnostic and surgical procedures.

▶ Obtain a list of the patient's current medications, including herbs, nutritional supplements, and nutraceuticals (see Appendix F).

▶ Review the procedure with the patient. Instruct the patient to rest for 1 hr before specimen collection. Inform the patient that specimen collection takes approximately 5 to 10 min. Address concerns about pain and explain that there may be some discomfort during the venipuncture.

▶ Instruct the patient to fast and to restrict fluids overnight. Instruct the patient not to ingest alcohol for 12 hr before the test. Protocols may vary among facilities.

Sensitivity to social and cultural issues, as well as concern for modesty, is important in providing psychological support before, during, and after the procedure.

▶ There are no medication restrictions unless by medical direction.

▶ Prepare an ice slurry in a cup or plastic bag to have on hand for immediate transport of the specimen to the laboratory.

INTRATEST:

▶ Ensure that the patient has complied with dietary restrictions and other pretesting preparations; ensure that food and liquids have been restricted for at least 12 hr prior to the procedure.

▶ If the patient has a history of allergic reaction to latex, avoid the use of equipment containing latex.

▶ Instruct the patient to cooperate fully and to follow directions. Direct the patient to breathe normally and to avoid unnecessary movement.

Observe standard precautions, and follow the general guidelines in Appendix A. Positively identify the patient, and label the appropriate specimen container with the corresponding patient demographics, initials of the person collecting the specimen, date, and time of collection. Instruct the patient *not* to clench and unclench fist immediately before or during specimen collection. Do not use a tourniquet. Perform a venipuncture. The tightly capped sample should be placed in an ice slurry immediately after collection. Information on the specimen label should be protected from water in the ice slurry by first placing the specimen in a protective plastic bag.

Remove the needle and apply direct pressure with dry gauze to stop bleeding. Observe/assess venipuncture site for bleeding or hematoma formation and secure gauze with adhesive bandage.

Promptly transport the specimen to the laboratory for processing and analysis.

POST-TEST:

A report of the results will be made available to the requesting HCP, who will discuss the results with the patient. Instruct the patient to resume usual diet and fluids, as directed by the HCP.

Nutritional Considerations: Instruct patients to consume water when exercising. Dehydration may occur when the body loses water during exercise. Early signs of dehydration include dry mouth, thirst, and concentrated dark yellow urine. If replacement fluids are not consumed at this time, the patient may become moderately dehydrated and exhibit symptoms of extreme thirst, dry oral mucus membranes, inability to produce tears, decreased urinary output, and lightheadedness. Severe dehydration manifests as confusion, lethargy, vertigo, tachycardia, anuria, diaphoresis, and loss of consciousness.

Reinforce information given by the patient's HCP regarding further testing, treatment, or referral to another HCP. Answer any questions or address any concerns voiced by the patient or family.

Depending on the results of this procedure, additional testing may be performed to evaluate or monitor progression of the disease process and determine the need for a change in therapy. Evaluate test results in relation to the patient's symptoms and other tests performed.

RELATED MONOGRAPHS:

Related laboratory tests include ALT, alveolar/arterial oxygen ratio, ammonia, analgesic and antipyretic drugs, anion gap, AST, biopsy liver, blood gases, CK, glucose, ketones, plethysmography, potassium, procalcitonin, pulse oximetry, and sodium.

Refer to the Cardiovascular, Endocrine, Hepatobiliary, Musculoskeletal, and Respiratory systems tables at the end of the book for related tests by body system.

Lactose Tolerance Test

SYNONYM/ACRONYM: LTT.

COMMON USE: To assess for lactose intolerance or other metabolic disorders.

SPECIMEN: Plasma (1 mL) collected in a gray-top (fluoride/oxalate) tube.

NORMAL FINDINGS: (Method: Spectrophotometry)

Change in Glucose Value*	Conventional Units	SI Units (Conventional Units × 0.0555)
Normal	Greater than 30 mg/dL	Greater than 1.7 mmol/L
Inconclusive	20–30 mg/dL	1.1–1.7 mmol/L
Abnormal	Less than 20 mg/dL	Less than 1.1 mmol/L

*Compared to fasting sample for infants, children, adults, and older adults.

DESCRIPTION: Lactose is a disaccharide found in dairy products. When ingested, lactose is broken down in the intestine by the sugar-splitting enzyme lactase, into glucose and galactose. When sufficient lactase is not available, intestinal bacteria metabolize the lactose, resulting in abdominal bloating, pain, flatus, and diarrhea. The lactose tolerance test screens for lactose intolerance by monitoring glucose levels after ingestion of a dose of lactose. There is also a noninvasive method to determine lactose intolerance using the hydrogen breath test. The breakdown of lactose by intestinal bacteria produces hydrogen gas. Before the administration of lactose, the patient breathes into a balloon. The concentration of hydrogen is measured from a sample of the gas in the balloon. After the administration of lactose, the patient breathes into a balloon at 15-min intervals over a period of 3 to 5 hr, and subsequent samples are measured for levels of hydrogen gas. The breath test is considered normal if the increase in hydrogen is less than 12 parts per million over the fasting or pretest level.

INDICATIONS

• Evaluate patients for suspected lactose intolerance

POTENTIAL DIAGNOSIS

Glucose Levels Increased In
• Normal response

Glucose Levels Decreased In
• Lactose intolerance (lactase is insufficient to break down ingested lactose into glucose)

CRITICAL FINDINGS

Glucose
Adults & Children
• Less than 40 mg/dL (SI: Less than 2.22 mmol/L)
• Greater than 400 mg/dL (SI: Greater than 22.2 mmol/L)

Note and immediately report to the health-care provider (HCP) any critically increased or decreased values and symptoms. Timely notification of critical values for lab or diagnostic studies is a role expectation of the professional nurse. Notification processes will vary among facilities. Upon receipt of the critical value the information should be read back to the caller to verify accuracy. Most policies require immediate notification of the primary HCP, hospitalist, or on-call HCP. Reported information includes the patient's name, unique identifiers, critical value, name of the person giving the report, and name of the person receiving the report. Documentation of notification should be made in the medical record with the name of the HCP notified, time and date of notification, and any orders received. Any delay in a timely report of a critical value may require completion of a notification form with review by Risk Management.

Symptoms of decreased glucose levels include headache, confusion, hunger, irritability, nervousness, restlessness, sweating, and weakness. Possible interventions include oral or IV administration of glucose, IV or intramuscular injection of glucagon, and continuous glucose monitoring.

Symptoms of elevated glucose levels include abdominal pain, fatigue, muscle cramps, nausea, vomiting, polyuria, and thirst. Possible interventions include subcutaneous or IV injection of insulin with continuous glucose monitoring.

INTERFERING FACTORS
- Numerous medications may alter glucose levels (see monograph titled "Glucose").
- Delayed gastric emptying may decrease glucose levels.
- Smoking may falsely increase glucose levels.
- Failure to follow dietary and activity restrictions before the procedure may cause the procedure to be canceled or repeated.

NURSING IMPLICATIONS AND PROCEDURE

PRETEST:
Positively identify the patient using at least two unique identifiers before providing care, treatment, or services.

Patient Teaching: Inform the patient this test can assist with evaluating tolerance to dairy products which contain lactose.

Obtain a history of the patient's complaints, including a list of known allergens, especially allergies or sensitivities to latex.

Obtain a history of the patient's gastrointestinal system, symptoms, and results of previously performed laboratory tests and diagnostic and surgical procedures.

Obtain a list of the patient's current medications, including herbs, nutritional supplements, and nutraceuticals (see Appendix F).

Review the procedure with the patient. Obtain the pediatric patient's weight to calculate dose of lactose to be administered. Inform the patient that multiple samples will be collected over a 90-min interval. Inform the patient that each specimen collection takes approximately 5 to 10 min. Address concerns about pain related to the procedure. Inform the patient that the test may produce symptoms such as cramps and diarrhea. Instruct the patient not to smoke cigarettes or chew gum during the test. Explain that there may be some discomfort during the venipuncture.

Sensitivity to social and cultural issues, as well as concern for modesty, is important in providing psychological support before, during, and after the procedure.

Inform the patient that fasting for at least 12 hr before the test is required and that strenuous activity should also be avoided for at least 12 hr before the test. Protocols may vary among facilities.

There are no medication restrictions unless by medical direction.

INTRATEST:
Ensure that the patient has complied with dietary and activity restrictions as well as other pretesting preparations; ensure that food has been restricted for at least 12 hr prior to the procedure.

If the patient has a history of allergic reaction to latex, avoid the use of equipment containing latex.

Administer lactose dissolved in a small amount of room temperature water (250 mL), over a 5- to 10-min period. Dosage is 2 g/kg body weight to a maximum of 50 g for patients of all ages. The requesting HCP may specify a lower challenge dose if severe lactose intolerance is suspected. One pound is equal to 0.45 kg; therefore, a weight of 50 lb is equal to 22 kg. The appropriate dosage of lactose in this example would be 45 g. Record body weight, dose administered, and time of ingestion. Encourage the patient to drink one to two glasses of water during the test.

▶ Instruct the patient to cooperate fully and to follow directions. Direct the patient to breathe normally and to avoid unnecessary movement.

▶ Observe standard precautions, and follow the general guidelines in Appendix A. Positively identify the patient, and label the appropriate specimen container with the corresponding patient demographics, initials of the person collecting the specimen, date, and time of collection. Perform a venipuncture. Samples should be collected at baseline, 15, 30, 60, 90, and 120 min. Record any symptoms the patient reports throughout the course of the test.

▶ Remove the needle and apply direct pressure with dry gauze to stop bleeding. Observe/assess venipuncture site for bleeding or hematoma formation and secure gauze with adhesive bandage.

▶ Promptly transport the specimen to the laboratory for processing and analysis. Glucose values change rapidly in an unprocessed, unpreserved specimen; therefore, if a Microtainer is used, each sample should be transported immediately after collection.

POST-TEST:

▶ A report of the results will be made available to the requesting HCP, who will discuss the results with the patient.

▶ Instruct the patient that resuming his or her usual diet may not be possible if lactose intolerance is identified. Educate patients on the importance

of following the dietary advice of a nutritionist to ensure proper nutritional balance.

Nutritional Considerations: Instruct the patient with lactose intolerance to avoid milk products and to carefully read labels on prepared products. Yogurt, which contains inactive lactase enzyme, may be ingested. The lactase in yogurt is activated by the temperature and pH of the duodenum and substitutes for the lack of endogenous lactase. Advise the patient that products such as Lactaid tablets or drops may allow ingestion of milk products without sequelae. Many lactose-free food products are now available in grocery stores.

▶ Recognize anxiety related to test results, and be supportive of concerns related to a perceived change in lifestyle. Discuss the implications of abnormal test results on the patient's lifestyle. Provide teaching and information regarding the clinical implications of the test results, as appropriate.

▶ Reinforce information given by the patient's HCP regarding further testing, treatment, or referral to another HCP. Answer any questions or address any concerns voiced by the patient or family.

▶ Depending on the results of this procedure, additional testing may be performed to evaluate or monitor progression of the disease process and determine the need for a change in therapy. Evaluate test results in relation to the patient's symptoms and other tests performed.

RELATED MONOGRAPHS:

▶ Related tests include D-xylose absorption, fecal analysis, and glucose.

▶ Refer to the Gastrointestinal System table at the end of the book for related tests by body system.

Laparoscopy, Abdominal

SYNONYM/ACRONYM: Abdominal peritoneoscopy.

COMMON USE: To visualize and assess the liver, gallbladder, and spleen to assist with surgical interventions, staging tumor, and performing diagnostic biopsies.

AREA OF APPLICATION: Abdomen and pelvis

CONTRAST: Carbon dioxide (CO_2).

DESCRIPTION: Abdominal or gastrointestinal (GI) laparoscopy provides direct visualization of the liver, gallbladder, spleen, and stomach after insufflation of carbon dioxide (CO_2). In this procedure, a rigid laparoscope is introduced into the body cavity through a 1- to 2-cm abdominal incision. The endoscope has a microscope to allow visualization of the organs, and it can be used to insert instruments for performing certain procedures, such as biopsy and tumor resection. Under general anesthesia, the peritoneal cavity is inflated with 2 to 3 L of CO_2. The gas distends the abdominal wall so that the instruments can be inserted safely. Advantages of this procedure compared to an open laparotomy include reduced pain, reduced length of stay at the hospital or surgical center, and reduced time off from work.

INDICATIONS

- Assist in performing surgical procedures such as cholecystectomy, appendectomy, hernia repair, hiatal hernia repair, and bowel resection
- Detect cirrhosis of the liver
- Detect pancreatic disorders
- Evaluate abdominal pain or abdominal mass of unknown origin
- Evaluate abdominal trauma in an emergency
- Evaluate and treat appendicitis
- Evaluate the extent of splenomegaly due to portal hypertension
- Evaluate jaundice of unknown origin
- Obtain biopsy specimens of benign or cancerous tumors
- Stage neoplastic disorders such as lymphomas, Hodgkin's disease, and hepatic carcinoma

POTENTIAL DIAGNOSIS

Normal findings in
- Normal appearance of the liver, spleen, gallbladder, pancreas, and other abdominal contents

Abnormal findings in
- Abdominal adhesions
- Appendicitis
- Ascites
- Cancer of any of the organs
- Cirrhosis of the liver
- Gangrenous gallbladder
- Intra-abdominal bleeding
- Portal hypertension
- Splenomegaly

CRITICAL FINDINGS
- Appendicitis

It is essential that critical diagnoses be communicated immediately to the appropriate health-care provider (HCP). A listing of these diagnoses varies among facilities. Note and immediately report to the HCP abnormal results and related symptoms. Timely notification of critical values for lab or diagnostic studies is a role expectation of the professional nurse. Notification processes will vary among facilities. Upon receipt of the critical value the information should be read back to the caller to verify accuracy. Most policies require immediate notification of the primary HCP, hospitalist, or on-call HCP. Reported information includes the patient's name, unique identifiers, critical value, name of the person giving the report, and name of the person receiving the report. Documentation of notification should be made in the medical record with the name of the HCP notified, time and date of notification, and any orders received. Any delay in a timely report of a critical value may require completion of a notification form with review by Risk Management.

INTERFERING FACTORS

This procedure is contraindicated for

* Patients who are pregnant or suspected of being pregnant, unless the potential benefits of the procedure far outweigh the risk of radiation exposure to the fetus.
* Patients with bleeding disorders, especially those associated with uremia and cytotoxic chemotherapy.
* Patients with cardiac conditions or dysrhythmias.
* Patients with advanced respiratory or cardiovascular disease.
* Patients with intestinal obstruction, abdominal mass, abdominal hernia, or suspected intra-abdominal hemorrhage.
* Patients with a history of peritonitis or multiple abdominal operations causing dense adhesions.

Factors that may impair clear visualization

* Gas or feces in the GI tract resulting from inadequate cleansing

or failure to restrict food intake before the study.
* Retained barium from a previous radiological procedure.
* Inability of the patient to cooperate or remain still during the procedure because of age, significant pain, or mental status.
* Metallic objects (e.g., jewelry, body rings) within the examination field, which may inhibit organ visualization and cause unclear images.

Other considerations

* The procedure may be terminated if chest pain or severe cardiac arrhythmias occur.
* Failure to follow dietary restrictions and other pretesting preparations may cause the procedure to be canceled or repeated.
* Patients who are in a hypoxemic or hypercapnic state will require continuous oxygen administration.
* Patients with acute infection or advanced malignancy involving the abdominal wall are at increased risk because organisms may be introduced into the normally sterile peritoneal cavity.

NURSING IMPLICATIONS AND PROCEDURE

PRETEST:

▶ Positively identify the patient using at least two unique identifiers before providing care, treatment, or services.
▶ *Patient Teaching:* Inform the patient this procedure can assist in assessing the abdominal organs.
▶ Obtain a history of the patient's complaints, including a list of known allergens, especially allergies or sensitivities to latex and anesthetics.
▶ Obtain a history of the patient's gastrointestinal and hepatobiliary systems, symptoms, and results of previously performed laboratory tests and diagnostic and surgical procedures.
▶ Ensure that this procedure is performed before any barium studies.

Record the date of the last menstrual period and determine the possibility of pregnancy in perimenopausal women.

Obtain a list of the patient's current medications, including anticoagulants, aspirin and other salicylates, herbs, nutritional supplements, and nutraceuticals, especially those known to affect coagulation (see Appendix F). Such products should be discontinued by medical direction for the appropriate number of days prior to a surgical procedure. Note the last time and dose of medication taken.

Review the procedure with the patient. Address concerns about pain related to the procedure and explain that some pain may be experienced during the test, and there may be moments of discomfort. Inform the patient that the procedure is performed in a surgery department, by an HCP, with support staff, and takes approximately 30 to 60 min.

Sensitivity to social and cultural issues, as well as concern for modesty, is important in providing psychological support before, during, and after the procedure.

Explain that an IV line may be inserted to allow infusion of IV fluids, anesthetics, analgesics, or IV sedation.

Inform the patient that a laxative and cleansing enema may be needed the day before the procedure, with cleansing enemas on the morning of the procedure, depending on the institution's policy.

Instruct the patient to remove jewelry and other metallic objects from the area to be examined prior to the procedure.

Instruct the patient to fast and restrict fluids for 8 hr prior to the procedure. Protocols may vary among facilities.

Make sure a written and informed consent has been signed prior to the procedure and before administering any medications.

INTRATEST:

Observe standard precautions, and follow the general guidelines in Appendix A. Positively identify the patient.

Ensure that the patient has complied with dietary, fluid, and medication

restrictions for at least 8 hr prior to the procedure.

Ensure the patient has removed all external metallic objects from the area to be examined.

Ensure that nonallergy to anesthesia is confirmed before the procedure is performed under general anesthesia.

Assess for completion of bowel preparation according to the institution's procedure.

Have emergency equipment readily available.

Instruct the patient to void prior to the procedure and to change into the gown, robe, and foot coverings provided.

Instruct the patient to cooperate fully and to follow directions. Instruct the patient to remain still throughout the procedure because movement produces unreliable results.

Obtain and record baseline vital signs.

Insert an IV line or venous access device at a low "keep open" rate.

Administer medications, as ordered, to reduce discomfort and to promote relaxation and sedation.

Place the patient on the laparoscopy table. If general anesthesia is to be used, it is administered at this time. Place the patient in a modified lithotomy position with the head tilted downward. Cleanse the abdomen with an antiseptic solution, and drape and catheterize the patient, if ordered.

The HCP identifies the site for the scope insertion and administers local anesthesia if that is to be used. After deeper layers are anesthetized, a pneumoperitoneum needle is placed between the visceral and parietal peritoneum.

CO_2 is insufflated through the pneumoperitoneum needle to separate the abdominal wall from the viscera and to aid in visualization of the abdominal structures. The pneumoperitoneum needle is removed, and the trocar and laparoscope are inserted through the incision.

After the examination, collection of tissue samples, and performance of therapeutic procedures, the scope is withdrawn. All possible CO_2 is evacuated via the trocar, which is then

L

removed. The skin incision is closed with sutures, clips, or sterile strips, and a small dressing or adhesive strip is applied.
- Observe/assess the incision site for bleeding, inflammation, or hematoma formation.

POST-TEST:

- A report of the results will be made available to the requesting HCP, who will discuss the results with the patient.
- Instruct the patient to resume usual diet, fluids, and medication, as directed by the HCP.
- Monitor vital signs and neurological status every 15 min for 1 hr, then every 2 hr for 4 hr, and as ordered. Take temperature every 4 hr for 24 hr. Monitor intake and output at least every 8 hr. Compare with baseline values. Notify the HCP if temperature is elevated. Protocols may vary among facilities.
- Instruct the patient to restrict activity for 2 to 7 days after the procedure.
- Instruct the patient in the care and assessment of the incision site.
- If indicated, inform the patient of a follow-up appointment for the removal of sutures.
- Inform the patient that shoulder discomfort may be experienced for 1 or 2 days after the procedure as a result of abdominal distention caused by insufflation of CO_2 into the abdomen and that mild analgesics and cold compresses, as ordered, can be used to relieve the discomfort.

- Emphasize that any persistent shoulder pain, abdominal pain, vaginal bleeding, fever, redness, or swelling of the incisional area must be reported to the HCP immediately.
- Recognize anxiety related to test results. Discuss the implications of abnormal test results on the patient's lifestyle. Provide teaching and information regarding the clinical implications of the test results, as appropriate.
- Reinforce information given by the patient's HCP regarding further testing, treatment, or referral to another HCP. Answer any questions or address any concerns voiced by the patient or family.
- Depending on the results of this procedure, additional testing may be needed to evaluate or monitor progression of the disease process and determine the need for a change in therapy. Evaluate test results in relation to the patient's symptoms and other tests performed.

RELATED MONOGRAPHS:

- Related tests include amylase, barium swallow, biopsy bone marrow, CBC, CBC WBC count and differential, CT abdomen, CT biliary tract and liver, CT pancreas, CRP, ESR, gallium scan, hepatobiliary scan, KUB, lipase, liver and spleen scan, lymphangiogram, MRI abdomen, MRI pelvis, peritoneal fluid analysis, US abdomen, and US pelvis.
- Refer to the Gastrointestinal and Hepatobiliary systems tables at the end of the book for related tests by body system.

Laparoscopy, Gynecologic

SYNONYM/ACRONYM: Gynecologic pelviscopy, gynecologic laparoscopy, pelvic endoscopy, peritoneoscopy.

COMMON USE: To visualize and assess the ovaries, fallopian tubes, and uterus toward diagnosing inflammation, malformations, cysts, and fibroids and to evaluate causes of infertility.

AREA OF APPLICATION: Pelvis.

CONTRAST: Carbon dioxide (CO_2).

DESCRIPTION: Gynecologic laparoscopy provides direct visualization of the internal pelvic contents, including the ovaries, fallopian tubes, and uterus, after insufflation of carbon dioxide (CO_2). It is done to diagnose and treat pelvic organ disorders as well as to perform surgical procedures on the organs. In this procedure, a rigid laparoscope is introduced into the body cavity through a 1- to 2-cm periumbilical incision. The endoscope has a microscope to allow visualization of the organs, and it can be used to insert instruments for performing procedures such as biopsy and tumor resection. Under general or local anesthesia, the peritoneal cavity is inflated with 2 to 3 L of CO_2. The gas distends the abdominal wall so that the instruments can be inserted safely. Advantages of this procedure compared to an open laparotomy include reduced pain, reduced length of stay at the hospital or surgical center, and reduced time off from work.

INDICATIONS
- Detect ectopic pregnancy and determine the need for surgery
- Detect pelvic inflammatory disease or abscess
- Detect uterine fibroids, ovarian cysts, and uterine malformations (ovarian cysts may be aspirated during the procedure)
- Evaluate amenorrhea and infertility
- Evaluate fallopian tubes and anatomic defects to determine the cause of infertility
- Evaluate known or suspected endometriosis, salpingitis, and hydrosalpinx
- Evaluate pelvic pain or masses of unknown cause
- Evaluate reproductive organs after therapy for infertility

- Obtain biopsy specimens to confirm suspected pelvic malignancies or metastasis
- Perform tubal sterilization and ovarian biopsy
- Perform vaginal hysterectomy
- Remove adhesions or foreign bodies such as intrauterine devices
- Treat endometriosis through electrocautery or laser vaporization

POTENTIAL DIAGNOSIS

Normal findings in
- Normal appearance of uterus, ovaries, fallopian tubes, and other pelvic contents

Abnormal findings in
- Ectopic pregnancy
- Endometriosis
- Ovarian cyst
- Ovarian tumor
- Pelvic adhesions
- Pelvic inflammatory disease
- Pelvic tumor
- Salpingitis
- Uterine fibroids

CRITICAL FINDINGS
- Ectopic pregnancy
- Foreign body
- Tumor with significant mass effect

It is essential that critical diagnoses be communicated immediately to the appropriate health-care provider (HCP). A listing of these diagnoses varies among facilities. Note and immediately report to the HCP abnormal results and related symptoms. Timely notification of critical values for lab or diagnostic studies is a role expectation of the professional nurse. Notification processes will vary among facilities. Upon receipt of the critical value the information should be read back to the caller to verify accuracy. Most policies require immediate notification of the primary HCP, hospitalist, or on-call HCP. Reported information includes the patient's name, unique identifiers, critical value, name of the person giving the report, and name of the person receiving the report. Documentation of notification should be made in the medical record with the name of the HCP notified, time and date of notification, and any orders received. Any delay in a timely report of a critical value may require completion of a notification form with review by Risk Management.

INTERFERING FACTORS

This procedure is contraindicated for

- Patients who are pregnant or suspected of being pregnant, unless the potential benefits of the procedure far outweigh the risks to the fetus and mother.
- Patients with bleeding disorders, especially those associated with uremia and cytotoxic chemotherapy.
- Patients with cardiac conditions or dysrhythmias.
- Patients with advanced respiratory or cardiovascular disease.
- Patients with intestinal obstruction, abdominal mass, abdominal hernia, or suspected intra-abdominal hemorrhage.

Factors that may impair clear visualization

- Gas or feces in the gastrointestinal (GI) tract resulting from inadequate cleansing or failure to restrict food intake before the study.
- Retained barium from a previous radiological procedure.
- Inability of the patient to cooperate or remain still during the procedure because of age, significant pain, or mental status.
- Metallic objects (e.g., jewelry, body rings) within the examination field, which may inhibit organ visualization and cause unclear images.

Other considerations

- The procedure may be terminated if chest pain or severe cardiac arrhythmias occur.

- Failure to follow dietary restrictions and other pretesting preparations may cause the procedure to be canceled or repeated.
- Patients who are in a hypoxemic or hypercapnic state will require continuous oxygen administration.
- Patients with acute infection or advanced malignancy involving the abdominal wall are at increased risk because organisms may be introduced into the normally sterile peritoneal cavity.

NURSING IMPLICATIONS AND PROCEDURE

PRETEST:

▸ Positively identify the patient using at least two unique identifiers before providing care, treatment, or services.

▸ *Patient Teaching:* Inform the patient this procedure can assist in assessing the abdominal and pelvic organs.

▸ Obtain a history of the patient's complaints, including a list of known allergens, especially allergies or sensitivities to latex and anesthetics.

▸ Obtain a history of the patient's reproductive system, symptoms, and results of previously performed laboratory tests and diagnostic and surgical procedures.

▸ Ensure that this procedure is performed before any barium studies.

▸ Record the date of the last menstrual period and determine the possibility of pregnancy in perimenopausal women.

▸ Obtain a list of the patient's current medications, including anticoagulants, aspirin and other salicylates, herbs, nutritional supplements, and nutraceuticals, especially those known to affect coagulation (see Appendix F). Such products should be discontinued by medical direction for the appropriate number of days prior to a surgical procedure. Note the last time and dose of medication taken.

▸ Review the procedure with the patient. Address concerns about pain related to the procedure and explain that some pain may be experienced during the test, and there may be moments of discomfort. Inform the patient that the procedure is performed in a surgery department by an HCP and support staff and takes approximately 30 to 60 min. *Sensitivity to social and cultural issues,* as well as concern for modesty, is important in providing psychological support before, during, and after the procedure.

Explain that an IV line may be inserted to allow infusion of IV fluids, anesthetics, analgesics, or IV sedation.

Inform the patient that a laxative and cleansing enema may be needed the day before the procedure, with cleansing enemas on the morning of the procedure, depending on the institution's policy.

Instruct the patient to remove jewelry and other metallic objects from the area to be examined prior to the procedure.

Instruct the patient to fast and restrict fluids for 8 hr prior to the procedure. Protocols may vary among facilities. *Make sure a written and informed consent has been signed prior to the procedure and before administering any medications.*

Observe standard precautions, and follow the general guidelines in Appendix A.

Positively identify the patient.

Ensure that the patient has complied with dietary, fluid, and medication restrictions for at least 8 hr prior to the procedure.

Ensure the patient has removed all external metallic objects from the area to be examined.

Ensure that nonallergy to anesthesia is confirmed before the procedure is performed under general anesthesia.

Assess for completion of bowel preparation according to the institution's procedure.

Have emergency equipment readily available.

Instruct the patient to void prior to the procedure and to change into the gown, robe, and foot coverings provided.

Instruct the patient to cooperate fully and to follow directions. Instruct the patient to remain still throughout the procedure because movement produces unreliable results.

Obtain and record baseline vital signs.

Insert an IV line or venous access device at a low "keep open" rate.

Administer medications, as ordered, to reduce discomfort and to promote relaxation and sedation.

Place the patient on the laparoscopy table. If general anesthesia is to be used, it is administered at this time. Place the patient in a modified lithotomy position with the head tilted downward. Cleanse the abdomen with an antiseptic solution, and drape and catheterize the patient, if ordered.

The HCP identifies the site for the scope insertion and administers local anesthesia if that is to be used. After deeper layers are anesthetized, a pneumoperitoneum needle is placed between the visceral and parietal peritoneum.

CO_2 is insufflated through the pneumoperitoneum needle to separate the abdominal wall from the viscera and to aid in visualization of the abdominal structures. The pneumoperitoneum needle is removed, and the trocar and laparoscope are inserted through the incision.

The HCP inserts a uterine manipulator through the vagina and cervix and into the uterus so that the uterus, fallopian tubes, and ovaries can be moved to permit better visualization.

After the examination, collection of tissue samples, and performance of therapeutic procedures (e.g., tubal ligation), the scope is withdrawn. All possible CO_2 is evacuated via the trocar, which is then removed. The skin incision is closed with sutures, clips, or sterile strips and a small dressing or adhesive strip is applied. After the perineum is cleansed, the uterine manipulator is removed and a sterile pad applied.

Observe/assess the incision site for bleeding, inflammation, or hematoma formation.

A report of the results will be made available to the requesting HCP, who will discuss the results with the patient.

- Instruct the patient to resume usual diet, fluids, and medication, as directed by the HCP.
- Monitor vital signs and neurological status every 15 min for 1 hr, then every 2 hr for 4 hr, and as ordered. Take temperature every 4 hr for 24 hr. Monitor intake and output at least every 8 hr. Compare with baseline values. Notify the HCP if temperature is elevated. Protocols may vary among facilities.
- Instruct the patient to restrict activity for 2 to 7 days after the procedure.
- Instruct the patient in the care and assessment of the incision site.
- If indicated, inform the patient of a follow-up appointment for the removal of sutures.
- Inform the patient that shoulder discomfort may be experienced for 1 or 2 days after the procedure as a result of abdominal distention caused by insufflation of CO_2 into the abdomen and that mild analgesics and cold compresses, as ordered, can be used to relieve the discomfort.
- Emphasize that any persistent shoulder pain, abdominal pain, vaginal bleeding, fever, redness, or swelling of the incisional area must be reported to the HCP immediately.
- Recognize anxiety related to test results. Discuss the implications of abnormal test results on the patient's lifestyle. Provide teaching and information regarding the clinical implications of the test results, as appropriate.
- Reinforce information given by the patient's HCP regarding further testing, treatment, or referral to another HCP. Answer any questions or address any concerns voiced by the patient or family.
- Depending on the results of this procedure, additional testing may be needed to evaluate or monitor progression of the disease process and determine the need for a change in therapy. Evaluate test results in relation to the patient's symptoms and other tests performed.

RELATED MONOGRAPHS:

- Related tests include cancer antigens, *Chlamydia* group antibody, CT abdomen, CT pelvis, HCG, MRI pelvis, Pap smear, progesterone, US pelvis, and uterine fibroid embolization.
- Refer to the Reproductive System table at the end of the book for related tests by body system.

Latex Allergy

SYNONYM/ACRONYM: N/A.

COMMON USE: To assess for allergic reaction to products containing latex.

SPECIMEN: Serum (1 mL) collected in a red-top tube.

NORMAL FINDINGS: (Method: Immunoassay) Negative.

POTENTIAL DIAGNOSIS

Positive findings in
Latex allergy

Negative findings in: N/A

CRITICAL FINDINGS: N/A

Find and print out the full monograph at DavisPlus (davisplus.fadavis.com, keyword Van Leeuwen).

Lead

SYNONYM/ACRONYM: Pb.

COMMON USE: To assess for lead toxicity and monitor exposure to lead to assist in diagnosing lead poisoning.

SPECIMEN: Whole blood (1 mL) collected in a special lead-free royal blue– or tan-top tube. Plasma (1 mL) collected in a lavender-top (EDTA) tube is also acceptable.

NORMAL FINDINGS: (Method: Atomic absorption spectrophotometry)

	Conventional Units	SI Units (Conventional Units × 0.0483)
Children and adults (WHO, CDC; environmental exposure)	Less than 10 mcg/dL	Less than 0.48 micromol/L
OSHA (occupational exposure standard)	Less than 40 mcg/dL	Less than 1.93 micromol/L

OSHA = Occupational Safety and Health Administration; WHO = World Health Organization; CDC = Centers for Disease Control and Prevention.

DESCRIPTION: Lead is a heavy metal and trace element. It is absorbed through the respiratory and gastrointestinal systems. It can also be transported from mother to fetus through the placenta. When there is frequent exposure to lead-containing items (e.g., paint, batteries, gasoline, pottery, bullets, printing materials) or occupations (mining, automobile, printing, and welding industries), many organs of the body are affected. Lead poisoning can cause severe behavioral and neurological effects. The blood test is considered the best indicator of lead poisoning, and confirmation is made by the lead mobilization test performed on a 24-hr urine specimen.

INDICATIONS
Assist in the diagnosis and treatment of lead poisoning

POTENTIAL DIAGNOSIS

Increased in
Heme synthesis involves the conversion of D-amino levulinic acid to porphobilinogen. Lead interferes with the enzyme that is responsible for this critical step in heme synthesis, amino levulinic acid dehydrase.

- Anemia of lead intoxication
- Lead encephalopathy
- Metal poisoning

Decreased in: N/A

CRITICAL FINDINGS ❋

- Levels greater than 30 mcg/dL (SI: Greater than 1.4 micromol/L) indicate significant exposure

• Levels greater than 60 mcg/dL (SI: Greater than 2.9 micromol/L) may require chelation therapy

Note and immediately report to the health-care provider (HCP) any critically increased values and related symptoms. Timely notification of critical values for lab or diagnostic studies is a role expectation of the professional nurse. Notification processes will vary among facilities. Upon receipt of the critical value the information should be read back to the caller to verify accuracy. Most policies require immediate notification of the primary HCP, hospitalist, or on-call HCP. Reported information includes the patient's name, unique identifiers, critical value, name of the person giving the report, and name of the person receiving the report. Documentation of notification should be made in the medical record with the name of the HCP notified, time and date of notification, and any orders received. Any delay in a timely report of a critical value may require completion of a notification form with review by Risk Management.

INTERFERING FACTORS

Contamination of the collection site and/or specimen with lead in dust can be avoided by taking special care to have the surfaces surrounding the collection location cleaned. Extra care should also be used to avoid contamination during the actual venipuncture.

NURSING IMPLICATIONS AND PROCEDURE

PRETEST:

▶ Positively identify the patient using at least two unique identifiers before providing care, treatment, or services.
▶ *Patient Teaching:* Inform the patient this test can assist in detecting lead exposure.

▶ Obtain a history of the patient's complaints, including a list of known allergens, especially allergies or sensitivities to latex.
▶ Obtain a history of the patient's hematopoietic system, symptoms, and results of previously performed laboratory tests and diagnostic and surgical procedures.
▶ Obtain a history of the patient's exposure to lead.
▶ Obtain a list of the patient's current medications, including herbs, nutritional supplements, and nutraceuticals (see Appendix F).
▶ Review the procedure with the patient. Inform the patient that specimen collection takes approximately 5 to 10 min. Address concerns about pain and explain that there may be some discomfort during the venipuncture.
▶ *Sensitivity to social and cultural issues,* as well as concern for modesty, is important in providing psychological support before, during, and after the procedure.
▶ There are no food, fluid, or medication restrictions unless by medical direction.

INTRATEST:

▶ If the patient has a history of allergic reaction to latex, avoid the use of equipment containing latex.
▶ Instruct the patient to cooperate fully and to follow directions. Direct the patient to breathe normally and to avoid unnecessary movement.
▶ Observe standard precautions, and follow the general guidelines in Appendix A. Positively identify the patient, and label the appropriate specimen container with the corresponding patient demographics, initials of the person collecting the specimen, date, and time of collection. Perform a venipuncture.
▶ Remove the needle and apply direct pressure with dry gauze to stop bleeding. Observe/assess venipuncture site for bleeding or hematoma formation and secure gauze with adhesive bandage.
▶ Promptly transport the specimen to the laboratory for processing and analysis.

POST-TEST:

A report of the results will be made available to the requesting HCP, who will discuss the results with the patient.

Reinforce information given by the patient's HCP regarding further testing, treatment, or referral to another HCP. Answer any questions or address any concerns voiced by the patient or family.

Depending on the results of this procedure, additional testing may be performed to evaluate or monitor progression of the disease process and determine the need for a change in therapy. Evaluate test results in relation to the patient's symptoms and other tests performed.

RELATED MONOGRAPHS:

Related tests include δ-aminolevulinic acid, CBC, CBC RBC morphology, erythrocyte protoporphyrin, and urine porphyrins.

Refer to the Hematopoietic System table at the end of the book for related tests by body system.

Lecithin/Sphingomyelin Ratio

SYNONYM/ACRONYM: L/S ratio.

COMMON USE: To assess for preterm infant fetal lung maturity to assist in evaluating for potential diagnosis of respiratory distress syndrome (RDS).

SPECIMEN: Amniotic fluid (10 mL) collected in a sterile amber glass or plastic tube or bottle protected from light.

NORMAL FINDINGS: (Method: Thin-layer chromatography)

	L/S Ratio
Mature (nondiabetic)	Greater than 2:1 in the presence of phosphatidyl glycerol
Borderline	1.5 to 1.9:1
Immature	Less than 1.5:1

DESCRIPTION: Respiratory distress syndrome (RDS) is the most common problem encountered in the care of premature infants. RDS, also called hyaline membrane disease, results from a deficiency of phospholipid lung surfactants. The phospholipids in surfactant are produced by specialized alveolar cells and stored in granular lamellar bodies in the lung. In normally developed lungs, surfactant coats the surface of the alveoli. Surfactant reduces the surface tension of the alveolar wall during breathing. When there is an insufficient quantity of surfactant, the alveoli are unable to expand normally and gas exchange is inhibited. Amniocentesis, a procedure by which fluid is removed from the amniotic sac, is used to assess fetal lung maturity.

Lecithin is the primary surfactant phospholipid, and it is

a stabilizing factor for the alveoli. It is produced at a low but constant rate until the 35th wk of gestation, after which its production sharply increases. Sphingomyelin, another phospholipid component of surfactant, is also produced at a constant rate after the 26th wk of gestation. Before the 35th wk, the lecithin/sphingomyelin (L/S) ratio is usually less than 1.6:1. The ratio increases to 2.0 or greater when the rate of lecithin production increases after the 35th wk of gestation. Other phospholipids, such as phosphatidyl glycerol (PG) and phosphatidyl inositol (PI), increase over time in amniotic fluid as well. The presence of PG indicates that the fetus is within 2 to 6 wk of lung maturity (i.e., at full term). Simultaneous measurement of PG with the L/S ratio improves diagnostic accuracy. Production of phospholipid surfactant is delayed in diabetic mothers. Therefore, caution must be used when interpreting the results obtained from a diabetic patient, and a higher ratio is expected to predict maturity.

INDICATIONS
- Assist in the evaluation of fetal lung maturity
- Determine the optimal time for obstetric intervention in cases of threatened fetal survival caused by stresses related to maternal diabetes, toxemia, hemolytic diseases of the newborn, or postmaturity
- Identify fetuses at risk of developing RDS

POTENTIAL DIAGNOSIS

Increased in
Evidenced by conditions that increase production of surfactant.

- Hypertension
- Intrauterine growth retardation
- Malnutrition
- Maternal diabetes
- Placenta previa
- Placental infarction
- Premature rupture of the membranes

Decreased in
Evidenced by conditions that decrease production of surfactant.

- Advanced maternal age
- Immature fetal lungs
- Multiple gestation
- Polyhydramnios

CRITICAL FINDINGS ◈
- An L/S ratio less than 1.5:1 is predictive of RDS at the time of delivery.

Note and immediately report to the health-care provider (HCP) any critically increased or decreased values and related symptoms. Infants known to be at risk for RDS can be treated with surfactant by intratracheal administration at birth. Timely notification of critical values for lab or diagnostic studies is a role expectation of the professional nurse. Notification processes will vary among facilities. Upon receipt of the critical value the information should be read back to the caller to verify accuracy. Most policies require immediate notification of the primary HCP, hospitalist, or on-call HCP. Reported information includes the patient's name, unique identifiers, critical value, name of the person giving the report, and name of the person receiving the report. Documentation of notification should be made in the medical record with the name of the HCP notified, time and date of notification, and any orders received. Any delay in a timely report of a critical value may require completion of a notification form with review by Risk Management.

INTERFERING FACTORS

Fetal blood falsely elevates the L/S ratio.

Exposing the specimen to light may cause falsely decreased values.

There is some risk to having an amniocentesis performed, and this should be weighed against the need to obtain the desired diagnostic information. A small percentage (0.5%) of patients have experienced complications including premature rupture of the membranes, premature labor, spontaneous abortion, and stillbirth.

NURSING IMPLICATIONS AND PROCEDURE

PRETEST:

Positively identify the patient using at least two unique identifiers before providing care, treatment, or services. *Patient Teaching:* Inform the parent this test can assist in obtaining an estimate of fetal lung maturity.

Obtain a history of the patient's complaints, including a list of known allergens, especially allergies or sensitivities to latex.

Obtain a history of the patient's reproductive and respiratory systems, symptoms, and results of previously performed laboratory tests and diagnostic and surgical procedures. Include any family history of genetic disorders such as cystic fibrosis, Duchenne's muscular dystrophy, hemophilia, sickle cell disease, Tay-Sachs disease, thalassemia, and trisomy 21. Obtain maternal Rh type. If Rh-negative, check for prior sensitization. A standard RhoGAM dose is indicated after amniocentesis; repeat doses should be considered if repeated amniocentesis is performed.

Record the date of the last menstrual period, and determine that the pregnancy is in the third trimester between the 28th and 40th wk.

Obtain a list of the patient's current medications, including herbs, nutritional supplements, and nutraceuticals (see Appendix F).

Review the procedure with the patient. Warn the patient that normal results do not guarantee a normal fetus. Assure the patient that precautions to avoid injury to the fetus will be taken by localizing the fetus with ultrasound. Address concerns about pain and explain that during the transabdominal procedure, any discomfort with a needle biopsy will be minimized with local anesthetics. Patients who are at 20 wk gestation or beyond should void before the test, because an empty bladder is less likely to be accidentally punctured during specimen collection. Encourage relaxation and controlled breathing during the procedure to aid in reducing any mild discomfort. Inform the patient that specimen collection is performed by an HCP specializing in this procedure and usually takes approximately 20 to 30 min to complete.

Sensitivity to social and cultural issues, as well as concern for modesty, is important in providing psychological support before, during, and after the procedure.

There are no food, fluid, or medication restrictions unless by medical direction.

Make sure a written and informed consent has been signed prior to the procedure and before administering any medications.

INTRATEST:

Ensure that the patient has voided before the procedure if gestation is 21 wk or more.

Have emergency equipment readily available.

Have patient remove clothes below the waist. Assist the patient to a supine position on the examination table with abdomen exposed. Drape the patient's legs, leaving the abdomen exposed. Raise her head or legs slightly to promote comfort and to relax abdominal muscles. If the uterus is large, place a pillow or rolled blanket under the patient's right side to prevent hypertension caused by great-vessel compression.

Instruct the patient to cooperate fully and to follow directions. Direct the

L

patient to breathe normally and to avoid unnecessary movement during administration of the local anesthetic and the procedure.

Record maternal and fetal baseline vital signs and continue to monitor throughout the procedure. Monitor for uterine contractions. Monitor fetal vital signs using ultrasound. Protocols may vary among facilities.

Observe standard precautions, and follow the general guidelines in Appendix A. Positively identify the patient, and label the appropriate specimen container with the corresponding patient demographics, initials of the person collecting the specimen, date, and time of collection.

Assess the position of the amniotic fluid, fetus, and placenta using ultrasound.

Assemble the necessary equipment, including an amniocentesis tray with solution for skin preparation, local anesthetic, 10- or 20-mL syringe, needles of various sizes (including a 22-gauge, 5-in. spinal needle), sterile drapes, sterile gloves, and foil-covered or amber specimen collection containers.

Cleanse suprapubic area with an antiseptic solution and protect with sterile drapes. A local anesthetic is injected. Explain that this may cause a stinging sensation.

A 22-gauge, 5-in. spinal needle is inserted through the abdominal and uterine walls. Explain that a sensation of pressure may be experienced when the needle is inserted. Explain to the patient how to use focusing and controlled breathing for relaxation during the procedure.

After the fluid is collected and the needle withdrawn, apply slight pressure to the site. Apply a sterile adhesive bandage to the site.

Monitor the patient for complications related to the procedure (e.g., premature labor, allergic reaction, anaphylaxis).

Place samples in properly labeled specimen container and promptly transport the specimen to the laboratory for processing and analysis.

POST-TEST:

A report of the results will be made available to the requesting HCP, who will discuss the results with the patient

✷ Fetal heart rate and maternal vital signs (i.e., heart rate, blood pressure, pulse, and respiration) must be compared to baseline values and closely monitored every 15 min for 30 to 60 min after the amniocentesis procedure. Protocols may vary among facilities.

Observe/assess for delayed allergic reactions, such as rash, urticaria, tachycardia, hyperpnea, hypertension, palpitations, nausea, or vomiting.

Observe/assess the amniocentesis site for bleeding, inflammation, or hematoma formation.

Instruct the patient to report any redness, edema, bleeding, or pain at the site.

Instruct the patient in the care and assessment of the amniocentesis site.

Instruct the patient to expect mild cramping, leakage of small amount of amniotic fluid, and vaginal spotting for up to 2 days following the procedure. Instruct the patient to immediately report moderate to severe abdominal pain or cramps, change in fetal activity increased or prolonged leaking of amniotic fluid from abdominal needle site, vaginal bleeding that is heavier than spotting, and either chills or fever to the HCP.

Instruct the patient to rest until all symptoms have disappeared before resuming normal levels of activity.

Administer standard dose of $Rh_o(D)$ immune globulin RhoGAM IM or Rhophylac IM or IV to maternal Rh-negative patients to prevent maternal Rh sensitization should the fetus be Rh-positive.

Administer mild analgesic and antibiotic therapy as ordered. Remind the patient of the importance of completing the entire course of antibiotic therapy, even if signs and symptoms disappear before completion of therapy.

Recognize anxiety related to test results, and offer support. Provide teaching and information regarding the clinical implications of the test results, as appropriate. Encourage the family to seek counseling if concerned with pregnancy termination or to seek genetic counseling if a chromosomal abnormality is determined. Decisions regarding elective abortion should take place in the presence of both parents. Provide a nonjudgmental, nonthreatening atmosphere for discussing the risks and difficulties of delivering and raising a developmentally challenged infant as well as for exploring other options (termination of pregnancy or adoption). It is also important to discuss feelings the mother and father may experience (e.g., guilt, depression, anger) if fetal abnormalities are detected. Reinforce information given by the patient's HCP regarding further testing, treatment, or referral to another HCP. Answer any questions or address any concerns voiced by the patient or family.

Instruct the patient in the use of any ordered medications. Explain the importance of adhering to the therapy regimen. As appropriate, instruct the patient in significant side effects and systemic reactions associated with the prescribed medication. Encourage her to review corresponding literature provided by a pharmacist.

Depending on the results of this procedure, additional testing may be performed to evaluate or monitor progression of the disease process and determine the need for a change in therapy. Evaluate test results in relation to the patient's symptoms and other tests performed.

RELATED MONOGRAPHS:

Related tests include amniotic fluid analysis, antibodies anticardiolipin, blood groups and antibodies, chromosome analysis, fetal fibronectin, α-fetoprotein, glucose, ketones, Kleihauer-Betke test, potassium, US biophysical profile obstetric, and UA.

Refer to the Reproductive and Respiratory systems tables at the end of the book for related tests by body system.

Leukocyte Alkaline Phosphatase

SYNONYM/ACRONYM: LAP, LAP score, LAP smear.

COMMON USE: To monitor response to therapy in Hodgkin's disease and diagnose other disorders of the hematological system such as aplastic anemia.

SPECIMEN: Whole blood (1 mL) collected in a lavender-top (EDTA) tube.

NORMAL FINDINGS: (Method: Microscopic evaluation of specially stained blood smears) 25 to 130 (score based on 0 to 4+ rating of 100 neutrophils).

DESCRIPTION: Alkaline phosphatase is an enzyme important for intracellular metabolic processes. It is present in the cytoplasm of neutrophilic granulocytes from the metamyelocyte to the segmented stage. Leukocyte alkaline phosphatase (LAP) concentrations may be altered by the presence of infection, stress, chronic inflammatory diseases, Hodgkin's disease, and hematological disorders. Levels are low in leukemic leukocytes and high in normal white blood cells (WBCs), making this test useful as a supportive test in the differential diagnosis of leukemia. It should be noted that test results must be correlated with the patient's condition because LAP levels increase toward normal in response to therapy.

INDICATIONS
• Differentiate chronic myelocytic leukemia from other disorders that increase the WBC count
• Monitor response of Hodgkin's disease to therapy

POTENTIAL DIAGNOSIS

Increased in
Conditions that result in an increase in leukocytes in all stages of maturity will reflect a corresponding increase in LAP.

• Aplastic leukemia
• Chronic inflammation
• Down's syndrome
• Hairy cell leukemia
• Hodgkin's disease
• Leukemia (acute and chronic lymphoblastic)
• Myelofibrosis with myeloid metaplasia
• Multiple myeloma
• Polycythemia vera *(increase in all blood cell lines, including leukocytes)*
• Pregnancy
• Stress
• Thrombocytopenia

Decreased in
• Chronic myelogenous leukemia
• Hereditary hypophosphatemia *(insufficient phosphorus levels)*
• Idiopathic thrombocytopenia purpura
• Nephrotic syndrome *(excessive loss of phosphorus)*
• Paroxysmal nocturnal hemoglobinuria *(possibly related to the*

absence of LAP and other proteins anchored to the red blood cell wall, resulting in complement-mediated hemolysis
• Sickle cell anemia
• Sideroblastic anemia

CRITICAL FINDINGS: N/A

INTERFERING FACTORS
Drugs that may increase the LAP score include steroids.

NURSING IMPLICATIONS AND PROCEDURE

PRETEST:
▶ Positively identify the patient using at least two unique identifiers before providing care, treatment, or services.
▶ *Patient Teaching:* Inform the patient this test can assist in evaluating for blood disorders.
▶ Obtain a history of the patient's complaints, including a list of known allergens, especially allergies or sensitivities to latex.
▶ Obtain a history of the patient's hematopoietic and immune systems, symptoms, and results of previously performed laboratory tests and diagnostic and surgical procedures.
▶ Obtain a list of the patient's current medications, including herbs, nutritional supplements, and nutraceuticals (see Appendix F).
▶ Review the procedure with the patient. Inform the patient that specimen collection takes approximately 5 to 10 min. Address concerns about pain and explain that there may be some discomfort during the venipuncture.
▶ *Sensitivity to social and cultural issues,* as well as concern for modesty, is important in providing psychological support before, during, and after the procedure.
▶ There are no food, fluid, or medication restrictions unless by medical direction.

INTRATEST:
▶ If the patient has a history of allergic reaction to latex, avoid the use of equipment containing latex.

Instruct the patient to cooperate fully and to follow directions. Direct the patient to breathe normally and to avoid unnecessary movement. Observe standard precautions, and follow the general guidelines in Appendix A. Positively identify the patient, and label the appropriate specimen container with the corresponding patient demographics, initials of the person collecting the specimen, date, and time of collection. Perform a venipuncture.

Remove the needle and apply direct pressure with dry gauze to stop bleeding. Observe/assess venipuncture site for bleeding or hematoma formation and secure gauze with adhesive bandage.

Promptly transport the specimen to the laboratory for processing and analysis.

POST-TEST:

A report of the results will be made available to the requesting health-care provider (HCP), who will discuss the results with the patient.

Instruct the patient to avoid exposure to infection if WBC count is decreased. Recognize anxiety related to test results, and be supportive of perceived loss of independence and fear of shortened life expectancy. Discuss the implications of abnormal test results on the patient's lifestyle. Provide teaching and information regarding the clinical implications of the test results, as appropriate. Educate the patient regarding access to counseling services.

Reinforce information given by the patient's HCP regarding further testing, treatment, or referral to another HCP. Answer any questions or address any concerns voiced by the patient or family.

Depending on the results of this procedure, additional testing may be performed to evaluate or monitor progression of the disease process and determine the need for a change in therapy. Evaluate test results in relation to the patient's symptoms and other tests performed.

RELATED MONOGRAPHS:

Related tests include biopsy bone marrow, calcium, CBC, CBC platelet count, CBC WBC count and differential, CT thoracic, gallium scan, Ham's test, Hgb electrophoresis, hemosiderin, IFE, immunoglobulins, iron, laparoscopy abdominal, liver and spleen scan, lymphangiogram, mediastinoscopy, phosphorus, and sickle cell screen.

Refer to the Hematopoietic and Immune systems tables at the end of the book for related tests by body system.

Lipase

SYNONYM/ACRONYM: Triacylglycerol acylhydrolase.

COMMON USE: To assess for pancreatic disease related to inflammation, tumor, or cyst, specific to the diagnosis of pancreatitis.

SPECIMEN: Serum (1 mL) collected in a red- or tiger-top tube. Plasma (1 mL) collected in a green-top (heparin) tube is also acceptable.

NORMAL FINDINGS: (Method: Enzymatic spectrophotometry)

Conventional & SI Units

Newborn–older adult
0–60 units/L

DESCRIPTION: Lipases are digestive enzymes secreted by the pancreas into the duodenum. Different lipolytic enzymes have specific substrates, but overall activity is collectively described as lipase. Lipase participates in fat digestion by breaking down triglycerides into fatty acids and glycerol. Lipase is released into the bloodstream when damage occurs to the pancreatic acinar cells. Its presence in the blood indicates pancreatic disease because the pancreas is the only organ that secretes this enzyme.

INDICATIONS

* Assist in the diagnosis of acute and chronic pancreatitis
* Assist in the diagnosis of pancreatic carcinoma

POTENTIAL DIAGNOSIS

Increased in

Lipase is contained in pancreatic tissue and is released into the serum when cell damage or necrosis occurs.

* Acute cholecystitis
* Obstruction of the pancreatic duct
* Pancreatic carcinoma (early)
* Pancreatic cyst or pseudocyst
* Pancreatic inflammation
* Pancreatitis (acute and chronic)
* Renal failure *(related to decreased renal excretion)*

Decreased in: N/A

CRITICAL FINDINGS: N/A

INTERFERING FACTORS

* Drugs that may increase lipase levels include acetaminophen, asparaginase, azathioprine, calcitriol, cholinergics, codeine, deoxycholate, diazoxide, didanosine, felbamate, glycocholate, hydrocortisone, indomethacin, meperidine, methacholine, methylprednisolone, metolazone, morphine, narcotics, nitrofurantoin, pancreozymin, pegaspargase, pentazocine, and taurocholate.
* Drugs that may decrease lipase levels include protamine and saline (IV infusions).
* Endoscopic retrograde cholangiopancreatography may increase lipase levels.
* Serum lipase levels increase with hemodialysis. Therefore, predialysis specimens should be collected for lipase analysis.

NURSING IMPLICATIONS AND PROCEDURE

PRETEST:

* Positively identify the patient using at least two unique identifiers before providing care, treatment, or services.
* *Patient Teaching:* Inform the patient this test can assist in diagnosing pancreatitis.
* Obtain a history of the patient's complaints, including a list of known allergens, especially allergies or sensitivities to latex.
* Obtain a history of the patient's gastrointestinal and hepatobiliary systems, symptoms, and results of previously performed laboratory tests and diagnostic and surgical procedures.
* Note any recent procedures that can interfere with test results.
* Obtain a list of the patient's current medications, including herbs, nutritional supplements, and nutraceuticals (see Appendix F).

▸ Review the procedure with the patient. Inform the patient that specimen collection takes approximately 5 to 10 min. Address concerns about pain and explain that there may be some discomfort during the venipuncture.

▸ *Sensitivity to social and cultural issues,* as well as concern for modesty, is important in providing psychological support before, during, and after the procedure.

▸ There are no food, fluid, or medication restrictions unless by medical direction.

NTRATEST:

▸ If the patient has a history of allergic reaction to latex, avoid the use of equipment containing latex.

▸ Instruct the patient to cooperate fully and to follow directions. Direct the patient to breathe normally and to avoid unnecessary movement.

▸ Observe standard precautions, and follow the general guidelines in Appendix A. Positively identify the patient, and label the appropriate specimen container with the corresponding patient demographics, initials of the person collecting the specimen, date, and time of collection. Perform a venipuncture.

▸ Remove the needle and apply direct pressure with dry gauze to stop bleeding. Observe/assess venipuncture site for bleeding or hematoma formation and secure gauze with adhesive bandage.

▸ Promptly transport the specimen to the laboratory for processing and analysis.

POST-TEST:

▸ A report of the results will be made available to the requesting health-care provider (HCP), who will discuss the results with the patient.

▸ *Nutritional Considerations:* Instruct the patient to ingest small, frequent meals if he or she has a gastrointestinal disorder; advise the patient to consider other dietary alterations as well. After acute symptoms subside and bowel sounds return, patients are usually prescribed a clear liquid diet, progressing to a low-fat, high-carbohydrate diet.

▸ Administer vitamin B_{12}, as ordered, to the patient with decreased lipase levels, especially if his or her disease prevents adequate absorption of the vitamin.

▸ Encourage the alcoholic patient to avoid alcohol and to seek appropriate counseling for substance abuse.

▸ Reinforce information given by the patient's HCP regarding further testing, treatment, or referral to another HCP. Answer any questions or address any concerns voiced by the patient or family.

▸ Depending on the results of this procedure, additional testing may be performed to evaluate or monitor progression of the disease process and determine the need for a change in therapy. Evaluate test results in relation to the patient's symptoms and other tests performed.

RELATED MONOGRAPHS:

▸ Related tests include ALT, ALP, amylase, AST, bilirubin, calcitonin stimulation, calcium, cancer antigens, cholangiography percutaneous transhepatic, cholesterol, CBC, CBC WCB count and diff, ERCP, fecal fat, GGT, hepatobiliary scan, magnesium, MRI pancreas, mumps serology, pleural fluid analysis, peritoneal fluid analysis, triglycerides, US abdomen, and US pancreas.

▸ Refer to the Gastrointestinal and Hepatobiliary systems tables at the end of the book for related tests by body system.

Lipoprotein Electrophoresis

SYNONYM/ACRONYM: Lipid fractionation; lipoprotein phenotyping; 3ga₁-lipoprotein cholesterol, high-density lipoprotein (HDL); β-lipoprotein cholesterol, low-density lipoprotein (LDL); pre-β-lipoprotein cholesterol, very-low-density lipoprotein (VLDL).

COMMON USE: To assist in categorizing lipoprotein as an indicator of cardiac health.

SPECIMEN: Serum (3 mL) collected in a red- or tiger-top tube.

NORMAL FINDINGS: (Method: Electrophoresis and 4°C test for specimen appearance) There is no quantitative interpretation of this test. The specimen appearance and electrophoretic pattern is visually interpreted.

Hyperlipoproteinemia: Fredrickson Type	Specimen Appearance	Electrophoretic Pattern
Type I	Clear with creamy top layer	Heavy chylomicron band
Type IIa	Clear	Heavy β band
Type IIb	Clear or faintly turbid	Heavy β and pre-β bands
Type III	Slightly to moderately turbid	Heavy β band
Type IV	Slightly to moderately turbid	Heavy pre-β band
Type V	Slightly to moderately turbid with creamy top layer	Intense chylomicron band and heavy β and pre-β bands

POTENTIAL DIAGNOSIS

• *Type I:* Hyperlipoproteinemia, or increased chylomicrons, can be primary, *resulting from an inherited deficiency of lipoprotein lipase,* or secondary, *caused by uncontrolled diabetes, systemic lupus erythematosus, and dysgammaglobulinemia.* Total cholesterol is normal to moderately elevated, and triglycerides (mostly exogenous chylomicrons) are grossly elevated. If the condition is inherited, symptoms will appear in childhood.

• *Type IIa:* Hyperlipoproteinemia can be primary, *resulting from*

inherited characteristics, or secondary, *caused by uncontrolled hypothyroidism, nephrotic syndrome, and dysgammaglobulinemia.* Total cholesterol is elevated, triglycerides are normal, and LDLC is elevated. If the condition is inherited, symptoms will appear in childhood.

• *Type IIb:* Hyperlipoproteinemia *can occur for the same reasons as in type IIa.* Total cholesterol, triglycerides, and LDLC are all elevated.

• *Type III:* Hyperlipoproteinemia can be primary, *resulting from inherited characteristics,* or secondary, *caused by hypothyroidism, uncontrolled diabetes, alcoholism, and dysgammaglobulinemia.* Total cholesterol and triglycerides are elevated, whereas LDLC is normal.

Type IV: Hyperlipoproteinemia can be primary, *resulting from inherited characteristics,* or secondary, *caused by poorly controlled diabetes, alcoholism, nephrotic syndrome, chronic renal failure, and dysgammaglobulinemia.* Total cholesterol is nor-

mal to moderately elevated, triglycerides are moderately to grossly elevated, and LDLC is normal.

• *Type V:* Hyperlipoproteinemia can be primary, *resulting from inherited characteristics,* or secondary, *caused by uncontrolled diabetes, alcoholism, nephrotic syndrome, and dysgammaglobulinemia.* Total cholesterol is normal to moderately elevated, triglycerides are grossly elevated, and LDLC is normal.

CRITICAL FINDINGS: N/A

Find and print out the full monograph at DavisPlus (davisplus.fadavis .com, keyword Van Leeuwen).

Liver and Spleen Scan

SYNONYM/ACRONYM: Liver and spleen scintigraphy, radionuclide liver scan, spleen scan.

COMMON USE: To visualize and assess the liver and spleen related to tumors, inflammation, cysts, abscess, trauma, and portal hypertension.

AREA OF APPLICATION: Abdomen.

CONTRAST: IV radioactive technetium-99m sulfur colloid.

DESCRIPTION: The liver and spleen scan is performed to help diagnose abnormalities in the function and structure of the liver and spleen. It is often performed in combination with lung scanning to help diagnose masses or inflammation in the diaphragmatic area. This procedure is useful for evaluating right-upper-quadrant pain, metastatic disease, jaundice, cirrhosis, ascites, traumatic infarction, and radiation-induced organ cellular necrosis. Technetium-99m (Tc-99m) sulfur

colloid is injected IV and rapidly taken up through phagocytosis by the reticuloendothelial cells, which normally function to remove particulate matter, including radioactive colloids in the liver and spleen. False-negative results may occur in patients with space-occupying lesions (e.g., tumors, cysts, abscesses) smaller than 2 cm. This scan can detect portal hypertension, demonstrated by a greater uptake of the radionuclide in the spleen than in the liver. Single-photon emission computed tomography (SPECT) has significantly improved the resolution and accuracy of liver scanning. SPECT enables images to be recorded from multiple angles around the body and reconstructed by a computer to produce images or "slices" representing the organ at different levels. For evaluation of a suspected hemangioma, the patient's red blood cells are combined with Tc-99m and images are recorded over the liver. To confirm the diagnosis, liver and spleen scans are done in conjunction with computed tomography (CT), magnetic resonance imaging (MRI), ultrasonography (US), and SPECT scans and interpreted in light of the results of liver function tests.

INDICATIONS

- Assess the condition of the liver and spleen after abdominal trauma
- Detect a bacterial or amebic abscess
- Detect and differentiate between primary and metastatic tumor focal disease
- Detect benign tumors, such as adenoma and cavernous hemangioma
- Detect cystic focal disease
- Detect diffuse hepatocellular disease, such as hepatitis and cirrhosis
- Detect infiltrative processes that affect the liver, such as sarcoidosis and amyloidosis
- Determine superior vena cava obstruction or Budd-Chiari syndrome
- Differentiate between splenomegaly and hepatomegaly
- Evaluate the effects of lower abdominal trauma, such as internal hemorrhage
- Evaluate jaundice
- Evaluate liver and spleen damage caused by radiation therapy or toxic drug therapy
- Evaluate palpable abdominal masses

POTENTIAL DIAGNOSIS

Normal findings in
- Normal size, contour, position, and function of the liver and spleen

Abnormal findings in
- Abscesses
- Cirrhosis
- Cysts
- Hemangiomas
- Hematomas
- Hepatitis
- Hodgkin's disease
- Infarction
- Infection
- Infiltrative process (amyloidosis and sarcoidosis)
- Inflammation of the diaphragmatic area
- Metastatic tumors
- Nodular hyperplasia
- Portal hypertension
- Primary benign or malignant tumors
- Traumatic lesions

CRITICAL FINDINGS
- Visceral injury

It is essential that critical diagnoses be communicated immediately to the appropriate health care provider (HCP). A listing of these diagnoses varies among facilities. Note and immediately report to the HCP abnormal results and related symptoms. Timely notification of critical values for lab or diagnostic studies is a role expectation of the professional nurse. Notification processes will vary among facilities. Upon receipt of the critical value the information should be read back to the caller to verify accuracy. Most policies require immediate notification of the primary HCP, hospitalist, or on-call HCP. Reported information includes the patient's name, unique identifiers, critical value ame of the person giving the report, nd name of the person receiving the eport. Documentation of notification hould be made in the medical record vith the name of the HCP notified, ime and date of notification, and any orders received. Any delay in a timely eport of a critical value may require ompletion of a notification form vith review by Risk Management.

NTERFERING FACTORS

This procedure is contraindicated for

Patients who are pregnant or suspected of being pregnant, unless the potential benefits of the procedure far outweigh the risks to the fetus and mother.

Factors that may impair clear imaging

Inability of the patient to cooperate or remain still during the procedure because of age, significant pain, or mental status.

Metallic objects (e.g., jewelry, body rings) within the examination field, which may inhibit organ visualization and cause unclear images.

Other nuclear scans done within the preceding 24 to 48 hr.

Other considerations

The scan may fail to detect focal lesions smaller than 2 cm in diameter.

Improper injection of the radionuclide may allow the tracer to seep deep into the muscle tissue, producing erroneous hot spots. Consultation with a health-care provider (HCP) should occur before the procedure for radiation safety concerns regarding younger patients or patients who are lactating.

Risks associated with radiation overexposure can result from frequent x-ray or radionuclide procedures. Personnel working in

the examination area should wear badges to record their level of radiation exposure.

NURSING IMPLICATIONS AND PROCEDURE

PRETEST:

▶ Positively identify the patient using at least two unique identifiers before providing care, treatment, or services.

Patient Teaching: Inform the patient this procedure can assist in evaluating liver and spleen function.

▶ Obtain a history of the patient's complaints, including a list of known allergens, especially allergies or sensitivities to latex, iodine, seafood, anesthetics, or contrast medium.

▶ Obtain a history of the patient's hematopoietic, hepatobiliary, and immune systems; symptoms; and results of previously performed laboratory tests and diagnostic and surgical procedures.

▶ Note any recent procedures that can interfere with test results, including examinations using iodine-based contrast medium.

▶ Record the date of the last menstrual period and determine the possibility of pregnancy in perimenopausal women.

▶ Obtain a list of the patient's current medications, including herbs, nutritional supplements, and nutraceuticals (see Appendix F).

▶ Review the procedure with the patient. Address concerns about pain related to the procedure and explain that some pain may be experienced during the test, or there may be moments of discomfort. Reassure the patient that the radionuclide poses no radioactive hazard and rarely produces side effects. Inform the patient the procedure is performed in a nuclear medicine department by an HCP specializing in this procedure, with support staff, and takes approximately 30 to 60 min.

Sensitivity to social and cultural issues, as well as concern for modesty, is important in providing psychological support before, during, and after the procedure.

▶ Instruct the patient to remove jewelry and other metallic objects from the area to be examined.

▶ There are no food, fluid, or medication restrictions unless by medical direction. *Make sure a written and informed consent has been signed prior to the procedure and before administering any medications.*

INTRATEST:

▶ Observe standard precautions, and follow the general guidelines in Appendix A. Positively identify the patient.

▶ Ensure that the patient has removed all external metallic objects from the area to be examined prior to the procedure.

▶ If the patient has a history of allergic reactions to any substance or drug, administer ordered prophylactic steroids or antihistamines before the procedure.

▶ Have emergency equipment readily available.

▶ Instruct the patient to void prior to the procedure and to change into the gown, robe, and foot coverings provided.

▶ Instruct the patient to cooperate fully and to follow directions. Instruct the patient to remain still throughout the procedure because movement produces unreliable results.

▶ Administer sedative to a child or to an uncooperative adult, as ordered.

▶ Place the patient in a supine position on a flat table with foam wedges, which help maintain position and immobilization.

▶ IV radionuclide is administered, and the abdomen is scanned immediately to screen for vascular lesions with images taken in various positions.

▶ Monitor the patient for complications related to the procedure (e.g., allergic reaction, anaphylaxis, bronchospasm).

▶ Remove the needle or catheter and apply a pressure dressing over the puncture site.

▶ Observe/assess the needle/catheter insertion site for bleeding, inflammation, or hematoma formation.

▶ The patient may be imaged by SPECT techniques to further clarify areas of suspicious radionuclide localization.

POST-TEST:

▶ A report of the results will be made available to the requesting HCP, who will discuss the results with the patient.

▶ Instruct the patient to resume usual medication and activity, as directed by the HCP.

▶ Unless contraindicated, advise patient to drink increased amounts of fluids for 24 to 48 hr to eliminate the radionuclide from the body. Inform the patient that radionuclide is eliminated from the body within 6 to 24 hr.

▶ No other radionuclide tests should be scheduled for 24 to 48 hr after this procedure.

▶ Instruct the patient in the care and assessment of the injection site.

▶ If a woman who is breastfeeding must have a nuclear scan, she should not breastfeed the infant until the radionuclide has been eliminated. This could take as long as 3 days. She should be instructed to express the milk and discard it during the 3-day period to prevent cessation of milk production.

▶ Instruct the patient to immediately flush the toilet and to meticulously wash hands with soap and water after each voiding for 24 hr after the procedure.

▶ Instruct all caregivers to wear gloves when discarding urine for 24 hr after the procedure. Wash gloved hands with soap and water before removing gloves. Then wash hands after the gloves are removed.

▶ *Nutritional Considerations:* A low-fat, low-cholesterol, and low-sodium diet should be consumed to reduce current disease processes. High fat consumption increases the amount of bile acids in the colon and should be avoided.

▶ Recognize anxiety related to test results, and be supportive of perceived loss of independent function. Discuss the implications of abnormal test results on the patient's lifestyle. Provide teaching and information regarding the clinical implications of the test results, as appropriate.

▶ Reinforce information given by the patient's HCP regarding further testing, treatment, or referral to another HCP.

Answer any questions or address any concerns voiced by the patient or family.

Depending on the results of this procedure, additional testing may be needed to evaluate or monitor progression of the disease process and determine the need for a change in therapy. Evaluate test results in relation to the patient's symptoms and other tests performed.

RELATED MONOGRAPHS:

Related tests include ALT, antibodies antimitochondrial, AST, bilirubin, biopsy liver, CT abdomen, CT biliary tract and liver, GGT, HAV, HBV, HCV, hepatobiliary scan, MRI abdomen, and US liver.
Refer to the Hematopoietic, Hepatobiliary, and Immune systems tables at the end of the book for related tests by body system.

Lung Perfusion Scan

SYNONYM/ACRONYM: Lung perfusion scintigraphy, lung scintiscan, pulmonary scan, radioactive perfusion scan, radionuclide lung scan, ventilation-perfusion scan, V/Q scan.

COMMON USE: To assess pulmonary blood flow to assist in diagnosis of pulmonary embolism.

AREA OF APPLICATION: Chest/thorax.

CONTRAST: IV radioactive material, usually macroaggregated albumin (MAA).

DESCRIPTION: The lung perfusion scan is a nuclear medicine study performed to evaluate a patient for pulmonary embolus (PE) or other pulmonary disorders. Technetium (Tc-99m) is injected IV and distributed throughout the pulmonary vasculature because of the gravitational effect on perfusion. The scan, which produces a visual image of pulmonary blood flow, is useful in diagnosing or confirming pulmonary vascular obstruction. The diameter of the IV-injected macroaggregated albumin (MAA) is larger than that of the pulmonary capillaries; therefore, the MAA temporarily becomes lodged in the pulmonary vasculature. A gamma camera detects the radiation emitted from the injected radioactive material,

and a representative image of the lung is obtained. This procedure is often done in conjunction with the lung ventilation scan to obtain clinical information that assists in differentiating among the many possible pathological conditions revealed by the procedure. The results are correlated with other diagnostic studies, such as pulmonary function, chest x-ray, pulmonary angiography, and arterial blood gases. A recent chest x-ray is essential for accurate interpretation of the lung perfusion scan. An area of nonperfusion seen in the same area as a pulmonary parenchymal abnormality on the chest x-ray indicates that a PE is not present; the defect may represent some other pathological condition, such as pneumonia.

INDICATIONS

- Aid in the diagnosis of PE in a patient with a normal chest x-ray
- Detect malignant tumor
- Differentiate between PE and other pulmonary diseases, such as pneumonia, pulmonary effusion, atelectasis, asthma, bronchitis, emphysema, and tumors
- Evaluate perfusion changes associated with congestive heart failure and pulmonary hypertension
- Evaluate pulmonary function preoperatively in a patient with pulmonary disease

POTENTIAL DIAGNOSIS

Normal findings in
- Diffuse and homogeneous uptake of the radioactive material by the lungs

Abnormal findings in
- Asthma
- Atelectasis
- Bronchitis
- Chronic obstructive pulmonary disease
- Emphysema
- Left atrial or pulmonary hypertension
- Lung displacement by fluid or chest masses
- Pneumonia
- Pneumonitis
- PE
- Tuberculosis

CRITICAL FINDINGS ❖

- PE

It is essential that critical diagnoses be communicated immediately to the appropriate health-care provider (HCP). A listing of these diagnoses varies among facilities. Note and immediately report to the HCP abnormal results and related symptoms. Timely notification of critical values for lab or diagnostic studies is a role expectation of the professional nurse. Notification processes will vary among facilities.

Upon receipt of the critical value the information should be read back to the caller to verify accuracy. Most policies require immediate notification of the primary HCP, hospitalist, or on-call HCP. Reported information includes the patient's name, unique identifiers, critical value, name of the person giving the report, and name of the person receiving the report. Documentation of notification should be made in the medical record with the name of the HCP notified, time and date of notification, and any orders received. Any delay in a timely report of a critical value may require completion of a notification form with review by Risk Management.

INTERFERING FACTORS

This procedure is contraindicated for
- Patients who are pregnant or suspected of being pregnant, unless the potential benefits of the procedure far outweigh the risks to the fetus and mother.
- Patients with atrial and ventricular septal defects, because the MAA particles will not reach the lungs.
- Patients with pulmonary hypertension.

Factors that may impair clear imaging
- Inability of the patient to cooperate or remain still during the procedure because of age, significant pain, or mental status.
- Metallic objects (e.g., jewelry, body rings) within the examination field, which may inhibit organ visualization and cause unclear images.
- Other nuclear scans done on the same day.

Other considerations
- Improper injection of the radionuclide may allow the tracer to seep deep into the muscle tissue, producing erroneous hot spots.

Consultation with an HCP should occur before the procedure for radiation safety concerns regarding younger patients or patients who are lactating.

Risks associated with radiation overexposure can result from frequent x-ray or radionuclide procedures. Personnel working in the examination area should wear badges to record their level of radiation.

NURSING IMPLICATIONS AND PROCEDURE

PRETEST:

Positively identify the patient using at least two unique identifiers before providing care, treatment, or services.

Patient Teaching: Inform the patient this procedure can assist in assessing blood flow to the lungs.

Obtain a history of the patient's complaints, including a list of known allergens, especially allergies or sensitivities to latex, iodine, seafood, contrast medium, anesthetics, or dyes.

Obtain a history of the patient's respiratory system, symptoms, and results of previously performed laboratory tests and diagnostic and surgical procedures.

Note any recent procedures that can interfere with test results, including examinations using iodine-based contrast medium.

Record the date of the last menstrual period and determine the possibility of pregnancy in perimenopausal women.

Obtain a list of the patient's current medications, including herbs, nutritional supplements, and nutraceuticals (see Appendix F).

Review the procedure with the patient. Address concerns about pain related to the procedure and explain that some pain may be experienced during the test, or there may be moments of discomfort. Reassure the patient that the radionuclide poses no radioactive hazard and rarely produces side effects. Inform the patient that the procedure is performed in a nuclear medicine department, by an HCP specializing in this procedure, with support staff, and takes approximately 60 min.

Sensitivity to social and cultural issues, as well as concern for modesty, is important in providing psychological support before, during, and after the procedure.

Instruct the patient to remove jewelry and other metallic objects from the area to be examined prior to the procedure.

There are no food, fluid, or medication restrictions unless by medical direction.

Make sure a written and informed consent has been signed prior to the procedure and before administering any medications.

INTRATEST:

Observe standard precautions, and follow the general guidelines in Appendix A. Positively identify the patient.

Ensure that the patient has removed all external metallic objects from the area to be examined prior to the procedure.

If the patient has a history of allergic reactions to any substance or drug, administer ordered prophylactic steroids or antihistamines before the procedure.

Have emergency equipment readily available.

Instruct the patient to void prior to the procedure and to change into the gown, robe, and foot coverings provided.

Record baseline vital signs and assess neurological status. Protocols may vary among facilities.

Instruct the patient to cooperate fully and to follow directions. Instruct the patient to remain still throughout the procedure because movement produces unreliable results.

Administer a sedative to a child or to an uncooperative adult, as ordered.

Place the patient in a supine position on a flat table with foam wedges, which help maintain position and immobilization.

IV radionuclide is administered, and the abdomen is scanned immediately to screen for vascular lesions with images taken in various positions.

▶ Monitor the patient for complications related to the procedure (e.g., allergic reaction, anaphylaxis, bronchospasm).

▶ Remove the needle or catheter and apply a pressure dressing over the puncture site.

▶ Observe/assess the needle/catheter insertion site for bleeding, inflammation, or hematoma formation.

POST-TEST:

▶ A report of the results will be made available to the requesting HCP, who will discuss the results with the patient.

▶ Unless contraindicated, advise patient to drink increased amounts of fluids for 24 to 48 hr to eliminate the radionuclide from the body. Inform the patient that radionuclide is eliminated from the body within 6 to 24 hr.

▶ No other radionuclide tests should be scheduled for 24 to 48 hr after this procedure.

▶ Monitor vital signs and neurological status every 15 min for 1 hr, then every 2 hr for 4 hr, and then as ordered by the HCP. Compare with baseline values. Protocols may vary among facilities.

▶ Instruct the patient to resume usual medication and activity, as directed by the HCP.

▶ Observe for delayed allergic reactions, such as rash, urticaria, tachycardia, hyperpnea, hypertension, palpitations, nausea, or vomiting.

▶ Instruct the patient to immediately report symptoms such as fast heart rate, difficulty breathing, skin rash, itching, chest pain, persistent right shoulder pain, or abdominal pain. Immediately report symptoms to the appropriate HCP.

▶ Observe/assess the needle/catheter insertion site for bleeding, inflammation, or hematoma formation.

▶ Instruct the patient in the care and assessment of the injection site.

▶ If a woman who is breastfeeding must have a nuclear scan, she should not breastfeed the infant until the radionuclide has been eliminated. This could take as long as 3 days. She should be instructed to express the milk and discard it during the 3-day period to prevent cessation of milk production.

▶ Instruct the patient to immediately flush the toilet and to meticulously wash hands with soap and water after each voiding for 24 hr after the procedure.

▶ Instruct all caregivers to wear gloves when discarding urine for 24 hr after the procedure. Wash gloved hands with soap and water before removing gloves. Then wash hands after the gloves are removed.

▶ Recognize anxiety related to test results, and be supportive of perceived loss of independent function. Discuss the implications of abnormal test results on the patient's lifestyle. Provide teaching and information regarding the clinical implications of the test results, as appropriate.

▶ Reinforce information given by the patient's HCP regarding further testing, treatment, or referral to another HCP. Answer any questions or address any concerns voiced by the patient or family.

▶ Depending on the results of this procedure, additional testing may be needed to evaluate or monitor progression of the disease process and determine the need for a change in therapy. Evaluate test results in relation to the patient's symptoms and other tests performed.

RELATED MONOGRAPHS:

▶ Related tests include α-1 AT, eosinophil count, ACE, alveolar/arterial gradient, angiography pulmonary, biopsy lung, blood gases, blood pool imaging, bronchoscopy, carbon dioxide, chest x-ray, CBC, CBC WBC count and differential, CT thoracic, culture and smear mycobacteria, culture blood, culture throat, culture sputum, culture viral, cytology sputum, ESR, IgE, gallium scan, lung ventilation scan, MRI chest, mediastinoscopy, plethysmography, pleural fluid analysis, PET heart, PFT, pulse oximetry, and TB skin tests.

▶ Refer to the Respiratory System table at the end of the book for related tests by body system.

Lung Ventilation Scan

SYNONYM/ACRONYM: Aerosol lung scan, radioactive ventilation scan, ventilation scan, VQ lung scan, xenon lung scan.

COMMON USE: To assess pulmonary ventilation to assist in diagnosis of pulmonary embolism.

AREA OF APPLICATION: Chest/thorax.

CONTRAST: Done with inhaled radioactive material (xenon gas or technetium-DTPA).

DESCRIPTION: The lung ventilation scan is a nuclear medicine study performed to evaluate a patient for pulmonary embolus (PE) or other pulmonary disorders. It can evaluate respiratory function (i.e., demonstrating areas of the lung that are patent and capable of ventilation) and dysfunction (e.g., parenchymal abnormalities affecting ventilation, such as pneumonia). The procedure is performed after the patient inhales air mixed with a radioactive gas through a face mask and mouthpiece. The radioactive gas delineates areas of the lung during ventilation. The distribution of the gas throughout the lung is measured in three phases:

* *Wash-in phase:* Phase during buildup of the radioactive gas
* *Equilibrium phase:* Phase after the patient rebreathes from a closed delivery system
* *Wash-out phase:* Phase after the radioactive gas has been removed

This procedure is usually performed along with a lung perfusion scan. When PE is present, ventilation scans display a normal wash-in and wash-out of radioactivity from the lung areas.

Parenchymal disease responsible for perfusion abnormalities will produce abnormal wash-in and wash-out phases. This test can be used to quantify regional ventilation in patients with pulmonary disease.

INDICATIONS

* Aid in the diagnosis of PE
* Differentiate between PE and other pulmonary diseases, such as pneumonia, pulmonary effusion, atelectasis, asthma, bronchitis, emphysema, and tumors
* Evaluate regional respiratory function
* Identify areas of the lung that are capable of ventilation
* Locate hypoventilation (regional), which can result from chronic obstructive pulmonary disease (COPD) or excessive smoking

POTENTIAL DIAGNOSIS

Normal findings in

* Equal distribution of radioactive gas throughout both lungs and a normal wash-out phase

Abnormal findings in

* Atelectasis
* Bronchitis

- Bronchogenic carcinoma
- COPD
- Emphysema
- PE
- Pneumonia
- Regional hypoventilation
- Sarcoidosis
- Tuberculosis
- Tumor

CRITICAL FINDINGS ◈
- PE

It is essential that critical diagnoses be communicated immediately to the appropriate health care provider (HCP). A listing of these diagnoses varies among facilities. Note and immediately report to the HCP abnormal results and related symptoms. Timely notification of critical values for lab or diagnostic studies is a role expectation of the professional nurse. Notification processes will vary among facilities. Upon receipt of the critical value the information should be read back to the caller to verify accuracy. Most policies require immediate notification of the primary HCP, hospitalist, or on-call HCP. Reported information includes the patient's name, critical value, name of the person giving the report, and name of the person receiving the report. Documentation of notification should be made in the medical record with the name of the HCP notified, time and date of notification, and any orders received. Any delay in a timely report of a critical value may require completion of a notification form with review by Risk Management.

INTERFERING FACTORS

This procedure is contraindicated for
- Patients who are pregnant or suspected of being pregnant, unless the potential benefits of the procedure far outweigh the risks to the fetus and mother.

Factors that may impair clear imaging
- Inability of the patient to cooperate or remain still during the procedure because of age, significant pain, or mental status.
- Metallic objects (e.g., jewelry, body rings) within the examination field, which may inhibit organ visualization and cause unclear images.
- Other nuclear scans done within the preceding 24 to 48 hr.

Other considerations
- The presence of conditions that affect perfusion or ventilation (e.g., tumors that obstruct the pulmonary artery, vasculitis, pulmonary edema, sickle cell disease, parasitic disease, emphysema, effusion, infection) can simulate a perfusion defect similar to PE.
- Consultation with a health-care provider (HCP) should occur before the procedure for radiation safety concerns regarding younger patients or patients who are lactating.
- Risks associated with radiation overexposure can result from frequent x-ray or radionuclide procedures. Personnel working in the examination area should wear badges to record their level of radiation exposure.

NURSING IMPLICATIONS AND PROCEDURE

PRETEST:

▶ Positively identify the patient using at least two unique identifiers before providing care, treatment, or services.
▶ *Patient Teaching:* Inform the patient this procedure can assist in assessing air flow to the lungs.
▶ Obtain a history of the patient's complaints, including a list of known allergens, especially allergies or sensitivities to latex, iodine, seafood, contrast medium, anesthetics, or dyes.

- Obtain a history of the patient's respiratory system, symptoms, and results of previously performed laboratory tests and diagnostic and surgical procedures.
- Note any recent procedures that can interfere with test results, including examinations using iodine-based contrast medium.
- Record the date of the last menstrual period and determine the possibility of pregnancy in perimenopausal women.
- Obtain a list of the patient's current medications, including herbs, nutritional supplements, and nutraceuticals (see Appendix F).
- Review the procedure with the patient. Address concerns about pain related to the procedure and explain that some pain may be experienced during the test, and there may be moments of discomfort. Reassure the patient that the radionuclide poses no radioactive hazard and rarely produces side effects. Inform the patient that the procedure is performed in a nuclear medicine department, usually by an HCP who specializes in this procedure, with support staff, and takes approximately 30 to 60 min.
- *Sensitivity to social and cultural issues,* as well as concern for modesty, is important in providing psychological support before, during, and after the procedure.
- Instruct the patient to remove jewelry and other metallic objects from the area to be examined.
- There are no food, fluid, or medication restrictions unless by medical direction.
- *Make sure a written and informed consent has been signed prior to the procedure and before administering any medications.*

INTRATEST:

- Observe standard precautions, and follow the general guidelines in Appendix A. Positively identify the patient.
- Ensure that the patient has removed all external metallic objects from the area to be examined prior to the procedure.
- If the patient has a history of allergic reactions to any substance or drug, administer ordered prophylactic steroids or antihistamines before the procedure.
- Have emergency equipment readily available.
- Instruct the patient to void prior to the procedure and to change into the gown, robe, and foot coverings provided.
- Record baseline vital signs and assess neurological status. Protocols may vary among facilities.
- Instruct the patient to cooperate fully and to follow directions. Direct the patient to remain still throughout the procedure because movement produces unreliable results.
- Administer sedative to a child or to an uncooperative adult, as ordered.
- Place the patient in a supine position on a flat table with foam wedges, which help maintain position and immobilization.
- The radionuclide is administered through a mask, which is placed over the patient's nose and mouth. The patient is asked to hold his or her breath for a short period of time while the scan is taken.
- Monitor the patient for complications related to the procedure (e.g., allergic reaction, anaphylaxis, bronchospasm).

POST-TEST:

- A report of the results will be made available to the requesting HCP, who will discuss the results with the patient.
- Unless contraindicated, advise patient to drink increased amounts of fluids for 24 to 48 hr to eliminate the radionuclide from the body. Inform the patient that radionuclide is eliminated from the body within 6 to 24 hr.
- No other radionuclide tests should be scheduled for 24 to 48 hr after this procedure.
- Evaluate the patient's vital signs. Monitor vital signs and neurological status every 15 min for 1 hr, then every 2 hr for 4 hr, and then as ordered by the HCP. Compare with baseline values. Protocols may vary among facilities.
- Instruct the patient to resume medication or activity, as directed by the HCP.
- If a woman who is breastfeeding must have a nuclear scan, she should

not breastfeed the infant until the radionuclide has been eliminated. This could take as long as 3 days. She should be instructed to express the milk and discard it during the 3-day period to prevent cessation of milk production.

Instruct the patient to immediately flush the toilet and to meticulously wash hands with soap and water after each voiding for 24 hr after the procedure.

Instruct all caregivers to wear gloves when discarding urine for 24 hr after the procedure. Wash gloved hands with soap and water before removing gloves. Then wash hands after the gloves are removed.

Nutritional Considerations: A low-fat, low-cholesterol, and low-sodium diet should be consumed to reduce current disease processes and/or decrease risk of hypertension and coronary artery disease.

Recognize anxiety related to test results, and be supportive of perceived loss of independent function. Discuss the implications of abnormal test results on the patient's lifestyle. Provide teaching and information regarding the clinical implications of the test results, as appropriate.

Reinforce information given by the patient's HCP regarding further testing, treatment, or referral to another HCP. Answer any questions or address any concerns voiced by the patient or family.

Depending on the results of this procedure, additional testing may be needed to evaluate or monitor progression of the disease process and determine the need for a change in therapy. Evaluate test results in relation to the patient's symptoms and other tests performed.

RELATED MONOGRAPHS:

Related tests include α-1 antitrypsin, alveolar/arterial ratio, ACE, angiography pulmonary, biopsy lung, blood gases, blood pool imaging, bronchoscopy, carbon dioxide, chest x-ray, CBC, CBC WBC count and differential, CT thorax, culture and smear mycobacteria, culture blood, culture sputum, culture throat, culture viral, cytology sputum, D-dimer, gallium scan, lung perfusion scan, MRI chest, mediastinoscopy, plethysmography, pleural fluid analysis, PET heart, PFT, TB skin tests, US venous Doppler extremity studies, and venography.

Refer to the Respiratory System table at the end of the book for related tests by body system.

Lupus Anticoagulant Antibodies

SYNONYM/ACRONYM: Lupus inhibitor phospholipid type, lupus antiphospholipid antibodies, LA.

COMMON USE: To assess for systemic dysfunction related to anticoagulation and assist in diagnosing conditions such as lupus erythematosus and fetal loss.

SPECIMEN: Plasma (1 mL) collected in a completely filled blue-top (3.2% sodium citrate) tube. If the patient's hematocrit exceeds 55%, the volume of citrate in the collection tube must be adjusted.

NORMAL FINDINGS: (Method: Dilute Russell viper venom test time) Negative.

DESCRIPTION: Lupus anticoagulant (LA) antibodies are immunoglobulins, usually of the immunoglobulin G class. They are also called lupus antiphospholipid antibodies because they interfere with phospholipid-dependent coagulation tests such as activated partial thromboplastin time (aPTT) by reacting with the phospholipids in the test system. They are not associated with a bleeding disorder unless thrombocytopenia or antiprothrombin antibodies are already present. They are associated with an increased risk of thrombosis. The combination of noninflammatory thrombosis of blood vessels, low platelet count, and history of miscarriage is termed *antiphospholipid antibody syndrome* and is confirmed by the presence of at least one of the clinical criteria (vascular thrombosis confirmed by histopathology or imaging studies; pregnancy morbidity defined as either one or more unexplained deaths of a morphologically normal fetus at or beyond the 10th week of gestation, one or more premature births of a morphologically normal neonate before the 34th week of gestation due to eclampsia or severe pre-eclampsia, or three or more unexplained consecutive spontaneous abortions before the 10th week of gestation) and one of the laboratory criteria (ACA, IgG, or IgM, detectable at greater than 40 units on two or more occasions at least 12 weeks apart; or LA detectable on two or more occasions at least 12 weeks apart; or anti-β_2 glycoprotein 1 antibody, IgG, or IgM, detectable on two or more occasions at least 12 weeks apart, all measured by a standardized ELISA, according to recommended procedures).

INDICATIONS
- Evaluate prolonged aPTT
- Investigate reasons for fetal death

POTENTIAL DIAGNOSIS

Positive findings in
- Antiphospholipid antibody syndrome *(LA are nonspecific antibodies associated with this syndrome)*
- Fetal loss *(thrombosis associated with LA can form clots that lodge in the placenta and disrupt nutrition to the fetus)*
- Raynaud's disease *(LA can be detected with this condition and can cause vascular inflammation)*
- Rheumatoid arthritis *(LA can be detected with this condition and can cause vascular inflammation)*
- Systemic lupus erythematosus *(related to formation of thrombi as a result of LA binding to phospholipids on cell walls)*
- Thromboembolism *(related to formation of thrombi as a result of LA binding to phospholipids on cell walls)*

Negative findings in: N/A

CRITICAL FINDINGS: N/A

INTERFERING FACTORS
- Drugs that may cause a positive LA test result include calcium channel blockers, heparin, hydralazine, hydantoin, isoniazid, methyldopa, phenytoin, phenothiazine, procainamide, quinine, quinidine, and Thorazine.
- Placement of a tourniquet for longer than 1 min can result in venous stasis and changes in the concentration of plasma proteins to be measured. Platelet activation may also occur under these conditions, causing erroneous results.
- Vascular injury during phlebotomy can activate platelets and coagulation factors, causing erroneous results.

- Hemolyzed specimens must be rejected because hemolysis is an indication of platelet and coagulation factor activation.
- Icteric or lipemic specimens interfere with optical testing methods, producing erroneous results.
- Hematocrit greater than 55% may cause falsely prolonged results because of anticoagulant excess relative to plasma volume.
- Incompletely filled collection tubes, specimens contaminated with heparin, clotted specimens, or unprocessed specimens not delivered to the laboratory within 1 to 2 hr of collection should be rejected.

NURSING IMPLICATIONS AND PROCEDURE

PRETEST:

Positively identify the patient using at least two unique identifiers before providing care, treatment, or services.
Patient Teaching: Inform the patient that this test can assist in evaluation of clotting disorders.

Obtain a history of the patient's complaints, including a list of known allergens, especially allergies or sensitivities to latex.

Obtain a history of the patient's hematopoietic, immune, musculoskeletal, and reproductive systems; symptoms; and results of previously performed laboratory tests and diagnostic and surgical procedures.

Obtain a list of the patient's current medications, including herbs, nutritional supplements, and nutraceuticals (see Appendix F).

Review the procedure with the patient. Inform the patient that specimen collection takes approximately 5 to 10 min. Address concerns about pain and explain that there may be some discomfort during the venipuncture.
Sensitivity to social and cultural issues, as well as concern for modesty, is important in providing psychological support before, during, and after the procedure.

Heparin therapy should be discontinued 2 days before specimen collection, with medical direction. Coumarin therapy should be discontinued 2 wk before specimen collection, with medical direction.

There are no food or fluid restrictions unless by medical direction.

INTRATEST:

Ensure that the patient has complied with pretesting preparations; assure that anticoagulant therapy has been restricted as required prior to the procedure.

If the patient has a history of allergic reaction to latex, avoid the use of equipment containing latex.

Instruct the patient to cooperate fully and to follow directions. Direct the patient to breathe normally and to avoid unnecessary movement.

Observe standard precautions, and follow the general guidelines in Appendix A. Positively identify the patient, and label the appropriate specimen container with the corresponding patient demographics, initials of the person collecting the specimen, date, and time of collection. Perform a venipuncture. Fill tube completely.
Important note: Two different concentrations of sodium citrate preservative are currently added to blue-top tubes for coagulation studies: 3.2% and 3.8%. The Clinical and Laboratory Standards Institute (CLSI; formerly the National Committee for Clinical Laboratory Standards [NCCLS]) guideline for sodium citrate is 3.2%. Laboratories establish reference ranges for coagulation testing based on numerous factors, including sodium citrate concentration, test equipment, and test reagents. It is important to ask the laboratory which concentration it recommends, because each concentration will have its own specific reference range. When multiple specimens are drawn, the blue-top tube should be collected after sterile (i.e., blood culture) tubes. Otherwise, when using a standard vacutainer system, the blue-top tube is the first tube collected. When a butterfly is used, due to the added tubing, an extra red-top tube should be collected before the

blue-top tube to ensure complete filling of the blue-top tube.

Remove the needle and apply direct pressure with dry gauze to stop bleeding. Observe/assess venipuncture site for bleeding or hematoma formation and secure gauze with adhesive bandage. Promptly transport the specimen to the laboratory for processing and analysis. The CLSI recommendation for processed and unprocessed samples stored in unopened tubes is that testing should be completed within 1 to 4 hr of collection. If the patient has a known hematocrit above 55%, adjust the amount of anticoagulant in the collection tube before drawing the blood according to the CLSI guidelines:

$$\text{Anticoagulant vol. } [x] = \\ (100 - \text{hematocrit})/(595 - \\ \text{hematocrit}) \times \text{total vol. of} \\ \text{anticoagulated blood required}$$

Example:

$$\text{Patient hematocrit} = 60\% = \\ [(100 - 60)/(595 - 60) \times 5.0] = \\ 0.37 \text{ mL sodium citrate for a} \\ 5\text{-mL standard drawing tube}$$

POST-TEST:

A report of the results will be made available to the requesting health-care provider (HCP), who will discuss the results with the patient.

Instruct the patient to resume usual medications, as directed by the HCP. Recognize anxiety related to test results, and offer support. Provide teaching and information regarding the clinical implications of the test results, as appropriate. It is also important to discuss feelings the mother and father may experience (e.g., guilt, depression, anger) if test results are abnormal. Educate the patient regarding access to counseling services. Provide contact information, if desired, for the Lupus Foundation of America (www .lupus.org).

Reinforce information given by the patient's HCP regarding further testing, treatment, or referral to another HCP. Answer any questions or address any concerns voiced by the patient or family.

Depending on the results of this procedure, additional testing may be performed to evaluate or monitor progression of the disease process and determine the need for a change in therapy. Evaluate test results in relation to the patient's symptoms and other tests performed.

RELATED MONOGRAPHS:

Related tests include antibody, anticardiolipin antibodies, anticyclic citrullinated peptide, ANA, arthroscopy, BMD, bone scan, CRP, ESR, FDP, MRI musculoskeletal, aPTT, protein S, PT/INR and mixing studies, radiography bone, RF, synovial fluid analysis, and US obstetric.

Refer to the Hematopoietic, Immune, Musculoskeletal, and Reproductive systems tables at the end of the book for related tests by body system.

Luteinizing Hormone

SYNONYM/ACRONYM: LH, luteotropin, interstitial cell–stimulating hormone (ICSH).

COMMON USE: To assess gonadal function related to fertility issues and response to therapy.

SPECIMEN: Serum (1 mL) collected in a red- or tiger-top tube. Plasma (1 mL) collected in a green-top (heparin) tube is also acceptable.

NORMAL FINDINGS: (Method: Immunoassay)

Concentration by Gender and by Phase (in Females)	Conventional and SI Units
Male	
Less than 2 yr	0.5–1.9 international units/mL
2–10 yr	Less than 0.5 international units/mL
11–20 yr	0.5–5.3 international units/mL
Adult	1.2–7.8 international units/mL
Female	
Less than 2–10 yr	Less than 0.5 international units/mL
11–20 yr	0.5–9 international units/mL
Phase in Females	
Follicular	1.7–15 international units/mL
Ovulatory	21.9–80 international units/mL
Luteal	0.6–16.3 international units/mL
Postmenopausal	14.2–52.3 international units/mL

DESCRIPTION: Luteinizing hormone (LH) is secreted by the anterior pituitary gland in response to stimulation by gonadotropin-releasing hormone, the same hypothalamic-releasing factor that stimulates follicle-stimulating hormone release. LH affects gonadal function in both men and women. In women, a surge of LH normally occurs at the midpoint of the menstrual cycle (ovulatory phase); this surge is believed to be induced by high estrogen levels. LH causes the ovum to be expelled from the ovary and stimulates development of the corpus luteum and progesterone production. As progesterone levels rise, LH production decreases. In males, LH stimulates the interstitial cells of Leydig, located in the testes, to produce testosterone. For this reason, in reference to males, LH is sometimes called interstitial cell–stimulating hormone. Secretion of LH is pulsatile and follows a circadian rhythm in response to the normal intermittent secretion of gonadotropin-releasing hormone. Serial specimens may be required to accurately demonstrate blood levels.

INDICATIONS

- Distinguish between primary and secondary causes of gonadal failure
- Evaluate children with precocious puberty
- Evaluate male and female infertility, as indicated by decreased LH levels
- Evaluate response to therapy to induce ovulation
- Support diagnosis of infertility caused by anovulation, as evidenced by lack of LH surge at the midpoint of the menstrual cycle

POTENTIAL DIAGNOSIS

Increased in
Conditions of decreased gonadal function cause a feedback response that stimulates LH secretion.

- Anorchia
- Gonadal failure
- Menopause
- Primary gonadal dysfunction

Decreased in
- Anorexia nervosa *(pathophysiology is unclear)*
- Kallmann's syndrome *(pathophysiology is unclear)*
- Malnutrition *(pathophysiology is unclear)*

- Pituitary or hypothalamic dysfunction *(these organs control production of LH; failure of the pituitary to produce LH or of the hypothalamus to produce gonadotropin-releasing hormone results in decreased LH levels)*
- Severe stress *(pathophysiology is unclear)*

CRITICAL FINDINGS: N/A

INTERFERING FACTORS

- Drugs and hormones that may increase LH levels include clomiphene, gonadotropin-releasing hormone, goserelin, ketoconazole, leuprolide, mestranol, nafarelin, naloxone, nilutamide, spironolactone, and tamoxifen.
- Drugs and hormones that may decrease LH levels include anabolic steroids, anticonvulsants, conjugated estrogens, cyproterone, danazol, digoxin, D-Trp-6-LHRH, estradiol valerate, estrogen/progestin therapy, finasteride, ganirelix, goserelin, ketoconazole, leuprolide, desogestrel/ethinylestradiol (Marvelon), medroxyprogesterone, megestrol, metformin, methandrostenolone, norethindrone, octreotide, oral contraceptives, phenothiazine, pimozide, pravastatin, progesterone, stanozolol, and tamoxifen.
- In menstruating women, values vary in relation to the phase of the menstrual cycle.
- LH secretion follows a circadian rhythm, with higher levels occurring during sleep.

NURSING IMPLICATIONS AND PROCEDURE

PRETEST:

- Positively identify the patient using at least two unique identifiers before providing care, treatment, or services.

Patient Teaching: Inform the patient this test can assist in assessing hormone and fertility disorders.

- Obtain a history of the patient's complaints, including a list of known allergens, especially allergies or sensitivities to latex.
- Obtain a history of the patient's endocrine and reproductive systems, symptoms, and results of previously performed laboratory tests and diagnostic and surgical procedures.
- Record the date of the last menstrual period and determine the possibility of pregnancy in perimenopausal women.
- Obtain a list of the patient's current medications, including herbs, nutritional supplements, and nutraceuticals (see Appendix F).
- Review the procedure with the patient. If the test is being performed to detect ovulation, inform the patient that it may be necessary to obtain a series of samples over a period of several days to detect peak LH levels. Inform the patient that specimen collection takes approximately 5 to 10 min. Address concerns about pain and explain that there may be some discomfort during the venipuncture.
- *Sensitivity to social and cultural issues,* as well as concern for modesty, is important in providing psychological support before, during, and after the procedure.
- There are no food, fluid, or medication restrictions unless by medical direction.

INTRATEST:

- If the patient has a history of allergic reaction to latex, avoid the use of equipment containing latex.
- Instruct the patient to cooperate fully and to follow directions. Direct the patient to breathe normally and to avoid unnecessary movement.
- Observe standard precautions, and follow the general guidelines in Appendix A. Positively identify the patient, and label the appropriate specimen container with the corresponding patient demographics, initials of the person collecting the specimen, date, and time of collection. Perform a venipuncture.

▶ Remove the needle and apply direct pressure with dry gauze to stop bleeding. Observe/assess venipuncture site for bleeding or hematoma formation and secure gauze with adhesive bandage.

▶ Promptly transport the specimen to the laboratory for processing and analysis.

POST-TEST:

▶ A report of the results will be made available to the requesting health-care provider (HCP), who will discuss the results with the patient.

▶ Reinforce information given by the patient's HCP regarding further testing, treatment, or referral to another HCP. Instruct the patient in the use of home ovulation test kits approved by the U.S. Food and Drug Administration, as appropriate. Answer any questions or address any concerns voiced by the patient or family.

▶ Depending on the results of this procedure, additional testing may be performed to evaluate or monitor progression of the disease process and determine the need for a change in therapy. Evaluate test results in relation to the patient's symptoms and other tests performed.

RELATED MONOGRAPHS:

▶ Related tests include ACTH, antisperm antibody, estradiol, FSH, progesterone, prolactin, and testosterone.

▶ Refer to the Endocrine and Reproductive systems tables at the end of the book for related tests by body system.

Lyme Antibody

SYNONYM/ACRONYM: N/A.

COMMON USE: To detect antibodies to the organism that causes Lyme disease.

SPECIMEN: Serum (1 mL) collected in a red-top tube.

NORMAL FINDINGS: (Method: Enzyme immunoassay) Less than 0.91 index; positives are confirmed by Western blot analysis.

DESCRIPTION: *Borrelia burgdorferi,* a deer tick–borne spirochete, is the organism that causes Lyme disease. Lyme disease affects multiple systems and is characterized by fever, arthralgia, and arthritis. The circular, red rash characterizing erythema migrans can appear 3 to 30 days after the tick bite. About one-half of patients in the early stage of Lyme disease (stage 1) and generally all of those in the advanced stage (stage 2—with cardiac, neurological, and rheumatoid manifestations) will have a positive test result. Patients in remission will also have a positive test response. The presence of immunoglobulin M (IgM) antibodies indicates acute infection. The presence of IgG antibodies indicates current or past infection. The Centers for Disease Control and Prevention (CDC) recommends a two-step testing process that begins with an immunofluorescence or enzyme-linked immunosorbent assay (ELISA) and is confirmed by using a Western blot test.

INDICATIONS

Assist in establishing a diagnosis of Lyme disease

POTENTIAL DIAGNOSIS

Positive findings in Lyme disease

Negative findings in: N/A

CRITICAL FINDINGS: N/A

INTERFERING FACTORS

• High rheumatoid-factor titers as well as cross-reactivity with Epstein-Barr virus and other spirochetes (e.g., *Rickettsia, Treponema*) may cause false-positive results.
• Positive test results should be confirmed by the Western blot method.

NURSING IMPLICATIONS AND PROCEDURE

PRETEST:

▶ Positively identify the patient using at least two unique identifiers before providing care, treatment, or services.
▶ *Patient Teaching:* Inform the patient this test can assist in diagnosing Lyme disease.
▶ Obtain a history of the patient's complaints, including a list of known allergens, especially allergies or sensitivities to latex.
▶ Obtain a history of the patient's immune and musculoskeletal systems, symptoms, a history of exposure, and results of previously performed laboratory tests and diagnostic and surgical procedures.
▶ Obtain a list of the patient's current medications, including herbs, nutritional supplements, and nutraceuticals (see Appendix F).
▶ Review the procedure with the patient. Inform the patient that several tests may be necessary to confirm diagnosis. Inform the patient that specimen collection takes approximately 5 to 10 min. Address concerns about pain and explain that there may be some discomfort during the venipuncture.

▶ *Sensitivity to social and cultural issues,* as well as concern for modesty, is important in providing psychological support before, during, and after the procedure.
▶ There are no food, fluid, or medication restrictions unless by medical direction.

INTRATEST:

▶ If the patient has a history of allergic reaction to latex, avoid the use of equipment containing latex.
▶ Instruct the patient to cooperate fully and to follow directions. Direct the patient to breathe normally and to avoid unnecessary movement.
▶ Observe standard precautions, and follow the general guidelines in Appendix A. Positively identify the patient, and label the appropriate specimen container with the corresponding patient demographics, initials of the person collecting the specimen, date, and time of collection. Perform a venipuncture.
▶ Remove the needle and apply direct pressure with dry gauze to stop bleeding. Observe/assess venipuncture site for bleeding or hematoma formation and secure gauze with adhesive bandage.
▶ Promptly transport the specimen to the laboratory for processing and analysis.

POST-TEST:

▶ A report of the results will be made available to the requesting health-care provider (HCP), who will discuss the results with the patient.
▶ Advise the patient to wear light-colored clothing that covers extremities when in areas infested by deer ticks and to check body for ticks after returning from infested areas.
▶ Recognize anxiety related to test results, and be supportive of impaired activity related to perceived loss of independence and fear of shortened life expectancy. Lyme disease can be debilitating and can result in significant changes in lifestyle. Discuss the implications of abnormal test results on the patient's lifestyle. Provide teaching and information regarding the clinical implications of the test results, as appropriate.

Educate the patient regarding access to counseling services.

Reinforce information given by the patient's HCP regarding further testing, treatment, or referral to another HCP. Emphasize the importance of reporting continued signs and symptoms of the infection. Provide information regarding vaccine-preventable diseases where indicated (e.g., anthrax, cervical cancer, diphtheria, encephalitis, hepatitis A and B, H1N1 flu, human papillomavirus, *Haemophilus influenza,* seasonal influenza, Lyme disease, measles, meningococcal disease, monkeypox, mumps, pertussis, pneumococcal disease, polio, rotavirus, rubella, shingles, smallpox, tetanus, typhoid fever, varicella, yellow fever). Provide contact information, if desired, for the CDC (www.cdc.gov/vaccines/vpd-vac). Answer any questions or address any concerns voiced by the patient or family.

Reinforce information given by the patient's HCP regarding further testing, treatment, or referral to another HCP. Warn the patient that false-positive test results can occur and that false-negative test results frequently occur. Answer any questions or address any concerns voiced by the patient or family.

Depending on the results of this procedure, additional testing may be performed to evaluate or monitor progression of the disease process and determine the need for a change in therapy. Evaluate test results in relation to the patient's symptoms and other tests performed.

RELATED MONOGRAPHS:

A related test is synovial fluid analysis.

Refer to the Immune and Musculoskeletal systems tables at the end of the book for related tests by body system.

Lymphangiography

SYNONYM/ACRONYM: Lymphangiogram.

COMMON USE: To visualize and assess the lymphatic system related to diagnosis of lymphomas such as Hodgkin's disease.

AREA OF APPLICATION: Lymphatic system.

CONTRAST: IV iodine-based contrast medium.

DESCRIPTION: Lymphangiography involves visualization of the lymphatic system after the injection of an iodinated oil–based contrast medium into a lymphatic vessel in the hand or foot. The lymphatic system consists of lymph vessels and nodes. Assessment of this system is important because cancer (lymphomas and Hodgkin's disease) often spreads via the lymphatic system. When the lymphatic system becomes obstructed, painful edema of the extremities usually results. The procedure is usually performed for cancer staging in patients with an established diagnosis of lymphoma or metastatic tumor. Injection into the hand allows visualization of the axillary and supraclavicular nodes. Injection into the foot allows visualization of the lymphatics of the leg, inguinal and iliac regions, and retroperitoneum up to the thoracic duct. Less commonly, injection into the foot can be used to visualize the cervical region (retroauricular area). This procedure can assess progression of the disease, assist in planning surgery, and monitor the effectiveness of chemotherapy or radiation treatment.

INDICATIONS

- Determine the extent of adenopathy
- Determine lymphatic cancer staging
- Distinguish primary from secondary lymphedema
- Evaluate edema of an extremity without known cause
- Evaluate effects of chemotherapy or radiation therapy
- Plan surgical treatment or evaluate effectiveness of chemotherapy or radiation therapy in controlling malignant tumors

POTENTIAL DIAGNOSIS

Normal findings in

- Normal lymphatic vessels and nodes that fill completely with contrast medium on the initial films. On 24-hr images, the lymph nodes are fully opacified and well circumscribed. The lymphatic channels are emptied a few hours after injection of the contrast medium

Abnormal findings in

- Abnormal lymphatic vessels
- Hodgkin's disease
- Metastatic tumor involving the lymph glands
- Nodal lymphoma
- Retroperitoneal lymphomas associated with Hodgkin's disease

CRITICAL FINDINGS: N/A

INTERFERING FACTORS

This procedure is contraindicated for

- ◆ Patients with pulmonary insufficiencies, cardiac diseases, or severe renal or hepatic disease.
- Patients with allergies to shellfish or iodinated dye. The contrast medium used may cause a life-threatening allergic reaction. Patients with a known hypersensitivity to the contrast medium may benefit from premedication with corticosteroids or the use of nonionic contrast medium.
- Patients who are pregnant or suspected of being pregnant, unless the potential benefits of the procedure far outweigh the risks to the fetus and mother.
- ◆ Elderly and other patients who are chronically dehydrated before the test, because of their risk of contrast-induced renal failure.
- ◆ Patients who are in renal failure.
- Young patients (17 yr and younger), unless the benefits of the x-ray diagnosis outweigh the risks of exposure to high levels of radiation.

Factors that may impair clear imaging

- Gas or feces in the gastrointestinal tract resulting from inadequate cleansing or failure to restrict food intake before the study.
- Retained barium from a previous radiological procedure.
- Metallic objects (e.g., jewelry, body rings) within the examination field, which may inhibit organ visualization and cause unclear images.
- Inability of the patient to cooperate or remain still during the procedure because of age, significant pain, or mental status.
- Inability to cannulate the lymphatic vessels.

Other considerations

- ◆ Be aware of risks associated with the contrast medium. The oil-based contrast medium may embolize into the lungs and will temporarily diminish pulmonary function. This can produce lipid pneumonia, which is a life-threatening complication.
- Consultation with a health-care provider (HCP) should occur before the procedure for radiation safety concerns regarding younger patients or patients who are lactating.
- Risks associated with radiation overexposure can result from frequent x-ray procedures. Personnel in the room with the patient should wear a protective lead apron, stand behind a shield, or leave the area while the examination is being done. Personnel working in the examination area should wear badges to record their level of radiation exposure.
- Failure to follow dietary restrictions and other pretesting preparations may cause the procedure to be canceled or repeated.

NURSING IMPLICATIONS AND PROCEDURE

PRETEST:

▸ Positively identify the patient using at least two unique identifiers before providing care, treatment, or services.
▸ *Patient Teaching:* Inform the patient this procedure can assist in assessing the lymphatic system.
▸ Obtain a history of the patient's complaints, including a list of known allergens, especially allergies or sensitivities to iodine, latex, seafood, anesthetics, or contrast mediums.
▸ Obtain a history of the patient's endocrine and immune systems, symptoms, and results of previously performed laboratory tests and diagnostic and surgical procedures.
▸ Note any recent procedures that can interfere with test results, including examinations using barium- or iodine-based contrast medium. Ensure that barium studies were performed more than 4 days before lymphangiography.
▸ Record the date of the last menstrual period and determine the possibility of pregnancy in perimenopausal women.
▸ Obtain a list of the patient's current medications, including herbs, nutritional supplements, and nutraceuticals (see Appendix F).
▸ Review the procedure with the patient Address concerns about pain and explain there may be moments of discomfort and some pain experienced during the test. Inform the patient that the procedure is performed by an HCF with support staff, and takes approximately 1 to 2 hr. Inform the patient tha he or she will have to return the next day, and the set of images taken upor return will take only 30 min.
▸ *Sensitivity to social and cultural issues,* as well as concern for modesty, is important in providing psychological support before, during, and after the procedure.
▸ Instruct the patient to remove jewelry and other metallic objects from the area to be examined prior to the procedure
▸ Instruct patient to withhold anticoagulant medication or to reduce dosage before the procedure, as ordered by the HCP.
▸ There are no food or fluid restrictions unless by medical direction.
▸ *Make sure a written and informed consent has been signed prior to the procedure and before administering any medications.*

INTRATEST:

▸ Observe standard precautions, and follow the general guidelines in Appendix A Positively identify the patient.
▸ Ensure the patient has complied with medication restrictions and pretesting preparations.
▸ Ensure the patient has removed all external metallic objects from the area to be examined.

If the patient has a history of allergic reactions to any substance or drug, administer ordered prophylactic steroids or antihistamines before the procedure. Use nonionic contrast medium for the procedure.

Have emergency equipment readily accessible.

Instruct the patient to void prior to the procedure and to change into the gown, robe, and foot coverings provided.

Instruct the patient to cooperate fully and to follow directions. Direct the patient to remain still throughout the procedure because movement produces unreliable results.

Obtain and record baseline vital signs, and assess neurological status.

Administer a mild sedative, as ordered.

Place the patient in a supine position on an x-ray table. Cleanse the selected area and cover with a sterile drape.

A local anesthetic is injected at the site, and a small incision is made or a needle inserted. A blue dye is injected intradermally into the area between the toes or fingers. The lymphatic vessels are identified as the dye moves. A local anesthetic is then injected into the dorsum of each foot or hand, and a small incision is made and cannulated for injection of the contrast medium.

The contrast medium is then injected, and the flow of the contrast medium is followed by fluoroscopy or images. When the contrast medium reaches the upper lumbar level, the infusion of contrast medium is discontinued.

X-ray images are taken of the chest, abdomen, and pelvis to determine the extent of filling of the lymphatic vessels. To examine the lymphatic nodes and to monitor the progress of delayed flow, 24-hr delayed images are taken.

Monitor the patient for complications related to the contrast medium (e.g., allergic reaction, anaphylaxis, bronchospasm).

Remove the needle or catheter and apply a pressure dressing over the puncture site.

Observe/assess the needle/catheter insertion site for bleeding, inflammation, or hematoma formation.

When the cannula is removed the incision is sutured and bandaged.

POST-TEST:

A report of the results will be made available to the requesting HCP, who will discuss the results with the patient.

Monitor vital signs and neurological status every 15 min for 30 min. Take temperature every 4 hr for 24 hr. Monitor intake and output at least every 8 hr. Compare with baseline values. Notify the HCP if temperature is elevated. Protocols may vary among facilities.

Observe/assess the cannula insertion site for bleeding, inflammation, or hematoma formation.

Observe for a delayed allergic reaction to contrast medium or pulmonary embolus, which may include shortness of breath, increased heart rate, pleuritic pain, hypotension, low-grade fever, and cyanosis.

Instruct the patient to immediately report symptoms such as fast heart rate, difficulty breathing, skin rash, itching, chest pain, persistent right shoulder pain, or abdominal pain. Immediately report symptoms to the appropriate HCP.

Instruct the patient in the care and assessment of the site.

Instruct the patient to apply cold compresses to the puncture site as needed to reduce discomfort or edema.

Instruct the patient to maintain bedrest up to 24 hr to reduce extremity swelling after the procedure, or as ordered.

Instruct the patient to resume usual medications, as directed by the HCP.

Recognize anxiety related to test results, and be supportive of perceived loss of independent function. Discuss the implications of abnormal test results on the patient's lifestyle. Provide teaching and information regarding the clinical implications of the test results, as appropriate.

Reinforce information given by the patient's HCP regarding further testing, treatment, or referral to another HCP. Answer any questions or address any concerns voiced by the patient or family.

Depending on the results of this procedure, additional testing may be needed to evaluate or monitor progression of the disease process and determine the need for a change in therapy. Evaluate test results in relation to the patient's symptoms and other tests performed.

RELATED MONOGRAPHS:

▸ Related tests include biopsy bone marrow, biopsy lymph nodes, CBC, CBC WBC count and differential, CT abdomen, CT pelvis, CT thoracic, gallium scan, laparoscopy abdominal, liver and spleen scan, MRI abdomen, mediastinoscopy, and US lymph nodes.

▸ Refer to the Endocrine and Immune systems tables at the end of the book for tests by related body system.

Magnesium, Blood

SYNONYM/ACRONYM: Mg^{2+}.

COMMON USE: To assess electrolyte balance related to magnesium levels to assist in diagnosis, monitoring diseases, and therapeutic interventions such as hemodialysis.

SPECIMEN: Serum (1 mL) collected in a red- or tiger-top tube.

NORMAL FINDINGS: (Method: Spectrophotometry)

Age	Conventional Units	SI Units (Conventional Units × 0.4114)
Newborn	1.7–2.5 mg/dL	0.7–1 mmol/L
Child	1.7–2.3 mg/dL	0.70–0.95 mmol/L
Adult	1.6–2.6 mg/dL	0.66–1.07 mmol/L

DESCRIPTION: Magnesium is required as a cofactor in numerous crucial enzymatic processes, such as protein synthesis, nucleic acid synthesis, and muscle contraction. Magnesium is also required for the use of adenosine diphosphate as a source of energy. It is the fourth most abundant cation and the second most abundant intracellular ion. Magnesium is needed for the transmission of nerve impulses and muscle relaxation. It controls absorption of sodium, potassium, calcium, and phosphorus; utilization of carbohydrate, lipid, and protein; and activation of enzyme systems that enable the B vitamins to function. Magnesium is also essential for oxidative phosphorylation, nucleic acid synthesis, and blood clotting. Urine magnesium levels reflect magnesium deficiency before serum levels. Magnesium deficiency severe enough to cause hypocalcemia and cardiac arrhythmias can exist despite normal serum magnesium levels.

INDICATIONS
- Determine electrolyte balance in renal failure and chronic alcoholism
- Evaluate cardiac arrhythmias (decreased magnesium levels can lead to excessive ventricular irritability)
- Evaluate known or suspected disorders associated with altered magnesium levels
- Monitor the effects of various drugs on magnesium levels

POTENTIAL DIAGNOSIS

Increased in
- Addison's disease *(related to insufficient production of aldosterone; decreased renal excretion)*
- Adrenocortical insufficiency *(related to decreased renal excretion)*
- Dehydration *(related to hemoconcentration)*
- Diabetic acidosis (severe) *(related to acid-base imbalance)*
- Hypothyroidism *(pathophysiology is unclear)*
- Massive hemolysis *(related to release of intracellular magnesium; intracellular concentration*

M

is three times higher than normal plasma levels)
- Overuse of antacids *(related to excessive intake of magnesium-containing antacids)*
- Renal insufficiency *(related to decreased urinary excretion)*
- Tissue trauma

Decreased in
- Alcoholism *(related to increased renal excretion and possible insufficient dietary intake)*
- Diabetic acidosis *(insulin treatment lowers blood glucose and appears to increase intracellular transport of magnesium)*
- Glomerulonephritis (chronic) *(related to diminished renal function; magnesium is reabsorbed in the renal tubules)*
- Hemodialysis *(related to loss of magnesium due to dialysis treatment)*
- Hyperaldosteronism *(related to increased excretion)*
- Hypocalcemia *(decreased magnesium is associated with decreased calcium and vitamin D levels)*
- Hypoparathyroidism *(related to decreased calcium)*
- Inadequate intake
- Inappropriate secretion of antidiuretic hormone *(related to fluid overload)*
- Long-term hyperalimentation
- Malabsorption *(related to impaired absorption of calcium and vitamin D)*
- Pancreatitis *(secondary to alcoholism)*
- Pregnancy
- Severe loss of body fluids *(diarrhea, lactation, sweating, laxative abuse)*

CRITICAL FINDINGS ◆

Adults
- Less than 1.2 mg/dL (SI: Less than 0.5 mmol/L)
- Greater than 4.9 mg/dL (SI: Greater than 2 mmol/L)

Children
- Less than 1.2 mg/dL (SI: Less than 0.5 mmol/L)
- Greater than 4.3 mg/dL (SI: Greater than 1.8 mmol/L)

Note and immediately report to the health-care provider (HCP) any critically increased or decreased values and related symptoms. Timely notification of critical values for lab or diagnostic studies is a role expectation of the professional nurse. Notification processes will vary among facilities. Upon receipt of the critical value the information should be read back to the caller to verify accuracy. Most policies require immediate notification of the primary HCP, hospitalist, or on-call HCP. Reported information includes the patient's name, unique identifiers, critical value, name of the person giving the report, and name of the person receiving the report. Documentation of notification should be made in the medical record with the name of the HCP notified, time and date of notification, and any orders received. Any delay in a timely report of a critical value may require completion of a notification form with review by Risk Management.

Symptoms such as tetany, weakness, dizziness, tremors, hyperactivity, nausea, vomiting, and convulsions occur at decreased (less than 1.2 mg/dL) concentrations. Electrocardiographic (ECG) changes (prolonged P-R and Q-T intervals; broad, flat T waves; and ventricular tachycardia) may also occur. Treatment may include IV or oral administration of magnesium salts, monitoring for respiratory depression and areflexia (IV administration of magnesium salts), and monitoring for diarrhea and metabolic alkalosis (oral administration to replace magnesium).

Respiratory paralysis, decreased reflexes, and cardiac arrest occur at grossly elevated (greater than 15 mg/dL) levels. ECG changes, such as prolonged P-R and Q-T intervals, and bradycardia may be seen. Toxic levels of magnesium may be reversed with the administration of calcium, dialysis treatments, and removal of the source of excessive intake.

INTERFERING FACTORS

- Drugs that may increase magnesium levels include acetylsalicylic acid and progesterone.
- Drugs that may decrease magnesium levels include albuterol, aminoglycosides, amphotericin B, bendroflumethiazide, chlorthalidone, cisplatin, citrates, cyclosporine, digoxin, gentamicin, glucagon, and oral contraceptives.
- Hemolysis results in a false elevation in values; such specimens should be rejected for analysis.
- Specimens should never be collected above an IV line because of the potential for dilution when the specimen and the IV solution combine in the collection container, falsely decreasing the result. There is also the potential of contaminating the sample with the substance of interest, if it is present in the IV solution, falsely increasing the result.

NURSING IMPLICATIONS AND PROCEDURE

PRETEST:

- Positively identify the patient using at least two unique identifiers before providing care, treatment, or services.
- *Patient Teaching:* Inform the patient this test can assist in the evaluation of electrolyte balance.
- Obtain a history of the patient's complaints, including a list of known allergens, especially allergies or sensitivities to latex.

- Obtain a history of the patient's cardiovascular, endocrine, gastrointestinal, genitourinary, and reproductive systems; symptoms; and results of previously performed laboratory tests and diagnostic and surgical procedures.
- Obtain a list of the patient's current medications, including herbs, nutritional supplements, and nutraceuticals (see Appendix F).
- Review the procedure with the patient. Inform the patient that specimen collection takes approximately 5 to 10 min. Address concerns about pain and explain that there may be some discomfort during the venipuncture.
- *Sensitivity to social and cultural issues,* as well as concern for modesty, is important in providing psychological support before, during, and after the procedure.
- There are no food, fluid, or medication restrictions unless by medical direction.

INTRATEST:

- If the patient has a history of allergic reaction to latex, avoid the use of equipment containing latex.
- Instruct the patient to cooperate fully and to follow directions. Direct the patient to breathe normally and to avoid unnecessary movement.
- Observe standard precautions, and follow the general guidelines in Appendix A. Positively identify the patient, and label the appropriate specimen container with the corresponding patient demographics, initials of the person collecting the specimen, date, and time of collection. Perform a venipuncture.
- Remove the needle and apply direct pressure with dry gauze to stop bleeding. Observe/assess venipuncture site for bleeding or hematoma formation and secure gauze with adhesive bandage.
- Promptly transport the specimen to the laboratory for processing and analysis.

POST-TEST:

- A report of the results will be made available to the requesting HCP, who will discuss the results with the patient.
- *Nutritional Considerations:* The Institute of Medicine's Food and Nutrition Board suggests 320 mg as the daily

recommended dietary allowance of magnesium for adult females age 31 to greater than 70 yr; 420 mg/d for adult males age 31 to greater than 70 yr; 310 mg/d for adult females age 19 to 30 yr; 400 mg/d for adult males age 19 to 30 yr; 360 mg/d for pregnant females age 31 to 50 yr; 350 mg/d for pregnant females age 19 to 30 yr; 400 mg/d for pregnant females under age 19 yr; 320 mg/d for lactating females age 31 to 50 yr; 310 mg/d for lactating females age 19 to 30 yr; 360 mg/d for lactating females under age 19 yr; 1,000 mg/d for lactating females under age 18 yr; 360 mg/d for female children age 14–18 yr; 410 mg/d for male children age 14 to 18 yr; 240 mg/d for children age 9 to 13 yr; 130 mg/d for children age 4 to 8 yr; 80 mg/d for children age 1 to 3 yr; 75 mg/d for children age 7 to 12 mo (recommended adequate intake); 30 mg/d for children age 0–6 mo (recommended adequate intake). Reprinted with permission from the National Academies Press, copyright 2013, National Academy of Sciences. Educate the magnesium-deficient patient regarding good dietary sources of magnesium, such as green vegetables, seeds, legumes, shrimp, and some bran cereals. Advise the patient that high intake of substances such as phosphorus, calcium, fat, and protein interferes with the absorption of magnesium.

▶ Instruct the patient to report any signs or symptoms of electrolyte imbalance,

such as dehydration, diarrhea, vomiting, or prolonged anorexia.

▶ Reinforce information given by the patient's HCP regarding further testing, treatment, or referral to another HCP. Answer any questions or address any concerns voiced by the patient or family. Educate the patient regarding access to nutritional counseling services. Provide contact information, if desired, for the Institute of Medicine of the National Academies (www.iom.edu).

▶ Depending on the results of this procedure, additional testing may be performed to evaluate or monitor progression of the disease process and determine the need for a change in therapy. Evaluate test results in relation to the patient's symptoms and other tests performed.

RELATED MONOGRAPHS:

▶ Related tests include ACTH, aldosterone, anion gap, antiarrhythmic drugs, AST, BUN, calcium, calculus kidney stone panel, CBC WBC count and differential, cortisol, CRP, CK and isoenzymes, creatinine, glucose, homocysteine, LDH and isoenzymes, magnesium urine, myoglobin, osmolality, PTH, phosphorus, potassium, renin, sodium, troponin, US abdomen, and vitamin D.

▶ Refer to the Cardiovascular, Endocrine, Gastrointestinal, Genitourinary, and Reproductive systems tables at the end of the book for related tests by body system.

Magnesium, Urine

SYNONYM/ACRONYM: Urine Mg^{2+}.

COMMON USE: To assess magnesium levels related to renal function.

SPECIMEN: Urine (5 mL) from a random or timed specimen collected in a clean plastic collection container with 6N hydrochloride as a preservative.

NORMAL FINDINGS: (Method: Spectrophotometry)

Conventional Units	SI Units (Conventional Units × 0.4114)
20–200 mg/24 hr	8.2–82.3 mmol/24 hr

DESCRIPTION: Magnesium is required as a cofactor in numerous crucial enzymatic processes, such as protein synthesis, nucleic acid synthesis, and muscle contraction. Magnesium is also required for the use of adenosine diphosphate as a source of energy. It is the fourth most abundant cation and the second most abundant intracellular ion. Magnesium is needed for the transmission of nerve impulses and muscle relaxation. It controls absorption of sodium, potassium, calcium, and phosphorus; utilization of carbohydrate, lipid, and protein; and activation of enzyme systems that enable the B vitamins to function. Magnesium is also essential for oxidative phosphorylation, nucleic acid synthesis, and blood clotting. Urine magnesium levels reflect magnesium deficiency before serum levels. Magnesium deficiency severe enough to cause hypocalcemia and cardiac arrhythmias can exist despite normal serum magnesium levels.

Regulating electrolyte balance is one of the major functions of the kidneys. In normally functioning kidneys, urine levels increase when serum levels are high and decrease when serum levels are low to maintain homeostasis. Analyzing these urinary levels can provide important clues as to the functioning of the kidneys and other major organs. Tests for electrolytes, such as magnesium, in urine usually involve timed urine collections over a 12- or 24-hr period. Measurement of random specimens may also be requested.

INDICATIONS
- Determine the potential cause of renal calculi
- Evaluate known or suspected endocrine disorder
- Evaluate known or suspected renal disease
- Evaluate magnesium imbalance
- Evaluate a malabsorption problem

POTENTIAL DIAGNOSIS

Increased in
- Alcoholism *(related to impaired absorption and increased urinary excretion)*
- Bartter's syndrome *(inherited defect in renal tubules that results in urinary wasting of potassium and magnesium)*
- Transplant recipients on cyclosporine and prednisone *(related to increased excretion by the kidney)*
- Use of corticosteroids *(related to increased excretion by the kidney)*
- Use of diuretics *(related to increased urinary excretion)*

Decreased in
- Abnormal renal function *(related to diminished ability of renal tubules to reabsorb magnesium)*
- Crohn's disease *(related to inadequate intestinal absorption)*
- Inappropriate secretion of antidiuretic hormone *(related to diminished renal absorption)*
- Salt-losing conditions *(related to diminished renal absorption)*

CRITICAL FINDINGS: N/A

INTERFERING FACTORS
- Drugs that may increase urine magnesium levels include cisplatin,

M

cyclosporine, ethacrynic acid, furosemide, mercaptomerin, mercurial diuretics, thiazides, torsemide, and triamterene.

- Drugs that may decrease urine magnesium levels include amiloride, angiotensin, oral contraceptives, parathyroid extract, and phosphates.
- Magnesium levels follow a circadian rhythm, and for this reason 24-hr collections are recommended.
- All urine voided for the timed collection period must be included in the collection, or else falsely decreased values may be obtained. Compare output records with volume collected to verify that all voids were included in the collection.

NURSING IMPLICATIONS AND PROCEDURE

PRETEST:

- Positively identify the patient using at least two unique identifiers before providing care, treatment, or services.
- *Patient Teaching:* Inform the patient this test can assist in evaluating magnesium balance.
- Obtain a history of the patient's complaints, including a list of known allergens, especially allergies or sensitivities to latex.
- Obtain a history of the patient's endocrine, gastrointestinal, and genitourinary systems; symptoms; and results of previously performed laboratory tests and diagnostic and surgical procedures.
- Obtain a list of the patient's current medications, including herbs, nutritional supplements, and nutraceuticals (see Appendix F).
- Review the procedure with the patient. Provide a nonmetallic urinal, bedpan, or toilet-mounted collection device. Address concerns about pain related to the procedure. Explain to the patient that there should be no discomfort during the procedure.

- Usually a 24-hr time frame for urine collection is ordered. Inform the patient that all urine must be saved during that 24-hr period. Instruct the patient not to void directly into the laboratory collection container. Instruct the patient to avoid defecating in the collection device and to keep toilet tissue out of the collection device to prevent contamination of the specimen. Place a sign in the bathroom to remind the patient to save all urine.
- Instruct the patient to void all urine into the collection device and then to pour the urine into the laboratory collection container. Alternatively, the specimen can be left in the collection device for a health-care staff member to add to the laboratory collection container.
- *Sensitivity to social and cultural issues,* as well as concern for modesty, is important in providing psychological support before, during, and after the procedure.
- Instruct the patient to avoid excessive exercise and stress during the 24-hr collection of urine.
- There are no food, fluid, or medication restrictions unless by medical direction.

INTRATEST:

- Ensure that the patient has complied with activity restrictions during the procedure.
- If the patient has a history of allergic reaction to latex, avoid the use of equipment containing latex.
- Instruct the patient to cooperate fully and to follow directions.
- Observe standard precautions, and follow the general guidelines in Appendix A. Positively identify the patient, and label the appropriate specimen container with the corresponding patient demographics, initials of the person collecting the specimen, date, and time of collection.

Random Specimen (Collect in Early Morning)
Clean-Catch Specimen
- Instruct the male patient to (1) thoroughly wash his hands, (2) cleanse the meatus, (3) void a small amount into the toilet, and (4) void directly into the specimen container.

Instruct the female patient to (1) thoroughly wash her hands; (2) cleanse the labia from front to back; (3) while keeping the labia separated, void a small amount into the toilet; and (4) without interrupting the urine stream, void directly into the specimen container.

Indwelling Catheter

Put on gloves. Empty drainage tube of urine. It may be necessary to clamp off the catheter for 15 to 30 min before specimen collection. Cleanse specimen port with antiseptic swab, and then aspirate 5 mL of urine with a 21- to 25-gauge needle and syringe. Transfer urine to a sterile container.

Timed Specimen

Obtain a clean 3-L urine specimen container, toilet-mounted collection device, and plastic bag (for transport of the specimen container). The specimen must be refrigerated or kept on ice throughout the entire collection period. If an indwelling urinary catheter is in place, the drainage bag must be kept on ice.

Begin the test between 6 and 8 a.m. if possible. Collect first voiding and discard. Record the time the specimen was discarded as the beginning of the timed collection period. The next morning, ask the patient to void at the same time the collection was started and add this last voiding to the container. Urinary output should be recorded throughout the collection time.

If an indwelling catheter is in place, replace the tubing and container system at the start of the collection time. Keep the container system on ice during the collection period, or empty the urine into a larger container periodically during the collection period; monitor to ensure continued drainage, and conclude the test the next morning at the same hour the collection was begun.

At the conclusion of the test, compare the quantity of urine with the urinary output record for the collection; if the specimen contains less than what was recorded as output, some urine may have been discarded, invalidating the test.

Include on the collection container's label the amount of urine, test start and stop times, and ingestion of any foods or medications that can affect test results.

Promptly transport the specimen to the laboratory for processing and analysis.

POST-TEST:

A report of the results will be made available to the requesting health-care provider (HCP), who will discuss the results with the patient.

Nutritional Considerations: The Institute of Medicine's Food and Nutrition Board suggests 320 mg as the daily recommended dietary allowance of magnesium for adult females age 31 to greater than 70 yr; 420 mg/d for adult males age 31 to greater than 70 yr; 310 mg/d for adult females age 19 to 30 yr; 400 mg/d for adult males age 19 to 30 yr; 360 mg/d for pregnant females age 31 to 50 yr; 350 mg/d for pregnant females age 19 to 30 yr; 400 mg/d for pregnant females under age 19 yr; 320 mg/d for lactating females age 31 to 50 yr; 310 mg/d for lactating females age 19 to 30 yr; 360 mg/d for lactating females under age 19 yr; 1,000 mg/d for lactating females under age 18 yr; 360 mg/d for female children age 14–18 yr; 410 mg/d for male children age 14 to 18 yr; 240 mg/d for children age 9 to 13 yr; 130 mg/d for children age 4 to 8 yr; 80 mg/d for children age 1 to 3 yr; 75 mg/d for children age 7 to 12 mo (recommended adequate intake); 30 mg/d for children age 0–6 mo (recommended adequate intake). Reprinted with permission from the National Academies Press, copyright 2013, National Academy of Sciences. Educate the magnesium-deficient patient regarding good dietary sources of magnesium, such as green vegetables, seeds, legumes, shrimp, and some bran cereals. Advise the patient that high intake of substances such as phosphorus, calcium, fat, and protein interferes with the absorption of magnesium.

Instruct the patient to report any signs or symptoms of electrolyte imbalance, such as dehydration, diarrhea, vomiting, or prolonged anorexia.

M

- Recognize anxiety related to test results. Discuss the implications of abnormal test results on the patient's lifestyle. Provide teaching and information regarding the clinical implications of the test results, as appropriate.
- Reinforce information given by the patient's HCP regarding further testing, treatment, or referral to another HCP. Answer any questions or address any concerns voiced by the patient or family.
- Depending on the results of this procedure, additional testing may be performed to evaluate or monitor progression of the disease process and determine the need for a change

in therapy. Evaluate test results in relation to the patient's symptoms and other tests performed.

RELATED MONOGRAPHS:

- Related tests include ACTH, aldosterone, angiography renal, anion gap, BUN, calcium, calculus kidney stone panel, CT renal, cortisol, creatinine, glucose, IVP, magnesium, osmolality, PTH, phosphorus, potassium, renin, renogram, sodium, troponin, UA, US kidney, and vitamin D.
- Refer to the Endocrine, Gastrointestinal, and Genitourinary systems tables at the end of the book for related tests by body system.

Magnetic Resonance Angiography

SYNONYM/ACRONYM: MRA.

COMMON USE: To visualize and assess blood flow in diseased and normal vessels toward diagnosis of vascular disease and to monitor and evaluate therapeutic interventions.

AREA OF APPLICATION: Vascular.

CONTRAST: Can be done with or without IV contrast (gadolinium).

DESCRIPTION: Magnetic resonance imaging (MRI) uses a magnet and radio waves to produce an energy field that can be displayed as an image. The magnetic field causes the hydrogen atoms in tissue to line up, and when radio waves are directed toward the magnetic field, the atoms absorb the radio waves and change their position. When the radio waves are turned off, the atoms go back to their original position; this change in the energy field is sensed by the equipment, and an image is generated by the attached computer

system. MRI produces cross-sectional images of the vessels in multiple planes without the use of ionizing radiation or the interference of bone or surrounding tissue.

Magnetic resonance angiography (MRA) is an application of MRI that provides images of blood flow and diseased and normal blood vessels. In patients who are allergic to iodinated contrast medium, MRA is used in place of angiography. MRA is particularly useful for visualizing vascular abnormalities, dissections, and other pathology.

Special imaging sequences allow the visualization of moving blood within the vascular system. Two common techniques to obtain images of flowing blood are time-of-flight and phase-contrast MRA. In time-of-flight imaging, incoming blood makes the vessels appear bright and surrounding tissue is suppressed. Phase-contrast images are produced by subtracting the stationary tissue surrounding the vessels where the blood is moving through vessels during the imaging, producing high-contrast images. MRA is the most accurate technique for imaging blood flowing in veins and small arteries (*laminar flow*), but it does not accurately depict blood flow in tortuous sections of vessels and distal to bifurcations and stenosis. Swirling blood may cause a signal loss and result in inadequate images, and the degree of vessel stenosis may be overestimated. Images can be obtained in two-dimensional (series of slices) or three-dimensional sequences.

INDICATIONS

- Detect pericardial abnormalities
- Detect peripheral artery disease (PAD)
- Detect thoracic and abdominal vascular diseases
- Determine renal artery stenosis
- Differentiate aortic aneurysms from tumors near the aorta
- Evaluate cardiac chambers and pulmonary vessels
- Evaluate postoperative angioplasty sites and bypass grafts
- Identify congenital vascular diseases
- Monitor and evaluate the effectiveness of medical or surgical treatment

POTENTIAL DIAGNOSIS

Normal findings in
- Normal blood flow in the area being examined, including blood flow rate

Abnormal findings in
- Aortic aneurysm
- Coarctations
- Dissections
- PAD
- Thrombosis within a vessel
- Tumor invasion of a vessel
- Vascular abnormalities
- Vessel occlusion
- Vessel stenosis

CRITICAL FINDINGS

- Aortic aneurysm
- Aortic dissection
- Occlusion
- Tumor with significant mass effect
- Vertebral artery dissection

It is essential that critical diagnoses be communicated immediately to the appropriate health-care provider (HCP). A listing of these diagnoses varies among facilities. Note and immediately report to the HCP abnormal results and related symptoms. Timely notification of critical values for lab or diagnostic studies is a role expectation of the professional nurse. Notification processes will vary among facilities. Upon receipt of the critical value the information should be read back to the caller to verify accuracy. Most policies require immediate notification of the primary HCP, hospitalist, or on-call HCP. Reported information includes the patient's name, unique identifiers, critical value, name of the person giving the report, and name of the person receiving the report. Documentation of notification should be made in the medical record with the name of the HCP notified, time and date of notification, and any orders received. Any delay in a timely report of a critical

M

value may require completion of a notification form with review by Risk Management.

INTERFERING FACTORS

This procedure is contraindicated for
- Patients with certain ferrous metal prosthetics, valves, aneurysm clips, inner ear prostheses, or other metallic objects.
- Patients with metal in their body, such as shrapnel or ferrous metal in the eye.
- Patients with cardiac pacemakers, because the pacemaker can be deactivated by MRI.
- Use of gadolinium-based contrast agents (GBCAs) is contraindicated in patients with acute or chronic severe renal insufficiency (glomerular filtration rate less than 30 mL/min/1.73 m^2). Patients should be screened for renal dysfunction prior to administration. The use of GBCAs should be avoided in these patients unless the benefits of the studies outweigh the risks and if essential diagnostic information is not available using non-contrast-enhanced diagnostic studies.
- Patients who are claustrophobic.
- Patients who are pregnant or suspected of being pregnant, unless the potential benefits of the procedure far outweigh the risks to the fetus and mother.

Factors that may impair clear imaging
- Metallic objects (e.g., jewelry, body rings, dental amalgams) within the examination field, which may inhibit organ visualization and cause unclear images.
- Inability of the patient to cooperate or remain still during the procedure because of age, significant pain, or mental status.

- Patients with extreme cases of claustrophobia, unless sedation is given before the study.

Other considerations
- If contrast medium is allowed to seep deep into the muscle tissue, vascular visualization will be impossible.

NURSING IMPLICATIONS AND PROCEDURE

PRETEST:

Positively identify the patient using at least two unique identifiers before providing care, treatment, or services.

Patient Teaching: Inform the patient this procedure can assist in assessing the vascular system.

Obtain a history of the patient's complaints, including a list of known allergens, especially allergies or sensitivities to latex, iodine, seafood, contrast medium, anesthetics, or dyes.

Obtain a history of the patient's cardiovascular system, symptoms, and results of previously performed laboratory tests and diagnostic and surgical procedures. Obtain a history of renal dysfunction if the use of GBCA is anticipated.

Ensure the results of BUN, creatinine, and eGFR (estimated glomerular filtration rate) are obtained if GBCA is to be used.

Determine if the patient has ever had any device implanted into his or her body, including copper intrauterine devices, pacemakers, ear implants, and heart valves.

Obtain occupational history to determine the presence of metal in the body, such as shrapnel or flecks of ferrous metal in the eye (which can cause retinal hemorrhage).

Note any recent procedures that can interfere with test results.

Record the date of the last menstrual period and determine the possibility of pregnancy in perimenopausal women.

Obtain a list of the patient's current medications, including herbs, nutritional supplements, and nutraceuticals (see Appendix F).

Review the procedure with the patient. Address concerns about pain related to the procedure and explain that no pain will be experienced during the test, but there may be moments of discomfort. Reassure the patient that if contrast is used, it poses no radioactive hazard and rarely produces side effects. Inform the patient the procedure is performed in an MRI department by an HCP who specializes in this procedure, with support staff, and takes approximately 30 to 60 min.

Inform the patient that the technologist will place him or her in a supine position on a flat table in a large cylindrical scanner.

Tell the patient to expect to hear loud banging from the scanner and possibly to see magnetophosphenes (flickering lights in the visual field); these will stop when the procedure is over.

Explain that an IV line may be inserted to allow infusion of IV fluids, contrast medium, or sedatives.

Sensitivity to social and cultural issues, as well as concern for modesty, is important in providing psychological support before, during, and after the procedure.

Instruct the patient to remove external metallic objects from the area to be examined prior to the procedure.

There are no food, fluid, or medication restrictions unless by medical direction.

INTRATEST:

Observe standard precautions, and follow the general guidelines in Appendix A. Positively identify the patient.

Ensure that the patient has removed external metallic objects from the area to be examined prior to the procedure.

If the patient has a history of allergic reactions to any substance or drug, administer ordered prophylactic steroids or antihistamines before the procedure.

Have emergency equipment readily available.

Instruct the patient to void prior to the procedure and to change into the gown, robe, and foot coverings provided.

Instruct the patient to cooperate fully and to follow directions. Instruct the patient to remain still throughout the procedure because movement produces unreliable results.

Supply earplugs to the patient to block out the loud, banging sounds that occur during the test. Instruct the patient to communicate with the technologist during the examination via a microphone within the scanner.

If an electrocardiogram or respiratory gating is to be performed in conjunction with the scan, apply MRI-safe electrodes to the appropriate sites.

Establish IV fluid line for the injection of emergency drugs and sedatives.

Administer an antianxiety agent, as ordered, if the patient has claustrophobia. Administer a sedative to a child or to an uncooperative adult, as ordered.

Place the patient in the supine position on an examination table.

If contrast is used, imaging can begin shortly after the injection.

Ask the patient to inhale deeply and hold his or her breath while the images are taken, and then to exhale after the images are taken.

Instruct the patient to take slow, deep breaths if nausea occurs during the procedure.

Monitor the patient for complications related to the procedure (e.g., allergic reaction, anaphylaxis, bronchospasm). Remove the needle or catheter and apply a pressure dressing over the puncture site.

Observe/assess the needle/catheter insertion site for bleeding, inflammation, or hematoma formation.

POST-TEST:

A report of the results will be made available to the requesting HCP, who will discuss the results with the patient.

Observe for delayed allergic reactions, such as rash, urticaria, tachycardia, hyperpnea, hypertension, palpitations, nausea, or vomiting.

Instruct the patient to immediately report symptoms such as fast heart rate, difficulty breathing, skin rash, itching, chest pain, persistent right shoulder pain, or abdominal pain. Immediately report symptoms to the appropriate HCP.

M

▶ Instruct the patient in the care and assessment of the injection site.

▶ Instruct the patient to apply cold compresses to the puncture site as needed to reduce discomfort or edema.

▶ Recognize anxiety related to test results. Discuss the implications of abnormal test results on the patient's lifestyle. Provide teaching and information regarding the clinical implications of the test results, as appropriate. Provide contact information, if desired, for the American Heart Association (www.americanheart.org), the NHLBI (www.nhlbi.nih.gov), or Legs for Life (www.legsforlife.org).

▶ Reinforce information given by the patient's HCP regarding further testing, treatment, or referral to another HCP. Answer any questions or address any concerns voiced by the patient or family.

▶ Depending on the results of this procedure, additional testing may be performed to evaluate or monitor progression of the disease process and determine the need for a change in therapy. Evaluate test results in relation to the patient's symptoms and other tests performed.

RELATED MONOGRAPHS:

▶ Related tests include angiography of the body area of interest, BUN, CT angiography, creatinine, US arterial Doppler carotid, and US venous Doppler.

▶ Refer to the Cardiovascular System table at the end of the book for related tests by body system.

Magnetic Resonance Imaging, Abdomen

SYNONYM/ACRONYM: Abdominal MRI.

COMMON USE: To visualize and assess abdominal and hepatic structures toward diagnosis of tumors, metastasis, aneurysm, and abscess. Also used to monitor medical and surgical therapeutic interventions.

AREA OF APPLICATION: Liver and abdominal area.

CONTRAST: Can be done with or without IV contrast medium (gadolinium).

DESCRIPTION: Magnetic resonance imaging (MRI) uses a magnet and radio waves to produce an energy field that can be displayed as an image. Use of magnetic fields with the aid of radiofrequency energy produces images primarily based on water content of tissue. The magnetic field causes the hydrogen atoms in tissue to line up, and when radio waves are directed toward the magnetic field, the atoms absorb the radio waves and change their position. When the radio waves are turned off, the atoms go back to their original position; this change in the energy field is sensed by the equipment, and an image is generated by the attached computer system. MRI produces cross-sectional images of the abdomen in multiple planes without the use of ionizing radiation or the interference of bone.

Abdominal MRI is performed to assist in diagnosing abnormalities of abdominal and hepatic structures. Contrast-enhanced imaging is effective for distinguishing peritoneal metastases from primary tumors of the gastrointestinal (GI) tract. Primary tumors of the stomach, pancreas, colon, and appendix often spread by intraperitoneal tumor shedding and subsequent peritoneal carcinomatosis. MRI uses the noniodinated contrast medium gadopentetate dimeglumine (Magnevist), which is administered IV to enhance contrast differences between normal and abnormal tissues.

Magnetic resonance angiography (MRA) is an application of MRI that provides images of blood flow and diseased and normal blood vessels. In patients who are allergic to iodinated contrast medium, MRA is used in place of angiography (see monograph titled "Magnetic Resonance Angiography").

INDICATIONS

- Detect abdominal aortic diseases
- Detect and stage cancer (primary or metastatic tumors of liver, pancreas, prostate, uterus, and bladder)
- Detect chronic pancreatitis
- Detect renal vein thrombosis
- Detect soft tissue abnormalities
- Determine and monitor tissue damage in renal transplant patients
- Determine the presence of blood clots, cysts, fluid or fat accumulation in tissues, hemorrhage, and infarctions
- Determine vascular complications of pancreatitis, venous thrombosis, or pseudoaneurysm
- Differentiate aortic aneurysms from tumors near the aorta
- Differentiate liver tumors from liver abnormalities, such as cysts, cavernous hemangiomas, and hepatic amebic abscesses
- Evaluate postoperative angioplasty sites and bypass grafts

- Monitor and evaluate the effectiveness of medical or surgical interventions and the course of the disease

POTENTIAL DIAGNOSIS

Normal findings in
- Normal anatomic structures, soft tissue density, and biochemical constituents of body tissues, including blood flow

Abnormal findings in
- Acute tubular necrosis
- Aneurysm
- Cholangitis
- Glomerulonephritis
- Hydronephrosis
- Internal bleeding
- Masses, lesions, infections, or inflammations
- Renal vein thrombosis
- Vena cava obstruction

CRITICAL FINDINGS
- Acute GI bleed
- Aortic aneurysm
- Infection
- Tumor with significant mass effect

It is essential that critical diagnoses be communicated immediately to the appropriate health-care provider (HCP). A listing of these diagnoses varies among facilities. Timely notification of critical values for lab or diagnostic studies is a role expectation of the professional nurse. Notification processes will vary among facilities. Upon receipt of the critical value the information should be read back to the caller to verify accuracy. Most policies require immediate notification of the primary HCP, hospitalist, or on-call HCP. Reported information includes the patient's name, unique identifiers, critical value, name of the person giving the report, and name of the person receiving the report. Documentation of notification should be made in the medical record with the name of the

M

HCP notified, time and date of notification, and any orders received. Any delay in a timely report of a critical value may require completion of a notification form with review by Risk Management.

INTERFERING FACTORS

This procedure is contraindicated for

- Patients with certain ferrous metal prostheses, valves, aneurysm clips, inner ear prostheses, or other metallic objects.
- ◈ Patients with metal in their body, such as shrapnel or ferrous metal in the eye.
- ◈ Patients with cardiac pacemakers, because the pacemaker can be deactivated by MRI.
- ◈ Use of gadolinium-based contrast agents (GBCAs) is contraindicated in patients with acute or chronic severe renal insufficiency (glomerular filtration rate less than 30 mL/min/1.73 m²). Patients should be screened for renal dysfunction prior to administration. The use of GBCAs should be avoided in these patients unless the benefits of the studies outweigh the risks and if essential diagnostic information is not available using non-contrast-enhanced diagnostic studies.
- Patients with intrauterine devices.
- Patients with iron pigments in tattoos.
- Patients who are claustrophobic.
- Patients who are pregnant or suspected of being pregnant, unless the potential benefits of the procedure far outweigh the risks to the fetus and mother.

Factors that may impair clear imaging

- Metallic objects (e.g., jewelry, body rings, dental amalgams) within the examination field, which may inhibit organ visualization and cause unclear images.
- Inability of the patient to cooperate or remain still during the procedure because of age, significant pain, or mental status.
- Patients with extreme cases of claustrophobia, unless sedation is given before the study or an open MRI is utilized.

Other considerations

- If contrast medium is allowed to seep deep into the muscle tissue, vascular visualization will be impossible.

NURSING IMPLICATIONS AND PROCEDURE

PRETEST:

▶ Positively identify the patient using at least two unique identifiers before providing care, treatment, or services.

▶ *Patient Teaching:* Inform the patient this procedure can assist in assessing the abdominal organs and structures.

▶ Obtain a history of the patient's complaints, including a list of known allergens, especially allergies or sensitivities to latex, iodine, seafood, contrast medium, anesthetics, or dyes.

▶ Obtain a history of the patient's gastrointestinal, genitourinary, and hepatobiliary systems; symptoms; and results of previously performed laboratory tests and diagnostic and surgical procedures. Obtain a history of renal dysfunction if the use of GBCA is anticipated.

▶ Ensure the results of BUN, creatinine, and eGFR (estimated glomerular filtration rate) are obtained if GBCA is to be used.

▶ Determine if the patient has ever had any device implanted into his or her body, including copper intrauterine devices, pacemakers, ear implants, and heart valves.

▶ Obtain occupational history to determine the presence of metal in the body, such as shrapnel or flecks of ferrous metal in the eye (which can cause retinal hemorrhage).

- Note any recent procedures that can interfere with test results, including examinations using barium- or iodine-based contrast medium.
- Record the date of the last menstrual period and determine the possibility of pregnancy in perimenopausal women.
- Obtain a list of the patient's current medications including herbs, nutritional supplements, and nutraceuticals (see Appendix F).
- Review the procedure with the patient. Address concerns about pain related to the procedure and explain that no pain will be experienced during the test, but there may be moments of discomfort. Reassure the patient that if contrast is used, it poses no radioactive hazard and rarely produces side effects. Inform the patient the procedure is performed in an MRI department by an HCP specializing in this procedure, with support staff, and takes approximately 30 to 60 min.
- Inform the patient that the technologist will place him or her in a supine position on a flat table in a large cylindrical scanner.
- Tell the patient to expect to hear loud banging from the scanner and possibly to see magnetophosphenes (flickering lights in the visual field); these will stop when the procedure is over.
- *Sensitivity to social and cultural issues,* as well as concern for modesty, is important in providing psychological support before, during, and after the procedure.
- Explain that an IV line may be inserted to allow infusion of IV fluids, contrast medium, or sedatives.
- Instruct the patient to remove jewelry and all other metallic objects from the area to be examined prior to the procedure.
- There are no food, fluid, or medication restrictions unless by medical direction.

INTRATEST:

- Observe standard precautions, and follow the general guidelines in Appendix A. Positively identify the patient.
- Ensure that the patient has removed all external metallic objects from the area to be examined prior to the procedure.
- If the patient has a history of allergic reactions to any substance or drug,

administer ordered prophylactic steroids or antihistamines before the procedure.
- Have emergency equipment readily available.
- Instruct the patient to void prior to the procedure and to change into the gown, robe, and foot coverings provided.
- Instruct the patient to cooperate fully and to follow directions. Instruct the patient to remain still throughout the procedure because movement produces unreliable results.
- Supply earplugs to the patient to block out the loud, banging sounds that occur during the test. Instruct the patient to communicate with the technologist during the examination via a microphone within the scanner.
- Establish an IV fluid line for the injection of emergency drugs and of sedatives.
- Administer an antianxiety agent, as ordered, if the patient has claustrophobia. Administer a sedative to a child or to an uncooperative adult, as ordered.
- Place the patient in the supine position on an examination table.
- If contrast is used, imaging can begin shortly after the injection.
- Ask the patient to inhale deeply and hold his or her breath while the images are taken and then to exhale after the images are taken.
- Instruct the patient to take slow, deep breaths if nausea occurs during the procedure.
- Monitor the patient for complications related to the procedure (e.g., allergic reaction, anaphylaxis, bronchospasm).
- Remove the needle or catheter and apply a pressure dressing over the puncture site.
- Observe/assess the needle/catheter insertion site for bleeding, inflammation, or hematoma formation.

POST-TEST:

- A report of the results will be made available to the requesting HCP, who will discuss the results with the patient.
- Observe for delayed allergic reactions, such as rash, urticaria, tachycardia, hyperpnea, hypertension, palpitations, nausea, or vomiting

M

- Instruct the patient to immediately report symptoms such as fast heart rate, difficulty breathing, skin rash, itching, chest pain, persistent right shoulder pain, or abdominal pain. Immediately report symptoms to the appropriate HCP.
- Instruct the patient in the care and assessment of the injection site.
- Instruct the patient to apply cold compresses to the puncture site as needed to reduce discomfort or edema.
- Recognize anxiety related to test results. Discuss the implications of abnormal test results on the patient's lifestyle. Provide teaching and information regarding the clinical implications of the test results, as appropriate.
- Reinforce information given by the patient's HCP regarding further testing, treatment, or referral to another HCP.

Answer any questions or address any concerns voiced by the patient or family.
- Depending on the results of this procedure, additional testing may be performed to evaluate or monitor progression of the disease process and determine the need for a change in therapy. Evaluate test results in relation to the patient's symptoms and other tests performed.

RELATED MONOGRAPHS:

- Related tests include angiography abdomen, BUN, CT abdomen, creatinine, GI blood loss scan, KUB study, US abdomen, and US liver and biliary system.
- Refer to the Gastrointestinal, Genitourinary, and Hepatobiliary systems tables at the end of the book for related tests by body system.

Magnetic Resonance Imaging, Brain

SYNONYM/ACRONYM: Brain MRI.

COMMON USE: To visualize and assess intracranial abnormalities related to tumor, bleeding, lesions, and infarct such as stroke.

AREA OF APPLICATION: Brain area.

CONTRAST: Can be done with or without IV contrast medium (gadolinium).

DESCRIPTION: Magnetic resonance imaging (MRI) uses a magnet and radio waves to produce an energy field that can be displayed as an image. Use of magnetic fields with the aid of radiofrequency energy produces images primarily based on water content of tissue. The magnetic field causes the hydrogen atoms in tissue to line up, and when radio waves are directed toward the magnetic field, the atoms absorb the radio waves and change their position. When the

radio waves are turned off, the atoms go back to their original position; this change in the energy field is sensed by the equipment, and an image is generated by the attached computer system. MRI produces cross-sectional images of pathological lesions of the brain in multiple planes without the use of ionizing radiation or the interference of bone or surrounding tissue.

Brain MRI can distinguish solid, cystic, and hemorrhagic

components of lesions. This procedure is done to aid in the diagnosis of intracranial abnormalities, including tumors, ischemia, infection, and multiple sclerosis, and in assessment of brain maturation in pediatric patients. Rapidly flowing blood on spin-echo MRI appears as an absence of signal or a void in the vessel's lumen. Blood flow can be evaluated in the cavernous and carotid arteries. Aneurysms may be diagnosed without traditional iodine-based contrast angiography, and old clotted blood in the walls of the aneurysms appears white. MRI uses the noniodinated contrast medium gadopentetate dimeglumine (Magnevist), which is administered IV to enhance contrast differences between normal and abnormal tissues.

Magnetic resonance angiography (MRA) is an application of MRI that provides images of blood flow and diseased and normal blood vessels. In patients who are allergic to iodinated contrast medium, MRA is used in place of angiography (see monograph titled "Magnetic Resonance Angiography").

INDICATIONS

Detect and locate brain tumors
Detect cause of cerebrovascular accident, cerebral infarct, or hemorrhage
Detect cranial bone, face, throat, and neck soft tissue lesions
Evaluate the cause of seizures, such as intracranial infection, edema, or increased intracranial pressure
Evaluate cerebral changes associated with dementia
Evaluate demyelinating disorders
Evaluate intracranial infections
Evaluate optic and auditory nerves

- Evaluate the potential causes of headache, visual loss, and vomiting
- Evaluate shunt placement and function in patients with hydrocephalus
- Evaluate the solid, cystic, and hemorrhagic components of lesions
- Evaluate vascularity of the brain and vascular integrity
- Monitor and evaluate the effectiveness of medical or surgical interventions, chemotherapy, radiation therapy, and the course of disease

POTENTIAL DIAGNOSIS

Normal findings in
- Normal anatomic structures, soft tissue density, blood flow rate, face, nasopharynx, neck, tongue, and brain

Abnormal findings in
- Abscess
- Acoustic neuroma
- Alzheimer's disease
- Aneurysm
- Arteriovenous malformation
- Benign meningioma
- Cerebral aneurysm
- Cerebral infarction
- Craniopharyngioma or meningioma
- Granuloma
- Intraparenchymal hematoma or hemorrhage
- Lipoma
- Metastasis
- Multiple sclerosis
- Optic nerve tumor
- Parkinson's disease
- Pituitary microadenoma
- Subdural empyema
- Ventriculitis

CRITICAL FINDINGS ✷
- Abscess
- Cerebral aneurysm
- Cerebral infarct
- Hydrocephalus
- Skull fracture or contusion
- Tumor with significant mass effect

It is essential that critical diagnoses be communicated immediately to the appropriate health-care provider (HCP). A listing of these diagnoses varies among facilities. Timely notification of critical values for lab or diagnostic studies is a role expectation of the professional nurse. Notification processes will vary among facilities. Upon receipt of the critical value the information should be read back to the caller to verify accuracy. Most policies require immediate notification of the primary HCP, hospitalist, or on-call HCP. Reported information includes the patient's name, unique identifiers, critical value, name of the person giving the report, and name of the person receiving the report. Documentation of notification should be made in the medical record with the name of the HCP notified, time and date of notification, and any orders received. Any delay in a timely report of a critical value may require completion of a notification form with review by Risk Management.

INTERFERING FACTORS

This procedure is contraindicated for

• Patients with certain ferrous metal prostheses, valves, aneurysm clips, inner ear prostheses, or other metallic objects.
• ❖ Patients with metal in their body, such as shrapnel or ferrous metal in the eye.
• ❖ Patients with cardiac pacemakers, because the pacemaker can be deactivated by MRI.
• ❖ Use of gadolinium-based contrast agents (GBCAs) is contraindicated in patients with acute or chronic severe renal insufficiency (glomerular filtration rate less than 30 mL/min/1.73 m^2). Patients should be screened for renal dysfunction prior to administration. The use of GBCAs should be avoided in these patients unless

the benefits of the studies outweigh the risks and if essential diagnostic information is not available using non-contrast-enhanced diagnostic studies.
• Patients with intrauterine devices.
• Patients with iron pigments in tattoos.
• Patients who are claustrophobic.
• Patients who are pregnant or suspected of being pregnant, unless the potential benefits of the procedure far outweigh the risks to the fetus and mother.

Factors that may impair clear imaging

• Metallic objects (e.g., jewelry, body rings, dental amalgams) within the examination field, which may inhibit organ visualization and cause unclear images.
• Inability of the patient to cooperate or remain still during the procedure because of age, significant pain, or mental status.
• Patients with extreme cases of claustrophobia, unless sedation is given before the study or an open MRI is utilized.

Other considerations

• If contrast medium is allowed to seep deep into the muscle tissue, vascular visualization will be impossible.

NURSING IMPLICATIONS AND PROCEDURE

PRETEST:

▶ Positively identify the patient using at least two unique identifiers before providing care, treatment, or services.
▶ *Patient Teaching:* Inform the patient this procedure can assist in assessing the brain.
▶ Obtain a history of the patient's complaints, including a list of known allergens, especially allergies or sensitivities to latex, iodine, seafood, contrast medium, anesthetics, or dyes.

Obtain a history of the patient's cardio-vascular and neuromuscular systems, symptoms, and results of previously performed laboratory tests and diag-nostic and surgical procedures. Obtain a history of renal dysfunction if the use of GBCA is anticipated.

Ensure the results of BUN, creatinine, and eGFR (estimated glomerular filtra-tion rate) are obtained if GBCA is to be used.

Determine if the patient has ever had any device implanted into his or her body, including copper intrauterine devices, pacemakers, ear implants, and heart valves.

Obtain occupational history to deter-mine the presence of metal in the body, such as shrapnel or flecks of fer-rous metal in the eye (which can cause retinal hemorrhage).

Note any recent procedures that can interfere with test results, including examinations using barium- or iodine-based contrast medium.

Record the date of the last menstrual period and determine the possibility of pregnancy in perimenopausal women. Obtain a list of the patient's current medications, including herbs, nutrition-al supplements, and nutraceuticals (see Appendix F).

Review the procedure with the patient. Address concerns about pain related to the procedure and explain that no pain will be experienced during the test, but there may be moments of discomfort. Reassure the patient that if contrast is used, it poses no radioactive hazard and rarely produces side effects. Inform the patient the procedure is performed in an MRI department, usually by an HCP who specializes in this procedure, with support staff, and takes approxi-mately 30 to 60 min.

Inform the patient that the technologist will place him or her in a supine posi-tion on a flat table in a large cylindrical scanner.

Tell the patient to expect to hear loud banging from the scanner and possibly to see magnetophosphenes (flickering lights in the visual field); these will stop when the procedure is over.

Sensitivity to social and cultural issues, as well as concern for modesty, is important in providing psychological support before, during, and after the procedure.

▸ Explain that an IV line may be inserted to allow infusion of IV fluids, contrast medium, or sedatives.

▸ Instruct the patient to remove jewelry and all other metallic objects from the area to be examined prior to the pro-cedure.

▸ There are no food, fluid, or medication restrictions unless by medical direction.

INTRATEST:

▸ Observe standard precautions, and fol-low the general guidelines in Appendix A. Positively identify the patient.

▸ Ensure that the patient has removed all external metallic objects from the area to be examined prior to the procedure.

▸ If the patient has a history of allergic reactions to any substance or drug, administer ordered prophylactic ste-roids or antihistamines before the pro-cedure.

▸ Have emergency equipment readily available.

▸ Instruct the patient to void prior to the procedure and to change into the gown, robe, and foot coverings provided.

▸ Instruct the patient to cooperate fully and to follow directions. Instruct the patient to remain still throughout the procedure because movement produc-es unreliable results.

▸ Supply earplugs to the patient to block out the loud, banging sounds that occur during the test. Instruct the patient to communicate with the tech-nologist during the examination via a microphone within the scanner.

▸ If an electrocardiogram or respiratory gating is to be performed in conjunc-tion with the scan, apply MRI-safe electrodes to the appropriate sites.

▸ Establish an IV fluid line for the injec-tion of emergency drugs and of seda-tives.

▸ Administer an antianxiety agent, as ordered, if the patient has claustropho-bia. Administer a sedative to a child or to an uncooperative adult, as ordered.

▸ Place the patient in the supine position on an examination table.

If contrast is used, imaging can begin shortly after the injection.

Ask the patient to inhale deeply and hold his or her breath while the images are taken and then to exhale after the images are taken.

Instruct the patient to take slow, deep breaths if nausea occurs during the procedure.

Monitor the patient for complications related to the procedure (e.g., allergic reaction, anaphylaxis, bronchospasm).

Remove the needle or catheter and apply a pressure dressing over the puncture site.

Observe/assess the needle/catheter insertion site for bleeding, inflammation, or hematoma formation.

POST-TEST:

A report of the results will be made available to the requesting HCP, who will discuss the results with the patient.

Observe for delayed allergic reactions, such as rash, urticaria, tachycardia, hyperpnea, hypertension, palpitations, nausea, or vomiting, if contrast medium was used.

Instruct the patient to immediately report symptoms such as fast heart rate, difficulty breathing, skin rash, itching, chest pain, persistent right shoulder pain, or abdominal pain. Immediately report symptoms to the appropriate HCP.

Instruct the patient to apply cold compresses to the puncture site as needed to reduce discomfort or edema.

Recognize anxiety related to test results. Discuss the implications of abnormal test results on the patient's lifestyle. Provide teaching and information regarding the clinical implications of the test results, as appropriate.

Reinforce information given by the patient's HCP regarding further testing, treatment, or referral to another HCP. Answer any questions or address any concerns voiced by the patient or family.

Depending on the results of this procedure, additional testing may be performed to evaluate or monitor progression of the disease process and determine the need for a change in therapy. Evaluate test results in relation to the patient's symptoms and other tests performed.

RELATED MONOGRAPHS:

Related tests include Alzheimer's disease markers, angiography of the carotids, BUN, CSF analysis, CT brain, creatinine, EMG, evoked brain potentials, and PET brain.

Refer to the Cardiovascular and Musculoskeletal systems tables at the end of the book for related tests by body system.

M

Magnetic Resonance Imaging, Breast

SYNONYM/ACRONYM: Breast MRI.

COMMON USE: To visualize and assess abnormalities in breast tissue to assist in evaluating structural abnormalities related to diagnoses such as cancer, abscess, and cysts.

AREA OF APPLICATION: Breast area.

CONTRAST: Can be done with or without IV contrast medium (gadolinium).

DESCRIPTION: Magnetic resonance imaging (MRI) uses a magnet and radio waves to produce an energy field that can be displayed as an image. Use of magnetic fields with the aid of radiofrequency energy produces images primarily based on water content of tissue. The magnetic field causes the hydrogen atoms in tissue to line up, and when radio waves are directed toward the magnetic field, the atoms absorb the radio waves and change their position. When the radio waves are turned off, the atoms go back to their original position; this change in the energy field is sensed by the equipment, and an image is generated by the attached computer system. MRI produces cross-sectional images of the pathological lesions in multiple planes without the use of ionizing radiation or the interference of surrounding tissue, breast implants, or surgically implanted clips.

MRI imaging of the breast is not a replacement for traditional mammography, ultrasound, or biopsy. This examination is extremely helpful in evaluating mammogram abnormalities and identifying early breast cancer in women at high risk. High-risk women include those who have had breast cancer, have an abnormal mutated breast cancer gene (BRCA1 or BRCA2), or have a mother or sister who has been diagnosed with breast cancer. Breast MRI is used most commonly in high-risk women when findings of a mammogram or ultrasound are inconclusive because of dense breast tissue or there is a suspected abnormality that requires further evaluation. MRI is also an excellent examination in the augmented

breast, including both the breast implant and the breast tissue surrounding the implant. This same examination is also useful for staging breast cancer and determining the most appropriate treatment. MRI uses the noniodinated contrast medium gadopentetate dimeglumine (Magnevist), which is administered IV to enhance contrast differences between normal and abnormal tissues.

INDICATIONS

- Evaluate breast implants
- Evaluate dense breasts
- Evaluate for residual cancer after lumpectomy
- Evaluate inverted nipples
- Evaluate small abnormalities
- Evaluate tissue after lumpectomy or mastectomy
- Evaluate women at high risk for breast cancer

POTENTIAL DIAGNOSIS

Normal findings in
- Normal anatomic structures, soft tissue density, and blood flow rate

Abnormal findings in
- Breast abscess or cyst
- Breast cancer
- Breast implant rupture
- Hematoma
- Soft tissue masses
- Vascular abnormalities

CRITICAL FINDINGS: N/A

INTERFERING FACTORS

This procedure is contraindicated for
- Patients with certain ferrous metal prostheses, valves, aneurysm clips, inner ear prostheses, or other metallic objects.

M

- ❖ Patients with metal in their body, such as shrapnel or ferrous metal in the eye.
- ❖ Patients with cardiac pacemakers, because the pacemaker can be deactivated by MRI.
- ❖ Use of gadolinium-based contrast agents (GBCAs) is contraindicated in patients with acute or chronic severe renal insufficiency (glomerular filtration rate less than 30 mL/min/1.73 m^2). Patients should be screened for renal dysfunction prior to administration. The use of GBCAs should be avoided in these patients unless the benefits of the studies outweigh the risks and if essential diagnostic information is not available using non-contrast-enhanced diagnostic studies.
- Patients with intrauterine devices.
- Patients with iron pigments in tattoos.
- Patients who are claustrophobic.
- Patients who are pregnant or suspected of being pregnant, unless the potential benefits of the procedure far outweigh the risks to the fetus and mother.

Factors that may impair clear imaging
- Metallic objects (e.g., jewelry, body rings) within the examination field, which may inhibit organ visualization and cause unclear images.
- Inability of the patient to cooperate or remain still during the procedure because of age, significant pain, or mental status.
- Patients with extreme cases of claustrophobia, unless sedation is given before the study or an open MRI is utilized.

Other considerations
- If contrast medium is allowed to seep deep into the muscle tissue, vascular visualization will be impossible.
- The procedure can be nonspecific; the examination is unable to image

calcifications that can indicate breast cancer, and there may be difficulty distinguishing between cancerous and noncancerous tumors.

NURSING IMPLICATIONS AND PROCEDURE

PRETEST:

▸ Positively identify the patient using at least two unique identifiers before providing care, treatment, or services.

▸ *Patient Teaching:* Inform the patient this procedure can assist in assessing the breast.

▸ Obtain a history of the patient's complaints, including a list of known allergens, especially allergies or sensitivities to latex, iodine, seafood, contrast medium, anesthetics, or dyes.

▸ Obtain a history of the patient's reproductive system, symptoms, and results of previously performed laboratory tests and diagnostic and surgical procedures. Obtain a history of renal dysfunction if the use of GBCA is anticipated.

▸ Ensure the results of BUN, creatinine, and eGFR (estimated glomerular filtration rate) are obtained if GBCA is to be used.

▸ Determine if the patient has ever had any device implanted into his or her body, including copper intrauterine devices, pacemakers, ear implants, and heart valves.

▸ Obtain occupational history to determine the presence of metal in the body, such as shrapnel or flecks of ferrous metal in the eye (which can cause retinal hemorrhage).

▸ Note any recent procedures that can interfere with test results, including examinations using barium- or iodine-based contrast medium.

▸ Record the date of the last menstrual period and determine the possibility of pregnancy in perimenopausal women.

▸ Obtain a list of the patient's current medications, including herbs, nutritional supplements, and nutraceuticals (see Appendix F).

▸ Review the procedure with the patient. Address concerns about pain related to the procedure and explain that no pain will be experienced during the test, but there may be moments of discomfort. Reassure the patient that if contrast is used, it poses no radioactive hazard and rarely produces side effects. Inform the patient that the procedure is performed in an MRI department by a health-care provider (HCP) who specializes in this procedure, with support staff, and takes approximately 30 to 60 min.

▶ Inform the patient that the technologist will place him or her in a prone position on a special imaging table in a large cylindrical scanner.

▶ Tell the patient to expect to hear loud banging from the scanner and possibly to see magnetophosphenes (flickering lights in the visual field); these will stop when the procedure is over.

▶ *Sensitivity to social and cultural issues,* as well as concern for modesty, is important in providing psychological support before, during, and after the procedure.

▶ Explain that an IV line may be inserted to allow infusion of IV fluids, contrast medium, or sedatives.

▶ Instruct the patient to remove jewelry and all other metallic objects from the area to be examined prior to the procedure.

▶ There are no food, fluid, or medication restrictions unless by medical direction.

▶ Observe standard precautions, and follow the general guidelines in Appendix A. Positively identify the patient.

▶ Ensure that the patient has removed all external metallic objects from the area to be examined prior to the procedure.

▶ If the patient has a history of allergic reactions to any substance or drug, administer ordered prophylactic steroids or antihistamines before the procedure.

▶ Have emergency equipment readily available.

▶ Instruct the patient to void prior to the procedure and to change into the gown, robe, and foot coverings provided.

▶ Instruct the patient to cooperate fully and to follow directions. Instruct the patient to remain still throughout the procedure because movement produces unreliable results.

▶ Supply earplugs to the patient to block out the loud, banging sounds that occur during the test. Instruct the patient to communicate with the technologist during the examination via a microphone within the scanner.

▶ Establish an IV fluid line for the injection of emergency drugs and of sedatives.

▶ Administer an antianxiety agent, as ordered, if the patient has claustrophobia. Administer a sedative to a child or to an uncooperative adult, as ordered.

▶ Place the patient in the prone position on a special examination table designed for breast imaging.

▶ If contrast is used, imaging can begin shortly after the injection.

▶ Ask the patient to inhale deeply and hold his or her breath while the images are taken and then to exhale after the images are taken.

▶ Instruct the patient to take slow, deep breaths if nausea occurs during the procedure.

▶ Monitor the patient for complications related to the procedure (e.g., allergic reaction, anaphylaxis, bronchospasm).

▶ Remove the needle or catheter and apply a pressure dressing over the puncture site.

▶ Observe/assess the needle/catheter insertion site for bleeding, inflammation, or hematoma formation.

▶ A report of the results will be made available to the requesting HCP, who will discuss the results with the patient.

▶ Observe for delayed allergic reactions, such as rash, urticaria, tachycardia, hyperpnea, hypertension, palpitations, nausea, or vomiting.

▶ Instruct the patient to immediately report symptoms such as fast heart rate, difficulty breathing, skin rash, itching, chest pain, persistent right shoulder pain, or abdominal pain. Immediately report symptoms to the appropriate HCP.

▶ Instruct the patient in the care and assessment of the injection site.

▶ Instruct the patient to apply cold compresses to the puncture site as needed to reduce discomfort or edema.

Recognize anxiety related to test results. Discuss the implications of abnormal test results on the patient's lifestyle. Provide teaching and information regarding the clinical implications of the test results, as appropriate. Educate the patient regarding access to counseling services.

Reinforce information given by the patient's HCP regarding further testing, treatment, or referral to another HCP. Decisions regarding the need for and frequency of breast self-examination, mammography, MRI breast, or other cancer screening procedures should be made after consultation between the patient and HCP. The most current guidelines for breast cancer screening of the general population as well as for individuals with increased risk are available from the American Cancer Society (www.cancer.org), the American College of Obstetricians and

Gynecologists (ACOG) (www.acog.org), and the American College of Radiology (www.acr.org). Answer any questions or address any concerns voiced by the patient or family.

Depending on the results of this procedure, additional testing may be performed to evaluate or monitor progression of the disease process and determine the need for a change in therapy. Evaluate test results in relation to the patient's symptoms and other tests performed.

RELATED MONOGRAPHS:

Related tests include biopsy breast, bone scan, BUN, cancer antigens, CT thorax, creatinine, ductography, mammogram, stereotactic biopsy breast, and US breast.

Refer to the Reproductive System table at the end of the book for related tests by body system.

Magnetic Resonance Imaging, Chest

M

SYNONYM/ACRONYM: Chest MRI.

COMMON USE: To visualize and assess pulmonary and cardiovascular structures toward diagnosing tumor, masses, aneurysm, infarct, air, fluid, and evaluate the effectiveness of medical, and surgical interventions.

AREA OF APPLICATION: Chest/thorax.

CONTRAST: Can be done with or without IV contrast medium (gadolinium).

DESCRIPTION: Magnetic resonance imaging (MRI) uses a magnet and radio waves to produce an energy field that can be displayed as an image. Use of magnetic fields with the aid of radiofrequency energy produces images primarily based on water content of tissue. The magnetic field causes the hydrogen atoms

in tissue to line up, and when radio waves are directed toward the magnetic field, the atoms absorb the radio waves and change their position. When the radio waves are turned off, the atoms go back to their original position; this change in the energy field is sensed by the equipment, and an image is generated by the attached computer system. MRI produces cross-sectional images of pathological lesions in multiple planes without the use of ionizing radiation or the interference of bone or surrounding tissue.

Chest MRI scanning is performed to assist in diagnosing abnormalities of cardiovascular and pulmonary structures. Two special techniques are available for evaluation of cardiovascular structures. One is the electrocardiograph (ECG)–gated multislice spin-echo sequence, used to diagnose anatomic abnormalities of the heart and aorta, and the other is the ECG-referenced gradient refocused sequence, used to diagnose heart function and analyze blood flow patterns.

Magnetic resonance angiography (MRA) is an application of MRI that provides images of blood flow and diseased and normal blood vessels. In patients who are allergic to iodinated contrast medium, MRA is used in place of angiography (see monograph titled "Magnetic Resonance Angiography").

INDICATIONS

Confirm diagnosis of cardiac and pericardiac masses

Detect aortic aneurysms

Detect myocardial infarction and cardiac muscle ischemia

Detect pericardial abnormalities

Detect pleural effusion

Detect thoracic aortic diseases

Determine blood, fluid, or fat accumulation in tissues, pleuritic space, or vessels

Determine cardiac ventricular function

Differentiate aortic aneurysms from tumors near the aorta

- Evaluate cardiac chambers and pulmonary vessels
- Evaluate postoperative angioplasty sites and bypass grafts
- Identify congenital heart diseases
- Monitor and evaluate the effectiveness of medical or surgical therapeutic regimen

POTENTIAL DIAGNOSIS

Normal findings in
- Normal heart and lung structures, soft tissue, and function, including blood flow rate

Abnormal findings in
- Aortic dissection
- Congenital heart diseases, including pulmonary atresia, aortic coarctation, agenesis of the pulmonary artery, and transposition of the great vessels
- Constrictive pericarditis
- Intramural and periaortic hematoma
- Myocardial infarction
- Pericardial hematoma or effusion
- Pleural effusion

CRITICAL FINDINGS
- Aortic aneurysm
- Aortic dissection
- Tumor with significant mass effect

It is essential that critical diagnoses be communicated immediately to the appropriate health-care provider (HCP). A listing of these diagnoses varies among facilities. Timely notification of critical values for lab or diagnostic studies is a role expectation of the professional nurse. Notification processes will vary among facilities. Upon receipt of the critical value the information should be read back to the caller to verify accuracy. Most policies require immediate notification of the primary HCP, hospitalist, or on-call HCP. Reported information includes the patient's name, unique identifiers, critical value, name of the person giving the report, and name of the person receiving the report.

M

Documentation of notification should be made in the medical record with the name of the HCP notified, time and date of notification, and any orders received. Any delay in a timely report of a critical value may require completion of a notification form with review by Risk Management.

INTERFERING FACTORS

This procedure is contraindicated for

• Patients with certain ferrous metal prostheses, valves, aneurysm clips, inner ear prostheses, or other metallic objects.

• ❖ Patients with metal in their body, such as shrapnel or ferrous metal in the eye.

• ❖ Patients with cardiac pacemakers, because the pacemaker can be deactivated by MRI.

• ❖ Use of gadolinium-based contrast agents (GBCAs) is contraindicated in patients with acute or chronic severe renal insufficiency (glomerular filtration rate less than 30 mL/min/1.73 m^2). Patients should be screened for renal dysfunction prior to administration. The use of GBCAs should be avoided in these patients unless the benefits of the studies outweigh the risks and if essential diagnostic information is not available using non-contrast-enhanced diagnostic studies.

• Patients with intrauterine devices.

• Patients with iron pigments in tattoos.

• Patients who are claustrophobic.

• Patients who are pregnant or suspected of being pregnant, unless the potential benefits of the procedure far outweigh the risks to the fetus and mother.

Factors that may impair clear imaging

• Metallic objects (e.g., jewelry, body rings, dental amalgams) within the examination field, which may inhibit organ visualization and cause unclear images.

• Inability of the patient to cooperate or remain still during the procedure because of age, significant pain, or mental status.

• Patients with extreme cases of claustrophobia, unless sedation is given before the study or an open MRI is utilized.

Other considerations

• If contrast medium is allowed to seep deep into the muscle tissue, vascular visualization will be impossible.

NURSING IMPLICATIONS AND PROCEDURE

PRETEST:

▸ Positively identify the patient using at least two unique identifiers before providing care, treatment, or services.

▸ *Patient Teaching:* Inform the patient this procedure can assist in assessing organs and structures inside the chest

▸ Obtain a history of the patient's complaints, including a list of known allergens, especially allergies or sensitivities to latex, iodine, seafood, contrast medium, anesthetics, or dyes.

▸ Obtain a history of the patient's cardiovascular and respiratory systems, symptoms, and results of previously performed laboratory tests and diagnostic and surgical procedures. Obtain a history of renal dysfunction if the use of GBCA is anticipated.

▸ Ensure the results of BUN, creatinine, and eGFR (estimated glomerular filtration rate) are obtained if GBCA is to be used.

▸ Determine if the patient has ever had any device implanted into his or her body, including copper intrauterine devices, pacemakers, ear implants, and heart valves.

▸ Obtain occupational history to determine the presence of metal in the body, such as shrapnel or flecks of ferrous metal in the eye (which can cause retinal hemorrhage).

Note any recent procedures that can interfere with test results, including examinations using barium- or iodine-based contrast medium.

Record the date of the last menstrual period and determine possibility of pregnancy in perimenopausal women.

Obtain a list of the patient's current medications, including herbs, nutritional supplements, and nutraceuticals (see Appendix F).

Review the procedure with the patient. Address concerns about pain related to the procedure and explain that no pain will be experienced during the test, but there may be moments of discomfort. Reassure the patient that if contrast is used, it poses no radioactive hazard and rarely produces side effects. Inform the patient the procedure is performed in an MRI department, usually by an HCP who specializes in these procedures, with support staff, and takes approximately 30 to 60 min.

Inform the patient that the technologist will place him or her in a supine position on a flat table in a large cylindrical scanner.

Tell the patient to expect to hear loud banging from the scanner and possibly to see magnetophosphenes (flickering lights in the visual field); these will stop when the procedure is over.

Sensitivity to social and cultural issues, as well as concern for modesty, is important in providing psychological support before, during, and after the procedure. Explain that an IV line may be inserted to allow infusion of IV fluids, contrast medium, or sedatives.

Instruct the patient to remove jewelry and all other metallic objects from the area to be examined prior to the procedure.

There are no food, fluid, or medication restrictions unless by medical direction.

INTRATEST:

Observe standard precautions, and follow the general guidelines in Appendix A. Positively identify the patient.

Ensure that the patient has removed all external metallic objects from the area to be examined prior to the procedure.

If the patient has a history of allergic reactions to any substance or drug, administer ordered prophylactic steroids or antihistamines before the procedure.

Have emergency equipment readily available.

Instruct the patient to void prior to the procedure and to change into the gown, robe, and foot coverings provided.

Instruct the patient to cooperate fully and to follow directions. Instruct the patient to remain still throughout the procedure because movement produces unreliable results.

Supply earplugs to the patient to block out the loud, banging sounds that occur during the test. Instruct the patient to communicate with the technologist during the examination via a microphone within the scanner.

If an electrocardiogram or respiratory gating is to be performed in conjunction with the scan, apply MRI-safe electrodes to the appropriate sites.

Establish an IV fluid line for the injection of emergency drugs and of sedatives.

Administer an antianxiety agent, as ordered, if the patient has claustrophobia. Administer a sedative to a child or to an uncooperative adult, as ordered.

Place the patient in the supine position on an examination table.

If contrast is used, imaging can begin shortly after the injection.

Ask the patient to inhale deeply and hold his or her breath while the images are taken and then to exhale after the images are taken.

Instruct the patient to take slow, deep breaths if nausea occurs during the procedure.

Monitor the patient for complications related to the procedure (e.g., allergic reaction, anaphylaxis, bronchospasm).

Remove the needle or catheter and apply a pressure dressing over the puncture site.

Observe/assess the needle/catheter insertion site for bleeding, inflammation, or hematoma formation.

POST-TEST:

A report of the results will be made available to the requesting HCP, who will discuss the results with the patient.

Observe for delayed allergic reactions, such as rash, urticaria, tachycardia,

M

hyperpnea, hypertension, palpitations, nausea, or vomiting.

▸ Instruct the patient to immediately report symptoms such as fast heart rate, difficulty breathing, skin rash, itching, chest pain, persistent right shoulder pain, or abdominal pain. Immediately report symptoms to the appropriate HCP.

▸ Instruct the patient in the care and assessment of the injection site.

▸ Instruct the patient to apply cold compresses to the puncture site as needed to reduce discomfort or edema.

▸ Recognize anxiety related to test results. Discuss the implications of abnormal test results on the patient's lifestyle. Provide teaching and information regarding the clinical implications of the test results, as appropriate.

▸ Reinforce information given by the patient's HCP regarding further testing, treatment, or referral to another HCP. Answer any questions or address any concerns voiced by the patient or family.

▸ Depending on the results of this procedure, additional testing may be performed to evaluate or monitor progression of the disease process and determine the need for a change in therapy. Evaluate test results in relation to the patient's symptoms and other tests performed.

RELATED MONOGRAPHS:

▸ Related tests include AST, BNP, blood gases, blood pool imaging, BUN, chest x-ray, CT cardiac scoring, CT thorax, CRP, CK and isoenzymes, creatinine, echocardiography, exercise stress test, Holter monitor, myocardial infarct scan, myocardial perfusion heart scan, myoglobin, pleural fluid analysis, PET scan of the heart, and troponins.

▸ Refer to the Cardiovascular and Respiratory systems tables at the end of the book for related tests by body system.

Magnetic Resonance Imaging, Musculoskeletal

M

SYNONYM/ACRONYM: Musculoskeletal (knee, shoulder, hand, wrist, foot, elbow, hip, spine) MRI.

COMMON USE: To visualize and assess bones, joints, and surrounding structures to assist in diagnosing defects, cysts, tumors, and fracture.

AREA OF APPLICATION: Bones, joints, soft tissues.

CONTRAST: Can be done with or without IV contrast medium (gadolinium).

DESCRIPTION: Magnetic resonance imaging (MRI) uses a magnet and radio waves to produce an energy field that can be displayed as an image. Use of magnetic fields with the aid of radiofrequency energy produces images primarily based on water content of tissue. The magnetic field causes the hydrogen atoms in tissue to line up, and when radio waves are directed toward the magnetic field, the atoms absorb the radio waves and change their position. When the radio waves are turned off, the atoms go back to their original position; this change in the energy field is sensed by the equipment, and an image is generated by the attached computer system. MRI produces cross-sectional images of bones and joints in multiple planes without the use of ionizing radiation or the interference of bone or surrounding tissue.

Musculoskeletal MRI is performed to assist in diagnosing abnormalities of bones and joints and surrounding soft tissue structures, including cartilage, synovium, ligaments, and tendons. MRI eliminates the risks associated with exposure to x-rays and causes no harm to cells. Contrast-enhanced imaging is effective for evaluating scarring from previous surgery, vascular abnormalities, and differentiation of metastases from primary tumors. MRI uses the noniodinated contrast medium gadopentetate dimeglumine (Magnevist), which is administered IV to enhance contrast differences between normal and abnormal tissues.

Magnetic resonance angiography (MRA) is an application of MRI that provides images of blood flow and diseased and normal blood vessels. In patients who are allergic to iodinated contrast medium, MRA is used in place of angiography (see monograph titled "Magnetic Resonance Angiography").

INDICATIONS

- Confirm diagnosis of osteomyelitis
- Detect avascular necrosis of the femoral head or knee
- Detect benign and cancerous tumors and cysts of the bone or soft tissue
- Detect bone infarcts in the epiphyseal or diaphyseal sites
- Detect changes in bone marrow
- Detect tears or degeneration of ligaments, tendons, and menisci resulting from trauma or pathology
- Determine cause of low back pain, including herniated disk and spinal degenerative disease
- Differentiate between primary and secondary malignant processes of the bone marrow
- Differentiate between a stress fracture and a tumor
- Evaluate meniscal detachment of the temporomandibular joint

POTENTIAL DIAGNOSIS

Normal findings in

- Normal bones, joints, and surrounding tissue structures; no articular disease, bone marrow disorders, tumors, infections, or trauma to the bones, joints, or muscles

Abnormal findings in

- Avascular necrosis of femoral head or knee, as found in Legg-Calvé-Perthes disease
- Bone marrow disease, such as Gaucher's disease, aplastic anemia, sickle cell disease, or polycythemia
- Degenerative spinal disease, such as spondylosis or arthritis
- Fibrosarcoma
- Hemangioma (muscular or osseous)
- Herniated disk
- Infection
- Meniscal tears or degeneration
- Osteochondroma
- Osteogenic sarcoma
- Osteomyelitis
- Rotator cuff tears
- Spinal stenosis
- Stress fracture
- Synovitis
- Tumor

CRITICAL FINDINGS: N/A

INTERFERING FACTORS

This procedure is contraindicated for

- Patients with certain ferrous metal prostheses, valves, aneurysm clips, inner ear prostheses, or other metallic objects.

M

- ✸ Patients with cardiac pacemakers, because the pacemaker can be deactivated by MRI.
- ✸ Use of gadolinium-based contrast agents (GBCAs) is contraindicated in patients with acute or chronic severe renal insufficiency (glomerular filtration rate less than 30 mL/min/1.73 m^2). Patients should be screened for renal dysfunction prior to administration. The use of GBCAs should be avoided in these patients unless the benefits of the studies outweigh the risks and if essential diagnostic information is not available using non-contrast-enhanced diagnostic studies.
- ✸ Patients with metal in their body, such as shrapnel or ferrous metal in the eye.
- Patients with intrauterine devices.
- Patients with iron pigments in tattoos.
- Patients who are claustrophobic.
- Patients who are pregnant or suspected of being pregnant, unless the potential benefits of the procedure far outweigh the risks to the fetus and mother.

Factors that may impair clear imaging
- Metallic objects (e.g., jewelry, body rings, dental amalgams) within the examination field, which may inhibit organ visualization and cause unclear images.
- Inability of the patient to cooperate or remain still during the procedure because of age, significant pain, or mental status.
- Patients with extreme cases of claustrophobia, unless sedation is given before the study or an open MRI is utilized.

Other considerations
- If contrast medium is allowed to seep deep into the muscle tissue, vascular visualization will be impossible.

NURSING IMPLICATIONS AND PROCEDURE

PRETEST:

▸ Positively identify the patient using at least two unique identifiers before providing care, treatment, or services.
▸ *Patient Teaching:* Inform the patient this procedure can assist in assessing bones, muscles, and joints.
▸ Obtain a history of the patient's complaints, including a list of known allergens, especially allergies or sensitivities to latex, iodine, seafood, contrast medium, anesthetics, or dyes.
▸ Obtain a history of the patient's musculoskeletal system, symptoms, and results of previously performed laboratory tests and diagnostic and surgical procedures. Obtain a history of renal dysfunction if the use of GBCA is anticipated.
▸ Ensure the results of BUN, creatinine, and eGFR (estimated glomerular filtration rate) are obtained if GBCA is to be used.
▸ Determine if the patient has ever had any device implanted into his or her body, including copper intrauterine devices, pacemakers, ear implants, and heart valves.
▸ Obtain occupational history to determine the presence of metal in the body, such as shrapnel or flecks of ferrous metal in the eye (which can cause retinal hemorrhage).
▸ Note any recent procedures that can interfere with test results, including examinations using barium- or iodine-based contrast medium.
▸ Record the date of the last menstrual period and determine the possibility of pregnancy in perimenopausal women.
▸ Obtain a list of the patient's current medications, including herbs, nutritional supplements, and nutraceuticals (see Appendix F).
▸ Review the procedure with the patient. Address concerns about pain related to the procedure and explain that no pain will be experienced during the test, but there may be moments of discomfort. Reassure the patient that if contrast is used, it poses no radioactive hazard and rarely produces side effects. Inform the patient the

M

procedure is performed in an MRI department, usually by a health-care provider (HCP) specializing in this procedure, with support staff, and takes approximately 30 to 60 min.

Inform the patient that the technologist will place him or her in a supine position on a flat table in a large cylindrical scanner.

Tell the patient to expect to hear loud banging from the scanner and possibly to see magnetophosphenes (flickering lights in the visual field); these will stop when the procedure is over.

Sensitivity to social and cultural issues, as well as concern for modesty, is important in providing psychological support before, during, and after the procedure.

Explain that an IV line may be inserted to allow infusion of IV fluids, contrast medium, or sedatives.

Instruct the patient to remove jewelry and all other metallic objects from the area to be examined prior to the procedure.

There are no food, fluid, or medication restrictions unless by medical direction.

INTRATEST:

Observe standard precautions, and follow the general guidelines in Appendix A.

Positively identify the patient.

Ensure that the patient has removed all external metallic objects from the area to be examined prior to the procedure.

If the patient has a history of allergic reactions to any substance or drug, administer ordered prophylactic steroids or antihistamines before the procedure.

Have emergency equipment readily available.

Instruct the patient to void prior to the procedure and to change into the gown, robe, and foot coverings provided.

Instruct the patient to cooperate fully and to follow directions. Instruct the patient to remain still throughout the procedure because movement produces unreliable results.

Supply earplugs to the patient to block out the loud, banging sounds that occur during the test. Instruct the patient to communicate with the

technologist during the examination via a microphone within the scanner.

▸ Establish an IV fluid line for the injection of emergency drugs and of sedatives.

▸ Administer an antianxiety agent, as ordered, if the patient has claustrophobia. Administer a sedative to a child or to an uncooperative adult, as ordered.

▸ Place the patient in the supine position on an examination table.

▸ If contrast is used, imaging can begin shortly after the injection.

▸ Ask the patient to inhale deeply and hold his or her breath while the images are taken and then to exhale after the images are taken.

▸ Instruct the patient to take slow, deep breaths if nausea occurs during the procedure.

▸ Monitor the patient for complications related to the procedure (e.g., allergic reaction, anaphylaxis, bronchospasm).

▸ Remove the needle or catheter and apply a pressure dressing over the puncture site.

▸ Observe/assess the needle/catheter insertion site for bleeding, inflammation, or hematoma formation.

POST-TEST:

▸ A report of the results will be made available to the requesting HCP, who will discuss the results with the patient.

▸ Observe for delayed allergic reactions, such as rash, urticaria, tachycardia, hyperpnea, hypertension, palpitations, nausea, or vomiting, if contrast medium was used.

▸ Instruct the patient to immediately report symptoms such as fast heart rate, difficulty breathing, skin rash, itching, chest pain, persistent right shoulder pain, or abdominal pain. Immediately report symptoms to the appropriate HCP.

▸ Instruct the patient in the care and assessment of the injection site.

▸ Instruct the patient to apply cold compresses to the puncture site as needed, to reduce discomfort or edema.

▸ Recognize anxiety related to test results, and be supportive of impaired activity related to anticipated chronic pain resulting from joint inflammation, impairment in mobility, musculoskeletal deformity, and loss of independence.

M

Discuss the implications of abnormal test results on the patient's lifestyle. Provide teaching and information regarding the clinical implications of the test results, as appropriate. Educate the patient regarding access to counseling services, as appropriate. Provide contact information, if desired, for the American College of Rheumatology (www.rheumatology.org) or for the Arthritis Foundation (www.arthritis.org).
Reinforce information given by the patient's HCP regarding further testing, treatment, or referral to another HCP. Answer any questions or address any concerns voiced by the patient or family.
Depending on the results of this procedure, additional testing may be performed to evaluate or monitor progression of the disease process and determine the need for a change in therapy. Evaluate test results in relation to the patient's symptoms and other tests performed.

RELATED MONOGRAPHS:

Related tests include anticyclic citrullinated antibodies, ANA, arthrogram, arthroscopy, bone mineral densitometry, bone scan, BUN, CRP, CT spine, creatinine, ESR, radiography of the bone, synovial fluid analysis, RF, and vertebroplasty.
Refer to the Musculoskeletal System table at the end of the book for related tests by body system.

Magnetic Resonance Imaging, Pancreas

SYNONYM/ACRONYM: Pancreatic MRI.

COMMON USE: To visualize and assess the pancreas for structural defects, tumor, masses, staging cancer, and evaluating the effectiveness of medical and surgical interventions.

AREA OF APPLICATION: Pancreatic/upper abdominal area.

CONTRAST: Can be done with or without IV contrast medium (gadolinium).

DESCRIPTION: Magnetic resonance imaging (MRI) uses a magnet and radio waves to produce an energy field that can be displayed as an image. Use of magnetic fields with the aid of radiofrequency energy produces images primarily based on water content of tissue. The magnetic field causes the hydrogen atoms in tissue to line up, and when radio waves are directed toward the magnetic field, the atoms absorb the radio waves and change their position. When the radio waves are turned off, the atoms go back to their original position; this change in the energy field is sensed by the equipment, and an image is generated by the attached computer system. MRI produces cross-sectional images of the abdominal area in multiple planes without the use of ionizing radiation or the interference of bone or surrounding tissue.

MRI of the pancreas is employed to evaluate small pancreatic adenocarcinomas, islet cell tumors, ductal abnormalities and calculi, or parenchymal abnormalities. A T1-weighted, fat-saturation series of images is probably best for evaluating the pancreatic parenchyma. This sequence is ideal for showing fat planes between the pancreas and peripancreatic structures and for identifying abnormalities such as fatty infiltration of the pancreas, hemorrhage, adenopathy, and carcinomas. T2-weighted images are most useful for depicting intrapancreatic or peripancreatic fluid collections, pancreatic neoplasms, and calculi. Imaging sequences can be adjusted to display fluid in the biliary tree and pancreatic ducts. MRI uses the noniodinated contrast medium gadopentetate dimeglumine (Magnevist), which is administered IV to enhance contrast differences between normal and abnormal tissues.

Magnetic resonance angiography (MRA) is an application of MRI that provides images of blood flow and diseased and normal blood vessels. In patients who are allergic to iodinated contrast medium, MRA is used in place of angiography (see monograph titled "Magnetic Resonance Angiography").

INDICATIONS

Detect pancreatic fatty infiltration, hemorrhage, and adenopathy
Detect a pancreatic mass
Detect pancreatitis
Detect primary or metastatic tumors of the pancreas and provide cancer staging
Detect soft tissue abnormalities
Determine vascular complications of pancreatitis, venous thrombosis, or pseudoaneurysm
Differentiate tumors from other abnormalities, such as cysts, cavernous hemangiomas, and pancreatic abscesses

• Monitor and evaluate the effectiveness of medical or surgical interventions and course of disease

POTENTIAL DIAGNOSIS

Normal findings in
• Normal anatomic structures and soft tissue density and biochemical constituents of the pancreatic parenchyma, including blood flow

Abnormal findings in
• Islet cell tumor
• Metastasis
• Pancreatic duct obstruction or calculi
• Pancreatic fatty infiltration, hemorrhage, and adenopathy
• Pancreatic mass
• Pancreatitis

CRITICAL FINDINGS: N/A

INTERFERING FACTORS

This procedure is contraindicated for
• Patients with certain ferrous metal prostheses, valves, aneurysm clips, inner ear prostheses, or other metallic objects.
• ✵ Patients with metal in their body, such as shrapnel or ferrous metal in the eye.
• ✵ Patients with cardiac pacemakers, because the pacemaker can be deactivated by MRI.
• ✵ Use of gadolinium-based contrast agents (GBCAs) is contraindicated in patients with acute or chronic severe renal insufficiency (glomerular filtration rate less than 30 mL/min/1.73 m^2). Patients should be screened for renal dysfunction prior to administration. The use of GBCAs should be avoided in these patients unless the benefits of the studies outweigh the risks and if essential diagnostic information is not available using noncontrast-enhanced diagnostic studies.

M

- Patients with intrauterine devices.
- Patients with iron pigments in tattoos.
- Patients who are claustrophobic.
- Patients who are pregnant or suspected of being pregnant, unless the potential benefits of the procedure far outweigh the risks to the fetus and mother.

Factors that may impair clear imaging

- Metallic objects (e.g., jewelry, body rings, dental amalgams) within the examination field, which may inhibit organ visualization and cause unclear images.
- Inability of the patient to cooperate or remain still during the procedure because of age, significant pain, or mental status.
- Patients with extreme cases of claustrophobia, unless sedation is given before the study or an open MRI is utilized.

Other considerations

- If contrast medium is allowed to seep deep into the muscle tissue, vascular visualization will be impossible.

NURSING IMPLICATIONS AND PROCEDURE

PRETEST:

- Positively identify the patient using at least two unique identifiers before providing care, treatment, or services.
- *Patient Teaching:* Inform the patient this procedure can assist in assessing the pancreas, organs, and structures inside the abdomen.
- Obtain a history of the patient's complaints, including a list of known allergens, especially allergies or sensitivities to latex, iodine, seafood, contrast medium, anesthetics, or dyes.
- Obtain a history of the patient's endocrine and hepatobiliary systems, symptoms, and results of previously performed laboratory tests and diagnostic and surgical procedures. Obtain a history of renal dysfunction if the use of GBCA is anticipated.

- Ensure the results of BUN, creatinine, and eGFR (estimated glomerular filtration rate) are obtained if GBCA is to be used
- Determine if the patient has ever had any device implanted into his or her body, including copper intrauterine devices, pacemakers, ear implants, and heart valves.
- Obtain occupational history to determine the presence of metal in the body, such as shrapnel or flecks of ferrous metal in the eye (which can cause retinal hemorrhage).
- Note any recent procedures that can interfere with test results, including examinations using barium- or iodine-based contrast medium.
- Record the date of the last menstrual period and determine the possibility of pregnancy in perimenopausal women.
- Obtain a list of the patient's current medications, including herbs, nutritional supplements, and nutraceuticals (see Appendix F).
- Review the procedure with the patient. Address concerns about pain related to the procedure and explain that no pain will be experienced during the test, but there may be moments of discomfort. Reassure the patient that if contrast is used, it poses no radioactive hazard and rarely produces side effects.
- Inform the patient that the procedure is performed in an MRI department by a health-care provider (HCP) specializing in this procedure, with support staff and takes approximately 30 to 60 min.
- Inform the patient that the technologist will place him or her in a supine position on a flat table in a large cylindrical scanner.
- Tell the patient to expect to hear loud banging from the scanner and possibly to see magnetophosphenes (flickering lights in the visual field); these will stop when the procedure is over.
- *Sensitivity to social and cultural issues,* as well as concern for modesty, is important in providing psychological support before, during, and after the procedure.
- Explain that an IV line may be inserted to allow infusion of IV fluids, contrast medium, or sedatives.
- Instruct the patient to remove jewelry and all other metallic objects from the

M

area to be examined prior to the procedure.

There are no food, fluid, or medication restrictions unless by medical direction.

INTRATEST:

- Observe standard precautions, and follow the general guidelines in Appendix A. Positively identify the patient.
- Ensure that the patient has removed all external metallic objects from the area to be examined prior to the procedure.
- If the patient has a history of allergic reactions to any substance or drug, administer ordered prophylactic steroids or antihistamines before the procedure. Have emergency equipment readily available.
- Instruct the patient to void prior to the procedure and to change into the gown, robe, and foot coverings provided.
- Instruct the patient to cooperate fully and to follow directions. Instruct the patient to remain still throughout the procedure because movement produces unreliable results.
- Supply earplugs to the patient to block out the loud, banging sounds that occur during the test. Instruct the patient to communicate with the technologist during the examination via a microphone within the scanner.
- Establish an IV fluid line for the injection of emergency drugs and of sedatives.
- Administer an antianxiety agent, as ordered, if the patient has claustrophobia. Administer a sedative to a child or to an uncooperative adult, as ordered.
- Place the patient in the supine position on an examination table.
- If contrast is used, imaging can begin shortly after the injection.
- Ask the patient to inhale deeply and hold his or her breath while the images are taken and then to exhale after the images are taken.
- Instruct the patient to take slow, deep breaths if nausea occurs during the procedure.
- Monitor the patient for complications related to the procedure (e.g., allergic reaction, anaphylaxis, bronchospasm).
- Remove the needle or catheter and apply a pressure dressing over the puncture site.

- Observe/assess the needle/catheter insertion site for bleeding, inflammation, or hematoma formation.

POST-TEST:

- A report of the results will be made available to the requesting HCP, who will discuss the results with the patient.
- Observe for delayed allergic reactions, such as rash, urticaria, tachycardia, hyperpnea, hypertension, palpitations, nausea, or vomiting.
- Instruct the patient to immediately report symptoms such as fast heart rate, difficulty breathing, skin rash, itching, chest pain, persistent right shoulder pain, or abdominal pain. Immediately report symptoms to the appropriate HCP.
- Instruct the patient in the care and assessment of the injection site.
- Instruct the patient to apply cold compresses to the puncture site as needed, to reduce discomfort or edema.
- Recognize anxiety related to test results. Discuss the implications of abnormal test results on the patient's lifestyle. Provide teaching and information regarding the clinical implications of the test results, as appropriate.
- Reinforce information given by the patient's HCP regarding further testing, treatment, or referral to another HCP. Answer any questions or address any concerns voiced by the patient or family.
- Depending on the results of this procedure, additional testing may be performed to evaluate or monitor progression of the disease process and determine the need for a change in therapy. Evaluate test results in relation to the patient's symptoms and other tests performed.

RELATED MONOGRAPHS:

- Related tests include amylase, angiography of the abdomen, BUN, calcitonin, cholangiopancreatography endoscopic retrograde, CT abdomen, creatinine, hepatobiliary scan, 5-hydroxyindoleacetic acid, lipase, peritoneal fluid analysis, US liver and biliary system, and US pancreas.
- Refer to the Endocrine and Hepatobiliary systems tables at the end of the book for related tests by body system.

M

Magnetic Resonance Imaging, Pelvis

SYNONYM/ACRONYM: Pelvis MRI.

COMMON USE: To visualize and assess the pelvis and surrounding structure for tumor, masses, staging cancer, and inflammation and to evaluate the effectiveness of medical and surgical interventions.

AREA OF APPLICATION: Pelvic area.

CONTRAST: Can be done with or without IV contrast medium (gadolinium).

DESCRIPTION: Magnetic resonance imaging (MRI) uses a magnet and radio waves to produce an energy field that can be displayed as an image. Use of magnetic fields with the aid of radiofrequency energy produces images primarily based on water content of tissue. The magnetic field causes the hydrogen atoms in tissue to line up, and when radio waves are directed toward the magnetic field, the atoms absorb the radio waves and change their position. When the radio waves are turned off, the atoms go back to their original position; this change in the energy field is sensed by the equipment, and an image is generated by the attached computer system. MRI produces cross-sectional images of the pelvic area in multiple planes without the use of ionizing radiation or the interference of bone or surrounding tissue.

Pelvic MRI is performed to assist in diagnosing abnormalities of the pelvis and associated structures. Contrast-enhanced MRI is effective for evaluating metastases from primary tumors. MRI is highly effective for depicting small-volume peritoneal tumors, carcinomatosis, and peritonitis and for determining the response to surgical and chemical therapies. MRI uses the noniodinated contrast medium gadopentetate dimeglumine (Magnevist), which is administered IV to enhance contrast differences between normal and abnormal tissues. Oral and rectal contrast administration may be used to isolate the bowel from adjacent pelvic organs and improve organ visualization.

Magnetic resonance angiography (MRA) is an application of MRI that provides images of blood flow and diseased and normal blood vessels. In patients who are allergic to iodinated contrast medium, MRA is used in place of angiography (see monograph titled "Magnetic Resonance Angiography").

INDICATIONS
- Detect cancer (primary or metastatic tumors of ovary, prostate, uterus, and bladder) and provide cancer staging
- Detect pelvic vascular diseases
- Detect peritonitis
- Detect soft tissue abnormalities
- Determine blood clots, cysts, fluid or fat accumulation in tissues, hemorrhage, and infarctions

Differentiate tumors from tissue abnormalities, such as cysts, cavernous hemangiomas, and abscesses

Monitor and evaluate the effectiveness of medical or surgical interventions and course of the disease

POTENTIAL DIAGNOSIS

Normal findings in

Normal pelvic structures and soft tissue density and biochemical constituents of pelvic tissues, including blood flow

Abnormal findings in

* Adenomyosis
* Ascites
* Fibroids
* Masses, lesions, infections, or inflammations
* Peritoneal tumor or carcinomatosis
* Peritonitis
* Pseudomyxoma peritonei

CRITICAL FINDINGS: N/A

INTERFERING FACTORS

This procedure is contraindicated for

Patients with certain ferrous metal prostheses, valves, aneurysm clips, inner ear prostheses, or other metallic objects.

Patients with metal in their body, such as shrapnel or ferrous metal in the eye.

Patients with cardiac pacemakers, because the pacemaker can be deactivated by MRI.

Use of gadolinium-based contrast agents (GBCAs) is contraindicated in patients with acute or chronic severe renal insufficiency (glomerular filtration rate less than 30 mL/min/1.73 m^2). Patients should be screened for renal dysfunction prior to administration. The use of GBCAs should be

avoided in these patients unless the benefits of the studies outweigh the risks and if essential diagnostic information is not available using non-contrast-enhanced diagnostic studies.

* Patients with intrauterine devices.
* Patients with iron pigments in tattoos.
* Patients who are claustrophobic.
* Patients who are pregnant or suspected of being pregnant, unless the potential benefits of the procedure far outweigh the risks to the fetus and mother.

Factors that may impair clear imaging

* Metallic objects (e.g., jewelry, body rings, dental amalgams) within the examination field, which may inhibit organ visualization and cause unclear images.
* Inability of the patient to cooperate or remain still during the procedure because of age, significant pain, or mental status.
* Patients with extreme cases of claustrophobia, unless sedation is given before the study or an open MRI is utilized.

Other considerations

* If contrast medium is allowed to seep deep into the muscle tissue, vascular visualization will be impossible.

M

NURSING IMPLICATIONS AND PROCEDURE

PRETEST:

Positively identify the patient using at least two unique identifiers before providing care, treatment, or services.

Patient Teaching: Inform the patient this procedure can assist in assessing the pelvis and surrounding structures.

Obtain a history of the patient's complaints, including a list of known allergens, especially allergies or sensitivities to latex, iodine, seafood, contrast medium, anesthetics, or dyes.

▸ Obtain a history of the patient's genitourinary system, symptoms, and results of previously performed laboratory tests and diagnostic and surgical procedures. Obtain a history of renal dysfunction if the use of GBCA is anticipated.

▸ Ensure the results of BUN, creatinine, and eGFR (estimated glomerular filtration rate) are obtained if GBCA is to be used.

▸ Determine if the patient has ever had any device implanted into his or her body, including copper intrauterine devices, pacemakers, ear implants, and heart valves.

▸ Obtain occupational history to determine the presence of metal in the body, such as shrapnel or flecks of ferrous metal in the eye (which can cause retinal hemorrhage).

▸ Note any recent procedures that can interfere with test results, including examinations using barium- or iodine-based contrast medium.

▸ Record the date of the last menstrual period and determine the possibility of pregnancy in perimenopausal women.

▸ Obtain a list of the patient's current medications, including herbs, nutritional supplements, and nutraceuticals (see Appendix F).

▸ Review the procedure with the patient. Address concerns about pain related to the procedure and explain that no pain will be experienced during the test, but there may be moments of discomfort. Reassure the patient that if contrast is used, it poses no radioactive hazard and rarely produces side effects. Inform the patient the procedure is performed in an MRI department by a health-care provider (HCP) specializing in this procedure, with support staff, and takes approximately 30 to 60 min.

▸ Inform the patient that the technologist will place him or her in a supine position on a flat table in a large cylindrical scanner.

▸ Tell the patient to expect to hear loud banging from the scanner and possibly to see magnetophosphenes (flickering lights in the visual field); these will stop when the procedure is over.

▸ *Sensitivity to social and cultural issues,* as well as concern for modesty, is important in providing psychological support before, during, and after the procedure.

▸ Explain that an IV line may be inserted to allow infusion of IV fluids, contrast medium, or sedatives.

▸ Instruct the patient to remove jewelry and all other metallic objects from the area to be examined prior to the procedure.

▸ There are no food, fluid, or medication restrictions unless by medical direction

INTRATEST:

▸ Observe standard precautions, and follow the general guidelines in Appendix A. Positively identify the patient.

▸ Ensure that the patient has removed all external metallic objects from the area to be examined prior to the procedure.

▸ If the patient has a history of allergic reactions to any substance or drug, administer ordered prophylactic steroids or antihistamines before the procedure.

▸ Have emergency equipment readily available.

▸ Instruct the patient to void prior to the procedure and to change into the gown, robe, and foot coverings provided.

▸ Instruct the patient to cooperate fully and to follow directions. Instruct the patient to remain still throughout the procedure because movement produces unreliable results.

▸ Supply earplugs to the patient to block out the loud, banging sounds that occur during the test. Instruct the patient to communicate with the technologist during the examination via a microphone within the scanner.

▸ Establish an IV fluid line for the injection of emergency drugs and of sedatives.

▸ Administer an antianxiety agent, as ordered, if the patient has claustrophobia. Administer a sedative to a child or to an uncooperative adult, as ordered.

Place the patient in the supine position on an examination table.

If contrast is used, imaging can begin shortly after the injection.

Ask the patient to inhale deeply and hold his or her breath while the images are taken and then to exhale after the images are taken.

Instruct the patient to take slow, deep breaths if nausea occurs during the procedure.

Monitor the patient for complications related to the procedure (e.g., allergic reaction, anaphylaxis, bronchospasm).

Remove the needle or catheter and apply a pressure dressing over the puncture site.

Observe/assess the needle/catheter insertion site for bleeding, inflammation, or hematoma formation.

POST-TEST:

A report of the results will be made available to the requesting HCP, who will discuss the results with the patient.

Observe for delayed allergic reactions, such as rash, urticaria, tachycardia, hyperpnea, hypertension, palpitations, nausea, or vomiting.

Instruct the patient to immediately report symptoms such as fast heart rate, difficulty breathing, skin rash, itching, chest pain, persistent right shoulder pain, or abdominal pain.

Immediately report symptoms to the appropriate HCP.

Instruct the patient in the care and assessment of the injection site.

Instruct the patient to apply cold compresses to the puncture site as needed, to reduce discomfort or edema.

Recognize anxiety related to test results. Discuss the implications of abnormal test results on the patient's lifestyle. Provide teaching and information regarding the clinical implications of the test results, as appropriate.

Reinforce information given by the patient's HCP regarding further testing, treatment, or referral to another HCP. Answer any questions or address any concerns voiced by the patient or family.

Depending on the results of this procedure, additional testing may be performed to evaluate or monitor progression of the disease process and determine the need for a change in therapy. Evaluate test results in relation to the patient's symptoms and other tests performed.

RELATED MONOGRAPHS:

Related tests include BUN, CT pelvis, creatinine, cystourethrography voiding, IVP, KUB study, renogram, and US pelvis.

Refer to the Genitourinary System table at the end of the book for related tests by body system.

M

Magnetic Resonance Imaging, Pituitary

SYNONYM/ACRONYM: Pituitary MRI, MRI of the parasellar region.

COMMON USE: To visualize and assess the pituitary and surrounding structures of the brain for lesions, hemorrhage, cysts, abscess, tumors, cancer, and infection.

AREA OF APPLICATION: Brain/pituitary area.

CONTRAST: Can be done with or without IV contrast medium (gadolinium).

DESCRIPTION: Magnetic resonance imaging (MRI) uses a magnet and radio waves to produce an energy field that can be displayed as an image. Use of magnetic fields with the aid of radiofrequency energy produces images primarily based on water content of tissue. The magnetic field causes the hydrogen atoms in tissue to line up, and when radio waves are directed toward the magnetic field, the atoms absorb the radio waves and change their position. When the radio waves are turned off, the atoms go back to their original position; this change in the energy field is sensed by the equipment, and an image is generated by the attached computer system. MRI produces cross-sectional images of the pituitary and parasellar region in multiple planes without the use of ionizing radiation or the interference of bone or surrounding tissue.

Pituitary MRI shows the relationship of pituitary lesions to the optic chiasm and cavernous sinuses. MRI has the capability of distinguishing the solid, cystic, and hemorrhagic components of lesions. Rapidly flowing blood on spin-echo MRI appears as an absence of signal or a void in the vessel's lumen. Blood flow can be evaluated in the cavernous and carotid arteries. Suprasellar aneurysms may be diagnosed without angiography, and old clotted blood in the walls of the aneurysms appears white. MRI uses the noniodinated contrast medium gadopentetate dimeglumine (Magnevist), which is administered IV to enhance contrast differences between normal and abnormal tissues.

Magnetic resonance angiography (MRA) is an application of MRI that provides images of blood flow and diseased and normal blood vessels. In patients who are allergic to iodinated contrast medium, MRA is used in place of angiography (see monograph titled "Magnetic Resonance Angiography").

INDICATIONS
- Detect microadenoma or macroadenoma of the pituitary
- Detect parasellar abnormalities
- Detect tumors of the pituitary
- Evaluate potential cause of headache, visual loss, and vomiting
- Evaluate the solid, cystic, and hemorrhagic components of lesions
- Evaluate vascularity of the pituitary
- Monitor and evaluate the effectiveness of medical or surgical interventions and course of disease

POTENTIAL DIAGNOSIS

Normal findings in
- Normal anatomic structures, density, and biochemical constituents of the pituitary, including blood flow

Abnormal findings in
- Abscess
- Aneurysm
- Choristoma
- Craniopharyngioma or meningioma
- Empty sella
- Granuloma
- Infarct or hemorrhage
- Macroadenoma or microadenoma
- Metastasis
- Parasitic infection

CRITICAL FINDINGS: N/A

INTERFERING FACTORS

This procedure is contraindicated for
- Patients with certain ferrous metal prostheses, valves, aneurysm clips,

inner ear prostheses, or other metallic objects.

* ❖ Patients with metal in their body, such as shrapnel or ferrous metal in the eye.
* ❖ Patients with cardiac pacemakers, because the pacemaker can be deactivated by MRI.
* ❖ Use of gadolinium-based contrast agents (GBCAs) is contraindicated in patients with acute or chronic severe renal insufficiency (glomerular filtration rate less than 30 mL/min/1.73 m²). Patients should be screened for renal dysfunction prior to administration. The use of GBCAs should be avoided in these patients unless the benefits of the studies outweigh the risks and if essential diagnostic information is not available using non–contrast-enhanced diagnostic studies.
* Patients with intrauterine devices.
* Patients with iron pigments in tattoos.
* Patients who are claustrophobic.
* Patients who are pregnant or suspected of being pregnant, unless the potential benefits of the procedure far outweigh the risks to the fetus and mother.

Factors that may impair clear imaging

* Metallic objects (e.g., jewelry, body rings, dental amalgams) within the examination field, which may inhibit organ visualization and cause unclear images.
* Inability of the patient to cooperate or remain still during the procedure because of age, significant pain, or mental status.
* Patients with extreme cases of claustrophobia, unless sedation is given before the study or an open MRI is utilized.

Other considerations

* If contrast medium is allowed to seep deep into the muscle tissue, vascular visualization will be impossible.

NURSING IMPLICATIONS AND PROCEDURE

PRETEST:

▸ Positively identify the patient using at least two unique identifiers before providing care, treatment, or services.

Patient Teaching: Inform the patient this procedure can assist in assessing the pituitary gland and surrounding brain tissue.

▸ Obtain a history of the patient's complaints, including a list of known allergens, especially allergies or sensitivities to latex, iodine, seafood, contrast medium, anesthetics, or dyes.

▸ Obtain a history of the patient's cardiovascular and endocrine systems, symptoms, and results of previously performed laboratory tests and diagnostic and surgical procedures. Obtain a history of renal dysfunction if the use of GBCA is anticipated.

▸ Ensure the results of BUN, creatinine, and eGFR (estimated glomerular filtration rate) are obtained if GBCA is to be used.

▸ Determine if the patient has ever had any device implanted into his or her body, including copper intrauterine devices, pacemakers, ear implants, and heart valves.

▸ Obtain occupational history to determine the presence of metal in the body, such as shrapnel or flecks of ferrous metal in the eye (which can cause retinal hemorrhage).

▸ Note any recent procedures that can interfere with test results, including examinations using barium- or iodine-based contrast medium.

▸ Record the date of the last menstrual period and determine the possibility of pregnancy in perimenopausal women.

▸ Obtain a list of the patient's current medications, including herbs, nutritional supplements, and nutraceuticals (see Appendix F).

▸ Review the procedure with the patient. Address concerns about pain related to the procedure and explain that no

M

pain will be experienced during the test, but there may be moments of discomfort. Inform the patient the procedure is performed in an MRI department by a health-care provider (HCP) specializing in this procedure, with support staff, and takes approximately 30 to 60 min.

▸ Inform the patient that the technologist will place him or her in a supine position on a flat table in a large cylindrical scanner.

▸ Tell the patient to expect to hear loud banging from the scanner and possibly to see magnetophosphenes (flickering lights in the visual field); these will stop when the procedure is over.

▸ *Sensitivity to social and cultural issues,* as well as concern for modesty, is important in providing psychological support before, during, and after the procedure.

▸ Explain that an IV line may be inserted to allow infusion of IV fluids, contrast medium, or sedatives.

▸ Instruct the patient to remove jewelry and all other metallic objects from the area to be examined prior to the procedure.

▸ There are no food, fluid, or medication restrictions unless by medical direction.

occur during the test. Instruct the patient to communicate with the technologist during the examination via a microphone within the scanner.

▸ Establish an IV fluid line for the injection of emergency drugs and of sedatives.

▸ Administer an antianxiety agent, as ordered, if the patient has claustrophobia. Administer a sedative to a child or to an uncooperative adult, as ordered.

▸ Place the patient in the supine position on an examination table.

▸ If contrast is used, imaging can begin shortly after the injection.

▸ Ask the patient to inhale deeply and hold his or her breath while the images are taken and then to exhale after the images are taken.

▸ Instruct the patient to take slow, deep breaths if nausea occurs during the procedure.

▸ Monitor the patient for complications related to the procedure (e.g., allergic reaction, anaphylaxis, bronchospasm).

▸ Remove the needle or catheter and apply a pressure dressing over the puncture site.

▸ Observe/assess the needle/catheter insertion site for bleeding, inflammation, or hematoma formation.

INTRATEST:

▸ Observe standard precautions, and follow the general guidelines in Appendix A. Positively identify the patient.

▸ Ensure that the patient has removed all external metallic objects from the area to be examined prior to the procedure.

▸ If the patient has a history of allergic reactions to any substance or drug, administer ordered prophylactic steroids or antihistamines before the procedure.

▸ Have emergency equipment readily available.

▸ Instruct the patient to void prior to the procedure and to change into the gown, robe, and foot coverings provided.

▸ Instruct the patient to cooperate fully and to follow directions. Instruct the patient to remain still throughout the procedure because movement produces unreliable results.

▸ Supply earplugs to the patient to block out the loud, banging sounds that

POST-TEST:

▸ A report of the results will be made available to the requesting HCP, who will discuss the results with the patient.

▸ Observe for delayed allergic reactions, such as rash, urticaria, tachycardia, hyperpnea, hypertension, palpitations, nausea, or vomiting.

▸ Instruct the patient to immediately report symptoms such as fast heart rate, difficulty breathing, skin rash, itching, chest pain, persistent right shoulder pain, or abdominal pain.

▸ Immediately report symptoms to the appropriate HCP.

▸ Instruct the patient in the care and assessment of the injection site.

▸ Instruct the patient to apply cold compresses to the puncture site as needed to reduce discomfort or edema.

▸ Recognize anxiety related to test results. Discuss the implications of abnormal test results on the patient's lifestyle. Provide teaching and information regarding the clinical implications of the test results, as appropriate.

Reinforce information given by the patient's HCP regarding further testing, treatment, or referral to another HCP. Answer any questions or address any concerns voiced by the patient or family.

Depending on the results of this procedure, additional testing may be performed to evaluate or monitor progression of the disease process and determine the need for a change in therapy. Evaluate test results in relation to the patient's symptoms and other tests performed.

RELATED MONOGRAPHS:

Related tests include ACTH and challenge tests, angiography brain, BUN, cortisol and challenge tests, CT brain, creatinine, EEG, MRI brain, and PET brain.

Refer to the Cardiovascular and Endocrine systems tables at the end of the book for related tests by body system.

Magnetic Resonance Venography

SYNONYM/ACRONYM: MRV.

COMMON USE: To visualize and assess blood flow in diseased and normal veins toward diagnosis of vascular disease and to monitor and evaluate therapeutic interventions.

AREA OF APPLICATION: Vascular.

CONTRAST: Can be done with or without IV contrast (gadolinium).

DESCRIPTION: Magnetic resonance imaging (MRI) uses a magnet and radio waves to produce an energy field that can be displayed as an image. The magnetic field causes the hydrogen atoms in tissue to line up, and when radio waves are directed toward the magnetic field, the atoms absorb the radio waves and change their position. When the radio waves are turned off, the atoms go back to their original position; this change in the energy field is sensed by the equipment, and an image is generated by the attached computer system. MRI produces cross-sectional images of the vessels in multiple planes without the use of ionizing radiation or the interference of bone or surrounding tissue.

Magnetic resonance venography (MRV) is an accurate, noninvasive technique used to detect deep vein thrombosis. This application of MRI provides images of blood flow in diseased and normal veins. In patients who are allergic to iodinated contrast medium, MRV is used in place of venography or computed tomography (CT) venography. MRV is particularly useful for visualizing vascular abnormalities, thrombosis, and other pathology. MRV can be accomplished with a contrast-enhanced (CE) or non–contrast-enhanced method. Special imaging sequences allow the visualization of moving blood within the venous system. Two common techniques to obtain images of flowing blood are time-of-flight (TOF) and steady-state free precession (SSFP). In TOF imaging, incoming blood makes the vessels appear bright, and surrounding tissue is suppressed. SSFP is generally used for assessment of veins in the chest, abdomen, and pelvis. Although the initial evaluation of the iliac and lower extremity veins is usually accomplished with sonography, MRV is more efficient in detecting venous thrombus in the pelvic and calf veins, especially in obese patients and those with chronic asymptomatic thrombus. MRV is now also being assessed as a surgical planning tool for brain tumors. Images can be obtained in two-dimensional (series of slices) or three-dimensional sequences.

INDICATIONS

- Detect peripheral vascular disease (PVD)
- Detect axillary vein disease
- Detect cerebral vein disease
- Detect pulmonary vein disease
- Evaluate iliac and lower-extremity vein disease
- Evaluate postoperative venous sites and bypass grafts
- Identify deep vein thrombus in postsurgical patients
- Monitor and evaluate the effectiveness of medical or surgical treatment

POTENTIAL DIAGNOSIS

Normal findings in
- Normal blood flow in the area being examined

Abnormal findings in
- Cerebral vein thrombosis
- Deep vein thrombosis
- Pulmonary emboli
- PVD
- Tumor invasion of a vein
- Vascular abnormalities

- Vein occlusion
- Vein stenosis

CRITICAL FINDINGS ◈

- Cerebral emboli
- Occlusion
- Pulmonary emboli
- Tumor with significant mass effect

It is essential that critical diagnoses be communicated immediately to the appropriate health-care provider (HCP). A listing of these diagnoses varies among facilities. Note and immediately report to the HCP abnormal results and related symptoms. Timely notification of critical values for lab or diagnostic studies is a role expectation of the professional nurse. Notification processes will vary among facilities. Upon receipt of the critical value the information should be read back to the caller to verify accuracy. Most policies require immediate notification of the primary HCP, hospitalist, or on-call HCP. Reported information includes the patient's name, unique identifiers, critical value, name of the person giving the report, and name of the person receiving the report. Documentation of notification should be made in the medical record with the name of the HCP notified, time and date of notification, and any orders received. Any delay in a timely report of a critical value may require completion of a notification form with review by Risk Management.

INTERFERING FACTORS

This procedure is contraindicated for
- Patients with certain ferrous metal prosthetics, valves, aneurysm clips, inner ear prostheses, or other metallic objects.
- Patients with metal in their body, such as shrapnel or ferrous metal in the eye.
- ◈ Patients with cardiac pacemakers, because the pacemaker can be deactivated by MRI.

◆ Use of gadolinium-based contrast agents (GBCAs) is contraindicated in patients with acute or chronic severe renal insufficiency (glomerular filtration rate less than 30 mL/min/1.73 m^2). Patients should be screened for renal dysfunction prior to administration. The use of GBCAs should be avoided in these patients unless the benefits of the studies outweigh the risks and if essential diagnostic information is not available using non-contrast-enhanced diagnostic studies.

• Patients who are claustrophobic.

• Patients who are pregnant or suspected of being pregnant, unless the potential benefits of the procedure far outweigh the risks to the fetus and mother.

Factors that may impair clear imaging

• Metallic objects (e.g., jewelry, body rings, dental amalgams) within the examination field, which may inhibit organ visualization and cause unclear images.

• Inability of the patient to cooperate or remain still during the procedure because of age, significant pain, or mental status.

• Patients with extreme cases of claustrophobia, unless sedation is given before the study.

Other considerations

• If contrast medium is allowed to seep deep into the muscle tissue, vascular visualization will be impossible.

NURSING IMPLICATIONS AND PROCEDURE

PRETEST:

▶ Positively identify the patient using at least two unique identifiers before providing care, treatment, or services.

▶ *Patient Teaching:* Inform the patient this procedure can assist in assessing the vascular system.

▶ Obtain a history of the patient's complaints, including a list of known allergens, especially allergies or sensitivities to latex, iodine, seafood, contrast medium, anesthetics, or dyes.

▶ Obtain a history of the patient's cardiovascular system, symptoms, and results of previously performed laboratory tests and diagnostic and surgical procedures. Obtain a history of renal dysfunction if the use of GBCA is anticipated.

▶ Ensure the results of BUN, creatinine, and eGFR (estimated glomerular filtration rate) are obtained if GBCA is to be used.

▶ Determine if the patient has ever had any device implanted into his or her body, including copper intrauterine devices, pacemakers, ear implants, and heart valves.

▶ Obtain occupational history to determine the presence of metal in the body, such as shrapnel or flecks of ferrous metal in the eye (which can cause retinal hemorrhage).

▶ Note any recent procedures that can interfere with test results.

▶ Record the date of the last menstrual period and determine the possibility of pregnancy in perimenopausal women.

▶ Obtain a list of the patient's current medications, including herbs, nutritional supplements, and nutraceuticals (see Appendix F).

▶ Review the procedure with the patient. Address concerns about pain related to the procedure and explain that no pain will be experienced during the test, but there may be moments of discomfort. Reassure the patient that if contrast is used, it poses no radioactive hazard and rarely produces side effects. Inform the patient the procedure is performed in an MRI department by an HCP who specializes in this procedure, with support staff, and takes approximately 30 to 60 min.

▶ Inform the patient that the technologist will place him or her in a supine position on a flat table in a large cylindrical scanner.

▶ Tell the patient to expect to hear loud banging from the scanner and possibly to see magnetophosphenes (flickering

M

lights in the visual field); these will stop when the procedure is over.

Explain that an IV line may be inserted to allow infusion of IV fluids, contrast medium, or sedatives.

Sensitivity to social and cultural issues, as well as concern for modesty, is important in providing psychological support before, during, and after the procedure.

Instruct the patient to remove external metallic objects from the area to be examined prior to the procedure.

There are no food, fluid, or medication restrictions unless by medical direction.

INTRATEST:

Observe standard precautions, and follow the general guidelines in Appendix A. Positively identify the patient.

Ensure that the patient has removed external metallic objects from the area to be examined prior to the procedure.

If the patient has a history of allergic reactions to any substance or drug, administer ordered prophylactic steroids or antihistamines before the procedure.

Have emergency equipment readily available.

Instruct the patient to void prior to the procedure and to change into the gown, robe, and foot coverings provided.

Instruct the patient to cooperate fully and to follow directions. Instruct the patient to remain still throughout the procedure because movement produces unreliable results.

Supply earplugs to the patient to block out the loud, banging sounds that occur during the test. Instruct the patient to communicate with the technologist during the examination via a microphone within the scanner.

If an electrocardiogram or respiratory gating is to be performed in conjunction with the scan, apply MRI-safe electrodes to the appropriate sites.

Establish IV fluid line for the injection of emergency drugs and sedatives.

Administer an antianxiety agent, as ordered, if the patient has claustrophobia. Administer a sedative to a child or to an uncooperative adult, as ordered.

Place the patient in the supine position on an examination table.

If contrast is used, imaging can begin shortly after the injection.

Ask the patient to inhale deeply and hold his or her breath while the images are taken, and then to exhale after the images are taken.

Instruct the patient to take slow, deep breaths if nausea occurs during the procedure.

Monitor the patient for complications related to the procedure (e.g., allergic reaction, anaphylaxis, bronchospasm).

Remove the needle or catheter and apply a pressure dressing over the puncture site.

Observe/assess the needle/catheter insertion site for bleeding, inflammation, or hematoma formation.

POST-TEST:

A report of the results will be made available to the requesting HCP, who will discuss the results with the patient.

Observe for delayed allergic reactions, such as rash, urticaria, tachycardia, hyperpnea, hypertension, palpitations, nausea, or vomiting.

Instruct the patient to immediately report symptoms such as fast heart rate, difficulty breathing, skin rash, itching, chest pain, persistent right shoulder pain, or abdominal pain. Immediately report symptoms to the appropriate HCP.

Instruct the patient in the care and assessment of the injection site.

Instruct the patient to apply cold compresses to the puncture site as needed to reduce discomfort or edema.

Recognize anxiety related to test results. Discuss the implications of abnormal test results on the patient's lifestyle. Provide teaching and information regarding the clinical implications of the test results, as appropriate.

Provide contact information, if desired, for the American Heart Association (www.americanheart.org), the NHLBI (www.nhlbi.nih.gov), or Legs for Life (www.legsforlife.org).

Reinforce information given by the patient's HCP regarding further testing, treatment, or referral to another HCP. Answer any questions

or address any concerns voiced by the patient or family.
▶ Depending on the results of this procedure, additional testing may be performed to evaluate or monitor progression of the disease process and determine the need for a change in therapy. Evaluate test results in relation to the patient's symptoms and other tests performed.

RELATED MONOGRAPHS:
▶ Related tests include angiography of the body area of interest, BUN, CT angiography, creatinine, US arterial Doppler carotid, US venous Doppler extremity studies, and venography lower extremity studies.
▶ Refer to the Cardiovascular System table at the end of the book for related tests by body system.

Mammography

SYNONYM/ACRONYM: Breast x-ray, mammogram.

COMMON USE: To visualize and assess breast tissue and surrounding lymph nodes for cancer, inflammation, abscess, tumor, and cysts.

AREA OF APPLICATION: Breast.

CONTRAST: None.

DESCRIPTION: Mammography, an x-ray examination of the breast, is most commonly used to detect breast cancer; however, it can also be used to detect and evaluate symptomatic changes associated with other breast diseases, including mastitis, abscess, cystic changes, cysts, benign tumors, masses, and lymph nodes. Mammography is usually performed with traditional x-ray film, but totally electronic image recording is becoming commonplace. Mammography can be used to locate a nonpalpable lesion for biopsy. Mammography cannot detect breast cancer with 100% accuracy. In approximately 15% of breast cancer cases, the cancer is not detected with mammography. To assist in early detection of nonpalpable breast lesions, computer-assisted diagnosis is currently being used. With this technique, a computer performs automated scanning of the mammogram before the healthcare provider (HCP) interprets the findings.

When a mass is detected, additional studies are performed to help differentiate the nature of the mass, as follows:

• Magnification views of the area in question
• Focal or "spot" views of the area in question, done with a specialized paddle-style compression device
• Ultrasound images of the area in question, which help differentiate between a fluid-filled cystic lesion and a solid lesion indicative of cancer or fibroadenomas

INDICATIONS
• Differentiate between benign and neoplastic breast disease

- Evaluate breast pain, skin retraction, nipple erosion, or nipple discharge
- Evaluate known or suspected breast cancer
- Evaluate nonpalpable breast masses
- Evaluate opposite breast after mastectomy
- Monitor postoperative and post–radiation treatment status of the breast
- Evaluate size, shape, and position of breast masses

POTENTIAL DIAGNOSIS

Normal findings in
- Normal breast tissue, with no cysts, tumors, or calcifications

Abnormal findings in
- Breast calcifications
- Breast cysts or abscesses
- Breast tumors
- Hematoma resulting from trauma
- Mastitis
- Soft tissue masses
- Vascular calcification

CRITICAL FINDINGS: N/A

INTERFERING FACTORS

This procedure is contraindicated for
- Patients who are pregnant or suspected of being pregnant, unless the potential benefits of the procedure far outweigh the risks to the fetus and mother.
- Patients younger than age 25, because the density of the breast tissue is such that diagnostic x-rays are of limited value.

Factors that may impair clear imaging
- Inability of the patient to cooperate or remain still during the procedure because of age, significant pain, or mental status.
- Metallic objects (e.g., jewelry, body rings) within the examination field,

which may inhibit organ visualization and cause unclear images.
- Application of substances such as talcum powder, deodorant, or creams to the skin of breasts or underarms, which may alter test results.
- Previous breast surgery, breast augmentation, or the presence of breast implants, which may decrease the readability of the examination.

Other considerations
- Consultation with an HCP should occur before the procedure for radiation safety concerns regarding infants of patients who are lactating.
- Risks associated with radiation overexposure can result from frequent x-ray procedures. Personnel in the room with the patient should wear a protective lead apron, stand behind a shield, or leave the area while the examination is being done. Personnel working in the examination area should wear badges to record their level of radiation exposure.

NURSING IMPLICATIONS AND PROCEDURE

PRETEST:

- Positively identify the patient using at least two unique identifiers before providing care, treatment, or services.
- *Patient Teaching:* Inform the patient this procedure can assist in assessing breast status.
- Obtain a history of the patient's complaints, including a list of known allergens, especially allergies or sensitivities to latex.
- Obtain a history of the patient's reproductive system, known or suspected breast disease, and family history of breast disease; symptoms; and results of previously performed laboratory tests and diagnostic and surgical procedures.

Record the date of the last menstrual period and determine the possibility of pregnancy in perimenopausal women.

Obtain a list of the patient's current medications, including herbs, nutritional supplements, and nutraceuticals (see Appendix F).

Review the procedure with the patient. Address concerns about pain related to the procedure. Inform the patient there may be discomfort associated with the study while the breast is being compressed, but the compression allows for better visualization of the breast tissue. Explain to the patient that the radiation dose will be kept to an absolute minimum. Inform the patient that the procedure is performed in the mammography department by a registered mammographer and takes approximately 15 to 30 min to complete.

Inform the patient that the best time to schedule the examination is 1 week after menses, when breast tenderness is decreased.

Sensitivity to social and cultural issues, as well as concern for modesty, is important in providing psychological support before, during, and after the procedure.

Inform the patient not to apply deodorant, body creams, or powders on the day of the procedure.

Instruct the patient to remove jewelry and other metallic objects from the area of examination.

There are no food, fluid, or medication restrictions unless by medical direction.

INTRATEST:

Observe standard precautions, and follow the general guidelines in Appendix A. Positively identify the patient.

Ensure that the patient has removed all jewelry and other metallic objects from the chest area.

Instruct the patient to void prior to the procedure and to change into the gown and robe provided.

Instruct the patient to cooperate fully and to follow directions. Instruct the patient to remain still throughout the procedure because movement produces unreliable results.

Assist the patient to a standing or sitting position in front of the x-ray machine, which is adjusted to the level of the breasts. Position the patient's arms out of the range of the area to be imaged.

Place breasts, one at a time, between the compression apparatus. Two images or exposures are taken of each breast. Ask the patient to hold her breath during each exposure. Additional images may be taken as requested by the radiologist before the patient leaves the mammography room.

POST-TEST:

A report of the results will be made available to the requesting HCP, who will discuss the results with the patient.

Determine if the patient has any further questions or concerns.

Recognize anxiety related to test results, and be supportive of fear of shortened life expectancy. Discuss the implications of abnormal test results on the patient's lifestyle. Provide teaching and information regarding the clinical implications of the test results, as appropriate. Educate the patient regarding access to counseling services. Provide contact information, if desired, for the American Cancer Society (www.cancer.org).

Reinforce information given by the patient's HCP regarding further testing, treatment, or referral to another HCP. Decisions regarding the need for and frequency of breast self-examination, mammography, MRI breast, or other cancer screening procedures should be made after consultation between the patient and HCP. The most current guidelines for breast cancer screening of the general population as well as individuals with increased risk are available from the American Cancer Society, the American College of Obstetricians and Gynecologists (ACOG) (www.acog.org), and the American College of Radiology (www.acr.org). Answer any questions or address any concerns voiced by the patient or family.

M

Depending on the results of this procedure, additional testing may be performed to evaluate or monitor progression of the disease process and determine the need for a change in therapy. Evaluate test results in relation to the patient's symptoms and other tests performed.

RELATED MONOGRAPHS:

Related tests include biopsy breast, cancer antigens, ductography, MRI breast, stereotactic biopsy breast, and US breast.

Refer to the Reproductive System table at the end of the book for related tests by body system.

Meckel's Diverticulum Scan

SYNONYM/ACRONYM: Ectopic gastric mucosa scan, Meckel's scan, Meckel's scintigraphy.

COMMON USE: To assess, evaluate, and diagnose the cause of abdominal pain and gastrointestinal bleeding.

AREA OF APPLICATION: Abdomen.

CONTRAST: IV radioactive technetium-99m pertechnetate.

DESCRIPTION: Meckel's diverticulum scan is a nuclear medicine study performed to assist in diagnosing the cause of abdominal pain or occult gastrointestinal (GI) bleeding and to assess the presence and size of a congenital anomaly of the GI tract. After IV injection of technetium-99m pertechnetate, immediate and delayed imaging is performed, with various views of the abdomen obtained. The radionuclide is taken up and concentrated by parietal cells of the gastric mucosa, whether located in the stomach or in a Meckel's diverticulum. Up to 25% of Meckel's diverticulum is lined internally with ectopic gastric mucosal tissue. This tissue is usually located in the ileum and right lower quadrant of the abdomen; it secretes acid that causes ulceration of intestinal tissue, which results in abdominal pain and occult blood in stools.

INDICATIONS
- Aid in the diagnosis of unexplained abdominal pain and GI bleeding caused by hydrochloric acid and pepsin secreted by ectopic gastric mucosa, which ulcerates nearby mucosa
- Detect sites of ectopic gastric mucosa

POTENTIAL DIAGNOSIS

Normal findings in
- Normal distribution of radionuclide by gastric mucosa at normal sites

Abnormal findings in
- Meckel's diverticulum, as evidenced by focally increased radioactive uptake in areas other than normal structures

CRITICAL FINDINGS: N/A

INTERFERING FACTORS

This procedure is contraindicated for
- Patients who are pregnant or suspected of being pregnant, unless

the potential benefits of the procedure far outweigh the risks to the fetus and mother.

Factors that may impair clear imaging
- Inability of the patient to cooperate or remain still during the procedure because of age, significant pain, or mental status.
- Metallic objects (e.g., jewelry, body rings) within the examination field, which may inhibit organ visualization and cause unclear images.
- Retained barium from a previous radiological procedure.
- Other nuclear scans done within the preceding 24 hr.

Other considerations
- Improper injection of the radionuclide may allow the tracer to seep deep into the muscle tissue, producing erroneous hot spots.
- Consultation with a health-care provider (HCP) should occur before the procedure for radiation safety concerns regarding younger patients or patients who are lactating.
- False-positive results may occur from nondiverticular bleeding, intussusception, duplication cysts, inflammatory bowel disease, hemangioma of the bowel, and other organ infections.
- Inadequate amount of gastric mucosa within Meckel's diverticulum can affect the ability to visualize abnormalities.
- Inaccurate timing for imaging after the radionuclide injection can affect the results.
- Failure to follow dietary restrictions before the procedure may cause the procedure to be canceled or repeated.
- Risks associated with radiation overexposure can result from frequent x-ray or radionuclide procedures. Personnel working in the examination area should wear

badges to record their level of radiation exposure.

NURSING IMPLICATIONS AND PROCEDURE

PRETEST:
- Positively identify the patient using at least two unique identifiers before providing care, treatment, or services.
- Inform the patient this procedure can assist in assessing gastrointestinal bleeding.
- Obtain a history of the patient's complaints, including a list of known allergens, especially allergies or sensitivities to latex, iodine, seafood, contrast medium, anesthetics, or dyes.
- Obtain a history of the patient's gastrointestinal system, symptoms, and results of previously performed laboratory tests and diagnostic and surgical procedures.
- Note any recent procedures that can interfere with test results.
- Record the date of the last menstrual period and determine the possibility of pregnancy in perimenopausal women.
- Obtain a list of the patient's current medications, including anticoagulants, aspirin and other salicylates, herbs, nutritional supplements, and nutraceuticals, especially those known to affect coagulation (see Appendix F). Such products should be discontinued by medical direction for the appropriate number of days prior to a surgical procedure. Note the last time and dose of medication taken.
- Review the procedure with the patient. Address concerns about pain and explain that some pain may be experienced during the test, but there may be moments of discomfort. Reassure the patient that the radionuclide poses no radioactive hazard and rarely produces side effects. Inform the patient that the procedure is performed in a nuclear medicine department by an HCP specializing in this procedure, with support staff, and takes approximately 60 min.
- *Sensitivity to social and cultural issues*, as well as concern for modesty, is

M

important in providing psychological support before, during, and after the procedure.

- Explain that an IV line may be inserted to allow infusion of IV fluids, contrast medium, dye, or sedatives. Usually normal saline is infused.
- Instruct the patient to remove jewelry and other metallic objects from the area to be examined.
- Instruct the patient to take a histamine blocker, as ordered, 2 days before the study to block GI secretion.
- *Make sure a written and informed consent has been signed prior to the procedure and before administering any medications.*
- The patient should fast and refrain from fluids for 8 hr prior to the procedure. Protocols may vary among facilities.

INTRATEST:

- Observe standard precautions, and follow the general guidelines in Appendix A. Positively identify the patient.
- Ensure that the patient has complied with dietary, fluid, and medication restrictions for 8 hr prior to the procedure.
- Ensure that the patient has removed all external metallic objects from the area to be examined prior to the procedure.
- Have emergency equipment readily available.
- Instruct the patient to void prior to the procedure and to change into the gown, robe, and foot coverings provided.
- Record baseline vital signs and assess neurological status. Protocols may vary among facilities.
- Instruct the patient to cooperate fully and to follow directions. Instruct the patient to remain still throughout the procedure because movement produces unreliable results.
- Place the patient in a supine position on a flat table with foam wedges, which help maintain position and immobilization.
- IV radionuclide is administered, and the abdomen is scanned immediately to screen for vascular lesions. Images are taken in various positions every 5 min for the next hour.
- Monitor the patient for complications related to the procedure (e.g., allergic reaction, anaphylaxis, bronchospasm).

- Remove the needle or catheter and apply a pressure dressing over the puncture site.
- Observe/assess the needle/catheter insertion site for bleeding, inflammation, or hematoma formation.

POST-TEST:

- A report of the results will be made available to the requesting HCP, who will discuss the results with the patient.
- Unless contraindicated, advise patient to drink increased amounts of fluids for 24 to 48 hr to eliminate the radionuclide from the body. Inform the patient that radionuclide is eliminated from the body within 6 to 24 hr.
- No other radionuclide tests should be scheduled for 24 to 48 hr after this procedure.
- Instruct the patient to resume usual diet, fluids, and medications, as directed by the HCP.
- Monitor vital signs and neurological status every 15 min for 1 hr, then every 2 hr for 4 hr, and then as ordered by the HCP. Take temperature every 4 hr for 24 hr. Monitor intake and output at least every 8 hr. Compare with baseline values. Notify the HCP if temperature is elevated. Protocols may vary among facilities.
- Observe for delayed allergic reactions, such as rash, urticaria, tachycardia, hyperpnea, hypertension, palpitations, nausea, or vomiting.
- Instruct the patient to immediately report symptoms such as fast heart rate, difficulty breathing, skin rash, itching, chest pain, persistent right shoulder pain, or abdominal pain. Immediately report symptoms to the appropriate HCP.
- Instruct the patient in the care and assessment of the injection site.
- If a woman who is breastfeeding must have a nuclear scan, she should not breastfeed the infant until the radionuclide has been eliminated. This could take as long as 3 days. She should be instructed to express the milk and discard it during the 3-day period to prevent cessation of milk production.
- Instruct the patient to immediately flush the toilet and to meticulously wash hands with soap and water after each voiding for 24 hr after the procedure.

Instruct all caregivers to wear gloves when discarding urine for 24 hr after the procedure. Wash gloved hands with soap and water before removing gloves. Then wash hands after the gloves are removed.

Nutritional Considerations: A low-fat, low-cholesterol, and low-sodium diet should be consumed to reduce current disease processes. High fat consumption increases the amount of bile acids in the colon and should be avoided.

Recognize anxiety related to test results, and be supportive of perceived loss of independent function. Discuss the implications of abnormal test results on the patient's lifestyle. Provide teaching and information regarding the clinical implications of the test results, as appropriate.

Reinforce information given by the patient's HCP regarding further testing, treatment, or referral to another HCP. Answer any questions or address any concerns voiced by the patient or family.

Depending on the results of this procedure, additional testing may be needed to evaluate or monitor progression of the disease process and determine the need for a change in therapy. Evaluate test results in relation to the patient's symptoms and other tests performed.

RELATED MONOGRAPHS:

Related tests include barium swallow, colonoscopy, CT abdomen, CT pelvis, esophageal manometry, EGD, fecal analysis, gastric acid stimulation, gastric emptying scan, gastrin stimulation, GI blood loss, MRI abdomen, MRI pelvis, and upper GI series.

Refer to the Gastrointestinal System table at the end of the book for related tests by body system.

Mediastinoscopy

SYNONYM/ACRONYM: N/A.

COMMON USE: To visualize and assess structures under the mediastinum to assist in obtaining biopsies for diagnosing and staging cancer and to evaluate the effectiveness of therapeutic interventions.

AREA OF APPLICATION: Mediastinum.

CONTRAST: None.

DESCRIPTION: Mediastinoscopy provides direct visualization of the structures that lie beneath the mediastinum, which is the area behind the sternum and between the lungs. The test is performed under general anesthesia by means of a mediastinoscope inserted through a surgical incision at the suprasternal notch. Structures that can be viewed include the trachea, the esophagus, the heart and its major vessels, the thymus gland, and the lymph nodes that receive drainage from the lungs. The procedure is performed primarily to visualize and obtain biopsy specimens of the mediastinal lymph nodes and to determine the extent of metastasis into the mediastinum for the determination of treatment planning in cancer patients.

INDICATIONS

- Confirm radiological evidence of a thoracic infectious process of an indeterminate nature, coccidioidomycosis, or histoplasmosis
- Confirm radiological or cytological evidence of carcinoma or sarcoidosis
- Detect Hodgkin's disease
- Detect metastasis into the anterior mediastinum or extrapleurally into the chest
- Determine stage of known bronchogenic carcinoma, as indicated by the extent of mediastinal lymph node involvement
- Evaluate a patient with signs and symptoms of obstruction of mediastinal lymph flow and a history of head or neck cancer to determine recurrence or spread

POTENTIAL DIAGNOSIS

Normal findings in

- Normal appearance of mediastinal structures
- No abnormal lymph node tissue

Abnormal findings in

- Bronchogenic carcinoma
- Coccidioidomycosis
- Granulomatous infections
- Histoplasmosis
- Hodgkin's disease
- *Pneumocystis jiroveci* (formerly *P. carinii*)
- Sarcoidosis
- Tuberculosis

CRITICAL FINDINGS: N/A

INTERFERING FACTORS

This procedure is contraindicated for

- Patients who have had a previous mediastinoscopy, because scarring can make insertion of the scope and biopsy of lymph nodes difficult.
- Patients who have superior vena cava obstruction, because this condition causes increased venous collateral circulation in the mediastinum.
- Patients who are pregnant or suspected of being pregnant, unless the potential benefits of the procedure far outweigh the risks to the fetus and mother.

Other considerations

- Failure to follow dietary restrictions before the procedure may cause the procedure to be canceled or repeated.

NURSING IMPLICATIONS AND PROCEDURE

PRETEST:

▸ Positively identify the patient using at least two unique identifiers before providing care, treatment, or services.

▸ *Patient Teaching:* Inform the patient this procedure can assist in assessing structure in the middle of the chest.

▸ Obtain a history of the patient's complaints or symptoms, including a list of known allergens, especially allergies or sensitivities to latex, iodine, seafood, contrast medium, and anesthetics.

▸ Obtain a history of the patient's immune and respiratory systems, symptoms, and results of previously performed laboratory tests and diagnostic and surgical procedures.

▸ Ensure that the results of blood typing and crossmatching are obtained and recorded before the procedure in the event that an emergency thoracotomy is required.

▸ Note any recent procedures that can interfere with test results. Ensure that this procedure is performed before an upper gastrointestinal study or barium swallow.

▸ Record the date of the last menstrual period and determine the possibility of pregnancy in perimenopausal women.

▸ Obtain a list of the patient's current medications, including herbs, nutritional supplements, and nutraceuticals (see Appendix F).

M

Review the procedure with the patient. Inform the patient that prophylactic antibiotics may be administered prior to the procedure. Address concerns about pain related to the procedure and explain that a general anesthesia will be administered to promote relaxation and reduce discomfort prior to the mediastinoscopy. Explain that some pain may be experienced after the test. Meperidine (Demerol) or morphine may be given as a sedative. Inform the patient that the procedure is performed in the operating room by a health-care provider (HCP) specializing in this procedure, with support staff, and usually takes 30 to 60 min to complete.

Sensitivity to social and cultural issues, as well as concern for modesty, is important in providing psychological support before, during, and after the procedure.

Explain that an IV line will be inserted to allow infusion of IV fluids, antibiotics, anesthetics, and analgesics.

Instruct the patient to remove jewelry and external metallic objects from the area to be examined prior to the procedure.

The patient should fast and restrict fluids for 8 hr prior to the procedure. Protocols may vary among facilities. Instruct the patient to avoid taking anticoagulant medication or to reduce dosage as ordered prior to the procedure. Number of days to withhold medication is dependent on the type of anticoagulant.

Make sure a written and informed consent has been signed prior to the procedure and before administering any medications.

INTRATEST:

Observe standard precautions, and follow the general guidelines in Appendix A. Positively identify the patient.

Ensure that the patient has complied with food, fluids, and medication restrictions for 8 hr prior to the procedure.

Ensure that the patient has removed jewelry and external metallic objects from the area to be examined prior to the procedure.

Have emergency equipment readily available.

Instruct the patient to void prior to the procedure and change into the gown, robe, and foot coverings provided.

Record baseline vital signs and assess neurological status. Protocols may vary among facilities.

Establish IV fluid line for the injection of emergency drugs and of sedatives.

Place electrocardiographic electrodes on the patient for cardiac monitoring. Establish baseline rhythm; determine if the patient has ventricular arrhythmias.

Avoid using morphine sulfate in patients with asthma or other pulmonary disease. This drug can further exacerbate bronchospasms and respiratory impairment.

Place the patient in the supine position. General anesthesia is administered via an endotracheal tube.

An incision is made at the suprasternal notch, and a path for the mediastinoscope is made using finger dissection. The lymph nodes can be palpated at this time. The lymph nodes on the right side of the mediastinum are most accessible and safest to biopsy by mediastinoscopy; the lymph nodes on the left side are more difficult to explore and biopsy because of their proximity to the aorta. Biopsy specimens of nodes on the left side of the mediastinum may need to be obtained by mediastinotomy, which involves performing a left anterior thoracotomy.

Place tissue samples in properly labeled specimen containers, and promptly transport the specimen to the laboratory for processing and analysis.

The scope is removed, and the incision is closed.

Observe/assess the incision site for bleeding, inflammation, or hematoma formation.

If the patient is stable and if no further surgery is immediately indicated, the patient is extubated.

POST-TEST:

A report of the results will be made available to the requesting HCP, who will discuss the results with the patient.

Do not allow the patient to eat or drink for 12 to 24 hr.

Instruct the patient to resume normal activity, medication, and diet in 24 hr or as tolerated after the examination, unless otherwise indicated.

The patient should remain in a semi-Fowler's position on either side until vital signs revert to preprocedure levels.

Monitor vital signs and neurological status every 15 min for 1 hr, then every 2 hr for 4 hr, and then as ordered by the HCP. Take temperature every 4 hr for 24 hr. Monitor intake and output, at least every 8 hr. Compare with baseline values. Notify the HCP if temperature changes. Protocols may vary among facilities.

Observe for delayed allergic reactions, such as rash, urticaria, tachycardia, hyperpnea, hypertension, palpitations, nausea, or vomiting.

Instruct the patient to immediately report symptoms such as fast heart rate, difficulty breathing, skin rash, itching, chest pain, persistent right shoulder pain, or abdominal pain. Immediately report symptoms to the appropriate HCP.

Instruct the patient in the care and assessment of the site.

Emphasize that any excessive bleeding; difficulty breathing; excessive coughing after biopsy; fever; or redness, swelling, or pain of the incisional area must be reported to the HCP immediately.

Recognize anxiety related to test results, and be supportive of perceived loss of independent function. Discuss the implications of abnormal test results on the patient's lifestyle. Provide teaching and information regarding the clinical implications of the test results, as appropriate.

Reinforce information given by the patient's HCP regarding further testing, treatment, or referral to another HCP. Answer any questions or address any concerns voiced by the patient or family. Depending on the results of this procedure, additional testing may be needed to evaluate or monitor progression of the disease process and determine the need for a change in therapy. Evaluate test results in relation to the patient's symptoms and other tests performed.

RELATED MONOGRAPHS:

Related tests include ACE, β_2-microglobulin, biopsy liver, biopsy lung, biopsy lymph node, blood gases, bronchoscopy, carbon dioxide, chest x-ray, CBC, CBC WBC count and differential, CT thoracic, culture and smear mycobacteria, gallium scan, Gram stain, laparoscopy abdominal, LAP, liver and spleen scan, lung perfusion scan, lung ventilation scan, lymphangiogram, MRI chest, platelet count, pleural fluid analysis, PFT, and TB skin tests.

Refer to the Immune and Respiratory systems tables at the end of the book for related tests by body system.

Metanephrines

SYNONYM/ACRONYM: N/A.

COMMON USE: To assist in the diagnosis of cancer of the adrenal medulla or to assess for the cause of hypertension.

SPECIMEN: Urine (25 mL) from a timed specimen collected in a clean amber plastic collection container with 6N hydrochloride as a preservative.

NORMAL FINDINGS: (Method: High-pressure liquid chromatography)

Age	Conventional Units	SI Units
Normetanephrines (Conventional Units × 5.07)		
3 mo–4 yr	54–249 mcg/24 hr	274–1,262 micromol/day
5–9 yr	31–398 mcg/24 hr	157–2,018 micromol/day
10–17 yr	67–531 mcg/24 hr	340–2,692 micromol/day
18–39 yr	35–482 mcg/24 hr	177–2,444 micromol/day
Greater than 40 yr	88–676 mcg/24 hr	446–3,427 micromol/day
Metanephrines, Total (Conventional Units × 5.07)		
3 mo–4 yr	79–345 mcg/24 hr	401–1,749 micromol/day
5–9 yr	49–409 mcg/24 hr	248–2,074 micromol/day
10–17 yr	107–741 mcg/24 hr	543–3,757 micromol/day
18–39 yr	94–695 mcg/24 hr	477–3,524 micromol/day
40–49 yr	182–739 mcg/24 hr	923–3,747 micromol/day
Greater than 50 yr	224–832 mcg/24 hr	1,136–4,218 micromol/day

DESCRIPTION: Metanephrines are the inactive metabolites of epinephrine and norepinephrine. Metanephrines are either excreted or further metabolized into vanillylmandelic acid. Release of metanephrines in the urine is indicative of disorders associated with excessive catecholamine production, particularly pheochromocytoma. Vanillylmandelic acid and catecholamines are normally measured with urinary metanephrines. Creatinine is usually measured simultaneously to ensure adequate collection and to calculate an excretion ratio of metabolite to creatinine.

INDICATIONS
- Assist in the diagnosis of suspected pheochromocytoma
- Assist in identifying the cause of hypertension
- Verify suspected tumors associated with excessive catecholamine secretion

POTENTIAL DIAGNOSIS

Increased in
- Ganglioneuroma
- Neuroblastoma
- Pheochromocytoma
- Severe stress

Decreased in: N/A

CRITICAL FINDINGS: N/A

INTERFERING FACTORS
- Drugs that may increase metanephrine levels include monoamine oxidase inhibitors and prochlorperazine.
- Methylglucamine in x-ray contrast medium may cause false-negative results.
- All urine voided for the timed collection period must be included in the collection or else falsely decreased values may be obtained. Compare output records with volume collected to verify that all voids were included in the collection.

NURSING IMPLICATIONS AND PROCEDURE

PRETEST:

Positively identify the patient using at least two unique identifiers before providing care, treatment, or services.

Patient Teaching: Inform the patient this test can assist in diagnosing adrenal gland health and hypertension.

Obtain a history of the patient's complaints, including a list of known allergens, especially allergies or sensitivities to latex.

Obtain a history of the patient's endocrine system, symptoms, and results of previously performed laboratory tests and diagnostic and surgical procedures. Note any recent procedures that can interfere with test results.

Obtain a list of the patient's current medications, including herbs, nutritional supplements, and nutraceuticals (see Appendix F).

Review the procedure with the patient. Provide a nonmetallic urinal, bedpan, or toilet-mounted collection device. Address concerns about pain and explain that there should be no discomfort during the procedure.

Usually a 24-hr time frame for urine collection is ordered. Inform the patient that all urine must be saved during that 24-hr period. Instruct the patient not to void directly into the laboratory collection container. Instruct the patient to avoid defecating in the collection device and to keep toilet tissue out of the collection device to prevent contamination of the specimen. Place a sign in the bathroom to remind the patient to save all urine.

Instruct the patient to void all urine into the collection device and then to pour the urine into the laboratory collection container. Alternatively, the specimen can be left in the collection device for a health-care staff member to add to the laboratory collection container.

At the conclusion of the test, compare the quantity of urine with the urinary output record for the collection; if the specimen contains less than what was recorded as output, some urine may have been discarded, thus invalidating the test.

Sensitivity to social and cultural issues, as well as concern for modesty, is important in providing psychological support before, during, and after the procedure.

Instruct the patient to avoid excessive exercise and stress during the 24-hr collection of urine.

There are no food, fluid, or medication restrictions unless by medical direction.

INTRATEST:

Ensure that the patient has complied with activity restrictions during the procedure.

If the patient has a history of allergic reaction to latex, avoid the use of equipment containing latex.

Instruct the patient to cooperate fully and to follow directions.

Observe standard precautions, and follow the general guidelines in Appendix A. Positively identify the patient, and label the appropriate specimen container with the corresponding patient demographics, initials of the person collecting the specimen, date, and time of collection.

Timed Specimen

Obtain a clean 3-L urine specimen container, toilet-mounted collection device, and plastic bag (for transport of the specimen container). The specimen must be refrigerated or kept on ice throughout the entire collection period. If an indwelling urinary catheter is in place, the drainage bag must be kept on ice.

Begin the test between 6 and 8 a.m. if possible. Collect first voiding and discard. Record the time the specimen was discarded as the beginning of the timed collection period. The next morning, ask the patient to void at the same time the collection was started and add this last voiding to the container. Urinary output should be recorded throughout the collection time.

If an indwelling catheter is in place, replace the tubing and container system at the start of the collection time. Keep the container system on ice during the collection period, or empty the urine into a larger container periodically during the collection period; monitor to ensure continued drainage, and conclude the test the next morning at the same hour the collection was begun.

At the conclusion of the test, compare the quantity of urine with the urinary output record for the collection; if the specimen contains less than what was recorded as output, some urine may have been discarded, invalidating the test.

M

▶ Include on the collection container's label the amount of urine and test start and stop times.

▶ Promptly transport the specimen to the laboratory for processing and analysis.

POST-TEST:

▶ A report of the results will be made available to the requesting health-care provider (HCP), who will discuss the results with the patient.

▶ Instruct the patient to resume usual activity, as directed by the HCP.

▶ Recognize anxiety related to test results, and be supportive of fear of shortened life expectancy. Discuss the implications of abnormal test results on the patient's lifestyle. Provide teaching and information regarding the clinical implications of the test results, as appropriate. Educate the patient regarding access to counseling services.

▶ Reinforce information given by the patient's HCP regarding further testing, treatment, or referral to another HCP. Answer any questions or address any concerns voiced by the patient or family.

▶ Depending on the results of this procedure, additional testing may be performed to evaluate or monitor progression of the disease process and determine the need for a change in therapy. Evaluate test results in relation to the patient's symptoms and other tests performed.

RELATED MONOGRAPHS:

▶ Related tests include angiography adrenal, cancer antigens, catecholamines, CT renal, HVA, renin, and VMA.

▶ Refer to the Endocrine System table at the end of the book for related tests by body system.

Methemoglobin

SYNONYM/ACRONYM: Hemoglobin, hemoglobin M, MetHb, Hgb M.

COMMON USE: To assess for cyanosis and hypoxemia associated with polycythemia, pathologies affecting hemoglobin, and potential inhaled drug toxicity.

SPECIMEN: Whole blood (1 mL) collected in green-top (heparin) tube. Specimen should be transported tightly capped and in an ice slurry.

NORMAL FINDINGS: (Method: Spectrophotometry)

Conventional Units	SI Units (Conventional Units × 155)
0.06–0.24 g/dL*	9.3–37.2 micromol/L*

*Percentage of total hemoglobin = 0.41–1.15%.
Note: The conversion factor of ×155 is based on the molecular weight of hemoglobin of 64,500 daltons (d), or 64.5 kd.

DESCRIPTION: Methemoglobin is a structural hemoglobin variant formed when the heme portion of the deoxygenated hemoglobin is oxidized to a ferric state rather than to the normal ferrous state, rendering it incapable of combining with and transporting oxygen to tissues. Visible cyanosis can result as levels approach 10% to 15% of total hemoglobin.

M

INDICATIONS

- Assist in the detection of acquired methemoglobinemia caused by the toxic effects of chemicals and drugs
- Assist in the detection of congenital methemoglobinemia, indicated by deficiency of red blood cell nicotinamide adenine dinucleotide (NADH)-methemoglobin reductase or presence of methemoglobin
- Evaluate cyanosis in the presence of normal blood gases

POTENTIAL DIAGNOSIS

Increased in

- Acquired methemoglobinemia (drugs, tobacco smoking, or ionizing radiation)
- Carbon monoxide poisoning *(carbon monoxide is a form of deoxygenated hemoglobin)*
- Hereditary methemoglobinemia *(evidenced by a deficiency of NADH-methemoglobin reductase or related to the presence of a hemoglobinopathy)*

Decreased in: N/A

CRITICAL FINDINGS ❖

Cyanosis can occur at levels greater than 10%.

Dizziness, fatigue, headache, and tachycardia can occur at levels greater than 30%.

Signs of central nervous system depression can occur at levels greater than 45%.

Death may occur at levels greater than 70%.

Note and immediately report to the health-care provider (HCP) any critically increased or decreased values and related symptoms. Timely notification of critical values for lab or diagnostic studies is a role expectation of the professional nurse.

Notification processes will vary among facilities. Upon receipt of the critical value the information should be read back to the caller to verify accuracy. Most policies require immediate notification of the primary HCP, hospitalist, or on-call HCP. Reported information includes the patient's name, unique identifiers, critical value, name of the person giving the report, and name of the person receiving the report. Documentation of notification should be made in the medical record with the name of the HCP notified, time and date of notification, and any orders received. Any delay in a timely report of a critical value may require completion of a notification form with review by Risk Management.

Possible interventions include airway protection, administration of oxygen, monitoring neurological status every hour, continuous pulse oximetry, hyperbaric oxygen therapy, and exchange transfusion. Administration of activated charcoal or gastric lavage may be effective if performed soon after the toxic agent is ingested. Emesis should never be induced in patients with no gag reflex because of the risk of aspiration. Methylene blue may be used to reverse the process of methemoglobin formation, but it should be used cautiously when methemoglobin levels are greater than 30%. Use of methylene blue is contraindicated in the presence of glucose-6-phosphate dehydrogenase deficiency.

INTERFERING FACTORS

- Drugs that may increase methemoglobin levels include acetanilid, amyl nitrate, aniline derivatives, benzocaine, dapsone, glucosulfone, isoniazid, phenytoin, silver nitrate, sulfonamides, and thiazolsulfone.

- Well water containing nitrate is the most common cause of methemoglobinemia in infants.
- Breastfeeding infants are capable of converting inorganic nitrate from common topical anesthetic applications containing nitrate to the nitrite ion, causing nitrite toxicity and increased methemoglobin.
- Prompt and proper specimen processing, storage, and analysis are important to achieve accurate results. Methemoglobin is unstable and should be transported on ice within a few hours of collection, or else the specimen should be rejected.

NURSING IMPLICATIONS AND PROCEDURE

PRETEST:

- Positively identify the patient using at least two unique identifiers before providing care, treatment, or services.
- *Patient Teaching:* Inform the patient this test can assist in identifying the cause of poor oxygenation.
- Obtain a history of the patient's complaints, including a list of known allergens, especially allergies or sensitivities to latex.
- Obtain a history of the patient's hematopoietic and respiratory systems, symptoms, and results of previously performed laboratory tests and diagnostic and surgical procedures.
- Note any recent procedures that can interfere with test results.
- Obtain a list of the patient's current medications, including herbs, nutritional supplements, and nutraceuticals (see Appendix F).
- Review the procedure with the patient. Inform the patient that specimen collection takes approximately 5 to 10 min. Address concerns about pain and explain that there may be some discomfort during the venipuncture.
- *Sensitivity to social and cultural issues,* as well as concern for modesty, is important in providing psychological support before, during, and after the procedure.
- There are no food, fluid, or medication restrictions unless by medical direction.
- Prepare an ice slurry in a cup or plastic bag to have on hand for immediate transport of the specimen to the laboratory.

INTRATEST:

- If the patient has a history of allergic reaction to latex, avoid the use of equipment containing latex.
- Instruct the patient to cooperate fully and to follow directions. Direct the patient to breathe normally and to avoid unnecessary movement.
- Observe standard precautions, and follow the general guidelines in Appendix A. Positively identify the patient, and label the appropriate specimen container with the corresponding patient demographics, initials of the person collecting the specimen, date, and time of collection. Perform a venipuncture.
- Remove the needle and apply direct pressure with dry gauze to stop bleeding. Observe/assess venipuncture site for bleeding or hematoma formation and secure gauze with adhesive bandage.
- Promptly transport the specimen to the laboratory for processing and analysis. The specimen should be placed in an ice slurry immediately after collection. Information on the specimen label should be protected from water in the ice slurry by first placing the specimen in a protective plastic bag.

POST-TEST:

- A report of the results will be made available to the requesting HCP, who will discuss the results with the patient.
- Instruct the patient to avoid carbon monoxide from firsthand or secondhand smoking, to have home gas furnace checked yearly for leaks, and to use gas appliances such as gas grills in a well-ventilated area.
- Reinforce information given by the patient's HCP regarding further testing, treatment, or referral to another HCP. Answer any questions or address any concerns voiced by the patient or family.

▶ Depending on the results of this procedure, additional testing may be performed to evaluate or monitor progression of the disease process and determine the need for a change in therapy. Evaluate test results in relation to the patient's symptoms and other tests performed.

RELATED MONOGRAPHS:

▶ Related tests include alveolar/arterial gradient, blood gases, carboxyhemoglobin, hemoglobin electrophoresis, and pulse oximetry.
▶ Refer to the Hematopoietic and Respiratory systems tables at the end of the book for related tests by body system.

Microalbumin

SYNONYM/ACRONYM: Albumin, urine.

COMMON USE: To assist in the identification and management of early diabetes in order to avoid or delay onset of diabetic associated renal disease.

SPECIMEN: Urine (10 mL) from a random or timed specimen collected in a clean plastic collection container.

NORMAL FINDINGS: (Method: Immunoassay)

Test	Conventional Units
Random microalbumin	Less than 0.03 mg albumin/mg creatinine
24-hr microalbumin	
Normal	Less than 30 mg/24 hr
Microalbuminuria	30–299 mg/24 hr
Clinical albuminuria	300 mg or greater/24 hr

Simultaneous measurement of urine creatinine or creatinine clearance may be requested. Normal ratio of microalbumin to creatinine is less than 30:1.

DESCRIPTION: The term *microalbumin* describes concentrations of albumin in urine that are greater than normal but undetectable by dipstick or traditional spectrophotometry methods. Microalbuminuria precedes the nephropathy associated with diabetes and is often elevated years before creatinine clearance shows abnormal values. Studies have shown that the median duration from onset of microalbuminuria to development of nephropathy is 5 to 7 yr.

INDICATIONS
- Evaluate renal disease
- Screen diabetic patients for early signs of nephropathy

POTENTIAL DIAGNOSIS

Increased in
Conditions resulting in increased renal excretion or loss of protein.

- Cardiomyopathy
- Diabetic nephropathy
- Exercise
- Hypertension (uncontrolled)
- Pre-eclampsia

- Renal disease
- Urinary tract infections

Decreased in: N/A

CRITICAL FINDINGS: N/A

INTERFERING FACTORS
- Drugs that may decrease microalbumin levels include captopril, dipyridamole, enalapril, furosemide, indapamide, perindopril, quinapril, ramipril, tolrestat, and simvastatin (Triflusal).
- All urine voided for the timed collection period must be included in the collection, or else falsely decreased values may be obtained. Compare output records with volume collected to verify that all voids were included in the collection.

NURSING IMPLICATIONS AND PROCEDURE

PRETEST:
- Positively identify the patient using at least two unique identifiers before providing care, treatment, or services.
- *Patient Teaching:* Inform the patient this test can assist in evaluating for early kidney disease.
- Obtain a history of the patient's complaints, including a list of known allergens, especially allergies or sensitivities to latex.
- Obtain a history of the patient's endocrine and genitourinary systems, symptoms, and results of previously performed laboratory tests and diagnostic and surgical procedures.
- Obtain a list of the patient's current medications, including herbs, nutritional supplements, and nutraceuticals (see Appendix F).
- Review the procedure with the patient. Provide a nonmetallic urinal, bedpan, or toilet-mounted collection device. Address concerns about pain and explain that there should be no discomfort during the procedure.
- Usually a 24-hr time frame for urine collection is ordered. Inform the patient

that all urine must be saved during that 24-hr period. Instruct the patient not to void directly into the laboratory collection container. Instruct the patient to avoid defecating in the collection device and to keep toilet tissue out of the collection device to prevent contamination of the specimen. Place a sign in the bathroom to remind the patient to save all urine.
- Instruct the patient to void all urine into the collection device and then to pour the urine into the laboratory collection container. Alternatively, the specimen can be left in the collection device for a health-care staff member to add to the laboratory collection container.
- *Sensitivity to social and cultural issues,* as well as concern for modesty, is important in providing psychological support before, during, and after the procedure.
- Instruct the patient to avoid excessive exercise and stress during the 24-hr collection of urine.
- There are no food, fluid, or medication restrictions unless by medical direction.

INTRATEST:
- Ensure that the patient has complied with activity restrictions during the procedure.
- If the patient has a history of allergic reaction to latex, avoid the use of equipment containing latex.
- Instruct the patient to cooperate fully and to follow directions.
- Observe standard precautions, and follow the general guidelines in Appendix A. Positively identify the patient, and label the appropriate specimen container with the corresponding patient demographics, initials of the person collecting the specimen, date, and time of collection.

Random Specimen (Collect in Early Morning)

Clean-Catch Specimen
- Instruct the male patient to (1) thoroughly wash his hands, (2) cleanse the meatus, (3) void a small amount into the toilet, and (4) void directly into the specimen container.
- Instruct the female patient to (1) thoroughly wash her hands; (2) cleanse the

labia from front to back; (3) while keeping the labia separated, void a small amount into the toilet; and (4) without interrupting the urine stream, void directly into the specimen container.

Indwelling Catheter

Put on gloves. Empty drainage tube of urine. It may be necessary to clamp off the catheter for 15 to 30 min before specimen collection. Cleanse specimen port with antiseptic swab, and then aspirate 5 mL of urine with a 21- to 25-gauge needle and syringe. Transfer urine to a sterile container.

Timed Specimen

Obtain a clean 3-L urine specimen container, toilet-mounted collection device, and plastic bag (for transport of the specimen container). The specimen must be refrigerated or kept on ice throughout the entire collection period. If an indwelling urinary catheter is in place, the drainage bag must be kept on ice.

Begin the test between 6 and 8 a.m. if possible. Collect first voiding and discard. Record the time the specimen was discarded as the beginning of the timed collection period. The next morning, ask the patient to void at the same time the collection was started and add this last voiding to the container. Urinary output should be recorded throughout the collection time.

If an indwelling catheter is in place, replace the tubing and container system at the start of the collection time. Keep the container system on ice during the collection period, or empty the urine into a larger container periodically during the collection period; monitor to ensure continued drainage, and conclude the test the next morning at the same hour the collection was begun.

At the conclusion of the test, compare the quantity of urine with the urinary output record for the collection; if the specimen contains less than what was recorded as output, some urine may have been discarded, invalidating the test.

Include on the collection container's label the amount of urine and test start and stop times.

General

Promptly transport the specimen to the laboratory for processing and analysis.

POST-TEST:

A report of the results will be made available to the requesting health-care provider (HCP), who will discuss the results with the patient.

Instruct the patient to resume usual activity, as directed by the HCP.

Instruct the patient and caregiver to report signs and symptoms of hypoglycemia or hyperglycemia.

Nutritional Considerations: Increased levels of microalbumin may be associated with diabetes. There is no "diabetic diet"; however, many meal-planning approaches with nutritional goals are endorsed by the American Dietetic Association. Patients who adhere to dietary recommendations report a better general feeling of health, better weight management, greater control of glucose and lipid values, and improved use of insulin. Instruct the patient, as appropriate, in nutritional management of diabetes. The American Heart Association's Therapeutic Lifestyle Changes (TLC) diet provides goals directed at people with specific risk factors and/or existing medical conditions (e.g., elevated LDL cholesterol levels, other lipid disorders, coronary artery disease [CAD], insulin-dependent diabetes, insulin resistance, or metabolic syndrome). The TLC approach also includes the use of plant stanols or sterols and increased dissolved fiber as an option for lowering LDL cholesterol levels; nutritional recommendations for daily total caloric intake; recommendations for allowable percentage of calories derived from fat (saturated and unsaturated), carbohydrates, protein, and cholesterol; as well as recommendations for daily expenditure of energy. The nutritional needs of each diabetic patient need to be determined individually (especially during pregnancy) with the appropriate health-care professionals, particularly professionals trained in nutrition.

Recognize anxiety related to test results, and be supportive of perceived loss of independence and fear of shortened life expectancy. Discuss the implications of abnormal test results on the patient's lifestyle. Provide teaching and information regarding the clinical implications of the test results, as appropriate. Emphasize, if indicated, that good glycemic control delays the onset and slows the progression of diabetic retinopathy, nephropathy, and neuropathy. Educate the patient regarding access to counseling services, as appropriate. Provide contact information, if desired, for the American Diabetes Association (www.diabetes .org) or the American Heart Association (www.americanheart.org).

▸ Reinforce information given by the patient's HCP regarding further testing, treatment, or referral to another HCP. Answer any questions or address any concerns voiced by the patient or family.

▸ Depending on the results of this procedure, additional testing may be performed to evaluate or monitor progression of the disease process and determine the need for a change in therapy. Evaluate test results in relation to the patient's symptoms and other tests performed.

RELATED MONOGRAPHS:

▸ Related tests include A/G ratio, angiography renal, blood pool imaging, BUN, CBC, cortisol, creatinine, creatinine clearance, culture urine, cystometry, cystoscopy, cytology urine, echocardiography, echocardiography transesophageal, EPO, fluorescein angiography, fundus photography, glucose, GTT, glycated hemoglobin, gonioscopy, Holter monitor, insulin, insulin antibodies, magnesium, protein total and fractions, renogram, UA, visual fields test, and voiding cystourethrography.

▸ Refer to the Endocrine and Genitourinary systems tables at the end of the book for related tests by body system.

Mumps Serology

SYNONYM/ACRONYM: N/A.

COMMON USE: To assist in diagnosing a present or past mumps infection.

SPECIMEN: Serum (1 mL) collected in a red-top tube.

NORMAL FINDINGS: (Method: Indirect immunofluorescence)

	IgM	Interpretation	IgG	Interpretation
Negative	0.89 index or less	No significant level of detectable antibody	Less than 5 IU/mL	No significant level of detectable antibody; indicative of nonimmunity
Indeterminate	0.9–1.0 index	Equivocal results; retest in 10–14 d	6–9 IU/mL	Equivocal results; retest in 10–14 d

(table continues on page 1006)

	IgM	Interpretation	IgG	Interpretation
Positive	1.1 index or greater	Antibody detected; indicative of recent immunization, current or recent infection	10 IU/mL or greater	Antibody detected; indicative of immunization, current or past infection

DESCRIPTION: Mumps serology is done to determine the presence of mumps antibody, indicating exposure to or active presence of mumps. Mumps, also known as *parotitis*, is an infectious viral disease of the parotid glands caused by a myxovirus that is transmitted by direct contact with or droplets spread from the saliva of an infected person. The incubation period averages 3 wk. Virus can be shed in saliva for 2 wk after infection and in urine for 2 wk after the onset of symptoms. Complications of infection include aseptic meningitis; encephalitis; and inflammation of the testes, ovaries, and pancreas. The presence of immunoglobulin M (IgM) antibodies indicates acute infection. The presence of immunoglobulin G (IgG) antibodies indicates current or past infection.

INDICATIONS
- Determine resistance to or protection against the mumps virus by a positive reaction or susceptibility to mumps by a negative reaction
- Document immunity
- Evaluate mumps-like diseases and differentiate between these and actual mumps

POTENTIAL DIAGNOSIS
Past or current mumps infection.

CRITICAL FINDINGS: N/A

INTERFERING FACTORS: N/A

NURSING IMPLICATIONS AND PROCEDURE

PRETEST:
- Positively identify the patient using at least two unique identifiers before providing care, treatment, or services.
- *Patient Teaching:* Inform the patient this test can assist in diagnosing a mumps infection.
- Obtain a history of the patient's complaints, including a list of known allergens, especially allergies or sensitivities to latex. Obtain a history of exposure.
- Obtain a history of the patient's immune system, symptoms, and results of previously performed laboratory tests and diagnostic and surgical procedures.
- Obtain a list of the patient's current medications, including herbs, nutritional supplements, and nutraceuticals (see Appendix F).
- Review the procedure with the patient. Inform the patient that several tests may be necessary to confirm diagnosis. Any individual positive result should be repeated in 7 to 14 days to monitor a change in detectable levels of antibodies. Inform the patient that specimen collection takes approximately 5 to 10 min. Address concerns about pain and explain that there may be some discomfort during the venipuncture.
- *Sensitivity to social and cultural issues,* as well as concern for modesty, is important in providing psychological support before, during, and after the procedure.
- There are no food, fluid, or medication restrictions unless by medical direction.

INTRATEST:
- If the patient has a history of allergic reaction to latex, avoid the use of equipment containing latex.

Instruct the patient to cooperate fully and to follow directions. Direct the patient to breathe normally and to avoid unnecessary movement. Observe standard precautions, and follow the general guidelines in Appendix A. Positively identify the patient, and label the appropriate specimen container with the corresponding patient demographics, initials of the person collecting the specimen, date, and time of collection. Perform a venipuncture. Remove the needle and apply direct pressure with dry gauze to stop bleeding. Observe/assess venipuncture site for bleeding or hematoma formation and secure gauze with adhesive bandage. Promptly transport the specimen to the laboratory for processing and analysis.

POST-TEST:

A report of the results will be made available to the requesting health-care provider (HCP), who will discuss the results with the patient.

Instruct the patient in isolation precautions during the time of communicability or contagion.

Emphasize that the patient must return to have a convalescent blood sample taken in 7 to 14 days.

Inform the patient that the presence of mumps antibodies ensures lifelong immunity.

▶ Reinforce information given by the patient's HCP regarding further testing, treatment, or referral to another HCP. Provide information regarding vaccine-preventable diseases where indicated (e.g., anthrax, cervical cancer, diphtheria, encephalitis, hepatitis A and B, H1N1 flu, human papillomavirus, *Haemophilus* influenza, seasonal influenza, Lyme disease, measles, meningococcal disease, monkeypox, mumps, pertussis, pneumococcal disease, polio, rotavirus, rubella, shingles, smallpox, tetanus, typhoid fever, varicella, yellow fever). Provide contact information, if desired, for the Centers for Disease Control and Prevention www.cdc.gov/vaccines/vpd-vac. Answer any questions or address any concerns voiced by the patient or family.

▶ Depending on the results of this procedure, additional testing may be performed to evaluate or monitor progression of the disease process and determine the need for a change in therapy. Evaluate test results in relation to the patient's symptoms and other tests performed.

RELATED MONOGRAPHS:

▶ Refer to the Immune System table at the end of the book for related tests by body system.

M

Myocardial Infarct Scan

SYNONYM/ACRONYM: PYP cardiac scan, infarct scan, pyrophosphate cardiac scan, acute myocardial infarction scan.

COMMON USE: To differentiate between new and old myocardial infarcts and evaluate myocardial perfusion.

AREA OF APPLICATION: Heart, chest/thorax.

CONTRAST: IV radioactive material, usually technetium-99m stannous pyrophosphate (PYP).

DESCRIPTION: Technetium-99m stannous pyrophosphate (PYP) scanning, also known as *myocardial infarct imaging*, reveals the presence of myocardial perfusion and the extent of myocardial infarction (MI). This procedure can distinguish new from old infarcts when a patient has had abnormal electrocardiograms (ECGs) and cardiac enzymes have returned to normal. PYP uptake by acutely infarcted tissue may be related to the influx of calcium through damaged cell membranes, which accompanies myocardial necrosis; that is, the radionuclide may be binding to calcium phosphates or to hydroxyapatite. The PYP in these damaged cells can be viewed as spots of increased radionuclide uptake that appear in 12 hr at the earliest.

PYP uptake usually takes place 24 to 72 hr after MI, and the radionuclide remains detectable for approximately 10 to 14 days after the MI. PYP uptake is proportional to the blood flow to the affected area; with large areas of necrosis, PYP uptake may be maximal around the periphery of a necrotic area, with little uptake being detectable in the poorly perfused center. Most of the PYP is concentrated in regions that have 20% to 40% of the normal blood flow.

Single-photon emission computed tomography (SPECT) can be used to visualize the heart from multiple angles and planes, enabling areas of MI to be viewed with greater accuracy and resolution. This technique removes overlying structures that may confuse interpretation of the results. With the availability of assays of troponins, myocardial infarct imaging has become less important in the diagnosis of acute MI.

INDICATIONS

- Aid in the diagnosis of (or confirm and locate) acute MI when ECG and enzyme testing do not provide a diagnosis
- Aid in the diagnosis of perioperative MI
- Differentiate between a new and old infarction
- Evaluate possible reinfarction or extension of the infarct
- Obtain baseline information about infarction before cardiac surgery

POTENTIAL DIAGNOSIS

Normal findings in
- Normal coronary blood flow and tissue perfusion, with no PYP localization in the myocardium
- No uptake above background activity in the myocardium (Note: when PYP uptake is present, it is graded in relation to adjacent rib activity)

Abnormal findings in
- MI, indicated by increased PYP uptake in the myocardium

CRITICAL FINDINGS: N/A

INTERFERING FACTORS

This procedure is contraindicated for
- Patients who are pregnant or suspected of being pregnant, unless the potential benefits of the procedure far outweigh the risk of radiation exposure to the fetus.
- Patients with hypersensitivity to the radionuclide.

Factors that may impair clear imaging
- Inability of the patient to cooperate or remain still during the procedure because of age, significant pain, or mental status.
- Metallic objects (e.g., jewelry, body rings) within the examination field, which may inhibit organ visualization and cause unclear images.

Other nuclear scans done within the previous 24 to 48 hr.

Conditions such as chest wall trauma, cardiac trauma, or recent cardioversion procedure.

Myocarditis.

Pericarditis.

Left ventricular aneurysm.

Metastasis.

Valvular and coronary artery calcifications.

Cardiac neoplasms.

Aneurysms.

Other considerations

Improper injection of the radionuclide may allow the tracer to seep deep into the muscle tissue, producing erroneous hot spots.

Consultation with a health-care provider (HCP) should occur before the procedure for radiation safety concerns regarding younger patients or patients who are lactating.

Risks associated with radiation overexposure can result from frequent x-ray or radionuclide procedures. Personnel working in the examination area should wear badges to record their level of radiation.

NURSING IMPLICATIONS AND PROCEDURE

PRETEST:

Positively identify the patient using at least two unique identifiers before providing care, treatment, or services.

Patient Teaching: Inform the patient this procedure can assess blood flow to the heart.

Obtain a history of the patient's complaints, including a list of known allergens, especially allergies or sensitivities to latex, iodine, seafood, contrast medium, anesthetics, or dyes.

Obtain a history of the patient's cardiovascular system, symptoms, and results of previously performed

laboratory tests and diagnostic and surgical procedures.

Note any recent procedures that can interfere with test results, including examinations using iodine-based contrast medium.

Record the date of the last menstrual period and determine the possibility of pregnancy in perimenopausal women.

Obtain a list of the patient's current medications, including herbs, nutritional supplements, and nutraceuticals (see Appendix F).

Review the procedure with the patient. Address concerns about pain related to the procedure and explain that some pain may be experienced during the test, and there may be moments of discomfort. Reassure the patient that the radionuclide poses no radioactive hazard and rarely produces side effects. Inform the patient that the procedure is performed in a nuclear medicine department by an HCP specializing in this procedure, with support staff, and will take approximately 30 to 60 min. Inform the patient that the technologist will administer an IV injection of the radionuclide and that he or she will need to return 2 to 3 hr later for the scan.

Sensitivity to social and cultural issues, as well as concern for modesty, is important in providing psychological support before, during, and after the procedure.

The patient should fast, restrict fluids, and refrain from smoking for 4 hr prior to the procedure. Instruct the patient to withhold medications for 24 hr before the procedure. Protocols may vary among facilities.

Make sure a written and informed consent has been signed prior to the procedure and before administering any medications.

Instruct the patient to remove jewelry and other metallic objects from the area to be examined.

INTRATEST:

Observe standard precautions, and follow the general guidelines in Appendix A. Positively identify the patient.

Ensure that the patient has complied with dietary and medication restrictions and other pretesting preparations.

M

Ensure that the patient has removed all external metallic objects prior to the procedure.

Have emergency equipment readily available.

Instruct the patient to void prior to the procedure and to change into the gown, robe, and foot coverings provided.

Instruct the patient to cooperate fully and to follow directions. Instruct the patient to lie very still during the procedure because movement will produce unclear images.

Place the patient in a supine position on a flat table with foam wedges to help maintain position and immobilization.

IV radionuclide is administered. The heart is scanned 2 to 4 hr after injection in various positions. In most circumstances, however, SPECT is done so that the heart can be viewed from multiple angles and planes.

Monitor the patient for complications related to the procedure (e.g., allergic reaction, anaphylaxis, bronchospasm).

Remove the needle or catheter and apply a pressure dressing over the puncture site.

Observe/assess the needle/catheter insertion site for bleeding, inflammation, or hematoma formation.

M

POST-TEST:

A report of the results will be made available to the requesting HCP, who will discuss the results with the patient.

Instruct the patient to resume normal activity and diet as directed by the HCP.

Unless contraindicated, advise the patient to drink increased amounts of fluids for 24 to 48 hr to eliminate the radionuclide from the body. Inform the patient that radionuclide is eliminated from the body within 6 to 24 hr.

No other radionuclide tests should be scheduled for 24 to 48 hr after this procedure.

Evaluate the patient's vital signs. Monitor vital signs and neurological status every 15 min for 1 hr, then every 2 hr for 4 hr, and then as ordered by HCP. Take temperature every 4 hr for 24 hr. Monitor intake and output at least every 8 hr. Compare with baseline values. Notify the HCP if temperature is elevated. Protocols may vary among facilities.

Observe for delayed allergic reactions, such as rash, urticaria, tachycardia, hyperpnea, hypertension, palpitations, nausea, or vomiting.

Instruct the patient to immediately report symptoms such as fast heart rate, difficulty breathing, skin rash, itching, chest pain, persistent right shoulder pain, or abdominal pain. Immediately report symptoms to the appropriate HCP.

Instruct the patient in the care and assessment of the injection site.

If the patient must return for additional imaging, advise the patient to rest in the interim and restrict diet to liquids before redistribution studies.

If a woman who is breastfeeding must have a nuclear scan, she should not breastfeed the infant until the radionuclide has been eliminated. This could take as long as 3 days. She should be instructed to express the milk and discard it during the 3-day period to prevent cessation of milk production.

Instruct the patient to flush the toilet immediately after each voiding following the procedure and to meticulously wash hands with soap and water after each voiding for 24 hr after the procedure.

Instruct all caregivers to wear gloves when discarding urine for 24 hr after the procedure. Wash gloved hands with soap and water before removing gloves. Then wash hands after the gloves are removed.

Nutritional Considerations: Abnormal findings may be associated with cardiovascular disease. The American Heart Association and National Heart, Lung, and Blood Institute (NHLBI) recommend nutritional therapy for individuals identified to be at high risk for developing coronary artery disease (CAD) or individuals who have specific risk factors and/or existing medical conditions (e.g., elevated LDL cholesterol levels, other lipid disorders insulin-dependent diabetes, insulin resistance, or metabolic syndrome). If overweight, the patient should be encouraged to achieve a normal weight. The NHLBI's National Cholesterol Education Program (NCEP) revised its dietary guidelines for reducing CAD in 2001. Guidelines for the Therapeutic Lifestyle Changes (TLC) diet are outlined in the Third Report of the Expert Panel on Detection, Evaluation, and Treatment of High Blood Cholesterol in Adults (Adult Treatment Panel III [ATP III]). The TLC diet emphasizes a reduction in foods high in saturated fats and cholesterol. Red meats, eggs, and dairy products are the major sources of saturated fats and cholesterol. If triglycerides also are elevated, the patient should be advised to eliminate or reduce alcohol and simple carbohydrates from the diet. The TLC approach also includes the use of plant stanols or sterols and increased dissolved fiber as an option for lowering LDL cholesterol levels; nutritional recommendations for daily total caloric intake; recommendations for allowable percentage of calories derived from fat (saturated and unsaturated), carbohydrates, protein, and cholesterol; as well as recommendations for daily expenditure of energy.

Nutritional Considerations: Overweight patients with high blood pressure should be encouraged to achieve a normal weight. Other changeable risk factors warranting patient education include strategies to safely decrease sodium intake, increase physical activity, decrease alcohol consumption, eliminate tobacco use, and decrease cholesterol levels.

Social and Cultural Considerations: Numerous studies point to the prevalence of excess body weight in American children and adolescents. Experts estimate that obesity is present in 25% of the population ages

6 to 11 yr. The medical, social, and emotional consequences of excess body weight are significant. Special attention should be given to instructing the child and caregiver regarding health risks and weight-control education.

▶ Recognize anxiety related to test results, and be supportive of fear of shortened life expectancy. Discuss the implications of abnormal test results on the patient's lifestyle. Provide teaching and information regarding the clinical implications of the test results, as appropriate. Educate the patient regarding access to counseling services. Provide contact information, if desired, for the American Heart Association (www.americanheart.org) or the NHLBI (www.nhlbi.nih.gov).

▶ Reinforce information given by the patient's HCP regarding further testing, treatment, or referral to another HCP. Answer any questions or address any concerns voiced by the patient or family.

▶ Depending on the results of this procedure, additional testing may be needed to evaluate or monitor progression of the disease process and determine the need for a change in therapy. Evaluate test results in relation to the patient's symptoms and other tests performed.

RELATED MONOGRAPHS:

▶ Related tests include angiography abdominal, AST, BNP, blood pool imaging, chest x-ray, CT abdominal, CT thoracic, CK and isoenzymes, culture viral, echocardiography, echocardiography transesophageal, ECG, MRA, MRI chest, myocardial perfusion scan, pericardial fluid analysis, and PET heart.

▶ Refer to the Cardiovascular System table at the end of the book for related tests by body system.

Myocardial Perfusion Heart Scan

SYNONYM/ACRONYM: Sestamibi scan, stress thallium, thallium scan.

COMMON USE: To assess cardiac blood flow to evaluate for and assist in diagnosing coronary artery disease and myocardial infarction.

AREA OF APPLICATION: Heart, chest/thorax.

CONTRAST: IV or oral radionuclide.

DESCRIPTION: Cardiac scanning is a nuclear medicine study that reveals clinical information about coronary blood flow, ventricular size, and cardiac function. Thallium-201 chloride rest or stress studies are used to evaluate myocardial blood flow to assist in diagnosing or determining the risk for ischemic cardiac disease, coronary artery disease (CAD), and myocardial infarction (MI). This procedure is an alternative to angiography or cardiac catheterization in cases in which these procedures may pose a risk to the patient. Thallium-201 is a potassium analogue and is taken up by myocardial cells proportional to blood flow to the cell and cell viability. During stress studies, the radionuclide is injected at peak exercise, after which the patient continues to exercise for several minutes. During exercise, areas of heart muscle supplied by normal arteries increase their blood supply, as well as the supply of thallium-201 delivery to the heart muscle, to a greater extent than regions of the heart muscle supplied by stenosed coronary arteries. This discrepancy in blood flow becomes apparent and quantifiable in subsequent imaging. Comparison of early stress images with images taken after 3 to 4 hr redistribution (delayed images) enables differentiation between normally perfused, healthy myocardium (which is normal at rest but ischemic on stress) and infarcted myocardium.

Technetium-99m agents such as sestamibi (2-methoxyisobutylisonitrile) are delivered similarly to thallium-201 during myocardial perfusion imaging, but they are extracted to a lesser degree on the first pass through the heart and are taken up by the mitochondria. Over a short period, the radionuclide concentrates in the heart to the same degree as thallium-201. The advantage to technetium-99m agents is that immediate imaging is unnecessary because the radionuclide remains fixed to the heart muscle for several hours. The examination requires two separate injections, one for the rest portion and one for the stress portion of the procedure. These injections can take place on the same day or preferably over a 2-day period. Examination quality is improved if the patient is given a light, fatty meal after the radionuclide is injected to facilitate hepatobiliary clearance of the radioactivity.

If stress testing cannot be performed by exercising, dipyridamole (Persantine) or adenosine, a vasodilator, can be administered orally or IV. A coronary vasodilator is administered before the thallium-201 or other radionuclide, and the scanning procedure is then performed. Vasodilators increase blood flow in normal coronary arteries twofold to threefold without exercise, and they reveal perfusion defects when blood flow is compromised by vessel pathology. Vasodilator-mediated myocardial perfusion scanning is reserved for patients who are unable to participate in treadmill, bicycle, or handgrip exercises for stress testing because of lung disease, neurological disorders (e.g., multiple sclerosis, spinal cord injury), morbid obesity, and orthopedic disorders (e.g., arthritis, limb amputation).

Single-photon emission computed tomography can be used to visualize the heart from multiple angles and planes, enabling areas of MI to be viewed with greater accuracy and resolution. This technique removes overlying structures that may confuse interpretation of the results.

INDICATIONS

Aid in the diagnosis of CAD or risk for CAD

Determine rest defects and reperfusion with delayed imaging in unstable angina

Evaluate the extent of CAD and determine cardiac function

Assess the function of collateral coronary arteries

Evaluate bypass graft patency and general cardiac status after surgery

Evaluate the site of an old MI to determine obstruction to cardiac muscle perfusion

- Evaluate the effectiveness of medication regimen and balloon angioplasty procedure on narrow coronary arteries

POTENTIAL DIAGNOSIS

Normal findings in
- Normal wall motion, coronary blood flow, tissue perfusion, and ventricular size and function

Abnormal findings in
- Abnormal stress and resting images, indicating previous MI
- Abnormal stress images with normal resting images, indicating transient ischemia
- Cardiac hypertrophy, indicated by increased radionuclide uptake in the myocardium
- Enlarged left ventricle
- Heart chamber disorder
- Ventricular septal defects

CRITICAL FINDINGS: N/A

INTERFERING FACTORS

This procedure is contraindicated for
- ❖ Patients who have taken sildenafil (Viagra) within the previous 48 hr, because this test may require the use of nitrates (nitroglycerin) that can precipitate life-threatening low blood pressure.
- Patients with bleeding disorders.
- Patients who are pregnant or suspected of being pregnant, unless the potential benefits of the procedure far outweigh the risk of radiation exposure to the fetus.
- Patients with hypersensitivity to the radionuclide.
- Patients with left ventricular hypertrophy, right and left bundle branch block, hypokalemia, and patients receiving cardiotonic therapy.
- Patients with anginal pain at rest or patients with severe atherosclerotic coronary vessels in whom dipyridamole testing cannot be performed.

M

• Patients with asthma, because chemical stress with vasodilators can cause bronchospasms.

Factors that may impair clear imaging

• Inability of the patient to cooperate or remain still during the procedure because of age, significant pain, or mental status.
• Medications such as digitalis and quinidine, which can alter cardiac contractility, and nitrates, which can affect cardiac performance.
• Single-vessel disease, which can produce false-negative thallium-201 scanning results.
• Conditions such as chest wall or cardiac trauma, angina that is difficult to control, significant cardiac arrhythmias, and recent cardioversion procedure.
• Suboptimal cardiac stress or patient exhaustion preventing maximum heart rate testing.
• Excessive eating or exercising between initial and redistribution imaging 4 hr later, which produces false-positive results.
• Improper adjustment of the radiological equipment to accommodate obese or thin patients, which can cause overexposure or underexposure and a poor-quality study.
• Patients who are very obese or who may exceed the weight limit for the equipment.
• Incorrect positioning of the patient, which may produce poor visualization of the area to be examined.
• Metallic objects (e.g., jewelry, body rings) within the examination field, which may inhibit organ visualization and cause unclear images.

Other considerations

• Failure to follow dietary restrictions before the procedure may cause the procedure to be canceled or repeated.
• Improper injection of the radionuclide that allows the tracer to seep deep into the muscle tissue produces erroneous hot spots.
• Inaccurate timing for imaging after radionuclide injection can affect the results.
• Consultation with a health-care provider (HCP) should occur before the procedure for radiation safety concerns regarding younger patients or patients who are lactating.
• Risks associated with radiation overexposure can result from frequent x-ray or radionuclide procedures. Personnel working in the examination area should wear badges to reveal their level of exposure to radiation.

NURSING IMPLICATIONS AND PROCEDURE

PRETEST:

▸ Positively identify the patient using at least two unique identifiers before providing care, treatment, or services.
▸ *Patient Teaching:* Inform the patient this procedure can assist in assessing blood flow to the heart.
▸ Obtain a history of the patient's complaints and symptoms, including a list of known allergens, especially allergies or sensitivities to latex.
▸ Obtain a history of the patient's cardiovascular system, symptoms, and results of previously performed laboratory tests and diagnostic and surgical procedures.
▸ Record the date of the last menstrual period and determine the possibility of pregnancy in perimenopausal women.
▸ Obtain a list of the patient's current medications, including herbs, nutritional supplements, and nutraceuticals (see Appendix F).
▸ Review the procedure with the patient. Address concerns about pain and explain that some pain may be experienced during the test, or there may be moments of discomfort. Inform the patient that the procedure is performed in a special department, usually in a radiology or vascular suite, by an HCP specializing in this procedure, with

support staff, and takes approximately 30 to 60 min.

Sensitivity to social and cultural issues, as well as concern for modesty, is important in providing psychological support before, during, and after the procedure.

Explain that an IV line may be inserted to allow infusion of IV fluids, contrast medium, dye, or sedatives. Usually normal saline is infused.

Instruct the patient to wear walking shoes (if treadmill exercise testing is to be performed), and emphasize the importance of reporting fatigue, pain, or shortness of breath.

Instruct the patient to remove dentures, jewelry, and other metallic objects from the area to be examined prior to the procedure.

Instruct the patient to fast for 4 hr, refrain from smoking for 4 to 6 hr, and withhold medications for 24 hr before the test. Instruct the patient to avoid taking anticoagulant medication or to reduce dosage as ordered prior to the procedure. Protocols may vary among facilities.

Make sure a written and informed consent has been signed prior to the procedure and before administering any medications.

This procedure may be terminated if chest pain, severe cardiac arrhythmias, or signs of a cerebrovascular accident occur.

INTRATEST:

Observe standard precautions, and follow the general guidelines in Appendix A. Positively identify the patient.

Ensure that the patient has complied with dietary, tobacco, and medication restrictions and other pretesting preparations for 4 to 6 hr prior to the procedure.

Ensure that the patient has removed external metallic objects from the area to be examined prior to the procedure.

Have emergency equipment readily available.

If the patient has a history of allergic reactions to any substance or drug, administer ordered prophylactic steroids or antihistamines before the procedure. Use nonionic contrast medium for the procedure.

Instruct the patient to void prior to the procedure and change into the gown, robe, and foot coverings provided.

Record baseline vital signs and assess neurological status. Protocols may vary among facilities.

Instruct the patient to cooperate fully and to follow directions.

Establish IV fluid line for the injection of emergency drugs and of sedatives.

Place electrocardiographic (ECG) electrodes on the patient for cardiac monitoring. Establish baseline rhythm; determine if the patient has ventricular arrhythmias. Monitor the patient's blood pressure throughout the procedure by using an automated blood pressure machine.

Assist the patient onto the treadmill or bicycle ergometer and ask the patient to exercise to a calculated 80% to 85% of the maximum heart rate, as determined by the protocol selected.

Wear gloves during the radionuclide injection and while handling patient's urine.

Thallium-201 is injected 60 to 90 sec before exercise is terminated, and imaging is done immediately in the supine position and repeated in 4 hr.

Patients who cannot exercise are given dipyridamole 4 min before thallium-201 is injected.

Inform the patient that movement during the resting procedure affects the results and makes interpretation difficult.

Monitor the patient for complications related to the procedure (e.g., allergic reaction, anaphylaxis, or bronchospasm).

Remove the needle or catheter and apply a pressure dressing over the puncture site.

Observe/assess the needle/catheter insertion site for bleeding, inflammation, or hematoma formation.

The results are recorded on film or in a computerized system for recall and postprocedure interpretation by the appropriate HCP.

POST-TEST:

A report of the results will be made available to the requesting HCP,

M

who will discuss the results with the patient.

- Instruct the patient to resume normal diet and activity, as directed by the HCP.
- Unless contraindicated, advise patient to drink increased amounts of fluids for 24 to 48 hr to eliminate the radionuclide from the body. Inform the patient that radionuclide is eliminated from the body within 6 to 24 hr.
- No other radionuclide tests should be scheduled for 24 to 48 hr after this procedure.
- Evaluate the patient's vital signs. Monitor vital signs and neurological status every 15 min for 1 hr, then every 2 hr for 4 hr, and then as ordered by HCP. Take temperature every 4 hr for 24 hr. Monitor intake and output at least every 8 hr. Compare with baseline values. Notify the HCP if temperature is elevated. Protocols may vary among facilities.
- Observe for delayed allergic reactions, such as rash, urticaria, tachycardia, hyperpnea, hypertension, palpitations, nausea, or vomiting.
- Instruct the patient to immediately report symptoms such as fast heart rate, difficulty breathing, skin rash, itching, chest pain, persistent right shoulder pain, or abdominal pain. Immediately report symptoms to the appropriate HCP.
- Instruct the patient in the care and assessment of the injection site.
- If the patient must return for additional imaging, advise the patient to rest in the interim and restrict diet to liquids before redistribution studies.
- If a woman who is breastfeeding must have a nuclear scan, she should not breastfeed the infant until the radionuclide has been eliminated. This could take as long as 3 days. She should be instructed to express the milk and discard it during the 3-day period to prevent cessation of milk production.
- Instruct the patient to flush the toilet immediately after each voiding following the procedure and to meticulously wash hands with soap and water after each voiding for 24 hr after the procedure.
- Instruct all caregivers to wear gloves when discarding urine for 24 hr after

the procedure. Wash gloved hands with soap and water before removing gloves. Then wash hands after the gloves are removed.

- *Nutritional Considerations:* Abnormal findings may be associated with cardiovascular disease. The American Heart Association and National Heart, Lung, and Blood Institute (NHLBI) recommend nutritional therapy for individuals identified to be at high risk for developing CAD or individuals who have specific risk factors and/or existing medical conditions (e.g., elevated LDL cholesterol levels, other lipid disorders, insulin-dependent diabetes, insulin resistance, or metabolic syndrome). If overweight, the patient should be encouraged to achieve a normal weight. Guidelines for the Therapeutic Lifestyle Changes (TLC) diet are outlined in the Third Report of the Expert Panel on Detection, Evaluation, and Treatment of High Blood Cholesterol in Adults (Adult Treatment Panel III [ATP III]). The TLC diet emphasizes a reduction in foods high in saturated fats and cholesterol. Red meats, eggs, and dairy products are the major sources of saturated fats and cholesterol. If triglycerides also are elevated, the patient should be advised to eliminate or reduce alcohol and simple carbohydrates from the diet. The TLC approach also includes the use of plant stanols or sterols and increased dissolved fiber as an option for lowering LDL cholesterol levels; nutritional recommendations for daily total caloric intake; recommendations for allowable percentage of calories derived from fat (saturated and unsaturated), carbohydrates, protein, and cholesterol; as well as recommendations for daily expenditure of energy.
- *Nutritional Considerations:* Overweight patients with high blood pressure should be encouraged to achieve a normal weight. Other changeable risk factors warranting patient education include strategies to safely decrease sodium intake, increase physical activity, decrease alcohol consumption, eliminate tobacco use, and decrease cholesterol levels.

Social and Cultural Considerations:
Numerous studies point to the prevalence of excess body weight in American children and adolescents. Experts estimate that obesity is present in 25% of the population ages 6 to 11 yr. The medical, social, and emotional consequences of excess body weight are significant. Special attention should be given to instructing the child and caregiver regarding health risks and weight-control education.

Recognize anxiety related to test results, and be supportive of fear of shortened life expectancy. Discuss the implications of abnormal test results on the patient's lifestyle. Provide teaching and information regarding the clinical implications of the test results, as appropriate. Educate the patient regarding access to counseling services. Provide contact information, if desired, for the American Heart Association (www.americanheart.org) or the NHLBI (www.nhlbi.nih.gov). Reinforce information given by the patient's HCP regarding further testing, treatment, or referral to another HCP.

Answer any questions or address any concerns voiced by the patient or family.

Depending on the results of this procedure, additional testing may be needed to evaluate or monitor progression of the disease process and determine the need for a change in therapy. Evaluate test results in relation to the patient's symptoms and other tests performed.

RELATED MONOGRAPHS:

Related tests include antiarrhythmic drugs, apolipoprotein A and B, AST, atrial natriuretic peptide, BNP, calcium, cholesterol (total, HDL, LDL), CT cardiac scoring, CRP, CK and isoenzymes, echocardiography, echocardiography transesophageal, ECG, exercise stress test, glucose, glycated hemoglobin, Holter monitor, homocysteine, ketones, LDH and isos, lipoprotein electrophoresis, magnesium, MRI chest, MI infarct scan, myoglobin, PET heart, potassium, triglycerides, and troponin.

Refer to the Cardiovascular System table at the end of the book for related tests by body system.

M

Myoglobin

SYNONYM/ACRONYM: MB.

COMMON USE: A general assessment of damage to skeletal or cardiac muscle from trauma or inflammation.

SPECIMEN: Serum (1 mL) collected in a red- or tiger-top tube.

NORMAL FINDINGS: (Method: Electrochemiluminescent immunoassay)

	Conventional Units	SI Units (Conventional Units × 0.571)
Male	28–72 ng/mL	16–41 nmol/L
Female	25–58 ng/mL	14.3–33.1 nmol/L

Values are higher in males.

DESCRIPTION: Myoglobin is an oxygen-binding muscle protein normally found in skeletal and cardiac muscle. It is released into the bloodstream after muscle damage from ischemia, trauma, or inflammation. Although myoglobin testing is more sensitive than creatinine kinase and isoenzymes, it does not indicate the specific site involved.

Timing for Appearance and Resolution of Serum/Plasma Cardiac Markers in Acute Myocardial Infarction

Cardiac Marker	Appearance (Hours)	Peak (Hours)	Resolution (Days)
AST	6–8	24–48	3–4
CK (total)	4–6	24	2–3
CK-MB	4–6	15–20	2–3
LDH	12	24–48	10–14
Myoglobin	1–3	4–12	1
Troponin I	2–6	15–20	5–7

INDICATIONS
• Assist in predicting a flare-up of polymyositis
• Estimate damage from skeletal muscle injury or myocardial infarction (MI)

POTENTIAL DIAGNOSIS

Increased in
Conditions that cause muscle damage; damaged muscle cells release myoglobin into circulation.

• Cardiac surgery
• Cocaine use *(rhabdomyolysis is a complication of cocaine use or overdose)*
• Exercise
• Malignant hyperthermia
• MI
• Progressive muscular dystrophy
• Renal failure
• Rhabdomyolysis
• Shock
• Thrombolytic therapy

Decreased in
• Myasthenia gravis
• Presence of antibodies to myoglobin, as seen in patients with polymyositis
• Rheumatoid arthritis

CRITICAL FINDINGS: N/A

INTERFERING FACTORS: N/A

NURSING IMPLICATIONS AND PROCEDURE

PRETEST:
Positively identify the patient using at least two unique identifiers before providing care, treatment, or services.
Patient Teaching: Inform the patient this test can assist in diagnosing cardiac or skeletal muscle damage.
Obtain a history of the patient's complaints, including a list of known allergens, especially allergies or sensitivities to latex.
Obtain a history of the patient's cardiovascular and musculoskeletal systems, symptoms, and results of previously performed laboratory tests and diagnostic and surgical procedures.
Obtain a list of the patient's current medications, including herbs, nutritional supplements, and nutraceuticals (see Appendix F).
Review the procedure with the patient. Inform the patient that specimen collection takes approximately 5 to 10 min. Address concerns about pain and explain that there may be some discomfort during the venipuncture.

Sensitivity to social and cultural issues, as well as concern for modesty, is important in providing psychological support before, during, and after the procedure.

There are no food, fluid, or medication restrictions unless by medical direction.

NTRATEST:

If the patient has a history of allergic reaction to latex, avoid the use of equipment containing latex.

Instruct the patient to cooperate fully and to follow directions. Direct the patient to breathe normally and to avoid unnecessary movement. Observe standard precautions, and follow the general guidelines in Appendix A. Positively identify the patient, and label the appropriate specimen container with the corresponding patient demographics, initials of the person collecting the specimen, date, and time of collection. Perform a venipuncture.

Remove the needle and apply direct pressure with dry gauze to stop bleeding. Observe/assess venipuncture site for bleeding or hematoma formation and secure gauze with adhesive bandage. Promptly transport the specimen to the laboratory for processing and analysis.

OST-TEST:

A report of the results will be made available to the requesting health-care provider (HCP), who will discuss the results with the patient.

Nutritional Considerations: Abnormal myoglobin levels may be associated with cardiovascular disease. The American Heart Association and National Heart, Lung, and Blood Institute (NHLBI) recommend nutritional therapy for individuals identified to be at high risk for developing coronary artery disease (CAD) or individuals who have specific risk factors and/or existing medical conditions (e.g., elevated LDL cholesterol levels, other lipid disorders, insulin-dependent diabetes, insulin resistance, or metabolic syndrome). If overweight, the patient should be encouraged to achieve a normal weight. Guidelines for the

Therapeutic Lifestyle Changes (TLC) diet are outlined in the Third Report of the Expert Panel on Detection, Evaluation, and Treatment of High Blood Cholesterol in Adults (Adult Treatment Panel III [ATP III]). The TLC diet emphasizes a reduction in foods high in saturated fats and cholesterol. Red meats, eggs, and dairy products are the major sources of saturated fats and cholesterol. If triglycerides also are elevated, the patient should be advised to eliminate or reduce alcohol and simple carbohydrates from the diet. The TLC approach also includes the use of plant stanols or sterols and increased dissolved fiber as an option for lowering LDL cholesterol levels; nutritional recommendations for daily total caloric intake; recommendations for allowable percentage of calories derived from fat (saturated and unsaturated), carbohydrates, protein, and cholesterol; as well as recommendations for daily expenditure of energy.

Nutritional Considerations: Overweight patients with high blood pressure should be encouraged to achieve a normal weight. Other changeable risk factors warranting patient education include strategies to safely decrease sodium intake, increase physical activity, decrease alcohol consumption, eliminate tobacco use, and decrease cholesterol levels.

Recognize anxiety related to test results, and be supportive of fear of shortened life expectancy. Discuss the implications of abnormal test results on the patient's lifestyle. Provide teaching and information regarding the clinical implications of the test results, as appropriate. Educate the patient regarding access to counseling services. Provide contact information, if desired, for the American Heart Association (www.americanheart.org) or the NHLBI (www.nhlbi.nih.gov).

Reinforce information given by the patient's HCP regarding further testing, treatment, or referral to another HCP. Answer any questions or address any concerns voiced by the patient or family.

Depending on the results of this procedure, additional testing may be

M

performed to evaluate or monitor progression of the disease process and determine the need for a change in therapy. Evaluate test results in relation to the patient's symptoms and other tests performed.

RELATED MONOGRAPHS:

‣ Related tests include antiarrhythmic drugs, apolipoprotein A and B, AST, ANP, blood gases, BNP, calcium, cholesterol (total, HDL, and LDL), CRP, CK and isoenzymes, CT cardiac scoring, echocardiography, echocardiography transesophageal, ECG, exercise stress test, glucose, glycated hemoglobin, Holter monitor, homocysteine, ketones LDH and isoenzymes, lipoprotein electrophoresis, magnesium, MRI chest, MI infarct scan, myoglobin, pericardial fluid analysis, PET heart, potassium, triglycerides, and troponin.

‣ Refer to the Cardiovascular and Musculoskeletal systems tables at the end of the book for related tests by body system.

M

Nerve Fiber Analysis

SYNONYM/ACRONYM: NFA.

COMMON USE: To assist in measuring the thickness of the retinal nerve fiber layer, to assist in diagnosing diseases of the eye such as glaucoma.

AREA OF APPLICATION: Eyes.

CONTRAST: N/A.

DESCRIPTION: There are over 1 million ganglion nerve cells in the retina of each eye. Each nerve cell has a long fiber that travels through the nerve fiber layer of the retina and exits the eye through the optic nerve. The optic nerve is made up of all the ganglion nerve fibers and connects the eye to the brain for vision to occur. As the ganglion cells die, the nerve fiber layer becomes thinner and an empty space in the optic nerve, called the cup, becomes larger. The thinning of the nerve fiber layer and the enlargement of the nerve fiber cup are measurements used to gauge the extent of damage to the retina. Significant damage to the nerve fiber layer occurs before loss of vision is noticed by the patient. Damage can be caused by glaucoma, aging, or occlusion of the vessels in the retina. Ganglion cell loss due to glaucoma begins in the periphery of the retina, thereby first affecting peripheral vision. This change in vision can also be detected by visual field testing. There are several different techniques for measuring nerve fiber layer thickness. One of the most common employs a laser that emits polarizing light waves. The laser's computer measures the change in direction of alignment of the light beam after it passes through the nerve fiber layer tissue. The amount of change in polarization correlates to the thickness of the retinal nerve fiber layer.

INDICATIONS

* Assist in the diagnosis of eye diseases
* Determine retinal nerve fiber layer thickness
* Monitor the effects of various therapies or the progression of conditions resulting in loss of vision

POTENTIAL DIAGNOSIS

Normal findings in
* Normal nerve fiber layer thickness

Abnormal findings in
* Glaucoma or suspicion of glaucoma
* Ocular hypertension

CRITICAL FINDINGS: N/A

INTERFERING FACTORS

Factors that may impair the results of the examination
* Inability of the patient to fixate on focal point.
* Corneal disorder that prevents proper alignment of the retinal nerve fibers.
* Dense cataract that prevents visualization of a clear nerve fiber image.
* Inability of the patient to cooperate or remain still during the test because of age, significant pain, or mental status.

N

NURSING IMPLICATIONS AND PROCEDURE

PRETEST:

▶ Positively identify the patient using at least two unique identifiers before providing care, treatment, or services.

Patient Teaching: Inform the patient this procedure can assist in diagnosing eye disease.

▶ Obtain a history of the patient's complaints, including a list of known allergens.

▶ Obtain a history of narrow-angle glaucoma. Obtain a history of known or suspected visual impairment, changes in visual acuity, and use of glasses or contact lenses.

▶ Obtain a history of the patient's known or suspected vision loss, including type and cause; eye conditions with treatment regimens; eye surgery; and other tests and procedures to assess and diagnose visual deficit.

▶ Obtain a history of symptoms and results of previously performed laboratory tests and diagnostic and surgical procedures.

▶ Obtain a list of the patient's current medications, including herbs, nutritional supplements, and nutraceuticals (see Appendix F).

▶ Instruct the patient to remove contact lenses or glasses, as appropriate. Instruct the patient regarding the importance of keeping the eyes open for the test.

▶ Review the procedure with the patient. Explain that the patient will be requested to fixate the eyes during the procedure. Address concerns about pain and explain that no pain will be experienced during the test, but there may be moments of discomfort. Explain to the patient that some discomfort may be experienced after the test when the numbness wears off from anesthetic drops administered prior to the test. Inform the patient that a health-care provider (HCP) performs the test and that to evaluate both eyes, the test can take 10 to 15 min.

Sensitivity to social and cultural issues, as well as concern for modesty, is important in providing psychological support before, during, and after the procedure.

▶ There are no food, fluid, or medication restrictions unless by medical direction.

INTRATEST:

▶ Observe standard precautions, and follow the general guidelines in Appendix A. Positively identify the patient.

▶ Instruct the patient to cooperate fully and to follow directions. Ask the patient to remain still during the procedure because movement produces unreliable results.

▶ Seat the patient comfortably. Instruct the patient to look straight ahead, keeping the eyes open and unblinking.

▶ Instill topical anesthetic in each eye, as ordered, and allow time for it to work. Topical anesthetic drops are placed in the eye with the patient looking up and the solution directed at the six o'clock position of the sclera (white of the eye) near the limbus (gray, semitransparent area of the eyeball where the cornea and sclera meet). Neither the dropper nor the bottle should touch the eyelashes.

▶ The equipment used to perform the test determines whether dilation of the pupils is required (OCT) or avoided (GDX).

▶ Request that the patient look straight ahead at a fixation light with the chin in the chin rest and forehead against the support bar. The patient should be reminded not to move the eyes or blink the eyelids as the measurement is taken. The person performing the test can store baseline data or retrieve previous images from the equipment. The equipment can create the mean image from current and previous data, and its computer can make a comparison against previous images.

POST-TEST:

▶ A report of the results will be made available to the requesting HCP, who will discuss the results with the patient.

▶ Recognize anxiety related to test results, and be supportive of impaired activity related to vision loss or anticipated loss of driving privileges.

Discuss the implications of abnormal test results on the patient's lifestyle. Provide teaching and information regarding the clinical implications of the test results, as appropriate. Provide contact information, if desired, for the Glaucoma Research Foundation (www.glaucoma.org).

Reinforce information given by the patient's HCP regarding further testing, treatment, or referral to another HCP. Instruct the patient in the use of any ordered medications, usually eye drops. Explain the importance of adhering to the therapy regimen, especially because glaucoma does not present symptoms. Instruct the patient in both the ocular side effects and systemic reactions associated with the prescribed medication. Encourage him or her to review corresponding literature provided by a pharmacist. Answer any questions or address any concerns voiced by the patient or family.

Depending on the results of this procedure, additional testing may be performed to evaluate or monitor progression of the disease process and determine the need for a change in therapy. Evaluate test results in relation to the patient's symptoms and other tests performed.

RELATED MONOGRAPHS:

Related tests include fundus photography, gonioscopy, pachymetry, slit-lamp biomicroscopy, and visual field testing.

Refer to the Ocular System table at the end of the book for related tests by body system.

Newborn Screening

SYNONYM/ACRONYM: NBS, newborn metabolic screening, tests for inborn errors of metabolism.

COMMON USE: To evaluate newborns for congenital abnormalities, which may include hearing loss; identification of hemoglobin variants such as thalassemias and sickle cell anemia; presence of antibodies that would indicate a HIV infection; or metabolic disorders such as homocystinuria, maple syrup urine disease (MSUD), phenylketonuria (PKU), tyrosinuria, and unexplained mental retardation.

AREA OF APPLICATION: Ears for hearing tests.

SPECIMEN: Whole blood for metabolic tests.

NORMAL FINDINGS: (Method: Thyroxine, TSH, and HIV—immunoassay; amino acids—tandem mass spectrometry; hemoglobin variants—electrophoresis)

Hearing Test	
Age	**Normal Findings**
Neonates–3 days	Normal pure tone average of –10 to 15 dB

Thyroid-Stimulating Hormone (TSH)		
Age	Conventional Units	SI Units (Conventional Units × 1)
Neonates–3 days	Less than 20 micro-international units/mL	Less than 20 milli-international units/L

Thyroxine, Total		
Age	Conventional Units	SI Units (Conventional Units × 12.9)
Neonates–3 days	11.8–22.6 mcg/dL	152–292 nmol/L

Hemoglobinopathies	Normal Hemoglobin Pattern
Blood spot amino acid analysis	Normal findings. Numerous amino acids are evaluated by blood spot testing, and values vary by method and laboratory. The testing laboratory should be consulted for corresponding reference ranges.
HIV antibodies	Negative

DESCRIPTION: Newborn screening is a process used to evaluate infants for disorders that are treatable but difficult to identify by direct observation of diagnosable symptoms. The testing is conducted shortly after birth and is mandated in all 50 states and U.S. territories through a collaborative effort between government agencies, local public health departments, hospitals, and parents. Testing is categorized as core tests and second-tier tests. The testing included in mandatory newborn screening programs varies among states and territories; testing of interest that is not included in the mandatory list can be requested by a health-care provider (HCP), as appropriate. Confirmatory testing is performed if abnormal findings are produced by screening methods. Properly

collected blood spot cards contain sufficient sample to perform both screening and confirmatory testing. Confirmatory testing varies depending on the initial screen and can include fatty acid oxidation probe tests on skin samples, enzyme uptake testing of skin or muscle tissue samples, enzyme assays of blood samples, DNA testing, gas chromatography/mass spectrometry, and tandem mass spectrometry. Testing for common genetically transferred conditions can be performed on either or both prospective parents by blood tests, skin tests, or DNA testing. DNA testing can also be performed on the fetus, in utero, through the collection of fetal cells by amniocentesis or chorionic villus sampling. Counseling and written, informed consent are recommended and sometimes required before genetic testing.

Every state and U.S. territory has a newborn screening program, which includes early hearing loss detection and intervention (EHDI). The goal of EHDI is to assure that permanent hearing loss is identified before 3 months of age, appropriate and timely intervention services are provided before 6 months of age, families of infants with hearing loss receive culturally competent support, and tracking and data management systems for newborn hearing screens are linked with other relevant public health information systems.

The adrenal glands are responsible for production of the hormones cortisol, aldosterone, and male sex androgens. Most infants born with congenital adrenal hyperplasia (CAH) make too much of the androgen hormones and not enough cortisol or aldosterone. The complex feedback loops in the body call for the adrenal glands to increase production of cortisol and aldosterone, and as the adrenal glands work harder to increase production, they increase in size, resulting in hyperplasia. CAH is a group of conditions. Most frequently, lack of or dysfunction of an enzyme called 21-hydroxylase results in one of two types of CAH. The first is a salt-wasting condition in which insufficient levels of aldosterone causes too much salt and water to be lost in the urine. Newborns with this condition are poor feeders and appear lethargic or sleepy. Other symptoms include vomiting, diarrhea, and dehydration, which can lead to weight loss, low blood pressure, and decreased electrolytes. If untreated, these symptoms can result in metabolic acidosis and shock, which in CAH infants is called an adrenal crisis. Signs of an adrenal crisis include confusion, irritability, tachycardia, and coma. The second most common type of CAH is a condition in which having too much of the androgen hormones in the blood causes female babies to develop masculinized or virilized genitals. High levels of androgens leads to precocious sexual development, well before the normal age of puberty, in both boys and girls.

Inadequate production of the thyroid hormone thyroxine can result in congenital hypothyroidism, which when untreated manifests in severely delayed physical and mental development. Inadequate production may be due to a defect such as a missing, misplaced, or malfunctioning thyroid gland. Inadequate production may also be due to the mother's thyroid condition or treatment during pregnancy or, less commonly encountered in developed nations, a maternal deficiency of iodine. Most newborns do not exhibit signs and symptoms of thyroxine deficiency during the first few weeks of life while they function on the hormone provided by their mother. As the maternal thyroxine is metabolized, some of the symptoms that ensue include coarse, swollen facial features; wide, short hands; respiratory problems; a hoarse-sounding cry; poor weight gain and small stature; delayed occurrence of developmental milestones such as sitting up, crawling, walking, and talking; goiter; anemia; bradycardia; myxedema (accumulation of fluid under the skin); and hearing loss. Children who remain untreated usually become mentally retarded and demonstrate physical disabilities; they may have an unsteady gait and lack coordination. Most demonstrate delays in development of speech, and some have behavioral problems.

Hemoglobin (Hgb) A is the main form of Hgb in the healthy adult. Hgb F is the main form of Hgb in the fetus, the remainder being composed of Hgb A_1 and A_2. Hgb S and C result from abnormal amino acid substitutions during the formation of Hgb and are inherited hemoglobinopathies. Hgb S results from an amino acid substitution during Hgb synthesis whereby valine replaces glutamic acid. Hemoglobin C Harlem results from the substitution of lysine for glutamic acid. Hgb electrophoresis is a separation process used to identify normal and abnormal forms of Hgb. Electrophoresis and high-performance liquid chromatography as well as molecular genetics testing for mutations can also be used to identify abnormal forms of Hgb. Individuals with sickle cell disease have chronic anemia because the abnormal Hgb is unable to carry oxygen. The red blood cells of affected individuals are also abnormal in shape, resembling a crescent or sickle rather than the normal disk shape. This abnormality, combined with cell-wall rigidity, prevents the cells from passing through smaller blood vessels. Blockages in blood vessels result in hypoxia, damage, and pain. Individuals with the sickle cell trait do not have the clinical manifestations of the disease but may pass the disease on to children if the other parent has the trait (or the disease) as well.

Amino acids are required for the production of proteins, enzymes, coenzymes, hormones, nucleic acids used to form DNA, pigments such as hemoglobin, and neurotransmitters. Testing for specific aminoacidopathies is generally performed on infants after an initial screening test with abnormal results. Certain congenital enzyme deficiencies interfere with normal amino acid metabolism and cause excessive accumulation of or deficiencies in amino acid levels. The major genetic disorders include phenylketonuria (PKU), maple syrup urine disease (MSUD), and tyrosinuria. Enzyme disorders can also result in conditions of dysfunctional fatty acid or organic acid metabolism in which toxic substances accumulate in the body and, if untreated, can result in death. Infants with these conditions often appear normal and healthy at birth. Symptoms can appear soon after feeding begins or not until the first months of life, depending on the specific condition. Most of the signs and symptoms of amino acid disorders in infants include poor feeding, lethargy, vomiting, and irritability. Newborns with MSUD produce urine that smells like maple syrup or burned sugar. Accumulation of ammonia, a by-product of protein metabolism, and the corresponding amino acids, results in progressive liver damage, hepatomegaly, jaundice, and tendency to bruise and bleed. If untreated, there may be delays in growth, lack of coordination, permanent learning disabilities, and mental retardation. Early diagnosis and treatment of certain aminoacidopathies can prevent mental retardation, reduced growth rates, and various unexplained symptoms.

Cystic fibrosis (CF) is a genetic disease that affects normal functioning of the exocrine glands, causing them to excrete large amounts of electrolytes. CF is characterized by abnormal exocrine secretions within the lungs, pancreas, small intestine, bile ducts, and skin. Some of the signs and symptoms that may be demonstrated by the newborn with CF include failure to thrive, salty sweat, chronic respiratory problems (constant coughing or wheezing, thick mucus, recurrent lung and sinus infections, nasal polyps), and chronic gastrointestinal problems (diarrhea, constipation, pain, gas, and greasy, malodorous stools that are bulky and pale colored). Patients with CF have sweat electrolyte levels two to five times normal. Sweat test values, with family history and signs and symptoms, are required to establish a diagnosis of CF. Clinical presentation may include chronic problems of the gastrointestinal and/or respiratory system. CF is more common in Caucasians than in other populations. Testing of stool samples for decreased trypsin activity has been used as a screen for CF in infants and children, but this is a much less reliable method than the sweat test. Sweat conductivity is a screening method that estimates chloride levels. Sweat conductivity values greater than or equal to 50 mEq/L should be referred for quantitative analysis of sweat chloride. The sweat electrolyte test is still considered the gold standard diagnostic for CF.

Biotin is an important water-soluble vitamin/cofactor that aids in the metabolism of fats, carbohydrates, and proteins. A congenital enzyme deficiency of biotinidase prevents biotin released during normal cellular turnover or via digested dietary proteins from being properly recycled and absorbed, resulting in biotin deficiency. Signs and symptoms of biotin deficiency appear within the first few months and can result in hypotonia, poor coordination, respiratory problems, delays in development, seizures, behavioral disorders, and learning disabilities. Untreated, the deficiency can lead to loss of vision and hearing, ataxia, skin rashes, and hair loss.

Lactose, the main sugar in milk and milk products, is composed of galactose and glucose. Galactosemia occurs when there is a deficiency of the enzyme galactose-1-phosphate uridyl transferase, which is responsible for the conversion of galactose into glucose. The inability of dietary galactose and lactose to be metabolized results in the accumulation of galactose-1-phosphate, which causes damage to the liver, central nervous system, and other body systems. Newborns with galactosemia usually have diarrhea and vomiting within a few days of drinking milk or formula containing lactose. Other early symptoms include poor suckling and feeding, failure to gain weight or grow in length, lethargy, and irritability. The accumulation of galactose-1-phosphate and ammonia is damaging to the liver, and symptoms likely to follow if untreated include hypoglycemia, seizures, coma, hepatomegaly, jaundice, bleeding, shock, and life-threatening bacteremia or septicemia. Early cataracts can occur in about 10% of children with galactosemia. Most untreated children eventually die of liver failure.

HIV is the etiological agent of AIDS and is transmitted through bodily secretions, especially by blood or sexual contact. The virus preferentially binds to the T4 helper lymphocytes and replicates within the cells. Current assays detect several viral proteins. Positive results should be confirmed by Western blot assay. This test is routinely recommended as part of a prenatal work-up and is required for evaluating donated blood units before release for transfusion. The Centers for Disease Control and Prevention (CDC) has structured its recommendations to increase identification of HIV-infected patients as early as possible; early identification increases treatment options, increases frequency of successful treatment, and can decrease further spread of disease.

| | Core Conditions Evaluated in Many states | | | |
Condition	Affected Component	Marker for Disease	Incidence	Potential Therapeutic Interventions	Outcomes of Therapeutic Interventions
Hearing loss	Damage to or malformations of the inner ear	Abnormal audiogram	1 in 5,000 births	Surgery, medications for infections, removal of substances blocking the ear canal, hearing aids	A shorter period of auditory deprivation has a positive impact on normal development.
Congenital adrenal hyperplasia (CAH) (classical)	Multiple types of CAH; majority have a deficiency of or nonfunctioning enzyme: 21-hydroxylase	17-hydroxyprogester-one (17-OHP)	1 in 25,000 births (75% have salt-wasting type; 25% have virilization type)	Oral cortisone administration, surgery for females with virilization	Patients who begin treatment soon after birth usually have normal growth and development.
Congenital hypothyroidism	Missing, misplaced, or malfunctioning thyroid gland resulting in insufficient thyroxine; insufficient thyroxine due to maternal thyroid condition or treatment with anti-thyroid medications during pregnancy	Thyroxine (total), thyroid-stimulating hormone	1 in 5,000 births	Administration of L-thyroxine	Patients who begin treatment soon after birth usually have normal growth and development.

Hemoglobinopathies	Variant hemoglobin	Hgb S: amino acid substitution of valine for glutamic acid in the beta-globin chain; Hgb C: amino acid substitution of lysine for glutamic acid in the beta-globin chain; thalassemia: loss of 2 amino acids in the alpha-globin chain or decreased production of the beta-globin chain	Hgb S: 1 in 5,000 births, 1 in 400 births for African Americans; Hgb S/C: 1 in 25,000 births; Hgb S/beta-thalassemia 1 in 50,000 births	Care of patients with Hgb S is complex, and the main goal is to prevent complications from infection, blindness from damaged blood vessels in the eye, anemia, dehydration, and fatigue. Some thalassemias may require iron supplementation.	The goal with treatment is to lessen symptoms. Treatment cannot cure the condition. Symptoms may occur in spite of good treatment.
Inborn errors of amino acid metabolism					
• Argininemia	Deficiency of or non-functioning enzyme: arginase	Arginine	Less than 1 in 100,000 births	Consultation with a dietician; low-protein diet supplemented by special medical foods and formula	Patients who begin treatment soon after birth and continue treatment throughout life usually have normal growth and development. Early treatment can help prevent high arginine and ammonia

(table continues on page 1030)

	Core Conditions Evaluated in Many states				
Condition	Affected Component	Marker for Disease	Incidence	Potential Therapeutic Interventions	Outcomes of Therapeutic Interventions
					levels. Accumulation of these substances can cause brain damage, resulting in lifelong learning problems, mental retardation, or lack of coordination.
• Citrullinemia type I	Deficiency of or non-functioning enzyme: argininosuccinate synthetase	Citrulline	Less than 1 in 100,000 births	Consultation with a dietician; low-protein diet supplemented by special medical foods and formula	Patients who begin treatment soon after birth and continue treatment throughout life usually have normal growth and development. Early treatment can help prevent high ammonia levels. Accumulation of ammonia can cause brain damage, resulting in lifelong

| Homocystinuria | Deficiency of or nonfunctioning enzyme: cystathionine beta-synthase | Methionine | Less than 1 in 100,000 births (found more often in white people from the New England region of the United States and in people of Irish ancestry) | Consultation with dietician; diet low in methionine supplemented by special medical foods; administration of vitamin B_6, vitamin B_{12}, folic acid, betaine, and L-cystine | learning problems, mental retardation, or lack of coordination. Patients who begin treatment soon after birth and continue treatment throughout life usually have normal growth and development. Treatment may lower the chance for blood clots, heart disease, and stroke. Treatment also lessens the chance of eye problems such as cataract or lens dislocation, which can often be corrected by surgery. |

(table continues on page 1032)

	Core Conditions Evaluated in Many states				
Condition	Affected Component	Marker for Disease	Incidence	Potential Therapeutic Interventions	Outcomes of Therapeutic Interventions
• Maple syrup urine disease (MSUD)	Deficiency of or nonfunctioning enzyme group: branched-chain ketoacid dehydrogenase	Leucine and isoleucine	Less than 1 in 100,000 births (found more often in Mennonite people in certain parts of the United States: about 1 in 380 babies of Mennonite background is born with MSUD; also found more often in people of French-Canadian ancestry)	Consultation with a dietician; diet low in branched-chain amino acids supplemented by special medical foods and formula, administration of thiamine; liver transplant	Patients who begin treatment soon after birth and continue treatment throughout life usually have normal growth and development. Untreated or delayed treatment results in brain damage and mental retardation.
• Phenylketonuria	Deficiency of or nonfunctioning enzyme: phenylalanine hydroxylase (PAH)	Phenylalanine	1 in 10,000–15,000 births	Consultation with a dietician; diet low in phenylalanine supplemented by special medical foods and formula; administration of BH4	Patients who begin treatment soon after birth and continue treatment throughout life usually have normal growth and development. Some patients may

experience delays in learning even after treatment, but without treatment or if treatment is delayed until after 6 mo of age, mental retardation usually results.

(tetrahydrobiopterin), which helps the PAH enzyme convert phenylalanine into tyrosine. Patients with this condition should avoid foods and vitamins containing the sugar substitute aspartame, which increases blood levels of phenylalanine

Disorder	Cause	Amino acid/substance	Incidence	Treatment	Outcome
• Tyrosinemia type 1	Deficiency of or non-functioning enzyme: fumarylacetoacetase	Tyrosine	Less than 1 in 100,000 births (found more often in people of French-Canadian ancestry)	Consultation with a dietician; diet low in tyrosine and phenylalanine supplemented by special medical foods and formula; administration of nitisinone to prevent liver and kidney damage; liver transplant	Patients who begin treatment soon after birth and continue treatment throughout life usually have normal growth and development. Without treatment, liver and kidney damage will occur.

(table continues on page 1034)

	Core Conditions Evaluated in Many states			
Condition	Affected Component	Marker for Disease	Incidence	Potential Therapeutic Interventions	Outcomes of Therapeutic Interventions
		Inborn errors of fatty acid metabolism			
• Carnitine uptake disorder	Deficiency of or nonfunctioning enzyme: carnitine transporter	Free and total carnitine	Less than 1 in 100,000 births	Consultation with a dietician; diet low in tyrosine and phenylalanine supplemented by special medical foods and formula;	Patients who begin treatment soon after birth and continue treatment throughout life usually have normal growth and development. Without treatment, infants may incur permanent brain damage resulting in learning disabilities or mental retardation.
• Long-chain L-3-hydroxyacyl-CoA dehydrogenase deficiency	Deficiency of or non-functioning enzyme: long-chain L-3-hydroxyacyl-CoA dehydrogenase	Acylcarnitines	Greater than 1 in 75,000 births (found more often in people of Finnish ancestry)	Consultation with a dietician; low-fat, high-carbohydrate diet supplemented by special medical	Patients who begin treatment soon after birth and continue treatment throughout life

• Medium-chain acyl-CoA dehydrogenase deficiency	Deficiency of or nonfunctioning enzyme: medium-chain acyl-CoA dehydrogenase	Octanoyl carnitine and acyl carnitine	Greater than 1 in 25,000 births (found more often in white people from Northern Europe and the United States)	Consultation with a dietician; low-fat, high-carbohydrate diet supplemented by special medical foods and formula consumed in small, frequent meals to avoid hypoglycemia; infants may need to be woken up to eat if they do not wake up on their own; administration of medium-chain triglyceride oil (MCT oil), L-carnitine and DHA (docosahexanoic acid) which may help prevent loss of eyesight	Patients who begin treatment soon after birth and continue treatment throughout life usually have normal growth and development. Continued episodes of hypoglycemia
				foods and formula consumed in small, frequent meals to avoid hypoglycemia; infants may need to be woken up to eat if they do not wake up on their own; administration of medium-chain triglyceride oil (MCT oil), L-carnitine and DHA (docosahexanoic acid) which may help prevent loss of eyesight	usually have normal growth and development. Continued episodes of hypoglycemia can lead to learning disabilities or mental retardation. With treatment, some people still develop vision, muscle, liver or heart problems.

(table continues on page 1036)

Core Conditions Evaluated in Many states

Condition	Affected Component	Marker for Disease	Incidence	Potential Therapeutic Interventions	Outcomes of Therapeutic Interventions
				avoid hypoglycemia; infants may need to be woken up to eat if they do not wake up on their own; administration of MCT oil and L-carnitine	can lead to lack of coordination, chronic muscle weakness, learning disabilities, or mental retardation.
• Trifunctional protein (TFP) deficiency	Deficiency of or nonfunctioning enzyme group: mitochondrial trifunctional protein	3-hydroxy-hexadec-anoylcarnitine	Less than 1 in 100,000 births	Consultation with a dietician; low-fat, high-carbohydrate diet supplemented by special medical foods and formula consumed in small, frequent meals to avoid hypoglycemia; infants may need to be woken up to eat if they do not wake up on their own; administration of MCT oil and L-carnitine	Most newborns with early TFP deficiency die of cardiac or respiratory problems, even when treated. Patients with childhood TFP deficiency who begin treatment soon after birth and continue treatment throughout life usually have normal growth and development. Continued episodes

of hypoglycemia can lead to lack of coordination, chronic muscle weakness, learning disabilities, or mental retardation. Patients with mild/muscle TFP deficiency who begin treatment soon after birth and continue treatment throughout life usually have normal growth and development. This form does not affect intelligence. Patients who begin treatment soon after birth and continue treatment throughout life usually have normal growth and development.

(table continues on page 1038)

	Deficiency of or non-functioning enzyme: very-long-chain acyl-CoA dehydrogenase	Tetradecenoylcarnitine	Greater than 1 in 75,000 births	Consultation with a dietician; low-fat, high-carbohydrate diet supplemented by special medical foods and formula consumed in small, frequent meals to avoid hypoglycemia; infants may
• Very-long-chain acyl-CoA dehydrogenase deficiency				

	Core Conditions Evaluated in Many states			
Condition	Affected Component	Marker for Disease	Incidence	Potential Therapeutic Interventions	Outcomes of Therapeutic Interventions
				need to be woken up to eat if they do not wake up on their own; administration of MCT oil and L-carnitine	
Inborn errors of organic acid metabolism					
• Glutaric acidemia Type 1	Deficiency of or nonfunctioning enzyme: glutaryl-CoA dehydrogenase	Glutarylcarnitine	Greater than 1 in 75,000 births (found more often in people of Amish background in the United States, the Ojibway Indian population in Canada, and people of Swedish ancestry)	Consultation with a dietician; diet high in carbohydrates, low in protein, especially lysine and tryptophan, supplemented by special medical foods and formula consumed in small, frequent meals; administration of riboflavin, carnitine	Patients who begin treatment soon after birth and continue treatment throughout life usually have normal growth and development.

• 3-hydroxy, 3-methylglutaric aciduria	Deficiency of or nonfunctioning enzyme: HMG CoA lyase	Acylcarnitines	Less than 1 in 100,000 births (found more often in people of Saudi Arabian, Portuguese, and Spanish ancestry)	Consultation with a dietician; diet high in carbohydrates, low in protein, especially leucine, supplemented by special medical foods and formula consumed in small, frequent meals; administration of carnitine	Patients who begin treatment soon after birth and continue treatment throughout life usually have normal growth and development.
• Isovaleric acidemia	Deficiency of or non-functioning enzyme: isovaleryl-CoA dehydrogenase	Isovaleryl carnitine	Less than 1 in 100,000 births	Consultation with a dietician; diet high in carbohydrates, low in protein, especially leucine, supplemented by special medical foods and formula consumed in small, frequent meals; administration of glycine, carnitine	Patients who begin treatment soon after birth and continue treatment throughout life usually have normal growth and development.

(table continues on page 1040)

Core Conditions Evaluated in Many states

Condition	Affected Component	Marker for Disease	Incidence	Potential Therapeutic Interventions	Outcomes of Therapeutic Interventions
• Methyl malonic acidemias (vitamin B_{12} disorders)	Deficiency of or non-functioning enzyme: methylmalonyl-CoA mutase combined with mutations causing defects in vitamin B_{12} metabolism	Propionylcarnitine	Less than 1 in 100,000 births	Consultation with a dietician; diet high in carbohydrates, low in protein, especially leucine, valine, methionine, and threonine, supplemented by special medical foods and formula consumed in small, frequent meals; administration of betaine, carnitine, vitamin B_{12}	Treatment may help some patients but not others. Some infants die even with treatment. Patients who begin treatment soon after birth and continue treatment throughout life may have permanent learning disabilities, psychiatric disorders, or mental retardation.
• Beta ketothiolase	Deficiency of or non-functioning enzyme: mitochondrial acetoacetyl-CoA thiolase	3-methylcrotonyl carnitine	Less than 1 in 100,000 births	Consultation with a dietician; diet high in carbohydrates, low in protein, supplemented by special medical foods and formula consumed in small,	Patients who begin treatment soon after birth and continue treatment throughout life usually have normal growth and development.

| Methyl malonic acidemias (methylmalonyl-CoA mutase) | Deficiency of or nonfunctioning enzyme: methylmalonyl-CoA mutase | Propionylcarnitine | Less than 1 in 75,000 births | frequent meals; administration of carnitine Consultation with a dietician; diet high in carbohydrates, low in protein, supplemented by special medical foods and formula consumed in small, frequent meals; administration of carnitine | Patients who begin treatment soon after birth and continue treatment throughout life usually have normal growth and development. Some patients, even with treatment, may have seizures, involuntary movement disorders, kidney failure, permanent learning disabilities, or mental retardation. Children who are not treated until after they have symptoms may have lasting physical and learning problems. |

(table continues on page 1042)

N

Core Conditions Evaluated in Many states

Condition	Affected Component	Marker for Disease	Incidence	Potential Therapeutic Interventions	Outcomes of Therapeutic Interventions
• Propionic acidemia	Deficiency of or nonfunctioning enzyme: propionyl-CoA carboxylase	Acylcarnitines	Greater than 1 in 75,000 births (found more often in people of Saudi Arabian ancestry and the Inuit Indian population of Greenland)	Consultation with a dietician; diet high in carbohydrates, low in protein, especially leucine, valine, methionine, and threonine, supplemented by special medical foods and formula consumed in small, frequent meals; administration of biotin, carnitine	Patients who begin treatment soon after birth and continue treatment throughout life usually have normal growth and development. Some patients, even with treatment, may have seizures, involuntary movement disorders, chronic infections, permanent learning disabilities, or mental retardation.
• Multiple carboxylase	Deficiency of or non-functioning enzyme: 3-methylcrotonyl-CoA carboxylase,	3-hydroxy-isovaleryl carnitine	Less than 1 in 100,000 births	Consultation with a dietician; diet high in carbohydrates, low in protein, sup-plemented by special medical foods and formula consumed	Patients who begin treatment soon after birth and continue treatment through

	2-methylbutyryl-CoA dehydrogenase			in small, frequent meals; administration of carnitine	out life usually have normal growth and development.
Other multisystem diseases					
Biotinidase deficiency	Deficiency of or nonfunctioning enzyme: biotinidase	Biotinidase	Greater than 1 in 75,000 births	Consultation with a dietician; diet supplemented by special medical foods and formula; administration of biotin	Patients who begin treatment soon after birth and continue treatment throughout life usually have normal growth and development.
Cystic fibrosis	Deficiency of or nonfunctioning protein: cystic fibrosis transmembrane conductance regulator protein	CF mutation analysis or immunoreactive trypsinogen	Greater than 1 in 5,000 births	Consultation with a dietician; higher calorie diet supplemented by special medical foods and formula, additional hydration, administration of pancreatic enzymes and vitamins; bronchodilators, antibiotics, mucus thinners; percussive therapy, ThAIRapy vest; gene therapy, lung transplant	Patients who begin treatment soon after birth and continue treatment throughout life usually have normal growth and development. The goal with treatment is to lessen symptoms. Treatment cannot cure the condition. Symptoms may occur in spite of good treatment.

(table continues on page 1044)

Core Conditions Evaluated in Many states

Condition	Affected Component	Marker for Disease	Incidence	Potential Therapeutic Interventions	Outcomes of Therapeutic Interventions
• Galactosemia (classical)	Deficiency of or nonfunctioning enzyme: galactose-1-phosphate uridyl transferase	Galactose-1-phosphate	Greater than 1 in 50,000 births	Consultation with a dietician; diet free of lactose and galactose supplemented by special medical foods and formula; administration of calcium, vitamin D, and vitamin K	Patients who begin treatment soon after birth and continue treatment throughout life usually have normal growth and development. Some patients may experience delays in learning even after treatment, but without treatment or if treatment is delayed until after 10 days of age, developmental delays and learning disabilities usually result.

INDICATIONS

Hearing Tests
- Screen for hearing loss in infants to determine the need for a referral to an audiologist

Blood Spot testing
- Assist in the diagnosis of CAH
- Assist in the diagnosis of congenital hypothyroidism
- Assist in the diagnosis of abnormal hemoglobins as with Hgb C disease, sickle cell trait or sickle cell disease, and thalassemias, especially in patients with a family history positive for any the disorders
- Assist in identifying the cause of hemolytic anemia resulting from G-6-PD enzyme deficiency
- Detect congenital errors of amino acid, fatty acid, or organic acid metabolism
- Detect congenital errors responsible for urea cycle disorders
- Screen for multisystem disorders such as CF, biotinidase deficiency, or galactosemia
- Test for HIV antibodies in infants who have documented and significant exposure to other infected individuals

POTENTIAL DIAGNOSIS

Abnormal findings in

Hearing Test
- Abnormal audiogram *(related to congenital damage or malformations of the inner ear, infections, residual amniotic fluid or vernix in the ear canal)*

Endocrine Disorders

Increased in
- Congenital hypothyroidism (TSH) *(related to decrease in total thyroxine hormone levels, which activates the feedback loop to increase production of TSH)*

- CAH (adrenocorticotropic hormone [ACTH] and androgens) *(related to an autosomal recessive inherited disorder that results in missing or malfunctioning enzymes responsible for the production of cortisol and which may result in a salt-wasting condition or virilization of female genitalia)*

Decreased in
- Congenital hypothyroidism (total T4) *(related to missing or malfunctioning thyroid gland resulting in absence or decrease in total thyroxine hormone levels)*
- CAH (21-hydroxylase) *(related to an autosomal recessive inherited disorder that results in missing or malfunctioning enzymes responsible for the production of cortisol and which may result in one of several conditions, including a salt-wasting condition or virilization of female genitalia)*
- CAH (cortisol) *(related to an autosomal recessive inherited disorder that results in missing or malfunctioning enzymes responsible for the production of cortisol and which may result in a salt-wasting condition or virilization of female genitalia)*
- CAH (aldosterone) *(related to an autosomal recessive inherited disorder that results in missing or malfunctioning enzymes responsible for the production of cortisol and which may result in a salt-wasting condition)*

Abnormal findings in

Hemoglobinopathies
- Hgb S: sickle cell trait or sickle cell anemia (most common variant in the United States; occurs with a frequency of about 8% among African Americans) *(related to an autosomal recessive inherited disorder that results in a genetic variation in the β-chain of hemoglobin,*

N

causing a conformational change in the bemoglobin molecule and affecting the oxygen-binding properties of bemoglobin, which results in sickle-shaped red blood cells)

- Hgb SC disease *(related to an autosomal recessive inherited disorder that results in the presence of an abnormal combination of Hgb S with Hgb C and presents a milder form of sickle cell anemia)*
- Hgb S/β-thalassemias *(related to an autosomal recessive inherited disorder that results in the presence of abnormal bemoglobin S/β-thalassemia, which combines the effects of thalassemia, a genetic disorder that results in decreased production of bemoglobin and sickle cell anemia, where sickled red blood cells lack the ability to combine effectively with oxygen)*

RBC Enzyme Defect

Decreased in

- G6PD deficiency *(usually related to an X-linked recessive inherited disorder that results in a deficiency of glucose-6-phosphate dehydrogenase, which causes a hemolytic anemia)*

Inborn Errors of Amino Acid Metabolism/Disorders of the Urea Cycle

- Aminoacidopathies *(usually related to an autosomal recessive inherited disorder that results in insufficient or nonfunctional enzyme levels; specific amino acids are implicated)*
- Disorders of the urea cycle; specifically argininemia, argininosuccinic acidemia, citrullinemia, and hyperammonemia/hyperornithinemia/homocitrullinemia *(usually related to an autosomal recessive inherited disorder that results*

in insufficient or nonfunctional enzyme levels; specific amino acids are implicated)

Inborn Errors of Organic Acid Metabolism

- Organic acid disorders *(usually related to an autosomal recessive inherited disorder that results in insufficient or nonfunctional enzyme levels; specific organic acids are implicated)*

Inborn Errors of Fatty Acid Metabolism

- Fatty acid oxidation disorders *(usually related to an autosomal recessive inherited disorder that results in insufficient or nonfunctional enzyme levels; specific fatty acids are implicated)*

Other Multisystem Diseases

- Biotinidase deficiency *(related to an autosomal recessive inherited disorder that results in deficiency of the enzyme biotinidase, which prevents absorption or recycling of the essential vitamin biotin)*
- Cystic fibrosis *(related to an autosomal recessive inherited disorder that results in insufficient or nonfunctional CF transmembrane conductance regulator protein, which results in poor transport of salts, especially sodium and chloride, and significantly impairs pulmonary and gastrointestinal function)*
- Galactosemia (classical) *(usually related to an autosomal recessive inherited disorder that results in insufficient or nonfunctional galactose-1-phosphate uridyl transferase enzyme levels*

Infectious Diseases

Positive findings in
- HIV-1 or HIV-2 infection

CRITICAL FINDINGS: N/A

INTERFERING FACTORS

• Specimens for newborn screening collected earlier than 24 h after the first feeding or collected from neonates receiving total parenteral nutrition may produce invalid results.

• Specimens for newborn screening that are improperly applied to the filter paper circles may produce invalid results.

• Touching blood spots after collection on the filter paper card may contaminate the sample and produce invalid results.

• Failure to let the filter paper sample dry may affect test results.

• Specimens for newborn screening collected after transfusion may produce invalid results.

• Nonreactive HIV test results occur during the acute stage of the disease, when the virus is present but antibodies have not sufficiently developed to be detected. It may take up to 6 mo for the test to become positive. During this stage, the test for HIV antigen may not confirm an HIV infection.

NURSING IMPLICATIONS AND PROCEDURE

PRETEST:

General

▸ Positively identify the patient using at least two unique identifiers before providing care, treatment, or services.

▸ *Patient Teaching:* Education regarding newborn screening should begin during the prenatal period and be reinforced at the time of preadmission testing. Many birthing facilities and hospitals provide educational brochures to the parents. Physicians and physician delegates are responsible to inform parents of the newborn screening process before discharge. Inform

the patient these procedures can assist in evaluating a number of congenital conditions, including hearing loss, thyroid function, adrenal gland function, and other metabolic enzyme disorders. Evaluation may also include HIV antibody testing if not performed prenatally or if otherwise clinically indicated.

▸ Obtain a history of the patient's complaints, including a list of known allergens, especially allergies or sensitivities to latex.

▸ Obtain a history of the patient's endocrine system, symptoms, and results of previously performed laboratory tests and diagnostic and surgical procedures.

▸ Obtain a list of the patient's current medications, including herbs, nutritional supplements, and nutraceuticals (see Appendix F).

Blood Tests

▸ Review the procedure with the parents or caregiver. Explain that blood specimens from neonates are collected by heel stick and applied to filter paper spots on the birth state's specific screening program card.

Hearing Test

▸ Review the procedure with the parents or caregiver. Address concerns about pain and explain that no discomfort will be experienced during the test. Inform the parents or caregiver that an audiologist or HCP trained in this procedure performs the test in a quiet room and that the test can take up 20 min to evaluate both ears. Explain that each ear is tested separately by using earphones and/or a device placed behind the ear to deliver sounds of varying intensities.

▸ *Sensitivity to social and cultural issues,* as well as concern for modesty, is important in providing psychological support before, during, and after the procedure.

▸ Most state regulations require screening specimens to be collected between 24 and 48 hr after birth to allow sufficient time after protein intake for abnormal metabolites to be detected, and preferably before blood product transfusion or physical transfer to another facility.

Hearing Test

Perform otoscopy examination to ensure that the external ear canal is free from any obstruction (see monograph titled "Otoscopy").

Test for closure of the canal from the pressure of the earphones by compressing the tragus. Tendency for the canal to close (often the case in children and elderly patients) can be corrected by the careful insertion of a small, stiff plastic tube into the anterior canal.

Start the test by providing a trial tone of 15 to 20 dB above the expected threshold to the ear for 1 to 2 sec to familiarize the patient with the sounds. If no response is indicated, the level is increased until a response is obtained, and then it is raised in 10-dB increments or until the audiometer's limit is reached for the test frequency. The test results are plotted on a graph called an audiogram using symbols that indicate the ear tested and responses using earphones (air conduction) or oscillator (bone conduction).

Air Conduction

In the air conduction test, the tone is delivered to an infant through insert earphones or ear muffins, and the auditory response is measured through electrodes placed on the infant's scalp. Air conduction is tested first by starting at 1,000 Hz and gradually decreasing the intensity 10 dB at a time until there is no response, indicating that the tone is no longer heard. The intensity is then increased 5 dB at a time until the tone is heard again. This is repeated until the same response is achieved at a 50% response rate at the same hertz level. The threshold is derived from the lowest decibel level at which the patient correctly responds to three out of six trials to a tone at that hertz level. The test is continued for each ear with tones delivered at 1,000 Hz, 2,000 Hz, 4,000 Hz, and 8,000 Hz, and then again at 1,000 Hz, 500 Hz, and 250 Hz to determine a second threshold. Results are recorded on a graph called an audiogram. Averaging the air conduction thresholds at the 500-Hz,

1,000-Hz, and 2,000-Hz levels reveals the degree of hearing loss and is called the pure tone average (PTA).

Bone Conduction

Bone conduction testing is performed in a similar manner to air conduction testing; a vibrator placed on the skull is used to deliver tones to an infant instead of earphones as in the air conduction test. The raised and lowered tones are delivered as in air conduction using 250 Hz, 500 Hz, 1,000 Hz, 2,000 Hz, and 4,000 Hz to determine the thresholds. An analysis of thresholds for air and bone conduction tones is done to determine the type of hearing loss (conductive, sensorineural, or mixed).

Otoacoustic Emissions

In otoacoustic testing, microphones are placed in the infant's ears. Nearby sounds should echo in the ear canal and be detected by the microphones if the infant's hearing is normal.

Filter Paper Test

Obtain kit and cleanse heel with antiseptic. Observe standard precautions, and follow the general guidelines in Appendix A. Use gauze to dry the stick area completely. Perform heel stick, gently squeeze infant's heel, and touch filter paper to the puncture site. When collecting samples for newborn screening, it is important to apply each blood drop to the correct side of the filter paper card and fill each circle with a single application of blood. Overfilling or underfilling the circles will cause the specimen card to be rejected by the testing facility. Additional information is required on newborn screening cards and may vary by state. Newborn screening cards should be allowed to air dry for several hours on a level, nonabsorbent, unenclosed area. If multiple patients are tested, do not stack cards. State regulations usually require the specimen cards to be submitted within 24 hr of collection. Observe/assess puncture site for bleeding or hematoma formation, and secure gauze with adhesive bandage.

POST-TEST:

▶ A report of the results will be made available to the requesting HCP, who will discuss the results with the parents or caregiver.

Nutritional Considerations: Instruct the parents or caregiver in special dietary modifications to treat deficiency, and refer parents or caregiver to a qualified nutritionist, as appropriate. Amino acids are classified as essential (i.e., must be present simultaneously in sufficient quantities), conditionally or acquired essential (i.e., under certain stressful conditions, they become essential), and nonessential (i.e., can be produced by the body, when needed, if diet does not provide them). Essential amino acids include lysine, threonine, histidine, isoleucine, methionine, phenylalanine, tryptophan, and valine. Conditionally essential amino acids include cysteine, tyrosine, arginine, citrulline, taurine, and carnitine. Nonessential amino acids include alanine, glutamic acid, aspartic acid, glycine, serine, proline, glutamine, and asparagine. A high intake of specific amino acids can cause other amino acids to become essential.

Social and Cultural Considerations: Recognize anxiety related to test results, and be supportive of parents' or caregiver's perceived loss of impaired activity or independence related to hearing loss or physical limitations and their fear of shortened life expectancy for the newborn. Discuss the implications of abnormal test results on the patient's lifestyle. Provide teaching and information regarding the clinical implications of the test results, as appropriate. Educate the parents and caregiver regarding access to genetic or other counseling services. Provide contact information, if desired, for the March of Dimes (www.marchofdimes.com), the National Library or Medicine (www.nlm.nih.gov/medlineplus/newbornscreening.html), general information (newbornscreening.info/Parents/facts.html), or the state department of health newborn screening program. There are numerous support groups and informational Web sites for specific conditions, including the National Center for Hearing Assessment and Management (www.infanthearing.org), the American Speech-Language-Hearing Association (www.asha.org), ABLEDATA (for assistive technology; sponsored by the National Institute on Disability and Rehabilitation Research [www.abledata.com]), the Sickle Cell Disease Association of America (www.sicklecelldisease.org), the Fatty Oxidation Disorders (FOD) Family Support Group (www.fodsupport.org), the Organic Acidemia Association (www.oaanews.org), the United Mitochondrial Disease Foundation (www.umdf.org), the Cystic Fibrosis Foundation (www.cff.org), and, for AIDS information, the National Institutes of Health (www.aidsinfo.nih.gov) and the CDC (www.cdc.gov).

▶ *Social and Cultural Considerations:* Inform parents or caregiver that positive neonatal HIV findings must be reported to local health department officials.

▶ *Social and Cultural Considerations:* Offer support, as appropriate, to parents who may be the victims of rape or sexual assault. Educate the parents regarding access to counseling services. Provide a nonjudgmental, nonthreatening atmosphere for a discussion during which risks of sexually transmitted diseases to the newborn are explained. It is also important to discuss problems the parents may experience (e.g., guilt, depression, anger).

▶ Reinforce information given by the patient's HCP regarding further testing, treatment, or referral to another HCP. Answer any questions or address any concerns voiced by the parents, family, or caregiver. Provide information regarding vaccine-preventable diseases where indicated (e.g., anthrax, cervical cancer, diphtheria, encephalitis, hepatitis A and B, H1N1 flu, human papillomavirus, *Haemophilus* influenza, seasonal influenza, Lyme disease, measles, meningococcal disease, monkeypox, mumps, pertussis, pneumococcal disease, polio, rotavirus, rubella, shingles, smallpox, tetanus, typhoid fever, varicella, yellow fever). Provide contact information, if desired, for the Centers for Disease Control and Prevention (www.cdc.gov/vaccines/vpd-vac).

N

▶ Depending on the results of these procedures, additional testing may be performed to evaluate or monitor progression of the disease process and determine the need for a change in therapy. Evaluate test results in relation to the patient's symptoms and other tests performed.

RELATED MONOGRAPHS:

▶ Related tests include amino acid screen, amniotic fluid analysis, audiometry hearing loss, biopsy chorionic villus, chloride sweat, chromosome analysis, CBC, evoked brain potential studies for hearing loss, glucose-6–phosphate dehydrogenase, hemoglobin electrophoresis, human immunodeficiency virus type 1 and type 2 antibodies, otoscopy, sickle cell screen, TSH, thyroxine total, and US thyroid.

▶ Refer to the Auditory, Endocrine, Genitourinary, Hematopoietic, Hepatobiliary, and Reproductive systems tables at the end of the book for related tests by body system.

N

Osmolality, Blood and Urine

COMMON USE: To assess fluid and electrolyte balance related to hydration, acid-base balance, and toxic screening; to assist in diagnosing diseases such as diabetes

SPECIMEN: Serum (1 mL) collected in a red- or tiger-top tube; urine (5 mL) from an unpreserved random specimen collected in a clean plastic collection container.

NORMAL FINDINGS: (Method: Freezing point depression)

	Conventional Units	SI Units (Conventional Units × 1)
Serum	275–295 mOsm/kg	275–295 mmol/kg
Urine		
Newborn	75–300 mOsm/kg	75–300 mmol/kg
Children and adults	250–900 mOsm/kg	250–900 mmol/kg

DESCRIPTION: Osmolality is the number of particles in a solution; it is independent of particle size, shape, and charge. Measurement of osmotic concentration in serum provides clinically useful information about water and dissolved-particle transport across fluid compartment membranes. Osmolality is used to assist in the diagnosis of metabolic, renal, and endocrine disorders. The simultaneous determination of serum and urine osmolality provides the opportunity to compare values between the two fluids. A normal urine-to-serum ratio is approximately 0.2 to 4.7 for random samples and greater than 3.0 for first-morning samples (dehydration normally occurs overnight). The major dissolved particles that contribute to osmolality are sodium, chloride, bicarbonate, urea, and glucose. Some of these substances are used in the following calculated estimate:

$$\text{Serum osmolality} = (2 \times Na^+) + (\text{glucose}/18) + (\text{BUN}/2.8)$$

Measured osmolality is higher than the estimated value. The osmolal gap is the difference between the measured and calculated values and is normally 5 to 10 mOsm/kg. If the difference is greater than 15 mOsm/kg, consider ethylene glycol, isopropanol, methanol, or ethanol toxicity. These substances behave like antifreeze, lowering the freezing point in the blood, and provide misleadingly high results.

INDICATIONS

Serum
- Assist in the evaluation of antidiuretic hormone (ADH) function
- Assist in rapid screening for toxic substances, such as ethylene glycol, ethanol, isopropanol, and methanol
- Evaluate electrolyte and acid-base balance
- Evaluate state of hydration

Urine
- Evaluate concentrating ability of the kidneys

- Evaluate diabetes insipidus
- Evaluate neonatal patients with protein or glucose in the urine
- Perform work-up for renal disease

POTENTIAL DIAGNOSIS

Increased in

- Serum
  Azotemia *(related to accumulation of nitrogen-containing waste products that contribute to osmolality)*
  Dehydration *(related to hemoconcentration)*
  Diabetes insipidus *(related to excessive loss of water through urination that results in hemoconcentration)*
  Diabetic ketoacidosis *(related to excessive loss of water through urination that results in hemoconcentration)*
  Hypercalcemia *(related to electrolyte imbalance that results in water loss and hemoconcentration)*
  Hypernatremia *(related to insufficient intake of water or excessive loss of water; sodium is a major cation in the determination of osmolality)*
- Urine
  Amyloidosis
  Azotemia *(related to decrease in renal blood flow; decrease in water excreted by the kidneys results in a more concentrated urine)*
  Congestive heart failure *(decrease in renal blood flow related to diminished cardiac output; decrease in water excreted by the kidneys results in a more concentrated urine)*
  Dehydration *(related to decrease in water excreted by the kidneys that results in a more concentrated urine)*
  Hyponatremia
  Syndrome of inappropriate antidiuretic hormone production (SIADH) *(related to decrease in water excreted by the kidneys that results in a more concentrated urine)*

Decreased in

- Serum
  Adrenocorticoid insufficiency
  Hyponatremia *(sodium is a major influence on osmolality; decreased sodium*

contributes to decreased osmolality)
  SIADH *(related to increase in water reabsorbed by the kidneys that results in a more dilute serum)*
  Water intoxication *(related to excessive water intake, which has a dilutional effect)*
- Urine
  Diabetes insipidus *(related to decreased ability of the kidneys to concentrate urine)*
  Hypernatremia *(related to increased water excreted by the kidneys that results in a more dilute urine)*
  Hypokalemia *(related to increased water excreted by the kidneys that results in a more dilute urine)*
  Primary polydipsia *(related to increase in water intake that results in dilute urine)*

CRITICAL FINDINGS

Serum

- Less than 265 mOsm/kg (SI: Less than 265 mmol/kg)
- Greater than 320 mOsm/kg (Greater than 320 mmol/kg)

Note and immediately report to the health-care provider (HCP) any critically increased or decreased values and related symptoms. Timely notification of critical values for lab or diagnostic studies is a role expectation of the professional nurse. Notification processes will vary among facilities. Upon receipt of the critical value the information should be read back to the caller to verify accuracy. Most policies require immediate notification of the primary HCP, hospitalist, or on-call HCP. Reported information includes the patient's name, unique identifiers, critical value, name of the person giving the report, and name of the person receiving the report. Documentation of notification should be made in the medical record with the name of the HCP

otified, time and date of notifica-
ion, and any orders received. Any
elay in a timely report of a critical
alue may require completion of a
otification form with review by
isk Management.

Serious clinical conditions may be
ssociated with elevated or decreased
erum osmolality. The following con-
itions are associated with elevated
erum osmolality:

Respiratory arrest: 360 mOsm/kg
Stupor of hyperglycemia: 385
mOsm/kg
Grand mal seizures: 420 mOsm/kg
Death: greater than 420 mOsm/kg

ymptoms of critically high levels
nclude poor skin turgor, listlessness,
cidosis (decreased pH), shock, sei-
ures, coma, and cardiopulmonary
rrest. Intervention may include
lose monitoring of electrolytes,
dministering intravenous fluids
ith the appropriate composition to
hift water either into or out of the
ntravascular space as needed, moni-
oring cardiac signs, continuing neu-
ological checks, and taking seizure
recautions.

TERFERING FACTORS
Drugs that may increase serum
osmolality include corticosteroids,
glycerin, inulin, ioxitalamic acid,
mannitol, and methoxyflurane.
Drugs that may decrease serum
osmolality include bendroflumethiazide, carbamazepine, chlorpromazine, chlorthalidone, cyclophosphamide, cyclothiazide, doxepin, hydrochlorothiazide, lor-
cainide, methyclothiazide, and
polythiazide.
Drugs that may increase urine
osmolality include anesthetic
agents, chlorpropamide, cyclophosphamide, furosemide, mannitol,
metolazone, octreotide, phloridzin,
and vincristine.

• Drugs that may decrease urine
osmolality include captopril, demeclocycline, glyburide, lithium,
methoxyflurane, octreotide, tolazamide, and verapamil.

NURSING IMPLICATIONS AND PROCEDURE

PRETEST:

- Positively identify the patient using at least two unique identifiers before providing care, treatment, or services.
- *Patient Teaching:* Inform the patient that the test is used to evaluate electrolyte and water balance.
- Obtain a history of the patient's complaints, including a list of known allergens, especially allergies or sensitivities to latex.
- Obtain a history of the patient's endocrine and genitourinary systems, symptoms, and results of previously performed laboratory tests and diagnostic and surgical procedures.
- Obtain a list of the patient's current medications, including herbs, nutritional supplements, and nutraceuticals (see Appendix F).
- Review the procedure with the patient. Inform the patient that blood specimen collection takes approximately 5 to 10 min; random urine collection takes approximately 5 min and depends on the cooperation of the patient. Urine specimen collection may also be timed. Address concerns about pain and explain that there may be some discomfort during the venipuncture; there will be no discomfort during urine collection.
- *Sensitivity to social and cultural issues,* as well as concern for modesty, is important in providing psychological support before, during, and after the procedure.
- There are no food, fluid, or medication restrictions unless by medical direction.

INTRATEST:

- Direct the patient to breathe normally and to avoid unnecessary movement during the venipuncture.

▶ Observe standard precautions, and follow the general guidelines in Appendix A. Positively identify the patient, and label the appropriate specimen container with the corresponding patient demographics, initials of the person collecting the specimen, date, and time of collection. Perform a venipuncture as appropriate.

Blood

▶ If the patient has a history of allergic reaction to latex, avoid the use of equipment containing latex.

▶ Perform a venipuncture.

▶ Remove the needle and apply direct pressure with dry gauze to stop bleeding. Observe/assess venipuncture site for bleeding or hematoma formation and secure gauze with adhesive bandage.

Urine

▶ Provide a nonmetallic urinal, bedpan, or toilet-mounted collection device.

▶ Either a random specimen or a timed collection may be requested. For timed specimens, a 12- or 24-hr time frame for urine collection may be ordered. Inform the patient that all urine must be saved during that 12- or 24-hr period. Instruct the patient not to void directly into the laboratory collection container. Instruct the patient to avoid defecating in the collection device and to keep toilet tissue out of the collection device to prevent contamination of the specimen. Place a sign in the bathroom to remind the patient to save all urine.

▶ Instruct the patient to void all urine into the collection device and then to pour the urine into the laboratory collection container. Alternatively, the specimen can be left in the collection device for a health-care staff member to add to the laboratory collection container.

Clean-Catch Specimen

▶ Instruct the male patient to (1) thoroughly wash his hands, (2) cleanse the meatus, (3) void a small amount into the toilet, and (4) void directly into the specimen container.

▶ Instruct the female patient to (1) thoroughly wash her hands; (2) cleanse the labia from front to back; (3) while keeping the labia separated, void a small amount into the toilet; and (4) without interrupting the urine stream, void directly into the specimen container.

Indwelling Catheter

▶ Put on gloves. Empty drainage tube of urine. It may be necessary to clamp off the catheter for 15 to 30 min before specimen collection. Cleanse specimen port with antiseptic swab, and then aspirate 5 mL of urine with a 21- to 25-gauge needle and syringe. Transfer urine to a sterile container.

Blood or Urine

▶ Promptly transport the specimen to the laboratory for processing and analysis.

POST-TEST:

▶ A report of the results will be made available to the requesting HCP, who will discuss the results with the patient.

▶ *Nutritional Considerations:* Decreased osmolality may be associated with overhydration. Observe the patient for signs and symptoms of fluid-volume excess related to excess electrolyte intake, fluid-volume deficit related to active body fluid loss, or risk of injury related to an alteration in body chemistry. (For electrolyte-specific dietary references, see monographs titled "Chloride," "Potassium," and "Sodium.")

▶ Increased osmolality may be associated with dehydration. Evaluate the patient for signs and symptoms of dehydration. Dehydration is a significant and common finding in geriatric and other patients in whom renal function has deteriorated.

▶ Recognize anxiety related to test results. Discuss the implications of abnormal test results on the patient's lifestyle. Provide teaching and information regarding the clinical implications of the test results, as appropriate. Educate the patient regarding access to counseling services. Provide contact information, if desired, for the National Kidney Foundation (www.kidney.org).

Reinforce information given by the patient's HCP regarding further testing, treatment, or referral to another HCP. Answer any questions or address any concerns voiced by the patient or family.

Depending on the results of this procedure, additional testing may be performed to evaluate or monitor progression of the disease process and determine the need for a change in therapy. Evaluate test results in relation to the patient's symptoms and other tests performed.

RELATED MONOGRAPHS:

- Related tests include ACTH, anion gap, ammonia, ADH, ANP, BNP, BUN, calcium, carbon dioxide, chloride, CBC hematocrit, CBC hemoglobin, cortisol, creatinine, echocardiography, echocardiography transesophageal, ethanol, glucose, ketones, lung perfusion scan, magnesium, phosphorus, potassium, sodium, and UA.
- Refer to the Endocrine and Genitourinary systems tables at the end of the book for related tests by body system.

Osmotic Fragility

SYNONYM/ACRONYM: Red blood cell osmotic fragility, OF.

COMMON USE: To assess the fragility of erythrocytes related to red blood cell lysis toward diagnosing diseases such as hemolytic anemia.

SPECIMEN: Whole blood (1 mL) collected in a green-top (heparin) tube and two peripheral blood smears.

NORMAL FINDINGS: (Method: Spectrophotometry) Hemolysis (unincubated) begins at 0.5 w/v sodium chloride (NaCl) solution and is complete at 0.3 w/v NaCl solution. Results are compared to a normal curve.

POTENTIAL DIAGNOSIS

Increased in

Conditions that produce RBCs with a small surface-to-volume ratio or RBCs that are rounder than normal will have increased osmotic fragility.

Acquired immune hemolytic anemias *(abnormal RBCs in size and shape; spherocytes)*

Hemolytic disease of the newborn *(abnormal RBCs in size and shape; spherocytes)*

Hereditary spherocytosis *(abnormal RBCs in size and shape; spherocytes)*

- Malaria *(related to effect of parasite on RBC membrane integrity)*
- Pyruvate kinase deficiency *(abnormal RBCs in size and shape; spherocytes)*

Decreased in

Conditions that produce RBCs with a large surface-to-volume ratio or RBCs that are flatter than normal will have decreased osmotic fragility.

- Asplenia *(abnormal cells are not removed from circulation due to absence of spleen; target cells)*
- Hemoglobinopathies *(abnormal RBCs in size and shape; target cells, drepanocytes)*

- Iron-deficiency anemia *(abnormal RBCs in size and shape; target cells)*
- Liver disease *(abnormal RBCs in size and shape; target cells)*

- Thalassemias *(abnormal RBCs in size and shape; target cells)*

CRITICAL FINDINGS: N/A

Find and print out the full monograph at DavisPlus (davisplus.fadavis.com, keyword Van Leeuwen).

Osteocalcin

SYNONYM/ACRONYM: Bone GLA protein, BGP.

COMMON USE: To assist in assessment of risk for osteoporosis and to evaluate effectiveness of therapeutic interventions.

SPECIMEN: Serum (1 mL) collected in a red-top tube.

NORMAL FINDINGS: (Method: Electrochemiluminescence)

Age and Sex	Conventional Units	SI Units (Conventional Units × 1)
6 mo–6 yr		
Male	39–121 ng/mL	39–121 mcg/L
Female	44–130 ng/mL	44–130 mcg/L
7–9 yr		
Male	66–182 ng/mL	66–182 mcg/L
Female	73–206 ng/mL	73–206 mcg/L
10–12 yr		
Male	85–232 ng/mL	85–232 mcg/L
Female	77–262 ng/mL	77–262 mcg/L
13–15 yr		
Male	70–336 ng/mL	70–336 mcg/L
Female	33–222 ng/mL	33–222 mcg/L
16–17 yr		
Male	43–237 ng/mL	43–237 mcg/L
Female	24–99 ng/mL	24–99 mcg/L
Adult		
Male	3–40 ng/mL	3–40 mcg/L
Female		
Premenopausal	5–30 ng/mL	5–30 mcg/L
Postmenopausal	9–50 ng/mL	9–50 mcg/L

DESCRIPTION: Osteocalcin is an important bone cell matrix protein and a sensitive marker in bone metabolism. It is produced by osteoblasts during the matrix mineralization phase of bone formation and is the most abundant noncollagenous bone cell protein. Synthesis of osteocalcin is dependent on vitamin K. Osteocalcin levels parallel alkaline phosphatase levels. Osteocalcin levels are affected by a number of factors, including the hormone estrogen. Assessment of osteocalcin levels permits indirect measurement of osteoblast activity and bone formation. Because it is released into the bloodstream during bone resorption, there is some question as to whether osteocalcin might also be considered a marker for bone matrix degradation and turnover.

INDICATIONS

Assist in the diagnosis of bone cancer
Evaluate bone disease
Evaluate bone metabolism
Monitor effectiveness of estrogen replacement therapy

POTENTIAL DIAGNOSIS

Increased in

Adolescents undergoing a growth spurt *(levels in the blood increase as the rate of bone formation increases)*

Chronic renal failure *(related to accumulation in circulation due to decreased renal excretion)*

Hyperthyroidism (primary and secondary) *(related to increased bone turnover)*

Metastatic skeletal disease *(levels in the blood increase as bone destruction releases it into circulation)*

Paget's disease *(levels in the blood increase as bone destruction releases it into circulation)*

Renal osteodystrophy *(related to bone degeneration secondary to hyperparathyroidism of chronic renal failure)*

- Some patients with osteoporosis *(levels in the blood increase as bone destruction releases it into circulation)*

Decreased in

- Growth hormone deficiency *(bone mineralization is stimulated by growth hormone)*
- Pregnancy *(increased demand by developing fetus results in an increase in maternal bone resorption)*
- Primary biliary cirrhosis *(related to increased bone loss)*

CRITICAL FINDINGS: N/A

INTERFERING FACTORS

- Drugs that may increase osteocalcin levels include anabolic steroids, calcitonin, calcitriol, danazol, nafarelin, pamidronate, parathyroid hormone, and stanozolol.
- Drugs that may decrease osteocalcin levels include alendronate, antithyroid therapy, corticosteroids, cyproterone, estradiol valerate, estrogen/progesterone therapy, glucocorticoids, hormone replacement therapy, methylprednisolone, oral contraceptives, pamidronate, parathyroid hormone, prednisolone, prednisone, raloxifene, tamoxifen, and vitamin D.

NURSING IMPLICATIONS AND PROCEDURE

PRETEST:

- Positively identify the patient using at least two unique identifiers before providing care, treatment, or services.
- *Patient Teaching:* Inform the patient this test can assist in evaluating for bone disease.
- Obtain a history of the patient's complaints, including a list of known allergens, especially allergies or sensitivities to latex.
- Obtain a history of the patient's musculoskeletal system, symptoms, and results of previously performed

laboratory tests and diagnostic and surgical procedures.

▶ Note any recent procedures that can interfere with test results.

▶ Obtain a list of the patient's current medications, including herbs, nutritional supplements, and nutraceuticals (see Appendix F).

▶ Review the procedure with the patient. Inform the patient that specimen collection takes approximately 5 to 10 min. Address concerns about pain and explain that there may be some discomfort during the venipuncture.

▶ *Sensitivity to social and cultural issues,* as well as concern for modesty, is important in providing psychological support before, during, and after the procedure

▶ There are no food, fluid, or medication restrictions unless by medical direction.

INTRATEST:

▶ If the patient has a history of allergic reaction to latex, avoid the use of equipment containing latex.

▶ Instruct the patient to cooperate fully and to follow directions. Direct the patient to breathe normally and to avoid unnecessary movement.

▶ Observe standard precautions, and follow the general guidelines in Appendix A. Positively identify the patient, and label the appropriate specimen container with the corresponding patient demographics, initials of the person collecting the specimen, date, and time of collection. Perform a venipuncture.

▶ Remove the needle and apply direct pressure with dry gauze to stop bleeding. Observe/assess venipuncture site for bleeding or hematoma formation and secure gauze with adhesive bandage.

▶ Promptly transport the specimen to the laboratory for processing and analysis.

POST-TEST:

▶ A report of the results will be made available to the requesting health-care provider (HCP), who will discuss the results with the patient.

▶ *Nutritional Considerations:* Increased osteocalcin levels may be associated with skeletal disease. Nutritional therapy is indicated for individuals identified

as being at high risk for developing osteoporosis. Educate the patient regarding the National Osteoporosis Foundation's guidelines, which include a regular regimen of weight-bearing exercises, limited alcohol intake, avoidance of tobacco products, and adequate dietary intake of vitamin D and calcium.

▶ *Nutritional Considerations:* Patients with abnormal calcium values should be informed that daily intake of calcium is important even though body stores in the bones can be called on to supplement circulating levels. The Institute of Medicine's Food and Nutrition Board suggests 1,200 mg as an adequate daily intake goal of dietary calcium for adult males and females age 51 to greater than 70 yr; 1,000 mg/d for adult males and females age 19 to 50 yr; 1,000 mg/d for pregnant and lactating females age 19 to 50 yr; 1,300 mg/d for pregnant and lactating females under age 19 yr; 1,300 mg/d for children age 9 to 18 yr; 800 mg/d for children age 4 to 8 yr; 500 mg/d for children age 1 to 3 yr; 270 mg/d for children age 7 to 12 mo; and 210 mg/d for children age 0 to 6 mo. Reprinted with permission from the National Academies Press, copyright 2013, National Academy of Sciences. Dietary calcium can be obtained from animal or plant sources. Milk and milk products, sardines, clams, oysters, salmon, rhubarb, spinach, beet green broccoli, kale, tofu, legumes, and fortified orange juice are high in calcium. Milk and milk products also contain vitamin D and lactose, which assist calcium absorption. Cooked vegetables yield more absorbable calcium than raw vegetables. Patients should be informed of the substances that can inhibit calcium absorption by irreversibly binding to some of the calcium, making it unavailable for absorption, such as oxalates, which naturally occur in some vegetables (e.g., beet greens, collards, leeks, okra, parsley, quinoa, spinach, Swiss chard) and are found in tea; phytic acid, found in some cereals (e.g., wheat bran, wheat germ); phosphoric acid, found in dark cola; and insoluble dietary fiber (in excessive amounts). Excessive protein intake can also negatively affect calcium absorption, especially if it is combined with foods high in phosphorus and in the presence of a reduced dietary calcium intake.

Nutritional Considerations: The Institute of Medicine's Food and Nutrition Board suggests 50 mcg/d as the tolerable upper limit for total daily intake of dietary vitamin D for males and females age 1 to greater than 70 yr; 50 mcg/d for pregnant and lactating females under age 18 through 50 yr and 25 mcg/d for children age 0 to 12 mo. Reprinted with permission from the National Academies Press, copyright 2013, National Academy of Sciences. Educate the patient with vitamin D deficiency, as appropriate, that the main dietary sources of vitamin D are fortified dairy foods and cod liver oil. Explain to the patient that vitamin D is also synthesized by the body, in the skin, and is activated by sunlight.

Nutritional Considerations: The Institute of Medicine's Food and Nutrition Board suggests 120 mcg/d as an adequate daily intake goal of dietary vitamin K for adult males age 19 to greater than 70 yr; 90 mcg/d for adult females age 19 to greater than 70 yr; 90 mcg/d for pregnant and lactating females age 19 to 50 yr; 75 mcg/d for pregnant and lactating females age under 18 yr; 75 mcg/d for children age 14 to 18 yr; 60 mcg/d for children age 9 to 13 yr; 55 mcg/d for children age 4 to 8 yr; 30 mcg/d for children age 1 to 3 yr; 2.5 mcg/d for children age 7 to 12 mo; and 2 mcg/d for children age 0 to

6 mo. Reprinted with permission from the National Academies Press, copyright 2013, National Academy of Sciences. Inform the patient with a vitamin K deficiency, as appropriate, that the main dietary sources of vitamin K are broccoli, cabbage, cauliflower, kale, spinach, leaf lettuce, watercress, parsley, and other raw green leafy vegetables, pork, liver, soybeans, mayonnaise and vegetable oils.

▶ Reinforce information given by the patient's HCP regarding further testing, treatment, or referral to another HCP. Answer any questions or address any concerns voiced by the patient or family. Educate the patient regarding access to nutritional counseling services. Provide contact information, if desired, for the Institute of Medicine of the National Academies (www.iom.edu).

▶ Depending on the results of this procedure, additional testing may be performed to evaluate or monitor progression of the disease process and determine the need for a change in therapy. Evaluate test results in relation to the patient's symptoms and other tests performed.

RELATED MONOGRAPHS:

▶ Related tests include ALP, biopsy bone, BMD, bone scan, calcium, collagen cross-linked N-telopeptide, MRI musculoskeletal, PTH, phosphorus, radiography bone, and vitamin D.

▶ Refer to the Musculoskeletal System table at the end of the book for related tests by body system.

Otoscopy

SYNONYM/ACRONYM: N/A.

COMMON USE: To visualize and assess internal and external structures of the ear to evaluate for pain or hearing loss.

AREA OF APPLICATION: Ears.

CONTRAST: N/A.

DESCRIPTION: This noninvasive procedure is used to inspect the external ear, auditory canal, and tympanic membrane. Otoscopy is an essential part of any general physical examination but is also done before any other audiological studies when symptoms of ear pain or hearing loss are present.

INDICATIONS

- Detect causes of deafness, obstruction, stenosis, or swelling of the pinna or canal causing a narrowing or closure that prevents sound from entering
- Detect ear abnormalities during routine physical examination
- Diagnose cause of ear pain
- Remove impacted cerumen (with a dull ring curette) or foreign bodies (with a forceps) that are obstructing the entrance of sound waves into the ear
- Evaluate acute or chronic otitis media and effectiveness of therapy in controlling infections

POTENTIAL DIAGNOSIS

Normal findings in
- Normal structure and appearance of the external ear, auditory canal, and tympanic membrane.
  Pinna: Funnel-shaped cartilaginous structure; no evidence of infection, pain, dermatitis with swelling, redness, or itching
- ***External auditory canal:*** S-shaped canal lined with fine hairs, sebaceous and ceruminous glands; no evidence of redness, lesions, edema, scaliness, pain, accumulation of cerumen, drainage, or presence of foreign bodies
  Tympanic membrane: Shallow, circular cone that is shiny and pearl gray in color, semitransparent whitish cord crossing from front to back just under the upper edge, cone of light on the

right side at the 4 o'clock position; no evidence of bulging, retraction, lusterless membrane, or obliteration of the cone of light

Abnormal findings in
- Cerumen accumulation
- Ear trauma
- Foreign bodies
- Otitis externa
- Otitis media
- Tympanic membrane perforation or rupture

CRITICAL FINDINGS: N/A

INTERFERING FACTORS

Factors that may impair the results of the examination
- Obstruction of the auditory canal with cerumen, dried drainage, or foreign bodies that prevent introduction of the otoscope.

NURSING IMPLICATIONS AND PROCEDURE

PRETEST:

- Positively identify the patient using at least two unique identifiers before providing care, treatment, or services.
- *Patient Teaching:* Inform the patient this procedure can assist in investigating suspected ear disorders.
- Obtain a history of the patient's complaints, including a list of known allergens, especially allergies or sensitivities to latex.
- Obtain a history of the patient's known or suspected hearing loss, including type and cause; ear conditions with treatment regimens; ear surgery; and other tests and procedures to assess and diagnose auditory deficit. Obtain a history of the patient's complaints of pain, itching, drainage, deafness, or presence of tympanotomy tube.
- Obtain a history of symptoms and results of previously performed laboratory tests, diagnostic and surgical procedures.

- Obtain a list of the patient's current medications, especially antibiotic regimen, as well as herbs, nutritional supplements, and nutraceuticals (see Appendix F).
- Review the procedure with the patient. Inform the caregiver that he or she may need to restrain a child in order to prevent damage to the ear if the child cannot remain still. Address concerns about pain and explain that no discomfort will be experienced during the test. Inform the patient that a healthcare provider (HCP) performs the test and that to evaluate both ears, the test can take 5 to 10 min.
- *Sensitivity to social and cultural issues,* as well as concern for modesty, is important in providing psychological support before, during, and after the procedure.
- There are no food, fluid, or medication restrictions unless by medical direction.
- Ensure that the external auditory canal is clear of impacted cerumen.

INTRATEST:

- Observe standard precautions, and follow the general guidelines in Appendix A. Positively identify the patient.
- Instruct the patient to cooperate fully and to follow directions. Ask the patient to remain still during the procedure because movement produces unreliable results.
- Administer ear drops or irrigation to prepare for cerumen removal, if ordered.
- Place adult patient in a sitting position; place a child in a supine position on the caregiver's lap. Request that the patient remain very still during the examination; a child can be restrained by the caregiver if necessary.
- Assemble the otoscope with the correct-size speculum to fit the size of the patient's ear, and check the light source. For the adult, tilt the head slightly away and, with the nondominant hand, pull the pinna upward and backward. For a child, hold the head steady or have the caregiver hold the child's head steady, depending on the age, and pull the pinna downward. Gently and slowly insert the speculum

into the ear canal downward and forward with the handle of the otoscope held downward. For the child, hold the handle upward while placing the edge of the hand holding the otoscope on the head to steady it during insertion. If the speculum resists insertion, withdraw and attach a smaller one.

- Place an eye to the lens of the otoscope, turn on the light source, and advance the speculum into the ear canal until the tympanic membrane is visible. Examine the posterior and anterior membrane, cone of light, outer rim (annulus), umbo, handle of the malleus, folds, and pars tensa.
- Culture any effusion with a sterile swab and culture tube (see "Culture, Bacterial, Ear," monograph); alternatively, an HCP will perform a needle aspiration from the middle ear through the tympanic membrane during the examination. Other procedures such as cerumen and foreign body removal can also be performed.
- Pneumatic otoscopy can be done to determine tympanic membrane flexibility. This test permits the introduction of air into the canal that reveals a reduction in movement of the membrane in otitis media and absence of movement in chronic otitis media.

POST-TEST:

- A report of the results will be made available to the requesting HCP, who will discuss the results with the patient.
- Administer ear drops of a soothing oil, as ordered, if the canal is irritated by removal of cerumen or foreign bodies.
- Recognize anxiety related to test results, and be supportive of impaired activity related to hearing loss. Discuss the implications of abnormal test results on the patient's lifestyle. Provide teaching and information regarding the clinical implications of the test results, as appropriate.
- Reinforce information given by the patient's HCP regarding further testing, treatment, or referral to another HCP. Answer any questions or address any concerns voiced by the patient or family.

▶ Depending on the results of this procedure, additional testing may be performed to evaluate or monitor progression of the disease process and determine the need for a change in therapy. Evaluate test results in relation to the patient's symptoms and other tests performed.

RELATED MONOGRAPHS:

▶ Related tests include antibiotic drugs, audiometry hearing loss, culture bacterial (ear), and Gram stain.
▶ Refer to the Auditory System table at the end of the book for related tests by body system.

Ova and Parasites, Stool

SYNONYM/ACRONYM: O & P.

COMMON USE: To assess for the presence of parasites, larvae, or eggs in stool to assist in diagnosing a parasitic infection.

SPECIMEN: Stool collected in a clean plastic, tightly capped container.

NORMAL FINDINGS: (Method: Macroscopic and microscopic examination) No presence of parasites, ova, or larvae.

DESCRIPTION: This test evaluates stool for the presence of intestinal parasites and their eggs. Some parasites are nonpathogenic; others, such as protozoa and worms, can cause serious illness.

INDICATIONS
• Assist in the diagnosis of parasitic infestation.

POTENTIAL DIAGNOSIS

Positive findings in
• Amebiasis—*Entamoeba histolytica* infection
• Ascariasis—*Ascaris lumbricoides* infection
• Blastocystis—*Blastocystis hominis* infection
• Cryptosporidiosis—*Cryptosporidium parvum* infection
• Enterobiasis—*Enterobius vermicularis* (pinworm) infection
• Giardiasis—*Giardia lamblia* infection

• Hookworm disease—*Ancylostoma duodenale, Necator americanus* infection
• Isospora—*Isospora belli* infection
• Schistosomiasis—*Schistosoma haematobium, S. japonicum, S. mansoni* infection
• Strongyloidiasis—*Strongyloides stercoralis* infection
• Tapeworm disease—*Diphyllobothrium, Hymenolepiasis, Taenia saginata, T. solium* infection
• Trematode disease—*Clonorchis sinensis, Fasciola hepatica, Fasciolopsis buski* infection
• Trichuriasis—*Trichuris trichiura* infection

CRITICAL FINDINGS: N/A

INTERFERING FACTORS
• Failure to test a fresh specimen may yield a false-negative result.
• Antimicrobial or antiamebic therapy within 10 days of test may yield a false-negative result.

Failure to wait 1 wk after a gastrointestinal study using barium or after laxative use can affect test results.

Medications such as antacids, antibiotics, antidiarrheal compounds, bismuth, castor oil, iron, magnesia, or psyllium fiber (Metamucil) may interfere with analysis.

NURSING IMPLICATIONS AND PROCEDURE

RETEST:

Positively identify the patient using at least two unique identifiers before providing care, treatment, or services.

Patient Teaching: Inform the patient that this test can assist in diagnosing a parasitic infection.

Obtain a history of the patient's complaints, including a list of known allergens. Document any travel to foreign countries.

Obtain a history of the patient's gastrointestinal and immune systems, symptoms, and results of previously performed laboratory tests and diagnostic and surgical procedures.

Note any recent therapies that can interfere with test results.

Obtain a list of the patient's current medications, including herbs, nutritional supplements, and nutraceuticals (see Appendix F).

Review the procedure with the patient. Instruct the patient on hand-washing procedures, and inform the patient that the infection may be contagious. Warn the patient not to contaminate the specimen with urine, toilet paper, or toilet water. Address concerns about pain and explain to the patient that there should be no discomfort during the procedure.

Sensitivity to social and cultural issues, as well as concern for modesty, is important in providing psychological support before, during, and after the procedure.

Instruct the patient to avoid medications that interfere with test results.

There are no food or fluid restrictions unless by medical direction.

INTRATEST:

Instruct the patient to cooperate fully and to follow directions.

Observe standard precautions, and follow the general guidelines in Appendix A. Positively identify the patient, and label the appropriate specimen container with the corresponding patient demographics, initials of the person collecting the specimen, date, and time of collection.

Collect a stool specimen directly into the container. If the patient is bedridden, use a clean bedpan and transfer the specimen into the container using a tongue depressor.

Specimens to be examined for the presence of pinworms are collected by the "Scotch tape" method in the morning before bathing or defecation. A small paddle with a piece of cellophane tape (sticky side facing out) is pressed against the perianal area. The tape is placed in a collection container and submitted to determine if ova are present. Sometimes adult worms are observed protruding from the rectum.

Promptly transport the specimen to the laboratory for processing and analysis.

POST-TEST:

A report of the results will be made available to the requesting health-care provider (HCP), who will discuss the results with the patient.

Recognize anxiety related to test results. Discuss the implications of abnormal test results on the patient's lifestyle. Provide teaching and information regarding the clinical implications of the test results, as appropriate.

Reinforce information given by the patient's HCP regarding further testing, treatment, or referral to another HCP. Educate the patient with positive findings on the transmission of the parasite, as indicated. Warn the patient that one negative result does not rule out parasitic infestation and that additional specimens may be required. Answer any questions or address any concerns voiced by the patient or family.

▶ Depending on the results of this procedure, additional testing may be performed to evaluate or monitor progression of the disease process and determine the need for a change in therapy. Evaluate test results in relation to the patient's symptoms and other tests performed.

RELATED MONOGRAPHS:

▶ Related tests include biopsy intestinal, biopsy liver, biopsy muscle, culture stool, fecal analysis, and IgE.
▶ Refer to the Gastrointestinal and Immune systems tables at the end of the book for related tests by body system.

Oxalate, Urine

SYNONYM/ACRONYM: N/A.

COMMON USE: To identify patients who are at risk for renal calculus formation or hyperoxaluria related to malabsorption.

SPECIMEN: Urine (25 mL) from a timed specimen collected in a clean plastic collection container with hydrogen chloride (HCl) as a preservative.

NORMAL FINDINGS: (Method: Spectrophotometry)

	Conventional Units	SI Units (Conventional Units × 11.4)
Children and adults	0–40 mg/24 hr	0–456 micromol/24 hr

DESCRIPTION: Oxalate is derived from the metabolism of oxalic acid, glycine, and ascorbic acid. Some individuals with malabsorption disorders absorb and excrete abnormally high amounts of oxalate, resulting in hyperoxaluria. Hyperoxaluria may be seen in patients who consume large amounts of animal protein, certain fruits and vegetables, or megadoses of vitamin C (ascorbic acid). Hyperoxaluria is also associated with ethylene glycol poisoning (oxalic acid is used in cleaning and bleaching agents). Patients who absorb and excrete large amounts of oxalate may form calcium oxalate kidney stones. Simultaneous measurement of serum and urine calcium is often requested.

INDICATIONS
- Assist in the evaluation of patients with ethylene glycol poisoning
- Assist in the evaluation of patients with a history of kidney stones
- Assist in the evaluation of patients with malabsorption syndromes or patients who have had jejunoileal bypass surgery

POTENTIAL DIAGNOSIS

Increased in
Conditions that result in malabsorption for any reason can lead to increased levels. Chronic diarrhea results in excessive loss of calcium

o bind oxalate. *Increased oxalate s absorbed by the intestine and xcreted by the kidneys.*

Bacterial overgrowth
Biliary tract disease
Bowel disease
Celiac disease
Cirrhosis
Crohn's disease
Diabetes
Ethylene glycol poisoning *(ethylene glycol is metabolized to oxalate and excreted by the kidneys; crystals are present in urine)*
Ileal resection
Jejunal shunt
Pancreatic disease
Primary hereditary hyperoxaluria (rare)
Pyridoxine (vitamin B$_6$) deficiency *(pyridoxine is a cofactor in an enzyme reaction that converts glyoxylic acid to glycine; deficiency results in an increase in oxalate)*
Sarcoidosis

Decreased in
Hypercalciuria *(related to formation of calcium oxalate crystals)*
Renal failure *(related to oxalate kidney stone disease)*

CRITICAL FINDINGS: N/A

INTERFERING FACTORS
Drugs and vitamins that may increase oxalate levels include ascorbic acid, calcium, and methoxyflurane.
Drugs that may decrease oxalate levels include nifedipine and pyridoxine.
Failure to follow dietary restrictions before the procedure may cause the procedure to be canceled or repeated.
Failure to collect sample in proper preservative may cause the procedure to be repeated. HCl helps keep oxalate dissolved in the urine. If the pH rises above 3.0, oxalate may precipitate from the sample, causing falsely decreased values. The acid also prevents oxidation of vitamin C to oxalate in the sample, causing falsely increased values.

NURSING IMPLICATIONS AND PROCEDURE

PRETEST:

- Positively identify the patient using at least two unique identifiers before providing care, treatment, or services.
- *Patient Teaching:* Inform the patient this test can assist in evaluating risk for kidney stones.
- Obtain a history of the patient's complaints, including a list of known allergens, especially allergies or sensitivities to latex.
- Obtain a history of the patient's gastrointestinal and genitourinary systems, symptoms, and results of previously performed laboratory tests and diagnostic and surgical procedures.
- Obtain a list of the patient's current medications, including herbs, nutritional supplements, and nutraceuticals (see Appendix F).
- Review the procedure with the patient. Provide a nonmetallic urinal, bedpan, or toilet-mounted collection device. Address concerns about pain and explain that there should be no discomfort during the procedure.
- *Sensitivity to social and cultural issues,* as well as concern for modesty, is important in providing psychological support before, during, and after the procedure.
- Usually a 24-hr time frame for urine collection is ordered. Inform the patient that all urine must be saved during that 24-hr period. Instruct the patient not to void directly into the laboratory collection container. Instruct the patient to avoid defecating in the collection device and to keep toilet tissue out of the collection device to prevent contamination of the specimen. Place a sign in the bathroom to remind the patient to save all urine.

Instruct the patient to void all urine into the collection device and then to pour the urine into the laboratory collection container. Alternatively, the specimen can be left in the collection device for a health-care staff member to add to the laboratory collection container.

There are no fluid or medication restrictions unless by medical direction.

Calcium supplements, gelatin, rhubarb, spinach, strawberries, tomatoes, and vitamin C should be restricted for at least 24 hr before the test. High-protein meals should also be avoided 24 hr before specimen collection. Protocols may vary among facilities.

INTRATEST:

Ensure that the patient has complied with dietary restrictions; assure that restricted foods have been avoided for at least 24 hr prior to the procedure.

If the patient has a history of allergic reaction to latex, avoid the use of equipment containing latex.

Instruct the patient to cooperate fully and to follow directions.

Observe standard precautions, and follow the general guidelines in Appendix A. Positively identify the patient, and label the appropriate specimen container with the corresponding patient demographics, initials of the person collecting the specimen, date, and time of collection.

Random Specimen (Collect in Early Morning)

Clean-Catch Specimen

Instruct the male patient to (1) thoroughly wash his hands, (2) cleanse the meatus, (3) void a small amount into the toilet, and (4) void directly into the specimen container.

Instruct the female patient to (1) thoroughly wash her hands; (2) cleanse the labia from front to back; (3) while keeping the labia separated, void a small amount into the toilet; and (4) without interrupting the urine stream, void directly into the specimen container.

Indwelling Catheter

Put on gloves. Empty drainage tube of urine. It may be necessary to clamp off the catheter for 15 to

30 min before specimen collection. Cleanse specimen port with antiseptic swab, and then aspirate 5 mL of urine with a 21- to 25-gauge needle and syringe. Transfer urine to a sterile container.

Timed Specimen

Obtain a clean 3-L urine specimen container, toilet-mounted collection device, and plastic bag (for transport of the specimen container). The specimen must be refrigerated or kept on ice throughout the entire collection period. If an indwelling urinary catheter is in place, the drainage bag must be kept on ice.

Begin the test between 6 and 8 a.m. if possible. Collect first voiding and discard. Record the time the specimen was discarded as the beginning of the timed collection period. The next morning, ask the patient to void at the same time the collection was started and add this last voiding to the container. Urinary output should be recorded throughout the collection time.

If an indwelling catheter is in place, replace the tubing and container system at the start of the collection time. Keep the container system on ice during the collection period, or empty the urine into a larger container periodically during the collection period; monitor to ensure continued drainage, and conclude the test the next morning at the same hour the collection was begun.

At the conclusion of the test, compare the quantity of urine with the urinary output record for the collection; if the specimen contains less than what was recorded as output, some urine may have been discarded, invalidating the test.

Include on the collection container's label the amount of urine, test start and stop times, and ingestion of any foods or medications that can affect test results.

General

Promptly transport the specimen to the laboratory for processing and analysis.

POST-TEST:

A report of the results will be made available to the requesting health-care provider (HCP), who will discuss the results with the patient.

Instruct the patient to resume usual diet, as directed by the HCP.

Nutritional Considerations: Consideration may be given to lessening dietary intake of oxalate if urine levels are increased. Encourage patients with abnormal results to seek advice regarding dietary modifications from a trained nutritionist. Magnesium supplementation may be recommended for patients with GI disease to prevent the development of calcium oxalate kidney stones. Recognize anxiety related to test results, and be supportive of fear of shortened life expectancy. Discuss the implications of abnormal test results on the patient's lifestyle. Provide teaching and information regarding the clinical implications of the test results, as appropriate. Educate the patient regarding access to counseling services.

Reinforce information given by the patient's HCP regarding further testing, treatment, or referral to another HCP. Answer any questions or address any concerns voiced by the patient or family.

Depending on the results of this procedure, additional testing may be performed to evaluate or monitor progression of the disease process and determine the need for a change in therapy. Evaluate test results in relation to the patient's symptoms and other tests performed.

RELATED MONOGRAPHS:

Related tests include calcium, calculus kidney stone panel, UA, urine uric acid, and vitamin C.

Refer to the Gastrointestinal and Genitourinary systems tables at the end of the book for related tests by body system.

O

Pachymetry

COMMON USE: To assess the thickness of the cornea prior to LASIK surgery and evaluate glaucoma risk.

AREA OF APPLICATION: Eyes.

CONTRAST: N/A.

DESCRIPTION: Pachymetry is the measurement of the thickness of the cornea using an ultrasound device called a pachymeter. Refractive surgery procedures such as LASIK (laser-assisted in-situ keratomileusis) remove tissue from the cornea. Pachymetry is used to ensure that enough central corneal tissue remains after surgery to prevent ectasia, or abnormal bowing, of thin corneas. Also, studies point to a correlation between increased risk of glaucoma and decreased corneal thickness. This correlation has influenced some health-care providers (HCPs) to include pachymetry as a part of a regular eye health examination for patients who have a family history of glaucoma or who are part of a high-risk population. African Americans have a higher incidence of glaucoma than any other ethnic group.

INDICATIONS

- Assist in the diagnosis of glaucoma (*Note:* the intraocular pressure in glaucoma patients with a thin cornea, 530 micron or less, may be higher than in patients whose corneal thickness is within normal limits)
- Determine corneal thickness in potential refractive surgery candidates
- Monitor the effects of various therapies using eye drops, laser, or filtering surgery

POTENTIAL DIAGNOSIS

Normal findings in
- Normal corneal thickness of 535 to 555 micron

Abnormal findings in
- Bullous keratopathy
- Corneal rejection after penetrating keratoplasty
- Fuchs' endothelial dystrophy
- Glaucoma

CRITICAL FINDINGS: N/A

INTERFERING FACTORS

Factors that may impair the results of the examination
- Inability of the patient to cooperate or remain still during the test because of age, significant pain, or mental status.
- Improper technique during application of the probe tip to the cornea.

NURSING IMPLICATIONS AND PROCEDURE

PRETEST:

▶ Positively identify the patient using at least two unique identifiers before providing care, treatment, or services.
▶ *Patient Teaching:* Inform the patient this procedure can assist in measuring the thickness of the cornea in the eye.
▶ Obtain a history of the patient's complaints, including a list of known allergens, especially allergies or sensitivities to latex.
▶ Obtain a history of narrow-angle glaucoma. Obtain a history of known or suspected visual impairment, changes

P

in visual acuity, and use of glasses or contact lenses.

Obtain a history of the patient's known or suspected vision loss, including type and cause; eye conditions with treatment regimens; eye surgery; and other tests and procedures to assess and diagnose visual deficit.

Obtain a history of symptoms and results of previously performed laboratory tests, diagnostic and surgical procedures.

Obtain a list of the patient's current medications, including herbs, nutritional supplements, and nutraceuticals (see Appendix F).

Instruct the patient to remove contact lenses or glasses, as appropriate. Instruct the patient regarding the importance of keeping the eyes open for the test. Review the procedure with the patient. Explain that the patient will be requested to fixate the eyes during the procedure. Address concerns about pain and explain that no pain will be experienced during the test, but there may be moments of discomfort. Explain that some discomfort may be experienced after the test when the numbness wears off from anesthetic drops administered prior to the test, or discomfort may occur if too much pressure is used during the test. Inform the patient that an HCP performs the test and that to evaluate both eyes, the test can take 3 to 5 min. *Sensitivity to social and cultural issues,* as well as concern for modesty, is important in providing psychological support before, during, and after the procedure. There are no food, fluid, or medication restrictions unless by medical direction.

INTRATEST:

Observe standard precautions, and follow the general guidelines in Appendix A. Positively identify the patient.

Instruct the patient to cooperate fully and to follow directions. Ask the patient to remain still during the procedure because movement produces unreliable results.

Seat the patient comfortably. Instruct the patient to look straight ahead, keeping the eyes open and unblinking. Instill topical anesthetic in each eye, as ordered, and allow time for it to work.

Topical anesthetic drops are placed in the eye with the patient looking up and the solution directed at the six o'clock position of the sclera (white of the eye) near the limbus (gray, semitransparent area of the eyeball where the cornea and sclera meet). Neither the dropper nor the bottle should touch the eyelashes.

▶ Request that the patient look straight ahead while the probe of the pachymeter is applied directly on the cornea of the eye. Take an average of three readings for each eye. Individual readings should be within 10 microns. Results on both eyes should be similar.

POST-TEST:

▶ A report of the results will be made available to the requesting HCP, who will discuss the results with the patient.

▶ Recognize anxiety related to test results. Encourage the family to recognize and be supportive of impaired activity related to vision loss, anticipated loss of driving privileges, or the possibility of requiring corrective lenses (self-image). Discuss the implications of test results on the patient's lifestyle. Reassure the patient regarding concerns related to impending cataract surgery. Provide teaching and information regarding the clinical implications of the test results, as appropriate. Provide contact information, if desired, for the Glaucoma Research Foundation (www.glaucoma.org).

▶ Reinforce information given by the patient's HCP regarding further testing, treatment, or referral to another HCP. Answer any questions or address any concerns voiced by the patient or family.

▶ Depending on the results of this procedure, additional testing may be performed to evaluate or monitor progression of the disease process and determine the need for a change in therapy. Evaluate test results in relation to the patient's symptoms and other tests performed.

RELATED MONOGRAPHS:

▶ Related tests include fundus photography, gonioscopy, intraocular pressure, and visual field testing.

▶ Refer to the Ocular System table at the end of the book for related tests by body system.

P

Papanicolaou Smear

SYNONYM/ACRONYM: Pap smear, cervical smear.

COMMON USE: To establish a cytological diagnosis of cervical and vaginal disease and identify the presence of genital infections, such as human papillomavirus, herpes, and cytomegalovirus.

SPECIMEN: Cervical and endocervical cells.

NORMAL FINDINGS: (Method: Microscopic examination of fixed and stained smear) Reporting of Pap smear findings may follow one of several formats and may vary by laboratory. Simplified content of the two most common formats for interpretation are listed in the table.

Bethesda System
Specimen type:
Smear, liquid-based, or other.
Specimen adequacy:
• *Satisfactory* for evaluation—endocervical transformation zone component is described as present or absent, along with other quality indicators (e.g., partially obscuring blood, inflammation).
• *Unsatisfactory* for evaluation—either the specimen is rejected and the reason given or the specimen is processed and examined but not evaluated for epithelial abnormalities and the reason is given.
General categorization:
• *Negative* for intraepithelial lesion or malignancy.
• *Epithelial cell abnormality* (abnormality is specified in the interpretation section of the report).
• *Other comments*
Interpretation/result:
1. Negative for intraepithelial lesion or malignancy
A. *List organisms causing infection:*
• *Trichomonas vaginalis;* fungal organisms consistent with *Candida* spp.; shift in flora suggestive of bacterial vaginosis; bacteria morphologically consistent with *Actinomyces* spp.; cellular changes consistent with herpes simplex virus
B. Other nonneoplastic findings:
• reactive cellular changes associated with inflammation, radiation, intrauterine device; glandular cell status post-hysterectomy; atrophy.
2. Epithelial cell abnormalities
A. *Squamous cell abnormalities*
• ASC of undetermined significance (ASC-US) cannot exclude HSIL (ASC-H)
• LSIL encompassing HPV, mild dysplasia, CIN 1
• HSIL encompassing moderate and severe dysplasia, CIS/CIN 2 and CIN 3 with features suspicious for invasion (if invasion is suspected)
• Squamous cell carcinoma

P

Bethesda System

- *Glandular cell*
  - Atypical glandular cells (NOS or specify otherwise)
  - Atypical glandular cells, favor neoplastic (NOS or specify otherwise)
  - Endocervical adenocarcinoma *in situ*
  - Adenocarcinoma
3. Other
   A. Endometrial cells (in a woman of 40 yr or greater)

Automated review:
Indicates the case was examined by an automated device and the results are listed along with the name of the device.

Ancillary testing:
Describes the test method and result.

Educational notes and suggestions:
Should be consistent with clinical follow-up guidelines published by professional organizations with references included.

ASC = atypical squamous cells; ASC-H = high-grade atypical squamous cells; ASC-US = atypical squamous cells undetermined significance; CIN = cervical intraepithelial neoplasia; CIS = carcinoma in situ; HSIL = high-grade squamous intraepithelial lesion; LSIL = low-grade squamous intraepithelial lesion.

DESCRIPTION: The Papanicolaou (Pap) smear is primarily used for the early detection of cervical cancer. The interpretation of Pap smears is as heavily dependent on the collection and fixation technique as it is on the completeness and accuracy of the clinical information provided with the specimen. The patient's age, date of last menstrual period, parity, surgical status, postmenopausal status, use of hormone therapy (including use of oral contraceptives), history of radiation or chemotherapy, history of abnormal vaginal bleeding, and history of previous Pap smears are essential for proper interpretation. Human papillomavirus (HPV) is the most common sexually transmitted virus and primary causal factor in the development of cervical cancer. Therefore, specimens for HPV are often collected simultaneously with the PAP smear. The laboratory should be consulted about the availability of this option prior to specimen collection because specific test kits are required to allow for simultaneous sample collection. HPV infection can be successfully treated once it has been identified. Gardasil, the first vaccine developed against HPV, is given in three doses, at 2 and 6 mo after the initial injection. The Centers for Disease Control and Prevention recommends vaccination for males and females age 11 and 12 yr. Vaccination is also recommended for females age 13 to 26 yr and males age 13 to 21 yr who have not been previously vaccinated. Cervarix is a second HPV vaccine available only for females.

A wet prep can be prepared simultaneously from a cervical or vaginal sample. The swab is touched to a microscope slide, and a small amount of saline is dropped on the slide. The slide is examined

P

by microscope to determine the presence of harmful bacteria or *Trichomonas*.

A Schiller's test entails applying an iodine solution to the cervix. Normal cells pick up the iodine and stain brown. Abnormal cells do not pick up any color.

Improvements in specimen preparation have added to the increased quality of screening procedures. Liquid-based Pap tests have largely replaced the traditional Pap smear. Cervical cells collected in the liquid media are applied in a very thin layer onto slides, using a method that clears away contaminants such as blood or vaginal discharge. Samples can be "split" so that questionable findings by cytological screening can be followed up with more specific molecular methods like nucleic acid hybridization probes, polymerase chain reaction, intracellular microRNA quantification, or immunocytochemistry to detect the presence of high-risk HPV. Computerized scanning systems are also being used to reduce the number of smears that require manual review by a cytotechnologist or pathologist.

There are now some alternatives to cone biopsy and cryosurgery for the treatment of cervical dysplasia. Patients with abnormal Pap smear results may have a cervical loop electrosurgical excision procedure (LEEP) performed to remove or destroy abnormal cervical tissue. In the LEEP procedure, a speculum is inserted into the vagina, the cervix is numbed, and a special electrically charged wire loop is used to painlessly remove the suspicious area. Postprocedure cramping and bleeding can occur. Laser ablation is another technique that can be employed for the precise removal of abnormal cervical tissue.

INDICATIONS
- Assist in the diagnosis of cervical dysplasia
- Assist in the diagnosis of endometriosis, condyloma, and vaginal adenosis
- Assist in the diagnosis of genital infections (herpes, *Candida* spp., *Trichomonas vaginalis,* cytomegalovirus, *Chlamydia,* lymphogranuloma venereum, HPV, and *Actinomyces* spp.)
- Assist in the diagnosis of primary and metastatic neoplasms
- Evaluate hormonal function

POTENTIAL DIAGNOSIS

Positive findings in
(See table [Bethesda system])

Decreased in: N/A

CRITICAL FINDINGS: N/A

INTERFERING FACTORS
- The smear should not be allowed to air dry before fixation.
- Lubricating jelly should not be used on the speculum.
- Improper collection site may result in specimen rejection. Samples for cancer screening are obtained from the posterior vaginal fornix and from the cervix. Samples for hormonal evaluation are obtained from the vagina.
- Douching, sexual intercourse, using tampons, or using vaginal medication within 24 hr prior to specimen collection can interfere with the specimen's results.
- Collection of other specimens prior to the collection of the Pap smear may be cause for specimen rejection.
- Contamination with blood from samples collected during the patient's menstrual period may be cause for specimen rejection.

NURSING IMPLICATIONS AND PROCEDURE

PRETEST:

- Positively identify the patient using at least two unique identifiers before providing care, treatment, or services.
- *Patient Teaching:* Inform the patient this procedure can assist in diagnosing disease of the reproductive system.
- Obtain a history of the patient's complaints, including a list of known allergens, especially allergies or sensitivities to latex.
- Obtain a history of the patient's immune and reproductive systems, symptoms, and results of previously performed laboratory tests and diagnostic and surgical procedures.
- Record the date of the last menstrual period and determine the possibility of pregnancy in perimenopausal women.
- Note any recent procedures that can interfere with test results.
- Obtain a list of the patient's current medications, including herbs, nutritional supplements, and nutraceuticals (see Appendix F).
- Review the procedure with the patient. Instruct the patient to avoid douching or sexual intercourse for 24 hr before specimen collection. Verify that the patient is not menstruating. Address concerns about pain and explain that there may be some discomfort during the procedure. Inform the patient that specimen collection is performed by a health-care provider (HCP) specializing in this procedure and takes approximately 5 to 10 min.
- *Sensitivity to social and cultural issues,* as well as concern for modesty, is important in providing psychological support before, during, and after the procedure.
- There are no food, fluid, or medication restrictions unless by medical direction.
- If the patient is taking vaginal antibiotic medication, testing should be delayed for 1 mo after the treatment has been completed.
- *Make sure a written and informed consent has been signed prior to the procedure and before administering any medications.*

INTRATEST:

- Have the patient void before the procedure.
- Have the patient remove clothes below the waist.
- Instruct the patient to cooperate fully and to follow directions. Ask the patient to breathe normally and to avoid unnecessary movement during the procedure.
- Observe standard precautions, and follow the general guidelines in Appendix A. Positively identify the patient, and label the appropriate specimen container with the corresponding patient demographics, initials of the person collecting the specimen, date, and time of collection.
- Assist the patient into a lithotomy position on a gynecological examination table (with feet in stirrups). Drape the patient's legs.
- A plastic or metal speculum is inserted into the vagina and is opened to gently spread apart the vagina for inspection of the cervix. The speculum may be dipped in warm water to aid in comfortable insertion.
- After the speculum is properly positioned, the cervical and vaginal specimens are obtained. A synthetic fiber brush is inserted deep enough into the cervix to reach the endocervical canal. The brush is then rotated one turn and removed. A plastic or wooden spatula is used to lightly scrape the cervix and vaginal wall.

Conventional Collection

- Specimens from both the brush and the spatula are plated on the glass slide. The brush specimen is plated using a gentle rolling motion, whereas the spatula specimen is plated using a light gliding motion across the slide. The specimens are immediately fixed to the slide with a liquid or spray containing 95% ethanol. The speculum is removed from the vagina. A pelvic and/or rectal examination is usually performed after specimen collection is completed.

ThinPrep Collection

- The ThinPrep bottle lid is opened and removed, exposing the solution. The brush and spatula specimens are then gently swished in the ThinPrep solution to remove the adhering cells. The brush and spatula are then removed from the ThinPrep solution, and the bottle lid is replaced and secured.

P

General

▶ Place samples in properly labeled specimen container and promptly transport the specimen to the laboratory for processing and analysis.

POST-TEST:

▶ A report of the results will be made available to the requesting HCP, who will discuss the results with the patient.
▶ Cleanse or allow the patient to cleanse secretions or excess lubricant (if a pelvic and/or rectal examination is also performed) from the perineal area. Provide a sanitary pad if cervical bleeding occurs.
▶ Recognize anxiety related to test results, and offer support. Discuss the implications of abnormal test results on the patient's lifestyle. Provide teaching and information regarding the clinical implications of the test results, as appropriate. Educate the patient regarding access to counseling services.
▶ Decisions regarding the need for and frequency of conventional or liquid-based Pap tests or other cancer screening procedures should be made after consultation between the patient and HCP. The most current guidelines for cervical cancer screening of the general population as well as of individuals with increased risk are available from the American Cancer Society (www.cancer.org) and the American College of Obstetricians and Gynecologists (ACOG) (www.acog.org).
▶ Reinforce information given by the patient's HCP regarding further testing,

treatment, or referral to another HCP. Provide information regarding vaccine-preventable diseases where indicated (e.g., anthrax, cervical cancer, diphtheria, encephalitis, hepatitis A and B, H1N1 flu, human papillomavirus, *Haemophilus influenza*, seasonal influenza, Lyme disease, measles, meningococcal disease, monkeypox, mumps, pertussis, pneumococcal disease, polio, rotavirus, rubella, shingles, smallpox, tetanus, typhoid fever, varicella, yellow fever). Provide contact information, if desired, for the Centers for Disease Control and Prevention (www.cdc.gov/vaccines/vpd-vac).
Answer any questions or address any concerns voiced by the patient or family.
▶ Depending on the results of this procedure, additional testing may be performed to evaluate or monitor progression of the disease process and determine the need for a change in therapy. Evaluate test results in relation to the patient's symptoms and other tests performed.

RELATED MONOGRAPHS:

▶ Related tests include biopsy cervical, cancer antigens, *Chlamydia* group antibody, colposcopy, culture anal/genital, culture throat, culture urine, culture viral, CMV, cytology urine, laparoscopy gynecologic, US pelvis, and UA.
▶ Refer to the Immune and Reproductive systems tables at the end of the book for related tests by body system.

Parathyroid Hormone

SYNONYM/ACRONYM: Parathormone, PTH, intact PTH, whole molecule PTH.

COMMON USE: To assist in the diagnosis of parathyroid disease and disorders of calcium balance. Also used to monitor patients receiving renal dialysis.

SPECIMEN: Serum (1 mL) collected in a red- or tiger-top tube. Specimen should be transported tightly capped and in an ice slurry.

NORMAL FINDINGS: (Method: Immunoassay)

Age	Conventional Units	SI Units (Conventional Units × 1)
Cord blood	Less than 3 pg/mL	Less than 3 ng/L
2–20 yr	9–52 pg/mL	9–52 ng/L
Adult	10–65 pg/mL	10–65 ng/L

DESCRIPTION: Parathyroid hormone (PTH) is secreted by the parathyroid glands in response to decreased levels of circulating calcium. PTH assists in the mobilization of calcium from bone into the bloodstream, promoting renal tubular reabsorption of calcium and depression of phosphate reabsorption, thereby reducing calcium excretion and increasing phosphate excretion by the kidneys. PTH also decreases the renal secretion of hydrogen ions, which leads to increased renal excretion of bicarbonate and chloride. PTH enhances renal production of active vitamin D metabolites, causing increased calcium absorption in the small intestine. The net result of PTH action is maintenance of adequate serum calcium levels. C-terminal and N-terminal assays were used prior to the development of reliable intact or whole molecule PTH assays. A rapid PTH assay has been developed specifically for intraoperative monitoring of PTH in the surgical treatment of primary hyperparathyroidism. Rapid PTH assays have proved valuable because the decision of whether the hyperparathyroidism involves one or multiple glands depends on measurement of circulating PTH levels. Surgical outcomes indicate that a 50% decrease or more in intraoperative PTH from baseline measurements can predict successful treatment with up to 97% accuracy. An intraoperative decrease of less than 50% indicates the need to identify and remove additional malfunctioning parathyroid tissue. In healthy individuals, intact PTH has a circulating half-life of about 5 min. N-terminal PTH has a circulating half-life of about 2 min and is found in very small quantities. Intact and N-terminal PTH are the only biologically active forms of the hormone. Ninety percent of circulating PTH is composed of inactive C-terminal and midregion fragments. PTH is cleared from the body by the kidneys.

INDICATIONS

- Assist in the diagnosis of hyperparathyroidism
- Assist in the diagnosis of suspected secondary hyperparathyroidism due to chronic renal failure, malignant tumors that produce ectopic PTH, and malabsorption syndromes
- Detect incidental damage or inadvertent removal of the parathyroid glands during thyroid or neck surgery
- Differentiate parathyroid and nonparathyroid causes of hypercalcemia
- Evaluate autoimmune destruction of the parathyroid glands
- Evaluate parathyroid response to altered serum calcium levels, especially those that result from malignant processes, leading to decreased PTH production
- Evaluate source of altered calcium metabolism

POTENTIAL DIAGNOSIS

Increased in

- Fluorosis *(skeletal fluorosis can cause a condition resembling secondary hyperparathyroidism,*

P

disruption in calcium homeostasis, and excessive PTH production)
- Primary, secondary, or tertiary hyperparathyroidism *(all result in excess PTH production)*
- Pseudogout *(calcium is lost due to deposits in the joint; decrease in calcium stimulates PTH production)*
- Pseudohypoparathyroidism
- Zollinger-Ellison syndrome *(related to poor intestinal absorption of calcium and vitamin D; decreased calcium stimulates PTH production)*

Decreased in
- Autoimmune destruction of the parathyroids *(related to decreased parathyroid function)*
- DiGeorge's syndrome *(related to hypoparathyroidism)*
- Hyperthyroidism *(related to increased calcium from bone loss; increased calcium levels inhibit PTH production)*
- Hypomagnesemia *(magnesium is a calcium channel blocker; low magnesium levels allow for increased calcium, which inhibits PTH production)*
- Nonparathyroid hypercalcemia (in the absence of renal failure) *(increased calcium levels inhibit PTH production)*
- Sarcoidosis *(related to increased calcium levels)*
- Secondary hypoparathyroidism due to surgery

CRITICAL FINDINGS: N/A

INTERFERING FACTORS
- Drugs that may increase PTH levels include clodronate, estrogen/progestin therapy, foscarnet, furosemide, hydrocortisone, isoniazid, lithium, nifedipine, octreotide, pamidronate, phosphates, prednisone, tamoxifen, and verapamil.

- Drugs and vitamins that may decrease PTH levels include alfacalcidol, aluminum hydroxide, calcitriol, diltiazem, magnesium sulfate, parathyroid hormone, pindolol, prednisone, and vitamin D
- PTH levels are subject to diurnal variation, with highest levels occurring in the morning.
- PTH levels should always be measured in conjunction with calcium for proper interpretation.
- Failure to follow dietary restrictions before the procedure may cause the procedure to be canceled or repeated.

NURSING IMPLICATIONS AND PROCEDURE

PRETEST:
- Positively identify the patient using at least two unique identifiers before providing care, treatment, or services.
- *Patient Teaching:* Inform the patient this test can assist in diagnosing parathyroid disease.
- Obtain a history of the patient's complaints, including a list of known allergens, especially allergies or sensitivities to latex.
- Obtain a history of the patient's endocrine system, symptoms, and results of previously performed laboratory tests and diagnostic and surgical procedures
- Obtain a list of the patient's current medications, including herbs, nutritional supplements, and nutraceuticals (see Appendix F).
- Review the procedure with the patient. Early-morning specimen collection is recommended because of the diurnal variation in PTH levels. Inform the patient that specimen collection takes approximately 5 to 10 min. Address concerns about pain and explain that there may be some discomfort during the venipuncture.
- *Sensitivity to social and cultural issues,* as well as concern for modesty, is important in providing psychological

support before, during, and after the procedure.

▸ The patient should fast for 12 hr before specimen collection. Protocols may vary among facilities.

▸ There are no fluid or medication restrictions unless by medical direction.

▸ Prepare an ice slurry in a cup or plastic bag to have on hand for immediate transport of the specimen to the laboratory.

INTRATEST:

▸ Ensure that the patient has complied with dietary restrictions; ensure that food has been restricted for at least 12 hr prior to the procedure.

▸ If the patient has a history of allergic reaction to latex, avoid the use of equipment containing latex.

▸ Instruct the patient to cooperate fully and to follow directions. Direct the patient to breathe normally and to avoid unnecessary movement.

▸ Observe standard precautions, and follow the general guidelines in Appendix A. Positively identify the patient, and label the appropriate specimen container with the corresponding patient demographics, initials of the person collecting the specimen, date, and time of collection. Perform a venipuncture.

▸ Remove the needle and apply direct pressure with dry gauze to stop bleeding. Observe/assess venipuncture site for bleeding or hematoma formation and secure gauze with adhesive bandage.

▸ Promptly transport the specimen to the laboratory for processing and analysis. The sample should be placed in an ice slurry immediately after collection. Information on the specimen label should be protected from water in the ice slurry by first placing the specimen in a protective plastic bag.

POST-TEST:

▸ A report of the results will be made available to the requesting health-care provider (HCP), who will discuss the results with the patient.

▸ Instruct the patient to resume usual diet, as directed by the HCP.

▸ *Nutritional Considerations:* Patients with abnormal parathyroid levels are also likely to experience the effects of calcium-level imbalances. Instruct the patient to report signs and symptoms of hypocalcemia and hypercalcemia to the HCP. (For critical values, signs, and symptoms of calcium imbalance and for nutritional information, see monographs titled "Calcium, Blood"; "Calcium, Ionized"; and "Calcium, Urine.")

▸ Reinforce information given by the patient's HCP regarding further testing, treatment, or referral to another HCP. Answer any questions or address any concerns voiced by the patient or family.

▸ Depending on the results of this procedure, additional testing may be performed to evaluate or monitor progression of the disease process and determine the need for a change in therapy. Evaluate test results in relation to the patient's symptoms and other tests performed.

RELATED MONOGRAPHS:

▸ Related tests include ALP, arthroscopy, calcitonin, calcium, collagen cross-linked telopeptides, evoked brain potentials, fecal fat, gastric emptying scan, gastric acid stimulation, gastrin stimulation test, parathyroid scan, phosphorus, RAIU, synovial fluid analysis, TSH, thyroxine, US thyroid and parathyroid, uric acid, UA, and vitamin D.

▸ Refer to the Endocrine System table at the end of the book for related tests by body system.

P

Parathyroid Scan

SYNONYM/ACRONYM: Parathyroid scintiscan.

COMMON USE: To assess the parathyroid gland toward diagnosing cancer and to perform postoperative evaluation of the parathyroid gland.

AREA OF APPLICATION: Parathyroid.

CONTRAST: IV technetium-99m (Tc-99m) pertechnetate, Tc-99m sestamibi, oral iodine-123, and thallium.

DESCRIPTION: Parathyroid scanning is performed to assist in the preoperative localization of parathyroid adenomas in clinically proven primary hyperparathyroidism; it is useful for distinguishing between intrinsic and extrinsic parathyroid adenomas. It is also performed after surgery to verify the presence of the parathyroid gland in children, and it is done after thyroidectomy as well.

The radionuclide is administered 10 to 20 min before the imaging is performed. The thyroid and surrounding tissues should be carefully palpated.

Fine-needle aspiration biopsy guided by ultrasound is occasionally necessary to differentiate thyroid pathology, as well as pathology of other tissues, from parathyroid neoplasia.

INDICATIONS
* Aid in the diagnosis of hyperparathyroidism
* Differentiate between extrinsic and intrinsic parathyroid adenoma but not between benign and malignant conditions
* Evaluate the parathyroid in patients with severe hypercalcemia or in patients before parathyroidectomy

POTENTIAL DIAGNOSIS

Normal findings in
* No areas of increased perfusion or uptake in the thyroid or parathyroid

Abnormal findings in
* Intrinsic and extrinsic parathyroid adenomas

CRITICAL FINDINGS: N/A

INTERFERING FACTORS

This procedure is contraindicated for
* Patients who are pregnant or suspected of being pregnant, unless the potential benefits of the procedure far outweigh the risks to the fetus and mother.

Factors that may impair clear imaging
* Inability of the patient to cooperate or remain still during the procedure because of age, significant pain, or mental status.
* Ingestion of foods containing iodine (e.g., iodized salt) and medications containing iodine (e.g., cough syrup, potassium iodide, vitamins, Lugol's solution, thyroid replacement medications), which can decrease uptake of the radionuclide.
* Other nuclear scans or iodinated contrast medium radiographic

studies done within the previous 24 to 48 hr.
- Metallic objects (e.g., jewelry, body rings) within the examination field, which may inhibit organ visualization and cause unclear images.

Other considerations
- Improper injection of the radionuclide that allows the tracer to seep deep into the muscle tissue produces erroneous hot spots.
- Consultation with a health-care provider (HCP) should occur before the procedure for radiation safety concerns regarding younger patients or patients who are lactating.
- Risks associated with radiation overexposure can result from frequent x-ray or radionuclide procedures. Personnel working in the examination area should wear badges to record their level of radiation exposure.

NURSING IMPLICATIONS AND PROCEDURE

PRETEST:

- Positively identify the patient using at least two unique identifiers before providing care, treatment, or services.
- *Patient Teaching:* Inform the patient this procedure can assist in diagnosing parathyroid disease.
- Obtain a history of the patient's complaints, including a list of known allergens, especially allergies or sensitivities to latex, iodine, seafood, contrast medium, or anesthetics.
- Note any recent procedures that can interfere with test results, including examinations using iodinated contrast medium or radioactive nuclides.
- Obtain a history of the patient's endocrine system, symptoms, and results of previously performed laboratory tests and diagnostic and surgical procedures.
- Record the date of the last menstrual period and determine the possibility of pregnancy in perimenopausal women.
- Obtain a list of the patient's current medications, including herbs, nutritional

supplements, and nutraceuticals (see Appendix F).
- Review the procedure with the patient. Address concerns about pain related to the procedure and explain that some pain may be experienced during the test. Inform the patient that the procedure is performed in a nuclear medicine department, usually by an HCP specializing in this procedure, with support staff, and takes approximately 30 to 60 min.
- *Sensitivity to social and cultural issues,* as well as concern for modesty, is important in providing psychological support before, during, and after the procedure.
- Instruct the patient to remove jewelry and other metallic objects from the area to be examined.
- There are no food, fluid, or medication restrictions unless by medical direction.
- *Make sure a written and informed consent has been signed prior to the procedure and before administering any medications.*

INTRATEST:

- Observe standard precautions, and follow the general guidelines in Appendix A. Positively identify the patient.
- Ensure that the patient has removed all external metallic objects from the area to be examined prior to the procedure.
- Instruct the patient to void prior to the procedure and to change into the gown, robe, and foot coverings provided.
- Instruct the patient to cooperate fully and to follow directions. Instruct the patient to remain still throughout the procedure because movement produces unreliable results.
- Technetium-99m (Tc-99m) pertechnetate is injected IV before scanning.
- Place the patient in a supine position under a radionuclide gamma camera. Images are preformed 15 min after the injection.
- With the patient in the same position, Tc-99m sestamibi is injected, and a second image is obtained after 10 min.
- Iodine-123 may be administered orally in place of Tc-99m pertechnetate; the imaging sequence, as described previously, is performed 24 hr later.

P

- Remove the needle or catheter and apply a pressure dressing over the puncture site.
- Observe/assess the needle/catheter insertion site for bleeding, inflammation, or hematoma formation.

POST-TEST:

- A report of the results will be made available to the requesting HCP, who will discuss the results with the patient.
- Observe/assess the needle/catheter insertion site for bleeding, inflammation, or hematoma formation.
- Instruct the patient in the care and assessment of the injection site.
- Advise the patient to drink increased amounts of fluids for 24 to 48 hr to eliminate the radionuclide from the body, unless contraindicated. Tell the patient that radionuclide is eliminated from the body within 6 to 24 hr.
- If a woman who is breastfeeding must have a nuclear scan, she should not breastfeed the infant until the radionuclide has been eliminated. This could take as long as 3 days. She should be instructed to express the milk and discard it during the 3-day period to prevent cessation of milk production.
- Instruct the patient to flush the toilet immediately and to meticulously wash hands with soap and water after each voiding for 24 hr after the procedure.

- Instruct all caregivers to wear gloves when discarding urine for 24 hr after the procedure. Wash gloved hands with soap and water before removing gloves. Then wash hands after the gloves are removed.
- Recognize anxiety related to test results, and be supportive of perceived loss of independent function. Discuss the implications of abnormal test results on the patient's lifestyle. Provide teaching and information regarding the clinical implications of the test results, as appropriate.
- Reinforce information given by the patient's HCP regarding further testing, treatment, or referral to another HCP. Answer any questions or address any concerns voiced by the patient or family.
- Depending on the results of this procedure, additional testing may be needed to evaluate or monitor progression of the disease process and determine the need for a change in therapy. Evaluate test results in relation to the patient's symptoms and other tests performed.

RELATED MONOGRAPHS:

- Related tests include calcitonin, calcium, CT thoracic and MRI chest, PTH, phosphorus, US thyroid and parathyroid, and vitamin D.
- Refer to the Endocrine System table at the end of the book for related tests by body system.

P

Partial Thromboplastin Time, Activated

SYNONYM/ACRONYM: aPTT, APTT.

COMMON USE: To assist in assessing coagulation disorders and monitor the effectiveness of therapeutic interventions.

SPECIMEN: Plasma (1 mL) collected in a completely filled blue-top (3.2% sodium citrate) tube. If the patient's hematocrit exceeds 55%, the volume of citrate in the collection tube must be adjusted.

NORMAL FINDINGS: (Method: Clot detection) 25 to 35 sec. The aPTT is normally prolonged in infants, up to 55 sec, and gradually decreases to the adult range by age 6 mo. Reference ranges vary with respect to the equipment and reagents used to perform the assay.

DESCRIPTION: The activated partial thromboplastin time (aPTT) coagulation test evaluates the function of the intrinsic (factors XII, XI, IX, and VIII) and common (factors V, X, II, and I) pathways of the coagulation sequence, specifically the intrinsic thromboplastin system. It represents the time required for a firm fibrin clot to form after tissue thromboplastin or phospholipid reagents similar to thromboplastin and calcium are added to the specimen. The aPTT is abnormal in 90% of patients with coagulation disorders and is useful in monitoring the inactivation of factor II effect of heparin therapy. The test is prolonged when there is a 30% to 40% deficiency in one of the factors required or when factor inhibitors (e.g., antithrombin III, protein C, or protein S) are present. The aPTT has additional activators, such as kaolin, celite, or elegiac acid, that more rapidly activate factor XII, making this test faster and more reliably reproducible than the partial thromboplastin time (PTT). The aPTT and prothrombin time (PT) tests assist in identifying the cause of bleeding or as preoperative tests to identify coagulation defects. A comparison between the results of aPTT and PT tests can allow some inferences to be made that a factor deficiency exists. A normal aPTT with a prolonged PT can occur only with factor VII deficiency. A prolonged aPTT with a normal PT could indicate a deficiency in factors XII, XI, IX, VIII, and VIII:C (von Willebrand factor). Factor deficiencies can also be identified by correction or substitution studies using normal serum. These studies are easy to perform and are accomplished by adding plasma from a healthy patient to a sample from a patient suspected to be factor deficient. When the aPTT is repeated and is corrected, or is within the reference range, it can be assumed that the prolonged aPTT is caused by a factor deficiency. If the result remains uncorrected, the prolonged aPTT is most likely due to a circulating anticoagulant. The administration of prophylactic low-dose heparin does not require serial monitoring of aPTT. (For more information on factor deficiencies, see monograph titled "Fibrinogen.")

INDICATIONS

- Detect congenital deficiencies in clotting factors, as seen in diseases such as hemophilia A (factor VIII) and hemophilia B (factor IX)
- Evaluate response to anticoagulant therapy with heparin or coumarin derivatives
- Identify individuals who may be prone to bleeding during surgical, obstetric, dental, or invasive diagnostic procedures
- Identify the possible cause of abnormal bleeding, such as epistaxis, hematoma, gingival bleeding, hematuria, and menorrhagia
- Monitor the hemostatic effects of conditions such as liver disease, protein deficiency, and fat malabsorption

P

POTENTIAL DIAGNOSIS

Prolonged in

- Afibrinogenemia *(related to insufficient levels of fibrinogen, which is required for clotting)*
- Circulating anticoagulants *(related to the presence of coagulation factor inhibitors, e.g., developed from long-term factor VIII therapy, or circulating anticoagulants associated with conditions like tuberculosis, systemic lupus erythematosus, rheumatoid arthritis, and chronic glomerulonephritis)*
- Circulating products of fibrin and fibrinogen degradation *(related to the presence of circulating breakdown products of fibrin)*
- Disseminated intravascular coagulation *(related to increased consumption of clotting factors)*
- Factor deficiencies *(related to insufficient levels of coagulation factors)*
- Hemodialysis patients *(related to the anticoagulant effect of heparin)*
- Severe liver disease *(insufficient production of clotting factors related to liver damage)*
- Vitamin K deficiency *(related to insufficient vitamin K levels required for clotting)*
- Von Willebrand's disease *(related to a congenital deficiency of clotting factors)*

CRITICAL FINDINGS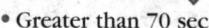

- Greater than 70 sec

Note and immediately report to the health-care provider (HCP) any critically increased values and related symptoms. Timely notification of critical values for lab or diagnostic studies is a role expectation of the professional nurse. Notification processes will vary among facilities. Upon receipt of the critical value the information should be read back to the caller to verify accuracy. Most policies require immediate notification of the primary HCP, hospitalist, or on-call HCP. Reported information includes the patient's name, unique identifiers, critical value, name of the person giving the report, and name of the person receiving the report. Documentation of notification should be made in the medical record with the name of the HCP notified, time and date of notification, and any orders received. Any delay in a timely report of a critical value may require completion of a notification form with review by Risk Management.

Important signs to note are prolonged bleeding from cuts or gums, hematoma at a puncture site, hemorrhage, blood in the stool, persistent epistaxis, heavy or prolonged menstrual flow, and shock. Monitor vital signs, unusual ecchymosis, occult blood, severe headache, unusual dizziness, and neurological changes until aPTT is within normal range.

INTERFERING FACTORS

- Drugs and vitamins such as anistreplase, antihistamines, chlorpromazine, salicylates, and ascorbic acid may cause prolonged aPTT.
- Anticoagulant therapy with heparin will prolong the aPTT.
- Copper is a component of factor V, and severe copper deficiencies may result in prolonged aPTT values.
- Traumatic venipunctures can activate the coagulation sequence by contamination of the sample with tissue thromboplastin and can produce falsely shortened results.
- Failure to fill the tube sufficiently to yield a proper blood-to-anticoagulant ratio invalidates the results and is reason for specimen rejection.
- Excessive agitation that causes sample hemolysis can falsely shorten the aPTT because the hemolyzed cells activate plasma-clotting factors.
- Inadequate mixing of the tube can produce erroneous results.

- Specimens left unprocessed for longer than 24 hr should be rejected for analysis.
- High platelet count or inadequate centrifugation will result in decreased values.
- Hematocrit greater than 55% may cause falsely prolonged results because of anticoagulant excess relative to plasma volume.
- Incompletely filled collection tubes, specimens contaminated with heparin, clotted specimens, or unprocessed specimens not delivered to the laboratory within 1 to 2 hr of collection should be rejected.

NURSING IMPLICATIONS AND PROCEDURE

PRETEST:

▸ Positively identify the patient using at least two unique identifiers before providing care, treatment, or services.

▸ *Patient Teaching:* Inform the patient this test can assist in evaluating the effectiveness of blood clotting.

▸ Obtain a history of the patient's complaints, including a list of known allergens, especially allergies or sensitivities to latex.

▸ Obtain a history of the patient's hematopoietic and hepatobiliary systems, especially any bleeding disorders and other symptoms, as well as results of previously performed laboratory tests and diagnostic and surgical procedures.

▸ Obtain a list of the patient's current medications, including anticoagulants, aspirin and other salicylates, herbs, nutritional supplements, and nutraceuticals (see Appendix F). Such products should be discontinued by medical direction for the appropriate number of days prior to a surgical procedure. If the patient is receiving anticoagulant therapy, note the time and amount of the last dose.

▸ Review the procedure with the patient. Inform the patient that specimen collection takes approximately 5 to 10 min. Address concerns about pain and explain there may be some discomfort during the venipuncture.

▸ *Sensitivity to social and cultural issues,* as well as concern for modesty, is important in providing psychological support before, during, and after the procedure. There are no food, fluid, or medication restrictions unless by medical direction.

INTRATEST:

▸ If the patient has a history of allergic reaction to latex, avoid the use of equipment containing latex.

▸ Instruct the patient to cooperate fully and to follow directions. Direct the patient to breathe normally and to avoid unnecessary movement.

▸ Observe standard precautions, and follow the general guidelines in Appendix A. Positively identify the patient, and label the appropriate specimen container with the corresponding patient demographics, initials of the person collecting the specimen, date, and time of collection. Perform a venipuncture. Fill tube completely. *Important note:* Two different concentrations of sodium citrate preservative are currently added to blue-top tubes for coagulation studies: 3.2% and 3.8%. The Clinical and Laboratory Standards Institute (CLSI; formerly the National Committee for Clinical Laboratory Standards [NCCLS]) guideline for sodium citrate is 3.2%. Laboratories establish reference ranges for coagulation testing based on numerous factors, including sodium citrate concentration, test equipment, and test reagents. It is important to ask the laboratory which concentration it recommends, because each concentration will have its own specific reference range. When multiple specimens are drawn, the blue-top tube should be collected after sterile (i.e., blood culture) tubes. Otherwise, when using a standard vacutainer system, the blue-top tube is the first tube collected. When a butterfly is used and due to the added tubing, an extra red-top tube should be collected before the blue-top tube to ensure complete filling of the blue-top tube.

▸ Remove the needle and apply direct pressure with dry gauze to stop bleeding. Observe/assess venipuncture site for bleeding or hematoma formation and secure gauze with adhesive bandage.

P

Promptly transport the specimen to the laboratory for processing and analysis. If delays in specimen transport and processing occur, it is important to consult with the testing laboratory. Whole blood specimens are stable at room temperature for up to 24 hr. Specimen stability requirements may also vary if the patient is receiving heparin therapy. Some laboratories require frozen plasma if testing will not be performed within 1 hr of collection. Criteria for rejection of specimens based on collection time may vary among facilities.

If the patient has a known hematocrit above 55%, adjust the amount of anticoagulant in the collection tube before drawing the blood according to the CLSI guidelines:

Anticoagulant vol. [x] = (100 − hematocrit) / (595 − hematocrit) × total vol. of anticoagulated blood required

Example:

Patient hematocrit = 60% = [(100 − 60) / (595 − 60) × 5.0] = 0.37 mL sodium citrate for a 5-mL standard drawing tube

POST-TEST:

A report of the results will be made available to the requesting HCP, who will discuss the results with the patient.

Instruct the patient to report severe bruising or bleeding from any areas of the skin or mucous membranes.

Inform the patient with prolonged aPTT values of the importance of taking precautions against bruising and bleeding, including the use of a soft bristle toothbrush, use of an electric razor, avoidance of constipation, avoidance of acetylsalicylic acid and similar products, and avoidance of intramuscular injections.

Inform the patient of the importance of periodic laboratory testing while taking an anticoagulant.

Reinforce information given by the patient's HCP regarding further testing, treatment, or referral to another HCP. Answer any questions or address any concerns voiced by the patient or family.

Depending on the results of this procedure, additional testing may be performed to evaluate or monitor progression of the disease process and determine the need for a change in therapy. Evaluate test results in relation to the patient's symptoms and other tests performed.

RELATED MONOGRAPHS:

Related tests include antithrombin III, bleeding time, coagulation factors, CBC, CBC platelet count, copper, D-dimer, FDP, plasminogen, protein C, protein S, PT/INR, and vitamin K.

Refer to the Hematopoietic and Hepatobiliary systems tables at the end of the book for related tests by body system.

P

Parvovirus B19 Immunoglobulin G and Immunoglobulin M Antibodies

SYNONYM/ACRONYM: N/A.

COMMON USE: To assist in confirming a diagnosis of a present or past parvovirus infection.

SPECIMEN: Serum (2 mL) collected in a red- or tiger-top tube.

NORMAL FINDINGS: (Method: Immunoassay)

Negative	Less than 0.8 index
Equivocal	0.8–1.2 index

DESCRIPTION: Parvovirus B19, a single-stranded DNA virus transmitted by respiratory secretions, is the only parvovirus known to infect humans. Its primary site of replication is in red blood cell precursors in the bone marrow. It is capable of causing disease along a wide spectrum ranging from a self-limited erythema (fifth disease) to bone marrow failure or aplastic crisis in patients with sickle cell anemia, spherocytosis, or thalassemia. Fetal hydrops and spontaneous abortion may also occur as a result of infection during pregnancy. The incubation period is approximately 1 wk after exposure. B19-specific antibodies appear in the serum approximately 3 days after the onset of symptoms. The presence of immunoglobulin M (IgM) antibodies indicates acute infection. The presence of immunoglobulin G (IgG) antibodies indicates past infection and is believed to confer lifelong immunity. Parvovirus B19 can also be detected by DNA hybridization using a polymerase chain reaction (PCR) method.

INDICATIONS
• Assist in establishing a diagnosis of parvovirus B19 infection

POTENTIAL DIAGNOSIS

Positive findings in
Parvovirus infection can be evidenced in a variety of conditions.

• Arthritis
• Erythema infectiosum (fifth disease)
• Erythrocyte aplasia
• Hydrops fetalis

Negative findings in: N/A

CRITICAL FINDINGS: N/A

INTERFERING FACTORS
• Immunocompromised patients may not develop sufficient antibody to be detected.

NURSING IMPLICATIONS AND PROCEDURE

PRETEST:

▶ Positively identify the patient using at least two unique identifiers before providing care, treatment, or services.
▶ *Patient Teaching:* Inform the patient this test can assist in diagnosing a viral infection.
▶ Obtain a history of the patient's complaints, including a list of known allergens, especially allergies or sensitivities to latex.
▶ Obtain a history of the patient's immune system, symptoms, and results of previously performed laboratory tests and diagnostic and surgical procedures.
▶ Obtain a list of the patient's current medications, including herbs, nutritional supplements, and nutraceuticals (see Appendix F).
▶ Review the procedure with the patient. Inform the patient that specimen collection takes approximately 5 to 10 min. Inform the patient that a subsequent sample will be required in 7 to 14 days. Address concerns about pain and explain that there may be some discomfort during the venipuncture.
▶ *Sensitivity to social and cultural issues,* as well as concern for modesty, is important in providing psychological support before, during, and after the procedure.
▶ There are no food, fluid, or medication restrictions unless by medical direction.

INTRATEST:

▶ If the patient has a history of allergic reaction to latex, avoid the use of equipment containing latex.

P

Instruct the patient to cooperate fully and to follow directions. Direct the patient to breathe normally and to avoid unnecessary movement.

Observe standard precautions, and follow the general guidelines in Appendix A. Positively identify the patient, and label the appropriate specimen container with the corresponding patient demographics, initials of the person collecting the specimen, date, and time of collection. Perform a venipuncture.

Remove the needle and apply direct pressure with dry gauze to stop bleeding. Observe/assess venipuncture site for bleeding or hematoma formation and secure gauze with adhesive bandage.

Promptly transport the specimen to the laboratory for processing and analysis.

POST-TEST:

A report of the results will be made available to the requesting health-care provider (HCP), who will discuss the results with the patient.

Recognize anxiety related to test results, and be supportive of impaired activity related to lack of neuromuscular control, perceived loss of independence, and fear of shortened life expectancy. Discuss the implications of abnormal test results on the patient's lifestyle. Provide teaching and information regarding the clinical implications of the test results, as appropriate. Educate the patient regarding access to counseling services.

Reinforce information given by the patient's HCP regarding further testing, treatment, or referral to another HCP. Emphasize the need for the patient to return to have a convalescent blood sample taken in 7 to 14 days. Answer any questions or address any concerns voiced by the patient or family.

Depending on the results of this procedure, additional testing may be performed to evaluate or monitor progression of the disease process and determine the need for a change in therapy. Evaluate test results in relation to the patient's symptoms and other tests performed.

RELATED MONOGRAPHS:

Related tests include CBC, CBC RBC morphology, and CBC WBC count and differential.

Refer to the Immune System table at the end of the book for related tests by body system.

Pericardial Fluid Analysis

SYNONYM/ACRONYM: None.

COMMON USE: To evaluate and classify the type of fluid between the pericardium membranes to assist with diagnosis of infection or fluid balance disorder.

SPECIMEN: Pericardial fluid (5 mL) collected in a red- or green-top (heparin) tube for glucose, a lavender-top (EDTA) tube for cell count, and sterile containers for microbiology specimens; 200 to 500 mL of fluid in a clear container for cytology. Ensure that there is an equal amount of fixative and fluid in the container for cytology.

NORMAL FINDINGS: (Method: Spectrophotometry for glucose; automated or manual cell count, macroscopic examination of cultured organisms, and microscopic examination of specimen for microbiology and cytology; microscopic examination of cultured microorganisms)

Pericardial Fluid	Reference Value
Appearance	Clear
Color	Pale yellow
Glucose	Parallels serum values
Red blood cell count	None seen
White blood cell count	Less than 300/mm³
Culture	No growth
Gram stain	No organisms seen
Cytology	No abnormal cells seen

DESCRIPTION: The heart is located within a protective membrane called the *pericardium*. The fluid between the pericardial membranes is called *serous fluid*. Normally only a small amount of fluid is present because the rates of fluid production and absorption are about the same. Many abnormal conditions can result in the buildup of fluid within the pericardium. Specific tests are usually ordered in addition to a common battery of tests used to distinguish a transudate from an exudate. *Transudates* are effusions that form as a result of a systemic disorder that disrupts the regulation of fluid balance, such as a suspected perforation. *Exudates* are caused by conditions involving the tissue of the membrane itself, such as an infection or malignancy. Fluid is withdrawn from the pericardium by needle aspiration and tested as listed in the previous and following tables.

Characteristic	Transudate	Exudate
Appearance	Clear	Cloudy or turbid
Specific gravity	Less than 1.015	Greater than 1.015
Total protein	Less than 2.5 g/dL	Greater than 3.0 g/dL
Fluid-to-serum protein ratio	Less than 0.5	Greater than 0.5
LDH	Parallels serum value	Less than 200 units/L
Fluid-to-serum LDH ratio	Less than 0.6	Greater than 0.6
Fluid cholesterol	Less than 55 mg/dL	Greater than 55 mg/dL
White blood cell count	Less than 100/mm³	Greater than 1,000/mm³

LDH = lactate dehydrogenase.

INDICATIONS

- Evaluate effusion of unknown etiology
- Investigate suspected hemorrhage, immune disease, malignancy, or infection

POTENTIAL DIAGNOSIS

Increased in
Condition/Test Showing Increased Result

- Bacterial pericarditis (red blood cell [RBC] count, white blood cell

[WBC] count with a predominance of neutrophils)
- Hemorrhagic pericarditis (RBC count, WBC count)
- Malignancy (RBC count, abnormal cytology)
- Post–myocardial infarction syndrome, also called Dressler's syndrome (RBC count, WBC count with a predominance of neutrophils)
- Rheumatoid disease or systemic lupus erythematosus (SLE) (RBC count, WBC count)
- Tuberculous or fungal pericarditis (RBC count, WBC count with a predominance of lymphocytes)
- Viral pericarditis (RBC count, WBC count with a predominance of neutrophils)

Decreased in

Condition/Test Showing Decreased Result

- Bacterial pericarditis (glucose)
- Malignancy (glucose)
- Rheumatoid disease or SLE (glucose)

CRITICAL FINDINGS

Positive culture findings in any sterile body fluid.

Note and immediately report to the health-care provider (HCP) positive culture results, if ordered, and related symptoms. Timely notification of critical values for lab or diagnostic studies is a role expectation of the professional nurse. Notification processes will vary among facilities. Upon receipt of the critical value the information should be read back to the caller to verify accuracy. Most policies require immediate notification of the primary HCP, hospitalist, or on-call HCP. Reported information includes the patient's name, unique identifiers, critical value, name of the person giving the report, and name of the person receiving the report. Documentation of notification should be made in the medical record with the name of the HCP notified, time and date of notification, and any orders received. Any delay in a timely report of a critical value may require completion of a notification form with review by Risk Management.

INTERFERING FACTORS
- Bloody fluid may be the result of a traumatic tap.
- Unknown hyperglycemia or hypoglycemia may be misleading in the comparison of fluid and serum glucose levels. Therefore, it is advisable to collect comparative serum samples a few hours before performing pericardiocentesis.
- Failure to follow dietary restrictions before the procedure may cause the procedure to be canceled or repeated.

NURSING IMPLICATIONS AND PROCEDURE

PRETEST:

- Positively identify the patient using at least two unique identifiers before providing care, treatment, or services.
- *Patient Teaching:* Inform the patient this procedure can assist with evaluating fluid around the heart.
- Obtain a history of the patient's complaints, including a list of known allergens, especially allergies or sensitivities to latex.
- Obtain a history of the patient's cardiovascular and immune system, especially any bleeding disorders and other symptoms, as well as results of previously performed laboratory tests and diagnostic and surgical procedures.
- Note any recent procedures that can interfere with test results.
- Record the date of the last menstrual period and determine the possibility of pregnancy in perimenopausal women.

Obtain a list of the patient's current medications, including anticoagulants, aspirin and other salicylates, herbs, nutritional supplements, and nutraceuticals (see Appendix F). Such products should be discontinued by medical direction for the appropriate number of days prior to the surgical procedure.

Review the procedure with the patient. Inform the patient that it may be necessary to remove hair from the site before the procedure. Address concerns about pain and explain that a sedative and/or analgesia will be administered to promote relaxation and reduce discomfort prior to needle insertion through the chest wall. Explain that any discomfort with the needle insertion will be minimized with local anesthetics and systemic analgesics. Explain that the anesthetic injection may cause a stinging sensation. Explain that after the skin has been anesthetized, a large needle will be inserted through the chest to obtain the fluid. Inform the patient that specimen collection is performed by an HCP specializing in this procedure and usually takes approximately 30 min to complete.

Explain that an IV line will be inserted to allow infusion of IV fluids, antibiotics, anesthetics, and analgesics.

Sensitivity to social and cultural issues, as well as concern for modesty, is important in providing psychological support before, during, and after the procedure.

Food and fluids should be restricted for 6 to 8 hr before the procedure, as directed by the HCP, unless the procedure is performed in an emergency situation to correct pericarditis. The requesting HCP may request that anticoagulants and aspirin be withheld. The number of days to withhold medication is dependent on the type of anticoagulant. Protocols may vary among facilities.

Make sure a written and informed consent has been signed prior to the procedure and before administering any medications.

INTRATEST:

Ensure that the patient has complied with dietary and fluids restrictions; assure that food and fluids have been restricted for at least 6 to 8 hr prior to the procedure.

Ensure that anticoagulant therapy has been withheld for the appropriate number of days prior to the procedure. Notify the HCP if patient anticoagulant therapy has not been withheld.

Have emergency equipment readily available.

Have the patient void before the procedure.

Have the patient remove clothes above the waist and put on a gown.

If the patient has a history of allergic reaction to latex, avoid the use of equipment containing latex.

Instruct the patient to cooperate fully and to follow directions. Direct the patient to breathe normally and to avoid unnecessary movement during the local anesthetic and the procedure.

Record baseline vital signs, and continue to monitor throughout the procedure. Protocols may vary among facilities.

Observe standard precautions, and follow the general guidelines in Appendix A. Positively identify the patient, and label the appropriate specimen container with the corresponding patient demographics, initials of the person collecting the specimen, date and time of collection, and site location.

Establish an IV line to allow infusion of IV fluids, anesthetics, analgesics, or IV sedation.

Assist the patient into a comfortable supine position with the head elevated 45° to 60°.

Prior to the administration of local anesthesia, clip hair from the site as needed, cleanse the site with an antiseptic solution, and drape the area with sterile towels. The skin at the injection site is then anesthetized.

The precordial (V) cardiac lead wire is attached to the cardiac needle with an alligator clip. The cardiac needle is inserted just below and to the left of the breastbone, and fluid is removed.

P

▶ Monitor vital signs every 15 min for signs of hypovolemia or shock. Monitor electrocardiogram for needle-tip positioning to indicate accidental puncture of the right atrium.

▶ The needle is withdrawn, and slight pressure is applied to the site. Apply a sterile dressing to the site.

▶ Monitor the patient for complications related to the procedure (e.g., allergic reaction, anaphylaxis).

▶ Place samples in properly labeled specimen containers, and promptly transport the specimens to the laboratory for processing and analysis.

POST-TEST:

▶ A report of the results will be made available to the requesting HCP, who will discuss the results with the patient.

▶ Instruct the patient to resume usual diet and medications, as directed by the HCP.

▶ Monitor vital signs and cardiac status every 15 min for the first hour, every 30 min for the next 2 hr, every hr for the next 4 hr, and every 4 hr for the next 24 hr. Take the patient's temperature every 4 hr for 24 hr. Monitor intake and output for 24 hr. Notify the HCP if temperature is elevated. Protocols may vary among facilities.

▶ Observe/assess the patient for signs of respiratory and cardiac distress, such as shortness of breath, cyanosis, or rapid pulse.

▶ Continue IV fluids until vital signs are stable and the patient can resume fluid intake independently.

▶ Inform the patient that 1 hr or more of bed rest is required after the procedure.

▶ Observe/assess the puncture site for bleeding or drainage and signs of inflammation each time vital signs are taken and daily thereafter for several days. Report to HCP if bleeding is present.

▶ Observe/assess for nausea and pain. Administer antiemetic and analgesic medications as needed and as directed by the HCP.

▶ Administer antibiotics, as ordered, and instruct the patient in the importance of completing the entire course of antibiotic therapy even if no symptoms are present.

▶ Recognize anxiety related to test results, and offer support. Discuss the implications of abnormal test results on the patient's lifestyle. Provide teaching and information regarding the clinical implications of the test results, as appropriate. Educate the patient regarding access to counseling services, if appropriate.

▶ Reinforce information given by the patient's HCP regarding further testing, treatment, or referral to another HCP. Answer any questions or address any concerns voiced by the patient or family.

▶ Depending on the results of this procedure, additional testing may be performed to evaluate or monitor progression of the disease process and determine the need for a change in therapy. Evaluate test results in relation to the patient's symptoms and other tests performed.

RELATED MONOGRAPHS:

▶ Related tests include AST, atrial natriuretic peptide, blood gases, B-type natriuretic peptide, cancer antigens, chest x-ray, CBC WBC count and differential, CK and isoenzymes, culture and smear mycobacteria, culture blood, culture fungal, culture viral, ECG, echocardiography, α_1-fetoprotein, homocysteine, LDH and isoenzymes, magnesium, MRI chest, MI scan, myoglobin, and troponin.

▶ Refer to the Cardiovascular and Immune systems tables at the end of the book for related tests by body system.

Peritoneal Fluid Analysis

SYNONYM/ACRONYM: Ascites fluid analysis.

COMMON USE: To evaluate and classify the type of fluid within the peritoneal cavity to assist with diagnosis of cancer, infection, necrosis, and perforation.

SPECIMEN: Peritoneal fluid (5 mL) collected in a red- or green-top (heparin) tube for amylase, glucose, and alkaline phosphatase; lavender-top (EDTA) tube for cell count; sterile containers for microbiology specimens; 200 to 500 mL of fluid in a clear container with anticoagulant for cytology. Ensure that there is an equal amount of fixative and fluid in the container for cytology.

NORMAL FINDINGS: (Method: Spectrophotometry for glucose, amylase, and alkaline phosphatase; automated or manual cell count, macroscopic examination of cultured organisms, and microscopic examination of specimen for microbiology and cytology; microscopic examination of cultured microorganisms)

Peritoneal Fluid	Reference Value
Appearance	Clear
Color	Pale yellow
Amylase	Parallels serum values
Alkaline phosphatase	Parallels serum values
CEA	Parallels serum values
Glucose	Parallels serum values
Red blood cell count	Less than 100,000/mm^3
White blood cell count	Less than 300/mm^3
Culture	No growth
Acid-fast stain	No organisms seen
Gram stain	No organisms seen
Cytology	No abnormal cells seen

DESCRIPTION: The peritoneal cavity and organs within it are lined with a protective membrane. The fluid between the membranes is called *serous fluid*. Normally only a small amount of fluid is present because the rates of fluid production and absorption are about the same. Many abnormal conditions can result in the buildup of fluid within the peritoneal cavity. Specific tests are usually ordered in addition to a common battery of tests used to distinguish a transudate from an exudate. *Transudates* are effusions that form as a result of a systemic disorder that disrupts the regulation of fluid balance, such as a suspected perforation. *Exudates* are caused by conditions involving the tissue of the membrane itself, such as an infection or malignancy. Fluid is withdrawn from the peritoneal cavity by needle aspiration and tested as listed in the previous and following tables.

P

INDICATIONS

* Evaluate ascites of unknown cause
* Investigate suspected peritoneal rupture, perforation, malignancy, or infection

Characteristic	Transudate	Exudate
Appearance	Clear	Cloudy or turbid
Specific gravity	Less than 1.015	Greater than 1.015
Total protein	Less than 2.5 g/dL	Greater than 3.0 g/dL
Fluid-to-serum protein ratio	Less than 0.5	Greater than 0.5
LDH	Parallels serum value	Less than 200 units/L
Fluid-to-serum LDH ratio	Less than 0.6	Greater than 0.6
Fluid cholesterol	Less than 55 mg/dL	Greater than 55 mg/dL
White blood cell count	Less than 100/mm³	Greater than 1,000/mm³

LDH = lactate dehydrogenase.

POTENTIAL DIAGNOSIS

Increased in

Condition/Test Showing Increased Result

* Abdominal malignancy (red blood cell [RBC] count, carcinoembryonic antigen, abnormal cytology)
* Abdominal trauma (RBC count greater than 100,000/mm³)
* Ascites caused by cirrhosis (white blood cell [WBC] count, neutrophils greater than 25% but less than 50%, absolute granulocyte count greater than 250/mm³)
* Bacterial peritonitis (WBC count, neutrophils greater than 50%, absolute granulocyte count greater than 250/mm³)
* Peritoneal effusion due to gastric strangulation, perforation, or necrosis (amylase, ammonia, alkaline phosphatase)
* Peritoneal effusion due to pancreatitis, pancreatic trauma, or pancreatic pseudocyst (amylase)
* Rupture or perforation of urinary bladder (ammonia, creatinine, urea)
* Tuberculous effusion (elevated lymphocyte count, positive acid-fast bacillus smear and culture [25% to 50% of cases])

Decreased in

Condition/Test Showing Decreased Result

* Abdominal malignancy (glucose)
* Tuberculous effusion (glucose)

CRITICAL FINDINGS

Positive culture findings in any sterile body fluid.

Note and immediately report to the health-care provider (HCP) positive culture results, if ordered, and related symptoms. Timely notification of critical values for lab or diagnostic studies is a role expectation of the professional nurse. Notification processes will vary among facilities. Upon receipt of the critical value the information should be read back to the caller to verify accuracy. Most policies require immediate notification of the primary HCP, Hospitalist, or on-call HCP. Reported information includes the patient's name, unique identifiers, critical value, name of the person giving the report, and name of the person receiving the report. Documentation of notification should be made in the medical record with the name of the HCP notified, time and date of notification, and any orders received. Any delay in a timely report of a critical value may require completion of a notification form with review by Risk Management.

INTERFERING FACTORS

- Bloody fluids may result from a traumatic tap.
- Unknown hyperglycemia or hypoglycemia may be misleading in the comparison of fluid and serum glucose levels. Therefore, it is advisable to collect comparative serum samples a few hours before performing paracentesis.

NURSING IMPLICATIONS AND PROCEDURE

PRETEST:

Positively identify the patient using at least two unique identifiers before providing care, treatment, or services.

Patient Teaching: Inform the patient this procedure can assist with evaluation of fluid surrounding the abdominal organs.

Obtain a history of the patient's complaints, including a list of known allergens, especially allergies or sensitivities to latex.

Obtain a history of the patient's gastrointestinal and immune system, especially any bleeding disorders and other symptoms, as well as results of previously performed laboratory tests and diagnostic and surgical procedures. Note any recent procedures that can interfere with test results.

Record the date of the last menstrual period and determine the possibility of pregnancy in perimenopausal women.

Obtain a list of the patient's current medications, including anticoagulants, aspirin and other salicylates, herbs, nutritional supplements, and nutraceuticals (see Appendix F). Such products should be discontinued by medical direction for the appropriate number of days prior to a surgical procedure.

Review the procedure with the patient. If patient has ascites, obtain weight and measure abdominal girth. Inform the patient that it may be necessary to remove hair from the site before the procedure. Address concerns about pain and explain that a sedative and/or analgesia will be administered to promote relaxation and reduce discomfort prior to needle insertion through the abdomen wall. Explain that any discomfort with the needle insertion will be minimized with local anesthetics and systemic analgesics. Explain that the anesthetic injection may cause an initial stinging sensation. Explain that after the skin has been anesthetized, a large needle will be inserted through the abdominal wall and a "popping" sensation may be experienced as the needle penetrates the peritoneum. Inform the patient that specimen collection is performed under sterile conditions by an HCP specializing in this procedure and usually takes approximately 30 min to complete. Explain that an IV line will be inserted to allow infusion of IV fluids, antibiotics, anesthetics, and analgesics.

Sensitivity to social and cultural issues, as well as concern for modesty, is important in providing psychological support before, during, and after the procedure.

There are no food or fluid restrictions unless by medical direction. The requesting HCP may request that anticoagulants and aspirin be withheld. The number of days to withhold medication is dependent on the type of anticoagulant.

Make sure a written and informed consent has been signed prior to the procedure and before administering any medications.

INTRATEST:

Ensure that anticoagulant therapy has been withheld for the appropriate number of days prior to the procedure. Notify the HCP if patient anticoagulant therapy has not been withheld.

Have emergency equipment readily available.

Have the patient void, or catheterize the patient to avoid accidental puncture of the bladder if he or she is unable to void.

Have the patient remove clothing and change into a gown for the procedure.

If the patient has a history of allergic reaction to latex, avoid the use of equipment containing latex.

Instruct the patient to cooperate fully and to follow directions. Direct the patient to breathe normally and to avoid unnecessary movement during the local anesthetic and the procedure.

Observe standard precautions, and follow the general guidelines in Appendix A. Positively identify the patient, and label the appropriate specimen container with the corresponding patient demographics, initials of the person collecting the specimen, date and time of collection, and site location.

▶ Record baseline vital signs and continue to monitor throughout the procedure. Protocols may vary among facilities.

▶ Establish an IV line to allow infusion of IV fluids, anesthetics, analgesics, or IV sedation.

▶ Assist the patient to a comfortable seated position with feet and back supported or in high Fowler's position. Prior to the administration of local anesthesia, clip hair from the site as needed, cleanse the site with an antiseptic solution, and drape the area with sterile towels. The skin at the injection site is then anesthetized.

▶ The paracentesis needle is inserted 1 to 2 in. below the umbilicus, and fluid is removed. If lavage fluid is required (helpful if malignancy is suspected), saline or Ringer's lactate can be infused via the needle over a 15- to 20-min period before the lavage fluid is removed. Monitor vital signs every 15 min for signs of hypovolemia or shock.

▶ No more than 1,500 to 2,000 mL of fluid should be removed at a time, even in the case of a therapeutic paracentesis, because of the risk of hypovolemia and shock.

▶ The needle is withdrawn, and slight pressure is applied to the site. Apply a sterile dressing to the site.

▶ Monitor the patient for complications related to the procedure (e.g., allergic reaction, anaphylaxis).

▶ Place samples in properly labeled specimen containers, and promptly transport the specimens to the laboratory for processing and analysis.

POST-TEST:

▶ A report of the results will be made available to the requesting HCP, who will discuss the results with the patient.

▶ Instruct the patient to resume usual medications, as directed by the HCP.

▶ Monitor vital signs every 15 min for the first hr, every 30 min for the next 2 hr, every hour for the next 4 hr, and every 4 hr for the next 24 hr. Take the patient's temperature every 4 hr for 24 hr. Monitor intake and output for 24 hr. Notify the HCP if temperature is elevated. Protocols may vary among facilities.

▶ Observe/assess the puncture site for bleeding or drainage and signs of inflammation each time vital signs are taken and daily thereafter for several days. Report to the HCP if bleeding is present.

▶ If a large amount of fluid was removed, obtain weight and measure abdominal girth.

▶ Inform the patient that 1 hr or more of bed rest is required after the procedure.

▶ Instruct the patient to immediately report severe abdominal pain. (*Note:* Rigidity of abdominal muscles indicates developing peritonitis.) Report to HCP if abdominal rigidity or pain is present.

▶ Observe/assess for nausea and pain. Administer antiemetic and analgesic medications as needed and as directed by the HCP.

▶ Administer antibiotics, as ordered, and instruct the patient in the importance of completing the entire course of antibiotic therapy even if no symptoms are present.

▶ Recognize anxiety related to test results, and offer support. Discuss the implications of abnormal test results on the patient's lifestyle. Provide teaching and information regarding the clinical implications of the test results, as appropriate. Educate the patient regarding access to counseling services, if appropriate.

▶ Reinforce information given by the patient's HCP regarding further testing, treatment, or referral to another HCP. Answer any questions or address any concerns voiced by the patient or family.

▶ Depending on the results of this procedure, additional testing may be performed to evaluate or monitor progression of the disease process and determine the need for a change in therapy. Evaluate test results in relation to the patient's symptoms and other tests performed.

RELATED MONOGRAPHS:

▶ Related tests include cancer antigens, CBC, CBC WBC count and differential, CT abdomen, CT biliary tract and liver, culture and smear mycobacteria, culture blood, culture fungal, culture viral, KUB studies, laparoscopy abdominal, liver and spleen scan, MRI abdomen, US abdomen, and US spleen.

▶ Refer to the Gastrointestinal and Immune systems tables at the end of the book for related tests by body system.

Phosphorus, Blood

SYNONYM/ACRONYM: Inorganic phosphorus, phosphate, PO_4.

COMMON USE: To assist in evaluating multiple body system functions by monitoring phosphorus levels in relation to other electrolytes. Used specifically to evaluate renal function in at-risk patients.

SPECIMEN: Serum (1 mL) collected in a red- or tiger-top tube. Plasma (1 mL) collected in green-top (heparin) tube is also acceptable.

NORMAL FINDINGS: (Method: Spectrophotometry)

Age	Conventional Units	SI Units (Conventional Units × 0.323)
0–5 day	4.6–8 mg/dL	1.5–2.6 mmol/L
1–3 yr	3.9–6.5 mg/dL	1.3–2.1 mmol/L
4–6 yr	4–5.4 mg/dL	1.3–1.7 mmol/L
7–11 yr	3.7–5.6 mg/dL	1.2–1.8 mmol/L
12–13 yr	3.3–5.4 mg/dL	1.1–1.7 mmol/L
14–15 yr	2.9–5.4 mg/dL	0.9–1.7 mmol/L
16–19 yr	2.8–4.6 mg/dL	0.9–1.5 mmol/L
Adult	2.5–4.5 mg/dL	0.8–1.4 mmol/L

Values may be slightly decreased in older adults due to dietary insufficiency or the effects of medications and the presence of multiple chronic or acute diseases with or without muted symptoms.

DESCRIPTION: Phosphorus, in the form of phosphate, is distributed throughout the body. Approximately 85% of the body's phosphorus is stored in bones; the remainder is found in cells and body fluids. It is the major intracellular anion and plays a crucial role in cellular metabolism, maintenance of cellular membranes, and formation of bones and teeth. Phosphorus also indirectly affects the release of oxygen from hemoglobin by affecting the formation of 2,3-bisphosphoglycerate. Levels of phosphorus are dependent on dietary intake.

Phosphorus excretion is regulated by the kidneys. Calcium and phosphorus are interrelated with respect to absorption and metabolic function. They have an inverse relationship with respect to concentration: Serum phosphorus is increased when serum calcium is decreased. Hyperphosphatemia can result in an infant fed only cow's milk during the first few weeks of life because of the combination of a high phosphorus content in cow's milk and the inability of infants' kidneys to clear the excess phosphorus.

INDICATIONS

* Assist in establishing a diagnosis of hyperparathyroidism
* Assist in the evaluation of renal failure

POTENTIAL DIAGNOSIS

Increased in

* Acromegaly *(related to increased renal absorption)*
* Bone metastases *(related to release from bone stores)*
* Diabetic ketoacidosis *(acid-base imbalance causes intracellular phosphorus to move into the extracellular fluid)*
* Excessive levels of vitamin D *(vitamin D promotes intestinal absorption of phosphorus; excessive levels promote phosphorus release from bone stores)*
* Hyperthermia *(tissue damage causes intracellular phosphorus to be released into circulation)*
* Hypocalcemia *(calcium and phosphorus have an inverse relationship)*
* Hypoparathyroidism *(related to increased renal absorption)*
* Lactic acidosis *(acid-base imbalance causes intracellular phosphorus to move into the extracellular fluid)*
* Milk alkali syndrome *(increased dietary intake)*
* Pseudohypoparathyroidism *(related to increased renal absorption)*
* Pulmonary embolism *(related to respiratory acid-base imbalance and compensatory mechanisms)*
* Renal failure *(related to decreased renal excretion)*
* Respiratory acidosis *(acid-base imbalance causes intracellular phosphorus to move into the extracellular fluid)*

Decreased in

* Acute gout *(related to decreased circulating calcium in calcium crystal–induced gout; calcium and phosphorus have an inverse relationship)*
* Alcohol withdrawal *(related to malnutrition)*
* Gram-negative bacterial septicemia
* Growth hormone deficiency
* Hyperalimentation therapy
* Hypercalcemia *(calcium and phosphorus have an inverse relationship)*
* Hyperinsulinism *(insulin increases intracellular movement of phosphorus)*
* Hyperparathyroidism *(parathyroid hormone [PTH] increases renal excretion)*
* Hypokalemia
* Impaired renal absorption *(decreases return of phosphorus to general circulation)*
* Malabsorption syndromes *(related to insufficient intestinal absorption of phosphorus)*
* Malnutrition *(related to deficient intake)*
* Osteomalacia *(evidenced by hypophosphatemia)*
* PTH-producing tumors *(PTH increases renal excretion)*
* Primary hyperparathyroidism *(PTH increases renal excretion)*
* Renal tubular acidosis
* Renal tubular defects *(related to decreased renal absorption)*
* Respiratory alkalosis
* Respiratory infections
* Rickets *(related to vitamin D deficiency)*
* Salicylate poisoning
* Severe burns
* Severe vomiting and diarrhea *(related to excessive loss)*
* Vitamin D deficiency *(related to vitamin D deficiency, which reduces intestinal and renal tubular absorption of phosphorus)*

CRITICAL FINDINGS ◈

Adults

* Less than 1.0 mg/dL (SI: Less than 0.3 mmol/L)

- Greater than 8.9 mg/dL (SI: Greater than 2.9 mmol/L)

Children
- Less than 1.3 mg/dL (SI: Less than 0.4 mmol/L)
- Greater than 8.9 mg/dL (SI: Greater than 2.9 mmol/L)

Note and immediately report to the health-care provider (HCP) any critically increased or decreased values and related symptoms. Timely notification of critical values for lab or diagnostic studies is a role expectation of the professional nurse. Notification processes will vary among facilities. Upon receipt of the critical value the information should be read back to the caller to verify accuracy. Most policies require immediate notification of the primary HCP, hospitalist, or on-call HCP. Reported information includes the patient's name, unique identifiers, critical value, name of the person giving the report, and name of the person receiving the report. Documentation of notification should be made in the medical record with the name of the HCP notified, time and date of notification, and any orders received. Any delay in a timely report of a critical value may require completion of a notification form with review by Risk Management. Interventions including IV replacement therapy with sodium or potassium phosphate may be necessary. Close monitoring of both phosphorus and calcium is important during replacement therapy.

INTERFERING FACTORS

- Drugs that may increase phosphorus levels include anabolic steroids, β-adrenergic blockers, ergocalciferol, furosemide, hydrochlorothiazide, methicillin (occurs with nephrotoxicity), oral contraceptives, parathyroid extract, phosphates, sodium etidronate, tetracycline (occurs with nephrotoxicity), and vitamin D.
- Drugs that may decrease phosphorus levels include acetazolamide, albuterol, aluminum salts, amino acids (via IV hyperalimentation), anesthetic agents, anticonvulsants, calcitonin, epinephrine, fibrin hydrolysate, fructose, glucocorticoids, glucose, insulin, mannitol, oral contraceptives, pamidronate, phenothiazine, phytate, and plicamycin.
- Serum phosphorus levels are subject to diurnal variation: They are highest in late morning and lowest in the evening; therefore, serial samples should be collected at the same time of day for consistency in interpretation.
- Hemolysis will falsely increase phosphorus values.
- Specimens should never be collected above an IV line because of the potential for dilution when the specimen and the IV solution combine in the collection container, thereby falsely decreasing the result. There is also the potential of contaminating the sample with the substance of interest if it is present in the IV solution, thereby falsely increasing the result.

NURSING IMPLICATIONS AND PROCEDURE

PRETEST:

- Positively identify the patient using at least two unique identifiers before providing care, treatment, or services.
- *Patient Teaching:* Inform the patient this test can assist in a general evaluation of body systems.
- Obtain a history of the patient's complaints, including a list of known allergens, especially allergies or sensitivities to latex.
- Obtain a history of the patient's endocrine, gastrointestinal, genitourinary, and musculoskeletal systems;

symptoms; and results of previously performed laboratory tests and diagnostic and surgical procedures.

▶ Obtain a list of the patient's current medications, including herbs, nutritional supplements, and nutraceuticals (see Appendix F).

▶ Review the procedure with the patient. Inform the patient that specimen collection takes approximately 5 to 10 min. Address concerns about pain and explain that there may be some discomfort during the venipuncture.

▶ *Sensitivity to social and cultural issues,* as well as concern for modesty, is important in providing psychological support before, during, and after the procedure.

▶ There are no food, fluid, or medication restrictions unless by medical direction.

INTRATEST:

▶ If the patient has a history of allergic reaction to latex, avoid the use of equipment containing latex.

▶ Instruct the patient to cooperate fully and to follow directions. Direct the patient to breathe normally and to avoid unnecessary movement.

▶ Observe standard precautions, and follow the general guidelines in Appendix A. Positively identify the patient, and label the appropriate specimen container with the corresponding patient demographics, initials of the person collecting the specimen, date, and time of collection. Perform a venipuncture.

▶ Remove the needle and apply direct pressure with dry gauze to stop bleeding. Observe/assess venipuncture site for bleeding or hematoma formation and secure gauze with adhesive bandage.

▶ Promptly transport the specimen to the laboratory for processing and analysis.

POST-TEST:

▶ A report of the results will be made available to the requesting HCP, who will discuss the results with the patient.

▶ *Nutritional Considerations:* The Institute of Medicine's Food and Nutrition Board suggests 700 mg as the daily recommended dietary allowance of phosphorus for adult males and females age 19

to greater than 70 yr; 700 mg/d for pregnant and lactating females age 31 to 50 yr; 1,250 mg/d for pregnant and lactating females under age 19 yr; 1,250 mg/d for children age 9 to 18 yr; 500 mg/d for children age 4 to 8 yr; 460 mg/d for children age 1 to 3 yr; 275 mg/d for children age 7 to 12 mo (recommended adequate intake); and 100 mg/d for children age 0 to 6 mo (recommended adequate intake). Reprinted with permission from the National Academies Press, copyright 2013, National Academy of Sciences. Severe hypophosphatemia is common in elderly patients or patients who have been hospitalized for long periods of time. Good dietary sources of phosphorus include meat, dairy products, nuts, and legumes. To decrease phosphorus levels to normal in the patient with hyperphosphatemia, dietary restriction may be recommended. Other interventions may include the administration of phosphate binders or calcitriol (the activated form of vitamin D).

▶ *Nutritional Considerations:* Vitamin D is necessary for the body to absorb phosphorus. The Institute of Medicine's Food and Nutrition Board suggests 50 mcg/d as the tolerable upper limit for total daily intake of dietary vitamin D for males and females age 1 to greater than 70 yr; 50 mcg/d for pregnant and lactating females under age 18 through 50 yr; and 25 mcg/d for children age 0 to 12 mo. Reprinted with permission from the National Academies Press, copyright 2013, National Academy of Sciences. Educate the patient with vitamin D deficiency, as appropriate, that the main dietary sources of vitamin D are cod liver oil and fortified dairy foods such as milk, cheese, and orange juice. Explain to the patient that vitamin D is also synthesized by the body, in the skin, and is activated by sunlight.

▶ Reinforce information given by the patient's HCP regarding further testing, treatment, or referral to another HCP. Answer any questions or address any concerns voiced by the patient or family. Educate the patient regarding access to nutritional counseling services. Provide contact information, if desired, for the Institute of

Medicine of the National Academies (www.iom.edu).

Depending on the results of this procedure, additional testing may be performed to evaluate or monitor progression of the disease process and determine the need for a change in therapy. Evaluate test results in relation to the patient's symptoms and other tests performed.

RELATED MONOGRAPHS:

Related tests include biopsy bone, blood gases, BUN, calcitonin, calcium, calculus kidney stone panel, carbon dioxide, chloride, collagen cross-linked N-telopeptides, CBC WBC count and differential, creatinine, fecal analysis, fecal fat, FDP, glucagon, glucose, GH, insulin, lactic acid, lung perfusion scan, lung ventilation scan, osmolality, osteocalcin, PTH, parathyroid scan, phosphorus urine, potassium, US abdomen, and vitamin D.

Refer to the Endocrine, Gastrointestinal, Genitourinary, and Musculoskeletal systems tables at the end of the book for related tests by body system.

Phosphorus, Urine

SYNONYM/ACRONYM: Urine phosphate.

COMMON USE: To assist in evaluating calcium and phosphorus levels related to use of diuretics in progression of renal disease.

SPECIMEN: Urine (5 mL) from an unpreserved random or timed specimen collected in a clean plastic collection container.

NORMAL FINDINGS: (Method: Spectrophotometry) Reference values are dependent on phosphorus and calcium intake. Phosphate excretion exhibits diurnal variation and is significantly higher at night.

Conventional Units	SI Units (Conventional Units × 0.0323)
400–1,300 mg/24 hr	12.9–42 mmol/24 hr

DESCRIPTION: Phosphorus, in the form of phosphate, is distributed throughout the body. Approximately 85% of the body's phosphorus is stored in bones; the remainder is found in cells and body fluids. It is the major intracellular anion and plays a crucial role in cellular metabolism, maintenance of cellular membranes, and formation of bones and teeth. Phosphorus also indirectly affects the release of oxygen from hemoglobin by affecting the formation of 2,3-bisphosphoglycerate. Levels of phosphorus are dependent on dietary intake.

Analyzing urinary phosphorus levels can provide important clues to the functioning of the kidneys and other major organs. Tests for phosphorus in urine usually involve timed urine collections over a 12- or 24-hr period. Measurement of random specimens may also be

P

requested. Children with thalassemia may have normal phosphorus absorption but increased excretion, which may result in a phosphorus deficiency.

INDICATIONS

- Assist in the diagnosis of hyperparathyroidism
- Assist in the evaluation of calcium and phosphorus balance
- Assist in the evaluation of nephrolithiasis
- Assist in the evaluation of renal tubular disease

POTENTIAL DIAGNOSIS

Increased in

- Abuse of diuretics *(related to increased renal excretion)*
- Primary hyperparathyroidism *(parathyroid hormone [PTH] increases renal excretion)*
- Renal tubular acidosis
- Vitamin D deficiency *(related to decreased renal reabsorption)*

Decreased in

- Hypoparathyroidism *(PTH enhances renal excretion; therefore, a lack of PTH will decrease urine phosphorus levels)*
- Pseudohypoparathyroidism *(PTH enhances renal reabsorption; therefore, a lack of response to PTH, as in pseudohypoparathyroidism, will decrease urine phosphorus levels)*
- Vitamin D intoxication *(vitamin D promotes renal excretion of phosphorus)*

CRITICAL FINDINGS: N/A

INTERFERING FACTORS

- Drugs and vitamins that can cause an increase in urine phosphorus levels include acetazolamide, acetylsalicylic acid, bismuth salts, calcitonin, corticosteroids, dihydrotachysterol, glucocorticoids, hydrochlorothiazide, mestranol, metolazone, parathyroid extract, and parathyroid hormone.
- Drugs that can cause a decrease in urine phosphorus levels include aluminum-containing antacids and diltiazem.
- Urine phosphorus levels are subject to diurnal variation: Output is highest in the afternoon, which is why 24-hr urine collections are recommended.
- All urine voided for the timed collection period must be included in the collection or else falsely decreased values may be obtained. Compare output records with volume collected to verify that all voids were included in the collection.

NURSING IMPLICATIONS AND PROCEDURE

PRETEST:

- Positively identify the patient using at least two unique identifiers before providing care, treatment, or services.
- *Patient Teaching:* Inform the patient this test can assist in evaluating calcium and phosphorus balance.
- Obtain a history of the patient's complaints, including a list of known allergens, especially allergies or sensitivities to latex.
- Obtain a history of the patient's endocrine and genitourinary systems, symptoms, and results of previously performed laboratory tests and diagnostic and surgical procedures.
- Obtain a list of the patient's current medications, including herbs, nutritional supplements, and nutraceuticals (see Appendix F).
- Review the procedure with the patient. Provide a nonmetallic urinal, bedpan, or toilet-mounted collection device. Address concerns about pain and explain that there should be no discomfort during the procedure.

- *Sensitivity to social and cultural issues,* as well as concern for modesty, is important in providing psychological support before, during, and after the procedure.
- Usually a 24-hr time frame for urine collection is ordered. Inform the patient that all urine must be saved during that 24-hr period. Instruct the patient not to void directly into the laboratory collection container. Instruct the patient to avoid defecating in the collection device and to keep toilet tissue out of the collection device to prevent contamination of the specimen. Place a sign in the bathroom to remind the patient to save all urine.
- Instruct the patient to void all urine into the collection device and then to pour the urine into the laboratory collection container. Alternatively, the specimen can be left in the collection device for a health-care staff member to add to the laboratory collection container.
- *Sensitivity to social and cultural issues,* as well as concern for modesty, is important in providing psychological support before, during, and after the procedure.
- Instruct the patient to avoid excessive exercise and stress during the 24-hr collection of urine.
- There are no food, fluid, or medication restrictions unless by medical direction.

NTRATEST:

- Ensure that the patient has complied with activity restrictions and pretesting preparations; assure that excessive exercise and stress have been restricted during the 24-hr procedure.
- If the patient has a history of allergic reaction to latex, avoid the use of equipment containing latex.
- Instruct the patient to cooperate fully and to follow directions.
- Observe standard precautions, and follow the general guidelines in Appendix A. Positively identify the patient, and label the appropriate specimen container with the corresponding patient demographics, initials of the person collecting the specimen, date, and time of collection.

Random Specimen (Collect in Early Morning)

Clean-Catch Specimen
- Instruct the male patient to (1) thoroughly wash his hands, (2) cleanse the meatus, (3) void a small amount into the toilet, and (4) void directly into the specimen container.
- Instruct the female patient to (1) thoroughly wash her hands; (2) cleanse the labia from front to back; (3) while keeping the labia separated, void a small amount into the toilet; and (4) without interrupting the urine stream, void directly into the specimen container.

Indwelling Catheter
- Put on gloves. Empty drainage tube of urine. It may be necessary to clamp off the catheter for 15 to 30 min before specimen collection. Cleanse specimen port with antiseptic swab, and then aspirate 5 mL of urine with a 21- to 25-gauge needle and syringe. Transfer urine to a sterile container.

Timed Specimen
- Obtain a clean 3-L urine specimen container, toilet-mounted collection device, and plastic bag (for transport of the specimen container). The specimen must be refrigerated or kept on ice throughout the entire collection period. If an indwelling urinary catheter is in place, the drainage bag must be kept on ice.
- Begin the test between 6 and 8 a.m. if possible. Collect first voiding and discard. Record the time the specimen was discarded as the beginning of the timed collection period. The next morning, ask the patient to void at the same time the collection was started and add this last voiding to the container. Urinary output should be recorded throughout the collection time.
- If an indwelling catheter is in place, replace the tubing and container system at the start of the collection time. Keep the container system on ice during the collection period, or empty the urine into a larger container periodically during the collection period; monitor to ensure continued drainage, and conclude the test the next morning at the same hour the collection was begun.

P

At the conclusion of the test, compare the quantity of urine with the urinary output record for the collection; if the specimen contains less than what was recorded as output, some urine may have been discarded, invalidating the test.

Include on the collection container's label the amount of urine, test start and stop times, and ingestion of any foods or medications that can affect test results.

General

Promptly transport the specimen to the laboratory for processing and analysis.

POST-TEST:

A report of the results will be made available to the requesting health-care provider (HCP), who will discuss the results with the patient.

Nutritional Considerations: The Institute of Medicine's Food and Nutrition Board suggests 50 mcg/d as the tolerable upper limit for total daily intake of dietary vitamin D for males and females age 1 to greater than 70 yr; 50 mcg/d for pregnant and lactating females under age 18 through 50 yr; and 25 mcg/d for children age 0 to 12 mo. Reprinted with permission from the National Academies Press, copyright 2013, National Academy of Sciences. Vitamin D is necessary for the body to absorb phosphorus. Educate the patient with vitamin D deficiency, as appropriate, that the main dietary sources of vitamin D are cod liver oil and fortified dairy foods such as milk, cheese, and orange juice. Explain to the patient that vitamin D is also synthesized by the body, in the skin, and is activated by sunlight.

Increased urine phosphorus levels may be associated with the formation of kidney stones. Educate the patient, if appropriate, on the importance of drinking a sufficient amount of water when kidney stones are suspected.

Recognize anxiety related to test results. Discuss the implications of abnormal test results on the patient's lifestyle. Provide teaching and information regarding the clinical implications of the test results, as appropriate.

Reinforce information given by the patient's HCP regarding further testing, treatment, or referral to another HCP. Answer any questions or address any concerns voiced by the patient or family.

Depending on the results of this procedure, additional testing may be performed to evaluate or monitor progression of the disease process and determine the need for a change in therapy. Evaluate test results in relation to the patient's symptoms and other tests performed.

RELATED MONOGRAPHS:

Related tests include ALP, calcitonin, calcium, calculus kidney stone panel, chloride, CT abdomen, cystoscopy, IVP, KUB studies, PTH, parathyroid scan, phosphorus blood, potassium, renogram, retrograde ureteropyelography, uric acid, and UA.

Refer to the Endocrine and Genitourinary systems tables at the end of the book for related tests by body system.

Plasminogen

SYNONYM/ACRONYM: Profibrinolysin, PMG.

COMMON USE: To assess thrombolytic disorders such as disseminated intravascular coagulation (DIC) and monitor thrombolytic therapy.

SPECIMEN: Plasma (1 mL) collected in a completely filled blue-top (3.2% sodium citrate) tube. If the patient's hematocrit exceeds 55%, the volume of citrate in the collection tube must be adjusted.

NORMAL FINDINGS: (Method: Chromogenic substrate for plasminogen activity and nephelometric for plasminogen antigen)

Plasminogen activity	80–100% of normal
Plasminogen antigen	7.5–15.5 mg/dL

Plasminogen activity in newborns is half of adult ranges.

DESCRIPTION: Plasminogen is a plasma glycoprotein produced by the liver. It is the circulating, inactive precursor to plasmin. Damaged tissues release a substance called *plasminogen activator* that initiates the conversion of plasminogen to plasmin. Plasmin participates in fibrinolysis and is capable of degrading fibrin, factor I (fibrinogen), factor V, and factor VIII. (For more information on fibrin degradation, see monograph titled "Fibrinogen.")

INDICATIONS

Evaluate the level of circulating plasminogen in patients with thrombosis or disseminated intravascular coagulation (DIC).

POTENTIAL DIAGNOSIS

Increased in

Pregnancy (late) *(pathophysiology is unclear)*

Decreased in

DIC *(related to increased consumption during the hyperfibrinolytic state by conversion to plasmin)*

Fibrinolytic therapy with tissue plasminogen activators such as streptokinase or urokinase *(related to increased consumption by conversion to plasmin)*

- Hereditary deficiency
- Liver disease *(related to decreased production by damaged liver cells)*
- Neonatal hyaline membrane disease *(possibly related to deficiency of plasminogen)*
- Postsurgical period *(possibly related to trauma of surgery)*

CRITICAL FINDINGS: N/A

INTERFERING FACTORS

- Drugs that may decrease plasminogen levels include streptokinase and urokinase.
- Hematocrit greater than 55% may cause falsely prolonged results because of anticoagulant excess relative to plasma volume.
- Incompletely filled collection tubes, specimens contaminated with heparin, clotted specimens, or unprocessed specimens not delivered to the laboratory within 1 to 2 hr of collection should be rejected.

P

NURSING IMPLICATIONS AND PROCEDURE

PRETEST:

- Positively identify the patient using at least two unique identifiers before providing care, treatment, or services.
- *Patient Teaching:* Inform the patient that this test can assist in evaluating the effectiveness of blood clotting.

▶ Obtain a history of the patient's complaints, including a list of known allergens, especially allergies or sensitivities to latex.

▶ Obtain a history of the patient's hematopoietic system, symptoms, and results of previously performed laboratory tests and diagnostic and surgical procedures.

▶ Obtain a list of the patient's current medications, including herbs, nutritional supplements, and nutraceuticals (see Appendix F).

▶ Review the procedure with the patient. Inform the patient that specimen collection takes approximately 5 to 10 min. Address concerns about pain and explain that there may be some discomfort during the venipuncture.

▶ *Sensitivity to social and cultural issues,* as well as concern for modesty, is important in providing psychological support before, during, and after the procedure.

▶ There are no food, fluid, or medication restrictions unless by medical direction.

INTRATEST:

▶ If the patient has a history of allergic reaction to latex, avoid the use of equipment containing latex.

▶ Instruct the patient to cooperate fully and to follow directions. Direct the patient to breathe normally and to avoid unnecessary movement.

▶ Observe standard precautions, and follow the general guidelines in Appendix A. Positively identify the patient, and label the appropriate specimen container with the corresponding patient demographics, initials of the person collecting the specimen, date, and time of collection. Perform a venipuncture. Fill tube completely. *Important note:* Two different concentrations of sodium citrate preservative are currently added to blue-top tubes for coagulation studies: 3.2% and 3.8%. The Clinical and Laboratory Standards Institute (CLSI; formerly the National Committee for Clinical Laboratory Standards [NCCLS]) guideline for sodium citrate is 3.2%. Laboratories establish reference ranges for coagulation testing based on

numerous factors, including sodium citrate concentration, test equipment, and test reagents. It is important to ask the laboratory which concentration it recommends, because each concentration will have its own specific reference range. When multiple specimens are drawn, the blue-top tube should be collected after sterile (i.e., blood culture) tubes. Otherwise, when using a standard vacutainer system, the blue-top tube is the first tube collected. When a butterfly is used and due to the added tubing, an extra red-top tube should be collected before the blue-top tube to ensure complete filling of the blue-top tube.

▶ Remove the needle and apply direct pressure with dry gauze to stop bleeding. Observe/assess venipuncture site for bleeding or hematoma formation and secure gauze with adhesive bandage.

▶ Promptly transport the specimen to the laboratory for processing and analysis. The CLSI recommendation for processed and unprocessed samples stored in unopened tubes is that testing should be completed within 1 to 4 hr of collection. If the patient has a known hematocrit above 55%, adjust the amount of anticoagulant in the collection tube before drawing the blood according to the CLSI guidelines:

$$\text{Anticoagulant vol. } [x] = (100 - \text{hematocrit}) / (595 - \text{hematocrit}) \times \text{total vol. of anticoagulated blood required}$$

Example:

$$\text{Patient hematocrit} = 60\%$$
$$= [(100 - 60) / (595 - 60) \times 5.0]$$
$$= 0.37 \text{ mL sodium citrate for a 5-mL standard drawing tube}$$

POST-TEST:

▶ A report of the results will be made available to the requesting health-care provider (HCP), who will discuss the results with the patient.

▶ Reinforce information given by the patient's HCP regarding further testing, treatment, or referral to another HCP. Answer any questions or address any concerns voiced by the patient or family.

Depending on the results of this procedure, additional testing may be performed to evaluate or monitor progression of the disease process and determine the need for a change in therapy. Evaluate test results in relation to the patient's symptoms and other tests performed.

RELATED MONOGRAPHS:

Related tests include AT-III, CBC platelet count, coagulation factors, FDP, fibrinogen, aPTT, protein S, and PT/INR.
Refer to the Hematopoietic System table at the end of the book for related tests by body system.

Platelet Antibodies

SYNONYM/ACRONYM: Antiplatelet antibody; platelet-bound IgG/IgM, direct and indirect.

COMMON USE: To assess for the presence of platelet antibodies to assist in diagnosing thrombocytopenia related to autoimmune conditions and platelet transfusion compatibility issues.

SPECIMEN: Serum (1 mL) collected in a red-top tube for indirect immunoglobulin G (IgG) antibody. Whole blood (7 mL) collected in a lavender-top (EDTA) tube for direct antibody.

NORMAL FINDINGS: (Method: Solid-phase enzyme-linked immunoassay) Negative.

DESCRIPTION: Platelet antibodies can be formed by autoimmune response, or they can be acquired in reaction to transfusion products or medications. Platelet autoantibodies are immunoglobulins of autoimmune origin (i.e., immunoglobulin G [IgG]), and they are present in various autoimmune disorders, including thrombocytopenias. Platelet alloantibodies develop in patients who become sensitized to platelet antigens of transfused blood. As a result, destruction of both donor and native platelets occurs along with a shortened survival time of platelets in the transfusion recipient. The platelet antibody detection test is also used for platelet typing, which allows compatible platelets to be transfused to patients with disorders such as aplastic anemia and cancer. Platelet typing decreases the alloimmunization risk resulting from repeated transfusions from random donors. Platelet typing may also provide additional support for a diagnosis of post-transfusional purpura.

INDICATIONS
- Assist in the detection of platelet alloimmune disorders
- Determine platelet type for refractory patients

P

POTENTIAL DIAGNOSIS

Increased in

Development of platelet antibodies is associated with autoimmune conditions and medications.

- AIDS *(related to medications used therapeutically)*
- Acute myeloid leukemia *(related to medications used therapeutically)*
- Idiopathic thrombocytopenic purpura *(related to development of platelet-associated IgG antibodies)*
- Immune complex diseases
- Multiple blood transfusions *(related in most cases to sensitization to PLA1 antigens on donor red blood cells that will stimulate formation of antiplatelet antibodies)*
- Multiple myeloma *(related to medications used therapeutically)*
- Neonatal immune thrombocytopenia *(related to maternal platelet–associated antibodies directed against fetal platelets)*
- Paroxysmal hemoglobinuria
- Rheumatoid arthritis *(related to medications used therapeutically)*
- Systemic lupus erythematosus *(related to medications used therapeutically)*
- Thrombocytopenias provoked by drugs (see monograph titled "Complete Blood Count, Platelet Count")

Decreased in: N/A

CRITICAL FINDINGS: N/A

INTERFERING FACTORS

- There are many drugs that may induce immune thrombocytopenia (production of antibodies that destroy platelets in response to the drugs). The most common include acetaminophen, gold salts, heparin (Type II HIT), oral diabetic medications, penicillin, quinidine, quinine, salicylates, sulfonamides, and sulfonylurea.
- There are many drugs that may induce nonimmune thrombocytopenia (effect of the drug includes bone marrow suppression or nonimmune platelet destruction). The most common include anticancer medications (e.g., bleomycin), ethanol, heparin (Type I HIT), procarbazine, protamine, ristocetin, thiazide, and valproic acid.
- Hemolyzed or clotted specimens will affect results.

NURSING IMPLICATIONS AND PROCEDURE

PRETEST:

- Positively identify the patient using at least two unique identifiers before providing care, treatment, or services.
- *Patient Teaching:* Inform the patient this test can assist in evaluating for issues related to platelet compatibility.
- Obtain a history of the patient's complaints, including a list of known allergens, especially allergies or sensitivities to latex.
- Obtain a history of the patient's hematopoietic and immune systems, especially any bleeding disorders and other symptoms, as well as results of previously performed laboratory tests and diagnostic and surgical procedures.
- Obtain a list of the patient's current medications, including anticoagulants, aspirin and other salicylates, herbs, nutritional supplements, and nutraceuticals (see Appendix F). Note the last time and dose of medication taken.
- Review the procedure with the patient. Inform the patient that specimen collection takes approximately 5 to 10 min. Address concerns about pain and explain that there may be some discomfort during the venipuncture.
- *Sensitivity to social and cultural issues,* as well as concern for modesty, is important in providing psychological support before, during, and after the procedure.

There are no food, fluid, or medication restrictions unless by medical direction.

NTRATEST:

If the patient has a history of allergic reaction to latex, avoid the use of equipment containing latex.

Instruct the patient to cooperate fully and to follow directions. Direct the patient to breathe normally and to avoid unnecessary movement.

Observe standard precautions, and follow the general guidelines in Appendix A. Positively identify the patient, and label the appropriate specimen container with the corresponding patient demographics, initials of the person collecting the specimen, date, and time of collection. Perform a venipuncture.

Remove the needle and apply direct pressure with dry gauze to stop bleeding. Observe/assess venipuncture site for bleeding or hematoma formation and secure gauze with adhesive bandage.

Promptly transport the specimen to the laboratory for processing and analysis.

POST-TEST:

A report of the results will be made available to the requesting health-care provider (HCP), who will discuss the results with the patient.

Note the patient's response to platelet transfusions.

Instruct the patient to report severe bruising or bleeding from any areas of the skin or mucous membranes.

Inform the patient who has developed platelet antibodies of the importance of taking precautions against bruising and bleeding, including the use of a soft bristle toothbrush, use of an electric razor, avoidance of constipation, avoidance of acetylsalicylic acid and similar products, and avoidance of intramuscular injections.

Reinforce information given by the patient's HCP regarding further testing, treatment, or referral to another HCP. Answer any questions or address any concerns voiced by the patient or family.

Depending on the results of this procedure, additional testing may be performed to evaluate or monitor progression of the disease process and determine the need for a change in therapy. Evaluate test results in relation to the patient's symptoms and other tests performed.

RELATED MONOGRAPHS:

Related tests include angiography abdominal, biopsy bone marrow, bleeding time, clot retraction, CBC platelet count, CT brain, Ham's test, hemosiderin, and LAP.

Refer to the Hematopoietic and Immune systems tables at the end of the book for related tests by body system.

P

Plethysmography

SYNONYM/ACRONYM: Impedance plethysmography, PVR.

COMMON USE: To measure changes in blood vessel size or changes in gas volume in the lungs to assist in diagnosing diseases such as deep vein thrombosis (DVT), chronic obstructive pulmonary disease (COPD), and some peripheral vascular disorders.

AREA OF APPLICATION: Veins, arteries, and lungs.

CONTRAST: None.

DESCRIPTION: Plethysmography is a noninvasive diagnostic manometric study used to measure changes in the size of blood vessels by determining volume changes in the blood vessels of the eye, extremities, and neck or to measure gas volume changes in the lungs.

Arterial plethysmography assesses arterial circulation in an upper or lower limb; it is used to diagnose extremity arteriosclerotic disease and to rule out occlusive disease. The test requires a normal extremity for comparison of results. The test is performed by applying a series of three blood pressure cuffs to the extremity. The amplitude of each pulse wave is then recorded.

Venous plethysmography, done with a series of cuffs, measures changes in venous capacity and outflow (volume and rate of outflow); it is used to diagnose a thrombotic condition that causes obstruction of the major veins of the extremity. When the cuffs are applied to an extremity in patients with venous obstruction, no initial increase in leg volume is recorded because the venous volume of the leg cannot dissipate quickly.

Body plethysmography measures the total amount (volume) of air within the thorax, whether or not the air is in ventilatory communication with the lung; the elasticity (compliance) of the lungs; and the resistance to airflow in the respiratory tree. It is used in conjunction with pulmonary stress testing and pulmonary function testing.

Impedance plethysmography is widely used to detect acute deep vein thrombosis (DVT) of the leg, but it can also be used in the arm, abdomen, neck, or thorax. Doppler flow studies now are used to identify DVT, but ultrasound studies are less accurate in examinations below the knee.

INDICATIONS

Arterial Plethysmography
- Confirm suspected acute arterial embolization
- Detect vascular changes associated with Raynaud's phenomenon and disease
- Determine changes in toe or finger pressures when ankle pressures are elevated as a result of arterial calcifications
- Determine the effect of trauma on the arteries in an extremity
- Determine peripheral small-artery changes (ischemia) caused by diabetes, and differentiate these changes from neuropathy
- Evaluate suspected arterial occlusive disease
- Locate and determine the degree of arterial atherosclerotic obstruction and vessel patency in peripheral atherosclerotic disease, as well as inflammatory changes causing obliteration in the vessels in thromboangiitis obliterans

Venous Plethysmography
- Detect partial or total venous thrombotic obstruction
- Determine valve competency in conjunction with Doppler ultrasonography in the diagnosis of varicose veins

Body Plethysmography
- Detect acute pulmonary disorders, such as atelectasis
- Detect or determine the status of chronic obstructive pulmonary disease (COPD), such as emphysema, asthma, or chronic bronchitis
- Detect or determine the status of restrictive pulmonary disease, such as fibrosis

Detect infectious pulmonary diseases, such as pneumonia

Determine baseline pulmonary status before pulmonary rehabilitation to determine potential therapeutic benefit

Differentiate between obstructive and restrictive pulmonary pathology

Impedance Plethysmography

Act as a diagnostic screen for patients at risk for DVT

Detect and evaluate DVT

Evaluate degree of resolution of DVT after treatment

Evaluate patients with suspected pulmonary embolism (most pulmonary emboli are complications of DVT in the leg)

POTENTIAL DIAGNOSIS

Normal findings in

Arterial plethysmography:

Normal arterial pulse waves: Steep upslope, more gradual downslope with narrow pointed peaks

Normal pressure: Less than 20 mm Hg systolic difference between the lower and upper extremities; toe pressure greater than or equal to 80% of ankle pressure and finger pressure greater than or equal to 80% of wrist pressure

Venous plethysmography:

Normal venous blood flow in the extremities

Venous filling times greater than 20 sec

Body plethysmography:

Thoracic gas volume: 2,400 mL

Compliance: 0.2 L/cm H_2O

Airway resistance: 0.6 to 2.5 cm H_2O/L per sec

Impedance plethysmography:

Sharp rise in volume with temporary occlusion

Rapid venous outflow with release of the occlusion

Abnormal findings in

COPD, restrictive lung disease, lung infection, or atelectasis (body plethysmography)

- DVT (arterial, venous, or impedance plethysmography)
- Incompetent valves, thrombosis, or thrombotic obstruction in a major vein in an extremity
- Small-vessel diabetic changes
- Vascular disease (Raynaud's phenomenon)
- Vascular trauma

CRITICAL FINDINGS

- DVT

It is essential that critical diagnoses be communicated immediately to the appropriate health-care provider (HCP). A listing of these diagnoses varies among facilities. Note and immediately report to the HCP abnormal results and related symptoms. Timely notification of critical values for lab or diagnostic studies is a role expectation of the professional nurse. Notification processes will vary among facilities. Upon receipt of the critical value the information should be read back to the caller to verify accuracy. Most policies require immediate notification of the primary HCP, hospitalist, or on-call HCP. Reported information includes the patient's name, unique identifiers, critical value, name of the person giving the report, and name of the person receiving the report. Documentation of notification should be made in the medical record with the name of the HCP notified, time and date of notification, and any orders received. Any delay in a timely report of a critical value may require completion of a notification form with review by Risk Management.

INTERFERING FACTORS

Arterial Plethysmography

Factors that may impair the results of the examination

- Cigarette smoking 2 hr before the study, which causes inaccurate results because the nicotine constricts the arteries.

P

- Alcohol consumption.
- Low cardiac output.
- Shock.
- Compression of pelvic veins (tumors or external compression by dressings).
- Environmental temperatures (hot or cold).
- Arterial occlusion proximal to the extremity to be examined, which can prevent blood flow to the limb.

Venous Plethysmography

Factors that may impair the results of the examination
- Low environmental temperature or cold extremity, which constricts the vessels.
- High anxiety level or muscle tenseness.
- Venous thrombotic occlusion proximal to the extremity to be examined, which can affect blood flow to the limb.

Body Plethysmography

Factors that may impair the results of the examination
- Inability of the patient to follow breathing instructions during the procedure.

Impedance Plethysmography

Factors that may impair the results of the examination
- Movement of the extremity during electrical impedance recording, poor electrode contact, or nonlinear electrical output, which can cause false-positive results.
- Constricting clothing or bandages.

NURSING IMPLICATIONS AND PROCEDURE

PRETEST:

▶ Positively identify the patient using at least two unique identifiers before providing care, treatment, or services.

Patient Teaching: Inform the patient this procedure can assist in evaluating blood vessel size and lung ventilation.
▶ Obtain a history of the patient's complaints including a list of known allergens, especially allergies or sensitivities to latex, iodine, seafood, contrast medium, or anesthetics.
▶ Obtain a history of the patient's cardiovascular and pulmonary systems, symptoms, and results of laboratory tests and diagnostic and surgical procedures.
▶ Record the date of the last menstrual period and determine the possibility of pregnancy in perimenopausal women.
▶ Obtain a list of the patient's current medications, including herbs, nutritional supplements, and nutraceuticals (see Appendix F).
▶ Review the procedure with the patient. Address concerns about pain related to the procedure and explain to the patient that no discomfort will be experienced during the test. Explain that there may be some discomfort during insertion of the nasoesophageal catheter if compliance testing is done. Inform the patient that the procedure is generally performed in a specialized area or at the bedside by an HCP who specializes in this procedure, with support staff, and usually takes 30 to 60 min.
▶ Assess the patient's ability to comply with directions given for rest, positioning, and activity before and during the procedure.
▶ For body plethysmography, record the patient's weight, height, and gender. Determine whether the patient is claustrophobic.
▶ *Sensitivity to social and cultural issues,* as well as concern for modesty, is important in providing psychological support before, during, and after the procedure.
▶ Instruct the patient to refrain from smoking for 2 hr prior to the procedure.
▶ There are no food, fluid, or medication restrictions unless by medical direction.

INTRATEST:

▶ Observe standard precautions, and follow the general guidelines in Appendix A. Positively identify the patient.

Ensure the patient has refrained from smoking for 2 hr before the procedure.

Instruct the patient to void prior to the procedure and to change into the gown, robe, and foot coverings provided.

Obtain and record baseline vital signs.

Instruct the patient to report any unexpected symptoms that occur during the test.

Arterial Plethysmography

Explain to the patient that cuffs are applied to the extremity to measure and compare blood flow.

Place the patient in a semi-Fowler's position on an examination table or in bed.

Ask the patient to notify medical personnel if he or she has unexpected symptoms during the test.

Instruct the patient to remain still during the procedure.

Apply three blood pressure cuffs to the extremity and attach a pulse volume recorder (plethysmograph), which records the amplitude of each pulse wave.

Inflate the cuffs to 65 mm Hg to measure the pulse waves of each cuff. When compared with a normal limb, these measurements determine the presence of arterial occlusive disease.

Venous Plethysmography

Explain to the patient that cuffs are applied to the extremity to measure and compare blood flow.

Place the patient in a semi-Fowler position on an examination table or in bed.

Instruct the patient to remain still during the procedure.

Apply two blood pressure cuffs to the extremity, one on the proximal part of the extremity (occlusion cuff) and the other on the distal part of the extremity (recorder cuff). Attach a third cuff to the pulse volume recorder.

Inflate the recorder cuff to 10 mm Hg, and evaluate the effects of respiration on venous volume: Absence of changes during respirations indicates venous thrombotic occlusion.

Inflate the occlusion cuff to 50 mm Hg, and record venous volume on the pulse monitor. Deflate the occlusion cuff after the highest volume is recorded in the recorder cuff. A delay in the return to preocclusion volume indicates venous thrombotic occlusion.

Body Plethysmography

Place the patient in a sitting position on a chair in the body box. Explain to the patient that the cuffs are applied to the extremities to measure and compare blood flow.

Position a nose clip to prevent breathing through the nose, and connect a mouthpiece to a measuring instrument.

Ask the patient to breathe through the mouthpiece.

Close the door to the box, and record the start time of the procedure. At the beginning of the study, instruct the patient to pant rapidly and shallowly, without allowing the glottis to close.

For compliance testing, a double-lumen nasoesophageal catheter is inserted, and the bag is inflated with air. Intraesophageal pressure is recorded during normal breathing.

Impedance Plethysmography

Explain to the patient that cuffs are applied to the extremity to measure and compare blood flow.

Place the patient on his or her back with the leg being tested above the heart level.

Flex the patient's knee slightly, and rotate the hips by shifting weight to the same side as the leg being tested.

Apply conductive gel and electrodes to the legs, near the cuffs.

Apply a blood pressure cuff to the thigh.

Inflate the pressure cuff attached to the thigh temporarily to occlude venous return without interfering with arterial blood flow. Expect the blood volume in the other calf to increase.

A tracing of changes in electrical impedance occurring during inflation and for 15 sec after cuff deflation is recorded.

With DVT, blood volume increases less than expected because the veins are already at capacity.

POST-TEST:

▸ A report of the results will be made available to the requesting HCP, who will discuss the results with the patient.
▸ Remove conductive gel and electrodes, as applied.
▸ Instruct the patient to resume usual activity and diet, as directed by the HCP.
▸ Monitor for severe ischemia, ulcers, and pain of the extremity after arterial, venous, or impedance plethysmography, and handle the extremity gently.
▸ Monitor respiratory pattern after body plethysmography, and allow the patient time to resume a normal breathing pattern.
▸ Monitor vital signs every 15 min until they return to baseline levels.
▸ Recognize anxiety related to test results, and be supportive of perceived loss of independent function. Discuss the implications of abnormal test results on the patient's lifestyle. Provide teaching and information regarding the clinical implications of the test results, as appropriate.
▸ Reinforce information given by the patient's HCP regarding further testing, treatment, or referral to another HCP. Answer any questions or address any concerns voiced by the patient or family.
▸ Depending on the results of this procedure, additional testing may be needed

to evaluate or monitor progression of the disease process and determine the need for a change in therapy. Evaluate test results in relation to the patient's symptoms and other tests performed.

RELATED MONOGRAPHS:

▸ Related tests include α_1-AT, angiography pulmonary, anion gap, arterial/alveolar oxygen ratio, AT-III, biopsy lung, blood gases, bronchoscopy, carboxyhemoglobin, cardiolipin antibodies, chest x-ray, chloride sweat, cold agglutinin, CBC, CBC hemoglobin, CBC WBC count and differential, CT angiography, CT thoracic, culture and smear for mycobacteria, culture bacterial sputum, culture viral, cytology sputum, D-dimer, echocardiography, ECG, EMG, ENG, fibrinogen, gram stain, IgE, lactic acid, lung perfusion scan, lung ventilation scan, lupus anticoagulant antibodies, MR angiography, MRI chest, osmolality, phosphorus, plasminogen, pleural fluid analysis, potassium, PET chest, PFT, pulse oximetry, sodium, TB skin test, and US arterial and venous Doppler of the extremities.
▸ Refer to the Cardiovascular and Pulmonary systems tables at the end of the book for related tests by body system.

Pleural Fluid Analysis

SYNONYM/ACRONYM: Thoracentesis fluid analysis.

COMMON USE: To assess and categorize fluid obtained from within the pleural space for infection, cancer, and blood as well as identify the cause of its accumulation.

SPECIMEN: Pleural fluid (5 mL) collected in a green-top (heparin) tube for amylase, cholesterol, glucose, lactate dehydrogenase (LDH), pH, protein, and triglycerides; lavender-top (EDTA) tube for cell count; sterile containers for microbiology specimens; 200 to 500 mL of fluid in a clear container with anticoagulant for cytology. Ensure that there is an equal amount of fixative and fluid in the container for cytology.

NORMAL FINDINGS: (Method: Spectrophotometry for amylase, cholesterol, glucose, LDH, protein, and triglycerides; ion-selective electrode for pH; automated or manual cell count; macroscopic and microscopic examination of cultured microorganisms; microscopic examination of specimen for microbiology and cytology)

Appearance	Clear
Color	Pale yellow
Amylase	Parallels serum values
Cholesterol	Parallels serum values
CEA	Parallels serum values
Glucose	Parallels serum values
LDH	Less than 200 units/L
Fluid LDH-to-serum LDH ratio	0.6 or less
Protein	3 g/dL
Fluid protein-to-serum protein ratio	0.5 or less
Triglycerides	Parallel serum values
pH	7.37–7.43
RBC count	Less than 1,000/mm^3
WBC count	Less than 1,000/mm^3
Culture	No growth
Gram stain	No organisms seen
Cytology	No abnormal cells seen

CEA = carcinoembryonic antigen; LDH = lactate dehydrogenase; RBC = red blood cell; WBC = white blood cell.

DESCRIPTION: The pleural cavity and organs within it are lined with a protective membrane. The fluid between the membranes is called *serous fluid*. Normally, only a small amount of fluid is present because the rates of fluid production and absorption are about the same. Many abnormal conditions can result in the buildup of fluid within the pleural cavity. Specific tests are usually ordered in addition to a common battery of tests used to distinguish a transudate from an exudate. *Transudates* are effusions that form as a result of a systemic disorder that disrupts the regulation of fluid balance, such as a suspected perforation. *Exudates* are caused by conditions involving the tissue of the membrane itself, such as an infection or malignancy. Fluid is withdrawn from the pleural cavity by needle aspiration and tested as listed in the previous and following tables.

Characteristic	Transudate	Exudate
Appearance	Clear	Cloudy or turbid
Specific gravity	Less than 1.015	Greater than 1.015
Total protein	Less than 2.5 g/dL	Greater than 3 g/dL
Fluid protein-to-serum protein ratio	Less than 0.5	Greater than 0.5
LDH	Parallels serum value	Less than 200 units/L

Characteristic	Transudate	Exudate
Fluid LDH-to-serum LDH ratio	Less than 0.6	Greater than 0.6
Fluid cholesterol	Less than 55 mg/dL	Greater than 55 mg/dL
WBC count	Less than 100/mm^3	Greater than 1,000/mm^3

LDH = lactate dehydrogenase; WBC = white blood cell.

INDICATIONS
- Differentiate transudates from exudates
- Evaluate effusion of unknown cause
- Investigate suspected rupture, immune disease, malignancy, or infection

POTENTIAL DIAGNOSIS
- *Bacterial or tuberculous empyema*: Red blood cell (RBC) count less than 5,000/mm^3, white blood cell (WBC) count 25,000 to 100,000/mm^3 with a predominance of neutrophils, increased fluid protein-to-serum protein ratio, increased fluid LDH-to-serum LDH ratio, decreased glucose, pH less than 7.3
- *Chylous pleural effusion:* Marked increase in both triglycerides (two to three times serum level) and chylomicrons
- *Effusion caused by pneumonia:* RBC count less than 5,000/mm^3, WBC count 5,000 to 25,000/mm^3 with a predominance of neutrophils and some eosinophils, increased fluid protein-to-serum protein ratio, increased fluid LDH-to-serum LDH ratio, pH less than 7.4 (and decreased glucose if bacterial pneumonia)
- *Esophageal rupture:* Significantly decreased pH (6.0) and elevated amylase
- *Hemothorax:* Bloody appearance, increased RBC count, elevated hematocrit
- *Malignancy:* RBC count 1,000 to 100,000/mm^3, WBC count 5,000 to 10,000/mm^3 with a predominance of lymphocytes, abnormal cytology, increased fluid protein-to-serum protein ratio, increased fluid LDH-to-serum LDH ratio, decreased glucose, pH less than 7.3
- *Pancreatitis:* RBC count 1,000 to 10,000/mm^3, WBC count 5,000 to 20,000/mm^3 with a predominance of neutrophils, pH greater than 7.3, increased fluid protein-to-serum protein ratio, increased fluid LDH-to-serum LDH ratio, increased amylase
- *Pulmonary infarction:* RBC count 10,000 to 100,000/mm^3, WBC count 5,000 to 15,000/mm^3 with a predominance of neutrophils, pH greater than 7.3, normal glucose, increased fluid protein-to-serum protein ratio, and increased fluid LDH-to-serum LDH ratio.
- *Pulmonary tuberculosis:* RBC count 10,000/mm^3, WBC count 5,000 to 10,000/mm^3 with a predominance of lymphocytes, positive acid-fast bacillus stain and culture, increased protein, decreased glucose, pH less than 7.3
- *Rheumatoid disease:* Normal RBC count, WBC count 1,000 to 20,000/mm^3 with a predominance of either lymphocytes or neutrophils, pH less than 7.3, decreased glucose, increased fluid protein-to-serum protein ratio, increased fluid LDH-to-serum LDH ratio, increased immunoglobulins
- *Systemic lupus erythematosus:* Similar findings as with rheumatoid disease, except that glucose is usually not decreased

CRITICAL FINDINGS

Positive culture findings in any sterile body fluid.

Note and immediately report to the health-care provider (HCP) positive culture results, if ordered, and related symptoms. pH 7.1 to 7.2 indicates need for immediate drainage. Timely notification of critical values or lab or diagnostic studies is a role expectation of the professional nurse. Notification processes will vary among facilities. Upon receipt of the critical value the information should be read back to the caller to verify accuracy. Most policies require immediate notification of the primary HCP, hospitalist, or on-call HCP. Reported information includes the patient's name, unique identifiers, critical value, name of the person giving the report, and name of the person receiving the report. Documentation of notification should be made in the medical record with the name of the HCP notified, time and date of notification, and any orders received. Any delay in a timely report of a critical value may require completion of a notification form with review by Risk Management.

INTERFERING FACTORS

Bloody fluids may be the result of a traumatic tap.

Unknown hyperglycemia or hypoglycemia may be misleading in the comparison of fluid and serum glucose levels. Therefore, it is advisable to collect comparative serum samples a few hours before performing thoracentesis.

NURSING IMPLICATIONS AND PROCEDURE

RETEST:

Positively identify the patient using at least two unique identifiers before providing care, treatment, or services.

Patient Teaching: Inform the patient this test can assist in identifying the type of fluid being produced within the body cavity.

▸ Obtain a history of the patient's complaints, including a list of known allergens, especially allergies or sensitivities to latex.

▸ Obtain a history of the patient's immune and respiratory systems, especially any bleeding disorders and other symptoms, as well as results of previously performed laboratory tests and diagnostic and surgical procedures.

▸ Note any recent procedures that can interfere with test results.

▸ Record the date of the last menstrual period and determine the possibility of pregnancy in perimenopausal women.

▸ Obtain a list of the patient's current medications, including anticoagulants, aspirin and other salicylates, herbs, nutritional supplements, and nutraceuticals (see Appendix F). Such products should be discontinued by medical direction for the appropriate number of days prior to a surgical procedure.

▸ Review the procedure with the patient. Inform the patient that it may be necessary to remove hair from the site before the procedure. Discuss with the patient that the requesting HCP may request that a cough suppressant be given before the thoracentesis. Address concerns about pain and explain that a sedative and/or analgesia will be administered to promote relaxation and reduce discomfort prior to needle insertion through the chest wall into the pleural space. Explain that any discomfort with the needle insertion will be minimized with local anesthetics and systemic analgesics. Explain that the local anesthetic injection may cause an initial stinging sensation. Meperidine (Demerol) or morphine may be given as a sedative. Inform the patient that the needle insertion is performed under sterile conditions by an HCP specializing in this procedure. The procedure usually takes about 20 min to complete.

▸ Explain that an IV line will be inserted to allow infusion of IV fluids, antibiotics, anesthetics, and analgesics.

P

Sensitivity to social and cultural issues, as well as concern for modesty, is important in providing psychological support before, during, and after the procedure.

There are no food or fluid restrictions unless by medical direction. The requesting HCP may request that anticoagulants and aspirin be withheld. The number of days to withhold medication is dependent on the type of anticoagulant.

Make sure a written and informed consent has been signed prior to the procedure and before administering any medications.

INTRATEST:

Ensure that anticoagulant therapy has been withheld for the appropriate number of days prior to the procedure. Notify the HCP if patient anticoagulant therapy has not been withheld.

Have emergency equipment readily available. Keep resuscitation equipment on hand in the case of respiratory impairment or laryngospasm after the procedure.

Avoid using morphine sulfate in those with asthma or other pulmonary disease. This drug can further exacerbate bronchospasms and respiratory impairment.

Have the patient remove clothing and change into a gown for the procedure.

Instruct the patient to cooperate fully and to follow directions. Direct the patient to breathe normally and to avoid unnecessary movement during the local anesthetic and the procedure.

Observe standard precautions, and follow the general guidelines in Appendix A. Positively identify the patient, and label the appropriate specimen container with the corresponding patient demographics, initials of the person collecting the specimen, date and time of collection, and site location.

Record baseline vital signs and continue to monitor throughout the procedure. Protocols may vary among facilities.

Establish an IV line to allow infusion of IV fluids, anesthetics, analgesics, or IV sedation.

Assist the patient into a comfortable sitting or side-lying position.

Prior to the administration of local anesthesia, clip hair from the site as needed, cleanse the site with an antiseptic solution, and drape the area with sterile towels. The skin at the injection site is then anesthetized. The thoracentesis needle is inserted, and fluid is removed.

The needle is withdrawn, and pressure is applied to the site with a petroleum jelly gauze. A pressure dressing is applied over the petroleum jelly gauze.

Monitor the patient for complications related to the procedure (e.g., allergic reaction, anaphylaxis).

Place samples in properly labeled specimen container, and promptly transport the specimen to the laboratory for processing and analysis.

POST-TEST:

A report of the results will be made available to the requesting HCP, who will discuss the results with the patient

Instruct the patient to resume usual medications, as directed by the HCP.

Monitor vital signs every 15 min for the first hr, every 30 min for the next 2 hr, every hour for the next 4 hr, and every 4 hr for the next 24 hr. Take the patient's temperature every 4 hr for 24 hr. Monitor intake and output for 24 hr. Notify the HCP if temperature is elevated. Protocols may vary among facilities.

Observe/assess the patient for signs of respiratory distress or skin color changes.

Observe/assess the thoracentesis site for bleeding, inflammation, or hematoma formation each time vital signs are taken and daily thereafter for several days.

Observe/assess the patient for hemoptysis, difficulty breathing, cough, air hunger, pain, or absent breathing sounds over the affected area. Report to HCP.

Inform the patient that 1 hr or more of bed rest (lying on the unaffected side) is required after the procedure. Elevate the patient's head for comfort.

Evaluate the patient for symptoms indicating the development of pneumothorax, such as dyspnea, tachypnea, anxiety, decreased breathing sounds, or restlessness. Prepare the patient for a chest x-ray, if ordered, to ensure that a pneumothorax has not occurred as a result of the procedure.

Observe/assess for nausea and pain. Administer antiemetic and analgesic medications as needed and as directed by the HCP.

Administer antibiotics, as ordered, and instruct the patient in the importance of completing the entire course of antibiotic therapy even if no symptoms are present.

Recognize anxiety related to test results, and offer support. Discuss the implications of abnormal test results on the patient's lifestyle. Provide teaching and information regarding the clinical implications of the test results, as appropriate. Educate the patient regarding access to counseling services, if appropriate.

Reinforce information given by the patient's HCP regarding further testing, treatment, or referral to another HCP. Answer any questions or address any concerns voiced by the patient or family. Depending on the results of this procedure, additional testing may be performed to evaluate or monitor progression of the disease process and determine the need for a change in therapy. Evaluate test results in relation to the patient's symptoms and other tests performed.

RELATED MONOGRAPHS:

Related tests include antibodies anti-cyclic citrullinated peptide, ANA, biopsy lung, blood gases, cancer antigens, chest x-ray, CBC WBC count and differential, CT thoracic, CRP, culture and smear mycobacteria, culture blood, culture fungal, culture viral, ECG, ESR, MRI chest, and RF.

Refer to the Immune and Respiratory systems tables at the end of the book for related tests by body system.

Porphyrins, Urine

SYNONYM/ACRONYM: Coproporphyrin, porphobilinogen, urobilinogen, and other porphyrins.

COMMON USE: To assess for porphyrias in the urine to assist with diagnosis of genetic disorders associated with porphyrin synthesis as well as heavy metal toxicity.

SPECIMEN: Urine (10 mL) from a random or timed specimen collected in a clean, amber-colored plastic collection container with sodium carbonate as a preservative.

NORMAL FINDINGS: (Method: High-performance liquid chromatography for porphyrins; spectrophotometry for δ-aminolevulinic acid and porphobilinogen)

Test	Conventional Units	SI Units
		(Conventional Units × 1.53)
Coproporphyrin I	0–24 mcg/24 h	0–34.3 nmol/24 hr
Coproporphyrin III	0–74 mcg/24 hr	0–113.2 nmol/24 hr

(table continues on page 1118)

Test	Conventional Units	SI Units
Uroporphyrins	0–24 mcg/24 hr	*(Conventional Units × 1.43)* 0–34.3 nmol/24 hr
Hexacarboxylporphyrin	Less than 1 mcg/24 hr	*(Conventional Units × 1.34)* Less than 1.34 nmol/24 hr
Heptacarboxylporphyrin	Less than 4 mcg/24 hr	*(Conventional Units × 1.27)* Less than 5.1 nmol/24 hr
Porphobilinogen	Less than 2.0 mg/24 hr	*(Conventional Units × 4.42)* Less than 8.8 micromol/24 hr
δ-Aminolevulinic acid	1.5–7.5 mg/24 hr	*(Conventional Units × 7.626)* 11.4–57.2 micromol/24 hr

DESCRIPTION: Porphyrins are produced during the synthesis of heme. If heme synthesis is disturbed, these precursors accumulate and are excreted in the urine in excessive amounts. Conditions producing increased levels of heme precursors are called *porphyrias*. The two main categories of genetically determined porphyrias are erythropoietic porphyrias, in which major abnormalities occur in red blood cell chemistry, and hepatic porphyrias, in which heme precursors are found in urine and feces. Erythropoietic and hepatic porphyrias are rare. Acquired porphyrias are characterized by greater accumulation of precursors in urine and feces than in red blood cells. Lead poisoning is the most common cause of acquired porphyrias. Porphyrins are reddish fluorescent compounds. Depending on the type of porphyrin present, the urine may be reddish, resembling port wine. Porphobilinogen is excreted as a colorless compound. A color change may occur in an acidic sample containing porphobilinogen if the sample is exposed to air for several hours.

INDICATIONS
- Assist in the diagnosis of congenital or acquired porphyrias characterized by abdominal pain, tachycardia, emesis, fever, leukocytosis, and neurological abnormalities
- Detect suspected lead poisoning, as indicated by elevated porphyrins

POTENTIAL DIAGNOSIS

Increased in
Accumulation of porphyrins or porphyrin precursors in the body is common to the various types of porphyrias. Excessive amounts of circulating porphyrins and precursors are excreted in the urine.

- Acute intermittent porphyria *(related to an autosomal dominant disorder resulting in a deficiency of the enzyme porphobilinogen deaminase and increased* excretion of porphobilinogen and delta-aminolevulinic acid [δ-ALA] in the urine)

- Acquired or chemical porphyrias (heavy metal, benzene, or carbon tetrachloride toxicity; drug induced) *(related to a disturbance in the heme biosynthetic pathway and increased excretion of delta-aminolevulinic acid in the urine)*
- ALAD deficiency porphyria *(related to an autosomal recessive disorder resulting in a deficiency of the enzyme delta-aminolevulinic acid dehydratase and increased excretion of δ-ALA in the urine)*
- Hepatoerythropoietic porphyria *(related to an autosomal recessive disorder resulting in a deficiency of the enzyme uroporphyrinogen decarboxylase and increased excretion of uroporphyrin and heptacarboxylporphyrin in the urine)*
- Hereditary coproporphyria *(related to an autosomal dominant disorder resulting in a deficiency of the enzyme coproporphyrinogen oxidase and increased excretion of porphobilinogen, δ-ALA, and coproporphyrin in the urine)*
- Porphyria cutanea tarda *(related to an acquired deficiency of the enzyme uroporphyrinogen decarboxylase activated by exposure to triggers such as iron, alcohol, hepatitis C virus, HIV, or estrogens and increased excretion of uroporphyrin, heptacarboxylporphyrin, and coproporphyrin in the urine)*
- Variegate porphyrias *(related to an autosomal dominant disorder resulting in a deficiency of the enzyme protoporphyrinogen oxidase and increased excretion of porphobilinogen, coproporphyrin, and δ-ALA in the urine during attacks; excretion of normal levels may be found between attacks)*

Decreased in: N/A

CRITICAL FINDINGS: N/A

INTERFERING FACTORS
- Drugs that may increase urine porphyrin levels include acriflavine, aminopyrine, ethoxazene, griseofulvin, hexachlorobenzene, oxytetracycline, and sulfonmethane.
- Numerous drugs are suspected as potential initiators of acute attacks, but drugs classified as unsafe for high-risk individuals include aminopyrine, aminoglutethimide, antipyrine, barbiturates, N-butylscopolammonium bromide, carbamazepine, carbromal, chlorpropamide, danazol, dapsone, diclofenac, diphenylhydantoin, ergot preparations, ethchlorvynol, ethinamate, glutethimide, griseofulvin, N-isopropyl meprobamate, mephenytoin, meprobamate, methyprylon, novobiocin, phenylbutazone, primidone, pyrazolone preparations, succinimides, sulfonamide antibiotics, sulfonethylmethane, sulfonmethane, synthetic estrogens and progestins, tolazamide, tolbutamide, trimethadione, and valproic acid.
- Exposure of the specimen to light can falsely decrease values.
- Screening methods are not well standardized and can produce false-negative results.
- Failure to collect all urine and store specimen properly during the 24-hour test period will interfere with results.

NURSING IMPLICATIONS AND PROCEDURE

PRETEST:
- Positively identify the patient using at least two unique identifiers before providing care, treatment, or services.
- *Patient Teaching:* Inform the patient this test can assist in evaluating for

conditions producing increased levels of heme precursors called porphyrias.

▸ Obtain a history of the patient's complaints, including a list of known allergens, especially allergies or sensitivities to latex.

▸ Obtain a history of the patient's hematopoietic system, symptoms, and results of previously performed laboratory tests and diagnostic and surgical procedures.

▸ Obtain a list of the patient's current medications, including herbs, nutritional supplements, and nutraceuticals (see Appendix F).

▸ Review the procedure with the patient. Provide a nonmetallic urinal, bedpan, or toilet-mounted collection device. Address concerns about pain and explain that there should be no discomfort during the procedure.

▸ Usually a 24-hr time frame for urine collection is ordered. Inform the patient that all urine must be saved during that 24-hr period. Instruct the patient not to void directly into the laboratory collection container. Instruct the patient to avoid defecating in the collection device and to keep toilet tissue out of the collection device to prevent contamination of the specimen. Place a sign in the bathroom to remind the patient to save all urine.

▸ Instruct the patient to void all urine into the collection device and then to pour the urine into the laboratory collection container. Alternatively, the specimen can be left in the collection device for a health-care staff member to add to the laboratory collection container.

▸ *Sensitivity to social and cultural issues,* as well as concern for modesty, is important in providing psychological support before, during, and after the procedure.

▸ There are no food, fluid, or medication restrictions unless by medical direction.

INTRATEST:

▸ If the patient has a history of allergic reaction to latex, avoid the use of equipment containing latex.

▸ Instruct the patient to cooperate fully and to follow directions.

▸ Observe standard precautions, and follow the general guidelines in

Appendix A. Positively identify the patient, and label the appropriate specimen container with the corresponding patient demographics, initials of the person collecting the specimen, date, and time of collection.

Random Specimen (Collect in Early Morning)

Clean-Catch Specimen

▸ Instruct the male patient to (1) thoroughly wash his hands, (2) cleanse the meatus, (3) void a small amount into the toilet, and (4) void directly into the specimen container.

▸ Instruct the female patient to (1) thoroughly wash her hands; (2) cleanse the labia from front to back; (3) while keeping the labia separated, void a small amount into the toilet; and (4) without interrupting the urine stream, void directly into the specimen container.

Indwelling Catheter

▸ Put on gloves. Empty drainage tube of urine. It may be necessary to clamp off the catheter for 15 to 30 minutes before specimen collection. Cleanse specimen port with antiseptic swab, and then aspirate 5 mL of urine with a 21- to 25-gauge needle and syringe. Transfer urine to a sterile container.

Timed Specimen

▸ Obtain a clean 3-L urine specimen container, toilet-mounted collection device, and plastic bag (for transport of the specimen container). The specimen must be refrigerated or kept on ice throughout the entire collection period. If an indwelling urinary catheter is in place, the drainage bag must be kept on ice.

▸ Begin the test between 6 and 8 a.m. if possible. Collect first voiding and discard. Record the time the specimen was discarded as the beginning of the timed collection period. The next morning, ask the patient to void at the same time the collection was started and add this last voiding to the container. Urinary output should be recorded throughout the collection time.

▸ If an indwelling catheter is in place, replace the tubing and container system at the start of the collection time. Keep the container system on ice during the collection period, or empty the urine into a larger container periodically during the collection period; monitor to ensure continued drainage, and conclude the test the next morning at the same hour the collection was begun. At the conclusion of the test, compare the quantity of urine with the urinary output record for the collection; if the specimen contains less than what was recorded as output, some urine may have been discarded, invalidating the test.

Include on the collection container's label the amount of urine, test start and stop times, and ingestion of any foods or medications that can affect test results.

General
Promptly transport the specimen to the laboratory for processing and analysis.

POST-TEST:

A report of the results will be made available to the requesting health-care provider (HCP), who will discuss the results with the patient.

Nutritional Considerations: Increased δ-ALA levels may be associated with an acute porphyria attack. Patients prone to attacks should eat a normal or high-carbohydrate diet. Dietary recommendations may be indicated and will vary depending on the condition and its severity; however, restrictions of or wide variations in dietary carbohydrate content should be avoided, even for short periods of time. After recovering from an attack, daily intake of carbohydrates should be 300 grams or more per day.

Recognize anxiety related to test results. Discuss the implications of abnormal test results on the patient's lifestyle. Provide teaching and information regarding the clinical implications of the test results, as appropriate. Educate the patient regarding access to counseling services. Provide contact information, if desired, for the American Porphyria Foundation (www.porphyria-foundation.com).

Reinforce information given by the patient's HCP regarding further testing, treatment, or referral to another HCP. Answer any questions or address any concerns voiced by the patient or family.

Depending on the results of this procedure, additional testing may be performed to evaluate or monitor progression of the disease process and determine the need for a change in therapy. Evaluate test results in relation to the patient's symptoms and other tests performed.

RELATED MONOGRAPHS:

Related tests include δ-aminolevulinic acid, erythrocyte protoporphyrin, and lead.

Refer to the Hematopoietic System table at the end of the book for related tests by body system.

P

Positron Emission Tomography, Brain

SYNONYM/ACRONYM: PET scan of the brain.

COMMON USE: To assess blood flow and metabolic processes of the brain to assist in diagnosis of disorders such as ischemic or hemorrhagic stroke or cancer and to evaluate head trauma.

AREA OF APPLICATION: Brain.

CONTRAST: IV radioactive material (fluorodeoxyglucose [FDG]).

DESCRIPTION: Positron emission tomography (PET) combines the biochemical properties of nuclear medicine with the accuracy of computed tomography (CT). PET uses positron emissions from specific radionuclides (oxygen, nitrogen, carbon, and fluorine) to produce detailed functional images within the body. After the radionuclide becomes concentrated in the brain, PET images of blood flow or metabolic processes at the cellular level can be obtained. Fluorine-18, in the form of fluorodeoxyglucose (FDG), is one of the more commonly used radionuclides. FDG is a glucose analogue, and because every cell uses glucose, the metabolic activity occurring in neurological conditions can be measured. There is little localization of FDG in normal tissue, allowing rapid detection of abnormal disease states. The brain uses oxygen and glucose almost exclusively to meet its energy needs, and therefore the brain's metabolism has been studied widely with PET.

The positron radiopharmaceuticals generally have short half-lives, ranging from a few seconds to a few hours, and therefore they must be produced in a cyclotron located near where the test is being done. The PET scanner translates the emissions from the radioactivity as the positron combines with the negative electrons from the tissues and forms gamma rays that can be detected by the scanner. This information is transmitted to the computer, which determines the location and its distribution and translates the emissions as color-coded images for viewing, quantitative measurements, activity changes in relation to time, and three-dimensional computer-aided analysis. Each radionuclide tracer is designed to measure a specific body process, such as glucose metabolism, blood flow, or brain tissue perfusion. The radionuclide can be administered IV or inhaled as a gas. PET has had the greatest clinical impact in patients with epilepsy, dementia, neurodegenerative diseases, inflammation, cerebrovascular disease (indirectly), and brain tumors.

The expense of the study and the limited availability of radiopharmaceuticals limit the use of PET even though it is more sensitive than traditional nuclear scanning and single-photon emission computed tomography. Changes in reimbursement and the advent of mobile technology have increased the availability of this procedure in the community setting.

INDICATIONS

- Detect Parkinson's disease and Huntington's disease, as evidenced by decreased metabolism
- Determine the effectiveness of therapy, as evidenced by biochemical activity of normal and abnormal tissues
- Determine physiological changes in psychosis and schizophrenia
- Differentiate between tumor recurrence and radiation necrosis
- Evaluate Alzheimer's disease and differentiate it from other causes of dementia, as evidenced by decreased cerebral flow and metabolism
- Evaluate cranial tumors pre- and postoperatively and determine stage and appropriate treatment or procedure
- Identify cerebrovascular accident or aneurysm, as evidenced by

decreased blood flow and oxygen use
* Identify focal seizures, as evidenced by decreased metabolism between seizures

POTENTIAL DIAGNOSIS

Normal findings in
* Normal patterns of tissue metabolism, blood flow, and radionuclide distribution

Abnormal findings in
* Alzheimer's disease
* Aneurysm
* Cerebral metastases
* Cerebrovascular accident
* Creutzfeldt-Jakob disease
* Dementia
* Head trauma
* Huntington's disease
* Migraine
* Parkinson's disease
* Schizophrenia
* Seizure disorders
* Tumors

CRITICAL FINDINGS

* Aneurysm
* Cerebrovascular accident
* Tumor with significant mass effect

It is essential that critical diagnoses be communicated immediately to the appropriate health-care provider (HCP). A listing of these diagnoses varies among facilities. Note and immediately report to the HCP abnormal results and related symptoms. Timely notification of critical values for lab or diagnostic studies is a role expectation of the professional nurse. Notification processes will vary among facilities. Upon receipt of the critical value the information should be read back to the caller to verify accuracy. Most policies require immediate notification of the primary HCP, hospitalist, or on-call HCP. Reported information includes the patient's name, unique identifiers, critical value, name of the person giving the report, and name of the person receiving the report. Documentation of notification should be made in the medical record with the name of the HCP notified, time and date of notification, and any orders received. Any delay in a timely report of a critical value may require completion of a notification form with review by Risk Management.

INTERFERING FACTORS

This procedure is contraindicated for
* Patients who are pregnant or suspected of being pregnant, unless the potential benefits of the procedure far outweigh the risks to the fetus and mother.

Factors that may impair clear imaging
* Inability of the patient to cooperate or remain still during the procedure because of age, significant pain, or mental status.
* Drugs that alter glucose metabolism, such as tranquilizers or insulin, because hypoglycemia can alter PET results.
* The use of alcohol, tobacco, or caffeine-containing drinks at least 24 hr before the study, because the effects of these substances would make it difficult to evaluate the patient's true physiological state (e.g., alcohol is a vasoconstrictor and would decrease blood flow to the target organ).
* Metallic objects (e.g., jewelry, body rings) within the examination field, which may inhibit organ visualization and cause unclear images.

Other considerations
* Failure to follow dietary restrictions before the procedure may cause the procedure to be canceled or repeated.
* Improper injection of the radionuclide that allows the tracer to seep deep into the muscle tissue produces erroneous hot spots.

P

- False-positive findings may occur as a result of normal gastrointestinal tract uptake and uptake in areas of infection or inflammation.
- Consultation with a HCP should occur before the procedure for radiation safety concerns regarding younger patients or patients who are lactating.
- Risks associated with radiation over-exposure can result from frequent x-ray or radionuclide procedures. Personnel working in the examination area should wear badges to record their level of radiation exposure.

NURSING IMPLICATIONS AND PROCEDURE

PRETEST:

▶ Positively identify the patient using at least two unique identifiers before providing care, treatment, or services.
▶ *Patient Teaching:* Inform the patient that this procedure can assist in assessing blood flow to the brain and brain tissue metabolism.
▶ Obtain a history of the patient's complaints, including a list of known allergens, especially allergies or sensitivities to latex, iodine, seafood, contrast medium, or anesthetics.
▶ Obtain a history of the patient's musculoskeletal system, symptoms, and results of previously performed laboratory tests and diagnostic and surgical procedures.
▶ Note any recent procedures that can interfere with test results, including examinations using barium- or iodine-based contrast medium.
▶ Record the date of the last menstrual period and determine the possibility of pregnancy in perimenopausal women.
▶ Obtain a list of the patient's current medications, including herbs, nutritional supplements, and nutraceuticals (see Appendix F).
▶ Review the procedure with the patient. Address concerns about pain related to the procedure and explain that some pain may be experienced during the test, or there may be moments of

discomfort. Reassure the patient that radioactive material poses minimal radioactive hazard because of its short half-life and rarely produces side effects. Inform the patient that the procedure is performed in a special department, usually in a radiology suite, by an HCP specializing in this procedure, with support staff, and takes approximately 60 to 120 min.

▶ *Sensitivity to social and cultural issues,* as well as concern for modesty, is important in providing psychological support before, during, and after the procedure.
▶ Sometimes FDG examinations are done after blood has been drawn to determine circulating blood glucose levels. If blood glucose levels are high, insulin may be given.
▶ Instruct the patient to remove jewelry and other metallic objects from the area to be examined prior to the procedure.
▶ Instruct the patient to avoid taking anticoagulant medication or to reduce dosage as ordered prior to the procedure.
▶ Instruct the patient to restrict food for 4 hr; restrict alcohol, nicotine, or caffeine-containing drinks for 24 hr; and withhold medications for 24 hr before the test. Protocols may vary among facilities.
▶ *Make sure a written and informed consent has been signed prior to the procedure and before administering any medications.*

INTRATEST:

▶ Observe standard precautions, and follow the general guidelines in Appendix A. Positively identify the patient.
▶ Ensure that the patient has complied with dietary, fluid, and medication restrictions and pretesting preparations
▶ Ensure the patient has removed all jewelry and external metallic objects from the area to be examined prior to the procedure.
▶ Have emergency equipment readily available.
▶ Instruct the patient to void prior to the procedure and to change into the gown robe, and foot coverings provided.

Instruct the patient to cooperate fully and to follow directions. Ask the patient to remain still throughout the procedure because movement produces unreliable results.

Record baseline vital signs and assess neurological status. Protocols may vary among facilities.

Place the patient in the supine position on an examination table.

The radionuclide is injected, and imaging is started after a 30-min delay. If comparative studies are indicated, additional injections may be needed. The patient may be asked to perform different cognitive activities (e.g., reading) to measure changes in brain activity during reasoning or remembering. The patient may be blindfolded or asked to use earplugs to decrease auditory and visual stimuli.

Monitor the patient for complications related to the procedure (e.g., allergic reaction, anaphylaxis, bronchospasm). Remove the needle or catheter and apply a pressure dressing over the puncture site.

Observe/assess the needle/catheter insertion site for bleeding, inflammation, or hematoma formation.

POST-TEST:

A report of the results will be made available to the requesting HCP, who will discuss the results with the patient.

Instruct the patient to resume pretest diet, fluids, medications, or activity.

Observe for delayed allergic reactions, such as rash, urticaria, tachycardia, hyperpnea, hypertension, palpitations, nausea, or vomiting.

Instruct the patient to immediately report symptoms such as fast heart rate, difficulty breathing, skin rash, itching, chest pain, persistent right shoulder pain, or abdominal pain. Immediately report symptoms to the appropriate HCP.

Observe/assess the needle/catheter insertion site for bleeding, inflammation, or hematoma formation.

Instruct the patient in the care and assessment of the injection site.

Instruct the patient to apply cold compresses to the puncture site as needed to reduce discomfort or edema.

Instruct the patient to drink increased amounts of fluids for 24 to 48 hr to eliminate the radionuclide from the body, unless contraindicated. Educate the patient that radionuclide is eliminated from the body within 6 to 24 hr.

Instruct the patient to flush the toilet immediately after each voiding and to meticulously wash hands with soap and water for 24 hr after the procedure.

Instruct all caregivers to wear gloves when discarding urine for 24 hr after the procedure. Wash gloved hands with soap and water before removing gloves. Then wash hands after the gloves are removed.

If a woman who is breastfeeding must have a nuclear scan, she should not breastfeed the infant until the radionuclide has been eliminated, about 3 days. Instruct her to express the milk and discard it during the 3-day period to prevent cessation of milk production.

No other radionuclide tests should be scheduled for 24 to 48 hr after this procedure.

Recognize anxiety related to test results, and be supportive of perceived loss of independent function. Discuss the implications of abnormal test results on the patient's lifestyle. Provide teaching and information regarding the clinical implications of the test results, as appropriate.

Reinforce information given by the patient's HCP regarding further testing, treatment, or referral to another HCP. Answer any questions or address any concerns voiced by the patient or family.

Depending on the results of this procedure, additional testing may be needed to evaluate or monitor progression of the disease process and determine the need for a change in therapy. Evaluate test results in relation to the patient's symptoms and other tests performed.

RELATED MONOGRAPHS:

Related tests include Alzheimer's disease markers, CT brain, EEG, MRI brain, and US arterial Doppler of the carotids.

Refer to the Musculoskeletal System table at the end of the book for related tests by body system.

P

Positron Emission Tomography, FDG

SYNONYM/ACRONYM: Fluorodeoxyglucose (FDG)-positron emission tomography (PET).

COMMON USE: To assist in assessment, staging, and monitoring of metabolically active malignant lesions in the breast, abdomen, brain, and heart, such as breast cancer, Parkinson's disease, and Alzheimer's disease.

AREA OF APPLICATION: Abdomen, brain, breast, heart, pelvis.

CONTRAST: IV radioactive material fluorodeoxyglucose (FDG).

DESCRIPTION: Fluorine-18, in the form of fluorodeoxyglucose (FDG), is one of the more commonly used radionuclides. FDG is a glucose analogue, and because every cell uses glucose, the metabolic activity occurring in neurological conditions can be measured. There is little localization of FDG in normal tissue, allowing rapid detection of abnormal disease states. The brain uses oxygen and glucose almost exclusively to meet its energy needs, and therefore the brain's metabolism has been studied widely with positron emission tomography (PET). The role of this procedure is to detect metabolically active malignant lesions. FDG-PET scan may also be used to stage and monitor the response to the malignant disease.

PET combines the biochemical properties of nuclear medicine with the accuracy of computed tomography (CT). PET uses positron emissions from specific radionuclides (oxygen, nitrogen, carbon, and fluorine) to produce detailed functional images within the body. The positron radiopharmaceuticals generally have short half-lives, ranging from a few seconds to a few hours, and therefore they must be produced in a cyclotron located near where the test is being done. The PET scanner translates the emissions from the radioactivity as the positron combines with the negative electrons from the tissues and forms gamma rays that can be detected by the scanner. This information is transmitted to the computer, which determines the location and its distribution and translates the emissions as color-coded images for viewing, quantitative measurements, activity changes in relation to time, and three-dimensional computer-aided analysis.

The expense of the study and the limited availability of radiopharmaceuticals limit the use of PET, even though it is more sensitive than traditional nuclear scanning and single-photon emission computed tomography. Changes in reimbursement and the advent of mobile technology have increased the availability of this procedure in the community setting.

INDICATIONS
- Detect Parkinson's disease and Huntington's disease, as evidenced by decreased metabolism
- Determine physiological changes in psychosis and schizophrenia

P

- Evaluate Alzheimer's disease and differentiate it from other causes of dementia, as evidenced by decreased cerebral flow and metabolism
- Evaluate coronary artery disease (CAD), as evidenced by decreased myocardial blood flow and myocardial perfusion
- Evaluate myocardial viability, as evidenced by low glucose metabolism
- Evaluate tumors preoperatively and postoperatively and determine grade, stage, and appropriate treatment or procedure
- Identify cerebrovascular accident or aneurysm, as evidenced by decreased blood flow and oxygen use
- Identify focal seizures, as evidenced by decreased metabolism between seizures

POTENTIAL DIAGNOSIS

Normal findings in

Normal patterns of tissue metabolism, blood flow, and radionuclide distribution

Abnormal findings in

Alzheimer's disease
Brain trauma
Breast cancer
Colorectal cancer
CAD
Epilepsy
Heart muscle dysfunction
Huntington's disease
Infections
Lung cancer
Lymphoma
Melanoma
Metastatic disease
Myeloma
Ovarian cancer
Pancreatic cancer
Parkinson's disease

CRITICAL FINDINGS: N/A

INTERFERING FACTORS

This procedure is contraindicated for

- Patients who are pregnant or suspected of being pregnant, unless the potential benefits of the procedure far outweigh the risks to the fetus and mother.

Factors that may impair clear imaging

- Inability of the patient to cooperate or remain still during the procedure because of age, significant pain, or mental status.
- Drugs that alter glucose metabolism, such as tranquilizers, sedatives, or insulin, because hypoglycemia can alter PET results.
- The use of alcohol, tobacco, or caffeine-containing drinks at least 24 hr before the study, because the effects of these substances, make it difficult to evaluate the patient's true physiological state (e.g., alcohol is a vasoconstrictor and would decrease blood flow to the target organ).
- Excessive exercise in the preceding 3 days, which can cause factitious uptake of the contrast material in the musculature.
- Excessive anxiety may affect valuation of brain function.
- Metallic objects (e.g., jewelry, body rings) within the examination field, which may inhibit organ visualization and cause unclear images.

Other considerations

- Failure to follow dietary restrictions before the procedure may cause the procedure to be canceled or repeated.
- Consultation with a health-care provider (HCP) should occur before the procedure for radiation safety concerns regarding younger patients or patients who are lactating.
- Risks associated with radiation overexposure can result from

P

frequent x-ray or radionuclide procedures. Personnel working in the examination area should wear badges to record their level of radiation exposure.

NURSING IMPLICATIONS AND PROCEDURE

PRETEST:

▶ Positively identify the patient using at least two unique identifiers before providing care, treatment, or services.
▶ *Patient Teaching:* Inform the patient this test can assist in assessing blood flow and tissue metabolism.
▶ Obtain a history of the patient's complaints, including a list of known allergens, especially allergies or sensitivities to latex, iodine, seafood, anesthetics, or contrast medium.
▶ Obtain a history of the patient's cardiovascular, hematopoietic, neuromuscular, and reproductive systems; symptoms; and results of previously performed laboratory tests and diagnostic and surgical procedures.
▶ Note any recent procedures that can interfere with test results, including examinations using barium- or iodine-based contrast medium.
▶ Record the date of last menstrual period and determine the possibility of pregnancy in perimenopausal women.
▶ Obtain a list of the patient's current medications, including herbs, nutritional supplements, and nutraceuticals (see Appendix F).
▶ Review the procedure with the patient. Address concerns about pain related to the procedure and explain that no pain will be experienced during the test, but there may be moments of discomfort. Reassure the patient the radionuclide poses no radioactive hazard and rarely produces side effects.
▶ Inform the patient that the procedure is performed in a nuclear medicine department, by an HCP specializing in this procedure, with support staff, and takes approximately 1 to 3 hr.
▶ *Sensitivity to social and cultural issues,* as well as concern for modesty, is important in providing psychological support before, during, and after the procedure.
▶ Instruct patients with diabetes to take their pretest dose of insulin at a meal 4 hr before the test.
▶ Sometimes FDG examinations are done after blood has been drawn to determine circulating blood glucose levels. If blood glucose levels are high, insulin may be given.
▶ Instruct the patient to remove jewelry and other metallic objects from the area to be examined prior to the procedure.
▶ Instruct the patient to restrict food for 4 to 6 hr; restrict alcohol, nicotine, or caffeine-containing drinks for 24 hr; and withhold medications for 24 hr before the test. The exception is that there are no dietary restrictions for patients undergoing cardiac imaging. Protocols may vary among facilities.
▶ *Make sure a written and informed consent has been signed prior to the procedure and before administering any medications.*

INTRATEST:

▶ Observe standard precautions, and follow the general guidelines in Appendix A. Positively identify the patient.
▶ Ensure that the patient has complied with dietary, fluid, and medication restrictions and pretesting preparations prior to the procedure.
▶ Ensure that the patient has removed external metallic objects from the area to be examined prior to the procedure.
▶ Have emergency equipment readily available.
▶ Instruct the patient to void prior to the procedure and to change into the gown, robe, and foot coverings provided.
▶ Instruct the patient to cooperate fully and to follow directions. Instruct the patient to remain still throughout the procedure because movement produces unreliable results.
▶ Record baseline vital signs and assess neurological status. Protocols may vary among facilities.
▶ Cardiac imaging patients may be asked to drink glucose prior to the radionuclide injection.
▶ Place the patient in the supine position on an examination table.

- The radionuclide is injected, and imaging is started after a 30-min delay. Images may be recorded for up to 3 hr postinjection.
- Monitor the patient for complications related to the procedure (e.g., allergic reaction, anaphylaxis, bronchospasm).
- Remove the needle or catheter and apply a pressure dressing over the puncture site.
- Observe/assess the needle/catheter insertion site for bleeding, inflammation, or hematoma formation.

POST-TEST:

- A report of the results will be made available to the requesting HCP, who will discuss the results with the patient.
- Instruct the patient to resume pretest diet, fluids, medications, and activity.
- Observe for delayed allergic reactions, such as rash, urticaria, tachycardia, hyperpnea, hypertension, palpitations, nausea, or vomiting.
- Instruct the patient to immediately report symptoms such as fast heart rate, difficulty breathing, skin rash, itching, chest pain, persistent right shoulder pain, or abdominal pain. Immediately report symptoms to the appropriate HCP.
- Observe/assess the needle/catheter insertion site for bleeding, inflammation, or hematoma formation.
- Instruct the patient in the care and assessment of the injection site.
- Instruct the patient to apply cold compresses to the puncture site as needed, to reduce discomfort or edema.
- Instruct the patient to drink increased amounts of fluids for 24 to 48 hr to eliminate the radionuclide from the body, unless contraindicated. Educate the patient that radionuclide is eliminated from the body within 6 to 24 hr.
- Instruct the patient to flush the toilet immediately after each voiding and to meticulously wash hands with soap and water for 24 hr after the procedure.
- Instruct all caregivers to wear gloves when discarding urine for 24 hr after the procedure. Wash gloved hands with soap and water before removing gloves. Then wash hands after the gloves are removed.

- If a woman who is breastfeeding must have a nuclear scan, she should not breastfeed the infant until the radionuclide has been eliminated, about 3 days. Instruct her to express the milk and discard it during the 3-day period to prevent cessation of milk production.

Nutritional Considerations: Abnormal findings may be associated with cardiovascular disease. The American Heart Association and National Heart, Lung, and Blood Institute (NHLBI) recommend nutritional therapy for individuals identified to be at high risk for developing CAD or individuals who have specific risk factors and/or existing medical conditions (e.g., elevated LDL cholesterol levels, other lipid disorders, insulin-dependent diabetes, insulin resistance, or metabolic syndrome). If overweight, the patient should be encouraged to achieve a normal weight. Guidelines for the Therapeutic Lifestyle Changes (TLC) diet are outlined in the Third Report of the Expert Panel on Detection, Evaluation, and Treatment of High Blood Cholesterol in Adults (Adult Treatment Panel III [ATP III]). The TLC diet emphasizes a reduction in foods high in saturated fats and cholesterol. Red meats, eggs, and dairy products are the major sources of saturated fats and cholesterol. If triglycerides also are elevated, the patient should be advised to eliminate or reduce alcohol and simple carbohydrates from the diet. The TLC approach also includes the use of plant stanols or sterols and increased dissolved fiber as an option for lowering LDL cholesterol levels; nutritional recommendations for daily total caloric intake; recommendations for allowable percentage of calories derived from fat (saturated and unsaturated), carbohydrates, protein, and cholesterol; as well as recommendations for daily expenditure of energy.

Nutritional Considerations: Overweight patients with high blood pressure should be encouraged to achieve a normal weight. Other changeable risk factors warranting patient education include strategies to safely decrease sodium intake, increase physical

P

activity, decrease alcohol consumption, eliminate tobacco use, and decrease cholesterol levels.

▸ No other radionuclide tests should be scheduled for 24 to 48 hr after this procedure.

▸ Recognize anxiety related to test results. Discuss the implications of abnormal test results on the patient's lifestyle. Provide teaching and information regarding the clinical implications of the test results, as appropriate.

▸ Reinforce information given by the patient's HCP regarding further testing, treatment, or referral to another HCP. Decisions regarding the need for and frequency of breast self-examination, mammography, magnetic resonance imaging (MRI) of the breast, or other cancer screening procedures should be made after consultation between the patient and HCP. The most current guidelines for breast cancer screening of the general population as well as of individuals with increased risk are available from the American Cancer Society (www.cancer.org), the American College of Obstetricians and Gynecologists (ACOG) (www.acog.org), and the American College of Radiology (www.acr.org). Answer any questions or address any concerns voiced by the patient or family.

▸ Depending on the results of this procedure, additional testing may be needed to evaluate or monitor progression of the disease process and determine the need for a change in therapy. Evaluate test results in relation to the patient's symptoms and other tests performed.

RELATED MONOGRAPHS:

▸ Related tests include AFP, Alzheimer's disease markers, amino acid screen, amylase, barium enema, biopsy breast, biopsy lung, bronchoscopy, calcitonin, cancer antigens, CBC WBC count and differential, CSF analysis, colonoscopy, CT abdomen, CT brain, CT pancreas, CT pelvis, cytology sputum, evoked brain potentials, exercise stress test, fecal analysis, gallium scan, laparoscopy abdominal, laparoscopy gyn, lymph-angiogram, mammography, MRI abdomen, MRI brain, MRI breast, MRI pelvis, myocardial perfusion heart scan, peritoneal fluid analysis, PET brain, PET heart, PET pelvis, proctosigmoidoscopy, stereotactic breast biopsy, US breast, US pancreas, US pelvis gyn, and WBC scan.

▸ Refer to the Cardiovascular, Musculoskeletal, and Reproductive systems tables at the end of the book for related tests by body system.

Positron Emission Tomography, Heart

SYNONYM/ACRONYM: PET scan of the heart.

COMMON USE: To assess blood flow and metabolic process of the heart to assist in diagnosis of disorders such as coronary artery disease, infarct, and aneurysm.

AREA OF APPLICATION: Heart, chest/thorax, vascular system.

CONTRAST: IV radioactive material (fluorodeoxyglucose [FDG]).

DESCRIPTION: Positron emission tomography (PET) combines the biochemical properties of nuclear medicine with the accuracy of computed tomography (CT). PET uses positron emissions from specific radionuclides (oxygen, nitrogen, carbon, and fluorine) to produce detailed functional images within the body. After the radionuclide becomes concentrated in the heart, PET images of blood flow or metabolic processes at the cellular level can be obtained. Fluorine-18, in the form of fluorodeoxyglucose (FDG), is one of the more commonly used radionuclides. FDG is a glucose analogue, and because every cell uses glucose, the metabolic activity occurring in heart conditions such as myocardial viability can be measured. There is little localization of FDG in normal tissue, allowing rapid detection of abnormal disease states.

The positron radiopharmaceuticals generally have short half-lives, ranging from a few seconds to a few hours, and therefore they must be produced in a cyclotron located near where the test is being done. The PET scanner translates the emissions from the radioactivity as the positron combines with the negative electrons from the tissues and forms gamma rays that can be detected by the scanner. This information is transmitted to the computer, which determines the location and its distribution and translates the emissions as color-coded images for viewing, quantitative measurements, activity changes in relation to time, and three-dimensional computer-aided analysis. Each radionuclide tracer is designed to measure a specific body process, such as glucose metabolism, blood flow, or tissue perfusion. The radionuclide can be administered IV or inhaled as a gas.

The expense of the study and the limited availability of radiopharmaceuticals limit the use of PET, even though it is more sensitive than traditional nuclear scanning and single-photon emission computed tomography. Changes in reimbursement and the advent of mobile technology have increased the availability of this procedure in the community setting.

INDICATIONS
- Assess tissue permeability
- Determine the effects of therapeutic drugs on malfunctioning or diseased tissue
- Determine localization of areas of heart metabolism
- Determine the presence of coronary artery disease (CAD), as evidenced by metabolic state during ischemia and after angina
- Determine the size of heart infarcts
- Identify cerebrovascular accident or aneurysm, as evidenced by decreasing blood flow and oxygen use

POTENTIAL DIAGNOSIS

Normal findings in
- Normal patterns of tissue metabolism, blood flow, and radionuclide distribution

Abnormal findings in
- Chronic obstructive pulmonary disease
- Decreased blood flow and decreased glucose concentration *(indicating necrotic, scarred tissue)*
- Enlarged left ventricle
- Heart chamber disorder
- Myocardial infarction *(indicating increased radionuclide uptake in the myocardium)*
- Pulmonary edema
- Reduced blood flow but increased glucose concentration *(indicating ischemia)*

CRITICAL FINDINGS: N/A

INTERFERING FACTORS

This procedure is contraindicated for

- Patients who are pregnant or suspected of being pregnant, unless the potential benefits of the procedure far outweigh the risks to the fetus and mother.

Factors that may impair clear imaging

- Inability of the patient to cooperate or remain still during the procedure because of age, significant pain, or mental status.
- Drugs that alter glucose metabolism, such as tranquilizers or insulin, because hypoglycemia can alter PET results.
- The use of alcohol, tobacco, or caffeine-containing drinks at least 24 hr before the study, because the effects of these substances would make it difficult to evaluate the patient's true physiological state (e.g., alcohol is a vasoconstrictor and would decrease blood flow to the target organ).
- Metallic objects (e.g., jewelry, body rings) within the examination field, which may inhibit organ visualization and cause unclear images.

Other considerations

- Failure to follow dietary restrictions before the procedure may cause the procedure to be canceled or repeated.
- Improper injection of the radionuclide that allows the tracer to seep deep into the muscle tissue produces erroneous hot spots.
- False-positive findings may occur as a result of normal gastrointestinal tract uptake and uptake in areas of infection or inflammation.
- Consultation with a health-care provider (HCP) should occur before the procedure for radiation safety concerns regarding younger patients or patients who are lactating.

- Risks associated with radiation overexposure can result from frequent x-ray or radionuclide procedures. Personnel working in the examination area should wear badges to record their level of radiation exposure.

NURSING IMPLICATIONS AND PROCEDURE

PRETEST:

- Positively identify the patient using at least two unique identifiers before providing care, treatment, or services.
- *Patient Teaching:* Inform the patient this procedure can assist in assessing blood flow to the heart.
- Obtain a history of the patient's complaints, including a list of known allergens, especially allergies or sensitivities to latex, iodine, seafood, contrast medium, or anesthetics.
- Obtain a history of the patient's cardiovascular and respiratory systems, symptoms, and results of previously performed laboratory tests and diagnostic and surgical procedures.
- Note any recent procedures that can interfere with test results, including examinations using barium- or iodine-based contrast medium.
- Record the date of the last menstrual period and determine the possibility of pregnancy in perimenopausal women.
- Obtain a list of the patient's current medications, including herbs, nutritional supplements, and nutraceuticals (see Appendix F).
- Review the procedure with the patient. Address concerns about pain related to the procedure and explain that some pain may be experienced during the test, or there may be moments of discomfort. Reassure the patient that radioactive material poses minimal radioactive hazard because of its short half-life and rarely produces side effects. Inform the patient that the procedure is performed in a special department, usually in a radiology suite, by an HCP specializing in this procedure, with support staff, and takes approximately 60 to 120 min.

P

Sensitivity to social and cultural issues, as well as concern for modesty, is important in providing psychological support before, during, and after the procedure.

Sometimes FDG examinations are done after blood has been drawn to determine circulating blood glucose levels. If blood glucose levels are high, insulin may be given.

Instruct the patient to remove jewelry and other metallic objects from the area to be examined prior to the procedure.

Instruct the patient to avoid taking anticoagulant medication or to reduce dosage as ordered prior to the procedure.

Instruct the patient to restrict food for 4 hr; restrict alcohol, nicotine, or caffeine-containing drinks for 24 hr; and withhold medications for 24 hr before the test. Protocols may vary among facilities.

Make sure a written and informed consent has been signed prior to the procedure and before administering any medications.

INTRATEST:

Observe standard precautions, and follow the general guidelines in Appendix A. Positively identify the patient.

Ensure that the patient has complied with dietary, fluid, and medication restrictions and pretesting preparations.

Ensure the patient has removed all jewelry and external metallic objects from the area to be examined prior to the procedure.

Have emergency equipment readily available.

Instruct the patient to void prior to the procedure and to change into the gown, robe, and foot coverings provided.

Instruct the patient to cooperate fully and to follow directions. Ask the patient to remain still throughout the procedure because movement produces unreliable results.

Record baseline vital signs and assess neurological status. Protocols may vary among facilities.

Place the patient in the supine position on an examination table.

The radionuclide is injected and imaging is done at periodic intervals, with continuous scanning done for 1 hr. If comparative studies are indicated, additional injections may be needed.

Monitor the patient for complications related to the procedure (e.g., allergic reaction, anaphylaxis, bronchospasm).

Remove the needle or catheter and apply a pressure dressing over the puncture site.

Observe/assess the needle site for bleeding, inflammation, or hematoma formation.

POST-TEST:

A report of the results will be made available to the requesting HCP, who will discuss the results with the patient.

Instruct the patient to resume pretest diet, fluids, medications, and activity.

Observe for delayed allergic reactions, such as rash, urticaria, tachycardia, hyperpnea, hypertension, palpitations, nausea, or vomiting.

Instruct the patient to immediately report symptoms such as fast heart rate, difficulty breathing, skin rash, itching, chest pain, persistent right shoulder pain, or abdominal pain. Immediately report symptoms to the appropriate HCP.

Observe/assess the needle/catheter insertion site for bleeding, inflammation, or hematoma formation.

Instruct the patient to apply cold compresses to the puncture site as needed, to reduce discomfort or edema.

Instruct the patient to drink increased amounts of fluids for 24 to 48 hr to eliminate the radionuclide from the body, unless contraindicated. Educate the patient that radionuclide is eliminated from the body within 6 to 24 hr.

Instruct the patient to flush the toilet immediately after each voiding and to meticulously wash hands with soap and water for 24 hr after the procedure.

Instruct all caregivers to wear gloves when discarding urine for 24 hr after the procedure. Wash gloved hands with soap and water before removing gloves. Then wash hands after the gloves are removed.

If a woman who is breastfeeding must have a nuclear scan, she should not

P

breastfeed the infant until the radionuclide has been eliminated, about 3 days. Instruct her to express the milk and discard it during the 3-day period to prevent cessation of milk production.

No other radionuclide tests should be scheduled for 24 to 48 hr after this procedure.

Nutritional Considerations: Abnormal findings may be associated with cardiovascular disease. The American Heart Association and National Heart, Lung, and Blood Institute (NHLBI) recommend nutritional therapy for individuals identified to be at high risk for developing CAD or individuals who have specific risk factors and/or existing medical conditions (e.g., elevated LDL cholesterol levels, other lipid disorders, insulin-dependent diabetes, insulin resistance, or metabolic syndrome). If overweight, the patient should be encouraged to achieve a normal weight. Guidelines for the Therapeutic Lifestyle Changes (TLC) diet are outlined in the Third Report of the Expert Panel on Detection, Evaluation, and Treatment of High Blood Cholesterol in Adults (Adult Treatment Panel III [ATP III]). The TLC diet emphasizes a reduction in foods high in saturated fats and cholesterol. Red meats, eggs, and dairy products are the major sources of saturated fats and cholesterol. If triglycerides also are elevated, the patient should be advised to eliminate or reduce alcohol and simple carbohydrates from the diet. The TLC approach also includes the use of plant stanols or sterols and increased dissolved fiber as an option for lowering LDL cholesterol levels; nutritional recommendations for daily total caloric intake; recommendations for allowable percentage of calories derived from fat (saturated and unsaturated), carbohydrates, protein, and cholesterol; as well as recommendations for daily expenditure of energy.

Nutritional Considerations: Overweight patients with high blood pressure should be encouraged to achieve a normal weight. Other changeable risk factors warranting patient education include strategies to safely decrease sodium intake, increase physical activity, decrease alcohol consumption, eliminate tobacco use, and decrease cholesterol levels.

Recognize anxiety related to test results, and be supportive of perceived loss of independent function. Discuss the implications of abnormal test results on the patient's lifestyle. Provide teaching and information regarding the clinical implications of the test results, as appropriate.

Reinforce information given by the patient's HCP regarding further testing, treatment, or referral to another HCP. Answer any questions or address any concerns voiced by the patient or family.

Depending on the results of this procedure, additional testing may be needed to evaluate or monitor progression of the disease process and determine the need for a change in therapy. Evaluate test results in relation to the patient's symptoms and other tests performed.

RELATED MONOGRAPHS:

Related tests for cardiac indications include anion gap, antiarrhythmic drugs, apolipoprotein A and B, arterial/alveolar oxygen ratio, AST, ANP, α_1-AT, biopsy lung, blood gases, blood pool imaging, BNP, bronchoscopy, calcium, ionized calcium, carboxyhemoglobin, chest x-ray, chloride sweat, cholesterol (total, HDL, and LDL), CRP, CBC, CT cardiac scoring, CT thoracic, CK and isoenzymes, culture and smear for mycobacteria, culture bacterial sputum, culture viral, cytology sputum, echocardiography, echocardiography transesophageal, ECG, electrolytes, exercise stress test, glucose, glycated hemoglobin, gram stain, Hgb, Holter monitor, homocysteine, ketones, LDH and isoenzymes, lipoprotein electrophoresis, magnesium, MRI chest, MI infarct scan, IgE, lactic acid, lung perfusion scan, lung ventilation scan, myocardial perfusion heart scan, myoglobin, osmolality, pericardial fluid analysis, phosphorus, plethysmography, pleural fluid analysis, PET heart, PFT, potassium, pulse oximetry, TB skin test, and triglycerides. Related tests for pulmonary indications include α_1-AT,

P

anion gap, arterial/alveolar oxygen ratio, biopsy lung, bronchoscopy, carboxyhemoglobin, chest x-ray, chloride sweat, CBC, CBC hemoglobin, CBC WBC count and differential, culture and smear for mycobacteria, culture bacterial sputum, culture viral, cytology sputum, electrolytes, gram stain, IgE, lactic acid, lung perfusion scan, lung ventilation scan, osmolality, phosphorus, plethysmography, pleural fluid analysis, and pulse oximetry.

Refer to the Cardiovascular and Respiratory systems tables at the end of the book for related tests by body system.

Positron Emission Tomography, Pelvis

SYNONYM/ACRONYM: PET scan of the pelvis.

COMMON USE: To assess blood flow and metabolism to the pelvis toward diagnosis of disorders such as colorectal tumor, assist in tumor staging, and monitor the effectiveness of therapeutic interventions.

AREA OF APPLICATION: Pelvis.

CONTRAST: IV radioactive material (fluorodeoxyglucose [FDG]).

DESCRIPTION: Positron emission tomography (PET) combines the biochemical properties of nuclear medicine with the accuracy of computed tomography (CT). PET uses positron emissions from specific radionuclides (oxygen, nitrogen, carbon, and fluorine) to produce detailed functional images within the body. After the radionuclide becomes concentrated in the pelvis, PET images of blood flow or metabolic processes at the cellular level can be obtained. Colorectal tumor detection, tumor staging, evaluation of the effects of therapy, detection of recurrent disease, and detection of metastases are the main reasons to do a pelvic PET scan. Fluorine-18, in the form of fluorodeoxyglucose (FDG), is one of the more commonly used radionuclides. FDG is a glucose analogue, and because every cell uses glucose, the metabolic activity occurring in pelvic conditions such as colorectal cancer can be measured. There is little localization of FDG in normal tissue, allowing rapid detection of abnormal disease states.

The positron radiopharmaceuticals generally have short half-lives, ranging from a few seconds to a few hours, and therefore they must be produced in a cyclotron located near where the test is being done. The PET scanner translates the emissions from the radioactivity as the positron combines with the negative electrons from the tissues and forms gamma rays that can be detected by the scanner. This information is transmitted to the computer, which determines the location and its distribution and translates the emissions as color-coded images for viewing, quantitative measurements, activity changes in relation to time, and three-dimensional

P

computer-aided analysis. Each radionuclide tracer is designed to measure a specific body process, such as glucose metabolism, blood flow, or tissue perfusion.

The expense of the study and the limited availability of radiopharmaceuticals limit the use of PET, even though it is more sensitive than traditional nuclear scanning and single-photon emission computed tomography. Changes in reimbursement and the advent of mobile technology have increased the availability of this procedure in the community setting.

INDICATIONS
- Determine the effects of therapy
- Determine the presence of colorectal cancer
- Determine the presence of metastases of a cancerous tumor
- Determine the recurrence of tumor or cancer
- Identify the site for biopsy

POTENTIAL DIAGNOSIS

Normal findings in
- Normal patterns of tissue metabolism, blood flow, and radionuclide distribution
- No focal uptake of radionuclide

Abnormal findings in
- Focal uptake of the radionuclide in pelvis
- Focal uptake in abnormal lymph nodes
- Focal uptake in tumor
- Focal uptake in metastases

CRITICAL FINDINGS: N/A

INTERFERING FACTORS

This procedure is contraindicated for
- Patients who are pregnant or suspected of being pregnant, unless the potential benefits of the procedure far outweigh the risks to the fetus and mother.

Factors that may impair clear imaging
- Inability of the patient to cooperate or remain still during the procedure because of age, significant pain, or mental status.
- Drugs that alter glucose metabolism, such as tranquilizers or insulin, because hypoglycemia can alter PET results.
- The use of alcohol, tobacco, or caffeine-containing drinks at least 24 hr before the study, because the effects of these substances would make it difficult to evaluate the patient's true physiological state (e.g., alcohol is a vasoconstrictor and would decrease blood flow to the target organ).
- Metallic objects within the examination field (e.g., jewelry, body rings), which may inhibit organ visualization and can produce unclear images.

Other considerations
- Failure to follow dietary restrictions before the procedure may cause the procedure to be canceled or repeated.
- Improper injection of the radionuclide that allows the tracer to seep deep into the muscle tissue produces erroneous hot spots.
- False-positive findings may occur as a result of normal gastrointestinal (GI) tract uptake and uptake in areas of infection or inflammation.
- Consultation with a health-care provider (HCP) should occur before the procedure for radiation safety concerns regarding younger patients or patients who are lactating.
- Risks associated with radiation overexposure can result from frequent x-ray or radionuclide procedures. Personnel working in the

examination area should wear badges to record their level of radiation exposure.

NURSING IMPLICATIONS AND PROCEDURE

PRETEST:

- Positively identify the patient using at least two unique identifiers before providing care, treatment, or services.
- *Patient Teaching:* Inform the patient this procedure can assist in assessing the pelvis related to abnormal organ function.
- Obtain a history of the patient's complaints, including a list of known allergens, especially allergies or sensitivities to latex, iodine, seafood, contrast medium, or anesthetics.
- Obtain a history of the patient's gastrointestinal system, symptoms, and results of previously performed laboratory tests and diagnostic and surgical procedures.
- Note any recent procedures that can interfere with test results, including examinations using barium- or iodine-based contrast medium.
- Record the date of the last menstrual period and determine the possibility of pregnancy in perimenopausal women.
- Obtain a list of the patient's current medications, including herbs, nutritional supplements, and nutraceuticals (see Appendix F).
- Review the procedure with the patient. Address concerns about pain related to the procedure and explain that some pain may be experienced during the test, and there may be moments of discomfort. Reassure the patient that radioactive material poses minimal radioactive hazard because of its short half-life and rarely produces side effects. Inform the patient that the procedure is performed in a special department, usually in a radiology suite, by an HCP specializing in this procedure, with support staff, and takes approximately 30 to 60 min.
- *Sensitivity to social and cultural issues,* as well as concern for modesty, is important in providing psychological support before, during, and after the procedure.
- Sometimes FDG examinations are done after blood has been drawn to determine circulating blood glucose levels. If blood glucose levels are high, insulin may be given.
- Instruct the patient to remove jewelry and other metallic objects in the area to be examined.
- Instruct the patient to avoid taking anticoagulant medication or to reduce dosage as ordered prior to the procedure.
- Instruct the patient to restrict food for 4 hr; restrict alcohol, nicotine, or caffeine-containing drinks for 24 hr; and withhold medications for 24 hr before the test. Protocols may vary among facilities.
- *Make sure a written and informed consent has been signed prior to the procedure and before administering any medications.*

INTRATEST:

- Observe standard precautions, and follow the general guidelines in Appendix A. Positively identify the patient.
- Ensure that the patient has complied with dietary, fluid, and medication restrictions and pretesting preparations.
- Ensure the patient has removed all jewelry and external metallic objects from the area to be examined prior to the procedure.
- Have emergency equipment readily available.
- Instruct the patient to void prior to the procedure and to change into the gown, robe, and foot coverings provided.
- Instruct the patient to cooperate fully and to follow directions. Ask the patient to remain still throughout the procedure because movement produces unreliable results.
- Record baseline vital signs and assess neurological status. Protocols may vary among facilities.
- Place the patient in the supine position on an examination table.
- The radionuclide is injected, and imaging is started after a 45-min delay. Continuous scanning may be done

for 1 hr. If comparative studies are indicated, additional injections of radionuclide may be needed.

▶ If required, the bladder may need to be lavaged via a urinary catheter with 2 L of 0.9% saline solution to remove concentrated radionuclide.

▶ Monitor the patient for complications related to the procedure (e.g., allergic reaction, anaphylaxis, bronchospasm).

▶ Remove the needle or catheter and apply a pressure dressing over the puncture site.

▶ Observe/assess the needle/catheter insertion site for bleeding, inflammation, or hematoma formation.

POST-TEST:

▶ A report of the results will be made available to the requesting HCP, who will discuss the results with the patient.

▶ Instruct the patient to resume pretest diet, fluids, medications, and activity.

▶ Observe for delayed allergic reactions, such as rash, urticaria, tachycardia, hyperpnea, hypertension, palpitations, nausea, or vomiting.

▶ Instruct the patient to immediately report symptoms such as fast heart rate, difficulty breathing, skin rash, itching, chest pain, persistent right shoulder pain, or abdominal pain. Immediately report symptoms to the appropriate HCP.

▶ Observe/assess the needle/catheter insertion site for bleeding, inflammation, or hematoma formation.

▶ Instruct the patient to apply cold compresses to the puncture site as needed, to reduce discomfort or edema.

▶ Instruct the patient to drink increased amounts of fluids for 24 to 48 hr to eliminate the radionuclide from the body, unless contraindicated. Tell the patient that radionuclide is eliminated from the body within 6 to 24 hr.

▶ Instruct the patient to flush the toilet immediately after each voiding and to meticulously wash hands with soap and water for 24 hr after the procedure.

▶ Tell all caregivers to wear gloves when discarding urine for 24 hr after the procedure. Wash gloved hands with soap and water before removing gloves. Then wash hands after the gloves are removed.

▶ If a woman who is breastfeeding must have a nuclear scan, she should not breastfeed the infant until the radionuclide has been eliminated, about 3 days. Instruct her to express the milk and discard it during the 3-day period to prevent cessation of milk production.

▶ No other radionuclide tests should be scheduled for 24 to 48 hr after this procedure.

▶ Recognize anxiety related to test results, and be supportive of perceived loss of independent function. Discuss the implications of abnormal test results on the patient's lifestyle. Provide teaching and information regarding the clinical implications of the test results, as appropriate.

▶ Reinforce information given by the patient's HCP regarding further testing, treatment, or referral to another HCP. Decisions regarding the need for and frequency of occult blood testing, colonoscopy, or other cancer screening procedures should be made after consultation between the patient and HCP. The most current guidelines for colon cancer screening of the general population as well as of individuals with increased risk are available from the American Cancer Society (www .cancer.org) and the American College of Gastroenterology (www.gi.org). Answer any questions or address any concerns voiced by the patient or family.

▶ Depending on the results of this procedure, additional testing may be needed to evaluate or monitor progression of the disease process and determine the need for a change in therapy. Evaluate test results in relation to the patient's symptoms and other tests performed.

RELATED MONOGRAPHS:

▶ Related tests include barium enema, biopsy intestinal, capsule endoscopy, cancer antigens, CT abdomen, fecal analysis, KUB, CT colonoscopy, MRI abdomen, and proctosigmoidoscopy.

▶ Refer to the Gastrointestinal System table at the end of the book for related tests by body system.

Potassium, Blood

SYNONYM/ACRONYM: Serum K^+.

COMMON USE: To evaluate fluid and electrolyte balance related to potassium levels toward diagnosing disorders such as acidosis, renal failure, dehydration, and monitor the effectiveness of therapeutic interventions.

SPECIMEN: Serum (1 mL) collected in a red- or tiger-top tube. Plasma (1 mL) collected in green-top (heparin) tube is also acceptable.

NORMAL FINDINGS: (Method: Ion-selective electrode)

Serum	Conventional & SI Units
Cord	5.6–12 mmol/L
1–12 hr	5.3–7.3 mmol/L
12–24 hr	5.3–8.9 mmol/L
24–48 hr	5.2–7.3 mmol/L
48–72 hr	5–7.7 mmol/L
3–7 days	3.2–5.5 mmol/L
8 days–1 mo	3.4–6 mmol/L
1–5 mo	3.5–5.6 mmol/L
6 mo–1 yr	3.5–6.1 mmol/L
2–19 yr	3.8–5.1 mmol/L
Adult–older adult	3.5–5.3 mmol/L

Note: Serum values are 0.1 mmol/L higher than plasma values, and reference ranges should be adjusted accordingly. It is important that serial measurements be collected using the same type of collection container to reduce variability of results from collection to collection. Older adults are at risk for hyperkalemia due to the decline in aldosterone levels, decline in renal function, and effects of commonly prescribed medications that inhibit the renin-angiotensin-aldosterone system.

DESCRIPTION: Electrolytes dissociate into electrically charged ions when dissolved. Cations, including potassium, carry a positive charge. Body fluids contain approximately equal numbers of anions and cations, although the nature of the ions and their mobility differs between the intracellular and extracellular compartments. Both types of ions affect the electrical and osmolar functions of the body. Electrolyte quantities and the balance among them are controlled by oxygen and carbon dioxide exchange in the lungs; absorption, secretion, and excretion of many substances by the kidneys; and secretion of regulatory hormones by the endocrine glands. Potassium is the most abundant intracellular cation. It is essential for the transmission of electrical impulses in cardiac and skeletal muscle. It also functions in enzyme reactions that transform glucose into energy and amino acids into proteins.

P

Potassium helps maintain acid-base equilibrium, and it has a significant and inverse relationship to pH: A decrease in pH of 0.1 increases the potassium level by 0.6 mmol/L.

Abnormal potassium levels can be caused by a number of contributing factors, which can be categorized as follows:

Altered renal excretion: Normally, 80% to 90% of the body's potassium is filtered out through the kidneys each day (the remainder is excreted in sweat and stool); renal disease can result in abnormally high potassium levels.

Altered dietary intake: A severe potassium deficiency can be caused by an inadequate intake of dietary potassium.

Altered cellular metabolism: Damaged red blood cells (RBCs) release potassium into the circulating fluid, resulting in increased potassium levels.

INDICATIONS

- Assess a known or suspected disorder associated with renal disease, glucose metabolism, trauma, or burns
- Assist in the evaluation of electrolyte imbalances; this test is especially indicated in elderly patients, patients receiving hyperalimentation supplements, patients on hemodialysis, and patients with hypertension
- Evaluate cardiac arrhythmia to determine whether altered potassium levels are contributing to the problem, especially during digitalis therapy, which leads to ventricular irritability
- Evaluate the effects of drug therapy, especially diuretics
- Evaluate the response to treatment for abnormal potassium levels
- Monitor known or suspected acidosis, because potassium moves from RBCs into the extracellular fluid in acidotic states
- Routine screen of electrolytes in acute and chronic illness

POTENTIAL DIAGNOSIS

Increased in
- Acidosis *(intracellular potassium ions are expelled in exchange for hydrogen ions in order to achieve electrical neutrality)*
- Acute renal failure *(potassium excretion is diminished, and it accumulates in the blood)*
- Addison's disease *(due to lack of aldosterone, potassium excretion is diminished, and it accumulates in the blood)*
- Asthma *(related to chronic inflammation and damage to lung tissue)*
- Burns *(related to tissue damage and release by damaged cells)*
- Chronic interstitial nephritis *(potassium excretion is diminished, and it accumulates in the blood)*
- Dehydration *(related to hemoconcentration)*
- Dialysis *(dialysis treatments simulate kidney function, but potassium builds up between treatments)*
- Diet *(related to excessive intake of salt substitutes or of potassium salts in medications)*
- Exercise *(related to tissue damage and release by damaged cells)*
- Hemolysis (massive) *(potassium is the major intracellular cation)*
- Hyperventilation *(in response to respiratory alkalosis, blood levels of potassium are increased in order to achieve electrical neutrality)*
- Hypoaldosteronism *(due to lack of aldosterone, potassium excretion is diminished, and it accumulates in the blood)*

- Insulin deficiency *(insulin deficiency results in movement of potassium from the cell into the extracellular fluid)*
- Ketoacidosis *(insulin deficiency results in movement of potassium from the cell into the extracellular fluid)*
- Leukocytosis
- Muscle necrosis *(related to tissue damage and release by damaged cells)*
- Near drowning
- Pregnancy
- Prolonged periods of standing
- Tissue trauma *(related to release by damaged cells)*
- Transfusion of old banked blood *(aged cells hemolyze and release intracellular potassium)*
- Tubular unresponsiveness to aldosterone
- Uremia

Decreased in
- Alcoholism *(related to insufficient dietary intake)*
- Alkalosis *(potassium uptake by cells is increased in response to release of hydrogen ions from cells)*
- Anorexia nervosa *(related to significant changes in renal function that result in hypokalemia)*
- Bradycardia *(hypokalemia can cause bradycardia)*
- Chronic, excessive licorice ingestion (from licorice root) *Licorice inhibits short-chain dehydrogenase/reductase enzymes. These enzymes normally prevent cortisol from binding to aldosterone receptor sites in the kidney. In the absence of these enzymes, cortisol acts on the kidney and triggers the same effects as aldosterone, which include increased potassium excretion, sodium retention, and water retention.*

- Congestive heart failure *(related to fluid retention and hemodilution)*
- Crohn's disease *(insufficient intestinal absorption)*
- Cushing's syndrome *(aldosterone facilitates the excretion of potassium by the kidneys)*
- Diet deficient in meat and vegetables *(insufficient dietary intake)*
- Excess insulin *(insulin causes glucose and potassium to move into cells)*
- Familial periodic paralysis *(related to fluid retention)*
- Gastrointestinal (GI) loss due to vomiting, diarrhea, nasogastric suction, or intestinal fistula
- Hyperaldosteronism *(aldosterone facilitates the excretion of potassium by the kidneys)*
- Hypertension *(medications used to treat hypertension may result in loss of potassium; hypertension is often related to diabetes and renal disease, which affect cellular retention and renal excretion of potassium respectively)*
- Hypomagnesemia *(magnesium levels tend to parallel potassium levels)*
- IV therapy with inadequate potassium supplementation
- Laxative abuse *(related to medications that cause potassium wasting)*
- Malabsorption *(related to insufficient intestinal absorption)*
- Pica (eating substances of no nutritional value, e.g., clay)
- Renal tubular acidosis *(condition results in excessive loss of potassium)*
- Sweating *(related to increased loss)*
- Theophylline administration, excessive *(theophylline drives potassium into cells, reducing circulating levels)*
- Thyrotoxicosis *(related to changes in renal function)*

P

CRITICAL FINDINGS ◈

Adults & children
- Less than 2.5 mmol/L
  (SI = Less than 2.5 mmol/L)
- Greater than 6.2 mmol/L
  (SI = Greater than 6.2 mmol/L)

Newborns
- Less than 2.8 mmol/L (SI = Less than 2.8 mmol/L)
- Greater than 7.6 mmol/L (SI = Greater than 7.6 mmol/L)

Note and immediately report to the health-care provider (HCP) any critically increased or decreased values and related symptoms, especially symptoms of fluid imbalance. Timely notification of critical values for lab or diagnostic studies is a role expectation of the professional nurse. Notification processes will vary among facilities. Upon receipt of the critical value the information should be read back to the caller to verify accuracy. Most policies require immediate notification of the primary HCP, hospitalist, or on-call HCP. Reported information includes the patient's name, unique identifiers, critical value, name of the person giving the report, and name of the person receiving the report. Documentation of notification should be made in the medical record with the name of the HCP notified, time and date of notification, and any orders received. Any delay in a timely report of a critical value may require completion of a notification form with review by Risk Management.

Symptoms of hyperkalemia include irritability, diarrhea, cramps, oliguria, difficulty speaking, and cardiac arrhythmias (peaked T waves and ventricular fibrillation). Continuous cardiac monitoring is indicated. Administration of sodium bicarbonate or calcium chloride may be requested. If the patient is receiving an IV supplement, verify that the patient is voiding.

Symptoms of hypokalemia include malaise, thirst, polyuria, anorexia, weak pulse, low blood pressure, vomiting, decreased reflexes, and electrocardiographic changes (depressed T waves and ventricular ectopy). Replacement therapy is indicated.

INTERFERING FACTORS
- Drugs that can cause an increase in potassium levels include ACE inhibitors, atenolol, basiliximab, captopril, clofibrate in association with renal disease, cyclosporine, dexamethasone, enalapril, etretinate, lisinopril in association with heart failure or hypertension, NSAIDs, some drugs with potassium salts, spironolactone, succinylcholine, and tacrolimus.
- Drugs that can cause a decrease in potassium levels include acetazolamide, acetylsalicylic acid, aldosterone, ammonium chloride, amphotericin B, bendroflumethiazide, benzthiazide, bicarbonate, captopril, cathartics, chlorothiazide, chlorthalidone, cisplatin, clorexolone, corticosteroids, cyclothiazide, dichlorphenamide, digoxin, diuretics, enalapril, foscarnet, fosphenytoin, furosemide, insulin, laxatives, metolazone, moxalactam (common when coadministered with amikacin), large doses of any IV penicillin, phenolphthalein (with chronic laxative abuse), polythiazide, quinethazone, sodium bicarbonate, tacrolimus, IV theophylline, thiazides, triamterene, and trichlormethiazide. A number of these medications initially increase the serum potassium level, but they also have a diuretic effect, which promotes potassium loss in the urine except in cases of renal insufficiency.
- Leukocytosis, as seen in leukemia, causes elevated potassium levels.
- False elevations can occur with vigorous pumping of the hand during venipuncture. Hemolysis of the sample and high platelet counts also

increase potassium levels, as follows: (1) Because potassium is an intracellular ion and concentrations are approximately 150 times extracellular concentrations, even a slight amount of hemolysis can cause a significant increase in levels. (2) Platelets release potassium during the clotting process, and therefore serum samples collected from patients with elevated platelet counts may produce spuriously high potassium levels. Plasma is the specimen of choice in patients known to have elevated platelet counts.

▸ False increases are seen in unprocessed samples left at room temperature because a significant amount of potassium leaks out of the cells within a few hours. Plasma or serum should be separated from cells within 4 hr of collection.

▸ Specimens should never be collected above an IV line because of the potential for dilution when the specimen and the IV solution combine in the collection container, falsely decreasing the result. There is also the potential of contaminating the sample with the substance of interest, if it is present in the IV solution, falsely increasing the result.

NURSING IMPLICATIONS AND PROCEDURE

PRETEST:

Positively identify the patient using at least two unique identifiers before providing care, treatment, or services.

Patient Teaching: Inform the patient this test can assist in evaluating electrolyte balance.

Obtain a history of the patient's complaints, including a list of known allergens, especially allergies or sensitivities to latex. Especially note complaints of weakness and confusion.

▸ Obtain a history of the patient's cardiovascular, endocrine, gastrointestinal, genitourinary, immune, and respiratory systems; symptoms; and results of previously performed laboratory tests and diagnostic and surgical procedures.

▸ Obtain a list of the patient's current medications, including herbs, nutritional supplements, and nutraceuticals (see Appendix F).

▸ Review the procedure with the patient. Inform the patient that specimen collection takes approximately 5 to 10 min. Address concerns about pain and explain that there may be some discomfort during the venipuncture.

Sensitivity to social and cultural issues, as well as concern for modesty, is important in providing psychological support before, during, and after the procedure.

There are no food, fluid, or medication restrictions unless by medical direction.

INTRATEST:

If the patient has a history of allergic reaction to latex, avoid the use of equipment containing latex.

Instruct the patient to cooperate fully and to follow directions. Direct the patient to breathe normally and to avoid unnecessary movement. Instruct the patient not to clench and unclench the fist immediately before or during specimen collection.

Observe standard precautions, and follow the general guidelines in Appendix A. Positively identify the patient, and label the appropriate specimen container with the corresponding patient demographics, initials of the person collecting the specimen, date, and time of collection. Perform a venipuncture.

▸ Remove the needle and apply direct pressure with dry gauze to stop bleeding. Observe/assess venipuncture site for bleeding or hematoma formation and secure gauze with adhesive bandage.

▸ Promptly transport the specimen to the laboratory for processing and analysis.

POST-TEST:

A report of the results will be made available to the requesting HCP, who will discuss the results with the patient.

Nutritional Considerations: The Institute of Medicine's Food and Nutrition Board suggests 4,700 mg as an adequate daily intake goal of dietary potassium for adults age 19 to greater than 70 yr; 4,700 mg/d for pregnant females under age 18 through 50 yr; 5,100 mg/d for lactating females under age 18 through 50 yr; 4,700 mg/d for children age 14 to 18 yr; 4,500 mg/d for children age 9 to 13 yr; 3,800 mg/d for children age 4 to 8 yr; 3,000 mg/d for children age 1 to 3 yr; 700 mg/d for children age 7 to 12 mo; and 400 mg/d for children 0 to 6 mo. Reprinted with permission from the National Academies Press, copyright 2013, National Academy of Sciences. Potassium is present in all plant and animal cells, making dietary replacement simple to achieve in the potassium-deficient patient.

Observe the patient for signs and symptoms of fluid volume excess related to excess potassium intake (hyperkalemia), fluid volume deficit related to active loss (hypokalemia), or risk of injury related to an alteration in body chemistry. Symptoms of hypokalemia and hyperkalemia include dehydration, diarrhea, vomiting, or prolonged anorexia. Increased potassium levels may be associated with dehydration. Evaluate the patient for signs and symptoms of dehydration. Dehydration is a significant and common finding in geriatric patients and other patients in whom renal function has deteriorated. The Institute of Medicine's Food and Nutrition Board suggests 3.7 L for adult males and 2.7 L for adult females age 19 to 70 yr as an adequate daily intake goal of total water; 3 L/d for pregnant females age 14 to 50 yr; 3.8 L/d for lactating females age 14 to 50 yr; 3.3 L/d for male and 2.3 L/d for female children age 14 to 18 yr; 2.4 L/d for male and 2.1 L/d for female children age 9 to 13 yr; 1.7 L/d for children age 4 to 8 yr; 1.3 L/d for children age 1 to 3 yr; 0.8 L/d for children age 7 to 12 mo; and 0.7 L/d (assumed to be from human milk) for children 0 to 6 mo. Reprinted with permission from the National Academies Press, copyright 2013, National Academy of Sciences.

Decreased potassium levels may occur in patients receiving digoxin or potassium-wasting diuretics. Potassium levels should be monitored carefully because cardiac arrhythmias can occur. Instruct the patient in electrolyte replacement therapy and changes in dietary intake that affect electrolyte levels, as ordered.

Reinforce information given by the patient's HCP regarding further testing, treatment, or referral to another HCP. Answer any questions or address any concerns voiced by the patient or family. Educate the patient regarding access to nutritional counseling services. Provide contact information, if desired, for the Institute of Medicine of the National Academies (www.iom.edu).

Depending on the results of this procedure, additional testing may be performed to evaluate or monitor progression of the disease process and determine the need for a change in therapy. Evaluate test results in relation to the patient's symptoms and other tests performed.

RELATED MONOGRAPHS:

Related tests include ACTH, aldosterone, anion gap, antiarrhythmic drugs, alveolar/arterial gradient, ANP, BNP, blood gases, BUN, calcium, carbon dioxide, chloride, complement, CBC hematocrit, CBC hemoglobin, CBC WBC count and differential, Coomb's antiglobulin (direct and indirect), cortisol, CK and isoenzymes, creatinine, DHEAS, echocardiography, echocardiography transesophageal, fecal fat, glucose, G6PD, Ham's test, haptoglobin, hemosiderin, insulin, ketones, lactic acid, lung perfusion scan, magnesium, osmolality, osmotic fragility, plethysmography, urine potassium, PFT, PK, renin, sickle cell screen, sodium, and US abdomen.

Refer to the Cardiovascular, Endocrine, Gastrointestinal, Genitourinary, Immune, and Respiratory systems tables at the end of the book for related tests by body system.

P

Potassium, Urine

SYNONYM/ACRONYM: Urine K$^+$.

COMMON USE: To evaluate electrolyte balance, acid-base balance, and hypokalemia.

SPECIMEN: Urine (5 mL) from an unpreserved random or timed specimen collected in a clean plastic collection container.

NORMAL FINDINGS: (Method: Ion-selective electrode)

Age	Conventional Units	SI Units (Conventional Units × 1)
6–10 yr		
Male	17–54 mEq/24 hr	17–54 mmol/24 hr
Female	8–37 mEq/24 hr	8–37 mmol/24 hr
10–14 yr		
Male	22–57 mEq/24 hr	22–57 mmol/24 hr
Female	18–58 mEq/24 hr	18–58 mmol/24 hr
Adult–older adult	26–123 mEq/24 hr	26–123 mmol/24 hr

Note: Reference values depend on potassium intake and diurnal variation. Excretion is significantly higher at night.
Potassium excretion declines in older adults due to the decline in aldosterone levels, decline in renal function, and effects of commonly prescribed medications that inhibit the renin-angiotensin-aldosterone system.

DESCRIPTION: Electrolytes dissociate into electrically charged ions when dissolved. Cations, including potassium, carry a positive charge. Body fluids contain approximately equal numbers of anions and cations, although the nature of the ions and their mobility differs between the intracellular and extracellular compartments. Both types of ions affect the electrical and osmolar functions of the body. Electrolyte quantities and the balance among them are controlled by oxygen and carbon dioxide exchange in the lungs; absorption, secretion, and excretion of many substances by the kidneys; and secretion of regulatory hormones by the endocrine glands. Potassium is the most abundant intracellular cation. It is essential for the transmission of electrical impulses in cardiac and skeletal muscle. It also functions in enzyme reactions that transform glucose into energy and amino acids into proteins. Potassium helps maintain acid-base equilibrium, and it has a significant and inverse relationship to pH: A decrease in pH of 0.1 increases the potassium level by 0.6 mEq/L.

Abnormal potassium levels can be caused by a number of contributing factors, which can be categorized as follows:

Altered renal excretion: Normally, 80% to 90% of the body's potassium is filtered out through the kidneys each day (the remainder is excreted in sweat and stool); renal disease can result in abnormally high potassium levels.

Altered dietary intake: A severe potassium deficiency can be caused by an inadequate intake of dietary potassium.

Altered cellular metabolism: Damaged red blood cells (RBCs) release potassium into the circulating fluid, resulting in increased potassium levels.

Regulating electrolyte balance is one of the major functions of the kidneys. In normally functioning kidneys, urine potassium levels increase when serum levels are high and decrease when serum levels are low to maintain homeostasis. The kidneys respond to alkalosis by excreting potassium to retain hydrogen ions and increase acidity. In acidosis, the body excretes hydrogen ions and retains potassium. Analyzing these urinary levels can provide important clues to the functioning of the kidneys and other major organs. Urine potassium tests usually involve timed urine collections over a 12- or 24-hr period. Measurement of random specimens also may be requested.

P

INDICATIONS
- Determine the potential cause of renal calculi
- Evaluate known or suspected endocrine disorder
- Evaluate known or suspected renal disease
- Evaluate malabsorption disorders

POTENTIAL DIAGNOSIS

Increased in
- Albright-type renal disease *(related to excessive production of cortisol)*

- Cushing's syndrome *(excessive corticosteroids, especially aldosterone levels, will increase urinary excretion of potassium)*
- Diabetic ketoacidosis *(insulin deficiency forces potassium into the extracellular fluid; excess potassium is excreted in the urine)*
- Diuretic therapy *(related to potassium-wasting effects of the medications)*
- Hyperaldosteronism *(excessive aldosterone levels will increase urinary excretion of potassium)*
- Starvation (onset) *(cells involved in providing energy through tissue breakdown release potassium into circulation)*
- Vomiting *(elevated urine potassium is a hallmark of bulimia)*

Decreased in
- Addison's disease *(reduced aldosterone levels will diminish excretion of potassium by the kidneys)*
- Potassium deficiency (chronic)
- Renal failure with decreased urine flow

CRITICAL FINDINGS: N/A

INTERFERING FACTORS
- Drugs and substances that can cause an increase in urine potassium levels include acetazolamide, acetylsalicylic acid, ammonium chloride, bendroflumethiazide, carbenoxolone, chlorthalidone, clopamide, corticosteroids, cortisone, diapamide, dichlorphenamide, diuretics, ethacrynic acid, fludrocortisone, furosemide, hydrochlorothiazide, hydrocortisone, intra-amniotic saline, mefruside, niacinamide, some oral contraceptives, thiazides, torsemide, triflocin, and viomycin.
- Drugs that can cause a decrease in urine potassium levels include anesthetic agents, felodipine, and levarterenol.

- A dietary deficiency or excess of potassium can lead to spurious results.
- Diuretic therapy with excessive loss of electrolytes into the urine may falsely elevate results.
- All urine voided for the timed collection period must be included in the collection, or else falsely decreased values may be obtained. Compare output records with volume collected to verify that all voids were included in the collection.
- Potassium levels are subject to diurnal variation (output being highest at night), which is why 24-hr collections are recommended.

NURSING IMPLICATIONS AND PROCEDURE

PRETEST:

- Positively identify the patient using at least two unique identifiers before providing care, treatment, or services.
- *Patient Teaching:* Inform the patient this test can assist in evaluating electrolyte balance.
- Obtain a history of the patient's complaints, including a list of known allergens, especially allergies or sensitivities to latex.
- Obtain a history of the patient's endocrine, gastrointestinal, and genitourinary systems; symptoms; and results of previously performed laboratory tests and diagnostic and surgical procedures.
- Obtain a list of the patient's current medications, including herbs, nutritional supplements, and nutraceuticals (see Appendix F).
- Review the procedure with the patient. Provide a nonmetallic urinal, bedpan, or toilet-mounted collection device. Address concerns about pain and explain that there should be no discomfort during the procedure.
- *Sensitivity to social and cultural issues,* as well as concern for modesty, is important in providing psychological support before, during, and after the procedure.

Usually a 24-hr time frame for urine collection is ordered. Inform the patient that all urine must be saved during that 24-hr period. Instruct the patient not to void directly into the laboratory collection container. Instruct the patient to avoid defecating in the collection device and to keep toilet tissue out of the collection device to prevent contamination of the specimen. Place a sign in the bathroom to remind the patient to save all urine.

Instruct the patient to void all urine into the collection device and then to pour the urine into the laboratory collection container. Alternatively, the specimen can be left in the collection device for a health-care staff member to add to the laboratory collection container.

There are no food, fluid, or medication restrictions unless by medical direction.

INTRATEST:

If the patient has a history of allergic reaction to latex, avoid the use of equipment containing latex.

Instruct the patient to cooperate fully and to follow directions.

Observe standard precautions, and follow the general guidelines in Appendix A. Positively identify the patient, and label the appropriate specimen container with the corresponding patient demographics, initials of the person collecting the specimen, date, and time of collection.

Random Specimen (Collect in Early Morning)

Clean-Catch Specimen

Instruct the male patient to (1) thoroughly wash his hands, (2) cleanse the meatus, (3) void a small amount into the toilet, and (4) void directly into the specimen container.

Instruct the female patient to (1) thoroughly wash her hands; (2) cleanse the labia from front to back; (3) while keeping the labia separated, void a small amount into the toilet; and (4) without interrupting the urine stream, void directly into the specimen container.

Indwelling Catheter

Put on gloves. Empty drainage tube of urine. It may be necessary to clamp off the catheter for 15 to 30 min before

P

specimen collection. Cleanse specimen port with antiseptic swab, and then aspirate 5 mL of urine with a 21- to 25-gauge needle and syringe. Transfer urine to a sterile container.

Timed Specimen

Obtain a clean 3-L urine specimen container, toilet-mounted collection device, and plastic bag (for transport of the specimen container). The specimen must be refrigerated or kept on ice throughout the entire collection period. If an indwelling urinary catheter is in place, the drainage bag must be kept on ice.

Begin the test between 6 and 8 a.m. if possible. Collect first voiding and discard. Record the time the specimen was discarded as the beginning of the timed collection period. The next morning, ask the patient to void at the same time the collection was started and add this last voiding to the container. Urinary output should be recorded throughout the collection time.

If an indwelling catheter is in place, replace the tubing and container system at the start of the collection time. Keep the container system on ice during the collection period, or empty the urine into a larger container periodically during the collection period; monitor to ensure continued drainage, and conclude the test the next morning at the same hour the collection was begun.

At the conclusion of the test, compare the quantity of urine with the urinary output record for the collection; if the specimen contains less than what was recorded as output, some urine may have been discarded, invalidating the test.

Include on the collection container's label the amount of urine, test start and stop times, and ingestion of any foods or medications that can affect test results.

General

Promptly transport the specimen to the laboratory for processing and analysis.

POST-TEST:

A report of the results will be made available to the requesting health-care provider (HCP), who will discuss the results with the patient.

Nutritional Considerations: The Institute of Medicine's Food and Nutrition Board suggests 4,700 mg as an adequate daily intake goal of dietary potassium for adults age 19 to greater than 70 yr; 4,700 mg/d for pregnant females under age 18 through 50 yr; 5,100 mg/d for lactating females under age 18 through 50 yr; 4,700 mg/d for children age 14 to 18 yr; 4,500 mg/d for children age 9 to 13 yr; 3,800 mg/d for children age 4 to 8 yr; 3,000 mg/d for children age 1 to 3 yr; 700 mg/d for children age 7 to 12 mo; and 400 mg/d for children 0 to 6 mo. Reprinted with permission from the National Academies Press, copyright 2013, National Academy of Sciences. Potassium is present in all plant and animal cells, making dietary replacement simple to achieve in the potassium-deficient patient.

Observe the patient for signs and symptoms of fluid volume excess related to excess potassium intake, fluid volume deficit related to active loss, or risk of injury related to an alteration in body chemistry. Symptoms include dehydration, diarrhea, vomiting, or prolonged anorexia. Instruct the patient in electrolyte replacement therapy and changes in dietary intake that affect electrolyte levels, as ordered.

Increased potassium levels may be associated with dehydration. Evaluate the patient for signs and symptoms of dehydration. Dehydration is a significant and common finding in geriatric patients and other patients in whom renal function has deteriorated. The Institute of Medicine's Food and Nutrition Board suggests 3.7 L for adult males and 2.7 L for adult females age 19 to 70 yr as an adequate daily intake goal of total water; 3 L/d for pregnant females age 14 to 50 yr; 3.8 L/d for lactating females age 14 to 50 yr; 3.3 L/d for male and 2.3 L/d for female children age 14 to 18 yr; 2.4 L/d for male and 2.1 L/d for female children age 9 to 13 yr; 1.7 L/d for children age 4 to 8 yr; 1.3 L/d for children age 1 to 3 yr; 0.8 L/d for children age 7 to 12 mo; and 0.7 L/d (assumed to be from human milk) for children 0 to 6 mo. Reprinted with permission from the National Academies Press, copyright 2013, National Academy of Sciences.

Patients receiving digoxin or diuretics should have potassium levels monitored carefully because cardiac arrhythmias can occur.

Increased urine potassium levels may be associated with the formation of kidney stones. Educate the patient, if appropriate, on the importance of drinking a sufficient amount of water when kidney stones are suspected.

Recognize anxiety related to test results. Discuss the implications of abnormal test results on the patient's lifestyle. Provide teaching and information regarding the clinical implications of the test results, as appropriate.

Reinforce information given by the patient's HCP regarding further testing, treatment, or referral to another HCP.

Answer any questions or address any concerns voiced by the patient or family.

Depending on the results of this procedure, additional testing may be performed to evaluate or monitor progression of the disease process and determine the need for a change in therapy. Evaluate test results in relation to the patient's symptoms and other tests performed.

RELATED MONOGRAPHS:

Related tests include ACTH, aldosterone, anion gap, BUN, calcium, calculus kidney stone panel, carbon dioxide, chloride, cortisol, creatinine, DHEAS, glucose, insulin, ketones, lactic acid, magnesium, osmolality, phosphorus, potassium, renin, sodium, and UA.

Refer to the Endocrine, Gastrointestinal, and Genitourinary systems tables at the end of the book for related tests by body system.

Prealbumin

SYNONYM/ACRONYM: Transthyretin.

COMMON USE: To assess nutritional status and evaluate liver function toward diagnosing disorders such as malnutrition and chronic renal failure.

SPECIMEN: Serum (1 mL) collected in a red- or tiger-top tube.

NORMAL FINDINGS: (Method: Nephelometry)

Age	Conventional Units	SI Units (Conventional Units × 10)
Newborn–1 mo	7–39 mg/dL	70–390 mg/L
1–6 mo	8.3–34 mg/dL	83–340 mg/L
6 mo–4 yr	2–36 mg/dL	20–360 mg/L
5–6 yr	12–30 mg/dL	120–300 mg/L
7 yr–adult/older adult	12–42 mg/dL	120–420 mg/L

DESCRIPTION: Prealbumin is a protein primarily produced by the liver. It is the major transport protein for triiodothyronine and thyroxine. It is also important in the metabolism of retinol-binding protein, which is needed for transporting vitamin A (retinol). Prealbumin has a short biological half-life of 2 days. This makes it a good indicator of protein status and an excellent marker for malnutrition. Prealbumin is often measured simultaneously with transferrin and albumin.

INDICATIONS
Evaluate nutritional status

POTENTIAL DIAGNOSIS

Increased in
- Alcoholism *(related to leakage of prealbumin from damaged hepatocytes and/or poor nutrition)*
- Chronic renal failure *(related to rapid turnover of prealbumin, which reflects a perceived elevation in the presence of overall loss of other proteins that take longer to produce)*
- Patients receiving steroids *(these drugs stimulate production of prealbumin)*

Decreased in
- Acute-phase inflammatory response *(prealbumin is a negative acute-phase reactant protein; levels decrease in the presence of inflammation)*
- Diseases of the liver *(related to decreased ability of the damaged liver to synthesize protein)*
- Hepatic damage *(related to decreased ability of the damaged liver to synthesize protein)*
- Malnutrition *(synthesis is decreased due to lack of proper diet)*
- Tissue necrosis *(prealbumin is a negative acute-phase reactant protein; levels decrease in the presence of inflammation)*

CRITICAL FINDINGS: N/A

INTERFERING FACTORS
- Drugs that may increase prealbumin levels include anabolic steroids, anticonvulsants, danazol, oral contraceptives, prednisolone, prednisone, and propranolol.
- Drugs that may decrease prealbumin levels include amiodarone and diethylstilbestrol.
- Fasting 4 hr before specimen collection is highly recommended. Reference ranges are often based on fasting populations to provide some level of standardization for comparison. The presence of lipids in the blood may also interfere with the test method; fasting eliminates this potential source of error, especially if the patient has elevated lipid levels.

NURSING IMPLICATIONS AND PROCEDURE

PRETEST:
- Positively identify the patient using at least two unique identifiers before providing care, treatment, or services.
- *Patient Teaching:* Inform the patient this test can assist in assessing nutritional status.
- Obtain a history of the patient's complaints, including a list of known allergens, especially allergies or sensitivities to latex.
- Obtain a history of the patient's endocrine, gastrointestinal, and hepatobiliary systems; symptoms; and results of previously performed laboratory tests and diagnostic and surgical procedures.
- Obtain a list of the patient's current medications, including herbs, nutritional supplements, and nutraceuticals (see Appendix F).
- Review the procedure with the patient. Inform the patient that specimen collection takes approximately 5 to 10 min. Address concerns about pain and explain that there may be some discomfort during the venipuncture.
- *Sensitivity to social and cultural issues,* as well as concern for modesty, is

important in providing psychological support before, during, and after the procedure.
▶ Instruct the patient to fast for 4 hr before specimen collection.
▶ There are no fluid or medication restrictions, unless by medical direction.

INTRATEST:

▶ Ensure that the patient has complied with dietary restrictions; ensure that food has been restricted for at least 4 hr prior to the procedure.
▶ If the patient has a history of allergic reaction to latex, avoid the use of equipment containing latex.
▶ Instruct the patient to cooperate fully and to follow directions. Direct the patient to breathe normally and to avoid unnecessary movement.
▶ Observe standard precautions, and follow the general guidelines in Appendix A. Positively identify the patient, and label the appropriate specimen container with the corresponding patient demographics, initials of the person collecting the specimen, date, and time of collection. Perform a venipuncture.
▶ Remove the needle and apply direct pressure with dry gauze to stop bleeding. Observe/assess venipuncture site for bleeding or hematoma formation and secure gauze with adhesive bandage.
▶ Promptly transport the specimen to the laboratory for processing and analysis.

POST-TEST:

▶ A report of the results will be made available to the requesting health-care provider (HCP), who will discuss the results with the patient.
▶ Instruct the patient to resume usual diet, as directed by the HCP.
▶ **Nutritional Considerations:** Nutritional therapy may be indicated for patients with decreased prealbumin levels. Educate the patient, as appropriate, that good dietary sources of complete protein (containing all eight essential amino acids) include meat, fish, eggs, and dairy products and that good sources of incomplete protein (lacking one or more of the eight essential amino acids) include grains, nuts, legumes, vegetables, and seeds.
▶ Reinforce information given by the patient's HCP regarding further testing, treatment, or referral to another HCP. Answer any questions or address any concerns voiced by the patient or family.
▶ Depending on the results of this procedure, additional testing may be performed to evaluate or monitor progression of the disease process and determine the need for a change in therapy. Evaluate test results in relation to the patient's symptoms and other tests performed.

RELATED MONOGRAPHS:

▶ Related tests include albumin, chloride, ferritin, iron/TIBC, potassium, protein, sodium, T_4, T_3, transferrin, and vitamin A.
▶ Refer to the Endocrine, Gastrointestinal, and Hepatobiliary systems tables at the end of the book for related tests by body system.

P

Procalcitonin

SYNONYM/ACRONYM: PCT.

COMMON USE: To assist in diagnosing bacterial infection and risk for developing sepsis.

SPECIMEN: Serum (2 mL) collected in a red- or tiger-top tube. Plasma (2 mL) collected in a lavender-top (EDTA) or a green-top (lithium or sodium heparin) tube is also acceptable.

NORMAL FINDINGS: (Method: Fluorescence immunoassay)

Age	Conventional Units	SI Units (Conventional Units × 1)
Newborn	Less than 2 ng/mL	Less than 2 mcg/L
18–20 hr	Less than 20 ng/mL	Less than 20 mcg/L
48 hr	Less than 5 ng/mL	Less than 5 mcg/L
3 days–adult	Less than 0.1 ng/mL	Less than 0.1 mcg/L

Interpretive Guidelines		
Interpretation	**Conventional Units**	**SI Units**
Bacterial infection absent or very unlikely	Less than 0.1 ng/mL	Less than 0.1 mcg/L
Bacterial infection possible; low risk for development of sepsis	Less than 0.5 ng/mL	Less than 0.5 mcg/L
Bacterial infection likely; development of sepsis is possible	0.5–2 ng/mL	0.5–2 mcg/L
Bacterial infection very likely; high risk for development of sepsis	2.1–9.9 ng/mL or greater	0.5–9.9 mcg/L or greater
Bacterial infection severe; septic shock is probable	10 ng/mL or greater	10 mcg/L or greater

DESCRIPTION: Sepsis is a very serious, potentially life-threatening systemic inflammatory response to infection. The host inflammatory reaction was termed *systemic inflammatory response syndrome* (SIRS) by the American College of Chest Physicians and the Society of Critical Care Medicine in 1992. SIRS is defined by documented clinical evidence of bacterial infection (e.g., culture results) in the presence of two of four other criteria: temperature greater than 100.4°F or less than 96.8°F, heart rate greater than 90 beats/min, hyperventilation (greater than 20 breaths/minute or $Paco_2$ less than 32 mm Hg), or white blood cell (WBC) count greater than 12 × 10^3/microL or less than 4 × 10^3/microL. The development of sepsis is initiated by the activation of circulating macrophages resulting from binding to receptors on the outer membrane of gram-negative or gram-positive bacteria. Other organisms, such as fungi, parasites, and viruses, are also capable of initiating SIRS, which can develop into sepsis. Severe sepsis involves a systemic inflammatory response that suppresses the immune system, activation of the coagulation process (reflected by prolonged PT and aPTT, elevated D-dimer, and deficiency of protein C), cardiovascular insufficiency, and multiple organ failure. The incidence of sepsis in hospitals is especially high in noncardiac intensive care units. Early-onset neonatal sepsis occurs in the first 72 hours of life with 85% of cases presenting in the first 24 hours. Early-onset neonatal sepsis is the result of colonization of the neonate from the mother as it moved through the birth canal before delivery. The Centers for Disease

Control and Prevention recommends universal screening for group B *Streptococcus* for all pregnant women at 35 to 37 weeks' gestation. Other organisms associated with early-onset neonatal sepsis include coagulase-negative *Staphylococcus*, *Escherichia coli*, *Haemophilus influenzae*, and *Listeria monocytogenes*.

Late-onset neonatal sepsis, during days 4 to 90, is acquired from the environment and has been associated with infection by *Acinetobacter*, *Candida*, coagulase-negative *Staphylococci*, *Enterobacter*, *E. coli*, group B *Streptococcus*, *Klebsiella*, *Pseudomonas*, *Serratia*, and *Staphylococcus aureus*, as well as some anaerobes. Normally procalcitonin, the precursor of the hormone calcitonin, is produced by the C cells of the thyroid. In SIRS, microbial toxins and inflammatory mediator proteins, including cytokines, tumor necrosis factor α, interleukin 1, prostaglandins, and platelet activating factor, may trigger the production of large amounts of procalcitonin by nonthyroidal, non-neuroendocrine cells throughout the body. Each phase of the inflammatory response creates another cascade of events that may conclude with septic shock and death. Procalcitonin is detectable within 2 to 4 hr after an SIRS-initiating event and peaks within 12 to 24 hr. Serial measurements are useful to monitor patients at risk of developing sepsis or to monitor response to therapy.

INDICATIONS

* Assist in the diagnosis of bacteremia and septicemia
* Assist in the differential diagnosis of bacterial versus viral meningitis
* Assist in the differential diagnosis of community-acquired bacterial versus viral pneumonia
* Monitor response to antibacterial therapy

POTENTIAL DIAGNOSIS

Increased in

* Bacteremia or septicemia *(related to SIRS induced overproduction of procalcitonin)*
* Major surgery *(related to inflammation in the absence of sepsis)*
* Multiorgan failure *(related to inflammation in the absence of sepsis)*
* Neuroendocrine tumors (medullary thyroid cancer, small-cell lung cancer, and carcinoid tumors) *(related to procalcitonin (PCT)-secreting tumor cells)*
* Severe burns *(related to inflammation in the absence of sepsis)*
* Severe trauma *(related to inflammation in the absence of sepsis)*
* Treatment with OKT3 antibodies (antibody used to protect a transplanted organ or graft from attack by T cells and subsequent rejection) and other drugs that stimulate the release of cytokines *(related to inflammatory response in the absence of sepsis)*

Decreased in: N/A

CRITICAL FINDINGS: N/A

INTERFERING FACTORS: N/A

NURSING IMPLICATIONS AND PROCEDURE

PRETEST:

▶ Positively identify the patient using at least two unique identifiers before providing care, treatment, or services.
▶ *Patient Teaching:* Inform the patient this test can assist in assessing for infection and response to antibiotic treatment.

▸ Obtain a history of the patient's complaints, including a list of known allergens, especially allergies or sensitivities to latex. The patient may complain of pain related to the inflammatory process in connective or other tissues.

▸ Obtain a history of the patient's immune system, symptoms, and results of previously performed laboratory tests and diagnostic and surgical procedures.

▸ Obtain a list of the patient's current medications, including herbs, nutritional supplements, and nutraceuticals (see Appendix F).

▸ Review the procedure with the patient. Inform the patient that specimen collection takes approximately 5 to 10 min. Address concerns about pain and explain that there may be some discomfort during the venipuncture. *Sensitivity to social and cultural issues,* as well as concern for modesty, is important in providing psychological support before, during, and after the procedure.

▸ There are no food, fluid, or medication restrictions unless by medical direction.

INTRATEST:

▸ If the patient has a history of allergic reaction to latex, avoid the use of equipment containing latex.

▸ Instruct the patient to cooperate fully and to follow directions. Direct the patient to breathe normally and to avoid unnecessary movement.

▸ Observe standard precautions, and follow the general guidelines in Appendix A. Positively identify the patient, and label the appropriate specimen container with the corresponding patient demographics, initials of the person collecting the specimen, date, and time of collection. Perform a venipuncture.

▸ Remove the needle and apply direct pressure with dry gauze to stop bleeding. Observe/assess venipuncture site for bleeding or hematoma formation and secure gauze with adhesive bandage.

▸ Promptly transport the specimen to the laboratory for processing and analysis.

POST-TEST:

▸ A report of the results will be made available to the requesting health-care provider (HCP), who will discuss the results with the patient.

▸ Answer any questions or address any concerns voiced by the patient or family.

▸ Depending on the results of this procedure, additional testing may be performed to evaluate or monitor progression of the disease process and determine the need for a change in therapy. Evaluate test results in relation to the patient's symptoms and other tests performed.

RELATED MONOGRAPHS:

▸ Related tests include ALKP, ALT, AST, antibiotic drugs, bilirubin total and fractions, coagulation factors, CBC, CBC platelet count, CBC WBC count and differential, creatinine, CRP, culture bacterial blood, culture bacterial anal/genital, culture bacterial urine, ESR, Gram stain, lactic acid, aPTT, PT, and Protein C.

▸ Refer to the Immune System table at the end of the book for related tests by body system.

Proctosigmoidoscopy

SYNONYM/ACRONYM: Anoscopy (anal canal), proctoscopy (rectum), flexible fiberoptic sigmoidoscopy, flexible proctosigmoidoscopy, sigmoidoscopy (sigmoid colon).

COMMON USE: To visualize and assess the colon, rectum, and anus to assist in diagnosing disorders such as cancer, inflammation, prolapse, and evaluate the effectiveness of medical and surgical therapeutic interventions.

AREA OF APPLICATION: Anus, rectum, colon.

CONTRAST: Air.

DESCRIPTION: Proctosigmoido-scopy allows direct visualization of the mucosa of the anal canal (anoscopy), rectum (procto-scopy), and distal sigmoid colon (sigmoidoscopy). The procedure can be performed using a rigid or flexible fiberoptic endoscope, but the flexible instrument is general-ly preferred. The endoscope is a multichannel device allowing visualization of the mucosal lin-ing of the colon, instillation of air, removal of fluid and foreign objects, obtainment of tissue biopsy specimens, and use of a laser for the destruction of tissue and control of bleeding. The endoscope is advanced approxi-mately 60 cm into the colon. This procedure is commonly used in patients with lower abdominal and perineal pain; changes in bowel habits; rectal prolapse dur-ing defecation; or passage of blood, mucus, or pus in the stool. Proctosigmoidoscopy can also be a therapeutic procedure, allowing removal of polyps or hemor-rhoids or reduction of a volvulus. Biopsy specimens of suspicious sites may be obtained during the procedure.

INDICATIONS
- Confirm the diagnosis of diverticu-lar disease
- Confirm the diagnosis of Hirschsprung's disease and colitis in children
- Determine the cause of pain and rectal prolapse during defecation
- Determine the cause of rectal itch-ing, pain, or burning
- Evaluate the cause of blood, pus, or mucus in the stool

- Evaluate postoperative anastomosis of the colon
- Examine the distal colon before barium enema (BE) x-ray to obtain improved visualization of the area, and after a BE when x-ray findings are inconclusive
- Reduce volvulus of the sigmoid colon
- Remove hemorrhoids by laser therapy
- Screen for and excise polyps
- Screen for colon cancer

POTENTIAL DIAGNOSIS

Normal findings in
- Normal mucosa of the anal canal, rectum, and sigmoid colon

Abnormal findings in
- Anal fissure or fistula
- Anorectal abscess
- Benign lesions
- Bleeding sites
- Bowel infection or inflammation
- Crohn's disease
- Diverticula
- Hypertrophic anal papillae
- Internal and external hemorrhoids
- Polyps
- Rectal prolapse
- Tumors
- Ulcerative colitis
- Vascular abnormalities

CRITICAL FINDINGS: N/A

INTERFERING FACTORS

This procedure is contraindicated for
- Patients with bleeding disorders, especially disorders associated with uremia and cytotoxic chemotherapy.
- Patients with cardiac conditions or arrhythmias.

- Patients with bowel perforation, acute peritonitis, ischemic bowel necrosis, toxic megacolon, diverticulitis, recent bowel surgery, advanced pregnancy, severe cardiac or pulmonary disease, recent myocardial infarction, known or suspected pulmonary embolus, large abdominal aortic or iliac aneurysm, or coagulation abnormality.

Factors that may impair clear imaging
- Inability of the patient to cooperate or remain still during the procedure because of age, significant pain, or mental status.
- Strictures or other abnormalities preventing passage of the scope.
- Barium swallow or upper gastrointestinal (GI) series within the preceding 48 hr.
- Severe lower GI bleeding or the presence of feces, barium, blood, or blood clots.

Other considerations
- Failure to follow dietary restrictions before the procedure may cause the procedure to be canceled or repeated.
- Use of bowel preparations that include laxatives or enemas should be avoided in pregnant patients or patients with inflammatory bowel disease unless specifically directed by a health-care provider (HCP).

NURSING IMPLICATIONS AND PROCEDURE

PRETEST:

▶ Positively identify the patient using at least two unique identifiers before providing care, treatment, or services.

▶ *Patient Teaching:* Inform the patient this procedure can assist in evaluating the rectum and lower colon for disease.

▶ Obtain a history of the patient's complaints, including a list of known allergens, especially allergies or sensitivities to latex, iodine, seafood, contrast medium, and anesthetics.

▶ Obtain a history of the patient's gastrointestinal system, symptoms, and results of previously performed laboratory tests and diagnostic and surgical procedures.

▶ Note any recent procedures that can interfere with test results. Ensure that this procedure is performed before an upper GI study or barium swallow.

▶ Record the date of the last menstrual period and determine the possibility of pregnancy in perimenopausal women.

▶ Obtain a list of the patient's current medications, including anticoagulants, aspirin and other salicylates, herbs, nutritional supplements, and nutraceuticals (see Appendix F). Such products should be discontinued by medical direction for the appropriate number of days prior to a surgical procedure. Note time and date of last dose.

▶ Note intake of oral iron preparations within 1 wk before the procedure because these cause black, sticky feces that are difficult to remove with bowel preparation.

▶ Review the procedure with the patient. Address concerns about pain related to the procedure and explain that some pain may be experienced during the test, and there may be moments of discomfort. Explain that a sedative and/or analgesia will be administered to promote relaxation and reduce discomfort prior to insertion of the anoscope. Inform the patient that the procedure is performed in a GI lab by an HCP specializing in this procedure, with support staff, and takes approximately 30 to 60 min.

▶ *Sensitivity to social and cultural issues,* as well as concern for modesty, is important in providing psychological support before, during, and after the procedure.

▶ Instruct the patient that a laxative may be needed the day before the procedure, with cleansing enemas on the morning of the procedure, depending on the institution's policy.

▶ Inform the patient that the urge to defecate may be experienced when the scope is passed. Encourage slow, deep breathing through the mouth to help alleviate the feeling.

- Inform the patient that flatus may be expelled during and after the procedure owing to air that is injected into the scope to improve visualization.
- Instruct the patient to eat a low-residue diet for 3 days prior to the procedure. Consume clear liquids only the evening before, and restrict food and fluids for 8 hr prior to the procedure. Protocols may vary among facilities.
- *Make sure a written and informed consent has been signed prior to the procedure and before administering any medications.*

INTRATEST:

- Observe standard precautions, and follow the general guidelines in Appendix A. Positively identify the patient.
- Ensure that the patient has complied with food, fluid, and medication restrictions and pretesting preparations.
- Administer two small-volume enemas 1 hr before the procedure.
- Have emergency equipment readily available.
- Instruct the patient to void prior to the procedure and change into the gown, robe, and foot coverings provided.
- Record baseline vital signs and continue to monitor throughout the procedure. Protocols may vary among facilities.
- Place the patient on an examination table in the left lateral decubitus position or the knee-chest position and drape with the buttocks exposed. The buttocks are placed at or extending slightly beyond the edge of the examination table or bed, preferably on a special examining table that tilts the patient into the desired position.
- The HCP visually inspects the perianal area and then performs a digital rectal examination with a well-lubricated, gloved finger. A fecal specimen may be obtained from the glove when the finger is removed from the rectum.
- A lubricated anoscope (7 cm in length) is inserted, and the anal canal is inspected (anoscopy). The anoscope is removed, and a lubricated proctoscope (27 cm in length) or flexible sigmoidoscope (35 to 60 cm in length) is inserted.

- The scope is manipulated gently to facilitate passage, and air may be insufflated through the scope to improve visualization. Suction and cotton swabs also are used to remove materials that hinder visualization.
- The patient is instructed to take deep breaths to aid in movement of the scope downward through the ascending colon to the cecum and into the terminal portion of the ileum.
- Examination is done as the scope is gradually withdrawn. Photographs are obtained for future reference.
- At the end of the procedure, the scope is completely withdrawn, and residual lubricant is cleansed from the anal area.
- Place fecal or tissue samples and polyps in properly labeled specimen containers, and promptly transport the specimen to the laboratory for processing and analysis.

POST-TEST:

- A report of the results will be made available to the requesting HCP, who will discuss the results with the patient.
- Monitor vital signs and neurological status every 15 min for 1 hr, then every 2 hr for 4 hr, and then as ordered by the HCP. Monitor temperature every 4 hr for 24 hr. Monitor intake and output at least every 8 hr. Compare with baseline values. Notify the HCP if temperature changes. Protocols may vary among facilities.
- Monitor for any rectal bleeding.
- Instruct the patient to resume diet, medication, and activity, as directed by the HCP.
- Instruct the patient to expect slight rectal bleeding for 2 days after removal of polyps or biopsy specimens, but heavy rectal bleeding must be immediately reported to the HCP.
- Instruct the patient that any abdominal pain, tenderness, or distention; pain on defecation; or fever must be reported to the HCP immediately.
- Inform the patient that any bloating or flatulence is the result of air insufflation.
- Encourage the patient to drink several glasses of water to help replace fluid lost during test preparation.

▶ Recognize anxiety related to test results, and be supportive of perceived loss of independence and fear of shortened life expectancy. Discuss the implications of abnormal test results on the patient's lifestyle. Provide teaching and information regarding the clinical implications of the test results, as appropriate. Educate the patient regarding access to counseling services.

▶ Reinforce information given by the patient's HCP regarding further testing, treatment, or referral to another HCP. Decisions regarding the need for and frequency of occult blood testing, colonoscopy, or other cancer screening procedures should be made after consultation between the patient and HCP. The most current guidelines for colon cancer screening of the general population as well as of individuals with increased risk are available from the American Cancer Society (www.cancer.org) and the American College of Gastroenterology (www.gi.org). Answer any questions or address any concerns voiced by the patient or family.

▶ Depending on the results of this procedure, additional testing may be needed to evaluate or monitor progression of the disease process and determine the need for a change in therapy. Evaluate test results in relation to the patient's symptoms and other tests performed.

RELATED MONOGRAPHS:

▶ Related tests include barium enema, capsule endoscopy, colonoscopy, CBC, CT abdomen, fecal analysis, fecal fat, GI blood loss scan, MRI abdomen, and US prostate transrectal.

▶ Refer to the Gastrointestinal System table at the end of the book for related tests by body system.

Progesterone

SYNONYM/ACRONYM: N/A.

COMMON USE: To assess ovarian function, assist in fertility work-ups, and monitor placental function during pregnancy related to disorders such as tumor, cysts, and threatened abortion.

SPECIMEN: Serum (1 mL) collected in a red- or tiger-top tube.

NORMAL FINDINGS: (Method: Immunochemiluminometric assay [ICMA])

Hormonal State	Conventional Units	SI Units (Conventional Units × 0.0318)
Prepubertal	7–52 ng/dL	0.2–1.7 nmol/L
Adult male	13–97 ng/dL	0.4–3.1 nmol/L
Adult female		
Follicular phase	15–70 ng/dL	0.5–2.2 nmol/L
Luteal phase	200–2,500 ng/dL	6.4–79.5 nmol/L
Pregnancy, first trimester	725–4,400 ng/dL	23–140 nmol/L

Hormonal State	Conventional Units	SI Units (Conventional Units × 0.0318)
Pregnancy, second trimester	1,950–8,250 ng/dL	62–262.4 nmol/L
Pregnancy, third trimester	6,500–22,900 ng/dL	206.7–728.2 nmol/L
Postmenopausal period	Less than 40 ng/dL	Less than 127.2 nmol/L

DESCRIPTION: Progesterone is a female sex hormone. Its function is to prepare the uterus for pregnancy and the breasts for lactation. Progesterone testing can be used to confirm that ovulation has occurred and to assess the functioning of the corpus luteum. Serial measurements can be performed to help determine the day of ovulation.

INDICATIONS

- Assist in the diagnosis of luteal-phase defects (performed in conjunction with endometrial biopsy)
- Evaluate patients at risk for early or spontaneous abortion
- Identify patients at risk for ectopic pregnancy and assessment of corpus luteum function
- Monitor patients ovulating during the induction of human chorionic gonadotropin (HCG), human menopausal gonadotropin, follicle-stimulating hormone/luteinizing hormone–releasing hormone, or clomiphene (serial measurements can assist in pinpointing the day of ovulation)
- Monitor patients receiving progesterone replacement therapy

POTENTIAL DIAGNOSIS

Increased in

- Chorioepithelioma of the ovary *(related to progesterone-secreting tumor)*
- Congenital adrenal hyperplasia *(related to excessive production of progesterone precursors)*
- Hydatidiform mole *(related to progesterone-secreting tumor)*
- Lipoid ovarian tumor *(related to progesterone-secreting tumor)*
- Ovulation *(related to normal production of progesterone)*
- Pregnancy *(related to normal production of progesterone)*
- Theca lutein cyst *(related to progesterone-secreting cyst)*

Decreased in

- Galactorrhea-amenorrhea syndrome *(progesterone is not produced in the absence of ovulation)*
- Primary or secondary hypogonadism *(related to diminished production of progesterone)*
- Short luteal-phase syndrome *(related to diminished time frame for production and secretion)*
- Threatened abortion, fetal demise, toxemia of pregnancy, pre-eclampsia, placental failure *(related to decreased production by threatened placenta)*

CRITICAL FINDINGS: N/A

INTERFERING FACTORS

- Drugs that may increase progesterone levels include clomiphene, corticotropin, hydroxyprogesterone, ketoconazole, mifepristone, progesterone, tamoxifen, and valproic acid.
- Drugs that may decrease progesterone levels include ampicillin, danazol, epostane, goserelin, and leuprolide.

P

NURSING IMPLICATIONS AND PROCEDURE

PRETEST:

▶ Positively identify the patient using at least two unique identifiers before providing care, treatment, or services.
Patient Teaching: Inform the patient this test can assist in evaluating hormone level during pregnancy.

▶ Obtain a history of the patient's complaints, including a list of known allergens, especially allergies or sensitivities to latex.

▶ Obtain a history of the patient's endocrine and reproductive systems, symptoms, and results of previously performed laboratory tests and diagnostic and surgical procedures.

▶ Record the date of the last menstrual period and determine the possibility of pregnancy in perimenopausal women.

▶ Obtain a list of the patient's current medications, including herbs, nutritional supplements, and nutraceuticals (see Appendix F).

▶ Review the procedure with the patient. Inform the patient that specimen collection takes approximately 5 to 10 min. Address concerns about pain and explain that there may be some discomfort during the venipuncture.
Sensitivity to social and cultural issues, as well as concern for modesty, is important in providing psychological support before, during, and after the procedure.

▶ There are no food, fluid, or medication restrictions unless by medical direction.

INTRATEST:

▶ If the patient has a history of allergic reaction to latex, avoid the use of equipment containing latex.

▶ Instruct the patient to cooperate fully and to follow directions. Direct the patient to breathe normally and to avoid unnecessary movement.

▶ Observe standard precautions, and follow the general guidelines in Appendix A. Positively identify the patient, and label the appropriate specimen container with the corresponding patient demographics, initials of the person collecting the specimen, date, and time of collection. Perform a venipuncture.

▶ Remove the needle and apply direct pressure with dry gauze to stop bleeding. Observe/assess venipuncture site for bleeding or hematoma formation and secure gauze with adhesive bandage.

▶ Promptly transport the specimen to the laboratory for processing and analysis.

POST-TEST:

▶ A report of the results will be made available to the requesting health-care provider (HCP), who will discuss the results with the patient.

▶ Recognize anxiety related to test results, and provide support. Provide teaching and information regarding the clinical implications of the test results, as appropriate. Provide a nonjudgmental, nonthreatening atmosphere for exploring other options (e.g., adoption). Educate the patient regarding access to counseling services, as appropriate.

▶ Reinforce information given by the patient's HCP regarding further testing, treatment, or referral to another HCP. Instruct the patient in the use of home pregnancy test kits approved by the U.S. Food and Drug Administration. Answer any questions or address any concerns voiced by the patient or family.

▶ Depending on the results of this procedure, additional testing may be performed to evaluate or monitor progression of the disease process and determine the need for a change in therapy. Evaluate test results in relation to the patient's symptoms and other tests performed.

RELATED MONOGRAPHS:

▶ Related tests include ACTH, AFP, amniotic fluid analysis, antibodies cardiolipin, biopsy chorionic villus, estradiol, fetal fibronectin, FSH, HCG, LH, prolactin, testosterone, and US BPP obstetric.

▶ Refer to the Endocrine and Reproductive systems tables at the end of the book for related tests by body system.

Prolactin

SYNONYM/ACRONYM: Luteotropic hormone, lactogenic hormone, lactogen, HPRL, PRL.

COMMON USE: To assess for lactation disorders and identify the presence of prolactin-secreting tumors to assist in diagnosing disorders such as lactation failure.

SPECIMEN: Serum (1 mL) collected in a red- or tiger-top tube. Specimen should be transported tightly capped and in an ice slurry.

NORMAL FINDINGS: (Method: Immunoassay)

Age	Conventional Units	SI Units (Conventional Units × 1)
Prepubertal males and females	3.2–20 ng/mL	3.2–20 mcg/L
Adult males	4–23 ng/mL	4–23 mcg/L
Adult females	4–30 ng/mL	4–30 mcg/L
Pregnant	5.3–215.3 ng/mL	5.3–215.3 mcg/L
Postmenopausal	2.4–24 ng/mL	2.4–24 mcg/L

DESCRIPTION: Prolactin is secreted by the pituitary gland. It is unique among hormones in that it responds to inhibition by the hypothalamus rather than to stimulation. The only known function of prolactin is to induce milk production in female breasts that are already stimulated by high estrogen levels. When milk production is established, lactation can continue without elevated prolactin levels. Prolactin levels rise late in pregnancy, peak with the initiation of lactation, and surge each time a woman breastfeeds. The function of prolactin in males is unknown.

INDICATIONS

- Assist in the diagnosis of primary hypothyroidism, as indicated by elevated levels
- Assist in the diagnosis of suspected tumor involving the lungs or kidneys (elevated levels indicating ectopic prolactin production)
- Evaluate failure of lactation in the postpartum period
- Evaluate sexual dysfunction of unknown cause in men and women
- Evaluate suspected postpartum hypophyseal infarction (Sheehan's syndrome), as indicated by decreased levels

POTENTIAL DIAGNOSIS

Increased in

- Adrenal insufficiency *(secondary to hypopituitarism)*
- Amenorrhea *(pathophysiology is unclear)*
- Anorexia nervosa *(pathophysiology is unclear)*

- Breastfeeding *(stimulates secretion of prolactin)*
- Chiari-Frommel and Argonz–Del Castillo syndromes *(endocrine disorders in which pituitary or hypothalamic tumors secrete excessive amounts of prolactin)*
- Chest wall injury *(trauma in this location can stimulate production of prolactin)*
- Chronic renal failure *(related to decreased renal excretion)*
- Ectopic prolactin-secreting tumors (e.g., lung, kidney)
- Galactorrhea *(production of breast milk related to prolactin-secreting tumor)*
- Hypothalamic and pituitary disorders
- Hypothyroidism (primary) *(related to pituitary gland dysfunction)*
- Pituitary tumor
- Polycystic ovary (Stein-Leventhal) syndrome
- Pregnancy
- Stress *(stimulates secretion of prolactin)*
- Surgery (pituitary stalk section)

Decreased in
- Sheehan's syndrome *(severe hemorrhage after obstetric delivery that causes pituitary infarct; secretion of all pituitary hormones is diminished)*

CRITICAL FINDINGS: N/A

INTERFERING FACTORS
- Drugs and hormones that may increase prolactin levels include amitriptyline, amoxapine, azosemide, benserazide, butaperazine, butorphanol, carbidopa, chlorophenylpiperazine, chlorpromazine, cimetidine, clomipramine, desipramine, diethylstilbestrol, enalapril, β-endorphin, enflurane, fenfluramine, fenoldopam, flunarizine, fluphenazine, fluvoxamine, furosemide, growth hormone–releasing hormone, haloperidol, hexarelin, imipramine, insulin, interferon-b, labetalol, loxapine, megestrol, mestranol, methyldopa, metoclopramide, molindone, morphine, nitrous oxide, oral contraceptives, oxcarbazepine, parathyroid hormone, pentagastrin, perphenazine, phenytoin, pimozide, prochlorperazine, promazine, ranitidine, remoxipride, reserpine, sulpiride, sultopride, thiethylperazine, thioridazine, thiothixene, thyrotropin-releasing hormone, trifluoperazine, trimipramine, tumor necrosis factor, veralipride, verapamil, and zometapine.
- Drugs and hormones that may decrease prolactin levels include anticonvulsants, apomorphine, bromocriptine, cabergoline, calcitonin, cyclosporine, dexamethasone, D-Trp-6-LHRH, levodopa, metoclopramide, morphine, nifedipine, octreotide, pergolide, ranitidine, rifampin, ritanserin, ropinirole, secretin, and tamoxifen.
- Episodic elevations can occur in response to sleep, stress, exercise, hypoglycemia, and breastfeeding.
- Venipuncture can cause falsely elevated levels.
- Prolactin secretion is subject to diurnal variation with highest levels occurring in the morning.
- Failure to follow dietary restrictions before the procedure may cause the procedure to be canceled or repeated.

NURSING IMPLICATIONS AND PROCEDURE

PRETEST:

Positively identify the patient using at least two unique identifiers before providing care, treatment, or services. *Patient Teaching:* Inform the patient that test can assist in evaluating breast feeding hormone level.

Obtain a history of the patient's complaints, including a list of known allergens, especially allergies or sensitivities to latex.

Obtain a history of the patient's endocrine and reproductive systems, symptoms, and results of previously performed laboratory tests and diagnostic and surgical procedures.

Obtain a list of the patient's current medications, including herbs, nutritional supplements, and nutraceuticals (see Appendix F).

Review the procedure with the patient. Specimen collection should occur between 8 and 10 a.m. Inform the patient that specimen collection takes approximately 5 to 10 min. Address concerns about pain and explain there may be some discomfort during the venipuncture.

Sensitivity to social and cultural issues, as well as concern for modesty, is important in providing psychological support before, during, and after the procedure.

The patient should fast for 12 hr before specimen collection because hyperglycemia can cause a short-term increase in prolactin levels.

There are no fluid or medication restrictions unless by medical direction.

Prepare an ice slurry in a cup or plastic bag to have on hand for immediate transport of the specimen to the laboratory.

INTRATEST:

Ensure that the patient has complied with dietary restrictions; ensure that food has been restricted for at least 12 hr prior to the procedure.

If the patient has a history of allergic reaction to latex, avoid the use of equipment containing latex.

Instruct the patient to cooperate fully and to follow directions. Direct the patient to breathe normally and to avoid unnecessary movement.

Observe standard precautions, and follow the general guidelines in Appendix A. Positively identify the patient, and label the appropriate specimen container with the corresponding patient demographics, initials of the person collecting the specimen, date, and time of collection. Perform a venipuncture.

Remove the needle and apply direct pressure with dry gauze to stop bleeding. Observe/assess venipuncture site for bleeding or hematoma formation and secure gauze with adhesive bandage.

Promptly transport the specimen to the laboratory for processing and analysis. The specimen should be placed in an ice slurry immediately after collection. Information on the specimen label should be protected from water in the ice slurry by first placing the specimen in a protective plastic bag.

POST-TEST:

A report of the results will be made available to the requesting health-care provider (HCP), who will discuss the results with the patient.

Instruct the patient to resume usual diet, as directed by the HCP.

Reinforce information given by the patient's HCP regarding further testing, treatment, or referral to another HCP. Answer any questions or address any concerns voiced by the patient or family.

Depending on the results of this procedure, additional testing may be performed to evaluate or monitor progression of the disease process and determine the need for a change in therapy. Evaluate test results in relation to the patient's symptoms and other tests performed.

RELATED MONOGRAPHS:

Related tests include ACE, BMD, CT pituitary, DHEAS, estradiol, FSH, GH, HCG, insulin, laparoscopy gynecologic, LH, MRI pituitary, progesterone, RAIU, TSH, and thyroxine.

Refer to the Endocrine and Reproductive systems tables at the end of the book for related tests by body system.

Prostate-Specific Antigen

SYNONYM/ACRONYM: PSA.

COMMON USE: To assess prostate health and assist in diagnosis of disorders such as prostate cancer, inflammation, and benign tumor and to evaluate effectiveness of medical and surgical therapeutic interventions.

SPECIMEN: Serum (1 mL) collected in a red- or tiger-top tube.

NORMAL FINDINGS: (Method: Immunoassay)

Gender	Conventional Units	SI Units (Conventional Units × 1)
Male	Less than 4 ng/mL	Less than 4 mcg/L
Post–radical prostatectomy (30–60 d)	Less than 0.1 ng/mL	Less than 0.1 mcg/L
Female	Less than 0.5 ng/mL	Less than 0.5 mcg/L

DESCRIPTION: Prostate-specific antigen (PSA) is produced exclusively by the epithelial cells of the prostate, periurethral, and perirectal glands. Used in conjunction with the digital rectal examination (DRE), PSA is a useful test for identifying and monitoring cancer of the prostate. Risk of diagnosis is higher in African American men, who are 61% more likely than Caucasian men to develop prostate cancer. Family history and age at diagnosis are other strong correlating factors. PSA circulates in both free and bound (complexed) forms. A low ratio of free to complexed PSA (i.e., less than 10%) is suggestive of prostate cancer; a ratio of greater than 30% is rarely associated with prostate cancer. New technology makes it possible to combine data such as analysis of molecular biomarkers and cellular structure specific to the individual's biopsy tissue, standard

tissue biopsy results, Gleason score, number of positive tumor cores, tumor stage, presurgical and postsurgical PSA levels, and postsurgical margin status with computerized mathematical programs to create a personalized report that predicts the likelihood of post-prostatectomy disease progression. Serial measurements of PSA in the blood are often performed before and after surgery. PSA velocity, the rate of PSA increase over time, is being used to identify the potential aggressiveness of the cancer. Approximately 15% to 40% of patients who have had their prostate removed will encounter an increase in PSA. Patients treated for prostate cancer and who have had a PSA recurrence can still develop a metastasis for as long as 8 years after the postsurgical PSA level increased. The majority of prostate tumors develop slowly and require minimal intervention, but patients with an increase in PSA greater than 2 ng/mL in a year are more likely to have an aggressive form of prostate cancer with a greater risk of death. Personalized medicine provides a technology to predict the progression of prostate cancer, likelihood of recurrence, or development of related metastatic disease. PSA is also produced in females, most notably in breast tissue. There is some evidence that elevated PSA levels in breast cancer patients are associated with positive estrogen and progesterone status. *Important note:* When following patients using serial testing, the same method of measurement should be consistently used.

INDICATIONS

Evaluate the effectiveness of treatment for prostate cancer (prostatectomy): Levels decrease if treatment is effective; rising levels are associated with recurrence and a poor prognosis

Investigate or evaluate an enlarged prostate gland, especially if prostate cancer is suspected

Stage prostate cancer

POTENTIAL DIAGNOSIS

Increased in

A breach in the protective barrier between the prostatic lumen and the bloodstream due to significant disease will allow measurable levels of circulating PSA.

Benign prostatic hypertrophy
Prostate cancer
Prostatic infarct
Prostatitis
Urinary retention

Decreased in: N/A

CRITICAL FINDINGS: N/A

INTERFERING FACTORS

• Drugs that decrease PSA levels include buserelin, dutasteride, finasteride, and flutamide.
• Increases may occur if ejaculation occurs within 24 hr prior to specimen collection. Increases can occur due to prostatic needle biopsy, cystoscopy, or prostatic infarction either by undergoing catheterization or the presence of an indwelling catheter; therefore, specimens should be collected prior to or 6 wk after the procedure. There is conflicting information regarding the effect of DRE on PSA values, and some health-care providers (HCPs) may specifically request specimen collection prior to DRE.

NURSING IMPLICATIONS AND PROCEDURE

PRETEST:

▶ Positively identify the patient using at least two unique identifiers before providing care, treatment, or services.

▶ *Patient Teaching:* Inform the patient this test can assist in assessing prostate health.

▶ Obtain a history of the patient's complaints, including a list of known allergens, especially allergies or sensitivities to latex.

▶ Obtain a history of the patient's genitourinary system, symptoms, and results of previously performed laboratory tests and diagnostic and surgical procedures.

▶ Note any recent procedures that can interfere with test results.

▶ Obtain a list of the patient's current medications, including herbs, nutritional supplements, and nutraceuticals (see Appendix F).

▶ Review the procedure with the patient. Inform the patient that specimen collection takes approximately 5 to 10 min. Address concerns about pain and explain that there may be some discomfort during the venipuncture.

P

Sensitivity to social and cultural issues, as well as concern for modesty, is important in providing psychological support before, during, and after the procedure.

There are no food, fluid, or medication restrictions unless by medical direction.

INTRATEST:

If the patient has a history of allergic reaction to latex, avoid the use of equipment containing latex.

Instruct the patient to cooperate fully and to follow directions. Direct the patient to breathe normally and to avoid unnecessary movement.

Observe standard precautions, and follow the general guidelines in Appendix A. Positively identify the patient, and label the appropriate specimen container with the corresponding patient demographics, initials of the person collecting the specimen, date, and time of collection. Perform a venipuncture.

Remove the needle and apply direct pressure with dry gauze to stop bleeding. Observe/assess venipuncture site for bleeding or hematoma formation and secure gauze with adhesive bandage.

Promptly transport the specimen to the laboratory for processing and analysis.

POST-TEST:

A report of the results will be made available to the requesting HCP, who will discuss the results with the patient.

Nutritional Considerations: There is growing evidence that inflammation and oxidation play key roles in the development of numerous diseases, including prostate cancer. Research also indicates that diets containing dried beans, fresh fruits and vegetables, nuts, spices, whole grains, and smaller amounts of red meats can increase the amount of protective antioxidants. Regular exercise, especially in combination with a healthy diet, can bring about changes in the body's metabolism that decrease inflammation and oxidation.

Recognize anxiety related to test results, and offer support. Counsel the patient, as appropriate, that sexual dysfunction related to altered body function, drugs, or radiation may occur. Discuss the implications of abnormal test results on the patient's lifestyle. Provide teaching and information regarding the clinical implications of the test results, as appropriate. Educate the patient regarding access to counseling services. Provide contact information, if desired, for the Prostate Cancer Foundation (www.prostatecancerfoundation.org).

Reinforce information given by the patient's HCP regarding further testing, treatment, or referral to another HCP. Answer any questions or address any concerns voiced by the patient or family. Decisions regarding the need for and frequency of routine PSA testing or other cancer screening procedures should be made after consultation between the patient and HCP. The most current guidelines for prostate cancer screening of the general population as well as of individuals with increased risk are available from the American Cancer Society (www.cancer.org) and the American Urological Association (www.aua.org).

Depending on the results of this procedure, additional testing may be performed to evaluate or monitor progression of the disease process and determine the need for a change in therapy. Evaluate test results in relation to the patient's symptoms and other tests performed.

RELATED MONOGRAPHS:

Related tests include biopsy prostate (including Gleason score), cystoscopy, cystourethrography voiding, PAP, retrograde ureteropyelography, semen analysis, and US prostate.

Refer to the Genitourinary System table at the end of the book for related tests by body system.

Protein, Blood, Total and Fractions

SYNONYM/ACRONYM: TP, SPEP (fractions include albumin, α_1-globulin, α_2-globulin, β-globulin, and γ-globulin).

COMMON USE: To assess nutritional status related to various disease and conditions such as dehydration, burns, and malabsorption.

SPECIMEN: Serum (1 mL) collected in a red- or tiger-top tube.

NORMAL FINDINGS: (Method: Spectrophotometry for total protein, electrophoresis for protein fractions)

Total Protein

Age	Conventional Units	SI Units (Conventional units × 10)
Newborn–5 days	3.8–6.2 g/dL	38–62 g/L
1–3 yr	5.9–7 g/dL	59–70 g/L
4–6 yr	5.9–7.8 g/dL	59–78 g/L
7–9 yr	6.2–8.1 g/dL	62–81 g/L
10–19 yr	6.3–8.6 g/dL	63–86 g/L
Adult	6–8 g/dL	60–80 g/L

Values may be slightly decreased in older adults due to insufficient intake or the effects of medications and the presence of multiple chronic or acute diseases with or without muted symptoms.

Protein Fractions

	Conventional Units	SI Units (Conventional Units × 10)
Albumin	3.4–4.8 g/dL	34–48 g/L
α_1-Globulin	0.2–0.4 g/dL	2–4 g/L
α_2-Globulin	0.4–0.8 g/dL	4–8 g/L
β-Globulin	0.5–1 g/dL	5–10 g/L
γ-Globulin	0.6–1.2 g/dL	6–12 g/L

Values may be slightly decreased in older adults due to insufficient intake or the effects of medications and the presence of multiple chronic or acute diseases with or without muted symptoms.

DESCRIPTION: Protein is essential to all physiological functions. Proteins consist of amino acids, the building blocks of blood and body tissues. Protein is also required for the regulation of metabolic processes, immunity, and proper water balance. Total protein includes albumin and globulins. Albumin, the protein present in the highest concentrations, is the main transport protein in the body. Albumin also significantly affects plasma oncotic pressure, which regulates the distribution of body fluid between blood vessels, tissues, and cells. α_1-Globulin includes α_1-antitrypsin, α_1-fetoprotein, α_1-acid glycoprotein, α_1-antichymotrypsin, inter-α_1-trypsin inhibitor, high-density lipoproteins, and group-specific component (vitamin D–binding protein). α_2-Globulin includes haptoglobin, ceruloplasmin, and α_2-macroglobulin. β-Globulin includes transferrin, hemopexin, very-low-density lipoproteins, low-density lipoproteins, β_2-microglobulin, fibrinogen, complement, and C-reactive protein. γ-Globulin includes immunoglobulin (Ig) G, IgA, IgM, IgD, and IgE. After an acute infection or trauma, levels of many of the liver-derived proteins increase, whereas albumin level decreases; these conditions may not reflect an abnormal total protein determination.

INDICATIONS
- Evaluation of edema, as seen in patients with low total protein and low albumin levels
- Evaluation of nutritional status

POTENTIAL DIAGNOSIS

Increased in
- α_1-Globulin proteins in acute and chronic inflammatory diseases
- α_2-Globulin proteins occasionally in diabetes, pancreatitis, and hemolysis
- β-Globulin proteins in hyperlipoproteinemias and monoclonal gammopathies
- γ-Globulin proteins in chronic liver diseases, chronic infections, autoimmune disorders, hepatitis, cirrhosis, and lymphoproliferative disorders

- Total protein:
  Dehydration *(related to hemoconcentration)*
  Monoclonal and polyclonal gammopathies *(related to excessive γ-globulin protein synthesis)*
  Myeloma *(related to excessive γ-globulin protein synthesis)*
  Sarcoidosis *(related to excessive γ-globulin protein synthesis)*
  Some types of chronic liver disease
  Tropical diseases (e.g., leprosy) *(related to inflammatory reaction)*
  Waldenström's macroglobulinemia *(related to excessive γ-globulin protein synthesis)*

Decreased in
- α_1-Globulin proteins in hereditary deficiency
- α_2-Globulin proteins in nephrotic syndrome, malignancies, numerous subacute and chronic inflammatory disorders, and recovery stage of severe burns
- β-Globulin proteins in hypo-β-lipoproteinemias and IgA deficiency
- γ-Globulin proteins in immune deficiency or suppression
- Total protein:
  Administration of IV fluids *(related to hemodilution)*
  Burns *(related to fluid retention, loss of albumin from chronic open burns)*
  Chronic alcoholism *(related to insufficient dietary intake; diminished protein synthesis by damaged liver)*
  Chronic ulcerative colitis *(related to poor intestinal absorption)*
  Cirrhosis *(related to damaged liver, which cannot synthesize adequate amount of protein)*
  Crohn's disease *(related to poor intestinal absorption)*
  Glomerulonephritis *(related to alteration in permeability that results in excessive loss by kidneys)*
  Heart failure *(related to fluid retention)*
  Hyperthyroidism *(possibly related to increased metabolism and corresponding protein synthesis)*

Malabsorption *(related to insufficient intestinal absorption)*

Malnutrition *(related to insufficient intake)*

Neoplasms

Nephrotic syndrome *(related to alteration in permeability that results in excessive loss by kidneys)*

Pregnancy *(related to fluid retention, dietary insufficiency, increased demands of growing fetus)*

Prolonged immobilization *(related to fluid retention)*

Protein-losing enteropathies *(related to excessive loss)*

Severe skin disease

Starvation *(related to insufficient intake)*

CRITICAL FINDINGS: N/A

INTERFERING FACTORS

• Drugs that may increase protein levels include amino acids (if given IV), anabolic steroids, angiotensin, anticonvulsants, corticosteroids, corticotropin, furosemide, insulin, isotretinoin, levonorgestrel, oral contraceptives, progesterone, radiographic agents, and thyroid agents.

• Drugs and substances that may decrease protein levels include acetylsalicylic acid, arginine, benzene, carvedilol, citrates, floxuridine, laxatives, mercury compounds, oral contraceptives, pentastarch, phosgene, pyrazinamide, rifampin, trimethadione, and valproic acid.

• Values are significantly lower (5% to 10%) in recumbent patients.

• Hemolysis can falsely elevate results.

• Venous stasis can falsely elevate results; the tourniquet should not be left on the arm for longer than 60 sec.

NURSING IMPLICATIONS AND PROCEDURE

PRETEST:

Positively identify the patient using at least two unique identifiers before providing care, treatment, or services.

Patient Teaching: Inform the patient this test can assist in assessing nutritional status related to disease process.

Obtain a history of the patient's complaints, including a list of known allergens especially allergies or sensitivities to latex.

Obtain a history of the patient's gastrointestinal, hepatobiliary, and immune systems; symptoms; and results of previously performed laboratory tests and diagnostic and surgical procedures.

Obtain a list of the patient's current medications, including herbs, nutritional supplements, and nutraceuticals (see Appendix F).

Review the procedure with the patient. Inform the patient that specimen collection takes approximately 5 to 10 min. Address concerns about pain and explain that there may be some discomfort during the venipuncture.

Sensitivity to social and cultural issues, as well as concern for modesty, is important in providing psychological support before, during, and after the procedure.

There are no food, fluid, or medication restrictions unless by medical direction.

INTRATEST:

If the patient has a history of allergic reaction to latex, avoid the use of equipment containing latex.

Instruct the patient to cooperate fully and to follow directions. Direct the patient to breathe normally and to avoid unnecessary movement.

Observe standard precautions, and follow the general guidelines in Appendix A. Positively identify the patient, and label the appropriate specimen container with the corresponding patient demographics, initials of the person collecting the specimen, date, and time of collection. Perform a venipuncture.

P

Remove the needle and apply direct pressure with dry gauze to stop bleeding. Observe venipuncture site for bleeding or hematoma formation and secure gauze with adhesive bandage.

Promptly transport the specimen to the laboratory for processing and analysis.

A report of the results will be made available to the requesting health-care provider (HCP), who will discuss the results with the patient.

Nutritional Considerations: Educate the patient, as appropriate, that good dietary sources of complete protein (containing all eight essential amino acids) include meat, fish, eggs, and dairy products and that good sources of incomplete protein (lacking one or more of the eight essential amino acids) include grains, nuts, legumes, vegetables, and seeds.

Reinforce information given by the patient's HCP regarding further testing, treatment, or referral to another HCP.

Answer any questions or address any concerns voiced by the patient or family.

Depending on the results of this procedure, additional testing may be performed to evaluate or monitor progression of the disease process and determine the need for a change in therapy. Evaluate test results in relation to the patient's symptoms and other tests performed.

RELATED MONOGRAPHS:

Related tests include albumin, ALP, ACE, anion gap, AST, biopsy liver, biopsy lung, calcium, carbon dioxide, chloride, CBC WBC count and differential, cryoglobulin, fecal analysis, fecal fat, gallium scan, GGT, IgA, IgG, IgM, IFE, liver and spleen scan, magnesium, mediastinoscopy, β_2-microglobulin, osmolality, protein urine total and fractions, PFT, radiography bone, RF, sodium, TSH, thyroxine, and UA.

Refer to the Gastrointestinal, Hepatobiliary, and Immune systems tables at the end of the book for related tests by body system.

Protein C

SYNONYM/ACRONYM: Protein C antigen, protein C functional.

COMMON USE: To assess coagulation function and assist in diagnosis of disorders such as thrombosis and protein C deficiency.

SPECIMEN: Plasma (1 mL) collected in a completely filled blue-top (3.2% sodium citrate) tube. If the patient's hematocrit exceeds 55%, the volume of citrate in the collection tube must be adjusted.

NORMAL FINDINGS: (Method: Clot detection) 70% to 140% activity. Values are significantly reduced in children because of liver immaturity. Levels rise to approximately 50% of adult levels by age 5 yr and reach adult levels by age 16 yr.

DESCRIPTION: Protein C is a vitamin K–dependent protein that originates in the liver and circulates in plasma. Protein C activation occurs on thrombomodulin receptors on the endothelial cell surface. Thrombin bound to thrombomodulin receptors preferentially activates protein C. Freely circulating thrombin mainly converts fibrinogen to fibrin. Other steps in the activation process require calcium and protein S cofactor binding (see monographs titled "Protein S" and "Fibrinogen"). Activated protein C exhibits potent anticoagulant effects by degrading activated factors V and VIII. Factor V Leiden is a genetic variant of factor V and is resistant to inactivation by protein C. Factor V Leiden is the most common inherited hypercoagulability disorder identified among individuals of Eurasian descent. There are two types of protein C deficiency:

Type I: Decreased antigen and function, detected by functional and antigenic assays
Type II: Normal antigen but decreased function, detected only by a functional assay

Functional assays are recommended for initial evaluation because of their greater sensitivity.

INDICATIONS
- Differentiate inherited deficiency from acquired deficiency
- Investigate the mechanism of idiopathic venous thrombosis

POTENTIAL DIAGNOSIS

Increased in: N/A

Decreased in
- Congenital deficiency
- Disseminated intravascular coagulation (DIC) *(related to increased consumption)*
- Liver disease *(related to decreased synthesis by the liver)*
- Oral anticoagulant therapy *(patients deficient in protein C may be at risk of developing Coumadin-induced skin necrosis unless an immediate-acting anticoagulant like heparin is administered until therapeutic Coumadin levels are achieved)*
- Septic shock *(related to increased consumption and decreased synthesis due to hepatic impairment)*
- Vitamin K deficiency *(related to production of dysfunctional protein in the absence of vitamin K)*

CRITICAL FINDINGS: N/A

INTERFERING FACTORS
- Drugs that may increase protein C levels include desmopressin and oral contraceptives.
- Drugs that may decrease protein C levels include coumarin and warfarin (Coumadin).
- Placement of tourniquet for longer than 60 sec can result in venous stasis and changes in the concentration of plasma proteins to be measured. Platelet activation may also occur under these conditions, causing erroneous results.
- Vascular injury during phlebotomy can activate platelets and coagulation factors, causing erroneous results.
- Hemolyzed specimens must be rejected because hemolysis is an indication of platelet and coagulation factor activation.
- Icteric or lipemic specimens interfere with optical testing methods, producing erroneous results.
- Hematocrit greater than 55% may cause falsely prolonged results because of anticoagulant excess relative to plasma volume.
- Incompletely filled collection tubes, specimens contaminated with heparin, clotted specimens, or unprocessed specimens not delivered to the laboratory within 1 to 2 hr of collection should be rejected.

P

NURSING IMPLICATIONS AND PROCEDURE

PRETEST:

▶ Positively identify the patient using at least two unique identifiers before providing care, treatment, or services.

▶ *Patient Teaching:* Inform the patient this test can assist in assessing anticoagulant function.

▶ Obtain a history of the patient's complaints, including a list of known allergens, especially allergies or sensitivities to latex.

▶ Obtain a history of the patient's hematopoietic and hepatobiliary systems, symptoms, and results of previously performed laboratory tests and diagnostic and surgical procedures.

▶ Obtain a list of the patient's current medications, including herbs, nutritional supplements, and nutraceuticals (see Appendix F).

▶ Review the procedure with the patient. Inform the patient that specimen collection takes approximately 5 to 10 min. Address concerns about pain and explain that there may be some discomfort during the venipuncture.

▶ *Sensitivity to social and cultural issues,* as well as concern for modesty, is important in providing psychological support before, during, and after the procedure.

▶ There are no food, fluid, or medication restrictions unless by medical direction.

INTRATEST:

▶ If the patient has a history of allergic reaction to latex, avoid the use of equipment containing latex.

▶ Instruct the patient to cooperate fully and to follow directions. Direct the patient to breathe normally and to avoid unnecessary movement.

▶ Observe standard precautions, and follow the general guidelines in Appendix A. Positively identify the patient, and label the appropriate specimen container with the corresponding patient demographics, initials of the person collecting the specimen, date, and time of collection. Perform a venipuncture. Fill tube completely. *Important note:* Two different

concentrations of sodium citrate preservative are currently added to blue-top tubes for coagulation studies: 3.2% and 3.8%. The Clinical and Laboratory Standards Institute (CLSI; formerly the National Committee for Clinical Laboratory Standards [NCCLS]) guideline for sodium citrate is 3.2%. Laboratories establish reference ranges for coagulation testing based on numerous factors, including sodium citrate concentration, test equipment, and test reagents. It is important to ask the laboratory which concentration it recommends, because each concentration will have its own specific reference range. When multiple specimens are drawn, the blue-top tube should be collected after sterile (i.e., blood culture) tubes. Otherwise, when using a standard vacutainer system, the blue-top tube is the first tube collected. When a butterfly is used and due to the added tubing, an extra red-top tube should be collected before the blue-top tube to ensure complete filling of the blue-top tube.

▶ Remove the needle and apply direct pressure with dry gauze to stop bleeding. Observe/assess venipuncture site for bleeding or hematoma formation and secure gauze with adhesive bandage.

▶ Promptly transport the specimen to the laboratory for processing and analysis. The CLSI recommendation for processed and unprocessed samples stored in unopened tubes is that testing should be completed within 1 to 4 hr of collection. If the patient has a known hematocrit above 55%, adjust the amount of anticoagulant in the collection tube before drawing the blood according to the CLSI guidelines:

Anticoagulant vol. [x] = (100 − hematocrit) / (595 − hematocrit) × total vol. of anticoagulated blood required

Example:

Patient hematocrit = 60% = [(100 − 60) / (595 − 60) × 5.0] = 0.37 mL sodium citrate for a 5-mL standard drawing tube

POST-TEST:

▶ A report of the results will be made available to the requesting health-care provider (HCP), who will discuss the results with the patient.

▶ Reinforce information given by the patient's HCP regarding further testing, treatment, or referral to another HCP. Answer any questions or address any concerns voiced by the patient or family.

▶ Depending on the results of this procedure, additional testing may be performed to evaluate or monitor progression of the disease process and determine the need for a change in therapy. Evaluate test results in relation to the patient's symptoms and other tests performed.

RELATED MONOGRAPHS:

▶ Related tests include antibody anticardiolipin, antithrombin III, calcium, CBC, coagulation factors (factor V), FDP, fibrinogen, lupus anticoagulant, aPTT, procalcitonin, protein S, PT/INR, and vitamin K.

▶ Refer to the Hematopoietic and Hepatobiliary systems tables at the end of the book for related tests by body system.

Protein S

SYNONYM/ACRONYM: Protein S antigen, protein S functional.

COMMON USE: To assess coagulation function, assist in the diagnosis of disorders such as disseminated intravascular coagulation (DIC), and evaluate oral anticoagulation therapy.

SPECIMEN: Plasma (1 mL) collected in a completely filled blue-top (3.2% sodium citrate) tube. If the patient's hematocrit exceeds 55%, the volume of citrate in the collection tube must be adjusted.

NORMAL FINDINGS: (Method: Clot detection)

	Conventional Units
Adult	70%–140% activity
Pediatric	12%–60% activity

Note: The low end of "normal" is lower in children younger than age 16 because of the immaturity of the liver.

DESCRIPTION: Protein S is a vitamin K–dependent protein that originates in the liver and circulates in plasma. It is a cofactor required for the activation of protein C (see monographs titled "Protein C" and "Fibrinogen"). Protein S exists in two forms: free (biologi-cally active) and bound. Approximately 40% of protein S circulates in the free form; the remainder is bound and is functionally inactive. There are two types of protein S deficiency:

Type I: Decreased antigen and function, detected by functional and antigenic assays
Type II: Normal antigen but decreased function, detected only by a functional assay

Functional assays are recommended for initial evaluation because of their greater sensitivity.

INDICATIONS

Investigate the cause of hypercoagulable states.

POTENTIAL DIAGNOSIS

Increased in: N/A

Decreased in
• Acute phase reactions *(related to increased levels of C4b-binding protein in response to inflammation, which decrease levels of available functional protein)*
• Congenital deficiency
• Disseminated intravascular coagulation (DIC) *(related to increased consumption)*
• Estrogen (replacement therapy, oral contraceptives, and pregnancy) *(elevated estrogen levels are associated with decreased protein levels; estrogen does not stimulate hypercoagulable states)*
• Liver disease *(related to decreased synthesis by the liver)*
• Oral anticoagulant therapy
• Vitamin K deficiency *(related to production of dysfunctional protein in the absence of vitamin K)*

CRITICAL FINDINGS: N/A

INTERFERING FACTORS
• Drugs that may decrease protein S levels include coumarin, estrogen, and warfarin (Coumadin).
• Placement of tourniquet for longer than 60 sec can result in venous stasis and changes in the concentration of plasma proteins to be measured. Platelet activation may also occur under these conditions, causing erroneous results.
• Vascular injury during phlebotomy can activate platelets and coagulation factors, causing erroneous results.
• Hemolyzed specimens must be rejected because hemolysis is an indication of platelet and coagulation factor activation.
• Icteric or lipemic specimens interfere with optical testing methods, producing erroneous results.
• Hematocrit greater than 55% may cause falsely prolonged results because of anticoagulant excess relative to plasma volume.
• Incompletely filled collection tubes, specimens contaminated with heparin, clotted specimens, or unprocessed specimens not delivered to the laboratory within 1 to 2 hr of collection should be rejected.

NURSING IMPLICATIONS AND PROCEDURE

PRETEST:

▸ Positively identify the patient using at least two unique identifiers before providing care, treatment, or services.
▸ *Patient Teaching:* Inform the patient this test can assist in assessing anticoagulant function.
▸ Obtain a history of the patient's complaints, including a list of known allergens, especially allergies or sensitivities to latex.
▸ Obtain a history of the patient's hematopoietic and hepatobiliary systems, symptoms, and results of previously performed laboratory tests and diagnostic and surgical procedures.
▸ Obtain a list of the patient's current medications, including herbs, nutritional supplements, and nutraceuticals (see Appendix F).
▸ Review the procedure with the patient. Inform the patient that specimen collection takes approximately 5 to 10 min. Address concerns about pain and explain that there may be some discomfort during the venipuncture.
▸ *Sensitivity to social and cultural issues,* as well as concern for modesty, is important in providing psychological support before, during, and after the procedure.
▸ There are no food, fluid, or medication restrictions unless by medical direction.

P

INTRATEST:

If the patient has a history of allergic reaction to latex, avoid the use of equipment containing latex.

Instruct the patient to cooperate fully and to follow directions. Direct the patient to breathe normally and to avoid unnecessary movement.

Observe standard precautions, and follow the general guidelines in Appendix A. Positively identify the patient, and label the appropriate specimen container with the corresponding patient demographics, initials of the person collecting the specimen, date, and time of collection. Perform a venipuncture. Fill tube completely. *Important note:* Two different concentrations of sodium citrate preservative are currently added to blue-top tubes for coagulation studies: 3.2% and 3.8%. The Clinical and Laboratory Standards Institute (CLSI; formerly the National Committee for Clinical Laboratory Standards [NCCLS]) guideline for sodium citrate is 3.2%. Laboratories establish reference ranges for coagulation testing based on numerous factors, including sodium citrate concentration, test equipment, and test reagents. It is important to ask the laboratory which concentration it recommends, because each concentration will have its own specific reference range. When multiple specimens are drawn, the blue-top tube should be collected after sterile (i.e., blood culture) tubes. Otherwise, when using a standard vacutainer system, the blue-top tube is the first tube collected. When a butterfly is used and due to the added tubing, an extra red-top tube should be collected before the blue-top tube to ensure complete filling of the blue-top tube.

Remove the needle and apply direct pressure with dry gauze to stop bleeding. Observe/assess venipuncture site for bleeding or hematoma formation and secure gauze with adhesive bandage.

Promptly transport the specimen to the laboratory for processing and analysis. The CLSI recommendation for processed and unprocessed samples stored in unopened tubes is that testing should be completed within 1 to 4 hr of collection. If the patient has a known hematocrit above 55%, adjust the amount of anticoagulant in the collection tube before drawing the blood according to the CLSI guidelines:

Anticoagulant vol. [x] = (100 − hematocrit) / (595 − hematocrit) × total vol. of anticoagulated blood required

Example:

Patient hematocrit = 60% = [(100 − 60) / (595 − 60) × 5.0] = 0.37 mL sodium citrate for a 5-mL standard drawing tube

POST-TEST:

A report of the results will be made available to the requesting health-care provider (HCP), who will discuss the results with the patient.

Reinforce information given by the patient's HCP regarding further testing, treatment, or referral to another HCP. Answer any questions or address any concerns voiced by the patient or family.

Depending on the results of this procedure, additional testing may be performed to evaluate or monitor progression of the disease process and determine the need for a change in therapy. Evaluate test results in relation to the patient's symptoms and other tests performed.

RELATED MONOGRAPHS:

Related tests include, anticardiolipin antibody, AT-III, calcium, CBC, coagulation factors (factor V), FDP, fibrinogen, lupus anticoagulant, aPTT, procalcitonin, protein C, PT/INR, and vitamin K.

Refer to the Hematopoietic and Hepatobiliary systems tables at the end of the book for related test by body system.

Protein, Urine: Total Quantitative and Fractions

SYNONYM/ACRONYM: None.

COMMON USE: To assess for the presence of protein in the urine toward diagnosing disorders affecting the kidneys and urinary tract, such as cancer, infection, and pre-eclampsia.

SPECIMEN: Urine (5 mL) from an unpreserved random or timed specimen collected in a clean plastic collection container.

NORMAL FINDINGS: (Method: Spectrophotometry for total protein, electrophoresis for protein fractions)

	Conventional Units	SI Units (Conventional Units × 0.001)
Total protein	30–150 mg/24 hr	0.03–0.15 g/24 hr

Electrophoresis for fractionation is qualitative: No monoclonal gammopathy detected. (Urine protein electrophoresis should be ordered along with serum protein electrophoresis.)

DESCRIPTION: Most proteins, with the exception of the immunoglobulins, are synthesized and catabolized in the liver, where they are broken down into amino acids. The amino acids are converted to ammonia and ketoacids. Ammonia is converted to urea via the urea cycle. Urea is excreted in the urine.

P

INDICATIONS
- Assist in the detection of Bence Jones proteins (light chains)
- Assist in the diagnosis of myeloma, Waldenström's macroglobulinemia, lymphoma, and amyloidosis
- Evaluate kidney function

POTENTIAL DIAGNOSIS

Increased in
- Diabetic nephropathy *(related to disease involving renal glomeruli, which increases permeability of protein)*
- Fanconi's syndrome *(related to abnormal protein deposits in the kidney, which can cause Fanconi's syndrome)*
- Heavy metal poisoning *(related to disease involving renal glomeruli, which increases permeability of protein)*
- Malignancies of the urinary tract *(tumors secrete protein into the urine)*
- Monoclonal gammopathies *(evidenced by large amounts of Bence Jones protein light chains excreted in the urine)*
- Multiple myeloma *(evidenced by large amounts of Bence Jones protein light chains excreted in the urine)*
- Nephrotic syndrome *(related to disease involving renal glomeruli, which increases permeability of protein)*

- Postexercise period *(related to muscle exertion)*
- Pre-eclampsia *(numerous factors contribute to increased permeability of the kidneys to protein)*
- Sickle cell disease *(related to increased destruction of red blood cells and excretion of hemoglobin protein)*
- Urinary tract infections *(related to disease involving renal glomeruli, which increases permeability of protein)*

Decreased in: N/A

CRITICAL FINDINGS: N/A

INTERFERING FACTORS
- Drugs and substances that may increase urine protein levels include acetaminophen, aminosalicylic acid, amphotericin B, ampicillin, antimony compounds, antipyrine, arsenicals, ascorbic acid, bacitracin, bismuth subsalicylate, bromate, capreomycin, captopril, carbamazepine, carbarsone, carbenoxolone, carbutamide, cephaloglycin, cephaloridine, chlorpromazine, chlorpropamide, chlorthalidone, chrysarobin, colistimethate, colistin, corticosteroids, cyclosporine, demeclocycline, 1,2-diaminopropane, diatrizoic acid, dihydrotachysterol, doxycycline, enalapril, gentamicin, gold, hydrogen sulfide, iodoalphionic acid, iodopyracet, iopanoic acid, iophenoxic acid, ipodate, kanamycin, corn oil (Lipomul), lithium, mefenamic acid, melarsonyl, melarsoprol, mercury compounds, methicillin, methylbromide, mezlocillin, mitomycin, nafcillin, naphthalene, neomycin, NSAIDs, oxacillin, paraldehyde, penicillamine, penicillin, phenolphthalein, phenols, phensuximide, phosphorus, picric acid, piperacillin, plicamycin, polymyxin, probenecid, promazine, pyrazolones, quaternary ammonium compounds, radiographic agents, rifampin, sodium bicarbonate, streptokinase, sulfisoxazole, suramin, tetracyclines, thallium, thiosemicarbazones, tolbutamide, tolmetin, triethylenemelamine, and vitamin D.
- Drugs that may decrease urine protein levels include benazepril, captopril, cyclosporine, diltiazem, enalapril, fosinopril, interferon, lisinopril, losartan, lovastatin, prednisolone, prednisone, and quinapril.
- All urine voided for the timed collection period must be included in the collection, or else falsely decreased values may be obtained. Compare output records with volume collected to verify that all voids were included in the collection.

NURSING IMPLICATIONS AND PROCEDURE

PRETEST:
- Positively identify the patient using at least two unique identifiers before providing care, treatment, or services.
- *Patient Teaching:* Inform the patient this test can assist in assessing the cause of protein in the urine.
- Obtain a history of the patient's complaints, including a list of known allergens, especially allergies or sensitivities to latex.
- Obtain a history of the patient's genitourinary and immune systems, symptoms, and results of previously performed laboratory tests and diagnostic and surgical procedures.
- Obtain a list of the patient's current medications, including herbs, nutritional supplements, and nutraceuticals (see Appendix F).
- Review the procedure with the patient. Provide a nonmetallic urinal, bedpan, or toilet-mounted collection device. Address concerns about pain and explain that there should be no discomfort during the procedure.
- Usually a 24-hr time frame for urine collection is ordered. Inform the patient

P

that all urine must be saved during that 24-hr period. Instruct the patient not to void directly into the laboratory collection container. Instruct the patient to avoid defecating in the collection device and to keep toilet tissue out of the collection device to prevent contamination of the specimen. Place a sign in the bathroom to remind the patient to save all urine.

▶ Instruct the patient to void all urine into the collection device and then to pour the urine into the laboratory collection container. Alternatively, the specimen can be left in the collection device for a health-care staff member to add to the laboratory collection container.

▶ *Sensitivity to social and cultural issues,* as well as concern for modesty, is important in providing psychological support before, during, and after the procedure.

▶ There are no food, fluid, or medication restrictions unless by medical direction.

INTRATEST:

▶ If the patient has a history of allergic reaction to latex, avoid the use of equipment containing latex.

▶ Instruct the patient to cooperate fully and to follow directions.

▶ Observe standard precautions, and follow the general guidelines in Appendix A. Positively identify the patient, and label the appropriate specimen container with the corresponding patient demographics, initials of the person collecting the specimen, date, and time of collection.

Random Specimen (Collect in Early Morning)

Clean-Catch Specimen

▶ Instruct the male patient to (1) thoroughly wash his hands, (2) cleanse the meatus, (3) void a small amount into the toilet, and (4) void directly into the specimen container.

▶ Instruct the female patient to (1) thoroughly wash her hands; (2) cleanse the labia from front to back; (3) while keeping the labia separated, void a small amount into the toilet; and (4) without interrupting the urine stream, void directly into the specimen container.

Indwelling Catheter

▶ Put on gloves. Empty drainage tube of urine. It may be necessary to clamp off the catheter for 15 to 30 min before specimen collection. Cleanse specimen port with antiseptic swab, and then aspirate 5 mL of urine with a 21- to 25-gauge needle and syringe. Transfer urine to a sterile container.

Timed Specimen

▶ Obtain a clean 3-L urine specimen container, toilet-mounted collection device, and plastic bag (for transport of the specimen container). The specimen must be refrigerated or kept on ice throughout the entire collection period. If an indwelling urinary catheter is in place, the drainage bag must be kept on ice.

▶ Begin the test between 6 and 8 a.m. if possible. Collect first voiding and discard. Record the time the specimen was discarded as the beginning of the timed collection period. The next morning, ask the patient to void at the same time the collection was started and add this last voiding to the container. Urinary output should be recorded throughout the collection time.

▶ If an indwelling catheter is in place, replace the tubing and container system at the start of the collection time. Keep the container system on ice during the collection period, or empty the urine into a larger container periodically during the collection period; monitor to ensure continued drainage, and conclude the test the next morning at the same hour the collection was begun.

▶ At the conclusion of the test, compare the quantity of urine with the urinary output record for the collection; if the specimen contains less than the recorded output, some urine may have been discarded, invalidating the test.

▶ Include on the collection container's label the amount of urine collected and test start and stop times.

General

▶ Promptly transport the specimen to the laboratory for processing and analysis.

A report of the results will be made available to the requesting health-care provider (HCP), who will discuss the results with the patient.

Recognize anxiety related to test results. Discuss the implications of abnormal test results on the patient's lifestyle. Provide teaching and information regarding the clinical implications of the test results, as appropriate.

Reinforce information given by the patient's HCP regarding further testing, treatment, or referral to another HCP. Answer any questions or address any concerns voiced by the patient or family.

Depending on the results of this procedure, additional testing may be performed to evaluate or monitor progression of the disease process and determine the need for a change in therapy. Evaluate test results in relation to the patient's symptoms and other tests performed.

RELATED MONOGRAPHS:

Related tests include amino acid screen, ACE, β_2-microglobulin, biopsy bladder, biopsy bone marrow, bladder cancer markers, BUN, calcium, CBC, CT pelvis, CT renal, creatinine, cryoglobulin, culture urine, cytology urine, cystometry, cystoscopy, glucose, glycated hemoglobin, Hgb electrophoresis, IgA, IgG, IgM, IFE, IVP, lead, LAP, MRI musculoskeletal, microalbumin, osmolality, porphyrins, protein blood total and fractions, renogram, sickle cell screen, US bladder, US spleen, UA, and voiding cystourethrography.

Refer to the Genitourinary and Immune systems tables at the end of the book for related tests by body system.

Prothrombin Time and International Normalized Ratio

SYNONYM/ACRONYM: Protime, PT.

COMMON USE: To assess and monitor coagulation status related to therapeutic interventions and disorders such as vitamin K deficiency.

SPECIMEN: Plasma (1 mL) collected in a completely filled blue-top (sodium citrate) tube.

NORMAL FINDINGS: (Method: Clot detection) 10 to 13 sec.
- International normalized ratio (INR) = Less than 2 for patients not receiving anticoagulation therapy, 2 to 3 for patients receiving treatment for venous thrombosis, pulmonary embolism, and valvular heart disease.
- INR = 2.5 to 3.5 for patients with mechanical heart valves and/or receiving treatment for recurrent systemic embolism.

P

DESCRIPTION: Prothrombin time (PT) is a coagulation test performed to measure the time it takes for a firm fibrin clot to form after tissue thromboplastin (factor III) and calcium are added to the sample. It is used to evaluate the extrinsic pathway of the coagulation sequence in patients receiving oral warfarin (Coumadin) anticoagulants. Prothrombin is a vitamin K–dependent protein produced by the liver; measurement is reported as time in seconds or percentage of normal activity.

The goal of long-term anticoagulation therapy is to achieve a balance between in vivo thrombus formation and hemorrhage. It is a delicate clinical balance, and because of differences in instruments and reagents, there is a wide variation in PT results among laboratories. Worldwide concern for the need to provide more consistency in monitoring patients receiving anticoagulant therapy led to the development of an international committee. In the early 1980s, manufacturers of instruments and reagents began comparing their measurement systems with a single reference material provided by the World Health Organization (WHO). The international effort successfully developed an algorithm to provide comparable PT values regardless of differences in laboratory methodology. Reagent and instrument manufacturers compare their results to the WHO reference and derive a factor called an international sensitivity index (ISI) that is applied to a mathematical formula to standardize the results. Laboratories convert their PT values into an international normalized ratio (INR) by using the following formula:

$$INR = (patient\ PT\ result/normal\ patient\ average)^{(ISI)}$$

PT evaluation can now be based on an INR using a standardized thromboplastin reagent to assist in making decisions regarding oral anticoagulation therapy.

The metabolism of many commonly prescribed medications is driven by the cytochrome P450 (CYP450) family of enzymes.

Genetic variants can alter enzymatic activity that results in a spectrum of effects ranging from the total absence of drug metabolism to ultrafast metabolism. Impaired drug metabolism can prevent the intended therapeutic effect or even lead to serious adverse drug reactions. Poor metabolizers (PM) are at increased risk for drug-induced side effects due to accumulation of drug in the blood, whereas ultra-rapid metabolizers (UM) require a higher-than-normal dosage because the drug is metabolized over a shorter duration than intended. In the case of prodrugs that require activation before metabolism, the opposite occurs: PM may require a higher dose because the activated drug is becoming available more slowly than intended, and UM may require less because the activated drug is becoming available sooner than intended. Other genetic phenotypes used to report CYP450 results are intermediate metabolizer (IM) and extensive metabolizer (EM). Genetic testing can be performed on blood samples submitted to a laboratory. The test method commonly used is polymerase chain reaction. Counseling and informed written consent are generally required for genetic testing. CYP2C9 is a gene in the CYP450 family that metabolizes prodrugs like the anticoagulant warfarin. Three major gene mutations are associated with warfarin response and are estimated to account for up to 45% of variations in Caucasians and up to 30% of variations in African Americans. The CYP450 genes are distributed differently and in predictable frequency among various ethnic groups; incidence of mutation in CYP2C9*2 allele in Caucasians is

8% to 19%, in Asians is less than 0% to 4%, and in African Americans is 0% to 12%; incidence of mutation in CYP2C9*3 allele in Caucasians is 5% to 16%, in Asians is 1% to 8%, and in African Americans is 0% to 6%; incidence of mutation in VKORC1 (as predicted by 1639G > A mutation) is 37% in Caucasians, 89% in Asians, and 14% in African Americans. CYP450 testing is available and should be used in conjunction with other factors, including all prescription and over-the-counter medications being used; mode of drug administration; use of tobacco products, foods, and supplements; age, weight, environment, activity level, and diseases with which the patient may be dealing.

Some inferences of factor deficiency can be made by comparison of results obtained from the activated partial thromboplastin time (aPTT) and PT tests. A normal aPTT with a prolonged PT can occur only with factor VII deficiency. A prolonged aPTT with a normal PT could indicate a deficiency in factors XII, XI, IX, and VIII as well as VIII:C (von Willebrand factor). Factor deficiencies can also be identified by correction or substitution studies using normal serum. These studies are easy to perform and are accomplished by adding plasma from a healthy patient to a sample from a suspected factor-deficient patient. When the PT is repeated and corrected, or within the reference range, it can be assumed that the prolonged PT is due to a factor deficiency (see monograph titled "Coagulation Factors"). If the result remains uncorrected, the prolonged PT is most likely due to a circulating anticoagulant.

INDICATIONS

- Differentiate between deficiencies of clotting factors II, V, VII, and X, which prolong the PT, and congenital coagulation disorders such as hemophilia A (factor VIII) and hemophilia B (factor IX), which do not alter the PT
- Evaluate the response to anticoagulant therapy with coumarin derivatives and determine dosage required to achieve therapeutic results
- Identify individuals who may be prone to bleeding during surgical, obstetric, dental, or invasive diagnostic procedures
- Identify the possible cause of abnormal bleeding, such as epistaxis, hematoma, gingival bleeding, hematuria, and menorrhagia
- Monitor the effects of conditions such as liver disease, protein deficiency, and fat malabsorption on hemostasis
- Screen for prothrombin deficiency
- Screen for vitamin K deficiency

POTENTIAL DIAGNOSIS

Increased in

- Afibrinogenemia, dysfibrinogenemia, or hypofibrinogenemia *(related to insufficient levels of fibrinogen, which is required for clotting; its absence prolongs PT)*
- Biliary obstruction *(related to poor absorption of fat-soluble vitamin K; vitamin K is required for clotting and its absence prolongs PT)*
- Disseminated intravascular coagulation *(related to increased consumption of clotting factors; PT is increased)*
- Hereditary deficiencies of factors II, V, VII, and X *(related to deficiency of factors required for clotting; their absence prolongs PT)*
- Liver disease (cirrhosis) *(related to decreased liver function, which results in decreased production of clotting factors and prolonged PT)*

- Massive transfusion of packed red blood cells (RBCs) *(related to dilutional effect of replacing a significant fraction of the total blood volume; there are insufficient clotting factors in plasma-poor, packed RBC products. Blood products contain anticoagulants, which compound the lack of adequate clotting factors in the case of massive transfusion)*
- Poor fat absorption *(tropical sprue, celiac disease, and chronic diarrhea are conditions that prevent absorption of fat-soluble vitamins, including vitamin K, which is required for clotting; its absence prolongs PT)*
- Presence of circulating anticoagulant *(related to the production of inhibitors of specific factors, e.g., developed from long-term factor VIII therapy or circulating anticoagulants associated with conditions like tuberculosis, systemic lupus erythematosus, rheumatoid arthritis, and chronic glomerulonephritis)*
- Salicylate intoxication *(related to decreased liver function)*
- Vitamin K deficiency *(vitamin K is required for clotting; its absence prolongs PT)*

Decreased in
- Ovarian hyperfunction
- Regional enteritis or ileitis

CRITICAL FINDINGS

INR
- Greater than 5

Prothrombin Time
- Greater than 27 sec

Note and immediately report to the health-care provider (HCP) any critically increased values and related symptoms. Timely notification of critical values for lab or diagnostic studies is a role expectation of the professional nurse. Notification processes will vary among facilities. Upon receipt of the critical value the information should be read back to the caller to verify accuracy. Most policies require immediate notification of the primary HCP, hospitalist, or on-call HCP. Reported information includes the patient's name, unique identifiers, critical value, name of the person giving the report, and name of the person receiving the report. Documentation of notification should be made in the medical record with the name of the HCP notified, time and date of notification, and any orders received. Any delay in a timely report of a critical value may require completion of a notification form with review by Risk Management.

Important signs to note are prolonged bleeding from cuts or gums, hematoma at a puncture site, hemorrhage, blood in the stool, persistent epistaxis, heavy or prolonged menstrual flow, and shock. Monitor vital signs, unusual ecchymosis, occult blood, severe headache, unusual dizziness, and neurological changes until PT is within normal range. Intramuscular administration of vitamin K, an anticoagulant reversal agent, may be requested by the HCP.

INTERFERING FACTORS
- Drugs that may increase the PT in patients receiving anticoagulation therapy include acetaminophen, acetylsalicylic acid, amiodarone, anabolic steroids, anisindione, anistreplase, antibiotics, antipyrine, carbenicillin, cathartics, chloral hydrate, chlorthalidone, cholestyramine, clofibrate, corticotropin, demeclocycline, dextrothyroxine, diazoxide, diflunisal, disulfiram, diuretics, doxycycline, erythromycin, ethyl alcohol, hydroxyzine, laxatives, mercaptopurine, miconazole, nalidixic acid, neomycin, niacin, oxyphenbutazone, phenytoin, quinidine, quinine, sulfachlorpyridazine, thyroxine, and tosylate bretylium.

- Drugs that may decrease the PT in patients receiving anticoagulation therapy include aminoglutethimide, amobarbital, anabolic steroids, antacids, antihistamines, barbiturates, carbamazepine, chloral hydrate, chlordane, chlordiazepoxide, cholestyramine, clofibrate, colchicine, corticosteroids, dichloralphenazone, diuretics, oral contraceptives, penicillin, primidone, raloxifene, rifabutin, rifampin, simethicone, spironolactone, tacrolimus, tolbutamide, and vitamin K.
- Traumatic venipunctures can activate the coagulation sequence by contaminating the sample with tissue thromboplastin and producing falsely shortened PT.
- Hematocrit greater than 55% may cause falsely prolonged results because of anticoagulant excess relative to plasma volume.
- Incompletely filled collection tubes, specimens contaminated with heparin, clotted or hemolyzed specimens, or unprocessed specimens not delivered to the laboratory within 24 hr of collection should be rejected.
- Excessive agitation causing sample hemolysis can falsely shorten the PT because the hemolyzed cells activate plasma-clotting factors.

NURSING IMPLICATIONS AND PROCEDURE

PRETEST:

- Positively identify the patient using at least two unique identifiers before providing care, treatment, or services.
- *Patient Teaching:* Inform the patient this test can assist in evaluating coagulation and monitor therapy.
- Obtain a history of the patient's complaints, including a list of known allergens, especially allergies or sensitivities to latex.
- Obtain a history of the patient's cardiovascular, hematopoietic, and

hepatobiliary systems, especially any bleeding disorders and other symptoms, as well as results of previously performed laboratory tests and diagnostic and surgical procedures.

- Obtain a list of the patient's current medications, including anticoagulants, aspirin and other salicylates, herbs, nutritional supplements, and nutraceuticals (see Appendix F). Such products should be discontinued by medical direction for the appropriate number of days prior to a surgical procedure. Note the last time and dose of medication taken.
- Review the procedure with the patient. Inform the patient that specimen collection takes approximately 5 to 10 min. Address concerns about pain and explain that there may be some discomfort during the venipuncture.
- *Sensitivity to social and cultural issues,* as well as concern for modesty, is important in providing psychological support before, during, and after the procedure.
- There are no food, fluid, or medication restrictions unless by medical direction.

INTRATEST:

- If the patient has a history of allergic reaction to latex, avoid the use of equipment containing latex.
- Instruct the patient to cooperate fully and to follow directions. Direct the patient to breathe normally and to avoid unnecessary movement.
- Observe standard precautions, and follow the general guidelines in Appendix A. Positively identify the patient, and label the appropriate specimen container with the corresponding patient demographics, initials of the person collecting the specimen, date, and time of collection. Perform a venipuncture. Fill tube completely. Important note: Two different concentrations of sodium citrate preservative are currently added to blue-top tubes for coagulation studies: 3.2% and 3.8%. The Clinical and Laboratory Standards Institute (CLSI; formerly the National Committee for Clinical Laboratory Standards [NCCLS]) guideline for sodium citrate is 3.2%. Laboratories establish reference ranges for coagulation testing based on numerous factors, including sodium citrate concentration, test equipment,

and test reagents. It is important to ask the laboratory which concentration it recommends, because each concentration will have its own specific reference range. When multiple specimens are drawn, the blue-top tube should be collected after sterile (i.e., blood culture) tubes. Otherwise, when using a standard vacutainer system, the blue-top tube is the first tube collected. When a butterfly is used and due to the added tubing, an extra red-top tube should be collected before the blue-top tube to ensure complete filling of the blue-top tube.

Remove the needle and apply direct pressure with dry gauze to stop bleeding. Observe/assess venipuncture site for bleeding or hematoma formation and secure gauze with adhesive bandage.

Promptly transport the specimen to the laboratory for processing and analysis. If delays in specimen transport and processing occur, it is important to consult with the testing laboratory. Whole blood specimens are stable at room temperature for up to 24 hr. Some laboratories will accept refrigerated whole blood samples up to 48 hr from the time of collection. Criteria for rejection of specimens based on collection time may vary among facilities.

If the patient has a known hematocrit above 55%, adjust the amount of anticoagulant in the collection tube before drawing the blood according to the CLSI guidelines:

Anticoagulant vol. [x] = (100 − hematocrit)/(595 − hematocrit) × total vol. of anticoagulated blood required

Example:

Patient hematocrit = 60% = [(100 − 60)/(595 − 60) × 5.0] = 0.37 mL sodium citrate for a 5-mL standard drawing tube

POST-TEST:

A report of the results will be made available to the requesting HCP, who will discuss the results with the patient.

Instruct the patient to report bleeding from any areas of the skin or mucous membranes.

Inform the patient with prolonged PT/INR of the importance of taking precautions against bruising and bleeding, including the use of a soft bristle toothbrush, use of an electric razor, avoidance of constipation, avoidance of aspirin products, and avoidance of intramuscular injections.

Inform the patient of the importance of periodic laboratory testing while taking an anticoagulant.

Nutritional Considerations: Foods high in vitamin K should be avoided by the patient on anticoagulant therapy. Foods that contain vitamin K include cabbage, cauliflower, chickpeas, egg yolks, green tea, pork, liver, milk, soybean products, tomatoes, mayonnaise, vegetable oils, and green leafy vegetables such as leaf lettuce, watercress, parsley, broccoli, brussels sprouts, kale, spinach, and turnip greens.

Nutritional Considerations: Avoid alcohol and alcohol products while taking warfarin because the combination of the two increases the risk of gastrointestinal bleeding.

Reinforce information given by the patient's HCP regarding further testing, treatment, or referral to another HCP. Instruct the patient in the use of home test kits for PT/INR approved by the U.S. Food and Drug Administration, as appropriate. Answer any questions or address any concerns voiced by the patient or family.

Depending on the results of this procedure, additional testing may be performed to evaluate or monitor progression of the disease process and determine the need for a change in therapy. Evaluate test results in relation to the patient's symptoms and other tests performed.

RELATED MONOGRAPHS:

Related tests include, ALP, ALT, ANA, AT-III, AST, bilirubin, biopsy liver, bleeding time, calcium, coagulation factors, CBC, CBC platelet count, CT liver and biliary tract, cryoglobulin, D-dimer, fecal analysis, fecal fat, FDP, fibrinogen, GGT, gastric acid emptying scan, hepatitis antibodies (A, B, C, D), liver and spleen scan, lupus anticoagulant, aPTT, plasminogen, protein C, protein S, US abdomen, US liver, and vitamin K.

Refer to the Cardiovascular, Hematopoietic, and Hepatobiliary systems tables at the end of the book for related tests by body system.

P

Pseudocholinesterase and Dibucaine Number

SYNONYM/ACRONYM: CHS, PCHE, AcCHS.

COMMON USE: To assess for pseudocholinesterase deficiency to assist in diagnosing a congenital deficiency. Special attention must be given to results for preoperative patients because positive results indicate risk for apnea with use of succinylcholine as an anesthetic agent.

SPECIMEN: Plasma (1 mL) collected in a lavender-top (EDTA) tube. Serum (1 mL) collected in a red-top tube is also acceptable.

NORMAL FINDINGS: (Method: Spectrophotometry, kinetic)

Test	Conventional Units
Pseudocholinesterase	
Males	3,334–7,031 IU/L
Females	2,504–6,297 IU/L

Dibucaine Number	Fraction (%) of Activity Inhibited
Normal homozygote	79%–84%
Heterozygote	55%–70%
Abnormal homozygote	16%–28%

POTENTIAL DIAGNOSIS

Increased in
Increased levels are observed in a number of conditions without specific cause.

- Diabetes
- Hyperthyroidism
- Nephrotic syndrome
- Obesity

Decreased in
The enzyme is produced in the liver, and any condition affecting liver function may result in decreased production of circulating enzyme.

- Acute infection
- Anemia (severe)
- Carcinomatosis
- Cirrhosis
- Congenital deficiency
- Hepatic carcinoma
- Hepatocellular disease
- Infectious hepatitis
- Insecticide exposure *(organic phosphate exposure decreases enzyme activity)*
- Malnutrition *(possibly related to decreased availability of transport proteins; condition associated with decreased enzyme activity)*
- Muscular dystrophy
- Myocardial infarction
- Plasmapheresis *(iatrogenic cause)*
- Succinylcholine hypersensitivity *(this chemical is a trigger in susceptible individuals)*
- Tuberculosis *(chronic infection is known to decrease enzyme activity)*
- Uremia *(pathological condition known to decrease enzyme activity)*

P

CRITICAL FINDINGS ✦

A positive result indicates that the patient is at risk for prolonged or unrecoverable apnea related to the inability to metabolize succinylcholine. Note and immediately report to the health-care provider (HCP) any critically increased values and related symptoms. Timely notification of critical values for lab or diagnostic studies is a role expectation of the professional nurse. Notification processes will vary among facilities. Upon receipt of the critical value the information should be read back to the caller to verify accuracy. Most policies require immediate notification of the primary HCP, hospitalist, or on-call HCP. Reported information includes the patient's name, unique identifiers, critical value, name of the person giving the report, and name of the person receiving the report. Documentation of notification should be made in the medical record with the name of the HCP notified, time and date of notification, and any orders received. Any delay in a timely report of a critical value may require completion of a notification form with review by Risk Management.

Notify the anesthesiologist if the test result is positive and surgery is scheduled.

Find and print out the full monograph at DavisPlus (http://davisplus.fadavis.com, keyword Van Leeuwen).

Pulmonary Function Studies

SYNONYM/ACRONYM: Pulmonary function tests (PFTs).

COMMON USE: To assess respiratory function to assist in evaluating obstructive versus restrictive lung disease and to monitor and assess the effectiveness of therapeutic interventions.

AREA OF APPLICATION: Lungs, respiratory system.

CONTRAST: None.

DESCRIPTION: Pulmonary function studies provide information about the volume, pattern, and rates of airflow involved in respiratory function. These studies may also include tests involving the diffusing capabilities of the lungs (i.e., volume of gases diffusing across a membrane). A complete pulmonary function study includes the determination of all lung volumes, spirometry, diffusing capacity, maximum voluntary ventilation, flow-volume loop (see figure), and maximum expiratory and inspiratory pressures. Other studies include small airway volumes.

Pulmonary function studies are classified according to lung volumes and capacities, rates of flow, and gas exchange. The exception is the diffusion test, which records the movement of a gas during inspiration and expiration. Lung volumes and capacities constitute the amount of air inhaled or exhaled from the lungs; this value is compared to normal reference values specific for the patient's age, height, and gender. The following are volumes and capacities measured by spirometry that do not require timed testing.

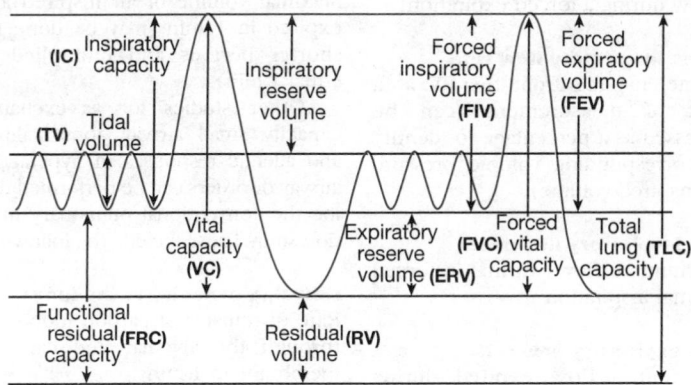

Tidal volume

Total amount of air inhaled and exhaled with one breath.

Residual volume (RV)

Amount of air remaining in the lungs after a maximum expiration effort (not measured by spirometry, but can be calculated from the functional residual capacity [FRC] minus the expiratory reserve volume [ERV]); this indirect type of measurement can be done by body plethysmography (see monograph titled "Plethysmography")

Inspiratory reserve volume

Maximum amount of air inhaled after normal inspirations

Expiratory reserve volume

Maximum amount of air exhaled after a resting expiration (can be calculated by the vital capacity [VC] minus the inspiratory capacity [IC])

Vital capacity

Maximum amount of air exhaled after a maximum inspiration (can be calculated by adding the IC and the ERV)

Total lung capacity

Total amount of air that the lungs can hold after maximal inspiration (can be calculated by adding the VC and the residual volume [RV])

Inspiratory capacity

Maximum amount of air inspired after normal expiration (can be calculated by adding the inspiratory RV and tidal volume)

Functional residual capacity

Volume of air that remains in the lungs after normal expiration (can be calculated by adding the RV and ERV)

The volumes, capacities, and rates of flow measured by spirometry that do require timed testing include the following:

Forced vital capacity in 1 sec

Maximum amount of air that can be forcefully exhaled after a full inspiration

Forced expiratory volume

Amount of air exhaled in the first second (can also be determined at 2 or 3 sec) of forced vital capacity (FVC, which is the amount of air exhaled in seconds, expressed as a percentage)

Maximal midexpiratory flow
Also known as forced expiratory flow rate (FEF$_{25-75}$), or the maximal rate of airflow during a forced expiration

Forced inspiratory flow rate
Volume inspired from the RV at a point of measurement (can be expressed as a percentage to identify the corresponding volume pressure and inspired volume)

Peak inspiratory flow rate
Maximum airflow during a forced maximal inspiration

Peak expiratory flow rate
Maximum airflow expired during FVC

Flow-volume loops
Flows and volumes recorded during forced expiratory volume and forced inspiratory VC procedures (see figure)

Maximal inspiratory-expiratory pressures
Measures the strength of the respiratory muscles in neuromuscular disorders

Maximal voluntary ventilation
Maximal volume of air inspired and expired in 1 min (may be done for shorter periods and multiplied to equal 1 min)

Other studies for gas-exchange capacity, small airway abnormalities, and allergic responses in hyperactive airway disorders can be performed during the conventional pulmonary function study. These include the following:

Diffusing capacity of the lungs
Rate of transfer of carbon monoxide through the alveolar and capillary membrane in 1 min

Closing volume
Measures the closure of small airways in the lower alveoli by monitoring volume and percentage of alveolar nitrogen after inhalation of 100% oxygen

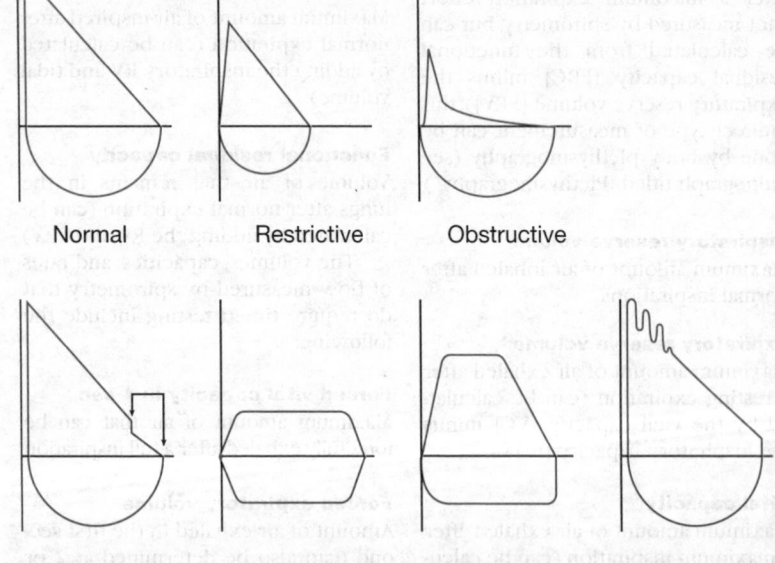

Normal   Restrictive   Obstructive

Small airway   Fixed upper   Variable upper   Sleep apnea
disease   airway obstruction   airway obstruction   disorder

Isoflow volume
Flow-volume loop test followed by inhalation of a mixture of helium and oxygen to determine small airway disease

Body plethysmography
Measures thoracic gas volume and airway resistance

Bronchial provocation
Quantifies airway response after inhalation of methacholine

Arterial blood gases
Measure oxygen, pH, and carbon dioxide in arterial blood

Values are expressed in units of mL, %, L, L/sec, and L/min, depending on the test performed.

INDICATIONS
- Detect chronic obstructive pulmonary disease (COPD) and/or restrictive pulmonary diseases that affect the chest wall (e.g., neuromuscular disorders, kyphosis, scoliosis) and lungs, as evidenced by abnormal airflows and volumes
- Determine airway response to inhalants in patients with an airway-reactive disorder
- Determine the diffusing capacity of the lungs (DCOL)
- Determine the effectiveness of therapy regimens, such as bronchodilators, for pulmonary disorders
- Determine the presence of lung disease when other studies, such as

x-rays, do not provide a definitive diagnosis, or determine the progression and severity of known COPD and restrictive pulmonary disease
- Evaluate the cause of dyspnea occurring with or without exercise
- Evaluate lung compliance to determine changes in elasticity, as evidenced by changes in lung volumes (decreased in restrictive pulmonary disease, increased in COPD and in elderly patients)
- Evaluate pulmonary disability for legal or insurance claims
- Evaluate pulmonary function after surgical pneumonectomy, lobectomy, or segmental lobectomy
- Evaluate the respiratory system to determine the patient's ability to tolerate procedures such as surgery or diagnostic studies
- Screen high-risk populations for early detection of pulmonary conditions (e.g., patients with exposure to occupational or environmental hazards, smokers, patients with a hereditary predisposition)

POTENTIAL DIAGNOSIS

Normal findings in
- Normal respiratory volume and capacities, gas diffusion, and distribution
- No evidence of COPD or restrictive pulmonary disease

Normal adult lung volumes, capacities, and flow rates are as follows:

TV	500 mL at rest
RV	1,200 mL (approximate)
IRV	3,000 mL (approximate)
ERV	1,100 mL (approximate)
VC	4,600 mL (approximate)
TLC	5,800 mL (approximate)
IC	3,500 mL (approximate)
FRC	2,300 mL (approximate)
FVC	3,000–5,000 mL (approximate)

(table continues on page 1190)

FEV$_1$/FVC	81%–83%
MMEF	25%–75%
FIF	25%–75%
MVV	25%–35% or 170 L/min
PIFR	300 L/min
PEFR	450 L/min
F-V loop	Normal curve
DCOL	25 mL/min per mm Hg (approximate)
CV	10%–20% of VC
V$_{iso}$	Based on age formula
Bronchial provocation	No change, or less than 20% reduction in FEV$_1$

Note: Normal values listed are estimated values for adults. Actual pediatric and adult values are based on age, height, and gender. These normal values are included on the patient's pulmonary function laboratory report. CV = closing volume; DCOL = diffusing capacity of the lungs; ERV = expiratory reserve volume; FEV$_1$ = forced expiratory volume in 1 sec; FIF = forced inspiratory flow rate; FRC = functional residual capacity; FVC = forced vital capacity in 1 second; F-V loop = flow-volume loop; IC = inspiratory capacity; IRV = inspiratory reserve volume; MMEF = maximal midexpiratory flow (also known as FEF$_{25–75}$); MVV = maximal voluntary ventilation; PEFR = peak expiratory flow rate; PIFR = peak inspiratory flow rate; RV = residual volume; TLC = total lung capacity; TV = tidal volume; VC = vital capacity; V$_{iso}$ = isoflow volume.

Abnormal findings in
- Allergy
- Asbestosis
- Asthma
- Bronchiectasis
- Chest trauma
- Chronic bronchitis
- Curvature of the spine
- Emphysema
- Myasthenia gravis
- Obesity
- Pulmonary fibrosis
- Pulmonary tumors
- Respiratory infections
- Sarcoidosis

CRITICAL FINDINGS: N/A

INTERFERING FACTORS
- The aging process can cause decreased values (FVC, DCOL) depending on the study done.
- Inability of the patient to put forth the necessary breathing effort affects the results.
- Medications such as bronchodilators can affect results.
- Improper placement of the nose clamp or mouthpiece that allows for leakage can affect volume results.

- Confusion or inability to understand instructions or cooperate during the study can cause inaccurate results.
- Testing is contraindicated in patients with cardiac insufficiency, recent myocardial infarction, and presence of chest pain that affects inspiration or expiration ability.
- Exercise caution with patients who have upper respiratory infections, such as a cold or acute bronchitis.

NURSING IMPLICATIONS AND PROCEDURE

PRETEST:

▶ Positively identify the patient using at least two unique identifiers before providing care, treatment, or services.

▶ *Patient Teaching:* Inform the patient this procedure can assist in assessing lung function.

▶ Obtain a history of the patient's complaints or symptoms, including a list of known allergens, especially allergies or sensitivities to latex, iodine, seafood, anesthetics, or contrast mediums.

Obtain a history of the patient's cardiovascular and respiratory systems, symptoms, and results of previously performed laboratory tests and diagnostic and surgical procedures.

Obtain a list of the patient's current medications, including herbs, nutritional supplements, and nutraceuticals (see Appendix F).

Review the procedure with the patient. Address concerns about pain related to the procedure and explain that no discomfort will be experienced during the test. Explain that the procedure is generally performed in a specially equipped room or in a health-care provider's (HCP's) office by an HCP specializing in this procedure and usually lasts 1 hr.

Sensitivity to social and cultural issues, as well as concern for modesty, is important in providing psychological support before, during, and after the procedure.

Record the patient's height and weight.

The patient should avoid bronchodilators (oral or inhalant) for at least 4 hr before the study, as directed by the HCP.

Instruct the patient to refrain from smoking tobacco or eating a heavy meal for 4 to 6 hr prior to the study. Protocols may vary among facilities.

INTRATEST:

Observe standard precautions, and follow the general guidelines in Appendix A. Positively identify the patient.

Ensure the patient has complied with dietary and medication restrictions and pretesting preparations.

Obtain an inhalant bronchodilator to treat any bronchospasms that may occur with testing.

Instruct the patient to void and to loosen any restrictive clothing.

Instruct the patient to cooperate fully and to follow directions.

Place the patient in a sitting position on a chair near the spirometry equipment.

Place a soft clip on the patient's nose to restrict nose breathing, and instruct the patient to breathe through the mouth.

Place a mouthpiece in the mouth and instruct the patient to close his or her lips around it to form a seal.

Tubing from the mouthpiece attaches to a cylinder that is connected to a computer that measures, records, and calculates the values for the tests done.

Instruct the patient to inhale deeply and then to quickly exhale as much air as possible into the mouthpiece.

Additional breathing maneuvers are performed on inspiration and expiration (normal, forced, and breath-holding).

POST-TEST:

A report of the results will be made available to the requesting HCP, who will discuss the results with the patient.

Assess the patient for dizziness or weakness after the testing.

Allow the patient to rest as long as needed to recover.

Instruct the patient to resume usual diet and medications, as directed by the HCP.

Recognize anxiety related to test results, and be supportive of perceived loss of independent function. Discuss the implications of abnormal test results on the patient's lifestyle. Provide teaching and information regarding the clinical implications of the test results, as appropriate.

Reinforce information given by the patient's HCP regarding further testing, treatment, or referral to another HCP. Answer any questions or address any concerns voiced by the patient or family.

Depending on the results of this procedure, additional testing may be performed to evaluate or monitor progression of the disease process and determine the need for a change in therapy. Evaluate test results in relation to the patient's symptoms and other tests performed.

RELATED MONOGRAPHS:

Related tests include α_1-AT, anion gap, arterial/alveolar oxygen ratio, biopsy lung, blood gases, bronchoscopy, carboxyhemoglobin, chest x-ray, chloride sweat, CBC, CBC hemoglobin, CBC WBC count and differential, CT

P

angiography, CT thoracic, culture and smear for mycobacteria, culture bacterial sputum, culture viral, cytology sputum, echocardiography, ECG, Gram stain, IgE, lactic acid, lung perfusion scan, lung ventilation scan, MR angiography, MRI chest, osmolality, phosphorus, plethysmography, pleural fluid analysis, potassium, PET chest, pulse oximetry, sodium, and TB skin test. Refer to the Cardiovascular and Respiratory systems tables at the end of the book for related tests by body system.

Pulse Oximetry

SYNONYM/ACRONYM: Oximetry, pulse ox.

COMMON USE: To assess arterial blood oxygenation toward evaluating respiratory status during ventilation, acute illness, activity, and sleep and to evaluate the effectiveness of therapeutic interventions.

AREA OF APPLICATION: Earlobe, fingertip; for infants, use the large toe, top or bottom of the foot, or sides of the ankle.

CONTRAST: None.

DESCRIPTION: Pulse oximetry is a noninvasive study that provides continuous readings of arterial blood oxygen saturation (SpO_2) using a sensor site (earlobe or fingertip). The SpO_2 equals the ratio of the amount of O_2 contained in the hemoglobin to the maximum amount of O_2 contained, with hemoglobin expressed as a percentage. The results obtained may compare favorably with O_2 saturation levels obtained by arterial blood gas analysis without the need to perform successive arterial punctures. The device used is a clip or probe that produces a light beam with two different wavelengths on one side. A sensor on the opposite side measures the absorption of each of the wavelengths of light to determine the O_2 saturation reading. The displayed result is a ratio, expressed as a percentage, between the actual O_2 content of the hemoglobin and the potential maximum O_2-carrying capacity of the hemoglobin.

INDICATIONS
- Determine the effectiveness of pulmonary gas exchange function
- Evaluate suspected nocturnal hypoxemia in chronic obstructive pulmonary disease
- Monitor oxygenation during testing for sleep apnea
- Monitor oxygenation perioperatively and during acute illnesses
- Monitor oxygenation status in patients on a ventilator, during surgery, and during bronchoscopy
- Monitor O_2 saturation during activities such as pulmonary exercise stress testing or pulmonary rehabilitation exercises to determine optimal tolerance

P

- Monitor response to pulmonary drug regimens, especially flow and O_2 content

POTENTIAL DIAGNOSIS

Normal findings in
- Greater than or equal to 95%

Abnormal findings in
- Abnormal gas exchange
- Hypoxemia with levels less than 95%
- Impaired cardiopulmonary function

CRITICAL FINDINGS: N/A

INTERFERING FACTORS

This procedure is contraindicated for
- Patients who smoke or have suffered carbon monoxide inhalation, because O_2 levels may be falsely elevated.

Factors that may result in incorrect values
- Patients with anemic conditions reflecting a reduction in hemoglobin, the O_2-carrying component in the blood.
- Excessive light surrounding the patient, such as from surgical lights.
- Impaired cardiopulmonary function.
- Lipid emulsion therapy and presence of certain dyes.
- Movement of the finger or ear or improper placement of probe or clip.
- Nail polish, artificial fingernails, and skin pigmentation when a finger probe is used.
- Vasoconstriction from cool skin temperature, drugs, hypotension, or vessel obstruction causing a decrease in blood flow.

Other considerations
- Accuracy for most units is plus or minus 4% with a standard deviation of 1%.

NURSING IMPLICATIONS AND PROCEDURE

PRETEST:
- Positively identify the patient using at least two unique identifiers before providing care, treatment, or services.
- *Patient Teaching:* Inform the patient this procedure can assist in monitoring oxygen in the blood.
- Obtain a history of the patient's complaints, including a list of known allergens, especially allergies or sensitivities to latex, iodine, seafood, contrast medium, or anesthetics.
- Obtain a history of the patient's cardiovascular and respiratory systems, symptoms, and results of previously performed laboratory tests and diagnostic and surgical procedures.
- Obtain a list of the patient's current medications, including herbs, nutritional supplements, and nutraceuticals (see Appendix F).
- Review the procedure with the patient. Address concerns about pain related to the procedure and explain that no pain is associated with the procedure. Inform the patient that the procedure is generally performed at the bedside, in the operating room during a surgical procedure, or in the office of a healthcare provider (HCP). Explain that the procedure lasts as long as the monitoring is needed and could be continuous.
- *Sensitivity to social and cultural issues,* as well as concern for modesty, is important in providing psychological support before, during, and after the procedure.
- If a finger probe is used, instruct the patient to remove artificial fingernails and nail polish.
- When used in the presence of flammable gases, the equipment must be approved for that specific use.
- Instruct the patient not to smoke for 24 hr before the procedure.
- There are no food, fluid, or medication restrictions unless by medical direction.

INTRATEST:
- Observe standard precautions, and follow the general guidelines in Appendix A. Positively identify the patient.

P

▶ Ensure that the patient has complied with pretesting instructions.
▶ If a finger probe is used, instruct the patient not to grip treadmill rail or bed rail tightly; doing so restricts blood flow.
▶ Instruct the patient to cooperate fully and to follow directions.
▶ Massage or apply a warm towel to the upper earlobe or finger to increase the blood flow.
▶ The index finger is normally used, but if the patient's finger is too large for the probe, a smaller finger can be used.
▶ If the earlobe is used, make sure good contact is achieved.
▶ The big toe, top or bottom of the foot, or sides of the heel may be used in infants.
▶ Place the photodetector probe over the finger in such a way that the light beams and sensors are opposite each other. Turn the power switch to the oximeter monitor, which will display information about heart rate and peripheral capillary saturation (SaO_2).
▶ Remove the clip used for monitoring when the procedure is complete.

POST-TEST:

▶ A report of the results will be made available to the requesting HCP, who will discuss the results with the patient.
▶ Closely observe SpO_2, and report to the HCP if it decreases to 90%.
▶ Recognize anxiety related to test results, and be supportive of perceived loss of independent function. Discuss the implications of abnormal test results on the patient's lifestyle. Provide teaching and information regarding the clinical implications of the test results, as appropriate.
▶ Reinforce information given by the patient's HCP regarding further testing, treatment, or referral to another HCP. Answer any questions or address any concerns voiced by the patient or family.
▶ Depending on the results of this procedure, additional testing may be performed to evaluate or monitor progression of the disease process and determine the need for a change in therapy. Evaluate test results in relation to the patient's symptoms and other tests performed.

RELATED MONOGRAPHS:

▶ Related tests include α_1-AT, anion gap, arterial/alveolar oxygen ratio, biopsy lung, blood gases, bronchoscopy, carboxyhemoglobin, chest x-ray, chloride sweat, CBC, CBC hemoglobin, CBC WBC count and differential, CT angiography, culture and smear for mycobacteria, culture bacterial sputum, culture viral, cytology sputum, ECG, Gram stain, IgE, lactic acid, lung perfusion scan, lung ventilation scan, MR angiography, MR chest, osmolality, phosphorus, plethysmography, pleural fluid analysis, potassium, pulmonary function tests, sodium, and TB skin test.
▶ Refer to the Cardiovascular and Respiratory systems tables at the end of the book for related tests by body system.

Pyruvate Kinase

SYNONYM/ACRONYM: PK.

COMMON USE: To assess for an enzyme deficiency to assist in diagnosis of hemolytic anemia.

SPECIMEN: Whole blood collected in yellow-top (acid-citrate-dextrose [ACD]) tube. Specimens collected in a lavender-top (EDTA) or green-top (heparin) tube also may be acceptable in some laboratories.

NORMAL FINDINGS: (Method: Spectrophotometry) 6 to 19 micromol NAD(H)$_2$/min/g hemoglobin (37°C).

POTENTIAL DIAGNOSIS

Increased in
Related to release of skeletal and cardiac specific isoenzymes of PK from damaged tissue cells.

- Carriers of Duchenne's muscular dystrophy
- Muscle disease
- Myocardial infarction

Decreased in
- Hereditary pyruvate kinase deficiency (evidenced by autosomal recessive trait for PK enzyme deficiency):
  Congenital nonspherocytic hemolytic anemia
- Acquired pyruvate kinase deficiency (related to interaction of medications used for therapy; related to release of leukocyte specific isoenzymes from damaged leukocytes):
  Acute leukemia
  Aplasias
  Other anemias

CRITICAL FINDINGS: N/A

Find and print out the full monograph at DavisPlus (http://davisplus.fadavis.com, keyword Van Leeuwen).

P

Radioactive Iodine Uptake

RAIU, thyroid uptake.

COMMON USE: To assess thyroid function toward diagnosing disorders such as hyperthyroidism and goiter.

AREA OF APPLICATION: Thyroid.

CONTRAST: Oral radioactive iodine.

DESCRIPTION: Radioactive iodine uptake (RAIU) is a nuclear medicine study used for evaluating thyroid function. It directly measures the ability of the thyroid gland to concentrate and retain circulating iodide for the synthesis of thyroid hormone. RAIU assists in the diagnosis of both hyperthyroidism and hypothyroidism, but it is more useful in the diagnosis of hyperthyroidism.

A very small dose of radioactive iodine-123 (I-123) or I-131 is administered orally, and images are taken at specified intervals after the initial dose is administered. The radionuclide emits gamma radiation, which allows external measurement. The uptake of radionuclide in the thyroid gland is measured as the percentage of radionuclide absorbed in a specific amount of time. The iodine not used is excreted in the urine. The thyroid gland does not distinguish between radioactive and nonradioactive iodine. Uptake values are used in conjunction with measurements of circulating thyroid hormone levels to differentiate primary and secondary thyroid disease, and serial measurements are helpful in long-term management of thyroid disease and its treatment.

INDICATIONS
- Evaluate hyperthyroidism and/or hypothyroidism
- Evaluate neck pain
- Evaluate the patient as part of a complete thyroid evaluation for symptomatic patients (e.g., swollen neck, neck pain, extreme sensitivity to heat or cold, jitters, sluggishness)
- Evaluate thyroiditis, goiter, or pituitary failure
- Monitor response to therapy for thyroid disease

POTENTIAL DIAGNOSIS
Normal findings in
- Variations in normal ranges of iodine uptake can occur with differences in dietary intake, geographic location, and protocols among laboratories:

Iodine Uptake	Percentage of Radionuclide
2-hr absorption	1%–13%
6-hr absorption	2%–25%
24-hr absorption	15%–45%

R

Abnormal findings in
- Decreased iodine intake or increased iodine excretion
- Graves' disease
- Iodine-deficient goiter
- Hashimoto's thyroiditis (early)
- Hyperthyroidism, increased uptake of radionuclide:
  Rebound thyroid hormone withdrawal
  Drugs and hormones such as barbiturates, diuretics, estrogens, lithium carbonate, phenothiazines, and thyroid-stimulating hormone
- Hypothyroidism, decreased uptake of 0% to 10% radionuclide over 24-hr period:
  Hypoalbuminemia
  Malabsorption
  Renal failure
  Subacute thyroiditis
  Thyrotoxicosis as a result of ectopic thyroid metastasis

CRITICAL FINDINGS: N/A

INTERFERING FACTORS

This procedure is contraindicated for
- Patients who are pregnant or suspected of being pregnant, unless the potential benefits of the procedure far outweigh the risks to the fetus and mother.

Factors that may impair clear imaging
- Inability of the patient to cooperate or remain still during the procedure because of age, significant pain, or mental status.
- Recent use of iodinated contrast medium for radiographic studies (within the last 4 wk) or nuclear medicine procedures done within the previous 24 to 48 hr.
- Iodine deficiency (e.g., patients with inadequate dietary intake, patients on phenothiazine therapy), which can increase radionuclide uptake.
- Certain drugs and other external sources of excess iodine, which can decrease radionuclide uptake, as follows:

Foods containing iodine (e.g., iodized salt)
Drugs such as aminosalicylic acid, antihistamines, antithyroid medications (e.g., propylthiouracil, iodothiouracil), corticosteroids, cough syrup, isoniazid, levothyroxine sodium/T$_4$, L-triiodothyronine, Lugol's solution, nitrates, penicillins, potassium iodide, propylthiouracil, saturated solution of potassium iodide, sulfonamides, thiocyanate, thyroid extract, tolbutamide, and warfarin
Multivitamins containing minerals
- Vomiting, severe diarrhea, and gastroenteritis, which can affect absorption of the oral radionuclide dose.
- Metallic objects (e.g., jewelry, body rings) within the examination field, which may inhibit organ visualization and cause unclear images.

Other considerations
- Failure to follow dietary restrictions before the procedure may cause the procedure to be canceled or repeated.
- Consultation with a health-care provider (HCP) should occur before the procedure for radiation safety concerns regarding younger patients or patients who are lactating.
- Risks associated with radiation overexposure can result from frequent x-ray or radionuclide procedures. Personnel working in the examination area should wear badges to record their level of radiation exposure.

NURSING IMPLICATIONS AND PROCEDURE

PRETEST:
▸ Positively identify the patient using at least two unique identifiers before providing care, treatment, or services.
▸ *Patient Teaching:* Inform the patient this test can assist in assessing thyroid function.
▸ Obtain a history of the patient's complaints, including a list of known

allergens, especially allergies or sensitivities to latex, iodine, seafood, contrast medium, anesthetics, or dyes.

Obtain a history of the patient's endocrine system, symptoms, and results of previously performed laboratory tests and diagnostic and surgical procedures. Note any recent procedures that can interfere with test results, including examinations using iodine-based contrast medium.

Ensure that this procedure is performed before all radiographic procedures using iodinated contrast medium.

Record the date of the last menstrual period and determine the possibility of pregnancy in perimenopausal women.

Obtain a list of the patient's current medications, including herbs, nutritional supplements, and nutraceuticals (see Appendix F).

Review the procedure with the patient. Address concerns about pain related to the procedure and explain that some pain may be experienced during the test, and there may be moments of discomfort. Inform the patient that the procedure is performed in a nuclear medicine department by an HCP who specializes in this procedure, with support staff, and takes approximately 15 to 30 min. Delayed images or data collection is needed 24 hr later.

Sensitivity to social and cultural issues, as well as concern for modesty, is important in providing psychological support before, during, and after the procedure.

Instruct the patient to remove jewelry and other metallic objects from the area to be examined.

Instruct the patient to fast and restrict fluids for 8 to 12 hr before the procedure. The patient may eat 4 hr after the injection unless otherwise indicated. Protocols may vary among facilities.

INTRATEST:

Observe standard precautions, and follow the general guidelines in Appendix A. Positively identify the patient.

Ensure the patient has complied with dietary, fluid, and medication restrictions for 8 to 12 hr before the procedure.

Ensure that the patient has removed all external metallic objects from the area to be examined prior to the procedure.

Instruct the patient to cooperate fully and to follow directions. Instruct the patient to remain still throughout the procedure because movement produces unreliable results.

Administer the I-123 orally (pill form).

Place the patient in a sitting or supine position in front of a radionuclide detector at 2, 6, and 24 hr after ingestion for uptake images.

POST-TEST:

A report of the results will be made available to the requesting HCP, who will discuss the results with the patient.

Instruct the patient to resume usual diet, as directed by the HCP.

Advise patient to drink increased amounts of fluids for 24 hr to eliminate the radionuclide from the body, unless contraindicated. Tell the patient that radionuclide is eliminated from the body within 24 to 48 hr.

If a woman who is breastfeeding must have a nuclear scan, she should not breastfeed the infant until the radionuclide has been eliminated. This could take as long as 3 days. She should be instructed to express the milk and discard it during the 3-day period to prevent cessation of milk production.

Instruct the patient to immediately flush the toilet and to meticulously wash hands with soap and water after each voiding for 24 hr after the procedure.

Instruct all caregivers to wear gloves when discarding urine for 24 hr after the procedure. Wash gloved hands with soap and water before removing gloves. Then wash hands after the gloves are removed.

Recognize anxiety related to test results, and be supportive of perceived loss of independent function. Discuss the implications of abnormal test results on the patient's lifestyle. Provide teaching and information regarding the clinical implications of the test results, as appropriate.

Reinforce information given by the patient's HCP regarding further testing, treatment, or referral to another HCP. Answer any questions or address any concerns voiced by the patient or family.

Depending on the results of this procedure, additional testing may be needed to evaluate or monitor progression of the disease process and determine the need for a change in therapy. Evaluate test results in relation to the patient's symptoms and other tests performed.

RELATED MONOGRAPHS:

Related tests include ACTH, albumin, ACE, antibodies antithyroglobulin, biopsy thyroid, BUN, CT spine, copper, creatinine, cystoscopy, fecal analysis, fecal fat, FSH, gastric emptying scan, GH, LH, PTH, protein, thyroglobulin, thyroid binding inhibitory immunoglobulins, thyroid scan, TSH, TSI, thyroxine, free T_4, triiodothyronine, free T_3, US thyroid, upper GI series, and UA.

Refer to the Endocrine System table at the end of the book for tests by related body system.

Radiofrequency Ablation, Liver

SYNONYM/ACRONYM: RFA, RF ablation.

COMMON USE: To assist in treating tumors of the liver that are too small for surgery or have poor response to chemotherapy.

AREA OF APPLICATION: Liver.

CONTRAST: Done without contrast.

DESCRIPTION: One minimally invasive therapy to eliminate tumors in organs such as the liver is called radiofrequency ablation (RFA). This technique works by passing electrical current in the range of radiofrequency waves between the needle electrode and the grounding pads placed on the patient's skin. A special needle electrode is placed in the tumor under the guidance of an imaging method such as ultrasound (US), computed tomography (CT) scanning, or magnetic resonance imaging (MRI). A radiofrequency current is then passed through the electrode to heat the tumor tissue near the needle tip and to ablate, or eliminate, it. The current creates heat around the electrode inside the tumor, and this heat spreads out to destroy the entire tumor but little of the surrounding normal liver tissue. The heat from radiofrequency energy also closes up small blood vessels, thereby minimizing the risk of bleeding. Because healthy liver tissue withstands more heat than a tumor, RFA is able to destroy a tumor and a small rim of normal tissue about its edges without affecting most of the normal liver. The dead tumor cells are gradually replaced by scar tissue that shrinks over time. Some liver tumors may have failed to respond to chemotherapy or have recurred after initial surgery, and they may be treated by RFA. If there are multiple tumor nodules, they may be treated in one or more sessions. In general, RFA

R

causes only minimal discomfort and may be done as an outpatient procedure without general anesthesia. RFA is most effective if the tumor is less than 2 in. in diameter; results are not as good when RFA is used to treat larger tumors. Similar therapy is being used to treat tumors in the kidney, pancreas, bone, thyroid, breast, adrenal gland, and lung.

INDICATIONS

- Ablation of metastases to the liver
- Ablation of primary liver tumors, with hepatocellular carcinoma
- Therapy for multiple small liver tumors that are too spread out to remove surgically
- Therapy for recurrent liver tumors
- Therapy for tumors that are less than 2 in. in diameter
- Therapy for tumors that have failed to respond to chemotherapy
- Therapy for tumors that have recurred after initial surgery

Risks

- May cause brief or long-lasting shoulder pain
- May cause inflammation of the gallbladder
- May cause damage to the bile ducts with resulting biliary obstruction
- May cause thermal damage to the bowel
- The patient may experience flu-like symptoms that appear 3 to 5 days after the procedure and last for approximately 5 days
- The patient may experience bleeding; if bleeding is severe, surgery may be needed

POTENTIAL DIAGNOSIS

Normal findings in

- Decrease in tumor size
- Normal size, position, contour, and texture of the liver

Abnormal findings in: N/A

CRITICAL FINDINGS: N/A

INTERFERING FACTORS

This procedure is contraindicated for

- Patients with bleeding disorders.
- Patients who are pregnant or suspected of being pregnant, unless the potential benefits of the procedure far outweigh the risks to the fetus and mother.

Factors that may impair clear imaging

- Metallic objects (e.g., jewelry, rings, surgery clips) within the examination field, which may inhibit organ visualization and cause unclear images.
- Inability of the patient to cooperate or remain still during the procedure because of age, significant pain, or mental status.

Other considerations

- Failure to follow dietary restrictions and other pretesting preparations before the procedure may cause the procedure to be canceled or repeated.
- Consultation with a health-care provider (HCP) should occur before the procedure for radiation safety concerns regarding younger patients or patients who are lactating.
- Risks associated with radiation overexposure can result from frequent x-ray procedures. Personnel in the room with the patient should wear a protective lead apron, stand behind a shield, or leave the area while the examination is being done. Personnel working in the examination area should wear badges to record their level of radiation exposure.

NURSING IMPLICATIONS AND PROCEDURE

PRETEST:

Positively identify the patient using at least two unique identifiers before providing care, treatment, or services.

Patient Teaching: Inform the patient this procedure can assist in assessing liver function.

Obtain a history of the patient's complaints, including a list of known allergens, especially allergies or sensitivities to latex, iodine, seafood, contrast medium, and anesthetics.

Obtain a history of the patient's hepatobiliary system, symptoms, and results of previously performed laboratory tests and diagnostic and surgical procedures.

Note any recent procedures that can interfere with test results, including barium examinations.

Record the date of the last menstrual period and determine the possibility of pregnancy in perimenopausal women.

Obtain a list of the patient's current medications, including anticoagulant therapy, aspirin and other salicylates, herbs, nutritional supplements, and nutraceuticals, especially those known to affect coagulation (see Appendix F). Such products should be discontinued by medical direction for the appropriate number of days prior to a surgical procedure. Note the last time and dose of medication taken.

Review the procedure with the patient. Address concerns about pain related to the procedure and explain that a sedative and/or analgesia will be administered to promote relaxation and reduce discomfort prior to the needle electrode insertion. Explain that any discomfort with the needle electrode will be minimized with local anesthetics and systemic analgesics. Inform the patient that the procedure is performed in the radiology department by an HCP, with support staff, and takes approximately 30 to 90 min.

Explain that an IV line may be inserted to allow infusion of IV fluids or sedatives. Usually normal saline is infused.

Sensitivity to social and cultural issues, as well as concern for modesty, is important in providing psychological support before, during, and after the procedure.

Instruct the patient to remove jewelry and other metallic objects from the area to be examined prior to the procedure.

This procedure may be terminated if chest pain or severe cardiac arrhythmias occur.

Instruct the patient to fast and restrict fluids for 8 hr prior to the procedure.

Instruct the patient to avoid taking anticoagulant medication or to reduce dosage as ordered prior to the procedure. Protocols may vary among facilities.

Make sure a written and informed consent has been signed prior to the procedure and before administering any medications.

INTRATEST:

Observe standard precautions, and follow the general guidelines in Appendix A. Positively identify the patient.

Ensure that the patient has complied with dietary, fluid, and medication restrictions and pretesting preparations.

Ensure that the patient has removed all external metallic objects from the area to be examined prior to the procedure.

Have emergency equipment readily available.

If the patient has a history of allergic reactions to any substance or drug, administer ordered prophylactic steroids or antihistamines before the procedure.

Instruct the patient to void and change into the gown, robe, and foot coverings provided.

Instruct the patient to cooperate fully and to follow directions. Instruct the patient to remain still throughout the procedure because movement produces unreliable results.

Record baseline vital signs and assess neurological status. Protocols may vary among facilities.

Establish an IV fluid line for the injection of emergency drugs and of sedatives.

R

Administer an antianxiety agent, as ordered, if the patient has claustrophobia. Administer a sedative to a child or to an uncooperative adult, as ordered.

Place electrocardiographic electrodes on the patient for cardiac monitoring. Establish baseline rhythm; determine if the patient has ventricular arrhythmias.

Place the patient in the supine position on an examination table. Cleanse the selected area, and cover with a sterile drape.

A local anesthetic is injected at the site, and a needle electrode is inserted under ultrasound, CT, or MRI guidance.

A radiofrequency current is passed through the needle electrode, and the tumor is ablated.

Instruct the patient to take slow, deep breaths if nausea occurs during the procedure. Monitor and administer an antiemetic agent if ordered. Ready an emesis basin for use.

The needle electrode is removed, and a pressure dressing is applied over the puncture site.

Observe/assess the needle electrode insertion site for bleeding, inflammation, or hematoma formation.

Monitor the patient for complications related to the procedure (e.g., allergic reaction, anaphylaxis, bronchospasm).

POST-TEST:

A report of the results will be made available to the requesting HCP, who will discuss the results with the patient.

Instruct the patient to resume usual diet, fluids, medications, and activity, as directed by the HCP.

Monitor vital signs and neurological status every 15 min for 1 hr, then every 2 hr for 4 hr, and as ordered. Take temperature every 6 hr for 24 hr. Compare with baseline values. Notify the HCP if temperature is elevated. Protocols may vary among facilities.

Observe for delayed allergic reactions, such as rash, urticaria, tachycardia, hyperpnea, hypertension, palpitations, nausea, or vomiting.

Instruct the patient to immediately report symptoms such as fast heart rate, difficulty breathing, skin rash, itching, chest pain, persistent right shoulder pain, or abdominal pain. Immediately report symptoms to the appropriate HCP.

Instruct the patient to immediately report bile leakage, inflammation, any pleuritic pain, persistent right shoulder pain, or abdominal pain.

Observe/assess the needle electrode insertion site for bleeding, inflammation, or hematoma formation.

Instruct the patient in the care and assessment of the site.

Instruct the patient to apply cold compresses to the puncture site as needed to reduce discomfort or edema.

Instruct the patient to maintain bed rest for 4 to 6 hr after the procedure or as ordered.

Recognize anxiety related to test results, and be supportive of impaired activity related to physical activity. Discuss the implications of abnormal test results on the patient's lifestyle. Provide teaching and information regarding the clinical implications of the test results, as appropriate.

Reinforce information given by the patient's HCP regarding further testing, treatment, or referral to another HCP. Answer any questions or address any concerns voiced by the patient or family.

Depending on the results of this procedure, additional testing may be performed to evaluate or monitor progression of the disease process and determine the need for a change in therapy. Evaluate test results in relation to the patient's symptoms and other tests performed.

RELATED MONOGRAPHS:

Related tests include angiography abdomen, AST, biopsy liver, CT liver, MRI abdomen, and US liver and biliary system.

Refer to the Hepatobiliary System tab at the end of the book for related tests by body system.

Radiography, Bone

SYNONYM/ACRONYM: Arm x-rays, bone x-rays, leg x-rays, rib x-rays, spine x-rays.

COMMON USE: To assist in evaluating bone pain, trauma, and abnormalities related to disorders or events such as dislocation, fracture, abuse, and degenerative disease.

AREA OF APPLICATION: Skeleton.

CONTRAST: None.

DESCRIPTION: Skeletal x-rays are used to evaluate extremity pain or discomfort due to trauma, bone and spine abnormalities, or fluid within a joint. Serial skeletal x-rays are used to evaluate growth pattern. Radiation emitted from the x-ray machine passes through the patient onto a photographic plate or x-ray film. X-rays pass through air freely and are mostly absorbed by the photographic media. Bones and tissues absorb the x-rays in varying degrees, thereby causing white and shades of gray on the x-ray recording media: Bones are very dense and therefore absorb most of the x-ray and appear white; organs are denser than air but not as dense as bone, so they appear in shades of gray. All metals absorb x-rays. Because the x-ray is absorbed or blocked, metal appears totally white on the film and thus facilitates the search for foreign bodies in the patient.

INDICATIONS

- Assist in detecting bone fracture, dislocation, deformity, and degeneration
- Evaluate for child abuse
- Evaluate growth pattern
- Identify abnormalities of bones, joints, and surrounding tissues
- Monitor fracture healing process

POTENTIAL DIAGNOSIS

Normal findings in
- *Infants and children:* Thin plate of cartilage, known as growth plate or epiphyseal plate, between the shaft and both ends
- *Adolescents and adults:* By age 17, calcification of cartilage plate; no evidence of fracture, congenital abnormalities, tumors, or infection

Abnormal findings in
- Arthritis
- Bone degeneration
- Bone spurs
- Foreign bodies
- Fracture
- Genetic disturbance (achondroplasia, dysplasia, dyostosis)
- Hormonal disturbance
- Infection, including osteomyelitis
- Injury
- Joint dislocation or effusion
- Nutritional or metabolic disturbances
- Osteoporosis or osteopenia
- Soft tissue abnormalities
- Tumor or neoplastic disease (osteogenic sarcoma, Paget's disease, myeloma)

CRITICAL FINDINGS: N/A

R

INTERFERING FACTORS

This procedure is contraindicated for

• Patients who are pregnant or suspected of being pregnant, unless the potential benefits of the procedure far outweigh the risks to the fetus and mother.

Factors that may impair clear imaging

• Retained barium from a previous radiological procedure.
• Metallic objects (e.g., jewelry, body rings) within the examination field, which may inhibit organ visualization and can produce unclear images.
• Inability of the patient to cooperate or remain still during the procedure because of age, significant pain, or mental status.

Other considerations

• Consultation with a health-care provider (HCP) should occur before the procedure for radiation safety concerns regarding younger patients or patients who are lactating.
• Risks associated with radiation overexposure can result from frequent x-ray procedures. Personnel in the room with the patient should wear a protective lead apron, stand behind a shield, or leave the area while the examination is being done. Personnel working in the examination area should wear badges to record their level of radiation exposure.

R

NURSING IMPLICATIONS AND PROCEDURE

PRETEST:

▶ Positively identify the patient using at least two unique identifiers before providing care, treatment, or services.
▶ *Patient Teaching:* Inform the patient this procedure can assist in examining bone structure.

▶ Obtain a history of the patient's complaints, including a list of known allergens, especially allergies or sensitivities to latex, iodine, seafood, anesthetics, or contrast medium.
▶ Obtain a history of the patient's musculoskeletal system, symptoms, and results of previously performed laboratory tests and diagnostic and surgical procedures.
▶ Record the date of the last menstrual period and determine the possibility of pregnancy in perimenopausal women.
▶ Obtain a list of the patient's current medications, including herbs, nutritional supplements, and nutraceuticals (see Appendix F).
▶ Review the procedure with the patient. Explain that numerous x-rays may be taken depending on the bones or joint affected. Address concerns about pain and explain that some pain may be experienced during the test, or there may be moments of discomfort. Inform the patient that the procedure is performed in the radiology department by an HCP, with support staff, and takes approximately 10 to 30 min.
▶ *Sensitivity to social and cultural issues,* as well as concern for modesty, is important in providing psychological support before, during, and after the procedure.
▶ Instruct the patient to inhale deeply and hold his or her breath while the image is taken. Warn the patient that the extremity's position during the procedure may be uncomfortable, but ask the patient to hold very still during the procedure because movement will produce unclear images.
▶ Instruct the patient to remove jewelry and other metallic objects from the area to be examined prior to the procedure.
▶ There are no food, fluid, or medication restrictions unless by medical direction.

INTRATEST:

▶ Observe standard precautions, and follow the general guidelines in Appendix A. Positively identify the patient.
▶ Ensure that the patient has removed all external metallic objects from the area to be examined prior to the procedure.

Have emergency equipment readily available.

Instruct the patient to void prior to the procedure and to change into the gown, robe, and foot coverings provided.

Place patient in a standing, sitting, or recumbent position in front of the image receptor.

Ask the patient to inhale deeply and hold his or her breath while the x-ray images are taken.

Instruct the patient to cooperate fully and to follow directions. Ask the patient to remain still throughout the procedure because movement produces unreliable results.

POST-TEST:

A report of the examination will be sent to the requesting HCP, who will discuss the results with the patient.

Recognize anxiety related to test results, and be supportive of impaired activity related to the perceived loss of daily function. Discuss the implications of abnormal test results on the patient's lifestyle. Provide teaching and information regarding the clinical implications of the test results, as appropriate. Provide contact information, if desired, for the American College of

Rheumatology (www.rheumatology.org) or for the Arthritis Foundation (www.arthritis.org).

Reinforce information given by the patient's HCP regarding further testing, treatment, or referral to another HCP. Explain the importance of adhering to the therapy regimen. Answer any questions or address any concerns voiced by the patient or family.

Depending on the results of this procedure, additional testing may be performed to evaluate or monitor progression of the disease process and determine the need for a change in therapy. Evaluate test results in relation to the patient's symptoms and other tests performed.

RELATED MONOGRAPHS:

Related tests include antibodies anticyclic citrullinated peptide, ANA, arthrogram, arthroscopy, biopsy bone, BMD, bone scan, calcium, CBC, CRP, collagen cross-linked telopeptides, CT spine, ESR, MRI musculoskeletal, osteocalcin, phosphorus, synovial fluid analysis, RF, vitamin D, and WBC scan.

Refer to the Musculoskeletal System table at the end of the book for related tests by body system.

Red Blood Cell Cholinesterase

SYNONYM/ACRONYM: Acetylcholinesterase (AChE), erythrocyte cholinesterase, true cholinesterase.

COMMON USE: To assess for pesticide toxicity and screen for cholinesterase deficiency, which may contribute to unrecoverable apnea after surgical induction with succinylcholine.

SPECIMEN: Whole blood (1 mL) collected in a lavender-top (EDTA) tube.

NORMAL FINDINGS: (Method: Spectrophotometry, kinetic)

Test	Conventional Units
RBC cholinesterase	5,300–10,000 international units/L

DESCRIPTION: There are two types of cholinesterase: *acetylcholinesterase (AChE)*, or "true cholinesterase," which is found in red blood cells (RBCs), lung, and brain (nerve) tissue; and *pseudocholinesterase*, which is mainly found in the plasma, liver, and heart. RBC AChE is highly specific for acetylcholine. RBC cholinesterase is used to assist in the diagnosis of chronic carbamate or organophosphate insecticide (e.g., parathion, malathion) toxicity. Organophosphate pesticides bind irreversibly with cholinesterase, inhibiting normal enzyme activity. Carbamate insecticides bind reversibly. Serum or plasma pseudocholinesterase is used more frequently to measure acute pesticide toxicity. Pseudocholinesterase is also the test used to indicate succinylcholine sensitivity (see monograph titled "Pseudocholinesterase and Dibucaine Number").

Patients with inherited cholinesterase deficiency are at risk during anesthesia if succinylcholine is administered as an anesthetic. Succinylcholine, a short-acting muscle relaxant, is a reversible inhibitor of acetylcholinesterase and is hydrolyzed by cholinesterase. Succinylcholine-sensitive patients may be unable to metabolize the anesthetic quickly, resulting in prolonged or unrecoverable apnea. This test, along with the pseudocholinesterase test, is also used to identify individuals with atypical forms of the enzyme cholinesterase. The prevalence of succinylcholine sensitivity is 1 in 2,000–4,000 homozygote and 1 in 500 heterozygote patients. There are more than 15 identified phenotypes; A, AS, S1, S2, F, AF, and FS are associated with prolonged apnea following the use of succinylcholine. Widespread preoperative screening is not routinely performed.

INDICATIONS
- Monitor cumulative exposure to organic phosphate insecticides
- Verify suspected exposure to organic phosphate insecticides

POTENTIAL DIAGNOSIS

Increased in
- Hemolytic anemias (e.g., sickle cell anemia, thalassemias, spherocytosis, and acquired hemolytic anemias) *(increased in hemolytic anemias as AChE is released from the hemolyzed RBCs)*

Decreased in
- Insecticide exposure *(organic phosphate insecticides inhibit AChE activity)*
- Late pregnancy *(related to anemia of pregnancy)*
- Paroxysmal nocturnal hemoglobinuria *(related to lack of RBC production by bone marrow)*
- Relapse of megaloblastic anemia *(related to underproduction of normal RBCs containing AChE)*

CRITICAL FINDINGS: N/A

INTERFERING FACTORS
- Drugs and substances that may increase RBC cholinesterase levels include echothiophate, parathion, and antiepileptic drugs such as carbamazepine, phenobarbital, phenytoin, and valproic acid.

• Improper anticoagulant; fluoride interferes with the measurement and causes a falsely decreased value.

NURSING IMPLICATIONS AND PROCEDURE

PRETEST:

• Positively identify the patient using at least two unique identifiers before providing care, treatment, or services.

• *Patient Teaching:* Inform the patient this test can assist in identification of pesticide poisoning.

• Obtain a history of the patient's complaints, including a list of known allergens, especially allergies or sensitivities to latex. Particularly important to report is exposure to pesticides causing symptoms including blurred vision, muscle weakness, nausea, vomiting, headaches, pulmonary edema, salivation, sweating, or convulsions. Obtain a history of exposure to occupational hazards and medication regimen. Obtain a history of the patient's hematopoietic system, symptoms, and results of previously performed laboratory tests and diagnostic and surgical procedures. Obtain a list of the patient's current medications, including herbs, nutritional supplements, and nutraceuticals (see Appendix F).

• Review the procedure with the patient. Inform the patient that specimen collection takes approximately 5 to 10 min. Address concerns about pain and explain that there may be some discomfort during the venipuncture. *Sensitivity to social and cultural issues,* as well as concern for modesty, is important in providing psychological support before, during, and after the procedure.

• There are no food, fluid, or medication restrictions, unless by medical direction.

INTRATEST:

• If the patient has a history of allergic reaction to latex, avoid the use of equipment containing latex.

• Instruct the patient to cooperate fully and to follow directions. Direct the patient to breathe normally and to avoid unnecessary movement.

• Observe standard precautions, and follow the general guidelines in Appendix A. Positively identify the patient, and label the appropriate specimen container with the corresponding patient demographics, initials of the person collecting the specimen, date, and time of collection. Perform a venipuncture.

• Remove the needle and apply direct pressure with dry gauze to stop bleeding. Observe/assess venipuncture site for bleeding or hematoma formation and secure gauze with adhesive bandage.

• Promptly transport the specimen to the laboratory for processing and analysis.

POST-TEST:

• A report of the results will be made available to the requesting health-care provider (HCP), who will discuss the results with the patient.

• The patient with decreased values should be observed for signs of fluid volume excess related to compromised regulatory mechanisms, decreased cardiac output related to decreased myocardial contractility or arrhythmias, and pain related to inflammation or ischemia.

• *Social and Cultural Considerations:* Recognize anxiety related to test results, and be supportive of impaired activity related to weakness and fear of shortened life expectancy. Discuss the implications of abnormal test results on the patient's lifestyle. Provide teaching and information regarding the clinical implications of the test results, as appropriate. Educate the patient regarding access to genetic counseling services and screening tests for other family members. Educate the patient regarding the use of a medic-alert bracelet to notify health-care workers of increased risk from exposure to medications that may lower cholinesterase activity.

• Reinforce information given by the patient's HCP regarding further testing, treatment, or referral to another HCP. Answer any questions or address any concerns voiced by the patient or family.

R

Depending on the results of this procedure, additional testing may be performed to evaluate or monitor progression of the disease process and determine the need for a change in therapy. Evaluate test results in relation to the patient's symptoms and other tests performed.

RELATED MONOGRAPHS:

Related tests include biopsy bone marrow, CBC, CBC RBC indices, CBC RBC morphology, Ham's test, pseudocholinesterase, sickle cell screen, and vitamin B_{12}. Refer to the Hematopoietic System table at the end of the book for related tests by body system.

Refraction

SYNONYM/ACRONYM: N/A.

COMMON USE: To assess the visual acuity of the eyes in patients of all ages, to evaluate visual acuity as required by driver licensing laws, and to assist in evaluating the eyes prior to therapeutic interventions such as eyeglasses, contact lenses, low vision aids, cataract surgery, or LASIK surgery.

AREA OF APPLICATION: Eyes.

CONTRAST: N/A.

DESCRIPTION: This noninvasive procedure tests the visual acuity (VA) of the eyes and determines abnormalities or refractive errors that need correction. Refractions are performed using a combination of different pieces of equipment. Refractive error can be quickly and accurately measured using computerized automatic refractors or manually with a viewing system consisting of an entire set of trial lenses mounted on a circular wheel (phoropter). A projector may also be used to display test letters and characters from Snellen eye charts for use in assessing VA. If the VA is worse than 20/20, the pinhole test may be used to quickly assess the best corrected vision. Refractive errors of the peripheral cornea and lens

can be reduced or eliminated by having the patient look through a pinhole at the vision test. Patients with cataracts or visual field defects will not show improved results using the pinhole test. The retinoscope is probably the most valuable instrument that can be used to objectively assess VA. It is also the only objective means of assessing refractive error in pediatric patients and patients who are unable to cooperate with other techniques of assessing refractive error due to illiteracy, senility, or inability to speak the same language as the examiner. Visual defects identified through refraction, such as hyperopia (farsightedness), in which the point of focus lies behind the retina; myopia (nearsightedness), in which the point of focus lies in front of the retina; and astigmatism, in which the refraction is unequal in different curvatures of the eyeball, can be corrected by glasses, contact lenses, or refractive surgery.

INDICATIONS

- Determine if an optical defect is present and if light rays entering the eye focus correctly on the retina
- Determine the refractive error prior to refractive surgery such as radial keratotomy (RK), photorefractive keratotomy (PRK), laser assisted in situ keratomileusis (LASIK), intracorneal rings (Intacs), limbal relaxing incisions (LRI), implantable contact lens (phakic intraocular lens [IOL]), clear lens replacement
- Determine the type of corrective lenses (e.g., biconvex or plus lenses for hyperopia, biconcave or minus lenses for myopia, compensatory lenses for astigmatism) needed for refractive errors
- Diagnose refractive errors in vision

POTENTIAL DIAGNOSIS

Visual Acuity Scale

Foot	Meter	Decimal
20/200	6/60	0.1
20/160	6/48	0.13
20/120	6/36	0.17
20/100	6/30	0.2
20/80	6/24	0.25
20/60	6/18	0.33
20/50	6/15	0.4
20/40	6/12	0.5
20/30	6/9	0.67
20/25	6/7.5	0.8
20/20	6/6	1
20/16	6/4.8	1.25
20/12	6/3.6	1.67
20/10	6/3	2

VA can be expressed fractionally in feet, fractionally in meters, or as a decimal where perfect vision of 20/20 feet or 6/6 meters is equal to 1. Comparing the fraction in feet or meters to the decimal helps demonstrate that acuity less than 20/20, or less than 1.0, is "worse" vision, and acuity greater than 20/20, or greater than 1.0, is "better." A patient who cannot achieve best corrected VA of 20/200 or above (greater than 0.1) in his or her better eye is considered legally blind in the United States.

Normal findings in

Normal visual acuity; 20/20 (with corrective lenses if appropriate).

Uncorrected Visual Acuity	Foot	Meter	Decimal
Mild vision loss	20/30–20/70	6/9–6/21	0.67–0.29
Moderate vision loss	20/80–20/160	6/24–6/48	0.25–0.13
Severe vision loss	20/200–20/400	6/60–6/120	0.1–0.05
Profound vision loss	20/500–20/1,000	6/150–6/300	0.04–0.02

Abnormal findings in
• Refractive errors such as astigmatism, hyperopia, and myopia.

CRITICAL FINDINGS: N/A

INTERFERING FACTORS

This procedure is contraindicated for
• Patients with narrow-angle glaucoma if pupil dilation is performed because dilation can initiate a severe and sight-threatening open-angle attack.
• Patients with allergies to mydriatics if pupil dilation using mydriatics is performed.

Factors that may impair clear imaging
• Improper pupil dilation may prevent adequate examination for refractive error.
• Inability of the patient to cooperate and remain still during the procedure because of age, significant pain, or mental status may interfere with the test results.
• Failure to follow medication restrictions before the procedure may cause the procedure to be canceled or repeated.

NURSING IMPLICATIONS AND PROCEDURE

PRETEST:

▶ Positively identify the patient using at least two unique identifiers before providing care, treatment, or services.

▶ *Patient Teaching:* Inform the patient this procedure can assist in assessing visual acuity.

▶ Obtain a history of the patient's complaints, including a list of known allergens, especially mydriatics if dilation is to be performed.

▶ Obtain a history of the patient's known or suspected vision loss; changes in visual acuity, including type and cause; use of glasses or contact lenses; eye conditions with treatment regimens; eye surgery; and other tests and procedures to assess and diagnose visual deficit.

▶ Obtain a history of symptoms and results of previously performed laboratory tests and diagnostic and surgical procedures.

▶ Obtain a list of the patient's current medications, including herbs, nutritional supplements, and nutraceuticals (see Appendix F).

▶ Instruct the patient to remove contact lenses or glasses, as appropriate. Instruct the patient regarding the importance of keeping the eyes open for the test.

▶ Review the procedure with the patient. Address concerns about pain and explain that mydriatics, if used, may cause blurred vision and sensitivity to light. There may also be a brief stinging sensation when the drop is put in the eye. Inform the patient that a healthcare provider (HCP) performs the test, in a quiet, darkened room, and that to evaluate both eyes, the test can take up 30 min (including time for the pupils to dilate before the test is actually performed).

▶ *Sensitivity to social and cultural issues,* as well as concern for modesty, is important in providing psychological support before, during, and after the procedure.

There are no food or fluid restrictions unless by medical direction.

The patient should withhold eye medications (particularly miotic eye drops which may constrict the pupil preventing a clear view of the fundus and mydriatic eyedrops in order to avoid instigation of an acute open angle attack in patients with narrow angle glaucoma) for at least 1 day prior to the test.

Ensure that the patient understands that he or she must refrain from driving until the pupils return to normal (about 4 hours) after the test and has made arrangements to have someone else be responsible for transportation after the test.

INTRATEST:

Observe standard precautions, and follow the general guidelines in Appendix A.

Positively identify the patient.

Ensure that the patient has complied with medication restrictions and pre-testing preparations; assure that eye medications, especially mydriatics, have been restricted for at least 1 day prior to the procedure.

Instruct the patient to cooperate fully and to follow directions. Ask the patient to remain still during the procedure because movement produces unreliable results.

If dilation is to be performed, administer the ordered mydriatic to each eye and repeat in 5 to 15 min. Drops are placed in the eye with the patient looking up and the solution directed at the six o'clock position of the sclera (white of the eye) near the limbus (gray, semitransparent area of the eyeball where the cornea and sclera meet). The dropper bottle should not touch the eyelashes. Ask the patient to place the chin in the chin rest and gently press the forehead against the support bar. The examiner will sit about 2 ft away at eye level with the patient. The retinoscope light is held in front of the eyes and directed through the pupil. Each eye is also examined for the characteristics of the red reflex, the reflection of the light from the retinoscope, which normally moves in the same direction as the light.

Request that the patient look straight ahead while the eyes are examined with the instrument and while different lenses are tried to provide the best corrective lenses to be prescribed. When optimal VA is obtained with the trial lenses in each eye, a prescription for corrective lenses is written.

POST-TEST:

A report of the results will be made available to the requesting HCP, who will discuss the results with the patient.

Instruct the patient to resume usual medications, as directed by the HCP.

Recognize anxiety related to test results, and be supportive of impaired activity related to vision loss, anticipated loss of driving privileges, or the possibility of requiring corrective lenses (self-image). Discuss the implications of abnormal test results on the patient's lifestyle. Provide teaching and information regarding the clinical implications of the test results, as appropriate. Provide contact information, if desired, for a general patient education Web site on the topic of eye care (e.g., www.allaboutvision.com).

Reinforce information given by the patient's HCP regarding further testing, treatment, or referral to another HCP. Inform the patient that visual acuity and responses to light may change. Suggest that the patient wear dark glasses after the test until the pupils return to normal size. Answer any questions or address any concerns voiced by the patient or family.

Depending on the results of this procedure, additional testing may be performed to evaluate or monitor progression of the disease process and determine the need for a change in therapy. Evaluate test results in relation to the patient's symptoms and other tests performed.

RELATED MONOGRAPHS:

Related tests include color perception test, intraocular muscle function, intraocular pressure, Schirmer tear test, and slit-lamp biomicroscopy.

Refer to the Ocular System table at the end of the book for related tests by body system.

R

Renin

SYNONYM/ACRONYM: Plasma renin activity (PRA).

COMMON USE: To assist in evaluating for a possible cause of hypertension.

SPECIMEN: Plasma (3 mL) collected in a lavender-top (EDTA) tube.

NORMAL FINDINGS: (Method: Radioimmunoassay)

Age and Position	Conventional Units	SI Units (Conventional Units × 1)
Newborn–12 mo	2–35 ng/mL/hr	2–35 ng/mL/hr
Supine, normal sodium diet		
1–3 yr	1.7–11.2 ng/mL/hr	1.7–11.2 mcg/L/hr
4–5 yr	1.0–6.5 ng/mL/hr	1.0–6.5 mcg/L/hr
6–10 yr	0.5–5.9 ng/mL/hr	0.5–5.9 mcg/L/hr
11–15 yr	0.5–3.3 ng/mL/hr	0.5–3.3 mcg/L/hr
Adult	0.2–2.3 ng/mL/hr	0.2–2.3 mcg/L/hr
Upright, normal sodium diet		
Adult–older adult	1.3–4 ng/mL/hr	1.3–4 mcg/L/hr

Values vary according to the laboratory performing the test, as well as the patient's age, gender, dietary pattern, state of hydration, posture, and physical activity.

DESCRIPTION: Renin is an enzyme that activates the renin-angiotensin system. It is released into the renal veins by the juxtaglomerular cells of the kidney in response to sodium depletion and hypovolemia. Renin converts angiotensinogen to angiotensin I. Angiotensin I is converted to angiotensin II, the biologically active form. Angiotensin II is a powerful vasoconstrictor that stimulates aldosterone production in the adrenal cortex. Angiotensin II and aldosterone increase blood pressure. Excessive amounts of angiotensin II cause renal hypertension. The renin assay screens for essential, renal, or renovascular hypertension. Plasma renin is expressed as the rate of angiotensin I formation per unit of time. The random collection of specimens without prior dietary preparations does not provide clinically significant information. Values should also be evaluated along with simultaneously collected aldosterone levels (see monographs titled "Aldosterone" and "Angiotensin-Converting Enzyme").

INDICATIONS
- Assist in the identification of primary hyperaldosteronism resulting from aldosterone-secreting adrenal adenoma
- Assist in monitoring patients on mineralocorticoid therapy
- Assist in the screening of the origin of essential, renal, or renovascular hypertension

POTENTIAL DIAGNOSIS

Increased in

Addison's disease *(related to hyponatremia, which stimulates production of renin)*

Bartter's syndrome *(related to hereditary defect in loop of Henle that affects sodium resorption; hyponatremia stimulates renin production)*

Cirrhosis *(related to fluid buildup, which dilutes sodium concentration; hyponatremia is a strong stimulus for production of renin)*

Congestive heart failure *(related to fluid buildup, which dilutes sodium concentration; hyponatremia is a strong stimulus for production of renin)*

Gastrointestinal disorders with electrolyte loss *(related to hyponatremia, which stimulates production of renin)*

Hepatitis *(related to fluid buildup, which dilutes sodium concentration; hyponatremia is a strong stimulus for production of renin)*

Hypokalemia *(related to decreased potassium levels, which stimulate renin production)*

Malignant hypertension *(related to secondary hyperaldosteronism that constricts the blood vessels and results in hypertension)*

Nephritis *(the kidneys can produce renin in response to inflammation or disease)*

Nephropathies with sodium or potassium wasting *(related to hyponatremia, which stimulates production of renin)*

Pheochromocytoma *(related to renin production in response to hypertension)*

Pregnancy *(related to retention of fluid and hyponatremia that stimulates renin production; normal pregnancy is associated with changes in the balance between renin and angiotensin)*

- Renin-producing renal tumors
- Renovascular hypertension *(related to decreased renal blood flow, which stimulates release of renin)*

Decreased in

- Cushing's syndrome *(related to excessive production of glucocorticoids, which increase sodium levels and decrease potassium levels, inhibiting renin production)*
- Primary hyperaldosteronism *(related to aldosterone-secreting adrenal tumor; aldosterone inhibits renin production)*

CRITICAL FINDINGS: N/A

INTERFERING FACTORS

- Drugs that may increase renin levels include albuterol, amiloride, azosemide, benazepril, bendroflumethiazide, captopril, chlorthalidone, cilazapril, cromakalim, desmopressin, diazoxide, dihydralazine, doxazosin, enalapril, endralazine, felodipine, fenoldopam, fosinopril, furosemide, hydralazine, hydrochlorothiazide, laxatives, lisinopril, lithium, methyclothiazide, metolazone, muzolimine, nicardipine, nifedipine, opiates, oral contraceptives, perindopril, ramipril, spironolactone, triamterene, and xipamide.
- Drugs and substances that may decrease renin levels include acetylsalicylic acid, angiotensin, angiotensin II, atenolol, bopindolol, bucindolol, carbenoxolone, carvedilol, clonidine, cyclosporin A, dexfenfluramine, glycyrrhiza, ibuprofen, indomethacin, levodopa, metoprolol, naproxen, nicardipine, NSAIDs, oral contraceptives, oxprenolol, propranolol, sulindax, and vasopressin.
- Upright body posture, stress, and strenuous exercise can increase renin levels.

R

- Recent radioactive scans or radiation can interfere with test results when radioimmunoassay is the test method.
- Diet can significantly affect results (e.g., low-sodium diets stimulate the release of renin).
- Hyperkalemia, acute increase in blood pressure, and increased blood volume may suppress renin secretion.
- Failure to follow dietary restrictions before the procedure may cause the procedure to be canceled or repeated.

NURSING IMPLICATIONS AND PROCEDURE

PRETEST:

▶ Positively identify the patient using at least two unique identifiers before providing care, treatment, or services.

▶ *Patient Teaching:* Inform the patient this test can assist in evaluating for high blood pressure.

▶ Obtain a history of the patient's complaints, including a list of known allergens, especially allergies or sensitivities to latex.

▶ Obtain a history of the patient's endocrine and genitourinary systems, symptoms, and results of previously performed laboratory tests and diagnostic and surgical procedures.

▶ Note any recent procedures that can interfere with test results.

▶ Obtain a list of the patient's current medications, including herbs, nutritional supplements, and nutraceuticals (see Appendix F).

▶ Review the procedure with the patient. Inform the patient or family member that the position required (supine or upright) must be maintained for 2 hr before specimen collection. Inform the patient that multiple specimens may be required. Inform the patient that specimen collection takes approximately 5 to 10 min. Address concerns about pain and explain that there may be some discomfort during the venipuncture.

▶ *Sensitivity to social and cultural issues,* as well as concern for modesty, is important in providing psychological support before, during, and after the procedure.

▶ The patient should be on a normal sodium diet (1 to 2 g sodium per day) for 2 to 4 wk before the test. Protocols may vary among facilities.

▶ By medical direction, the patient should avoid diuretics, antihypertensive drugs, herbals, cyclic progestogens, and estrogens for 2 to 4 wk before the test.

▶ Prepare an ice slurry in a cup or plastic bag to have ready for immediate transport of the specimen to the laboratory.

INTRATEST:

▶ Ensure that the patient has complied with diet and medication restrictions and pretesting dietary preparations; ensure that specific medications have been restricted for at least 2 to 4 wk prior to the procedure.

▶ If the patient has a history of allergic reaction to latex, avoid the use of equipment containing latex.

▶ Instruct the patient to cooperate fully and to follow directions. Direct the patient to breathe normally and to avoid unnecessary movement.

▶ Observe standard precautions, and follow the general guidelines in Appendix A. Positively identify the patient, and label the appropriate tubes with the corresponding patient demographics, date, and time of collection. Specify patient position (upright or supine) and exact source of specimen (peripheral vs. arterial). Perform a venipuncture after the patient has been in the upright (sitting or standing) position for 2 hr. If a supine specimen is requested on an inpatient, the specimen should be collected early in the morning before the patient rises.

▶ Remove the needle and apply direct pressure with dry gauze to stop bleeding. Observe/assess venipuncture site for bleeding or hematoma formation and secure gauze with adhesive bandage.

▶ The sample should be placed in an ice slurry immediately after collection. Information on the specimen label should be protected from water in the

R

ice slurry by first placing the specimen in a protective plastic bag. Promptly transport the specimen to the laboratory for processing and analysis.

A report of the results will be made available to the requesting health-care provider (HCP), who will discuss the results with the patient.

Instruct the patient to resume usual medications, as directed by the HCP.

Nutritional Considerations: Instruct the patient to notify the requesting HCP of any signs and symptoms of dehydration or fluid overload related to abnormal renin levels or compromised sodium regulatory mechanisms. Fluid loss or dehydration is signaled by the thirst response. Decreased skin turgor, dry mouth, and multiple longitudinal furrows in the tongue are symptoms of dehydration. Fluid overload may be signaled by a loss of appetite and nausea. Excessive fluid also causes pitting edema: When firm pressure is placed on the skin over a bone (e.g., the ankle), the indentation will remain after 5 sec.

Nutritional Considerations: Educate patients of the importance of proper water balance. The Institute of Medicine's Food and Nutrition Board suggests 3.7 L for males and 2.7 L for females as the daily intake goal of total dietary water for adults age 19 to greater than 70 yr; 3 L/d for pregnant females age 14 to 51 yr; 3.8 L/d for lactating females age 14 to 51 yr; 3.3 L/d for male and 2.3 L/d for female children age 14 to 18 yr; 2.4 L/d for male and 2.1 L/d for female children age 9 to 13 yr; 1.7 L/d for children age 4 to 8 yr; 1.3 L/d for children age 1 to 3 yr; 0.8 L/d for children age 7 to 12 mo; and 0.7 L/d (assumed to be from human milk) for children 0 to 6 mo. Reprinted with permission from the National Academies Press, copyright 2013, National Academy of Sciences. In buildings with hard water, untreated tap water contains minerals such as calcium, magnesium, and iron. Water-softening systems replace these minerals with sodium, and therefore patients on a low-sodium diet should

avoid drinking treated tap water and drink bottled water instead.

Nutritional Considerations: Renin levels affect the regulation of fluid balance and electrolytes. If appropriate, educate patients with low sodium levels that the major source of dietary sodium is found in table salt. Many foods, such as milk and other dairy products, are also good sources of dietary sodium. Most other dietary sodium is available through the consumption of processed foods. Patients on low-sodium diets should be advised to avoid beverages such as colas, ginger ale, sports drinks, lemon-lime sodas, and root beer. Many over-the-counter medications, including antacids, laxatives, analgesics, sedatives, and antitussives, contain significant amounts of sodium. The best advice is to emphasize the importance of reading all food, beverage, and medicine labels. The Institute of Medicine's Food and Nutrition Board suggests 1,200 mg as an adequate daily intake goal of dietary sodium for adult males and females greater than age 70 yr; 1,300 mg/d for adult males and females age 51 to 70 yr; 1,500 mg/d for adult males and females age 19 to 50 yr; 1,500 mg/d for pregnant and lactating females under age 18 through 50 yr; 1,500 mg/d for children age 9 to 18 yr; 1,200 mg/d for children age 4 to 8 yr; 1,000 mg/d for children age 1 to 3 yr; 370 mg/d for children age 7 to 12 mo; and 120 mg/d for children age 0 to 6 mo. Reprinted with permission from the National Academies Press, copyright 2013, National Academy of Sciences. The requesting HCP or nutritionist should be consulted before the patient on a low-sodium diet begins using salt substitutes. The Institute of Medicine's Food and Nutrition Board suggests 4,700 mg as the daily intake goal of dietary potassium for adults age 19 to greater than 70 yr; 4,700 mg/d for pregnant females under age 18 through 51 yr; 5,100 mg/d for lactating females under age 18 through 51 yr; 4,700 mg/d for children age 14 to 18 yr; 4,500 mg/d for children age 9 to 13 yr; 3,800 mg/d for children age 4 to 8 yr; 3,000 mg/d for children age 1 to 3 yr; 700 mg/d for

R

children age 7 to 12 mo; and 400 mg/d for children 0 to 6 mo. Reprinted with permission from the National Academies Press, copyright 2013, National Academy of Sciences. Potassium is present in all plant and animal cells, making dietary replacement fairly simple to achieve.

▸ Reinforce information given by the patient's HCP regarding further testing, treatment, or referral to another HCP. Answer any questions or address any concerns voiced by the patient or family.

▸ Depending on the results of this procedure, additional testing may be performed to evaluate or monitor progression of the disease process and determine the need for a change in therapy. Evaluate test results in relation to the patient's symptoms and other tests performed.

RELATED MONOGRAPHS:

▸ Related tests include ACTH, ALT, aldosterone, ACE, AST, ANP, BNP, bilirubin, biopsy kidney, BUN, calcium, chloride, cortisol, creatinine, DHEAS, fecal fat, GGT, glucose, GTT, magnesium, metanephrines, potassium, protein total and fractions, renogram, sodium, UA, and VMA.

▸ Refer to the Endocrine and Genitourinary systems tables at the end of the book for related tests by body system.

Renogram

SYNONYM/ACRONYM: Radioactive renogram, renocystography, renocystogram, renal scintigraphy.

COMMON USE: To assist in diagnosing renal disorders such as embolism, obstruction, infection, inflammation, trauma, stones, and bleeding.

AREA OF APPLICATION: Kidneys.

CONTRAST: IV radioactive material.

DESCRIPTION: A renogram is a nuclear medicine study performed to assist in diagnosing renal disorders, such as abnormal blood flow, collecting-system defects, and excretion dysfunction. Because renography uses no iodinated contrast medium, it is safe to use in patients who have iodine allergies or compromised renal function.

After IV administration of the radioisotope, information about the structures of the kidneys is obtained. The radioactive material is detected by a gamma camera, which can detect the gamma rays emitted by the radionuclide in the kidney. Renography simultaneously tracks the rate at which the radionuclide flows into *(vascular phase)*, through *(tubular phase)*, and out of *(excretory phase)* the kidneys. The times are plotted on a graph and compared to normal parameters of organ function. Differential estimates of left and right kidney contributions to glomerular filtration rate and effective renal plasma flow can be calculated. With the use

R

of diuretic stimulation during the excretory phase, it is possible to differentiate between anatomic obstruction and nonobstructive residual dilation from previous hydronephrosis. All information obtained is stored in a computer to be used for further interpretation and computations. Renal function can be monitored by serially repeating this test and comparing results.

INDICATIONS

- Aid in the diagnosis of renal artery embolism or renal infarction causing obstruction
- Aid in the diagnosis of renal artery stenosis resulting from renal dysplasia or atherosclerosis and causing arterial hypertension and reduced glomerular filtration rate

Aid in the diagnosis of renal vein thrombosis resulting from dehydration in infants or obstruction of blood flow in the presence of renal tumors in adults

Detect renal infectious or inflammatory diseases, such as acute or chronic pyelonephritis, renal abscess, or nephritis

Determine the presence and effects of renal trauma, such as arterial injury, renal contusion, hematoma, rupture, arteriovenous fistula, or urinary extravasation

Determine the presence, location, and cause of obstructive uropathy, such as calculi, neoplasm, congenital disorders, scarring, or inflammation

Evaluate acute and chronic renal failure

Evaluate chronic urinary tract infections, especially in children

Evaluate kidney transplant for acute or chronic rejection

Evaluate obstruction caused by stones or tumor

POTENTIAL DIAGNOSIS

Normal findings in

- Normal shape, size, position, symmetry, vasculature, perfusion, and function of the kidneys
- Radionuclide material circulates bilaterally, symmetrically, and without interruption through the renal parenchyma, ureters, and urinary bladder, with 50% of the radionuclide excreted within the first 10 min

Abnormal findings in

- Acute tubular necrosis
- Congenital anomalies (e.g., absence of a kidney)
- Decreased renal function
- Diminished blood supply
- Infection or inflammation (pyelonephritis, glomerulonephritis)
- Masses
- Obstructive uropathy
- Renal failure, infarction, cyst, or abscess
- Renal vascular disease, including renal artery stenosis or renal vein thrombosis
- Trauma

CRITICAL FINDINGS: N/A

INTERFERING FACTORS

This procedure is contraindicated for

- Patients who are pregnant or suspected of being pregnant, unless the potential benefits of the procedure far outweigh the risks to the fetus and mother.

Factors that may impair clear imaging

- Inability of the patient to cooperate or remain still during the procedure because of age, significant pain, or mental status.
- Serum creatinine levels greater than or equal to 3 mg/dL (depending on the radionuclide used), which can decrease renal perfusion.

R

- Other nuclear medicine studies done within the previous 24 to 48 hr.
- Medications such as antihypertensives, angiotensin-converting enzyme (ACE) inhibitors, and β-blockers taken within 24 hr of the test.
- Dehydration, which can accentuate abnormalities, or overhydration, which can mask abnormalities.
- Metallic objects (e.g., jewelry, body rings) within the examination field, which may inhibit organ visualization.

Other considerations

- Consultation with a health-care provider (HCP) should occur before the procedure for radiation safety concerns regarding younger patients or patients who are lactating.
- Risks associated with radiation overexposure can result from frequent x-ray or radionuclide procedures. Personnel working in the examination area should wear badges to record their level of radiation exposure.
- Inaccurate timing of imaging after the radionuclide injection can affect the results.

NURSING IMPLICATIONS AND PROCEDURE

PRETEST:

- Positively identify the patient using at least two unique identifiers before providing care, treatment, or services.
- *Patient Teaching:* Inform the patient this procedure can assist in assessing the renal system.
- Obtain a history of the patient's complaints, including a list of known allergens, especially allergies or sensitivities to latex, iodine, seafood, anesthetics, or contrast medium.
- Obtain a history of the patient's genitourinary system, symptoms, and results of previously performed laboratory

tests and diagnostic and surgical procedures.
- Record the date of the last menstrual period and determine the possibility of pregnancy in perimenopausal women.
- Obtain a list of the patient's current medications, including herbs, nutritional supplements, and nutraceuticals (see Appendix F).
- Review the procedure with the patient. Address concerns about pain related to the procedure and explain that some pain may be experienced during the test, and there may be moments of discomfort. Reassure the patient that radioactive material poses minimal radioactive hazard because of its short half-life and rarely produces side effects. Inform the patient that the procedure is performed in a nuclear medicine department by an HCP and usually takes approximately 60 to 90 min, and that delayed images are needed 2 to 24 hr later. The patient may leave the department and return later to undergo delayed imaging.
- *Sensitivity to social and cultural issues,* as well as concern for modesty, is important in providing psychological support before, during, and after the procedure.
- Instruct the patient to remove jewelry and other metallic objects from the area to be examined prior to the procedure.
- Inform the patient that he or she will be asked to drink several glasses of fluid before the study for hydration, unless the patient has a restricted fluid intake for other reasons.
- There are no food or medication restrictions unless by medical direction.

INTRATEST:

- Observe standard precautions, and follow the general guidelines in Appendix A. Positively identify the patient.
- Ensure that the patient has removed external metallic objects from the area to be examined prior to the procedure.
- Instruct the patient to void and change into the gown, robe, and foot coverings provided.
- Administer sedative to a child or to an uncooperative adult, as ordered.

Place the patient in a supine position on a flat table with foam wedges to help maintain position and immobilization.

The radionuclide is administered IV, and the kidney area is scanned immediately with images taken every minute for 30 min.

During the flow and static imaging, the diuretic furosemide (Lasix) or ACE inhibitor (captopril) can be administered IV and images obtained.

Urine and blood laboratory studies are done after the renogram to correlate findings before diagnosis.

If a study for vesicoureteral reflux is done, the patient is asked to void, and a catheter is inserted into the bladder. The radionuclide is instilled into the bladder, and multiple images are obtained during bladder filling. The patient is then requested to void, with the catheter in place or after catheter removal, depending on department policy. Imaging is continued during and after voiding. Reflux is determined by calculating the urine volume and counts obtained by imaging.

Gloves should be worn during the radionuclide administration and while handling the patient's urine.

Remove the needle or catheter and apply a pressure dressing over the puncture site.

Observe/assess the needle/catheter insertion site for bleeding, inflammation, or hematoma formation.

OST-TEST:

A report of the results will be made available to the requesting HCP, who will discuss the results with the patient. Unless contraindicated, advise patient to drink increased amounts of fluids for 24 hr to eliminate the radionuclide from the body. Inform the patient that radionuclide is eliminated from the body within 6 to 24 hr.

Instruct the patient to immediately flush the toilet and to meticulously wash

hands with soap and water after each voiding for 24 hr after the procedure.

Instruct all caregivers to wear gloves when discarding urine for 24 hr after the procedure. Wash gloved hands with soap and water before removing gloves. Then wash ungloved hands after the gloves are removed.

Observe/assess the needle/catheter site for bleeding, hematoma formation, and inflammation.

Instruct the patient in the care and assessment of the site.

Instruct the patient to apply cold compresses to the puncture site as needed to reduce discomfort or edema.

Recognize anxiety related to test results. Discuss the implications of abnormal test results on the patient's lifestyle. Provide teaching and information regarding the clinical importance of the test results, as appropriate.

Reinforce information given by the patient's HCP regarding further testing, treatment, or referral to another HCP. Answer any questions or address any concerns voiced by the patient or family.

Depending on the results of this procedure, additional testing may be needed to evaluate or monitor progression of the disease process and determine the need for a change in therapy. Evaluate test results in relation to the patient's symptoms and other tests performed.

RELATED MONOGRAPHS:

Related tests include angiography renal, antibodies anti-glomerular basement membrane, biopsy kidney, bladder cancer markers, BUN, calculus kidney stone panel, C4, CT abdomen, CT pelvis, CT renal, creatinine, creatinine clearance, cystoscopy, IVP, KUB studies, MRA, MRI abdomen, retrograde ureteropyelography, strep group A, US abdomen, US kidney, and UA.

Refer to the Genitourinary System table at the end of the book for related tests by body system.

R

Reticulocyte Count

SYNONYM/ACRONYM: Retic count.

COMMON USE: To assess reticulocyte count in relation to bone marrow activity toward diagnosing anemias such as pernicious, iron deficiency, and hemolytic to monitor response of therapeutic interventions.

SPECIMEN: Whole blood (1 mL) collected in a lavender-top (EDTA) tube.

NORMAL FINDINGS: (Method: Automated analyzer or microscopic examination of specially stained peripheral blood smear)

Age	Reticulocyte Count %
Newborn	2%–4.8%
7–30 days	0.4%–2.8%
31–60 days	0.9%–3.8%
3 mo–18 yr	0.8%–2.1%
Adult–older adult	0.8%–2.5%
	Reticulocyte Count (absolute number)
Birth–older adult	0.02–0.10 (10^6 cells/mm^3)
	Immature Reticulocyte Fraction %
Birth	2.5%–6.5%
Newborn–older adult	2.5%–17.0%
	Reticulocyte Hemoglobin
Birth	22–32 pg/cell
Newborn–18 yr	23–34 pg/cell
Adult–older adult	30–35 pg/cell

DESCRIPTION: Normally, as it matures, the red blood cell (RBC) loses its nucleus. The remaining ribonucleic acid (RNA) produces a characteristic color when special stains are used, making these cells easy to identify and enumerate. Some automated cell counters have the ability to provide a reticulocyte panel, which includes the enumeration of circulating reticulocytes as an absolute count and as a percentage of total RBCs; the immature reticulocyte fraction (IRF), which reflects the number of reticulocytes released into the circulation within the past 24 to 48 hours; and the reticulocyte hemoglobin (Ret-He) content, which reflects the amount of iron incorporated into the maturing RBCs. The presence of reticulocytes is an indication of the level of erythropoietic activity in the bone marrow. The information provided by the reticulocyte panel is useful in the evaluation of anemias, bone marrow response to therapy, degree of bone marrow engraftment following transplant, and the effectiveness of altitude training

R

in high-performance athletes. In abnormal conditions, reticulocytes are prematurely released into circulation. (See monographs titled "Complete Blood Count, RBC Count" and "Complete Blood Count, RBC Morphology and Inclusions.")

INDICATIONS

- Evaluate erythropoietic activity
- Monitor response to therapy for anemias

POTENTIAL DIAGNOSIS

The reticulocyte production index (RPI) is a good estimate of RBC production. The calculation corrects the count for anemia and for the premature release of reticulocytes into the peripheral blood during periods of hemolysis or significant bleeding. The RPI also takes into consideration the maturation time of large polychromatophilic cells or nucleated RBCs seen on the peripheral smear:

RPI = % reticulocytes × [patient hematocrit (Hct) / normal Hct] × (1 / maturation time)

As the formula shows, the RPI is inversely proportional to Hct, as follows:

Hematocrit (%)	Maturation Time (days)
45	1
35	1.5
25	2
15	2.5

Increased in
Conditions that result in excessive RBC loss or destruction stimulate a compensatory bone marrow response by increasing production of RBCs.

- Blood loss
- Hemolytic anemias
- Iron-deficiency anemia
- Megaloblastic anemia

Decreased in

- Alcoholism *(decreased production related to nutritional deficit)*
- Anemia of chronic disease
- Aplastic anemia *(related to overall lack of RBC)*
- Bone marrow replacement *(new marrow fails to produce RBCs until it engrafts)*
- Endocrine disease *(hypometabolism related to hypothyroidism is reflected by decreased bone marrow activity)*
- RBC aplasia *(related to overall lack of RBCs)*
- Renal disease *(diseased kidneys cannot produce erythropoietin, which stimulates the bone marrow to produce RBCs)*
- Sideroblastic anemia *(RBCs are produced but are abnormal in that they cannot incorporate iron into hemoglobin, resulting in anemia)*

CRITICAL FINDINGS: N/A

INTERFERING FACTORS

- Drugs that may increase reticulocyte counts include acetanilid, acetylsalicylic acid, amyl nitrate, antimalarials, antipyretics, antipyrine, arsenicals, corticotropin, dimercaprol, etretinate, furaltadone, furazolidone, levodopa, methyldopa, nitrofurans, penicillin, procainamide, and sulfones.
- Drugs that may decrease reticulocyte counts include azathioprine, dactinomycin, hydroxyurea, methotrexate, and zidovudine.
- Reticulocyte count may be falsely increased by the presence of RBC inclusions (Howell-Jolly bodies, Heinz bodies, and Pappenheimer bodies) that stain with methylene blue.

R

- Reticulocyte count may be falsely decreased as a result of the dilutional effect after a recent blood transfusion.
- Specimens that are clotted or hemolyzed should be rejected for analysis.

NURSING IMPLICATIONS AND PROCEDURE

PRETEST:

▶ Positively identify the patient using at least two unique identifiers before providing care, treatment, or services.
Patient Teaching: Inform the patient this test can assist in assessing for anemia.

▶ Obtain a history of the patient's complaints, including a list of known allergens, especially allergies or sensitivities to latex.

▶ Obtain a history of the patient's hematopoietic system, symptoms, and results of previously performed laboratory tests and diagnostic and surgical procedures.

▶ Note any recent procedures that can interfere with test results.

▶ Obtain a list of the patient's current medications, including herbs, nutritional supplements, and nutraceuticals (see Appendix F).

▶ Review the procedure with the patient. Inform the patient that specimen collection takes approximately 5 to 10 min. Address concerns about pain and explain that there may be some discomfort during the venipuncture.
Sensitivity to social and cultural issues, as well as concern for modesty, is important in providing psychological support before, during, and after the procedure.

▶ There are no food, fluid, or medication restrictions unless by medical direction.

INTRATEST:

▶ If the patient has a history of allergic reaction to latex, avoid the use of equipment containing latex.

▶ Instruct the patient to cooperate fully and to follow directions. Direct the

patient to breathe normally and to avoid unnecessary movement.

▶ Observe standard precautions, and follow the general guidelines in Appendix A. Positively identify the patient, and label the appropriate specimen container with the corresponding patient demographics, initials of the person collecting the specimen, date, and time of collection. Perform a venipuncture.

▶ Remove the needle and apply direct pressure with dry gauze to stop bleeding. Observe/asses venipuncture site for bleeding or hematoma formation and secure gauze with adhesive bandage.

▶ Promptly transport the specimen to the laboratory for processing and analysis.

POST-TEST:

▶ A report of the results will be made available to the requesting health-care provider (HCP), who will discuss the results with the patient.

▶ Reinforce information given by the patient's HCP regarding further testing, treatment, or referral to another HCP. Answer any questions or address any concerns voiced by the patient or family.

▶ Depending on the results of this procedure, additional testing may be performed to evaluate or monitor progression of the disease process and determine the need for a change in therapy. Evaluate test results in relation to the patient's symptoms and other tests performed.

RELATED MONOGRAPHS:

▶ Related tests include biopsy bone marrow, complement, CBC, CBC hematocrit, CBC hemoglobin, CBC RBC count, CBC RBC indices, CBC RBC morphology, Coomb's antiglobulin direct and indirect, erythropoietin, iron/TIBC, ferritin, folate, G6PD, Ham's test, Hgb electrophoresis, lead, osmotic fragility, PK, sickle cell screen, and vitamin B_{12}.

▶ Refer to the Hematopoietic System table at the end of the book for related tests by body system.

Retrograde Ureteropyelography

SYNONYM/ACRONYM: Retrograde.

COMMON USE: To assess the urinary tract for trauma, obstruction, stones, infection, and abscess that can interfere with function.

AREA OF APPLICATION: Renal calyces, ureter.

CONTRAST: Radiopaque iodine-based contrast medium.

DESCRIPTION: Retrograde ureteropyelography uses a contrast medium introduced through a ureteral catheter during cystography and radiographic visualization to view the renal collecting system (calyces, renal pelvis, and urethra). During a cystoscopic examination, a catheter is advanced through the ureters and into the kidney; contrast medium is injected through the catheter into the kidney. This procedure is primarily used in patients who are known to be hypersensitive to IV injected iodine-based contrast medium and when excretory ureterography does not adequately reveal the renal collecting system. The incidence of allergic reaction to the contrast medium is reduced because there is less systemic absorption of the contrast medium when injected into the kidney than when injected IV. Retrograde ureteropyelography sometimes provides more information about the anatomy of the different parts of the collecting system than can be obtained by excretory ureteropyelography. The procedure is not hampered by impaired renal function, but it carries the risk of urinary tract infection and sepsis.

INDICATIONS
- Evaluate the effects of urinary system trauma
- Evaluate known or suspected ureteral obstruction
- Evaluate placement of a ureteral stent or catheter
- Evaluate the presence of calculi in the kidneys, ureters, or bladder
- Evaluate the renal collecting system when excretory urography is unsuccessful
- Evaluate space-occupying lesions or congenital anomalies of the urinary system
- Evaluate the structure and integrity of the renal collecting system

POTENTIAL DIAGNOSIS

Normal findings in
- Normal outline and opacification of renal pelvis and calyces
- Normal size and uniform filling of the ureters
- Symmetrical and bilateral outline of structures

Abnormal findings in
- Congenital renal or urinary tract abnormalities
- Hydronephrosis
- Neoplasms
- Obstruction as a result of tumor, blood clot, stricture, or calculi
- Obstruction of ureteropelvic junction
- Perinephric abscess

R

- Perinephric inflammation or suppuration
- Polycystic kidney disease
- Prostatic enlargement
- Tumor of the kidneys or the collecting system

CRITICAL FINDINGS: N/A

INTERFERING FACTORS

This procedure is contraindicated for

- Patients with allergies to shellfish or iodinated dye. The contrast medium used may cause a life-threatening allergic reaction. Patients with a known hypersensitivity to the contrast medium may benefit from premedication with corticosteroids or the use of non-ionic contrast medium.
- Patients who are pregnant or suspected of being pregnant, unless the potential benefits of the procedure far outweigh the risks to the fetus and mother.
- Elderly and other patients who are chronically dehydrated before the test, because of their risk of contrast-induced renal failure.
- Patients who are in renal failure.
- Patients with renal insufficiency, indicated by a blood urea nitrogen value greater than 40 mg/dL, because contrast medium can complicate kidney function.
- Young patients (17 yr and younger), unless the benefits of the x-ray diagnosis outweigh the risks of exposure to high levels of radiation.
- Patients with multiple myeloma, who may experience decreased kidney function subsequent to administration of contrast medium.

Factors that may impair clear imaging

- Gas or feces in the gastrointestinal tract resulting from inadequate cleansing or failure to restrict food intake before the study.

- Retained barium from a previous radiological procedure.
- Metallic objects (e.g., jewelry, body rings) within the examination field, which may inhibit organ visualization and cause unclear images.
- Inability of the patient to cooperate or remain still during the procedure because of age, significant pain, or mental status.

Other considerations

- Consultation with a health-care provider (HCP) should occur before the procedure for radiation safety concerns regarding younger patients or patients who are lactating.
- Risks associated with radiation overexposure can result from frequent x-ray procedures. Personnel in the room with the patient should wear a protective lead apron, stand behind a shield or leave the area while the examination is being done. Personnel working in the examination area should wear badges to record their level of radiation exposure.
- Failure to follow dietary restrictions and other pretesting preparations may cause the procedure to be canceled or repeated.

NURSING IMPLICATIONS AND PROCEDURE

PRETEST:

▶ Positively identify the patient using at least two unique identifiers before providing care, treatment, or services.
▶ *Patient Teaching:* Inform the patient this procedure can assist in assessing the urinary tract.
▶ Obtain a history of the patient's complaints, including a list of known allergens, especially allergies or sensitivities to latex, iodine, seafood, anesthetics, or contrast medium.
▶ Obtain a history of the patient's genitourinary system, symptoms, and results

of previously performed laboratory tests and diagnostic and surgical procedures.

Note any recent procedures that can interfere with test results, including examinations using barium.

Record the date of the last menstrual period and determine the possibility of pregnancy in perimenopausal women.

Obtain a list of the patient's current medications, including herbs, nutritional supplements, and nutraceuticals (see Appendix F).

Patients receiving metformin (Glucophage) for non–insulin-dependent (type 2) diabetes should discontinue the drug on the day of the test and continue to withhold it for 48 hr after the test. Failure to do so may result in lactic acidosis.

Review the procedure with the patient. Address concerns about pain related to the procedure and explain that some pain may be experienced during the test, or there may be moments of discomfort. Inform the patient that the procedure is performed in a special department, usually in a radiology or vascular suite, by an HCP, with support staff, and takes approximately 30 to 60 min.

Sensitivity to social and cultural issues, as well as concern for modesty, is important in providing psychological support before, during, and after the procedure.

Inform the patient that he or she may receive a laxative the night before the test and an enema or a cathartic the morning of the test, as ordered.

Explain that an IV line may be inserted to allow infusion of IV fluids, contrast medium, or sedatives. Usually normal saline is infused.

Inform the patient that if a local anesthetic is used, the patient may feel (1) some pressure in the kidney area as the catheter is introduced and contrast medium injected and (2) the urgency to void.

Instruct the patient to remove jewelry and other metallic objects from the area to be examined prior to the procedure.

Instruct the patient to fast and restrict fluids for 8 hr prior to the procedure.

Instruct the patient to avoid taking anticoagulant medication or to reduce dosage as ordered prior to the procedure. Protocols may vary among facilities.

This procedure may be terminated if chest pain, severe cardiac arrhythmias, or signs of a cerebrovascular accident occur.

Make sure a written and informed consent has been signed prior to the procedure and before administering any medications.

INTRATEST:

Observe standard precautions, and follow the general guidelines in Appendix A. Positively identify the patient.

Ensure that the patient has complied with dietary, fluid, and medication restrictions for 8 hr prior to the procedure.

Ensure the patient has removed all external metallic objects from the area to be examined prior to the procedure.

If the patient has a history of allergic reactions to any substance or drug, administer ordered prophylactic steroids or antihistamines before the procedure. Use nonionic contrast medium for the procedure.

Have emergency equipment readily available.

Instruct the patient to void prior to the procedure and to change into the gown, robe, and foot coverings provided.

Instruct the patient to cooperate fully and to follow directions. Instruct the patient to remain still throughout the procedure because movement produces unreliable results.

Record baseline vital signs and assess neurological status. Protocols may vary among facilities.

Establish an IV fluid line for the injection of emergency drugs and of sedatives.

Administer an antianxiety agent, as ordered, if the patient has claustrophobia. Administer a sedative to a child or to an uncooperative adult, as ordered.

Place electrocardiographic electrodes on the patient for cardiac monitoring. Establish baseline rhythm; determine if the patient has ventricular arrhythmias.

Place patient supine on the table in the lithotomy position.

A kidney, ureter, and bladder (KUB) or plain image is taken to ensure that no barium or stool will obscure visualization of the urinary system. The patient may be asked to hold his or her breath to facilitate visualization.

The patient is given a local anesthetic, and a cystoscopic examination is performed and the bladder is inspected.

A catheter is inserted, and the renal pelvis is emptied by gravity. Contrast medium is introduced into the catheter. Inform the patient that the contrast medium may cause a temporary flushing of the face, a feeling of warmth, or nausea.

X-ray images are made and the results processed. Inform the patient that additional images may be necessary to visualize the area in question.

Additional contrast medium is injected through the catheter to outline the ureters as the catheter is withdrawn.

The catheter may be kept in place and attached to a gravity drainage unit until urinary flow has returned or is corrected.

Additional x-ray images are taken 10 to 15 min after the catheter is removed to evaluate retention of the contrast medium, indicating urinary stasis.

Remove the needle or catheter and apply a pressure dressing over the puncture site.

Observe/assess the needle/catheter insertion site for bleeding, inflammation, or hematoma formation.

POST-TEST:

A report of the results will be made available to the requesting HCP, who will discuss the results with the patient.

Instruct the patient to resume usual diet, fluids, medications, and activity, as directed by the HCP. Renal function should be assessed before metformin is resumed.

Monitor vital signs and neurological status every 15 min for 1 hr, then every 2 hr for 4 hr, and then as ordered. Take temperature every 4 hr for 24 hr. Monitor intake and output at least every 8 hr. Compare with baseline values. Notify the HCP if temperature is elevated. Protocols may vary among facilities.

Observe for delayed allergic reactions, such as rash, urticaria, tachycardia, hyperpnea, hypertension, palpitations, nausea, or vomiting.

Instruct the patient to immediately report symptoms such as fast heart rate, difficulty breathing, skin rash, itching, chest pain, persistent right shoulder pain, or abdominal pain. Immediately report symptoms to the appropriate HCP.

Observe/assess the needle/catheter insertion site for bleeding, inflammation, or hematoma formation.

Instruct the patient in the care and assessment of the site.

Instruct the patient to apply cold compresses to the puncture site as needed to reduce discomfort or edema.

Monitor for signs of sepsis and severe pain in the kidney area.

Maintain the patient on adequate hydration after the procedure. Encourage the patient to drink lots of fluids to prevent stasis and to prevent the buildup of bacteria.

Recognize anxiety related to test results, and be supportive of perceived loss of independent function. Discuss the implications of abnormal test results on the patient's lifestyle. Provide teaching and information regarding the clinical implications of the test results, as appropriate.

Reinforce information given by the patient's HCP regarding further testing, treatment, or referral to another HCP. Answer any questions or address any concerns voiced by the patient or family.

Instruct the patient in the use of any ordered medications. Explain the importance of adhering to the therapy regimen. As appropriate, instruct the patient in significant side effects and systemic reactions associated with the prescribed medication. Encourage him or her to review corresponding literature provided by a pharmacist.

Depending on the results of this procedure, additional testing may be needed to evaluate or monitor progression of the disease process and determine the need for a change in therapy.

Evaluate test results in relation to the patient's symptoms and other tests performed.

RELATED MONOGRAPHS:

▸ Related tests include angiography renal, BUN, calculus kidney stone panel, CT abdomen, creatinine, cystoscopy, IVP, KUB, MRI abdomen, PT/INR, PSA, renogram, US kidney, UA, and voiding cystourethrography.

▸ Refer to the Genitourinary System table at the end of the book for related tests by body system.

Rheumatoid Factor

SYNONYM/ACRONYM: RF, RA.

COMMON USE: To primarily assist in diagnosing rheumatoid arthritis.

SPECIMEN: Serum (1 mL) collected in a red-top tube.

NORMAL FINDINGS: (Method: Immunoturbidimetric) Less than 14 international units/mL. Elevated values may be detected in healthy adults 60 years and older.

DESCRIPTION: Rheumatoid arthritis (RA) is a chronic, systemic autoimmune disease that damages the joints. Inflammation caused by autoimmune responses can affect other organs and body systems. The American Academy of Rheumatology's current criteria focuses on earlier diagnosis of newly presenting patients who have at least one swollen joint unrelated to another condition. The criteria includes four determinants: joint involvement (number and size of joints involved), serological test results (rheumatoid factor [RF] and/or anticitrullinated protein antibody [ACPA]), indications of acute inflammation (C-reactive protein [CRP] and/or erythrocyte sedimentation rate [ESR]), and duration of symptoms. A score of 6 or greater defines the presence of RA. Patients with longstanding RA, whose condition is inactive, or whose prior history would have satisfied the previous classification criteria by having four of seven findings—morning stiffness, arthritis of three or more joint areas, arthritis of hand joints, symmetric arthritis, rheumatoid nodules, abnormal amounts of rheumatoid factor, and radiographic changes—should remain classified as having RA. The study of RA is complex, and it is believed that multiple genes may be involved in the manifestation of RA. Individuals with RA harbor a macroglobulin-type antibody called *rheumatoid factor* in their blood. Patients with other diseases (e.g., systemic lupus erythematosus [SLE] and occasionally tuberculosis, chronic hepatitis, infectious mononucleosis, and subacute bacterial endocarditis) may also test positive for RF. RF antibodies are usually immunoglobulin (Ig) M but may also be IgG or IgA. Women are two to

R

three times more likely to develop RA than men. While RA is most likely to affect people aged 35 to 50, it can affect all ages.

INDICATIONS

Assist in the diagnosis of rheumatoid arthritis, especially when clinical diagnosis is difficult

POTENTIAL DIAGNOSIS

Increased in

Pathophysiology is unclear, but RF is present in numerous conditions, including rheumatoid arthritis.

- Chronic hepatitis
- Chronic viral infections
- Cirrhosis
- Dermatomyositis
- Infectious mononucleosis
- Leishmaniasis
- Leprosy
- Malaria
- Rheumatoid arthritis
- Sarcoidosis
- Scleroderma
- Sjögren's syndrome
- SLE
- Syphilis
- Tuberculosis
- Waldenström's macroglobulinemia

Decreased in: N/A

CRITICAL FINDINGS: N/A

INTERFERING FACTORS

- Older healthy patients may have higher values.
- Recent blood transfusion, multiple vaccinations or transfusions, or an inadequately activated complement may affect results.
- Serum with cryoglobulin or high lipid levels may cause a false-positive test and may require that the test be repeated after a fat-restriction diet.

NURSING IMPLICATIONS AND PROCEDURE

PRETEST:

▸ Positively identify the patient using at least two unique identifiers before providing care, treatment, or services.
▸ *Patient Teaching:* Inform the patient this test can assist in diagnosing arthritic disorders.
▸ Obtain a history of the patient's complaints, including a list of known allergens, especially allergies or sensitivities to latex.
▸ Obtain a history of the patient's immune and musculoskeletal systems, symptoms, and results of previously performed laboratory tests and diagnostic and surgical procedures.
▸ Obtain a list of the patient's current medications, including herbs, nutritional supplements, and nutraceuticals (see Appendix F).
▸ Review the procedure with the patient. Inform the patient that specimen collection takes approximately 5 to 10 min. Address concerns about pain and explain that there may be some discomfort during the venipuncture.
▸ *Sensitivity to social and cultural issues,* as well as concern for modesty, is important in providing psychological support before, during, and after the procedure.
▸ There are no food, fluid, or medication restrictions unless by medical direction.

INTRATEST:

▸ If the patient has a history of allergic reaction to latex, avoid the use of equipment containing latex.
▸ Instruct the patient to cooperate fully and to follow directions. Direct the patient to breathe normally and to avoid unnecessary movement.
▸ Observe standard precautions, and follow the general guidelines in Appendix A. Positively identify the patient, and label the appropriate specimen container with the corresponding patient demographics, initials of the person collecting the specimen, date, and time of collection. Perform a venipuncture.
▸ Remove the needle and apply direct pressure with dry gauze to stop

bleeding. Observe venipuncture site for bleeding or hematoma formation and secure gauze with adhesive bandage.

▶ Promptly transport the specimen to the laboratory for processing and analysis.

POST-TEST:

▶ A report of the results will be made available to the requesting health-care provider (HCP), who will discuss the results with the patient.

▶ Recognize anxiety related to test results, and be supportive of impaired activity related to anticipated chronic pain resulting from joint inflammation, impairment in mobility, musculoskeletal deformity, and loss of independence. Discuss the implications of abnormal test results on the patient's lifestyle. Provide teaching and information regarding the clinical implications of the test results, as appropriate. Educate the patient regarding access to counseling services, as appropriate. Provide contact information, if desired, for the American College of Rheumatology (www.rheumatology .org) or for the Arthritis Foundation (www.arthritis.org).

▶ Reinforce information given by the patient's HCP regarding further testing, treatment, or referral to another HCP.

Advise the patient, as appropriate, that additional studies may be undertaken to determine treatment regimen or to determine the possible causes of symptoms if the test is negative for RA. Answer any questions or address any concerns voiced by the patient or family.

▶ Depending on the results of this procedure, additional testing may be performed to evaluate or monitor progression of the disease process and determine the need for a change in therapy. Anemia is a common complication of RA. Evaluate test results in relation to the patient's symptoms and other tests performed.

RELATED MONOGRAPHS:

▶ Related laboratory tests include antibodies anticyclic citrullinated peptide, ANA, arthrogram, arthroscopy, biopsy bone, BMD, bone scan, calcium, collagen cross-linked telopeptides, CBC, CT spine, CRP, ESR, MRI musculoskeletal, osteocalcin, phosphorus, radiography bone, synovial fluid analysis, uric acid, vitamin D, and WBC scan.

▶ Refer to the Immune and Musculoskeletal systems tables at the end of the book for related tests by body system.

Rubella Antibodies, IgG and IgM

SYNONYM/ACRONYM: German measles serology.

COMMON USE: To assess for antibodies related to rubella immunity or for presence of rubella infection.

SPECIMEN: Serum (1 mL) collected in a red-top tube.

NORMAL FINDINGS: (Method: Chemiluminescent immunoassay)

	IgM	Interpretation	IgG	Interpretation
Negative	0.9 index or less	No significant level of detectable antibody	Less than 8 U/mL	No significant level of detectable antibody; indicative of nonimmunity
Indeterminate	0.91–1.09 index	Equivocal results; retest in 10–14 d	8–12 U/mL	Equivocal results; retest in 10–14 d
Positive	1.1 index or greater	Antibody detected; indicative of recent immunization, current or recent infection	Greater than 12 U/mL	Antibody detected; indicative of immunization, current or past infection

DESCRIPTION: Rubella, commonly known as German measles, is a communicable viral disease transmitted by contact with respiratory secretions and aerosolized droplets of the secretions. The incubation period is 14 to 21 days. This disease produces a pink, macular rash that disappears in 2 to 3 days. Rubella infection induces immunoglobulin (Ig) G and IgM antibody production. This test can determine current infection or immunity from past infection. Rubella serology is part of the TORCH (*to*xoplasmosis, *r*ubella, *c*ytomegalovirus, and *h*erpes simplex type 2) panel routinely performed on pregnant women. Fetal infection during the first trimester can cause spontaneous abortion or congenital defects. Ideally, the immune status of women of childbearing age should be ascertained before pregnancy, when vaccination can be administered to provide lifelong immunity. The presence of IgM antibodies indicates acute infection. The presence of IgG antibodies indicates current or past infection. Susceptibility to rubella is indicated by a negative reaction. Many laboratories use a qualitative assay that detects the presence of both IgM and IgG rubella antibodies. IgM- and IgG-specific enzyme immunoassays are also available to help distinguish acute infection from immune status. Either the rubella-combined or IgG-specific assay should be used in routine prenatal testing of maternal serum.

INDICATIONS
- Assist in the diagnosis of rubella infection
- Determine presence of rubella antibodies
- Determine susceptibility to rubella, particularly in pregnant women
- Perform as part of routine prenatal serological testing

R

POTENTIAL DIAGNOSIS

Positive findings in
• Rubella infection (past or present)

CRITICAL FINDINGS

A nonimmune status in pregnant patients may present significant health consequences for the developing fetus if the mother is exposed to an infected individual.

Note and immediately report to the health-care provider (HCP) pregnant patients with rubella nonimmune status. Timely notification of critical values for lab or diagnostic studies is a role expectation of the professional nurse. Notification processes will vary among facilities. Upon receipt of the critical value the information should be read back to the caller to verify accuracy. Most policies require immediate notification of the primary HCP, hospitalist, or on-call HCP. Reported information includes the patient's name, unique identifiers, critical value, name of the person giving the report, and name of the person receiving the report. Documentation of notification should be made in the medical record with the name of the HCP notified, time and date of notification, and any orders received. Any delay in a timely report of a critical value may require completion of a notification form with review by Risk Management.

INTERFERING FACTORS: N/A

NURSING IMPLICATIONS AND PROCEDURE

PRETEST:

  Positively identify the patient using at least two unique identifiers before providing care, treatment, or services.
  Patient Teaching: Inform the patient this test can indicate rubella infection or immunity.

  Obtain a history of the patient's complaints, including a list of known allergens, especially allergies or sensitivities to latex.
  Obtain a history of exposure to rubella.
  Obtain a history of the patient's immune and reproductive systems, symptoms, and results of previously performed laboratory tests and diagnostic and surgical procedures.
  Obtain a list of the patient's current medications, including herbs, nutritional supplements, and nutraceuticals (see Appendix F).
  Review the procedure with the patient. Inform the patient that several tests may be necessary to confirm diagnosis. Any individual positive result should be repeated in 7 to 14 days to monitor a change in detectable level of antibody. Inform the patient that specimen collection takes approximately 5 to 10 min. Address concerns about pain and explain that there may be some discomfort during the venipuncture.
  Sensitivity to social and cultural issues, as well as concern for modesty, is important in providing psychological support before, during, and after the procedure.
  There are no food, fluid, or medication restrictions unless by medical direction.

INTRATEST:

  If the patient has a history of allergic reaction to latex, avoid the use of equipment containing latex.
  Instruct the patient to cooperate fully and to follow directions. Direct the patient to breathe normally and to avoid unnecessary movement.
  Observe standard precautions, and follow the general guidelines in Appendix A. Positively identify the patient, and label the appropriate specimen container with the corresponding patient demographics, initials of the person collecting the specimen, date, and time of collection. Perform a venipuncture.
  Remove the needle and apply direct pressure with dry gauze to stop bleeding. Observe/assess venipuncture site for bleeding or hematoma formation and secure gauze with adhesive bandage.
  Promptly transport the specimen to the laboratory for processing and analysis.

R

POST-TEST:

A report of the results will be made available to the requesting HCP, who will discuss the results with the patient.

Vaccination Considerations: Record the date of the last menstrual period and determine the possibility of pregnancy prior to administration of rubella vaccine to female rubella-nonimmune patients. Instruct patient not to become pregnant for 1 mo after being vaccinated with the rubella vaccine to protect any fetus from contracting the disease and having serious birth defects. Instruct the patient on birth control methods to prevent pregnancy, if appropriate. Delay rubella vaccination in pregnancy until after childbirth, and give immediately prior to discharge from the hospital.

Recognize anxiety related to test results, and provide emotional support if results are positive and the patient is pregnant. Encourage the family to seek counseling if concerned with pregnancy termination. Provide teaching and information regarding the clinical implications of the test results, as appropriate. Decisions regarding elective abortion should take place in the presence of both parents. Provide a nonjudgmental, nonthreatening atmosphere for discussing the risks and difficulties of delivering and raising a developmentally challenged infant as well as for exploring other options (e.g., termination of pregnancy or adoption). Educate the patient regarding access to counseling services, as appropriate.

Reinforce information given by the patient's HCP regarding further testing, treatment, or referral to another HCP. Instruct the patient in isolation precautions during time of communicability or contagion. Emphasize the need to return to have a convalescent blood sample taken in 7 to 14 days. Provide information regarding vaccine-preventable diseases where indicated (e.g., anthrax, cervical cancer, diphtheria, encephalitis, hepatitis A and B, H1N1 flu, human papillomavirus, *Haemophilus influenza*, seasonal influenza, Lyme disease, measles, meningococcal disease, monkeypox, mumps, pertussis, pneumococcal disease, polio, rotavirus, rubella, shingles, smallpox, tetanus, typhoid fever, varicella, yellow fever). Provide contact information, if desired, for the Centers for Disease Control and Prevention (www.cdc.gov/vaccines/vpd-vac). Answer any questions or address any concerns voiced by the patient or family.

Depending on the results of this procedure, additional testing may be performed to evaluate or monitor progression of the disease process and determine the need for a change in therapy. Evaluate test results in relation to the patient's symptoms and other tests performed.

RELATED MONOGRAPHS:

Related tests include culture viral, CMV, rubeola, *Toxoplasma,* and varicella antibody.

Refer to the Immune and Reproductive systems tables at the end of the book for related tests by body system.

R

Rubeola Antibodies

SYNONYM/ACRONYM: Measles serology.

COMMON USE: To assess for a rubeola infection or immunity.

SPECIMEN: Serum (1 mL) collected in a red-top tube.

NORMAL FINDINGS: (Method: Enzyme immunoassay)

	IgM	Interpretation	IgG	Interpretation
Negative	0.79 AU or less	No significant level of detectable antibody	0.89 index or less	No significant level of detectable antibody; indicative of nonimmunity
Indeterminate	0.8–1.2 AU	Equivocal results; retest in 10–14 d	0.9–1.0 index	Equivocal results; retest in 10–14 d
Positive	1.3 AU or greater	Antibody detected; indicative of recent immunization, current or recent infection	1.1 index or greater	Antibody detected; indicative of immunization, current or past infection

DESCRIPTION: Measles is caused by a single-stranded ribonucleic acid (RNA) paramyxovirus that invades the respiratory tract and lymphoreticular tissues. It is transmitted by respiratory secretions and aerosolized droplets of the secretions. The incubation period is 10 to 11 days. Symptoms initially include conjunctivitis, cough, and fever. Koplik's spots develop 4 to 5 days later, followed by papular eruptions, body rash, and lymphadenopathy. The presence of immunoglobulin (Ig) M antibodies indicates acute infection. The presence of IgG antibodies indicates current or past infection. Susceptibility to measles is indicated by a negative reaction. Many laboratories use a qualitative assay that detects the presence of both IgM and IgG rubeola antibodies. IgM- and IgG-specific enzyme immunoassays are also available to help distinguish acute infection from immune status.

INDICATIONS
• Determine resistance to or protection against measles virus

• Differential diagnosis of viral infection, especially in pregnant women with a history of exposure to measles

POTENTIAL DIAGNOSIS

Positive findings in
• Measles infection

CRITICAL FINDINGS: N/A

INTERFERING FACTORS: N/A

NURSING IMPLICATIONS AND PROCEDURE

PRETEST:
▸ Positively identify the patient using at least two unique identifiers before providing care, treatment, or services.
▸ *Patient Teaching:* Inform the patient this test is to assess for measles.
▸ Obtain a history of the patient's complaints, including a list of known allergens, especially allergies or sensitivities to latex.
▸ Obtain a history of exposure to measles.
▸ Obtain a history of the patient's immune system, symptoms, and results of previously performed laboratory tests and diagnostic and surgical procedures.

- Obtain a list of the patient's current medications, including herbs, nutritional supplements, and nutraceuticals (see Appendix F).
- Review the procedure with the patient. Inform the patient that several tests may be necessary to confirm the diagnosis. Any individual positive result should be repeated in 7 to 14 days to monitor a change in detectable levels of antibody. Inform the patient that specimen collection takes approximately 5 to 10 min. Address concerns about pain and explain that there may be some discomfort during the venipuncture.
- *Sensitivity to social and cultural issues,* as well as concern for modesty, is important in providing psychological support before, during, and after the procedure.
- There are no food, fluid, or medication restrictions, unless by medical direction.

INTRATEST:

- If the patient has a history of allergic reaction to latex, avoid the use of equipment containing latex.
- Instruct the patient to cooperate fully and to follow directions. Direct the patient to breathe normally and to avoid unnecessary movement.
- Observe standard precautions, and follow the general guidelines in Appendix A. Positively identify the patient, and label the appropriate specimen container with the corresponding patient demographics, initials of the person collecting the specimen, date, and time of collection. Perform a venipuncture.
- Remove the needle and apply direct pressure with dry gauze to stop bleeding. Observe/assess venipuncture site for bleeding or hematoma formation and secure gauze with adhesive bandage.
- Promptly transport the specimen to the laboratory for processing and analysis.

POST-TEST:

- A report of the results will be made available to the requesting health-care provider (HCP), who will discuss the results with the patient.
- *Vaccination Considerations:* Record the date of the last menstrual period and determine the possibility of pregnancy prior to administration of rubeola vaccine to female rubeola-nonimmune patients. Instruct patient not to become pregnant for 1 mo after being vaccinated with the rubeola vaccine to protect any fetus from contracting the disease. The danger of contracting measles while pregnant include the possibilities of miscarriage, stillbirth, or preterm delivery. Instruct the patient on birth control methods to prevent pregnancy, if appropriate. Delay rubella vaccination in pregnancy until after childbirth, and give immediately prior to discharge from the hospital.
- Reinforce information given by the patient's HCP regarding further testing, treatment, or referral to another HCP. Instruct the patient in isolation precautions during time of communicability or contagion. Emphasize the need to return to have a convalescent blood sample taken in 7 to 14 days. Provide information regarding vaccine-preventable diseases where indicated (e.g., anthrax, cervical cancer, diphtheria, encephalitis, hepatitis A and B, H1N1 flu, human papillomavirus, *Haemophilus influenza*, seasonal influenza, Lyme disease, measles, meningococcal disease, monkeypox, mumps, pertussis, pneumococcal disease, polio, rotavirus, rubella, shingles, smallpox, tetanus, typhoid fever, varicella, yellow fever). Provide contact information, if desired, for the Centers for Disease Control and Prevention (www.cdc.gov/vaccines/vpd-vac). Answer any questions or address any concerns voiced by the patient or family.
- Depending on the results of this procedure, additional testing may be performed to evaluate or monitor progression of the disease process and determine the need for a change in therapy. Evaluate test results in relation to the patient's symptoms and other tests performed.

RELATED MONOGRAPHS:

- Related tests include culture viral, rubella, and varicella.
- Refer to the Immune System table at the end of the book for related tests by body system.

Schirmer Tear Test

COMMON USE: To assess tear duct function.

AREA OF APPLICATION: Eyes.

CONTRAST: N/A.

DESCRIPTION: The tear film, secreted by the lacrimal, Krause, and Wolfring glands, covers the surface of the eye. Blinking spreads tears over the eye and moves them toward an opening in the lower eyelid known as the punctum. Tears drain through the punctum into the nasolacrimal duct and into the nose. The Schirmer tear test simultaneously tests both eyes to assess lacrimal gland function by determining the amount of moisture accumulated on standardized filter paper or strips held against the conjunctival sac of each eye. The Schirmer test measures both reflex and basic secretion of tears. The Schirmer II test measures basic tear secretion and is used to evaluate the accessory glands of Krause and Wolfring. The Schirmer test is performed by instilling a topical anesthetic before insertion of filter paper. The topical anesthetic inhibits reflex tearing of major lacrimal glands by the filter paper, allowing testing of the accessory glands. The Schirmer II test is performed by irritating the nostril with a cotton swab to stimulate tear production.

INDICATIONS

- Assess adequacy of tearing for contact lens comfort
- Assess suspected tearing deficiency

POTENTIAL DIAGNOSIS

Normal findings in
- 10 mm of moisture on test strip after 5 min. It may be slightly less than 10 mm in elderly patients.

Abnormal findings in
- Tearing deficiency related to aging, dry eye syndrome, or Sjögren's syndrome
- Tearing deficiency secondary to leukemia, lymphoma, or rheumatoid arthritis

CRITICAL FINDINGS: N/A

INTERFERING FACTORS

Factors that may impair the results of the examination
- Inability of the patient to remain still and cooperative during the test may interfere with the test results.
- Rubbing or squeezing the eyes may affect results.

NURSING IMPLICATIONS AND PROCEDURE

PRETEST:

- Positively identify the patient using at least two unique identifiers before providing care, treatment, or services.
- *Patient Teaching:* Inform the patient this procedure can assist in evaluating tear duct function.
- Obtain a history of the patient's complaints, including a list of known allergens, especially topical anesthetic eyedrops.

S

- Obtain a history of the patient's known or suspected vision loss; changes in visual acuity, including type and cause; use of glasses or contact lenses; eye conditions with treatment regimens; eye surgery; and other tests and procedures to assess and diagnose visual deficit.
- Obtain a history of the patient's symptoms and results of previously performed laboratory tests and diagnostic and surgical procedures.
- Obtain a list of the patient's current medications, including herbs, nutritional supplements, and nutraceuticals (see Appendix F).
- Instruct the patient to remove contact lenses or glasses, as appropriate.
- Instruct the patient regarding the importance of keeping the eyes open for the test.
- Review the procedure with the patient. Address concerns about pain and explain that no pain will be experienced during the test, but there may be moments of discomfort. Explain to the patient that some discomfort may be experienced after the test when the numbness wears off from anesthetic drops administered prior to the test. Inform the patient that the test is performed by a health-care provider (HCP) and takes about 15 min to complete.
- *Sensitivity to social and cultural issues,* as well as concern for modesty, is important in providing psychological support before, during, and after the procedure.
- There are no food, fluid, or medication restrictions unless by medical direction.

INTRATEST:

- Observe standard precautions, and follow the general guidelines in Appendix A. Positively identify the patient.
- Instruct the patient to cooperate fully and to follow directions. Ask the patient to remain still during the procedure because movement produces unreliable results.
- Seat the patient comfortably. Instruct the patient to look straight ahead, keeping the eyes open and unblinking.
- Instill topical anesthetic in each eye,

as ordered, and provide time for it to work. Topical anesthetic drops are placed in the eye with the patient looking up and the solution directed at the six o'clock position of the sclera (white of the eye) near the limbus (gray, semitransparent area of the eyeball where the cornea and sclera meet). Neither the dropper nor the bottle should touch the eyelashes. Insert a test strip in each eye. The strip should be folded over the midportion of both lower eyelids. Instruct the patient to gently close both eyes for approximately 5 minutes then remove the strips and measure the amount of moisture on the strips.

POST-TEST:

- A report of the results will be made available to the requesting HCP, who will discuss the results with the patient.
- Assess for corneal abrasion caused by patient rubbing the eye before topical anesthetic has worn off.
- Instruct the patient to avoid rubbing the eyes for 30 min after the procedure.
- If appropriate, instruct the patient not to reinsert contact lenses for 2 hr.
- Recognize anxiety related to test results, and be supportive of pain related to decreased lacrimation or inflammation. Discuss the implications of abnormal test results on the patient's lifestyle. Provide teaching and information regarding the clinical implications of the test results, as appropriate. Provide contact information, if desired, for a general patient education Web site on the topic of eye care (e.g., www.allaboutvision.com).
- Reinforce information given by the patient's HCP regarding further testing, treatment, or referral to another HCP. Answer any questions or address any concerns voiced by the patient or family.
- Instruct the patient in the use of any ordered medications. Explain the importance of adhering to the therapy regimen. As appropriate, instruct the patient in significant side effects and

systemic reactions associated with the prescribed medication. Encourage him or her to review corresponding literature provided by a pharmacist. Depending on the results of this procedure, additional testing may be performed to evaluate or monitor progression of the disease process and determine the need for a change in therapy. Evaluate test results in relation to the patient's symptoms and other tests performed.

RELATED MONOGRAPHS:

Related tests include antibodies ANA, refraction, rheumatoid factor, and slit-lamp biomicroscopy.

Refer to the Ocular System table at the end of the book for related tests by body system.

Semen Analysis

SYNONYM/ACRONYM: N/A.

COMMON USE: To assess for male infertility related to disorders such as obstruction, testicular failure, and atrophy.

SPECIMEN: Semen from ejaculate specimen collected in a clean, dry, glass container known to be free of detergent. The specimen container should be kept at body temperature (37°C) during transportation.

NORMAL FINDINGS: (Method: Macroscopic and microscopic examination)

Test	Normal Result
Volume	2–5 mL
Color	White or opaque
Appearance	Viscous (pours in droplets, not clumps or strings)
Clotting and liquefaction	Complete in 15–20 min, rarely over 60 min
pH	7.2–8
Sperm count	Greater than 15 million/mL
Total sperm count	Greater than 39 million/ejaculate
Motility	At least 40% at 60 min
Vitality (membrane intact)	At least 58%
Morphology	Greater than 25–30% normal oval-headed forms

The number of normal sperm is calculated by multiplying the total sperm count by the percentage of normal forms.

DESCRIPTION: Semen analysis is a valid measure of overall male fertility. Semen contains a combination of elements produced by various parts of the male reproductive system. Spermatozoa are produced in the testes and account for only a small volume of seminal fluid. Fructose and other nutrients are provided by fluid produced in the seminal vesicles. The prostate gland provides acid phosphatase and other enzymes required for coagulation and liquefaction of semen. Sperm motility depends on the presence of a sufficient level of ionized calcium. If the specimen has an abnormal appearance (e.g., bloody, oddly colored, turbid), the patient may have an infection. Specimens can be tested with a leukocyte esterase strip to detect the presence of white blood cells.

INDICATIONS

- Assist in the diagnosis of azoospermia and oligospermia
- Evaluate infertility
- Evaluate effectiveness of vasectomy
- Evaluate the effectiveness of vasectomy reversal
- Support or disprove sterility in paternity suit

POTENTIAL DIAGNOSIS

There is marked intraindividual variation in sperm count. Indications of suboptimal fertility should be investigated by serial analysis of two to three samples collected over several months. If abnormal results are obtained, additional testing may be requested.

Abnormality	Test Ordered	Normal Result
Decreased count	Fructose	Present (greater than 150 mg/dL)
Decreased motility with clumping	Male antisperm antibodies	Absent
Normal semen analysis with infertility	Female antisperm antibodies	Absent

Increased in: N/A

Decreased in
- Hyperpyrexia *(unusual and abnormal elevation in body temperature may result in insufficient sperm production)*
- Infertility *(related to insufficient production of sperm)*
- Obstruction of ejaculatory system
- Orchitis *(insufficient sperm production usually related to viral infection, rarely bacterial infection)*
- Postvasectomy period *(related to obstruction of the vas deferens)*
- Primary and secondary testicular failure *(congenital, as in Klinefelter's syndrome, or acquired via infection)*

- Testicular atrophy (e.g., recovery from mumps)
- Varicocele *(abnormal enlargement of the blood vessels in the scrotal area eventually damages testicular tissue and affects sperm production)*

CRITICAL FINDINGS: N/A

INTERFERING FACTORS

- Drugs and substances that may decrease sperm count include arsenic, azathioprine, cannabis, cimetidine, cocaine, cyclophosphamide, estrogens, fluoxymesterone, ketoconazole, lead, methotrexate, methyltestosterone, nitrofurantoin, nitrogen mustard, procarbazine, sulfa-salazine, and vincristine.

- Testicular radiation may decrease sperm counts.
- Cigarette smoking is associated with decreased production of semen.
- Caffeine consumption is associated with increased sperm density and number of abnormal forms.
- Delays in transporting the specimen and failure to keep the specimen warm during transportation are the most common reasons for specimen rejection.

NURSING IMPLICATIONS AND PROCEDURE

PRETEST:

Positively identify the patient using at least two unique identifiers before providing care, treatment, or services.

Patient Teaching: Inform the patient this test can assess for infertility.

Obtain a history of the patient's complaints, including a list of known allergens, especially allergies or sensitivities to latex.

Obtain a history of the patient's immune and reproductive systems, symptoms, and results of previously performed laboratory tests and diagnostic and surgical procedures.

Obtain a list of the patient's current medications, including herbs, nutritional supplements, and nutraceuticals (see Appendix F).

Note any recent procedures that can interfere with test results.

Review the procedure with the patient. Instruct the patient to refrain from any sexual activity for 3 days before specimen collection. Instruct the patient to bring the specimen to the laboratory within 30 to 60 min of collection and to keep the specimen warm (close to body temperature) during transportation. The requesting health-care provider (HCP) usually provides the patient with instructions for specimen collection. Address concerns about pain and explain that there should be no discomfort during the procedure.

Sensitivity to social and cultural issues, as well as concern for modesty, is important in providing psychological support before, during, and after the procedure.

There are no food, fluid, or medication restrictions unless by medical direction.

INTRATEST:

Instruct the patient to cooperate fully and to follow directions.

Observe standard precautions, and follow the general guidelines in Appendix A. Positively identify the patient, and label the appropriate specimen container with the corresponding patient demographics, initials of the person collecting the specimen, date, and time of collection.

Ejaculated Specimen

Ideally, the specimen is obtained by masturbation in a private location close to the laboratory. In cases in which the patient expresses psychological or religious concerns about masturbation, the specimen can be obtained during coitus interruptus, through the use of a condom, or through postcoital collection of samples from the cervical canal and vagina of the patient's sexual partner. The patient should be warned about the possible loss of the sperm-rich portion of the sample if coitus interruptus is the collection approach. If a condom is used, the patient must be instructed to carefully wash and dry the condom completely before use to prevent contamination of the specimen with spermicides.

Cervical Vaginal Specimen

Assist the patient's partner to the lithotomy position on the examination table. A speculum is inserted, and the specimen is obtained by direct smear or aspiration of saline lavage.

Specimens Collected From Skin or Clothing

Dried semen may be collected by sponging the skin with a gauze soaked in saline or by soaking the material in a saline solution.

S

General
▸ Promptly transport the specimen to the laboratory for processing and analysis.

POST-TEST:

▸ A report of the results will be made available to the requesting HCP, who will discuss the results with the patient.
▸ Recognize anxiety related to test results. Provide a supportive, nonjudgmental environment when assisting a patient through the process of fertility testing. Discuss the implications of abnormal test results on the patient's lifestyle. Provide teaching and information regarding the clinical implications of the test results, as appropriate. Encourage the patient or family to seek counseling and other support services if concerned with infertility.
▸ Reinforce information given by the patient's HCP regarding further testing, treatment, or referral to another HCP. Answer any questions or address any concerns voiced by the patient or family.
▸ Depending on the results of this procedure, additional testing may be performed to evaluate or monitor progression of the disease process and determine the need for a change in therapy. Evaluate test results in relation to the patient's symptoms and other tests performed.

RELATED MONOGRAPHS:

▸ Related tests include antisperm antibodies, cancer antigens, *Chlamydia* group antibodies, estradiol, FSH, hysterosalpingography, laparoscopy gynecologic, LH, testosterone, and US scrotal.
▸ Refer to the Immune and Reproductive systems tables at the end of the book for related tests by body system.

Sialography

SYNONYM/ACRONYM: Salivary gland studies.

COMMON USE: To assess parotid, submaxillary, sublingual, and submandibular ducts for structure, tumors, and inflammation related to pain, swelling, and tenderness.

AREA OF APPLICATION: Base of the tongue, mandible, parotid gland, submandibular gland, sublingual gland.

CONTRAST: Water-soluble iodinated contrast medium.

DESCRIPTION: Sialography is the radiographic visualization of the salivary glands and ducts. These glands secrete saliva into the mouth, and there are three pairs of salivary glands: the parotid, the submandibular, and the sublingual. Sialography involves the introduction of a water-soluble contrast agent into the orifices of the salivary gland ducts with a small cannula, followed by a series of radiographic images. The evaluation of the salivary glands is usually done with computed tomography or magnetic resonance imaging; however, sialography is the method of choice when a definite diagnosis is required for pathology such as sialadenitis (inflammation of the salivary glands) or if the oral component of Sjögren's syndrome is a concern.

INDICATIONS

- Evaluate the presence of calculi in the salivary glands
- Evaluate the presence of tumors in the salivary glands
- Evaluate narrowing of the salivary ducts

POTENTIAL DIAGNOSIS

Normal findings in

- Normal salivary ducts with no indication of gland abnormalities

Abnormal findings in

- Calculi
- Fistulas
- Mixed parotid tumors
- Sialectasia (dilation of a duct)
- Strictures of the ducts

CRITICAL FINDINGS: N/A

INTERFERING FACTORS

This procedure is contraindicated for

- Patients with allergies to shellfish and iodinated dye. The contrast medium used may cause life-threatening allergic reaction. Patients with a known hypersensitivity to the contrast medium may benefit from premedication with cortico-steroids or the use of nonionic contrast medium.

Factors that may impair clear imaging

- Inability of the patient to cooperate or remain still during the test because of age, significant pain, or mental status may interfere with the test results.

Other considerations

- Risks associated with radiation overexposure can result from frequent x-ray procedures. Personnel in the room with the patient should wear a protective lead apron, stand behind a shield, or leave the area while the examination is being done. Personnel working in the examination area should wear badges to record the level of radiation exposure.

NURSING IMPLICATIONS AND PROCEDURE

PRETEST:

▶ Positively identify the patient using at least two unique identifiers before providing care, treatment, or services.

▶ *Patient Teaching:* Inform the patient that this procedure can assist in assessing duct glands in the neck and mouth.

▶ Obtain a history of the patient's complaints, including a list of known allergens, especially allergies or sensitivities to latex, iodine, seafood, contrast medium, anesthetics, or dyes.

▶ Obtain a history of the patient's endocrine system, symptoms, and results of previously performed laboratory tests and diagnostic and surgical procedures.

▶ Record the date of last menstrual period and determine the possibility of pregnancy in perimenopausal women.

▶ Obtain a list of the patient's current medications, including anticoagulants, aspirin and other salicylates, herbs, nutritional supplements, and nutraceuticals (see Appendix F).

▶ Instruct the patient to remove dentures or removable bridgework prior to examination.

▶ Review the procedure with the patient. Inform the patient that the procedure is usually done with the patient awake and laying on a table. Address concerns about pain and explain that the patient may be asked to suck on a lemon slice to dilate the salivary orifice, and a local anesthetic spray or liquid may be applied to the throat to ease with insertion of the cannula. Inform the patient that the procedure is performed in a radiology department by a health-care provider (HCP) specializing in this procedure, with support staff, and takes approximately 15 to 30 min.

▶ *Sensitivity to social and cultural issues,* as well as concern for modesty, is

S

important in providing psychological support before, during, and after the procedure.

There are no food, fluid, or medication restrictions unless by medical direction.

Make sure a written and informed consent has been signed prior to the procedure and before administering any medications.

INTRATEST:

Observe standard precautions, and follow the general guidelines in Appendix A. Positively identify the patient.

Ensure that the patient has removed dentures and removable bridgework prior to the procedure.

If the patient has a history of severe allergic reactions to any substance or drug, administer ordered prophylactic steroids or antihistamines before the procedure. Use nonionic contrast medium for the procedure.

Have emergency equipment readily available.

Instruct the patient to cooperate fully and to follow directions. Instruct the patient to remain still throughout the procedure because movement produces unreliable results.

Place the patient in the supine position on an examination table. Instill ordered topical anesthetic in the throat, as ordered, and allow time for it to work.

The salivary duct is located and dilated. Following insertion of the cannula, the contrast medium is injected, and a series of images is taken. Delayed images may be taken to examine the ducts in cases of ductal obstruction.

Ask the patient to inhale deeply and hold his or her breath while the x-ray images are taken, and then to exhale after the images are taken.

Monitor the patient for complications related to the procedure (e.g., allergic reaction, anaphylaxis, bronchospasm).

Remove the needle or cannula.

Observe/assess the needle/cannula insertion site for bleeding or inflammation.

POST-TEST:

A report of the results will be made available to the requesting HCP, who will discuss the results with the patient.

Instruct the patient to wait until the numbness in the throat wears off before attempting to eat or drink following the procedure.

Observe for delayed allergic reactions, such as rash, urticaria, tachycardia, hyperpnea, hypertension, palpitations, nausea, or vomiting.

Instruct the patient to immediately report symptoms such as fast heart rate, difficulty breathing, skin rash, itching, chest pain, persistent right shoulder pain, or abdominal pain. Immediately report symptoms to the appropriate HCP.

Observe/assess the needle/cannula insertion site for bleeding or inflammation.

Instruct the patient in the care and assessment of the site.

Instruct the patient to apply cold compresses to the puncture site as needed to reduce discomfort or edema.

Recognize anxiety related to test results. Discuss the implications of abnormal test results on the patient's lifestyle. Provide teaching and information regarding the clinical implications of the test results, as appropriate.

Reinforce information given by the patient's HCP regarding further testing, treatment, or referral to another HCP. Answer any questions or address any concerns voiced by the patient or family.

Depending on the results of this procedure, additional testing may be needed to evaluate or monitor progression of the disease process and determine the need for a change in therapy. Evaluate test results in relation to the patient's symptoms and other tests performed.

RELATED MONOGRAPHS:

Related tests include CT brain, MRI brain, and radiography bone.

Refer to the Endocrine System table at the end of the book for related tests by body system.

Sickle Cell Screen

SYNONYM/ACRONYM: Sickle cell test.

COMMON USE: To assess for hemoglobin S to assist in diagnosing sickle cell anemia.

SPECIMEN: Whole blood (1 mL) collected in a lavender-top (EDTA) tube.

NORMAL FINDINGS: (Method: Hemoglobin high-salt solubility) Negative.

DESCRIPTION: The sickle cell screen is one of several screening tests for a group of hereditary hemoglobinopathies. The test is positive in the presence of rare sickling hemoglobin (Hgb) variants such as Hgb S and Hgb C Harlem. Electrophoresis and high-performance liquid chromatography as well as molecular genetics testing for beta-globin mutations can also be used to identify Hgb S. Hgb S results from an amino acid substitution during Hgb synthesis whereby valine replaces glutamic acid. Hemoglobin C Harlem results from the substitution of lysine for glutamic acid. Individuals with sickle cell disease have chronic anemia because the abnormal Hgb is unable to carry oxygen. The red blood cells of affected individuals are also abnormal in shape, resembling a crescent or sickle rather than the normal disk shape. This abnormality, combined with cell-wall rigidity, prevents the cells from passing through smaller blood vessels. Blockages in blood vessels result in hypoxia, damage, and pain. Individuals with the sickle cell trait do not have the clinical manifestations of the disease but may pass the disease on to children if the other parent has the trait (or the disease) as well.

INDICATIONS
- Detect sickled red blood cells
- Evaluate hemolytic anemias

POTENTIAL DIAGNOSIS

Positive findings in
Deoxygenated Hgb S is insoluble in the presence of a high-salt solution and will form a cloudy turbid suspension when present.

- Combination of Hgb S with other hemoglobinopathies
- Hgb C Harlem anemia
- Sickle cell anemia
- Sickle cell trait
- Thalassemias

Negative findings in: N/A

CRITICAL FINDINGS: N/A

INTERFERING FACTORS
- Drugs that may increase sickle cells in vitro include prostaglandins.
- A positive test does not distinguish between the sickle trait and sickle cell anemia; to make this determination, follow-up testing by Hgb electrophoresis should be performed.
- False-negative results may occur in children younger than 3 mo of age.
- False-negative results may occur in patients who have received a recent blood transfusion before specimen collection, as a result of the dilutional effect.

S

- False-positive results may occur in patients without the trait or disease who have received a blood transfusion from a sickle cell–positive donor; this effect can last for 4 mo after the transfusion.
- Test results are unreliable if the patient has pernicious anemia or polycythemia.

NURSING IMPLICATIONS AND PROCEDURE

PRETEST:

▶ Positively identify the patient using at least two unique identifiers before providing care, treatment, or services.
▶ *Patient Teaching:* Inform the patient this test can assist in diagnosing anemia.
▶ Obtain a history of the patient's complaints, including a list of known allergens, especially allergies or sensitivities to latex.
▶ Obtain a history of the patient's hematopoietic system, symptoms, and results of previously performed laboratory tests and diagnostic and surgical procedures.
▶ Note any recent procedures that can interfere with test results.
▶ Obtain a list of the patient's current medications, including herbs, nutritional supplements, and nutraceuticals (see Appendix F).
▶ Review the procedure with the patient. Inform the patient that specimen collection takes approximately 5 to 10 min. Address concerns about pain and explain that there may be some discomfort during the venipuncture.
▶ *Sensitivity to social and cultural issues,* as well as concern for modesty, is important in providing psychological support before, during, and after the procedure.
▶ There are no food, fluid, or medication restrictions unless by medical direction.

INTRATEST:

▶ If the patient has a history of allergic reaction to latex, avoid the use of equipment containing latex.

▶ Instruct the patient to cooperate fully and to follow directions. Direct the patient to breathe normally and to avoid unnecessary movement.
▶ Observe standard precautions, and follow the general guidelines in Appendix A. Positively identify the patient, and label the appropriate specimen container with the corresponding patient demographics, initials of the person collecting the specimen, date, and time of collection. Perform a venipuncture.
▶ Remove the needle and apply direct pressure with dry gauze to stop bleeding. Observe/assess venipuncture site for bleeding or hematoma formation and secure gauze with adhesive bandage.
▶ Promptly transport the specimen to the laboratory for processing and analysis.

POST-TEST:

▶ A report of the results will be made available to the requesting health-care provider (HCP), who will discuss the results with the patient.
▶ Advise the patient with sickle cell disease to avoid situations in which hypoxia may occur, such as strenuous exercise, staying at high altitudes, or traveling in an unpressurized aircraft. Obstetric and surgical patients with sickle cell anemia are at risk for hypoxia and therefore require close observation: Obstetric patients are at risk for hypoxia during the stress of labor and delivery, and surgical patients may become hypoxic while under general anesthesia.
▶ Recognize anxiety related to test results, and offer support, as appropriate. Discuss the implications of abnormal test results on the patient's lifestyle. Provide teaching and information regarding the clinical implications of the test results, as appropriate. Educate the patient regarding access to counseling services (www.sicklecelldisease.org).
▶ Reinforce information given by the patient's HCP regarding further testing, treatment, or referral to another HCP. Inform the patient that further testing may be indicated if results are positive.

Answer any questions or address any concerns voiced by the patient or family. Depending on the results of this procedure, additional testing may be performed to evaluate or monitor progression of the disease process and determine the need for a change in therapy. Evaluate test results in relation to the patient's symptoms and other tests performed.

RELATED MONOGRAPHS:

▶ Related tests include biopsy bone marrow, CBC, CBC RBC morphology, CBC RBC indices, ESR, Hgb electrophoresis, hemosiderin, LAP, MRI musculoskeletal, newborn screening, RBC cholinesterase, and US spleen.

▶ Refer to the Hematopoietic System table at the end of the book for related tests by body system.

Slit-Lamp Biomicroscopy

SYNONYM/ACRONYM: Slit-lamp examination.

COMMON USE: To detect abnormalities in the external and anterior eye structures to assist in diagnosing disorders such as corneal injury, hemorrhage, ulcers, and abrasion.

AREA OF APPLICATION: Eyes.

CONTRAST: N/A.

DESCRIPTION: This noninvasive procedure is used to visualize the anterior portion of the eye and its parts, including the eyelids and eyelashes, sclera, conjunctiva, cornea, iris, lens, and anterior chamber, and to detect pathology of any of these areas of the eyes. The slit lamp has a binocular microscope and light source that can be adjusted to examine the fluid, tissues, and structures of the eyes. Special attachments to the slit lamp are used for special studies and more detailed views of specific areas. Dilating drops or mydriatics may be used to enlarge the pupil in order to allow the examiner to see the eye in greater detail. Mydriatics work either by temporarily paralyzing the muscle that makes the pupil smaller or by stimulating the iris dilator muscle. Blue or hazel eyes dilate faster than brown eyes.

INDICATIONS

- Detect conjunctival and corneal injuries by foreign bodies and determine if ocular penetration or anterior chamber hemorrhage is present
- Detect corneal abrasions, ulcers, or abnormal curvatures (keratoconus)
- Detect deficiency in tear formation indicative of lacrimal dysfunction causing dry eye disease that can lead to corneal erosions or infection
- Detect lens opacities indicative of cataract formation
- Determine the presence of blepharitis, conjunctivitis, hordeolum, entropion, ectropion, trachoma, scleritis, and iritis
- Evaluate the fit of contact lenses

S

POTENTIAL DIAGNOSIS

Normal findings in

- Normal anterior tissues and structures of the eyes

Abnormal findings in

- Blepharitis
- Conjunctivitis
- Corneal abrasions
- Corneal ulcers
- Ectropion
- Entropion
- Hordeolum
- Iritis
- Keratoconus (abnormal curvatures)
- Lens opacities
- Scleritis
- Trachoma

CRITICAL FINDINGS: N/A

INTERFERING FACTORS

- Patients with narrow-angle glaucoma if pupil dilation is performed, because dilation can initiate a severe and sight-threatening open-angle attack.
- Patients with allergies to mydriatics if pupil dilation using mydriatics is performed.
- Inability of the patient to cooperate and remain still during the procedure because of age, significant pain, or mental status may interfere with the test results.
- Failure to follow medication restrictions before the procedure may cause the procedure to be canceled or repeated.

NURSING IMPLICATIONS AND PROCEDURE

PRETEST:

▸ Positively identify the patient using at least two unique identifiers before providing care, treatment, or services.

▸ *Patient Teaching:* Inform the patient this procedure can assist in evaluating the structures of the eye.

▸ Obtain a history of the patient's complaints, including a list of known allergens, especially mydriatics if dilation is to be performed.

▸ Obtain a history of the patient's known or suspected vision loss, changes in visual acuity, including type and cause; use of glasses or contact lenses; eye conditions with treatment regimens; eye surgery; and other tests and procedures to assess and diagnose visual deficit.

▸ Obtain a history of the patient's symptoms and results of previously performed laboratory tests and diagnostic and surgical procedures.

▸ Obtain a list of the patient's current medications, including herbs, nutritional supplements, and nutraceuticals (see Appendix F).

▸ Instruct the patient to remove contact lenses or glasses, as appropriate, unless the study is being done to check the fit and effectiveness of the contact lenses. Instruct the patient regarding the importance of keeping the eyes open for the test.

▸ Review the procedure with the patient. Address concerns about pain and explain that mydriatics, if used, may cause blurred vision and sensitivity to light. There may also be a brief stinging sensation when the drop is put in the eye. Inform the patient that a healthcare provider (HCP) performs the test in a quiet, darkened room, and that to evaluate both eyes, the test can take up 30 min (including time for the pupils to dilate before the test is actually performed).

▸ *Sensitivity to social and cultural issues,* as well as concern for modesty, is important in providing psychological support before, during, and after the procedure.

▸ There are no food or fluid restrictions unless by medical direction.

▸ The patient should withhold eye medications (particularly miotic eye drops which may constrict the pupil preventing a clear view of the fundus and mydriatic eyedrops in order to avoid instigation of an acute open angle attack in patients with narrow angle glaucoma) for at least 1 day prior to the procedure.

S

Ensure that the patient understands that he or she must refrain from driving until the pupils return to normal (about 4 hr) after the test and has made arrangements to have someone else be responsible for transportation after the test.

INTRATEST:

Observe standard precautions, and follow the general guidelines in Appendix A. Positively identify the patient.

Ensure that the patient has complied with medication restrictions and pre-testing preparations; assure that eye medications, especially mydriatics, have been restricted for at least 1 day prior to the procedure.

Instruct the patient to cooperate fully and to follow directions. Ask the patient to remain still during the procedure because movement produces unreliable results.

Seat the patient comfortably. If dilation is to be performed, administer the ordered mydriatic to each eye and repeat in 5 to 15 min. Drops are placed in the eye with the patient looking up and the solution directed at the six o'clock position of the sclera (white of the eye) near the limbus (gray, semitransparent area of the eyeball where the cornea and sclera meet). Neither dropper nor bottle should touch the eyelashes.

Ask the patient to place the chin in the chin rest and gently press the forehead against the support bar.

The HCP places the slit lamp in front of the patient's eyes in line with the examiner's eyes. The external structures of the eyes are inspected with the special bright light and microscope of the slit lamp. The light is then directed into the patient's eyes to inspect the anterior fluids and structures and is adjusted for shape, intensity, and depth needed to visualize these areas. Magnification of the microscope is also adjusted to optimize visualization of the eye structures.

Special attachments and procedures can also be used to obtain further diagnostic information about the eyes. These may include, for example, a camera to photograph specific parts,

gonioscopy to determine anterior chamber closure, and a cobalt-blue filter to detect minute corneal scratches, breaks, and abrasions with corneal staining.

POST-TEST:

A report of the results will be made available to the requesting HCP, who will discuss the results with the patient.

Instruct the patient to resume usual medications, as directed by the HCP.

Recognize anxiety related to test results, and encourage the family to recognize and be supportive of impaired activity related to vision loss, anticipated loss of driving privileges, or the possibility of requiring corrective lenses (self-image). Discuss the implications of the abnormal test results on the patient's lifestyle. Provide contact information, if desired, for a general patient education Web site on the topic of eye care (e.g., www.allaboutvision.com).

Reinforce information given by the patient's HCP regarding further testing, treatment, or referral to another HCP. Inform the patient that visual acuity and responses to light may change. Suggest that the patient wear dark glasses after the test until the pupils return to normal size. Answer any questions or address any concerns voiced by the patient or family.

Depending on the results of this procedure, additional testing may be performed to evaluate or monitor progression of the disease process and determine the need for a change in therapy. Evaluate test results in relation to the patient's symptoms and other tests performed.

RELATED MONOGRAPHS:

Related tests include color perception test, fluorescein angiography, gonioscopy, intraocular muscle function, intraocular pressure, nerve fiber analysis, refraction, Schirmer tear test, and visual field testing.

Refer to the Ocular System table at the end of the book for related tests by body system.

Sodium, Blood

SYNONYM/ACRONYM: Serum Na$^+$.

COMMON USE: To assess electrolyte balance related to hydration levels and disorders such as diarrhea and vomiting and to monitor the effect of diuretic use.

SPECIMEN: Serum (1 mL) collected in a red- or tiger-top tube. Plasma (1 mL) collected in a green-top (heparin) tube is also acceptable.

NORMAL FINDINGS: (Method: Ion-selective electrode)

Age	Conventional Units	SI Units (Conventional Units × 1)
Cord	126–166 mEq/L	126–166 mmol/L
1–12 hr	124–156 mEq/L	124–156 mmol/L
12–24 hr	132–159 mEq/L	132–159 mmol/L
24–48 hr	134–160 mEq/L	134–160 mmol/L
48–72 hr	139–162 mEq/L	139–162 mmol/L
Newborn	135–145 mEq/L	135–145 mmol/L
7 d–1 mo	134–144 mEq/L	134–144 mmol/L
2 mo–5 mo	134–142 mEq/L	134–142 mmol/L
6 mo–1 yr	133–142 mEq/L	133–142 mmol/L
Child-Adult–older adult	135–145 mEq/L	135–145 mmol/L

Note: Older adults are at increased risk for both hypernatremia and hyponatremia. Diminished thirst, illness, and lack of mobility are common causes for hypernatremia in older adults. There are multiple causes of hyponatremia in older adults, but the most common factor may be related to the use of thiazide diuretics.

DESCRIPTION: Sodium is the most abundant cation in the extracellular fluid and, together with the accompanying chloride and bicarbonate anions, accounts for 92% of serum osmolality. Sodium plays a major role in maintaining homeostasis in a variety of ways, including maintaining the osmotic pressure of extracellular fluid, regulating renal retention and excretion of water, maintaining acid-base balance, regulating potassium and chloride levels, stimulating neuromuscular reactions, and maintaining systemic blood pressure. *Hypernatremia* (elevated sodium level) occurs when there is excessive water loss or abnormal retention of sodium. *Hyponatremia* (low sodium level) occurs when there is inadequate sodium retention or inadequate intake.

INDICATIONS

• Determine whole-body stores of sodium, because the ion is predominantly extracellular

- Monitor the effectiveness of drug therapy, especially diuretics, on serum sodium levels

POTENTIAL DIAGNOSIS

Increased in

- Azotemia *(related to increased renal retention)*
- Burns *(hemoconcentration related to excessive loss of free water)*
- Cushing's disease
- Dehydration
- Diabetes *(dehydration related to frequent urination)*
- Diarrhea *(related to water loss in excess of salt loss)*
- Excessive intake
- Excessive saline therapy *(related to administration of IV fluids)*
- Excessive sweating *(related to loss of free water, which can cause hemoconcentration)*
- Fever *(related to loss of free water through sweating)*
- Hyperaldosteronism *(related to excessive production of aldosterone, which increases renal absorption of sodium and increases blood levels)*
- Lactic acidosis *(related to diabetes)*
- Nasogastric feeding with inadequate fluid *(related to dehydration and hemoconcentration)*
- Vomiting *(related to dehydration)*

Decreased in

- Central nervous system disease
- Congestive heart failure *(diminished renal blood flow due to reduced cardiac capacity decreases urinary excretion and increases blood sodium levels)*
- Cystic fibrosis *(related to loss from chronic diarrhea; poor intestinal absorption)*
- Excessive antidiuretic hormone production *(related to excessive loss through renal excretion)*
- Excessive use of diuretics *(related to excessive loss through renal excretion; renal absorption is blocked)*
- Hepatic failure *(hemodilution related to fluid retention)*
- Hypoproteinemia *(related to fluid retention)*
- Insufficient intake
- IV glucose infusion *(hypertonic glucose draws water into extracellular fluid and sodium is diluted)*
- Mineralocorticoid deficiency (Addison's disease) *(related to inadequate production of aldosterone, which results in decreased absorption by the kidneys)*
- Nephrotic syndrome *(related to decreased ability of renal tubules to reabsorb sodium)*

CRITICAL FINDINGS

- *Hyponatremia:* Less than 120 mmol/L (SI: Less than 120 mmol/L)
- *Hypernatremia:* Greater than 160 mmol/L (SI: Greater than 160 mmol/L)

Note and immediately report to the health-care provider (HCP) any critically increased or decreased values and related symptoms especially fluid imbalance. Timely notification of critical values for lab or diagnostic studies is a role expectation of the professional nurse. Notification processes will vary among facilities. Upon receipt of the critical value the information should be read back to the caller to verify accuracy. Most policies require immediate notification of the primary HCP, hospitalist, or on-call HCP. Reported information includes the patient's name, unique identifiers, critical value, name of the person giving the report, and name of the person receiving the report. Documentation of notification should be made in the medical record with the name of the HCP notified, time and date of notification, and any orders received. Any delay in a timely report of a critical value may require completion of a notification form with review by Risk Management.

Signs and symptoms of hyponatremia include confusion, irritability, convulsions, tachycardia, nausea, vomiting, and loss of consciousness. Possible interventions include maintenance of airway, monitoring for convulsions, fluid restriction, and performance of hourly neurological checks. Administration of saline for replacement requires close attention to serum and urine osmolality.

Signs and symptoms of hypernatremia include restlessness, intense thirst, weakness, swollen tongue, seizures, and coma. Possible interventions include treatment of the underlying cause of water loss or sodium excess, which includes sodium restriction and administration of diuretics combined with IV solutions of 5% dextrose in water (D_5W).

INTERFERING FACTORS

- Drugs that may increase serum sodium levels include anabolic steroids, angiotensin, bicarbonate, carbenoxolone, cisplatin, corticotropin, cortisone, gamma globulin, and mannitol.
- Drugs that may decrease serum sodium levels include amphotericin B, bicarbonate, cathartics (excessive use), chlorpropamide, chlorthalidone, diuretics, ethacrynic acid, fluoxetine, furosemide, laxatives (excessive use), methyclothiazide, metolazone, nicardipine, quinethazone, theophylline (IV infusion), thiazides, and triamterene.
- Specimens should never be collected above an IV line because of the potential for dilution when the specimen and the IV solution combine in the collection container, falsely decreasing the result. There is also the potential of contaminating the sample with the substance of interest, if it is present in the IV solution, falsely increasing the result.

NURSING IMPLICATIONS AND PROCEDURE

PRETEST:

▶ Positively identify the patient using at least two unique identifiers before providing care, treatment, or services.
▶ *Patient Teaching:* Inform the patient this test can assist in evaluating electrolyte balance.
▶ Obtain a history of the patient's complaints, including a list of known allergens, especially allergies or sensitivities to latex.
▶ Obtain a history of the patient's cardiovascular, endocrine, and genitourinary systems; symptoms; and results of previously performed laboratory tests and diagnostic and surgical procedures.
▶ Obtain a list of the patient's current medications, including herbs, nutritional supplements, and nutraceuticals (see Appendix F).
▶ Review the procedure with the patient. Inform the patient that specimen collection takes approximately 5 to 10 min. Address concerns about pain and explain that there may be some discomfort during the venipuncture.
▶ *Sensitivity to social and cultural issues,* as well as concern for modesty, is important in providing psychological support before, during, and after the procedure.
▶ There are no food, fluid, or medication restrictions unless by medical direction.

INTRATEST:

▶ If the patient has a history of allergic reaction to latex, avoid the use of equipment containing latex.
▶ Instruct the patient to cooperate fully and to follow directions. Direct the patient to breathe normally and to avoid unnecessary movement.
▶ Observe standard precautions, and follow the general guidelines in Appendix A. Positively identify the patient, and label the appropriate specimen container with the corresponding patient demographics, initials of the person collecting the specimen, date, and time of collection. Perform a venipuncture.

▶ Remove the needle and apply direct pressure with dry gauze to stop bleeding. Observe/assess venipuncture site for bleeding or hematoma formation and secure gauze with adhesive bandage.

▶ Promptly transport the specimen to the laboratory for processing and analysis.

POST-TEST:

▶ A report of the results will be made available to the requesting HCP, who will discuss the results with the patient.

▶ *Nutritional Considerations:* Evaluate the patient for signs and symptoms of dehydration. Decreased skin turgor, dry mouth, and multiple longitudinal furrows in the tongue are symptoms of dehydration. Dehydration is a significant and common finding in geriatric and other patients in whom renal function has deteriorated. The Institute of Medicine's Food and Nutrition Board suggests 3.7 L for adult males and 2.7 L for adult females age 19 to 70 yr as an adequate daily intake goal of total water; 3 L/d for pregnant females age 14 to 50 yr; 3.8 L/d for lactating females age 14 to 50 yr; 3.3 L/d for male and 2.3 L/d for female children age 14 to 18 yr; 2.4 L/d for male and 2.1 L/d for female children age 9 to 13 yr; 1.7 L/d for children age 4 to 8 yr; 1.3 L/d for children age 1 to 3 yr; 0.8 L/d for children age 7 to 12 mo; and 0.7 L/d (assumed to be from human milk) for children 0 to 6 mo. Reprinted with permission from the National Academies Press, copyright 2013, National Academy of Sciences.

▶ *Nutritional Considerations:* If appropriate, educate patients with low sodium levels that the major source of dietary sodium is found in table salt. Many foods, such as milk and other dairy products, are also good sources of dietary sodium. Most other dietary sodium is available through the consumption of processed foods. Patients on low-sodium diets should be advised to avoid beverages such as colas, ginger ale, sports drinks, lemon-lime sodas, and root beer. Many over-the-counter medications, including antacids, laxatives, analgesics, sedatives, and antitussives, contain significant amounts of sodium. The best advice is to emphasize the importance of reading all food, beverage, and medicine labels. The Institute of Medicine's Food and Nutrition Board suggests 1,200 mg as an adequate daily intake goal of dietary sodium for adult males and females greater than age 70 yr; 1,300 mg/d for adult males and females age 51 to 70 yr; 1,500 mg/d for adult males and females age 19 to 50 yr; 1,500 mg/d for pregnant and lactating females under age 18 through 50 yr; 1,500 mg/d for children age 9 to 18 yr; 1,200 mg/d for children age 4 to 8 yr; 1,000 mg/d for children age 1 to 3 yr; 370 mg/d for children age 7 to 12 mo; and 120 mg/d for children age 0 to 6 mo. Reprinted with permission from the National Academies Press, copyright 2013, National Academy of Sciences.

▶ Reinforce information given by the patient's HCP regarding further testing, treatment, or referral to another HCP. Answer any questions or address any concerns voiced by the patient or family. Educate the patient regarding access to nutritional counseling services. Provide contact information, if desired, for the Institute of Medicine of the National Academies (www.iom.edu).

▶ Depending on the results of this procedure, additional testing may be performed to evaluate or monitor progression of the disease process and determine the need for a change in therapy. Evaluate test results in relation to the patient's symptoms and other tests performed.

RELATED MONOGRAPHS:

▶ Related tests include ACTH, aldosterone, anion gap, ANP, BNP, blood gases, BUN, calculus kidney stone panel, BUN, calcium, carbon dioxide, chloride, chloride sweat, cortisol, creatinine, DHEAS, echocardiography, glucose, insulin, ketones, lactic acid, lung perfusion scan, magnesium, osmolality, potassium, renin, US abdomen, urine sodium, and UA.

▶ Refer to the Cardiovascular, Endocrine, and Genitourinary systems tables at the end of the book for related tests by body system.

S

Sodium, Urine

SYNONYM/ACRONYM: Urine Na$^+$.

COMMON USE: To assist in evaluating for acute renal failure, acute oliguria, and to assist in the differential diagnosis of hyponatremia.

SPECIMEN: Urine (5 mL) from an unpreserved random or timed specimen collected in a clean plastic collection container.

NORMAL FINDINGS: (Method: Ion-selective electrode)

Age	Conventional Units	SI Units (Conventional Units × 1)
6–10 yr		
Male	41–115 mEq/24 hr	41–115 mmol/24 hr
Female	20–69 mEq/24 hr	20–69 mmol/24 hr
10–14 yr		
Male	63–177 mEq/24 hr	63–177 mmol/24 hr
Female	48–168 mEq/24 hr	48–168 mmol/24 hr
Adult–older adult	27–287 mEq/24 hr	27–287 mmol/24 hr

Values vary markedly depending on dietary intake and hydration state.

DESCRIPTION: Sodium balance is dependent on a number of influences in addition to dietary intake, including aldosterone, renin, and atrial natriuretic hormone levels. Regulating electrolyte balance is a major function of the kidneys. In normally functioning kidneys, urine sodium levels increase when serum levels are high and decrease when serum levels are low to maintain homeostasis. Analyzing these urinary levels can provide important clues to the functioning of the kidneys and other major organs. There is diurnal variation in excretion of sodium, with values lower at night. Urine sodium tests usually involve timed urine collections over a 12- or 24-hr period. Measurement of random specimens may also be requested.

INDICATIONS
- Determine potential cause of renal calculi
- Evaluate known or suspected endocrine disorder
- Evaluate known or suspected renal disease
- Evaluate malabsorption disorders

POTENTIAL DIAGNOSIS

Increased in
- Adrenal failure *(inadequate production of aldosterone results in decreased renal sodium absorption)*

S

- Dehydration *(related to decreased water excretion, which results in higher concentration of the urine constituents)*
- Diabetes *(increased glucose levels result in hypertonic extracellular fluid; dehydration from excessive urination can cause hemoconcentration)*
- Diuretic therapy *(medication causes sodium to be lost by the kidneys)*
- Excessive intake
- Renal tubular acidosis *(related to diabetes)*
- Salt-losing nephritis *(related to diminished capacity of the kidneys to reabsorb sodium)*
- Syndrome of inappropriate antidiuretic hormone secretion *(related to increased reabsorption of water by the kidneys, which results in higher concentration of the urine constituents)*

Decreased in

- Adrenal hyperfunction, such as Cushing's disease and hyperaldosteronism *(overproduction of aldosterone and other corticosteroids stimulate renal absorption of sodium decreasing urine sodium levels)*
- Congestive heart failure *(decreased renal blood flow related to diminished cardiac output)*
- Diarrhea *(related to decreased intestinal absorption; a decrease in blood levels will cause sodium to be retained by the kidneys and will lower urine sodium levels)*
- Excessive sweating *(excessive loss of sodium through sweat; sodium will be retained by the kidneys)*
- Extrarenal sodium loss with adequate hydration
- Insufficient intake
- Postoperative period (first 24 to 48 hr)
- Prerenal azotemia
- Sodium retention *(premenstrual)*

CRITICAL FINDINGS: N/A

INTERFERING FACTORS

- Drugs that may increase urine sodium levels include acetazolamide, acetylsalicylic acid, amiloride, ammonium chloride, azosemide, benzthiazide, bumetanide, calcitonin, chlorothiazide, clopamide, cyclothiazide, diapamide, dopamine, ethacrynic acid, furosemide, hydrocortisone, hydroflumethiazide, isosorbide, levodopa, mercurial diuretics, methyclothiazide, metolazone, polythiazide, quinethazone, spironolactone, sulfates, tetracycline, thiazides, torasemide, triamterene, trichlormethiazide, triflocin, verapamil, and vincristine.
- Drugs that may decrease urine sodium levels include aldosterone, anesthetics, angiotensin, corticosteroids, cortisone, etodolac, indomethacin, levarterenol, lithium, and propranolol.
- Sodium levels are subject to diurnal variation (output being lowest at night), which is why 24-hr collections are recommended.

NURSING IMPLICATIONS AND PROCEDURE

PRETEST:

- Positively identify the patient using at least two unique identifiers before providing care, treatment, or services.
- *Patient Teaching:* Inform the patient this test can assist in evaluating kidney function.
- Obtain a history of the patient's complaints, including a list of known allergens, especially allergies or sensitivities to latex.
- Obtain a history of the patient's endocrine and genitourinary systems, symptoms, and results of previously performed laboratory tests and diagnostic and surgical procedures.

▸ Obtain a list of the patient's current medications, including herbs, nutritional supplements, and nutraceuticals (see Appendix F).

▸ Review the procedure with the patient. Provide a nonmetallic urinal, bedpan, or toilet-mounted collection device. Address concerns about pain and explain that there should be no discomfort during the procedure.

▸ *Sensitivity to social and cultural issues,* as well as concern for modesty, is important in providing psychological support before, during, and after the procedure.

▸ Usually a 24-hr time frame for urine collection is ordered. Inform the patient that all urine must be saved during that 24-hr period. Instruct the patient not to void directly into the laboratory collection container. Instruct the patient to avoid defecating in the collection device and to keep toilet tissue out of the collection device to prevent contamination of the specimen. Place a sign in the bathroom to remind the patient to save all urine.

▸ Instruct the patient to void all urine into the collection device and then to pour the urine into the laboratory collection container. Alternatively, the specimen can be left in the collection device for a health care staff member to add to the laboratory collection container.

▸ There are no food, fluid, or medication restrictions unless by medical direction.

INTRATEST:

▸ If the patient has a history of allergic reaction to latex, avoid the use of equipment containing latex.

▸ Instruct the patient to cooperate fully and to follow directions.

▸ Observe standard precautions, and follow the general guidelines in Appendix A. Positively identify the patient, and label the appropriate specimen container with the corresponding patient demographics, initials of the person collecting the specimen, date, and time of collection.

Random Specimen (Collect in Early Morning)

Clean-Catch Specimen

▸ Instruct the male patient to (1) thoroughly wash his hands, (2) cleanse the meatus, (3) void a small amount into the toilet, and (4) void directly into the specimen container.

▸ Instruct the female patient to (1) thoroughly wash her hands; (2) cleanse the labia from front to back; (3) while keeping the labia separated, void a small amount into the toilet; and (4) without interrupting the urine stream, void directly into the specimen container.

Indwelling Catheter

▸ Put on gloves. Empty drainage tube of urine. It may be necessary to clamp off the catheter for 15 to 30 min before specimen collection. Cleanse specimen port with antiseptic swab, and then aspirate 5 mL of urine with a 21- to 25-gauge needle and syringe. Transfer urine to a sterile container.

Timed Specimen

▸ Obtain a clean 3 L urine specimen container, toilet-mounted collection device, and plastic bag (for transport of the specimen container). The specimen must be refrigerated or kept on ice throughout the entire collection period. If an indwelling urinary catheter is in place, the drainage bag must be kept on ice.

▸ Begin the test between 6 and 8 a.m., if possible. Collect first voiding and discard. Record the time the specimen was discarded as the beginning of the timed collection period. The next morning, ask the patient to void at the same time the collection was started and add this last voiding to the container. Urinary output should be recorded throughout the collection time.

▸ If an indwelling catheter is in place, replace the tubing and container system at the start of the collection time. Keep the container system on ice during the collection period, or empty the urine into a larger container periodically during the collection period; monitor to ensure continued drainage, and conclude the test the next morning at the same hour the collection was begun.

▸ At the conclusion of the test, compare the quantity of urine with the urinary output record for the collection; if the specimen contains less than what was recorded as output, some urine may have been discarded, invalidating the test.

▸ Include on the collection container's label the amount of urine, test start and stop times, and any foods or medications that can affect test results.

General

▸ Promptly transport the specimen to the laboratory for processing and analysis.

POST-TEST:

▸ A report of the results will be made available to the requesting health-care provider (HCP), who will discuss the results with the patient.

▸ Instruct the patient to resume usual diet, fluids, medications, and activity, as directed by the HCP.

▸ **Nutritional Considerations:** If appropriate, educate patients with low sodium levels that the major source of dietary sodium is found in table salt. Many foods, such as milk and other dairy products, are also good sources of dietary sodium. Most other dietary sodium is available through the consumption of processed foods. Patients on low-sodium diets should be advised to avoid beverages such as colas, ginger ale, sports drinks, lemon-lime sodas, and root beer. Many over-the-counter medications, including antacids, laxatives, analgesics, sedatives, and antitussives, contain significant amounts of sodium. The best advice is to emphasize the importance of reading all food, beverage, and medicine labels. The Institute of Medicine's Food and Nutrition Board suggests 1,200 mg as an adequate daily intake goal of dietary sodium for adult males and females greater than age 70 yr; 1,300 mg/d for adult males and females age 51 to 70 yr;

1,500 mg/d for adult males and females age 19 to 50 yr; 1,500 mg/d for pregnant and lactating females under age 18 through 50 yr; 1,500 mg/d for children age 9 to 18 yr; 1,200 mg/d for children age 4 to 8 yr; 1,000 mg/d for children age 1 to 3 yr; 370 mg/d for children age 7 to 12 mo; and 120 mg/d for children age 0 to 6 mo. Reprinted with permission from the National Academies Press, copyright 2013, National Academy of Sciences.

▸ Recognize anxiety related to test results. Discuss the implications of abnormal test results on the patient's lifestyle. Provide teaching and information regarding the clinical implications of the test results, as appropriate.

▸ Reinforce information given by the patient's HCP regarding further testing, treatment, or referral to another HCP. Answer any questions or address any concerns voiced by the patient or family.

▸ Depending on the results of this procedure, additional testing may be performed to evaluate or monitor progression of the disease process and determine the need for a change in therapy. Evaluate test results in relation to the patient's symptoms and other tests performed.

RELATED MONOGRAPHS:

▸ Related tests include ACTH, aldosterone, anion gap, ANP, BNP, blood gases, BUN, calcium, calculus kidney stone panel, carbon dioxide, chloride, chloride sweat, cortisol, creatinine, DHEAS, echocardiography, glucose, insulin, ketones, lactic acid, lung perfusion scan, magnesium, osmolality, potassium, renin, sodium, and UA.

▸ Refer to the Endocrine and Genitourinary system tables at the end of the book for related tests by body system.

S

Spondee Speech Recognition Threshold

SYNONYM/ACRONYM: SRT, speech reception threshold, speech recognition threshold.

COMMON USE: To evaluate for hearing loss related to speech discrepancies.

AREA OF APPLICATION: Ears.

CONTRAST: N/A.

DESCRIPTION: This noninvasive speech audiometric procedure measures the degree of hearing loss for speech. The speech recognition threshold is the lowest hearing level at which speech can barely be recognized or understood. In this test, a number of spondaic words are presented to the patient at different intensities. Spondaic words, or spondees, are words containing two syllables that are equally accented or emphasized when they are spoken to the patient. The SRT is defined as the lowest hearing level at which the patient correctly repeats 50% of a list of spondaic words. Examples are airplane, hot dog, outside, ice cream, and baseball.

INDICATIONS
• Determine appropriate gain during hearing aid selection
• Determine the extent of hearing loss related to speech recognition, as evidenced by the faintest level at which spondee words are correctly repeated
• Differentiate a real hearing loss from pseudohypoacusis
• Verify pure tone results

POTENTIAL DIAGNOSIS

Normal findings in
• Normal spondee threshold of about 6 to 10 dB (decibels) of the normal pure tone threshold with 50% of the words presented being correctly repeated at the appropriate intensity (see monograph titled "Audiometry, Hearing Loss")
• Normal speech recognition with 90% to 100% of the words presented being correctly repeated at an appropriate intensity

Abnormal findings in
• Conductive hearing loss
• Impacted cerumen
• Obstruction of external ear canal *(related to presence of a foreign body)*
• Otitis externa *(related to infection in ear canal)*
• Otitis media *(related to poor eustachian tube function or infection)*
• Otitis media serus *(related to fluid in middle ear due to allergies or a cold)*
• Otosclerosis
• High-frequency hearing loss *(normal hearing range is 20 Hz to 20,000 Hz; high-frequency range begins at 4,000 Hz)*
• Presbycusis *(related to gradual hearing loss experienced in advancing age, which occurs in the high-frequency range)*
• Noise induced *(related to exposure over long periods of time)*
• Sensorineural hearing loss (acoustic nerve impairment)

- Congenital damage or malformations of the inner ear
- Ménière's disease
- Ototoxic drugs *(aminoglycosides, e.g., gentamicin or tobramycin; salicylates, e.g., aspirin)*
- Presbycusis *(related to gradual hearing loss experienced in advancing age)*
- Serious infections *(meningitis, measles, mumps, other viral, syphilis)*
- Trauma to the inner ear *(related to exposure to noise in excess of 90 dB or as a result of physical trauma)*
- Tumor *(e.g., acoustic neuroma, cerebellopontine angle tumor, meningioma)*
- Vascular disorders

CRITICAL FINDINGS: N/A

INTERFERING FACTORS

Factors that may impair the results of the examination

- Inability of the patient to cooperate or remain still during the procedure because of age or mental status may interfere with the test results.
- Unfamiliarity with the language in which the words are presented or with the words themselves will alter the results.
- Improper placement of the earphones and inconsistency in frequency of word presentation will affect results.

NURSING IMPLICATIONS AND PROCEDURE

PRETEST:

▶ Positively identify the patient using at least two unique identifiers before providing care, treatment, or services.
▶ *Patient Teaching:* Inform the patient this procedure can assist in measuring hearing loss related to speech.

▶ Obtain a history of the patient's complaints, including a list of known allergens.
▶ Obtain a history of the patient's known or suspected hearing loss, including type and cause; ear conditions with treatment regimens; ear surgery; and other tests and procedures to assess and diagnose hearing deficit.
▶ Obtain a history of the patient's symptoms and results of previously performed laboratory tests and diagnostic and surgical procedures.
▶ Obtain a list of the patient's current medications, including herbs, nutritional supplements, and nutraceuticals (see Appendix F).
▶ Review the procedure with the patient. Ensure that the patient understands words and sounds in the language to be used for the test. Inform the patient that a series of words that change from loud to soft tones will be presented using earphones and that he or she will be asked to repeat the word. Explain that each ear is tested separately. Address concerns about pain and explain that no discomfort will be experienced during the test. Inform the patient that a health-care provider (HCP) performs the test, in a quiet, soundproof room, and that the evaluation takes 5 to 10 min.
▶ *Sensitivity to social and cultural issues,* as well as concern for modesty, is important in providing psychological support before, during, and after the procedure.
▶ There are no food, fluid, or medication restrictions unless by medical direction.

INTRATEST:

▶ Observe standard precautions, and follow the general guidelines in Appendix A. Positively identify the patient.
▶ Instruct the patient to cooperate fully and to follow directions. Ask the patient to remain still during the procedure because movement produces unreliable results.
▶ Seat the patient on a chair in a soundproof booth. Place the earphones on the patient's head and secure them over the ears. The audiometer is set at 20 dB above the known pure tone threshold obtained from audiometry.

S

The test represents hearing levels at speech frequencies of 500, 1,000, and 2,000 Hz.

The spondee words are presented to the ear with the best auditory response using a speech audiometer. The intensity is decreased and then increased to the softest sound at which the patient is able to hear the words and respond correctly to 50% of them. The procedure is then repeated for the other ear.

POST-TEST:

A report of the results will be made available to the requesting HCP, who will discuss the results with the patient.

Recognize anxiety related to test results, and be supportive of activity related to impaired hearing and perceived loss of independence. Discuss the implications of abnormal test results on the patient's lifestyle. Provide teaching and information regarding the clinical implications of the test results, as appropriate. Educate the patient regarding access to counseling services. Provide contact information, if desired, for the American Speech-Language-Hearing Association (www.asha.org).

Reinforce information given by the patient's HCP regarding further testing, treatment, or referral to another HCP. Answer any questions or address any concerns voiced by the patient or family.

Depending on the results of this procedure, additional testing may be performed to evaluate or monitor progression of the disease process and determine the need for a change in therapy. Evaluate test results in relation to the patient's symptoms and other tests performed.

RELATED MONOGRAPHS:

Related tests include antimicrobial drugs, analgesic and antipyretic drugs, audiometry hearing loss, culture bacterial (ear), and Gram stain.

Refer to the Auditory System table at the end of the book for related tests by body system.

Stereotactic Biopsy, Breast

SYNONYM/ACRONYM: N/A.

COMMON USE: To assess suspicious breast tissue for cancer.

SPECIMEN: Breast tissue or cells.

NORMAL FINDINGS: (Method: Macroscopic and microscopic examination of tissue) No abnormal cells or tissue.

S

DESCRIPTION: A stereotactic breast biopsy is helpful when a mammogram or ultrasound examination shows a mass, a cluster of microcalcifications (tiny calcium deposits that are closely grouped together), or an area of abnormal tissue change, usually with no lump being felt on a careful breast examination. A number of biopsy instruments and methods are utilized with x-ray guidance. They include core biopsy, which uses a large-bore needle to remove a generous sample of breast tissue, and a vacuum-assisted needle biopsy device. As an alternative to an open-core surgical biopsy, which removes an entire breast lump for microscopic analysis, a narrow needle may be passed through the skin into the area under investigation. This is accomplished with the help of special breast x-rays. Images of the breast are obtained with a mammography machine, and the images are recorded in a computer. An initial x-ray locates the abnormality, and two stereo views are obtained, each angled 15° to either side of the initial image. The computer calculates how much the area of interest has changed with each image and determines the exact site in three-dimensional space. A small sample of breast tissue is obtained and can show whether the breast mass is cancerous. A pathologist examines the tissue that was removed and makes a final diagnosis to allow for effective treatment.

INDICATIONS

* A mammogram showing a suspicious cluster of small calcium deposits
* A mammogram showing a suspicious solid mass that cannot be felt on breast examination
* Evidence of breast lesion by palpation, mammography, or ultrasound
* New mass or area of calcium deposits present at a previous surgery site
* Observable breast changes such as "peau d'orange" skin, scaly skin of the areola, drainage from the nipple, or ulceration of the skin
* Patient preference for a nonsurgical method of lesion assessment

* Structure of the breast tissue is distorted

POTENTIAL DIAGNOSIS
* Positive findings in carcinoma of the breast

CRITICAL FINDINGS: N/A

INTERFERING FACTORS
* This procedure is contraindicated in patients with bleeding disorders.

Factors that may impair clear imaging
* Failure to restrict food intake before the study.
* Metallic objects (e.g., jewelry, body rings, dental amalgams) within the examination field, which may inhibit organ visualization and cause unclear images.
* Inability of the patient to cooperate or remain still during the procedure because of age, significant pain, or mental status.

Other considerations
* Complications of the procedure include hemorrhage, infection at the insertion site, and cardiac arrhythmias.
* Failure to follow dietary restrictions before the procedure may cause the procedure to be canceled or repeated.
* Consultation with a health-care practitioner (HCP) should occur before the procedure for radiation safety concerns regarding younger patients or patients who are lactating.
* Risks associated with radiation overexposure can result from frequent x-ray procedures. Personnel in the room with the patient should wear a protective lead apron, stand behind a shield, or leave the area while the examination is being done. Personnel working in the examination area should wear badges to record their level of radiation exposure.

S

NURSING IMPLICATIONS AND PROCEDURE

PRETEST:

▶ Positively identify the patient using at least two unique identifiers before providing care, treatment, or services.

▶ *Patient Teaching:* Inform the patient this procedure can assist in assessing breast health.

▶ Obtain a history of the patient's complaints, including a list of known allergens, especially allergies or sensitivities to latex or anesthetics.

▶ Obtain a history of the patient's reproductive system, symptoms, and results of previously performed laboratory tests and diagnostic and surgical procedures. Note any recent procedures that can interfere with test results.

▶ Record the date of the last menstrual period and determine the possibility of pregnancy in perimenopausal women.

▶ Obtain a list of the patient's current medications, including anticoagulant therapy, aspirin and other salicylates, herbs, nutritional supplements, and nutraceuticals, especially those known to affect coagulation (see Appendix F). It is recommended that use be discontinued 14 days before surgical procedures. The requesting HCP and laboratory should be advised if the patient regularly uses these products so that their effects can be taken into consideration when reviewing results.

▶ Review the procedure with the patient. Address concerns about pain related to the procedure and explain that some pain will be experienced during the test, or there may be moments of discomfort. Inform the patient that the procedure is performed in a special room, usually a mammography suite, by an HCP specializing in this procedure, with support staff, and takes approximately 30 to 60 min.

▶ *Sensitivity to social and cultural issues,* as well as concern for modesty, is important in providing psychological support before, during, and after the procedure.

▶ Explain that an IV line may be inserted to allow infusion of IV fluids or sedatives. Usually normal saline is infused.

▶ Instruct the patient to remove jewelry and other metallic objects from the area of the procedure.

▶ Instruct the patient to avoid taking anticoagulant medication or to reduce dosage as ordered prior to the procedure. Number of days to withhold medication is dependent on the type of anticoagulant.

▶ Instruct the patient to fast and restrict fluids for 4 hr prior to the procedure. Protocols may vary among facilities.

▶ Make sure a written and informed consent has been signed prior to the procedure and before administering any medications.

▶ The procedure may be terminated if chest pain or severe cardiac arrhythmias occur.

INTRATEST:

▶ Ensure that the patient has complied with dietary and medication restrictions for 4 hr prior to the procedure.

▶ Ensure that anticoagulant therapy has been withheld for the appropriate number of days prior to the procedure. Number of days to withhold medication is dependent on the type of anticoagulant. Notify the HCP if patient anticoagulant therapy has not been withheld.

▶ Ensure the patient has removed all external metallic objects from the area to be examined prior to the procedure.

▶ Have emergency equipment readily available.

▶ If the patient has a history of severe allergic reactions to any substance or drug, administer ordered prophylactic steroids or antihistamines before the procedure.

▶ Instruct the patient to void and change into the gown, robe, and foot coverings provided.

▶ Observe standard precautions, and follow the general guidelines in Appendix A. Positively identify the patient, and label the appropriate specimen containers with the corresponding patient demographics, date and time of collection, and site location (left or right breast).

▶ Instruct the patient to cooperate fully and to follow directions. Instruct the patient to remain still throughout the procedure because movement produces unreliable results.

▶ Record baseline vital signs and assess neurological status. Protocols may vary among facilities.

S

Establish an IV fluid line for the injection of emergency drugs and of sedatives.

Place the patient in the prone or sitting position on an examination table. Cleanse the selected area, and cover with a sterile drape.

A local anesthetic is injected at the site, and a small incision is made or a needle inserted.

Instruct the patient to inhale deeply and hold his or her breath while the images are taken, and then to exhale after the images are taken.

Instruct the patient to take slow, deep breaths if nausea occurs during the procedure. Monitor and administer an antiemetic agent if ordered. Ready an emesis basin for use.

Monitor the patient for complications related to the procedure (e.g., allergic reaction, anaphylaxis, bronchospasm).

Remove the needle or catheter and apply a pressure dressing over the puncture site.

Observe/assess the needle/catheter insertion site for bleeding, inflammation, or hematoma formation.

Place tissue samples in properly labeled specimen containers, and promptly transport the specimens to the laboratory for processing and analysis.

POST-TEST:

A report of the results will be made available to the requesting HCP, who will discuss the results with the patient.

Instruct the patient to resume usual diet and medications, as directed by the HCP.

Monitor vital signs and neurological status every 15 min for 1 hr, then every 2 hr for 4 hr, and then as ordered by the HCP. Take temperature every 4 hr for 24 hr. Monitor intake and output at least every 8 hr. Compare with baseline values. Notify the HCP if temperature is elevated. Protocols may vary among facilities.

Observe for delayed allergic reactions, such as rash, urticaria, tachycardia, hyperpnea, hypertension, palpitations, nausea, or vomiting.

Instruct the patient to immediately report symptoms such as fast heart rate, difficulty breathing, skin rash, itching, chest pain, persistent right shoulder pain, or abdominal pain.

Immediately report symptoms to the appropriate HCP.

Observe/assess the biopsy site for bleeding, inflammation, or hematoma formation.

Instruct the patient in the care and assessment of the site.

Recognize anxiety related to test results, and be supportive of the potential perceived loss of body image. Discuss the implications of abnormal test results on the patient's lifestyle. Provide teaching and information regarding the clinical implications of the test results, as appropriate. Educate the patient regarding access to counseling services. Provide contact information, if desired, for the American Cancer Society (www.cancer.org).

Reinforce information given by the patient's HCP regarding further testing, treatment, or referral to another HCP. Decisions regarding the need for and frequency of breast self-examination, mammography, magnetic resonance imaging (MRI) of the breast, or other cancer screening procedures should be made after consultation between the patient and HCP. The most current guidelines for breast cancer screening of the general population as well as of individuals with increased risk are available from the American Cancer Society (www.cancer.org), the American College of Obstetricians and Gynecologists (ACOG) (www.acog.org), and the American College of Radiology (www.acr.org). Answer any questions or address any concerns voiced by the patient or family.

Depending on the results of this procedure, additional testing may be performed to evaluate or monitor progression of the disease process and determine the need for a change in therapy. Evaluate test results in relation to the patient's symptoms and other tests performed.

RELATED MONOGRAPHS:

Related tests include biopsy breast, cancer antigens, ductography, mammography, MRI breast, and US breast.

Refer to the Reproductive System table at the end of the book for related tests by body system.

S

Synovial Fluid Analysis

SYNONYM/ACRONYM: Arthrocentesis, joint fluid analysis, knee fluid analysis.

COMMON USE: To identify the presence and assist in the management of joint disease related to disorders such as arthritis and gout.

SPECIMEN: Synovial fluid collected in a red-top tube for antinuclear antibodies (ANAs), complement, crystal examination, protein, rheumatoid factor (RF), and uric acid; sterile (red-top) tube for microbiological testing; lavender-top (EDTA) tube for mucin clot/viscosity, complete blood count (CBC) and differential, gray-top (sodium fluoride [NaFl]) tube for glucose; green-top (heparin) tube for lactic acid and pH.

NORMAL FINDINGS: (Method: Macroscopic evaluation of appearance; spectrophotometry for glucose, lactic acid, protein, and uric acid; Gram stain, acid-fast stain, and culture for microbiology; microscopic examination of fluid for cell count and evaluation of crystals; ion-selective electrode for pH; nephelometry for RF and C3 complement; indirect fluorescence for ANAs).

Test	Normal Result
Color	Colorless to pale yellow
Clarity	Clear
Viscosity	High
ANA	Parallels serum level
C3	Parallels serum level
Glucose	Less than 10 mg/dL of blood level
Lactic acid	5–20 mg/dL
pH	7.2–7.4
Protein	Less than 3 g/dL
RF	Parallels serum level
Uric acid	Parallels serum level
Crystals	None present
RBC count	None
WBC count	Less than $0.2 \times 10^3/mm^3$ (or $200/mm^3$)
Neutrophils	Less than 25%
WBC morphology	No abnormal cells or inclusions
Gram stain and culture	No organisms present
AFB smear and culture	No AFB present

AFB = acid-fast bacilli; ANA = antinuclear antibodies; C3 = complement; RBC = red blood cell; RF = rheumatoid factor; WBC = white blood cell.

DESCRIPTION: Synovial fluid analysis is performed via arthrocentesis, an invasive procedure involving insertion of a needle into the joint space. Synovial effusions are associated with disorders or injuries involving the joints. The most commonly aspirated joint is the knee, although samples also can be obtained from the shoulder, hip, elbow, wrist, and ankle if clinically indicated. Joint disorders can be classified into five categories: noninflammatory, inflammatory, septic, crystal-induced, and hemorrhagic. The mucin clot test is used to correlate the qualitative assessment of synovial fluid viscosity with the presence of hyaluronic acid. The test is performed by mixing equal amounts of synovial fluid and 5% acetic acid solution on a glass slide and grading the ropiness of the subsequent clot as good, fair, or poor. Long, ropy strands are seen in normal synovial fluid.

INDICATIONS

- Administration of anti-inflammatory medications by injection
- Assist in the diagnosis of arthritis
- Assist in the evaluation of joint effusions
- Assist in the diagnosis of joint infection
- Differentiate gout from pseudogout

POTENTIAL DIAGNOSIS

Fluid values increased in

- Acute bacterial infection: White blood cell (WBC) count greater than $50 \times 10^3/mm^3$, marked predominance of neutrophils (greater than 90% neutrophils), positive Gram stain, positive cultures, possible presence of rice bodies, increased lactic acid (produced by bacteria), and complement levels paralleling those found in serum (may be elevated or decreased)

- *Gout:* WBC count variable: $(0.5–200) \times 10^3/mm^3$ with a predominance of neutrophils (90% neutrophils), presence of monosodium urate crystals, increased uric acid, and complement levels paralleling those of serum (may be elevated or decreased)

- *Osteoarthritis, traumatic arthritis degenerative joint disease:* WBC count less than $3 \times 10^3/mm^3$ with less than 25% neutrophils and the presence of cartilage cells

- *Pseudogout:* Presence of calcium pyrophosphate crystals

- *Rheumatoid arthritis:* WBC count $(3–50) \times 10^3/mm^3$ with a predominance of neutrophils (greater than 70% neutrophils), presence of ragocyte cells and possibly rice bodies, presence of cholesterol crystals if effusion is chronic, increased protein, increased lactic acid, and presence of rheumatoid factor

- *Systemic lupus erythematosus (SLE):* $(3–50) \times 10^3/mm^3$ with a predominance of neutrophils, presence of SLE cells, and presence of antinuclear antibodies

- *Trauma, joint tumors, or hemophilic arthritis:* Elevated RBC count, increased protein level, and presence of fat droplets (if trauma involved)

- *Tuberculous arthritis:* WBC count $(2–100) \times 10^3/mm^3$ with a predominance of neutrophils (up to 90% neutrophils), possible presence of rice bodies, presence of cholesterol crystals if effusion is chronic, in some cases a positive culture and smear for acid-fast bacilli (results frequently negative), and lactic acid

Fluid values decreased in (analytes in parentheses are decreased)

- Acute bacterial arthritis (glucose and pH)
- Gout (glucose)

S

- Rheumatoid arthritis (glucose, pH, and complement)
- SLE (glucose, pH, and complement)
- Tuberculous arthritis (glucose and pH)

CRITICAL FINDINGS ✤

Positive culture findings in any sterile body fluid. Timely notification of critical values for lab or diagnostic studies is a role expectation of the professional nurse. Notification processes will vary among facilities. Upon receipt of the critical value the information should be read back to the caller to verify accuracy. Most policies require immediate notification of the primary HCP, hospitalist, or on-call HCP. Reported information includes the patient's name, unique identifiers, critical value, name of the person giving the report, and name of the person receiving the report. Documentation of notification should be made in the medical record with the name of the HCP notified, time and date of notification, and any orders received. Any delay in a timely report of a critical value may require completion of a notification form with review by Risk Management.

INTERFERING FACTORS

- Blood in the sample from traumatic arthrocentesis may falsely elevate the RBC count.
- Undetected hypoglycemia or hyperglycemia may produce misleading glucose values.
- Refrigeration of the sample may result in an increase in monosodium urate crystals secondary to decreased solubility of uric acid; exposure of the sample to room air with a resultant loss of carbon dioxide and rise in pH encourages the formation of calcium pyrophosphate crystals.

NURSING IMPLICATIONS AND PROCEDURE

PRETEST:

Positively identify the patient using at least two unique identifiers before providing care, treatment, or services.

Patient Teaching: Inform the patient this procedure can assist in assessing joint health.

Obtain a history of the patient's complaints, including a list of known allergens, especially allergies or sensitivities to latex.

Obtain a history of the patient's immune and musculoskeletal systems, especially any bleeding disorders and other symptoms, and results of previously performed laboratory tests and diagnostic and surgical procedures.

Note any recent procedures that can interfere with test results.

Record the date of the last menstrual period and determine the possibility of pregnancy in perimenopausal women.

Obtain a list of the patient's current medications, anticoagulants, aspirin and other salicylates, herbs, nutritional supplements, and nutraceuticals (see Appendix F). Such products should be discontinued by medical direction for the appropriate number of days prior to a surgical procedure.

Review the procedure with the patient. Inform the patient that it may be necessary to remove hair from the site before the procedure. Address concerns about pain and explain that a sedative and/or analgesia will be administered to promote relaxation and reduce discomfort prior to needle insertion through the joint space. Explain that any discomfort with the needle insertion will be minimized with local anesthetics and systemic analgesics. Explain that the anesthetic injection may cause an initial stinging sensation. Explain that, after the skin has been anesthetized, a large needle will be inserted through the joint space and a "popping" sensation may be experienced as the needle penetrates the joint. Inform the patient that the procedure is performed by a healthcare provider (HCP) specializing in this

S

procedure. The procedure usually takes approximately 20 min to complete.

Sensitivity to social and cultural issues, as well as concern for modesty, is important in providing psychological support before, during, and after the procedure.

There are no fluid restrictions unless by medical direction. Fasting for at least 12 hr before the procedure is recommended if fluid glucose measurements are included in the analysis. Instruct the patient to avoid taking anticoagulant medication or to reduce dosage as ordered prior to the procedure. Protocols may vary among facilities.

Make sure a written and informed consent has been signed prior to the procedure and before administering any medications.

INTRATEST:

Ensure that the patient has complied with dietary and medication restrictions and pretesting preparations; assure that food has been restricted for at least 12 hr prior to the procedure. Ensure that anticoagulant medications and aspirin have been withheld, as ordered.

Assemble the necessary equipment, including an arthrocentesis tray with solution for skin preparation, local anesthetic, a 20-mL syringe, needles of various sizes, sterile drapes, and sterile gloves for the tests to be performed.

Instruct the patient to cooperate fully and to follow directions. Direct the patient to breathe normally and to avoid unnecessary movement during the local anesthetic and the procedure.

Observe standard precautions, and follow the general guidelines in Appendix A. Positively identify the patient, and label the appropriate specimen container with the corresponding patient demographics, initials of the person collecting the specimen, date and time of collection, and site location, especially, right or left knee, shoulder, hip, elbow, wrist, or ankle.

Assist the patient into a comfortable sitting or supine position, as appropriate.

Prior to the administration of general or local anesthesia, use clippers to remove hair from the site, cleanse the site with an antiseptic solution, and drape the area with sterile towels.

After the local anesthetic is administered, the needle is inserted at the collection site, and fluid is removed by syringe. Manual pressure may be applied to facilitate fluid removal.

If medication is injected into the joint, the syringe containing the sample is detached from the needle and replaced with the one containing the drug. The medication is injected with gentle pressure. The needle is withdrawn, and digital pressure is applied to the site for a few minutes. If there is no evidence of bleeding, a sterile dressing is applied to the site. An elastic bandage can be applied to the joint.

Monitor the patient for complications related to the procedure (allergic reaction, anaphylaxis).

Place samples in properly labeled specimen containers and promptly transport the specimens to the laboratory for processing and analysis. If bacterial culture and sensitivity tests are to be performed, record on the specimen containers any antibiotic therapy the patient is receiving.

POST-TEST:

A report of the results will be made available to the requesting HCP, who will discuss the results with the patient.

Instruct the patient to resume usual diet and medications, as directed by the HCP.

After local anesthesia, monitor vital signs and compare with baseline values. Notify the HCP if temperature is elevated. Protocols may vary among facilities.

Observe/assess puncture site for bleeding, bruising, inflammation, and excessive drainage of synovial fluid approximately every 4 hr for 24 hr and daily thereafter for several days.

Instruct the patient to report excessive pain, bleeding, or swelling to the requesting HCP immediately. Report to HCP if severe pain is present or the patient is unable to move the joint.

Observe/assess for nausea and pain. Administer antiemetic and analgesic medications as needed and as directed by the HCP.

Instruct the patient to apply an ice pack to the site for 24 to 48 hr.

Administer antibiotics, as ordered, and instruct the patient in the importance of completing the entire course of antibiotic therapy even if no symptoms are present.

Recognize anxiety related to test results, and be supportive of impaired activity related to anticipated chronic pain resulting from joint inflammation, impairment in mobility, musculoskeletal deformity, and loss of independence. Discuss the implications of abnormal test results on the patient's lifestyle. Provide teaching and information regarding the clinical implications of the test results, as appropriate. Educate the patient regarding access to counseling services, as appropriate. Provide contact information, if desired, for the American College of Rheumatology (www.rheumatology.org) or for the Arthritis Foundation (www.arthritis.org).

Reinforce information given by the patient's HCP regarding further testing, treatment, or referral to another HCP.

Instruct the patient or caregiver to handle linen and dispose of dressings cautiously, especially if septic arthritis is suspected. Instruct the patient to avoid excessive use of the joint for several days to prevent pain and swelling. Instruct the patient to return for a follow-up visit as scheduled. Answer any questions or address any concerns voiced by the patient or family.

Depending on the results of this procedure, additional testing may be performed to evaluate or monitor progression of the disease process and determine the need for a change in therapy. Evaluate test results in relation to the patient's symptoms and other tests performed.

RELATED MONOGRAPHS:

Related tests include antibodies anti-cyclic citrullinated, ANA, arthrogram, arthroscopy, BMD, bone scan, CRP, cholesterol, CBC, CBC WBC count and differential, ESR, MRI musculoskeletal, radiography bone, RF, synovial fluid analysis, and uric acid.

Refer to the Immune and Musculoskeletal systems tables at the end of the book for related tests by body system.

Syphilis Serology

SYNONYM/ACRONYM: Automated reagin testing (ART), fluorescent treponemal antibody testing (FTA-ABS), microhemagglutination–*Treponema pallidum* (MHA-TP), rapid plasma reagin (RPR), treponemal studies, Venereal Disease Research Laboratory (VDRL) testing.

COMMON USE: To indicate past or present syphilis infection.

SPECIMEN: Serum (1 mL) collected in a red- or tiger-top tube.

NORMAL FINDINGS: (Method: Dark-field microscopy, rapid plasma reagin, enzyme-linked immunosorbent assay [ELISA], microhemagglutination, fluorescence) Nonreactive or absence of treponemal organisms.

DESCRIPTION: Syphilis is a sexually transmitted disease with three stages. On average, symptoms start within 3 weeks of infection but can appear as soon as 10 days or as late as 90 days after infection. The primary stage of syphilis is usually marked by the appearance of a single sore, called a chancre, at the site where the organism entered the body. The chancre is small and round in appearance, is firm, and is usually painless. The chancre lasts 3 to 6 weeks and heals with or without treatment. If untreated, the infection progresses to the secondary stage as the chancre is healing or several weeks after the chancre has healed. The secondary stage is characterized by a skin rash and lesions of the mucous membranes. Other symptoms may include fever, swollen lymph glands, sore throat, patchy hair loss, headaches, weight loss, muscle aches, and fatigue. As with the primary stage, the signs and symptoms of secondary syphilis will resolve either with or without treatment. If untreated, the infection will progress to the latent or hidden stage in which the infection and ability to transmit infection is present even though the infected person is asymptomatic. The latent stage begins when the primary and secondary symptoms disappear, and it can last for years. About 15% of people in the latent stage, who have not been treated, will develop late-stage syphilis, which can appear 10 to 20 years after infection. Untreated disease at this stage can result in significant damage to the brain, nerves, eyes, heart, blood vessels, liver, bones, and joints—damage serious enough to cause death. Signs and symptoms of the late stage of syphilis include difficulty coordinating muscle movements, numbness, paralysis, blindness, and dementia.

There are numerous methods for detecting *Treponema pallidum*, the gram-negative spirochete bacterium known to cause syphilis. Syphilis serology is routinely ordered as part of a prenatal workup and is required for evaluating donated blood units before release for transfusion. Selection of the proper testing method is important. Automated reagin testing (ART), rapid plasma reagin (RPR), and Venereal Disease Research Laboratory (VDRL) testing have traditionally been used for screening purposes. These nontreponemal assays detect antibodies directed against lipoidal antigens from damaged host cells. Nontreponemal assays can produce false-positive results, which are associated with older age or conditions unrelated to syphilis, such as autoimmune disorders or injection drug use, and require confirmation by a treponemal test method. Fluorescent treponemal antibody testing (FTA-ABS), microhemagglutination–*Treponema pallidum* (MHA-TP), and *Treponema pallidum* by particle agglutination (TP-PA) are confirmatory methods for samples that screen positive or reactive. Some laboratories have begun using a reverse-screening approach. Highly automated, rapid-testing treponemal enzyme immunoassays (EIA) and chemiluminescent assays (CIA) detect antibodies directed against T. pallidum proteins. These assays detect early primary infections as well as past treated infections. The problem with the EIAs and CIAs is that they are very sensitive but less specific; therefore, positive test results should be confirmed using a nontreponemal assay. If reverse screening is used, the Centers for

S

Disease Control and Prevention recommends (1) positive EIA/CIA be confirmed using the RPR and reactive RPR test results should be reported as the endpoint titer of reactivity; (2) a positive EIA/CIA followed by a nonreactive RPR should be tested by a direct treponemal assay such as the TP-PA or FTA-ABS to ensure a false-positive result is not reported and acted upon. Cerebrospinal fluid should be tested only by the FTA-ABS method. Cord blood should not be submitted for testing by any of the aforementioned methods; instead, the mother's serum should be tested to establish whether the infant should be treated.

INDICATIONS
- Monitor effectiveness of treatment for syphilis
- Screen for and confirm the presence of syphilis

POTENTIAL DIAGNOSIS

Positive findings in
- Syphilis

False-positive or false-reactive findings in screening (RPR, VDRL) tests
- Infectious:
  Bacterial endocarditis
  Chancroid
  Chickenpox
  HIV
  Infectious mononucleosis
  Leprosy
  Leptospirosis
  Lymphogranuloma venereum
  Malaria
  Measles
  Mumps
  Mycoplasma pneumoniae
  Pneumococcal pneumonia
  Psittacosis
  Relapsing fever
  Rickettsial disease
  Scarlet fever
  Trypanosomiasis
  Tuberculosis
  Vaccinia (live or attenuated)
  Viral hepatitis
- Noninfectious:
  Advanced cancer
  Advancing age
  Chronic liver disease
  Connective tissue diseases
  IV drug use
  Multiple blood transfusions
  Multiple myeloma and other immunological disorders
  Narcotic addiction
  Pregnancy

False-positive or false-reactive findings in confirmatory (FTA-ABS, MHA-TP) tests
- Infectious:
  Infectious mononucleosis
  Leprosy
  Leptospirosis
  Lyme disease
  Malaria
  Relapsing fever
- Noninfectious:
  Systemic lupus erythematosus

False-positive findings in confirmatory (TP-PA) tests
- Infectious:
  Pinta
  Yaws

Negative findings in: N/A

CRITICAL FINDINGS: N/A

INTERFERING FACTORS: N/A

NURSING IMPLICATIONS AND PROCEDURE

PRETEST:
▸ Positively identify the patient using at least two unique identifiers before providing care, treatment, or services.
▸ *Patient Teaching:* Inform the patient this test can assist in diagnosing syphilis.

▶ Obtain a history of the patient's complaints, including a list of known allergens, especially allergies or sensitivities to latex.
▶ Obtain a history of exposure.
▶ Obtain a history of the patient's immune and reproductive systems, symptoms, and results of previously performed laboratory tests and diagnostic and surgical procedures.
▶ Obtain a list of the patient's current medications, including herbs, nutritional supplements, and nutraceuticals (see Appendix F).
▶ Review the procedure with the patient. Inform the patient that specimen collection takes approximately 5 to 10 min. Address concerns about pain and explain that there may be some discomfort during the venipuncture.
▶ *Sensitivity to social and cultural issues,* as well as concern for modesty, is important in providing psychological support before, during, and after the procedure.
▶ There are no food, fluid, or medication restrictions unless by medical direction.

INTRATEST:

▶ If the patient has a history of allergic reaction to latex, avoid the use of equipment containing latex.
▶ Instruct the patient to cooperate fully and to follow directions. Direct the patient to breathe normally and to avoid unnecessary movement.
▶ Observe standard precautions, and follow the general guidelines in Appendix A. Positively identify the patient, and label the appropriate specimen container with the corresponding patient demographics, initials of the person collecting the specimen, date, and time of collection. Perform a venipuncture.
▶ Remove the needle and apply direct pressure with dry gauze to stop bleeding. Observe/assess venipuncture site for bleeding or hematoma formation and secure gauze with adhesive bandage.
▶ Promptly transport the specimen to the laboratory for processing and analysis.

POST-TEST:

▶ A report of the results will be made available to the requesting health-care provider (HCP), who will discuss the results with the patient.
▶ Recognize anxiety related to test results, and offer support. Counsel the patient, as appropriate, regarding the risk of transmission and proper prophylaxis, and reinforce the importance of strict adherence to the treatment regimen. Inform the patient that positive findings must be reported to local health department officials, who will question him or her regarding sexual partners. Provide teaching and information regarding the clinical implications of the test results, as appropriate. Educate the patient regarding access to counseling services.
▶ Reinforce information given by the patient's HCP regarding further testing, treatment, or referral to another HCP. Inform the patient that repeat testing may be needed at 3-mo intervals for 1 yr to monitor the effectiveness of treatment. Provide information regarding vaccine-preventable diseases where indicated (e.g., anthrax, cervical cancer, diphtheria, encephalitis, hepatitis A and B, H1N1 flu, human papillomavirus, Haemophilus influenza, seasonal influenza, Lyme disease, measles, meningococcal disease, monkeypox, mumps, pertussis, pneumococcal disease, polio, rotavirus, rubella, shingles, smallpox, tetanus, typhoid fever, varicella, yellow fever). Provide contact information, if desired, for the CDC (www.cdc.gov/vaccines/vpd-vac). Answer any questions or address any concerns voiced by the patient or family.
▶ Offer support, as appropriate, to patients who may be the victim of rape or sexual assault. Educate the patient regarding access to counseling services. Provide a nonjudgmental, nonthreatening atmosphere for a discussion during which risks of sexually transmitted diseases are explained. It is also important to discuss problems the patient may experience (e.g., guilt, depression, anger).

S

Depending on the results of this procedure, additional testing may be performed to evaluate or monitor progression of the disease process and determine the need for a change in therapy. Evaluate test results in relation to the patient's symptoms and other tests performed.

Related tests include acid phosphatase, cerebrospinal fluid analysis, *Chlamydia* group antibody, culture bacterial anal, Gram stain, hepatitis B, hepatitis C, HIV, and β_2-microglobulin.

Refer to the Immune and Reproductive systems tables at the end of the book for related tests by body system.

Testosterone, Total

SYNONYM/ACRONYM: N/A.

COMMON USE: To evaluate testosterone to assist in identification of disorders related to early puberty, late puberty, and infertility while assessing gonadal and adrenal function.

SPECIMEN: Serum (1 mL) collected in a red- or tiger-top tube. Plasma (1 mL) collected in green-top (heparin) tube is also acceptable.

NORMAL FINDINGS: (Method: Immunochemiluminometric assay [ICMA])

Age	Conventional Units	SI Units (Conventional Units × 0.0347)
Cord blood		
Male	17–61 ng/dL	0.59–2.12 nmol/L
Female	16–44 ng/dL	0.56–1.53 nmol/L
1–5 mo		
Male	1–177 ng/dL	0.03–6.14 nmol/L
Female	1–5 ng/dL	0.03–0.17 nmol/L
6–11 mo		
Male	2–7 ng/dL	0.07–0.24 nmol/L
Female	2–5 ng/dL	0.07–0.17 nmol/L
1–5 yr		
Male and female	0–10 ng/dL	0.00–0.35 nmol/L
6–7 yr		
Male	0–20 ng/dL	0.00–0.69 nmol/L
Female	0–10 ng/dL	0.00–0.35 nmol/L
8–10 yr		
Male	0–25 ng/dL	0.00–0.87 nmol/L
Female	0–30 ng/dL	0.00–1.0 nmol/L
11–12 yr		
Male	0–350 ng/dL	0.00–12.1 nmol/L
Female	0–50 ng/dL	0.00–1.74 nmol/L
13–15 yr		
Male	15–500 ng/dL	0.52–17.35 nmol/L
Female	0–50 ng/dL	0.00–1.74 nmol/L
Adult–older adult		
Male	241–827 ng/dL	8.36–28.70 nmol/L
Female	15–70 ng/dL	0.52–2.43 nmol/L

Tanner Stage		
	Male	Female
I	2–23 ng/dL	2–10 ng/dL
II	5–70 ng/dL	5–30 ng/dL
III	15–280 ng/dL	10–30 ng/dL
IV	105–545 ng/dL	15–40 ng/dL
V	265–800 ng/dL	10–40 ng/dL

T

DESCRIPTION: Testosterone is the major androgen responsible for sexual differentiation. In males, testosterone is made by the Leydig cells in the testicles and is responsible for spermatogenesis and the development of secondary sex characteristics. In females, the ovary and adrenal gland secrete small amounts of this hormone; however, most of the testosterone in females comes from the metabolism of androstenedione. In males, a testicular, adrenal, or pituitary tumor can cause an overabundance of testosterone, triggering precocious puberty. In females, adrenal tumors, hyperplasia, and medications can cause an overabundance of this hormone, resulting in masculinization or hirsutism.

INDICATIONS
* Assist in the diagnosis of hypergonadism
* Assist in the diagnosis of male sexual precocity before age 10
* Distinguish between primary and secondary hypogonadism
* Evaluate hirsutism
* Evaluate male infertility

POTENTIAL DIAGNOSIS

Increased in
* Adrenal hyperplasia *(oversecretion of the androgen precursor dehydroepiandrosterone [DHEA])*
* Adrenocortical tumors *(oversecretion of the androgen precursor DHEA)*
* Hirsutism *(any condition that results in increased production of testosterone or its precursors)*
* Hyperthyroidism *(high thyroxine levels increase the production of sex hormone–binding protein,*
which increases measured levels of total testosterone)*
* Idiopathic sexual precocity *(related to stimulation of testosterone production by elevated levels of luteinizing hormone [LH])*
* Polycystic ovaries *(high estrogen levels increase the production of sex hormone–binding protein, which increases measured levels of total testosterone)*
* Syndrome of androgen resistance
* Testicular or extragonadal tumors *(related to excessive secretion of testosterone)*
* Trophoblastic tumors during pregnancy
* Virilizing ovarian tumors

Decreased in
* Anovulation
* Cryptorchidism *(related to dysfunctional testes)*
* Delayed puberty
* Down syndrome *(related to diminished or dysfunctional testes)*
* Excessive alcohol intake *(alcohol inhibits secretion of testosterone)*
* Hepatic insufficiency *(related to decreased binding protein and reflects decreased measured levels of total testosterone)*
* Impotence *(decreased testosterone levels can result in impotence)*
* Klinefelter's syndrome *(chromosome abnormality XXY associated with testicular failure)*
* Malnutrition
* Myotonic dystrophy *(related to testicular atrophy)*
* Orchiectomy *(testosterone production occurs in the testes)*
* Primary and secondary hypogonadism
* Primary and secondary hypopituitarism
* Uremia

CRITICAL FINDINGS: N/A

INTERFERING FACTORS

- Drugs that may increase testosterone levels include barbiturates, bromocriptine, cimetidine, flutamide, gonadotropin, levonorgestrel, mifepristone, moclobemide, nafarelin (males), nilutamide, oral contraceptives, rifampin, and tamoxifen.
- Drugs that may decrease testosterone levels include cyclophosphamide, cyproterone, danazol, dexamethasone, diethylstilbestrol, digoxin, D-Trp-6-LHRH, fenoldopam, goserelin, ketoconazole, leuprolide, magnesium sulfate, medroxyprogesterone, methylprednisone, nandrolone, oral contraceptives, pravastatin, prednisone, pyridoglutethimide, spironolactone, stanozolol, tetracycline, and thioridazine.

NURSING IMPLICATIONS AND PROCEDURE

PRETEST:

- Positively identify the patient using at least two unique identifiers before providing care, treatment, or services.
- *Patient Teaching:* Inform the patient this test can assist with evaluating hormone levels.
- Obtain a history of the patient's complaints, including a list of known allergens, especially allergies or sensitivities to latex.
- Obtain a history of the patient's endocrine and reproductive systems, symptoms, and results of previously performed laboratory tests and diagnostic and surgical procedures.
- Obtain a list of the patient's current medications, including herbs, nutritional supplements, and nutraceuticals (see Appendix F).
- Review the procedure with the patient. Inform the patient that specimen collection takes approximately 5 to 10 min. Address concerns about pain and explain that there may be some discomfort during the venipuncture.

- *Sensitivity to social and cultural issues,* as well as concern for modesty, is important in providing psychological support before, during, and after the procedure.
- There are no food, fluid, or medication restrictions unless by medical direction.

INTRATEST:

- If the patient has a history of allergic reaction to latex, avoid the use of equipment containing latex.
- Instruct the patient to cooperate fully and to follow directions. Direct the patient to breathe normally and to avoid unnecessary movement.
- Observe standard precautions, and follow the general guidelines in Appendix A. Positively identify the patient, and label the appropriate specimen container with the corresponding patient demographics, initials of the person collecting the specimen, date, and time of collection. Perform a venipuncture.
- Remove the needle and apply direct pressure with dry gauze to stop bleeding. Observe/assess venipuncture site for bleeding or hematoma formation and secure gauze with adhesive bandage.
- Promptly transport the specimen to the laboratory for processing and analysis.

POST-TEST:

- A report of the results will be made available to the requesting health-care provider (HCP), who will discuss the results with the patient.
- Recognize anxiety related to test results, and offer support, as appropriate.
- Discuss the implications of abnormal test results on the patient's lifestyle. Provide teaching and information regarding the clinical implications of the test results, as appropriate. Educate the patient regarding access to counseling services.
- Reinforce information given by the patient's HCP regarding further testing, treatment, or referral to another HCP. Answer any questions or address any concerns voiced by the patient or family.
- Depending on the results of this procedure, additional testing may be performed to evaluate or monitor

T

progression of the disease process and determine the need for a change in therapy. Evaluate test results in relation to the patient's symptoms and other tests performed.

RELATED MONOGRAPHS:

▶ Related tests include angiography adrenal gland scan, ACE, antibodies antisperm, biopsy thyroid, chromosome analysis, CT renal, DHEAS, estradiol, FSH, LH, PTH, RAIU, semen analysis, thyroid scan, TSH, thyroxine, and US scrotal.

▶ Refer to the Endocrine and Reproductive systems tables at the end of the book for related test by body system.

Thyroglobulin

SYNONYM/ACRONYM: Tg.

COMMON USE: To evaluate thyroid gland function related to disorders such as tumor, inflammation, structural damage, and cancer.

SPECIMEN: Serum (1 mL) collected in a red- or tiger-top tube.

NORMAL FINDINGS: (Method: Chemiluminescent enzyme immunoassay)

Age	Conventional Units	SI Units (Conventional Units × 1)
Premature infant		
1 day	107–395 ng/mL	107–395 mcg/L
3 days	49–163 ng/mL	49–163 mcg/L
Cord blood	5–65 ng/mL	5–65 mcg/L
1 day	6–93 ng/mL	6–93 mcg/L
10 days	9–148 ng/mL	9–148 mcg/L
1 mo	17–63 ng/mL	17–63 mcg/L
7–12 yr	20–50 ng/mL	20–50 mcg/L
12–18 yr	9–27 ng/mL	9–27 mcg/L
Adult–older adult	0–50 ng/mL	0–50 mcg/L

DESCRIPTION: Thyroglobulin is an iodinated glycoprotein secreted by follicular epithelial cells of the thyroid gland. It is the storage form of the thyroid hormones thyroxine (T_4) and triiodothyronine (T_3). When thyroid hormones are released into the bloodstream, they split from thyroglobulin in response to thyroid-stimulating hormone. Values greater than 55 ng/mL are indicative of tumor recurrence in athyrotic patients.

INDICATIONS

• Assist in the diagnosis of subacute thyroiditis
• Assist in the diagnosis of suspected disorders of excess thyroid hormone
• Management of differentiated or metastatic cancer of the thyroid

- Monitor response to treatment of goiter
- Monitor T_4 therapy in patients with solitary nodules

POTENTIAL DIAGNOSIS

Increased in

Thyroglobulin is secreted by normal, abnormal, and cancerous thyroid tissue cells.

- Differentiated thyroid cancer
- Graves' disease (untreated) *(autoimmune destruction of thyroid tissue cells)*
- Surgery or irradiation of the thyroid *(elevated levels indicate residual or disseminated carcinoma)*
- T_4-binding globulin deficiency
- Thyroiditis *(related to leakage from inflamed, damaged thyroid tissue cells)*
- Thyrotoxicosis

Decreased in

- Administration of thyroid hormone *(feedback loop suppresses production)*
- Congenital athyrosis (neonates) *(related to insufficient synthesis)*
- Thyrotoxicosis factitia

CRITICAL FINDINGS: N/A

INTERFERING FACTORS

- Drugs that may decrease thyroglobulin levels include neomycin and T_4.
- Autoantibodies to thyroglobulin can cause decreased values.
- Recent thyroid surgery or needle biopsy can interfere with test results.

NURSING IMPLICATIONS AND PROCEDURE

PRETEST:

- Positively identify the patient using at least two unique identifiers before providing care, treatment, or services.
- *Patient Teaching:* Inform the patient this test can assist in assessing the thyroid gland.

- Obtain a history of the patient's complaints, including a list of known allergens, especially allergies or sensitivities to latex.
- Obtain a history of the patient's endocrine system, symptoms, and results of previously performed laboratory tests and diagnostic and surgical procedures.
- Obtain a list of the patient's current medications, including herbs, nutritional supplements, and nutraceuticals (see Appendix F).
- Review the procedure with the patient. Inform the patient that specimen collection takes approximately 5 to 10 min. Address concerns about pain and explain that there may be some discomfort during the venipuncture.
- *Sensitivity to social and cultural issues,* as well as concern for modesty, is important in providing psychological support before, during, and after the procedure.
- There are no food, fluid, or medication restrictions unless by medical direction.

INTRATEST:

- If the patient has a history of allergic reaction to latex, avoid the use of equipment containing latex.
- Instruct the patient to cooperate fully and to follow directions. Direct the patient to breathe normally and to avoid unnecessary movement.
- Observe standard precautions, and follow the general guidelines in Appendix A. Positively identify the patient, and label the appropriate specimen container with the corresponding patient demographics, initials of the person collecting the specimen, date, and time of collection. Perform a venipuncture.
- Remove the needle and apply direct pressure with dry gauze to stop bleeding. Observe/assess venipuncture site for bleeding or hematoma formation and secure gauze with adhesive bandage.
- Promptly transport the specimen to the laboratory for processing and analysis.

POST-TEST:

▸ A report of the results will be made available to the requesting health-care provider (HCP), who will discuss the results with the patient.

▸ Reinforce information given by the patient's HCP regarding further testing, treatment, or referral to another HCP. Answer any questions or address any concerns voiced by the patient or family.

▸ Depending on the results of this procedure, additional testing may be performed to evaluate or monitor progression of the disease process and determine the need for a change in

therapy. Evaluate test results in relation to the patient's symptoms and other tests performed.

RELATED MONOGRAPHS:

▸ Related tests include ACTH, albumin, ACE, antibodies thyroglobulin, biopsy thyroid, copper, follicle-stimulating hormone, growth hormone, luteinizing hormone, PTH, protein, RAIU, TBII, thyroid scan, TSH, TSI, T_4, free T_4, T_3, free T_3, and US thyroid.

▸ Refer to the Endocrine System table at the end of the book for related tests by body system.

Thyroid-Binding Inhibitory Immunoglobulin

SYNONYM/ACRONYM: Thyrotropin receptor antibodies, thyrotropin-binding inhibitory immunoglobulin, TBII.

COMMON USE: To assist in diagnosing Graves' disease related to thyroid function.

SPECIMEN: Serum (1 mL) collected in a red-top tube.

NORMAL FINDINGS: (Method: Electrochemiluminescence) 0.0–1.75 units/L.

POTENTIAL DIAGNOSIS

Increased in
Evidenced by antibodies that block the action of TSH and result in hyperthyroid conditions.

• Graves' disease
• Hyperthyroidism (various forms)

• Maternal thyroid disease
• Neonatal thyroid disease
• Toxic goiter

Decreased in: N/A

CRITICAL FINDINGS: N/A

Find and print out the full monograph at DavisPlus (http://davisplus.fadavis.com, keyword Van Leeuwen).

Thyroid Scan

SYNONYM/ACRONYM: Iodine thyroid scan, technetium thyroid scan, thyroid scintiscan.

COMMON USE: To assess thyroid gland size, structure, function, and shape toward diagnosing disorders such as tumor, inflammation, cancer, and bleeding.

AREA OF APPLICATION: Thyroid.

CONTRAST: Oral radioactive iodine or IV technetium-99m pertechnetate.

DESCRIPTION: The thyroid scan is a nuclear medicine study performed to assess thyroid size, shape, position, and function. It is useful for evaluating thyroid nodules, multinodular goiter, and thyroiditis; assisting in the differential diagnosis of masses in the neck, base of the tongue, and mediastinum; and ruling out possible ectopic thyroid tissue in these areas. Thyroid scanning is performed after oral administration of radioactive iodine-123 (I-123) or I-131 or IV injection of technetium-99m (Tc-99m). Increased or decreased uptake by the thyroid gland and surrounding area and tissue is noted: Areas of increased radionuclide uptake ("hot spots") are caused by hyperfunctioning thyroid nodules, which are usually nonmalignant; areas of decreased uptake ("cold spots") are caused by hypofunctioning nodules, which are more likely to be malignant. Ultrasound imaging may be used to determine if the cold spot is a solid, semicystic lesion or a pure cyst (cysts are rarely cancerous). To determine whether the cold spot depicts a malignant neoplasm, however, a biopsy must be performed.

INDICATIONS
- Assess palpable nodules and differentiate between a benign tumor or cyst and a malignant tumor
- Assess the presence of a thyroid nodule or enlarged thyroid gland
- Detect benign or malignant thyroid tumors
- Detect causes of neck or substernal masses
- Detect forms of thyroiditis (e.g., acute, chronic, Hashimoto's)
- Detect thyroid dysfunction
- Differentiate between Graves' disease and Plummer's disease, both of which cause hyperthyroidism
- Evaluate thyroid function in hyperthyroidism and hypothyroidism (analysis combined with interpretation of laboratory tests, thyroid function panel including thyroxine and triiodothyronine, and thyroid uptake tests)

POTENTIAL DIAGNOSIS

Normal findings in
- Normal size, contour, position, and function of the thyroid gland with homogeneous uptake of the radionuclide

Abnormal findings in
- Adenoma
- Cysts
- Fibrosis

T

- Goiter
- Graves' disease (diffusely enlarged, hyperfunctioning gland)
- Hematoma
- Metastasis
- Plummer's disease (nodular hyperfunctioning gland)
- Thyroiditis (Hashimoto's)
- Thyrotoxicosis
- Tumors, benign or malignant

CRITICAL FINDINGS: N/A

INTERFERING FACTORS

This procedure is contraindicated for

- Patients who are pregnant or suspected of being pregnant, unless the potential benefits of the procedure far outweigh the risks to the fetus or mother.

Factors that may impair clear imaging

- Inability of the patient to cooperate or remain still during the procedure because of age, significant pain, or mental status.
- Other nuclear scans or iodinated contrast medium radiographic studies done within the previous 24 to 48 hr.
- Ingestion of foods containing iodine (iodized salt) or medications containing iodine (cough syrup, potassium iodide, vitamins, Lugol's solution, thyroid replacement medications), which can decrease the uptake of the radionuclide.
- Antithyroid medications (propylthiouracil), corticosteroids, antihistamines, warfarin, sulfonamides, nitrates, corticosteroids, thyroid hormones, and isoniazid, which can decrease the uptake of the radionuclide.
- Increased uptake of iodine in persons with an iodine-deficient diet or who are on phenothiazine therapy.
- Vomiting and severe diarrhea, which can affect absorption of orally administered radionuclide.

- Gastroenteritis, which can interfere with absorption of orally administered radionuclide.
- Metallic objects (e.g., jewelry, body rings) within the examination field, which may inhibit organ visualization and cause unclear images.

Other considerations

- Improper injection of the radionuclide that allows the tracer to seep deep into the muscle tissue can produce erroneous hot spots.
- Consultation with a health-care provider (HCP) should occur before the procedure for radiation safety concerns regarding younger patients or patients who are lactating.
- Risks associated with radiation overexposure can result from frequent x-ray or radionuclide procedures. Personnel working in the examination area should wear badges to record their level of radiation exposure.

NURSING IMPLICATIONS AND PROCEDURE

PRETEST:

▶ Positively identify the patient using at least two unique identifiers before providing care, treatment, or services.

▶ *Patient Teaching:* Inform the patient this procedure can assist in evaluating the thyroid glands structure and function.

▶ Obtain a history of the patient's complaints, including a list of known allergens, especially allergies or sensitivities to latex, iodine, seafood, contrast medium, anesthetics, or dyes.

▶ Obtain a history of the patient's endocrine system, symptoms, and results of previously performed laboratory tests and diagnostic and surgical procedures.

▶ Ensure thyroid blood tests are completed prior to this procedure.

▶ Note any recent procedures that can interfere with test results, including

T

examinations using iodinated contrast medium or radioactive nuclides.

▸ Ensure that this procedure is performed before all radiographic procedures using iodinated contrast medium.

▸ Record the date of the last menstrual period and determine the possibility of pregnancy in perimenopausal women.

▸ Obtain a list of the patient's current medications, including herbs, nutritional supplements, and nutraceuticals (see Appendix F).

▸ Review the procedure with the patient. Address concerns about pain related to the procedure and explain that some pain may be experienced during the test. Inform the patient that the procedure is performed in a nuclear medicine department, usually by an HCP specializing in this procedure, with support staff, and takes approximately 30 to 60 min.

▸ *Sensitivity to social and cultural issues,* as well as concern for modesty, is important in providing psychological support before, during, and after the procedure.

▸ Instruct the patient to remove jewelry and other metallic objects from the area to be examined.

▸ The patient should fast for 8 to 12 hr prior to the procedure. Protocols may vary among facilities.

▸ *Make sure a written and informed consent has been signed prior to the procedure and before administering any medications.*

INTRATEST:

▸ Observe standard precautions, and follow the general guidelines in Appendix A. Positively identify the patient.

▸ Ensure that the patient has complied with dietary restrictions for 8 to 12 hr prior to the procedure.

▸ Ensure that the patient has removed all external metallic objects from the area to be examined prior to the procedure.

▸ Instruct the patient to void prior to the procedure and to change into the gown, robe, and foot coverings provided.

▸ Instruct the patient to cooperate fully and to follow directions. Ask the patient to lie still during the procedure

because movement produces unclear images.

▸ Administer sedative to a child or to an uncooperative adult, as ordered.

▸ Tc-99m pertechnetate is injected IV 20 min before scanning.

▸ If oral radioactive nuclide is used instead, administer I-123 24 hr before scanning.

▸ Place the patient in a supine position on a flat table to obtain images of the neck area.

▸ Remove the needle or catheter and apply a pressure dressing over the puncture site.

▸ Observe/assess the needle/catheter insertion site for bleeding, inflammation, or hematoma formation.

POST-TEST:

▸ A report of the results will be made available to the requesting HCP, who will discuss the results with the patient.

▸ Observe/assess the needle/catheter insertion site for bleeding, inflammation, or hematoma formation.

▸ Instruct the patient in the care and assessment of the injection site.

▸ Advise the patient to drink increased amounts of fluids for 24 to 48 hr to eliminate the radionuclide from the body, unless contraindicated. Tell the patient that radionuclide is eliminated from the body within 6 to 24 hr.

▸ If a woman who is breastfeeding must have a nuclear scan, she should not breastfeed the infant until the radionuclide has been eliminated. This could take as long as 3 days. She should be instructed to express the milk and discard it during the 3-day period to prevent cessation of milk production.

▸ Instruct the patient to flush the toilet immediately and to meticulously wash hands with soap and water after each voiding for 24 hr after the procedure.

▸ Instruct all caregivers to wear gloves when discarding urine for 24 hr after the procedure. Wash gloved hands with soap and water before removing gloves. Then wash hands after the gloves are removed.

▸ Recognize anxiety related to test results, and be supportive of perceived loss of independent function. Discuss the implications of abnormal test results on the patient's lifestyle. Provide teaching and information regarding the clinical implications of the test results, as appropriate.

▶ Reinforce information given by the patient's HCP regarding further testing, treatment, or referral to another HCP. Answer any questions or address any concerns voiced by the patient or family.

▶ Depending on the results of this procedure, additional testing may be needed to evaluate or monitor progression of the disease process and determine the

need for a change in therapy. Evaluate test results in relation to the patient's symptoms and other tests performed.

RELATED MONOGRAPHS:

▶ Related tests include ACTH, angiography adrenal, biopsy thyroid, calcium, CT renal, cortisol, glucose, radioactive iodine uptake, sodium, thyroglobulin, thyroid antibodies, TBII, thyroid scan, TSH, TT_3, T_4, FT_4, and US thyroid.

▶ Refer to the Endocrine System table at the end of the book for related tests by body system.

Thyroid-Stimulating Hormone

SYNONYM/ACRONYM: Thyrotropin, TSH.

COMMON USE: To evaluate thyroid gland function related to the primary cause of hypothyroidism and assess for congenital disorders, tumor, cancer, and inflammation.

SPECIMEN: Serum (1 mL) collected in a red- or tiger-top tube; for a neonate, use filter paper.

NORMAL FINDINGS: (Method: Immunoassay)

Age	Conventional Units	SI Units (Conventional Units × 1)
Neonates–3 days	Less than 20 micro-international units/mL	Less than 20 milli-international units/L
2 wk–5 mo	1.7–9.1 micro-international units/mL	1.7–9.1 milli-international units/L
6 mo–20 yr	0.7–6.4 micro-international units/mL	0.7–6.4 milli-international units/L
21–54 yr	0.4–4.2 micro-international units/mL	0.4–4.2 milli-international units/L
55–87 yr	0.5–8.9 micro-international units/mL	0.5–8.9 milli-international units/L

T

DESCRIPTION: Thyroid-stimulating hormone (TSH) is produced by the pituitary gland in response

to stimulation by thyrotropin-releasing hormone (TRH), a hypothalamic-releasing factor. TRH regulates the release and circulating levels of thyroid hormones in response to variables such as cold, stress, and increased metabolic need. Thyroid and pituitary function can be evaluated by TSH measurement. TSH exhibits diurnal variation, peaking between midnight and 4 a.m. and troughing between 5 and 6 p.m. TSH values are high at birth but reach adult levels in the first week of life. Elevated TSH levels combined with decreased thyroxine (T_4) levels indicate hypothyroidism and thyroid gland dysfunction. In general, decreased TSH and T_4 levels indicate secondary congenital hypothyroidism and pituitary hypothalamic dysfunction. A normal TSH level and a depressed T_4 level may indicate (1) hypothyroidism owing to a congenital defect in T_4-binding globulin or (2) transient congenital hypothyroidism owing to hypoxia or prematurity. Early diagnosis and treatment in the neonate are crucial for the prevention of cretinism and mental retardation.

INDICATIONS

- Assist in the diagnosis of congenital hypothyroidism
- Assist in the diagnosis of hypothyroidism or hyperthyroidism or suspected pituitary or hypothalamic dysfunction
- Differentiate functional euthyroidism from true hypothyroidism in debilitated individuals

POTENTIAL DIAGNOSIS

Increased in
A decrease in thyroid hormone levels activates the feedback loop to increase production of TSH.

- Congenital hypothyroidism in the neonate (filter paper test)

- Ectopic TSH-producing tumors (lung, breast)
- Primary hypothyroidism *(related to a dysfunctional thyroid gland)*
- Secondary hyperthyroidism owing to pituitary hyperactivity
- Thyroid hormone resistance
- Thyroiditis (Hashimoto's autoimmune disease)

Decreased in
An increase in thyroid hormone levels activates the feedback loop to decrease production of TSH.

- Excessive thyroid hormone replacement
- Graves' disease
- Primary hyperthyroidism
- Secondary hypothyroidism *(related to pituitary involvement that decreases production of TSH)*
- Tertiary hypothyroidism *(related to hypothalamic involvement that decreases production of TRH)*

CRITICAL FINDINGS: N/A

INTERFERING FACTORS

- Drugs and hormones that may increase TSH levels include amiodarone, benserazide, erythrosine, flunarizine (males), iobenzamic acid, iodides, lithium, methimazole, metoclopramide, morphine, propranolol, radiographic agents, TRH, and valproic acid.
- Drugs and hormones that may decrease TSH levels include acetylsalicylic acid, amiodarone, anabolic steroids, carbamazepine, corticosteroids, glucocorticoids, hydrocortisone, interferon-alfa-2b, iodamide, levodopa (in hypothyroidism), levothyroxine, methergoline, nifedipine, T_4, and triiodothyronine (T_3).
- Failure to let the filter paper sample dry may affect test results.

T

NURSING IMPLICATIONS AND PROCEDURE

PRETEST:

▶ Positively identify the patient using at least two unique identifiers before providing care, treatment, or services.

▶ *Patient Teaching:* Inform the patient this test can assist in evaluating thyroid function.

▶ Obtain a history of the patient's complaints, including a list of known allergens, especially allergies or sensitivities to latex.

▶ Obtain a history of the patient's endocrine system, symptoms, and results of previously performed laboratory tests and diagnostic and surgical procedures.

▶ Obtain a list of the patient's current medications, including herbs, nutritional supplements, and nutraceuticals (see Appendix F).

▶ Review the procedure with the patient. Inform the patient that specimen collection takes approximately 5 to 10 min. Address concerns about pain and explain that there may be some discomfort during the venipuncture.

▶ *Sensitivity to social and cultural issues,* as well as concern for modesty, is important in providing psychological support before, during, and after the procedure. There are no food, fluid, or medication restrictions unless by medical direction.

INTRATEST:

▶ If the patient has a history of allergic reaction to latex, avoid the use of equipment containing latex.

▶ Instruct the patient to cooperate fully and to follow directions. Direct the patient to breathe normally and to avoid unnecessary movement.

▶ Observe standard precautions, and follow the general guidelines in Appendix A. Positively identify the patient, and label the appropriate specimen container with the corresponding patient demographics, initials of the person collecting the specimen, date, and time of collection. Perform a venipuncture.

▶ Remove the needle and apply direct pressure with dry gauze to stop bleeding. Observe/assess venipuncture site for bleeding or hematoma formation and secure gauze with adhesive bandage.

▶ Promptly transport the specimen to the laboratory for processing and analysis.

Filter Paper Test (Neonate)
Obtain kit and cleanse heel with antiseptic. Observe standard precautions, and follow the general guidelines in Appendix A. Use gauze to dry the stick area completely. Perform heel stick, gently squeeze infant's heel, and touch filter paper to the puncture site. When collecting samples for newborn screening, it is important to apply each blood drop to the correct side of the filter paper card and fill each circle with a single application of blood. Overfilling or underfilling the circles will cause the specimen card to be rejected by the testing facility. Additional information is required on newborn screening cards and may vary by state. Newborn screening cards should be allowed to air dry for several hours on a level, nonabsorbent, unenclosed area. If multiple patients are tested, do not stack cards. State regulations usually require the specimen cards to be submitted within 24 hr of collection.

POST-TEST:

▶ A report of the results will be made available to the requesting health-care provider (HCP), who will discuss the results with the patient.

▶ Reinforce information given by the patient's HCP regarding further testing, treatment, or referral to another HCP. Answer any questions or address any concerns voiced by the patient or family.

▶ Depending on the results of this procedure, additional testing may be performed to evaluate or monitor progression of the disease process and determine the need for a change in therapy. Evaluate test results in relation to the patient's symptoms and other tests performed.

RELATED MONOGRAPHS:

▶ Related tests include albumin, antibodies antithyroglobulin, biopsy thyroid, copper, newborn screening, PTH, protein, RAIU, thyroglobulin, TSI, TBII, thyroid scan, T_4, free T_4, T_3, free T_3, and US thyroid.

▶ Refer to the Endocrine System table at the end of the book for related tests by body system.

T

Thyroid-Stimulating Immunoglobulins

SYNONYM/ACRONYM: Thyrotropin receptor antibodies, TSI.

COMMON USE: To differentiate between antibodies that stimulate or inhibit thyroid hormone production related to disorders such as Graves' disease.

SPECIMEN: Serum (1 mL) collected in a red-top tube.

NORMAL FINDINGS: (Method: Animal cell transfection with luciferase marker) Less than 130% of basal activity.

DESCRIPTION: There are two functional types of thyroid receptor immunoglobulins: *thyroid-stimulating immunoglobulin (TSI)* and *thyroid-binding inhibitory immunoglobulin (TBII)*. TSI reacts with the receptors, activates intracellular enzymes, and promotes epithelial cell activity that operates outside the feedback regulation for thyroid-stimulating hormone (TSH); TBII blocks the action of TSH and is believed to cause certain types of hyperthyroidism (see monograph titled "Thyroid-Binding Inhibitory Immunoglobulin"). These antibodies were formerly known as *long-acting thyroid stimulators*. High levels in pregnancy may have some predictive value for neonatal thyrotoxicosis: A positive result indicates that the antibodies are stimulating (TSI); a negative result indicates that the antibodies are blocking (TBII). TSI testing measures thyroid receptor immunoglobulin levels in the evaluation of thyroid disease.

INDICATIONS

- Follow-up to positive TBII assay in differentiating antibody stimulation from neutral or suppressing activity
- Monitor hyperthyroid patients at risk for relapse or remission

POTENTIAL DIAGNOSIS

Increased in
- Graves' disease *(this form of hyperthyroidism has an autoimmune component; the antibodies stimulate release of thyroid hormones outside the feedback loop that regulates TSH levels)*

Decreased in: N/A

CRITICAL FINDINGS: N/A

INTERFERING FACTORS

- Lithium may cause false-positive TBII results.

NURSING IMPLICATIONS AND PROCEDURE

PRETEST:

- Positively identify the patient using at least two unique identifiers before providing care, treatment, or services.
- *Patient Teaching:* Inform the patient this test can assist in assessing thyroid gland function.
- Obtain a history of the patient's complaints, including a list of known allergens, especially allergies or sensitivities to latex.
- Obtain a history of the patient's endocrine system, symptoms, and results of previously performed laboratory tests and diagnostic and surgical procedures.

T

Obtain a list of the patient's current medications, including herbs, nutritional supplements, and nutraceuticals (see Appendix F).

Review the procedure with the patient. Inform the patient that specimen collection takes approximately 5 to 10 min. Address concerns about pain and explain that there may be some discomfort during the venipuncture.

Sensitivity to social and cultural issues, as well as concern for modesty, is important in providing psychological support before, during, and after the procedure.

There are no food, fluid, or medication restrictions unless by medical direction.

INTRATEST:

If the patient has a history of allergic reaction to latex, avoid the use of equipment containing latex.

Instruct the patient to cooperate fully and to follow directions. Direct the patient to breathe normally and to avoid unnecessary movement.

Observe standard precautions, and follow the general guidelines in Appendix A. Positively identify the patient, and label the appropriate specimen container with the corresponding patient demographics, initials of the person collecting the specimen, date, and time of collection. Perform a venipuncture.

Remove the needle and apply direct pressure with dry gauze to stop bleeding.

Observe/assess venipuncture site for bleeding or hematoma formation and secure gauze with adhesive bandage.

Promptly transport the specimen to the laboratory for processing and analysis.

POST-TEST:

A report of the results will be made available to the requesting health-care provider (HCP), who will discuss the results with the patient.

Reinforce information given by the patient's HCP regarding further testing, treatment, or referral to another HCP. Answer any questions or address any concerns voiced by the patient or family.

Depending on the results of this procedure, additional testing may be performed to evaluate or monitor progression of the disease process and determine the need for a change in therapy. Evaluate test results in relation to the patient's symptoms and other tests performed.

RELATED MONOGRAPHS:

Related tests include albumin, antibodies antithyroglobulin, biopsy thyroid, copper, PTH, protein, RAIU, thyroglobulin, TBII, thyroid scan, TSH, T_4, free T_4, T_3, free T_3, and US thyroid.

Refer to the Endocrine System table at the end of the book for related tests by body system.

Thyroxine-Binding Globulin

SYNONYM/ACRONYM: TBG.

COMMON USE: To evaluate thyroid hormone levels related to deficiency or excess to assist in diagnosing disorders such as hyperthyroidism and hypothyroidism.

SPECIMEN: Serum (1 mL) collected in a red- or tiger-top tube.

NORMAL FINDINGS: (Method: Immunochemiluminometric assay [ICMA])

Age	Conventional Units	SI Units (Conventional Units × 10)
0–1 wk	3–8 mg/dL	30–80 mg/L
1–12 mo	1.6–3.6 mg/dL	16–36 mg/L
14–19 yr	1.2–2.5 mg/dL	12–25 mg/L
Greater than 20 yr	1.3–3.3 mg/dL	13–33 mg/L
Pregnancy, third trimester	4.7–5.9 mg/dL	47–59 mg/L
Oral contraceptives	1.5–5.5 mg/dL	15–55 mg/L

DESCRIPTION: Thyroxine-binding globulin (TBG) is the predominant protein carrier for circulating thyroxine (T_4) and triiodothyronine (T_3). T_4-binding prealbumin and T_4-binding albumin are the other transport proteins. Conditions that affect TBG levels and binding capacity also affect free T_3 and free T_4 levels.

INDICATIONS
• Differentiate elevated T_4 due to hyperthyroidism from increased TBG binding in euthyroid patients
• Evaluate hypothyroid patients
• Identify deficiency or excess of TBG due to hereditary abnormality

POTENTIAL DIAGNOSIS

Increased in
• Acute intermittent porphyria *(pathophysiology is unclear)*
• Estrogen therapy *(TBG is increased in the presence of exogenous or endogenous estrogens)*
• Genetically high TBG (rare)
• Hyperthyroidism *(related to increased levels of total thyroxine available for binding)*
• Infectious hepatitis and other liver diseases *(pathophysiology is unclear)*
• Neonates
• Pregnancy *(TBG is increased in the presence of exogenous or endogenous estrogens)*

Decreased in
• Acromegaly
• Chronic hepatic disease *(related to general decrease in protein synthesis)*
• Genetically low TBG
• Major illness *(related to general decrease in protein synthesis)*
• Marked hypoproteinemia, malnutrition *(related to general decrease in protein synthesis)*
• Nephrotic syndrome *(related to general increase in protein loss)*
• Ovarian hypofunction *(TBG is decreased in the absence of estrogens)*
• Surgical stress *(related to general decrease in protein synthesis)*
• Testosterone-producing tumors *(TBG is decreased in the presence of testosterone)*

CRITICAL FINDINGS: N/A

INTERFERING FACTORS
• Drugs and hormones that may increase TBG levels include estrogens, oral contraceptives, perphenazine, and tamoxifen.
• Drugs that may decrease TBG levels include anabolic steroids, androgens, asparaginase, corticosteroids, corticotropin, danazol, phenytoin, and propranolol.

T

NURSING IMPLICATIONS AND PROCEDURE

PRETEST:

- Positively identify the patient using at least two unique identifiers before providing care, treatment, or services.
- *Patient Teaching:* Inform the patient this test can assist in assessing thyroid gland function.
- Obtain a history of the patient's complaints, including a list of known allergens, especially allergies or sensitivities to latex.
- Obtain a history of the patient's endocrine system, symptoms, and results of previously performed laboratory tests and diagnostic and surgical procedures.
- Obtain a list of the patient's current medications, including herbs, nutritional supplements, and nutraceuticals (see Appendix F).
- Review the procedure with the patient. Inform the patient that specimen collection takes approximately 5 to 10 min. Address concerns about pain and explain that there may be some discomfort during the venipuncture.
- *Sensitivity to social and cultural issues,* as well as concern for modesty, is important in providing psychological support before, during, and after the procedure.
- There are no food, fluid, or medication restrictions unless by medical direction.

INTRATEST:

- If the patient has a history of allergic reaction to latex, avoid the use of equipment containing latex.
- Instruct the patient to cooperate fully and to follow directions. Direct the patient to breathe normally and to avoid unnecessary movement.

- Observe standard precautions, and follow the general guidelines in Appendix A. Positively identify the patient, and label the appropriate specimen container with the corresponding patient demographics, initials of the person collecting the specimen, date, and time of collection. Perform a venipuncture.
- Remove the needle and apply direct pressure with dry gauze to stop bleeding. Observe/assess venipuncture site for bleeding or hematoma formation and secure gauze with adhesive bandage.
- Promptly transport the specimen to the laboratory for processing and analysis.

POST-TEST:

- A report of the results will be made available to the requesting health-care provider (HCP), who will discuss the results with the patient.
- Reinforce information given by the patient's HCP regarding further testing, treatment, or referral to another HCP. Answer any questions or address any concerns voiced by the patient or family.
- Depending on the results of this procedure, additional testing may be performed to evaluate or monitor progression of the disease process and determine the need for a change in therapy. Evaluate test results in relation to the patient's symptoms and other tests performed.

RELATED MONOGRAPHS:

- Related tests include antibodies antithyroglobulin, thyroglobulin, TBII, thyroid scan, TSH, TSI, T_3, free T_3, T_4, free T_4, and US thyroid.
- Refer to the Endocrine System table at the end of the book for related tests by body system.

T

Thyroxine, Free

SYNONYM/ACRONYM: Free T_4, FT_4.

COMMON USE: A complementary laboratory test in evaluating thyroid hormones levels related to deficiency or excess to assist in diagnosing hyperthyroidism and hypothyroidism.

SPECIMEN: Serum (1 mL) collected in a red- or tiger-top tube. Plasma (1 mL) collected in a green-top (heparin) tube is also acceptable.

NORMAL FINDINGS: (Method: Immunoassay)

Age	Conventional Units	SI Units (Conventional Units × 12.9)
Newborn	0.8–2.8 ng/dL	10–36 pmol/L
1–12 mo	0.8–2 ng/dL	10–26 pmol/L
1–18 yr	0.8–1.7 ng/dL	10–22 pmol/L
Adult–older adult	0.8–1.5 ng/dL	10–19 pmol/L
Pregnancy (1st trimester)	0.9–1.4 ng/dL	12–18 pmol/L
Pregnancy (2nd trimester)	0.7–1.3 ng/dL	9–17 pmol/L

DESCRIPTION: Thyroxine (T_4) is a hormone produced and secreted by the thyroid gland. Newborns are commonly tested for decreased T_4 levels by a filter paper method (see monograph titled "Thyroxine, Total"). Most T_4 in the serum (99.97%) is bound to thyroxine-binding globulin (TBG), prealbumin, and albumin. The remainder (0.03%) circulates as unbound or free T_4, which is the physiologically active form. Levels of free T_4 are proportional to levels of total T_4. The advantage of measuring free T_4 instead of total T_4 is that, unlike total T_4 measurements, free T_4 levels are not affected by fluctuations in TBG levels; as a result, free T_4 levels are considered the most accurate indicator of T_4 and its thyrometabolic activity. Free T_4 measurements are useful in evaluating thyroid disease when thyroid-stimulating hormone (TSH) levels alone provide insufficient information. Free T_4 and TSH levels are inversely proportional. Measurement of free T_4 is also recommended during treatment for hyperthyroidism until symptoms have abated and levels have decreased into the normal range.

INDICATIONS
- Evaluate signs of hypothyroidism or hyperthyroidism
- Monitor response to therapy for hypothyroidism or hyperthyroidism

POTENTIAL DIAGNOSIS

Increased in
- Hyperthyroidism *(thyroxine is produced independently of stimulation by TSH)*

- Hypothyroidism treated with T_4 *(laboratory tests do not distinguish between endogenous and exogenous sources)*

Decreased in

- Hypothyroidism *(thyroid hormones are not produced in sufficient quantities regardless of TSH levels)*
- Pregnancy (late)

CRITICAL FINDINGS: N/A

INTERFERING FACTORS

- Drugs that may increase free T_4 levels include acetylsalicylic acid, amiodarone, halofenate, heparin, iopanoic acid, levothyroxine, methimazole, and radiographic agents.
- Drugs that may decrease free T_4 levels include amiodarone, anabolic steroids, asparaginase, methadone, methimazole, oral contraceptives, and phenylbutazone.

> **NURSING IMPLICATIONS AND PROCEDURE**

PRETEST:

- Positively identify the patient using at least two unique identifiers before providing care, treatment, or services.
- *Patient Teaching:* Inform the patient this test can assist in assessing thyroid gland function.
- Obtain a history of the patient's complaints, including a list of known allergens, especially allergies or sensitivities to latex.
- Obtain a history of the patient's endocrine system, symptoms, and results of previously performed laboratory tests and diagnostic and surgical procedures.
- Obtain a list of the patient's current medications, including herbs, nutritional supplements, and nutraceuticals (see Appendix F).
- Review the procedure with the patient. Inform the patient that specimen collection takes approximately 5 to

10 min. Address concerns about pain and explain that there may be some discomfort during the venipuncture. *Sensitivity to social and cultural issues,* as well as concern for modesty, is important in providing psychological support before, during, and after the procedure.
- There are no food, fluid, or medication restrictions unless by medical direction.

INTRATEST:

- If the patient has a history of allergic reaction to latex, avoid the use of equipment containing latex.
- Instruct the patient to cooperate fully and to follow directions. Direct the patient to breathe normally and to avoid unnecessary movement.
- Observe standard precautions, and follow the general guidelines in Appendix A. Positively identify the patient, and label the appropriate specimen container with the corresponding patient demographics, initials of the person collecting the specimen, date, and time of collection. Perform a venipuncture.
- Remove the needle and apply direct pressure with dry gauze to stop bleeding. Observe/assess venipuncture site for bleeding or hematoma formation and secure gauze with adhesive bandage.
- Promptly transport the specimen to the laboratory for processing and analysis.

POST-TEST:

- A report of the results will be made available to the requesting health-care provider (HCP), who will discuss the results with the patient.
- Reinforce information given by the patient's HCP regarding further testing, treatment, or referral to another HCP. Answer any questions or address any concerns voiced by the patient or family.
- Depending on the results of this procedure, additional testing may be performed to evaluate or monitor progression of the disease process and determine the need for a change in therapy. Evaluate test results in relation to the patient's symptoms and other tests performed.

T

RELATED MONOGRAPHS:

Related tests include albumin, antibodies antithyroglobulin, biopsy thyroid, copper, PTH, prealbumin, protein, RAIU, thyroglobulin, TBII, thyroid scan,

TSH, TSI, T_4, T_3, free T_3, and US thyroid.

Refer to the Endocrine System table at the end of the book for related tests by body system.

Thyroxine, Total

SYNONYM/ACRONYM: T_4.

COMMON USE: A first look at thyroid function and a tool to evaluate the effectiveness of therapeutic thyroid therapy.

SPECIMEN: Serum (1 mL) collected in a red- or tiger-top tube. Plasma (1 mL) collected in a green-top (heparin) tube is also acceptable.

NORMAL FINDINGS: (Method: Immunoassay)

Age	Conventional Units	SI Units (Conventional Units × 12.9)
Cord blood	6.6–17.5 mcg/dL	85–226 nmol/L
1–3 days	5.4–22.6 mcg/dL	70–292 nmol/L
1 wk–23 mo	5.4–16.6 mcg/dL	70–214 nmol/L
2–6 yr	5.3–15 mcg/dL	68–194 nmol/L
7–11 yr	5.7–14.1 mcg/dL	74–182 nmol/L
12–19 yr	4.7–14.6 mcg/dL	61–188 nmol/L
Adult	4.6–12 mcg/dL	59–155 nmol/L
Pregnant female	5.5–16 mcg/dL	71–206 nmol/L
Over 60 yr	5–10.7 mcg/dL	64–138 nmol/L

DESCRIPTION: Thyroxine (T_4) is a hormone produced and secreted by the thyroid gland. Newborns are commonly tested for decreased T_4 levels by a filter paper method. Most T_4 in the serum (99.97%) is bound to thyroxine-binding globulin (TBG), prealbumin, and albumin. The remainder (0.03%) circulates as unbound or free T_4, which is the physiologically active form. Levels of free T_4 are proportional to levels of total T_4. The advantage of measuring free T_4 instead of total T_4 is that, unlike total T_4 measurements, free T_4 levels are not affected by fluctuations in TBG levels; as a result, free T_4 levels are considered the most accurate indicator of T_4 and its thyrometabolic activity (see monograph titled "Thyroxine, Free").

T

INDICATIONS

- Evaluate signs of hypothyroidism or hyperthyroidism and neonatal screening for congenital hypothyroidism (required in all 50 states)
- Evaluate thyroid response to protein deficiency associated with severe illnesses
- Monitor response to therapy for hypothyroidism or hyperthyroidism

POTENTIAL DIAGNOSIS

Increased in

- Acute psychiatric illnesses *(pathophysiology is unknown, although there is a relationship between thyroid hormone levels and certain types of mental illness)*
- Excessive intake of iodine *(iodine is rapidly taken up by the body to form thyroxine)*
- Hepatitis *(related to decreased production of TBG by damaged liver cells)*
- Hyperthyroidism *(thyroxine is produced independently of stimulation by TSH)*
- Obesity
- Thyrotoxicosis due to Graves' disease *(thyroxine is produced independently of stimulation by TSH)*
- Thyrotoxicosis factitia *(laboratory tests do not distinguish between endogenous and exogenous sources)*

Decreased in

- Decreased TBG *(nephrotic syndrome, liver disease, gastrointestinal protein loss, malnutrition)*
- Hypothyroidism *(thyroid hormones are not produced in sufficient quantities regardless of TSH levels)*
- Panhypopituitarism *(dysfunctional pituitary gland does not secrete enough thyrotropin to stimulate the thyroid to produce thyroxine)*
- Strenuous exercise

CRITICAL FINDINGS

- *Hypothyroidism:* Less than 2 mcg/dL (SI: Less than 25.8 nmol/L)
- *Hyperthyroidism:* Greater than 20 mcg/dL Greater than 258 nmol/L)

Note and immediately report to the health-care provider (HCP) any critically increased or decreased values and related symptoms. Timely notification of critical values for lab or diagnostic studies is a role expectation of the professional nurse. Notification processes will vary among facilities. Upon receipt of the critical value the information should be read back to the caller to verify accuracy. Most policies require immediate notification of the primary HCP, hospitalist, or on-call HCP. Reported information includes the patient's name, unique identifiers, critical value, name of the person giving the report, and name of the person receiving the report. Documentation of notification should be made in the medical record with the name of the HCP notified, time and date of notification, and any orders received. Any delay in a timely report of a critical value may require completion of a notification form with review by Risk Management.

At levels less than 2 mcg/dL, the patient is at risk for myxedema coma. Signs and symptoms of severe hypothyroidism include hypothermia, hypotension, bradycardia, hypoventilation, lethargy, and coma. Possible interventions include airway support, hourly monitoring for neurological function and blood pressure, and administration of IV thyroid hormone.

At levels greater than 20 mcg/dL, the patient is at risk for thyroid storm. Signs and symptoms of severe hyperthyroidism include hyperthermia, diaphoresis, vomiting, dehydration, and shock. Possible interventions include supportive treatment for shock, fluid and electrolyte replacement for dehydration, and administration of antithyroid drugs (propylthiouracil and Lugol's solution).

INTERFERING FACTORS

- Drugs that may increase T_4 levels include amiodarone, amphetamines, corticosteroids, ether, fluorouracil, glucocorticoids, halofenate, insulin, iobenzamic acid, iopanoic acid, ipodate, levarterenol, levodopa, levothyroxine, opiates, oral contraceptives, phenothiazine, and prostaglandins.

- Drugs, substances, and treatments that may decrease T_4 levels include acetylsalicylic acid, aminoglutethimide, aminosalicylic acid, amiodarone, anabolic steroids, anticonvulsants, asparaginase, barbiturates, carbimazole, chlorpromazine, chlorpropamide, cholestyramine, clofibrate, cobalt, colestipol, corticotropin, cortisone, cotrimoxazole, cytostatic therapy, danazol, dehydroepiandrosterone, dexamethasone, diazepam, diazo dyes (e.g., Evans blue), dinitrophenol, ethionamide, fenclofenac, halofenate, hydroxyphenylpyruvic acid, interferon alfa-2b, iothiouracil, iron, isotretinoin, liothyronine, lithium, lovastatin, methimazole, methylthiouracil, mitotane, norethindrone, penicillamine, penicillin, phenylacetic acid derivatives, phenylbutazone, potassium iodide, propylthiouracil, reserpine, salicylate, sodium nitroprusside, stanozolol, sulfonylureas, tetrachlorothyronine, tolbutamide, and triiodothyronine (T_3).

NURSING IMPLICATIONS AND PROCEDURE

PRETEST:

- Positively identify the patient using at least two unique identifiers before providing care, treatment, or services.
- *Patient Teaching:* Inform the patient this test can assist in assessing thyroid gland function.

- Obtain a history of the patient's complaints, including a list of known allergens, especially allergies or sensitivities to latex.
- Obtain a history of the patient's endocrine system, symptoms, and results of previously performed laboratory tests and diagnostic and surgical procedures.
- Obtain a list of the patient's current medications, including herbs, nutritional supplements, and nutraceuticals (see Appendix F).
- Review the procedure with the patient. Inform the patient that specimen collection takes approximately 5 to 10 min. Address concerns about pain and explain that there may be some discomfort during the venipuncture.
- *Sensitivity to social and cultural issues,* as well as concern for modesty, is important in providing psychological support before, during, and after the procedure.
- There are no food, fluid, or medication restrictions unless by medical direction.

INTRATEST:

- If the patient has a history of allergic reaction to latex, avoid the use of equipment containing latex.
- Instruct the patient to cooperate fully and to follow directions. Direct the patient to breathe normally and to avoid unnecessary movement.
- Observe standard precautions, and follow the general guidelines in Appendix A. Positively identify the patient, and label the appropriate specimen container with the corresponding patient demographics, initials of the person collecting the specimen, date, and time of collection. Perform a venipuncture.
- Remove the needle and apply direct pressure with dry gauze to stop bleeding. Observe/assess venipuncture site for bleeding or hematoma formation and secure gauze with adhesive bandage.
- Promptly transport the specimen to the laboratory for processing and analysis.

POST-TEST:

- A report of the results will be made available to the requesting HCP, who will discuss the results with the patient.

T

▸ Reinforce information given by the patient's HCP regarding further testing, treatment, or referral to another HCP. Answer any questions or address any concerns voiced by the patient or family.

▸ Depending on the results of this procedure, additional testing may be performed to evaluate or monitor progression of the disease process and determine the need for a change in therapy. Evaluate test results in relation to the patient's symptoms and other tests performed.

RELATED MONOGRAPHS:

▸ Related tests include albumin, antibodies antithyroglobulin, biopsy thyroid, copper, newborn screening, PTH, prealbumin, protein, RAIU, thyroglobulin, TBII, thyroid scan, TSH, TSI, free T_4, T_3, free T_3, and US thyroid.

▸ Refer to the Endocrine System table at the end of the book for related tests by body system.

Toxoplasma Antibody

SYNONYM/ACRONYM: Toxoplasmosis serology, toxoplasmosis titer.

COMMON USE: To assess for a past or present toxoplasmosis infection and to assess for the presence of antibodies.

SPECIMEN: Serum (1 mL) collected in a red-top tube.

NORMAL FINDINGS: (Method: Chemiluminescent immunoassay)

	IgM	Interpretation	IgG	Interpretation
Negative	0.89 index or less	No significant level of detectable antibody	6.4 IU/mL or less	No significant level of detectable antibody; indicative of nonimmunity
Indeterminate	0.9–1 index	Equivocal results; retest in 10–14 d	6.5–7.9 IU/mL	Equivocal results; retest in 10–14 d
Positive	1.1 index or greater	Antibody detected; indicative of recent immunization, current or recent infection	8 IU/mL or greater	Antibody detected; indicative of immunization, current or past infection

T

DESCRIPTION: Toxoplasmosis is a severe, generalized granulomatous central nervous system disease caused by the protozoan *Toxoplasma gondii*. Transmission to humans occurs by ingesting undercooked meat or handling contaminated matter such as cat litter. Immunoglobulin (Ig) M antibodies develop approximately 5 days after infection and can remain elevated for 3 wk to several months. IgG antibodies develop 1 to 2 wk after infection and can remain elevated for months or years. *T. gondii* serology is part of the TORCH (*t*oxoplasmosis, *r*ubella, *c*ytomegalovirus, and *h*erpes simplex type 2) panel routinely performed on pregnant women. Fetal infection during the first trimester can cause spontaneous abortion or congenital defects. Immunocompromised individuals are also at high risk for serious complications if infected. The presence of IgM antibodies indicates acute or congenital infection; the presence of IgG antibodies indicates current or past infection.

INDICATIONS

- Assist in establishing a diagnosis of toxoplasmosis
- Document past exposure or immunity
- Serological screening during pregnancy

POTENTIAL DIAGNOSIS

Positive findings in
- *Toxoplasma* infection

CRITICAL FINDINGS: N/A

INTERFERING FACTORS: N/A

NURSING IMPLICATIONS AND PROCEDURE

PRETEST:

- Positively identify the patient using at least two unique identifiers before providing care, treatment, or services.
- *Patient Teaching:* Inform the patient this test can assist in assessing for toxoplasmosis infection.
- Obtain a history of the patient's complaints, including a list of known allergens, especially allergies or sensitivities to latex.
- Obtain a history of exposure.
- Obtain a history of the patient's immune and reproductive systems, a history of other potential sources of exposure, symptoms, and results of previously performed laboratory tests and diagnostic and surgical procedures.
- Obtain a list of the patient's current medications, including herbs, nutritional supplements, and nutraceuticals (see Appendix F).
- Review the procedure with the patient. Inform the patient that several tests may be necessary to confirm the diagnosis. Any individual positive result should be repeated in 3 wk to monitor a change in detectable level of antibody. Inform the patient that specimen collection takes approximately 5 to 10 min. Address concerns about pain and explain that there may be some discomfort during the venipuncture.
- *Sensitivity to social and cultural issues,* as well as concern for modesty, is important in providing psychological support before, during, and after the procedure.
- There are no food, fluid, or medication restrictions unless by medical direction.

INTRATEST:

- If the patient has a history of allergic reaction to latex, avoid the use of equipment containing latex.
- Instruct the patient to cooperate fully and to follow directions. Direct the patient to breathe normally and to avoid unnecessary movement.
- Observe standard precautions, and follow the general guidelines in Appendix A. Positively identify the patient, and label the appropriate specimen container

T

with the corresponding patient demographics, initials of the person collecting the specimen, date, and time of collection. Perform a venipuncture.

▶ Remove the needle and apply direct pressure with dry gauze to stop bleeding. Observe/assess venipuncture site for bleeding or hematoma formation and secure gauze with adhesive bandage.

▶ Promptly transport the specimen to the laboratory for processing and analysis.

POST-TEST:

▶ A report of the results will be made available to the requesting health-care provider (HCP), who will discuss the results with the patient.

▶ Recognize anxiety related to test results, and provide emotional support if results are positive and the patient is pregnant and/or immunocompromised. Discuss the implications of abnormal test results on the patient's lifestyle. Provide teaching and information regarding the clinical implications of the test results, as appropriate. Educate the patient regarding access to counseling services.

▶ Reinforce information given by the patient's HCP regarding further testing, treatment, or referral to another HCP. Instruct the patient in isolation precautions during time of communicability or contagion. Emphasize the need to return to have a convalescent blood sample taken in 3 wk. Answer any questions or address any concerns voiced by the patient and family.

▶ Depending on the results of this procedure, additional testing may be performed to evaluate or monitor progression of the disease process and determine the need for a change in therapy. Evaluate test results in relation to the patient's symptoms and other tests performed.

RELATED MONOGRAPHS:

▶ Related tests include CMV, fetal fibronectin, rubella, and viral culture.

▶ Refer to the Immune and Reproductive systems tables at the end of the book for related tests by body system.

Transferrin

SYNONYM/ACRONYM: Siderophilin, TRF.

COMMON USE: To assess circulating iron levels related to dietary intake to assist in diagnosing disorders such as iron deficiency anemia or hemochromatosis.

SPECIMEN: Serum (1 mL) collected in a red- or tiger-top tube.

NORMAL FINDINGS: (Method: Nephelometry)

Age	Conventional Units	SI Units (Conventional Units × 0.01)
Newborn	130–275 mg/dL	1.3–2.75 g/L
1–9 yr	180–330 mg/dL	1.8–3.3 g/L
10–19 yr	195–385 mg/dL	1.95–3.85 g/L
Adult		
Male	215–365 mg/dL	2.2–3.6 g/L
Female	250–380 mg/dL	2.5–3.8 g/L

DESCRIPTION: Transferrin is a glycoprotein formed in the liver. It transports circulating iron obtained from dietary intake and red blood cell breakdown. Transferrin carries 50% to 70% of the body's iron; normally it is approximately one-third saturated. Inadequate transferrin levels can lead to impaired hemoglobin synthesis and anemia. Transferrin is subject to diurnal variation, and it is responsible for the variation in levels of serum iron throughout the day. (See monograph titled "Iron-Binding Capacity [Total], Transferrin, and Iron Saturation.")

INDICATIONS

- Determine the iron-binding capacity of the blood
- Evaluate iron metabolism in iron-deficiency anemia
- Evaluate nutritional status
- Screen for hemochromatosis

POTENTIAL DIAGNOSIS

Increased in

- Estrogen therapy *(estrogen stimulates the liver to produce transferrin)*
- Iron-deficiency anemia *(the liver produces transferrin in response to decreased iron levels)*
- Pregnancy *(the liver produces transferrin in response to anemia of pregnancy)*

Decreased in

- Acute or chronic infection *(a negative acute-phase reactant protein whose levels decrease in response to inflammation)*
- Cancer (especially of the gastrointestinal tract) *(related to malnutrition)*
- Excessive protein loss from renal disease *(related to increased loss from damaged kidney)*
- Hepatic damage *(related to decreased synthesis in the liver)*
- Hereditary atransferrinemia
- Malnutrition *(related to a protein-deficient diet that does not provide the nutrients required for synthesis)*

CRITICAL FINDINGS: N/A

INTERFERING FACTORS

- Drugs that may increase transferrin levels include carbamazepine, danazol, mestranol, and oral contraceptives.
- Drugs that may decrease transferrin levels include cortisone and dextran.
- Transferrin levels are subject to diurnal variation and should be collected in the morning, when levels are highest.
- Failure to follow dietary restrictions before the procedure may cause the procedure to be canceled or repeated.

NURSING IMPLICATIONS AND PROCEDURE

PRETEST:

- Positively identify the patient using at least two unique identifiers before providing care, treatment, or services.
- *Patient Teaching:* Inform the patient this test can assist in evaluating for anemia.
- Obtain a history of the patient's complaints, including a list of known allergens, especially allergies or sensitivities to latex.
- Obtain a history of the patient's hematopoietic system, symptoms, and results of previously performed laboratory tests and diagnostic and surgical procedures.
- Obtain a list of the patient's current medications, including herbs, nutritional supplements, and nutraceuticals (see Appendix F).
- Review the procedure with the patient. Inform the patient that specimen collection takes approximately 5 to

10 min. Address concerns about pain and explain that there may be some discomfort during the venipuncture.

Sensitivity to social and cultural issues, as well as concern for modesty, is important in providing psychological support before, during, and after the procedure.

- Instruct the patient to fast for at least 12 hr before specimen collection.
- There are no fluid or medication restrictions unless by medical direction.

INTRATEST:

- Ensure that the patient has complied with dietary restrictions; ensure that food has been restricted for at least 12 hr prior to the procedure.
- If the patient has a history of allergic reaction to latex, avoid the use of equipment containing latex.
- Instruct the patient to cooperate fully and to follow directions. Direct the patient to breathe normally and to avoid unnecessary movement.
- Observe standard precautions, and follow the general guidelines in Appendix A. Positively identify the patient, and label the appropriate specimen container with the corresponding patient demographics, initials of the person collecting the specimen, date, and time of collection. Perform a venipuncture.
- Remove the needle and apply direct pressure with dry gauze to stop bleeding. Observe/assess venipuncture site for bleeding or hematoma formation and secure gauze with adhesive bandage.
- Promptly transport the specimen to the laboratory for processing and analysis.

POST-TEST:

- A report of the results will be made available to the requesting health-care provider (HCP), who will discuss the results with the patient.
- Instruct the patient to resume usual diet, as directed by the HCP.

Nutritional Considerations: The Institute of Medicine's Food and Nutrition Board suggests 8 mg as the daily recommended dietary allowance of iron for adult males and females age 51 to greater than 70 yr; 18 mg/d for adult females age 19 to 50 yr; 8 mg/d for adult males age 19 to 50 yr; 27 mg/d for pregnant females under age 18 through 50 yr; 9 mg/d for lactating females age 19 to 50 yr; 10 mg/d for lactating females under age 18 yr; 15 mg/d for female children age 14 to 18 yr; 11 mg/d for male children age 14 to 18 yr; 8 mg/d for children age 9 to 13 yr; 10 mg/d for children age 4 to 8 yr; 7 mg/d for children age 1 to 3 yr; 11 mg/d for children age 7 to 12 mo; and 0.27 mg/d for children age 0 to 6 mo (recommended adequate intake). Reprinted with permission from the National Academies Press, copyright 2013, National Academy of Sciences. Educate the patient with abnormal iron values that numerous factors affect the absorption of iron, enhancing or decreasing absorption regardless of the original content of the iron-containing dietary source. Patients must be educated to either increase or avoid intake of iron and iron-rich foods depending on their specific condition; for example, a patient with hemochromatosis or acute pernicious anemia should be educated to avoid foods rich in iron. Consumption of large amounts of alcohol damages the intestine and allows increased absorption of iron. A high intake of calcium and ascorbic acid also increases iron absorption. Iron absorption after a meal is also increased by factors in meat, fish, and poultry. Iron absorption is decreased by the absence (gastric resection) or diminished presence (use of antacids) of gastric acid. Phytic acids from cereals, tannins from tea and coffee, oxalic acid from vegetables, and minerals such as copper, zinc, and manganese interfere with iron absorption.

- Reinforce information given by the patient's HCP regarding further testing, treatment, or referral to another HCP. Answer any questions or address any concerns voiced by the patient or family. Educate the patient regarding access to nutritional counseling services. Provide contact information, if desired, for the Institute of Medicine of the National Academies (www.iom.edu).

Depending on the results of this procedure, additional testing may be performed to evaluate or monitor progression of the disease process and determine the need for a change in therapy. Evaluate test results in relation to the patient's symptoms and other tests performed.

RELATED MONOGRAPHS:

Related tests include A/G, cancer antigens, CBC, CBC RBC count, CBC RBC indices, CBC RBC morphology, ferritin, iron/TIBC, prealbumin, and total protein.

Refer to the Hematopoietic System table at the end of the book for related tests by body system.

Triglycerides

SYNONYM/ACRONYM: Trigs, TG.

COMMON USE: To evaluate triglyceride levels to assess cardiovascular disease risk and evaluate the effectiveness of therapeutic interventions.

SPECIMEN: Serum (1 mL) collected in a red- or tiger-top tube. Plasma (1 mL) collected in a green-top (heparin) tube is also acceptable.

NORMAL FINDINGS: (Method: Spectrophotometry)

ATP III Classification	Conventional Units	SI Units (Conventional Units × 0.0113)
Normal	Less than 150 mg/dL	Less than 1.7 mmol/L
Borderline high	150–199 mg/dL	1.7–2.2 mmol/L
High	200–499 mg/dL	2.2–5.6 mmol/L
Very high	Greater than 500 mg/dL	Greater than 5.6 mmol/L

DESCRIPTION: Triglycerides (TGs) are a combination of three fatty acids and one glycerol molecule. They are necessary to provide energy for various metabolic processes. Excess triglycerides are stored in adipose tissue, and the fatty acids provide the raw materials needed for conversion to glucose (gluconeogenesis) or for direct use as an energy source. Although fatty acids originate in the diet, many are also derived from unused glucose and amino acids that the liver converts into stored energy. Beyond triglyceride, total cholesterol, high-density lipoprotein (HDL), and low-density lipoprotein (LDL) cholesterol values, other important risk factors must be considered. The Framingham algorithm can assist in estimating the risk of developing coronary artery disease (CAD) within a 10-yr period. The National Cholesterol Education Program (NCEP) also provides important guidelines. The latest NCEP guidelines for target lipid levels, major risk factors, and

T

therapeutic interventions are outlined in Adult Treatment Panel III (ATP III). Triglyceride levels vary by age, gender, weight, and race:

Levels increase with age.

Levels are higher in men than in women (among women, those who take oral contraceptives have levels that are 20 to 40 mg/dL higher than those who do not).

Levels are higher in overweight and obese people than in those with normal weight.

Levels in African Americans are approximately 10 to 20 mg/dL lower than in whites.

INDICATIONS

- Evaluate known or suspected disorders associated with altered triglyceride levels
- Identify hyperlipoproteinemia (hyperlipidemia) in patients with a family history of the disorder
- Monitor the response to drugs known to alter triglyceride levels
- Screen adults who are either over 40 yr or obese to estimate the risk for atherosclerotic cardiovascular disease

POTENTIAL DIAGNOSIS

Increased in

- Acute myocardial infarction *(elevated TG is identified as an independent risk factor in the development of CAD)*
- Alcoholism *(related to decreased breakdown of fats in the liver and increased blood levels)*
- Anorexia nervosa *(compensatory increase secondary to starvation)*
- Chronic ischemic heart disease *(elevated TG is identified as an independent risk factor in the development of CAD)*
- Cirrhosis *(increased TG blood levels related to decreased breakdown of fats in the liver)*

- Glycogen storage disease *(G6PD deficiency, e.g., von Gierke's disease, results in hepatic overproduction of very-low-density lipoprotein [VLDL] cholesterol, the TG-rich lipoprotein)*
- Gout *(TG is frequently elevated in patients with gout, possibly related to alterations in apolipoprotein E genotypes)*
- Hyperlipoproteinemia *(related to increase in transport proteins)*
- Hypertension *(associated with elevated TG, which is identified as an independent risk factor in the development of CAD)*
- Hypothyroidism *(significant relationship between elevated TG and decreased metabolism)*
- Impaired glucose tolerance *(increase in insulin stimulates production of TG by liver)*
- Metabolic syndrome *(syndrome consisting of obesity, high blood pressure, and insulin resistance)*
- Nephrotic syndrome *(related to absence or insufficient levels of lipoprotein lipase to remove circulating TG and to decreased catabolism of TG-rich VLDL lipoproteins)*
- Obesity *(significant and complex relationship between obesity and elevated TG)*
- Pancreatitis *(acute and chronic; related to effects on insulin production)*
- Pregnancy *(increased demand for production of hormones related to pregnancy)*
- Renal failure *(related to diabetes; elevated insulin levels stimulate production of TG by liver)*
- Respiratory distress syndrome *(related to artificial lung surfactant used for therapy)*
- Stress *(related to poor diet; effect of hormones secreted under stressful situations that affect glucose levels)*

T

- Syndrome X *(metabolic syndrome consisting of obesity, high blood pressure, and insulin resistance)*
- Werner's syndrome *(clinical features resemble syndrome X)*

Decreased in

- End-stage liver disease *(related to cessation of liver function that results in decreased production of TG and TG transport proteins)*
- Hyperthyroidism *(related to increased catabolism of VLDL transport proteins and general increase in metabolism)*
- Hypolipoproteinemia and abetalipoproteinemia *(related to decrease in transport proteins)*
- Intestinal lymphangiectasia
- Malabsorption disorders *(inadequate supply from dietary sources)*
- Malnutrition *(inadequate supply from dietary sources)*

CRITICAL FINDINGS: N/A

INTERFERING FACTORS

- Drugs that may increase triglyceride levels include acetylsalicylic acid, aldatense, atenolol, bisoprolol, β blockers, bendroflumethiazide, cholestyramine, conjugated estrogens, cyclosporine, estrogen/progestin therapy, estropipate, ethynodiol, etretinate, furosemide, glucocorticoids, hydrochlorothiazide, isotretinoin, labetalol, levonorgestrel, medroxyprogesterone, mepindolol, methyclothiazide, metoprolol, miconazole, mirtazapine, nadolol, nafarelin, oral contraceptives, oxprenolol, pindolol, prazosin, propranolol, tamoxifen, thiazides, ticlopidine, timolol, and tretinoin.
- Drugs and substances that may decrease triglyceride levels include anabolic steroids, ascorbic acid, beclobrate, bezafibrate, captopril, carvedilol, celiprolol, celiprolol, chenodiol, cholestyramine, cilazapril, ciprofibrate, clofibrate, colestipol, danazol, dextrothyroxine, doxazosin, enalapril, eptastatin (type IIb only), fenofibrate, flaxseed oil, fluvastatin, gemfibrozil, halofenate, insulin, levonorgestrel, levothyroxine, lifibrol, lovastatin, medroxyprogesterone, metformin, nafenopin, niacin, niceritrol, Norplant, pentoxifylline, pinacidil, pindolol, pravastatin, prazosin, probucol, simvastatin, and verapamil.
- Failure to follow dietary restrictions before the procedure may cause the procedure to be canceled or repeated.

NURSING IMPLICATIONS AND PROCEDURE

PRETEST:

- Positively identify the patient using at least two unique identifiers before providing care, treatment, or services.
- *Patient Teaching:* Inform the patient this test can assist in monitoring and evaluating lipid levels.
- Obtain a history of the patient's complaints, including a list of known allergens, especially allergies or sensitivities to latex.
- Obtain a history of the patient's cardiovascular system, symptoms, and results of previously performed laboratory tests and diagnostic and surgical procedures.
- Obtain a list of the patient's current medications, including herbs, nutritional supplements, and nutraceuticals (see Appendix F).
- Review the procedure with the patient. Inform the patient that specimen collection takes approximately 5 to 10 min. Address concerns about pain and explain that there may be some discomfort during the venipuncture.
- *Sensitivity to social and cultural issues,* as well as concern for modesty, is important in providing psychological support before, during, and after the procedure.
- The patient should fast for 12 hr before specimen collection. Ideally, the patient should be on a stable diet for 3 wk

and avoid alcohol consumption for 3 days before specimen collection. Protocols may vary among facilities. There are no medication restrictions unless by medical direction.

INTRATEST:

Ensure that the patient has complied with dietary restrictions and other pre-testing preparations; assure that food has been restricted for at least 12 hr prior to the procedure.

If the patient has a history of allergic reaction to latex, avoid the use of equipment containing latex.

Instruct the patient to cooperate fully and to follow directions. Direct the patient to breathe normally and to avoid unnecessary movement.

Observe standard precautions, and follow the general guidelines in Appendix A. Positively identify the patient, and label the appropriate specimen container with the corresponding patient demographics, initials of the person collecting the specimen, date, and time of collection. Perform a venipuncture.

Remove the needle and apply direct pressure with dry gauze to stop bleeding. Observe/assess venipuncture site for bleeding or hematoma formation and secure gauze with adhesive bandage.

Promptly transport the specimen to the laboratory for processing and analysis.

POST-TEST:

A report of the results will be made available to the requesting health-care provider (HCP), who will discuss the results with the patient.

Instruct the patient to resume usual diet, as directed by the HCP.

Nutritional Considerations: Increased triglyceride levels may be associated with atherosclerosis and CAD. The American Heart Association and National Heart, Lung, and Blood Institute (NHLBI) recommend nutritional therapy for individuals identified to be at high risk for developing CAD or individuals who have specific risk factors and/or existing medical conditions (e.g., elevated LDL cholesterol levels,

other lipid disorders, insulin-dependent diabetes, insulin resistance, or metabolic syndrome). If overweight, the patient should be encouraged to achieve a normal weight. Guidelines for the Therapeutic Lifestyle Changes (TLC) diet are outlined in the Third Report of the Expert Panel on Detection, Evaluation, and Treatment of High Blood Cholesterol in Adults (Adult Treatment Panel III [ATP III]). The TLC diet emphasizes a reduction in foods high in saturated fats and cholesterol. Red meats, eggs, and dairy products are the major sources of saturated fats and cholesterol. If triglycerides also are elevated, the patient should be advised to eliminate or reduce alcohol and simple carbohydrates from the diet. The TLC approach also includes the use of plant stanols or sterols and increased dissolved fiber as an option for lowering LDL cholesterol levels; nutritional recommendations for daily total caloric intake; recommendations for allowable percentage of calories derived from fat (saturated and unsaturated), carbohydrates, protein, and cholesterol; as well as recommendations for daily expenditure of energy.

Nutritional Considerations: Overweight patients with high blood pressure should be encouraged to achieve a normal weight. Other changeable risk factors warranting patient education include strategies to safely decrease sodium intake, increase physical activity, decrease alcohol consumption, eliminate tobacco use, and decrease cholesterol levels.

Sensitivity to social and cultural issues: Numerous studies point to the increased prevalence of excess body weight in American children and adolescents. Experts estimate that obesity is present in 25% of the population ages 6 to 11 yr. The medical, social, and emotional consequences of excess body weight are significant. Special attention should be given to instructing the pediatric patient and caregiver regarding health risks and weight control.

Recognize anxiety related to test results, and be supportive of fear of shortened life expectancy. Discuss the implications of abnormal test results on the patient's lifestyle. Provide teaching and information regarding the clinical implications of the test results, as appropriate. Educate the patient regarding access to counseling services. Provide contact information, if desired, for the American Heart Association (www.americanheart.org) or the NHLBI (www.nhlbi.nih.gov).

Reinforce information given by the patient's HCP regarding further testing, treatment, or referral to another HCP. Answer any questions or address any concerns voiced by the patient or family.

Depending on the results of this procedure, additional testing may be performed to evaluate or monitor progression of the disease process and determine the need for a change in therapy. Evaluate test results in relation to the patient's symptoms and other tests performed.

RELATED MONOGRAPHS:

Related tests include antiarrhythmic drugs, apolipoprotein A and B, AST, atrial natriuretic peptide, blood gases, BNP, calcium (total and ionized), cholesterol (total, HDL, and LDL), CT cardiac scoring, C-reactive protein, CK and isoenzymes, echocardiography, glucose, glycated hemoglobin, Holter monitor, homocysteine, ketones, LDH and isoenzymes, lipoprotein electrophoresis, magnesium, MRI chest, myocardial infarct scan, myocardial perfusion heart scan, myoglobin, PET heart, potassium, and troponin.

Refer to the Cardiovascular System table at the end of the book for related tests by body system.

Triiodothyronine, Free

SYNONYM/ACRONYM: Free T_3, FT_3.

COMMON USE: A complementary adjunct to evaluate thyroid hormone levels primarily related to hyperthyroidism and to assess causes of hypothyroidism.

SPECIMEN: Serum (1 mL) collected in a red- or tiger-top tube.

NORMAL FINDINGS: (Method: Immunoassay)

Age	Conventional Units	SI Units (Conventional Units × 0.0154)
0–3 days	2–7.9 pg/mL	0.03–0.12 pmol/L
4–30 days	2–5.2 pg/mL	0.03–0.08 pmol/L
1–23 mo	1.6–6.4 pg/mL	0.02–0.1 pmol/L
2–6 yr	2–6 pg/mL	0.03–0.09 pmol/L
7–17 yr	2.9–5.1 pg/mL	0.04–0.08 pmol/L
Adults and older adults	2.6–4.8 pg/mL	0.04–0.07 pmol/L
Pregnant women (4–9 mo gestation)	2–3.4 pg/mL	0.03–0.05 pmol/L

T

DESCRIPTION: Unlike the thyroid hormone thyroxine (T_4), most T_3 is converted enzymatically from T_4 in the tissues rather than being produced directly by the thyroid gland (see monograph titled "Thyroxine, Total"). Approximately one-third of T_4 is converted to T_3. Most T_3 in the serum (99.97%) is bound to thyroxine-binding globulin (TBG), prealbumin, and albumin. The remainder (0.03%) circulates as unbound or free T_3, which is the physiologically active form. Levels of free T_3 are proportional to levels of total T_3. The advantage of measuring free T_3 instead of total T_3 is that, unlike total T_3 measurements, free T_3 levels are not affected by fluctuations in TBG levels. T_3 is four to five times more biologically potent than T_4. This hormone, along with T_4, is responsible for maintaining a euthyroid state. Free T_3 measurements are rarely required, but they are indicated in the diagnosis of T_3 toxicosis and when certain drugs are being administered that interfere with the conversion of T_4 to T_3.

INDICATIONS
- Adjunctive aid to thyroid-stimulating hormone (TSH) and free T_4 assessment
- Assist in the diagnosis of T_3 toxicosis

POTENTIAL DIAGNOSIS

Increased in
- High altitude
- Hyperthyroidism *(triiodothyronine is produced independently of stimulation by TSH)*
- T_3 toxicosis

Decreased in
- Hypothyroidism *(thyroid hormones are not produced in sufficient quantities regardless of TSH levels)*
- Malnutrition *(related to protein or iodine deficiency; iodine is needed for thyroid hormone synthesis and proteins are needed for transport)*
- Nonthyroidal chronic diseases
- Pregnancy (late)

CRITICAL FINDINGS: N/A

INTERFERING FACTORS
- Drugs that may increase free T_3 include acetylsalicylic acid, amiodarone, and levothyroxine.
- Drugs that may decrease free T_3 include amiodarone, methimazole, phenytoin, propranolol, and radiographic agents.

NURSING IMPLICATIONS AND PROCEDURE

PRETEST:

- Positively identify the patient using at least two unique identifiers before providing care, treatment, or services.
- *Patient Teaching:* Inform the patient this test can assist in assessing thyroid gland function.
- Obtain a history of the patient's complaints, including a list of known allergens, especially allergies or sensitivities to latex.
- Obtain a history of the patient's endocrine system, symptoms, and results of previously performed laboratory tests and diagnostic and surgical procedures.
- Obtain a list of the patient's current medications, including herbs, nutritional supplements, and nutraceuticals (see Appendix F).
- Review the procedure with the patient. Inform the patient that specimen collection takes approximately 5 to 10 min. Address concerns about pain and explain that there may be some discomfort during the venipuncture.
- *Sensitivity to social and cultural issues,* as well as concern for modesty, is important in providing psychological support before, during, and after the procedure.

T

▶ There are no food, fluid, or medication restrictions unless by medical direction.

INTRATEST:

▶ If the patient has a history of allergic reaction to latex, avoid the use of equipment containing latex.

▶ Instruct the patient to cooperate fully and to follow directions. Direct the patient to breathe normally and to avoid unnecessary movement.

▶ Observe standard precautions, and follow the general guidelines in Appendix A. Positively identify the patient, and label the appropriate specimen container with the corresponding patient demographics, initials of the person collecting the specimen, date, and time of collection. Perform a venipuncture.

▶ Remove the needle and apply direct pressure with dry gauze to stop bleeding. Observe/assess venipuncture site for bleeding or hematoma formation and secure gauze with adhesive bandage.

▶ Promptly transport the specimen to the laboratory for processing and analysis.

POST-TEST:

▶ A report of the results will be made available to the requesting health-care provider (HCP), who will discuss the results with the patient.

▶ Reinforce information given by the patient's HCP regarding further testing, treatment, or referral to another HCP. Answer any questions or address any concerns voiced by the patient or family.

▶ Depending on the results of this procedure, additional testing may be performed to evaluate or monitor progression of the disease process and determine the need for a change in therapy. Evaluate test results in relation to the patient's symptoms and other tests performed.

RELATED MONOGRAPHS:

▶ Related tests include albumin, antibodies antithyroglobulin, biopsy thyroid, copper, PTH, prealbumin, protein, RAIU, thyroglobulin, TBII, thyroid scan, TSH, TSI, T_4, free T_4, T_3, and US thyroid.

▶ Refer to the Endocrine System table at the end of the book for related tests by body system.

Triiodothyronine, Total

SYNONYM/ACRONYM: T_3.

COMMON USE: To assist in evaluating thyroid function primarily related to diagnosing hyperthyroidism and monitoring the effectiveness of therapeutic interventions.

SPECIMEN: Serum (1 mL) collected in a red- or tiger-top tube. Plasma (1 mL) collected in a green-top (heparin) tube is also acceptable.

NORMAL FINDINGS: (Method: Immunoassay)

T

Age	Conventional Units	SI Units (Conventional Units × 0.0154)
Cord blood	14–86 ng/dL	0.22–1.32 nmol/L
1–3 days	100–292 ng/dL	1.54–4.5 nmol/L
4–30 days	62–243 ng/dL	0.96–3.74 nmol/L
1–12 mo	105–245 ng/dL	1.62–3.77 nmol/L
1–5 yr	105–269 ng/dL	1.62–4.14 nmol/L
6–10 yr	94–241 ng/dL	1.45–3.71 nmol/L
16–20 yr	80–210 ng/dL	1.23–3.23 nmol/L
Adult	70–204 ng/dL	1.08–3.14 nmol/L
Older adult	40–181 ng/dL	0.62–2.79 nmol/L
Pregnant woman (last 4 mo gestation)	116–247 ng/dL	1.79–3.8 nmol/L

DESCRIPTION: Unlike the thyroid hormone thyroxine (T_4), most T_3 is converted enzymatically from T_4 in the tissues rather than being produced directly by the thyroid gland (see monograph titled "Thyroxine, Total"). Approximately one-third of T_4 is converted to T_3. Most T_3 in the serum (99.97%) is bound to thyroxine-binding globulin (TBG), prealbumin, and albumin. The remainder (0.03%) circulates as unbound or free T_3, which is the physiologically active form. Levels of free T_3 are proportional to levels of total T_3. The advantage of measuring free T_3 instead of total T_3 is that, unlike total T_3 measurements, free T_3 levels are not affected by fluctuations in TBG levels. T_3 is four to five times more biologically potent than T_4. This hormone, along with T_4, is responsible for maintaining a euthyroid state.

INDICATIONS

Adjunctive aid to thyroid-stimulating hormone (TSH) and free T_4 assessment.

POTENTIAL DIAGNOSIS

Increased in
- Conditions with increased TBG *(e.g., pregnancy and estrogen therapy)*
- Early thyroid failure
- Hyperthyroidism *(triiodothyronine is produced independently of stimulation by TSH)*
- Iodine-deficiency goiter
- T_3 toxicosis
- Thyrotoxicosis factitia *(laboratory tests do not distinguish between endogenous and exogenous sources)*
- Treated hyperthyroidism

Decreased in
- Acute and subacute nonthyroidal disease *(pathophysiology is unclear)*
- Conditions with decreased TBG *(TBG is the major transport protein)*
- Hypothyroidism *(thyroid hormones are not produced in sufficient quantities regardless of TSH levels)*
- Malnutrition *(related to insufficient protein sources to form albumin and TBG)*

CRITICAL FINDINGS: N/A

T

INTERFERING FACTORS

- Drugs that may increase total T_3 levels include amiodarone, amphetamine, benziodarone, clofibrate, fluorouracil, halofenate, insulin, levothyroxine, methadone, opiates, oral contraceptives, phenothiazine, phenytoin, prostaglandins, and T_3.
- Drugs that may decrease total T_3 levels include acetylsalicylic acid, amiodarone, anabolic steroids, asparaginase, carbamazepine, cholestyramine, clomiphene, colestipol, dexamethasone, fenclofenac, furosemide, glucocorticoids, hydrocortisone, interferon alfa-2b, iobenzamic acid, iopanoic acid, ipodate, isotretinoin, lithium, methimazole, netilmicin, oral contraceptives, penicillamine, phenylbutazone, phenytoin, potassium iodide, prednisone, propranolol, propylthiouracil, radiographic agents, sodium ipodate, salicylate, sulfonylureas, and tyropanoic acid.

NURSING IMPLICATIONS AND PROCEDURE

PRETEST:

- Positively identify the patient using at least two unique identifiers before providing care, treatment, or services.
- *Patient Teaching:* Inform the patient this test can assist in assessing thyroid gland function.
- Obtain a history of the patient's complaints, including a list of known allergens, especially allergies or sensitivities to latex.
- Obtain a history of the patient's endocrine system, symptoms, and results of previously performed laboratory tests and diagnostic and surgical procedures.
- Obtain a list of the patient's current medications, including herbs, nutritional supplements, and nutraceuticals (see Appendix F).
- Review the procedure with the patient. Inform the patient that specimen collection takes approximately 5 to 10 min. Address concerns about pain and explain that there may be some discomfort during the venipuncture. *Sensitivity to social and cultural issues,* as well as concern for modesty, is important in providing psychological support before, during, and after the procedure.
- There are no food, fluid, or medication restrictions unless by medical direction.

INTRATEST:

- If the patient has a history of allergic reaction to latex, avoid the use of equipment containing latex.
- Instruct the patient to cooperate fully and to follow directions. Direct the patient to breathe normally and to avoid unnecessary movement.
- Observe standard precautions, and follow the general guidelines in Appendix A. Positively identify the patient, and label the appropriate specimen container with the corresponding patient demographics, initials of the person collecting the specimen, date, and time of collection. Perform a venipuncture.
- Remove the needle and apply direct pressure with dry gauze to stop bleeding. Observe/assess venipuncture site for bleeding or hematoma formation and secure gauze with adhesive bandage.
- Promptly transport the specimen to the laboratory for processing and analysis.

POST-TEST:

- A report of the results will be made available to the requesting health-care provider (HCP), who will discuss the results with the patient.
- Reinforce information given by the patient's HCP regarding further testing, treatment, or referral to another HCP. Answer any questions or address any concerns voiced by the patient or family.
- Depending on the results of this procedure, additional testing may be performed to evaluate or monitor progression of the disease process and determine the need for a change in

therapy. Evaluate test results in relation to the patient's symptoms and other tests performed.

RELATED MONOGRAPHS:

Related tests include albumin, antibodies antithyroglobulin, biopsy thyroid, copper, PTH, prealbumin, protein, RAIU, thyroglobulin, TBII, thyroid scan, TSH, TSI, T_4, free T_4, free T_3, and US thyroid.

Refer to the Endocrine System table at the end of the book for related tests by body system.

Troponins I and T

SYNONYM/ACRONYM: Cardiac troponin, cardiac troponin I (cTnI), cardiac troponin T (cTnT).

COMMON USE: To assist in evaluating myocardial muscle damage related to disorders such as myocardial infarction.

SPECIMEN: Serum (1 mL) collected in a red- or tiger-top tube. Plasma (1 mL) collected in a green-top (heparin) tube is also acceptable. Serial sampling is highly recommended. Care must be taken to use the same type of collection container if serial measurements are to be taken.

NORMAL FINDINGS: (Method: Enzyme immunoassay)

Troponin I	
0–30 d	Less than 4.8 ng/mL
1–3 mo	Less than 0.4 ng/mL
3–6 mo	Less than 0.3 ng/mL
7–12 mo	Less than 0.2 ng/mL
1–18 yr	Less than 0.1 ng/mL
Adult	Less than 0.05 ng/mL
Troponin T	Less than 0.2 ng/mL

Normal values can vary significantly due to differences in test kit reagents and instrumentation. The testing laboratory should be consulted for comparison of results to the corresponding reference range.

DESCRIPTION: Troponin is a complex of three contractile proteins that regulate the interaction of actin and myosin. Troponin C is the calcium-binding subunit; it does not have a cardiac muscle–specific subunit. Troponin I and troponin T, however, do have cardiac muscle–specific subunits. They are detectable a few hours to 7 days after the onset of symptoms of myocardial damage. Troponin I is thought to be a more specific marker of cardiac damage than troponin T. Cardiac troponin I begins to rise 2 to 6 hr after myocardial infarction (MI). It has a biphasic peak: It initially peaks at 15 to 24 hr after MI and then exhibits a lower peak after 60 to 80 hr. Cardiac troponin T levels rise 2 to 6 hr after MI and remain elevated. Both proteins return to the reference range 7 days after MI.

T

Timing for Appearance and Resolution of Serum/Plasma Cardiac Markers in Acute MI

Cardiac Marker	Appearance (hr)	Peak (hr)	Resolution (days)
AST	6–8	24–48	3–4
CK (total)	4–6	24	2–3
Cardiac Marker	Appearance (hr)	Peak (hr)	Resolution (days)
CK-MB	4–6	15–20	2–3
LDH	12	24–48	10–14
Myoglobin	1–3	4–12	1
Troponin I	2–6	15–20	5–7

AST = aspartate aminotransferase; CK = creatine kinase; CK-MB = creatine kinase MB fraction; LDH = lactate dehydrogenase.

INDICATIONS

- Assist in establishing a diagnosis of MI
- Evaluate myocardial cell damage

POTENTIAL DIAGNOSIS

Increased in

Conditions that result in cardiac tissue damage; troponin is released from damaged tissue into the circulation.

- Acute MI
- Minor myocardial damage
- Myocardial damage after coronary artery bypass graft surgery or percutaneous transluminal coronary angioplasty

Unstable angina pectoris

Decreased in: N/A

CRITICAL FINDINGS: N/A

INTERFERING FACTORS: N/A

NURSING IMPLICATIONS AND PROCEDURE

PRETEST:

Positively identify the patient using at least two unique identifiers before providing care, treatment, or services. *Patient Teaching:* Inform the patient this test can assist in evaluating heart damage.

- Obtain a history of the patient's complaints, including a list of known allergens, especially allergies or sensitivities to latex.
- Obtain a history of the patient's cardiovascular system, symptoms, and results of previously performed laboratory tests and diagnostic and surgical procedures.
- Obtain a list of the patient's current medications, including herbs, nutritional supplements, and nutraceuticals (see Appendix F).
- Review the procedure with the patient. Inform the patient that a number of samples will be collected. Collection at time of admission, 2 to 4 hr, 6 to 8 hr, and 12 hr after admission are the minimal recommendations. Additional samples may be requested. Inform the patient that specimen collection takes approximately 5 to 10 min. Address concerns about pain and explain that there may be some discomfort during the venipuncture.
- *Sensitivity to social and cultural issues,* as well as concern for modesty, is important in providing psychological support before, during, and after the procedure.
- There are no food, fluid, or medication restrictions unless by medical direction.

INTRATEST:

- If the patient has a history of allergic reaction to latex, avoid the use of equipment containing latex.
- Instruct the patient to cooperate fully and to follow directions. Direct the

patient to breathe normally and to avoid unnecessary movement.

▸ Observe standard precautions, and follow the general guidelines in Appendix A. Positively identify the patient, and label the appropriate specimen container with the corresponding patient demographics, initials of the person collecting the specimen, date, and time of collection. Perform a venipuncture.

▸ Remove the needle and apply direct pressure with dry gauze to stop bleeding. Observe/assess venipuncture site for bleeding or hematoma formation and secure gauze with adhesive bandage.

▸ Promptly transport the specimen to the laboratory for processing and analysis.

POST-TEST:

▸ A report of the results will be made available to the requesting HCP, who will discuss the results with the patient.

▸ *Nutritional Considerations:* Increased troponin levels are associated with coronary artery disease (CAD). The American Heart Association and National Heart, Lung, and Blood Institute (NHLBI) recommend nutritional therapy for individuals identified to be at high risk for developing CAD or individuals who have specific risk factors and/or existing medical conditions (e.g., elevated LDL cholesterol levels, other lipid disorders, insulin-dependent diabetes, insulin resistance, or metabolic syndrome). If overweight, the patient should be encouraged to achieve a normal weight. Guidelines for the Therapeutic Lifestyle Changes (TLC) diet are outlined in the Third Report of the Expert Panel on Detection, Evaluation, and Treatment of High Blood Cholesterol in Adults (Adult Treatment Panel III [ATP III]). The TLC diet emphasizes a reduction in foods high in saturated fats and cholesterol. Red meats, eggs, and dairy products are the major sources of saturated fats and cholesterol. If triglycerides also are elevated, the patient should be advised to eliminate or reduce alcohol and simple carbohydrates from the diet. The TLC approach also includes the use of plant stanols or sterols and increased dissolved fiber as an option for lowering LDL cholesterol levels; nutritional recommendations for daily total caloric intake; recommendations for allowable percentage of calories derived from fat (saturated and unsaturated), carbohydrates, protein, and cholesterol; as well as recommendations for daily expenditure of energy.

▸ *Nutritional Considerations:* Overweight patients with high blood pressure should be encouraged to achieve a normal weight. Other changeable risk factors warranting patient education include strategies to safely decrease sodium intake, increase physical activity, decrease alcohol consumption, eliminate tobacco use, and decrease cholesterol levels.

▸ *Social and Cultural Considerations:* Numerous studies point to the prevalence of excess body weight in American children and adolescents. Experts estimate that obesity is present in 25% of the population ages 6 to 11 yr. The medical, social, and emotional consequences of excess body weight are significant. Special attention should be given to instructing the child and caregiver regarding health risks and weight-control education.

▸ Recognize anxiety related to test results, and be supportive of fear of shortened life expectancy. Discuss the implications of abnormal test results on the patient's lifestyle. Provide teaching and information regarding the clinical implications of the test results, as appropriate. Educate the patient regarding access to counseling services. Provide contact information, if desired, for the American Heart Association (www.americanheart.org) or the NHLBI (www.nhlbi.nih.gov).

▸ Reinforce information given by the patient's HCP regarding further testing, treatment, or referral to another HCP. Answer any questions or address any concerns voiced by the patient or family.

▸ Depending on the results of this procedure, additional testing may be performed to evaluate or monitor progression of the disease process and determine the need for a change in therapy. Evaluate test results in relation to the patient's symptoms and other tests performed.

RELATED MONOGRAPHS:

- Related tests include antiarrhythmic drugs, apolipoprotein A and B, AST, ANP, blood gases, blood pool imaging, BNP, calcium, ionized calcium, cholesterol (total, HDL, and LDL), CRP, CT cardiac scoring, CK and isoenzymes, culture viral, echocardiography, echocardiography transesophageal, ECG, exercise stress test, glucose, glycated hemoglobin, Holter monitor, homocysteine, ketones, LDH and isoenzymes, lipoprotein electrophoresis, magnesium, MRI chest, MI infarct scan, myocardial perfusion heart scan, myoglobin, pericardial fluid analysis, PET heart, potassium, and triglycerides.
- Refer to the Cardiovascular System table at the end of the book for related tests by body system.

Tuberculosis: Skin and Blood Tests

SYNONYM/ACRONYM: TST, TB tine test, PPD, Mantoux skin test, QuantiFERON-TB Gold blood test (QFT-G), QuantiFERON-TB Gold In-Tube test (QFT-GIT), T-SPOT.TB test (T-SPOT).

COMMON USE: To evaluate for current or past tuberculin infection or exposure.

SPECIMEN: Whole blood (5 mL) collected in a green-top (LiHep) tube (QuantiFERON-TB Gold and T-SPOT.TB blood tests), 1 mL whole blood collected in each of 3 special (Nil, Antigen and Mitogen) specimen containers (QuantiFERON-TB Gold In-Tube test).

NORMAL FINDINGS: (Method: Intradermal skin test, enzyme-linked immunosorbent assay [ELISA] blood test for QuantiFERON assays, enzyme-linked immunoSpot [ELISPOT] for T-SPOT.TB test) Negative.

DESCRIPTION: Tuberculin skin tests are done to determine past or present exposure to tuberculosis (TB). The multipuncture or tine test, a screening technique, uses either purified protein derivative (PPD) of tuberculin or old tuberculin. A positive response at the puncture site indicates cell-mediated immunity to the organism or a delayed hypersensitivity caused by interaction of the sensitized T lymphocytes. Verification of the patient's positive response to the multipuncture test is done with the more definitive Mantoux test using Aplisol or Tubersol administered by intradermal injection. The Mantoux test is the test of choice in symptomatic patients. It is also used in some settings as a screening test. A negative result is judged if there is no sign of redness or induration at the site of the injection or if the zone of redness and induration is less than 5 mm in diameter. A positive result is evidenced by an area of erythema and induration at the injection site that is greater than

10 mm. A positive result does not distinguish between active and dormant infection. A positive response to the Mantoux test is followed up with chest radiography and bacteriological sputum testing to confirm diagnosis.

The QuantiFERON-TB Gold (QFT-G), QuantiFERON-TB Gold In-Tube (QFT-GIT), and T-SPOT.TB interferon release blood tests are approved by the U.S. Food and Drug Administration for all applications in which the TB skin test is used. The blood tests are procedures in which T lymphocytes from the patient, either in whole blood or harvested from whole blood, are incubated with a reagent cocktail of peptides that simulate two or three proteins, ESAT-6, CFP-10, and TB7.7, made only by *Mycobacterium tuberculosis*. These proteins are not found in the blood of previously vaccinated individuals or individuals who do not have TB. The blood test offers the advantage of eliminating many of the false reactions encountered with skin testing, only a single patient visit is required, and results can be available within 24 hr. The blood tests and skin tests are approved as indirect tests for *Mycobacterium tuberculosis*, and the Centers for Disease Control and Prevention (CDC) recommends their use in conjunction with risk assessment, chest x-ray and other appropriate medical and diagnostic evaluations.

INDICATIONS

* Evaluate cough, weight loss, fatigue, hemoptysis, and abnormal x-rays to determine if the cause of symptoms is TB
* Evaluate known or suspected exposure to TB, with or without symptoms, to determine if TB is present
* Evaluate patients with medical conditions placing them at risk for TB (e.g., AIDS, lymphoma, diabetes)
* Screen infants with the tine test at the time of first immunizations to determine TB exposure
* Screen populations at risk for developing TB (e.g., health-care providers [HCPs], nursing home residents, correctional facility personnel, prison inmates, and residents of the inner city living in poor hygienic conditions)

POTENTIAL DIAGNOSIS

Positive findings in
* Pulmonary TB

CRITICAL FINDINGS ◈
* Positive results

Note and immediately report to the HCP positive results and related symptoms.

INTERFERING FACTORS

General
* Each of the blood and skin tests evaluate different facets of the immune response and use different methodologies and reagents; interpretations may not be interchangeable.

Skin Test
* Drugs such as immunosuppressive agents or steroids can alter results.
* Diseases such as hematological cancers or sarcoidosis can alter results.
* Recent or present bacterial, fungal, or viral infections may affect results. False-positive results may be caused by the presence of nontuberculous mycobacteria or by serial testing.
* False-negative results can occur if sensitized T cells are temporarily decreased. False-negative results also can occur in the presence of bacterial infections, immunological deficiencies, immunosuppressive

agents, live-virus vaccinations (e.g., measles, mumps, varicella, rubella), malnutrition, old age, overwhelming TB, renal failure, and active viral infections (e.g., chickenpox, measles, mumps).

- Improper storage of the tuberculin solution (e.g., with respect to temperature, exposure to light, and stability on opening) may affect the results.
- Improper technique when performing the intradermal injection (e.g., injecting into subcutaneous tissue) may cause false-negative results.
- Incorrect amount or dilution of antigen injected or delayed injection after drawing the antigen up into the syringe may affect the results.
- Incorrect reading of the measurement of response or timing of the reading may interfere with results.
- ❖ It is not known whether the test has teratogenic effects or reproductive implications; the test should be administered to pregnant women only when clearly indicated.
- ❖ The test should not be administered to a patient with a previously positive tuberculin skin test because of the danger of severe reaction, including vesiculation, ulceration, and necrosis.
- The test does not distinguish between current and past infection.

Blood Test

- The performance of these blood tests has not been evaluated in large studies with patients who have impaired or altered immune function, have or are highly likely to develop TB, are younger than 17, are pregnant, or have diseases other than TB. These individuals are either immunosuppressed, immunocompromised, or have immature immune function and may not produce sufficient numbers of T lymphocytes for accurate results. The

testing laboratory should be consulted for interpretation of results or limitations for use with patients in these categories.
- False-negative results are possible due to exposure or infection prior to development of detectable immune response.
- False-positive results are possible due to some cross-reactivity to some strains of environmental mycobacteria.
- False-negative results are possible due to exposure or infection prior to development of detectable immune response.

NURSING IMPLICATIONS AND PROCEDURE

PRETEST:

Blood and Skin Tests

Positively identify the patient using at least two unique identifiers before providing care, treatment, or services.

Patient Teaching: Inform the patient this test can assess for a tuberculin infection or exposure.

Obtain a history of the patient's complaints, including a list of known allergens, especially allergies and sensitivities to latex.

Obtain a history of the patient's immune and respiratory systems, symptoms, and results of previously performed laboratory tests and diagnostic and surgical procedures. Obtain a history of TB or TB exposure, signs and symptoms indicating possible TB, and other skin tests or vaccinations and sensitivities.

Obtain a list of the patient's current medications, including herbs, nutritional supplements, and nutraceuticals (see Appendix F).

Review the procedure with the patient.

Skin Test

Before beginning the test, ensure that the patient does not currently have TB and has not previously had a positive skin test. Do not administer the test if the patient has a skin rash or other

T

eruptions at the test site. Inform the patient that the procedure takes approximately 5 min. Address concerns about pain and explain that a moderate amount of pain may be experienced when the intradermal injection is performed.

Emphasize to the patient that the area should not be scratched or disturbed after the injection and before the reading.

Blood Test

Inform the patient that specimen collection takes approximately 5 to 10 min. Address concerns about pain and explain that there may be some discomfort during the venipuncture.

Blood and Skin Tests

Sensitivity to social and cultural issues, as well as concern for modesty, is important in providing psychological support before, during, and after the procedure.

There are no food, fluid, or medication restrictions unless by medical direction.

INTRATEST:

Observe standard precautions, and follow the general guidelines in Appendix A. Positively identify the patient.

Blood and Skin Tests

If the patient has a history of allergic reaction to latex, avoid the use of equipment containing latex.

Instruct the patient to cooperate fully and to follow directions. Direct the patient to breathe normally and to avoid unnecessary movement.

Skin Test

Have epinephrine hydrochloride solution (1:1,000) available in the event of anaphylaxis.

Cleanse the skin site on the lower anterior forearm with alcohol swabs and allow to air-dry.

Multipuncture Test

Remove the cap covering the tines and stretch the forearm skin taut. Firmly press the device into the prepared site, hold it in place for 1 sec, and then remove it. Four punctures should be visible. Record the site, and remind the patient to return in 48 to 72 hr to have the test read. At the time of the reading,

use a plastic ruler to measure the diameter of the largest indurated area, making sure the room is sufficiently lighted to perform the reading. A palpable induration greater than or equal to 2 mm at one or more of the punctures indicates a positive test result.

Mantoux (Intradermal) Test

Prepare PPD or old tuberculin in a tuberculin syringe with a short, 26-gauge needle attached. Prepare the appropriate dilution and amount for the most commonly used intermediate strength (5 tuberculin units in 0.1 mL) or a first strength usually used for children (1 tuberculin unit in 0.1 mL). Inject the preparation intradermally at the prepared site as soon as it is drawn up into the syringe. When properly injected, a bleb or wheal 6 to 10 mm in diameter is formed within the layers of the skin. Record the site, and remind the patient to return in 48 to 72 hr to have the test read. At the time of the reading, use a plastic ruler to measure the diameter of the largest indurated area, making sure the room is sufficiently lighted to perform the reading. Palpate for thickening of the tissue; a positive result is indicated by a reaction of 5 mm or more with erythema and edema.

Blood Test

Observe standard precautions, and follow the general guidelines in Appendix A. Positively identify the patient, and label the appropriate specimen container with the corresponding patient demographics, initials of the person collecting the specimen, date, and time of collection. Perform a venipuncture.

Remove the needle and apply direct pressure with dry gauze to stop bleeding. Observe/assess venipuncture site for bleeding or hematoma formation and secure gauze with adhesive bandage.

Promptly transport the specimen to the laboratory for processing and analysis.

POST-TEST:

A report of the results will be made available to the requesting HCP, who will discuss the results with the patient.

Recognize anxiety related to test results and be supportive of perceived loss of independence and fear of shortened life expectancy. Discuss the implications of abnormal test results on the patient's lifestyle. Provide teaching and information regarding the clinical implications of the test results, as appropriate. Counsel the patient, as appropriate, regarding the risk of transmission and proper prophylaxis, and reinforce the importance of strict adherence to the treatment regimen. Inform the patient that positive findings must be reported to local health department officials, who will question him or her regarding other persons who may have been exposed through contact. Educate the patient regarding access to counseling services.

Reinforce information given by the patient's HCP regarding further testing, treatment, or referral to another HCP. Emphasize to the patient who receives skin testing of the need to return and have the test results read within the specified time frame of 48 to 72 hr after injection. Inform the patient that the effects from a positive response at the site can remain for 1 wk. Educate the patient that a positive result may put him or her at risk for infection related to impaired primary defenses, impaired gas exchange related to decrease in effective lung surface, and intolerance to activity related to an imbalance between oxygen supply and demand. Answer any questions or address any concerns voiced by the patient or family.

Depending on the results of this procedure, additional testing may be performed to evaluate or monitor progression of the disease process and determine the need for a change in therapy. Evaluate test results in relation to the patient's symptoms and other tests performed.

RELATED MONOGRAPHS:

Related tests include alveolar/arterial gradient, angiography pulmonary, biopsy lung, blood gases, bronchoscopy, calcium, carbon dioxide, chest x-ray, CBC WBC count and differential, CT thoracic, culture and smear mycobacteria, culture blood, culture sputum, cytology sputum, eosinophil count, ESR, gallium scan, Gram stain, lung perfusion scan, lung ventilation scan, mediastinoscopy, pleural fluid analysis, PFT, and zinc.

Refer to the Immune and Respiratory systems tables at the end of the book for related tests by body system.

Tuning Fork Tests

SYNONYM/ACRONYM: Bing test, Rinne test, Schwabach test, Weber test.

COMMON USE: To assess for and determine type of hearing loss.

AREA OF APPLICATION: Ears.

CONTRAST: N/A.

DESCRIPTION: These noninvasive assessment procedures are done to distinguish conduction hearing loss from sensorineural hearing loss. They may be performed as part of the physical assessment examination and followed by hearing loss audiometry for confirmation of questionable results. The tuning fork tests described in this monograph are named for the four German otologists who described their use. Tuning fork tests are used less frequently by audiologists in favor of more sophisticated electronic methods, but presentation of the tuning fork test methodology is useful to illustrate the principles involved in electronic test methods.

A tuning fork is a bipronged metallic device that emits a clear tone at a particular pitch when it is set into vibration by holding the stem in the hand and striking one of the prongs or tines against a firm surface. The Bing test samples for conductive hearing loss by intermittently occluding and unblocking the opening of the ear canal while holding a vibrating tuning fork to the mastoid process behind the ear. The occlusion effect is absent in patients with conductive hearing loss and is present in patients with normal hearing or with sensorineural hearing loss. The Rinne test compares the patient's own hearing by bone conduction to his or her hearing by air conduction to determine whether hearing loss, if detected, is conductive or sensorineural. The Schwabach test compares the patient's level of bone conduction hearing to that of a presumed normal-hearing examiner. The Weber test has been modified by many audiologists for use with electronic equipment. When the test is administered, the patient is asked to tell the examiner the location of the tone heard (left ear, right ear, both ears, or midline) in order to determine whether the hearing loss is conductive, sensorineural, or mixed.

INDICATIONS
- Evaluate type of hearing loss (conductive or sensorineural)

- Screen for hearing loss as part of a routine physical examination and to determine the need for referral to an audiologist

POTENTIAL DIAGNOSIS

Normal findings in
- Normal air and bone conduction in both ears; no evidence of hearing loss
- Bing test: Pulsating sound that gets louder and softer when the opening to the ear canal is alternately opened and closed (*Note:* This result, observed in patients with normal hearing, is also observed in patients with sensorineural hearing loss.)
- Rinne test: Longer and louder tone heard by air conduction than by bone conduction (*Note:* This result, observed in patients with normal hearing, is also observed in patients with sensorineural hearing loss.)
- Schwabach test: Same tone loudness heard equally long by the examiner and the patient
- Weber test: Same tone loudness heard equally in both ears

Abnormal findings in
- Conduction hearing loss related to or evidenced by:
  Impacted cerumen
  Obstruction of external ear canal **(presence of a foreign body)**
  Otitis externa **(infection in ear canal)**
  Otitis media **(poor eustachian tube function or infection)**
  Otitis media serous **(fluid in middle ear due to allergies or a cold)**
  Otosclerosis
  Bing test: No change in the loudness of the sound
  Rinne test: Tone louder or detected for a longer time than the air-conducted tone
  Schwabach test: Prolonged duration of tone when compared to that heard by the examiner
  Weber test: Lateralization of tone to one ear, indicating loss of hearing on that

T

side (*i.e., tone is heard in the poorer ear*)

- Sensorineural hearing loss related to or evidenced by:

Congenital damage or malformations of the inner ear

Ménière's disease

Ototoxic drugs (aminoglycosides, e.g., gentamicin or tobramycin; salicylates, e.g., aspirin)

Presbycusis (gradual hearing loss experienced in advancing age)

Serious infections (meningitis, measles, mumps, other viral, syphilis)

Trauma to the inner ear (related to exposure to noise in excess of 90 dB or as a result of physical trauma)

Tumor (e.g., acoustic neuroma, cerebellopontine angle tumor, meningioma)

Vascular disorders

Bing test: Pulsating sound that gets louder and softer when the opening to the ear canal is alternately opened and closed

Rinne test: Tone heard louder by air conduction

Schwabach test: Shortened duration of tone when compared to that heard by the examiner

Weber test: Lateralization of tone to one ear indicating loss of hearing on the other side (i.e., tone is heard in the better ear)

CRITICAL FINDINGS: N/A

INTERFERING FACTORS

Factors that may impair the results of the examination

- Poor technique in striking the tuning fork or incorrect placement can result in inaccurate results.
- Inability of the patient to understand how to identify responses or unwillingness of the patient to cooperate during the test can cause inaccurate results.
- Hearing loss in the examiner can affect results in those tests that utilize hearing comparisons between patient and examiner.

NURSING IMPLICATIONS AND PROCEDURE

PRETEST:

- Positively identify the patient using at least two unique identifiers before providing care, treatment, or services.
- *Patient Teaching:* Inform the patient this procedure can assist in assessing for hearing loss.
- Obtain a history of the patient's complaints, including a list of known allergens.
- Obtain a history of the patient's known or suspected hearing loss, including type and cause; ear conditions with treatment regimens; ear surgery; and other tests and procedures to assess and diagnose auditory deficit.
- Obtain a history of the patient's symptoms and results of previously performed laboratory tests and diagnostic and surgical procedures.
- Obtain a list of the patient's current medications, including herbs, nutritional supplements, and nutraceuticals (see Appendix F).
- Review the procedure with the patient. Address concerns about pain and explain that no discomfort will be experienced during the test. Inform the patient that a health-care provider (HCP) performs the test in a quiet, darkened room, and that to evaluate both ears, the test can take 5 to 10 min.
- Ensure that the external auditory canal is clear of impacted cerumen.
- There are no food, fluid, or medication restrictions unless by medical direction.

INTRATEST:

- Observe standard precautions, and follow the general guidelines in Appendix A. Positively identify the patient.
- Instruct the patient to cooperate fully and to follow directions. Instruct the patient to remain still throughout the procedure because movement produces unreliable results.
- Seat the patient in a quiet environment positioned such that the patient is comfortable and is facing the examiner. A tuning fork of 1,024 Hz is used because it tests within the range of human speech (400 to 5,000 Hz).

T

Bing test: Tap the tuning fork handle against the hand to start a light vibration. Hold the handle to the mastoid process behind the ear while alternately opening and closing the ear canal with a finger. Ask the patient to report whether he or she hears a change in loudness or softness in sound. Record the result as a positive Bing if the patient reports a pulsating change in sound. Record as a negative Bing if no change in loudness is detected.

Rinne test: Tap the tuning fork handle against the hand to start a light vibration. Have the patient mask the ear not being tested by moving a finger in and out of the ear canal of that ear. Hold the base of the vibrating tuning fork with the thumb and forefinger of the dominant hand and place it in contact with the patient's mastoid process (bone conduction). Ask the patient when the sound is no longer heard. Follow this with placement of the same vibrating tuning fork in front of the ear canal (air conduction) without touching the external part of the ear. Ask the patient which of the two has the loudest or longest tone. Repeat the test in the other ear. Record as Rinne positive if air conduction is heard longer and Rinne negative if bone conduction is heard longer.

Schwabach test: Tap the tuning fork handle against the hand to start a light vibration. Hold the base of the tuning fork against one side of the patient's mastoid process and ask if the tone is heard. Have the patient mask the ear not being tested by moving a finger in and out of the ear canal of that ear. The examiner then places the tuning fork against the same side of his or her own mastoid process and listens for the tone. The tuning fork is alternated on the same side between the patient and examiner until the sound is no longer heard, noting whether the sound ceased to be heard by both the patient and the examiner at the same point in time. The procedure is repeated on the other ear. If the patient hears the tone for a longer or shorter time, count and note this in seconds.

Weber test: Tap the tuning fork handle against the hand to start a light vibration. Hold the base of the vibrating tuning fork with the thumb and forefinger of the dominant hand and place it on the middle of the patient's forehead or at the vertex of the head. Ask the patient to determine if the sound is heard better and longer on one side than the other. Record as Weber right or left. If sound is heard equally, record as Weber negative.

POST-TEST:

A report of the results will be made available to the requesting HCP, who will discuss the results with the patient.

Recognize anxiety related to test results, and be supportive of impaired activity related to hearing loss and perceived loss of independence. Discuss the implications of abnormal test results on the patient's lifestyle. Provide teaching and information regarding the clinical implications of the test results, as appropriate. Educate the patient regarding access to counseling services. Provide contact information, if desired, for the American Speech-Language-Hearing Association (www.asha.org).

Reinforce information given by the patient's HCP regarding further testing, treatment, or referral to another HCP. As appropriate, instruct the patient in the use, cleaning, and storing of a hearing aid. Answer any questions or address any concerns voiced by the patient or family.

Depending on the results of this procedure, additional testing may be performed to evaluate or monitor progression of the disease process and determine the need for a change in therapy. Evaluate test results in relation to the patient's symptoms and other tests performed.

RELATED MONOGRAPHS:

Related tests include antibiotic drugs, analgesic and antipyretic drugs, audiometry hearing loss, culture bacterial (ear), Gram stain, evoked brain potential studies for hearing loss, otoscopy, and spondee speech reception threshold.

Refer to the Auditory System table at the end of the book for related tests by body system.

Ultrasound, Abdomen

SYNONYM/ACRONYM: Abdominal ultrasound, abdomen sonography.

COMMON USE: To visualize and assess the solid organs of the abdomen, including the aorta, bile ducts, gallbladder, kidneys, pancreas, spleen, and other large abdominal blood vessels. This study is used to perform biopsies and assist in diagnosing disorders such as aortic aneurysm, infections, fluid collections, masses, and obstructions. This procedure can also be used to evaluate therapeutic interventions such as organ transplants.

AREA OF APPLICATION: Abdomen from the xiphoid process to the umbilicus.

CONTRAST: Done without contrast.

DESCRIPTION: Ultrasound (US) procedures are diagnostic, non-invasive, and relatively inexpensive. They take a short time to complete, do not use radiation, and cause no harm to the patient. Abdominal US is valuable in determining aortic aneurysms, the internal components of organ masses (solid vs. cystic), and for evaluating other abdominal diseases, ascites, and abdominal obstruction. High-frequency sound waves of various intensities are delivered by a transducer, a flashlight-shaped device, pressed against the skin. The waves are bounced back, converted to electrical energy, amplifi by the transducer, and displayed on a monitor. Abdominal US can be performed on the same day as a radionuclide scan or other radiological procedure and is especially valuable in patients who have hypersensitivity to contrast medium or are pregnant. It does not rely on the injection of contrast medium to obtain a diagnosis. The procedure is indicated for evaluation after an organ transplant and is used as a guide for biopsy and other interventional procedures, abscess drainage, or tube placements. Abdominal US may be the diagnostic examination of choice because no radiation is used and, in most cases, the accuracy is sufficient to make a diagnosis without any further imaging procedures.

INDICATIONS

- Determine the patency and function of abdominal blood vessels, including the abdominal aorta; vena cava; and portal, splenic, renal, and superior and inferior mesenteric veins
- Detect and measure an abdominal aortic aneurysm
- Monitor abdominal aortic aneurysm expansion to prevent rupture
- Determine changes within small aortic aneurysms pre- and postsurgery
- Evaluate abdominal ascites
- Evaluate size, shape, and pathology of intra-abdominal organs

POTENTIAL DIAGNOSIS

Normal findings in

- Absence of ascites, aortic aneurysm, cysts, obstruction, or tumors
- Normal size, position, and shape of intra-abdominal organs and associated structures

Abnormal findings in

- Abdominal abscess, ascitic fluid, or hematoma
- Aortic aneurysm greater than 4 cm

U

- Congenital absence or malplacement of organs
- Gallbladder or renal calculi
- Tumor or cyst in kidney, liver, spleen, or retroperitoneal space

CRITICAL FINDINGS
- Aortic aneurysm measuring 5 cm or more in diameter.

It is essential that critical diagnoses be communicated immediately to the appropriate health-care provider (HCP). A listing of these diagnoses varies among facilities. Note and immediately report to the HCP abnormal results and related symptoms. Timely notification of critical values for lab or diagnostic studies is a role expectation of the professional nurse. Notification processes will vary among facilities. Upon receipt of the critical value the information should be read back to the caller to verify accuracy. Most policies require immediate notification of the primary HCP, hospitalist, or on-call HCP. Reported information includes the patient's name, unique identifiers, critical value, name of the person giving the report, and name of the person receiving the report. Documentation of notification should be made in the medical record with the name of the HCP notified, time and date of notification, and any orders received. Any delay in a timely report of a critical value may require completion of a notification form with review by Risk Management.

INTERFERING FACTORS

This procedure is contraindicated for
- Patients with open abdominal wounds

Factors that may impair clear imaging
- Attenuation of the sound waves by the ribs, which can impair clear imaging of upper abdominal structures.

- Incorrect placement of the transducer over the desired test site.
- Retained gas or barium from a previous radiological procedure.
- Metallic objects (e.g., jewelry, body rings) within the examination field, which may inhibit organ visualization and cause unclear images.

Other considerations
- Failure to follow dietary and fluid restrictions and other pretesting preparations may cause the procedure to be canceled or repeated.
- Inability of the patient to cooperate or remain still during the procedure because of age, significant pain, or mental status may interfere with the test results.

NURSING IMPLICATIONS AND PROCEDURE

PRETEST:
- Positively identify the patient using at least two unique identifiers before providing care, treatment, or services.
- Inform the patient this procedure can assist in assessing abdominal abnormalities.
- Obtain a history of the patient's complaints, including a list of known allergens, especially allergies or sensitivities to latex.
- Obtain a history of results of the patient's cardiovascular, gastrointestinal, genitourinary, and hepatobiliary systems, symptoms, and results of previously performed laboratory tests, diagnostic and surgical procedures.
- Note any recent procedures that can interfere with test results (i.e., barium procedures, surgery, or biopsy). There should be 24 hours between administration of barium and this test.
- Endoscopic retrograde cholangiopancreatography, colonoscopy, and computed tomography of the abdomen, if ordered, should be scheduled after this procedure.
- Obtain a list of the patient's current medications, including herbs,

nutritional supplements, and nutraceuticals (see Appendix F).

Review the procedure with the patient. Address concerns about pain related to the procedure. Explain to the patient that there may be moments of discomfort experienced during the test. Inform the patient that the procedure is performed in a ultrasound department, by a health-care provider (HCP) specializing in this procedure, with support staff, and takes approximately 30 to 60 minutes.

Sensitivity to social and cultural issues, as well as concern for modesty, is important in providing psychological support before, during, and after the procedure.

Instruct the patient to remove jewelry and other metallic objects in the area to be examined.

There are no food or fluid restrictions for US of the aorta. Restrictions for US studies of other abdominal organs may be imposed by medical direction.

INTRATEST:

Observe standard precautions, and follow the general guidelines in Appendix A. Positively identify the patient.

Ensure that food and fluids have been restricted, if required, prior to the procedure.

Ensure that the patient has removed external metallic objects prior to the procedure.

Instruct the patient to void prior to the procedure and to change into the gown, robe, and foot coverings provided.

Instruct the patient to cooperate fully and to follow directions. Instruct the patient to remain still throughout the procedure because movement produces unreliable results.

Place the patient in the supine position on an examination table. The right- or left-side-up positions may be used to allow gravity to reposition the liver, gas, and fluid to facilitate better organ visualization.

Expose the abdominal area and drape the patient.

Conductive gel is applied to the skin, and a Doppler transducer is moved over the skin to obtain images of the area of interest.

Ask the patient to breathe normally during the examination. If necessary for better organ visualization, ask the patient to inhale deeply and hold his or her breath.

POST-TEST:

A report of the results will be sent to the requesting HCP, who will discuss the results with the patient.

When the study is completed, remove the gel from the skin.

Instruct the patient to resume usual diet and fluids, as directed by the HCP.

Nutritional Considerations: A low-fat, low-cholesterol, and low-sodium diet should be consumed to reduce current disease processes and/or decrease risk of hypertension and coronary artery disease.

Recognize anxiety related to test results. Discuss the implications of abnormal test results on the patient's lifestyle. Provide teaching and information regarding the clinical implications of the test results, as appropriate.

Reinforce information given by the patient's HCP regarding further testing, treatment, or referral to another HCP. Answer any questions or address any concerns voiced by the patient or family.

Depending on the results of this procedure, additional testing may be needed to evaluate or monitor progression of the disease process and determine the need for a change in therapy. Evaluate test results in relation to the patient's symptoms and other tests performed.

RELATED MONOGRAPHS:

Related tests include ACTH and challenge tests, albumin, ALKP, ALT, amylase, angiography abdomen, AST, biopsy intestinal, biopsy liver, bilirubin and fractions, BUN, calcium, calculus kidney stone panel, cancer antigens, carbon dioxide, CBC, CBC hematocrit, CBC hemoglobin, CBC WBC and differential, chloride, cortisol and challenge tests, creatinine, CT abdomen, GGT, HCG, hepatobiliary scan, infectious mononucleosis, IVP, KUB, LDH, lipase, magnesium, MRI

U

abdomen, peritoneal fluid analysis, phosphorus, potassium, PT/INR, renogram, sodium, US kidney, US liver and biliary, US pancreas, US spleen, uric acid, urinalysis, and WBC scan.

▶ Refer to the Cardiovascular, Gastrointestinal, Genitourinary, and Hepatobiliary systems tables at the end of the book for related tests by body system.

Ultrasound, Arterial Doppler, Carotid Studies

SYNONYM/ACRONYM: Carotid Doppler, carotid ultrasound, arterial ultrasound.

COMMON USE: To visualize and assess blood flow through the carotid arteries toward evaluating risk for stroke related to atherosclerosis.

AREA OF APPLICATION: Arteries.

CONTRAST: Done without contrast.

DESCRIPTION: Ultrasound (US) procedures are diagnostic, non-invasive, and relatively inexpensive. They take a short time to complete, do not use radiation, and cause no harm to the patient. Using the duplex scanning method, carotid US records sound waves to obtain information about the carotid arteries. The amplitude and waveform of the carotid pulse are measured, resulting in a two-dimensional image of the artery. Carotid arterial sites used for the studies include the common carotid, external carotid, and internal carotid. Blood flow direction, velocity, and the presence of flow disturbances can be readily assessed. The sound waves hit the moving red blood cells and are reflected back to the transducer, a flashlight-shaped device, pressed against the skin. The sound emitted by the equipment corresponds to the velocity of the blood flow through the vessel. The result is

the visualization of the artery to assist in the diagnosis (i.e., presence, amount, location) of plaque causing vessel stenosis or atherosclerotic occlusion affecting the flow of blood to the brain. Depending on the degree of stenosis causing a reduction in vessel diameter, additional testing can be performed to determine the effect of stenosis on the hemodynamic status of the artery.

The ankle-brachial index (ABI) can also be assessed during this study. This noninvasive, simple comparison of blood pressure measurements in the arms and legs can be used to detect peripheral artery disease (PAD). A Doppler stethoscope is used to obtain the systolic pressure in either the dorsalis pedis or the posterior tibial artery. This ankle pressure is then divided by the highest brachial systolic pressure acquired after taking the blood pressure in both of the patient's arms. This index should be greater than 1. When the index falls below 0.5, blood flow impairment is considered significant. Patients should be scheduled for a vascular consult for an abnormal ABI. Patients with diabetes or kidney disease, and some elderly patients, may have a falsely elevated ABI due to calcifications of the vessels in the ankle causing an increased systolic pressure. The ABI test approaches 95% accuracy in detecting PAD. However, a normal ABI value does not absolutely rule out the possibility of PAD for some individuals, and additional tests should be done to evaluate symptoms.

INDICATIONS

- Assist in the diagnosis of carotid artery occlusive disease, as evidenced by visualization of blood flow disruption
- Detect irregularities in the structure of the carotid arteries
- Detect plaque or stenosis of the carotid artery, as evidenced by turbulent blood flow or changes in Doppler signals indicating occlusion
- Evaluate PAD

POTENTIAL DIAGNOSIS

Normal findings in
- Normal blood flow through the carotid arteries with no evidence of occlusion or narrowing

Abnormal findings in
- Carotid artery occlusive disease (atherosclerosis)
- PAD
- Plaque or stenosis of carotid artery
- Reduction in vessel diameter of more than 16%, indicating stenosis

CRITICAL FINDINGS: N/A

INTERFERING FACTORS

Factors that may impair clear imaging
- Attenuation of the sound waves by bony structures, which can impair clear imaging of the vessels.
- Incorrect placement of the transducer over the desired test site.
- Metallic objects (e.g., jewelry, body rings) within the examination field, which may inhibit organ visualization and cause unclear images.
- Inability of the patient to cooperate or remain still during the procedure because of age, significant pain, or mental status.

NURSING IMPLICATIONS AND PROCEDURE

PRETEST:

- Positively identify the patient using at least two unique identifiers before providing care, treatment, or services.
- *Patient Teaching:* Inform the patient this procedure can assist in assessing the carotid arteries in the neck.
- Obtain a history of the patient's complaints, including a list of known allergens, especially allergies or sensitivities to latex.
- Obtain a history of the patient's cardiovascular system, symptoms, and results of previously performed laboratory tests and diagnostic and surgical procedures.
- Note any recent procedures that can interfere with test results (i.e., barium or iodine-based contrast procedures, surgery, or biopsy). There should be 24 hr between administration of barium or iodine contrast medium and this test.
- Obtain a list of the patient's current medications, including anticoagulants, aspirin and other salicylates, herbs, nutritional supplements, and nutraceuticals. (see Appendix F). Such products should be discontinued by medical direction for the appropriate number of days prior to a surgical procedure.

Review the procedure with the patient. Address concerns about pain related to the procedure and explain that some pain may be experienced during the test, and there may be moments of discomfort. Inform the patient that the procedure is performed in a US department by a health-care provider (HCP) who specializes in this procedure, with support staff, and takes approximately 30 to 60 min.

Sensitivity to social and cultural issues, as well as concern for modesty, is important in providing psychological support before, during, and after the procedure.

Instruct the patient to remove jewelry and other metallic objects from the area to be examined.

There are no food, fluid, or medication restrictions unless by medical direction.

INTRATEST:

Observe standard precautions, and follow the general guidelines in Appendix A. Positively identify the patient.

Ensure that the patient has removed all external metallic objects from the area to be examined prior to the procedure.

Instruct the patient to void and change into the gown, robe, and foot coverings provided.

Instruct the patient to cooperate fully and to follow directions. Ask the patient to remain still throughout the procedure because movement produces unreliable results.

Place the patient in the supine position on an examination table; other positions may be used during the examination.

Expose the neck and drape the patient.

Conductive gel is applied to the skin, and a Doppler transducer is moved over the skin to obtain images of the area of interest.

Ask the patient to breathe normally during the examination. If necessary for better organ visualization, ask the patient to inhale deeply and hold his or her breath.

POST-TEST:

A report of the results will be made available to the requesting HCP,

who will discuss the results with the patient.

When the study is completed, remove the gel from the skin.

Instruct the patient to continue with diet, fluids, and medications, as directed by the HCP.

Nutritional Considerations: Abnormal findings may be associated with cardiovascular disease. The American Heart Association and National Heart, Lung, and Blood Institute (NHLBI) recommend nutritional therapy for individuals identified to be at high risk for developing coronary artery disease (CAD) or individuals who have specific risk factors and/or existing medical conditions (e.g., elevated LDL cholesterol levels, other lipid disorders, insulin-dependent diabetes, insulin resistance, or metabolic syndrome). If overweight, the patient should be encouraged to achieve a normal weight. Guidelines for the Therapeutic Lifestyle Changes (TLC) diet are outlined in the Third Report of the Expert Panel on Detection, Evaluation, and Treatment of High Blood Cholesterol in Adults (Adult Treatment Panel III [ATP III]). The TLC diet emphasizes a reduction in foods high in saturated fats and cholesterol. Red meats, eggs, and dairy products are the major sources of saturated fats and cholesterol. If triglycerides also are elevated, the patient should be advised to eliminate or reduce alcohol and simple carbohydrates from the diet. The TLC approach also includes the use of plant stanols or sterols and increased dissolved fiber as an option for lowering LDL cholesterol levels; nutritional recommendations for daily total caloric intake; recommendations for allowable percentage of calories derived from fat (saturated and unsaturated), carbohydrates, protein, and cholesterol; as well as recommendations for daily expenditure of energy.

Nutritional Considerations: Overweight patients with high blood pressure should be encouraged to achieve a normal weight. Other changeable risk factors warranting patient education include strategies to safely decrease sodium intake, increase physical activity, decrease alcohol consumption, eliminate tobacco use, and decrease cholesterol levels.

Social and Cultural Considerations:
Numerous studies point to the prevalence of excess body weight in American children and adolescents. Experts estimate that obesity is present in 25% of the population ages 6 to 11 yr. The medical, social, and emotional consequences of excess body weight are significant. Special attention should be given to instructing the child and caregiver regarding health risks and weight-control education.

Recognize anxiety related to test results, and be supportive of fear of shortened life expectancy and perceived loss of independent function. Discuss the implications of abnormal test results on the patient's lifestyle. Provide teaching and information regarding the clinical implications of the test results, as appropriate. Educate the patient regarding access to counseling services. Provide contact information, if desired, for the American Heart Association (www. americanheart.org), the National Heart, Lung, and Blood Institute (www.nhlbi .nih.gov), or the Legs for Life (www .legsforlife.org).

Reinforce information given by the patient's HCP regarding further testing, treatment, or referral to another HCP. Answer any questions or address any concerns voiced by the patient or family.

Instruct the patient in the use of any ordered medications. Explain the importance of adhering to the therapy regimen. As appropriate, instruct the patient in significant side effects and systemic reactions associated with the prescribed medication. Encourage him or her to review corresponding literature provided by a pharmacist.

Depending on the results of this procedure, additional testing may be performed to evaluate or monitor progression of the disease process and determine the need for a change in therapy. Evaluate test results in relation to the patient's symptoms and other tests performed.

RELATED MONOGRAPHS:

Related tests include angiography carotid, angiography coronary, antiarrhythmic drugs, apolipoprotein A & B, AST, blood gases, calcium, cholesterol (total, HDL, LDL), CT angiography, CT cardiac scoring, echocardiography, CRP, CK and isoenzymes, glucose, glycated hemoglobin, Holter monitor, homocysteine, ketones, LDH and isoenzymes, lipoprotein electrophoresis, magnesium, MRI angiography, MRI chest, MRI venography, myocardial infarction scan, myocardial perfusion heart scan, myoglobin, PET heart, triglycerides, troponin, US arterial Doppler upper and lower extremities, and US venous Doppler extremity.

Refer to the Cardiovascular System table at the end of the book for related tests by body system.

Ultrasound, Arterial Doppler, Lower and Upper Extremity Studies

SYNONYM/ACRONYM: Doppler, arterial ultrasound, duplex scan.

COMMON USE: To visualize and assess blood flow through the arteries of the upper and lower extremities toward diagnosing disorders such as occlusion and aneurysm and evaluate for the presence of plaque and stenosis. This procedure can also be used to assess the effectiveness of therapeutic interventions such as arterial graphs and blood flow to transplanted organs.

U

AREA OF APPLICATION: Arteries of the lower and upper extremities.

CONTRAST: Done without contrast.

DESCRIPTION: Ultrasound (US) procedures are diagnostic, non-invasive, and relatively inexpensive. They take a short time to complete, do not use radiation, and cause no harm to the patient. Using the duplex scanning method, arterial leg US records sound waves to obtain information about the arteries of the lower extremities from the common femoral arteries and their branches as they extend into the calf area. The amplitude and waveform of the pulses are measured, resulting in a two-dimensional image of the artery. Blood flow direction, velocity, and the presence of flow disturbances can be readily assessed, and for diagnostic studies, the technique is done bilaterally. The sound waves hit the moving red blood cells and are reflected back to the transducer, a flashlight-shaped device, pressed against the skin. The sound that is emitted by the equipment corresponds to the velocity of the blood flow through the vessel. The result is the visualization of the artery to assist in the diagnosis (i.e., presence, amount, and location) of plaque causing vessel stenosis or occlusion and to help determine the cause of claudication. Arterial reconstruction and graft condition and patency can also be evaluated.

In arterial Doppler studies, arteriosclerotic disease of the peripheral vessels can be detected by slowly deflating blood pressure cuffs that are placed on an extremity such as the calf, ankle, or upper extremity. The systolic pressure of the various arteries of the extremities can be measured. The Doppler transducer can detect the first sign of blood flow through the cuffed artery, even the most minimal blood flow, as evidenced by a swishing noise. There is normally a reduction in systolic blood pressure from the arteries of the arms to the arteries of the legs; a reduction exceeding 20 mm Hg is indicative of occlusive disease (deep vein thrombosis) proximal to the area being tested. This procedure may also be used to monitor the patency of a graft, status of previous corrective surgery, vascular status of the blood flow to a transplanted organ, blood flow to a mass, or the extent of vascular trauma.

The ankle-brachial index (ABI) can also be assessed during this study. This noninvasive, simple comparison of blood pressure measurements in the arms and legs can be used to detect peripheral artery disease (PAD). A Doppler stethoscope is used to obtain the systolic pressure in either the dorsalis pedis or the posterior tibial artery. This ankle pressure is then divided by the highest brachial systolic pressure acquired after taking the blood pressure in both of the patient's arms. This index should be greater than 1. When the index falls below 0.5, blood flow impairment is considered significant. Patients should be scheduled for a vascular consult for an abnormal ABI. Patients with diabetes or kidney disease, and some elderly patients, may have a falsely elevated ABI due to calcifications of the vessels in the ankle causing an increased

U

systolic pressure. The ABI test approaches 95% accuracy in detecting PAD. However, a normal ABI value does not absolutely rule out the possibility of PAD for some individuals, and additional tests should be done to evaluate symptoms.

INDICATIONS

- Aid in the diagnosis of small or large vessel PAD
- Aid in the diagnosis of spastic arterial disease, such as Raynaud's phenomenon
- Assist in the diagnosis of aneurysm, pseudoaneurysm, hematoma, arteriovenous malformation, or hemangioma
- Assist in the diagnosis of ischemia, arterial calcification, or plaques, as evidenced by visualization of blood flow disruption
- Detect irregularities in the structure of the arteries
- Detect plaque or stenosis of the lower extremity artery, as evidenced by turbulent blood flow or changes in Doppler signals indicating occlusion
- Determine the patency of a vascular graft, stent, or previous surgery
- Evaluate possible arterial trauma

POTENTIAL DIAGNOSIS

Normal findings in

- Normal blood flow through the lower extremity arteries with no evidence of vessel occlusion or narrowing
- Normal arterial systolic and diastolic Doppler signals
- Normal reduction in systolic blood pressure (i.e., less than 20 mm Hg) when compared to a normal extremity
- Normal ABI (greater than 0.85)

Abnormal findings in

- ABI less than 0.85, indicating significant arterial occlusive disease within the extremity
- Aneurysm
- Arterial calcification or plaques
- Embolic arterial occlusion
- Graft diameter reduction
- Hemangioma
- Hematoma
- Ischemia
- PAD
- Pseudoaneurysm
- Reduction in vessel diameter of more than 16%, indicating stenosis
- Spastic arterial occlusive disease, such as Raynaud's phenomenon

CRITICAL FINDINGS: N/A

INTERFERING FACTORS

This procedure is contraindicated for

- Patients with an open or draining lesion.

Factors that may impair the results of the examination

- Attenuation of the sound waves by bony structures, which can impair clear imaging of the vessels.
- Cold extremities, resulting in vasoconstriction, which can cause inaccurate measurements.
- Occlusion proximal to the site being studied, which would affect blood flow to the area.
- Cigarette smoking, because nicotine can cause constriction of the peripheral vessels.
- An abnormally large leg, making direct examination difficult.
- Incorrect placement of the transducer over the desired test site.
- Metallic objects (e.g., jewelry, body rings) within the examination field, which may inhibit organ visualization and cause unclear images.
- Inability of the patient to cooperate or remain still during the

procedure because of age, significant pain, or mental status.

NURSING IMPLICATIONS AND PROCEDURE

PRETEST:

- Positively identify the patient using at least two unique identifiers before providing care, treatment, or services.
- *Patient Teaching:* Inform the patient this procedure can assist in assessing blood flow to the upper and lower extremities.
- Obtain a history of the patient's complaints, including a list of known allergens, especially allergies or sensitivities to latex.
- Obtain a history of the patient's cardiovascular system, symptoms, and results of previously performed laboratory tests and diagnostic and surgical procedures.
- Report the presence of a lesion that is open or draining; maintain clean, dry dressing for the ulcer; protect the limb from trauma.
- Note any recent procedures that can interfere with test results (i.e., barium or iodine-based contrast procedures, surgery, or biopsy). There should be 24 hr between administration of barium or iodine contrast medium and this test.
- Obtain a list of the patient's current medications, including herbs, nutritional supplements, and nutraceuticals (see Appendix F).
- Review the procedure with the patient. Address concerns about pain related to the procedure and explain that some pain may be experienced during the test, and there may be moments of discomfort. Inform the patient that the procedure is performed in a US department by a health-care provider (HCP) specializing in this procedure, with support staff, and takes approximately 30 to 60 min.
- *Sensitivity to social and cultural issues,* as well as concern for modesty, is important in providing psychological support before, during, and after the procedure.

- Instruct the patient to remove jewelry and other metallic objects from the area to be examined.
- There are no food, fluid, or medication restrictions unless by medical direction.

INTRATEST:

- Observe standard precautions, and follow the general guidelines in Appendix A. Positively identify the patient.
- Ensure that the patient has removed all external metallic objects from the area to be examined prior to the procedure.
- Instruct the patient to void and change into the gown, robe, and foot coverings provided.
- Instruct the patient to cooperate fully and to follow directions. Ask the patient to remain still throughout the procedure because movement produces unreliable results.
- Place the patient in the supine position on an examination table; other positions may be used during the examination.
- Expose the area of interest and drape the patient.
- Place blood pressure cuffs on the thigh, calf, and ankle.
- Apply conductive gel to the skin over the area distal to each of the cuffs to promote the passage of sound waves as a Doppler transducer is moved over the skin to obtain images of the area of interest.
- Inflate the thigh cuff to a level above the patient's systolic pressure found in the normal extremity.
- Place the Doppler transducer in the gel, distal to the inflated cuff, and slowly release the pressure in the cuff.
- When the swishing sound of blood flow is heard, record it at the highest point along the artery at which it is audible. The test is repeated at the calf and then the ankle.

POST-TEST:

- A report of the results will be made available to the requesting HCP, who will discuss the results with the patient.
- When the study is completed, remove the gel from the skin.
- Instruct the patient to continue diet, fluids, and medications, as directed by the HCP.

Nutritional Considerations: A low-fat, low-cholesterol, and low-sodium diet should be consumed to reduce current disease processes and/or decrease risk of hypertension and coronary artery disease.

Recognize anxiety related to test results, and be supportive of perceived loss of independent function. Discuss the implications of abnormal test results on the patient's lifestyle. Provide teaching and information regarding the clinical implications of the test results, as appropriate. Provide contact information, if desired, for the American Heart Association (www.americanheart .org), the National Heart, Lung, and Blood Institute (www.nhlbi.nih. gov), or the Legs for Life (www.legs-forlife.org).

Reinforce information given by the patient's HCP regarding further testing, treatment, or referral to another HCP. Answer any questions or address any concerns voiced by the patient or family.

Depending on the results of this procedure, additional testing may be performed to evaluate or monitor progression of the disease process and determine the need for a change in therapy. Evaluate test results in relation to the patient's symptoms and other tests performed.

RELATED MONOGRAPHS:

Related tests include alveolar/arterial ratio, ANA, angiography pulmonary, aPTT, blood gases, CBC platelet count, CT angiography, D-Dimer, FDP, fibrinogen, lung perfusion scan, lung ventilation scan, MRI abdomen, MRI angiography, plethysmography, PT/INR, US venous Doppler lower extremities, and venography lower extremity.

Refer to the Cardiovascular System table at the end of the book for related tests by body system.

Ultrasound, A-scan

SYNONYM/ACRONYM: Amplitude modulation scan, A-scan ultrasound biometry.

COMMON USE: To assess for ocular tissue abnormality related to lens replacement in cataract surgery.

AREA OF APPLICATION: Eyes.

CONTRAST: N/A.

DESCRIPTION: Diagnostic techniques such as A-scan ultrasonography can be used to identify abnormal tissue. The A-scan employs a single-beam, linear sound wave to detect abnormalities by returning an echo when interference disrupts its straight path. When the sound wave is directed at lens vitreous, the normal homogeneous tissue does not return an echo; an opaque lens with a cataract will produce an echo. The returning waves produced by abnormal tissue are received by a microfilm that converts the sound energy into electrical impulses that are amplified and displayed on an oscilloscope as an ultrasonogram or echogram. The A-scan echo can be used to indicate the position of the cornea and retina. The A-scan is most commonly used to measure the axial length of the eye. This measurement is used to determine the power requirement for an intraocular lens used to replace the abnormal, opaque lens of the eye removed in cataract surgery. There are two different methods currently in use. The applanation method involves placement of an ultrasound (US) probe directly on the cornea. The immersion technique is more popular because it does not require direct contact and compression of the cornea. The immersion technique protects the cornea by placement of a fluid layer between the eye and the US probe. The accuracy of the immersion technique is thought to be greater than applanation because no corneal compression is caused by the immersion method. Therefore, the measured axial length achieved by immersion is closer to the true axial length of the cornea.

INDICATIONS

• Determination of power requirement for replacement intraocular lens in cataract surgery.

POTENTIAL DIAGNOSIS

Normal findings in
• Normal homogeneous ocular tissue

Abnormal findings in
• Cataract

CRITICAL FINDINGS: N/A

INTERFERING FACTORS

Factors that may impair the results of the examination
• Inability of the patient to cooperate and remain still during the procedure may interfere with the test results.
• Rubbing or squeezing the eyes may affect results.
• Improper placement of the probe tip to the surface of the eye may produce inaccurate results.

NURSING IMPLICATIONS AND PROCEDURE

PRETEST:

▶ Positively identify the patient using at least two unique identifiers before providing care, treatment, or services.
▶ *Patient Teaching:* Inform the patient this procedure determines the strength of the lens that will be replaced during cataract surgery.
▶ Obtain a history of the patient's complaints, including a list of known allergens, especially topical anesthetic eyedrops.
▶ Obtain a history of the patient's known or suspected vision loss; changes in visual acuity, including type and cause; use of glasses or contact lenses; eye conditions with treatment regimens; eye surgery; and other tests and procedures to assess and diagnose visual deficit.
▶ Obtain a history of symptoms and results of previously performed laboratory tests and diagnostic and surgical procedures.
▶ Obtain a list of the patient's current medications, including herbs, nutritional supplements, and nutraceuticals (see Appendix F).
▶ Instruct the patient to remove contact lenses or glasses, as appropriate.
▶ Instruct the patient regarding the importance of keeping the eyes open for the test.
▶ Review the procedure with the patient. Explain that the patient will be requested

U

to fixate the eyes during the procedure. Address concerns about pain and explain that no discomfort will be experienced during the test but that some discomfort may be experienced after the test when the numbness wears off from the anesthetic drops administered prior to the test. Inform the patient that a health-care provider (HCP) performs the test in a quiet, darkened room and that evaluation of the eye upon which surgery is to be performed can take up 10 min.

▶ *Sensitivity to social and cultural issues,* as well as concern for modesty, is important in providing psychological support before, during, and after the procedure.

▶ There are no food, fluid, or medication restrictions unless by medical direction.

INTRATEST:

▶ Observe standard precautions, and follow the general guidelines in Appendix A. Positively identify the patient.

▶ Instruct the patient to cooperate fully and to follow directions. Ask the patient to remain still during the procedure because movement produces unreliable results.

▶ Seat the patient comfortably. Instruct the patient to look straight ahead, keeping the eyes open and unblinking.

▶ Instill topical anesthetic in each eye, as ordered, and provide time for it to work. Topical anesthetic drops are placed in the eye with the patient looking up and the solution directed at the six o'clock position of the sclera (white of the eye) near the limbus (gray, semitransparent area of the eyeball where the cornea and sclera meet). Neither the dropper nor the bottle should touch the eyelashes.

▶ Ask the patient to place the chin in the chin rest and gently press the forehead against the support bar. When the

US probe is properly positioned on the patient's surgical eye, a reading is automatically taken.

▶ Multiple measurements may be taken in order to ensure that a consistent and accurate reading has been achieved. Variability between serial measurements is unavoidable using the applanation technique.

POST-TEST:

▶ A report of the results will be made available to the requesting HCP, who will discuss the results with the patient.

▶ Recognize anxiety related to test results, and be supportive of impaired activity related to vision loss, anticipated loss of driving privileges, or the possibility of requiring corrective lenses (self-image). Discuss the implications of test results on the patient's lifestyle. Reassure the patient regarding concerns related to the impending cataract surgery. Provide teaching and information regarding the clinical implications of the test results, as appropriate.

▶ Reinforce information given by the patient's HCP regarding further testing, treatment, or referral to another HCP. Answer any questions or address any concerns voiced by the patient or family.

▶ Depending on the results of this procedure, additional testing may be performed to evaluate or monitor progression of the disease process and determine the need for a change in therapy. Evaluate test results in relation to the patient's symptoms and other tests performed.

RELATED MONOGRAPHS:

▶ Related tests include refraction and slit-lamp biomicroscopy.

▶ Refer to the Ocular System table at the end of the book for related tests by body system.

U

Ultrasound, Biophysical Profile, Obstetric

SYNONYM/ACRONYM: BPP ultrasound, fetal age sonogram, gestational age sonogram, OB sonography, pregnancy ultrasound, pregnancy echo, pregnant uterus ultrasonography.

COMMON USE: To visualize and assess the fetus in utero to monitor fetal health related to growth, congenital abnormalities, distress, and demise. Also used to identify gender and multiple pregnancy and to obtain amniotic fluid for analysis.

AREA OF APPLICATION: Pelvis and abdominal region.

CONTRAST: N/A.

DESCRIPTION: Ultrasound (US) procedures are diagnostic, noninvasive, and relatively inexpensive. They take a short time to complete, do not use radiation, and cause no harm to the patient. Obstetric US uses high-frequency waves of various intensities delivered by a transducer, a flashlight-shaped device, pressed against the skin or inserted into the vagina. The waves are bounced back, converted to electrical energy, amplified by the transducer, and displayed on a monitor to visualize the fetus and placenta. This procedure is done by a transabdominal or transvaginal approach, depending on when the procedure is performed (first trimester [transvaginal] vs. second trimester [transabdominal]). It is the safest method of examination to evaluate the uterus and determine fetal size, growth, and position; fetal structural abnormalities; ectopic pregnancy; placenta position and amount of amniotic fluid; and multiple gestation. Obstetric US is used to secure different types of information regarding the fetus, varying with the trimester during which the procedure is

done. This procedure may also include a nonstress test (NST) in combination with Doppler monitoring of amniotic fluid volume, fetal heart, gross fetal movements, fetal muscle tone, and fetal respiratory movements to detect high-risk pregnancy. The procedure is indicated as a guide for amniocentesis, cordocentesis, fetoscopy, aspiration of multiple oocytes for in vitro fertilization, and other intrauterine interventional procedures. Because the pregnant uterus is filled with amniotic fluid, ultrasonography is an ideal method of evaluating the fetus and placenta; it is also the diagnostic examination of choice because no radiation is used and, in most cases, the accuracy is sufficient to make the diagnosis without any further imaging procedures.

The biophysical profile (BPP) considers five antepartum parameters measured to predict fetal wellness. The BPP is indicated in women with high-risk pregnancies to identify a fetus in distress or in jeopardy of demise. It includes fetal heart rate (FHR) measurement, fetal breathing movements, fetal body movements, fetal muscle tone, and amniotic fluid volume. Each of the five parameters is assigned a score of either 0 or 2, allowing a maximum or perfect score of 10. The

NST is an external US monitoring of FHR performed either as part of the BPP or when one or more of the US procedures have abnormal results. The NST is interpreted as either reactive or nonreactive.

BPP Parameter	Normal: Score = 2	Abnormal: Score = 0
Fetal heart rate reactivity	Two or more movement-associated FHR accelerations of 15 or more beats/min above baseline, lasting 15 sec, in a 20-min interval	One or no movement-associated FHR accelerations of 15 or more beats/min above baseline in a 20-min interval
Fetal breathing movements	One or more breathing movements lasting 20–60 sec in a 30-min interval	Absent or no breathing movements lasting longer than 19 sec in a 30-min interval
Fetal body movements	Two or more discrete body or limb movements in a 30-min interval	Less than two discrete body or limb movements in a 30-min interval
Fetal muscle tone	One or more episodes of active limb extension and return to flexion (to include opening and closing of hand)	Absent movement, slow extension with partial return to flexion, partial opening of hand
Amniotic fluid volume	One or more pockets of fluid that are 2 cm or more in the vertical axis	No pockets of fluid or no pocket measuring at least 2 cm in the vertical axis

A contraction stress test (CST or oxytocin challenge test) may be requested in the event of an abnormal fetal heart rate in the BPP or NST. The CST is used to assess the fetus's ability to tolerate low oxygen levels as experienced during labor contractions. The CST includes external FHR monitoring by US and measurement of oxytocin (Pitocin)-induced uterine contractions. Pressure changes during contractions are monitored on an external tocodynamometer. Results of the two tests are interpreted as negative or positive. A negative or

normal finding is no late decelerations of FHR during three induced contractions over a 10-min period. A positive or abnormal finding is identified when frequent contractions of 90 sec or more occur and FHR decelerates beyond the time of the contractions. The amniotic fluid index (AFI) is another application of US used to estimate amniotic fluid volume. The abdomen is divided into four quadrants using the umbilicus to delineate upper and lower halves and linea nigra to delineate the left and right halves. The numbered score is determined by adding the

U

sum in centimeters of fluid in pockets seen in each of the four quadrants. The score is interpreted in relation to gestational age. The median index is considered normal between 8 and 12 cm. Oligohydramnios (too little amniotic fluid) is associated with an index between 5 and 6 cm, and polyhydramnios (too much amniotic fluid) with an index between 18 and 22 cm.

INDICATIONS

- Detect blighted ovum (missed abortion), as evidenced by empty gestational sac
- Detect fetal death, as evidenced by absence of movement and fetal heart tones
- Detect fetal position before birth, such as breech or transverse presentations
- Detect tubal and other forms of ectopic pregnancy
- Determine and confirm pregnancy or multiple gestation by determining the number of gestational sacs in the first trimester
- Determine cause of bleeding, such as placenta previa or abruptio placentae
- Determine fetal effects of Rh incompatibility due to maternal sensitization
- Determine fetal gestational age by uterine size and measurements of crown-rump length, biparietal diameter, fetal extremities, head, and other parts of the anatomy at key phases of fetal development
- Determine fetal heart and body movements and detect high-risk pregnancy by monitoring fetal heart and respiratory movements in combination with Doppler US or real-time grayscale scanning
- Determine fetal structural anomalies, usually at the 20th week of gestation or later
- Determine the placental size, location, and site of implantation
- Differentiate a tumor (hydatidiform mole) from a normal pregnancy
- Guide the needle during amniocentesis and fetal transfusion
- Measure fetal gestational age and evaluate umbilical artery, uterine artery, and fetal aorta by Doppler examination to determine fetal intrauterine growth retardation
- Monitor placental growth and amniotic fluid volume

POTENTIAL DIAGNOSIS

Normal findings in

- Normal age, size, viability, position, and functional capacities of the fetus
- Normal placenta size, position, and structure; adequate volume of amniotic fluid
- BPP score of 8 to 10 is considered normal. Each of the fetal movements evaluated in the BPP is related to oxygen-dependent activities that originate from the central nervous system. Their presence is assumed to indicate normal brain function and absence of systemic hypoxia.

Abnormal findings in

- Abruptio placentae
- Adnexal torsion
- Cardiac abnormalities
- Ectopic pregnancy
- Fetal death
- Fetal hydrops
- Fetal malpresentation (breech, transverse)
- Hydrocephalus
- Intestinal atresia
- Myelomeningocele
- Multiple pregnancy
- Placenta previa
- Renal or skeletal defects
- BPP score between 4 and 6 is considered equivocal. Gestational age is important in determining intervals for retesting and/or a decision to deliver.

CRITICAL FINDINGS ✦

- Abruptio placentae
- Adnexal torsion
- BPP score between 0 and 2 is abnormal and indicates the need for assessment and immediate delivery.
- Ectopic pregnancy
- Fetal death
- Placenta previa

It is essential that critical diagnoses be communicated immediately to the appropriate health-care provider (HCP). A listing of these diagnoses varies among facilities. Note and immediately report to the HCP abnormal results and related symptoms. Timely notification of critical values for lab or diagnostic studies is a role expectation of the professional nurse. Notification processes will vary among facilities. Upon receipt of the critical value the information should be read back to the caller to verify accuracy. Most policies require immediate notification of the primary HCP, hospitalist, or on-call HCP. Reported information includes the patient's name, unique identifiers, critical value, name of the person giving the report, and name of the person receiving the report. Documentation of notification should be made in the medical record with the name of the HCP notified, time and date of notification, and any orders received. Any delay in a timely report of a critical value may require completion of a notification form with review by Risk Management.

INTERFERING FACTORS

This procedure is contraindicated for

- Patients with latex allergy; use of the vaginal probe requires the probe to be covered with a condom-like sac, usually made from latex. Latex-free covers are available.

Factors that may impair clear imaging

- Incorrect placement of the transducer over the desired test site.
- Retained gas or barium from a previous radiological procedure.
- Dehydration, which can cause failure to demonstrate the boundaries between organs and tissue structures.
- Insufficiently full bladder, which fails to push the bowel from the pelvis and the uterus from the symphysis pubis, thereby prohibiting clear imaging of the pelvic organs in transabdominal imaging.
- Metallic objects (e.g., jewelry, body rings) within the examination field, which may inhibit organ visualization and cause unclear images.
- Improper adjustment of the US equipment to accommodate obese or thin patients, which can cause a poor-quality study.
- Patients who are very obese, who may exceed the weight limit for the equipment.

Factors that may result in incorrect values

- Absence of activity in a particular parameter of the BPP may be related to fetal sleep pattern; gestational age less than 33 wk or greater than 42 wk; maternal ingestion of glucose, nicotine, or alcohol; maternal administration of magnesium or medications; artificial or premature rupture of membranes; and/or labor.

Other considerations

- Inability of the patient to cooperate or remain still during the procedure because of significant pain or mental status may interfere with the test results.

U

NURSING IMPLICATIONS AND PROCEDURE

PRETEST:

- Positively identify the patient using at least two unique identifiers before providing care, treatment, or services.
- *Patient Teaching:* Inform the patient this procedure can assess abdomen and pelvic organ function.
- Obtain a history of the patient's complaints, including a list of known allergens, especially allergies or sensitivities to latex.
- Obtain a history of the patient's reproductive system, symptoms, and results of previously performed laboratory tests and diagnostic and surgical procedures.
- Note any recent procedures that can interfere with test results (i.e., barium procedures, surgery, or biopsy). There should be 24 hr between administration of barium and this test.
- Endoscopic retrograde cholangiopancreatography and colonoscopy, if ordered, should be scheduled after this procedure.
- Record the date of the last menstrual period. Obtain a history of menstrual dates, previous pregnancy, and treatment received for high-risk pregnancy.
- Obtain a list of the patient's current medications, including herbs, nutritional supplements, and nutraceuticals (see Appendix F).
- Review the procedure with the patient. Address concerns about pain related to the procedure and explain that some pain may be experienced during the test, and there may be moments of discomfort. Inform the patient the procedure is performed in a US department, usually by an HCP specializing in this procedure, and takes approximately 30 to 60 min.
- For the transvaginal approach, inform the patient that a sterile latex- or sheath-covered probe will be inserted into the vagina.
- *Sensitivity to social and cultural issues,* as well as concern for modesty, is important in providing psychological support before, during, and after the procedure.

- Instruct the patient receiving transabdominal US to drink five to six glasses of fluid 90 min before the procedure, and not to void, because the procedure requires a full bladder. Patients receiving transvaginal US only do not need to have a full bladder.
- Instruct the patient to remove jewelry and other metallic objects from the area to be examined prior to the procedure.
- There are no food or medication restrictions unless by medical direction. The test may be scheduled in relation to mealtime because fetal activity is highest 1 to 3 hr after the mother ingests a meal.

INTRATEST:

- Observe standard precautions, and follow the general guidelines in Appendix A. Positively identify the patient.
- Ensure that the patient has removed all external metallic objects from the area to be examined prior to the procedure.
- Ensure that the patient receiving transabdominal US drank five to six glasses of fluid and has not voided.
- Instruct the patient to change into the gown, robe, and foot coverings provided.
- Instruct the patient to cooperate fully and to follow directions. Ask the patient to remain still throughout the procedure because movement produces unreliable results.
- Place the patient in the supine position on an examination table. The right- or left-side-up position may be used to allow gravity to reposition the liver, gas, and fluid to facilitate better organ visualization.
- Expose the abdominal area and drape the patient.
- *Transabdominal approach:* Conductive gel is applied to the skin, and a transducer is moved over the skin while the bladder is distended to obtain images of the area of interest.
- *Transvaginal approach:* A lubricated, covered probe is inserted into the vagina and moved to different levels to obtain images.
- Ask the patient to breathe normally during the examination. If necessary for

U

better organ visualization, ask the patient to inhale deeply and hold her breath.

POST-TEST:

▶ A report of the results will be made available to the requesting HCP, who will discuss the results with the patient. Allow the patient to void, as needed.

▶ When the study is completed, remove the gel from the skin.

▶ Recognize anxiety related to test results. Discuss the implications of abnormal test results on the patient's lifestyle. Provide teaching and information regarding the clinical implications of the test results, as appropriate. Encourage the family to seek appropriate counseling if concerned with pregnancy termination and to seek genetic counseling if a chromosomal abnormality is determined. Decisions regarding elective abortion should take place in the presence of both parents. Provide a nonjudgmental, nonthreatening atmosphere for discussing the risks and difficulties of delivering and raising a developmentally challenged infant and for exploring other options (termination of pregnancy or adoption). It is also important to discuss problems the mother and father may experience (guilt, depression, anger) if fetal abnormalities are detected.

▶ Reinforce information given by the patient's HCP regarding further testing, treatment, or referral to another HCP. Answer any questions or address any concerns voiced by the patient or family.

▶ Depending on the results of this procedure, additional testing may be performed to evaluate or monitor progression of the disease process and determine the need for a change in therapy. Evaluate test results in relation to the patient's symptoms and other tests performed.

RELATED MONOGRAPHS:

▶ Related tests include amniotic fluid analysis, biopsy chorionic villus, blood groups and antibodies, chromosome analysis, culture bacterial anal/genital, culture viral, fetal fibronectin, α_1-fetoprotein, hexosaminidase A and B, human chorionic gonadotropin, KUB, Kleihauer-Betke test, lecithin/sphingomyelin ratio, MRI abdomen, and prolactin.

▶ Refer to the Reproductive System table at the end of the book for related tests by body system.

Ultrasound, Bladder

SYNONYM/ACRONYM: Bladder sonography.

COMMON USE: To visualize and assess the bladder toward diagnosing disorders such as retention, obstruction, distention, cancer, infection, bleeding, and inflammation.

AREA OF APPLICATION: Bladder.

CONTRAST: Done without contrast.

DESCRIPTION: Ultrasound (US) procedures are diagnostic, noninvasive, and relatively inexpensive. They take a short time to complete, do not use radiation, and cause no harm to the patient.

U

Bladder US evaluates disorders of the bladder, such as masses or lesions. Bladder position, structure, and size are examined with the use of high-frequency waves of various intensities delivered by a transducer, a flashlight-shaped device, pressed against the skin. Methods for imaging include the transrectal, transurethral, and transvaginal approach. The waves are bounced back, converted to electrical energy, amplified by the transducer, and displayed on a monitor to evaluate the structure and position of the contents of the bladder. The examination is helpful for monitoring patient response to therapy for bladder disease. Bladder images can be included in ultrasonography of the kidneys, ureters, bladder, urethra, and gonads in diagnosing renal/neurological disorders. Bladder US may be the diagnostic examination of choice because no radiation is used and, in most cases, the accuracy is sufficient to make the diagnosis without any further imaging procedures.

INDICATIONS

- Assess residual urine after voiding to diagnose urinary tract obstruction causing overdistention
- Detect tumor of the bladder wall or pelvis, as evidenced by distorted position or changes in bladder contour
- Determine end-stage malignancy of the bladder caused by extension of a primary tumor of the ovary or other pelvic organ
- Evaluate the cause of urinary tract infection, urine retention, and flank pain
- Evaluate hematuria, urinary frequency, dysuria, and suprapubic pain

- Measure urinary bladder volume by transurethral or transvaginal approach

POTENTIAL DIAGNOSIS

Normal findings in
- Normal size, position, and contour of the bladder

Abnormal findings in
- Bladder diverticulum
- Cyst
- Cystitis
- Malignancy of the bladder
- Tumor
- Ureterocele
- Urinary tract obstruction

CRITICAL FINDINGS: N/A

INTERFERING FACTORS

This procedure is contraindicated for
- Patients with latex allergy; use of the vaginal probe requires the probe to be covered with a condom-like sac, usually made from latex. Latex-free covers are available.

Factors that may impair clear imaging
- Incorrect placement of the transducer over the desired test site.
- Retained gas or barium from a previous radiological procedure.
- Dehydration, which can cause failure to demonstrate the boundaries between organs and tissue structures.
- Insufficiently full bladder, which fails to push the bowel from the pelvis and the uterus from the symphysis pubis, thereby prohibiting clear imaging of the pelvic organs in transabdominal imaging.
- Metallic objects (e.g., jewelry, body rings) within the examination field, which may inhibit organ visualization and cause unclear images.

Other considerations

- Failure to follow pretesting preparations may cause the procedure to be canceled or repeated.
- Inability of the patient to cooperate or remain still during the procedure because of age, significant pain, or mental status may interfere with the test results.

NURSING IMPLICATIONS AND PROCEDURE

PRETEST:

Positively identify the patient using at least two unique identifiers before providing care, treatment, or services.

Patient Teaching: Inform the patient this procedure can assist in assessing the bladder and pelvic organs.

Obtain a history of the patient's complaints, including a list of known allergens, especially allergies or sensitivities to latex.

Obtain a history of the patient's genitourinary system, symptoms, and results of previously performed laboratory tests and diagnostic and surgical procedures.

Note any recent procedures that can interfere with test results (i.e., barium procedures, surgery, or biopsy). There should be 24 hr between administration of barium and this test.

Endoscopic retrograde cholangiopancreatography, colonoscopy, and computed tomography of the abdomen, if ordered, should be scheduled after this procedure.

Record the date of the last menstrual period and determine the possibility of pregnancy in perimenopausal women.

Obtain a list of the patient's current medications, including herbs, nutritional supplements, and nutraceuticals (see Appendix F).

Review the procedure with the patient. Address concerns about pain related to the procedure. Explain to the patient that some pain may be experienced during the test, and there may be moments of discomfort. Inform the patient that the procedure is performed in a US department by a health-care provider (HCP), with support staff, and takes approximately 30 to 60 min.

Sensitivity to social and cultural issues, as well as concern for modesty, is important in providing psychological support before, during, and after the procedure.

Inform the patient for the transvaginal approach, that a sterile latex- or sheath-covered probe will be inserted into the vagina.

Instruct the patient receiving transabdominal US to drink five to six glasses of fluid 90 min before the procedure, and not to void, because the procedure requires a full bladder. Patients receiving transvaginal US only do not need to have a full bladder.

Instruct the patient to remove jewelry and other metallic objects from the area to be examined.

There are no food, fluid, or medication restrictions unless by medical direction.

INTRATEST:

Observe standard precautions, and follow the general guidelines in Appendix A. Positively identify the patient.

Ensure that the patient has removed all external metallic objects from the area to be examined prior to the procedure.

Ensure that the patient receiving transabdominal US drank five to six glasses of fluid and has not voided.

Instruct the patient to change into the gown, robe, and foot coverings provided.

Instruct the patient to cooperate fully and to follow directions. Instruct the patient to remain still throughout the procedure because movement produces unreliable results.

Place the patient in the supine position on an examination table. The right- or left-side-up positions may be used to allow gravity to reposition the liver, gas, and fluid to facilitate better organ visualization.

Expose the abdominal area and drape the patient.

Transabdominal approach: Conductive gel is applied to the skin, and a transducer is moved over the skin while the bladder is distended to obtain images of the area of interest.

Transvaginal approach: A covered and lubricated probe is inserted into the vagina and moved to different levels during scanning.

Ask the patient to breathe normally during the examination. If necessary for better organ visualization, ask the patient to inhale deeply and hold his or her breath.

If the patient is to be examined for residual urine volume, ask the patient to empty the bladder; repeat the procedure and calculate the volume.

POST-TEST:

A report of the results will be made available to the requesting HCP, who will discuss the results with the patient.

Allow the patient to void, as needed.

When the study is completed, remove the gel from the skin.

Recognize anxiety related to test results. Discuss the implications of abnormal test results on the patient's lifestyle. Provide teaching and information regarding the clinical implications of the test results, as appropriate.

Reinforce information given by the patient's HCP regarding further testing, treatment, or referral to another HCP. Answer any questions or address any concerns voiced by the patient or family.

Depending on the results of this procedure, additional testing may be performed to evaluate or monitor progression of the disease process and determine the need for a change in therapy. Evaluate test results in relation to the patient's symptoms and other tests performed.

RELATED MONOGRAPHS:

Related tests include bladder cancer markers urine, CT pelvis, cystoscopy, IVP, KUB study, and MRI pelvis.

Refer to the Genitourinary System table in the end of the book for related tests by body system.

Ultrasound, Breast

SYNONYM/ACRONYM: Mammographic ultrasound.

COMMON USE: Used in place of or in conjunction with mammography to assist in diagnosing disorders such as tumor, cancer, and cysts.

AREA OF APPLICATION: Breast.

CONTRAST: Done without contrast.

DESCRIPTION: Ultrasound (US) procedures are diagnostic, noninvasive, and relatively inexpensive. They take a short time to complete, do not use radiation, and cause no harm to the patient. When used in conjunction with mammography and clinical examination, breast US is indispensable in the diagnosis and management of benign and malignant process. Both breasts are usually examined during this procedure. The examination uses high-frequency waves of various intensities delivered by a transducer, a flashlight-shaped device, pressed against the skin. The waves are bounced back, converted to electrical energy, amplified by the transducer, and displayed on a monitor to determine the presence of palpable and nonpalpable masses and their size and structure. This procedure is useful in patients with an abnormal mass on a mammogram because it can determine whether the abnormality is cystic or solid; that is, it can differentiate between a palpable, fluid-filled cyst and a palpable, solid breast lesion (benign or malignant). It is especially useful in patients with dense breast tissue and in those with silicone prostheses, because the US beam easily penetrates in these situations, allowing routine examination that cannot be performed with x-ray mammography. The procedure can be done as an adjunct to mammography, or it can be done in place of mammography in patients who refuse x-ray exposure or those in whom it is contraindicated (e.g., pregnant women, women less than 25 yr). The procedure is indicated as a guide for biopsy and other interventional procedures and as a means of monitoring disease progression or the effects of treatment.

INDICATIONS

- Detect very small tumors in combination with mammography for diagnostic validation
- Determine the presence of nonpalpable abnormalities viewed on mammography of dense breast tissue and monitor changes in these abnormalities
- Differentiate among types of breast masses (e.g., cyst, solid tumor, other lesions) in dense breast tissue
- Evaluate palpable masses in young (less than age 25), pregnant, and lactating patients

- Guide interventional procedures such as cyst aspiration, large-needle core biopsy, fine-needle aspiration biopsy, abscess drainage, presurgical localization, and galactography
- Identify an abscess in a patient with mastitis

POTENTIAL DIAGNOSIS

Normal findings in

- Normal subcutaneous, mammary, and retromammary layers of tissue in both breasts; no evidence of pathological lesions (cyst or tumor) in either breast

Abnormal findings in

- Abscess
- Breast solid tumor, lesions
- Cancer (ductal carcinoma, infiltrating lobular carcinoma, medullary carcinoma, tubular carcinoma, and papillary carcinoma)
- Cystic breast disease
- Fibroadenoma
- Focal fibrosis
- Galactocele
- Hamartoma (fibroadenolipoma)
- Hematoma
- Papilloma
- Phyllodes tumor
- Radial scar

CRITICAL FINDINGS: N/A

INTERFERING FACTORS

Factors that may impair clear imaging

- Incorrect placement of the transducer over the desired test site.
- Metallic objects (e.g., jewelry, body rings) within the examination field, which may inhibit organ visualization and cause unclear images.
- Excessively large breasts.
- Inability of the patient to cooperate or remain still during the procedure because of age, significant pain, or mental status.

U

NURSING IMPLICATIONS AND PROCEDURE

PRETEST:

▶ Positively identify the patient using at least two unique identifiers before providing care, treatment, or services.

▶ *Patient Teaching:* Inform the patient this procedure can assist in assessing the breast.

▶ Obtain a history of the patient's complaints, including a list of known allergens, especially allergies or sensitivities to latex.

▶ Obtain a history of the patient's reproductive system, symptoms, and results of previously performed laboratory tests and diagnostic and surgical procedures.

▶ Obtain a list of the patient's current medications, including herbs, nutritional supplements, and nutraceuticals (see Appendix F).

▶ Review the procedure with the patient. Address concerns about pain related to the procedure and explain that some pain may be experienced during the test, and there may be moments of discomfort. Inform the patient that the procedure is performed in a US department by a health-care provider (HCP) who specializes in this procedure, with support staff, and takes approximately 30 to 60 min.

▶ *Sensitivity to social and cultural issues,* as well as concern for modesty, is important in providing psychological support before, during, and after the procedure.

▶ Instruct the patient not to apply lotions, deodorant, bath powder, or other substances to the chest and breast area before the examination.

▶ Instruct the patient to remove jewelry and other metallic objects from the area to be examined.

▶ There are no food, fluid, or medication restrictions unless by medical direction.

INTRATEST:

▶ Observe standard precautions, and follow the general guidelines in Appendix A. Positively identify the patient.

▶ Ensure that the patient has not applied lotions, deodorant, bath powder, or other substances to the chest and breast area before the examination.

▶ Ensure that the patient has removed all external metallic objects from the area to be examined prior to the procedure.

▶ Instruct the patient to change into the gown and robe provided.

▶ Instruct the patient to cooperate fully and to follow directions. Instruct the patient to remain still throughout the procedure because movement produces unreliable results.

▶ Place the patient in the supine position on an examination table. The right- and left-side-up positions are also used during the scan to facilitate better organ visualization.

▶ Expose the breast area and drape the patient.

▶ Conductive gel is applied to the skin and a transducer is moved over the skin to obtain images of the area of interest.

▶ Ask the patient to breathe normally during the examination. If necessary for better organ visualization, ask the patient to inhale deeply and hold her breath.

POST-TEST:

▶ A report of the results will be made available to the requesting HCP, who will discuss the results with the patient.

▶ When the study is completed, remove the gel from the skin.

▶ Recognize anxiety related to test results. Discuss the implications of abnormal test results on the patient's lifestyle. Provide teaching and information regarding the clinical implications of the test results, as appropriate. Educate the patient regarding access to counseling services. Provide contact information, if desired, for the American Cancer Society (www.cancer.org).

▶ Reinforce information given by the patient's HCP regarding further testing, treatment, or referral to another HCP. Decisions regarding the need for and frequency of breast self-examination, mammography, MRI breast, or other cancer screening procedures should be made after consultation between the patient and HCP. The most current guidelines for breast cancer screening

of the general population as well as of individuals with increased risk are available from the American Cancer Society (www.cancer.org), the American College of Obstetricians and Gynecologists (ACOG) (www.acog.org), and the American College of Radiology (www.acr.org). Answer any questions or address any concerns voiced by the patient or family.
▸ Depending on the results of this procedure, additional testing may be performed to evaluate or monitor progression of the disease process and determine the need for a change in therapy. Evaluate test results in relation to the patient's symptoms and other tests performed.

RELATED MONOGRAPHS:
▸ Related tests include biopsy breast, cancer antigens, chest x-ray, CT thorax, ductograpy, mammogram, MRI breast, and stereotactic biopsy breast.
▸ Refer to the Reproductive System table at the end of the book for related tests by body system.

Ultrasound, Kidney

SYNONYM/ACRONYM: Renal ultrasound, renal sonography.

COMMON USE: To visualize and assess the kidneys, to perform biopsies, and assist in diagnosing disorders such as tumor, cancer, stones, and congenital anomalies. This procedure can also be used to evaluate therapeutic interventions such as transplants.

AREA OF APPLICATION: Kidney.

CONTRAST: Done without contrast.

DESCRIPTION: Ultrasound (US) procedures are diagnostic, noninvasive, and relatively inexpensive. They take a short time to complete, do not use radiation, and cause no harm to the patient. Renal US is used to evaluate renal system disorders. It is valuable for determining the internal components of renal masses (solid vs. cystic) and for evaluating other renal diseases, renal parenchyma, perirenal tissues, and obstruction. US uses high-frequency waves of various intensities delivered by a transducer, a flashlight-shaped device, pressed against the skin. The waves are bounced back, converted to electrical energy, amplified by the transducer, and displayed on a monitor to evaluate the structure, size, and position of the kidney. Renal US can be performed on the same day as a radionuclide scan or other radiological procedure and is especially valuable in patients who are in renal failure, have hypersensitivity to contrast medium, have a kidney that did not visualize on intravenous pyelography (IVP), or are pregnant. It does not rely on renal function or the injection of contrast medium to obtain a diagnosis. The procedure is indicated for evaluation after a

U

kidney transplant and is used as a guide for biopsy and other interventional procedures, abscess drainage, and nephrostomy tube placement. Renal US may be the diagnostic examination of choice because no radiation is used and, in most cases, the accuracy is sufficient to make the diagnosis without any further imaging procedures.

INDICATIONS

- Aid in the diagnosis of the effect of chronic glomerulonephritis and end-stage chronic renal failure on the kidneys (e.g., decrease in size)
- Detect an accumulation of fluid in the kidney caused by backflow of urine, hemorrhage, or perirenal fluid
- Detect masses and differentiate between cysts or solid tumors, as evidenced by specific waveform patterns or absence of sound waves
- Determine the presence and location of renal or ureteral calculi and obstruction
- Determine the size, shape, and position of a nonfunctioning kidney to identify the cause
- Evaluate or plan therapy for renal tumors
- Evaluate renal transplantation for changes in kidney size
- Locate the site of and guide percutaneous renal biopsy, aspiration needle insertion, or nephrostomy tube insertion
- Monitor kidney development in children when renal disease has been diagnosed
- Provide the location and size of renal masses in patients who are unable to undergo IVP because of poor renal function or an allergy to iodinated contrast medium

POTENTIAL DIAGNOSIS

Normal findings in

- Absence of calculi, cysts, hydronephrosis, obstruction, or tumor
- Normal size, position, and shape of the kidneys and associated structures

Abnormal findings in

- Acute glomerulonephritis
- Acute pyelonephritis
- Congenital anomalies, such as absent, horseshoe, ectopic, or duplicated kidney
- Hydronephrosis
- Obstruction of ureters
- Perirenal abscess or hematoma
- Polycystic kidney
- Rejection of renal transplant
- Renal calculi
- Renal cysts, hypertrophy, or tumors
- Ureteral obstruction

CRITICAL FINDINGS: N/A

INTERFERING FACTORS

Factors that may impair clear imaging

- Attenuation of the sound waves by the ribs, which can impair clear imaging of the kidney.
- Incorrect placement of the transducer over the desired test site.
- Retained gas or barium from a previous radiological procedure.
- Metallic objects (e.g., jewelry, body rings) within the examination field, which may inhibit organ visualization and cause unclear images.

Other considerations

- Inability of the patient to cooperate or remain still during the procedure because of age, significant pain, or mental status may interfere with the test results.

NURSING IMPLICATIONS AND PROCEDURE

PRETEST:

▶ Positively identify the patient using at least two unique identifiers before providing care, treatment, or services.

▶ *Patient Teaching:* Inform the patient this procedure can assist in assessing kidney function.

▶ Obtain a history of the patient's complaints, including a list of known allergens, especially allergies or sensitivities to latex.

▶ Obtain a history of the patient's genitourinary system, symptoms, and results of previously performed laboratory tests and diagnostic and surgical procedures.

▶ Note any recent procedures that can interfere with test results (i.e., barium procedures, surgery, or biopsy). There should be 24 hr between administration of barium and this test.

▶ Endoscopic retrograde cholangiopancreatography, colonoscopy, and computed tomography of the abdomen, if ordered, should be scheduled after this procedure.

▶ Record the date of the last menstrual period and determine the possibility of pregnancy in perimenopausal women.

▶ Obtain a list of the patient's current medications, including herbs, nutritional supplements, and nutraceuticals (see Appendix F).

▶ Review the procedure with the patient. Address concerns about pain related to the procedure. Explain to the patient that some pain may be experienced during the test, and there may be moments of discomfort. Inform the patient that the procedure is performed in a US department, usually by a health-care provider (HCP), with support staff, and takes approximately 30 to 60 min.

▶ *Sensitivity to social and cultural issues,* as well as concern for modesty, is important in providing psychological support before, during, and after the procedure.

▶ Instruct the patient to remove jewelry and other metallic objects from the area to be examined.

▶ There are no food, fluid, or medication restrictions unless by medical direction.

INTRATEST:

▶ Observe standard precautions, and follow the general guidelines in Appendix A. Positively identify the patient.

▶ Ensure that the patient has removed all external metallic objects from the area to be examined prior to the procedure.

▶ Instruct the patient to void and change into the gown, robe, and foot coverings provided.

▶ Instruct the patient to cooperate fully and to follow directions. Instruct the patient to remain still throughout the procedure because movement produces unreliable results.

▶ Place the patient in the supine position on an examination table. The right- or left-side-up positions may be used to allow gravity to reposition the liver, gas, and fluid to facilitate better organ visualization.

▶ Expose the abdominal and kidney area and drape the patient.

▶ Conductive gel is applied to the skin, and a transducer is moved over the skin to obtain images of the area of interest.

▶ Ask the patient to breathe normally during the examination. If necessary for better organ visualization, ask the patient to inhale deeply and hold his or her breath.

POST-TEST:

▶ A report of the results will be made available to the requesting HCP, who will discuss the results with the patient.

▶ When the study is completed, remove the gel from the skin.

▶ Recognize anxiety related to test results. Discuss the implications of abnormal test results on the patient's lifestyle. Provide teaching and information regarding the clinical implications of the test results, as appropriate.

▶ Reinforce information given by the patient's HCP regarding further testing, treatment, or referral to another HCP. Answer any questions or address any concerns voiced by the patient or family.

▶ Depending on the results of this procedure, additional testing may be

performed to evaluate or monitor progression of the disease process and determine the need for a change in therapy. Evaluate test results in relation to the patient's symptoms and other tests performed.

RELATED MONOGRAPHS:

▶ Related tests include angiography renal, anti-glomerular basement membrane antibody, biopsy kidney, BUN, calculus kidney stone panel, CT abdomen, creatinine, creatinine clearance, cytology urine, erythropoietin, group A streptococcal screen, IVP, KUB study, MRI abdomen, renogram, retrograde ureteropyelography, UA, and US abdomen.

▶ Refer to the Genitourinary System table at the end of the book for related tests by system.

Ultrasound, Liver and Biliary System

SYNONYM/ACRONYM: Gallbladder ultrasound, liver ultrasound, hepatobiliary sonography.

COMMON USE: To visualize and assess liver and gallbladder structure and function, assist in obtaining a biopsy, and diagnose disorders such as gallstones, cancer, tumors, cysts, and bleeding. Also used to evaluate the effectiveness of therapeutic interventions.

AREA OF APPLICATION: Liver, gallbladder, bile ducts.

CONTRAST: Done without contrast.

DESCRIPTION: Ultrasound (US) procedures are diagnostic, non-invasive, and relatively inexpensive. They take a short time to complete, do not use radiation, and cause no harm to the patient. Hepatobiliary US uses high-frequency waves of various intensities delivered by a transducer, a flashlight-shaped device, pressed against the skin. The waves are bounced back, converted to electrical energy, amplified by the transducer, and displayed on a monitor to evaluate the structure, size, and position of the liver and gallbladder in the right upper quadrant (RUQ) of the abdomen. The gallbladder and biliary system collect, store, concentrate, and transport bile to the intestines to aid in digestion. This procedure allows visualization of the gallbladder and bile ducts when the patient may have impaired liver function, and it is especially helpful when done on patients in whom gallstones cannot be visualized with oral or IV radiological studies. Liver US can be done in combination with a nuclear scan to obtain information about liver function and density differences in the liver. The procedure is indicated as a guide for biopsy and other interventional procedures. Hepatobiliary US may be the diagnostic examination of choice

U

because no radiation is used and, in most cases, the accuracy is sufficient to make the diagnosis without any further imaging procedures.

INDICATIONS

* Detect cysts, polyps, hematoma, abscesses, hemangioma, adenoma, metastatic disease, hepatitis, or solid tumor of the liver or gallbladder, as evidenced by echoes specific to tissue density and sharply or poorly defined masses
* Detect gallstones or inflammation when oral cholecystography is inconclusive
* Detect hepatic lesions, as evidenced by density differences and echopattern changes
* Determine the cause of unexplained hepatomegaly and abnormal liver function tests
* Determine cause of unexplained RUQ pain
* Determine patency and diameter of the hepatic duct for dilation or obstruction
* Differentiate between obstructive and nonobstructive jaundice by determining the cause
* Evaluate response to therapy for tumor, as evidenced by a decrease in size of the organ
* Guide biopsy or tube placement
* Guide catheter placement into the gallbladder for stone dissolution and gallbladder fragmentation

POTENTIAL DIAGNOSIS

Normal findings in
* Normal size, position, and shape of the liver and gallbladder as well as patency of the cystic and common bile ducts

Abnormal findings in
* Biliary or hepatic duct obstruction/dilation

* Cirrhosis
* Gallbladder inflammation, stones, carcinoma, polyps
* Hematoma or trauma
* Hepatic tumors, metastasis, cysts, hemangioma, hepatitis
* Hepatocellular disease, adenoma
* Hepatomegaly
* Intrahepatic abscess
* Subphrenic abscesses

CRITICAL FINDINGS: N/A

INTERFERING FACTORS

Factors that may impair clear imaging
* Attenuation of the sound waves by the ribs, which can impair clear imaging of the right lobe of the liver.
* Incorrect placement of the transducer over the desired test site.
* Gas or feces in the gastrointestinal tract resulting from inadequate cleansing or failure to restrict food intake before the study.
* Retained barium from a previous radiological procedure.
* Metallic objects (e.g., jewelry, body rings) within the examination field, which may inhibit organ visualization and can produce unclear images.
* Inability of the patient to cooperate or remain still during the procedure because of age, significant pain, or mental status.

Other considerations
* Failure to follow dietary restrictions may cause the procedure to be canceled or repeated.

NURSING IMPLICATIONS AND PROCEDURE

PRETEST:
▶ Positively identify the patient using at least two unique identifiers before providing care, treatment, or services.

Patient Teaching: Inform the patient this procedure can assist in assessing liver and biliary function.

Obtain a history of the patient's complaints, including a list of known allergens, especially allergies or sensitivities to latex.

Obtain a history of the patient's hepatobiliary system, symptoms, and results of previously performed laboratory tests and diagnostic and surgical procedures.

Note any recent procedures that can interfere with test results (i.e., barium procedures, surgery, or biopsy). There should be 24 hr between administration of barium and this test.

Endoscopic retrograde cholangiopancreatography, colonoscopy, and computed tomography of the abdomen, if ordered, should be scheduled after this procedure.

Obtain a list of the patient's current medications, including herbs, nutritional supplements, and nutraceuticals (see Appendix F).

Review the procedure with the patient. Address concerns about pain related to the procedure and explain that some pain may be experienced during the test, and there may be moments of discomfort. Inform the patient that the procedure is performed in a US department, usually by a health-care provider (HCP) who specializes in this procedure, with support staff, and takes approximately 30 to 60 min.

Sensitivity to social and cultural issues, as well as concern for modesty, is important in providing psychological support before, during, and after the procedure.

Instruct the patient to remove jewelry and other metallic objects from the area to be examined.

The patient should fast and restrict fluids for 8 hr prior to the procedure. Protocols may vary among facilities.

INTRATEST:

Observe standard precautions, and follow the general guidelines in Appendix A. Positively identify the patient.

Ensure that food and fluids have been restricted for at least 8 hr prior to the procedure.

Ensure that the patient has removed all external metallic objects from the area to be examined prior to the procedure.

Instruct the patient to void and change into the gown, robe, and foot coverings provided.

Instruct the patient to cooperate fully and to follow directions. Instruct the patient to remain still throughout the procedure because movement produces unreliable results.

Place the patient in the supine position on an examination table. The right- or left-side-up positions may be used to allow gravity to reposition the liver, gas, and fluid to facilitate better organ visualization.

Expose the abdominal area and drape the patient.

Conductive gel is applied to the skin, and a transducer is moved over the skin to obtain images of the area of interest.

Ask the patient to breathe normally during the examination. If necessary for better organ visualization, ask the patient to inhale deeply and hold his or her breath.

POST-TEST:

A report of the results will be made available to the requesting HCP, who will discuss the results with the patient.

When the study is completed, remove the gel from the skin.

Instruct the patient to resume usual diet and fluids, as directed by the HCP.

Recognize anxiety related to test results. Discuss the implications of abnormal test results on the patient's lifestyle. Provide teaching and information regarding the clinical implications of the test results, as appropriate.

Reinforce information given by the patient's HCP regarding further testing, treatment, or referral to another HCP. Answer any questions or address any concerns voiced by the patient or family.

Depending on the results of this procedure, additional testing may be performed to evaluate or monitor progression of the disease process and determine the need for a change in therapy. Evaluate test results in relation to the patient's symptoms and other tests performed.

RELATED MONOGRAPHS:
Related tests include ALP, ALT, AST, bilirubin, biopsy liver, cholangiography, colonoscopy, CT abdomen, endoscopy, ERCP, GGT, haptoglobin, hepatitis (A, B, C antigens and/or antibodies), hepatobiliary scan, laparoscopy abdominal, MRI abdomen, radiofrequency ablation liver, and US abdomen.
Refer to the Hepatobiliary System table at the end of the book for related tests by body system.

Ultrasound, Lymph Nodes and Retroperitoneum

SYNONYM/ACRONYM: Lymph node sonography.

COMMON USE: To visualize and assess for lymph node enlargement related to disorders such as infection, abscess, tumor, and cancer. Also used as a tool to biopsy and evaluate the progress of therapeutic interventions.

AREA OF APPLICATION: Abdomen, pelvis, and retroperitoneum.

CONTRAST: Done without contrast.

DESCRIPTION: Ultrasound (US) procedures are diagnostic, noninvasive, and relatively inexpensive. They take a short time to complete, do not use radiation, and cause no harm to the patient. Lymph node US uses high-frequency waves of various intensities delivered by a transducer, a flashlight-shaped device, pressed against the skin. The waves are bounced back, converted to electrical energy, amplified by the transducer, and displayed on a monitor to evaluate the structure, size, and position of the lymph nodes to examine the retroperitoneum and surrounding tissues. This procedure is used for the evaluation of retroperitoneal pathology, usually lymph node enlargement. US is the preferred diagnostic method because this area is inaccessible to conventional radiography in diagnosing

lymphadenopathy, although it can be used in combination with lymphangiography, magnetic resonance imaging, and computed tomography (CT) to confirm the diagnosis. The procedure may be used for monitoring the effect of radiation or chemotherapy on the lymph nodes. Lymph node US may be the diagnostic examination of choice because no radiation is used and, in most cases, the accuracy is sufficient to make the diagnosis without any further imaging procedures.

INDICATIONS
- Detect lymphoma
- Determine the location of enlarged nodes to plan radiation and other therapy
- Determine the size or enlargement of aortic and iliac lymph nodes
- Evaluate the effects of medical, radiation, or surgical therapy on the

U

size of nodes or tumors, as evidenced by shrinkage or continued presence of the mass or nodes

POTENTIAL DIAGNOSIS

Normal findings in
• Normal retroperitoneal and intrapelvic node size of 1.5 cm in diameter

Abnormal findings in
• Infection or abscess
• Lymphoma
• Retroperitoneal tumor

CRITICAL FINDINGS: N/A

INTERFERING FACTORS

Factors that may impair clear imaging
• Incorrect placement of the transducer over the desired test site.
• Gas or feces in the gastrointestinal tract resulting from inadequate cleansing or failure to restrict food intake before the study.
• Retained barium from a previous radiological procedure.
• Dehydration, which can cause failure to demonstrate the boundaries between organs and tissue structures.
• Insufficiently full bladder, which fails to push the bowel from the pelvis and the uterus from the symphysis pubis, thereby prohibiting clear imaging of the pelvic organs in transabdominal imaging.
• Metallic objects (e.g., jewelry, or body rings) within the examination field, which may inhibit organ visualization and cause unclear images.

Other considerations
• Failure to follow dietary/fluid instructions and other pretesting preparations may cause the procedure to be canceled or repeated.
• Inability of the patient to cooperate or remain still during the procedure

because of age, significant pain, or mental status may interfere with the test results.

NURSING IMPLICATIONS AND PROCEDURE

PRETEST:

▸ Positively identify the patient using at least two unique identifiers before providing care, treatment, or services.
▸ *Patient Teaching:* Inform the patient this procedure can assist in assessing the lymph nodes and surrounding tissue.
▸ Obtain a history of the patient's complaints, including a list of known allergens, especially allergies or sensitivities to latex.
▸ Obtain a history of the patient's immune system, symptoms, and results of previously performed laboratory tests and diagnostic and surgical procedures.
▸ Note any recent procedures that can interfere with test results (i.e., barium procedures, surgery, or biopsy). There should be 24 hr between administration of barium and this test.
▸ Endoscopic retrograde cholangiopancreatography, colonoscopy, and CT of the abdomen, if ordered, should be scheduled after this procedure.
▸ Obtain a list of the patient's current medications, including herbs, nutritional supplements, and nutraceuticals (see Appendix F).
▸ Review the procedure with the patient. Address concerns about pain related to the procedure and explain that some pain may be experienced during the test, and there may be moments of discomfort. Inform the patient that the procedure is performed in a US department by a health-care provider (HCP) who specializes in this procedure, with support staff, and takes approximately 30 to 60 min.
▸ *Sensitivity to social and cultural issues,* as well as concern for modesty, is important in providing psychological

U

support before, during, and after the procedure.

▶ Instruct the patient to remove jewelry and other metallic objects from the area to be examined.

▶ The patient should fast and restrict fluids for 8 hr prior to the procedure. Inform the patient that transabdominal US requires a full bladder. Protocols may vary among facilities.

▶ Instruct the patient to drink five to six glasses of fluid 90 min before the procedure, and not to void before the procedure.

INTRATEST:

▶ Observe standard precautions, and follow the general guidelines in Appendix A. Positively identify the patient.

▶ Ensure that food and fluids have been restricted for at least 8 hr prior to the procedure.

▶ Ensure that the patient receiving transabdominal US drank five to six glasses of fluid and has not voided.

▶ Ensure that the patient has removed all external metallic objects from the area to be examined prior to the procedure.

▶ Instruct the patient to change into the gown, robe, and foot coverings provided.

▶ Instruct the patient to cooperate fully and to follow directions. Ask the patient to remain still throughout the procedure because movement produces unreliable results.

▶ Place the patient in the supine position on an examination table; other positions may be used during the examination.

▶ Expose the abdominal area and drape the patient.

▶ Conductive gel is applied to the skin, and a transducer is moved over the skin while the bladder is distended to obtain images of the area of interest.

▶ Ask the patient to breathe normally during the examination. If necessary for better organ visualization, ask the patient to inhale deeply and hold his or her breath.

POST-TEST:

▶ A report of the results will be made available to the requesting HCP, who will discuss the results with the patient.

▶ Allow the patient to void, as needed.

▶ When the study is completed, remove the gel from the skin.

▶ Instruct the patient to resume usual diet and fluids, as directed by the HCP.

▶ Recognize anxiety related to test results. Discuss the implications of abnormal test results on the patient's lifestyle. Provide teaching and information regarding the clinical implications of the test results, as appropriate.

▶ Reinforce information given by the patient's HCP regarding further testing, treatment, or referral to another HCP. Answer any questions or address any concerns voiced by the patient or family.

▶ Depending on the results of this procedure, additional testing may be performed to evaluate or monitor progression of the disease process and determine the need for a change in therapy. Evaluate test results in relation to the patient's symptoms and other tests performed.

RELATED MONOGRAPHS:

▶ Related tests include angiography abdomen, biopsy bone marrow, biopsy lymph nodes, CBC, CBC hemoglobin, CBC RBC count, CBC RBC morphology and inclusions, CT abdomen, CT colonoscopy, ESR, gallium scan, KUB study, laparoscopy abdominal, lymphangiogram, and MRI abdomen.

▶ Refer to the Immune System table at the end of the book for related tests by body system.

U

Ultrasound, Pancreas

SYNONYM/ACRONYM: Pancreatic ultrasonography.

COMMON USE: To visualize and assess the pancreas toward diagnosing disorders such as tumor, cancer, obstruction, and cysts. Also used as a tool for biopsy and to evaluate the effectiveness of therapeutic interventions.

AREA OF APPLICATION: Pancreas and upper abdomen.

CONTRAST: Done without contrast.

DESCRIPTION: Ultrasound (US) procedures are diagnostic, noninvasive, and relatively inexpensive. They take a short time to complete, do not use radiation, and cause no harm to the patient. Pancreatic US uses high-frequency waves of various intensities delivered by a transducer, a flashlight-shaped device, pressed against the skin. The waves are bounced back, converted to electrical energy, amplified by the transducer, and displayed on a monitor to determine the size, shape, and position of the pancreas; determine the presence of masses or other abnormalities of the pancreas; and examine the surrounding viscera. The procedure is indicated as a guide for biopsy, aspiration, and other interventional procedures. Pancreatic US may be the diagnostic examination of choice because no radiation is used and, in most cases, the accuracy is sufficient to make the diagnosis without any further imaging procedures; however, it is usually done in combination with computed tomography (CT) or magnetic resonance imaging of the pancreas.

INDICATIONS

- Detect anatomic abnormalities as a consequence of pancreatitis
- Detect pancreatic cancer, as evidenced by a poorly defined mass or a mass in the head of the pancreas that obstructs the pancreatic duct
- Detect pancreatitis, as evidenced by pancreatic enlargement with increased echoes
- Detect pseudocysts, as evidenced by a well-defined mass with absence of echoes from the interior
- Monitor therapeutic response to tumor treatment
- Provide guidance for percutaneous aspiration and fine-needle biopsy of the pancreas

POTENTIAL DIAGNOSIS

Normal findings in
- Normal size, position, contour, and texture of the pancreas

Abnormal findings in
- Acute pancreatitis
- Calculi
- Pancreatic duct obstruction
- Pancreatic tumor
- Pseudocysts

CRITICAL FINDINGS: N/A

INTERFERING FACTORS

Factors that may impair clear imaging

- Attenuation of the sound waves by the ribs, which can impair clear imaging of the pancreas.
- Incorrect placement of the transducer over the desired test site.
- Gas or feces in the gastrointestinal (GI) tract resulting from inadequate cleansing or failure to restrict food intake before the study.
- Retained barium from a previous radiological procedure.
- Metallic objects (e.g., jewelry, body rings) within the examination field, which may inhibit organ visualization and cause unclear images.

Other considerations

- Failure to follow dietary and fluid restrictions and other pretesting preparations may cause the procedure to be canceled or repeated.
- Inability of the patient to cooperate or remain still during the procedure because of age, significant pain, or mental status may interfere with the test results.

NURSING IMPLICATIONS AND PROCEDURE

PRETEST:

▶ Positively identify the patient using at least two unique identifiers before providing care, treatment, or services.

▶ *Patient Teaching:* Inform the patient this procedure can assist in assessing pancreatic function.

▶ Obtain a history of the patient's complaints, including a list of known allergens, especially allergies or sensitivities to latex.

▶ Obtain a history of the patient's gastrointestinal system, symptoms, and results of previously performed laboratory tests and diagnostic and surgical procedures.

▶ Note any recent procedures that can interfere with test results (i.e., barium procedures, surgery, or biopsy). There should be 24 hr between administration of barium and this test.

▶ Endoscopic retrograde cholangiopancreatography, colonoscopy, and CT of the abdomen, if ordered, should be scheduled after this procedure.

▶ Record the date of the last menstrual period and determine the possibility of pregnancy in perimenopausal women.

▶ Obtain a list of the patient's current medications, including herbs, nutritional supplements, and nutraceuticals (see Appendix F).

▶ Review the procedure with the patient. Address concerns about pain related to the procedure and explain that some pain may be experienced during the test, and there may be moments of discomfort. Inform the patient that the procedure is performed in a US department, usually by a health-care provider (HCP) specializing in this procedure, with support staff, and takes approximately 30 to 60 min.

▶ *Sensitivity to social and cultural issues,* as well as concern for modesty, is important in providing psychological support before, during, and after the procedure.

▶ Instruct the patient to remove jewelry and other metallic objects from the area to be examined.

▶ The patient should fast and restrict fluids for 8 hr prior to the procedure. Protocols may vary among facilities.

INTRATEST:

▶ Observe standard precautions, and follow the general guidelines in Appendix A. Positively identify the patient.

▶ Ensure that food and fluids have been restricted for at least 8 hr prior to the procedure.

▶ Ensure that the patient has removed all external metallic objects from the area to be examined prior to the procedure.

▶ Instruct the patient to void and change into the gown, robe, and foot coverings provided.

▶ Instruct the patient to cooperate fully and to follow directions. Ask the patient to remain still throughout the procedure because movement produces unreliable results.

Place the patient in the supine position on an examination table. The right- or left-side-up position may be used to allow gravity to reposition the liver, gas, and fluid to facilitate better organ visualization.

Expose the abdominal area and drape the patient.

Conductive gel is applied to the skin, and a transducer is moved over the skin to obtain images of the area of interest.

Ask the patient to breathe normally during the examination. If necessary for better organ visualization, ask the patient to inhale deeply and hold his or her breath.

POST-TEST:

A report of the results will be made available to the requesting HCP, who will discuss the results with the patient.

When the study is completed, remove the gel from the skin.

Instruct the patient to resume usual diet and fluids, as directed by the HCP.

Recognize anxiety related to test results. Discuss the implications of abnormal test results on the patient's lifestyle. Provide teaching and information regarding the clinical implications of the test results, as appropriate.

Reinforce information given by the patient's HCP regarding further testing, treatment, or referral to another HCP. Answer any questions or address any concerns voiced by the patient or family.

Depending on the results of this procedure, additional testing may be needed to evaluate or monitor progression of the disease process and determine the need for a change in therapy. Evaluate test results in relation to the patient's symptoms and other tests performed.

RELATED MONOGRAPHS:

Related tests include amylase, cancer antigens, CT abdomen, CT pancreas, C peptide, ERCP, KUB study, laparoscopy abdominal, lipase, MRI abdomen, MRI pancreas, peritoneal fluid analysis, and US abdomen.

Refer to the Gastrointestinal System table at the end of the book for related tests by body system.

Ultrasound, Pelvis (Gynecologic, Nonobstetric)

SYNONYM/ACRONYM: Lower abdominal ultrasound, pelvic gynecologic (GYN) sonogram, pelvic sonography.

COMMON USE: To visualize and assess the pelvis for disorders such as uterine mass, tumor, cancer, cyst, and fibroids. This procedure can also be useful in evaluating ovulation and fallopian tube function related to fertility issues.

AREA OF APPLICATION: Pelvis and appendix region.

CONTRAST: Done without contrast.

DESCRIPTION: Ultrasound (US) procedures are diagnostic, noninvasive, and relatively inexpensive. They take a short time to complete, do not use radiation, and cause no harm to the patient. Gynecologic US uses high-frequency sound waves of various intensities delivered by a transducer, a flashlight-shaped device, pressed against the skin or inserted into the vagina. The waves are bounced back, converted to electrical energy, amplified by the transducer, and displayed on a monitor in order to determine the presence, size, and structure of masses and cysts and determine the position of an intrauterine contraceptive device (IUD); evaluate postmenopausal bleeding; and examine other abnormalities of the uterus, ovaries, fallopian tubes, and vagina.

This procedure is done by a transabdominal or transvaginal approach. The transabdominal approach provides a view of the pelvic organs posterior to the bladder. It requires a full bladder, thereby allowing a window for transmission of the US waves, pushing the uterus away from the pubic symphysis, pushing the bowel out of the pelvis, and acting as a reference for comparison in the evaluation of the internal structures of a mass or cyst being examined. The transvaginal approach focuses on the female reproductive organs and is often used to monitor ovulation over a period of days in patients undergoing fertility assessment. This approach is also used in obese patients or in patients with retroversion of the uterus because the sound waves are better able to reach the organ from the vaginal site. Transvaginal images are significantly more accurate compared to anterior transabdominal images in identifying paracervical, endometrial, and ovarian pathology, and the transvaginal approach does not require a full bladder. The procedure is indicated as a guide for biopsy and other

interventional procedures. Pelvic US may be the diagnostic examination of choice because no radiation is used and, in most cases, the accuracy is sufficient to make the diagnosis without any further imaging procedures.

INDICATIONS

- Detect and monitor the treatment of pelvic inflammatory disease (PID) when done in combination with other laboratory tests
- Detect bleeding into the pelvis resulting from trauma to the area or ascites associated with tumor metastasis
- Detect masses in the pelvis and differentiate them from cysts or solid tumors, as evidenced by differences in sound-wave patterns
- Detect pelvic abscess or peritonitis caused by a ruptured appendix or diverticulitis
- Detect pregnancy, including ectopic pregnancy
- Detect the presence of ovarian cysts and malignancy and determine the type, if possible, as evidenced by size, outline, and change in position of other pelvic organs
- Evaluate the effectiveness of tumor therapy, as evidenced by a reduction in mass size
- Evaluate suspected fibroid tumor or bladder tumor
- Evaluate the thickness of the uterine wall
- Monitor placement and location of an IUD
- Monitor follicular size associated with fertility studies or to remove follicles for in vitro transplantation

POTENTIAL DIAGNOSIS

Normal findings in
- Normal size, position, location, and structure of pelvic organs (e.g., uterus, ovaries, fallopian tubes,

vagina); IUD properly positioned within the uterine cavity

Abnormal findings in
• Abscess
• Adnexal torsion
• Appendicitis
• Ectopic pregnancy
• Endometrioma
• Fibroids (leiomyoma)
• Infection
• Nonovarian cyst
• Ovarian cysts
• Ovarian tumor
• Pelvic abscess
• Peritonitis
• PID
• Uterine tumor or adnexal tumor

CRITICAL FINDINGS
• Abscess
• Adnexal torsion
• Appendicitis
• Ectopic pregnancy
• Infection
• Tumor with significant mass effect

It is essential that critical diagnoses be communicated immediately to the appropriate health-care provider (HCP). A listing of these diagnoses varies among facilities. Note and immediately report to the HCP abnormal results and related symptoms. Timely notification of critical values for lab or diagnostic studies is a role expectation of the professional nurse. Notification processes will vary among facilities. Upon receipt of the critical value the information should be read back to the caller to verify accuracy. Most policies require immediate notification of the primary HCP, hospitalist, or on-call HCP. Reported information includes the patient's name, unique identifiers, critical value, name of the person giving the report, and name of the person receiving the report. Documentation of notification should be made in the medical record with the name of the HCP notified, time and date of notifi-

cation, and any orders received. Any delay in a timely report of a critical value may require completion of a notification form with review by Risk Management.

INTERFERING FACTORS

This procedure is contraindicated for
• Patients with latex allergy; use of the vaginal probe requires the probe to be covered with a condom-like sac, usually made from latex. Latex-free covers are available.

Factors that may impair clear imaging
• Incorrect placement of the transducer over the desired test site.
• Gas or feces in the gastrointestinal tract resulting from inadequate cleansing or failure to restrict food intake before the study.
• Retained barium from a previous radiological procedure.
• Dehydration, which can cause failure to demonstrate the boundaries between organs and tissue structures.
• Insufficiently full bladder, which fails to push the bowel from the pelvis and the uterus from the symphysis pubis, thereby prohibiting clear imaging of the pelvic organs in transabdominal imaging.
• Metallic objects (e.g., jewelry, body rings) within the examination field, which may inhibit organ visualization and cause unclear images.

Other considerations
• Failure to follow dietary/fluid instructions and other pretesting preparations may cause the procedure to be canceled or repeated.
• Inability of the patient to cooperate or remain still during the procedure because of age, significant pain, or mental status, may interfere with the test results.

NURSING IMPLICATIONS AND PROCEDURE

PRETEST:

Positively identify the patient using at least two unique identifiers before providing care, treatment, or services.

Patient Teaching: Inform the patient that this procedure can assist in assessing pelvic organ function.

Obtain a history of the patient's complaints, including a list of known allergens, especially allergies or sensitivities to latex.

Obtain a history of the patient's reproductive system, symptoms, and results of previously performed laboratory tests and diagnostic and surgical procedures.

Note any recent procedures that can interfere with test results (i.e., barium procedures, surgery, or biopsy). There should be 24 hr between administration of barium and this test.

Endoscopic retrograde cholangiopancreatography, colonoscopy, and computed tomography of the abdomen, if ordered, should be scheduled after this procedure.

Record the date of the last menstrual period and determine the possibility of pregnancy in perimenopausal women.

Obtain a list of the patient's current medications, including herbs, nutritional supplements, and nutraceuticals (see Appendix F).

Review the procedure with the patient. Address concerns about pain related to the procedure and explain that some pain may be experienced during the test, and there may be moments of discomfort. Inform the patient that the procedure is performed in a US department by an HCP who specializes in this procedure, with support staff, and takes approximately 30 to 60 min.

Sensitivity to social and cultural issues, as well as concern for modesty, is important in providing psychological support before, during, and after the procedure.

Instruct the patient to remove jewelry and other metallic objects from the area to be examined.

Instruct the patient that a latex or sterile sheath-covered probe will be inserted into the vagina for the transvaginal approach.

The patient should fast and restrict fluids for 8 hr prior to the procedure. Protocols may vary among facilities.

Instruct the patient receiving transabdominal US to drink three to five glasses of fluid 90 min before the examination and not to void, because the procedure requires a full bladder. Patients receiving transvaginal US only do not need to have a full bladder.

INTRATEST:

Observe standard precautions, and follow the general guidelines in Appendix A. Positively identify the patient.

Ensure that food and fluids have been restricted for at least 8 hr prior to the procedure.

Ensure that the patient receiving transabdominal US drank three to five glasses of fluid and has not voided.

Ensure that the patient has removed all external metallic objects from the area to be examined prior to the procedure.

Instruct the patient to change into the gown, robe, and foot coverings provided. Remind her not to void before the procedure. Patients receiving transvaginal US do not need to have a full bladder.

Instruct the patient to cooperate fully and to follow directions. Ask the patient to remain still throughout the procedure because movement produces unreliable results.

Place the patient in the supine position on an examination table. The right- or left-side-up positions may be used to allow gravity to reposition the liver, gas, and fluid to facilitate better organ visualization.

Expose the abdominal and pelvic area and drape the patient.

Transabdominal approach: Conductive gel is applied to the skin, and a transducer is moved over the skin while the bladder is distended to obtain images of the area of interest.

Transvaginal approach: A covered and lubricated probe is inserted into the vagina and moved to different levels. Images are obtained and recorded.

Ask the patient to breathe normally during the examination. If necessary for

U

better organ visualization, ask the patient to inhale deeply and hold her breath.

POST-TEST:

▶ A report of the results will be made available to the requesting HCP, who will discuss the results with the patient.
▶ Allow the patient to void, as needed.
▶ When the study is completed, remove the gel from the skin.
▶ Instruct the patient to resume usual diet and fluids, as directed by the HCP.
▶ Recognize anxiety related to test results. Discuss the implications of abnormal test results on the patient's lifestyle. Provide teaching and information regarding the clinical implications of the test results, as appropriate. Educate the patient regarding access to counseling services. Provide contact information, if desired, for the American Cancer Society (www.cancer.org).

▶ Reinforce information given by the patient's HCP regarding further testing, treatment, or referral to another HCP. Answer any questions or address any concerns voiced by the patient or family.
▶ Depending on the results of this procedure, additional testing may be needed to evaluate or monitor progression of the disease process and determine the need for a change in therapy. Evaluate test results in relation to the patient's symptoms and other tests performed.

RELATED MONOGRAPHS:

▶ Related tests include cancer antigens, colposcopy, CT abdomen, hysterosalpingography, KUB study, laparoscopy gynecologic, MRI abdomen, Pap smear, and PET pelvis.
▶ Refer to the Reproductive System table at the end of the book for related tests by body system.

Ultrasound, Prostate (Transrectal)

SYNONYM/ACRONYM: Prostate sonography.

COMMON USE: To visualize and assess the prostate gland as an adjunct of prostate-specific antigen (PSA) blood testing and examination to assist in diagnosing disorders such as tumor and cancer. Also used to assist in guiding biopsy of the prostate.

AREA OF APPLICATION: Prostate, seminal vesicles.

CONTRAST: Done without contrast.

DESCRIPTION: Ultrasound (US) procedures are diagnostic, noninvasive, and relatively inexpensive. They take a short time to complete, do not use radiation, and cause no harm to the patient. Prostate US is used for the evaluation of disorders of the prostate, especially in response to an elevated concentration of

prostate-specific antigen (PSA) on a blood test and as a complement to a digital rectal examination. It uses high-frequency sound waves of various intensities delivered by a transducer, a candle-shaped device, which is lubricated, sheathed with a condom, and inserted a few inches into the rectum. The waves are bounced back,

U

converted to electrical energy, amplified by the transducer, and displayed on a monitor to evaluate the structure, size, and position of the contents of the prostate (e.g., masses) as well as other prostate pathology. It aids in the diagnosis of prostatic cancer by evaluating palpable nodules and is useful as a guide to biopsy. This procedure can evaluate prostate tissue, the seminal vesicles, and surrounding perirectal tissue. It can also be used to stage carcinoma and to assist in radiation seed placement. The examination is helpful in monitoring patient response to therapy for prostatic disease. Micturition disorders can also be evaluated by this procedure. Prostate US may be the diagnostic examination of choice because no radiation is used and, in most cases, the accuracy is sufficient to make the diagnosis without any further imaging procedures.

INDICATIONS
* Aid in the diagnosis of micturition disorders
* Aid in prostate cancer diagnosis
* Assess prostatic calcifications
* Assist in guided needle biopsy of a suspected tumor
* Assist in radiation seed placement
* Determine prostatic cancer staging
* Detect prostatitis

POTENTIAL DIAGNOSIS

Normal findings in
* Normal size, consistency, and contour of the prostate gland

Abnormal findings in
* Benign prostatic hypertrophy or hyperplasia
* Micturition disorders
* Perirectal abscess
* Perirectal tumor
* Prostate abscess
* Prostate cancer
* Prostatitis
* Rectal tumor
* Seminal vesicle tumor

CRITICAL FINDINGS: N/A

INTERFERING FACTORS

This procedure is contraindicated for
* ❖ Patients with latex allergy; use of the rectal probe requires the probe to be covered with a condom, usually made from latex. Latex-free covers are available.

Factors that may impair clear imaging
* Attenuation of the sound waves by the pelvic bones, which can impair clear imaging of the prostate.
* Incorrect placement of the transducer over the desired test site.
* Gas or feces in the gastrointestinal tract resulting from inadequate cleansing or failure to restrict food intake before the study.
* Retained barium from a previous radiological procedure.
* Metallic objects (e.g., jewelry, body rings) within the examination field, which may inhibit organ visualization and cause unclear images.

Other considerations
* Failure to follow pretesting preparations may cause the procedure to be canceled or repeated.
* Inability of the patient to cooperate or remain still during the procedure because of age, significant pain, or mental status may interfere with the test results.

NURSING IMPLICATIONS AND PROCEDURE

PRETEST:
▶ Positively identify the patient using at least two unique identifiers before providing care, treatment, or services.

Patient Teaching: Inform the patient this procedure can assist in evaluating the prostate gland.

Obtain a history of the patient's complaints, including a list of known allergens, especially allergies or sensitivities to latex.

Obtain a history of the patient's genito-urinary system, symptoms, and results of previously performed laboratory tests and diagnostic and surgical procedures.

Note any recent procedures that can interfere with test results (i.e., barium procedures, surgery, or biopsy). There should be 24 hr between administration of barium and this test.

Colonoscopy and computed tomography of the abdomen, if ordered, should be scheduled after this procedure.

Obtain a list of the patient's current medications, including herbs, nutritional supplements, and nutraceuticals (see Appendix F).

Review the procedure with the patient. Address concerns about pain related to the procedure and explain that some pain may be experienced during the test, and there may be moments of discomfort. Inform the patient that the procedure is performed in a US department by a health-care provider (HCP) who specializes in this procedure, with support staff, and takes approximately 30 to 60 min.

Inform the patient that a sterile latex- or sheath-covered probe will be inserted into the rectum.

Sensitivity to social and cultural issues, as well as concern for modesty, is important in providing psychological support before, during, and after the procedure.

There are no food, fluid, or medication restrictions unless by medical direction.

INTRATEST:

Observe standard precautions, and follow the general guidelines in Appendix A. Positively identify the patient.

Instruct the patient to void and change into the gown, robe, and foot coverings provided.

Instruct the patient to cooperate fully and to follow directions. Ask the patient to remain still throughout the procedure because movement produces unreliable results.

Place the patient on the examination table on his left side with his knees bent toward the chest; other positions may be used during the examination.

Expose the rectal area and drape the patient.

Cover the rectal probe with a lubricated condom and insert it into the rectum. Inform the patient that he may feel slight pressure as the transducer is inserted. Water may be introduced through the sheath surrounding the transducer.

Ask the patient to breathe normally during the examination. If necessary for better organ visualization, ask the patient to inhale deeply and hold his breath.

POST-TEST:

A report of the results will be made available to the requesting HCP, who will discuss the results with the patient.

When the study is completed, remove the gel from the skin.

Nutritional Considerations: There is growing evidence that inflammation and oxidation play key roles in the development of numerous diseases, including prostate cancer. Research also indicates that diets containing dried beans, fresh fruits and vegetables, nuts, spices, whole grains, and smaller amounts of red meats can increase the amount of protective antioxidants. Regular exercise, especially in combination with a healthy diet, can bring about changes in the body's metabolism that decrease inflammation and oxidation.

Recognize anxiety related to test results. Discuss the implications of abnormal test results on the patient's lifestyle. Provide teaching and information regarding the clinical implications of the test results, as appropriate. Educate the patient regarding access to counseling services. Provide contact information, if desired, for the National Cancer Institute (www.cancer.gov) or the Prostate Cancer Foundation (www.prostatecancerfoundation.org).

Reinforce information given by the patient's HCP regarding further testing,

treatment, or referral to another HCP. Answer any questions or address any concerns voiced by the patient or family. Decisions regarding the need for and frequency of routine PSA testing or other cancer screening procedures should be made after consultation between the patient and HCP. The most current guidelines for cervical cancer screening of the general population as well as of individuals with increased risk are available from the American Cancer Society (www.cancer.org) and the American Urological Association (www.aua.org).

▶ Depending on the results of this procedure, additional testing may be needed

to evaluate or monitor progression of the disease process and determine the need for a change in therapy. Evaluate test results in relation to the patient's symptoms and other tests performed.

RELATED MONOGRAPHS:

▶ Related tests include biopsy prostate, CT pelvis, cystoscopy, cystourethrography voiding, IVP, KUB study, MRI pelvis, proctosigmoidoscopy, PSA, renogram, retrograde ureteropyelography, and semen analysis.
▶ Refer to the Genitourinary System table at the end of the book for related tests by body system.

Ultrasound, Scrotal

SYNONYM/ACRONYM: Scrotal sonography, ultrasound of the testes, testicular ultrasound.

COMMON USE: To visualize and assess scrotum structure and function toward diagnosing disorders such as tumor, cancer, undescended testes, and chronic inflammation.

AREA OF APPLICATION: Scrotum.

CONTRAST: Done without contrast.

DESCRIPTION: Ultrasound (US) procedures are diagnostic, noninvasive, and relatively inexpensive. They take a short time to complete, do not use radiation, and cause no harm to the patient. Scrotal US is used for the evaluation of disorders of the scrotum. It is valuable in determining the internal components of masses (solid vs. cystic) and for the evaluation of the testicle, extratesticular and intrascrotal tissues, benign and malignant tumors, and other scrotal pathology. It uses high-frequency sound waves of various

intensities delivered by a transducer, a flashlight-shaped device, which is pressed against the skin. The waves are bounced back, converted to electrical energy, amplified by the transducer, and displayed on a monitor to evaluate the structure, size, and position of the contents of the scrotum. Scrotal US can be performed before or after a radionuclide scan for further clarification of a testicular mass. Extratesticular lesions such as hydrocele, hematocele (blood in the scrotum), and pyocele (pus in the scrotum) can be

U

identified, as can cryptorchidism (undescended testicles). Scrotal US may be the diagnostic examination of choice because no radiation is used and, in most cases, the accuracy is sufficient to make the diagnosis without any further imaging procedures.

INDICATIONS

- Aid in the diagnosis of a chronic inflammatory condition such as epididymitis
- Aid in the diagnosis of a mass and differentiate between a cyst and a solid tumor, as evidenced by specific waveform patterns or the absence of sound waves respectively
- Aid in the diagnosis of scrotal or testicular size, abnormality, or pathology
- Aid in the diagnosis of testicular torsion and associated testicular infarction
- Assist guided needle biopsy of a suspected testicle tumor
- Determine the cause of chronic scrotal swelling or pain
- Determine the presence of a hydrocele, pyocele, spermatocele, or hernia before surgery
- Evaluate the effectiveness of treatment for testicular infections
- Locate an undescended testicle

POTENTIAL DIAGNOSIS

Normal findings in
- Normal size, position, and shape of the scrotum and structure of the testes

Abnormal findings in
- Abscess
- Epididymal cyst
- Epididymitis
- Hematoma
- Hydrocele
- Infarction
- Microlithiasis
- Orchitis
- Pyocele
- Scrotal hernia
- Spermatocele
- Testicular torsion
- Tumor, benign or malignant
- Tunica albuginea cyst
- Undescended testicle (cryptorchidism)
- Varicocele

CRITICAL FINDINGS
- Testicular torsion

It is essential that critical diagnoses be communicated immediately to the appropriate health-care provider (HCP). A listing of these diagnoses varies among facilities. Note and immediately report to the HCP abnormal results and related symptoms. Timely notification of critical values for lab or diagnostic studies is a role expectation of the professional nurse. Notification processes will vary among facilities. Upon receipt of the critical value the information should be read back to the caller to verify accuracy. Most policies require immediate notification of the primary HCP, hospitalist, or on-call HCP. Reported information includes the patient's name, unique identifiers, critical value, name of the person giving the report, and name of the person receiving the report. Documentation of notification should be made in the medical record with the name of the HCP notified, time and date of notification, and any orders received. Any delay in a timely report of a critical value may require completion of a notification form with review by Risk Management.

INTERFERING FACTORS

Factors that may impair clear imaging
- Incorrect placement of the transducer over the desired test site.

- Metallic objects (e.g., jewelry, body rings) within the examination field, which may inhibit organ visualization and cause unclear images.
- Inability of the patient to cooperate or remain still during the procedure because of age, significant pain, or mental status.

NURSING IMPLICATIONS AND PROCEDURE

PRETEST:

▶ Positively identify the patient using at least two unique identifiers before providing care, treatment, or services.

▶ *Patient Teaching:* Inform the patient this procedure can assist in assessing the scrotum.

▶ Obtain a history of the patient's complaints, including a list of known allergens, especially allergies or sensitivities to latex.

▶ Obtain a history of the patient's reproductive system, symptoms, and results of previously performed laboratory tests and diagnostic and surgical procedures.

▶ Note any recent procedures that can interfere with test results (i.e., surgery or biopsy).

▶ Colonoscopy and computed tomography of the abdomen, if ordered, should be scheduled after this procedure.

▶ Obtain a list of the patient's current medications, including herbs, nutritional supplements, and nutraceuticals (see Appendix F).

▶ Review the procedure with the patient. Address concerns about pain related to the procedure and explain that some pain may be experienced during the test, and there may be moments of discomfort. Inform the patient that the procedure is performed in a US department, by an HCP who specializes in this procedure, with support staff, and takes approximately 30 to 60 min.

▶ *Sensitivity to social and cultural issues,* as well as concern for modesty, is important in providing psychological support before, during, and after the procedure.

▶ Instruct the patient to remove jewelry and other metallic objects from the area to be examined.

▶ There are no food, fluid, or medication restrictions unless by medical direction.

INTRATEST:

▶ Observe standard precautions, and follow the general guidelines in Appendix A. Positively identify the patient.

▶ Ensure that the patient has removed all external metallic objects from the area to be examined prior to the procedure.

▶ Instruct the patient to void and change into the gown, robe, and foot coverings provided.

▶ Instruct the patient to cooperate fully and to follow directions. Ask the patient to remain still throughout the procedure because movement produces unreliable results.

▶ Place the patient in the supine position on an examination table; other positions may be used during the examination.

▶ Expose the abdomen/pelvic area and drape the patient.

▶ Lift the penis upward and gently tape it to the lower part of the abdomen. Elevate the scrotum with a rolled towel or sponge for immobilization.

▶ Conductive gel is applied to the skin, and a transducer is moved over the skin to obtain images of the area of interest.

▶ Ask the patient to breathe normally during the examination. If necessary for better organ visualization, ask the patient to inhale deeply and hold his breath.

POST-TEST:

▶ A report of the results will be made available to the requesting HCP, who will discuss the results with the patient.

▶ When the study is completed, remove the gel from the skin.

▶ Recognize anxiety related to test results. Discuss the implications of abnormal test results on the patient's lifestyle. Provide teaching and information regarding the clinical implications of the test results, as appropriate.

▶ Reinforce information given by the patient's HCP regarding further testing,

U

treatment, or referral to another HCP. Answer any questions or address any concerns voiced by the patient or family.

▶ Depending on the results of this procedure, additional testing may be needed to evaluate or monitor progression of the disease process and determine the need for a change in therapy. Evaluate test results in relation to the patient's symptoms and other tests performed.

RELATED MONOGRAPHS:

▶ Related tests include AFP, CT pelvis, KUB study, MRI pelvis, and semen analysis.
▶ Refer to the Reproductive System table at the end of the book for related tests by body system.

Ultrasound, Spleen

SYNONYM/ACRONYM: Spleen ultrasonography.

COMMON USE: To visualize and assess the spleen for abscess, trauma, rupture, cancer, and tumor. Also used to evaluate the effectiveness of therapeutic interventions and assist with guided biopsy.

AREA OF APPLICATION: Spleen/left upper quadrant.

CONTRAST: Done without contrast.

DESCRIPTION: Ultrasound (US) procedures are diagnostic, noninvasive, and relatively inexpensive. They take a short time to complete, do not use radiation, and cause no harm to the patient. Spleen US uses high-frequency waves of various intensities delivered by a transducer, a flashlight-shaped device, pressed against the skin. The waves are bounced back, converted to electrical energy, amplified by the transducer, and displayed on a monitor to evaluate the structure, size, and position of the spleen. This test is valuable for determining the internal components of splenic masses (solid vs. cystic) and evaluating other splenic pathology, splenic trauma, and left upper quadrant perisplenic tissues. It can be performed to supplement a radionuclide scan or computed tomography (CT). It is especially valuable in patients who are in renal failure, are hypersensitive to contrast medium, or are pregnant, because it does not rely on adequate renal function or the injection of contrast medium to obtain a diagnosis. The procedure may also be used as a guide for biopsy, other interventional procedures, and abscess drainage. Spleen US may be the diagnostic examination of choice because no radiation is used and, in most cases, the accuracy is sufficient to make the diagnosis without any further imaging procedures.

INDICATIONS

• Detect the presence of a subphrenic abscess after splenectomy
• Detect splenic masses; differentiate between cysts or solid tumors (in

U

combination with CT), as evidenced by specific waveform patterns or absence of sound waves respectively; and determine whether they are intrasplenic or extrasplenic
- Determine late-stage sickle cell disease, as evidenced by decreased spleen size and presence of echoes
- Determine the presence of splenomegaly and assess the size and volume of the spleen in these cases, as evidenced by increased echoes and visibility of the spleen
- Differentiate spleen trauma from blood or fluid accumulation between the splenic capsule and parenchyma
- Evaluate the effect of medical or surgical therapy on the progression or resolution of splenic disease
- Evaluate the extent of abdominal trauma and spleen involvement, including enlargement or rupture, after a recent trauma
- Evaluate the spleen before splenectomy performed for thrombocytopenic purpura

POTENTIAL DIAGNOSIS

Normal findings in
- Normal size, position, and contour of the spleen and associated structures

Abnormal findings in
- Abscess
- Accessory or ectopic spleen
- Infection
- Lymphatic disease; lymph node enlargement
- Splenic calcifications
- Splenic masses, tumors, cysts, or infarction
- Splenic trauma
- Splenomegaly

CRITICAL FINDINGS: N/A

INTERFERING FACTORS

Factors that may impair clear imaging
- Attenuation of the sound waves by the ribs and an aerated left lung, which can impair clear imaging of the spleen.
- Masses near the testing site, which can displace the spleen and cause inaccurate results if confused with splenomegaly.
- Dehydration, which can cause failure to demonstrate the boundaries between organs and tissue structures.
- Incorrect placement of the transducer over the desired test site.
- Gas or feces in the gastrointestinal tract resulting from inadequate cleansing or failure to restrict food intake before the study.
- Retained barium from a previous radiological procedure.
- Metallic objects (e.g., jewelry, body rings) within the examination field, which may inhibit organ visualization and can produce unclear images.

Other considerations
- Failure to follow dietary restrictions and other pretesting preparations may cause the procedure to be canceled or repeated.
- Inability of the patient to cooperate or remain still during the procedure because of age, significant pain, or mental status may interfere with the test results.

NURSING IMPLICATIONS AND PROCEDURE

PRETEST:
Positively identify the patient using at least two unique identifiers before providing care, treatment, or services.
Patient Teaching: Inform the patient this procedure can assist in assessing the function of the spleen.

Obtain a history of the patient's complaints, including a list of known allergens, especially allergies or sensitivities to latex.

Obtain a history of the patient's hematopoietic system, symptoms, and results of previously performed laboratory tests and diagnostic and surgical procedures.

Note any recent procedures that can interfere with test results (i.e., barium procedures, surgery, or biopsy). There should be 24 hr between administration of barium and this test.

Endoscopic retrograde cholangiopancreatography, colonoscopy, and CT of the abdomen, if ordered, should be scheduled after this procedure.

Obtain a list of the patient's current medications, including herbs, nutritional supplements, and nutraceuticals (see Appendix F).

Review the procedure with the patient. Address concerns about pain related to the procedure and explain that some pain may be experienced during the test, and there may be moments of discomfort. Inform the patient that the procedure is performed in a US department by a health-care provider (HCP) who specializes in this procedure, with support staff, and takes approximately 30 to 60 min. *Sensitivity to social and cultural issues,* as well as concern for modesty, is important in providing psychological support before, during, and after the procedure.

Instruct the patient to remove jewelry and other metallic objects in the area to be examined.

The patient should fast and restrict fluids for 8 hr prior to the procedure. Protocols may vary among facilities.

INTRATEST:

Observe standard precautions, and follow the general guidelines in Appendix A. Positively identify the patient.

Ensure that food and fluids have been restricted for at least 8 hr prior to the procedure.

Ensure that the patient has removed all external metallic objects in the area prior to the procedure.

Instruct the patient to void and change into the gown, robe, and foot coverings provided.

Instruct the patient to cooperate fully and to follow directions. Ask the patient to remain still throughout the procedure because movement produces unreliable results.

Place the patient in the supine position on an examination table. The right- or left-side-up position may be used to allow gravity to reposition the liver, gas, and fluid to facilitate better organ visualization.

Expose the abdominal area and drape the patient.

Conductive gel is applied to the skin, and a transducer is moved over the skin to obtain images of the area of interest.

Ask the patient to breathe normally during the examination. If necessary for better organ visualization, ask the patient to inhale deeply and hold his or her breath.

POST-TEST:

A report of the results will be made available to the requesting HCP, who will discuss the results with the patient.

When the study is completed, remove the gel from the skin.

Instruct the patient to resume usual diet and fluids, as directed by the HCP.

Recognize anxiety related to test results. Discuss the implications of abnormal test results on the patient's lifestyle. Provide teaching and information regarding the clinical implications of the test results, as appropriate.

Reinforce information given by the patient's HCP regarding further testing, treatment, or referral to another HCP. Answer any questions or address any concerns voiced by the patient or family.

Depending on the results of this procedure, additional testing may be performed to evaluate or monitor progression of the disease process and determine the need for a change in therapy. Evaluate test results in relation to the patient's symptoms and other tests performed.

RELATED MONOGRAPHS:

Related tests include angiography abdomen, biopsy bone marrow, CBC platelet count, CBC WBC and differential, CT abdomen, KUB study, liver and spleen scan, MRI abdomen, sickle cell screen, US abdomen, and WBC scan.

Refer to the Hematopoietic System table at the end of the book for related tests by body system.

Ultrasound, Thyroid and Parathyroid

SYNONYM/ACRONYM: Parathyroid sonography, thyroid echo, thyroid sonography.

COMMON USE: To visualize and assess the thyroid and parathyroid glands for tumor, cancer, and cyst. Also used to stage cancer, guide biopsies, and monitor the effectiveness of therapeutic interventions.

AREA OF APPLICATION: Anterior neck region, parathyroid, thyroid.

CONTRAST: Done without contrast.

DESCRIPTION: Ultrasound (US) procedures are diagnostic, noninvasive, and relatively inexpensive. They take a short time to complete, do not use radiation, and cause no harm to the patient. Thyroid and parathyroid US uses high-frequency sound waves of various intensities delivered by a transducer, a flashlight-shaped device, pressed against the skin. The waves are bounced back, converted to electrical energy, amplified by the transducer, and displayed on a monitor to determine the position, size, shape, weight, and presence of masses of the thyroid gland; enlargement of the parathyroid glands; and other abnormalities of the thyroid and parathyroid glands and surrounding tissues. The primary purpose of this procedure is to determine whether a nodule is a fluid-filled cyst (usually benign) or a solid tumor (possibly malignant). This procedure is useful in evaluating the glands' response to medical treatment or assessing the remaining tissue after surgical resection. The procedure may be indicated as a guide for biopsy, aspiration, or other interventional procedures. Thyroid and parathyroid US may be the diagnostic examination of choice because no radiation is used and, in most cases, the accuracy is sufficient to make the diagnosis without any further imaging procedures; it is clearly the procedure of choice when examining the glands of pregnant patients. This procedure is usually done in combination with nuclear medicine imaging procedures and computed tomography of the neck. Despite the advantages of the procedure, in some cases it may not detect small nodules and lesions (less than 1 cm), leading to false-negative findings.

U

INDICATIONS

- Assist in determining the presence of a tumor, as evidenced by an irregular border and shadowing at the distal edge, peripheral echoes, or high- and low-amplitude echoes, depending on the density of the tumor mass; and diagnosing tumor type (e.g., benign, adenoma, carcinoma)
- Assist in diagnosing the presence of a cyst, as evidenced by a smoothly outlined, echo-free amplitude except at the far borders of the mass
- Assist in diagnosis in the presence of a parathyroid enlargement indicating a tumor or hyperplasia, as evidenced by an echo pattern of lower amplitude than that for a thyroid tumor
- Determine the need for surgical biopsy of a tumor or fine-needle biopsy of a cyst
- Differentiate among a nodule, solid tumor, or fluid-filled cyst
- Evaluate the effect of a therapeutic regimen for a thyroid mass or Graves' disease by determining the size and weight of the gland
- Evaluate thyroid abnormalities during pregnancy (mother or baby)

POTENTIAL DIAGNOSIS

Normal findings in
- Normal size, position, contour, and structure of the thyroid and parathyroid glands with uniform echo patterns throughout the glands; no evidence of tumor cysts or nodules in the glands

Abnormal findings in
- Glandular enlargement
- Goiter
- Graves' disease
- Parathyroid tumor or hyperplasia
- Thyroid cysts
- Thyroid tumors (benign or malignant)

CRITICAL FINDINGS: N/A

INTERFERING FACTORS

Factors that may impair clear imaging
- Attenuation of the sound waves by the ribs, which can impair clear imaging of the parathyroid.
- Incorrect placement of the transducer over the desired test site.
- Metallic objects (e.g., jewelry, body rings) within the examination field, which may inhibit organ visualization and cause unclear images.

Other considerations
- Nodules less than 1 cm in diameter may not be detected.
- Nonthyroid cysts may appear the same as thyroid cysts.
- Inability of the patient to cooperate or remain still during the procedure because of age, significant pain, or mental status may interfere with the test results.

NURSING IMPLICATIONS AND PROCEDURE

PRETEST:

- Positively identify the patient using at least two unique identifiers before providing care, treatment, or services.
- *Patient Teaching:* Inform the patient this procedure can assist in assessing thyroid and parathyroid gland function.
- Obtain a history of the patient's complaints, including a list of known allergens, especially allergies or sensitivities to latex.
- Obtain a history of the patient's endocrine system, symptoms, and results of previously performed laboratory tests and diagnostic and surgical procedures.
- Note any recent procedures that can interfere with test results (i.e., barium procedures, surgery, or biopsy). There should be 24 hr between administration of barium and this test.

U

▶ Obtain a list of the patient's current medications, including herbs, nutritional supplements, and nutraceuticals (see Appendix F).

▶ Review the procedure with the patient. Address concerns about pain related to the procedure and explain that some pain may be experienced during the test, and there may be moments of discomfort. Inform the patient that the procedure is performed in a US department by a health-care provider (HCP), with support staff, and takes approximately 30 to 60 min. *Sensitivity to social and cultural issues,* as well as concern for modesty, is important in providing psychological support before, during, and after the procedure.

▶ Instruct the patient to remove jewelry and other metallic objects from the area to be examined.

▶ There are no food, fluid, or medication restrictions unless by medical direction.

INTRATEST:

▶ Observe standard precautions, and follow the general guidelines in Appendix A. Positively identify the patient.

▶ Ensure that the patient has removed all external metallic objects from the area to be examined prior to the procedure.

▶ Instruct the patient to void and change into the gown, robe, and foot coverings provided.

▶ Instruct the patient to cooperate fully and to follow directions. Ask the patient to remain still throughout the procedure because movement produces unreliable results.

▶ Place the patient in the supine position on an examination table; other positions may be used during the examination.

▶ Expose the neck and chest area and drape the patient.

▶ Hyperextend the neck, and place a pillow under the patient's shoulders to maintain a comfortable position. (An alternative method of imaging includes the use of a bag filled with water or gel placed over the neck area.)

▶ Conductive gel is applied to the skin, and a transducer is moved over the skin to obtain images of the area of interest.

▶ Ask the patient to breathe normally during the examination. If necessary for better organ visualization, ask the patient to inhale deeply and hold his or her breath.

POST-TEST:

▶ A report of the results will be made available to the requesting HCP, who will discuss the results with the patient.

▶ When the study is completed, remove the gel from the skin.

▶ Recognize anxiety related to test results. Discuss the implications of abnormal test results on the patient's lifestyle. Provide teaching and information regarding the clinical implications of the test results, as appropriate.

▶ Reinforce information given by the patient's HCP regarding further testing, treatment, or referral to another HCP. Answer any questions or address any concerns voiced by the patient or family.

▶ Depending on the results of this procedure, additional testing may be performed to evaluate or monitor progression of the disease process and determine the need for a change in therapy. Evaluate test results in relation to the patient's symptoms and other tests performed.

RELATED MONOGRAPHS:

▶ Related tests include antibodies antithyroglobulin, biopsy thyroid, chest x-ray, CT thorax, MRI chest, newborn screening, PTH, parathyroid scan, radioactive iodine uptake, thyroidbinding inhibitory immunoglobulin, thyroglobulin, thyroid scan, TSH, thyroxine free, thyroxine total, triiodothyronine free, and triiodothyronine total.

▶ Refer to the Endocrine System table at the end of the book for related tests by body system.

U

Ultrasound, Venous Doppler, Extremity Studies

SYNONYM/ACRONYM: Venous duplex, venous sonogram, venous ultrasound.

COMMON USE: To assess venous blood flow in the upper and lower extremities toward diagnosing disorders such as deep vein thrombosis, venous insufficiency, causation of pulmonary embolism, varicose veins, and monitor the effects of therapeutic interventions.

AREA OF APPLICATION: Veins of the upper and lower extremities.

CONTRAST: Done without contrast.

DESCRIPTION: Ultrasound (US) procedures are diagnostic, noninvasive, and relatively inexpensive. They take a short time to complete, do not use radiation, and cause no harm to the patient. Peripheral venous Doppler US records sound waves to obtain information about the patency of the venous vasculature in the upper and lower extremities to identify narrowing or occlusions of the veins or arteries. In venous Doppler studies, the Doppler identifies moving red blood cells (RBCs) within the vein. The US beam is directed at the vein and through the Doppler transducer while the RBCs reflect the beam back to the transducer. The reflected sound waves or echoes are transformed by a computer into scans, graphs, or audible sounds. Blood flow direction, velocity, and the presence of flow disturbances can be readily assessed. The velocity of the blood flow is transformed as a "swishing" noise, audible through the audio speaker. If the vein is occluded, no swishing sound is heard.

For diagnostic studies, the procedure is done bilaterally. The sound emitted by the equipment corresponds to the velocity of the blood flow through the vessel occurring with spontaneous respirations. Changes in these sounds during respirations indicate the possibility of abnormal venous flow secondary to occlusive disease; the absence of sound indicates complete obstruction. Compression with a transducer augments a vessel for evaluation of thrombosis. Noncompressibility of the vessel indicates a thrombosis. Plethysmography may be performed to determine the filling time of calf veins to diagnose thrombotic disorder of a major vein and to identify incompetent valves in the venous system. An additional method used to evaluate incompetent valves is the Valsalva technique combined with venous duplex imaging.

The ankle-brachial index (ABI) can also be assessed during this study. This noninvasive, simple comparison of blood pressure measurements in the arms and legs can be used to detect peripheral vascular disease (PVD). A Doppler stethoscope is used to obtain the systolic pressure in either the dorsalis pedis or the posterior tibial artery. This ankle pressure is then divided by the highest brachial systolic pressure acquired after taking the blood pressure in both of the patient's arms. This index should be greater than 1.00. When the index falls below 0.5, blood flow impairment is considered significant. Patients should be scheduled for a vascular consult for an abnormal ABI. Patients with diabetes or kidney disease, and some elderly patients, may have a falsely elevated ABI due to calcifications of the vessels in the ankle causing an increased systolic pressure. The ABI test approaches 95% accuracy in detecting PVD. However, a normal ABI value does not absolutely rule out the possibility of PVD for some individuals, and additional tests should be done to evaluate symptoms.

INDICATIONS

- Aid in the diagnosis of venous occlusion secondary to thrombosis or thrombophlebitis
- Aid in the diagnosis of superficial thrombosis or deep vein thrombosis (DVT) leading to venous occlusion or obstruction, as evidenced by absence of venous flow, especially upon augmentation of the extremity; variations in flow during respirations; or failure of the veins to compress completely when the extremity is compressed
- Detect chronic venous insufficiency, as evidenced by reverse blood flow indicating incompetent valves
- Determine if further diagnostic procedures are needed to make or confirm a diagnosis
- Determine the source of emboli when pulmonary embolism is suspected or diagnosed
- Determine venous damage after trauma to the site
- Differentiate between primary and secondary varicose veins
- Evaluate the patency of the venous system in patients with a swollen, painful leg
- Evaluate PVD
- Monitor the effectiveness of therapeutic interventions

POTENTIAL DIAGNOSIS

Normal findings in

- Normal Doppler venous signal that occurs spontaneously with the patient's respiration
- Normal blood flow through the veins of the extremities with no evidence of vessel occlusion

Abnormal findings in

- Chronic venous insufficiency
- Primary varicose veins
- PVD
- Recannulization in the area of an old thrombus
- Secondary varicose veins
- Superficial thrombosis or DVT
- Venous narrowing or occlusion secondary to thrombosis or thrombophlebitis
- Venous trauma

CRITICAL FINDINGS

- DVT

It is essential that critical diagnoses be communicated immediately to the appropriate health-care provider (HCP). A listing of these diagnoses varies among facilities. Note and immediately report to the HCP abnormal results and related symptoms. Timely notification of critical values for lab or diagnostic studies is a role expectation of the professional nurse. Notification processes will vary among facilities. Upon receipt of the critical value the information should be read back to the caller to verify accuracy. Most policies require immediate notification of the primary HCP, hospitalist, or on-call HCP. Reported information includes the patient's name, unique identifiers, critical value, name of the person giving the report, and name of the person receiving the report. Documentation of notification should be made in the medical record with the name of the HCP notified, time and date of notification, and any orders received. Any delay in a timely report of a critical value may require completion of a notification form with review by Risk Management.

INTERFERING FACTORS

This procedure is contraindicated for
• Patients with an open or draining lesion.

Factors that may impair clear imaging
• Attenuation of the sound waves by bony structures, which can impair clear imaging of the vessels.
• Cigarette smoking, because nicotine can cause constriction of the peripheral vessels.
• Incorrect placement of the transducer over the desired test site.
• Metallic objects (e.g., jewelry, body rings) within the examination field, which may inhibit organ visualization and cause unclear images.
• Cold extremities, resulting in vasoconstriction that can cause inaccurate measurements.
• Occlusion proximal to the site being studied, which would affect blood flow to the area.
• An abnormally large or swollen leg, making sonic penetration difficult.
• Incorrect positioning of the patient, which may produce poor visualization of the area to be examined.

Other considerations
• Inability of the patient to cooperate or remain still during the procedure because of age, significant pain, or mental status.

NURSING IMPLICATIONS AND PROCEDURE

PRETEST:

▸ Positively identify the patient using at least two unique identifiers before providing care, treatment, or services.
▸ *Patient Teaching:* Inform the patient this procedure can assist in assessing the veins.
▸ Obtain a history of the patient's complaints, including a list of known allergens, especially allergies or sensitivities to latex.
▸ Obtain a history of the patient's cardiovascular system, symptoms, and results of previously performed laboratory tests and diagnostic and surgical procedures.
▸ Report the presence of a lesion that is open or draining; maintain clean, dry dressing for the ulcer; protect the limb from trauma.
▸ Note any recent procedures that can interfere with test results (i.e., barium procedures, surgery, or biopsy). There should be 24 hr between administration of barium- or iodine-based contrast medium and this test.
▸ Endoscopic retrograde cholangiopancreatography, colonoscopy, and computed tomography of the abdomen, if ordered, should be scheduled after this procedure.
▸ Obtain a list of the patient's current medications, including herbs, nutritional supplements, and nutraceuticals (see Appendix F).
▸ Review the procedure with the patient. Address concerns about pain related to the procedure and explain that some pain may be experienced during the test, and there may be moments of discomfort. Inform the patient that the procedure is performed in a US department by an HCP who specializes in this procedure, with support staff, and takes approximately 30 to 60 min.

Sensitivity to social and cultural issues, as well as concern for modesty, is important in providing psychological support before, during, and after the procedure.

► Instruct the patient to remove jewelry and other metallic objects from the area to be examined.

► There are no food, fluid, or medication restrictions unless by medical direction.

INTRATEST:

► Observe standard precautions, and follow the general guidelines in Appendix A. Positively identify the patient.

► Ensure that the patient has removed all external metallic objects from the area to be examined prior to the procedure.

► Instruct the patient to void and change into the gown, robe, and foot coverings provided.

► Instruct the patient to cooperate fully and to follow directions. Ask the patient to remain still throughout the procedure because movement produces unreliable results.

► Place the patient in the supine position on an examination table; other positions may be used during the examination.

► Expose the area of interest and drape the patient.

► Conductive gel is applied to the skin, and a transducer is moved over the area to obtain images of the area of interest. Waveforms are visualized and recorded with variations in respirations. Images with and without compression are performed proximally or distally to an obstruction to obtain information about a venous occlusion or obstruction. The procedure can be performed for both arms and legs to obtain bilateral blood flow determination.

► Do not place the transducer on an ulcer site when there is evidence of venous stasis or ulcer.

► Ask the patient to breathe normally during the examination. If necessary for better organ visualization, ask the patient to inhale deeply and hold his or her breath.

POST-TEST:

► A report of the results will be made available to the requesting HCP, who will discuss the results with the patient.

► When the study is completed, remove the gel from the skin.

► Instruct the patient to continue diet, fluids, and medications, as directed by the HCP.

► *Nutritional Considerations:* Abnormal findings may be associated with cardiovascular disease. The American Heart Association and National Heart, Lung, and Blood Institute (NHLBI) recommend nutritional therapy for individuals identified to be at high risk for developing coronary artery disease (CAD) or individuals who have specific risk factors and/or existing medical conditions (e.g., elevated LDL cholesterol levels, other lipid disorders, insulin-dependent diabetes, insulin resistance, or metabolic syndrome). If overweight, the patient should be encouraged to achieve a normal weight. Guidelines for the Therapeutic Lifestyle Changes (TLC) diet are outlined in the Third Report of the Expert Panel on Detection, Evaluation, and Treatment of High Blood Cholesterol in Adults (Adult Treatment Panel III [ATP III]). The TLC diet emphasizes a reduction in foods high in saturated fats and cholesterol. Red meats, eggs, and dairy products are the major sources of saturated fats and cholesterol. If triglycerides also are elevated, the patient should be advised to eliminate or reduce alcohol and simple carbohydrates from the diet. The TLC approach also includes the use of plant stanols or sterols and increased dissolved fiber as an option for lowering LDL cholesterol levels; nutritional recommendations for daily total caloric intake; recommendations for allowable percentage of calories derived from fat (saturated and unsaturated), carbohydrates, protein, and cholesterol; as well as recommendations for daily expenditure of energy.

► *Nutritional Considerations:* Overweight patients with high blood pressure should be encouraged to achieve a normal weight. Other changeable risk factors warranting patient education include strategies to safely decrease sodium intake, increase physical activity, decrease alcohol consumption, eliminate

U

tobacco use, and decrease cholesterol levels.

Social and Cultural Considerations: Numerous studies point to the prevalence of excess body weight in American children and adolescents. Experts estimate that obesity is present in 25% of the population ages 6 to 11 yr. The medical, social, and emotional consequences of excess body weight are significant. Special attention should be given to instructing the child and caregiver regarding health risks and weight-control education.

Recognize anxiety related to test results, and be supportive of fear of shortened life expectancy. Discuss the implications of abnormal test results on the patient's lifestyle. Provide teaching and information regarding the clinical implications of the test results, as appropriate. Educate the patient regarding access to counseling services. Provide contact information, if desired, for the American Heart Association (www.americanheart.org), the NHLBI (www.nhlbi.nih.gov), or the Legs for Life (www.legsforlife.org).

Reinforce information given by the patient's HCP regarding further testing, treatment, or referral to another HCP. Answer any questions or address any concerns voiced by the patient or family.

Depending on the results of this procedure, additional testing may be needed to evaluate or monitor progression of the disease process and determine the need for a change in therapy. Evaluate test results in relation to the patient's symptoms and other tests performed.

RELATED MONOGRAPHS:

Related tests include alveolar/arterial ratio, angiography pulmonary, blood gases, CBC platelet count, CT angiography, D-dimer, FDP, fibrinogen, lung perfusion scan, lung ventilation scan, MRI abdomen, MRI angiography, aPTT, plethysmography, PT/INR, US arterial Doppler lower and upper extremity studies, and venography lower extremities.

Refer to the Cardiovascular System table at the end of the book for related tests by body system.

Upper Gastrointestinal and Small Bowel Series

SYNONYM/ACRONYM: Gastric radiography, stomach series, small bowel study, upper GI series, UGI.

COMMON USE: To assess the esophagus, stomach, and small bowel for disorders related to obstruction, perforation, weight loss, swallowing, pain, cancer, reflux disease, ulcers, and structural anomalies.

AREA OF APPLICATION: Esophagus, stomach, and small intestine.

CONTRAST: Barium sulfate.

DESCRIPTION: The upper gastrointestinal (GI) series is a radiological examination of the esophagus, stomach, and small intestine after ingestion of barium sulfate, which is a milkshake-like, radiopaque substance. A combination of x-ray and fluoroscopy techniques is used to record the study. Air may be instilled to provide double contrast and better visualization of the lumen of the esophagus, stomach, and duodenum. If perforation or obstruction is suspected, a water-soluble iodinated contrast medium is used. This test is especially useful in the evaluation of patients experiencing dysphagia, regurgitation, gastroesophageal reflux (GER), epigastric pain, hematemesis, melena, and unexplained weight loss. This test is also used to evaluate the results of gastric surgery, especially when an anastomotic leak is suspected. When a small bowel series is included, the test detects disorders of the jejunum and ileum. The patient's position is changed during the examination to allow visualization of the various structures and their function. The images are visualized on a fluoroscopic screen, recorded, and stored electronically or on x-ray film for review by a physician. Drugs such as glucagon may be given during an upper GI series to relax the GI tract; drugs such as metoclopramide (Reglan) may be given to accelerate the passage of the barium through the stomach and small intestine.

When the small bowel series is performed separately, the patient may be asked to drink several glasses of barium, or enteroclysis may be used to instill the barium. With enteroclysis, a catheter is passed through the nose or mouth and advanced past the pylorus and into the duodenum. Barium, followed by methylcellulose solution, is instilled via the catheter directly into the small bowel.

INDICATIONS
- Determine the cause of regurgitation or epigastric pain
- Determine the presence of neoplasms, ulcers, diverticula, obstruction, foreign body, and hiatal hernia
- Evaluate suspected GER, inflammatory process, congenital anomaly, motility disorder, or structural change
- Evaluate unexplained weight loss or anemia
- Identify and locate the origin of hematemesis

POTENTIAL DIAGNOSIS

Normal findings in
- Normal size, shape, position, and functioning of the esophagus, stomach, and small bowel

Abnormal findings in
- Achalasia
- Cancer of the esophagus
- Chalasis
- Congenital abnormalities
- Duodenal cancer, diverticula, and ulcers
- Esophageal diverticula, motility disorders, ulcers, varices, and inflammation
- Foreign body
- Gastric cancer, tumors, and ulcers
- Gastritis
- Hiatal hernia
- Perforation of the esophagus, stomach, or small bowel
- Polyps
- Small bowel tumors
- Strictures

CRITICAL FINDINGS ◈
- Foreign body
- Perforated bowel
- Tumor with significant mass effect

It is essential that critical diagnoses be communicated immediately to the appropriate health-care provider (HCP). A listing of these diagnoses varies among facilities. Note and

U

immediately report to the HCP abnormal results and related symptoms. Timely notification of critical values for lab or diagnostic studies is a role expectation of the professional nurse. Notification processes will vary among facilities. Upon receipt of the critical value the information should be read back to the caller to verify accuracy. Most policies require immediate notification of the primary HCP, hospitalist, or on-call HCP. Reported information includes the patient's name, unique identifiers, critical value, name of the person giving the report, and name of the person receiving the report. Documentation of notification should be made in the medical record with the name of the HCP notified, time and date of notification, and any orders received. Any delay in a timely report of a critical value may require completion of a notification form with review by Risk Management.

INTERFERING FACTORS

This procedure is contraindicated for

- Patients who are pregnant or suspected of being pregnant, unless the potential benefits of the procedure far outweigh the risks to the fetus and mother.
- Patients with an intestinal obstruction.
- Patients suspected of having upper GI perforation, in whom barium should not be used.

Factors that may impair clear imaging

- Inability of the patient to cooperate or remain still during the procedure because of age, significant pain, or mental status.
- Metallic objects (e.g., jewelry, body rings) within the examination field, which may inhibit organ visualization and cause unclear images.

Other considerations

- Failure to follow dietary restrictions before the procedure may cause the procedure to be canceled or repeated.
- Patients with swallowing problems may aspirate the barium, which could interfere with the procedure and cause patient complications.
- Possible constipation or partial bowel obstruction caused by retained barium in the small bowel or colon may affect test results.
- This procedure should be done after a kidney x-ray (IV pyelography) or computed tomography of the abdomen or pelvis.
- Consultation with the appropriate HCP should occur before the procedure for radiation safety concerns regarding younger patients or patients who are lactating.
- Risks associated with radiation overexposure can result from frequent x-ray procedures. Personnel in the room with the patient should wear a protective lead apron, stand behind a shield, or leave the area while the examination is being done. Personnel working in the examination area should wear badges to record their level of radiation exposure.

NURSING IMPLICATIONS AND PROCEDURE

PRETEST:

▶ Positively identify the patient using at least two unique identifiers before providing care, treatment, or services.

▶ *Patient Teaching:* Inform the patient this procedure can assist in assessing the esophagus, stomach, and small intestine.

▶ Obtain a history of the patient's complaints, including a list of known allergens, especially allergies or sensitivities to latex, iodine, seafood, anesthetics, or contrast medium.

U

▶ Obtain a history of the patient's gastrointestinal system, symptoms, and results of previously performed laboratory tests and diagnostic and surgical procedures.

▶ Ensure that this procedure is performed before a barium swallow.

▶ Record the date of the last menstrual period and determine the possibility of pregnancy in perimenopausal women.

▶ Obtain a list of the patient's current medications, including anticoagulants, aspirin and other salicylates, herbs, nutritional supplements, and nutraceuticals, especially those known to affect coagulation (see Appendix F).

▶ Review the procedure with the patient. Address concerns about pain and explain that there may be moments of discomfort and some pain experienced during the procedure. Inform the patient that the procedure is usually performed in a radiology department by an HCP, with support staff, and takes approximately 30 to 60 min.

▶ *Sensitivity to social and cultural issues,* as well as concern for modesty, is important in providing psychological support before, during, and after the procedure.

▶ Explain to the patient that he or she will be asked to drink a milkshake-like solution that has an unpleasant chalky taste.

▶ Instruct the patient to remove jewelry and other metallic objects from the area to be examined prior to the procedure.

▶ Instruct the patient to fast and restrict fluids for 8 hr prior to the procedure. Protocols may vary among facilities.

INTRATEST:

▶ Observe standard precautions, and follow the general guidelines in Appendix A. Positively identify the patient.

▶ Ensure that the patient has complied with dietary and fluid restrictions for 8 hr prior to the procedure.

▶ Ensure that the patient has removed all external metallic objects from the area to be examined prior to the procedure.

▶ Have emergency equipment readily available.

▶ Instruct the patient to void prior to the procedure and to change into

the gown, robe, and foot coverings provided.

▶ Instruct the patient to cooperate fully and to follow directions. Ask the patient to remain still throughout the procedure because movement produces unreliable results.

Upper Gastrointestinal Series

▶ Place the patient on the x-ray table in a supine position, or ask the patient to stand in front of a fluoroscopy screen.

▶ Instruct the patient to take several swallows of the barium mixture through a straw while images are taken of the pharyngeal motion. An effervescent agent may also be administered to introduce air into the stomach.

Small Bowel Series

▶ If the small bowel is to be examined after the upper GI series, instruct the patient to drink an additional glass of barium while the small intestine is observed for passage of barium. Images are taken at 30- to 60-min intervals until the barium reaches the ileocecal valve. This process can last up to 5 hr, with follow-up images taken at 24 hr.

POST-TEST:

▶ A report of the results will be made available to the requesting HCP, who will discuss the results with the patient.

▶ Instruct the patient to resume usual diet and fluids, as directed by the HCP.

▶ Monitor for reaction to iodinated contrast medium, including rash, urticaria, tachycardia, hyperpnea, hypertension, palpitations, nausea, or vomiting, if iodine is used.

▶ Instruct the patient to immediately report symptoms such as fast heart rate, difficulty breathing, skin rash, itching, chest pain, persistent right shoulder pain, or abdominal pain. Immediately report symptoms to the appropriate HCP.

▶ Instruct the patient to take a mild laxative and increase fluid intake (four glasses) to aid in the elimination of barium unless contraindicated.

▶ Inform the patient that his or her stool will be white or light in color for 2 to 3 days. If the patient is unable to

U

eliminate the barium, or if the stool does not return to normal color, the patient should notify the HCP.

Recognize anxiety related to test results, and be supportive of perceived loss of independence and fear of shortened life expectancy. Discuss the implications of abnormal test results on the patient's lifestyle. Provide teaching and information regarding the clinical implications of the test results, as appropriate. Educate the patient regarding access to counseling services.

Reinforce information given by the patient's HCP regarding further testing, treatment, or referral to another HCP. Answer any questions or address any concerns voiced by the patient or family.

Depending on the results of this procedure, additional testing may be needed to evaluate or monitor progression of the disease process and determine the need for a change in therapy. Evaluate test results in relation to the patient's symptoms and other tests performed.

RELATED MONOGRAPHS:

Related tests include barium enema, barium swallow, capsule endoscopy, CT abdomen, endoscopic retrograde cholangiopancreatography, esophageal manometry, fecal analysis, gastric acid stimulation test, gastric emptying scan, gastrin stimulation test, gastroesophageal reflux scan, *H. pylori* antibody, KUB study, MRI abdomen, and US pelvis.

Refer to the Gastrointestinal System table at the end of the book for related tests by body system.

Urea Breath Test

SYNONYM/ACRONYM: PY test, C-14 urea breath test, breath test, pylori breath test, UBT.

COMMON USE: To assist in diagnosing a gastrointestinal infection and ulceration of the stomach or duodenum related to a *Helicobacter pylori* infection.

AREA OF APPLICATION: Stomach.

CONTRAST: Radioactive C-14 urea in capsule form.

DESCRIPTION: The C-14 urea breath test (UBT) is used to assist in the diagnosis of *Helicobacter pylori* infection. *H. pylori* is a bacteria that can infect the stomach lining. It has been implicated as the cause of many gastrointestinal conditions, including the development of duodenal and gastric ulcers. The UBT is a simple, noninvasive diagnostic nuclear medicine procedure that requires the patient to swallow a small amount of radiopharmaceutical C-14–labeled urea in a capsule with lukewarm water. In the presence of urease, an enzyme secreted by *H. pylori* in the gut, the urea in the capsule is broken down into nitrogen and C-14–labeled carbon dioxide (CO_2). The labeled CO_2 is absorbed through the stomach lining into the blood and excreted by the lungs. Breath samples are collected and trapped in a Mylar balloon. The C-14 urea is counted and quantitated with a liquid scintillation counter. The UBT can also be used to indicate the elimination of *H. pylori* infection after treatment with antibiotics. Other tests used to detect the presence of *H. pylori* include a blood *H. pylori* antibody test, a stool antigen test, and stomach biopsy.

INDICATIONS
- Aid in detection of *H. pylori* infection in the stomach
- Monitor eradication of *H. pylori* infection following treatment regimen
- Evaluation of new-onset dyspepsia

POTENTIAL DIAGNOSIS

Normal findings in
- Negative for *H. pylori:* Less than 50 dpm (disintegrations per minute)

Abnormal findings in
- Indeterminate for *H. pylori:* 50 to 199 dpm
- Positive for *H. pylori:* Greater than 200 dpm

CRITICAL FINDINGS: N/A

INTERFERING FACTORS

This procedure is contraindicated for
- Patients who are pregnant or suspected of being pregnant, unless the potential benefits of the procedure outweigh the risks to the fetus and the mother.
- Patients who have taken antibiotics, Pepto-Bismol, or bismuth in the past 30 days.
- Patients who have taken sucralfate in the past 14 days.
- Patients who have used a proton pump inhibitor within the past 14 days.

Other considerations
- Consultation with a health-care provider (HCP) should occur

before the procedure for radiation safety concerns regarding younger patients or patients who are lactating.
- Failure to follow dietary restrictions and other pretesting preparations may cause the procedure to be canceled or repeated.
- Patients who have had resective gastric surgery have the potential for resultant bacterial overgrowth (non-*H. pylori* urease), which can cause a false-positive result.
- Achlorhydria can cause a false-positive result.

NURSING IMPLICATIONS AND PROCEDURE

PRETEST:
▸ Positively identify the patient using at least two unique identifiers before providing care, treatment, or services.
▸ *Patient Teaching:* Inform the patient this procedure can assist in diagnosing an infection of the stomach or intestine.
▸ Obtain a history of the patient's gastrointestinal system, symptoms, and results of previously performed laboratory tests and diagnostic and surgical procedures.
▸ Record the date of the last menstrual period and determine the possibility of pregnancy in premenopausal women.
▸ Obtain a list of the patient's current medications, including herbs, nutritional supplements, and nutraceuticals (see Appendix F).
▸ Review the procedure with the patient. Reassure the patient that the radionuclide poses no radioactive hazard and rarely produces side effects. Address concerns about pain and explain that there should be no discomfort during the procedure. Inform the patient that the procedure is done in the nuclear medicine department by technologists and support staff and usually takes approximately 30 to 60 min.
▸ *Sensitivity to social and cultural issues,* as well as concern for modesty, is important in providing psychological support before, during, and after the procedure.

U

Instruct the patient to fast, restrict fluids, and, by medical direction, withhold medication for 6 hr prior to the procedure. Protocols may vary among facilities.

INTRATEST:

Observe standard precautions, and follow the general guidelines in Appendix A. Positively identify the patient.

Ensure the patient has complied with dietary and medication restrictions and pretesting preparations; assure that food, fluids, and medications have been restricted for at least 6 hr prior to the procedure.

Instruct the patient to blow into a balloon prior to the start of the procedure to collect a sample of breath.

Instruct the patient to swallow the C-14 capsule directly from a cup, followed by 20 mL of lukewarm water. Provide an additional 20 mL of lukewarm water for the patient to drink at 3 min after the dose.

Breath samples are taken at different periods of time by instructing the patient to take in a deep breath and hold it for approximately 5 to 10 sec before exhaling through a straw into a Mylar balloon.

Samples are counted on a liquid scintillation counter (LSC) and recorded in disintegrations per minute.

POST-TEST:

A report of the results will be made available to the requesting HCP, who will discuss the results with the patient.

Instruct the patient to resume usual diet and medication, as directed by the HCP.

Unless contraindicated, advise patient to drink increased amounts of fluids for 12 to 24 hr to eliminate the radionuclide from the body.

If a woman who is breastfeeding must have a breath test, she should not breastfeed the infant until the radionuclide has been eliminated. She should be instructed to express the milk and discard it during a 3-day period to prevent cessation of milk production.

Recognize anxiety related to test results. Discuss the implications of abnormal test results on the patient's lifestyle. Provide teaching and information regarding the clinical implications of the test results, as appropriate.

Reinforce information given by the patient's HCP regarding further testing, treatment, or referral to another HCP. Answer any questions or address any concerns voiced by the patient or family.

Depending on the results of the procedure, additional testing may be performed to evaluate or monitor progression of the disease process and determine the need for change in therapy. Evaluate test results in relation to the patient's symptoms and other tests performed.

RELATED MONOGRAPHS:

Related tests include EGD, gastric emptying scan, *H. pylori* antibody, KUB study, and UGI.

See the Gastrointestinal System table at the end of the book for related tests by body system.

Urea Nitrogen, Blood

U

SYNONYM/ACRONYM: BUN.

COMMON USE: To assist in assessing for renal function toward diagnosing disorders such as kidney failure and dehydration. Also used in monitoring the effectiveness of therapeutic interventions such as hemodialysis.

SPECIMEN: Serum (1 mL) collected in a red- or tiger-top tube. Plasma (1 mL) collected in a green-top (heparin) tube is also acceptable.

NORMAL FINDINGS: (Method: Spectrophotometry)

Age	Conventional Units	SI Units (Conventional Units × 0.357)
Newborn–3 yr	5–17 mg/dL	1.8–6.1 mmol/L
4–13 yr	7–17 mg/dL	2.5–6.1 mmol/L
14 yr–adult	8–21 mg/dL	2.9–7.5 mmol/L
Adult older than 90 yr	10–31 mg/dL	3.6–11.1 mmol/L

DESCRIPTION: Urea is a nonprotein nitrogen compound formed in the liver from ammonia as an end product of protein metabolism. Urea diffuses freely into extracellular and intracellular fluid and is ultimately excreted by the kidneys. Blood urea nitrogen (BUN) levels reflect the balance between the production and excretion of urea. BUN and creatinine values are commonly evaluated together. The normal BUN/creatinine ratio is 15:1 to 24:1. (e.g., if a patient has a BUN of 15 mg/dL, the creatinine should be approximately 0.6 to 1 mg/dL). BUN is used in the following calculation to estimate serum osmolality: $(2 \times Na^+) + (glucose/18) + (BUN/2.8)$.

INDICATIONS
- Assess nutritional support
- Evaluate hemodialysis therapy
- Evaluate hydration
- Evaluate liver function
- Evaluate patients with lymphoma after chemotherapy (tumor lysis)
- Evaluate renal function
- Monitor the effects of drugs known to be nephrotoxic or hepatotoxic

POTENTIAL DIAGNOSIS

Increased in
- Acute renal failure *(related to decreased renal excretion)*
- Chronic glomerulonephritis *(related to decreased renal excretion)*
- Congestive heart failure *(related to decreased blood flow to the kidneys, decreased renal excretion, and accumulation in circulating blood)*
- Decreased renal perfusion *(reflects decreased renal excretion and increased blood levels)*
- Diabetes *(related to decreased renal excretion)*
- Excessive protein ingestion *(related to increased protein metabolism)*
- Gastrointestinal (GI) bleeding *(excessive blood protein in the GI tract and increased protein metabolism)*
- Hyperalimentation *(related to increased protein metabolism)*
- Hypovolemia *(related to decreased blood flow to the kidneys, decreased renal excretion, and accumulation in circulating blood)*
- Ketoacidosis *(dehydration from ketoacidosis correlates with decreased renal excretion of urea nitrogen)*
- Muscle wasting from starvation *(related to increased protein metabolism)*
- Neoplasms *(related to increased protein metabolism or to decreased renal excretion)*

U

- Nephrotoxic agents *(related to decreased renal excretion and accumulation in circulating blood)*
- Pyelonephritis *(related to decreased renal excretion)*
- Shock *(related to decreased blood flow to the kidneys, decreased renal excretion, and accumulation in circulating blood)*
- Urinary tract obstruction *(related to decreased renal excretion and accumulation in circulating blood)*

Decreased in

- Inadequate dietary protein *(urea nitrogen is a by-product of protein metabolism; less available protein is reflected in decreased BUN levels)*
- Low-protein/high-carbohydrate diet *(urea nitrogen is a by-product of protein metabolism; less available protein is reflected in decreased BUN levels)*
- Malabsorption syndromes *(urea nitrogen is a by-product of protein metabolism; less available protein is reflected in decreased BUN levels)*
- Pregnancy
- Severe liver disease *(BUN is synthesized in the liver, so liver damage results in decreased levels)*

CRITICAL FINDINGS ✦

Adults

- Greater than 100 mg/dL (SI: Greater than 35.7 mmol/L) (nondialysis patients)

Children

- Greater than 55 mg/dL (SI: Greater than 19.6 mmol/L) (nondialysis patients)

Note and immediately report to the health-care provider (HCP) any critically increased or decreased values and related symptoms especially fluid imbalance. Timely notification of critical values for lab or diagnostic studies is a role expectation of the professional nurse. Notification processes will vary among facilities. Upon receipt of the critical value the information should be read back to the caller to verify accuracy. Most policies require immediate notification of the primary HCP, hospitalist, or on-call HCP. Reported information includes the patient's name, unique identifiers, critical value, name of the person giving the report, and name of the person receiving the report. Documentation of notification should be made in the medical record with the name of the HCP notified, time and date of notification, and any orders received. Any delay in a timely report of a critical value may require completion of a notification form with review by Risk Management.

A patient with a grossly elevated BUN may have signs and symptoms including acidemia, agitation, confusion, fatigue, nausea, vomiting, and coma. Possible interventions include treatment of the cause, administration of IV bicarbonate, a low-protein diet, hemodialysis, and caution with respect to prescribing and continuing nephrotoxic medications.

INTERFERING FACTORS

- Drugs, substances, and vitamins that may increase BUN levels include acetaminophen, alanine, aldatense, alkaline antacids, amphotericin B, antimony compounds, arsenicals, bacitracin, bismuth subsalicylate, capreomycin, carbenoxolone, carbutamide, cephalosporins, chloral hydrate, chloramphenicol, chlorthalidone, colistimethate, colistin, cotrimoxazole, dexamethasone, dextran, diclofenac, doxycycline, ethylene glycol, gentamicin, guanethidine, guanoxan, ibuprofen, ifosfamide, ipodate, kanamycin, mephenesin, metolazone, mitomycin, neomycin, phosphorus, plicamycin, tertatolol, tetracycline, triamterene, triethylenemelamine, viomycin, and vitamin D.

•Drugs that may decrease BUN levels include acetohydroxamic acid, chloramphenicol, fluorides, paramethasone, phenothiazine, and streptomycin.

NURSING IMPLICATIONS AND PROCEDURE

PRETEST:

▶ Positively identify the patient using at least two unique identifiers before providing care, treatment, or services.

▶ *Patient Teaching:* Inform the patient this test can assist in assessing kidney function.

▶ Obtain a history of the patient's complaints, including a list of known allergens, especially allergies or sensitivities to latex.

▶ Obtain a history of the patient's genitourinary and hepatobiliary systems, symptoms, and results of previously performed laboratory tests and diagnostic and surgical procedures.

▶ Obtain a list of the patient's current medications, including herbs, nutritional supplements, and nutraceuticals (see Appendix F).

▶ Review the procedure with the patient. Inform the patient that specimen collection takes approximately 5 to 10 min. Address concerns about pain and explain that there may be some discomfort during the venipuncture.

▶ *Sensitivity to social and cultural issues,* as well as concern for modesty, is important in providing psychological support before, during, and after the procedure.

▶ There are no food, fluid, or medication restrictions unless by medical direction.

INTRATEST:

▶ If the patient has a history of allergic reaction to latex, avoid the use of equipment containing latex.

▶ Instruct the patient to cooperate fully and to follow directions. Direct the patient to breathe normally and to avoid unnecessary movement.

▶ Observe standard precautions, and follow the general guidelines in Appendix A. Positively identify the patient, and label the appropriate specimen container with the corresponding patient demographics, initials of the person collecting the specimen, date, and time of collection. Perform a venipuncture.

▶ Remove the needle and apply direct pressure with dry gauze to stop bleeding. Observe/assess venipuncture site for bleeding or hematoma formation and secure gauze with adhesive bandage.

▶ Promptly transport the specimen to the laboratory for processing and analysis.

POST-TEST:

▶ A report of the results will be made available to the requesting HCP, who will discuss the results with the patient.

▶ Monitor intake and output for fluid imbalance in renal dysfunction and dehydration.

▶ *Nutritional Considerations:* Greater than 100 Nitrogen balance is commonly used as a nutritional assessment tool to indicate protein change. In healthy individuals, protein anabolism and catabolism are in equilibrium. During various disease states, nutritional intake decreases, resulting in a negative balance. During recovery from illness and with proper nutritional support, the nitrogen balance becomes positive. BUN is an important analyte to measure during administration of total parenteral nutrition (TPN). Educate the patient, as appropriate, in dietary adjustments required to maintain proper nitrogen balance. Inform the patient that the requesting HCP may prescribe TPN as part of the treatment plan.

▶ *Nutritional Considerations:* An elevated BUN can be caused by a high-protein diet or dehydration. Unless medically restricted, a healthy diet consisting of the five food groups of the food pyramid should be consumed daily. Water consumption should include six to eight 8-oz glasses of water per day, or water consumption equivalent to half of the body's weight in fluid ounces (32 fl oz = 1 qt; 34 fl oz = 1 L).

Recognize anxiety related to test results. Discuss the implications of abnormal test results on the patient's lifestyle. Provide teaching and information regarding the clinical implications of the test results, as appropriate.

Reinforce information given by the patient's HCP regarding further testing, treatment, or referral to another HCP. Answer any questions or address any concerns voiced by the patient or family.

Depending on the results of this procedure, additional testing may be performed to evaluate or monitor progression of the disease process and determine the need for a change in therapy. Evaluate test results in relation to the patient's symptoms and other tests performed.

RELATED MONOGRAPHS:

Related tests include anion gap, antibiotic drugs, biopsy kidney, calcium, calculus kidney stone panel, CT spleen, creatinine, creatinine clearance, cytology urine, cystoscopy, electrolytes, gallium scan, glucose, glycated hemoglobin, 5–HIAA, IVP, ketones, magnesium, MRI venography, microalbumin, osmolality, oxalate, phosphorus, protein total and fractions, renogram, US abdomen, US kidney, UA, urea nitrogen urine, and uric acid.

Refer to the Genitourinary and Hepatobiliary systems tables at the end of the book for related tests by body system.

Urea Nitrogen, Urine

SYNONYM/ACRONYM: N/A.

COMMON USE: To assess renal function related to the progression of disorders such as diabetes, liver disease, and renal disease.

SPECIMEN: Urine (5 mL) from an unpreserved random or timed specimen collected in a clean plastic collection container.

NORMAL FINDINGS: (Method: Spectrophotometry)

Conventional Units	SI Units (Conventional Units × 35.7)
12–20 g/24 hr	428–714 mmol/24 hr

DESCRIPTION: Urea is a nonprotein nitrogen compound formed in the liver from ammonia as an end product of protein metabolism. Urea diffuses freely into extracellular and intracellular fluid and is ultimately excreted by the kidneys. Urine urea nitrogen levels reflect the balance between the production and excretion of urea.

INDICATIONS
- Evaluate renal disease
- Predict the impact that other conditions, such as diabetes and liver disease, will have on the kidneys

POTENTIAL DIAGNOSIS

Increased in
- Diabetes *(related to increased protein metabolism)*
- Hyperthyroidism

•Increased dietary protein *(related to increased protein metabolism)*
•Postoperative period

Decreased in
•Liver disease *(BUN is synthesized in the liver, so liver damage results in decreased levels)*
•Low-protein/high-carbohydrate diet *(urea nitrogen is a by-product of protein metabolism; less available protein is reflected in decreased BUN levels)*
•Normal-growing pediatric patients *(increased demand for protein; less available protein is reflected in decreased BUN levels)*
•Pregnancy *(increased demand for protein; less available protein is reflected in decreased BUN levels)*
•Renal disease *(related to decreased renal excretion)*
•Toxemia *(related to hypertension and decreased renal excretion)*

CRITICAL FINDINGS: N/A

INTERFERING FACTORS
•Drugs that may increase urine urea nitrogen levels include alanine and glycine.
•Drugs that may decrease urine urea nitrogen levels include furosemide, growth hormone, insulin, and testosterone.
•All urine voided for the timed collection period must be included in the collection or else falsely decreased values may be obtained. Compare output records with volume collected to verify that all voids were included in the collection.

NURSING IMPLICATIONS AND PROCEDURE

PRETEST:
▶ Positively identify the patient using at least two unique identifiers before providing care, treatment, or services.

▶ *Patient Teaching:* Inform the patient this test can assist in assessing kidney function.
▶ Obtain a history of the patient's complaints, including a list of known allergens, especially allergies or sensitivities to latex.
▶ Obtain a history of the patient's genitourinary and hepatobiliary systems, symptoms, and results of previously performed laboratory tests and diagnostic and surgical procedures.
▶ Obtain a list of the patient's current medications, including herbs, nutritional supplements, and nutraceuticals (see Appendix F).
▶ Review the procedure with the patient. Provide a nonmetallic urinal, bedpan, or toilet-mounted collection device. Address concerns about pain and explain that there should be no discomfort during the procedure.
▶ Usually a 24-hr time frame for urine collection is ordered. Inform the patient that all urine must be saved during that 24-hr period. Instruct the patient not to void directly into the laboratory collection container. Instruct the patient to avoid defecating in the collection device and to keep toilet tissue out of the collection device to prevent contamination of the specimen. Place a sign in the bathroom to remind the patient to save all urine.
▶ Instruct the patient to void all urine into the collection device and then to pour the urine into the laboratory collection container. Alternatively, the specimen can be left in the collection device for a health-care staff member to add to the laboratory collection container.
▶ *Sensitivity to social and cultural issues,* as well as concern for modesty, is important in providing psychological support before, during, and after the procedure.
▶ There are no food, fluid, or medication restrictions unless by medical direction.

INTRATEST:
▶ If the patient has a history of allergic reaction to latex, avoid the use of equipment containing latex.
▶ Instruct the patient to cooperate fully and to follow directions.

U

Observe standard precautions, and follow the general guidelines in Appendix A. Positively identify the patient, and label the appropriate specimen container with the corresponding patient demographics, initials of the person collecting the specimen, date, and time of collection.

Random Specimen (Collect in Early Morning)
Clean-Catch Specimen

Instruct the male patient to (1) thoroughly wash his hands, (2) cleanse the meatus, (3) void a small amount into the toilet, and (4) void directly into the specimen container.

Instruct the female patient to (1) thoroughly wash her hands; (2) cleanse the labia from front to back; (3) while keeping the labia separated, void a small amount into the toilet; and (4) without interrupting the urine stream, void directly into the specimen container.

Indwelling Catheter

Put on gloves. Empty drainage tube of urine. It may be necessary to clamp off the catheter for 15 to 30 min before specimen collection. Cleanse specimen port with antiseptic swab, and then aspirate 5 mL of urine with a 21- to 25-gauge needle and syringe. Transfer urine to a sterile container.

Timed Specimen

Obtain a clean 3-L urine specimen container, toilet-mounted collection device, and plastic bag (for transport of the specimen container). The specimen must be refrigerated or kept on ice throughout the entire collection period. If an indwelling urinary catheter is in place, the drainage bag must be kept on ice.

Begin the test between 6 and 8 a.m. if possible. Collect first voiding and discard. Record the time the specimen was discarded as the beginning of the timed collection period. The next morning, ask the patient to void at the same time the collection was started and add this last voiding to the container. Urinary output should be recorded throughout the collection time.

If an indwelling catheter is in place, replace the tubing and container system at the start of the collection time. Keep the container system on ice during the collection period, or empty the urine into a larger container periodically during the collection period; monitor to ensure continued drainage, and conclude the test the next morning at the same hour the collection was begun.

At the conclusion of the test, compare the quantity of urine with the urinary output record for the collection; if the specimen contains less than what was recorded as output, some urine may have been discarded, invalidating the test.

Include on the collection container's label the amount of urine, test start and stop times, and ingestion of any medications that can affect test results.

General

Promptly transport the specimen to the laboratory for processing and analysis.

A report of the results will be made available to the requesting health-care provider (HCP), who will discuss the results with the patient.

Nutritional Considerations: An elevated BUN can be caused by a high-protein diet or dehydration. Unless medically restricted, a healthy diet consisting of the five food groups of the food pyramid should be consumed daily. Water consumption should include six to eight 8-oz glasses of water per day, or water consumption equivalent to half of the body's weight in fluid ounces (32 fl oz = 1 qt; 34 fl oz = 1 L).

Recognize anxiety related to test results. Discuss the implications of abnormal test results on the patient's lifestyle. Provide teaching and information regarding the clinical implications of the test results, as appropriate.

Reinforce information given by the patient's HCP regarding further testing, treatment, or referral to another HCP. Answer any questions or address any concerns voiced by the patient or family.

Depending on the results of this procedure, additional testing may be

performed to evaluate or monitor progression of the disease process and determine the need for a change in therapy. Evaluate test results in relation to the patient's symptoms and other tests performed.

▶ Related tests include anion gap, antibiotic drugs, biopsy kidney, BUN, calcium, calculus kidney stone panel, CT spleen, creatinine, creatinine clearance, cytology urine, cystoscopy, electrolytes, gallium scan, glucose, glycated hemoglobin, 5–HIAA, IVP, ketones, magnesium, microalbumin, osmolality, oxalate, phosphorus, protein total and fractions, renogram, US kidney, UA, and uric acid.

▶ Refer to the Genitourinary and Hepatobiliary systems tables at the end of the book for related tests by body system.

Urethrography, Retrograde

SYNONYM/ACRONYM: N/A.

COMMON USE: To assess urethral patency in order to evaluate the success of surgical interventions on patients who have urethral structures or other anomalies that interfere with urination.

AREA OF APPLICATION: Urethra.

CONTRAST: Radiopaque contrast medium.

DESCRIPTION: Retrograde urethrography is performed almost exclusively in male patients. It uses contrast medium, either injected or instilled via a catheter into the urethra, to visualize the membranous, bulbar, and penile portions, particularly after surgical repair of the urethra to assess the success of the surgery. The posterior portion of the urethra is visualized better when the procedure is performed with voiding cystourethrography. In women, it may be performed after surgical repair of the urethra to assess the success of the surgery and to assess structural abnormalities in conjunction with an evaluation for voiding dysfunction.

INDICATIONS
- Aid in the diagnosis of urethral strictures, lacerations, diverticula, and congenital anomalies

POTENTIAL DIAGNOSIS

Normal findings in
- Normal size, shape, and course of the membranous, bulbar, and penile portions of the urethra in male patients
- If the prostatic portion can be visualized, it also should appear normal

Abnormal findings in
- Congenital anomalies, such as urethral valves and perineal hypospadias
- False passages in the urethra
- Prostatic enlargement
- Tumors of the urethra
- Urethral calculi

U

- Urethral diverticula
- Urethral fistulas
- Urethral strictures and lacerations

CRITICAL FINDINGS: N/A

INTERFERING FACTORS

This procedure is contraindicated for

- ✦ Patients with allergies to shellfish or iodinated contrast medium. The contrast medium used may cause a life-threatening allergic reaction. Patients with a known hypersensitivity to the contrast medium may benefit from premedication with corticosteroids or the use of nonionic contrast medium.
- Patients who are pregnant or suspected of being pregnant, unless the potential benefits of the procedure far outweigh the risks to the fetus and mother.
- ✦ Elderly and other patients who are chronically dehydrated before the test, because of their risk of contrast-induced renal failure.
- ✦ Patients who are in renal failure.

Factors that may impair clear imaging

- Inability of the patient to cooperate or remain still during the procedure because of age, significant pain, or mental status.
- Metallic objects (e.g., jewelry, body rings) within the examination field, which may inhibit organ visualization and cause unclear images.

Other considerations

- Consultation with a health-care provider (HCP) should occur before the procedure for radiation safety concerns regarding younger patients or patients who are lactating.
- Risks associated with radiation overexposure can result from frequent x-ray procedures. Personnel in the room with the patient should wear a protective lead apron, stand behind a shield, or leave the area while the examination is being done. Personnel working in the examination area should wear badges to record their level of radiation exposure.

> # NURSING IMPLICATIONS AND PROCEDURE
>
> **PRETEST:**
>
> ▶ Positively identify the patient using at least two unique identifiers before providing care, treatment, or services.
> ▶ *Patient Teaching:* Inform the patient this procedure can assist in assessing the urethral patency.
> ▶ Obtain a history of the patient's complaints, including a list of known allergens, especially allergies or sensitivities to latex, iodine, seafood, anesthetics, or contrast medium.
> ▶ Obtain a history of the patient's genitourinary system, symptoms, and results of previously performed laboratory tests and diagnostic and surgical procedures.
> ▶ Ensure that this procedure is performed before an upper gastrointestinal study or barium swallow.
> ▶ Record the date of the last menstrual period and determine the possibility of pregnancy in perimenopausal women.
> ▶ Obtain a list of the patient's current medications, including herbs, nutritional supplements, and nutraceuticals (see Appendix F).
> ▶ Review the procedure with the patient. Address concerns about pain and explain that there may be moments of discomfort and some pain experienced during the procedure. Inform the patient that the procedure is performed in a cystoscopy room by an HCP, with support staff, and takes approximately 30 min.
> ▶ *Sensitivity to social and cultural issues,* as well as concern for modesty, is important in providing psychological

U

support before, during, and after the procedure.

▶ Inform the patient that some pressure may be experienced when the catheter is inserted and contrast medium is instilled.

▶ Instruct the patient to remove jewelry and other metallic objects from the area to be examined prior to the procedure.

▶ There are no food or fluid restrictions unless by medical direction.

Make sure a written and informed consent has been signed prior to the procedure and before administering any medications.

INTRATEST:

▶ Observe standard precautions, and follow the general guidelines in Appendix A. Positively identify the patient.

▶ Ensure the patient has removed all external metallic objects from the area to be examined prior to the procedure.

▶ Instruct the patient to void prior to the procedure and to change into the gown, robe, and foot coverings provided.

▶ Instruct the patient to cooperate fully and to follow directions. Ask the patient to lie still during the procedure because movement produces unclear images.

▶ Obtain and record the patient's baseline vital signs.

▶ Place the patient on the table in a supine position.

▶ A single plain film is taken of the bladder and urethra.

▶ A catheter is filled with contrast medium to eliminate air pockets and is inserted until the balloon reaches the meatus. Inform the patient that the contrast medium may cause a temporary flushing of the face, a feeling of warmth, urticaria, headache, vomiting, or nausea.

▶ After three-fourths of the contrast medium is injected, another image

is taken while the remainder of the contrast medium is injected.

▶ The procedure may be done on female patients using a double balloon to occlude the bladder neck from above and below the external meatus.

POST-TEST:

▶ A report of the results will be made available to the requesting HCP, who will discuss the results with the patient.

▶ Instruct the patient to resume usual activities, as directed by the HCP.

▶ Monitor vital and neurological signs every 15 min until they return to pre-procedure levels.

▶ Monitor fluid intake and urinary output for 24 hr after the procedure. Decreased urine output may indicate impending renal failure.

▶ Monitor for signs and symptoms of sepsis, including fever, chills, and severe pain in the kidney area.

▶ Instruct the patient to drink plenty of fluids to prevent stasis and to prevent the buildup of bacteria.

▶ Reinforce information given by the patient's HCP regarding further testing, treatment, or referral to another HCP. Answer any questions or address any concerns voiced by the patient or family.

▶ Depending on the results of this procedure, additional testing may be needed to evaluate or monitor progression of the disease process and determine the need for a change in therapy. Evaluate test results in relation to the patient's symptoms and other tests performed.

RELATED MONOGRAPHS:

▶ Related tests include CT abdomen, CT pelvis, cystometry, cystoscopy, IVP, MRI abdomen, PSA, renogram, retrograde ureteropyelography, urinalysis, and voiding cystourethrography.

▶ Refer to the Genitourinary System table at the end of the book for related tests by body system.

U

Uric Acid, Blood

SYNONYM/ACRONYM: Urate.

COMMON USE: To monitor uric acid levels during treatment for gout and evaluation of tissue destruction, liver damage, renal function, and monitor the effectiveness of therapeutic interventions.

SPECIMEN: Serum (1 mL) collected in a red- or tiger-top tube. Plasma (1 mL) collected in a green-top (heparin) tube is also acceptable. Note: Rasburicase will rapidly decrease uric acid in specimens left at room temperature. If patients are receiving this medication, collect the blood sample in a prechilled green-top (heparin) tube and transport in an ice slurry.

NORMAL FINDINGS: (Method: Spectrophotometry)

Age	Conventional Units	SI Units (Conventional Units × 0.059)
1–30 d		
Male	1.3–4.9	0.08–0.29 mmol/L
Female	1.4–6.2	0.08–0.37 mmol/L
1–3 mo		
Male	1.4–5.3	0.08–0.31 mmol/L
Female	1.4–5.8	0.08–0.34 mmol/L
4–12 mo		
Male	1.5–6.4	0.09–0.38 mmol/L
Female	1.4–6.2	0.08–0.37 mmol/L
1–3 yr		
Male & female	1.8–5	0.11–0.3 mmol/L
4–6 yr		
Male & female	2.2–4.7	0.13–0.28 mmol/L
7–9 yr		
Male & female	2–5	0.12–0.3 mmol/L
10–12 yr		
Male & female	2.3–5.9	0.14–0.35 mmol/L
13–15 yr		
Male	3.1–7	0.18–0.41 mmol/L
Female	2.3–6.4	0.14–0.38 mmol/L
16–18 yr		
Male	2.1–7.6	0.12–0.45 mmol/L
Female	2.4–6.6	0.14–0.39 mmol/L
19 yr–Adult		
Male	4–8 mg/dL	0.24–0.47 mmol/L
Female	2.5–7 mg/dL	0.15–0.41 mmol/L
Adult older than 60 yr		
Male	4.2–8.2 mg/dL	0.25–0.48 mmol/L
Female	3.5–7.3 mg/dL	0.21–0.43 mmol/L

Therapeutic target for patients with gout: Less than 6 mg/dL (SI: Less than 0.4 mmol/L).

U

DESCRIPTION: Uric acid is the end product of purine metabolism. Purines are important constituents of nucleic acids; purine turnover occurs continuously in the body, producing substantial amounts of uric acid even in the absence of purine intake from dietary sources such as organ meats (e.g., liver, thymus gland and/or pancreas [sweetbreads], kidney), legumes, and yeasts. Uric acid is filtered, absorbed, and secreted by the kidneys and is a common constituent of urine. Serum urate levels are affected by the amount of uric acid produced and by the efficiency of renal excretion. Values can vary based on diet, gender, body size, level of exercise, level of stress, and regularity in consumption of alcohol. Elevated uric acid levels can indicate conditions of critical cellular injury or destruction; hyperuricemia has an association with hypertension, hypertriglyceridemia, obesity, myocardial infarct, renal disease, and diabetes. Rasburicase is a medication used in the treatment and prevention of acute hyperuricemia related to tumor lysis syndrome in children and for leukemias and lymphomas related to the toxic effects of chemotherapy. Rasburicase is a recombinant form of uricase oxidase, an enzyme that converts uric acid to allantoin, a much more soluble and effectively excreted substance than uric acid.

INDICATIONS
- Assist in the diagnosis of gout when there is a family history (autosomal dominant genetic disorder) or signs and symptoms of gout, indicated by elevated uric acid levels

- Determine the cause of known or suspected renal calculi
- Evaluate the extent of tissue destruction in infection, starvation, excessive exercise, malignancies, chemotherapy, or radiation therapy
- Evaluate possible liver damage in eclampsia, indicated by elevated uric acid levels
- Monitor the effects of drugs known to alter uric acid levels, either as a side effect or as a therapeutic effect

POTENTIAL DIAGNOSIS

Increased in
Conditions that result in high cellular turnover release nucleic acids into circulation, which are converted to uric acid by the liver.
- Acute tissue destruction as a result of starvation or excessive exercise *(related to cellular destruction)*
- Alcoholism
- Chemotherapy and radiation therapy *(related to high cellular turnover)*
- Chronic lead toxicity *(cellular destruction related to hemolysis)*
- Congestive heart failure *(related to cellular destruction)*
- Diabetes *(decreased renal excretion results in increased blood levels)*
- Down syndrome
- Eclampsia
- Excessive dietary purines *(purines are nucleic acid bases converted to uric acid by the liver)*
- Glucose-6-phosphate dehydrogenase deficiency *(cellular destruction related to hemolysis)*
- Gout *(usually related to excess dietary intake)*
- Hyperparathyroidism
- Hypertension *(related to effects on renal excretion)*
- Hypoparathyroidism *(related to disturbances in calcium and phosphorus homeostasis)*

U

- Lactic acidosis *(cellular destruction related to shock)*
- Lead poisoning *(cellular destruction related to hemolysis)*
- Lesch-Nyhan syndrome *(related to disorder of uric acid metabolism)*
- Multiple myeloma *(related to high cell turnover)*
- Pernicious anemia *(cellular destruction related to hemolysis)*
- Polycystic kidney disease *(related to decreased renal excretion, which results in increased blood levels)*
- Polycythemia *(related to increased cellular destruction)*
- Psoriasis
- Sickle cell anemia *(cellular destruction related to hemolysis)*
- Tumors *(related to high cell turnover)*
- Type III hyperlipidemia

Decreased in
- Fanconi's syndrome *(related to increased renal excretion)*
- Low-purine diet *(related to insufficient nutrients for liver to synthesize uric acid)*
- Severe liver disease *(uric acid synthesis occurs in the liver)*
- Wilson's disease *(affects normal liver function and is related to impaired tubular absorption)*

CRITICAL FINDINGS

Adults
- Greater than 13 mg/dL
  (SI: Greater than 0.8 mmol/L)

Children
- Greater than 12 mg/dL
  (SI: Greater than 0.7 mmol/L)

Note and immediately report to the health-care provider (HCP) any critically increased or decreased values and related symptoms especially fluid imbalance. Timely notification of critical values for lab or diagnostic studies is a role expectation of the professional nurse. Notification processes will vary among facilities. Upon receipt of the critical value the information should be read back to the caller to verify accuracy. Most policies require immediate notification of the primary HCP, hospitalist, or on-call HCP. Reported information includes the patient's name, unique identifiers, critical value, name of the person giving the report, and name of the person receiving the report. Documentation of notification should be made in the medical record with the name of the HCP notified, time and date of notification, and any orders received. Any delay in a timely report of a critical value may require completion of a notification form with review by Risk Management.

Symptoms of acute renal dysfunction and/or failure associated with hyperuricemia include altered mental status, nausea and vomiting, fluid overload, pericarditis, and seizures. Prophylactic measures against the development of hyperuricemia should be undertaken before initiation of chemotherapy. Possible interventions include discontinuing medications that increase serum urate levels or produce acidic urine (e.g., thiazides and salicylates); administration of fluids with sodium bicarbonate as an additive to IV solutions to promote hydration and alkalinization of the urine to a pH greater than 7; administration of allopurinol 1 to 2 days before chemotherapy; monitoring of serum electrolyte, uric acid, phosphorus, calcium, and creatinine levels; and monitoring for ureteral obstruction by urate calculi using computed tomography or ultrasound studies. Possible interventions for advanced renal insufficiency and subsequent renal failure may include peritoneal dialysis or hemodialysis.

INTERFERING FACTORS
- Drugs and substances that may increase uric acid levels include acetylsalicylic acid (low doses), aldatense, aminothiadiazole,

anabolic steroids, antineoplastic agents, atenolol, azathioprine, aza-thymine, azauridine, chlorambucil, chlorthalidone, cisplatin, corn oil, cyclosporine, cyclothiazide, cytara-bine, diapamide, diuretics, ethacry-nic acid, ethambutol, ethoxzolamide, flumethiazide, hydrochlorothiazide, hydroflumethiazide, ibufenac, ibu-profen, levarterenol, mefruside, mercaptopurine, methicillin, metho-trexate, methoxyflurane, methyclo-thiazide, mitomycin, morinamide, polythiazide, prednisone, pyrazin-amide, quinethazone, salicylate, spi-ronolactone, tacrolimus, theophylline, thiazide diuretics, thioguanine, thio-tepa, triamterene, trichlormethia-zide, vincristine, and warfarin.

- Drugs that may decrease uric acid levels include allopurinol, aspirin (high doses), azathioprine, benzbro-maron, benziodarone, canola oil, chlorothiazide (given IV), chlor-promazine, chlorprothixene, cin-chophen, clofibrate, corticosteroids, corticotropin, coumarin, dicumarol, enalapril, fenofibrate, flufenamic acid, guaifenesin, iodipamide, iodo-pyracet, iopanoic acid, ipodate, lisinopril, mefenamic acid, mersalyl, methotrexate, oxyphenbutazone, phenindione, phenolsulfonphtha-lein, probenecid, radiographic agents, rasburicase, seclazone, sul-finpyrazone, and verapamil.

- Rasburicase will rapidly decrease uric acid in specimens left at room temperature. Specimens must be collected in prechilled tubes, trans-ported in an ice slurry, and tested within 4 hr of collection.

NURSING IMPLICATIONS AND PROCEDURE

PRETEST:

▶ Positively identify the patient using at least two unique identifiers before providing care, treatment, or services.

▶ *Patient Teaching:* Inform the patient this test can assist in diagnosing gout and assessing kidney function.

▶ Obtain a history of the patient's com-plaints, including a list of known aller-gens, especially allergies or sensitivities to latex. Especially note pain and edema in joints and great toe (caused by precipitation of sodium urates), headache, fatigue, decreased urinary output, and hypertension.

▶ Obtain a history of the patient's genito-urinary, hepatobiliary, and musculoskel-etal systems; symptoms; and results of previously performed laboratory tests and diagnostic and surgical proce-dures.

▶ Obtain a list of the patient's current medications, including herbs, nutritio-nal supplements, and nutraceuticals (see Appendix F).

▶ Review the procedure with the patient. Inform the patient that specimen col-lection takes approximately 5 to 10 min. Address concerns about pain and explain that there may be some discomfort during the venipuncture.

▶ *Sensitivity to social and cultural issues,* as well as concern for modesty, is important in providing psychological support before, during, and after the procedure.

▶ There are no food, fluid, or medication restrictions unless by medical direction.

INTRATEST:

▶ If the patient has a history of allergic reaction to latex, avoid the use of equipment containing latex.

▶ Instruct the patient to cooperate fully and to follow directions. Direct the patient to breathe normally and to avoid unnecessary movement.

▶ Observe standard precautions, and follow the general guidelines in Appendix A. Positively identify the patient, and label the appropriate specimen container with the corre-sponding patient demographics, initials of the person collecting the specimen, date, and time of collection. Perform a venipuncture.

▶ Remove the needle and apply direct pressure with dry gauze to stop bleed-ing. Observe/assess venipuncture site for bleeding or hematoma formation

and secure gauze with adhesive bandage.
- Promptly transport the specimen to the laboratory for processing and analysis.

POST-TEST:

- A report of the results will be made available to the requesting health-care provider (HCP), who will discuss the results with the patient.
- *Nutritional Considerations:* Increased uric acid levels may be associated with the formation of kidney stones. Educate the patient, if appropriate, on the importance of drinking a sufficient amount of water when kidney stones are suspected.
- *Nutritional Considerations:* Increased uric acid levels may be associated with gout. Nutritional therapy may be appropriate for some patients identified as having gout. Educate the patient that foods high in oxalic acid include caffeinated beverages, raw blackberries, gooseberries and plums, whole-wheat bread, beets, carrots, beans, rhubarb, spinach, dry cocoa, and Ovaltine. Foods high in purines include organ meats, which should be restricted. In other cases, the requesting HCP may not prescribe a low-purine or purine-restricted diet for treatment of gout because medications can control the condition easily and effectively.
- Recognize anxiety related to test results. Discuss the implications of abnormal test results on the patient's lifestyle. Provide teaching and information regarding the clinical implications of the test results, as appropriate.
- Reinforce information given by the patient's HCP regarding further testing, treatment, or referral to another HCP. Answer any questions or address any concerns voiced by the patient or family.
- Depending on the results of this procedure, additional testing may be performed to evaluate or monitor progression of the disease process and determine the need for a change in therapy. Evaluate test results in relation to the patient's symptoms and other tests performed.

RELATED MONOGRAPHS:

- Related tests include arthroscopy, biopsy bone marrow, calcium, calculus kidney stone panel, cholesterol, collagen cross-linked telopeptide, CBC, CBC RBC count, CBC RBC indices, CBC RBC morphology, creatinine, creatinine clearance, gastrin stimulation, G6PD, lactic acid, lead, PTH, parathyroid scan, phosphorus, sickle cell screen, synovial fluid analysis, UA, US abdomen, and uric acid urine.
- Refer to the Genitourinary, Hepatobiliary, and Musculoskeletal systems tables at the end of the book for related tests by body system.

Uric Acid, Urine

SYNONYM/ACRONYM: Urine urate.

COMMON USE: To assist in confirming a diagnosis of gout, assess renal function, evaluate for genetic defects related to uric acid levels, and monitor the effectiveness of therapeutic interventions.

SPECIMEN: Urine (5 mL) from a random or timed specimen collected in a clean plastic, unrefrigerated collection container. Sodium hydroxide preservative may be recommended to prevent precipitation of urates.

NORMAL FINDINGS: (Method: Spectrophotometry)

Gender	Conventional Units*	SI Units (Conventional Units × 0.0059)
Male	250–800 mg/24 hr	1.48–4.72 mmol/24 hr
Female	250–750 mg/24 hr	1.48–4.43 mmol/24 hr

*Values reflect average purine diet.

DESCRIPTION: Uric acid is the end product of purine metabolism. Purines are important constituents of nucleic acids; purine turnover occurs continuously in the body, producing substantial amounts of uric acid even in the absence of purine intake from dietary sources such as organ meats (e.g., liver, thymus gland and/or pancreas [sweetbreads], kidney), legumes, and yeasts. Uric acid is filtered, absorbed, and secreted by the kidneys and is a common constituent of urine. The ratio of 24-hr urine uric acid to creatinine can be used as a test for detection of the Lesch-Nyhan syndrome, a disorder of uric acid metabolism associated with absence of the enzyme hypoxanthine-guanine phosphoribosyltransferase. The ratio in healthy patients is reported to range from 0.21 to 0.59. Patients with partial or complete enzyme deficiency can have ratios from 2 to 5.

INDICATIONS
- Compare urine and serum uric acid levels to provide an index of renal function
- Detect enzyme deficiencies and metabolic disturbances that affect the body's production of uric acid
- Monitor the response to therapy with uricosuric drugs
- Monitor urinary effects of disorders that cause hyperuricemia

POTENTIAL DIAGNOSIS

Increased in
- Disorders associated with impaired renal tubular absorption, such as Fanconi's syndrome and Wilson's disease
- Disorders of purine metabolism
- Excessive dietary intake of purines
- Gout
- Neoplastic disorders, such as leukemia, lymphosarcoma, and multiple myeloma *(related to increased cell turnover)*
- Pernicious anemia *(related to increased cell turnover)*
- Polycythemia vera *(related to increased cell turnover)*
- Renal calculus formation *(related to increased urinary excretion)*
- Sickle cell anemia *(related to increased cell turnover)*

Decreased in
- Chronic alcohol ingestion *(related to decreased excretion)*
- Hypertension *(related to decreased excretion)*
- Severe renal damage *(possibly resulting from chronic glomerulonephritis, collagen disorders, diabetic glomerulosclerosis, lactic acidosis, ketoacidosis, or alcohol abuse)*

CRITICAL FINDINGS: N/A

INTERFERING FACTORS
- Drugs that may increase urine uric acid levels include acetohexamide, ampicillin, ascorbic acid, azapropazone, benzbromarone, chlorpromazine, chlorprothixene, corticotropin,

coumarin, dicumarol, ethyl biscou-macetate, iodipamide, iodopyracet, iopanoic acid, ipodate, mannose, mer-barone, mercaptopurine, mersalyl, methotrexate, niacinamide, nifedip-ine, phenindione, phenolsulfonphtha-lein, phenylbutazone, phloridzin, probenecid, salicylates (long-term, large doses), seclazone, sulfinpyr-azone, and verapamil.

- •Drugs that may decrease urine uric acid levels include acetazolamide, allopurinol, angiotensin, benzbroma-rone, bumetanide, chlorothiazide, chlorthalidone, ethacrynic acid, eth-ambutol, ethoxzolamide, hydrochlo-rothiazide, levarterenol, niacin, pyrazinoic acid, and thiazide diuretics.
- •All urine voided for the timed col-lection period must be included in the collection or else falsely decreased values may be obtained. Compare output records with vol-ume collected to verify that all voids were included in the collection.

NURSING IMPLICATIONS AND PROCEDURE

PRETEST:

▶ Positively identify the patient using at least two unique identifiers before providing care, treatment, or services.
▶ *Patient Teaching:* Inform the patient this test can assist in diagnosing gout and kidney disease.
▶ Obtain a history of the patient's com-plaints, including a list of known aller-gens, especially allergies or sensitivities to latex.
▶ Obtain a history of the patient's genito-urinary system, symptoms, and results of previously performed laboratory tests and diagnostic and surgical pro-cedures.
▶ Obtain a list of the patient's current medications, including herbs, nutritio-nal supplements, and nutraceuticals (see Appendix F).
▶ Review the procedure with the patient. Provide a nonmetallic urinal, bedpan,

or toilet-mounted collection device. Address concerns about pain and explain that there should be no dis-comfort during the procedure.
▶ Usually a 24-hr time frame for urine collection is ordered. Inform the patient that all urine must be saved during that 24-hr period. Instruct the patient not to void directly into the laboratory collec-tion container. Instruct the patient to avoid defecating in the collection device and to keep toilet tissue out of the collection device to prevent con-tamination of the specimen. Place a sign in the bathroom to remind the patient to save all urine.
▶ Instruct the patient to void all urine into the collection device and then to pour the urine into the laboratory collection container. Alternatively, the specimen can be left in the collection device for a health-care staff member to add to the laboratory collection container.
▶ *Sensitivity to social and cultural issues,* as well as concern for modesty, is important in providing psychological support before, during, and after the procedure.
▶ There are no food, fluid, or medication restrictions unless by medical direction.

INTRATEST:

▶ If the patient has a history of allergic reaction to latex, avoid the use of equipment containing latex.
▶ Instruct the patient to cooperate fully and to follow directions.
▶ Observe standard precautions, and follow the general guidelines in Appendix A. Positively identify the patient, and label the appropriate specimen containers with the corre-sponding patient demographics, initials of the person collecting the specimen, date, and time of collection.

Random Specimen (Collect in Early Morning)

Clean-Catch Specimen
▶ Instruct the male patient to (1) thorou-ghly wash his hands, (2) cleanse the meatus, (3) void a small amount into the toilet, and (4) void directly into the specimen container.
▶ Instruct the female patient to (1) thorou-ghly wash her hands; (2) cleanse the

labia from front to back; (3) while keeping the labia separated, void a small amount into the toilet; and (4) without interrupting the urine stream, void directly into the specimen container.

Indwelling Catheter

Put on gloves. Empty drainage tube of urine. It may be necessary to clamp off the catheter for 15 to 30 min before specimen collection. Cleanse specimen port with antiseptic swab, and then aspirate 5 mL of urine with a 21- to 25-gauge needle and syringe. Transfer urine to a sterile container.

Timed Specimen

Obtain a clean 3-L urine specimen container, toilet-mounted collection device, and plastic bag (for transport of the specimen container). The specimen must be refrigerated or kept on ice throughout the entire collection period. If an indwelling urinary catheter is in place, the drainage bag must be kept on ice.

Begin the test between 6 and 8 a.m. if possible. Collect first voiding and discard. Record the time the specimen was discarded as the beginning of the timed collection period. The next morning, ask the patient to void at the same time the collection was started and add this last voiding to the container. Urinary output should be recorded throughout the collection time.

If an indwelling catheter is in place, replace the tubing and container system at the start of the collection time. Keep the container system on ice during the collection period, or empty the urine into a larger container periodically during the collection period; monitor to ensure continued drainage, and conclude the test the next morning at the same hour the collection was begun.

At the conclusion of the test, compare the quantity of urine with the urinary output record for the collection; if the specimen contains less than what was recorded as output, some urine may have been discarded, invalidating the test.

Include on the collection container's label the amount of urine, test start and stop times, and any medications that can affect test results.

General

Promptly transport the specimen to the laboratory for processing and analysis.

POST-TEST:

A report of the results will be made available to the requesting health-care provider (HCP), who will discuss the results with the patient.

Increased uric acid levels may be associated with the formation of kidney stones. Educate the patient, if appropriate, on the importance of drinking a sufficient amount of water when kidney stones are suspected.

Nutritional Considerations: Increased uric acid levels may be associated with gout. Nutritional therapy may be appropriate for some patients identified as having gout. Educate the patient that foods high in oxalic acid include caffeinated beverages, raw blackberries, gooseberries and plums, whole-wheat bread, beets, carrots, beans, rhubarb, spinach, dry cocoa, and Ovaltine. Foods high in purines include organ meats, which should be restricted. In other cases, the requesting HCP may not prescribe a low-purine or purine-restricted diet for treatment of gout because medications can control the condition easily and effectively.

Recognize anxiety related to test results. Discuss the implications of abnormal test results on the patient's lifestyle. Provide teaching and information regarding the clinical implications of the test results, as appropriate.

Reinforce information given by the patient's HCP regarding further testing, treatment, or referral to another HCP. Answer any questions or address any concerns voiced by the patient or family.

Depending on the results of this procedure, additional testing may be performed to evaluate or monitor progression of the disease process and determine the need for a change in therapy. Evaluate test results in relation to the patient's symptoms and other tests performed.

RELATED MONOGRAPHS:

Related tests include arthroscopy, biopsy bone marrow, calcium, calculus

U

kidney stone panel, cholesterol, collagen cross-linked telopeptide, CBC, CBC RBC count, CBC RBC indices, CBC RBC morphology, creatinine, creatinine clearance, gastrin stimulation, G6PD, lactic acid, lead, oxalate, PTH, parathyroid scan, phosphorus, sickle cell screen, synovial fluid analysis, UA, and uric acid blood.

▶ Refer to the Genitourinary System table at the end of the book for related tests by body system.

Urinalysis

SYNONYM/ACRONYM: UA.

COMMON USE: To screen urine for multiple substances such as infection, blood, sugar, bilirubin, urobilinogen, nitrates, and protein to assist in diagnosing disorders such as renal and liver disease as well as assess hydration status.

SPECIMEN: Urine (15 mL) from an unpreserved, random specimen collected in a clean plastic collection container.

NORMAL FINDINGS: (Method: Macroscopic evaluation by dipstick and microscopic examination) Urinalysis comprises a battery of tests including a description of the color and appearance of urine; measurement of specific gravity and pH; and semiquantitative measurement of protein, glucose, ketones, urobilinogen, bilirubin, hemoglobin, nitrites, and leukocyte esterase. Urine sediment may also be examined for the presence of crystals, casts, renal epithelial cells, transitional epithelial cells, squamous epithelial cells, white blood cells (WBCs), red blood cells (RBCs), bacteria, yeast, sperm, and any other substances excreted in the urine that may have clinical significance. Examination of urine sediment is performed microscopically under high power, and results are reported as the number seen per high-power field (hpf). The color of normal urine ranges from light yellow to deep amber. The color depends on the patient's state of hydration (more concentrated samples are darker in color), diet, medication regimen, and exposure to other substances that may contribute to unusual color or odor. The appearance of normal urine is clear. Cloudiness is sometimes attributable to the presence of amorphous phosphates or urates as well as blood, WBCs, fat, or bacteria. Normal specific gravity is 1.001 to 1.029.

Dipstick

pH	5–9
Protein	Less than 20 mg/dL
Glucose	Negative
Ketones	Negative
Hemoglobin	Negative
Bilirubin	Negative
Urobilinogen	Up to 1 mg/dL
Nitrite	Negative
Leukocyte esterase	Negative
Specific gravity	1.001–1.029

U

Microscopic Examination

Red blood cells	Less than 5/hpf
White blood cells	Less than 5/hpf
Renal cells	None seen
Transitional cells	None seen
Squamous cells	Rare; usually no clinical significance
Casts	Rare hyaline; otherwise, none seen
Crystals in acid urine	Uric acid, calcium oxalate, amorphous urates
Crystals in alkaline urine	Triple phosphate, calcium phosphate, ammonium biurate, calcium carbonate, amorphous phosphates
Bacteria, yeast, parasites	None seen

DESCRIPTION: Routine urinalysis, one of the most widely ordered laboratory procedures, is used for basic screening purposes. It is a group of tests that evaluate the kidneys' ability to selectively excrete and reabsorb substances while maintaining proper water balance. The results can provide valuable information regarding the overall health of the patient and the patient's response to disease and treatment. The urine dipstick has a number of pads on it to indicate various biochemical markers. Urine pH is an indication of the kidneys' ability to help maintain balanced hydrogen ion concentration in the blood. Specific gravity is a reflection of the concentration ability of the kidneys. Urine protein is the most common indicator of renal disease, although there are conditions that can cause benign proteinuria. Glucose is used as an indicator of diabetes. The presence of ketones indicates impaired carbohydrate metabolism. Hemoglobin indicates the presence of blood, which is associated with renal disease. Bilirubin is used to assist in the detection of liver disorders. Urobilinogen indicates hepatic or hematopoietic conditions. Nitrites and leukocytes are used to test for bacteriuria and other sources of urinary tract infections (UTIs). Most laboratories have established criteria for the microscopic examination of urine based on patient population (e.g., pediatric, oncology, urology), unusual appearance, and biochemical reactions.

INDICATIONS

- Determine the presence of a genitourinary infection or abnormality
- Monitor the effects of physical or emotional stress
- Monitor fluid imbalances or treatment for fluid imbalances
- Monitor the response to drug therapy and evaluate undesired reactions to drugs that may impair renal function
- Provide screening as part of a general physical examination, especially on admission to a health-care facility or before surgery

U

POTENTIAL DIAGNOSIS

Unusual Color

Color	Presence of
Deep yellow	Riboflavin
Orange	Bilirubin, chrysophanic acid, phenazopiridine, santonin
Pink	Beet pigment, hemoglobin, myoglobin, porphyrin, rhubarb
Red	Beet pigment, hemoglobin, myoglobin, porphyrin, uroerythrin
Green	Oxidized bilirubin, Clorets (breath mint)
Blue	Diagnex, indican, methylene blue
Brown	Bilirubin, hematin, methemoglobin, metronidazole, nitrofurantoin, metabolites of rhubarb, senna
Black	Homogentisic acid, melanin
Smoky	Red blood cells

Test	Increased in	Decreased in
pH	Ingestion of citrus fruits	Ingestion of cranberries
	Vegetarian diets	High-protein diets
	Metabolic and respiratory alkalosis	Metabolic or respiratory acidosis
Protein	Benign proteinuria owing to stress, physical exercise, exposure to cold, or standing	N/A
	Diabetic nephropathy	
	Glomerulonephritis	
	Nephrosis	
	Toxemia of pregnancy	
Glucose	Diabetes	N/A
Ketones	Diabetes	N/A
	Fasting	
	Fever	
	High-protein diets	
	Isopropanol intoxication	
	Postanesthesia period	
	Starvation	
	Vomiting	
Hemoglobin	Diseases of the bladder	N/A
	Exercise (march hemoglobinuria)	
	Glomerulonephritis	
	Hemolytic anemia or other causes of hemolysis (e.g., drugs, parasites, transfusion reaction)	
	Malignancy	
	Menstruation	

U

Test	Increased in	Decreased in
	Paroxysmal cold hemoglobinuria	
	Paroxysmal nocturnal hemoglobinuria	
	Pyelonephritis	
	Snake or spider bites	
	Trauma	
	Tuberculosis	
	Urinary tract infections	
	Urolithiasis	
Urobilinogen	Cirrhosis	Antibiotic therapy (suppresses normal intestinal flora)
	Heart failure	
	Hemolytic anemia	
	Hepatitis	Obstruction of the bile duct
	Infectious mononucleosis	
	Malaria	
	Pernicious anemia	
Bilirubin	Cirrhosis	N/A
	Hepatic tumor	
	Hepatitis	
Nitrites	Presence of nitrite-forming bacteria (e.g., *Citrobacter, Enterobacter, Escherichia coli, Klebsiella, Proteus, Pseudomonas, Salmonella,* and some species of *Staphylococcus*)	N/A
Leukocyte esterase	Bacterial infection	N/A
	Calculus formation	
	Fungal or parasitic infection	
	Glomerulonephritis	
	Interstitial nephritis	
	Tumor	
Specific gravity	Adrenal insufficiency	Diuresis
	Congestive heart failure	Excess IV fluids
	Dehydration	Excess hydration
	Diabetes	Hypothermia
	Diarrhea	Impaired renal concentrating ability
	Fever	
	Proteinuria	
	Sweating	
	Vomiting	
	Water restriction	
	X-ray dyes	

U

Formed Elements in Urine Sediment

Cellular Elements

- Clue cells (cell wall of the bacteria causes adhesion to epithelial cells) are present in nonspecific vaginitis caused by *Gardnerella vaginitis, Mobiluncus cortisii,* and *M. mulieris.*
- RBCs are present in glomerulonephritis, lupus nephritis, focal glomerulonephritis, calculus, malignancy, infection, tuberculosis, infarction, renal vein thrombosis, trauma, hydronephrosis, polycystic kidney, urinary tract disease, prostatitis, pyelonephritis, appendicitis, salpingitis, diverticulitis, gout, scurvy, subacute bacterial endocarditis, infectious mononucleosis, hemoglobinopathies, coagulation disorders, heart failure, and malaria.
- Renal cells that have absorbed cholesterol and triglycerides are also known as oval fat bodies.
- Renal cells come from the lining of the collecting ducts, and increased numbers indicate acute tubular damage as seen in acute tubular necrosis, pyelonephritis, malignant nephrosclerosis, acute glomerulonephritis, acute drug or substance (salicylate, lead, or ethylene glycol) intoxication, or chemotherapy, resulting in desquamation, urolithiasis, and kidney transplant rejection.
- Squamous cells line the vagina and distal portion of the urethra. The presence of normal squamous epithelial cells in female urine is generally of no clinical significance. Abnormal cells with enlarged nuclei indicate the need for cytological studies to rule out malignancy.
- Transitional cells line the renal pelvis, ureter, bladder, and proximal portion of the urethra. Increased numbers are seen with infection, trauma, and malignancy.
- WBCs are present in acute UTI, tubulointerstitial nephritis, lupus nephritis, pyelonephritis, kidney transplant rejection, fever, and strenuous exercise.

Casts

- Granular casts are formed from protein or by the decomposition of cellular elements. They may be seen in renal disease, viral infections, or lead intoxication.
- Large numbers of hyaline casts may be seen in renal diseases, hypertension, congestive heart failure, or nephrotic syndrome and in more benign conditions such as fever, exposure to cold temperatures, exercise, or diuretic use.
- RBC casts may be found in acute glomerulonephritis, lupus nephritis, and subacute bacterial endocarditis.
- Waxy casts are seen in chronic renal failure or conditions such as kidney transplant rejection, in which there is renal stasis.
- WBC casts may be seen in lupus nephritis, acute glomerulonephritis, interstitial nephritis, and acute pyelonephritis.

Crystals

- Crystals found in freshly voided urine have more clinical significance than crystals seen in a urine sample that has been standing for more than 2 to 4 hr.
- Calcium oxalate crystals are found in ethylene glycol poisoning, urolithiasis, high dietary intake of oxalates, and Crohn's disease.
- Cystine crystals are seen in patients with cystinosis or cystinuria.
- Leucine or tyrosine crystals may be seen in patients with severe liver disease.
- Large numbers of uric acid crystals are seen in patients with urolithiasis, gout, high dietary intake of foods rich in purines, or who are receiving chemotherapy (see monograph titled "Uric Acid, Urine").

CRITICAL FINDINGS ◈

Possible critical values are the presence of uric acid, cystine, leucine, or tyrosine crystals.

The combination of grossly elevated urine glucose and ketones is also considered significant.

Note and immediately report to the health-care provider (HCP) any critical values and related symptoms. Timely notification of critical values for lab or diagnostic studies is a role expectation of the professional nurse. Notification processes will vary among facilities. Upon receipt of the critical value the information should be read back to the caller to verify accuracy. Most policies require immediate notification of the primary HCP, hospitalist, or on-call HCP. Reported information includes the patient's name, unique identifiers, critical value, name of the person giving the report, and name of the person receiving the report. Documentation of notification should be made in the medical record with the name of the HCP notified, time and date of notification, and any orders received. Any delay in a timely report of a critical value may require completion of a notification form with review by Risk Management.

INTERFERING FACTORS

- Certain foods, such as onion, garlic, and asparagus, contain substances that may give urine an unusual odor. An ammonia-like odor may be produced by the presence of bacteria. Urine with a maple syrup–like odor may indicate a congenital metabolic defect (maple syrup urine disease).
- The various biochemical strips are subject to interference that may produce false-positive or false-negative results. Consult the laboratory for specific information regarding limitations of the method in use and a listing of interfering drugs.
- The dipstick method for protein detection is mostly sensitive to the presence of albumin; light-chain or Bence Jones proteins may not be detected by this method. Alkaline pH may produce false-positive protein results.
- Large amounts of ketones or ascorbic acid may produce false-negative or decreased color development on the glucose pad. Contamination of the collection container or specimen with chlorine, sodium hypochlorite, or peroxide may cause false-positive glucose results.
- False-positive ketone results may be produced in the presence of ascorbic acid, levodopa metabolites, valproic acid, phenazopyridine, phenylketones, or phthaleins.
- The hemoglobin pad may detect myoglobin, intact RBCs, and free hemoglobin. Contamination of the collection container or specimen with sodium hypochlorite or iodine may cause false-positive hemoglobin results. Negative or decreased hemoglobin results may occur in the presence of formalin, elevated protein, nitrite, ascorbic acid, or high specific gravity.
- False-negative nitrite results are common. Negative or decreased results may be seen in the presence of ascorbic acid and high specific gravity. Other causes of false-negative values relate to the amount of time the urine was in the bladder before voiding or the presence of pathogenic organisms that do not reduce nitrates to nitrites.
- False-positive leukocyte esterase reactions result from specimens contaminated by vaginal secretions. The presence of high glucose, protein, or ascorbic acid concentrations may cause false-negative results. Specimens with high specific gravity may also produce false-negative results. Patients with neutropenia (e.g., oncology patients) may also

have false-negative results because they do not produce enough WBCs to exceed the sensitivity of the biochemical reaction.

• Specimens that cannot be delivered to the laboratory or tested within 1 hr should be refrigerated or should have a preservative added that is recommended by the laboratory. Specimens collected more than 2 hr before submission may be rejected for analysis.

• Because changes in the urine specimen occur over time, prompt and proper specimen processing, storage, and analysis are important to achieve accurate results.

Changes that may occur over time include:

Production of a stronger odor and an increase in pH (bacteria in the urine break urea down to ammonia)

A decrease in clarity (as bacterial growth proceeds or precipitates form)

A decrease in bilirubin and urobilinogen (oxidation to biliverdin and urobilin)

A decrease in ketones (lost through volatilization)

Decreased glucose (consumed by bacteria)

An increase in bacteria (growth over time)

Disintegration of casts, WBCs, and RBCs

An increase in nitrite (overgrowth of bacteria)

NURSING IMPLICATIONS AND PROCEDURE

PRETEST:

▸ Positively identify the patient using at least two unique identifiers before providing care, treatment, or services.

▸ *Patient Teaching:* Inform the patient this test can assist in assessing for disease, infection, and inflammation and evaluate for dehydration.

▸ Obtain a history of the patient's complaints, including a list of known allergens, especially allergies or sensitivities to latex.

▸ Obtain a history of the patient's endocrine, genitourinary, immune, hematopoietic, and hepatobiliary systems; symptoms; and results of previously performed laboratory tests and diagnostic and surgical procedures.

▸ Obtain a list of the patient's current medications, including herbs, nutritional supplements, and nutraceuticals (see Appendix F).

▸ Review the procedure with the patient. If a catheterized specimen is to be collected, explain this procedure to the patient, and obtain a catheterization tray. Address concerns about pain and explain that there should be no discomfort during the procedure. Inform the patient that specimen collection takes approximately 5 to 10 min.

▸ *Sensitivity to social and cultural issues,* as well as concern for modesty, is important in providing psychological support before, during, and after the procedure.

▸ There are no food, fluid, or medication restrictions unless by medical direction.

INTRATEST:

▸ If the patient has a history of allergic reaction to latex, avoid the use of equipment containing latex.

▸ Instruct the patient to cooperate fully and to follow directions. Direct the patient to breathe normally and to avoid unnecessary movement.

▸ Observe standard precautions, and follow the general guidelines in Appendix A. Positively identify the patient, and label the appropriate specimen container with the corresponding patient demographics, initials of the person collecting the specimen, date, and time of collection.

Random Specimen (Collect in Early Morning)

Clean-Catch Specimen

▸ Instruct the male patient to (1) thoroughly wash his hands, (2) cleanse the meatus, (3) void a small amount into the toilet, and (4) void directly into the specimen container.

Instruct the female patient to (1) thoroughly wash her hands; (2) cleanse the labia from front to back; (3) while keeping the labia separated, void a small amount into the toilet; and (4) without interrupting the urine stream, void directly into the specimen container.

Pediatric Urine Collector

Put on gloves. Appropriately cleanse the genital area, and allow the area to dry. Remove the covering over the adhesive strips on the collector bag, and apply the bag over the genital area. Diaper the child. When specimen is obtained, place the entire collection bag in a sterile urine container.

Indwelling Catheter

Put on gloves. Empty drainage tube of urine. It may be necessary to clamp off the catheter for 15 to 30 min before specimen collection. Cleanse specimen port with antiseptic swab, and then aspirate 5 mL of urine with a 21- to 25-gauge needle and syringe. Transfer urine to a sterile container.

Urinary Catheterization

Place female patient in lithotomy position or male patient in supine position. Using sterile technique, open the straight urinary catheterization kit and perform urinary catheterization. Place the retained urine in a sterile specimen container.

Suprapubic Aspiration

Place the patient in a supine position. Cleanse the area with antiseptic and drape with sterile drapes. A needle is inserted through the skin into the bladder. A syringe attached to the needle is used to aspirate the urine sample. The needle is then removed and a sterile dressing is applied to the site. Place the sterile sample in a sterile specimen container.

Do not collect urine from the pouch from the patient with a urinary diversion (e.g., ileal conduit). Instead, perform catheterization through the stoma.

General

Include on the collection container's label whether the specimen is clean catch or catheter and any medications that may interfere with test results.

Promptly transport the specimen to the laboratory for processing and analysis.

POST-TEST:

A report of the results will be made available to the requesting HCP, who will discuss the results with the patient.

Instruct the patient to report symptoms such as pain related to tissue inflammation, pain or irritation during void, bladder spasms, or alterations in urinary elimination.

Observe/assess for signs of inflammation if the specimen is obtained by suprapubic aspiration.

Recognize anxiety related to test results. Discuss the implications of abnormal test results on the patient's lifestyle. Provide teaching and information regarding the clinical implications of the test results, as appropriate. Instruct the patient with a UTI, as appropriate, on the proper technique for wiping the perineal area (front to back) after a bowel movement. UTIs are more common in women who use diaphragm/spermicide contraception. These patients can be educated, as appropriate, in the proper insertion and removal of the contraceptive device to avoid recurrent UTIs.

Reinforce information given by the patient's HCP regarding further testing, treatment, or referral to another HCP. Instruct the patient to begin antibiotic therapy, as prescribed, and instruct the patient in the importance of completing the entire course of antibiotic therapy even if symptoms are no longer present. Answer any questions or address any concerns voiced by the patient or family.

Depending on the results of this procedure, additional testing may be performed to evaluate or monitor progression of the disease process and determine the need for a change in therapy. Evaluate test results in relation to the patient's symptoms and other tests performed.

RELATED MONOGRAPHS:

Related tests include amino acids, angiography renal, antibodies, antiglomerular basement membrane, biopsy bladder, biopsy kidney, bladder cancer

U

marker, BUN, calcium, calculus kidney stone panel, CBC, creatinine, culture urine, cystometry, cystoscopy, cysto-urethrography voiding, cytology urine, electrolytes, glucose, glycated hemoglobin, IFE, IVP, ketones, KUB study, microalbumin, osmolality, oxalate, protein total, phosphorus, renogram, retrograde ureteropyelography, urea nitrogen urine, uric acid (blood and urine), and US abdomen.

▸ Refer to the Endocrine, Genitourinary, Immune, Hematopoietic, and Hepatobiliary systems tables at the end of the book for related tests by body system.

Uterine Fibroid Embolization

SYNONYM/ACRONYM: UFE; uterine artery embolization.

COMMON USE: A less invasive modality used to assist in treating fibroid tumors found in the uterine lining, heavy menstrual bleeding, and pelvic pain.

AREA OF APPLICATION: Uterus.

CONTRAST: IV iodine based.

DESCRIPTION: Uterine fibroid embolization (UFE) is a way of treating fibroid tumors of the uterus. Fibroid tumors, also known as myomas, are masses of fibrous and muscle tissue in the uterine wall that are benign but that may cause heavy menstrual bleeding, pain in the pelvic region, or pressure on the bladder or bowel. Using angiographic methods, a catheter is placed in each of the two uterine arteries, and small particles are injected to block the arterial branches that supply blood to the fibroids. The fibroid tissue dies, the mass shrinks, and the symptoms are relieved. This procedure, which is done under local anesthesia, is less invasive than open surgery done to remove uterine fibroids. Because the effects of uterine fibroid embolization on fertility are not yet known, the ideal candidate is a premenopausal woman with symptoms from fibroid tumors who no longer wishes to become pregnant. This technique is an alternative for women who do not want to receive blood transfusions or do not wish to receive general anesthesia. This procedure may be used to halt severe bleeding following childbirth or caused by gynecological tumors.

INDICATIONS
- Treatment for anemia from chronic blood loss
- Treatment of fibroid tumors and tumor vascularity, for both single and multiple tumors
- Treatment of tumors in lieu of surgical resection

POTENTIAL DIAGNOSIS

Normal findings in
- Decrease in uterine bleeding
- Decrease of pelvic pain or fullness

Abnormal findings in
• No reduction in size of fibroid

CRITICAL FINDINGS: N/A

INTERFERING FACTORS

This procedure is contraindicated for

• ◈ Patients with allergies to shellfish or iodinated contrast medium. The contrast medium used may cause a life-threatening allergic reaction. Patients with a known hypersensitivity to contrast medium may benefit from premedication with corticosteroids or the use of nonionic contrast medium.

• Patients with bleeding disorders.

• Patients who are pregnant or suspected of being pregnant, unless the potential benefits of the procedure far outweigh the risks to the fetus and mother.

• Patients in whom cancer is a possibility or who have inflammation or infection in the pelvis.

• ◈ Elderly and other patients who are chronically dehydrated before the procedure, because of their risk of contrast-induced renal failure.

• ◈ Patients who are in renal failure.

Factors that may impair clear imaging

• Gas or feces in the gastrointestinal tract resulting from inadequate cleansing or failure to restrict food intake before the study.

• Retained barium from a previous radiological procedure.

• Metallic objects (e.g., jewelry, body rings) within the examination field, which may inhibit organ visualization and cause unclear images.

Other considerations

• Complications of the procedure include hemorrhage, infection at the insertion site, and cardiac arrhythmias.

• The procedure may be terminated if chest pain or severe cardiac arrhythmias occur.

• Inability of the patient to cooperate or remain still during the procedure because of age, significant pain, or mental status, may interfere with the test results.

• Failure to follow dietary restrictions before the procedure may cause the procedure to be canceled or repeated.

• Consultation with a health-care provider (HCP) should occur before the procedure for radiation safety concerns regarding younger patients or patients who are lactating.

• Risks associated with radiation overexposure can result from frequent x-ray procedures. Personnel in the room with the patient should wear a protective lead apron, stand behind a shield, or leave the area while the examination is being done. Personnel working in the examination area should wear badges to record their level of radiation exposure.

• A small percentage of women may pass a small piece of fibroid tissue after the procedure. Women with this problem may require a procedure called a D & C (dilatation and curettage).

• Some women may experience menopause shortly after the procedure.

NURSING IMPLICATIONS AND PROCEDURE

PRETEST:

▸ Positively identify the patient using at least two unique identifiers before providing care, treatment, or services.

▸ *Patient Teaching:* Inform the patient this procedure can assist in assessing and treating the uterus.

▸ Obtain a history of the patient's complaints, including a list of known allergens, especially allergies or sensitivities to latex, iodine, seafood, anesthetics, or contrast medium.

▶ Obtain a history of the patient's reproductive system, symptoms, and results of previously performed laboratory tests and diagnostic and surgical procedures.

▶ Note any recent procedures that can interfere with test results; include examinations utilizing barium- or iodine-based contrast medium.

▶ Record the date of the last menstrual period and determine the possibility of pregnancy in perimenopausal women.

▶ Obtain a list of the patient's current medications, including anticoagulants, aspirin and other salicylates, herbs, nutritional supplements, and nutraceuticals, especially those known to affect coagulation (see Appendix F). Such products should be discontinued by medical direction for the appropriate number of days prior to a surgical procedure. Note the last time and dose of medication taken.

▶ If contrast medium is scheduled to be used, patients receiving metformin (Glucophage) for non–insulin-dependent (type 2) diabetes should discontinue the drug on the day of the test and continue to withhold it for 48 hr after the test. Failure to do so may result in lactic acidosis.

▶ Review the procedure with the patient. Address concerns about pain and explain that there may be moments of discomfort and some pain experienced during the test. Explain that a sedative and/or anesthetic may be administered before the procedure to promote relaxation. Inform the patient that the procedure is performed in a radiology or vascular department by an HCP, with support staff, and takes approximately 30 to 120 min.

▶ *Sensitivity to social and cultural issues,* as well as concern for modesty, is important in providing psychological support before, during, and after the procedure.

▶ Explain that an IV line may be inserted to allow infusion of IV fluids, contrast medium, or sedatives. Usually normal saline is infused.

▶ Inform the patient that a burning and flushing sensation may be felt throughout the body during injection of the contrast medium. After injection of the contrast medium, the patient may experience an urge to cough, flushing, nausea, or a salty or metallic taste.

▶ Instruct the patient to remove jewelry and other metallic objects from the area to be examined prior to the procedure.

▶ Instruct the patient to fast and restrict fluids for 8 hr prior to the procedure. Instruct the patient to avoid taking anticoagulant medication or to reduce dosage as ordered prior to the procedure. Protocols may vary among facilities.

▶ Make sure a written and informed consent has been signed prior to the procedure and before administering any medications.

▶ This procedure may be terminated if chest pain, severe cardiac arrhythmias, or signs of a cerebrovascular accident occur.

INTRATEST:

▶ Observe standard precautions, and follow the general guidelines in Appendix A Positively identify the patient.

▶ Ensure the patient has complied with dietary, fluid, and medication restrictions for 8 hr prior to the procedure.

▶ Ensure the patient has removed all external metallic objects from the area to be examined prior to the procedure.

▶ If the patient has a history of allergic reactions to any substance or drug, administer ordered prophylactic steroids or antihistamines before the procedure. Use nonionic contrast medium for the procedure.

▶ Have emergency equipment readily available.

▶ Instruct the patient to void prior to the procedure and to change into the gown, robe, and foot coverings provided.

▶ Instruct the patient to cooperate fully and to follow directions. Instruct the patient to remain still throughout the procedure because movement produces unreliable results.

▶ Record baseline vital signs and assess neurological status. Protocols may vary among facilities.

Establish an IV fluid line for the injection of emergency drugs and of sedatives.

Administer an antianxiety agent, as ordered, if the patient has claustrophobia. Administer a sedative to an uncooperative adult, as ordered.

Place electrocardiographic electrodes on the patient for cardiac monitoring. Establish baseline rhythm; determine if the patient has ventricular arrhythmias.

Using a pen, mark the site of the patient's peripheral pulses before angiography; this allows for quicker and more consistent assessment of the pulses after the procedure.

Place the patient in the supine position on an examination table. Cleanse the selected area, and cover with a sterile drape.

The contrast medium is injected, and a rapid series of images is taken during and after the filling of the vessels to be examined. Delayed images may be taken to examine the vessels after a time and to monitor the venous phase of the procedure.

Ask the patient to inhale deeply and hold her breath while the x-ray images are taken, and then to exhale after the images are taken.

Instruct the patient to take slow, deep breaths if nausea occurs during the procedure. Monitor and administer an antiemetic agent if ordered. Ready an emesis basin for use.

Particles are injected through the catheter to block the blood flow to the fibroids. The particles include polyvinyl alcohol, gelatin sponge (Gelfoam), and microspheres.

The needle or catheter is removed, and a pressure dressing is applied over the puncture site.

Monitor the patient for complications related to the procedure (e.g., allergic reaction, anaphylaxis, bronchospasm). Observe/assess the needle/catheter insertion site for bleeding, inflammation, or hematoma formation.

POST-TEST:

A report of the results will be made available to the requesting HCP, who will discuss the results with the patient.

Instruct the patient to resume usual diet, fluids, medications, or activity, as directed by the HCP. Renal function should be assessed before metformin is resumed.

Monitor vital signs and neurological status every 15 min for 1 hr, then every 2 hr for 4 hr, and then as ordered by the HCP. Take temperature every 4 hr for 24 hr. Monitor intake and output at least every 8 hr. Compare with baseline values. Notify the HCP if temperature is elevated. Protocols may vary among facilities.

Observe for delayed allergic reactions, such as rash, urticaria, tachycardia, hyperpnea, hypertension, palpitations, nausea, or vomiting.

Instruct the patient to immediately report symptoms such as fast heart rate, difficulty breathing, skin rash, itching, chest pain, persistent right shoulder pain, or abdominal pain. Immediately report symptoms to the appropriate HCP.

Patients may experience pelvic cramps for several days after the procedure and possible mild nausea and fever.

Assess extremities for signs of ischemia or absence of distal pulse caused by a catheter-induced thrombus.

Instruct the patient in the care and assessment of the injection site.

Instruct the patient to apply cold compresses to the puncture site as needed, to reduce discomfort or edema.

Recognize anxiety related to test results, and be supportive of impaired activity related to genitourinary system. Discuss the implications of abnormal test results on the patient's lifestyle. Provide teaching and information regarding the clinical implications of the test results, as appropriate. Educate the patient regarding access to counseling services.

Reinforce information given by the patient's HCP regarding further testing, treatment, or referral to another HCP. Answer any questions or address any concerns voiced by the patient or family.

Instruct the patient in the use of any ordered medications. Explain the importance of adhering to the therapy regimen. As appropriate, instruct the patient in significant side effects and systemic reactions associated with the prescribed medication. Encourage her to review corresponding literature provided by a pharmacist.

▸ Depending on the results of this procedure, additional testing may be performed to evaluate or monitor progression of the disease process and determine the need for a change in therapy. Evaluate test results in relation to the patient's symptoms and other tests performed.

RELATED MONOGRAPHS:

▸ Related tests include CBC, CT angiography, CT pelvis, hysterosalpingography, laparoscopy, MRA, MRI pelvis, PT/INR, and US pelvis.

▸ Refer to the Reproductive System table at the end of the book for related tests by body system.

U

Vanillylmandelic Acid, Urine

SYNONYM/ACRONYM: VMA.

COMMON USE: To assist in the diagnosis and follow up treatment of pheochromocytoma, neuroblastoma, and ganglioblastoma. This test can also be useful in evaluation and follow-up of hypertension.

V

SPECIMEN: Urine (25 mL) from a timed specimen collected in a clean plastic collection container with 6N hydrochloric acid as a preservative.

NORMAL FINDINGS: (Method: High-pressure liquid chromatography)

Age	Conventional Units	SI Units (Conventional Units × 5.05)
3–6 yr	1–2.6 mg/24 hr	5–13 micromol/24 hr
7–10 yr	2–3.2 mg/24 hr	10–16 micromol/24 hr
11–16 yr	2.3–5.2 mg/24 hr	12–26 micromol/24 hr
17–83 yr	1.4–6.5 mg/24 hr	7–33 micromol/24 hr

DESCRIPTION: Vanillylmandelic acid (VMA) is a major metabolite of epinephrine and norepinephrine. It is elevated in conditions that also are marked by over production of catecholamines. Creatinine is usually measured simultaneously and to calculate an excretion ratio of metabolite to creatinine.

INDICATIONS
• Assist in the diagnosis of neuroblastoma, ganglioneuroma, or pheochromocytoma
• Evaluate hypertension of unknown cause

POTENTIAL DIAGNOSIS

Increased in
Catecholamine-secreting tumors will cause an increase in VMA.

• Ganglioneuroma
• Hypertension secondary to pheochromocytoma
• Neuroblastoma
• Pheochromocytoma

Decreased in: N/A

CRITICAL FINDINGS: N/A

INTERFERING FACTORS
• Drugs that may increase VMA levels include ajmaline, chlorpromazine, glucagon, guaifenesin, guanethidine, isoproterenol, methyldopa, nitroglycerin, oxytetracycline, phenazopyridine, phenolsulfonphthalein, prochlorperazine, rauwolfia, reserpine, sulfobromophthalein, and syrosingopine.
• Drugs that may decrease VMA levels include brofaromine, guanethidine, guanfacine, imipramine, isocarboxazid, methyldopa, monoamine oxidase inhibitors, morphine, nialamide (in patients with schizophrenia), and reserpine.
• Stress, hypoglycemia, hyperthyroidism, strenuous exercise, smoking, and drugs can produce elevated catecholamines.
• Recent radioactive scans within 1 wk of the test can interfere with test results.

• Failure to collect all urine and store 24-hr specimen properly will result in a falsely low result.
• Failure to follow dietary restrictions before the procedure may cause the procedure to be canceled or repeated.

NURSING IMPLICATIONS AND PROCEDURE

PRETEST:

▸ Positively identify the patient using at least two unique identifiers before providing care, treatment, or services.

▸ *Patient Teaching:* Inform the patient this test can assist in evaluating or the presence of tumors.

▸ Obtain a history of the patient's complaints, including a list of known allergens, especially allergies or sensitivities to latex.

▸ Obtain a history of the patient's endocrine system, symptoms, and results of previously performed laboratory tests and diagnostic and surgical procedures.

▸ Obtain a list of the patient's current medications, including herbs, nutritional supplements, and nutraceuticals (see Appendix F).

▸ Review the procedure with the patient. Provide a nonmetallic urinal, bedpan, or toilet-mounted collection device. Address concerns about pain and explain that there should be no discomfort during the procedure.

▸ *Sensitivity to social and cultural issues,* as well as concern for modesty, is important in providing psychological support before, during, and after the procedure.

▸ Usually a 24-hr time frame for urine collection is ordered. Inform the patient that all urine must be saved during that 24-hr period. Instruct the patient not to void directly into the laboratory collection container. Instruct the patient to avoid defecating in the collection device and to keep toilet tissue out of the collection device to prevent contamination of the specimen. Place a sign in the bathroom to remind the patient to save all urine.

▸ Instruct the patient to void all urine into the collection device and then to pour the urine into the laboratory collection container. Alternatively, the specimen can be left in the collection device for a health-care staff member to add to the laboratory collection container.

▸ There are no fluid restrictions unless by medical direction.

▸ Instruct the patient to abstain from smoking tobacco for 24 hr before testing.

▸ Inform the patient of the following dietary, medication, and activity restrictions in preparation for the test (protocols may vary among facilities):

The patient should not consume foods high in amines for 48 hr before testing (bananas, avocados, beer, aged cheese, chocolate, cocoa, coffee, fava beans, grains, tea, vanilla, walnuts, and red wine).

The patient should not consume foods or fluids high in caffeine for 48 hr before testing (coffee, tea, cocoa, and chocolate).

The patient should not consume any foods or fluids containing vanilla or licorice.

The patient should avoid self-prescribed medications (especially aspirin) and prescribed medications (especially pyridoxine, levodopa, amoxicillin, carbidopa, reserpine, and disulfiram) for 2 wk before testing and as directed.

The patient should avoid excessive exercise and stress during the 24-hr collection of urine.

INTRATEST:

▸ Ensure that the patient has complied with dietary, medication, and activity restrictions and pretesting preparations prior to the procedure.

▸ If the patient has a history of allergic reaction to latex, avoid the use of equipment containing latex.

Instruct the patient to cooperate fully and to follow directions.

Observe standard precautions, and follow the general guidelines in Appendix A. Positively identify the patient, and label the appropriate specimen container with the corresponding patient demographics, initials of the person collecting the specimen, date, and time of collection.

Timed Specimen

Obtain a clean 3-L urine specimen container, toilet-mounted collection device, and plastic bag (for transport of the specimen container). The specimen must be refrigerated or kept on ice throughout the entire collection period. If an indwelling urinary catheter is in place, the drainage bag must be kept on ice.

Begin the test between 6 and 8 a.m. if possible. Collect first voiding and discard. Record the time the specimen was discarded as the beginning of the timed collection period. The next morning, ask the patient to void at the same time the collection was started and add this last voiding to the container. Urinary output should be recorded throughout the collection time.

If an indwelling catheter is in place, replace the tubing and container system at the start of the collection time. Keep the container system on ice during the collection period, or empty the urine into a larger container periodically during the collection period; monitor to ensure continued drainage, and conclude the test the next morning at the same hour the collection was begun.

At the conclusion of the test, compare the quantity of urine with the urinary output record for the collection; if the specimen contains less than what was recorded as output, some urine may have been discarded, invalidating the test.

Include on the collection container's label the amount of urine, test start and stop times, and ingestion of any foods or medications that can affect test results.

Promptly transport the specimen to the laboratory for processing and analysis.

POST-TEST:

A report of the results will be made available to the requesting health-care provider (HCP), who will discuss the results with the patient.

Instruct the patient to resume usual diet, fluids, medications, and activity, as directed by the HCP.

Nutritional Considerations: Instruct the patient to avoid foods or drinks containing caffeine. Over-the-counter medications should be taken only under the advice of the patient's HCP.

Recognize anxiety related to test results, and be supportive of fear of shortened life expectancy. Discuss the implications of abnormal test results on the patient's lifestyle. Provide teaching and information regarding the clinical implications of the test results, as appropriate. Educate the patient regarding access to counseling services.

Reinforce information given by the patient's HCP regarding further testing, treatment, or referral to another HCP. Answer any questions or address any concerns voiced by the patient or family.

Depending on the results of this procedure, additional testing may be performed to evaluate or monitor progression of the disease process and determine the need for a change in therapy. Evaluate test results in relation to the patient's symptoms and other tests performed.

RELATED MONOGRAPHS:

Related tests include angiography adrenal, calcium, catecholamines, CT renal, homovanillic acid, metanephrines, and renin.

Related to Endocrine System table at the end of the book for related tests by body system.

V

Varicella Antibodies

SYNONYM/ACRONYM: Varicella-zoster antibodies, chickenpox, VZ.

COMMON USE: To assist in diagnosing chickenpox or shingles related to a varicella-zoster infection and to assess for immunity.

SPECIMEN: Serum (1 mL) collected in a red-top tube.

NORMAL FINDINGS: (Method: Enzyme immunoassay)

	IgM	Interpretation	IgG	Interpretation
Negative	0.89 index or less	No significant level of detectable antibody	0.89 index or less	No significant level of detectable antibody; indicative of nonimmunity
Indeterminate	0.9–1.0 index	Equivocal results; retest in 10–14 d	0.9–1.0 index	Equivocal results; retest in 10–14 d
Positive	1.1 index or greater	Antibody detected; indicative of recent immunization, current or recent infection	1.1 index or greater	Antibody detected; indicative of immunization, current or past infection

DESCRIPTION: Varicella-zoster is a double-stranded DNA herpes virus that is responsible for two clinical syndromes: chickenpox and shingles. The incubation period is 2 to 3 wk, and it is highly contagious for about 2 wk beginning 2 days before a rash develops. It is transmitted in respiratory secretions. The primary exposure to the highly contagious virus usually occurs in susceptible school-age children. Adults without prior exposure and who become infected may have severe complications, including pneumonia. Neonatal infection from the mother is possible if exposure occurs during the last 3 wk of gestation. Shingles results when the presumably latent virus is reactivated. The presence of immunoglobulin (Ig) M antibodies indicates acute infection. The presence of IgG antibodies indicates current or past infection. A reactive varicella antibody result indicates immunity but does not protect an individual from shingles. There are also polymerase chain reaction methods that can detect varicella-zoster DNA in various specimen types.

INDICATIONS
• Determine susceptibility or immunity to chickenpox

POTENTIAL DIAGNOSIS

Positive findings in
• Varicella infection

Negative findings in: N/A

CRITICAL FINDINGS: N/A

INTERFERING FACTORS: N/A

NURSING IMPLICATIONS AND PROCEDURE

PRETEST:

▶ Positively identify the patient using at least two unique identifiers before providing care, treatment, or services.
▶ *Patient Teaching:* Inform the patient this test can assist in assessing for a viral infection or immunity.
▶ Obtain a history of the patient's complaints, including a list of known allergens, especially allergies or sensitivities to latex.
▶ Obtain a history of exposure to varicella.
▶ Obtain a history of the patient's immune and reproductive systems, symptoms, and results of previously performed laboratory tests and diagnostic and surgical procedures.
▶ Obtain a list of the patient's current medications, including herbs, nutritional supplements, and nutraceuticals (see Appendix F).
▶ Review the procedure with the patient. Inform the patient that several tests may be necessary to confirm diagnosis. Any individual positive result should be repeated in 7 to 14 days to monitor a change in detectable level of antibody.

Inform the patient that specimen collection takes approximately 5 to 10 min. Address concerns about pain and explain that there may be some discomfort during the venipuncture.
▶ *Sensitivity to social and cultural issues,* as well as concern for modesty, is important in providing psychological support before, during, and after the procedure.
▶ There are no food, fluid, or medication restrictions unless by medical direction.

INTRATEST:

▶ If the patient has a history of allergic reaction to latex, avoid the use of equipment containing latex.
▶ Instruct the patient to cooperate fully and to follow directions. Direct the patient to breathe normally and to avoid unnecessary movement.
▶ Observe standard precautions, and follow the general guidelines in Appendix A. Positively identify the patient, and label the appropriate specimen container with the corresponding patient demographics, initials of the person collecting the specimen, date, and time of collection. Perform a venipuncture.
▶ Remove the needle and apply direct pressure with dry gauze to stop bleeding. Observe/assess venipuncture site for bleeding or hematoma formation and secure gauze with adhesive bandage.
▶ Promptly transport the specimen to the laboratory for processing and analysis.

POST-TEST:

▶ A report of the results will be made available to the requesting health-care provider (HCP), who will discuss the results with the patient.
▶ *Vaccination Considerations:* Record the date of last menstrual period and determine the possibility of pregnancy prior to administration of varicella vaccine to female varicella-nonimmune patients. Instruct patient not to become pregnant for 1 mo after being vaccinated with the varicella vaccine to protect any fetus from contracting the disease and having serious birth defects. Instruct on birth control methods to prevent pregnancy, if appropriate.

V

Recognize anxiety related to test results, and provide emotional support if results are positive and the patient is pregnant. Inform the patient with shingles about access to pain management. Discuss the implications of abnormal test results on the patient's lifestyle. Provide teaching and information regarding the clinical implications of the test results, as appropriate. Educate the patient regarding access to counseling services.

Reinforce information given by the patient's HCP regarding further testing, treatment, or referral to another HCP. Instruct the patient in isolation precautions during the time of communicability or contagion. Emphasize the need to return to have a convalescent blood sample taken in 7 to 14 days. Provide information regarding vaccine-preventable diseases where indicated (e.g., anthrax, cervical cancer, diphtheria, encephalitis, hepatitis A and B, H1N1 flu, human papillomavirus,

Haemophilus influenza, seasonal influenza, Lyme disease, measles, meningococcal disease, monkeypox, mumps, pertussis, pneumococcal disease, polio, rotavirus, rubella, shingles, smallpox, tetanus, typhoid fever, varicella, yellow fever). Provide contact information, if desired, for the Centers for Disease Control and Prevention (www.cdc.gov/vaccines/vpd-vac). Answer any questions or address any concerns voiced by the patient or family.

Depending on the results of this procedure, additional testing may be performed to evaluate or monitor progression of the disease process and determine the need for a change in therapy. Evaluate test results in relation to the patient's symptoms and other tests performed.

RELATED MONOGRAPHS:

Refer to the Immune and Reproductive systems tables at the end of the book for related tests by body system.

Venography, Lower Extremity Studies

SYNONYM/ACRONYM: Lower limb venography, phlebography, venogram.

COMMON USE: To visualize and assess the venous vasculature in the lower extremities related to diagnosis of deep vein thrombosis and congenital anomalies.

AREA OF APPLICATION: Veins of the lower extremities.

CONTRAST: IV iodine based.

DESCRIPTION: Venography allows x-ray visualization of the venous vasculature system of the extremities after injection of an iodinated contrast medium. Lower extremity studies identify and locate thrombi within the venous system of the lower limbs. After injection of the contrast medium, x-ray images are taken at timed intervals. Usually both extremities are studied, and the unaffected side is used for comparison with the side suspected of having deep vein thrombosis (DVT) or other venous abnormalities, such as congenital malformations or incompetent valves. Thrombus formation usually occurs in the deep calf veins and at the venous junction and its valves. If DVT is not treated, it can lead to femoral and iliac venous occlusion, or the thrombus can become an embolus, causing a pulmonary embolism. Venography is accurate for thrombi in veins below the knee.

INDICATIONS

• Assess deep vein valvular competence
• Confirm a diagnosis of DVT
• Determine the cause of extremity swelling or pain
• Determine the source of emboli when pulmonary embolism is suspected or diagnosed
• Distinguish clot formation from venous obstruction
• Evaluate congenital venous malformations
• Locate a vein for arterial bypass graft surgery

POTENTIAL DIAGNOSIS

Normal findings in

No obstruction to flow and no filling defects after injection of radiopaque contrast medium; steady opacification of superficial and deep vasculature with no filling defects

Abnormal findings in

• Deep vein valvular incompetence
• DVT
• Pulmonary embolism
• Venous obstruction

CRITICAL FINDINGS

• DVT

It is essential that critical diagnoses be communicated immediately to the appropriate health-care provider (HCP). A listing of these diagnoses varies among facilities. Note and immediately report to the HCP abnormal results and related symptoms. Timely notification of critical values for lab or diagnostic studies is a role expectation of the professional nurse. Notification processes will vary among facilities. Upon receipt of the critical value the information should be read back to the caller to verify accuracy. Most policies require immediate notification of the primary HCP, hospitalist, or on-call HCP. Reported information includes the patient's name, unique identifiers, critical value, name of the person giving the report, and name of the person receiving the report. Documentation of notification should be made in the medical record with the name of the HCP notified, time and date of notification, and any orders received. Any delay in a timely report of a critical value may require completion of a notification form with review by Risk Management.

INTERFERING FACTORS

This procedure is contraindicated for

• Patients with allergies to shellfish or iodinated dye. The contrast medium used may cause a life-threatening allergic reaction. Patients with a known hypersensitivity to the contrast medium may benefit from premedication with corticosteroids or the use of non-ionic contrast medium.
• Patients who are pregnant or suspected of being pregnant, unless the potential benefits of the procedure far outweigh the risks to the fetus and mother.
• Elderly and other patients who are chronically dehydrated before the test, because of their risk of contrast-induced renal failure.
• Patients who are in renal failure.
• Patients with bleeding disorders.

Factors that may impair clear imaging

• Metallic objects (e.g., jewelry, body rings) within the examination field, which may inhibit organ visualization and cause unclear images.
• Movement of the leg being tested, excessive tourniquet constriction, insufficient injection of contrast medium, and delay between injection and the x-ray.
• Severe edema of the legs, making venous access impossible.

Other considerations

• Improper injection of the contrast medium that allows it to seep deep into the muscle tissue.
• Inability of the patient to cooperate or remain still during the procedure because of age, significant pain, or mental status, may interfere with the test results.
• Consultation with a HCP should occur before the procedure for radiation safety concerns regarding younger patients or patients who are lactating.
• Risks associated with radiation overexposure can result from frequent x-ray procedures. Personnel in the room with the patient should wear a protective lead apron, stand behind a shield, or leave the area while the examination is being done. Personnel working in the examination area should wear badges to record their level of radiation exposure.

NURSING IMPLICATIONS AND PROCEDURE

PRETEST:

▶ Positively identify the patient using at least two unique identifiers before providing care, treatment, or services.
▶ *Patient Teaching:* Inform the patient this procedure can assist in assessing the veins in the lower extremities.

▶ Obtain a history of the patient's complaints, including a list of known allergens, especially allergies or sensitivities to latex, iodine, seafood, contrast medium, anesthetics, and contrast medium.
▶ Note any recent procedures that can interfere with test results, including examinations using barium- or iodine-based contrast medium.
▶ Obtain a history of the patient's cardiovascular and respiratory systems, symptoms, and results of previously performed laboratory tests and diagnostic and surgical procedures.
▶ Record the date of the last menstrual period and determine the possibility of pregnancy in perimenopausal women.
▶ Obtain a list of the patient's current medications, including anticoagulants, aspirin and other salicylates, herbs, nutritional supplements, and nutraceuticals, especially those known to affect coagulation (see Appendix F). Such products should be discontinued by medical direction for the appropriate number of days prior to a surgical procedure. Note the last time and dose of medication taken.
▶ Patients receiving metformin (Glucophage) for non–insulin-dependent (type 2) diabetes should discontinue the drug on the day of the test and continue to withhold it for 48 hr after the test. Failure to do so may result in lactic acidosis.
▶ Review the procedure with the patient. Address concerns about pain and explain to the patient that there may be moments of discomfort and some pain experienced during the procedure. Inform the patient that the procedure is usually performed in a radiology or vascular suite by an HCP, with support staff, and takes approximately 30 to 60 min.
▶ *Sensitivity to social and cultural issues,* as well as concern for modesty, is important in providing psychological support before, during, and after the procedure.
▶ Explain that an IV line may be inserted to allow infusion of IV fluids, contrast medium, or sedatives. Usually normal saline is infused.
▶ Inform the patient that a burning and flushing sensation may be felt throughout the body during injection of the

contrast medium. After injection of the contrast medium, the patient may experience an urge to cough, flushing, nausea, or a salty or metallic taste.

▶ Instruct the patient to remove jewelry and other metallic objects from the area to be examined prior to the procedure.

▶ Instruct the patient to fast and restrict fluids for 8 hr prior to the procedure. Protocols may vary among facilities.

▶ *Make sure a written and informed consent has been signed prior to the procedure and before administering any medications.*

▶ This procedure may be terminated if chest pain, severe cardiac arrhythmias, or signs of a cerebrovascular accident occur.

INTRATEST:

▶ Observe standard precautions, and follow the general guidelines in Appendix A. Positively identify the patient.

▶ Ensure the patient has complied with dietary, fluid, and medication restrictions for 8 hr prior to the procedure.

▶ Ensure the patient has removed all external metallic objects from the area to be examined prior to the procedure.

▶ If the patient has a history of allergic reactions to any substance or drug, administer ordered prophylactic steroids or antihistamines before the procedure. Use nonionic contrast medium for the procedure.

▶ Have emergency equipment readily available.

▶ Instruct the patient to void prior to the procedure and to change into the gown, robe, and foot coverings provided.

▶ Instruct the patient to cooperate fully and to follow directions. Ask the patient to remain still throughout the procedure because movement produces unreliable results.

▶ Record baseline vital signs, and continue to monitor throughout the procedure. Protocols may vary among facilities.

▶ Establish an IV fluid line for the injection of emergency drugs and of sedatives.

▶ Administer an antianxiety agent, as ordered, if the patient has claustrophobia. Administer a sedative to a child or to an uncooperative adult, as ordered.

▶ Place electrocardiographic electrodes on the patient for cardiac monitoring. Establish baseline rhythm; determine if the patient has ventricular arrhythmias.

▶ Using a pen, mark the site of the patient's peripheral pulses before venography; this allows for quicker and more consistent assessment of the pulses after the procedure.

▶ Place the patient in the supine position on an examination table. Cleanse the selected area, and cover with a sterile drape.

▶ A local anesthetic is injected at the site, and a small incision is made or a needle inserted.

▶ The contrast medium is injected, and a rapid series of images is taken during and after the filling of the vessels to be examined.

▶ Instruct the patient to inhale deeply and hold his or her breath while the x-ray images are taken, and then to exhale.

▶ Instruct the patient to take slow, deep breaths if nausea occurs during the procedure.

▶ Monitor the patient for complications related to the procedure (e.g., allergic reaction, anaphylaxis, bronchospasm).

▶ The needle or catheter is removed, and a pressure dressing is applied over the puncture site.

▶ Observe/assess the needle/catheter insertion site for bleeding, inflammation, or hematoma formation.

POST-TEST:

▶ A report of the results will be made available to the requesting HCP, who will discuss the results with the patient.

▶ Instruct the patient to resume diet, fluids, and medications, as directed by the HCP. Renal function should be assessed before metformin is resumed.

▶ Monitor vital signs and neurological status every 15 min for 1 hr, then every 2 hr for 4 hr, and then as ordered by the HCP. Take temperature every 4 hr for 24 hr. Monitor intake and output at least every 8 hr. Compare with baseline values. Notify the HCP if temperature is elevated. Protocols may vary among facilities.

V

▸ Observe for delayed allergic reactions, such as rash, urticaria, tachycardia, hyperpnea, hypertension, palpitations, nausea, or vomiting.

▸ Instruct the patient to immediately report symptoms such as fast heart rate, difficulty breathing, skin rash, itching, chest pain, persistent right shoulder pain, or abdominal pain. Immediately report symptoms to the appropriate HCP.

▸ Assess extremities for signs of ischemia or absence of distal pulse caused by a catheter-induced thrombus.

▸ Instruct the patient in the care and assessment of the site.

▸ Instruct the patient to apply cold compresses to the puncture site as needed to reduce discomfort or edema.

▸ Instruct the patient to maintain bed rest for 4 to 6 hr after the procedure or as ordered.

▸ Recognize anxiety related to test results, and be supportive of perceived loss of independent function. Discuss the implications of abnormal test results on the patient's lifestyle. Provide teaching and information regarding the clinical implications of the test results, as appropriate.

▸ Reinforce information given by the patient's HCP regarding further testing, treatment, or referral to another HCP. Answer any questions or address any concerns voiced by the patient or family.

▸ Depending on the results of this procedure, additional testing may be needed to evaluate or monitor progression of the disease process and determine the need for a change in therapy. Evaluate test results in relation to the patient's symptoms and other tests performed.

RELATED MONOGRAPHS:

▸ Related tests include alveolar/arterial gradient, angiography pulmonary, antibodies anticardiolipin, antithrombin III, blood gases, CT angiography, D-dimer, FDP, lactic acid, lung perfusion scan, lung ventilation scan, MRA, MRI abdomen, plethysmography, PT/INR, renogram, US peripheral Doppler, and US venous Doppler extremity studies.

▸ Refer to the Cardiovascular and Respiratory systems tables at the end of the book for related tests by body system.

Vertebroplasty

SYNONYM/ACRONYM: None.

COMMON USE: A minimally invasive procedure to treat the spine for disorders such as tumor, lesions, osteoporosis, vertebral compression, and pain.

AREA OF APPLICATION: Spine.

CONTRAST: None.

DESCRIPTION: Vertebroplasty is a minimally invasive, nonsurgical therapy used to repair a broken vertebra and to provide relief of pain related to vertebral compression in the spine that has been weakened by osteoporosis or tumoral lesions. Osteoporosis affects over 10 million women in the United States and accounts for

V

over 700,000 vertebral fractures per year. This procedure is usually successful at alleviating the pain caused by a compression fracture less than 6 mo in duration with pain directly referable to the location of the fracture. Secondary benefits may include vertebra stabilization and reduction of the risk of further compression. This procedure is usually performed on an outpatient basis. The procedure involves injection of orthopedic cement mixture through a needle into a fracture site. Injection is visualized with guidance from radiological imaging. Vertebroplasty may be the preferred procedure when patients are too elderly or frail to tolerate open spinal surgery or if bones are too weak for surgical repair. Patients with a malignant tumor may benefit from vertebroplasty. Other possible applications include younger patients whose osteoporosis is caused by long-term steroid use or a metabolic disorder. This procedure is recommended after basic treatments such as bedrest and orthopedic braces have failed or when pain medication has been ineffective or caused the patient medical problems, including stomach ulcers.

INDICATIONS

- Assist in the detection of nonmalignant tumors before surgical resection.
- Repair of compression spinal fractures of varying ages. Fractures older than 6 mo will respond but at a slower rate. Fractures less than 4 wk old should be given a chance to heal without intervention unless they are associated with disabling pain or hospitalization.
- Repair of spinal problems due to tumors.

POTENTIAL DIAGNOSIS

Normal findings in
- Improvement in the ability to ambulate without pain
- Relief of back pain

Abnormal findings in
- Failure to reduce the patient's pain
- Failure to improve the patient's mobility

CRITICAL FINDINGS: N/A

INTERFERING FACTORS

This procedure is contraindicated for
- Patients with allergies to shellfish or iodinated dye. The contrast medium used may cause a life-threatening allergic reaction. Patients with a known hypersensitivity to the contrast medium may benefit from premedication with corticosteroids or the use of nonionic contrast medium.
- Pain that is primarily radicular in nature.
- Patients with bleeding disorders.
- Patients who are pregnant or suspected of being pregnant, unless the potential benefits of the procedure far outweigh the risks to the fetus and mother.
- Pain that is improving or that has been present and unchanged for years.
- Imaging procedures that suggest no fracture is present or that the fracture is remote from the patient's pain.

Factors that may impair clear imaging
- Gas or feces in the gastrointestinal tract resulting from inadequate cleansing or failure to restrict food intake before the study.
- Retained barium from a previous radiological procedure.
- Metallic objects (e.g., jewelry, body rings) within the examination field, which may inhibit organ visualization and cause unclear images.

Other considerations

- Complications of the procedure include hemorrhage, infection at the insertion site, and cardiac arrhythmias.
- The procedure may be terminated if chest pain or severe cardiac arrhythmias occur.
- Inability of the patient to cooperate or remain still during the procedure because of age, significant pain, or mental status, may interfere with the test results.
- Failure to follow dietary restrictions before the procedure may cause the procedure to be canceled or repeated.
- Consultation with a health-care provider (HCP) should occur before the procedure for radiation safety concerns regarding younger patients or patients who are lactating.
- Risks associated with radiation overexposure can result from frequent x-ray procedures. Personnel in the room with the patient should wear a protective lead apron, stand behind a shield, or leave the area while the examination is being done. Personnel working in the examination area should wear badges to record their level of radiation exposure.

NURSING IMPLICATIONS AND PROCEDURE

PRETEST:

▶ Positively identify the patient using at least two unique identifiers before providing care, treatment, or services.
▶ *Patient Teaching:* Inform the patient this procedure can assist in improving spinal cord function.
▶ Obtain a history of the patient's complaints, including a list of known allergens, especially allergies or sensitivities to latex, iodine, seafood, contrast medium, anesthetics, or contrast medium.

▶ Note any recent procedures that can interfere with test results, including examinations using barium- or iodine-based contrast medium.
▶ Obtain a history of the patient's musculoskeletal system, symptoms, and results of previously performed laboratory tests and diagnostic and surgical procedures.
▶ Record the date of the last menstrual period and determine the possibility of pregnancy in perimenopausal women.
▶ Obtain a list of the patient's current medications, including anticoagulants, aspirin and other salicylates, herbs, nutritional supplements, and nutraceuticals, especially those known to affect coagulation (see Appendix F). Such products should be discontinued by medical direction for the appropriate number of days prior to a surgical procedure. Note the last time and dose of medication taken.
▶ Review the procedure with the patient. Address concerns about pain and explain that there may be moments of discomfort and some pain experienced during the test. Inform the patient that the procedure is usually performed in the radiology department by an HCP, with support staff, and takes approximately 30 to 90 min.
▶ *Sensitivity to social and cultural issues,* as well as concern for modesty, is important in providing psychological support before, during, and after the procedure.
▶ Explain that an IV line may be inserted to allow infusion of IV fluids, contrast medium, or sedatives. Usually normal saline is infused.
▶ Instruct the patient to remove jewelry and other metallic objects from the area to be examined prior to the procedure.
▶ Instruct the patient to fast and restrict fluids for 8 hr prior to the procedure. Protocols may vary among facilities.
▶ *Make sure a written and informed consent has been signed prior to the procedure and before administering any medications.*
▶ This procedure may be terminated if chest pain or severe cardiac arrhythmias occur.

INTRATEST:

Observe standard precautions, and follow the general guidelines in Appendix A. Positively identify the patient.

Ensure the patient has complied with dietary, fluid, and medication restrictions for 8 hr prior to the procedure.

Ensure the patient has removed all external metallic objects from the area to be examined.

If the patient has a history of allergic reactions to any substance or drug, administer ordered prophylactic steroids or antihistamines before the procedure. Use nonionic contrast medium for the procedure.

Have emergency equipment readily available.

Instruct the patient to void prior to the procedure and to change into the gown, robe, and foot coverings provided.

Instruct the patient to cooperate fully and to follow directions. Ask the patient to remain still throughout the procedure because movement produces unreliable results.

Record baseline vital signs, and continue to monitor throughout the procedure. Protocols may vary among facilities.

Establish an IV fluid line for the injection of emergency drugs and of sedatives.

Administer an antianxiety agent, as ordered, if the patient is claustrophobia. Administer a sedative to a child or to an uncooperative adult, as ordered.

Place electrocardiographic electrodes on the patient for cardiac monitoring. Establish baseline rhythm; determine if the patient has ventricular arrhythmias.

Place the patient in the prone position on an examination table. Cleanse the selected area, and cover with a sterile drape.

A local anesthetic is injected at the site, and a small incision is made or a needle inserted under fluoroscopy.

Orthopedic cement is injected through the needle into the fracture.

Ask the patient to inhale deeply and hold his or her breath while the images are taken, and then to exhale.

Instruct the patient to take slow, deep breaths if nausea occurs during the procedure.

Monitor the patient for complications related to the procedure (e.g., allergic reaction, anaphylaxis, bronchospasm).

The needle or catheter is removed, and a pressure dressing is applied over the puncture site.

Observe/assess the needle/catheter insertion site for bleeding, inflammation, or hematoma formation.

POST-TEST:

A report of the results will be made available to the requesting HCP, who will discuss the results with the patient.

Instruct the patient to resume usual diet, fluids, medications, or activity, as directed by the HCP. Renal function should be assessed before metformin is resumed.

Monitor vital signs and neurological status every 15 min for 1 hr, then every 2 hr for 4 hr, and then as ordered by the HCP. Take temperature every 4 hr for 24 hr. Monitor intake and output at least every 8 hr. Compare with baseline values. Notify the HCP if temperature is elevated. Protocols may vary among facilities.

Observe for delayed allergic reactions, such as rash, urticaria, tachycardia, hyperpnea, hypertension, palpitations, nausea, or vomiting.

Instruct the patient to immediately report symptoms such as fast heart rate, difficulty breathing, skin rash, itching, chest pain, persistent right shoulder pain, or abdominal pain.

Immediately report symptoms to the appropriate HCP.

Instruct the patient and caregiver in the care and assessment of the site.

Instruct the patient's caregiver to apply cold compresses to the puncture site as needed to reduce discomfort or edema.

Instruct the patient to maintain bedrest for 4 to 6 hr after the procedure or as ordered.

Recognize anxiety related to test results, and be supportive of impaired activity related to physical activity. Discuss the implications of abnormal test results on the patient's lifestyle. Provide teaching and information regarding the clinical implications of the test results, as appropriate.

V

Reinforce information given by the patient's HCP regarding further testing, treatment, or referral to another HCP. Answer any questions or address any concerns voiced by the patient or family.

Depending on the results of this procedure, additional testing may be performed to evaluate or monitor progression of the disease process and determine the need for a change in therapy. Evaluate test results in relation to the patient's symptoms and other tests performed.

RELATED MONOGRAPHS:

Related tests include bone mineral densitometry, bone scan, CT spine, EMG, and MRI musculoskeletal.

Refer to the Musculoskeletal System table at the end of the book for related tests by body system.

Visual Fields Test

SYNONYM/ACRONYM: Perimetry, VF.

COMMON USE: To assess visual field function related to the retina, optic nerve, and optic pathways to assist in diagnosing visual loss disorders such as brain tumors, macular degeneration, and diabetes.

AREA OF APPLICATION: Eyes.

CONTRAST: N/A.

DESCRIPTION: The visual field (VF) is the area within which objects can be seen by the eye as it fixes on a central point. The central field is an area extending 25° surrounding the fixation point. The peripheral field is the remainder of the area within which objects can be viewed. This test evaluates the central VF, except within the physiological blind spot, through systematic movement of the test object across a tangent screen. It tests the function of the retina, optic nerve, and optic pathways. VF testing may be performed manually by the examiner (confrontation VF examination) or by using partially or fully automated equipment (tangent screen, Goldman, Humphrey VF examination). In the manual VF test, the patient is asked to cover one eye and fix his or her gaze on the examiner. The examiner moves his or her hand out of the patient's VF and then gradually brings it back into the patient's VF. The patient signals the examiner when the hand comes back into view. The test is repeated on the other eye. The manual test is frequently used for screening because it is quick and simple. Tangent screen or Goldman testing is an automated method commonly used to create a map of the patient's VF and is described in greater detail in this monograph.

INDICATIONS

• Detect field vision loss and evaluate its progression or regression

POTENTIAL DIAGNOSIS

Normal findings in

• Normal central vision field extends in a circle approximately 25–30° on all sides of central fixation and out 60° superiorly (upward), 60° nasally (medially), 75° inferiorly (downward), and 90° temporally (laterally). There is a normal physio-logical blind spot, 12° to 15° temporal to the central fixation point and approximately 1.5° below the horizontal meridian which is approximately 7.5° high and 5.5° wide. The patient should be able to see the test object throughout the entire central vision field except within the physiological blind spot.

Abnormal findings in

• Amblyopia
• Blepharochalasis
• Blurred vision
• Brain tumors
• Cerebrovascular accidents
• Choroidal nevus
• Diabetes with ophthalmic manifestations
• Glaucoma
• Headache
• Macular degeneration
• Macular drusen
• Nystagmus
• Optic neuritis or neuropathy
• Ptosis of eyelid
• Retinal detachment, hole, or tear
• Retinal exudates or hemorrhage
• Retinal occlusion of the artery or vein
• Retinitis pigmentosa
• Subjective visual disturbance
• Use of high-risk medications
• VF defect
• Vitreous traction syndrome

CRITICAL FINDINGS: N/A

INTERFERING FACTORS

Factors that may impair clear imaging

• An uncooperative patient or a patient with severe vision loss who has difficulty seeing even a large vision screen may have test results that are invalid.
• Assess and make note of the patient's cooperation and reliability as good, fair, or poor, because it is difficult to evaluate factors such as general health, fatigue, or reaction time that affect test performance.

NURSING IMPLICATIONS AND PROCEDURE

PRETEST:

▶ Positively identify the patient using at least two unique identifiers before providing care, treatment, or services.
▶ *Patient Teaching:* Inform the patient this procedure assesses visual field function and vision loss.
▶ Obtain a history of the patient's complaints, including a list of known allergens.
▶ Obtain a history of the patient's known or suspected vision loss; changes in visual acuity, including type and cause; use of glasses or contact lenses; eye conditions with treatment regimens; eye surgery; and other tests and procedures to assess and diagnose visual deficit.
▶ Obtain a history of symptoms and results of previously performed laboratory tests and diagnostic and surgical procedures.
▶ Obtain a list of the patient's current medications, including herbs, nutritional supplements, and nutraceuticals (see Appendix F).
▶ Measurement of visual acuity with and without corrective lenses prior to testing is highly recommended. Instruct the patient to wear corrective lenses if appropriate and if worn to correct for distance vision. Instruct the patient regarding the importance of keeping the eyes open for the test.

Review the procedure with the patient. Address concerns about pain and explain that no discomfort will be experienced during the test. Inform the patient that a health-care provider (HCP) performs the test in a quiet, darkened room and that to evaluate both eyes, the test can take up 30 min.

Sensitivity to social and cultural issues, as well as concern for modesty, is important in providing psychological support before, during, and after the procedure.

There are no food, fluid, or medication restrictions unless by medical direction.

INTRATEST:

Observe standard precautions, and follow the general guidelines in Appendix A. Positively identify the patient.

Instruct the patient to cooperate fully and to follow directions. Ask the patient to remain still during the procedure because movement produces unreliable results.

Seat the patient 3 ft away from the tangent screen with the eye being tested directly in line with the central fixation tangent, usually a white disk, on the screen. Cover the eye that is not being tested. Ask the patient to place the chin in the chin rest and gently press the forehead against the support bar. Reposition the patient as appropriate to ensure the eye(s) to be tested are properly aligned in front of the VF testing equipment. While the patient stares at the disk on the screen, the examiner moves an object toward the patient's visual field. The patient signals the examiner when the object enters his or her visual field. The patient's responses are recorded, and a map of the patient's VF, including areas of visual defect, can be drawn on paper manually or by a computer.

POST-TEST:

A report of the results will be made available to the requesting HCP, who will discuss the results with the patient.

Recognize anxiety related to test results, and be supportive of impaired activity related to vision loss, perceived loss of driving privileges, or the possibility of requiring corrective lenses (self-image). Discuss the implications of the test results on the patient's lifestyle. Provide contact information, if desired, for a general patient education Web site on the topic of eye care (e.g., www.allaboutvision.com). Provide contact information regarding vision aids, if desired, for ABLEDATA (sponsored by the National Institute on Disability and Rehabilitation Research [NIDRR], available at www.abledata.com). Information can also be obtained from the American Macular Degeneration Foundation (www.macular.org), the Glaucoma Research Foundation (www.glaucoma.org), and the American Diabetes Association (www.diabetes.org).

Reinforce information given by the patient's HCP regarding further testing, treatment, or referral to another HCP. Answer any questions or address any concerns voiced by the patient or family.

Instruct the patient in the use of any ordered medications. Explain the importance of adhering to the therapy regimen. As appropriate, instruct the patient in significant side effects and systemic reactions associated with the prescribed medication. Encourage him or her to review corresponding literature provided by a pharmacist.

Depending on the results of this procedure, additional testing may be performed to evaluate or monitor progression of the disease process and determine the need for a change in therapy. Evaluate test results in relation to the patient's symptoms and other tests performed.

RELATED MONOGRAPHS:

Related tests include CT brain, EEG, evoked brain potentials, fluorescein angiography, fructosamine, fundus photography, glucagon, glucose, glycated hemoglobin, gonioscopy, insulin, intraocular pressure, microalbumin, plethysmography, PET brain, and slit-lamp biomicroscopy.

Refer to the Ocular System table at the end of the book for related tests by body system.

Vitamin B$_{12}$

SYNONYM/ACRONYM: Cyanocobalamin.

COMMON USE: To assess vitamin B$_{12}$ levels to assist in diagnosing disorders such as pernicious anemia and malabsorption syndromes.

SPECIMEN: Serum (1 mL) collected in a red- or tiger-top tube.

NORMAL FINDINGS: (Method: Immunochemiluminescent assay)

Age	Conventional Units	SI Units (Conventional Units × 0.738)
Newborn–11 mo	160–1,300 pg/mL	118–959 pmol/L
Adult	200–900 pg/mL	148–664 pmol/L

Values tend to decrease in older adults.

DESCRIPTION: Vitamin B$_{12}$ has a ringed crystalline structure that surrounds an atom of cobalt. It is essential in DNA synthesis, hematopoiesis, and central nervous system (CNS) integrity. It is derived solely from dietary intake. Animal products are the richest source of vitamin B$_{12}$. Its absorption depends on the presence of intrinsic factor. Circumstances that may result in a deficiency of this vitamin include the presence of stomach or intestinal disease as well as insufficient dietary intake of foods containing vitamin B$_{12}$. A significant increase in red blood cells (RBCs) mean corpuscular volume may be an important indicator of vitamin B$_{12}$ deficiency.

INDICATIONS

- Assist in the diagnosis of CNS disorders
- Assist in the diagnosis of megaloblastic anemia
- Evaluate alcoholism
- Evaluate malabsorption syndromes

POTENTIAL DIAGNOSIS

Increased in

Increases are noted in a number of conditions; pathophysiology is unclear.

- Chronic granulocytic leukemia
- Chronic obstructive pulmonary disease
- Chronic renal failure
- Diabetes
- Leukocytosis
- Liver cell damage (hepatitis, cirrhosis) *(stores in damaged hepatocytes are released into circulation; synthesis of transport proteins is diminished by liver damage)*
- Obesity
- Polycythemia vera
- Protein malnutrition *(lack of transport proteins increases circulating levels)*
- Severe congestive heart failure
- Some carcinomas

Decreased in

- Abnormalities of cobalamin transport or metabolism
- Bacterial overgrowth *(vitamin is consumed and utilized by the bacteria)*

V

- Crohn's disease *(related to poor absorption)*
- Dietary deficiency *(related to insufficient intake, e.g., in vegetarians)*
- Diphyllobothrium (fish tapeworm) infestation *(vitamin is consumed and utilized by the parasite)*
- Gastric or small intestine surgery *(related to dietary deficiency or poor absorption)*
- Hypochlorhydria *(related to ineffective digestion resulting in poor absorption)*
- Inflammatory bowel disease *(related to dietary deficiency or poor absorption)*
- Intestinal malabsorption
- Intrinsic factor deficiency *(required for proper vitamin B_{12} absorption)*
- Late pregnancy *(related to dietary deficiency or poor absorption)*
- Pernicious anemia *(related to dietary deficiency or poor absorption)*

CRITICAL FINDINGS: N/A

INTERFERING FACTORS

- Drugs that may increase vitamin B_{12} levels include chloral hydrate.
- Drugs that may decrease vitamin B_{12} levels include alcohol, aminosalicylic acid, anticonvulsants, ascorbic acid, cholestyramine, cimetidine, colchicine, metformin, neomycin, oral contraceptives, ranitidine, and triamterene.
- Hemolysis or exposure of the specimen to light invalidates results.
- Specimen collection soon after blood transfusion can falsely increase vitamin B_{12} levels.
- Failure to follow dietary restrictions before the procedure may cause the procedure to be canceled or repeated.

NURSING IMPLICATIONS AND PROCEDURE

PRETEST:

- Positively identify the patient using at least two unique identifiers before providing care, treatment, or services.
- *Patient Teaching:* Inform the patient this test can assist in diagnosing a vitamin toxicity or deficiency.
- Obtain a history of the patient's complaints, including a list of known allergens, especially allergies or sensitivities to latex.
- Obtain a history of the patient's gastrointestinal and hematopoietic systems, symptoms, and results of previously performed laboratory tests and diagnostic and surgical procedures.
- Obtain a list of the patient's current medications, including herbs, nutritional supplements, and nutraceuticals (see Appendix F).
- Review the procedure with the patient. Inform the patient that specimen collection takes approximately 5 to 10 min. Address concerns about pain and explain that there may be some discomfort during the venipuncture.
- *Sensitivity to social and cultural issues,* as well as concern for modesty, is important in providing psychological support before, during, and after the procedure.
- Instruct the patient to fast for at least 12 hr before specimen collection. Protocols may vary among facilities. There are no fluid or medication restrictions unless by medical direction.

INTRATEST:

- Ensure that the patient has complied with dietary restrictions; assure that food has been restricted for at least 12 hr prior to the procedure.
- If the patient has a history of allergic reaction to latex, avoid the use of equipment containing latex.
- Instruct the patient to cooperate fully and to follow directions. Direct the patient to breathe normally and to avoid unnecessary movement.
- Observe standard precautions, and follow the general guidelines in Appendix A. Positively identify the patient, and label the appropriate specimen container with the corresponding patient

demographics, initials of the person collecting the specimen, date, and time of collection. Perform a venipuncture. Protect the specimen from light.

▸ Remove the needle and apply direct pressure with dry gauze to stop bleeding. Observe/assess venipuncture site for bleeding or hematoma formation and secure gauze with adhesive bandage.

▸ Promptly transport the specimen to the laboratory for processing and analysis.

POST-TEST:

▸ A report of the results will be made available to the requesting health-care provider (HCP), who will discuss the results with the patient.

▸ Instruct the patient to resume usual diet, as directed by the HCP.

▸ *Nutritional Considerations:* The Institute of Medicine's Food and Nutrition Board suggests 2.4 mcg as the daily recommended dietary allowance of vitamin B_{12} for adult males and females age 19 to greater than 70 yr; 2.6 mcg/d for pregnant females less than age 18 through age 50 yr; 2.8 mcg/d for lactating females less than age 18 through age 50 yr; 2.4 mcg/d for children age 14 to 18 yr; 1.8 mcg/d for children age 9 to 13 yr; 1.2 mcg/d for children age 4 to 8 yr; 0.9 mcg/d for children age 1 to 3 yr; 0.5 mcg/d for children age 7 to 12 mo (recommended adequate intake); and 0.4 mcg/d for children age 0 to 6 mo (recommended adequate intake). Reprinted with permission from the National Academies Press, copyright 2013, National Academy of Sciences. Instruct the patient with vitamin B_{12} deficiency, as appropriate, in the use of vitamin supplements. Inform the patient, as appropriate, that the best dietary sources of vitamin B_{12} are meats, fish, poultry, eggs, and milk.

▸ Reinforce information given by the patient's HCP regarding further testing, treatment, or referral to another HCP. Answer any questions or address any concerns voiced by the patient or family. Educate the patient regarding access to nutritional counseling services. Provide contact information, if desired, for the Institute of Medicine of the National Academies (www.iom.edu).

▸ Depending on the results of this procedure, additional testing may be performed to evaluate or monitor progression of the disease process and determine the need for a change in therapy. Evaluate test results in relation to the patient's symptoms and other tests performed.

RELATED MONOGRAPHS:

▸ Related tests include CBC, CBC RBC count, CBC RBC indices, CBC RBC morphology, CBC WBC count and differential, folate, gastric acid stimulation, gastrin stimulation, homocysteine, and intrinsic factor antibodies.

▸ Refer to the Gastrointestinal and Hematopoietic systems tables at the end of the book for related tests by body system.

Vitamin D

SYNONYM/ACRONYM: Cholecalciferol, vitamin D 1,25-dihydroxy.

COMMON USE: To assess vitamin D levels toward diagnosing disorders such as vitamin toxicity, malabsorption, and vitamin deficiency.

SPECIMEN: Serum (1 mL) collected in a red-top tube. Plasma (1 mL) collected in a green-top (heparin) tube is also acceptable.

NORMAL FINDINGS: (Method: High-performance liquid chromatography)

Form	Conventional Units	SI Units (Conventional Units × 2.496)
Vitamin D 25-dihydroxy	20–100 ng/mL	49.9–249.6 nmol/L
Deficient	Less than 20 ng/mL	Less than 49.9 nmol/L
Insufficient	20–30 ng/mL	49.9–74.9 nmol/L
Optimal	Greater than 30 ng/mL	Greater than 74.9 nmol/L
Vitamin D 1,25-dihydroxy	15–60 pg/mL	37.4–149.8 pmol/L

DESCRIPTION: Vitamin D is a group of interrelated sterols that have hormonal activity in multiple organs and tissues of the body, including the kidneys, liver, skin, and bones. There are two metabolically active forms of vitamin D: vitamin D 25-dihydroxy and vitamin D 1,25-dihydroxy. Ergocalciferol (vitamin D_2) is formed when ergosterol in plants is exposed to sunlight. Ergocalciferol is absorbed by the stomach and intestine when orally ingested. Cholecalciferol (vitamin D_3) is formed when the skin is exposed to sunlight or ultraviolet light. Vitamins D_2 and D_3 enter the bloodstream after absorption. Vitamin D_3 is converted to vitamin D 25-dihydroxy by the liver and is the major circulating form of the vitamin. Vitamin D_2 is converted to vitamin D 1,25-dihydroxy (calcitriol) by the kidneys and is the more biologically active form. Vitamin D acts with parathyroid hormone and calcitonin to regulate calcium metabolism and osteoblast function. The effects of vitamin D deficiency have been studied for many years, and continued research indicates a link between vitamin D deficiency and the development of diseases such as heart failure, stroke, hypertension, cancer, autism, multiple sclerosis, type 2 diabetes, systemic lupus erythematosus, depression, and immune function.

The amount of vitamin D_3 produced by exposure of the skin to UV radiation depends on the intensity of the radiation as well as the duration of exposure. The use of lotions containing sun block significantly decreases production of vitamin D_3.

INDICATIONS
- Differential diagnosis of disorders of calcium and phosphorus metabolism
- Evaluate deficiency or suspected toxicity
- Investigate bone diseases
- Investigate malabsorption

POTENTIAL DIAGNOSIS

Increased in
- Endogenous vitamin D intoxication *(in conditions such as sarcoidosis, cat scratch disease, and some lymphomas, extrarenal conversion of 25-dihydroxy to 1,25-dihydroxy vitamin D occurs with a corresponding abnormal elevation of calcium)*
- Exogenous vitamin D intoxication

Decreased in
- Bowel resection *(related to lack of absorption)*
- Celiac disease *(related to lack of absorption)*
- Inflammatory bowel disease *(related to lack of absorption)*
- Malabsorption *(related to lack of absorption)*

- Osteomalacia *(related to dietary insufficiency)*
- Pancreatic insufficiency *(lack of digestive enzymes to metabolize fat-soluble vitamin D; malabsorption)*
- Rickets *(related to dietary insufficiency)*
- Thyrotoxicosis *(possibly related to increased calcium loss through sweat, urine, or feces with corresponding decrease in vitamin D levels)*

CRITICAL FINDINGS

Vitamin toxicity can be as significant as problems brought about by vitamin deficiencies. The potential for toxicity is especially important to consider with respect to fat-soluble vitamins, which are not eliminated from the body as quickly as water-soluble vitamins and can accumulate in the body. Most cases of toxicity are brought about by oversupplementing and can be avoided by consulting a qualified nutritionist for recommended daily dietary and supplemental allowances. Signs and symptoms of vitamin D toxicity include nausea, loss of appetite, vomiting, polyuria, muscle weakness, and constipation.

INTERFERING FACTORS

- Drugs that may increase vitamin D levels include pravastatin.

NURSING IMPLICATIONS AND PROCEDURE

PRETEST:

- Positively identify the patient using at least two unique identifiers before providing care, treatment, or services.
- *Patient Teaching:* Inform the patient this test can assist in diagnosing vitamin toxicity or deficiency.
- Obtain a history of the patient's complaints, including a list of known allergens, especially allergies or sensitivities to latex.
- Obtain a history of the patient's gastrointestinal and musculoskeletal systems, symptoms, and results of previously performed laboratory tests and diagnostic and surgical procedures.
- Obtain a list of the patient's current medications, including herbs, nutritional supplements, and nutraceuticals (see Appendix F).
- Review the procedure with the patient. Inform the patient that specimen collection takes approximately 5 to 10 min. Address concerns about pain and explain that there may be some discomfort during the venipuncture.
- *Sensitivity to social and cultural issues,* as well as concern for modesty, is important in providing psychological support before, during, and after the procedure.
- There are no food, fluid, or medication restrictions unless by medical direction.

INTRATEST:

- If the patient has a history of allergic reaction to latex, avoid the use of equipment containing latex.
- Instruct the patient to cooperate fully and to follow directions. Direct the patient to breathe normally and to avoid unnecessary movement.
- Observe standard precautions, and follow the general guidelines in Appendix A. Positively identify the patient, and label the appropriate specimen container with the corresponding patient demographics, initials of the person collecting the specimen, date, and time of collection. Perform a venipuncture.
- Remove the needle and apply direct pressure with dry gauze to stop bleeding. Observe/assess venipuncture site for bleeding or hematoma formation and secure gauze with adhesive bandage.
- Promptly transport the specimen to the laboratory for processing and analysis.

POST-TEST:

- A report of the results will be made available to the requesting health-care provider (HCP), who will discuss the results with the patient.

Nutritional Considerations: The Institute of Medicine's Food and Nutrition Board suggests 50 mcg as the tolerable upper limit for total daily intake of dietary vitamin D for males and females age 1 to greater than 70 yr; 50 mcg/d for pregnant and lactating females under age 18 through 50 yr; and 25 mcg/d for children age 0 to 12 mo. Reprinted with permission from the National Academies Press, copyright 2013, National Academy of Sciences. Educate the patient with vitamin D deficiency, as appropriate, that the main dietary sources of vitamin D are fortified dairy foods and cod liver oil. Explain to the patient that vitamin D is also synthesized by the body, in the skin, and is activated by sunlight. Reinforce information given by the patient's HCP regarding further testing, treatment, or referral to another HCP. Answer any questions or address any concerns voiced by the patient or family. Educate the patient regarding access to nutritional counseling services. Provide contact information, if desired, for the Institute of Medicine of the National Academies (www.iom.edu).

Depending on the results of this procedure, additional testing may be performed to evaluate or monitor progression of the disease process and determine the need for a change in therapy. Evaluate test results in relation to the patient's symptoms and other tests performed.

RELATED MONOGRAPHS:

Related tests include amylase, ANCA, biopsy intestinal, calcium, capsule endoscopy, colonoscopy, fecal analysis, fecal fat, antibodies gliadin antibodies, kidney stone panel, laparoscopy abdominal, lipase, osteocalcin, oxalate, phosphorus, and proctosigmoidoscopy.

Refer to the Gastrointestinal and Musculoskeletal systems tables at the end of the book for related tests by body system.

Vitamin E

SYNONYM/ACRONYM: Tocopherol.

COMMON USE: To assess vitamin E levels to assist in diagnosing vitamin toxicity, malabsorption, neuromuscular disorders, and vitamin deficiency.

SPECIMEN: Serum (1 mL) collected in a red- or tiger-top tube.

NORMAL FINDINGS: (Method: High-performance liquid chromatography)

Age	Conventional Units	SI Units (Conventional Units × 2.322)
Newborn	1–3.5 mg/L	2.3–8.1 micromol/L
Neonate	2.5–3.7	5.8–8.6
2–5 mo	2–6	4.6–13.9
6–12 mo	3.5–8	8.1–18.6
1–6 yr	3–9	7.0–20.9

Age	Conventional Units	SI Units (Conventional Units × 2.322)
7–12 yr	4–9 mg/L	9.3–20.9 micromol/L
13–19 yr	6–10 mg/L	13.9–23.2 micromol/L
Adult	5–18 mg/L	11.6–41.8 micromol/L

Values tend to decrease in older adults.

DESCRIPTION: Vitamin E is a powerful fat-soluble antioxidant that prevents the oxidation of unsaturated fatty acids, which can combine with polysaccharides to form deposits in tissue. For this reason, vitamin E is believed to reduce the risk of coronary artery disease. Vitamin E reserves in lung tissue provide a barrier against air pollution and protect red blood cell (RBC) membrane integrity from oxidation. Oxidation of fatty acids in RBC membranes can result in irreversible membrane damage and hemolysis. Studies are in progress to confirm the suspicion that oxidation also contributes to the formation of cataracts and macular degeneration of the retina. Because vitamin E is found in a wide variety of foods, a deficiency secondary to inadequate dietary intake is rare. Alpha-tocopherol appears to be the most plentiful and important form of eight vitamin E antioxidants; there are four tocopherols (alpha-, beta-, gamma-, and delta-) and four tocotrienols (alpha-, beta-, gamma-, and delta-).

INDICATIONS
• Evaluate neuromuscular disorders in premature infants and adults
• Evaluate patients with malabsorption disorders
• Evaluate suspected hemolytic anemia in premature infants and adults
• Monitor patients on long-term parenteral nutrition

POTENTIAL DIAGNOSIS

Increased in
• Obstructive liver disease *(related to malabsorption associated with obstructive liver disease)*
• Vitamin E intoxication *(related to excessive intake)*

Decreased in
• Abetalipoproteinemia *(rare inherited disorder of fat metabolism evidenced by poor absorption of fat and fat-soluble vitamin E)*
• Hemolytic anemia *(related to deficiency of vitamin E, an important antioxidant that protects RBC cell membranes from weakening)*
• Malabsorption disorders, such as biliary atresia, cirrhosis, cystic fibrosis, chronic pancreatitis, pancreatic carcinoma, and chronic cholestasis

CRITICAL FINDINGS ◈
Vitamin toxicity can be as significant as problems brought about by vitamin deficiencies. The potential for toxicity is especially important to consider with respect to fat-soluble vitamins, which are not eliminated from the body as quickly as water-soluble vitamins and can accumulate in the body. Most cases of toxicity are brought about by oversupplementing and can be avoided by consulting a qualified nutritionist for recommended daily dietary and supplemental allowances. *Note:* Excessive supplementation of vitamin E (greater than 60 times the recommended dietary allowance over a period of 1 yr or longer) can result in excessive

bleeding, delayed healing of wounds, and depression.

INTERFERING FACTORS

- Drugs that may increase vitamin E levels include anticonvulsants (in women).
- Drugs that may decrease vitamin E levels include anticonvulsants (in men).
- Exposure of the specimen to light decreases vitamin E levels, resulting in a falsely low result.

NURSING IMPLICATIONS AND PROCEDURE

PRETEST:

▸ Positively identify the patient using at least two unique identifiers before providing care, treatment, or services.
▸ *Patient Teaching:* Inform the patient this lab test can assist in evaluating vitamin toxicity or deficiency.
▸ Obtain a history of the patient's complaints, including a list of known allergens, especially allergies or sensitivities to latex.
▸ Obtain a history of the patient's cardiovascular, gastrointestinal, hematopoietic, and hepatobiliary systems; symptoms; and results of previously performed laboratory tests and diagnostic and surgical procedures.
▸ Obtain a list of the patient's current medications, including herbs, nutritional supplements, and nutraceuticals (see Appendix F).
▸ Review the procedure with the patient. Inform the patient that specimen collection takes approximately 5 to 10 min. Address concerns about pain and explain that there may be some discomfort during the venipuncture.
▸ *Sensitivity to social and cultural issues,* as well as concern for modesty, is important in providing psychological support before, during, and after the procedure.
▸ There are no food, fluid, or medication restrictions unless by medical direction.

INTRATEST:

▸ If the patient has a history of allergic reaction to latex, avoid the use of equipment containing latex.
▸ Instruct the patient to cooperate fully and to follow directions. Direct the patient to breathe normally and to avoid unnecessary movement.
▸ Observe standard precautions, and follow the general guidelines in Appendix A. Positively identify the patient, and label the appropriate specimen container with the corresponding patient demographics, initials of the person collecting the specimen, date, and time of collection. Perform a venipuncture.
▸ Positively identify the patient, and label the appropriate specimen container with the corresponding patient demographics, initials of the person collecting the specimen, date, and time of collection. Perform a venipuncture.
▸ Remove the needle and apply direct pressure with dry gauze to stop bleeding. Observe/assess venipuncture site for bleeding or hematoma formation and secure gauze with adhesive bandage.
▸ Promptly transport the specimen to the laboratory for processing and analysis.

POST-TEST:

▸ A report of the results will be made available to the requesting health-care provider (HCP), who will discuss the results with the patient.
▸ *Nutritional Considerations:* The Institute of Medicine's Food and Nutrition Board suggests 15 mg as the daily recommended dietary allowance for dietary vitamin E for adult males and females age 19 to greater than 70 yr; 15 mg/d for pregnant females less than age 18 through 50 yr; 19 mg/d for lactating females less than age 18 through 50 yr; 15 mg/d for children age 14–18 yr; 11 mg/d for children age 9 to 13 yr; 7 mg/d for children age 4 to 8 yr; 6 mg/d for children age 1 to 3 yr; 5 mg/d for children age 7 to 12 mo (adequate intake); and 4 mg/d for children age 0 to 6 mo (adequate intake). Reprinted with permission from the National Academies Press, copyright 2013,

National Academy of Sciences. Educate the patient with a vitamin E deficiency, if appropriate, that the main dietary sources of vitamin E are vegetable oils (including olive oil), whole grains, wheat germ, nuts, milk, eggs, meats, fish, and green leafy vegetables. Vitamin E is fairly stable at most cooking temperatures (except frying) and when exposed to acidic foods.

Reinforce information given by the patient's HCP regarding further testing, treatment, or referral to another HCP. Answer any questions or address any concerns voiced by the patient or family. Educate the patient regarding access to nutritional counseling services. Provide contact information, if desired, for the Institute of Medicine of the National Academies (www.iom.edu).

Depending on the results of this procedure, additional testing may be performed to evaluate or monitor progression of the disease process and determine the need for a change in therapy. Evaluate test results in relation to the patient's symptoms and other tests performed.

RELATED MONOGRAPHS:

Related tests include amylase, antibodies gliadin, biopsy bone marrow, biopsy intestinal, capsule endoscopy, colonoscopy, complement, CBC, CBC hematocrit, CBC hemoglobin, CBC RBC count, CBC RBC indices, CBC RBC morphology, Coomb's antiglobulin direct and indirect, fecal analysis, fecal fat, Ham's test, Hgb electrophoresis, laparoscopy abdominal, lipase, osmotic fragility, and proctosigmoidoscopy.

Refer to the Cardiovascular, Gastrointestinal, Hematopoietic, and Hepatobiliary systems tables at the end of the book for related tests by body system.

Vitamin K

SYNONYM/ACRONYM: Phylloquinone, phytonadione.

COMMON USE: Assessment of vitamin K levels to assist in diagnosing bleeding disorders where etiology is unknown, identify vitamin toxicity, and evaluate symptoms related to chronic antibiotic use.

SPECIMEN: Serum (1 mL) collected in a red-top tube.

NORMAL FINDINGS: (Method: High-performance liquid chromatography)

Conventional Units	SI Units (Conventional Units × 2.22)
0.13–1.19 ng/mL	0.29–2.64 nmol/L

DESCRIPTION: Vitamin K is one of the fat-soluble vitamins. It is essential for the formation of prothrombin; factors VII, IX, and X; and proteins C and S. Vitamin K also works with vitamin D in synthesizing bone protein and regulating calcium levels (see monograph titled "Vitamin D.") Vitamin K levels are not often requested, but vitamin K is often prescribed as a medication.

Approximately one-half of the body's vitamin K is produced by intestinal bacteria; the other half is obtained from dietary sources. There are three forms of vitamin K: vitamin K_1, or phylloquinone, which is found in foods; vitamin K_2, or menaquinone, which is synthesized by intestinal bacteria; and vitamin K_3, or menadione, which is the synthetic, water-soluble, pharmaceutical form of the vitamin. Vitamin K_3 is two to three times more potent than the naturally occurring forms.

INDICATIONS
Evaluation of bleeding of unknown cause (e.g., frequent nosebleeds, bruising).

POTENTIAL DIAGNOSIS

Increased in
• Excessive administration of vitamin K

Decreased in
• Antibiotic therapy *(related to decreased intestinal flora)*
• Chronic fat malabsorption *(related to lack of digestive enzymes and poor absorption)*
• Cystic fibrosis *(related to lack of digestive enzymes and poor absorption)*
• Diarrhea (in infants) *(related to increased loss in feces)*
• Gastrointestinal disease *(related to malabsorption)*
• Hemorrhagic disease of the newborn *(newborns normally have low levels of vitamin K; neonates at risk are those who are not given a prophylactic vitamin K shot at birth or those receiving nutrition strictly from breast milk, which has less vitamin K than cow's milk)*
• Hypoprothrombinemia *(related to insufficient levels of prothrombin, a vitamin K–dependent protein)*

• Liver disease *(interferes with storage of vitamin K)*
• Obstructive jaundice *(related to insufficient levels of bile salts required for absorption of vitamin K)*
• Pancreatic disease *(related to insufficient levels of enzymes to metabolize vitamin K)*

CRITICAL FINDINGS
Vitamin toxicity can be as significant as problems brought about by vitamin deficiencies. The potential for toxicity is especially important to consider with respect to fat-soluble vitamins, which are not eliminated from the body as quickly as water-soluble vitamins and can accumulate in the body. The naturally occurring forms, vitamins K_1 and K_2, do not cause toxicity. Signs and symptoms of vitamin K_3 toxicity include bleeding and jaundice. Possible interventions include withholding the source.

INTERFERING FACTORS
• Drugs and substances that may decrease vitamin K levels include antibiotics, cholestyramine, coumarin, mineral oil, and warfarin.

NURSING IMPLICATIONS AND PROCEDURE

PRETEST:
▸ Positively identify the patient using at least two unique identifiers before providing care, treatment, or services.
▸ *Patient Teaching:* Inform the patient this test can assist in evaluating vitamin toxicity or deficiency.
▸ Obtain a history of the patient's complaints, including a list of known allergens, especially allergies or sensitivities to latex.
▸ Obtain a history of the patient's hematopoietic and hepatobiliary systems, symptoms, and results of previously performed laboratory tests and diagnostic and surgical procedures.

V

- Obtain a list of the patient's current medications, including herbs, nutritional supplements, and nutraceuticals (see Appendix F).
- Review the procedure with the patient. Inform the patient that specimen collection takes approximately 5 to 10 min. Address concerns about pain and explain that there may be some discomfort during the venipuncture.
- *Sensitivity to social and cultural issues,* as well as concern for modesty, is important in providing psychological support before, during, and after the procedure.
- There are no food, fluid, or medication restrictions unless by medical direction.

INTRATEST:

- If the patient has a history of allergic reaction to latex, avoid the use of equipment containing latex.
- Instruct the patient to cooperate fully and to follow directions. Direct the patient to breathe normally and to avoid unnecessary movement.
- Observe standard precautions, and follow the general guidelines in Appendix A. Positively identify the patient, and label the appropriate specimen container with the corresponding patient demographics, initials of the person collecting the specimen, date, and time of collection. Perform a venipuncture.
- Remove the needle and apply direct pressure with dry gauze to stop bleeding. Observe/assess venipuncture site for bleeding or hematoma formation and secure gauze with adhesive bandage.
- Promptly transport the specimen to the laboratory for processing and analysis.

POST-TEST:

- A report of the results will be made available to the requesting health-care provider (HCP), who will discuss the results with the patient.
- *Nutritional Considerations:* The Institute of Medicine's Food and Nutrition Board suggests 120 mcg as an adequate daily intake goal of dietary vitamin K for adult males age 19 to greater than 70 yr; 90 mcg/d for adult females age 19 to greater than 70 yr; 90 mcg/d for pregnant and lactating females age 19 to 50 yr; 75 mcg/d for pregnant and lactating females age less than 18 yr; 75 mcg/d for children age 14 to 18 yr; 60 mcg/d for children age 9 to 13 yr; 55 mcg/d for children age 4 to 8 yr; and 30 mcg/d for children age 1 to 3 yr; 2.5 mcg/d for children age 7 to 12 mo; and 2 mcg/d for children age 0 to 6 mo. Reprinted with permission from the National Academies Press, copyright 2013, National Academy of Sciences. Inform the patient with a vitamin K deficiency, as appropriate, that the main dietary sources of vitamin K are broccoli, cabbage, cauliflower, kale, spinach, leaf lettuce, watercress, parsley, and other raw green leafy vegetables, pork, liver, soybeans, mayonnaise and vegetable oils.

- Instruct the patient to report bleeding from any areas of the skin or mucous membranes.
- Inform the patient of the importance of taking precautions against bleeding or bruising, including the use of a soft bristle toothbrush, use of an electric razor, avoidance of constipation, avoidance of aspirin products, and avoidance of intramuscular injections.
- Reinforce information given by the patient's HCP regarding further testing, treatment, or referral to another HCP. Answer any questions or address any concerns voiced by the patient or family. Educate the patient regarding access to nutritional counseling services. Provide contact information, if desired, for the Institute of Medicine of the National Academies (www.iom.edu).
- Depending on the results of this procedure, additional testing may be performed to evaluate or monitor progression of the disease process and determine the need for a change in therapy. Evaluate test results in relation to the patient's symptoms and other tests performed.

RELATED MONOGRAPHS:

- Related tests include ALT, antithrombin III, AST, bilirubin, chloride sweat, CBC, fecal analysis, fecal fat, GGT, and PT/INR.
- Refer to the Hematopoietic and Hepatobiliary systems tables at the end of the book for related tests by body system.

V

Vitamins A, B₁, B₆, and C

SYNONYM/ACRONYM: Vitamin A: retinol, carotene; vitamin B_1: thiamine; vitamin B_6: pyroxidine, P-5 -P, pyridoxyl-5-phosphate; vitamin C: ascorbic acid.

COMMON USE: To assess vitamin deficiency or toxicity to assist in diagnosing nutritional disorders such as malabsorption; disorders that affect vision, skin, and bones; and other diseases.

SPECIMEN: Serum (1 mL) collected in a red-top tube each for vitamins A and C; plasma (1 mL) collected in a lavender-top (EDTA) tube each for vitamins B_1 and B_6.

NORMAL FINDINGS: (Method: High-performance liquid chromatography)

Vitamin	Age	Conventional Units	SI Units
Vitamin A			*(Conventional Units × 0.0349)*
	Birth–1 yr	14–52 mcg/dL	0.49–1.81 micromol/L
	1–6 yr	20–43 mcg/dL	0.7–1.5 micromol/L
	7–12 yr	26–49 mcg/dL	0.91–1.71 micromol/L
	13–19 yr	26–72 mcg/dL	0.91–2.51 micromol/L
	Adult	30–120 mcg/dL	1.05–4.19 micromol/L
Vitamin B_1			*(Conventional Units × 29.6)*
		0.21–0.43 mcg/dL	6.2–12.7 micromol/L
Vitamin B_6			*(Conversion Factor × 4.046)*
		5–30 ng/mL	20–121 nmol/L
Vitamin C			*(Conventional Units × 56.78)*
		0.6–1.9 mg/dL	34.1–107.9 micromol/L

Vitamin B_1, vitamin B_6, and vitamin C levels tend to decrease in older adults.

DESCRIPTION: Vitamin assays are used in the measurement of nutritional status. Low levels indicate inadequate oral intake, poor nutritional status, or malabsorption problems. High levels indicate excessive intake, vitamin intoxication, or absorption problems. Vitamin A is a fat-soluble nutrient that promotes normal vision and prevents night blindness; contributes to growth of bone, teeth, and soft tissues; supports thyroxine formation; maintains epithelial cell membranes, skin, and mucous membranes; and acts as an anti-infection agent. Vitamins B_1, B_6, and C are water soluble. Vitamin B_1 acts as an enzyme and plays an important role in the Krebs cycle of cellular metabolism. Vitamin B_6 is important in heme synthesis and functions as a coenzyme in amino acid metabolism and glycogenolysis. It includes pyridoxine, pyridoxal, and pyridoxamine. Vitamin C promotes collagen synthesis, maintains capillary strength, facilitates release of iron from ferritin to form hemoglobin, and functions in the stress response.

INDICATIONS

Vitamin A
- Assist in the diagnosis of night blindness
- Evaluate skin disorders
- Investigate suspected vitamin A deficiency

Vitamin B₁
- Investigate suspected beriberi
- Monitor the effects of chronic alcoholism

Vitamin B₆
- Investigate suspected malabsorption or malnutrition
- Investigate suspected vitamin B₆ deficiency

Vitamin C
- Investigate suspected metabolic or malabsorptive disorders
- Investigate suspected scurvy

POTENTIAL DIAGNOSIS

Increased in
- Vitamin A:
  Chronic kidney disease
  Idiopathic hypercalcemia in infants
  Vitamin A toxicity

Decreased in
- Vitamin A:
  Abetalipoproteinemia *(related to poor absorption)*
  Carcinoid syndrome *(related to poor absorption)*
  Chronic infections *(vitamin A deficiency decreases ability to fight infection)*
  Cystic fibrosis *(related to poor absorption)*
  Disseminated tuberculosis *(related to poor absorption)*
  Hypothyroidism *(condition decreases ability of beta carotene to convert to vitamin A)*
  Infantile blindness *(related to dietary deficiency)*
  Liver, gastrointestinal (GI), or pancreatic disease *(related to malabsorption or poor absorption)*

Night blindness *(related to chronic dietary deficiency or lack of absorption)*
Protein malnutrition *(related to dietary deficiency)*
Sterility and teratogenesis *(related to dietary deficiency)*
Zinc deficiency *(zinc is required for generation of vitamin A transport proteins)*

- Vitamin B₁:
  Alcoholism *(related to dietary deficiency)*
  Carcinoid syndrome *(related to dietary deficiency or lack of absorption)*
  Hartnup's disease *(related to dietary deficiency)*
  Pellagra *(related to dietary deficiency)*

- Vitamin B₆ *(this vitamin is involved in many essential functions, such as nucleic acid synthesis, enzyme activation, antibody production, electrolyte balance, and RBC formation; deficiencies result in a variety of conditions):*
  Alcoholism *(related to dietary deficiency)*
  Asthma
  Carpal tunnel syndrome
  Gestational diabetes
  Lactation *(related to dietary deficiency and/or increased demand)*
  Malabsorption
  Malnutrition
  Neonatal seizures
  Normal pregnancies *(related to dietary deficiency and/or increased demand)*
  Occupational exposure to hydrazine compounds *(enzymatic pathways are altered by hydralazines in a manner that increases excretion of vitamin B₆)*
  Pellagra *(related to dietary deficiency)*
  Pre-eclamptic edema
  Renal dialysis
  Uremia

- Vitamin C:
  Alcoholism *(related to dietary deficiency)*
  Anemia *(related to dietary deficiency)*
  Cancer *(related to dietary deficiency or lack of absorption)*

Hemodialysis *(vitamin C is lost during the treatment)*

Hyperthyroidism *(related to dietary deficiency and/or increased demand)*

Malabsorption

Pregnancy *(related to dietary deficiency and/or increased demand)*

Rheumatoid disease

Scurvy *(related to dietary deficiency or lack of absorption)*

CRITICAL FINDINGS

Vitamin toxicity can be as significant as problems brought about by vitamin deficiencies. The potential for toxicity is especially important to consider with respect to fat-soluble vitamins (A, D, E, and K), which are not eliminated from the body as quickly as water-soluble vitamins and can accumulate in the body. Most cases of toxicity are brought about by oversupplementing and can be avoided by consulting a qualified nutritionist for recommended daily dietary and supplemental allowances. Signs and symptoms of vitamin A toxicity may include headache, blurred vision, bone pain, joint pain, dry skin, and loss of appetite.

INTERFERING FACTORS

- Drugs and substances that may increase vitamin A levels include alcohol (moderate intake), oral contraceptives, and probucol.
- Drugs and substances that may decrease vitamin A levels include alcohol (chronic intake, alcoholism), allopurinol, cholestyramine, colestipol, mineral oil, and neomycin.
- Drugs that may decrease vitamin B_1 levels include glibenclamide, isoniazid, and valproic acid.
- Drugs that may decrease vitamin B_6 levels include amiodarone, anticonvulsants, cycloserine, disulfiram, ethanol, hydralazine, isoniazid, levodopa, oral contraceptives,

penicillamine, pyrazinoic acid, and theophylline.

- Drugs and substances that may decrease vitamin C levels include acetylsalicylic acid, aminopyrine, barbiturates, estrogens, heavy metals, oral contraceptives, nitrosamines, and paraldehyde.
- Chronic tobacco smoking decreases vitamin C levels.
- Various diseases may affect vitamin levels (see Potential Diagnosis section).
- Diets high in freshwater fish and tea, which are thiamine antagonists, may cause decreased vitamin B_1 levels.
- Long-term hyperalimentation may result in decreased vitamin levels.
- Exposure of the specimen to light decreases vitamin levels, resulting in a falsely low results.

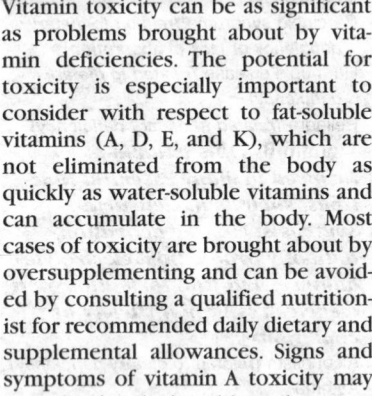

NURSING IMPLICATIONS AND PROCEDURE

PRETEST:

- Positively identify the patient using at least two unique identifiers before providing care, treatment, or services.
- *Patient Teaching:* Inform the patient this test can assist in evaluating vitamin toxicity or deficiency.
- Obtain a history of the patient's complaints, including a list of known allergens, especially allergies or sensitivities to latex.
- Obtain a history of the patient's gastrointestinal, genitourinary, hepatobiliary, immune, and musculoskeletal systems; symptoms; and results of previously performed laboratory tests and diagnostic and surgical procedures.
- Obtain a list of the patient's current medications, including herbs, nutritional supplements, and nutraceuticals (see Appendix F).
- Review the procedure with the patient. Inform the patient that specimen collection takes approximately 5 to

10 min. Address concerns about pain and explain that there may be some discomfort during the venipuncture. *Sensitivity to social and cultural issues,* as well as concern for modesty, is important in providing psychological support before, during, and after the procedure.

▶ Instruct the patient to fast for at least 12 hr before specimen collection for vitamin A.

▶ There are no fluid or medication restrictions unless by medical direction.

INTRATEST:

▶ Ensure that the patient has complied with dietary restrictions; assure that food has been restricted for at least 12 hr prior to the vitamin A test.

▶ If the patient has a history of allergic reaction to latex, avoid the use of equipment containing latex.

▶ Instruct the patient to cooperate fully and to follow directions. Direct the patient to breathe normally and to avoid unnecessary movement.

▶ Observe standard precautions, and follow the general guidelines in Appendix A. Positively identify the patient, and label the appropriate specimen container with the corresponding patient demographics, initials of the person collecting the specimen, date, and time of collection. Perform a venipuncture.

▶ Remove the needle and apply direct pressure with dry gauze to stop bleeding. Observe/assess venipuncture site for bleeding or hematoma formation and secure gauze with adhesive bandage.

▶ Promptly transport the specimen to the laboratory for processing and analysis.

POST-TEST:

▶ A report of the results will be made available to the requesting health-care provider (HCP), who will discuss the results with the patient.

▶ *Nutritional Considerations:* Educate patient with a specific vitamin deficiency,

as appropriate, regarding dietary sources of these vitamins. Advise the patient to ask a nutritionist to develop a diet plan recommended for his or her specific needs.

Vitamin A

Nutritional Considerations: The Institute of Medicine's Food and Nutrition Board suggests 900 mcg as the daily recommended dietary allowance for vitamin A for males age 14 to greater than 70 yr and 700 mcg/d for females age 14 to greater than 70 yr; 770 mcg/d for pregnant females age 19 to 50 yr; 750 mcg/d for pregnant females under age 19 yr; 1,300 mcg/d for lactating females age 19 to 50 yr; 1,200 mcg/d for lactating females under age 18 yr; 600 mcg/d for children age 9 to 13 yr; 400 mcg/d for children age 4 to 8 yr; 300 mcg/d for children age 1 to 3 yr; 500 mcg/d for children age 7 to 12 mo (recommended adequate intake); and 400 mcg/d for children age 0 to 6 mo (recommended adequate intake). Reprinted with permission from the National Academies Press, copyright 2013, National Academy of Sciences. Educate the patient with vitamin A deficiency, as appropriate, that the main dietary source of vitamin A is carotene, a yellow pigment noticeable in most fruits and vegetables, especially carrots, sweet potatoes, squash, apricots, and cantaloupe. It is also present in spinach, collards, broccoli, and cabbage. This vitamin is fairly stable at most cooking temperatures, but it is destroyed easily by light and oxidation.

Vitamin B₁

Vitamin B₁ is the most stable with respect to the effects of environmental factors. Nutritional Considerations: The Institute of Medicine's Food and Nutrition Board suggests 1.2 mg as the daily recommended dietary allowance for dietary vitamin B₁ for males age 14 to greater than 70 yr and 1.1 mg/d for females age 19 to greater than 70 yr; 1.4 mg/d for pregnant and lactating females less than age 18 through 50 yr; 1 mg/d for females age 14 to 18 yr; 0.9 mg/d for children age 9 to 13 yr; 0.6 mg/d for children age 4 to 8 yr; 0.5 mg/d for children age 1 to 3 yr; 0.3 mg/d for children age 7 to 12 mo (recommended adequate intake); and 0.2 mg/d for children age 0 to 6 mo (recommended adequate intake). Reprinted with permission from the National Academies Press, copyright 2013, National Academy of Sciences. Educate the patient with vitamin A deficiency, as appropriate, that the main dietary sources of vitamin B_1 are meats, coffee, peanuts, and legumes. The body is also capable of making some vitamin B_1 by converting the amino acid tryptophan to niacin.

Vitamin B_6

Nutritional Considerations: The Institute of Medicine's Food and Nutrition Board suggests 1.7 mg as the daily recommended dietary allowance for dietary vitamin B_6 for adult males and 1.5 mg/d for adult females age 51 to greater than 70 yr; 1.3 mg/d for adult males and females age 19 to 50 yr; 1.9 mg/d for pregnant females less than age 18 through 50 yr; 2.0 mg/d for lactating females less than age 18 through 50 yr; 1.3 mg/d for male children and 1.2 mg/d for female children age 14 to 18 yr; 1.0 mg/d for children age 9 to 13 yr; 0.6 mg/d for children age 4 to 8 yr; 0.5 mg/d for children age 1 to 3 yr; 0.3 mg/d for children age 7 to 12 mo (recommended adequate intake); and 0.1 mg/d for children age 0 to 6 mo (recommended adequate intake). Reprinted with permission from the National Academies Press, copyright 2013, National Academy of Sciences. Educate the patient with vitamin B_6 deficiency, as appropriate, that the main dietary sources of vitamin B_6 include meats (especially beef and pork), whole grains, wheat germ, legumes (beans, peas, lentils), potatoes, oatmeal, and bananas. As with other water-soluble vitamins, it is best preserved by rapid cooking, although it is relatively stable at most cooking temperatures (except frying) and when exposed to acidic

foods. This vitamin is destroyed rapidly by light and alkalis.

Vitamin C

Nutritional Considerations: The Institute of Medicine's Food and Nutrition Board suggests 90 mg as the daily recommended dietary allowance for dietary vitamin C for adult males and 75 mg/d for adult females age 19 to greater than 70 yr; 85 mg/d for pregnant females age 19 to 50 yr; 80 mg/d for pregnant females under age 19 yr; 120 mg/d for lactating females age 19 to 50 yr; 115 mg/d for lactating females under age 19 yr; 75 mg/d for male children and 65 mg/d for female children age 14 to 18 yr; 45 mg/d for children age 9 to 13 yr; 25 mg/d for children age 4 to 8 yr; 15 mg/d for children age 1 to 3 yr; 50 mg/d for children age 7 to 12 mo (recommended adequate intake); 40 mg/d for children age 0 to 6 mo (recommended adequate intake). Reprinted with permission from the National Academies Press, copyright 2013, National Academy of Sciences. Educate the patient with vitamin C deficiency, as appropriate, that citrus fruits are excellent dietary sources of vitamin C. Other good sources are green and red peppers, tomatoes, white potatoes, cabbage, broccoli, chard, kale, turnip greens, asparagus, berries, melons, pineapple, and guava. Vitamin C is destroyed by exposure to air, light, heat, or alkalis. Boiling water before cooking eliminates dissolved oxygen that destroys vitamin C in the process of boiling. Vegetables should be crisp and cooked as quickly as possible.

General

Reinforce information given by the patient's HCP regarding further testing, treatment, or referral to another HCP. Answer any questions or address any concerns voiced by the patient or family. Educate the patient regarding access to nutritional counseling services. Provide contact information, if desired, for the Institute of Medicine of the National Academies (www.iom.edu).

▶ Depending on the results of this procedure, additional testing may be performed to evaluate or monitor progression of the disease process and determine the need for a change in therapy. Evaluate test results in relation to the patient's symptoms and other tests performed.

RELATED MONOGRAPHS:

▶ Related tests include amylase, BUN, chloride sweat, CBC, creatinine, lipase, prealbumin, TSH, FT_4, and zinc.

▶ Refer to the Gastrointestinal, Genitourinary, Hepatobiliary, Immune, and Musculoskeletal systems tables at the end of the book for related tests by body system.

White Blood Cell Scan

SYNONYM/ACRONYM: Infection scintigraphy, inflammatory scan, labeled autologous leukocytes, labeled leukocyte scan, WBC imaging.

COMMON USE: To assist in identification of abscess, infection, and inflammation of the bone, bowel, wound, and skin.

AREA OF APPLICATION: Whole body.

CONTRAST: IV radionuclide combined with white blood cells.

DESCRIPTION: Because white blood cells (WBCs) naturally accumulate in areas of inflammation, the WBC scan uses radiolabeled WBCs to help determine the site of an acute infection or confirm the presence or absence of infection or inflammation at a suspected site. A gamma camera detects the radiation emitted from the injected radionuclide, and a representative image of the radionuclide distribution is obtained and recorded or stored electronically. Because of its better image resolution and greater specificity for acute infections, the WBC scan has replaced scanning with gallium-67 citrate (Ga-67). Some chronic infections associated with pulmonary disease, however, may be better imaged with Ga-67. The WBC scan is especially helpful in detecting postoperative infection sites and in documenting lack of residual infection after a course of therapy.

INDICATIONS

- Aid in the diagnosis of infectious or inflammatory diseases
- Differentiate infectious from noninfectious process
- Evaluate the effects of treatment
- Evaluate inflammatory bowel disease (IBD)
- Evaluate patients with fever of unknown origin
- Evaluate postsurgical sites and wound infections
- Evaluate suspected infection of an orthopedic prosthesis
- Evaluate suspected osteomyelitis

POTENTIAL DIAGNOSIS

Normal findings in
- No focal localization of the radionuclide, along with some slight localization of the radionuclide within the reticuloendothelial system (liver, spleen, and bone marrow)

Abnormal findings in
- Abscess
- Arthritis
- Infection
- Inflammation
- IBD
- Osteomyelitis

CRITICAL FINDINGS: N/A

INTERFERING FACTORS

This procedure is contraindicated for
- Patients who are pregnant or suspected of being pregnant, unless the potential benefits of the procedure far outweigh the risks to the fetus and mother.

Factors that may impair clear imaging
- Inability of the patient to cooperate or remain still during the procedure because of age, significant pain, or mental status.

W

- Retained barium from a previous radiological procedure, which may inhibit visualization of an abdominal lesion.
- Metallic objects (e.g., jewelry, body rings) within the examination field, which may inhibit organ visualization and cause unclear images.
- Other nuclear scans done within 48 hr and Ga-67 scans within 4 wk before the procedure.
- Lesions smaller than 1 to 2 cm, which may not be detectable.
- A distended bladder, which may obscure pelvic detail.

Other considerations

- Improper injection of the radionuclide that allows the tracer to seep deep into the muscle tissue produces erroneous hot spots.
- Patients with a low WBC count may need donor WBCs to complete the radionuclide labeling process; otherwise, Ga-67 scanning should be performed instead.
- False-negative images may be a result of hemodialysis, hyperglycemia, hyperalimentation, steroid therapy, and antibiotic therapy.
- The presence of multiple myeloma or thyroid cancer can result in a false-negative scan for bone abnormalities.
- Consultation with a health-care provider (HCP) should occur before the procedure for radiation safety concerns regarding younger patients or patients who are lactating.
- Risks associated with radiation overexposure can result from frequent x-ray or radionuclide procedures. Personnel working in the examination area should wear badges to record their level of radiation exposure.

NURSING IMPLICATIONS AND PROCEDURE

PRETEST:

▷ Positively identify the patient using at least two unique identifiers before providing care, treatment, or services.

▷ *Patient Teaching:* Inform the patient this test can assist in assessing for the presence of infection or inflammation.

▷ Obtain a history of the patient's complaints, including a list of known allergens, especially allergies or sensitivities to latex, iodine, seafood, contrast medium, or anesthetics.

▷ Obtain a history of the patient's immune system, symptoms, and results of previously performed laboratory tests and diagnostic and surgical procedures.

▷ Note any recent procedures that can interfere with test results, including barium examinations.

▷ Record the date of the last menstrual period and determine the possibility of pregnancy in perimenopausal women.

▷ Obtain a list of the patient's current medications, including anticoagulant therapy, aspirin and other salicylates, herbs, nutritional supplements, and nutraceuticals (see Appendix F). Note the last time and dose of medication taken.

▷ Review the procedure with the patient. Address concerns about pain related to the procedure and explain that some pain may be experienced during the test, and there may be moments of discomfort. Reassure the patient that the radionuclide poses no radioactive hazard and rarely produces side effects. Inform the patient that the procedure is performed in a nuclear medicine department by an HCP. It usually takes approximately 1 to 6 hr, and delayed images are needed 24 hr later. The patient may leave the department and return later to undergo delayed imaging.

▷ *Sensitivity to social and cultural issues,* as well as concern for modesty, is important in providing psychological

W

support before, during, and after the procedure.

▶ Instruct the patient to remove jewelry and other metallic objects from the area to be examined.

▶ There are no dietary or medication restrictions prior to the procedure, unless by medical direction.

Make sure a written and informed consent has been signed prior to the procedure and before administering any medications.

INTRATEST:

▶ Observe standard precautions, and follow the general guidelines in Appendix A. Positively identify the patient.

▶ Ensure the patient has removed all external metallic objects prior to the procedure.

▶ If the patient has a history of allergic reactions to any substance or drug, administer ordered prophylactic steroids or antihistamines before the procedure.

▶ Have emergency equipment readily available.

▶ Instruct the patient to void prior to the procedure and to change into the gown, robe, and foot coverings provided.

▶ Administer sedative to a child or to an uncooperative adult, as ordered.

▶ On the day of the test, draw a 50- to 80-mL sample of blood for separating the WBCs from the blood and an in vitro process of labeling with radionuclide.

▶ IV radionuclide-labeled autologous WBCs are administered.

▶ Images are recorded 1 to 6 hr post-injection depending on the radionuclide used. Delayed images may be required at 24 hr after the injection.

▶ Remove the needle or catheter and apply a pressure dressing over the puncture site.

▶ Observe/assess the needle/catheter insertion site for bleeding, inflammation, or hematoma formation.

▶ If abdominal abscess or infection is suspected, laxatives or enemas may be ordered before delayed imaging.

POST-TEST:

▶ A report of the results will be made available to the requesting HCP, who will discuss the results with the patient.

▶ Unless contraindicated, advise patient to drink increased amounts of fluids for 24 to 48 hr to eliminate the radionuclide from the body. Inform the patient that radionuclide is eliminated from the body within 6 to 24 hr.

▶ No other radionuclide tests should be scheduled for 24 to 48 hr after this procedure.

▶ Observe/assess the needle/catheter insertion site for bleeding, inflammation, or hematoma formation.

▶ Instruct the patient in the care and assessment of the injection site.

▶ If a woman who is breastfeeding must have a nuclear scan, she should not breastfeed the infant until the radionuclide has been eliminated. This could take as long as 3 days. She should be instructed to express the milk and discard it during the 3-day period to prevent cessation of milk production.

▶ Instruct the patient to immediately flush the toilet and to meticulously wash hands with soap and water after each voiding for 24 hr after the procedure.

▶ Instruct all caregivers to wear gloves when discarding urine for 24 hr after the procedure. Wash gloved hands with soap and water before removing gloves. Then wash hands after the gloves are removed.

▶ Recognize anxiety related to test results, and be supportive of perceived loss of independent function. Discuss the implications of abnormal test results on the patient's lifestyle. Provide teaching and information regarding the clinical implications of the test results, as appropriate.

▶ Reinforce information given by the patient's HCP regarding further testing, treatment, or referral to another HCP. Answer any questions or address any concerns voiced by the patient or family.

▶ Depending on the results of this procedure, additional testing may be needed to evaluate or monitor progression of the disease process and determine the need for a change in therapy. Evaluate test results in relation to the patient's symptoms and other tests performed.

RELATED MONOGRAPHS:

Related tests include angiography pulmonary, bone scan, colonoscopy, CBC, CBC WBC count and differential, CT abdomen, CT pelvis, CT spine, culture (blood, skin, wound), ESR, fecal analysis, gallium scan, GI blood loss scan, KUB, MRI musculoskeletal, MRI pelvis, MRI spine, proctosigmoidoscopy, radiography bone, US abdomen, US pelvis, and vitamin D.

Refer to the Immune System table at the end of the book for related tests by body system.

W

Zinc

SYNONYM/ACRONYM: Zn.

COMMON USE: To assist in assessing for vitamin deficiency or toxicity, monitor therapeutic interventions, and assist in diagnosing disorders such as acrodermatitis enteropathica.

SPECIMEN: Serum (1 mL) collected in a trace element-free, royal blue-top tube.

NORMAL FINDINGS: (Method: Atomic absorption spectrophotometry)

Age	Conventional Units	SI Units (Conventional Units × 0.153)
Newborn–6 mo	26–141 mcg/dL	4–21.6 micromol/L
6–11 mo	29–131 mcg/dL	4.4–20 micromol/L
1–4 yr	31–115 mcg/dL	4.7–17.6 micromol/L
4–5 yr	48–119 mcg/dL	7.3–18.2 micromol/L
6–9 yr	48–129 mcg/dL	7.3–19.7 micromol/L
10–13 yr	25–148 mcg/dL	3.8–22.6 micromol/L
14–17 yr	46–130 mcg/dL	7–19.9 micromol/L
Adult	70–120 mcg/dL	10.7–18.4 micromol/L

DESCRIPTION: Zinc is found in all body tissues, but the highest concentrations are found in the eye, bone, and male reproductive organs. Zinc is involved in RNA and DNA synthesis and is essential in the process of tissue repair. It is also required for the formation of collagen and the production of active vitamin A (for the visual pigment rhodopsin). Zinc also functions as a chelating agent to protect the body from lead and cadmium poisoning. Zinc is absorbed from the small intestine. Its absorption and excretion seem to be through the same sites as those for iron and copper. The body does not store zinc as it does copper and iron. Untreated zinc deficiency in infants may result in a condition called acrodermatitis enteropathica. Symptoms include growth retardation, diarrhea, impaired wound healing, and frequent infections. Adolescents and adults with zinc deficiency exhibit similar adverse effects on growth, sexual development, and immune function, as well as altered taste and smell, emotional instability, impaired adaptation to darkness, impaired night vision, tremors, and a bullous, pustular rash over the extremities.

INDICATIONS
- Assist in confirming acrodermatitis enteropathica
- Evaluate nutritional deficiency
- Evaluate possible toxicity
- Monitor replacement therapy in individuals with identified deficiencies
- Monitor therapy of individuals with Wilson's disease

POTENTIAL DIAGNOSIS

Increased in
Zinc is contained in and secreted by numerous types of cells in the body. Damaged cells release zinc into circulation and increase blood levels.

- Anemia *(related to competitive relationship with copper; copper deficiency is associated with decreased production of red blood cells)*

Decreased in

This trace metal is an essential component of enzymes that participate in protein and carbohydrate metabolism. It is involved in DNA replication, insulin storage, carbon dioxide gas exchange, cellular immunity and healing, promotion of body growth, and sexual maturity. Deficiencies result in a variety of conditions.

- Acrodermatitis enteropathica *(congenital abnormality that affects zinc uptake and results in zinc deficiency)*
- AIDS
- Acute infections
- Acute stress
- Burns
- Cirrhosis
- Conditions that decrease albumin *(related to lack of available transport proteins)*
- Diabetes
- Long-term total parenteral nutrition
- Malabsorption
- Myocardial infarction
- Nephrotic syndrome
- Nutritional deficiency
- Pregnancy *(related to increased uptake by fetus; related to excessive levels of iron and folic acid prescribed during pregnancy and which interfere with absorption)*
- Pulmonary tuberculosis

CRITICAL FINDINGS: N/A

INTERFERING FACTORS

- Drugs that may increase zinc levels include auranofin, chlorthalidone, corticotropin, oral contraceptives, and penicillamine.

- Drugs that may decrease zinc levels include anticonvulsants, cisplatin, citrates, corticosteroids, estrogens, interferon, oral contraceptives, and prednisone.

NURSING IMPLICATIONS AND PROCEDURE

PRETEST:

- Positively identify the patient using at least two unique identifiers before providing care, treatment, or services.
- *Patient Teaching:* Inform the patient this test can assist in evaluating for disorders associated with abnormal zinc levels and monitor response to therapy.
- Obtain a history of the patient's complaints, including a list of known allergens, especially allergies or sensitivities to latex.
- Obtain a history of the patient's gastrointestinal, hepatobiliary, immune, and musculoskeletal systems; symptoms; and results of previously performed laboratory tests and diagnostic and surgical procedures.
- Obtain a list of the patient's current medications, including herbs, nutritional supplements, and nutraceuticals (see Appendix F).
- Review the procedure with the patient. Inform the patient that specimen collection takes approximately 5 to 10 min. Address concerns about pain and explain that there may be some discomfort during the venipuncture.
- *Sensitivity to social and cultural issues,* as well as concern for modesty, is important in providing psychological support before, during, and after the procedure.
- There are no food, fluid, or medication restrictions unless by medical direction.

INTRATEST:

- If the patient has a history of allergic reaction to latex, avoid the use of equipment containing latex.
- Instruct the patient to cooperate fully and to follow directions. Direct the patient to breathe normally and to avoid unnecessary movement.

▶ Observe standard precautions, and follow the general guidelines in Appendix A. Positively identify the patient, and label the appropriate specimen container with the corresponding patient demographics, initials of the person collecting the specimen, date, and time of collection. Perform a venipuncture.

▶ Remove the needle and apply direct pressure with dry gauze to stop bleeding. Observe/assess venipuncture site for bleeding or hematoma formation and secure gauze with adhesive bandage.

▶ Promptly transport the specimen to the laboratory for processing and analysis.

POST-TEST:

▶ A report of the results will be made available to the requesting health-care provider (HCP), who will discuss the results with the patient.

▶ *Nutritional Considerations:* Topical or oral supplementation may be ordered for patients with zinc deficiency. The Institute of Medicine's Food and Nutrition Board suggests 11 mg as the daily recommended dietary allowance for dietary zinc for males age 14 to greater than 50 yr; 8 mg/d for adult females age 19 to greater than 50 yr; 11 mg/d for pregnant females age 19 to 50 yr; 12 mg/d for pregnant females age 14 to 18 yr; 12 mg/d for lactating females age 19 to 50 yr; 13 mg/d for lactating females age 14 to 18 yr; 9 mg/d for females age 14 to 18 yr; 8 mg/d for children age 9 to 13 yr; 5 mg/d for children age 4 to 8 yr; 3 mg/d for children age 7 mo to 3 yr; 2 mg/d for children age 0 to 6 mo.

Reprinted with permission from the National Academies Press, copyright 2013, National Academy of Sciences. Dietary sources high in zinc include shellfish, red meat, wheat germ, nuts, and processed foods such as canned pork and beans and canned chili. Patients should be informed that phytates (from whole grains, coffee, cocoa, or tea) bind zinc and prevent it from being absorbed. Decreases in zinc also can be induced by increased intake of iron, copper, or manganese. Vitamin and mineral supplements with a greater than 3:1 iron/zinc ratio inhibit zinc absorption.

▶ Reinforce information given by the patient's HCP regarding further testing, treatment, or referral to another HCP. Answer any questions or address any concerns voiced by the patient or family. Educate the patient regarding access to nutritional counseling services. Provide contact information, if desired, for the Institute of Medicine of the National Academies (www.iom.edu).

▶ Depending on the results of this procedure, additional testing may be performed to evaluate or monitor progression of the disease process and determine the need for a change in therapy. Evaluate test results in relation to the patient's symptoms and other tests performed.

RELATED MONOGRAPHS:

▶ Related tests include albumin, CBC, CBC WBC and differential, copper, iron, and vitamin A.

▶ Refer to the Gastrointestinal, Immune, Hepatobiliary, and Musculoskeletal systems tables at the end of the book for related tests by body system.

System Tables

Auditory System

Laboratory Tests Associated With the Auditory System

Antimicrobial drugs—aminoglycosides: amikacin, gentamicin, tobramycin; tricyclic glycopeptide: vancomycin, 139–144
Culture, bacterial, anal/genital, ear, eye, skin, and wound, 565–571
Newborn screening, 1023–1050
Zinc, 1446–1448

Diagnostic Tests Associated With the Auditory System

Audiometry hearing loss, 170–174
Computed tomography, brain, 479–484
Evoked brain potentials, 679–682
Magnetic resonance imaging, brain, 983–987
Otoscopy, 1059–1062
Spondee speech reception threshold, 1256–1258
Tuning fork tests, 1313–1316

Cardiovascular System

Laboratory Tests Associated With the Cardiovascular System

Alveolar/arterial gradient, 33–36
Anion gap, 87–89
Antiarrhythmic drugs, 90–97
Apolipoproteins; A, B, and E, 154–158
Aspartate aminotransferase, 165–169
Atrial natriuretic peptide, 169–170
Blood gases, 253–264
B-type natriuretic peptide, 287–290
Calcium, blood, 294–299
Calcium, ionized, 299–303
Carbon dioxide, 317–321
Chloride, blood, 347–351
Cholesterol, HDL and LDL, 367–372
Cholesterol, total, 372–376
Complete blood count, 410–419
Complete blood count, hematocrit, 420–426
Complete blood count, hemoglobin, 426–432
Complete blood count, RBC count, 439–446
C-reactive protein, 539–542
Creatine kinase and isoenzymes, 542–546
D-Dimer, 616–618
Digoxin, 90–97
Disopyramide, 90–97
Erythrocyte sedimentation rate, 664–668
Fibrinogen degradation products, 709–712
Flecainide, 90–97
Homocysteine and methylmalonic acid, 813–816
International normalized ratio (INR), 1179–1184
Lactate dehydrogenase and isoenzymes, 889
Lactic acid, 890–893
Lidocaine, 90–97
Lipoprotein(a), 372–376
Lipoprotein electrophoresis, 916
Magnesium, blood, 941–944
Myoglobin, 1017–1020
Pericardial fluid analysis, 1086–1090
Potassium, blood, 1139–1144
Procainamide, 90–97
Prothrombin time and INR, 1179–1184
Quinidine, 90–97
Sodium, blood, 1248–1251
Triglycerides, 1297–1301
Troponins I and T, 1306–1309
Vitamin E, 1433–1435

SYS

Diagnostic Tests Associated With the Cardiovascular System

Angiography, abdomen, 60–64
Angiography, carotid, 69–73
Angiography, coronary, 73–77
Angiography, pulmonary, 78–81
Blood pool imaging, 270–275
Chest x-ray, 341–344
Computed tomography, angiography, 470–475
Computed tomography, cardiac scoring, 484–488
Echocardiography, 632–635
Echocardiography, transesophageal, 636–640
Electrocardiogram, 640–646
Exercise stress test, 682–687
Holter monitor, 810–812
Magnetic resonance angiography, 948–952
Magnetic resonance imaging, brain, 956–960
Magnetic resonance imaging, chest, 964–968

Magnetic resonance imaging, venography, 983–987
Myocardial infarct scan, 1007–1011
Myocardial perfusion heart scan, 1012–1017
Plethysmography, 1107–1112
Positron emission tomography, fluorodeoxyglucose, 1121–1125
Positron emission tomography, heart, 1130–1135
Pulmonary function studies, 1186–1192
Pulse oximetry, 1192–1194
Ultrasound, abdomen, 1317–1320
Ultrasound, arterial Doppler, carotid studies, 1320–1323
Ultrasound, arterial Doppler, lower and upper extremity studies, 1323–1327
Ultrasound, venous Doppler, extremity studies, 1368–1372
Venography, lower extremity studies, 1414–1418

Endocrine System

Laboratory Tests Associated With the Endocrine System

Adrenocorticotropic hormone (and challenge tests), 8–14
Aldosterone, 22–26
Angiotensin-converting enzyme, 86–87
Anion gap, 87–89
Antibodies, antithyroglobulin and antithyroid peroxidase, 114–116
Antidiuretic hormone, 136–139
Biopsy, thyroid, 246–249
Calcitonin and calcitonin stimulation tests, 291–294
Calcium, urine, 303–307
Catecholamines, blood and urine, 324–330
Chloride, blood, 347–351
Chloride, sweat, 352–356
Cortisol and challenge tests, 531–536
C-peptide, 536–539

Dehydroepiandrosterone sulfate, 618–621
Dexamethasone suppression test, 532
Estradiol, 678
Follicle-stimulating hormone, 719–721
Fructosamine, 722–724
Glucagon, 750–753
Glucose (fasting, random, 2-hour postprandial), 753–760
Glucose tolerance tests, 763–769
Glycated hemoglobin, 770–773
Growth hormone, stimulation and suppression tests, 781–783
Homovanillic acid, 817–819
Human chorionic gonadotropin, 819–823
5-Hydroxyindoleacetic acid, 831–833

Laboratory Tests Associated With the Endocrine System

Insulin and insulin response to glucose, 856–860
Insulin antibodies, 860–862
Ketones, blood and urine, 880–882
Lactic acid, 890–893
Luteinizing hormone, 931–934
Magnesium, blood, 941–944
Magnesium, urine, 944–948
Metanephrines, 996–999
Metyrapone stimulation, 532
Microalbumin, 1002–1005
Newborn screening, 1023–1050
Osmolality, blood and urine, 1051–1055
Parathyroid hormone, 1074–1077
Phosphorus, blood, 1095–1099
Phosphorus, urine, 1099–1102
Potassium, blood, 1139–1144
Potassium, urine, 1145–1149
Prealbumin, 1149–1151
Progesterone, 1158–1160
Prolactin, 1161–1163
Renin, 1212–1216
Sodium, blood, 1248–1251
Sodium, urine, 1252–1255
Testosterone, total, 1271–1274
Thyroglobulin, 1274–1276
Thyroid-binding inhibitory immunoglobulin, 1276
Thyroid-stimulating hormone, 1280–1282
Thyroid-stimulating immunoglobulins, 1283–1284
Thyroxine-binding globulin, 1284–1286
Thyroxine, free, 1287–1289
Thyroxine, total, 1289–1292
Triiodothyronine, free, 1301–1303
Triiodothyronine, total, 1303–1306
Urinalysis, 1396–1404
Vanillylmandelic acid, urine, 1409–1411

SYS

Diagnostic Tests Associated With the Endocrine System

Adrenal gland scan, 5–7
Angiography, adrenal, 65–68
Computed tomography, pituitary, 502–505
Lymphangiography, 936–940
Magnetic resonance imaging, pancreas, 972–976
Magnetic resonance imaging, pituitary, 979–983
Parathyroid scan, 1078–1080
Radioactive iodine uptake, 1197–1199
Sialography, 1240–1242
Thyroid scan, 1277–1280
Ultrasound, thyroid and parathyroid, 1365–1367

Gastrointestinal System

Laboratory Tests Associated With the Gastrointestinal System

Albumin and albumin/globulin ratio, 17–20
Amylase, 53–56
Antibodies, antineutrophilic cytoplasmic, 104–105
Antibodies, gliadin (immunoglobulin G and immunoglobulin A), endomysial (immunoglobulin A), tissue transglutaminase (immunoglobulin A), 119–122
Biopsy, intestinal, 215–217
Calcium, blood, 294–299
Calcium, ionized, 299–303
Cancer antigens, 310–313
Cholesterol, total, 372–376
Complete blood count, 410–419
Complete blood count, hematocrit, 420–426
Complete blood count, hemoglobin, 426–432

(table continues on page 1452)

Laboratory Tests Associated With the Gastrointestinal System

Complete blood count, RBC count, 439–446

Complete blood count, RBC indices, 446–449

Complete blood count, RBC morphology and inclusions, 450–455

Culture, bacterial, stool, 581–583

Culture, viral, 593–596

D-Xylose tolerance test, 628–631

Endomysial antibodies (immunoglobulin G and immunoglobulin A), 119–122

Fecal analysis, 687–689

Fecal fat, 690–693

Folate, 716–718

Fructosamine, 722–724

Gastric analysis and gastric acid stimulation test, 733–737

Gastrin and gastrin stimulation test, 740–743

Gram stain, 776–778

Helicobacter pylori antibody, 787–788

5-Hydroxyindoleacetic acid, 831–833

Intrinsic factor antibodies, 871–873

Iron, 873–877

Lactose tolerance test, 893–896

Lipase, 913–915

Magnesium, blood, 941–944

Magnesium, urine, 944–948

Ova and parasites, stool, 1062–1064

Oxalate, urine, 1064–1067

Peritoneal fluid analysis, 1091–1094

Phosphorus, blood, 1095–1099

Potassium, blood, 1139–1144

Potassium, urine, 1145–1149

Prealbumin, 1149–1151

Protein, blood, total and fractions, 1167–1170

Transglutaminase antibodies (immunoglobulin G and immunoglobulin A), 116–119

Triglycerides, 1297–1301

Vitamin B_{12}, 1425–1427

Vitamin D, 1427–1430

Vitamin E, 1433–1435

Vitamins A, B_1, B_6, and C, 1436–1441

Zinc, 1446–1448

Diagnostic Tests Associated With the Gastrointestinal System

Barium enema, 179–182

Barium swallow, 182–185

Capsule endoscopy, 314–317

Cholangiography, percutaneous transhepatic, 356–360

Cholangiography, postoperative, 360–363

Cholangiopancreatography, endoscopic retrograde, 363–367

Colonoscopy, 395–399

Computed tomography, abdomen, 465–469

Computed tomography, colonoscopy, 489–493

Computed tomography, pancreas, 493–497

Computed tomography, pelvis, 497–502

Esophageal manometry, 670–674

Esophagogastroduodenoscopy, 674–677

Gastric emptying scan, 737–740

Gastroesophageal reflux scan, 743–746

Gastrointestinal blood loss scan, 746–750

Hydrogen breath test, 893–895

Kidney, ureter, and bladder study, 883–886

Laparoscopy, abdomen, 897–900

Magnetic resonance imaging, abdomen, 952–956

Meckel's diverticulum scan, 990–993

Positron emission tomography, pelvis, 1135–1138

Proctosigmoidoscopy, 1154–1158

Ultrasound, abdomen,

Ultrasound, pancreas, 1317–1320

Upper gastrointestinal and small bowel series, 1372–1376

Urea breath test, 1376–1378

Genitourinary System

Laboratory Tests Associated With the Genitourinary System

Acetaminophen, 57–60
Acid phosphatase, prostatic, 4
Albumin and albumin/globulin ratio, 17–20
Aldosterone, 22–26
Amikacin, 139–44
Amino acid screen, blood, 40–41
Amino acid screen, urine, 41–42
Anion gap, 87–89
Antiarrhythmic drugs, 90–97
Antimicrobial drugs, 139–144
Antibodies, anti–glomerular basement membrane, 100–101
Antibodies, antineutrophic cytoplasmic, 104–105
Anticonvulsant drugs, 122–129
Antidepressant drugs, 131–135
Antidiuretic hormone, 136–139
Antipsychotic drugs, 144–148
β_2-Microglobulin, blood and urine, 175–178
Biopsy, bladder, 190–193
Biopsy, kidney, 218–221
Biopsy, prostate, 237–242
Bladder cancer markers, urine, 249–251
Blood gases, 253–264
Calcium, blood, 294–299
Calcium, ionized, 299–303
Calcium, urine, 303–307
Calculus, kidney stone panel, 307–310
Carbon dioxide, 317–321
Chloride, blood, 347–351
Complete blood count, 410–419
Complete blood count, hematocrit, 420–426
Complete blood count, hemoglobin, 426–432
Complete blood count, RBC count, 439–446

Creatinine, blood, 547–551
Creatinine, urine, and creatinine clearance, urine, 551–556
Culture, bacterial, urine, 587–590
Culture, viral, 595–596
Cyclosporine, 848–854
Cytology, urine, 611–613
Erythropoietin, 611–613
Gentamicin, 139–144
Gram stain, 776–778
Lithium, 144–148
Magnesium, blood, 941–944
Magnesium, urine, 944–948
Methotrexate, 848–854
Microalbumin, 1002–1005
Newborn screening, 1023–1050
Osmolality, blood and urine, 1051–1055
Oxalate, urine, 1064–1067
Phosphorus, blood, 1095–1099
Phosphorus, urine, 1099–1102
Potassium, blood, 1095–1099
Potassium, urine, 1139–1144
Prostate-specific antigen, 1145–1149
Protein, urine: total quantitative and fractions, 1176–1179
Renin, 1212–1216
Salicylate, 57–60
Sodium, blood, 1248–1251
Sodium, urine, 1252–1255
Tobramycin, 139–144
Urea nitrogen, blood, 1378–1382
Urea nitrogen, urine, 1382–1385
Uric acid, blood, 1388–1392
Uric acid, urine, 1392–1396
Urinalysis, 1396–1404
Vancomycin, 139–144
Vitamins A, B_1, B_6, and C, 1436–1441

Diagnostic Tests Associated With the Genitourinary System

Angiography, renal, 82–86
Computed tomography, pelvis, 497–502
Computed tomography, renal, 506–510
Cystometry, 596–599

Cystoscopy, 600–603
Cystourethrography, voiding, 603–606
Electromyography, pelvic floor sphincter, 653–655

(table continues on page 1454)

Diagnostic Tests Associated With the Genitourinary System

Intravenous pyelography, 868–871
Kidney, ureter, and bladder study, 883–886
Magnetic resonance imaging, abdomen, 952–956
Magnetic resonance imaging, pelvis, 976–979
Renogram, 1216–1219

Retrograde ureteropyelography, 1223–1227
Ultrasound, abdomen, 1317–1320
Ultrasound, bladder, 1335–1338
Ultrasound, kidney, 1341–1344
Ultrasound, prostate, 1356–1359
Urethrography, retrograde, 1385–1387

SYS

Hematopoietic System

Laboratory Tests Associated With the Hematopoietic System

11–Dehydrothromboxane B2, 999–1012
δ-Aminolevulinic acid, 42–44
Anion gap, 87–89
Antibodies, cardiolipin, immunoglobulin A, immunoglobulin G, and immunoglobulin M, 116–119
Antithrombin III, 148–150
β-2 Glycoprotein 1, 116–119
Biopsy, bone marrow, 194–197
Bleeding time, 252–253
Blood groups and antibodies, 265–270
Calcium, blood, 294–299
Calcium, ionized, 299–303
CD4/CD8 enumeration, 330–333
Clot retraction, 380
Coagulation factors, 381–388
Complete blood count, 410–419
Complete blood count, hematocrit, 420–426
Complete blood count, hemoglobin, 426–432
Complete blood count, platelet count, 433–439
Complete blood count, RBC count, 439–446
Complete blood count, RBC indices, 413
Complete blood count, RBC morphology and inclusions, 450–455
Complete blood count, WBC count and differential, 455–464

Coombs' antiglobulin, direct, 523–525
Coombs' antiglobulin, indirect, 526–528
Copper, 528–533
CYP2C19, 433–439
D-Dimer, 616–618
Eosinophil count, 659–662
Erythrocyte protoporphyrin, free, 662–664
Erythrocyte sedimentation rate, 664–668
Erythropoietin, 668–670
Ferritin, 693–696
Fibrinogen degradation products, 709–712
Fibrinogen, 706–709
Folate, 716–718
Glucose-6-phosphate dehydrogenase, 761–763
Ham's test for paroxysmal nocturnal hemoglobinuria, 784
Haptoglobin, 784–786
Hemoglobin electrophoresis, 789–791
Hemosiderin, 791–793
Homocysteine and methylmalonic acid, 813–816
Immmunofixation electrophoresis, blood and urine, 840–842
Immunoglobulins A, D, G, and M, 844–848
International normalized ratio (INR), 1179–1184
Intrinsic factor antibodies, 871–873

Laboratory Tests Associated With the Hematopoietic System

Iron, 873–877
Iron-binding capacity (total), transferrin, and iron saturation, 877–879
Kleihauer-Betke test, 886–888
Lactate dehydrogenase and isoenzymes, 889–890
Lead, 905–907
Leukocyte alkaline phosphatase, 911–913
Lupus anticoagulant antibodies, 928–931
Methemoglobin, 999–1002
Osmotic fragility, 1055
Partial thromboplastin time, activated, 180–184

Plasminogen, 1102–1105
Platelet antibodies, 1105–1107
Porphyrins, urine, 1117–1121
Protein C, 1170–1173
Protein S, 1173–1175
Prothrombin time and INR, 1179–1184
Pyruvate kinase, 1194–1195
Red blood cell cholinesterase, 1205–1208
Reticulocyte count, 1220–1222
Sickle cell screen, 1243–1245
Transferrin, 1294–1297
Urinalysis, 1396–1404
Vitamin B_{12}, 1425–1427
Vitamin E, 1430–1435
Vitamin K, 1433–1435

Diagnostic Tests Associated With the Hematopoietic System

Computed tomography, spleen, 514–519
Liver and spleen scan, 917–921
Lymphangiography, 939–940
Ultrasound, spleen, 1362–1365

Hepatobiliary System

Laboratory Tests Associated With the Hepatobiliary System

Acetaminophen, 57–60
Acetylsalicylic acid, 57–60
Alanine aminotransferase, 14–16
Albumin, 17–20
Aldolase, 21
Alkaline phosphatase and isoenzymes, 26–30
Amino acid, blood, 40–41
Amino acid, urine, 41–42
Amitriptyline, 131–135
Ammonia, 45–47
Amylase, 53–56
Antibodies, actin (smooth muscle), and mitochondrial M2, 101–103
Antibodies, antineutrophilic cytoplasmic, 104–105

α_1-Antitrypsin and α_1-antitrypsin phenotyping, 151–154
Aspartate aminotransferase, 165–169
Bilirubin and bilirubin fractions, 185–190
Biopsy, liver, 221–225
Calcium, blood, 294–299
Calcium, ionized, 299–303
Carbamazepine, 122–126
Ceruloplasmin, 339–341
Cholesterol, total, 372–376
Coagulation factors, 380–388
Complete blood count, 410–419
Complete blood count, hematocrit, 420–426
Complete blood count, hemoglobin, 426–432

(table continues on page 1456)

Laboratory Tests Associated With the Hepatobiliary System

Complete blood count, RBC count, 439–446

Complete blood count, RBC morphology and inclusions, 450–455

Copper, 528–531

Desipramine, 131–135

Diazepam, 131–135

Doxepin, 131–135

Ethosuximide, 122–129

Fibrinogen, 706–708

δ-Glutamyltransferase, 731–733

Haloperidol, 144–148

Haptoglobin, 784–786

Hepatitis A antibody, 793–795

Hepatitis B antigen and antibody, 795–798

Hepatitis C antibody, 798–800

Hepatitis D antibody, 801

Hepatitis E antibody, 801–803

Imipramine, 131–135

Infectious mononucleosis screen, 854–856

International normalized ratio (INR), 1179–1184

Lactate dehydrogenase and isoenzymes, 889–890

Lactic acid, 890–893

Lipase, 913–915

Lipoprotein(a), 362–364

Newborn screening, 1023–1050

Nortriptyline, 131–135

Partial thromboplastin time, activated, 1080–1084

Phenobarbital, 122–129

Phenytoin, 122–129

Prealbumin, 1149–1151

Primidone, 122–129

Protein, blood, total and fractions, 1167–1170

Protein C, 1170–1173

Protein S, 1173–1175

Prothrombin time and INR, 1179–1184

Pseudocholinesterase, 1185–1186

Urea nitrogen, blood, 1378–1392

Uric acid, blood, 1388–1392

Urinalysis, 1396–1404

Valproic acid, 122–129

Vitamin E, 1430–1433

Vitamin K, 1433–1435

Zinc, 1446–1448

Diagnostic Tests Associated With the Hepatobiliary System

Cholangiography, percutaneous transhepatic, 356–360

Cholangiography, postoperative, 360–363

Cholangiopancreatography, endoscopic retrograde, 363–367

Computed tomography, abdomen, 465–469

Computed tomography, biliary tract and liver, 475–479

Computed tomography, pancreas, 493–497

Hepatobiliary scan, 803–806

Laparoscopy, abdomen, 897–900

Liver and spleen scan, 917–921

Magnetic resonance imaging, abdomen, 952–956

Magnetic resonance imaging, pancreas, 972–975

Radiofrequency ablation, liver, 1119–1203

Ultrasound, abdomen, 1317–1320

Ultrasound, liver and biliary system, 1344–1347

Immune System

Laboratory Tests Associated With the Immune System

(table continues on page 1458)

SYS

Laboratory Tests Associated With the Immune System

Eosinophil count, 659–662
Erythrocyte sedimentation rate, 664–668
α₁-Fetoprotein, 698–703
Gentamicin, 139–144
Gram stain, 776–778
Group A streptococcal screen, 779–780
Haptoglobin, 784–786
Hepatitis A antibody, 793–795
Hepatitis B antigen and antibody, 795–798
Hepatitis C antibody, 798–800
Hepatitis D antibody, 801
Hepatitis E antibody, 800–803
Human chorionic gonadotropin, 819–823
Human immunodeficiency virus type 1 and type 2 antibodies, 823–826
Human leukocyte antigen B27, 827–828
Human T-lymphotropic virus type I and type II antibodies, 829–831
5-Hydroxyindoleacetic acid, 831–833
Hypersensitivity pneumonitis, serology, 834
Immunofixation electrophoresis, blood and urine, 840–842
Immunoglobulin E, 842–844
Immunoglobulins A, D, G, and M, 844–848
Infectious mononucleosis screen, 854–856
Insulin antibodies, 860–862
Latex allergy, 904
Leukocyte alkaline phosphatase, 911–913
Lupus anticoagulant antibodies, 928–931

Lyme antibody, 934–936
Mumps serology, 1005–1007
Ova and parasites, stool, 1062–1064
Papanicolaou smear, 1070–1074
Parvovirus B19 immunoglobulin G and immunoglobulin M antibodies, 1084–1086
Pericardial fluid analysis, 1086–1090
Peritoneal fluid analysis, 1091–1094
Platelet antibodies, 1105–1107
Pleural fluid analysis, 1112–1117
Potassium, blood, 1139–1144
Procalcitonin, 1151–1154
Protein, blood, total and fractions, 1167–1170
Protein, urine: total quantitative and fractions, 1176–1179
Rheumatoid factor, 1227–1229
Rubella antibodies, IgG and IgM, 1229–1232
Rubeola antibodies, 1232–1234
Semen analysis, 1237–1240
Streptococcal screen, rapid, 779–780
Synovial fluid analysis, 1262–1266
Syphilis serology, 1266–1270
Tissue transglutaminase antibodies, 296
Tobramycin, 139–144
Toxoplasma antibody, 1292–1294
Tuberculosis: skin and blood tests, 1309–1313
Urinalysis, 1396–1404
Vancomycin, 139–144
Varicella, 1412–1414
Vitamins A, B₁, B₆, and C, 1436–1441
Zinc, 1446–1448

Diagnostic Tests Associated With the Immune System

Bronchoscopy, 282–287
Gallium scan, 728–730
Liver and spleen scan, 917–921
Lymphangiography, 936–940

Mediastinoscopy, 993–996
Ultrasound, lymph nodes and retroperitoneum, 1347–1349
White blood cell scan, 1442–1445

Musculoskeletal System

Laboratory Tests Associated With the Musculoskeletal System

Diagnostic Tests Associated With the Musculoskeletal System

Nutritional Considerations

Laboratory Tests With Nutritional Considerations

Albumin and albumin/globulin ratio, 17–20
Calcium, blood, 294–299
Chloride, blood, 347–351
Cholesterol, HDL and LDL, 367–372
Cholesterol, total, 372–376
Copper, 528–531
Folate, 716–718
Glucose, 753–760
Insulin and insulin response to glucose, 857–860
Iron, 873–877

Magnesium, blood, 941–944
Oxalate, urine, 1064–1067
Phosphorus, blood, 1095–1099
Potassium, blood, 1139–1144
Sodium, blood, 1248–1251
Triglycerides, 1297–1301
Uric acid, blood, 1388–1392
Vitamin B_{12}, 1425–1427
Vitamin D, 1427–1430
Vitamin E, 1430–1433
Vitamin K, 1433–1435
Vitamins A, B_1, B_6, and C, 1436–1441

Ocular System

Laboratory Tests Associated With the Ocular System

Antiarrhythmic drugs: amiodarone, digoxin, disopyramide, flecainide, lidocaine, procainamide, quinidine, 90–97
Antibodies, antinuclear, anti-DNA, anticentromere, antiextractable nuclear antigen, and antiscleroderma, 106–109
Anticonvulsant drugs: carbamazepine, ethosuximide, lamotrigine, phenobarbital, phenytoin, primidone, valproic acid, 122–129

C-peptide, 536–539
Culture, bacterial, anal/genital, ear, eye, skin, and wound, 565–571
Fructosamine, 722–724
Glucagon, 750–753
Glucose, 753–760
Glycated hemoglobin A_{1C}, 770–773
Insulin and insulin response to glucose, 856–860
Microalbumin, 1002–1005
Rheumatoid factor, 1227–1229
Vitamins A, B_1, B_6, and C, 1436–1441

Diagnostic Tests Associated With the Ocular System

Color perception test, 400–401
Computed tomography, brain, 479–484
Evoked brain potentials, 679–682
Fluorescein angiography, 712–716
Fundus photography, 724–727
Gonioscopy, 773–776
Intraocular muscle function, 862–864
Intraocular pressure, 865–867

Magnetic resonance imaging, brain, 956–960
Nerve fiber analysis, 1021–1023
Pachymetry, 1068–1069
Plethysmography, 1107–1112
Refraction, 1208–1211
Schirmer test, 1235–1237
Slit-lamp biomicroscopy, 1245–1246
Ultrasound, A-scan, 1327–1330
Visual fields test, 1422–1424

SYS

Reproductive System

Laboratory Tests Associated With the Reproductive System

Acid phosphatase, prostatic, 4
Amino acid screen, blood, 40–41
Amino acid screen, urine, 41–42
Amniotic fluid analysis, 47–53
Antibodies, antisperm, 110–112
Antibodies, cardiolipin, immunoglobulin A, immunoglobulin G, and immunoglobulin M, 116–119
β-2 Glycoprotein 1, 116–119
Biopsy, breast, 203–207
Biopsy, cervical, 207–211
Biopsy, chorionic villus, 211–214
Cancer antigens, 310–313
Chlamydia group antibody, IgG and IgM, 344–345
Chromosome analysis, blood, 376–379
Collagen cross-linked N-telopeptide, 391–395
Culture, bacterial, anal/genital, 565–571
Culture, viral, 593–596
Cytomegalovirus, immunoglobulin G, and immunoglobulin M, 613–615
Estradiol, 678
Fern test, 49
Fetal fibronectin, 696–698
α_1-Fetoprotein, 698–703
Follicle-stimulating hormone, 719–721
Gram stain, 776–778
Her-2/neu oncoprotein, 203–207
Hexosaminidase A and B, 807–810
Human chorionic gonadotropin, 819–823
Human immunodeficiency virus type 1 and type 2 antibodies, 823–826
Human papillomavirus, 1070–1074
Inhibin-A, 701
Ki67, 203–207
Kleihauer-Betke test, 886–888
Lecithin/sphingomyelin ratio, 907–911
Lupus anticoagulant antibodies, 928–930
Luteinizing hormone, 931–934
Magnesium, blood, 941–944
Newborn screening, 1023–1050
P53, 203–207
Papanicolaou smear, 1070–1074
Placental alpha microglobulin-1 protein, 49
Proliferating cell nuclear antigen, 203–207
Progesterone, 1158–1160
Prolactin, 1161–1163
Rubella antibodies, IgG and IgM, 1228–1232
S-phase fraction, 203–207
Semen analysis, 1237–1240
Syphilis serology, 1266–1270
Testosterone, total, 1271–1274
Toxoplasma antibody, 1292–1294
Urinalysis, 1396–1404
Varicella antibodies, 1412–1414

Diagnostic Tests Associated With the Reproductive System

Colposcopy, 402–404
Computed tomography, pelvis, 497–502
Contraction stress test, 1331
Ductography, 625–628
Fetoscopy, 703–705
Hysterosalpingography, 834–837
Hysteroscopy, 838–839
Laparoscopy, gynecologic, 900–904
Magnetic resonance imaging, breast, 960–964
Magnetic resonance imaging, pelvis, 976–979
Mammography, 987–990
Nonstress test, 1331
Positron emission tomography, FDG, 1226–1130
Stereotactic biopsy, breast, 1258–1261
Ultrasound, biophysical profile, obstetric, 1330–1335
Ultrasound, breast, 1338–1341
Ultrasound, pelvic, gynecologic, 1352–1356
Ultrasound, scrotal, 1359–1362
Uterine fibroid embolization, 1404–1408

Respiratory System

Laboratory Tests Associated With the Respiratory System

Allergen-specific immunoglobulin E, 31–35

Alveolar/arterial gradient and arterial/alveolar oxygen ratio, 33–36

Angiotensin-converting enzyme, 86–87

Anion gap, 87–89

Antibodies, anti–glomerular basement membrane, 1100–1101

α_1-Antitrypsin and α_1-antitrypsin phenotyping, 151–154

Biopsy, lung, 225–230

Blood gases, 253–264

Carbon dioxide, 317–320

Carboxyhemoglobin, 321–324

Chloride, blood, 347–351

Chloride, sweat, 352–356

Cold agglutinin titer, 389–391

Complete blood count, 410–419

Complete blood count, hematocrit, 420–446

Complete blood count, hemoglobin, 426–432

Complete blood count, RBC count, 439–446

Complete blood count, RBC indices, 413

Complete blood count, WBC count and differential, 454–464

Culture and smear, mycobacteria, 559–565

Culture, bacterial, sputum, 575–580

Culture, bacterial, throat, 584–586

Culture, viral, 593–596

Cytology, sputum, 606–611

D-Dimer, 616–618

Eosinophil count, 659–662

Erythrocyte sedimentation rate, 646–668

Fecal fat, 690–693

Gram stain, 776–778

Group A streptococcal screen, 779–780

Hypersensitivity pneumonitis, serology, 834

Immunoglobulin E, 842–844

Lactic acid, 890–893

Lecithin/sphingomyelin ratio, 907–911

Methemoglobin, 999–1002

Pleural fluid analysis, 1112–1117

Potassium, blood, 1139–1144

Rapid streptococcal screen, 779–780

Tuberculosis: skin and blood tests, 1309–1313

Diagnostic Tests Associated With the Respiratory System

Angiography, pulmonary, 78–81

Bronchoscopy, 282–287

Chest x-ray, 341–344

Computed tomography, thoracic, 519–522

Endoscopy, sinus, 658–659

Lung perfusion scan, 921–924

Lung ventilation scan, 925–928

Magnetic resonance imaging, chest, 964–968

Mediastinoscopy, 993–996

Plethysmography, 1107–1112

Positron emission tomography, heart, 1030–1035

Pulmonary function studies, 1186–1192

Pulse oximetry, 1192–1194

Venography, lower extremity studies, 1414–1418

Therapeutic Drug Monitoring and Toxicology

Laboratory Tests Associated With Therapeutic Drug Monitoring and Toxicology

Acetaminophen, 57–60
Acetylsalicylic acid, 57–60
Albumin, 17–20
Alcohol, ethyl, 621–625
Amikacin, 139–144
Amiodarone, 90–97
Amitriptyline, 131–135
Amphetamines, 621–625
Cannabinoids, 621–625
Carbamazepine, 122–129
Cocaine, 621–625
Cyclosporine, 848–853
CYP 450, 121–129, 131–135, 144–148
Diazepam, 621–625
Digoxin, 90–97
Disopyramide, 90–97
Doxepin, 131–135
Ethanol, 621–625
Ethosuximide, 122–129
Everolimus, 848–853
Gentamicin, 139–144

Haloperidol, 144–148
Imipramine, 141–135
Lamotrigene, 122–129, 131–135
Lead, 905–907
Lidocaine, 90–97
Lithium, 144–148
Methotrexate, 848–853
Nortriptyline, 131–135
Opiates, 621–625
Protriptyline, 131–135
Sirolimus, 848–853
Tacrolimus, 848–853
Phencyclidine, 621–625
Phenobarbital, 122–129
Phenytoin, 122–129
Primidone, 122–129
Procainamide, 90–97
Quinidine, 90–97
Tobramycin, 139–144
Tricyclic antidepressants, 147
Valproic acid, 122–129
Vancomycin, 139–144

SYS

Patient Preparation and Specimen Collection

PATIENT PREPARATION BEFORE DIAGNOSTIC AND LABORATORY PROCEDURES

The first step in any laboratory or diagnostic procedure is patient preparation or patient teaching before the performance of the procedure. This pretesting explanation to the patient or caregiver follows essentially the same pattern for all sites and types of studies and includes the following:

- *Statement of the purpose of the study.* The level of detail provided to patients about the test purpose depends on numerous factors and should be individualized appropriately in each particular setting.

- *Description of the procedure, including site and method.* It is a good idea to explain to the patient that you will be wearing gloves throughout the procedure. The explanation should help the patient understand that the use of gloves is standard practice established for his or her protection as well as yours. Many institutions require hand washing at the beginning and end of each specimen collection encounter and between each patient.

- *Description of the sensations, including discomfort and pain, that the patient may experience during the specimen collection procedure.* Address concerns about pain related to the procedure and suggest breathing or visualization techniques to promote relaxation. For pediatric patients, a doll may be used to "show" the procedure. Where appropriate, the use of sedative or anesthetizing agents may assist in allaying anxiety the patient may experience related to anticipation of pain associated with the procedure. Sensitivity to cultural and social issues, as well as concern for modesty, is important in providing psychological support.

- *Instruction regarding pretesting preparations related to diet, liquids, medications, and activity as well as any restrictions regarding diet, liquids, medications, activity, known allergies, therapies, or other procedures that might affect test results.* To increase patient compliance, the instructions should include an explanation of why strict adherence to the instructions is required.

- *Recognition of anxiety related to test results.* Provide a compassionate, reassuring environment. Be prepared to educate the patient regarding access to the appropriate counseling services. Encourage the patient to ask questions and verbalize his or her concerns.

Specific collection techniques and patient preparation vary by site, study required, and level of invasiveness. These techniques are described in the individual monographs.

- It is essential that the patient be positively and properly identified before providing care, treatment, or services. Specimens should always be labeled with the patient's name, date of birth (or some other unique identifier), date collected, time collected, and initials of the person collecting the sample.

- Orders should be completed accurately and submitted per laboratory policy.

BLOOD SPECIMENS

Most laboratory tests that require a blood specimen use venous blood. Venous blood can be collected directly from the vein or by way of capillary puncture. Capillary blood can be obtained from the fingertips or earlobes of adults and smal

APP

children. Capillary blood can also be obtained from the heels of infants. The circumstances in which the capillary method is selected over direct venipuncture include cases in which:

- The patient has poor veins.
- The patient has small veins.
- The patient has a limited number of available veins.
- The patient has significant anxiety about the venipuncture procedure.

Venous blood also can be obtained from vascular access devices, such as heparin locks and central venous catheters. Examples of central venous catheters include the triple-lumen subclavian, Hickman, and Groshong catheters.

Fetal blood samples can be obtained, when warranted, by a qualified health-care provider (HCP) from the scalp or from the umbilical cord.

Arterial blood can be collected from the radial, brachial, or femoral artery if blood gas analysis is requested.

Some general guidelines should be followed in the procurement and handling of blood specimens:

- The practice of an overnight fast before specimen collection is a general recommendation. Reference ranges are often based on fasting populations to provide some level of standardization for comparison. Some test results are dramatically affected by foods, however, and fasting is a pretest requirement. The presence of lipids in the blood also may interfere with the test method; fasting eliminates this potential source of error, especially if the patient already has elevated lipid levels. The laboratory should always be consulted if there is a question whether fasting is a requirement or a recommendation.
- Gloves and any other additional personal protective equipment indicated by the patient's condition should always be worn during the specimen collection process. Appendix G provides a more detailed description of standard precautions.
- Stress can cause variations in some test results. A sleeping patient should be gently awakened and allowed the opportunity to become oriented before collection site selection. Comatose or unconscious patients should be greeted in the same gentle manner because, although they are unable to respond, they may be capable of hearing and understanding. Anticipate instances in which patient cooperation may be an issue. Enlist a second person to assist with specimen collection to ensure a safe, quality collection experience for all involved.
- Localized activity such as the application of a tourniquet or clenching the hand to assist in visualizing the vein can cause variations in some test results. It is important to be aware of affected studies before specimen collection.
- Hemoconcentration may cause variations in some test results. The tourniquet should never be left in place for longer than 1 min.
- Previous puncture sites should be avoided when accessing a blood vessel by any means to reduce the potential for infection.
- Specimens should never be collected above an IV line because of the potential for dilution when the specimen and the IV solution combine in the collection container, falsely decreasing the result. It is also possible that substances in the IV solution could contaminate the specimen and result in falsely elevated test results.
- Changes in posture from supine to erect or long-term maintenance of a supine posture causes variations in some test results. It is important to be

APP

aware of this effect when results are interpreted and compared with previous values.

- Collection times for therapeutic drug (peak and trough) or other specific monitoring (e.g., chemotherapy, glucose, insulin, or potassium) should be documented carefully in relation to the time of medication administration. It is essential that this information be communicated clearly and accurately to avoid misunderstanding of the dose time in relation to the collection time. Miscommunication between the individual administering the medication and the individual collecting the specimen is the most frequent cause of subtherapeutic levels, toxic levels, and misleading information used in the calculation of future therapies.

- The laboratory should be consulted regarding minimum specimen collection requirements when multiple tube types or samples are required. The amount of serum or plasma collected can be estimated using assumptions of packed cell volume or hematocrit. The packed cell volume of a healthy woman is usually 38% to 44% of the total blood volume. If a full 5-mL red-top tube is collected, and the hematocrit is 38% to 44%, approximately 2.8 to 3.1 mL, or [5 – (5 × 0.44)] to [5 – (5 × 0.38)], of the total blood volume should be serum. Factors that invalidate estimation include conditions such as anemia, polycythemia, dehydration, and overhydration.

- The laboratory should be consulted regarding the preferred specimen container before specimen collection. Specific analytes may vary in concentration depending on whether the sample is serum or plasma. It is strongly recommended that when serial measurements are to be carried out, the same type of collection container be used so that fluctuations in values caused by variations in specimen type are not misinterpreted as changes in clinical status. Consultation regarding collection containers is also important because some laboratory methods are optimized for a specific specimen type (serum versus plasma). Also, preservatives present in collection containers, such as sodium fluoride, may exhibit a chemical interference with test reagents that can cause underestimation or overestimation of measured values. Other preservatives, such as EDTA, can block the analyte of interest in the sample from participating in the test reaction, invalidating test results. Finally, it is possible that some high-throughput, robotic equipment systems require specific and standardized collection containers.

- Prompt and proper specimen processing, storage, and analysis are important to achieve accurate results. Specimens collected in containers with solid or liquid preservatives or with gel separators should be mixed by inverting the tube 10 times immediately after the tube has been filled. Handle the specimen gently to avoid hemolysis. Specimens should always be transported to the laboratory as quickly as possible after collection.

Results that are evaluated outside the entire context of the preparatory, collection, and handling process may be interpreted erroneously if consideration is not given to the above-listed general guidelines.

Site Selection

Capillary Puncture: Assess the selected area. It should be free of lesions and calluses, there should be no edema, and the site should feel warm. If the site feels cool or appears pale or cyanotic, warm compresses can be applied over 3 to

5 min to dilate the capillaries. For fingersticks, the central, fleshy, distal portions of the third or fourth fingers are the preferred collection sites (Fig. A–1). For neonatal heel sticks, the medial and lateral surfaces of the plantar area are preferred to avoid direct puncture of the heel bone, which could result in osteomyelitis (Fig. A–2).

Venipuncture of Arm: Assess the arm for visibly accessible veins. The selected area should not be burned or scarred, have a tattoo, or have hematoma present. Even after the tourniquet is applied, not all patients have a prominent median

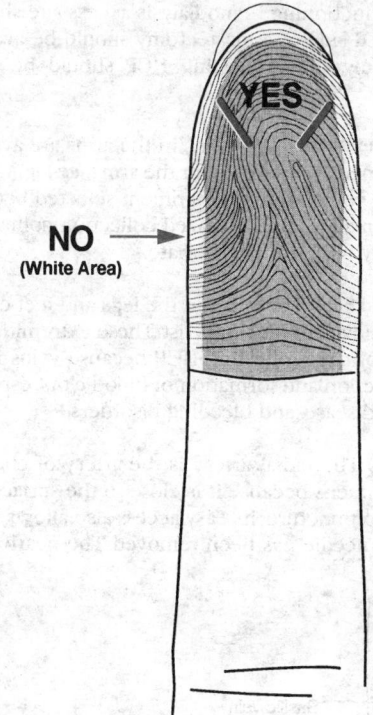

Figure A–1 Site selection. Capillary puncture of the finger.

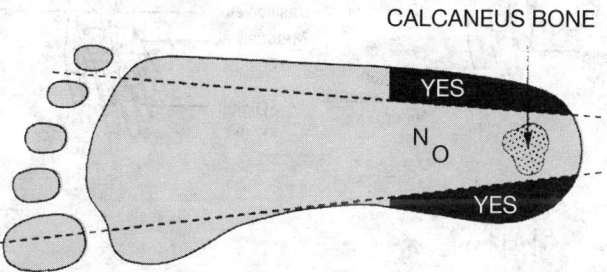

Figure A–2 Site selection. Capillary puncture of the heel.

cubital, cephalic, or basilic vein. Both arms should be observed because some patients have accessible veins in one arm and not the other. The median cubital vein in the antecubital fossa is the preferred venipuncture site. The patient may be able to provide the best information regarding venous access if he or she has had previous venipuncture experience (Fig. A–3). Alternative techniques to increase visibility of veins may include warming the arm, allowing the arm to dangle downward for a minute or two, tapping the antecubital area with the index finger, or massaging the arm upward from wrist to elbow. The condition of the vein also should be assessed before venipuncture. Sclerotic (hard, scarred) veins or veins in which phlebitis previously occurred should be avoided. Arms with a functioning hemodialysis access site should not be used. The arm on the affected side of a mastectomy should be avoided. In the case of a double mastectomy, the requesting HCP should be consulted before specimen collection.

Venipuncture of Hand and Wrist: If no veins in the arms are available, hands and wrists should be examined as described for the arm (see Fig. A–3). Consideration should be given to the venipuncture equipment selected because the veins in these areas are much smaller. Pediatric-sized collection containers and needles with a larger gauge may be more appropriate.

Venipuncture of Legs and Feet: The veins in the legs and feet can be accessed as with sites located on the arm, hand, or wrist. These extremities should be used only on the approval of the requesting HCP because veins in these locations are more prone to infection and formation of blood clots, especially in patients with diabetes, cardiac disease, and bleeding disorders.

Radial Arterial Puncture: The radial artery is the artery of choice for obtaining arterial blood gas specimens because it is close to the surface of the wrist and does not require a deep puncture. Its easy access also allows for more effective compression after the needle has been removed. The nearby ulnar artery can

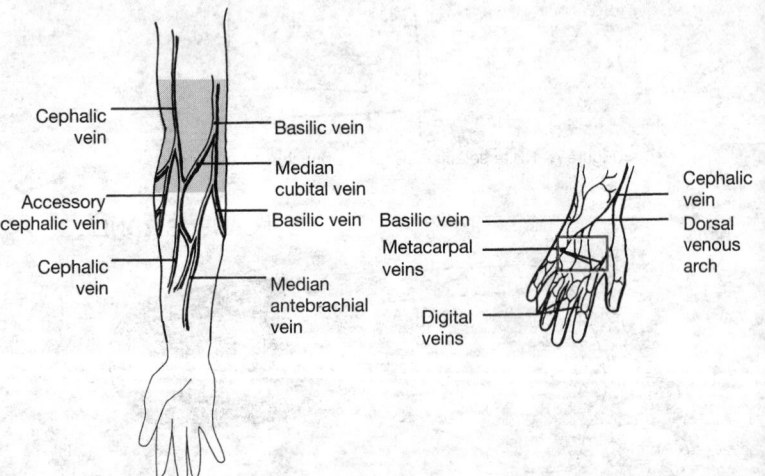

Figure A–3 Site selection. Venipuncture arm/hand.

provide sufficient collateral circulation to the hand during specimen collection and postcollection compression (Fig. A-4).

Percutaneous Umbilical Cord Sampling: The blood is aspirated from the umbilical cord under the guidance of ultrasonography and using a 20- or 22-gauge spinal needle inserted through the mother's abdomen.

Postnatal Umbilical Cord Sampling: The blood is aspirated from the umbilical cord using a 20- or 22-gauge needle and transferred to the appropriate collection container.

Fetal Scalp Sampling: The requesting HCP makes a puncture in the fetal scalp using a microblade, and the specimen is collected in a long capillary tube. The tube is usually capped on both ends immediately after specimen collection.

Locks and Catheters: These devices are sometimes inserted to provide a means for the administration of fluids or medications and to obtain blood specimens without the need for frequent venipuncture. The device first should be assessed for patency. The need for heparinization, irrigation, or clot removal depends on the type of device in use and the institution-specific or HCP-specific protocols in effect. Use sterile technique because these devices provide direct access to the patient's bloodstream. When IV fluids are being administered via a device at the time of specimen collection, blood should be obtained from the opposite side of the body. If this is not possible, the flow should be stopped for 5 min before specimen collection. The first 5 mL of blood collected should be discarded.

APP

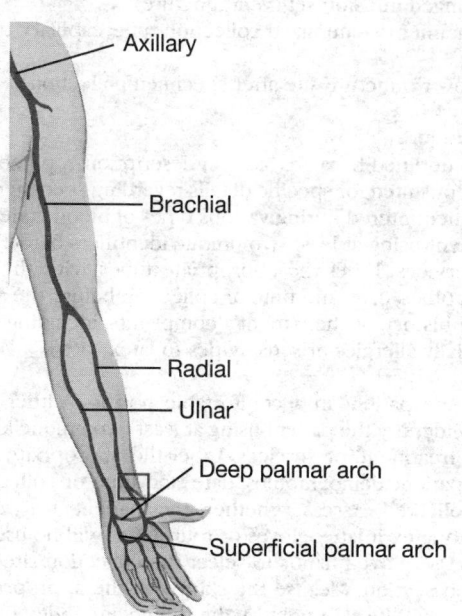

Figure A–4 Site selection. Arterial arm/hand.

Selection of Blood Collection Equipment

In many cases when a blood sample is required, serum is the specimen type of choice. Plasma may be frequently substituted, however. Specimen processing is more rapid for plasma samples than serum samples because the anticoagulated sample does not need to clot before centrifugation. Plasma samples also require less centrifugation time to achieve adequate separation. Consult with the testing laboratory regarding recommended specimen types. The basic blood collection tubes are shown on the inside cover of this book. Consider latex allergy when selecting the collection equipment appropriate for each patient. Equipment used in specimen collection includes:

- Gloves and other personal protective equipment depending on the situation
- Tourniquet
- Materials to cleanse or disinfect the collection site (alcohol preparations [70% alcohol], povidone-iodine solution [Betadine], or green soap are the most commonly used materials)
- Gauze (to wipe collection site dry after cleansing)
- Sterile lancet (capillary puncture)
- Syringe and needle (arterial puncture or venipuncture)
- Vial of heparin and syringe or heparin unit dose
- Sterile normal saline in 50-mL syringe (for indwelling devices such as Groshong catheter)
- Sterile cap or hub (for indwelling devices when the cap or hub will be replaced after specimen procurement)
- Needle and holder for vacuumized collection tube system (arterial puncture or venipuncture)
- Butterfly or winged infusion set (venipuncture)
- Collection container (vacuumized collection tube, capillary tube, or Microtainer)
- Bandage (to cover puncture site after specimen collection)

Collection Procedure

The procedures outlined here are basic in description. A phlebotomy or other item should be consulted for specific details regarding specimen collection and complications encountered during various types of blood collection. Positively identify the patient using at least two unique identifiers before providing care, treatment, or services. Label the appropriate tubes with the corresponding patient demographics, date, and time of collection before the specimen is collected. Obtain a history of the patient's complaints, including a list of known allergens, especially allergies or sensitivities to latex.

Capillary: Place the patient in a comfortable position either sitting or lying down. Positively identify the patient using at least two unique identifiers before providing care, treatment, or services. Label the appropriate tubes with the corresponding patient demographics, date, and time of collection before the specimen is collected. Assess whether the patient has allergies to the disinfectant or to latex if latex gloves or tourniquet will be used in the collection procedure. Use gloved hands to select the collection site as described in the site selection section. Cleanse the skin with the appropriate disinfectant and dry the area. Pull the skin tight by the thumb and index finger of the nondominant hand on either side of the puncture site and move them in opposite directions. Puncture the skin with a sterile lancet to a depth of approximately 2 mm, using a quick, firm motion. Wipe the first drop of blood away using the gauze. If flow is poor, the site should not be squeezed or the specimen may become contaminated with tissue fluid. Do not allow the collection container to touch the puncture site. Collect the sample in the capillary tube or Microtainer. The capillary tube should be held in a horizontal position to avoid the introduction of air bubbles into the sample. Microtainer tubes should be held in a downward-slanted direction to facilitate the flow of blood into the capillary scoop of the collection device. If a smear is required, allow a drop of blood to fall onto a clean microscope slide. Gently spread the drop across the slide using the edge of another slide. Apply slight pressure to the puncture site with a clean piece of gauze until bleeding stops, and then apply a bandage. Safely dispose of the sharps. Transport properly labeled specimens immediately to the laboratory.

Venipuncture Using a Syringe or Vacuumized Needle and Holder System: Place the patient in a comfortable position either sitting or lying down. Positively identify the patient using at least two unique identifiers before providing care, treatment, or services. Label the appropriate tubes with the corresponding patient demographics, date, and time of collection before the specimen is collected. Assess whether the patient has allergies to the disinfectant or to latex if latex gloves or tourniquet will be used in the collection procedure. Use gloved hands to select the collection site as described in the Site Selection section. Locate the vein visually, then by palpation using the index finger. The thumb should not be used because it has a pulse beat and may cause confusion in site selection or in differentiating a vein from an artery. Select the appropriate collection materials (needle size, butterfly, syringe, collection container size) on the basis of the vein size, vein depth, appearance of the collection site, patient's age, and anticipated level of cooperation. Cleanse the skin with the appropriate disinfectant and dry the area. Select the appropriate collection tubes. If blood cultures are to be collected, disinfect the top of the collection containers as directed by the testing laboratory. Be sure to have extra tubes within easy reach in case the vacuum in a collection tube is lost and a substitute is required. Apply the tourniquet 3 to 4 in. above the selected collection site. Remove the sterile needle cap, and inspect the tip of the needle for defects. Pull the skin tight by placing the thumb of the nondominant hand 1 or 2 in. below the puncture site and moving the thumb in the opposite direction. The thumb is placed below the puncture site to help avoid an accidental needle stick if the patient moves suddenly. Ensure that the needle is bevel up and held at an angle of approximately 15° to 30° (depending on the depth of the vein) (Fig. A–5).

Puncture the skin with a smooth, firm motion using a sterile needle held by the dominant hand. A reduction in pressure is achieved when the needle has penetrated the vein successfully. Be sure to release the tourniquet within 1 min of application. Fill the vacuumized collection containers in the prescribed order of draw for the studies ordered. Tubes with anticoagulants can be gently mixed with the free nondominant hand as they are filled. When the required containers have been filled, withdraw the needle and apply pressure to the collection site until the bleeding stops. In most cases, a piece of gauze can be placed on the collection site and the arm bent upward to hold it in place while attention is given to disposing of the sharps safely. In cases in which a syringe

Figure A–5 Venipuncture needle placement at insertion.

is used, the barrel of the syringe should be gently pulled back during specimen collection and gently pushed in during the transfer to collection tubes. The vacuum in the collection container should not be allowed to suck the sample into the container, but rather the speed of entry should be controlled by the pressure applied to the barrel. The blood should gently roll down the side of the tube to prevent hemolysis. Transport properly labeled specimens immediately to the laboratory.

Radial Artery Puncture: Place the patient in a comfortable position either sitting or lying down. Positively identify the patient using at least two unique identifiers before providing care, treatment, or services. Label the appropriate tubes with the corresponding patient demographics, date, and time of collection before the specimen is collected. Assess whether the patient has allergies to the disinfectant or to latex if latex gloves or tourniquet will be used in the collection procedure. Assess if the patient has an allergy to local anesthetics, and inform the HCP accordingly. Glove the hands, and select the collection site as described in the site selection section. Ensure that the patient has adequate collateral circulation to the hand if thrombosis of the radial artery occurs after arterial puncture by performing an Allen test before puncture. The Allen test is performed by occlusion of the ulnar and radial arteries on the palmar surface of the wrist with two fingers. The thumb should not be used to locate these arteries because it has a pulse. Compress both arteries, and ask the patient to open and close the fist several times until the palm turns pale. Release pressure only on the ulnar artery. Color should return to the palm within 5 sec if the ulnar artery is functioning. If color returns above the wrist the Allen test is positive. The Allen test also should be performed on the opposite hand. The wrist to which color is restored fastest has better circulation and should be selected as the site for blood gas collection. Be sure to explain to the patient that an arterial puncture is painful. The site may be anesthetized with 1% to 2% lidocaine (Xylocaine) before puncture. The index finger of the nondominant hand is placed over the site where the needle will enter the artery, not the site where the needle will penetrate the skin. The specimen is collected in an air-free heparinized syringe, which is held like a dart in the dominant hand and inserted slowly, bevel up, about 5 to 10 mm below the palpating finger at a 45° to 60° angle. When blood enters the needle hub, arterial pressure should cause blood to pump into the syringe. When enough specimen has been collected, the needle is withdrawn from the arm, and pressure is applied to the collection site for a minimum of 5 to 10 min. Immediately after the needle has been withdrawn safely from the arm, the exposed end of the syringe should be stoppered.

Samples should be gently and well mixed to ensure proper mixing of the heparin with the sample. The heparin prevents formation of small clots that result in rejection of the sample. The tightly capped sample should be placed in an ice slurry immediately after collection. Information on the specimen label should be protected from water in the ice slurry by first placing the specimen in a protective plastic bag. Transport properly labeled specimens immediately to the laboratory.

Indwelling Devices: Positively identify the patient using at least two unique identifiers before providing care, treatment, or services. Label the appropriate tubes with the corresponding patient demographics, date, and time of collection before the specimen is collected. Indwelling devices are either heparinized or irrigated after specimen collection. Before specimen collection, prepare the heparin in a syringe, if required. Allow the heparin (unit dose or prepared solution in the syringe) to equilibrate at room temperature during specimen collection. Cleanse the catheter cap or hub with povidone-iodine and 70% alcohol over 2 min. Using sterile gloves, remove the cap and attach a 5- or 10-mL syringe to the connector. Withdraw 5 mL of blood to be discarded. Clamp the catheter. (The Groshong catheter does not require clamping because it has a special valve that eliminates the need for clamping.) Attach another 5- or 10-mL syringe and begin collecting blood for transfer to the collection tubes. After the required specimen has been withdrawn, the device is heparinized by slowly injecting the heparin into the cap or hub of the device. Clamp the device 2 in. from the cap, remove the needle, and unclamp the device. Attach a new sterile cap or hub if the old one has been discarded. Groshong catheters are irrigated rather than heparinized. Irrigation of a Groshong catheter is accomplished by gently injecting 20 to 30 mL of sterile normal saline through the cap with moderate force. Remove the needle using some positive pressure (pressing down on the plunger) to prevent the solution from backing up into the syringe. Transport properly labeled specimens immediately to the laboratory.

Order of Draw for Glass or Plastic Tubes (Reflects Current CLSI [formerly NCCLS] Guideline: Recommended Order of Draw, H3-A6, [Vol 27, No 26])
Note: Always follow your facility's protocol for order of draw.

- First—Blood culture and other tests requiring sterile specimen (yellow or yellow/black stopper); blood culture bottle first, followed by sodium polyethanol sulfonate (SPS) tube for acid-fast bacilli specimens.
- Second—Coagulation studies (light blue [sodium citrate] stopper); sodium citrate forms calcium salts to remove calcium, and this prevents specimen clotting. *Note:* When using a winged blood or vacutainer collection set and the blue-top tube is the first tube drawn, a nonadditive red-top or coagulation discard tube should be collected first and discarded. The amount of blood in the discard tube needs to be sufficient to fill the winged collection set tubing's "dead space" or fill one-quarter of the discard tube. This is done to ensure complete filling of the blue-top tube. The blue-top tube to be used for testing must be filled to ensure the proper ratio of blood to additive in the test specimen blue-top tube.
- Third—Plain or nonadditive (red or red/gray [gel] stopper); red/gray-top serum separator tube (SST) contains a gel separator and clot activator. SSTs are not appropriate for all testing requiring a serum specimen. They are

generally unacceptable for therapeutic drug monitoring and serology studies. The laboratory should be consulted if there are questions regarding the use of SSTs.

• Fourth—Additive tubes in the following order:

Green stopper: Tube contains sodium heparin or lithium heparin anticoagulant (heparin inactivates thrombin and thromboplastin, and this prevents specimen clotting). For ammonia levels, use sodium or lithium heparin. For lithium levels, use sodium heparin.

Lavender stopper: Tube contains K_3 EDTA (tripotassium EDTA forms calcium salts to remove calcium from the sample, and this prevents specimen clotting while preserving the integrity of the red blood cell wall).

White stopper: Tube contains K_3 EDTA with gel (this preservative is intended for polymerase chain reaction [PCR] and branched DNA amplification [bDNA] techniques used in molecular diagnostics testing).

Blue/black stopper: Tube contains sodium citrate or sodium heparin with gel (this tube should be collected after EDTA but before any tube containing a liquid additive; this tube is intended for separation and harvesting of mononuclear cells from the whole blood matrix for use in molecular diagnostics testing).

Gray stopper: Tube contains potassium oxalate/sodium fluoride (the potassium oxalate acts as an anticoagulant, and the sodium fluoride prevents glycolysis).

Clear stopper: Tube contains PAXgene blood RNA preservative solution (this tube should always be collected last, and if no other tubes are collected, a discard tube should be collected first and discarded; this tube is preferred for subsequent isolation and purification of intracellular RNA from whole blood for PCR used in molecular diagnostics testing).

URINE SPECIMENS

The patient should be informed that improper collection, storage, and transport are the primary reasons for specimen rejection and subsequent requests for recollection. If the specimen is to be collected at home, it should be collected in a clean plastic container (preferably a container from the testing laboratory). Many studies require refrigeration after collection. If the collection container includes a preservative, the patient should be made aware of the contents and advised as to what the precaution labels mean (caution labels such as caustic, corrosive, acid, and base should be affixed to the container as appropriate). When a preservative or fixative is included in the container, the patient should be advised not to remove it. The patient also should be told not to void directly into the container. The patient should be given a collection device, if indicated, and instructed to void into the collection device. The specimen should be carefully transferred into the collection container. Urinary output should be recorded throughout the collection time if the specimen is being collected over a specified time interval. Some laboratories provide preprinted collection instructions tailored to their methods. The specimen should be transported promptly to the laboratory after collection.

Wear gloves and any other additional personal protective equipment indicated by the patient's condition. See Appendix G for a more detailed description of standard precautions. Assess whether the patient has allergies to the disinfectant or anesthetic, or to latex if latex gloves or catheter will be used in the procedure.

Random: These samples are mainly used for routine screening and can be collected at any time of the day. The patient should be instructed to void either directly into the collection container (if there is no preservative) or into a collection device for transfer into the specimen container.

First Morning: Urine on rising in the morning is very concentrated. These specimens are indicated when screening for substances that may not be detectable in a more dilute random sample. These specimens are also necessary for testing conditions such as orthostatic proteinuria, in which levels vary with changes in posture.

Second Void: In some cases, it is desirable to test freshly produced urine to evaluate the patient's current status, as with glucose and ketones. Explain to the patient that he or she should first void and then drink a glass of water. The patient should be instructed to wait 30 min and then void either directly into the collection container or into a collection device for transfer into the collection container.

Clean Catch: These midstream specimens are generally used for microbiological or cytological studies. They also may be requested for routine urinalysis to provide a specimen that is least contaminated with urethral cells, microorganisms, mucus, or other substances that may affect the interpretation of results. Instruct the male patient first to wash hands thoroughly, then cleanse the meatus, void a small amount into the toilet, and void either directly into the specimen container or into a collection device for transfer into the specimen container. Instruct the female patient first to wash hands thoroughly, and then to cleanse the labia from front to back. While keeping the labia separated, the patient should void a small amount into the toilet, and then, without interrupting the urine stream, void either directly into the specimen container or into a collection device for transfer into the specimen container.

Catheterized Random or Clean Catch: "Straight catheterization" is indicated when the patient is unable to void, when the patient is unable to prepare properly for clean-catch specimen collection, or when the patient has an indwelling catheter in place from which a urine sample may be obtained. Before collecting a specimen from the catheter, observe the drainage tube to ensure that it is empty, and then clamp the tube distal to the collection port 15 min before specimen collection. Cleanse the port with an antiseptic swab such as 70% alcohol and allow the port to dry. Use a needle and syringe (sterile if indicated) to withdraw the required amount of specimen. Unclamp the tube.

Timed: To quantify substances in urine, 24-hr urine collections are used. They are also used to measure substances whose level of excretion varies over time. The use of preservatives and the handling of specimens during the timed collection may be subject to variability among laboratories. The testing laboratory should be consulted regarding specific instructions before starting the test. Many times the specimen must be refrigerated or kept on ice throughout the entire collection period. Explain to the patient that it is crucial for *all* urine to be included in the collection. Urinary output should be recorded throughout the collection time if the specimen is being collected over a specified time interval. The test should begin between 6 and 8 a.m. if possible. Instruct the patient to collect the first void of the day and discard it. The start time of the collection period begins at the time the first voided specimen was discarded and should be recorded along with the date on the collection container. The patient should be instructed to void at the same time the following morning and to add this last voiding to the container. This is the end time of the collection and should be recorded along with the date on the container. For patients who are in the hospital, the urinary output should be compared with the volume measured in the completed collection container. Discrepancies between the two volumes indicate that a collection might have been discarded. A creatinine level often is requested along with the study of interest to evaluate the completeness of the collection.

Catheterized Timed: Instructions for this type of collection are basically the same as those for timed specimen collection. The test should begin by changing the tubing and drainage bag. If a preservative is required, it can be placed directly in the drainage bag, or the specimen can be removed at frequent intervals (every 2 hr) and transferred to the collection container to which the preservative has been added. The drainage bag must be kept on ice or emptied periodically into the collection container during the entire collection period if indicated by the testing laboratory. The tubing should be monitored throughout the collection period to ensure continued drainage.

Suprapubic Aspiration: This procedure is performed by inserting a needle directly into the bladder. Because the bladder is normally sterile, the urine collected should also be free from any contamination caused by the presence of microorganisms. Place the patient in a supine position. Cleanse the area with antiseptic and drape with sterile drapes. A local anesthetic may be administered before insertion of the needle. A needle is inserted through the skin into the bladder. A syringe attached to the needle is used to aspirate the urine sample. The needle is then removed and a sterile dressing is applied to the site. Place the sterile sample in a sterile specimen container. The site must be observed for signs of inflammation or infection.

Pediatric: Specimen collection can be achieved by any of the above-described methods using collection devices specifically designed for pediatric patients. Appropriately cleanse the genital area and allow the area to dry. For a random collection, remove the covering of the adhesive strips on the collector bag and apply over the genital area. Diaper the child. When the specimen is obtained, place the entire collection bag in the specimen container (use a sterile container as appropriate for the requested study). Some laboratories may have specific preferences for the submission of urine specimens for culture. Consult the laboratory before collection to avoid specimen rejection.

BODY FLUID, STOOL, AND TISSUE

Wear gloves and any other additional personal protective equipment indicated by the patient's condition. See Appendix G for a more detailed description of standard precautions. Assess whether the patient has allergies to the disinfectant or anesthetic or to latex if latex gloves will be used in the procedure.

Specific collection techniques vary by site, study required, and level of invasiveness. These techniques are described in the individual monographs.

DIAGNOSTIC TESTING

Wear gloves and any other additional personal protective equipment indicated by the patient's condition. See Appendix G for a more detailed description of standard precautions. Assess whether the patient has allergies to the disinfectant, anesthetic, contrast material, or medications or to latex if latex gloves, catheter, or tourniquet will be used in the procedure.

A sleeping patient should be gently awakened and allowed the opportunity to become oriented before preparation for the selected study. Comatose or unconscious patients should be greeted in the same gentle manner because, although they are unable to respond, they may be capable of hearing and understanding. Anticipate instances in which patient cooperation may be an issue. Enlist a second person to help with preparing the patient for the procedure to ensure a safe, quality testing experience for all involved.

Specific techniques and patient preparation vary by site, study required, and level of invasiveness. These techniques are described in the individual monographs.

APP

Appendix B

Potential Nursing Diagnoses Associated with Laboratory and Diagnostic Testing

PRETEST PHASE

Anxiety related to undiagnosed health problems

Anxiety related to perceived threat to health status

Anxiety and fear related to anticipated diagnostic results

Anxiety and fear related to perception of diagnostic procedure as frightening or embarrassing

Powerlessness related to unfamiliar procedure, equipment, environment, or personnel

Knowledge deficit related to lack of information or possible misinterpretation of information provided about the procedure

Knowledge deficit related to informed consent, legal implications of testing

Potential for noncompliance with test protocols related to inability to understand or follow instructions

Potential for noncompliance with test protocols related to presence of high anxiety, confusion, or denial

Potential for noncompliance with test protocols related to lack of knowledge or appropriate instruction

Potential for noncompliance with test protocols related to confusion, weakness, and other individual factors

Positive health-seeking behavior related to willingness to submit to diagnostic testing

At-risk health behavior related to refusal to participate in diagnostic testing

INTRATEST PHASE

Risk for injury related to developmental age, psychological factors, and test procedures

Risk for infection or allergic reaction related to altered immune function, history of chronic illness, allergens, or infectious agent

Risk for latex allergy response associated with test equipment

Pain, nausea, vomiting, or diarrhea related to laboratory and diagnostic procedures

Injury, actual or risk for, related to invasive procedure associated with laboratory or diagnostic testing

Risk for infection related to invasive procedures

Risk for bleeding associated with altered bleeding tendencies related to invasive procedures

Fatigue related to diagnostic procedure

Anxiety and fear related to arterial puncture or venipuncture

Risk for injury, bleeding, hematoma, or infection related to arterial puncture or venipuncture

Pain related to arterial puncture or venipuncture

Risk for impaired skin integrity

Potential impairment of gas exchange associated with test procedure

POST-TEST PHASE

Knowledge deficit related to significance of test results and potential need for further testing

Knowledge deficit related to test outcome deviation that may necessitate medication or lifestyle alterations

Anxiety and fear related to test outcome that may necessitate medication or lifestyle alterations

Ineffective coping related to test outcome and potential for other interventional techniques or procedures

Anticipatory grieving related to test outcome

Anticipatory or actual grieving related to perceived loss of health or threat of death associated with diagnostic outcome

Decisional conflict related to test outcome and potential for interventional procedures

Potential alteration in tissue perfusion: cerebral, cardiopulmonary, or peripheral

Knowledge deficit related to care after procedure

Potential for caregiver strain or interrupted family process related to laboratory or diagnostic results

Self-image disturbance related to altered ability to perform activities of daily living due to diagnostic findings

Spiritual distress related to unfavorable diagnostic study results

Caregiver-role strain related to anticipated increased care responsibilities associated with unfavorable laboratory or diagnostic study results

Appendix C

Guidelines for Age-Specific Communication

Effective communication between the health-care provider and the patient is influenced by the patient's cognitive abilities, sensory development or deprivation, level of stress, and environment. Effective communication with individuals at any stage of life is possible if one recognizes that it is essential to employ age-specific communication techniques based on an understanding of the continuum of human development as highlighted here.

INFANT (BIRTH TO 18 MO)

Developmental Stage: Trust versus Mistrust
Developing trust in others, demonstrated by consistent reliable care with love and affection
Lack of positive interactions leads to mistrust
Feeding is an important event at this developmental age

Physical
Rapid gains in height and weight
Gradual shift from reflexive movements to intentional actions

Motor and Sensory
Responds to light and sound
Progresses to raising and turning head, bringing hand to mouth, rolling over, sitting upright, and standing

Cognitive
Learns by imitation
Progresses to recognize familiar objects and people
Advances to speaking three or four words

Psychosocial
Significant persons are parents or primary caregivers
Develops sense of trust and security if needs are met
May show fear of strangers
May exhibit separation anxiety

Nursing Implications
Keep a parent or primary caregiver in view
Face the infant when providing care
Involve significant persons in care if appropriate
Complete intrusive or uncomfortable interventions last when possible
Use soothing nonverbal communication, such as holding, rocking, and cuddling
Check environment for safety hazards
Take precautions to prevent rolling off of surfaces
Maintain safety and keep crib side rails up at all times
Provide consistency in health-care staff to limit the number of strangers
Assess immunizations

TODDLER (2 TO 3 YR)

Developmental Stage: Autonomy versus Shame and Doubt
Becoming independent and self-reliant
Failure to do so results in self-doubt and shame
Potty training is an important event at this developmental age

Physical
Learning bladder and bowel control
Temporary teeth erupt
Physiological systems mature

Motor and Sensory
Developing a higher level of manual dexterity (builds towers with blocks)
Progresses to walking, jumping, and climbing
Loves to experiment

Cognitive
Has a short attention span
Understands simple directions and requests

Psychosocial

Significant persons are parents
Asserts independence
Understands ownership
Does not always understand sharing
Attached to security objects
Knows own gender
Plays simple games

Nursing Implications

Face the toddler during interactions
Give one direction at a time
Tie words to action (toddlers learn by example)
Use firm, direct approach; avoid harsh/excited words or actions
Use distraction techniques
Use soothing nonverbal communication, such as rocking, cuddling, and holding
Communicate through play (dolls, puppets, music)
Prepare shortly before a procedure
Allow choices when possible
Encourage mother or parent to stay with the child as appropriate
Encourage parents to participate in care as appropriate (e.g., child may be more easily examined when sitting in parent's lap)
Maintain safety and keep crib side rails up at all times

PRESCHOOL (3 TO 5 YR)

Developmental Stage: Initiative versus Guilt

Exploration and control of the environment while seeking answers to the world around them
Initiative that is rewarded results in a sense of purpose
Disapproval results in guilt and shame
Exploration is an important event at this developmental age

Physical

Birth length doubles
Bladder and bowel control achieved
Immune system is still immature

Motor and Sensory

Progresses in dressing self and lacing own shoes
Able to use pencil and scissors

Improving motor skills
Difficulty in judging distances predisposes to accidents

Cognitive

Thinking is concrete
Memory improves
Uses an active imagination
Able to ask for help

Psychosocial

Knows primary colors
Can count to five
Thinks anything that moves is alive
Concerned over small injuries
Egocentric thought and behavior
Able to help with simple chores

Nursing Implications

Provide simple explanations
Allow child to participate during physical examinations to encourage cooperation
Recognize that even small procedures (rectal temperature, IV start, etc.) are distressing
Recognize that postprocedure teaching is more meaningful than preprocedure teaching

SCHOOL AGE (6 TO 11 YR)

Developmental Stage: Industry versus Inferiority

Achievement of academic goals, including problem-solving and mastering tasks
Success leads to a sense of industry and failure to a sense of inferiority
School attendance is an important event at this developmental age

Physical

Growth is slow and regular
Permanent teeth erupt
Pubescent changes start
May experience growing pains
May experience fatigue

Motor and Sensory

Skips and hops
Dresses and undresses independently
Throws and catches a ball
Uses common utensils and tools
Draws, paints, and likes quiet as well as active games

APP

Cognitive

Major cognitive skill is communication
Understands numbers and can count
Constructs sentences and asks questions
Capable of logical thinking and can reason
Takes pride in accomplishments
Develops increased attention span

Psychosocial

Significant persons are parents, siblings, peers, teachers (prefers friends to family)
Increases independence and begins to assert self (may be physically aggressive)
Masters new tasks and acquires new skills
Behavior can be modified by rewards and punishment
Works hard to be successful

Nursing Implications

Clearly define and reinforce behavior limits
Tell jokes and play games with rules
Check for special words used to identify parents, body parts, or body functions
Explain procedures in advance, using simple explanations and correct terminology
Use dolls or puppets for explanations when performing procedures
Provide privacy
Protect modesty during examination
Involve whenever possible
Allow child to have some control
Promote independence
Praise for good behavior
Acknowledge fear, pain, or family separation
Educate about hygiene
Keep immunizations up to date

ADOLESCENT (12 TO 18 YR)

Developmental Stage: Identity versus Role Confusion

Separating self from parents and developing an individual identity
Learning to cope with who they are, how they fit in, ongoing body changes, and relationships with the opposite sex
Success leads to a strong sense of self and failure to role confusion
Development of social relationships is an important task

Physical

Growth in skeletal size is rapid
Reproductive system matures
Vital signs approximate those of an adult

Motor and Sensory

Easily fatigued
May need more rest and sleep in early adolescence
Awkwardness in gross motor activity
Demonstrates improving fine motor skills

Cognitive

Increased ability to use abstract thought and logic
Able to handle hypothetical situations and thoughts
Shows growth in self-esteem but is challenged by bouts of insecurity
Avoids asking questions for fear of appearing unintelligent

Psychosocial

Develops sexual identity
Shows interest in and confusion with own development
Develops concern with physical appearance
Establishes critical need for privacy
Values belonging to peer group
Perceives self as invincible
Identity is threatened by hospitalization

Nursing Implications

Recognize that adolescent likes to be treated as an adult
Do not talk to others about the patient in front of him or her
Do not ask questions about drugs, sex, or use of tobacco in front of parents
Provide information about routines and therapy with rationale
Provide privacy
Protect modesty during examination
Supplement information with rationale
Encourage questions
Allow to maintain control
Involve in planning and making decisions for own care
Allow for expression of fear, such as fear of bodily injury and loss of control
Encourage collaboration between adolescent and health-care team
Provide guidance in health-care decisions

YOUNG ADULT (19 TO 40 YR)

Developmental Stage: Intimacy versus Isolation

Forms intimate, loving relationships with others

Success leads to strong personal relationships, and failure leads to loneliness

Relationship building is the most important developmental task at this age

Physical

Reaches physical and sexual maturity

Prone to health problems related to an inability to cope with new responsibilities

Nutritional needs for maintenance rather than growth

Health-care needs related to preventative medicine

Motor and Sensory

Skills are fully developed

Full sensory development

Cognitive

Focuses on time constraints and wants to learn only what is practical for him or her

May be dual caregiver (i.e., parents and children)

Is a problem-solver

May seek intellectual experiences

May acquire new work skills

Psychosocial

Experiences emotional stress secondary to mate selection, vocational selection, assuming occupational roles, marriage, childbearing, financial pressure, and independence

Becomes more comfortable with body image

Becomes independent of parents

Chooses career and begins work life

Develops intimate relationships

Creates personal set of values

Reaches psychosocial maturity

Demonstrates interest in community and world affairs

Nursing Implications

Provide privacy

Respect personal values

Provide information regarding treatment plan

Provide rationale for adhering to treatment plan

Provide information and support to make health-care decisions

Encourage questions and concerns, and address them respectfully

Provide education to family as appropriate

Understand that impact on income may influence care decisions

Provide care that emphasizes strengths rather than limitations

Provide honest and supportive care

Understand that some adjustment to family roles may be necessary due to illness

Understand that unknown factors may affect behavior

MIDDLE ADULTHOOD (40 TO 65 YR)

Developmental Stage: Generativity versus Stagnation

Goal is developing a positive change in others through caring and nurturing

Success leads to a sense of accomplishment and failure to a sense of being uninvolved

Work and parenting are the most important developmental tasks at this age

Physical

Decrease in bone density

Decrease in height with age

Decrease in muscle tone

Adjustment to menopause (women) and sexual dysfunction (men)

Decrease in physical endurance

Motor and Sensory

Decreasing visual acuity

Hearing may begin to deteriorate

Changes in smell and taste

Cognitive

Assists children to become independent

Begins to prepare for death emotionally

Seeks further education

Psychosocial

Experiences becoming a grandparent

Maintains contact with extended family

Engages in adult leisure activities

Prepares for retirement

Recognizes aging process

APP

Nursing Implications

Inform of treatment plan

Involve in planning care

Recognize that family roles may need adjustments due to illness

Recognize that family stress may occur due to illness

Understand that support income may be affected by illness

LATE ADULTHOOD (65 YR AND OLDER)

Developmental Stage: Ego Integrity versus Despair

Reflection of the life lived

Acceptance of how own life was lived leads to feelings of success

Despair, bitterness, and regret occur if, upon reflection, own life seems to be a failure

Life review and reflection is the most important developmental task at this age

Physical

Ages gradually and individually

Experiences decreased tolerance to heat/cold

Encounters declining cardiac and renal function

Experiences skeletal changes (bones become more prominent, shrinkage in vertebral disks, stiff joints)

Becomes subject to increased susceptibility to infection and to high blood pressure

Undergoes skin changes

Motor and Sensory

Experiences decrease in mobility, visual acuity, ability to respond to stimuli, hearing, and motor skills

Cognitive

Experiences decrease in memory, slowing of mental functions, slowness in learning, and drop in performance

Psychosocial

Encounters lifestyle changes secondary to children leaving home, children providing grandchildren, re-establishing a relationship as a couple, and retirement/hobbies

Develops increased concern for health and financial security

Accepts concept of own mortality

Faces decreased authority and autonomy

Experiences depression related to decreased physical, motor, and cognitive abilities

Nursing Implications

Give respect and provide privacy

Explain instructions well to patient and family

Include patient in conversation/activity to prevent social isolation

Review important points repeatedly

Ask questions to verify understanding

Focus on strengths, not limitations

Respect preference for independence

Encourage to talk about feelings

Provide information and support regarding end-of-life decisions

Avoid assuming loss of abilities

Seek information as necessary to deal with impairments

Provide teaching for safety

Monitor closely to avoid falls

Keep room clutter-free and call bell within reach

Consider additional lighting at night

Control room temperature for comfort

Consider need for changes in diet and activity

Provide teaching for medications and test preparations

Watch for signs of drug toxicity; medications may require smaller doses

Transfusion Reactions: Laboratory Findings and Potential Nursing Interventions

These reactions are mainly associated with the transfusion of leuko-reduced packed red blood cells.

CATEGORIES:

I. Acute (Less Than 24 hr) Immune-Mediated Transfusion Reactions
   a. ABO and non-ABO acute hemolytic
   b. Febrile nonhemolytic
   c. Urticarial/allergic reaction
   d. Anaphylactic reaction

II. Acute (Less Than 24 hr) Non–Immune-Mediated Transfusion Reactions
   a. Transfusion-related acute lung injury
   b. Circulatory overload
   c. Metabolic complications
   d. Hypothermia
   e. Hypotension associated with angiotensin-converting enzyme inhibition
   f. Embolism (air and particulate)
   g. Nonimmune hemolysis

III. Delayed (Greater Than 24 hr) Immune-Mediated Transfusion Reactions
   a. Hemolytic
   b. Alloimmunization to red blood cell, white blood cell, platelet, and protein antigens
   c. Graft versus host

IV. Delayed (Greater Than 24 hr) Non–Immune-Mediated Transfusion Reactions
   a. Iron overload

I. Acute Immune-Mediated Transfusion Reactions

a. ABO and non-ABO	Dramatic, severe, and can be fatal; incidence of acute hemolytic is 1:38,000 to 1:70,000 units; result of reaction between antibodies in the patient's plasma and the corresponding antigen being present on the donor's cells; severity affected by amount of patient antibody present, quantity of antigen on transfused cells, volume of blood transfused
Symptoms	Anxiety, chills, fever, flushing, generalized bleeding, hemoglobinuria, hypotension, lower back pain, nausea, pain or oozing at the infusion site, renal failure with oliguria, tachycardia, vomiting
Laboratory findings	Positive DAT; elevated: indirect bilirubin (5–7 hr posttransfusion), LDH, BUN, creatinine, PT, aPTT; decreased: anti-A and anti-B titers, haptoglobin; hemoglobinemia; hemoglobinuria; hypofibrinogenemia; thrombocytopenia; positive urinary hemosiderin; presence of spherocytes and RBC fragments on peripheral smear

(table continues on page 1486)

I. Acute Immune-Mediated Transfusion Reactions (continued)

Treatment	Immediately stop transfusion, maintain airway, oxygen therapy as needed, maintain renal flow at greater than 100 mL/hr by use of osmotic and diuretic agents (e.g., Lasix, furosemide); monitor for development of DIC (uncontrolled bleeding, decreasing platelet count, prolonged PT/PTT); future transfusion with O-negative packed cells
b. Febrile nonhemolytic	Most common type of transfusion reaction; incidence is 1:200 to 1:17 (0.5%–6.0%); repeat occurrences are uncommon; result of antileukocyte, antiplatelet, or anti-HLA antibodies
Symptoms	Chills, cough, fever, headache, rigors, tachycardia, vomiting
Laboratory findings	Negative DAT; transient leukopenia
Treatment	Immediately stop transfusion; administer non-salicylate-containing antipyretics (steroids in severe cases); meperidine by injection may be useful in patients with rigors; transfuse with leukocyte-reduced blood after two documented febrile nonhemolytic reactions
c. Urticarial/allergic reaction	Second-most common type of reaction; incidence 1:100 to 1:33 (1%–3%); histamine-mediated reaction of allergin + IgE fixed on mast cells
Symptoms	Hives, itching, local erythema, usually no fever
Laboratory findings	Negative DAT
Treatment	Immediately stop transfusion; keep line open; administer antihistamines (e.g., diphenhydramine 25–50 mg); resume transfusion when symptoms subside; for future transfusions, premedicate with antihistamines; consider future transfusion with washed or deglycerized frozen RBCs after recurrent allergic reaction
d. Anaphylactic reaction	Occurs rapidly with 10 mL or less; 1 in 700 individuals are IgA deficient and 25% have anti-IgA antibodies that will react to donor's plasma proteins; incidence is 1:20,000 to 1:50,000
Symptoms	Abdominal cramping, anxiety, bronchospasm, cyanosis, circulatory collapse, dyspnea, flushing, hypotension, laryngeal edema, loss of consciousness, shock, substernal pain, tachycardia, urticaria, wheezing
Laboratory findings	Negative DAT, presence of IgG class anti-IgA antibodies or undetectable level of IgA
Treatment	Treat for anaphylaxis with epinephrine, steroid therapy as needed, maintain airway, oxygen therapy as needed, Trendelenburg position, fluids; for future transfusions, premedicate with antihistamines and transfuse with IgA-deficient donor blood or autologous blood

APP

II. Acute Non–Immune-Mediated Transfusion Reactions

a. Transfusion-related acute lung injury	Incidence of reaction to anti-WBC antibodies in donated whole blood–derived platelets, 1:432; in plasma-containing blood component, 1:2,000; in blood component, 1:5,000; fresh frozen plasma, 1:7,900
Symptoms	Cyanosis, fever, hypotension, hypoxemia, respiratory failure, tachycardia
Laboratory findings	Positive WBC antibody screen (donor or recipient), incompatible WBC crossmatch, normal BNP can help differentiate from circulatory overload
Treatment	Supportive care until recovered, maintain airway, oxygen therapy as needed, treat hypotension; implicated donors should be deferred from future donation
b. Circulatory overload	Incidence less than 1%; result of volume overload
Symptoms	Cough, dyspnea, headache, hypertension, orthopnea, tachycardia
Laboratory findings	Abnormal increase in BNP level can help differentiate from TRALI
Treatment	Upright posture; maintain airway, oxygen therapy as needed, diuretic; administer blood slowly; phlebotomy (250-mL increments)
c. Metabolic complications	Hypocalcemia resulting from rapid massive infusion of citrate; incidence dependent on clinical setting
Symptoms	Arrhythmia, paresthesia, tetany
Laboratory findings	Elevated ionized calcium level, prolonged Q-T interval on EKG
Treatment	Slow calcium infusion, oral calcium supplement for mild symptoms; monitor ionized calcium levels (severe symptoms)
d. Hypothermia	Result of rapid infusion of cold blood
Symptoms	Cardiac arrhythmia
Laboratory findings	N/A
Treatment	Utilize blood warmer
e. Hypotension associated with ACE inhibition	Patients on ACE inhibitors receiving leukocyte-reduced packed cells have experienced hypotension (believed to be the result of an interaction between the ACE inhibitor and the kinin/prekallikrein system); incidence is dependent on the clinical setting.
Symptoms	Flushing, hypotension
Laboratory findings	Positive DAT, hemolyzed intra- or post-transfusion specimen
Treatment	Avoid bedside leukocyte filtration
f. Embolism (air and particulate)	Result of air infusion via line; incidence is rare
Symptoms	Acute cyanosis, cardiac arrhythmia, cough, hypotension, pain, sudden shortness of breath

APP

(table continues on page 1488)

II. Acute Non–Immune-Mediated Transfusion Reactions (continued)

Laboratory findings	N/A
Treatment	Position patient on left side with legs elevated above head and chest
g. Nonimmune hemolysis	Result of physical or chemical destruction of RBCs (e.g., heating, freezing, hemolytic drug, solution added to blood); incidence is rare
Symptoms	Hemoglobinuria
Laboratory findings	Positive plasma-free hemoglobin, positive DAT, obvious hemolysis in unit containing the blood
Treatment	Identify and eliminate cause

III. Delayed Immune-Mediated Transfusion Reactions

a. Hemolytic	Anamnestic immune response to RBC antigens; incidence 1:11,000 to 1:50,000
Symptoms	Anemia, fever, mild jaundice
Laboratory findings	Positive antibody screen, urinary hemosiderin and DAT; increased LDH, bilirubin
Treatment	Identify antibody and transfuse compatible blood as needed
b. Alloimmunization to RBC, WBC, platelet, and protein antigens	Immune response to RBC, WBC, or platelet antigens; incidence 1:100
Symptoms	Delayed hemolytic reaction
Laboratory findings	Positive antibody screen and DAT
Treatment	Avoid unnecessary transfusions; give leukocyte-reduced blood if transfusion is necessary
c. Graft versus host	Donor lymphocytes attack recipient's host tissue; incidence is rare
Symptoms	Anorexia, diarrhea, erythroderma, fever, hepatitis, maculopapular rash, nausea, pancytopenia, vomiting; symptoms typically appear 8–10 days following transfusion but may appear as soon as 3 or as later as 30 days posttransfusion, rapid progression of symptoms with almost 100% mortality
Laboratory findings	Abnormal skin biopsy, incompatible HLA typing
Treatment	Immunosuppressant therapy (methotrexate, corticosteroids, IV immune globulin); transfuse with irradiated blood products; stem cell transplant

IV. Delayed Non–Immune-Mediated Transfusion Reactions

a. *Iron overload*	Result of chronic transfusions (greater than 100)
Symptoms	Symptoms associated with cardiomyopathy, cirrhosis, diabetes
Laboratory findings	Increased iron levels
Treatment	Desferioxamine

ACE = angiotensin-converting enzyme; BNP = B-type natriuretic peptide; BUN = blood urea nitrogen; DAT = (Coombs') direct antiglobulin test; DIC = disseminated intravascular coagulation; ECG = electrocardiogram; HLA = human leukocyte antigen; Ig = immunoglobulin; LDH = lactate dehydrogenase; N/A = not applicable; PT = prothrombin time; PTT = partial thromboplastin time; RBC = red blood cell; TRALI = transfusion-related acute lung injury; WBC = white blood cell.

APP

Appendix E

Introduction to CLIA

The acronym *CLIA* stands for Clinical Laboratory Improvement Amendments. In 1988, Congress passed CLIA to establish quality standards that would apply to laboratory testing nationwide. The standards ensure that, regardless of location, all clinical testing on human specimens is performed with accuracy, reliability, and timeliness. In 1992, CLIA's final regulations distinguished between levels of test complexity. Three categories were established: waived complexity, moderate complexity (includes the subcategory of provider-performed microscopy [PPM]), and high-complexity testing. Permission to perform clinical laboratory testing in any or all categories requires the laboratory director to submit an application to enroll in the CLIA program, pay the applicable fee, and meet quality requirements that correspond to the type of certificate that is obtained. The 10-1-04 edition of 42 CFR Ch. IV, Part 493, the most current version of CLIA regulations, is the source used to write this introduction (available at wwwn.cdc.gov/clia/pdf/42cfr493_2004.pdf).

A Certificate of Waiver (COW) obtained by the appropriate health-care provider (HCP) allows qualified nursing or other health-care personnel to perform procedures classified as waived testing in an HCP's office or in a hospital nursing unit. Waived testing includes tests that are cleared by the U.S. Food and Drug Administration (FDA) for home use, have manufacturers' instructions to follow, and pose no harm to the patient if testing is performed incorrectly. The testing process utilizes controls. Examples of waived testing include dipstick urinalysis, fecal occult blood, ovulation testing, urine pregnancy tests, erythrocyte sedimentation rate (nonautomated), hemoglobin (copper sulfate method), blood glucose (on glucose meters cleared by the FDA), spun hematocrit, and hemoglobin by single analyte instruments that are self-contained with direct measurement and readout. Over 100 analytes, used in a variety of test systems and that can be performed on eight different specimen types, have been waived. Specific information can be obtained at www.accessdata.fda.gov/scripts/cdrh/cfdocs/cfClia/analyteswaived.cfm.

In addition to waived testing, PPM testing can be performed in an HCP's office. A PPM certificate obtained by a physician or midlevel practitioner allows the practitioner to perform PPM testing on specimens obtained during the patient's office visit. A midlevel practitioner can perform this type of testing under the direct supervision of a physician or in independent practice if authorized by the state. A microscope is utilized to view the specimens during the patient's office visit. PPM tests are performed on specimens in situations in which the accuracy of the findings would be compromised if a delay in testing were to occur. The testing process has no available controls. Examples of PPM testing include urine sediment examinations; potassium hydroxide preparations; pinworm examinations; fern tests; nasal smears for granulocytes; fecal leukocyte examinations; qualitative semen analysis (limited to determining the presence or absence of sperm and detection of motility); postcoital direct qualitative examinations of vaginal or cervical mucus; and wet-mount testing for the presence or absence of bacteria, fungi, parasites, and cellular elements.

Hospital and reference laboratories perform tests of moderate and high complexity. The laboratory director must obtain the corresponding CLIA certificate and have personnel qualified to perform tests of moderate and high complexity.

Effects of Natural Products on Laboratory Values

The use of natural products has increased significantly, but to date, their preparation is unregulated. Their actions can affect normal and abnormal physiological processes as well as interact with prescription medications. Their presence in the body, alone or in combination with over-the-counter products or prescription medications, may physiologically affect the intended target or cause analytical interference in such a way that the test result is affected. For this reason, it is important to note their use. The natural products listed here are contraindicated or are recommended for use with caution in patients with body system disorders or patients taking medications for these disorders. The requesting health-care provider (HCP) and laboratory should be advised if the patient is regularly using these products so that their potential effects can be taken into consideration when reviewing results.

APP

This list is not all-inclusive. Questions regarding the potential benefits and contraindications of natural products should be referred to the appropriate HCP. As a general recommendation, natural products and nutraceuticals are contraindicated during pregnancy and lactation.

NATURAL PRODUCTS THAT MAY AFFECT CARDIOVASCULAR DISORDERS OR INTERACT WITH THERAPEUTICS (INCLUDING HYPERTENSION AND HYPOTENSION)

Natural Products

Adonis
Aloe
Bromelain
Buckthorn
Cascara
Chinese rhubarb
Coleus
Dong quai
Elder
Ephedra
Ergot
Frangula
Garlic
Ginseng
Goldenseal
Green tea (with caffeine)
Henbane
Horsetail
Lily of the valley
Ma-huang
Reishi
Senna
Squill
Tylophora
Valerian
Yohimbe bark

NATURAL PRODUCTS AND NUTRACEUTICALS THAT MAY AFFECT ENDOCRINE DISORDERS OR INTERACT WITH THERAPEUTICS

Natural Products

Bilberry
Bitter melon
Bladderwrack
Blupleurum
Bugleweed
Echinacea
Ephedra
Fenugreek
Garcinia
Garlic
Ginseng
Goat's rue
Green tea (with caffeine)
Guggul
Licorice
Marshmallow
Olive leaf
Psyllium
Tylophora

Minerals
Chromium
Nutraceuticals
Dehydroepiandrosterone
α-Lipoic acid
Para-aminobenzoic acid
Thyroid extract

NATURAL PRODUCTS AND NUTRACEUTICALS THAT MAY AFFECT GASTROINTESTINAL DISORDERS OR INTERACT WITH THERAPEUTICS

Natural Products
Bromelain
Cascara
Chinese rhubarb
Dandelion
Psyllium
Senna

Nutraceuticals
Betaine hydrochloride

NATURAL PRODUCTS AND NUTRACEUTICALS THAT MAY AFFECT GENITOURINARY DISORDERS OR INTERACT WITH THERAPEUTICS

Natural Products
Aloe
Arabinoxylane
Bladderwrack
Buckthorn
Cascara
Chinese rhubarb
Dandelion
Echinacea
Ephedra
Ergot
Frangula
Ginseng
Guarana
Horse chestnut
Horsetail
Licorice
Parsley oil (high doses)
Saw palmetto
Senna
Stinging nettle
White oak
White willow

Nutraceuticals
Creatine
Modified citrus pectin

NATURAL PRODUCTS AND NUTRACEUTICALS THAT MAY AFFECT BLEEDING DISORDERS OR INTERACT WITH THERAPEUTICS

Natural Products
Arnica
Astragalus
Bilberry
Bromelian
Cat's claw
Cayenne
Coleus
Cordyceps
Devil's claw
Dong quai
Evening primrose
Feverfew
Garlic
Ginger
Gingko
Ginseng
Grape seed
Green tea (with caffeine)
Guggui
Horse chestnut
Papaya
Red clover
Red yeast rice
Reishi
Turmeric
White willow

Nutraceuticals
Docosahexaenoic acid (DHA)
Fish oils (the omega-3 fatty acids: EPA and DHA)

NATURAL PRODUCTS AND NUTRACEUTICALS THAT MAY AFFECT HEPATOBILIARY DISORDERS OR INTERACT WITH THERAPEUTICS

Natural Products
Alkanet
Alpine ragwort
Coltsfoot
Comfrey

APP

Dusty miller
Forget-me-not
Germander
Groundsel
Olive leaf
Parsley oil (large doses)
Pennyroyal
Peppermint
Ragwort
Red yeast rice
Sweet clover
White oak
White willow

Nutraceuticals
Creatine

NATURAL PRODUCTS AND AMINO ACIDS THAT MAY AFFECT IMMUNE DISORDERS OR INTERACT WITH THERAPEUTICS

Natural Products
Astragalus
Black cohosh

Echinacea
Saw palmetto

Amino Acids
Arginine

NATURAL PRODUCTS THAT MAY AFFECT RESPIRATORY DISORDERS OR INTERACT WITH THERAPEUTICS

Natural Products
Artichoke
Cayenne
Chamomile
Cordyceps
Echinacea
Feverfew
Garlic
Peppermint oil
White willow

APP

Appendix G

Standard Precautions

Recommendations for Isolation Precautions in Hospitals*

RATIONALE FOR ISOLATION PRECAUTIONS IN HOSPITALS

Transmission of infection within a hospital requires three elements: a source of infecting microorganisms, a susceptible host, and a means of transmission for the microorganism.

Source

Human sources of the infecting microorganisms in hospitals may be patients, personnel, or, on occasion, visitors, and may include persons with acute disease, persons in the incubation period of a disease, persons who are colonized by an infectious agent but have no apparent disease, or persons who are chronic carriers of an infectious agent. Other sources of infecting microorganisms can be the patient's own endogenous flora, which may be difficult to control, and inanimate environmental objects that have become contaminated, including equipment and medications.

Host

Resistance among persons to pathogenic microorganisms varies greatly. Some persons may be immune to infection or may be able to resist colonization by an infectious agent; others exposed to the same agent may establish a commensal relationship with the infecting microorganism and become asymptomatic carriers; still others may develop clinical disease. Host factors such as age, underlying diseases; certain treatments with antimicrobials, corticosteroids, or other immunosuppressive agents; irradiation; and breaks in the first line of defense mechanisms caused by such factors as surgical operations, anesthesia, and indwelling urinary and central venous catheters (urinary catheters and central venous catheters) may render patients more susceptible to infection.

Transmission

The classic definition of *transmission* is an appraisal of how classes of pathogens cause infection. Simply stated, microorganisms are transmitted in hospitals by several routes, and the same microorganism may be transmitted by more than one route. There are three common modes of transmission: contact, droplet, and airborne. Within this context, health-care providers need to differentiate between nosocomial infection and health-care-associated infection (HAI). The term *nosocomial infection* refers to those infections that are acquired in a hospital, whereas an HAI can be acquired from delivery of care in multiple settings, including, hospitals, long-term care, ambulatory care, or home care. The difference between the two terms is that in nosocomial infections we know the infection was acquired in the hospital. With HAI we know that the infection was acquired somewhere along the health-care path, we are just not sure exactly when or where. An example would be an individual who moves from home care, to acute care, to long-term care. Additional modes of transmission are common vehicle and vectorborne, which will be discussed briefly for the purpose of this guideline as neither play a significant role in the typical nosocomial or HAI infections.

1494

. *Contact transmission,* the most important and frequent mode of transmission of nosocomial or HAI infections, is divided into two subgroups: direct-contact transmission and indirect-contact transmission.

1a. *Direct-contact transmission* involves a direct body surface-to-body surface contact and physical transfer of microorganisms between a suscep-tible host and an infected or colonized person. In the health-care setting, this occurs most frequently between patient and health-care personnel through a mucous membrane crack or ungloved patient contact with infected/infested skin. Examples of such contacts can include turning a patient, giving a patient a bath, or performing other patient-care activities that require direct contact. Direct-contact transmission also can occur between two patients, with one serving as the source of the infectious microorganisms and the other as a susceptible host.

1b. *Indirect-contact transmission* involves contact of a susceptible host with a contaminated intermediate object, usually inanimate, such as contam-inated instruments, needles, dressings, or shared patient care devices such as glucose monitoring machines. For children, those inanimate objects can even include toys. Other sources are insufficient hand hygiene, or gloves that are not changed between patients, as well as soiled clothing such as uniforms or laboratory coats have been found to be a source for indirect-contact transmission. Multidrug-resistant organisms (MDRO) are a special concern in health-care settings. Transmission usually occurs patient-to-patient by the hands of health-care workers.

Droplet transmission, theoretically, is a form of contact transmission. However, the mechanism of transfer of the pathogen to the host is quite distinct from either direct- or indirect-contact transmission. Therefore, drop-let transmission is considered a separate route of transmission in this guide-line. Historically droplet size is defined as being 5 µm or greater. Droplets are generated from the source person primarily during coughing, sneezing, and talking, and during the performance of certain procedures such as suction-ing and bronchoscopy. Transmission occurs when droplets containing micro-organisms generated from the infected person are propelled a short distance through the air and deposited on the host's conjunctivae, nasal mucosa, or mouth. The general rule of thumb has been that droplets will travel approxi-mately 3 ft from the source to the host. However, studies suggest that drop-lets from organisms such as smallpox and severe acute respiratory distress syndrome (SARS) can travel a distance of 6 ft or more from source to host. Therefore the suggested distance of 3 ft is considered to be a recommenda-tion rather a mandate. As a result, distance should not be the only criteria used to decide whether or not the use of a mask is appropriate. Because droplets do not remain suspended in the air, special air handling and ventila-tion are not required to prevent droplet transmission; that is, droplet trans-mission *must not* be confused with airborne transmission.

Airborne transmission occurs by dissemination of either airborne droplet nuclei (small-particle residue [5 µm or smaller in size] of evaporated drop-lets containing microorganisms that remain suspended in the air for long periods of time) or dust particles containing the infectious agent. Microorganisms carried in this manner can be dispersed widely by air cur-rents and may become inhaled by a susceptible host within the same room or over a longer distance from the source patient, depending on environ-mental factors; therefore, special air handling and ventilation such as an airborne infection isolation room are required to prevent airborne transmission. Microorganisms transmitted by airborne transmission include *Mycobacterium tuberculosis, Aspergillus spp.,* and the rubeola and varicella viruses.

4. *Common vehicle transmission* applies to microorganisms transmitted by contaminated items such as food, water, medications, devices, and equipment

5. *Vector-borne transmission* occurs when vectors such as mosquitoes, flies, rats, and other vermin transmit microorganisms; this route of transmission is of less significance in hospitals in the United States than in other regions of the world.

Isolation precautions are designed to prevent transmission of microorganisms by these routes in hospitals. Because agent and host factors are more difficult to control, interruption of transfer of microorganisms is directed primarily at transmission. This goal can be more readily achieved by having an infection control nurse assist in the implementation of policies at the unit level; adequate staff with minimal use of outside staff; clinical laboratory support to promptly report important organisms or outbreak concerns; implementation of a culture of safety within the organization; adherence of health-care workers to recommended infection control guidelines; surveillance for HAIs; and continuing education of health-care workers, patients, and families. The recommendations presented in this guideline are based on this concept.

Placing a patient on isolation precautions, however, often presents certain disadvantages to the hospital, patients, personnel, and visitors. Isolation precautions may require specialized equipment and environmental modifications that add to the cost of hospitalization. Isolation precautions may make frequent visits by nurses, physicians, and other personnel inconvenient, and they may make it more difficult for personnel to give the prompt and frequent care that sometimes is required. The use of a multi-patient room for one patient uses valuable space that otherwise might accommodate several patients. Moreover, forced solitude deprives the patient of normal social relationships and may be psychologically harmful, especially to children. These disadvantages, however, must be weighed against the hospital's mission to prevent the spread of serious and epidemiologically important microorganisms in the hospital.

FUNDAMENTALS OF ISOLATION PRECAUTIONS

A variety of infection control measures are used for decreasing the risk of transmission of microorganisms in hospitals. These measures make up the fundamentals of isolation precautions. Examples of personal protective equipment (PPE) used in infection control include gloves, gowns, masks, goggles, and shoe covers.

Hand Hygiene and Gloving

Hand hygiene is frequently called the single most important measure to reduce the risks of transmitting organisms from one person to another or from one site to another on the same patient. The concept of hand hygiene includes hand washing, or in the absence of visible soiling, the use of approved alcohol-based products for hand disinfecting. The scientific rationale, indications, methods, and products for hand washing are delineated in other publications.

Hand washing or the use of alcohol-based products should be completed as promptly and thoroughly as possible between patient contacts and after contact with blood, body fluids, secretions, and excretions. Hand hygiene should also occur after contact with equipment or articles contaminated by blood, fluids, secretions, or excretions. Such hygiene is an important component of infection control and isolation precautions. In addition to hand hygiene, gloves play a key role in reducing the risks of microorganism transmission. The effectiveness of hand hygiene can be reduced by health-care workers wearing artificial nails as they can harbor pathogenic organisms. It is recommended that health-care workers who provide direct patient care be restricted from wearing these nails.

Gloves are worn for three important reasons in hospitals. First, gloves are worn to provide a protective barrier and to prevent gross contamination of the hands when touching blood, body fluids, secretions, excretions, mucous membranes, and nonintact skin; the wearing of gloves in specified circumstances to reduce the risk of exposures to bloodborne pathogens is mandated by the Occupational Safety and Health Administration (OSHA) bloodborne pathogens final rule. Second, gloves are worn to reduce the likelihood that microorganisms present on the hands of personnel will be transmitted to patients during invasive or other patient-care procedures that involve touching a patient's mucous membranes and nonintact skin. Third, gloves are worn to reduce the likelihood that hands of personnel contaminated with microorganisms from a patient or a fomite can transmit these microorganisms to another patient. In this situation, gloves must be changed between patient contacts and hands washed after gloves are removed.

Wearing gloves does not replace the need for hand hygiene, because gloves may have small, inapparent defects or may be torn during use, and hands can become contaminated during removal of gloves. Changing gloves is recommended when provision of care requires touching equipment that is moved from room to room. Failure to change gloves between patient contacts is an infection control hazard.

Patient Placement

Appropriate patient placement is a significant component of isolation precautions. A private room is important to prevent direct- or indirect-contact transmission when the source patient has poor hygienic habits, contaminates the environment, or cannot be expected to assist in maintaining infection control precautions to limit transmission of microorganisms (e.g., infants, children, and patients with altered mental status). When possible, a patient with highly transmissible or epidemiologically important microorganisms is placed in a private room with hand washing and toilet facilities to reduce opportunities for transmission of microorganisms.

When a private room is not available, an infected patient is placed with an appropriate roommate. Patients infected by the same microorganism usually can share a room, provided they are not infected with other potentially transmissible microorganisms and the likelihood of reinfection with the same organism is minimal. Such sharing of rooms, also referred to as cohorting patients, is useful especially during outbreaks or when there is a shortage of private rooms. When a private room is not available and cohorting is not achievable or recommended, it is very important to consider the epidemiology and mode of transmission of the infecting pathogen and the patient population being served in determining patient placement. Under these circumstances, consultation with infection control professionals is advised before patient placement. Moreover, when an infected patient shares a room with a noninfected patient, it also is important that patients, personnel, and visitors take precautions to prevent the spread of infection and that roommates are selected carefully.

Guidelines for construction, equipment, air handling, and ventilation fo isolation rooms are delineated in other publications. A private room wit appropriate air handling and ventilation is particularly important for reducing the risk of transmission of microorganisms from a source patient to susceptible patients and other persons in hospitals when the microorganism is spread b airborne transmission. Some hospitals use an isolation room with an anteroom as an extra measure of precaution to prevent airborne transmission. Adequat data regarding the need for an anteroom, however, is not available. Ventilatio recommendations for isolation rooms housing patients with pulmonary tube culosis have been delineated in other Centers for Disease Control an Prevention (CDC) guidelines.

Transport of Infected Patients

Limiting the movement and transport of patients infected with virulent epidemiologically important microorganisms and ensuring that such patient leave their rooms only for essential purposes reduces opportunities for tran mission of microorganisms in hospitals. When patient transport is necessary, is important that (1) appropriate barriers (e.g., masks, impervious dressing are worn or used by the patient to reduce the opportunity for transmission pertinent microorganisms to other patients, personnel, and visitors and reduce contamination of the environment; (2) personnel in the area to whic the patient is to be taken are notified of the impending arrival of the patie and of the precautions to be used to reduce the risk of transmission of infe tious microorganisms; and (3) patients are informed of ways by which the can assist in preventing the transmission of their infectious microorganisms others.

Masks, Respiratory Protection, Eye Protection, Face Shields

Various types of masks, goggles, and face shields are worn alone or in com nation to provide barrier protection. A mask that covers both the nose and t mouth, as well as goggles or a face shield are worn by hospital personnel d ing procedures and patient-care activities that are likely to generate splash or sprays of blood, body fluids, secretions, or excretions to provide protecti of the mucous membranes of the eyes, nose, and mouth from contact transm sion of pathogens. The use of masks also protects the patient from exposu to organisms from health-care workers during sterile procedures, and prote health-care workers and others from exposure to coughing patients. The we ing of masks, eye protection, and face shields in specified circumstances reduce the risk of exposures to bloodborne pathogens is mandated by t OSHA bloodborne pathogens final rule. A surgical mask generally is worn hospital personnel to provide protection against spread of infectious lar particle droplets that are transmitted by close contact and generally tra only short distances (up to 3 ft) from infected patients who are coughing sneezing.

An area of major concern and controversy over the last several years been the role and selection of respiratory protection equipment and the im cations of a respiratory protection program for prevention of transmission tuberculosis in hospitals. Traditionally, although the efficacy was not prove surgical mask was worn for isolation precautions in hospitals when patie were known or suspected to be infected with pathogens spread by the airborne route of transmission. In 1990, however, the CDC tuberculosis guidelines stated that surgical masks may not be effective in preventing the inhalation of droplet nuclei and recommended the use of disposable particulate respirators, despite that the efficacy of particulate respirators in protecting persons from the inhalation of *M. tuberculosis* had not been demonstrated. By definition, particulate respirators included dust-mist (DM), dust-fume-mist (DFM), or high-efficiency particulate air (HEPA) filter respirators certified by the CDC National Institute for Occupational Safety and Health (NIOSH); because the generic term "particulate respirator" was used in the 1990 guidelines, the implication was that any of these respirators provided sufficient protection.

In 1993, a draft revision of the CDC tuberculosis guidelines outlined performance criteria for respirators and stated that some DM or DFM respirators might not meet these criteria. After review of public comments, the guidelines were finalized in October 1994, with the draft respirator criteria unchanged. At that time, the only class of respirators that were known to consistently meet or exceed the performance criteria outlined in the 1994 tuberculosis guidelines and that were certified by NIOSH (as required by OSHA) were HEPA filter respirators. Subsequently, NIOSH revised the testing and certification requirements for all types of air-purifying respirators, including those used for tuberculosis control. The new rule, effective in July 1995, provides a broader range of certified respirators that meet the performance criteria recommended by the CDC in the 1994 tuberculosis guidelines. NIOSH has indicated that the N95 (N category at 95% efficiency) meets the CDC performance criteria for a tuberculosis respirator. Current recommendations encourage health-care care workers to undergo fit-testing. The goal of fit-testing is to ensure that the health-care worker's respirator (N95 mask) fits well during job performance. The frequency of fit-testing has not been specified. Generally fit-testing should be repeated when there is a change in facial features, a change in mask model or sizing, and for any condition effecting the health-care worker's respiratory function. During testing, it is important to assess theses salient points, mask positioning and fit across the nose, cheeks, and chin, with room for eye protection, and room to talk. Additional information on the evolution of respirator recommendations, regulations to protect hospital personnel, and the role of various federal agencies in respiratory protection for hospital personnel has been published.

Gowns and Protective Apparel

Various types of gowns and protective apparel are worn to provide barrier protection and to reduce opportunities for transmission of microorganisms in hospitals. Gowns are worn to prevent contamination of clothing and to protect the skin of personnel from blood and body fluid exposures. Gowns specially coated to make them impermeable to liquids, leg coverings, boots or shoe coverings provide greater protection to the skin when splashes or large quantities of infective material are present or anticipated. Gowns should cover the arms, torso, and legs to mid-thigh, providing complete coverage of these areas. Remove gowns cautiously to prevent contamination of clothing. Gowns and all other PPE should be removed and discarded prior to leaving the patient's room. The wearing of gowns and protective apparel under specified circumstances to reduce the risk of exposures to bloodborne pathogens is mandated by the OSHA bloodborne pathogens final rule (Categories IB/IC).

Gowns are also worn by personnel during the care of patients infected with epidemiologically important microorganisms to reduce the opportunity for transmission of pathogens from patients or items in their environment to other patients or environments; when gowns are worn for this purpose, they are removed before leaving the patient's environment and hands are washed. Adequate data regarding the efficacy of gowns for this purpose, however, are not available.

Patient-Care Equipment and Articles

Many factors determine whether special handling and disposal of used patient-care equipment and articles are prudent or required, including the likelihood of contamination with infective material; the ability to cut, stick, or otherwise cause injury (needles, scalpels, and other sharp instruments [sharps]); the severity of the associated disease; and the environmental stability of the pathogens involved. Some used articles are enclosed in containers or bags to prevent inadvertent exposures to patients, personnel, and visitors and to prevent contamination of the environment. Used sharps are placed in puncture-resistant containers; other articles are placed in a bag. One bag is adequate if the bag is sturdy and the article can be placed in the bag without contaminating the outside of the bag; otherwise, two bags are used.

The scientific rationale, indications, methods, products, and equipment for reprocessing patient-care equipment are delineated in other publications. Contaminated reusable critical medical devices or patient-care equipment (i.e., equipment that enters normally sterile tissue or through which blood flows) or semicritical medical devices or patient-care equipment (i.e., equipment that touches mucous membranes) are sterilized or disinfected (reprocessed) after use to reduce the risk of transmission of microorganisms to other patients; the type of reprocessing is determined by the article and its intended use, the manufacturer's recommendations, hospital policy, and any applicable guidelines and regulations.

Noncritical equipment (i.e., equipment that touches intact skin) contaminated with blood, body fluids, secretions, or excretions is cleaned and disinfected after use, according to hospital policy. Contaminated disposable (single-use) patient-care equipment is handled and transported in a manner that reduces the risk of transmission of microorganisms and decreases environmental contamination in the hospital; the equipment is disposed of according to hospital policy and applicable regulations.

Linen and Laundry

Although soiled linen may be contaminated with pathogenic microorganisms, the risk of disease transmission is negligible if it is handled, transported, and laundered in a manner that avoids transfer of microorganisms to patients, personnel, and environments. Rather than rigid rules and regulations, hygienic and common sense storage and processing of clean and soiled linen are recommended. The methods for handling, transporting, and laundering of soiled linen are determined by hospital policy and any applicable regulations.

Dishes, Glasses, Cups, and Eating Utensils

No special precautions are needed for dishes, glasses, cups, or eating utensils. Either disposable or reusable dishes and utensils can be used for patients in isolation precautions. The combination of hot water and detergents used ospital dishwashers is sufficient to decontaminate dishes, glasses, cups, and ating utensils.

outine and Terminal Cleaning

he room, or cubicle, and bedside equipment of patients on Transmission-ased Precautions are cleaned using the same procedures used for patients on andard Precautions, unless the infecting microorganism(s) and the amount of wironmental contamination indicates special cleaning. In addition to thor-igh cleaning, adequate disinfection of bedside equipment and environmental irfaces (e.g., bedrails, bedside tables, carts, commodes, doorknobs, faucet indles) is indicated for certain pathogens, especially enterococci, which can rvive in the inanimate environment for prolonged periods of time. Patients Imitted to hospital rooms that previously were occupied by patients infected colonized with such pathogens are at increased risk of infection from con-minated environmental surfaces and bedside equipment if they have not en cleaned and disinfected adequately. The methods, thoroughness, and fre-iency of cleaning and the products used are determined by hospital policy.

SPITAL INFECTION CONTROL PRACTICES ADVISORY COMMITTEE (HICPAC))LATION PRECAUTIONS

iere are two tiers of HICPAC isolation precautions: first Standard Precautions, d second Transmission-Based Precautions. In the first, and most important, r are those precautions designed for the care of all patients in hospitals, ;ardless of their diagnosis or presumed infection status. Implementation of ·se "Standard Precautions" is the primary strategy for successful nosocomial ·ection control. In the second tier are precautions designed only for the care specified patients. These additional "Transmission-Based Precautions" are for :ients known or suspected to be infected by epidemiologically important hogens spread by airborne or droplet transmission or by contact with dry n or contaminated surfaces.

indard Precautions

indard Precautions synthesize the major features of Universal Precautions ') and Body Substance Isolation (BSI) under the premise that transmissible ·ctions agents can be contained in multiple care situations and apply to all ients receiving care in any health-care setting, regardless of their diagnosis presumed infection status. Standard Precautions apply to (1) blood; (2) all iy fluids, secretions, and excretions except sweat, regardless of whether y contain visible blood; (3) nonintact skin; and (4) mucous membranes. idard Precautions are designed to reduce the risk of transmission of micro-inisms from both recognized and unrecognized sources of infection in pitals. Basic Standard Precautions include the use of gown, mask, gloves, goggles or face shield as appropriate. Three new recommendations ised on patient protection have been added to Standard Precaution guide-: (1) Respiratory Hygiene/Cough Etiquette, (2) mask use for catheter ·rtion/injection (spinal, epidural), and (3) safe injection practices. Respiratory Hygiene/Cough Etiquette was developed as a response to SARS ising on patients and family members who enter the health-care setting a undiagnosed respiratory symptoms including cough, congestion, runny ·, and productive secretions. There are five basic goals associated with iiratory Hygiene/Cough Etiquette: (1) to educate interceding staff, family, patients, and visitors when a high-risk patient enters the health-care settin[g] with regard to description of respiratory symptoms, the importance of repor[t]ing symptoms, description of the types and use of PPE; (2) to communicat[e] information regarding respiratory hygiene and cough etiquette via poste[r] instructions in appropriate languages; (3) to enforce source control measure[s] (covering mouth when coughing or sneezing, proper disposal of contaminate[d] tissues, appropriate use of surgical masks by the coughing individual); (4) [to] enforce effective hand hygiene; and (5) to maintain a distance of 3 to 6 ft [or] more from source person if PPE is not being used.

Protection with mask use during spinal procedures (epidural injection [or] catheter placement) is recommended to prevent contamination from oroph[a]ryngeal droplets causing infection. The October 2005 HICPAC concluded th[at] there is sufficient evidence to support this recommended change in practic[e.]

Safe injection focuses on preventing pathogen outbreaks from ineffecti[ve] infection control practice. Conceptually, emphasis is placed on aseptic tec[h]nique with use of sterile single-use needles and syringes, use of disposab[le] needles, use of single rather than multiple dose vials, and prevention of co[n]tamination of injection devices and medication. Emphasis is placed on th[e] training and retraining of aseptic technique and infection control practices.

Transmission-Based Precautions

Transmission-Based Precautions are designed for patients documented or s[us]pected to be infected with highly transmissible or epidemiologically importa[nt] pathogens for which additional precautions beyond Standard Precautions a[re] needed to interrupt transmission in hospitals. There are three types [of] Transmission-Based Precautions: Airborne Precautions (or Airborne Infecti[on] Isolation Precautions [AIIR]), Droplet Precautions, and Contact Precautio[ns.] They may be combined for diseases that have multiple routes of transmissi[on.] When used either singularly or in combination, they are to be used in addit[ion] to Standard Precautions.

Airborne Precautions are designed to reduce the risk of airborne transm[is]sion of infectious agents. Airborne transmission occurs by dissemination [of] either airborne droplet nuclei (small-particle residue [5 μm or smaller in si[ze] of evaporated droplets that may remain suspended in the air for long peri[ods] of time) or dust particles containing the infectious agent. Microorganisms [car]ried in this manner can be dispersed widely by air currents and may beco[me] inhaled by or deposited on a susceptible host within the same room or ov[er a] longer distance from the source patient, depending on environmental fact[ors;] therefore, special air handling and ventilation are required to prevent airbo[rne] transmission. Airborne Precautions apply to patients known or suspected t[o be] infected with epidemiologically important pathogens that can be transmi[tted] by the airborne route.

Droplet Precautions are designed to reduce the risk of droplet transmiss[ion] of infectious agents. Droplet transmission involves contact of the conjuncti[va] or the mucous membranes of the nose or mouth of a susceptible person w[ith] large-particle droplets (larger than 5 μm in size) containing microorgani[sms] generated from a person who has a clinical disease or who is a carrier of [the] microorganism. Droplets are generated from the source person primarily du[ring] coughing, sneezing, or talking and during the performance of certain pr[oce]dures such as suctioning and bronchoscopy. Transmission via large-par[ticle] droplets requires close contact between source and recipient persons beca[use] droplets do not remain suspended in the air and generally travel only short distances. General rule of thumb has been that droplets will carry through the air a distance of usually 3 or fewer feet. However, evidence suggests that some droplets such as chickenpox or SARS can carry as far as 6 ft from their source. Therefore the suggested distance of 3 ft should be considered an example of how far a droplet can carry from the source to the host rather than an exact measurement. Because droplets do not remain suspended in the air, special air handling and ventilation are not required to prevent droplet transmission. Droplet Precautions apply to any patient known or suspected to be infected with epidemiologically important pathogens that can be transmitted by infectious droplets.

Contact Precautions are designed to reduce the risk of transmission of epidemiologically important microorganisms by direct or indirect contact. Contact precautions also apply in the presence of fecal incontinence, excessive wound drainage, and any other body secretions that may indicate a contamination/transmission risk. Direct-contact transmission involves skin-to-skin contact and physical transfer of microorganisms to a susceptible host from an infected or colonized person, such as occurs when personnel turn patients, bathe patients, or perform other patient-care activities that require physical contact. Direct-contact transmission also can occur between two patients (e.g., by hand contact), with one serving as the source of infectious microorganisms and the other as a susceptible host. Indirect-contact transmission involves contact of a susceptible host with a contaminated intermediate object, usually inanimate, in the patient's environment. Contact Precautions apply to specified patients known or suspected to be infected or colonized (presence of microorganism on or in patient but without clinical signs and symptoms of infection) with epidemiologically important microorganisms than can be transmitted by direct or indirect contact.

EMPIRIC USE OF AIRBORNE, DROPLET, OR CONTACT PRECAUTIONS

In many instances, the risk of nosocomial transmission of infection may be highest before a definitive diagnosis can be made and before precautions based on that diagnosis can be implemented. The routine use of Standard Precautions for all patients should greatly reduce this risk for conditions other than those requiring Airborne, Droplet, or Contact Precautions. Although it is not possible to prospectively identify all patients needing these enhanced precautions, certain clinical syndromes and conditions carry a sufficiently high risk to warrant the empiric addition of enhanced precautions (Transmission-Based Precautions), whereas a definitive diagnosis is pursued and test recommendations are required to institute Transmission-Based Precautions in these instances until test results are obtained.

Read and print out the full appendix at DavisPlus (http://davisplus.fadavis.com, keyword Van Leeuwen).

Laboratory Critical Findings

Monograph Title	Critical Finding (Conventional Units)	Critical Finding (SI)
Therapeutic Drugs		
Analgesic and Antipyretic Drugs		
Acetaminophen	Greater than 200 mcg/mL (4 hr postingestion)	Greater than 1,324 micromol/L (4 hr postingestion)
Acetylsalicylic acid	Greater than 40 mg/dL	Greater than 2.9 mmol/L
Antiarrhythmic Drugs		
Amiodarone	Greater than 2.5 mcg/mL	Greater than 4 micromol/L
Digoxin	Greater than 2.5 ng/mL	Greater than 3.2 nmol/L
Disopyramide	Greater than 7 mcg/mL	Greater than 20.6 micromol/L
Flecainide	Greater than 1 mcg/mL	Greater than 2.41 micromol/L
Lidocaine	Greater than 6 mcg/mL	Greater than 25.6 micromol/L
Procainamide	Greater than 10 mcg/mL	Greater than 42.3 micromol/L
N-Acetyl Procainamide	Greater than 40 mcg/mL	Greater than 169.2 micromol/L
Quinidine	Greater than 6 mcg/mL	Greater than 18.5 micromol/L
Antimicrobial Drugs		
Aminoglycosides: Amikacin	Greater than 10 mcg/mL	Greater than 17.1 micromol/L
Aminoglycosides: Gentamicin	Peak greater than 12 mcg/mL, trough greater than 2 mcg/mL	Peak greater than 25.1 micromol/L, trough greater than 4.2 micromol/L
Aminoglycosides: Tobramycin	Peak greater than 12 mcg/mL, trough greater than 2 mcg/mL	Peak greater than 25.1 micromol/L, trough greater than 4.2 micromol/L
Tricyclic Glycopeptide: Vancomycin	Trough greater than 30 mcg/mL	Trough greater than 20.7 micromol/L
Anticonvulsant Drugs		
Carbamazepine	Greater than 20 mcg/mL	Greater than 84.6 micromol/L
Ethosuximide	Greater than 200 mcg/mL	Greater than 1,416 micromol/L
Lamotrigine	Greater than 20 mcg/mL	Greater than 78.1 micromol/L

Monograph Title	Critical Finding (Conventional Units)	Critical Finding (SI)
Phenobarbital	Greater than 60 mcg/mL	Greater than 258.6 micromol/L
Phenytoin	Greater than 40 mcg/mL	Greater than 158.4 micromol/L
Primidone	Greater than 15 mcg/mL	Greater than 68.7 micromol/L
Valproic Acid	Greater than 200 mcg/mL	Greater than 1,386 micromol/L
Antidepressant Drugs (Cyclic)		
Amitriptyline	Greater than 500 ng/mL	Greater than 1,805 nmol/L
Nortriptyline	Greater than 500 ng/mL	Greater than 1,900 nmol/L
Protriptyline	Greater than 500 ng/mL	Greater than 1,900 nmol/L
Doxepin	Greater than 500 ng/mL	Greater than 1,790 nmol/L
Imipramine	Greater than 500 ng/mL	Greater than 1,785 nmol/L
Antipsychotic Drugs and Antimanic Drugs		
Haloperidol	Greater than 42 ng/mL	Greater than 84 nmol/L
Lithium	Greater than 2 mEq/L	Greater than 2 mmol/L
Immunosuppressants		
Cyclosporine	Greater than 400 mcg/mL	Greater than 332.8 nmol/L
Methotrexate	Greater than 1 micromol/L after 48 hr with high-dose therapy; greater than 0.02 micromol/L after 48 hr with low-dose therapy	
Tacrolimus	Greater than 25 ng/mL	
Alphabetical Listing		
Bilirubin and Bilirubin Fractions	*Adults & children*: total bilirubin: greater than 15 mg/dL; *newborns*: total bilirubin: greater than 13 mg/dL	*Adults & children*: total bilirubin: greater than 257 micromol/L; *newborns*: total bilirubin: greater than 222 micromol/L
Biopsies	Assessment of clear margins after tissue excision; classification or grading of tumor; identification of malignancy	
Biopsy, Chorionic Villus	Identification of abnormalities in chorionic villus tissue	

(table continues on page 1506)

Monograph Title	Critical Finding (Conventional Units)	Critical Finding (SI)
Bleeding Time	Greater than 14 min	
Blood Gases	*Adults* & *children*: pH less than 7.20 or greater than 7.60; HCO_3 less than 10 or greater than 40 mmol/L; Pco_2 less than 20 or greater than 67 mm Hg; Po_2 less than 45 mm Hg; *newborns*: Po_2 less than 37 mm Hg or greater than 92 mm Hg	*Adults* & *children*: pH less than 7.20 or greater than 7.60; HCO_3 less than 10 or greater than 40 mmol/L; Pco_2 less than 2.7 or greater than 8.9 kPa; Po_2 less than 6.0 kPa; *newborns*: Po_2 less than 4.9 or greater than 12.2 kPa
Blood Groups and Antibodies	Note and immediately report to the health-care provider any signs and symptoms associated with a blood transfusion reaction	
Calcium, Blood	Less than 7 mg/dL or greater than 12 mg/dL	Less than 1.8 or greater than 3 mmol/L
Calcium, Ionized	Less than 3.2 mg/dL or greater than 6.2 mg/dL	Less than 0.8 or greater than 1.6 mmol/L
Carbon Dioxide	Less than 15 mmol/L or greater than 40 mmol/L	Less than 15 mmol/L or greater than 40 mmol/L
Carboxyhemoglobin	30%–40%: dizziness, muscle weakness, vision problems, confusion, increased heart rate, increased breathing rate; 50%–60%: loss of consciousness, coma; greater than 60%: death	
Cerebrospinal Fluid Analysis	Positive Gram stain, India ink preparation, or culture; presence of malignant cells or blasts; elevated WBC count; *Adults*: glucose less than 37 mg/dL or greater than 440 mg/dL; *children*: less than 31 mg/dL or greater than 440 mg/dL	Positive Gram stain, India ink preparation, or culture; presence of malignant cells or blasts; elevated WBC count; *Adults*: glucose less than 2 mmol/L or greater than 24.4 mmol/L; *children*: less than 1.7 mmol/L or greater than 24.4 mmol/L

Monograph Title	Critical Finding (Conventional Units)	Critical Finding (SI)
Chloride, Blood	Less than 80 mmol/L or greater than 115 mmol/L	Less than 80 mmol/L or greater than 115 mmol/L
Chloride, Sweat	20 yr or younger: greater than 60 mmol/L considered diagnostic of cystic fibrosis; older than 20 yr: greater than 70 mmol/L considered diagnostic of cystic fibrosis	20 yr or younger: greater than 60 mmol/L considered diagnostic of cystic fibrosis; older than 20 yr: greater than 70 mmol/L considered diagnostic of cystic fibrosis
Complete Blood Count, Hematocrit	*Adults* & *children*: less than 19.8% or greater than 60%; *newborns*: less than 28.5% or greater than 66.9%	*Adults* & *children*: less than 0.2 L/L or greater than 0.6 L/L; *newborns*: less than 0.28 L/L or greater than 0.67 L/L
Complete Blood Count, Hemoglobin	*Adults* & *children*: less than 6.6 g/dL or greater than 20 g/dL; *newborns*: less than 9.5 g/dL or greater than 22.3 g/dL	*Adults* & *children*: less than 66 g/L or greater than 200 g/L; *newborns*: less than 95 g/L or greater than 223 g/L
Complete Blood Count, Platelet Count	Less than 50×10^3/microL greater than $1,000 \times 10^3$/microL	Less than 50×10^9/L; greater than $1,000 \times 10^9$/L
Complete Blood Count, RBC Morphology and Inclusions	The presence of abnormal cells, other morphological characteristics, or cellular inclusions may signify a potentially life-threatening or serious health condition and should be investigated. Examples are the presence of sickle cells, moderate numbers of spherocytes, marked schistocytosis, oval macrocytes, basophilic stippling, nucleated RBCs (if the patient is not an infant), or malarial organisms	

(table continues on page 1508)

APP

Monograph Title	Critical Finding (Conventional Units)	Critical Finding (SI)
Complete Blood Count, WBC Count and Differential	Less than 2.5 WBC × 10³/mm³; greater than 30 WBC × 10³/mm³	Less than 2.5 × 10⁹/L; greater than 30 × 10⁹/L
Creatinine, Blood	*Adults*: potential critical value is greater than 7.4 mg/dL (nondialysis patient); *children*: potential critical value is greater than 3.8 mg/dL (nondialysis patient)	*Adults*: potential critical value is greater than 654.2 micromol/L (nondialysis patient); *children*: potential critical value is greater than 336 micromol/L (nondialysis patient)
Creatinine, Urine, and Creatinine Clearance, Urine	Degree of impairment—marked: less than 28 mL/min/1.73 m²	Degree of impairment—marked: less than 0.5 mL/s/1.73 m²
Cultures	Positive for acid-fast bacillus, *Campylobacter*, *Clostridium difficile*, *Corynebacterium diphtheriae*, *Escherichia coli* O157:H7, influenza, *Legionella*, *Listeria*, methicillin-resistant *Staphylococcus aureus*, respiratory syncytial virus, rotavirus, *Salmonella*, *Shigella*, vancomycin-resistant enterococcus, varicella, *Vibrio*, and *Yersinia*. Positive findings in any sterile body fluid such as amniotic fluid, blood, pericardial fluid, peritoneal fluid, pleural fluid. Lists of specific organisms may vary by facility; specific organisms are required to be reported to local, state, and national departments of health	
Cytology, Sputum and Urine	Identification of malignancy	
δ-Aminolevulinic Acid	Greater than 20 mg/24 hr	Greater than 152.5 micromol/24
Fibrinogen	Less than 80 mg/dL	Less than 2.4 micromo

Monograph Title	Critical Finding (Conventional Units)	Critical Finding (SI)
Glucose	*Adults* & *children*: less than 40 mg/dL; greater than 400 mg/dL; *newborns*: less than 32 mg/dL; greater than 328 mg/dL	*Adults* & *children*: less than 2.22 mmol/L; greater than 22.2 mmol/L; *newborns*: less than 1.8 mmol/L; greater than 18.2 mmol/L
Gram Stain	Any positive results in blood, cerebrospinal fluid, or any body cavity fluid	
Iron	Serious toxicity: greater than 400 mcg/dL; lethal: greater than 1,000 mcg/dL	Serious toxicity: greater than 71.6 micromol/L; lethal: greater than 179 micromol/L
Ketones, Blood and Urine	Strongly positive test results for ketones	
Lactic Acid	*Adults*: greater than 31 mg/dL; *children*: greater than 37 mg/dL	*Adults*: greater than 3.4 mmol/L; *children*: greater than 4.1 mmol/L
Lead	Levels greater than 30 mcg/dL indicate significant exposure; levels greater than 60 mcg/dL may require chelation therapy	Levels greater than 1.4 micromol/L indicate significant exposure; levels greater than 2.9 micromol/L may require chelation therapy
Lecithin/Sphingomyelin Ratio	An L/S ratio less than 1.5:1 is predictive of respiratory distress syndrome at the time of delivery	
Magnesium, Blood	*Adults*: less than 1.2 mg/dL; greater than 4.9 mg/dL; *children*: less than 1.2 mg/dL; greater than 4.3 mg/dL	*Adults*: less than 0.5 mmol/L; greater than 2 mmol/L; *children*: less than 0.5 mmol/L; greater than 1.8 mmol/L
Methemoglobin	Signs of central nervous system depression can occur at levels greater than 45%; death may occur at levels greater than 70%	
Osmolality, Blood	Less than 265 mOsm/kg; greater than 320 mOsm/kg	Less than 265 mmol/kg; greater than 320 mmol/kg

(table continues on page 1510)

Monograph Title	Critical Finding (Conventional Units)	Critical Finding (SI)
Partial Thromboplastin Time (PTT)	Greater than 70 sec	
Pericardial Fluid	Positive culture findings in any sterile body fluid	
Peritoneal Fluid	Positive culture findings in any sterile body fluid	
Phosphorus, Blood	*Adults*: less than 1 mg/dL; greater than 8.9 mg/dL; *children*: less than 1.3 mg/dL; greater than 8.9 mg/dL	*Adults*: less than 0.3 mmol/L; greater than 2.9 mmol/L; *children*: less than 0.4 mmol/L; greater than 2.9 mmol/L
Pleural Fluid	Positive culture findings in any sterile body fluid	
Potassium, Blood	*Adults* & *children*: less than 2.5 mmol/L; greater than 6.2 mmol/L; *newborns*: less than 2.8 mmol/L; greater than 7.6 mmol/L	*Adults* & *children*: less than 2.5 mmol/L; greater than 6.2 mmol/L; *newborns*: less than 2.8 mmol/L; greater than 7.6 mmol/L
Prothrombin Time and International Normalized Ratio	PT greater than 27 sec; INR greater than 5	
Pseudocholinesterase and Dibucaine Number	A positive result indicates that the patient is at risk for prolonged or unrecoverable apnea related to the inability to metabolize succinylcholine	
Rubella Antibodies	A nonimmune status in pregnant patients may present significant health consequences for the developing fetus if the mother is exposed to an infected individual	
Sodium, Blood	Less than 120 mmol/L; greater than 160 mmol/L	Less than 120 mmol/L greater than 160 mmol/L
Synovial Fluid	Positive culture findings in any sterile body fluid	
Thyroxine, Total	Less than 2.0 mcg/dL; greater than 20.0 mcg/dL	Less than 25.8 nmol/L greater than 258 nmol/L
Tuberculin Skin Tests	Positive results	

Monograph Title	Critical Finding (Conventional Units)	Critical Finding (SI)
Urea Nitrogen, Blood	*Adults*: greater than 100 mg/dL (nondialysis patients); *children*: greater than 55 mg/dL (nondialysis patients)	*Adults*: greater than 35.7 mmol/L (nondialysis patients); *children*: greater than 19.6 mmol/L (nondialysis patients)
Uric Acid, Blood	*Adults*: greater than 13 mg/dL; *children*: greater than 12 mg/dL	*Adults*: greater than 0.8 mmol/L; *children*: greater than 0.7 mmol/L
Urinalysis	Presence of uric acid, cystine, leucine, or tyrosine crystals; the combination of grossly elevated urine glucose and ketones is also considered significant	
Vitamins D, E, K	Vitamin toxicity can be as significant as problems brought about by vitamin deficiencies. The potential for toxicity is especially important to consider with respect to fat-soluble vitamins, which are not eliminated from the body as quickly as water-soluble vitamins and can accumulate in the body	

Appendix I

Diagnostic Critical Findings

Monograph Title	Critical Finding
Angiography, Abdomen	Abscess; aneurysm
Angiography, Coronary	Aneurysm; aortic dissection
Angiography, Pulmonary	Pulmonary embolism
Blood Pool Imaging	Myocardial infarction
Chest X-Ray	Foreign body; malposition of tube, line, or post-operative device (pacemaker); pneumonia; pneumoperitoneum; pneumothorax; spine fracture
Computed Tomography, Abdomen	Abscess; acute gastrointestinal (GI) bleed; aortic aneurysm; appendicitis; aortic dissection; bowel perforation; bowel obstruction; mesenteric torsion; significant solid organ laceration; tumor with significant mass effect; visceral injury
Computed Tomography, Angiography	Brain or spinal cord ischemia; emboli; hemorrhage; leaking aortic aneurysm; occlusion; tumor with significant mass effect
Computed Tomography, Brain	Abscess; acute hemorrhage; aneurysm; infarction; infection; tumor with significant mass effect
Computed Tomography, Pelvis	Ectopic pregnancy; tumor with significant mass effect
Computed Tomography, Spine	Cord compression; fracture; tumor with significant mass effect
Computed Tomography, Spleen	Abscess; hemorrhage; laceration
Computed Tomography, Thoracic	Aortic aneurysm; aortic dissection; pneumothorax; pulmonary embolism
Ductography	Ductal carcinoma in situ (DSIS); invasive breast cancer
Echocardiography	Aneurysm; infection; obstruction; tumor with significant mass effect
Echocardiography, Transesophageal	Aneurysm; aortic dissection
Electrocardiogram	Adult: Acute changes in ST elevation may indicate acute myocardial infarction or pericarditis; asystole; heart block, second an third degree with bradycardia less than 60 beats per min; pulseless electrical activity pulseless ventricular tachycardia; PVCs greater than three in a row, pauses greater than 3 sec, or identified blocks; unstable tachycardia; ventricular fibrillation

Monograph Title	Critical Finding
Electrocardiogram	Pediatric: Asystole; bradycardia less than 60 beats per minute; pulseless electrical activity; pulseless ventricular tachycardia; supraventricular tachycardia; ventricular fibrillation
Electroencephalography	Abscess; brain death; head injury; hemorrhage; intracranial hemorrhage
Esophagogastroduodenoscopy	Presence and location of acute GI bleed
Gastrointestinal Blood Loss Scan	Acute GI bleed
Kidney, Ureter, and Bladder Study	Bowel obstruction; ischemic bowel; visceral injury
Laparoscopy, Abdominal	Appendicitis
Laparoscopy, Gynecologic	Ectopic pregnancy; foreign body; tumor with significant mass effect
Liver and Spleen Scan	Visceral injury
Lung Perfusion Scan	Pulmonary embolism
Lung Ventilation Scan	Pulmonary embolism
Magnetic Resonance Angiography	Aortic aneurysm; aortic dissection; occlusion; tumor with significant mass effect; vertebral artery dissection
Magnetic Resonance Imaging, Abdomen	Acute GI bleed; aortic aneurysm; infection; tumor with significant mass effect
Magnetic Resonance Imaging, Brain	Abscess; cerebral aneurysm; cerebral infarct; hydrocephalus; skull fracture or contusion; tumor with significant mass effect
Magnetic Resonance Imaging, Chest	Aortic aneurysm; aortic dissection; tumor with significant mass effect
Magnetic Resonance Imaging, Venography	Cerebral embolus; pulmonary embolus; occlusion; tumor with significant mass effect
Plethysmography	Deep vein thrombosis
Positron Emission Tomography, Brain	Aneurysm; cerebrovascular accident; tumor with significant mass effect
Ultrasound, Abdomen	Aneurysm 5 cm or greater
Ultrasound, Biophysical Profile, Obstetric	Abruptio placentae; adnexal torsion; biophysical profile score between 0 and 2 is abnormal and indicates the need for assessment and immediate delivery; ectopic pregnancy; fetal death; placenta previa
Ultrasound, Pelvis (Gynecologic, Nonobstetric)	Abscess; adnexal torsion; appendicitis; ectopic pregnancy; infection; tumor with significant mass effect
Ultrasound, Scrotal	Testicular torsion
Ultrasound, Venous Doppler, Extremity Studies	Deep vein thrombosis

(table continues on page 1514)

Monograph Title	Critical Finding
Upper Gastrointestinal and Small Bowel Series	Foreign body; perforated bowel; tumor with significant mass effect
Venography, Lower Extremity Studies	Deep vein valvular incompetence; deep vein thrombosis; pulmonary embolism; venous obstruction

Bibliography

1997 Update of the 1982 American College of Rheumatology revised criteria for classification of systemic lupus erythematosus. (n.d.). Retrieved from www.rheumatology.org/practice/clinicalclassification/SLE/1997_update_of_the_1982_acr_revised_criteria_for_classification_of_sle.pdf.

AABB. (2011). Technical manual. Bethesda, MD: American Association of Blood Banks.

AABB. (2009). Circular of information. Retrieved from www.aabb.org/resources/bct/Documents/coi0809r.pdf.

Abramson, N., & Melton, B. (2000). Leukocytosis: Basics of clinical assessment. American Family Physician, 62(9):2053–2060.

ACOG. (2006, Reaffirmed 2010). Committee Opinion Number 348. Umbilical cord blood gas and acid base analysis. Obstetrics and Gynecology, 108(5):1319–1322.

ACOG. (2011). Committee Opinion Number 504. Screening and diagnosis of gestational diabetes. Retrieved from www.acog.org/~/media/Committee%20Opinions/Committee%20on%20Obstetric%20Practice/co504.pdf?dmc=1&ts=20120304T2032008591.

ADA. (2011). Standards of medical care in diabetes—2012. Retrieved from http://care.diabetesjournals.org/content/35/Supplement_1/S11.full.pdf+html.

Adler, A., & Carlton, C. (2012). Introduction to radiologic sciences and patient care (5th ed.). St. Louis, MO: Elsevier Science Health Science.

Aetna Clinical Policy Bulletins. (2011). Urea breath testing for H. pylori infection. Retrieved from www.aetna.com/cpb/medical/data/100_199/0177.html.

Albany Medical Center. (n.d.). Lymphocyte subset reference ranges (Addendum IV). Retrieved from www.amc.edu/pathology_labservices/addenda/addenda_documents/Lymphocyte_Subset_Reference_Ranges__4_2.pdf.

Alexander, D. (Ed.). (2011, January 13). Pseudocholinesterase deficiency. Retrieved from http://emedicine.medscape.com/article/247019-overview.

American Cancer Society. (2012, March 5). Guidelines for the early detection of cancer. Retrieved from www.cancer.org.

American College of Rheumatology (2010). The 2010 ACR-EULAR classification criteria for rheumatoid arthritis. Retrieved from www.rheumatology.org/practice/clinical/classification/ra/ra_2010.asp.

American Diabetes Association. (2012, January). Standards of medical care in diabetes—2012. Diabetes Care, 35(S1):S11–S61.

American Heart Association. (n.d.). Classification of functional capacity and objective assessment. Retrieved from http://americanheart.org/presenter.jhtml?identifier=4569.

American Heart Association. (2006, June 19). Diet and lifestyle recommendations revision 2006: A scientific statement from the American Heart Association Nutrition Committee. Retrieved from http://circ.ahajournals.org/content/114/1/82.full.pdf.

American Heart Association. (n.d.). Symptoms and diagnosis of PAD. Retrieved from www.heart.org/HEARTORG/Conditions/More/PeripheralArteryDisease/Symptoms-and-Diagnosis-of-PAD_UCM_301306_Article.jsp#.T0E6gfmwXJ4.

American Society of Health-System Pharmacists. (2012). AHFS drug information 2012. Bethesda, MD: American Society of Health-System Pharmacists.

American Society for Clinical Laboratory Science. (2003, July 26). Role of the clinical laboratory in response to an expanding geriatric population. Retrieved from www.ascls.org/?page=Pos_Pap_Ex&hhSearchTerms=role+and+of+and+the+and+clinical+and+laboratory+and+in+and+response+and+to+and+an+and+expanding+and+geriatric+and+population.

American Speech-Language-Hearing Association. (2004). Guidelines for audiologic assessment of children from birth to 5 years of age. Retrieved from www.asha.org/docs/pdf/GL2004-00002.pdf.

Amin, M., Grignon, D., Humphrey, P., & Srigley, J. (2004). Gleason grading of prostate cancer: A contemporary approach. Philadelphia: Lippincott Williams & Wilkins.

Amniotic fluid and the biophysical profile. (2012). Retrieved from www.gynob.com/biopamfl.htm.

Analytes and their cutoffs. (2010, October 1). Retrieved from www.workplace.samhsa.gov/drugtesting/pdf/2010guidelinesanalytescutoffs.pdf.

Andersen-Berry, A., Rosenkrantz, T. (Ed.), Bellig, L., & Ohning, B. (2011, December 1). Neonatal sepsis. Retrieved from http://emedicine.medscape.com/article/978352-overview.

Andolina, V., Lille, S., & Willison, K. (2010). Mammographic imaging, a practical guide (3rd ed.). Baltimore: Lippincott Williams & Wilkins.

Angelini, D. (2003, June 9). Update on non-obstetric surgical conditions in pregnancy: Pancreatitis. Retrieved from www.medscape.com/viewarticle/452759

ARUP Laboratories. (2006–2012). Test directory. Retrieved from www.aruplab.com/Testing-Information/lab-test-directory.jsp.

Assessing coagulation. (n.d.). Retrieved from www.anaesthetist.com/icu/organs/blood/coag.htm.

Athena Diagnostics. (2012). Test directory. Retrieved from www.athenadiagnostics.com/content/test-catalog.

Baker, J., & Schumacher, R. (2010). Update on gout and hyperuricemia. Retrieved from www.medscape.com/viewarticle/716203.

Baurmash, H. (2004). Submandibular salivary stones: Current management modalities. Retrieved from www.exodontia.info/files/JOMS_2004._Submandibular_Salivary_Stones_-_Current_Management_Modalities.pdf.

Becker, C. (2003). Clinical evaluation for osteoporosis. Retrieved from www.ncbi.nlm.nih.gov/pubmed/12916288.

Becker, M., Visser, L., van Schaik, R., Hofman, A., Uitterlinden, A., & Stricker, B. (2009, February 19). Genetic variation in the multidrug and toxin extrusion 1 transporter protein influences the glucose-lowering effect of metformin in patients with diabetes: A preliminary study. Retrieved from http://diabetes.diabetesjournals.org/content/58/3/745.

Becton Dickinson. (2004). Understanding additives: Heparin. Retrieved from www.bd.com/vacutainer/labnotes/2004winterspring/additives_heparin.asp.

Becton Dickinson. (2004). BD Vacutainer® order of draw for multiple tube collections. Retrieved from www.bd.com/ca/pdfs/VS5729-4%20Order%20of%20Draw%20Jun%2004.pdf.

Bernstein, M., & Luggen, A. (2010). Nutrition for the older adult. Sudbury, MA: Jones & Bartlett.

Bishop, M., Fody, E., & Schoeff, L. (Eds.). (2009). Clinical chemistry techniques, principles, correlations (6th ed.). Philadelphia: Lippincott Williams & Wilkins.

Blocki, F. (2009). Vitamin D deficiency. Retrieved from http://laboratory-manager.advanceweb.com/Article/Vitamin-D-Deficiency-4.aspx.

Bleustein, B., Despres, N., Belenky, A., Ghani, F., & Armstrong, E. (2003, April 1). BNP in diagnosis of heart failure. Advance for Administrators of the Laboratory, 12(4):65.

Borazanci, E. (2009). Interpreting abnormal PT, aPTT times. Retrieved from http://lib.sh.lsuhsc.edu/am_rpt/media/files/09242009.pdf.

Bouma, B., & Meijers, J. (2000). Role of blood coagulation factor XI in downregulation of fibrinolysis. Current Opinion in Hematology 7(5):266–272.

Branson, B., Handsfield, H., Lampe, A., et al. (2006, September 22). Revised recommendations for HIV testing of adults, adolescents, and pregnant women in health-care settings. Retrieved from www.cdc.gov/mmwr/preview/mmwrhtml/rr5514a1.htm.

Brayden, R. (2011). Transcutaneous bilirubin measurement. Retrieved from www.cpnonline.org/CRS/CRS/pa_tranbili_pep.htm.

Briggs, C., Grant, D., & Machin, S. (2001). Comparison of the automated reticulocyte counts and immature reticulocyte fraction measurements obtained with the ABX Pentra 120 Retic Blood Analyzer and the Sysmex XE-2100 Automated Hematology Analyzer. Retrieved from http://mmserver.cjp.com/gems/labhem/7.2.Briggs.pdf.

Briggs, C., Kunka, S., Hart, D., Oguni, S., & Machin, S. (2004). Assessment of an immature platelet fraction (IPF) in peripheral thrombocytopenia. Retrieved from http://onlinelibrary.wiley.com/doi/10.1111/j.1365-2141.2004.04987.x/full.

Burtis, C., & Ashwood, E. (1999). Tietz textbook of clinical chemistry (3rd ed.). Philadelphia: WB Saunders.

Buttarello, M., Bulian, P., Farina, G., et al. (2002). Five Fully automated methods for performing immature reticulocyte fraction. Comparison in diagnosis of bone marrow aplasia. Retrieved from http://ajcp.ascpjournals.org/content/117/6/871.full.pdf.

Bushong, S. (2003). Magnetic resonance imaging-physical and biological principles (3rd ed.). St. Louis, MO: Mosby.

Cantwell, C., Cradock, A., Bruzzi J., et al. (2006). MR venography with true fast imaging with steady-state precession for suspected lower-limb deep vein thrombosis. Journal of Vascular Interventional Radiology, 17(11): 1763–1769.

Carlton, R., & Alder, A. Principles of radiographic imaging (4th ed.). (2006). Clifton Park, NY: Delmar Thomson.

Cassels, C. (2008, April 3). FDG-PET imaging allows early detection of Alzheimer's, other dementia types. Retrieved from www.medscape.com/viewarticle/572505.

Cavanaugh, B. Nurses' manual of laboratory and diagnostic tests (4th ed.). (2003). Philadelphia: FA Davis.

Centers for Disease Control and Prevention. (2012, February 22). Vaccine information statement. HPV vaccine. Retrieved from www.cdc.gov/vaccines/pubs/vis/downloads/vis-hpv-gardasil.pdf.

Centers for Medicare and Medicaid Services. (2012). CLIA program: Clinical laboratory improvement amendments. Retrieved from https://www.cms.gov/CLIA/.

Centre for Digestive Diseases. (2009). Urea Breath Test. Retrieved from www.cdd.com.au/pages/procedures/urea_breath_test.html.

Crawford, I., Türkeri, L., Ozveri, H., Ilker, Y., & Akda, A. (1996). Short-term effect of digital rectal exam on serum prostate-specific antigen levels: A prospective study. Retrieved from www.ncbi.nlm.nih.gov/pubmed/8791045.

Chang, C., & Kass, L. (1997). Clinical significance of immature reticulocyte fraction determined by automated reticulocyte counting. Retrieved from www.ncbi.nlm.nih.gov/pubmed/9208980.

Chelation therapy. (2008). Retrieved from www.cancer.org/Treatment/TreatmentsandSideEffects/ComplementaryandAlternativeMedicine/PharmacologicalandBiologicalTreatment/chelation-therapy.

Chua, W., Tan, L., Kamaraj, R., Chiong, E., Liang, S., & Esuvaranathan, K. (2010). The use of NMP22 and urine cytology for the surveillance of patients with superficial bladder cancer. Retrieved from www.ispub.com/journal/the-internet-journal-of-urology/volume-6-number-2/the-use-of-nmp22-and-urine-cytology-for-the-surveilance-of-patients-with-superficial-bladder-cancer.html.

Classification criteria for the diagnosis of systemic lupus erythematosus (SLE). (2010, January 22). Retrieved from www.medicalcriteria.com/criteria/sle_print.htm.

CLR: Table of critical limits. (2011–2012). Retrieved from www.clr-online.com.

Clinical and Laboratory Standards Institute. (2009). Sweat testing: Sample collection and quantitative chloride analysis; approved guideline (3rd ed.). Wayne, PA: Clinical and Laboratory Standards Institute.

Contraction Stress Test. (2010, December, 9). Retrieved from www.webmd.com/baby/contraction-stress-test.

Cornforth, T. (2010, March 29). Hysteroscopy FAQ. Retrieved from http://womenshealth.about.com/cs/surgery/a/hysteroscopyqa.htm.

Davidson, M., London, M., & Ladewig, P. (2011). Olds' maternal-newborn nursing & women's health across the lifespan (9th ed.). Upper Saddle River, NJ: Prentice Hall.

Department of Health and Human Services, Office of Disease Prevention and Health Promotion. (2012). Healthy people 2020. Retrieved from www.healthypeople.gov/2020/default.aspx.

Department of Health and Human Services, Panel on Anti-retroviral Guidelines for Adults and Adolescents. (2011, October 14). Guidelines for the use of anti-retroviral agents in HIV infected adults and adolescents. Retrieved from www.aidsinfo.nih.gov/ContentFiles/AdultandAdolescentGL.pdf.

Dietary reference intake: electrolytes and water. (2011, September 13). Retrieved

from www.iom.edu/Global/News%20
announcements/~/media/442A08B899
F44DF9AAD083D86164C75B.ashx.

DiPiro, J., Talbert, R., Yee, G., Matzke, G., Wells, B., & Posey, L. (2011). Pharmacotherapy: A pathophysiologic approach (8th ed.). New York: McGraw-Hill.

Disorders of neuromuscular transmission. (2008). Retrieved from www.merck-manuals.com/professional/neurologic_disorders/peripheral_nervous_system_and_motor_unit_disorders/disorders_of_neuromuscular_transmission.html.

Dooley, W. (2009). Breast ductoscopy and the evolution of the intra-ductal approach to breast cancer. Retrieved from www.ncbi.nlm.nih.gov/pubmed/19775336.

Drug cutoff concentrations. (2010). Retrieved from http://workplace.samhsa.gov/DrugTesting/pdf/2010GuidelinesAnalytesCutoffs.pdf.

Dubin, D. (2000). Rapid interpretation of EKGs (6th ed.). Tampa, FL: Cover Publishing Company.

Dungan, K., Buse, J., Largay, J., et al. (2006, February 21). 1,5-Anhydroglucitol and postprandial hyperglycemia as measured by continuous glucose monitoring system in moderately controlled patients with diabetes. Retrieved from http://care.diabetesjournals.org/content/29/6/1214.full.

Dugdale, D. (2010, July 7). Lactose tolerance tests. Retrieved from www.nlm.nih.gov/medlineplus/ency/article/003500.htm.

Eastman, G., Wald, C., & Crossin, J. (2005). Getting started in clinical radiology: From image to diagnosis. New York: Thieme Medical Publishers.

Eby, C. (2009). Warfarin dosing. Should labs offer pharmacogenetic testing? Clinical Laboratory News, 35(6). Retrieved from www.aacc.org/publications/cln/2009/June/Pages/series0609.aspx#.

Esposito K., & Giugliano, D. (2003). The metabolic syndrome and inflammation: association or causation? Retrieved from www.ncbi.nlm.nih.gov/pubmed/15673055.

Eustice, C. (2011, June 29). What is rheumatoid factor? Retrieved from www.arthritis.about.com/od/radiagnosis/a/rheumfactor.htm.

Farid-Moayer, M., Lowe, S., Martin, B., Talavera, F., Goldberg, E., & Mechaber, A.

(2003). Microscopic polyangiitis. Retrieved from www.emedicine.com/med/topic2931.htm.

Flemming, T. (Ed.). (2000). PDR for herbal medicines (2nd ed.). Montvale, NJ: Thomson Medical Economics.

Framingham Heart Study. (2012). Coronary heart disease. Retrieved from www.framinghamheartstudy.org/risk/coronary.html.

Frank, E., Long, B., & Smith, B. (2012). Merrill's atlas of radiographic positions and radiologic procedures (12th ed.). St. Louis, MO: Mosby.

Fritsche, H., Grossman, B., Lerner S., & Sawczuk, I. (n.d.). National Academy of Clinical Biochemistry Guidelines for the use of tumor markers in bladder cancer. Retrieved from www.aacc.org/SiteCollectionDocuments/NACB/LMPG/tumor/chp3h_bladder.pdf.

Gearhart, P., Sehdev, H., & Ritchie, W. (2011, April 11). Ultrasonography in biophysical profile. Retrieved from http://emedicine.medscape.com/article/405454-overview.

Gill, K. (2001). Abdominal ultrasound: A practioner's guide. Philadelphia: WB Saunders.

Glockner, J., & Lee, C. (2010). Magnetic resonance venography. Retrieved from www.thefreelibrary.com/_/print/PrintArticle.aspx?id=231094248.

Goldenberg, W. (2011). Myasthenia gravis Retrieved from http://emedicine.medscape.com/article/793136-overview.

Goldfarb, D., Stein, B., Shamszadeh M., & Petersen, R. (1986). Age related change in tissue levels of prostatic acid phosphatase and prostate specific antigen. Retrieved from www.ncbi.nlm.nih/pubmed/2430115.

Golish, J. (1992). Diagnostic procedure handbook with key word index. Cleveland, OH: Lexi-Company.

Goolsby, Mary J., & Grubbs, L. (2006). Advanced assessment: Interpreting findings and formulating differential diagnoses. Philadelphia: FA Davis.

Graff, L. (1983). A handbook of urinalysi Philadelphia: Lippincott Williams & Wilkins.

Greer, J., Foerster, J., Rodgers, G., et al (Eds.) . (2008). Wintrobe's clinical hematology (12th ed.). Philadelphia: Lippincott Williams & Wilkins.

Gregersen, P. (2007). The genetics behind rheumatoid arthritis: Five susceptibility genes and counting. Retrieved from www.arthritis.org/genetics-ra.php.

Grimmer, T., Riemenschneider, M., Förstl, H., et. al. (2009, June 1). Beta amyloid in Alzheimer's disease: Increased deposition in brain is reflected in reduced concentration in cerebrospinal fluid. Biological Psychiatry, 65(11):927–934.

Gunderman, R. (2006). Essential radiology (2nd ed.). New York: Thieme Medical Publishers.

Hearing Assessment. (2012). Retrieved from www.asha.org/public/hearing/testing/assess.htm.

Heller, G., & Hendel, R. (2010). Nuclear cardiology: Practical applications. (2nd ed.). New York: McGraw-Hill.

Henderson, Z., & Ecker, J. (2003). Fetal scalp blood sampling—limited role in contemporary obstetric practice: Part II. Laboratory Medicine, 34(8):594–600.

Hennerici, M., & Neiserberg-Heusler, D. (2005). Vascular diagnosis with ultrasound (2nd ed. revised). New York: Thieme Medical Publishers.

Hicks, J., & Boeckx, R. (1984). Pediatric clinical chemistry. Philadelphia: WB Saunders.

Hoeltke, L: Phlebotomy: The clinical laboratory manual series. Albany, NY: Delmar Thomson Learning.

Hoover, K., & Park, I. (2011). Reverse sequence syphilis screening. An overview by CDC. Retrieved from www.cdc.gov/std/syphilis/syphilis-webinar-slides.pdf.

Hopfer Deglin, J., & Hazard Vallerand, A. (2011). Davis's drug guide for nurses (12th ed.). Philadelphia: FA Davis.

Hopper, K. (2005). The modern coagulation cascade and coagulation abnormalities associated with sepsis. Retrieved from www.ivis.org/proceedings/scivac/2005/Hopper1_en.pdf?LA=1.

Hormone disorders. (n.d.). Retrieved from www.healthinaging.org/agingintheknow/chapters_print_ch_trial.asp?ch=48.

How is bone cancer diagnosed? (2012, January 5). Retrieved from www.cancer.org/cancer/bonecancer/detailedguide/bone-cancer-diagnosis.

HPV vaccine information for young women. (2011). Retrieved from www.cdc.gov/std/hpv/stdfact-hpv-vaccine-young-women.htm.

Hughes, V. (2002). How does jaundice affect breast feeding? Retrieved from www.mynursingwear.com/html/BreastfeedingInfo/English/jaundice.pdf.

Hultén, M., Dhanjal, S., & Pertl, B. (2003). Rapid and simple prenatal diagnosis of common chromosome disorders: Advantages and disadvantages of the molecular methods FISH and QF–PCR. Retrieved from www.reproduction-online.org/content/126/3/279.full.pdf.

Indman, P. (2012). Hysteroscopy. Retrieved from www.gynalternatives.com/hsc.htm.

Initiating antiretroviral therapy in treatment-nave patients. (2011, January, 10). Retrieved from www.aidsinfo.nih.gov/Guidelines/HTML/1/adult-and-adolescent-treatment-guidelines/10/initiating-antiretroviral-therapy-in-treatment-naive-patients.

Inoue, S. (2010). Leukocytosis. Retrieved from http://emedicine.medscape.com/article/956278-overview.

International Medicine Clinic Research Consortium. (1995). Effect of digital rectal examination on serum prostate antigen in a primary care setting. Retrieved from http://archinte.ama-assn.org/cgi/content/abstract/155/4/389.

International Warfarin Pharmacogenetics Consortium. (2009). Estimation of the warfarin dose with clinical and pharmacogenetic data. Retrieved from www.nejm.org/doi/full/10.1056/NEJMoa0809329.

Interpretations of decreased visual acuity. (2011). Retrieved from www.fpnotebook.com/eye/sx/DcrsdVslActy.htm (accessed 6/17/09).

Izbicki, G., Rudensky, B., Na'amad, M., Hershko, C., Huerta, M., & Hersch, M. (2004). Transfusion-related leukocytosis in critically ill patients. Critical Care Medicine, 32(2):439-442.

Jacobs, D. S., DeMott, W. R., & Oxley, D. K. (2001). Laboratory test handbook (5th ed.). Hudson, OH: LexiComp.

Jhang, J. Abnormal basic coagulation testing. (n.d.). Retrieved from www.pathology.columbia.edu/education/residency/coag.pdf.

Kaushansky, K., Lichtman, M., Beutler, E., Kipps, T., Prchal, J., & Seligsohn, U. (2010). Williams hematology (8th ed.). New York: McGraw-Hill.

Kawamura, D., & Lunsford, B. (2012). Diagnostic medical sonography—Abdomen and superficial structures (3rd ed.). Baltimore: Lippincott Williams & Wilkins.

Kiechle, F. (Ed.). (2010, August). How useful are immature granulocytes in an automated differential cell count? Retrieved from www.cap.org/apps/cap.portal?_nfpb=true&cntvwrPtlt_actionOverride=%2Fportlets%2Fconte ntViewer%2Fshow&_windowLabel= cntvwrPtlt&cntvwrPtlt%7BactionForm. contentReference%7D=cap_ today%2F0810%2F0808_QA.html&_ state=maximized&_ pageLabel=cntvwr.

Kimball, S. (2011, March 25). Speech audiometry. Retrieved from http:// emedicine.medscape.com/ article/1822315–overview.

Krinsky, G., & Zhang, J. (2011). Magnetic resonance imaging—Vascular application tips. Retrieved from www.med .nyu.edu/mri/vascular/app_tips_ mrvenography.html.

Kunjumoideen, K. (n.d.). Drugs causing thrombocytopenia or low platelet count. Retrieved from www.medicineworld.org/physicians/hematology/ thrombocytopenia.html.

Kusuma, B., & Schulz, T. (2009). Acute disseminated intravascular coagulation. Retrieved from www.turner-white .com/memberfile.php?PubCode= hp_mar09_coagulation.pdf.

LabCorp. (n.d.) Test menu. Retrieved from www.labcorp.com/wps/portal/ provider/testmenu/.

LaRosa, S. (2010, August 1). Sepsis. Retrieved from www.clevelandclinicmeded.com/medicalpubs/diseaseman-agement/infectious-disease/sepsis/.

LaValle, J., Krinsky, D., & Hawkins, E. (2002). Natural therapeutics pocket guide (2nd ed.). Hudson, OH: Lexi-Comp.

Lee, F. (2011, March 1). The tau protein. Retrieved from www.web-books.com/ eLibrary/Medicine/Neurological/ Alzheimer_Tau.htm.

Lehman, C. (1998). Saunders manual of clinical laboratory science. Philadelphia: WB Saunders.

Lein, M., Kwiatkowski, M., Semjonow, A., et al. (2003). The effect of digital rectal examination on the serum prostate specific antigen concentration: results of a randomized study. Retrieved from www.mendeley.com/ research/multicenter-clinical-trial-complexed-prostate-specific-antigen-low-prostate-specific-antigen-concentrations/.

Lewis, S., Ruff Dirksen, S., Heitkemper, M., Bucher, L., & Camera, I. (2010). Medical surgical nursing assessment and management of clinical problems (8th ed.). St. Louis, MO: Mosby.

Licorice. (2011, September 18). Retrieved from en.wikipedia.org/wiki/liquorice.

Lotan, T., & Epstein, J. (2010). Gleason grading system. Retrieved from www .nature.com/nrurol/journal/v7/n3/full/ nrurol.2010.9.html.

Lutz, C., & Przytulski, K. (2010). Nutrition and diet therapy (4th ed.). Philadelphia FA Davis.

Madison, J. (2002). Transcutaneous bilirubin measurement is as effective as laboratory serum bilirubin measurements at detecting hyperbilirubinemia. Retrieved from www.med.umich.edu/ pediatrics/ebm/cats/bili.htm.

Magnetic resonance venography (MRV). (n.d.). Retrieved from http://professionalradiology.com/magnetic-resonance-venography-mrv.php.

Maher, K. (2008). Against the grain: A celiac disease review. Medical Laboratory Observer, 40(8):22–27.

Martin, F., & Clark, J. (2011). Introduction to audiology (11th ed.). Boston: Allyn & Bacon.

Mawuenyega, K., Sigurdson, W., Ovod, V., et al. (2010, December 9). Decreased clearance of CNS β-amyloid in Alzheimer's disease. Science, 330(6012):1774.

Mazurek, G., Jereb, J., Vernon, A., LoBue, P., Goldberg, S., & Castro, K. (2010, June 25). Updated guidelines for using interferon gamma release assays to detect mycobacterium tuberculosis infection—United States, 2010. Retrieved from www.cdc.gov/mmwr/pdf/rr/ rr5905.pdf.

McCall, R., & Tankersly, C. (2011). Phlebotomy essentials (5th ed.). Philadelphia: Lippincott Williams and Wilkins.

McGee, K., & Baumann, N. (2009). Procalcitonin: Clinical utility in diagnosing sepsis. Retrieved from www.aacc.org/publications/cln/2009/july/Pages/series0709.aspx#.

McPherson, R., & Pincus, M. (2011). Henry's clinical diagnosis and management by laboratory methods (22nd ed.). Philadelphia: WB Saunders.

Merck manual of geriatrics. (2011). App I, Laboratory values. Retrieved from www.merck.com/mkgr/mmg/appndxs/app1.jsp.

Mesters, R., Mannucci, P., Coppola, R., Keller, T., Ostermann, H., & Kienast, J. (1996). Factor VIIa and antithrombin III activity during severe sepsis and septic shock in neutropenic patients. Retrieved from http://bloodjournal.hematologylibrary.org/content/88/3/881.full.pdf.

Miyazak, M., & Lee, V. (n.d.). Nonenhanced MR angiography. Retrieved from http://radiology.rsna.org/content/248/1/20.full (accessed 11/08/11).

Miyakis S., Lockshin M., Atsumi T., et al. (2006). International consensus statement on an update of the classification criteria for definite antiphospholipid syndrome (APS). Journal of Thrombosis and Haemostasis, 4(2):295–306.

Morbidity and Mortality Weekly Report. (2011, February 11). Discordant results from reverse sequence syphilis screening—Five laboratories, United States, 2006–2010. Retrieved from www.cdc.gov/mmwr/preview/mmwrhtml/mm6005a1.htm?s_cid=mm6005a1_w.

Morris, E., & Liberman, L. (2005). Breast MRI: Diagnosis and intervention. New York: Springer.

Morris, R. (n.d.). New highly specific autoantibody markers in RA. Present status and future prospects. Retrieved from www.rdlinc.com/pdf/articles/AutoantibodiesRA-DrMorris-10-5-06_4.pdf.

Moses, S. (2007, October 21). Fetal scalp pH. Retrieved from www.fpnotebook.com/ob/lab/ftlsclpph.htm.

Moses, S. (2007, October 21). Umbilical cord blood gas analysis. Retrieved from www.fpnotebook.com/ob/lab/umblcclcrdbldgsanlys.htm.

MRI Registry Review Program. (2011). Clifton, NJ: Medical Imaging Consultants.

Myasthenia Gravis Foundation of America. (2010). Retrieved from www.myasthenia.org/LivingwithMG/InformationalMaterials.aspx.

National Academy of Clinical Biochemistry (2008). Thyroid disease. Retrieved from www.aacc.org/members/nacb/Archive/LMPG/ThyroidDisease/Pages/ThyroidDiseasePDF.aspx#.

National Institute of Neurological Disorders and Stroke. (2011). Myasthenia gravis fact sheet. Retrieved from www.ninds.nih.gov/disorders/myasthenia_gravis/detail_myasthenia_gravis.htm.

NCCN Guidelines for patients. (2010). Retrieved from www.memorialcare.org/medical_services/breast-care/pdf/nccn-guidelines-breast.pdf.

Neonatal handbook. (n.d.). Retrieved from www.netsvic.org.au/nets/handbook/index.cfm?doc_id=460.

New York State Department of Health. (n.d.). Newborn screening program. Retrieved from www.wadsworth.org/newborn/babhealth.htm#1.

New York State Department of Health. (n.d.). Newborn screening in New York State: A guide for health professionals. Retrieved from www.wadsworth.org/newborn/pdf/phyguidelines.pdf.

NYHA classification—The stages of heart failure. (2002). Retrieved from www.abouthf.org/questions_stages.htm.

O'Riordan, M. (2004). Update to the NCEP ATP III guidelines recommends aggressively treating LDL cholesterol levels in high-risk patients. Retrieved from www.theheart.org/article/148997.do.

Otten, J., Hellwig, J., & Meyers, L. (Eds.). (2006). Dietary reference intakes: The essential guide to nutrient requirements. Washington, DC: The National Academies Press.

Palkuti, H. (1995). International normalized ratio (INR): Clinical significance and applications. Retrieved from www.biodatacorp.com/library/reference/International_Normalized_Ratio.pdf.

Patel, D., Presti J., McNeal, J., Gill, H., Brooks, J., & King, C. (2005). Preoperative PSA velocity is an independent prognostic factor for relapse after radical prostatectomy. Retrieved from http://jco.ascopubs.org/content/23/25/6157.full.pdf.

Peart, O. (2008). Lange Q&A: Mammography examination (2nd ed.). New York: McGraw-Hill.

Penman, J. (2010). Procalcitonin evaluation & use in Victoria B.C. Retrieved from www.bcsls.net/pages/documents/Penman-Procalcitonin.pdf.

Peripheral vascular disease (PVD)/Peripheral artery disease (PAD). (n.d.). Retrieved from http://stanfordhospital.org/clinicsmedServices/COE/surgicalServices/vascularSurgery/patientEducation/peripher.html.

Plaut, D. (2008). Detection of colon cancer. Advance for Administrators of the Laboratory 17:10.

Pokorski, R. (1990). Laboratory values in the elderly. Retrieved from www.aaimedicine.org/journal-of-insurance-medicine/jim/1990/022-02-0117.pdf.

Pomerance, J. (2002). Umbilical cord blood gas casebook. Journal of Perinatology, 22(6):504–505.

Porter, R. (Ed.). (2011). The Merck manual of diagnosis and treatment (19th ed.). Whitehouse Station, NJ: Merck Sharp & Dohme Corp.

Prechota, W., & Staszewski, A. (1992). Reference ranges of lipids and apolipoproteins in pregnancy. Retrieved from www.ncbi.nlm.nih.gov/pubmed/1618359.

Pregnancy and pancreatitis. (2006). Retrieved from http://pregnancyand-pancreatitis.blogspot.com.

Prostate-specific antigen best practice statement update panel. (2009). Prostate-specific antigen best practice statement 2009 update. Retrieved from www.auanet.org/content/guidelines-and-quality-care/clinical.../psa09.pdf.

Quanta Lite CCP IgG ELISA package insert. (2011). Retrieved from www.inovadx.com/Products/di_files/708790.html.

Quest Diagnostics (2000–2012). Test menu. Retrieved from www.questdiagnostics.com/hcp/qtim/testMenuSearch.do.

Quinley, E. (2010). Immunohematology principles and practice (3rd ed.). Philadelphia: Lippincott Williams & Wilkins.

Reichel, W., Gallo, J., Busby-Whitehead, J., Rabins, P., Sillman, R., & Murphy, J. (1999). Reichel's care of the elderly. Clinical aspects of aging (5th ed.). New York: Cambridge University Press.

Renne, T., & Gailani, R. (2007). Role of factor XII in hemostasis and thrombosis:

Clinical implications. Retrieved from www.ncbi.nlm.nih.gov/pubmed/17605651.

Reynolds, D. (1997). Apolipoprotein E. Retrieved from wwwchem.csustan.edu/chem4400/sjbr/dawn971.htm.

Renuart, A., Mistry, R., Avery, R., et. al. (2011). Reference range for cerebrospinal fluid protein concentration in children and adolescents. Retrieved from www.abstracts2view.com/pas/view.php?nu=PAS11L1_2135.

Rhophylac®. (2012). Retrieved from http://rhophylac.com/includes/pdf/PI%20Information%20Chart.pdf.

Riddel, J, Aouizerat, B., Miaskowski, C., & Lillicrap, D. (2007). Theories of blood coagulation. Journal of Pediatric Hematology/Oncology Nurses, 24(3):123-131.

Riley, R., & Tidwell, A. (2005). D-dimer assays. Retrieved from www.pathology.vcu.edu/clinical/coag/D-Dimer.pdf.

Roche Diagnostics (2009–2010). Rheumatoid factors II (V 7 EN). Indianapolis, IN: Roche Diagnostics.

Rogaeva, E. (2008). The genetic profile of Alzheimer's disease: PS1 on chromosome 14q24.3 and PS2 genes on chromosome 1q31-q42. Retrieved from www.medscape.com/viewarticle/586756_3.

Rowlett, R. (2011). SI units for clinical data. Retrieved from www.unc.edu/~rowlet/units/scales/clinical_data.html.

Runge, V. (1996). Contrast-enhanced clinical magnetic resonance imaging. Lexington: University Press of Kentucky.

Ryan, K., Ray, C., Ahmad, N., Drew, W., & Plorde, J. (2010). Sherris medical microbiology, (5th ed.). Columbus, OH: McGraw-Hill.

Sabin, C. (2010). When should antiretroviral therapy be started in HIV-positive persons? Retrieved from http://f1000.com/reports/m/2/81/.

Saladin, K. (2007). Human anatomy. New York: McGraw-Hill.

Schull, P. (Ed.). (1998). Illustrated guide diagnostic tests (2nd ed.). Springhouse, PA: Springhouse Publishing.

Screening, Technology, and Research in Genetics. (2009). Newborn screening. Retrieved from http://newbornscreening.info/index.html.

Seeram, E. (2008). Computed tomography: Physical principles, clinical application, and quality control (3rd ed.). Philadelphia: WB Saunders.

Select normal pediatric laboratory values. (n.d.). Retrieved from http://wps.prenhall.com/wps/media/objects/354/362846/London%20App.%20B.pdf.

Senthilnayagam, B., Kumar, T., Sukumaran, J., Jeya M., & Ramesh Rao K. (2012). Automated measurement of immature granulocytes: Performance characteristics and utility in routine clinical practice. Retrieved from www.ncbi.nlm.nih.gov/pmc/articles/PMC3289863/.

Shackett, P. (2008). Nuclear medicine technology: Procedures and quick reference. Philadelphia: Lippincott Williams & Wilkins.

Sharp, P., Gemmell, H., & Murray, A. (Eds.). (2005). Practical nuclear medicine (3rd ed.). New York: Springer.

Shimeld, L. (1999). Essentials of diagnostic microbiology. Albany, NY: Delmar Thomson Learning.

Shiner, J. (2010). Sepsis: Definitions, epidemiology, etiology and pathogenesis. Retrieved from www.chestnet.org/accp/pccsu/sepsis-definitions-epidemiology-etiology-and-pathogenesis?page=0,3.

Slopek, A. (2006). Fundamentals of special radiographic procedures (5th ed.). St. Louis, MO: WB Saunders.

Society of Nuclear Medicine. (2001). Procedure guidelines for C-14 urea breath test. Retrieved from http://interactive.snm.org/docs/pg_ch07_0403.pdf.

Sokoll, L., Remaley, A., Sena, et al. (2010). Intraoperative parathyroid hormone. Retrieved from www.aacc.org/siteCollectionDocuments/NACB/LMPG/POCT/Chapter%2010.pdf.

Soldin, S., Brugnara, C., & Wong, E. (Eds.). 2003). Pediatric reference ranges (4th ed.). Washington, DC: AACC Press.

Sperling, J. (2005). Cardiac biomarkers: Past, present and future. Retrieved from mrp.ouhsc.edu/sites/oumedicine/uploads/images/CardiacBiomarkers.ppt.

Quill, W., Wade, W., & Cobb, H. (2007). Estimating glomerular filtration rate with a modification of diet in renal disease equation: Implications for pharmacy. Retrieved from www.medscape.com/viewarticle/555611.

Stein, H., & Stein, R. (2006). The ophthalmic assistant: A guide for ophthalmic personnel (8th ed.). St. Louis, MO: Mosby.

Strasinger, S., & Dilorenzo, M. (2008). Urinalysis and body fluids (5th ed.). Philadelphia: FA Davis.

Strasinger, S., & Di Lorenzo, M. (1996). Phlebotomy workbook for the multi-skilled healthcare professional. Philadelphia: FA Davis.

Sunderland, T., Linker, G., Mirza, N., et. al. (2003). Decreased beta-amyloid 1-42 and increased tau levels in cerebrospinal fluid of patients with Alzheimer disease. Retrieved from www.ncbi.nlm.nih.gov/pubmed/12709467.

Terris, D., Weinberger, P., Farrag, T., Seybt, M., & Oliver, J. (2011). Restoring point-of-care testing during parathyroidectomy with a newer parathyroid hormone assay. Retrieved from http://oto.sagepub.com/content/145/4/557.

Thaler, L., & Blevens, L. (1998, August). The low dose (1-microg) adrenocorticotropin stimulation test in the evaluation of patients with suspected central adrenal insufficiency. [abstract] Journal of Clinical Endocrinology & Metabolism, 83(8):2726-2729.

The ankle-brachial index. (n.d.). Retrieved from www.vdf.org/diseaseinfo/pad/anklebrachial.php.

The BTA TRAK® assay. (n.d.). Retrieved from www.btastat.com/bta_trak_test.html.

Transcutaneous bilirubin measurement. (n.d.). Retrieved from www.newbornwhocc.org/pdf/tran.pdf.

ThermoScientific. (2012). PCT & sepsis. Retrieved from http://procalcitonin.com/default.aspx?tree=_2_4&=aboutpct4.

Thomas, D., & Wolinski, A. (2002). Submandibular calculus on conventional sialography. Retrieved from www.eurorad.org/case.php?id=1446.

Thrombocytopenia—drug induced. Retrieved from http://pennstatehershey.adam.com/content.aspx?productId=117&pid=1&gid=000556.

TNM staging system. Retrieved from www.cancer.gov/cancertopics/factsheet/detection/staging.

Torres, L., Dutton, A., & Linn-Watson, T. (2009). Patient care in imaging technology (Basic medical techniques and patient care in imaging technology)

(7th ed.). Philadelphia: Lippincott Williams & Wilkins.

Type, degree and configuration of hearing loss. (2011). Retrieved from www .asha.org/uploadedFiles/AIS-Hearing-Loss-Types-Degree-Configuration.pdf.

Understanding Gleason grading. (2008). Retrieved from http://prostatecancerin-folink.net/treatment/staging-grading/gleason-grading/.

Urden, L., Stacy, K., & Lough, M. (2009). Critical care nursing: Diagnosis and management (6th ed). St. Louis, MO: Mosby.

U.S. Food and Drug Administration. (2010). Information for healthcare professionals gadolinium-based contrast agents for magnetic resonance imaging (marketed as Magnevist, MultiHance, Omniscan, OptiMARK, Prohance). Retrieved from www.fda.gov/Drugs/DrugSafety/PostmarketDrugSafetyInformationforPatientsandProviders/ucm142884.htm (accessed 7/23/08).

Van Dyne, R. (1998, Oct.). Diagnosing common bleeding disorders. Advance for the Administrators of the Laboratory, 74.

Van Leeuwen, A., & Perry, E. (2000). Basic principles of chemistry: Techniques using alternate measurements. Denver, CO: Colorado Association for Continuing Medical Laboratory Education.

Venes, D. (Ed.). (2009). Taber's cyclopedic medical dictionary (21st ed.). Philadelphia: FA Davis.

Verstraete, A. (2004). Detection times of drugs of abuse in blood, urine, and oral fluid. Retrieved from www.labmed .yale.edu/Images/detection%20times%20in%20urine%20rev_tcm45-9313.pdf.

Von Schulthess, G. (2001). Clinical positron emission tomography. Philadelphia: Lippincott Williams & Wilkins.

Warell, D., Cox, T., & Firth, J. (Eds.). (2005). Oxford textbook of medicine. New York: Oxford University Press.

WebMD. Hysteroscopy. (2010). Retrieved from www.webmd.com/infertility-and-reproduction/guide/hysteroscopy-infertility.

WebMD. Sarcoidosis. (2010, February 20). Retrieved from www.webmd.com/lung/arthritis-sarcoidosis.

Widman, F., & Ittani, C. (1998). An introduction to clinical immunology and serology. Philadelphia: FA Davis.

Wikipedia. (2011). LEEP procedure. Retrieved from http://en.wikipedia.org/wiki/Loop_electrical_excision_procedure.

Wikipedia. (2012). Newborn screening. Retrieved from http://en.wikipedia.org/wiki/Newborn_screening.

Wilk, A., & van Venrooj, W. (2003). The use of anti-cyclic citrullinated peptide (anti-CCP) antibodies in RA. Retrieved from www.rheumatology.org/publications/hotline/1003anticcp.asp.

Willey, J., Sherwood, L., & Woolverton, C. (2010). Prescott's microbiology. Columbus, OH: McGraw-Hill.

Wilson, D., & Hockenberry, M. (2011). Wong's clinical manual of pediatric nursing (8th ed.). St. Louis, MO: Mosby.

World Health Organization. (2010). Laboratory manual for the examination and processing of human semen. Retrieved from http://whqlibdoc.who.int/publications/2010/9789241547789_eng.pdf.

Workowski, K., & Berman, S. (2010, December 17). Sexually transmitted diseases. Treatment guidelines 2010. Retrieved from www.cdc.gov/std/treatment/2010/STD-Treatment-2010-RR5912.pdf.

Wu, A. (Ed.). (2003). Cardiac markers (2nd ed.). Totowa, NJ: Humana Press.

Wu, A. (Ed.). (2006). Tietz clinical guide to laboratory tests (4th ed.). St. Louis, MO: WB Saunders.

Yamamoto, D., Shoji, T., Kawanishi H., et (2001). A utility of ductography and fiberoptic ductoscopy for patients wi nipple discharge. Retrieved from www .ncbi.nlm.nih.gov/pubmed/11768599

Yeomans, E., Hauth J., Gilstrap L., & Strickland, D. (1985). Umbilical cord pH, Pco_2, and bicarbonate following uncomplicated term vaginal deliverie American Journal of Obstetrics and Gynecology, 151(6):798–800.

Young, D. (2000). Effects of drugs on clical laboratory tests (5th ed.). Washington, DC: AACC Press.

Young, D., & Friedman, R. (2001). Effe of disease on clinical laboratory tes (4th ed.). Washington, DC: AACC Press.

Zhang, Y., Thompson, R., Zhang, H., & Xu, H. (2011, January 7). APP proce ing in Alzheimer's disease. Molecu Brain, 4(1):3.

IN

IND

IN

IND

IND

IND

ND

IND

IND

IND

IND

IND

IND

IND

IND

IND

IND

IND

IND

IND

IND

IND

IND

IND

IND

IND

IND

IND

IND

IND

IND

IND

IND

IND

IND

IND

IND

IND

IND